TEMPLE FIELDING

FIELDING'S
Travel Guide
to Europe

1977 EDITION

Chapter headings illustrated by Lombard C. Jones

mum,

Armchair travelling can be fun too – e.g. page 533. Things not to buy.

love &f x

FIELDING PUBLICATIONS
105 MADISON AVENUE, NEW YORK, N.Y. 10016
In association with William Morrow & Company, Inc.
Publishers: New York

Printed in the United States of America.
Library of Congress Catalog Card No. 59-7408

ISBN 0-688-61188-5

Map by Dyno Lowenstein

To my brother,

Captain Dodge Fielding, F. A.
(Philippines, April 30, 1945)

Ever enchanted by travel, he
took the Big Trip with his
usual smile.

Nancy and Temple Fielding

ABOUT THE FIELDING TEAM

TEMPLE FIELDING

A native of New York City who grew up in Stamford, Conn., TEMPLE FIELDING has lived with his wife Nancy and son Dodge on the island of Mallorca for more than 25 years.

The idea for *Fielding's* sprang from an orientation booklet and Lieutenant (later Major) Fielding—just out of Princeton—was ordered to write for incoming recruits at Fort Bragg. The booklet was so successful that it was adapted by other camps, and over 2-million copies were distributed. Then he was assigned to special intelligence with guerrilla forces in North Africa, Italy, and the Balkans, spending several months behind enemy lines in Yugoslavia with Tito.

After the war, FIELDING, by this time a budding foreign correspondent, was working in Europe and found that there was no really practical travel guide available. Nancy suggested that he write his own, using the same highly readable style as in the Fort Bragg manual. And so he did, and so it changed his life and the lives of millions of travelers.

Fielding's was the first of its kind—a practical what-to, where-to, how-to European guide that avoided what the author calls "the tinsel illusions of Graustarkian fairyland peopled by picturesque native dancers" and also steered clear of the "deadly tedious cathedrals-and-cobblestones" approach of the Baedekers. The first edition—only about 1/10th the size of the present one—was an immediate hit, and FIELDING soon gave up his other writing assignments to devote all his time to the Guide.

Glamour job? Not so says FIELDING. "Only our editors and we can have an inkling of the job's demands upon our legs, digestions, energies, and lives in general. It is ruthless." Last year the team inspected approximately 3180 hotels or pensions, dined in some 1200 restaurants, inspected 850 shops, explored at least 500 nightclubs, and visited hundreds of incidental attractions during their rigorous 6-month research rounds.

Up to 150,000 words of *Fielding's* are revised or rewritten every year. Although the Central Offices are in a neighboring town, much of his writing is done at Villa Fielding, a dazzling white house perched on a mountainside in Mallorca. There he works at an oversize, U-shaped desk painted his favorite color—marine blue—with his only 4-footed "Editorial Assistant," his beloved St. Bernard, sprawled at his feet. With a grin, he tells people that Baby and he often hold heated discussions on arcane or esoteric points of syntax.

TEMPLE FIELDING'S 24 foreign decorations or awards for his work include 2 Knight Commanderships and 5 Knighthoods.

NANCY PARKER FIELDING

Famed international hostess, epicurean cook, imaginative decorator, crossword fiend, and hopelessly soft touch for pets of all shapes and sizes, gifted and glamorous Nancy Fielding lived an unusually happy childhood with her silver-designing family in Newburyport, Mass. After matriculating at Bradford Junior College, Pembroke (Brown University) and Katherine Gibbs, for 2 years she was initiated into her future vocations as an assistant to massively productive author-publisher Fulton Oursler. Several months after she had joined Fulton's sister-in-law as a junior partner in a New York literary agency venture, the boss married and turned over the struggling business to her. So dew-fresh at 23 that the editors fondly dubbed her "Betty Co-Ed with the braids," she sallied forth to build the renamed Nancy Parker Agency into one of the most highly respected authors' representatives in America.

In 1941, through the matchmaking machinations of a *Readers Digest* editor, she met a young Carolina-based Army officer named Temple Fielding and signed him up as the lowest ranking client on her totem pole. After 5 dates in 2 months they were married. The early pressure following the enormously successful debut of the *Travel Guide* became so overwhelming that in 1950 she took a sabbatical abroad to rescue him. Quickly they became an inseparable team, visiting more than 155 countries together. Co-author of 2 of the annual Fielding books, she is a former columnist for The Hall Syndicate and foreign correspondent for a number of magazines and newspapers. In addition to numerous other honors and awards, she has been elevated by Spain's government to the rank of Dame of the high Order of Mérito Civil.

Her cookbook collection contains more than 1000 volumes. She also collects perfumes, passionately follows football, baseball, and other sports, plays dangerous poker and kalookie, and produces a continuous parade of utterly useless geegaws in needlepoint.

JOSEPH A. RAFF

Joseph A. Raff, affectionately known as Tio Pepe ("Uncle Joe") in the Fielding circle, first came to Mallorca in 1961 to assist Temple on a complex and difficult one-shot project. Their professional marriage clicked so happily and their friendship rooted so rapidly that within weeks Joe was enlisted as a permanent member of the staff. Today he is the President of Fielding Publications. When not in orbit, the Raffs base themselves at a 350-year-old farmhouse which they have enchantingly reconstructed on a verdant hillside overlooking the ancient village of Pollensa and the sea.

Though born in New York, Joe spent most of his younger years in the South. A graduate of the University of North Carolina at Chapel Hill, his further studies in International Relations took him to Indiana, Ohio, and Harvard Universities. Journalism has always been his pursuit. Starting with school papers, he moved to become a Wire Editor of the Associated Press, a reporter for 3 top newspapers in North Carolina, the Automotive Editor for *Sports Illustrated*, and then, after leaping the Atlantic, the Managing Editor of the *Rome Daily American*. It was from the Eternal City that the Fielding travel interests lured him. Indefatigably to maintain the balance between the changing tastes of the Fielding readers and the changing scenes of Europe has long been Joe's vocational lifeblood and Golden Fleece.

Nonprofessionally his joy in sports also keeps him moving. Although Judy has persuaded him to give up auto racing, regularly he descends Europe's fastest ski runs, plays expert tennis, and captains his beloved deepwater Danish sloop.

DODGE TEMPLE FIELDING

Dodge Fielding has inhaled and exhaled travel from infancy. After becoming a permanent European resident at the age of 5, his Seven League Boots have spanned more than 29 times Marco Polo's mileage. His present tally of countries, territories, and possessions visited is 89. He speaks 4 languages without accent and 4 others fluently.

Vocationally and avocationally his background is characteristically in keeping as a Fielding. Born in New York and matriculated at Dutch, Spanish, and Danish primary schools, he advanced through Massachusetts' Governor Dummer Academy and the World Campus Afloat to a B.A. from Hamilton College in Clinton, N.Y.

From childhood he has been immutably wedded to the creative pen. At 10 he composed and bylined 7 of his father's syndicated columns. At 14 he wrote feature interviews in Spanish for 2 Madrid newspapers. At 17 he made his debut with the company in an independent research sweep through 28 cities in 18 nations to provide students' information for the maiden edition of *Fielding's Low-Cost Europe*. As fruit of the comprehensive 7-year training period with Fielding Publications, including a 2-year technical hiatus with an international airline and major travel agency in Manhattan, Dodge added his own perennial to the clan's list of guidebooks.

In addition to his normal share of duties, he produced the anually-revised volume, *Fielding's Selected Favorites: Hotels & Inns, Europe*, after inspecting and plucking the pick of 3,846 foreign hostelries. Then he formed the Swiss-based Fielding Corporation, of which he is the President, dedicated to the expansion of the group's nonpublishing interests in the travel industry.

When not on the road or behind his desk, at 31 this bon vivant bachelor can be found on a tennis court, a karate mat, a sandtrap on a golf course, or in the cockpit of a Beechcraft Bonanza.

JUDY RAFF

Judy Raff came to the Fielding team as a bonus—and what a sage, gracious, scintillating one she is! While Joe was being broken in with Temple in the early sixties, her keen, ever-questing mind became restless for the challenges of new horizons. Nancy and Joe immediately made capital of her sharp eyes, impeccable taste, and unusual intuition by first training her in professionally evaluating the merchandise and fashion worlds for the *Shopping Guide*. From this sphere she progressed rapidly to gathering, weighing, and reporting on every major field of activity covered in all of the Fielding series, splitting her concentration neatly among 3 of its annually-revised volumes. Since 1964 she has been Chief Researcher of the company.

Her U.S. venue is the desert country of the Southwest; the family residence is in Las Vegas. Born in Philadelphia into the broadcasting world, she followed the air waves to New York (where as a child she was a Quiz Kid), to North Carolina (where she handled programming and radio station schedules in the Tar Heel capital), and finally to Europe (where her frequent and arduous cross-continental forays with Joe provide double coverage of their beats). Her education is a nomadic moveable feast provided by the Connecticut College for Women, the University of North Carolina at Chapel Hill, and New York University, where she took a B.A. in history plus graduate courses in art history. Apart from her career with the Fielding clan, Judy has also been active in the fields of architecture, home-living, and magazine redesign.

Like Nancy, she is widely known as an outstanding international hostess. Her chief avocations are the happy pursuit of culinary exotica within the score of nations she regularly visits, zealous tennis, resolute skiing, and crewing aboard the Danish sloop which is the Raffs' beloved second home.

Europe

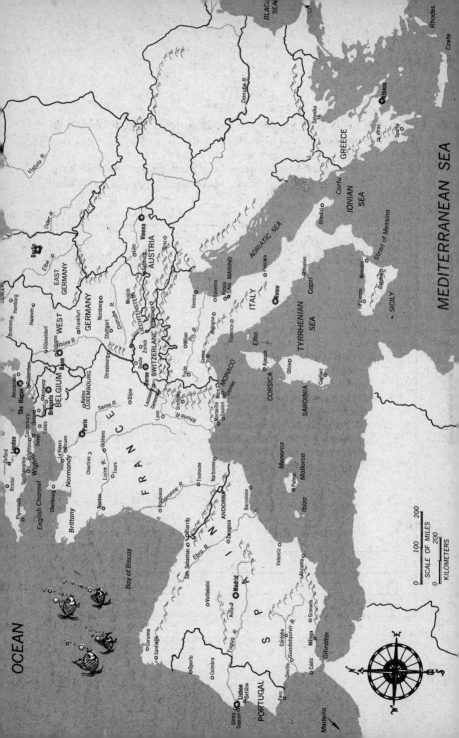

Other Fielding Travel Guides are available from your bookseller or from William Morrow and Company.

When ordering, add 50¢ postage and handling for the first book, plus 15¢ for each additional book. Make checks payable to William Morrow & Co.

To: William Morrow & Co., Inc.
6 Henderson Dr.
West Caldwell, N.J. 07006

Please send me:

Quantity		Price
_____	Fielding's Travel Guide to Europe, 1977	_____
_____	Fielding's Shopping Guide, 1977	_____
_____	Fielding's Guide to the Caribbean, 1977	_____
_____	Fielding's Guide to Traveling with Children	_____
_____	Speaking You English?	_____
_____	Fielding's Conversation Guide to Europe	_____
	Postage	_____
	Sales tax if applicable	_____
	Total	_____

NAME _____

STREET _____

CITY   STATE   ZIP

(For prices, see inside back cover.)

Contents

20

Me To You
(The Confession Box)

Readers are sometimes curious about the backstage operations of this *Guide*. Who gathers the information? Who collaborates? Do we travel under our own names? How much freeloading and "compliments of the management" can we squeeze? What kind of a rakeoff do we get from merchants and other businesses we recommend?

Here's a quick glimpse at the inside picture:

First, once upon a time the name "Fielding" enveloped all of the literary clankings and wheezings of a six-armed one-man band. During ensuing years a host of warmhearted but uninformed souls has proliferated the legend that I, a larger-than-life Lone Ranger, annually swoop through all of the cities and boondocks of 23 European nations to root out and to report every single current touristic development on this panoramic scene. Not so. Please, please not so! Long ago "Fielding" became a generic word shared in total measure by the most finely honed, smoothly functioning team it has ever been my joy and my privilege to encounter. As mentioned briefly in the respective biographical sketches, the production demands on this author became so hopelessly overwhelming that after the publication of 2 editions of this *Guide* my Nancy sold her New York literary agency in 1950 to become my first Chief of Staff, researcher and, full-time collaborator abroad. In love, in work, in life, we complement each other so completely that our joint unification in every emotion and endeavor has always been and continues to be astonishing. Without her ever-continuous and ever-intensive total participation, today our whole series would lie fallow as dustily buried history. After an unsuccessful 2-year experiment with an editorial assistant when the load became too heavy for us to bear together, in 1961 prophetic fate brought us the golden sunlight of Joe and Judy Raff. Lengthy, meticulous, and arduous training trips brought out their mettle. In temperaments, in professional gifts, in ever-sparkling personalities they fit with perfection into the extraordinary special demands which this exacting

25

field requires. Then, following a string of new and inadequately motivated editorial assistants, our Marco Polo son Dodge attained the maturity to move into and to take full command of the job for which he had been actively training for 7 years. At once he joined hands with Nancy, Judy, Joe, and me in contributing his remarkable aptitude, talents, and background to research and to write major shares of all of the 3 titles revised annually by this clan. In 1972 he produced a fourth—his own highly successful perennial, *Fielding's Selected Favorites: Hotels & Inns, Europe.* Next he formed the Swiss-based Fielding Corporation, of which he is the President, to expand the group's nonpublishing interests in the travel industry. He is a dynamo who ideally rounds out the circle. To have generated what we have for more than the past decade without the mind-boggling labors, savvy, and dedication of this entire team would be unthinkable. Our Administrative Vice President, Estanislao ("Stan") de la Cruz, whose half-Chinese, half-Spanish bloodline brings out all the grace, loyalty, sparkle, and nobility of both nationalities, with the alert assistance of faithful Jaime Sebastian, has for the 14th year been a tower of strength in running his department and in coordinating the enormous mass of raw material which was ultimately fed into these pages. Our adored New York-based anchor, Eunice Riedel, has long drawn this group's ringing vote as the best Editor in the U.S. publishing industry. She, her competent associate Allan Garshman, and her X-ray-vision gals continue to dedicate their professional hearts, souls, expertise, and élan to the gargantuan task of keeping on the track of each of the millions of words, spellings, punctuation marks, collations, and other far more technical challenges in the 13 separate volumes produced by our company. In sum, this all-for-all cohesion works out in the very special happy harmony which can be built only through mutual respect, toil, and devotion.

Necessity has dictated that each member of our basic quintet is a Jack or Jacqueline of all trades. He or she is equipped to handle—and *does* handle whenever required—every single phase of every single one of our projects. Although each has his or her pet titles (e.g., Nancy and Judy with the *Shopping Guide*, Dodge with the *Hotels Guide*), no "specialist" exists. Conversely, in the balances of its ages and outlooks, it might be pertinent to compare its constituents to those of a mini, aggressively successful, pro football team. Joe, Dodge, and Judy brim with the vitality, the dash, the daring, the constant flow of the new ideas, new approaches, new planning patterns of youth; Nancy and I are the cool-eyed veterans who know most of the tricks of protecting our flanks. This is one important reason why we jell so efficiently as a unit.

Hundreds of scattered friends and thousands of kind readers have also provided a priceless flow of facts and advice. (If you should write and then not hear from us for months, it's only because we're traveling, we're swamped, and we're so tired at the end of those days that no juice is left for correspondence. Still, we try our damndest eventually to express our appreciation, even if it's delayed until a year from next Tuesday!.

But the key factor must always be this: The 5 of us have got to remain the *only* ones upon whom the responsibility of this *Guide* rests, with me as the final authority. It was often necessary to override all other opinions, ranging from those of colleagues or "outsiders" closest to us to those of well-meaning but adamant strangers who insisted that François' Coffee Pot is every bit as good as the Tour d'Argent. In this way, a united single level of judgment can be maintained from cover to cover, encouraging you, the reader, to measure your tastes against ours and to make your own uniform adjustment throughout. As a corollary, the sole way to keep this standard alive is for all of those qualified to get out and see those spots for ourselves. Excluding some of Dodge's hideaways, we in the clan have personally covered perhaps 98% of the establishments listed, and, for the rest, it's clear when we haven't.

Third, none of us ever introduces himself or herself until the check has been paid or the work has been done. No one ever knows our schedules except the next hotelier—if we haven't walked in cold, in hopes of snagging a room. Our primary obsession is to be accepted as Mr. and Mrs. John Smith, routine American tourists, who apparently speak nothing but English, who are typically easygoing, and who might be somewhat baffled by it all (which is often too true!). Sometimes we lose our little game by being spotted and identified—but the frequency with which we win it, especially after retrudging so much of the same ground time and time again, continues to astound us.

Fourth, this book is 100% independent and 100% clean. Through its 30 years of existence, we've stuck to one inflexible rule *always:* No payola, commissions, rakeoffs, cuts, kickbacks, or outside compensation in any form —from *anybody*. From time to time, skeptical travelers have scoffed at this claim. Here's our answer: Let anyone open this book, pick the name of any hotel, restaurant, shop, or local attraction from any page, and go straight to the source for his own checkup. We're proud to say that we've always been faithful to our principles as working reporters—and we're going to stay that way.

Fifth, we pick up our checks wherever we go—often under strenuous protest from the people we write about. In case anyone cares, the ledgers of our 2 companies show that we spent $112,190.14 last year in travel and operating expenses. Opportunities for freeloading are endless for any accredited travel writer—but *only* by paying our way can we (1) call the shots as we see them, and (2) maintain the total independence which is so important to this type of book.

Sixth, we work continuously, the calendar round, to try to keep our *Guides* up to the minute. Our year normally breaks down into 6 months on the road and 6 months of committing to manuscript the new facts and impressions gathered along the way. Our firsthand coverage of the foreign scene is exhaustive—and sometimes darned exhausting, too. All of us switch routes every year. On a basis of physical fact, with no impertinence or self-assertion, we just haven't come across anyone else in the travel world

—author, travel agent, transportation official, or otherwise—who could spare the time or expend the energy to visit *personally* even 25% of this number of European facilities.

Seventh, you and we are bound to have violent disagreements at times, due to the necessarily arbitrary structure of this kind of writing. You'll probably call some of our advice fatheaded and many of our conclusions noxious. Just who do these conceited characters think *they* are, pushing you around and telling you with insulting flatness that that 3rd-rate hash joint is the *only* good place in town? But today's voyager, thank goodness, has notably high intelligence and notably strong views. Only a moron could agree with every sentence on every page—and that's not you, this year's sharp-eyed, travelwise pilgrim! So please regard the *Guide* merely as a broad, general tool for your touring pleasure—not as an encyclopedia with all the final answers.

Eighth, sundry skimmers of this opus have accused us of concentrating entirely upon deluxe sites that offer breast of nightingale and liveried footmen as standard equipment. This is nonsense. In these pages you'll find thousands upon thousands upon thousands of suggestions for every economic level of traveler. You'll come across bargains galore in this *Guide*—legions of them so low in price that your wallet will whistle. But if you're a *serious* economizer who seeks ONLY the bottom-budget lodgings and facilities of the Continent, our annually revised paperback, *Fielding's Low-Cost Europe*, has been tailor-made to s-t-r-e-t-c-h every penny of your journey until it hollers. There simply isn't space in the *Travel Guide* to list more tight-economy places than are already there—so we created this specialized book, now in its 11th voluminously revised and updated annual edition, to blanket these thousands of additional entries. Important: Exactly the same criteria of decency, cleanliness, and integrity have been applied in both volumes.

Last, as you will see, we are ruthless in our coverage of clip joints, tourist traps, conniving taxi drivers, hucksters who pay under-the-counter commissions on voyagers' purchases, storekeepers with a special set of prices for U.S. neophytes, and all foreign agencies that deceive or swindle the cheerfully honest North American. In a less venomous way, we're sharply critical of what we believe is a dirty restaurant, a punk hotel, an overpriced merchant, mediocre food, and an overrated sightseeing attraction, or any facility which, in our most thoughtful observation, doesn't deliver full value for the traveler's hard-earned dollar. Because nobody wants to read an opinion that his establishment robs the customer or is overrun with bedbugs, this policy has made scores of bitter enemies over the years. There has even been an anonymous death threat mailed to our home. Here's the crux: You, our reader, are our *only* consideration in this text. We did not write it for the benefit of hotels, restaurants, airlines, shops, or any other agencies, good or bad. Instead, your protection and your interests are not only paramount to us, but exclusive. Trite as it might sound, your travel happiness is our modest but utterly sincere personal crusade.

For trouble-free journeying, time is a crucial ingredient in this volume or any like it. We *do* know what we're talking about here. After a 1-year period, *almost ¼th of the Guide's* wordage has been ripped out and re-newed. Would you buy stocks today by using last summer's *Wall Street Journal?* So when you're finished with this, we advise—nay, implore—you not to make it a cheap hand-me-down for friends. Just loosen up a few bucks, buy them the accurate, up-to-the-minute, spanking-new edition con-taining all the changes—and earn their gratitude rather than their grumbles. Now—even though this counsel might conjure up suspicions of publishers' cash registers ringing away, that's incidental. Nobody hates money, including indigent travel reporters—but nobody wants readers swearing at him or her for bum information that is dismally outdated, either.

The public relations pressures on this *Guide* by American manufacturers who sought plugs for their products became intolerable. That is why, starting with the 1965 issue, we dropped *all* references to *all* U.S. brand names—including to our sorrow, many innocents who never put the slightest sus-picion of any squeeze on us. You'll read about these same articles, but you'll just have to play guessing games about their brands.

Here's a tip suggested to us by one of France's leading restaurateurs. Whenever you enter any dining place in Europe, do as the *Guide Michelin* has advised its travelers for many years: Take this book with you and dis-play it openly on your table as a silent weapon against indifference or bad treatment. When the management spots it, frequently you'll be surprised how your cuisine and your service will suddenly pick up.

Errors, bloopers, boners? With any good fisherman, editor, or author, a few big ones (sometimes horrifyingly big!) are bound to get away—and you'll find them, sure as shooting. If you'll pause to consider the sheer number and bulk of facts in this nearly 1-million-word treatise on the NOW living patterns of 26 independent nations or key tourist areas, perhaps we'll be forgiven if the occasional but inevitable howler should let you down. As Polydorus said, 2 millenniums ago, "Perfection is unthinkable—except for a beautiful woman." Hence, all we can do is sweat, try like hell, cross our fingers until the knuckles crack, and then brace ourselves our hardest.

But this jubilee anniversary edition which now sits in your hand is the distillation of 30 years of solid work, more than 2¾ths-million European miles, countless hours of editorial polishing, and actual field trial by mil-lions upon millions of pilgrims abroad. It has come a long, long way from the slender manuscript we so timidly introduced to the traveler back in '48. Therefore, we're especially happy for the chance to make this offering by far the most complete and by far the most useful we've ever produced.

Our fondest hope is that your trip—even if it's in your armchair—gives your half the fun and half the delight that Lombard Jones had with his illustrations and we had with the text of this good-humored companion.

/ T.H.F.

Europe, the United Kingdom, Ireland . . . Formentor, Mallorca,
Balearic Isles.

FIELDING'S
Travel Guide to Europe

1977 EDITION

Let's Get Ready

Exactly 35,852 chores stare you coldly in the eye before departure. That's natural. But you're bound for Europe, not for the headwaters of the Zambezi River by dugout canoe. No lions, tigers, or exotic dangers lurk in the jungles of mankind's most civilized and highly cultured continent—only wolves, who are usually amusing company and pretty good dancers, too. Sure, things are different—but not *that* different; a street is a street, a waiter is a waiter, and a radish is a radish whether it's in London, Lucerne, or Little Falls. If you're at all fluttery, remember that 17-jillion travelers have blazed your trail without harm to themselves or, more important, to the local populations. So relax.

Let's go over your trip, step by step. Some of these preliminaries will be old stuff to you—but use them as a check list. Maybe they'll remind you of something you've forgotten. Or maybe, if we're lucky, you'll pick up a fact or two. If 300 of the minor details should slip your mind, such as winding the cat or drowning the milkman, don't think a *thing* about it. There isn't a voyager alive who doesn't get distracted, because any transatlantic trek carries an extra emotional jolt.

COSTS Take the elastic band off your bankroll, because the first leg of your trip will cost you plenty.

Please turn to the end of the book for our last-minute roundup of basic fares, regulations, and further transportation lore.

By air, overocean rates on all scheduled carriers (except Icelandic Airlines and International Air Bahama) are exactly the same. An organization called the International Air Transport Association (IATA) is responsible for this questionable practice; more later about this controversial octopus. At current writing, Alice might take one glance at the frightening crazy quilt of fare tables, hedgings, and wishy-washy compromises—and then dive straight back Through the Looking Glass to seek the sage advice of the Mad Hatter.

Steamship rates are generally more expensive than airway rates. If you cross in the Aga Khan's suite and demand a special diet of Rocky Mountain Peacock Tongues Flambés, you can pay a lot more. If you don't mind sharing a dormitory with the population of Podunk—all of whom snore—you can pay a lot less. For specific prices, see your travel agent.

The cost of living still varies—but, in almost every country, the specter of inflation is rampant. You can forget about the "cheap" Europe of yore, with its $2 rooms, 75¢ meals, and 25¢ drinks, because it has now dwindled to the point of virtual extinction. Roughly (a personal evaluation), here is a scale of present comparisons:

Most expensive are Germany, Switzerland, France, Belgium, Monaco, Denmark, Sweden, Norway, and Finland. Second in expensiveness are Austria, England, Italy, Portugal, the Netherlands, San Marino, and Luxembourg. Least expensive are Spain, Greece, and Ireland. Today NOT ONE of the capital cities is "cheap"; conversely, many small towns and villages still are.

If you're an oilman from Texas or a woman who holds more than 5 department store charge accounts—in other words, rich—count on a minimum of $120 per couple per day (transportation extra) to keep the wolves away. *If you wish to maintain the normal and everyday living standards of America's dominant mid-income group—not the student or the excessively-tight-budget level—do not attempt a trip this year to metropolitan Europe on a budget of less than $45 per person or $80 per twosome for actual daily expenses.* Superficial dream peddlers will assure you that you can blithely breeze through the Continent and the British Isles—even holidaying in paralyzingly priced Paris, for God's sake!—on a perfectly ridiculous number of dollars per day. Because my Nancy and I are so shocked and so disgusted by the false illusions that some of them build—and by the number of innocent readers who find themselves literally stranded abroad—we produced our own *Fielding's Low-Cost Europe.* The 11th edition of this money-saver, published in paperback every winter, offers serious economizers who must guard every penny our *realistic* appraisals of thousands of bottom-budget establishments and facilities which space limitations prevent us from including in the *Travel Guide.* But, for the aforementioned dominant mid-income group (who are not involved in a package plan), that's why our $45 or $80 averages are recommended to those independent travelers who want to live decently, tip generously, shop reasonably, and not worry too much about buying that extra martini. And what the hell—it's for the fun of it that you're going, isn't it?

A good trick few sky travelers know about is to take No-Show, and you should be out within 72 hours. The explanation is simple: Every carrier is plagued by wise guys who make duplicate or multiple bookings for the same crossing—and then leave all but 1 company in the lurch. So notify the airline you're ready to pull out at a minute's notice!

And don't forget to *reconfirm* every ticket everywhere not less than 72 hours in advance of departure, or you might lose your space. Also be sure to spell your name for the airline attendant. Since computers are too often fallible, don't risk losing your seat because the programmer misperceived your familiar handle.

PASSPORTS AND VISAS   The passport is the document that seems to combine the best features of the U.S. Constitution, the Message to Garcia, and the Ark of the Covenant. Guard it more carefully than your wallet—or your spouse. Without them you can move, but without the passport you're finished. In dire cases it might mean days of catastrophic delay.

Enormous streamlining measures have been wrought by our on-the-ball (but criminally State-Department-mistreated) Passport Office during the past few years. Now all touristic passports are valid for 5 years from date of issue, after which a new one may be obtained. Certain post offices handle the paper work. Ask if yours is one. If you are really in a remote corner and don't fall into one of the categories listed below, your "Application for Passport by Mail," *must* be accompanied by your most recent passport, 2 signed identical photos of your glowing countenance (taken within 6 months of licking the stamps), and a verdant $10. Forward them either to your nearest Passport Agency or to the Passport Office, Washington, D.C. 20524.

First-timers may not use the mails. They must appear in person before an Agent of the Department of State, a clerk of any federal court or state court of record, a judge or clerk of any probate court, or a postal employee designated by the Postmaster at selected Post Offices. Bring along evidence of citizenship (a certified birth certificate should be submitted as proof of birth in the U.S.), personal identification, those same 2 photos of y-o-u, and that everlovin' $10-bill—plus 3 additional bucks as an execution fee. Others ineligible for postal exchange are (1) anyone who can't provide his most recent passport issued in his own name within the past 8 years, (2) any whippersnapper whose earlier travel document was issued before the 18th birthday, (3) any candidate for official or diplomatic papers, or (4) any supplicant wanderer seeking a wholesale rate for his family. Yep, you may wrap up the entire brood in 1 package—husband, wife, and 16 children if you have them—thereby saving a whole string of individual payments. But if a feud should break out en route, somebody's going to find himself or herself stuck in Zwartsluis, Holland.

Special note to wayfaring brides and gay new divorcées: The passport-by-mail will be granted only in the name under which the previous passport was recorded. To skirt this one, you can send in an original or certified copy of a court order or marriage license showing the name change.

Look in the phone books of New York, Philadelphia, Washington, D.C., Boston, Chicago, Miami, New Orleans, Los Angeles, Seattle, San Francisco, and Honolulu under United States Government, Department of State, Passport Agency. Application forms may be had not only from these offices, but from the 4000 authorized Clerks of Court and post offices through the nation, from your travel agent or international airline.

For those abroad, petitions for new passports must be made *in person* at the nearest American Embassy or Consulate. Your old, dog-eared, canceled friend will be returned as a souvenir when the new one is issued.

One MUST: Before you go tootling off, be sure to check this vital companion and follow religiously the fine print on the inside covers.

Yet another word of caution: Don't DARE to try to leave America without a *valid* passport. A number of foreign countries have become so hot under their T-shirts about travelers' increasing demands for entry without valid passports that they are cracking down by holding these truants at the airport or dock and shipping them straight back home by the first available transport. If you're in *genuine* trouble, nobody can be a better friend than the Passport Office—but don't try to fool either it or its foreign counterparts.

Frances G. Knight, our charming and brilliantly competent Passport Director, has revolutionized the Office during her tenure of 2 decades. Because this outstanding executive places the interest of the traveling public first, her innovations have been remarkable despite the burgeoning demand and the stupid shortsightedness of Foggy Bottom bureaucrats who are thwarting her pleas for adequate personnel.

First, *provided that all documents are correctly submitted,* approximately 2 weeks is the normal maximum issuance. Second, the series of brochures *(You and Your Passport, Now That You Have A Passport,* etc.) has been rewritten in a friendly, chatty style; all are free of charge. Third, Miss Knight inaugurated the optional use of color pictures, urging voyagers to *"Get a good picture.* The Passport Office welcomes photographs that depict the applicant as a relaxed, smiling person . . ."* Fourth, they are released in 3 versions: (1) a Liberty Bell-ringer in its flag-blue cover, for tourists, with silver lettering and a fresh face for bicentennial celebrants; (2) in-the-red maroon cover, for Government employees traveling on official business; and (3) cloak-and-dagger black cover, for members of the diplomatic service.

Some (rare) photographers will give you a list of each country's picture requirements. *As insurance, always be sure to get 5 or 6 extra photos;* later they might save hours and headaches.

Now—visas. For stays generally up to 3 months, every nation in Western Europe has eliminated this formality for U.S. visitors. To enter Russia, most of the Iron Curtain satellites, most of the Middle East, most of Africa, and practically all of Asia or the Pacific, however, visas are still demanded. If you're extending your tour, ask your travel agent or airline representative to sally forth into the lush forests of red tape. He'll also furnish the forms for police certificates, health certificates, and other special documents.

Visa fees range from zero to $30, depending upon the country. You may pick up the later ones during the first stages of your wanderings on the other side—but it's far, far easier to check out all of these requirements before leaving home. Any questions? *Visa Requirements of Foreign Governments* (Brochure M-264) is the Passport Office gospel on the subject.

Denmark, Finland, Iceland, Norway, and Sweden operate a 1-entry, 1-exit "free" zone within their combined borders—harbinger of the pleasant trend toward fewer European frontier stations stamping visitors' credentials. When the Traveler's Holy Grail—the simple International Identity Card—becomes a reality, the battle of documents will be won, thank goodness.

If you are not an American citizen, and if you intend to return to the States at the end of your voyage, a *Sailing Permit* is a must; you may pick up one from the nearest Internal Revenue office. Noncitizens who are permanent U.S. residents may go abroad and return to an established residence after an absence *not exceeding 1 year;* all they do is to present their Alien Registration Receipt cards. If they plan to stay more than 12 months, however, they've got to get an *Immigration Service Reentry Permit* before departure from American soil—or else. Your travel agent will handle it.

§PASSPORT TIPS FROM MISS KNIGHT:

Double-check the expiration date to make certain it will not run out just as you bound up the gangway to make an international connection.

Don't use it as a notebook, scrapbook, or autograph book—in fact, never touch your pen to it, save in its listed requirements.

Don't fiddle with the photo. Above all, don't "accidentally" spill nail polish or ink on your birth date, because it can become invalid.

Never use it as collateral or pledge—and always register it if you send it through the mails.

Never lend it to a stranger—or even to a friend.

Always carry it on your person when you head for a new country—never in your luggage, which can so easily go astray.

And *always* GUARD IT AGAINST THEFT. Thousands of U.S. passports vanish each season under mysterious circumstances (about 1000 per year in France alone!); many filter into unauthorized or even enemy hands. The going rate in the underworld ranges from $500 to $2500 per copy.

Finally, the Passport Office scrupulously checks into cases of so-called "lost" documentation (now approaching 30,000 per year!) because of the dramatic rise in crimes involving identity fraud. You can help control this seamy foreign and domestic corruption by carefully protecting your passport *at all times.*

SHOTS   The smallpox-vaccination certificate is demanded by U.S. authorities solely of travelers from nations where this disease is endemic (none in Free Europe). Typhoid, tetanus-diphtheria, cholera, and polio immunization wouldn't hurt (your resistance, not your arm!)—if you're timid or if you're hitting the southern rim in summer. A booster of improved flu vaccine and one gamma globulin injection to help ward off hepatitis are smart though rarely crucial preventive measures, too.

But if you plan to poke through any odd places around the Mediterranean (including *all* of North Africa, the Middle East, the bottom of Italy, and most of the islands)—or if you're heading for deep Africa or Asia—for heaven's sake be brave and let your doctor shoot the works. Europe, generally speaking, is safe and sound; they've got good public-health officials, fine doctors, and the latest drugs. These hotter lands, though, still crawl with 77-zillion varmints—and nothing is more dismal than hospitalization thousands of miles from home.

Dr. W. Price Fitch of Mamaroneck, N.Y., the internationally famous authority on travel health, recommends the following series of inoculations and vaccinations for the latter group of voyagers:

Type of Immunization	Time Consumed
Smallpox	1 visit
Tetanus and Diphtheria	1 visit
Cholera	1 or 2 visits
Typhus	2 visits, 7 days apart
Typhoid	2 visits, 7 days apart
Polio (Oral triple)	1 visit
Influenza	1 visit

Yellow fever serum is so delicate to process and difficult to keep that it can be found in only 1 place in most cities—in New York, for example, at the U.S. Public Health Service, 67 Hudson St. Hours: 1:30 P.M. and 2:30 P.M., 5 days a week, no charge. Only parts of Africa and Asia plus 1 South American nation require this. Certificates are good for 10 years.

Malaria is also still prevalent in some regions, including Morocco, Algeria, and much of the Middle East. Dr. Fitch recommends Aralen as an effective combatant. The World Health Organization also endorses Avloclor, Nivaquine, and Resochin. Plague immunization is still tricky and ineffectual. It is not recommended unless the visited country demands it.

Complete information on foreign immunization laws and U.S. reentry rules can be found in U.S. Public Health Service publication No. 384, *Immunization Information for International Travel* (U.S. Government Printing Office, 30¢).

Please consult your own physician if any special problems should arise.

§TIPS: Allow 8 weeks for the bulk of your shots.

If you are diabetic, allergic to penicillin, or have any physical condition that may require emergency care, *please don't fail to turn ahead to "Let's Be European"* for details on the lifesaving diagnostic tags of peerless, nonprofit Medic-Alert. Literally, it might mean your life.

LUGGAGE?   Take as little as possible. Pare down our following suggested list as far as your individual requirements will stand it—because the less you carry to Europe, the happier you'll travel and the more you can bring back.

A suitcase in good condition doesn't need reinforcement—but if your bag is at all old or fragile, it's mighty good sense to wrap a leather strap or belt tightly around the outside.

Nancy always tucks a 2-lb. folding canvas "Last Minute" case into her luggage at the start of every journey. It's shaped like a horse's feedbag, packs flat, and the weight is negligible. Gifts and bulky items collected on the road go into this special container—and her personal wearables and requisites are never jumbled or crowded. (If you can't find this, a routine military-style duffel bag will do.)

Since between 1% and 2% of *all* passengers' luggage carried by international airlines are misshipped or lost forever, tape your name and address on the upper *inside* lid of every piece you carry. Thus, if you disembark in Lisbon, but 1 bag should stay on the plane to Rome, the searchers there can spot it at once and fly it back to you instantly.

Finally, a timesaving and thief-parrying trick is to mark *all* your bags (even the overnight ones!) with your own private symbol in adhesive or miracle tape. The airport or hotel porter can then pull them out of the pile in a flash —and you're home free while others are bird-dogging.

FOR THE AIR TRAVELER: MALE   What clothes does a man take to today's Europe? What should he leave behind? How can he squeeze the last free ounce from his 66- or 44-lb. limit?

These questions—and many more—we have carefully studied with clothing experts and tested through years of field trial.

Now for our complete *cold-weather* wardrobe, *including all garments on the person of the passenger:*

  1 topcoat (see following paragraph)
  1 folding plastic raincoat, featherweight, sufficiently roomy to be slipped
    over topcoat
  2 wool knit or woven business suits (one dark) or 1 leisure suit and one
    business one
  1 sport jacket
  1 pair slacks, double-knit, flannel, or worsted
  2 pair shoes
  7 broadcloth or 3 drip-dry shirts
  9 pair socks
 15 handkerchiefs
  7 neckties
  6 sets underwear, shorts and tops
  3 pairs of pajamas
  1 robe, foulard or synthetic
  1 pair slippers, folding
  1 belt
  1 hat, neutral or dark shade, crushable (if worn)
  1 cashmere sweater
    Toilet kit
    Medicines and miscellaneous (see "Five-Star Indispensables")
    (Optional) Dinner coat and trousers, dress shoes, black socks, soft evening
    shirt, black tie, cuff links. Recommended *only* for extra-social types. The
    turtleneck fashion for evening wear has now faded away in Europe. Ruffles
    are A-okay from the Raffles to the Ritz.

If you're the *average* visitor who plans to stick to the major cities, a light, warm, cashmere-type topcoat will serve you infinitely better than a clumsy, bulky, stiff overcoat.

Double-knit cloth is especially recommended. It requires little or no pressing and is outstandingly durable. Jackets should have 2 inside pockets.

The sport jacket should be warm, wrinkle-resistant (little pressing), and of a dark pattern (no cleaning). A 3-button, easy-fitting model is the most comfortable; the extra inside pocket is helpful. If your trip is jet-propelled, take only drip-dry shirts. But if you're on a more routine schedule and staying in good hotels, the laundry is so fast (anywhere from 4 to 48 hours) that broadcloth is neater as the bulk of your supply. However, hotel laundry bills abroad can be downright wicked.

Leave your silk pajamas at home. The laundries might ruin them.

New shoes might make blisters. Tuck in an old, comfortable pair, too.

Ever try nonslip, waterproof full soles and heels, by the way? They're wonderful for international travel.

Sweater? Full-length sleeves. They'll feel mighty good at times.

For the *summer* or *warm-weather* traveler, here are the recommended substitutions:

If you're bound for North or Central Europe, or the mountains, nights will probably be so cool you'll want 1 *lightweight* wool suit—not winter weight.

In Mediterranean and southerly areas, at least 1 quick-dry suit is not only advised, but urged.

Tropical dinner clothes (only for socialites).

If desired, add bathing trunks.

The rest of the list should be your selections from the same items.

Paging all transatlantic-bound fellow-males—IMPORTANT!! In every large city in Europe and the British Isles, the mode of dress is strikingly more formal and conservative than in our casual and easygoing homeland. Rural sightseeing excursions are one thing—but if you're over 21, *never* stroll the boulevards of London, Paris, Rome, Madrid, or any other major center in your shirtsleeves.

FOR THE AIR TRAVELER: FEMALE A woman's international air wardrobe calls for even more ingenuity and flexibility than a man's. The following *basic* air wardrobe is recommended. As major building blocks, most seasoned transatlantic commuters swear by no-press dresses and separates for summer, knits and suits for winter, and a sheath dress year round. This list includes all the clothing worn by the traveler:

 1 coat
 1 suit
 1 pantsuit (if suitable to your figure)
 1 cocktail dress
 1 dress, stretch silk or similar "smashable"
 1 dress, "smashable" knit or wool
 3 pairs of shoes
 2 blouses
 1 bra and panties
 2 slips
 1 girdle (optional)
 2 nightgowns
12 pair stockings or panty hose
 1 sweater
 2 scarves
 1 hat
 1 robe
 1 pair slippers, folding
12 handkerchiefs
 3 purses
   Toilet articles and cosmetics
   Jewelry
   (Optional) Dinner dress and accessories

Naturally, your wardrobe must be designed for *your* travel needs. Based on this list, you can be smartly, freshly attired 24 hours a day.

§TIPS: Assuming that 1 outfit of the basic ensemble is worn, the balance should (but probably won't!) weigh, with suitcases, about 42 lbs.

Stick as closely as you can to 1 color scheme to mix and match for variety.

Use separate transparent plastic bags for gloves, bras, slips, hosiery, scarves, handkerchiefs, nighties—everything but dresses.

Wear your heaviest suit on the airplane.

Except specifically for beach or mountain resort use, don't take slacks or miniskirts unless you're built like Britt Ekland. On fat or plump gals (even in sun or snow centers), Europeans hate 'em!

Coats: Take an all-purpose coat and fur jacket (strictly optional). Carry them over your arm (in a zippered bag) or wear them so that they won't count on your allowance.

The "smashables" and "stretchables" are a boon to the woman traveler. Concentrate almost exclusively on these miracle fabrics for your overseas wardrobe.

For winter, tuck in 1 pair of woollies; for summer, don't forget your bathing suit.

Always include that "good little black dress" *(sic!)*—preferably the one with short sleeves in a "smashable." You'll need it for cocktail dates, dinner parties, and special occasions.

Wise travelers say *shoes* are the most important item. Take 2 pairs for walking and 1 pair for glamour, even to Paris or London. And be sure that at least 1 is an old, comfortable, and thoroughly broken-in low-heel model.

The quality of your clothes should be carefully considered. If, your oldest non-"smashable" suit is in good condition, don't pick up something newer—and of poorer material—just for the trip. Travel is hard on clothes; be sure yours are durable and will hold their shape.

Sweaters, scarves, and jewelry are invaluable. A cashmere and/or synthetic sweater set is especially recommended. With 2 scarves and your jewelry, you can do a lot of tricks in changing your appearance.

A soft crushable hat packs easily; so do turbans.

Cosmetics: If not packaged this way, transfer your makeup to plastic containers. Squeezing the sides of the container a bit as you put on the top creates suction and makes it more leakproof. Most women travelers overload on beauty preparations; don't fall into this trap, because you can buy practically anything you need from one end of Europe to the other.

Back to luggage. Take 2 bags—plus 1 makeup kit (heartily unrecommended, unless you can't stand life without it)—and not a single piece more.

Pocketbook? Get a *big* purse. Don't buy the horse's feedbag type; everything sloshes around the bottom. Stick to the kind with ample zippered compartments and side pockets.

FIVE-STAR INDISPENSABLES—AND TUCK-INS Far, far too many transatlantic travelers—especially first-timers—pack their bags as if they were checking into the Ritz in Paris for a month or trekking from Malawi to Burundi. This parade of pretty, shiny, useless junk is pathetic—cruelly expensive in overweight charges, and a built-in booby trap to touring comfort and freedom.

Today's Europe is *loaded* with luxury and utility goods of almost every description. Most cities now offer almost anything the visitor might wish. U.S. name brands are sold at a premium—but if you're willing to go along with foreign (particularly Common Market) counterparts, you can save plenty of headaches, space, and money. This applies to soap, cosmetics, chocolates, reading material, toilet articles, liquor—nearly everything.

A few typically American products are either difficult or impossible to find abroad, however—and these are the ones that are either mandatory or pleasant to take along if a corner can be spared.

Here, to us, are the absolute *musts*—urgently recommended to all overseas vacationers, regardless of routings or budgets:

A copy of *Speaking You English?* by Kenneth R. Morgan (Fielding Publications, $6.95), the funniest and most unorthodoxly helpful travel book we have ever enjoyed in our lives. Its highly personalized style is wickedly critical whenever deserved, consistently hilarious, irresistibly readable, and remarkably uninhibited in its attack on the genteel touristic hypocrisies which face any voyager abroad. It parades a robust appetite for life and an irreverence for prevailing pieties while upholding an impeccable standard of literary judgment. Even after nearly 3 decades of globetrotting, we find it not only delightful but invaluable. Please don't miss it!

An extra pair of spectacles (and the prescription!), if you use 'em.

The most reputable, most famous, American-made windproof lighter you can buy. Matches are often hard to get, and this heavy-duty lighter is an absolute must for the traveler. (Slip a few extra flints inside, under its top roll of stuffing.) Various similar U.S. makes, gas jobs and others simply aren't built to deliver the goods when you are fighting to light a cigarette on a breezy esplanade.

A money clip. European bills are often too large for an American wallet.

An electric shaver can be a trial abroad unless you are equipped to cope with current-and-socket problems. If you are about to buy a new one, choose an international model which allows you to switch from 110 to 220 to (sometimes) an intermediate voltage; the cordless type is yet another convenient slayer of whiskers. Remember that you might need at least 2 types of adapter plugs. Your American product must have one of several adapter kits available. Repair is available for most makes in major cities, from private, not company-operated, agencies.

A soap container and a bar of toilet soap which fits it. Some European hotels below Deluxe category do not furnish this necessity—merely custom, because plenty is available everywhere. You can restock abroad.

A pencil or key-ring flashlight—strictly pocket-size. European illumination isn't American illumination, and this might come in handy.

If they insist upon U.S products, enough intimate supplies for the ladies of the party to last the entire trip. But similarly designed and equally reliable local brands, as well as our own, are easily available all over the Continent.

Kao-Con (concentrated Kaopectate in a plastic bottle or, even better, the tablet form if you can find it) and a medicinal corker labeled Polymagma, or whatever product your own doctor might prescribe (hopefully his choice will be one which is available from druggists on the Continent). Chances are good that you'll pick up diarrhea from change of diet or change of water (tainted food is rare these days). If you don't have one of these compounds to use instantly, you'd be in trouble. An old-timer, Entero-Vioform, has been linked by Japanese scientists to severe nerve and ocular disorders. The American Medical Association advises caution—as well as the avoidance of local drinking water whenever one is in doubt. (WARNING: Please, please take heed that many of these drugs are lethal to pets.)

Head-cold miseries? Sinutab or Emprazil might do wonders to fluff up the spirits and buck up the patient. Actifed, a sniffle-fighter used by our Astronauts, is an excellent nasal decongestant.

Sleeping pills—if you're the type who flirts with the Sandman.

Tongue-tied? Blue Cross publishes a handy pamphlet titled *A Foreign Language Guide to Health Care* which can convert your anglicized aches or pains into pelucid French, German, Italian, or Spanish laments. With this you can find out what ails you in 4 dimensions. Ask for it through Blue Cross or Blue Shield.

Smokers should pack the maximum permissible limit of cigarettes, cigars, or pipe tobacco, except if they cross on TWA or the scant other airlines which sell them aboard tax-free. Ask your travel agent. You'll find U.S. cigarettes in every nation—at up to $2.25 per package. Pipe tobacco is sometimes almost impossible to find. (Spain, is one example).

For *tuck-ins,* 1 or 2 of the following might strike your fancy. *None of them is a necessity, in any sense*—but if weight and other factors permit, selected samples might add to your touring comfort:

A special wallet for your passport—excellent protection against misplacement or loss. At the better leather-goods shops from $15.

A travel-type alarm clock or watch. See *Fielding's Selective Shopping Guide to Europe* ($3.50) for our comments about these.

Five or 6 extra passport photos, in case you should need a driver's license, visa, ski-lift card, or goodness knows *what* strange document.

Toilet paper? Here, from Dr. Kenneth R. Morgan's hilarious *Speaking You English? A Lighthearted Guide to World Travel,* published by Fielding Publications, Inc., is this deadly accurate description of the more common European varieties: "Foreign toilet paper falls into 3 categories: (A) wrapping-paper type, (b) crepe-paper type, and (c) wax-paper type. It is therefore very useful for (a) wrapping small packages, (b) Christmas decorations, or (c) storing food in the refrigerator." If your hotel stock comes in these forms, almost always locally you can buy something softer than #5-grade sandpaper. Some take a roll along, crushing it flat—but today this is unneccessary.

A purse-size tape measure, with both inches and centimeters. Most gals buy European linens, for example—and whipping out one of these will forestall endless yakety-yak and scribblings about feet, yards, and meters.

A tiny, self-inking rubber stamp bearing your name and stateside address, for foreign envelopes, hotel registers, and other documents en route. Available in major stationery stores; timesaving for the gadget-minded.

A soothing antacid such as Mylanta, in liquid or tablet form (the latter travels better). Wine tends to sour the stomachs of travelers not accustomed to it, and you'll probably drink plenty before you're through.

A couple of dozen (or more!) tiny, nearly weightless envelopes of a facial freshener and invigorator—exactly the thing for sticky hands, grimy faces, and stiff necks at the end of a tiring train, plane, or bus trip. A 2nd type has been saturated with a cleansing, antiseptic, and deodorant lotion for those difficult days (it does not function as a substitute for the sanitary napkin); also practical for toilet seats and doorknobs of public restrooms abroad.

At least 1 box (20 foil-wrapped, 1-shot packages) of a *cold*-water detergent. Find a brand which *prefers* cold water and which will dissolve instantly in brick-hard liquid.

A sleep shade and wax earplugs—helpful for light sleepers on the transatlantic flight and in the noisier European hotels.

For walkers, vigorous shophounds and sightseers, and heavy perspirers, an antiseptic foot powder. Salt tablets (ask your druggist) are also splendid for reviving flagging energies in Mediterranean regions during the summer.

For rural excursionists in hot countries, an insect-repellent.

Carry one of the most indispensable items—a corkscrew.

A collapsible cup, outdoorsman's-style, for that railway compartment, excursion bus, or other thirsty moments when there are Bottles Only.

For the very latest developments in hot-from-the-factory travel gadgets, drop in at wonderful Hammacher Schlemmer (145 E. 57th St., N.Y.) and have a chat with President Dominic Tampone who spends much of his day on the sales floors. He happily gives his personal welcome to friends of this *Guide.*

Gifts? The U.S. or Canadian "smashables" and "stretchables" in women's wear, plus drip-dry items of all types, are greeted with smiles all over the Continent. At this writing, they are still relatively costly abroad. New gadgets of *any* kind—for the house, car, office, sports, anything—are almost bound to be successful: if you make sure that it's new, that it's streamlined, that it rattles, pops, grunts, roars, lights up, or plays music, that's it. Unusual beachwear (bathing caps, robes, bags, and the like) is appreciated; so are gift subscriptions to such U.S. magazines as *National Geographic, Vogue, Harper's Bazaar,* and *House and Garden,* or those with a format for the hobbies of your recipient, such as *Gourmet, Mechanix Illustrated, Travel and Leisure,* and *Field & Stream*—or, if his or her hobby is more biological, *Playboy* (banned in Spain) or *Cosmopolitan,* perhaps.

Actually, over the years, the most consistently welcome small gift we've ever found to please European friends is the famous aforementioned wind-proof lighter with the recipient's signature engraved across its front. Many nations have match monopolies; this makes the possession of a lighter almost mandatory for the smoker—and how they love it, when it bears their own handwriting! The price for the whole works is around $5. A ½-dozen plain ones, without engraving, might also be carried for an expression of appreciation to officials or citizens abroad who have broken their backs to be helpful (as some will!)—and who won't accept money. (In 3 decades of roaming we've found this such a hit that we asked the factory how many we had purchased at full price and given away all over the world. To our amazement, the answer was "more than 1000." THAT'S how much we like it—so much, in fact, that we're going to dent our rigid rule against listing brand names of U.S. products by dropping the hint that this lighter starts with Zip—oh, you've got it!) Urgent tip: *The transparent plastic type of lighter should not be used in flight.* Pressure variations can turn it into a torch.

Declare all your gifts as personal property; as presents, most foreign Customs will hook you with a fat gift tax.

MISCELLANEOUS TIPS No magazines, if you're flying. They weigh plenty, and you'll find all you can read on the plane.

When bound for the airport, stuff your pockets (or pocketbook) to over-flowing with the heaviest items you can find. If you're really in a jam with excess pounds, seal up the sleeves of your topcoat or raincoat with safety pins and fill up the arms; it's cheating, but you might get away with it. Then, just before you weigh in, throw *all* your coats over your shoulders, so that you are technically "wearing" them. It may look ridiculous to the spectators, but ignore 'em (One extra-skinny—or is it skinflint?—reader even goes as far as suggesting that men's socks stuffed with the weightiest possessions be tied to an under-belt around the waist!) The point is this: *You* don't count, but every ounce of your baggage is a pearl beyond price.

After your U.S. return, *don't* send cigarette lighters, liquor, synthetics, expensive mechanical gadgets, or similar items in appreciation for courtesies extended during your trip. *If* European Customs will admit them (liquor and lighters by mail are almost universally prohibited, for example), the duties might be murderous for your friends.

MONEY   At this writing it no longer pays, in most cases, to try to beat other local rates of exchange by outside bank purchases in countries where the currency is strong. The European market nowadays simply is too fickle for safe speculation in sizable amounts. But in parts of Africa or practically anywhere in the Far East, it would help to pick up the maximum amounts you can legally carry across these borders, before your departure from the United States. You can save anywhere from 5% to 50%—extra cash dropped into your lap, for extra fun en route.

All European airports have 24-hour banks where you can exchange dollars or traveler's checks for local currency. If you can't wait for tipping change, cab fare, or some folding money, hike to Perera Company, Inc., 636 Fifth Ave. (Rockefeller Center), New York, or the downtown office at 29 Broadway for one of their "Pre-Packs" containing applicable coins and notes. Their whopping commission is 10%, but it's soothing if you're the worrying kind. This company, also has dispenser machines at Kennedy and maintains an office in the main lobby. We've received howls of outrage from departing travelers that these devices too often don't function properly. Because of the aforementioned 24-hour airport banks abroad, please don't overbuy.

A few foreign currencies (subject to change) are mutually "convertible." This means, quite simply, that in exchange for your American traveler's checks within these nations, you may draw any hard monies including our greenbacks. You may also buy traveler's checks valid in francs, marks, or others at foreign-exchange houses in the major cities of the U.S. or Canada, or at most U.S. international airports.

Always cash your checks at a bank abroad, not in your hotel. The hotel's rakeoff can be 20% or even 25%.

But we still find it easier and wiser to carry about $200 in U.S. currency, and the balance in (1) traveler's checks, (2) free-market foreign currencies for those countries not party to these currency reforms, and (3) personal checks. Internationally recognized credit cards (American Express, Diners' Club, etc.) have become almost "must" items in these days of volatile currency reforms. Warning: Although legions upon legions of hotels, restaurants, shops, and other establishments abroad will accept at least one of them, many top-line places still turn thumbs down on all.

CURRENCY AND METRIC CONVERTER   Now for the conversion of

foreign money, and a solution—*Fielding's World Currency and Metric Converter*—that instantly translates U.S. and foreign currencies *anywhere in the world,* and is so flexible that it will *never go out of date!* Wherever you go in foreign lands, the man-across-the-counter will smile blandly and mutter, "You owe me 1675 francs," or "29 guilders," or "22,380 lire," or something equally baffling. The poor American traveler, particularly the country-hopping variety, goes into a spin like this: "If 1 escudo is worth 3.35¢, call it 3¢, divide 3 into 878 escudos . . ." and out come the pencil and the shiny little beads of perspiration.

So many readers of this book found themselves stymied that they wrote in to ask for a shortcut, and we've finally come up with a device that does the job with gratifying efficiency.

This pocket-size gadget quickly converts the currency of any country in the world into dollars—or dollars into any foreign currency. Operation of the low-cost *Fielding's World Currency Converter* is simple: You merely set a sliding scale so that the U.S. dollar is aligned with the foreign currency unit —and read across to convert any amount. Because the sliding scale can be set for any exchange rate, floating currencies are no problem—you simply reset the scale as exchange rates change.

As a supplement, on the reverse side you'll find *Fielding's World Metric Converter,* which instantly converts U.S. and metric measurements in the most common categories you'll encounter as a traveler: miles, pounds, ounces, gallons, inches, yards, and temperature.

You should find this red-white-and-blue converter beside the cash register of your local bookshop—if not, ask them to stock it for the convenience of other travelers as well.

YOUR TRAVEL ARRANGEMENTS Now let's lay aside all the rich excitement and glamour surrounding your journey—gently, so that we don't bruise or hurt it!—and get down to actual mechanics: By which travel method are you planning to go?

There are 3 choices open to you—as a trailblazer, as a so-called F.I.T., or as a member of an escorted tour. Let's examine each of these carefully, because your decision here might make or break your trip:

As a trailblazer (a term coined for convenience), you'd be 100% on your own. If you already know Europe well—and, most important, *if you nail down and copper-rivet every routing, date, transportation booking, and hotel reservation before your departure from America*—you'll probably have a wonderful holiday, with fun most or all of the way. But if this is your first trip abroad you're almost bound to run into certain headaches, snarls, and disappointments. In Off Season it's relatively easy—but in today's High Season rat race, particularly in the popular tourist spots, the well-meaning but fumbling amateur is often licked before departure. *And* "High Season" has now spread into early spring and late autumn!

The F.I.T. category (trade jargon for "Foreign Independent Trip") is ideal for the first-time or unsure new vacationer who wants freedom of movement combined with expert protection. Here's how this works: Merely tell your travel agent where you want to go, how many days you can spare, and how much you can pry out of the piggy bank for the expedition. That's all. When you leave, he'll hand you your complete string of tickets, a tailor-made itinerary that lists dates, times, train numbers, hotels, transfers, the works, and a book of voucher coupons with which you'll "pay" practically every bill you'll encounter. If you wish to have a friendly face greet you at each airport or station and take over your burdens, that's easy too. Naturally, since you're the boss, you'll be booked exactly where and how you specify—and you've a far better chance, especially in High Season, of getting into the most desirable places than you generally have. You'll pay a percentage more if you go as an F.I.T., of course—but you've got professional brains guarding your interests every hour of every day, and the headaches it saves are beyond price.

On an escorted tour, you don't even have to know that Paris is in France or that the Matterhorn isn't a tuba. It's that simple. If you're a stranger to the Continent, or if you're lonely, lazy, gregarious, fun-loving, or shy—any of 10-dozen reasons—here might be the perfect answer for your requirements. Parties run from 15 to 30, with 25 about average. A lump sum must be paid in advance. This usually takes care of the entire trip—every blessed thing except your tips, wines, liquors, laundry, gambling, gifts, snacks between meals, and 1759 other extras which always pop up to plague you.

It can be a beautifully serene way to go, because all of your problems are supposed to be solved by an experienced third party, the company official in charge of the group. If things are working right, *he* will fight with porters, scream at taxi drivers, bludgeon room clerks when reservations are snafued. Everything is arranged, down to your last Mona Lisa. At the end of the trip, incidentally, don't forget to give the tour conductor either a healthy tip or a decent gift—the nature and the value depending upon the price category of the tour, its duration, and the personality, kindness, and attention involved. Both the sponsoring company and your native tact should help your decision here.

Scores of agencies specialize in this field of travel. Prices vary. If you pick the right operator, you can see more of Europe under better conditions for less money than you could possibly do alone—a bargain which no individual tourist could touch. It has just *got* to be cheaper for any firm to set up a tour for 25 simultaneous bookings: Hotels, railways, restaurants, and other facilities give special discounts, 1 truck and 2 men can handle 50 suitcases, 1 bus can do the work of 10 taxis, and so on. Of course you're paying an extra fee for the services of your group shepherd and for the tremendous organizational work which goes into the project, but when this is watered down to your share, 1/25th of the total, it's a mosquito bite. There are dozens of fine houses in the field which function on small margins and which deliver the goods. If you should pick a greedy operator, however, you might pay as much as 30% to 40% more than you would by covering the same ground on an independent basis. Once again, it's all a matter of (1) choosing the right travel agent, and (2) making sure he books you with the right tour company.

PICKING YOUR TRAVEL AGENT   As in all major fields of commerce, the travel-agency business has every type of operator, from superfine to bad.

First in size and in renown are the giants: American Express, Thomas Cook, and AAA World-Wide Travel, Inc. Some carpers feel that (1) their F.I.T. facilities are spotty—excellent in some countries but miserable in others, (2) personalization of their services sometimes suffers gravely because the client is just 1 more name on a roster of thousands, and (3) some (not all) of their charges are steep. On banking matters, the first 2 are so superb that they brook no competition abroad. And not even their severest critic could deny that they're vastly widespread, their integrity is unquestioned, and they're as solid as Mount Everest.

Next in importance and in solidity are the 25 or 30 Old Reliable tour companies—the pacesetters, the Elder Statesmen of this highly complex trade. Most of them are members of a potent regulatory organization called the Creative Tour Operators Association. In any of these you'll find expert guidance, heavy experience, and absolute honesty.

Then comes the backbone and bulk of the field—the small, earnest, hard-working retail agencies in almost every city or town of North America. Maybe it's not as venerable or as big as the Giants or the Old Reliables, but as their local representative it can always call upon them for advice. Most break their backs to add a large helping of happiness to its clients' holidays. With few exceptions, it'll steer you right for standard fees. See this hometown operator first, once you're satisfied that he's not a fly-by-night—because you'll have face-to-face attention, which is always the best.

Finally there are the sharpies, deadbeats, and thieves—fortunately rare. This breed is few in number, but if one of them gets you in his grasp, probabilities are high that these villains will milk you for fantastic charges, ruin your trip, and break your heart.

Which operator should you select? Here are several broad yardsticks:

The first criterion you should look for is membership in the American Society of Travel Agents (ASTA). This venerable, nonprofit federation of top travel and transportation companies is the standard-bearer of the industry. Its 7500-member roster is broken down into regional and local chapters, so that all new applicants can be judged by their peers instead of by a remote headquarters; candidates are hand-picked, and requirements are stringent. No one could say that *all* good agents belong to ASTA, because there are dozens of reputable houses which don't; somewhere within this non-ASTA classification, however, you'll find most of the newcomers, mavericks, border-line operators, and out-and-out wolves. By the same token, membership in ASTA isn't a flat guarantee that at least 1 member won't try hard to pry the gold fillings right out of your mouth; it's just a mighty good *indication* of the soundness of the operator. *Look for the ASTA seal*—a big, cross-hatched globe with "ASTA" emblazoned across its face—whenever you visit a travel agent's office. If he hasn't got it, possibly he's still all right—but an outside checkup is suggested, just to make certain you haven't fallen from that 97% bracket of square shooters into that 3% bracket of racketeers.

The second criterion is membership in other professional organizations—International Air Transport Association, Trans-Atlantic Conference, and so on. This may mean exactly zero. The slipperiest, most unsavory firm I ever found in the travel industry (now bankrupt and soiling the trade no more, thank heavens!) belonged for nearly 10 years to IATA, ATC, TAPC, TPC, and WHPC—until IATA far too late, caught up with it. Here was an extreme case, admittedly, but the police powers of these alliances are all sadly inadequate when it comes to expelling the occasional bunko artist. So don't count too much on the string of letters after an agent's name.

The third criterion is local reputation: Other businessmen, your Chamber of Commerce, or your Better Business Bureau can tell you in general whether he's substantial or fly-by-night.

The fourth is price: Are his charges routine, or does he scale them up? A little shopping around can determine this if any dark suspicions in this direction should cross your mind when he quotes the costs. (Airline ticketing today, however, is so complex that even airline reservations personnel frequently commit bloopers on billings.)

The fifth is his familiarity with the area he is selling: Does he have *current, firsthand knowledge,* or is he glibly rephrasing a pamphlet he has read? This is important, because last year's European picture is fantastically different from this year's picture—to which, as one minor example, each annual 200-thousand-word-plus revision of this book attests.

The sixth—always the soundest one—is contact with a previous client. If he did a bangup job for Mabel and Bob Smith last year, chances are excellent he'll repeat it for you. If you are *sure* that your hometown travel agent fulfills all the above requirements, he's the man you should visit straightaway, because he can unquestionably do the best job for you.

If you're not sure, here's an alternate suggestion that might help you. After successive years of pleasant association with 2 illustrious and fine houses, I've now switched to a small group of dynamic experts whose first love is *individual itineraries*—a step which seems better in line with the requirements of readers of this book.

From the top candidates, without hesitation we have picked Don Travel Service, Inc., Suite 1904, 375 Park Ave., N.Y. 10022 (Telephone 212 PL2–4020). In honest analysis, this company is probably no more reliable, hard-working, or alert than a dozen of its high-level competitors. What excites us here, instead, is its combination of rare qualities which seem tailor-made for friends of the *Guide* who happen to like what we like:

By offering higher employee incentives than any agency we know, hand-some, dynamic, warm Founder-Owner-President Charles E. Benisch 17 years ago fielded a ball-bearing-oiled team whose experience, vigor, and interest in the traveler is extraordinary. They know, and they *care*. Europe is their most special love. They try to learn everything pertinent about each prospective tripper before suggesting his or her totally personalized journey. Topping their affiliations with correspondent-agents throughout the world, full-time Don Travel experts are permanently based in London, Paris, and Brussels to be at your call. Their roster of clients who either go for fun or combine business with pleasure is probably the most distinguished on the Eastern Seaboard. They are large enough to swing important weight but small enough so that you would be a staffwide worry, not another faceless unit on the production line.

If you'd prefer to join a group instead of striking out alone, Don Travel Service can easily handle this too. In today's blizzard of package propaganda, these whiz-bangs sift out the dross. Your own selection is the result of tireless consultation, research, and rechecking by artisans in a highly specialized and often dangerously devious craft. The sum is contented, pretested grazing for you—anywhere you roam.

This operation impresses us so much that I recently accepted the unpaid honor of a seat on its Board of Directors and to become an active consultant and working associate. Naturally your inquiries cost nothing—but once you might involve these busy and highly paid specialists in spending their hours in making up your individualized itineraries and in otherwise dispensing their detailed wisdom, the normal $25 deposit, subtracted when your plans are finalized, would be requested. If your own travel agent (whom you should consult first) doesn't happen to come up with what you want, write to Mr. Benisch, or drop in to see him if you visit New York. You won't get the millennium or a miracle, but he, his on-the-ball associates, and we will give you everything all of us know.

TAKEOFF BY PLANE   New York, Boston, Chicago, Los Angeles, San Francisco, Dallas, Washington, Houston, Detroit, Philadelphia, Miami, and Montreal are among the major North American stations for transatlantic air traffic. You can fly direct from any of these, without changing planes.

The New York East Side Airlines Terminal is on First Avenue between 37th and 38th Streets. Here's the midtown center for most major carriers.

From Montreal and Toronto there are frequent schedules by Air Canada, BA, KLM, and Air France. If you're from the southern states, this is a slick way to go because it gives you a look at our great northern neighbor.

At the appointed time (probably in midafternoon, and try to arrive fresh because "jet fatigue" from switching time zones can sap your energies far faster than you might think), you'll report to the meeting place designated by your carrier. The Passenger Service representative takes over from here; you should (but sometimes won't) find him affable, courteous, and cooperative. Your ticket is inspected; countermen weigh and check your baggage. Hang on to your overnight bag; here's the place they'll try to grab it for cargo.

The special bus service to Kennedy Airport gets you there on time, come hell or high water. The fare is $4 out of *your* pocket, not the airline's, and travel time to the International Terminal is normally from 45 to 60 minutes. (Don't park your own car out here because garage fees alone could almost buy you another country on your itinerary.)

For the average tripper there is no outgoing Customs inspection. (Items purchased for the commercial use of others, or items being exported under a bill of lading, must be cleared, however.) It's just about as easy as climbing aboard a flight for Dallas or Miami.

§TIPS: Traveler's insurance and baggage insurance? We'd strongly advise— no, urge—you to take out both merely as routine, if you'll forgive us for being so bold. For *international flight insurance,* there are many choices, including comprehensive accident protection anywhere in the world—24 hours per day, land, sea, or air. The *baggage* insurance policies are, as usual, full of fine-print "buts," "excepts," "doesn't apply," and "valid ONLY if lost by a cross-eyed Mongolian coolie aboard a sampan."

Don't count on the prolonged existence of insurance counter service at airports. The Pilots' Association has now activated a powerful campaign to push these facilities completely out, because "They make it too easy for crackpots to get spur-of-the-moment ideas," in its opinion. Who'll win? Our money is on the skippers.

Camera: If you're taking along a Contax, Rolleiflex, or *any* photo apparatus of foreign manufacture, register it with your nearest United States Customs or with the Bureau at the airport or dock. No charge. Otherwise you might pay 15% to 20% import duty on return. American cameras are exempt.

Leica is a bit tricky. While the stateside company warmly assists the traveler who takes his U.S.-purchased Leica abroad, *only* 1 European-purchased Leica with 1 attached lens may be brought back by each voyager.

Pets: Through the A.S.P.C.A.'s Animalport at Kennedy, you can arrange to ship your pet, be it a dog, cat, baboon, or hippopotamus, to your overseas destination, where it will be awaiting your arrival. Or you can take it with you on the same plane as excess baggage. Be sure to check quarantine regulations of the countries you will visit. Your boxer or Siamese, for example, will now pine its heart out for *one year* in a cage in the United Kingdom; in Denmark, the term is 6 months. Department stores, specialists, or the A.S.P.-C.A. will furnish you with a crate. Daily board at the Animalport runs from pennies for a bird to heftier charges for an elephant. Air-cargo rates are infinitely cheaper than those for excess baggage. As a final suggestion, consult the A.S.P.C.A. or Pan Am's *Petiquette* booklet for further information and hints.

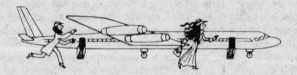

Reminders: Don't tip on airlines. Following special kindnesses from employees, write a note of appreciation to the president of the company, instead.

If you should be stuck by bad weather at Gander, Shannon, or elsewhere, that's hard luck for the carrier's exchequer, not yours. They'll pay your hotel bill, extra meals, all basic incidentals, praise be—regardless of the class of your flight. For information on possible recovery of damages for being "bumped off" a flight, please turn to "Let's Go By Plane."

All set? Okay, now that you're ready, let's think about being European.

Let's Be European

Europe is a fascinating checkerboard. Each nation has its own customs, its own quirks. It's just as if between Austin and Amarillo you were to find 3 languages and 3 cultures—each new. (Even Texas isn't *that* different!)

Here are a few generalities for today's traveler. They were learned the hard way—so careful reading is suggested.

PERMISSION TO BREATHE All Western European countries allow U.S. citizens free entry for *maximum visits of 2 to 6 months; 3 is the average.* If you plan to stay longer *anywhere, check with your concierge about visa requirements before your first 60 days are up.*

MONEY As mentioned earlier, we recommend that your funds be broken down 4 ways: (1) U.S. currency, (2) dollar traveler's checks, (3) free-market currencies purchased in America, Switzerland, or Lebanon for countries not party to recent reforms, and (4) personal checks on your hometown bank.

Credit cards? At this writing, the wickedest brawl in the travel industry continues to rage over control of the burgeoning European market. With battle lines still so fluid, we're compelled to abstain from making one overall recommendation. Personally, we use American Express and Diner's Club regularly, and both play helpful roles in our marathon journeyings. Despite tub-thumping advertising claims, no one—repeat, no one—yet offers a "universal" credit card, or anything that remotely approaches it. We have also previously noted that a substantial number of Europe's most distinguished institutions still won't touch any of these fine organizations. Some honor only Eurocard, a newish venture which, according to them, takes a smaller bite from their exchequers. Incidentally, if you hold an Amexco card (or if you book through them), you can still receive mail from home at the overseas American Express branches. Otherwise this lifesaving service has been curtailed. What a pity!

If your references are impeccable, your aura is prosperous, and you don't illuminate the lobby with a hula-hula sport shirt, hotel credit managers abroad will sometimes (not always!) accept your personal check. Since $5000 in traveler's checks costs a fat $50, here's a smart potential saving.

But *some* dollar traveler's checks are a necessity—and you should buy *only* from the biggest of big-name institutions. Dozens of international financial houses are reliable, but you might have the devil's own time proving it to hotelkeepers and department-store managers. The top-line giants are known to most of the little people; there's seldom any question about their validity.

For cash transfers, if all goes normally, nothing matches American Express' fast and efficient cable service; in hours, not days, they can and do forward funds to travelers in any part of the world—except, possibly, Spain. (Spanish banking laws are so snarled that transfers of U.S. traveler's checks take up to 5 weeks!) Because every foreign or domestic office is staffed by human beings, goofs *do* occur—but these are refreshingly rare. If your problems are special ones, go to their New York office at 61 West 51 St.; it has saved the lives of many frantic voyagers.

§TIP: When you enter a country, your greenbacks will take care of your expenses until you reach a bank. (Air passengers can almost always convert currencies at airports, but rail trippers aren't always so lucky. Incidentally, don't change *all* of your lucre at the airport; we've discovered that the midtown banks often offer a better rate). When you leave a country, a little folding money will handle your breakfast, taxi, porters, and small outgoing expenses. Since traveler's checks come in units of $10 or more, you're not stuck with a fistful of leftover bills.

Leftover European *change* is a far thornier problem. Surplus bills can normally be passed in the next country, but people just sniff at your foreign change. Get rid of *all* coins (except souvenirs) before crossing the border.

CUSTOMS OFFICIALS Most Customs officials are human beings, even as you and I; a few of them are skunks. None is very fussy with American tourists these days; you might sail through your entire tour through the "Nothing To Declare" gatepaths, if you're lucky, without 1 bag being checked. The speed of your clearance usually depends upon the inspector's state of digestion. Here are some helpful hints:

"Name, rank, and serial number *only,*" as they used to say in the Army. Be affable and cooperative, but button your lip. Their sole interest is to get rid of you; if you keep your mouth shut, things will move twice as fast.

Hold your U.S. passport casually in hand—don't flaunt it!—so that the inspector can identify you. (This might sound absurd, but sometimes it's surprisingly helpful.) And speak English solely, *not* a foreign language.

Liquor in your luggage: Break the seals before you get to Customs. In some lands (British Isles excepted) this may get around the import duty. Some countries forbid more than 1. If you have an extra, stick it in the pocket of the overcoat that hangs "carelessly" over your arm.

The Common Market nations have upped and standardized travelers' allowances on duty-free items. Now officially they permit 300 cigarettes, 1½ liters of hard liquor (2 "fifth" bottles should pass), 3 liters (¾-gallon) of wine, 1⅓ lbs. of coffee, and ¼ lb. of tea. However, they are seldom closely scanned.

Gifts for European friends: Let Customs assume they're personal belongings (unless you don't mind paying a tax on each item). In any case, make them ask *you* the status of the articles.

U.S. Customs men are astonishingly conscientious and cheerful, considering the fact that 10-thousand of them do the job that it should take 25-thousand to achieve. They have the legal right to examine *every* piece of luggage carried by *every* traveler; generally, however, they'll spot-check your possessions. To save their time (and get you through faster), carry all your European purchases in 1 bag—and don't cheat a penny's worth, because they're experts at snaring fibbers.

These experts are probing deeper than ever before into hidden corners in a deliberate move to control skyjacking and halt the inflow of narcotics from abroad. "Blitz" checks are being made to control and discourage the tidal flood of drugs. Naturally, you might be delayed by these vital measures, but any traveler of goodwill will certainly cooperate 100% with these overloaded officials.

Major reforms in clearance procedures have been made. An oral declaration system is in effect at all international airports under U.S. jurisdiction, including San Juan Airport. (Now you'll also find it abroad in London, Amsterdam, Zürich, Geneva, and many other major points of entry.) Under this innovation the traveler simply fills out a short form identifying himself, the carrier, accompanying members of the family, and the date—that's all. Only total purchases abroad exceeding $100 per person must be listed. In the terminus choose between the "Nothing To Declare" lane and walk straight out—or the conventional one. (Perhaps unknown to them, people are watched closely in the former.) If the baggage is inspected, they should start by telling the agent how they have exceeded the limitation. In addition, single-officer inspection (to consolidate all matters of immigration, Customs, agriculture, and public health) has cut down processing time at Kennedy. Other changes such as taxing all articles at a single percentage rate, ending "every bag" inspection except in cases of criminal suspicion, and eliminating the "unnecessary harassment" of foreigners have also been recommended. The commissioner, Vernon D. Acree, a genial fair-but-tough 3-decade-plus IRS veteran with an outstanding law enforcement and administrative background, is injecting even more vitality into the veins of this semisclerotic 180-odd-year-old agency. He's doing a commendable job for which he should be congratulated.

Anyone out of the States for more than 48 hours may bring in $100 (retail value) in merchandise without charge. These goods must accompany you personally on your return. Your free importation of wines or booze is 1 quart per person 21 years or over—a monument to the enormous power of the U.S. liquor lobby in Washington. Most states admit more than a quart if a modest duty is paid on the overage; others, such as California, confiscate all extra spirits. (Since beverages, regardless of quantity, are part of your $100 deduction, this odorous damned foolishness has absolutely no bearing on the balance-of-payments question—and the traveler is made the sucker.) Here are a few points to remember: (1) To repeat: *Each individual* is given the maximum amount. You may pool with any member of your family, including infants-in-arms. (2) You may continue to send an unlimited number of under-$10 (fair retail value) gifts from abroad to U.S. friends (more about this below). (3) Most important, European prices are often sufficiently lower so that you can slap down full duty on many of your purchases and *still* save money. As of now, approximate tariffs are: Cameras (if lens is not chief value) are taxed at only 7½% (6% for motion picture cameras), cut but unset stones only 0% to 5%, wooden furniture only 5% (chairs 8.5%), "temporarily" strung cultured pearls, *without a Hachea clasp,* only 2.5%—and many more items are pegged at the same moderate levels. A foreign-born typewriter, incidentally, is admitted without any tax bite. The '77 edition of *Fielding's Shopping Guide to Europe* ($3.50) contains further listings and details; sorry, space is too tight here. Your U.S. merchant must pay exactly the same duties as you pay, plus high brokerage fees, transportation, and agency profit margins—before adding his own markup of 40%, 70%, or even 100%. By the time you buy it from him, therefore, it's most often fatally higher than if you'd bought it yourself at the source and paid duty.

HELP, PLEASE! If you have any blind friends or relatives, we would be profoundly grateful if you would tell them that they can now get their talented hands on a braille edition of "Customs Hints for Returning U.S. Residents" in which the allowances, rules, and exemptions are explained. All Customs regional offices and 50 libraries in the U.S. that cooperate with the blind and the handicapped stock these booklets in braille. Deepest thanks!

Regarding other regulations, here are some key facts and suggestions: (1) Go easy on those Coronas for the boss or that bubble water for the blonde or blond, because 100 cigars and one quart per person of alcoholic beverages are all you may import without fee (*foreign-made* cigarettes are unlimited, however)—and remember they'll grab your liquor if they think you're going to use it in violation of your local state or county laws. With certain limitations, booze may be "shipped to follow." (2) Foreign fruits, meats, plants, and vegetables are the kiss of death. Because that harmless-looking salami or those shiny grapes or that beautiful little potted shamrock might carry pests which could destroy millions of dollars in livestock, food, forests, or ornamentals, virtually all are confiscated. Most foreign-made eatables are banned unless all ingredients are printed on the label. (3) Your exemptions may include alterations or repairs on anything you originally took abroad; if your car throws a piston or your watch gets a dunking en route, charge off the cost of making them tick again. (4) Antiques 100 years old (exceptions: rugs and carpets made after 1700) are unrestricted. They include furniture, hardware, brass, bronze, marble, terra cotta, porcelain, chinaware, and "any object considered to have artistic value." Be sure to bring certificates of verification, if available. As a side note, insurance coverage may save you endless headaches. We're hearing about more and more cases of dockside theft, particularly of small articles—so this added protection is a bargain at *any* price. (5) Original works of art (*not* copies)—paintings, drawings, and sculptures of any age—and stamps are duty-free. So are books, prints, lithographs, and maps over 20 years old. (6)

Gifts costing less than $10 may be mailed from abroad on a duty-free basis, with no effect on your exemptions. Alcohol, tobacco, and perfume are ineligible. No 1 person may receive more than 1 gift in 1 day; plainly mark the package "Gift—Value Under $10." Because our Bureau is cracking down hard on violators, for heaven's sake, DON'T let that chiseling European merchant (or your own misguided sense of thrift) forward a $20 or $25 item under this guise. If it is seized, *you're* liable to be retaining a Philadelphia lawyer for this open-and-shut Customs violation. Officials are especially wary of bundles from France, Italy, and Denmark, countries where so many fast workers try to slip through that little something extra. (7) Certain trade-marked articles—especially watches, perfumes, optical goods, musical instruments, and phonograph records—require written permission of the foreign manufacturer or U.S. distributor before they may be cleared intact (accordions are especially hairy). A few well-known manufacturers (Revlon, Nivea, Maybelline) and some lesser-known (have you ever heard of Ot-Val Grove, Armorskin-Hormona, or Herr. Gahn-Henrick Gahns Aktiebolag?) are so stingy that nothing may be imported without their documentary consent. Most companies, however, allow bona fide tourists to bring back at least 1 unit as a souvenir. The way around it? Remove or obliterate the trademark. (8) If you sell some articles within 3 years after importation on a duty-free basis, you'll be fined double the normal quotation. But you *are* permitted to sell anything that was initially purchased for your personal or household use. Original intent is the key factor. (9) Everything in your baggage must be for your personal use or the use of your immediate family, or for gifts; samples and other merchandise will be taxed. (10) Finally, French postcards, egret feathers, ammunition, narcotics, sultry redheads without passports, and various other demoralizing commodities are contraband.

Be especially careful of items made from the skins of crocodile, spotted cat, or other endangered species. The list of God's creatures which are rapidly vanishing from our planet is dismayingly long—too lengthy (and stretching day by day) for us to include here for purposes of up-to-the-minute accuracy. Be sure to ask U.S. Customs before departure for a summary of those species which are especially fragile—and please remember that critters that are dispatched in a brutal fashion are also under protection and thus these pelts too can be seized by officials. Arrests for violations are not unknown; moreover, ignorance of the law is, as usual, no excuse.

On the European side, cigarettes are usually what officials look for first— if they look at all. Above the prescribed number, there's a fat duty to be paid. In some cases the excess will be confiscated, or (in England) the levy must be paid on the entire supply. Most wink at a reasonable excess. If in doubt, here's the best way to handle the tough ones:

When asked how many you're carrying, be casual—and vague. You don't know—3 or 4 packs, you "guess." Being bewildered is often helpful.

Stuff as many packs as you can into the pockets of your suit and overcoat. Normally the only personal search is confined to hijack security measures.

Don't pack the excess at the bottom of the bag; that's where they'll head, straight as a plumb bob. Put it halfway down, and chances are they'll skip them.

At least 50 cigars *or* 1 lb. of pipe tobacco are okay nearly everywhere.

If you have 3 or 4 parcels, your inquisitor has been trained to inspect the one wrapped with the greatest care. Likewise, if there is a choice between a bag and an independent package or a case, he will usually examine the latter.

Some officials are straight; some are as crooked as an anteater's nose. Don't play with the Americans, British, Irish, Dutch, Scandinavians, or Swiss.

If the duty is too high, or if you're carrying a taxable item to a 2nd or 3rd country, the Customs will hold it in escrow at the border for your return, without charge—and it's usually safe. One or 2 lands won't do this.

Carry a pen wherever you go. You'll be astonished at the number of immigration, currency, and health forms you'll be asked to fill out.

A backbreaking number of *unexpected* expenses are inevitable. Example: Some international airports surprise the unwary with a "departure tax" of 80¢ to $5 per passenger. (They're often incorporated in your ticket price so you may not be aware of them.) These bites, plus the endless nitpicks in hotels and elsewhere, can add as much as $100 to an extended European tour.

Be patient. You'll idle away many a dull hour at Customs counters—*and, as we've repeatedly pointed out, quite possibly not once will you be asked to open a single bag!* There's not one darned thing you can do about it—so why not relax and catch up on the latest whodunit?

§TIP: Separate shipment home of European gifts and purchases? *Watch out!* Breakage and forwarding pitfalls are the bane of thousands of innocents.

Merchandise is often jammed into a shoebox and blithely sent on its way; on arrival it's flat as a pancake and in 322 pieces. Unless the merchant guarantees, *in writing* (oral promises aren't enough!), safe delivery or free replacement for everything which arrives smashed, don't take the chance.

Many stores turn over their stateside shipments to commercial Customs brokers—and this is murder to anyone's bank account. In the U.S.A. it is transferred from Customs to a private warehouse—which collects a full month of storage charges whether it's there for 10 hours or 30 days. This, plus big commissions and handling fees for both the forwarding agent abroad and the U.S. broker runs up your tariffs to astronomical levels. *The Travel Agent* magazine reports a case in which the voyager was charged $65 on a $100 purchase of perfume—making the total more than she or he would have paid if originally purchased on Fifth Avenue.

The only sure method is to carry everything with you. Second best is to ship *by parcel post*—NOT through a Customs broker. You *must* impress the shopkeeper that it *must* go by parcel post (if your purchase is not too bulky), because often he'll give you his assurances, and then nonchalantly put it in the clutches of his forwarding agent. If neither method is practicable, ask the local American Express branch to refer you to the best local packer or shipper; sadly, the baggage forwarding services of this worldwide institution have been discontinued.

URGENT!! DRUG ARRESTS ABROAD Here is a cold-turkey summary of this grisly scene. We are reporters, not reformers, lecturers, or bleeding-heart advisers. Our job is to inform, not to moralize. In this spirit, now we are compelled to spell out to various damnfool innocents among the traveling public that *at this writing approximately 1500 Americans, most in their late teens or early twenties, are serving terms in foreign jails as drug smugglers, with sentences ranging from 2 years to 7 years or even LIFE imprisonment—often pronounced after months and months of helpless languishing in a cell or "tank" while awaiting trial.* Hash is the most common troublemaker; nearly all of the Customs and judicial authorities regard it almost as seriously as horse. The imperiling amounts can be pathetically small—2 ounces hidden in a matchbox or a bra, for example. Bail? In most places, what's that? U.S. Consular assistance? To the hair-tearing frustration of this splendid body of diplomats, all of the help permitted to the vast majority of offenders, no matter how naïve, are heartfelt but useless words of sympathy.

Confinement is often made to "detoxification asylums" (a euphemism for mental hospitals). The aforementioned pretrial delays and the penal conditions in all-too-many nations stagger the imagination.

One of the most vicious aspects is the tolerance—even the encouragement! —of "legal entrapment" methods which would instantly be thrown out of any court in any of our 50 states. As an illustration, selected pushers are permitted to sell as much of whatever plant, narcotic, or other illegal compound as they please—provided they're very, very careful to furnish the officials with every possible detail about every buyer in every transaction. Interpol (the world police organization) is then alerted.

Once the alarm is out, God help anyone who conceals "just a couple of joints" to cross an international border!

Hence, to update the popular World War II question in an infinitely sinister context, "Is this trip *really* necessary?"

TIPPING Here are 2 important continental practices which baffle most new American visitors: (1) *The bulk of the tip is usually included in the bill,* and (2) *extra tips are usually distributed at checkout time.*

Most hotels and restaurants automatically add a service charge to your statement of from 10% to 20%, depending upon the country. Watch this.

In your hotel the only people customarily tipped *before* the final-hour reckoning are (1) the porter who carries your bags to the room (see individual countries for suggested amounts); (2) the *piccolo, botones,* or *chasseur*—equivalent to the young U.S. bellboy—who brings the occasional message to your door (small change only); (3) the doorman who snags your taxis. Don't shell out to anyone else until you're ready to leave.

On departure from any Deluxe or First-class European hostelry, however, certain *extra* gratuities are *always* expected. Specific recommendations follow, for each land. In general, give the day concierge (Hall Porter) a minimum of $1.50, never less; stretch this to perhaps $7 if your visit has lasted more than a week. (Often the night concierge and he do not pool their tips.) Give the maid some small change (50¢ per day should do); give the room waiter and the valet slightly more, if you have used them. In the new 1000-room houses now blanketing Europe, you can reduce or even eliminate some tips completely. (If there's a shoeshine machine in the corridor, why throw away money?) Similarly, when concierge desks become peopled by an impersonal battery of 6 to 10 lieutenants, we leave only a token amount; a sizable one would not say "thank you" any better to this faceless throng. In smaller hotels the porter (bellboy) who handles your baggage is usually the man who has shined the shoes you have left by your door; he rates 50¢ to $1 when you move in and when you move out. *Never give a concierge a lump sum for distribution to the rest,* because he may keep too much of it for himself; the hotel manager, however, normally may be trusted implicitly as your banker. Second-class or tourist rates are proportionately less.

In restaurants give substantial tips only if your waiter has been unusually attentive. Some local diners let things ride with the service charge on the check. The majority leaves small change on the table.

A good average for miscellaneous services is 15%; if the bill is less than $1, bump it into 20%.

Washroom attendants are always tipped with the smallest coin or coins of the currency; so are theater ushers, except in 1 or 2 countries.

Cigarettes used to be largess for extraordinary service, but their importance has long been zero. Forget them.

Don't be browbeaten just because you're a tourist. Many Italian and Belgian taxi drivers, for example, have the vicious habit of extracting their own tips before they return your change. They know better. If this happens, demand the full amount, step out of the cab—and tell them to go to hell.

Continental servants are usually 100% better trained, better polished, and more interested in their patrons' welfare than American servants. You'd be surprised what a smile and a pleasant word will do for these excellent people —because not all Europeans treat them as human beings.

Urgent: Wherever you are and whatever you do, always carry a pocketful of assorted small change. Cash a large bill (or 2) each day before setting forth; by always having the EXACT tip on hand, the time and money you'll save will be phenomenal. Please give extra-serious consideration to this suggestion, because we find it one of the most practical in this book.

LANGUAGE   In today's Europe language is no barrier. As long as you've got a tongue, 3 or 4 hands, and an active imagination, you'll get along fine.

English is understood in just about every large hotel, restaurant, shop, nightclub, and major sightseeing facility abroad. Only in rural districts should you find any serious difficulties.

Have no fears about going to a linguistically strange country. Plenty of North Americans have been there before, to break the ice for you.

§TIP: When you're talking English and Mr. Native is talking Zulu, watch the volume of your voice. If your interlocutor doesn't speak your language, there's a ludicrous tendency on both parts to shout.

SMÖRGASBORD AND CRÊPES SUZETTE   While it's true that an occasional European refrigerator might be substandard, today's continental traveler runs across almost no tainted food. If he does, chances are better than even he has found it in some little hole-in-the-wall instead of the average or high-class restaurant or hotel. Europeans feed Europeans too. Cuisine is taken much more seriously than it is in the States. So don't harbor any notions you're going to be poisoned, because you aren't.

Some of the Classic Traveler's Complaint stems from plain, old-fashioned overfatigue and overexcitement—because it's common sense that the human physique isn't built for the extraordinary stimulation and abuse stemming from body-clock resettings and high-tension hopscotch across 5 or 10 foreign lands. At home, who would dream of stuffing the stomach with 2 huge meals daily, washed down with wine—and then compounding the strain with the crazy hours compounded by the jet lag plus such strenuous sightseeing and shopping? Of course, cases of *turista* also come from bacteria (strains of *Escherichia coli*, if you want to curse them by name) and changes of water. *In* ALL *European capitals and in* MOST *larger cities, engineering advances now make it perfectly safe to drink right out of the tap.* It's sensible to stick to bottled water where the supply sources are questionable (for names of traditional brands in still and sparkling varieties, see later)—but it's the height of absurdity in any major metropolis today to waste money on this at perhaps 75¢ per liter, when the drinks you're knocking down so happily are made with local ice. Ask that everything be cooked in butter (a major operation, sometimes). These basic precautions should help.

Quite possibly you'll pick up diarrhea anyhow, if only from tension and excitement. Don't worry about amoebae or the bad forms, though; if you pick up something, 99½% of the time it will be temporary and strictly harmless. If you get it, we suggest that you use one of the medicines listed in "Five-Star Indispensables" in "Let's Get Ready," and we urge that you take *nothing* else by mouth until the intestinal organs are comfortable. Then start gradually on liquids (no milk, no citrus juices). "Flat" cola, strong tea, bouillon, jello, salt crackers, and small portions of starchy bland foods are all good. If the diarrhea recurs, go back to nothing by mouth and start over again. *Be sure* to consult a physician if the diarrhea still persists.

If you dine in small, primitive spots, here are some pointers:

Watch the milk in the Mediterranean lands. Even ice cream or the cream in your coffee can be dangerous. Big hotels and restaurants normally take ample precautions, but sometimes little joints don't.

Watch hamburger, sausage, stew, hash, cannelloni, and the like. If they don't have the cheeseburger you order, they might accommodate you smilingly by tossing Dobbin, Fido, or the cat into the grinder.

If your lobster, *écrevisse,* or similar crustacean has a tight tail, his death was so sudden that he was probably alive when he hit boiling water—a fairly reliable guarantee he's safe to eat. But if his tail is loose, *don't touch!*

Since pollution is also widespread abroad, beware of clams, oysters, and other shell-shockers that could nest near sewage flows.

Watch ice cubes if you suspect they're made from well water or suspect the purity of the source. Incidentally, *never* drink from a well or stream in Europe, no matter where you are or how thirsty you are.

If you're stuck in a beanery so repulsive it shivers your hair, order just hardboiled eggs, yogurt, or toast. The bugs can't do much to these items (as long as you get a piece from the inside of the loaf!).

In the Middle East, Far East, North and Central Africa, and similar hot spots, special precautions are absolutely mandatory. Consult your travel agent or airline for hints on these.

TAKING THE PLUNGE   *Important!!* In these days of spoilage of our rivers, lakes, and coasts, no American in his right mind would even think of dipping his recreational toes into the waters of, say, New York's East River, or Hoboken's shores, or San Diego Bay, the Detroit River, or the myriad repositories and sewerways of our industrial waste. Similarly, no sane European would consider taking a swim in the Rhine, the harbor of Marseille, the bilge-blackened ports of Bremen, Bremerhaven, Southhampton, Naples, or certain regions that fill with pollutants at particular times of the year. As a guideline to European aquatic pastimes and pleasures, we suggest that you exercise the same sea-horsesense that you would use at home. Moreover, if you ever have any doubts, why not play it extra safe and use a hotel or municipal pool to get on an athlete's footing with the rest of us?

METRIC MEASUREMENT   The metric system used in every European country (but not extensively in the British Isles) is still confusing to most Americans; it won't be soon, because, of course, we are adopting it.

Here are a few translations. Conquer these 5 and you'll get along fine:

A kilometer (pronounced kill-OM-eter by the "mile"-minded British and Irish and KILL-o-meter by the continentals) is roughly 6/10ths of a mile. Multiply by 6, knock off 1 decimal point, and you've got it in miles.

A kilo or kilogram (potatoes and onions) is 2.2 pounds.

A meter (dress material) and a liter (gasoline, beer) are both roughly 11/10ths—one of a yard, the other of a quart. (There are about 2½ centimeters to 1 inch.)

A gram (airmail letters) is very tiny. There are about 28 to the ounce.

If you don't like arithmetic, our handy *Fielding's World Currency and Metric Converter* will instantly convert U.S. and metric measurements in all the above categories, plus temperature.

Now, for those who don't have their copy of our up-to-the-minute, pocket-size *Shopping Guide to Europe*, here are some conversions which might come in handy. Since sizes are not standardized, this is a fairly rough yardstick. Try on the items whenever possible.

Junior Misses

American	9	11	13	15	17
European	34	36	38	40	42

Women's Clothing

American	10-30	12-32	14-34	16-36	18-38	20-40
European	40	42	44	46	48	50

Women's Shoes

American	4	5	6	7	8	9
European	34	35	36	37	38	39

Children's Dresses and Suits

American	2	4	6	8	10	12
European	40-45	50-55	60-65	70-75	80-85	80-95
English	16-18	20-22	24-26	28-30	32-34	36-38

Men's Sweaters

American	Small	Medium	Large	Extra Large
European	44	46-48	40	52-54
English	34	36-38	50	42-44

Men's Shirts

American	14	14½	15	15½	16	16½	17
European	36	37	38	39	41	42	43

(Men's shirt, hat, pajamas, and suit sizes are identical in U.S. and England.)

Men's Shoes

American	5	6	7	8	9	10	11	12
European	38	39	40	41	42	43	44	45

Last, here's a refresher on how to change Centigrade temperatures into Fahrenheit. The classic method is to take 9/5ths of the *Centigrade* temperature (the reading on European thermometers) and add 32. A much easier way, suggested by a kindly Tulsa friend of the *Guide*, is to double the Centigrade reading, deduct 10%, and add the same 32. Example: Let's imagine that the mercury says 15°. Twice 15 is 30, and 10% of 30 is 3. Taking 3 from 30 leaves 27. Add 32 to 27, and you'll have the Yankee version of 59°. In print it looks complicated—but in practice it's so simple that almost any traveler can do it in his head. Try it and see!

TEMPERATURE CONVERSION TABLE

CENTIGRADE	FAHRENHEIT
+ 100	+ 212
50	122
35	95
30	86
25	77
20	68
15	59
10	50
+ 5	41
0	32
− 5	− 23
10	14
15	+ 5
18	0
− 20	− 4

CROOKS AND SAINTS   The honesty and integrity in Scandinavia, Switzerland, and other smaller nations shame even America and England. Spain is generally one of the most trustworthy of all.

But there are all too many lands where constant petty thievery is sickening. Italy is the most flagrant offender in Western Europe, and France is second. Tourists are fair game to unscrupulous hotel, restaurant, taxi, shop, and scads of other people; once something disappears, it's usually gone for good.

In descending order, currency, jewelry, traveler's checks, cameras, passports, tobacco, perfume, candy, and light articles of clothing are the most frequent targets. *Lock your suitcase; leave your valuables in the hotel safe.*

Never let your luggage out of sight when traveling by rail (unless you check it in one of the new luggage bins at the head of the train). When you go to the restaurant car, either ask your fellow-passengers to keep an eye on it, or, if they dine at the same time, get the car attendant or conductor to lock the compartment. Stay with it on airlines as long as you can, too.

Try not to leave it unguarded in a waiting taxi or in the custody of a strange porter, except at the largest hotels.

Never leave items of worth in an unwatched car, especially a convertible —even if locked. When you park at night, especially in Italy, leave your glove compartment wide open to show that its contents are valueless.

Watch your coat as if it were studded with rubies.

If you're grounded at a strange airport, leave nothing—not even the time of day—in the airplane.

Always keep a duplicate laundry list. Socks, shorts, and handkerchiefs will dwindle if you don't.

Check the bulk of your funds and precious jewelry with the hotel cashier when you register. You can draw from him daily—and you've got 2 strikes on pickpockets. Unfortunately, however, the third pitch may be a strike on you. Since the recent rash of hotel holdups, these lockboxes are no longer always guaranteed safe by the hostelry.

Be extra-careful in North Africa, Italy, and France.

TRAINS AND EURAILPASS   One of the fattest bargains in Europe is the Eurailpass ("Your-rail-pass"). Any *resident* of North, Central, or South America may roam wherever and whenever desired on any continental train (not British; they have a separate Thrift Rail Plan) without further payment except for routine sleeper or *couchette* supplements. It offers 7 days for $90, 2 weeks of unlimited travel for $145, 21 days for $180, 1 month for $220, 2 months for $300, and 3 months for $360. Acceptable in First class (including

Trans-Europ-Express and extra-fare runs) by railroads of Austria, Belgium, Bulgaria, Denmark, France, Italy, Luxembourg, the Netherlands, Norway, Portugal, Spain, Sweden, Switzerland, and West Germany; English Channel crossings to London linking into the continental system (BritRail operates its own thrift package, so see under "England"); also honored on certain lake or river steamers, ferry services, bus routes, and private railways. In most lands children under 4 years are free and tykes between 4 and 12 go ½-fare. *You must buy it before heading for Europe, because it is not sold abroad. To secure confirmed reservations booked through U.S. agencies is tricky unless application is made long in advance.* For further inquiries, see your travel agent or write to Eurailpass, Box 90, Bohemia, New York 11716. (First Class is often jammed with foresighted backpackers. There's also a 2-month, Second-class Student Railpass for $195!)

Swiss, Scandinavian, German, French, and Dutch railways are excellent. Spanish, Italian, Portuguese, Belgian, and even some British trains are occasionally terrible. They are all overcrowded in High Season, so make your reservations *now* or as soon as you reach Europe.

The Trans-Europ-Express (TEE) is a high-speed, main-line rocket linking the major cities of 9 nations—Italy, France, Monaco, Holland, Belgium, West Germany, Austria, Switzerland, and Luxembourg. If your destination is within 250 miles, your door-to-door travel time will probably be less than if you bid for airline travel—and at nearly ¼th the cost! Moreover, in winter or foggy periods, rail is far more reliable. The trains are mostly self-propelled diesel units (autorails in France). Tickets are one class only; a 15% to 20% supplement is added unless you have a Eurailpass; air conditioning is standard; cars have smoking and nonsmoking divisions; advance seat reservations are mandatory; no standing room is sold. Average running speed is about 80 mph; as examples of their high-stepping gait, Paris–Brussels is only 2 hours, 22 minutes (3½ hrs. by air *et al.* from midtown-to-midtown), and Paris–Zürich is only 6 hours. Dining facilities are always on hand; frontier formalities have been streamlined to a minimum; conductors and uniformed hostesses or stewards wear TEE insignia and are multilingual. Teleprinter reservations can be made in 15 minutes *if* available—but be safe by requesting them 3 weeks before departure. Here's the greatest step forward in foreign railroading since the Wagons-Lit dining-car people discovered that the Animal Kingdom provides other meats besides veal. Important: Always take your luggage on board with you. If you check it through, it might be put onto a "regular" train and reach your destination much later than you do.

On all other trains abroad make sure *first* that there's a diner. We got stuck again, foolishly, because we neglected to find out that restaurant cars are not carried through the Simplon Tunnel (except on TEE, they never cross borders). Advance knowledge will give you time to improvise your own picnic —much better than the station platform vendors' snacks.

There is drinking water on about 1% of the local trains of Europe. Carry your own bottle unless you're riding a mainliner.

When you leave your seat for a meal, put some bulky possession (your spouse, for example?) on the cushion. Otherwise, the first incoming passenger is liable to take over, leaving you the worst place and lousiest view.

Dining cars? Here's the procedure: Usually there are 2 (sometimes 3) separate servings. First the Steward will come to your compartment, learn your time preference, and give you a table-booking slip which must be returned when he greets you in his own domain. Although a few meager à la carte items are available, probably 98% of the customers consume the standard, fixed meal at the standard, fixed price (usually $6.50 to $9). Course after course is served on a 1-shot, universal basis; everybody eats the soup, the veal (1 gets you 10 that it still *is* veal, too!), the salad, the cheese, and the fruit from the same service platters. When the whole car has finished, the cashier presents the check. Either don't tip or keep it below 5%.

Sleeping cars? Wagons-Lits offer 3 First-class and 2 Second-class categories. First class consists of regular 1-berth or 2-berth accommodations, plus "Specials" for shorter runs (20 small single compartments per car). Second class offers the new T-2 berthing with 18 double-decked twin compartments per car; these are gradually supplementing the older 3-bunk units. France has the Second-class *couchette*—a minimum-price 6-seat (or 6-berth) compartment in which passengers may lie down without undressing. It's great for yoga apprentices or paratroopers.

If you share your wagon-lit with a stranger, unhappily it'll be a man if you're male or a woman if you're female. (Fascinating booking mistakes sometimes happen, however, to passengers with ambiguous first names such as Sydney, Evelyn, Clare, Leigh, or Temple.) It's good manners to stand in the outside passageway while he shaves or she dresses.

No portable radios may be played on French, Swiss, and Swedish railways.

When you turn in a ticket, it is sometimes necessary to wait 3 months before you can get your money back. Fantastic red tape, that's all.

Check the date of expiration of your round-trip ticket. On short rides in some countries they expire within 24 hours.

YOUR OWN CAR   If you're planning to ship your car across the Atlantic, we'd recommend 2 standard documents: (1) a valid U.S. Driving License, and (2) an American International Driving Permit ($3, nine languages, no longer mandatory but still useful for remote motoring) issued through the AAA. United States license plates may be used for all countries.

The transatlantic passage is still a juicy source of revenue for steamship operators. This situation remains an absolute disgrace—a racket which gouges the innocent traveler ruthlessly. It is rigged so that a round trip costs only a trifling sum more than a 1-way run, and the total often exceeds the price of the passenger ticket! Since the car occupies measly dead space and makes no demands, the companies should hide their heads in shame for milking the helpless international motorist in this way. Atop the whopping $450 to $700 basic ticket (depending on the distance and the weight of the car), and the almost mandatory insurance against damage by those damnably reckless, slam-bang stevedores, lighterage fees must be added for ports without adequate docks. Be *sure* to draw a special marine insurance policy (the 3-A's has one) against damage en route.

Normal freight rates for 1-way shipment eastbound vary with the destination and are subject to seasonal fluctuation. The exact price cannot be determined until the car has been measured at the pier. Brokerage charges, covering actual shipment, are additional to freight rates. Because sailings are subject to cargo demands, they may be weekly, semimonthly, or monthly.

Since your gas tank will be drained when you deliver your buggy to the wharf, try to leave the sons-of-guns only a cupful.

Third Party Insurance (Public Liability and Property Damage) is compulsory throughout Europe. *Be sure to get complete coverage*—fire, theft, damage to yourself, the works—*wherever you go on the Continent.* If there's an accident, no matter how trivial, you'll be up to your neck in gendarmes, red tape, and A.D. 1066 legal procedures—and it's the devil to prove that the other fellow is wrong when you have to shout him down in a strange language. Ask the AAA or the agency where you make your purchase.

If there isn't an AAA office nearby, write to *AAA World-Wide Travel, Inc.,* 8111 Gatehouse Rd., Falls Church, Va. 22042. The Foreign Motoring Service division here is normally very patient, and helpful.

Straight rental of a car in Europe? If this comes as part of your travel agent's package—fine; you're buying his know-how, his service, and your touring convenience. But if you're making your own arrangements independently, *we recommend you wait until you've crossed the Atlantic instead of setting up any advance reservations in the States.* Here is our reasoning:

Every good-size city on the Continent has scads of excellent rental cars, both self-drive and chauffeur-driven. Nobody, but nobody, has a true Europe-wide chain of auto-hire offices; everybody makes use of a string of local operators. What you're riding isn't a Hertz or Avis or National car, in most cases; it's actually a Schmidt or Delamain, or Angelotti car under a U.S. name.

While we have no special quarrel with this setup, we'd personally prefer the privilege of (1) selecting our own local outfit, (2) examining what we are paying for, before agreeing to take it, and (3) making our own deal.

It is our honest opinion that the caliber of their selected firms varies considerably. In some cities we think they're unparalleled, but in others we don't go along. When booked by any U.S. company, however, you get what you get.

No single local outfit can stock every kind of car. Before leaving home, you might *think* you want a Ford or Opel or Simca, but after on-the-spot comparative shopping, that cute little Porsche or that sleek little Fiat might be far closer to your personal taste. Seeing is better.

Prices are supposed to be standard—but they aren't, please believe us. If you do your own talking, particularly in Off Season, you can end up with quotations substantially under the "official" rates.

Therefore, we earnestly believe that your best bet is to walk in cold abroad and strike your own bargains for exactly the car which pleases you most for that section of your tour. A recognized credit card will be a help; today many agents feel that cash deposits are not enough to prevent car thieves from driving off and never returning with the vehicle.

Outright purchase of an auto in Europe, for (1) shipment home, or for (2) eventual resale to the original foreign dealer on the guaranteed repurchase plan? Make sure that your car meets American specifications for glass, safety features, muffler, and headlights; later conversion can be costly.

There's also a guaranteed repurchase scheme in which the agency buys back the vehicle at the termination of your journey, at a price mutually agreed upon in advance. Where the horse trading comes in, of course, is on the repurchase part of any agreement—and that's just routine business. American offices which offer these services are normally reliable and fair-dealing. But since even the best of them are subject to human frailties, we do not assume responsibility for their performance.

Please remember that (1) the U.S. duty on automobiles is 3% *ad valorem*, plus a possible State surcharge; (2) all English cars must be exported from Great Britain within 12 months; (3) France, with its comparatively low tax of 20%, is the only European country where *private* sale of an automobile is practical (unless you want to drive to "free" Andorra and take a chance on getting a tiny fraction of its value from those sharper-than-sharp dealers); (4) payments usually must be made in dollars; the tag may be hiked slightly because of required U.S. safety standards; (5) many foreign insurance companies won't accept applicants under 21 years of age; (6) it's wise to inquire *first* whether the car you're getting is brand-new or so-called "new," which is often "used"; and (7) as stated above, transatlantic shipment costs a hell of a lot more than those steamship robbers should charge for it.

As automobiles purchased abroad cannot be driven legally in the U.S. with foreign license plates, it is best to make advance arrangements to have your home-state plates awaiting you at the pier. If you fail to do this, however, a 30-day in-transit vehicle permit may be purchased for $5 from the New York State Department of Motor Vehicles at 155 Worth St., N.Y.; you must apply in person, and present proof of ownership and of liability insurance coverage.

§TIPS: At this writing, Americans may drive in any country in Eastern or Western Europe, with one exception—Albania. Motoring in other Iron Curtain lands is complicated; travel by private auto in East Germany is *not* recommended. You cannot take your automobile from West Berlin to East Berlin; if you're granted the Transit Visa through the Communist sector, you'll be required to stay on one ill-kept autobahn only.

European railways will now "piggyback" your steed all over the place. The 11 rail networks that web most of Europe will almost certainly continue the fare-reduction program begun a few years back. In an effort to lay off some of the expense of returning their often-empty flatcars and sleepers to the country of origin, price cuts of up to 60% were instituted. Here is a bargain-basement boon to the time-pressed driver who can cover vast stretches of tough or dull terrain, save on hotel bills, and avoid highway dangers when fatigue strikes. Consult your travel agent or the national tourist offices about this. We've personally had excellent luck and superior comfort on many of these services, while other highway pilots have honked about the lack of deluxe facilities on a few isolated treks.

If you can avoid it, don't buy French or Italian insurance. Persuading some of their companies to acknowledge liability can become a full-time occupation which will keep you pitching until 2001. If you buy an Italian-made chariot in Italy, however, you must draw a local policy.

With minor exceptions, road signs are standard. There are 3 basic categories: (1) triangular, to indicate danger (intersection, railway crossing, slippery road, etc.), (2) circular, to lay down prohibitions (road closed, 1-way street, no passing, etc.), (3) rectangular, to provide information (garage ahead, telephone ahead, first-aid station ahead, etc.). They are easy to learn.

Don't glance at the map, turn to your companion, and casually announce, "We're going to make 350 miles tomorrow!"—because in most cases you're not, anywhere in Europe, unless you're prepared for total exhaustion. Compared to U.S. driving conditions, continental roads are generally so antiquated your eyes might pop in disbelief. Relatively few superhighways or thruways exist. Germany, Italy, France, Denmark, and Holland have the most. "Progressive" nations such as Switzerland and England are still so appallingly behind times that it's ludicrous. So please be careful not to bite off more distance than you can comfortably—or safely—chew, because usually 500 U.S. miles amount to 250 or 300 over there.

Gasoline rings up at about twice the U.S. price. The fuel crisis created some stalls in '74 but later gas flowed abundantly everywhere. In most countries a top speed limit of 110 to 130 kilometers per hour is imposed for freeway traffic with 90 kilometers per hour set for secondary highway runs, and 50 to 60 kph pegged for suburban cruising; though this precautionary conservation measure may be lifted by the time of your arrival, why not follow it anyway and enjoy the ride while saving money? (As the speed limits are not uniform, be sure to ask at each frontier concerning that nation's rules.)

Left-hand traffic? Only in Great Britain and Ireland. In all other countries you'll drive as you do at home. (At least that's their hope!)

Finally—and we can't repeat the warning often enough—your chances of being killed or maimed, or clobbering a third party, are 300% greater in Europe than in the U.S. You'll see why as soon as those Italian, French, Belgian, and other charming maniacs start buzzing around you.

STUDENTS, TEACHERS, AND BUDGETEERS   You might be interested to know that my Nancy and I are publishing the 11th annually revised edition of our paperback, *Fielding's Low-Cost Europe*. Years of personal on-the-spot research and countless hours of writing and editorial time have been poured into its creation and its vast new '77 updatings. The results are thousands upon thousands of money-saving facts and field-tested observations gathered exclusively for the careful budgeteer. Its twin aims: (1) to save $$$$$$$ for you, and (2) to give you a darned good time. The bargain hotels, pensions, dining spots, sightseeing targets, night places, shopping buys, and other facilities in every major hub of Western Europe are covered in far, far greater detail than the space limitations of this *Travel Guide* permit us.

Therefore, in order to conserve precious linage here and to offer you infinitely more complete coverage, we have shifted all travel lore for academicians and for the especially thrift-conscious to this handy and inexpensive paperback.

ODD FACTS—SOME IMPORTANT! The American term "First class" becomes "Deluxe" abroad; "First class" is American "Second class."

URGENT: The contrast between European-style hotelkeeping and U.S.-style overseas hotelkeeping is *enormous.* There can be no "right" or "wrong" answer; it is 101% dependent upon your own preferences. Newer continental-owned imitations of our Yankee concepts are not considered in these evaluations. Here, in broad and general terms (you will find numerous exceptions), are the assets and the debits of these conflicting schools of operations: (1) *Overall Aura:* The big U.S. chains frequently export their stateside flamboyance and impersonality. Despite their scatterings of regional touches, if you don't look out of the windows, you might just as well be registered in a Los Angeles, Little Rock, or Louisville hotel. On the other hand, foreign establishments normally radiate an old-fashioned charm and grace which project the flavor of participating in European living. If typical and good, they are much more friendly, intimate, and ingratiating. (2) *Accommodations:* The construction of the American-type hostelry is standardized from the ground up—a tremendous advantage over traditional Old Country competition. Its bedrooms, precisely identical within their price groupings, break down into only 3 to 5 standardized categories. As a result, the least expensive chamber in the building usually offers adequate elbowroom, good mattresses, and a convenient array of jet-age gadgets. Conversely, the sleeping facilities of the continental, British, and Irish enterprises, unless very new or newish, are most often wildly uneven in square footage and comfort. The quality houses of this family run a confused gamut from suites more opulent than those of their U.S. colleagues (even to duplexes with private elevators!), to better doubles, to poorer doubles, and finally to a quota of miserably cramped, miserably furnished quarters known to the trade as "the mother-in-law rooms." (If you should draw one of the latter, heavens prevent, ask the Reception Chief to change you if alternate space is available. Then make a personal inspection before moving in.) Curiously, the private bathrooms of the American installations, while efficiently designed, tend to be far less commodious and inviting than those of the more luxurious foreign counterparts. (3) *Service:* In the American troupe, attendance to the guest is not only slower but almost invariably mechanical. For plantwide efficiency, the staff ratio normally is cut down to vary between ¾ths and 1 employee to 1 occupant. For room service guests must telephone a central complex which usually adjoins or is a part of the far-distant kitchen. It is possible that you will never be served twice by the same man from downstairs. This eliminates the foundation of a cordial rapport, and it also complicates the tipping problem. In contrast, the Boniface abroad extends much warmer, faster, much more individual attention. The staff ratio in his best hotels ranges from 1½ to 2½ employees to each guest. Because most operate efficient service pantries on every floor of bedrooms, the traveler merely pushes the service buttons on the night table, and the maid or waiter (based within hovering distance) should appear almost instantly.

Their kindly faces will be with you for the duration of your visit. If you are the characteristically cordial overseas pilgrim, you'll soon be heartened to hear that Carmen, the chambermaid, has finally married off her eldest daughter, or that Felix, the night waiter, at last has made a down payment on a summer house in the Tyrol. To them, you are a person, not a semianonymous room number. When they become your friends, through this small enrichment you will be given a happier and warmer taste of your host country. (4) *Cuisine:* U.S. chains gear their grills and dining rooms to the steak-and-potato addict. Their brand of cookery cuts corners ruthlessly. Practically every item on every plate is expertly cost-accounted. Nearly without exception, they dish up mass fare of medium—often poor—standards and quality. By comparison, Continentals generally scorn this "kitchen factory" level. A much wider selection of foreign specialties customarily is featured. No bookkeepers check the weight and dimensions of your lamb chops or roast chicken. As a broad rule of thumb, they present more careful, more savory skilletwork, because of their greater culinary heritage and pride. (5) *Prices:* In tariffs, both groups are almost entirely competitive within their own categories. . . . Now, given these pros and cons, it is entirely your own option to pick the chocolate or the vanilla. *You* pays *your* money, so *you* takes YOUR choice!

Wherever you overnight abroad, it's wise to be fire-conscious about your accommodations. Most emphatically, we do not wish to trouble your peace of mind in any way, because you'll find most of the better-grade hotels 100% safe—but once in a million times conflagrations *do* bring disaster. In too many of the less-expensive places, you'll find open stairwells, inflammable furnishings, no fire escapes, or other potential hazards. In these, as a standard practice and small precaution which just might save your life, analyze in advance your possible escape route. If there is none, and if the building should look dangerous, accept only a lower-floor room.

When you register in most European hotels save in Germany, "Joe Jones, Tuscaloosa, U.S.A." won't satisfy that gimlet-eyed clerk. You'll be given a form as long as your arm. Neat trick, if he falls for it: Scrawl your name on the bottom, hand over your passport, and ask *him* to do the work. Sometimes he won't bite, though—so *memorize the number and date of issue of your passport for just such occasions.* In some lands this document will be held overnight at the desk for registration with the local police. If so, pleee-se don't forget to pick it up when you check out!

Be sure to indicate your date of arrival *and* departure when you apply for accommodations abroad. Should you omit the latter, a little man in a large claw-hammer coat might step up, smile apologetically, and bounce you out into the cold, cruel world—routine European practice.

Foreign chambermaids take delight in hiding your pajamas or nightgown under the pillow or actually between the sheets (Scandinavia). But this innocent pastime pales beside the Slipper Game—that ancient major sport of challenging guests to find their slippers on the top closet shelf, in the bedside cabinet which holds the chamber pot, or elsewhere. By dogged diligence and luck, my Nancy and I have managed to bat 1.000 over the years on these contests. Shamefully we must confess, however, that we've lost at least half a dozen sets of nightclothes!

Practically every European hotel has a Grand Panjandrum who is known as the concierge (pronounced "con-see-air-sssh"); in the U.K. and Ireland he is called the Hall Porter. He is the head contact man with the clients—boss of the bellhops, mail clerks, key clerks, nearly everybody on the street-floor service staff except the dining-room-and-bar help. He wears a pair of gold crossed keys ("Clefs d'Or") on his lapels—and he's not to be confused with the striped-pants, pearl-stickpin people at the Reception counter in the lobby. Use him for everything—stamps, outside errands, complaints, reservations for trains, theaters, or restaurants, and, most important of all, questions and advice about what's what in the city. And be sure to tip him when you check out—a minimum of $1 per day per couple in Deluxe or First-class houses, and perhaps 50¢ per day in lesser ones. This tip is pooled for the whole desk (2 to 10 individuals who have served you), and it's cheap at the price. Since setups vary from place to place, it's always safest to ask him what specific areas your gratuity covers. Incidentally, never tip the lofty Reception gents.

Nearly every continental hostelry offers what is called the Pension ("Pawn-see-ahn," not "Pen-shun") Plan, which quotes room and board at one flat daily or weekly rate. It generally breaks down into 3 choices: Full Pension (room and all meals), Demipension (room and 2 meals), and Bed-and-Breakfast. Some countries require that you state your choice on registration; some hotels require that you take Full Pension only. *Be sure to find out what is included and what is not included, as soon as you check in*—or you might be paying twice for your lunch or dinner, without being aware of it until they give you the bill.

Watch out for "supplements"—those devilish little sneak-charges which constantly rise to plague the innocent traveler. If you're operating under one of the Pension Plans, for example, most hotels give you the traditional continental breakfast as part of the contract—coffee or tea, toast, jam, butter, and a small pitcher of what is laughingly called cream. This will ordinarily be eaten in your room, because downstairs is most often closed. But when the waiter smiles and asks if Madame and Monsieur would like some orange juice, some fruit, some cereal, an egg perhaps?—these are on *your* bill, not the hotel's. When you sit down to dine, they'll allow you only the dishes-of-the-day—a rigid list—and if you order *anything* extra, that's socked onto your account, too. If you don't watch these supplements carefully, they can absolutely murder any carefully planned budget.

Almost nowhere abroad will a bellhop appear at Reception to wrassle your luggage. It is normal to separate you from your bags at the entrance—and later to bring them independently up to your room.

Some hotels below Deluxe category do not furnish soap to guests—not poverty or stinginess, but a difference of customs. Try to have your own supply.

The bidet, an institution in European bathrooms, is less known in North America. It's a shallow, kidney-shape porcelain apparatus, which might at first sight be a flat hopper; faucets at one end control the flow and temperature of the water. Our description in earlier editions of the *Guide* was so timid and uninformative that it drew a protest from Dr. Kenneth R. Morgan, the Bridgeport, Conn., physician, whose aforementioned *Speaking You English?*

A Lighthearted Guide to World Travel is the most wickedly witty, fun-filled, down-to-earth travel book in which we have ever delighted. Here are the good Doctor's merry but highly useful observations on this subject: "Since the average American looks at it and says, 'What the hell do you do with it?', I propose to explain. Since the average travel writer approaches the subject with such delicacy as to leave the reader in total ignorance, I intend to approach [the bidet] with such vulgarity as to leave no doubt as to its purpose. Its primary use is to wash off your bottom, which, with the strange variety of johns you've been visiting on daytime excursions, probably needs it. In practical use, one fills the little tub with warm water and sits on it facing the wall, a sensation somewhat akin to forgetting to put the seat down before sitting on the john. Europeans probably only do this when stark naked. Ignorant Americans emerge with wet nylons and shoes full of water. The European female or male may subsequently proceed to take a complete sponge bath from ears to toes, either because there is no bathtub or they are too lazy to get into one. The bidets with little fountains in the middle are old-fashioned and are, sad to say, gradually being replaced. Too bad, because they are lots of fun. The spray, if turned full on, goes right up to the ceiling. The technique here is to adjust the spray to a height of about 8 inches or so and allow it to play merrily over your navel. You can also balance a Ping-Pong ball on it; it will stay for hours. As a substitute for an actual douche (American, not French) it is perfectly hopeless, which is why this type of bidet has gone out of style." Anyone for questions?

Finally, whenever you have a truly serious complaint about any hotel, insist upon taking it up personally with the Director—no one else! And if his underlings should try to block you from seeing him, tell them flatly and firmly that you are following specific instructions given in this *Guide*.

Continental weather, especially in Northern and Central Europe, is often terrible until May 15 or later. Off Season travelers should schedule itineraries with big-city events, not scenic tours of the countryside.

Pompeii, the Vatican, the Louvre, and other cultural meccas fairly crawl with Roman numerals. If antiquities are your dish, it won't hurt to relearn your MCMLMM's in advance.

Always print, not handwrite, your name and address—especially in mail orders. Trying to decipher our American scrawl drives Europeans just as crazy as we are driven trying to interpret theirs.

Send off all thank-you notes before leaving each city. This will prevent giant-size headaches later, when you've misplaced that damned address.

Dates are written differently in Europe: Our form of 6/30/77, for example, becomes 30/6/77.

Here's an oddity of language, too: Corn (European) is the name for wheat (American), while corn (American) becomes maize abroad.

Carry lots of calling cards—preferably engraved ones, since these are *the* status symbol in the Arrived Set Abroad. Although you may leave a paper trail that would be the envy of Hansel and Gretel, this subtle puff might smooth a VIP path of rose petals and red carpeting for you.

Most restaurants abroad (1) levy a special price for the bread you eat and (2) don't serve drinking water unless specifically requested. At some places (normally either the costliest or cheapest ones) you'll also pay extra for the tablecloth and napkins—the origin of "cover charge."

Store hours are a nuisance. Most shops close at noon and reopen at 2 P.M. —always the period you plan to do your buying. In hot countries such as Spain or Italy, the siesta lasts until 4 or 4:30 P.M., but the doors remain open until 7 P.M. or later. In England, Scandinavia, and other northern climes, however, they go straight through from perhaps 9 A.M. to 5:00 or 5:30.

One institution that nearly always petrifies the overseas visitor is the coeducational toilet room—a facility standard from one end of the Continent to the other. Here's the typical arrangement: One common washroom with washbowls and towels serves all comers. Leading off this, are 2 adjoining cubicles, marked "Men" or "Ladies." Sometimes these booths are separated by a partition which extends only from the knees to the top of the head, with yawning gaps at floor and ceiling level. You'll find this disturbing architecture at topnotch places too! More primitive establishments often offer the Turkish Toilet—2 size-14½ molded concrete feet strategically placed in front of a large hole chopped right through the floor—that's all! And for men, here's one more tidbit: Don't let sudden paralysis freeze the works if a woman attendant should blithely be knitting smack in the center of the men's room. If she can stand it (which she can), just drop a coin in her dish, give her a smile, tip your hat, and relax.

The majority of professional guides in Europe bitterly hate this book and savagely slander its author; once we even received a Death Threat from an anonymous Madrid–Toledo guide. Their rage is based on the fact that for many years we have continued to expose and to campaign against their dirty kickback racket. Here's how they'll try to sting you: This chiseler will ferret out 2nd-rate or 3rd-rate shopkeepers willing to pay a commission (generally 10% to 25%) on suckers who can be persuaded to load up on shoddy, sleazy goods *which have been marked up to cover the guide's rakeoff.* Most bizarre and insulting of all is that many of the "local" goods are production-line-produced elsewhere. Result: They get junk, and they pay from 10% to 25% more for the privilege of being rooked. Remember that *no* decent, legitimate shop anywhere in Europe would *dream* of stooping to such shady practice, any more than would Neiman-Marcus or Tiffany; there's one price for every-body. In Paris, Rome, Brussels, Madrid, Nice, Barcelona—yes, even in honest Amsterdam!—this shabby practice flourishes with the tacit knowledge of agency officials. So, (1) *you* pick the stores, (2) be sure that they're the big ones, and (3) don't let the person talk you into patronizing some quaint little hole-in-the-wall which is "positively the best place in town!" Also, when they curse this book, and pledge on their mother's memory that they've personally watched That Man Fielding accept big bribes from rascally merchants, please reach for a large grain of salt.

The *café filtre,* that satanic device endorsed by French, Belgian, and other backers of the Perfect Perpetual Motion Principle, has doubtless poleaxed thousands of strangers. Its tiny pot is crowned by a metal gimmick through which the water drips in microscopic droplets, until the supply and you are equally exhausted. Horn-handed veterans speed the process by removing the lid and milking their palm over its top to create additional suction; newcomers are advised to attempt this only with gloves. If time counts, you'll soon find yourself asking the waiter to deliver your demitasse with your soup.

Since lots of metropolitan railway stations abroad are deadends, don't panic when you roll off in the exact opposite direction from your destination.

Many hotel rooms have locks which demand 2 turns of the key instead of one. These must be twisted until both tumblers snap into place (easily audible); if only one is engaged, you have only 50% security against thieves.

In hand-operated elevators (called "lifts" abroad), keep your finger on your destination-button as you close the gates or doors, or you might go up and down the shaft like a monkey on a stick at the summons of 32 impatient Europeans who have beat you to the punch! And please close those doors tightly when you step out, or no one will be able to use it.

For a list of about 200 motels of the European Motel Federation, write to Secretary, E.M.F., Dapplesweg 17, Berne, Switzerland.

Restaurant search while passing through small towns or villages? Silvino Trompetto, the globally esteemed Master Executive Chef of London's illustrious Savoy Hotel, recommends that strangers ask a good-sized chemist (drugstore manager), who will probably know the grade of the raw fare and the hygienic conditions of every eating place.

Foreign table etiquette: A Miami Beach Guidester asks for table tips abroad. Here goes: (1) The man or the host (if it is a party) always leads the way to the table, following the Maître and followed by his guest or guests, including ladies. (2) The fish knife and fish fork are easily recognizable by their distinctive shapes. The former resembles a large butter knife, and the latter has a broad cutting edge on one tine. (3) When you're faced with a multiplicity of knives and forks, always reach for the outside ones, farthest away from the plate. (4) The dessert implements are placed *above* the plate —not to the sides. (5) The clamplike instrument sometimes presented with asparagus first captures the stalk and is then lifted directly to the mouth. (6) The special pincers for snails are employed to hold the shell firmly while forking out the beastie with the other hand. (7) You might be asked if you prefer your oysters to be served "without beard." The "beard" is the dark circumference surrounding the nugget; most Americans prefer it "with beard." (8) The toothpick is used with abandon abroad. The more discreet diner at least has the grace to manipulate it with his napkin as a screen. When 2 people at the same table are engaged in this comic prophylaxis, it resembles the childhood game of peekaboo. (9) European hand-eating is just about confined to bread. Our American practice of picking up fried chicken with the fingers, peeling fruit Tarzan-style, and touching other comestibles is frowned upon. Continentals almost always use knives and forks.

Foreign theater etiquette: Which way do you face when you try to slither unobtrusively into your center-of-the-row seats? Europeans consider it rude for the latecomer to force them to face YOUR proscenium. They prefer the navel-to-eyeball confrontation. So go in facing the rear of the theater and the citizenry in your row. And who knows? You might even meet the violet eyes of a good-looking and unescorted friend for the rest of the evening!

Shoeshine: Before retiring for the night, drop your clodhoppers just outside your threshold, in the hall (except in Finland). They'll shine 'em free—part of the hotel-service charge (but you must add a small tip when you leave). Not much chance that your neighbor will steal them.

Service: When the telephone-use for room service isn't applicable, press the proper button on the gadget on your bedside table (or on the wall by the entrance). A light will flash outside your door; each button lights its own color, so the waiter and porter won't come when you want the maid. If you can't read the language, there is a clever drawing of each functionary beside his particular button. Sometimes there is a third system: An extra button on the base of the phone which, when pushed, summons the maid.

Bath: If it's down the hall, notify the maid a few minutes in advance. She has to unlock it and clean it up for you. In some countries every time you think of the word "bathtub," you're out another 50¢-or-so (baths are extra).

Letters: The accordion foldup international air form is available nearly everywhere. Prolific letter writers love 'em because (1) they save up to a third in postage, and (2) they run out of space just after ". . . wish you were here."

Hotel Postage: When you turn over your correspondence to the concierge's lads with instructions that it be airmailed, stand right there until they put on the stamps. Otherwise it might arrive by ordinary postage, with the desk people pocketing the difference. Always stamp postcards yourself, because too many go into the wastebasket. This is a routine petty racket markedly in smaller hotels.

Cameras: Be wary about leaving them in your room or putting them down anywhere. "Still" types are passed by most Customs, but movie types can cause infuriating difficulties (see "Customs" under individual countries).

Film: Color film is available in all major cities. Supplies are often spotty during the summer rush. Take your own, as insurance, especially if you are not going to be at any one stop long enough to have European-purchased film processed in Europe. (American developing of foreign negatives often gives negative results due to differences in chemicals.) Plenty of good black-and-white in all sizes practically everywhere. During these times of skyjack scares, it might be wiser to hand-carry all of your film (stills or even cinema types), since the new luggage x-raying equipment at international airports can alter the balance of unexposed *and* exposed keepsakes.

Sexy blonde: Take a good look at her these days; she might leave you a souvenir. The venereal rate abroad is again a red-alert epidemic. Not only has syphilis made a devastating comeback, but there's a strain of gonorrhea so hardy that it eats penicillin for breakfast. Plenty of willing, gorgeous women in half the cafés and railway station districts in Europe—but it's a chance, nearly always. Gigolos are liable to be infected, too.

Long-distance telephone: Except as specified below, *never make any international or transatlantic calls from your hotel, because you'll pay a surcharge of up to 300% if you do.* For decades it has been common and disgraceful tradition in virtually every hostelry abroad to tack its own "service fee" onto your bill for the casual, simple, normal use of its operator and the instrument. When checkout time comes, travelers are aghast to find that the $8.80 chat with the family in Connecticut has cost them $35.20 or that the $21.55 business talk with their Chicago partner has hooked them for $86.20. Deeply alarmed by this violation against public interest, AT&T's brilliant Long Lines

President Richard R. Hough and forceful Director-Overseas Administration E. E. Carr have recently inaugurated a towering counter-campaign named "Teleplan." In return for huge advertising and public relations expenditures on both sides of the ocean to bring massive new long-distance business to foreign telephone companies, their *quo* for this *quid* is that fair and reasonable maximum supplements be rigidly imposed upon all hotels or other 3rd parties in countrywide prohibitions. Already Ireland and Israel have adopted the "Teleplan" system. By the time you read these words, Scandinavia will probably—not positively—be in the fold. Nation by nation these progressive executives are patiently chopping away to eliminate these cruel excesses. Although Government Post Office ownerships or equipment inadequacies rule out adoption in such lands as France and Italy for the foreseeable future, eventually this team in benevolent Ma Bell may well integrate this project into a quasi-Pan European network and give fantastic savings to permanent or transient users overseas. . . . If you MUST make an emergency call from your bedroom, there are 2 ways to avoid all extra levies: (1) use your AT&T credit card (no others valid) or (2) reverse the charges. Otherwise, except in the aforementioned locations, pocket the price of a bottle or a magnum of champagne by putting them through at any local telephone center. . . . Almost everywhere you might wander these days in the civilized areas of the Old Continent, you may direct-dial to technically advanced points all over the world. As in North America, toll connections are made almost instantaneously.

Cables: Expensive, but increasingly accurate and dependable, except perhaps in Spain. Telex also is widely available, and it costs much less.

Maps: Not only indispensable after you get there, but timesaving and great fun before you leave. Stateside navigators might wish to send for the interesting catalogue offered by Richards European City Maps, 6311 Yucca Street, Hollywood, CA. 90028. Discounts of 5% and 10% are made on orders of more than 5 and 10. Good.

Who's Where: Celebrity Service, Inc., brainchild and *opera major* of the inimitable Earl Blackwell, operates full-scale field headquarters in Paris, London, and Rome. If you wish to locate any prominent personality abroad—peripatetic VIP or continental resident—you need only ask the concierge to query these mother hens. For an additional small fee you may subscribe to Ringmaster B's *Celebrity Bulletin,* a daily publication that tells you which film stars, TV luminaries, playwrights, Pulitzer Prize winners, and international socialites are between the sheets in your hotel (but not with whom!).

Office facilities en route: Manpower, Inc., has been set up in more than 325 metropolises on 5 continents. One of its 100-thousand assistants can be found in almost any major European city. Check the local phone books under this name or MAS.

Also for the businessman, a bonanza of free information is available through our U.S. Department of Commerce in Washington, D.C. Frequently, if you send this agency your itinerary and list of needs, the answers to your questions will be waiting at the proper one of its 40 offices abroad. These experts can save you priceless cargoes of time and smooth out a sea of wrinkles—but give Uncle Sam about 6 weeks' notice to yield tiptop results.

Budget meals: Self-service restaurants are now in every key center. Because you carry your own tray with your $2.50 to $5 meal, potential language problems with your waiter are eliminated. See *Fielding's Low-Cost Europe* for hundreds of listings.

Medical precaution: Medic Alert Foundation renders an invaluable non-profit service to travelers who suffer from any serious medical problem. It furnishes lifesaving emblems of 10-karat gold-filled ($25), of sterling silver ($9), or of stainless steel ($7) to be worn around the neck or wrist—or to be hung from a charm bracelet. Should the patient be unable to talk, medical personnel or law-enforcement officials are instantly informed of dangers inherent in standard treatment. The tag carries such warnings as "DIABETIC," "ALLERGIC TO PENICILLIN," "TAKING ANTICOAGULANTS," "WEARING CONTACT LENSES," "NECK BREATHER," or whatever difficulty. It also bears the telephone number of the Medic-Alert headquarters in California to which anyone may call "Collect" from anywhere in the world at any hour of day or night for additional file material about the individual case. This laudable project is the charitable mission of Marion Collins, M.D., who almost lost his teen-age daughter when she was given an antitetanus injection following an automobile accident (a preventive which would be administered routinely if the physician were not warned). If you'll pardon our paraphrase, no traveler should *ever* be caught alive without one of these emblems. For more information about this splendid organization (donations are tax deductible), write to Medic-Alert Foundation International, Turlock, Calif.

If a personal emergency involving catastrophe or possible death should occur when regular transportation is not available, ask the American Consulate or Embassy about MAC (Military Airlift Command). It is the world's largest airline. Its Communications, Weather, Rescue, Photographic, and other Defense services are invaluable—but when it steals so many thousands of overseas passengers from legitimate commercial carriers, you, as a bruised and contused taxpayer, might as well cash in on your investment if disaster should strike. U.S. military planes and pilots, with daily schedules to every corner of Europe; extremely low fares.

American Military Cemeteries: Gold Star travelers whose gallant sons or daughters rest in military cemeteries abroad may obtain geographical and other information from the American Battle Monuments Commission, Forrestal Building, 1000 Independence Ave. s.w., Washington, D.C. 20314, or from this organization's office in our Paris, Rome, or London embassies.

Reservation: This simply can't be emphasized enough: Next to your passport, your hotel reservation is the *most vital part of your trip. Reserve in advance; before you go, wait for confirmation.* Also be specific when booking! In some countries a bath is a bath is a bath, which may not include a water closet as well. Except in Deluxe establishments, it is best to request a room with "bath *and* toilet," if you want these amenities.

Miscellaneous tips: Change your shoes at least twice a day, every day that you're abroad. This is better than yogurt and wheat germ to make the traveler Last Longer, Look Younger, and Feel Peppier.

Unless yours is an ultramodern hotel, keep your windows closed, even on the muggiest day. In most European buildings, inside temperatures are considerably lower than outside ones, due to the thickness of the walls—and the fresh-air fiend not only lets in the heat but a new army of flies.

If your accommodation is air-conditioned, ask your baggage porter how to operate the controls before he leaves the room. Otherwise, you might find yourself taking a sauna instead of a siesta on an August afternoon.

Plan your schedule so that your day breaks into 2 or 3 different and unrelated parts. Eight hours of unrelieved sightseeing, shopping, or exploring on foot at one clip becomes leg-heavy work. A sensible itinerary, for example, would cover the museums and cultural interests in the morning, take you to an open-air restaurant for lunch (to clear the mental cobwebs), and send you out refreshed for the afternoon of shopping.

Whenever a lady visits a European cathedral, long sleeves (or a cardigan) and a head scarf are still regarded as good form, despite the fact the Vatican recently decided that such dress is no longer required. (NEVER miniskirts, p-l-e-a-s-e!) Likewise, men should not enter without jackets or in Bermudas. Ignoring this is such bad manners that it's a direct insult to the religion and to the local people. For ladies wandering at random, it's a good idea to tuck a scarf into your pocket or purse.

If there's any choice about the location of your bedchamber, here are 2 points to remember: (1) In general, take the highest possible floor (less noise, fewer flies, cleaner air), and (2) always try to face either east or north (a northeast corner room above the 6th or 7th floor is perfect—unless it's on a heavily traveled artery or you're missing great hunks of local scenery.)

Take a nap whenever you can steal a moment; after luncheon is the best time. This will recharge your batteries and lessen that terrible travel fag.

Boarding a taxi? Keep your map of the city handy, so that if the hackie plays "no speak," you can pinpoint your destination to him.

Plan to keep a few coins handy when using the Italian turnpikes or the German autobahns, or some English pennies for the motorways in Britain. They are also an indispensable—especially for the ladies—in the public conveniences en route. Their slogan: "No dough, No go!"

Briefly and broadly, that's the general travel picture in today's Europe. We hope your trip will give you pleasure beyond price—that you will have happiness and a bounty of thrills—and that it will always pay you off in the currency of cobwebs and dreams.

We hope, too, that both Europe and this book are faithful when called upon for your friendship.

Austria

No country on the Continent guarantees the footloose wanderer more breath-taking mountains, a larger helping of enchanting beauty, or a warmer welcome from its people. In Vienna, Salzburg, and Innsbruck you'll find the fingerprints, footprints, and bottle prints of migrations of outlanders who have long savored its heady lures; in smaller centers you will experience a sample of living which has remained undisturbed since the days of Franz Josef (well, er, at least since last winter's visit of the Baltimore Ski Club). The popularity of this rollicking republic is romping along at break-the-bank pace. Don't ever confuse Austria with Germany; they're as far apart in customs, attitudes, and culture as are Italy and France.

When the skies turn peekaboo-blue, that's the signal for the lemming crush to begin. In the capital today, there's scarcely a letup from Maytime until the October rains. The countryside offers a few available kips when cosmopolites are touring the major festivals and fairs, but who wants to spend all his days in the clover? Ironclad hotel reservations, therefore, are an absolute must; *don't go without confirmation!* Despite the whopping national increase of 175-thousand new beds in about a decade (Austrian chamber-*Mädchen* puff up about 600-thousand pillows), she still hasn't enough facilities to cope with the flood of foreign visitors during halcyon days—or even in the fringe seasons. For skiers, the first weekend in January to the first weekend in February is the choice period if you don't have a previous booking; before and after, the resorts are filled to the rafters. And don't be surprised if you find the gates locked and the caretaker curled up in the sack when you visit a castle or a museum during scheduled sightseeing hours, because formal organization (discounting that of the splendid Austrian National Tourist Office) is often slightly slaphappy. But as compensation you will get a warm, hearty, individual welcome—much less commercial than that of the Swiss. You may range from such deluxe pleasure domes of sport as the Arlberg's Zürserhof to a simple mode of village living that is comfortable enough for anyone but the fussiest type of traveler, who ought to stick to the largest cities. France is the country in which to parade that mink coat and that new Dior; milady may do the same at Austria's chic resorts or at the music festivals, but in general Austria is where you let down your hair and have fun.

ATTITUDE TOWARD TOURISTS   The Austrians couldn't be nicer. For detailed holiday information on this enticing nation, write, phone, or call in person at the **Austrian National Tourist Office**, 545 Fifth Ave., N.Y. 10017. Its dynamic young Director, Dr. Heinz Patzak, has the lore of his native land at his fingertips; you'll find him a gold mine of advice, facts, and guidance.

The home office of this organization is doing an outstanding job. The official **Tourist Information Office** in the capital handles all routine holiday questions. On any extraordinary difficulties or puzzles get in touch with the **Österreichische Fremdenverkehrswerbung** (Austrian National Tourist Office) at Hohenstaufengasse 3-5, Vienna I. The knowledgeable and capable Comanagers, Dr. Helmut Zolles and Dkfm. Frank Kübler, are its moving forces. There are 9 **Landesverkehrsämter** (Provincial Tourist Offices), as well as propaganda stations, tourist boards, and spa administrations in Austrian tourist centers. Branches are maintained in 18 foreign capitals.

In local health resorts, ask for the *Kurdirektor;* in other hamlets, try the *Verkehrsamt* (regional aid stations).

Special for winter sports: This season 15 mountain resorts will inaugurate a welcoming program titled "American Skiers' Best Friends." In each upland station there will be an official national host who is there to greet visiting Yanks, tell them where the snow is best, and generally serve as an amiable Austrian helpmate and companion to fellow countrymen-and-women on their slopes. *Danke vielmals!*

MONEY AND PRICES   The principal monetary unit is the schilling. At this writing it is worth about 5½¢, or call it 18 schillings to $1. Below this is the groschen; since its value is only 1/20th of a cent, toss these around as carelessly as chicken feed—with an expenditure of 11½¢.

There are now coins for 2, 5, 10, and 50 groschen, and 1, 5, 10, 25, and 50 schillings. Notes are in denominations of 20, 50, 100, 500, and 1000 schillings.

The Added Value Tax of 18%, which touches the human animal at almost every turn, is the latest unpleasant jolt to everyone's bank balance.

§TIP: A few 100-schilling commemorative coins are minted annually—handsome souvenirs. Check with any national bank.

CUSTOMS AND IMMIGRATION   Sensible regulations. Visitors are permitted to bring in unlimited amounts of foreign currency and/or schillings; *export* is restricted to 15,000 Austrian schillings.

On normal occasions Customs officials are gentle, gracious, and good hosts. Since 80% of all tourists arrive by car and peak-period traffic jams are horrendous, the inspectors virtually shoo motorists through. That honest-Johan look below your eyebrows should sail you through.

But if you happen to hit one of the rare spot checks, they are apt to strip your baggage down to the last comic book. Wayfarers to and from Germany most often get this Z treatment.

Ordinarily, however, you'll like your welcome to Austria.

HOTELS   For far more comprehensive information on certain Austrian hostelries than space limitations permit here, interested travelers are referred to *Fielding's Selected Favorites: Hotels and Inns, Europe* ($4.95) by our ever-roving son, Dodge Temple Fielding. The revised edition, in which a total of 300-odd favored possibilities were hand-picked from the 5000-plus personally inspected, will be at your bookstore early this year.

New hotels have brought a lot more glamour to the current picture. It comes at a wowing cost, however; tariffs have climbed so abruptly and combustively that they are a shock to returning pilgrims. *This season, the normal range is from $33 to $60 for a twin with bath. In the better stops, you'll be lucky to get away for less than $50.* One amelioration is the all-inclusive price scale —no pesky extra charges for service, taxes, heating, bread, *couvert,* and the like. This is small consolation, however, for the Great Leap Forward.

Today *Vienna* claims its very own **Hilton**, a city in itself that offers 700 latchkeys, a quartet of restaurants, shops, and—most convenient of all—the main city air terminal smack under its hangar-wide roof. The mayor here is General Manager Rupert Huber, whom we haven't yet met. We'll rate his striking white candidate after it has had a season or so to adjust to its surroundings. How this metropolis is growing!

Warning: Save in the Intercontinental (which has its own facilities), avoid all laundering and dry cleaning in major Viennese hotels if your wardrobe can possibly hold out until your next stop. Often our things have been hideously butchered by the reigning outside near-monopoly.

The century-old but split-second-fresh **Imperial** is the blue-ribbon choice for the client who wants grandeur, suavity, and action with his million-$ elegance. This beautiful, imposing, 200-room, fully air-conditioned hostelry has now achieved near-perfection in every department. Choice of ultramodern or classic-style rooms, all handsomely decorated; Royal Suites—truly "Royal"—with palatial opulence at a palatial rate; Suite #202–203, considerably less formal and less expensive, is so indescribably appealing in its exquisite comfort that to us it is among the happiest nests we've found ANYWHERE. Spotless maintenance; flawless taste; 2 superkind, crack-trained staffers to each client; Concierge Willi Lache and his minions standouts. A Chicago Guidester says, "You feel like *somebody* at the *Imperial!*" Demipension is required at intervals, but the cuisine is extraordinarily delicious. The famous Director Karl-Peter Littig rates palms and salaams for his magnificent job here; Manager Heinke also deserves Imperial laurels. We regard it not only as the best hotel in Austria, but (as does *Fortune Magazine*) also as one of the The Eleven Greatest Hotels of the World.

The **Bristol**, under the Imperial wand and with similar tariffs, has risen majestically to our second slot. Its restyled restaurant is *the* after-theater-and-opera gathering spot in the capital. Enormous changes made with all traditional grace notes carefully retained; well-appointed silk-lined bedchambers where the suites and the singles shine with a special pride; all in all, extremely chic in every element of its decorative scheme. Under the baton of Gerhard Paul, an able protégé of Grand Master Littig, the orchestration becomes more and more a symphony of delight every year. Highly recommended on every score.

The **Sacher** trades on its global reputation for Old Worldliness. Turn-of-the-century furnishings, high ceilings, oil paintings, and statuary abound; modern touches elsewhere have enhanced its efficiency. Its drawbacks, however, are equally significant. In our judgment, most of its accommodations are painfully small for transatlantic travelers with ample luggage; the house policy of not accepting *any* credit cards seems ill-advised; better sound-proofing should be installed on all streetfront units; we again received pushy service during an after-opera meal when the waiters wanted to leave; moreover the cuisine was not up to our former meals here. Undoubtedly here is an aristocrat—of that there's no question; but whether you are lured by its personality depends upon you. We've seen this hotel long enough to be convinced that it is changeless, timeless, and fine in its very own way. Our very own way, however, is different enough to incline us preferentially toward the Imperial and the Bristol with the Sacher chasing closely at their heels. Very special and as the French would say, *"Chacun à son goût."*

The **Krantz-Ambassador**, while not advancing, is maintaining its standards. It has long been the Vienna home of kings, heads of state, giants of the musical world, and others who shun the spotlight. Dual entrances from 2 avenues; twin lobbies; mulberry silk throughout; full air-chilling; handsome, spacious accommodations with comfortable bathrooms; small dining room (for clients only) with superb cuisine; unusually friendly attention; one of the few hotels in Vienna that never requires demipension.

The **Hotel Im Palais Schwarzenberg** (Schwarzenbergplatz 9), a charming island of serenity, occupying the right wing of one of Vienna's most beautiful baroque palaces, exudes the feeling that the visitor is ensconced in a provincial mansion. Garden and plaza setting just off the Ringstrasse, 5 minutes from the central whirl; client capacity increased to 50. All 34 rooms have private bath and individual décor, either antique or modern; 8 fresh kips in new wing; some units in the chalet extension featuring neat little kitchenettes. Manager Ivo Mohrenschildt is displaying a masterful grasp of town-and-country inn-keeping. Different and excellent.

The 14-story, $12,000,000, 500-room **Intercontinental** is an edifice from the impersonal cookie mold that makes guests wonder whether they are in Vienna, Abidjan, Auckland, or Rawalpindi. At last, however, it seems to be warming up here and there. Sleek-modern exterior; quiet but not inconvenient situation near the Wienfluss and Stadtpark; orange-shaded Brasserie for quick meals; excellent, all-you-can-lap-up noon-to-3 P.M. buffet daily; other conveniences. General Manager John Edmair is continuing the company's efforts to give this huge installation more of a human pulse beat. Still more muscle than heart, but very strong indeed in its own particular way.

The **Bellevue** is drawing an increasing number of stateside travelers. Space for 7-score guests, but only 2-score with private bath or shower; décor a mixture of modern furnishings, crystal chandeliers, chintz bed-puffs, and frilled lampshades; enclosed garage; interior garden. As one of Vienna's oldest hostelries it is as clean as the day it was born. Fair enough.

The 77-room **President** is well groomed by Directress Sylvia Seyrling. Some twins with a 3rd bed; smartly furnished; summer breakfast garden; Nordic dining salon. We prefer this one to the **Strudlhof,** which also is new, modern, and economically priced.

The conveniently-sited, 121-unit **Astoria** stepped out of the beauty parlor in a futile attempt to show that her non-Waldorf salad days are over. Dowager wrinkles sadly confessing her fresh makeup; 2 elevators; extensive and tasteful bath renewals; dreary corridors; ancient furnishings "modernized" rather than replaced; solid, but lacking even 1 twinkle of spark. What we do love, however, is the space in her bedchambers. More of a dedicated (or resigned) spinster than a Carnaby cuddlebug.

The centrally located **Europa**, more sassy and peppy, gets downright skimpy when it comes to elbowroom. Ingratiating dining strip overlooking the street; twentieth-century accouterments in all bedchambers; shoulder-squeezing baths; #802 or #702 offer the widest angles for duos. Rather commercial but indeed tolerable if you happen to be a rich elf.

Am Parkring is club-sandwiched on the 11th to 13th floors of a commercial office building. Quiet, viewful units; excellent maintenance overlorded by Manager Ernst Stockinger; tiny singles with half-bathtubs; small, functional, tasteful doubles; cramped luggage space; Lilliputian balconies on the top 2 floors; demipension is mandatory. Modern, utilitarian architecture and motif.

The **Parkhotel Schoenbrunn**, facing the palace grounds, can take pride in its lobby, lounges, shops, and a pleasant garden wing; many groups feather-nest here. The **De France** (slipping again) and the **Prinz Eugen** (7th and 8th floors rear the best) are members of the same corporation. The **Erzherzog Rainer** is coming back to life these days. Special emphasis on its dining facilities; extra-attentive service; renewed public rooms; improved bed-chambers. On the jump again, we're happy to report. Then come the **Am Stephan-platz** (opposite the cathedral; aged but increasingly graceful), the **Tyrol** (a perked-up cutie), the **Kummer, Royal** (excellent rooftop solarium; kind-hearted people; magnificent views from upper quarters), **Clima**, and the **Zen-trum**. The **Tourotel**, not unlike its sister chain-links elsewhere, adheres to the standard pattern of clean, narrow-dimensioned, moderately priced accommo-dations, modern-gauged public facilities, Wienerwald-quality cuisine (same ownership as the restaurant amalgam), and an outlying situation better suited for self-drive motorists than for taxi-borne thrifties. Our thumbs still turn straight down on the **Regina** and the **Graben.** For apartment digs lasting 2 weeks or more, try the **Capricorno** or the **Hietzinger Hof.**

Now for that "special something": **Schloss Laudon.** Here is a work of love as cloistered as a rare gem. It is set in the Vienna Woods only 30 minutes by car or hotel bus shuttle when traffic is heavy. The fortress site, dating back to 1130, was fully restored a few years ago. And how lavish it is for this little land! You'll find a verdant rolling estate with a lake for fishing, moat and gondolas for romantic paddling, bridle paths, stables, swimming pool, tennis courts, supervised playground and recreation room, bowling, sauna, library, ice-skating and horse-drawn sleigh-riding in winter, and so much peace and tranquility that even the swans have been charged to glide softly in the ponds. Tastefully preserved interior; hunters' lodge café-restaurant; Grill inside the Old Mill; watchful service under the stewardship of kind, soft-spoken Manager Peter Laszlo; expensive cuisine which sometimes mangles classic international recipes but shines in national specialties. Delightful bedchambers in the main hostelry but less agreeable kips in an outskirting lodge; décor divided among Baroque, Biedermeier, Empire, and Peasant modes, most of them gracefully appointed. Highest recommendation nationally among its type. STOP PRESS: As we go to press, word has just reached us that Schloss Laudon has closed.

The **Kahlenberg**, also a sizable haul by car from the center, is an appendage of the gigantic pretzel and suds palace of the same name. Ultramodern décor; total of 33 cramped rooms with balconies; regular bus service. Because of the atrocious skilletcraft and service we've noted at this state-owned feedery, we wouldn't stay here on a bet—but for an enthralling panorama of the metropolis, the Vienna Woods, and the Danube, it's absolutely tops.

Pensions? The **Atlanta** is our favorite. Others we find worthy are **Opernring, Elite, Arenburg,** and **Schneider.**

Dedicated budgeteers? Since we're too bottlenecked here for additional entries, please consult *Fielding's Low-Cost Europe,* our annually revised paperback, which lists scads more bargain hotels or pensions and money-saving tips for serious economizers.

Salzburg offers several good choices—each for a different taste. If charm and local color are your targets, the country-tavern-style **Goldener Hirsch,** which boasts more than 400 years of nubile grace, is small, intimate, and delightful. After midnight you can usually hear the original Gold Hart or some other attractive 2-legged animal prancing upstairs on the creaky floors in the older segment; the newer wing, which almost doubles its capacity, combines Old Goldener Hirsch-flavored garniture with twentieth-century architecture, with nary a squeak to be heard. This one is ably managed by the personable young Count Johannes Walderdorf. Superb maintenance; ultrakind Concierge Erich Volk; s-m-o-o-t-h drinks by Kurt Bayer, an amateur musicologist who knows more about Wolfgang than did Frau Mozart. Cuisine? Good but not splendid. Traditionally the city's number one, but check before booking because there has been some talk in the trade about its changing hands in the near future. True? **Österreichischer Hof**'s renovations are striking. The more conventional wanderer might prefer this one to the above. Glass-front "Panorama" floor with fresh furnishings, private baths, air conditioning, and river view; each unit in its own distinctive décor; all 5 restaurants with waterside terraces; dramatically improved cookery; additional refurbishings continuing. Over the century mark, but still looking trim and sailing smartly. The **Winkler** was physically colorful during our recent winks, but it has an extremely commercial air possibly pinned to the fact that it has been taken over by a travel agency. We imagine that Manager Müller must feel obliged to favor clients sent by the mother company, but let's wait a season or so before rendering any conclusive judgment on this t'Winkler. Even though its administrative reins seem a bit tangled of late, we are still receiving happy tidings from travelers who've paused recently at the **Bristol.** On the spiritual side, we are delighted to report that it retains its famed hospitality, cordiality, and easy homespun graces. On the physical side, despite its new elevator and touchups, it impressed us as clinging nostalgically to many arthritic furnishings, frayed textiles, and mixed-period decorative whims. The 20 new units are best; front billets can be very noisy. Closed in winter. Okay, but miles from a Ritz. The **Parkhotel Mirabell** is for the ultramodern school; much thought, time, and money went into the construction of this imposing structure, but the sloppy maintenance we've repeatedly observed might well be riding this racer to ruin. Lilliputian rooms; gadgets galore; singles with coffin-size bath and shower; connecting indoor swimming pool; staff eager but slow. We'd call this one grossly overpriced. To round out the leaders, the **Kobenzl,** 2500 feet above the city on the Judenbergalpe, is a bargain. Host Rupert Herzog and his beautiful wife—*what* a charmer!—lovingly operate this gorgeously refashioned, spectacularly situated aerie. Spotlessly maintained; bubble-happy swimming pool that's heated; sauna; panoramic restaurant; proud of its table—and properly so; amiable, wide-angle lodgings and newly spaced-out bathrooms; annex with sun terrace open year round while the main house sleeps in winter; no demipension required at any time. Chair lift to outskirts of city until 5:30 P.M. but not in bad weather; 10 minutes by car from the center, with 2 daily free runs or independent hire for perhaps $3.50. Except for a few minor nit-picks, here is a heavenly setting run by good people who deserve their success in this unique upland retreat.

Haus Ingeborg, about 10 minutes out, is a 4-century-old cutie that oozes Tyrolean grace. Very small, very select, and very much to be recommended to inn-mates with wheels. Open March 1 to October 30.

The others? (1) **Schlosshotel St. Rupert** (55-pillow renovated castle 1½ miles out; lovely gardens; quiet; open Apr.-Oct.), (2) **Fondachhof** (attractive suburban villa; pool; limited menu; for tranquillity lovers), (3) **Schlosswirt** (huge country manse in nearby *Anif;* 20 of its 40 rooms in annex; outstanding cookery; likewise peaceful), (4) **Friesacher** (also in *Anif;* handsome rustic restaurant; book in the main building only), (5) **Kasererhof** (overall taste and startlingly high tariffs here kill it for us), (6) **Europa** (a 15-story eyesore marring the valley profile; to us, grim, commercial, and cold as an Arctic cod). Second class: (1) **Pitter** (bustling with conventions; good for its type; improving steadily), (2) **Auersperg,** (3) **Stieglbrau,** (4) **Kasererbräu,** (5) **Markus Sittikus,** (6) **Zum Hirschen.** We hear abundant praise for the not-yet-inspected **Weisse Taube.** Third class: (1) **Elefant** (pachyderm born in A.D. 1200; inviting ground-floor Stube; 40 clean, nice rooms), (2) **Eibenhaus** (near Friesacher in *Anif;* captivating view in fresh-air surroundings; basic at best), (3) **Blaue Gans,** (4) **Mitteregg** (above the Kobenzl; strictly for sporting, rawboned budgeteers who want to cash in on a million-dollar vista). Pensions: (1) **Radauer,** (2) **Fürstenweg;** nearly all the better ones are slightly out of town. The **Airport Hotel** is functional and little else.

Looking for something very Austrian and very unusual? Two praiseworthy bets: (1) **Schloss Fuschl** at *Fuschl,* 15 miles due east, is a glorious oasis for the moneyed traveler of taste. Enlarged terrace seating 80; Winter Garden;

9-hole golf course; automatic bowling alley. Total of 64 rooms and 38 baths; patrician furnishings; swimming, horseback riding, boating, lake or stream fishing. Two romantic suites and a bungalow lakeside; 2 simple hillside guest-houses (one a l-o-n-g hike); Manager Pischl, with a big assist from his nice wife, is moving mountains here. Normally open from early May to late October, but check if you're a snowcat or bunny. Like the Goldener Hirsch in Salzburg, this fine house also may be changing proprietors soon. PS: If this Schloss is closed or filled, try the **Jagdhof** which flanks the entry road to the aristocratic Fuschl estate. Same ownership but simple hunter-style accommodations instead of ultraposh amenities; perhaps the world's largest pipe collection. A worthy lower-cost alternative, especially for families on wheels. (2) **Schloss Sighartstein,** a 600-year-old castle with the baronial charm of the Franz Josef era, is a wonder and delight to travelers who appreciate tradition. Overlooking Lake Wallersee at *Neumarkt,* only 16 miles from Salzburg; capacity for 18 guests; all main meals served at 1 big table, with the titled proprietors as your host and hostess; children are welcome, BUT they'd better be well-mannered. A friendly Texas Guidester writes, "Countess Uiberacker and Count and Countess Palffy were the most delightful hosts in all Austria." Neither a hotel nor an inn (even though it does have an elevator), but an old-fashioned country mansion; April 1 to end-October only. Inquiries: Graf Palffy, Schloss Sighartstein, Post Neumarkt, Salzburg. Guarantee: You'll fall in love with this noble-ranked and noble-hearted family, too.

In *Innsbruck,* the handsome, colorful, comfortable **Tyrol** is tops for the region; King of the Mountain Erwin Gutwinski has wrought mighty changes during his tenure. Entirely redecorated from foothills to summit; many artful touches including rich textiles, porcelain sconces, chandeliers, and waiters in local costume; every unit with bath or shower. Except for Noël, it is *closed in winter,* when clients are shuttled across the street to the snow-bright **Europa.** This one was transformed by the Gutwinski wand a short while back; it is kept in top form; the dining salon was recently refashioned in gold and purple. Heavy play from group bookings; in season, folk dancing, singing, and revelry buckle the walls of its inviting Barocksaal. Here's a stand-up model of what sharp-eyed management and generous infusions of schillings can do. The **Holiday Inn,** a tall midtown edifice, linked itself into the international chain recently. The bedchambers are the star attractions by far, for comfort, scenic rewards, and modern conveniences. Public sectors are a weakness, in our judgment; the cuisine, if you're lucky, easily can be forgotten. Service? Though poor, it's likely to improve with seasoning. The **Mariabrunn,** 2½ miles out, is 1000 feet high on the north slope of the mountain range; exhilarating vista; cellar-sited Kupferstuben in stone and timber (nights only). Adequate. The neighboring balcony-clad **Bellevue,** owned by the same family, is a recent entry with space for 50 nappers. Okay but not truly Belle. The **Goldener Adler,** founded in 1390, comes up with oodles of authentic antiquity at all-too-authentic twentieth-century tariffs. Restyled public rooms; Director Karl Pokorny is trying hard. Now worthy to nest in one of the oldest corners of Austria. The **Grauer Bär** also specializes in package trippers; 147 plain accommodations and 48 baths; almost impossible to get in, unless you bring your charter club, Boy Scout troop, or affinity clause with you. The 30-room

Greif, with a low bath ratio, is no longer as sparkling as it should be—or was; comparatively lightweight rates. The **Clima**'s bargain-basement taste is not appealing to us. **Touringhaus,** connected to the Tyrol and supervised by the Gutwinski clan, boasts an excellent situation. Butter-fresh breakfast room and snack bar; space for 55 clients; only 1 private bath; be sure to bid for one of the back rooms facing the Nordkette for a superb view (your next-door neighbor at the Tyrol is paying 8 times more for the very same vista!). A budgeteer's delight. The **Roter Adler** was totally refashioned not too far back. The **Alpenmotel,** in our judgment, is too remote and too unattractive to be considered. The ever-crowded **Goldener Stern** is a sleeping factory on the "out"-side of the Inn River. Obviously a Goldener Mine for somebody, but fool's gold in our value-conscious opinion.

In most choicely sited *Igls* (pronounced "Eagles"), a 10-minute drive above Innsbruck, the **Sporthotel** is just the ticket for the luxury sport buffs. Smooth rusticity; dancing to orchestral lilts nightly; sauna plus hydropathic treatments; pine-and-glass-lined indoor-outdoor pool; another exclusively for fresh-air paddlers; free ski lift; individual garages. Comfortable units with bath; demi-suites (the nicest in the new wing) slightly higher. Its Beck family operators have now spiffed up the nearby **Schlosshotel Igls.** Huge rooms; sumptuous appointments in the finest tradition of highborn Tyrolean life-styles; space for only 30 patricians. We can't wait to try it on for size. The **Park,** almost completely rebuilt and wearing a penthouse swimming pool as its chapeau, is another bucolic hillsider to which we lost our hearts. Glorious setting in a spruce-d-up pinewood; less costly and more tranquil than the leader; ice rink and 4 ski lifts nearby; no foreign tour groups EVER, states ever-kind Proprietress Balzar; 62 spacious bedrooms, most with balcony and 44 with private bath. Lovely for the older or more sedate wanderer. **Iglerhof** has now returned to its original family ownership. Magnificent perch above a mountain meadow, but to us oh-so-sour when compared to the sweet charm of the Park or the flavorful grooming of the Sporthotel. Will it improve?

Badgastein's innkeepers make up some 7000 beds daily in the summer season (cures and medical treatments) and the winter season (skiing), but between mid-October and mid-December, as in most similar resorts, the spooks wear the sheets in this ghost town. Nothing, but nothing, is open. The balconied, 200-room **Parkhotel Bellevue** garners the affluent young and the twinkling old. Completely renewed; lodge-style downstairs bar *the* social nucleus in winter; music nightly by a trio of orchestras; excellent management by smiling, evergreen Proprietor S. J. Wührer. The colorful **Bellevue-Alm** is a chalet pleasure dome 400 meters above the main installation. Accessible by chair lift from below or a morning's ski from the upper slopes; hot lunches, group barbecues, après-ski nuzzling, poolside lounging, or rustic overnighting in its 14 bedchambers. Highly recommended for the spirited. Below this one, the **Kaiserhof,** of ancient vintage, has been renovated; well maintained and getting better. Luxury standards but the quality of its unquestioned refine-ment seemed a bit heavy for our taste. The **Elisabethpark** has been perked up smartly, enlarged once again, and given a thermal swimming pool. A Lizzie on the go which some rank as the regina of the vale. We certainly were impressed by its sprightly mien on our recent inspection. Highly recommended. The **Straubinger** is now getting too old-fashioned to suit us. The **Grand Hotel de l'Europe** still was closed on our latest look. The **Germania** and **Mozart** have been skidding in our estimation. **Haus Hirth** has a distinct sanitarium personality, at least in our eyes. In the budget category, we prefer (1) **Schillerhof** (2) **Sporthotel** (3) **Wildbad** (perhaps now enjoying year-round operation), (4) **Eden**, (5) **Regina**, and (6) **Savoy**. The **Alpenhof** is an economizer's delight. Ownership by (and connected to) the Parkhotel Bellevue; lovely situation; guests may use *all* the facilities of its opulent sister. Golden bangles at brass-bed tariffs.

In *Kitzbühel,* Falk Volkhart, the Pharaoh of Munich's great Bayerischer Hof, took over the **Tenne** and is creating an upland haven in "alpine deluxe" motif. Space for about 70; 10 rooms with open fires, rich in *gemütlich* atmosphere; sauna; timber-lined grill. Please avoid the annex. Overall, we like it. We haven't seen the **Hirzingerhof,** but we hear nice things about it. The Tyrolean-style, 55-room, 55-bath **Goldener Greif** offers heated-water, interior swimming pool, restaurant, grill, and casino. Here's the traditional social hub of the valley—but for how long will it continue to be the leading lady in this role? Very good indeed. The imposing **Grand** has undergone no major changes. The redecorated **Weisses Rössl** boasts 80 units and 40 baths; very well maintained; pleasant atmosphere; tennis court, center-of-town situation. Kindly proprietor Hirnsberger will see to your every comfort. The chalet-style **Reischhof** is the same as it was—which isn't special. The **Lutzenberg** is another wide-bodied chalet. The public rooms feature open timbers; so does the pool. Not expensive, but you'll need your own transportation—whether in wheel form or on skis. **Schloss Lebenberg,** a recently expanded castle on a hillock 5 minutes from town, offers a fresh wing, glass-enclosed swimming pool, elegantly perked-up décor, and fairly steep prices. If you are searching for a refined and somewhat formal address, here it is. **Schlosshotel Münichau,** a 1200-year-old matron meticulously restored by the Goldener Greif directors, has come back to life with flair and vitality. Two miles from the center in pastoral farm country; 50 units, all with bath; attractive dining room plus a 2-story Grill annex and outdoor dining patio for summer meals; same rates as the mother hotel in town. A haven for the let's-get-away-from-it-all traveler. *All of the above close at various slack periods;* the modest **Klausnerhof**, near the station, is the only hostelry that operates year round.

Linz's **Tourotel** is linked to the new convention center, Bruckner Halle. It is just what you might expect. Out on the skirts of town, the **Crest** digs are better for overnighting motorists than for lingerers. The **Schwechater Hof** takes pride in its highly regarded restaurant. Its 54 bedchambers are supplied with only 7 baths and 6 showers; a general overhauling has been realized. Old-fashioned, but recommendable for budgeteers.

Zürs am Arlberg's leading house—and one of the top spots on the European winter sport circuit—is the merrily rich **Zürserhof**. Beautiful appointments in Peasant Baroque; sumptuous wing of suites, all with working fireplaces; a living museum of fine regional furnishings; full range of facilities for skiers; soothing comforts provided by Proprietor Ernst Skardarasy, president of the Austrian Hotel Association; the hitching post of many international notables. Elegant and good. The **Lorünser,** with more sporting *Gemüt-*

lichkeit and a younger clientele, boasts a permafrost-to-pitched-roof renovation. Its set-meal gastronomy (with options, plus a policy of answering requests for special dishes) is one of the best we've experienced in the alps. Now 70 rooms; Manager Herbert Jochum, a former Olympic trainer, and his dee-lovely wife, Inge, couldn't be nicer. They and their cordial staff made our recent week's skiing sojourn here pure Vorarlberg-high bliss. Heaven for serious athletes—outdoor variety. The **Alpenrose** is a bouquet of petals; swimming pool and sauna; 2 bars; tea dancing daily plus nightly revels. Somewhat more prickly-commercial in tone than the top blossoms, but a handsome haven for highlanders. **Edelweiss** is simple, cozy, and bustling. Its *Stubli*, where we yum-yumed over a sinfully delicious *Backhendl* (fried chicken, Austrian version), is always jammed. The hillbound **Alpenhof,** now grown to 50 units, is infused with the giant-size grace of the owning Thurnherr family. Intimacy is the pivotal word here—with all the comforts of home-sweet-home, including much of that feeling, too. The village-*centrum* **Albona** seems to be a chalet that just couldn't cease growing. The popular discothèque plus the doin's in the nearby Mara wrap up nearly 99.999% of the nightlife in this sleepy vale. If you're after action and treed landscape, try the next-door townlet in the following paragraph.

Lech, 10 minutes from Zürs am Arlberg, comes up with the (1) **Gasthof Post** (brightly decorated 3-story chalet; extensive antique collection; substantial amenities; ingratiating atmosphere where you might see a queen, a prince, or even a lowly travel writer sipping a crisp Bloody Mary in its convivial nookeries); (2) **Schneider** (across the covered bridge from the frontrunner; razed and rebuilt as one of the slickest mock-ups of rustication we've seen lately; indoor swimming pool; impressive, even dramatically imposing, but somehow too contrived and polished to suit our personal tastes); (3) **Kristberg** (conceived by the legendary Egon Zimmerman who originally put up a tiny house on a tiny knoll; pleasant view; attractive and smashingly successful Egon's Scotch Club with dancing nightly); (4) **Kristiania** (similar in personality to the Kristberg; owned by Othmar Schneider; a traveler's reward if you are seeking pension instead of hotel atmosphere); (5) **Krone** (almost in the belfry of the town chapel; still fairly comfortable, but becoming seedier with advancing age; now a bit campy, in our opinion); (6) **Arlberg** (new entrance and that's about all); (7) **Berghof** (a cozy corner for medium-budget sporting types). If you don't want the bustle of Lech or the relative isolation of Zürs, then why not try **Oberlech?** It can be reached from the main center by cableway. For us, here is the best of both worlds. The lodgings are all pretty rawboned. **Sonnenburg** seems to be the most sophisticated. About 60% bath ratio; stimulating cookery; friendly people; swimming pool. The **Montana** is noted for its kitchen and the **Goldener Berg** is comfortable. The **Petersboden,** despite its spartan simplicity, is our favorite. Fabulous welcome by Otto Stundner; good vittles by Annie; mecca of scads of celebrities; not for the persnickety, but definitely for dedicated sportsmen and snowbunnies.

Here's a rundown on other centers popular with Americans:

Baden: (1) **Parkhotel** (many recommendations by helpful readers; service and cuisine reportedly outstanding), (2) **Kurhotel Esplanade** (highly regarded cure center; excellent swimming pool), (3) **Herzoghof**. The freshly tapped-out

Papst, is also blue ribbon. *Bad Ischl*: (1) Post, (2) **Goldenes Schiff,** (3) Freischütz. *Dornbirn*: Park (management by Paul Eder). *Feldkirch*: **Alpenrose** (tiny, charming, very Austrian). *Graz*: (1) Daniel, (2) Steirerhof, (3) Weitzer, (4) Parkhotel. *Hochgurgl*: (1) Hochgurgl, (2) Hochland, (3) Angerer Alm. *Mallnitz*: Pension Bellevue (if it's 1/12th as good as a friendly wanderer quoths so enthusiastically, it's the Promised Land). *Saalbach*: (1) Sporthotel, (2) Kristall, and (3) Saalbacherhof; all unknown to us personally. *Schruns*: Kurhotel Montafon (top-class international spa a skip-and-jump from the Swiss and Liechtenstein frontiers; rich and celebrated clientele; medical supervision). The brand-new **Löwen** is said to be a lovely rustic-mooded contender here. *Seefeld*: (1) Klosterbrau, (2) Philipi, (3) Larchenhof, (4) Tyrol, (5) Astoria, (6) Eden. *St. Anton am Arlberg* is one of Europe's capitals of winter sport. Here's our rating: (1) Post, (2) Schwarzer Adler, (3) Arlberg. All village hotels are noisy in season. Over at *Stuben,* another Arlberg ski station, the **Hubertushof** would be our pick of the spare harvest. *St. Wolfgang*: Weisses Rössl is the world-famous restaurant onto which has been added sleeping space for 100; Easter to mid-October only; no elevators; #28 is the choicest. *Velden am Wörthersee*: (1) Schloss Velden (ownership by the same family who command the famous Three Hussars in Vienna), (2) **Seehotel-Mösslacher-Veldenerhof** (nice vistas; friendly staff; few outlanders; music in the evenings). *Ybbs-on-Danube* offers another **Weisses Rössl**. Baroque restaurant; Franconian wine cellar with gypsy and Schrammel music; modern; clean; reportedly very pleasant. The province of Styria (near *Frohnleiten*) boasts the medieval cliffhugging **Schloss Rabenstein,** which one loyal reader calls "wonderful." Golf nearby; located on the main Vienna-Graz line.

The **Galina,** Austria's first motel, rolled in on Bundesstrasse #1 (Federal Highway #1) at Kilometer Stone #599 near *Frastanz,* a few miles from the Swiss and Liechtenstein borders. It was followed by a second entry near *Vöcklabruck* (30 rooms, 2 baths, 6 showers; raw, clean, cheap), 30-odd miles from Salzburg on the same Bundesstrasse #1 toward Linz and Vienna. Now, at least 8 others have sprung up, the pick of which are the **Huemer** in *Schwanenstadt,* operated by Frau Hilde Titze, and the **Crest** at *Linz.* The **Grossglockner** (near *Lienz*) is no longer recommended.

Tips from the turrets: Schloss-hoppers will quite possibly be pleased with the **Drassburg** near *Eisenstadt* and the **Pichlarn** near *Stainach-Irdning.* The latter is large, airy, and far from the personal sort of castle most wayfarers seek for overknighting. The indoor-outdoor pool complex is a dream. Closed November 1 to December 15.

Other well-known castle-hotels are **Feyregg** (at Bad Hall between Salzburg and Vienna), the aforementioned **Velden, Bernstein,** and **Jormannsdorf** (near the Hungarian frontier).

The **Parkhotel** at *Pörtschach am Wörthersee* is considered by various observers to be one of the better havens in the nation. Others vigorously disagree. It is quietly sited on a 56,200-square-yard promontory, surrounded by the famous flower-beaches of the region and well-tended parks. Tennis courts; health baths; cozy Weinstube; 25 suites and 147 bedchambers, all with bath, balcony, and unimpaired view. Worth it? In the same village, **Schloss Seefels,** with more modest facilities and few private baths, is also said to be a tranquil corner for lakeside relaxing.

The **Hotel Schloss Itter,** near *Wörgl,* is again perking. It is one of the most exciting entries of all architecturally, dating from A.D. 1532. Somewhat remote location; adequate comfort; heated pool; uneven standards; high tabs. The setting is truly postcard country.

For other towns or villages, consult the Austrian National Tourist Office or your travel agent. Far too many for this limited space, sorry to say.

§TIP: **Huetteldorf Youth Hostel,** just outside the capital with a view of the Vienna Woods, is the first of a new series of guesthouses for teen-agers. Beds 50 in 8-place dormitories; reasonable meals. The **Pötzleinsdorf Hostel** is also said to be worthy. More on these in *Fielding's Low-Cost Europe.*

FOOD   American breakfast averages $2 to $4; a memorable lunch and dinner in pleasing surroundings normally go from $7.50 to $18. With champagne and imported cognac you may run the latter up considerably. Wonderful food, too—steaks, chops, shellfish, fresh trout, pastries galore, the works —most often delicately prepared and graciously served. Each region has its own specialties. In the capital, try to work in a sampling of Frittaten (consommé with thinly sliced pancakes in it), Viennese Tafelspitz (boiled beef with a cream and chive mantel plus a side dish of horseradish mixed with applesauce), and Topfenknödel (a sweetish sphere of baked cottage cheese glazed with sugar, wading in a light syrup and plum gravy). For adventure and variety, here's one of the best gastronomic lands we've found.

Warning: Any good Austrian flies into a trauma of acute bookkeeperitis whenever he picks up a pencil. Everything is charged separately in this literal-minded nation: You'll be individually billed for your bread by the slice, butter by the pat, rolls by the count—and the soda in your Scotch!

RESTAURANTS   *Vienna's* number one establishment and perhaps the tops in all of Central Europe, in our opinion, is still **The Three Hussars** (Zu Den Drei Husaren, Weihburggasse 4, about a block from the Krantz-Ambassador). Although our face is so well known here that we cannot avoid the hated Red Carpet treatment, last time everybody seemed to be drawing the same superbly deft service. Classic atmosphere; topflight international cuisine under the direction of aristocratic Egon von Fodermayer; smooth drinks by Anton; reserve in advance. A famous and delicious feature is the mammoth selection of hors d'oeuvres on rolling carts. *Dinner only;* closed mid-July through August; ask for Maître Hans; this charming, sophisticated landmark *can* give you the most distinguished meal in Austria if it puts itself out.

The *rear* room of **Stadtkrug,** directly across the street, offers a grand piano, and 16 candlelit tables in ruby-red Renaissance surroundings with moire tapestries, upholstery, and old paintings. Now serving both lunch and dinner; closed July, August, and every Sunday; to repeat, reserve ahead in the Sakristei Room, *ignore the simple entrance segment, and walk straight through to the back.* On our most recent rounds, unfortunately the quality of this leading contender, while good, seemed miles behind that of its more celebrated neighbor.

The most dramatic, but hardly the most sparkling, light on the dining horizon stands 820 feet above the capital in the **Danube Tower,** a radio-TV mast which sports a revolving crow's nest. Your tummy can be regulated to twirl at 1 revolution every 52, 39, or 26 minutes, while the city, the river, the Vienna Woods, Schönbrunn Palace, and the profile of the Carpathian Mountains silently glide across your eyeballs. It might unwind and possibly collapse, however, as soon as you start your meal. Every nibble of ours, sad to relate, was uniformly tasteless if not downright wretched—and with taxi fares it's very expensive. It seems to be the inexorable fate of 90% of us visiting firemen to be taken or guided here by hyperzealous Viennese—but if you can feign plague, pyrexia, or lockjaw, PLEASE use ANY excuse to avoid going. A marvelous Tinkertoy for the spirit but not the body.

The **Belvedere Stöckl** (Prinz-Eugen-Strasse 25) borders the Belvedere Palace gardens on one side and the busy boulevard on the other. Ocher stucco mansion; 15 tables with a long handsome culinary display as its centerpiece attraction; friendly, sophisticated attention; urbane décor employing gold damask, muted colors, and the soft sparkle of well-set *couverts.* For the appearance and gastronomy, the tariffs are quite reasonable for its category. En route toward becoming a standard bearer.

Franziskaner, on the Platz of the same name, offers a cozy mien and a beguiling décor—but, in our most serious judgment, the cuisine still misses and the establishment still doesn't jell as a warm, attractive composite. Sorry, but still not recommended. **Rauchkuchl** (Schweglerstrasse 37, about 10 minutes from the center) bills itself as "Vienna's Only Medieval Restaurant"— a cheerful overstatement, because (save for its Lilliputian upstairs loft for winter revelry) it's about as Middle-Aged as a turnpike Howard Johnson's. Its reception, cookery, and service were all absolutely foul in our opinion on our incognito try. Nix for the nonce.

For local color, the municipally owned, redecorated, immense **Wiener Rathauskeller** (Rathausplatz, in City Hall) shouldn't be missed. Here's that very rare exception: A government-operated institution that really shines. Vast and immaculate fully automatic kitchen, the largest in the land; 4 distinctively different dining areas, each a gem in its way, which one should examine before being seated; 2 open for lunch as well as post-7:30 dinner. The cookery is certainly not the most delicate in the world, but for a huge restaurant complex of this type, few can top it. Surprisingly reasonable tariffs; first-quality ingredients; service that was perfection—and friendly, to boot. For any pocketbook, here should be a winner.

The **Paulusstube** (Walfischgasse 7, a 1-minute aria from the opera) is a midtown transplant of a Grinzing *Heuriger* (see below). Handsome façade; shabbily comfortable interior; vaulted ceilings; strolling musicians; friendly but uninspired service; dreary regional dishes. Now only fair at best, in our revised opinion.

Coq d'Or (Führichgasse 1, around the corner from the Krantz-Ambassador), has tumbled precipitously again in our pecking order. We found medium-price, substandard skilletry not worth even the modest outlay.

Wegenstein (be sure to take a taxi) yields some of the best wild-game platters locally on call. Very small dimensions; definitely "in" among the Hunting Set; reserve ahead; plan to eat fairly early, because the chef whips off his cap at 10:30 P.M. **Falstaff** (Währingerstrasse 67) is similar in girth and nutrients, but it doesn't have a garden and it does have a grill. This Pantagruel fed well for a moderate number of sovereigns. **Marchfelderhof** (25 minutes out at *Deutsch-Wagram*) is a mixed bag of touristic playfulness. About a dozen halls, dens, crannies, cafés, or caverns; gimmicky but fun with your own throng; lonely for solos. We can take it or leave it.

The café and restaurant in **Auersperg Palais,** one of Vienna's masterpieces of baroque architecture, are spectacularly soothing to the eye—but oh, oh, oh, those puffed-up prices! The costs for its indifferently cooked fare seem ludicrously inflated by local criteria. For us, once was *genug,* but perhaps you'll take exception.

The intimate and charming little **Zum Weissen Rauchfangkehrer** (Weihburggasse 4) is a favorite of actors, artists, and journalists. Classic German décor, tinkling piano, friendly reception, rough service, decent food for the price. Closed Sundays, all of July and August, and many holidays. **H. Stiedl's Beerklinik** (Steindelg 4) seats about 350 customers overall, in the amusing cellar or in the Biedermeier restaurant; budgeteers love it. Open every day of the year; no music; reasonable tabs. The **Griechenbeisl** (Fleischmarkt 11), where the Olde Taverne atmosphere has been laid on with a trowel, is larger, noisier, and poorly ventilated; what they served us was atrocious.

The **Balkan Grill** (Brunnengasse 13, about 15 minutes from the center) is an on-or-off enterprise which, if "on," can be delightful. Restaurant and roofed garden-side terrace; waiters in Bosnian costumes; strolling musicians. Start with a straight-from-the-carafe Barack apricot brandy (the martinis are repulsive); order the Serbian hors d'oeuvres first, and then please don't miss the Siskebab à la Jenghiz Khan for 1, 2, or 3 persons. Finally, you'll be given a serving of Turkish paste; tuck a piece between your molars and cheek in the Balkan way, and sip your coffee mumps-style. *Evenings only,* from 6:30 P.M. to 1 A.M.; medium expensive; closed Sunday. This place is a find—IF you hit it right.

Csardasfürstin is a smaller splash on the goulash circuit. Two levels; off-key gypsy melodizing; low-key cookery featuring Cevapcici (peppery meat patties skewered and served on a flaming rack) and Töltöt Kàposzta (a stuffed cabbage that lost something in the translation). First-rate theater, but reportorial conscience compels us to pan the Pots & Pans Department. **Feuervogel** (Alserbachstrasse 21) is one of the oldest Russian feederies in town. Painted up in geometric florals; lamps in cookie jars; amiable rotund host; fair culinary art, but no rave. Our twin dinner came to about $30. **Au Gaststaette** (Danube Park) still is nothing special, in our opinion. The **Winzerhaus,** on the Rotenturmstrasse, features Polish cookery straight from the banks of the Vistula. Stained-glass-and-timber-dark atmos-shmeer; high-backed carved booths; commendable kitchen; a dandy Danzig delight.

Kervansaray (Mahlerstrasse) serves Döner Kebab, Yoghurt Sour Yayla, Moussaka, and other Turkish tempters in luxurious surroundings. If you enjoy this cuisine, here's a blue-ribbon candidate. **Ming Court** (Kärntner

Strasse) is our Chinese choice. It must be one of the most visually endearing restaurants in Central Europe. Our abalone salad and piquant Sacha Pork, served with puff-bread, sauces, nuts, and greens, were gastronomic landmarks. Not expensive but very deluxe in every respect. **China-Pavillion** (corner of Mariahilfer Strasse—Winkelmannstrasse) is no longer worth the costly taxi ride from the center, in our judgment. So solly.

Sunny weather? Here's a Vienna Woods pilgrimage my Nancy and I never fail to make: Fischerhaus for lunch, followed by coffee *only* (no food) at Kahlenberg. **Fischerhaus,** high in the hills at *Hermannskogel,* is about 30 minutes from the heart of Vienna. Its quality and sophistication are now such that here is really the *only* recommendable stop for lunch or dinner in the entire area. Small, attractive country mansion with terrace; garden totally transformed; dining under a sheltering roof; fine but not extraordinary view; elaborate menu featuring the specialties of 10 nations. We like especially the Austrian Bauernschmaus ("Farmers' Plate") and the roast duckling. Warmhearted Proprietor M. R. Gura is so understaffed when there's a full house that you might fulminate. Therefore, please *always* reserve in advance and please *always* try it either earlier or later than normal—especially on weekends. Better and better.

Kahlenberg, perched on a mountaintop a skip-and-a-jump away, is fabulously situated; from its colossal East Veranda and dining-terrace, the city, the Danube, and a large slice of Czechoslovakia are at your feet. Accommodations for 2000 munchers, sippers, or Czech-pointers; open every day; adjoining small hotel previously mentioned. A visible cloud of food odors hung in all the rooms we inspected except the "luxury" restaurant during our latest cold-weather visit. The service is amiable (least frenzied on the glassed-in veranda); it struck us, however, that a team of half-trained chimpanzees could scarcely be more addled. It seems obvious that Government ownership accounts for the slackness. But its scenic grandeurs make it a *must,* and that is why it is urged that you share them with lunch already under your belt.

Hübner's Cobenzl, closer to town on the same highway, has always been a major disappointment to us—including on our most recent recheck. Even the coffee didn't taste very good. Could it be that this is a favorite of many car-hire chauffeurs because of favors received from the management? No insinuation is intended here in this innocent question. Sorry, still not recommended.

Burg Greifenstein, in Niederösterreich, a former castle of the Prince of Liechtenstein, is another high-over-the-Danube site reachable by too many steps for elderly or ailing adventurers. Typical enthralling *schloss*-top vistas; better service and cuisine than at most other Hübner hubs—which to us, at least, doesn't mean much. We were fascinated by the arms museum, but *they* were fascinated by our mixocology lesson in building a Bloody Mary, a concoction previously unknown to them. Youngsters like the downstairs Knappenstube, a colorful corner of fun.

Alternate excursions? Please don't forget about the lovely **Schloss Laudon** (see "Hotels"). Its cuisine might be forgettable, but the experience won't. Then there's the sylvan **Tyrolean Gardens,** fringing the Gloriet of Schönbrunn Palace. If little ones are in tow, the adjoining zoo is fun.

The Viennese coffee houses, one of Austria's greatest traditions, are fast waning from the onslaught of the brash, Nedick-style café-espresso bars which have crept up from Italy. Worthy old-style survivors are the **Mozart,** the **Landtmann,** and the **Prückel.**

The legendary *Konditoreien* ("confection shops," for want of a better word) are still rolling along merrily, thanks to Allah. Emperor of this realm—for the time being anyway—remains **Demel** (Kohlmarkt 14), where grateful citizenry have been stuffing themselves cross-eyed since A.D. 1813. In an alleged double cross, the son of Franz Sacher, Metternich's pastry chef, is said to have sold his father's $1,000,000 Sacher Torte recipe to this house. The 25-year *Kriegspiel* was finally compromised by a court verdict: The hotel may now vend the "Original Sacher Cake," while Demel may purvey simply the "Demel Sacher Cake"! If you enjoy aspics, cookies, salads, sandwiches, cold meats, iced juices, chocolate puffs overflowing with Chantilly, and Viennese coffee (black coffee, sugar, and hot milk stirred into a king-size cup, topped by great blobs of whipped cream), from 30 seconds to 3000 minutes later a countergirl will bring your plate to your tiny table. The service is sweet, but horribly, maddeningly disorganized, especially at peak hours—so go just before noon, if you can. Wickedly expensive; open every day, but poor selection on Sundays; ask for the English-speaking Frau Gretl; if money is a secondary consideration, recommended with our tongues slapping our chests. Other outstanding examples are **Lehmann** and **Heiner.**

For a more commercial type of operation, pop in at one of the 19 **Aïda** shops. All guarantee tiptop freshness that only a volume operation can turn out at such lowdown tariffs. Ownership by the dynamic Felix Prousek, one of the fastest-rising tycoons in Austria. *Terrific.*

Finally, Vienna is famous for its *Heuriger*—the "new-wine" or "fresh-wine" gardens. The most celebrated of these establishments are in Grinzing, 15 to 25 minutes by taxi. Look for the garland of pine twigs and vine leaves over the door, and bring your own cold meat, butter, cheese, and bread, if you wish to follow the local custom. Or try their old-time specialty, if you can find it in this less-enlightened era—Backhendl, which is very young, milk-fed chicken, breaded in a unique way. Typical, sound examples are **Leopold Kurtz-Manhart** at Cobenzlgasse 15 (the oldest in Grinzing; don't miss the cellar), Walter Rode's **Heuriger** (Himmelstrasse 4), **Rode's "Altes Haus"** (where we had a delicious meal), the **Musil,** the **Hauermandl,** the **Figmüller,** the **Backhendlstation** (Grinzingerstrasse 50), **Martinkovits** (Bellevuestrasse 4), **Franz Mayer Pfarrplatz,** and **Reinprecht** (3 entries: Cobenzlgasse 20, 22, and 28). Locals now feel Grinzing is becoming too touristic; many are moving over to the Brunnergasse in Perchtoldsdorf, about 30 minutes by taxi. The **Spiegelhofer** (Hochstrasse 75) would be our top winery here. All shut down intermittently, whenever the barrels run out; light buffet and wine only except where noted, with no spirits or beer. For even less money, the **Wienerwald** chain (about 500 restaurants in more than 125 European cities, plus 8 in New York) boasts 10 links in the capital. All are slickly rustic, and all turn out unusually savory fare. Quite a money-saver and quite good for its category.

Dedicated budgeteers? Since we're too bottlenecked here for additional entries, please consult *Fielding's Low-Cost Europe,* our annually revised paperback, which lists scads more bargain dining spots and tips.

In *Salzburg* the **Peterskeller** is the traditional showplace if not the pulsing magnet of the tour operators. Never a shrine of gastronomy, its cookery seldom matches the excellence of its wines. Regional dishes only; dim Old World atmosphere; low price tags; supervision by the savvy Benedictine monks who own it; no beer. **Schlosswirt,** in the neighboring village of *Anif,* is a favorite of many motorborne trippers (taxis are lethally expensive here). Country manse with cottage specialties; garden dining in summer; very reasonable tabs. This simple place is ably administered by Mr. and Mrs. Graf. **Weinrestaurant Moser** features 3 rooms in solid tones. Vaulted ceilings; amiable staff; substantial local selections only. We now prefer it to the Peterskeller. The rebuilt **Winkler Café** (no longer operated by the midtown hotel) offers lunch plus dinner dancing from May to October only; casino portion due to open this season; *what* a fantastic view it has! Although **Weisses Roessl** ("White Horse," at Linzergasse 15) has gone down in the Mouth Department it is still popular. Worth a look if you're looking, but not a bite.

For elegance among the independents, **Alt Salzburg,** behind the Goldener Hirsch, wins our bouquet of orchids. Arched alleyway entrance flanked by flags of various nations; Frenchy bar just inside; twin inner sancta under brick vaults. Several Italian specialties are spotlighted on the menu but Austrian fare predominates; the latter can be uneven in quality. Service is variable. Highish tabs.

In **Die Bastey,** near Mozartplatz, reservations are an absolute m-u-s-t. Our one vital demurrer: The ventilation we found was absurdly inadequate. Long, booth-filled room; sweating waiters; merry guests. Sound cookery, but oh that air!

Nearby, the **K & K** is modern, clean, fair in price, zestless visually, but highly popular.

Then there's the **Zinnkrug** ("Pewter Pot") on the 4th floor of a building across the street from the Österreichischer Hof. Attractive view over the river and rooftops; overworked minions in regional costume. The chicken in a creamed curry bath was delicious; the gypsy-art grill was pleasant and abundant; the Crêpes Costello might have been pranks by the shades of the Marx Brothers team. Otherwise we enjoyed it.

The **Zum Eulenspiegel** (Hagenauerplatz 2), in the fifteenth-century city gatehouse, has 3 floors, sophisticated tavern-type ambiance, and hungry tourists 6-deep. The jokes and proverbs on the walls are so earthy that we hope your German is academic rather than colloquial. The Proprietor and his staffers are virtuosos at giving the customer the Suave Sell on that extra cocktail, that highest-price item, and that rarest bottle. While it is still passable, we believe that the cuisine and service attitudes have fallen off noticeably.

Festungsrestaurant in the Festung (castle) and **Stieglkeller** (Festungsgasse 10) are more famous for folk dancing (summer only) than for groceries; check your concierge first, because on some evenings nothing happens; the latter spot, designed vaguely like the inside of a beer barrel, is the only place we've ever found where the purple-faced customer climbs 5 flights of stairs to get to the cellar. The **Augustinerbräustüberl** (Augustinergasse 4), a mammoth, old-fashioned beer hall and chestnut-tree garden which can handle 2000 merrymakers without blowing off the suds, is almost unknown to foreigners. Self-service throughout; cold plates and snacks only; opens daily at 3 P.M.; personnel about as lunkheaded as the *Mad* boy, with practically nobody caring a hoot; colorful and amusing, despite the oafs in attendance.

Helbrunn Castle, a costly taxi jaunt from the center, offers practical jokes and squirt tricks with its famous fountains, as well as delicious Châteaubriand and typical Tyrolean folk music. Kids from 5 to 95 love the charming wild-animal preserve on the grounds. **Café Glockenspiel** rings up a sterling peep at the Mozartplatz, but the vittles are only passing fair for the passing parade. **G'würzmühl** is slickly rustic in décor and slick enough in its skillet skills. **Weisses Kreuz** has good Balkan dishes—and the irritating feeling that they're rushing the hell out of you. **Salzachkeller** in the Hotel Österreichischer Hof is in the high-price league; noteworthy fare; often jammed in High Season; amiable if you can squeeze in.

The **Goldener Hirsch**, once a superstar for hotel cookery, for us now ranks as only substantial. Our latest repasts here have not been equal to earlier ones. Good, but not great. The **Europa** gives us a pain somewhere between the neck and the knees; the medium-range **Stein** is just okay. The **Goldene Sonne,** in an old house that was renovated, comfortized, and reopened by Mr. Dachs, former manager of Schloss Fuschl, is a sweet little haven in any of its precincts. Ground floor snackery plus L-shape dining salon; several cozy upstairs bins; cordial service; medium prices; savory dishes; next to the elevator leading to the Mönchsberg. We like it.

Finally, the **Casino Alm** (see "Nightclubs") offers a restaurant wing called the Stadl. Open rafters, lamps dangling over tables from hayloft rigs, and hopsacking napery; bar-discothèque segment. The owner can be rightfully proud of the chef, but he should clamp his table staff in irons. Recommended for cuisine, but fie on those curmudgeons in black.

Innsbruck's kitchens churn out nutrition and little else. The most dressed-up evening you'll have will probably be in your own hotel—and as local innkeeping goes, the **Tyrol** goes best. **Europastüberl** (across the street, with a separate entrance around the corner from the Europa) pans out very worthy vittles. At the latter, the unique Innsbruckerschnitzel is topped with cheese; the Tesener Kastanieneis is chestnut ice cream bathed in applesauce. Ummmmm. **Goldener Adler's** fare has picked up notably. Flambé specialties prepared close enough to singe the nap off your funnybone; 1 unit for fondues only, isolating its odor; attentive service. Surely no tour de force for culinary crafts, but carloads better than the addled Adler of yore. **Bergisel** is simple, savory, and schilling-saving; be sure to try Mrs. Gerö's scintillating strudel. We haven't tried the **Holiday Inn.**

Among the independents, the **Stiftskeller** is still drawing howls from dissatisfied readers. It rose to the top, slumped, climbed back to number one ranking—and now we opine that it is skidding again. If you'd like to chance it and are adventurous, try the red-hot Paprika Hatschec, a combustible liquid of Hungarian origin with the flash point and chemical characteristics of napalm. Grasp both ears firmly before you sip it, because they'll spin as fast as propellers if you don't. **Stiegelbrau,** our leading candidate a while back, is still atmospheric; the cooking is good, but the selections are very limited. Bierstüberl on one side, exclusively for males; nonsegregated dining facilities across the hall, with a relaxed, comfortable, middle-class patronage; rolls and *blatte* (delicious unleavened bread) automatically appear. **Altes Haus Delevo** is a Quaint-y Inn-y built with both eyes cocked on the tourist trade with 5 rooms on 2 floors. Balkan grills the specialty; prices high; cuisine above average; pleasant. The **Palette** is next door to the Touringhaus; steaks are the specialty. The **Feldkirchner** is tops for snacks; modern-rustic surroundings. **Tabasco** has a lot of pepper too, but the service burned us up. The town has a **Wienerwald** which is okay for its type. **Weisses Kreuz** once played host to Mozart when he performed for the Empress; we haven't been back to the minuet since 1787.

A café occupies the upper level of the **Bacchus,** and the chic (by Innsbruck standards) **Restaurant-Weinstube** is in the cellar. Because there's an orchestra in the latter they call it a "nightclub"—which it isn't. The cuisine is above average, but the tables are so tiny and the elbowroom so cramped that we find it on the uncomfortable side. Closed Sunday. Students congregate at **Papillon** (Meranerstrasse) for beer-drinking, wine-bibing, and song.

The **Wilder Mann** (4 miles out) is in the beguiling little village of *Lans,* a lovely drive via Igls. You'll find 4 small rooms here which might have been lifted from a mythical Austrian edition of *House and Garden*—and your interest will be whetted still more when you see the spotless kitchen, the apple-cheeked country girls who are the waitresses, and the assemblage of rural folk in Tyrolean garb. Substantial, appetizing fare; hot dogs with horseradish so fresh it will make your eyes water; tiny ice-cream cones on a bed of whipped cream; other choices. Proprietress Frau Schöpf is heart and soul. Rewarding if you don't expect glamour.

Elsewhere we've enjoyed the following: In *Linz,* the **Kremsmünsterer Weinstube,** in the Old Town, has a bar leading to 3 vaulted dining rooms with ancient atmosphere; good regional food, but rather heavy. In *Kitzbühel,* try the **Tenne** for fun or the little **Chizzo** for snacks and savory Serbian nuggets. In *Badgastein,* the Grill of the **Parkhotel Bellevue** is the unchallenged leader. The **Straubinger Stüberl** offers a pleasant couplet of rooms, costumed waitresses, and unexciting cookery. The **Kaiser-Friedrich-Laube,** under the Gasteiner Hotel aegis, presents local trappings and traditional dishes. Enterprising local interests operate an ambitious restaurant-café in the congress center. For summer motorists, the **Grüner-Baum** is said to be a pleasant outdoor valley haven. In most Austrian ski stations, sporting appetites must be satisfied with your pension-plan hotel fare. Lunches are either picnics on the slopes or obtained through a meal voucher at an upland hut.

For restaurants in other cities, check with the Austrian National Tourist Office or your concierge. Incidentally, the **Konditorei Zauner** in *Bad Ischl* rivals Vienna's Demel as the most tempting *confiserie* of the civilized world.

NIGHTCLUBS   In *Vienna, Moulin Rouge* (Walfischgasse 1), Austria's pale carbon copy in the Latin Quarter department, is a-spin. Two-tier circular room with excellent viewing potential; B-gals aplenty; ample strips, magic acts, and similar variety wheezes more-or-less continuously through the evening. On our visit Sandy Schweppes effer-divested herself of apparel intermittently until the house went flat at 6 A.M. If the double-barreled entrance fee doesn't put you into an immediate catatonic state, perhaps your whisky at $6 per slug, beer at $3.75 per mug, or Dom Perignon champagne at $70 per jug will. Ouch! For Texas oilmen only. By contrast, you should pay between $3 and $5.75 per Scotch in most other places, with door charges skittering between zero and $2 per reveler. **Fledermaus** (Spiegelgasse 2) has only a dime-or-so admission nibble. Long, well-ventilated room; 5 alcoves for intimate sipping; danceable combo; friendly atmosphere; large drinks; cabarets in German at 11 P.M. and 2 A.M., which can be dull if one doesn't understand the language; smooth operation ably steered by local Music Man Gerhard Bronner. We like it. **Eve** (next to the Astoria Hotel) is also moving up in the harem. Ownership by the Blatzheim interests which now blanket the German nightscape; snuggly ambiance; 2 orchestras; sleek houris eternally disrobing —all in the tradition of chiffon by the bolt. Good hunting ground for the lone male Nimrod. Not bad. **Chez Nous** (Kärntner Strasse 10), a modest entry run by an ex-waiter from Maxim's, is one hole we detest with consummate passion. Here's a very good one—to avoid with utmost care. The **Sir Winston Club** is an amusing pub for chitchat, suds, and snacks. **Gerard** draws a nice young following for music and dance. The **New Splendid Bar** (Jasomirgottstrasse 3) is a curiously shaped 3-tier, off-circular room with upbeat music; larger than most and quite attractive; our only carp here is that our later bill, when we dropped in again, illegally carried the music charge on each of our drinks rather than on our first consumption only. **Eden Bar** (Liliengasse 2) is THE perch for chic Viennese night owls. Ho-hum décor; excellent 4-piece combo; no pickups; closed Sundays from May to July and various holidays. Go late. The **Take Five** is a hard-driving disk joint. Twin bars flank the small dance floor; dim lights. So-so. **Atrium** is divided into 4 celler quadrants with 3 bars. Good music and liquids. The **Schaukelpferd Bar** (Kegelgasse 30) features stucco walls, wood beams, and fireplace. Nice. **Steckenpferd** (Dorotheergasse) is similar in tone; quiet dance music is the theme. Unusual architecture is a feature of the **Loos Bar** (Kärntner Durchgang near Stephansplatz). On our "never again" roster is the **B.B.-Bar** (adjoining Messe Palace); miserable décor, miserable atmosphere, and miserable patrons.

Jazz hounds? **Die Tenne** (Annagasse 3) is a barn-like dance hall which rocks for the Jean Set. Modest prices; frequently filled with youngsters who would rather dance than eat. The **Koralle** (Porzellangasse 39) and the plaid-fad **Scotch-Bar** (Ringstrasse) are also jammed with kids. **Maryland** is a tiny state of mind for similar notes and bars.

Down around navel level come **Casbah** (Naglergasse 23) and **Café Renz** (Zirkusgasse 50). Soberingly ugly house girls (perhaps that's why they give serious scholars a free booklet of cutie photos when they enter); rough patrons from this roughest district of Vienna; "separates" available. Both are *really* dumps.

Even lower on this circuit's anatomy is **Opium Höhle** (Habsburgergasse 4), a rugged cellar joint For Gents Only. Décor faintly reminiscent, to us, of High

Chinese Bordello circa the Wan Hong Crooked Period of the Tartar philosophers; adjoining Champagne Room is so much darker that customers are obliged to put aside their newspapers for concentration on more sociable activities, such as games involving digital skills. Go about 11:30 P.M., and leave your wife in the hotel with a copy of Henry Miller. Interesting as a curiosity only. (Not incidentally in these modern times, its name is a hallucinogenic put-on; the strongest thing we saw being smoked here was a filter-tip Kool.)

In **Salzburg,** there's gambling at the plush **Casino Salzburg.** Handsome furnishings; 1 baccarat and 5 roulette tables; pleasant bar; open from 7 P.M. to 2 A.M. (4 A.M. on weekends) except on Christmas Eve and religious holidays; small entrance fee, from which you are presented a chip to start your play. *Remember to take along your passport, or you won't be admitted.* As a wise Los Angeles physician wryly comments, "If you don't speak fluent German and if you don't quite understand the meaning of the word 'Manque,' take Jimmy the Greek along."

The aforementioned **Winkler Café** (not to be confused with the hotel and no longer under the same ownership), atop the cliff by special elevator, offers summertime dancing on its lovely terrace, as well as in its Las Vegas night-club. Face-lifting due; higher-than-average prices. Let's hope it improves. The **Half Moon** and the **Old Grenadier** are patronized by young discophiles. The **Cocktail Club** has fallen off so dramatically it can no longer be recommended. The **Hexenturm** ("Witches' Tower") in the Elmo Hotel is an amusing brew for shaveless shavers; expensive modern furnishings; late hours; snacks. Perfect for disk addicts with unslipped disks. Also for the youth patrol, **Rendez-vous** and **Shubert-Diele** are routine and less-than-routine, respectively. The **Casino Alm,** a few minutes from the center, is a miniature 5–ring circus. Bowling alley; Stadl restaurant; cheerful rustic nightclub. It also offers swimming (day and night), tennis (day and night), minigolf (day), table tennis (day and night), steeplechasing (day), and a surprisingly energetic smile (day and night). Amusing. The **Friesacher Stadl** in neighboring **Anif** offers a somewhat similar setup; discothèque; action from 9 P.M. to 4 A.M.; pleasant merrymaking here in a building disguised as an old barn.

Casanova is seedy, 2nd-rate Broadway with Austrian rural overtones; not for us. The **Winkler Alm** features an Alpine-style floor show nightly; rather expensive; production-line fun. Finally, if you tire of the noise and smoke and clatter, the wonderful old **Café Bazar** (the coffeehouse opposite Lanz, at the bridge), with marble tables, newspaper racks, and dignity, will give solace and balm to your soul. The venerable **Tomaselli** (Alter Markt) and the bustling modern **Glockenspiel** (Mozartplatz) are popular runners-up.

In **Innsbruck,** the Keller (cellar, not the terrace) of the **Greifkeller** has crazy Tyrolean ceilings, cow-stall booths, tavern-type bar; tiny dance floor, 2–piece band, occasional entertainment on Saturdays in season; go after 11 P.M. and reserve in advance; this little joint can jump. For the inn crowd, the **Clima Hotel** now has its own Club in the cellar. Cleverly in tune with the tempo. The **Hofgarten,** in the park, has agreeable terrace-dancing in summer and moves into sterile, brash, typical honky-tonk-style quarters in winter. Average but worth a look. **Palette** is drawing the royal share of young swingers; it's a cellar with the rage of the age.

For other cities, here's a quick check list: **St. Anton:** (1) **Hotel Post,** (2) **Hotel Arlberg,** or (3) any spot that's "in" on your week-to-ski. **Badgastein:** (1) **Schafflinger Skialm** (mountain-log-cabin motif; full meals and dancing; favorite of favorites among the piste bashers), (2) **Mühlhäusl** (old-tavern setting; popular for dancing and light bites), (3) **Park Bellevue,** (4) **Casino Bar.** **Kitzbühel:** The **Tenne** in the Guido Reisch (see "Hotels") has now been perked up; it's a honey. Then, we'd rate 'em, (1) **Goldene Gams** (best band, biggest floor, attractive bar), (2) Sportklause at the **Goldener Greif,** (3) **Praxmair,** (4) **Weisses Rössl,** (5) **Alte Kitz.** **Zürs:** (1) **Zürserhof,** (2) **Edelweiss,** (3) **Alpenrose,** or (4) soaking in a hot tub. **Seefeld-in-Tirol:** (1) **Karwendelkeller,** (2) **Eden Bar.** **Linz:** (1) **Central Bar,** (2) **Metropol Bar,** (3) **Orient Bar.** **Graz:** (1) **Barock Bar,** (2) **Kabaret Kärntnerhof,** (3) **Ring Bar,** (4) **Triumph Bar.**

In smaller towns, ask the concierge of your hotel.

Gambling casinos? **Salzburg**'s is already mentioned; the same fine chain also operates in **Badgastein, Kitzbühel, Velden am Wörthersee, Baden bei Wien, Riezlern, Bregenz,** and **Seefeld-in-Tirol.** **Vienna**'s Cercle Wien is up 1-flight in the Palais Esterházy (Kärntner Strasse)—directly above the Adlmüller shop. Roulette, chemin de fer, and—now—blackjack comprise the play-for-pay; moderate admission. Take your passport to all of these!

Feminine companionship? Plenty. They cluster like pigeons in their favorite cotes (your concierge will steer you). Generally, they're at selected cafés between 5 P.M. and 7 P.M. or in the nightclub bars later. Specific streets in the center of Vienna are loaded—positively loaded!—with them just before midnight, but the corner of Kärntner Strasse and Krugerstrasse (if the subway construction hasn't chased them off) is the safest place to negotiate. More remote sites draw the less-attractive trulls and invite danger. Caution: Once you shut the door, the damsel will explain that her quoted fee covers merely a few minutes; a longer engagement will cost much more. Sometimes (not always) medical control, with weekly checkups by physicians (one should ask to see the dated stamp on her official card); gratis hygienic devices required by law; as cold-bloodedly commercial as an arbitrage sale. Major Austrian cities have licensed bordellos (1 in Vienna, 2 in Salzburg, and 2 in Innsbruck, for example); ask any taxi driver or porter.

§TIPS: The nightclub "separate" has a separate meaning here of togetherness. These are small private rooms tucked away in the inner recesses of such Viennese hot spots as Chez Femme, Casbah, Café Renz, and Opium Höhle. They are usually available from 2 A.M. to 6 A.M. Amorous roosters select the chickens in the bar. Since John Law forbids doors on these schilling-filling stations, 3 sets of heavy draw-drapes bar the entries and muffle the groans. The furnishings invariably consist of a small chaise longue, 1 or 2 armless chairs, and a tiny table for the champagne always demanded by the professionally dehydrated babe. Your tab for the champagne is the standard price; the girls hopefully ask for a 1000–schilling fee, but if the evening is lean, the goods can be priced at 500 schillings. Because the nightclub per se is closed, there is little-or-no chance some blundering yokel might mistake a "separate" for the men's room and interrupt the proceedings. This is sex at its most raw and most deep-frozen—worse, most uncomfortable!—level. But it's there, *if* you've just returned from a 3-year fossil hunt in the fastness of Tin-Zaouaten Oasis in the Sahara.

"Bar" has 2 interpretations in Austria: (1) saloon-style, as the American corner tavern, and (2) nightclub for dancing.

TAXIS   All modern cars these days. In Vienna's fleet of about 1650 vehicles, roughly 1600 are driven by men and 60 by women. Once we drew a Brünn-hilde with a size 17½ collar and muscles more rippling than John Wayne's; her cowboy driving homogenized us 20 years in 20 yards. But most of the representatives of both genders are courtly, and their prices are still fair.

Unless you're either stony-drunk or desperate, never take a taxi in *Innsbruck* or *Salzburg*. Although all cabs now have meters, these are the fastest ticking and flipping mechanisms we have ever boggled at in our travels. Absolutely outrageous; strictly for suckers or invalids.

CAR HIRE   Our pick of the crop in *Vienna* is a small but profoundly conscientious organization called **Erhart Car Hire & Travel**, 25 Zwoelfer-gasse (out-of-the-way 15th district; tel.: 83–23–22). All of our recent capital rounds have been enormously enhanced by its knowledgeable corps of drivers. Furthermore, Proprietor Walther Erhart has volunteered to be a general factotum, consultant, and Dutch uncle to any *Guide* reader who has problems in his nation or who may be traveling into Eastern Europe. His services are wide, varied, and supremely courteous. He will even romp over the ski zones with special winter-sport holiday packages if you have a large family or small party in tow. Airport pickup and delivery of arriving or departing visitors at rates far below the taxi bite (the terminus is almost 1 hour outside the city); multichoice, inexpensive to opulent chauffeur- or self-drive; tantalizing tours to Hungary (2 days, passport and 2 photos required), an overnight jaunt to Salzburg, a full day in the Wachau wine district—you name it and he, his staff, or his fine travel agency in the city will fix it for you in a jitney or a jiffy. AND there's that wonderful comfort of a dependable new friend in town who will pull strings to snag you a better hotel room, tickets to the Opera, entry into the always-oversold Spanish Riding School, a babysitter, or help with almost any legitimate and reasonable need. English-speaking pilots, of course. Competitive tariffs; highest recommendation, especially for the pervading brand of Erhart-inspired kindness that envelops this dynamic little company. It also operates a branch in *Salzburg* (10 Dariogasse, tel: 20400), masterfully guided by Hans Erhart, his brother. This one is every bit as professionally sound, ethical, and smooth as the alma mater; it does not, however, have self-drive vehicles.

TRAINS   Most of the international trains are comfortable; complaints have reached us lately about the *Arlberg Express*. The majority have sleepers and dining facilities; all serve drinks. The modern autorail cars (example: The air-conditioned *Blaue Blitz*) are good, too. All interior main lines have electric traction, and a number of diesel types chug point-to-point in many areas.

There is a small surcharge on Expresses. The 50% reduction for the Junior Set stops at their 15th birthday.

The **Austria Ticket** is a new wrinkle in rod-riding (also includes bus links) which is valid for 8 to 15 days and saves sizable chunks of *geld* from the traveler's pouch. It provides other money-saving favors as well.

And don't forget Austria is included in that remarkable transportation bargain, the "Eurailpass" (described in "Let's Be European").

AIRLINE Austrian Airlines (AUA) no longer offers any domestic air bridges. The fleet of DC–9's, with each plane named after a famous composer, now fans out to 33 cities in 22 European, Middle Eastern, and North African countries. We recently stepped off another AUA loop as hotter converts to this company than we'd ever been before. Its highly skilled administrators have custom-built superb service, kindness, and s-m-o-o-t-h thoroughness into just about every aspect which affects the passenger. For airborne cookery, the cuisine was so beautifully presented that we could scarcely believe our eyes—and it tasted even better than it looked!

AUA's slogan is "The Friendly Airline." This strikes us as being far too modest a claim for what such legions of admiring travelers, including us, regard as one of the finest smaller carriers flying today.

DRINKS Wines are your best bet. Prices average $3.50 to $10 per bottle and $1 to $2.25 for ¼-liter.

While Klosterneuburger is perhaps the best white wine, if you stick to a brand with the equally jaw-cracking name of Gumpoldskirchner (available in most places), you'll always be safe—and very probably pleased. Keep in mind "gum," and "Leopold," and it will stand out on the wine list. Other dependable and sound labels are Kremser, Duernsteiner, Hohenwarther, and Nussberger. The finest red wine we've ever tasted is Vöslauer; red wines from Baden are most often superb. From the Wachau district along the Danube, Suedbahn and Burgenland pressings win the local medals.

Of the beers, Gösser Bräu is a rich brew made in Styria. It's full-bodied and fine; choice of light or dark. Schwechater is tops in Vienna.

With 1 exception, imported potables are relatively expensive. Bourbon and rye are now amply abundant. The happiest bargain is Beefeater gin—locally licensed and bottled, it sells for around $7.50. Other foreign supplies are limited, and there's practically no choice of brands. Strictly for nickel-plated gullets, there's a local rum which puts life in afternoon tea, a "club whisky" which will lift the hat right off your head, and a schnapps which you'll find still delicately flaked with enamel from the bathtub. If you can take it like Dean Martin, there's also the local plum brandy or slivovitz. Enzian is another brandy, distilled from the roots of the tall curious yellow (not blue) gentian. Verdict: At some indeterminate point between (1) mildly repugnant, (2) actively repulsive, and (3) totally unswallowable. Finally, Bowle is a delicious summer punch made of cognac, white wine, champagne or curaçao, and fresh fruits: served from a bowl at perhaps 75¢ per glass.

§**TIPS:** When you order a martini, be sure to specify "Beefeater" (cheaper) or "Gordon's"; the ordinary Austrian gin is best applied to arrest baldness.

Every restaurant, tavern, or bar in the nation—1 to every 200 inhabitants —must levy a 20% surtax on wines and spirits. Half of this is an alcohol nip while another gulp of 10% is decanted for beverages in general, whether they be coffee, tea, or *milk,* if you please!

THINGS TO SEE   Enough to keep the tourist busy for a year. In *Vienna,* your primary targets will probably be (1) a look at the Ringstrasse, the famous boulevard circling the city, (2) a ride through the woods immortalized by Johann Strauss (pick your tour carefully, because Guidesters again have complained about ramshackle loudspeaker systems and wheezy guides who droned indistinctly in all 4 languages), (3) for tradition only, a look at the far-from-blue Danube, and (4) a peek at the whole picture from the pike's peak of the Danube Tower, an 840-foot TV-radio mast (see "Restaurants"). Then you might try (1) a performance at the ultimate glory of this world music capital, the magnificently rebuilt Opera House (closed July and Aug.; 200 seats per performance allotted to local travel agents for foreign visitors), (2) the eye-popping Spanish Riding School (precision horse-training rehearsals every weekday morning except Mon. for the fabulous full-dress Sun. morning show or Wednesday nightriders; early Mar. to end-June and early Sept. to mid-Dec. only; *book through a travel agency or theater ticket office well ahead and don't miss it!),* (3) the Theatre an der Wien (light opera), (4) the venerable St. Stephen's Cathedral, (5) Schönbrunn Palace (ancient summer castle of the double-eagle monarchy), (6) the Secular and Ecclesiastical Treasure Rooms in the Hofburg, where the crown jewels are on opulent display (no English-speaking guides, alas), and (7) the Clock Museum (near St. Stephen's Cathedral; more than 3000 specimens on silent exhibit—without a single cuckoo in the lot), and (8) the house where Beethoven wrote his "Heiligenstadt Testament" in 1802 (Probusgasse 6). Then there's the "Music and Light Around Belvedere Palace" spectacle (held in German at this famed baroque structure which has played such an important role in the nation's history), concerts in various palaces in summer (consult local tip sheets for when and where), Auersperg Palace (which Richard Strauss immortalized in *Der Rosenkavalier*), and the splendid Brueghel collection and other *rarae aves* in the Kunsthistorisches Museum (Museum of Fine Arts). Plenty of 1st-rate art galleries, other museums, and other Baedeker attractions in and around this center—but remember that music, especially opera and more especially Mozart, is the staff of life to any properly formed Viennese ear. For information *and* reservation of rooms go to Vienna Western Station (Westbahnhof), the Vienna Southern Station (Südbahnhof), the office at the Opera underpass, or Vienna Airport. In addition, during the summer season, you may apply at Purkersdorf, Highway #1, or Inzersdorf, Highway #17, or Praterkai, station for the Danube steamers. Posted conspicuously here and on other main roads leading to the capital are modern information kiosks with official hostesses.

A ride on the Danube? (1) Daily passenger service in summer from the German frontier to Vienna is as popular as ever—and it's a delightful experience to climb aboard at Passau for the 7 A.M. sailing, lunch after the noon stop at Linz, dine in the lingering sunset on the river, and slip into the capital at 7:45 P.M. If this haul is too long for your tastes, the *Stadt Wien,* the *Stadt*

Passau, the *Johann Strauss,* and the *Schoenbrunn* may be boarded in the late morning at the railway hub of Linz. Should your car present a problem, a professional chauffeur is on tap to "pilot" it from Passau to Linz or from Passau to Vienna—both at moderate fees. Staterooms available; ample restaurant and bar facilities; modest prices; more beguiling than the Rhine excursion because it's not so cut-and-dried. (2) From Vienna, you may sail up to Linz for a postmidnight arrival and a return the following day in time for a late dinner. (3) Special moonlight cruises (Vienna to Vienna) are sometimes promoted, too. Don't forget that the above services are operated *from May to September only.* (4) Although the Austrian *Theodor Körner* makes occasional cruises downstream (normally it links Vienna and Passau), only the Soviets have a regular run between Vienna and Odessa, docking at such Iron Curtain points as Budapest, Belgrade, Ruse, Giurgiu, and Ismail, with City sightseeing excursions en route. The *Dnjepr* and the *Wolga* ply from Vienna all the way to Yalta, the Black Sea resort. They offer a 13–day round trip to 7 countries. (5) The Austrian hydrofoil *Delphin* and the Hungarian hydrofoil *Sirály* ("Seagull") zip between Vienna, Linz, and Budapest from early May until mid-September; departure and return days vary. For all of the more distant ports, find out whether you'll need a standard or transit visa. And do it early!

Salzburg ? In addition to the many classic-type attractions such as Mozart's birthplace and the Mozart Museum, do visit the enchanting Salzburg Marionette Theater—probably the best-known company of its kind on the boards today. For kids from 5 to 90—definitely including us! The Salzburg Festspielhaus, like the Vienna State Opera House, ranks at the top in theatrical facilities. This supermodern 7–unit structure contains 2340 seats—none more than 115 feet from that beauty spot on the contralto chin! Equally interesting to music-lovers are the Palace Concerts, now scheduled for most of the year. Movie fans might give 5 bells to Hans Erhart's **Sound of Music Tour** that reels them over the landmarks of that famous film. And finally, let's not forget the cable car, 9 miles out, which zips up 6170 feet of Alp (the Dürrnberg) in 8 minutes, for a commendably modest price per dizzy head. While in the region you can visit the Hallein Salt Mine, plus the Giant Ice Caves at Werfen (May to Oct.).

Now, in quick summary, here is our rating of outstanding attractions to the North American traveler:

1. Vienna.
2. The drive over the Grossglockner, which no visitor to Austria should miss. There is a 900-car silo garage at the 8000-foot pass. Pretty little Lienz is an ideal target for overnighting.
3. Salzburg and surroundings.
4. The Austrian Danube cruise (see above), including the Wachau excursion via delightful little Dürnstein and the noted monastery at Melk.
5. The Salzkammergut lake country—Bad Ischl, Bad Aussee, Wolfgangsee, Traunsee, Mondsee, Hallstätter See, Gosausee.
6. Drive, by car or bus, from Bad Aussee through the Gesäuse, the narrowest part of the Enns Valley, and the Salza Valley to Mariazell; from there go via the Seeberg to Graz, branching off at Stainach-Irdning to Schlad-

ming-Ramsau, Austriahütte at the foot of the Dachstein Massif, and at Hieflau to Eisenerz with its famous lake.

7. In winter, any of these—again with our previous admonition that your fun or fracture-count is relative to the depth and frequency of your sitzmarks: Zürs, Lech, St. Anton am Arlberg, and Stuben; Obergurgl; Hochsölden; Igls; Seefeld; Kitzbühel; Zell am See; Saalbach; Badgastein; Hofgastein; the Radstädter Tauern; Mallnitz. Austria is often credited with breeding some of the most daring, the speediest, and the most demanding skiers under God's gray sky, so be sure to pick an address in your appropriate league.

8. For Alpine scenery in summer: Zell am See (cable railway to the Schmittenhöhe and its hotel at 6000 ft.), Salzkammergut lake district near Salzburg, and Badgastein; the remarkable Silvretta High Alpine Road and the Hochtannberg Road in Vorarlberg, among the most thrilling larger highways of Europe. Other outstanding mountain views abound on the Katschberg road (Salzburg—Klagenfurt), the Pötschenpass road (Styria—Upper Austria) and the Wechselbundesstrasse east of the Semmering (Lower Austria—Styria).

9. Winter *and* summer skiing? The Kitzsteinhorn, via the cable car from Kaprun, the cable lift to Zell am See, the glacier at Dachstein, or the Tyrolian ice packs at Neustift-Stubaital.

10. Ötztal, Ausserfern, Zillertal, and Achensee, all in the Tyrol.

11. Velden and Pörtschach, both on Wörthersee in Carinthia.

12. The quiet, family-type resorts of Weissensee in Carinthia.

13. The baroque monastery of St. Florian (Bruckner organ) near Linz.

14. Semmering, the mountain health resort 3000 feet up—only a 2-hour drive from Vienna. Bus excursions are operated in season.

15. The Burgenland, 1 hour from Vienna, with its many castles, Neusiedler Lake, Haydn's resting place, and colorful inns with gypsy music.

Pamphlets on these regions are available at the usual sources, notably the Austrian National Tourist Office and the local tourist offices. If Salzburg is one of your goals, the *Official Guide* (published by Karl Gordon Co.) is sold at most newsstands and is more than worth its small charge.

Roads? At too long last, many improvements. The Salzburg—Vienna autobahn is the most noteworthy and the most traveled. The expressway over the Brenner Pass between Innsbruck and Italy is negotiable, but check in fringe seasons because the weather can close it down. The 6-lane highway from Vienna southward has crawled just beyond Wiener Neustadt; construction is proceeding between Wiener Neustadt and Tarvisio (Italy) via Styria and Carinthia; the link between Innsbruck and Kufstein is now finished. Until all of the proposed links are in operation, sometimes (not always!) you'll continue to find yourself frustrated by some of the most narrow, crooked, choked, potholed, antiquated arteries in today's Europe.

Good service stations in practically every city, town, and hamlet. Gas here, as everywhere in Europe, is increasingly expensive.

Jaywalking is considered a heinous crime in metropoli; if you're stopped, the fine may be a fast buck, collectable on the spot. Don't protest; pay up, since you're licked. (Incidentally, if you are an incurable in this sport, travel in your shabbiest duds, because penalties are often based on the official's judgment of the offender's financial status.)

§TIP: If you understand German, bird-dog Vienna's 28 special phone services which run the gamut from kitchen recipes to a tuning tone for musicians.

FESTIVALS   The **Salzburg Festival**, Austria's most famous, is held from the latter part of July to the end of August. The average program includes 8 operas—by Mozart, Strauss, Verdi and others, plus a world première—in 27 performances. Other events: Major orchestra concerts, Mozart chamber opera, instrumental recitals, Mozart matinees, serenades, lieder, ballet and sacred music. While it is on, the visitor will feel as if he had set up a cot next to the Information Booth in Grand Central Station; *don't attempt it without confirmed reservations in advance.* (This holds for the Easter Festival as well.) If you can't find space (as is probable), and if you're sufficiently desperate, write to the Landesreisebüro or the Stadt-verkehrsbüro in Salzburg, either of which will try to find a private family with an extra pallet.

Other most illustrious events are the **Vienna Festival** (mid-May to mid-June; a glory of operas, operettas, concerts, and plays), the **Bregenz Festival** (late July to late Aug.; performances on a gigantic floating stage on Lake Constance), and the **Graz Steirischer Herbst Festival** (Oct.; modern music and art exhibits).

Consult the Austrian National Tourist Office for details about these.

TIPPING   The mysterious word "Trinkgeld" will pop up like the Old Man of the Sea during your Austrian journey. It means "tip." Here is a rough guide of the *extra* gratuities which you, as an American, will be expected to give:

Waiter—10% extra (to the man who serves you, not to the headwaiter); bartender—10% of drinks; maid—10 schillings per night; washroom attendant—2 schillings; taxi driver—10% to 15% of fare; theater usher—1 schilling; doorman—3–5 schillings; porter and bellboy—5–10 schillings.

If someone gives you extra extra attention with an extra, extra smile, you may wish to bump these up a notch or 2.

THINGS TO BUY   Except for leather, lederhosen, ski togs and equipment, and regional handicrafts, *Vienna* seems to offer the shopper the greatest variety, highest quality, and lowest prices—straight down the line.

The city fathers have now set aside 6 malls for pedestrians only which are lined with benches, transplanted trees, and new lighting patterns. These traffic-free islands of serenity include Kantnerstrasse (the main shopping street), Cobenzlgasse (in the Grinzing section), Schönlaterngasse, Favoriten, and the 2 latest additions of Naglergasse and Jodok Fink Square. They are a delight.

Petit point is the first yen of many trippers—and the **J. Jolles Studios** (Andreasgasse 6), largest producer of this item in the world, as well as Grand Prix winner at the Brussels World's Fair, gets our vote as the leader of the industry. It's a factory, with 8 master painters, 70 specialized craftsmen, and more than 1000 home workers—plus (if we may be forgiven for a wincing alliteration that happens to be true) the jolly Jolles staff, who delight in welcoming American callers and in showing off the techniques of their absorbing work. All goods are assembled and sold on the premises—at a 10% discount, we might add. If you want the Jolles name, you've got to go to the source, because the management never authorizes outside representation. In addition to its bottomless supply of petit point articles, gay summer handbags and travel bags are also offered at interesting prices—sketched, traced, and mounted to traditional handcut jewelers' frames. Enlarged quarters; global mailing service with free postage on all purchases; studio and store open weekdays (not Saturdays) during routine local shopping hours; ask for courtly Paul Nowak. Highest recommendation.

A.E. Koechert (Neuer Markt 15, across from the taxi entrance of the Hotel Krantz-Ambassador) is worth the time of anyone who likes extraordinarily fine brooches, rings, clips, bracelets, necklaces, and original creations in the renowned Viennese style. Austrian handwork in precious metals and gems not only has its distinctive flavor, but labor costs are so low that only Portugal can offer such comparatively modest price levels in this specialty. This particular shop, founded in 1814 by the great-great-grandfather of the present proprietors, was designated by successive Emperors as Crown Jewelers to the Imperial Court—an honor which involved, among other things, the stewardship and maintenance of the fabulous Royal Treasure Chamber, still a major sightseeing attraction of the Imperial Palace. Dazzlingly opulent pieces are available to the millionaire trade, but for travelers like us who haven't much to spend, Koechert also shines with equal radiance. Their selection of exclusively designed clips and other items in the forms of flowers, dogs, sunbursts, fish, and ferns made of cut crystal, precious stones, and brilliants runs from $100 to $150. There's an intangible quality and spirit in them which makes them as characteristically Viennese as gold filigree carving is characteristically Portuguese. This ethereal, special, different beauty is impossible for us to describe; all we know is that we love it and that you won't find it elsewhere. The gentlemanly Mr. Wilfrid, Gotfrid, or Dietrich Koechert will take personal care of you. A treasure house.

Boutique with outstanding Viennese handcrafts? **Elfi Müller & Co.** (Kärntner Strasse 53, opposite the Opera House) is a FIND for handmade clothing and Austrian mementos. Talented, twinkling Mrs. Müller creates her celebrated designs in enamel, brass, wood, gold, and silver. Very fair prices; ask personally for Mrs. Müller. Recommended for many, many years by the American Embassy and by us.

Wiener Porzellanfabrik Augarten (3 outlets: Stock-Im-Eisenplatz 3, Mariahilfer Strasse 99, and the Schloss Augarten) has magnificent Spanish Riding School figurines, some knockout dinner settings, and other top-class creations. Formerly we were lukewarm about this world-famous institution; now we are red hot in our esteem for it.

Porcelain and glass? **Rasper & Söhne** (Graben 15) has a large shop featuring these items, including a charming "Drop In Boutique" and many unusual items for the home. This company operates on a national level, with branches in Salzburg and several other regional centers. Solidly run, solidly recommended. **Lobmeyrs,** (Kärtner Strasse 26) is also dead-on the bull's-eye of distinction with its crystal specialities, Herend china from Hungary, and other *belles tournures.* **Bakalovits** (Spiegelgasse 3) stocks the best chandeliers in the city.

Leather goods? **Mädler** (Graben 17 and Mariahilfer Strasse 24) has dominated the field since this Zurich-based firm expanded to Vienna in 1973. For one and one-quarter centuries this fine house has been hide-bound to the concept of quality. Here you will find a sumptuous selection of suitcases, carry-on bags, handbags, vanity cases, briefcases, and scores upon scores of stunning, hard-to-find gift items. The styling is attractive; the price range is appealing; the workmanship is superior. Personable Director Schintag (at the Graben branch) will see to your needs. We love these 2 shops—and we bet you will too!

Regional clothes? **Loden-Plankl** (Michaelerplatz 6) is one of the oldest, most respected, and most dependable establishments in the trade today. Custom-tailored suits require 2 fittings, 2 weeks, and approximately $225 of your shopping budget. Sweaters also available for children ($25 to $35) and adults ($50 to $100) of both genders. Mr. Plankl himself will greet you with warmth and graciousness. **Tostmann** (Schottengasse) is highly regarded for its dirndls. **Lanz** (Kärntner Strasse 10) is also very, very good.

Chic sportswear for women? **Resi Hammerer** (Kärntner Strasse 29–31) has been The Latest Word in Austrian fashion for 26 years. Mrs. Hammerer, the former ski champion, has channeled her expertise into a full line of medal-winning models: everything from hats to blouses to slacks to skirts to suits to shoes to full-length coats—all coordinated to delight the eye, the wearer, and the pocketbook. Matching this dazzling array are the smiles of her alert staff. Here's a sterling value in a post-Silver Anniversary year.

Textiles? **Boecker** (Kärtner Strasse) offers a wide selection, plus conventional garments.

A perennial favorite in Vienna is the classic age-old Austrian-style *Weinheber* (wine siphon), set neck down so that upward pressure from your glass activates the valve. Before buying one, however, make triply sure they check the mechanism with water while you watch. Try **Österreichische Werkstätten** (Kärntner Strasse 6).

Department store? **Steffl** on Kärtner Strasse, opposite the Ambassador Krantz Hotel, sells everything from Scotch tape to that extra suitcase, at usual department store prices.

Finally, please don't miss the enormously intriguing **Dorotheum Auction,** if it's operating while you're there. Four large and 6 small lengthy merry-go-rounds annually; furniture, clocks, jewelry, coins, stamps, classic and modern objets d'art in copious profusion, plus scads of other categories even including cars (!); reserve prices by neutral experts tagged on all merchandise; open mornings for buyers' pre-examinations; professional bidders available to you for flea-bite fee. Full details on this fascinating landmark and how best to handle yourself for the greatest fun and greatest bargains (which are often fantastic) are outlined step by step in *Fielding's Shopping Guide to Europe.* Paris' Flea Market 1000 times enhanced!

In *Salzburg,* here are our best bets:

Slezak (Markartplatz 8) lighted its 100th birthday candle in '73. Here is the highest quality and widest selection we've found in the nation—finer than the best in Vienna, in our opinion. Ladies' handbags for city, travel, country, and sport; gold-embroidered evening bags and belts; all styles, sizes, and types of leather suitcases; roomy attaché and briefcases; Nécessaire cases and overnight bags; gorgeous first, first quality cashmere and Shetland sweaters at equal to or lower than English or Scottish tariffs (a European Free Trade Association bonus); gloves, tasteful souvenirs and accessories. Wonderful men's wallets, too; we've used them for years. A paradise for mailing gifts to the U.S. Prices? 100% decent. Owner Mrs. Gertrude Michel and her gentle staff will all charm you with their Austrian sweetness. Unrivaled nationally in its field for taste and integrity.

Lederhosen and leather wearables? **Jahn-Markl** (Residenzplatz 3) always comes up with top quality at ridiculously low costs—and thanks to the radiant warmth of friendly Irving Markl, there's a cozy feeling about this ancient little place.

Regional wear? We're very happy with **Trachten Wenger** (Munzgasse 2). Their wonderful assortment of dirndls and their foursquare prices are 2 compelling reasons for our patronage. Recommended.

The **Salzburger Heimatwerk** (Residenzplatz, near Jahn Markl) is tops for handicrafts in the area. The best word for this shop is "sweet": sweet merchandise, sweet minions, sweet ambiance. Be sure to ask for young, energetic Toni Reiser, whose courteous counsel awaits you. Fine in every respect.

Lanz is in Salzburg at the end of the main bridge (see *Vienna* shopping). Antiques? Wonderful browsing on Goldgasse. Try M. H. Grotjan (Goldgasse 13) or R. G. Oberholzner, farther up the street. Jewelry? **Eligius Scheibl** (Griesgasse 3). Candles of all varieties? **Ferdinand Weber** (Getreidegasse 3).

In *Innsbruck,* we found far slimmer pickings than in other centers; you may disagree, but we feel the shopping is comparatively poor here.

Regional (e.g. Tyrolean) apparel is one of 2 conspicuous exceptions. **Lodenbaur** (Brixner Strasse 4) is our unequivocal choice. Handsome, urbane Fritz Baur runs this splendid house with keenness, competence, and charm. Very worthy indeed.

Tiroler Glashuette KG is the other must for discerning shoppers. Crystal is the medium, Professor Riedel is the *maestro,* and a line of exquisite—truly exquisite—bowls, glasses, ashtrays, sculptures, and other articles for the home is the fabulous result. The 3-tiered rose-vase set is one of the most striking works of art (for that is what it is) that we've seen. Shipping is done directly from the factory, 20 minutes out of the city. *Wunderbar!*

Handicrafts? **Tiroler Heimatwerk** (Meranerstrasse 2) now seems to us a bit dreary. We prefer **Handwerkskunst** on Wilhelm Greilstrasse. **Lanz**, also fine, has opened a branch on the same street.

Buying hours? *Vienna:* Weekdays from 8 or 9 A.M. to 6 P.M.; generally no noon closing; shuttered Saturdays at 12:30 P.M. *Other cities:* 8 to 9 A.M. openings, closing hours variable.

Dedicated shophounds? Space is too tight here for further listings—so consult this year's edition of *Fielding's Shopping Guide to Europe* for more stores, more details, and more lore.

WHAT NOT TO BUY   All American mass-produced items (pens and the like) have such monstrous import taxes slapped on them that their cost is far out of proportion to their value. Unless it's an emergency, you'll probably prefer to do without until you come home.

While high-quality Austrian souvenirs are world-famous, most of the gimcracks marked "Souvenir of Hochland, High in the Edelweiss"—those little horrors for Uncle Charlie's mantle—are a miserable waste of money.

LOCAL RACKETS   Should you patronize the lower-grade nightclubs, you are practically asking for padded checks and other crudities too gloomy to mention. Even the top-line nighteries indulge in one-upmanship. A common clip is for your hotel concierge to offer you a so-called cut-rate entry ticket. It will be printed, for example, "45 schillings," for which you will happily pay 35 schillings. Later, when you arrive at the club, you'll find that your "bargain" is the standard admission fee.

Much too often, ticket purchasing by travelers to Vienna is a classic illustration of caveat emptor. As a preliminary, commissions on sales to the opera, sports events, the Spanish Riding School, and other popular events have been boosted to 30%—plus additional small bites. Almost habitually your hotel or your agency will give you the sob story that "only the most expensive seats are left." (And why not, since their cut is bigger?) Nonsense! At 7 of the 8 major performances we attended during a recent visit, literally scores of satisfactory but less-costly seats went begging after we had been told to expect a sellout. Thus, always apply first, in person, at the sales window of the arena, theater, or opera. If *they* tell you that the situation is SRO, *then* retreat to your outside sources, which may be holding admissions up their sleeves.

Petty rackets are growing up in places where there are enough U.S. tourists to make it worthwhile, but none of them has been particularly costly or particularly serious up to now.

In general, the Austrians are forthright and honest people, to whom the trickery of some of their Latin neighbors is completely incomprehensible.

Belgium

Belgium is a tiny land—but its sinews are huge and its power is enormous. The size of the State of Maryland, here is one of the most densely populated countries in Europe.

The Flemings are the Nawth'n Yankees; the Walloons are the Southern Cuhn'ls; Brussels, like Washington, is just about the only place they'll speak to each other. The language question has been the hottest issue since the Dutch occupation of 1815. About 30 years ago the country was formally divided into 2 linguistic areas—Flanders, where Flemish (or Dutch) is used in administration, state schools, and courts by about 5 million, and the Walloon section, former dominion of the Carolingian monarchy, where French is the official tongue of a minority of 3 million. In the capital, the sole neutral ground, it continued to be a case of who could talk the loudest. The recent fights over proposed new language boundaries precipitated serious Flemish riots which nearly wrecked the nation. New legislation finally sanctioned Flemish in the North and French in the South—stranding pockets of both groups on alien soil. Next came an effort to further harmonize the 2 autonomous cultural and administrative entities by establishing 3: a 55% Flemish region, a 33% French district, and a 12% tutti-frutti mixture of the Brussels enclave. This proposal, bogged down by political triple-talk, led to vicious words, then to hurled bricks and paving stones—and tumbled the Government. Less violent donnybrooks continue to occur periodically.

CITIES *Brussels* is where you'll probably start. It's the center of government, industry, business, and culture. It's a city of tomorrow and a city of the past—1¼-million people, a fascinating hodgepodge of New York, Middletown, and a farmer's market of A.D. 900. For some time it had been enjoying the wildest construction boom of any capital in Europe—a Low Country that swiftly became an ultra-High-Riser. It boasts a good airport, 4 railroad stations, a new subway, plenty of excellent hotels, restaurants, movies, and shops. This metropolis is practically crawling with history (turn to "Things to See").

Antwerp is one of the greatest ports on the European continent—yet it's 54 miles from the smell of salt water. The Scheldt River is the answer: 50-thousand barges and 12-thousand ocean ships tie up to the 30 miles of docks every year. The 6-lane, 2000-foot-long, $62,000,000 John F. Kennedy Tunnel eases train and car traffic under the river; it forms a vital part of the E-3 highway which, France willing, eventually will link Stockholm with Lisbon. In the port area alone, $600,000,000 in corporate investment was recently Scheldt out by river bank-ers. Flemish is the regional language; the Rubens mansion is a sightseeing must, along with the "Mad Meg" (Mayer van der Bergh) Museum, the 9th-century-old National Maritime Museum, and the Plantin Moretus Museum (patrician house with ancient printing plant); so is the magnificent statue in the Grand Place of the Roman centurion who saved the town, thus providing the legend from which the metropolis took its name. The Zoo includes an aquarium in the gardens, a delphinarium, a unique aviary, and a nocturama. Rather commercial atmosphere by day; nightowling that is beginning to ruffle the feathers of the municipal fathers.

Liège, close to the German border, is third in rank. Embraced by the Meuse basin, which long ago inspired the masters of Mosan art, today it has become a student center and a springboard to the Ardennes. The legendary FN-Browning small arms plant, plus 20 smaller but fine competitors (obtain entrance to some through the local Tourist Office) are also in this city; it has been an armament hub since the Middle Ages The panorama from the Cointe is particularly worth enjoying. Liège folk have been known for generations for their special brand of friendly hospitality.

Bruges, a medieval city now less than 1 hour from the capital, is the favorite of most Americans, including us. If you're in Belgium on Ascension Day, the world-famous Procession of the Holy Blood here should not be missed. The ancient architecture is intact; no one can build a new chicken coop unless it adheres to Flemish style. Handmade lace and the wonderful little local pastries are the industries of greatest interest to the tourist. A pleasant thing to do is to hire a little motorboat and laze at random along the canals, which have been successfully sanitized through a major depollution program. It's a delightful town; a visit is highly recommended.

Ghent now takes a second place to Bruges—at least in our oft-contested opinion. Culture, beauty, and charm still exist, of course, but so many commercial aspects have now crept in that much of its color seems to have evaporated. Our local chums insist, however, that dyed-in-the-woolies antiquarians will be rewarded more profoundly here by ardent searching than they will by cursory rubbernecking in the more obvious targets. Probably we're callous boobs, but scholars we ain't.

Ostend, very maritime in feeling, is one of Belgium's most famous sea coast resorts and seafood shrines (one of the very best we've found in the North). It is the summer retreat of the royal family—plus thousands of less exalted bathers who crowd its golden sands. On the scenic, speedy superhighway from Brussels, you can stop at Bruges and Ghent, and then breeze up here in practically nothing flat. The Kursaal is among the world's handsomest gambling casinos (more about this later). Zeebrugge and Knokke-Heist are just up the pike.

Bastogne, way down in the Ardennes Forest, is now officially known as "The Nuts City." General McAuliffe's classic utterance (it was actually a ruder and more pungent word!) is something the nation can't forget. Site of the magnificent Mardasson Monument, dedicated to American troops lost in the Battle of the Bulge. Dull town but fine memorial.

Namur (prettiest girls!), **Dinant**, and the pastoral **Meuse Valley** offer an especially pleasant answer to the traveler in search of peace.

MONEY AND PRICES   The Belgian franc is the medium of exchange. It's worth about 2½ ¢. The smaller unit is the centime; at this writing (subject to change), figure 100 of these to 1 franc.

Price levels this year? Up, up, and away. Rampaging trans-European inflation is plunging hands into pockets and purses at at least a 15% faster rate nowadays-and-nights. Until March 31 (and perhaps afterward, so be sure to check), the pain can be offset slightly by a "Bonus Day" offer promoted by the Belgian National Tourist Office. Residents of the U.S. and Canada qualify for a grab bag of sightseeing and accommodation benefits if they make Brussels their first or last stop in Europe on a direct scheduled transatlantic flight. Let's hope they'll extend it for the full year!

ATTITUDE TOWARD TOURISTS   The **Commissariat Général au Tourisme**, Central Station, Brussels, is the official tourist office. Under the aegis of Arthur Haulot, potentate of the entire skein of tourist commissions, this group and associated bodies do a splendid job for the American visitor. M. Haulot, former President of the famed International Union of Official Travel Organizations, has had years of fruitful experience in this field, and he is personally responsible for the universal tourist-mindedness among the people of his friendly nation. Keenly intelligent Jean Gyory, his Press and Public Relations Officer, is an ex-newspaperman and ex-editor who also has outstanding charm and abilities. Both of these likable gentlemen speak perfect English. If you have any special (not routine) problems, drop in for a chat with either—and you'll get instant and sympathetic attention. Before leaving New York, it might also be wise to check your itinerary with the metropolitan branch, the **Belgian Tourist Bureau**, 589 Fifth Avenue. Director De Maerel and Tourist Adviser Mrs. Nadine de Bary are walking encyclopedias of travel lore on the lanes and by-lanes of their nation.

§TIPS: If you wish to move around cheaply, it would be the height of wisdom to pick up a low-cost Tourist Card in the capital. This entitles you to 2 days of unlimited tram and bus travel—2 of the least exciting but safest forms of surface transportation in this taxi-mad, motor-crazed town. Several sources sell them, but the handiest would probably be the **Tourist Information Center** at 12 rue de la Colline (Grand' Place).

CUSTOMS AND IMMIGRATION   Excellent. Courteous, friendly, and highly efficient. Bona fide tourists are passed without so much as a peek. Only travelers with commercial items or declarable wares need visit the hawkshaws. They are most interested in cigarettes (300 maximum), spirits (2 bottles will probably get by), wine, and perfume.

Tips for convenience: The control of passports has been limited to the outer frontiers of the Common Market countries. For motorists, the same wise action may be applied to "green cards" (international liability insurance).

HOTELS For far more comprehensive information on certain Belgian hostelries than space limitations permit here, interested travelers are referred to *Fielding's Selected Favorites: Hotels and Inns, Europe* ($4.95) by our son, Dodge Temple Fielding. The revised edition, in which a total of 300-odd favored possibilities were hand-picked from the 4000-plus personally inspected, will be at your bookstore early this year.

The standard houses in this nation are clean, impersonal, and efficient. Although tariffs in Brussels are already very high, whispers hint darkly that the levels may be raised significantly—and perhaps by this season—to cover spiraling costs, salary hikes, and that aforementioned Value-Added Tax. *A double room (no meals or extras) at a good metropolitan address jogs along at between $30 and $60, with singles keeping pace from $24 to $36, and suites sprinting ahead in the $85 to $200 area.* Quotations elsewhere are slightly lower. And, please don't forget that whopping 28% addition for taxes and service!

In **Brussels**, the construction bug is getting time-and-a-half for overtime. In the resulting epidemic, a rash of new hostelries surfaced and more may soon bubble up—even though there is a glut of space now in this city. (Some, in fact, are doomed to failure due to a lack of sufficient traffic.) All-in-all, it portends a mighty battle—with the traveler as the winner.

The new, 500-room **Sheraton**—in our opinion, the handsomest link in the European division of this chain—has had its share of teething pains, but if it hangs in there, we believe it will soon be acclaimed as the luxury address of Brussels. Midcity venue with ample public oases; a fringe benefit of boutiques; gracious lobby; sumptuous Le Comtes de Flandre Grill; medieval evenings in the Table du Roy restaurant; Louis d'Or dining quarter, plus a coffee "pavillon," a cocktail lounge, and a discothèque; a pool due for unveiling after our recent inspection. Generous bedchamber dimensions (some twin units even with 3 beds); yellows, browns, and orange tones in textiles; radio and color TV (latter with 2 closed-circuit films provided each day for stay-at-homes); small tubs; 45 excellent suites which stoke up kitchenettes. Though the plant is physically stunning, the management and service will pose dual question?marks? for visitors over the ensuing months. If the text of this Yankee-bred book lives up to the promise of its smart-looking cover, then the Sheraton should be a best seller. Let's see.

We are becoming increasingly fond of the young and muscular **Royal Windsor**. There's a darkling cozy richness in all the gathering nooks and a gleaming fresh welcome in the private accomodations. Stately exterior topped by a handsome gabled roof; Victorian-mood mezzanine chophouse; Wellington Pub plus the Waterloo Club for liquids and chitchat; quick-service coffee shop; 300 bedchambers with private bath, hushabye soundproofing (a boon since it is so central), radio, TV (on request), and air conditioning. Though the tariffs may seem exaggeratedly high, they are in line with the competition. What's equally important, the value is there. Royal salutes of welcome to this Windsor!

The high-capacity **Hilton**, though now showing wear as a result of extreme popularity through recent years, swings in with such button-poppers as the ruggedly handsome Maison du Boeuf Grill (at treetop level overlooking the Egmont Gardens and the Royal Palace, offering beef flown in from America), the splendid En Plein Ciel ("High in the Sky") Supper Club with a combo-notion for dancers, the 27th-story cocktail lounge, Le Bar with exploration theme and piano melodizing, delightfully beautified coffee shop, and oodles of quiet corners for sips and salubrious chitchat, plus one of the finest sauna baths in which we've roasted anywhere south of Copenhagen (see "Tip" under "Nightclubs" for the sobering facts on this gem). Accommodations with the usual Hiltonations; 1 entire floor (16th) devoted exclusively to 4 VIP suites, with multiple-connecting bedchambers, kitchenettes, and everything except a redheaded lap-warmer; guidance by soft-spoken, sharp-eyed General Manager Wille Sprokkreeff, who also captains all of this chain's Benelux interests. Chief Concierge Frans Anthoons and his highly charged brigade (Roland, Jacques, Geraard, Willy, Raymond) are superb travelers' aides. Overall, a stalwart contender.

The **Palace**, on the other hand, might be superior for the visitor who seeks continental rather than Made-in-U.S.A. atmosphere. Here is the keystone of the famous Les Grands Hôtels Européens chain. Every room with bath and shower, most topnotch, but a few clinkers in the stack; 2 dining precincts with excellent food; attractive little bar; beauty parlor and barbershop. Try to reserve on the Park, not on the Square. Hardworking, go-getting Manager Robert Ramaekers is kind; he maintains this very sound establishment as 1 of the nation's pacesetters.

The **Westbury**, alas, has closed its hotel doors—a victim of the boom that fizzled. The **Lendi** also bid farewell to the innkeepers' race.

The **Atlanta** is once more a Confederate winner, after lagging behind for a few years. Its new wing is a splendid attraction, boosting its room count to 244 and adding a vast shopping enclave plus a Day-Glo rooftop breakfast oasis. Amply appointed throughout for efficient use of its rigid space limitations; 6-channel radios now stock equipment; telephones in all bathrooms; all streetside units with acoustic ceilings. Max and Charles Gmür, the veteran Swiss proprietors, deserve salutes for their generous investment in comfort and brightness; here is a cheery, friendly, and informal stop, especially for those who travel with children. So good we can say with confidence that this Atlanta has risen again with all flags flying.

The **MacDonald** pipes in with a bagful of colorful high notes. Its sourest chords in a baser clef, however, rent the air with bleats about flat service standards. Reason? We blame it on the mini-mini back-of-the-house facilities, with the kitchen and staff areas so horribly cramped and inefficient that the people must almost step on one another's toes. Graceful upbeat flair; entrance leading to an interior bridge across a miniature pool and tinkling waterfall; masculine Horseshoe Bar, split-level La Causerie coffee shop, and copper-hued Ember Grill jowl-by-cheek-by-jowl; bubbling Champagne Room on the

11th floor for dining in Art Nouveau surroundings; rouge-tone Le Gong nightclub for dancing; overall clean-lined elegance. The full complement is only 76 bedchambers, about ½ of which have "wall-o-beds," a fancy term for the space-saving Murphy variety (but we doff our cap to the errant word-huckster, because these are especially clever in design); all units with full bath, separate W.C., radio, TV, stocked refrigerator, bar, and air conditioning. If the laird of this MacDonald household had rapped the knuckles of the architect for planning that stupid behind-the-scenes Lilliput, this would be a bonnie choice indeed.

The **Ramada** charges less than the Sheraton for its 200 U.S.-chain-fed accommodations; the exterior strikes us as architecturally boring; inside (sic) there's the Garden Restaurant for light grazing and the Mexican Club (no South-of-the-Border cuisine but Mex-cellent in tone) for really donning the feedbag, both of which are brimming with eye appeal. If you like the Ramada life-style in the U.S. of A., then you'll probably feel at home here. (Is that why you came?)

The **Plaza**, after a hiatus of discontent, has popped back as a happy little wonder. Central location, with interior tranquillity; a rainbow of fresh pastels chirp their welcomes, from the flocks of refeathered nests upstairs. A satisfactory rejuvenation that was urgently needed. Now recommended with heartier cheers than those of yore.

The totally restyled **Mayfair** also beckons with renewed radiance. Quietly modern in tone; bar in brass and rust-color leatherette; small conference facilities; boutique; hairdresser; parking; 106 bedchambers in timeless ambiance. A welcome change which gets our salaams.

The **Amigo**, behind the City Hall (and behind the Jail, too, where cater-wauling new arrivals sometimes make *enemigos* of dozing guests), offers an austere flagstone lobby and Seville-style bar in contrived Belgian-Spanish mélange. The beds, chairs, and other furniture seem almost miniature—just not man-size either to the eye or the fanny—but the tariffs for doubles seem too fat for what's there. Its management, also busy with Amigos in **Namur, Mons,** and **Verviers**, is considering expanding into a neighboring building (not the hoosegow!), so the carpenters may be banging away by the time you check in. Better for Benelux businessmen than for U.S. vacationers, in our opinion. You might well disagree.

The new **Brussels Europe** was imported from England as a novitiate in the Grand Metropolitan chain. While its accouterments boast ample allure and its staff already seem to have mastered their jobs, we feel that it is too far from the center for the convenience of shoppers and sightseers. Winning Dukes Restaurant surrounding a fish pond, with brick walls, fern-filled planter boxes, and red rush-bottom chairs; elegant Beefeater eatery ornately decorated with oil portraits on paneled backdrops; inviting, snugglesome bedrooms featuring rich textiles, dark-wood furniture, and high-grade fittings and garnishment. Since Brussels is a businessman's hub, this hostelry is aiming unabashedly for that trade. Nevertheless, if you don't mind the long taxi hop to the doin's, we think that joy-seeking holiday spirits might warmly like it too.

The **Métropole** houses 500 suites or bedchambers in a spacious, rambling structure; because conventions and tour groups are urgently needed to fill its vast space, the fun of the independent wanderer is sometimes a bit dampened. Even so, more than half the rooms have lately been respiced; the public precincts have been shifted about and face-lifted in a becoming traditional fashion; scads of baths have been replaced; TV's are switching on everywhere; carpets and streamlining appear on every floor. Old in style but becoming younger in spirit by the hour.

The 63-room-and-bath **President Nord** wins our vote for reasonable value at relatively reasonable prices. No restaurant, but pleasant English Bar and snack room; clean, bright atmosphere; cordial staff headed by hardworking Manager A. Formisani. The midtown address is another feather in its sweet little chapeau. Very worthy for the outlay.

Its newer running mate, the **President Centre**, reflects the success of the first-termer. This administration, furthermore, does offer a restaurant plus an air of greater prosperity. The levies, however, are about the same. Our double-barreled recommendation to this pair.

The **Brussels Residence Hotel**, which recently unwrapped 50 fresher bedchambers, also has been doing an outstanding job with its 40 older duplex apartments. The décor throughout is so colorful it is almost Scandinavian. Famous restaurant on ground floor augmented by 2 more, 1 Japanese, 1 Hawaiian; Cub Room nightclub; garage; a good buy, provided your architectural tastes are avant-garde.

The **Astoria** is continuing its new Old-World ambiance for the benefit of nostalgic wayfarers who may again enjoy its solid comforts. More than 100 rooms and 80 modernized baths; stuffed with crystal chandeliers and white furniture. Especially recommendable to senior travelers.

The **Siru**, which we used to feel was a good value for higher-bracket economy pilgrims, has been freshened up and given a smart new entrance. Courteous attention a major goal of personable Director Pierre Halkin; French cuisine in the popular La Gousse d'Ail ("Clove of Garlic") restaurant. The **Arenberg** is a strong challenger now. The **Bedford** (added wing with private baths) fits in about here on our checklist. Next in line are the **Charlemagne, La Cascade, De France, Central, Vendôme, Residence** and **Noga**, none of which keep Conrad Hilton awake nights; take your pick, because we'd rate them about on a par.

Holiday Inn is a welcome addition at the airport. Chandeliered lobby often sharing space with advertising promotions; congress facilities; 2 outdoor tennis courts; enclosed pool; 2 saunas plus biceptual gym. Second-stage Waterloo Tavern, dim but colorfully fitted with toy soldier regimentalia; adjoining Les 9 Provinces restaurant (weekday buffet); bright Café Holiday for preflight bites or heavier cargo. All 300 soundproofed rooms with bath, shower, radio, color TV, air cooling, direct-dial phone, and other Space Age gimmickery; excellent w-i-d-e beds with gaily striped spreads; gold carpeting; nonskid tubs; unattractive open wardrobes. At your service is a shuttle service (request it at the Avis counter in the terminal), plus city hops hourly by minibus from 8 A.M. to midnight. Nearby is the French-bred **Novotel**, its 160 sleepers wrapped around a central swimming pool. Motel space concepts but, like its neighbor, particularly useful for airborne short-timers. We haven't yet parked at the new **Jacques Borel** out at *Wepion*, close to Namur, but we're told it counts 130 latchkeys, private baths, air cooling, 2 restaurants, and a heated indoor-outdoor pool. Sounds pretty good.

Dedicated budgeteers? Since we're too bottlenecked here for additional entries, please consult *Fielding's Low-Cost Europe*, our annually revised paperback, which lists scads more bargain hotels or pensions and money-saving tips for serious economizers.

In *Antwerp*, the hotel boom is finally bottoming out. Among the contemporary contenders, we'd pick the sleekly elegant, midcity **De Keyser**. It evokes a clean modern air enhanced by quality appurtenances. Refined Old Masters restaurant; chummy Paint Pot coffee corner with raffia lamps suspended over tables; the blessed advent of efficient soundproofing in the accomodations; radio-TV consoles; compact but well concieved. Our choice for up-to-daters. The **Eurotel** makes a splash with a good-size swimming pool and a spacious parking lot (important in this traffic-choked anthill). The dining salon is a colorful creation of wood, polished metal, and bright textiles; the café served us (albeit in pleasant surroundings) what was perhaps our most repelling ingestion ever on Belgian soil. Bedrooms are substantial but not inspired. **Esso**, about a mile out on the E-3 pike, greets motorists with several interesting tapestries in its entry hall. Airy Wellington restaurant and coffee shop; chipper Campaign Bar; 5 attractive penthouse suites; more than 300 look-alike chambers stacked in a high-rise configuration. Dedicated conventioneers will feel at home. On the same highway, the 180-room **Quality Inn** is known for its restaurant; it also features a pool and sauna. The **Antwerp Tower** and the **Empire**, both back in town, are appealing. So are the **Theatre**, the **Plaza**, and the **City Park**, if you are seeking a modern mood. The **GB Motor Hotel**, on the route to Brussels, isn't bad for wheelborne travelers, but the industrial neighborhood should encourage after-dark arrivals. Also in the suburbs, the **Antwerp Docks**, with 80 rooms and 80 beds, has a terrible superhighway location in a complex of dunes and factories; some doubles are passable, but others are totally unrecommendable; huge family-style café on the ground floor. There's a **Novotel** in the harbor district. If you still prefer being out of the city, the totally renovated **Kasteel van Brasschaat** (often called the Park) is a semiluxurious country hideaway 15 minutes toward Breda (Netherlands). Lovely converted estate with lakes for boating and swimming, ponds, and arcadian peace; some baronial accommodations with mirrored doors 10-feet high; other disconcerting touches of cheap plastic. Here's the weekend haven of many local G.M. executives. Don't bother with the **Dennenhof Motel** in the same vicinity. Nice outside, but horrid interior, in our opinion.

In *Bruges*, the pert **Holiday Inn** is stealing the local thunder nowadays. It was developed with disarming flair from the assemblage of several ancient houses. The cunning meld of new and old is balm to the travel-weary wayfarer. After this one, the **Portinari** should be its closest rival in quality. Its 50 rooms, all with bath *or* shower, are neo-Scandinavian in tone; nice dining room and bar; improved cuisine; carpark; breakfast, balky service, sagging beds, and taxes included with the price of the room. The **Duc de Bourgogne** is world-famous as a restaurant. The lobby and the dining areas, literally chockablock with great paintings, are lovely; the upstairs now offers a colorful palette of improvements. Pillow space for a mere 22 sleepyheads; 10 private baths; canalside sweetness in an ancient inn that we somehow find reminiscent of New York's Frick gallery. Chiefly for cozy-corner seekers and pigment addicts. Another oddity? Try the "botel" called **De Barge-Westhinder**, an 18-stateroom ship anchored at the Komvest. The galley is unusually good; the bunks are comfortable for their type; the cost of passage is right. Frankly, we're as salty as Popeye, so the whole saline concept appeals to us even if it is a bit kooky. The **Bryghia** provides an agreeable modern aura at modest tariffs. Very clean surroundings and garniture; 18 rooms and 18 baths; breakfast only. We like the waterway shoulders and the peek at the courtyard where Master Memling's are always on tap. The neighboring **Europ** again serves naught but the morning repast; more tour-oriented than the Bryghia; fewer bathrooms. The **Bridge**, also nearby, seems more inviting from the outside than it does upon closer examination. Only 2 private baths for 37 nervous occupants. As we said, we like the exterior, but our innards tremble. **Sablon** has 55 rooms and 28 baths; main structure dates from 1772, with new wing added in '59 (1959, that is!); full or demipension required in season; so oppressively old-fashioned it gives us the megrims. The **Londres** is no better—in fact, even a shade or so grimmer. The **Park** is parked in Zand Square, offering 40 rooms with bath, radio, and TV-on-request. In the village of *Oostkamp* (4 miles out, on the Courtrai road), the **het Schaak** is a worthwhile stop for motorists who prefer a do-it-yourself setup to the more elaborate service of a metropolitan hostelry. The **Lodewijk van Male**, at St. Kruis (Malesteenweg 488), is a bucolic country estate with a river and park at its rear doorstep. The best of its 18 units face Mother Nature rather than the highway. The cuisine alone is worth a linger.

In *Ghent*, the clean-lined, modernistic **Europa** wins the day. Moreover, its canalside situation in a residential district near St.-Pieters Station affords much more P & Q than any of the midcity turnstiles. Two-tone brick and glass exterior; broad window-wrapped lounge with warming Persian carpets; ingratiating colonial restaurant; stained glass counterpointing the turn-of-the-century bar. Again the bedchambers use to full advantage the outdoorsy feeling with floor-to-ceiling windows; all 40 units are adorned with thick rugs, fluffy spreads, radio, phone, and private bath. Definitely recommended when the sojourn isn't too long. **Holiday Inn** presented its U. S. passport-to-comfort very recently. It is a bit out of the center. While we can recommend the physical plant, we'd suggest that you take your vittles elsewhere. Best for resting—and for dieting, in our view. The **Cour St.-Georges**, on the other jaw, is suggested only for its Old World restaurant, which is an interesting period piece. The hotel itself was founded in A.D. 1228—and when you see it you'll believe it. The **Carlton** is a drive-inn owned by the Terminus (see below). Not much public space, but passable for pit-stoppers to whom sleep is the main concern. The **Park** unfolds its withered vines to reveal 37 bedrooms, more than ½ of which claim some kind of hygienic device for part or all of the human anatomy. Noisy, midintersection location; basic, in a traditionally moth-eaten way. The station-sited **Terminus** is even more exquisite. Ugh!

Liège offers the tiny 8-room hillside **Le Clou Doré** (Mont-St.-Martin 33),

above the restaurant of the same name. Small but elegantly outfitted with fine
Flemish paintings. The service and maintenance standards in the hotel (not
the restaurant) segment are notably substandard by comparison, but despite
this debit we enjoy parking here. Be warned that the number of accommodations is so limited that wise wanderers will reserve early.

An American-born, waterfront **Holiday Inn** (200 units plus heated pool)
caters pretty heavily to conference confabs since it is located so near to the
congress hall. We personally prefer the newer **Ramada Inn** (100 air-conditioned rooms; good cookery), which greatly resembles its sister operation in
the capital. The 100-chamber **Post House** is a motel with such added facilities as a pool, a grill, and conference centers. The first 2 U.S. imports come
on very strong for comfort, efficiency, and convenience. Both are fine additions to the Liège scene. (Incidentally, we wonder if you won't agree with us
that Belgium's Ramada master draftsman *really* knows how to produce a
boring exterior. Happily, they belie what you'll discover inside.)
De la Couronne, hard by the station, draws a choochoo clientele. It has
been vastly improved, but *still* only rates so-so on our score sheet.

In **Bastogne**, the century-old, pink-faced **Lebrun** is just about the only
show in town. Ardennaise dining room; antlers and a boar's head rampant
in its lounge-bar; covered tea garden with climbing plants, aviary, and aquarium. Not great.

In **Ostend**, everyone now seems to head from the ferry landing straight
over to the pertly modern, spanking-fresh **Melinda**. Only 40 units (with bath),
but prime it is for this little port. The old **Palais des Thermes**, a big seafront
bath establishment, is City owned and privately operated. The 30-room **Bero**
comes with a full bath count. It is a fresh challenger. Opposite the Kursaal,
the 50-room-and-bath **Riff** rafts in with a cheerful flair that's rare on this
coast. Pick a front unit and we think you'll be as happy as an Ostend clam.
In the city, the **Imperial** offers a degree of comfort; rooms ending with "0,"
"1," or "2" have ocean views. The **Ter Streep** ("At the Stripe," or the line
where the sea stopped 3 centuries ago) copies the Hilton idea of innkeeping
down to a modest T. Now we'd call it the best bet locally. The **Wellington**
is just barely better than the **Palais**, *if* you snag one of its premium waterfront
accommodations. Otherwise it seemed to us a sand-bit nightmare. The rebuilt
Westminster, under the Riff aegis, is strictly riffraff in our book. We can't get
on the beam with the **Telstar**, either. They're a coaxial bust as far as these
viewers are concerned.

Knokke-Heist's **Sofitel Thalassa-La Réserve** is probably the leading
resort hotel in the nation. Situated on the shores of a little lake 200 yards from
the sea, it directly faces the Casino. Beautiful interior; 8 tennis courts; minigolf; swimming pool; water skiing; fitness center and health clinic to be added;
general atmosphere tends toward elegance. One unique feature is that every
bedroom bears the individual stamps of a Flemish, Walloon, Dutch, or
French artist—including Roger Nellens, the son of the owner. The *haute
cuisine* is an extra strong point here. Highly recommended. Open *daily* from
Easter to November 1 and *weekends only* in winter. The modernized **Lugano**
might be a possible alternative; we haven't seen the renewed structure.

For detailed information, consult the Belgian Tourist Bureau's excellent (and imaginatively titled) booklet, "Belgian Hotels." You'll find the addresses, facilities, and prices of every registered hotel or pension in the nation.

RESTAURANTS   If you can pay the price, you'll get fat fast in Belgium. In its ranking establishments gustatory standards are so high they challenge the best in France.

In *Brussels*, **Villa Lorraine** (avenue du Vivier-d'Oie 75) remains a glory. It is presently another "must" candidate for anyone's list of romantic lunches or big nights out. Parkland situation bordering the Bois de la Cambre, about 10 minutes by taxi from the center; converted mansion resplendent with deep-pile carpets, rich brocades, and colossal floral decorations; wooden bar with leaded stained-glass doors leading to an open, bower-shaded terrace; sumptuous, even regal, interior dining room with champagne moiré-silk wall coverings, gilt chandeliers and sconces, and a crackling hearth; captivating flower-girt garden patio, glass-lined for dining with nature on inclement days. Sadly but realistically, the prices match the rewards in every way. Very costly, but very, very special indeed. Highly recommended.

The **Parc Savoy** (place Marie-José 9) could almost be considered a miniature Villa Lorraine. Enchanting sylvan setting; flowers bordering the paneled entrance and the patio of the Cercle Privé cocktail lounge; inner Cercle overlooking the greensward; several dining nookeries including the main rotunda, a mirrored alcove ringing one side, and a conservatory-style glassed-in terrace which is extra-extra-charming when the days are halcyon. The service, overseen masterfully by English-speaking Maître César, is as polished as the enormous silver duck press that dominates the pivotal area. Specialties run from $6 to $16; a full meal with wine goes for about $24 on the average. (And does it go down smoothly!!!) Our banquet was nothing short of superb. Exquisite, discerning, and totally aristocratic.

The midtown **Ravenstein** (rue Ravenstein 1) is a wondrous restoration from the fourteenth and fifteenth centuries. Moreover, it was a restaurant even before this century was born. A single hearth-front salon with about 8 tables plus an upper welcoming loge; magnificent crystal chandelier; fine linens; leaded windows; polished beams and wooden dado enhanced by a rouge-and-gold textile wall covering; masterly oil paintings. The cuisine and the service are the perfect complement to its patrician atmosphere. If you happen to be in Belgium in early March please try the delicate poached-egg dish with nibbles of hops, a seasonal delight. At other times the Soufflé St. Jacques (or with lobster) is also ambrosial. One of the oldest and finest addresses in the capital. And, of course, blue-ribbon in prices too.

One of the most illustrious and delightful contenders in the plush league traditionally has been **La Maison du Cygne** (Grand' Place 9). It was sold a while back, and some complaints began to fall upon our desk. Now we are happy to report that these have dried up and we are receiving letters of praise again for the chic restaurant and the ground-floor l'Ommegang clubroom. We think that Mr. Theo's new administration today has restored the former glories of this beautiful landmark. When passing in or out, don't forget to rub the arm of the little Everard t'Serclaes statue in the building's façade and make 3 wishes; it has dispensed good luck since A.D. 1320. Head straight for the little elevator and ride upstairs, where you'll find paneled walls, luxurious bottle-green banquettes, and a huge rôtisserie grill at one end; 3 sectional divisions lend a feeling of intimacy here. The menu is handsomely presented inside an original engraving by Brussels' beloved artist, Nicole Ickx (ask if you can buy one as a stunning souvenir of the Belgian townscape; or, if you're *really* ready for an artful adventure, why not visit her studio at 34 rue de la Paille, which is nearby? Call first, however, to make sure this gracious lady can receive you: Tel. 5115437).

L'Écailler du Palais Royal (rue Bodenbroek 18, near the Grand Sablon) is the newest venture of M. Marcel Kreusch, who is doing such wonders at Villa Lorraine. This one specializes in seafood. Main ground-floor room with green plaid walls, brass sconces, ocean-toned textiles, and a restful oil painting dominating one side; 12-stool counter dominating the other. Upstairs outfitted in burnt orange, brown, and rich polished woods, swinging saloon doors, hurricane lamps, and a handsome painting of a schooner. Pincushions provided for spearing the gratis snails in tiny beakers; white wine poured into beautiful prefrosted glasses. The shellfish were Atlantic-fresh (oysters are a house pride, with good reason); our grilled Turbot with anchovy butter was one of the most succulent catches we've ever hooked into in this sea-soned land. Closed Sundays and bank holidays. Again, cheers and salutes.

In this district, **Au Vieux St.-Martin**, on the Grand-Sablon #38, is outstanding for typical Belgian fare, sausages, and hardy dishes. If you're not too hungry, go in the evening for snacks.

For elegance, the **Carlton** (boulevard de Waterloo 28) still gets our vote, although some Guidesters recently have begun to demur. Tasteful redecoration which generates opulently subdued atmosphere; sparkling direction by Dante Farinone. Bright summer garden for lunching or dining; piano lilts after dark; Saturday night dancing medium to high. For gastronomes who relish big restaurants, still a reasonably sound candidate.

La Couronne (Grand' Place 28) is chichi, urbane, and expensive. The cookery, however, can be variable. Warm reception enhanced by the appearance of cocktail niblets plus other on-the-house tidbits throughout the meal (peanuts, olives, crackers, Pâté Maison in jelly with celery salad, and a broad selection of petits fours); our martini must have had a U.S. birth certificate, because it was so perfect and so authentic. Try for a window seat in summer; avoid the topmost floor always.

Brussels Restaurant (avenue Louise 319) is strong on design. Its indirect lighting, candelabra, piano music, and other suave touches blend to create a nonaggressive modernity, pointed up here and there by judicious use of woods. We only wish the chef could do as much for us as the architect does.

Comme Chez Soi (place Rouppe 23) is high on the culinary controversy list. Some lucky ducks and ganders quack that it's easily the city's leading feedery for cookery, service, and finesse. Other feathered friends grouse that you must be known by the proprietor before you will be treated as even tolerably human. There's no view to speak of; the atmosphere is busy and tensive; the tabs are strictly platinum-tinged. For cuisine, it should be applauded, but our professional and personal sympathies, as always, remain resolutely with the ordinary traveler, not with the smart-aleck flunkies, starched minions, or negligent patrons. This one's on you, because we disclaim all possible responsibility for leading you to it.

Chalet Robinson, on the tiny Ile du Bois de la Cambre, 10 minutes from town by car and reached via a storybook cable-ferry, has become a self-service feedery under its new management.

We offer top orchids to **La Maison du Seigneur**, 15 minutes out the Chaussée de Tervuren (#189). It is a white brick farmhouse with stables for riders; there's a bar and lounge plus a provincial L-shape dinning room. The cuisine is worthy of any *grand seigneur*—at tabs that jab close to $20 per *tête*. Closed Tuesday.

A longtime reader who lived in Brussels for 3 years put **Pierre Romayer** high up on his menu after 6 satisfying seatings. At this point he tipped us off —and we quite agree. Meats top our list of the commodities; the tabs are modest for the quality; the portions are almost massive. It is out of town near Val Vert and Père Moulliard. Worth the journey.

Seafood? **L'Huitrière** (20 quai aux Briques) cops the title among First-class candidates. (The aforementioned L'Écailler du Palais Royal, if you recall, is a Deluxe entry and is thus more costly.) Main-floor room wood paneled, with inset tiles and enough coffee grinders to send Messrs. Chase & Sanborn into ecstasies; less inspired but more polished upstairs dining salon for overflow traffic (of which there is always plenty); a favorite at midday of local businessmen and in the evenings of sea-savvy families. Our Bisque de Homard was among the best we've *ever* sipped anywhere. The oysters were so fresh they winked up from their half shells; the stewed eel—yep, stewed eel, which sounds so repugnant—was d-eel-ightful; the Coquilles St. Jacques were heavenly; the Crêpes Grand Marnier were succulent. More recently we were enraptured by a Lobster Thermidor, and the love affair still lingers to haunt our musing idylls. Wild fowl, grills, and other terra firma critters also available, but it would be a pity not to bid for the ocean offerings. Closed Monday; reserve ahead through Maître René. So g-o-o-d! The same proprietress, Mme. De Smet, recently unshucked another shell-ter at nearby *Ganshoren* called **Au Chaudron d'Or**, which dates back to the 17th century. It's good, too, but we prefer the *alma mater* for our shell games.

If L'Huitrière is full, **François**, just a few doors away, is a formidable alternative. You'll find a 2-story, madeover residential home with leaded windows, linoleum floors, rosé drapes and pelmets, pencil-yellow linens, and mirrors scattered higgledy-piggledy. Our starter of mussels (we counted 20) on an iced platter was a repast in itself. Moreover, the serving of Turbot Dugleré was so huge that it might have been hacked from a whale. The fried shrimps ordered by another member of our party were a little disappointing. Also popular with locals; also not too costly; also quite recommendable.

Vincent is about as colorful as they come. It is on the narrow rue des Dominicains, just off the even narrower Petite rue des Bouchers in the most shoulder-squeezing quarter of the Old Town. Its wide street-front window is hung with beef and paved with fish. Entry via the kitchen; steamy atmosphere crowded with jocular activity; 2 segments, one leaning toward maritime outfittings and the other inclined toward an *auberge* theme. Our twin gridiron of entrecôte was about the size of a football; with salad, beer, coffee, and dessert the bill came to $18 for 2. You won't fall asleep over your meal—and that, good friend, is a gilt-edged guarantee!

Le Londres (rue de l'Ecuyer 23) holds the title as Brussels' most ancient dining establishment. Bright—almost too well watt-ed—cheerful, rectangular room with yellow napery, verdant flora, mirrored walls, and red banquettes; voluminous menu that may be outpricing the value on the plate nowadays. The wine card goes back to Château Haut-Bailly Graves, '19! The ventilation is a little close; the surroundings are not too chic.

L'Eperon d'Or (rue des Eperonniers 8) specializes in cuddlesome dimensions, brass chandeliers, burgundy tones, and blue-stocking tabulations. Although our wedge of steer is a tender memory, our teeth still rattle at the overall cost for full-meal ingestion. Ouch!

Shanghai (27 rue des Bouchers), said to be ballyhooed by some visitors (Soviets, perhaps?) as the best Chinese spot in town, did not poison us—but after the pain our tummies experienced, we almost wished they had. Its aftermath was a night of horrors. PLEASE AVOID IT. Disrecommended with a passion. We had agreeable vittles at **Ming's** (rue du Grand Cerf 9–11), a 2-minute totter from the Hilton. To us it resembles a Swiss *Stubli* with Cantonese overtones. As possible alternative bets, good words have come our way regarding the **Porte d'Or** (boulevard Adolphe Max 158) and the **Golden Dragon** (avenue Louise 291). Both **Le Mandarin** (rue au Beurre 21) and **Le Mandarin II** (avenue Brugmann 510) were suggested to us for their Chinese-Indonesian kitchens.

Arche de Noé ("Noah's Ark," at rue du Beau Site 27) offers an eye-popping, free-choice menu in small and plain surroundings. The Rognon du Veau is exceptional, especially if you come in 2-by-2.

The **Rôtisserie du Vieux Strasbourg** (boulevard du Jardin Botanique 2) is a gem that now seems to us to be losing its luster. Grill atmosphere; no cocktails, no beer, no beef here; you gits what you gits. This saddens us personally, because we've been so fond of it over so many prior years.

Shopping nibbles? **Watney's Pub Louise**, inside the charming Garden Stores district, is just what its name implies. The entire works—from globe sconces, to frosted mirrors, to beer-pump handles—was imported from "Jolly Olde England"—quotes and all. Attractive Edwardian main-floor restaurant with comfortable booths; downstairs Circle Privé Bar serving only sandwiches and beverages; maximum set-lunch menu in the $6.50 Circle. Affected, mincing waiters in foulard waistcoats, dainty shirts, and painfully tight pants. Amusing for a sudsy laugh. The **Ji Snack**, also in the same complex, turns on a psychedelic mood. Tidbits for farthings; a handy feedbag for light biters. Our double-barreled verdict? We don't hate 'em, but we sure don't love 'em, either. **Copenhagen Tavern**, a few doors from the Hilton, turns on mighty savory Danish snacks in elegant precints. Soft sconce illumination reflects from ochre velvet walls. Open both day and late into the evening. A cheerful "Skål" to this one.

The typical and delightful **bistros** along Petite rue des Bouchers are kind to budgets. Emphasize the word *Petite* when giving the address to the taxi driver. No great shakes as epicurean palaces, but pleasant bargains. A glowing report about a place in the vicinity called **Léon's** tempted us to try it, and we agree that the Moules au Vin Blanc are sufficiently good and numerous for you to "eat yourself into a coma." Go here if you feel like musseling around. At **Aux Armes de Bruxelles** in this same district, we didn't clam to that oh-so-no service or so-so cookery by one nip.

In **Chez Marius en Provence** (place du Petit Sablon 1), the proprietor seemingly couldn't care less what we ate, and the prices seemed all out of proportion to our investigative eye; this one also impressed us not a bit. Another *Chez* to *Cherchez*? Okay: **Chez Stan's** (*sic*) whomps up championship steaks in a crumbling, darkly nostalgic tavern. Also esteemed are the pot-au-feu and the fried scampi. Two friendly waiters; paper table "cloths"; old-line mien that is simple, honest, and worthy. It's at rue des Dominicains 12. Just opposite, incidentally, **Ogenblik** does pleasant things with piscatorial pickin's.

Handholding? If you can't make notable progress after 15 minutes of pitching at **Au Bon Vieux Temps** (rue Marché-aux-Herbes 12), brother, you might as well turn it in for a new model. We've only cocktailed here, so we don't know anything about the food. **De Bellemolen**, on the Ghent pike, is another romantic target. It is situated in an old mill. There's also a garden for—well, milling around. Bad jokes aside, the cookery is worth the distance.

Game for a small expedition? An assortment of 9 choices, varying in quality:

(1) The famous **Atomium Restaurant** which we've already mentioned; it's one of the few unrazed structures from the World's Fair. Zoom by high-speed elevator to the top ball of this fabulous Tinkertoy; get your table on the lower of the 2 levels; be prepared to pay a mint; the management has really pulled up its plutonium. The view alone is in the megaton range. An experience not to be missed.

(2) The colorful **Auberge du Chevalier**, at *Beersel* (7 miles from the heart of Brussels), is a small hunting-lodge-style inn adjoining a moated castle. Smoky timbered ceilings, medieval furniture, huge fireplace, pewter, silver, and copper utensils; wine and beer only; cuisine above average once again, on our incognito visit; fairly steep prices. Sit under the big willow on the terrace for your apéritifs, then move inside for vittles. Lovely in sunshine, dull in rain. Important: *Be sure* to get exact road directions from your hotel concierge, because it's a murderous place for any American motorist to find in this Flemish-speaking (not French-speaking) region.

(3) Don't forget the glorious **Villa Lorraine** mentioned earlier in this section. It's not exactly an "excursion" target, but it *is* out of the center and it *is* out of this world.

(4) **L'Abreuvoir**, at place St.-Job in *Uccle*, is moving up strongly. This might be a better alternative. (And if this one's full, try **Brasier** in the same village.)

(5) **Le Pré au Bois**, on the main pike toward Waterloo, is now in the capable hands of the former maître at Villa Lorraine and the chief barman at Maîson du Cygne. Only a 20-minute ride and well worth the jaunt.

(6) **Château de Groenendael**, at *Groenendael*, is also in the woods; eighteenth-century baronial atmosphere too seldom broken by the appearance of a waiter. We haven't had much luck with the gastronomy either lately.

(7) The **Au Prince d'Orange** (avenue du Prince d'Orange 1, about 5 miles out toward Waterloo) used to be princely, but it seems to us to have lost some status under its latest change of sovereign. English-country-inn motif; open rôtisserie-grill; terrace-dining under the trees in season; bar at entrance; cozy tearoom with fireplace; open all year.

(8) **Le Fond'Roy** at *Uccle*, 9 miles by car, gives us the impression it has skidded into a slump. Still, the setting is appealing.

(9) **Père Mouillard**, in *Hoeilaart* (near the Groenendael Station), is a warmly conceived *auberge* with chillingly high tariffs. If your lady companion is built like Anita Ekberg, you might enjoy it—the restaurant, that is, or both, we hope!

Dedicated budgeteers? Since we're too bottlenecked here for additional entries, please consult our annually revised paperback, *Fielding's Low-Cost Europe,* which lists scads more bargain dining spots and money-saving tips.

In *Antwerp*, the previously mentioned **De Keyser Hotel** stokes up enviable cookery at its ovens. The Old Masters segment is ingratiating if you want to dine in formal surroundings. The Paint Pot provides a more casual atmosphere and lighter fare.

Among straight restaurants, **Rôtisserie Cigogne d'Alsace** (Wiegstraat 9) is the unchallenged sachem. Here *is* a charmer. Cozy 10-table, ground-floor dining room with live-trout tank, canopied display case for meats, beamed ceiling, leaded windows, and gaily flowered wallpaper; a spectacular wooden stairway leads to upstairs annex which isn't quite as attractive. Outstanding wine list; 5-course menu bearing a vast number of choices; big à la carte selection, not cheap; cuisine piping hot and excellent. Reserve in advance; open all year; top recommendation.

St.-Jacob In Galicië (Braderijstraat 12-16) has blessed the tummies of a devoted following of disciples. Old-City richness in an ancient structure; panels, overhead timbers, tilework, brass-studded leather chairs, rustic bar and open grill; 10 tables; thick-caloried French cookery with medium-range fixed menus, plus à la carte; Patron M. Doyen is the Saint-in-Residence.

Another upper-crust address is the tower perch of **Sir Anthony Van Dyck.** It is located at 16 Oude Koornmarkt ("Old Grain Market") in an assemblage of 16th-century buildings called the Vlaaikensgang. The scenery alone makes this one worthwhile, but happily, too, the gastronomy is first-rate. A towering recommendation for this pillar of local culinations.

De Zeven Schaken ("The Seven Shields"), a rustic corner in the lovely Grote Markt, accents light bites for late romantics. It offers brick and cane walls, stucco and beamed ceiling, bottle-jug illumination, curved bar, open hearth, and all the trappings of a snugglesome nook. Onion soup and steaks seem to command the most attention. No rave for cookery, but fun for the lighthearted and spirited.

The **Rade** (Van Dijckkaai 8) has the edge over the **Critérium** (De Keyserlei 25)—small, Flemish décor, Belgian cooking, and medium bracket. Between October 1 and May 15, *La Pérouse* is a luxuriously interesting novelty. It's the dining salon of the *Flandria XVI,* which is moored between these dates at the Flandria Co. dock on the Scheldt River. (In summer the boat makes daily Tourist-class shuttles between Antwerp and Flushing.) Recently refitted wooden deck; interior décor dotted with gay flowers; à la carte menu only; piano music at night; amusing in sunlight or starlight, but not advised during rain, fog, or storms. Closed Monday. The smaller *Flandria XVII* is used for private parties and charters, plus summer toots to Rotterdam. Finally, **Au Gourmet sans Chiqué** (Vestingstraat 3) offers 10 tables, an old-fashioned air, immaculate cleanliness, and an excellent 6-course menu; closed 3 weeks in summer, when Patron Louis T. Verhoeven retreats from his skillets. Pleasant.

Sunny day excursion? Try the **Hôtel du Parc**, between Antwerp and Ghent near the town of **Lokeren**. It's as famous for its food as it is for its architecture. Timber and antique atmosphere; superior cuisine and service; especially captivating on a summer day. In **Boom**, the **Linden Hof** is another hotshot to keep in mind.

In **Bruges**, the **Duc de Bourgogne** (Huidevettersplaats 12) wins the romance-and-vista sweepstakes in a walk. It is enchanting to the eye, reasonably satisfying to the palate, and not unduly merciless on the wallet; here's a charming lovely canalside oasis. The **Portinari** is also pleasant, especially if you raise potted plants; excellent vittles. Shoppers like the tempting pâtisserie called **Van den Berge's** (on market square), which comes up with cold buffet, sandwiches, and light refreshments; a haven when the dogs start barking from too much walking. **Baeyens** (8 Wollestraat) is also a sweetie. There's one country restaurant of unusual aspect which seems to have special appeal to hungry Americans—**By Lamme Goedzak at Damme**. Extensive decorative talents were employed in the restoration of these fourteenth-century cellars and this ancient building. The result is a handsome rural tavern, with steaks the specialty. Take route N-67 toward Knokke for 5 miles from the center of Bruges. When you see the "Bezoekt Damme" sign, turn right and cross the bridge into the village, where you'll find this hard-to-locate restaurant; return via the **Bruges–Sluis** canal for more direct motoring and a change of scenery. Closed at odd times, so be sure to make advance reservations. Urbane, highly priced, and pleasant. At **Oostkerke**, a mile away, the **Siphon** pumps up gushers of foodstuffs for droplets of francs. Old Flemish surroundings; open rôtisserie with crackling meats; waterway specialty of eel in a yummy cream sauce (a wiggly bonanza, if you squirm for such dishes). A perfect stop on the economy circuit. A delightful fair-weather alternative is **Goedendag**! ("Good Day!") in **Lissewege**, 6½ miles from Bruges. New proprietor Roger Toon has turned on all the sophisticated-rustic charm and sylvan wiles he knows. White cottage-like structure on Hoogstraat; bar at entrance; large open copper grill; eye-appealing board of salads, ham racks, and other dishes greet Ye Hungry Guest; a fireman's staircase spirals above the cashier counter. Tariffs in line with the tops in the metropolis; courteous staff, cuisine that is positively delicious. The **Romboudt** and the **Oosthoek**, both within a bivalve's squirt, are also attractive, but they lack that final touch of élan that made us fall for Goedendag. At **Zeebrugge**, **Le Chalut**, peering at fisherman's wharf through broad windows, is fashionable these days. The rich tariffs don't do anything to deny it, either. Waiters in middy blouses; charts on walls; ocean-size choice of briny critters. Our Turbot was as fluffy as a

Rinso ad; the $33 twin tab for a modest lunch gave us a whitewashed sensation, too. This one's a question of net worth *vs.* net wares.

In **Liège**, **Le Clou Doré** (33 Mont-St.-Martin), overlooking the distant cathedral and miniature townscape, is the Deluxe den of local gastronomes. Elegant manner blending dusty mulberry and Empire-gold trim with antique timbers and glass; intimate anteroom for quiet toasting; outdoor tea terrace for summer sipping; 10 large tables surrounding a central fountain; reception by Hosts Souveryns and Olaerts. Attentive minions who tend to push the house specialties; minuscule wine list and limited menu. But we go for it warmly, despite notable service and administrative drawbacks. **Le Vieux Liège**, sometimes called Maison Havart (41 quai de la Goffé), muses nostalgically on the banks of the Meuse. Strikingly handsome sixteenth-century structure of brick and cross-hatched timbers; 2 floors with candles, brass chandeliers, flowers, tilework, and copperware; extremely inviting rustic milieu; reasonably good cookery which can develop the chills while being run up and down that busy staircase. The *patron* here is the former maître of Le Clou Doré; we hope he can invest just a dash more professional knowhow into this worthy and historic plant, because with proper supervision it could become one of the gastronomic landmarks of the Old World. Costly. For regional specialties, try either **Mamé vi cou** (9 rue de la Wache) or **La Ripaille** (rue de la Goffe). The chef of the new **Ramada** knows his skillets; let's hope he keeps up the good cookery.

In **Bastogne**, the chef at the **Hotel Lebrun** takes the cupcake. Choose between the rich Ardennaise dining room or the greenery-filled covered garden. The plain, clean, and friendly **Restaurant Borges** is second in line.

At nearby **Noirefontaine**, **L'Auberge du Moulin Hideux** has been ballyhooed by a baker's dozen of our Belgian brethren—whose only debate is whether it's a charming 15-room hotel with a superb restaurant, or vice-versa. We've oft tilted with this happy windmill and must agree with both opinions. The rose-colored house nestles in a sleepy hollow, offering homey comforts, crackling fires, open beams, and river views through cottage windows. We fairly glowed from savoring the mousse of woodcock and Ardennes ham and a Ballotine de Volaille wafer thin and sprinkled with pistachio nuts; one look at the dessert trolley is enough to encourage anyone to embrace obesity for a lifetime. The prices, however, will repeal your hedonistic tendencies and return you safely to ascetic ideals. An experience to be lived.

In **Ghent** (are you set for a spelling lesson?) our first choice is **'tPatijntje**, located at Gordunakaai 99. If you stumble at this mouthful (who doesn't?), retreat to the 2nd-ranking **Cigogne-d'Alsace** at Koningin Astridlaan 52. **Cour de St. Georges** is okay for hotel fare. (Easier to pronounce, too.) Newcomers include the **Horse Shoe, Vieux Strasbourg,** and **Barracuda.** We don't know these.

In **Ostend**, we recently rereenjoyed another superb seafood meal, and we highly recommend that you try this modest house before seeking out fancier digs. **Belgica** is 1 of the perhaps 30 harborfront candidates fighting tooth-and-fin for attention. There's no décor to speak of—but oh, my, what delicious things swim out of that tiny little kitchen! Two enormous heavenly soles, dessert, a small bottle of wine, and coffee cost our duo a reasonable $13.50.

No tricks with fancy recipes; honest fare we are confident you will never forget; hardworking ownership by M. Rottier, who is likely to be the only one aboard who speaks English. Just drive along the port frontage until you come to this house, stop, enter, and prepare yourself for an Atlantic-size treat. Odds are 5 to 1 that you won't be disappointed! Although favorable comments have reached us about the rivaling **Petit Breton**, **Le Vigneron**, **Le Périgord**, **Charles V**, **Lusitania**, and **Prince Albert**, we know where WE'RE going for the next 164 visits to this community.

For other restaurants, consult any branch of the official Tourist Office.

NIGHTCLUBS In *Brussels*, most of the pack (not counting the 2 or 3 largest ones) are out-and-out clip joints—bare-bosom floor shows, large orchestras, predatory young ladies at the bar, and champagne at $30 to $50 per bottle—nonvintage at that. This capital hasn't run out of the genus known as the B-girl—the type who sips tea while the sucker across the table pays $7 for her "whisky"—but it ain't what it used to be. You can recognize the pros around the smaller bars of the Gare du Nord section, but beware of the demure lassies on the boulevards who'll take you to a little winery where the tab could be $30 for the same *vin blanc* which sells for a-buck-a-bottle at the corner store. Fortunately, the average Belgian "hostess" is easy to pick out. Hard, shrill, she has a couple of gold teeth, dresses like Sadie Thompson, slaps on cosmetics with a bricklayer's trowel, and has a faster eye for a franc than a Strasbourg banker—a recognizable dog, and a greedy one. Never have we seen such a contrast between the "good" girls (who are charming, chic, and pretty) and the "bad" girls of any city.

In short, Brussels after dark devotes a lot of its energies to bachelorhood (temporary or otherwise), with mechanical fun designed for the outlander. Leave the bulk of your traveler's checks in the hotel, but take along at least $75 if you plan to have a whirl—because it will cost you plenty. (For additional comments on prostitution dangers please turn to the end of this section.)

Chez Paul au Gaity (rue Fossé-aux-Loups 18) remains the leader in after-dark entertainment. Always-fresh décor; better than average floor show featuring fast-paced "singles" and plenty of nudity. Naturally, you'll find it expensive. Advance reservations are suggested if you want a ringside table. A leading night light for many and many a moon.

P.S.: Don't allow any taxi hack to steer you to a joint called **Le Shako** on the pretext that he misunderstood your French pronunciation of Chez Paul. This sleazy trick was twice pulled on us, despite our implicitly clear and specific directions. If you are carrying this book, show the driver the name and address—or write it down on a slip of paper before setting out. Our blood steams at this brazen rapacity—and so would yours, to be taken for such an idiot.

Le Crazy (rue Crespel 15), just a quick stagger from Hilton's portals, provides a pale replica of Paris's Crazy Horse Saloon. The show is amusing and well mounted by a bevy of leggy beauties. The combo is smooth, the stereo not too loud, the air fresh, and the drinks legitimate. There's less of a variety-show quality here than you'll see at Chez Paul, and frankly, we think the pulchritude is more abundant. Maybe you'll disagree—but *what* argument could ever be more engaging? **Cabaret of Geraldine** (16 rue des Dominicains) seems to be on the rise. It sometimes features gay performances with group singing and flights of fancy by the audience. A dollop of spirits may ring up $7.50 or so at the register. These are followed by **Funny Horse** (rue de Pepin), which attracts a younger crowd for uninhibited rollicking. Somewhere along this belt, **El Poncho** (rue de la Fourche) deserves a notch in the *noche* if cabaret is your bag.

The **Fashion Club** (avenue Louise, near the Bois) is à la mode this minute with a fad-mad following. High jinks for low tabs; chiefly designed for young singles on a cool prowl or old marrieds of 20 or 21.

Golden Gate, in the Galerie Louise, is said to swing chiefly for the upper *Crustacea* of Brussels' Café society. We haven't sampled this newcomer yet. (In fact, on our latest prowls, we couldn't even *find* it on 3 separate nights of searching. It did exist, however.) Good luck, if you try.

Mainly for dancing? **St. Louis** (35 rue Defacqz), **Elite Club** (3 rue Jourdan) and **L'Interdit** (47 rue Livourne) seem to draw the nicest traffic.

Finally, the private club in the MacDonald Hotel slides in with a suave mien for elegant romancing. House residents are admitted by a card provided by the management; if you're staying elsewhere, perhaps a soft, kind word to the concierge might win your entry. It's lovely and worth a try—especially when your ladyfriend is lovely and worth a try. Also in the hotel milieu, the Hilton's rooftop **En Plein Ciel** provides a patrician atmosphere for wooful wanderers. No entrance formalities are required here; just wear shoes—*and* take your wallet.

§TIP: If your dawn comes up like thunder, Dr. Fielding can prescribe no better post-night-owl remedy than a therapeutic descent to the **Hilton** basement's splendid sauna—one of the cleanest and most elegant broilers we've ever seen for soaking away one's sins. Evergreen and ever-smiling Proprietress Helga Wilke and her staff provide fluffy peignoirs, huge leather-upholstered "executive" chaise lounges, the latest *Playboy,* soft lighting, soft music, and soft hands applied by 2 massage-specializing lovelies (a blonde or brunette, take your pick), who will gently towel you down as you emerge from the shower. Operating hours: 9 A.M. to 9 P.M. on weekdays, 9 A.M. to 7 P.M. on Saturdays, and 9 A.M. to noon on holidays; closed Christmas and, alas, New Year's Day. Ladies are accepted by appointment only. The saunas cost about $7 and the massages at least double; this might seem expensive, but we assure repentants that it is worth every droplet and groan. We love it—even when we're sober. Blue-ribbon pampering À La King.

Random Randies? A word of grave warning: A sort of gang-bang-bang war currently is being waged on the rueful *rues* of Brussels these nights. Several men have met violent death in the conflicts which have pitted imported call girls against local *poules.* The home-grown (and Italian) trollops charge about 1/10th the fees of the Dutch or French connections. (The latter squeeze out $60 to $125 per 15-minute trick. One Parisienne took in $5600 in 40 days . . . er, nights, while her 50-or-so colleagues regularly earn about $240,000 per month.) The high-priced action seems to have cornered the market around rue Stassart near the fashionable tenderloins of the Avenue Louise, while the bargain-basement trulls trudge along the opposite end of Avenue Louise near the Gare du Nord. As occasional shootouts do occur, avoid the risk of crossfire and, if you must, rely on old Ma Bell—use the telephone. Incidentally, here is one instance in which it it is *not* economical to employ migratory workers.

In **Antwerp**, unless you're a sailor, a discophile, or a habitué of waterfront joints, you'll probably be muffling your yawns along afterdark row. Each sunset brings new hot spots, but by dawn most of them are cool and heading for a just oblivion. Please excuse this text, therefore, if one of these hyperperishable roosts has vanished by the time you alight. Possibly the best guidance we can provide that may still be current by the time you arrive, is to head for Market Square ("Stadswaag") and simply shop around. This is the main nocturnal gathering ground for night hawks and the nesting place for many clubs, whether for students, swells, or *matelots*. **Villa d'Este** on Grand' Place, with its typical nightclub wheeze and single acts every 20 minutes, has been the most popular. The **Kilt**, launched by the same owner, is less lavish; central location; same show schedule and price scale. **Scotch Club** can't even hold a tartan to it. **L'Abbaye** is blessed with a fair sampling of naked flesh; similar tithings as Villa d'Este, its alter ego in the night circuit. **Sans Souci** is only a few doors away physically and not far behind spiritually. **Play Boys**, near the De Keyser Hotel, is the leader for dancing; small cabaret; a bevy of playmates on tap that Hugh Hefner wouldn't enjoin even for a game of leapfrog. **Whisky-A-Gogo** (just off Grand' Place) is for disks and sips only. **Club 13** (rue Anneessens 13) offers a bar, piano, and singer, but no terpsichore; lonely males may have luck here finding the better class of pickups. **Nostradamus**, about 30 yards from the Cathedral, has about 25 seats, a bar, a pianist, and casual entertainment from time to time. Pleasant around 10:30 P.M., after the movies are out.

The discothèque is very fashionable here. **Little Club** was the in-vogue tub-thumper of the lot. L-shape room swaddled in emerald-green silk; long bar with long drinks; music swinging from hot to cool; "society" nook supposedly for members only, but anyone with pockets can enter. Unchallenged. **No Club** also nods *si-si* to the hoi polloi, despite its seemingly private status and discouraging name. **Phare-Choc** is pure candy to the Young Set. No B-maidens in any of these, but all fairly bristle with available dancing partners. Skip **Asterix**, **Match Club**, and **Kings Road**, a cluster of ho-hummers near the Grand' Place that couldn't be more routine if they hired a specialist in boredom. Strictly for An-twerps.

To wrap up (or unwrap down), there are 2 or 3 joints in the Club 13 area which display photos of performers at their entrances (merely sucker bait, because there's no show), peddle bad champagne at $40 per bottle, and condone the most ruthless type of B-girl. Run, don't walk, in the opposite direction. The Quartier Latin and the Habor Area have many small cafés which cater to sailors—who, poor fellows, are victims of the machine age. With improvements in cargo-handling machinery, their shore leaves have been cut to the point where they must run through their social activities as fast as rabbits.

In *Liège*, the **Tabarin** (en Bergerue 14) surveys the top of a very small heap. Modern interior with illuminated glass dance floor; movie-screen projections with a scattering of nudes among the projected images; human strips between film strips; comfortable chairs and good ventilation. You'll find more B-girls here than you can muster from the 2nd-letter pages of the Manhattan Telephone Directory. Coolish but pleasant atmosphere. **La Dolce Vita** (rue St. Adalbert 7) is a dancing-to-disks hideaway; the choice among a poor lot. **Au 1900** and **Wild West** (both on rue d'Amay) are chiefly for students (particularly freshmen). Loud, dim, and beer-soaked—but fun if you still check the mirror every morning to see if any new whiskers have budded. The leading private clubs are **La Cave, La Rhumerie,** and **Les Champs Elysée**; ask locally how you can join. P.S.: Unless your stomach is cast iron and your wallet is spun gold, stay out of the jernts along the rue Pot d'Or. There's more High Season shearing here than in Queensland in October.

TAXIS   Be careful.

Since beginning our annual trek through this country back in '46, we have undergone hassle after hassle with various local drivers. In the capital, or elsewhere in Belgium, you might find courteous and honest hackies—or, alas, you might meet some of the most exasperating and frustrating service personnel you'll ever encounter abroad. The worst of the lot may not return the proper change, insist on inflated tips, and even browbeat and curse their passengers. If your pilot "forgets" to put down the flag on his meter, remind him loudly and instantly.

Incidentally, Belgian taxi fares are the highest in the world. Service (such as it may be) is included, *so don't bother with any further voluntary doles.*

TRAINS   Very good nowadays. There's even a car-train that will take your auto from Brussels to Munich, Avignon, St. Raphaël, Villach, and Narbonne for peanut-size outlays.

The 5-day-minimum Tourist Card ("abonnement") is perfect for rod-riding excursioners. The costs? $13 for 5 days, $18 for 10 days, and $23 for 15 days of almost unlimited railroading within the country. (Unless you're Casey Jones, 5 days should be sufficient to cover this little land.) The Brussels International Airport line is privately operated, so you'll pay separately for this 15-min. run. Nevertheless it's worth those few extra cents for the convenience of going to or from the center of town so easily. Also available is a 1-day plan called "Un Beau Jour" that is a real money-saver for quick trippers.

AIRLINE   With a sleek fleet of 30 aircraft and 140-thousand miles of far-flung routes, Sabena is one of the more important and most respected carriers in the industry, with an annual average of more than 1½-million ticketholders.

The glittering fleet of Boeing 707 and 747 and Douglas DC-10 jets is employed on the Brussels–America (New York, Montreal, Mexico City, Montevideo, Guatemala, Buenos Aires, and Santiago), Brussels–Africa, and

Brussels–Orient (to Tokyo, Jakarta, and Singapore via the North Pole or via Southeast Asia) links, while Boeing 737's serve the shorter-haul destinations.

From Brussels, Sabena planes fan out to 70 cities on 4 continents. Brussels International Airport is the base airport and headquarters. At check-in time here, you can now register for the seat of your choice on your outgoing aircraft. Ask at the counter for this thoughtful service.

Recommendation: On our recent Sabena rides we were again delighted in every particular. The aircraft were comfortable, beautifully appointed, and beautifully flown; food was superb; service was exceptionally suave and pleasant. Sabena is an efficient, well-established carrier with an excellent record and a progressive attitude. We find it outstanding and recommend it heartily.

§TIPS: At the Brussels International Airport, tax-free shops offer tobacco, liquor, liqueur, camera, watches, perfumes, and selected manufactured goods.

There's also a 15-room Aérohotel. Units available day *and* night at low rates.

If you're going to town and loathe the abominable taxi drivers as heartily as we do, there are superb electric train connections; low tariffs; follow the signs from the disembarking ramps; only 15 minutes to the city.

For the Distaff Side Only: If you need advice or assistance in the Belgian capital, consult the kindhearted damsels here who represent the Sabena Welcome Club. They will help you to find anything from a baby sitter to a poodle to an English-language confessor.

DRINKS   Trappist beer is unique and cheap. There are 2 types: "Double" (the normal variety) and "Triple" (hard to find). Both are different from anything brewed anywhere—vague Coca-Cola overtones, believe it or not, which 50% of first-timers loathe and 50% are wild about; a curiosity. (One Guidester wisecracked, "Not 'Cola' beer—just *bum* beer!") The Rochefort monks produce a 3rd kind from oranges, which is also a fluid oddity. Other national quaffs (Goud-Ster, Elberg, Artois, Haecht, Gueuze-Lambic, Duke, Ginder Ale *(sic!),* and the like) aren't quite up to Danish or Dutch standards, but they're infinitely superior to that bottled froggy water sold to the unwary in France. A good 1/3 rd of the nation's 189 breweries bubble in Brabant and each one throughout the land produces 5 or 6 separate types of malt beverage. The native brew of Brussels is Le Lambic; sipped naturally, it will put a pucker on your kisser that will make you the talk of the harem; many locals add sugar; we suggest about 328 heaping tablespoons per glass. The locals also down Kriek-Lambic, a cherry beverage found only in the oldest taverns. The saturated Belgian is perennially one of the world's heartiest beer drinkers.

All kinds of spirits and wines are available in profusion for just about what we'd spend for them at home.

But don't forget to try that Trappist beer whether you enjoy it or not, even though those monks will never convert Mr. Schlitz to their mixology.

§TIP: "Gin Martini" on a menu isn't that dry, before-dinner solace that warms the marrow in the U.S. It is plain vermouth. For the cocktail, simply let your tongue hang out about 9 inches and mumble one word: "Dry."

THINGS TO SEE   In a 1-day walk around any Belgian city, it's possible to see the history of Belgian civilization. Unlike London, Paris, and Rome, things are relatively close together—a happy bonus for the sightseer.

In **Brussels**, after strolling the glorious Grand' Place (where autos have been banned, thank heaven), every American tourist seems to head for the Manneken-Pis—probably because he or she wants to be shocked. It's the famous bronze statue of the boy doing you-know-what; one story goes that a king wanted to immortalize his son in the last position he saw him just before the youngster was accidentally killed. Another is that he was lost—and the searchers found him in that particular pose. He has been stolen 4 times; a brand-new little squirt was created from the original mold after his most recent kidnaping in the mid-60's. A Tokyo newspaper and an Indian prince are among the 80 bemused parties who have donated costumes to cover his nakedness—all of which may be viewed at the Maison du Roi. His miniature in various forms of dress is one of Belgium's most popular souvenirs to visiting firemen. Although he may disappoint you, see the "Oldest Citizen of Brussels" anyway, just for the record.

Plenty of cathedrals (Belgium is almost entirely Catholic), including Sts. Michel et Gudule (generally called Ste. Gudule). Other standbys are the King's Palace, the Courts of Justice, Théâtre Royal de la Monnaie with the lavish "Ballet of the XXth Century," and wonderful winter concerts with top-line artists—plus all the museums and art galleries any classicist could wish for.

The permanent center of Belgian entertainment life is the Palais des Beaux-Arts, an underground labyrinth which contains a huge concert hall (3000 seats), several small theaters, a movie house, a king-size exhibition hall for paintings, a restaurant, and headquarters of most of the artistic associations.

For some of the most thrilling Flemish art, go to the richly endowed, vastly expanded, and freshly renovated Musée de l'Art Ancien, rue de la Régence, near the Beaux-Arts building. Today it is one of the finest in Europe.

Waterloo Battlefield is not recommended. It is one of the sorriest, poorest tourist sights of Europe. You'll ride a bus or car for a wearisome stretch, and when you get there, ordinary cow pastures and a heap of dirt will greet you. Don't waste your money on this one.

La Hulpe, a Brussels suburb, is famed for its orchids. The Royal Palace at **Laeken** is another worthy target for green thumbs. Furthermore, flower shows exist in **Lochristi** (near Ghent), **Sainte-Marie-sur-Semois**, and at **Spa**, but check on the dates before you leave the capital.

Ghent and **Bruges**, less than 1 hour from Brussels on the superhighway, are the cities which draw the most Americans. If you want to cover a lot of territory fast, here's a once-over-lightly itinerary which can be comfortably done in 1 highly active day: By private car, start from Brussels at the uncivilized hour of 8:30 A.M. Take the expressway straight to the Bruges turnoff and Bruges (ignoring Ghent, which you'll be seeing later). Head for Van den Berge's attractive pâtisserie on the market square for your coffee break. Have a little boat ride on a canal, sightsee where you will, and then amble down either the expressway or Route N-10 (distances about even) to Ostend.

Your main target here should be the **Kursaal**—one of the most modern and efficient gambling casinos in the world. Baccarat, roulette, swimming, 2500-seat concert hall, restaurant, nightclub—the works; 35¢ minimum play in the Grand Salle, 75¢ minimum play in the Sporting Room, and a $600 single play limit in both. Foreigners who bring their passports are admitted to both *salles* on a special 2-day arrangement for a $2.25 fee which can later be credited toward a Season Card; admission to all else is public. You may be interested in the budgeteer's weekend, which includes dinner, a hotel room for 1 night, and Sunday-morning breakfast—all for about $20. (No such bargains, however, during the summer months.) Quite a buy.

If there's time, you might then wish to run out to **Knokke**, Belgium's most chichi seaside resort and site of the World Poetry Biennial, a few miles along the coast to the north. If not, perhaps you'd be happier to head straight for lunch. Either the charming Goedendag at **Lissewege**, 6½ miles from Bruges, or the By Lamme Goedzak at **Damme**, 5 miles from Bruges, or even the economical Siphon, a mile from Damme at **Oostkerke** (see "Restaurants"), is suggested; make advance reservations, for sure. Then climb back on the expressway to the Ghent turnoff and **Ghent** for a view of Van Eyck's immortal "Holy Lamb" at the **Cathedral**; follow this with tea at the ramshackle Cour St.-Georges, oldest hotel in the north; the rooms are poor but the dining facilities passable (we *still* can't pronounce the best independent restaurant). Those with extra fortitude may want to run out to the **Castle of Laarne** for a peek at its $2,000,000 silver collection, its tapestries, its furniture, and the spook who haunts its grandiose halls. The expressway will have you back in the capital by dinnertime—dogtired but (we hope) reasonably well pleased with your comprehensive excursion.

If you should go to **Antwerp**, there's one sight about halfway between the cities (12 miles from Brussels, on the main road) which most visitors miss. This is **Fort Breendonk**, one of the most infamous Nazi concentration camps in Europe. It has been preserved intact as a national museum; even the torture chambers are still there, in all their horror. Some travelers might wish to make a thorough inspection of this grim relic of a dark period of history; personally, it's too heart-tearing for us.

Another outstanding attraction is the **Grottos of Han**, about 3 hours from the capital. The underground streams are interesting, the colors are exquisite, and the rooms are so huge that opera used to be presented in them. Admission is chickenfeed and the train fare is peanuts.

Newer magnets for tourists are the Sound-and-Light *(Son et Lumière)* spectacles from May 1 through September 30 in the courtyards of medieval castles at **Bouillon**, **La Roche**, **Ghent**, **Bruges**, **Antwerp**, **Tournai**, and other locations. **Liège** has come up with a panoramic entertainment called "Forms and Light," in which a 175-foot mobile and the glass walls of the Palais des Congrès serve as a huge screen for luminous, colored images reflected in the River Meuse. Its creators claim they have invented a unique art expression. In any case, it's way out, man, but *way*. Summer only.

The **Carnival** de **Binche** (pronounced "Bahn-ssh") is worth a 500-mile detour from any set itinerary, if you happen to be in Europe in early March. Started by Maximilian in the sixteenth century, the pseudo-Peruvian costumes are fantastically colorful—with hats 4½ feet tall. On the climax day,

5000 participants "dance" the grand parade. *Wear your oldest clothes if you go to this*—blue jeans, if possible—because the crowd will kiss you, hit you painlessly with air-filled skin bags, and throw oranges at you, all simultaneously. About an hour's drive from Brussels; unreservedly recommended; ask the Belgian Tourist Bureau for the exact date.

For Art and Architecture Addicts: Good King Baudouin recently threw open the massive doors to dozens of Belgium's most beautiful (and never-before-public) chateaux, including his own palace in Brussels. In the last, you can see rare Beauvais tapestries, Napoleonic furniture, and regal porcelain, plus the monarch's marble Staircase of Honor and Throne Room. Court is held for you 9:30 A.M. to 4 P.M. from about July 22 to mid-September. You also might wish to savor rural manors with their priceless treasures. Ticket prices differ; most are in the neighborhood of $2. Be sure to check with the Belgian Tourist Office or Sabena for the full list before you leave. If you're already in Brussels, the Commissariat Général au Tourisme will supply all necessary details.

For further information on sightseeing, folklore, and other data of interest to the overseas visitor, the official Tourist Office has issued a gem of a booklet imaginatively called *Belgium*. Written succinctly by ex-newspaperman Jean Gyory, it's of enormous value to every stranger. Available only through its New York office (589 Fifth Ave.), and free of charge.

THINGS TO BUY   Lace, gold craftsmanship, charms, and crystal are the top buys, with pipes, infants' wear, copper, ceramics, firearms, and diamonds.

As of our press-time these costs we quote are correct, but because of the possible supplement in the form of the aforementioned Added Value Tax, they might be slightly higher when you are ready to fill your shopping bag. Thus, if these quotations don't quite match the tags on the merchandise when you arrive, please don't blame us.

Lace is the biggest bargain—and it's a racketeer's jungle. *Go alone and unheralded,* because it's common practice to kick back a percentage of what you spend to the man who sent you—including not only hotel concierges but guides of 2 of the world's most famous travel agencies.

Far and away the finest house in Europe for lace is **Maria Loix** (handsome headquarters at rue d'Arenberg 52-54, 1 block below the front of St. Michael Church). *Insist* on going here, despite what chiseling local concierges, taxi drivers, guides, and envy-ridden competitors might tell you about its being "out of business" or "closed," because in this racket-ridden industry, the Loix firm has always been the lighthouse of quality, variety, square prices, and impeccable reliability. Since the deaths of the radiant Mme. Maria and her sweet sister Mme. Bertha, both octogenarians, daughter Mme. Georgette, who worked with them for decades, is carrying on everything unchanged. Stunning handworked lace blouses for $46 to $54 which Saks or Bergdorf couldn't duplicate for $100; all sizes of lace or lace-linen tablecloths (napkins to match) in Princess, Duchess, Flanders, Venetian, or a score of Brussels patterns; bridge cloths and placemats with matching napkins; wedding veils in scores of designs, and delicate fingertip veils; round, square, oval, or rectangular doilies in all sizes and types of laces; fans, mantillas, butterflies, other small gift remembrances. To repeat, no matter *how* the local gangsters try to steer you to inferior dealers through phony sales talks or downright lies —in order to collect their secret commissions on what YOU buy—send them running. There is only one Maria Loix.

Diamonds, charms, jewels, silverware, and gifts? For lovers of beautiful things, **Wolfers Frères** (ave. Louise 82–84) is as important a Belgian sightseeing attraction as the Grand' Place or the King's Palace. Its stunning new theater, with lacquered walls and bronze pillars enclosing a garden with clerestory for daylight viewing of its gems and creative treasures, was an inspiration of the fabulous Monsieur Cognard. Visitors from 5 continents drop in to marvel at its vast collection of flea-size to boulder-size diamonds —Belgium being the world's largest producer of cut varieties, and Wolfers offering competitive prices to any in Europe. They also come to "oh" and to "ah" at its superrich jewelry, splendid silverware, and exquisite craftsmanship in precious metals. Of special interest to Yankee bargain hunters is Wolfers' $$$$$-saving arrangement with famous old Gorham (Providence, R. I.) and Wallace (Lancaster, Pa.) to supply all their flat- and hollow-ware lines anywhere in America at 25% below U.S. retail tabs. Here, too, is the only dealer in the nation where you can buy such top-ranking watches as Piaget, Patek Philippe, and Chopard at Swiss tabs or even less. But despite its regal array of treasures, this does NOT mean you need last Tuesday's cash balance of the Morgan Guaranty before presuming to walk through its doors. Unique gold charms are a Wolfers' trademark. Ask for Freddy Wolfers by name (you'll find him urbane, charming, handsome, and a delightfully personable spirit). Although this Great House caters to unthinkably rich clients, you'll always be warmly welcomed to browse to your heart's content. A paradise.

Val St. Lambert crystal and glassware is gorgeous, and it costs a mint. Hard-to-find factory near Liège; small extra charge for U.S. shipments; safe delivery guaranteed. Lovely, lovely stuff, grossly unappreciated by some of their listless, lunkheaded, couldn't-care-less salesgirls.

Sumptuous and unusual chocolates? **Godiva** (Grand' Place 22, boulevard Adolphe Max 87, Brussels Hilton, and several other branches) beguiles the senses while tickling one's sweet tooth. Its cleverly wrapped "shotgun cartridges," for instance, substitute the house's deee-licious creamy specialty for powder and shot. Golfers and tennis players are similarly favored. Fun, fanciful, and fabulously fattening.

Cutlery? Wonderful **Henckels** ("The Twins") of Germany has a branch at boulevard Anspach 10; surprisingly inexpensive; personable English-speaking Manager Jeschke is there to show you the world's best quality.

Delplace, rue de la Régence 11, internationally known and respected, is the leading antique dealer; rue Lebeau, rue Watteau, and rue Ernest Allard are the favorite streets for the antique hound. Prices? High.

Smith and Son, with its large stock of hardcover titles and more than 2000 paperbacks, is the only British or American bookshop in the capital.

Department stores? **L'Innovation**, razed by a catastrophic fire several years back, is now operating again in spacious, attractive, nonflammable premises on rue Neuve; again we rate it as the finest in the nation. Next down the line is **Galeries Anspach**. This impresses us as routine; so do the local 5-and-10's.

Marché-aux-Puces (the Flea Market, in the place du Grand-sablon) can be great fun. Officially, it's known as the "Antique Market," but the colloquial term fits better. Saturday and Sunday mornings are best, from 9 A.M. to noon. You'll find clothing, watches, statues, books, junk galore—and you must *always* wrangle until your face is purple, because prices can come down as much as 50%. In winter, huge eatable snails are sold from pushcarts here (3 for 20¢!), thus fortifying the habitués with sufficient vitamins to scream and wave their arms until the final whistle. Plenty of laughs if you're a bargain hunter.

There's a curbside **Bird Market** on Sunday mornings in the Grand' Place.

In *Liège*, the historic **Batte Sunday Market** notably outshines its Brussels competitor in color, versatility, and serious interest to buyers. Encyclopedic variety of merchandise; haggle just as hard for the same rewards; go earliest possible between 9 A.M. and noon. *Formidable!*

Shopping hours are generally 9 A.M. to noon and 2 P.M to 6 P.M. (Friday until 9 P.M.).

Dedicated shophounds? Space is too tight here for further listings—so consult this year's edition of *Fielding's Shopping Guide to Europe* for more stores, more details, and more lore.

THINGS NOT TO BUY   Shoes (the lasts are wrong for us), "bargain" Swiss watches (they're made in Italy and what they *don't* have in common with their Swiss look-alikes is their cheesiness), perfume and wine (buy these in France), stockings, nylon underwear (poorer quality than U. S. products). Today it's nearly impossible for the average traveling lady to have clothes made for her here, since the few fine couturières are generally sewed up by their own Belgian clientele. (Besides, they are very, *very* expensive.)

HAIRDRESSERS   Sanitary, well equipped, expert (so they tell me). If time is short, appointments can be made on a few minutes' notice. A "set" costs about $9 (shampoo included). **Antoine**, rue de Namur 68, seems to draw the loudest cheers from chic visitors. **Roger** (avenue Louise 88) is hairdresser to Princess Paola, so you might get the royal treatment.

LOCAL RACKETS   Leave the clip joints alone. They're expensive—and often dangerous. The B-girls will drink colored water for "cognac"—and when you've spent all your money, they'll move along to the next customer. Your American clothes are an engraved invitation to the bartender, too; in this type of place his smoothest cocktail is the Mickey Finn.

Here's one which continues to grow fast: On several side streets leading off Boulevard Adolphe Max (the main drag through the center), beautifully made-up tootsies in décolleté white dresses frame themselves in picture windows and beckon to passing males with Circean allure. When the randy reuben enters and asks, "How much?", she sweetly murmurs "$50 with a bottle of champagne." (She can be bargained down to $35.) The bubbling rotgut is then produced, paid for, and consumed. But before the sucker can take off his coat, she smiles equally sweetly and says "Goodbye!" Should he protest this bum's rush, a heavyweight as muscular as George Foreman will magically appear, sometimes accompanied by a very hungry Alsatian or Doberman. So what sheep ever argues this shearing?

For automotive repairs, go to the dealer who represents Ford, Buick, Chevrolet, Cadillac, or whatever you are driving. *Be careful about patronizing the small garages* in Belgium, because often a chiseler will charge you the price of the car to get it out. If you're stuck, make your deal *first,* before allowing them to move one finger on the job.

Finally, to repeat, don't let anyone feed you the phony-baloney (see "Things to Buy") that the Maria Loix shop is "closed," "on vacation," or "at a different address." It's there, it's *always* open except Sundays and holidays, and Mme. Georgette or her son will welcome you!

Berlin

The Black Forest, the Rhine, and probably 50 other localities of today's Germany have greater beauty and more spectacular scenery than Berlin. Yet, political eruptions aside, if we were forced to limit any German tour to a single goal, we'd pick Berlin in a walk.

First, let's get the Big Question out of the way. As we write this, at least, the masters of the Orwellian-termed German Democratic Republic (DDR for short) are still observing the nonagression, nonmolestation multilateral treaty which was signed in '72. West Berlin continues to be trouble-free. In the Communist-ruled areas, visitors continue to be safe *as long as they stay within the proper boundaries.*

The city is divided into 4 Sectors (don't call them "Zones," because that is the national, not local, term for apportionment). The Western Sectors have a population of 2.1-million, and the remaining 1.1 million are under Soviet control. Within Free Berlin are 12 districts; since each may exercise its civic pride by naming its own streets; one famous interdistrict thoroughfare has no less than 8 different titles from place to place. The Berliner, always noted for his un-Teutonic lightness, gaiety, and rapier wit, is America's best friend in Germany.

East of the newly augmented and heightened Wall, more than 3 decades of 5-year programs are finally beginning to show. In the last spurt, approximately 130-thousand new apartments were built. Although they are look-alike prefabricated monotonous monoliths, thousands of East Berliners now have a real address instead of a nest carved out of crumbling rubble. Streets are being paved, State-operated stores line the main boulevard, a handful of skyscraping hotels have appeared to house the delegations from Minsk to Sinkiang, and there is more stir and bustle than ever before in the postwar era. During our recent survey, however, again we found that this is nothing more than a costly, highly contrived, and pathetic sham. Hardly a soul has

138

the money to shop in those stores. The hotels are drab even though they are modern. The avenues may be smooth but the few vehicles on them are usually government-owned. Behind these rows of apartment buildings is the gray, frightful carcass of a neglected and helpless society. On a guided tour by sunlight, it seems to represent real achievement. On our own, it was another story. After dark, it is a dreary, suffocating nightmare. West of the Wall, there's always light, action, fun, progress, and—you will sense it right to the tips of your toes—*freedom*. Nowhere on earth can the difference be felt so dramatically. A few yards from bleakness, one of Europe's most sparkling glass-and-aluminum cities has sprung up in phoenix fashion. Most visitors never realize that this metropolis has now become Germany's largest industrial center; approximately 86% of her wares are exported. The contrast between the trim, graceful, orderly West Berlin of today and its neighbor across the line will hit you as savagely as a bludgeon.

Here, in capsule form, is a quick roundup of pertinent facts for the voyager. Please keep in mind that this information is accurate only up to *Guide* deadline, subject to later changes. Since conditions could again be volatile despite the treaty, you should check with your travel agent, who can advise you of up-to-the-minute developments:

TRAVEL DOCUMENTS   A valid U.S. passport is all you need. Baggage examination is waived except on commercial merchandise. If you're driving, be sure to have ownership, registration, insurance, and a car identity plaque showing country of origin. Incidentally, youngsters under 16 are not permitted to enter the East without an adult leader or guardian.

TRANSPORTATION   By air is best. It's cheaper, too, than comparable flights to other destinations; ticket prices have been slashed to attract more visitors to the isolated city (see Germany: "Airlines"). Pan Am (using Boeing 727's) and British Airways fly heavy shuttle schedules (almost hourly) to Hanover, Hamburg, Bremen, Cologne/Bonn, Düsseldorf, Stuttgart, Nürnberg, Frankfurt am Main, and Munich. Air France makes a Paris–Berlin–Paris round each day, while BA does the same for London, Manchester, and Glasgow trippers. Now that Tempelhof is being used solely as a U.S. military base, be sure your plane is scheduled to land at the modern, orange-colored Tegel Airport (with a duty-free shop ready for your crisp new Deutsche Marks) in the French sector of West Berlin, *not Schoenefeld Airport in the East German Zone* (outside the city); while the Communists have not yet substantially interfered with transients who have made this mistake, you'd be subjected to unfriendly passport controls and forced to pay for the special visa. From Tegel, city bus #9 leaves every 10 minutes and runs right through the center of town with pauses along the route; the price is a mere 10 DM, plus luggage; you can also grab the very same service from metropolitan stops out to the airport.

If you plan to enter and depart at 2 different road gateways or rail stations, officials should be apprised of your itinerary. For U.S. motorists, the Munich–Berlin and the Helmstedt–Marienborn–Berlin autobahns, among others, are authorized 2-way routes at this writing; at the outgoing Baltic checkpoints of

Warnemünde, Sassnitz, and Zinnwald, fees are collected. The East German stop is at Dreilinden, utilized for the routes between Helmstedt and Marienborn and between Munich, Rudolphstein, and Hirschberg. You're forbidden to stray one inch from them; the Soviet sections are badly maintained. You should have a full tank of gas, despite the fact service stations have opened along this path; they're especially marked; payment *must* be made in West German Deutsche Marks. Hence, our advice is to leave your auto in Hanover, buy a round trip by plane, and take the 35-minute hop to West Berlin. If you are under 22 years of age or over 65, inquire about the 25% discount for junior and senior citizens that was in operation last year. Perhaps it will be renewed for both categories this year. Now available are the DB's flat-rate round trips to Berlin which include Second-class travel on express trains and up to 6 nights in a hotel or pension with breakfast. Buses are also possible, and they're modern.

HOTELS   For far more comprehensive information on certain Berlin hostelries than space limitations permit here, interested travelers are referred to *Fielding's Selected Favorites: Hotels and Inns, Europe* ($4.95) by Dodge Temple Fielding, our globe-circling son. The revised edition, in which a total of 300-odd favored possibilities were handpicked from the 4000-plus personally inspected, will be at your bookstore early this year.

An amazingly short time ago, Berlin counted a mere 3000 guest beds; today her chambermaids fluff up perhaps 16-thousand pillows. Here is one of the few remaining continental hubs in which one can usually find nonreserved space in High Season; in winter the middle-bracket wayfarer can pull on his nightcap for 20% less than in summer. Generally the quality is outstanding; the newer candidates, however, hew the narrowest line possible when it comes to adequate living space. A common wheeze has it that a pitifully crippled Münchener was seen one morning by his friend, hobbling along the Kurfürstendamm. *"Gott im Himmel!"* cried the Berliner. "What happened to you? Were you hit by a freight train?" "No," replied the friend from Munich, "I just spent a night in your most modern hotel." Calling them "cramped" would be akin to dismissing the Himalayas as "tall."

The **Kempinski** has rocketed up under the savvy handling of Chief Astronaut Rudolf Münster, one of Germany's leading and most personable hosts. Superb public areas; outstanding grill; fun-filled bar with dancing; sparkling, oh-zoned jetstream pool and sauna; tiptop service. Tower units now fully air-conditioned; all accommodations glowing with rosy-cheeked illumination, comfortable beds, radios, Frigobars, and good baths with double basins and Italian ceramic tiles; eye-popping Presidential Suite with kitchen for a mini-ransom per chief-of-stately-night. Highest accolades for its big-city concept.

Thanks to heaping doses of dollars and determination, the **Hilton,** under the new general managership of Reinhold Aignherr, continues to rebound after years of decline. Renewed public facilities include the conservatory-style Die Gartenlaube in green and white for breakfast and snacks, the Zum Hugenotten restaurant with its ceramic oven and burgundy-rose tones, the frosted-glass, art-nouveau Pavillon Bar, and the rooftop Panorama Bar with its palm haven supper club. Accommodations, many in Sandman tan and fitted with new tables and chairs, color TV, and other pepper-uppers, come in 5 varieties: standard studios, with beds placed askew; conventional-twins with 2 beds and a grand-alliance headboard (our preference) and alcove-twins or demisuites; a sprinkling of more lavish suites, capped by the posh Presidential apartment. We believe that *all* the baths and many of the rooms are too, too tiny for true comfort, but this is a criticism shared with many hostelries in the Divided City. Nevertheless, this one's now solid for the '70's.

The 175-unit **Palace**, sited conveniently in the Europa Center, is thick in the decorator department. Spacious, elegant lobby; adjoining dark-hued bar combining English Establishment with Erstwhile Empire; numerous vitrines recalling images of The Old Curiosity Shop; woody ground-floor grill with open rôtisserie; restaurant up 1 flight-of-fancy to a soft green and rich blue haven; easy access to the nearby public pool and other thermic therapies. Manager Karl Stiehle is laboring overtime to create a Palace of comfort here.

The **Ambassador** has been rising rapidly to challenge the pack. Director Rachfahl is its latest envoy. Beautiful public rooms, perhaps the most alluring in the metropolis; entrance lounge with spherical copper hearth; captivating canopied dining quarter with deftly prepared but comparatively high-priced culinations; popular bar and grill with quiet patio, flowered chairs, and garden setting; terrace-rimmed Coffee Shop for nibblers; modern penthouse swimming pool with slide-away roof, plus adjoining sauna, massage parlors, and solarium; beauty salon; eye-catching murals in corridors; woody tones throughout; TV with every latchkey. Somewhat expensive, but not unreasonable considering the rewards in color, flair, comfort, and service.

The **Savoy** is an excellent buy for traditionalists. Large, l-a-r-g-e, L-A-R-G-E rooms, all with bath and shower and most with twin basins; doubles ending in "10" particularly worthy; new casual-style restaurant and bar with snacks available; courteous concierge and reception staffs; management by Mr. Rudigkeit. Very good indeed for Old World seekers. Our own recent 5-day sojourn here ranks among the nicest we've experienced for moderatlely priced dwelling space.

The quiet, residential-style **Parkhotel Zellermayer** is a delight for nonbusiness types and families seeking a noninstitutional retreat within the frenetic metropolis. Recent expansion program augmented by around-the-calendar updatings; all bedchambers with bath or shower; fine restaurant; friendly snack corner; Jockey Bar; tranquil interior courtyard with babbling fountain; underground garage. If you are so-in-love, ask especially for 1 of the 2 units with a large bed snuggling in a great wicker basket—ooooo, la, la! Here's a cozy nook, if we ever spied one. Warm recommendation for its ingratiating charm.

The steadily growing **Schweizerhof** struts an imposing stance across the street from the Hilton. It is always so jammed with conventioneers and commercial wayfarers that it has added a wing for 350 more occupants, (total capacity now at 900!), plus the Old Marketplace restaurant with cobblestones, streetlamps, and fountain, Le Mascaron nightspot and bar, a banquet hall, and its very own swimming pool. Handsomely renewed lobby; expanded reception area; spacious corner-sited breakfast garden; wood-shingled salon; chalet-style Grill with adjoining 3-table Schützenstübli and the Zunftstube extension; Wappen Bar with Swiss heraldry; 2 garages; 100% air-chilled; full range of contemporary trappings from Naugahyde furniture to multichannel radios. If the studio units in the new section seem too small for your brood, 1000 Marks a night will secure the Presidential Suite. (Parents will appreciate its triple-glazed, bulletproof windows!). Actually, the revamped 7th-floor accommodations are now amply wide-angled. New Manager Klaus Stolle is giving this Swiss house Alpine helpings of worthy projects and charm.

The 5-story, 130-unit **Sylterhof** provides an overall feeling of Frenchyness rather than Germanic heaviness. White, clean-lined restaurant; posh Casino Bar; corridors with handsome bas-relief panels, heavy draperies, and mirrors; colored towels furled in pea-pod-size bathrooms; sleek appointments that are beginning to show some wear. Here's a superior bet for any Man or Woman of the Times. Recommended.

The heart of the 82-room **Seehof** seems to us to have sclerotic inner chambers. Blue and white checkerboard façade; enchanting situation with restaurant, lamplit terrace, bar, and covered, glass-lined swimming pool all oriented toward the lovely Lietzensee (town lake); fresh rustic tones cunningly conjured up by its architect owner and his artist wife. It is so thoroughly winning in so many, many ways that we wonder how the designer possibly could have sketched its accommodations in such ridiculously paltry dimensions.

The youthful **Hamburg** is next. Red canopied entrance; large blue-carpeted lounge; nice copper-tone bar; fresh dining salon; quick-meal corner; flowers everywhere for brighteners. Its 240 units also were planned for overly small-boned trippers. Worthy if you can wrap all your travel possessions into a lady's handkerchief.

After the above, our choices would run as follows: **Europäischer Hof** (noncentral situation near the bus terminus, but handy to the international exhibitions at the Funkturm), **Bremen** (peaking above a filling-station complex, useful midcity site; penthouse breakfast room with open terrace for snacks; no bar or restaurant; 44 of its 48 units earmarked as singles; the other 4 with TV and Frigobar), **Berlin** (dimly lit, brick-lined Grill with delicious cuisine for the outlay; active bar; some units with tiny balconies; fair but not special), **Am Zoo** (Weinkrüger restaurant quite agreeable), **Studio** (a study in miniaturism; clean as a surgeon's pinkie; low rates; conscientious management by ever-kind Directress Dähmcke), **President** (behind the Sylterhof in an area of urban growth; supermodernistic in structure and efficiency), **Arosa** (appealing, but surely one of the narrowest-gauge hostelries we've ever, ever, ever inspected; for no-hipped striplings exclusively), **Hervis** (a 10-minute stroll from Checkpoint Charlie; ample lebensraum; '68 vintage instrumentation; very kind staff), **Plaza** (140 rooms, all with bath or showers; low tabs in Low Seasons; all in all, pretty slim pickin's), **Savigny** (to our peepers, better for geriatrics than peripatetics), **Dom** (in a fast-fading district; tailor-made for traveling parties and tour packages of foreign origin; not recommended by us), **Steinplatz** (somewhat austere in atmosphere, but trying to loosen up; a favorite of many actresses and single ladies), either the **Lichtburg** or its sister the **Franke** (substantial but commercial), and **Arosa Airline Hotel** (good location but little else; slipping). The rooms at the **Thober** are no longer tolerable, in our view. The **Gehrhus** is in a special category, occupying a suburban site about 20 minutes from Action Central in the Grunewald district. Here's a castle structure that recently was brightened up and touched up in a most ingratiating way, revealing the best of its aristocratic origins.

Apartment dwelling? The 12-tier **Stössensee**, beside its namesake lake and a warbler's chirp from Grunewald's greenery, comes up with 2-score functional but uninspired abodes. Water sports (lake or covered pool), tennis, and sauna close by; adjoining supermarket; spartan lobby; midget bar; limp restaurant-*cum*-clubroom; somber, linoleum-lined corridors. All units are decorated in the Middle Mundane Modern Mode; #1001, for example, provides orange walls, a beige carpet, tartan chairs and sofa, an indestructible table, a minikitchenette, and an alcove sleeping nook. Minimum stay 2 weeks; 40% discount applied to a month or more; buses #92 and #94 routed down Kaiserdamm to the doin's. A fair bet for wallet-watching wanderers.

RESTAURANTS   The robust **Ritz**, a decorously beaded string of 3 small rooms, retains its position as one of the best dining bets in the Divided City. Some of the dishes that surely will dally delightfully with your fancy include the Gordon's Gin Tomato soup, the Blinis, the Scallops in Sweet Basil Broth, and the Rack of Venison. The versatile monarch of the ovens also cooks up a mélange of dishes from all over the globe; Chinese egg rolls, Russian ragout, palm-wine soup served in a ceramic molding of an Oriental girl's head, Indonesian Nasi Goreng—goodness knows what else. Its maintenance has improved notably; service is polite, but waiters tend to push the most expensive dishes. Again, *always* reserve in advance; closed Sunday; very well liked by U.S. wanderers, including this writer. Also in the top bracket is the **Maître**. French ownership and French chef; 3 salons, of which we prefer the Paris Room in the evening; interesting and varied menu, with prices listed on the host's card only; superb wines in this club center for champagne connoisseurs; unusually attentive service; presentation of match covers with the client's name inscribed in gold; surprisingly reasonable tariffs. Open for lunch and dinner; *always* book your table ahead. *Vive Le Maître!*

In the charm department, top marks—and D-Marks, too!—go to **Le Popote**, a relative newcomer that is quite chic at the moment. Of its 2 cozy roomlets, we prefer the one to the rear. Bar near the entrance; black wooden carnival horses mounted on the coral-colored walls; about 10 obsidian-hued enamel tables; sprays of explosive color in dried-flower arrangements; cuisine imaginative and well presented. We hope its popularity thrives.

A candidate we liked even more, but which is far more modest in concept as well as in price, is the **Big Window**. Since it is known only by the Berlin cognoscenti, we include its address and phone number: 49 Joachim-Friedrich Str., Tel. 886 58 36—and *be sure to reserve in advance*. The whole shebang is only about 10 yards deep with tables on either side of a center aisle, kitch on the walls, and wonders from the kitchen. The affable proprietor will explain (in English) his native Armenian specialties as well as his own adaptations of them. But please take our rapturous word for it and try the spareribs followed by his Lule Kebab with Lavasch. The latter is composed of seasoned strips of marinated meat grilled inside a large crêpe. Tear off a morsel of the bread, enfold a nibble of lamb, sprinkle on the dust of dried levantine berries, and prepare your taste buds for a culinary treat that you will long remember. The entire experience for us was numbingly delicious and we are forever grateful to Berlin gastronomes Joe and Jacqui Diedrich for introducing us to this favorite hideaway of theirs. Splendid! The **Tessiner Stuben** and the **Chalet Suisse** both evoke, of course, the muses of Helvetian tummyware. Decoratively, too, the inspiration is reenforced by rough stucco walls, wrought iron, copper pots, garlic garlands, and other touches of Alpine lore. The cookery is substantial though not thrilling. We do recommend this upland pair, but more for atmosphere than for skilletcraft. **Zlata Praha**, once one of our beloved Czech-Points, seems to have slipped a notch or so on our recent sampling. We pray that it will pull itself together and resume its status of esteem very soon. Two simple chambers; waiters in trim waistcoats and velvet cummerbunds; little English spoken. Slovakian specialties, including Prague Ham in a pastry shell, Pussta Hirtenfleisch (Shepherd's Meat with Dumplings), and Rumpsteak Lecso (with hot peppers); fascinating Sirner Paska dessert (a cheese loaf with a chilled tutti-frutti complex). Try—if you dare—the ultrabitter Pilsner Urquell beer which takes 10 to 15 minutes to draw from the tap (the Slavic toast is "Eschi Shigeria"). **Alexander** with 6 rooms on 2 floors is recommendable for its cozy ambiance but no longer for its cookery. Front section in traditional dress; middle unit with horseshoe counter for quick feedbagging; back segment in hunting-lodge motif; additional corners for private parties. Highish tabs and lowish cuisine, think we. **Conti-Fischstuben** is a prime catch for seafood anglers; although it's rather costly, here's a happy pole-bender for finny-philes. **Schultheiss Brauhaus**, across from the Kempinski, is a sparkling candidate in the midprice league —especially for such a centrally sited establishment. Terrace entrance invitingly splashed with garden greenery; inner landscape charmingly wrought of huge beer barrels hewn into cozy booths, rustic beams, wide windows, and provincial trimmings. Gargantuan portions for reasonable outlays; he-man steaks presented appetizingly on wooden platters. The formula is winning. So is a South American version off the same grill: the **Churrasco**, an Argentinian harnessmate of similar *ranchos* in Frankfurt, Munich, Hamburg, and Bremen. The penthouse **I-Punkt**, just below the revolving Mercedes Star emblem crowning the Europa Center, is tops for view but not for flavor. Glass-lined ring of tables; breathtaking vista; sky-high tabs for basement-level cookery, in our opinion; the eyes—not the palate—have it here. In the same building, the Cologne-based Blatzheim interests have sponsored a quintet of caloric consumerism. It consists of (1) the **Edelweiss** (beer-hall atmosphere including an oooompah band), (2) the **Alt-Berlin** (for hometown boosters), (3) the **Europa-Snack** (for guess what?), (4) the **Europa-Terrassen** (lovely in summer), and (5) the **Twenty-five** (dancing and friendly nibbles). It may seem strange, but after a trial of each, we found the entire package uniformly poor in quality and 2nd-rate in concept and décor. Any resemblance to urbane service seemed purely coincidental. In the same architectural complex, you'll find the **Tokyo** (with oh-so-feeble stabs at that noble Japanese cuisine), the fine little **English Pub** (for short orders), a **Danish** niche (for smørrebrød), and such a multitude of bars and snackeries that they could occupy a month of sampling and fill 100 tummies the size of the *Graf Zeppelin.* The **Holland-Stübl** cooks up nutrients drawn from the traditional Dutch and Indonesian tables. The **Hardy Wine Restaurant** is a veteran from yesteryear. Limited menu but unlimited grape larder; enchanting turn-of-the-century atmosphere; go late when it zings. This one can be fun if you are with a German-speaking group. **Le Bou Bou** rates as a full-scale booboo, in our opinion. It tries to recall an earlier era with modern affectations. We found slaphappy service and larrikin attitudes. In the hotel category, the Grill of the **Kempinski** often dishes out some mighty savory viands (especially those sautéed *scampi*). In the hotel dining room do us—and yourself—a favor by ordering the heavenly Kalbfleischröllchen (tender veal niblets bathed in a Boursin cheese and whipped-spinach sauce). Even Ali MacGraw can't beat *that* for tempting calf. Schade & Wolff's **"Funkturm"** is Berlin's answer to the Eiffel Tower restaurant of Paris; about 150 feet up a steel structure by elevator; magnificent view; definitely worth a visit by everyone, if only for tea or a snack. The same management has opened a second Fair Grounds establishment called **Palais am Funkturm**; mass-production service in a cavernous exhibition hall. **Huth-macher** is young, crowded, and reminiscent of Schrafft's in tone; big restaurant upstairs with agreeable décor, and bakery-coffee shop downstairs; piano and violin at teatime. **Drei Bären** is coming up rapidly; now particularly well liked for its sidewalk terrace whenever the sunbeams glow. For steaks, **Heinz Holl** hits the steer's eye; flavorful filets (for Germany) on a wooden platter; chummy ambiance; only 6 tables; candles in hurricane lamps; sand-colored banquettes. Your waitress will serve you with taurine grace. The **Black Angus** also specializes in grills. Solid value, but little in the way of atmosphere. The **Hong Kong**, followed by the **Lingnan**, is said to offer the best Chinese cookery in town; neither is a rave by top U.S. standards, according to sinophiles. A merry group of local friends detoured us to the **Lung Fung** instead. Surprisingly, its management found itself short of chopsticks. The last one in the group (yours truly) was handed one solitary stick—a digital trial-by-fire which we defy even our own "Wily Oriental" colleague, Stan de la Cruz, to pull off with aplomb. Clumsily, but with fierce determination, we finally jabbed our way through a mediocre repast. **Alt Nürnberg** is about average. For kosher meals, there's a restaurant at the **Jewish Community Center** (Fasanenstrasse 79); there's another called **Shalom,** but we didn't have the mazel to go by here either. There are many, many more candidates in this Baltic-size pool from which to choose, so joyful hunting to you!

Among the *Bierstuben, the Alt-Berliner Biersalon,* a skip and a jump from the Kempinski, is a baronial beer hall with Yorkville or Milwaukee overtones; sidewalk café; mass-production food and service, with adequate fodder for a moderate investment. Across the *damm,* just opposite, the **Bierpalast** raises a toast with brew, vittles, live shows, big-name acts, terpsichore, and table telephones, all set in a tableau of Prussian décor. The former Bräustübl at the **Hotel Steinplatz** was modernized, sanitized, and made aseptic; its charm, sad to say, has gone-mit-dem-wind. *Quick snack?* Try the ground-floor counter in the **Bilka** department store; full restaurant 1-flight up. The **"Quick "** operation has slowed to a walk; no longer recommended. The **Aschinger** chain, with table *or* self-service, is a happy economy bet; bean soup, 2 wieners, and bread for around a buck. *Sunny day?* Drive out to a lakeside establishment called **Wannsee-Terrassen**, in the Wannsee District (25 minutes and about 24 DM each way by taxi from the center, or 1/10th the price by bus #s-4); heavenly, open, 3-tiered terrace on a hill, lovely panorama, and mediocre cookery at modest prices; don't miss it, despite its poor kitchen, if the weather is fair. You can have a swim at a sandy beach here, too. Another excursion point for summer is the lakefront, split-log **Blockhaus Nikolskoe** at the Havel, near the frontier. It was built for Tsar Nicholas's visit to Berlin; you can even putt-putt out by ferry in warm months, a good economy move since the taxi ride is quite expensive. Very scenic inside and out, but not as spectacular in the culinary sector. **Bahnhofs-Terrassen**, at the Zoo Station, is strictly for the birds, in our opinion; outdoor terrace with view of the zoological garden. *Weinstuben?* **Habel**, near Am Roseneck is the choice, with **Koelsch** second. We've also heard good things about the **Neumann** (very well liked locally), but we've never emptied glasses here. Don't forget the previously mentioned Hardy, which is a winehouse with a difference. *Cafés?* The **Caroussel**, on the boulevard side of the Kempinski, takes the honors; excellent for snacks. The **Kranzler** is very good; from its perch you can command an excellent view of the Kurfürstendamm and Joachimstaler Strasse. The **Mozart-Terrassen**, on the corner of the K-damm and Leibnizstrasse, is a pleasant reminder of Vienna. The **Delfter Kachel** continues as a standby.

Dedicated budgeteers? Since we're too bottlenecked here for additional entries, please consult our annually revised paperback, *Fielding's Low-Cost Europe,* which lists scads more bargain hotels, pensions, dining spots, and money-saving tips for serious economizers.

NIGHTCLUBS A plethora. There are about 220 honest-to-no-goodness nighteries in the heart of the city alone. Counting bars and hideaways in the outlying suburbia, approximately 500 owl-ing stations swing. The entrance fees or cover charges hover between $2 and $6, roughly paralleling the cost of a Scotch-and-Soda. As in most after-dark dens, beer is cheap and champagne is hell on the budget.

Among the "In-Set" disco-hubs, the innermost clique gather at **Annabel's**, unrelated to the London shrine of nightlife that bears the same name. Smart crowd; modish music; reasonable prices. Maybe you can pry your way in if it is not a busy status-Saturday night. The **Onasis** would be the next ship in this fleet, followed by **Joy**, mainly for an older assemblage of café society.

The **Resi**, always a big attraction for visiting firemen, now seems routine. Concept more appealing to the Old Guard rather than Young-Lancers; 250 telephone and pneumatic tube installations, 1 at each table; call up or write an appetizing note to any savory dish who smiles (the majors play only on weekends); huge main room and cellar room; water-plays on stage at 10:30 P.M. and 12:30 A.M.; closed Monday. Fun for some but a bore for others. The **Palais Madame** bounces up with an intriguingly named gimmick called the "Ball Paradox." When it comes time to dance, guess? Girl picks boy! If you enjoy oddballs, you'll have one here. **Keese** offers the same turnabout. Should you know its counterpart-ner in Hamburg, this one's better. **Chez Romy Haaq** is currently the SRO gayest blade in town. While the show reflects deviant preferences, the audience is drawn from the general public. So popular that it is difficult to get in, especially on weekends. **Chez Nous** has 2 elaborately decorated rooms with quilted and draped walls and ceilings in the style of what might be called Louis XIV½. You'll find fancy candelabra, a gold grand piano, a bar, and—incongruously—a bright honky-tonk jukebox not quite concealed between the 2 ornate sancta. Think thrice here before reaching for the hand of that beautiful blonde, because "she" might turn out to be a blond; some of the patrons we saw were gay boys attired in exquisitely modish gowns. **Chez André**, formerly called Cherchez la Femme, is similar; you'll *cherchez* all night, but we doubt you'll find one. Dogleg bar in beige, white, and black; dance area in flat black and red. The comedians (comediennes?) lean more heavily on national themes here than they do at that *chez* called Nous. **Le Clou** also tries to get its share of the same traffic, but we think this one should be renamed Le Clip. **Fifty-fifty** has become a competitor in this 50-50 league. **Kleist Casino** (fondly labeled "K.C." by the *pervertamento*) has been redone in the gayest of moods. **Wu Wu**, across the street, also woowoos you-know-whowhos. **Neuve Trocadero** comes hither with the less modish *belles* of the *belle*-bottomed populace. Incidentally, there are about 55 homosexual clubs in this city. **Big Eden** (Kurfürstendamm at Knesebeckstrasse, and not the same as the next spot we mention) is chiefly for kids; inexpensive; huge dimensions; a 400-speaker stereo unit. **New Eden Saloon** (different building) offers a glass-lined sidewalk café and a spacious interior with ultradim illumination and iron-lung ventilation; 2 midget bars; a sprinkling of B-girls; ear-rending music so raucous it chased us out before show time; intermittent melodies by a 5-piece combo (all of whom are surely deaf by now, poor fellows). Okay, if you bring your earmuffs. **Rendez-Vous** 19 has nonstop strip and other talents of the routine nightscape; nothing special. **Eierschale** ("Eggshell"), with 2-watt lights and low-cost cokes, crawls with all kinds of characters; the Firestoners, Louisiana Hot Seven, or Spree City Stompers give with everything from Dixie to Slop; man, it jaunts and jactitates. **Coupé 77** remains one of our favorite local watering places. Interior designed as an antique railroad coach; brass lamps, polished woods, quilted leather benches; disk music only; inexpensive drinks. Toots of praise for this little caboose. **Mari Posa** (with adolescent *ondines* in a shallow pool) to us exudes a boisterous decibel-count, bust-rous and topless disk jockettes, and crummy atmosphere. **Dorett** is an okay corral for show-timing and dancing. **Cabaret** provides a fair strip that should suit some gents to a T-ease. **Big Apple** (this time not from the same paradise) is a center for the Teenie Bopper Set; hot music, cokes, beer—plus enough long hair for a complete camouflage job on the Brandenburg Gate. The **Cheetah** appeals to the avant-est of the avant-garde. A fairly expensive taxi ride from the center to its jungle lair; entrance through a looooooooong and madly painted tunnel; interior resembling a 3-dimensional atomic structure; radar dishes behind the frizzy-headed orchestra; orange toadstool lamps; multilevel pods for nonjiggers; clear-plastic cushioned chairs on lilypad platforms. Loud as sin, of course. Not our earful, but perhaps the kids will love it. The **English Pub,** in the décor you'd expect, is a more sedate station for quaffs and suds. **Chateau** draws a nice following of young people to its semicircular bar. Attractive and inexpensive. The **Hofbräu Haus**, sited near the zoo, is now said by one savvy wag to cater "to Turks, Arabs, and assorted cameldrivers." We have no desire to mount it. The **Gallerie** cools it with modern notes only; the chords are no longer live, but on tape or wax.

Sobering Facts: The $1,600,000 **Thermen** in the Europa Center should cure any hangover. This grandiose health haven contains a swimming pool, a sauna, Russian and Roman baths, massage parlors, a gym, a medicinal hydro-therapy salon, sun rooms, a beauty parlor, plus summer terraces and a restaurant. An all-day sweat can be had extremely reasonably; its hours are from 10 A.M. to 11 P.M. from Monday through that heavenly Day of Rest.

Berlin now has its very own **Casino** in the Europa Center rolling from 3 P.M. to 5 A.M. Roulette and blackjack are available, too. Entry is 5 DM.

Porn? Stay away from the live shows as they are often sham acts. Film theaters—myriad in number, vast in choice—change from 6 to 10 D.M. for about as much pepper as you can take—and are *they* hot stuff. Wow!

Narcotics? We found no permanent drug scene, except perhaps the odd exchange in subway stations. Don't horse around in this league whatever you do.

Play for pay? The most popular rendezvous is now the midriff of Kurfür-stendamm, near Lehniner Platz and Uhlandstrasse. It is most heavily patron-ized from 11:30 P.M. onward. Mobilized *Mädchens* usually cruise along Strasse des 17 Juni. While the standard fee is about 50 marks, the unknowing visitor is often persuaded to part with a higher figure. In general, the caliber of this group is brassy, coarse, and very, very tough. Other pickups may be found in such places as the **Scotch 13**, **La Strada**, and **Mambo**. Striptease shows in all; clip practices prevailing and often perilous for visitors; B-gals housebound until dawn's early light, but free-lancers usually available RIGHT NOW. We do not advise anyone—repeat, *anyone*—to hit this some-times-dangerous circuit, so please be warned if you do.

TAXIS AND CAR RENTALS   The city is well accommodated by a 4500-car fleet, mostly composed of comfortable Mercedes diesels; ½ of them are linked to a central exchange by radio-telephone. Drivers are courteous—so nice, in fact, that they consider a tip a gratuity and express their apprecia-tion politely. Here it's really silly to rent a self-drive vehicle, because your area of free movement is peanut-size. If you plan a tour, we'd suggest hiring a taxi or a private chauffeur-driven car. Of the latter, we think the prices are not only outrageous for Germany but high for anywhere in Europe.

Tip for the Tipsy: Drink too much and reluctant to drive? Just telephone 313–40–54 (if you can), and any one of 400 available students (who also will serve as baby sitters) will come to your rescue as chauffeur, crutch, and fellow philosopher. The cost is about $5 per hour; the pickup service works in a matter of minutes.

THINGS TO SEE   Since the Soviets put up their evil Wall-of-China in Berlin, conditions have been so fluid and uncertain that we urge you to consult your travel agent before scrambling off to possible disappointment. Highlights of special interest that are accessible or visible at this moment include the following—and "new" is the operative word as you skim down this paragraph: (1) a circuit of the western side of **The Wall** (your heart will weep, because here is one of the most profoundly moving jolts of anyone's travel life. To try to counter the shock of viewing this monstrous horror, the East Germans have now completed construction on a new wall with revolving tubing on top to prevent a solid grip when scaling, a whitewashed surface—because moving targets show up better—and concrete watchtowers to house and hide machine-gun nests. Surrounding it is a no-man's-land bristling with camouflaged fortifications and obstacles as a replacement for the propaganda-damaging visible battlements and barbed wire); (2) the repaired, Red-sentried **Brandenburg Gate**; (3) the **Soviet War Memorial** 300 yards *inside* Free Berlin from this Gate—a *Soviet*-controlled and guarded monument containing stones from the former Reichs Chancellery (called "the Last Plunderer" by the wisecracking Berliners), the 2 first T-34 tanks to enter the city, and masses of phony flowers; (4) the famous **Freedom Bell** (in Schöneberg Town Hall), which rings for 3 minutes daily at noon; (5) the **Kaiser-Wilhelm Memorial Church**, around the war ruins of which, after years of debate, a modern building designed by Professor Egon Eiermann has been raised; popular organ recitals, brief meditation services at 5:30 P.M. and 6 P.M., Monday through Friday; (6) **Charlottenburg Castle**, reconstructed in the original baroque as the only structure in the Western Sectors which still bears the architectural tradition of the Prussian kingdom; while here, don't miss the Arts and Handicrafts Museum, the Museum of Pre-and-Proto-history and the Egyptian Museum housing the 3000-year-old bust of the Egyptian Queen Nefertiti; (7) **Ethnology Museum** in Dahlem, our bid as the world leader in this field; nowhere have we seen items so intelligently and engagingly displayed; (8) **Ernst-Reuter-Platz**, named for the late, great burgomaster, where a 61-jet fountain gives a jazz-ballet effect amid rising modern skyscrapers in one of Europe's largest traffic circles; (9) the **Congress Hall** in the Tiergarten, designed by U.S. Architect Hugh A. Stubbins and built from joint funds of the Benjamin Franklin Foundation and the German Federal Republic; (10) the **Art Gallery** at Dahlem, with 600 valuable paintings from the thirteenth to the eighteenth century; (11) the **Academy of Arts**, built with $2,000,000 contributed by Berlin-born Philadelphian Henry H. Reichhold to house the creative arts (includes theater, studios, halls, snack bars, and cafés); (12) the stupendous **Neue Nationalgalerie** on Potsdamer Platz in the Tiergarten, (13) the **Hansa Quarter**, site of the '57 International Building Exhibition and transformed into a 1600-apartment residential section by 54 architects from all over the globe; (14) the 1936 **Olympic Stadium**; (15) the **West Berlin Zoo**, largest in Europe, with its 3200-plus mammals and 9500 reptiles; (16) the **Aquarium**, a superb midtown treat containing one of the most extensive finny collections on the globe; (17) **Potsdamer Platz**—the junction of the U.S., British, and Soviet Sectors; and (18) a **Waterway Tour** on the Havel River and its cozy coves; 6 departures daily beginning at 9:30 A.M. from Wannsee; refreshment bars aboard. Well worth hearing is the **Berlin Philharmonic Orchestra** in its dazzling concert hall (next to the National Galleries) designed by Architect Hans Scharoun. If your visit corresponds with the dates of the city's Performing Arts Festival, don't miss these outstanding cultural events at the **Deutsche Oper Berlin**. There are 18 playhouses in the city, including the popular **Freie Volksbühne**. For facts about the vast flock of other museums (Botanical, History, Childrens', Antiques, Musical, Radio, others) and routine attractions, consult the official **Tourist Office** (open from 7:30 A.M. to 10:30 P.M. at Hardenbergstr. 20) or inquire at the **Information Center**; the latter now has 22 specialists equipped to answer any questions on recreational, artistic, or commercial topics—in English, naturally. While at the Tourist Office, be sure to pick up the free Bummel ("Stroller's") Pass. This handout contains coupons which entitle the visitor to discounts up to 33⅓% on hosts of things he or she may do in the city. Valid for 1 full year; a marvelous guideline for seeing and saving. And now for a final word of caution before closing this section: Please exercise the utmost care when you approach that treacherous dividing line. Conditions vacillate from second to second here, and it's best to apply to this turbulent situation the same warning you find at beaches where there are similar undercurrents: NEVER SWIM ALONE.

TOURS TO EAST BERLIN   Combined excursions which cover both sides of the wall take 4 and 5 hours, cost from $8 to $10, and offer English-speaking guides. They originate from the intersection of Kurfürstendamm and Uhlandstrasse; from the Kaiser-Wilhelm Memorial Church; and from the corner of Meinekestrasse at the Kurfürstendamm. The crossover point for foot, car, or bus traffic is at the junction of Friedrichstrasse and Zimmerstrasse (you may know it as "Checkpoint Charlie"). We strongly recommend you book onto a circuit that includes the awesome Pergamon Museum (usually only a ½-hour stop, so try to get back for a longer browse) and the birch-lined Russian Cemetery. The loop that highlights the enormous communications tower is a mockery of Soviet bearish bureaucracy. While the view is magnificent, you'll pay for it through the admission charge. Only cold meals are served, at a minimum of close to $5 when we were last there; a cake-and-coffee nibble nipped us for $3; all comestibles we saw were barely edible; and, finally—get this—after you've spent *precisely* 1 hour in the rotating restaurant (it's on a 60-minute cycle), the guards march in and give you the boot. To employ an irresistible word play, comes the revolution and out you go! Itineraries usually contain a coffee break and a postcard snoop in the Berolina Hotel, so you won't perish from hunger or thirst en route. Subway entry into the East (watch for the submachine guns bristling in the abandoned platforms through No Man's Land) may be made by taking the train from Zoo Station. While you may enter with no more documentation than a valid passport (or normal motoring papers, if you go by car), we must stress and restress that there *is* risk in parting the Iron Curtain with anything less than an organized touring group. All currency, incidentally, must be declared on entry; all Sovietside expenditures must also be accounted for on departure.

Other Eastern targets? We've recently disembarked from a 6-hour spin to neighboring Potsdam by motor coach. On this trip, 2 hours each way were consumed by frontier formalities and relentless fisheyed surveillance by Russian military martinets. Passing the time in the halted buses, we witnessed passenger cars being gutted by suspicious inspectors at the border. The official docket was composed of a shuffle through Frederik the Great's crumbling Sanssouci Castle (you don enormous felt slippers so that your shoes won't mar the flooring) and a whisk through the Tudor-style Cecilienhof Mansion (where the Potsdam Agreement was signed in 1945). Your reward? A slab of tasteless cake and a cup of insipid coffee at the mile-long tables of the Interhotel (meant to be a showcase of Eastern innkeeping,but pathetically 3rd-rate by Western guidelines—at least, so sayeth this *Guide*). If you ever, ever, ever wish to confirm the free-press reports of Red tape, grimness, and bathetic spiritless life beyond the Wall, then this is the tour to snatch. Otherwise, don't be tempted. Dresden, Meissen, and Leipzig also can be absorbed on a 2-day swing, but our pores were too saturated to consider it for 2 seconds. All, incidentally, are relatively inexpensive. The reason is obvious.

THINGS TO BUY   The prices of most commodities in West Berlin now correspond with those in the rest of Free Germany; local prosperity has negated most of the need for the Federally-sponsored 4% discount. For porcelains, **Staatliche Porzellan-Manufaktur Berlin** carries the most interesting specialties; beautiful dinner sets; go to the factory (Wegelystrasse 1) or salesroom (Kurfürstendamm 205) for 25% to 50% off on 2nd and 3rd qualities. Optical goods? Wonderful **Söhnges** (see "Things to Buy" in *Munich*) now has branches at Kurfürstendamm 139, Reichsstrasse 83, and at "Europa Center"; a world leader. For department-store shopping, a toss-up between Kurfürstendamm's new **Wertheim** and the more traditional **KaDeWe** ("Kaufhaus des Westens"); if you pick the latter, don't miss walking up (not riding up!) at least 3 floors; a local institution. For cutlery, **J. A. Henckels** (see "Things to Buy" in *Frankfurt*) offers a branch at Kurfürstendamm 33; Mr. Böhm is the local manager. For antiques Keithstrasse is the street, with 12 or 14 shops nearly in a row; we liked an establishment called **Reta** (Keithstrasse 8 and Kurfürstendamm 204) particularly. For books, **Marga Schoeller Bücherstube** (Knesebeckstrasse 33) and **Kiepert** (Hardenbergstrasse 4-5) are attractive and versatile; scores of new U.S. titles and reprints.

TRAVEL INFORMATION   The **Berlin Tourist Office** (Fasanenstrasse ⅞, Charlottenburg), directed by the efficient, hardworking, charming Dr. Ilse Wolff, is outstanding for its help to the traveler. Offices are maintained at key points to dispense advice, brochures, and every type of assistance to any voyager; there's even a branch at the airport, to greet the visitor as he steps off the plane! Write or contact the dedicated Dr. Wolff if any problem should plague you—or, in her absence, her assistants, Mr. Binek and Mrs. Dieterici, who spring eternal. The ever-helpful, keen-eyed Mr. Karl-Bernhard Ulbrecht is another member of this brilliant staff. They'll go all out to make your stay a happy and comfortable one!

Denmark

Don't miss it! Of the 100-odd foreign lands we've visited, Denmark is closest to a 3-ring circus—and closest, too, to our travel hearts.

This mighty midget has something no other nation can quite duplicate. Nothing is bigger, deeper, taller, wider, more spectacular, more rugged, or more awe-inspiring here than anywhere else. Yet for delight and enchantment for the U.S. traveler on holiday, we think that it stands alone, head and shoulders above the rest of the handsome pack.

There are 3 secrets to this extraordinary charm. First is the serene beauty of its rural countryside—cool green forests, tranquil sunny fields, crazy thatched cottages in brilliant whites or soft pastels, endless miles of tidy, eye-soothing scenery straight from a calendar picture. Bisected by running brooks, carpeted with flowers, and dotted with ancient castles on its hilltops, the rolling terrain has a sweet and happy quality of its own.

Second is its gaiety and its polish. Unlike more serious-minded Sweden, more isolated Norway, or more somber Finland, Denmark is so cosmopolitan that it takes its pleasures in a carefree, sophisticated, and urbane way. Paris has traditionally been the amusement and dining capital of Europe; in miniature, Copenhagen offers as much (or possibly more!) brightness and fun.

Third—most important—is its people. Because they laugh at our jokes, look at life with our eyes, share the same robust love for food, drink, sex, speed, gadgets, music, painting, and the other lively arts, Danes are temperamentally closer to Americans than any other Continentals. They are fonder of us than of any other visitors, and their welcome proves it.

This kinship of humor is particularly important. Don't take your *Hamlet* too seriously—because if there's a single Melancholy Dane left, we haven't met him. The practical joke is their special delight—as long as it's harmless. Nothing gives them (or the visitor) more pleasure than a good belly laugh. They're the Pucks of Scandinavia.

Cleanliness is a national fetish. Cockroaches? Bedbugs? Silverfish? Lice?

We'll buy you a snaps for every one you find in your hotel or restaurant in Denmark.

Traveling with kids? Park your whole brood in Copenhagen, called the "Children's capital of the World," or in any of the nearby camps for tyke-size Vikings—and enjoy the rest of your European ramblings without those darling little millstones constantly lousing up your freedom. This fairy-tale land of Hans Christian Andersen is a paradise for young fry. In addition to baby-sitting and/or board and/or room, special outings to Tivoli Gardens amusement park, Copenhagen Zoo, Benneweis Circus, and other high spots can readily be arranged. Solid, nutritious Danish food; healthy exercise and spotless quarters; English-speaking guardians; loving care by a people born to handle youngsters. What's more, your offspring would probably be 165 times happier here than being dragged around and force-fed on deadly churches and museums by Ol' Mom, and Ol' Pop. See your travel agent or the Danish Tourist Board for further information.

In social welfare the Danes are extraordinarily committed—but this costs money, LOTS of money. Accordingly, taxes are wickedly high. The Dane now must pay anywhere from 5% to 25% more for virtually everything that he or she eats, smokes, wears, buys, or sleeps in (but not with, thank goodness!). For You the Visitor, there remains one happy escape valve: All purchases which are EXPORTED by foreigners are granted a deduction of 13% (see "Things to Buy").

CITIES *Copenhagen*, the 800-year-old city of 7 mayors, *is* metropolitan Denmark. Pronounce it to rhyme with "Haig & Haig," not "jog" or "bog"; the latter is strictly the German way. More than ¼ th of the 5-million national population live and work here. Government, industry, the international airport, the best hotels, restaurants, shops, and amusements are all here. So is one of the finest zoos in Europe. So, too, is the Princess of the harbor, the adored Little Mermaid. You simply *can't* go to Denmark without seeing this charming, gracious capital.

Aarhus, next in importance, is 1/10th Copenhagen's size. A vacation city, a university city, it boasts a unique open-air museum—a complete medieval town rebuilt with original bricks and timber. Once one of our least favorite Danish centers, this harbor has perked up commendably in recent times. It's still too commercial and port-oriented for most holidaymakers, however. The hotel facilities are recommendable as YOURhus in AARhus. Restaurants have improved, night life has flowered a bit, and the people extend a warmer-than-former greeting. Not much for Jutland high jinks, but jiggling up in our jottings.

Odense, 3rd on the list, is Hans Christian Andersen's hometown; his top hat and his trunk, lovingly preserved, rate as high with local burghers as the Holy Grail. In this major port, rich in industry, you may also find King Canute's famous monument in the market square and the A.D. 1090 crypt which contains the ashes of some of Denmark's greatest kings.

Aalborg, magnet of many industrial fairs, manufactures akvavit (the national hard drink)—and is also the most successful Fun Manufacturer on the Peninsula.

These 4 are the only cities larger than Stamford, Conn. *Ebeltoft*, a cobblestoned sweetie, is characteristic of many of the mini-minopoli; this tot governs itself from the world's tiniest town hall, where it is opined that "the mayor alone constitutes a crowd". **Legoland** is indeed a genuine toyland. **Ribe** is a paragraph out of the Middle Ages. **Vejle** nuzzles the banks of a deep fjord. **Aerøskøbing**, **Rudbøl**, and a peeping galaxy of tiny hamlets are only a few of the sparklers at which to blink, many of which we shall examine under our microscope in "Things to See" further along.

MONEY AND PRICES

Two kinds of money here: øre and kroner. Øre is the chicken feed—100 units to the krone. Subject to change, as we go to press a krone (Danish for crown) is worth about 16¢. Øre come in coins of 5, 10, and 25; there are coins for 1 and 5 Kr., but larger amounts are in bills. Other presstime quotations:

$$
\begin{aligned}
6 \text{ øre} &= 1¢ \\
100 \text{ øre} &= 1 \text{ krone} = 16¢ \\
6 \text{ kroner} &= 98¢
\end{aligned}
$$

The costs of certain items (specifically spirits, wines, tobacco, and car purchase) are murderous. Others are only slightly maiming to the wallet; if you go as an average tourist, you may be sure that they'll treat you fairly, except for alcohol and tobacco levies. In almost every case, however, each kroner that you invest will reward you with inordinate quality, taste, merriment, or beauty—be it textile, ceramic, plastic, or blonde.

ATTITUDE TOWARD TOURISTS

Denmark gives tourists the biggest, heartiest welcome in the continent.

The **Danish Tourist Board** (Danmarks Turistråd), at Banegårdspladsen 2, considered by many to be the most efficient official bureau in tourism today, aids pilgrims by selecting and registering the best of thousands of private homes it has inspected in Copenhagen. Requirements are rigid: Cleanliness, comfort, a telephone, and a separate entrance. If you can't get a hotel reservation in the capital, try the city's Tourist Association (Central Railway Station Kiosk "P") *after* you arrive. To avoid competition with your travel agent, it will not handle mail reservations—but it guarantees absolutely that you won't be propping up your tired tootsies on a bench in Mutual Park when you climb off that plane or train in Copenhagen. SAS proffers the very same service at Kastrup Airport. These simple but excellent accommodations will normally set you back anywhere from $7 to $9 per person.

Sven Acker is the National Tourist Chief. With the experienced help of Vice Director Jørgen Helweg, this network of several foreign branches and 160 domestic offices ticks as smoothly as a 21-jewel watch. (Incidentally, this organization operates a Complaint Bureau at the headquarters. Since it opened, 90% of the squawks from visitors, no matter how outlandish, have been settled to the satisfaction of these travelers. To our knowledge, at this writing it is the only national facility of its type in the world—and an *enormous* help to the stranger. Leave it to Mr. Acker and his Danes!) See any of these goodhearted, good-natured executives if special problems should arise, because they're all there to help you in their very best ways.

The **Danish National Travel Office** branch in New York merged with the tourist offices of Norway, Sweden, and Finland at 75 Rockefeller Plaza, N.Y. 10019; its Director for Denmark, Axel Dessau, is another witty, warm charmer of vast experience and savvy, to whose droll personality you will instantly succumb. Your inquiries about his beloved country, whether by letter or in person, are welcomed. In Los Angeles, offices are at 3600 Wilshire Blvd., Los Angeles, Calif. 90010.

Students seeking inexpensive shelter should write the **Herbergsringen** (Youths Hostels Association), Vesterbrogade 35, DK-1620 Copenhagen V, for knapsacks full of tips..

CUSTOMS AND IMMIGRATION
The American entering Denmark gets a 3-inch smile, a token poke at a bag or 2, and the all-important salute which means we-trust-you.

Cigarettes and liquor are their main worry—but don't be too concerned about the exact legal limits. Present regulations allow "a sufficient amount for your stay"—a maximum of 400 cigarettes or 200 cigarillos or 100 cigars and 1 jug of spirits (or 2 of a dessert wine plus 2 of a table wine).

§TIPS: Better check with your nearest Danish consulate or the Danish Tourist Board before leashing up Fido or Tom Cat for a Scandinavian romp. The authorities may alter the quarantine rules soon, but at this writing the pet-iquette points are moot. (This also applies to Greenland, Bozo!)

Your U.S. driving license is valid in Denmark.

HOTELS
For far more comprehensive information on certain Danish hostelries than space limitations permit here interested travelers are referred to *Fielding's Selected Favorites: Hotels and Inns, Europe* ($4.95) by our son, Dodge Temple Fielding. The revised edition, in which a total of 300-odd favored possibilities were handpicked from the 4000-plus personally inspected, will be at your bookstore early this year.

In general, the hotels are admirable—spotless, comfortable—and nearly always with delicious food. Service is usually cordial, but hoteliers (not unlike their colleagues in other lands) are plagued by staff limitations and untrained personnel. *Without meals, but including official increments, a single runs anywhere from about $18 to $42 and a double from about $29 to as high as $85.*

In *Copenhagen*, the building contractors while away their evenings flipping through brochures for Cadillacs, Chris-Crafts, and summer homes on the Riviera. A daisy meadow of hostelries is sprouting while older plants are being refertilized.

The **Plaza**, one such product of a mighty and elegant transformation (it was the modest Terminus, a station hotel), has made its breathtakingly successful bid on the side of classic traditionalism. What a splendid achievement has been wrought by Proprietor Jørgen Tønnesen, the kingmaker of the Kong Frederik (see below), and General Manager Pelle Saaek, who also served as his Court Chamberlain there! The change has been so eye-popping and it was executed with such princely resolve blended with fine taste that virtually no vestige of the roundhouse days remains. Our own happy conclusions about this rejuvenated candidate are underscored almost daily by letters to us from cosmopolitan readers who sing its praises. For more orchids, please see our comments in the "Restaurants" section further along, in which we describe its exquisite dining precincts. The bar, in the form of an English private library, is, in our judgment, one of the most graceful rooms in the north of Europe. It is enhanced by handsome oil paintings, candle and lamp illumination, brass fixtures, leather furnishings, and richly bound tomes. The brace of larger apartments and the several junior suites carry out the patrician theme. In every way, here is a thing of beauty. Superb!!

The **Royal**, backed by the Scandinavian Airlines System, has been soaring so sweetly that this year we are again rubbing our eyes. Until the new Scandinavia (also funded partly by SAS) undergoes a thorough shakedown —which could consume perhaps another season—this smoothy is likely to remain higher in our pecking order, in large part because of its indomitable royal roost of administrators. The imposingly modern 22-story, 292-room skyscraper breaks down into 3 units: the hostelry, the flight terminal, and the 120-car garage. Entirely air-conditioned; magnificent view from its higher sections; spacious lobby and restaurant; Orchid Bar; the not-to-be-missed "Candlelight Dinner" every Wednesday evening in winter; excellent sauna and massage facilities. Thanks to the endless patience, hard work, and wizardry of crack veteran Alberto Kappenberger of Zürich's Baur au Lac fame (helped tirelessly by his beautiful wife Ruth), every department—service, kitchen, concierge desk, switchboard, the works—operates so frictionlessly that this whole house seems to run on ball bearings.

Swooping out of the wild blue yonder, the sleek, smartly preened, 537-nest **Scandinavia** is almost twice the size of its Royal stepsister. Modernity was born in the Land of Woden; this sky-high streamliner ably reflects its noble heritage. Tranquil but handy off-bridgehead location, a pleasant but longish stroll (or free shuttle) to Tivoli Gardens; trim lobby with equally trim area for well-presented light bites; plush, panoramic 25th-floor restaurant and cocktail lounge; Artillery Bar; health center with saunas, gymnasium, indoor pool, and expert supervision. The comfortable dwelling space is broken down into the following pattern: 4 master suites, 41 junior suites, 147 deluxe doubles, 200 standard duos, 21 singles, and 124 *grand lit* (double-bed spreads for twin or solo occupancy). General Manager Philip Hughes commands the helm here; Assistant Manager Timothy Whitehead, a personable Englishman, ably unfolded his wings at the Savoy and at Brown's in London; voyagers from just about everywhere will spot Paul Moen, for 12 years the concierge of the Royal and one of the best Chief Hall Porters in the profession. We are especially impressed by the agreeable, clean-lined décor, the outstanding cuisine, and the almost universal warmth and friendliness of the staff. Here is one of the top luxury addresses in the entire boreal skein.

The fine old **d'Angleterre** has been a monument for more than 2 centuries. The handsome, urbane Dreyer brothers who own it (Dines, pronounced "Dee-ness," handles the hotel properties, while Peter controls the wine companies) are continuing to pour about $250,000 annually into modernizations and improvements. Their latest prides include the Tranque Bar, with porce-

lain capping by Royal Copanhagen for the decoration, and the brand-new
Reine Pedauque restaurant, with live music and à la carte and fixed-price
selections that also incorporate a free-flowing supply of Burgundy in mag-
nums. Management reins are now in the hands of Eigil Hummelgaard, formerly of the Royal and the Europa, who is so fascinated by the enormously
important behind-the-scenes technical operations that the clients seldom see
him—and more's the pity for those who miss this house's traditionally warm
Danish welcome. The staff is generally one of the most fiercely loyal, deeply
experienced, proudest, and kindest in the north of Europe. We are assured
by the progressive administration that the handful of outdated bedchambers
are being pepped up or phased out. Lots of renewal dust is flying and lots more
is promised—a happy development which reaffirms our 30-year love affair
with this Grand Old Dowager. Long may she live and prosper!

The **Kong Frederik** has skyrocketed since its doorknob-to-bedpost revamping under the aegis of Jørgen Tønnesen, the genius who lately refashioned the
now-gorgeous Plaza (see above). Good location just off Town Hall Square;
"traditional" lobby paneled in Caucasian nutwood, lined with paintings of all
9 Frederiks, and backed by a sweet little library. Off-lobby Queens Restaurant
with 20 tables, comfortable chairs, and elegant clublike décor; Old-English-
style grill and pub up front, seating about 60, for inexpensive snacks and sips
(both open for late-hour nutrients); intimate, leather-lined elevator; small
booknooks with pan-linguistic selections in all corridors. Size of the bedchambers, once a severe handicap, has been increased slightly by breaking up a
dozen double rooms into spacious singles. Full count of 70 units, all with bath
or shower, with the better ones outfitted with peignoirs, shower caps, soap
powder, and other unexpected amenities. The front units, tuned in on the
everlasting street clangor, vitally need double windows; piped music soothes
your temper if you can't find space to open that 2nd suitcase. Manager Eggert
Møller has things well in hand and gives you an excellent value for your
kroner in this high-price-hotel nation. Just the stop if you don't hanker for
wide-open spaces.

The once-proud **Palace**, which tumbled down our ladder several years ago,
still cannot be recommended by us this year. The harborside **Codan**, skip-
pered by Leif la Cour, remains a sound bark though it now functions at a more
modest tide level; the prices have been reduced in the process.

The **Hafnia** was gutted in '73 by a raging conflagration which resulted in
the deaths of 35 guests or staffers, 18 of whom were American travelers. Here
is an all-too-graphic reminder of the vitally, vitally urgent dicta we earlier
advanced in "Let's Be European": (1) *Always* analyze in advance your possible escape route from every bedroom you plan to occupy, and (2) *always*
switch immediately to the lowest possible floor if you can't find a safe way
out. A totally reconstructed Hafnia may appear in time for this season.

The **Tre Falke** ("Three Falcons") feathers an attractive, chirpy bank of
roosts. Superb indirect lighting; moteless cleanliness; firm, modern beds
upholstered in imitation leather; plastic desks that we defy you to discern
from wood. Some units are extra-tiny but efficiently arranged (a rooftop water
tank prevents altering the vertical superstructure). Through intelligent study
by General Manager Jørgen Bertelsen, this house has been warmed up by use

of more harmonious colors and different furniture combinations—little amenities in the main, which make all the difference. Tasteful, soothing lobby; intimate restaurant with cute little summer garden (possibly a change in chefs, however, because our latest meal here wasn't up to the standards it should have commanded); nice bar; superior service; big, big windows but Lilliputian baths; an oh-so-welcome parking lot directly in front where harried motorists can leave their lizzies. This establishment would rate a lot higher on our score sheet if so many of its chambers were not so minuscule.

The **Richmond** recently was purchased by a tour agency, so we must wait a bit to discern whether it will adapt itself to a new role or continue hosting independent travelers. The handsome, captivating little Snack Bar, with white fiber-glass chairs, copper cones of flowers, yellow napery, and modernistic trim, is one of the sweetest drop-in spots in Copenhagen; the main dining room is in natural Oregon-pine louvres with highlights of gray-green and peacock blue; new reception and perked-up lounges. Upstairs color schemes based on soothing earthy hues; 5 lovely suites with individual refrigerators; many other graceful touches added. Improving.

The **Imperial** wheels in under the sponsorship of the Royal Danish Automobile Club. There is a bustling, commercial feel to its rather severe lobby. All doubles with bath, toilet, and radio, small and starkly furnished; singles uncomfortably tiny for travelers with transatlantic luggage; every bathroom we inspected, very poor indeed; no suites available, and none contemplated. Our latest lunch was easy on the palate; happily the service overall seems to have improved. Fair.

The **Penta**, formerly the Europa, has joined the fleet of the giant Møller Shipping Line (Denmark's biggest), which along with its European partners is still pouring money into it and pitching as best it knows how—but there's still a long voyage ahead. Outer hull chipped, scraped, and freshened; inner bulkheads repainted; main deck's Bistro enlarged and bar added; forward cabins refitted. Toning up smartly; this one soon may be a spanker.

As for the 1000-bed **Sheraton**, it was born in '73 and, in our opinion, remains sadly undeveloped in several major respects. The exterior architecture is faceless; the lobby provoked a zero from our aesthetic senses; the King's Court restaurant is enchanting; the Felix Brasserie recalls the flapper era; the penthouse bar commands a wondrous view of the cityscape. Shops adjoin the lounges; there's a sauna, plus hairdressing facilities; there's also a 1250-car garage. The cubicles are look-alike products stamped from the Sheraton cookie mold; the prices, however, incline more toward Crêpes Suzette levels. Yes, it's big and it's very central—and young as it is, it has even been partially refashioned—but we can't yet wax enthusiastic about its virtues. Sorry, but we feel that this often-splendid U.S.-based chain presently has a clinker on its hands in this Copenhagen operation.

The youthful **71 Nyhavn** (same address and name) bristles with personality. It is a converted "New Harbor" warehouse hard by the docks—an especially desirable mooring for saltier voyagers. The timber-and-stucco interior is the ubiquitous servant of its 1804 construction. Inn-gratiating atmosphere; kind-hearted staff; attractive candle-lit restaurant with appealing low-cost cuisine; no tubs (only showers) in its grim, cramped baths (again owing to the architectural shoals); small bedchambers in the $47 range; larger viewful junior suites for roughly twice the price. Adequate space is a problem here. Chiefly for seafarers.

The **Mercur,** taken over by the same local travel agency that now runs the Richmond, also remains open to the independent client. Some of its 115 accommodations are peanut-size and many of its doubles are "combinations" (daybed and couch, instead of 2 full-breadth beds); newer havens are much more generous in living space; today's best picks of rooms include #'s 205, 206, 218, 616, and 618. All units with private bath and dual-pane windows with transom ventilators; new Golden Tournedos grill; new Baggrunden cocktail lounge (open till 5 A.M.); outdoor tennis court (sic); snack shop; cinema. Substantial physical improvements but still mercurial. In general moving up in our esteem.

The midtown, 65-room **Alexandra** is a cheery corner house. Its kips and baths are fresh; only breakfasts are served; the lounge jumps the barrier in an equestrian theme; now closed December to March as an economy move. Best perches are the spacious 3-window corner doubles; handy garage next door.

The **Astoria**, a station hotel, strikes us as being off its runners. We found cold reception, an amateurish staff, and abominable service; there are a few fair-size bedrooms. Distinctly not the Waldorf. The **Osterport**, near the Langelinie Promenade and literally floating on a foundation of cork, is a fair haul from Town Hall Square—but it's worth it if you're watching those pennies and if you can get into the newer section rather than the old part. The food (enormous smørrebrød and a fantastic Danish all-you-can-eat breakfast for almost unbelievably low tariffs) is exceptional. Manager Finn Pedersen does a good job with this admittedly modest house by the side of the tracks. The **Grand** shines klieg lights on its silk-swathed, old-fashioned dining room which is summa cum laude for comfort and as bright as a Victorian silver dollar. On the other side of this coin, however, its accommodations are only passable. Here's the pity.

The **Opera** warbles in with only 26 rooms and 8 suites. Central situation behind the Royal Theatre; Den Kongelige restaurant on the ground floor; very costly tariffs for the best stalls in the house. Not a prima donna, but to us an unjustifiably high-priced chorus voice.

The 35-room-and-bath, midtown **Ascot** is a recent entry on the capital track. Only breakfast is offered at this converted eighteenth-century address.

The (watch this spelling) **Hotel Aviv** used to feature a Kosher kitchen, but now serves breakfast only. The rooms are modest; the disappearance of the meals, once a *mitzvah* for ethnic dieters, gives ample cause for *tsores. Oy-vay.*

The 6-story, 272-room **Danhotel** resides just 10 minutes by foot from Kastrup Airport. Danish-modern lobby with "Muzak," bank, souvenir shop, cute circular bar, writing area, all of them surrounding a central restaurant. Its 17 "Deluxe" doubles, adequately sized, offer every needed comfort (save for shower curtains in the baths); the "standard" bedrooms are in the "studio" mood, suitable for overnighting but not for fortnighting; 10 additional "family" accommodations sleep 4 on 2 single beds and 2 convertible couches. Winter rates sink by about 30% per category. Very recommendable for its price levels, in local comparisons. Other Kastrup kandidates inklude the SAS-sponsored **Globetrotter** and the **Bel Air**. They share a similar transient personality. The **Arthur Frommer** hostelry is also appropriate for flocks; more about this one in *Fielding's Low-Cost Europe*.

In the direction of **Elsinore**, not far from the capital, the huge **Marienlyst** was breathtakingly and extensively beautified not long ago. Vast 500-seat dining room which can be expanded to 1400 *couverts;* recreational "Happyland" open each evening, with pinball machines and other diversions targeted for the 18-to-30-year group; 6 bowling alleys; minicar track with 12 speedsters; basketball court; trap shooting; discothèque for young fry; small stakes roulette wheels, which are the only Government-approved spinneries in Denmark; "Veranda" cafeteria for hungry sports; health studio with 3 saunas (each with its own pool, into which an automatic ice-cube machine dispenses frozen pine-oil cubes); 12 exercise machines for 12 masochists at a time; artificial wave-maker swimming pool, with the degree of openings of its slide-away ceiling and fade-away walls controlled by solar intensities. Water babies are continuously bathed by an ultraviolet "sun," guaranteeing tan 365 days of the year. All in all, here's an expensive, enjoyable—and exhausting, if you wish—blue-ribbon suburban hideaway.

The 76-room **Marina** at **Vedbaek**, just across the Strandvejen and looking to the harbor, is purebred Scandinavian Modern—perhaps too cool for some. Sleek white concrete-and-glass structure; viewful outdoor terrace; bar, counter, and snack corner all connected to the airline-terminal-type dining room; sauna, billiard parlor, and good-size garage. All bedchambers with efficiency baths, radios, telephones, studio beds, sailing-theme photomurals, and crow's-nest balconies; tariffs slightly higher than the Marienlyst, a comparison which seems considerably out of line for the relative value; frequent changes of management in its short life which have been no help to staff morale. Good if you go-go-go for the twenty-first century, but otherwise only so-so-so. As for other popular choices near Copenhagen, the reopened **Hvide Hus** at **Frederiksdal** near **Lyngby**, on a lake 20 minutes northwest of the capital, is a link in the "White House" chain which is standard in character with its 45 units and well-respected restaurant. Prices are at economy level now—and so may be its service. The sleekly modern, 50-room-and-bath **Trouville** at **Hornbaek,** past Elsinore, now remains open through the 4 seasons; it is known for its kitchen. The **StoreKro**, near **Fredensborg**, offers several new baths and redecoration of most of its rooms, and is once again attracting tourists like clusters of bees. A more modest favorite of ours— virtually unknown to North Americans—is the revivified **Vinhuset** at **Naestved**. Plain but comfortable accommodations; village charm, not city slick; winsomely Danish public rooms; extrasavory food; Paul Rasmussen, the manager, is really doing a job here. **Køge** has the **Hvide Hus**, 7 miles south on E-4 to Rødby; there's also the delightfully revamped **Sonnerup Old Inn**, with its charcoal grill, rôtisserie, and smiling chef ready for a bustling business; our recent peek told us why.

In **Aarhus**, Denmark's 2nd city, the young **Marselis** easily wins the laurels. Outskirts situation in a wooded grove at the lap of the sea; brick exterior carried over into the lobby décor; attractive ceramic art inset along walls and corridors; waterside restaurant with piano melodies counterpointing the beat of the waves; simple but comfortable units with a nautical view through full-length windows; gray or soft-blue fabrics throughout. If peace is your motive, look no farther. Highly recommended. The **Atlantic**, smack in the middle of the busy port, is another high-tide contender. Modern lobby, amusing Fisherman's Pub, popular Tøf-Tøf ("Choo-Choo") bar and discothèque, eyeful 10th-floor restaurant with live music from 7 P.M. to midnight, and handy garage for motorists. All doubles are small but comfy, with baths and tiny balconies; all singles in the back; 6 suites with a minimum of froufrou; price tags slightly below the Marselis bracket. Norwegian-bound travelers find their ferry tied up practically at the doorstep. Also worthy. The **Royal,** in midcity, is spavined, tired, and commercial. Breakfast only now that its restaurant is closed. The **Ansgar** now seems as stale aesthetically as it does from a service point of view. In need of a spiritual uplift, quoth we. The **Ritz** has tapped on a scattered amount of plumbing and plans to add more to match its updated bedchambers; renewed restaurant; better maintained than the Royal. Manager Finn Enevoldsen is eager to perk this one up. The **Mercur,** in the Viby suburb, occupies the first 3 floors of a college building. The **Three Oaks** sprouted not too long ago in neighboring *Brabrand.* Two miles north on Route #10 is the unpretentious Motel La Tour (see below).

In *Odense*, the **Grand** is the grandest—and it's getting grander all the time. Fine restaurant, popular bar, and cabaret dancing nightly in season. Solid value for your money. **Motel Brasilia**, at the outskirts on the road to Middelfart, is a charmer. Extra-pleasant surroundings enhanced by ducks, swans, and a family of deer as your neighbors; décor of brick-faced walls, motoring-theme wallpaper, and good carpets; attractive restaurant; try #37, a quiet gardenside suite-nik with a refrigerator and a little sitting room. Rates about half those at the Grand. **Motel Odense**, on the Nyborg pike, is a half-timber farmhouse that is more alluring on the outside than in. Sleeping setup with toe-to-toe bed arrangement (ideal for playing footsie but a puzzling challenge to Don Juans); linoleum floors and throw rugs; splash-all showers (with those beds, this almost guarantees athlete's footsie-tootsie as your memory of Odense). Given a few quarts of financial plsama, this could be one of the lovelies of the North; now it's pretty much of an Ugly Duckling. The **Windsor** offers nice rooms but only 11 pipe in with private bath or shower. Fair.

In *Aalborg*, the **Phønix** is one of Jutland's outstanding addresses. It has been continuously operated for more than a century in a building that predates the American Revolution. Colorfully executed and carefully maintained; 135 rooms, about ½ with simple bath or shower; delightful 3-table, 6-stool bar; 36-room wing with 100% bath count; eye-soothing green and blue color scheme; radiant heating. The **Hvide Hus** in Kilden Park specializes in congresses. Third-floor heated swimming pool; sauna; shops; tinkling and crackling bar with icy sips by an open fireplace; snack center plus panoramic penthouse grill; 202 rooms in efficiency style, each with private balcony and refrigerator. Strictly for modernists—or congressmen. The **Hafnia** and **Park** are both station hotels which are clean, adequate, and routine. The **Central,** with a few modernized bedchambers and a renewed dining room, still cries for the services of a regiment of carpenters, painters, and plumbers; mediocre.

On the **Jutland Peninsula**, from the German border working north, here are our bids for the 8 most pleasant candidates: (1) Søgaardhus ("Stork's Nest House," 7 minutes from **Krusaa**, the German–Danish frontier station) is a godsend to the international motorist who prefers the overland route to the Puttgarden–Rødby Havn water route. Tidy, neat, and comfortable; Danish charm as creamy and as savory as Danish butter; outstanding cuisine; separate 8-room motel annex, but the main building is nicer. We grow crazier about this little gem and its friendly staff every year. (In this immediate area, the **Am Gränze** and the **Europa**, both on the German side, are contemporary, functional, and without 1/1000th of the feather-nesting features of the "Stork." Even the **Krusaagard** and the tiny, tiny **Holdbikro**, on Danish soil, are more affluent in human warmth than these 2.) At **Abenrå**, about 20 minutes north of Søgaardhus, the low and linear **White House** is a worthy fjord-stop on Highway A-10. A couple of miles south of **Haderslev**, the **Syd** catches unknowing customers before they arrive at the even better, glass-bound, sleek-lined **BP Motel**, which is a honey for twentieth-century highwaymen-and-women. (2) In **Kolding**, the **Saxildhus** is attractive and immaculate; excellent restaurant; 50 rooms, 30 baths; the singles, even without shower, are cozy. Worthy on every count. The **Trocadero** appears to be an inn, but it's really a night spot for dancing and snacks. (3) just outside **Vejle**, on the brow of a hill overlooking the fjord and forests, the **Munkebjerg** is one of the best in the region. This former monastic site is now a low linear retreat for the merry laity. Rough-brick and wood-lined corridors; window-girt dining room; fireside lounges; dancing to live music; sauna; hairdresser; comfortable modern-provincial bedchambers, all facing the pines; warmhearted but equally provincial service; poor cuisine on our overnight stop. A celestial "Monk's Mountain," but certainly ascetic in its culinary habits. In the town itself, the 11-story, austere **Australia** boasts a better chef, but here the rooms are more like twentieth-century cells. Director Kaj Olsen has a big and difficult plant to nourish. Only fair. (4) One-half mile from **Skanderborg**, the slick-rustic **Skanderborghus** provides a skandalously beautiful woodland-and-lake view. It has 43 small rooms, all with toilet plus bath or shower (#22, #23, #122, and #123 are corner units with more space). Connected restaurant-lounge-bar wing as an independent entity, to preserve a modicum of quiet for sleeping guests (sit at the far end for the best vista); excellent cuisine, presentation, and service; Finnish-type sauna bath; fishing privileges. Inexpensive and mightily gratifying for a weekend, a week, or an era. (5) In **Ebeltoft**, northeast of Aarhus off the prime north–south artery, you'll find the **Hvide Hus** (yet another "White House"). Here is an ultramodern, terrace-lined Arcadia soughing in a glen several hundred yards from the edge of the Kattegat. Only 53 rooms spread along 4 floors of a long stratiform configuration. Every unit with bath, all facing the sea and all with private balcony and seating area; 44-inch beds for spacious comfort, painted hessian-covered walls; annex and 4 extra-nice, extra-soul-soothing cottages also available; small bar-nightclub; nearby stables, sailing port, and 18-hole golf course; 5 minutes' walk to a not-so-hot beach; sauna; service a bit unseasoned; bales and bales of peace except for a nostalgic moment each evening when the town watchman carols the hour as he walks his rounds—and even *that* is down in the town. Manager Jorgen Guldstrøm is its Chief Executive. Should this happen to be full, the nearby **Motel Vibaek** might be able to take you; it's also modern and a honey, as well—but do reserve in advance at either. (6) In *Randers*, the **Randers** calls itself the "Leaping Salmon Hotel"—and it's a reasonably good catch for the provinces. Considerable updatings completed; heated garage; 90 units, each with private bath; same direction as the Imperial in Copenhagen. The 100-room-and-bath **Kongen Ege** ("Royal Oaks") spreads its limbs in a 20-acre park at the town's edge. A stalwart. (7) At the *Rebild Bakker* turnoff from Highway A-10, 16 miles south of Aalborg, the **Rold Stor-Kro** is a laudable entry. Lovely situation on the fringe of Denmark's largest forest, on the heather of which the Danish-American July 4th celebrations take place annually. Helmsmanship by Manager Jørgen Pedersen; sprawling sun terrace; 2-tier restaurant with oversize windows; snug downstairs bar with TV; children's playroom; most imposing wine cellar in Jutland. All accommodations, most of them with bath and shower, face the wood; a few so-called cabin rooms with double-decker beds are available for students or the Junior Set; the color and eye-appeal of the public quarters is not carried into the sleeping sections. (8) The **Hanstholm,** under the same aegis, takes its name from its headland setting on the lighthouse cape about 70 miles west of *Aalborg* and 15 miles north of *Thisted*. Perched on a lime rock 125 feet above the North Sea; nearby harbor entrance, Denmark's only year-round ice-free port; game preserve, beach, and wilderness all in your hip pocket.

Other possibilities? At *Billund,* the **Vis-a-Vis** is a very pleasant entry across from the toy town of *Legoland* (refer to "Things to See").

In the *Herning* area, the 30-bed **Karup** is a country address. Even though the shelter is modest, the food is mighty satisfying.

In *Silkeborg*, the midtown **Dania** is the easy champ. Viewful dining room with delicious cuisine and careful service; Alley Cat Bar meowing from 4 P.M. to 2 A.M.; most units with foot-to-foot twin bed arrangement. Not bad—if you've just had a pedicure. On the outskirts, the **Impala** (2 miles northeast on Highway #15) leapt onto the landscape after our latest safari. Cellar pool, sauna, and bar; ornithological theme; 42 rooms, mostly with private bath. Sounds chipper.

About 2 miles southeast of *Ans* (a village 20 minutes southwest of *Viborg* and 15 minutes north of *Silkeborg*, the **Kongensbro Kro** nestles cozily just off the highway intersection, down by the edge of a lovely lake. Old-style inn restored in the Danish tradition by the proprietary family; forest-green dining room with excellent skillet skills on our feast; cellar-cited tiny pub and TV nook; 32 bedchambers, including a handful of modern units; high bath count boasting plumbing that really works. If you're in the region, make an effort to search out this little gem. We have a hunch you might fall in love with it.

In *Esbjerg*, ferry-port for England, try your derndest to look pretty for the **Britannia's** reception chief, Mr. Herlufsen. He is your Open Sesame to what our eyes and itchy hides regard as the only decent, appetizing, and immaculately clean treasure-trove in this busy center. To our dismay, it was fully booked on our latest try. After fighting for space elsewhere, winning a couple of berths, and scratching all night, we'd recommend skipping this harbor altogether unless you get the green light from our number-one choice. The facilities are modern, the cookery is delicious (especially the finny fare), and the prices are right. Managing Director Jens Petersen, formerly of the Richmond in Copenhagen, runs a tight ship. **Bang's**? That's a hotel—or so they say. We stayed here and can't believe it. The **Esbjerg** struck us as being equal to it in every visible way. Plan your trip to arrive just before boat time so that you may have the option of moving farther eastward if the Britannia is full.

In **Grenå**, a ferry stop from Hundested (Zealand) and Varberg (Sweden) 31 miles east of Randers, the **Du Nord** comes up with a 100% bath count, good vittles, and good service. Be sure to check before booking, because there is talk that this one might be sold to the town as a congress center.

In **Ribe**, it's the **Dagmar**. Its dining room is a grace note of Old World harmony. Now some bedchambers have been given a dash of New World convenience.

Island of Falster : In **Nykøbing Falster**, the **Baltic** heretofore has been winning everybody's sweepstakes. Now we're told that it presently employs . . . not 1, not 2, not 3, but *4* managers and is run "collectively"! True or falster? *This* we've got to see.

Island of Fyn : **Odense**'s choices have been listed above. In **Svendborg**, it's the well-regarded **Svendborg**; 56 rooms and 56 baths; good food and service; dinner music; very pleasant indeed. At **Nyborg**, don't miss at least a meal, a sip, or a snooze at the waterside **Hesselet**—to us, one of the most charming isles of enchantment in the nation. Two levels, trimly composed of wood, brick, and glass; forested tonsure with an apron of green reaching to the sea; golf course within chipping distance; sauna; sedate library plus a "garden room" for tranquil hours. Ultra-handsome wood-and-glass-lined Tranquebar Grill; costumed Japanese waitresses serving their well-prepared native dishes plus fine Danish cuisine; mulberry tablecloths; hot wet napkins offered before the meal; lovely porcelain by Royal Copenhagen. Both food and attention were superb—the best culinary experience, in fact, of a recent Danish reel. Accommodations sumptuously outfitted with grass-woven wall coverings or textiles, divans, easy chairs, and Oriental art works. The doubles are nice, but the suites are exquisite. Full- or half-pension plan available; prices on the high side, but aptly suited to the rewards. Could this be the finest resort hostelry on the island? Easily—and perhaps in the entire country, as well. Highest recommendation. The **Nyborg Strand**, nearby, is a bulky relic of a bygone era. Traditional in tone except for a few minor updatings; pool and sauna; a favorite with families and their chillun' for Sunday's lunch out. Near **Middelfart**, at the other end of the island, the **Staurby** is better than average for motoring Vikings and their broods. Look for it on the *Lille Baelt*.

Some of these aren't elaborate, but they're all clean, reasonably comfortable, and full of warm Danish smiles.

Motels? They're springing up as thickly as poppies these days—but don't expect U.S. standards. To Danes, the motel is a simple, functional, convenient roadside stop—for a price. Some offer private toilets and washbasins; some come up with private showers; some even are equipped with private baths.

No piped music, no gaudy swimming pools, no fancy balconies for elegant breakfasting—but no $50 tariffs, either. Here's a selected list for the road traveler, some of which we've seen and some of which we've merely heard about:

Approaching Denmark from Germany via the island of *Fehmarn*, the Teuton ferry station of *Puttgarden* offers the basic **Baltic** and the better blue-and-gray **Dansk** (next to the toll gate); on the Danish side is the **Danhotel**; all are efficiency minded.

Island of Zealand, including Copenhagen area: There are 4, *not* rated in order of attractiveness. (1) **Wittrup Motel**, 20 minutes from the capital on Highway #1 (toward Roskilde, at *Albertslund*). Forty-eight doubles and 8 singles, all with shower and toilet; including service; utilitarian rather than fancy. (2) The quieter **BP Motel**, also on Highway #1 near *Roskilde*, 19 miles west of Copenhagen; space for 72 pillow-talkers; 14 units with shower and toilet; restaurant, cafeteria, bar, and lounge; okay if you don't mind the distance from the doin's. (3) The **Halsskov Motel** at the Halsskov car-ferry station (*Korsør*, 65 miles along the main trans-Denmark route to Fyn and Jutland); 24 showers or baths for 30 accommodations; fair restaurant. (4) The **Motel Søvilla**, on the Copenhagen–Gedser highway at kilometer stone #32, has installed baths, toilets, and telephones in 8 of its 16 doubles; restaurant, lounge, and carports. We've inspected neither the **Crest** of *Glostrup*, at the E-4–A-1 junction, nor the **Risø**, north of *Roskilde,* near the atomic research station (go off A-1, through the town, and 20 minutes into the sticks). The remaining establishments on Zealand are more primitive.

Jutland Peninsula—Vejle area: Motel **Bøgekroen**, 2 miles south of Vejle on Highway #18, is so spartan it's only for bottom-budget wanderers or students. **Lindved Motel**, 6 miles north of Vejle on Highway #13 to Viborg, might afford good training for marine recruits boot-camping on the Bolivian *anteplano,* but not for you. At *Haderslev*, south of Kolding on E-3, the glass-bound **Haderslev** is a glazed peach for modernists; nice restaurant; very slick. Avoid the aforementioned **Syd**; keep going to the **BP Motel** farther into town. *Aarhus area*: Motel **La Tour**, just north of Aarhus on Highway A-10, has a 20-room-and-bath addition which doubles its capacity; very pleasant, modern lounge-restaurant-bar with an interior "garden"; a cut above average, but not luxury level. *Ebeltoft area*: Motel **Lyngsbaek** is a converted farmstead in half-timber style; sea-and-hills views; beach ½-mile away; all rooms with showers; sound basic comforts in tranquil, no-sound surroundings. *Aalborg area*: Motel **Aalborg** (Scheelsminde is its alternate name), just south of town on Highways E-3 and A-10, rates well above at least 95% of its Danish confreres in charm and appeal. Small restaurant with piano music on weekends; 65 rooms, all with showers, toilets, and washbasins; colorless ambiance in a growing industrial zone, but good carpeting, cleanliness, and comfort; very satisfactory indeed. The **Europa**, farther south at *Svenstrup*, is another possibility; only fair, but modern. *Frederikshavn area*: Motel **Lisboa** has 18 doubles with toilet, shower, and telephone; we think it's pretty poor; for the desperate only. The newer **Jutlandia** is said to be better. Medium tariffs; up-to-the-instant Danish décor; sounds like it might be the pick of the local crop. **Hoffman's,** in town, is a tale of 39 rooms, 7 baths,

a pleasant dining room and bar, and a generally grim aspect. We much prefer
the **Viking** at *Saeby*, 7 miles south, with a fresher mien and an expansive
sea view. If you're driving north, the 48-room **Skagen**, a wink from the
lighthouse, might turn you on. Sport and relaxation are the main themes on
those far-flung dunes.

Dedicated budgeteers? Since we're too bottlenecked here for additional
entries, please consult our annually revised paperback, *Fielding's Low-Cost
Europe,* which lists scads more bargain hotels or pensions and money-saving
tips for serious economizers.

FOOD   In France and Belgium the food is most often extraordinary; in
Denmark it's most often incomparable. The finest restaurants of New York,
Paris, or Rome can't touch the variety and price values of some of the
Copenhagen establishments.

One Danish quirk is their dislike of piquant or sour comestibles. Pickles,
garlic, and pungent spices are almost entirely ignored by their cooks. Yet their
culinary magic is so great that you'll hardly ever miss them.

If you're reducing, buy yourself size-72 blinders before you go to Denmark.

RESTAURANTS   Nearly always good, even the hotdog stands.

In *Copenhagen* let's take a look first at the hotel dining rooms. Due to
the increased cost of labor and food, now these are frequently your best bet;
today hoteliers often use their restaurants as loss leaders in attracting customers.

This year, in our considered estimation, the **Plaza** is the finest and most
beautiful gastronomic shrine in the capital. We've already described its 3500-
book Library Bar under "Hotels." The adjoining dining sectors are equally
engaging and delightful. While its special fish and game segment still remains
a "must" on our trip list, the **Baron of Beef** is a delight to the senses.
Handsome wood finish; yard-high brass candlesticks especially designed by
the famous Bjørn Wiinblad); sand-hued napery; bone-handled cutlery; choir-
back chairs; tapestries set into private alcoves, flanked by delicate wall
sconces. Outstanding reception, service, and presentation; enormous broad-
side menu leaning predominantly toward meats; one of the most complete
wine cards we've studied outside of Gaul. (Incidentally, the former general
manager of the hotel, the enterprising Hans Jørgen Eriksen, and his extraordinarily talented Chef, Søren Gericke, have just joined their considerable
forces to open the new Anatole, at Gothersgade 35, which we are just itching
and twitching to try.) The **d'Angleterre** turns on a handsomely reconstructed,
partially glassed-in sidewalk café in season which is enormously popular with
upper-circle Copenhageners and visitors; the dining room now seems to waver
between formality and informality, therefore, giving us the impression that,
in view of today's rivals, it doesn't quite know what it wants or where it should
go. The **Palace**, in our opinion, now is so dismal that we avoid it strenuously.
The enclosed patio of the **Imperial**, with its removable roof, sun umbrellas,
and charming mien, wins gastronomic honors; the service standards have
been perked up, too. In addition, the Fielding left foot has long been cozily

familiar with the rail at the Imperial Bar; it is also recommended to all other portside hooves. While the new **Scandinavia**'s off-lobby restaurant is pleasant for light things, the 25th-floor spread (closed on Sunday) is oh-so-nice for scenic luncheons and big-nighting; the drinks, the panorama, and the skilletry are superb. The **Royal** gives the traveler the option of a 180-place restaurant or a 70-place Snack Bar Grill; both serve up top-rate fare in their respective realms. And please don't forget those beautifully romantic, winter-only, Wednesday-evening "Candlelight Dinners" which are STUNNING for sophisticated dining and dancing (see "Hotels"). Den Kongelige in the **Hotel Opera** has tumbled drastically in our ratings. No longer recommended. The **Tre Falke** nibblings rate as only fair. The restaurant of the **Østerport** specializes in smorgasbord. We again recently ate one of its bargain-basement whoppers (lunch only—don't fail to try the novel Blue Castello cheese), and we're still searching for our belt buckle. Breakfast, incidentally, also features a jumbo-size groaning board—if you can face so much sinning so early of a morn. The **Grand** now puts its emphasis on cuisine and the results tell the happy tale—whether in its dining room, its adjoining economy-minded Ziwago Grill, or in its Le Kilt restaurant. The **Kong Frederik**'s Queens Restaurant is a wood-lined beauty with comfortable armchairs and plenty of built-in ease. The adjoining pub is alive with camaraderie and good cheer; snacks only.

Among the independents, the new **Anatole**, which we've just mentioned, *must* be among the front-runners judging from the personnel involved in its creation. How we envy you for tucking in your inaugural napkin before we do.

Au Coq d'Or (H.C. Andersen's boulevard 13) used to be virtually the undisputed epicurean leader among the nation's dining places. It declined for a while, was revived, and now has hit the gastronomic and service skids again, in our opinion. Too bad, too.

Pistolkaelderen (Ny Østergade 9, through the passageway next to Bee Cee on the Pedestrian Mall) is part of the complex developed in Birger Christensen's ancient and splendid hideaway enclave which used to contain his storehouses. (Bjørn Wiinblad's fairyland shop is another.) Vice President Tom Mesereau of W.R. Grace & Co., the elder son-in-law of legendary Gene Leone of New York's Mamma Leone's fame, who spent many years of personal training under the Maestro—has built a terrific, repeat *terrific,* intimate steak house in a maze of cozy rooms down one flight. Louisa, his lovely, gifted wife, has decorated it so attractively that it oozes with charm. As for the quality of the fare, U.S. Southwestern tycoons Rudy Ortiz and A. Bob Jordan chorused during our chance meeting in Denmark, "Here's the most fantastic steak we've ever had in Europe, with the most delicate Béarnaise we've ever eaten anywhere—period." *Olé!* Simple but tantalizing menu spotlighting the main attraction plus a selection of hors d'oeuvres, cheeses, desserts, and beverages; lighter fare available at noon; moderate prices for what you'll get. What a glorious little jewel in every way!

For seafarers, it's still a tossup between **Krogs Fiskerestaurant** (Gammel Strand 38) and **Fiskehusets** (Gammel Strand 34), both facing the docks across the street from Denmark's famous fisherwomen peddlers. In the main, more tourists seem to gravitate to the former and more local residents to the latter. Over the eons, we've been fond of Krogs, the specialties of which are lobster salad and filet of sole steamed in white wine —and our latest try of this quiet, unpretentious establishment was again satisfactory. (We have heard one scorching complaint from a New England family who allege rude treatment and begrudging service, perhaps due to the presence of their young children.) At Fiskehusets, next door, we found our Filet de Plaice Tout Paris well cooked, the décor renewed but retaining its traditional warm aura, the kitchen totally modernized, and the service kind in spirit. Both are surprisingly simple for their piscatorial reputations—and both proudly serve the best fish dishes in the capital.

The **7 Små Hjem** ("7 Small Homes"), at Jernbanegade 4, showed marked improvement in the quality of its cuisine on our recent visit. For years, this has been our only major demurrer to this charmingly decorated architectural jumble of pint-size rooms—one of the most ingratiating interiors of any restaurant we know. You still won't get anything that begins to approach the palate or tummy satisfaction of more substantial houses, in our opinion, because this place is frankly and unabashedly designed for the tourist trade rather than for Danes. But a manful job has been done in injecting more substance into its former slick-but-hollow, promotion-style fare. A big asset: Drinks are relatively cheap.

Heering (Pilestraede 19) is the French-mode chef-d'oeuvre of young Thomas Heering, who assembled restaurant, buffet, and takeout facilities under one neat *toit*. Locals are flocking in.

Not long ago Frascati again changed its personality. Now it is an Italian venture called **Bella Napoli**—a culinary mutation which we mourn. It remains conveniently perched beside the Town Hall Square.

Glyptoteket (Stormgade 35), with its courageous blind owner and its proximity to the celebrated sculpture museum of the same name, is a perennial port-o'-call of visitors.

The **Langelinie Pavillionen**, in a park-and-seaside setting overlooking Copenhagen's famous "Little Mermaid," is a few minutes from the center of town. Its large, modern, glass-concrete-and-wood dining room seating several hundred guests is gaining in beauty as the walls mellow to an older, warmer tone; impressive entrance, lush banquet rooms; mass capacity and big turnover; food sharply improved. Skilled management by veteran Kaj Jørgensen, former Director of the Palace Hotel; medium-expensive for Denmark; pleasant as a short excursion on a sunny day. P.S. to sportsmen: Upstairs you'll find the lounges and dining room of the Danish Royal Yacht Club, which is one of the finest sailing anchorages in Europe. Your own local club card will probably admit you—but if not, beg a friend who is a member, because this is a "must" for yachtsmen. Toots, hoots, and salutes!

Arne Cohn's (Rørholmsgade 2) is the first choice of the Chosen People in Denmark—the sole independent kosher restaurant in the land. It also happens to be our enthusiastic choice for these wonderful Danish comestibles. Entrance through a bustling small butcher shop with yummy displays; small room to one side with exactly 2 tables (a 4-seater and a 2-seater) and counter service. Order the day's home-cooked specialties, or step up to the cold cases and point your pinkie at whatever appeals to you (most of it will!). Our palate danced a happy hora over the chopped chicken liver, meatballs, matzo-ball soup, gefilte fish, sausages, potato salad, garlic pickles, homemade cookies, and the coffee. All were *delicious*. One of the cheeriest assets here is the beaming, Haifa-honey-sweet welcome from the ladies of the small staff. As a contrast to the superspecial Danish cuisine which offers almost nothing sour, here you will find the piquancy which the traveler's palate often craves. No Manischewitz or other alcohols served (butcher shops cannot be licensed); open 9 A.M. to 5 P.M. Monday through Thursday; closed 1 P.M. Friday and all day Saturday; CARE packages available for Shabbath which are perfect for a Philistine or a Saturday picnic, too—but if you share our brand of fun, you'll Passover a weekday and gorge on the scene. Highly recommended—from one Temple to another.

Escoffier (Dronningens Tvaergade 43) waxes both generous and jejune. Here's the only place in Scandinavia, to our knowledge, where portions are served in 2 sizes—large if you're hungry, small if you're not. No carpets in its 4 paneled rooms; dark-green leather chairs and wall banquettes; no-nonsense aura; poor ventilation. Proprietor Fritz Petersen's cookbook is dog-eared at the pages describing Gallic sauces and French and Italian oddments. Cuisine so uneven that you should consult the zodiac to decide what to order.

Frederiksberg Raadhuskaelder, near the Tre Falke Hotel, is Denmark's only *Ratskeller*. Domed ceiling; sidewalk café; rather dull décor; good wine cellar; substantial but unglamorous fare at reasonable tariffs.

Tivoli Gardens (May to mid-Sept.) has a number of first-class restaurants. Here's our latest evaluation: **Belle Terasse, Divan I, Divan II**, and **Perlen** (very modern) lead our list. Down a bit comes **Grøften** (perhaps the most Danish of all in personality). If you want glorious flowers, open patios, and truly relaxed dining when the weather is fair, wonderful Tivoli itself is the place to go. The Copenhagen Zoo offers everything from picnic tables to snack bars to garden dining. All prices, all tastes, all good. **Gilleleje** (Nyhavn 10) is a captivating anchorage amply decked out with sailors' mementos from around the globe: ceremonial machetes, beads, African and Polynesian masks, a marvelous butterfly collection, and dozens more curiosities. Be sure to toot in advance if you want a slip. A trim little bark. **Nyhavns Faergekro** (5 Nyhavn) is not. It purports to be the oldest restaurant (1728) in the city. After seeing it and trying it, we'll certainly not fight with this claim.

Josty (Pileallé 14-A) is a pleasant indoor-outdoor spot. Sprawling converted mansion in a midtown park; several rooms of varying degrees of formality; informal glass-enclosed interior garden for winter munching and hedge row alfresco tables on a summer day; medium tabs; medium-to-poor service; medium-to-good cooking. The young fry will love the skittle alley and the woods for romping. Open every day, all the year round. Okay.

For a whippet-fast, bankroll-painless choice of dishes, **Cheval Blanc** (Mikkelbryggersgade 6, behind the Palace Hotel) specializes in light bites, open sandwiches, and grills; counter in front, plus a lineup of bleached-wood tables. Colorful, clean, easy, and inexpensive. Here's *just* the place to economize after purchasing that white mink jacket from Birger Christensen. Nearby, the **Stedet** (Lavendelstraede 13–15) means "The Place" in Danish. Lightning service; frequent changes of dishes; tiptop quality foodstuffs. Just The Place for shoppers. **La Cuisine** (Nørreport) is a blithe spirited medium–low-cost corner. And are those waitresses pretty. Yum-Yum!

Both the new **Fiskekaelderen** (Ved Stranden 18, facing the fish market) and the **Prag** (Amagerbrogade 37) are said to be pleasantly revamped offerings. We'll try both next fling around.

Perhaps the best restaurant buy in Copenhagen for lacerated budgets can be found at the **K.A.R**. operation at Frederiksberggade 24. K.A.R. is the local abbreviation for "Women's Alcohol-Free Restaurant"—but for goodness' sake don't let this awful name discourage you from trying this one; it's clean, simple, surprisingly attractive, and serves genuine Danish dishes unobtainable in fancy places. AND it has introduced Tuborg and Carlsberg beers to the "dry" menu of earlier days. *Ave!*

If you're making the North Zealand "castle" excursion, there are several stops for your noon meal. **Store-Kro**, near *Fredensborg*, romps up with a large, semipaneled, gold-pillared room in smooth but coldish international rather than Danish décor. The **Marienlyst** at *Elsinore* is suave, chichi, and international; personally, we prefer dinner to lunch in this now-gorgeous resort. We're also fond of the charming little **Søllerød Kro**, in the village of *Søllerød* (about 25 minutes out of the capital toward Elsinore). Cream-colored stucco building, thatched roof, a quiet rockbound pond in front, cottage windows, painted doors, and a lovely presentation of food that perfectly matches the fairy-tale surroundings. The tariffs are reasonable in this flavorful little dream world. **Torup Kro**, 45 minutes from Copenhagen at *Torup*, is another scene from a reverie. This one is white and also sports a thatched chapeau. Inside the ceilings are as low as the prices, and the quality is as high as your spirits should be after you dine. Marvelous 12-item cold platter, plus hot fish and ham courses, plus vegetables, plus cheese, plus cake, plus, plus, plus, plus . . . plus a minus-minded bill of only $23 for 2 happily stuffed tummies. Our Easter luncheon was so overwhelming we could barely make the Ascension from our table. We can't wait for a Second Coming. **Bregnerød Kro**, another charmer within short commuting distance in the direction of Hillerød, is a reborn country tavern about 20 minutes from Town Hall Square. Its red roadside building, with 2 freshly thatched roofs, has offered food and/or lodging to the hungry and/or the weary for more than 3 centuries. In late '67, it was purchased and renovated by Hans Goldbach (formerly of the Hotel Phønix in Aalborg and the Hotel Imperial in Copenhagen). Low ceilings with beams and gilded epigrams; green-paneled walls with tastefully painted coffers; intimate illumination by coach lights, 3-unit, red-shaded student lamps, and tapers; color-blends uniquely Danish; casement windows; flowers; cunningly contrived table mats. The cuisine is good but not spectacular, because it dishes up simple country fare—just that.

In *Aalborg*, the **Italiano** still brooks no argument on its 1st-place ranking. Three chic, intimate rooms in which Danish color skills are gaily blended with Latin liveliness; tranquil atmosphere with piano softly tinkling in the background; Vatikanet cell with Roman statuary; 1 of the largest and most impressive menus on the Scandinavian circuit; enviable cuisine; outstanding service; very expensive for Denmark. We liked this one a lot. **Ambassadeurs** is composed of the following: the Mexicana with dinner dancing and 3 tequila troughs, and the Galejen for recorded music in a marine mood. Take your pick. For snacks, the **Bistro**, a few doors from the Phønix, or the **Cafeteria Aalborg**, one block from the bridge, should soothe light appetites agreeably. Finally, in summer, the splendid view from the **Skydepavillonen** makes this candidate a popular choice among 1st-time visitors.

Between **Aalborg** and **Aarhus**, on the Mariager road (not the main highway) above **Randers**, try not to miss the superbly colorful and charming **Hvidsten Kro**. This one is a knockout. A 5-course standard banquet, called "Gudrun's Recipe," has been served in this country inn for elephants' years; the price is remarkably low, and we'll guarantee it'll be one of the unique dining experiences of your travel life. Just ask the sweet, regionally costumed lass who serves your table for the "Recipe" by name, and she'll do the rest. Suggestion: Nibble at *all* offerings until the sausage course comes, because the gargantuan quantity has been known to pop the eardrums of innocent initiates. One of the world's most interesting bets for the price.

In **Aarhus**, soar falcon-straight to **Aarhus-Hallen** for your first evening; no other target can remotely touch it. The concept is stunning: 6 tiers, very attractively architected, in eye-appealing Danish color blends; big dance floor; a bar occupies the peak of this merry Mount Everest. Small menu; food appetizingly presented but poorly cooked. Here is one of the top night places in the North. **Klostergaarden** has praiseworthy cuisine, but (1) the atmosphere is yawnfully dull and conventional, and (2) the Direction caters so extensively to private parties and banquets that we have the feeling it doesn't care too much about the independent client. **Varna**, open the year round, is said to be tiptop. **Sjette Frederiks Kro** reportedly whips up vittles that are okay but not exciting. The **Marselis** has the leading hotel kitchen in town. The **Atlantic** provides a viewful rooftop peek at the port. **Cabana** is modern and said to be a swinger.

In **Silkeborg**, all roads lead to **La Strada**. Curiously, this small, pleasant town, smack in the center of Jutland, draws gastronomes to sample such specialties as Vol au Vent Pommery, Malay Chicken, Saltimbocca alla Sebastiano, Paella Valenciana, or Bombay Toast. Flemming Kubel, the merry maestro, masterfully monitors his munchers, minions, and munificent menu. Central location; no view; worth a special detour. The kitchen of the **Hotel Dania** also draws accolades for a job well done. The **Hotel Faergegaarden** at **Svejbaek**, about 15 minutes out, is a heavenly expedition for sunny day or starlit evening. Lovely lakeside situation; spotless napery and kindly attention; charming rural mien. Country-style fried eel with creamed potatoes is the specialty here—and don't turn up your nose, because no fried chicken ever tasted better! The drive through the majestic forest is alone worth the price of a feast.

Odense's traditional leader is the dining room of the **Grand**. Among the independents, the **Old Inn** has an interesting atmosphere and excellent fare. An ancient cellar has been tricked out as a cocktail lounge and coffee nook for post-gustatory sipping. The **Ugly Duckling**, near the H.C.A. House, is a decorative delight. Unthinkably antique building with painted heraldry on the timber and stucco façade; smoky-lantern mien; single room divided by a ceiling-high wine cradle; fresh flowers everywhere. Despite the visual spell it weaves, we continue to receive many quacks of outrage concerning barnyard service and hey-rube reception. **Hos Bang** offers sandwiches only, plus a goodly serving of music and dance from 9 P.M. to 5 A.M. As a switch, **Den Fynske Landsby** ("The Funen Village"), a very-junior Danish Williamsburg 5 miles out, has a country-style *koldt bord* ("Cold table") that is certified to bust every button and strain every zipper. Simple, typical, and oh so solid!

Svendborg's **Hotel Svendborg** and *Faaborg*'s venerable **Rasmussen's Hotel** are classics for Danish country fare. If you're motoring near *Frederikshavn*, the sweet little thatch-roofed **Svalereden**, a couple of miles south of town, is a cutie; weekend smørrebrød; a rural delight.

Dedicated budgeteers? Since we're too bottlenecked here for additional entries, please consult our annually revised paperback, *Fielding's Low-Cost Europe,* which lists scads more bargain dining spots and money-saving tips for serious economizers.

NIGHTCLUBS   The Danes have a droll sense of humor. They sanction public drinking around the clock—but a citizen reckless enough to take advantage of this broad-mindedness is forced by law to get fresh air at intervals. The Government figures this way: If the customer sits and sits, he might get drunk—but if he is forced by a staggered system of closing times to change places, at some point he's bound to go home.

A total of 35 restaurants or gin mills in Copenhagen (plus a few in Odense, Aarhus, and Aalborg) have been granted special permission to remain open until 5 A.M.—the precise moment, incidentally, when workmen's bars are pulling up their shutters for prebreakfast topers. Most (not all) of the establishments listed below belong to this extra-late group.

Door charges at the better portals toll in at between $1.50 and $3, depending on the night of the week. Scottish libations are decanted for slightly less than the cost of an equivalent quantity of U235. Champagne? Say "gulp" right now and save a small fortune.

The Palmehaven, once the leading contender in the elegance circuit, reconsidered its calling and resumed life as Le Carrousel, then went through yet another self-appraisal and appeared as the Hard Rock, only to switch once again to become **Daddy's Dance Hall**. The neonostalgic theme locks onto the Marilyn Monroe and Chuck Berry era, with music drawn from Early Beatlemania. The 2 young, spirited owners often enjoy sellout nights—but for how long?—*that's* the question.

Chat Noir (called Valencia in its former life) also has been totally revamped by its new proprietor. Improved kitchen; now with striptease and floor show; today's music for today's dancing.

We hear that the **Tordenskjold** is now the city's most distinguished discothèque, but this entry on Kongens Nytorv is still untested by us personally. Sorry.

Lorry draws the Danish butter-and-egg man, his ever-loving family, and tour groups by the chattering busloads. Here you may dine at 6 P.M. in one spot, move to the big cabaret between 8 P.M. and 12, and move again to its

Seven-Nine Club (heaven forbid!) to wind up at 5 A.M.; you've really got Character if you can stand the din that long. A sign over the door reads "The One Who Can Say No Is The Strongest"—and the management isn't kidding. Clientele composed of openmouthed gawks or loudmouthed whelps on almost every one of our Lorry-rides; not our mug of beer at any time, but perhaps you'll have better luck on your try—if you go. Younger spirits seem to like the adjoining **Grock**, which also specializes in dark circles under red eyes.

Raadhus Kaelderen ("Vin og Ølgod"), at the site of the Old Town Hall (A.D. 1200), throbs with very special, very Danish zest. Capacity for 400 merrymakers on 3 different levels; separate segments successively devoted to an English pub, a Portuguese *bodega,* a Ratskeller, a Grill-Rôtisserie, and a whopping Main Hall. Emphasis on drinking, snacking, and musical revelry; more frolicking by adults than by teen types; oompah band; songbooks at each place setting; locked-arms singing; "dancing" on the benches whenever the spirit moves. Low prices; active daily from 8 P.M. to 2 A.M. or later. Heaps of hilarity for the fancy-free of all ages. Highly recommended for its delightful, authentic Copenhagen color.

Madame Arthur and the neighboring **Why Not** seem to attract a sexually versatile clientele—and, why not? **Club 10** is for antiques as ancient as 25-or-so. This crock liked it. Club de Paris rose from the ashes of its fire a while back to become the Ali Baba. Then it changed hands 3 more times and when we last looked (a week from last Tuesday) it was again called **Club de Paris**. (On Thursdays, Fridays, and Saturdays, we're told, it becomes a transvestite discothèque.)

Nimb used to spell early-evening glamour to the Junior Set. It still features dancing but we're not enthusiastic about it.

In Tivoli Gardens, **Taverna** is the leading light. Among the hotels, the Sheraton's **Penthouse** and the Scandinavia's **Artilleri Bar** are worthy beacons in the night.

One joint which used to scare the pants off us is **Kakadu** ("Cockatoo"). With our respected friend and colleague, Herb Caen, whose sparkle makes him one of America's best-loved columnists, we have long had a running gag about this saloon—and he never failed to tease us gently about "old-maidishness." Time was when a visitor could have lost a couple of front teeth through some drunken Scandinavian mariner's haymaker. Now it is peopled by businessmen in 3-button gray flannels and business girls in no-button gowns. The latter invoice the former about $135 per share of their common stock. (Along toward dawn's early light, the price sinks to about $60 across the street at **Maxim**'s, but we still consider this place to be too rugged for anyone but Popeye or Clyde Barrow.) Dark, snugglesome, ground-floor hideaway with piano-melodizing, a copper grill, bar, and figures moving languorously in the shadows; upstairs (small entrance fee) with smooth combo; Moorish-arched dance corner; Mitch-Miller-trained bartenders who sip-along with the clients (and don't always hold it as well). Now yours for a cockatoo or a bachelor-do. Move over, Herb; I'm joining your club, chum.

For the more staid businessman on the loose, **Wonderbar** is also well-known for unattached girls in search of companionship. These ladies are older crows compared to the Kakadu chicks, and they charge less for reviewing gents' portfolios. Intimate and cheerful, with pleasant salon furnishings and almost prudishly decorous atmosphere; open until 5 A.M. and occasionally absolutely dead; ask for Mr. Pedersen.

Santa Fe (which was Lover's Lane, which was Paradise, which was the Adam & Eve, which was the Adlon), has been taken over by yet another lover and converted into a music, strip, and dance parlor. Go between 9 P.M. and 4 A.M.—and you'd better go fast or it might switch careers again. **Trocadero** we wouldn't recommend to anybody with less than the consolidated toughness of the National Hockey League. Even then, we'd still have our doubts. For music buffs, **La Fontaine** (swing and contemporary bars), **Vingaarden** (Dixie and blues to mod-sounds), and **De Tre Musketerer** (New Orleans beats) are the current hot spots, featuring some of the best itinerant U.S. and continental combos. **Cap Horn** in Nyhavn, alas, has become just another discothèque—and not a very good one at that. Gone are the nights of its New Orleans jazz, only to be supplanted by a pendulous disc-jockette who swings in topless rhythm behind a pane of glass. **Pussy Cat, Bonaparte** (open very late) and **Star Club** specialize in youthful revels. **La Cubana**, across from Lorry, is the loudest pulser for the Teen Team. Ground-floor cluster of 3 bars and numerous pine-paneled alcoves; modern dance band; quieter upstairs lair for steam-heated romantics; rope-swing bar "stools" and barmaids so grateful when you leave a tip that they might ring a cowbell audible in Sweden. Everything up-and-up; fine for the Junior Set. Among the other rendezvous is the previously mentioned **Seven-Nine** at Lorry, which we happen to regard as appalling.

You'll have kegs of fun in Copenhagen. It's known far and wide as the "Paris of the North"—but that's wrong. For our money, that's as unfair as calling Paris the "Copenhagen of the South."

PORNOtations After a slump had set in, Copenhagen regained her dominance as Scandinavia's sex queen, rivaling even wicked Hamburg. More recently, however, officials shuttered many of the shops and movie haunts—not on morals charges (heavens forbid!) but because many of the operators neglected to pay their taxes or the fees for their licenses. A number still exist even on the most exclusive shopping streets, but if anybody has trouble finding one, any taxi driver or concierge can point out their locations. Some newsstands still groan—even moan—with a surfeit of sizzling salacity, libidinous literature, and cranked-out carnality. English-language directories limn the lusty listings for all of the unblushing bawdiness in the city: film shows, live shows, mixed shows, audience-participation shows, intimate massage services, socially oriented saunas, sex stores-clubs-libraries, even porn beer showing nudes on the labels (from Sweden)—brother, just name your bag and it's in this sensualists' grab bag. If any eyebrows are raised, they might be yours alone.

On our latest visit to this capital, mine climbed my forehead for the initial 10 minutes or so in the minitheater of the **Porno Supermarket** (Frederiksberggade 6, about 3 blocks down the Pedestrian Shopping Street from Town Hall Square). For about $5, I had been admitted to the continuous rerun of 20 short movies, mostly in color, spliced together into large reels. Despite the many varieties of subjects and postures, its monotony very quickly made it a totally dull bore. But because those rascals made no announcements about the 9-minute segments still to come, and because my curiosity made me fear that I'd miss something interesting, this stupid travel-writing nerd sat impatiently through the entire 3-hour program.

The Danes themselves regard this exhibitionism with mildly curious amusement—if they regard it at all. But to the visiting outlander they yawn, "If that's what you want, it's here for the asking"—and nobody looks askance.

Out of the capital, **Elsinore**'s **Marienlyst**, which faces the Danish-Swedish straits and Hamlet's Castle, boasts the redecorated, elegant Casino Bar, which draws the cream of Danish and Swedish "Riviera" society for its entertainment and dancing—plus chicken-feed roulette. Worth the 1-hour (each way) excursion on a bonny August evening. **Aalborg** offers the **Ambassadeurs** (see "Restaurants"). **Aarhus** comes up with the newish **Cabana**, about 5 minutes from the Royal Hotel. Orchestra; modern décor; small cabaret nightly. Okay. Its only worthy alternate is the **Maritza**, which is split into 2 totally dissimilar segments. In front, the cozy Bluebird Room attracts middle-age citizens who can count 25 birthdays or more; little band, tiny floor, quiet ambiance, charming for the buildup with Her. In back, there's a big, pleasantly decorated, Munich-type *Bierstube,* with 4 tiers of tables and (if the university is in session) regiments of merry students who lock arms and sing until the rafters tremble. If you shave twice per day or wear a girdle, recommended only if crowded and if you're in the mood for a sophomoric jag. **Aarhus-Hallen** is once again a topliner. The **Atlantic Hotel** now splashes ashore with 2 breakers; both ebb at 5 A.M.

§TIP: The only full-blown clip joints in Denmark are in the dock area of Copenhagen. Leave some of your money (enough to get home on) at your hotel if you want to go slumming here, which you probably won't. Some of the little bars give you local red-eye for Scotch, but perhaps this is to be expected. You might as well save time by ordering straight Kreml.

TAXIS   Better than they were, but still not plentiful when it rains or at theater time. Usually you must get them by telephone; your hotel porter, or anyone in the store or restaurant you are in will do it for you.

A taxi ride is pretty costly, but it includes an automatic tip. Even though many drivers now speak English, it's wise to jot down your destination in advance. As a group they're among the most gracious hackies in the world.

TRAINS AND FERRIES   Pride of the Danes are the *Lyntog,* crack trains which fan out from Copenhagen to the major cities. The *Englaenderen* ("Englishman") Boat Special, fastest and best of all, runs from the capital to Esbjerg (port for England) and back. The service and facilities are excellent—but trains are as crowded as Macy's basement, so make your reservations ahead of time. Fares are still a bargain. Incidentally, the overnight ferry between

Esbjerg and the British coast was extremely comfortable on our recent voyage.

Most of your local excursions, however, will be made by boat, car or bus; these are the short-hop conveyances in Denmark.

The "Bird Line" project—called "Bee Line" by locals, in the ever-green battle of the birds and the bees—is the rail-and-superhighway seam from Copenhagen to the southern tip of the archipelago. A train-and car-ferry handles the 1-hour, 11-mile gusset between Denmark and the West German island of Fehmarn. Smart drivers get advance reservations for their auto, giving them priority when the pickaback train ferries are loaded. From here, a bridge joins the mainland—and you're off running!

The 500 islands of this maritime nation are linked by the cleanest, most efficient, most attractive ferries (many with space for cars) that we have ever encountered. You can also ride the rails, bus routes, or ferry lanes at reduced prices. The "Rover" ticket, a 10-day package of unlimited gamboling, cost about $115 for First-class or close to $80 for Second-class travels. The "Rover" is obtainable only, however, in the U. K., Germany, France, or Norway. It's a splendid bargain for insatiable adventurers.

AIRLINES For general information, see "Scandinavian Airlines System."

SAS reins for Denmark are in the hands of our dear old SAS chum, Johannes Nielsen, who has been directing the airline's affairs in Italy for so many years; if this merry and courtly executive is out of town, take your problems to the SAS City Terminal Manager Erlander.

Air service to the Faeroe Islands, the group of 21 islands between Iceland and the Shetlands belonging to Denmark, was inaugurated by Faeroe Airways some time back and is now under the SAS burgee. Fokker Friendships do all the flapping to and fro.

Danair recently lifted off as a domestic carrier. It services all home territories except the routes between Copenhagen and Greenland, Aarhus, Aalborg, and Rønne, which SAS continues to visit. We've not yet had an opportunity to climb aboard.

DRINKS Beer, beer, beer—wonderful, rich, foaming beer, everywhere you turn. Danes are among the greatest beer drinkers on earth. In '70, Carlsberg and Tuborg put their heads together in one of the best marriages conceivable. Though now merged commercially, they continue to produce their own delightful formulae. Order either—or both—and you'll see why we consider these the most soothing and delicious brews ever made. The products of the smaller Wiibroe Brewery up in Elsinore are also fine. If you don't like the stronger "Export" (Gold or Silver Cap) grade, there are at least 7 or 8 types to choose from; the dry, pale "Green" Tuborg or "Hof" Carlsberg (never exported) and the Carlsberg bock-style are perennial favorites. Incidentally, you have an open invitation to visit either of these celebrated Copenhagen landmarks; each is twice as big as Radio City, and each offers copious free samples.

Akvavit (snaps) is the national "hard" drink. King of akvavits is the "Aalborg" brand, surpassing all Swedish and Norwegian types. It looks like water, smells like cough medicine, tastes like anisette, and kicks like a broad-side of 16-inch naval guns. It's terrific. Drink it *ice-cold* and chase it with beer, as the Danes do—but treat it with proper respect.

Peter Heering, formerly called Cherry Heering, is marvelous. Of all the fine liqueurs made today, this ruby elixir happens to be our personal favorite of favorites. It has been a Danish national institution since the first Peter Heering mixed the magic formula in 1818. On only 1 of the country's 500 islands —Zealand—can the dark, rich cherries with their special flavor be found. Debonair cosmopolite Peter Heering IV, the present entrepreneur, ably and skillfully carries on the strict traditions of the family business. It is not a cherry cordial, not a cherry drink—it is a formula from the Family Heering, unique and delightful. Be sure it's served cold, cold, COLD from the refriger-ator—then try it and see. You might also enjoy this company's new mild and golden Christianshavner Snaps, which, unlike other akvavits, is recom-mended for serving at only a moderately chilly temperature rather than iceberg gelid.

A superduper Danish liqueur specialty has been produced for generations from choice sun-ripened black currants infused with fine West Indian rums. The generic name is "Solbaerrom"—and the brand to be *certain* to ask for is Bestle. Here's a delectable accompaniment to the famous Danish open sandwiches, cheese courses, hot pancakes, apple dumplings, and other sweets. Serve it chilled—and be sure it's Bestle's!

Genuine absinthe is sold over the counter or by the drink in Denmark— one of the few countries in the world which still permits it. Try one for size, because you'll have a hard time sampling it elsewhere.

Imported Scotch, rye, bourbon, vodka, and gin are all available—with rum, rye, and bourbon only in the more popular tourist places, because Danes seldom drink them. Because of the brutal taxes, bottled spirits and wines cost considerably more than we pay at home. At bars, the prices alone are enough to produce a mile-wide hangover.

SKÅL

This is one of the friendliest, most gracious national customs in the world. In Denmark and in all of Scandinavia it is faithfully followed; good manners dictate that you become familiar with the ceremony.

It's a toast, of course—and the rules are rigid. Here's what you do: Wait until somebody gives the signal, then raise your glass, look the recipient in the eye, nod, and say loudly "Skål" (pronounced "skawl"). Drink bottoms up, never permitting your eyes to waver from the eyes of the recipient. When you finish, raise your glass again and bow slightly; only then can your fixed gaze be lowered.

If you are host, you must "Skål" each of your guests individually at some point during the meal; a guest may "Skål" anyone at any time at any part of the table, with 2 exceptions—the hostess (throughout Scandinavia) and the host (Norway and Sweden). In Denmark you may salute the host with this gesture, because the Danes are less formal than their Nordic brothers, but it is horribly bad manners everywhere to salute the lady. If the party were a large one, she'd be drunk in 10 minutes.

No custom is more heartwarming to the visiting stranger.

THINGS TO SEE   Of the sightseeing attractions in Copenhagen, **Tivoli**, which is more than 130 years young, should be your priority stop. It's incomparable: Central Park, the Botanical Gardens, the Atlantic City Boardwalk, the Flower Show, and a tiny European-style Disneyland rolled into one. The setting and décor are magnificent; the location is smack in the center of Copenhagen. Admission varies between 2- and 6-bits, depending upon the time of day and the day of the week. For this ridiculously small change you can hear a 54-piece symphony orchestra and Europe's greatest soloists in the stunning Concert Hall. At midnight on certain evenings there are marvelous fireworks; you'll be bowled over by their originality and beauty. Visiting Copenhagen without seeing Tivoli is like visiting Manhattan without seeing Times Square and Radio City. *Open May 1 to mid-September.*

Behind Tivoli is the renowned **Glyptothek**, outstanding art galleries built, believe it or not, on millions of mugs of beer. Many years ago, the public-spirited Carlsberg brewery endowed a National Foundation for development and furtherance of Danish painting, sculpture, literature, and fine art. Glyptothek is one of the results, and it is a joy to the soul. The totally renewed **National Museum of Fine Arts** is proudly showing its prizes now. It's said to be a thing of beauty. The **Zoological Museum** and the **Music Historical Museum** also tune in on tourists.

The **Little Mermaid**, Denmark's most beloved and most photographed lassie, who had her 60th birthday in '73, looks as fresh, sweet, and charming as she did when the Carlsberg brewery commissioned Edward Eriksen to sculpt her in 1913. She sits and muses at Langelinie Quay, in the port area.

Then, if your taste runs to it, there's **Rosenborg Palace**, with crown jewels and private collections of art, clothing, furniture, and paraphernalia used by Danish kings through many centuries.

And don't forget the **Zoo**, one of the world's best, with more than 700 species of wild animals on 30 well-planned acres of choice ground. This is one of the highest points in Copenhagen; from the big platform you can see Sweden on a clear day. Visited by more than 1½-million people per year; good restaurants; lots of fun.

Another *must* is a **Danish bath**—if you are male. We don't care where you've been or who has scrubbed you—you've never had anything like it. The Copenhagen Baths (Badeanstalten Köbenhavn, Studiestraede 63) is a fair example. The ladies' section is a private club, but 2 floors remain for men. The penthouse sauna in the Royal Hotel (21st floor) offers fewer facilities but in more chic surroundings. Open weekdays only from 9 A.M. to 9 P.M.; sparklingly clean cubicles and kind personal attention by Chief Rub-a-Dub-Dubber Mrs. Eskildsen, and a charming twosome of Japanese ladies who'll knead the flesh of any occidental Mikado or Madame Butterfly (3 individual hot spots for distaffers). Always be sure to call first for an appointment, because this one is much smaller. As a straight sauna, it is excellent—but we much prefer to be cooked the more elaborate and fun-filled way unique to Denmark.

At least 8 metropolitan and 5 suburban or rural **sightseeing tours** are now sponsored and operated by all the top travel agencies. Within the capital, their durations vary from 1½ to 2¾ hours, their prices range from $4.50 to twice as much, and the majority are offered during the warmer months only. Among the most popular examples are the Royal Tour (Changing of the Guard ceremony, the Crown Jewels, Christiansborg Palace, etc.), the World of Tomorrow Tour (Denmark's social institutions in action in everyday life, from kindergartens to schools to homes for the aged), the Arts and Crafts Tour (visits to the Georg Jensen silversmithy, the porcelain factories, Den Permanente, etc.), and the Industrial Art Tour. Half-day to whole-day tours range from $10.50 to $27. The provincial excursions strike out for points as distant as Odense. Starting point for all is the statue of the Lure Horn Blowers in Town Hall Square. For specific dates and details consult the nearest office of the Danish Tourist Board—or, when you are in the capital, check with the Information Office at Banegårdspladsen 2. Once on the hoof, don't forget to wear your most comfortable shoes.

For covering Copenhagen by boat, Copenhagen at night, the Carlsberg or Tuborg breweries, North or South Zealand (Zealand is also known as Seeland or Sjaelland), or a ½-dozen other local options, your hall porter will again be your St. Peter. He knows all the agencies and what's best at what season.

Finally, **hydrofoil boats** now whisk commuters or sightseers between Copenhagen and Malmö (Sweden) in 35 minutes. Hourly departures; ask your hotel porter for tickets and information.

In the suburbs of Copenhagen, the **North Zealand circuit** is particularly recommended. *Pièce de résistance* here, of course, is Hamlet's Castle (known to the Danes as Kronborg Castle) at Elsinore. You'll also see Frederiksborg Castle, lovely little lakes and forests, stork nests, fairy-tale cottages in warm pastels, and all sorts of intriguing things—with a pause for refreshment at either the splendid Marienlyst hotel-restaurant or the ultrafuturistic "Pearl of the Coast," or both.

Louisiana, the nation's most modern art gallery, is also north of the capital —20 miles, to be exact, on a private estate at Humlebaek. This creation of philanthropic Knud W. Jensen was opened as a noncommercial locus (despite the entrance fee) for the best in Danish avant-garde paintings, sculpture, graphic arts, crafts, and design. Everything possible has been done to maintain an atmosphere of natural beauty and of privacy; there are no petty regulations and no uniformed guards; its coffee shop will nourish your mortal coil. A delight to the eyes and to the spirit.

No late June or early July visitor should dream of missing the world-famous **Viking Plays** at the "Viking Town" of Frederikssund, 24 miles north-west of Copenhagen. Here is what might be called the Scandinavian Oberammergau, minus religious aspects and plus Hellzapoppin'. We've been itching to see this festival for eons, but since it has been impossible to adapt our travel schedule to it, our friend Kaj Larsen has written us the following witty and informative report: "Each summer there's a different authentic tale, splendid old stories like *Roar And Helge, Uffe The Meek,* or *Starkad The Mighty.* All the actors—150 to 200 persons—are townsfolk with either a lot or a little ham in their souls. One universal rule is that they must let their beards grow (though only for the male parts, we must confess). The play takes place in the open air, on a very beautiful stage. While these sagas always have a highly dramatic content, the big fighting scenes always give the audience the best thrill (castles are burned down, scoundrels are murdered, and the good always seem to survive). After the performance, everybody gathers in Valhallá, a Viking Guild Hall, where roast chicken and beer are offered and a group of Vikings entertain in various languages. If you, as you write, 'have never met a sour Dane,' we can tell you that we have never said goodbye to a sour tourist." Again, turn to the Danish Tourist Board for full information.

For a 3-day ramble by motor coach through the untrammeled charms of rural Denmark, the famous **Fairytale Tour** is an institution. Thousands of Americans have already enjoyed its leisurely progress from Copenhagen through Funen to North Jutland. (Incidentally, we have had some beefs about the inconvenience of connections on the southbound circuit.) First-class all the way; English-speaking guide; a lovely journey in every respect. Daily or 5-times-weekly departures from early May to mid-September. If you can make it over to *Jelling* (near Vejle), be sure to look at Denmark's "birth certificate"—the rune stone erected by Harald Bluetooth in A.D. 940 and dedicated to the ancestors of the present sovereigns. This is also the oldest pictorial representation of Christ as a Viking. The chapel cemetery goes back even further, however—to 40 years earlier, when "Gorm The Old and Thyra, His Queen" were buried. There's a small *Kro* (tavern) next to the churchyard for a meal or a coffee break en route.

The spot-of-spots for us, however, is missed by the Fairytale Tour. This is enchanting little **Aerøskøbing**, capital of the tiny island of Aerø, where the houses resemble frosting on a wedding cake, the key to the jail hangs by the door so that everyone may use it, and the fabulous Ships-In-Bottles Museum (also displaying pipes and every Danish stamp ever printed) would make even the Sphinx break into a grin. The lone hotel has no curtains on its windows, but never mind that. Lately the islanders have been encouraging a plan to make Aerø the "Hong Kong of the North"—a tax-free zone to woo more visitors and shoppers. Some houses and boats now fly their own local flag. Who knows? Before long there may be a Home Rule movement afoot in Lilliput! Never in our European travel lives has any village so captivated our hearts. Improved train and ferry connections now make it only about a 6-hour journey from the capital.

The 2- to 3-day **Circle Tour** covers a multitude of delightful sins—and you'll commit them by bus and ship. You'll see everything except Count Griffenfeld's pajamas. For further details and booking, apply to any local travel agent or the Danish Tourist Board.

Offbeat attractions? (1) For the young-in-heart of any age, a trip to **Lego-land** at **Billund** is an Eldorado of vacation fun. The famous Lego toy enterprise has created a miniature wonderland on some 40-thousand square yards of Tiny Tim-like terrain. There are more than 600 buildings, ships, and other structures, surrounded by canals, electric trains, and functioning replicas of urban life; at nightfall, 30-thousand windows light up in the Oz-like dream. As if this weren't enough, there's a real driving school for tots, utilizing electric automobiles and monitored by control towers and traffic lights, and a guiding voice tells the kiddie when he's infracted a law. The streets resemble a shrunken version of your own suburbia. There's a picnic campsite with a feathered Indian chief to oversee the grilling of hot dogs and hamburgers. You'll also find 2 beautiful restaurants—a cafeteria for inexpensive meals or a posh, deep-carpeted dining room. Spotted in the arcade of fine modern buildings adjoining the outdoor exhibits is one of the most entertaining puppet theaters we've ever giggled through. Concurrently, young ladies are enchanted by the collection of 30 doll houses containing authentic antique specimens dating from around 1580 to 1900. In our own childlike excitement, we might have forgotten some other joyful thriller—but go for yourself and see. Open every day from May 1 to September 30 from 10 A.M. to 10 P.M.; less than a dollar entrance for grown-ups and about half as much for children. By car from Copenhagen it takes about 4½ hours on the Vejle highway. SAS has put on 4 flights per day in either direction; air taxis make the journey in about an hour (slightly longer than the big birds). The airport is almost beside the Legoland doorstep, so local transportation is no problem. Across the road, the toymakers operate a stunning motel named (appropriately) **Vis-a-Vis**, with attractive dining facilities, making accommodation almost as easy as Little Jack Horner's pie. (P.S. to Mom and Pop: Any Lego toy on display can be ordered here and shipped to the little ones for birthdays, Christmas, or when you wish; the museum-piece dolls can't.) Don't miss it. (2) While in this region, take the roaring side trip to **Vejle Zoo's Lion Park** at *Givskud.* You can stalk around in your own car on an escorted 30-minute photo-safari where 33 tawny cats will wink right in your shutter. The jungle is open daily in summer from 10 A.M. to shortly before sunset. Again, the admission fee is peanuts—but don't lose your arm feeding them to the lions! (3) Then there are the 700 fantastic sixteenth-century skeletons at the Cistercian Abbey of Øm, near Rye (Aarhus is the closest terminal), and (4) Bundgaard's startling statuary in the depths of a chalk mine (ask directions in Rebild for the Thingbaek Kalkvaerk & Mine, just off main Highway #10 about 5 minutes north, toward Aalborg). Doctors of medicine find Øm particularly interesting.

CAR RENTAL   **Hertz** (Kastrup Airport, Hotel Royal, Falkoner Alle 7, in Copenhagen, and an outlet in Aalborg) is the giant of the Danish car-hire field. Its fleet includes Volvos (wonderful in snow and ice), Opels, Taunuses, BMW's, Fords, Porsches, and Volkswagens. Highly reliable.

U-Drive Volkswagens, popular with younger people or family groups, are the specialty of **Autourist**, (headquarters at Halmtorvet 11 in Copenhagen). They have 5 European branches. Other cars (Mercedes, Volvos, Opels, some American imports, and Caravans) available.

Avis is also in the swim (head office at Østerbrogade 62, plus another city hub and one at Kastrup). While numerous models are always on tap, this house features Simca in its lineup, a coach which personally does not enthuse us. Prices and services are competitive, however.

The most courteous, pleasant, and efficient chauffeur-guide we've found in Copenhagen is **Ronald Haworth** (Vejrøgade 2), a kindly Britisher who came back after World War II to marry a Danish girl. His fleet is available round the clock, every day of the year; just call him at 15-16-05 and tell him your needs. Should your arrangements be impromptu, phone his wife at 18-04-24, and she will transmit your message immediately by short-wave radio to his car. If he is engaged, she will summon another dependable English-speaking driver from his pool, 8 of whom also speak our tongue (and are at home anywhere in Europe, as well). Large, clean, comfortable automobiles, including Chryslers, Pontiacs, Dodges, Plymouths, Impalas, plus some 7-place broughams; standard rates. Here's an organization that is not only a courier service but a booking agent, a baggage nanny, and a Dutch Uncle to boot.

If his cars are reserved, try **Copenhagen Limousine Service** (Danasvej 4; Tel. 31-12-34) for a s-t-r-e-t-c-h-e-d C-a-d-i-l-l-a-c, a l-o-n-g L-i-n-c-o-l-n, a c-o-o-l C-h-r-y-s-l-e-r, or any of 9 other luxury carriages. All drivers speak English, of course. Its affiliate, **Pitzner Auto** (Trommesalen 4; Tel. 11-12-34) rents new self-drive automobiles on similar terms to those of Autourist. Our own experience with this organization has been very satisfactory indeed. Recommended.

TIPPING   The best-organized system in Europe. In restaurants the tip is automatically extracted (an extra penny, for example, is often added to the price of a glass of beer). In many situations, however, you are expected to do the honors. Make it a flat 15% always—but inquire first, or you may be tipping twice. Tip concierge, room waiter, and maid according to what they do for you, if you like. The baggage porter gets about 25¢ per suitcase, which is included on your bill (but a small additional coin is always appreciated).

One happy thing: You won't find the average Dane with his hand out. Whether you tip him or not, you'll get a warm smile and expert help.

THINGS TO BUY   Scores of Americans consider the shopping in Denmark the finest on the Continent. Most of the merchandise is outstandingly tasteful in the special Danish way. The aforementioned 15% "MOMS" tax is effective on a national scale *within* the country. But *ALL EXPORTED MERCHANDISE* is granted a deduction of 13.04%. Therefore, make arrangements with your shops to ship your major purchases (1) direct to your home, or (2) for pickups by you, direct to your Danish point of exit.

Two extraordinary establishments should be the first targets of any visitor: **Den Permanente** (Vesterport Building) and Illums Bolighus, Center of Modern Design (Amagertorv 10). Den Permanente is the so-called "Permanent Exhibition"—the show, sample, and sales rooms for practically all established firms or individual craftsmen in the nation. Every piece on the spacious, appealingly decorated floors—each approved by the jury elected by its 250 participants—is Danish. Small artisans from the most remote hinterlands exhibit beside the largest industrial art concerns. You'll find contemporary furniture designed by such renowned Grand Masters as Poul Kjaerholm, Kaare Klint, Hans J. Wegner, Børge Mogensen, Arne Jacobsen, and other leaders. Leading the parade of other products for your home and your personal use are curtains, cutlery, dinnerware, jewelry (you can choose from the work of 60 silversmiths), and textiles. Atop the arresting new staircase, the 2nd floor features everything from 50¢ mementos to stainless-steel and silver flatware to handblocked print dresses to fabrics—a collection which is not only 99% certain to intrigue *you* for your own personal picks, but which is also a potential gold mine for your Christmas and birthday gifts. Den Permanente is proud of its wholesale department for foreign retailers and of its contract division which undertakes complete furnishings of private homes and institutions. Its shipping department boasts such experts in dispatching even its most delicate merchandise all over the world that yours will be handled with meticulous care. The combination of expertise in arts and crafts, and expertise in administrative complexities, is rare indeed—but Managing Director Ivan Engel has it, and he is doing wonders to ease your buying path. Unique.

Illums Bolighus, Center of Modern Design (Amagertorv 10), is the closest we've ever found to being *the* dream shop of any American host or hostess. The level of artistry, quality, and technical soundness throughout its 4 sweepingly dramatic, air-conditioned floors is electrifying. True-life displays replace counters. You'll find everything for the home in this one-and-only "Home House," more radiant than ever with the unveiling of its top floor (with a top quality but inexpensive roof-garden restaurant that's a knockout!), plus "Mini-Illums" branches at the Hotel Scandinavia and Kastrup Airport. Graceful Danish furniture galore, with guaranteed safe delivery through its flourishing weekly container shipping service to U.S. at a net 40% under U.S. prices (same saving on scores more buys); the nation's longest shelves of porcelain, rustic stoneware, and faïence; Fashion Department with exclusive dresses and accessories; Fur Department; Gastronomic Department; the famous Wooden Articles Department; the Arts and Crafts Department; Fairy Tale Department (DON'T MISS exploring this supercharming favorite of ours). And these, all tax-free if shipped, are only the beginning! Fireball Jørgen Basse, whose impressive international background includes Bullock's in America and Harrods in London, is in taut, zesty, imaginative command. See for yourself!

Exquisite porcelain? Celebrated **Bing & Grøndahl** (Amagertorv 4, on the pedestrian mall at the capital's Stork Fountain hub) traces its roots to A.D. 1830. This is the pioneer which at the turn of the century revolutionized the industry by achieving the final historic breakthrough of *under*glaze decoration techniques. Whenever their cherished objects in our own home conjure up reminiscences of their vast ground-floor trove, even to each other it is impossible to put into words the qualities of gentleness, of tenderness, of magic enchantment which in their consummate artistry they have conveyed to their soaring birds, swimming fishes, friendly dogs, and sweet children of Hans Christian Andersen figurines. You will also discover the same elements to the same or a lesser degree in their vases, ashtrays, stoneware in the contemporary mode, and even in their "annual plates" which commemorate such events as Christmas—and in heavy emphasis, as well, among the plethora of lovely one-and-only pieces. How much? Anywhere from $1 to $2100, as little or as much as you choose. Up one flight the Dinnerware Department unfolds its lures. The more than 100 separate patterns on display constitute the largest selection of Bing & Grøndahl dinner services in the world. Interestingly, among the trio of the most sought-after designs, "Seagull," "Empire," and "Snowflower," the first 2 were created by lady artists in the late 1800's; the 104-unit "Empire" set flowed from the brush of Mrs. Harriet Bing, wife of the then-proprietor who originally brought global fame to the firm by seeking out and signing up a roster of big-name painters. Here you'll find a range from gift articles at less than $1 to superfancy, super-precious plates at $600 each. Because of their 87 years of trailblazing in the underglaze field, all of their porcelain is amazingly resistant to all kinds of soaps, detergents, and acids. The 1300+ employees are justly proud of the organization's Appointments to the Royal Courts of Denmark, Great Britain, and Sweden. Ask for Manager Per Simonsen, who loves his treasures and who is dedicated to his clients. Unbeatable!

Royal Copenhagen, a few steps away, is also venerable, highly distinguished, and universally respected. **Frøsig** (Nørrebrogade 9) is a small, crowded center for "seconds" and replacement pieces of all leading factories. *Please* get all of your porcelain while you're on Danish soil, because the markup in North America for exactly the same items is staggering.

Silver? While world-famous Georg Jensen has gorgeous displays and the biggest name, we are *not* enthusiastic about his prices. In our most carefully considered professional opinions—and perhaps you'll disagree—this house is squeezing every extra penny the tourist traffic will tolerate through the snob value of its prestigious reputation. Our own personal leading choice is **Hans Hansens Sølv** (Amagertorv 16, on the pedestrian mall), which we regard as the most intimately tasteful silver store in all of Denmark. During our painstaking comparison shopping for 5 pieces of similar weight and purity, their entries ran from 8% to 22% under the Jensen prices—and we defy any average hostess or guest in her home to pick out the piece which cost 22% less or 22% more. The design and craftsmanship in this 3rd-generation landmark are perfection, combining the skills of honest masters with the dynamic forms of the sculptor's art. Mr. Peder Mikkelsen will help you in this fairyland of temptation. The greatest, say we!

Handblown, handmade glassware? The nation's only producer is **Holmegaard** (main newly expanded shop: Østergade 15), which since 1825 has triumphantly combined traditional craftsmanship with excitingly different ideas which reflect stunning individuality. Dozens of free brochures; kindly Manager Henning Lundsgaard will be your oracle. A glittering wonderland.

Furs? More high-grade mink is raised in Denmark than in any other foreign land—and the quality and savings are unbeatable. By far the most eye-gleaming assortment, in our opinion, can be found at the 108-year-old house of **Birger Christensen** (Østergade 38). Purveyors By Appointment to no less than 3 Royal Courts and to most of the important foreign embassies, they offer a reservoir of the largest stocks and widest fur choices in Europe. They are so understated and so *different* that many customers now walk in to ask without specifying for "a fur coat"—simply because they want a Birger Christensen styling and label. The specialty here is their world-famous Saga mink in a color galaxy of 20 mutations. Since the Copenhagen mink auctions are traditionally lower, the lucky foreigner *still* pays ENORMOUSLY less than the identical pieces would cost in the U.S.—without luxury tax, too! The inventory is deliberately umbrellaed to cover all age and economic groups from the finest at the top, to the lovely brand-new 700 BC contemporary line starting at $600, to more modestly priced Fun Furs in coats, capes, jackets, hats, you-name-it for less opulent, chic, sophisticated swingers. The alert, gifted, and charming Birger Christensen, Jr. has now set up outlets at the Hotel Royal and the Hotel Scandinavia, as well as his own departments in New York's Bloomingdale's, the West Coast's I. Magnin, St. Louis' Stix, Baer & Fuller, Washington's Garfinckel's, Pittsburgh's Joseph Horne, Houston's Sakowitz, Chicago's Stanley Korshak—and now Tokyo's ultrafine Prince International Shopping Arcade. As the only major house in the world to create new collections twice yearly, its fashion shows have been smash successes from coast to coast in U.S.A., Paris (exclusively for Hermès), Gstaad, Saudi Arabia, Zürich, Montreal, Kuwait, and now Tokyo. This debonair entrepreneur also operates the highly successful Bee Cee boutique (see below). Ask for the dynamic, instantly likable Mr. Christensen in person. Dreamy, dreamy, dreamy!

A. C. Bang, across the street, is also chic and highly reputable. Although considerable improvement has been shown lately, we, at least, still don't think their creations reflect quite the same genius in fashion and styling and flair as those of the One-And-Only Mr. Christensen.

Fabrics? **Per Reumert** (handsome quarters at Hyskenstraede 1 on the Amagertorv corner) and **Gera Stoffer** (Østergade 36-38, adjoining Birger Christensen) are now the kings of this field. Heaven for fashion hounds.

Nifty boutique? **Bee Cee** (Østergade 24) stands for the ubiquitous Birger Christensen—and by now you should know that this name hallmarks q-u-a-l-i-t-y. The spirit throughout is so gay and youthful that the chic buyer of any age finds it irresistible à la mode. Here, as well as in its Hotel Scandinavia, Royal Hotel, and suburban Lyngby branches, are selected Birger Christensen furs, eye-arresting sportswear, casual clothes, accessories, blouses, Hermès scarves, and other temptations, plus stunning new lines of from-cradle-up male and female Danish hand-knitted sweaters (your own pattern also custom-woven by elderly homebodies) from $25 to $75 and all sizes, brad-studded wooden clogs in white, blue, yellow, red, brown, or black for $15 to $25 which are currently a high-vogue rage. The English-speaking staff are all the Aaa Bee Cee of kindness and fun. A dilly for discerning dollies!

Mostly for men? Ever hear of a legend called Brooks Brothers? Well, if the airline ticket in your pocket didn't prove otherwise, you could believe you were in that revered American institution the moment you step into **Brødrene Andersen** (Østergade 7-9) in the heart of Copenhagen's Old Town. This Danish house has been a stitch in time for well over a century, stylishly attiring the Establishment fraternity—including, we might add, the Royal Danish Court since its more recent princes were in knee pants. Many of its materials are purchased on London's stately Savile Row—the sort that even make women look twice (and then usually with envy). Andersen's conservative wood-lined interior is rich in masculine character—and so is its debonair clothing. Proprietor Frithiof Nexøe-Larsen opens a sesame of sartorial treasures—cashmere coats and jackets from Hobson and Chester Barrie plus Burberry classics, Danish sweaters and cardigans, and 100% hand-tailored outfits. A custom, 3-fitting suit can be meticulously constructed in from 2 to 3 weeks. When spun from the one-fitting ring system, however, the price drops markedly. And don't despair, ladies; you can turn waiting time to profit in Andersen's small but recently expanded and well-stocked women's department, where there are troves of lovely sweaters, slacks, and skirts from Jaeger, Pringle, Celine, and Luisa Spagnoli. Cashmere by the yard from Edinburgh's Harrisons can be selected here and sent to you directly from Scotland; the 15% purchase tax may also be avoided by dispatching all goods to your home. General Manager Jørgen Bruun is your impeccable host. His aides, Mr. Jorgen Nexøe-Larsen (3rd generation) and Mr. Nielsen on the ground floor, Mrs. Brandt in the ladies' department, and Mr. Hansen and Mr. Gulløv upstairs, also speak English and also are the souls of kindness. Princely—and that's only the half of it!

Bjørn Wiinblad Hus (Ny Østergade 11, is hidden away in a newly restored cluster of historic buildings on elfin Pistolstraede, a few steps down this ministreet bordering the Bee Cee boutique. In this merry atmosphere are Wiinblad's extraordinary ceramics, his marvelous tables, many of his most celebrated posters, reproductions of his sketches for ballets and plays, his deliciously deft greeting cards, and other inspired creations—all bearing the unique, cunning, instantly recognizable Wiinblad artistry. A captivating fun house for tots of all ages.

Flowers? **Svend Schaumann** (Kongens Nytorv, adjoining d'Angleterre Hotel) is our candidate for the top florist in Europe. His flair for beautiful arrangements is inimitable. Purveyor to the Royal Court, Denmark's social elite, and distinguished visitors.

Denmark is one of the handiest countries in which to restock your supplies of stateside books and magazines. Both the **English Bookshop** (adjoining the Palace Hotel) and **Boghallen** (up one block) carry new titles, paperback reprints, lithographs, fine art impressions, and souvenirs. Both are topflight.

§TIP: The **Gateway Store** in the Free Zone Waiting Room of Copenhagen's Kastrup Airport stocks 121 brands of choice liquors and liqueurs, U.S. cigarettes, and other goodies—all at those wonderfully low tax-free prices. Anyone bound out of Denmark for anywhere, including other Scandinavian lands, may purchase up to the limits prescribed by Customs at his destination merely by producing his Aircraft Boarding Card as identification.

Dedicated shophounds? Space is too tight here for further listings—so consult this year's edition of *Fielding's Shopping Guide to Europe* ($3.50) for more stores, more details, and more lore.

LOCAL RACKETS   We've run across only 2—and the latter isn't even Danish. One we'd watch is the substitution of Cloc whisky for Scotch—at Scotch prices—in some cheap spots. The other is the influx of counterfeit 100-kroner bills—from Mallorca, no less! Since all legal 100-kroner notes begin with "A" and this funny money (at least so far) has started with other letters, it's easy to spot them. Denmark is a land of honorable, honest people.

BELIEVE IT OR NOT   You should raise your hat to any Danish friend you see on the street. Men doff their hats to men—a national custom.

When you meet a Danish friend after he has entertained you or been kind to you, your first words should not be "Hello!" or "How are you?" Rigid good manners dictate that your greeting be "Tak for sidst!"—"Thanks for the last time we were together!" As the thankingest people in the world, they also have variations of "Tak" ("Thanks!") for meals, tea, coffee, drinks, the day, the fun, the ride, and just about every human act.

It's unheard of to refuse a Skål. Even if you don't drink, go through the ceremony. Be sure to touch the glass to your lips.

Danish women have a taste for cigars and handle them with finesse.

Denmark is the only land in Europe which celebrates the Fourth of July on a gigantic scale. At Rebild, a forest-and-heather area, more than 50-thousand U.S.-loving Danes and Danish-Americans gather to hear distinguished speakers and to watch the huge fireworks display at Aalborg. If you're within shooting distance of any part of Scandinavia around this time, don't miss it!

If you'll stand outside Au Coq d'Or restaurant way out toward the curb on H. C. Andersen's boulevard and gaze upward to a famous statue atop a nearby building, you'll share a naughty sight from the far edge of this corner, which for years has been a source of merriment to Copenhageners.

England

Not all the British are English. The United Kingdom has 4 distinct peoples, about as dissimilar as a horse, a bull, a mule, and a deer. The Scots (say "Scotch" only when you're thirsty!) are geniuses with their hands, sticklers for thrift, conscientious workers who think like the French. The Irish are mercurial, whimsical, stubborn, mystical. The Welsh are shrewd, deep, intense, music-prone, hewn from their native granite. We're concerned here with the English. They're the ones you must know longest, probe deepest, understand best before you can catch glimmerings of their unique greatness.

There's a childlike quality to their spirit—a charming, puckish, stubborn refusal to grow up. When you dig under their shell, you'll find passion, gaiety, richness, all the warm, human values of your next-door neighbor.

More than 25 American presidents had British blood. Almost 30-million Americans can find their roots in Britain. While dozens of nationalities have contributed heroic shares to America's greatness, here's a fact: The foundation of our culture—language, law, customs, behavior—is essentially British.

The Queen isn't just the figurehead many Americans take her for. On the contrary, she is the symbolic expression of national unity. She can sample a pudding in a farmer's kitchen without lowering her exalted station or her immense personal dignity. She is "family" to many of her people, just the way a few lucky screen stars are "family" to Middletown, U.S.A.

Great Britain sets its watch to Greenwich Mean Time (GMT) in the winter; this means that Tired Tommy gets out of bed an hour earlier than Lucky Pierre who lives across the Channel. However, British Summer Time (BST) allows everyone on both sides to yawn in unison.

The 55-million people—New York, California, Illinois, Michigan, and Wisconsin combined—find things pretty crowded; on their 93-thousand square miles they have less living space than do citizens of highly concentrated Connecticut. Few of the forests remain. There is good farm and grazing land in the south and in parts of Scotland; this is where that renowned fat, tender beef is grown. Rivers and streams abound. The coastline is so tortuous, so full of inlets into which big ships can travel, that no point in Scotland, for example, is more than 60 miles from the sea. If the natural contours weren't that way, we might be living in a far less pleasant world; we can thank this lucky geographic freak for the creation and existence of the British Navy.

Climate? Don't believe the travel posters; on the average it's pretty awful. New York has far more uncomfortable extremes; here the Gulf Stream plugs up both ends of the thermometer. It's seldom unbearably hot or unbearably cold, despite common latitude with Labrador and the Baltic States, but its dampness is enough to give chronic rhinitis to a cigar-store Indian. Remember Browning's classic line, "Oh, to be in England, now that April's there"? For our money, however, June is usually tops. May, September, and October are its next best months; go then if you can possibly arrange it. One asset is the duration of daylight on spring and summer evenings; in Scotland you can often play golf at 10 P.M. March and November fogs are not as frequent visitors as they used to be; winter sunshine has increased by 70% in London since '62 because of laudably stringent air pollution laws. The miserable pall of smoke over some industrial areas is being controlled to some degree in a network of "smokeless zones." Take warm clothing with you whenever you go to these changeable islands—particularly in summer, when you think you need it least!

You won't freeze in England, despite the scarcity of that twentieth-century device, the central-heating unit; neither will you roast, despite the paucity of air conditioning. But you may barely escape both: On a good fall day, it's windy at 9, raining at 11, sunny at 3, foggy at 5, and snowing at seven.

For national good manners, here is perhaps the most courteous society in the world. Their philosophy is a simple and gracious one: Since most human beings are already insecure, why make things worse? Courtesy starts at the cradle; British children are so much better disciplined than U.S. youngsters that there's no comparison. The story goes that an aristocratic mother once went to the nursery and found it empty. Peering out the window, she saw her 4-year-old son sliding down the drainpipe. "Richard!" she said severely—and the little boy promptly slid up again.

CITIES *Greater London* is a Tale of Two Cities: King's City and Merchants' City. They were invaded by the Romans in A.D. 43, but the story prior to that is still a mystery. She is the grandmother of capitals, almost 8-million strong and 610 miles square, vying with New York and Tokyo as the largest urbanized area in the world.

More and more, her midtown sections profile the rude invasion of steel-and-glass monoliths. Hardly a week passes without announcements of another new skyscraper to lance into her cardiac zone—the heartbeat nucleus obliquely called the Greater London Council, consisting of the City of London, Westminster, the Royal Borough of Kensington and Chelsea, and 30 other metropolitan boroughs. Even London Bridge, which was *truly* falling down, recently became a $6,000,000 tourist attraction in Arizona's Lake Havasu City. Meanwhile, the mother city has replaced it with a $9,600,000, 6-lane span.

Despite this frenzy of growth, for ages visitors have thought that London's streets must have been planned by the Mad Hatter or by wandering cows; they wind helter-skelter in 10-thousand directions. But there's beauty about this eccentric old dowager, a sweep to her 5 central parks (St. James's, Green, Hyde, Kensington, and Regent's), a dignity about her Portland-stone buildings, white with weathering or black with soot, and a charm about her pageantry, her pomp, her leisurely Victorian pace.

Transportation? Wonderful subways ("undergrounds" or "tubes"); pulsing London (Heathrow) Airport (currently being re-engineered, thank goodness) jammed by 16.4-million passengers on nearly 300-thousand flights per year, plus Gatwick to alleviate its raging blood pressure, plus a 3rd international terminus to be ready in 1980 at Maplin in Essex. The Thames, their Hudson River, makes its friendly way through the Port, 3000 acres of wharves and docks; the "City" (Wall Street), Westminster (Capitol Hill), the West End (Times Square and Fifth Avenue), Soho and Chelsea (Greenwich Village), Mayfair (Park Avenue), and many other districts split the metropolis into its components. You'll be enchanted by London. Write for the value-packed 12-month "Season Ticket to the History of Britain" ($2.45 at the Department of the Environment, Neville House, Page Street, London, S.W. 1P 4LS) which will admit you to the Tower of London and 649 other eye-poppers in the United Kingdom. Or ask the British Tourist Authority (64 St. James's Street, London, S.W.1A 1NF) for the $7.00, month-long "Open to View" pass which lowers the drawbridge onto all Department of Environment properties, plus those in the National Trust and about 200 others that are privately owned. Bring your passport. A tour of Britain could be planned around these monuments. If you're economy-minded, choose among the $1.50 "Red Bus Rover" ticket (unlimited one-day travel on all central red buses), $1.60-per-day "Green Rover" ticket (unlimited travel for one day on London country bus routes but not on Green Line Coaches), "Golden Rover" romper at $2.50 (unlimited one-day loops on Green Line Coaches *and* green London Country Buses) or the 4-day ($10), 7-day ($13), or monthly ($45) "Go As You Please" teasers (unlimited bus or subway use, with Green Line coaches excepted). Youngsters under 14 roll for less than ½ fare on the first 2. If you're a zoo fan, take the water buses, which ply along the Regent's Canal between Paddington and Camden Town, to this famous institution (mid-Mar. to end-Sept. only). But to us the best sightseeing fun of all here is from the Thames—not to be missed by *any* pilgrim of *any* age if humanly possible. This is the 45-minute boat ride (50 pence one way or 80 pence round trip) from Westminster Pier, Abbey Embankment or Charing Cross Pier to the lovely outlying suburban center of nautical Greenwich. All services are operative at 20-minute intervals between April and November. While you glide down the river, you'll be painlessly filled with enchanting facts and tidbits which most native Londoners don't even know. After landing and inspecting the original *Cutty Sark* clipper in drydock, ohing and ahing at the Gypsy Moth Conservatory, admiring the magnificently architected and groomed

College grounds, and idling through the charming streets of the town, have lunch at the Trafalgar Tavern, which is directly on the bank, a short skip from where you'll dock. Reserve in advance; delightful ambiance; French-type cuisine; prices highish; Navy-size portions; more oaken-hearted valiance needed in the kitchen; closed Sunday nights and holidays. You may return either by the way you came or by double-decker bus. What a grand, grand excursion on a sunny day! Nelson's Column and Trafalgar Square, Buckingham Palace, Parliament, Hyde Park, Westminster Abbey, the Tower of London (with the Crown Jewels), the stunning new National Theatre, and Madame Tussaud's wax museum are, individually, the top targets for visitors. There is a marvelous, magic kaleidoscope of literally hundreds more. But what you'll like most is the color of everyday life along these crooked, crazy, sweet little streets.

Birmingham, with 80 square miles and 1-million people, is the second city of England. The irascible Dr. Johnson found a wife here—no trick for any man, we can assure you, so long as he throws in the promise to take her away from this iron and steel center. Its face is changing radically. The modern Rotunda Building in midcity resembles a stack of concrete hotcakes; the so-called Bull Ring is one of the nation's most dramatic urban renewal projects; New Street Station was rebuilt over 7 downtown acres. However, it remains a Detroit rather than a San Francisco to the traveler.

Liverpool, the size of St. Louis, is third. Substitute docks, freighters, and railway tunnels for steel mills, foundries, and lofts, and you have a smaller Birmingham. It, too, is modernizing—but, sad to say, at a far slower pace.

Manchester, the textile center and fourth city, is connected with the sea by a 36-mile ship canal. The 14-story, 264-room, $4,800,000 Hotel Piccadilly made its midtown debut a while back, as one pod of a skyrocketing development program. The $6,720,000 air terminal building is an heir-conditioned offspring of its booming rebirth pains. Although here is one of the principal centers of political, literary, scientific, and musical advancement, most Yankee sightseers find it commercial and unrewarding.

Sheffield (cutlery, steel) and **Leeds** (woolens), next in line, also are humdrum to the vacationing American. Incidentally, natives of the latter are called "Leeds Loiners." Good Yorkshiremen, they—rough, tough, and gruff on the surface but, like purebred bull terriers, gentle as lambs under their bristling exteriors. **Coventry**, home of Jaguar cars (Lady Godiva chose a local hayburner instead), is another bolt in the boiler belt. Its proudest attraction is the controversial modern rose-gray sandstone Cathedral which stands beside the bombed shell of the 5-centuries-old cathedral. The town, and a dull one it is, has roughly the population of Denver.

The charm of the United Kingdom is not in her industrial cities. Go to the moors, the heaths, the dales, and lakes, the hamlets. Run out to Cambridge or Oxford for an excursion (but avoid the latter on the first Mon. and Tues. of Sept., when the annual St. Giles' Fair turns it into a shambles). Try the Shakespeare country in Warwickshire; try Canterbury in Kent, one of the ecclesiastical matrixes of civilization, or Rye and Dorking for simple village charm; try Winchester, the former capital of the realm, for a permeation of history harking back to the Knights of the Round Table; try the 35-mile-square Lake District, a miniature Switzerland in Cumberland, Westmorland, and Lancashire; try the cathedrals and serene stone villages of Gloucestershire; try rugged Cornwall, the Hardy country of Dorset and Wiltshire, Raleigh's Devon, the castles of Snowdonia, the poetic Cotswolds, the Derbyshire peaks, the Yorkshire moors, the Scottish Highlands, the hot springs of Harrogate, the unbelievably broad beaches of Southport, the renowned antiquities in the valleys of the Usk and the Wye. Around every bend in the road you'll find an ever-changing landscape, with customs, dialects, ways of life new to you, but as old to the culture as Chaucer and Malory. London is unique, but skip Birmingham, Liverpool, Manchester, and Leeds. Look for the real England at the roots of her grass.

MONEY AND PRICES   British currency, which for centuries has bedeviled North Americans and most other foreigners, was changed in 1971 from the traditional system to one based on decimals similar to ours. The pound (£) is now divided into 100 pence ("pennies" or p's"), just as our dollar breaks into 100 cents. As we go to press, the floating rate for £1 is less than $1.80, making the sterling zone an unusually good travel and shopping bargin for dollar-fed vacation budgets. The coins are half new penny, 1 new pence, 2 new pence, 5 new pence, 10 new pence, and 50 new pence. Until the old mintings have been phased out completely, it will pay to remember that 5 new pence is interchangeable with the old shilling (sometimes called a "bob" and still in free circulation). It follows logically then that 10 new pence is the same as 2 shillings, while 50 new pence can be swapped for (you guessed it) 10 shillings. Also gradually being withdrawn is the sixpence ("tanner"). Now—if you've got all that please relax, because the worst is over.

Concerning your folding money, the £1, £5, and £10 denominations will continue to roll along unchanged. A new note for £20 pictures the Queen and Shakespeare.

In metropolitan centers, prices are on a level with U.S. living, but you'll be pleasantly surprised how much purchasing elastic there is in your '77 greenbacks due to the falling pound and the strengthening dollar. Deluxe hostelries charge about the highest rates abroad today (see "Hotels"). Medium-class shelter, plus a typical English breakfast, can be had from $14 to $25 per guest. Staple foods aren't too expensive, particularly out of London, but luxuries such as game and fish will run up your bill and your temperature. Whisky (due to staggering taxation) is murder all over the country, even in the Scottish heather where the dew is gathered—about $1.25 for a nip which wouldn't give a buzz to a teetotaling elf.

The VAT started bubbling in Britain in 1973, when the so-called *V*alue *A*dded *T*ax went into effect. Initial chaos and confusion have now given way to abiding anger, particularly among hoteliers, restaurateurs, and their deftly-sheared customers. Your hotel room, restaurant, movie, play, cigars, and top quality liquor bounced higher than a pogo stick in this Sea of Storms. What you won't see, though, is how your host has incorporated higher maintenance costs into the room rate, since plumbers, electricians, decorators, and even lawyers benefit from the upstart levy. Aggravating Anomaly Department: A sandwich is taxed 8% if you eat it in the restaurant, but it's untaxed if you carry it out; chocolates are un-VATed on the grocer's shelf, but not at the candy counter in a movie theater (unless, of course, you eat them in the lobby . . .). The few hostelries that don't hit you with that 12 1/2% service tab *also don't levy VAT,* bless 'em.

ATTITUDE TOWARD TOURISTS

The American offices of the **British Tourist Authority** do outstandingly good work, thanks to U.S. General Manager James T. Turbayne, O.B.E. For his solid achievements, this unusually able and attractive executive has received the decoration of Officer of the Order of the British Empire from Queen Elizabeth—and well merited it was! If the pleasant ladies at his Information Counter at 680 Fifth Ave., N.Y. 10019, or the branch personnel at his Chicago or Los Angeles outlets can't solve your problem, write or call either Mr. Turbayne in person or his charming, razor-quick assistant, Mrs. Helen Newman. Here's a star pair.

The Canadian office is at 151 Bloor St. West, Toronto 5. There are also European branches in Paris, Amsterdam, Brussels, Rome, Madrid, Copenhagen, Stockholm, Zürich, Oslo, and Frankfurt-am-Main.

If you'll pop into the **Tourist Information Centre** at 64/65 St. James's St., or the **London Tourist Board** at 4 Grosvenor Gardens, SW1W ODU, you'll find a veritable font of courtesy and assistance.

CUSTOMS AND IMMIGRATION

As in France, almost everything is forbidden but nearly everything is allowed. This paradox is the "tolerance" system; the law says no, but the kindly Customs authorities say yes.

Legally, you may claim very little—but if your luggage accompanies you the inspectors will pass without levy a *reasonable* amount of dutiable effects *for your personal use.*

Technically they can slap *Customs duties* on new clothing (purchased in the U.S. or continental Europe) of 17½% to 33%, on cigarettes of $5 per carton, on spirits of $5 to $6 per fifth (ouch!), on jewelry of 25% to 36%, and so on. Should you be nasty, they can wreck a 4-figure bank account in 4 minutes flat.

But, luckily for all, these officials are among Britain's best ambassadors of good will. They are intelligent, polite, and efficient. If you are frank and well-mannered in replying to their frank and well-mannered questions (you'll be asked, for example, the purpose of your visit and your proposed length of stay), chances are they'll never even peep into your bags. On only 6 of our last 32 visits did they ask us to open a piece of luggage—and this seems to be the normal approach toward the average American visitor.

London's Heathrow Airport, in fact, has set up 2 portals—one for those with nothing to declare and another for travelers with taxable items. Let your conscience be your guide!

Prohibited articles include dogs, muskrats (got one in your suitcase?), weapons, narcotics, egret feathers, and naughty French postcards. The restrictions on pets are now being strictly enforced, with penalties for animal smuggling ranging from confiscation to destruction to unlimited fines for owners and even up to a year's imprisonment for offenders.

Don't declare your gifts as gifts until they ask you.

Always say, when queried, that you are a tourist traveling for pleasure, unless you intend to apply for a work permit.

Follow the hints under "Customs Officials" in "Let's Be European". They'll come in handy.

Export licenses are mandatory for some items. These include manuscripts over 70 years old, archaeological material, diamonds or articles set or mounted with diamonds—almost anything more than 100 years old with an individual value of more than £4000. The British Government has now increased the value of works of art more than 100 years old which can be exported without a special license. You can pick up required documents at the Department of Trade and Industry, Export Licensing Branch, Norman Shaw North Building, Derby Gate, Victoria Embankment, London S.W.1A 2JB.

You'll probably like your reception in England—and, in the same sense, your departure, too. Almost without exception, the Customs officials are a fine body of men with whom to do business.

§HERE'S AN IMPORTANT TIP: You may *bring in* unlimited amounts of sterling, dollars, francs, and other currencies (declare them all!)—but you may *take out a maximum of only £25 in British bank notes*. They're hard as nails about this; plead all you like, but they'll confiscate every penny of your surplus.

HOTELS For far more comprehensive information on certain British hostelries than space limitations permit here, interested travelers are referred to *Fielding's Selected Favorites: Hotels and Inns, Europe* ($4.95) by Dodge Temple Fielding, who just happens to be our very own son. The revised edition, in which a total of 300-odd favored possibilities were handpicked from the 4000-plus personally inspected, will be at your bookstore early this year.

In England, excellent service; facilities improving by leaps and bounds; murderously expensive.

In **London**, *a mere single in a posh pad may ring up $40 or so; twin billings bong in at a resounding $65 for bed, breakfast, service, and taxes; make it $95 for a small suite or at least $130 for a large one. Medium-bracket innkeepers charge only about 20% less than their patrician peers, which means that ordinary London lodgings now sock the traveler for about as much as the finest palace-type houses on the Continent.* In sum, however, although you'll pay plenty for a latchkey, we'll also bet that your fun will be the merriest in many a year.

Now for our breakdown of the individual hotels. Because of the swelling flood of newcomers, we feel it is not appropriate to rank the Old Guard with the Avant-Garde. We have, therefore, divided our ratings into "Traditional," "Contemporary," and "Assorted" brackets. The candidates surrounding Heathrow Airport and in outlying districts are covered separately toward the end of this section.

TRADITIONAL HOTELS:

Claridge's, Brook St., W.1: There is still tremendous snob appeal in this last stronghold of nearly vanished British wealth, particularly if Burke's *Landed*

Gentry carries your name or if you sport an old-school tie. However, General Manager Lund Hansen has somewhat softened its formerly stiff mien. Crown jewel of the fabulous Savoy Hotels empire; no bar, no dancing; the ultimate in luxury, urbanity, and prices, but aura so autocratic that it's not for the average visitor looking for a home away from home. A gem, at Cartier prices. Better and better.

Savoy, Strand, W.C.2: Here, to our minds, is the greatest large hotel of the world, bar none—tailor-made to the best taste of the American abroad. Five-hundred rooms with bath, all instantly convertible into suites; 100 apartments; vast majority of units impeccable, but a scattering of poorly executed "mother-in-law" units allotted to the less fortunate when the house is jam-packed; staff of 1500, at least 3 to every "client" (for you're always a "client," not a "guest"). Superb cuisine; refashioned Savoy Grill in white marble with yew paneling, which some visitors find cooler than the former shrine of diners; new shopping arcade linking Grill to the poly-chrome-striped main bar; Savoy Restaurant, with dancing and headline en-tertainers, also the exclusive earldom of the superlatively great Maître Chef Trompetto; crack Public Relations staff mistress-minded by Canadian-born Prudence Emery; TV in many rooms; telephones in all bedrooms, sitting rooms, and bathrooms. If money is no object, the Presidential Suite (chris-tened by Mr. Truman in '56) at a President's ransom is one of the most discreetly opulent accommodations on the other side of the Atlantic. Hand-some, dedicated General Manager Beverley Griffin operates this 7-ring show with commanding flair. Highest recommendation of any big hotel we know for the discriminating U.S. voyager.

Berkeley, Wilton Place, S.W. 1: Pronounced "Barkley"; this Savoy Hotels landmark resides on a lovely site edging Hyde Park in the fashionable Bel-gravia district. We aver that here might be the last truly super-deluxe hotel in the world to be built as a cunningly modernized showcase in the supremely gracious traditional style. At your command are such features as the opulent Lilac Restaurant, the fine-feathered Le Perroquet luncheon salon *cum* night-time disco (see "Restaurants"), the mellow Bar, the soooo comfy, 68-seat Mineva minicinema, the gorgeous penthouse pool with sliding roof, refresh-ment facilities, and sauna—a galaxy. There are 25 regal suites and 156 knock-out doubles; the flawless demisuites among the latter group are our favorites in the house for our personal requirements. Best of all is the fact that beloved General Manager Charles Fornara has one of the finest staffs under any London roof; Chief Hall-Porter Goodberry is among his collection of special prizes. A noble, graceful, remarkably beautiful oasis.

Dorchester, Park Lane, W.1: This one remains a favorite with thousands of loyalists around the globe—and with very good reason, too. Her radiant wardrobe glistens with fresh carpets and furnishings, larger windows, and added balconies; the public rooms, now air-conditioned, are so immaculate they require only normal upkeep. The Oliver Messel, the Harlequin, and the other superduper suites, the lobby, the American Bar, the Grill, and the alfresco summer dining-terrace are delightful; the service is superb in every regard. Now even the rather old-fashioned baths are showing some sparkle, with Delft tilework as highlights. Overall, the major improvements merit warmest praise. We pray that its new owners, a consortium of Middle Eastern investors, and its new director, Peter Stafford, will keep up the excellent work here.

Connaught, Carlos Place, W.1: This spell-weaving old-timer couldn't be a more felicitous choice for the traveler in search of comfort and tranquillity in the homespun way—provided, of course, that you live in a palatially homespun mansion. If you desire a spacious room, flawless service, a superior restaurant and grill, a faintly English-Manor-House atmosphere, no orchestras, no dancing, no radio, no TV (except in suites), and quiet British gentility which is nearly Edwardian in tone, here is surely the place for you. Kindly, mannerly, attentive staff, from Head Hall Porter John to Head Barman Tony to the youngest employee; Savoy Hotels, Ltd. ownership, but independent administration. Respectable U.S.-style martinis; the cuisine in the Grill vies with the most exalted in the capital. Again we couldn't have been happier in what might well be compared in aura to a top-ranking London club. Book l-o-n-g in advance.

Grosvenor House, Park Lane, W.1: Virtually everything was swept away and replaced in this house's recent $7,250,000 rejuvenation—excepting the spit-and-polish efficiency of the staff and the somewhat commercial aura of its purposeful functionalism. Two fresh restaurants and the revamped lounges are its proudest button-poppers. We much prefer the colorful decorative schemes on the even-numbered floors, but perhaps you'll disagree. The management is continuing the policy of catering heavily to the affluent businessman, with banquets and conventions a specialty; many tourists like it as their London headquarters, too. Moving up notably and landably.

Brown's, Dover St., W.1: Since 1837, this old-timer has been one of the most famous hostelries in the British Empire. The Trust House people with their Forte partners unleashed a Trust fund for improvements; they also brought in General Manager John Donnithorne, one of the most gifted Trustees on the chain's roster, as its helmsman. Façade recently painted; lobby and public rooms freshened, with more updatings to come; extensive recarpeting; maze-like corridors, a result of linking 11 townhouses together to create this composite; older units beautified, given Edwardian-style wardrobes, and homey profiles; 142 rooms and 5 suites; 70% bath ratio; an overall feeling of slow-motion activity among antebellum furnishings. Almost all accommodations are comfortable and the baths include some very nice touches indeed; its price scale makes it one of the best upper-crust bargains in London today. Improving steadily and now recommended.

Dukes, St. James's Place, S.W.1: This 1908 model has been fitted out to recapture the gaslight-era clatter of horseless carriages over its cobblestone court. Wrought-iron entrance; clubby brown and green lobby; tiny leather bar; St. James's restaurant with moderately priced, reasonably varied menu. Total of 52 tiny fiefs (29 named for illustrious duchies), some of which are in a separate enclave; soft, earth-tone carpeting; bath, telephone, TV, 3-channel radio; suites sweetened with fireplaces, fully equipped kitchens, scales, and even electric toothbrushes. Manager Proquitte's crisp staff not only will try to address you by name, Milord, but will stock your castle with fresh flowers, a salver of fruit, and a warmed copy of the *Times*. Its rates are extremely reasonable for its value, provided you don't mind the paltry space in some of its dukedoms. A quiet, dignified, and charming monument to another day.

Ritz, Piccadilly, W.1: Many U.S. readers and Londoners vilify it. Other travelers—from how it appears to us, a distinct minority—view it as St. Peter's sacred gift to innkeeping. It has just been taken over by a group that intends to enhance its luster and add sparkle to its marketing approach. Grandly conceived main floor with pillared corridors, chandeliered lobby, palm-court lounge for tea-timing, and huge, column-lined rotunda dining salon displaying gilded garlands of laurel; many upstairs rooms equally sumptuous and spacious, with satin spreads on brass beds; deep-pile flowered carpeting; enormous fixtures in baths that are reminiscent of your rich grandma's house; others dingy and unimaginative, in our rueful view; kind attention by floor personnel who are nearly all old-liners; indifferent-to-haughty reception crew, according to a growing pile of Guidester complaints; less helpful Hall Porters, on our recent test encounter. The cookery? Wildly divergent opinions from residents and wayfarers continue. If you like this aging veteran, naturally you're the decision-maker, but as far as we're concerned we'll wait until the promised revisions by its new owners have been effected before passing judgment.

Hyde Park, Knightsbridge, S.W.1: Here the Trust Houses Forte organization has taken this former Victorian mastodon under its wing and, as easily as we mix a metaphor, it is turning this once-molting relic into a slicker chick. You'll find an invigorated lounge with comfortable black-leather banquettes, a face-lifted adjoining writing room, the classic mulberry-and-purple-toned dining salon with French windows facing the park, a tavern-style Grill down one flight, and the rather plain Horseshoe Bar also down at hoof level. This one has a tutti-frutti mixture of 200 bedchambers; our favorite is #504-508, a redone corner suite with a canary and turquoise sitting room. Most of the changes here have been and will continue to be in conservative taste; the architect's biggest advantage, however, is in the availability of ample living space. Not flashy, but intimately more solid in its division.

Park Lane, Piccadilly, W.1: After deteriorating rather sadly, some of this mainliner's historic urbanity has been recaptured—only *some,* however in our renewed opinion. It still has a long Park Lane to hoe. Here's a thoroughly mixed bag which, unless soon revivified, might be in danger of becoming simply an *old* bag. Guidesters generally either love it or loathe it. Personally, we are no longer among its fans.

May Fair, Berkeley St., W.1: There is a busy commercial air about this one augmented by a package-group personality. Still, the accommodations are adequate and amply sized, and the staff are pleasant. The Beachcomber Restaurant and bar add some color (even though we prefer Trader Vic's in the Hilton); the Candlelight Room doesn't impress us too much. Basically sound and fundamentally agreeable, but there are many others we enjoy more.

Charing Cross, Strand, W.C.2: This adjunct to Trafalgar Square couldn't be more central if it tried. Strangely enough, the Charing Cross Station-side rooms are quieter than those fronting on the busy street. Some updatings from *tempus-to-tempus;* newish entrance; 100% bath ratio; 5th and 6th floors clinical but viewful; prices modest and in line with the rewards. For reasonable space in what impresses us as a Formica-lined barn, here 'tis.

De Vere, De Vere Gardens, W.8: Our overnight here not long ago was a disappointing experience. Manager B. R. Constable wrote us afterwards that many changes would bring new graces to its doorstep. We hope so, but on our 2 follow-up inspections (incognito, of course) we could find spare evidence of what we think we should experience as a fully satisfied customer. Perhaps more updatings are in the pipeline.

CONTEMPORARY HOTELS:

Inn on the Park, Park Lane, W.1: Canada's sumptuous bid for the well-heeled wanderer is poised in splendor on a triangle of 14-karat real estate across from the Hilton. Its small but richly appointed lobby has wood paneling, crystal illumination, sandy-beige marble flooring, and a tooled leather table where guests sit, rather than stand, to register. Secluded enclave of shops; mezzanine dining complex composed of the window-lined Four Seasons Restaurant (vast menu at reasonable prices) and bar; the modern-lined Vintage Grill; the pin-lit, rouge-hued bar-lounge; and a glass-sheathed, cool room for wines and foods. Two sizes of twin-occupancy accommodations with the slightly more expensive billets by far the better ones; Empire furnishings in blue, ocher, or brown schemes; TV's set into stately highboys; single-basin marblesque baths. Its 20 suites vary in motif and mood while their prices are universally stratospheric; occasionally the sitting rooms are disproportionately better than the sleeping segments. Very costly, very appealing to the eye—and especially liked by rich, sophisticated, spirited clientele.

Park Tower, Knightsbridge, S.W.1: Here's an import from Canada, a slice of blue from the same Skyline group that operates our leading Heathrow Airport entry (below). Cylindrical, 18-story concrete-and-glass building affording all-around restful views of Hyde Park; wide bay windows; impressive travertine lobby enriched with wood, modern tapestries, orange-textiled furniture, metal sculpture, and cunning illumination; starburst rotunda lounge with a colossal flower-filled copper vat as its centerpiece; darkly inviting Henry VIII Grill with brick dividers, heavy chairs, diptych menus, and pewter settings; spring-daubed Le Café Jardin coffee shop (also called "Trianon") in dusty rose and grass green. Crowning this galaxy of public rooms and its powerful towerful of 300 superb bedchambers is the stunningly panoramic Top of the Park lounge which no sybaritic nature lover should miss. To some it may seem flamboyant, or ostentatious, or even overwhelming. We are betting, however, that most registrants (many of them Middle Eastern jillionaires) will find the comfort so abundant, the attention so wholehearted, and the concept so fresh that they will enjoy every facet of this well-staged production.

The **Churchill**, 30 Portman Sq., W.1: Loew, the American movie moguls, raised the curtain on a 500-room London premiere. The Adam-inspired lobby is an immediate indicator of this new era in mass-minded innkeeping; we were instantly struck by the fact that as many as 1000 souls can live here at the same time. With predictable silver-screen audacity, the public rooms have been dressed out for costume roles: The Number Ten Dining Room with tented eaves and a leopard-spot carpet (a godsend to clumsy waiters); the Bar surrounded by Japanese murals; the Greenery Coffee Shop dominated by a tiled niche and a porcelain fountain; and the Regency Lounge (sunken, *mais oui*). Dynamic General Manager Gordon Webb and kindhearted Reception Chief Kelegerides have an enormous plant with which to work; we don't envy them their inevitable headaches in getting an enterprise of this magnitude on rails. Service is currently its haunting concern. We wish it "V" for victory.

The brand-new, air-conditioned, sparkling-bright **Intercontinental** resides in the same convenient hotel cluster as the Hilton, the Inn on the Park, and other top-line contemporary stalwarts. The coolness of its entrance and lobby belie the easy grace, the rich colorations, and the luxurious comfort provided by its bedchambers. Interior, somewhat stuffy Le Soufflé reataurant in dusty-rouge tones; Coffee House for all-hour snacks and breakfast; viewful 7th-floor discothèque in *art rétro*, for sipping and dancing; griddle-hot sauna and cool-off pool with ever-friendly Ted at the valves (available for massage); excellent beauty salon and barber; select boutiques; underground parking. You'll find wonderfull shaggy textiles, stocked Frigobar, radio, color TV with provision for in-house showing of first-run films, and the usual scanty IHC bathroom—a design borne of this chain's evident conviction that human beings all are descended from Lilliputians. The better, costlier units face Hyde Park (with the dual-glaze windows shut, they are quiet); extra-light sleepers may opt for a vistaless courtside address. Veteran Director Max Blouet, 74, was summoned to inaugurate this 500-room show; skilled and amiable General Manager Graham Jeffrey carries the fire and professional knowhow to keep it ticking smoothly on a day-to-night basis; Chief Concierge Denicolo is another reliable name on the roster. In spite of its youthfulness, which inevitably bedevils earlybird patrons, our just-ended fortnight could hardly have been better or more pleasurable. Off to a splendid start! Let's see how it goes.

Athenaeum, Piccadilly, W.4: Our first impression of this patrician was that we were looking at a smaller (100-room) version of our first choice in this category—a sort of Innlet on the Park. If there can be such a thing as no-nonsense beauty, this Rank-run, first-rank hostelry has it. The restaurant is called "The Restaurant"; the bar is called "The Bar"; the appointments are tiptop in quality, bright with floral patterns, and selected for restful color blends. Spiced as it is with piquant discernment, we could only guess that discriminating clientele will love it. As one might expect, the tariffs are pretty zesty, too. Not for any old (or young) run-of-the-millionaire, but for those who sincerely cherish subdued graciousness.

London Hilton, Park Lane, W.1: Not to be confused with its new, lower-cost, Kensington cousin, this transplant of purebred Americana cracked out of its shell bright and sassy in '63. Frenzied lobby atmosphere bustling with U.S. colonists, conventioneers (there's even a Business Firm Service Desk), seas of conducted tour trippers, and hypertense gumchewers; 4 restaurants, including a handsome roof plateau for dining and supper dancing, and a downstairs Trader Vic's Polynesian thatchery (miserable!); popular Scandinavian Sandwich Shop with Wiinblad porcelains atwinkle; 5 bars, plus the sip-and-dance 007 nightclub; underground parking for 350 cars; every unit with radio and TV; one Y-shape wing houses studio-style accommodations only. In all but a few the décor follows a Eurasian theme; bedchambers are generally large, gracious, comfortable, and have thoughtfully executed closet space; well-designed bathrooms. Here, in general, is perhaps the closest version of a "hotel machine" that America could export.

Montcalm, Great Cumberland Place, W.1H.: If you have a passion for brown, here is your own true love. Sand, beige, sable, fawn, sorrel, umber, cocoa, chestnut—you'll find them all within these precincts. Well, what's dun is dun. Most of the ground-floor walls are upholstered in suede; furnishings are in leather; even the elevator has kidding around it; baths are carpeted; rooms have ice-water taps, back-lit mirrors, and thermal controls. Suites feature spiral staircases and attractive 1½-story windows; ordinary twins are not spacious, but they are passable if your stay isn't a long one. We wonder if you will agree with us that the restaurant's portraits are so awful that they border on the comic. The staff couldn't be nicer; the service is gracious; we liked it in most regards.

Westbury, New Bond St., W.1: This Knott Corporation house, inaugurated in '55 and billed as the "first American hotel in London," has mellowed and matured impressively. A crippling lack of space—the biggest bugaboo in former years—cunningly has been alleviated by ripping out hundreds of built-in, floor-to-ceiling, room-consuming cupboards and replacing them with slim-line but sufficient-size dressers. The closet areas have been rearranged; basic reds, blues, and greens also lend an eye-expanding illusion; the baths remain bruisingly narrow-sided. It is convenient for shopping and theater going. Still not the wide open spaces, but much, much improved and now recommended.

Royal Garden, Kensington High St., W.8: This 500-room, T-shape giant opened in '65 on a 1-acre site overlooking Kensington Gardens and Hyde Park. Much of its physical plant is well designed, comfortable, and appealing to the eye, including the revamped Royal Roof and Garden Room dining dens and bar; all upstairs nests have been refeathered with bright new tweeds and convenient telephone stands; during our peek, tour groups were homing in like swallows returning to you-know-where. So many reports from Guidesters wail about the staff attitudes that once again service remains a big ???.

The Gloucester, Harrington Gardens, S.W.7: What Rank Hotels believed it could do in a small way with the previously mentioned, 100-room Athenaeum, it has repeated with nearly as much style in this grander, splashier, zippy 571-unit star-spangled spectacular. The spatial concepts are so cleverly executed that the untrained observer could scarcely guess that a thousand souls are sharing his address. Fresh lobby arcade rising to a mezzanine level; clubby Grill; sumptuous lounge; Le Château Wine Bar (upstairs portion with tables; cellar section with counter libations), a very popular fad in present-day London; sauna; hairdressing facilities for men and women. The accommodations, though extremely well equipped, seemed rather spare in dimensions. The prices, however, are in the medium range while the rewards nudge firmly into luxury levels.

Curzon, Stanhope Row, Park Lane, W.1.: Tucked into a handy cul-de-sac shouldering the Hilton, this little entry and the **Londonderry**, Park Lane, W.1, which is across the street from the Hilton, used to be excellent bright-eyed tykes which we recommended. Our enthusiasm has declined to a yawn. Now both are quite poor, in our opinion, for their highish tabs.

Royal Lancaster, Hyde Park, W.2: This 400-room, 18-story gong-beater for the booming Rank organization made its bow in 1967. The lobby now boasts the addition of Hal's Bar; the Beefeater Restaurant has a moss-green carpet, mellow yellows, and spring-like tones to complement the branch-top vistas from its wide windows; the Mediterranean Café features a lovely centerpiece pillar forming a ceramic tree; the Pub glows with burgundy undertones. The viewful premium bedrooms come with grass-fiber wall coverings, raw-silk spreads, terrific music-news-and-TV consoles, and such thoughtful fillips as fresh flowers in a vase beside the bathtub and, under the sprinkler, a tiny mirror at shower-cap height for ladies. Very amiable and able staff; management now in the hands of Jonathan Dale-Roberts; excellent parking facilities; among the gilt-edged peerage in its prices.

Carlton Tower, Sloane St., S.W.1: This 18-story U.S. export, offering 307 rooms with bath, shower, TV, and radio, opened in '61. Bedrooms in restful gray, gold, and other soft tones; attractive public rooms, including cleverly illuminated lobby in tile, marble, and wood, and 2 knockout dining rooms. But the sleeping accommodations are so small that Mr. Pullman would give their designer a medal. In our size 11's, we paced off a single to the guess-and-God measurements of 10 x 12 feet—a disgrace at the stadium-size price level. All in all, we're surprised that either its builders or its later owners would condone such a frugal policy in this high-price unit. Ground-floor Rib Room, rich-looking in a ruby haze, serves an 11-ounce, diet-busting monolith of yumptious roast beef, a baked potato, and a big salad bowl for a very reasonable outlay. Substantial, especially for small-boned pilgrims.

The **Bristol**, 1 Berkeley St., W1X 6NE: This 200-unit entry, set only a block from Piccadilly Circus smack in the center of the West End's choicest shops, was built on the site of the prestigious "old" Berkeley. Clean-lined marble-and-wood reception and foyer; costly and suave white-and-gold Louis XV restaurant; adjoining cream and green cocktail area tinkling with pianotations; Eden-like florist displays burgeoning near entrance; superconvenient underground parking pad; round-the-clock room service; efficient, friendly staff; tiptop Hall Portering by amiable Ted Cooper. The sancta cunningly complement the downstairs French theme: Most are expansively proportioned (ask for a large unit); they are provided with unobtrusive twentieth-century gadgets that His Most Gracious Majesty, King Louis, would have swapped his best coach to possess. We've just spent a week here and found it to be a quietly tasteful charmer in every respect.

The **Portman**, 22 Portman Sq., W.1: This British Airways-Intercontinental speedster landed 2 blocks from Marble Arch in '71. Hangar-like lobby less ingratiating than cabins at loftier altitudes; Captain's Galley providing in-flight comestibles around the clock; runway-level Rôtisserie Normande offering Gallic fillips in an ambitious menu; alfresco terrace for teaing-off when the visibility is unlimited; Captain's Bar instrumented for piano-accompanied refueling; hairdresser, barber, boutiques, garage, and other support elements flying in tight formation. Accommodations are stacked in 2 carefully controlled towers, one with 85 compact solo units, the other with 175 tandems and 16 suites; accouterments come standardized and include TV and air cooling plus generously proportioned closets and baths. We think this swept-wing bird is right on course.

The Selfridge, Orchard St., W.1.: If shopping is your bag, what better shopping bag could you fill but Selfridges? This one is tucked right into the middle of the famous department store. Handsome wood, glass, and burnished-metal entry and foyer; paneled lounge; cobble-paved Fletcher's Restaurant with a vendor's barrow of garden produce to tempt incomers; charming oaken Stoves Bar recalling the days of Dickens; chipper Victorian Picnic Basket coffee shop open from 7 A.M. to 1 A.M. Its 330 units feature room-wide windows which provide an impression of space when, in fact, little exists. Fitted Empire furniture enhances the clever maximizing of minimum dimensions. Very appealing in general and reasonably priced, but if you do a lot of purchasing, don't drag the packages back to your narrow digs.

Portobello, 22 Stanley Gardens, W.11: This 20-room, 5-suite sweetie is just plain fun. A handsome pair of Victorian homes have been joined in harmonious wedlock by Tim and Cathy Herring, an affable, young, and talented couple who enjoy the self-same status. Palms abound, cheer pervades, and good taste is in evidence down to the smallest detail. Its main drawback is in the miniature baths, which really are too small for sultans of ablution. Artfully chic clientele who enjoy its special élan and off-beat personality.

Penta, Cromwell Rd., S.W.7: Almost adjoining the West End Terminal, this jumbo, piloted by Grand Metropolitan Hotels, is owned by a consortium of international airlines and banks. It is zooming toward success not only because of the jet thrust from its sponsors, but because it is a model of what keen administration, smart budgeting, and shrewd architecture can do. As one simple example, the pictures in the lounge, which people seldom study carefully, are all colorful but inexpensive prints in nice frames, but the chairs in the Pub of Pubs, which you will touch and linger in, are upholstered in the finest polished leather. While the bedrooms are cramped (the brochure is a triumphant illustration of what a wide-angle lens can do for a microscopic subject), the prices are at bedrock level for these cheerful surroundings. On balance, we give it high marks for its unabashed production-line concept.

Cavendish, Jermyn St., S.W.1: Speaking of airliners and airlines, here is a 255-unit, "First-class" (not "Deluxe") midtowner that bears a striking resemblance to our own Pan American Building on Park Avenue in Manhattan. Personable Manager Mereweather is a gracious and capable host. Attractive public rooms including the 24-hour Ribblesdale Restaurant, dark-tone Sub Rosa Bar (named after the original Cavendish's famed Rosa Lewis), and mezzanine lounge-bar; sensible distribution of accommodations, with a smattering of penthouse suites and doubles, normal twins in 2 distinct styles, and lookalike singles. All bedchambers with tiny baths, bedside radio and TV controls; limited luggage space; building-wide fresh-air ventilation; poor pressing service; round-the-clock laundry at standard town prices (a considerable saving); only continental breakfast or snacks served in the rooms. We prefer nests ending in "21." Its simple, clean-lined efficiency is almost Scandinavian in tone.

The Holiday Inn-keepers recently made a 3-point landing in London and its environs. The one carrying the company's green-and-yellow banner into the dogfight at Heathrow is described with its airport competitors at the end of this section. Following are our evaluations of both city entries:

Marble Arch Holiday Inn, George St., W.1: Since this house is more conveniently sited than its crosstown counterpart (see below), its designers opted for fewer frills as inducement to register; the accent is therefore on functional simplicity. Sedate restaurant effectively employing ersatz foliage and clever lighting; plain-as-plain coffee shop encased in green tiles; Tyburn Bar with soft illumination and possibly the most tiddily low-backed chairs on which we've lately tippled; heated pool and sauna gurgling and steaming underground; parking for 100 autos. The 240 pads, all tastefully toned in blue, pink, and beige, come with either 1 or 2 double beds, bath and shower, phone, radio, color TV, individual climate control, and other standard Inn-ovations. One of the better-forged of this firm's foreign links.

Swiss Cottage Holiday Inn, King Henry's Rd., N.W.3: Sorry, but this one is not an Alpine chalet lifted lock, stock, and yodel from Zermatt. Instead it's named after its neighborhood, which nudges suburban Hampstead and is a 10-minute tube toot from Action Central. Architecture and décor? Arabesque, with persistent use of arches, vaulting, tiles, and carpets. Henry VIII Restaurant, overlooking a garden, tuned more to Aladdin's taste than that of the rotund royalist; attractive King Henry Bar, studded with director's chairs and potted palmery, a short swizzle from the indoor pool; soft-drink and free-ice machines stationed like stoic sentinels on each floor. All 300 chambers duel with the din on 2 main arteries; all sport goatee-sized balconettes, reasonable closet, bureau, and breathing space, and the other standard amenities of these stops. The slightly lower tabs here, versus those of its downtown cousin, can be nullified with the flick of a taxi flag. Moor-or-less too far out in too many ways.

Britannia, Grosvenor Sq., W.1: This relative newcomer is set back in a brick-lined courtyard directly across from the U.S. Embassy. The handsome exterior is far better than the 436 inner sancta, in our opinion. Fresh-from-the-sticks migrations of bug-eyed package groups milling in the lobby on our visit; others occupying every chair in anticipation of some miraculous "happening" —or even a punctual tour guide; rows of shops; a pub nestling in one bin; dining room pulsing with trippers; food not inviting to our eye (our taster didn't sample the wares); Regency Bar not aged in bond; spooky-red, leather-sheathed elevators. Bedchambers with darkwood furniture, predominantly blue-and-green textiles, radio-TV-clock combo, direct-dial phones, and elbow-battering baths that are miniaturized even in the suites. In general, it is well laid out but drearily executed by the decorators.

Royal Kensington, Kensington High St., W. 14: This once-proud entry now seem to be skidding, in our opinion. Its far-out location also is not in its favor. Handy TWA terminal at ground elevation; no lobby to speak of; squeezed-up reception cabin; Beef Encounter Restaurant; l'Apéritif and Cockpit Bars; Coffee Shop; stylings based upon a fine Scandinavian sensitivity for color and texture, but the housekeeping standards now are so scandalous, in our view, that we cannot recommend it until it picks up its socks.

Europa, Grosvenor Square, W.1: This 273-room, giant Georgian sentinel is a typical product of modern-day market research. It is designed almost exclusively for tours; furniture and fabrics are precisely the same throughout; living space and staff attention are both in short supply; rates are steepish. All-in-all, no great shakes.

Lowndes, 19–21 Lowndes St., S.W.1: This 80-chamber monument to quiet elegance, set practically around the corner from Harrods and other chic emporia, could, with sharper administration, be one of the stars of the luxury galaxy. Our recent stay here, however, was a disappointment, owing to what we considered poor maintenance and slack service attitudes—all at whiplash price tags, too. What a pity, since it has such a fine location and so much potential.

Howard, Temple Place, W.C.2: From its perch on the Strand, this deluxe newcomer overlooks the Thames. Same administration as Lowndes; eighteenth-century décor; 150 bedrooms; penthouse suites; Quai d'Or French restaurant; terraced apron of gardens. Let's hope the management grooms this pacer better than it does its above harness mate.

Kennedy, Cardington St., N.W.1: This 207-roomer boasts many vote-getting awards and a few lost precincts that could be serious handicaps. It is convenient to Euston Station, nicely situated beside St. James's Gardens, but huddled neglectedly in a metropolitan backwater that we doubt many travelers will like. Okay for its moderate tabs, however.

Imperial, Russell Sq., W.C.1: This 461-cell pueblo, adjoining and in the same consortium as the President (see below), won't ever be a worry to the Savoy chain. Entrance cupped in a fountain court; s-p-a-a-a-a-c-i-o-u-s lobby pointing clients to cubicles in 3 wings; mass-production dining room; achingly tiny bedchambers outfitted with what appeared to us to be box-crate furnishings of the cheapest order; unbelievably cramped baths in which the w.c.'s and bidets are separated from the basins. This big boy is *really* tuned in on the jumbo era. Imperial? Not in our forum.

President, Russell Square, W.C.1: This 7-story candidate, inaugurated with 200 units and 246 more now added, was a lame duck for us until we saw the results of its reelection campaign. All of its formerly miserable rooms now spruced up with gold and brown carpeting, fresh wallpaper, and lively curtains; remodeled dining room toned in a salmon-and-moss-green color scheme; quick-service, saw-toothed counter also available. If the bathrooms and elfin tubs are brought up to current standards we'll predict that this President will win a 3rd term.

Bedford, Southampton Row, W.C.1: Here's what might be dubbed a 180-room Vice President. Same pattern of its busy-busy carpet; similarly conceived lounge and dining room, but pleasant garden adjoins; minuscule bathrooms with separate toilet; closets (this time not water) also mite-y small. Also routine, except for its friendly staff.

Washington, 6 Curzon St., W.1: As an importation of American hotel technique, 60% enlarged by a streamlined wing, for us it still doesn't come off. Neither does the staff, who seemed to prefer being elsewhere. The public rooms have been redecorated and air-conditioned; ground floor, including the tangerine lounge and a quartet of banquet salons, enlarged and perked up; Hussar Bar uncorked; a flock of bedchamber renewals now so worn and battered that the Salvation Army might refuse them as a gift; to our eyes, the newer wing is miserable in space and appointments; the glass-mosaic-aluminum-and-tubular-chair motif strikes us, at least, as being more at home in Pittsburgh than in Old Lady London. Not for us in this flavorful capital, but perhaps you'll disagree.

Bloomsbury Centre, Coram St., W.C.1: Here's a lackluster commercial pod that occupies part of an office building near Russell Square. In our professional judgment, this dreary number is better suited to traveling salesmen than holidaymakers. Its late-blossoming sister operation, the **Regent Centre** near Regent's Park, peeps from its garden with 350 budrooms—each cross-pollinated to resemble the original plant. Same ownership for both.

Uncle Conrad's 2nd London venture, the 610-room **Kensington Hilton** (way out on Holland Park Ave., near Shepherd's Bush) is offered to Hiltonians at nearly ⅓rd off the the deluxe rates of the Park Lane entry. While it is handsomely decorated in richly textured materials, the location is unfortunate because today's taxi fares can push daily expenditures up to top-line levels. If, however, you don't mind using public transport, the subway (tube) and bus stops are practically at your doorstep. Buff brick facade; Nipponese restaurant; weekly medieval feasts planned in the Tudor Tavern; individually adjustable thermostats in all units; likewise refrigerator/bar and color TV. Very well presented; here's a concept which we laud. The question is, will the public buy it?

Cunard steamed up with bunk space for 1300 mariners moored far out on Talgarth Road. Even though it strains to incorporate a maritime theme, the project is so group oriented that we found nary a trace of personality. The 826-bedchamber **Tower** on St. Katharine's Way reflects all of the charm of the World Trade Center it was meant to complement. This whopper is one of the largest in the British Isles. Not for this congressman. Finally, the economy-priced **Metropole**, on Edgware Road near Marble Arch, counts a mere 555 accommodations. The entrance is so awkward for motorists that they would find it much easier to drive only to the back portals. We like the efforts made here to stoke up decorative warmth in the public rooms. The sleepers, however, remain little more than body-size cubicles. The **Royal National** opened its 350 units recently; it functions chiefly for groups. Reasonable prices; reasonable rewards.

ASSORTED HOTELS:

Here is a grab bag that we won't even attempt to classify. Some of its entries are big, some tiny, some brand-new, some with a sprinkling of modernizations, some ancient and flavorful, some downright decrepit. Because of these myriad variables and the added factor of personal taste which would make one house appealing to one traveler and absolutely hideous to another, we will only describe them briefly and let you be the judge. Now let's pull open the strings and see what we've snared. . . . or, what's snared us!

Capital, Basil St., S.W.3: Our recent week's sojourn here couldn't have been smoother in comfort, service, cuisine, and midtown convenience (only a few steps from Harrods). The restaurant, not particularly strong on eye appeal, has generated a mighty following of culinary loyalists among London's well-heeled cognoscenti; we must count ourselves among the chef's disciples. No real lobby to speak of, merely a Hall Porter's desk and reception counter staffed by smiling professionals; cozy-corner bar; vaguely French bedchamber décor employing blond-wood furniture and cream-yellow color trends; compact, efficient baths; no historic or sylvan vistas from any of its

60 windows. For the outlay, we think it is one of the best buys in the dwelling-space market of Olde London Towne. Warmly recommended for metropolophiles.

Chesterfield, 34 Charles St., W.1: Here's another youngster with flair. It comprises the union of 2 old houses, incorporating charm, varilevel stair climbing, nice rooms, a Buttery spread with reasonable food buys, and a restaurant that glows with a Regency tradition. It has a distinctive character that many will praise. We are among them. Very central.

Dolphin Square, Chichester St., S.W.1: Here, to us at least, is the stop which offers the *very* best value for the traveler's £ in today's London. It is one of the 2 largest blocks of apartments outside of the United States and the Soviet Union. A total of 1050 privately leased units are contained in a quadrangle of houses, each named after a British naval personage. Rodney House is the operative nexus and the site for 150 transient accommodations, available by the day, week, or month. Quiet, convenient location; Hall Porter, Reception, Key and Cashier counters; extraordinarily well planned and executed shopping arcade, with grocer, liquor store, baker, butcher, fruiterer, druggist, stationer-newsvendor, hairdresser, and bank concentrated in 1 corridor (plus a valet-laundry service in the basement); overlooking the heated indoor pool is a pleasant, popular-price restaurant open from 7:30 A.M. to midnight 7 days a week; 2 bars; 8 squash courts; Finnish log saunas for boys and girls; 350-car underground garage; travel bureau cum theater-ticket agency; attractive gardens; 26 automatic elevators. Not long ago more than $1,000,000 was spent for improvements. Here's the structural breakdown: Approximately 25 three-room apartments; 100 two-room apartments; 25 one-room apartments; 30 so-called Guest Rooms for younger, hardier voyagers (public toilets and tubs). Tabs amazingly low for the value; discounts usually given for stays of a week or more; most accommodations fully equipped with kitchenette (stove, refrigerator, sink, linens, dishes, glasses, table silver, etc.); TV installed upon request for a small additional charge; free maid service 6 days per week (and what a fine, friendly corps they are!). Units ending in "25" are very good, as are the "03's" and "16's". Extra beds or cots can be provided at nominal cost. Pets are banned—but this is unimportant, since Fido or Pussy must spend eons in quarantine before being admitted to Britain. Here is one enormous advantage: *You can bring along your wife, and the savings effected in 11 days by both of you in Dolphin Square over your otherwise lonely single in any of London's Deluxe hotels will more than pay for her scheduled airline transatlantic transportation.* To any money-minded pilgrim who wants to play house in tranquillity and comfort, with every imaginable facility available by telephone, our highest recommendation.

White House, Albany St., N.W.1: This former apartment-style abode was transformed into a medium-budget hotel. Oval lobby retained but now crammed with kiosks and vitrines; elbow-to-elbow restaurant currently floating over the former pool; chophouse cooking where that eatery originally stood; sharply angular bar presently red-faced and, to us, uncozy. Of the rooms that had been redecorated by our visit, all reflected a Danish air; each contained a small sitting area, condensed narrow beds, a pair of chairs, a small TV table, and tiny, bare-ly tolerable baths. If the present administration continues to improve its current platform, this conveniently situated, bargain-priced White House should be worthy of many a term in office.

The **Stafford**, St. James's Place, S.W.1: This entry is a converted manse tucked away in a little mews. In tone it resembles Brown's, one of our favorite "traditional" candidates; today it sparkles with renewed vigor, perfect maintenance, and a distinctive personality that evokes the flavor of fine English values. Handy location that is quiet, though the house is merely 100 yards from Piccadilly; private-homelike lounge; expanded dining salon; graceful bar (from which, it is vowed, the first martini was exported to the Colonies); classical décor; 47 ample-size units, all with bath; not for bargain hunters. Definitely for the discriminating.

St. George's, Langham Place, W.1: Somewhat remote situation, but easily (and economically) within reach of the visceral midsections of the city; split-personality building shared with B.B.C. headquarters (a boon for communications types); ground-floor entrance; 14th-story lobby; adjoining panoramic Octave Restaurant (à la carte and ooolala for cuisine); bar-lounge combination; all units with truly spectacular townscape vistas through huge full-wall windows. The accommodation we are crazy about is the so-called Bed-Sitting Room, which is enormous and plushly outfitted. Highly recommended in its upper-medium category.

Elizabetta, Cromwell Rd., S.W.5: This debutante came out in '72, but has aged rapidly since that bright day, we are sad to report. Bustling, relatively far-out location one block from the British Airways West Terminal; boxy, 7-tiered exterior; silver slipper-sized bar-lounge star-studded with red, black, and gold damask-like wallpaper plus gilded candelabra and sconces; miniaturized restaurant with Middle Eastern cuisine. Recently it changed hands, so perhaps it will take a while longer to recapture some of that early charm.

The **Chelsea**, Sloane St., W.1: This 220-unit midtowner features a swimming pool in its courtyard overlooked by the Bohemian Bar and the blue-and-leather-toned France & Choiseul Restaurant. Unfortunately, here is another quick starter that has faded in the stretch. Vaulted coffee den plus wine bar; 4 penthouse suites; 100-car parking spread (what a blessing in this eye of the traffic typhoon). Room-width windows with no special views on the lower floors; book away from Sloane St. if you insist on quiet. What a dream house this could be, in our opinion, if the whole operation were tauter.

Wilbraham, Wilbraham Place, S.W.1: This neighbor is older in style but fresh in appearance. Le Beurre Fondue restaurant and the intimate lounges provide their own brand of cozyness. Varying assortment of 57 rooms, 34 with bath; substantial and nice as a London town house. Prices are surprisingly low for the reward.

Kensington Palace, De Vere Gardens, W.8: This house is still moving up the ladder; the results we've seen are heartening indeed. Lobby tastefully restyled and air-conditioned; lounge shifted; coffee shop bubbling from 7 A.M. to 12:30 A.M.; good maintenance; heavy business from conducted tours. About ¼ th of its accommodations in dismal studio motif; conventional twins much better by comparison; nearly all sleeping space revamped. Not Deluxe, but a fair-enough First-class bet if you draw a refeathered nest.

Piccadilly, Piccadilly, W.1: Now for a house which gives its guests a ringside seat at the Circus that puts shoppers right in the limey-light. It revamped baths or added them where none existed previously; it also reupholstered the furniture à la 16-Ounce Boxing Glove. Old-stock, traditional lobby; large, comfortable rooms as British as plum duff; bid for the quieter rear side. Rates? Its bloated price for doubles strikes us as being almost as overstuffed as its sofas. Late reader reports fairly froth with rage about the reception, Hall Porter's desk, and general staff attitudes. These are, however, in tune with the Broadwayesque nature of the plant and its clientele. Far from the dilly-of-the-pick.

Royal Trafalgar, Whitcomb St., W.C.2: This 110-box bastion of busily bounding barnstormers, tucked behind its namesake square, is excellently positioned for addicted sightseers—but that's about that, as far as we're concerned. Tiny lobby where we saw throngs almost as dense as Attila's troops; Angus Steak House concession plus Battle of Trafalgar Pub for beefing and brewing. All rooms seem to have been thoughtfully proportioned so that guests can reach almost anything from dead center; all come with bath, radio, TV, and round-the-clock service. Here, to us, is a strictly commercial, unpretentious shelter reasonably priced for what it offers. Revamping plans soon may alter it appreciably.

Leinster Towers, a community of several former houses, offers 165 accommodations under one roof. Hodgepodge interior; Gilded Cage basement restaurant with bargain-basement décor on our last peek awhile back; all units with weensie private baths and ⅔rds with cooking facilities; possibly the narrowest beds we've seen since Fort Bragg. Better for lean, long-residing dwarfs than for normally proportioned overnight visitors, in our estimation. Too costly in comparison with the comforts of many similar hostelries.

The **Ryan**, Gwynne Pl., Kings Cross Rd., W.C.1: This typical Ryan's Daughter resides 5 minutes from the calamitous cacophonics of Kings Cross Station on a site that's inconvenient for wheel-less nomads. Block-long structure; twinkling Irish colleens at reception; longish lounge, restaurant, and Victorian Bar; 215 billets (some family units) with bath, central heating, phone, radio, and TV. Because its accent is so strong on group traffic, and since its tabs nudge those of the Holiday Inn at Swiss Cottage, we are compelled to nominate this transplanted Dubliner as a strictly overnight stop.

Strand Palace, Strand, W.C.2, **Regent Palace**, Piccadilly Circus, W.1: Chrome steel, imitation leather, typically modern-American in motif. If you like the sterile, brash surroundings of the Edison in New York or the Baker in Dallas, these 2 are for you.

Cumberland, Marble Arch, W.1: Here is a one-price, glacially commercial house for the tourist on a budget. American-style service; barnlike Carvery restaurant, with meats and chef searing in the middle of the room; skull-throbbing public-address system eternally bleating in the lobby; a fat piece of change gives you a depressingly barebones single with bath; some readers have squawked about allegedly callous reservations attitude. The upkeep is good, but this frenetic ant colony is totally impersonal.

International, Cromwell Rd., S.W.5, opposite the British Airways West Terminal: Although this 425-compartment jumbo took off in '70, to us it looked as if it might have been hauling cargoes of kangaroos from the Outback during the past few seasons. Cavernous marble lobby; Cavalier Room and Cromwell Coffee Shop for pack'em-stack'em feedings; Stuart Bar, a dimly lighted water hole; small, modernistic yet seemingly ill-kempt cages while we were there. Sadly, here is one to Buck, in our Beatty-eyed view.

Post House, Bayswater Rd., W.2, operated by the Trust Houses Forte organization, has completed its expansion and modernization with grim results, say we. Too bad because we once liked it very much. The nearby **Embassy** (150 Bayswater Rd., W.2) blends modernisms with period themes in a happy meld of 2 distinct ideas. The medium tariffs and the all-out effort of the staff on our recent visit make us think that foreign envoys will enjoy being in its diplomatic circle. The **Averard** (Lancaster Gate, W.2) seems to be slipping, in our opinion; mainly for the bargain hunter. **Mt. Royal** (Marble Arch, W.1) is a commercial colossus of 695 identical shoe-boxy cubicles, all with bath, telephone, and radio. An up-only escalator rises from the street to the lobby; functionality on every hand, by the factory load; so-so maintenance; swarming with tour groups. The **Londoner** (Welbeck St., W.1), is less frenetic but just as mercantile. Black and white marble lobby with steel trim, reminiscent of your familiar First National Bank; downstairs Four Seasons restaurant; 125 rooms and baths, all reasonably sized and modern if not worn in tone; 4 suites; front accommodations noisy. The **Waldorf** (Aldwych, W.C.2) was renewed in a quasi-Edwardian fashion. It seemed very expensive for the value; moreover, we're not too fond of the Covent Garden district for residential purposes. The **Ramada** (20 Chesham Pl., S.W.1) strikes us as being an old Jekyll in a new Hyde. Neither pelt thrills us, however. **Harrington Hall**, about 15 minutes from Piccadilly in Harrington Gardens, which we stumbled across on a recent London digging-of-the-digs, has a cozy grill, cheery breakfast nook, and attractive basement Chez Cleo French restaurant; all of its 30 singles and 45 doubles with private baths (even these boast wall-to-wall carpets); 2 fair suites; nice staff. Too many recent wails from Guidesters who complained of hammock-like beds and high-crowned prices. No longer the bargain of yore. **Hyde Park Towers** (Inverness Terrace, W.2) gave its 120 rooms (105 with bath or shower) a face-lifting; restaurant with dancing; coffee shop; commercial but sound. **Parkway** (Inverness Terrace, W.2) also has a Bayswater address some 10 minutes from Piccadilly. About 80 rooms divided among 3 separate houses; approximately ⅓rd with private bath, mostly on the first floor; each bedchamber with radio, telephone, and coin box for individual heating unit. Tour groups toddle in here by the score. **Park Plaza** (Lancaster Gate, W.2), opposite Hyde Park, is an amiable bet for families, provided the children are carefully watched whenever they cross traffic-clogged Bayswater Road. Loving care (not to mention $450,000 in renovation work) was lavished on this house before it was sold to the Strand interests. A solid value, particularly since you now have 70 additional units to choose from. **Mandeville** (Mandeville Place, W.1) is a 163-room warren which might bring to your mind a run for captive conducted-tour rabbits. We'd rate it as a mixture of hare-raising grimness and a bare minimum of cottontail comforts. **Stratford Court** (Oxford St., W.1) could have done with some suds and polish when we saw it. Attractive dining room; 135 bedchambers with private bath; noisy, commercial air in a traditional showcase. The

Alexandra National at Finsbury Park is in such a remote and miserable neighborhood that we don't recommend it.

The **Clive** (Primrose Hill Rd., Hampstead) boasts a medium-size, glass-sheathed structure expanded by 38 units and a garage. Unless you can find no roof in town or unless you prefer to nest way out here near Euston Station in the suburbs, we think this is too remote for most holidaymakers. **Astor Lodge** (St. John's Wood) is ½-apartment house; nice staff, but nothing special, in our opinion.

St. Ermin's (Caxton St., S.W.1) has been extensively revamped and given baths throughout. We're still not too enthusiastic, but the management seems to be trying to perk it up. **Fleming's** (Half Moon St., W.1) shines pretty weakly on our charts. **Berners** (Berner St., W.1) glows even lower on our burner. **Mt. Pleasant** has a mighty pleasant covey of charming receptionists, but it is so poorly situated in a railway-postal complex that most U.S. travelers, we believe, would find it unappealing.

The hotel blips which we pick up on our radar from the fringes of **London Airport** have just about tripled of late. All are a boon to flight-weary travelers as transient hole-ups.

Most luxurious is the 355-unit, Canadian-born **Skyline**, which formally touched down in '71—a sisterly precursor of the lovely Park Tower in midcity, which we've already described. Our reconnaissance revealed the following: Caribbean Patio featuring large pool, with bar shrouded in palms and exotic flora; Diamond Lil's reincarnated Gold Rush Saloon with honky-tonk ivories and bouncing banjos; Colony Room, an Edwardian dine-and-dancer; never-say-dry Café Jardin; excellent maintenance throughout. All traditionally furnished skyliners come with bath and shower, color TV, individually controlled thermostats, and other Age of Apollo instrumentation; the ultracostly Vice Regal Suite is the plushest airport pad we've seen in any airfield-complex shelter in the world. There are bus links to the terminal or town. In keeping with its unrivaled stature the rates are the steepest of the cluster.

The **Heathrow**, which rolled out in '73 as the only squadron member actually parked on airport turf, is a sprawling, 4-level, concrete-colored structure hangaring 725 mono-, bi-, and tri-placers. Sweeping lobby-lounge with black marble floor, red rugs, circular settees, low mirrored ceiling, and ponderous cross-stick chandeliers; expansive polar-frosted Rib Room; The Flying Machine and Sir Francis Drake Bars with respective aero-nautical gimmickry; round-the-clock-alert coffee shop; tailspinning discothèque; indoor pool, bar, and sauna bordered by flowers and fountains. All of its sound-proofed chambers provide vivid hues, TV, air conditioning, and kooky, perilous-looking (but absolutely safe) "Bell Captain Bar-lettes" which double as breakfast warmers; many feature Paul Bunyanesque beds but Tom Thumbish tubs; ramps facing the nearest runway are pegged highest (an entertainment surcharge?). Pilot Allen Deeslam is doing a commendable job of navigating this conventional jumbo which, by our dead reckoning, is better suited to groups and congresses than to soloing families.

The **Holiday Inn**, splayed like a 3-bladed prop, yelled "contact" in '73; it roared in ahead of its sister ship, 10 miles away at Slough. Piper Cubby-hole green-and-beige lobby; pale-ish Blue Ribbon feedery revving till 2 A.M.; tan and hearty Beefeater Bar; never-snoozing Satellite Coffee Shop; health center embracing pool, sauna, massagery, gym, and tennis courts; golf links. All 300 low-clearance units sport smallish but practical baths and showers, the standard entertainment package, floor-to-ceiling panes, and annoying open wardrobes; kids under 12 ride on their parents' ticket. Warning: If you try brewing your own tea or coffee with the Frankensteinian apparatus provided for that purpose, first-timers will cringe at what must be a DC-9 endeavoring earnestly to separate you from your hat—but please fear not. It's simply the steam innocently venting its spleen.

The **Sheraton-Heathrow** taxis in on a mile-distant pasture that overlooks an unsightly factory. Low-profile concrete building; protruding blocks suggesting to us a nasty case of architectural hives; cockpit-size lobby in Buck Rogers Gothic; raised bar; Cranford Restaurant for seafood and grills which we did not try. The Footlights nightery, staged as a Victorian pub, also offers vittles. In-'n-out swimmery plus steam room; poolside snacks; frequent double-decker bus connection to Knightsbridge. The 440 private launch pads, swathed mostly in purple and maroon, plug into color TV's, radios, electric trouser presses, and the aforementioned bar-lettes; they're passably comfortable, well proportioned, functional, and unfrivolous. So much for hoeing that row on this heath.

The older **Excelsior**, a Trust Houses Forte operation, is still superior for its purpose and still richly priced for its league. Its nonstop coffee shop, pub-style Tavern Bar, brick-bound sunken Rôtisserie, and posh Draitone Manor restaurant are further pluses on its manifest. The last, in opulent post-Victorian décor, exhibits black-trimmed scarlet walls, a carved wood ceiling, cushy leather chairs, and mirrors; an impressive seafood display is the major culinary attraction. Adjoining this, there's the 8-table "Library" with crystal glasses, superb cookery, and genuine bookery. All 660 of it's small-boned but efficient accommodations have private bath, air conditioning, soundproofing, wall-to-wall carpeting, TV, piped music, and Jet-Age gadgetry. Moreover, there's a beauty salon, a sauna, car hire service, a heated pool, and ample parking facilities. General Manager Genero keeps his craft in trim. Here's another highly suitable hangar for tired airmen or airwomen. **Skyway**, also a relative veteran, now has 450 rooms, including 9 suites, all with bath, telephone and TV; facilities nearly always open, with restaurant on 24-hour and Snack Bar on 20-hour basis (our New York-cut sirloin and filet in the former were excellent); heated, floodlit, open-air pool; shopping arcade; flight transportation provided to terminus. The efficient, amiable service standards are a blessing both to you and to new Chief Skyway Blazer Davidson, whom we've not yet met. We like it. **Ariel**, opened in '61, is a 184-room, doughnut-shape structure designed to give you that flying-saucer feeling. Soundproofed, air-conditioned bedrooms; showers in each bath; TV and radio; free transportation to and from the airport; a specialty restaurant on the homing beam night and day. Tickets here are more costly than at the Sheraton, but we'd give the latter the edge in spite of it.

The 600-slot **Post House**, another Trust Houses Forte flier, is practically a self-service sanctuary. Imposing 10-tier house posted on 15 acres; vast lobby bordering on the brash; supermarket carts for transporting your own baggage. Great Britain Grill, Buttery, and Bar all in tribute to I. K. Brunel, the nineteenth-century marine wizard; pool, bank, boutiques, and news kiosk rounding out the public precincts. All cubbies are standardly furnished and are available in 8 color schemes; a continental breakfast will be left *outside* your door; offspring under 16 slumber gratis if they share the parental billet. Low price tags reflect a policy of minimum service. We'd suggest that you file your flight plan well in advance if you expect to land here. If you're motoring, set your inertial navigation system as follows: The M-4 highway to Junction 4, then onto B-379 Staines Rd., and finally onto Sipson Rd. (that should leave your compass spinning faster than a chopper prop). The **Centre** is the cheapest of the lot. Its 300 standard quarters and 60 flatlets (bedroom, salon, kitchenette, and bath) are listlessly strung out in a long, low, functional configuration. Simple, brown-carpeted reception; Globetrotter Bar only 800 feet from a runway; lusterless Silver Table restaurant. Look-alike sleepers with gray carpet, rust spreads, radios, phones, adjustable air cooling and reportedly the only triple-glaze panes in or around London. We saw evidence of slipshod maintenance in the wake of heavy tour group traffic around it's control tower. On our scale, undesirable for the investment.

Coming in on a wing and without a prayer of finding a kip, a sip, and a hot dip? The **Berkeley Arms**, smack in the middle of Cranford, a hamlet 2 miles from touchdown but linked to London by subway, might fill the bill. The charmingly Tudorized inn is attached to a newer slabular structure in which may be the most incongruous alliance since W. C. Fields faced Baby Leroy. Open kitchen with grill; blithe coffee nook in orange and bronze; 4 hefty imbiberies; radiant enclosed garden; ice machines on each floor; automatic alarms in each room; décor conceivably by Mr. Howard Johnson. Recommended only for one-night-standing in a pinch. The distant **Heathrow Ambassador**? We'd rather cuddle in a diplomatic pouch.

At Gatwick Airport, we'd pick the **Copthorne** over the **Piccadilly**, but both should be considered only as emergency hanger space at best.

If you're ever stuck for a place to stay, the nonprofit Accommodation Service of the **London Tourist Board** (tel.: 01 730 9845) or the **HOTAC Accommodation Service** (tel.: 01 935 2555) will fly to your rescue when they can.

Dedicated budgeteers? About 10-dozen stopping places in London are listed and rated in this *Travel Guide* which you now hold in your hand. Since there simply isn't space here for additional entries, please consult our annually revised paperback, *Fielding's Low-Cost Europe,* for more bargain hotels, boardinghouses, rock-bottom-cost institutions, and money-saving tips for serious economizers.

For the provinces, a fresh harvest of the best plums on the tourist tree follows below. You'll also find a list of suggested country hotels and eating places in "Country Dining Near London," at the end of the "Restaurants" section. Otherwise, consult the National Information Bureau, your travel agent, or refer to the fat "Hotels and Restaurants in Britain" directory issued free of charge by the British Travel Association's American offices.

§TIPS: The so-called **Trust Houses Forte** chain is often your best bet for country lodging. This federation of more than 200 rural hostelries scattered all over the U.K. is not luxury class, but scrupulous cleanliness, comfortable beds, more and more private baths yearly, relatively low tariffs, and the best available local food are guaranteed. A company-wide, credit-card plan is operative. Write Trust Houses Forte Ltd., 166 High Holborn, London, W.C.1, for the official listings and ratings.

Falcon Inns, a selective flock of a newer feather, also provides some of the best nests in the U.K. Armed with beaks full of capital, this energetic and discriminating outfit has started buying historically or scenically sound hostelries which often have suffered from neglect and then bringing them back to life through careful restoration and expensive decorating. Some of their finished products are listed below, with more on the way. While their tariffs tend to be a shade higher than Trust Houses Forte entries, we think in most cases that the perch is worth the difference.

Now for our alphabetical rundown of your candidates in the chief cities, towns, and villages on the holiday route:

Aston Clinton: The eighteenth-century **Bell** chimes on both sides of the A-41 London-Oxford trunk road. Restaurant-*cum*-inn, compleat with courtyard on one flank; rustic brick-and-beam dining salon with bar, pea-green banquettes, silver candelabra, and French wine-district maps juxtaposed to Bavarian Chef Jaques Dick's Gallic creations; Pavilion for private parties across the pike. Although charming, the main house's mere 5 over-the-kitchen accommodations are Tinkerbell small; we'd therefore opt for any of the 16 spacious apartments across the yard; #16, a luxury suite with side-by-side tubs for dual rub-a-dub-dubs, is our pick of these belle-ringers. For whom does this Bell toll? Energetic Michael Harris and his mum, Daphne, assure us it tolls for you.

Bath: The **Francis**, a Trust Houses Forte member, leads the pack. Total renewal a short while back; 70 rooms all with private plumbing; clean and pleasant; friendly staff; spectacularly accoutered restaurant with cuisine that pales by comparison. Since the front faces a lovely park, but also borders a noisy street, light sleepers should bid for the back of the house. The **Priory** is noted for its culinary glories. It also plays host to overnighters. Small, intimate, and quality conscious. **Lansdown Grove**, high in the city, is tranquil; it sets a fair table, too. **Royal York** is getting a bit fusty, in our opinion. Some redecorations recently, but still too long in the tooth for us. The **Cliffe**, 5 miles out on A-36, is a stone-shelled sweetie; a wonderful site in a quiet valley; 8 bedrooms and baths; careful supervision by Roy and Freda Donaldson, its resident proprietors. In the village of **Limpley Stoke**, the **Limpley Stoke** is larger, less cozy, but just as hushaby; the cookery is also pretty good by suburban standards. The **Northey Arms**, on the A-4, is chiefly a pub, but its duet of bedchambers are button-cute. For a luxury alternative, the tinkling little **Bell House** at nearby **Sutton Benger** (outside Chippenham) is a delight. Cozy complement of 17 rooms, ½ with private facilities and many with balconies; each bed with its own rolling table for pajama breakfasts; superior comfort; book away from the roadside for serious snoozing; one of the finest kitchens away from the gourmet centers of London; not scenic in its locale, but an excellent rural headquarters for touring Wiltshire and Somerset. Expensive but worthy. The freshly expanded **Manor House**, at the neighboring Dr. Doolittle village of **Castle Combe**, is a spellbinder. It's only a minute's walk from the main road; the hamlet, incidentally, has been voted the prettiest habitat in all of England, and we couldn't agree more fervently, even though it's virtually trampled by rubberneckers on Sundays and holidays. It was also the site where Shakespeare's Falstaff lived and where the first woolen blanket was woven. Historians are still trying to find the connection. Lovely apron of grass edging a stream and murmuring fall, surrounding forests, tiers of flowers; antique shop plus furnishings inside the hotel marked for sale to visitors; superb accommodations, with the best views from #4 or #2; Garden Wing not up to the original edifice. Our recent stay was as peaceful as anything St. Peter could produce because the house is so well insulated from those rubbernecking throngs down in the village. Highly recommended. The **Castle**, on the town square, is also attractive. Lounge ceiling beams so low that one timber is inscribed "Duck. . .or grouse!" The food here is outstanding and varied, but the living space is more limited than in the Manor. If you have a car, try not to miss this hidden jewel of Britain.

Birmingham : The sleekly modern, 9-story, strataform **Albany**, in the heart of this booming industrial city, is a Lyon's bred-cub (London's Strand Palace and Regent Palace are others). Clean, well run, and usually busy; handsome Gun Room downstairs for midday snacks and to while away evenings; bar and adjoining dining room with blue banquettes (dancing on Sat. nights); 100% air conditioning; 254 rooms, all with radio and duo-pane windows; nicely outfitted baths with tubs, showers, and facial-tissue dispensers; 3 penthouse suites; tasteful doubles in the medium-price range; excellent studio singles. This one's a bonanza, considering the competition. The **Midland** is old-fashioned, creaky, and sprawling. The **Imperial Centre** has an advantage of sharper-eyed sanitation among the traditional candidates—or so it seemed to us. **Plough & Harrow**, with 40 sleeping units, is better for food than for shelter. The 140-room **Royal Angus** grazes with tender twin rates. Here might be a bully choice. The **Holiday Inn**-keepers have unveiled a candidate here; it's a welcome addition to this hotel-poor metropolis.

Bournemouth: The Deluxe-category **Royal Bath** makes the biggest splash. Gorgeous garden situation; small, kidney-shaped swimming pool; well-stacked casino; as clean and fresh as a wind from the Wight. Top recommendation for seaside somnolence, particularly if your quarter faces the water. The **Carlton**, also by Poole Bay and also in the same official bracket, is another worthy choice. No pool, but elevator service down the cliff face to the breakers; dining room plus Causerie; bar; 100 doubles and 20 singles, all with private facilities. Good, but not up to the high-water mark of the Royal Bath on our measuring rod. Down a notch, **Palace Court** is a pleasant stop for families. Dining salon with adjoining dance quadrant; modern bar; 102

rooms and baths; many couriers' chambers without plumbing; front units with balconies. A sound value. Among the Second-class houses, we like **Highcliff**, **Marsham**, and **Savoy**—in that order. The **Round House** has been a-round only a short time, but long enough for us to get loco-motion sickness at the thought of it. Cacophonous locale between major roads; piled poker-chip architecture; frosty dealers at the front desk while we visited; appropriately named Blandford Restaurant; trio of much-needed bars; 100 pastel-toned Late Formica Period boxes. The traffic din and lack of air conditioning mean you choose between ventilation with intonation or modulation with stagnation. To us, a round house-of-cards.

Brighton: The better nests stretch along the beach strip 2 miles from town. Most of these hostelries (1) adhere to the Georgian or Regency periods or (2) entertain a fervent addiction for British aluminum (oops, aluMINium), Pullman-car upholstery, and hand-greased velvets. The **Metropole** is possibly now the lone exception. Modern, panoramic Starlit Room 150 feet up, with dancing nightly and boasted *"haute cuisine"* (what else could it be at this altitude?); winter and summer casino; slick Monaco Bar; public children's pool and community beach in front; ground level refashioned (and how it needed it!). Complex of 275 modernized units that frankly leave us as cold as a display-case Dover sole; loaded to its soul-less gills with conventions in winter. *The* social nucleus of vintage-car buffs and highborne holidaymakers, but inexplicably cheerless to us. The parent company also runs the **Bedford** at the site of the original relic of the same name. This year's model is a functional, neo-Scandinavian 16-decker. The Dickens Bar (after all, he DID stay here and he DID rewrite *Bleak House* here) was the only concession to interest we could find. All 130 units come with bath, radio, and what we rate as icebergs of . . . brrrr. **Royal Albion** is next on the roster. Excellent Albion Grill with open rôtisserie; updated seafront bar; dour Tudor Bar downstairs; renovated accommodations that are starkly beachy but far from peachy. Passable for this gritty resort. **Royal Crescent**, on the high road above the cliffs, is our choice among the East Beach hostelries. Here's a lovely perch for sea musings. The **Old Ship** has 122 staterooms; 55 heads; forequarters with small balconies; newer units with less space but much better décor and comfort. Modest but worthy. The **Grand** is a misnomer.

Bristol: *This* **Grand** is the cream of the local sherry cask. Total redecoration program piped out; alluring Plimsol Bar downstairs, with the sunlight of Jerez on tap; Newmarket Bar, across the street, for snacks in a paddock atmosphere; attractive lounge and adjacent restaurant; handsome Grill; 155 renewed bedchambers; 70 freshly constructed, smaller units with built-in furniture; suite #104-105 usually booked by celebrities or wine moguls. Easily the vintage leader. The **Unicorn**, at dockside, takes the honors for modernists; the Rank organization is the guiding force behind this one. All 196 rooms with bath, shower, radio, TV, and phone; Copperfield Cocktail, and Waterfront bars; continental breakfasts served in rooms, but English repasts only in the restaurant. Clean and vitally needed here. The **Royal** struck us as commercial and seedy. **Hawthorne**'s is suggested only for times of dire distress. The **Holiday Inn** should be a boon to this hotel-starved community, as might the new **Ramada**, or even the **Dragonara**, reportedly backed by the biggest gambling syndicate in the country. We'll place our bets, however, after our next gamboling session here.

Cambridge: The **University Arms** has been modernized—but totally depersonalized in the process. Statler-style exterior; building chocked up on stilts, with parking space beneath; dining room facing the Green; 126 units, 58 of them newish; 82 private baths; host to multitudes of special interest groups. Our recent sleep-over was no Arms-load of embraces. The **Royal Cambridge** has also wrapped up a construction program. Interior gutted and rebuilt from the foundation up; rotunda lobby; downstairs Western Bar; main floor Royal Bar; plain dining room; barbershop and beauty parlor; parking lot (a blessing in this traffic-choked city); 30 accommodations added, boosting the overall total to 91. Now pretty good. The **Blue Boar,** a midvillage Trust Houses Forte link, is rooting for fatter acorns. Vaulted lobby totally restyled; lounge reshaped; bar remixed; staff unruffled by the presence of clients; sedately antique dining room; most accommodations similarly stripped of beauty by stuffing them thickly with vinyl, plastics, ugly bakelite and other synthetics. *What* a Boar it was to us, we're Blue to report! The **Gonville** may soon be razed and replaced with 100 new rooms. "May" is the operative word here. The **Cambridgeshire**, on the other hand, *has* 100 new rooms plus 18 equally new golf holes. It's touted as a "leisure hotel." Sounds not only needed but a value as well. The **Bath** offers limited amenities but good cuisine.

Canterbury: **Slatters** tells the best tale of all. Rebuilt in 1963; modernized Forum Restaurant on the foundations of a Roman amphitheater; Founder's room for popular-price vittles; central heating; full carpeting; small bedchambers. Clean and worthy. The **Chaucer**, with 47 rooms and 30 private baths, is surprisingly comfortable. The **County** dates back to the 1500's. Wooden floors; beguiling lobby breakfront; paneled dining room; low bath count has now been somewhat augmented. Fair. **Abbots Barton**, along the Dover road, depressed us; its amenities are basic; its flair is zero.

Carlisle: The **Crown and Mitre** reigns supreme at this key hub on the road to Scotland. Birth announcement penned in 1906 but few antique vestiges left by its New Rule School tutors; lobby-level Coffee Shop for light bites; cranberry-colored Belowstairs Restaurant accurately named and adequately provisioned; Edwardian Peace & Plenty Pub; Jonesian Railway Tavern (Casey, that is). All 80 units boast carpeting, TV, and 2-channel radio; 70 sprout sprinklers and tubs. The front singles were the tiniest catchalls we'd seen since our toybox days; others, however, were spaciously sized and flairfully outfitted; twentieth-century ice and shoeshine machines are (alas) stationed conveniently on each floor. Deserving of its local crown and modern mitre. The 60-sancta **Cumbria**, in its final grooming during our romp through this realm not long ago, could become a serious pretender.

Chester: The graciously imposing **Grosvenor** walks away with the honors. Smart public rooms; rich leather-padded Arkle Bar; coolish dining salon; 102 comfortable, fully carpeted bedchambers in tasteful color blends; newish baths throughout. Chief Hall Porter Fred Jones, an invaluable fixture here for eons, knows his Chester-fields bush by bush; mixmaster George is his barnone counterpart. A giant multilevel garage is available for parking immediately behind the hotel. Recommended. The **Blossoms**, which had been fading perceptibly, is beginning to bloom again under the fertile management of Barry Williment. The staff still needs pruning in places, however. Entrance moved to the sidestreet facade; downstairs Buttery and coffee shop; public rooms pleasant; corridors refreshened but occasionally serving as the conduits of strong cooking odors; bedchambers inclined toward motelish motivations, though varying in size and bouquet. The **Queen** recently appeared in new raiments fitted by her Trust Houses Forte tailors. Facilities? Eighty-two rooms and 70 baths; meal vouchers for other tables in the royal family; definitely not high regency, but a noble effort indeed. Both the **Washington** and the **Westminster** have been modernized in this era; both are small, near the station, have ingratiating bars, and are good bets for budgeteers.

Coventry: The **Leofric** is, to us at least, the only decent stop in town. Modern building with cool functional overtones; 3 restaurants; 2 bars; snack corner; 101 rooms; 75% bath ratio; top-floor units with TV; careful maintenance. Despite its assets, this one gives us the feeling of loitering in a moviehouse lobby. Acceptable but commercial.

Dover: The **White Cliffs** is the sole house we would rate as climbable. Seafront porch and glassed-in terrace; 62 rooms in the main building, plus a few more in the annex; 18 private baths; #95 is a nice double. Reasonably good comfort for the cliff dweller. The **Dover Stage**? Candidly, we think it's a horror. It seemed to us that the rooms were designed as cabins for one-night stands, and the whole just slung together, despite being presentable on the outside. Packed solid during our recent journey; fully booked every High Season night for 1½ years ahead. Heartily disrecommended by this *Guide*. There's yet another fresh **Holiday Inn**-undation down here. We'll check its tide level soon, but early voyagers tell us that it is the best of all for the ebb and flow of tourism.

Durham: The 47-room **Royal County** is sweet in its homey fashion. Handsome fifteenth-century staircase; superior cookery for the region; doubles, including breakfast, in the moderate range; thoughtfully equipped, down to that hot-water bottle in your bed. The **Three Tuns**, owned by the same company, is also nicely maintained.

Falmouth: Slim pickin's in the town itself, but flanking it is a dual bonanza. **Tresanton**, across the bay in sleepy *St. Mawes*, might have been spirited from the sunny Mediterranean. Three slopeside buildings are partly hidden from the main road. The first contains a reception parlor in granny dress plus 4 plain rooms; the 2nd, called the Anchorage, harbors 5 Victorian units, including bay-windowed #1, with an almost sensational view of the bay. Finally, there's the Avalon, with 19 choice chambers, a rose-covered stone terrace, a homey drawing room, and the partitioned, wicker-chaired, beautifully muraled dining den. In the latter, Chef Francois Guglerie whomps up Falmouth-melting native and Gallic specialties. Yvette Oliver, as gracious as she is beautiful, is its driving force. Super. **Meudon**, 12 miles out via a narrow, twisty road, is embraced by such breathtaking gardens that even Green Thumb Set's digits should grow even greener in envy. Three-hundred-year-old manor house handsomely grafted onto the younger, larger main building; terraced, flora-lined patio; stately lounge crackling cheerily in winter; airy restaurant a pane away from Eden. The somewhat withered peapod bedchambers vitally need a dose of Vigaro and more careful pruning, in our opinion. Otherwise, Chief Gardener Pilgrim has cultivated a horticultural heaven for botany buffs.

Grasmere The invigorated, sassy **Swan** has nipped the Prince of Wales's royal assets (see below) and now swims in for first-place honors. White stucco abode framed by tulips in season; raftered hearth-warmed lounge; flintlocks in its small chummy bar; garden-edged restaurant mellowed by oaken beams and copper lamps. Of its 35 chambers, 11 tap into tubs (8 of them in the new, centrally heated, and therefore preferable extension); all feature thick broadloom, radio, and amiable stirrings of country life. Proprietress Gertrude Gibson and intrepid Manager Peter Coward are doing an outstanding job of keeping their fine-feathered fowl on course. Closed for preening November to March. Further down upon this swany river, the **Prince of Wales** dog-paddles in with Regency public quarters; that seems to be the limit of its princeliness. There's an active cellar pub; the dwelling units strike us as having lived too long in exile. And where does the **Red Lion** place in this swimming meet? Do cats hate water?

Harrogate: The **Majestic**—for position *only*. It's Trust Houses Forte's treasury has spent what we consider to be an insufficient sum on a renovation program. While the lobby, bar, 2 elevators, and carpets have been renewed, our inside bedchamber seemed to face more tubing than might have been seen at an Apollo launching pad. Try elsewhere first. The **Crown** takes our coronet for comfort once again. Amiable Manager Douglas Pearcey has refeathered one entire wing, restyled the lounge, and refashioned the dining room; he is adding 18 new baths annually until all 114 accommodations boast private facilities; everything is sparkly clean. Chief Hall Porter Mr. Thwaites is a walking encyclopedia—and a mighty friendly one. Recommended. The **Old Swan**, hatched in 1679, is fun for antiquarians. Now with central heating for your winter Swan-downing; comfortable, unthinkably ancient bar; skylighted Bramham dining room; very popular Oyster Bar (microwave cooker, yet!) for crackling snacks until 11 P.M.; total of 140 units and 90 baths; 3 attractive suites; book only the newer rooms here. Two unique fillips: (1) Each bedchamber contains a handsome, knowledgeable guide to Yorkshire (a *printed* guide, regretfully, ladies) and (2) in summer, a leather-lunged minion with a king-size posthorn blows a tantara to announce the arrival of new guests. Very worthy indeed—if you'll toot your own bugle sufficiently loud to ring down one of the better units. The 145-room **Cairn**, a Trust Houses Forte marker, is situated across the garden from Harrogate College. Marble arch-and-pillar lobby; attractive but overpowering Ionic dining room; hearthside bar decorated cleverly with textile printing blocks; VIP suite that could have leapt from a Hilton blueprint; bedchambers that are typically Trust-worthy, Loyal, Helpful, Friendly, Courteous, Kind, etc. etc. We like it more, however, for its public rooms than for its upstairs Merit Badge amenities. Finally, for a lovely daylight excursion or an overnight in the country, we highly recommend a jaunt to the **Devonshire Arms** at **Bolton Abbey**—15 miles across the Yorkshire dales through some of the most glorious countryside in fair Albion. Charming inn with a dozen sleeping quarters and hardly any private plumbing; delicious food and excellent service; cozy dining room overlooking the glistening Wharfe River; friendly rustic atmosphere that any open-hearted traveler would adore for its simple good cheer. After lunch, walk through the back gate and across the meadow to the riverbank; turn left and stroll a ½-mile up to the beautiful ruins of the abbey itself; then return along the highway, where glimpses of the hills and bright water peep through openings in the moss-gathered graystone walls. The prices are extremely moderate, of course. Here is the true pastoral flavor of Olde England—and you will never forget its joy.

Helmsley: The **Black Swan**, a 400-year-old whooper now cared for by the new-as-tomorrow Trust Houses keepers, is the pick of the gaggle in these parts. Nicely scrambled Georgian-Tudor-Moderne cote overlooking the town's market; series of earthy lounges with stone and brick fireplaces and split-rail trimmings; solidly British restaurant with bay windows almost caressing the lawn and garden; 3 bars. Total of 38 nooks, including those in the rear wing; all commonly denominated by ample space, central heating, bathrooms with hotshot towel racks, TV, radio, and a tea-coffee cooker. Manager Dennis Hopper has trained his pet to trumpet fortissimo.

Hereford: The **Green Dragon**, another attraction in the ubiquitous Trust Houses menagerie, is the local fire-breather. Eighteenth-century white structure; large dining room paneled in oak that was chopped and planed in 1600; adjoining cocktail cranny; popular ground-floor Offa Bar. All 100 units with full plumbing; the carpeting and the complete electric entertainment package are standard; #234, the lone suite, is a commodious choice and a sound buy. Here's one beastie that isn't dragin' its feet.

Keswick: **Armathwaite Hall** is one of the most imposing sylvan retreats in the entire Lake District. Venerable estate 7½ miles out of town, at the north end of Bassenthwaite Lake; beautiful green apron sloping to the water's edge; L-shape castle; baronial furnishings; solid, but in our estimation uninspirational cookery; closed November to April. Luxurious, but somewhat austere—in the latter regard, not entirely unlike how we found Manager Stanley Phillips and oodles of his starchy underlings. **Castle Inn**, a nicely restyled, personally run year-rounder, is also up at this end of the lake. Crossroads situation; clean, attractive appointments; modest rates. For motorists in search of a cozy 1-night hitching post. **Lodore Swiss**, on the outskirts across the road from the lake, generates a younger, more sprightly aura. Building in gray Borrowdale stone; heated swimming pool; 2 saunas; 2 gyms with impulse showers; sun lounge; masseuse; tennis court; dancing twice weekly; film showings; nursery with resident nanny. Fresh, well-appointed public rooms; modern entrance; bright lounges (one in avant-garde purple); cheerful bar; waterfront dining salon; La Cascade Grill; 73 comfortable accommodations and 65 baths. Proprietor England and his Swiss wife take pride in their well-trained staff and ingratiating house. The young and the restless (or travelers with children) would probably prefer its greater informality. The **Keswick** is smack-dab beside the old station *cum* railroad museum. Lovely manicured garden; 75 renewed (or nearly so) bedchambers in a mansion that is again seeing better days; formerly stiff-upper-crusted aura now softened with a bar, attractive conservatory, acres of broadloom, and an added TV lounge. Its Falcon owners are working wonders with this aerie. The repolished **Royal Oak** stays open year round. Careful Trust Householding by Manageress Mrs. M.T. McVarish; coolish front desk crew; electric blankets (*below* you, not above you!); bathrooms equipped with plastic spoons (a thoughtful touch, although damned if we can figure out w-h-y); basic but pleasant enough for the quick bird of passage, especially in its newer nests. The **Skiddaw** added a wing in which the architect thought it unnecessary to install plumbing; that has now been rectified, bringing the overall count to 12 units and as many tubs. GOOD SHOW! The **George** reeks with antiquity, among other things; nice people, however. The **Derwentwater** has an excellent position but an invasion of bus tours spoils its peace. The **Scafell** attracts many climbers with its new-fangled "showers" and other modern amenities. The **Borrowdale** has 7 private baths; it lacks central heating. **Borrowdale Gates** is even more old-fashioned. Nix.

King's Lynn: The 3-century-old **Globe** prides itself on its dining facilities: the Apéritif Bar, the Steak Bar (in Routine Rustic, with savory main courses plus light bites), and the Chicken Bar (more uppity, less attractive, and bigger meals). This house is a toper's dream; because it has 9—repeat, 9—bars, there's never the slightest need to get one's feet wet by stepping outside. Its quarters include 49 rooms, 1 suite, and 6 private baths. Amusing in concept. The handsome **Duke's Head**, also on Market Place, comes up with 75 bedchambers, more than half of them lately constructed and with fresh baths. Well run by its Trust Houses Forte managers.

Leeds: The **Queen's** belies its 10-story graystone facade which reminds us of a cross between Ataturk's Tomb and the Kremlin Wall. Dignified oval lobby; aloof reception phalanx; split-level, octagonal, and columned Harewood Restaurant; Knave's Coffee House plus 2 bars; sauna and massage cells. All 200 pads are dabbed in lugubrious chromatics; all are equipped with bathroom, double-glazed panes, phones, and TV; the fronts are the pick of the litter. The queen of Leeds, but almost agonizingly straight-laced to our shoestring impressions. Next is the new **Dragonara**, with another 200 bath-, TV-, and radio-riddled upstairs complex. This one is distinctly "with it," but we'll wait awhile to be sure *we* are. We haven't seen the **Ramada**, a U.S. export. Finally, there's the **Merrion**, about as commercial as Rank can file 'em.

Lincoln: The **White Hart**, across from the cathedral, leaps with a captivating grace in living. Rich furnishings; emphasis on walnut; many fine examples of Chippendale; leaded windows; a historic lounge in which a conclave of brass hats conceived the first modern fighting tank. Almost all its 60 rooms with carpeted private baths; 12 new suites added recently, not including the sumptuous Brownlow Suite (single, double, sitting room, and 2 baths); #36 is our choice of the twins; management by capable Geoffrey Townend; polished olde inn flavor and hospitable air. Very, very good. **Eastgate**, also near the cathedral, was opened in '65. Modern in tone; lilac-shaded dining room; adjoining bar and outdoor terrace; Buttery open until 10:30 P.M.; 70 ample-size rooms with bath, radio, individual heating control, and TV for hire; #330 a beguiling treetops double. Totally different ambiance from the White Hart, but worthy if you prefer twentieth-century appointments.

Liverpool: In this large and prominent port-metropolis, only the **Adelphi** is recommendable. Lime Street site near the station; British Transport ownership; pleasant Grill; attractive French restaurant; well maintained and comfortable. **St. George's**, a Trust Houses Forte fortress, lines up 157 chambers and a like number of baths. We haven't yet presented arms, but it should be a welcome addition to this Liverpudlian pool. So should the latest entry by the **Holiday Inn** operators on Paradise Street and the Thistle Group's **Atlantic Tower**.

Manchester: The $7,000,000, 14-story **Piccadilly** is the undisputed champion of the featherweight lot. Locally, nothing can lay a glove on it. While it is clean, collected, and efficient, it also seems as sterile as a missile center. Circular ramp entrance to a cantilever lobby done in pine-louvered wood, Sicilian white marble, and icelike mosaics; 5 bars (the Plaza and the bale-filled—but not baleful—King Cotton nooks are the pick); dining room; Grill; 24-hour Coffee Shop with miserable service standards and punishing price tabs; 50 doubles and 205 singles (an obvious guidepost to its commercial intent); small bedrooms with nice furnishings and textiles. Very good except for its formidable impersonality. The **Midland** is the oldest in town; still well maintained; highly respected French restaurant. Unfortunately, age is beginning to tattle here. The **Grand** is said to live up to its moniker; we missed it, sad to say.

Midhurst: This medieval hamlet, similar to Rye and overrun with equal numbers of summer package tours, is proud of its twin-winged A.D. 1430 and A.D. 1650 **Spread Eagle**. White Tudor facade; skylit entrance; beamed dining room with copper-clad hearth and talon-to-talon tables affording fine views of the courtyard. Trio of bars including the vaulted Coal Hole; a dart room; heavily timbered hunting theme lounge; the Cromwell nook, where The Protector hanged his adversaries (possibly for not picking up the tab?). The 20-chamber **Angel** might be heaven for those seeking a more central location, more informality, less deliberate charm, and less pretention than its more famous opponent.

Moretonhampstead: **Manor House**, with its incredibly beautiful softly rolling acres of manicured grass and gardens 12 miles from *Exeter*, is the lord of its well-mannered fief. Iron gate-to-front-door drive fringing the 18-hole golf course; tennis courts; 2 trout streams; rhododendrons, azaleas, willows, and elms galore; long, gray, 3-level stone structure; somewhat austere dining room with white columns, leaded windows, and sound cuisine. Heaven for duffers, anglers, shutterbugs, horticulturists, and dedicated lazybones.

Newcastle-upon-Tyne: The **Gosforth Park**, overlooking the racecourse, romps over the finish line by at least several lengths. Handsome Brandling Grill; adjoining Silver Ring Bar; 101 bedrooms and 5 suites; double this amount now being readied plus barber and beauty salons, a sauna, boutiques, and a riding school; small baths; radio, remote-control TV (wired for color); phones near tubs; thick carpets; studio-twins predominating. Definitely in our winner's circle, but v-e-r-y expensive. **Five Bridges**, at *Gateshead*, has slipped in the stretch. Increasingly mercantile in tone; décor of the ultramodern mechanical engineer's school; dramatic Bewick's Bar outfitted to resemble the inside of a gearbox; Engine Room public bar; Tynesider Steak Bar for signalmen-in-a-hurry; window-lined dining room; shops at street level; public rooms air-conditioned; rooftop parking space (a godsend in this city). All 108 units with private bath, piped music, TV and radio. Okay, but now our pick to place not to win. The **Royal Station** in midcity offers solid comfort in rather dull surroundings. Public rooms recently updated; pastel doors facing the corridors. We were told that a certain Miss Taylor purchased one of its beds and that a certain Mr. Burton bought one of its pillows. (Just for fun, we tried them, and they didn't seem all *that* comfortable!) *Tertium quid?* Perhaps. The reshod **County**, in the Gosforth stable, is a mod-lined shoo-in for its moderate stakes. The 8-story **Swallow** is close on its heels in the same filly's match. Swallow-taled restaurant; shopping plaza; plenty of heat. Okay. The **Royal Turk's Head** wears a turban provided by its Thistle proprietors; this one, too, runs in the money. We haven't seen the new 151-unit **Holiday Inn.** Newcastle is nearly always jammed with business travelers and conventioneers. Be sure your booking is confirmed before toting your own coal to this commercial hub; otherwise, you may share our irritation at having to drive to a remote country inn through the gloom of night.

New Milton: **Chewton Glen**, a stately Georgian mansion growing within a sea of flowers 90 miles southwest of London, is now one of the finest inns in England. Red brick edifice sprinkled with green shutters; recently revamped homey lobby; thickly carpeted, book-lined Sun Lounge; Marryat Restaurant with cozy-rosy napery and justifiably renowned fare; Garden Room dinery with hunting scenes on grass-green walls; redecorated Cocktail Bar opening onto terrace-tial flora. The old section snuggles 8 airy attic-type doubles with antiquated bathrooms; the best accommodations are in the new wing, all with eye-popping views, remote-control lighting, radio, TV, and today's tubs; chambers ending with digits from 0 to 4 are the picks of the pack. Proprietor Martin Skan, a young dynamo, is working wonders here. Lovely! (Incidentally, if you are making your way between Southampton and London, here is a gracious alternative to England's dismal port city. More on this further along.)

Oxford: The **Randolph** is a dealer's choice. Continual modernizations under Trust Houses Forte aegis; dining room reproportioned and ceiling lowered; fresh hall for private parties; Ox-in-the-Cellar Buttery; some up-to-date units in plain but passable taste; many Gothic touches; next-door garage which motorists cheer. Better every season. The renovated **Eastgate** is clean, neat, and small. For budgeteers, the **Tackley**, on High Street, is old-fashioned but sparkling; the **Melville** and the **Isis**, both on Iffley Road, are worthy alternates. Pilgrims on wheels usually aim for the **Excelsior Motor Lodge**, on the outskirts toward Woodstock. It is modern and appealing; best of all, it offers the blessing of keeping your car out from possibly the most traffic-snarled city in the British Isles. Nothing really wins our Blue in this important center.

Rye: The **Mermaid** is a masterpiece of feudalism fused with modern provincial comfort. Long stucco-and-timber ivy-clad building topped with chimney pots; oaken dining den; Dr. Syn's Chamber paneled and branded with aphorisms from the Bard of Avon; Giant's Fireplace Bar (look up the flue which was once used by smugglers); tranquil courtyard. Eighteen of the 26 accommodations come fully plumbed; no suites; all tend toward the diminutive but are jam-packed with Elizabethan emollients such as 4-poster beds and brassy lamps. Our only demurrer here concerns the attitudes we encountered of some smug and all-too-brassy staff members, who possibly have been conditioned by the seas of tourists who flood Rye in high-tide season. Nevertheless, the Mermaid floats.

Salisbury: The Trust-Houses-Forte-held **White Hart** provides the greatest comfort for your pence; a while back it came through its Hart-felt renovation program in White-hot condition. Woody highlights in bedroom décor; good baths; 25-unit annex. We are still charmed by the original parking lot sign that lists the prices for feeding the horses and washing the carriages. The **Red Lion**, which dates back to the seventeenth century, comes up with a handsome antique dining room, full carpeting, a later wing in which the rooms are smaller than the older ones. Total of 50 units and 30 baths; very nice staff; enjoyable if you're unapprehensive of beamed ceilings and floors which sag with your footsteps. The **Rose & Crown** added to its petals in '68; its site by the river is peaceful. **King's Arms**, also old-fashioned, has a Tudor façade and a matching interior. It almost adjoins the White Hart. The **County Hotel** compiles a curious set of statistics: 32 rooms, 2 private baths, 3 restaurants, and 7—yes, 7—bars. At a tiny hostelry called the **Cathedral** long ago we encountered our first barefoot receptionist (a novitiate, perhaps?). She was better-heeled on our latest look, having gone through 3 changes of ownership and a renovation—the hotel, that is, not the lady. If you prefer the suburbs, why not drive 8 miles farther to the sweet little **Antrobus Arms** at **Amesbury** (near Stonehenge)? Reasonably comfortable inn; inviting bar; oh-so-rustic TV lounge *(sic);* fine restaurant with the maître in a swallow-tailed coat and his pencil alertly poised. All 18 bathed accommodations are named for regions; we stayed in the "North Devon," a *grand-lit* double; it was delightful. This one is recommended for country living.

Southampton: Crack-off-the-bat, we'd strongly urge that you NOT overnight here. If possible, take a taxi to **Winchester** (13 miles) and book into the **Wessex** (prior reservations advised). For your first or last night in glorious Britain, Winchester (see separate paragraph to follow) will provide a much more colorful introduction or memory than will this cold, grimy, industrial port. Similarly, we also can recommend the previously mentioned Chewton Glen at New Milton (18 miles). Curiously, the **Skyway** is not near the airport but down by the docks. While its glass-lined Solent Restaurant serves appetizing fish dishes, we dined beside some of the most *mal-de-mer* -provoking oil-painted seascapes we've ever seen. Handsome Habour Bar; penthouse Polynesian deck for snacks and after-dark revels; large car park. The bedchambers could be termed, charitably, as routine, but since the traffic is so heavy at this crossroads, advance reservations are a must. Better for a meal en route than an overnight. The **Dolphin** has been modernized to the scant limits of its antique facilities by the proprietary Trust Houses Forte group; 70 rooms and baths; plenty of creaks. The **Polygon**, a large, bulky structure, strikes us as being about as frumpish as a damp wool ulster; some newer units merely passable; public rooms recently smartened up, with a possibility of more bedchambers next. The **Royal** is too commercial for our taste. The intimate **Berkeley**, tucked away in the interior of the city, is comfortable and has a commendable table. It's more of a family inn than a full-blown hotel.

Stratford-upon-Avon: The 260-chamber **Hilton**, clinging discordantly to more than 4 acres of carefully Tudored riverside garden, made its entrance just before the Ides of March, 1973. Long, low structure that is manifestly upstaged by its tucked-away neighbor, the Royal Shakespeare Theatre; sets composed of beams, brick, stone, and sterner stuff; hearth-warmed reception; green, gold, and orange-accented Warwick Grill serving up platters which pleased us not; octagonal Actor's Bar performing a soliloquy on the patio; news kiosk and shops cueing off the lobby; ballroom for 350 bartering balladeers. There's a hotel barge that shuttles guests to all performances; there are also parking facilities for 250 coaches, a godsend in this traffic-jammed vale. All nests are twin-bedded, reasonably proportioned, and festooned with Falstaffian flourishes; each offers an individually controlled thermostat, a radio, taped melodies, and a direct-dial phone. General Manager Kenneth S. Kennedy must forthwith mor sternlee instructe his troupe according to their separate artes, that they may serve with keener measure and stouter hearts. The venerable **Welcombe**, on Warwick Road, an inconvenient 3 miles outside the village, is the best-known luxury house in the region. Sprawling park surroundings; originally constructed so there would be 1 window for every day of the year (we secretly believe there are as many chimneys, too); British Transport ownership; 3 suites, 92 rooms, and 81 baths; expensive tariffs. The Direction proudly told us that Teddy Roosevelt stopped here in 1910 and occupied #121 (double bed, no bathroom for this Rough Rider). Because of its remoteness, Guidesters have complained of difficulties in securing theater tickets from the busy marketplaces in town. Despite its outstanding reputation, we find it dull and old hat. In the center, the **Shakespeare** is much more fun for younger globe-trotters. Charming Tudor architecture replete with gables, open timbers, leaded windows, and hanging flowerpots; gimmicky names for the bar ("Measure For Measure"), the dining room ("As You Like It"), and the bedchambers—all of which bear the title of a play, a poem, or one of the Bard's characters (we can't tell if the bridal suite is "Romeo and Juliet," "A Lover's Complaint," "Much Ado About Nothing," or "Love's Labour's Lost"). Here's a smooth professional operation that blends antique charm with a fair share of twentieth-century comfort. Recommended for its type. **Alveston Manor**, a Trust Houses Forte interest, has perked up in direct proportion to the fine talents of General Manager Cassini and to the reinvigoration of its genial personnel. Fine old main building which contains only 1/6th of the complement; 100 rooms in newer Charlecote and Warrick wings with simple billets; sound plant, more courtly staff. The **Falcon** has refeathered its nest. Timber-and-stucco house revamped; central heating added; motel section now functioning; reputedly superior cuisine. A few seasons back, the Tudor-style **White Swan** stirred up breakers in the pond by installing its first baths since the fifteenth century. Total of 60 units, 7 with that glorious newfangled plumbing; we like #5, a cozy double with the typically thoughtful Trust Houses Forte touch of a hot-water bottle in the bed. Pleasant. The **Haytor** is more a residence-cum-hotel. Quiet suburban situation (and don't think *that* isn't a joy in this bustling hamlet!). Artistic décor throughout; attractive red map-lined dining room; all bedchambers color-blended down to the linens and blankets; all of the loving touches and pampering amenities of a fine private home; dancing twice weekly; happily modest prices for such fruitful rewards. Proprietor and Mrs. Tagg, who prune every limb in the 2-acre garden and polish every facet of the cut crystal, also supply theater tickets at normal box-office prices. (This is a tremendous asset, because prominent local citizens can always snag the best seats for crowded performances—but please ask for them well in advance, just to be safe.) No groups ever accepted. Tiny, charming, and our highest recommendation for its type. The **Red Horse**, where Washington Irving penned his *Sketch Book*, has been regroomed. Now a polished, modest but praiseworthy budget bet. It is one of the few hotels in Stratford that will accept reservations by telephone instead of by mail. Predictably nice personnel; it knows its task and performs it well; ample indeed for the lightly bankrolled pilgrim. The **Swan's Nest** counts very few private birdbaths, but its cuisine is far from fowl stuff —creditably worth honking about, in fact. **Ravenhurst** is the choice of many dollarwise travelers; lodging for reasonable prices; many personal attentions; quite satisfactory. Information about the 2 youth hostels in town can be garnered from the local tourist office; charming Mrs. B. G. Browne is a walking (and smiling) encyclopedia of Avon-side news, ticket information, private housing, and transportation (address: 20 Chapel St.).

Many first-timers blindly insist on residing in Stratford while attending the Shakespeare performances or touring the countryside. Seasoned wayfarers with their own transportation more shrewdly avoid the crush of this touristic hub by finding the true Arcadian solace of rural England in the neighboring *Cotswolds*. The distances are short and cover some of the most inspiring landscape under Merlin's wand. For a minichapter on this region which has such enormous appeal to wanders, please see the comments that follow in the latter part of this "Hotels" section.

Torquay: The **Imperial** was started the year the American Civil War ended. Now part of the Trust Houses Forte empire; reputedly trustworthy restaurant; air conditioning; swimming pool; beauty and barber shops; 2 Imperially supreme saunas. The 45 singles, 110 duos, and 2 suites have a private bath apiece. Sound. Perhaps even more so is the new, sea-fronted **Grand**, which will welcome you with a Regency Restaurant, Caribbean Bar, golf, riding, a pool, sauna, and tennis.

Warwick: The **Lord Leycester** offers a tartan Grill, a masculine wood-lined bar, damask-clad corridors, 45 comfortable, fully carpeted rooms, and 6 private baths; its best doubles with plumbing aren't at all expensive, if you can hook one. Not bad. The **Warwick Arms** comes up with 45 units, 2 baths, and yet another proprietor who may change things soon. We're waiting. **Saxon Mill**, 10 minutes along Kenilworth Road, is for dining rather than for overnighting; poor and cocky service on our try; famous, but we found it very ordinary; food that edges on being overpriced. **De Monfort** is a newer one opened by the Devere interests. It's modern in concept, if not downright chilly in tone. Look for it in neighboring *Kenilworth*, a short spin from town.

Wells: The elfin, 10-room, 5-bath **Crown** takes the throne, but it could easily be unseated by a stalwart sovereign if one were to march in, we'd avow. Legend has it that William Penn once gave a speech standing at one of its windows. The **Star** shines brightest in its Tudor dining room, Grill, and friendly lounges; 22 second-magnitude Star chambers; grand sum of 3 private baths; kindly staff; worthy if you don't hanker for your own plumbing. **Gate House**, the oldest hostelry in this ancient town, is built right into the cathedral walls; the situation is handy for clerics, but it offers only basic amenities. The **Swan** seems Routine Antiquity to our eyes; somewhat molted when compared with the smarter chicks of similar vintage.

Winchester: As aforementioned, if you are arriving by ship, this town (or, as stated earlier, New Milton) creates a far better first impression of England than does grimy Southampton. The modern-lined, 91-room **Wessex**, built over a Roman well, is the pacesetter for miles around. Situated across the lawn from the world-famous cathedral; twentieth-century architecture which does not clash, odd as it might seem, with the moss-raked edifice; sound restaurant overlooking the hallowed resting places of some of Albion's greatest personages; cozy Buttery for late-hour snacks; well-appointed rooms with blessed space to unkink after shipboard snugness; full bath count. If you reserve in advance and specify details of your arrival (both strongly advised), the hotel will arrange for a car to meet you at the dock. Highest recommendation.

Windermere: The **Belsfield** recently rang up almost $2,000,000 in refurbishing bills while chiming in as this area's top clapper. The belfry knells the arrival of a new wing by its Falcon management, plus a new restaurant, a revamped lobby, a library, game chamber, and dining room, as well as ample behind-the-scenes tollings. Most of its 85 accommodations now boast baths, radios, pants presses, and other amenities. The hard-working Nugent family also avow there's an indoor pool in your future here. Unquestionably the leader. The **Old England** has slipped largely because of its convention trafficking, think we. Nice terrace above the water, overlooking the small-boat docks; mixture of Victorian and Flash Gordon appointments; modern lakefront wing bringing capacity up to the 100 mark, the latest of which are the best. Nirvana for the Skruggs Brush Co., Ltd. annual gala, but no longer for ours. The **Hydro** is big and rambling, but some Regency touchups have helped; it specializes in group traffic. **St. Martin's**, across from Old England, is a tiny, clean economy stop. *Ambleside*, a midget's skip from Windermere, is one of the most panoramic vantage points in the Lake District. The **Langdale Chase Hotel** is stubbornly Victorian in its old-fashioned atmosphere; enough wood carvings to have kept 100 whittlers busy for 20 years; buckle-bending teas for hikers' appetites; 36 rooms and 20 baths; the Boathouse, the prime buy, is closed Dec. 8 to Feb. 1. Proprietress Dalzell tries hard to provide a lot for your pounds; we like the garden and the kindness, but some Pilgrims may find the décor as overpowering as a 3-week holiday in Hagia Sophia. Otherwise warmly recommended. The sprawling **Salutation** is 2nd (many package tours); it is stalked closely by the **White Lion**. **Low Wood**, on the outskirts, is a fair bet for budgeteers; it has been expanded to 141 bedchambers; bid for the newest ones.

Woodstock: The 750-year-old **Bear**, a short lope from Oxford, rears up as the 4th-oldest inn in Albion. Its 3 structures face the town market, the most ancient comprising a thickly beamed and happily hearthed lounge-bar, a taper-lit dining room further brightened by flowers and mellowed by pewter and brass, and a tally-ho cocktail nook. The adjoining 2-tiered Park Suite annex, enveloping 6 of the 32-den total, is a lazy ursine's delight. The Stable Block, across the courtyard, is another cozy cubby hole, if you can believe Mr. and Mrs. R. Burton, who have hibernated here. Koalas of kudos to likable and energetic Manager Jeremy Porter, Head Porter Leslie, and Barman Keith, who make it a major light in the Woodstock sky.

York: The **Royal Station Hotel** chugs in first. We're losing our head of steam for it, however, now that we're receiving so many complaints from New Yorkers. Basic comforts in the so-called Grand Tradition; some units with modern teak furniture; front perches which overlook the garden fountain and the Minster. Its manager had better get busy stoking up some Station-ary charms. Not so Royal any more. The **Chase** greets guests with a 6-foot-tall saddle at its entrance. (Yorkshire wags claim, "Aye, they've never found a jockey to fit it!"). Ugly pipes on the façade proclaim its introduction to the Age of Indoor Plumbing; central heating; extensive reconstructions which provide smaller bedrooms than in the original building. We'd choose #26, a large double with bath that offers a railbird's peek at the racetrack behind the house. This one places, not wins—but it's still in the money. The **Elm Bank** is a living museum of Art Nouveau—one of the finest and most complete collections of the décor of 1897; scholars often come to study it. Should you stay here, however, you might think, as we did, that the chambermaid hasn't popped in since the turn of the century. Total of 55 grim rooms plus 3 more annexed; 24 raw baths or showers; 1 newer floor. If you walk in as a curiosity-seeker, ask to see the fabulous Regency bed in room #44 (for which antiquarians have offered startling sums). Here's a lodgings' oddity we can recommend only if you harbor a driving interest in the culture of this period. If you do, it's heaven; if you don't, you might think you've stepped into a Beardsley nightmare. The tidy, sparkling **Viking**, a midtown candidate, moors down beside the Ouse River. The backers bankrolling it churned up 106 First-class stalls aimed at conventioneers.

THE COTSWOLDS:

This microdomain is (1) such a charmer and (2) so concentrated that we will consolidate its attractions into this single subchapter. To view its treasures properly an automobile is a necessity. Although the majority of its most intimate corners can be absorbed within 2 or 3 days, lingering for a week brings rich rewards—especially in spring, summer, or autumn.

Broadway is perhaps the most logical springboard from which to plunge. It is only 15 miles from Stratford-upon-Avon, 25 miles or so from Warwick Castle, Kenilworth Castle, Banbury and its cross, Sulgrave Manor (ancestral home of George Washington, where you'll find the original Stars and Stripes), the Duke of Marlborough's Blenheim Palace where Winston Churchill was born, Worcester with its cathedral and its porcelain works, and a host of closer storybook hamlets with poetic names such as Upper and Lower Slaughter, Bourton-on-the-Water (the "Venice of the Cotswolds"), Moreton-in-Marsh, Stow-on-the-Wold, Chipping Campden, and many more. The **Lygon Arms**, in our opinion, is one of the finest inns in England. Aside from a few thickheaded waiters or waitresses, this 400-year-old hostelry is always a pleasure to our senses. Dynamic Director Douglas Barrington, a kindhearted and dedicated hotelier, has provided living space for modernists as well as for traditionalists. In its way, the twentieth-century wing is every bit as appealing as is the very room where Cromwell courted the sandman. This house wins our top accolade. The half-timbered and stone **Broadway**, across the main pike, is more modest. Lower rates; amiable family atmosphere; handsome 2-story lounge and adjoining gardens. At *Banbury*, **Whately Hall** bounds away with local thunder; its downstairs dining room is a special Hall-mark of pride, as is the brick bar room. The building has hosted Benjamin Franklin. Guiding light is Patrick Salmon; Michael Blanchard, the previous proprietor is now elsewhere with this hostelry's new Falcon chain owners. Please note that this bustling center is not as quiet as most of the other toyland hideaways. *Moreton-in-Marsh* boasts the **Redesdale Arms** crackling an invitation with its open hearths, the larger chef-blessed **Manor House**, and the slightly commercial **White Hart**. All 3 delight the souls of antique hunters. *Stow-on-the-Wold* 's bid comes from the **Old Farmhouse**, with each of its quintet of bedrooms sweeter than the next. A dining tip comes to us about the **Unicorn**, with French cuisine prepared by Robert and Brenda Maynaud. Sounds like a winner. *Bibury* fluffs up the previously mentioned **Swan** for country living and perhaps some trout casting from the banks of the Coln. **Bibury Court** is a fair catch, too. *Burford* tucks the **Lamb Inn** into a cozy corner of the townlet. While tranquillity is present, its fleece could use a little combing now and then. This home lives for teatime—a sip of which we richly enjoyed. *Chipping Campden* chips in with the **Kings Arms**. The village is more appealing than these sheltering arms, but for short stoppers who spend their days out sightseeing, it is more than adequate. Nearby *Sutton Benger* and *Castle Combe*, on the Cotswold fringes, are covered earlier under "Bath." At *Cleeve Hill*, near Cheltenham, the **Malvern View** is a refined cleeveage for golfers, who'll find the links and the Severn Valley a perfect 2 for tee. At *Bourton-on-the-Water* the **Old New Inn** plunks all 24 of its bedchambers on the ground floor. It also is a popular target for its amusing model village, which tickles the fancy of all of us middle-age children. Even the kids like it!

Don't expect many private baths or Statler-style concepts in any of these hostelries. They are all inns. Most of them date back to the middle fifteenth-century. Most of them are operated by good-hearted people who think that you've come to *see* how they live not *change* how they live. The cookery may evoke fond yearnings for a hardboiled egg or a snack from your picnic survival kit, but perhaps this is a good way to start that overdue diet. But one thing is certain: from the *Forest-of-Dean* to *Shipton-under-Wych-wood* and from *White Ladies Aston* to *Tintern Abbey*, we'll wager that you'll be as enchanted as we always are by this uniquely colorful loop in the British skein.

As for miscellaneous county cousins not previously listed, here's a selection from our town-and-country grab bag:

Berkshire: **Sunninghill**'s recently crowned **Royal Berkshire** ascended to its throne smartly; reliable sources already call it a Queen Anne mansion with 5-star standards and tariffs to match. Total of 52 sumptuous chambers, all with color TV and refrigerators; Olympian gamut of sports facilities on its 15 manicured acres. Excellent.

Cornwall: We recommend **Tregenna Castle** at *St. Ives* for sports buffs and photographers: tennis, golf, fishing, and boating for the former, and Land's End plus St. Ives harbor for the latter. The 55-unit **St. Ives Bay** recently underwent revampings which included 2 dining rooms, a new elevator, sauna, and beds; the shower count still is stalled at 1/3rd of the available units; suite #8 crests best for wave watchers. At *Gunnislake*, we take little stock in the **Tavistock**.

Devonshire: In *Honiton*, we'd pick **Deer Park** and the **Greyhound.** The latter old dog's new tricks include a wagtail restaurant and bar but no private plumbing in its 10 puppy-size cubicles. Mr. and Mrs. Brain mastermind this Fido. At *Fairy Cross,* it's the **Portledge Arms**.

Dorsetshire: **Dormy House** in *Ferndown* tees off as a smashing handicapper for the golfing set; phalanx of 80 on-par doubles and 14 singles, most with bath or shower; 2 secluded cottages for nonclubhouse activists.

Durham: In *Blanchland*, we're happily haunted by the *Lord Crewe Arms*, a twelfth-century inn in a ghost village. Ch-ch-ch-charming.

Kent: In *Pembury*, it's the **Priory** or the sleekly modern **Great Danes** near *Maidstone* with an indoor heated swimming pool that is a blessing. In the border town of *Melrose*, Roxburghshire (in Scotland but on the English motoring circuit), it's the **George & Abbotsford**. The **Leicester Arms** at *Penshurst* looked to us on our checkout as if its furnishings might have been selected from a Green Stamp catalogue. Nix.

Norfolk: In *Thetford* you'll find the unpretentious **Bell**, a blend of the modern and the ancient.

Northumberland: Otterburn's pacesetter is the stucco-coated **Percy Arms**, with its pleasant window-lined dining room, 2 bars, and ample comforts. Second, we'd pick **Otterburn Tower**, a converted castle with too few private baths. In nearby *Corbridge*, there's the modest but adequate **Angel Inn**; an angelic host of pipe smokers reads and nods in its lounge. In *Berwick-on-Tweed*, it's the **King's Arms**, where the death of the lamb to furnish our cutlets we considered a needless atrocity; there's also the **Castle** aside the northern approach to the city.

Nottinghamshire: In *Nottingham* the Rank-operated **Bridgford** has an excellent site on the Trent but small bedchambers.

Oxfordshire: In *Newbridge*, we distinctly favor **The Rose Revived**, a sweet inn at the juncture of the Thames and the Windrush; very good kitchen.

Shropshire: The **Feathers** in *Ludlow* fluffs up a half-timbered facade, a bevy of bedchambers dripping with history (and even tubs), and an oak-and-brick restaurant that should take you back to 1565 faster than the Shrewsbury Stage. At *Hopton Castle,* fringing the Clun Forest, the **Lower House Country Lodge** is an intimate hideaway with the personality of a private home. John and Sally Dann are hosts at this restored medieval estate. Prices seem very reasonable for what we are told is solid value. We'll look in soon.

Sussex: In *Arundel*, settle for the **Norfolk Arms**. In *Uckfield*, it's the manorial *Buxted Park* which provides health and hydro facilities which we've yet to try.

Wiltshire: In **Swindon**, the **Wiltshire** enfolds 85 newfangled units with bath, radio, TV, and central heating, plus a streamlined dining room and bar; its Oddenino ownership is another plus. Although the **Old Ship**, berthed at **Mere** attains flank speed with its galley, we'd rate its cabins as Dead Slow. Mere-ly one skipper's opinion, however.

Worcestershire: In **Worcester**, our pick is the newish **Gifford** followed by the **Star** and then the **Crown**. The **Raven** quoths well for nearby *Droit-wich*—and boasts 18 singles and 30 doubles, 40 of which have private bird-sized baths. Beak-satisfying cuisine of plain English dishes; fair tariffs that include morning birdseed. Manageress Betty Boughten flies steadily here.

Yorkshire: The **Punch Bowl** at *Low Row* in the heart of the hills and dales, ladles out 17 drops in the main house and peaceful annex, the choices of a beaming 6-table eatery, and the delights of a sound wine cellar. Proprietor Roughton's very young son cannily dispenses the drinks. (Is this how the inn got its name?) The **Londesborough Arms** at *Selby* offers 17 almost Spartan nooks with 14 splashers and intercoms in lieu of phones; one night seems maximum right.

If you range as far as Wales, 2 stops in the north are outstanding. The first is *Portmeirion*, a cottage-laced village on a private peninsula overlooking Cardigan Bay, only a few miles from *Penrhyndeudraeth*—and don't ask us to pronounce that, please! (Okay, if you insist, it sounds vaguely like "penny-headdress," said with a lisp.) The entire complex seems to have been built from an Italian dream sequence. Travelers can cozy themselves into either the hotel or the bungalows. Fireplaces galore; kindness by the shipload; exquisite sea- and landscape vistas; delicious food. Only the main building and 2 cottages are open all year, so check ahead. This is a marvelous retreat for anyone seeking the peace and loveliness of the Welsh byways. The second is **Ruthin Castle**, at *Ruthin*, not on the sea. This comfortized fortress special-izes in medieval banquets every night except Sunday. The waitresses are in costume; there's authentic folk singing and clog dancing; there's cuisine done in the manner of the Middle Ages; there are tour groups almost scaling the turrets. Surprisingly high living standards, but not too rewarding after the novelty has worn off and the Clywd Valley sights have been seen. With few hotels for miles in any direction, be sure to wander with an easy itinerary and firm reservations.

Obviously you'll find scores and scores more. These represent a broadly comprehensive, hand-picked assemblage of the better ones which we've re-cently either overnighted in or inspected. Half of the fun is in digging up little inns for yourself, to discover later that the lavatory is in the washshed and that the w.c. is down on Lower 40, where heifers peep at you through the crescent-shape window in the door.

Motels? Popping up as fast as a berserk automatic toaster. All are modern, since investors saw a potential market only within the past few years. The **Watney-Lyon** group is one of the trailblazers, with a gross of operations now and more in blueprint. Samples are at *Epping* (*Essex*), *Matford* (*Devon*, 1½ miles from Exeter on the bypass), *Ower* (*Hampshire*, on London–Bourne-mouth road, a convenient stop for Southampton arrivals), *Newingreen* (*Kent*, near Hythe and in easy reach of Dover), and *Frome* (*Somerset*). **Trust Houses-Forte Ltd.** has constructed units at *Alveston* (near Bristol), *Chip-*

penham (Wiltshire), **Sherborne** *(Dorset)*, and **Epping** *(Essex).*, **Norman Cross** *(Huntingdonshire)*, and **Boroughbridge** (*Yorkshire*, between London and Edinburgh on the Great North Road). At **Plymouth**, the **Holiday Inn** planners have unveiled 224 bedrooms and sited other links at **Leicester** and **Slough-Windsor**, plus the ones that we've already pinpointed. The Forte group has unwrapped the previously mentioned **Excelsior Motor Lodge** and Autogrill 2 miles north of **Oxford**. Then there are the **Boulter's Lock** at **Maidenhead** and **Bridge House** at **Reigate**, both under the watchful eye of Tom Cressy, the wayfarers' friend. Finally, just 1½ miles from **London Airport**, the **Master Robert Motel** awaits (ask how it got its name; bet you 10 to 1 you can't guess!) and **Crest** has unveiled a 115-roomer in London (at Wembley Park).

Special facilities for children? The British Tourist Authority suggests **Childminders** (67 Marlebone High St.). Others include **Universal Aunts** (36 Walpole St.), **Visitors Welcome** (17 Radley Mews), and **Junior Jaunts** (13A Harriet Walk). Nanny's rates usually are calculated by the hour and vary according to time of day. **The House on the Hill** (33 Hoop Lane, N.W. 11) and **Walton Day Nursery** (239 Knightsbridge) will take care of toddlers all day long, and the latter by the week. Outside London, **Norland Nursery Training College** (Hungerford, *Berkshire*) will board small fry, and **Holiday Parents** (Petersfield, *Hampshire*) will place them in English homes (temporarily!).

Overnight in a castle or a country house? You might query an organization called **Country Homes & Castles** in Great Britain, which lists more than 100 addresses (mostly fine estates rather than historic fortresses). We haven't yet sampled its offerings, but many look worthy. For the photo-filled brochure write to David Morse, Oak Leaf Enterprises, Ltd., 41 Dover St., London W.1.

Check-out time in Great Britain is usually noon.

Most hotels take a rakeoff when they cash your traveler's checks—sometimes a stiff one, too. Ask about this difference first, because a trip to the nearest bank may be worth the energy.

Watch out for a stupid, irritating custom called "corkage"—which charges the guest perhaps £1 for drinking out of his own bottle in his own room. To bypass this silly business, don't deposit empties in the wastebasket—and hide the liquor when the waiter or maid is present.

Within the U.K., be sure to have confirmed reservations *in advance* wherever you wander. Space at certain times of the year can be so tight that you may be sorry if you don't.

FOOD Notably improved over the past decade—and much more variety, too. The fine restaurants offer delectable food; where you'll continue to need your Tums by the gross is in the smaller, cheaper places run by gentle ladies or gentry with palates of Portland stone. Among the constellation of fashionable new stops there is a tendency among chefs to confuse richness with excellence; a surfeit of cream seems to find its unwheyward way into nearly every whip or fold from the kitchen.

Certain items have always been good: Roasts, grills, salmon, Yorkshire ham, Stilton cheese, bacon, and 2 or 3 others. Routine British cookery, however, has been scandalously poor since WW I—a shocking national indifference to the kitchen which nothing but sheer boredom with the subject can explain. With an encouraging new interest in food among young housewives and an ever-growing circle of British gourmets, standards are definitely on the rise.

Meal hours are fixed. Breakfast used to be heavy, but now it is comparatively light; lunch, seldom taken before 1 o'clock, is substantial; tea, at 4:30 P.M., is a sacred ritual in every walk of life; dinner, between 7 P.M. and 8:30 P.M., is the biggest repast of all. As in Norway, the local schedule calls for 4 meals per day; some may not cook well, especially at rural addresses, but the English eat as heartily as do most Americans.

§TIPS: English oysters are expensive but superb. Imperials (available all of the "R" months) are considered the finest; the larger Colchesters (Oct. to Jan.) are also exquisite. Don't miss them if you're a bivalve fan.

In case you're as baffled by the difference between these so-typical lookalikes as we were, steak-and-kidney *pie* is made with pastry crust, while steak-and-kidney *pudding* ("pud" to the locals) is made with a suet dumpling top which is indigestably deelishus.

Check the prices of all delicacies offered as side dishes. Most are flown in from points as remote as South Africa—so if your maître suggests "a nice piece of melon," for example, it might come from Israel and it might cost $5. Even a portion of humble asparagus might rock you $6.50!

RESTAURANTS AND NIGHTCLUBS   Pick your spot, and you'll be fed beautifully; wander into an untried establishment, no matter how quaint it appears, and you'd possibly give your shirt to be back in Chock Full O'Nuts in New York.

In *London*, the Mayfair and Soho districts have the best and most interesting places, with Chelsea making an increasingly strong bid as the local Left Bank. Mayfair is chichi and costly, like New York's gilded East Side; Soho and Chelsea are closer to Greenwich Village in flavor, although the tabs can run plenty high here too. Remember: *Most* major independent restaurants and hotel grillrooms (not hotel dining rooms) are shut tight on Sundays. And remember especially, please, that it's *always* wise to make advance reservations in London, regardless of the place or hour; they call it "booking."

At long last more places are staying open for after-theater dining. Choose your spot before setting out for the evening, and NEVER ask any taxi driver to suggest an oasis in the capital. After the sun sets in this stronghold of the British Empire, the slick practices are more myriad than the stars above. At least 1½-dozen clubs personally known to us pay commissions to taximen for delivering warm bodies to their doorsteps—and then clip the client unmercifully. We heard of one case in which a woman was held for "ransom" until the husband went back to his hotel and retrieved money enough to pay a thumpingly padded bill. If you're hooked, don't fight, because physical danger lurks too often. It's much safer to try to compromise with the management if you're given a loaded check. See the police later if the amount is important enough, but save your skin, your molars, and your pretty blue peepers first. Mayfair is most often racket-free, but Soho—from end-to-end—is a viper pit.

Official sources list about 400 so-called quality establishments in the capital. Here is the numbing, leg-wearying Grand Total of more than 200 which we have tried *personally* (unless otherwise indicated)—representing practically every type, style, and price bracket. Let's first report by category the ones we recommend, then follow with a roundup of those we found indifferent or disappointing.

For *fashionable dining without dancing (average meal $8 to $18),* here are our choices.

If a restaurant can be born with a pedigree, then young **Waltons of Walton Street** (121 Walton St.) certainly qualifies splendidly. It was conceived by personable young Malcolm Livingston, formerly the manager of Carrier's (see below); Headwaiter Michael Catsanis came from Inigo Jones; the cutlery is Georg Jensen; the china is Royal Copenhagen. The cuisine, not incidentally, is straight from heaven. Breeding shows, too, in the restful décor which melds traditional Trianon-gray, pale-yellow, and lavender textiles with handsomely wrought stainless-steel valances and drilled globe table lamps—an intermarriage that sounds peculiar but jibes beautifully. Georgian windows overlooking the quiet street had to be boarded up because of the insanity of an IRA bombing; a smoked-mirror-clad inner nook is available for more intimacy (better after theater); the set meals (lunch available in 3 or 4 courses, at $8.75 or $11.25, dinner at $15 and a late supper at midday tariffs) are changed about every 3 weeks as seasonal items come to market. On 5 recent test visits we sampled such inventive creations as a lightly whipped camembert mousse; sole with orange and cream sauce (an eighteenth-century recipe); Veal Paupiettes (thin slices) filled with spinach and smoked ham; a salad of yogurt, mushroom, and celeriac; cream-cheese pie; and a baseball-size melon flavored with cassis. The wines also disclose their patrician bearing; our superb Pernaud-Vergelesses '57 was only one entry among many excellent Beaunes, not to mention the vast selection of other aristocratic vintages from France, Germany, and elsewhere. Service from the friendly barman, from the knowledgeable sommelier, and from the waiters, and the attention from Mr. Livingston (I presume) himself, are the ultimate in cordiality and refinement. As bloodlines go, this one is true blue. A fervent recommendation from us that grows even warmer as this youngster matures.

Parkes Restaurant & Mr. Benson's Bar (4 Beauchamp Place) remains a red-hot rage among a discreet group of London socialites who know their gastronomy. Messrs. Tom Benson, J. L. Chamberlain, and 3 skilled chef-associates are carrying on the late founder's tradition with imagination and distinction. Cozy dimensions in menu-lined cellar of an old domicile; 21 tables seating 66 lucky clients; no bar, but spirits and extra-fine wines available; jungle of flora. The selections are limited to what the partners find to be the quality shopping bets on that day, but the variety is always extensive. Four-course fixed-price lunch (several choices at each stage) from noon to 3 P.M.; more elaborate fixed-price dinner which may include such originals as sweetbreads with cognac, mussels in a mustard soup, baby turkey with cherries and chestnuts, a salad with Roquefort pâté, or a succulent, flower-surrounded peach filled with lemon sherbet; Chefs Clarke, Gregori, and Coyle form a triple-threat that's nigh impossible to beat in this towne. Always jammed to its scuppers; impossible to wander in and find a table at *any* time; so popular that dozens are turned away nightly; thus, *nail down that reservation well in advance!* On several trips (not all) over the past decade or so, we have found our very best meal here of these London rounds; the prices are proportionally (but rightfully) among the loftiest in the Kingdom.

Mirabelle (56 Curzon St.), dressy and chichi, bears the reputation of the most sophisticated straight restaurant in Great Britain—but a disturbing number of Guidesters have not been too happy here. Despite these comments, here's one of the most attractive atmospheres to be found anywhere. The air-conditioned, flower-banked, semigarden patio is delightful in rainy or sunny weather. Superior kitchen; fine buffet in summer; clientele of international bluebloods. But remember that it will cost you plenty, and that your welcome may not be as gracious as it could be. Recommended despite these reservations.

The Empress (15 Berkeley St., opposite the May Fair Hotel), is under the same directorial aegis as L'Écu de France. Handsomely decorated room in gray-blue and cherry-red, with wraparound interior balcony for hand-holders. About 40 tables; small, companion-piece cocktail lounge, mural panels, gentle lighting, and piano musings blend in a judicious mixture; costly selections, often featuring first-of-the-season vegetables; occasional hard-sell efforts by fast-talking captains; cuisine normally excellent, but off days do occur. General Manager G. Negri is chief consort of both this and of L'Écu (you can also ask for Mr. Torres or Mr. Moroni); always open except for Saturday lunch. If you hit it right, you might fall in love with it.

Carrier's (2 Camden Passage, Islington) is a dynamic entry by go-getting North American Robert Carrier whose cookbooks and recipe-card packets are the "in" dishes in many an international home kitchen. His "Take Away" shop, a few doors away in the chic antique quarter called "The Angel," is a distilled toyland for U.S. homemakers or snack-timers. One tier for his "Supper by Candlelight" (4 scrumptious courses served from 10:30 P.M. to 11:15 P.M.); intimate-to-almost-cramped dimensions; 6-table main-floor dining room with plum and fireman-red tablecloths and paisley napkins; green textile-covered walls and deep-sea carpeting; homey white-painted brick; upstairs unit (which we prefer for its bonus of quiet) with Ferrari color scheme; a few outdoor tables "greenhoused" with foliage rotating by season; tiny bar and split-level cocktail lounge, serving those dreadful deep-saffron-colored British-style martinis (we finally supervised our own formula). The set menu includes 4 courses and an open wine. (Sample: a Smoked Salmon Quiche, French onion tart, or delicious Brabande of Smoked Trout to start, followed by an herb-scented meat or grilled wildfowl, button mushrooms à la Grecque, and a topper of Moroccan Orange Salad, Lemon Posset, or Chocolate Fancy. Sound scrumptious? You bet.) The carafe of Sancerre, selected from the barrel in France by Mr. Carrier, is sensational for its low cost. Our splendid and continuing feasts couldn't be better in presentation, in concept, and in the basic soundness of an *haute cuisine* enhanced with intelligence and imagination. Be absolutely certain to reserve in advance. If you can arrange it, try to go on a Saturday, when the antique market is galloping full tilt—a nourishing afternoon for inveterate shop hounds. Happy recommendation as one of the top gastronomic centers in the metropolis today—and lots of fun too. P.S. —*Out* of the metropolis near Ipswich, you can find yet another dalliance at the Maestro's Hintlesham Hall (see "Country Dining near London").

Frederick's, also in Camden Passage, may be only a few doors away geographically, but this younger entry (which we'd label as a would-be imitator) was light-years away in quality during our orbit. Now we hear that it may be on the rebound. Two unusually attractive dining levels, with the upper one more formal; lower segment, down a few steps, fronted by tall wide windows overlooking a garden patio; white brick walls; slate flooring. We've always maintained that with a coordinated effort, not to mention a better staff, this could be a little trove. Perhaps it finally is mellowing. We'll see soon.

Lacy's (26 Whitfield St.) lends excitement to the London culinary scene through the efforts of the hospitable and talented husband-and-wife team Bill Lacy (a childhood protégé of Escoffier) and Margaret Costa (a respected oenologist and frequent contributer to *Gourmet* magazine). Ground-floor reception with restaurant downstairs under white stucco vaults; tile floors, a bit cool to the tootsies; paintings for warmth; fascinating wine list which accents interesting, somewhat remote *crus* that are inexpensive and more than adequate. Our chilled avocado soup was one of the finest servings we've sampled in many an eve; our partner's ladle of watercress, lettuce, and almonds also was outstanding. Here is a champion without pretentions.

Ma Cuisine (113 Walton St.) is another serious contender, tiny though the precincts may be. A mere 7 tables; timber-lined wall on one side; burnt-orange textile on the other; brass and copper pans for décor. Warmharted reception by Lucette, the charming wife of the Chef-Proprietor Mouilleron, one of the leading proponents of French gastronomy on English soil. Open weekdays only for lunch and dinner. Our repast was as delicate as a St.-Tropezian zephyr.

La Croisette (168 Ifield Rd.) also recalls a Rivera mood, contrived as it is with service personnel in oystermen's sweatshirts, iced seafood displays, and artwork of the Côte d'Azur. We thought the entrance tatty; it lead down a chipped and scruffy spiral staircase to a miserably ventilated arched cellar. Extremely cordial reception; immediate offer of an apperitif, gratis; abundant and superior $14 set meal, plus rather expensive wines. It is highly fashionable at the moment, but we found the close atmosphere uncommodious for true dining pleasure. Perhaps you will have another impression. Closed Mondays and lunchtime, except on Sundays.

La Napoule (8–10 N. Audley St., Grosvenor Sq.) also lacks eye appeal but to our palate it approached the quintessence of gastronomic pleasure. Busy, noisy, jovial ambiance; bar at entrance rubbing elbows with the cloakroom activity; long 2-tier room in dull brown; clouded windows on one side, mirrored alcoves on the other, and greenery growing down the middle. The Vichyssoise was perfect; the Quenelles of Smoked Salmon were as light as a dream of minuets; the Scampi Timbale also was so weightless it could have wafted from the kitchen by itself; the duck with mint was bizarre, but essentially good; the sauces were carefully prepared without tricks or gimmickry; the wine list is mammoth. An outstanding meal will clobber your bank balance; of this you can be sure. Strictly for the cognoscenti of the table to whom cost is secondary.

Venerable **Tiddy Dols Eating House** (2 Hertford St., Sheperd Market), named after the legendary eighteenth-century gingerbread man, is a delightfully inviting cluster of 6 ancient rooms, 2 bars, and a minstrels' gallery in 9 contiguous domiciles highlighted by Hogarth prints, tastefully muted Old English décor, pert young waitresses in Elizabethan costume, and unusually fine fare—counterpointed by strolling balladeers. It is serene and thoroughly ingratiating—with a no-tipping policy that *really* works. Now there's also live entertainment from 7 to 11 P.M. and dancing from 11 to 3. Staples include steak-and-kidney pudding, steak in a copper pot, fisherman's pie, and many other more unique tempters. *Always* book in advance; especially enticing for after-theater suppers. If you don't choose gingerbread for dessert, which would be a mistake, please have a go at the Pippin Tansy. Open 6 P.M. to 3 A.M. We're all out for this quaint, charm-loaded establishment, but we do urge you to check your bill extra-carefully here.

L'Écu de France (111 Jermyn St.) knows its gastronomy. Now that it has recovered from its serious slump, this house is really clicking again. When you receive that Écu-brand of overbustling but kindly service, we think you will agree that here is one of the leading French restaurants on British soil. Tasteful, lively, not spectacular or chichi; business clientele predominant at lunchtime; large handwritten menus in the Gallic tradition; outstanding vintage wines somewhat overpriced, served by sommeliers in cellarmen's smocks; bar chairs uncomfortably tiny, but dining-room facilities excellent; management by Mario Borlenghi, with Nick masterminding the bar. It is closed for lunch on Saturdays, but open for Sunday dinner. Once more it merits ringing cheers and *santés.*

Drones (1 Pont St.), we hear, recently was ruined by a conflagration; we don't know if it will be rebuilt but we hope so.

Le Gavroche ("The Gamin," 61 Lower Sloane St.) could have been forgiven in its initial stages if occasionally serious culinary efforts were supplanted by the new breed of London's hoked-up theatrical cookery. Now, however, the latter seems to prattle front-and-center while the spotlight has dimmed on more masterful gastronomy. Foyer with 2 tables and a floor-to-ceiling wine rack directly behind the bar (a perfect way to sour fine vintages; our claret was off, while its contemporary bottlings are almost universally sound); angular, V-shape room adjoining, with sound-softened ceiling, tobacco-tan walls, ocher banquettes, and 18 tables with shaded candlesticks; extensive wine card with tabs startlingly higher than those of nearly all of the other top establishments. The cuisine on our latest repeat performance was still benighted by exaggerated spicing and cloying infusions of superheavy cream; and dishes, when served, immediately flashed into our minds the imagery of a haughtily vainglorious ham-actor chef posturing in the kitchen. (This was based solely on the mental reactions of those moments; we have never seen the gentleman in question.) The pretentious pose of our French-speaking maître was a trifle gagging when we consider that he is playing 99% of the time to a monolingual

English audience. This time the price for 2 persons nudged the $45 mark, including tips and beverages. Here, to us, is a classic example of a restaurant replete with dramatic gimmicks to impress tinsel lovers whose familiarity with high cuisine is at the 5th-grade level. The true gastronome, in our opinion, should strenuously avoid it.

Also very Gallic in flavor is **Le Bressan** (14 Wrights Lane), where the heavy scarlet damask, satin, and brocade belie the lightness of the culinary side. Dinner is best, but plan to bid *adieu* to $40 or so if you arrive in tandem.

Julie's (137 Portland Rd.) currently is in with the innermost circle of young aristocratic funlovers. Only the jovial wine bar (with small lunches) is open at midday. Furnishings and décor drawn from various periods of English antiquity; a small forest of potted palms; taped classical music; quite cuddlesome in concept, perhaps even cliquish insofar as an outsider's impressions may be concerned. The food is as appealing as the surroundings. Artfully conceived and out of the ordinary as restaurants go. We enjoyed it, but we're not sure everyone will.

Inigo Jones (14 Garrick St.) is tucked away in a former mission house in the heart of the theatrical district. Look for its entrance beside what appears to be a chapel door but is now the portal of an office building. Impressively handsome interior employing many fine touches left over from its era as a stained-glass factory; bar up front with live harpsichord music nightly; antique-brick walls spotted with illuminated cathedral windows; carved medieval gargoyles which made even *us* look good to our lady companion; tangerine-and-plum linens; cellar den less interesting than the ground level. So-so attention is given by waiters gaily attired in Edwardian waistcoats, ruffled cuffs, skintight trews, and some with shoulder-length tresses. Although the presentation was superb, somehow the culinary substance did not live up to the appetizing promise we had anticipated. But it's not too costly—and certainly here's a reward for the hungry eye. Recommended, if you don't expect Litri to prepare your vittles.

Le Carrosse (19-21 Elystan St., S.W.3) has been creating a cross fire of chitchat lately. Textile wall coverings; matching curtains; coach wheels over the doorway; huge centerpiece of dried flowers; yokes and other tack hung here and there; trappings a little shabby; so was our service. The cookery was suprisingly delectable, but because of the dismal location and tacky trim, we are not too enthusiastic. We think it's a fad that will eventually fade.

Popote (3 Walton St.), to us, at least, goes overboard into the aesthetic seas. A trio of dainty roomettes usually abubble with dainty people relaxing nervously in its delicate atmosphere. French conservatory ambiance; draped ceiling; candles and flowers on tables; gilt chairs; giltless menu of limited size; main dishes about $6 and fair to our tastebuds; sweetie-pie reception and service. John Wayne would probably feel uneasy here, but Tiny Tim might adore it.

Alonso's (32 Queenstown Rd., S.W.8) is a bit off the beaten path, but the with-it crowd quickly spotted this crazy lair. Childlike watercolors on matburgundy walls; dark carpet; candles and flowers on its several tables; inventive, almost playful menu that discloses a disdain for culinary convention; fixed-price card in the $10 range without wine. It will be interesting to see if

Mr. Alonso has the sticking power to remain popular with the oh-so-fickle, unsettled, young executive set.

Andrea's (Blacklands Terrace, a backlands alley off King's Road) splits its hearty but unpretentious personality between Italian and French cuisine. Perhaps 16 tables up front plus one typically Latin cranny out back; open wine rack opposite entrance; rainbow of red, yellow, and blue-hued checkered cloths with matching napery; dessert-and-cheese display tray with 4-wheel drive; efficient, friendly staff. We're extremely high on this house's tempting array of easy-on-the-wallet traditional dishes, the gratis Turkish paste offered with coffee, and the welkin of welcomes. Solid through and through.

Old Russia (9 Dean Bradley House, Horseferry Rd.) is a labor of love by Mme. Elena Konstantinovna, who transported all 52 tons of it (only the carpeting is British) from the Far East. The 3 dining rooms recreate the moods of Odessa, Moldavia, and Siberia. If you munch your Marinovanaia Ribba (fish cooked in vegetables) in the last one, please don't be alarmed if you find an old woman sleeping on the mantelpiece—merely a provincial method of keeping warm. When the Proprietress explains her selections, she is proud to point out that some of them are no longer served elsewhere. Our Blinis, Ukranian Borscht, Beef Strogonoff, and Marojenoie (rainbow ice cream) were happy conventional choices. The white Russian wine (its color, not its politics!) was an interesting change. Two set menus are available including the Zahouski Dinner, a ruble-saving series of Tsar-iffic hors d'oeuvres (try this with one of her 3 specially blended vodkas). Closed Sunday. A Russian Rhapsody.

Barracuda (1D Baker St., off Portman Square), in a suavely styled subterranean setting, just may dish out the most savory Italian delicacies in London. Plush bar to the right of the stairs for prepasta persuasions; catacomb setting; thick carpet; indirect green illumination which Transylvanians would probably adore; discreetly hidden combo alternating with piped melodies; streamlined tables and chairs; equally streamlined clientele. Our Quaglie Bell'Antonio (boned quail with Parma ham wrapped in flaky pastry) was a bird of paradise; the service was prompt and proper; the tabs have the bite of a hungry Barracuda. Gilt-edged costs, but still in the swim.

A flaming-hot fad that faded is **Leith's** (92 Kensington Park Rd.) To us, here's another revealing example of how Would-Be Fashionable Sheep follow the lead of other Would-Be Fashionable Sheep. Ugly multiformed dining segments hewn from a converted apartment in a low-rent district; drab walls; miserable lighting; a more disciplined maître than the earlier clown is now on duty. When Prudence Leith is present we can see the reason for its local popularity, but at other times our enthusiasm is nil, null, and nix. (She wasn't on hand on a recent and disappointing sampling, but she was during our latest incognito trial; the latter, we say with Prudence, was quite satisfactory gastonomically.)

For *medium-priced dining without dancing (average meal $7 to $12),* we are very favorably impressed by the food at **Overtons St. James's** (5 St. James's St.), which offers seafood specialties plus a goodly store of grills and meats in modern surroundings. Two floors; excellent oyster bar; noisy; tourist-trammeled; big after-theater trade; 1 wail of bitterness from a Long Island Guidester who complained of service snippishness, sullen attitudes, and an improper regard for sanitary food handling and presentation; closed Sundays. **Vendôme** (20 Dover St.) is also catnip for those with piscatorial palates. Separate counter for bivalve fanciers; eighteenth-century French décor; Manager John Rusbridge is your hardworking host; closed Saturday; pleasant. **La Terrazza** (19 Romilly St.) still remains a hot rendezvous for fashionable, mannerly swingers. Double necklace of small rooms in 2 strands (ground level and cellar); tiny tables with elbow-to-elbow relationships among adjoining parties; personable and charming Italian-born directorial team of Mario and Franco, who also operate the same-style **Tiberio** (22 Queen St.; see later) and the equally chichi Kensington swinger called **Mario & Franco's Trattoo** (2 Abingdon Rd.). The only drawback—a big one—was the substandard quality of our latest pseudo-Peninsular-style dinner. Although it might have passed as fair for London, it was a very weak carbon copy of the genuine article. But who cares about the food here, anyway? Enormously popular, so be sure to book *allegretto*. **Café Royal** (68 Regent St.) has come back with a bang. This famous Bohemian hangout with the flavor of Delmonico's at the turn of the century again offers the discriminating diner everything it should. Service leans toward the hurry-hurry school; our recent try produced good substantial cuisine; the presentation was superb. Be sure to sit in the Grill Room (closed Sun.).

L'Étoile (30 Charlotte St.) started off nobly when this century was in diapers. How it continues to get better, we'll never understand—but it does. The French-based cuisine is, in fact, more delicate than that of some of the biggest names in Paris. The wines are exquisite and treated with grace and solemnity by one of the finest sommeliers on either side of the Channel. Highly skilled waiters in swallowtail coats; yellow walls ending at a ruby border; red figured carpet. The same clientele keeps coming back delightful year after delightful decade—and so will we. For the medium bracket, here's deluxe gastronomy. Again, highly recommended—and be sure to reserve in advance. **Isola Bella** (15 Frith St.) has been taken over by a former waiter of this house; he now aims the skillets at chiefly French recipes. Very good; closed Sunday. **White Tower** (1 Percy St.) is a north-of-Soho standby, with the Greek hospitality of John Stais to welcome you. Two floors eternally busy (and often a 3rd, as well); walls lined with fez-topped braves and decorative plates; superb service; wonderful Dolmades, stuffed eggplant, Moussaka, and other fully developed Levantine delights, plus "retsina" and French wines. We love it. **Frank's Italian Restaurant** (63 Jermyn St.) whips up savory pasta, risotto, and other Latin delicacies for a modest number of lire. Big lunch traffic of clients from the business district; quiet at night; more for good food than for good looks. **Leoni's Quo Vadis** (Dean St.) used to be one of our favorites, but we've gone off it of late. **Marquis** (121A Mount St.) is described by one gracious lady as "splendid for the dinner you wish you could have had at home." We've recently emerged from a checkup, and this friendly tipster couldn't be more correct. Lovely presentation of French and Italian dishes (especially the veal and the duck); smart clientele who were obviously enjoying its luxury surroundings at medium prices. The small pine-planked quad-

rant in the rear is chiefly for private parties. Thank you, kind Madame, for
the lead! **Martinez** (25 Swallow St.), now with sporadic guitar strumming in
both the bar and dining room, also has Spanish tiles, Iberian specialties, and
smiling attention; don't expect Escoffier to prepare your dinner, but for what
you pay, it's one of the better reasonably priced choices in the capital.

Chelsea has gained its very own place in the sun. Now it's the grazing
ground for London's younger avant-garde set—angry young achievers post-
blue-jeans, Medium Fry, poets, painters, and phrase makers. Its momentum
began with the espresso bars, many of which soon developed into 50 or more
new feederies. **Alvaro's** (124 King's Rd.), the head of the pack 10 seconds ago,
now seems vedy old chapeau. Close atmosphere; white walls; plain settings;
damnably uncomfortable for long lingering or lounging. Food? Ho-hum—but
if you care, you miss the whole point. Alvaro himself left and has opened
I Paparazzi (54 Dean St.) and **La Famiglia** (7 Langton St.), both of which
are unknown to us. **Nick's Diner** (88 Ifield Rd.) was leased by Proprietor
Nicholas Clarke to his staff while he uncorked a neighboring bistro called
Nikitas (65 Ifield Rd.) with a ground-level bar, a cellar cell with gold-papered
walls, icon fixtures, and dim lighting. Everyone in our party was disappointed
by their cookery, but we all agreed that the wide selection and service of the
imported vodkas was excellent. Not for dining, but for imbibing. Other Chelsea chummeries? **Alexander's** (also on King's Rd.) is in the Old Guard of the
candlewax-and-gingham gang. It has been so successful that the management
now boasts an Alexandrian duet, with the newer branch nearby. **Chez Luba**
(Yeoman's Row) is a converted stable that was so excruciatingly popular
yesterday that we wouldn't be caught sober in it tonight. Pssssssst! . . . **Borgo
San Frediano** (62 Fulham Rd.), whispered to be *buonissimo*, we found just
plain awful in kitchen skills and service standards on our very recent try.
Though many tout it, we'd prefer to ignore it.

For *English traditional* dining, **Stone's Chop House** (Panton St., off The
Haymarket), in our opinion, generally continues as a felicitous exponent of
the national art. Handsome décor, warm and delightful, with updated Regency predominant; stone-floor cocktail lounge in black and red leather with
hunting motif; wood paneling with windows bordered in stained glass; natural
timber pillars; clever soft-sell illumination; lovely mural of a Canaletto harbor
scene. The upstairs Domino Lounge leads to a large, charmingly irregular
room in brick and tile, with marble statuary; Pebble Bar adjoining booths
along the periphery. Ask for charming General Manager M.C. Williams, who
will receive you warmly. No fancy French or "International" cuisine here—
just superb English stick-to-the-rib roast grills, "puds," and "Dover Sole that
brings tears to the eyes for grief that anything so innocent and tender should
have to yield up its life." This quotation was penned by another guidebook
scrivener about 75 years ago. All we can add, 7 decades later, is "Hear! Hear!"
Simpson's-in-the-Strand (100 Strand), around the corner from the Savoy, is
regaining its stride after riding too hard on its long and distinguished reputation. Men's Bar in cellar and venerable, paneled, ground-floor restaurant
(ladies admitted to latter only Sats.); rich, decorous, comfortable main restaurant up 1 flight (ladies always welcome). It serves almost the same classic

dishes as Stone's, but a further comparison between the 2 would not yet be felicitous, in our opinion. We passionately avoid its potted shrimps, however. Closed Sunday; mandatory to reserve in advance for lunch; don't forget the custom of tipping your carver. Two oddities: (1) Gentlemen are requested not to smoke their pipes in the dining room, and (2) tea is available but politely discouraged here (Simpson's avows it's for teatime *only*—an hour when its portals are shut). **Kettners** (Romilly St., Soho, W.1), a dining staple since 1867, lived up to its plus-and-minus slogan on our try: "No music, but the best of food." Its cornerstone of quality is ample reason for its century-plus of success. Scattered complaints to us continue about slipping service, sloppy waiters, and skimpy portions. Twin-segment bar sprinkled with intimate perches; a duet of dining rooms down a few steps; gold tapestry-clad walls; a warm touch in burgundy overdrapes highlighted by white scrim curtains; a happy nest of 3-dozen tables sparkling with starched blue-and-white linens. Lunch from noon to 3 P.M.; dinner from 6 to 11:30 P.M., when the last order is taken; Sunday schedules slightly shorter for each mealtime. Closed on Christmas only. Also improving. **Rules** (35 Maiden Lane), also a short hike from the Savoy Hotel, presents a charming Edwardian impression of seediness. Creaky, rippled floors; dimensions so cozy that you can 'ear every *h* drop 'ard at the next table; overchummy but friendly welcome. Game, pies, mutton chops, the hearty fare (and feel!) of Old England; no roast beef, but our latest steak was handled with dutiful respect. Our bill for 1 (sirloin, fruit, and a ½-bottle of claret) was in the $12 range. This ancient landmark, popular for after-theater suppers, is closed Sundays. **The Baron of Beef** (Gutter Lane, Gresham St.) is another retreat where the Aberdeen Angus is deified. Odd-shape, low-ceiling room with stuffy ventilation; décor pleasant but undistinguished; elbow-type tables with sleigh-type seats; service as cheerful and benign as the vases of flowers; very noisy when full. Despite its outstandingly savory beef and extra-courteous attention, not worth the long trek to London's financial district if you're closer to Stone's or the Rib Room (see below). **Cowcross** (6–7 Cowcross St.) is in the center of Smithfield, Europe's largest wholesale meat market—and *that* is exactly why you should order one of its bovine selections. Clublike atmosphere; hunt scenes on walls; wonderful grills; poor desserts; medium prices. The area is fun; so is the meal—if you're not a vegetarian. If you are herbivorous, try **Crank's** (Marshall St. near Regent St.), where we recently devoured one of the most savory repasts that botany can provide. Juice bar; cafeteria; health-food kiosk; delicious cookery in nice simple surroundings. A welcome change of viands. The **Wig & Pen Club** (229-230 Strand), built in 1625, is the beloved oasis of upper-echelon newsmen from neighboring Fleet Street. Here is the only building on this famous avenue to survive both the Great Fire of London and the subsequent invasion of hungry managing editors and thirsty foreign correspondents. Proprietor Dick Brennan, however, is his own Great Fire as a host—one of the most genial, eager-to-cheer bonifaces we know. He willingly serves as the Good Samaritan for virtually scores of Yankee pilgrims seeking advice on transportation, hotel space, or any legitimate wayfarer's headache. A number of doll-size dining rooms radiate from the 4 crooked flights of stairs; the trispire penthouse roof garden features lobster and other selections in hot weather; 5 bars dispense smiles in season; pine-lined Inns of Court Room for the "hospitality hour"; never expect to find so much as a frozen carrot here, since the chef scorns anything but the natural savor of earth-fresh vegetables. Dick promises us that any faithful Guidester will be issued a Temporary Membership Card FREE, valid for the duration of his London visit. Hallelujah! Open until 11 P.M. weekdays except Saturdays until 6 P.M., not at all on Sundays. **The Hunting Lodge** (16 Lower Regent St.) is one of the most ambitious, sumptuous, and elegant projects of the mighty Trust Houses Forte interests. Modern aura, subdued and delightfully pleasant; oak panels, indirect lighting, teak tables, black-leather chairs and banquettes; 5 murals painted for charity by Peter Thorneycroft, the Realm's ex-Minister of Defense. A dark-brick open grill commands the central focus, producing the mainstays of its now-disappointing British fare. Fascinating menu listing such items as Smoked Bloater, Cottage Pie, and Finnan Haddie; roast beef and steaks (our latest one again was positively wretched) are the noon features, with roast lamb spotlighted at night; both are dispensed from rolling trolleys. Enormous wine cellar with *only* blue-ribbon vintages (no mere Beaujolais or lesser pressings in evidence)—at prices that seem just plain outrageous. Unless you're totally determined to go, or unless you are winking at the roast with an expense-account voucher in your pocket, we just don't think that the enormous gap in cost is worth it any longer. Perhaps you'll disagree. Pimm's now has only 1 of its former 4 branches currently in operation: **Ye Olde Dr. Butler's Head** (Mason's Ave.). This institution inspired the famous Pimm's Cups; known the world over. Closed Saturday to Monday. **Guinea Grill Room** (30 Bruton Place), a 400-year-old converted stable located in a tiny mews, serves only meats (grills particularly), vegetables, salads, and desserts. Entrance via the kitchen; bypass the 9-table "inside" dining room and aim straight for the arbor-bowered "garden" with red walls, a dozen candlelit tables, and a cozy throng of diners—generally Colonists from our shores rather than Redcoats (but more of the latter taking the cue). There's a saloon up front if you want to detour for a nip. Extremely popular—and with good reason!—so be sure to book in advance. Our big, big demurrer here—shared by a number of equally innocent Guidesters—is that no prices are listed for either the comestibles or the wines; on a recent visit the check was so high we were stunned by its nasty surprise. Open for lunch and dinner on weekdays, dinner only on Saturdays, and never on Sundays.

The **Blue Boar Inn**, on Leicester Square (how more conveniently located could it be?), had lost some of its flair on our latest check. The Jousting Bar, at ground level, is a run-of-the-spigot pub, with nothing to distinguish it from hundreds of its fellows. But down one flight, the venturer finds (1) a candlelit cocktail bar, (2) the Robin Hood Tavern, an optional dining place separated by wrought iron and crossed pikes over its "doorway" from (3) the main restaurant. Medieval English motif, with handsome arched ceilings; fat candles for every group; flaming "torchlights" as wall fixtures; artful color blends; perhaps 35 tables; good service. Still popular with its essentially British clientele; convenient to the cluster of first-run movie theaters in this area. **Wilton's** (27 Bury St.), a turn-of-the-century period piece, appeals to traditionalists. Although roast beef is *not* the main attraction, it is always available and nearly always excellent. For decades this busy bistro has been famed for its piscatorial splendors, which are now featured less and less but which retain the highest quality. Prices are often not listed. In the main stream, and excellent for its type. **Massey's Chop House** (38 Beauchamp Place) features similar high-protein products, but only a fraction of the atmosphere. This old Forte forge is better for dinner than for lunch. The **Paramount Grill** (14-15 Irving St.) is not paramount with us for grills; many U.S. military types form ranks here; a chow line at best. The **George and Vulture** (3 Castle Court) is a 2-story, open-grill rough-and-ready chophouse, with ancient, friendly waiters and a near-medieval setting; it claims title as the oldest tavern in existence, founded in A.D. 1175; our salad easily could have dated from the same year; our melon was harder than a tempered cannonball; our steak was rewarding, however. Open for lunch only, Monday through Friday; go before 1 P.M. or after 1:45 P.M., because its regular stockbroker clientele keeps it jammed. Medium prices for no-nonsense cookery; more British than the British; you may have to share a table. Not spectacular, but veddy, veddy Plantagenet. **Mrs. Beeton's Hungry Horse** (196 Fulham Rd.) offers standard fodder at stable tariffs. Simple surroundings in a whitewashed basement rick; fair-withered clientele of Smart Set fillies, stallions, and perhaps a few geldings; pleasant for a long-shot diversion. **Mr. Fogg**, an annex of the previously described Café Royal, permits you to grill your own steak at tableside, leaving the chef free to preside over his salad bowl. The prices are inviting, but the atmosphere is, well . . . Foggy. Very convenient, but short on eye appeal.

For *seafood,* the capital of this salty island has splendid versatility. **Scott's** (20 Mount St.) is decked out with raspberry-damask wall coverings, marble columns, Spy prints on white brick, bas-relief panels, and crystal chandeliers. Swallowtail-coated Manager Luigi has labored valiantly to please, and he merits kudos aplenty. Every morsel of our latest meal was delicious, and our service was impeccable. We enjoyed it thoroughly, and it is our hope you will, too. **Cunningham's** (17B Curzon St.) has changed its décor for something resembling Gaulish Boudoir. The vittles and attention were worth the fishing expedition, but the billings seemed baleen to this Poseidon. **Wheeler's** (19 Old Compton St.), original link in the worthy chain that includes Vendôme and 5 others, features Dover sole in 23 ways, lobster in 12 ways, and scallops in 5 ways; closed Sundays. Surely among the front sailors of the regatta. **Carafe** (15 Lowndes St.), now part of the Wheeler's group, offers 14-table intimacy, service that often rankles, so-so cuisine, a clientele of theatrical or business VIPs, and exactly the same menu as its bigger brother we've just mentioned; closed Monday. **Manzi's** (corner Lisle and Leicester Sts., W.C.2) is the oldest maritime den in London; reasonable tabs; grilled sole the specialty; unusually rewarding and money-saving. **Bentley's** (11 Swallow St.) swims in as a firmly fleshed midtown wiggler. Busy ground-floor bar and oyster counter; one-room upstairs restaurant with azalea-red walls hung with paintings; unwatchful disattention by frumpy waitresses; rush-rush atmosphere. Cookery that is almost *too* simple (some would say "bland"); reasonable-to-rich prices. A quality nook—but we won't go out of our way for our next try. **Bill Bentley's**

(31 Beauchamp Place), not to be confused with the above, features wine from the copious cave of B-B Himself. Subterranean sherry bar; ground-level pub for sips and nibbles; globe-lit, blue-trimmed upstairs dining area. The herring in heavy cream reaped net profits for our piscatorial speculation; our skewered medallions of turbot, ham, and green peppers, served on a bed of rice and capers, added another dividend. An otherwise pleasant repast was marred only by the sight of waiters gorging themselves on mussels and clams when they weren't attending to the clients. Ah, well . . . a small carp, really. Closed Sunday. Going into heavier poundage, the midtown, Med-mooded **Golden Carp** (8a Mount St.) is done up in fishnets, maritime paintings, raw-wood tables, and ship lanterns. Huge portions of better than average cookery; not cheap; quick service; same ownership as the aforementioned Marquis, which makes it a solid bottom feeder.

For *hotel dining,* to select only a handful from the carloads, the renewed yew-tree-and-white-marble **Savoy Grill** is an international legend; not only is it the acme of chichi and sophistication, but scores of serious gourmets maintain that it serves the best-prepared food in the United Kingdom. Famous Maître Luigi now manages Claridge's Restaurant, and Vercelli, who used to be at the Berkeley Grill, now rules in collaboration with Maestro Silvano Trompetto, the greatest chef in the United Kingdom. The **Connaught Grill** is on a par. We like each in its own way, however, so they are neck-and-neck in our ratings. Urbane, cozy atmosphere; impeccable from service to presentation to cuisine. Also especially warranted for after-theater supping. The **Capital** capitalizes on a well deserved reputation for distinguished continental fare. Our Mousseline de Coquille St. Jacques and Carré d'Agneau were nothing short of splendid. Few tables, so reserve ahead; small adjoining lounge; smooth service. Surely one of the finest in today's London. The aforementioned Le Perroquet in the **Berkeley** is the nexus for an excellent luncheon. This sleek-feathered entry, which flaps into a chirping discothèque at night, provides a table-buckling buffet within one of the most decorative cages around. A galaxy of cold meats, salads, and piping hot dishes is available for as many courses as your conscience (and belt) will permit, all at a remarkable $9 or so. Should this large display not pique your appetite, a selection of soups and salads (avocado, chicken with cranberry dressing, ham and orange, hollowed apple, and others) is available. Tempting, tasteful, and thrifty. The air-conditioned **Dorchester Grill** is smart for lunch; very social, very urbane; cuisine only so-so, in our opinion. At **Claridge's,** the main dining room has been given a shot of adrenalin, plus better lighting, and the chipper little cosmos known as the Causerie has an ample smörgåsbord selection (lunch and dinner this time), including mineral water, wine, or beer. General Manager Hansen is a Dane; he was wise enough to install one of his countrymen as the chef here; now both beam with national pride. Reserve well in advance, even if you are a hotel guest. Our recent meal in the main restaurant was perfect in every regard. Worth a visit. The **Carlton Tower's Rib Room**? Shut your ears to its broad-A accents, and you'll swear you're in flat-A Manny Wolf's Manhattan Chophouse or Arthur's in Dallas. Attractive red décor and restful lighting; reception, service, and staff attitude eager but sometimes fickle; succulent Prime Angus beef sliced in mammoth Yankee-style slabs; menu loaded with Madison Avenue superlatives which horrify staid Tories (*e.g.*, "Gourmet Adam Rib Cut, a veritable Beefeater's Bonanza"). Huge plates that dwarf the foil-baked potato; routine salad; ice water at every table; ventilation on the stuffy side. The barman needs a governor on his stirring arm, because twice our martinis came back with too much Thames and too little Gordon's. The Chelsea Room is 1-flight up. Both can be tremendous or disappointing, depending upon how you happen to hit them. The **Park Tower**'s Henry VIII haven is rich in décor for disciples of beef eating and lobster cracking. The **Inn on the Park**'s parking places are mentioned under "Hotels." The **Royal Lancaster**'s Mediterranean Café is one of the best budget moorings on the London shoreline, for our pound of sterling or pounds of flesh. The new **Intercontinental**'s Le Soufflé still needs maturing, in our opinion. The preparations in the Coffee House impressed us as uninspired. The **Strand Hotels** group (Regent Palace, Strand Palace, and Cumberland) offers so-called Carveries in each of these locations. Here you carve your own cuts of beef, ham, or lamb (as much as you want, as often as you want). Be sure to check their hours, because their openings and closings vary. The Beachcomber at the **May Fair** is a flash that fizzled into a cornball South Sea Island luau. At the same hotel, but worlds above the low-tide Beachcomber, you'll find patrician dining at the Châteaubriand. The **Hyde Park Grill** and the **St. George's** (viewful penthouse vista) are also well known for their kitchens. The **Ritz** boasts one of the most gorgeous rotunda rooms in Europe, but to us That Man in the Kitchen needs culinary lessons.

❧

Dining and/or dancing? London's nightscape—as in Paris, New York, Hamburg, and a host of other cities where the moon is better known than the sun—*is one of the fastest-changing in the world.* Entertainment establishments rise and fall so swiftly that even the most up-tonight tip sheets have difficulty keeping *au courant.* Therefore, please do not bet your last dollar on the accuracy of our survey here.

Talk of the Town still wins the brass ring on the Times-Square-style merry-go-round. Tycoon Charles Forte and Deputy H. Henry preside over this $425,000 conversion of the old Hippodrome on Leicester Square, which is now one of the most stunning theater-restaurants we've ever visited. Immense stage and music pit, sectionalized into mobile units; one huge, fast show nightly, followed by performances at 11 P.M. of international cabaret stars; 2 oversize, flawlessly integrated orchestras; tables seating a total of 625 have replaced all theater-style chairs. Fixed-price, 3-course dinner for around $18 Monday through Thursday (maybe $2 more on Fri. and Sat.) mandatory for all customers; typical but eatable production-line fare. Open from 8 P.M. to 1:15 A.M.; book in advance for either the balcony or the rear of the main floor for a better view of the spectacles. The Lido in Paris is larger and more elaborate, but for London this Colossal Evening at such reasonable cost is an almost unbelievable phenomenon. If you're a Latin Quarter fan, don't miss it.

The extensively redecorated **Royal Roof** of the Royal Garden Hotel gracefully combines sophistication and well-trained minions with a fine flair for theatrics. Beautiful presentation of The Royal Strings, a harmonic blend of 7 violins, a guitar, and an accordion which plays en masse for several numbers, then the musicians individually stroll among the diners while maintaining perfect melodic unison; 20-minute performances at 11 P.M. and midnight. Selective, small menu with 10th-floor prices; overpriced wine carte, no admission or cover charge. Here's a lovely, romantic, handholding ambiance, with dim lights, a chic conception, and a wonderful view—BUT pad your wallet, because you can drop a bundle of greenstuff. Tallyho!

Hatchett's Piccadilly, bought and reconstructed by the Restaurant Associates organization, is now a multilevel, multipurpose caravanserai straight off the drawing boards of the twenty-first century. Ground-floor coffee shop lined with giant posters that provide an affectation of early times; stingingly modern main restaurant with silvered walls, steel-braced emerald chairs, and *i*-dot tables so tiny a pair of canaries might feel cramped at feeding time; pale-orange bar to one side that repeats its motif-in-stainless; downstairs discothèque featuring an icy flower theme but heated up by one of the hottest combos in town; mediocre to poor cookery.

Tiberio (22 Queen St., Mayfair) is a touch of La Bella Roma. Peninsular cookery and décor; entrance through a below-stairs tiled bar to a gracious vaulted dining room; low-hanging lamps, 22 pink-clad tables, rush-bottom chairs; nice use of flowers; kitchen shielded by red-tinted glass. Very fine skillet work and service to match; lunch from noon to 3 P.M.; dinner from 7 P.M. to midnight; supper dancing from 11:30 P.M. to 3:30 A.M.; closed Sunday; expensive. An upbeat little swinger that is snatching a lot of business away from the competition. We say *bravissimo!*

Quaglino's (16 Bury St.) served us a pleasant meal and an eveningful of danceable music in the conventional (not modern) mood. Its inner heart glitters with reflections from lovely antique mirrors. Far from cheap, but a fair late-night-out for traditionalists.

La Dolce Notte (55 Jermyn St.) is no longer as sweet as the nights of yore; Italian cookery; dancing; a listless lump from the Dolce Vita (Frith St.; see below) sugar bowl.

L'Hirondelle (Swallow St.) is a cellar-bration spot with about 30 tables; floor shows with 5 chorines and a couple of "singles" at 10:30 P.M. and 1 A.M.; dancing until 3:45 A.M. Minimum dinner of 3 routine courses for lofty money; a cover charge appears if you do not order the vittles. Average.

Latin Quarter (13–17 Wardour St., Piccadilly Circus, W.1) exercises a sincere effort to imitate its historic New York namesake of yore—and the price tags more than achieve that noble end. Rectangular chamber; tables set on the sunken floor; Toulouse-Lautrec Bar; wide-angle stage; wide-angle babes frolicking at 11 P.M. and 1 A.M.; dinner dancing to 2 orchestras from 8:30 P.M. until the 3:30 closing.

Élysée (13 Percy St.) is a haven which effuses a Hellenic charm all its own. The décor is routine, but when the crowd is right it's delightfully lively. Big Greek patronage—and what people are merrier?—who richly enjoy the hospitality of host George Karageorgis. Ground floor with 15 tables, a small bar and dance floor, 3 to 4 musicians (*bouzouki* and accordion), and a singing Athena—all imported from Aegean shores. Far more fun, however, is watching supple and handsome George balance up to 7 full glasses atop his head, climbing on and off a stripped table every time the next one is added to the stack. Summer roof garden for nearly 100 midday or evening munchers, some of whom spontaneously leap up to provide impromptu entertainment; hours noon to 3 P.M. and 6:30 P.M. to 3 A.M. Noisy, cheerful, getting more expensive, not at all romantic—but often (not always) hilarious if you bring the right mood. Go on the late side.

La Dolce Vita (10 Frith St., Soho) is another target for the bargain hunter —but as we said, its Angus Steak Housekeepers seem to have sapped a lot of its former sauce. Italian cuisine, roman-tically decorated and executed; upstairs dining room for à la carte selections, guitar strummings, and higher tabs; more cozy *caverna* downstairs with fixed menu (28 dishes); ho-hum atmosphere. Open noon to 3 P.M. and 6 P.M. to midnight, 7 days a week; no dancing on Monday. Fair enough for *paesani* who value their lire, but we find it more and more *lento, di notte a notte*. Among the hotels, the **Savoy**, the **Inn on the Park** (Vintage Room only), the **Dorchester** (beautiful Terrace Room, as we mentioned before), the **Hilton**, and **Grosvenor House** all offer the Light Fantastic in their restaurants (separate from their Grills); Claridge's doesn't believe in all that jazz. The penthouse of the **Park Tower** vies with heaven itself for breathtaking vistas.

Many of the so-called *Membership Clubs* offer extremely attractive facilities for the visitor in search of dining, wining, and excitement. They are organized on a "private" basis to skirt the liquor laws. Local residents must pay nominal annual "dues" of perhaps £2, but travelers with valid foreign passports are usually issued a special card and admitted free.

The "Clubmanship Plan" is a gigantic chowder made up of nearly 400 separate clubs in 57 different cities and stirred into one enormous dining pool. For the full list, from Wales to Tewkesbury, write The Clubman, 5 Avery Rd., W.1.

As for **Les Ambassadeurs** (5 Hamilton Place), there are many surface charms including Le Cercle casino on the top floor with roulette and chemin de fer—but the most tiresome gamble is the process of getting into the joint. Starting way, way back, owner John Mills's quixotic entrance policies alienated so many *Guide* travelers that it fairly turns our stomach. One reader angrily stated (apparently based on our condemnation of this establishment in previous *Guide* editions), "You are due a round of cheers, because on our bill of £5 or so, three waiters demanded from my confused husband 20% (£1), and then extracted £2 from him. No itemization whatsoever on our bills.

J. Mills doesn't think you are so hot—and we don't think he is!" Once again, not recommended to any user of this book—and if any further slanderous nonsense from Mr. Mills or any of his employees reaches our ears, such as his alleged pearl of wisdom that "Fielding will recommend anyone for a free meal," we're going to take a great deal of pleasure in hauling this gentleman to court.

The **Hispaniola Restaurant Ship** is a newer splash in the pond. This one is a converted ferry moored Thames-side near the Charing Cross subway station. The entrance is not at all shipshape, but don't let it discourage you. Interior effectively deck-orated; recently rigged bar; upper level exclusively à la carte; fish is the specialty, and ours was much too saucy for our palate. Braces of MP's and businessmen customarily lunch here; the theater crowd takes over in the evening. Open year round. Better for ambiance than for fare.

The **White Elephant** (28 Curzon St.) is still frequented by its allotment of theatrical pashas, business tycoons, and would-be's—but again, speaking personally, we're mystified by whatever mystique draws them here. Brocade-and-velvet Regency with a gilt-complex; bar to the left of entrance; tables so small that one's elbow inadvertently becomes an offensive weapon while dining. Entrance by member introduction (a letter will do); à la carte menu; no entertainment. Mixed French- and Italian-style cuisine; our meal was not only wretched, but we will never forgive the villain who dumped ordinary, caffeine-loaded Nescafé into the showy caffeine-free Nescafé tin (he'd apparently run out of the latter), thus giving my 3-cup Nancy and me an entire sleepless night. We don't think you trekked all the way to Britain to spend your time and hard-earned cash on this type of pachyderm. Thus, we suggest passing it by without even a howdah.

The dine-and-dance-until-one-ayem **Wellington Club** (116 Knightsbridge) is a sound bet where you'll have little trouble becoming a Temporary Member. We have recently come from a whirl at the **New Yorker Club** (36 Park Lane) and we were not impressed—except unfavorably. Nix as our picks.

Nightclub high-or-low jinks? For early or wee-hours fun and games à la international gin mill, our number one favorite continues to stand fast: Frisky, hyperthyroid **Churchill's of Bond Street** (160 New Bond St.)—and please don't confuse it with the mammoth Churchill Hotel on Portman Sq. Jam-packed with film stars, oil sheiks, maharajahs, high politicos, playboys and other celebrities. Atmosphere just raffish enough to be intriguing; illumination tailor-made for Passive Pitches; 1¼-hour, 40-artist floor shows early, midevening, and late; moderately steep cover charge, and drinks at Paris prices (above average U.S. prices); don't try it unless you expect to spend plenty, because your evening will be *very* expensive. If you're a man and alone, you should have no trouble finding a beautiful and amusing companion, to whom it is gracious to offer a gift as "taxi fare," (£5 to £10 is the going rate) for her conversational company. Dinner begins at 8 P.M. (delay it until about 9:30)—and man, *what* a dinner! If you are a funloving insomniac, breakfasts are always on the house for everyone. (The management hasn't any interest in making profits from its food because it makes enough from its drinks.) Midnight is the best playtime, though. Be sure to ask for that dapper bantyrooster with twinkling eyes and a gigantic "guardee" (handlebar) mustache, Host Harry Meadows, because he always gives friends of this book a very special red-carpet welcome. Don't miss this waggish refueling depot if you're looking for afterdark stimulation with a cheerful, nicely naughty aura. So much better than any similar oasis in this lusty, uninhibited league that there's no serious rival for the big spender.

The **Georgian Club** (10 Bury St.), formerly known more graphically as the Georgian Pussy Club, is sometimes an entertaining alley for the visiting tomcat. Membership nip for overseas tiger-types payable at the door; small main room with striped chairs and "star" ceiling; only 12 tables; drinking nook adjoining, with 4 *double* barstools. Dancing to a hot little combo; cabaret; flocks of girls who sometimes bother the customers even if they want to be alone; drinks very costly indeed; don't take your wife. There's an ample à la carte menu; its hours are from 7 P.M. to midnight. Because of the early closing, gentlemen who successfully make the pitch may take the lady out for further revelries at other gin mills. Recommended, but expensive. The **Stork Room** (99 Regent St.) is another tranquilizer for lonesome or amorous gents; dim, dim lights; hostesses by the platoon; tiny dance floor and cabaret; tariffs very high for values received; "specialized" might be the word for this one. The **New Bagatelle** (Conduit St.) impressed us not a bit. What did we say after our latest play? Nay, nay, NAY!!

WARNING: England's lower, more greedy clip joints are among the worst in the Western World. Government intervention was kicked off by 3 foreign visitors who spent 15 minutes drinking nothing but fruit juice in one of London's baser dives and received a bill for $75.60. A bill now requires nightclubs to display a price list for drinks, forbids overcharging, and bans harpies from the doorways of these establishments, where formerly they attempted to lure customers inside with vague "good time" promises. Operators who break the rules now face stiff penalties. The intent is laudable, but enforcement is dismally lax. So pursue your merriment with care!

Gambling high-or-low jinks? For the moment, it's in a state of flux. The Government clamped down on casinos in 1970; now the existing houses nationwide number a mere 45 or so, a thundering falloff from the 1200 of yesteryear. At the same time a ban was placed on cabaret and other live entertainment in major establishments—a move aimed at eliminating the drift of people into gambling who may have come chiefly for the shows and music. The prospects for reopening them are bleak, but a movement is afoot to try to convince the authorities that this will only drive much gambling underground and thus create a speakeasy subculture in the U.K. There is evidence that just this is happening. In the officially approved ones that remain, almost everything goes except pitch-and-toss—a game played by miners which all too quickly can involve staggering sums. Horses, dogs, football, the gender of an expected royal heir—just name it, and somebody will snap up your wager.

CAUTION: No State or Municipal controls exist on the tables or wheels. No self-imposed code of honesty of the Las Vegas type exists, either, because there is no communal organization to draw up any rules. Thus, many games suddenly become crooked as soon as the stakes get large. *Pick your place carefully, especially if you roll 'em high!*

The capital, of course, is the heartbeat of action. Before the embargo, its 400-plus clubs used to turn over an estimated $30,000,000 weekly. The shuttering of approximately 90% of the gameries plus the imposition of a tax to axe the gaming rooms has hurt the fringe operators, but efforts to dampen the national fever have failed flagrantly. As of our press time, this information is entirely accurate. However, with so much crackling in Great Britain over the new legislation, we can not guarantee exactly what you can expect at the moment you arrive. Therefore, we'd advise that you hedge your bets with last-minute, on-the-scene information. Now let's review the odds on our latest gambol through the gamble-inns.

The **Victoria Sporting Club** (150-162 Edgware Rd., W.2), the largest contender in the British Isles *or* Europe, might be termed a "gambling factory." Production-belt operation that woos "mass" (*vs.* "class") patronage; 1st floor featuring dice, blackjack, roulette, and chemin de fer; 2nd level offering gin rummy and *kaluki* (13-card rummy); 2 slot machines; restaurant service from lunch to breakfast. This house is cashing in b-i-g. Extremely popular at the F. W. Woolworth—not the Cartier—level.

The **Clermont Club** (44 Berkeley Square) has been mentioned above—see Annabel's.

Historic and famous **Crockford's** (16 Carlton House Terrace) was shuttered in the late '60's, allegedly for sinister reasons. Now it has been taken over by Curzon House (below) and reopened. Again a high roller.

Curzon House Club (Curzon St.) draws about the same type of clientele as Crockford's, and wraps them in a sedate and chilly ambiance. It dwells in the former manse of the 4th Earl Howe, followed by the Duke and Duchess of York (who later became King George VI and Queen Elizabeth). Lavish restaurant with enormous menu and delicious cuisine; Buffet Bar; racing room; choice of blackjack, bridge, poker, *kaluki,* gin rummy, chemin de fer, and roulette; bedrooms available for members' use. Not up to the Clermont, in our opinion—but solid competition, nonetheless.

Olympic Casino (79 Queensway) has been redecorated, but its ultraserious Olympian competitors will scarcely see the change. Packed with gamesters from the Levant; not at all for amateurs; expensive.

Other choices in this group include the **Playboy Club** on Park Lane (a 6-story, $4-million, 100-bunny warren with eating, drinking, and, yes, even sleeping facilities, plus official playpens for blackjack, chemin de fer, dice, and roulette; very popular and very worthwile for the lone male who likes to look at—touching is taboo—curvacious representatives of the rabbit family); **Charlie Chester Casino** at 12 Archer St. (functioning noon to you-name-it, with roulette, blackjack, and Las Vegas dice); and the **Golden Nugget** at 22 Shaftesbury Avenue (6 types of play). None of these (except the Playboy, which is special,) measures up to the establishments listed above, in our opinion. Still other boxcar candidates where we have yet to roll the dice include **Palm Beach Club** in the old ballroom of the May Fair Hotel (French croupiers); **Le Cercle** at 5 Hamilton Place (built-in barbershop and sauna);

the **Sportsman** (3 Tottenham Ct. Rd., W.1); the **International Sporting Club** (Berkeley Hotel); the **Knightsbridge Sporting Club** (163 Knightsbridge), which provides French and U.S.-style casinos and free breakfast, and on and on and on.

Discothèque jinks? These, of course, are among the most perishable of all institutions in the entertainment field. They pop up quickly (generally with insufficient investment capital), stay "in" for a short lifetime, and fold up when the "chic" crowd takes its fickle fancies elsewhere.
Burlesque (14 Bruton Place, formerly called Revolution) seemed to be rolling along during our earlier capital rounds. With its combo-notion of recorded and live music, it was also the noisiest. Friday nights come on the jammiest; prices are average. Here is a straight, unpretentious disco which will rivet your eardrums to the back of your chair. **Tramp's** (Jermyn St.) draws a chic young following. Worth going. **La Valbonne** (62 Kingly St.) is averred to stage topless waitresses around a swimming pool. That's one way to make a splash. **Miranda**, across the street, is popular at lunchtime with gents from the financial district. They apparently attend the anatomy lessons to reassure themselves that mankind is mammalian. **Flicka** (Swallow St.) is still fun.
Among the even more volatile contenders, **Speakeasy** (48 Margaret St.) speaks the easiest. Here's the home of the so-called Wow-Girls, a fractious flummox on the go-go theme (which, if heard, must already be extinct). It's the very navel of Carnabystanding. Next comes the **Saddle Room** (1-A Hamilton Mews). Gussied-up tack stall; rustic paneling; main dance floor plus upper tier for the mezzanine peerage; running strong from 10 P.M. to 4 A.M.; better than it was. The Fielding name is not popular here; just say Duncan Hines sent you, and see how that works. **Lulu's** (9 Young St.) is aptly sited; very "with it" for "young" devotées of Owner Louis Brown who operates 9 spots *in toto,* several of which are listed in this section.
. Then there is **Raffles** (287 King's Rd.), with a library complex, open hearths with crackling fires, and Old English décor. Some "outs" yearning to get "in" even claim it's a mini-Annabel's—but then they're not members of Annabel's, are they? **Edelweiss** (19 Oxford St.) is still flowering as an Alpine tavern, attracting all ages and all species for grazing. **Samantha's Psychedelic** (3 New Burlington St.) is another scene for cooling it in the nether world. **Le Kilt** (60 Greek St.) is proud of its "Swinging Sounds and Pub Prices" and of its widely advertised comforter "Where a Young Lady May Go Unescorted and Be Completely at Her Ease!" (Not *our* Young Lady, if we had one.)
At least a score of similar places exist, most of them in the same atonal, eardrum-shattering ambiance. We repeat our warning to the dedicated: Since the fad vacillates so rapidly—almost monthly—please do not depend too heavily on these suggestions. They can wilt as swiftly as cotton candy in a cloudburst. But authoritative *What's On in London,* issued weekly as the most comprehensive entertainment guide in the capital, will help keep you abreast of the action on a weekly basis. Here's virtually a *must* for you dayflies and nightowls.

Nudity and low jinks? There has been an enormous recent change in Britain's entertainment picture. Several years back some smart operator discovered that the law requiring nude or seminude performers to freeze in a motionless position did not apply in private clubs. Overnight, the Take-It-Off boom raced through Soho and Stepney as fast as St. Elmo's fire. The carnage was terrific—until the police stepped in to eliminate some of the riper smut huts.

Then, several seasons ago, the Greater London Council pantingly granted the appeal to peel in public, so now—again—anything goes. Before the ban was lifted, the strip had become so unfashionable, most of the small places which featured it deteriorated into rank, dismal, and rapacious clip joints. Now it will take time—no one can tell how long—to recover the uncover market of daze gone bye-bye. (One farsighted promoter, however, immediately unswaddled a snackery with topless waitresses—doing his part, no doubt, to put London out in Front.) At present, we think the action is more uninhibited, unabashed, and far, far broader (in both senses) in the mammoth concentration of Hamburg's Reeperbahn. London swings with girlishly adolescent hips, but it certainly doesn't swing with either the freedom or the abandon of those St. Pauli *Fraülein*. (Just the playgirls and B-girls there make more than $25,000,000 per year!) Nevertheless, in England there's still a hint of what's meant—and more is on the way. If you stick to the 3 exponents listed below (provided they're still going), you'll be safe—and perhaps amused.

"Membership," in the past, has been the key gimmick. You had to (and may still have to) "join" by paying a moderate initiation fee. The law is unclear to us, but we believe (possibly erroneously) that *48 hours must still elapse before you may be admitted*. In a number of them, on every visit you must pay an entrance fee of approximately £1.50 per person; guests may be invited for the same tariff per person.

There are 2 categories of clubs. The 3 mentioned below are among the dwindling strip-and-clip joints, which are fly-by-nighters—most of them easily identified by their jukebox wheeze and their small herd of bovine babes as graceless as heifers. In both categories, the caliber of talent varies from herbivorous, gum-chewing manatee-types (par for the course), to vivacious, chattering monkey-types (the "talkers"), on up to a small handful of exquisite English beauties.

In the "National" spots we list, the ladies wear G-strings right up to that final instant before blackout—then off goes the net—and in the quickest wink you've ever blinked, out go the lights. We've seen butterfly collections that were sexier. All these theaters have music-hall seats and tables for bar service.

The attrition rate among these establishments is so fast and so unpredictable that today's leaders are tomorrow's duds. As we write this, the best by far is still **Raymond Revuebar** (Brewer St.). Entrance fee abolished, but memberships vary with the proximity of your seat to the action—thus a bargain for farsighted voyeurs. ("Life Members" getting the choice perches). These billings all grant admission to a frenetic, jumbo-size lounge, bar, and dance floor. Adjoining is a tier-table, music-hall theater, with fast-moving shows increasingly dominated by singles acts and strippers (5 performances nightly, beginning at 8:20 P.M. and ending with the 1:15 A.M. "Topless" caper), in which the ladies cavort on a raised stage for unimpaired inspection. Best of its type in London; be sure to book in advance; not at all cheap, because you can see a Manhattan musical for the same outlay. Incidentally, Mr. Raymond recently announced plans to reopen the celebrated **Windmill Theatre,** and, after a $500,000 tilt with the decorators, he intends to stage 2 shows per nude-filled night. Since the Strip King took out a 114-year lease on the house, we'll still have time to get by for a peek and a follow-up report to you.

Casino de Paris Club (5–7 Denman St.) was redecorated as a minitheater with a runway sprinting almost the full length of the aisle. It's one of the few legitimate, decent places of its type featuring a "continuous" show (breaks of perhaps 20 minutes between each) from 2:30 P.M.—yep, that's "P." M. (!)—to 10:30 P.M. Excellent choreography; elaborate costumes; sexillated strippers and show girls; all seats £3. We don't quite agree with the B.B.C. reviewer who stated, "Purists and Puritans may scream, but I thought it great fun"—because we do not find it *this* naughty. We do concur, however, that it can be uplifting for the dedicated girl watcher—and we recommend it.

Third on our list is the **Nell Gwynne Club** (Dean St.). Ascend via a Lilliputian elevator and you'll find yourself in its sky-high (for London), refurbished cluster of bar, diminutive theater, and tiny stage. She also caters to the late afternoon gentry; low bars; strip from 6 P.M. Worth a peek only as a curiosity.

One drawback to the nudity on most of this circuit: With the exception of the above establishments and a scattershot of others, the girls are so graceless and witless they'll bore you to death. As an illustration, on a round with 3 other seasoned nighthawks, the verdict was unanimous: (1) save for one single stop, we felt we had been viewing an excruciatingly dull series of Bare-Bottom Amateur Nights, and (2) the performers were so sexless that not one of our quartet got even one mild tingle from the acres of flesh paraded about as thrillingly as a bathtub of jello.

A further informational point: The Wolfenden Law was designed to end sidewalk soliciting, but Parliament and the police have learned the hard way that You Can't Keep A Bad Girl Down (or is it "Up"?). Frustrated gents to whom taste is no barrier may meet (with less frequency these days) the former pavement pounders by consulting "business cards" on street bulletin boards, or joining various afterdark bus queues which are used as blinds for pickups (if accused of loitering, what better alibi than "I'm whyting for a bus, officer"?). The direct and flagrant 60¢ *Ladies Directory* ("Young Amanda, 36-20-35, will be pleased to consider offerings . . ."), dried up when its publisher received 9 months in the clink. But the public relations topper to end all toppers was the quick-witted British lass who boldly advertised her expertise in several ultrarespectable newspapers as a "Demolition and Erection Specialist." T-i-m-b-e-r!!

As in so many parts of today's United States, permissiveness is so great that in Soho, within a 10- to 15-minute walk from Piccadilly Circus, the visitor can find the same style of "bookstores" which sell the hardest-of-hard-core photographs, cartoons, underground magazines, and 8-mm reels of motion-picture film (color and black-and-white). The front sections of these establishments, some of which display samples of pornography, also display legitimate current publications. But just push your way through the door to the rear marked "Private," and you'll find yourself engulfed in slime. Candid photograph sets, priced at New York rates or slightly more for 4 different exposures, line the shelves in classified groupings of every imaginable approach to *amour:* "straight," sadism ("snuffies" in which the wench is slaughtered and the newer "munchies" in which she's butchered and devoured), masochism, lesbianism, fetishism, male homosexuality, "circuses," and the lot. The movie films (sited in smelly phone-booth-size cubicles wherein you'll feed endless shillings into a coinbox just to see a shoe removed) and cartoons run the same gamut. Most of these salacious tableaux are only "simulated," not true-blue encounters.

On a more upbeat note, the flock of *escort agencies* supplying birds-by-the-hour to lone eagles is proliferating faster than a flight of fire-fed phoenixes. Customers customarily cull newspaper ads or rely on word-of-beak, select their aviary, and then come in on a wing and a prayer to choose their canaries from displays of snapshots. Before you can say "12 O'Clock High" (or, more usually, "8 O'Clock Sharp"), she's at your door, ready to step out. Rates flap at about $35 an hour plus taxi fare; your companion keeps perhaps $15. Be sure to check on check-in time, since fees soar much higher after the bewitching hour. Although a 2 A.M. curfew is standard, it can be stretched if the nightingale takes a moonshine to you. An offer she can't refuse? She probably will—but there again it's a matter of you and the mood and the music. *Bon chance!*

For *dining oddities,* perhaps the zaniest meal in London can be found at the Elizabethan Room of the **Gore Hotel** (189 Queen's Gate)—an experience for every visitor (just once). Owner Robin Howard, a scholar and gourmet, has duplicated every detail of a banquet served in the time of Queen Bess and has reproduced the renowned Seven Star Chamber in the basement, where other Olde Worlde flights of fancy take place. Among the dishes you'll be served are Sturgeon or Lobster Pie, Peacock Pâté, Boar's Head Salad, Salmagundi, Good King Henry (wild spinach), Syllabub—all sorts of authentic but odd things, and they're washed down with mead and mulled claret. Wooden plates; 2 old-style table utensils only; clay pipes; straw on the floor; waitresses in Elizabethan costumes who may be pinched at will (or so Mr. Howard says—but please don't take *our* word, because we've never had either the yen or the nerve). Foodwise, you won't dance with enjoyment when you've finished; funwise, however, it's a great experience—to repeat, just once. **Flanagan's** (100 Baker St., 37 St. Martin's Lane, and 11 Kensington High St.), harks back only as far as the Gay Nineties. Sawdust floors; honky-tonk piano; costumed waitresses; beverage posters of the 1800's on the walls; patrons following lyrics printed on the napkins join the community sings. The cookery is indifferent, but in this mesmeric clime, who cares? Beer kegs of joviality 7 days a week until 12:30 A.M. Happily recommended. Pick and choose? **Justin de Blank** (54 Duke St., W.1) is a sort of do-it-yourself delicatessen for the celebrity set. Our quiche was dee-liche! Cute and costly. The **Barbican** (Lee House, London Wall), in the skyrocketing Barbican development, is what might be termed a Caesarean section of the past. Roman highlights in a posh modern setting; top positions held by former Dorchester and Hatchetts personnel; costly à la carte dishes; closed Saturdays, Sundays, and bank holidays; chiefly for expense-account business lunches. Good, but not for the budgeteering merrymaker. For a change of pace in an entirely different category, the nonprofit **Mermaid Theatre** (Puddle Dock and Upper Thames St.) offers 500 seats, many of them priced so that 2 people may have food and entertainment for a very reasonable outlay. Riverside restaurant; curtainless stage without proscenium arch on which Founder Bernard Miles presents everything from Shakespeare to Maxwell Anderson to opera to music hall to lunchtime concerts to film shows to 1-act plays. The City of London encouraged lease of the site by a token rent, and contributions from both sides of the Atlantic have added more than $168,000 to its operating capital. Evening performances at 6 P.M. and 8:40 P.M.; an interesting and courageous venture which merits support. Poor mouth? Here's one that's so cheap, so rawboned, and so down-right crumbling that we hesitate to mention it at all—but is the food ever g-o-o-d! The name is **Five-five-five** (555 Battersea Park Rd., S.W.11). It's way the hell-and-gone out in the sticks of London's industrial backwaters. About 5 tables attended by Vera, the Polish chef's wife; sign on the door announcing that it is closed (a ploy to keep out the streetside drunks); dinner only; selection limited to what Master Stan Nawrat decides is the best for that day. Marvelous sauces created for meats and wild game; savory homemade pâtés and sausages; heavenly for the palate, but catastrophically uncomfortable, cramped, and poorly ventilated. The prices are rock-bottom for such quality cuisine. The Royal Family has dined at its oilcloth tables and tolerated the palsy-walsy, backslapping, dirty-joketelling hospitality of its proprietor (often his softspoken spouse cringes in the corner). We recommend it *to the adventurous only*. Be sure to reserve ahead (tel.: 228 7011), take your best brand of humor, and be prepared for a feast you'll never forget. Unusual, but interesting. **Sheekey's** (29–31 St. Martin's Court) is another for the broad-minded cognoscenti. Steamed seafood only (an oddball lease prohibits frying the fish). Impossible to reserve, so you takes your chances; open noon to 8:30 P.M. weekdays and 3 P.M. on Saturdays; closed Sundays; inexpensive; superb, within its limitations. **Le Cellier du Midi** (Church Row in Hampstead) is an outskirts oasis introduced to us by those discerning London gourmets, Rudi and Vera Freimuth, who are also our dear friends and summer neighbors in Formentor. They love it for its atmosphere and for its reasonable cookery, as a family retreat—and we couldn't agree more. Dark, snugglesome bracelet of several cellar rooms; candles on rustic plank tables; garlands of garlic hanging from rough walls; wonderful terrine spiked with brandy; succulent white veal with cream and onion sauce; mouth-melting boiled beef with capers au gratin; no beverage license, so the wines (if you don't bring your own bottle) are imported from a nearby pub. The service is informal, but careful and ever-so-friendly. We richly enjoyed every morsel and moment—and we think you might, too. A honey for its type.

Now let's look into the nationalities grab bag. Kosher cookery? **Bloom's** (blossoming at 90 Whitechapel High St.) is a no-nonsense ethnic paradise. Take-out order section and stand-up counters near the entrance where legions of ravenous lunchtime *landsleit* joyously celebrate the glories of pastrami, corned beef, roast beef, chopped liver, tongue, and other inspired deli-cacies; table area with napery as white as a bar mitzvah boy's collar also jammed with midday mavens munching blintzes, gefilte fish, kreplach, and other traditional tempters; health foods such as chicken soup always available. While the waiters are extra kind, you should know that they're also faster than Yeshiva basketball players dribbling against Notre Dame. Rituals of the Beth Din and Kashrus Commission are scrupulously (and scrumptiously) observed; rabbi and religious supervisor are on the premises daily (and not just for a snack, either). Second-generation management by Sidney Bloom, the warm and soooo-conscientious son of the 1920 founder, who now sends trucks out for home delivery and stocks the shelves of the best shops in the U.K. with his famous name-brand canned products. Because of the teeming luncheon throngs and the no-reservations policy, we prefer dinner here. Closed Saturdays, of course. Our sincere mazel tov to this, the finest Bloom on the orthodox stem. (Although there's a branch at 130 Golder's Green Rd., we enjoy the original plant a bit more.) **Isow's** seems to us to concentrate on high-pressure treatment from a snippish battery of waiters. And that so-called sommelier? We suspect that Gen. Dayan wouldn't even wish him on Mr. Yasir Arafat. Spanish savors? The aforementioned **Martinez** (Swallow St.); there's a sweet little patio for your pleasure. East Indian curries and specialties? Try **Jamshid** (6 Glendower Place, S. Kensington); here's the best Oriental fare we've found in the British Isles. Our choices are the Chicken Curry or the Chicken Dhansak served with Papadams (sun-dried lentil flour bread), and those wonderful Jelibies for dessert. Or try the very much larger and more famous **Veeraswamy's** (99-101 Regent St., with entrance on Swallow St.), which has been sold and is now directed by R. N. Kapur; our recent veer toward this swami's table was delightful. **Omar Khayyam** (177 Regent St.) is just plain awful, in this sheik's opinion; unpalatable food; preposterous belly dancing by a pathetic tub-tummied wiggler; clientele of rednecked oglers. We prefer a book of verse, a flask of wine, and thou. The fad for Tandoori now seems to be—and deservingly so—on the tip of every Asian-aimed tongue. This is an overnight marinade of chicken and kebabs baked in a special Indian oven (the "tandoori") and followed by the curry course. **Gaylord** (79 Mortimer St.), a branch of the New Delhi and Bombay trees, is the plushiest exponent of this particular type of cookery. **Agra** (137 Whitfield St.), with a different ambiance but similar cuisine, can pan out Tandoori, curry, and an Indian dessert plus coffee for very reasonable rupees, Sahib. **Shezan** (16 Cheval Pl.) is said to be a winner, but we haven't seen it. Chinese food? This yum-yum fever which for several years overwhelmed England is giving way to the rage for so-called Italian-style *trattorie;* nearly all the Cathay ventures are currently moving out from the center. Compared with the Hong Kong or American variety, however, we think them discouragingly 2nd-rate— mainly because the English climate is too windy and too cold to grow the essential greens and vegetables. If you must, **Fu Tong** (29 Kensington High St.) used to be the best bet in the metropolis, but now we think it has gone off. Attractive slick-modern décor; service chop-chop and rush-rush; clean and bright as a bubble. Perhaps you'll rate it higher. The celebrated Soho establishment, **Lee Ho Fook,** has a split personality; it is divided into 2 segments. Though the fancy address at 15–16 Gerrard St. wins a star in *Michelin*'s U.K. edition, we've always much preferred the modest and cheaper family nookery just around the corner at 41–43 Wardour St. Look into both, pay your money, and take your choice. **Lotus House** (61–69 Edgware Rd., W.2) has soothed that yen of many show-biz types, but as with Fu Tong, we feel it has reached its zenith and may now be descending. **China Garden** (66 Brewer St.), which blossoms under the same Lotus management, greets its guests with unusual Eastern décor; attractive. **Good Friends** (139 Salmon Lane, E.14) , in the tough Limehouse orchard, serves Cantonese dishes at reasonable tariffs. Dull, no-nonsense ambiance; on Sundays, Chinese Embassy personnel jam it tighter than an egg roll. **Kuo Yuan** (259 High Road, Willesden Green, N.W.10) strikes us as one of the best Peking-style contenders in Londontown; book in advance. The **Sailing Junk** (59 Marloes Rd.) specializes in the same type of cookery. It hides behind a sign saying only "Restaurant," which may be the understatement of the year. Our 9-course dinners and delicious Chinese red wine, sampled unhurriedly amid red lanterns, cane, and a jungle of greenery, made our hearts and tummies croon. So did the check which was presented in a conch. We also are fond of the **Whistling Junk** which smartly sails in with 9 courses from the galley—a set feast that is delectable and surprisingly reasonable in cost as well. Our recent repast here as guests of London gourmets Ken and Vera Hawes (who know a fine table when they sit down to one) was even more rewarding than earlier visits. **Lee Yuan** (40 Earls Court Rd., W.8) gets our favorable nod. So does **Loon Fung's** (37–38 Gerrard St.), where typically no-nonsense décor belies a staggering 127 choices of *Oriental* rather than Chinese-American fare. Piped melodies straight from the pagoda; air conditioning; open noon to 11:30, including Sundays. **Gallery Rendezvous** (55 Beak St., W.1), despite its unlikely name, specializes in northern fare; it is one of our favorites, as is the same-ownership **Dumpling Inn** (15A Gerrard St.), although the staff in the latter seemed to think it was bestowing a favor by serving us. (**Soho Rendezvous** is yet another member of this tong.) **Chelsea Rendezvous** (4 Sydney St.) specializes in Shanghai cuisine at medium-hai prices; mostly it is attended by London's Shang-Hai-Society. **Mr. Chow** (151 Knightsbridge) remains a pacesetter for London's current Trendy Set. A Great Wall exists, in our opinion, between its skilled kitchen staff and its low-powered battery of waiters who, on our visit, seemed grossly deficient not only in basic etiquette, but in the use of the abacus. Henceforth we'll chow elsewhere. Turkish delight? Try **Gallipoli** (Bishopsgate Churchyard, E.C.2), which could fatten any sultan; plush décor; open until 3 A.M.; dancing every night (both Western and belly types); surprisingly authentic, say the eunuchs in the harem. Viennese? **Old Vienna** (94 New Bond St., W.1) waxes schmaltzy, with Owner Joszi and his troupe gussied up in lederhosen; group singing to accordionotations; party atmosphere; well worth the outlay if you're feeling not ritzy but fritzy. French comestibles? The still-growing **Le Français** (259 Fulham Rd., S.W.3) burns hotter than a Languedoc skillet. Proprietorship by a pair of Gauls who do the marketing, whip the sauces, and welcome the patrons; ask for Bernard; an "in" spot for Francophiles; unknown to us as yet. **La Terrasse Tio Pepe** (13

Shepherd's Place, not to be confused with Shepherd Market), despite its Iberian handle, strums up only Gallic dishes; attentive service, quiet ambiance, soft guitarrangements; handy to the U.S. Embassy. Even our own "Uncle Joe" (see "Me to You") tips his sombrero to this "Uncle Joe." It's especially salubrious to dine alfresco here during the summer months. **Fontainebleau** (3 Northumberland Ave., W.C.2), **Le Lavandou** (15 Blandford St., W.1), and the neighboring **Auberge d'Artagnan** (19 Blandford St., W.1) are 3 freshets we'll be anxious to sample on our next promenade. **L'Opera** (32 Great Queen St., W.C.2) is only fair, in our opinion. The prices are reasonable and the atmosphere is cheerful, but our cuisine lacked zest. Never, please, *never* let them seat you in the lonely downstairs grotto. The after-theater fun is to be found at ground level. Imperial settings? **Villa dei Cesari** (135 Grosvenor Rd., S.W.1) boasts a river view; waiters in centurian garb, and dancing until 2:30 A.M.; closed Monday, but one of the few that features food, music, and dancing on the Sabbath. Very Rome-antic. Finally, you might brave the rotating restaurant atop the 620-foot **Post Office Tower,** close to Tottenham Court Road. Robert Butlin (the spinoffspring of his prominent daddy, Billy Butlin, of holiday camp fame) is the whirling dervish in the catering department; revolving 7 days a week for lunch and dinner, and already so popular with tourists, businessmen, their out-of-town clients, and "Hey-Martha-Looka-here" rubberneckers that in peak season it's useless even to *hope* to get in without a reservation made 3 days ahead. (If you do try, ask for Manager Gustav at The Top of The Tower.) Poorly arranged circular bar which doesn't properly utilize the spectacular view; one-flight higher to the restaurant. It is set for one revolution every 23 minutes—much too fast, we found, for our digestive comfort. (Others on the Continent creep at closer to one full turn per hour, a pace which is better for the tummy, more romantic, and easier on vertigo sufferers.) The décor screams of tacky institutionality. Three-course table d'hôte; à la carte dinner selections; wretchedly rushed 2-seating system (no leisurely musings here); ludicrously, if not malevolently, expensive for the production-line glop we tried that pretended to be *haute cuisine*.

Snacks? The capital is now peppered with imitations of the typical American hamburger joint with typically American prices. The only comestibles in this category certified Triple-A by us are dished up at **The Great American Disaster** (335 Fulham Rd. and 9 Beauchamp Place) 17—count'em, 17— different styles of burgers are served. Our thick ½-pounder, shrouded in melted American cheese and accompanied by French fries and crisp salad, reminded us so nostalgically of their best U.S. cousins that we nearly stood up and saluted. Skip the original location, which is hellandgone away; hie to the newer Beauchamp ("Beecham") Place operation. The latter is a long paneled room lined with step-up booths; the kitchen with its charcoal grill is to the rear; *New York Times* page-one reprints of great American disasters hang balefully on one wall. Since the waiters are young, long-haired, casual, and friendly, and since tapes of pop singers are amplified—but AMPLIFIED —to paralyzing levels, old crocks over 30 are hereby warned. Sirloin steak sandwiches, *delicious* cheesecake, "Real American" apple pie (sold out during our visit), banana splits, and hearty milkshakes round out the picture (and probably your tummy, too). Hours are from 11 A.M. to midnight Sunday to

Thursday, but until 1 A.M. on Friday and Saturday. Go before 7 or after 10 to avoid the queues (*lines*, mate)—and please remember that, for the category, it's very expensive. Next in order on our ABC (Authentic Burger Chart) are: **The Hungry Years** (Earls Court Rd.), **Yankee** (newer offering at 22 Brompton Rd. preferable to the original at 26–28 Binney St.) and, sputtering down the pike in last place, **The Long Island Expressway** (Escalade Department Store, Brompton Rd.)

The **Golden Egg** is scrambling all over West End. Numerous shell-ters for pecking; Italic décor; quite a string of chicks. Roast-beef sandwich? The publike **Running Footman** (corner Charles St. and Berkeley Square) is superduper in this department. The **Square Rigger** (corner Arthur and King William Sts., near London Bridge) has a lunch counter plus 2 small dining nooks; whaling-ship motif; minnow-size tabs; weekdays only; well liked by many. Continental-style espresso bars are a nickel a dozen in today's London; you'll find them all over the city, as a reaction against rising food prices. Among the better ones are **Cul de Sac** (43 Brompton Rd.) and **Les Enfants Terribles** (93 Dean St.). **Troubadour** (265 Old Brompton Rd.) is not recommended by this *Guide*. Most of these are not up to U.S. snack-bar standards by a long shot—and relatively expensive against the cost of an average full meal in a restaurant—but (with the exception of the Troubadour) satisfactory all the same. A somewhat more elaborate version is **Sands** (33 New Bond St.), a modern lite-bitery for shoppers. Meal with a hole in it? Not 1, but 2 U.S. firms now perk on London soil. Both **Dunkin' Donuts** and **Mr. Donut** have realized plans to invade Her Majesty's Realm. (We can already hear, " 'Ave a doughnut with yer cuppa, ducks?")

High tea at the **Ritz**? Posh, yes. Expensive, no. For a glimpse of the Stately London of yore, drop in between 4 P.M. and 5:30 P.M. at the spacious, gracious, changeless ground-floor lounge of this old-fashioned landmark. Its assorted finger sandwiches are excellent; specify your preferences to your swallow-tail-coated waiter. The average cost is perhaps $2.50 per person. Gentlemen are required to wear jackets and neckties. If you've reached a certain age and have had a good lunch, this may well serve as your supper.

For *public houses (pubs) and pub-crawling,* please turn farther along to the section headed "Drinks."

Dedicated budgeteers? As previously mentioned, more than 200 London establishments embracing all price categories are listed in these pages—and we just do not have the space for more. But if you want the lowdown on dozens of additional bargain dining spots which we can't include here, please consult our annually revised *Fielding's Low-Cost Europe,* tailor-made for the serious economizer *only.*

For *country dining near London*—all easy excursions on a sunny day— more than a dozen widely known candidates present themselves. To us, one of the better sancta, despite its longer-than-average haul, is Robert Carrier's **Hintlesham Hall** in *Hintlesham*, Suffolk, an ancient hamlet near Ipswich and Colchester. This world-renowned culinary authority (see "Restaurants,

London") purchased the gone-to-seed Great Hall and its sylvan grounds in 1971. With close to $750,000 and tankards of his heart's blood, he totally restored the mansion and then converted it into a stunningly beautiful landmark. Mr. Carrier's 4-course luncheon (fixed-price choice of perhaps 32 dishes, many original) runs close to $15, a sum many antiquarians would gladly pay just for the privilege of viewing the premises. Brandade of Smoked Trout, Chilled Bouillabaisse Salad, Fingers of Sole Rémoulade, Trio of Lamb Chops with Green Butter, Charcoal Grilled Scotch Sirloin with Roquefort Butter, Ragoût of Lamb à la Bourguignonne, and Sorbet au Cassis with Blackcurrant Sauce are but random samplings. Debonair Manager Paul Lewis will offer you the choice of quaffing or savoring in the Long Hall, the Bar, the Blue Room, the Red Room, the China Room, or the 2-story-high Great Saloon. As a bonus, "Festival Events"—concerts, recitals, wine-tasting regales, and more—are held from early June to mid-July. If at all possible, PUL-EEZE ask your hotel concierge to telephone Mr. Carrier's London namesake restaurant, not only to find out what's on at Hintlesham Hall, but to make a reservation for you even if only the culinations are cooking. Most famous, perhaps, is **The Compleat Angler**, at **Marlow**, *Buckinghamshire* (31 miles), with 40 bedrooms and private baths. This opulent inn, which sits beside a peaceful view on the Thames reaches a pinnacle of pastoral beauty. Goodness, is it attractive! Sadly, however our cocktails and service in its bar were even more slipshod than the appallingly low-grade à la carte cookery at which we then picked with such embarrassment in the slick-rustic, leaded-window dining room. Perhaps its relatively heavy bus excursion trade might be partially responsible. If the full potential of this gorgeous setting were to be realized through administrative reorganization—including the hiring of a far superior chef—to us here would be one of the most celestial rural havens in the world. As it stands, we find it so overpriced and so disappointing that we consider it a waste of time. **Ye Olde Bell**, **Hurley**, *Berkshire* (32 miles; about ½-hour beyond Northold on M-4), dates from A.D. 1135, and it's also very popular and also comparatively costly; for overnighters, 9 rooms and 9 baths. Here's one of the "inn"-spots outside of town, oozing with lazy charm, fashionable clientele, relaxing ambiance; sound but not top-London-class fare; limited selections but a substantial meal; *reserve ahead* here too. Happily recommended. **The Orchard**, **Ruislip**, *Middlesex* (16 miles), is a large, pukka establishment where the dancing is a gnat's eyelash better than the food and, like the food, is served every night of the year; Saturday evening it is *black tie only*. Modern mien; immaculate kitchen; drinks served on the umbrella-dotted lawn; in season, gala-night bookings must be made 5 weeks in advance. John Lambourne operates this sophisticated Tudor mansion and continues to offer special warm welcomes to Guidesters. **Gravetye Manor**, **East Grinstead**, *Sussex* (30 miles), is an impressive Elizabethan mansion (built in 1598) crowning 30 acres of magnificent gardens, woodland, and lake. However, much remains to be done with the interior of this hotel and Country Club. (Members have their own bar, special prices, and certain privileges, such as trout fishing on the lake.) It reminds us of a fine British Colonial hotel of 40 years ago, with little changed in either décor or ambiance. High ceilings; handsome woodwork; lounge with overstuffed chairs, sofas, and pukka sahib

Colonels and their Ladies; pleasant reception and service, but dining room unimaginative in furnishings and cuisine unimaginative in execution; expensive. Our old friend Peter Herbert, formerly of London's Gore Hotel and its famous Elizabethan Room, still has a fairly long hike to make his ambitious venture appealing to today's North Americans as well as to vintage English gentry. To get there, take A-22 (the Eastbourne Road); about 7 miles past Godstone, at the crossroads, turn right on B-2028 to Turner's Hill. The drive out is so lovely and the surroundings are so beautiful that, despite its drawbacks, we recommend an expedition on a benign day. *Advance reservations advised.*

Others of above-average stature are as follows: In *Berkshire,* (a) **Hind's Head** and **Monkey Island** hotels, both in *Bray* (28 miles); the former, operated by Mrs. Kelly, has a terrace and features unabashed English catering competently done; the latter is an eighteenth-century fishing lodge on a tiny island in the Thames. The **Waterside Inn,** in the same village, features more-French-style cuisine—and at nearly Parisian-style tariffs! It, too, overlooks the river; closed Mondays; big rewards for big prices. (b) **Milton Ernest Hall Hotel**, near *Bedford* (45 miles), is a bucolic restoration of the house designed by William Butterfield, the famous Victorian architect. It's also now the 25-hour-a-day hobby of Mr. and Mrs. Harmar-Brown, who hawkeye their chefs and personally select its choice wines. Our great-and-good pals, *Time*'s Chief Photographer Ben Martin and his ravishing actress-wife, Kathryn, say this is a "must" for its glorious décor, cookery, and friendliness. (c) **White Hart** and **French Horn**, both in *Sonning-on-Thames* (36 miles), a captivating rural village; in the former you may enjoy country roast beef while watching the boats skim past, and in the latter (more costly), across the bridge, you'll find an even better river view, but the specialties are more continental and not as appetizing. (d) **Boulter's Inn**, *Maidenhead* (27 miles), has a lovely riverbank situation at Boulter's Lock; 13 rooms and 1 private bath. Direction by Tom Cressy, who also operates the previously mentioned Bridge House Motel at Reigate, resident management by John Moses, who led his own exodus from the same Bridge House; recent $120,000 modernization; 3-piece combo for dancing nightly. Much improved; now considered by many to be the best suburban target near the capital. The (e) **King's Head** at *Little Marlow* (5 miles from Maidenhead) is still another potential charmer, with Major John Nichols and his wife in command; we missed it on our latest loop. (f) The **Little Angel** in *Remenham* (36 miles) is a cozy and genial retreat across the bridge from Henley; solid, unelaborate cookery; nice clientele; operated by an ex-RAF officer who turned in his wings for this pocket-size seraph. (g) **Skindle's Hotel**, *Maidenhead* (27 miles), once the pick of the area, has skidded so rapidly downhill that our enthusiasm has now completely waned; the old crew has fled, and a gaming room has been installed; no longer the charmer of old. In *Buckinghamshire,* (a) the **Bell Hotel**, *Aston Clinton* (36 miles), resembles a routine pub; when we tried Gerry Harris' viands some time back, they were extra good—but now we're getting reports that they aren't worth the ride; if you go, always call for advance reservations on weekends. (b) The **Jolly Farmer**, *Chalfont Saint Peter* near Gerrards Cross (23 miles), is a renowned pub which makes to order 401 varieties of sandwiches; top-quality ingredients selected by Proprietors Tom and Lucille Davies; full menu and wine list; reasonable tariffs; a find. In *Essex,* the **Old Mill** at **Harlow** (25 miles) offers French and English dishes prepared personally by Owner Bronson; not spectacular but good. We've heard nice compliments about **Harlow Hill.** In *Surrey,* (a) **Mayflower Hotel**, **Cobham** (19 miles), is a plushy oasis for the Hungry Man run by Charles, ex-Savoy and Berkeley majordomo; also nice here is the **Talbot,** which boasts ownership of Nelson's chair. (b) **Whyte Harte**, **Bletchingley** (22 miles), a fourteenth-century inn with old beams, open fireplaces, and better-than-routine vittles supervised by C. H. Mathews. (c) The **Old Bell,** **Oxted** (22 miles), another inn of the same vintage without quite the flavor of the Whyte Harte, but very pleasant all the same. (d) **Onslow Arms**, **West Clandon** near Guildford (about 30 miles), an A.D. 1623 roadside hostelry thick with atmosphere, and mellow with its Free House varieties of beer, ale, and porter. (e) **Great Fosters**, **Egham** (18 miles) features unique 4-centuries-old gardens and 23 guest rooms for lovers of antiquities and service. In *Sussex,* **The Maltravers**, **Arundel** (58 miles), which leads the country with its gastronomic delights, its furnishings of rare antiques and fine paintings, and its unusual policy, for rural establishments, of staying open until 11 P.M. or after; closed Monday; now under new management, but still as good as ever, in our opinion. In *Northamptonshire,* near the border of *Oxfordshire,* **The Cartwright Arms**, **Aynho** near Banbury (62 miles), a famous old coach house that has been renovated; dine in candlelight on mahogany, at the most savory table in the district.

For *other dining spots in the provinces of England,* let's run down the list of the ones we tried (or which drew exceptional praise) on our recent county-by-county circuit. Space is so limited that there is no point in repeating some of the dining spots associated with Albion's ubiquitous inns; for the best bets among these, please check back to our "Hotels" section.

Bristol: **Bristol**: (1) **Llandoger Trow**, (2) **John Harvey's**, (3) **Chateaubriand,** (4) **Grand Hotel Grill Room.** Out at nearby **Thornbury,** Kenneth Bell's sixteenth-century **Thornbury Castle** is one of the region's proudest gastronomic shrines. Here a meal is an event..

Cambridgeshire: **Cambridge**: (1) **Coach & Horses** (outskirts, in **Trumpington**), (2) **Turk's Head**, (3) **Sylder**, (4) **The Green Man** (across from Coach & Horses), (5) **Garden House Hotel**, (6) **Pagoda** (Oriental, of course), (7) **Arts Theatre**, (8) **Bistro Italiano.**

Cheshire: **Chester**: (1) **Grosvenor Arms**, (2) **Plantation Inn**, (3) **Abbot's Well,** (4) **Steak House** ; the **Kardomah** for snacks; the **Chanticleer,** the **Yen Hong**, the **Green Dragon** for Chinese food, and the **Courtyard,** in that order.

Ledsham: **Craxton Wood Country Club**.

Prestbury: **Bridge Hotel**.

Cornwall: **Budock Vean**: Budock Vean Hotel.
  St. Ives: Tregenna Castle Hotel.
  St. Mawes: Ship and Castle, The Tresanton.

Cumberland: **Keswick**: Armathwaite Hall Hotel.

Derbyshire: **Rowsley**: Peacock Hotel.

Devonshire: **Brixham: Randall's** (no lunch served; Gallic dishes predominating; expensive but worthy).
  Fairy Cross (near **Bideford**): *Portledge Hotel.*
  Hatherleigh, North Devon: **The George**.
  Moretonhampstead: Manor House Hotel.
  Torquay: Imperial Hotel.

Dorset: **Ferndown** (8 miles from **Bournemouth**): Dormy Hotel.

Gloucestershire: **Bibury**: The Swan (try the trout from the River Coln outside your window, or the duck with cherry sauce, finishing with a "flummery," a celestial mousse).
  Moreton-in-Marsh: The Redesdale Arms.
  Old Sodbury: Cross Hands Hotel.

Hampshire: **Bournemouth**: (1) South Western Hotel, (2) **Rancheros** (3) San Marco. Outside of town: (1) **Harbour Heights *at Poole***, (2) Rose & Crown (in the New Forest). Ask locally about the rash of new tiny family-run eateries in the interior of the town. Don't forget the above-mentioned **Dormy Hotel** at Ferndown.
  Portsmouth: Keppel's Head.
  Winchester: (1) Elizabethan, (2) Wessex Hotel, (3) Royal Hotel.

Isle of Wight: **Yarmouth**: The George.

Kent: **Boughton Aluph** (11 miles from **Canterbury**): Flying Horse Inn (NOT recommended this year). **Canterbury**: (1) Duck Inn, (2) Slatters Hotel (a few recent bleats from Guidesters concerning dining room service and cleanliness), (3) **The Castle**.
  Dover: Coachotel (also called Dover and Stage), famous but not recommended.
  Folkestone: Burlington Hotel.

Lancashire: **Manchester**: (1) Café Royal, (2) French Restaurant in the Midland Hotel, (3) Gourmet.
  Liverpool: Reece's.

Lincolnshire: **Lincoln**: White Hart Hotel.

Northumberland: **Newcastle-upon-Tyne**: (1) Gosforth Park, (2) Royal Station, (3) Five Bridges Hotel, (4) Dante's. Lindsay's is no longer recommended.

Oxfordshire: **Oxford**: (1) Elizabeth, (2) Roebuck. Among pubs: (1) The Bear, (2) Turf Tavern, (3) The Trout Inn (outside at **Godstow**, near the village of Wolvercote).
Woodstock: The Bear.

Somerset: **Bath**: (1) Hole-in-Wall, (2) Popjoys, (3) Mario's, (4) Lansdown Grove Hotel. The best dinner and fun may be had at The George, a 600-year-old pub 10 minutes out; be sure to see "Hanging Judge" Jeffries' gallows and medieval prison memorabilia—and reserve, OR ELSE!
Wells: The Miner's Arms in the neighboring village of Priddy (please get careful directions to this Paul Leyton enterprise).

Suffolk: **Aldeburgh**: The Wentworth.

Sussex: **Brighton**: (1) Starlit Room of the Metropole Hotel, (2) La Mascotta, (3) Wheeler's Sheridan (fish), (4) English's Oyster Bar.
Cooden: Cooden Beach Hotel.
Eastbourne: Chez Maurice.
Lewes: White Hart Hotel.
Rye: Mermaid.

Warwickshire: **Birmingham**: (1) Carosel, (2) Burlington, (3) The Plough and Harrow, (4) Albany Hotel, (5) Lambert Court Hotel (3 miles out on the Hagley Rd.).
Coventry: Leofric Hotel.
Stratford-upon-Avon: (1) The Dirty Duck (so named by the extraordinarily charming proprietor of this outstanding drop-in spot in the vicinity as a parody on "The White Swan.") (2) The Beefeater, (3) Hong Kong. Among hotels: (1) The Welcombe, (2) The Hilton, (3) The Shakespeare, (4) The Falcon, (5) The Swan's Nest. The upstairs restaurant of the Shakespeare Theatre opens the curtain on a 4-star steak production for about $4. Worthy indeed as an encore to spiritual feasts onstage downstairs. Be sure to book your table in advance.
Warwick: (1) Spencer's West Gate Arms (one of the tops for looks, flavor, and price in the entire region), (2) Aylesford (one of the most wretched in the nation *if* its maître is as rude to you as he was to us), (3) the Grill of the Lord Leycester Hotel. The Saxon Mill (10 minutes along the Kenilworth Rd.) now seems to be slipping. Our recent meal was poorly served, routinely prepared, and relatively costly. Still, it is very attractive to the eye.

Wiltshire: **Colerne**: The Vineyard.
Salisbury: The Haunch of Venison.

Worcestershire: **Broadway**: (1) **Hunter's Lodge**, (2) **Lygon Arms**, (3) **Dower House**.

Ilkley: **Box Tree** (one of the most talked-about spots in England—and almost all the chat is good).

Yorkshire: **South Stainley**: **Red Lion Inn**.
Walshford: **Bridge Inn**.
York: (1) **Terry's**, (2) **Betty's**, (3) **De Grey Rooms**, (4) **Windmill**, (5) **Marshall & Snellgrove** (snacks).

TAXIS   The quaint, dignified, celebrated horseless carriages have finally pushed the controversial "minicabs" off the track; the former now rein nearly alone, offering stately privacy as their proudest product. Passengers are hidden from pedestrians' views as their ancestors were hidden in the cabbies of the gaslight era. A few newer hacks, however, are less colorful and closed. The tough and economical diesel-engine models now are being exported to America, where they already are rolling in Detroit, Philadelphia, Boston, and San Francisco. In our view, they're the finest, most comfortable, best-designed taxis in the world.

The minimum fare is roughly 60¢. An average trip in the center of the city runs from $1.50 to $2.50. For each additional rider above one person, there's an extra charge of about a dime. All have meters, so look for the flag lever or the light on the roof; if the former is up and the latter is illuminated, the car is for hire.

The minicabs, which for years caused bitterness and violence between their owners and those of the conventional fleets because they had muscled into the Big Boys' domain, are now prohibited from cruising (although much to the consternation of regular hacks, too many still do). They must operate as "cars for hire," which means that they now can be summoned only by telephone.

If you're traveling between the capital and Heathrow Airport, you can at last forget about those grim days when you often had to make your bargain in advance. Stern legislation now limits the hop to whatever is shown on the meter (it should average about £5). If you should be fleeced on this 14-mile drive, the British Airports Authority wants to be told. The cabbies are so hopping mad about the meter rate, however, that they may suddenly become invisible when they see you emerge from your hotel with a suitcase in one hand and an airline ticket in the other. If you can't find one ranked up at the Airport, buses leave frequently for the city.

§TIP: After theater, at rush hours, or when it's raining, you might as well unpack your pogo stick to hop back to your hotel. During the hyper-busy or nocturnal slack periods, this is easily one of the most exasperating metropoli in the world. We have waited literally hours and walked miles, on a recent London circuit, in search of hacks. Concierges, we discovered to our surprise, now usually won't bother to telephone for you. Doormen often have as many as 20 customers waiting for them to hail a rover. The *only* suggestions we can offer are (1) again, hire a car and driver if it's a big night out, (2) do not stray far from the population pockets or theater districts if you hope to get home at a reasonable time, and (3) telephone the Radio Taxi service (272 3030) or Owner Drivers service (286 4848), which might not answer the phone if the cabs are occupied. With public transportation closing down around 12:30 A.M., hundreds of innocents and their shivering ladies are hopelessly stranded in this otherwise sophisticated city every night. Most cabbies simply won't work during the late hours—it's a shocking development.

TRAINS   Because Britain invented railways, it has more track per square mile than any other nation and a station for every 5 miles of line. Most main lines radiate from London, and all are improving these days. Intercity trains —often air-conditioned now and with sleepers on night express runs—are usually fine. In this group are the rockets that can hit 100 mph and can average better than 70 mph flashing across Albion. (The prototype of a 125-mph streaker has been sundering the air between London and Bristol lately.) The proudest pacesetters include the famous *Liverpool, Manchester, Yorkshire, and Tees-Tyne Pullmans.* Other favorites are the *Flying Scotsman* (393 miles between London and Edinburgh in 345 minutes), the *Cornish Riviera Express,* and the *Royal Scot.*

If you plan to do a lot of moving around in the U.K., the BritRail Pass will buy 8, 15, 21, or 30 days of unlimited rail travel at bargain rates. Go to the British Railways Offices in New York, Los Angeles, Vancouver, or Toronto for details on these. Remember, please, that these are ONLY for sale in North America. There's also a special BritRail Youth Pass for 8, 15, or 30 days that's even cheaper than the standard version; you've got to be between 14 and 22 to qualify. Again, pick it up BEFORE you leave.

Should you land there without these money-savers, get your passage from the local "booking clerk" at the "booking office" in the "booking hall." Your big baggage ("luggage") travels separately in the "luggage van"—unless it consists of 1 or 2 normal suitcases, in which case you'll carry it in your compartment. Get a porter wherever you go; everybody does. To facilitate your program, chug right over to any British Rail Travel Centre in central London.

Compartments are of 4 major types: First-class and Second-class, Smoking and Nonsmoking. The "open-plan saloon carriage" also appears frequently for long dry runs. Seats are often bookable in advance on the main circuits (always on Pullmans); if you see a slip of paper on the back cushion, you're out of luck—unless it's your reservation!

§TIPS: Crossing to Ireland on a British Rail vessel used to be a voyage any traveler would yearn to forget. Not long ago, the officials realized this and began to brighten up the fleet. Now the "Sealink" network makes rail, ship, or car connections pleasant, convenient, and economical. It hooks into numerous U.K. destinations as well as into continental gateways. If you're in a hurry, the "Seaspeed" ferrytale is a yarn spun out by a growing fleet of Hovercraft.

We've recently unwound from Swedish-Lloyd's 36-hour car-ferry spin between Southampton–Bilbao (Spain) aboard the *Patricia,* a clean, well organized, and fully stabilized steamer. While it eliminates your weary wheel hours, it does not save time or money for Iberia-bound voyagers—and it denies motorists the pleasures of the French countryside and adventures in Gallic cuisine.

The "Motorail" trains (from the special terminal at Kensington) will whisk you and your automobile almost anywhere in the nation (40 separate services and 125,000 car spaces by day and night all year round). Strides have been strode recently to improve creature comforts on these—exchanging benches for sprung mattresses, providing linen instead of only blankets, and furnishing (a proud boast nowadays) HOT WATER. There are also Train-Your-Car services from London (avoiding the crowded Exeter bypass) to both Totnes (Devon) and St. Austell (Cornwall), for lazy westbound motorists. All are less expensive than one might think.

A helpmate for the rod-riding wayfarer is BR's timetable, obtainable for a little over a dollar apiece from the Publicity Department, British Railways Board, Melbury House, Melbury Terrace, London, N.W.1, or from bookshops or station kiosks.

AIRLINES With the exception of British Caledonian Airways and several independent operators who exist upon charters, cargo, and a wee ration of passenger trade, the British Government owns and controls (in practical effect) virtually all important scheduled air service within the United Kingdom. In 1974, its 2 huge fleets—BOAC (British Overseas Airways Corporation) and BEA (British European Airways)—were merged into one giant national flag carrier: **British Airways**, circling the globe though a ½-million-mile network that now calls at 163 airports in 81 countries. Its flock of more than 220 planes is among the world's largest; moreover, last year it introduced the 1350-mph Concorde on regular supersonic runs.

British Caledonian was hatched in 1970. As it only recently cut out its VC-10 service across the Atlantic, its U.K. fleet now consists of shiny BAC III's and Boeing 707 Intercontinentals, based at Gatwick (near London). Today it flies only charters between the U.S. and home. Internally, it stirs the air all over the U.K. We wouldn't turn a hair if this outfit's Golden Lion emblem were to appear on a moon shuttle before long, thanks to hard-driving Chairman Adam Thomson, whose imagination encompasses everything from ordering multimillion-dollar jets to plaid kilts for the line's pretty, polite, and highly polished hostesses. He is pushing Scottish-type hospitality and amenities with full force and enormous success. Our intra-European jaunts have ranged from excellent to superb.

British Airways' European Division fairly blankets the U.K., with hookups throughout the Continent, the Middle East, and North Africa. Its international equipment consists of Tristar air buses, Tridents, BAC III's and Super-III's. A regular helicopter service chops a swath between Penzance and the Scilly Islands.

After a series of teeth-gnashing and hair-tearing experiences with the former BEA in recent times, our latest hops between Brussels, London, Edinburgh, and Mallorca revealed a welcome improvement—a breath of fresh airways as cheering as a carrier's new prospects. In general, the ground personnel couldn't have been friendlier or more helpful. All 3 lunches aloft were superior to any we've previously tried from their caterers; the aircrews showed genuine consideration for the customer, paying special attention to children traveling alone. We also feel safer on BA than on much of its competition, because British technical competence and thoroughness are 2nd to none in the aviation world. Hence, it is a pleasure to report that we were more favorable impressed than ever before by the reorganized squadron's courtesy, skill, and smart flying trim. Let's hope that it maintains this upward course.

The Overseas Division (formerly BOAC) is another nest of professional falcons, with in-flight comforts so pleasant that we're happy to ride it any day to any destination. This hard-driving enterprise was first with jet propulsion in commercial service (1952), first with propjets on transatlantic schedules (1957), first to fly the paying passenger over the ocean on pure jets (1958), and first (in conjunction with Air France) to launch commercial aviation into the supersonic era via the Concorde (1976). Round-the-world services were inaugurated in '59; step aboard in London, and in less than 60 hours you may circle the globe.

Since some time back this contender joined the Jumbo fracas, now the welkin buzzes with its own Boeing-747 hummings-and-goings. It also takes pride in its fleet of Boeing 707's and Vickers Super VC-10's (117 passengers). We've recently deplaned from the latter after hightailing it across the Atlantic —and what honeys these babies are! The cuisine is superb in *both* classes; despite IATA's chokes on what operators can offer budget travelers, these crafty chefs present food so masterfully it seems a Lucullan feast. The service is best-British in attentiveness, friendliness, and watchfulness—in step with the nation's centuries of heartwarming good manners. Salutes, toots, and fond salaams to this splendid airplane and her staffs!

§TIPS: For wander-woes, a gentleman who will receive you cordially is BA's Overseas Division Customer Relations Manager, David Creedy, at the British Airways Terminal, Buckingham Palace Road, London, S.W.1.

Unfortunately, for regional and European flights you can no longer check in either yourself or your luggage at the West London Terminal. (Transoceanic passengers can register at the Buckingham Palace Road Air Terminal in town.) Now the traveler is responsible for getting himself to the airport on time, so be sure to allow for this; flights to some politically sensitive areas require as much as 95 minutes advance check-in. Buses leave the West London terminal for Heathrow every 10 minutes, but a flight will not be held if your bus is delayed.

Air-car-rail ferry systems can whisk you and your car to or from the Continent in a jiffy (see below).

CAR TIPS   Car-ferrying across the English Channel has become Big Business—and it's mushrooming yearly. With the 2219-ton former *Normannia* completely rebuilt, the *Lord Warden,* the *Maid of Kent,* and the aforementioned *Dover* (200 cars, 1000 passengers) now added to the Dover–Boulogne line, the *Londoner* (roulette, bingo, and dancing) now gamboling between Tilbury–Calais, the *Compiègne* and other sizable vessels now in service between Dover–Calais—in addition to the present well-stocked fleets—approximately ½-million automobiles a year are toted between British and continental ports. In peak season, about 70 sailings a day link Britain with France or the Belgian headlands at Ostend. A drive-on-and-off car-ferry service with 3 ships shuttles between Newhaven and Dieppe (103 miles from Paris)—ideal for motorists pointing for southwestern France, Spain, or Portugal. For the connection with Bilbao (Spain), please see our earlier comment under "Trains." **Normandy Ferries** operates between Rosslare (Ireland) and Le Havre, providing separate hookups between Southampton and Le Havre; **Southern Ferries** weighs anchor with drive-on vessels such as the *Eagle* between Southampton and Lisbon or Tangier. Hovercraft now fan out year round between Ramsgate and Calais; you'll be floating on air for a mere 40 minutes; conventional luggers take 3 times longer. Most of these "flying" boats can carry only 36 people, but more recently the *Mountbatten* made its first commando raid from Dover to Boulogne toting 250 S.O.B.'s (souls on board), plus 30 cars. Several more of these ultranoisy, $4,000,000 blowhards also now have taken to the waves. Channel conditions hardly ever bother these skimmers, unless there is unusually heavy weather. They are, however, constantly battling a multitude of gremlins in the machinery.

By air, British Air Ferries' fleet of Carvairs (nose-loading, 5-car, 22-passenger DC-4's) regularly drone between Southend Airport (40 miles from London) and Ostend (45 min.), Le Touquet (35 min.), Basle (150 min.), and Rotterdam (65 min.), saving at least 4 hours of travel time. Rates compare favorably with the sea route. Once on the Continent, you can board excellent car-sleeper service to almost any European rail hub. Be sure to book your reservations *early* in High Season.

§Conversion to left-side driving and traffic in the British Isles (due to change in the dim and misty future) is a lot trickier than you might think—especially in 90° turns, traffic circles, and passing (oops, "overtaking" is the proper word there!). Gradually, international road-sign symbols are replacing traditional English ones—but for some time, both will be in existence. For the first few hundred miles, most American drivers don't dare relax for an instant.

§The Automobile Association and Royal Automobile Club are our candidates for the most alert organizations of their type. Official motorcyclists and service trucks patrol main roads to lend an experienced hand, without charge, to any of the 3,689,422 members who may be stalled or in distress. Don't move an inch in Britian without first joining the AA; your card will also be honored in Germany, Scandinavia, Ireland, and the Benelux lands.

§The British gallon is nearly 1/5th larger than the U.S. gallon. Incidentally, this is the only area north of Africa (except perhaps for Gibraltar) where miles are employed instead of kilometers.

§Spot a fast-moving woman driver in your rearview mirror? Slow down! It's likely to be a Scotland Yard bobbette patrolling the highway in a 120-mph sports car. How fiendish can life get in this motorized age? Limits, incidentally, are 70 mph on expressways, 60 mph on 4-laners, and 50 mph on 2-lane pikes. Better wear your seatbelt buckled, too.

DRINKS The celebrated Public House—"pub," for short—traditionally has been the heartbeat of England. In the old-timers, there are no jukeboxes, no bustling bartenders, no feelings of haste in your average pub. It's a social center, a place to relax and talk over the latest heavyweight contender, to play darts for a brace of pints. It's wonderful.

But in the pubs, as almost everywhere else, change is in the wind. The British Government is now seriously considering extention of the hour when the jolly publican calls "Time, Gentlemen, Time!" Generally, the saloon doors swing open at 11 A.M. and are fastened shut at 11 P.M. The lawmakers also want to eliminate the 3 P.M. to 5 P.M. closure—a cruel hiatus that parches many a fine British throat. Furthermore, there's a foot-on-the-rail movement to lower the age below 18 for entry into these establishments. All this may be realized by the time you arrive. What already has started, however, fills us with deep regret because it strikes at the very heart of the institution itself: the epidemic growth of the so-called Singing Pub or Entertainment Pub. The classic types (a few listed below) are being overtaken rapidly by these mod-mooded newcomers; within a couple of decades, we fear, the old ones may become extinct. In the capital, **Holsten Bierkeller** (34 Brook St.) is typical of the trend away from quiet conversation and traditional British folkways. In this example, the ambiance is that of a German beer cellar—rowdy, noisy, packed with young swingers, and specializing in Teutonic fare, with an inexpensive 3-course "meal". The **Redcliffe Hotel** (268 Fulham Rd.) asks a cover charge daily except on Mondays and Wednesdays; it features a discothèque (shiver me timbers!). For those who relished the Old England of Yore, these are mournful mutations indeed.

The traditional ones that remain are, like the amoeba, self-divided. On one side you'll find the Public Bar—plain, utilitarian, for drinkers who want no nonsense. On the other side, with a separate entrance, is the Saloon Bar—better decorated, more comfortable, the one you'll probably head for. Prices are usually a trifle higher in the latter.

Then, of course, there are 3 styles of classic pubs: City Tavern (spirits and wine featured above draught beers), Gin Palace (typically Victorian if authentic), and Alehouse (plain, ancient, and historic). (The proliferating "wine bars" are another story altogether; these are more like continental bistros, for sips, chats, and nibbles of cheese and tidbits.)

As for what to order, there are 3 major British brews: Mild ale ("mild"), a medium-sweet, medium-brown, inexpensive choice which is becoming more rare in Central London; bitter beer ("bitter"), a pale brown, heavier variety; and Burton ("old"), which is deep brown, quite sweet, and richest of all. English drinkers like to mix these basic types to suit their individual preferences. But remember Burton is available September and June only. If you want straight mild ale, *don't* step right up, as one did in the Good Old Days, and ask for a "wallop"; now you might suddenly sprout a cauliflower ear.

Of heroes, England has more than her share. One of them, The Society for the Preservation of Beers from the Wood, is spreading swiftly across the isle. Says Good Banker Arthur Millard, the Chairman, who protests loudest against brews in tin cans: "We are being avalanched with beer drinkers who dislike the sealed dustbin stuff that pubs throw at you nowadays." We, too, join the chorus by lending our hearty bass to "Roll Out the Barrel"!

§TIPS: After-hours, if you order a beer with your meal, the waiter is apt to shake his head righteously and offer you cider instead. Accept the "cider," because more than likely it will be your beer—a "mistake"!

Delicious *English* wine? The versatile cellars of London's luxury **Dorchester Hotel** come up with this phenomenem, thanks to the connoisseur's palate of General Manager Robin Oldland—Adgestone from the Isle of Wight. Since the vines are ½ German and ½ French, the result is a fresh, clear, interesting product of a Moselle. Please try it!

§WARNING: *Don't drive a car if you have consumed even as little as 2 pints of beer!!* Under the mercilessly stringent provisions of the Road Safety Act, the vehicle operator doesn't have to be drunk to face fines up to $250, 4 months in the pokey (or both), and loss of his or her license for one year. Suspects are required to take a roadside "Breathalyser" test; if the crystals in the plastic bag turn green (even that 2nd pint will do it for some people), it is scientific proof that 80 milliliters of their blood contains more than 80 milligrams of alcohol. There is no recourse for either resident or visitor. The police are so tough that business in some pubs immediately dropped by 50% or more. So ask a teetotaling companion to take over the wheel when you want to live it up—or hie yourself back and forth by taxi, bus, or underground.

P.S. This applies everywhere within the United Kingdom.

As we promised, here are some characteristic pubs (even though a few of these, too, are now trending toward the fashions of Britain's continuing hippie culture):

Cockney Pride (Jermyn St.) has been transformed into one of the most "in" houses on the London scene today. Large cellar room colorfully festooned with authentic Victorianisms; old-fashioned horseshoe bar offering such Olde Englande standards as faggots (mincemeat-and-peas pudding), toad-in-the-hole (sausages in batter pudding), shepherd's pie, and many more historic tidbits—all priced at a pittance. Waiters in fancy vests and bowlers; waitresses in long Gay Nineties gowns; player piano tinkling in the background; normal pub hours (from 11 P.M. to midnight you must order food with drink). Very noisy, very crowded, amusing; a fun place for a pint, a snack, or even a meal (if you can stand the din that long). Here's an artful recreation of Good Queen Vickie's day; deservedly popular.

The **Red Lion** (48 Parliament St.), is a favorite with students from Guys Hospital. The Public Bar is on Parliament Street, the Saloon Bar on Derby Gate. Downstairs is best; no darts; ladies welcome. We noted the addition of a piano and vocalist on Sundays, plus an increasing sing-along quality in its atmosphere. It will probably roar even louder soon.

Antelope (Eaton Terrace) is a gem—not too moldy, not too chichi, a gentle introduction to the science of pubbery. Prices higher than average, but *still* low; excellent for a plain, cheerful dinner; one of our favorites.

The **Prospect of Whitby** (57 Wapping Wall), like the Cheshire Cheese (where you should be sure to sit at Samuel Johnson's table) and the previously mentioned George and Vulture (see "Restaurants"), is a tavern rather than a true pub. It has installed a Hawaiian band and a singer—to us, the ultimate abomination in these ancient English surroundings. Hangout of students who are sometimes rowdy. Dock area; rambling, helter-skelter building raised in 1520; Pepys Room for dining; stuffed alligator, human skull, and other oddities suspended over bar. Closed Sunday.

The **Sherlock Holmes Tavern** (Northumberland St.) is a latecomer in the Whitbread Brewery's series of so-called museum taverns. On the ground floor, you'll find the main bar, a scattering of tables, and, as wall decorations, a fascinating collection of "memorabilia" from his most famous "cases" (a plaster mold of a "paw print" of the hound of the Baskervilles, Detective Lestrade's "handcuffs," the "code" used in the story of the dancing men, etc.); to the side there's a painfully plain little nook for the earnest toper. Upstairs is the Grill, with tapestried wall coverings and white banquettes; to the rear of this section is a glassed-off montage of the famous fictional sitting room shared by the great sleuth and Dr. Watson at "221-B Baker St." Food adequate for pub (not restaurant) level; our tab for 3 was comparatively expensive. Recommended as a novelty for Holmes fans—and who isn't one?

The **Buccaneer** (Leicester Square) is an imposing example of its namesake. There's a galleon theme floating on a Polynesian undercurrent.

Nag's Head (Covent Garden), now plinking along with folk singers on Sunday evenings, **Samuel Pepys'** (Brooks Wharf, Upper Thames St.), **World's End** (King's Rd.)—the list of names and addresses is long, if you're not too choosy. You'll find them scattered everywhere.

All of the above satisfactory for the dilettante who has come to see a few *other* sights in the nation. But for the serious-minded suds-buff who would make girl scouts out of the ghosts of Brendan Behan, Dylan Thomas, and W. C. Fields, nothing beats the guidance of that camel-bellied specialist of all publicans, Alan Reeve-Jones, author of *London Pubs.* Together with his ever-faithful cast-iron liver, Mr. Reeve-Jones consumed 11 happy years visiting 1500 drinking stations, only to list and to recommend a mere 166. Here are a few of his candidates, but don't stop with these. Track down Mr. R-J's tome and find your own particular pot-o'-gold! Examples: For visual appeal the Admiral Codrington (Mossop St.); for film makers, the Intrepid Fox (Wardour St.); for doctors, the Crown (in Chelsea); for world travelers, the Fitzroy (Charlotte St.); for Egyptologists, the Museum Tavern (Great Russell St.); for Members of Parliament, the St. Stephen's Tavern, just a skip from Westminster (listen for the bell—a signal that a vote is about to be taken in the Commons). Any thirsty merrymaker will find this a guidebook with a real head on it.

Beer, gin, rum, and liqueurs are plentiful and good; Scotch is costly. You'll pay from $1 for a "small" (Understatement of the Year) and from $1.60 for a "large" (junior-size) portion in today's London. The bottle price has been nudged up again, bringing your outlay to around $12 for most proprietary brands. Remember, too, that British Scotch is somewhat weaker than ours.

To the average Englishman, ice used to be that strange, transparent, cold-to-the-touch substance upon which the fishmonger chilled his halibut. Now that so many visiting Americans have insisted that whisky requires the stuff, he'll often go along by dropping 1 small cube—or 2, at the most—into his drink. British lager is customarily served (not always!) at room temperature —but, as the ever-delightful C. V. R. Thompson wrote before his death, the room is usually so cold that the beer is delicious. My Nancy and I, however, are such barbarians about liking our brews cold, cold, COLD that we order Carlsberg or Tuborg (both Danish) draft whenever we can find them in restaurants—which, to our joy, is now surprisingly often in the larger cities.

THINGS TO SEE   Impossible to cover in this limited space. There's as much to see in the United Kingdom as in other countries 5 times as big. For broad, generalized hints only, turn to the sections on "Cities" and "Miscellaneous." As a starter, don't forget the previously mentioned "Season Ticket to the History of Britain" or the British Tourist Authority's "Open to View" grabbag (see "Cities").

Another tiptop, low-cost suggestion is the **Grey-Green Coach** organization, which operates excellent budget-level bus tours. The vehicles are immaculately maintained; excursions fan out on 2-to-8-day loops touching the historic and scenic heartbeats of the U.K., some even skipping over to the Continent. The packages are too detailed to cover here, but drop a note to the ever-friendly chairman, Henry Ewer, who will send you one of the comprehensive brochures filled with tempting itineraries, dates, accommodations, prices, and true-to-life photos. His address is Grey-Green Coaches Ltd., 53 Stamford Hill London, N16 5TD. Here's a genuine money-stretcher in a world of shrinking values.

Possibly the greatest provincial attractions to U.S. travelers are the 960 **castles, homes, and gardens** which have been opened to the public, on payment of a modest fee. The National Trust, a nonofficial, nonprofit body, now owns 200. Of the grand total, 40 are "Great Houses"; the balance consists of stately mansions, country manors, abbeys, and sentimental shrines such as Rudyard Kipling's former residence. Most popular and most outstanding is Woburn Abbey and Zoo Park (42 miles from London, 54 miles from Stratford-upon-Avon); 1.5-million guests per year "oh" and "ah" at the 3000 deer, the safariland of African animals, the multimillion-dollar art collection, 3000 acres of enchanting parkland, the model village, the cable car system, the exhibition of 17,000 toy soldiers, the Zoo restaurant, and the splendid antique furnishings of this "Most English of the Palaces." High in popularity is Chatsworth (on the River Derwent 33 miles southeast of Manchester), which is renowned for its magnificent gardens with water effects. The Duke of Norfolk's Arundel (near Brighton), the Duke of Marlborough's Blenheim Palace (8 miles north of Oxford), where Sir Winston Churchill was born, Beaulieu Abbey and Palace House, with a fine vintage-automobile museum (14 miles from Southampton), and the Marquess of Bath's Longleat where 50 African lions roam the ancestral park (24 miles from Bristol) are also favorite tourist targets. The later home of Sir Winston, Chartwell (2 miles from

Westerham, in Kent), will undoubtedly become a beloved monument to the history of our own lifetimes. Only recently opened to the public, it maintains the flavor of the period between the wars—the happiest years of the great statesman's life. My Lord Montagu's (*sic*) estate at Beaulieu chugs along on the strength of its Motor Museum, which car buffs love to horn in on. For hours, prices, descriptions, and transportation data on 818 of these sites, the annually revised *Historic Houses, Castles and Gardens* is available in limited supply at the British Book Centre, 996 Lexington Ave., N.Y. 10021, or at T. Scott Martin Books, 527 Sutter St., San Francisco. The price is $1.50.

What must be the most blue-blooded conference since Runnymede was attended by 600 British dukes, marquesses, earls, and other noblemen who own aristocratic homes in England. Their purpose? To form—please get this —a "trade union" to plan new ways for attracting visitors to their estates. Long live *noblesse oblige* (or is that guild-ing their lily?).

Guidesters interested in modern art should visit the still controversial **Coventry Cathedral**. Designed by Sir Basil Spence, it contains the largest tapestry in the world (the work of Graham Sutherland), sculpture by Sir Jacob Epstein, and stained glass by John Piper.

On the other slipper, traditionalists usually love the **Antique Dealers' Fair and Exhibition**, normally held from mid- to late-June each year at Grosvenor House, Park Lane, London, W.1. Most items are up for sale; experts authenticate every one of the displays; all are pre-1830. Always popular with the English—from the Royal Family to Agatha Applemore of Amesbury. Highly recommended.

Canal and river cruising has undergone a renaissance among U.S. visitors. Inland Waterway Holiday Cruises (Preston Brook, Runcorn, Cheshire) and Inland Cruising Co. (The Marina, Braunston, Daventry, Northamptonshire) churn up a wide variety of excursions along much of the country's canal network from midspring to midautumn. Here is about the ultimate in leisurely touring, most of it along narrow, winding arroyos that lap Oxford, Chester, Rugby, Rickmansworth, Warwick, Nottingham, and more than a dozen other shady wadies between London and Manchester. Rates are by the week; see your travel agent for bookings, but be sure to nail them down early. For briefer forays, Thames Launches and Thames Motor Boat Co. provide 1-hour, 2-hour, and all-day journeys from Tower Pier to the Tower of London and upstream to Putney, Kew, Richmond, and Hampton Court, plus special 2-hour evening sojourns. Yet another 2½-hour canalization (with lunch) can be had aboard the *Fair Lady* of Camden Lock, Chalk Farm Road, Camden Town.

The overwhelming sublimity of the little **Chapels Royal** is virtually a secret to all foreign visitors except a relative handful who reside in the Commonwealth. The reason? Unless the tourist dresses conservatively and is quietly mannerly, he or she is not wanted by the vicars and the congregations. As a further illustration, cameras are banned. These gloriously beautiful places of worship are tucked away in a number of the most famous and most historic monuments of the United Kingdom—settings that are incredible to the uninitiated. All are sponsored by the Crown. Some date back to the eleventh or twelfth century. The Sunday services normally start at 11 A.M. The choirs are limited in number but magnificent in voice. Should you wish to attend, you'll find a listing of the locations and the hours in Saturday's better-grade London newspapers. Wear a church-going-type suit or dress (not sports clothes), arrive at least 15 minutes early, and regardless of your religious persuasion (save if you're agnostic) you should find it one of the richest experiences of your journey abroad—an indelible lifetime memory.

Sound and Light spectacles *(Son et Lumière)* have crossed the English Channel from France and caught on fast. So far they have been presented at the Tower of London, Buxton, Canterbury, Carrickfergus Castle, Dover Castle, Eltham Palace, Kenilworth Castle, Greenwich Palace, Cardiff Castle, Gloucester Cathedral, Southwark Cathedral, Ragley Hall, York Minster, and Norwich Cathedral in Norfolk, and Greys Court in Henley-on-Thames; there's also one aboard the *H.M.S. Victory* in Portsmouth, plus others at Pembroke and Stirling Castles; at Winchester, Worcester, and Durham Cathedrals; at Bury St. Edmunds, Hampton Court Palace, (as a droll aside, the Associated Press reported that when the searchlights were turned on for the opening night's show at Ragley Hall, the Marquess was, by accident, vividly and embarrassingly silhouetted in his bathroom), Rochester, St. Paul's and Lichfield Cathedrals, and Sherborne and Tewkesbury Abbeys. Consult your nearest British Travel office for last-minute information on the whens and wheres.

The **Chichester Drama Festival** presents an interesting Greek-Elizabethan playhouse. Directed by Sir John Clements, it draws such stellar performers as Dame Edith Evans, Sir John Gielgud, and Margaret Leighton. The theater, situated in a 43-acre park, is 62 miles southwest of London. In summer, special trains will whisk you back to Victoria Station by midnight; schedules also geared for matinées; express buses also make the journey; for particulars consult your Hall Porter. Tickets average the price of a movie back home; those who hunger for more than the arts may dine at the Theatre Restaurant. The pre-curtain smörgåsbord is said to be excellent, but we've never said skål to this particular table. If you want to make a night of it, you might find diggings of a sort at Woodend House (West Stoke), the 12-acre manor formerly occupied by one of Nelson's commanders at Trafalgar and by Lily Langtry; 11 rooms; tennis and horses; reasonable rates. A laudable venture.

Stratford-upon-Avon is a living shrine that no serious Anglophile should miss. Hardly any do, since during performance weeks (4 programs annually between Mar. and Dec.) and in midsummer it is packed to its rafters with wide-eyed disciples—95% of them Americans. The Royal Shakespeare Theatre—largely endowed by funds from U.S. citizens—is, of course, the be-all and end-all of local attractions. If you haven't nailed down your matinee or evening tickets in London beforehand *(which is a virtual "must"),* go immediately to the window in the theater foyer or to the below-mentioned tourist office; sometimes a few last-minute cancellations turn up. Each year the Bard's birthday is commemorated here on April 23. Despite the crush of seething humanity, much of the feeling of Elizabethan times remains in the stucco-and-beam buildings that line its narrow, flower-dotted flagstone streets. Favorite targets in town include Shakespeare's Birthplace, Anne Hathaway's Cottage, The New Place (the poet's retirement home), the adjoining sunken Knott Garden, Hall's Croft, and (for Cantabs) Harvard House, where the university founder lived. Excursions into the nearby environs should encompass a visit to Mary Arden's House at Wilmcote, Warwick Castle, Kenilworth, or to such sweet little hamlets as Honington, Temple Grafton, Bourton-on-the-Water, Stanton, Chipping Campden, and those mentioned in our earlier "Cotswolds" roundup. Hotels and restaurants (see separate sections) run from fair to adequate to promising; almost all, however, are replete with eye-appealing bonuses for the culturally alert pilgrim. Since tourism is this village's chief occupation, *be certain to have your room reservation confirmed in writing.* And if you have any travel problems, shoot arrow-straight for the tourist office (20 Chapel St.) where Mrs. B. G. Browne will gently and patiently erase your woes. Here is more than a Measure for Measure reward to all who cherish our language and literature.

TIPPING   Railway porters get 25¢ per bag; when there are 3 pieces or more, cut this to 20¢ each. Taxi drivers get 15%, or a minimum of 20¢. The hotel service charge has been discussed previously; bellboys, doorkeepers, bartenders, and others who give you special attention receive separate consideration, with 10% or a minimum of 5 pence.

THINGS TO BUY   Cashmeres, tartans, Burberrys, smoking supplies, food delicacies, silver, sporting equipment, Lock's hats for men, English flower perfumes, Loewe leather goods, rare books, Toplet fashions for ladies, Liberty silks, and antique bric-a-brac are the best bets.

Five-star***** "find" for ladies? Here is one of the hottest bargains for the traveling gal in London if you hit its stocks on the right day—and you won't find it outside the pages of the Fielding books. World-famous **Toplet Knitwear Ltd.** (new location in lovely air-conditioned Regency mews house at 18 Bruton Place—*not* Bruton St.!—off Berkeley Square), the London designer in knitwear and jersey which distributes solely through the most elegant stores on Fifth Avenue, Wilshire Boulevard, rue du Faubourg-St.-Honoré, and similar fashion temples, historically has adhered to its wholesale-only policy. In '68, through our deep personal friendship with Owner-President Rudi Freimuth, a unique arrangement emerged. This privilege can be extended to *overseas visitors only*, who *must* produce a copy of our *Guide* for admission. Then Mr. Freimuth, his handsome son Thomas, and Sales Director Mrs. Kane will permit you to select any part or parts of its latest collection at WHOLESALE prices—savings as much as 70% below their U.S. levels. The summer-wear models in noncrushable drip-dry, no-ironing fabrics are gorgeous. (There's an exquisitely tailored wool line for the cold months, too.) Its ingenious 6-piece coordinated "Top Set" of knitwear and jersey (skirt, sweater, jacket, dress, shirt, and slacks), which makes 12 different combinations all packable in your own attaché case, is yours for an astonishing $100 to $150. You'll also find superb cocktail gowns (shorts $55 to $75, longs $65 to $89); top quality polyester suits and dresses ($45 to $69); shimmering hostess outfits, chic sportswear, gay prints, and lots, lots more. Open Monday through Friday *(not Sat.)* from 9 A.M. to 1 P.M. and 2 P.M. to 5 P.M.; closed on normal holidays; if in doubt, call 499-3110 or 499-3119. Run, don't walk; REALLY special!

Cashmeres, tartans, and materials? Our number one candidate is **W. Bill, Ltd**.—the finest woolen specialist we've ever found in the British Isles. This 130-year-old firm, the first to introduce Irish and Welsh tweeds to England, has 2 branches (93 New Bond St. and 28 Old Bond St., London W.1.)—and don't be fooled by the smallness of their stores, because the stocks are not only gorgeous but inexhaustible. Purest, softest cashmere sweaters, Shetland knitwear with matching tweeds at attractive prices; cashmere suitings and coatings $50 up per yard; handwoven Harris and Shetland tweeds at $8 to $10 per yard; choice worsteds, flannels, and tropicals at $25 to $70 per yard (tailored, if required); Scotch tartans and tailored skirts from $21; downy mohair throws from $50 and wraps from $17; silk squares at $8; tartan cashmere travel rugs at $65 (ours has been worth its weight in gold since 1950); men's jackets, men's hats made from their own tweeds by Lock & Co., and other regional temptations. Both houses offer exactly the same expert knowledge and attention. Personable Brian Bill (4th generation) is your oracle at 28 Old Bond St., while John Milton and Mr. Olliver will greet you at 93 New Bond St. The demand for impeccable custom tailoring is growing fast at each; if time fleets, large stocks of ready-made jackets for men and tweed skirts and tartan kilts for ladies are on tap. Legions of sage absentee shophounds write to Mr. Hammett or Miss Smith for their eye-popingly illustrated mail-order catalogue. All merchandise is interchangeable between branches within minutes. Far superior, in our personal opinions, to all competitors. Square-shooting, solid, and utterly reliable.

Burberrys rainwear and topcoats? "Burberrys" is a familiar word to millions of shoppers—and well it should be, because Thomas Burberry, who invented the first weatherproof cloth, is immortalized in his living monument, the **House of Burberry** at 18 Haymarket, near American Express. Here countless U.S. pilgrims make their selections from probably the most comprehensive range of foul-weather apparel, suits, and casuals anywhere under the sun—*or* clouds. Up-to-the-minute-styled Burberrys are also extremely popular in wool or Terylene-and-cotton gabardines. The latest addition to its ever-increasing spectrum is the travel luggage with matching umbrellas in the classic Burberry check. Next you'll find the world-famous Burberry Reversibles. Among the vast forests of topcoats, wonderful tweeds of every conceivable type await; if you're feeling extra-flush, you may also treat yourself to a rich, luxurious, 100% camelhair or 100% cashmere. (If you're not feeling quite so flush, they accept Diners Club, American Express, Master Charge, and Eurocard credit cards.) Featured in the ladies department, along with the full range of waterproofs, is a distinguished selection of casuals and knitwear, with a vast selection of cashmere, Shetland, and lamb's-wool sweaters (for both genders); beautiful English worsteds, tweeds, tartans, and cashmeres also available by the meter. Speaking personally, I find the Burberry raincoat such a durable investment that I wonder how these good people make money on it; after 17 years of wearing or packing my model over perhaps 2-million miles, today it is as stylish, as unwrinkled, and as good as new! Ask for Retail Director Mr. Lack or Store Manager Mr. Horne, both of whom know our U.S. tastes and will go all out to be helpful (as, in fact, will all of the Burberry sales staff).

Pipes, smokers' requisites, gift articles, ladies' accessories, men's toiletries?

Dunhill (30 Duke St., St. James's, S.W.1) should need no introduction to anyone, because no other establishment anywhere has ever offered more consistently fine quality in its merchandise. Gentlemanly, dignified Mr. Chad or Assistant Manager Mr. Adam will attend your regular wants, and they'll bring sweet memories of happier eras to you. So richly British that it shouldn't be missed. Stunning branches in *New York* (620 Fifth Ave.) and *Paris* (15 rue de la Paix).

Magnificent leather goods? Fabulous 131-year-old **Loewe**, Spain's revered leather master, met such an overwhelmingly successful reception in London that quickly it moved to expanded, oh-so-chic premises at 25 Old Bond St. and has a boutique in the Hilton. With its 2 Iberian factories, 18 deluxe salons, 750 employees, a Royal Court appointment, and several international Gold Medals, this peerless house is proud of its deserved reputation for producing some of the most exquisite works of art in its field anywhere on earth today. Suède garments, bags, gloves, shoes, billfolds, wallets, luggage, the entire line —all with the finish of a precious gem. For the addresses of its peninsular outlets, consult the "Things to Buy" section under "Spain." Important bonus: *25% discount on all articles chosen in London and shipped to you from Spain.* Although remarkable craftsmanship in leather has been a British tradition for centuries, nobody in today's U.K. can touch Loewe's style, workmanship, and quality.

Fortnum & Mason, on Piccadilly, is the only store we know where the clerk who fetches your can of celery soup wears a cutaway coat and striped pants. It used to be one of the greatest centers for delicacies in existence—but now, in genuine sadness, nostalgia, and reluctance, we feel that it is skidding downward at a rate which alarms us. It is rumored that its wearables and all other departments above the ground floor (comestibles, wines, spirits, restaurants) either have been or might be sold; true? In any case, today's fantastic Fauchon of Paris (see "France") has pulled so far ahead as *the* epicurean center of the world, in our opinion that we'd find it impossible to compare them in the same breath. Actually, the splendid Food Halls in Harrods and Selfridges win our local blue ribbon for versatility.

English flower perfumes and toiletries? To cross the threshold of 89 Jermyn Street is to take a fascinating step into English history. **The House of Floris**, a family institution established in 1730 and Perfumers to H.M. The Queen, is irresistibly alluring with its heavenly arrays of traditional English fragrances in an unhurried atmosphere of unique Victorian elegance. There are singularly special and different Perfumes, Toilet Waters, Bath Essences, Soaps, and Powders in Jasmine, Lily of the Valley, Ormonde (their exclusive "Bouquet" fragrance), Rose Geranium, Sandalwood, our own favorite Stephanotis, and many more. A selection from their exquisite collection of filled Pomanders and Pot-Pourri Jars in Ceramics and English Bone China makes inexpensive and delightfully unusual take-home gifts. Male shoppers should investigate the extensive "No. 89 for Men" range of Toiletries and its ever-popular c-o-o-l costar, Limes Toilet Water. Direct Postal Export Scheme and mail-order services are available. Enchanting!

Silver or jewelry? It is our most urgent recommendation that you head straight to **Garrard & Co., Ltd.**—not to any lesser purveyor. Garrard (the

"Gar" rhymes with "care," not "jar") are Crown Jewellers to Her Majesty Queen Elizabeth II. The list of British and foreign royalty whose court appointments it holds is a miniature *Almanach de Gotha*. In keeping with its station, this old-line landmark, founded in 1721, offers impeccable standards of design and quality that are universally recognized—plus a reputation for service that is unsurpassed anywhere on the globe. And what a Palace of Treasures it is! Start your fascinating tour in the ground floor Silver Department, where you'll find seemingly inexhaustible stocks of beautiful flatware and hollowware, both modern and antique. Next, step across the main aisle to see the new, rare, fascinatingly different, 3-dimensional jeweled pictures by William Tolliday—a Garrard exclusive. Then allow yourself to be dazzled by the most elegant gems and other precious objects in the Commonwealth, many designed and fashioned by the same craftsmen who take care of Great Britain's Crown Jewels. Finally, stroll up to the mezzanine to be intrigued by the magnificent display of watches and clocks for any occasion and any surroundings. Armchair travelers from all over the free world write to Garrard for its "Gifts," "Silver," or "Watch" catalogues. Ask for the Showroom Manager. You'll be welcomed—so browse to your heart's content!

Sporting equipment, sportswear, and quality miscellany? If you're an Abercrombie & Fitch fan, you'll revel in its overseas twin, **Lillywhites**, the best-known and most exciting center of its type abroad. Unparalleled.

Men's furnishings? **Hilditch & Key Ltd.** (73 Jermyn St.) is a sturdy, versatile, and reliable old-timer. Even more appealing to our personal tastes are the reasonably priced custom-made and ready-made shirts, blazers, sport coats, and slacks at **Turnbull and Asser,** a few steps away at 71–72 Jermyn St. Why not try both?

Shoes? **Alan McAfee** (5 Cork St.) purveys some of its beautiful products through Saks Fifth Avenue—which, because of import duties, shipping expenses, and other costs, naturally must charge a lot more in the States. Personally, we've found their creations to be smartly styled, durable, and surprisingly reasonable for their high standards of quality. Be sure to ask for Mr. Smith, who takes special care of our clan. Strongly commended to discriminating transatlantic voyagers. **T. Elliot & Sons** (76 New Bond St.) has been recommended to us by a number of shophounds. We're eager to visit it.

Young designers and boutiques? A flood of fresh, provocative talent is changing the face of traditional British *haute couture*. So many small, chic shops have sprung up that it is impossible to enumerate them in this limited space. See our *Shopping Guide* for more than 3 dozen of our favorites.

Books? As most travelers know, **Foyle's** (119–125 Charing Cross Road) is not only the world's biggest bookshop, but it's the most fun, too. From a teen-agers' business started nearly 75 years ago in the kitchen of their parents' home the astonishing Foyle brothers expanded it to an inventory of 4-million volumes. Besides the stock of everything from *Tarzan of the Apes* to (we suppose) a First Folio Shakespeare, the major delight about this sprawling jumble of buildings, stacks, and staircases is its total informality. Here is a haven, a retreat, a window-shopper's clubhouse, a place to idle the motor when the day's problems are too much for you. While there, we'd suggest that you inquire about the famous monthly Literary Luncheons at the Dorchester, which feature celebrated visiting authors from Prime Ministers to Nobel Laureates, and which no U.S. booklover should *think* of missing. Wonderful!

Arrestingly charming stationery, diaries, address books, and selected gift items? **Frank Smythson Limited** (54 New Bond St.), which holds the Royal Warrant of Stationers to Her Majesty the Queen, is a delight in its atmosphere, its tastes and its friendly welcome to browsers. Courtly General Manager Thomas Neale would help you to enjoy your visit. For ourselves we've discovered more than a dozen enchanting originals here.

Finest men's hats, umbrellas, and special apparel? Continuously since 1759, there has existed only one top-ranking center in the western world—**James Lock & Co., Ltd.** (6 St. James's St.). The Nelson Room ships a cargo of tempters—superbly styled topcoats, rainwear, blazers, sports jackets, and slacks, all bearing either the famous Lock label or made especially for Lock by the prestigious House of Rodex. Also at hand are its luxurious, exclusive ladies' silk scarves. But the topper, the capper, the lid on this prize package is the hat—every conceivable male headgear for formal or leisure wear. There is also a superb collection of umbrellas, belts, ties, billfolds, and leather attaché cases. No purchase tax on exports; be sure to ask for the ever-cordial Messrs. Priest or Brine, who best know the needs of overseas visitors. *The* one-and-only!

Shotguns? **Purdey** (57-58 S. Audley St.)—but only if your banker calls you "Mr. Niarchos," because that storied "pair of Purdeys" will set you back at least $16,000. **Holland & Holland**, also remarkable, comes next on the ladder.

Silks? **Liberty** (Regent St.) is outstanding for misses' linen dresses, beachwear, and party things—but the Liberty silks are still the best buy (provided you're not bound for Italy).

Department stores? **Harrods, Marks & Spencer, Peter Jones, Selfridges, John Lewis & Co., Peter Robinson, D. H. Evans & Co., Bourne & Hollingsworth, Dickins & Jones, Harvey Nichols & Co**. Your taxi driver can find them. The first 3 are the finest, although the Harrods and Selfridges Food Halls are wonderlands which, to many including us, decisively top all of their big-time competition.

Antiques, china, glass, and gift items? The **General Trading Company (Mayfair) Ltd.**, (144 Sloane St., Sloane Square) is our happiest British Discovery in years—"discovery" being a remonstrance to these very dumb authors, because just where had we been since 1920 or so? This one is a joy, really a joy—the largest retail shop of its kind in the world, occupying elegant headquarters in 4 spacious, serene, redecorated Edwardian mansions. The 4th, more recently purchased and totally refurbished, not only vastly broadens its space and its scope, but its lovely garden and attractively thought-out touches also reinforce the enchantment of its character. Trashy "fillers" are scorned by Director David Part and his associates. In antiques, English period pieces (Sheraton, Regency, Hepplewhite, and the like), china, and *objets d'art* are the specialties. Comprehensive displays of modern bone china for the table (no figurines) and pottery (Royal Worcester, Spode, Crown Staffordshire, Wedgwood, and other leading wares); fine table glass in quantities; big and versatile Gift Department of handicrafts, leather work, china vases, placemats, bar accessories, French porcelain *cachepots,* picnic accessories, and goodness knows *what* other temptingly lovely items on parade; Soft Furnishings Department with imaginative and tasteful fabrics for contemporary or period decoration; enlarged complex with EVERYTHING for the gardener. All prices are plainly marked by this family-managed concern, and you'll find tempters here from $1 up to whatever you wish to pay. Be sure to ask for the gentle and delightful Mr. Part in person. Safe shipment is guaranteed to any place on the globe, even to R. T. (Republic of Texas). Super.

If General Trading shouldn't have what you're hunting for, try famous and fine **Asprey** (165–169 New Bond St.) for anything from an Adam fireplace to a gold swizzle stick to Ringo-Starr-designed chess and backgammon sets to historical figures in porcelain.

For antiques, after the above General Trading Company, the **Portobello Road Market** (Sat. only), the **Old Caledonian Market** *(go on Friday mornings)*, and **Camden Passage** in the suburb of *Islington* are currently the hottest bets among hunters In The Know. **Fulham Road** and **King's Road**, Chelsea, are for those who can afford sentimentality in the more expensive bracket; **Beauchamp Place** (pronounced "Beecham"), just off Knightsbridge, is for zillionaires; **Kensington Church Street** and **Notting Hill Gate** remain popular-price playgrounds. For further data and tips on this enormous field, *we* always forget—so we use *Fielding's Shopping Guide to Europe.*

Saddlery, equine equipment, and riding habits? **W. & H. Gidden Limited** (15 New Clifford St., New Bond St.), established in 1806, is 7th Heaven for the equestrian, with a seemingly limitless galaxy of top-quality saddles, bridles, bits, harnesses, horse clothing, horse boots and other accessories, whips, tools such as curry combs and hoof picks, brushes, stable equipment, veterinary products, and beautifully chic riding outfits for both genders. Ask for likable expert Mr. J. Dennett.

Auctions? **Sotheby's** (34-35 New Bond St.) and **Christie's** (8 King St., St. James's) are the world's greatest auction rooms, as everybody knows. Seventy percent of all items they sell go for under $240; feel free to seek the happily shared expertise (gratis) of their staffs. Consult their listings in the London newspapers for what is coming up during your visit. A number of smaller and more specialized houses are also described in our *Shopping Guide*; no space here.

Men's made-to-measure? There are so many superb tailors in London that it's hard to make a choice. Among the select houses are **Anderson & Sheppard** (30 Savile Row), which now also caters to ladies; **Benson, Perry & Whitley** (9 Cork St.); **Hawes & Curtis** (43 Dover St.); **Henry Poole** (10 Cork St.); **Huntsman** (11 Savile Row); **James & James** (11 Old Burlington St.); **Wyser & Bryant** (45 Maddox St.). Not all the leaders are on this list, again because of lack of room—but here's a good cross section of the standard-bearers. Prices have skyrocketed shockingly. In the top establishments, you'll easily pay $500, depending upon the choice of material and the work required. (That's why I now confine all of my patronage to the Brioni and Angelo firms in Rome, who do an equally handsome and careful job in a substantially lower range.

§TIPS: Every tailor has his own cutting style. Don't ask for pegged pants or knee-length pleats, because he won't stand for major alterations of his special hallmark. And display every tooth you own in a gigantic smile the moment you meet the cutter; if he doesn't like your personality, it might be 47¼ years before delivery.

Your own Coat of Arms in decorative heraldry? **Mullins of London** (Bond St.) Ltd. (9 New Bond St.) has long been a world leader in strikingly decorative heraldic plaques, parchments, scrolls, door knockers, car badges, blazer-pocket badges and the like, hand fashioned in your own family's coat of arms at startlingly low prices. Catalogue and major mail-order facilities with guaranteed delivery; Miss Lee-Dunne and Miss McLaren your friendly mentors; Heraldic Heritage branch at Heathrow Airport. Unusually interesting, pride-inducing, and worthy.

Recent leniency: All goods, regardless of value, may now be purchased by *overseas visitors* without the 5% to 33% British Purchase Tax. Because most establishments charge a fee for making the necessary arrangements, it is both sensible and timesaving to pay it in full on all trifling acquisitions.

Shopper's reconnaissance? At the **Design Centre** (28 Haymarket) or the **Crafts Centre** (43 Earlham St.), you'll find samples, pictures, and information about more than 1000 British products; free admission; nothing sold on the premises; good first stop for the neophyte.

Baggage, parcel, or car shipment? Again we have tried **Robert Fisher (Shipping) Ltd.** (32 Lexington St.) in forwarding 5 or 6 crates of miscellaneous personal possessions from London to our home in Mallorca. They packed it so beautifully that even its most fragile items arrived in perfect condition. Our salutes!

Shopping hours: London, in general, 9 A.M. to 5:30 P.M. with some Saturday closings at 1 P.M. and others at 5:30 P.M.; large department stores open one specific weeknight (Thurs. on Oxford St., Weds. at Harrods, etc.); smaller shops in Chelsea, Soho, and similar districts close at 1 P.M. on Thursday, but are usually open all day Saturday; everything shuttered on Sunday except a few delicatessens, 1 or 2 other food shops (mornings only), and a handful of all-night drugstores ("chemists"). It's advisable to check before setting out. The National Chamber of Trade is currently investigating the possibility of a 5-day shopping week.

Dedicated shophounds? Space is too tight here for further listings—so consult the purse-size '77 edition of *Fielding's Shopping Guide to Europe* for more stores, more details, and more lore.

BEAUTY PARLORS **René** (66 S. Audley St.) can make you ravishing; appointments required. **Raymond** (18 Grafton St., a Knightsbridge salon, and many provincial branches) caters to Royalty and scads of film stars; special priority reported for overseas visitors' bookings; personally unknown to us, but comments are favorable. The **Cadogan Club** (182 Sloane St.) is suggested by Rose Hughes, the radiant spouse of Publishing Potentate Larry Hughes, our own William Morrow associate. Chic clientele in small busy surroundings; decidedly expensive, but if you meet Rose, you'll see that it's worth it! If you can't get in these, try **Rubinstein**, **Antoine**, **Bouchard**, or any good shop along New Bond, Albemarle, or Dover Streets.

Tip about 15%. On a $5 job, for example, 20 Pence for the maestro and 15 Pence for the assistants are ample.

MISCELLANEOUS   Bus travel? A minimum of 5¢ a mile, and often pretty rugged. Try your hotel Hall Porter for schedules. (Don't forget our Grey-Green suggestion in "Things To See.")

Sightseeing information and tourists' Events of the Day? Dial 246-8041, and an official service will give you full details on hours and locations of important London sightseeing events, art exhibitions, theatrical performances, and What's Going On. This "Teletourist" assistance is also available in French (246-8043), Spanish (246-8047), or German (246-8045). And speaking of British telephones, a credit-card service (cost: 60¢) has been inaugurated, permitting the accepted subscriber to pick up any phone in the world and charge the call to his own number.

"Gentleman Guide"? Cambridge and Oxford students, replete with dark suits, bowlers, and carnations, double as tour leaders through **Undergraduate Tours, Ltd.** (6 South Molton St., W.1), a division of British Tours Ltd. A flock of Guidesters continue to sing their praises. They are selected not only for their knowledge of the country, their personalities, and their background, but also for the quality of their cars—which transport you! Some preplanned itineraries available, but you may always roam whenever and wherever your spirit moves. British Tours also offer "Lilliput Tours" for children. They operate year round. A similar curriculum is offered by the **Take-a-Guide** organization (11 Old Bond St.).

Lazy? Tired? **Miss Grace Slater**, former Shopping Consultant to *Shopping Magazine* and *The Londoner,* has a service that will line up your most difficult needs, ready for your inspection in a matter of hours. Ask her for any sizable *specialized* item (from a Chippendale chair to a set of old Wedgwood to a Georgian silver tooth mug to Scottish bagpipes), and it'll be there. Don't bother her, however, about ordinary merchandise which is available everywhere, because she's too busy to fool with it. No markups; her commissions are from merchants only. Phone 624-6215 for an appointment, or write your requirements in advance to her at 29 Abercorn Place, London, N.W.8.

Changing of the Guard ? Because of the manpower shortage (!), the ceremony no longer takes place daily at Buckingham Palace at 11:30 A.M. Alas! The Undersecretary of the Army has officially stated that in the winter it will be intermittent but that from April to September, whenever the Queen is in residence there, "every effort will be made" to restore its age-old scheduling. The situation is equally chancy with the Horse Guards at Whitehall, where the Mounted Squadron of the Household Cavalry Regiment usually changes at 11 A.M. on weekdays and an hour earlier on Sunday. Call the above-mentioned English-language number for further directions. Times occasionally vary.

Windsor Castle ? Before any excursion here, check *first* as to whether it's open; requirements of the Court usually (but not always) result in the closing of the State Apartments during April and substantial portions of March, May, and June. The Tower of London will be receiving weekdays (10 A.M. to 5 P.M.) and on Sunday, beginning around April 1 and running through early October (2 P.M. to 5 P.M.).

LOCAL RACKETS   Cockney guides can sometimes lie with the artistry of a Munchausen. Any old house is a "castle"; any old street is "where

Dickens played as a child." Result: The tourist pays money, but sees and learns nothing. Book your tours only through a reliable agency—or get registered guides through the British Tourist Authority.

The occasional taxi driver will offer to "show London to the American gentleman"—and charge the fee on the meter, which will be astronomical. Don't fall for it; make your arrangements through a reputable company.

Whenever you cash a traveler's check in a hotel, make it a point to inquire *first* about the hotel's percentage on the transaction. If it's too big a bite (it frequently is!), you'll save a chunk by going to the nearest bank. Even more important, don't make international telephone calls from your hotel because of the appalling house charges which most of them levy; go to the Central Exchange instead.

Guard your wallet carefully in crowds these days—particularly aboard jammed buses or subway ("underground") cars—because pickpocketing is increasing radically. On the transportation scene, often one man will carry on a loud (and distracting) argument with the conductor while his confederate jostles the victim and deftly does the job.

The so-called key swindle is still unlocking portals of woe. This is the vintage con game in which a Soho B-girl or a "hostess" in a 4th-rate booze joint will slip the sucker the alleged key to her apartment, on deposit of perhaps £5 "for good faith." When he arrives at the rendezvous, either it's a phony address or she never shows up. A similar racket was worked recently on a sophisticated American bachelor, who should have known better than to be "taken" by the owner of one of the dingy, sleazy sex-cinema theaters in the Leicester Square area. After showing an innocuous movie, this entrepreneur persuaded the Yankee and 3 Englishmen in the audience to pay £15 *in advance* to see an "exhibition" a few blocks away. The address turned out to be a vacant lot. When the suckers returned to demand that their money be refunded, the racketeer, then surrounded by bodyguards, smiled benignly and asked, "*WHAT* money?" Be wary of any approaches by sly, whisper-keen slickers in Soho and similar districts; please don't *ever* give any "down payments" or "faith" money on any promised reward. It almost always leads to loss and sorrow if you are lured into this trap.

If your ignorance of British currency is apparent, there are sharpers who will deliberately underchange you. This has become much more prevalent with the monetary shift into Pence and with the migrations of foreign workers into the hotel, restaurant, and service industries. Also watch railway ticket clerks, who'll mumble about "new fare tables" when you catch them. Bus ticket-sellers are also becoming great palming artists; on our recent month-long London rounds, this writer *never* was given the correct change on any of the numerous bus rides. Know what you gave—and keep your hand extended until all of the proper coins come back. Please learn the system, as described under "Money"; with a little practice (especially under the decimal system), you'll find it quite easy.

Finland

The word is *sisu*. It doesn't mean "bravura." It doesn't mean "strong-arm toughness." It doesn't mean "steely nerves." It doesn't mean "tenacity." It doesn't even mean "guts."

What it means is ALL of these—tripled in spades.

Sisu is the remarkable combination of courage, stubbornness, and never-say-die which is the remarkable hallmark of the remarkable Finns.

To most foreigners, Suomi, the Finns' own name for Finland (which you'll see on its postage stamps and other printed matter), evokes more misguided conceptions and stereotypes than any other nation in this *Guide*.

Examples?

The Finn is a big, jolly, platinum-blond Scandinavian.

Not true.

In the first place (he will argue hard with you about this!), he is not a genuine Scandinavian. Exempting his 6% minority of Swedish ancestry, he is a member of the Finno-Ugric language group which is closely related to Estonian, less so to Hungarian. He's as different from the Danes, Norwegians, and Swedes as a balalaika is from a bugle. Next, he is a lot smaller than the average North American. Next, he is jolly—but chiefly in his very private way. Finally, up to 70% of the platinum blondes are bleached.

Secondary misconceptions are that he dresses warmly and gaily and lives in a Santa Claus toyland of low prices.

Again not true.

Actually, the Finns' everyday attire is as colorless and drab as in Leningrad. Next, it will cost you more to live in Helsinki than in Albany, Atlanta, or Albuquerque.

This most northerly Republic in the world—⅓rd of her anatomy is above the Arctic Circle—sprawls over an area which would hold 16 New Jerseys. The nicest thing is that she is the most unspoiled nation in Europe. Her

285

60-thousand lakes and 200-thousand islands give her map the strikingly beautiful zigzag venation of blue and white. Most of her terrain is low-lying; some regions are a broken jumble of hillocks, fells, ridges, and hollows, while others are monotonously flat for seemingly endless miles. Prizewinning Danish author Willy Breinholst put it lyrically when he wrote, "70% of her countryside is covered by forests, 30% by lakes, and 100% by skies." To my Nancy, the dominant impression of Finland's spring is pearl-pink and mulberry-blue.

North Carolina could swap houses with her population of slightly better than 4½ million. Most of her 50 cities and 30 towns cling to her coasts.

Forestry is the basis of her economy; shipping is her lifeline. Agriculture and industry split the rest of the occupational pie.

Freedom of worship has been law since 1923. The Evangelical Lutheran faith claims an overwhelming 93.1%. The next largest congregation is Greek Orthodox (1.6%). All others—Catholics, Jews, non-Lutheran Protestants, Moslems, atheists, the lot—total 5.3%.

Education—curiously for such an advanced people—is compulsory for only 9 years; there are, however, 11 universities and 13 other institutions of higher learning. Universal military service during wartime—please duck when you read *this* one!—is required of all able-bodied males between 17 and SIXTY.

Finland has had 42 wars with Russia. Despite the extraordinary bravery and tenacity of her warriors, she has lost them all. This 130-thousand-square-mile country is so close to the 8.6-million-square-mile vastness of the U.S.S.R. that it has always walked a perilously taut tightrope between West and East. The interacting of this dissonant David with the Slavic Goliath—plus the amazing tolerance of this Goliath for this David—is such a vital factor in nearly every aspect of Finnish life that you, as a wayfarer, should be made aware of these undercurrents which less perceptive U.S. pilgrims might fail to sense or to see.

Here, in a thimble, is the paradox: While the policy of fanatical neutrality was, is, and will be the only deterrent to stop Russia from gobbling up Finland, there is no such thing as a truly neutral Finn.

Most of the population, in private, is ardently oriented toward the West. They remember being bludgeoned into paying the colossal blackmail of $300,000,000 at market level for so-called reparations of WW II. They remember the heartcrushing loss in 2 wars of 1 fighting man out of every 4.

Except for the dead of winter, forget about buying a set of Dr. Denton's as your Finnish garb. The Gulf Stream is so benign that in the lower and middle reaches of the nation you may dress as you would for an Ohio February or a Northern California July. In the south there is snow for only about 5 months; in Lapland this stretches to 7 months. And don't bring your skis to Helsinki for that Christmas outing—because, sport, it jest *ain't* that cool for Yule. The midsummer sun is a fascinating phenomenon. In Helsinki, your midsummer days will last 19 hours. At Utsjoki, on the northern tip of Lapland, there is continuous daylight for 73 days.

A sure way of slapping a Finnish friend in the face is to refuse his or her invitation to a sauna. The classic version takes place in a 2-cubicled log cabin on the shore of the coldest damn lake that could ever possibly quick-freeze Mr. Birdseye's most precious jewels. The stripped participants proceed to a split-level, spruce-lined room. Since the coolest portion of this Arctic Hades is frequently above 240°F., its upper tiers should be left exclusively to cloven-hoofed veterans. At intervals your host or hostess (mixed saunas, customary among marrieds, are not exactly unknown among unmarrieds) will pitch ladles of cold water over a bed of blast-furnace-heated stones—and the resulting clouds of sizzling steam will poach you scarlet, white, and sapphire. Then the conductor will beat the bejesus out of you with leafy birch branches—"just to start up your circulation." Finally, the party bursts forth from this inferno, breaks the world's sprint record to the water's edge, and pushes aside the larger chunks of ice with their right feet so that they won't fracture their skulls when they dive into the lake.

This variety is murder.

But for the stranger who visits metropolitan climes, the citified version is, by comparison, a sophisticated, gentle, glorious physical experience. Most hotels in the larger centers feature sauna installations so elaborate, handsome, and comfortable that newcomers cannot believe their eyes. They are so popular (1 sauna per 6 steaming Finns) that, to be sure you savor this northland treat, you should book your sauna even before your hotel room. As in Sweden, 1 or 2 old crones, who have examined many a better man than you or I (let's admit that might be possible), will lead you by the hand through every stage of the parboiling—even to the extent of towling you, placing your feet in heated wooden clogs, and tucking you tenderly between crisp sheets for your post-sauna nap.

If you value your dignity and your hide, NEVER volunteer for a back-woods sauna. (Being trapped is a different story.) But please don't leave Finland without treating yourself to the luxury, the therapy, and the relaxa-tion of the civilized version. If you do, you will foolishly bypass one of the most delightfully hedonistic rituals of today's world.

CITIES   If the map of Finland were an inkblot, the shade of Dr. Rorschach might interpret its general shape as a rough facsimile of a snowman whose right arm is waving westward and whose overcaloried bottom has been slightly misshapen by the melting rays of the sun.

Lapland starts at the broomstraws in his hair and drops to the buttons on his chest. Only a handful of settlements occupy his midriff. Nearly all the nation's cities and towns are grouped between his thighs and his toes. It is almost an axiom that the farther south a city is located, the more important it is.

Helsinki (**Helsingfors** to the founding Swedes; pronounce it with the accent on "Hel"), at the same latitude as Oslo and Leningrad, is the capital, the main port, the lodestone for slightly more than a ½-million toilers, and the heartbeat of the land. It is as distinct in character as the other northern capitals.

Its peninsula, flecked by a lovely archipelago, juts nearly due south to be surrounded on 3 sides by the sea. Architecturally, it's a mishmash of Empire, New York Public Library, Byzantine, and the futuristic fantasies of Aalto, Rewell, and the Siréns; except around the harbor, we felt the distinct overall impression of grimness. It offers an improved hotel scene; scads of comfortable, commodious restaurants, snack bars, and cafés for excellent dining; transportation plentiful and expensive; a fine airport; modern subway in the blueprint stage; enchanting Linnanmäki amusement park and adjoining island zoo; glorious shopping, offering some of the most original and captivating designs you will ever see; opera house, Finlandia Hall for concerts, 13 theaters, 2 botanical gardens, and—glory be!—more museums than the Brothers Baedeker could waddle through in 7 months of Sundays; painless, low-cost, easy-to-arrange excursions by boat, bus, rail, or car to dozens of nearby points of interest. At first sight you may not fall in love with this metropolis—but its beauty, ugliness, gaiety, dourness, incredible skein of contrasts and contradictions are guaranteed to leave you with the impression that here is one of the most fascinating hubs of the Western World.

Tampere, 109 miles northwest of bottom-situated Helsinki and encompassed by lakes, is 2nd in size. This so-called Pittsburgh of Finland keeps the majority of its 170-thousand citizens out of mischief in its steel, paper, pulp, linen, and textile factories, plus its university. Despite so much heavy industry, it is a green city replete with parks. Since there are 4 girls to every 3 men here, Finnish males often smile musingly when its name is mentioned. Perhaps its next proudest boast is possession of a 1000-seat outdoor auditorium which revolves somewhat less rapidly than a merry-go-round; it spins in season only. One of the nation's biggest hotels—operated by the YMCA—is sited here; to the despair of one of the thirstiest populations in Free Europe, it is dry. Tampere is visited by many travelers because it is a prize pearl on one of the most popular sightseeing strings.

Turku, a skip and a jump due west of Helsinki, is Finland's cultural center, fourteenth-century capital, original seat of its tradition-rich A.D. 1640 university, and an important passenger port for Sweden. Shipbuilding, foodstuffs, and ceramics lead its commerce. The Handicraft Museum, one of the few building complexes to survive the great fire of 1827, is especially worth visiting. Not yet much of a tourist magnet, but coming along fast.

Lahti, a 65-mile inland ride from the capital, was a market crossroads for hundreds of years. With fantastic suddenness, less than 6 decades ago it sprang into a mushrooming parish which now supports 92-thousand population and a striving industrial dynamism. Because of its youth, and consequent adaptability, architecturally it is a Design for Tomorrow. It is not surprising that many visitors call it "the most American city in Finland." Not only is Lahti proud of the Mallasjuoma Brewery (claimed to be even larger than mighty Carlsberg or Tuborg before they merged), it also brags it is the biggest furniture-making center on the Continent. Lahti's key travel attraction is its twice-daily hydrofoil service arrow-straight up the lake to Jyväskylä. The one-way ride takes 3 hours, and it is so lovely in good weather that it shouldn't be missed.

Oulu, on the west coast about 400 miles due north of Helsinki, is the shopping, trading, medical, and educational matrix for thousands of square miles of the midriff of our mythical snowman. This dominant rail and road junction stands on a group of islands at the mouth of the Oulujoki River. The first island contains the very modern, swiftly expanding new city, the second a stadium and sports center, and the third a carefully planned community for public entertainment. There's a famous quip that the buildings of its recently founded university are spread out so haphazardly that the Dean of Architecture once stepped out for a cup of coffee and was never seen again. This town draws mainly business traffic.

Pori, peaking the isosceles triangle 70 miles above its base of Tampere and Turku, is another west-coast port for the wealthy farming country surrounding it. Very few foreigners pause here, unless $$$$ are involved.

All other settlements within these 130-thousand-square-mile precincts are towns, villages, or hamlets of less than 60 thousand.

Now let's take a quick look at the smaller, more colorful targets which are of special interest to footloose vacationers from abroad.

Aulanko, 3 miles from Sibelius' birthplace of Hämeenlinna, is the most glittering sapphire in the bracelet of western lakes. This is a lodestar for the holiday-minded—accessible by car (slightly over an hour on the highway from Helsinki), by train, or by the Silver Line water coach that glides between Hämeenlinna and Tampere. Capital-ists run out here for golfing, tennis, boating, swimming, water-skiing, horseback riding, broiling their hides in its log-cabin sauna, sightseeing from the top of its 100-foot granite needle, or just communing with some of the most glorious natural scenery in the northlands. You will also see the ski lift and downhill slope recently added to the winter facilities. The **Hotel Aulanko** boasts a balcony for each accommodation, private baths, a so-so restaurant for 700 clients, a bar, a sauna, and a resident orchestra. The **Youth Hostel** at Lake Aulangonjärvi affords more modest shelter for the overflow summer throngs. To gild the lily, there's a daily lake cruise for the restless—restaurant aboard—which touches other nearby beauty ports.

Kuopio is the touristic capital of the Eastern Lake District, just about knee-high on our hypothetical snowman. Here is the jumping-off point for the renowned lake excursions which ripple out in various directions. Dominating the settlement is a big hill that is crowned by a tower with a revolving restaurant at its tippity-top. Try to visit this center, if you can, in the January Market Days. (The stands in Market Place function year around on weekdays and are fun for visiting, too.) Not unimportantly for everyone concerned, the natives of Kuopio speak such a difficult dialect that not even the other Finns can understand it—and THIS, dear friends, automatically awards them the diamond-studded Lavoris Cup for Phonetic Mouthwash.

The curious, unique, and legendary Greek Orthodox church and monastery near Kuopio is worth a special journey—especially in summer when you can do it by boat.

Jyväskylä is the northern harbor for the aforementioned 3-hour hydrofoil cruise up the lake from Lahti. This nucleus of central Finland, an ancient cultural community which is now industrialized by big neighboring pulp, paper, and engineering works, is another departure station for expeditions in all directions. Many structures of this unusually eye-appealing town were blueprinted by the late, globally celebrated Professor Alvar Aalto.

Hanko, a sleepy seacoast town, draws the elite to savor its southern summer charms.

Discounting Lapland—in its entirety one of the greatest touristic drawing points on the Continent—its gateway of *Rovaniemi* (turn to "Hotels" *et seq.*) and the towns *Savonlinna* and *Porvoo* attract more vacationers every year.

MONEY AND PRICES

If you're North American, formally call the currency unit Finnmark (FMK)—but informally just mark. If you're Finnish, it's markka (pronounced mark-ah). The abbreviation is MK. As soon as it twins, triples, or otherwise pluralizes, the lonesome markka adds another *a* to become markkaa.

Today's approximate values:

| 1 | markka = 26¢ U.S. | 1 | dollar = 4 markkaa |
| 1 | markka = 100 penniä | | |

The denominations are 1, 5, 10, 20, and 50 in the penniä bracket; there are also 1- and 5-markka coins. Markka notes come in 1, 5, 10, 50, 100, and 500.

Prices? Despite recent small-bore revisions, they remain high. Taxes and export fees on nearly everything you can name, swallow, or fondle have absorbed almost 3/5ths of what would have been savings for foreign visitors. Expect Finland to be rough on the bank account.

In the best hotels, a good double averages perhaps $30 to $50 plus 15% in surcharges. A respectable dinner in one of the better restaurants is at least $10, not including drinks or extras. A custom-made man's suit—unstylishly cut to most North Americans—runs from $100 to $200. Finnish-licensed, Finnish-manufactured, American-style cigarettes are a reasonable 65¢ to 85¢—but if they are U.S.-made, they'll furnish that morning cough for up to $2.25 per pack. Local snaps is $1.15 per wallop in the average bar—but the minute you switch to whisky it's about $2 per 2 fingers, PLUS 60¢ for your soda.

To borrow the old bromide—" 'Tain't cheap, McGee!" But hell's fire. For your unique thrills, joys, and memories of these twinkling lakes and sleeping forests, we'll bet you're not going to regret 1 markka spent in this lovely land.

ATTITUDE TOWARD TOURISTS

Because this nation has drawn fewer foreign vacationers than any other major European land, we are delighted by the farsightedness with which these industrious Finns are attacking the complexities of (1) attracting outlanders and (2) providing facilities for them.

First off, the **Finnish Travel Association**, Kalevankatu 1, Helsinki, is the master organization, guidepost, and Dear Abby for the network. We haven't had the pleasure of meeting its Director, Heikki Maki, but we have made good friends with Bengt Pihlström, Secretary General of the Tourist Board. This personable, capable Finn, who couldn't be more cooperative and whose English is flawless, will be happy to answer any urgent queries if he's in town, but for your average run-of-the-nation puzzlers, simply call on the helpful minions of the FTB who headquarter at Kluuvikatu 8 (3rd floor).

Second, there's an 11-office skein of Travel Information Bureaus in various key cities abroad. If you're a New Yorker, hie yourself to the **Finnish National Tourist Office** (now merged with Denmark, Sweden, and Norway into one central office), Scandinavia House, at 75 Rockefeller Plaza, N.Y. 10019. There is also a joint Scandinavian font at 3600 Wilshire Blvd., Los Angeles, Calif. 90010. Overseas offices are in London, Paris, Stockholm, Amsterdam, Zürich, Hamburg, West Berlin, and Munich.

Third, the cheerful, friendly staff of the live-wire **City Tourist Office**, at Pohjoisesplanadi 19, in Helsinki can be of enormous on-the-scene assistance. Their kindliness toward bewildered visitors is limitless. Here is a splendid source for information concerning not only the capital and its environs, but the entire nation. They will even try to furnish baby-sitters to the papoose-trapped—so go to them for any problem, beat or offbeat.

Fourth, most major municipalities provide their own information facilities. Just inquire locally for the City Tourist Office.

Finally, Finland's greatest blessing for foreign businessmen in any field is the **Finnfacts Institute**, which publishes the superb newsletter *Finnfacts*. It's sponsored by the most important branches of Finland's economic life, every facet of which the publication's subject matter reflects. Should any industrial or economic questions plague you, just drop *Finnfacts* a line at Unioninkatu 14A 00130 Helsinki 13, in the capital, or, if you are in town, ask for Managing Director Matti Kohva or PR Officer Teuvo Tikkanen. All of its staff is dedicated to your cause.

CUSTOMS AND IMMIGRATION   Among the easiest and most pleasant in Free Europe. Although regulations exist, you'll possibly be waved through without a peek or poke—but with a broad smile of welcome.

Portable typewriters, radios, phonographs, tape recorders, cameras, and binoculars must—again, technically—be entered on the passport. Dogs and other pets must have an entry authorization from the veterinary surgeon of the Ministry of Agriculture. Shotguns require a permit.

You may bring in an unlimited amount of any currency you wish, but you are supposed to exit with a maximum in Finnish money of what you imported in foreign exchange.

They'll look at your passport as identification—but, conforming to their block agreement with Denmark, Iceland, Norway, and Sweden, they'll stamp it only if Finland is either your incoming or outgoing Nordic gateway.

Formalities for motorists are identical to those of Norway. After 3 months in the nation, you must register the car.

Good people!

HOTELS   The picture today has radically improved over the inn-digent scene of a few short seasons ago. Although at peak periods space can still be a will-o'-wisp, at last competition has become so keen that your new or spruced-up accommodation will probably please you. In any case, the wise voyager is urgently advised *to be sure,* SURE, *SURE—especially in summer —to have ALL Finnish hotel reservations confirmed and reconfirmed IN AD-VANCE.*

If you haven't, the **Hotellikeskus** ("Hotel Booking Center") *might* be able to bail you out. This office is located in the Helsinki Railway Station. The telephone is 11-13-3, and it is open 9 A.M. to 9 P.M. on weekdays; on Saturday from 9 A.M. to 7 P.M., and on Sunday from noon to 7 P.M.

Prices vary widely across this land. In the capital, barely adequate singles start at $18, with doubles going at around $28, and an occasional triple at $30. Twin accommodations in the top hotels on our list range between $33 and $53, with a few suites bounding up to around $125.

Helsinki recently enjoyed a hotel boom—a condition for which all of us have been itching for many an indolent year. The co-leader in the capital is the spry 300-unit **Intercontinental** which faces a lovely sylvan park, backs on the Finnair city terminal, and shoulders the developing Congress House. Ten-story plant vaguely resembling the ICH edifices in Hanover, Cologne, and Düsseldorf; viewful, red-hued, rooftop Ambassador Club with dance orchestra and bar; excellent saunas and glass-lined pool at the same altitude; Brasserie for light nibbling; standardized bedchambers spacious for a today-type hostelry; wide-angle suites. Substantial for the outlay.

Next door, the equally proud, also-Deluxe **Hesperia** has come up so dramatically that it is a vital challenger for the lead. Except in size, the rooms it has harvested are nearly the same as those of its neighbor. Main restaurant plus a Steakhouse and Coffee Corner; subterranean nightclub with submarine atmosphere; distinct focus on the "with-it" mood; a quartet of saunas, a gym, and a swimming pool with an adjoining fire-lit snackery. The accommodations accent Finnish modernity, efficiency, somewhat limited dimensions, and low-line, narrowish beds. You may pluck its golden apples with assurance, Hera.

The **Marski** is still pitching as hard as ever. This '62 entry is a typical example of what one might term segmented Erector Set architecture. Main bar in lobby corner; copper-ceilinged dining room with dance band until 11:30 P.M.; another vast, well-illuminated restaurant up one-flight. On the higher levels, 3 suites, 160 rooms, 151 baths, and 12 showers await with attractive pastel hues, comfortable furniture, and harmonious décor; baths ample-size in doubles but small in loners; all singles convertible to double occupancy. There are the swinging cellar-sited M Club (open to members and hotel residents only) and a thoughtfully planned dining scheme which allows ½-pension guests to eat meals at any of the Polar Hotel chain restaurants (Casino, Kalastajatorppa, and Sillankorva). All in all, a contender as the best hostelry in the land.

The fresh **Torppa**, frequently lengthened to **Kalastajatorppa** by those articulate locals who love their syllables, made its debut under the aegis of this same famous Finnish chain. It's a First-class operation from the tip of its flagstaff to the bottom tiles in its indoor pool. Sauna; nightclub; excellent new wing; rooms with private bath and a seaview; rates in the Marski range. The 10-minute taxi ride out to it adds to your outlay, but the advantages for tranquillity seekers should be worth this vexation. Out here you'll also find the 150-room **New Torppa** a little farther away from Laajalahti Bay. A happy complex for uncomplicating souls.

The **Palace** provides a magnificent harbor setting with panorama of city and archipelago. Small, unimpressive ground floor lobby; immense, low-price, snack-barish, window-wrapped grill up one flight; luxurious, panoramic, popular 10th-floor dining room with red (not blue) ribbon cuisine; the most luxurious sauna this side of Hades, where you'll never regret your reckless extravagance in asking for Dressing Room #1. Plush Finnish-style décor on 9th floor, containing total of 60 rooms with bath *or* shower (50% double, 50% single, 12 facing the harbor); larger versions delightfully livable; rear units generally tiny; smiling, willing, eager-to-please staff with almost no knowledge of English. An excellent mooring for port-siders.

The midcity **Vaakuna** has been rocketing up with spectacular speed. Recently completed round-the-house renewal program supervised by General Manager Paul Borgstrom; modern grill open until midnight; penthouse bar and snackery featuring frequent changes of national themes; Scotch Bar; 2 saunas; rich dark-wood singles; grandly modern Presidential Suite; good baths. We like the touches of art in the lodgings and the Sunday movies for children. After a successful lift-off, steadily soaring.

The youthful **Merihotelli** looms modernistically for seaside meri-makers. Like the neighboring Ursula (see below), it is a fairly long run from the whirl of midtown, rendering it slightly expensive for gadabout sightseers. Grill-Bar and 300-seat restaurant with green plants galore and a magnificent panorama; waterfront terrace; white-brick, nautical Pontus Night Club in the cellar with dancing until 3 A.M. plus meals for night owls; 2 beautiful rooftop saunas with plate-glass windows; 87 rooms, with the best facing the tiny harbor and its reeling colony of airborne gulls (we prefer #311; it's even better, we think, than the same-price #312); 7 suites with accordion door dividers; light but small baths throughout. Seaworthy and see-worthy—especially for salty types.

The vastly redecorated **Helsinki** is now owned by the same burgeoning SOK group that holds the keys to the above pair plus the Hesperia. It, too, is an amiable choice. If you want its best double, try for a so-called "superior" accommodation with new furnishings, upholstered bedsteads, and soft colorizations (most of these are on the 3rd and 4th floors). This 115-room house (including 6 suites) offers 115 baths or showers. Nightclub called the "Helsinki-By-Night Club" (*sic*), open until 3 A.M.; 9th-floor sauna that is out of this temperate world. Likeable.

The **Olympia** has gone over to the rapidly extending SOK hands, so we can't be sure how the gloves (or soks) will fit in '77. Although it is a 10-minute ride from the center, the big advantage here is that it shares the building with the Sport Palace (Finland's down-the-nose answer to the bleak, windowless Communist-owned House of Culture). Total of 47 very-small-but-cozy rooms; all doubles with elf-size baths and all singles with leprechaun-size showers; English inconveniently unfamiliar; service almost an unknown quantum. Fair—but only if you speak Finnish and are reasonably self-sustaining.

The **Ursula** is close to the Meri, but without the same glorious waterfront view. Chinesey avant-garde lobby a mini-hallmark of its space concepts; clinical breakfast room stocked with magazines, a TV set (plus schedule), and books; bedchambers that fairly sparkle with cleanliness and flair; colorful touches of plaids, blues, and orange. The rock-bottom rates are excellent for the value; #606 is a superb buy as a suitenik for 2 or for a small family. Again, fundamentally austere and do-it-yourself, but not at all bad for hard-line budgeteers. Recommended as such.

The **Torni** has been taken over by the Helsinki Hotels people who perhaps by now have changed it for the better—in fact, the only way it could have been changed, in our opinion.

Out at suburban *Tapiola*, the 82-room **Garden** provides modern compact shelter, a pool, a sauna, and 2 dining decks. The fundamentals are here, but we feel it's too far from the bright lights.

Although in our view none of the following win blue ribbons for excellence, here's the way we'd rate the rest of the pack: **Seurahuone** (refreshed while retaining its old style), **Klaus Kurki, Hospiz (YMCA), Perho, Academica, Satakuntatalo,** and, out of town, the **Otaniemi**. We are not familiar with the **Hotel Uusimaa** or the **Hotel Metro** since they both came under new ownership. The Finnish National Travel Offices in New York or Los Angeles will be happy to furnish further information.

Dedicated budgeteers? Since we're too bottlenecked here for additional entries, please consult our annually revised paperback, *Fielding's Low-Cost Europe,* which lists scads more bargain hotels or pensions and scads more money-saving tips for serious budget-watchers.

In *Tampere*, the **Tammer** gets our 1st vote. Old-fashioned English colonial ambiance; central situation; partially modernized; 60 rooms; most doubles with private bath; pleasant but not great. The 2nd-place **Kaupunginhotelli**, constructed in the early '60s, is owned by a cooperative store. Also centrally located; smaller rooms but service on the same friendly par; not exciting but clean and adequate. The renovated **Victoria** shed its Victorian age and now is quite a substantial medium-bracket entry. **Hospiz Emmaus**, the 240 rooms of which make it Finland's 2nd-largest hostelry, is YMCA-operated and—as usual—as dry as a squeezed and sunbaked salted herring. *All* genders of clients accepted; restaurant absolutely miserable; loaded with cheap tour groups from Eastern-bloc countries; not for any wayfarer who demands his or her amenities.

Turku's menu comes up with the venerable **Seurahuone/Societetshuset**. (Note its split Finnish-Swedish official name; its local English nomenclature is "Sausage House.") Delightfully cozy bar; excellent cookery, with special accent on seafood; thoughtful, warm service; 55 rooms which (if not reconstructed) tend to be larger than the competitions'. We think you might say "Hot Dog!" for this one (speaking frank-ly!). Next off the griddle (natch) comes the antebellum **Hamburger Börs**, with its thick walls, high ceilings, and nineteenth-century appurtenances. Also famous for its food; occasional single-act entertainment in its restaurant; not up to the leader. The tasteless, unattractive **Turku** is a pale turkey. Badly conceived modern décor in which nothing seems to jell; largest lobby in town; simple appointments; bustling with conducted tours. We haven't seen the young **Marina Palace**, but we do like the mother company. The **Ruissalo** is a clean-lined, fresh-faced sea-sider which to us resembles a block of studio apartments. **Ylioppilastalo**, a student dormitory in winter which becomes a 293-room hotel in summer, could scarcely be more basic—but WHAT a bargain with its flat daily rate for 2 costing the price of a New York movie for one! The **Ikituuri** also welcomes *tuurists* in suummer only. A mere 1800 beds in this uurbanization; all uunits with shower; 5 restaurants; very *tuuri* indeed is this Iki. The American Holiday Inn-keepers might now have action here.

Lahti offers the much improved **Seurahuone**, on its main street; it was built in the '20s but has since undergone various modernizations. Pleasant restaurant; 90 rooms; worthy. **Valtakulma** and **Jukola** are our next picks in this heavily traveled but disappointingly hotel-poor community.

In **Oulu**, the **Tervahovi** is the only hostelry worth your patronage (perhaps you'll disagree when you see the new **Vaakuna**, which we haven't yet inspected). You won't find any peacocks' tongues, but at least you'll be decently comfortable. The **Kauppahotelli**, considerably larger but somewhat less expensive, is a boon for the locals, but we don't think it's for you or for us. The 3rd-ranking **Arina** is a cooperative venture which has possibilities, but which to us has absolutely no appeal in its present state.

Kuopio has sparse pickings for the pampered. Its leader—which isn't saying much—is the **Atlas**. Finnish guests love to intertwine its name with the word *allas,* which means "bathtub"; when they express their intention to overnight here, they pun that they're "going to take the plunge." Situated on the main market square; 45 rooms with limited plumbing; dismiss all fears of taking any plunge into the twenty-first century if you are bound for here. No better than so-so. The 55-room **Puijonsarvi** is commercial and routine. The **Kalla** and the **Kaupunginhotelli** are lower-ranking alsorans.

Pori boasts the **Juhana Herttua** ("Duke John"). We hear that this 55-unit house is conveniently situated, pleasantly staffed, and nicely executed. The newer **Cumulus** has come up with 54 rooms with bath or shower, a pool, a sauna, and a cellar restaurant. We're cloudy on its service standards. The **Rantasipi** beckons from the dunes of **Yyteri Beach**, a delightful location for a resort hotel, but its amenities are unknown to us. Its chain, however, is a recommendable one in general. The **Satakunta** and **Otava** are yet 2 other reasons why we must hop out to Pori when the thaws come.

In **Jyväskylä**, the 120-chamber **Jyväshovi**, on the main shopping street, could scarcely be more routine. The Rantasipi steamboaters have chugged up with the sylvan **Laajavuori**, which looks like a honey of a spot for relaxing. It seems to be cosponsored by Mother Nature. Recommended site seen and sight unseen. All others here are small, simple, and spartan.

In **Savonlinna**, we'd select the vastly refashioned and enlarged **Tott** over the 32-room **Seurahuone**. Their rates are about the same, but neither will call back the wraith of César Ritz bearing a silver salver in homage. The new 32-room **Spa Casino** also isn't the soul of inn-spiration, but it is adequate.

Hanko, the seaside resort, offers the delightful little **Regatta Hotel**. Since its proprietor owns a TV factory, all its 20 rooms are equipped with his latest models. Charming décor; swimming pool; high but not exorbitant tariffs for the values. Exceptionally good.

Rovaniemi, gateway to Lapland but still a long way south of the

main ranges and camping sites, comes up with the famous but well-used
Polar Hotel. Lobby-level bar dominated by huge copper fireplace with
chimney, reindeer mural, and entire polar-bear skin displayed solely to
frighten the kiddies away from those snaps (it doesn't); 4th-floor dining
room with a Klondike personality and poor cuisine. Total of 36 spacious
bedchambers, each with small bathroom and cheerful furnishings; singles
okay as singles but overcramped and uncomfortable when converted into
temporary "doubles." Again, book as far ahead as possible. (Sportsmen,
incidentally, might be interested in the Polar's 10-person, log-lined **Bear's
Den**, a guest lodge 18 miles north on the shores of Bear Lake ["Kar-
hujärvi"]. Fully equipped for angling and all sorts of huffing-and-puffing;
inquire through the hotel.) The **Pohjanhovi** ("Nordic Court") is looking
courtlier now that it has been totally renovated and a new wing has been
added. Its position on the banks of the broad and beautiful river is far
superior to that of the Polar—and its cookery is far more savory too. The
Motel Ounasvaara rolls out a jumbo-size restaurant and 38 pedestrian
kips. You've braked at better.

In the *Kemijärvi* district, 60 miles east, the 70-room **Suomutunturi** boasts
a dining room with the Arctic Circle running right through its middle.
Handmade furnishings; facilities for winter and summer sports. Since this one
is an architectural duplicate of a herdsman's hut, it classifies as a real Lapp-
warmer.

§TIPS: It cannot be sufficiently reiterated that hotel staffs could scarcely be
warmer, kinder, and sweeter as human beings—but we would lay odds that
less than 10% of them know 20 words of English (all put together!).

It might be helpful for newcomers to turn to the section on "Tipping,"
because gratuities are handled differently in this country than in most.

In Finland, do NOT place your shoes outside your door before you retire.
Nobody will steal them—BUT, 99.99% of the time nobody will shine them
either. This is the only country in Western Europe in which this service is
not common custom.

FOOD   It's finny fare for the Finns. This Far North kitchen puts its heaviest
accent on fish dishes. Although an increasing amount of meat is appearing
on the plate, the East Arctic version of our Mid-Atlantic adage is still, "A
herring a day keeps the doctor away."

The Suomis take their table seriously. Although they show a healthy respect for hearty, solid, no-nonsense sustenance, its preparation is interesting
and its presentation is almost always attractive. Their sturdy piscatorial diet
is made up of sprats, whitefish, pike, bream, flounder, and salmon, which may
swim to your table grilled, pickled, fried, boiled, salted, smoked, baked,
poached, creamed, stuffed, in batter, or vulcanized.

Try not to miss that glorious midsummer gustatory treat called rapuja (the
minisize freshwater crayfish which the Swedes know as kräftor). The waiter
will studiously tie you in a paper bib from larynx to pelvis and then panto-
mime meticulous instructions on how to extract every tender morsel of meat
and suck every heavenly drop of nectar from this dill-seasoned-and-decorated
crustacean—a dill-icious dilly of a dill-ightful dish!

The Finnish interpretation of smörgåsbord (see "Food" under "Sweden") is called *voileipäpöytä,* or *pitopöytä* for short(er). As with all such North Country festive boards, always eat your herring first, other cold fish next, then cold meats, and finally tackle the hot niblets—all on separate plates, of course. It's gastronomic heresy to mix sea and land on one platter.

In reminiscence, our own tongues shoot out with the alacrity of a New Year's Eve favor when we conjure up the delights of such specialties as Sillisalaatti (herring salad), Smoked Poronliha (reindeer), Kesäkeitto (fresh vegetable soup with milk), Sauna Sausages (munched after *you* bake in the baths), or such "normally" hot dishes as Kalakukko (fish and pork pie with salt-baked potatoes—and if you want your tonsils to last 7450 years after you're interred, just eat the skins of those spuds), a creation called Jansson's Temptation (a gooey casserole of potatoes, onions, cream, and herbs), Karjalanpiirakat (piping-hot Karelian pastries), Maksalaatikko (liver pudding), Lanttulaatikko (turnip casserole), Punajuuri Salaattia (beetroot salad), and Paistetut Sienet (fried wild mushrooms). The hungry citizenry here normally wash these down with Piimää (buttermilk) or Kalja (nonalcoholic beer); personally, whenever we stare at these 2 beverages, other ideas flow with amazing freedom. Wild game? The most popular candidates include grouse, wild duck, ptarmigan (try it roasted as Riekkopaisti—yum YUM!), venison, and the national favorite, Reindeer tongue (Poron Kieli).

For the perfect finish to your local repast, there are scads of luscious fruit soups made from the wild or cultivated berries of Finland—the lingonberry, cloudberry, brambleberry, bilberry (similar to our huckleberry), and others. These taste gems also garnish pancakes or bejewel the savorful, wondrous, ever-so-tempting Pähkinäkakku (nut cake)—and 2 of them (see "Drinks") are bases for the most popular national liqueurs. For your cheese plate, experiment with the Romadur variety of the local interpretation of Camembert. There are more than 2-dozen types, but the one most favored by the Finns has a flavor, color, and texture similar to Edam.

Finland's epicurean choices—while oriented chiefly around the lakes, rivers, and sea—are wide enough for most holidaying connoisseurs. There is a delicacy in their makeup, plus the eye-appeal common to all Nordic tables. And for most visiting palates, there is enough exoticism and interest to regale your dutifully listening friends for hours on end.

RESTAURANTS AND NIGHT LIFE   Often they are one and the same. The Finns nourish their bodies while stoking their high spirits, since the majority of Suomi dining spots are what would constitute nightclubs in most other lands. If you stuff your tummy in the first group of oases mentioned below at midday—and merely nibble and tipple before midnight at the second selection of hitching posts—you can save a feedbag full of green folding fodder.

And, speaking of green, the baize tables of roulette have been legalized for restaurants in 11 cities and on some Finnish ships. In the capital, the wheels of fortune spin in a total of 8 establishments. It is similar to the practice in Sweden, where the stakes are only penni-ante.

Helsinki offers the best and most varied culinary havens in the nation— AND the most expensive.

Leading the parade of *independent restaurants without dancing* is **Motti** (Töölöntorinkatu 2), a mellow-minded fount where most of the local business nabobs and palate-savvy politicians gather regularly. Smooth, soothing, sub-dued décor; split-level floor plan; comfortable black leather chairs; 5 booth-bound banquettes; flowers and lamps softly enhance the settings. Cuisine excellent, with service to match; all maîtres English-speaking, but menus (and waitresses) in the patois of Finland and Sweden only; 11 A.M. commencement weekdays (noon on Sun.) to 1 A.M. each morn. A tasteful delight in every way. Top recommendation.

White Lady (Mannerheimintie 93) happens to strike us (you might dis-agree, of course) as Motti's closest rival. About 10 minutes out; windowed-terrace scheme with cascades of ivy; greenery cunningly upstaging the chef for attention; about 20 tables with napery whiter than Lapland in March; Musical Department nightly from Mr. Steinway. Extra-savory morsels exqui-sitely presented; multitude of selections seldom found in Norway, Denmark, or Sweden; lunch from noon to 4 P.M.; dinner from 4 P.M. to 7 P.M., with à la carte until 1 A.M.; *closed Saturday and Sunday.* Nearly a neck-and-neck pacer with Motti; more popular by daylight than after gloaming. This chic, vivacious, appealing White Lady is (as they say back in Brooklyn) A Real Dish.

König (Mikonkatu 4, just off the Esplanade, 5 minutes' stroll from the Hotel Marski) is strategically paced by Runar ("Pixen") Björklöf, the re-nowned ex-international-½-miler. Here used to be a favorite haven of Sibelius and ranking artists of the turn-of-the-century. Today, in strikingly attractive and tasteful contemporary garb, it is a photo-Finnish contender with the 2 independent leaders. Toddle down one-flight; charming bar to the right; dramatic décor (our only objection: the too-dazzling reflection of lights on the shiny gold tabletops); excellent cuisine; try the Pheasant Titania if in season. Probably the most expensive midday (not dinner) stop of all, but an 18-karat joy—and ALWAYS, ALWAYS booked at peak hours, so reserve in advance, for sure!

The century-old **Kappeli**, on Market Sq., was renewed and opened after our latest loop; we hear that it is a *must* for the foreign tourist.

Savoy (Eteläesplanadi 14) attracts visiting dignitaries and government lead-ers to its aerie atop a midtown office building. Sophisticated atmosphere highlighted with stress-form plywood furniture designed by Alvar Aalto; white-brick and timber surroundings; brass lamps over flower settings; about 25 tables; international cookery predominating, intertwined with local fare; we especially liked the Forsmac (minced lamb and herring, served at lunch-time only with a potato baked in salt—but DON'T eat the jacket!). Reserve your chair between noon and 2 P.M. or from 7 P.M. to 10 P.M. Another top-of-the-Mark oasis.

Royal (Esplanaadikatu 2), at the park end of the Swedish Theater but not under its management, features a lovely alfresco terrace for seasonal munch-ing. Entrance through a large bar and café; formal dining room partitioned by 4 chubby square pillars; clean, stiffish, chandelierish decoration in beige, gray, and red. Beyond this nucleus, facing the greensward and the heart of the city, is the semienclosed, opaque-glass-roofed patio. Cuisine good but not outstanding; service warm; expensive, but delightful under the Arctic sunlight. Half of it turns into the Royal Club each nocturne, with the militant ukase that *only "quiet" music will be played* for terpsichore.

Among the *restaurants with dancing at night*—many featuring small floor shows—the most famous summerization stop is **Kalastajatorppa** ("Fisherman's Cottage" or, more popularly, "Hut"), which also gives its name to the hotel at this site. Large, sprawling mansion in a sylvan-waterside setting about 10 minutes by taxi from the city; starkish rotunda-style main dining room with windows round about, an enormous central chandelier, and some 40 tables edging the 30-foot dance circle; mezzanine level containing perhaps 3-dozen more tables. Peppery 5-piece combo spicing up the digesting hours; cheek-to-cheek melodies afterward. Kiddie-size table utensils; pleasantly presented food which we think is definitely overpriced for its quality, quantity, and value. Downstairs there's a grand-scale, candlelit haven, much more cheerful and colorful; undulating bar snaking around ¼ th of the wall; polychromatic glass panels; no action except at the cocktail hour and after 11 P.M.; rhythmic trio in season. EVENINGS ONLY (no lunch); winter hours in the dining room from 6 P.M. to 2 A.M.; closes one hour earlier during the summer season; downstairs room open to 4 A.M. in summer and to 3 A.M. in winter. With the later-mentioned M Club as a rival, here is probably *the* most expensive place in Finland—and that's the biggest hook in this Fisherman's Hut.

Espilä (Fredrikinkatu 56) lures funlovers up a staircase lined with a map of Europe, highlighting beer mugs, national dancers, and everything except the family Maytag. Long, multipillared main room in railway-flat dimensions split asunder by a wee turntable for dancing; seating for perhaps 80 parties; jammed with unaccompanied pro or nonpro females and couples. To the left is the miniaturized Cocktail Bar, an 18-stool doughnut for 100-proof dunking; here's a gimmicky revolving parasol overhead advertising house potables. We can't say much for its locally touted hors d'oeuvres or 15-minute lunch, but as a nocturnal choice it can be very lively when gaiety reigns. Operable 7 P.M. to 3 A.M. (Sun. 4 P.M. to midnight), so go early; shows 10 P.M., 11 P.M., and midnight; shuttered Mondays. Swingingest joint in town.

Kaivohuone (Kaivopuisto), or "Well Room," occupies the top of a small knoll in a parkland setting. Unhappily, it still leaves us as cold as a 90-year-old Lapp's libido. Huddle of ruby-red rooms, with the restaurant and bar angling to face the bandstand; well-worn velvet chairs; candles on tables in a vain attempt for warmth. Our late light bite was gnashingly expensive for the niblets presented to us. With them came the worst cabaret we've witnessed since our last grammar school variety show.

Fennia (Mikonkatu 17) offers a spacious, airy, lozenge-shape salon paneled with compressed seaweed to absorb the din of revelry; and painted red to match everything else in the room—including the clients' eyeballs. About 30 petit round tables; 10-stool bar; main restaurant-cabaret under a trio of arches; dance rectangle down one rung and music several steps lower in quality. We don't know the fare, but we *do* like the roominess and aura of this haven, after so many smoke-filled, narrow-gauge, and clangorous competitors. Door charge less than the price of a drink; brief floor shows 10 P.M. and 1 A.M.; rollicks best after 10:30 P.M.; but doors part at 7 P.M. and swing shut at 3 A.M.;

clusters of finely formed Finnish females (not attached to the house) on tap for a jig and a jug; operative summers. Discounting strictly dancing spots such as Teatteri Grilli or M Club, this is definitely, to our taste, *the* leading light among the cabaret-restaurants.

Adlon (Fabianinkatu 14) sham-facedly says "hello" with a phonyed up medieval mien, a red-brick courtyard, and fake little semicircular balconies around its upper periphery. Through another door is the principal hall in 1920-ish décor. Orchestra thump-and-bumptious on our whirl; dinner show so awful at our latest sitting that *we* were embarrassed; lunch Monday through Friday, with so-so smörgåsbord; remains a host until 3 A.M. Yet the bar to starboard is one of the chummiest and most tasteful drinking troughs in Helsinki, in contrast to the big-time emporium adjoining.

M Club, downstairs in the Marski Hotel and open only to members or to hotel residents, is usually packed with funloving Jet Setters, Finnish species. We had to paw the carpeted turf at the entrance for nearly ½-hour because it was so jam-packed. Long, rather narrow, recently refashioned basement room; service harassed, haphazard, and perspiring (but cordial); supper snacks available; open every night from 9 P.M. to 4 A.M.. Very active, fashionable, and expensive—but, sorry, we much prefer the similarly styled and similarly chic Teatteri Grilli. Still in hotel circles, the nocturnal doin's in the **Hesperia** seem to draw loyal local flocks of discerning nighthawks. Its cuisine needs upping.

Sillankorva (Pitkänsillanranta 3) is another candidate in the Marski ménage. This one, coolishly modern in décor and atmosphere, is extremely popular for evening meals. Businessmen flock here for midday nutrition. But the Suomi concept of dining in a big, brightly illuminated hall that is noisy, bustling, and totally lacking in intimacy somehow doesn't reach our sense of pleasure. While the food and prices are in order, we just can't buy it.

The adjoining **Mobile** is something else. We like it a lot for evening revels. These 2 share the same cloakroom, but that's all. Handsome leather-upholstered bar in an independent niche; 3 segments radiating from a central dance floor (one in red, one in blue, one in yellow; take your pick, ladies); knee-height-to-ceiling windows overlooking a quiet waterway; possibly the best orchestra in town drawing what seemed to us the highest grade of young and middle-age clientele; fair nightclub food at moderate tariffs; excellent service (even without English). It was recently augmented by the **Dixie** (Western style, padhner) and the **Neckar** (West German style, Max)—territories for inexpensive snacks, redeye, and snaps. Very good for its type.

The popular **Arkadia** (Fredrikinkatu 48) is, however, dominated by a highly commercial ambiance. Highly regarded, but not by us.

On our visit, **Ostia** (Hämeentie 33), in one of the modest districts of town, seemed to have corralled every no-necked hick south of St. Nick's capital. We discovered that "ladies can invite men in the afternoon"—but for what, we never learned. Entrance up one-flight in a modern office building; sardine-jammed, mirror-lined room with suspended red lamps, smoke-filled atmosphere, and (if you could bottle it) enough noise to shatter the contents of a large glass factory. If you go, bring your brass knucks and jet-ground-crew earmuffs.

Casino (Kulosaari/Brändö, a 15-minute taxi ride from the center) is presented on the rocks. Magnificent seascape view; rollicking summer bounce; specialty of the house is the Casino Salad with Caspian Caviar, giant Pacific crab, shrimp and tuna enriched with mushrooms, asparagus, and sundry vegetable tidbits. Better order a table in advance; occasional shows presented.

The **Helsinki Club**, in the basement of the Helsinki Hotel, creates an enticing atmosphere enhanced by walls of gold briquettes, deep-emerald draperies, rouge paintwork, black padded semicircular booths, white plastic tulip chairs, and a neighboring bar in a mulberry hue. Its greatest appeal is to young romantics who are well mannered, well dressed, and well heeled. Quiet in tone and intimate for dancers who obviously consider this only the first leg of a long, lingering, and lovely evening.

In the *miscellaneous category*, **Orfeus** (Yrjönkatu 30) is a tiny cellar with piano titillations after dark. Settings for about 70; baby bar; inexpensive lunch and dinner. Well respected. For Russian calories, hop onto tiny **Troika** first, followed by **Kasakka** or **Saslikki**, all comrades under the same garlic-scented proprietary banner. **Havis Amanda** (Unioninkatu 23) is a fish specialty house that seems to net happy schools of local diners. **Budapest**, in one of the least savory parts of the capital, is chiefly for the younger set. Downstairs mostly for college-age pickups; upstairs restaurant with good-for-its-type Hungarian dishes, wines, and pseudo-Magyar melodies. So-so cookery; ho-hum ambiance. **Esplanaadikappeli**, near the flower market, has been newly restyled; now open the year around. **Fazer** (Kluuvikatu 3), a sort of English tearoom, is the IN-most cozy corner for—what else?—tea. Light bites, beer, and wine also; mostly for ladies, who love it. There's a newer branch in the City Center, but the original is more our cuppa. As for other candidates, this *Guide* does NOT recommend **Vaakuna**, **Bellevue**, **Elite**, **New Angleterre**, **Tullin Puomi**, **Monte Carlo**, or the **HOK** to any North American traveler.

In the hotel league, our most elegant orchids go to the **Intercontinental**. The **Hesperia** is in full bloom, but the culinary standards don't impress us too favorably. The **Marski** and the **Palace** gather bowers of flowers. The **Meri** wins a bouquet too. **Perho** (a hotel-school restaurant) rates about a B-minus to C-plus on our report card. The **Helsinki** is unspectacular but solid and okay. We haven't sampled the fare in the restaurant of the **Finlandia Hall**, but reports are reasonably favorable.

Inexpensive dining? **Chez Marius** (Mikonkatu 1) is so tiny that one Finnish wag quipped, "There's no room for dancing. The idea here is to keep breathing." French cuisine tenderly administered by M. Marius Raichi, formerly of the local film industry and an Oscar-winning personality. No alcohol; *lunch only!!!* Reserve in advance. **Fen Kuan** (Eerikinkatu 14) offers such startling Finno-Ugric delights as Nasi Goreng and Sukiyaki. Re-markka-ble bar creations from "Ox on the Rocks" to "Yellow River" to "Fini"; menu listing such tempters as "Chicken with Eight Jewels" or "Chicken with 100 Flowers"; 7th-heavenly Mandarin Rolls. Exotic coolie-nary skills in exotic culi-national surroundings. Not the Oriental recipes to which we Occidentals are accustomed, but nevertheless a sweet-and-sour treat in this northerly clime. Snacklovers will probably enjoy the coffee shop atmosphere of such chain operations as **Café de Colombia**, **Primula**, and **Nissen**. Don't bother with the **Pika-Pala**.

Two excursion points? **Dipoli**, about 15 minutes out by taxi at Otaniemi, is a *must* for any traveler who has interest in architecture. Its modern design and decorative concepts have lured students from all over the world. While the tables might capture your eye, the cookery is secondary. The **Old Sea Fortress** ("Valhalla"), on the island of Suomenlinna, is said to be a rewarding choice for summer sailors, but we were here when the sea was frozen and the castle was icebound. Small café for light bites (no lunch in the fort); open from 5 P.M. to I A.M. when the straits are navigable; continental cuisine for dinner; dancing within the embrace of its ancient stone walls; motor-launch departures every 15 minutes from Kauppatori. Sounds as if it's towers of fun.

For pickup pickin's, the best hunting grounds in the metropolis are **Espilä**, **Kaivohuone**, and **Fennia**.

Prostitution scarcely exists in Finland. Since there is virtually no discrimination by gender (*e.g.*, 80% of the dentists are women), practically no female needs to solicit to make a living. Whatever exists is done almost exclusively for fun. Thus, instead of baldly presented cash, a "gift" of about $35, tactfully given to the average semipro (for rendering "average" services, of course), is considered a courteous talisman. Chicken-hawks won't even find a low district where this traffic centers. Since ice-cold play-for-pay is not a popular local sport, all you need do is muster your courage and then make your pitch —in lilting, lyrical Finnish. Good luck, chum!

As in parts of Sweden, custom permits males to approach escorted or unescorted females with invitations to the dance. She may, of course, refuse —but generally she won't, unless the gentleman (1) smells like a moose, or (2) resembles a 16-point reindeer buck.

In restaurants—not bars or nightclubs—don't be surprised if your eyesight begins to fail in the wee hours. As a signal that the *spiritus fermenti* will cease to flow in most establishments 45 minutes before closing time, proprietors blink the houselights. Those with thirsts are wise to order their next ration at this warning sign to reorder.

Outside the capital, your best bet for dining will probably be your hotel. In most Finnish hostelries, however, full or demipension is not required.

§TIPS: Here it pays the toper to review his ABC's. Restaurants with "A" rights are licensed to serve all categories of spirits. Those with "B" classification serve only wines. All "C" category spots limit their libations to lager. These certifications generally parallel their respective price brackets with ceilings imposed by the government. The cheaper houses, quickie joints, and self-service eateries most often (except in the proprietor's personal lower-righthand desk drawer) do not have one drop of alcohol in their precincts.

The separate service charges on your bills add only a soothing 13% of your total. Waiters are seldom given more than 50¢. (see "Tipping").

Now for a startler: Most First-class dining establishments open their portals at II A.M. All—except those which also feature nightclubs—have a thriving business by high noon. Standard dinner menus blossom as early as 4 P.M. and wane by 8 P.M. But now the warning: Then, and for the rest of the evening, you must pay those astronomical Finnish prices—everything, of course, on an à la carte basis. As we mentioned earlier, you can save a packet by eating a large midday meal and then coasting on the nighttime nutrients.

Never try to rush that waitress (yes, almost never "waiter") in Finland.

She's an expert at flouncing away from the finger-snapping, antsy-pantsy, gobble-it-up patron. And if you have an appointment, it might save up to 60 minutes if you ask for your bill when you order your soup.

Most menus are printed in the 2 official languages: Finnish and Swedish. A few progressive restaurateurs now add French, English, or German, depending upon their clientele. Incidentally, the lower-case letters "x.à." following the name of a dish mean "2 portions minimum."

Always go late to savor Helsinki night life (except to Espilä, which wraps up the evening at 1 A.M.). The gear shifts of merriment seldom mesh into overdrive before 11 P.M.—and from then onward, they're off and racing.

Odd Finnish law: (a) Nobody who shows even a clue of having consumed so much as a teaspoonful of Fletcher's Castoria can be admitted to any night spot—the explanation for the clusters of drunks or semidrunks outside the entrances late in the evening. (b) BUT once inside, practically speaking, there is no limit to the quantities permitted to be swallowed. That is why you'll see these 6-fisted Finnish topers getting ⅞ths embalmed once they reach the inner sanctum. And all the people you'll meet, even so potted they rock-'n'-roll while seated next to you at a bar or at an adjoining table, will probably be so friendly, hospitable, and open-handed toward you, as a North American or Western visitor, that their avuncular beaming is sure to touch your heart.

Dedicated budgeteers? Since we're too bottlenecked here for additional entries, please consult our annually revised paperback, *Fielding's Low-Cost Europe,* which lists scads more bargain dining spots and money-saving tips for serious economizers.

DRINKS On a recent Saturday morning at 8:30 A.M., 2 Finnish brothers cleared away the remnants of their breakfast and placed 6 quarts of snaps on the table. Two hours later, without a word, they attacked the 2nd jug. At 3:20 P.M., still in total silence, they uncorked number three. When the grandfather clock struck 5 P.M., the younger brother glanced up and said, "Pretty chimes, eh, Urpo?" Urpo scowled fiercely, slammed down his glass, and shouted, "For God's sake, Mikko, are we *talking* or are we *drinking?*"

The Finns, as a group, are just about the wettest Wets or the dryest Drys we've ever encountered. The polite 2-sherry or 1-whisky sipper is practically unknown, except among the ladies. Like his Swedish cousin, the Finn subscribes to the principle that when a man drinks, he DRINKS.

Prohibition was tried and abolished. In its place, the State formed the alcohol monopoly, "Alkoholiliike" ("Alko" for short) to centralize control of all intoxicating beverages and to hard-sell the advantages of beer and wine. Its stocks are large and well chosen; its prices range from steep to outlandish —income from the monopoly accounts for 1/6th of Finland's total budget! (For some screwball reason, soda water is sometimes almost as expensive as the amber in your glass. If you want to economize, take yours on the rocks or with plain, flat H$_2$O.) In Helsinki alone, Alko boasts about 25 retail outlets. If you like your weekend tipple, remember that these are open on most weekdays from 10 A.M. to 5 P.M., an hour later on Friday, plus 10 A.M. to 2 P.M. on Saturday.

Authorized hotels and restaurants ladle hooch from noon to 1 A. M. Room service in hotels stops earlier—but please blame the waiters' union, not the barmaid, for this. For teetotalers there are a sizable number of dry hotels, spearheaded by the powerful YMCA chain. Cafés and many restaurants are not granted licenses.

After vodka, Jaloviina (the generic term for snaps) is the Finns' favorite hard likker. There are 5 major types. Pöytäviina and Vaakuna, both distilled WOOD alcohol, are cheap; when you burp after more than 3 ounces, don't be surprised if you should light that gentleman's cigarette 20 feet away. Tähkäviina, made from grain, is costlier and less combustible. Koskenkorva is what might be termed the "standard" snaps of the land; its flavor is reminiscent of Denmark's Aalborg. Finally, Alko's '62 brainstorm of sponsoring a superior product called "Finnish Dry Vodka" has met with fantastic success both at home and abroad. It offers a far smoother, cleaner, less pungent taste than any of the others, selling for about $9.50 per jug.

Though soberingly expensive ($20 per ordinary fifth), whisky is popular among the more cosmopolitan inhabitants. Curiously, Finns drink more cognac than do the citizens of any other nation.

Two national liqueurs of consequence present themselves to the connoisseur. Lakka, made from Arctic cloudberries, draws cheers and 5 stars from these samplers as one of the most delicious *digestifs* we have ever enjoyed in our travel lives. It is expensive because of the shortage of these berries. *Don't miss it*—but make certain you get it WELL CHILLED!

Mesimarja is the other. This smooth, syrupy, near-ruby-red beverage has an equally distinctive impact upon the palate. Often it is extremely hard to find, due to the even more limited supply of the Arctic brambleberry which forms its essence. Please be sure this one is hard-chilled too.

Finland boasts 23 major breweries. The aforementioned Mallasjuoma at Lahti is the largest. Helsinki's kingpin is Koff; you may quaff at least 14 other brands here. Turku's Aura is perhaps the third-runner.

Only 3 types of beer are vatted. Pilsner, the lightest, guarantees less than 2.2% alcohol. The most popular choice, "3rd Class" (so named from a taxation gimmick), goes for about the same as its Milwaukee cousins. Strongest and best is "A" ("Atomic"), the export variety. Always order this one, even though it costs a little more. Imports carry a premium, naturally. Finns can now buy it at their grocery stores, at dairies (yep, that's the pap), and even at cafés.

§TIPS: Finnish toasts? *Skål* is the most common; *Hei* ("Hey") is the most friendly, relaxed, and familiar; *Kippis* is the one usually taught to foreigners.

Local law enforces a one-at-a-time clause on the imbiber. Snaps and beer can be mated (with foodstuffs only), but otherwise no 2 glasses of spirits are permitted on your table at the same time (for example, you must finish your Scotch before your cognac can be served). Double drinks are also prohibited —and your waitress is held answerable to the Alko authorities. But in everyday (or everynight) practice, the better watering spots will bend this law if you are a good-natured, presentable, and reasonably sober foreigner—or if you are with Finnish clients whom the proprietor knows.

Hangover clinics have been opened in Helsinki and 6 other Finnish towns. Signs at their entrances announce "FIRST AID POST FOR HANGOVERS.

HOURS: 6:30 A.M. to 8:30 A.M. WEEKDAYS." Patients are treated with a choice of vitamins, bouillon, fruit juices, tranquilizers, kindness, understanding—and, in a few far-gone cases, stimulants. Curiously, the customer count is always heavier on Tuesday than on Monday. Ask Your Friendly Concierge for the address of the nearest branch.

Finally, please, please—even if you're DESPERATE—ponder deeply our recommendation to avoid a concoction named Hochmann's. Great balls of lightning! This nuclear explosive, named for the druggist who first compounded it, consists of 96% pure alcohol plus ether. Lapps make this home brew for reindeer roundup time. After castrating the calves with their teeth, they swill Hochmann's (1) as a mouth cleanser, (2) as an antiseptic for the animals, and (3) for the simple purpose of becoming roaring drunk. (We don't object to the alcohol; it's the hors d'oeuvre that kill us.)

P.S. Since Alko shops are freezingly scarce up in remote Lapland, and since money means nothing to those far-northern herders, a fifth of booze can win you a loving Lapp forevermore. Freakishly, his favorite tipple is Ballantine's Scotch or Remy Martin cognac. *Hei! Hei!*

TAXIS   When your eyes hit this astounding tidbit, please don't faint dead away, because we love you.

Ready?

Ready for sure?

Nobody tips ANY taxi driver in ALL of Finland.

Helsinki has granted 1200 operative medallions, so the authorities are mighty persnickety. If the driver's car isn't clean—or if he himself isn't well groomed—he may lose his license. Most vehicles are owner-operated. As a group, drivers are extremely cordial, honest, and good-natured. We've heard many stories about efforts by these pilots to trace their passengers to return personal possessions (including thousands of dollars in currency or traveler's checks) left behind in their cabs.

Most of today's cars are Mercedes diesels and the smaller U.S. makes. You may either pick one up from its stand or flag an empty cruiser on the street. Tariffs are fairly steep by European norms. From 11 P.M. to 6 A.M. there is a night supplement of 1 FMK; the same is added all day on Sundays.

§TIPS: Three passengers cost more than 2—but only a trifling sum.

Since so few of the drivers speak English, *be sure* to have handy a written slip from your concierge which bears the address of your destination.

AIRLINE   No country is more custom tailored to air travel than Finland.

Finnair, the lion's share of which is nationally owned, is its perfect answer. This half-century-old carrier offers the second densest domestic network (next to Iceland) in Europe—plus the lowest domestic flying rates.

In its ground and in-flight passenger service, Finnair strongly and repeatedly—on flight after flight—continues to impress us as a well-meaning but unsophisticated SAS. (As one amusing example, domestic aircraft sport advertising cards on the cabin interiors à la bus and subway ads in our country.) But its personnel couldn't be more friendly, kindly, or obliging.

If you should have any special Finnair problems, dump them into the capable and kind hands of our ever-helpful, relentlessly striving-to-please friend Veli Virkkunen, a tall and handsome model of Finnish hospitality and good nature. He may be reached at the Finnair Building in the capital.

In 1966, Finnair broke new ground in the European aviation industry by abolishing baggage weigh-in on *domestic routes;* 3 pieces of luggage are carried free of charge regardless of weight on flights within Finland, with a minimal charge for any additional bags. (For passengers to or from international flights, these liberalized regulations apply *only* on the domestic leg of the journey, and *only* if a stopover is made in Helsinki.)

Recommendation: Finnair adds up to a crackerjack feeder airline which we like, respect, and would fly any day. But, for its ticketholders' comfort, it still has much to learn from the more savvy, world-experienced Big Boys.

§TIPS: Finnair offers a $120 **Holiday Ticket** to non-Scandinavian tourists, permitting 15 days of unlimited use of all domestic airlanes. Be sure to check with your travel agent, because this bargain, if it is still cooking by your arrival, is much too good to miss.

TRAINS   Fair to excellent.

The Finnish State Railways are government owned and operated. Their total trackage is a surprisingly small 3210 miles. Although a 10-year electrification program is now under way, most trains are still diesel-hauled. It is interesting to note that an undisclosed number of wood-burning steam engines are in storage for emergency use. Since the nation has no coal or oil deposits, these could be instantly "de-mothballed" for facing that 43rd war with you-know-who.

Traffic between Finland and Sweden is severely hampered because the sizes of the track gauges differ—thus necessitating transfers of all ticket-holders and cargo at the frontier. That is one reason most of Suomi's freight and passenger flow with the outside world is by sea or air. At last, however, negotiators are sharpening their brains and their pencils to resolve the discrepancy.

The railways offer a galaxy of enticing thrills via the Tourist Ticket and Finnrail Pass systems (train-bus-boat) at astonishingly reasonable prices. You'll find more about these in "Things to See."

TIPPING   Finland, bless its heart, is one of the least gratuity-conscious nations in the world. Service personnel seemingly could not care less whether you ignore their ministrations or reward them lavishly for their attentions.

The bountiful diner will sometimes make a Diamond-Jim-Brady-style gesture and leave as much as 50¢—but more often the waiter receives no tip above the 13% service charge on the bill. Neither does your doorman, hairdresser, shoeshine boy, theater usher, or railroad helpmates—including your porter, stewards, dining car waiter, or bartender (whether anchored or on wheels).

As we said before, don't tip your taxi driver. Your concierge should receive a token *only* for special performances—not for his routine functions. Curiously, cloakroom attendants pull down a big 2 bits for just checking your hat and coat; how *this* anomaly came about, goodness only knows. Hotel baggage porters earn from 1 to 2 markkaa, depending upon the number of pieces they tote. Since it is not Finnish custom to leave your shoes outside your hotel room for polishing, your chambermaid should win at least 1 markka for this extra favor—and more for any other exceptional kindnesses.

Here's Heaven for us pigeons who are normally such fat, ripe targets in the Lands of the Itching Palms.

PERSONAL SERVICES Hairdressers? Finland's better beauty salons are so crowded that it is absolutely, completely, totally, vitally, absorbingly (enough adverbs?) necessary to arrange advance appointments in summer *or* winter. Generally their hours are from 8 A.M. to 5 P.M., with Saturday closings at 4 P.M. In Helsinki, my Nancy finds **Elsa Arento** (Mikonkatu 8 and Annankatu 15) first and **M. Heikki** (P. Roobertinkatu 10C) next.

Barbers? Actually, many are Barberellas—yep, that's right, they're women, and quite able at their work.

THINGS TO SEE In *Helsinki*, our immediate and urgent suggestion would be for you to drop in to see the **City Tourist Office** (Pohjois Esplanaadikatu 19), so close to the harbor you can practically park your birch-bark canoe at its door. (In case your taxi driver doesn't get the message, its German name is "Städtisches Fremdenverkehrsamt"—and damned if we can even *spell* the CTO's Finnish name.) The hospitable staff will offer you so many pamphlets, brochures, suggestions, and goodies that you can immediately proceed to select what *you* want to see. To us, this makes a lot more sense than limiting your sightseeing program to whatever your concierge or that well-intentioned fellow-voyager might suggest.

For a starter you might be offered any of several **tours by bus** which operate in summer, carry English-speaking guides, and cover just about every standard attraction one might wish to visit. Last time we checked, these particular ones originated at Simonkatu 1 (tel. 645–883).

A number of **boat excursions** are available for groups. There are also coastal cruisers from cozy types to Baltic-crossers such as the 1200-passenger car-ferry, *Finlandia*. However, if you should wish to go-it-alone in the capital or in any other major port, "water taxis" of all sizes are available by the hour or day. An indefatigable local friend chartered one of them for 28 of his intimates at approximately $5 per 60 minutes. Go to the end of Aleksanterinkatu, look the craft over, and take your choice. If you're interested, ask the CTO to arrange one for you wherever you wander along the coast or the lakes. The extra fee for an English-speaking guide, also procurable through the CTO, is about $7 per hour. Members of U.S. yacht clubs may share Finnish yacht club privileges nearly everywhere; if you make the proper connections, you can borrow or rent a speedboat this way.

An outstanding target in Helsinki is the **zoo** on Korkeasaari ("High Island"), a ¼-hour ferry ride away or reachable via the new Kamaa Bridge. This venerable landmark, with its "cat" area isolated by sunken pit barriers, is one of Finland's biggest drawing cards for resident and visitor alike.

You should also get a boot out of the **Open Market**. To find it, just follow the Esplanade down to the base of the harbor near the Palace Hotel. The best time is 7 A.M. until 10 A.M. Here is a colorful cross-sectional slice of Grade-A Finland.

First-timers are often enamored of the special **tram tour** which makes a figure 8 through the heart of the metropolis. The streetcar number is #3-T (for goodness' sake, don't climb aboard any other!), and the cost is 7 FMK. No guides are supplied, but special pamphlets, printed in several languages, are issued so that you may sort the Mineralogical Museum of the Geographical Survey of Finland from the Public Toilets as you roll. (Loudspeakers provide commentary en route during the summer months in English as well as in several other idioms.) A good place to start and to finish is the Open Market. You will then be permitted to take any other of its cars or buses for the rest of the day—absolutely free of charge. (There's also the 10-journey card which rings up 13 FMK.)

With the zoo, **Linnanmäki Amusement Park** is the hub's best-liked magnet for merrymakers. This highest point (270 feet) of the city might be likened, in a much more modest way, to a smaller Tivoli. It offers its funloving patrons the biggest roller coaster in Europe, lots of other rides, variety shows— something for just about everybody. Open only on Saturday and Sunday from early to mid-May, but thenceforth daily except Monday from May 15 to September 1.

Another recommended excursion is to **Seurasaari**, 10 minutes from the center on an island connected by a bridge. Awaiting you is a fascinating collection of authentic Finnish country houses from various provinces, some of them many centuries old. All have been scouted out on their original sites, disassembled log by log and nail by nail, and reassembled with love. The guides are dressed in regional costumes. Folk dancing is featured in season. Here's the best place of all in which to spend the Midsummer Eve holiday.

Culture seekers can easily cultivate onion-size bunions in Helsinki's 30-odd museums, art galleries, and similar institutions. The CTO will give you all the listings, hours, admission charges, and other details of interest. One of them names the most illustrious statuary within the capital, from a number called "Ilmatar and the Duck" to a number called "Kullervo Addresses His Sword." In Off Season, 3- and 4-day "Lifeseeing Tours" are available for visitors with specialized interest in the arts, education, and welfare.

The perfect helpmate for any newcomer to the city is Pan Am's splendid, free, little bulletin, "**This Week in Helsinki**," published year round. Available at all hotels, department stores, travel agencies.

Finally, one of the best bets is the Helsinki Tourist Association's no-cost 4-language weekly-in-summer publication, "**Helsinki This Week**" (in Finnish, "Helsingin Viikko"). Your hotel porter should have a stack of copies prominently displayed; if he hasn't, ask him to send out for one. Here's an excellent source on what's showing at the flicks and similar subjects of equal gravity.

Starving for the latest news in English? Dial 018 for a taped 24-hour free service. The 5 P.M. to 6 P.M. evening bulletin is the most complete. Topical tourist suggestions? Ring 058 for an English synopsis of "Helsinki Today," sponsored by the CTO

In the environs only 6 miles out, you might be staggered by what is probably the finest modern planned community in the world today—*Tapi-ola*. About 2 decades ago, the Housing Foundation, a private nonprofit organization, commenced the development of 670 virgin acres of lovely sea vistas ringed by birches and dense pine forests. In a competition involving hundreds, 12 of Finland's top architects were selected to design the town center and to blend the natural contours of the land. This still-unfinished masterpiece—not a housing project or a suburb, but a miniature community —is broken down into 3 independent neighborhoods, each with its own shopping centers and schools, and each serving from 5000 to 6000 inhabi-tants. For outlanders interested in a twenty-first-century projection of city planning, here is a marvel that can't be found elsewhere. You can snack at either the viewful Tapiontorni or the Linnunrata tower cafeteria; the previ-ously mentioned Dipoli, a far-out architectural wonder, exists chiefly for stu dents and conferences.

Hvitträsk, former home and studio of Saarinen, Lindgren, and Gesellius, is also captivating to architecture buffs. It was one of the earliest serious (and gracious) attempts to blend structure into landscape. Near the stone and log complex there's a superb free swimming beach, plus a good restaurant. Con-nections by bus (platform 55) and taxi are best. The nearest train depot is *Luoma*—a mile hike unless you can flag down a cab. A charmer!

When the sun is shining, the excursion to *Porvoo* is popular with the restless. The steamer *J. L. Runeberg* departs Wednesdays, Fridays and week-ends from the Helsinki Market Square. You may eat aboard en route, or save your appetite for the modern (but so-so, sad to say) Crystal Restaurant at the destination or at the nearby luxury Haikon Kartano Hotel in *Haikko*.

Another lovely SUNday trip is to the Regatta Hotel in *Hanko* (see "Ho-tels"). Its only drawback is the 90-mile pull each way. Closer to your Helsinki base is *Aulanko* and neighboring *Hämeenlinna* (see "Cities")—and once there, we'll bet you will want to stay several days. A Hotel Aulanko bus meets trains at the Hämeenlinna depot or returns guests to the station any time between 8 A.M. and 11 P.M. in season. This one's a *special* honey.

For provincial pioneering, no less than 9 different companies offer no less than 50 different **tours** within the nation. Your best bet, as we previously suggested, is to sort them out in the Finnish Tourist Board in Helsinki, where brochures with complete information on all are available.

The most sought-after regional excursion in Finland is along the so-called Silver Line. Of the many choices at your command, we'd select a candidate called **Blue White Silverline Tour**, which covers the rich south of the nation, with stops at the Hotel Aulanko (the country's leading tourist resort), Tam-pere (the 2nd largest city), and several other attractions. Highlight is a ½-day cruise by water coach from Aulanko. The duration is 2 days; departures are frequent from early June through late August, and the reasonable price includes transportation, transfers, sightseeing, hotels, meals, English-speak-ing guide, entrance fees, and tips.

The 4-day, **Blue White Lakeland Tour** includes stops at Mikkeli, Savon-linna (famous for its water-bounded castle), and Imatra; it departs Wednes-days in summer.

It is hopeless for this *Guide* to attempt to describe the almost countless permutations of sightseeing routes among the most important 200 or 300 of Finland's 60-thousand lakes. Just go to your travel agent, and he'll bury you up to your eyebrows in an Erie-Ontario-Huron of brochures.

The tourist lodestone which radiates the greatest color, magnetism, and fairy-tale fascination is, of course, **Lapland**. For the comfort-conscious and better-heeled, our top recommendation is the **Lapland North Cape Tour**. This flies you from Helsinki to Rovaniemi (Lapland's gateway; note that the airport's welcoming sign is spelled out in antlers), where you climb aboard a motor coach to strike out almost due north for Enontekiö. From here you proceed still farther north to Alta (how we love this world's-end settlement!) and finally to Ultima Thule—Hammerfest, Norway, the most northerly city in the world. After overnights here and at remote Inari, you are driven back to Rovaniemi, bedded down in the Polar Hotel, and flown back to Helsinki the following morning. This 7-day, 2-country junket departs every Sunday, Monday, and Wednesday from mid-June to mid-August. Highly recommended. Finnair's **Midnight Sun Flight**, which lasts a night and a day, leaves Helsinki every day from June 10 to July 10 visiting Rovaniemi on the Artic Circle.

For winter sportsmen, the facilities in Lapland are made-to-measure for rawboned pioneers of new slopes and resorts. **Rukatunturi**, a herringbone below the Arctic Circle in eastern Finland, boasts a slalom track, 2 lifts, lights on downhill runs, and the longest jumps in Scandinavia. For experts. **Pallastunturi**, mostly for beginners, provides a special Christmas program, including a gift from Old St. Nick—free skiing instructions. The Finnish Travel Association can fill you in. We've never tried 'em.

To tie up this Finnish package in bright ribbons, one of the capital's happiest surprises is its **Tourist Ticket** plan that lets you choose your destinations at will and then slices off the normal rates. The lowdown on this economizer, plus the Finnrail Pass for unlimited 8-day-to-month-long rod riding, may be obtained through any Finnish National Tourist Office branch, the City Tourist Office of Helsinki, or your own travel agent—and not a single detail regarding time, length, price, and conditions of each individual journey will be omitted. Tickets are sold through travel bureaus and all Finnish railway stations. The duration is year round, and passages are valid for 60 days. Children under 12 (in your custody) ride the railways at ½-fare. Nearly all the circuits are limited to southern and middle Finland; only one touches Rovaniemi, the most northerly terminus. Best liked among foreigners is the 6- to 8-day swing through the southern lake district. Your transportation for this 730-mile journey is so cheap that we won't spoil the surprise by telling you.

Final admonition, 70 times repeated: The Finnish provinces offer simple, unspoiled, delightful comforts to you—but please never, never, never expect to find the travel amenities of older, less virginal, more cynical lands.

THINGS TO BUY   The Finnish eye for form and the Finnish flair for originality are so exciting that in many creative fields the Finns surpass their northern neighbors.

In *Helsinki*, before buying even a 2-penny toothbrush, we recommend—

nay, urge!—every shopper to head straight for the Finnish Design Center (Kasarmikatu 19). Here is where the nation's greatest artists and artisans—in weaving, glass, textiles, furniture, silver, the gamut—display their masterpieces. You cannot purchase a single item here—but this nonprofit organization will direct you, upon request, to the appropriate atelier, studio, or retailer to which you have taken a fancy.

Weaving? **Neovius** (City Passage and other addresses) is our purl among pearls. Lovely, lovely rugs, wall hangings, cushions, and the like; Miss Leena Laajamo speaks no English (except through her lovely eyes). **Friends of Finnish Handicraft** (Lönnrotinkatu 4) is a close contender. Without any hint of hyperbole or exaggeration, the finer products of both houses are works of art. Larger rugs from $100 to $400; patterns, wools, and weave-it-yourself kits available in each. The word is Dreamy.

Jewelry and Arctic gems? A tossup between **Kaunis Koru Oy** (Intercontinental Hotel) and **Kalevala Koru** (Keskuskatu 4). Distinguished and interesting stocks; competitive prices; in spectrolites and other semiprecious stones mined only above Finland's Arctic Circle, wide range from ridiculously inexpensive to fairly costly silver brooches, bracelets, men's cuff links, necklaces, and rings. While the latter offers better display facilities, the enchanting English-speaking Mrs. Ritvanen of Kaunis Koru understands her jewels and projects her knowledge gracefully and helpfully to the traveler. **A. Tillander** has a fine old name as a conventional jeweler, but he finesses Finnish specialization.

Women's fashion? World-famous **Marimekko** has 4 different outlets: (1) Marimekko-Vintti (Keskuskatu 3), the main store in which you'll find most of its range, (2) Marimekko-Muksula (Eerikinkatu 8), which specializes in clothing for the younger set, (3) a new branch at Pohjoisesplanadi 31, and (4) Marimekko-Mittamari (Pursimiehenkatu 9), with custom-mades only, from evening dresses to a complete travel wardrobe to matching outfits for the entire family. Extra-fine.

Furniture? In **Artek** (Keskuskatu 3) look for the late Alvar Aalto's globally revered designs for grownups and children; the other items here didn't impress us very much.

China? **Arabia** rides the steed. In comparison, the rest are scrub stock.

Handicrafts? In **Sokeain Myymälä** (Mannerheimintie 20 and branches), absolutely everything—baskets, furniture, souvenirs, a little jewelry, other items—is made by the blind. It's so worthy that we profoundly wish it could be more fascinating.

Department store? World-famous **Stockmann** (Aleksanderinkatu) is Finland's largest retail operation—a northern Saks-Field's-Magnin's-Macy's rolled into one. This landmark for more than a century is a national institution, with branches in *Tampere*, *Turku*, and *Pietarsaari*. If you're in a rush, you can centralize all of your marketing here, with an English-speaking guide to help you. Its Finnish arts and crafts are especially fine. The merchandise runs the gamut from distinguished to routine, depending on its price tags. Warning: A Guidester was told that its branch in the airport was a duty-free shop. Upon investigating his outraged complaint, we found that it was NOT. Recommended. **Sokos, Elanto,** and **Pukeva** are solid alternatives.

Shopping hours: Weekdays, 8:30 A.M. to 5 P.M., plus 8 P.M. on Monday and

Friday; Saturday, 8:30 A.M. to 4 P.M. in winter, with 3 P.M. closings in summer.

Tip: There is a handy shopping complex under Helsinki's Railroad Station, with most of its many stores open on weekdays from 10 A.M. to 10 P.M. and Sundays(!) from noon to 10 P.M.

THINGS NOT TO BUY   Imported items (silks, mechanical gadgets, and the like) are saddled with colossal import duties. Gold is worked almost exclusively in 18 karats, and it is therefore for Croesus. Nearly all antiques have either been snapped up or used for firewood. Leather goods (except shoes) are fiendishly high—probably due to the same Customs chomp. Many paper products, to our astonishment (we still do not understand the economics of this), carry exorbitant price tags. As we previously warned, a pack of cigarettes not locally manufactured under Finnish license will rock you about $2. Finally, due to such high-quality standards versus such low production quotas, an increasing supply of cheap, junky "handicrafts" are imported from Japan or Germany—so make sure their source is Finnish before you shell out your beans.

LOCAL RACKETS   Practically none. After exhaustive inquiry among Finnish friends, we finally managed to pin down 2 minor cautions:

In the lowest-class dives, sometimes you won't get the brand of whisky you order. But it will be *genuine whisky* always (never altered, adulterated, or falsified)—because the state-operated Alcohol Monopoly would slice off the proprietor's pouring arm if it weren't. Literally, it can put him in jail.

It is always wise to lock your car, because no law has yet been entered on Finland's law books under which joy-riding kids may be prosecuted.

Otherwise—to repeat—these people are so honest that some country inns still issue no keys to any of the rooms. Who, in today's world, can match this?

France

For 13 centuries the French have offered the world a puzzling, provocative personality, as multiple and unpredictable as a psychiatric patient. You'll be baffled by the combination of emotion and logic. There's a conflict between generosity and niggardliness, idealism and cynicism, fieriness and apathy, gaiety and shrewdness, which can be found in no other civilized people. Many foreign travelers like the French people on first sight and become hair-tearingly exasperated with them on second sight. Some, such as my Nancy and I, finally fall in love with them, never to waver—while others never graduate from dislike and disappointment. It's a black-or-white picture, in which halfway attitudes are rare. If you are able to understand the age-old, mercurial, Gallic temperament, you'll find that this national group can be highly stimulating companions and wonderfully loyal, durable friends, with warmth and hospitality which will overwhelm you. It would be tragic for any American tourist abroad to miss at least a sampling of France's innumerable attractions, most of which cannot be duplicated in any other country. And, best of all, this year—illuminated by Valéry Giscard d'Estaing's sagacious and sympathetic presidency—should offer one of the best opportunities in history to end your visit to France with warmth for its citizens in your heart.

Our own most recent *tours de France* have been by far the happiest we've personally experienced in years. The people-in-the-street have seemed motivated by amity rather than animosity. We found them phenomenally ready to give of themselves to the stranger from abroad. Now please hold your chapeau: As an example, on nearly *all* of our rides in Paris and other cities, the drivers even thanked US for our tips and wished US *"un bon séjour"* ("a pleasant stay") in France!

While your greeting should be enthusiastic, it will still come at a price that may jolt you to the heels. To be fair, however, this economic virus is spreading in epidemic proportions to every other nation of Western Europe. We have already commented in "Let's Get Ready" that NOT ONE of the capital cities of the Continent has escaped its own vicious inflation.

April in Paris can be lovely—but August in Paris, except for the howling mobs of foreign tourists, is as dead as last week's lobster soufflé. This is the time of the *congé payé*, when approximately 1¾-million Parisians pack their bags, suntan oil, and mosquito lotion, and swarm from the capital like lemmings to the sea. At the Spanish frontier early last August, motorists sat at their wheels for 5 hours waiting in line to cross the border. French labor unions legalized this paid vacation some years ago. It has caught on so successfully that if it weren't for the floodtide of outlanders, the capital would be a semi-ghost-town (similar to Madrid from Aug. 1 to Sept. 15) for 31 days. More than 2800 of the existing 4200 bakeries are boarded up; so are hundreds of restaurants, cafés, grocers, pharmacies, laundries, plumbers, doctors' offices, shops, and other service institutions. As a result, nearly everything unwinds to a state of suspended animation. Most U.S. residents of our acquaintance there adore its somnolence then—and you might too. But if you're looking for the real thing, don't visit this beautiful old city while she's packed in mothballs; for the fullest travel satisfaction, plan your stay for any other month.

Despite major, laudable, and continuing reforms and streamlining, French bureaucracy and red tape will drive you out of your mind. It's even worse than Darkest Washington. The Government is the top employer, siphoning off an incredible 17% of the total industrial work force and a staggering number of civil servants who yawn away their days as official charges, and controlling ⅓rd of all buying and selling within the nation—virtually an economic stranglehold. Don't ever be foolish enough to set out bravely but alone to redeem a railway ticket, pick up a postage-due package, or fight through any official transaction; before being waved away at 23 windows on 16 different floors, exhaustion and frustration will utterly consume you. Noble advances have been made in Customs, Immigration, and similar agencies where the tourist-appreciation threshold is strongest—but if you can't persuade your hotel concierge or some innocent dupe to play patsy for you on other administrative chores, it's a lot easier and more sensible to forget them.

Wherever you roam on the Old Continent, the *International Herald Tribune* will be your faithful informant and companion. This cosmopolitan publishing landmark is far zippier, fresher, and more readable than any other English-language newspaper abroad. From Bergen to Lisbon to Athens to Davos to Ruritania, direct your hotel concierge to deliver it to your room daily. To my Nancy and me, and to thousands of news-starved wanderers, it's the best low-cost investment in Europe.

CITIES *Paris* still has such old-time institutions as the Eiffel Tower, fabulous perfumes, Cartier jewels, Fauchon gastronomies, Sorbonne, Folies Bergère, Arc de Triomphe, Notre-Dame, Mona Lisa, and 10-dozen others—

plus some shiny new ones, including a lofty crop of controversial high-rise office titans that punctuate (if not dominate) the traditional skyline. Paris boasts 3-million people, hundreds of hotels, 10 railway stations, 3 airports, 2 heliports, 362 art galleries, 25 museums, magnificent cuisine, nightclubs galore, charm and local color in many corners. One side of Paris' face remains ancient and grimy, while the other offers sweeping boulevards, broad parks, splendid statuary, and architectural dignity. This year (IF you can afford it) you'll want plenty of time in this metropolis—so save for it, both days and dollars.

Marseille, larger than Milwaukee or St. Louis, and the oldest city of France, is 2nd in importance. (New excavations date it back to Grecian times, when it was called "Massalia.") It's the chief port, with heavy Italian influence, routine-to-poor hotels, superb restaurants, Château d'If (Monte Cristo's famous island prison, an interesting 30-minute boat ride away), practically no major monuments except l'Abbaye de St. Victor or the Basilica of Notre-Dame de la Garde, plenty of color, new construction, and a frenetic atmosphere. The ancient harbor town is brightening to make its bid as the principal anchorage for tourists in southern France. The enlarged airport represents a jet-propelled start in this direction. If you succumb to the wooing, be sure to stay out of the Algerian Quarter (rue Ste.-Barbe, rue des Chaneliers, etc.) after dark, because it's one of the most rugged, dangerous slums in the world.

Lyon, with nearly the same population as Buffalo or Seattle, is the junction of 2 rivers (Rhône and Saône) and 2 worlds (central and northern Europe). This apex between the Alps and Burgundy has been called "the Scotland of France," due to the fogs generated by the confluence of the streams, and to the reputedly dour nature of its residents. Renowned for its silks and its stupendous dining establishments; mediocre hotels, by metropolitan standards; heavy industry; proud, clean-lined Sports Palace, containing one of Europe's largest enclosed tracks; huge convention center to keynote its commercial tone; some Roman antiquities, châteaux, cultural attractions, but a way station rather than a primary target for most travelers.

Toulouse, the size of Oklahoma City, is strictly routine—but at last its hotel picture is improving. *Nice* is 5th. More about this city plus *Cannes* and their environs in the "French Riviera." *Bordeaux*, with ¼ million, is 6th; it's an inland port on the estuary of the Garonne, and, except for its Romanesque cathedral, its wine, theater, opera, and May music festival, there's little of interest to the visitor.

Lille, way up north by Belgium, *Strasbourg*, chief French port on the Rhine, and *Nantes*, near the mouth of the Loire, are next in size. Of the 3 we would choose Strasbourg; the others are pocket-size replicas of Marseille, and not much fun for the tourist.

Grenoble, with all of her streets ending at the base of a mountain, is a provincial industrial hub and staging chute for skiers heading up the slopes.

Deauville and *Trouville* are tête-à-tête resorts linked by a bridge over the Touques River. The former is a head taller than her less glamorous twin —a patrician lady with a flair for *la vie joyeuse*. Her amorous perfume draws tryst-minded, off-the-record weekenders, because she offers all the accouterments of High-Life leisure—yachting, racing, polo, golf, aero-clubbiness,

gambling, curling (the outdoor variety, too), a $2,000,000 covered pool for
year-round dipping, a wide flower-lined beach, and an annual $200,000 enter-
tainment budget that headlines some of the world's greatest entertainers. The
famous New Brummel nightclub of the Casino, and the ultracozy winter
Casino, are all part-and-pleasant-parcel of the night scene. Efforts are being
made to stoke the popular image now on a 4-seasonal basis instead of merely
in strawberry time. Trouville, a less opulent refuge, has fewer pretensions of
gentility and refinement. Parisians, who can make the drive in about 3 hours,
crowd both in increasing numbers.

   Biarritz, *Cap d' Antibes*, and *St.-Jean-de-Luz* are favorites with
vacationers—justly so; winter sports in *Megève*, *Chamonix*, *Val d'Isère*
(Savoie), *Courchevel*, *Alpe d'Huez* (the most lively neighbor of Grenoble), and 30 other upland retreats, boasting more than 1750 resort hotels, are
booming.

   France offers an enormous choice, from barhopping in Paris to mountain
climbing in the Alps to toasting your toes on the Riviera to rusticating in 2000
specially listed villages off the beaten track. The **National Office for Tourist
Information** at 127 avenue Champs-Élysées, the **Tourist Headquarters** at 8
avenue de l'Opéra, both in Paris (or the **French Government Tourist Office**,
610 Fifth Ave., N.Y. 10020; 9401 Wilshire Blvd., Los Angeles, Calif. 90210;
323 Geary St., San Francisco, Calif., 111 N. Wabash Ave., Chicago, Ill.; and
1840 ouest rue Sherbrooke, Montreal), will give you further details.

MONEY   Barring any last-minute currency alterations, today your dollar
will buy a little less than 5 francs—minus a few centimes by the time your
particular exchange house takes its cut and allowing for daily fluctuations
related to France's floating monetary system.

   Following endless complications, French coinage stands at 1, 2, 5, 10, and
20 in the centime range, and 1, 2, 5, and 20 in franc pieces; those which are
issued but which you are not likely to see in circulation include the "demifranc," the 10 F silver medallion (so swiftly gobbled up that its going collectors' rate was actually 13 F on a late check), and the even more elusive 50 F
rara avis. Both the 5- and 10-centime pieces have all but vanished; the "old"
1- and 2-franc chips still remain; the 20-franc piece is being freshly minted in
a new issue of silver alloy; the 20-centime coin is a yellowish blend of copper
and aluminum; the "demifranc" is engraved in nickel. Banknotes have been
rounded at 5, 10, 50, 100, and 500 F.

ATTITUDE TOWARD TOURISTS   Dynamic Gerard Ducray is Secretary of State for Tourism. His powers over hotel, transportation, and associated industries have been radically broadened. A National Tourism Fund
to underwrite large-scale facilities is gaining force; under way are a national
parks system, a special commission on mountain resorts, a "nautical tourism"
program, moves to enliven the "dead" Paris of July and August, another
"Welcome to France" promotion that offers special touristic bargains between November 1 and March 31, and a campaign to promote interest in the
charms of less-known rural areas, villages, and hamlets. Under this "welcome" mat you can realize significant savings in hotel accommodation too,

but your travel agent must validate your certificate before you leave North America. We hope with all our hearts that M. Ducray can avoid being bogged down by the numbing bureaucracy which eventually defeated all his predecessors.

For the baffled traveler, the **National Office for Tourist Information** can be found at 127 avenue Champs-Élysées. Guidance may also be sought at the **Commissariat Général au Tourisme**, 8 avenue de l'Opéra.

The City of Paris has set up its own **Information Bureau**, also at 127 avenue Champs-Élysées, linked by Telex to similar centers in other French cities. At your service are an exchange office, accredited representatives of touring agencies, and hotel reservations facilities. Even the Paris Prefecture of Police is in on the hospitality act; foreigners who seek a *permis de séjour* or wish to straighten out an official problem are escorted by gray-uniformed hostesses to pleasantly decorated private offices. *Formidable!*

In North America (New York, Chicago, San Francisco, Beverly Hills, and Montreal), the **French Government Tourist Offices** continue their fruitful assistance to the stateside or Canadian visitor. The Canadian Chief is Max Chamson. In New York, Georges Sauvayre is the U.S. Director-General for French tourism overall, while George Hern, Jr., is the gifted Director of Public Relations. The expert to consult about planning your trip is Marie-France Baudry, who has just taken over the new Information Center on the 6th floor of Rockefeller Center. Here you will also find inquiry desks manned by the French National Railroad, and Air France. Address for information, brochures, and the like: 610 Fifth Ave., New York, N.Y. 10020.

CUSTOMS AND IMMIGRATION French Customs regulations specifically forbid the traveler to import anything but his naked epidermis. But since the mechanics of enforcement *do* present certain practical difficulties, they let down the bars on a "tolerance" basis.

Technically there are specific limitations on items such as liquor (3 bottles of wine and 1 of hardware), still cameras (2 of differing styles), movie cameras (1 portable), 10 rolls of film for each, a tape recorder with 2 reels or 10 records, a portable radio, a portable typewriter, tobacco (2 cartons of cigarettes for the intercontinental visitor, but 1 carton only for travelers from European points, or 125 cigars, or 1 lb. of pipe tobacco—the last 2 allowed men only), and other commodities. In practice, however, the *average* American gets a "Vous n'avez rien à déclarer?", a grunt, a scribbling of chalk—and he's through without opening one piece of luggage.

No limits on your currency imports. The export limit is 500 F.

No export restrictions on gifts or personal purchases except antiques or works of art—and here they're tough. If the artist is living, or if the work was executed after 1921, you may arrange an exchange liability at the Comité Professionel des Galeries d'Art, 3 rue du Faubourg-St.-Honoré, Paris. Better still, let your dealer get it for you—and *always insist on being given a bill for Customs reference.* Actually, it's wise to have this document for even a 49¢ lithograph of *The Vanishing Indian,* because some of the intellectual giants at the counters don't know the difference between Renoir, Renault, and Raincoat—thus setting things up for a possible delay. *Allow a minimum of*

48 hours for this. Except for these 2 categories, you can load up on everything you want; your only concern is U.S. entry.

VISAS   For visitors who plan to stay more than 3 months, French Consulates in New York, Chicago, Los Angeles, San Francisco, New Orleans, Boston, or St. Louis provide visas. Take your passport and photos.

HOTELS   For far more comprehensive information on certain French hostelries than space limitations permit here, interested travelers are referred to *Fielding's Selected Favorites: Hotels and Inns, Europe* by our Marco Polo son, Dodge Temple Fielding. The revised edition, in which a total of 300-odd favored possibilities were handpicked from the 4000-plus personally inspected, will be at your bookstore early this year. Generally speaking, Gallic hotels are now quite good. In the provinces, improvements are now healthy and continuous. Still, don't be surprised if your regional hostelry turns out to be vintage 1893, with hot-and-cold running proprietor complete with seedy vest and toothpick.

Recently the Government finally put sharp teeth in its official rating system. Contrary to its lax, carefree prior practice, this innovation is effective because it directly involves the police. All hostelries considered to be worthy of receiving outlanders are classed as *Hôtels de Tourisme.* These are broken down into 5 categories: Deluxe, 4-star, 3-star 2-star, and 1-star. The last trio are urther subdivided into "A," "B," and "C." The same applies to the *Relais de Tourisme* (suburban stops) and *Motels de Tourisme* (on major highways). As stated below, price controls cover only the lowest 3 groups. All have been painstakingly reinspected. (One proprietor complained to us that the inspector studied his 46-room establishment for 2½ days and then wrote a 24-page report of its deficiencies.) Therefore, in order to qualify, every physical plant must now conform in every detail to the standards of the rating for which it has reapplied—the ratios of private bathrooms to bedrooms, the presence of adequate breakfast rooms with the specified numbers of seats, the toilets separated by their own individual doors, and scores of similar ukases. Legions of hoteliers frantically—some in panic!—rebuilt and repainted so that they wouldn't be dropped to the next lower category and thus diminish their earnings. This supervision applies to lodging charges only; in "pension" (meal) arrangements, legally the sky is the limit.

Don't forget the requirement of 10% to 30% extra for service charge *(majoration)* and taxes—no matter where you go. Taxes are now included by law in all quotations, but for service and supplements it's still almost a case of "anything goes." The amount depends upon the location and category— *so be certain this total has been calculated in the summation before you sign the register.* It can give you a nasty surprise if you're caught.

The Government has stepped into the travel picture in another way, too. Now French hoteliers can be held liable for the theft of a registrant's possessions—either from the hotel or from the hostelry's parking lot. The law, at least, ought to influence the selection of staff and create better safeguards throughout.

In Paris tariffs are the same or even higher than those in the larger U.S.

cities, despite all Government efforts to hold down the upward spiral. As we've stated, the cost of accommodations has more than tripled within the past decade and the squeeze this year, in seasoned travelers' opinions, is frankly scandalous. Deluxe and First-class establishments set their own charges—which are always as high, naturally, as Old Dobbin Customer will stand without bursting his traces and bolting. One of the biggest dodges is that when space for one is "unavailable," the lone traveler may be charged for double occupancy. *At one extreme, the leaders run perhaps $27 minimum for a single, $44 minimum for a double, and $90 minimum for a suite. At the other, budget vacationers can find scores of tatterdemalion slow-water antiquities around the Étoile, the Opéra, and on the Left Bank for $18 per day—and mighty, mighty basic, at that. Between these limits, houses of the "popular" tourist category, such as the Grand, Scribe, Commodore, and the like, offer minimum doubles with bath, service, taxes, and breakfast for perhaps $35. Off Season tabs (in the resorts, not in the main centers) can be 10% to 20% lower.*

One caution: When you eat your breakfast in your room (most visitors follow this continental tradition), items such as fruit juice, cereal, eggs, or sausages are not included in the house quotation for the standard coffee or tea *complet*. They cost like the devil and add up fast.

All French Government Tourist Offices have definitive lists of Gallic stopping places everywhere, free of charge. A splendid bet for the less well-heeled vacationer is the *Logis de France Guide*—a roundup of more than 2500 clean, modest country and resort hotels, hand-picked by the **Fédération Nationale des Logis de France**; available at this organization's Paris headquarters, 25 rue Jean Mermoz, for $1; although tariffs have edged upward to the average full-pension range of $12 to $16, their selections are still generally less expensive than competitive ones. For more opulent tastes, the **Relais de Campagne-Route du Bonheur Association** (also nonprofit) offers a superb 5-language compilation of perhaps 150 leading French or foreign-owned rural oases—châteaux, manor houses, converted monasteries, and the like—all with well-known restaurants (a few entries are for dining only). Although a handful are substandard, the majority offer dependable quality. What a splendid group it is too! For details drop by the information office at 17 place Vendôme in Paris. King and Queen of the field, however, remain the indispensable **Guide Michelin** and **Guide Kléber-Colombes**, both of which no serious traveler in France should ever be without.

The previously mentioned **City of Paris Tourist Information Bureau**, at 127 avenue Champs Élyseés, will spring to your rescue in emergencies by finding you a room within a 60-mile radius of Cannes, Nice, Marseille, Reims, Lourdes, Strasbourg, Tours, Rouen, Lyon, Vichy, Dijon, Aix-les-Bains, or (of course) the capital. Reservations guaranteed for one night only (this avoids competition with travel agencies); direct connection with Paris Welcome Information Offices at main railway stations, with lovely Hostesses of Paris on tap; Telex network, currency exchange, and similar services; open 9 A.M. to midnight including Sunday. No fees.

Paris at peak times can be one of the tightest accommodations bottlenecks in Europe. But this squeeze is fast in the process of being not only loosened but virtually eliminated for well stuffed wallets only—*NOT* for lower-spending wanderers. Officially, at least, a massive campaign has been launched to assist responsible professionals through low-interest loans and perhaps grants for the fastest possible proliferation exclusively of 2-star hotels and motels along France's highways—badly needed economy lodgings which will be a godsend to the budget traveler.

In *Paris*, our Big 10 lead off this year with what is essentially a 3-way tie at the top; the Bristol, the Ritz and the Plaza-Athénée are pounding down the homestretch neck-and-neck-and-neck. On the rail and challenging fast are the Crillon, Meurice, Lancaster, and Prince de Galles, followed closely by such favorites as the Intercontinental, the Hilton, and the George V.

The **Bristol** (112 rue du Faubourg-St.-Honoré) has been booted home to the winner's circle season after season. Already it has become a totally independent island within the city; with its own electrical power, water, and food storehouses, it can sit out any strike or municipal shutdown with complete equanimity. Very recently, dynamic and attractive Pierre Jammet, who teams on all operations with his lovely wife Heidi, embarked upon a $3,000,000 reconstruction program. New parking, sipping, dining, banqueting, and garden facilities plus 2-dozen new bedchambers have been unrolled from the Bristol blueprints. Ground floor filled with Gobelins and rare paintings; stunning oval dining room with special gastronomic repasts offered on Wednesdays; refreshments served in the lobby and lounge by eighteenth-century-clad butlers. More than 50% suites or apartments, many air-conditioned; giddily opulent duplex penthouse for VIP's and/or Houstonites, with private elevator, 5 rooms, 3 baths, 2 flower-bedecked terraces, and art treasures, in the trifling neighborhood of $375 per day; #204-207 remodeled into one of the world's handsomest sitting rooms (fine bedroom connecting), for ordinary millionaires who can afford its $200 rate. Delicious, award-winning cuisine; air-chilled beauty parlor and barbershop among the most expensively wrought in the capital; masseur; many other services and attractions. For the convenience of its U.S. following, the Bristol has opened an exclusive booking office at 19 E. 73rd St., New York; immediate confirmation can now be made on our own home soil.

The **Ritz** (15 place Vendôme) is still the rallying point of the Old Guard. Basically it remains a fine structure with luxurious facilities and an eminently distinguished clientele. It boasts an unbeatably central location, tons of venerable marble and mellowed woodwork, the ghosts of countless patrician guests, and 80% American patronage. The top-to-bottom 5-year grand restoration plan finally has been wrapped up. Much of the credit for its color blendings and modern innovations goes to Mme. Charles Ritz and her artistic husband. With or in its 50 living rooms and 210 bedchambers you'll now find superefficient baths, 5-channel piped music, and color TV outlets for employment upon request; there's a fine beauty salon and a barbershop; the bar is coming back into a style that faded and is now recovering. Again the skilletry (but not the service) in its Espadon Grill drew sighs of disappointment from us. Here presently, under the baton of debonair Director Janusz Zembrzuski, is an urbane meld of yesterday and today: While its administration painfully winces at the thought of refrigerators in the sleeping quarters, specially made small carpets are available for dogs! To the delight of its loyal following, who have sworn by it for decades, this monument has made a comeback which, almost strictly in the classic rather than the contemporary sense, again qualifies it as *A Ritz as Big as a Diamond*.

For decades the **Plaza-Athénée** (25 avenue Montaigne) has catered with conspicuous success to inconspicuously wealthy travelers, people who have wanted the best in fashionable and reasonably quiet surroundings. But ever since London's Charles Forte interests acquired this landmark in the late '60s, a $6,000,000 revolution has been discreetly taking place to update its old-fashioned splendor by transforming it into one of the most tastefully and elegantly flair-filled hostelries on the Continent; going a bit further into blue-sky territory, it could be considered today as one of the 3 greatest hotels in the world. The most active achiever in its renaissance is General Manager Paul Bougenaux, formerly its famous concierge, who has spent more than 30 years on the premises. He recently redid the whole house on a quarter-by-quarter basis, redecorated the bedchambers throughout in Louis XV or Louis XVI, and knocked down walls on the 2 penultimate floors to double room dimensions. Illustrious M. Roland of Tour d'Argent celebrity now supervises the Very First Rank cuisine; try his globally renowned lobster soufflé. While the courtyard restaurant (3 full-time florists!) has now been tailored for year-round operation, its vivid blooms, pools, bridge, free-flying songbirds, gay red parasols, and polka-dotted tablecloths create the impression of Eternal Spring. Every room offers a good bath, an excellently stocked refrigerator, color TV, 4-channel piped music, and news broadcasts in English; the penthouse is composed of 4 supersuites. Cheers, salutes, and salaams to M. Bougenaux and his fine staff for their virtuoso performance!

The **Crillon** (10 place de la Concorde), home of most top American diplomats during conferences of State, has taken such gigantic strides under Director Claude Lemercier that now it has become a full-fledged member of Paris' élite group. Every one of its 220 accommodations has been given a completely fresh face. A smart Grill and the ultramodern, 2-room Le Concord Bar have been added (the latter is radically out of character with its historic image but very nice per se). You'll ride elevators with leather interiors by Hermès; there's also a handsomely keyed-in 3-cabin Telex room. Convenient site next to the U.S. Embassy; lobby 100% refurbished, with tasteful shopping vitrines; all corridors remade. While the bedchambers are chipper, bright, and well equipped, they maintain the traditional tone; all baths have been revivified, most of them with thermal taps in tubs and showers, and some with a mock-wood motif. Wayfaring Yankees (who comprise 75% of its registrations) are fond of the night menu (alas, not around the clock) of cold selections and the he-man breakfasts. Though expensive, this house provides *beaucoup* return for your francs.

The **Meurice** (228 rue de Rivoli) is now owned by the prestigious Grand Hotels of Italy Corporation (CIGA), which so beautifully administers such beloved pacesetters as the Grand and the Excelsior in Rome, the Grand and the Excelsior in Florence, the Gritti Palace in Venice, and a number of other dazzlers. (In the same transaction, it also bought Paris' Prince de Galles and Grand, both of which are listed below, plus the 146 local buildings belonging to Tycoon Rente Foncière, among which it will retain only the choicest locations.) New administration by General Manager Claude Ginella. Vast reconstructions are now on the boards, probably to include a new gastronomic restaurant with 60 couverts and an overall spruce-up of the bedchambers. In the meantime, this plant offers stylish public rooms, the clublike Copper Bar and Grill in unusually appealing masculine tones which is geared for faster-than-normal meals if desired, all accommodations facing the park and 140 bathrooms freshly revivified, a recently recoiffed beauty salon, a noted kitchen, minibar service to all clients, and scores of other well-executed features in its deeply rooted tradition of grace and comfort. When CIGA pours more money into it in CIGA's unique way, it should be not only great but fabulous.

The **Lancaster** (7 rue de Berri) recently was purchased by London's Savoy Hotels Ltd., the superlative innkeeping chain that includes the golden links of Claridge's, the Berkeley, the Connaught, and, of course, the Savoy. A more perfect commercial marriage can scarcely be visualized, because all parties are on the same wavelength in spoiling the wayfarer with old-fashioned *personalized* attention and satisfaction supreme. Young, winning John Iversen, handsome enough to be a film star, took over with subtle but socko command; aided by his Savoy and Reid's (Madeira) background, he is exactly the type to be at the helm here. Deftly and skillfully he introduced masses upon masses of major and minor improvements which have exorcised its slowly creeping geriatric aura without impinging upon its extraordinary feeling of privacy, tranquillity, and intimacy as a large and lovely town house. Most of the rooms are so exquisite but comparatively so small in their dimensions (yet still comfort-plus) that we believe their appeal is greater to ladies than to men; no 2 of them are outfitted alike. Our only demurrer, with which you might totally disagree, lies in what seems to us to be substandard cuisine for such an otherwise exalted haven; we think that it is time that the chef, who has performed here for 30-odd years, should be turned out to pasture and that more appetizing fare should be presented in its charming little hideaway garden. Extra-special for travelers who indulge their extra-special tastes.

For traditionalists the fine old **Prince de Galles** ("Prince of Wales"), cheek-by-jowl with its fading rival, the George V, has long been a cordial, attractive, and comfortable haven. Now that the previously mentioned Grand Hotels of Italy Corporation (CIGA) has absorbed it into their mighty fold, this already *soigné* nobleman may or may not be crowned as the Parisian king of the new empire—or perhaps its masters will select the Meurice for this honor. Nobody yet seems to know. In any case, huge sums of money are being pumped into both. New General Manager Marguerie is the fireman at pump. Two floors per annum completely redone in a 6-year cycle; good beverage-stocked refrigerator in every shelter; about 80% of baths with twin washbasins and wallpapered ceilings; corridors particularly fresh, cheerful, and ingeniously colorful; outstanding gastronomy; chic and sheikish Moorish courtyard for terrace dining in summer. Chief Concierge Joseph Monti is a mountain of strength, as were all of the staff we met during our latest visit. Already far superior to the George V, in our evaluation—with an even greater future already budding under the dynamic CIGA banner.

The venerable Continental was purchased by the Intercontinental Hotels chain and renamed the **Intercontinental Paris**. This then-tawdry relic was closed for 6 months and gutted so completely that only its outside shell remained. Excellent central location embracing the original but now refashioned Garden Court; canopied terrace on one side overlooking a central pond for seasonal outdoor dining; lobby a strikingly attractive mixture of nineteenth-century and Cape Kennedy appurtenances-of-tomorrow; many grace notes in its chamber-music ensemble boldly melded with jazzy footnotes; intimate Rôtisserie Rivoli, curiously shaped with 6 alcoves and seating the grand sum of 180; Le Bistro for lighter biting and libations to music (piped from noon until a pianist comes on from 9 P.M. to 2 A.M.); Bar Rivoli with an after-gloaming harpist; Coffee Shop. During our latest visit its public rooms were bustling with approximately 50% group traffic. A normal concomitant of this—and we don't believe this Paris I.H.C. is an exception—is that service often can be distressingly indifferent. Full air conditioning; double-pane windows for silent-nighting; ample space in rooms with soft-view hues in blue, gray, green, or burnt orange; wall-to-wall carpeting; so-so furnishings; typically tiny baths; all singles with *grands lits*. As the disparate elements are further integrated, it is bound to improve even more.

The T-shape, 11-story **Paris Hilton**—with a Tinkertoy called the Eiffel Tower standing in its backyard—opened its Left Bank portals in '66, the first Deluxe hotel to be illuminated in the City of Light since the George V was switched on in '33. Outlying situation requiring a taxi hop for every midtown errand, shopping jag, or sightseeing jaunt; marvelous vista from Seine-side rooms; dreary claustrophobic view from rear windows, overlooking the Atomic Energy Commission complex. Mélange-happy lobby lined with shops; convenient 300-car underground garage; 6 refreshment centers (see "Restaurants"). Price tags nudge $75 to $90 per day per couple, which is getting up into real *argent,* even for Paris. The gargantuan task of coping with this giant has fallen to tiger-quick, Swiss-born General Manager Pierre Jaquillard, who molded the Athens landmark and is now the Hilton veep in charge of company projects in France, Spain, Portugal, Morocco, and Tunisia. In sum, here is another chain reaction: Good for those who like it. (The Orly Hilton, a smaller brother, is covered separately at the conclusion of the Paris "Hotels" section.)

We think the **George V**, part of the package taken over by the London Charles Forte interests a few years back, should borrow, devour, and set into practice the principles delineated in the Management Manual of its sister acquisition, the Plaza-Athénée. So much recent mail from Guidesters had flooded in that on our Parisian rounds this author (as we did earlier) again slipped unnoticed through the lobby to an elevator, spent nearly 2 hours roaming from floor to floor (innocently helped by chambermaids through unoccupied rooms), prowled all of the public rooms downstairs, and then lunched alone in its garden restaurant—totally unidentified all the way. The result of this unusual study was a mixture of delight and despair. The bar, with its 1930's mien and a 1000-lamp chandelier, is a beauty spot—a graceful touch indeed. The staff attitudes impressed us as improving generally, with only occasional manifestations from personnel who insist on remaining insouciant and careless. My light meal, again very expensive, was well presented and enjoyable. There is no doubt about it being one of the capital's capital addresses, but we wonder sometimes whether the capital outlays are equal to the rewards.

Below the Big 10, the degree varying slightly, is a cluster with fine facilities and distinctive qualities. Let's lead off this next category with a recent entry that is certainly "big" in its own way.

The fresh-faced **Méridien**, with over *1000* latchkeys, is really more of a hotel-city than an inn in the traditional sense. The Porte Maillot enclave, directly opposite the Congress Hall, is a design for the times. Its lobby, only slightly smaller than the state of Delaware, is dominated by thickets of easy chairs and illuminated by a tubular forest of suspended lamps; a gelid stainless-steel bar chills the nether reaches leading to the cool courtside Clos Longchamps restaurant. Colorful Arlequin Rôtisserie; Japanese Yamoto corner; cellar-sited circular café; nightclub—well, you name it and it's probably there. The look-alike bedchambers feature one flank clad in the same carpeting that cloaks the floor; their other facilities include semifitted furniture, radio console and TV, air conditioning, comfortable beds, Bell-Captain refrigerated bars, baths with space-age tubs and cleverly designed glass splashplates for showers, and maximum utilization of limited elbowroom. Take your problems to Concierge Robert Lissardy, one of the nicest and most competent hall porters in the City of Light. This jumbo, largely fueled by Air France financing, is piloted by able Ernst Etter, who switched cockpits from the Pan Am-icable Paris Intercontinental. Basically sound, but with a chill-factor associated purely with the twentieth century.

The equally new **P.L.M. Saint-Jacques** is another Orwellian creation—this one with a mere 812 accommodations. It is handy to the major train stations and the route to Orly Airport (shuttle every ¼-hour), and not too far from Montparnasse. (Our taxi fare to the Étoile totaled nearly $7, however.) Impressive cubistic façade; 15 floors of windows angled port and starboard; airy blue-and-white lobby with greenery, a fountain, and drilled steel columns; once again the full panoply of restaurants (including a Japanese one and a Polynesian bar), boutiques, and tourist services; narrow, efficient, pentagonal bedchambers in orange, blue, or brown tones; sparrow-size baths with marble-top basins and dip-your-toe tubs. A novel touch is the hotel's credit card system whereby guests charge round-the-house expenditures to a central computer. Now being managed by our long-term friend, the skilled veteran hotelier Jean Burca, who will be bending every effort to warm it up.

The giant new **Concorde-Lafayette**, sponsored by the Concorde group (Crillon, Lutecia, and other well-regarded local oases), connects with the Paris Convention Hall, which seats 4000. Its first 2-dozen tiers cater exclusively to groups, with no room service available. The next 8 levels stack up for independent bookings; these come with coral textiles, matched furnishings, brown carpets, and dimensions which seem a shade smaller than those of the above entry. Comfort standards, however, are about the same. General Manager Leclercq's crowning joy is the panoramic penthouse restaurant and bar. Another 1000-room colossus, but segmented in such a clever way that both groupies and soloists share the rewards—with, perhaps, never the twain to meet.

The **Royal Monceau** presently is enjoying a total, well-planned renaissance under the masterful guidance of skilled and personable Jean Hennocq, one of the tops in his craft. Lobby festooned with the graceful dignity to match its stately facade; corridors refashioned; all backstage support facilities shaken up or shaken out. This year you'll discover an ingratiating patio-garden restaurant in season, many modernized accommodations and baths, carefully prepared cuisine, kindhearted reception by Philippe Juredieu, cordial attention by a well-trained staff, and heavy group traffic during the tourist months. Its ancient milieu misses the distilled elegance of our Big 10 candidates, but tariffs are about 30% cheaper. Given another few seasons, M. Hennocq will wring even more wonders from this dowager. Very good indeed for its semi-aristocratic bearing and solid value.

The **Grand,** despite its convenient central address, strikes us as being by far the least desirable 3rd of the hotels package purchased by the Grand Hotels of Italy Corporation, better known as CIGA. As it stands, it is well on the way to achieving its goal as a convention hotel. Robert Vernay instituted extensive revampings here. The exterior has been brightened with glass and burnished metal. Ceilings have been lowered (but, alas, the prices have moved in the other direction). Careful attention has been accorded to illumination techniques throughout the building. There's the zippier lobby leading to the bar and Café de la Paix (another part of the acquisition), the fresh Pacific Room for quick meals, a refashioned terrace, and much more sparkle. Manager Marcelin is a gentleman who bears the stamp of the true professional. Strongly we fear that no matter how proven-superb the skills of the CIGA innkeepers, because of its size and basic construction, this must always be a mass-production-belt house with frigid impersonality.

On recent rounds we reinspected the **Hotel de la Trémoille,** smallest of the trio taken over by England's Charles Forte interests in the late '60s (including the Plaza-Athénée and the George V). When we previously were there, it impressed us as being down at the heels. Today, the public rooms have maintained their distinguished character, about 60 bedchambers have been refashioned, and a lot of color has been sprinkled in. The 100-unit **Frontenac,** also in this stable, has been perked up, too, and now is quite a handsome second choice. About 50% of its accommodations were renewed nicely, so be sure to ask for one of these.

L'Hôtel (13 rue des Beaux-Arts, on the Left Bank) is dramatically unorthodox. French actor Guy Louis Duboucheron and Texas architect Robin Westbrook spent 27 months transforming the seedy, moldy, 30-room, 3-bath Hôtel Alsace—its only pale distinction that Oscar Wilde died there—into a luxury-class operation of 2 suites, 25 rooms, and 27 baths. To the rear of its Lilliputian lobby its greenhouse-style terrace restaurant presents a tiny fountain, 2 caged monkeys, parrots, drawable curtains under its light-well ceiling, a mass of vines, blue tablecloths, and 2 dirty rugs. The cuisine—which impressed my Nancy as being notably substandard—is whoppingly expensive à la carte. The wine card, although versatile, is also overpriced, in her opinion. The bedrooms, each different and some air-conditioned, are all decorated in exquisite taste. The cellar-to-roof drawback here is that all of its dimensions have been telescoped into such super-compactness, including luggage space, that any large-framed guest would find this doll's house uncomfortably cramped. Here seems to be a truly lovely Parisian haven for *lady* travelers of means—not for average males, who require vastly greater Lebensraum.

The **Raphaël**, 2 blocks from the Arc de Triomphe, exudes an air of understated grace and dignity. Its salons are filled with beautiful oil paintings and its bedrooms evoke the grandeur of a manor house. However, for what is now to us an alarmingly long time, a number of disturbing reader reports have filtered onto our desk, complaining chiefly of a falloff in maintenance which our own eyes confirmed on our very recent stopover. What a pity, because fundamentally this is a charming plant.

The **Brighton** brightens its enviable site on the convenient rue de Rivoli. Traditional rooms with full carpeting, French windows, brass beds, and good illumination; superb maintenance; ample comfort and coziness; #410 an excellent 3-bed corner accommodation; back units quiet. No restaurant, but a spread for breakfast; nice personnel who truly seem to care. It is, in our opinion, just what a small, medium-priced hostelry should be.

As for the new 200-room **Suffren La Tour**, sponsored by the French Railways, the accent is on the Suffren. Too much *argent* for too little reward, in our opinion.

The **Hotel France et Choiseul** (rue St. Honoré across from place Vendôme) is making the most of its near-perfect address. The British-based Adda Hotels group bought this veteran, gutted it down to its most basic walls, and then virtually rebuilt the entire structure. Untouched, however, remain its Louis XVI Emperatrice-style foyer, the muraled walls of the main salon, and the courtyard—all ruled inviolable by the French National Art Commission. Upstairs its 135 nests are pretty standard in their somewhat limited elbowroom and their accouterments: Dark brown furniture, dark brown rugs, built-in wardrobes, no pictures (we were told the probable fairytale that they had been spirited away by larcenous guests), and no frills except an outside doorbell, a computerized awakening system, and a minibar. General Manager Armand Benichou is an interested host. Too often, however, his guests arrive in van-filled migrations. The fresh **Napoleon,** near the Etoile, is much better now in a modernized Regency manner. Looking up (as Bonaparte might) and very well sited. The Rank-run **Westminster** seemed to us to be blistering overpriced for its bedroom talents. The Tudor salon, Bulldog Restaurant and Empire bar, however, are appealing. Now let's dip into the grab-bag of assorted capital hostelries:

The **Lotti** is now under the able guidance of General Manager Hector Berger and Resident Manager Jacques Massot. Pleasant bar and grill adjoining the small restaurant; revamped 6th floor, plus 10 new units on every other level; some garret-style accommodations; acres of new carpets. An intimate type of house that we like a lot.

The **Commodore**, at a convenient midcity site, used to be a good commercial-style bet. Although the management has cleaned up its lobby and unchipped most of its corridors, we repeatedly saw soiled hand-marks on doors and along the walls. Some frayed carpets have now been replaced or repaired. No longer a bargain.

The **Sofitel-Bourbon** was decanted in '69 at a spiritless address in the feckless VIIe arrondissement. The proof of its modern lobby tasted so weak to our palate that any one of 250 hotels we had inspected directly preceding this one stirred our corpuscles with greater zing. Amiably zesty 40-seat dining room; deep-frozen bar; valiant-to-eye-throbbing color schemes in accommodations; a cocktail shaker of assets and debits in space arrangements, with most dimensions small; minibaths with microtubs. We have never been fond of the French chain in which this entry is one of its recent links, and here we feel pity for Director Marcel Côte, an old friend and a fine hotelier. Not our cup of Mumm—or even our Bourbon Sour. The same group operates the 630-unit **Sofitel de Paris**. It is across the *rue* from the capital's Parc des Expositions—which gives you a pretty fair idea of its fair-minded function. After our very latest rounds, yet another giant was due to rise: The 32-story, $30,000,000, 800-room, red-toned **Nikko.** Its domain, under the stewardship of Shiro Mikura, is southwest of the Eiffel Tower on the shore of the Seine at 61 quai de Grenelle. We'll have a full report next edition.

The 75-room-and-bath-or-shower **Celtic**, just off the Étoile, doesn't seem to have lived up to its restyling promises—at least not to our eyes anyway. Our favorite double here is #13. Our formerly chilly reaction has warmed up by several degrees. The **Victoria Palace** occupies a silent setting. Friendly reception from a covey of lovely French quails; equally ingratiating staff directed by M. Di Domenico; renewed dining room with quality cooking; streetside bar; 3 lounges; well maintained. A solid value for the money.

The **Club Méditerranée**, out of the center and for members only, is such an antihotel concept that we couldn't buy it even if we belonged to this worldwide organization. Room service does not even exist; each morning your "breakfast" is delivered through a chute from the corridor—instant coffee plus a thermos of hot water, no less. Regardless of its handy site and successful restaurant, never, never, never for these Mallorca Mediterraneanites.

The **Grand Hôtel Littré** is in the hands of Proprietor Albert Schmitt (former President of the French Hotels Association) and his charming wife, who also own the Victoria Palace. Since these houses are back-to-back, a hallway connects them, and their tariffs are identical. Before reopening the former, they tore it apart and put it back together again in a commendably clean, fresh, and attractive way. Charming bar; 3-tier lobby; TV room; 2 small but comfortable lounges; sparkling dining room to brighten the visitor's welcome. The chef is rightfully proud of his Gallic *haute cuisine.* All 4 suites and 120 rooms come with adequately spacious private baths. The décor is restful and practical; try to reserve on the courtyard for sun and tranquillity. These good people, including Manager Baer, have now turned this into an excellent bet for the price. **La Résidence du Bois**, just a totter from the Étoile on rue Chalgrin, is an 18-room hideaway with quietude, luxury, and no fireworks. Operated in a dignified homespun manner by Banker-Turned-Boniface Henry Desponts; no full restaurant, but light meals available; minimum twins for around $60; 3 suites; one 2-story nest with private entrance; all accommodations tastefully appointed and cheerful; #10 and #23 best for silent siestas. Recommendable on many counts. **San Regis** offers 2 duplex suites, 12 normal suites, and 42 rooms (all with private plumbing), with the better, redecorated units to the rear. Sadly missed is its former restaurant, now converted into a 5-table short-order operation. Not bad, but not good either. The **Normandy** has been invaded by carpenters and plasterers—all 7 floors, all 130 rooms (of which we prefer the "07" series). Ask to see an accommodation before booking if you can, because some are small while others are generous in dimensions. Coming up smartly.

Hôtel La Pérouse (40 rue La-Pérouse), sited in a quiet neighborhood belying its 2-block distance from the Arc de Triomphe, now seems to be in a slump, in our opinion. Small lobby, calm and reserved; dining room colored in lemon and beautified by green velour chairs and rose-flowered rug. Its 8 suites and 40 rooms, all with private bath and shower, are ample in size. Fair overall, but becoming in need of stimulants.

The **Royal Hôtel** (33 avenue Friedland in a tranquil situation near the Étoile) was eminently worth the search. Midget lobby newly refashioned; all-new 6th floor; new heating system installed; tour groups never accepted; side-street locations the quietest, despite double windows on the Avenue side; everything spotless. All accommodations we have either stayed in or inspected over the years, while small and costly for the category, have looked pert and have smelled as fresh as a mountain pine grove. Each and every face —from Jean's at reception, Gaston's as Chief Concierge, the housecleaning women's, and amiable, courtly, highly likeable Director André Lebrun's— wears a size-48 smile that will make you glow in response. The **Vernet** is also a 2-minute stroll from the Étoile. Quiet side-street harbor (rue Vernet) in the *coeur* of Paris; friendly family atmosphere nourished by the Percepied brothers; bar and pleasant restaurant; 63 Gallic bedchambers; only 2 without private bath. Aside from its economy in this 24-karat city, this one's greatest asset is its oasis of calm in the eye of the hurricane whirl. The **Hôtel De Stockholm**, across the street, reflects the tastes of its French/Scandinavian commercial clientele. While the leather chairs in the Swedish-style lobby look well-sat-in, the overall upkeep is good. It offers 55 small, functional rooms of no particular flair, all with bath and shower. Satisfactory choice for businessmen. **Hôtel de Castiglione** has a grandmotherly ambiance. Smallish lobby; appetizing dining room and handsome tartanesque bar up 1 flight; clean and well illuminated; 110 units, most with private baths. Comfortable. The 29-nest **Lido**, well-scrubbed and polished, offers many thoughtful minutiae. Fairly tranquil considering its proximity to Place de la Madeleine; bright, modern lobby; no restaurant; s-l-o-w elevator; carpeted corridors; large wallpapered bedrooms. Aim high for *les toits de Paris* view. LidOkay.

The European Hotel Corporation's **Penta** under management contract to the Grand Metropolitan's experienced specialists, made its debut next to the Paris Exhibition Hall at La Défense, about 2 miles west of the Arc de Triomphe. Since here is today's most modern business section in the metropolis or its environs, naturally this venture has been keyed to heavy commercial traffic. The sister operation in London is doing a fine job in its medium category. Eventually this one will, too, we think, despite some early complaints concerning greenhorn staffers and the accompanying handicaps of growing pains.

The 32-story **Sheraton** is a-bustling on the Left Bank—yes, *Left Bank*—

one block from the Montparnasse Railway Station and just above the subway stop. A total of 1000 smallish bedchambers; plastic galore in the lobby but more warmth upstairs; every convention facility imaginable; other features which make it a larger-than-usual but otherwise typical Sheraton installation. Surprisingly for such a vast hostelry, the service is good. General Manager Raymond Marcelin runs the show.

Madeleine-Palace (8 rue Cambon) has been zestlessly restyled. Total of 116 accommodations and no baths or showers; we saw soiled carpeting throughout; package trippers galore; adjoining King Charles Restaurant, in attractive burnt-orange and panels. A mixed bag. The recently expanded **Madeleine-Plaza**, directly on the place de la Madeleine, has pea-pod rooms that glisten; top floor the most tranquil in this traffic-choked zone; 18 newer units perhaps a few centimeters more spacious. Especially warm greeting for *Guide*-toting wanderers. The **St. James et d'Albany** is no longer recommended by us. The **Hôtel de Castille** is creaky but comfy.

Claridge, smack on the Champs-Élysées, seemed to us to be drawing some pretty unsavory traffic on out latest reinspection. Not our cup of bubbly. The **Terminus St.-Lazare-Concorde** should, in our opinion, bring blushes to the cheeks of the otherwise discerning Concorde chain executives whose showcase is the splendid Crillon. This grandpop's-era railway-terminus-style lodging operation, fairly crawling with flockers from other lands during our recent scrutiny, might be viewed as a gimmicked-up Hotel Grand which, as has been intimated, we regard with all the affection we would give a giant bus station. The **Ambassador**, which shoots for the same patronage, offers some bedchambers as grim as a Wagnerian stage, many furnishings as Old-Fashioned as muddled sugar, lemon peel, whisky, and Angostura, plus service either indifferent (especially from the concierge) or dum-dum (from the receptionist); horrid cuisine; cleaned up somewhat on our latest visit; but for its address and highish tabs, we still consider this one an unworthy plenipotentiary. The venerable **California**, opposite the *International Herald Tribune* building, is still Franco-American-commercial in tone. While we are warmly nostalgic about the Eric Hawkins' Corner in its Golden Gate Bar (he was the *Trib*'s late, great Editor Emeritus), and while the restaurant was recently improved in a bright but not exciting way, to us the rest continues to leave much too much to be desired.

We remain fond of the **Scandinavia** (27 rue Tournon, 2 blocks from the Sorbonne), a historic inn built during the reign of Louis XIII, which features authentic period furnishings and paintings; no elevator; 22 petite rooms and baths with beamed ceilings, velvet curtains, wall-to-wall carpets, elfin beds, and bits of medieval lore; gracious minions, headed by English-speaking Directress Collette Thibault. But—and this is an important "but"—no restaurant, no bar service, no alcohol sold on the premises; breakfast only. They've built a snack bar next door, however. So small and so popular that reservations *must* be nailed down in advance. **Hôtel de l'Université**, near St.-Germain-des-Prés, is a newcomer with flair. Only 27 small rooms in an old house converted by Mr. and Mrs. Bergmann. Handsome wrought iron staircase; twelfth-century bar; twentieth-century Club 22 for snacks; wooden beams, vaults, marble, textiles, and stucco blending into a tasteful composite in which no 2 units are the same. Simple furnishings; reasonable prices that vary with the particular accommodation; again, no restaurant. Another Left Banker that we feel is worth the investment. The **Cécilia**, where the kindly manager and wife are putting lots of heart into remodeling, is a friendly but unostentatious port for voyaging families. Exceptionally good for wayfarers who seek a sympathetic house without fancy frills. The **Bradford**, a 5-minute hike from the Champs-Élysées in a quiet backwater, has taken such a dive of late, in our opinion, that it is no longer a worthy choice. Sorry to see it sinking. **Scribe,** the traditional transient newspaperman's hangout, is ideal in the Circulation Department, but 2nd-rate in Layout and Makeup. About 15% of units and baths recently reset, but still a tabloid, in our judgment.

Vendôme, boasting a situation similar to the Ritz, has been moving ahead manfully. Empire décor plus brass bedsteads; oldish corridors; ample space provided; smilingly helpful staff. We like its slipper-style comfort. The **Madison**, opposite the St.-Germain-des-Prés church, is tops in its vicinity. Fresh lobby; 12 bedchambers revamped each year; front units nicest and largest; okay at best. As for the **Burgundy**, we've received so many reports of dregs in the bottle that we are putting this one on the shelf for a season or so. The **Grand Hotel des Principautes Unies,** facing a half-razed edifice on the Luxembourg Gardens, is far more ingratiating once you are inside. No restaurant but 27 fresh-faced accommodations. Substantial for the outlay.

One of the top bets in the lower priced category is **Régence-Étoile,** so close to the Arc de Triomphe that you'll feel monumentally Gallic. Tiny cubicles that experience merely a nodding acquaintance with the housekeeper, we would guess; 18 cozy-corner bathrooms; breakfast only. A good buy by Parisian standards. **Édouard VII**, next to Brentano's on avenue de l'Opéra, has 90 old but adequate rooms, 80 baths, steel beds, an abundance of stained-glass windows in the upstairs halls, and a bustling impersonal mien; not special. **Louvois**, 5 minutes from the Opéra, is about the same. **Royal St.-Honoré, Harvey,** and **Bellman** fall into the routine bracket. Good staffs in all. **Lutetia,** one of the few big hotels on the Left Bank, is favored by French senators from the provinces. Some love it, while others don't appreciate its dated mien. The **Saint-Simon**, also on this *rive,* is chiefly for tranquillity seekers; family-run pension atmosphere in which no meals are served; no concierge; no elevator; small cellar bar; pleasant for that specialized client who seeks its milieu. **Grand Hôtel du Mont-Blanc**, near Notre-Dame, seems haphazard and far from Grand; not our pony of Pernod. **Astor** (breakfast only) and **Mapotel Pont Royal** are average. The latter is enhanced by Les Antiquaires restaurant. The **Montalembert**, its neighbor, is similar in price but better in *quid pro quo.* Its 60 units with bath or shower recently were refashioned with verve. Much improved and well managed today. **Cayré** is coming up, too. Now okay for the outlay. **Richmond**, in the 9th arrondissement, is for shelter-seekers only. **Vermont** is even more simple, with no lobby or lounge, meager plumbing facilities, and small sleeping cells. For unfinicky pilgrims only. In the same category and equally inhabitable are the finely honed 23-room-and-bath **Masséna**, the cozy **Tronchet** with 2 atelier units under the eaves, and the patio-sweet **Régent's Garden Hotel**; each has distinctive color and charm as well as its particular drawback, but in all 3 your happiness depends on which bedroom you draw. The **Régina** is old, comfy, and clean; another candidate for wanderers with large broods. **Pavillon Henry IV**, at St.-Germain-en-Laye (closed Dec. through Feb.) is suburban and lovely for a rest. Nearby there's the **Cazaudehore**, a 24-chamber, charming hostelry which forms a part of the country estate; comfort is princely in La Forestiere segment; the expensive cuisine is superb in the dining portion. Warmly recommended.

At *Versailles,* the beautiful, period-piece **Trianon Palace,** with its classic décor, is not as august as it was. Only 10 rooms renewed recently (and gracefully), with hopes to tackle the remaining 90 soon; 68 baths; much scruffiness visible on this look; savory cuisine and elegant presentation, but, to us at least, bumptious, inept service. For its highborn tariffs, no longer the aristocrat of yore—at least in our opinion.

Student digs? Drop a line to **l'Office du Tourisme Universitaire**, 137 boulevard St.-Michel, and it will send you a list of moderately priced shelters. The **French Cultural Services**, 972 Fifth Ave., New York, N.Y. 10021, which offers a free booklet on summer schools, might also be helpful.

Naturally, there are hundreds more—far too many to attempt to list in this type of book. The ones we've selected, however, are either the best known or the cream of their categories—a wide-ranging cross section.

Dedicated budgeteers? Since we're too bottlenecked here for additional entries, please consult our annually revised paperback, *Fielding's Low-Cost Europe,* which lists scads more bargain hotels or pensions and money-saving tips for economizers.

Airport lodgings? Aside from those abuilding at Orly, there are 4 major choices. We rate one excellent. The **Orly Hilton** is 20 to 30 minutes from the heart of the city (take a bus to economize), directly across the street from the main terminal building. Modern sawtooth exterior with double windows, soundproofed ceilings and walls, and 100% air conditioning that will never fret the Jet Set; 120-unit wing where the Queen-size beds are especially targeted for singles or lovers; totally refurbished lobby; long, wide corridors opening onto 2 lounges, a beauty parlor and barbershop, plus other commercial niches; cunning series of vitrine-like ponds and gardens leading to a separate fuselage containing (1) Le Coffee Shop (gay stripe-and-mural décor; excellent sandwiches and light dishes at reasonable tabs; open 6:30 A.M. to 11 P.M. daily), (2) L'Atelier Bar (also colorful in an abstract fashion; 12-seat counter; tiny dance floor), and (3) La Louisiane Restaurant (service now smooth and cordial); management by Jean Claude Noel. Mostly conventional twins among the 268 rooms in the original structure; some Deluxe corner locations excellent; studio configurations are smallest and poorest; all baths typically Pinchpenny Hiltonian; adequate living room but pipsqueak luggage space for overseas migrators; up-to-the-minute electro-nic-knacks from 3-channel radio, to piped music, to the Almighty TV. Free hotel-terminal shuttle service is offered. Staff now smiling, eager, and helpful (especially the doormen, shuttle drivers, and floor personnel). Service glitches were manifest in abundance during our very recent overnight; we hope that these inconveniences will be remedied under the direction of Manager Noel.

The 3-star, 600-unit **Bagnolet,** a Novotel enterprise, is operative overlooking the freeway at a median point between the city and Orly Airport, an $8 to $9 taxi ride or 15 minutes by the Métro to the hub of the urban action. Its high-rise neighborhood is unattractive; bleak, stark efficiency is its bag; tolerable but certainly not happy-making for the pilgrim who seeks a money-saving place of repose. The **Orly P.L.M.**, the airess of its landed big-city sister, makes few pretensions toward luxury. Efficiency and commerce are its prime motivations.

The **Airhôtel** draws our top scallions. We wouldn't sleep here on a bet. The **Frantel**, looking through lozenge-shape windows upon a roadside heath, is for the fogbound only, in our view. We list it here merely as a convenience, not as a recommendation. **Holiday Inn**-vaded the nearby industrial suburb of Rungis with 180 chambers. (This will add to H-I plans for another 90-room unit at Porte de Versailles and still another H-I newcomer out at Roissy's Charles de Gaulle Airport.)

Speaking of Roissy, the **Jacques Borel** offers 352 soundproofed kips which, in our opinion, are nothing more than in-transit overnighters. Rooms we inspected were agonizingly cramped for anyone with ambitions to stretch out after a transatlantic flight. Unless you simply *must* bunk out here, we'd advise you to skip right off to the City of Light. On the 9th floor, incidentally, you'll find the viewful Les Valois restaurant.

Selections in the Provinces are as follows (also please see the separate regional subsections at the end of this chapter):

Aix-en-Provence: (1) **Cézanne** (tucked into a quiet nook of the mid-city district; lovely paintings in lobby; intimate in concept and not many accommodations, so be sure to book in advance), (2) **Hôtel du Roy René** (good physical plant; grand in approach, but a bit frayed in presentation; nice staff if you drive, empty your car of all valuables for the night if it is parked out front), (3) **Riviera "Le Pigonnet"**.

Aix-les-Bains: (1) **Splendide et Royal** (unchallenged leader), (2) **Astoria**, (3) **Albion**. All summer season only.

Amiens: (1) **Grand**, (2) **Nord-Sud**, (3) **Univers** (no restaurant), (4) **Carlton-Belfort**.

Albi: **Hostellerie Saint-Antoine** was our pick of the modest in-town selection. Out of the city, the same administration runs the rustically posh **La Reserve**, which is a polished Tarnside gem.

Antibes, *Nice*, *Cannes*, etc.: See section on "The Riviera."

Arles: All disappointing. **Jules César** best of inferior lot but cuisine good. A friendly Los Alamos couple recommend a "blissfully quiet gem" called the **Select** (35 blvd. G. Clemenceau). We'll be anxious to sample their generous —and probably select—suggestion.

Asnières-sur-Nouère: **Moulin du Maine Brun** (a quiet hideaway crooked into "the elbow of Cognac").

Auch: **Hotel de France** (between Folix and Biarritz in Gascogne).

Avallon: (1) **Poste** (famous provincial inn with 24 rooms and 20 baths; Napoleon snoozed alone in #3—a single with w.c.; glorious comforts in #6, a canopy-bed double; magnificent and costly cuisine; attractive décor; reception much improved on our recent hitching-Poste; compulsory charges on facilities which are normally optional; closed Dec. to mid-Feb.), (2) **Chapeau Rouge** (routine).

Avignon: (1) **Le Prieuré** (formerly a small rural gem, at Villeneuve-les-Avignon, which may be beginning to slip, according to very recent reader letters; closed Dec. to mid-Feb.), (2) **Europe** (in town; reports of lumpy mattresses on some beds; recommendable kitchen, with an A-plus rating for the roast lamb).

Avranches: See "Normandy Beachheads."

Barbizon: **Bas-Bréau** (expensive, homey, woodland stop only 45 minutes from the capital).

Bayeux: **Lion d'Or** (small, quiet, amiable; extensive renovations and additions completed; ably but modestly run by Manager Jouvin-Bessiere; no reservations held after 8 P.M.; closed Dec. 21 to Jan. 11).

Beaune: **de la Poste** (Chevillot management; superior restaurant specializing in Jambon de Dijon Burgundy with green herbs).

Belfort: **Hostellerie du Château** (plush period furnishings; delicious food.)

Biarritz: (1) **Palais** (municipal ownership; 200 bedrooms, stunning swimming pool with chic cabanas, all luxuries; sumptuous and lethally expensive), (2) **Miramar** (slightly larger, with 250 accommodations, this Bermond Group house still has a big name and is excellent), (3) **Régina et Golf** (between golf course and sea; closed Oct. through May; good), (4) **Plaza** (midtown situation; the only major hostelry open all year; 20% of its small but comfortable units redecorated each season, on a continuing cycle; not dazzling; kind and efficient administration), (5) **El Mirador** (1st floor renewed; sweeping sea vistas from front windows; Coq Hardi restaurant at ground level), (6) **Marbella** (modest and reasonable). For student digs, tops is the **Beaulieu**, followed by the **Belvédère**. Still cheaper and offering sweet sheltering arms are the pension-style **Central, Monguillot,** and **Washington**. The teenie-tiny **Patio**, open year round, is another cheerful bet for budgeteers. Most of the aforementioned are open in summer only; most insist upon full pension.

Bordeaux: (1) **Normandie** (no dining room), (2) **Splendid** (pleasant dining salon and public rooms; yokelesque cellar nightclub; gray-dismal but physically comfortable accommodations), (3) **Grand** (100 units; many recent refreshenings; so-so), (4) **Royal Gascogne** (colorful bedchambers; attractive Old World scheme gone somewhat to seed; only fair), (5) **Terminus,** and (6) **Montré**. **Chapon Fin** is a passable economy stop.

Brest: (1) **Continental,** (2) **Moderne** (no restaurant). Both for the birds.

Caen: See "Normandy Beachheads."

Cahors: **Le Château de Mercuès** (5 miles from the center on a hilltop in the Lot Valley; Deluxe amenities; excellent cuisine; one of the true beauty spots of *La Belle France;* seasonal so check first and book in advance; be certain to drive over to the wonderful prehistoric caves of **Pech-Merle** near **Cabrerets** which will surely be one of the cultural highlights of your visit to Europe).

Calais: (1) **Meurice** (good kitchen, but rooms basic), (2) **Sauvage** (also basic). Skip the rest.

Carcassonne: (1) **Cité** (interestingly situated in the medieval Old City,

high above the "new"; veteran traveler Robert M. Hodes, Vice-President of
Edgar Rice Burroughs, Inc., recently chided us on our previous criticisms of
this house—it has been closed during our last several visits—commenting,
"We were treated to perhaps the finest service during this entire 6-week trip";
open Apr. to Sept. only; the leader), (2) **Terminus** (antebellum and clean;
when we saw the 4′ 11″, 75-lb. maid who had been sent out to wrassle our 2
king-size suitcases, we lugged them up ourselves; passable but not distinguished), (3) **Central** (some urgently needed updatings; still poor. The food?
Urp, gag, ugh! We suffered 3 days from 1 meal). Finesse the rest.

   Chamonix: (1) **Croix Blanche** (midvillage situation that can be noisy;
main dining room with copper-and-iron hood drawing sparks up the chimney;
"modern" rooms with beds lower than your ski bottoms; "traditional" accommodations better; all units with baths; 4-season operation; nice staff;
recommended), (2) **Mont-Blanc** (charming split-level round-the-hearth dining room; gardenside terrace bar; tennis court; pine-lined bedchambers; attentive direction by kindly, ever-helpful M. Morand; a favorite with Americans,
with good reason), (3) **Carlton** (big and old-fashioned; superior personnel;
substandard furnishings and comforts), (4) **Bellevue** on the main drag; woody
atmosphere; smoothly operated; a charmer for the price), (5) **La Sapinière**,
(6) **Les Charmoz**, (7) **Des Alpes** (every room with private bath, but most with
shabby carpets and furniture). Down the line in attractiveness come **Albert
et Milan** and **Hermitage-Paccard**. **Au Bon Coin** is a dainty little corner with
lots of heart plus soothing tabs. If none of these suits your taste, there are
approximately 100 others on the immediate and nearby slopes. All of these
will probably be welcoming guests when you arrive.

   Chateaulin (near Port-Launay): **Au Bon Accueil** (chiefly for its table
salmon and its salmon-fishermen clientele).

   Cherbourg: (1) **Sofitel** (from what we know of miserable existing competition and of the Sofitel in Strasbourg, this *has* to be the leading light, even
though we have not seen it. Total of 80 rooms, all with bath or shower, radio,
and available TV; beach-and-harbor-view dining room; bar; parking area;
handy to the car-ferry dock; a modern Messianic miracle for this port). Then
(2) **Moderne et Terminus**, (3) **Louvre et Marine**, and (4) **Grand** (no restaurant)—all beyond our pale.

   Courchevel: (1) **Pralong 2000** (as the name suggests, it's as modern as
the day after tomorrow), (2) **Carlina** (pick of the older snow crop; several
slalom-pikes ahead of any contenders from yesteryear), (3) **Le Lana** and (4)
Grand (both similar prices but lower quality).

   Deauville: (1) **Normandy** is one of France's finest. Fronted by tennis
courts and sea; Grand Siècle architecture, partially modernized; some rooms
in exquisite taste; the only hotel we've visited where the liners in the wastebas-
kets matched the curtains, chair fabrics, and wallpaper. Young, alert M.
Crauffron will receive you gracefully and see to any needs, whims, or comforts. Stratospheric rates; open all year; terrific for a weekend, even with your
own wife. (2) **Royal** is also excellent. (3) **Golf** has a 1st-rate view and extra-
good cuisine; popular with golfers and the older generation. (4) **Arcades** and
(5) **La Fresnaye** (seasonal). **Castel Normand** was shuttered during our Off
Season round.

Dieppe : (1) **Univers** (Palm Sun. through Nov.), (2) **Aguado** (closed Feb.). We haven't seen the 52-room **La Présidence**, but it could well be the hottest contender on the Dieppe doorstieppe today; we hope you like it on your next trieppe.

Digne : **Ermitage Napoléon** (now slipping; no dining room; smallest brother of Les Grands Hôtels Européens organization). The 50-room **Paris** is reported to be modest but adequate; they say its fish-specialty restaurant is its strongest point.

Dijon : Not so hot. Try (1) **La Cloche**, (2) **Chapeau Rouge** (fine table), (3) **Central**, (4) **Ducs de Bourgogne**. If you like red and white running wine in your room, M. Victor Maillard's unique innovation at the **Terminus** should intrigue you. Heading north (10 miles) toward Paris, **Hostellerie Val-Suzon**, at ***Val-Suzon***, might be a worthy alternative. We detect good vibrations on this one.

Divonne-les-Bains : Although French, this resort suburb of Geneva (only 20 minutes out) is so closely linked to its Swiss hub that we've given it full coverage under "Switzerland."

Dunkerque : **Victoria** is *it;* not advised if avoidable.

Évian-les-Bains : (1) **La Verniaz et ses Chalets**, (2) **Royal**, (3) **Splendide**, and (4) **Ermitage**. Three-month season.

Fère-en-Tardenois : **Hostellerie du Château** (about 1½ hours from Paris and well worth the jaunt).

Grenoble : (1) **Park** (automatic temperature controls, automatic elevators, bathroom telephones, and stocked electric refrigerators in all rooms), (2) **Alpotel** (in the same administrative range as the Park), (3) **Terminus** (no restaurant), (4) **Trois Dauphins**, (5) **Savoie**. All except Park and Alpes (and perhaps Trois Dauphins) uninvitingly commercial; about 40 other ho-hum hostelries to choose from. About 4 miles out, the **Rostang** provides 4-star comfort and a delightful table which is warmly recommended to us by best-selling author-gourmet Paul Gallico. We can't wait to try it, Paul.

La Baule : (1) **Hermitage**, by all means (vast 300-room modernization program lately completed; 1st-rank management by Gérard Mauger, ably assisted by his lovely wife, both formerly of the famous Château d'Artigny at Montbazon). Then, (2) **Marie-Louise** (guests may take some meals at the Hermitage), and (3) **Royal**. This top triumvirate is owned by the same company; all face the sea; all are comfortable. Next come (4) **Cecil**, (5) **Pléiades** (attractivelyrenewed),(6)**Hélios** (not as stylish, but better food). **Bretagne**, with its downstairs dining room, down-in-the-mouth aspect, and 1850 sanitarium atmosphere, has the best name for a winter stop. We much prefer to overnight in the modest but cozy **Auberge de la Chaumière**, with its park setting; 10 minutes from the sea. **Concorde** and **Beau Rivage** are basic; best for freshmen on senior allowance. In nearby ***Pornichet***, the 35-room, garden-bound **Fleur de Thé** is said to be a particularly pleasant Teahouse of the August Moon; we haven't sipped its savor, but it sounds salubrious. Farther up the estuary, at ***St. Nazaire***, Le Bretagne offers simple but clean shelter for one-night wayfarers; definitely not for lingering.

La Muse (Aveyron) : **Grand Hotel du Rozier et de la Muse** (hook a trout from the River Tarn and bask in the sweet lack of pollution).

Le Havre: Passable but not more. (1) **Normandie** is the choice; 2nd-line. (2) **Celtic** and (3) **États-Unis** have no restaurants and are rugged. We gather from favorable reader reports that **Grand Hôtel de Bordeaux,** with no restaurant, may be worth trying, but we don't know it personally.

Le Touquet-Paris-Plage: (1) **Westminster** (big, classic French resort style), (2) **Mer**, (3) **Le Centre**, (4) **Bristol**, (5) **Alexandra**. All seasonal only.

Les Baux: The word "sensational" has been grossly overabused by Broadway and Hollywood—but when applied to **Baumanière** the fit is such perfection that we are impelled to use it. For affluent motorists who seek the cream-of-the-cream on the Paris–Riviera run, this relatively small, elegant, high-price oasis is indisputably one of the world's Better Mousetraps. It crowns a rugged, rock-tortured valley less than 2 hours northwest of Marseille. We rate it as 1 of our 2 top dining choices of France. On an unforgettable incognito visit we had Foie Gras Maison, Gigot d'Agneau en Croûte, Banon (a local cheese similar to Stilton), and a bottle of Romanée Conti '45. It was the happiest investment of that entire tour. (Such a repast today would cost perhaps $35 per person, without figuring in the wine.) Recently we pushed away from another such feast, and it remains the same superlative treat at approximately the same tariff. Gastronomic heaven! Patio service in season, with a lovely sweep of the valley; *cave* of 25-thousand bottles; friendly country staff, tennis club, swimming pool, and horseback riding. The main building has 10 charming regional-style rooms; there's an adjoining annex with a few more, as well as the Cabro d'Or project ½-mile down the slope, with its own dining room and extra-tranquil privacy. Accommodations in the former cost almost double the tariffs of the latter; they're worth it to the well-heeled pilgrim. Our cheers and our bows to M. Thuilier and his extraordinary—yes, "sensational!"—creation.

Lille: (1) The air-conditioned, romantically situated, air-minded, **Novotel** at—wh-air else?—the airport. (2) The traditional **Royal**. (3) The **Carlton**, which barely makes the Junior Varsity.

Limoges: The First-class **Royal-Limousin** boasts its Le Renoir restaurant and 76 well-equipped bedchambers. The hands-down champ for miles around.

Loué: Ricordeau (see "Normandy Beachheads").

Lourdes: See section on "Lourdes."

Lyon: The **Sofitel** unwrapped 200 bedrooms, a panoramic restaurant, and 2 bars which we've sampled and thoroughly enjoyed. Director Pierre Denis is doing a splendid job with this twentieth-century plant. The **Royal**, a giant step down the ladder, would normally come next. However, a Houston reader who spent one "agonizing" night on the floor here (she preferred it to her bed) opines that we are *still* not emphatic enough about the size of that step. PS: She also avows that the check-out time on her visit was 8:30 A.M.! After these, there are the **Grand Hôtel et Nouvel** (with the only hotel brochure we've ever seen featuring a color photograph of the furnace room; central heating *ça va sans dire!*) and the **Beaux-Arts** (no restaurant). The business-oriented **Terminus** is in the P.L.M. chain. Fair. In the **Carlton** we were ruthlessly cheated by 2 sharpies behind the bar and later given a padded bill by the room clerk; a steaming report from a similarly bilked reader came in later. The **Eurotel** interests have announced the launching of a 369-room house with a viewful restaurant and a 300-car garage sometime very soon. One rave report flashed in from a Portland Guidester who was enraptured by the fresh, 60-room, air-conditioned **Le Roosevelt**. He describes 4 styles of interior décor, a fine grill, medium rates, and superlative charm as well as luxurious comfort; another missive from a Golden Gater found it very disappointing. Now *we* are the eager Beavers who want to try it! For outskirters **La Réserve** at nearby **Lissieu** looks dreamy as a manse-in-the-meadow; reportedly**** service and all the accouterments of God's Little Acre. Another on our list.

Mâcon: **Frantel** (by the Saône; first of a new chain reaction).

Marseille: The newish **Concorde Prado** (now the local pacesetter), (2) **Grand Hôtel et Noailles** (try to stay in the original Grand Hôtel section), (3) **Splendide** (pick a back nest for quieter snoozing), (4) **Terminus** (private sancta better than public rooms), (5) **L'Arbois**, (6) **Beauvau**, (7) **Genève** (may be improved since our last peek). (8) **Astoria**, (9) **Rome et St.-Pierre**, (10) **Victoria**, (11) **Sélect**, (12) **St.-Georges**, (13) **Paris-Nice**, and (14) **Castellane** (perhaps a lucky number for thrifty but tiny voyagers). For the moment, the **Bristol** is not recommended. Otherwise, this port traditionally has offered such limited comfort in lodgings that well-heeled U.S. motorists heretofore have found infinitely greater pleasure in pushing along to wonderful Baumanière at Les Baux (see above) for their overnight stay.

Megève: Choice of more than 100 establishments with over 2000 accommodations from Christmas to Easter and July through August. (1) **Mont d'Arbois** (a few minutes above the town; nearby mountaintop airport for 25-minute flights to Geneva; 18-hole golf course; ski slopes, horseback riding, tennis; thermopane-lined heated pool, overlooking snow-draped peaks, a wonder of modern architecture; gymnasium; sauna and massage; shops; Lorca hairdresser; dining room plus downstairs Rôtisserie Grill and snack center; renovated main building; 96-unit Clubhouse wing offering smaller bedrooms, all with private balcony or terrace; outbuildings including La Taverne Bavaroise, plus 1 individual 13-bedroom chalet with private bar and dining room which remains open even when the hotel is shuttered at slack periods; seasonal and oh-so-lovely), (2) **Duc de Savoie** (newer Deluxe candidate on the same alp as the Mont d'Arbois; more modern in concept than the leading house; 2 pools, sauna, and full resort amenities; service and cuisine still suffering), (3) **Hermitage** (also highborne; small, with wall-to-wall carpets and ceiling-to-floor warmth and charm; 64 units; try for #33, with double exposure and patio; closed May and Nov.), (4) **Mont Blanc** (the heartbeat of midvillage; 2 rollicking horses out front; beaucoup frolicking clients inside; rather expensive for value received), (5) **Mont-Joly** (modernized and expanded; fine perked-up dining room and improved bedchambers; cozy ambiance; seasonal), (6) **Coin du Feu** (same size; no restaurant; very popular; we've never stopped at its hearthside), (7) **Beau Site** (situated below Mont d'Arbois; 30 rooms, extra-savory vittles, low prices; Proprietor Besson exudes kindness; a sweet haven).

Metz: Try the '62-vintage **Carlton**; 45 rooms and baths; quiet setting; reasonable rates; superior to the **Royal**.

Modane: **Hôtel de France**, midway between Turin and Grenoble, is a handy refuge from Alpine storms; 18 rooms, with one bath to each floor.

Montargis : **Auberge des Templiers** (thatched-roof cottage-style dwelling in the tranquil Loiret district).

Mont-de-Marsan (in Landes province): **Le Bois Fleuri** (opened '64; park setting, swimming pool, and tennis; 12 apartments with kitchen and private terrace.

Montpellier : About 3 miles out on avenue de Lodève, **Les Violettes** is reputed to be the pick of the patch. The centrally sited, 116-room **Frantel** is newer, if you prefer being in town.

Mont-St.-Michel : (1) **Du Guesclin** (2) **Mère Poulard**, (3) **Terrasses**. All very simple; seasonal only (April. 1 to end-Oct.); the highest decibel-count in rural France; tourists galore. **Auberge St.-Michel** in **Avranches** (13 miles) is a good alternate.

Mulhouse : Steel yourself for the singular **Parc**, if you must; Basle, Switzerland, offers far better. A **Frantel** should be chuffing near the station; our choochoo hasn't paused here lately.

Nancy : (1) **Grand**, (2) **Theirs**, (3) **Excelsior et d'Angleterre**. All commercial.

Nantes : (1) **Central** (best for comfort; thoroughly redecorated with fresh, gay colors, wall coverings, and furniture; fully carpeted; all rooms with bath or shower—*and* glass-dimpled bathroom doors; inviting Crémaillère restaurant; many improvements), (2) **Duchesse Anne** (opposite the château and best for situation), (3) **France et Voyageurs** (poorer location; improving amenities).

Narbonne : Skip it if you can—but if stuck, you'll probably be happiest in **La Résidence**; **Languedoc** and **La Dorade** are routine. Many are seasonal.

Nîmes : (1) **Impérator** is good, and (2) **Cheval Blanc et Arènes** is fair.

Orléans : After (1) **Ste. Catherine** (run-of-the-grist), plus (2) **Arcades** and (3) **Les Cèdres** (both small, unimpressive, and without restaurants), just spin the wheel. No winners here!

Perpignan : Pretty dreary. If you must halt, we'd pick them this way: (1) **De France** (on the main drag; enclosed, sidewalk-sited L'Échanson; cheery, solid qualities in many of the bedchambers), (2) **Grand** (higher category, higher tariffs, but lower charm level, in our opinion), (3) **Catalogne** (under the Grand sway; the only air-conditioned hostelry in the city), (4) **Park**, and (5) **Windsor**. If you are heading toward Barcelona (NB: the Spanish frontier closes at midnight in winter), there are many new candidates by the seaside. None will wow you, but you might prefer one of those, at vastly lower tariffs, to this Hicksville, France.

Pessac-l'Aloutte : **La Reserve** (one of the more rewarding residential pauses in the Bordeaux region).

Pléven : If you do not share our rejection of administrative haughtiness, you might deign to sample the enchanting fifteenth-century **Manoir du Vaumadeuc**. Madame de Pontbriand, its manorly innkeeper, is selective in her clientele and somewhat chary about Americans, in general. Many discriminating French friends praise its voluminous physical charms and superior cuisine, but our discriminations run another course. Sorry, but this one's on you.

Poitiers : The **France** is the pick of the patch.

Reims: Squalid for a city its size and for the marketplace of the luxury champagne commerce. (1) **De La Paix** (you won't write home about its illustriousness), (2) **Le Bristol** (satisfactory *if* you draw one of its colorful rooms; clean and reasonably priced; nice people; no dining salon), (3) **Grand Hôtel du Nord** (so designed that some of the shower stalls are smack by your pillow), (4) **Continental** (enough globes in its restaurant to recall the I-told-you-so Shade of Edward II; otherwise cold and Shade-less). Before spending a night in almost any of these 2nd-run houses, guzzle a gallon of the local bubbly to temper the temples. The 2-story, chilly **Novotel** (2½ miles out) is motelish in feeling. All 125 units set up for 3 people; coin-operated photostat machine in the lobby (why?); shopping center across the pike; grill room surrounding the bar; an air of boredom surrounding everything else. We're told the **Royal Champagne** (20 minutes toward Epernay, at *Champillon*) might be a passable alternate. At nearby *Fère-en-Tardenois*, the **Hostellerie du Château** is a back-country beauty.

Rennes: (1) **Du Guesclin** (good food, simple rooms), (2) **Angelina** (without restaurant).

Rouen: (1) **Poste**, (2) **Astrid**, without restaurant, modest and cheap.

St.-Étienne: (1) **Grand**, (2) **France** (no restaurant), (3) **Cheval Noir**. None inspiring

St.-Jean-de-Luz: (1) **Chantaco** (flamingo-colored estate about 10 minutes out; adjoins marsh and golf course; lovely terrace and Spanish garden; tennis; parking; elegant country hideaway that is better than par; we hope, oh how we hope, that the superhighway almost at its doorstep will not destroy your tranquillity here); (2) **Miramar** (hilltop situation looking to sea and pinewood; Basque furnishings; pleasant; most suitable for older peace-seeking pilgrims; nice staff); (3) **Modern** (big, white, typically French seaside resort hotel; faces water, with many balconies; some halfhearted improvements; decidedly not Modern). In the town, the **Madison** is a small and cozy house smoothly run by M. Robert Pateau and his wife. The once-bubbling **Édouard VII** is no longer 7-Up; it has gone flat. **Les Motels Basques** (rond-point Ste.-Barbe), resembling a Pueblo village that has seen hard times, is passable at best for motorists; we'd prefer to make it firmly passable on our itinerary. The petit **Donibane**, on the outskirts, offers a gleamingly clean but modest hitching post for short-term budgeteers.

St.-Malo: (1) **France et Châteaubriand** (Apr. through Oct. only), (2) **Central** (all year).

St.-Nazaire: Ouch! See *La Baule*—or pause only briefly at **Le Bretagne.**

Strasbourg: (1) **Terminus-Gruber** (colors that will either delight or fell you; each floor in another hue-and-cry scheme; richly attractive Cour de Rosemont dining room, plus a second restaurant with less charm; very good for avant-garde travelers who like those busy-dizzy-busy decorator shades), (2) **Sofitel's St.-Pierre-le-Jeune** (modernistic structure, suggestive of a better-grade Statler; coolish bar and Le Châteaubriand restaurant; indoor-outdoor patio; underground carpark; 180 rooms, all with bath, radio, telephone, and pastel bed linens; pay-as-you-chill air conditioning; pleasant, but you might as well be lodging in any up-to-date hotel anywhere in the world), (3) **Grand** (extensive renovations; new units smaller and more expensive than more comfortable traditional ones; no restaurant; fair value without oomph), (4) **Maison Rouge** (attractive, fresh Le Chambord restaurant for foie gras goose-stuffers; bad case of the creaks), (5) **Monopole-Métropole** (inviting hunting-lodge dining room its most worthy feature; kindly staff; most bedrooms now halfheartedly renovated, but many remain with makeshift baths and shift-less space). About 4 miles out, at the Rhine frontier bridge between France and Germany, the freshly expanded **Motel du Pont de l'Europe** spans a gap with 100 nests; the adjoining Kronenbourg brasserie, however, is not a favorite nibble nook of ours. Perhaps you'll disagree. Finally, the rapidly lengthening **Novotel** chain has forged a 30-room motel with pool at the Colmar Airport.

Toulon: The **Frantel** has replaced the former Tour Blanche; about 10 minutes out, it has a stunning situation. Superior restaurant; Le Surcouf Bar; pool, gardens, most units with balcony and sea view. Other hostelries here are not so hot.

Toulouse: (1) **Les Comtes de Toulouse** (150 rooms with private baths; blue-ribbon quality throughout; superb comfort and among the most courteous service we've ever encountered on an overnight bivouac in the provinces), (2) **Concorde** (100 accommodations; more commercial in feeling, but very good indeed), (3) **Grand Hôtel et Tivollier** (above average), (4) **France** (no restaurant), (5) **Cie Midi**. **Ours Blanc** is small and unpretentious. (How's yours?)

Tours: See "Châteaux Country."

Trouville: (1) **Bellevue** (opposite Casino), (2) **La Résidence** (off the beachfront Promenades des Planches), (3) **La Plage** (faces Casino and best known for its restaurant), (4) **La France** (on blvd. F. Moureaux, overlooking the Touques River), (5) **Chatham** (nearest the beach). None exceptional.

Val-d'Isère: (1) **Solaise** (Alpine garden setting with ski slopes at the back door; 3-story rustic wooden structure; 45 bedrooms and many private balconies; comfort for snow buffs, (2) **Christiania** (50 fresh accommodations; tariffs less than ½ the Solaise tabs; good), (3) **Edelweiss** (superior kitchen, we're told; best for budgeteers). Ski nostalgics will probably Head in a direct downhill traverse to the Kastle of Jean-Claude Killy's father, **La Bergerie**. We've never stemmed the gates here, but it's said to be as delightful and cozy as the inside of a Porsche. Sounds as if it might win a gold medal. Another house that we are anxious to sample is **Le Kern** run by the ever-smiling Michel Jeanbin and his hospitable wife, Yvette, who do it all as a hobby. Their La Grange restaurant already has one of the best reputations in the highlands. It's small, friendly, and simple, according to reliable voyagers who have snoozed here before we could, the lucky ducks.

Varetz: **Château de Castel Novel** is a lovely ancient haven with a new annex overlooking the pool. Nice people and excellent cuisine at satisfying prices. If you're near it, stop here.

Vézelay: **La Poste et le Lion** is a charmer. Then, over at *St.-Père-sous-Vézelay,* **l'Espérance** wins the orchids.

Vichy: Dozens, all loaded with holidaying French families. We haven't taken the waters here lately, but we'd judge they line up this way: (1) **Ambassadeurs** (agreeable atmosphere), (2) **Pavillon Sévigné** (nice setting and gardens), (3) **Queens**, (4) **Albert Ier** (good Le Patio restaurant). All seasonal.

Vittel: The summer-only **Grand** is outstanding, with the **Pavillon Cérès** and **Continental** (both also seasonal) as runners-up.

§TIPS: *Always* check every item on every bill. The chiseling of many French hotels is disgraceful; big fat "mistakes" are as common as dandelions.

Prefer an apartment? The 161 real estaters who formed the **Fédération Nationale des Agents Immobiliers** (163 rue St.-Honoré, Paris 1) are girded to attack all the formalities and then plunk you into a chalet, villa or most any other sort of dwelling you select. Though we have never tried this organization, its reputation for reliability and competence is excellent.

Or a farmhouse? Write to **Gîte de France** which can send you prices, locations, and other particulars on renting an abode in rural Gaul. While we haven't hoed this row, friends who have say it is an enriching, low-cost experience for adventurous types. Address: 34 rue Godot de Mauroy, 75009 Paris.

FOOD Terrific—if you can pay the price. Goodness knows, you'll pay plenty for what you get—but in no other place in the world can you eat as well. And in 1977 there are exhilarating changes in the aromatic wind.

Girth-conscious chefs are now catering to slimmer waistlines among their svelte patronage. The amazing thing is that flavors remain intense or are even purer than in the classic richer preparations. This year every kitchen sorcerer and saucerer's apprentice will be undercooking at least a few showcase dishes and even serving some viands raw, only mellowed in natural impact by marinades. Also for the first time, women are being accorded reluctant honors as master chefs in a country where male chauvinism dominates the professional ovens. Though the hesitant, still-feeble movement has only just begun, it is charged with the sort of controversy one might expect in a land that idolizes its nutrients as much as it prizes its womanhood—and from a population that adores debate on *both* of these topics. Anyway that you toss this spring-green salad, gastronomically speaking, France is more exciting today than it has been in many a year.

Truffles from Périgord, saffron from Langres, foie gras from Strasbourg, small duck foie gras or *confits d'oie* from Quercy, mustard from Dijon, mackerel from Nantes, hams from Bayonne, conserves from Normandy, more than 200 registered cheeses—all are unique. Even flowers are eaten— Tulip Stem Salad in the Eiffel Tower Restaurant (never go tulip picking on a holiday here, because it's a monumental crush!), Lime Blossom Poached Chicken in Lasserre's, Violets Soufflé in the Tour d'Argent, plus acacia-filled fritters and other novelties elsewhere.

To get the menu, ask for the *carte;* "menu" in French generally means the fixed-price meal of the day—not the list of choices to which we are accustomed at home. The *carte* carries all of these clusters of independent dishes, from available appetizers and soups through its desserts ("à la carte").

If a dish is marked "à la Provençale" or "à la Niçoise," garlic and olive oil will raise their lovely, rugged heads.

Hors d'oeuvres are an excellent bet in almost every restaurant.

Never order a sandwich in a top restaurant. If you do, the chef is liable to challenge you to a duel.

Try foie gras with truffles as a first course. Don't confuse it with pâté de foie gras (goose-liver leftovers mixed with pork)—or *any* other commercial pâté. The real stuff, a Rolls-Royce among delicacies, is expensive even in France but shouldn't be missed. Prices, however, may topple before too long. Very recently a way was found to "mass-produce" enlarged livers in these fowl, instead of force-feeding them by hand. A new surgical approach destroys the area in the brain that controls hunger. Thus through auto-ingestion, the goose crams itself cockeyed by overindulging. Pigs were next on the Gallic operating tables. Any bleats from the S.P.C.A.?

Don't touch milk or cream in unsavory places. Quite possibly they might be unpasteurized—and untrustworthy. Even Parisians are wary of microbes lurking in much of their ice cream.

Whenever your tab is stamped "Service Not Included," make sure the waiter hasn't surreptitiously added the service charge anyway. Cafés along the Champs-Élysées are especially villainous in this practice.

You'll ask 6 times for a glass of water before you can sell the idea to the waiter. It upsets his stomach to watch you drink it. As for its purity, a red-hot disagreement flared among Paris hygiene experts—one group claiming categorically that "most of the faucet water in the capital is unfit for human consumption," and the other saying, "Yes, it's bad, but not all *that* bad."

Many diners stick to the bottled variety. Order Évian if you want the noncarbonated type; Perrier is the classic carbonated mixer for your Scotch, because it offers the most bubbles; Vichy, which comes in several types, is equally famous and somewhat less effervescent. According to our French friends, all of these are therapeutic for everything from pinkeye to clubfeet. Tap water is *l'eau naturelle,* and—with Paris a question mark—it is relatively safe in French metropolises.

Because of a different roasting process, most U.S. travelers feel that French coffee should be used for filling O'Cedar bottles. It's bitter, it's different, but the quality, per se, is as fine as you'll find on the shelves of your gourmet foodshop at home. If your Nescafé runs out (it comes caffeine-free too), you can buy a fresh can at almost any French grocer. But if you don't want to bother about instant coffee, refuse the local offering the moment your gullet will no longer contract, and drink tea, as we do.

The French apéritif often has the sweetness of a liqueur or a dessert wine. If you like your drinks dry, be sure to order carefully.

RESTAURANTS   More than 13,000 in **Paris** alone, with a fantastic range of specialties and prices. The smaller places may charge $6 to $10 for a delicious fixed-price meal; the larger ones usually run, on the same arrangement, from $18 to $30 per person; if you order à la carte in the Great Establishments, your dinner might go up even to $50 or $75 without pausing for breath.

As a general rule the capital is far more expensive than the provinces. In Paris, lunchtime customers in the costlier shrines are often businessmen on generous expense accounts; rarely is a woman seen alone. In the country it is still possible to dine well for a reasonable outlay. As a curiosity, you might wish to notice the difference in clientele on your next trip. We'll bet you'll find a difference in the bill, too.

A while back inflation squelchers abolished the automatic cover charge (the price you paid for the privilege of eating with a knife, fork, spoon, and table linen) with triumphant political pomp. It was supposed to be replaced with an overall 10% increase—and that was to be the absolute limit. But this "control" is a sorry travesty, because it can never be enforced in a thousand years.

One way to beat the system—sometimes, at least—is to take advantage of the little-publicized *Restaurants de Tourisme* plan. Government-sponsored and promoted through the National Hotel and Restaurant Association, this setup offers a so-called Tourist Menu in every French establishment you're likely to visit; expansion to other Common Market countries is planned. Thus you may enter nearly any restaurant and be fed a full meal, including wine, service, and taxes, for about $2.50 to $7.50, depending upon the official category of the institution. In theory you won't be given pressed duck and Haut Brion '61 for this investment, but you will get a substantial and savory repast.

In practice, this scheme has 1 big pitfall: When the foreigner innocently orders the $2.50 dinner, he's all too likely to draw the table by the coal chute, the busboy for his waiter, and the Country Cousin treatment from his soup to his toothpicks. Personally, I'd no more stroll into Tour d'Argent, Lasserre, Pyramide, or a similar gastronomic shrine and ask for the "Tourist Menu" than I'd make amorous cries to a wild moose—and I hope you wouldn't. The most common ploy everywhere is to present the à la carte menu without comment, thus forcing the client to ask for the blue-plate special. But if your appetite is on the light side, and you exercise discretion in time and place, it *is* an excellent plan, and it *can* save you a hatful of money.

Here's another suggestion: If the restaurant is an elaborate and well-known one, telephone for your own reservation. Somebody is bound to speak English there—and you'll save the kickback your concierge would normally pocket for making the call.

Third, if you're an August visitor in the capital, *check beforehand* to make certain your place is open. Hundreds of establishments shutter during the 31 days of the *congé payé* ("paid vacation") peak.

Finally—and this is IMPORTANT!!!—never, but *never,* get hooked by knavish taxi drivers (of whom there are many), who tell you the gastronomic shrine you have selected is "closed," "under repairs," or any similar guff. Their game is to steer you to an address where they can collect a commission —which almost certainly will be a joint. If you nail down your reservation in advance, then you're on solid ground to insist the hackie take you there and *only* there. This racket is deplorably prevalent in Paris today.

Now—got your bib on? Okay, here we go:

In the *expensive indoor* group, it is our conviction that when everything is normal, the **Tour d'Argent** (15 quai de la Tournelle) cannot be surpassed by any restaurant in the world. Stunningly redecorated; penthouse setting over the Seine; brilliant spotlighted vista of Notre-Dame at 9:30 P.M. every night except Monday (municipally furnished illumination on weekends, but paid for privately by this establishment on other evenings solely for the added pleasure of its clients); predinner cocktails or postmeal cordials in its cozy, gracious, ground-floor Gastronomic Museum by prearrangement only. Because the presence of more than 20 visitors per day now disbalances the temperature of its wine cellars, you must also apply in advance for candlelit samplings in these romantic surroundings—and please don't forget to give a modest gratuity to the Master of the *Cave*. Upstairs a heaven-sent aroma of delicately chafed sauces greets the entering guest. No longer satirically labeled the "duck joint," for although you may still watch your Caneton Tour d'Argent being pressed on an elevated sideboard, the variety of other specialties is now broad enough to stagger a Lucullus. Wear your best duds; reserve in advance; ask for friendly Director of the Table Jean Joulia or Jacques; we much prefer lunch to dinner here, because the pace is more *lento* and the relaxation is better. (For private luncheons of 10 to 50 persons, an enclave of special dining suites has been opened; ask to see its oh-so-tempting menu suggestions.) Because the aforementioned wine cellars are among the greatest in the world, it is correct dining form to disregard water and to order a vintage wine from Sommelier Christian. If you're host, only your menu will carry prices; none appear on those of your guests. Handsome, debonair, razor-sharp Owner-Author Claude Terrail and his entire staff are to be congratulated for reestablishing their Silver Tower as one of the best-run, most satisfactory epicurean centers in business today. Closed Monday.

Lasserre (17 avenue Franklin-D.-Roosevelt) also has been one of our tip-tip-tip-of-the-top Parisian candidates since '59. For more than a decade we have walked in cold annually, always to find a reception which couldn't have been warmer, service which couldn't have been smoother, and cuisine so delicious that our taste buds stood up and sang the "Marseillaise." Sumptuous décor, brightened by flowers, greens, and the Maestro's proudest toy—a sliding roof which opens at the touch of a button to admit sunlight or moonbeams; gold-rimmed service plates, silver-necked carafes, antique silver vases, the finest of appointments; chic, sleek international clientele; outstanding original specialties, including Steak Dumas avec Moelle (a garnish of delicate sauce and marrow) and a dessert (which shouldn't be missed) called Pannequet Soufflé Flambé; occasional raffles in which live doves carry the lucky numbers. How this group continues to outdo themselves from one year to the next is a mystery to us. The great Maestro himself, ever-gracious Maître Pierre (whose English is probably better than mine), and their ever-suave minions take pride in wrapping their clients in warmed, fluffy cotton. Please attempt no reservations by mail, because these people aren't set up to cope with their tidal wave of desired advance bookings through correspondence; make them instead by telephone instantly after your arrival on French soil. Closed Sundays and the last 3 weeks of August; always nail down your table ahead of time.

Maxim's ? With the increased diversification of Owner Louis Vaudable's interests, this once most-glamorous restaurant in the world seemed to us to fall apart at the seams. Now we have lunched or dined here with sufficient frequency to become positive, in our opinion, that the general quality of its cookery falls lamentably short of its reputation. If you, the client, were permitted to inspect its kitchen (which as a rule is obstinately off limits to strangers), you might wonder, as we do, how these old-fashioned, over-cramped, unattractive premises can possibly produce top epicurean fare. And the prices—wow! Monsieur Vaudable is one of the greatest geniuses in public relations whom we have ever met; on the other hand, we cannot classify him as being even remotely close to one of the greatest gastronomic technicians of our acquaintance. To us, Maxim's remains a glittering showcase of *haute couture* and celebrated countenances (especially on the rue Royale frontage), to which many people go primarily to see or to be seen.

Lucas-Carton (9 place de la Madeleine) embraces the visitor with warm, beautiful, ageless French elegance in food, in spirit, and in ambiance. Nothing has faded from the classic glory of this venerable landmark. Flawlessly maintained décor of dark orange-red banquettes, mirrored walls, sparklingly polished woodwork, and the other ingredients of Gallic tradition; the service, ever-alert (when it is not too crowded), spotlessly clad in well-cut tailcoats (even the young boys); cuisine normally excellent but occasional complaints nowadays are coming to our desk. We recently received an ultra-hot stinger concerning some alleged legerdemain in the handling and billing of an expensive wine. (The reporters are trusted friends and highly intelligent world travelers.) It is ideally situated for well-heeled shoppers in search of an oasis of calm for their lunch. Our bill for 2, including a bottle of fine wine and all tips, nudged $65. Open every day.

Taillevent (15 rue Lamennais) has long, long continued to radiate its glories in the Very Very First Rank of Gallic spiritual and atmospheric gastronomic tradition. Fantastic *cave;* the wine list carries a staggering 502 choices, with 145-thousand bottles to back it up. If you happen to be in town around wine-tasting time (mid-Mar.), try to attend the formal *La Paulée*—a sampling of several dozen new wines; the restaurant closes except to those who wish to engage in this special sport (just ask André Vrinat, who is a Director of France's venerable Academy of Wines); dinner and the deluge of beverages for about $30; a heavenly skylark for anyone. Excellent kitchen; friendly reception; convenient location near Champs-Élysées; high tariffs; closed Sunday; *always* phone beforehand for your table. And, if you can, book here at night, since the Vrinat masters bleed that their high-powered business-executive clients at lunch do not have the time to be served with the attention they so winningly lavish on each guest. Hallelujah!

Concerning the equally noble **Vivarois** (Avenue Victor-Hugo 192), may we be forgiven if we expose, with not the slightest presumption intended, a small ray of pride? When this venture was in its swaddling clothes in 1968, the kind readers who accepted our wildly enthusiastic evaluation from then until 1973 helped it over its rough introductory bumps, when so many French gourmets refused to take it seriously because of their dislike of its nontraditional, clean-lined, modern décor. But 5 seasons back, *Michelin* and *Kléber* both raised it to the top of their respective national categories. Its working proprietors are M. and Mme. Claude Peyrot; even in his relative youth (well, under 40) he is a virtuoso, a Grand Master of gastronomic genius. (In all of our experience of sitting behind napkins or talking with chefs, we have met only

5 others who even began to approach the art of *haute cuisine* with the same total dedication as M. Peyrot. Here is a very, very special man in this era.) Pastel-yellow or sage clothed tables too close together; charcoal-hued banquettes; white Knoll chairs with cushions; 2 avant-garde murals woven by Belgian Monk Dom Robert; beautiful, gleaming, superefficient kitchen. In honor of his years as a pupil at the fabulous Pyramide in Vienne, M. Peyrot now offers Dodine de Canard Truffé à la Façon de Fernand Point—and DO we recommend this to all comers!!! His feather-light Sole Soufflé with Lobster Sauce and his Tarte Tatin are additional never-to-be-forgotten taste treats. Once our party was extraordinarily fortunate to strike his Le Loup Farci de Quelle du Brochet as the *plat du jour* during our visit; this marvelous epicurean adventure may be special-ordered a day or so in advance. Charming Mme. Peyrot has a fair command of English. They are closed Sunday night, all Monday, and normally from July 15 to September 10. We are ever-grateful to our cherished friend Georges Prade, the world-famous epicure and connoisseur, for steering us here. Always reserve in advance, because the same local gastronomes who used to sniff superciliously at it are now phoning up to 2 weeks ahead for space—and *don't miss it!*

Lamazère (23 rue de Ponthieu, also close to the Champs-Elysées), a *grand luxe* contender, has entered the scene as what is possibly the most expensive dining establishment in the city today. Owner Lamazère is in love with truffles, foie gras, and cassoulets. So are jillions of others, including us—but, during his 14-year proprietorship of the Proust, his amour extended to experimentation in new blends of these delights. While at least 50 other dishes are always on his card, these are the highest triumphs of his extremely high cuisine. A recent move to encourage late dining seems to be of little interest to the cassoulet, foie gras, and truffle traffic. We found the décor pretentious, the attention urbane, the tariffs astronomical, and the quality aristocratic.

Ledoyen (Carré des Champs-Élysées) occupies a position in the circle of blue bloods, though we personally feel that it may be slipping somewhat. Marvelous park setting (convenient for motorists) and handsome entrance; enclosed terrace dining room banked in rose velvet, with rose-velvet upholstered ceiling beams and star-spangled draped chiffon; large plate-glass windows; sumptuous brocaded sink-in armchairs; low candelabra; ruffled lace mantles over sateen tablecloths; antique silver tureens for flowers; gold service; soft piano lilts filtering through chiffon and chandeliers. In the private-party sections, entire walls (lighting sconces and all) vanish in a hush when more space is needed. A bit precious, extraordinarily chic, and decidedly among the exalted addresses in Paris.

Les Belles Gourmandes (5 rue Paul-Louis-Courier) is another example of what France's "new chefs" are up to. It tries to produce a similar tone with its mod-mooded styling and hard-driving attentions by the Fourgeron chef-hostess team. Front room with 14 tables; smaller back nookery for private parties; 4-stool bar; Regency lighting; velvet touch-ups; plum-red ceiling; unattractive brown chairs uncomfortable for most men (bid for a banquette if you're built like Tarzan). Lovely glasses, tableware, and accouterments; ample wine card; cuisine fine, but not as glorious by half as that of Vivarois. Again, reservations are mandatory. Closed Sundays and all of August.

L'Archestrate (84 rue de Varenne) is a recently opened "discovery" from a recent tour of the tables. And is it a honey! A small, attractive chamber is the site in which Proprietor-Chef Alain Senderens stirs the magic of his craft. Ocher-tone textile walls; high-back chairs with ruby and gold stripes; matching curtains and carpet; 2 blue-and-white porcelain chandeliers; baronial atmosphere that is in no way austere; flowers almost wherever the eye turns; ingratiating reception. Our merry-go-round began with the customary house gift of a delicious *pipérade*. The party then launched into cream-bathed snails with herbs (but no garlic), a marvelous raspberry-color Sea Bass in red (sic) wine sauce (Bouzy of the Champagne district), and a platter of oh-so-sinfully delectable hot duck livers topped with marble-size apples. Service uneven; appropriately expensive price tags; a totally enjoyable gustatory experience which we hope to repeat for many visits to come. Closed Sundays and holidays. As the French exclaim—ooo-la-la!

Grand Véfour (17 rue de Beaujolais) is a thing unto itself—and a very expensive thing it is, too. We have the suspicion that self-important, publicity-conscious Owner Raymond Oliver might fancy himself, given the provocation, as Virlogeux' heaven-picked Emissary in mortal guise. We regret that our own tastes differ in this regard. Classic lush décor that is a pinch less than baroque; fine old bas-relief ceilings; interior orientation that might dismay claustrophobes; frequent change of managers. Cookery? Passable but, in our most considered opinion, far below the quality one might expect for such princely prices.

Escargot-Montorgueil (38 rue Montorgueil), owned by the sister of the Tour d'Argent's Claude Terrail, has been a gourmets' favorite for more than 150 years. Serene but not plush atmosphere; good attention, as long as you aren't placed in the inadequately staffed upstairs section. Closed Monday and all of August. Traditionally well regarded.

Les Armes de Bretagne (108 av. du Maine) is in a neighborhood in the throes of urban renewal, but do not let this dissuade you; inside it is elegance itself. Two sectors, one with sidewalk windows, another in an apse with interior orientation; textiled cognac-color walls; polished blackamoor sconces; art deco paintings; malacca chairs; lace curtains. Courageous Chef André Laurier treated us with 2 new-concept creations from his culinary lab; we thoroughly enjoyed the experiments (though we are not sure everyone else will): the first, slivers of raw sea bass marinated in vinaigrette; the second, roast duck in a sauce of pink Chinese peppercorns; both unique taste experiences. We also were grateful for his Terrine de Tourbot à la Mousse de Rascasse—*formidable!* Kindhearted Maître Roland Boyer will lead you amiably through the thickets of the "new" cuisine or consult with you carefully on conventional dishes. An important restaurant for serious gastronomes.

Two excellent women chefs regaled us very recently with masterworks of their respective kitchens. Though they are often the targets of male-chef vilification in the French media, their consummate skill with the skillets will, in our most serious judgment, resist any trivial carping and gender-motivated criticism. Mme. Marie Trama is already bringing fame to her small, rustic, ingratiating **Chez Tante Madée** (11 rue Dupin). Her Oysters Florentine are superb, almost a meal in themselves. Two tiny rooms separated by a rough-timber divider; stone and brick walls; intimate atmosphere that complements the personalized cooking. **Veronique Cuisinière** (9 rue de Pontoise) is perhaps even more attractive to the eye while being a joy to the palate as well. Beige textiled walls; seventeenth-century oil paintings; exquisite furnishings and antiques; pewter fixtures; clay-toned mantles over cream undercloths on tables; fixed-price meal about $20 per person—and an extraordinary one it is, too! Never have we savored better vegetable purées than those from the modest kitchen of talented and attractive Veronique, a protégé, incidentally, of food-purist Michel Guérard. STOP PRESS: We hear, alas, that Veronique may close or change location; please check before starting out. Both excellent; both deserve respect and attention.

Drouant (place Gaillon) splits its personality between a grill (left) and a more formal 2-room dining spread (right). The former harks back to the style of the Twenties; the latter seems a bit stiff with beige marble walls, white linen, and mirrors. The English language, sadly, is not one of its best-selling commodities. We suggest the fish (especially Turbot soufflé) over the meat platters, because our party found all of the hoofware rather plodding. The grill functions daily while the other half relaxes on Saturdays. Okay, but not what it was in former years.

Lapérouse (51 quai des Grands-Augustins—Left Bank) was sold recently and may even be resold by the time you read these words. Like Grand Véfour, this landmark also seems to lean mightily on customer recognition.

Chez Denis (10 rue Gustave Flaubert), despite its earlier publicity, impresses us as losing rather than gaining ground. Somewhat unattractive Pergola interior with floral bowers; capacity of about 30 guests; admirable wine selection which seemed superprohibitively overpriced to us; unusually high number of dishes marked "s.g.," plus other curious billing procedures which can enrich the tab rapidly. (One reader howled—and we concur—over an unexceptional 3-person dinner that he reported rang up $120! And, of course, you've read about *N.Y. Times*man Craig Claiborne's notorious $4000 meal for 2.) Bordeaux-born Patron Denis glides among the diners soft-selling his 18-karat items; if you're not on guard he might sweet-talk you into ransoming a woodcock, a truffle, or a sautéed salamander—in addition to persuading you, in his smooth and personable way, to order his fanciest vintages (Bordeaux, especially).

Nicolas (12 rue de la Fidélité), one of the oldest restaurants in Paris, is owned and operated by our good friend, Julien François, President of France's Restaurateurs, a Commander of the Cordon Bleu, and a Commander of the Legion d'Honneur. As he is the elected spokesman for every dining establishment in the nation, his haven darned well ought to be super—and it is, at astonishingly modest tariffs for such scrumptious fare. Patronage heavily Gallic; always full; smiling invitation to visit the kitchen. The Maestro is ably assisted by his enchanting English-speaking daughter, Mme. Nicole, and her handsome husband, M. Daniel; Maîtres Christian and Maurice also parleyvoo in our parlance. The foie gras is possibly the finest you will ever experience anywhere. (The kitchen prepares about 18 tons of it per year!) Copper-rivet your advance reservations; rare bonus of staying open on Sunday (except in July); closed Saturday instead. To us and to countless other devotees, absolutely unbeatable in its category.

Le Train Bleu, which began life as Le Buffet in 1901, recently changed its name—but it is still in the Gare de Lyon and still one of the dining delights of contemporary as well as nostalgic Paris. Although the sumptuous salons overlook the comings and goings of trains, from this point on its resemblance to any other station restaurant in the world is totally absent. The staircase is a gracious wonder; huge chandeliers hang from gold-leafed ceilings; walls are decorated with carvings; superb woodwork and brassware are abundant.

And before we get off this track, **Le Relais Paris-Est** (in the station at Gare de l'Est) still seems to us to be running out of steam. One of the several points which elicited our disfavor was the flashy, showy, and gimmicky listing of century wines that are completely undrinkable. This is Lesson Number 1 in oenology, and we are frankly puzzled how any knowledgeable diner could be taken in by such an obvious ploy. Not for us, at those prices—and especially with Le Train Bleu (see above) cannonballing down the rails as a competitor.

Les 3 Moutons (63 avenue F. D. Roosevelt) and **Les 3 Limousins** (8 rue de Berri) both specialize in grills—the former on sheep, of course, and the latter on steer. Same shared management; similar trimmings and fixtures; same sort of chuck-wagon attitudes mixed with obvious capital gains for city slickers; each displays a life-size stuffed representative of its wares—neither of which is nearly so inflated as are the prices, however. Of the pair, we prefer the first. Twin midtowners for rich range rovers.

L'Orangerie (28 rue St.-Louis-en-l'Ile) seems to be getting marginally better. Here is its concept: select clientele of "SEE-ME!" nabobs; self-generating egotism a pillar as a promotional come-on; more value of late for your greenbacks; somewhat limited choice of main-course and fringe dishes. Rustic trappings in a single chamber 4 yards wide and 20 yards long; candle illumination; timber beams; "spoken" menu with pick of ½-dozen entrées, a dessert, a wine (either open Beaujolais or Bordeaux), and coffee at a fixed price. If you like the juice of this Orangerie, the squeeze is part of the parcel.

Relais Bisson (37 quai Grands-Augustins) currently seems to blow hot or cold—with the emphasis on the latter, we regret to pen. One thing that remains consistent, however, is the bill—thumpingly high. The décor—an Eden of greenery surrounded by beige and orange pastels—is lovely, but nice as it is, it does not make up for the prices we paid for so-so service and only fair cookery.

Chez Albert (122 avenue de Maine) let us down last time. While the Coquille St. Jacques is reputed to be tops in the city, our companion's was filled with the liquor they may well have failed to put in her pre-lunch cocktail. Deadly serious atmosphere overlorded by the Beaumont family; fish and lobster specialties; main room draped in canvas à la sidewalk café; our foursome draped with a franc-heavy wallpaper job for an unimpressive meal. Don't be lured into the costly trap of ordering the ancient white wines. Closed Mondays and August. Chic clientele, but not our choice of *chez* from the foaming California shores to the rockbound côte of the avenue de Maine.

Relais Louis XIII (8 rue des Grands-Augustins) is a colorful, *intime*, stone-and-timber-lined corner of Paris, where the ambiance is soothingly relaxed, the management is strictly professional, and the food is good. The squire of the kitchen, André Marfeuille, presents a limited but tempting selection; the fine art collection tastefully augmented; air conditioning added; all salons delightful in their separate ways. Appealing to all of the senses.

Chez Allard (41 rue St.-André-des-Arts) is currently so "in" that smart bistro habitués—as at the aforementioned l'Orangerie—must reserve 2 or 3 days ahead to be "in." Its 2 formerly tiny, jam-packed rooms have been expanded for the comfort of the identical capacity of diners; virtually no décor —but ooooooh those sauces, and ahhhhh that house wine, Bonnesmares! Fairly steep for the surroundings, but excellent fare prepared by Mme. Allard, who is generally regarded as the top female chef in Paris. Closed Sundays and holidays. A winner.

Jamin (32 rue de Longchamp) is a treasure—a tiny trove with flowers, coziness, and 14-karat price tags. Increasingly costly (which might explain why we've noted fewer and fewer clients of late); suavely polished; comfortable; delectable omelets embracing shrimp, lobster, sea urchins, truffles, and other exotic dainties; marvelous duck livers. Here's one to enjoy if you can afford it.

Here's a midcity quartet which we recently reviewed afresh: **Chez Ramponneau** (21 avenue Marceau), near the Étoile, reflects a tavern air with line-drawn murals, cartwheel fixtures, and an atmosphere that doesn't quite live up to its intent, in our opinion. The billings, however, are exceedingly sincere. **La Toque Lorraine** (9 rue de l'Echelle), fringing the Louvre district, is now in the able hands of M. and Mme. Michel Thiebaut who redistribute the culinary wealth of Lorraine to lucky Parisians. The coinage in some recipes goes back to the 1750's. A nice 10-table "find." The **Pavillon Louis XIV** (8 blvd. St.-Denis) probably is spacious enough to entertain the court of its namesake. It is crowded, lively, and friendly—but not intimate. Closed June through August plus every Tuesday. Average prices for above average quality. **La Bourgogne** (6 avenue Basquet), peeking up at the Eiffel Tower, sets about 20 tables in an L-configuration, sets partitions between them, and sets flowers upon them. The cuisine seemed very expensive for the return, but the heavenly desserts almost make you forgive the cash register. Closed August and Sundays.

Au Vieux Berlin (32 avenue George V), across the street from the George V and Prince de Galles hotels, is delightful for romancers—or even for holding hands with your wife (if you enjoy *talking* with her!). This urbane, candlelit establishment, with soft piano notes in its background (plus an adjoining snack counter), is a semiofficial German *pied-à-terre* in Paris. Its choice of viands is happily balanced. If your palate feels Frenchy, its Gallic yen will be handsomely satisfied—but if it should be your moment for Herring Hausfrau, sausages, potato salad, and draft Löwenbräu, these are also at your command in a flash. Closed Sundays and most holidays. Recommended.

The **Copenhague** (142 avenue Champs-Élysées, part of Denmark House) is moving up dramatically as an exponent of fine Danish fare. Today we think most well-heeled travelers will enjoy its presentation and its skilletcrafts on sight. Bar downstairs, garden dining in summer; urbane atmosphere; good cold buffet in the Copenhagen tradition; excellent wines; prices climbing ominously; licensed and supervised by the Danish Government; open every day; be sure to ask for alert and friendly Maître d'Hôtel René Bernard.

La Marée (1 rue Daru) makes the stylish inner circle—and it is gaining ground steadily. Animated atmosphere created by a chic (and often beautiful) clientele; soft glow provided by chapel-glass stained panels and Edwardian globe fixtures on mirrored sconces; split-level construction (we prefer the sunken zone nearer the front); ruby-hue velvet banquettes; fresh flowers on tables; enormous broadside menu; service improved. The prices are in line with its quality and appealing ambiance.

Hostellerie de Nicolas Flamel (51 rue de Montmorency in the 3rd arrondissement, not to be confused with boulevard de Montmorency in the 16th arrondissement) is perhaps the oldest house in town (A.D. 1438). It was once occupied by the alchemist Pernelle. Medieval atmosphere, natch; fixed-price meal (about $22 inclusive)—an advantage, because the client knows in advance how much he will spend. Lunch and dinner served; adequate but not extraordinary cookery; reserve ahead. Worthy.

Chaumière de l'Isle offers dinner only, with 3—sometimes 4—choices of entrée every day of the year except April 7. Your reception is growing more careless in direct proportion to its mounting success. It's so chock-full that reservations must be made 24 hours in advance (except on Apr. 6). Try to conduct your relations with the cordial mother of the house rather than with the daughter whom we found so chilly.

Île de France, a youthful entry which toots only on weekends, is moored opposite 32 quai de New-York, between Debilly footbridge and the Pont d'Iéna. This former barge of the Compagnie Générale Transatlantique has been transformed into what might be termed a midstream diner. The galley produces just the fare you might expect from a Gallic interpretation of a Mississippi steamboat. We found it duller than the stern of a paddle-wheeler, but perhaps we cruised in on an off night.

In the *medium-to-moderately-expensive* group, **St. Moritz** (a few steps off the Étoile, adjoining the Royal Hotel) is a handsome contender. Sleek interior highlighted by pale wooden coffers inset with wall plates; colorful, well-appointed décor; cuisine substantial, but not in the Grand category; the *fruits de mer* (seafood) platter a good catch; closed Sunday and all of August. Rewarding to the eye and the palate.

Coconnas (2 bis place des Vosges), now renewed, is agreeably situated in an ancient flower market which Louis XII later converted into his personal pavilion. Long, narrow room with 20 wooden tables; simple décor; immaculately clean; special attention to pâtés, a dish called Merlan en Colère ("a whiting biting his own tail"), and Poule au Pot; average check now in the $18 range; becoming more and more expensive, unfortunately. Guy is the host. Master Restaurateur Claude Terrail (Tour d'Argent) is the owner. Closed Tuesday.

Rôtisserie de la Reine Pédauque (6 rue de la Pépinière, near Gare St.-Lazare) had faltered quite a bit, but now that it is under new management we must get back for another try. **L'Assiette au Beurre** (11 rue St. Benoit) strikes us as being so put-on that we gnash our molars in the presence of such posturing. We feel almost as strongly about **Chez Benoit** (20 rue St. Martin), which plays its poor little heart out for the ultrapampered Nescafé Society

of Paris. Slum-district location which the fad followers find irresistibly chic;
2 drab rooms; no décor; passable cookery; plenty of smoke. Bah, not for us.

Chez Raffatin et Honorine (16 boulevard St.-Germain) in its simple way
is once again a celebration for the senses. The small staff really seem to care.
Glass-enclosed sidewalk tables; aislelike room hung with sausages and ham;
8-foot buffet serving as one wall; rusticity galore. A friendly spot for relaxation and good value.

D'chez Eux (2 avenue Lowendal), a 2-minute ride from the Hilton, is
almost exactly the same, since M. and Mme. A. Court followed up their
St.-Germain project listed directly above (and which they've since sold) with
this even more colorful version. Again, an enclosed sidewalk tonsure; similar
kitchen crafts for a somewhat higher $-riddled per-person outlay; closed
Sunday.

Cochon d'Or (192 avenue Jean-Jaurés) is a rather long ride out to Pont de
Pantin. Several rooms, of which we prefer the 1st-floor salon with mirrored
walls and a low ceiling; our light tandem dinner, including wine, came to $36,
and we found it unexciting to the point of boredom. Don't go out of your way,
but if you are in the neighborhood when starvation strikes it will do.

Our sentiments are about the same for the **Bistro Barriere de Clichy** (11 rue
de Paris), which resides 20 minutes from the center in a dreary suburb.
Cuisine uneven; stark interior; exceptional bargains in wines. Ho-hum.

La Boule d'Or (13 boulevard La Tour-Maubourg) seemed to be the answer
to the Jackie Gleason appetites. WOW! Each table was practically sway-
backed with nibbling items just to hold you over until the real feed began:
pickles, rolls, and chunks of farmhouse butter the size of the Arc de Triomphe; enormous rillette portion containing at least a pound of meat—merely
a starter! Blanquette de Veau designed to quell the hunger pangs of Olympic
decathlon champions (we've seldom seen a male in the place who weighed less
than 200 lbs.!); desserts from cabbage-size pears in nests of cream and pastry,
to towering soufflés, to shells of sweets so tempting that ladies' corsets split
asunder at the sight of a passing tray. On our stuffings we paid about $20 each.
Just the thing for size-99 tummies.

We wouldn't bother with **Pierre Traiteur** (10 rue de Richelieu) since it is
mainly a Gallic businessmen's haunt. Fair skilletry but no joys otherwise, at
least to us.

Maisonnette Russe (6 rue d'Armaille) is a moderately priced high-stepper.
Dim chamber with faded aristocratic air; antique lamps; maroon velour and
leather chairs; 2 boars' heads glaring at diners. Borscht with perhaps half a
steer in each bowl; Russian vodka by the iceberg; desserts for dreaming: spun
sugar nests and chocolate cake resembling a long ton of chilled fudge. Not
for diet watchers; surprisingly rewarding for presentation, cuisine, service,
and atmosphere.

Pharamond (24 rue de la Grande-Truanderie in Les Halles) draws a midday businessman patronage and an elegant evening clientele to its old-fashioned precincts (born in 1832). Excellent cuisine, especially its famed Tripes
à la mode de Caen. Better now than a few years ago.

Auberge de l'Argoat (27 avenue Reille, in the 14th arrondissement) offers
a rural Breton inn atmosphere. Outskirts situation about 20 minutes by taxi

from the Étoile; wooden-gate entrance; charcoal fireplace surrounded by laboriously contrived trappings such as a boar's head and a hammerlock rifle; 10 tables under a beamed ceiling; red and white napery; king-size wineglasses as big as Cyclopean eyecups. More for touristy visual appeal than for Inner Man treats.

Chez les Anges (54 blvd. de Latour-Maubourg) and the **Ambassade d'Auvergne & du Rouergue** (22 rue de Grenier) both exude a pleasant rustic charm. We prefer the former which, unfortunately, runs about 20% higher in its billings. Your profits, however, appear on the platters which we think are perhaps 50% more savory. Both are fun, however.

Paul Chêne (123 rue Lauriston) is à la mode for residents of this silk-stocking neighborhood; Calcuttas of golfers use this as their 19th green. Clean, typical-bistro décor; about 50 couverts; able young chef from Lyon—a recommendation in itself. That ever-savvy Prince of the Mumm champagne domain, Georges Prade, calls its Poule au Pot "intelligently served." In response to this, an equally distinguished and globally renowned gourmet retorted the following to us by mail: "I agree with our friend Georges Prade to say that the Poule au Pot is 'intelligently served,' but I do not agree regarding the quality of the Poule au Pot." Gentlemen, choose your weapons! A winning family house, with careful and honest cooking—*and* a highly controversial Poule au Pot!

Galiote (rue Gamboust) turned on a memorable meal during recent Paris rovings. Three segmented rooms, pleasant but in no way elegant; wood paneling and brass chandeliers; informal but attentive service. (The proprietor was wearing a sweater and no tie on the afternoon of our visit.) Outstanding hors d'oeuvres display; nice wines; full-dress fare in the medium-cost range. Our light veal-chop lunch with *cèpes* was better than average. Sound for value.

Le Petit Colombier (42 rue des Acacias) is a bit off the beaten track—a few minutes by taxi beyond the Arc de Triomphe. But if you're wandering in this neighborhood, you might find this small house amiable. Go upstairs for a window table, if available; especially good carafe wines. Average check $17 or so; not worth a special pilgrimage, but satisfactory for the price.

Joseph (56 rue Pierre-Charron) is peopled by top French executives and a smart lunch crowd. It is also handy for travelers who stay in either the George V or Prince de Galles hotels. Friendly, unelaborate atmosphere; routine prices; closed Sunday. We've always found them working hard and well.

Auberge de France (1 rue du Mont-Thabor), located between Place Vendôme and the Tuileries, is a seventeenth-century-style entry which also features a *raclette stübli* in the cellar (for Swiss cheese dishes). Manager Ferrié, a former chef schooled by Fauchon, is revealing respectable culinary skills in the classical tradition. Though we haven't sampled either, raptures have been broadcast around the town about the piscatorial Sea-Wolf Ali-Baba and the Musketeer Sherbert. Our recent steerage was superb but our partner's duck was just fair. Worth an experiment, for sure.

Berlioz (135 avenue Malakoff) on our latest visit decanted a delicious wine which was far too good for the listless cuisine. Attractive long room with yellow textiles in a bright mien; one of the best sommeliers on the circuit;

almost empty this time. Perhaps we hit it on an off day, but we were singularly unimpressed. Closed Saturday.

Lucien (12 rue Sourcouf) is straight Gallic, with mixed French and Yankee colony clientele. Simple ambiance; 8 tables; a nervous, hardworking owner who knows food; if he has moules, pheasant, and soufflé on the menu, you should rise to Cloud Nine. Expensive for its setting; reservations a must; closed Monday; sturdy and dependable.

The **Quai d'Orsay** (Left Bank, near rue Fabert) claims many happy disciples. The elbow-to-elbow bistro character is so popular—especially with a young assemblage of chatterers—that bookings must be made a day ahead. The stuffed neck of duck is the stuff of dreams—perhaps not for the *canard,* but it was for this happy waddler.

Café de la Paix (12 boulevard Capucines)? This Paris landmark has just been reopened, and—praise to Allah—it remains in the former 19th-century style. The restoration is a joy to any nostalgic Francophile.

For hotel dining, space prohibits a special rundown here, so please refer back to our "Hotels" section where we've tried to describe the more noteworthy tables.

Chez l'Ami Louis, Rôtisserie de la Table du Roy, Aux Lyonnais, and **Michelle** form a quartet over which we are not too enthusiastic even though they have certain admirable points. Service and cookery at Chez l'Ami Louis impressed us as having become careless, if not downright slovenly. Its slum neighborhood might be considered "colorful" by some, but your interests and safety are too much of a concern for us to suggest it. On our last 3 visits, Table du Roy crawled with so many Americans we could shut our eyes and swear we were back in Howard Johnson's. Aux Lyonnais served us delicious scallops in mustard sauce, but the modest surroundings and the immodest prices turned us off; it does evoke a deep-French atmosphere, however. Michelle, we think, has gone off. The last shouldn't be confused with **Chez Michel** (10 rue de Belzunce), a specialty bistro where the haute quality matches its haute tariffs.

In the *outdoor* group, one of the most attractive places for a summer lunch (no dinner served), had been **Pré Catelan**, in the Bois de Boulogne—when one of its all-too-frequent business conventions, wedding receptions, or group functions was not overrunning the premises. Because this one now caters almost primarily to this patronage, we feel it has lost much of its charm for the independent pilgrim.

A woodland alternate in the same district is **La Grande Cascade** which is slightly less costly and creates pleasant conflagrations with its kidneys flambé.

Pavillon Royale nibbles at the bank of a sylvan lake. **Samantha** is its nightclub portion.

Auberge du Vert-Galant (42 quai des Orfèvres, Île de la Cité) sits on the bank of the ancient island in the Seine and offers a memorable panorama of the river and the Left Bank. Firmly sustained by lawyers, because it is just a tort's (or tart's) throw from the Palais de Justice. Adequate but not spectacular kitchen actions; high but not exorbitant fees; when the weather is right, not a plaintiff to be found.

La Mère Catherine, another well-known alfresco establishment, is *not* recommended for either its food or its attitudes—at least as we sampled them.

In the *inexpensive group*, **Dominique** (19 rue Bréa), annually updated and refreshed during the month of June when it is closed, is just as satisfactory today as when we first stumbled across it in '46. At the counters near the entrance you can eat nobly for about $12 or so. This includes a choice of soup, *plat du jour*, cheese, and dessert. For a special treat, we suggest the grilled sturgeon and the blintzes with caviar; borsch à la crème, or Shashlik Karsky. Dining in the intimate room in the rear or upstairs costs more for 4 courses plus a small bottle of wine; à la carte service also is available. Dominique and son Gary always provide a lot for your money, with some excellent Russian specialties and sound French dishes. Recommended for its friendly spirit.

Chez Joséphine (117 rue du Cherche-Midi) couldn't be more typical, as a middle-class bistro. Don't expect plush seats or fancy service. The well-known skillets are mastered by Chef Jean Dumonet, who is beloved for his Truffled Andouillettes, his Ballottines, his sweetbreads with morels, and his rabbit in mustard sauce—all for reasonable sums. The heart of France.

Chez Maître Paul (corner of rue M.-le-Prince and rue Casimir Delavigne) is a honey of a little place for economy trippers. The Man Himself does all the cooking, and he features a wine called Bourgueil from his own vineyard in Touraine. Always full—so reserve in advance. Closed Tuesday.

Au Pactole (44 boulevard St.-Germain) draws many businessmen at lunchtime and families in the evening. Enclosed sidewalk terrace; 7-table interior sanctum with gold wallpaper, oil paintings, and flowers; agonizingly slow service on our visit. The set menus are the star attractions here—a 4-course one and a 5-plate spread with more selections available. Fair enough, even as the tabs now seem to be rocketing upward.

Au Petit Riche (125 rue le Peletier) turns back the mechanism of timelessness to before this century began. If you've got a kink for globes, polished wood, and the décor of saloons in ships that were retired long, long ago, then you may dig this artifact. Go early; on our first attempt they would not serve us at the wicked hour of 9:15 P.M. Closed August as well as Sundays and holidays.

Chez André (53 boulevard St.-Marcel) holds a special attraction for journalists and exquisite mannequins from the couturier precincts which it flanks. (Personally, darned if we can think of a nicer combination.) Paper "tablecloths"; noisy room with old-fashioned partitions; busy enough to encourage early or late arrival by the wisest diners; no reservations taken. Footnote: The gamin stake is delightful.

Le Berthoud (1 rue Valette) is a splendid stop for rubbing the nap off the elbows. It's more engaging than a barrel full of people—and that's just how you'll feel when coffee time rolls around. Fascinating, inexpensive egg dishes bobbling in pools of melted butter or cream or both; Moujik (Russian tasties) worthy of anybody's lip service; gay heaps of salad; wee sausages to lion-share steaks for moderate outlays; calories-be-damned desserts. If you enjoy humanity at close quarters, we think you might relish this community plate.

Vieux Paris (2 rue de l'Abbaye), also on the Left Bank, features Algerian and Middle Eastern fare. You may sample Greek Souvlaki (Shishkebab),

Egyptian rice, Arabian Couscous (Wednesday only), and all sorts of exotic preparations. A popular low-cost choice.

The **Bar de Théâtre** (catercorner to the Plaza-Athénée) is a noon and after-theater gossip-and-groceries hangout for young dress designers, high-fashion salesgirls, and models who haven't quite reached the pinnacle. Tiny tables for these tiny appetites; passable fare; slow service; reasonable tariffs. Can be fun for Twiggies.

Au Beaujolais (19 quai de la Tournelle), across from the famous Tour d'Argent, is ultramodest. Meats hanging from the ceiling; butchers' aprons hanging from the shirt-sleeved waiters; happy bellies hanging from some of the best-fed clients in Paris. About as atmospheric as a pilot's ready room; tantalizing menu; ask for English-speaking Bernard; always reserve in advance. If you must wait for a table, be sure to pass the time with a *kir*, the house cocktail—white wine with a shot of Cassis. For pure-but-simple eating, this one's tough to beat. Closed Monday and in August. Recommended.

Chez René (around the corner at 14 boulevard St.-Germain) has the same sort of personality. Even noisier (if such a thing is possible) than Au Beaujolais; same prices; similar but less refined cookery; this comparison is also true for the customers, we think. You can stuff yourself for about $10.50, except on Sunday. Bring earplugs.

Chez Marius (30 rue des Fossés-St.-Bernard), taken over by Jacques Chalvet, surges with new energy to upgrade its beloved reputation. Two floors which are as simple as π; mouth-melting Coq au Vin; juicy grills. Extra-savvy Parisian gourmets who can afford much more often dine here and often bring their associates. This haven is easy on the expense account and nice on the palate. Functions every day but Sunday. Sound.

Le Marigny (avenue Marigny, around the corner from the Bristol Hotel) is a simple corner nook for cornering simple cookery. Our latest Coeur de Filet with French fries was particularly savory and modestly priced. For such a high-price district of such a high-price city, here is a budgeteer's find. Recommended.

La Pomme Soufflé (37 bis rue Ponthieu) is designed in the shape of a lollipop, with tables along the stem and a jamup of noisy diners in the "pop" division. Light bites and quick service are the specialties of this busy beehive. Fair, but distressingly cacophonous.

La Quetsch (6 rue Capucines) is a restaurant-delicatessen which once pleased us greatly but now deeply saddens us. Sorry.

Le Boccador (7 rue Boccador, near the Plaza-Athénée) has changed proprietors. It has not, however, changed its mandate on excellence. The value is still there, we are pleased to report.

Le Dahu (10 rue de la Trémoille, very close by) has smoother décor, great charm, and high tabs. Large cellar dining room; open grill; garlands of garlic, red-check lampshades, cheeses, copperware, beamed ceiling, fruit and vegetable baskets, and other slick-rustic oddments; dishes and atmosphere from the Haute-Savoie. M. Cambin and his family know their fondues and highland fare. This one is so highly regarded, crowded, and close that you'll literally rub—and we mean rub—your anatomy with your boonfellows. Contusin' but amusin'.

No other book, not even *Michelin,* or *Kléber,* can begin to tackle the hundreds upon hundreds of good bistros in Paris, so please forgive the necessary omissions of countless worthy examples. The best fun of all is to put on your walking shoes and explore for yourself.

Among the *restaurant curiosities,* **Caviar Kaspia** (17 place de la Madeleine) is beguiling. Above this prominent specialty establishment are 3 tiny rooms à la teashop—but fresh caviar, smoked salmon, smoked trout, smoked eel, and 2 or 3 other delicacies make up its wares. The capacity is similarly limited —a mere 9 tables and munching space at the bar for about 9. Hot borscht is always available. The blinis are the stuff of dreams, and you may choose your own size, grade, and color of the caviar "berry" (trade lingo for "egg"). Chilled French or Alsatian white wines, vodka, and champagne are the only potables. Deft reception and attention by Guy Loup; open weekdays continuously from 9 A.M. to 8:15 P.M.; closed Sunday. A heavenly haven for odd-hour refreshment when your feet and soul are bruised from shopping. One reminder: Don't grow faint when the *patron* presents his neck-snapping bill for "that simple little snack." Caviar is caviar; literally, its cost per ounce is higher than sterling silver nearly anywhere on earth save in Iran or the Soviet Union. Thus your check will be very, very high. As with all delicious morsels in life, the best costs money—whether you marry it or just nibble it.

Au Mouton de Panurge (17 rue de Choiseul) is startlingly pornographic. The takeoff point for the bawdy décor and strange menu is the commemoration of humorist-and-satirist Rabelais; from here, some of the house developments are only vulgar while some are just plain repulsive. The rolls are baked in the shape of a male organ, which also appear as a bottle stopper in the even more organic wine jugs. Others, as well, are right out of the barnyard. Spicy murals; a live sheep which drinks wine; an out-and-out tourist trap in conception and tone, but the new owner seems to be making an effort to improve its overall quality. Still kinky.

Then, let's not forget that famous institution partway up the **Eiffel Tower** by elevator. Glorious panorama of Paris (that's the Hilton, next door); grill open for lunch year round; main restaurant closed November 15 to Easter. The big news here is that the first-floor establishment now features headliners of the entertainment world 6 evenings per week (see "Nightclubs"). Cuisine? On all of our earlier scales it was fully satisfactory—but now more and more complaints from Guidesters have found their ways to our mailbox, topped by a wail from a Greenwich Village pilgrim who wrote, "It was plainly REAL BAD." Conversely, other Guidesters whose palates we trust continue to sing its praises in 5×5 enthusiasm. In any case, the setting of this expensive dining place is matchless.

Inside the **Louvre Museum**, there is a self-service restaurant with an outdoor terrace (good weather) overlooking the Carrousel and Tuileries Gardens. Light meals from 10 A.M. to 5 P.M. for as little as $3; drinks and tea to alleviate those hunger pangs and to nurture your search for culture. A 2nd is also operating in another gallery.

Like cheese? The restaurant adjoining **Androuët's Cheese Shop** (41 rue d'Amsterdam, near Gare St.-Lazare) will make you pleasantly cheesy on the cheesiest assortment of dishes and samples in this cheese-loving nation. Marvelous munching if you're as mouselike in tastes as we are. We *adore* this fascinating complex!

For *seafood*, **Le Duc** (243 boulevard Raspail), where we've joyfully taken the hook, line, and sinker, offered the yummiest bait we've snapped at in a long, long time. Its maritime mood is fashioned of 15 flower-decked tables, varnished bulkheads, prints of old ships, brass lamps in gimbals, and hints of its Mediterranean origins. Indeed, its skipper is from Marseilles; when the markets of Paris cannot provide the catches he desires, he simply closes and refuses customers! Luckily for us, his haul was plentiful on our try. Our iced shellfish platter was so overwhelming in amplitude, arrangement, and variety that it almost constituted a graduate course in oceanography. This should have served as a generous meal by itself. However, our follow-up order of grilled *loup* (rockfish) for 2 was also unforgettable in both eye- and palate-appeal. The service was skilled but busy, the atmosphere was talkative, and the billings are blue-ribbon. Devotees of saltwater fare, however, should not permit themselves to miss it. Outstanding—and that's an understatement.

La Méditerranée (2 place de l'Odéon), down several pegs in cost, has gay map-lined tablecloths, a large menu, and great charm. Small terrace; our latest incognito lunch here was adequate but no rave; ambiance so cheery and warmth of Proprietor Jean Subrenat so winning that at practically every meal some film luminary or other VIP can be depended upon to show up. Excellent ambiance.

La Coquille (6 rue du Débarcadère), near the Meridien Hotel, is short on eye-appeal and atmosphere, but the cookery is superb for its bistro character. Trouble is our billings seemed far too high for our fillings. Otherwise M. Blache and his daughter do a sterling job.

Le Chalut (94 boulevard Batignolles) swims one of the strongest races for the fancier of fine finny fare. Its décor could not be more unattractive and less inspired if it had been designed by a haddock. But oooooooooolaLA, that wondrously huge menu of marine masterpieces—so special, so delectable, and so perfect that gourmets from miles around leap troutlike to get in. Owner Bernardy produces his feasts for high-medium rewards. Pack-jammed, especially on Friday; closed from May 30 to September 1. For the self-chosen few who *really* pamper their palates.

Rech (62 avenue des Ternes) gradually has grown more Rech-ed, in our opinion. We now prefer a bright little young sprat called **La Pêcherie** (24 rue Pierre Lescot) with a white-and-violet theme and a bubbling fountain to greet you. Strong in visual chic.

Prunier (9 rue Duphot and branch on 16 avenue Victor-Hugo) is *still* no top banana, in our estimation—although a number of readers disagree. The Duphot division appealed more to us for its ambiance than for its culinary charms. At the Victor-Hugo address our fish was delicious—outstandingly so, in fact. But the wine was poorly served, the atmosphere was drearily vacuous, and at 9:30 on a Saturday evening there were practically no other customers. Sorry, but we continue to muster absolutely no enthusiasm for this Paris landmark.

For kosher cookery we like (1) **Le Sportif** (24 rue Vieille-du-Temple), (2) **Eden** (36 boulevard Bonne-Nouvelle), (3) **Flambaum** (37 rue Faubourg-Montmartre; closed Jan. to Apr.), and (4) **Henri** (9 passage Basfoi). For a quickie bite of Gefilte Fish (or maybe a corned beef sandwich), try the **Goldenberg Delicatessen** (69 avenue de Wagram) which stays open 7 days a week from 8 A.M. to midnight. Oy-vay, is *that* good!

Le Canyon, formerly La Trinquette (1 rue Gustave-Courbet), draws ranks of Yanks to its 1-room, 2-tier, all-American precincts. Only 5 tables and a 4-stool bar-counter; paneled in Old West motif with desert scenes on the walls. Available are such nostalgic goods as Southern Fried Chicken, spareribs, T-bone steak, Idaho potatoes, apple pie, and many other lip-smackers. Prices are minimal; we enjoyed our ham steak with pineapple on our recent sampling. Neither a whiz nor a rave, but fun for home-away-from-homers. Canadians may prefer the **Québecoise**, a few steps off the Champ-Élysées, where steaks and even bear meat are flown in from the new world. While the prices seemed lofty to us, the overall tone didn't appeal to our senses.

Soul food? **Haynes** (3 rue Clauzel, a few steps from place Pigalle) features U.S. Deep South cookery skillfully supervised by Leroy Haynes, the black former secretary of the Urban League in Atlanta who turned restaurateur and part-time movie actor. Almost 100% American clientele, well attired and well behaved, on our visit; bustling sweet service by pert Scandinavian or African waitresses; about a dozen tables; rough stucco walls; flattering illumination; daily specialties including such classics as Chicken 'n' Dumplings, Barbecued Ribs, and Jambalaya; nutrients from 6 P.M. to 1:30 A.M. only; lights out at 2 A.M.; closed Sunday, but open on weekday holidays. To us, the Haynes personality is even a bigger attraction than the comestibles.

For others, here's how we'd pick them in order of desirability: *Spanish:* **Chez José**, avenue Jean Moulin. *Basque:* **Auberge Basque**, 51 rue Verneuil, is a touch of the Pyrenees; between dishes, the waiters double as singing guitarists; nobody speaks English, but the atmosphere is so vivacious, who cares? Closed Sundays and July 15 through September 4. *Italian:* (1) **Toscana**, 7 rue Ponthieu, leaves a good taste on the palate as well as on the spirit, thanks to the skill and kindness of its owner-host; only 10 tables, but each filled with devoted loyalists. (2) **Conti**, 72 rue Lauriston, also deserves a gastronomic bravo; more and more popular. (3) **Peppo** (115 avenue de Villiers) dispenses substantial groceries at lower prices. *Russian:* Don't forget **Maisonnette Russe** and **Dominique** which we've already written "Da! Da!" about. *Indian:* **Annapurna**, 32 rue de Berri, curries favor with a multitude of followers. Two small rooms containing 8 tables each; attractive Asian décor; open year round. *Chinese:* **China-Town** receives our bow for day-to-day Orientations. For superluxury, **Tong Yen**, 1 bis rue Jean Mermoz, is drawing a heavy trade in expense-account Mandarins who never check the opulent scores from the abacus. Although it does not serve the type of Chinese fare to which we are accustomed in the States, here is unquestionably the leader of this culinary school in Paris. **L'Ambassadeur,** 30 rue de Longchamp, also scores high in the subgum league. *Japanese:* **Miki**, 3 rue d'Artois, appears to be the rising sun in this heaven. **Chez Hanafousa**, 4 passage de la Petite-Boucherie, also glows, especially for its meats. There are now about 50 such ethnic contenders in this city. *Swedish:* **Relais de Suède**, 125 avenue Champs-Élysées, offers perhaps the only smörgasbord in Paris—reputedly almost as good as any in Sweden. *German:* **Au Vieux Berlin**, opposite the George V and Prince de Galles hotels, has been previously described. It is *wunderbar! Health foods* (Yep, in Paris!): **Veggie**, 38 rue de Verneuil, caters to clear-eyed Tarzans, Janes, and assorted bushy-tailed buffs of botany.

Snacks and quick fare? Snack bars and light-lunch places are mushrooming so fast that, in most tourist districts, all the visitor has to do is to wander down the closest boulevard. First and most interesting, famous old **Fauchon** (28 place de la Madeleine) operates a stand-up "Cafeteria" which serves honest-to-goodness Maxwell House coffee (plus French, Italian, Swiss, and Turkish blends), Schlitz beer, superb fresh fruit, various juices, sandwiches, cottage cheese, hot specialties, pastries, and c-r-e-a-m-y ice cream. This latest append-age to France's most celebrated fancy foods center is a boon to homesick stateside tummies. Recommended with our tongue slapping our chest. A more opulent example to the eye is **Le Drug Store** (133 avenue Champs-Élysées, near Arc de Triomphe) which to our taste can't compare in quality or value. To augment this, a *Wagon-Lits* movieland version reels in adjoining the busy Place de l'Opéra and there's yet a newer one on the Rond Point. And if you miss that trio of midtown swingers, there's still another branch in St.-Germain-des-Prés.

More typical is **Le Grill-Shop** (67 avenue Champs-Élysées), which is small and bustling and has a clean U.S.-style décor in bright yellow with mirrors. Our order here was for one "Hot Dog sur Toast." But up came one "Super Hot Dog Garni," which consisted of 2 embarrassingly naked and hollow-chested wieners with a plate of potato chips, 2 rolls which any well-groomed American frankfurter would sneer at, and 2 dabs of butter—a total of almost $3, with the coffee—an imitation so pale it couldn't be peddled for 50¢ in a Little League ball park at home. But some of the French-based items being served looked quite appetizing.

For Jehovah's sake, we'd avoid the huge **Pizza Pino** which glows spectacu-larly on the Champs-Élysées. Our recent expensive "Pizza Chef" preparation we'd call nothing but a disgusting swill of limp pasta soaking languidly in a polychromatic infusion of runny eggs, tomato broth, and the faintest hint of cheese, the surface charged with some unidentifiable extruded meat that seemed to pose as a distant relative of sausage. One taste and we fled. Ugh!

Jour et Nuit (2 rue de Berri, just off the Champs-Élysées) is open every *jour et nuit;* okay for that last bite before you tuck in.

The **Wimpy** chain, whose luncheonettes are dotted all over London and sprinkled around Germany, Belgium, and Italy, has also invaded Paris, Mar-seille, Nice, Bordeaux, Lille, Toulouse, and Lyon. France's king of chain feederies, Jacques Borel, is the chef, of course. "Wimpy-burgers," advertised as *"Repas complets dans un pain rond"* ("Complete meals on a bun"), are the main feature—but here they serve them with a small bottle of red wine.

Le Snack has become so popular, in fact, that 1-channel specialists are beginning to pop up. **Chez Aron Fils de Tunis** (19 boulevard Montmartre) spotlights ultrasweet fritters from Africa called Beignet. **Les Écuries Wash-ington** (5 rue Washington) flips oddball-filled *crêpes* or plain old honey-capped flapjacks, from $1 to $2. **La Boutique à Sandwich** (a totter off the Champs-Élysées on rue du Colisée) builds you-know-whats in 30 different styles. **La Maisonnette du Caviar** (directly across the street) stirs up Russian delights at prices calculated not to hurt any fellow-traveler. The **Bazar** (corner of rue St.-Benoît and rue Guillaume Apollinaire) is an automat-style feedery that is capable of filling 600 mouths at one time. Through its Horn-and-Hardart-type dispensing panels, you can purchase everything from hot cross buns to packaged stockings. Bring a pocketful of coins.

If you don't insist on Howard Johnson's—or even U.S. lunch-cart—standards, you'll find most of these counter-type spots adequate.

Dedicated budgeteers? Since we're too bottlenecked here for additional entries, please consult our annually revised *Fielding's Low-Cost Europe,* which lists scads more bargain dining spots and money-saving tips for serious economizers.

Orly Airport area? In the terminal building, most jetters gobble their calories at the punk drugstore-type counter on the ground floor without ever being aware that the structure also contains the **Trois Soleils**, the **Rôtisserie Le Tournebroche** and a popular-price corner called **Les Horizons.** Infinitely better, in our opinion, is the **Orly Hilton** trio, a 2-minute walk (if you live to dodge the traffic). We like and heartily recommend both its Le Coffee Shop and L'Atelier Bar, the secondary lights in this U.S. oasis. Especially at night, La Louisiane Restaurant represents a romantic bayou attempt to reproduce Olde New Orleans. Cajun-based cuisine which shows imagination and, in some dishes, honors the Crescent City with skillful skilletry; the personnel are now disciplined, kind, and helpful. We haven't touched down at the **Maxim's** hangar at Orly Ouest. Local high-flyers praise it warmly. The new Charles de Gaulle Airport (utilized almost exclusively for trans-atlantic flights) also provides refueling by Maxim's—and expensive it is! This is a catering affiliate of the city shrine. It was too early on our trial to make a firm and fair judgment of quality and service.

Good restaurants in the provinces are as thick as Fido's fleas. To cover them all here is impossible, due to the space limitations; in any case, the wonderful *Guide Michelin* and *Guide Kléber* already list and rate them by the thousands, in the world's most dependable mass surveys. Below are some of the better (or best) tables of France; consult *Michelin* or *Kléber* for more modest selections. Most of these offer cookery at its highest, usually (not always) with prices to match:

Near Paris:
　　Bougival (11 miles): (1) **Coq Hardi** (a high U.S. Treasury Dept. official howls at its unfavorable exchange rate levied on dollars; we'll watch this one carefully from now on), (2) **Le Camelia** (blossoming better than ever under the tender tenure of another "new chef" in this national trend, M. Delaveyne).
　Chennevières-sur-Marne (11 miles): Écu de France.

Louveciennes (10 miles): **L'Auberge du Coeur Volent** (very "in" with the Jet Settlers).

    Pontchartrain (24 miles): (1) **L'Aubergade**, (2) **Chez Sam**.

    Port-Royal-des-Champs (21 miles): **Chez Denise**.

    St.-Germain-en-Laye (15 miles): **Pavillon Henri IV**.

Bordeaux Coast and environs:

Biarritz: **Relais de Parme**, at the airport, is one of the best in the region; view of Anglet; modern décor; open all year; same ownership as the midtown leader. In the city, it's (1) **Café de Paris** (aviary entrance, with hearth on one side and Atlantic on the other; friendly but forgetful service; closed in Feb.; expensive; father-and-son Pierre and Robert LaPorte alternate between managing this house and the Relais de Parme), (2) **Rôtisserie Coq Hardi** (glorious command of coast from window tables; listless attention; inconsistent cookery; our Coquilles St. Jacques was superb in taste but microscopic in size), (3) **Le Link** (golf course situation; lunch only; rushed atmosphere; same Café de Paris ownership; closed Feb.).

    Down the pike, vaguely north of Pau (about 25 miles), in the department of Landes, the noted monarch of modern chefs, Michel Guérard, practices his alchemy at ***Eugénie-les-Bains***, located in the health center known as the **Hôtel des Sources et des Prés**. For low-caloried masterworks here indeed is a dining shrine. Always reserve in advance, especially if you plan to overnight in the 40-room establishment; closed winters; ovens begin stoking in April. A marvel of inventive new cuisine.

Bidart (Biarritz 4 miles): (1) **Chistera** (no special décor; good dining) and **Relais Franco-Espagnol** (change of management; slipping further and further in our ratings).

Bordeaux: (1) **Château Trompette**, (2) **Réserve Etche Ona** (5 miles out at L'Alouette), (3) **Toque Blanche**, (4) **Hôtel Splendid**. **Dubern** had slipped badly, in our opinion. Now we hear that it is making a dramatic comeback. We'll be anxious to try it anew. **Chapon Fin** is now for snacks only.

Meschers-sur-Gironde (Royan 7 miles): **Chantecler**.

St.-Jean-de-Luz: (1) **Au Chipiron** (cozy as a *grand lit des huîtres;* tiny and delectable), (2) **Petit Grill Basque** (also small, with more emphasis on cookery than surroundings; closed Jan. to mid-Feb.), (3) **Pigeon Blanc** (we prefer the main rustic room to the annex; only for regional dishes; best for budgeteers). **Taverne Basque**, next door, has skidded down and down on our scoresheet. So has **Bar Basque**. El Bravo, in the Hotel Madison, is a valiant contender. Out of the city, the restaurant of the **Hôtel Chantaco** takes the laurel wreath for elegant dining. Also, don't forget the Chistera in neighboring ***Bidart***.

Burgundy and environs:

Avallon: (1) **Poste** (it lost 1 of its 3 stars in *Michelin* several seasons back, but our subsequent meals could not have been better. Perhaps because the famous French arbiter has been cutting down its out-of-the-way spots "worthy of a special detour"—and a new major highway puts this one off the main line—this is the reason it was dropped a notch. We, on the other hand, continue to recommend it with all-out enthusiasm), (2) **Moulin des Ruats** (1 mile out), (3) **Relais Fleuri** (2½ miles out).

Dijon: (1) **Chapeau Rouge**, (2) **Val-Suzon** (3 miles out), (3) **Ducs de Bourgogne**, (4) **Hôtel de la Cloche**. A late visit to the **Pré aux Clercs et Trois Faisans** was a sad disappointment.

Montbard: **Hôtel de la Gare** (the local trout and ham are superb—not to mention the wine!).

Saulieu (Avallon 25 miles, and thus also off the prime auto traffic grid): **Côte d'Or** is no longer what it was now that M. and Mme. François Minot, the young proprietor-chef team who gave it such fame, have departed.

Channel Coast and environs:

Channel crossers to/from **Calais**, **Boulogne**, **Le Touquet** : Gourmet Michael Lawrence, long a French resident, writes, "Next time PLEASE go out of your way to try a meal or stopover at **Le Relais Guillaume de Normandy** in **St.-Valery**, 11½ miles northwest of Abbeville. It's a glorious delight, with supreme hospitality, excellent cuisine, and a *patron* who speaks English 22% better than I do. No other book lists this little paradise."

Brest : **Voyageurs**.

Deauville-Trouville : (1) The **Casino Grill** for summer, (2) **La Malibran** (Winter Casino) for the colder months, (3) **Ciro's** on the beach promenade for lunch year round. All have Normandy Hotel supervision, the same chef, and high-quality administration by Maître Paul-Jean. The 1st is big and nobly bred; the 2nd is cozy with its champagne-velvet banquettes and deluxe intimacy; the 3rd is a glass-faced beachfront haven for delectable seafood specialties. Down the line: (4) **La Crémaillère** (saloon ambiance, scarlet carpet, wine-cask table, and copperware galore; menu based on the local finny harvests), (5) **Castel Normand**, (6) **Chatham**, (7) **Le Grand Large**, (8) **Golf** (closed in winter). Tops for hotel fare, of course, is the **Normandy**. The **Royal,** also good, has Empire furnishings and a cool atmosphere. Finally, be sure to slip on your espadrilles and hike out to the little restaurants along the Touques River for the petite and delicious *crevettes grises*—the best shrimps in all Gaul.

Honfleur (Deauville 9 miles): **Ferme St.-Siméon** (*very* expensive).

Le Havre : (1) **Le Grand Large**, (2) **Monaco**. We are deeply grateful for a missive on our desk which reads, "Since your restaurant suggestions for Le Havre were so negligible, we started to seek one and quite by accident we 3 priests came upon **L'Etable**. . . . It is such a delight: rustic interior and steaks over a wood fire. I thought I'd died and gone to heaven, they were so delicious." Thank you, Father. *Non sibi, sed omnibus.*

Le Touquet : (1) **Ambassadeurs et Grill Room**, (2) **L'Escale**.

Les Ponts-Neufs (St. Malo 21 miles): **Lorand-Barre**.

Orbec (main road Chartres–Verneuil–Deauville, 12 miles southeast of Lisieux): **Caneton** (superb fixed-price lunch; don't miss it!).

Pont-Audemer (Deauville 24 miles): **Auberge Vieux Puits**. We haven't been back here for too long an interval, but veteran Guidester Bradley Gaylord reports, "Utter perfection and charm. . . . Dedicated ownership by M. and Mme. Jacques Foltz. . . . Fantastically fine 4-course lunch. . . . The most charming spot on our entire trip. . . . My brother is head of Bell Aerospace. Can I send you a helicopter?" Yes, Brad, YES, YES, YES!!

Pont-Aven (Quimperlé 10 miles): **Moulin Rosmadec**.

Rouen : (1) **Relais Fleuri**, (2) **Couronne**, (3) **Michel**, (4) **L'Ecu de France**.

Trouville : (1) **La Régence**, (2) **À la Sole Normande**, (3) **Chatham**.

Villerville (Deauville 3 miles): **Chez Mahu** seems to be rolling on. If closed, try **Manoir de Grand Bec**.

Châteaux Country (see separate section).

Languedoc (west of Provence):
 Lamastre : **Midi**.
 Roquefort : **Grand Hôtel**.

Lyon and environs:
 Bourg-en-Bresse : (1) **Auberge Bressane**, (2) **Chalet de Brou** (both ½-mile out in the village of **Brou**, opposite the church; the latter is an economy stop).
 Condrieu (Vienne 8 miles): **Beau Rivage**.
 Lyon : Possibly still a 1st-place tie between **Mère Brazier** (atop Col de la Luère, 13 miles out) and Paul Bocuse's **Auberge Bocuse** (at Collonges-au-Mont-d'Or, 5½ miles out). Down the line come: (2) **Mère Guy**, (3) **Vignard Chez Juliette**, (4) **Vettard** (also called Café Neuf), (5) **Nandron**, (6) **La Sauvagie** (3 miles out).
 Mionnay : **Chez La Mère Charles** (a *Chez* that is known to all serious French tummies).
 Roanne : **Troisgros** (Scallope de Saumon or, if that's out of season, Poisson St.-Pierre à l'Oseille; both the culinary masterworks).
 Valence (south of Vienne): **Pic** is the Pic of the lot.
 Vienne : **Pyramide** (once rated as the world's finest, we find its luster fading to a certain degree).

Provence and environs:
 Aix-en-Provence: Le Charvet (L-shape-room; terribly hot in warm months; heavy, rich décor; delicious cuisine; small selection; numbingly expensive; closed Mon. and Aug.).
 Avignon : (1) **Hiely**, (2) **Auberge de France**. At **Noves** (7 miles out): **Auberge de Noves**. At **Les Angles** (2 miles): **Ermitage-Meissonnier**. At **Villeneuve** : **Le Prieuré**.

Carcassonne : (1) **Logie de Trencavel**, (2) **La Rôtisserie Périgourdine**
(both closed during winter). **Auter** has an attractive atmosphere but
grossly unappetizing cuisine; it was the most disappointing meal on a
recent trek through France.

Les Baux (Avignon 19 miles): The great **Baumanière** (see under Les
Baux in "Hotels" section).

Marseille : See below.

Montélimar: La Relais de la Napoule.

Solliès-Toucas (Toulon 10 miles): **Chez Garin**. (Grand Maestro
Georges Garin has closed his Parisian landmark to concentrate entirely upon this less elaborate but still expensive First Category
hobby.)

Reims:
(1) **Le Florence** (especially good chicken in champagne sauce and
Gratin du Sole), (2) **La Paix** (plain surroundings; substantial cookery
at reasonable prices), (3) **La Coupole** (many tour groups; expensive for
value; specialty is lobster), (4) **Boyer** (said to be excellent; somehow
we've always missed it, darn it). At nearby ***Epernay***, try the **Hotel
Berceaux**.

Riviera: see separate section, the "French Riviera."

Savoie (Swiss border):
Arbois (actually in the Jura): **Hôtel de Paris** (noted for its wines).

Chamonix : (1) **Le Royal** in the Casino (Park Avenue living-room
ambiance; glass-enclosed view of illuminated garden; elegant), (2)
Lion d'Or, (3) **Le Lutetia**, (4) **Le Choucas** (for snacks), (5)**Le Crèperie**
(for crepes of all types). The best hotel dining is at the **Carlton**, which
has begun to skid.

Courchevel : Not much. (1) **Hôtel Carlina**, (2) that apple in your
pocket.

Évian-les-Bains : (1) **La Verniaz**, (2) **Casino** restaurant, (3) **Hôtel
Lumina** (one mile out), (4) **Hôtel Royal**.

Megève: (1) **Capucin Gourmand** (blessings bestowed on this patrician
by that connoisseur of calories, Edmond Bory, the doge of Fauchon
in Paris), (2) **Hôtel du Mont d'Arbois** (enormous selection in 4 dining quarters at varying price ranges; lovely views), (3) **Toque
Blanche**, (4) **Le Refuge** (one of the finest exclusively seafood restaurants we've sampled recently; small bamboo-clad room bursting with
flowers, including an especially high pansy count; limited menu but
everything flawless; open ski season only), (5) **Viking** (with dancing
and a club atmosphere; grills best; expensive; go late), (6) **La Géren-
tière**, (7) **Mont-Joly Hôtel** (highly respected by the local high life,
but our repast was down in the valley, the valley so low). We haven't
sampled the wares at the **Duc de Savoie Hotel**.

Talloires : **Auberge du Père Bise**.

Strasbourg and environs:

Colmar (20 minutes north at Illhaeusern): The enlarged and beautified **Auberge de l'Ill**, on the banks of the Haut-Rhin, is now one of the top stops in the nation. We are thrilled to report that all of our earlier demurrers have been swept away by the Haeberlin brothers and their conscientious staff; they now provide blue-ribbon quality in every respect. Cuisine excellent, but heavy in the Sauce Department (remember this is Alsatian fare, not Classic French). Damned good Turbot Soufflé with lobster sauce, Noisettes de Chevreuil, and ice cream; perfect attention from an alert corps of captains and waiters. Closed Tuesday. Summary: Superb for country dining! Prices here, not incidentally, are not punishingly high for the quality. They're not cheap either, mind you. In Colmar itself, the much less expensive **Maison des Têtes** provides highly satisfactory fare.

Strasbourg: (1) **Au Crocodile**, (2) **Au Gourmet Sans Chique**, (3) **Le Bristol**, (4) **Coq d'Alsace** (5) **l'Aubette**, (6) **Valentin Sorg**.

Wantzenau (10 minutes north): (1) **Zimmer** (rustic), (2) **Au Moulin** (open air; closed Tues. and from mid-July to early Aug.).

Marseille deserves special attention because of its importance as a crossroads and jumping-off point. We shouldn't forget, either, that it's almost universally conceded to be France's foremost seafood center. Our number one candidate here is **Le Caribou** (place Thiers, in the little square behind Surcouf Restaurant). The atmosphere is rustic, colorful, and appetizing. Zingo-checkered tablecloths are a visual highlight. Add the small tables and little balcony, and you have a perfect setting for the savory cuisine. Droolingly we recommend *La Spécialité Qui Plaît Aux Gourmets;* try these yummy hot and cold specials, which are a full meal in themselves. Shellfish in profusion during the R-months; meats and fowl always on tap. Tops for urbanity and variety. **Brasserie des Catalans** (6 rue Catalans) angles its spotlight almost exclusively on sea fare. Go here for absolutely the finest bouillabaisse in the region. The service is rough, the décor strictly utilitarian, and there's no view (except for the vision of the chef!). Master of things briny. **Surcouf**, nipping at the yacht gangplanks on quai de Rive-Neuve, comes up with a mock-elegant mien but ultrasavory vittles. Our recent Délices des Fruits de Mer (sea niblets folded in a luscious sauce-bathed pancake) again was a marvel for a soothingly low outlay. Professional service assiduously overseen by Manager Pierre Chargueraud. Good. The **New York** is also highly regarded by hungry locals who haunt the Old Port, but the reception we received gave us the feeling we were inconveniencing the staff by spending our money here. Red awning-covered entrance boasting open-air oyster bar to preview coming attractions; chic-but-no-nonsense atmosphere of hanging iron lamps and damask panels; jam-packed when the meal gong sounds. Passable. **Cintra**, next door, offers a crow's-nest peek at the ship's spars from its 1st-floor deck; ground level for snacks only. Best for its panorama. **Au Pescadou**, inland at place Castellane, will give you the greatest shellshock of your culinary lifetime. We counted no less than 54 types and grades of crustaceans at the market-stall entrance; just point your pinkie at any one of them, and it will be yours. Almost anything that swims, frolics, or creeps in the Mediterranean is here. Noisy; rough service; ghastly décor—but, my, what a piscatorial paradise! **Chez Fredo**'s fame is built on its pizza; decorated simply and plainly in the Corsican and Provençal moods; much better for French-speaking pilgrims than for those who don't "parley-voo." Outside of town, we'd pick Chef Berot's **l'Ercole**.

That winds it up—and please don't be surprised if that "darling little restaurant—the one everybody goes to!" isn't here. Of the 300-or-so we've staggered through in Paris alone, nearly half are listed here—and that leaves us with only about 11,900 to go. So don't get an inferiority complex if you should miss that little gem your friends rave about, because how can they expect you to visit more than 10 or 20 of the enormous total?

NIGHTCLUBS

NIGHTCLUBS Practically on every corner. You have your choice of a $75 dinner, a watusi, a sophisticated bar, a 50—count 'em—50-leg show, a strip at 11:30 A.M. or P.M., a prostitute, a gigolo, an "exhibition," a glass of beer, a team of acrobats, or a Mickey Finn. Take your pick, because Paris has them all.

But let's never forget, for one minute here, that some of the most cold-blooded, ruthless poachers of the evening world have set you up as their top-priority target. You're nothing but a big, fat, ripe American chump who will drink any rotgut with a "champagne" label, applaud any tired old bag sans her usually necessary brassière, and pay a triple king's ransom for the "privilege." Most Parisian cabaret operators are downright vicious toward the suckers who keep them alive—and this includes innocents from Belgium, England, Holland, Egypt, Zululand, or anywhere. Taxes, steeper than Mont Blanc, contribute materially to this psychology. According to a government official quoted by a U.S.-owned periodical, they're so outrageously discriminatory that these rookeries are *forced* to exploit customers to stay alive —and the police wink at corrupt practices out of sympathy for the owners. Thus while there are notable exceptions, I *make no blanket guarantee whatever* on the spots listed below. So please remember, when you tour these bright lights, you're on your own. Please also remember that names, owners, and addresses change so rapidly here that our now-accurate listings may not even be in operation by the time you set out for the evening. This is perhaps the most perishable copy in this book.

The big brassy places are tourist favorites. Some charge $5 or so admission per person (a flat rate at the door), and most refuse to serve anything but champagne at $18 to $60 per bottle at the tables; if you do manage to ransom a Scotch and soda here, it might fizz in for around $12 per cup. Such beverages on a drink-by-drink basis, however, normally can be had only if you stand at the bar, where each will ring up $7-or-so for the comptroller. All the big ones are out for the indiscriminate spender who won't bother to check the bill.

The **Lido**, more formal in its showmanship than ever before, stages what is probably the most elaborate Ziegfeld-type spectacle on earth today. It stuns the customers with its ensemble of at least 50 dancers, showgirls, seminudes, and headline international acts. But it also levies a bare-chested minimum—

repeat, minimum—of 95 F per person for either a ½-bottle of so-called champagne or 2 drinks. Guests who sit through both the 11 P.M. and 1:15 A.M. performances (they are almost identical) are walloped with exactly double these figures, theatrically and financially. The architectural layout is so flat that, behind the first few rows or the numerous wide-girth pillars, the spectator needs a periscope (2 eyepieces, please) or a portable x-ray unit to see what jiggles below the shoulders. Although you can garner a pale notion of the motion from the bar (thus conserving money), most visitors hie themselves here for its fair-to-poor dinner and a better chance at a ringside seat. But, as a long-suffering Assistant Professor of the University of New Hampshire so rightfully reminds us, "This means a compulsory 147 F for this indifferent meal plus the ½-bottle of terrible champagne or 2 small drinks— and there is no escaping it, when one dines. You should underline their charges in bright red ink!" About 9 P.M. is the best time to go. Here's strictly a dealer's choice as to whether or not this globally famous mecca of dazzle is worth its investment to you.

The almost equally renowned **Moulin Rouge**, immortalized by Toulouse-Lautrec and later known for its can-can by generations of wide-eyed spinsters, has been taken over by the Lido. Although the tariffs are just about the same, it is purposely geared to a lower category. Huge, tiered, theaterlike hall; bar atop the pyramid; lavish show with some seminudes. Here again we have the TV "spectacular," with mammary glands the twin features, plus enough feathers and chiffon to bury the Gare du Nord. Old egret to most travelers —except, of course, first-timers.

The **Eiffel Tower** adds its gleam to the City of Light with a dinner show in the first-floor restaurant. Supper begins at 8 sharp; the show is at 9:30 P.M., concluding 2 hours later; the elevators stop elevating at midnight, but there is little to let you down in the entire evening of refined relaxation and fun. It goes every night but Sunday. Recommended.

Olympia, a music hall fixture since 1893, has been snatched from the brink of oblivion by its tenacious director, Bruno Coquatrix. The house that hosted such luminaries as Maurice Chevalier and Mistinguette promises to hang on in spite of what it protested as a confiscatory tax situation. We wish it continued success.

The **Crazy Horse Saloon** (12 avenue George V) continues to draw masses of U.S. tourists with wives, U.S. tourists with oo-la-la nonwives, U.S. tourists solo, and U.S. tourists. Contrived, occasionally salacious, sometimes entirely nude striptease, cleverly aided by projected images (we're talkin' about FILM projections, Sam!); many of which are underexposed; thunderously loud musical assists; rapid, knock-'em-back service; your 1st drink at the bar will pour for close to $10; if you are seated at a table the cost will be considerably more; it is open every night year round. Perhaps we're being stuffy or miserly, but at these prices, for what is there, we always have the feeling of being such suckers that the place just doesn't appeal to us. Scads of Guidesters disagree. If you go, be double-sure to watch your billings and to check your change (especially the folding money).

For the revue type of attraction, the **Folies Bergére,** with its 40 tableaux displaying 1600 costumes, is the most glamorous, though its quality is a far

cry from what it used to be. It is booked for days or weeks in advance, for
—with the aforementioned Lido—it is about as popular with Americans as
the World's Series; make reservations through your hometown travel agent
if you're determined to see it. If you land in Paris without tickets, here are
2 tricks which *might* work: Either cross the palm of your hotel concierge with
beaucoup silver immediately after arrival, or go to the Theater Office at
American Express at exactly 5 P.M. on performance day and hope for cancellations (which are frequent). **Casino de Paris,** also for outlanders and also
usually jammed, is runner-up in this category.

Was anyone speaking of a fascinating study called s-x? If so, the "Sex-
yrama" at small, crowded, ruby-velvet **Sexy** (68 rue Pierre Charron) offers
a parade of s-xy-looking dames and oily muscular male escorts on a tiny stage
between 10:30 P.M. and 12:30 A.M. nightly. Oh-so-friendly-nuzzling atmosphere; numerous darkened nooks to discuss French economics with yumptious and pleasant B-girls with a marathon state of thirst. This one is stuffed
with slack-jawed, bug-eyed gents. Provocative but expensive.

Lucky Strip (4 rue Arsène-Houssaye, a minute from the Étoile) is the type
of place where you could take your children—*if* they happened to be junior
delinquents. Bar at entrance; tiered "orchestra" section with armchairs and
tables stair-stepping down to the proscenium; peppery combo zinging from
10:30 P.M. until the last customer weaves out; attractive B-girls who struck
us as more rapacious (at least on our recent visit) than a pack of starving
hyenas; knavery from the fang-tooth barmaid who tried to hide the "official"
house prices from our view. Because of the jackal-jaded attitude encountered
by us we cannot recommend it to any Guidester. Go strictly at your own risk.

The **Fifty-Fifty** (26 rue Fontaine), seems to start its sexes at the 50-50
degree and then move them up to more complex ratios. This time the house
featured "Les Mini-Boys et Les Mini-Girls"—but we didn't see mini of either,
if we must be specific. The manager impressed us as being almost as scruffy
as one of his well-worn carpets. The area is dangerous. Approach with caution
—in every respect. **Madame Arthur** (75 bis rue des Martyrs, near Sacré-
Coeur), with its horrible orange façade and rococo pillars, draws a number
of madames named Arthur; female impersonators are its feature; don't pinch
anything here, because it might pinch back. **Elle et Lui** (31 rue Vavin) bills
itself as "The sensational Night Club of Montparnasse Where the Woman is
'King'." It seemed to us to be more elle et elle and lui et lui. Although we
heard that for a time it was operated as a private club, we suspect the only
people turned away might have been those without billfolds or purses. Open
every night—unfortunately. The side-by-side **Le Carrousel** struck us as being
a perfect study hall for sociologists and geneticists. Here's Lapland in Paris.

Shéhérazade (3 rue de Liège), a traditionalist, now has gone so commercial
that we no longer applaud it. The service is kind—but at $15 per drink it ought
to be almost loving. (A jug of Chivas sells for a mere $110!) To have your
fortune told you must grease Madame Monika's palm with $25—quite a
handout. Its décor is seedy and overwhelmingly rococo. The cuisine is White
Russian, not distinguished but adequate—and quite costly. It operates 7
nights per week. And "operates" is the operative word.

The tariffs at **Chez Raspoutine** (58 rue de Bassano) are OUTRAGEOUS.

Previously we have reported about our own clipping here—but this was somewhat less gross than the indignity just suffered by our esteemed friend and *bon vivant*, Senior Editor Dennis McEvoy of the *Reader's Digest*. No entrée was ordered. His bill for 2 blinis with smoked salmon, 2 cups of borscht, a double soufflé, 2 vodkas, and a bottle of the cheapest wine on the menu? $153.16!!! Now that he and we have been so brutally sheared, this joint is on our Black Books forevermore. **Tsarevitch** (1 rue des Colonels-Renard) is a posh pad for passionate pashas. Doorman who is an exact duplicate of Harpo Marx à la astrakhan; wall coverings in old gold damask; mauve-draped ceiling; incarnadine silk tablecloths bearing silver candelabra with red (but White) Russian tapers; a royal Tartar portrait commands the rich Slavic scene. Cuisine heavy in both quality and cost (only the host sees those aristocratic menu prices); coffee and champagne (the latter pushed strongly) served on a sterling doily; friendly professional attention; performers (some excellent) every 20 minutes throughout the evening; zither, accordion, and string ensembling between singles' acts. Better, in our opinion, than any of the above Russian trio. How long it can last at its present tariff level is hard to say. Recommendable—but check your bill carefully. Even more costly is **Reginskaïa** (128 rue La Boétie), a fairly recent space probe into the wallets of Parisian fad cultists by the famous Régine (see *Discothèques*). May we assume that you value your travel funds too dearly to shell out anywhere from $130 to $170 for a twin dinner and a brush with her cabaret cabals? Even with its superior cuisine, fine orchestra, and rich ambiance, we think this is the straw to break any hedonist's backbone. No thanks; not for us. **Monseigneur** (94 rue d'Amsterdam) has been renovated; emphasis now on high-life violin serenades, high prices, and high controversy as to whether it can survive. Well done, but costly. You can also find gypsy strings and the Hungarian spirit of yore at **Paprika** (14 rue Chauchat), especially after midnight; fodder as spicy as the name. **Franc-Pinot** (1 quai de Bourbon) shouldn't fool you by its unpretentious entrance; down the narrow staircase you'll find an intimate seventeenth-century *cave* in soft mulberry and fairly oozing with character; mirrors, tiers of tables, air conditioning, and an intermittent floor show from 10:30 P.M. onward, alternating with dancing to a 3-piece combo; music and dinner commence at 9 P.M., with supper available until dawn. Hospitality carefully supervised by kindly, young, English-speaking Yves Sénié. First-timers usually like this one. **La Tête de l'Art** (5 avenue de l'Opera) provides an artfully heady night out, with a sound dinner, champagne, and an excellent show for under $60. Naturally, you'd enjoy the comedy acts more if your French is as facile as the wit employed. Good but special. **Alcazar** (62 rue Mazarine) offers a gay-oriented evening to its followers. Turn-of-the-century atmosphere; singing, jesting waiters; kooky diversions plus a zesty parade of entertainment. **Michou** (80 rue des Martyrs) does a similar thing in its own more modest way. **Étoile de Moscou** (6 rue Arsène-Houssaye, near the Étoile), is a semicircular family-type club with loud singers (a Russian chorus, maybe?). Hosting by Igor and Vava in this nucleus or in the **Au Stéréo Club**, a bar and discothèque on the same property; same ownership as Tsarevitch. **Villa d'Este** (a few doors away and also tied in with its neighbor) seemed to us to draw a cheaper clientele even though they are asked to pay considerably higher tariffs; open for the cocktail hour and tea dancing from 4:30 P.M. on Saturday and Sunday—and always from 9 P.M. until morn. We quaffed but did not sup. **Topless** (2 rue Coustou) is earning bra-vos from goggle-eyed gents these evenings. On our swing down this mammary lane a number of males seemed to be doing a good job of pouring their Martinis down their natty wide lapels as they watched. For no man who is in his cups. **Pussy Cat** (22 rue Quentin Beauchart) used to be the Grisby, which we also couldn't stomach.

Visit a quarter of this list, and you'll need a new oil well to cover your checks.

Discothèques? As in London and all of the major continental cities, they wax and wane with such astonishing rapidity that yesterday's vogue might be tomorrow's bane. If possible, they are even more volatile than the "traditional" night spots. Therefore, a number of the following places might well be out of business by the time of your arrival.

Regine's (74 rue de Ponthieu) is the offspring of the ever-fertile, eternally verdant Regine, creator of the aforementioned Reginskaïa and New Jimmy's (see below). As if you hadn't already guessed, this *dame* never does anything on the cheap. A twin outing here could easily kiss adieu to $180. Entrance down several flights of stairs; mirrored ceiling; well-faked marble dressing; soft illumination across paneled walls and potted palms. You may be interested to see the Pop-Art kitchen. Though the dance *piste* evokes notions of a sophisticated moonscape, the overall tone is that of the flapper era. Excellent band; generous and genuine libations; sparkling clientele. We recommend it, but mainly to Middle Eastern émirs with oily gushers at their gateposts.

The **St. Hilaire** (74 rue de Rennes, not to be confused with the rue Vavin or rue Geoffroy-St.-Hilaire installations) is a private club; visitors are welcomed, however, by prearrangement with concierges at leading hotels. Restaurant segment directed by Alan Senderens of Archestrade fame (see "Restaurants"); space for 50 diners behind glass-sheathed walls; disco portion in long narrow room with oval dance floor; open all week, with meals surrendered on Sundays. Nod hello to the silver stork on the staircase for us. Discreet, chic, and another one that is wickedly expensive.

Chez Castel was still very much "in" during our latest visit. It is in a slum quarter grandly and euphemistically named rue de Princesse. Ground-floor waiting room lined with creepy rejects who were praying for enough prominence to earn a table downstairs; same-level cozy grill and fin-de-siècle bar; grubbed-out subterranean pub; canopied entrance where the more esteemed lemurs played, danced, dallied, and imbibed; supper rooms and a relatively serene bar. The best, in our opinion, of this curiously popular species. On the same *rue*, **Le Club d'O** *rue*fully longs for as much traffic. To get it, the portals seem to be open to just about anyone with pockets or purse. Bizarre-to-eerie interior; curi-form pillars; fiendishly dim illumination; beverages seemed to be conjured up by clever alchemists. Popular among wizards, sorcerers, nighthawks, and tradesmen in nocturnal bitchcraft? **King's Club** (rue de l'Echaudé), impressed us as being as gussied up as the study of Mad King Ludwig. Wall-to-wall carpets, but not on the floors—on the walls, naturally, where they belong; weirdly shaped lighting fixtures; speakers, or plutonium extractors (God knows which) around the ceiling; a hairy-underarmed, porridge-faced female record spinner in the corner; handsome waiters who bob, weave, double-shuffle, bump, grind, and jerk with the music as they transport your liquids. **New Jimmy's** (125 boulevard Montparnasse) is still popular, but it's no longer a monumental effort to jimmy your way into its sacred precincts. Inside, the aforementioned *Doyenne* of the Dandies, Régine herself, occasionally waddles, slops, and swoops among her chosen people. Dark surroundings that almost sequester the features of its clientele; black-tile décor; black-and-blue patrons contusing on the eensy dance floor while trying to maintain their conscious chic; jammed with youthful blue bloods whose red corpuscles hover at 102° F. Going down, in our opinion. **Number One** is so *privé* that you'll have to collar a local prince-in-exile to help you storm its social barricades. We did, and found it hardly worth the effort. François-Patrice's *other* **St. Hilaire** (24 rue Vavin) tops the expected facilities with a restaurant terrace. We prefer the Hilaireity more at the rue de Rennes address (see above). **Abreuvoir St.-Hilaire** (7 rue Geoffroy-St.-Hilaire) serves inexpensive fare in its dining room and reasonable drinks in its bar, with its gyrations confined to its basement. **Le Boeuf sur le Toit** ("The Steer on the Roof"), now operated along the same lines as a student hangout, is highly cliquish. The **Bus Paladium** (6 rue Fontaine) is in the rugged and avaricious Pigalle district. For a time it was shut down for being too noisy. Orchestra; matinées Sundays and holidays. Watch your hat, coat, wallet and—if necessary—your molars. The cellar-sited **Ecossais** surrounds itself in red Scotch plaids, Tiffany lamps, and tinseled ceilings. Upstairs is the Kilt, which is less fashionable. Both serve as pick-up centers for under-25's. **Montparnasse 2000** (28 rue Vavin) makes us yawn well into the next century.

For cocktails (6:30 P.M. to 8:30 P.M. are the usual French hours), the **Ritz Bar** on the rue Cambon side is the most chic. The **George V Bar** is the most frenetic; the flower-lined Garden Bar of the **Lancaster** may still be the most soothing; the tartan-seat **Plaza-Athénée Bar** and the **Meurice Bar** are among the most discreet. **Harry's Bar** (5 rue Daunou) couldn't be more Main Street-U.S.A. if it imported Schlitz beer and TV wrestling matches; now beloved by French as well as old-time American clientele. **La Calavados** (40 avenue Pierre Ier de Serbie, around the corner from the George V) is sophisticated, fashionable, and crowded; this one is open until 6 A.M., and it's one of the most popular places in Paris for a late, late, LATE supper. The food is far from epicurean, but the welcome is warm, the tempo is lively and the atmosphere is pleasant. We like it. Another pleasant appetite quencher in the darkling hours is **La Mendigotte** (quai de l'Hôtel-de-Ville), which offers a friendly little dining room, an open fire during the chilly months, adequate fare, and an intimate floor show. Sidewalk or terrace oases include the renowned **Café de la Paix** (which has reopened in its original style and is better than before, in our renewed opinon), **Fouquet's** (99 Champs-Élysées), **Colisée** (44 Champs-Élysées; served us a heavenly mixed-shellfish platter around midnight recently), **Alexandre** (53 avenue George V), **Club de Paris** (3 avenue Matignon), and scores of others.

For after dinner, there are also dozens of drop-in places—casual bars or *boîtes* for a quick look and one drink. The **Ascot,** next to the George V, suavely recalls an appropriate racecourse theme. Soft lights and soft piano melodizing; sedate, patrician, and expensive. About 2 blocks away, **Le Brummel's** (50 rue François 1er) is comprised of twin rooms on 2 levels. Attractive for friendly persuasions. **La Calavados**, mentioned above, is one of our favorites. For seekers of serene local color, the perennial **Au Lapin Agile** ("Agile Rabbit") at 4 rue des Saules still serves brandied cherries, still offers the same 9 tables in the same smoky, low-ceilinged room, and still features spouting poets, venerable musicians, ancient instruments, and some of the best folk songs of the capital; touristy but interesting; closed Monday. The **Mars Club** (4 rue Robert-Estienne) is noted for its hot-and-cool piano; smoky, jammed, a mecca for celebrated visiting musicians, and employees who seemingly couldn't care less about finding your space or taking your beverage order; if you're full of good cheer and John Haig's Best, here's real rhythm, man. But if you're our kind of jazz cat, you might like the **Artois** (27 rue d'Artois), formerly called the Mod Club, and before that the Blue Note. It offered fair talent, cheerful atmosphere, pleasant décor, a nice staff, and enough air; no cabaret, no B-girls, nothing but good drinks and extra-mellifluous music. **Slow Club** (130 rue de Rivoli) beats out perhaps the most consistently high-grade Dixieland in the city. Loaded with the Younger Set on weekends; surely no place to sit and scarcely any space to stand; closed Monday. For serious listeners who can survive the discomfort, it is superb—but for tailgate dilettantes, it is strictly disrecommended.

§TIPS: Don't wander into Montmartre unless you are with French friends, preferably *tough* French friends. Some cabbies in this district cannot be trusted. Bases such as the Shéhérazade, Monseigneur, and Au Lapin Agile continue to be relatively safe, but exercise *utmost* caution on the "joint" circuit, which is not only a fiscal chopping block but can be physically dangerous as well.

Post-mortem tip: There's a Turkish Bath at the Claridge Hotel.

Post-post-mortem tip: The Golden Cross Association has opened the first of a chain of *sans Alcool* "bars." (*Entre nous,* dear chickens, we've never tried it, don't know where it is, and don't plan to investigate one inch further. But it's there!)

Got a problem, sweetie? France is offering a velvet glove to the lovelorn or confused (or even infected) swain or lass who needs advice. A free counseling service by phone (544–5646) provides expert guidance to anonymous callers on legal matters, contraception, abortion, puberty, marriage, or whatever. Leave it to the French!

Any hotelkeeper who rents a room to a prostitute is guilty, by national ordinance, of procuring—and this carries a stiff fine, a possible prison term, and even loss of property for repeaters. As a result, there has been a rush for apartments in the areas where tourist swarms are thickest: Champs-Élysées, Madeleine, and the Opéra. The 5-to-10-thousand professionals still in action scoff at this so-called Operation Virtue and claim that business was never better. So many "Rosemarys" are picking up customers in their sleek sports cars and whisking them to the parks that the Bois de Boulogne—one of 10 zones designated as "operating areas" by the Sin Syndicate—is popularly dubbed "The Green Grass Hotel." "Organization" prostitutes administer other zones so strictly that interlopers who propound cheaper labor are discouraged by classic gangster methods. Many B-girls in the better nightclubs or strip joints are "union" practitioners of the trade (who went on strike for 2 weeks last springtime!)—and it's wise to remember that these particular pigeons are normally forbidden to leave before the closing time of 2 A.M. to 6 A.M. Also, if anyone's flesh should ever be weak, he should (1) make certain he's not steered to lodgings which would entangle him with this law, and (2) harbor the chilly reminder that the infection rate of syphilis and other forms of venereal disease in French cities and industrial areas has jackrabbited frighteningly. (Have you thought about a holiday in the country lately?)

TAXIS   At night, when it rains, during meal hours, and at the peak of the rush, Paris' 14,500 taxis are as elusive as ever. From the discovery of the gasoline engine until a few years ago, cabbies just plain quit as soon as the clock struck lunch or dinner—and all the pedestrian got was assorted gestures of men-stuffing-their-mouths-with-food. But now, legally at least, they're supposed to take you where *you* want to go, instead of only in the direction of their garage or home. Unhappily, few additional vehicles seem to be available during these key periods.

Cabs are smaller but tabs are bigger. There are set fees for the airports (and don't let them charge you for the return leg to the city, which is included in the lump sum), the racetrack, and other suburban destinations, so be sure to check these flat rates to avoid a possible clip.

§TIP: Stay away from large, luxurious taxis without meters which roam the gin-mill areas at night. They'll take the fillings right out of your teeth!

If the chauffeur who takes you home demands an exorbitant price (very frequent after midnight), here's how to handle him: (1) Note and remember the sum on the meter, (2) give him your sweetest smile, (3) tell him you've got to break a 100-franc note with the hotel cashier, and (4) head straight for the concierge. Then explain the situation to this official and let *him* not only pay the legal amount but also spit in the bandit's eye with your compliments. (Your knowledge of the meter reading is important here, because if the concierge thinks you haven't checked it, *he* might bilk you too!)

Before climbing into any taxi in Paris, be sure that the meter is set at the starting rate (except if you've telephoned for the carriage, of course, when the pickup distance is separate). Otherwise you'll be paying for the last customer's ride in addition to your own. Especially widespread at night.

TRAINS   The French National Railroads (SNCF), a state-controlled network that is 80% electrified, are among the best in Europe. They're also the fastest in the world, *averaging* more than 75 mph over 4250 miles daily, and more than 65 mph over 50-thousand miles. Regular routings also include 125 mph cannonballing along numerous strips of trackage.

If you plan much train travel, take advantage of the Eurailpass (see "Let's Be European").

Routine fares, fast-train supplements, sleeping car supplements, dining car charges, seat reservations, and baggage rates have increased in the past few seasons. So have round trip or circular journeys up to 900 miles (1500 km) —but between 900 and 1200 miles they're 20% less, and over 1500 miles there's a 30% saving. Children between 4 and 10 go at ½-fare; babies ride free. Stopovers are permitted, and groups of 10 or more are given 30% to 40% reductions. For excursions from Paris, 1-day Sunday tickets and 3-day week-end tickets for destinations within roughly 50 miles of the capital come at a 30% to 50% bargain. Dogs cost the same as Junior does.

Fixed meals are served on diners, unspectacular in quality but reasonable in price. You may obtain reservations for 1st, 2nd, or 3rd sitting before departure on the platform in front of the restaurant car, or from the roving steward aboard. You may also be seated without prior arrangements after all reservations holders have been accommodated.

Better still for the budget rider, self-service, cafeteria-style "Cafés à Go-Go" on rails have been introduced. The average price was estimated to be 50% less than a normal repast in the traditional dining car.

There are 3 ways to sleep: Coach, couchette, and *wagon-lit*. The coach is for the birds. The couchette, a French development, offers 6 bunks per unit; you may stretch out but not undress. The *wagon-lit* is the Pullman of Europe; you'll pay for your (1) railroad ticket, (2) berth, (3) reservation, and (4) service tax. It's worth the difference! An improvement on this is the 18-pod (9 uppers, 9 lowers) "T2" car—a cozy his-and-hers arrangement available even with a Second-class rail ticket. The first ones made overnight scoots from Paris to —where else?—the Riviera.

Crack expresses are an important part of the system—Deluxe specials such as *Le Mistral* (Paris–Nice) or the *Simplon* (Paris–Milan) or the *Orient* (Paris–Vienna)—not to mention the *Trans-Europe-Express* runs. The international ones are excellent while you're in France—but when you cross the border, they're liable to become highly erratic. Autorail Rapides, motorcoaches on rails, are the flashiest wrinkle. Usually they're extra fare.

Increasingly the French are employing the "turbotrain"—a fan-driven fuselage riding on a cushion of air and directed by a T-shape track. These streakers zip along the Strasbourg–Lyons, Tours–Nantes–Limoges–Bordeaux routes, ultimately to whoosh to Marseille.

"Snack Cars" (quick-bite dining in the $4 range), "Express Trays" (airline-style "meal" served at your seat), Club Car telephones, dancing cars, movie compartments, Telex, public address systems, bubble-top scenic coaches, and other innovations are appearing on more hauls.

Nine separate stations in Paris, spread all over the map. Eliminate the baggage transfer headache by using the *Transit Cloakroom Service*, which connects the 3 main depots. Cost: 2 F for each piece, for pickup on departure at the station cloakroom. Double-check your terminus before consigning your bags, and check again before leaving your hotel.

Redcaps are bluecaps, and are addressed as "porteur." Although there is a fixed fee for each bag, they will *always* expect an extra tip to top it. If your suitcases are too large, they must be deposited in the rack at the end of the car. Make sure they are placed there, and then look again at major stations to be sure no "mistake" is made by a departing passenger.

Tickets are collected after you get off the train. Don't toss yours away, or you may pay double.

Reserve your seat when you purchase your passage. This precaution will cost you about an extra half-dollar (or $1 if you book it in the U.S.), but it's worth $200 not to be forced to fight the mobs.

A package deal called "Service Complet"—tickets, seats, diningcar space, sleeper, hired car, everything but love and beer—is also offered by the railroads. Your travel agent can fix this up for you too.

Except for the Eurailpass, tickets are valid for varying periods from 10 to 30 days. If your trip is postponed, make sure of the expiration date for the return trip to salvage your investment.

Once you buy a ticket, brother, you're stuck. They've never heard of immediate redemption; you'll wait 1 to 3 months for your money—and when you're back in America you'll get it in francs. French bureaucracy again of the most maddening sort.

TIP: If you prefer wings to rods, this year you will be able to ride the rails between the Paris-North Station and Charles de Gaulle Airport in 19 minutes; this new rail linkup runs every ¼-hour.

AIRLINE Air France bridges all 5 continents with more than 300-thousand miles of unduplicated routes; it ranks 2nd in Europe and 9th in the world. Every 2½ minutes a modern, up-to-date Air France liner arrives or departs somewhere in the world.

At Air France destinations all over the map, "Welcome Service" desks have been staffed with multilingual personnel especially trained to lend advice and assistance to travelers. At Kennedy, Charles de Gaulle, and Orly airports, nursery facilities are available; at the Paris airports, there are First-class and VIP lounges. Most transatlantic flights (including the new Concorde supersonic swifties) and many connecting ones depart and arrive at Charles de Gaulle; however, there are several each day which still utilize Orly, so be sure to note whether you have to make an airport transfer (about $4 twixt CDG and ORY). CDG is 14 miles north of Paris; it offers drive-in-check-in services (as well as check-in positions at entryways); the 30-minute ride leaving for Porte Maillot every 15 minutes costs about $2.50. Buses to Orly gear up at Les Invalides every 15 minutes; they take usually less than one hour and cost $2.50. Both city terminals are equipped with shops, restaurants, bars, car rentals, ticket bureaus for theater and sightseeing, barber and beauty parlors, and new baggage-handling equipment. Aloft, among the Air France cachets for the customers' comforts are kosher and special diet meals, infant hammocks, baby foods, and disposable diapers. In addition, the company is following the in-flight entertainment trend by providing first-run color movies in 2 languages and 10-channel musical offerings for transatlantic and other long-distance jetters. Screens are the giant overhead type, with audio portions transmitted through earphones.

Board Chairman Pierre Giraudet has long been a guiding light in the French transportation industry; Gilbert Pérol is the line's president; Roland Hawkins, an American from Iowa, ably oversees his realm of the North and Central American Division.

French cabin service is traditionally excellent. On all of our most recent hops, the crews in both First class and Economy class were absolutely outstanding in every regard in seeming to *care* about the welfare and happiness of their charges. Without exception, the *Chefs de Cabine* and the stewards were grave, courteous, and extra-thoughtful. The oh-so-charming hostesses, although clad in unbecoming Balenciaga uniforms topped by clumsy peaked caps, overcame this sartorial handicap through their natural chic and size-36 smiles.

In food Air France flies an erratic course. In the past, their European flights have provided us with more pleasure than have the transatlantic Gaulic galley. Now, however, the long-range gastronomy is tiptop in quality and presentation too.

If scheduling difficulties or other special problems should plague you, take them at once to American-born Ed Tourtellotte at Air France, 1350 Avenue of the Americas, New York, N.Y. He is the airline's Manager of Public Relations, North and Central American Division. In our years as travel reporters, we have never met a faster thinking, more dependable, more patient, and more cheerful PR executive anywhere.

In summary, we like the new Air France that we've been patronizing. What's more, we predict you will, too.

§TIPS: At Orly blue-uniformed baggage handlers of the Elan company tried to extract tips from us on 3 separate arrivals for loading our luggage into the airport–town bus. Don't fall for it because they're already paid very well for operating this concession. But *do* be sure that they put your suitcase inside the bus before it grinds into first gear.

Also at Orly, PLEASE WATCH YOUR STEP! The flooring, as slippery as a Marseille gigolo, can all too easily give you a dangerous tumble. Though local doctors have repeatedly advised airport administrators of the danger, nothing had been done to our press time. One Paris osteopath reports, "American travelers at Orly fall and break bones at the minimum rate of 3 or 4 times a week, and sometimes every day." So forget your flying worries; it's the *walking* that is fearsome here!

DRINKS   Each region proudly offers its own distinctive wine. If you're not particular (or if you're a tried-and-true traveler), much of the time you'll stick to *vin ordinaire,* the routine carafe table wine. It's eminently satisfactory.

Broadly speaking, it's *red* with meat or game, *white* with fish, fowl, oysters, or hors d'oeuvres. If the meat is heavy, gamy, or spicy, Burgundy is usually chosen over Bordeaux.

Never follow a sweet wine by a dry wine, or a heavy wine by a light wine.

Champagne is the only type correctly served through all courses of a meal. Have you ever tried Mumm's Cordon Rosé, the best of the celebrated "pink" varieties? Delicious! "Bubbly" is the customary beverage to be ordered in all upper-bracket nightclubs. Never horrify discerning French by using a swizzle stick—a barbarity to many despite its recent comeback in fad circles; if you don't like its effervescence, take a dry white wine instead. And if the cork pops too loudly, the temperature is wrong; send it back, without delay, for further chilling.

Add water to your ordinary table wine, if you choose (many people do it) —but never, never, *never* dilute a vintage of character.

When in France, (1) don't fill a wineglass up to its brim (the bouquet is hampered by a full glass), and (2) leave a few drops at the end, even if they seem too good to waste (you might drink the harmless but unpleasant dregs).

As a result of the new "fast-aging" techniques, wine comes to maturity much earlier than in former times—the whites usually ahead of the reds. Among red Bordeaux, the last best 1/2 dozen vintages include the '71, '70, '69, '67, '66, and '64 pressings; among whites, try the '71, '70, '67, '62, '61, and '59 offerings. Red Burgundy follows the red Bordeaux pattern, with the addition of 1973; you can skip the '69 white Burgundy, otherwise following the red Burgundian scheme. The better recent Rhônes reward '73, '71, '70, '69, '67, and '66. The Loire produced splendid beverages from '69 through '73, with the exception of '72, which was poor everywhere. For your champagnes, look for a dated bottle, because that is the signal from the producer that it is worthy of being identified by year; you'll bubble best with '69, '66, '64, '62, '61, and '59. Got that? Okay, *santé!*

Here are our personal favorites among France's leading varieties. These are the very top classification, and they're expensive examples of their types:

Red Burgundy: Romanée-Conti
White Burgundy (dry): Chevalier-Montrachet
Red Bordeaux: Château Haut-Brion
Sauterne (very sweet): Château d'Yquem
Côtes-du-Rhône: Châteauneuf-du-Pape
Alsatian: Gewürztraminer
Rosé: Château Bellet
"Demi" Champagne: Crémant de Crémant

A special word about this last entry: Here is an elixir of great delicacy and rarity made by Mumm, so small in supply that it is sold or given as gifts only to pet restaurant proprietors of this topflight vintner. Halfway between a "full" and a "still" champagne in effervescence, it offers the connoisseur a lovely bouquet and just enough bubbles to add its very distinguishable tang and zest. Our plea: In some deluxe house where you know the *patron* well, sidle up and whisper in his ear—and *hope!*

Among the lower-price red wines, Beaujolais is usually an excellent bet, though fraudulent jugglings are becoming more prevalent in questionable establishments. It should be ordered young. Get either Brouilly, Moulin-à-Vent, Juliénas, Morgon, or Fleurie (the sub-names on the label) if you can. Other old standbys in this range are the less-exalted varieties of St.-Julien, St.-Emilion, Médoc, Pomerol, and St.-Estèphe. Unless you're gilded with gold sovereigns, these should be more than adequate for ordinary dining.

Among inexpensive white wines, Chablis is very tricky, due to minuscule supplies of sound types. If you like your whites dry, as most of us do, Pouilly Blanc Fumé, Pouilly-Fuissé, or Muscadet should do the trick without breaking the bank—and they are *delightful.* What passes for genuine Chavignol in many places today is horrid. But Traminer, from Alsace, still has an affinity for a good filet of sole. Algerian wines are no longer under French control. Consequently, they have swapped their potency (the sugar is vital) for acidity (necessary for aging). "French" table varieties, however, are cut as much as 50% with this African import or "strong" Italian or other "sunny" types; the higher alcohol content (which comes from sugar) is required to satisfy current tastes and pocketbooks. Today more and more bottles of low-grade foreign wines are finding their way onto Gallic grocery-store shelves—and perhaps even into the glass at your bistro's table.

Lasting favorites at tables around the world are:

Anjou	Chambertin (extra fine)
Beaune	Cheval-Blanc (extra fine)
Château Ausone	Corton
Château Lafite (extra fine)	Haut-Bailly
Château Latour (extra fine)	Hermitage
Château Margaux (extra fine)	Meursault
Clos d'Estournel	Pommard
Clos Fourtet	Richebourg (extra fine)

Naturally, this is only skimming the surface. There are scores more.

Order Vouvray or *vin mousseux* (sparkling wine) if you want to save money. Though cheaper than champagne, they have attractive similarities. Reason: The champagne name is patented, and these varieties originate outside the legal district.

Finally—and don't collapse if you see it—France now markets substantial quality wine in *tin cans.*

Whiskies from Scotland are plentiful. About 60 brands now fight for the national market. Gordon-type gin goes for less money, of course (French varieties are awful); the import quota on bourbons and ryes is soaring to the point that the French are considering restoring the Bourbon dynasty. Most North American bottled "hard " ware is available in clubs and stores nowadays.

Your best buy is cognac, fine types of which sell for as little as $5. This is the national "hard" drink, spoken of as *fine* (feen); reputable French cognac and Armagnac are magnificent. The people of Normandy are weaned on Calvados, a pungent applejack that can do wondrous things when it's old and warmed. True-blue Normands claim that if sipped between courses it "reams a hole in the belly to make room for more food." Grand Marnier is the standard cordial. Liqueurs such as Bénédictine, Crème de Menthe, Cointreau, Pernod, Crème Yvette, Crème de Cassis, Triple Sec, and Pastis are exclusively French; they are the originals, and all others are imitations or branches of the distilleries (Spain).

Most of the beer is frightful—bitter, watery, with an aftertaste of liver-fed pollywogs—but you'll see a lot of it because it's cheap. Fortunately, some Alsatian types ably contradict this statement. In the past decade, beer has lost its north-France identity; countrywide quaffing has shot up 55%. Always ask for "bee-air," because "beer" to the French waiter means "Byrrh," a popular red vermouth-type apéritif. (For serious quaffers of malt-and-hops, a benevolent publican now offers the brews of Gaul, Scandinavia, England, Belgium, Germany, Ireland, Luxembourg, Czechoslovakia, Japan, and several other nations in his recently tapped out brasserie named **Au Général La Fayette**, at 52 rue La Fayette in Paris.) Cocktails are often mixed with thimbles instead of legitimate shot glasses. In most international establishments they're expensive but excellent; in the average provincial hotel or restaurant, however, they're little in demand.

Psssst! Never tell a Frenchman this (he'll either deny it or reply with an uppercut!)—but over the recent past, border-to-border tastes have been turning to fruit juices (a market increase of 85%) and mineral water (up by 34%). And how is *your* liver, Alphonse?

THINGS TO SEE   France is a 20-ring circus, with 239 animals performing simultaneously. Your travel agent or the French Government Tourist Office will have to block it out in detail for you, because there's too much to cover for this book.

In *Paris*, to orient yourself, first hop onto a morning or afternoon sightseeing tour on a **Cityrama** double-decker bus; hourly departures 9 A.M. through 5 P.M., 3-hour duration, phone 260–8430 for details. For about $7 you can be guided past the major sights, the ones you've known since grade school: Notre-Dame, Bastille, Conciergerie, Ste.-Chapelle, Sorbonne, Panthéon, Latin Quarter, Montparnasse, Hôtel des Invalides (now with an English version for its *Son et Lumière*—er, "Sound and Light"), Eiffel Tower, Madeleine, the boulevards, Louvre, Tuileries, Palais de Chaillot, the place de la Concorde, Champs-Élysées, Arc de Triomphe, Sacré-Coeur, Montmartre, and other points. Corny? Certainly—but broad coverage and good fun (1) *if* you can successfully look over, under, or around the 5-inch hearing disks and seat-conduits that block your vision, (2) *if* the sound tapes aren't too worn to be audible (which frequently they are), and (3) *if* that canned voice isn't describing a famous striptease center just as you pass the Chamber of Deputies.

Bird's-eyeing over the city may be yours at Air Paris, Orly Airport, for a swoop over the city or the Châteaux Country; special charters for other nearby regions also are available.

For budget trippers, **Paris Transport Company** (RATP) offers a special low-price "Tourist Ticket" valid for unlimited rides, during 7 consecutive days, on any Métro train (subway), metropolitan bus, and certain suburban carriers. On flashing your U.S. passport, you may buy it at various RATP offices in the capital (53 bis quai des Grands-Augustins is one bureau), or before your U.S. departure, at the French National Railroads, 610 Fifth Ave., N.Y. 10027.

Strong-legged wanderers enjoy the **"Rambles in Paris"** walking tours—a series which covers the maximum of interesting places with the minimum of pedestrian effort. Sunday, it's the Île de la Cité and Île St.-Louis; Monday, the Palais Royal, Louvre, and Tuileries; Tuesday, Montmartre; Wednesday, the Bastille and Marais; Thursday, the Latin Quarter; Friday, St.-Germain-des-Prés; and Saturday, wait and see, *chérie!* Starting time is 3 P.M., at the rendezvous point for the day; the cost is trifling; telephone KEL 2405 between 8 A.M. and 11 A.M. for particulars. Here's the way the inquisitive stranger can *really* see the City of Light; highly recommended to all who like to stroll.

The **Eiffel Tower**, which sports a "hat"—a big television mast—is perennially the visitor's number one target in France. It was built as a temporary structure for the Paris World's Fair of 1889—not by the man who invented the Tinker Toy, but by the man who designed the Brooklyn Bridge. Open from 10:30 A.M. to 5 P.M. daily; $2 admission to top platform, with lower prices for lower platforms; panoramic restaurant (closed Nov. 15 to Easter, due to fog and cold winds that can freeze the hydraulic fluid in the elevator pumps), plus popular grill (operates all year). If someone should sidle up and offer to sell you a "piece" of this structure, don't whistle for the gendarmes. Unlike the Woolworth Building, which has been "sold" to hayseeds since Grandpappy's day, Eiffel Tower stock is traded on the open market. Secret note to gentlemen: Please consult the "Tip" at the end of this section.

American Express "**Paris By Night** " conducted tours, at about $25 per person, are a good value for the uninitiated. They're on the mechanical side, as they'd almost have to be, but you're as safe as if you were doing the town with an F.B.I. man. Worthy for first-timers—unless they'd prefer to shift for themselves.

Just-for-fun boat tours on the Seine have been Big Business for eons. Entrepreneur Jean Bruel's "**Bateaux Mouches**" fleet includes *La Patache* (theater, TV, 800 capacity), the *Galiote* (theater, dance floor, same general facilities), the *Jean-Sébastien Mouche* (flagship with 300-place restaurant), *Le Coche d'Eau* (self-service restaurant), and the *Parisien* (the best cookery of the 5). You have your choice of 2½- or 1¼-hour rides; frequent departures from morning through evening; full of kids before noon, businessmen at lunchtime, tourist mobs in midafternoon, romantics at 5 P.M., and international celebrities after dark; boarding tickets range from around $2 to $5. Meals are served on 12:30 P.M. and 8:30 P.M. voyages, but we thought the cuisine was on about the level of an Albanian army mess hall (for buck privates, that is); we wouldn't pay $4 for the so-called $28 Gourmet Dinner, even at Paris prices. Departures from a Right Bank wharf between Pont des Invalides and Pont de l'Alma; ask your concierge for schedules, or phone BAL 9610. **Vedettes Paris-Tour Eiffel** operate small rivercraft at 20-minute intervals from the wharf near the Eiffel Tower; 90-minute duration, $2.25 fare, optional visit to historic wine cellars for a little extra. Now paddling is its 5-hour, $25 circuit, which also incorporates lunch or dinner at the restaurant in the Tower. This one and the **Vedettes Pont-Neuf** are not as good for visibility nor are they as comfortable as the "Bateaux Mouches," but they are pleasant all the same. A delightful experience, if you happen to hit a sailing without too many Ladies' SPCA Societies from Ketchikan, Killarney, or Kokomo.

Minicar tours operated by the "**Auto-Mouche** " division provide compact vehicles with taped broadcasts corresponding to prescribed itineraries throughout the city. They even tell you where to find a parking space, which should be recompense enough to warrant *any* rental cost!

A brush with necrology? The world's largest repository of human bones has been unearthed for hardened spirits. The remains of 4-to-5-million souls are stacked along 2700 feet of catacombs near the Place Denfert-Rocherau in Montparnasse. To lend even more spookiness to this macabre nether-nether-land, visitors are issued candles for the long gloomy circuit.

A semiprofessional guide service is offered by the municipally operated **Bureau Officiel de Placement des Guides**, 83 rue Taitbout. Most of its personnel are university students. Daily rates, when we last heard, were about $12 for a guide-interpreter, perhaps a buck more for a First-class Courier, and $10 or so for a Second-class Courier—all, of course, plus tip. Probably these costs have gone up. Specify an English-speaking guide if you don't "parleyvoo." Another bet might be the **Association Connaître et Aimer la France,** 400 rue St.-Honoré. Identical idea as London's popular Undergraduate Tours, Ltd.; ½-day Paris rate of about $25; double that for a full day; choice of several out-of-town excursions. We haven't tried this one, but if the lads perform as well as their English counterparts, it should be well worth every franc.

Too many visitors miss the **smaller museums** such as the Cluny (Gothic exterior and medieval collection), the Carnavalet (hodgepodge of authentic artifacts of Parisian history), the Gobelins (tapestry), the Rodin (works of the sculptor in a home and garden), the Military (near the Gare des Invalides), the Opéra (part of the famous landmark; separate entrance), the Jacquemart-André (across the street from the Café de la Paix, specializing in Italian Renaissance as well as eighteenth century), the Victor-Hugo (place des Vosges, a relatively untrammeled highpoint), and the Hunting Museum (60 rue des Archives) for city-bound nimrods. This year, in the Beaubourg district, the ambitious National Center for Art and Culture is due to be unveiled; it will contain just what its name implies. For peripatetic philatelists, there's the Musée Postal (exhibits on the history of stamps and how they are made).

The **Louvre** has been rejuvenated inside and outside. The work cost some $20,000,000. Twenty-six new exhibit halls were opened, plus a panoramic sightseeing terrace on the roof of one wing. We are especially fond of the Orangerie, with so many lovely Utrillos, Cézannes, Monets, and other gems set in the atmosphere of a private collector's apartment. Art lovers can replenish lost vitamins at the self-service snack counters not only in the Louvre, but in the Jeu de Paume Museum (Tuileries Gardens), the Museum of Modern Art (13 avenue du Président Wilson), and the Château at Versailles. They may nibble on hors d'oeuvres, cold cuts, cheese, pastries, and the like for about $2. Mona Lisa's smile possibly comes from confidence that even she could cook better.

Enghien-les-Bains, 20 minutes out, features a spa and a casino where fun-lovers may risk a variety of games of chance. Parklike surroundings, outdoor dining; dancing and scheduled entertainments; thermal baths to soak up that travel fatigue and "ti many martoonis." We've *still* never run out here, but we'll try our luck one day. Season: April 1 to December 31. Not expensive.

Another delight is to take a carriage ride through ***St.-Germain-en-Laye.*** This forest is one of the most sloth-provoking in Europe, and there is a magnificent, mile-long terrace with a view of the capital when the weather is clear.

Bas-Bréau at *Barbizon*, 43 miles out, used to be the home of Robert Louis Stevenson; now it's a cheerful and expensive little hotel-restaurant, the favorite of many film and stage luminaries. Garden; open fireplace for winter; interesting village; happy for lunch or dinner on a sunny day.

There are many other attractions on the outskirts of, or reasonably near, Paris: *Fontainebleau* (François I's palace—now totally renovated—where Napoléon signed his abdication; magnificent forest), *St.-Cloud* (park and especially good view of Paris), *St.-Denis* (abbey church, tombs of the kings of France), *Chantilly* (horse racing in June-July, château, museum, forest), *Chartres* (lovely drive through the wheat-gold Beauce Plain and across the Eure River to a hillock famed for its impressive cathedral with windows dating from 6 to 7 centuries ago), *Compiègne* (Armistice signed in WW I), *Reims* (world-famous cathedral), and *Château-Thierry* (American battleground, museum). *Versailles* offers a snack bar adjoining the museum; fountains turned on and admission prices halved on Sundays during the warm months; open 10 A.M. to 5 P.M. every day except Tuesday; remarkably restored theater, with even the eighteenth-century cut-velvet patterns duplicated on hand looms; no heating in winter so climb into your woollies or your flask of Remy Martin. All easily reached by bus, train, or automobile; most offer conducted tours.

RATP, the Paris bus line, operates special ½-day and full-day guided excursions through the Île de France region, with regular departures from place de la Madeleine. It also runs multiday junkets to the Loire Valley Châteaux Country, to Normandy, and to the D-Day beachheads, from late April to the end of October.

§FIVE-STAR TIP*****: If you're in Paris, steal a day to take the 2½-hour drive over good roads (via Soissons) to *Reims*. By train it's only a 1½-hour zip from the Gare de l'Est. Here, through a very special arrangement between the Mumm champagne moguls and this *Guide,* you can enjoy one of the tours of your lifetime. As an outgrowth of long and deep personal ties with my Nancy and this author, President René Lalou (who died in '73 in his vigorous 90's) and World Sales Director Georges Prade proposed that a remarkable and unforgettable private welcome be extended to readers of this book. No commissions, kickbacks, or monkey business are involved, naturally—only warm and privileged friendship, as always. The only hook: because outsiders must be prevented from horning in on this expensive welcome by Mumm, you *must* show your copy of the *Travel Guide* to the authorities there. If you go to Mumm on rue du Champ-de-Mars and ask for Director of the Cellars M. Bernard Geoffroy, you will be given a red-carpet excursion through the premises in which America's most popular champagne (1.5-million bottles annually of the 5-million total sales for the industry) is created, aged, and handled with such love. Hours: 9 A.M. to 11 A.M. and 2 P.M. to 5 P.M., *but no tours on Saturday and Sunday between November 1 and February 28.* Here is the Cordon Rouge and Cordon Rosé of charted exploration into a captivating new realm to most travelers—so please try not to miss this very special opportunity to listen to Mumm's word right from the bottle's mouth. *Santé!*

§TIP FOR MEN ONLY: How to impress your *chérie?* Truffles and breast of nightingale at Tour d'Argent? A Jeroboam of Mumm Cordon Rouge '47? A planeload of posies from Nice? But how unimaginative can you get, chum? Now you can floodlight the skyscraping Eiffel Tower for 1 whole hour as a solo expression of passion for you *amour*—and if *that* doesn't knock her off her heels, you'd better turn in your medals. Notice must be given 48 hours in advance to the Service de l'Éclairage Publique in City Hall any time after October 15 (when this edifice is not illuminated as a standard tourist attraction). The cost? A mere $85 for a stunt that would make noodle soup out of a blank check at Cartier. Bargain Basement Lotharios may kindle the Arch of Triumph for a piddling $50 an hour and other landmarks for even less. And as we write this, a mischievously wicked (but delightfully delicious) thought occurs to us: Why not telephone *several* of the most luscious *Parisiennes* listed in your little black book, tell each that you are suddenly tied up in a business conference, and that at 9:03½ o'clock, on-the-dot, the tower will burst into radiance as a trifling homage to your love for "her and her alone"? (We'll bet you 50 francs you'll *really* be busy tomorrow night!)

Independent, self-sustaining sections covering the *Châteaux Country, Lourdes,* and the *Normandy Beachheads* follow.

CHÂTEAUX COUNTRY   Renaissance France flourished at the peak of its elegance in this region. Because of its serene beauties and proximity to Paris, kings, courtiers, and courtesans relaxed here in dazzling luxury. Strongholds were built, aristocracy thrived, and culture was unfettered. To this day, linguistic scholars point out, the nation's purest tongue is spoken in the Loire Valley.

The tumbrels of the Reign of Terror swept away the actors of this historic drama, but little of their glorious handwork was despoiled. Still preserved are 46 great castles or mansions.

From June to end-September, 6 châteaux are further embellished with *Son et Lumière* ("Sound and Light") programs. At least 2-dozen others are flood-lit nightly or on weekends for nocturnal excursionists. However, the presentations (except at Chenonceaux) are given in French—a pleasure-dampening, needless hardship to thousands of foreign visitors. Most nations offering *Son et Lumière* schedule English-language versions at least once a week; France doesn't generally, and it's a pity.

First off the bat, don't rush. Even to begin to savor its charms, you'll need 3 to 5 days; a week will pay dividends.

Second, it would be helpful to read up as much as possible in advance of your arrival. The Anglicized edition of Michelin's *Châteaux de la Loire* offers the greatest detail of any publication we've found; suggested trips from 1 to 5 days are also outlined. *Châteaux of the Loire,* distributed by England's Automobile Association (Fanum House, New Coventry St., London W.1), strings together a 450-mile itinerary. Michelin's sectional map No. 64 is indispensable to the motorist.

Your key base should be *Tours* or its vicinity, because this central point is less than 25 miles from most of the principal châteaux.

Our candidates for the 4 most interesting structures in this cluster are Chenonceaux, Amboise, Azay-le-Rideau, and Villandry. Cheverny (see below) is in a special category.

Chenonceaux, a breathtakingly graceful castle, straddles the Cher River. Beautiful formal gardens extend from its sides. Within the trussed-arch building are tapestries and other seventeenth century treasures. Although finishing touches weren't applied until 1634, Diane de Poitiers, beloved mistress of Henri II, occupied it nearly 100 years earlier. Many Americans vote this one as their favorite.

Amboise, the burial place of Leonardo da Vinci, is smaller and less spectacular—but hardly less rewarding. At this writing, it offers a spectacle called "The Cradle of the Renaissance," which draws upon music from the fifteenth and sixteenth centuries. Here you may also visit the illuminated terraces, the chapel, and the gardens—all for less than $1. **Azay-le-Rideau**, charmingly sited over the Indre River and surrounded by groves, is now a Fine Arts Museum; from the French point of view, this one is possibly the most dramatic of all. **Villandry** is noted for its magnificent 3-tier gardens, as well as for its history; the top level has a 7500-square-yard lake, the middle level formal horticulture, and the bottom level a grandly conceived layout of vegetables!

Cheverny, tucked away at *Loir-et-Cher,* is one of the most perfectly conceived and best preserved edifices in the region. It is thriving as an occupied homestead under the aegis of the Marquis de Vibraye. Entry around $1; only ½-dozen rooms open to the public, but these are exquisite; fabulous Hunting Museum dating back through centuries of royal hunts (secretly we wonder if the Marquis has assembled more horns than Henry Ford II). Don't miss this imposing beauty with its tonsure of precisely maintained gardens and parkland. As a living example of ancient manor-isms, here is a dream come true.

Others of note include **Chambord** (largest; 40 miles north of Tours), **Langeais** (privately owned and lived in; another with a beautifully preserved interior; no Sound and Light; 15 miles), and **Loches** (so medieval that it's an Olympus for antiquarians and a bore to travelers with no architectural interests; 15 miles). One of the most exciting from the theatrical point of view is **Château du Lude** (32 miles), with a twice-weekly pageant—in season—of 400 characters in costume, prancing horses, boats, dancers, and singers. This one captured the 1964 Prize for Tourism. The oration is in French, *bien sûr!*

From Tours you can visit **Chenonceaux** (19 miles) and **Amboise** (16 miles) in 1 evening. Buses leave the below-mentioned Syndicat d'Initiative at 8:15 or 9 P.M. and return at midnight; the all-inclusive excursion is around $10 per person. Scads of additional bus departures to your choice of other châteaux are available both daytimes and evenings at the Tours railway station; costs vary from $3 to $6, plus entrance fees.

Spot and floodlighting are employed on various occasions at châteaux in the following places: Ainay-le-Vieil; Bourges (the Mansion of Jacques-

Coeur and the Cathedral of St.-Étienne here), Châteaubriant; Châteauneuf-sur-Loire; Culan; La Ferté-St.-Aubin; Fontevrault; Gien; Nantes; Sully-sur-Loire; Tours (with musical program); Valençay.

The châteaux which must be seen by daylight are Beauregard, Chaumont, Cheverny, Chinon, Cinq-Mars-la-Pile, Langeais, Lavardin, Luynes, Ménars, Meung-sur-Loire, Montgeoffroy, Moncontour, Montoire, Montreuil-Bellay, Montsoreau, Poncé, Romorantin, St.-Aignan-sur-Cher, Saumur, Talcy, Ussé (inspiration for "The Sleeping Beauty"), Vaux-le-Vicomte, Villandry. We haven't yet unhitched our coach-and-six at the "new" Courtanvaux, the castle of the Duke of Fezensac, scion of the oldest family in France. This 500-year-old, 112-room estate is at Besse-sur-Braye, between Tours and Le Mans.

One *must* stop for newcomers—the earlier, the better!—is the Tours Syndicat d'Initiative, an ultramodern, round, glass-bound facility on place de la Gare. It is linked by Telex to Cannes, Nice, Paris, and 11 other centers, in case your later reservations have gone awry; it will change your money when the banks are closed (Sun., Mon., and after 6 P.M.); it comes up with brochures by the yard and regional information by the bushel. From mid-March to mid-October, this voyager's gold mine is open from 9 A.M. to 9 P.M. (10 P.M. on weekends), with a lunch hour shuttering between 1 P.M. and 2 P.M. Be sure to ask for vivacious, attractive, highly knowledgeable Mme. Tandeau.

HOTELS   One of the happier aspects of life in the Loire Valley is that you can take your choice, among the top-liners, of a huge château or a little one. Let's start small. The lovingly restored **Château de Marçay**, set in an enchanting estate dating back to the fifteenth century, is only a few minutes from *Chinon* by car. The lounges are intimate and sumptuous, with brass chandeliers, painted beams, rich textiles, and oil paintings; the dining salon is a masterpiece of refined rusticity, featuring a handsome hearth, thick timbers, exquisite table settings, and the finest cuisine we encountered on our most recent gustatory fossick through this sector of France. The service was kindhearted and impeccable. For quiet country living at its most discriminating level, this gem really glisters.

At the other end of the scale, and certainly even more imposing in its larger, grandiose concept, is the **Château d'Artigny**, which stands watch over the Indre Valley on National Highway No. 10 in *Montbazon* (7 miles from Tours). Here you'll find a twentieth-century entry conceived in pure eighteenth-century style. The site, once the palace of the King's Treasurer, was razed in 1769 and rebuilt over 2 decades beginning in 1912 by the perfumer François Coty, who lavished so much money on his pet avocation that he even installed cold-vaults so that visiting ladies could safely store their furs! Imposing view, especially on the meandering river side; manicured gardens and 50 acres of private woodland, swimming pool, tennis, riding, and fishing; hunting, shooting, golfing, rowing, sport-flying facilities or clubs all within easy reach, and even chamber music ensembles on selected winter evenings. Grand-but-cold entrance hall leading to stately lounges; richly carved library; next-door chapel with 4 exceptionally cozy duplex apartments. Total of 56 extra-spacious bedchambers; #5, on the river, is fit for royalty (many chiefs-of-state stop here); #31 features a bath that was the former pastry kitchen, and it's one of the nicest on the garden side; don't let them shunt you over to the so-called "pavilion", a down-the-road annex used for overflow bus groups or late arrivals. In general, the cuisine tries hard, but still comes well short of perfection, in our opinion. Manager Alain Rabier has improved the service, but running such a palatial monument indeed must be taxing. Certainly one of the most impressive addresses in the nation.

Domaine de Beauvois, at *Luynes* (9 miles west of Tours), is also owned by the d'Artigny musketeers. Structurally and decoratively it, too, is an architectural paradise. There is, for us at least, more coziness here, but then perhaps you're looking for grandeur. Both are reccommendable in their respective manorisms.

Château de Beaulieu, at *Joué-les-Tours*, is more modest. This one seems to draw bouquets of orchids and bunches of onions from Guidesters, some of whom love it and others of whom abhor it. Enormous grounds and homey surroundings in a garden setting; swimming pool; tennis courts; alfresco terrace for summer dining; open every day the calender round. *Beau* it is.

Le Domaine da la Tortinière, also near *Montbazon* (turn left 1 mile toward Tours), is a century-old mansion astride a hill in a sylvan private park. The terrace, shaded by red umbrellas, overlooks the peacefully winding Indre River. The cuisine on our very recent 4-day passage was nothing short of splendid, but the rooms did not give off the sparkle that one might expect and the service, while cordial, was a bit slack. Overall, it was an enjoyable stopover.

The **Bon Laboureur et du Château**, at *Chenonceaux*, is a knockout for gustation, but merely functional for overnighting. The tariffs are quite reasonable, too.

Le Choiseul at *Amboise* (15 miles from Tours) has been brought back to life gloriously—both as a gourmet oasis and as an elegant hostelry—by new owners, Nicola and Jacqueline Diaferio. This vigorous, spirited, and ever-smiling couple have inspired this house with their own zest and vitality. The dining room, with its captivating view of the river, is especially recommendable for lunch. Better and better.

Next in preference—for geographic reasons *only*—come the hotels of *Tours*. In general, they're a cheerless, scruffy lot, considering this city's importance as a sightseeing mecca.

The 5-story, 125-room **Meridien** is a link in the old chain that has its big-sister operation in the capital. La Crémaillère grill, with alfresco terrace for summer; cookery simply awful on our sampling; adjoining La Bergerie bar; pool and tennis. The site, just off the busy highway, murders any semblance of tranquility, but it is convenient for the caravans of buses that roll in here to disgorge the throngs who arrive in migratory proportions. To us, crass and blatantly commercial.

The **Univers** has at last swallowed 4 or 5 lovely-pills, but it needs to take the rest of the bottle. Complement of 85 pleasant units with bath; #232 spacious and quiet; 42 without bath; 29 recently revamped in Tour-ist style; top-rate singles seemed cruelly expensive for the value; minimum cells are available, however. From New Year's Day until March 15 the restaurant is closed; hungry guests are either left on their own or shuttled over to the Hôtel Métropole.

The group-minded **Métropole** offers 70 bedchambers. Now most accommodations lean toward the Directoire school of decoration. The tavern-style dining salon and bar are clean but uninspired. This hostelry introduced us to what we now call the "Murphy bidet"—a curious streamlined contraption that swings out from its disguised recess in the wall by fingertip control. The **Central** is a recently revitalized vintage landmark. Still no restaurant; almost spotless housekeeping; 45 rooms, 15 baths, and 5 showers; mile-high ceilings; simple but agreeable sleeping quarters. A few baths are conventional, but others have that awful peekaboo, where-are-your-earmuffs-darling, half-partition arrangement. Improved to the point where the French would call it "a proper place." The **Grand**, a station hotel, provides reasonable shelter but chug-chug staffwork. **Bordeaux** has been modernized; ho hum. The **Foch**, with 14 rooms and 2 private baths, is a value for budgeteers. So is **Le Rabelais**, which is okay as a tiny nest. **De l'Europe's** 51 rooms are scrubbed, but that's about all that can be said about them. **Mondial**, over the Buré Restaurant (no connection), is not recommended for U.S. patronage. The **Mayflower** seemed more wretched, and **Le Moderne** is at the bottom of our barrel.

Other stopping places in the Château Country or Loire region, some good and some poor, are as follows:

Angers : **Boule d'Or, Croix de Guerre, Anjou**.
Blois : **Château, Médicis** (the latter 4 miles out, at St.-Denis).
Chambord : **St.-Michel**.
Charité-sur-Loire : **Le Grand Monarque**. .
Chinon : **France, Boule d'Or**.
Gien : **Rivage**.
Loches : **France, Tour St.-Antoine**.
Orléans : **Arcades**.
Saumur : **Budan, Roi René, Hostellerie du Prieuré**.
Valençay : **Espagne**.
Vendôme : **Grand Vendôme, Commerce**.

RESTAURANTS   In the Tours area, **Le Nègre** (often called "Barrier"), directly across the bridge at *St.-Symphorien*, is world famous, but our own most recent repast here was a severe disappointment—at a price that can easily jolt a headbone from the neckbone. We've heard other complaints, too, so we can only caution you from our own findings and from what we've picked up lately from Guidesters. In fairness, many still swear by M. Barrier and his kitchen magic. Not this reporter, however.

For château dining, the previously mentioned **Marçay** would be our pick among the thoroughbreds. **Le Choiseul**, at *Amboise*, and **Domaine de la Tortinière**, near *Montbazon*, usually are tiptop too, followed by **d'Artigny** for its aristocratic bearing. .

Lyonnais (48 rue Nationale, in *Tours* itself) is quite satisfactory if you want to be among the brighter lights of the city. Modern mien, with tile floors which would chill the visitors' bones if they weren't offset by the kindliness of the hostess and the friendliness of the staff; excellent fare, at tariffs considerably lower than those of Le Nègre. Recommended. **Rôtisserie Tourangelle** (23 rue Commerce), the next contender, has a leisurely, old-fashioned air, shy but eager-to-please personnel, and praiseworthy cookery. **Buré** (street floor of Hotel Mondial) is adequate but routine. **La Trattoria** is fair if you seek a change-of-pasta. **Meridien** makes us gag at the very thought.

Please don't forget the previously mentioned **Bon Laboureur et du Château** at *Chenonceaux*, which is a rustic dream spot with heavenly cuisine. At *Amboise*, the little **Auberge du Mail**, behind the river dike and beyond the center of town, offers less costly menus. Sweet postage-stamp-size patio with 9 red-clothed tables under a grape arbor; plain, clean, no-nonsense interior; Gallic family management. Not plushy but substantial. The riverside **Bellevue** served us a very decent and inexpensive tourist lunch which we enjoyed on a recent stop; simple but nice. The nearby, more-attractive **Lion d'Or** is very appealing if you are not expecting gourmet-level cuisine. We enjoyed our recent lunch here.

The **Château de Pray**, 1½ miles up the river, is a hillside mansion with a spacious front terrace offering a fine view of the Loire. Sixteen rooms in pseudo-Renaissance motif; deluxe food and prices; numerous Guidesters have complained about tabs coming up higher than they bargained for, so be sure to check your bill before payment; closed January 5 through February 10. Elegant and pleasant.

In *Langeais*, the **Duchesse Anne** has a beguiling garden in which a cote of snow-white doves will puff up and preen at the first sign of a paying client; their fantails are so disciplined that we have dark suspicions of managerial sorcery. About 50 tables outside, 20 more in the modern dining room, and large windows between the sites. Savory vittles and engaging atmosphere; see-for-yourself kitchen, where the white caps are in constant flurry. Definitely worth a try. The **Hôtel Hosten**, almost directly across the street, has a less attractive patio adjoining its Charles VIII bar. Piquant; hospitable attention from the owners; coming up steadily.

In *Guécélard*, 10 miles south of Le Mans on Route N-23, **La Botte d'Asperges** is a slender, long-fronted pit stop with a tiny front terrace that provides a panorama of passing cars and trucks and the *BoucherieCharcuterie* across the highway. In the rear, however, there's a sleepy little garden with even sleepier goldfish, where you may drowse over your Noix de Veau.

If you plan a visit to the previously mentioned Château de Cheverny, you can stoke up at the **Hôtel des Trois Marchands.** It is in the heart of the toy village, edging on the church square. It also has skidded to appalling depths, in our opinion, but is now offered as an emergency refueling pit for famished motorists.

Other alternatives of varying magnitude are:

Angers: Le Vert d'Eau (closed Fri.), **Hostellerie Château** (6 miles).
Bracieux: Le Relais.
Chartre-sur-le-Loir: France.

Château-la-Vallière: Écu.

Chaumont-sur-Loire: Hostellerie du Château.

Les Bezards: Auberge des Templiers.

Montoire-sur-le-Loir: Cheval Rouge.

Orléans: Auberge St.-Jacques, Auberge de la Montespan, Jeanne-d'Arc, Aux Canotiers.

Poiters: The people here are spoiled rotten, in our opinion, by the migrations of tourists who sate their gluttonous coffers with a supererogation of international skekels. Though old-fashioned, the **Hotel France** was the *only* place where we were greeted with courtesy and where any effort was made on behalf of human decency. For this alone we are grateful.

Final suggestion: During High Season (which now includes May and June), the Châteaux Country is deluged by sightseers of umpteen dozen nationalities. April and September are perhaps the best months, because everything is open but traffic is slightly thinner. Whenever you go, however, try to wrap up ALL your reservations *in advance*.

LOURDES   In 1858, 14-year-old Bernadette Soubirous knelt by Massabielle Rock in Lourdes and received the 1st of her 18 visions. Since then, what is probably the 2nd most famous Catholic shrine in existence has sprung up around the site. More than 1-million pilgrims congregate annually at the grotto where the Virgin Mary started the waters flowing during Bernadette's 9th vision.

Transportation to Lourdes has never been easy because of its off-trail setting near the Spanish border. You may make the 555-mile journey from Paris by rail in 9¼ hours, or you may fly in High Season via Air France, Aer Lingus, or a number of other regular and charter carriers. In winter the best connection is from Paris. Flights arrive at Ossun International Airport, about 4 miles out of town.

Unfortunately, the atmosphere of Lourdes has become sickeningly commercial. On our recent loop we saw a sign reading "Visitez Les Grottes de Bethlehem." It was hanging over a Jolly Roger pinball machine in the Snack Bar Parisien. Shoppers gush through the Maison Catholique and the Palais du Rosare—the local market centers of claptrap—to purchase such items as cry-baby Jesus dolls and "l'Apparition" plastic hip-flasks for carrying away the local holy water. (A jigger-type screw-cap on the latter, however, suggests it may also be used for other curatives.) This sort of thing is a shock to the devout, and well it might be. This shrine city has been sadly victimized by opportunistic souvenir-mongers. But for sincerely religious travelers of any faith, Lourdes can be a deeply moving experience, despite the commercial shoddiness of its fringes.

There are approximately 420 hotels in and around the city. Though some are on the expensive side, their quality ranges from low-mediocre to downright-miserable. In most, full pension (room *and* meals) is either obligatory or pushed as hard as they can push it. Since the restaurants we've tried here are all poor, however, this practice isn't quite as outrageous as it would be in centers with higher gastronomic standards. And, since they know they've got you hooked, you usually must pay *full menu prices for the first 3 days.* After that you qualify for the reduced half- or full-pension rates.

Best of the lukewarm lot, in our opinion, is the **Grand Hôtel de la Grotte,** with meals compulsory. Down the line come **Ambassadeurs** (dripping with souvenir stands), **Impérial**, **Moderne**, (a misnomer if we ever spied one) and **Chapelle et Paro**—all seasonal, some noisy, and none exciting. We hear that the **Hostellerie de l'Astazou** is homey, but we haven't tried it. For budgeteers, a happy report has come in from a friendly reader about the **Windsor;** he liked his accommodations, was delighted by staff attitudes, raved about the cuisine, and called its low, low tariffs "a fantastic value"; this one was closed on our attempt to check it out for you, but it looked pretty fair from the outside.

§TIP: Frankly, we found the city so crass and repulsive in all its touristic aspects that we were determined to find some small tranquil haven where we could escape from its hurly-burly sideshow. To our relief, on about a 20-minute easy drive into the Pyrénées we found the mountain-hugged ski station of *Cauterets*. It is peacefully embraced in the lowest point of the Lutour Valley and splashed by a dozen waterfalls, the largest being the Cascade de Cerisey. No hotels are outstanding in this snugglesome sylvan retreat, but somehow any of them seemed better than the best in Lourdes. The **Parc** harks the biggest name, but we prefer the **Chalet**—which *looks* like a chalet. The fresh-faced **Mouré** is very central; it's a skip and a slip to the ski lift. The **Ambassadeurs**, old but improving, boasts the best cuisine in town. As a sign of its provinciality, the rambling, white-stuccoed, red-windowed **Bordeaux**, where we recently placed our sitzmark, advertises Ping-Pong on its stationary —a "first" for us. The **Victoria** is solid yet creaky, as only the French can make 'em. Nice people, however. About 6 miles toward Lourdes, in the village of *Argelès-Gazost*, the **Miramont** and the **Pyrénées** draw the big-city spenders, but **Mon Cottage** would draw little old *moi*—chiefly for its solace. If you want to be reminded of God's majesty up among the cathedral spires of the Hautes-Pyrénées, we believe you'd prefer either of these 2 tiny hermitages to the blare and screech of the major attraction.

NORMANDY BEACHHEADS   In quiet salt breezes blowing softly over St.-Laurent-sur-Mer, you can stand beside the magnificent polychrome plaque which marks the spot where the first wave of U.S. troops doggedly fought their way up the sand banks to achieve what was to become the most planet-shaking mass military movement in the annals of mankind. Below, in serene majesty, lies the full sweep of Omaha Beach and the sun-twinkled waters of the Channel. To the rear is a beautiful chapel, an impressive *rondure* with the names of the fallen, and a trim reception center for pilgrims. To your flank stretches the immaculate greensward and tidy white crosses of the far-flung cemetery, in which 2 Roosevelts are buried beside thousands of their brave comrades.

If you're motoring, strike out first for *Arromanches-les-Bains* (roughly 38 miles from Deauville), strategic center of the British zone of attack and site of the only remaining "Mulberry" artificial harbor. The string of ships deliberately sunk to form the breakwater has been raised, but the mammoth concrete pierheads and a large stranded landing craft remain in its sands. A stretch of highway with telescopes, charts, and listening devices enhances the historic site. Be sure to visit the fascinating Musée du Débarquement (loosely translated as "Invasion Museum"), where battle memorabilia and autographed photos of the commanders are on display, where movies of the fighting taken by combat cameramen are shown frequently during the day, and where an ingenious diorama reconstructs the action on a grand scale. Transatlantic visitors are greeted by ever-kind, English-speaking Antoinette de Berenger.

Then move along to the previously described memorial and cemetery at Omaha Beach in **St.-Laurent-sur-Mer** (perhaps 7 miles). From this U.S. fountainhead, take the several-hundred-yard skip to the seaward road marked St.-Laurent-sur-Mer (par la Côte). This detour, about 1½ miles long, permits you to drive directly along Omaha for a snail's eye view. At the north end you may inspect a small complex of Nazi pillboxes.

The most dramatic terrain of all is Pointe du Hoc (7 miles from central Omaha), where Colonel Rudder's American Rangers stormed its incredibly perilous cliff, seized and held its death-spewing German fortifications for 48 hours in which all but 14 of these heroes were killed or wounded—to find later that they had attacked the wrong promontory!

Utah Beach, about 20 miles farther along, holds little of sightseeing interest today—unless, of course, there are personal reasons for visiting it.

With these stirring battlegrounds behind you, swing down to the base of the peninsula to fabulous Mont-St.-Michel, southeast to Tours and the Châteaux Country of the Loire (see separate section), and then up through Joan of Arc's Orléans (or several alternate routes) to Paris. Distances from point-to-point are short; this entire trip, which can be taken in either direction, of course, should total less than 450 miles—and it's a honey. Whenever you are faced with a choice between a major highway or an off trail by-lane, always take the smaller road. The latter are well paved, and it is on them you will find the essence of the people and the nation.

Hotels and restaurants in Normandy are generally simple and 2nd line. **Caen**'s **Malherbe**, in the center but overlooking a wide prairie, was the pacesetter. Check first to make sure it is in operation by the time of your Norman invasion. The modest **Moderne** offers dining facilities; it is a suitable alternate during this hiatus. The **Metropole** and **Place Royal** come up with breakfast only. The **Gourmet** is said to be okay for budgeteers. For independent dining, **Alcide**, an ivy-covered modern bower, served us a delicate meal at a very reasonable price—considering the high quality of the fare. Outside of a visit to the Abbey, previously we had recommended **Mont-St.-Michel** as a meal stop only. But a number of Guidesters, including an especially sweet and enthusiastic lady from East Paterson, N.J., have reported a splendid renaissance at the **Mère Poulard**, with fresh paint, good plumbing, and a massive overhaul. Cheers to them and to it! Closed from October to April. However, the tiny 2nd-place **Du Guesclin** is still too raw. In winter, the 21-room **Mouton Blanc** is almost the only show in town;

our hardy and well-cooked fixed-meal consisted of 6 Portuguese oysters, a huge omelet, leg of lamb, beans, potatoes, and apple tart; we haven't room to describe the à la carte choices. Even though here is one of the most astonishing architectural wonders of any civilization, it's so noisy and so glutted with excursionists in season that restful sleep is at a premium. You'll also have to climb by foot to your destination, because no cars are permitted on its narrow steep streets. Be sure not to wander off the causeway over the shoal, especially if you're traveling with children; the tides rise so fast that the sands can be dangerous. Nearby **Avranches** has the little **Auberge St.-Michel**, opposite the statue of General George Patton. This one, however, now seems to be in retreat, according to frontline reports from our scouts. During cold months, the creaky-but-kindly **France et Londres** is worthy only for the sweeter-than-sweet Bertheaume family and staff. **Croix d'Or**, also in the same family but seasonal only, has 17 extra-nice rooms, a 50% bath count, many redecorations, and the finest cuisine of all contenders (especially the hors d'oeuvres and the duckling). **Bellevue**, across from the Auberge St.-Michel, is another possible bet in the modest-shelter category. In **Vire**, the **Cheval Blanc**, fronted by a garden plaza, is the pacesetter, both for its comfort and for its table. In **Bayeux**, the **Lion d'Or** roars about its gay but modest dining room, with a "Mathilde" frieze; simple yet adequate bedchambers; nice personnel; a favorite of our old friends, the international oil-company pilgrims Charlie and Alice McWilliams, who always use it as a base for their Invasion Coast wanderings. **Lisieux**? We hear sweet murmurings about the **Espérance**, but we can't verify them from personal experience.

If you happen to be as far east as **Orbec** (13 miles from Lisieux)—or even as far east as Tokyo (6132 miles)—be sure to plan a meal at **Caneton,** a heavenly little rustic tempter that makes us drool in retrospect. Proprietor Joseph Ruaux stuffed us fuller—and happier—than a Christmas goose on the morning of Dec. 24. Our repast of Timbale de Langouste (lobster in a succulent port sauce), plain roast duck, cheese, and a mulled, very old Calvados were all the stuff from which culinary dreams are made. We won't tell you more. Just go, and we will accept your supplicant gratitude for the rest of our envious lives. Closed Tuesday and October. Reserve ahead.

When en route to the Châteaux Country (or to the wonderful Benedictine Abbey at **Solesmes**, world famous for its Gregorian chants), try to plan a lunch break—or a night's stay, if time permits—at the **Ricordeau** in **Loué** (3 miles off N-157, about ⅔rds of the way from Laval toward Le Mans). This high-class but not elaborate provincial hotel is worth a detour; its cuisine rates our ardent cheers. Seventeen small, tranquil, and agreeable rooms; high-ceilinged, traditional dining salon; terrific wine cellar (even Romanée-Conti '28 available!).

TIPPING   Every human being who serves you will proffer a hand with stunning rapidity. You can't beat the Egyptians, French, and Italians: They've got a unique nose for the gratuity. At the movies, if you don't tip, the usherette will probably flash her light into your eyes until you do—normal procedure, and nothing can be done about it! (Besides, her income is based on the alms she garners from you and not on the chicken feed she knocks down as "salary.") There's no use bucking the system. The French don't overtip the French as we do, but their own upper classes get taken too, because that's the tradition.

Hotels add up to 30% in service charges and taxes, depending on class and location. "Restaurants de Tourisme"—most of the better-known places fall into this official category—automatically take a 15% service bite (as previously mentioned, the cover charge has been officially abolished), to which Americans are expected to add another 5% to 7% for the waiter. Where this does not apply (read the bottom of the check), give the waiter 15% to 20%, the checkroom attendant ½-franc (50 centimes), the washroom attendant ½-franc, and the wine steward (if you use him) 2 francs. Taxi drivers get a franc or two, depending upon the length of the ride; hotel doormen (when calling a taxi) get about the same, ordinarily, and more if they go out in the rain to capture your vehicle.

At the theater you buy your program but you don't have to tip (if you don't mind getting a dirty look). The local residents strongly resent giving anything on top of the purchase price. The above-mentioned usherette gets 50 centimes—rigid custom—and the washroom attendant about equal.

Bartenders expect about 20% on each drink they serve you.

THINGS TO BUY

The automatic 17% to 20% discount offered by shopkeepers on hard currency traveler's or foreign personal checks (not banknotes) has been curbed by the French Government. Under the revised rules the visitor must produce his or her passport at the store. If the purchases exceed NF 400 in value (or NF 690 if you are from a Common Market country), you may carry them with you and still receive the discount. Smaller purchases are discounted only if shipped abroad. Any currency, including francs, is now accepted. The amount of the discount ranges between 10% and 25%, depending on the category of the item. All of the merchandise accompanied in person must fit into your luggage. Travelers who leave by train or car must follow specified rail or highway routes, as well as an explicit procedure, to be eligible. The seller may opt between giving the buyer the discount on his premises (thus taking the appreciable risk that the voyager will forget to surrender the forms at the border), or mailing the discount money to the buyer after Customs has returned the forms (thus creating an equally appreciable risk for the tourist if the shop should be dishonest or if the documents should stray during their peregrinations). This red tape reaches a new height in silliness—but who hates a reduction of up to ¼ th of the entire purchase price?

This year, by law, all goods except certain perishable comestibles sold in bulk must display a price tag—a bonus of protection and fair dealing for you and a device for curbing inflation for the government.

For women: Gloves, undergarments, silk flowers, bags, perfume, boutique items, glassware, umbrellas, hats, fine jewelry, and high-fashion clothes. For men: Luggage and leather accessories, cigarette holders, lighters, razors, cologne, novelty jewelry, steak knives, and neckties (pick your shop). For both: Gourmet food items, wines, spirits, and books.

Gloves and scarves? **Denise Francelle** (244 rue de Rivoli) has been our favorite since '46—and she gets better every year. Inside this beautiful modern façade, there is room for exactly 5½ customers—and it's always crowded!—but her selection is so smart and her prices are so sensible that her vast international clientele couldn't care less. Somewhere on the premises, though, she must have a colossal storage room—because in gloves alone (not to mention other specialties) she carries all sizes of about 400 different models in each of the popular colors. You'll find Kislav exclusives, plain, fancy, daytime, evening, barbecue—styles for every mood. One popular gimmick is her beaded or Beauvais gloves with bag to match. Full assortment of scarves—square or long, printed, hand-painted, or brocaded—from Cardin, Balenciaga, Jean Patou, Lanvin, and others. Handmade beaded or attractive Beauvais bags in all colors, too. The latest additions are her lovely umbrellas. Problem-solving dividend, even when you're back in the States: for a nominal postage fee, Madame will AIRMAIL one pair of gloves per box to your Christmas or Special Occasion designee. And what a sensation they cause—direct from Denise Francelle Paris! Ask for sweet Mlle. Brigitte. Reliable and excellent.

For the most fabulous leather goods in France, don't miss a look at famous old **Hermès** (24 rue du Faubourg-St.-Honoré). Everything imaginable; most items are hand-fashioned on the premises. High price tags for superquality.

Boutique items? The princely French institution of **Lubin** (11 rue Royale, near Maxim's), makers of dee-licious *Idole* and other regal perfumes, features $5 to *haute élégance* gift items that excite the feminine soul. *Formidable!* **Roger & Gallet** (62 rue du Faubourg-St. Honoré) has doubled in size and stocks of outstandingly attractive accessories for both genders. Literally hundreds of others line the center.

Sexy fragrances? **Charles Blair** (374 rue St.-Honoré) is the benevolent sorcerer who, in 1934, invented what *both* members of this writing team—and their legions of friends who have since become addicts—regard as the world's sexiest bath essence. (It is THE secret weapon, deliberately never admitted, of an inner circle of America's and Europe's most devastating celebrities.) Now a whole bath line of other libidinous man-traps has been added: Toilet Water, Toilet Soap, and Perfumed Flannel, all with this inimitable fragrance—plus, if you please, a Toilet Water called For Men for Him, as well as for Her a new perfume called "*Medea*," which is positively dangerous in its provocation. This magician has also installed the pick of the ultra-fashionable Givenchy Gentlemen, Inc. line of masculine accessories (shirts, ties, sweaters, etc.) on these same premises. A find. Open weekdays from 10 A.M. to 1 P.M. and 2 P.M. to 6 P.M.; closed Saturday, Sunday, and holidays; mail orders welcomed.

Books? **Brentano's** (37 avenue de l'Opéra) and **W. H. Smith & Son** (248 rue de Rivoli) offer the gamut from the newest Fifth Avenue bestseller to hundreds of 25¢ paperbacks to the naughty but amusing antics of literate ladies-for-hire like Miss Fanny Hill. In the former, an especially sweet Irish colleen, Mrs. Dorothy Vlaccot (yes, the Greeks have discovered the Emerald Isle!), will help you around the shelves. Smith's has a good English tearoom upstairs.

Inimitable crystal? After **Baccarat** (30 bis rue de Paradis) had successfully petitioned Louis XV in 1765 for creation of the nation's first art glass, for over 3 centuries it swept gold medals, grand prizes, and 24 other awards in every prestigious national or international competition, as well as its homeland's Grand Prix for its workers' social welfare. Don't be mistakenly overawed because it has made official State services for all later kings, presidents, or maharajahs of France, Latin America, and India, as well as for shahs of Iran, emperors of Japan and Ethiopia, Presidents Teddy Roosevelt and JFK, and a host of others. Its specialities with greatest buying appeal to us less exalted travelers are the eye-popping bar decanters ($40 up), wine and liqueur glasses ($12 up), vases ($30 up), animals ($25 up), paperweights and ashtrays ($30 up)—all glorious, all reasonable for their exquisite perfection. While there, PLEASE don't miss the fantastic museum so lovingly nurtured by Baccarat's debonair, gifted director, Count René de Chambrun. Refund of 16.66% on all over-$100 orders; closed Sundays and holidays only; branch in N.Y.C. A glittering fairyland.

Jewelry and gold objects? **Chaumet** (12 place Vendôme), Crown Jeweler to most of the royal courts of Europe, is so distinctive and vital in its design and creative skills that unquestionably in our minds it stands heads, coronets, and tiaras above any of its great Gallic competitors. Its origins trace back to when Napoleon shopped here. Today there are no French purveyors in the field who, in our fervent opinions, nearly so excitingly lend their artistry to the classic traditions as well as to the dynamism of contemporary stylings as do Jacques and Pierre Chaumet. Their gems are of the same sovereign quality which this house crafted into Bonaparte's coronation crown and the parures of Empress Marie-Louise. Although its prices follow international levels, Chaumet provides certain unbeatable financial concessions which bear serious inquiry. The chicness of its mountings is unsurpassed anywhere. Pocket lighters in semiprecious stones, $150 to $200; new ashtray and bowl designs in malachite, sodalite, and other beauties with vermeil motifs, $200 to $400; lovely semiprecious-stone rings $300, and with a few diamonds, $350 to $460; new-vogue short gold necklaces with colored gems and diamonds, $1300 to $2000; glorious gold chains with multicolored beads; bowls, cups, and sculptures. And, ah . . . be sure to ask the Chaumets to show you the Baccarat castoffs—leftover crystal extrusions out of which their artisans have fashioned gleaming animal forms by applying gold manes, muzzles, jeweled eyes, or whatever their imaginations dictated. How exquisite they are! If you're the average modernist of taste, we virtually guarantee that you'll melt at the Arcade-Chaumet next door. Downstairs you are invited to witness one of the most imaginative merchandising presentations we've ever seen—a multiple-screen film parade of special objets d'art and personal jewelry. This show alone is worth a flight of fancy across the Atlantic. Chaumet's English branch is at 178 New Bond St., London. For patrician pamperings and distinguished talismans of eternal splendor, don't miss Chaumet. Here is indeed an international Wonder of Wonders.

Perfumes? Be careful, because the retail end of this industry is one of the biggest rackets on the Continent today. *Never be swayed by any shopkeeper's "recommendation." To be safe, buy only the products of established manufacturers.* A favorite trick in this swindler-infested business is to hard-sell a "house" abomination or an unknown brand—with neither staying power nor one iota of merit—as "outstanding," offering the sucker a huge "discount" on a 10th-rate bottle which has already been rigged to yield a 75% to 85% profit. When in Paris, we always buy our personal supplies of perfume at **Fauchon** (see below), because here's one house we know is 1000% reliable.

Remember, please, that *most* (not all) of the leaders are "restricted brands" in the U.S. Customs. Whenever this applies, your importation into the States is limited to one bottle of the same type *per person* (in a few types either the 3-oz. size or 2 bottles are standard). Here's where husbands come in handy, for a change. Have him declare the excess! Direct-mail shipment to America is sometimes prohibited. Be sure to check these restrictions before you buy, because excess amounts are automatically confiscated by our Lads in Blue.

For a comprehensive roundup of the newest scents plus our categories and rankings of France's top 46 perfume manufacturers—insufficient space here!—see *Fielding's Shopping Guide to Europe.*

Perfumes, gourmet foods, liquors, gifts? If you like to eat, to drink, to sniff, and to savor as much as we do, a walk through famous **Fauchon** (24-26-28 place de la Madeleine) should be one of the most fascinating sensory experiences of your shopping life. For 90+ years Fauchon has been France's number one center for fancy foodstuffs, wines, and spirits—with perfumes and selected gift items adding luster to its crown. One floor up, in the newly enlarged boutique, you'll find the 90 top essences of the nation at unbeatable prices. Adjoining, you'll find (1) the modernized "Kingdom of Foie Gras and Caviar" so cherished for its 10% dividends to outlanders; (2) the *nec plus ultra* Epicure Department, and (3) the popular Liquor Department, where the staff will forward purchases to your embarkation point at 15% below the price-tag figures. With its inimitable parade of finest champagnes, rare liqueurs, pâtés, cognac-tinged tangerines, glazed chestnuts, and hundreds of other exotics, Fauchon is the world's most glittering Ali Baba's Cave for French *and* foreign gourmet treasures. Across the street the "Sweet Corner" has delicious candies (15% discount when shipped), petits fours, and ice cream; the all-day Cafeteria dispenses American-style refreshments—even Maxwell House coffee! English-speaking staff constantly in circulation, including 1 smilingly helpful, purebred Yankee salesman, Mr. Chris. Huge mail-order business; flawless service and integrity throughout. Hours: Boutique-Perfumery, 9:15 to 6:30, closed on Monday; other food sections, 9:15 to 6:30 including Saturday but not Monday; Cafeteria, same but including Monday. Brilliant General Manager Edmond Bory should glow with pride. Wonderful!

Lingerie? **Cordelia** (21 rue Cambon) features many items from the Dior line. The female member of this writing team thinks of them as "yummy." The male member of this writing team thinks of them—often. Ask for Mme. Saëz. Exceptionally fine.

Unbelievably exquisite silk flowers? **Trousselier** (73 boulevard Haussmann) wears the crown as the finest creator of artificial flowers in silk anywhere in the world. When we asked how many species they could produce, we were told "every one nature produces." Without exception, everything on the shelves—Peace and American beauty roses, anemones, tulips, water irises, lots more—has been lovingly handcrafted. Ask for Miss Paule. A one and only.

Art galleries? Literally hundreds. Among the most tried-and-true landmarks are **Galerie de France** (3 rue du Faubourg-St.-Honoré), **Galerie Claude Bernard** (3 rue des Beaux-Arts), **Karl Flinker** (34 rue du Bac), **Drouand-David** (52 rue du Faubourg-St.-Honoré), **Katia Granof** (place Beauveau), **Alex Maguy** (69 rue du Faubourg-St.-Honoré), **Lucie Weil** (6 rue Bonaparte), **Maeght** (13 rue de Téhéran), and **Galerie Bellier** (32 avenue Pierre-Ier-de-Serbie). Serious devotees should first pick up a current copy of *l'Officiel des Galeries* (15 rue de Temple), the definitive source of information about which painters and sculptors are being shown where in the whole nation.

Costume jewelry and trinkets? Try the above **Lubin** (special items only) or **Roger & Gallet**—then **Line Vautrin** (3 rue de l'Université) or **Burma** (16 rue de la Paix and 2 branches).

Colorful Paris markets? Most famous is the **Flea Market** ("Marché aux Puces," Porte de Clignancourt), part of which has already been condemned to make way for new construction. Currently it is so overrun with tourists that it has the faint aura of an A & P supermarket or a Baltimore auction. So has the renowned **Swiss Village.** You'll probably pay more in both than you would in a legitimate shop—but they're fun just the same if you've never dickered for those reindeer antlers or busted Louis XIV ear trumpets. Go Saturday, Sunday, or Monday only to the former (the best time to buy is Sat. morning); the latter is open every day except Tuesday and Wednesday. **Marché Biron** boasts approximately 250 stands and perhaps the most varied—if not most fascinating—collection of European antiques available today. **Marché St. Pierre**, the textiles-and-remnants market (rue Charles-Nodier, foot of Sacré-Coeur church), is a maze of stalls which work during the ordinary business hours. The **Dog Market** (106 rue Brancion, and nothing to do with the Flea Market!), with everything from friendly mongrels to snooty canine royalty, operates from 2 P.M. to 4 P.M. on Sunday (it's the Horse Market the rest of the time!). The **Bird Market** cheeps along on Sunday, too, in the then-bare Flower Market on Île de la Cité. The **Stamp Market** is perforated with philatelic bugs on Thursdays, Sundays, and holidays along avenue Gabriel (between avenues Matignon and Marigny). Then, many of the stalls of legendary **Les Halles**, the bulk of which has been moved to the outskirts, have very recently been taken over by hippie-type artisans who peddle old furniture, maxidresses, shoes, costume trinkets, and the like at prices which are often absurdly high because of this colony's current vogue. (You may still make this neighborhood your 5 A.M. stop for onion soup before hitting the sack, but don't go at dawn on Mon.) There are flower markets all over the metropolis.

Virtually all of the merchandise we saw in the 80-plus shops which make up the **Tour-Main-Montparnasse Commercial Center** was so trashy that we regretted making the trek.

Auctions? In '76 the **Hôtel Drouot Rive Gauche** moved into the aristo-cratic and high-cost Faubourg St. Germain neighborhood. Here continues the top center of this traditionally regulated industry. (Private auctions are forbidden in France.) Beacuse its new quarters are cleaner and better located, its patronage has jumped by at least 20%; many of its seedier previ-ous Flea Market buyers have given way to a more affluent general public. In these square, red-fabric-decorated rooms, you'll find diamonds, china, rec-ords, silver, pianos, first-folio Molières, and old tennis shoes—just about anything ever created for sale by man. Faithful clients include Greek zil-lionaire Stavros Niarchos, former French Premier Mendès-France, Charles Boyer, and goodness knows who. Inspection of articles from 10 A.M. to 11 A.M. daily and all day Saturday; sales from 2 P.M. to 6 P.M. Monday through Friday; *closed in August* and closed Sunday too. Flee to the up-stairs Secretariat for English-speaking assistance. A field day for those who strike it right.

Furs? Big houses are outrageously steep, and small houses are often tricky; Denmark is the place to buy. But why not *rent* a chic coat, stole, or jacket in mink or other varieties at **Laude** (1 rue de Paradis)? Prices range from about $18 to $40 for a full weekend; take your passport, and prepare your hotel concierge to vouch for you. Crummy building, but patronized by such luminaries as Brigitte Bardot.

Department stores? **Galeries Lafayette** is now our preference, because of its smarter stylings, followed by **Trois-Quartiers** and **Au Printemps**. They're so close together that you won't need a taxi to cover them all. **Au Printemps-Nation**, a 5-story branch of the last, has recently been opened on Paris' eastern edge, for suburban shoppers. **Bon Marché**, near the Hôtel Lutetia on the Left Bank, is the biggest and cheapest.

Store hours? Completely screwy. We'll do our damnedest to explain them, but anyone who can follow the next few sentences gets a Gold Key to the Flea Market door: Plush jewelers, dressmakers, hatmakers, and chi-chi operators close on Saturday but are open on Monday. Hairdressers al-most always stay open all day Saturday but close all day Monday. Food stores are also open all day Saturday, but they put up their shutters until 2:30 P.M. on Monday. Department stores stay open all day Saturday *and* Monday during the summer rush but close on Monday during the rest of the year. As for the noon hours daily, some of the big fellows work right through, without a lunch break—but the vast majority operate only from 9 A.M. to 12-or-12:30 P.M., and later from 2 P.M. to 6-or-6:30 P.M. Better count on lunch all the way from noon to 2 P.M., because otherwise it's easy to be frustrated.

The **Airport Shops** in the International Zone at Orly? Watch out! Very, very few items of their merchandise are tax-free.

Dedicated shophounds? Space is too tight here for further listings—so consult this year's newly revised purse-size edition of *Fielding's Shopping Guide to Europe* for more stores, more details, and more lore.

THINGS NOT TO BUY Low-price mechanical things, such as fountain pens and novelty gadgets. Shoes are a bad bet; they seldom fit American feet. Most inexpensive apparel is sleazy in this custom-made culture.

Don't buy a dress in any but the leading shops. Fashions are patented for a 2-year period; when smaller places finally get the pattern, it's more dowdy than last Easter's hat.

Actually, you're better off not buying anything readymade. The ones who purchase clothing off the rack are low-income workers; almost always you'll find bad tailoring, poor quality, and sudden bulges where they shouldn't be.

Leave French nylons strictly alone. A run a minute seems to be par. My Nancy's report, after testing 3 of the most expensive brands: "Not really sheer—quality poor—bad heels—they bag at the knees and run."

Much silk today isn't up to former standards. If you are going to Italy, stock up there. Or if you must have the French variety, be sure it's "Lyon," because this is as fine as can be found north of Milan and Como.

HAIRDRESSERS In Paris, *this* year's place is still **Alexandre** (120 rue du Faubourg-St.-Honoré); here's where the world's most famous beauties now migrate. The immediate predecessor, **Guillaume** (5 avenue Matignon), is still fine, too; phone ELY 2866 and ask for Mme. Labbe. Both very social, both filled with capable light-footed gents, and both expensive as all get-out. **Jacques Dessanges** (37 avenue Franklin-D.-Roosevelt) is less costly but thoroughly satisfactory. **Serge Simon** (7 rue de Ponthieu) is also good for a curl. **Mme. Pascale** in the Hotel Bristol is even better, in our opinion. **Roger Pasquier** (40 avenue Pierre 1er de Serbie) can be a life-saving discovery because he is open on Mondays from 9:15 A.M. straight through to 6 P.M.— a notable rarity when 99% habitually are closed all of that day.

This nation has long been a leader in the art of hairdressing.

PERSONAL SERVICES Dentist? **Dr. S. Holzmann** (8 rue de la Paix) has been recommended by bright-smiling California Guidesters who offer to share him with any unfortunate pilgrims who may need dental services. They say that he is kind, gentle, and speaks English fluently; moreover, they vow that you won't gnash your teeth when he gives his bill. We can't say that we're looking forward to our first visit, but we're grateful for the tip. Many thanks!

LOCAL RACKETS Plenty. To many an unscrupulous Frenchman, the American tourist is the ripest rube in the world.

Petty thievery is common. Don't leave *any* valuables in your hotel room; toss your cigarettes in your bag, and lock it. Watch your coat and hat in restaurants. In general, the French are an honest people but the incidence of chicanery, particularly in the cities, is high.

Again as in our own U.S., automobile thievery has risen to shocking proportions. A high-echelon insurance executive, who estimates that more than 2000 cars disappear in Cannes anually, has informed us that his company pays off more theft policies in France than in any other European nation—adding that "In Italy or elsewhere, they more often steal the contents, while here they more often steal the vehicle." Thus, please take the same precautions that you do at home.

"Steerers" often don't steer. When a seedy-looking man sidles up to you with promises of wickedness, don't pay him a sou until he's produced the proof. The same goes for snapshot photographers who can do wonders with their empty cameras. The proof is in the proof—so be negative to avoid being film-flammed.

When a Paris taxi driver tells you your favorite restaurant is "closed for repairs" or similar drivel, regard this as his first move toward suggesting his own "superb hideaway where the cuisine is better than Tour d'Argent, Lasserre, or any other place in the city." Nonsense! He's just hungry for his rakeoff from the dump. Make your own reservation by phone beforehand—and insist the hackie drive you where *you* want to go. We color scarlet with rage when we hear about so many innocent visitors being sucked in on this ploy.

Mickey Finns or muggings are far from uncommon in the lowest dives. Stay away from them unless you bring your own football team.

When you flash a big bankroll you're asking for trouble in king-size portions. Paris is full of hungry pickpockets; if you check tomorrow's money with the hotel cashier you're ahead of the game.

Stay out of the disreputable Algerian sections, especially at night. They often mix murder with their larceny.

French hotels and waiters—*even those in the top brackets*—can load your bill more deftly and artistically than can their colleagues in Europe. *Always* demand an itemized bill; *always* check every item and the total.

No matter how dazzling the offer, puh-LEEEZE don't change any money on the streets. When *anyone* offers you 7 francs to the dollar, you can be *certain* you're about to be duped. These operators (sometimes aided by eye-popping girls in miniskirts) are so convincing that a Pennsylvania Chief of County Detectives was talked out of a bundle of dollars—and he still doesn't know how it was done.

Sidewalk photographers in the tourist areas are a plague. They'll demand up to $6 for *one* Polaroid candid print. Through some crazy quirk of jurisprudence, it's even quasi-legal. The heaviest infestations seem to be on the Champs-Élysées and just outside the Louvre. Remedy: Make a stone face and totally ignore them as you pass by.

If your new 5-franc coin feels coarse, just drop it casually on the counter before you accept it. Should it sound flat, ask for another. Silver coins—worth nearly one buck in Uncle Sam's currency—make a clear ring when they're okay.

An amusing dodge—almost surefire with the curious American male—is the Art Studies Pitch. Street hawkers will sidle up to you with offers of "hot nude photographs" for 30 francs. After 5 blocks of running argument you can beat them down, as I did, to 2 francs—and they will slip the photos into your pocket and disappear. When you examine the collection you'll find you have Art Studies, all right—photographic reproductions of works by gentlemen named Rubens, Goya, and Rembrandt, straight from the walls of the very best museums.

Don't buy whisky at "bargain" prices, unless you're sure of the source. It's more likely to be Lipton's Prime Pekoe, or something far less attractive.

Last, a New York Assistant District Attorney has issued an urgent warning to unsuspecting amateur art lovers (and to experts who should know better) that "originals" with phony signatures of Europe's masters are flooding into America. Recently, when conferring with Louvre officials he was told that 100 fake Utrillos had been confiscated by French customs men. A deluge of other forgeries was revealed to the public only a short time later.

# French Riviera

The sunbathed strip of French soil closest to Corsica and North Africa should have been named "The Gold Coast," because of its glittering sheen, its flawlessness, and its 24-karat prices in comparison to lesser Gallic resorts. Instead, from the color of the bordering Mediterranean, it is called Côte d'Azur, the Azure Coast. Brilliant whites, greens, and yellows predominate; the only blues the visitor will find are the sea, the sky, and the figures at the bottom of many of his tabs.

He might see red, however, whenever he tries to buck the exasperating traffic. From June 20 to September 20 when the vacation recess of France's schools coincides with High Season, the logjam is catastrophic. As a novel though costly method of circumventing this automotive mob scene, the Heli-Sud Co., which bases two helicopters at Cannes' Mandelieu Airport, has choppered into the picture with an air-taxi service for pleasure and cargo flights, and other charter work. Train connections and the carriages also have improved notably of late down here.

The once-frantic building boom is continuing to level out. For yachtsmen, marinas are corking up quicker than Chris can christen new Crafts. Hotel rooms and even tent space have become so impossibly rare during the summer months that the Government is opening a 100-mile "Second Riviera," along the neglected yet nevertheless expensive Languedoc coastline between the mouth of the Rhône and the Spanish frontier. They have already poetically dubbed this stretch of sand the "Vermilion Coast." If they can scare up $300,000,000, drain the swamps to kill the Jersey-size mosquitoes, and reforest the adjoining hills to harness the incessant winds (already under way), at least 800-thousand Côte d'Azur vacationers could be wooed annually.

CITIES *Nice*, the capital, is the largest. She is a metropolitan center, with the same dress size as Miami or El Paso; her contrast with smaller, more

403

sophisticated Cannes seems sharper every year. Nevertheless, she offers her acolytes a race track, an opera house, the nearby Matisse Museum, night-clubs, tennis, speedboating, water-skiing, and scores of hotels and restaurants. Her new $15,000,000 Ruhl Casino seeks to outruhl and outroll neighboring Monte Carlo's baizeworks with a personality patterned on our own Las Vegas gambols. Her Promenade des Anglais, extending for miles along the sparkling waterfront, beats Miami Beach's Collins Avenue 40 ways. Her more recent additions include the Convention and Exposition Hall, the esplanade flanking the Paillon River, a fascinating Museum of Shells (many alive), the Chagall Museum, and a slew of new municipal parking spreads. A huge marina near the airport, with accommodations for 1200 yachts, is a beaut. Because the beaches are comparatively poor and pebbly (a fact not advertised by the local tourist office), winter is the best season. King Carnival will be burned for the 92nd spring season this year on the day before Ash Wednesday, in a spectacle rivaling Mardi Gras. Mid-January to March is the most rewarding time to go, whereas November and early December are the worst. At any period, however, it is wise to stay in the city itself rather than in the airport environs, where planes boom in at an ear-throbbing 115 decibels (a din that registers 45 units above continued human tolerance!). In recognition of this jangling fact, all jet traffic has been eliminated between 11 P.M. and 6 A.M.

Cannes, normally about 45 minutes from Nice, is much higher in the social scale. This resort is so popular in High Season that it can be uncomfortably overcrowded. Now there's a magnificent 2nd yacht harbor, called Port Canto, at the eastern extremity of the bay, with 450-car parking lot adjoining; it's connected to a second car park west of these piers by a free bus shuttle service. This auxiliary nautical port-of-sport boasts a clubhouse, restaurant, grill, heated pool, exhibition hall, card rooms, and bowling facilities—the works. The quay itself—big enough to accommodate 450 pleasure boats—furnishes electricity in 3 voltages, telephone, T.V., running-water connections at each mooring, and guarded access (all night, too) from the shore walks. It follows close on the heels of the expanded Croisette, the main boulevard that separates the beach from the more lush hotels. Overlooking the city and illuminated at night is the tenth-century Castrum Canoîs with the Museum of Mediterranean Civilization in its dungeon. Smack in the center of town is the original yacht basin, crowned by the Maritime Station; big ships must be reached by lighter, however, because of the harbor's relatively narrow and shallow conformation. Boats run frequently to the Lérins, where the fifth-century Monastery of the Cistercians was St. Patrick's starting point for evangelizing Europe; it is open to women visitors, too. At the Royal Fort on Île Ste-Marguerite, you might like to visit the cell which has inspired stories, plays, and movies by the ream—once occupied, they say, by the Man in the Iron Mask. The beaches surrounding Cannes (summer bathing only) are the best east of St.-Tropez, despite the occasional blight of oil from passing tankers or other transient pollutions. The Palais des Festivals, tripled in size to accommodate 4000 people, has been reopened. There are 3 casinos—the Municipal house (Nov. 1 to May 31), the Palm Beach (June 1 to Oct. 31; extensively enlarged and revised), and the Casino des Fleurs (all year); a Sports Palace; an active polo green; 3 golf courses; an annual Film Festival, automobile *Rallye,* and other events; Super-Cannes, with its spectacular vista; a spate of luxurious hotels; a collection of villas unequaled in France; a continuous parade of suntanned celebrities; a busy sidewalk trade in sex (of any inclination); and a gala almost every night. It's a lesson in self-denial to remain a stranger after an hour or 2 near some of those Venuses or Tarzans in an inch or 2 of bathing suit. Much more lively and fashionable than metropolitan Nice.

Juan-les-Pins and **Cap d'Antibes** are on the opposite sides of an oyster-shaped peninsula—geographically close, but socially so far apart they barely nod to each other. The former is a vast vacation center on the popular level, with its own Jazz Festival in July. The latter, site of the historic and illustrious Hôtel du Cap and Eden Roc Restaurant, is a more sheltered retreat which caters to the rich. Commodores will now find a better yacht basin than ever before. A 5-star attraction is the Château Grimaldi, the reconstructed medieval fortress filled with Picassos—a *must* for every sightseer. Since parking is difficult here, you'd be wise to leave the car below and to hike to its portals on foot. Perhaps even more interesting is the newer Escoffier Museum, a few miles inland at **Villeneuve-Loubet**. This shrine to one of France's master chefs also is used as a center of culinary education, technology, research, and historical reference dating back to the fourteenth century. Much of the support for the foundation and reopening of the birthplace of the gastronomic genius came from French chefs living in America.

Grasse, a skip and a jump from both Nice and Cannes, is worth visiting because of its production of essential oils for perfumes. Think twice before you load up on the local brands of scents here, however. (See "Shopping.")

Cagnes-sur-Mer, halfway between Antibes and Nice, is proud of its perky little parimutuel racetrack. It's called Hippodrome de la Côte d'Azur, and it's open from mid-December to mid-March, and during most of July and August (night races only, because of the heat). Cultural touts also praise the neighboring Renoir Museum. Nearby, at the **Biot** turnoff on RN7, you'll find a Marineland splashing with a gay flotilla of flippery fellows. Regular performances begin at 2 P.M.

La Napoule, 5 miles west of Cannes, is the proud owner of the beautiful and interesting Château de la Napoule Art Foundation. Two large, well-lighted galleries with capacity of up to 100 paintings; guided tours from 3 P.M. to 5 P.M. every day except Tuesday; courtyard recitals during the summer; chamber music concerts and small theatrical performances from time to time. Another interesting development here is the recently opened 550-yacht marina. It is already aflutter with burgees of discerning skippers from all over the Mediterranean.

St.-Paul-de-Vence is the proud custodian of the Maeght Foundation, an art museum-cum-park which alone is worth a transatlantic journey. If you are anywhere on this coast do make an effort to experience this celebration of the senses.

St.-Tropez merits bravos for not succumbing to the characters who have tried to whittle it down to their level. In winter it's still a sweet little port. In season, however, it crawls with oddballs—especially on weekends. But why not, since it boasts what are probably the finest beaches of the province? At

Port Grimaud, 3 miles to the southeast, a more residential colony of sun seekers has set up aweigh of life. Topless sunning is legally indulged in especially on the Tahiti or Salins beaches, but an anything-goes-off attitude exists nearly everywhere despite a recent effort by gimlet-eyed police to levy fines on bottomless baskers of both sexes. Unless you are a swinger, you probably won't cotton to it during Pandemonium Time.

The rest of the Azure Coast sparkles with small coastal or mountainside settlements—some unattractive, many overbursting with humanity during the warm months, but most scenically charming.

HOTELS   For far more comprehensive information on certain Riviera hostelries than space limitations permit here, interested travelers are referred to *Fielding's Selected Favorites: Hotels and Inns, Europe* by Dodge Temple Fielding (son of yours truly). Its annually revised edition, in which a total of 300-odd favored possibilities were handpicked from the 4000-plus personally inspected, will be at your bookstore early this year.

Now, to minimize confusion, let's start near the Italian border and work our way west along the coast to St.-Tropez and beyond—with the group of inland possibilities between Nice and Cannes treated as a separate block. (Some of the smaller ones in the latter group will be found in "Restaurants.")

Menton, east of the Monaco enclave, offers as its leader the year-round, 40-room **Napoléon** on the quai Laurenti. Each medium size unit with private bath and loggia; Sun Roof Grill with a commanding view of the Old Town. The **Viking**, under Swedish management and down a notch in price and quality, has 34 units with bath, 20 with their own cooking facilities. Top nightclub in the city (which often makes its early-to-bedders howl about the disturbance); handsome sweep of the Italian Riviera, the mountain, and Cap Martin from its cost-accounted dining salon. The renovated **Prince de Galles** has 65 bedrooms; homey feeling, with down-to-earth comforts. **Vendôme**, an updated old-timer, provides lots of elbowroom, good management, and perhaps the best kitchen in the area. The **Victoria** occupies one floor in an apartment building. Nothing outstanding but not disagreeable—which amply sums up all of Menton's facilities.

At **Roquebrune**, high above Cap Martin, the **Vistaéro** provides one of the most breathtaking views this side of a NASA space capsule. From one side you can look down practically every chimney in Monte Carlo, from the other you can see the blue-mist haze of the Italian Rivera. To enhance the panorama, almost every inch of seafront wall space is plate glass—in public rooms as well as in bedchambers. Some complaints, in fact, have trickled in that the eye-filling restaurant charges "50% for the menu and 50% for the sights"—a bargain, we'd say, even if it served grubworms and seaweed (which it doesn't). Colorful mezzanine with chirping birds and a babbling fishpond; quality furnishings; 30 bedrooms, all with bath and balcony; suite #22-23, with its canopied bed, outstandingly attractive; another pair of apartments also very good; pool agurgle for simmertime splashers. We hope you will share our enthusiasm for it. Tiptop.

Down at **Cap Martin** itself, the sea-level **Victoria** rules the ripples in a modest pond. Lobby plus main-floor bar, but no restaurant; 32 units with good private bath; 22 with balcony; classical décor highlighted by silks and brocaded walls. Fair value for your franc. The **Alexandra**, with Le Sporting nightclub directly in front, is less prepossessing. Never exposed to the sun— a crucial drawback to most holidaymakers; all units with small loggias; fully air-conditioned and carpeted. Okay in execution, but no rave.

In *Beaulieu*, **La Réserve** is a jewel which shimmers more beautifully than ever. Its special atmosphere of intimacy, luxury, and elegance was masterfully preserved through its major reconstruction. Among epicures its world-famous restaurant has long been one of France's most *distingué* landmarks —and now its hotel section matches its superb cuisine. Beguiling lobby; lovely, lovely lounge restyled as a replica of the best reception room in Rome's Farnese Palace; richly appointed bar; beautiful summer patio for alfresco dining when the wind is low; dining salon segmented into 3 parts, with the center portion the private domain of Réserve residents; many new balconies; 5 suites and 54 rooms, all with bath and most with fresh, tasteful refurbishing; 2-story annexed "pavilion" with viewless accommodation close to the highway (used mostly for overflow); fully air-conditioned; a Telex board. The large pool area, extending into the bay, incorporates a sun-restaurant, 3 saunas, a massage room, de-tension hydrotherapy with high-pressure hose, 38 dressing rooms, a bar, and an inside restaurant; this complex is also reserved for the exclusive use of hotel guests. Suave, warmhearted Director Jean Potfer merits salutes and salaams for continuing to operate the perfect retreat for travelers who seek tranquillity, easeful living, exquisite food, and impeccable attention on their Côte d'Azur holiday. The adjoining, air-conditioned **Métropole**, situated in a 2½-acre, flower-girted park directly bordering the surf, is also proud of its revisions, although they are not as sumptuous as those of the neighboring La Réserve. Professional guidance by veteran Manager Badrutt whose experience is your guarantee of holiday satisfaction. Heated pool, barette, and seaside summer restaurant on a terrace above its rock "beach"; quiet ambiance; traditional furnishings; bubble-bright dining room; sumptuous new lounges; refreshed rooms, suites, and baths. Very pleasant indeed, but still overshadowed by its great neighbor.

In sight, around the curve of the bay at *St.-Jean-Cap-Ferrat*, the Deluxe **La Voile d'Or** ("The Golden Sail") is similar architectually to La Réserve— the work of the same designer. Total of 50 rooms, each with a distinctive decorative theme; bid for a portside unit only if you're feeling affluent; superb marble baths; full air conditioning and soundproofing; waterfront restaurant nuzzling the yacht harbor; excellent beach; pool on a raised garden platform; oodles of beauteous terraces. This one is in the same price bracket as La Réserve; its clientele now leans heavily toward Italian patronage. A smoothly sailing vessel. The nearby **Grand** seems to be suffering from a lack of financial plasma. Dismaller and dismaller, as Alice might say.

Villefranche-sur-Mer has the fading **Versailles**, a post-debutante smack on the main highway leading up the Corniche. In a topsy-turvy arrangement, the lobby, restaurant, and bar are at road level; an elevator drops you down to your accommodations. About 50 small, functional, rather sterile rooms, all with bath, radio, and individual balcony; small sun terrace with excellent view of the passing hubcaps. Rates which we consider overpriced; ringside at the Indianapolis "500" is a lot more fun.

Nice's hotel picture boasts an exciting future—and even an impressive present with such imposing names as **Hilton, Sheraton, Holiday Inn,** and **Novotel** on the upcoming roster. While the 200-room **Frantel** now nods hello from the av. Notre-Dame, several more may fling open their portals before these words are read by you, so be sure to have your travel agent keep you posted on exact debut dates. The 444-unit **Meridien** is the latest to appear in this new generation. Sited on hotel row adjoining the Albert Ier Gardens, it provides a heated pool, 2 restaurants, an open-air café, full air conditioning, and the ice-cool chill of a purely commercial institution, almost expressly designed to pack in busloads of sun seekers and gamesters. (It shares the same edifice as the Ruhl Casino.) The rates seem quite reasonable. As we write this, of course, it is too early to snuggle the other incubating premies into our rankings. Next year we'll survey the flock anew.

The **Negresco** remains among the most distinguished stopping places on the coast. The dining is shared by 3 separate sections: (a) The Salon Louis XIV, with its gorgeous antique, Louvre-restored ceiling from the Mancini Castle and a huge white stone fireplace, (b) Le Trianon dining room in Regency décor, and (c) an adjoining salon, similar in tone. Every bedchamber with bath; 1st and 4th floors freshly restyled; 7 new suites ready or on the way; revampings scheduled from lobby to cupolas by Manager Michel Palmer, a young hard-driving pro; air conditioning, music consoles, TV, and minibars throughout; large, handsome, lively bar; French renaissance uniforms for key staffers, including knee breeches for the elevator operators; first-rate concierge in verteran Léon Cinci. Its winningly farsighted, personable, and progressive Maître-President Paul Augier is one of the top hoteliers on the Continent. Now open year round. Head, shoulders, and Napoléonic hat above everything else in town; highest recommendation in Nice.

The **Plaza** has been entirely revamped and air-conditioned. Built-in water-fall in the lounge; off-lobby bar; bedchambers ending with "12" with views of the Albert Ier Gardens and the sea. The comfort and appurtenances of its 12 suites and 160 nests, all with private bath, vary sharply. Its Concierge, Louis Bianco, will work hard to please you. Okay, but quite a step down from Negresco's heavenly climes.

The 137-room, 8-story, fully air-conditioned **Splendid** also occupies a town site rather than a beach location. Warmhearted Director Henry Tschann, who was born within its premises, is the 3rd generation of his family to hold its reins (the 4th generation is in the wings); although he operates on friendly agreement with the Sofitel chain, he is the boss, and that's clear; one illustration is that most of his staff has been with him for 20 years or longer. Rooftop swimming (the only pool in the city reserved exclusively for its hotel clients); kiddies' pool and cascade; solarium and sauna; no restaurant, but handsome grill-bar (thus no forced-feeding policy); 40-car garage, barbershop, beauty parlor, bank, and travel agency. Bless 'em, every one! Tastefully modern rooms; soft, restful tone; multichannel radios. Mr. Tschann and his good people provide a lot for your francs in First-class (not Deluxe by intention) returns. We like this one very much, and we recommend it very highly indeed.

The **Park** greets callers with a street-level complex which includes 6 airline desks; garage to ease midtown parking; garishly dramatic lobby with fire-place, a fountain, and flickering gaslights as eternal lighting; bar reshaken;

breakfast room now doubling as conference room. Top-floor sleepers under its mansard roof the best bet; others a cocktail of good, fair, and poor. Approximately 60% of the traffic in this house consists of conducted tour groups. The end product is no great shakes, despite all the recent efforts for its resurrection. Generally, however, it is better than passable.

The **Westminster Concorde** is fuddy-duddy in concept, but the location alone accords it several points over other lackluster entries. Updatings may be on the way.

The **West-End**, beautifully situated with one side to the sea and another facing a lovely garden, has employed its share of carpenters, plasterers, and painters over the past half-dozen years. Most bedsteads have been replaced with carved wooden frames; #417 is an exceptionally nice twin; #419 is a commodious triple; units glancing sidewise at the garden or the sea are tranquil and viewful; the back is quiet but bereft of scenery. Considerably more agreeable; a good value in the medium stratum.

The **Atlantic** redid some of its units in plasticy-tacky themes. We'd place it as a toss-up between the very old-timers and the very mods—of neither of which are we too fond.

The **Georges** is almost unbelievably sumptuous for its modest category and bargain-basement costs. Tiny, spotless structure on the hard-to-find rue Henri-Cordier (a few doors from the École Hôtelière); all units with private bath; high-level appointments, including picture windows, chandeliers, crystal sconces, satin spreads, and good furnishings; no restaurant; small lounge. This one is a hobby of a gentleman named Vidal and his English-speaking son, both of whom like doing things right.

In midcity, the **Harvey** is wound with Gordian skill into the tightest traffic snarls of this car-crammed metropolis. Its St. Germain restaurant is pleasant; so are some of its small, modern, air-chilled rooms, but overall it would not be one of our leading choices. Nevertheless, this Harvey is hopping.

Near the access road to Nice Airport, up in the hills and in the vicinity of St. Paul-de-Vence, there's the much heralded, new, air-conditioned **Mas d'Artigny,** a sister operation to the Château d'Artigny in the Loire Valley at Montbazon. It's a dreamland, too, for romantic types who enjoy being in luxury while off the beaten pathways of the coastal mash. Suites with individual swimming pools and private entrances from your own garden; main pool and terrace on a tier below the dining salon and lounges; tennis and 16 acres of hillside for strolling. Every convenience available for a restful, honeymoonful holiday. A beaut—with prices to match.

Cap d'Antibes is crowned, at the tip of the point, by the famed **Hôtel du Cap** and the **Eden Roc** restaurant. The former, which recently lighted its 100th birthday candle, is a baronial, Second-Empire-style structure that counts among its guests the wealthiest and most ultrachic travelers in the world. Nearly every room in the house has been redone exquisitely; full air conditioning has been installed; the staff-client ratio is an almost unheard of 3 to 1; J. C. Irondelle, the young, gracious, and attractive General Manager, is outstandingly competent. Both du Cap and Eden Roc are open from Easter to late September only. What a glorious place it is! Next in line is the **Résidence du Cap**, sited in 5 acres of garden away from the sea. Its best amenities are a lovely swimming pool with bar, a tennis court, corridors replete with paintings on exhibition, and an Italian patio for breakfast. Its 3 suites and 40 other accommodations, all with private bath, are simply but cheerfully furnished; demipension is obligatory from June 15 to September 15. Mrs. Fay, the owner, is to be commended for making it more and more desirable every year. Clients are received from March to October. Because it is so sedate, it appeals to travelers in search of gentle tranquillity—not to swingers.

In *Antibes*, try the **Royal** first followed by the tiny **Josse**.

In *Juan-les-Pins*, **Belles Rives**, open from April to October, is proudest of its seaside situation, its charming beach restaurant with a fabulous built-in vista, and its boating facilities for water skiing or sailing. Splendid terrace; furnishings colorful and attractive; repainted halls; immaculate mien. Now that its rooms have been pepped up, here is a formidable contender. The **Juana** is forging ahead encouragingly. The lobby, stairs, dining room, bar, and all of its refashioned bedrooms have been lately carpeted; the pleasant terrace garden in front has been made even more tempting for lunching or dining; its German clientele seems to be increasing. Hard work which shows happy results. The 220-unit **Le Provençal** has improved markedly under Manager Arpino, whom we haven't met. We can now recommend this house with reasonable confidence. The little **Astoria** stays open all year. Of its 53 rooms, 32 come with bath, 21 come with shower, and only 5 lack balcony. A coffee shop and bar are operative; the use of a nearby private beach is part of your package. While it is modest in its dimensions and décor within its category, the hospitality of Proprietor Virgili Brancaleoni and his sons, Raymond and Marcel, couldn't come straighter from their hearts.

In *Cannes*, the Casino-owned **Majestic** has parlayed a $250,000,000 gamble into a bonanza jackpot. And what a sleek-lined filly she is! The fortune poured into improving her performance has produced not only some of the finest accommodations along the Riviera, but comfort and beauty standards that vie with the best on the Continent. Here are samples of her ground-level innovations: an elegant high-ceiling, marble-clad lobby and reception area; a smartly restyled dining salon, with its terrace shifted from the Croisette to the garden side; a Grill in modern coolish tones; a handsome teal-blue bar with an antique-auto theme; a crescent-shape, heated seawater swimming pool in the romantic palm grove (meal service on its aprons); a beauty parlor and barbershop; an underground parking station; a total reorganization of the "unseen" service features which pump the plasma through the entire operation. Upstairs, her reconstructed units are outfitted with sumptuous creature comforts and costly engineering details, more of which are being added each happy season. Jacques Bardet, the dedicated, charming, extraordinarily able General Manager has made a difficult (and to us, wise) decision in concentrating his sizable stake on a series of limited but painstakingly planned targets. By doing so, he has established a criterion of taste that could conceivably restore the Côte d'Azur to its former glories. Our highest recommendation —but book your room far, far, far in advance, and only in the revitalized quarters. By the time of your arrival, the same group will have opened the totally rebuilt **Montfleury**, which in the final stages of its 225-room construction looked appealing to us. Ask your travel agent for last-minute details.

The **Carlton**, which earlier was in a state of flux, has made such stunning advances under its Grand Metropolitan proprietors that we are delighted to rank it as another premier coastal oasis. Today, almost all of the formerly forlorn pockets of fecklessness have fled, with numerous freshenings supplanting them. Personally, our favorite haven here would be in the west wing because of the quiet, the lovely foliage, and the breathtaking vista of the Riviera sunsets. (Please check this out with the reservations desk first, however, because we've heard that approval has been given for an 8-story building nearby—and it *could* be right next to your pillow!) The dining facilities seem to be the only weak points in this remade palace. Otherwise, again this is a splendid pad for the poshest of pashas.

The **Grand** provides a set-back garden situation; it was erected by Master Hotelier Paul Augier of the Negresco interests in Nice. Ultramodern L-shape structure with all-glass fronts for every accommodation; 90 rooms with sea-view terraces; 300 studios and apartments available for long-term rentals. The bar, snack foyer, and public quarters are a mushroom patch of Saarinen chairs and white-top tables; the cozy little Grill (now run by the famous Lamour family) is best after dusk. The penthouse has an exotic cluster of 10 demisuites with curtains which separate the beds from the sitting areas; these are absolutely enchanting in twenty-first-century stylizations. The "normal" sleeping chambers have ersatz-leather furnishings, low beds, silk watermark wall coverings and dominant hues of mustard, salmon, lagoon blue, and Formica white; garage, parking space, sun lounge, and private beach are at your command. Hiltonites generally love it. Very good indeed.

Gray d'Albion has been sold and probably will be under reconstruction at the time of your arrival. Scratch it for the nonce. **Le Fouquet's**, with a mere 10 rooms, also has been rebuilt; it gives us the impression of being a deluxe gemstone. We'll see next visit.

The new **Victoria**, under the same administrative commonweal as the Canberra, is winsome but costly. Gracious overall décor introduced by its English-style lobby; wood-toned bar; captivating garden with a small swimming pool; front units with terraces and striped awnings; flowered carpets; silk bedspreads and padded headboards; baths with basins in alcoves; radio and electrically controlled shutters; no restaurant. It has so much style that we think it will quickly acquire many Victorian vassals within its Gallic realm.

The **Martinez-Concorde**, with 15 suites, 400 bedchambers, and 415 baths, is one of France's largest resort havens. Dynamic new Manager Michel Dissat, its new pilot, is considering a thorough overhaul, but for the moment we are not sure exactly what its future will hold. Central situation which streetwalkers seem to find convenient, judging from the curbstone traffic during our stopover; theater-type entrance and commercial aura; snack corner for light bites; outdoor terrace restaurant; very pleasant L'Amiral bar extending to Croisette. Private beach with restaurant, circular bar and water skiing (with or without instruction). Conventions galore during the colder months; a few conducted tours from April to October. Here's a huge, simply furnished, somewhat impersonal beehive.

The 60-unit **Savoy** (directly in back of the Carlton, one short block from the waterfront) is set in a lovely little garden. Its squeaky floors, comfortable living dimensions, and old-fashioned furnishings (including brass beds) betray its 4 decades of existence—but its housekeeping is spotless, and eye-appealing fresh paint is nearly everywhere. Just off the side entrance, a flight below the lobby, you will find a sparkling little restaurant. In High Season both a 3-day minimum stay and demipension are required. There's a feeling of leisure in this venerable place which appeals to many Quiet Americans—yet the action is less than 5 minutes away. Recommended to the tranquil type of vacationer.

The **Méditerranée**, at the edge of the Old Port and a public beach, has taken beauty pills. It is now a link in the ever-lengthening Sofitel chain. The façade has been spiffed up smartly; the lobby has been brightened by a camouflage of flowers and plants. Viewful maritime lounge; amiable outdoor terrace; gay yellow-and-white La Louisiane Restaurant; partially air-conditioned; piped music. Its upstairs has also been refashioned; accommodations are now ample in size, with fresh furnishings and bright ambiance; try to book #312. This corner is very noisy, of course, but so is practically every other bayside site in Cannes. Improved so vastly that the administration merits applause.

The **Canberra**, with its sweet garden and separate parking area, has no restaurant but offers agreeable living. Try to stay on the garden side, because the din from rue Antibes is often disturbing; #104 is the pick of the house. The price range is about the same as that of the Savoy, but it draws a much livelier clientele. Generally satisfactory.

The **Port Canto Yacht Harbor**? This one lately has been linked into the British Trust Houses-Forte chain. Physically, it's a dream—but let's see how it functions under its new U.K. harbormasters. Early reports are favorable.

Good accommodations in Cannes at low prices? These are rare birds on these high-flying shores. Perhaps you'll have luck at the **Belle Plage**, about 150 yards off the Plage du Midi (Cannes' other beach). Although you'll probably be asked for a demipension arrangement, you may be able to wrangle a bed-and-breakfast rate if you *both* talk fast. Otherwise, there's the value-packed **Villa Palma**, near the Martinez, and the downtown **Athénée** in a nice plant. The **Mondial** is sinking, in our opinion.

La Napoule-Plage, 8 miles west of Cannes, offers the **Ermitage du Riou** (swimming and golf). Seafront construction has given this one a backseat location. All rooms are large and comfortable; those on the rear, overlooking the river, are less noisy. A favorite among the mashie-and-putter set.

Miramar-Esterel is blessed by the **St.-Christophe** on its Red-Roc Beach. Same ownership as Paris' San Regis; 5-tier building with 5 front locations per floor; all rooms with terrace; nice pool; Easter to October only. Tranquil isolation.

St.-Raphaël 's **Continental** is nearest the beach. It's noisy and no rave in any sense. **Beau Séjour** is pleasant enough. The **Hôtel au Golf de Vallescure**, 6 miles out, has been thoroughly updated over recent years; it now emits a beckoning glow. Through a series of slipups—both technical and personal—our text has failed to note the many and continuing virtues of this house. On our next coastal romp, we will certainly make a point of trying to stay here as a client. In the meantime, our apologies go to General Manager

Percepied, a gentleman who seems to be extra-anxious to please the traveling public.

St.-Tropez ' flashiest bidder is the expensive anti-hotel called **Le Byblos,** slightly below the Citadel, with a distant view of the harbor. Its overall concept strenuously fights against conventional hotel-keeping. Irregular configuration suggesting a casbah mystique; swimming pool in a palm court; dining room ceiling in Persian carpeting; a leopard-skin (genuine) bar; snack facilities for bathing-suited nibblers where the client should rear up on hind legs if they attempt the old racket of trying to overpressure him or her into ordering a huge repast; decorative highlights featuring paisley brocades, gold embroideries, heavy damask, rich mosaics, and hammered brass; numerous raw stone walls and open beams; 59 bedrooms; some split-level suites; baths with brick tiles and wooden panels. The cramped dimensions of some of the accommodations might present a vexing problem to the long-term visitor. For those who can afford its wincingly high tariffs, here's a fascinating—perhaps too overwhelming—layout.

La Pinède is another costly but ingratiating San-Trop hideaway. Proprietors M. and Mme. Jean Michel have added one new wing consisting of a glass-fronted dining flank and bar plus sleeping facilities, each of the last boasting its own crescent-shape terrace, alcove beds, rheostat illumination, and a coin-operated vibrator-belt machine (1 franc per 3-minute jiggle). At water's edge is a tiny 4-cell tower which Audrey Hepburn, Michele Morgan, Françoise Sagan, and Raquel Welch, among other cupcakes, have used as a retreat; surrounding this is a small private beach. For taste and peace by the shipload, this one should be the stuff of which dreams are made. But we balked strenuously on our layover when we found it was impossible to order anything less than a full meal at lunchtime; nothing à la carte was ever available, in fact. Such shortsighted lack of flexibility in an establishment where the twin rate is equal to or higher than that of the Byblos struck us as sheer folly—especially in a resort where well-tended waistlines are scrutinized by connoisseurs, measured by micrometers, and admired by all. We hope that this offensive, expensive, caloric overglut will have been changed by the time of your arrival. Aside from it, however, here is a blue-ribbon port-o'-call.

L'Ermitage, next to the Byblos, offers the disadvantage of remoteness balanced by the same asset of tranquillity. Only 32 units, many with baths and showers which share the bedroom with you; lots of kooky charm that can be fun for the open-minded. Mr. and Mrs. Jean Bremond (he's an excellent painter) runs their house in such an aggressively personalized manner that many travelers love it (and others abhor it). We happen to like it for its slaphappy-artsy mien. **Mas Bellevue**, about 2 miles out between Tahiti and Salins beaches, is a pink structure overlooking the bay and a tumbling boscage of Mediterranean foliage. Somewhat raw but satisfactory for the let's-get-away-from-it-all traveler. **Lou Troupelen** comes on in similar style. While it is slightly more polished, we are not so fond of its situation. On our investigation, **Tahiti**, at the site of the same name, seemed replete with bare-breasted gals sans sunsuits, and beefcake bruisers who might have been plucked directly from the cartoons of *Playboy*'s "Little Annie Fanny." Hardly a discriminating oasis, in our carefully lingering view. The **Coste**, with 30 look-alike bedchambers, is too dreary for our tastes. If you must, bid for the back rooms only, which face the bay and sport private balconies. Closed November and December. The **Paris**, operative from April to September, is too noisy for all but the deef. The **Giraglia** in *Port Grimaud* is moored in a quiet anchorage where no automotive traffic is permitted beyond the gates of this private canal-laced village. Wood-on-stucco construction; maritime décor; tacky undertones but generally amusing in concept and presentation. A bonanza for boating buffs who are seekers of the bizarre. The 50-room **Le Kilal**, at *Grimaud*, is smack in the village with views oriented toward the seaward valley. Gorgeous setting; delightful dining room or patio at poolside; perfect accommodations. Capable backing should assure a happy holiday here. A stunner in a hilltown showcase. Forget the rest—but don't forget to RESERVE IN ADVANCE in all.

Croix Valmer (10 miles from St.-Tropez) has the quiet, clean **Hotel Restaurant Saint-Michel**. Breathtaking view of the Bay of Cavalaire. A discriminating Swiss friend says it offers "excellent bourgeois cuisine." Open April 10 to early October.

The mountainsides and the valleys inland from the coast are dotted with stops. Since the vast majority offer limited sleeping facilities (or none), and since their primary function is culinary in nature, you will find them listed in "Restaurants."

Finally, the **Hôtel de Paris** and other great landmarks of *Monte Carlo* are covered in the "Monaco" section.

RESTAURANTS Again for your geographic convenience, let's start close to the Italian border and work our way west in as orderly a point-to-point route as we can contrive. The inland stops between Nice and Cannes will be delineated last, in a separate grouping.

At *Cap Martin*, 4 miles from Monte Carlo, **Le Pirate** is executed in phony gypsy-encampment style with a roaring fire, flamenco dancers, bare-chested waiters, and gimmickry galore. Photos of many celebrities line its walls. Rickety structure which impresses us as being a gussied-up nest of packing cases; prices so high that we think they are outrageous; lunch starting at 1 P.M. and dinner from 9 P.M. onward. Cartiers of ultrarich notables still tie up here, but darned if we can puzzle out how this particular scene attracts them and their satellites.

Menton has a secret. It's **Francine**, located at the port. Some dear friends shared this treasure with us and now we'll pass it along to you. Francine does the cooking; the place is simple but nice; no English is spoken (who cares?); the prices are low for the value. Remember—it's a secret.

In *Roquebrune*, high above Cap Martin, **Au Grand Inquisiteur** STILL makes us Grandly Inquisitive, because when we huffed and puffed our way up to it on May 13, a sign on the door informed us it didn't open for its season until May 15. It is situated on a hillside lane in this lovely tenth-century village, most of which must be penetrated on foot through dipping, soaring, crazily winding footpaths between its buildings. Although this one is billed as an inn, its main function is obviously that of a restaurant. Even if its cuisine should prove indifferent, the fortress-hamlet itself would be worth the excursion. Warning: Cardiac patients, the infirm, or the elderly would be ill-advised to select it, because for them the gradients might prove dangerously steep.

The **Chèvre d'Or** at *Èze Village*, halfway between Nice and Monaco on the Middle Corniche, used to be one of our favorite perches for full plates and rich panoramas. It was sold, declined for a while, and now seems to be on the happy comeback trail. Still not as it was, but much better. How genuinely we hope it can be restored to the glories of yore!

At *Beaulieu* (a few minutes from Nice), **La Réserve** is a gourmet's delight. Physically, as well, its 3-part seafront dining room is lovelier than ever. In this superb establishment (see "Hotels"), everything runs as smoothly as a Silver Cloud. Your meal will cost a lot, but the cookery and the surroundings are so blissfully soothing that the investment should be painless. Another asset: The staff is so suave and urbane that every time the waiter glides by we expect to see him tenderly clutching 2 warmed soup spoons. Choose a sunny day or starlit evening for splurging here. One of our most enthusiastic recommendations in France.

Château Madrid, on the Middle Corniche above *Beaulieu*, towers on the lip of a cliff that drops 300 feet straight down—and your heart might plunge the same distance when they hand you that check. The panorama is soul-stirring. The enterprising son of longtime Proprietor Sarti is in command, and the quality of its fare is now superior to what it has been for years. Superb —but is it yet worth its exalted tariffs?

St.-Jean-Cap-Ferrat's finest offering is **La Voile d'Or**. Our latest lunch on its gaily umbrellaed, grass patio over the little harbor was excellent in every way; the service was skilled and attentive; the bill was, of course, quite steep. Sommelier André Melkonian, who wears the 5-star insigne of his 2000-member Association as the '68 Champion of France, introduced us to Château Bellet Rosé, the finest of its type we have savored in our travel lives. As we have previously commented in the "Hotels" section, here is a splendid choice for the Action Set.

Villefranche-sur-Mer (3 miles from Nice) might provide an entertaining change of pace. It's way down a winding road which ends at the bay. **La Mère Germaine** has climbed back to first rank here. Alfresco terrace-dining for 100 in season is vexingly rushed; hearty Salade Niçoise; bouillabaisse without a smidgen of vitally-necessary rouille (saffron-garlic paste) until *you yourself* add and blend it from your personal sidedish; closed November 15 to December 20 and every Wednesday in winter; open for lunch *only* on summer Wednesdays. **Bidou,** formerly Le Potis Chez Veidou, is next, followed by **La Frégate-Chez Irene** and **Le Corsaire**; this trio is also agreeable. But not all the happy possibilities are at harborside. Up on the Grande Corniche, **Le Rustique** (La Ferme St.-Michel) is a charmer for the eye, but now we hear that both service and cuisine have fallen off drastically. Terrace for ruminating or hunting-room interior snugly glass-wrapped; checked cloths; quilted green ceiling; candle beams, piped music, and intimacy. We'll recheck the comestibles very soon.

In *Nice*, our beloved friends Rose and Mortimer Sachs enthusiastically steered us to **Le Périgord** (7 ave. Georges-Clemenceau), assuring us that "it now out-dazzles everything here." (These 2-decade veteran Guidesters should know, because their exquisite taste is responsible for the European-style gaiety and charm now rampant throughout the 1/3rd of Palm Beach's famous Worth Avenue which they own.) Timber-toned dining room; handsome hearth adorned with pewter cups; copperware and carved-wood trim; sweet, tree-shaded patio. Chef-Owner Jean Hebrard, aided by his wife, turns on truffles in pastry shells, smoked goose and duck, Gratin of Sole Filets, and similar delights, with superb Bellet and Château Minuty wines. Two set menus are offered, plus à-la-carte specialties, which of course can jingle up to much more. Although it is quite expensive, we found it worth every centime of our outlay. Bouquets to the Sachses and the Hebrards for one of the most memorable gastronomic feasts of that very recent year. *Formidable!*

Another culinary spellbinder is **L'Ane Rouge**, a seafood tieup that's smack in the port. Sidewalk terrace on the viewful Quai des Deux-Emmanuel, under blue-and-white striped awning; planter boxes; azure tablecloths; polished open beams in 2 rooms. Tears of gratitude may issue from your soul if you order the Moules Farcies, the creamy fish stew called Bourride, and the achingly, sinfully, oh-I-can't-stand-it-it's-so-good homemade chocolate cake. The Vidalot family has created a little gem here that no serious gastronome should miss. If you really want to pamper your palate (while ignoring your budget) do try this one.

Chez Puget "Le Petit Brouant" (4 bis rue Deloye) is yet another splendid independent dining establishment. Bar at entrance; about 25 tables; handsomely redecorated dining room with Burgundy touches, paintings, plates on walls, and a small fountain—all of them made brilliant with flowers and made charming with Provence paneling circa 1875. Three standard menus are at hand: one with 3 courses, one with 6 choices of main course accompanied by all trimmings, and the third a full-dress banquet. For an appetizer, try the mouth-melting Dodine de Canard aux Vieille France (duck pâté); then, if a light, low-calorie but savory dish should appeal to you, launch into the delicious Sole Meunière. The service is savvy, kind, and warm; ask for Madame Marie Thérâse, the English-speaking daughter-in-law of the proprietor. Urban location with no view; adjoining outdoor terrace; closed Mondays and all of June.

La Poularde Chez Lucullus (across the street at 9 rue Deloye) might be its closest local contender. Bar near door; L-shape premises with beamed ceiling and Baccarat-rose-colored banquettes; semiopen kitchen to rear; perhaps 15 tables. The culinary level is high; the menu is versatile and interesting; with one exception, every dish (all different) for our party of 4 was turned out with loving care. Tours-born Proprietor Normand supervises on cat feet, pleasantly and genially. Here again is a high-level entry with good, earnest, dedicated people. However, its illumination is so overbright, its ventilation so inadequate, and its noise level so high when the house is full that we much prefer the serenity and atmosphere (not necessarily the cookery) of Chez Puget.

Chez Don Camillo (5 rue des Ponchettes), serene and comfortable, has placed its 8 round tables so thoughtfully that no one can overhear your private whispers. Smiling welcome and attention; limited menu featuring Italian specialties; veal, veal, and more veal its pride. Our sommelier-waiter, an Italianate Frenchman who couldn't have been kinder, first poured our ½-bottle of wine to both of us without prior tasting by me; then he poured the second ½-bottle into our partially filled glasses. To us, a pleasant but not distinguished hideaway.

St.-Moritz (5 rue du Congrès, adjoining the Casino de la Méditerranée) turns out mouth-watering Swiss specialties; chalet atmosphere that can seem touristy. Excellent cookery.

La Bourride (6 rue de Rivoli) is a tiny, tiny establishment with a capacity for 1 man (without Adler heels), 3 small boys, and a dwarf—but it's so well-liked that people queue up on the street to squeeze into it; try to go just before noon, or 1 P.M., 7 P.M. or 8 P.M.

Dinner for 2 and the show at the **Ruhl Casino** will gobble up a quick $100 —and possibly you will have difficulty trying to recall a more tasteless repast. The pure quantity on our visit was gargantuan, but there was a total absence of savor, in our opinion. Therefore, the question is: Are the high kickers worth the high-stepping tariffs? Up to you.

"Fish Row" is what we term the cluster of restaurants which line the eastern end of the quai États-Unis, the boulevard along the seafront. Most of them have "terraces" which, for obvious reason, are glass-enclosed. The traffic is so heavy, the road is so high-crowned, and the cars so close that timid souls at their front tables cringe when the Gallic motorized cowboys zip literally within 10 feet of their Salade Niçoise. Proceeding outward from the center, you'll find **Hublet**, **La Maison Rouge**, *Le Scampi* and **Raynaud** (same management and same kitchen; the latter is one of the largest and most popular along the boulevard—railroad-apartment layout; about 70 tables; service forgetful but kind), **Prince's**, **Le Bouée**, **Le Fort**, **Le Marée**, and **La Girelle Royale**. They are pointedly tourist-oriented; their service is too often harried. In our opinion, Raynaud and La Girelle Royale are the picks of this mass-production lot.

Other nocturnal lairs include **La Chunga** (related to the fine little night spot in Cannes; shellfish display outside; discothèque downstairs), **Cave Niçoise**, **La Coquille** (solid medium-bracket stop), the Hotel Westminster's **Il Pozzo** (superb Italian fodder), and **Taverne Bavaroise**.

Snacks and casual libations **Le Tramway** (Lamartine 11) is an amusing novelty which overflows with the local Smart Set—an ancient converted trolley car which used to run between Nice and Marseille. Enterprising Piero Terrot bought it in the boneyard, inserted it intact into the building, and refashioned its interior in a bizarre and entertaining manner. It now contains 7 green-leather booths each for 4 persons, a tiny kitchen, and such appurtenances as street mural photographs on both sides to give the illusion of motion, display ads above, and subway-style handstraps for nervous standees. Normally packed at lunchtime and around 9 P.M.; closed Sundays, holidays, and all of August. Fun.

Le Koudou (on the Promenade, a few steps from Negresco, West-End, and Westminster) boasts an agreeable terrace with tables; attractively modern ambiance of blond woods and black leather chairs or banquettes; piped music; appetizers, salads, eggs, sandwiches, vast choice of crêpes, ice cream, and all types of beverages available. During High Season it is open from 1 P.M. to midnight 7 days per week; from November 1 to December 1 it is shuttered. So tastefully executed that we like it.

The **Negresco**'s 3-part dining complex is a stellar attraction for well-heeled visitors—and its dramatic La Rotonde (see "Hotels") is one of Nice's most popular stops for the voyager-in-a-hurry.

Ciel d'Azur at Nice Airport is one of the higher fliers in the local skies. It is a deluxe candidate; a snack bar and medium-priced restaurant are also available in the same flight plan.

About 15 minutes above Nice (by car, not by plane) atop the mountain ridge, you'll find the garden-terraced **Rôtisserie de St. Pancrace**, run by Marccau Teillas, who often cooks for the finest chefs on the coast when they take a day off. It is heaven-scent country (beacuse of its altitude, no doubt); dining under the trees is a sylvan gift; the Royale de Poissons, Sweetbreads en Croute, and duck with morilles must have been handed down to Chef Teillas by the gods themselves. While the cookery is from the welkin, the prices are down to earth considering such extraordinary quality. Go only on a sun-filled day for the fullest rhapsody of the heights.

Haut de Cagnes, in the walled city above Cros-de-Cagnes, has such narrow, hilly streets that even the visitor in the smallest European-made car must scramble up 3 challenging flights of steps to reach **La Cagnard**. Here is a little charmer which commands a splendid view of the valley and a glimpse of the sea. Twelve small and tastefully but simply decorated rooms, all with bath, are available for overnighters. For the strong-legged, worth the climb.

Near *Antibes*, on the main Nice-Cannes line, is probably the most famous independent dining establishment of the Côte d'Azur—**La Bonne Auberge**. We lauded it, for perhaps a decade—but, when its cuisine started to slide downward in perhaps '62 and continued to strike us as having plummeted lower and lower on all our subsequent incognito visits, reluctantly we panned it with increasing intensity. Last year, however, the following word came in from the late Paul Gallico, a resident of Antibes and the perennial best-selling author who was the finest amateur chef whose skilletry we have ever enjoyed: "Under its new owners, it is once more a deluxe restaurant definitely in Michelin's 2-star or 3-star category. Ginny and I went there for our anniversary dinner last night. We had no reservation, we were not known, but we received the utmost of courtesy and kindness. . . . I cannot tell you the difference between the place today compared to the one which you and I so thoroughly disliked when we repeatedly tried it together. The food has become superb, but what makes the evening even more pleasant is the ambiance, the service, and how it is run. . . . Our mutual chum Freddy Heineken [the Dutch brewer] was there with his family last night, too, and they expressed themselves as satisfied as we. . . . I promise you that you can now recommend it as tops in this district . . ." Hurrah! Physically this expensive oasis has always been so stunning that after this expert's reevaluation we can scarcely wait to get back!

In town, **Les Vieux Murs** fires the biggest gun from its site on a cannon point of the ancient seagirt ramparts. Lovely antique setting as permanent as time itself; stucco walls; arched ceilings; colorful regional interior. Fish soup and Lobster Thermidor are the house prides; it is popular with a savvy set of gastronomes. Very worthy. **L'Oursin** (rue de la République) is also a winner. Fresh, fresh shellfish during the R-months; a good catch. Book ahead to be safe.

At *Golfe Juan*, a bit farther along the coast, the simple, family-run **Chez Tétou** is indisputably outstanding for finny fare. Alfresco terrace with 9 tables; enclosed terrace with 8 tables; open kitchen to right of entrance; main room unadorned; scrubbed wood tables. Dozen-item seafood menu, with the Sole Meunière and the bouillabaisse especially enjoyable. Friendly, informal atmosphere; open day and night in summer, but only at noon in winter. Mumm Champagne Prince Georges Prade rightfully raves about this one, because it is very special indeed.

Mougins (a short ride up from Golfe Juan) is attracting the reverent attention of nabobs from miles around because of its newly revivified **Le Moulin de Mougins**. When Monsieur Mouine recently sold it to Monsieur Vergé, within weeks its cuisine was changed from flatulent to terrific. This one is set beside a running stream in the valley below the village. It is composed of a loosely linked bracelet of dining niches, the most desirable being the glass-fronted veranda, which is usually booked by favored customers. The atmosphere of the entire establishment is charmingly esthetic. Tariffs run from wincing, to twitching, to paralyzing. **Mas Candille** is pitched more toward its resident guests than toward outsiders. Patio dining in summer; fireside munching in chilly weather. Excellent day-to-day skilletcraft, but not a candidate for That Big Night Out. The **France** has just been taken over by André Surmain, a former Mallorca neighbor and, prior to that, the driving force behind the costly Lutèce in New York. We wish you *mucha suerte* and renewed fortunes, André.

In *Cannes*, the colorful **La Reine Pédauque** (in the center at 4 rue Mar.-Joffre) delighted us with one of the most carefully prepared, graciously served, and gastronomically gratifying meals that we have consumed in many a year along this azure coast. Single room with figured-tile floor; oil paintings; brass and copperware hanging from the ceiling; chairs with cut-velvet upholstery; fresh flowers abounding. The repast is introduced with a gratis offering of tiny hot canapés. Bountiful hors-d'oeuvres cart, sporting even Caviar Niçoise (a ground-olive curiosity); oh-so-heavenly, helium-light Mousseline de Rascasse; butter-soft pepper-filet in either wine or cream sauce; fluffy Ris de Veau in a pastry shell; additional specialties including Langouste Gastronome and Filet d'Agneau en Croûte, which we didn't sample (darn it; there wasn't room!). Chef Dorange and the dedicated little tribe who collectively make this such a delightful culinary outing, deserve Big E's for Efforts Well Done. Surely a leading light within many miles, in our judgment. Closed Mondays and from June 28 to July 19.

Le Festival (55 blvd. Croisette, opposite Palais des Festivals) just has been taken over by former Parisian interests with Chef Claude Rocher, previously of the capital's Plaza-Athénée, at the stoves. Gay colors; fresh décor; animated, high-decibel atmosphere; choice of sidewalk or interior placement in an all-new edifice. If the sun is shining and the bikinis are jiggling, enjoy a lazy noonday meal in the open section. If you hit it right, superior for its resort-style type.

The Municipal Casino houses the charming **Brummel** for intimate dining; red velvet walls and banquettes; black pillars, dim illumination by fat Christmas candles on each table; drinks (legitimate) for perhaps $7. The **Le Bistingo** pans out year-around vittles at garden level; there's also a tier up one flight over the Jetée Albert Edward. **Ambassadeurs,** with its vast dimensions, rising dance floor, and well-mounted shows, features a 15-piece orchestra and attractions on Friday, Saturday, and Sunday from December to end-May; superb wines are available at approximately ⅓rd less than for corresponding vintages in smaller independent restaurants. Very sound cuisine, too. The **Palm Beach Casino**, also restyled, sparkles anew. This one is a frond-swept dream on a summer's eve. Closed in winter. The **Bistrot** is dressed up just as its name implies. The 2 rooms have access directly onto the Albert Edouard quay.

Chez Félix (between the Carlton and the Miramar) is spirited, touristy, and well patronized by the motion-picture people and such dissolute characters as guidebook authors and journalists; closed mid-November to mid-December; Americans like it because they can eat one dish if they choose. The food is only so-so, but the kindness they'll show you overrides its listlessness. Félix —now enjoying a deserved retirement—had his public relations down to a science, and his droll son, an equally engaging host, is a chip-off-the-old-gallant. Very popular, so nail down your table in advance. **La Chunga** (across from the Martinez) is a jovial den with more of a nightclub than restaurant personality. Simple dishes, but more than satisfactory if you're in a funloving mood. **Gaston et Gastounette** (6 quai St.-Pierre) served us an unexciting lunch when we munched here incognito. Two nights later, when we were the guests of prominent Cannes citizens, the dinner fairly sizzled with zest and sparkle. Travelers have complained lately of being given the à la carte menu and having to demand the fixed-price card; others squawk about waiters who are marvels at addition (they seem to keep adding, ADDING, and A-D-D-D-D-D-D-I-N-G). Check your bill carefully here. Variable. **Voile au Vent** (17 quai St.-Pierre) sails in with a bar and restaurant, side by side, reached through individual street entrances. Chef Polo conjures up simple magic with his skillets; active Frenchy atmosphere; smooth administration by Mme. Ducrot, who has a special warm welcome for Guidesters. One of the best culinary buys in town. The **Laurent** (12 rue Macé) was a happy discovery on a recent Cannery cutup. Laurent and wife Michele minister to diners in the tranquil, antique-cutlery surroundings of their "museum of the table." Moderate tariffs; careful preparations; ingratiating hosts; recommended. The expanded **Blue Bar** in the Palais des Festivals, is almost a carbon copy of Chez Félix—except that it hasn't been discovered by the Jet Set. Lower tabs, slick service; recommendable when we popped in, but a management switch could alter things considerably. **Meridien** (near the Hotel Méditerranée) is a charmer for daydreaming, sea-gazing, and sipping at snack time; a winner in the outdoor league, but the attention can sometimes be strictly low tide. In the clubhouse at the previously mentioned **Port Canto** yacht basin, **La Pêcherie** is in British hands today. Its galley was untested by us on our anchorage, but physically it was most attractive to our weather eye. Navigate carefully, mates, and please don't confuse this one with the **Moby Dick**, which is also in the new port area. The latter is for crews and the general boating public, while the former had been only for the Reefer Coat Set and their invited guests. In the vicinity of the station, a trio of smart bets stand in a cluster on rue 24-Août. These are: **Au Bec Fin, Le Monaco**, and **Bougourne**. All moderately priced; all with respectable wares; all right. **Da Bouttau** (10 rue St.-Antoine) is an atmospherey little retreat where they sketch your order (instead of writing it) on your paper tablecloth and dining check; much of the spark was lost with the death of the owner, because neither the uncle nor the daughter has his zip; rôtisseried chicken is its specialty; big-beamed, cozy, colorful room, with lipstick-smeared names covering the walls; guitar and accordion music; other branches in Nice and Évian; cookery good but not stupendous; reserve ahead during summer. **Toque Blanche** (3 rue Lafontaine) has skidded to the point where the quality of its fare matches—and no longer makes up for—its frenetic and haphazard service, in our opinion. Off our list. **Denis** (10 rue de Bône) is a pleasant grill adjoining the Embassy Hotel. This family operation strives to satisfy—and we think that it achieves its purpose amply and for only a moderate quota of funds. Solid. **Vesuvio** (on the Croisette near Hotel Martinez) erupts with pizza poofs. Full of fire and flair; always packed; right for *bastante pasta*. **Le Pingouin** (36 rue Jean-Jaurès) has a laudable table d'hôte. Clean and pleasant; slightly tearoomy in feeling; closed in November. **Le Coq Hardi** (just off quai St.-Pierre) is in the same low price bracket, and it's also cheerful, well scrubbed, and recommendable as a good little "find." **La Poêle d'Or** (23 rue États-Unis), is noted for its soufflé of trout and Bresse chicken, prepared carefully by Proprietor-chef Chartier. **Au Foie Gras**, once a favorite of ours, was been taken over by Britishers Pascal and Freda Cozzolino, who are assisted by their Savoy-trained son George. While not a single friend in Cannes had a kind word to say about it, our own meal, taken from the fixed menu, was remarkably worthwhile for a modest outlay. Busy, elbow-to-elbow ambiance; extremely pleasant family; savory repast from snails to sole to vegetables to dessert. We cannot fault it in any way, except to regret that the hooligans who hang out at the adjoining bowling alley are so rowdy in the street. We'd call it a fine value for the price. **Le Maschou** (17 bis rue St.-Antoine) has been suggested with enthusiasm by a discriminating Guidester from Gotham; we're always delighted by his suggestions, so we're looking forward to our first sampling of this one. Light bites? **La Boite à Sandwich** (3 Galeries Fleuries), to our sad, sad professional and personal disappointment, has been absorbed by a huge 2-block real-estate construction complex which took over its name in the process. Now this former little wonder cannot be recommended by this *Guide* under any circumstances.

La Napoule-Plage (8 miles west of Cannes) offers the deservedly famous **L'Oasis**, once again paradise for our palates—but its reception and client attention before, during, and after this meal were below par for such a gastronomic shrine. Entrance beside a somnolent tree-arched pool; recently restyled and expanded single room with several 2- or 3-table adjuncts radiating from it; flowers, wrought-iron fixtures, and understated provincialism; new, spotless kitchen; owned by the Outhier family, who try to give it their all. One absolute must: PLEASE try the Brioche de Foie Gras, in its feather-light disk of pastry. Reserve ahead; closed Tüesday. Great for its glorious cuisine—but disappointing to us in its staffwork.

Mère Terrats, at one time equally as revered, to us now seems to be in a prolonged slump. How we hope it can regain its former status, because this one could be a dream spot.

La Brocherie II, at the boat basin, sails in with a lovely vista, fair skilletry, and yachtsman prices. Here's another lovely anchorage for launching or lunching.

St.-Tropez represents **Da Lolo** as *the* most fashionable stop. Roughhewn sturdy interior clearly in contrast to the fragile squadron of pixilated waiters soaring through the ozone; close atmosphere redolent with Gigot aux 7 Herbes; on our latest try some time back, everything from lamb to our partner's steak to salad apparently floating in the very same sauce. Only open house-wine was available, which we recognized as Spanish (later confirmed by the maître); custard dessert tasted as if it had been put together with a packaged mix. Not overcostly, but not overgood, either. Far better, in our opinion, is **Les Mouscardins**. Glorious panoramic situation at end of the port quay. It's busy, bustling, attractive, but not fancy, and expensive. Closed mid-Oct. to Feb. 1. The next challenger is **Auberge des Maures** (4 rue des Lices); also costly; shuttered Nov. to mid-Dec. This one tries to create the atmosphere of a gypsy pad, and it does so in an amusing way. The walls are decked with cast-off items and sentimental knickknacks; the dimensions (except for the portions, which are huge) are cozy; the waitresses are tricked out in regional costumes. Outside there's a dawdle-and-dine, arbor-covered patio which is attractive in season. The special cookery of Provence is its *raison d'être*. Prices trending upward, but well worth the investment for quality and friendly service. It evokes a sense of comin'-through-the-wry.

For casual dining or drinking, there are several resorty hangouts along the waterfront. Each features an awning-covered apron partially exposed to the sun, the stars, and the stares of the passing parade; back of this sits a more interior "exterior" patio; finally comes the inner sanctum itself—a tiny culinary enclave big enough for perhaps 3 tables, a small-boned waiter, and the inevitable bowl of fruit. **L'Escale** is still the harbor master, with a prix fixe docking fee; **Le Girelier** specializes in simple fish plates and matching tariffs; **La Rascasse** isn't bad; neither are **Tante Marie**, **L'Équipage**, and **L'Adventure**; **La Goûtade** *is*—at least we think so after our latest supper here. For drinking only, **Sénéquier** hosts some of the tightest-hipped gals' slacks on the coast. Deep lounge chairs for loafing from sunup to moonrise—or the reverse. The ONLY place to go if you have 14 or 15 hours to kill, plus a cast-iron liver. As for the rest, **La Belle Isnarde** (40 bis rue Allard) is typical of the less-costly digs in town, while the very rich (those who can cough up taxi fare) sometimes venture up to **Fenière**, a garden restaurant near the Citadel, or out to suburban **Grimaud** (**Les Santons** is costly but excellent in Port Grimaud), **Ramatuelle**, **La Bonne Fontaine**, or **Gassin**. The cuisine at the **Le Byblos Hôtel** is Deluxe—in cost, but less than patrician in savor.

Inland attractions between Nice and Cannes? The route to **St. Paul de Vence** and **Vence** is an ideal excursion target on a sunny day or starlit night. Rural restaurants and inns are as thick as fleas, so if you make the right selection, your Inner Man or Woman will glow. Here are the best ones, starting upward from Cagnes-sur-Mere:

L'Abbaye Joseph at **Colle-sur-Loup** is a good-sized family-operated establishment which oozes with charm. Historic building; lovely garden terraces; beautiful small chapel decorated by Michel Marie Pulain, the well-known French artist; stalagmites of accumulated candles on rock piles and dividers nearly everywhere one looks. Although lunch is served, it is more pleasant to take dinner on its flower-filled court or in 1 of its 3 interior rooms. Its gay Gallic ambiance in the evening is heightened by a strolling accordionist and guitarist. The atmosphere is happy, the portions are large, and the food is average rather than outstanding. **Toque Blanche**, the next one, is suggestive of a tavern house. Nice little patio with a middling view; semiopen kitchen; about 12 tables; better-than-average wine card for the region. Not special— but not expensive, either. **Les Oliviers**, perhaps 300 yards farther along, serves the most distinguished cuisine in the immediate neighborhood. Big open-air rôtisserie next to an orange tree in the garden; flowers abounding; beautiful open patio (no view); awnings and glass façade protecting its immaculate row of canary-yellow tablecloths; small terrace with another file of tables running along one wall; 4 menus standard; sizable à la carte. To the rear is a pleasant and tranquil 10-room "hotel" in a separate building. We'd rate this as one of the best establishments in the entire area, but not up to Le Mas des Serres (see below). Closed from November 15 to December 15.

Now **St.-Paul-de-Vence** will loom up before you. This walled feudal hamlet has streets which resemble tunnels, coats-of-arms on its houses, a lovely fountain, and a feeling of profound serenity when it's not overrun by outlanders. The previously mentioned **La Mas d'Artigny** is super for suiteniks or idle bathers and lunchers. The cuisine is outstanding, and, of course, it is not inexpensive. Then there's **Colombe d'Or** (Golden Dove), with an ultrawarm reception, relaxed patio dining under parasols when the sun is shining, an interior cluster of cozy rooms reflecting slick rusticity, an outstanding collection of paintings, a fine swimming pool, and a magnetic physical allure. The selection is ample, but though the food is served atop a lovely mountain peak it still falls short of *haute cuisine*. The nearby **Vieux Moulin** is ground out with contrived millings from Claude Laurent, "The dangerous man for your figure." We are forced to agree with him. In **Vence** itself, there's the little Hostellerie Lion d'Or which enlarged its name to **Hostellerie et Auberge des Seigneurs et du Lion d'Or** when it remodeled the upstairs to provide its handful of rooms with baths. Its view is nil—but when we last checked it sometime back, we liked its simple milieu and fare. Fartherest along is the internationally renowned **Le Château du Domaine St. Martin,** which commands an eagle's-eye sweep of the countryside. The lobby is a hodgepodge of needlepoint, cretonne, and brocade; the overall effect is one of a well-intentioned effort which in our eyes simply does not jell. Heart-shape bicarbonatized swimming pool (possibly for indigestion sufferers); well-tended sylvan grounds; tower accommodations for the steady-in-balance; some rooms agreeable; others not so hot. The restaurant-dining room, with 3 sides of glass opening to its stupendous vista, is the main attraction. Its ambiance is lovely; its cookery and service standards are now on par with the finest in the land. Here's a stunning project on a stunning site.

On the same road, you'll find **Les Collettes**, where Auguste Renoir did his painting from 1908 until his death in 1919. It is now a museum. At nearby **Verrerie de Biot**, the widow of **Fernand Léger** has opened to the public an impressive building which houses more than 200 of this great modern's works. You may wish to study the glass creations here. In the area, you will also find the gemlike **Matisse Chapel** (open Tues. and Thurs. only) and the impressive **Maeght Foundation**, already mentioned, with its splendid collection of mobiles, sculpture, Impressionist mementoes, and abstract paintings.

Seven miles up the Corniche in the hamlet of *La Gaude* (near Vence), the **Hostellerie L'Hermitage** definitely merits a try. Window-lined dining room overlooking a lovely landscape of farm-girt hills and the valley of the River Cagnes; strawberry linens, tropical plants, and the chirping of caged birds. New ownership but equally superior fare. For a good unpretentious meal in inexpensive arcadian comfort, this spot is hard to beat in the area. Closed November and December. A pacesetter in the nonsumptuous bracket.

On the alternate road from St.-Paul-de-Vence down to the coast, **Hostellerie du Piol**, 1 mile south of the village, has a hilltop site and a panorama to match. The patio accommodates 120 for lunch or dinner. Small tables; dancing nightly to recorded music; swimming pool, sauna, and tennis court. Inside, you'll find a cheerful hearth, colorful tablecloths, tiled floors, a petite bar, and a pool from which big goldfish normally stare back. Total of 22 rooms; immaculate modern kitchen. If you like the atmosphere of Spanish missions, you will probably bask in this one.

Le Mas des Serres, 1½ miles from the village, falls last in this listing—but we find it by far the best. Enclosing the whole property is a handsome cypress hedge. The twin main buildings form 2 sides of a garden which bursts with flowers and flowering shrubs. Its bedrooms in the converted farmhouse and the long "bungalow" row are all different; named rather than numbered, they are comfortably, tastefully (but not overlavishly) furnished. During the week, there is a good choice of viands; on Sunday, only the all-inclusive menu is available. It is without question the feeling of being *chez soi* that impresses us most here—an ease of living that one would be hard put to find elsewhere. Mme. Marité Saucourt will welcome you with superlative grace. Wonderful!

NIGHT LIFE?   In *Nice* head first to the new and glittering **Ruhl Casino**, where the main interest is gambling. It mounts big busty shows in the Las Vegas tradition and, as one commentator quipped, "The lights are bright enough to permit minor surgery on the craps tables." We've already described its culinary shortcomings, so don't expect gourmandism from this quarter. The **Mécart** is by far the swingingest discothèque in the elegance circuit. If you're hungry, try the restaurant to the side of the gaming room; good food and not too expensive; Maître Invert is a charmer. The next siren is the **Thistle Club** (6 rue Halévy); the French call it "Chez les Ecossais." One of Scotland's whisky giants opened this pure distillate of after-dark sparkle, but now private management has taken over. You'll find tartans everywhere, and a map of the motherland at the entrance delineates the country clans. Spectacularly attractive and tasteful planning and décor, with 3 bars festooning its double-decker motif. Closed Thursday. Recommended with *slainthevas!*

On a par with these, but not in the mainstream of midnight traffic, **La Pignata** in the hills above Nice is a honey for romancers. Dancing, small cabaret, and outdoor restaurant in summer; mini-*corrida* for sun-filled *picadores;* open all year, but best in season. **Pizzaiolo**, in the Old Town, is i-t for young fry. Modest show; good music; dinner available; cramped for space, but popular with the tolerant. In neither of these are neckties required, since they are much more informal than metropolitan digs.

The girlie cabarets, in the next category, to us smell the same as their older sisters in Paris—tailor-made for butter-and-egg men with fistfuls of francs and a fine lack of interest in who grabs them. **Brummel** (place Masséna) stands at least a swizzle-stick higher than any other *genus nightclubus in corpore.* The show time seems to be determined by the traffic. Our whisky was uncut, but don't take this for gospel. **Folies Club** (place Masséna) is the largest independent operator; there's dancing from 5 P.M. to 7:30 P.M. and from 9 P.M. to 2:30 a.m. Two shows: 11:30 P.M. and 12:45 A.M., with 10 to 15 performers. Crowded during July, August, holidays, and Carnival time. Tables in tiers; bar-ette to one side; atmosphere reminiscent of the '20s, except for the whisky which tasted legit. **Tcha-Tcha** (rue Masséna) is a cellar-bration gin mill where 45 pairs of dilated pupils strain into Stygian darkness. After a brief singles act every 15 minutes, the lights flicker off and you're again paddling on the Styx. A local sidekick and I—both of us exactly 20-million miles from being Apollos—weren't there 2 minutes before the waiter brought a note in English from a thirsty mademoiselle which read, "Both of you are so devastatingly handsome that I *cannot* resist you. I love handsome Americans! I will come to your table and you will give me champagne, yes?" When we answered that we were naught but simple, humble U.S. journalists whose parsimonious editors *(sic!)* didn't pay us enough to buy champagne, she abruptly developed the swoons for another devastatingly handsome customer—this one a bald, balloon-bellied, 5'5" French Hercules with a face like a toad's. And don't thirst for Scotland's best, because our libation never saw dawn over the heather. Plenty of "hostesses" in all of these joints, but remember that here and elsewhere, *the girls are required to stay on the premises until closing time;* so don't let yourself be conned for a string of hideously expensive drinks without keeping this in mind.

In *Cannes*, the **Municipal Casino** draws most of the smart night owls to its gaming rooms (redone in Pakistan onyx and Carrara marble), to its grand-style Ambassadeurs (shows and dancing), and to its sleek Brummel Room (quiet intimations; see "Restaurants"). Director Banwarth has moved alps to bring this house up to peak performance; every cranny reflects his professional touch. Now tops in local sophisticated night life. The **Palm Beach Casino**, which opens in summer on the exact day that this one closes, is a stunner, as well. **Whisky à Gogo** (115 avenue de Lérins, near Palm Beach Casino) has perhaps taken leadership in the animation league. Lovely setting under a vine-clad arbor; cane chairs with bright cushions; mixed crowd and sufficient noise; open April to October. **La Chunga** features guitar pickin's from the *pampas;* saddles and tack for décor; high-stirrup society roundup on busy nights; not too expensive, and chic. **St. James**, formerly called the Moulin Rouge Hi-Fi Club, starts perking nightly at 10 P.M., and there's a Sunday Matinée from 4 P.M. to 8 P.M.; striptease, other acts, paper favors; drinks relatively inexpensive, with no cover or minimum. You've seen better. **Maxim's de Cannes** couldn't be more typical of its type. The **Playgirl Club,** formerly called Playboy Club before Chief Surgeon Hugh Hefner altered its gender with a juridical scalpel, is back in business again. If it plays in the same old ways of yore, we'd call it too costly for all but consenting adults. Nix, in our unabashed opinion.

Antibes offers a caravansary of attractions in its eye-popping **La Siesta**. This amusement center (which has also opened a casino), 7 miles from Cannes and 12 miles from Nice, adjoins the highway bridge over the Brague River. A sign at its entrance reads "The only conditions for admission to this establishment are ELEGANCE and GOOD EDUCATION . . ." Among the facilities open to those who pass the test as patrician scholars are adult Go-Karting, infant Go-Karting, bowling, swimming, water skiing, trampolines, a restaurant, a rôtisserie, a pizzeria, and a nightclub. The main building of this mélange contains such bizarre touches as 3 large bats in a large pansy-ringed cage and wagon-wheel cocktail tales with spokes filled with peppercorns, maize niblets, pine nuts, and a couple of similar products we could not identify. On Saturday nights during the Season it is almost too crowded to move; teen-agers invade in regiments. During the rest of the week, however, it's lively, merry, and patronized by all age groups. At this writing everything except the Go-Karting is shuttered from October till April, but serious consideration is being given to no siestas the year round for anything. Go about 8 P.M.—and bring your Sloan's Liniment.

In *St.-Tropez*, night life becomes formal when the customer wears shoes. **Papagayo**, with orchestra from June to September and stereo in the fringe weeks, has routine décor and no show. On a busy night here, you'll find more shaggy heads than at a conference of Kalahari tribesmen. **Club 55** is the fashion center where planter's hats, hot pants, and *longuette* rags were raging the instant we popped in—and surely became as dated as buttonhooks by dawn. **Esquinade** is a noisy cluster of 3 cellars; records only; for budding gentlemen-to-be who can get by on 2 shaves per week; same ownership as the Megève pop-spot of the same name. **Woom-Woom** was still boom-booming for the small fry on our most recent zoom-zoom through town. **Yeti** appeared an abominable snow-woman when we peeked in—strictly for "the girls" (well groom-groomed). **Les Caves du Roy** has turned on the charm and tuned up an orchestra; it was very much in vogue, at least as of last week. **Le Gorille** is still the stop for that predawn breakfast and early-morning-cap. If these don't fill the bill, try **Café de Paris**, a summer meeting place of the famous, or the other café bars we mentioned earlier.

In *Villefranche*, we are told the **Tiki-Club** peddles a pseudo-Tahitian atmosphere and a small hula-hula-type show. Small; reasonably priced; drinks and snacks only.

TAXIS AND CAR RENTALS?　Taxi fares on the Riviera are exorbitant. The zoning of the fares from district to district within these cities is so outrageous it will drive you up the wall; as soon as the car crosses these invisible lines, the fares shoot up in colossal jumps. The meters, which are detachable, are on the cabbie's side, placed so that it is almost impossible for the passengers to read them. Often you will find they have lifted them from their brackets and deposited them on the front floor of the vehicle. Therefore, walk whenever you can or use a privately hired car.

In **Cannes,** the best car rental agency we found is **Cannes-Tourisme**, 8 Grand blvd. de Super Cannes. If you telephone 385417 or 381536, you'll have a fine automobile with an English-speaking driver at your hotel portal in a flash—or you may rent a self-drive vehicle for your roving. Ask for our friend Louis Lemaire or for Guy or Roger who form a trinity of helpfulness. **Garage Plaza** in **Nice** perhaps tops that list for chauffeur-driven chariots as well as for self-drive vehicles. Then too you'll find the big international agents in both cities (**Avis, Hertz, Eurocar,** or **Siter**—the last for Citroëns only) and at Nice airport.

SHOPPING Please see the boxed text above the "Things to Buy" section in "France" for information about the discounts available on purchases made by foreigners.

Perfume is supposed to be one of the best buys—but our enthusiasm for some of the much-touted distillations of this region, notably Grasse, is very much on the dim side. These products all have their virtues and advantages, which are excellent *within the limits of their categories.* But don't let anybody tell you that they're the same as the Big Name brands, because definitely, emphatically, and conclusively, they're NOT!

And don't let them con you, either (as several friends reported last year), that we are any less disgusted by various local pitchmen and pitchwomen and that we have "changed our minds." We are NOT—and we have NOT!

What boobs or rubes do these people take us tourists for? A low-grade moron knows that a $240 dune buggy is *like* a Cadillac, in that it has 4 wheels, an engine, and a chassis; equally, these scents are *like* the others, in that they smell good and add to a woman's allure. But they just aren't in the same league, because the top operators spend thousands of dollars to develop and to protect their own secret masterpieces. Your $5 bill here will bring you exactly $5 worth of merchandise—not $10 or $20, as some sellers are prone to indicate. As 3rd-line gifts for the home folks, samples of these local varieties might do the job, because they're cheap, they're pretty, and nobody can deny that they're French. But the sales practices impress us as being so slippery, misleading, and morally vile that we personally want no truck with them. In the future, we will never touch these lower-quality imitations again.

Negrescorama in **Nice**'s elegant Hotel Negresco makes a perfect 1st stop for the visitor. Here, in one grand circle, you will find the cream-of-the-cream of products from all over France, as well as handpicked imports. Boutique ready-to-wear; boutique jewelry; finest Limoges china; Lalique crystal; perfume; silk scarves from Dior, Hermès, Balmain and others; silver and 18-carat-gold charms; exclusive men's gifts; *haute couture* ties; fine toys; beguiling local handicrafts and souvenirs; lots, lots more. Technical Counselor Jean F. Raviola ringmastered a similar shopping circus for 8 years in the Caribbean; his charming wife Andrée is the arbiter of all the merchandise in the entire complex. *Completely duty free*; no city tax; experienced worldwide shipment; credit cards honored; open 365 days per year from 9 A.M. to 8:30 P.M. Our top recommendation on the entire coast.

In proven big-name perfumes—not junk—**Rimay** in *Cannes* (46 rue d'Antibes) offers splendid stocks. The charming M. and Mme. Taillebois are completely truthworthy and ethical in every respect. Here's where we always make our purchase when we're on the Riviera.

Tax-free, duty-free wines, liquors, and other products are delivered to your stateroom by a company called **E.G.P.** (6 rue St.-Honoré, *Cannes*, back of the Majestic Hotel)—at billings which amount to a steal. Exportation only. Are we jealous of your lot as you toss down buckets of $7 a Cordon Rouge Vintage across the blue Mediterranean? Not much; we just jump into our water wings every time a passing boat whistles. But please remember: U.S. Customs now has that 1-quart free limit per traveler, above which there's a moderate duty per bottle.

The **Riviera Airport** (which has, incidentally, a delightful open-air restaurant and restrooms with showers) also offers a special shop to passengers bound for any country except France. It's a great place to load up on spirits, at tariffs which can't be touched domestically. But are the perfumes tax-free, as a clerk so blithely assured us, or are they priced the same as in Nice or Cannes? Payments in foreign hard currencies only (no francs).

Otherwise, we're strictly lukewarm about shopping possibilities along this entire coast, except for branches of a few ultrachic Paris landmarks. The average local stores seem poor and the stocks disappointingly limited for such a supposedly glamorous resort center.

FURTHER INFORMATION   Try either the **Services du Tourisme de la ville de Cannes**, at the Palais des Festivaux (on the Croisette; ask for Max Vitu), or the **Welcome Information Service** branches in Nice and Cannes. The first offers an Information Desk, an English-speaking staff (including hostesses who have lived in the States), a greeting service (at that hideous Maritime Station) which meets every incoming ocean liner, and other aids. It keeps 2 girls in touch with all hotels and pensions to find space for new arrivals. It's open every day until midnight during this rush season. The 2nd comes up with the same type of aid, plus a helping hand to locate immediate hotel accommodations for stranded travelers. It is connected by Telex to 12 companion bureaus in major cities. Both have absolutely nothing to sell; their only aim is to assist you so that you'll get the best possible impression of the Côte d'Azur.

For your *bookings,* however (the Services du Tourisme makes no reservations for planes, trains, buses, local sightseeing, etc.), we cheerfully recommend 2 top-ranking centers: **Agence Havas** (5 rue Maréchal Foch) and **Agent Cannes** (Building du Casino)—both in Cannes. R. Fleury, mogul of the latter, possesses vast experience, excellent judgment, and a formidable reputation for honesty, patience, and amiability. These gracious people may be depended upon 100%.

 # Germany

The miracle of today's Western Germany must be seen to be believed. Probably no other nation in the history of the world has made such enormous strides in so short a time.

This year's visitor will find every conceivable amenity save one (the penalty of success): Service standards are disturbingly low—almost as poor as ours in the U.S. Thousands of bellhops, porters maids, bus drivers, waiters, and similar jobholders seem to rue their present occupations, covet higher earnings for less work, and occasionally (not too often, to date) vent their splenetic dissatisfaction on the people they attend, including the visitor. To balance this, the traveler will find luxurious hotels, delicious food, an unrivaled transportation network, and all the pleasures or comforts of meticulously organized tourist facilities. In blue-ribbon havens, he will also see the glimmerings of the broad smile and the warm welcome which hark back to a more gentle era. He will discover teeming, bustling, kinetically supercharged cities—tidy, colorful, immaculate villages—grim, austere industrial complexes which stretch for miles—and rugged grandeur or bucolic tranquillity in rural areas which are so beautiful they will often take his breath away.

CITIES   Aside from political factors, *Berlin* is one of the most interesting and rewarding single tourist targets in Germany. A completely separate and independent section on this magnet is found earlier in the *Guide*.

Frankfurt am Main is pretty impersonal—except for the lovely Old Town, the beauty of the Römer, and the fun to be had sipping *appelwoi* (apple wine) in the colorful taverns of Sachsenhausen, the most ancient district of this modern metropolis. Overall you might not like it as much as other cities (it has never been a particular favorite of tourists). But it is the transportation hub, the banking center, the leading Trade Fair center, and the home of one of Europe's busiest jumbo jetports—so there's a good chance you'll spend at least one night in this bustling hive of 700-thousand. One dazzler is a rotating restaurant perched 332 feet up the world's tallest silo. Another is its 1085-foot TV tower, the highest building in the Federal Republic. A third is the restored Opera House. Theater, concerts, Goethe's house, outstanding zoo, a full range of hotels, fine restaurants, tempting shopping, a "Welcome Service" for motorists, a host-and-hostess fillip for bewildered sightseers. The Rhine Main airport terminus is replete with the latest facilities and trimmings. Escalators convey passengers to platforms for trains which whisk them to the Central Station in 11 minutes.

Hamburg, with approximately 2-million population, is Western Germany's first seaport and largest city. It too spins a 890-foot-tall TV spindle that also has a rotating restaurant. Next, it will proudly welcome the airs and airesses of the Soaring Seventies with its Holstenfeld Airport—a project so mammoth it will vie with the Dallas-Ft. Worth complex. Dine in the famous Ratsweinkeller, stroll through Planten un Blomen Park, shop along Alster Lake, visit one of Germany's largest collections of fine paintings at the Art Gallery (50 showrooms!), take a whirl through that naked, rowdy Reeperbahn night district, ride a steamer to Blankenese on the Elbe River, or to the war-famous island of Helgoland (great for lobsters, but oh those prices!), see Hagenbeck's renowned zoo with its Troparium to display its apes, snakes, crocodiles, and other exotic critters in natural surroundings—and you'll come home with happy memories for the rocking chair.

Munich, the Bavarian capital, is the southern apex of industry, commerce, U.S. soldiery, and at least 1 foreign visitor for each 1 of the 1-million permanent population. Its touristic gears whirled in double time for the '72 Olympics, on the city's outskirts where the main stadium boasts a capacity for 80-thousand spectators. The typical Bavarian is a better host than the typical northerner; his beer steins are bigger and his smiles are broader. In addition, here's the number one art center; the celebrated "Pinakothek" with its magnificent collection of 7000 German, Florentine, Venetian, Dutch, Flemish, and other fourteenth-to-eighteenth-century masters flowers from May to October each year; in the Haus der Kunst there are additional works belonging to the Bavarian State Art Collection. Residenzmuseum (historic crowns, tiaras, and treasures of royalty) and adjoining Schatzkammer (perfectly preserved ancient theater) are so fabulous that no wanderer should miss them. There are a Beer Museum (now with a new head on it), the "Museum of Blooming Nonsense" (Valentin-Musäum), and the 951-foot IVA television tower with a spiraling elevator and a neighboring 100-foot "Space station," plus a pavilion. The glitteringly reconstructed State Opera House is an acoustically perfect 6-tier showcase resembling the original *belle époque* marvel of 3 decades ago. The theaters, the Zeiss Planetarium, and other cultural attractions are outstanding. So are the fabled Oktoberfest (late Sept. through early Oct.) and the Fasching (Jan. and Feb.). The local adage states that the former is for beer and laughs, while the latter is for sex and Sekt (German "champagne"). Need proof? (1) The peak annual birthrate is during September and October, precisely 9 months after the January-February revels. (2) Besides, who feels like making Oktoberfest love after consuming 3.3-million quarts of beer and 700-thousand weenies? Three times each year the Auer Dult sales on the Mariahilfsplatz keep bargain-seekers hopping at the local version of Paris' Flea Market. Plenty of good restaurants and bright lights the calendar round, too. You'll probably want to stay here as long as you can.

Cologne's modern midtown towers contrast dramatically with its beautifully preserved Cathedral, a magnificent structure, the largest Gothic building in the world. A 6-lane bridge spanning the Rhine provides the final link between the city and the Ruhr–Frankfurt autobahn—as an alternate, of course, to the more exciting 6½-minute swing on the aerial ropeway (altitude 165 feet!). The redesigned Cologne-Bonn Airport is zipped into the speedway circuit, making it far more handy to air travelers. Much of the excavation for a metropolitan subway system has been completed. The hotel situation shows laudable recent improvement, but good accommodations are still somewhat short in High Season. The big draws are the Cathedral, the stunning theater-opera house, the playhouse, the Roman Germanistic Museum surrounding the Dionysus Mosaic, plus a splendid gem display, and Phantasialand, the local answer to the Disney realms. Inquire at the city's Tourist Office about the "Meet-the-People Teas" (5 P.M., except Sat., Sun., and holidays), which are opening many homes to foreign visitors. Tickets for this hospitality service, plus free eau de Cologne (the real thing), city guides, maps, and color slides, are also available at the Hotel Excelsior Ernst, a 2-minute skip from the tourist headquarters.

Bonn, its neighbor, now stretches out into several suburban hamlets. Its population was more than doubled by its absorption of 10 adjoining communities, pushing up the headcount to 300-thousand. It boasts Poppelsdorf Palace, the Rhenish Land Museum, the versatile Zoological Research Institute and Museum, and Beethoven as its most famous son—but the streets (on which $150,000,000 are finally being spent) are a rat race. Such a frenetic and impersonal atmosphere pervades that we'll take central Detroit anytime. An incredible number of cars jam its streets en route to other destinations; 36 times per day, 3 railway crossings halt traffic for an average of 20 minutes each hour. (To relieve this maddening congestion a *2nd* bridge across the Rhine is now operative, thank goodness); 36-thousand vehicles per day funnel through and clog the Koblenzer Gate along the main north-south link between Cologne and Coblenz. And if this isn't enough, rain falls on its unfortunate inhabitants 162 days per year!

Bremen, the 2nd-largest seaport, is a typical *Hanse* (medieval merchants' union) city. Fine Ratskeller, marketplace, golf course, 600-year-old City Hall statue of Roland, and a rather gnu zoo, and the tavern-studded Schnoor district for sipping, shopping, or browsing. *Kassel*, *Aachen* (with its engrossing International Press Museum), *Schweinfurt*, *Landshut*, and *Ingolstadt* are among the handful of centers which still suffer from their wartime semidestruction—and which can probably never be the same, despite intensive rebuilding. *Essen* is a railroad hub, an iron and steel community, a virtual Krupp fief. It is also the home of a well-stocked art museum, and it borders Gruga Park, the so-called Garden Spot of the Ruhr. Not worth a touring detour, but improving year by year.

Hanover, basically an attractive mercantile mart, boasts a marvelous jam-free street system—but where do people go? In the State Opera and the

Herrenhausen Park and Palace, however, you'll find 1st-quality music and theater. Out at **Hodenhagen,** there's also a wildlife park with numerous residents of Serengeti shivering under the weak northern sun.

Stuttgart takes pride in its pleasant location, mineral springs, eye-popping 692-foot Fernsehturm (TV tower) restaurant, German Antiques Fair, dramatically modern Liederhalle for concerts, an art collection acquired from Norwegian shipping executive Ragnar Moltzau, "Sunny" (the performing chimp at the Wilhelma Zoo and Botanical Gardens), and such important factories as Daimler-Benz, Porsche, Kodak-Germany, and Bosch-Germany. Literally translated, the name of the city is "Stud Farm"—a term most servicemen stationed here would call euphemistic. Too many industrial plants and too much commerce; not very exciting for touring humans—*or* stallions.

Heidelberg ("Heather Hill"), scene of *The Student Prince,* is a sad example of what happens to a glorious, tailor-made sightseeing target when it is overrun by hordes of rubberneckers. It boasts an enchanting situation astride a riverbank, the world's largest wine barrel (58-thousand gallons), Karzer Prison for obstreperous fifteenth-century students of its celebrated university, the Lion Gate, undergraduate dueling clubs (now revived), the dazzling $7,000,000 railway station, and the 127-foot TV tower (observation platform open to the public). It is also the seat of the U.S. European Army Headquarters, with 25-thousand bored soldiers housed in a suburban area. Please beware of the trolley cars here; the streets are so narrow they practically cannonball down the sidewalks. Heidelberg is guilty of nothing except an excess of beauty and historic charm; the only thing wrong with it is the rabble of Japanese, French, Italian, Belgian, Scandinavian, Indian, Greek, North American, Latin American, and Hottentot tourists who spoil it in Season. But in good weather during the slowest months—*wunderbar!*

Lübeck, "Queen of the Hanse," is so rich in monuments, antiquities, paintings, and antique salt-storage houses that it's a great favorite of serious-minded voyagers—and **Travemünde**, the neighboring Baltic resort, balances the ledger by offering a gambling casino and plenty of excitement in summer to the frivolous. **Kiel**, nearby, was the marine host for the sailing contests of the Olympics. Worth a visit, particularly by old salts.

Baden-Baden splashes in with its famous Lichtentaler Allee, Roman baths and thermal ablutions. The 3-story Congress Hall, with its main-floor restaurant and flowering terrace, has been inaugurated at nearby Augustaplatz; the more youthful, jazzed-up casino with a recreational wing, spa gardens, 300-car underground garage, racetrack, and other enticements, is drawing discriminating vacationers. Its "Grand Week" of big-time horse racing (late Aug. to early Sept.) is internationally known. Enthusiastically recommended for rural resort lazing.

Düsseldorf is Germany's center of *haute couture;* beautiful clothes (on beautiful mannequins). The main street, called "Kö," runs along a lovely waterway; hotel development booming; good restaurants, Benrath Castle, scads of churches and art galleries, a modern 4-story apartment-style bordello with 228 "tenants" and 8000 "visitors" a day (see "Nightclubs"), cosmopolitan citizens, and handsome environs, one of which includes the $5,000,000 Minidomm, elf-size scaledowns of world-famous architectural wonders from

Gothic cathedrals to Kennedy Airport (open daily from 9 A.M. to II P.M.; between Düsseldorf and Mülheim).

Nürnberg is a charming example of the once-moated medieval metropolis. Its walls, towers, and ancient landmarks have been almost completely restored (one tower stands 1000 feet tall beaming TV pictures thoughout the area); the impressive Kaiserburg (Imperial Palace), dominating the local landscape, is 100% in trim again—this time without the "Iron Maiden" and other historic instruments of torture; the kids love the Grimms' Witch Cottage at the castle entrance (totally covered with eatable gingerbread at yuletide); the Meistersingerhalle is a handsome stride forward. Dürer's 5-century-old dwelling, and the St. Lorenz and St. Sebaldus churches are the most popular sights; the Grand Hotel is above average for comfort.

Garmisch-Partenkirchen, is an Alpine resort with strong tourist appeal and backup facilities sprouting everywhere—so much so, in fact, that much of its charm is swiftly vanishing. Magnificent panorama of the German and Austrian Alps; bracing climate; restyled casino; winter sports galore, with ski runs and lifts, bobsledding, cable cars, a glass-lined public swimming pool, and much more. Take the train for a short roll, then whistle up the 8-minute cable ride to the 9730-foot crown of Zugspitze Mountain; it's an eyeful you'll never forget.

Oberammergau, having played its Passion in '70, will now snooze somnolently for the better part of an uneventful decade. Meanwhile, the townsfolk will be cooling off in the new complex of swimming pools.

Augsburg, home of the Rennaissance commercial leaders named Fugger, boasts the oldest socialized housing project in the world. If you're an opera lover, don't miss the open-air performances at the famous Rotes Tor ("Red Gate"). Nothing much else of special interest.

The smaller towns, villages, and hamlets are the true jewels of Germany's crown; here's where you'll find the travel-poster scenery and glamour. Wonderful little **Dinkelsbühl**, walled, moated, and fortified in A.D. 928, is one example; medieval **Rothenburg** continues its all-out *Putsch* against motor traffic and parked vehicles in certain areas, thus preserving its ancient charm. We are almost equally entranced by **Nördlingen**, **Schongau**, **Landsberg**, and **Füssen** (also along the so-called Romantic Road), **Celle**, **Lüneburg, Goslar**, **Stade**, **Schleswig**, and dozens of others. Then there are the historic German spas, among the best known of which are **Wiesbaden** (rheumatism), **Bad Harzburg** (internal ailments), **Bad Nauheim** (heart disease), **Bad Homburg** (gambling casino to raise the patients' metabolisms), **Badenweiler** (rheumatism), **Bad Reichenhall** (asthma—plus being the terminus of the oldest pipeline in Europe: 350 years old, made of wood and lead, and used to carry salt water for curative purposes between here and **Traunstein**, 20 miles away), **Bad Kissingen** (gastric ailments), the previously mentioned **Baden-Baden**, and at least 20-dozen others which we haven't space to list.

The Roman-built **Moselle Valley** route from the Luxembourg border to Coblenz, where the Moselle joins the Rhine, remains one of the most pleasant drives or river cruises of Europe; its wine hamlets such as **Cochem** are enchanting. So is the **Rhine Valley**, when you're allowed to ignore its traffic-choked segments; you may also cover it in either direction between Coblenz and Wiesbaden/Mainz on the renowned steamer excursions (turn to "Things to See"). Driving is the most fun, though, if you like medieval castles —of which Marksburg, near **Braubach**, will probably intrigue you the most.

For information on other places, consult the German Tourist Offices or your travel agent.

MONEY AND PRICES
Basic units are the Pfennig and the Deutsche Mark. If you run out of either, the Deutsche Bundesbank makes special accommodation loans to hard-up tourists.

The currency is so strong that it keeps on being revalued. Some observers believe that this *still* isn't enough and that it will soon be followed by yet another rise in relation to the 7 European monetary systems to which it is linked.

One pfennig is worth around 1/3¢; 1 mark (abbreviated DM) now swaps for about 39¢. There are coins for 1, 2, 5, 10, and 50 pfennigs, plus 1, 2, and 5 marks. Notes appear in 5, 10, 20, 50, 100, and 500-mark denominations; the 1000-mark whopper bears the 2nd highest value of any monetary unit in Europe.

Currently you may bring into or take out of West Germany all of the frozen currencies *or* marks that you can possibly squeeze out of your wife.

In cities and tourist centers, prices are steep. Dinner in a top restaurant runs $17 to $27; $11 should buy a good meal in almost any routine establishment. A double room with bath usually rings up $30 to $60 or more; a single starts at about $23. A Scotch-and-soda in a decent nightclub might cost from perhaps $3.50 to $7.50, (small admission charge extra). In the villages and hamlets, however, levels are much cheaper.

CUSTOMS AND IMMIGRATION
All Foreign visitors may bring in the following without duty: (1) articles for personal use, (2) 1 fifth of your favorite potable for personal use in an *opened* (not sealed) bottle (2 or 3 would probably get by), (3) sufficient foodstuffs—no coffee or tea, however—to take you *only* as far as your German destination (amounts discretionary with the individual Customs officer, and (4) 400 cigarettes *or* 100 cigars *or* 500 grams of pipe tobacco, provided you're an overseas resident (not European national) and at least 15 years old.

If you've got Fido on a leash or Felix in a basket, you must show a health certificate for your canine or feline companion. This can be a statement by a veterinarian that the pet reveals no symptoms of illness and that, 3 months prior to issuance of the paper, no cases of rabies were registered in your hometown or area. Since this document is valid for only 20 days after issuance, if you're planning a long holiday you'd better leave your shaggy friend behind.

One gracious wrinkle, which more nations should copy, has been introduced especially for the ladies. If you're shy, if you're coy, or if your Little Things show Tattletale Gray from the rigors of your trip, your baggage at German frontiers may be inspected in privacy.

When you carry purchases from other countries on a noncommercial basis, they will not be affected. The limit on personal gifts, other than food, has been boosted to DM100). Overseas travelers may export, duty-free, up to DM2000), but Europeans are limited to 1/5th that sum.

Most of the time the inspectors will be satisfied with an oral declaration of the nature of your luggage. You merely tell them what you have, and they'll let you pass after a token poke at your bags. For more than a dozen years now, they have not even been stamping passports on entry or exit unless you request it as a souvenir.

But occasionally they'll cross you up, just to make things interesting. If this happens, you'll find them thorough, polite, and typically Germanic in attention to detail.

HOTELS   For far more comprehensive information on certain hostelries than space limitations permit here, interested travelers are referred to the annually revised *Fielding's Selected Favorites: Hotels and Inns, Europe* by our son, Dodge Temple Fielding. The latest edition, in which a total of 300-odd favored possibilities were handpicked from the 4000-plus personally inspected, will be at your bookstore early this year.

On the average, the quality nationally is fair to excellent. Its best ones would hold their own anywhere in the world.

Tourist centers are *all* so jammed during the season that *it is imperative to make your reservations in advance.* In the metropolises, plumbing nearly always comes with your hotel room key; private baths are at a premium, however, in small towns. Garages are available almost without exception. The average spa or health resort offers warm mineral baths as part of its service.

Fair warning: One-piece mattress addicts often have to settle for something not quite the same in German hotels. Although our home-grown variety now appears in more tourist-route stops, you're still likely to find 3 mattresses on 1 board—devilishly placed so that your fanny is squeezed into a crack.

Identification papers or documents are no longer required of the guest at registration time—such bold common sense that the Ministers of the Interior who abolished this nuisance should be awarded the Order of the Golden Scissors, with Crossed Laurels of Shredded Red Tape. Cheers for them—and let's hope that other nations soon follow!

Accommodations begin at about $33 for a bare-boned twin unit with bath; singles start about 30% less; topline lodging will cost anywhere from $35 to $60 or more for 2, while normal suites command rates of approximately $100 on up to 3 times more for the Presidential spreads. At most addresses, breakfast —perhaps even a sausage or a wedge of cheese—may be wrapped into the overall bill.

While **Frankfurt am Main** is one of Germany's key spots for visitors, its hotels are geared for the commercial traveler rather than the tourist. (The Schlosshotel Kronberg is a notable exception; see further along, please.) In this strongbox of more than 1000 banks, 80% of its transients are on missions of commerce, and the remaining 20% are merely changing planes or waiting to go elsewhere. As a result, you're more likely to find a cool, businesslike approach than a warm welcome. A prime example is the **Frankfurter Hof**, in every way a fine, no-nonsense address in the middle of a no-nonsense city. General Manager Curt Peyer has done almost all that is possible to create an atmosphere of robust vigor. You'll find the spectacular, Old Frankfurt cellar restaurant (called the "Stubb") with vaulted ceilings, each segment dedicated to a particular phase of the city's history; it pans out authentic nineteenth-century local recipes balanced to suit modern diets and tastes. Charming Restaurant Français in Empire II and rich emerald tones; less appealing wicker-and-wood Grill with iron firebacks; Apéritif Bar, with squat leather easy chairs; handsome Lipizzaner Bar. The Peyer Project further includes numerous modernized bedchambers, all now with hush-the-traffic windows; good parking facilities; direct-dial telephone system; color TV now in suites and eventually to be throughout. Service attitudes? In the past, too rushed to care; under Mr. Peyer's special training program, they are vastly better. Still a busy-busy-busy beehive, but its many new blossoms now give this one a Meissen bowl of welcome new honey.

The **Hessischer Hof** is smaller, more sedate, and less colorful. Mixture of older and newer rooms in varying segments; so-so service; thoroughfare situation, with extra-ply windows to shut out the noises. Cellar bar for romantic couples; zestless dining room; tiny summer café; winter garden with sliding roof; bedchambers roomy and uncozy, with ample closet space; large baths. Now quite recommendable.

The air-conditioned, 21-story **Intercontinental** commands an ideal site beside the Main River. On an adjoining plot, there's a newer 20-floor, 300-unit annex plus a swimming pool; this addition—connected to its alma mater by a tunnel and an escalator—jostles the overall room count up to more than 800 accommodations with exactly the same narrow dimensions and routine décor. The refashioned Rôtisserie is richly garbed in wood and brocade. The ground-level bar and breakfast room have been re-formed amiably. A Wine Room, off the Brasserie, is a novel cup. The annex restaurant and shops are going full steam ahead under the direction of Guy Frey. Concierge Koehler knows his job perfectly and is a blessing to any Frankfurt-stationed traveler. But in an establishment of this enormous size, it is technically impossible—especially in reservations handling—for genuine personalized attention to exist. An institution, but a good one which is fast improving.

The new, towering, glassy **Plaza** only was nearing completion on our recent swing, so we can't tell you very much about it. The location, across from the Messe (fair grounds) will be an asset to exhibitors. Canadian Pacific is the host; luxury is the category; service will be the focus. We wish it luck.

The 2-part **Park** was taken over by the group holding the keys to the Berlin Hotel in Berlin. Handsome entrance, dining room ideal for business tête-à-têtes; superb cuisine and overall service standards; late-model glass-and-stone wing in linear form; every fresh unit with private bath or shower; currently so popular that the reception desk turns away as many as 30 or 40 potential clients a day. Agreeable, but not luxurious. The **Savoy** is a bright addition with lots of hospitality fixin's: Sauna, pool, open grill, attractive bar, night-club, and restaurant, plus the able direction of Ernst Bloemers. For its moderate tabs, very sound, even if the living space is limited.

The **Airport Hotel**, backed by the Steigenberger people (owners of the

Frankfurter Hof), made its 350-point landing at the edge of the runways a while back. The hospital-modern, 10-story, Y-shape structure jets in with a full bath count, air conditioning, soundproofing, a large pool under a glass dome for all-season splashing, a sauna, a nightclub, a coffee shop, and a country-club grill plus a conventional restaurant. Exceptionally well done for its particular type. The new, 9-story, S-shape, air-conditioned, 560-room **Sheraton**, even closer to the terminal, is linked to it by a pedestrian bridge. There are a pool, a sauna, 3 restaurants, the Red Baron nightery, parking for 7000 (sic) cars, a subway station beneath you (10 minutes to town) and a first-rate concierge in dynamic Eric Plant. Cool, big, but efficient. A 312-pit **Esso** station recently made its debut, as well as a 300-unit innery by the **Holiday Inn**-keepers (well out on the Main–Taunus pike), plus yet another European entry for **Ramada** (near the H-I, but with more zest, in our opinion) and a reasonably nice commercial house called the **Arabella** out in the industrial suburb of *Neiderrad*.

The **Gravenbruch** is a charmingly cozy nook. Its chief disadvantage is that it is located 15 minutes from the heart of the city—a short hop from the airport and only a few seconds off the north-south autobahn intersection called Frankfurter Kreuz (a handy pull-off for motorists). Pleasant man-made lakeside site; captivating rustic dining room with forest-viewing windows and a crackling open hearth; well-appointed bedrooms; ground-floor units with direct access to the gardens; 2nd-floor duos with balconies. An excellent choice for wheelborne families.

Next is the peaceful, well-run **National**. Nurtured with love by its hardworking proprietor, it shines as brightly as the flecks in *Goldwasser;* softspoken Manager Steier is as easygoing—yet as efficient—as the domain he commands. Pleasant restaurant; bedchambers modernized in a thoughtful way; most suitable for the maturer wayfarer. Gentility and homey kindness are the biggest assets here.

The **Baseler Hof**, the **Hamburger Hof**, and the **Savigny** are off our list.

The 95-room **Monopol-Metropole**, hard by the station and in the Excelsior roundhouse, has been chugging along at a sprightly clip—and its carloads of improvements show. The **Excelsior** has forgotten to take its charm pills for too long now, in our opinion. The carpets in the lounges, elevator, and other public centers were not quite as dirty as the floor of a cattle car, but they were in strong competition when we saw them. Its commercial air was mixed pungently with the aromas of cooking grease and blue cigar smoke. As Longfellow might have scriven about it, "A banner with the strange device, Excelsior!"

The **Continental** seemed worn out when we inspected it; its few recent updatings were colored in greens and purples. 'Nuff said.

The little **Hotel am Zoo** (across from the Zoo garden) is clean, bright, and okay for small-boned travelers; somewhat expensive. **Württemberger Hof**, with 16 added singles and baths, is less costly, but less comfortable; students might like it. **Haus Marina** offers 27 rooms with small bathrooms; breakfast only; quiet situation and good-humored ambiance; not bad for the price if some much needed retouchings are effected soon. In the meantime, the **Diana**, in the same league, might be a cozier nest. The **West End** and the **Hübner** also are pleasant tykes. The **Luxor** and the **Jaguar** are contenders in Second-class; the latter seems to have more spring to its gait. The **Westfälinger Hof** is chiefly for the merchant trade; the back rooms are quieter. The **Palace**, **Rex**, and **Gloria**, also in this category, are commercial, commercial—oo-la-la, are they commercial; no place for Guidesters, in our opinion. The **Zeppelin**, deflated some time ago, is filling up again. Best for young balloonists, who would probably call it a gasser for the price.

For limousine motorists and golfers, the **Schlosshotel Kronberg** is a knock-out on the Carriage Trade Circuit. It's 10 miles (about 25 minutes) from the center of Frankfurt at *Kronberg*, seat of the Hesse Empire and the baronial headquarters of the proprietor, the Prince of Hesse. (His ancestors once conquered Frankfurt.) After its recent fortune-consuming restoration and expansion, the Schloss is better than ever before—a dream come true. (Avoid the top floor if you hanker for antiquity.) This original Tudor castle of Empress Friedrich III, the eldest daughter of Queen Victoria, still retains its grand terrace, its priceless tapestries, its art masterpieces (Titian and Holbein paintings in the dining room), and its beautiful furnishings which so deftly have been combined with up-to-the-minute amenities. Personable, handsome Director Gian Luigi Zanotti (formerly of the wonderful Splendido of Portofino in Italy) who also oversees the Hessischer Hof in Frankfurt for its noble landlords, should be congratulated. Exquisite—a heritage preserved. The nearby **Viktoria** is a less expensive carpark for buckboarders seeking a Kronberg address but simpler shelter. Total of 30 starkly modern, unadorned bedchambers; golfing privileges, so duffers can dig their divots with the Kronberg Klan. Fair for the fairways, but only so-so at the 19th hole. The historic **Ritters Park-Hotel** in *Bad Homburg* (30 minutes out) is a mediocre alternative. Unprepossessing dining room; a bedraggled plant that could use some Vigoro in the way of capital improvements; perhaps Director Wilfried Brusius, formerly of Venice's Bauer Grünwald and Park hotels and Rome's Caesar Augustus, has the green thumb to make it thrive again. Definitely not in the same league with the klassy Kronberg.

Munich, as we've already mentioned, fielded 10-thousand visitors during the '72 Olympic Pillow Case Race. Although the roar of the crowds is now only an echo in the colorful history of the Games, its hotelathon will provide you with many more 1st-, 2nd-, and 3rd-string kips than existed before the starter's gun went off.

The **Bayerischer Hof** is a zillion-dollar champion that keeps improving with age. Brightest baubles include a Trader Vic's restaurant (noteworthy for drinks, décor, and now quality cuisine), an 850-capacity festival hall, the Tirolian Stube adjoining the Palais Keller for local atmosphere and short-order regional cookery, a 200-ton sliding-roofed swimming pool, a health center with adjoining bar, and the Grill—arches, bottle-glass windows, tile-lined rôtisserie, and adjoining garden-terrace. If perfection is your order of the day, try the adjoining Palais Montgelas, an elegant classic serving as sort of a Bavarian cousin to the Waldorf Towers. The tariffs there are only slightly more than in the main building (a few units there could use a perk-up), but from private receptionist to golden bathroom taps, everything here is even more patrician. Both personally and professionally, we are hopelessly in love with #43, a one-of-a-kind atelier which brought us such joy during our most recent stay. In the cellar there's the finest and liveliest nightclub in Bavaria for 200. If money's no object, Suites #328-329 and #428-429 in the original structure offer a gold *double* bathtub, piped music in the bathroom, a fine bar in the sitting room, and wide-angle comfort; #705 and #770 are rustic renditions of the same sweet song, with open fireplaces, stereos, and tonight's-the-night terraces. As if this weren't enough, there's now a kilometer-long Mercedes-600 limousine parked at your front door for special airport shuttles, weddings, special events, or private hire. Costly revampings behind the scenes also contribute toward an improvement in quicker and more tightly controlled room service in this vast establishment. Concierges Stoess and Freytag are outstandingly warm, kind, and efficient. Owner Falk Volkhart merits kudos for his zingingly spirited supervision.

The splendidly refashioned **Vier Jahreszeiten**, a stalwart of the Old Guard, today easily shares the Munich throne. It is a beauty that radiates nobility, hospitality, and good taste. The entrance is a glistering introduction in glass and buffed bronze; the reception and concierge desks are broad, handsome, and efficient; the lobby provides 2 tiers of wood-paneled Edwardian charm; carpets everywhere are fresh, deep, and colorful. The white-and-gold Walter-speil restaurant, for perhaps a half-century a gathering place of discerning international gourmets, is *the* focal point of the area's gastronomy. To one side is the intimate English bar serving soft dance melodies with sips and sups; on the other flank is the Eck ("Corner"), a window-lined nookery that already has become famous for its Friday-Saturday buffets; the rooftop pool and sun terrace offer breakfast, lunch and the very same panorama provided by the ultraplush Presidential Suite. Other fillips include the sauna, massage center, hairdressing salons, elevators, and a 2-level underground garage. Though every bedchamber was totally remade, key pieces of the finest older furniture were retained for tradition's sake. They are replete with every technical and human comfort they could conjure. Concierges Jakob Pfanzelt and Peter Kruppel are only 2 of the superb staff members whom Manager Mass a-masses at his willing command. Recommended any winter, summer, spring, or autumn. Our all-out congratulations to the Four Seasonal team!

The **Continental** is sumptuous in both its newer and its revamped older segments. Spacious lounges; glorious azure-tiled winter roof garden bursting with flowers; 2 small outdoor parks for summer dining; corridors (some skylighted) with Gothic antiques worthy of the world's finest museums. Handsome popular Conti Grill with 2000-year-old fountain; cuisine which many residents and travelers praise but which we've found mediocre on our several tries. We are especially fond of its late-model courtside demisuites outfitted in rich textiles, elegantly etched mirror panels and sixteenth-century oil paintings. Proprietor Billig, who has spent both a fortune and a lifetime collecting these treasures, spared absolutely not one pfennig in cultivating this tasteful setting. Likable Manager Staschik ably commands his decorous silk-stocking realm—but staff problems are his Cross to Bear, just as they are throughout topflight German hoteleries. The attractions far, far outweigh the debits in this normally fine establishment.

Holiday Inn, a 3-part giant in the Schwabing district, leaped into the fray swinging a cluster of 400 door keys. Its trio of buildings contains rather limited but colorful space for 600; all of the singles have been decked out with double beds. Modernistic interior; lobby and reception in the central edifice; handsome Old Munich Bar under brick arches; dining salon, grill, and coffee shop; Yellow Submarine nightclub; beverage and ice machines on the various floors; swimming pool. Moderate prices that we believe will draw many pilgrims to its rather remote portals. Most Holidaymakers would probably find a happy home here.

The 500-unit **Hilton**, sited near the English Gardens and thus also a fair fling from midtown, reveals a lobby possessing all the charms to our eyes, at least, of a bank lounge in Zug. Ground floor Asian cookery; dimly viewful roof restaurant with dinner dancing; Marco Polo Bar moored nearby; year-round swimmery plus sauna. Although every accommodation is fitted with the now-standard bath, direct-dial phone, radio, and TV, we found them as short on decorative flair, quality furnishings, and warmth as they were long on gadgetry. So-so.

In this hotel pennant race, we are sorry to report that the outskirting **Sheraton** shows significant promise of striking out—at least in the considered opinion of these scouts who not only have watched it from the bleachers but have faced it from a home-plate field box. To our disappointment, the reception and concierge desks have balked almost every time we've watched them pitch; the snack bar and restaurant have consistently fanned out; the silver-foiled Vibraphon nightspot we diagnose as an easy victim of the inside curve; lucky line drives were registered by the pool, sauna, and massage center; the shoeshine and ice machines in the corridors of such a high-priced stadium seemed to us to be far more appropriate in dugout-style facilities. Our hatbox double was worthy of a farm club, and our bathroom—well, we'd send it to the showers, too. As rookies go, we'd give it a lowly .110 batting average. *Adios.*

The 250-room **Eden-Wolff** boasts a fine plant that we feel is being neglected through poor maintenance. Wood-lined lobby, lounge, and adjoining trellis-work bar; ski-lodge dining room with knotty timbers, stone arch, and Brueghel mural; colorful yet rapidly fading sleeping quarters, many featuring alcove beds; garage. From its swallow-tailed concierge to its smallest cranny, this midtowner could stand proud and mighty if the lazy housekeepers would get cracking. The station-sited **Bundesbahn** continues to win our Silver Medals for Old World Charm and Modern Comfort. All chambers soundproofed and air-cooled; newer entries plugged into TV's and bountiful baths; immaculate maintenance; #507, just under the joists, double-teams for pleasant dreams. Although the **Excelsior** is also hard by the train terminal, it is a surprising island of quiet. Contemporary Christmas-card lobby in wood and stained glass; appealing Sankt Hubertus restaurant in 3 tiers and hunting motif; 100 spotless units, including penthouse suites, encircling a peaceful courtyard; some sancta cheery and others dull. A decent value. The air-conditioned **Königshof**, under the same ownership, has been totally reborn as an attractive and unusual colorama; lovely restaurant; cozy hideaway bar at rear of lobby; bid for the 5th-floor rooms—huge windows, piped music, and a maze of convenience-gadgetry. Thanks to the tirelessly successful labors of

Prexy Geisel, now plush instead of utilitarian. The sparkling **Ambassador** offers 62 little studios with the beds, only 28 of which are doubles, partitioned off by drapes; private baths and kitchenettes throughout; TV and radio in every room; Persian rugs atop wall-to-wall monotone carpets to raise the BTUs on the personality scale. Chief attaché to this diplomat is Director G. Zillibiller. Comfortable and functional for families with children. The new, low-cost, 600-unit **Penta**, a sister to the airline consortium hostelries of the same name in London and Paris, is functional. Happily, the subway (S-Bahn) stops at its door on Rosenheimer Platz.

The 150-room **Arabella**, in a satellite suburb that's a costly taxi ride from the bright lights, is—like the Sheraton, its neighbor—probably too remote for the average North American merrymaker and shopper. The **Morizet**, even newer and colorfully cloaked in Frenchy tones, is only as distant as Schwabing; it's a much more rewarding choice in many ways. We are especially fond of the Basco wine room and its Parisianne Restaurant. The nearby **International** seemed too aggressively mod-minded to suit us. The 400-bed **Palace** is another outskirter, this one on the route to Garmisch. Most suitable for 2-suitors. **Esso** fuels up 155 capsules that are air-conditioned and Baverian-modern in style.

The **Deutscher Kaiser**, a toot from the railroad station, is a skyscraping resurrection from the war years. Commercial and clean; 180 rooms and 110 baths within its 18 stories; reserve high for wide-window eyefuls and silence. Okay as an overnight caboose. **Drei Löwen** ("Three Lions") is a favorite of well-bred Bavarian gentry who visit the metropolis. Extensive modernizations and expansions; 2 attractive dining rooms; cheery retreats. Recommended for its warmhearted personnel and matching clientele. The **Europäischer Hof** is no longer operated by Sisters of the Holy Family. We must check it again after this defrocking. Jokes aside, we will reinspect it soon. The pink-faced **Amba** hosts numerous tour packages within its 90-room shell. The **Platzl**, opposite the beer-weary Hofbräuhaus, is most definitely not recommended. The **Ariston** recently popped up; it serves breakfast only. The **Palace** is another late bloomer; it's far from the action. The **Metropol** is stiff, dour, and institutional; icy-cold lobby halfheartedly brightened by tropical flora; routine bedchambers; about as charming as a plastic pterosaur. The **Stachus**, **Esplanade**, and **Luitpold** strike us as being grim, grimmer, and grimmest—in that order. Last, and we think in many respects least, is the boxy **Tourotel**. Distant location in an industrial forest of smokestacks; plasticky reception and lobby; Naugahyde-and-formica restaurant and bar; pool and sauna. While the kind staff remains the big plus here, in our opinion the minuses have it.

Hamburg offers a mixed bag. Here are our evaluations of the prime runners in the field:

The high-tide **Atlantic** exchanges nightly reflections across the lake with the Vier Jahreszeiten (see below). It is completely comfortable and elegant; it is also the center of The Action from sunup to cock's crow. Its Poseidon is tall, amiable Kurt Walterspiel; the staff manager is bright young Jochen Geweyer. You'll find Die Brücke restaurant for quick meals, the Edwardian-modern Rendez-vous Bar with piano music, a dining room with orchestrated dinner dancing, an expanded grill, air conditioning in all public quadrants, an indoor pool-massage-sauna complex, and 105 rooms freshly turned out and furnished anew. For pasha-level living, our favorites among the updated suites are #311–315; regular doubles are also generally (not always) superb; all can be T-Viewed at no charge. A 3-story garage adjoins; excellent concierge team of Hägermann, Schweser, and Bistram are the Answer Men for your Hamburg puzzles. An urbane beautifully run colossus that we highly recommend.

The exquisite, lakefront **Vier Jahreszeiten** is a salubrious choice for the discriminating voyager who prefers subtle tapers to bright lights. This patrician is a dreamy haven for tranquility seekers, with luxury, finesse, and extraordinary maintenance. Its 200 units offer 200 baths and showers (many with colorful tile mosaics); some small but nicely decorated singles, some luxurious and spacious single-suites or alcove-twins, and some viewless inside units. Excellent cuisine; delightfully serene grill with open hearth; dining room beautified; charming hand-holders' bar adjoining the sleepy-looking dance-bar which has music from 9 P.M. to 2 A.M. The Condi Café features split-level lunching and a candy shop on the ground floor. Personable Director Karl Willman now is the Chief Gardener of the entire 4-season operation. The 2 radiant daughters of the late proprietor, Fritz Haerlin, also lend grace notes to this joyful composition: Anne conducts hotel matters, while Thekla usually adds her sweetness to the Candy Corner. Again we give this one our fond long-standing plaudits of praise.

The 32-tier **Plaza**—spliced neatly into the new municipal convention center—boasts of being the Federal Republic's highest hostelry. We hear that Canadian Pacific now runs this show following a transfer from Loews. Beige slab-u-lar structure with tinted windows; escalator ushering ticket holders to its marble bijou lobby; brick-and-board regional Vierlander Stuben; tapestried English Grille; nautical Galleon Bar; Blue Satellite discothèque; glass-sheathed sauna and pool; battery of boutiques; garage. Its cloying peppermint-striped corridors lead to 570 look-alike units; most are cookie-mold-standard doubles or twins; all are powdered in variations of brown and white accented by red or yellow; the boxy coffee tables, plastic chairs, globe lamps, and abstract paintings remind us of a Creative Playthings school. Air conditioning, direct-dial phones, remote-control lighting, 5-channel radios, and color TV are standard; the windowsills are a tall 4 feet above carpet level; the wake-up-your-eyes bathrooms—wowee!—are jazzed up in silver, white, and yellow patterned wallpaper. The producers of this Hanseatic spectacular predict that the bulk of its audience will be North European businessmen. We agree with that forecast. *Und gesundheit!*

The **Prem** is a renovated mansion made prem-and-proper through many recent improvements. The entrance and lobby, with its adjoining paneled bar, broadened and perked up smartly; corridors repainted; excellent cookery; warm service; parking lot and individual garages unveiled; all units brightened. We thoroughly enjoyed a 4-night stay in #14, a good-size Louis XV-style double facing the placid garden. Very nice indeed. The neighboring **Bellevue** boasts 85 bedchambers and an 85% bath ratio. Coming up, in our estimation. The **Berlin**, a Y-shape structure, is convenient for motorists who weary near the autobahn junction of Bremen and Lübeck-Kiel. Overall, it's tasteful and well maintained; the run-of-the-mill doubles are small and cluttered. The oval restaurant is O-kay but not inspiring; the underground garage parks 100 cars. The **Crest Motel** in the *"City North"* district is styled for the year 2000. It's one of the better links of an already excellent chain reaction. Superb physical facilities, but weak in service and culinary points. The **Parkhochhaus** is another candidate designed for motorists on the go-go circuit. Handsome restaurant in Swedish modern is open until 2 A.M.; gay yellow breakfast room with balcony; spotlessly clean; efficiency-type doubles with shower or full bath; 14 nests with private balconies; garage space for all guests. We admire its hardworking administration and its conscientious efforts to please, especially as spotlighted by General Manager Fritz Rahn and Reception Chief Hermann Hoth, who nurture a particular warmth for Guidesters. The **Falck** also leans to Scandinavian simplicity, but what it reveals in starkness it fails to recover in personality. The 135-room **Ambassador** struts in with a swimming pool, a sauna, a happily plaid-clad dining room, and a rustic bar. The tiny bedchambers in this converted office building are its chief handicap. Non-central and only fair. The **Reichshof**, a station hotel, has a lobby as sterile as a gelded herring. The **Europäischer Hof** also comes up with an assembly-line personality; 500 rooms with a high proportion of singles; 75% bath or shower ratio, all weenie-small; lobby as austere as a morgue's foyer; conventioneers galore. We wouldn't bother with either the **Pacific** or the **Motel Hamburg**. Ugh. The **Royal**, near the Atlantic, is for students, serious budgeteers, or self-abnegating eremites. The **Alsterhof** has 80 varying accommodations, 2 so-called penthouse suites (possibly because one gets that pent-up feeling in them), and 21 of the most minuscule baths outside a U-boat; #211 and #212, among the latest batch of improved units, are exceptions, with twin basins and adequate tubs. Maintenance is picking up. We're happy to say that this one's now right for the price.

Pensions? **Zeyn** (Rothenbaumchaussee 177), across from the Funkturm, is tuned in on hospitality. No English is spoken here, but these simple householders are kindly and most helpful. Clean; only 1 room with bath. **Marlyta**, across the way, is smaller but also amiable. As for other pensions, it's a good general rule to steer clear of the station and the St. Pauli areas because of their heavier-than-average patronage by prostitutes.

Düsseldorf? Both the **Hilton** and the **Intercontinental** open their shiny portals in an outskirting commercial subdivision. Due to their remoteness, we'll evaluate these ultracontemporary houses at the end of this roundup. For traditionalists—as opposed to modernists—nothing in the city proper can beat the **Breidenbacher Hof**, a classic that is smoothly run by Renate Linsenmeyer. This one, from cellar to roof, is a little jewel. Brand-new reception; glorious, elegant lobby salon; new bar-lounge with wood paneling, black leather and pastoral paintings; marvelous, cozy Eck ("corner") restaurant in Art Deco, with beaded lamps, salmon textiles, iced-glass partitions, and imaginative selections on a small menu. Fine concierge and staff; grill-lounge as easy on the optic nerves as it is on the tummy, with VSOP cognac walls and fine Italian mahogany furniture; quartet of gorgeous suites; many little touches so many German houses lack. The **Park-Hotel** has been stung ouch-ouch-hard by the competition hornet. Lobby usually achatter with businessmen; dining room enriched with wood carvings; Étoile Bar. All bedrooms with adequate furnishings and full carpeting; 99% of the baths revamped and at last good; all units with radio; suites with TV and refrigerator. Coolish, but eminently satisfactory. The **Savoy** is First-class rather than Deluxe. Restaurant with adjoining bar; all 95 units on the small side except for a few corner doubles with wraparound windows and ample space. Stereotyped. The **Esplanade**, in the same category and under the Savoy banner, recently emerged from a roundhouse revamping, adding about 50% more rooms in the process. Quieter situation; similar to the Savoy in most aspects of its insti-Teutonic atmosphere; heated indoor swimming pool available to guests at no extra charge (a privilege shared by the next-door **Atlantik**, which is lower priced and might be a worthy bet for budgeteers); sauna (supplement added); woody restaurant-cum-grill; grandmotherly breakfast quarter; 85 units, 75% of which claim private baths. As solid as a Deutsche Mark, but just about as passionless to the touch. The **Börsen,** a breakfast-only hostelry, is in the same chain; it employs the same decorator, but it thrills us even less. The **Eden** flowers with 90 small but fresh-faced pods, and 70 private baths. We are especially fond of #264, a corner double with roco-collaborations. The **Uebachs** attracts an older clientele of loyal German wayfarers. We like its overall feeling of cleanliness and puffy-pillow snap.

Now for our outlying stalwarts: The 12-story, 383-room, fully air-conditioned **Hilton** took root adjacent to the Congress Hall. Expansive off-lobby shopping gallery; sauna; health center; beauty parlor; swimming pool; thumpingly expensive turn-of-the-century San Francisco Restaurant that just isn't worth the outlay, in our opinion; coffee shop; 1890 Night Club in burgundy velvet, happily a-jiggle with luscious costumed hostesses; inviting Düssel Bar for quiet libations; bedchambers poured from the familiar Conrad cookie mold; typically narrowlined baths. While our enthusiasm is dipping for this one, that shouldn't turn away big spenders who love Hiltoniana.

The neighboring **Intercontinental**, in the same heavyweight class, has not matured as fully as its contemporary opponent, in our referee's judgment, but hopefully the management can pep it up. Cleverly conceived public rooms highlighting an Old Rhenish motif in the ground-floor dining and sipping segments; ultimate finesse reflected in the penthouse Belle Epoque restaurant and bar, where the cost of its Champagne Dinner, a special feature, was enough to levitate our own roof; fanciful appointments which to us sputter disappointingly; expensively outfitted accommodations; more space than is at the Hilton, but not employed to its best advantage; excellent concierge; snail-pace room service. It has basically the same upper-level tariffs and structural facilities as its peer, but we don't find it quite as appealing in our overall estimate. Perhaps you'll disagree.

Ramada now has joined the fray with a muscular entry across the river from the city. Taverny public rooms; English country-life feeling which provides a dark nesting quality; bed-roosts rather compact; medium price range. The nearby **Penta** has similar tariffs, but overall we find it cool and institutional. Its leading features include the restaurant and bar as well as the pool and sauna.

Further out, the **Schloss Hotel Hugenpoet**, a 25-minute ride along the pike to Essen, dates back to before the fifteenth century. Local citizens venture here for weekend repasts, wedding parties, and strolls around its historic frog ponds. Only 25 antique rooms, most with private bath; #28, a single, featuring a 300-year-old bed; #27, the bridal chamber, boasting newer springs and a softer mattress (thank heavens!); spooky corridors. We enjoyed our recent meal in the ancient castle dining hall. Out at the airport, the **Wartburg** will shelter you in perfunctory fashion if you are fogged in.

Heidelberg ? Number one is the **Europäischer Hof** (sometimes called "Europe"). It makes continuous updatings in the most tasteful of traditional Germanic themes. Its latest bauble is a spanking-new, 20-room wing with shops, conference salons, and a cellar garage. Total of more than 120 units; terrace-dining (season), or upgraded Kurfürstenstube Grill (local specialties and beguiling color); attractive bar. So fine in every department that we're always anxious to return. **Park-Hotel Haarlass**, out of town overlooking the Neckar, has zoomed up in our esteem as a result of the enormous refashionings wrought here. Lovely window-lined resaurant apart from main building; new bar; all acommodations restyled; all with new baths; carpets, wallpaper, oil paintings in superb frames; cordial staff. Medium prices reflect heavy group trade. Coming up zestily. **Stiftsmühle**, on the same river, has a much better basic plant, but, alas, it seems to us to be riding on its laurels. Baronial in tone but the aristocracy appears to be fading. Too bad because it could be a winner. Both of these require a car for ease in mobility. The **Schrieder** is a mélange of large, medium, and small bedchambers, some good, some fair, and some poor. The **Ritter**, which planted its first cornerstone in 1952, is growing newer by the moment. Shucks! Except for the restaurant, almost every speck of its once-rich antiquity has been erased. Very central, and now very ordinary. **Neckar,** on the waterside in the city, is an awkward building dappled with bright modern hues and functional furniture. Four doubles and 2 baths added, bringing the total to 34 rooms, 14 with plumbing; décor ranging from fair to substandard; breakfast only. The blue-tile **Kurfürst** offers 47 clean but spare bedrooms, 11 baths, 8 showers, and slaphappy service that discloses unpolished management and a poorly trained staff. Very limited. **Crest** operates a 68-room motel here. Cocktail lounge, 2 restaurants, ample space, and tip-top quality throughout. Incidentally, a **Holiday Inn** is out at nearby *Walldorf*. And, at *Ludwigshafen-Heidelberg*, the U.S.-bred **Ramada** organization has uncorked some competition.

In *Bremen*, the **Park** is majestically situated on 500 acres of Hanseatic real estate, fronted by a small lake and backed by a prairie-size lawn. Just 5 minutes from the station, but celestially quiet; 100 rooms and a trio of suites on the Paul Bunyan scale; dancing nightly in the Halali Bar; the thinking is so lavish there's even a special alfresco "Hund Bar" to furnish tidbits to your dogs. Unquestionably the leader, and a beautiful one. Next, the **Crest** probably offers the most comfort. The drawback here, however, is that it is out of the city heartbeat, so a car would be required. **Columbus,** in a century-old shell, offers an appealing lobby plus a few updatings; 170 units with 110 baths; singles so tiny they should remove the buttons from your jacket when you ask for your key; corner demisuites ending in "07" a reasonable buy for what you get; 2 restaurants and bar; very commercial; designed for extra-skinny transients. The next-door **Zur Post,** darker than its neighbor, is adequate but nothing more. **Overseas**, in the same category, is smack in the center and oh-so-noisy. The latter rents many accommodations with 3 beds; mostly for families or the *ménage à trois.*

Bremerhaven, 45 miles north, offers the **Nordsee** with 85 rooms and nearly a full bath count. Stark lobby in functional simplicity; cheerful breakfast quarter filled with greenery; men's bar; large clean doubles. A better-than-average buy for skippers who dock at eventide. **Naber**, a cut lower, comes up with rou-teeny roomery. The less-attractive **Metropole** completes the roundup.

Hanover 's youthful 8-story, 300-unit **Intercontinental** is, for the moment anyway, a golden turret of this global network; it rates—with us, at least—among the top modern-style hostelries on the Continent. Ideal situation, with the City Hall (magnificently illuminated at night), town lake, and shopping center almost at your doorstep; orange-canopied entrance beside a pool and fountain; glittery lobby warmed by rosewood panels and glamorous movie-TV stars who make this their offstage greenroom; Calenberger Bar with candlelight, red-leather trim, rich appointments, a terrific combo, and perfectly concocted drinks; dancing every night but Monday. Delicious cuisine in the dramatically decorated Prinz Tavern (lunch and dinner), the open-rôtisseried Grill segment, the cheerful Brasserie (6 A.M. to 11 P.M.), and the chummy, rustic *Bierstube* (snacks and suds from noon to midnight); pastry shop; 300-car garage; office space for transients; curvilinear secretaries available for executive suite-niks. The sleeping accommodations contain so many agré-mens we can't even begin to describe them. One carp: The baths are much too cramped. Otherwise, enthusiastically recommended. The 220-room **Kastens Hotel and Luisenhof**, with a lobby as frigid as a bathhouse foyer, has been hit hard by its uncontended competitor. Attractive wood, copper, and brick grill, where you can watch your steaks sizzle; air-conditioned; traditional bedrooms. While reasonable shelter is offered, it's not even a light jab on the biceps of the champ. Within the city, this is followed, successively, by the **Grand Hotel Mussmann** with its fresh restaurant and Tessiner Bar, and the **Europäischer Hof**. Outside of town, the **Esso** motel is superb in its category, except in 2 departments. Pleasant Bristol Grill, plus a coffee shop; summer terrace overlooking an enchanting deer park; each well-made unit with balcony and solid first-class comfort; low rates for high standards. We found the service wretched, and the food was on a par with what you might find in any Esso filling station in the States. What a shame, in face of its many assets! **Parkhotel-Motel Kronsberg** (yep, that's its true name) features a restaurant with 5 dining rooms plus a *Bierstube,* each one contributing mightily to the aroma of sauerkraut that was so redolent from portals to penthouse when we walked in. Well furnished and color-accented; slightly more expensive than the Crest; not bad as a 2nd choice if you have a heavy cold. Our recent fly-in to the airport-sited **Holiday Inn** left us wondering why we didn't book on the next flight out. The large comfortable beds and color TV did little to ameliorate the myriad problems we found at hand. One of the weaker outlets of this empire, in our estimation. About 25 miles northeast, at the medieval village of *Celle*, the **Parkhotel Fürstenhof** would seem to be a boreal dream if one can believe the publicity material. We plan to take a look at Manager Brühl's seventeenth-century baroque mansion and dwelling-annex very soon.

Cologne's foremost address, in our renewed opinion, is the stately and famous **Excelsior Ernst**, facing the Cathedral square. Continual updating campaigns; appealing polished-wood, oh-so-richly elegant Hanse Stuben grill, one of the nicest rooms in all Germany; new lobby also in Hanseatic tones; every bedchamber refashioned. Antebellum décor; cozy twins and nice apartments; frenetic atmosphere; on the commercial side, but smoothly managed. Concierge Brehm is the perfect man to answer 4711 of your Cologne questions. An aristocratic contender. Pan-Am's **Intercontinental** globespanner, which unlocked its 280 portals in '71, has already established itself as the local leader for modernists. Wood-pillared lobby glowing with globe lamps and cushy accoutrements; savvy front-desk team; ground-floor Brasserie and Interview Imbibery dispensing succulent Thüringer sausage and potent martinis, respectively and respectfully; vistaful rooftop Belvedere Restaurant and Bar with terpsichore on tap; pool, solarium, sun terrace, and sizzling sauna; bevy of boutiques; subterranean parking quarters. Unless the rising amount of tour traffic (30% on our last check) boils over the brim, here's a house that should continue bubbling happily.

The **Dom**, Dom-inated by hardworking Proprietor-Director Edgar Lührs, remains one of the better traditional hostelries in the region. In this traffic-occluded town, its 650-car underground garage, with direct entry to the hotel, comes as a blessing to anyone on wheels. Generous infusions of freshness everywhere; cheery restaurant; pleasant summer terrace; spacious accommodations, all with radio; TV on request; excellent direct-dial telephone installation; tariffs quite reasonable for the deluxe rewards; corner-sited #105, #206, and #306 pick of the litter. Excellent location and recommended. The **Mondial** caters especially to motorists and tour groups. Ground-floor garage topped by 150 units, each with bath and shower; some larger quarters available; overall functionality, but rates rather steep for the high level of chill. The **Senats-Hotel**, in a noisy location, boasts 70 fully carpeted rooms with floor-to-ceiling windows, 70 baths with curtain partitions, a dining room, and simple amenities. A sizable bundle of shortcomings, but passable if you arrive equipped with an indulgent nature. The **Europa** would be a decent hole-up if only someone would read the riot act to at least ½ of its personnel. We'd suggest they start with the front desk and then move on massively. Unh-unh. The 55-room **Ambassador** was sold after its inauguration; this one is having its troubles, according to local rumor. It gave us the impression of overrushed construction and cheap materials. The **Ramada** is located out at the industrial community of **Leverkusen**; the plant is fine but unless business required that we locate out here we'd prefer to be in Cologne. Back in the city, the 53-room **Cardinal** tweets sweetly; full bath or shower count; morning meal only; an inexpensive nest, central and cozy. **Atlantic**, associated with the Europa, serves breakfast only; its sister relationship is enough to make us fly its coop. **Breslauer Hof,** near the station, is a diminutive little dandy. **Berlin** is not recommended by this *Guide*. The **Adria**, at Hohe Pforte (which you might never find) in the midtown area, is a satisfactory economy stop. Modern, but so tight in dimensions you'll feel more snug than a knackwurst in a frankfurter roll. The **Regent** is too far into the outskirts to bother about. The **Crest** is out there, too; motorists are its bag.

Wiesbaden is a scenic spa and an excellent springboard for your Romantic Road-running. Bright feathers in the cap of the handsome **Schwarzer Bock** include the Le Capricorne French Restaurant (with nearly a ½-acre of priceless fifteenth-century wood carvings), and a newer wing boasting 30 rooms and 10 suites. Classic, tasteful atmosphere; lovely 5th-floor roof garden with grill, Chinese tearoom, restaurant, sundeck, and cocktail terrace; fizzy indoor swimming pool filled with sparkling water from local springs; highly skilled concierge in Tony Leyendecker; minimum rooms very small, but each has 2 washbasins in its bathroom and other urbane touches. For color and action, you can hardly do better locally. Although the **Nassauer Hof** is quieter, it is equally top drawer in comfort and luxury. Enormous input achieved recently by friendly Manager John Van Daalen; new entry and lobby; superb hall-portering by keen Heino Reichard; new bar with copper hearth; modern TV quarter; spacious grill with windows facing the casino and the bowling green; first-rate cuisine; pool and sauna. Everyone knows his or her assignment to perfection and performs it deftly, properly, and cheerfully. Warmly recommended.

The Intercontinental chain has linked up its 168-room, medium-budget **Forum**. Heated pool; restaurant; buffet breakfast; lounge and bar; direct-dial phones; air conditioning. Too cool for the vacationer, in our view. The **Blum**, though noisy, again seems to be satisfying a number of Guidesters this year; very popular coffee shop and mezzanine restaurant; 100% air conditioning; radio in all units; worn patches in many carpets; nothing special, but reasonably worthy. The **Park** offers a diverse bag of bedrooms along with a generally commodious atmosphere. The 100-room, 50-bath **Taunus** is thumbs down to us. The pleasantly situated **Klee** comes up with 50 kips, all with private bath; breakfast is the only meal; no bar; #34 with 2 balconies and a gay mien is a good buy. Rather informal. The **Grüner Wald**, another Second-class hostelry, has grown too creaky for all but the sparest of budgets. Passable at best. The midtown **Badhaus Bären** put on a new face; it also added a pool; many furnishings old-fashioned; overpriced for the value, say we. The aged **Goldenes Ross und Goldene Kette** is a dandy dip for penny-pinchers; no private baths, but a fine spa facility with one of the oldest thermal taps in the city; rock-bottom prices. Good for what ails you—especially if your aches are in your wallet. The **Eden** and the **Sabini**? Never. Finally, in the outskirts at *Östrich*, the ancient and colorful **Schwan** is one of the nation's best-known country inns; set-back Rhine-side location with enchanting view; savory regional cookery; friendly service. Ask for room #27 (with 7 riverview windows) or #21 (cute as a dollhouse); both sunny; operated by the Winkel-Wenckstern family since A.D. 1628; ideal for tranquillity; legendary for its wines; open March 1 to December 1 only. Be sure not to confuse it with the one in *Erbach*, which is 4 miles closer to Wiesbaden, because it's nowhere nearly as Sch-wanderful. The road-clinched, castle-hotel **Reinhartshausen**, in the same riverside neighborhood, was a disappointment to us. As one example of its bizarre motif, the Teutonic vaulted cellar restaurant was filled with good old Rheingau Scottish tartans. If you're stuck, ask for room #100; the terrace adjoining it is the size of a tennis court. We've seen better.

Mainz ? The **Hilton**, ably managed by Eric Moerscher, is by far the leader locally. Open V-shape structure nipping at the banks of the Rhine; adjacent to the 3000-capacity Rheingoldhalle congress center; so cunningly sited it is equally convenient for air travelers, rail rodders, motorists, or riverboat excursionists. Specialty restaurant suggestive of a steamer (overlooking the Rhine too); brick-walled Weinstube; Bierstube; cocktail lounge; full air conditioning; garage; car rental facility; beauty parlor; barbershop. All 251 rooms with bath, shower, radio, TV, and direct dial telephone; stretch-out space very limited. Considering the local competition, we wouldn't be at all surprised if Mainz were to deify Uncle Conrad soon. The **Mainzer Hof**, long one of our least favorite retreats, drops into the 2nd slot. The lobby has been refreshed and a new entry unveiled; a bit more style has been introduced; the people are nicer now, too. It's sound, solid, and basic, but we can't get very excited by it. The **Europahotel** is a good value for the price. Total of 69 rooms, all with balcony or loggia, bath, TV outlets, radio, dumbwaiter (guests order by pneumatic tube), and other modern appurtenances, including accommodations for Bozo; 5 doubles named and decorated in the styles of the 5 continents; 3 separate dining spots, one of them now a grill; 200 yards from the railway station.

Stuttgart 's 8-story **Am Schlossgarten** is an asset to this Detroit of Germany. Its courteous service and friendly atmosphere are fostered by Manager Bachstein, formerly of the excellent Alte Post Restaurant. Good cuisine in its glass-lined dining salon or parkside sun terrace; Swabian tavern with paneled, leather-ceilinged bar; 125 rooms adequate for short stays; small "efficiency" baths; no full suites; pleasant, angular construction with nice touches of wood. Worthy, especially for the staff kindness. The **Graf Zeppelin**, is operated by the ubiquitous Steigenberger chain which has now strengthened this link with an expansion program. Longer-term visitors may find larger accommodations here, plus a goodly supply of suites; double windows; excellent air-conditioning system; refinished Zeppelin-Stüble restaurant; rejiggered bar with handsome wood paneling; fresh carpets; other improvements; a Zeppelin that is definitely flying high, wide, and handsome. **Parkhotel**, 10 minutes out in Villaberg Park, offers 85 bedrooms, 54 baths, and generally bathetic styling. The surroundings are restful except when the tours pour in. This one *could* shine, but it would take about a million marks to polish it. The 100-unit **Royal** has donned some fresh raiments. Pleasant suites, with #117 our choice of the crop; poor vistas throughout; TV available on request. Pick only the newer nests here. **Schloss Solitude** is a 15-minute scoot from town via the highway that periodically becomes the world-famous sports-car racing course. Its main function (except to coddle Porsche-bred nostalgics who rally out to whip through a few gears) is to serve as a nexus for scores of weddings, meetings, and back-slapping reunions. Complement of 37 rooms, 4 baths, and 13 showers; 2 suites; small restaurant; kitchen off the lobby. While there are a few commendable facets here, it is too remote and hushaby for most lively trippers —unless "I do!" or "I don't!" are on the tip of your tongue. Neither the **Ketterer** (groups galore from Europe's backwaters) nor the **Reichsbahn** (adjoining the station and about as noisy as a Rolling Stone) will ever put London's Savoy out of business. The **Airport Hotel** glides in with a cargo of flair in its soft-toned, window-lined dining room, its adjoining bar, and the mod-mooded lobby. All 128 rooms with bath, radio, beds with vibrators, and telephone; bus and even a helicopter service for the Stuttgart environs. Public areas are air-conditioned, but bedchambers are only soundproofed. Simple but ample for short-haulers. Within sight, the 200-unit **Hotel Stuttgart International** raises its proud head just off Highway 27 at **Möhringen**, 5 minutes from the airport and a fairly expensive taxi hop from the center of town. Dining facilities include a cafeteria, breakfast room, banquet hall, Swiss feedery, rooftop aerie, garden nutrition nook, and a ground-floor nightclub; there are also a pool, sauna, bowling lanes, underground garage, beauty parlor, bank, doctor, dentist, and a travel agency. Superb furnishings in all bedrooms, demisuites, and full apartments. Very well appointed. An outstanding candidate for anyone wishing to be away from midcity.

In **Nürnberg**, the **Grand** is still the Old Guard leader. Now 130 baths for 160 bedrooms; cocktail lounge; Walliser Kanne restaurant created from a dismantled Swiss chalet; private 60-car garage. Although the housekeeper needs a smack on the fanny, this is otherwise a smooth-running oasis for the more mature traveler. The vivacious **Carlton** is almost the same size. Richly attractive emerald restaurant enhanced by a burgundy carpet and wrought-iron fixtures; headwaiters in tails; handsome tartan bar and black executive chairs under a gold ceiling; amiable doubles; modern suites. More active wayfarers will probably prefer this one to the Grand. Very good. **Am Sterntor**'s public rooms and corridors dseemed to this Jonah as dreary as the inside of a whale, although the bedchambers are contrastingly fresh and cheery. The **Victoria**'s exterior and downstairs, on the other hand, belie what you'll find when you open your bedroom door: heavy, dismal, grim cells. The Concierge speaks no English; it is adequate for overnighting—if all the benches in the bus station are occupied, that is. **Kaiserhof** impressed us as being too rickety for its stiff tariffs. **Am Ring**, situated in the eye of an intersecting traffic hurricane, is bright, clean, and satisfactory; breakfast only; noisier than a 3-Am-Ring circus. **Reichshof** evokes a commercial feel, with furniture that looks as if it were borrowed from a nightclub; okay if you can take floozie froufrou. Personally, if we had wheels and were only passing through, we'd pick the **Crest Motel** in a jiffy or a jitney. Handy site for road-runners near the exit to the Berlin–Munich and Frankfurt–Nürnberg autobahns; 6 stories containing a specialty restaurant, the Puppengrill for international fare, the Oldtimer Bar, and 92 bedrooms or suites, each with bath or shower, telephone, and radio. Fill 'er up?

In **Bonn**, the Steigenberger chain (Frankfurter Hof and a peck of others) has opened its sleeping factory in the aggressively ugly City Center—a crassful, classless urban subdivision which reflects far more haste than taste. Although the massive **Steigenberger** functions as an efficient institution, it performs with so little inspiration that it was a letdown to us. Passably interesting vista from the 18th-floor Ambassador Restaurant (where the window tables are usually reserved for diplomats); adjoining bar and neighboring swimming pool; Atrium Coffee Shop a tepid and listless decorative blend; a megalopolis of boutiques, kiosks, and service facilities skirting the ground level. Spacious studio singles—a tradeMark of German hostelries where the solitary executive roams interminably in homeless tangents; light, well-furnished, mod-school doubles, especially roomy in the corner accommodations; the twins ending in "23" are best. While nothing is overtly offensive here, our impression is one of consuming boredom. The **Königshof**, more traditional in tone, shoulders the riverbank. Adequate shelter that will never excite your aesthetic senses. The midvillage **Stern** is sternly cold. The midtown **Schlosspark** is small and clean; it boasts a swimming pool that might be described in the same way. In the diplomatic enclave of *Bad Godesberg,* a mile or so along "Embassy Row," the **Rheinhotel Dreesen** has a beautiful riverscape command but a lead-heavy Teutonic air. The redecorated **Rheinland** offers 50 bedrooms with private bath; another routine hatrack. The **Eden** is fair, but the 80-room-and-bath **Arera** is choicer in this price Arera. The **Parkhotel Zum Kurfürsten**, at *Frankenthal* on the Bonn–Strasbourg highway, got high but well-spent marks from an Austrian Guidester who raves about its "food, service, and exceptional standards." For additional Bonn-*mots,* please look back to our remarks on nearby Cologne—to our palate, a sweeter bonbon any day or night. At *Königswinter*, the modest, town-owned **Düsseldorfer Hof** is open the calendar round. Director Dieter Schäfer knows his *Hofs.*

Baden-Baden has the **Brenner's Park**, which is a classic. Rhapsodic location in a sylvan grove with a terraced stream and fountain exchanging sweet babblings; fast and friendly service; lounge music nightly, but most clients are wrapped in the arms of Morpheus long before midnight. To woo a younger following, it has splashed up a breathtakingly attractive, classically Roman indoor swimming pool with a view of the park, a party room, and—but of course—a beauty parlor. Faithful old-timers, however, still clamor so vigorously to get in here that its management has had to establish a 3- to 4-week limit-of-stay for all guests—depending, naturally, on the length of their cure. To relieve some of the pressure, it opened the summer-only adjoining Villa Stephanie with its own dining salon and 20 superb rooms, including 4 extra-comfortable suites. World-famous for its high standards—and deservedly so. The more commercial **Europäischer Hof** is the hub of activity for the swinging affluent set. Just a toss of the dice from the Casino; charming streamside dining room; candlelight dining on weekends; revivified bar with piano lilts until after midnight; low personnel-to-client ratio. Its 60 doubles front the park; 90 singles are to the rear; most have private bath. Alive and thriving. The faun-colored **Bellevue** has a garden setting, lovely awning-covered balconies, set-back alcoves, and a conflict of heavy Teutonic traditionalism with twentieth-century aluminum extrusions. A new pool may be ready for your toe-testing soon. Coolish bar, potted-palm atmosphere downstairs; 90 rooms and 72 baths; #214-215 is a choice double. Closed from November 1 to early April. This one might appeal more to European tastes than to ours. The **Badischer Hof**, owned by the Europäischer Hof people, is built as a 4-story atrium. Total of 90 attractive modern bedrooms; all 70 bathrooms equipped with thermal water taps. Sound, but you pay a hefty premium for that special H_2O. **Peter's Bad-Hotel Zum Hirsch** has been in the same family for more than 300 years. Busy location; part of its triangular structure spans a street that cuts an isosceles swath through the courtyard. Inviting reception area, restaurant, bar, and elevator; connecting annex comfortably renovated; Manager Brück knows his innkeeping. Many of its accommodations have private balconies and thermal water taps; all units warmed with original oil paintings; demipension not required in season. The **Atlantic**, on the Oos-side (Oos is *not* a commentary but the stream that runs through the town), offers a lovely terrace for dining; all units with rivulet-fronting balconies, and a disappointing fustiness. Regrettably slow-paced renovation program. The **Holland** has added an indoor pool and exercise parlor, renovated all its bedchambers, and generally updated itself. For golfing buffs, the lovely First-class **Waldhotel Selighof** is a linkside, chalet-style siren that effuses allure. Magnificent hill-bound, timber-lined course; private swimming pool and tennis courts; improved entrance; brightened breakfast terrace. Since comfort is in its righteous domain, top recommendation for the Sporting Set. The nearby **Golf Hotel** is a sprawling, gable-garbled, and gaunt example of typical old-fashioned resort innkeeping; the later wing is somewhat ameliorative; the indoor swimmery with jet stream, sauna, massage, plus solarium segments, and added private baths, (bringing the count up to 100%) may have thawed its cool overall demeanor. Both are about 2½ miles from the center of Baden-Baden and, in their respective categories, a satisfactory Two for Tee. In *Herrenalb*, 12 miles into the fringing wineland of the Black Forest, the rugged-but-refined **Post Hotel** has quietly played host to tranquillity seekers from the late Duke of Windsor to the Maharaja of Baroda. Ideal for a pastoral excursion or a restorative holiday. Cuisine that vies with some of the best we have ever tasted in Germany; pleasant but not overdone décor, touched up with rich antiques; cozy twelfth-century Klosterschränke Grill, with beams, stucco, and stone; 2 dining rooms and garden sipping nook; bar; heated pool; 50 comfortable units, most with shower and/or bath. Proprietor Mönch is its courtly Boniface. Here is an isle of bucolic calm where the value of peace is understood to its very core. Top recommendation for those who enjoy the luxurious brand of quietness.

Garmisch-Partenkirchen hasn't been reviewed by us in much too long, we are ashamed to confess. We plan to rectify this error pronto; in the meantime we hope you will be indulgent with us in this particular resort. The **Alpina** some time ago had invested an alp's-worth of high-fashion hotel baubles. It proved to be a re-*mark*-able move in every way. Exquisite garden and pool area, with a battery of $100 chaise longues; inviting public rooms; 40 Deluxe bedchambers; superior cuisine on our try. The centrally located **Marktplatz** offers a charming chalet exterior with geranium-laden balconies. Uplifted lobby, lounge, dining-room annex, bar, breakfast nook, garage, and elevator; gay in-and-outdoor terrace for summer meals; cookery that seems to be fair one day and poor the next. Its ancient *Bierstube* has rich masculine appeal. Total of 47 rooms and 28 baths; 2 suites; tastefully furnished and spotlessly maintained; operated year round. Very good indeed. The expanded **Wittelsbach** is wiggling with renewed vigor. Newer south-side wing with balconies, bringing the overall total to 56 units, all with bath or shower; indoor swimming pool; eye-rejoicing flower garden; bedrooms in native tones with *Bauhaus* fixtures that may seem outdated to modernists. Solid and recommendable. The **Riessersee**, 2 miles from the center, commands a lovely hilltop view of the valley. Large sprawling structure; tennis courts, minigolf, sauna and thermal water treatments; attractive public rooms; about ½ its 100 units have private bath. Pleasant for rural relaxation. The 300-year-old **Clausing's Posthotel**, back in town, attracts chiefly a European clientele. If you are looking for that Old World atmosphere with scarcely a Colonist in sight, you'll most likely find it here. **Golf Sonnenbichl** is stroking par today. The excellent eyeful from its frontside balconied rooms, the viewful Blue Restaurant, the Zirbelstube for highland hilarity and yodeling, and its Delft-style bar are all pluses. Managing-Proprietor Georg Bader is doing a Bader-than-average job making things gooder every year. Closed October 1 to December 20. The **Partenkirchener Hof** has a similar personality, and one of the best tables in the valley for the medium budget. The **Obermühle** makes a splash with its indoor pool. The 45-room **Garmischer Hof**, a breakfast-only hostelry, has had many improvements; approximately ⅓rd of its units have private bath. The **Neu-Werdenfels** also provides reasonably good shelter for budget travelers. Outstanding pensions are (1) **Leiner**, (2) **Schell**, (3) **Flora** (expanded to semihotel proportions), and (4) the young **Gästehaus Georgenhof**. More? Take your pick of the other 172 hotels, inns, pensions, and guest houses —and *viel Glück!*

Want to get away from it all? Atop the 9730-foot Zugspitze, masons in crampons have constructed the miraculous **Hotel Schneefernerhaus**, with its lovely winter garden overlooking the top of the world. Basic accommodations for ski buffs, scenic buffs, and yeti; a wonder of engineering. The tragic avalanche which struck the sun terrace of this hostelry some years back underscores the danger of Alpine thaws—so if you travel in the uplands in spring, please be extra-cautious of the snow-cliffs above you. (As skiers know, the greatest danger comes after a rain that freezes and is followed by snowfall; the ice below serves as a death-dealing sliding board to chute tons of new surface snow down the slopes when even a slight noise or a ½-degree change of temperature breaks the pack.) On the Austrian side, a few yards away, the 50-bed **Alpenhotel der Tiroler** may be another candidate. If this one is functioning, both are accessible via the cog-rail route or the bone-chilling cable-car ride to the summit. High life at low tariffs—but please *do* be careful in spring!

Oberammergau is at peace again after 1970's Passion Play. The leading candidate is still the ancient **Alois Lang**. Quiet situation enhanced by a no-tour-group policy (rare in this frenetic hive); 51 rooms; all units with private balcony and most with bath; fresh carpeting throughout. Its 3 dining rooms serve up savory vittles. Manager Ranges is trying extra-hard to please Americans—and he seems to be doing it, day-after-day. Recommended as a pleasant but unfancy hitching post. The **Wolf** offers more charm in its bedchambers (especially the top-floor Bavarian rooms), but its central situation and busy-busy public areas give it a somewhat commercial feel. Flowers and colorful touches everywhere; prices lower than the leader; very good value. **Alte Post** comes up with cheery accommodations but a very low bath count. **Böld** plays host to battalions of G.I.'s during ski season; not bad for the basic-minded sportsman. The **Wittelsbach** turns over more tourists, it seems, than does Mr. Cook. Going bach-ward Wittel-by-Wittel. In neighboring *Et-*

tal, also in Oberbayern, the barnish **Ludwig der Bayer** has a big name locally, but to us it seems as cold as a penguin's pinfeather; if you burrow into its icebergs, take the newer wing only. We dislike this one with or without a Passion.

The Romantic Road? First off, here is a smattering of its history. What you seek, of course, is preserved obsolescence. You'll discover exactly that. This fascinating route was a vital and thriving lifeline during the Middle Ages, when a military link between fortresses was imperative for survival. The word "Hof," which is suffixed to the names of so many modern German hotels, literally derives from the walled and safe "courtyard" where travelers could rest while passing from stronghold to stronghold. Initially, they slept in their carriages or under their horses. Soon drink was provided. Later food was served. Finally overnight shelters were constructed. When the wars ended and transportation lanes were shifted, these great installations became superannuated. Not until recent times did historic interest regenerate their unique touristic allure.

Now to the practical side. Even though the authentic Romantic Way begins in the Würzburg environs, we'd suggest you spend your first night in either **Mainz** (the Hilton is a far cry from a "Hof") or in **Wiesbaden** (where accommodations are better than anything you'll find en route, with the exception of Rothenburg ob der Tauber). If you insist upon **Würzburg**, however, we'd recommend the old-fashioned **Lämmle** (convenient, because it's beside the Market Square), the much better **Erbachshof** (4 miles out of town; good food; a bit costly), or even the **Grundmühle** (about the same distance from the center; converted mill in a lovely valley; also outstanding cuisine for the region). **Bad Mergentheim** is no longer lauded as a scenic attraction; today it's more famous as a spa, with the top watering spot the modernistic **Viktoria**. Now zip through **Weikersheim** and **Creglingen** to **Rothenburg ob der Tauber** for the best and most exciting overnight of the entire loop. This antique sparkler is the gem of the bracelet, so we urge that you concentrate most of your time, calories, and shut-eye here. As for hotels, we'd rate them as follows: (1) **Eisenhut** (this famous "Iron Hat" offers a stunning terrace-restaurant over the Tauber, an expanded dining room and an added wing; 2 adjoining buildings recently purchased and 1-unit façade extended; some accommodations perked up, but still flairless in the older sections; room #102 is praised as one of the *most* "romantic" on the entire "road" by one gallant knight of the nightscape; much improved cuisine that can be inconsistent; a surfeit of haughty staffers; very high tabs), (2) **Goldener Hirsch** (superb view; lower rates and a special greeting for 1st-and-2nd honeymooners; some newer units with baths; Blue Terrace dining room in Louis XVI mood; new elevator; very good; very friendly), (3) the colorful 13-unit **Adam** (gay *Weinstube;* far better bedchambers than the older ones in the Eisenhut at twice the bite), and (4) the cozy 30-room **Markusturm** (group-minded in season). Moving on through **Feuchtwangen** to **Dinkelsbühl**, the **Rose** is nonperfumed to our sniffer; the next-door **Deutsches Haus** is passable at best; the little **Palmengarten**, though without a restaurant, now seems to be the number one frond. **Nördlingen** is nörd for lingering, and **Donauwörth** is nau worthwhile; both should be daylight pauses only. In **Augsburg**, the most

august is the **Drei Mohren** ("Three Moors"); the **Lamm** baaaas up to our 2nd
slot; the newer **Alpen** peaks in for show money. None will really wow you.
In *Landsberg*, the once-pleasant **Goggl** is no-Goggl, as far as we're concerned. In *Regensburg*, the **Avia** flies away with the prize; it's a pipit.
Rottenbuch, Wies, Steingaden and world-renowned *Schwangau*
strike us as being miserable for creature comforts, but thrilling for rubbernecking. Wayfarers may bunk at the **Hirsch** in nearby *Füssen*, which boasts
50 rooms, 10 baths, a listless restaurant, and a cozy country-style *Stube* for
beer, wine, and trencherman fare. Frankly, if we were heading this way for
the purpose of seeing the Neuschwanstein and Hohenschwangau castles, we'd
opt for either the road-hugged, tiny **Lisl und Jägerhaus** or the 40-room
Müller at the base of the path leading up to the summits. The latter recently
renewed; some chambers attractively finished in pinewood; snack bar; tavern;
not bad if you can sweet-talk private plumbing from the reception people.

   To capsule what's left, in *Constance*, it's the cloistered, totally rebuilt
Insel, a former monastery, and, according to a savvy friend, the **Bayerischer
Hof**, on the nearby island resort of *Lindau*; in *Freiburg*, the smoothly
administered **Colombi** (7 stories of comfortable modernity; better than average cookery; try the Black Forest Farmer's Soup for a tummy hoedown); the
115-kip-and-bath **Stadt Freiburg** is said to be a solid, strictly functional shelter
with the bonus of a 700-car garage; in *Hinterzarten* in the Black Forest,
the **Adler** steals the loving cup as one of the beauty queens of Germany
(glorious parkland and flower-girt setting; glass-enclosed swimming pool for
year-round dipping; tennis, minigolf, *boccia* court, water sports on Lake
Titisee, ice skating, curling rink, toboggan run, nearby ski lifts and golf
course; baronial appointments; sumptuous comfort; owned by the Riesterer
family since 1446; only 13 miles from Freiburg; an arcadia of *Hochschwarzwal-
dian* peace); in *Ulm*, the recently built **Bundesbahnhotel**; in *Bad Kissingen*,
the **Kurhaus-Hotel**; in *Mannheim*, the **Mannheimer Hof**, with 183 rooms,
160 baths, and 2 bowling alleys, plus the expanded **Wartburg-Hospiz**; in
Kassel, 4 miles up toward the last Kaiser's castle, the tastelessly modernistic
Schlosshotel Wilhelmshöhe (61 balconied rooms, 50 baths or showers, patio
dining and dancing nightly in summer; cheerless, commercial, convention-
aerie) or, the 155-bed **Holiday Inn** luring motorists near the east exit of the
autobahn; in *Kaiserslautern*, the **President** for modernists; in *Ettlingen*,
the enlarged Beverly-Hills-rustic **Erbprinz**, a handsomely sophisticated and
worthy lunch stop between Frankfurt and Munich; in *Duisburg*, the 135-
room **Duisburg Hof** (each unit given individual personality, with large baths,
king-size beds, flawless service); for *Celle* see "Hanover"; in *Coblenz*,
Hohenstaufen barely paces a pasty pack; in *Cochem*, the **Alte Thorschenke**
for a sweet little inn with an excellent wine restaurant, the **Germania** for a
grander atmosphere, or the **Brixiade** for sleeker twentieth century fixin's
(pick your room carefully because traffic noise can be a menace to light
sleepers); near *Bargteheide* (Schleswig-Holstein), the antique-lovely
Schloss Tremsbüttel, ranging from ultraposh to downright dowdy; on Palm-
berg Mountain (43 miles west of Munich toward *Ampfing*) the 40-guest
Schloss Geldern, a medieval fief; in *Oberstdorf/Allgäu*, near Garmisch,
the **Adula** for cures and skiers—but in which order, we can't say (vast linear

chalet structure; reportedly outstanding cuisine; a rapidly developing sports area with this entry as the lance corporal); in **Ravensburg**, the 14-story **Europa**, with an Alpine lake view from its roof garden; in **Triberg,** the **Park Wehrle,** a rich, hearty, German colonial establishment in the hands of the same family since 1707, with a mouth-watering English-language menu; in **Kehl**, across the Rhine from Strasbourg, the 7-story **Europa** with 50 units and 32 baths or showers; in **Lübeck,** the freshly unwrapped **Lysia**; at **Puttgarden**, on the island of **Fehmarn** (auto route to Copenhagen), the low-lined blue-and-gray **Dansk** or the basic **Baltic**, 10 minutes south of the toll-gates (across the frontier at **Rødby Havn**, the fresh clean **Danhotel** and the **Motel Rødby Havn**; see "Denmark" for more); in **Karlsruhe**, the **Park** and **Schwarzwald** in Karlsruhe-Rüppurr. **Rüdesheim?** So many booze-soaked revelers in season and such clattery freight trains almost in your room that we'd advise Rhine trippers to avoid overnighting here; skip up to the **Krone** in **Assmannshausen**, instead. We haven't practiced with our Zippo in the **Ewige Lampe** ("Eternal Light"), which guttered out as a restaurant and has been rekindled as a hostelry.

Berlin hotels are listed in this city's independent section toward the front of this book.

Finally, at least 50 feudal palaces and knights' castles have been converted into hotels—Gothic vaults, moats, battlements, ghosts, and all. Some are luxury class, some are plainer. The northern Rhineland, the Palatinate, Franconia, Upper Bavaria, Hesse, and Württemberg-Baden are especially thick with them. Too scattered to list here, due to space limitations, but you'll usually find one within shooting distance of most major points of the nation. Great fun for motorists, as a change of pace; try at least one, if only for the experience. The **German National Tourist Association** (see "Information on Germany") will gladly send you a special folder containing a full list plus particulars. **Schloss Auel** (16 miles from **Bonn**) and the aforementioned **Schloss Kronberg** (10 miles from **Frankfurt am Main**) are especially outstanding.

For further data on accommodations not mentioned above (outlying motels for example), consult the local **Tourist Office** in any of the larger cities or towns. They are usually at or near the railway stations, and will gladly try to answer your needs.

Youth hostels? The **German Youth Hostels Association** offers 75-thousand beds in more than 700 branches, most of them in the Rhineland region; some perking-up of accommodations has been done in the hiking areas. A building spree is putting up hostels in or near the larger cities and cultural centers.

Dedicated budgeteers in Frankfurt, Munich, and Berlin? Since we're too bottlenecked here for additional entries in these key hubs, please consult our annually revised paperback, *Fielding's Low-Cost Europe*, which lists scads more bargain hotels or pensions and money-saving tips for serious economizers.

FOOD AND RESTAURANTS   First-class restaurant meals currently average $11 to $19 without wine, coffee, and spirits. Beef has become so costly that an official campaign has just been launched to raise deer for slaughtering. (It is not so dear.) If you want to do yourself well, with caviar, lobster, Prague ham, or other gustatory delights, your bill may run into the Wild, Wild Blue Yonder. But if you are content to eat in the small, family-type establishments (plenty available; most of them completely satisfactory), your tab should be close to perhaps $8. In country inns you can sometimes have a 3-course feast for as little as $3.50.

Coffee and tea are higher than in America. There are at least 7 different brews and strengths of coffee, ranging from the insipid, prune-juice-colored Mokka to the popular Kaffee Hag (nearly caffeine-free) to Italian-style Espresso. "Filter," sometimes known as "Karlsbader Kaffee" from the machine in which it's made, is closest to American-style; Double Mokka, grainy and strong, is a good man's drink. You'll be safest if you always specify your type to the waiter.

National custom dictates that tables be shared by 2 or more parties if the restaurant or nightclub is crowded. Quite often you might find yourself sitting with strangers—fortunately, most of the time in a courteous but remote "please pass the salt" relationship rather than one of compulsory small talk and yak-yak. If you wish to yatter, fine—but if you're tired, they'll generally confine their conversation to their own group.

Contrary to legend (and the myopic standards of some otherwise reliable gourmets), German regional cooking is often light, delicate, and highly inventive.

Frankfurt am Main is in a culinary slump. Why this should occur in a city with more than 1000 banks, with one of the busiest international airports in the world, with congresses, trade fairs, and exhibits year round, and with a commerce that turns over more money annually than many national budgets, is a puzzle to us and a blot upon its citizens. The **Taverne Royale** now wears the crown among the independent regency. Decorative doors with sabers for handles; large room with a rustic well, Venetian lanterns, balcony, copper pot-stills, centurion helmets, coach lamps, and candles; comfortable semicircular bleached-wood booths with plum-colored textiles; rôtisserie under a tiled cupola; stucco walls with a hunting mural. (Strange as it might seem, this kooky combination jells.) The menu lists a phenomenal 89 dishes, not including salads and vegetables; the 2 main courses we tried were quite satisfactory, though far from *Larousse Gastronomique* standards. With its soft music, smooth service, appealing but mixed-up scenery, and laudably low tariffs for the cookery, we'd say this should rate high on anyone's local list. **Alt Copenhagen** is thoroughly appealing to the eye—in the style of an ancient Danish tavern—but the cookery on our latest try was enough to bring out the Viking in our temper. Perhaps you might like it for a snack when you're not hungry, or when you've got a head cold 3 miles wide. The **Faust** is a ground-level chorus boy in the Opera—a flairless after-theater retreat; the downstairs Paprika, in our opinion, has become just another goulash pit. For color and atmosphere so thick you can almost scrape it off your lapels, **Brückenkeller** (Schützenstrasse 6) is fun. Every stop on the console has been pulled to romanticize this medieval-type cellar with its fine arched ceilings; 20 candlelit tables; each with a bright little azalea plant, are banked in 3 tiers; soft

mood-music swells from hidden record player into deeper sancta with perhaps 50 more tables; large, elaborately carved wine barrel, illuminated by
candles, is *pièce de résistance* of decoration scheme; harried service, 80-item
menu and 200,000-bottle wine subcellar; good-but-not-great food at decent
prices; cool and pleasant in summer. So untypical of Frankfurt restaurants
in the warmth and coziness of its ambiance that we like it a lot and recommend it unhesitatingly, despite the schmaltz. Or why not cross the river and
go over to the old quarter of Sachsenhausen, where the apple wine taverns
offer their special flavor and revelry? There are many scattered around, so the
custom is to roam from one to another taking small dishes at each. Our
favorite is **Klaane Sachsehäuser** (Neuerwall 11), where our party delighted in
the Schneegestöber ("snow flurry") of camembert-like cheese mixed with
chopped onion, and the Ripchen, a smoked pork chop. Community tables at
all; singing as the mood commands; lots of laughter and jovial fraternizing.
But more on this further along. (We included this one here just to tease your
appetite with the unconventional.) The **Mövenpick** (Opernplatz 2), continues
to sizzle as the hottest skillet among local socialites—with tariffs to match.
Cuddlesome personality but snail-pace attention; about 400 seats in several
sections (including a "Quick-Pick"); soft lighting and pink napery that melds
with the copper highlights; cuisine improved under the energetic chain-driven
supervision that produces such happy tummies in Switzerland. Its adjoining
Café Opera invites fair-weather small talk on a wide garden-fronted terrace.
Still another link has been forged at a shopping center 4 miles from midtown.
This one is called **Rôtisserie Baron de la Mouette**. Same foodstuffs, very
nicely presented among wood-slat walls and apple-red textiles. Perhaps the
best nutrients in this city today can be digested in hotel dining rooms; we have
always found them consistent, at least—and that, in itself, is something. For
a well-prepared novelty, be sure not to miss the Old Frankfurt (or "Stubb")
in the cellar of the **Frankfurter Hof**. General Manager Curt Peyer carried his
chef on the payroll a full year ahead of its opening date, solely to experiment
with its genuine nineteenth-century Hessian dishes. A team of experts combined talents to authenticate every detail from culinary selections to the most
minor decorative touches in each of the 11 rooms. Vitrines in white stucco
walls displaying artifacts; each corner different in personality, yet melding
nicely into a harmonious whole. Friendly reception by a smiling hostess in
period attire; open kitchen where only a portion of the dishes are prepared;
ambiance of congenial vitality rather than stuporous dignity. The cookery is
not to be confused with that of sophisticated gustatory shrines; it is almost
cottage fare in its straightforward hardiness, and it is good. Several of the
hostesses speak English. This one is a highlight for the city and a "must" for
any venturesome visitor. On the same premises you'll find the chic Restaurant
Français for international cuisine and the he-man Grill (Maine lobsters flown
in regularly); both are highly touted by local taste-makers. We've also
snatched a snack at the comfortable Apéritif Bar, and it was delicious. The
Intercontinental Hotel provides perhaps the city's richest mood in its lovely,
river-view Rôtisserie—a delight to the aesthetic senses. For light bites and
sipping, we like the Brasserie, the Wine Room, and the Oyster Bar. Its Sunday
buffet has almost become a ritual among Frankfurters. The **Gravenbruch**,

outside of town, is a delight for agrestic sleekness and fireside dining. Set meals, plus à la carte; dollar-size children's menu; just the spot for sylvan wiles. Don't skip the tiny boutique that purveys local sausages, cheeses, and handicraft items; even if you don't buy, it's worth a peek. The **Parkhotel** boasts a good kitchen; the hors d'oeuvres merit a blue ribbon. The **Patrizier**, near the Frankfurter Hof, is a small, Old German place with simple food at relatively low prices; menu in English; so-so. **Peking**, opposite the same hotel and often touted by its concierge as a good Chinese eatery, impressed us as being a pet promotion project of modern Maoists from that Oriental city. We were sitting Cantonese Ducks for this one; from now on we'll be more hawkish. Not recommended. We found the **Asia** reasonable for curry; our abalone with Chinese mushrooms was excellent; otherwise you've got a choice of about 250 items. In aforementioned Sachsenhausen Borough, across the Main, nonacrophobics may dine in **Henninger**'s rotating **Tower Restaurant** mounted on a 396-foot-high circular structure. Wow! You may sit and stuff while 360° of landscape passes before your eyes. We've just come from a feeding in the more expensive Panorama tier where, upon careful considera-tion we gladly would serve our chef with what we think he possibly most deserves—defenestration! For budgeteers, it offers the twirling **Drehscheibe** circle which orbits in the opposite direction to the Panorama ring, thus making it possible for an adventurous diner to unwind on one level and wind up his meal on another. Verdict: If you don't mind dining miserably and expensively in a slow-motion centrifuge, you'll probably be awed by this impressive turn of events. The midtown **Schwarzer Stern** (Kalbächer Gasse 8) offers hardy fare in the earthy surroundings of a decorator's barn. Timber-and-stucco walls in both downstairs snackery and 2nd-story dining room; trimmings of pewterware, copper knickknacks, grain flails, and a wine press; regional cooking (and language) only; appetizing nutrients and mountainous servings. If you aren't stung by the crush of busy-bee diners in this little hive, the value for your marks should be returned. Now—as promised—back to the typical *Apfelweinstuben* ("Apple wine rooms"). **Grauer Bock**, on the other side of the river, is another neighborhood tavern to end neighborhood taverns: Wooden tables, grimy floors, smoky walls, pretzel vendors, great color and animation; hot dogs, sauerkraut, beer, sandwiches, and a redoubta-ble affair called "Handkäs mit Musik"—"Handkäs" being the cheese, with vinegar, oil, paprika, onions, and kümmel combined on top to make the "Musik." BROTHER! The smaller **Gemaltes Haus** ("Painted House") and the **Blauer Engel** are also fine examples of this school. Among the equally typical wine restaurants, **Rheinpfalz Weinstuben**-Hahnhof has a sweet ter-race and a Palatinate-rural-inn ambiance of scrubbed tables and woodcarv-ings; you can have an excellent dinner with delectable Forster Jesuitengarten Riesling Auslese; thoroughly enjoyable on a balmy summer's night; central location. **Stadt Wien**, formerly called Pfälzer Weinstube (at the Cathedral), and **Bacchus** are also attractive, but Rheinpfalz has them all licked. **Maier Gustl's**, also on Münchenerstrasse, is said to have more than its share of lederhosen, knobby knees, musik—*die werks.*

For light refreshments, **Café Hauptwache** has a modern production-line restaurant facing the esplanade on its lower floor and a marvelous coffee and pastry parlor at ground level. Go to the latter for extraheavy calories and a peek at the painted figures on the walls. A sweetie.

If the sun is shining and transportation is at hand, the best luncheon expedition one can make in the area is the drive to the former castle of Empress Friedrich III—the **Schlosshotel Kronberg** (see "Hotels"). Gorgeous 200-foot open terrace for dining; expensive; so relaxing it's a *must* for anyone who can do it. The taxi price, unhappily, is robbery. Open all year. The happiest "discovery" of one of our recent local huntings was **Gutsschänke Neuhof**, 20 minutes out at the settlement of *Neuhof.* Self-contained farming village at work continuously since 1499; locally harvested and husbanded flora and fauna; packaged products sold at the Alte Backstube outbuilding (sausages, dairy goods, sweets, nuts, wines, plus some touristy craft items). Restaurant in the handsome half-timber manor house; 2 floors of compartmentalized dining rooms; outdoor terrace for summer daydreaming; warm, cozy atmosphere; flowers on every table; attentive waiters in cranberry waistcoats; able management by Mr. Bilz. Our twin lunches consisting of herring, soup, a risotto, ham steak, a celestial slice of cherry cake, coffee, with an ambrosial Moselle wine totaled nearly $21, including tip—and it couldn't have filled 2 midriffs with greater contentment. Be sure to reserve well in advance here, because savvy Frankfurters love this one with a passion. Tops for its type. Next most amusing is the **Tennis Bar** (restaurant) in the Kurpark at *Bad Homburg.* Covered porch, same prices as Kronberg, select menu, snail-like service; closeup view of the courts and players; closed Mondays from November through April. Between Frankfurt and Kronberg, there's **Bad Soden** for an outdoor tea stop or light terrace-dining. Pleasant, but a straw hut compared to the Schloss. The **Unterschweinstiege** at the Airport Hotel is a beauty for grill buffs, but we took off before our tongue could savor its crackles; the conventional dining room is less appealing—at least to the eye, in our view.

Munich offers a wide and exciting variety of dining haunts. The best establishment, in our opinion, is **Boettner** (Theatinerstr. 8). The dinner that was just served 2 of these incognito travelers was so exquisite that in memory we still savor every dish. Only 9 tables in rear of a small wine and gourmet-item shop; pleasant but not ornate atmosphere; close attention by staff who *care;* shuttered on Sundays; very expensive but worth every pfennig. Be certain to make your advance reservation in this extraordinary nook. For the most fun along with overwhelming variety and sparkling culinations, the **Käfer Schänke** (Schumannstrasse/Prince Regentstrasse) is the Barnum & Bailey and Bulgari of Munich gastronomy. Its enormous success springs largely from its quality. This one grew out of (and above) a patrician delicacy shop. Most of the tempters for first courses and appetizers are displayed in cafeteria-style chilling cabinets. Diners are invited to take their plate and select from the dozens of handsomely presented salads, gelatins, timbales, pâtés, croûtes, coldcut tidbits, treasures of the briny, and a trove of other 14-carrot nibbles; pick as much or as little as your appetite or diet dictates; the staff keeps a running record for your billing. Their prices are astonishingly low. Later a flock of waiters serves the main dishes, beverages, cheeses, sweets or other platters at your table or at rustic counters that resemble a Texas version of a Walgreen's or a Rustlers' Rexall store. The atmosphere is gay with laughter and bustling with activity. We enjoyed our repast as much as any informal feast we've experienced in Germany in many a year. Don't expect lacework and cut crystal; here the accent is on food and frolic. Always jammed, so be sure to call for a table. Excellent for its type. Now, returning to the silk-stocking precincts, the dining room of the **Vier Jahreszeiten** unquestionably retains its high repute in the hands of the Intercontinental chain (see "Hotels"). Excellent soft music is rendered with the comestibles in the intimate bar annex. The Friday-Saturday buffets in the Eck ("Corner") of the lovely dining salon are becoming famous with German epicures. The overall supervision remains under the legendary Walterspiel wand, a name that has become synonymous with fine fare throughout this neck of the *Wald*. The **Bayerischer Hof** rafts ashore with its Trader Vic's, which is keeping the jungle drums busy beating out exciting drinks, delicious Polynesian fixin's, and amiable professional service; the traditional favorite here has always been the Grill. The latter, with an intimate Stube, has substantial cookery, nightly zither melodies, and competent management. **Zur Kanne** (Maximilianstrasse 36), while deservedly popular for both lunch and dinner, is most chic when it becomes an after-theater rendezvous for the opera group; 6 small rooms linked by twilight illumination, enchantment, and tranquillity; subdued chintz banquettes and walls doodled with cartoons, photos, and programs; excellent wine-restaurant menu. We like this one a lot. The romantic little **Bazaar** (Marktstrasse 3), a dimly glowing Ottoman nook, is caparisoned with striped banquettes, perforated brass lamps, and a tucked-away bar for extra-private weavers of mystic spells, potions, and charms. You'll be soothed by such taped Byzantine hits as "I Wish I Was In Love Again" and "My Heart Belongs to Daddy"; our recently repeated Turkish delight consisted of 2 gigantic succulent porterhouse steaks (the specialty), 2 delicious salads, a bottle of French wine, and 2 Irish coffees; all were memorable. Expensive, but worth every Ottoman lire; recommended to any Lothario, Beefeater, or Sultan with an occidental palate. **Romanoff** (Bauerstrasse 2) marches in as another costly but quality-minded aristocrat. Friendly atmosphere configured into an L-form; bar at the L's elbow; gas lamps; one raised tier of banquettes; tempting selection of blinis, borscht, main dishes, and side nibbles from the Old Country, plus vodka served in a block of ice. Although local friends report that the waiters often can be snippish, our meal was a pleasure in every respect. **Datscha** (Kaiserstrasse) is a poor-mouth attempt to copy high-Steppeing cookery, in our opinion. The décor is wonderfully cozy, but the service, presentation, preparation, and general lack of finesse were enough to put us off henceforth and forevermore. One thing to say for it—it's cheap. **La Cave** (Maximilianstrasse) now seems to have lost some of its fad-rage status. Entrance via a copper-plated chute; stairway handrail made from a musket; cellar cells under vaulted ceiling; candles on tables; warm service; food miserably presented and matchingly prepared on our try; ear-stabbing music that never let up throughout the course of that long, agonizing, fretful feed. High on the In Set's snob list, but not our grotto right from the outset. No thanks. **Tantris** (Johan Fichtelstrasse 7) is said to be a fine addition to the Schwabing culinary scene. We were too stuffed to brave it. For other stake-outs, we must tie up at steak houses **Ochs'n Willi** and **Ochs'n Sepp**, which are also reputed to mix up a nightly mess of old-fashioned Oklahoma spare-ribs. This same group runs the **Beim Haberer** local-style wine cellar, the modern **Spatenhaus**, and **Max 2** for snacks in a *fin de siècle* setting. For medium-price dining, **Goldene Stadt** (Oberanger 44) whipped up one of the best meals of a recent teutonic trot—including those sampled at restaurants of infinitely higher cost and fame. Four adjoining rooms; main segment adorned with a photomural of the bridge over the Moldau in central Prague; beautiful and respectful reception, the like of which one seldom experiences in this timeless era; careful service by German-speaking waiters; family ambiance that blends sophistication with a gentle informal ease. The Slavic and local dishes are all prepared by highly skilled Dušan Hubácek, the white-smocked owner-chef. Be sure to top off his feast with a shot of Barack offered in a stovepipe glass. Here is our top rating as the finest Czech-point this side of the Iron Curtain. **Humplmayr** has impressed us for many years as being uneven, an observation which we've long reported. Now, on our latest visit, we hit such a flagrant off day that we were not only disappointed but dismayed. While it can still come up with exceptionally fine meals at costly tariffs when everyone is pulling together, what we found this time was such vivid lack of consistency that our former high esteem for this landmark has markedly diminished.

Next to the ranking Ratskeller (see below), the **Peterhof Gaststätten** complex (Marienplatz) is our pick for good, solid, inexpensive Bavarian fare—far outshining Donisel or the numerous other family-frequented places which dot this central area. Two-floor Peterhof from ground level in clean-lined regional décor and with plenty of space between its tables and big booths; basement Peterskeller for beer and oompah band between 5 and 12:30; slightly more costly Hock Café on 5th floor with lovely view of the square and of the historic moving figures in the Town Hall which enchant big crowds at 11 A.M. and 5 P.M.; both restaurants open continuously from 9 A.M. to midnight. Salt of the earth. The **Ratskeller** was closed over several months recently (including the span of our visit) for vast renewals and renovations. Local friends in the know believed that this already-splendid example of its genre would emerge as the finest in the nation. **Kuenstlerhaus** has been taken over by the fast-expanding **Mövenpick** interests; we suppose it will conform to the usual fine Swiss-bred pattern of this network. **Schwarzwälder**, also now part of a chain, is superb; **Bei Milan** is pleasant; so are the artist-and-film hangouts of **Kasak** and **Haxenbauer. Csarda Piroschka**, a Hungarian cellar beneath the Haus der Kunst (Art Museum), is about as gimmick-ridden as they come—but enjoyable if your mood is right. Walls dripping with painted florals; menus presented in wooden toy houses; cymbal-throbbing gypsy melodies by a high-strung court of costumed musicians; very kind reception; busy but attentive service; cookery that is strictly from Hunger-y. Popular among first-timers—just once. **Walliser Stuben** (Leopoldstrasse), a Swiss Valais cave, is very attractive; garden-dining in summer; no lunch; bowling alley; straight from Zermatt, and fun. The midcity **Chesa Ruegg** (behind the Vier Jahreszeiten) comes up with another ladle of Helvetia: beamed ceiling, copper pans, and pottery; small sidewalk terrace and moderate tabs. **Mifune** (Ismaninger Strasse 136), named for the Japanese heroine of the film *Paper Tiger*, is run in conjunction with the local Japanese tourist office. Toshiro Mifune and her gracious English-speaking son, Shiro, almost always are on hand. Attractive Oriental flavored (and fragranced) décor; longish bar; large counter service section with Nipponese bell-shaped grills for the Steak Teppanyaki specialty; 2 western dens with about 7 tables; tea room for ceremonial purposes. Two suggestions: Either reserve 1 of the 3 Japanese salons (4 to 8 persons), leave your shoes at its entrance, sit on the floor, and order from the kimono-clad waitresses the special 5-course lunch or dinner menu at $26; or try the delicious à la carte Makunouchi, a red lacquered, covered, compartmented picnic box which contains rice topped by onions, fish, steak, shrimp, pork, egg flan, 4 different types of salads, and pickles. Hours: 11:30 to 2 and 6 to midnight the calendar around, except on Mondays when Mifune rests.

Alois Dallmayr is reminiscent of Paris' fabulous Fauchon but considerably larger. On the vast ground floor is one of the world's most distinguished food centers with a staggering variety of German and imported delicacies including an aromatic coffee department, a tea department, a marvelous selection of cheeses, fish, hams, vegetables, pastries—name your yum-yum. Upstairs is a 4-room skein of charming light-bite restaurants. Adjoining is a very distinguished gift boutique. The food is expensive but superb. *The* sophisticates of Munich patronize this establishment, as well they should. **Kreutzkamm**, near the Bayerischerhof on Maffeistrasse, is an excellent *Konditorei* for nibblings; it is open the whole shopping day. Homemade desserts and candies are main features. Also chic clientele, but more out-of-towners. The tripartite **Café Luitpold** (Briennerstrasse 11) is a splendid midtown oasis for all pocketbooks. Its divisions are the café section, the grill with counter seating, and the pâtisserie-confection shop. Fast service, good food, and lip-smacking snacks; ask for the handsome young Manager, Mr. Pollman. Highly recommended. Italian fixin's? **Galleria** (Sparkassenstrasse across from Haxenbauer) is a narrow, white, stucco, real-life *galleria* hung with a movable feast of paintings and carved polychromatic carriage yokes. Six candle-topped tables and chamber music contribute to the air of unhurried refinement; perhaps 12 pastas and half as many entrées, all bigger than your eyes and masterfully composed, bless the menu; the Santa Cristina chianti plays perfect counterpoint; Giuseppe Perni plays perfect host. **Picadore** and **Circus**, both rolling along on Occamstrasse, pound pleasing pizzas for sidewalk revelers and budgeteering nighthawks. The **Conti Grill** of the Hotel Continental is loaded with rustic charm, but our meat a while back was tougher than Batman's bicep. Perhaps other trippers have had better luck—or stronger choppers—because since that try several Guidesters waxed enthusiastic both for it and for Maître Berhog; so we dutifully returned for an all-out sampling on our subsequent Munich rounds—only to repeat our earlier experiences. Maybe what we need is a new dentist. Finally, the **Kaiser Stube** in the Hotel Deutscher Kaiser might be worth a casual visit.

Sightseeing thrill? Head out to the $5,500,000, 951-foot **Olympia Tower**, a TV spike looming over the site of the Olympic Games and an enormous ice rink. From its upper tiers the Alps (65 miles away) are easily visible on a clear day. Small entrance fee; ground-floor Atrium Restaurant with wood panels, suspended "gas" lamps, and a chicken-roost wall decoration (the poultry-

minded Wienerwald chain operates the food interests here); rocket-thrust
ascent via the fastest elevator in Europe (you might swallow your tummy as
you rise 7 meters per second); revolving 3-speed, 32-table panoramic dining
ring that is breathtaking; stationary snack bar; upper-level observation deck,
plus a children's platform still higher (with low but thick walls to prevent
parental coronaries when the little ones venture near the edge). Cuisine
typical of the Wienerwald kitchens: savory in a few simple dishes, bland in
many others, inexpensive, and 1st-rate quality in ingredients, presentation,
and handling. For about $5 by taxi, pennies by tram (#3 or #7), or special
bus from the station, this is a *must* for any first-timer to Munich. If it's a
glaring or bright day, be sure to bring sunglasses for your fullest enjoyment.

For beer gardens or beer cellars in the city proper, **Mathaeser Beer City**,
which bills itself as the "largest beer-tavern in the world," is managed by
young, hyperactive Peter Reiss. The open-air garden upstairs normally operates during the 3 warmest months. Concerts in main section at 10:30 to 4 and
from 4:30 to 12 with a bigger band; open every day except December 24; good
hearty food. For an atmosphere-filled and gratifyingly inexpensive meal,
Nürnberger Bratwurstglorkl, opposite the Dom, should be mentioned. The
dumplings, as well as the wursts, are triumphs. **Platzl**, opposite the Hofbräuhaus and a few steps from the Vier Jahreszeiten, might be called a
Bavarian Music Hall; a lively show (in German) goes on throughout your
dinner every day of the week. Also clean, also sound cookery, also typical.
The **Franziskaner** has a similar personality. **Löwenbräukeller**, a gigantic
building and garden, can handle 8000 customers at a sitting; strictly mass
production for local workers of modest means; 2nd-rate in food, service,
atmosphere, and feel. **Augustiner-Keller** offers kegs of action in summer and
a bunged-out zero in winter. The internationally renowned **Hofbräuhaus**,
which has a capacity for 7000 tipplers, seems to have been the target for every
tourist since Genghis Khan. A $500,000 revision was undertaken to eliminate
what Bavarian State Secretary Franz Lippert termed "its prison character"
and "beer-dampened floor." On our latest inspection, we could detect a
considerable degree of improvement. There was roughhouse tussling on 2
recent pop-ins, but these altercations usually are directed onto the street
where police haul away the combatants. Have a drink, a peek, and a listen
to the oooom-pah band. If you do it just once, that's enough.

Wine restaurant? Try the modest **Weinstadl** (Burgstrasse 5), an Old City
tavern virtually unchanged since the day it opened more than 5 centuries ago.
Here is Munich's most ancient house, the site where town scribes scratched
out the first municipal records at long wooden tables. Main floor plus cellar;
vaulted ceilings of brick and mortar; nothing fancy and nothing pretended;
heavy play from local clientele of blue-collar workers; open daily from 10 A.M.
to midnight. Fun as a change of pace.

Outskirts? On a summer evening the **Forsthaus Wörnbrunn**, in the Grünwald forest, is said to promote friendly persuasions with a salubrious setting
and pleasant dining. We haven't had the pleasure of anyone's company here
yet, but we're anxious to do so soon.

There's one custom that's a *must* in Bavaria—especially in Munich. According to local legend, Weisswürste, the renowned white sausage, must be

consumed "before the church bells ring." So that the belfries won't take offense, everyone ritualistically winds up the evening's toot by stuffing his own casing with this specialty. A typical Würste-house is **Donisl** (across from City Hall), where they serve 373 miles of this blanched-veal delight on a slow morning. You'll S-link home—happily!

In *Hamburg*, the baronial **Ratsweinkeller**, pride of the municipality, is one of the best of its type in Germany. Elaborate and suave décor; dignified and cosmopolitan atmosphere; service sputtering, as almost everywhere these days. Try its Nordsee-Steinbutt Gekocht mit Zerlassener Butter if you're a jet-propelled turbot-fan. For romancers, **Die Insel**, should heat up any tryst. Red-canopy entrance; tented rectangular bar with stools, secretarial chairs, coach lights, and a view of the adjoining dance floor; fireside lounge with stone walls, dim lamps, deep divans, and a living room ambiance; small dining annex featuring a copper-hooded rôtisserie, ruby carpet, patterned napery, and white furniture. Limited menu for midday munching, bigger and better choices for evening; recorded music only; always packed in the evenings, so reserve ahead. Frankly costly, but very pleasant if your jeans have both genes and plenty of jingle. Proprietor Ramon Preuss also runs **La Bonne Auberge** (zum Goldenen Stern, toward the airport), a daily farmhouse feedery that is again riding high. **Wein-Restaurant J. H. C. Ehmke** is g-astronomically expensive by German standards. The cuisine is good but not grand; some vegetables are insipid; better for sea-faring than steer-age; closed Sundays. Nice sampling of the Old World if you can stand the New World prices. **W. Schümann's Austernkeller** ("Oyster Cellar"), Jungfernstieg 34, is a page out of the memoirs of Kaiser Wilhelm. Ground-floor situation belies its subterranean title; photos of celebrities so elegantly bearded they would challenge Commander Whitehead; high-backed booths and chairs; stained-glass touches; 7 private dining roomettes with closable door for business conferences or monkey-business conferees; bustling but friendly attention. For skilletry we prefer this one to Ehmke. Recommended. **Jacob**, 20 minutes out at *Hamburg-Nienstedten*, is a riverbank mansion that served its first guest on April 1, 1791. Now it wears a fresh wardrobe that is said to be charming. We'll give it another whirl on our forthcoming whirlings. The hilltop **Süllberg**, in nearby *Blankenese*, might be another worthy alternative. **Bavaria Blick** is a split-level, glass-lined aerie topping the St. Pauli Brewery. Suave reception for its prosperous clientele; 25 flower-clad tables; dishes as appealing to the eye as to the palate; the house pride is its finny fare; coffee comes up with a snooker of double-rich whipped cream; it seems to improve every time we go. Don't forget to ask your waiter for binoculars, to put yourself right on the bridge of that freighter piloting up the Elbe. A high spot, both geographically and gastronomically. The **Uberseebrücke** (auf der Uberpromenade) almost could be its twin. Situated adjacent to the river; tall, wide windows on 3 sides; 101-item menu; child's plate "For Our Little Guests" at less than half the adult billings (but what boy could eat with all of those boats passing right under his nose?); exquisite presentation and culinary performance, but portions too large for most Yankee middies (midriffs, that is). Costly but definitely rewarding. **Riper** (Grosse Reichenstrasse 56) is an amusing old-time establishment where the Hamburg Card Playing Society meets nightly. Family ownership since the first cut of the deck; "hot pots" and typical local fare for penny-ante prices; fun as a change of pace. So is the **Fursthof**, a tavern in which you can fetch your own vittles. **Panorama**, appropriately perched in a penthouse, comes next. Care for the address? Get set: It's Glockengiesserwall Ecke Ferdinandtor 1 im Kunsthaus, Hamburg 1. Whew! Simple glass-bound nest overlooking the Alster, the boats, cars, trains, and Hamburgers below; illumination by pods of long plastic icicles; padded cupcake-shape chairs and placemats on tables; bustling café-type service and cookery that was surprisingly good; eel soup is a specialty, and it is deeeeel-ishous. The daytime is best in summer; evenings are nicest in winter. A recommendable lookout—*if* you spend a working day memorizing its name and site. In the same vicinity, **Alsterpavillon**, the large semicircular building with the sprawling sidewalk café and tiers of terraces over the lake, is so central and so obvious that most visitors at least see it in passing; plush dining room upstairs, tearoom downstairs, snacks in the open; attractive and good. Hermann Sellmer's **Fischereihafen-Restaurant**, on a quay overlooking the busy Norder Elbe waterway, has excellent salmon, sole, and other fruit of the sea. Reserve in advance; go upstairs; quite expensive; don't order lobster or crab, because the tab will kill you. **Alsterschiff**, a small ship permanently anchored in the Inner Lake (center of town), offers 11 tables in the tiny cabin for dining afloat; amusing experience, but the galley's not the best. **Coelln** is famous for its oysters (expensive!) during the winter months. **Mühlenkamper Fährhaus** (Osterbekstrasse 1, a few minutes out from the center) again and again has served us perfectly splendid gastronomy. Our latest sampling was so superior in every respect that we are convinced this is one of the best dining spots in the North. Atmosphere almost homey in execution; padded red-leather booths for sink-in comfort; oil paintings, brass chandeliers, and warm wood paneling; excellent-to-extraordinary service masterminded by all Hiller-sheims plus Maître Otto, a real pro. While there are several rooms upstairs, we prefer the main level for coziness and action. Delicious slivers of smoked salmon and sturgeon were delivered on individual wooden platters and gar-nished with fresh salad tidbits. Our sweet-and-sour goose was so tender, flavorful, and handsomely presented that we still go into a roc-style flap when we think of it. We also purloined a slice of our partner's lamb with chive and cream sauce (and nearly had an arm chopped off in the process); it was so succulent that we bow to her aggressiveness. (She wasn't my Nancy, by the way.) Our Raspberry Romanoff (a Hamburg specialty of smooth, tart gelatin folded in cream) was a dessert fit for the czars. Nothing faltered. A dinner for 2 will jiggle into the high-tariff range with cocktails, wine, liqueur, and coffee, but we can practically promise you it will be one of the most memora-ble repasts of your national journey. Yum! **Peter Lembcke** (Holzdamm 49) is another diet-buster that turns out irresistible calories for Hamburg's cog-noscenti. Here is a 2nd example of the "secret" corners which too often resist international fame; it is, however, well known and loved by discriminating locals. Proprietor-Chef Karl Krause oversees his domain, his skillets, and his guests while wandering broodingly in a floor-length laboratory technician's gown. Godawful fittings which constitute no décor at all; worn, tattered, and utterly charmless surroundings in a creaky town house; only a 3-minute waddle from the Atlantic Hotel; poor ventilation; such fine old-fashioned Teutonic cuisine that none of these obvious shortcomings really matter. For our money, the steaks have no peer anywhere in the city. The prices are surprisingly modest. Not at all for impressing a lady friend, but a serious wooer for the Hungry Man. **Blockhouse** (Dorotheenstrasse) is named for Herr Block, its beefeating proprietor. Attractive interior featuring timbered ceilings, sycamore-green carpets, colored windowpanes, and candle lights; active convivial bar to left of entrance; overly seasoned Western-style steaks; good baked potatoes and salads; young waitresses who struggle valiantly and vainly, yet sweetly, with the English language. More colorful than Lembcke's, but its steerage can't begin to compare with that specialist, in our opinion. Most suitable for young romantics. **Franziskaner**, around the corner from the Vier Jahreszeiten, is a sound budget bet for local vittles. Heavily wooded den with moss banquettes, beige walls, and brassy bar; spotlessly clean; fleet-footed service. Nürnberger sausages over sauerkraut go fastest here. **Churrasco** (Ferdinandstrasse 61) is an Argentine steak-out that will probably make you wish you'd stayed down on the pampas. Some in this chain are okay, but this'un ain't for us'ns. The **Finland Restaurant** in Finland House is very much in the swim these days. Its very highly regarded for its buffet table—and with ample reason. So is **Kon Tiki** in the Hotel Norge, where for a set price voyagers can stuff down a raft of ship's stores. Keep sailing back for seconds or thirds at no extra charge; beverages are separate. **Zillertal** is the leading *Bierstube*—only fair—and **Münchener Hofbräuhaus** is pretty vulgar and unappealing; the latter has convenient hours, however, because it dishes out light bites and soup until 3 A.M. We haven't sampled the new 300-seat **Orpheus**, which reportedly serves jazz, folklore, and frolic with its comestibles. For snacks, try the spotlessly modern "K.B." chain, a self-service operation, or **Edelweiss**, where the quality is usually excellent. Among the hotels, the **Atlantic** and the **Vier Jahreszeiten** duel in dual combat for a *touché;* we'd give the edge to the former. The **Parkhochhaus** is inexpensive and cheerful, but passable only for its à la carte selections.

Like so many other German metropolises, Hamburg has its own TV tower *cum* revolving restaurant, dubbed the **Fernsehturm**. The 60-minute, live-and-in-color special rates a minus-ate on our gustatory scale. Lower-level cafeteria with formica tables and seemingly dizzy scouring crew; top-tier dining ring with color-keyed booths set on a moving floor; stationary bar at the axis. The whip cracks for dinner at 6:30 sharp; then the herd stampedes in like bulls thundering through the streets of Pamplona. Its management seemingly prefers to work tightly packed grazers rather than strays; therefore they loaded up communal boards even when tables stood empty elsewhere. Our "Angus", billed euphemistically as the "Best in Town," did not specify *which* town—and we'd wager that they couldn't have meant . . . well, anyone for a Hamburger?

In *Cologne*, the Hanse Stuben in the **Excelsior Ernst** is easily our choice as the most elegant spot (see "Hotels"). The cuisine more than matches the glorious setting. Among the independents, **Die Bastei** is so spectacular it shouldn't be missed. Elevated, glassed-in, ¾-circle building jutting out almost into the waters of the Rhine; split-level dining; French, Belgian, Swiss, Aus-

trian, and German specialties, all identified on the menu by national license-
plate markings ("CH" for Switzerland, etc.); tea music through the gloaming,
dinner chords from 7:30 P.M. to 10 P.M., and dance melodies thereafter; vastly
improved service and culinations on our latest foray; steep tariffs. A must for
its revitalized skilletry, unusual architecture, and striking Rhine view. **Wolff's
Wine House,** in a less glamorous urban location, is as strong on cuisine
but weaker on vista. Uninteresting, windowless composite of 2 poorly ventilated rooms; on a recent circuit we could not even stand it long enough to
order, because a trio of leather-lunged cigar smokers were puffing up so much
blue air that our companion asked to leave. Peppy service (when it finally
comes!); menu in German only. Our latest meal was once again up to its
former standards, but the prices were much higher—too high, we think, for
what you get. **Le Pot-Flambé**, to go into reverse again, is better for eye appeal
than for palate satisfaction. Entrance enhanced by a wooden-trough cattle-
fountain; barn décor with sausage-hung wooden beams, Swiss farmhouse
lanterns, red napery, and drip-draped waxed bottles for candle illumination;
wine served in crockery drinking pitchers. Highly embroidered busboys; zith-
er-plucked melodies; food heavily seasoned and undistinguished. Can be fun
if you're in a tolerant mood. The **Schweizer Stube** brews up a similar ambiance and very little Swiss bliss from the kitchen. The twin-room **Balkan Grill**,
one link in a chain, comes up with a superior brand of national cookery.
Trout tank at entrance; wood paneling; brass chandelier; Adriatic patterns on
linens; generally informal air. Our Grill-Teller (composed of Cevapcici, Raz-
nijici, and other native meats) and our partner's Djuwetsch (pork with paprika, rice, onions, tomatoes, and herbs) were very good indeed, and the
portions were piled almost as high as a Dinaric Alp; other novel touches were
the Balkan salad and the Yugoslavian red wine. Surprisingly inexpensive;
recommended. **Weinhaus im Walfisch**, the choice of many U.S. service families, offers 2 floors and tavernish, 2-fisted cookery. Built in 1750, it has been
a restaurant continuously since 1837. For local color, the **Früh** (to the rear
of the Dom-Hotel) or the **Päffgen** couldn't be more characteristic; waiters in
dark-blue shirts; no tablecloths, no fripperies; crowded with *Herren* and
Hausfrauen drinking wine or special Cologne beer, and gossiping like mad;
go to either for a sausage, a beer, and to watch the locals unwind. **Im Hahnen**
is a slightly more refined version of this ilk. **Alt Köln**, next to the Excelsior
Ernst, slaps on Old Cologne in 4711 predictable ways. Aromatic of spit-roasted
bantams; fun if your tastes run to corny; poor service; chicken-feed prices. A
mixed grill. (On the other flank of the same hostelry, you'll find an American-
bred **MacDonald**'s.) **Treppchen** ("Little Staircase") of the Hotel Europa is
a charming wine cellar for sipping and snacks; music but no dancing; closed
Wednesday; late afternoon or evening only; not quite up to its former glories.
These are the best in their respective leagues, in our opinion. Travel-wise
Guidester Kurt Luhn sends us words of praise for the outskirting **Gaststätte
Marienbild**. His observations are so keen that we pass this entry along to you
unhesitatingly. We're anxious to try it, too. A friendly resident of this city,
moreover, now advises us that we have committed a sin of omission by failing
to list an inn called **Altenberger Hof**, east of town in the Bergischer hills.
We'd never heard of it or even of the "famous Altenberger Dom" which it

apparently faces. So live and learn. Out at **Köln-Mergeim** the **Golderner Pflug** is said to whip up commendable French cuisine in a private house. More for evening than for midday.

In **Heidelberg**, the versatile facilities and fine cookery in the perked up Kurfürstenstube of the **Europäischer Hof** top them all. The **Ritter**, which dates back to 1592, comes up with above-average vittles and authentic Old German surroundings. The suit of armor which we almost mistook for the maître has now been removed, possibly to save other reubens from making the same mistake. Two adjoining rooms; blossoms on each table; English menu; informal ambiance; inexpensive. Sound, but not what one might call thrilling. The **Museum Restaurant** is a delight. Entry through large portals that face a court and a sylvan park beyond; interior with heavy beams supported by carved tree trunks; 2 rooms separated by red granite pillars and ancient arches; windows with stained glass inserts; bronze chandeliers. The menu is enticing, the service sound, and the prices in the medium bracket. In every way, we enjoyed it. **Molkenkur**, reachable by car or tiny funicular, has a magnificent mountainside 100-foot terrace, well *above* the Schloss (castle); 3 rows of tables and glorious view; attractive inside dining room; expensive and they try hard; a worthy bet, especially in good weather. (The Schloss is closed to the public.) As you might expect, tourists often swarm the precincts. **Königstuhl**, way-way-way up at the mountaintop TV tower, broadcasts only so-so-so cookery—BUT that nonvideo view is worth those coaxial impulses in your tummy. **Schinderhannes**, on Theatrestrasse, is fun as a wine restaurant; it is open only for dinner and late revels. For light bites, there are miles of spaghetti factories and endless rounds of pizzerias along the Hauptstrasse in the center of town. **Haarlass Terrace**, across the river, is lovely when the sun shines but often choked with bus-crowds. **Kupferkanne** is agreeable; **Goldener Hecht**, at the corner of the Old Bridge, is old, colorful, and a favorite among artists and students (they proudly informed us that Goethe *nearly* spent a night here!). **Perkeo**, once a favorite, is no longer recommended. As for the highly publicized student taverns, the **Red Ox** has the greatest fame, but we found its food miserable, its service glacial, and its atmosphere commercially touristy; try **Seppl**, which seems a far more authentic mirror of undergraduate life—but remember that these places are strictly for sightseers except during the school terms. Those predatory sophomores are past masters at cadging drinks, so button your pockets! If you're driving down to Munich from Frankfurt am Main and seek a lunch stop, the previously described **Hotel Erbprinz** at **Ettlingen** is a joy; highly recommended. We're told that you can sup medievally, but not evilly, at the hotel **Zum Ritter** in nearby **Neckargemünd**, where ancient-style dishes are served in bowls and attacked solely with Gothic daggers. We'll schedule a night-out here soon.

In **Düsseldorf**, the new Eck in the **Breidenbacher Hof** would be our choice for any daytime meal, while the grill is nicer for evening. The **Hilton**'s San Francisco Room to us is now more show than value. The neighboring **Intercontinental** leans (natch) to continental cuisine at its penthouse restaurant. Again, costly for the rewards. Among the independents, the prize easily goes to the wickedly cost-be-damned **Orangerie**, with red textile walls, candle

sconces, mirrored coach lamps and orchard color intonations. Only the host
receives the prices on his menu, so if you notice a transfixed glaze on his eyes
and the beginnings of paralysis setting in, you'll know why. (Our *very light*
meal for 2—*no* cocktails, *no* dessert, and a *modest* wine came to $60.) Perfect
service; superb French cuisine; very stylish, but oh those tabs! Next in the fleet
comes **Bateau Ivre** ("Tipsy Ship"), at Kurzestrasse 11, in the Old Town—a
5-minute swagger from the Breidenbacher Hof. Gangway entrance; Maritime
Bar; impressive nautical interior with polished-wood bulkheads, portholes,
riveted supports, canvas and lapstreak topsides, carpeted deck, a brass binnacle, a telescope, and a holdful of salty lore; gob-ishly overworked but seaworthy waiters in navy-and-orange middy blouses; leather seats; candlescent
tones. Reserve well in advance, because it's a dinghy in size compared to its
whaleboat popularity. Closed Sunday. **Walliser Stuben**, centrally located,
struck us as gimmicky and lethally expensive for the return in nutrients.
Doorway bar leading to 3 chalet-style rooms; split-timber and stucco walls;
Blue Ox cowbells; alcohol lamplighting; enormous 12-page menu and rather
poor wine card. Our verdict? More for the tourist's eye than the connoisseur's
tummy. **Zum Schiffchen**, like Früh in Cologne, is the Real McCoy for local
flavor; big regional menu; no tablecloths; home town beer a feature; simple,
inexpensive, unelaborate, and a good value for budgeteers. Quite sound and
still improving. The Düsseldorf water table is such that historically this city
has never had a cellar restaurant *("Ratskeller");* this is the closest thing to
it here. Back in the Old City, the **Schneider-Wibbel-Stuben** is a sound up-one-
flight operation for fish specialties, sausages, and beer. **Zum Kurfürst** 's cookery impressed us as having gone off to the point where we can no longer
recommend it. "**M & F** " is large, bustling, noisy—a beehive of upper-bracket
office people and toilers-in-a-hurry; not for the tranquil or peace loving.
Schnellenburg, about 15 minutes from the center, sprawls handsomely on the
bank of the Rhine; modern, country-inn atmosphere; watch the boats putt-
putt by as you sit on its terrace; the cuisine would be tops if the chef would
use his herb-shelf more liberally. A delight, *if* you pick your weather. For
another pleasant excursion, please see our report on **Schloss Hugenpoet** ; it's
listed under "Hotels."

Garmisch-Partenkirchen's **Marktplatz Hotel** is renowned for its dining room, but it seems to have good days and bad. Old-fashioned atmosphere
inside, with a lighter, brighter feel to its newer annex; gay in-and-outdoor
terrace for warm weather munching; medium tabs. Variable. **Bräustüberl**,
operated by a brewery, is smallish, and its aura is Bavarian; low prices and
solid fare. **Post Hotel** has a larger Bavarian-style restaurant which we don't
happen to care for. Riender's Grill in the **Partenkirchner Hof** is the choice
of many locals—with very good reason. Moderate outlays for rich inlays.
Way, way up at the tippy-top of 9730-foot Zugspitze Mountain, masons have
erected a 1000-seat self-service restaurant which is Germany's loftiest. To
reach it, take the high-strung express cableway, or the slower cog railroad.
Broad windows and a huge terrace command a view of the Wetterstein Range
and the Central Alps. More elegant (but not sophisticated) fodder is served
up in the **Hotel Schneefernerhaus**, which shares the real estate on this dizzy-
ing summit. Don't even consider the insipid cookery (this pilgrim didn't),

because you'll hardly look once at your plate. And please remember our caution (see "Hotels") about the dangerous spring thaws in this area.

In **Stuttgart**, the **Fernsehturm** (TV tower) is a sensation—for view, not for gastronomy. Atop a hill, it's a 692-foot-high needle which impales a tapered aluminum and glass "cork" at the 558-foot level—and this cork is a 4-story restaurant, TV transmission point, observation platform, kitchen, and wine cellar. The elevator takes 35 seconds to get up there—but if you're the cowardly character that I am, your heart will need only ½-second to climb past your teeth at your first downward look. Lunch moderately priced; dinner more expensive; food decidedly not the main feature here (my stomach got lost). Director Max Schaber tries hard, but some of the many other TV tower restaurants now scraping German skies are better than this original edifice. Back in the city proper, we've always been addicted to the colorful and charming **Alte Post**. If you're neither an eagle nor a landlubber, perhaps **Lukullus** might titillate your fancy. This floating restaurant is a converted excursion liner moored on the Neckar at **Stuttgart-Bad Cannstatt**. Capacity for more than 500 passengers—er, diners; meals served on several deck levels, with special accommodations for winter rigors; Schifferstube ("Skipper's Bar") up forward with lantern fixtures and other rigging. As for the galley, sorry, mates, we're completely at sea. The **Scheffelstuben** (Haussmannstrasse 5) and the rustic-style **Waldhotel Schatten** (near the Solitude race course) are under the same managerial aegis. The latter offers a substantial and inexpensive Sunday buffet. The **Schwabenbräu** was tapped out by a brewery. Typical food of the region (plus suds, of course). A **Mövenpick**, with its woodlined Rôtisserie Baron de la Mouette, now sizzles on the Kleiner Schlossplatz. This Swiss chain knows its vittles. **Traube**, about 5 minutes from the airport, is described by one jovial Guidester as "Black Forest baroque" in décor. Superb gastronomy; extensive wine selection (and well treated, too); lots of country-style atmosphere to spur on the appetite. We think you'll like it, but be sure to phone first to reserve a table.

Bremen, never a gastronome's city, is beginning to flower. The blossomking is still **Essig Haus**, with its venerable Hanseatic woodwork; ownership by the Parkhotel. **Schnoor 2**, which takes its name from its address, is extremely well regarded by Bremen-and-women; 400-year-old gabled house in snazzy rustic tones; certainly tops in eye appeal, with cookery just a chef's pinch less savory than Essig Haus. **Belgrad**, a skip away at Schnoor 12, specializes in gypsy music and atmosphere; open for lunch and then until 2 A.M. The **Balkan Grill**, at Am Herzogenkamp 32, in the suburb of **Horn**, repeats the same kitchen, the same hours, the same music, the same ambiance —and, oh yes, the same management. Also take a peek or a nibble at the historic and good **Ratskeller**, where the Faust legend is said to have been originated centuries ago. The **Alt-Bremen**, recalling the city from 1750 to 1850, sounds touristy, but it could be fun. Too much bustle and commerce in this metropolis for truly comfortable dining leisure.

Hanover's surest all-around bet can be placed smack on the nose of the **Intercontinental** (see "Hotels"). The Prinz Tavern, with cozy clusters of booths plus open tables, crackling grill, wood paneling, painted screens, pewter service plates, handsome ceramics, and waiters in good-looking Lower

Saxony costumes, is as delightful to the eye as to the palate. Its Brasserie is ideal for coffee shop habitués. The woody *Bierstube* wins the cup for suds and snacking. Light bites are also available in that wonderful Calenberger Bar, where some of the most glamorous starlets on the German TV screen unwind their long luscious limbs and let down their golden locks while spiral-eyed males swallow club sandwiches whole. Very well run in every department; recommended for any category of taste, hunger, or thirst—from sip to sup to señorita. The attractive **Wichmann** (about 10 minutes along the Hildesheimer pike) could be a paradise—if only the chef knew his *assiette* from his aspic. From any aspect, gastronomically our saddle of hare could scarcely have been more clumsily dismounted (poor thing, it must have died miserably); our sauce was ghastly; our wine was foul; our service was bumbling. What a shame, because this thatched-roof farmer's cottage, with cozy individual rooms, candlelight, and a pleasant ambiance, could be a sparkler in the right hands. Perhaps you'll have better luck—but somehow we doubt it. **La Bonne Auberge** is the leading independent choice in midcity. Straw-covered booths with checkered tablecloths and storm lamps; saddles, copper fixin's, and stableware set the scene; waitresses in Basque costumes. A board with 35 hors d'oeuvres selections greets the newcomer; handsome presentation of appetizing fodder; fair prices. A good little hitching post. The **Dubrovnik**, on the Hotel Europa's 5th floor, is a U-shape Dalmation creation that's almost guaranteed to change the shape U're in, but fast. Rather leaden Balkan backdrop; dark wood tables; window-sited booths; moss-and-maroon velvet drapery; suspended orange lamps; exceptionally kind personnel. Our servings from Serbia (mixed grill) consisted of a lamb shish kebab—dee-lish-shish pork chop, hamburger, liver, rice, French fries (what, you never heard of Croatian potatoes?), cabbage, tomato, hot peppers, onion, and lettuce; this we wetted down with a carafe of the house's semisweet Yugoslavian red wine. With fixin's so fine and tabs so low, here's a buy for the adventurous diner. **Herrenhaüser**, 2 blocks from the Intercontinental, bespeaks easygoing neighborliness from 5:30 P.M. until 5 A.M. Small counter up front; plain tables and chairs at the rear; wallpaper possibly dating back to the heyday of Bismark. Since most selections tend to fall into the *wurst* family, no normal repast edges past $5.50. Marginal. If you have 20 seconds to pronounce it, **Brauereigaststaetten** is 20 minutes out the main pike to Bremen. This atmospheric choice is located in a suburban brewery; the skillets know only the most toothsome samplings of regional fare. Not costly. Recommended highly for its type. Insomniacs' delight? **Am Kamin** serves grills and frills around the clock. On my next Hanovernight when I can't sleep, Am Kamin right on down here for a lil ole snack; then Am gwan straight back to bed.

Baden-Baden's **Brenner's Park Hotel** is classified in the nation's highest gastronomic category by savvy Teutons. And well it might be, because here is an Old World Diadem. Richly elegant décor, not overstressed, in off-white, crystal, and gold; red and flaxen carpeting; flowers in silver vases; sweetly bucolic vistas from dining room or gardenside summer terrace; service that anticipates your slightest whim; cuisine as smooth and gentle as the attention you receive. Here is solace for the discriminating nabob. *Wunderbar!* The auditorium-size **Casino Restaurant** draws crowds in season but no plaudits from us the year around. Instead, within the same building, we prefer the **Mirabelle**, which is linked to the more popular-priced **Boulevard Terrace** as well as to the attractive **Paddock Bar**, with a pianist from 7 to midnight; downstairs is the Club Tavern disco-restaurant. **Stahlbad** (Lichtentaler Strasse 27), a 3-minute walk from the Brenner's Park, provides 2 adjoining rooms tricked out with hanging lamps, copper cake-molds, an emerald-tile fireplace, and gaily painted plates. Menu in German, but a color photo album of the selections is on hand to ease your ordering perplexities. Hard working, white-jacketed-and-capped Owner-Chef Schwank prepares most of the dishes at your tableside—such High German specialties as Sukiyaki, Risi-Bisi, and "Hollywoodsteak." For dessert, please try his half-melted sherbet served in a giant brandy snifter. Theatrical and very, very expensive—but viable and fun if the Mark is no object. The **Baden Wine Cellar** is pleasant for a sip and snack. The **Mandarin**, with both Cantonese and Peking perkings, pans out only fair Oriental fare. We suspect the chef was born a little west of the Yangtze—somewhere between Karlsruhe and Pforzheim, for example. In nearby *Herrenalb*, the **Post Hotel** is a dream (see "Hotels"). Former twelfth-century monastery; Klosterschänke Grill, with beamed braces in stone and stucco walls or arches; flowers and candles on each table; the bread is served in 2-foot-long baskets. Our consommé, smoked trout with whipped horseradish sauce, and saddle of venison washed down by local wine, was a deliciously memorable repast. Not too costly, and *what* a delight! **Schloss Neuweier** turns on a reasonably good kitchen in an atmosphere of antiquity. At *Oberbeuern*, the **Wald Hotel Fischkultur** is really a trout ranch, so you can guess at the specialty. **Burg Windeck** perches about ½-hour from Baden-Baden above the village of *Bühl*. This rebuilt castle site is a small hostelry and restaurant. Breathtaking vista from wide windows overlooking the vine-draped hills, the rilling Rhine Valley, the cobalt horizon with the peaks of the Vosges Mountains, and the frontiers of France. (That's Strasbourg twinkling in the sunlight.) Regional dishes only; delicious local wines; handsome rustic interior décor ignorable for the panorama. If you should lunch late or on a weekend, there's a fair chance you'll be joined at your table by a clutch of dumpy *Hausfrauen* in bullet hats who clutch their eternal umbrellas. These ladies will examine the entire menu, comment extensively on each item, contemplate as deeply as a Hindu guru, and finally order a wedge of whip-creamy cake with a glass of cold water. Their gab will be incessant until sunset or moonrise. They are a sociological fact of life in many German dining rooms —the Vestal Matrons of a Bombazine Goddess. May they never perish! When the sun is glowing and so are you, try to sample the unique flavor of the Black Forest. Ride out to nearby villages in the vineyard country—preferably by any route other than the autobahn. Hamlets such as *Varnhalt* (Hotel Katzenberger 's Adler), *Umweg* (Boxbeutel), and *Neuweier* (the previously mentioned **Schloss, Lamm,** or **Rebenhof**) are just a few of the many oases within a 10-mile radius of Baden-Baden. Don't miss a drive through this region—perhaps a longer excursion down to *Hinterzarten*'s captivating **Hotel Adler.** Here you will savor the peace, the silence, the majesty, and the pastoral loveliness of the romantic *Schwarzwald*.

In *Nürnberg*, let us lead off with our first choice of THE place to avoid:

The famous **Goldenes Posthorn**. This self-appointed temple of gastronomy claims to be both the oldest wine cellar in Germany (A.D. 1498) and very nearly the finest restaurant on both hemispheres. With as much charity as we can muster, let us simply impart that our views hardly coincide with those of its management. Pure fun and authentic local color? We adore the **Bratwurst-Herzle**. Community tables; standard pewter plate, heart-shape platter of fingerling sausages, sauerkraut and horseradish (about a buck), beer, cheese —and that's all; always packed. In the same category, **Schranke, Bratwurst-Häusle**, and **Bärle** are also worthy but offer less flair. The **Spital**, spanning the river on 2 giant arches, is a typical wine restaurant that dishes up typically awesome German proportions. **Nassauer Keller** has better cookery.

Wiesbaden boasts the renowned **Mutter Engel**—a hollow bruit, as far as we're concerned. There are 2 sancta of no decorative significance, one with clay-color walls and the other in green; the waiters were far too busy with bookwork, preening, and self-importance to serve the worthy offerings of the able chef. Basically sound, if some lion tamer would snap the whip at those cats in black. We much prefer the circular grill room at the **Nassauer Hof** (see "Hotels"). The **Hotel de France** also serves up tempting viands. **Am Kamin** bases its reputation chiefly on steaks. **Müller's Weinstube** toasts visitors only in the evenings. The **Mövenpick** is across from the Casino; it's okay for medium-priced dining in this high-priced town. **Lessing Stuben** and **Pfeffermühle** are local in style and typical in cookery. **Yuen's China-Restaurant** is a converted beer hall gone Cantonese.

In *Berchtesgaden*, the **Geiger** will probably register the loudest beeps on your counter, even though its skillets are only mildly atomic. Our steak dinners produced sighs from contented waistlines; 70 beds available for overnighters. This town, for our money, is a brass-plated tourist trap.

Bonn's leader is **Im Alten Hut** (Meckenheimer Strasse 27). Plenty of atmosphere; medium-expensive; evenings only; closed Sunday. The **Hansa am Kaiserplatz** (Kaiserplatz 18) is our 2nd choice; international cuisine; not very special. **Salvator** (Sürststrasse) wins the beer mug for typical German fare. **Em Höttche** is headed by a brewery. Main square situation with main-line cookery. The viewful salon aloft the **Steigenberger Hotel** in the Bonn Center can be fun when it offers one of its frequent "gastronomic weeks." Otherwise it's pretty routine. **Am Tulpenfeld**, nearby, seemed better for day-in-night-out cookery. In neighboring *Bad Godesberg*, **Maternus** is the most popular rendezvous of the diplomatic set.

Berlin suggestions are listed in the independent chapter on this city.

Finally, if you're bound down the *east* bank of the Rhine, the famous old **Krone Hotel-Restaurant** at *Assmannshausen* (21 miles from Wiesbaden and 42 miles from Frankfurt am Main) is an enchanting choice for lunch when sunbeams are dancing on the river. Terrace-dining on the warmer days, under a grapevine "roof"; long, paneled, inside salon with low ceilings and ancient spirits; quite expensive; red-wine specialties are Assmannshäusener and a sparkling burgundy-type called Schäumender Special Roter Cuvée; open mid-March to mid-November. There's so much flavor here that it's worth a short (but not too time-consuming) detour. On the main road beside the stream; you can't miss spotting it from your car.

Motoring? There are oodles of self-service cafeterias on the nation's high-speed autobahns—and more are popping up by the minute. American-style snacks are their stock in trade. Simple, low-price, functional tummy-filling fare that is a boon to hungry wayfarers.

Like France, Germany has so many hundreds of interesting eating places there simply isn't space to attempt to cover them all here. For information on other centers or villages, consult the local Tourist Offices everywhere.

§TIPS: If in doubt about a good place to eat in a strange town, head straight as Supermouse for the nearest *Ratskeller*. The word means "council cellar" and it's the place (usually the cellar of the town hall) where in the Middle Ages municipal officials received guests. There is one in most communities; part of the *Ratskeller* is known as the *Ratstrinkstube* (council drinking room). The tradition of quality is stoutly upheld in most of these; some are better than others, but as a whole they are thoroughly dependable.

What to call the waiter? That's an amusing puzzle. Some old-fashioned Germans address him as "Kellner," which means, quite simply and logically, "Waiter." Certain others give a boost to this toiler's ego by shortening "Ober-kellner," which means "Headwaiter," to "Ober"—and spreading this one around to all comers. But now, in these less discriminating times—or more flattering ones (what you will)—nearly everyone expects to be addressed as "Herr Ober"—"Mr. Headwaiter."

Dedicated budgeteers? Since we're too bottlenecked here for additional entries, please consult our annually revised paperback, *Fielding's Low-Cost Europe,* which lists scads more bargain dining spots and money-saving tips for serious economizers.

NIGHTCLUBS Booming! You can find whatever you're after—innocent, interestingly naughty, or wicked—in almost every big city.

It continues to be our conviction that, for the most rugged, down-to-bare-facts night life, **Hamburg** holds the diamond-studded G-string over any other European metropolis by at least 6 bumps and 24 grinds. The Reeper-bahn and its sidestreets are brilliant from dusk to dawn with the neon entice-ments of dozens of girlie-joints. Some of the flesh marts, with elaborate cabarets and slick décors, are sufficiently respectable for family trade. Others, however, are for men only—and that means *for men only.* In these, generally 3 to 12 "artistes" perform solo or in tandem in the seminude or nude.

The local alphabet begins and ends with B—not only for the regiments of B-girls who quaff so-called double-gin fizzes at a 10-spot each (it's the most expensive drink), but also because the area is the B-all and end-all of orga-nized eroticism. Sex Unabashed permeates the atmosphere.

In this twilight zone, 3000 of the 13-thousand residents are prostitutes. Until the '64 reform, nearly 100% of the local shills, pimps, strippers, and associated tradesmen were under the iron fist of a ruthless syndicate called "The Black Gang." Extortion, beatings, and bullyboy tactics were so com-monplace that Hamburg Security Chief Kurt Falck flexed his muscles. "We shall make it a place where men can seek pleasure without fear or danger!" thundered a spokesman—who simultaneously was careful to hedge that "the

district will not be converted into a convent school for 15-year-old girls."
(What priory, after all, ever earned a gainful income of $25,000,000 per year?)
Despite pronunciamentos, mobster elements are still in the saddle. Although
the cleanup crusade initiated by reputable operators and supported by such
influential newspapers as *Bild-Zeitung* has begun to make inroads, much of
this area still is NOT safe for visitors.

If you'll stick to the places recommended below, your wallet and your
molars *should* be safe (no blanket guarantees by us). The best fun, of course,
is to make the rounds of as many as possible, with 1 drink and 15 minutes in
each. As a rule, there's a $1.50 door bite, another 2 bits for your coat check
(never tip here), and no minimum charge; Scotch (much of it falsified) runs
up to $10 per slug. *But don't wander elsewhere under any circumstances.*

PS for budgeteers: A rash of porno cinema halls is sweeping the city as we
pen these words. The shows are varied, long, cheap, and even more revealing
than much of the live action on stage in the cabarets. Ask locally for the flick
of the moment.

Among the smaller strip depots, **Colibri** (Grosse Freiheit 34) is absolute
tops. Now with mirrors, pink satin, and pleated rouge wall hangings; one of
the few offering live music; coveys of girls who have earned their major-
sports'-letter "B" in the professional leagues. One excessively well-endowed
barmaid actually offers an uddermost private part for the boggle-eyed gentleman to kiss (a new nightclub high or low, depending upon how one regards
such brazenry). Jammed with lone males; 45-minute shows from 8 P.M. to 4
A.M. (5 A.M. on Sat. night), with a 10-minute breather between each; young,
accomplished, good-looking strippers who eventually become barefoot up to
their coiffures; amorous themes seldom included in the Boy Scout Manual
("love" between ladies is almost a ritual); unmonkeyed-with whisky; beer plus
schnapps for reasonable tabs (a mandatory combination not sold separately).
Intimate dimensions; go late for the least inhibited theatrics; for the insatia-
bles, the small protruding stage is ringed by stools. Should you have trouble
getting in, because of its popular appeal, tell Albert, the tall bumper-faced
bouncer at the door (whose heart is gold), that you "read Fielding's." For
some unfathomable reason he will bend over backward to slip you in. If you're
in the mood for a stroll down mammary lane, here's THE spot. **Salambo**,
across the street, was aflutter with transvestites on our peep-show look;
off-and-on slide projections superimposed on nude models; one bell only, and
very few belles otherwise. **Erotica**, next door, is one of those which we've
mentioned that deals in free-reelers. "Blue" films; beer the most popular
beverage; no entry fee; as raw as they come. **Safari** was renewed from doorknobs to knockers sometime in the recent past. Expandable interior glazed
by a colossal onstage sun; iridescent flora on the ceiling; starboard bar with
unbroken view of the action; disturbingly handsome bar girls. (We heard
some have undergone surgery to reverse their gender.) Good spirits; good
shows; swinging for the broad-minded. **Tabu** drums up a pleasantly cozy
mien, but its whisky comes in sampler bottles with their seals already broken;
the product is just what you'll think it is—or worse! Tabu on our score sheet.
For pickups, connoisseurs usually consider that **Mehrer Café** stocks the
choicest and safest dainties; the admission fee is about $3, which may be used

to buy a Coke; the going rate for those other sweets, during our reportorial shopping, was 70 DM or so as the "gift" to the lady; the hotel room rents for about half that outlay, and the normal check-out time is 2 hours after initial entry. The **Casino de Paris** resembles a mock-luxury-class dance hall; it teams with pros, semipros, and sandlotters, many of whom are not employed by the house; don't bother. **Lausen**, with no show, performs the same function. Typical of the dozens of 1-cylinder lairs is **Atlantis**, which gave up its bunny club for hareline respectability; 3 strips per knight; okay. The **Barcelona** features a cabaret in which it would be difficult for even a gynecologist to distinguish between the señoritas and the señores. A spot named **Kesse** bounces out its so-called Ball Paradox nightly. **Koenigin** has become a disk spinner. **Zillestal**, a beer garden, also taps out terpsichore; wives are tolerated (even if not always by their spouses). **Die Dubarry**'s checkered career is all too well known to the authorities; not recommended. **Lolita** is now a 44th-class clip trap, in our opinion; although we spotted no sheep-shearing scissors on the premises, it wouldn't have startled us if we had. **Moonlight**, now under the Safari banner, during our visit was loaded with transvestites, odd sexes, and nonsexes; here was one of the dirtiest, rottenest, most tasteless shows we've ever seen anywhere, anytime. On one loop, we heard that a trio of Japanese visitors was zapped $820 for 45 minutes of drinking. If true, that's either one helluva thirst or one helluva condemnation. We won't say which. Ugh! The **X-Club** is working its way backward through the alphabet; now it earns straight "A's" for what it is. A ½-dozen strippers; intimate ambiance; relatively honest; worth a peekaboo. **Maxim**'s, which was closed by the cops, reopened as a western-style pub. Locals have commented to us that it's *alles Käse* or "all cheese" (low German slang for "it stinks"); we don't know, however, from our own sniffer. **Petite Fleur** is recommended if you like blue; the Boys in Blue, at a guess, possibly swoop in 6 or 7 times per week. In utmost seriousness, please stay far, f–a–r, f—a—r away from this Little Flower. And while you're *not* at it, also please skip **Zum Silbersack** and **Haifisch**. These can be physically dangerous.

So can the **Piraten Cabaret** (a few doors off the mainstream, on Talstrasse). Avoid this one above all others is our advice.

In many cases, the syndicates have hired jail-hardened scum to take over in areas being threatened with extinction by cleanup patrols and by the city's responsible citizenry. One fulcrum is the infamous, eye-popping Herbert-strasse, a 1-block street just off the main drag, where harlots sit in showcase windows facing the sidewalks. Unless the gangland bosses win the war for wickedness, it is due for demolition before very long. Here the prostitutes ask about $35 per encounter. Another is the Fish Market district, where the scales fall even lower for a squalid catch. Frequently their milieu is the back seat of a car. These areas are as riddled with peril as they are with disease.

To combat them with an officially supervised competitor, private sources have erected a $1,000,000 play-for-pay mill on the Reeperbahn. Dubbed the Eros Center, it provides "office space" for 136 pros under a city-sanctioned philosophy endorsing that solon of sex, Mae West, who declaimed, "A girl in the house is worth two on the street." The U-shape structure was thoughtfully conceived: A "contact courtyard" with infrared heating for winter solicitation, an underground garage, a beauty parlor, 9 R-&-R rooms (where only the ladies may meet), and comfortable apartments equipped with kitchens. (We were amused on our chaste browsings to discover, in the red-lamplit corridor leading to the "courtyard," coin-operated machines which dispense dirty postcards and pornographic books—perhaps for those who wish to jot a note to the folks back home?) In these confines, rates nip from $25 to $40 for a short meeting; full-night lingerings are not encouraged. At the adjoining ground-floor snack bar of the Café Mira, the toll is about $60 per hour; the turnabout for a full nocturn (negotiable here and *not* discouraged) soars into the $250 range. Extensive precautions are taken to insure sanitation, including regular checkups by doctors. Tax officials, as well as local government authorities, are duty-bound to be among the Center's regular visitors.

As for run-of-the-Hun streetwalkers, please, PLEASE avoid ALL contact with these babes—the dregs of the port—who have more fancy rackets on tap than Mr. Spalding has balls—tennis, bowling, cue, golf, or any others you'd care to name. Remember always that none of the bar or taxi girls in the St. Pauli area may leave before the doors close—and that's 4 A.M. or later. Final stop for 'most everybody is **Blauer Peter**, *open from 4 A.M. to 10 A.M. only;* no show; 5-piece combo for dancing; all kinds of light food and all materials for that nightcap; very pleasant.

In other sections of the city, **Die Insel** ("The Isle"), previously mentioned under "Restaurants," is recommended for romancers; suave terrace or candlelit dining, wining, and dancing to recorded music. Proprietor Ramon Preuss also turns the night lights on at his **Ambassador Club** (snacks, drinks, and quiet diplomacy), his newer **Stork Club** at Am Schlump 15 (baby bites and discothèque), and the earlier-noted **La Bonne Auberge** (converted farmhouse restaurant). **Kleine Komödie**, **Rendezvous**, and **Hansa-Theatre** are all entertaining—but you have to speak good German to enjoy them. The last boasts the oldest reigning variety show in Germany (a dubious honor), but it is amusing for snacks, sips, and an exposure to the ho-hummery of the Hanseatic.

Gambling? You'll find roulette, baccarat, blackjack, and slot machines at the new Casino in ***Hittfeld***, about ½-hour by car or by train. Tables open at 2 P.M. daily. *Glück und Glas wie bald bricht das!*

Frankfurt am Main is a good play town too—if you hit it right. Locally the jernts are known as *"Nepp"* (a loose translation of "clip," which has now been adopted universally throughout Germany), so take it from there as to what you can expect. A current sucker technique is the "champagne racket" (described under "Tips" at the end of this section). Unlike in Hamburg, the authorities are not maintaining as firm a grip on the operators. Within 1 year we have seen previously friendly, legitimate clubs and bars degenerate into some of the most rapacious fleecing dens this side of the Bangkok waterfront. Even a number of the finest hubs have gone so predatory that if you are not careful, they'll peck your eyes from their sockets. **Imperial** still has the biggest name. A short chug from the station, in the nightlife district; scarlet velvet semicircle with banquettes and picture-gallery booths; full head of steam at 10:30 P.M.; only clusters of bored, yawning males on our latest sleepwalk; anything's likely to appear, from jigglers to jugglers; waitresses in short skirts and lo-o-o-ong necklines. During one late round, an eyewitness told us of a customer whose surprise bill was close to $500 in champagne chits; when the client did not have sufficient funds on him to clear the cuff, the management is alleged to have sent strong-arm lads with him in the wee hours to his hotel for total collection. So caution is advised. **Europa Cabaret** is a rising challenger. Spacious eye-scanning interior; happy atmosphere in Frenchy tones; ro-busty show; tantalizing strips. A wee tot of whisky rings up an eye-popping tab. The red-hued Europa Bar is its cozier downstairs nook with booths on one side and a counter on the other. Not bad, if the Frankfurt-by-Night tours don't usurp the fun. The **Casino de Paris** lies in wait with an alcove-lined main room fully equipped with tiger-toothed babes. Entrance gouge from a jerk who apparently can't count and obviously had convinced himself that our change should be short; the stairway from this portal leads to a convenient hotel above; whisky costs are higher than a laddy's kilt in a full gale. Sorry, but we detest this dive. The square-sided **BB Club**, a longish taxi ride from the center, is infinitely better for persuasive exchanges. Arcade décor with small balcony; tiny band cooing sweet nothings to match your own or hers; friendly bar and reasonable tariffs. Pleasant as a hideaway. **Black Jack,** the draw of the deck for under-21 disco-types, can easily be trumped—if you'll excuse our gamefully mixed metaphor. For fun and sophistication, **St. John's** would evoke almost any intimate confession. This pub-style hermitage was canonized for candlelight worshipers and TV-escapists; smiling redeemers sit comfortably at a horseshoe bar with built-in piano, or at low cocktail tables with dwarf-size captain's chairs. Pretty waitresses in tartans; white-painted brick wall; woody touches; fireplace crackling during cold months; fine ventilation; dartboard usually in use by males throwing for drinks; well-dressed clientele of Frankfurt's young to middle-age High Society, plus most of the other Beautiful People in town. St. John himself, a topnotch showman, takes to the mike, cues the piano, and belts out tuneful swing-songs at ½-hour intervals. As proprietor, host, and focal point for his loyal disciples, he's a tough act to follow. Delicious snacks and light meals are available at reasonable tithings. Good fun and amiability are the rules; worth a pilgrimage anytime. **Jimmy's Bar**, downstairs in the Hessischer Hof Hotel, is another pleasant dew-drop-inn for liquids and chitchat. **Taverna Bar** decants a rather distinguished atmosphere. Cellar situation in an office building; excellent orchestra enhanced by harp strains; tile dance floor; yellow and black striped banquettes; good drinks; well ventilated and clean; no shows. Could be romantic if you bring your own companion. **Swing Bar** is slightly better than routine—but very slightly. **Pik Dame** specializes in lesbian acts and other more pathetic charades. Skip the next-door **Riz**, 'cause 't'ain't Rizy and it is risky. **Parisiana** is done in the inevitable rouge hues; lowdown show of 15 strippers or seminudes plus a ½-dozen solos; the dancing girls mix with the baldies, but all the talent is rooted until 4 A.M.; a chomp for admission; the proprietor doesn't tolerate cottonmouths, for even the teetotaler must order an unfortified "Sport Cocktail." We wish we'd saved that excursion for our barber, because we sure got clipped here. **Erotica** also offered us a 1st-class crew cut; they will murder your faith in the Boy Scout Oath. **Ellis Elliot**, once the leader in the girlie league, now has such poor talent and horrible lack of exhaust fans that it has become to us an economy-size disappointment. For pickups, the **Café Express** turns on the steam at its central Kaiserstrasse address. If it's a quick belt you're after, ankle over one block from the station to the **Lili Franz Bar**, **New York City Bar**, **Kasino Bar**, **Cocett Bar**, or several dozen more to quell that raging thirst. Never, incidentally, rendezvous at the **Rendezvous Bar**. A friend of this *Guide* reports that the ladies here all hold Ph.D.'s in the later-described "champagne racket." The **Star Cabaret** shines in a similar magnitude, but the next-door **Sex Theatre** is fair enough for raw, no-nonsense overdoses of gut-and-creaky grinds. **Dr. Müller's**, with several midtown sites, purveys porn to the masses. It is possibly the most reliable spot of all for unknotting any kinks, too.

An unsavory sample of many a Frankfurter's night life can be encountered on the selected streets where "taxi girls" ply their winsome trade (there are no meters in the vehicles, however!). Kaiserstrasse and Taunusstrasse are 2. of the busiest lovers' lanes that traffic in this rolling sport. The Mossellestrasse and Elbestrasse also are reasonably safe; these areas are policed to some degree. At ALL costs, avoid the shanties in the so-called Gypsy Court. These are murder—and we are not just employing a figure of speech. More details under "Tips" at the end of this section.

Munich has quite a variety of night spots. Our number one choice is the subterranean lode of the **Hotel Bayerischer Hof**. Split-level gem with the bar and wraparound tables mounted high and a dance circle below; brick and timber décor; central heating by some of the hottest bands on the Continent; appetizing snacks and good honest drinks; steady clientele of the prettiest natives and most discerning night wanderers from afar. Tops in Bavaria. The **Hilton** features pana-romantics and dancing on its 15th floor. Also in hotel circles, the Holiday Inn's **Yellow Submarine** packs a lot of firepower. Don't flinch when a shark swims by your porthole—strong drink when you're in this drink. Our independent nominee is **Eve**, a sophisticated lady who is tastefully ornamented. Continuous show beginning at 11:30 P.M.; the inevitable door snip; at tables, the house policy requires a bottle of champagne (expensive to astronomical) or a ½-bottle of whisky; individual drinks grudgingly served at bar; teetalers find themselves in the squeezer, with orange juice at nectar price levels per cup (and it's been cut!). Without straining a whit, your eyes normally can't miss a clutch of one-dozen Grade-A B-girls. **Ba-ba-lu**, in Schwabing, draws the Smart Young Set, plus a heavy Italian patronage. Now refashioned and fresher than ever; electrified and electrifying combo turned on at top volume; popular bar where they ask your preference in brands of whisky; no cabaret; you, the client, do the performing. Lots of fun IF your eardrums are made of Bessemer steel. The nearby **Big Apple** pulls in the same youth market; its core is more seedy, however. **Käuzchen** takes us back to the bearcat-and-raccoon-coat days. Parisian ambiance woven through 2 adjoining garret-style rooms; color-paned skylight; dark, cozy, and informal; one of the liltingest Memphis jazz bands we've ever eared (the man on that licorice stick was blowing pure candy). If you're in that heyday mood, here's a "Couch" that is the cat's pajamas. The neighboring **Scotch Kneipe** scotched us as a woody, airless den hacked out in zestless log manorisms; not our lodge, but quite popular. **Die Spritz'n** is even smaller, closer, and thus "with it" tonight.

Nibbles available at both. **Capt'n Cook** ran a trimmer ship, say we. The skipper is plastered-in-Paris on the main deck; polished interior and polished passenger list; a cargo of pleasure. **Gaslight Club**, a 50-yard stagger from Ba-ba-lu, struck us as one of the better examples of the city's teen-type discothèques. Wooden sawtooth ceiling; twin plank bars; excellent spirits tumbled into a hefty tumbler. Smart, gay, and popular—but almost exclusively for youngbloods. **Nachteule** is also chiefly for those who haven't begun to vote. **Schwabylon**, a multicolored mechanical colossus of a fun factory, resides next to the Holiday Inn. Look for this wildly painted "aircraft carrier superstructure"—but then *who could miss it?* Wow! **Luna** shines brightest for GI's. **Gisela** is jumping up; it's fun again for a more senior following. **Bongo** drums up a tropical never-never-land atmosphere. If whisky is your sauce, you must hike up at 1 of its 4—count 'em, 4—bars staffed by native houris; if you want to glim the show, a bottle of wine (how suave!) is SOP; 2 dance floors; intermittent entertainment. Also one of the best of its league in Germany. **Intermezzo** is popular with a young crowd. Small show that's a sizzler; our beverage was served in a Haig & Haig bottle, but some villain had "pinched" the genuine article; smooth band; aging ladies of the evening. Take pocket change, because the barmaid made it clear she considers it a mortal sin to break big bills. Our former favorite for soft serenades and persuasive sipping was **St. James Club.** Now that the John Begg barrel has been debunged, the warm furniture moved out, the excellent combo replaced by 8-track tapes, cows go a-mooing at the bar steerage, and staffers with arithmetical deficiencies hired—it fills us with sorrow. Closed Sunday. **P-1** has a more charming atmosphere, except the cocktail lounge still looked moth-eaten on our latest night flight. Inner sanctum with timber and oil paintings; same bar design as St. James' had before it lost its saintliness, plus a balcony as well. Very "In" tonight, but tomorrow, who knows? **Cin-Cin**, near the Four Seasons, is pleasant, too. Circular bar, semicircular booths, no circular women, but very sleek, chic Executive Setters and slim German Pointers. A cozy niche for swanky-panky. Some of the student hangouts in Schwabing, Munich's "Little Montmartre," are amusing and colorful; typical examples are **Heuboden**, a tramcar known as the **Subway** which was formerly called Käfig (the best), **Siegesgarten**, and **Badewanne**. **Hängematte** is so heavy and so grimly joyous it's not for Americans; miserable ventilation too. **Lola Montez**, across from the Hofbräuhaus, seemed routine. Tillbury, in the same district, was a socko decorative success, but now it has become rather routine as a steak-joint-*cum*-disco-club titled the **Come-In**. We Walked-Out. **Domicile** is the hottest and coolest stop for jazz. **Jack's Bar** is another jernt where the gals have mastered the "champagne racket"; hold your hat. As for **Moulin Rouge**, they sheared us here just like dull-witted sheep, efficiently, neatly, and ruthlessly. Just the place to whine when you dine; champagne at the alto-stratospheric stratum; not recommended even to Fidel Castro. Flower power? **Blow Up** blew up and blew out. This same corporation later opened a sequel in its **Citta 2000** complex. Restaurants, shops, bowling lanes, a discothèque —almost anything except a much-needed clinic for ruptured eardrums. The theme, in our opinion, is pure claptrap, whether it be musical, sartorial, visual, or gustatory.

The prostitutes who used to line the aptly-named Nymphenburgerstrasse (and were banned several years ago) are back again. But now they parade Landsberger Strasse, near the outskirts of the city, and Josephspitalstrasse, where they must remain in doorways or passages to avoid arrest for "street-walking." From $35 to $70 is the customary fee (not counting, of course, the medical treatment which usually follows). Anyone who touches this group is a con-genital idiot and imbecile. Hausfrauen? In our advanced age of techno-logical nomenclature, the most famous name in the local trade is **Mex Haus** (112 Hohenzollernstrasse). The state winks at its hygienically (we hear) useful function. No credit cards accepted. P.S. When it was inaugurated, its name was Imex Haus, but shortly afterward it changed its moniker because of a complaint from a corporation that bore the same title. (We can imagine the peculiar customer mail *that* company undoubtedly received!)

Düsseldorf 's more finely feathered night owls generally alight, become a-lit, and trip a light-fantastic evening at the **Hilton's** 1890 Club (see "Ho-tels"). Slightly older fowl and slower of wing usually perch at the Belle Epoque of the **Intercontinental**. The migrations of additional afterdark revel-ers have their choice of about 50 so-called dancing-bars—small drop-ins with glib bar girls who pour the drinks (often from tampered stocks), hostesses who cannot leave before 5 A.M., dim lights, postage-stamp dance floors, and music of sorts. Their vogue changes from year to year. **Salome** and **Queen**, jointly (no pun) owned, specialize in luscious dehydrated B-girls, elegant dimness, and white-hot price tags. Be careful. Disco-haunts include the **Barcelona** (a Wild West saloon ambiance, plus a loooong bar), the **Lord Nelson** (nautical rig; snacks and light meals from the galley), and the **Big Apple** (youthful and green). **Rio-Rita** is on the comeback trail—but there's still a long, long trail a-winding. **Kokette** is small, *intime,* slick, and coquettish; sexy loners on a lily-pad stage; whisky crudely cut—and at a surgeon's billing per slice; teem-ing with attractive yum-yums. **Klamotte** is replete with baubles, bangles, and beady-eyed babes; the ladies will provide conversation in depth; the customer must provide his wallet's ceiling. A rough spot. We'd prefer to court those same kicks with **Erotica**—that is, if we'd already finished reading the last issue of the *Plumbers' Quarterly. Klein Paris* would serve almost the same function. **Black Bottom** is for dancing; bottom drawer, in our opinion. **Das Kommödchen** is amusing for topical humor, all of it in German, *natürlich. Fatty's Atelier* is deep, narrow, and lamplit; fun for a sip, but nothing more. **Charley's**, the **Old Fashioned**, and **Bonbonnière** are bars within an olive's throw of each other; all are respectable *if* you respect their normal quota of sucker tactics and other perils. **New Orleans** (for dancing) and **Der Pferde-stall** (for nuzzling) are both owned by the stylish, high-quality Bateau Ivre (see "Restaurants"); they are okay. The niches along Hunsrückstrasse near the corner of Bolkerstrasse are mostly for late late libations and sweepup operations after the evening is spent—and so are you.

Cologne's leading nightspot for the young executive set is **Big Ben**—at this point in time, that is. **Love Story** also tells a similar tale. For lone males, **Kokett** takes a cupcake. Intimate as the inside of a Turk's tent; draped walls; mirrored panels; drumhead dance pad. A prude might say that the waitresses' black costumes are cut too low where they should be high (and vice versa) —but we wouldn't. Sex-elating strips by delicious "singles," and good whisky.

Fine for cozy cornerings. **Chez Nous** offers *vous* about 12 tables backed by a tiny bar, short "shows" every 20 minutes, shorter but untampered-with libations, and comparatively bundled-up B-girls. Okay for snorting, but not for serious cavorting. **Goldener Spiegel** reflects a boudoir mood. Tiny bar at entrance; larger one farther back; candlelight and frilly wrought-ironwork; well-wrought bar girls who were not predatory on our swing; smooth trio for dancing; snuggling in the Frenchy booths at the periphery. Pretty good for its type. In the same neighborhood, nighthawks can also wing in at **Westminster**. **Play Boy**, **Black Horse** and **P-7** spin for discothèque-niks.

Hanover's afterdark scene perks brightly. Sophisticates don their dandiest duds and shoot straight for the **Calenberger Bar** of the Intercontinental (see "Hotels"). Cabaret addicts usually prefer **Eve** first (pickups available, but house girls chained to the bar stools until 5 A.M.), **Pigalle** second, and **Jenseits** third (former showman Jens behind the bar periodically breaks into song-and-joke sessions for the happy throng). **Ex** is the leading dance oasis and discothèque. Glass-bulb décor; fascinating vitrine with a montage of musical instruments; plaid bar; rouge carpets; quite nice. **Pendel**, across the street, is under the same ownership; it has an interesting clock theme, which unfortunately seems to be running down. The **Journal** wins our cup for strictly quaffing; it's a 2nd home for newspapermen or writers who happen to be in town. **Löwenbräu** shouldn't be missed by seekers of local color; typically Germanic; sudsy to its core. Avoid all streetwalkers in this city, chaps. They ply through the Steintor area at from $50 to $100 per car-hop. These babes too often work in cahoots with strong-arm gangmen who poise in the shadows until the strategic moment, and then the ponce will pounce.

In *Bonn*, the Old Fashion, near the Old Town Hall, now calls herself **Eve** but what's in a name? Brass stools; electrified "kerosene" lamps; copper dance floor; an ancient bicycle hanging from the ceiling; these and other curios form the décor. Supper available, recorded music only. You won't weep if you miss it. The **Carlton** is another one that doesn't turn us on. Why not drop in at the **Steigenberger Hotel** for a nip or drive over to Cologne if insomnia strikes and if there's an itch that *really* needs scratching?

Wiesbaden's leader is the prim and proper **Park**; afternoon openings with magic acts and jugglers, then growing riper as the day grows older. **Intermezzo** spotlights buff-tone strippers. **Parisiana Bar** comes up with revues and booze, but little to amuse.

When *Nürnberg*'s night shadows fall and masculine temperatures rise, **Chérie** is the most popular root of their fever; they quaff costly libations to see women who don't even wear clothes, poor things. **Erotica** follows suit in this suitless art. Many similar spots line Luitpoldstrasse, if anyone is a glutton for torture.

For *Berlin*, see its independent chapter earlier in the *Guide*. In other centers, consult the local Tourist Office or your hotel concierge for the necessary information. You'll usually find plenty of action in the larger towns, because Germans love excitement after the working day is over.

§TIPS: There are 3 types of bar girls: those who pour the drinks and stay in back of the bar (few men handle this work in nightclubs), those who sit with the customers along the front of the bar, and those who do both. Most of them drink real liquor instead of tea; most expect a sizable tip on top of their drinks; few, if any, are permitted to leave before closing time.

The overspilling "Champagne Racket" is one the lonesome or randy sucker is likely to meet in almost any 2nd-rate hideaway. Here's how the Teutonic treatment works: Amiable Homo-*sap*- iens picks up a cuddlesome companion in a bar. The flaxen Saxon suggests they buy a bottle of bubbly and retire to her apartment, where they can "relax." The Sekt appears at the table—preopened—so of course they *must* drink it before leaving the joint. Then a 2nd jug appears by magic—also preopened—and the 3rd one the babe smashes by "accident" on the floor! By this time, if Mr. Jerko doesn't realize he's getting Sekt without sex, he deserves Jug Number Four.

As a footnote to our previous comments about Frankfurt, the upper crust of the Sex-for-Marks Circuit has banded together in what might facetiously be called a loosely run co-op. Each speaks at least one foreign language, maintains a plush apartment, and drives an elegant car. If the gentleman meets a blonde but prefers a brunette, he is passed along to the coiffure hue of his choice. Most engagements are arranged through hotel bellhops.

Are you a *Playboy, Oui,* or *Penthouse* subscriber? If so, you'll undoubtedly spy your favorite centerfold teaser billed into the sleaziest bars of almost any city. These tempting photos are used to lure suckers inside on a vague promise that these come-on dollies are stripping for the fellas. Since it's all nothing but bait, of course, please read the fine print outside all clubs before jackrabbiting inside.

TAXIS   In the larger cities, taxis are fairly plentiful. Lots of new ones, because competition is tough; most are in the Mercedes, Opel, or Datsun size and they're comfortable. They're cheap when compared, for example, with the Swiss or Belgian brotherhood.

TRAINS   The German Federal Railways surpass almost any other system in Europe today. Trains are punctual, clean, and comfortable. New DB (for "Deutsche Bundesbahn") sleepers offer individually adjustable air conditioning, broad beds with foam-rubber mattresses, quilts, folding walls, electric razor outlets, shower-baths, and many other innovations; DB diners are efficient and reasonably priced; Trans-Europ-Express and Intercity electric locomotives which can average 125 mph on certain runs are painted a distinctive cream-and-burgundy (others are cream and turquoise). Prides of the line are the *Helvetia*, the *Wilhelm Busch*, the *Porta Westfalica*, the *Münchner Kindl*, the all-sleeper *Komet*, the *Roland*, the *Blue Gentian*, the *Rheinpfeil*, and the *Gambrinus*. During summer months, the fabled *Orient Express* connects Paris with Bucharest. But Germany's slickest choochoo is the crack *Rheingold*, with its elevated, air-conditioned observation dome. The *Blauer Enzian* (without a dome), is its near-twin. The *Parsifal* is still another speedy contender. All of these stars now are linked into a First-class-only grid called Intercity. After the network's quick-lunch counters on wheels—buffet units that serve low-cost meals and snacks—became big hits, DB forged out 28 more with lower counters and seats à la U.S. drugstore style. Air-conditioned dining cars are attached to most of these trains today.

Almost all German trackage and switches have now undergone the so-called seamless-welding process; the rhythmic clickety-clack of the wheels is a nostalgic memory nearly everywhere.

Tariffs are more than reasonable, by U.S. standards. And don't forget that great travel bargain—the Eurailpass (see "Let's Be European").

First-class is worth the investment. Second-class, usually quite crowded, is cheaper and sometimes agreeable. Buy your international railway tickets and railway agency coupons *outside* Germany, because you'll save money. On domestic rail travel, substantial reductions (especially on summer weekdays) are available. Consult the German Tourist Offices or your travel agent about these. Within the country, many stations now provide computer data print-outs; just punch the key coded with your destination and out pops all the scoop on departure times, connections, arrival and cost.

§TIPS: On most of the better cars (not necessarily the streamlined ones) seats which to the eye are completely ordinary can be lowered like a barber's chair by an ingenious mechanical arrangement.

"Bunk cars" *(Liegewagen)* are available to budgeteers on many intra-German and some international night runs. They're sort of "Economy Pull-mans," with no curtains and 3 decks of 6 bunks per compartment; the passenger sleeps (if he can) in his clothes. Far, far better than sitting up, even in those newfangled chairs.

For sufferers of compartment-claustrophobia, the Frankfurt–Vienna sleeper connection has long had roomier dimensions with wider beds. Air conditioning can be regulated by each individual by use of bunkside knobs. These cars are appearing on many other runs today—oops, tonight.

On medium-short hauls (*e.g.,* Cologne–Frankfurt), the better trains are now beating the airliners' time—airport-to-city coverage considered.

Several fast trains offer continuous telephone service en route and more are getting it.

For tired motorists, piggyback service rides your car along with you between various international and domestic points. These destinations have become so numerous they literally pepper the European map. They require too much space for us to include them here. Please check with your travel agent for the latest details. Sleepers and bunk cars carried; reservations later than one week in advance accepted on space-available basis only; comparatively high prices, varying with bumper-to-bumper measurements.

Luggage problems? Get rid of your heavy pieces by registering them through to your destination; fees are in the flea-bite class. Since most centers offer this service, you can forward your possessions direct to your lodgings by rail and post bus; it costs only a little more than the railway shipping charge. Actually, the most painless method is to turn over all your bags to your hotel porter at check-out time—and he'll forward them direct to your room in your next hotel, probably via the train which you ride. Wonderful for lone ladies or lazy folks like us! A score of depots now feature self-service hand carts, just as in your supermarket, into which you may pile your effects and roll them to the taxi or tram platforms; they display signs reading *Für Ihr Gepäck* ("For Your Baggage"); free of charge to date, and so popular they'll soon be universal.

BUSES AND CARS　Most long-haul buses, particularly in sightseeing districts, are modern—and gentle to the area in contact with the seat. Many offer adjustable chairs, public-address system, radio loudspeakers, and sliding or glass tops for maximum visibility. The German Federal Railways, the German Federal Post, and the German Touring Company all run good ones. If it weren't for the fiendish traffic in most urban centers, this would be a delightful way to cover the country.

Although we still haven't had a chance to try them, dozens of kind readers have sent rave reports about motor-coach tours of the Bavarian Alps, the Allgäu Alps, the Black Forest roads, and other scenic high spots. Some of them even go to Salzburg and the Tyrol in Austria. These tours are astonishingly cheap; all agree that the buses are excellent, service is frequent, and the routes are glorious.

Automobiles to hire? The German Federal Railways inaugurated an admirable service: When the traveler buys his train ticket at any of 130 major stations, for a small returnable deposit he may order a self-drive or chauffeur-driven car to meet him at any of 10 important destinations (Düsseldorf, Frankfurt am Main, Hamburg, Munich, Bonn, Cologne, Heidelberg, and the like). Approved private companies are used locally; rates vary with the type of car, but all are comparatively reasonable; no profits accrue to the railroads. If you shouldn't want to bother with this more generalized facility, we've had complete satisfaction for years from the firm of **Philipp Keller** (Schlossstrasse 32-36) in *Frankfurt am Main*. Our good friend Peter, as Mr. Keller is known, has 8 chauffeur-driven cars with English-speaking drivers—plus a close working affiliation with the best self-drive company in the Frankfurt area. Careful, reputable, thoughtful service; highest recommendation. In *Munich*, we've also had good luck over the years with **Auto-Sixt** (Seitzstrasse 9-11). This efficient outfit, Germany's largest car-hire company, offers more than 400 self-drive or chauffeur-drive vehicles to the motorist—all brand-new or very late models in perhaps a dozen different makes (including a splendid Mercedes 600 with TV, sliding roof, and a constantly replenished cocktail bar). Write to genial Erich or Regina Sixt, both of whom speak fluent English and who offer a special warmth to Guidesters, for further details. **Severin & Luer** is the best we've come across that is rooted in *Hamburg.*

ADAC and AvD, the 2 most important German automobile clubs, offer tour information in most cities. In the ports of Hamburg and Bremerhaven, and at a number of key frontier crossings, they and the German Tourist Association have set up special bureaus to help foreign visitors plan their trips. No charge. There's also a free motorists' aid service for outlanders stranded on the autobahns. Just flag down a red or yellow patrol car or get to one of the telephones set 7 miles apart throughout the network. (Berlin offers the same, but until we see what effect the new East–West agreements have, we still discourage driving to—or having a car in—the Divided City.) In the Alps, the ADAC rents snow chains to winter trippers; your small deposit is refunded when you return 'em. Postscript for families: Children under 12 must ride in the back seat, but an exception is made if there is an overflow of offspring.

AIRLINE   Lufthansa, the German National Airline, boasts an all-jet fleet of Boeing 747's, 707's, 727's, and 737's, plus the DC-10 and the Airbus.

Stewardesses are generally pleasant; all speak English. Some stewards, however, can turn into snippy, officious smart-alecks at times. On one recently completed Hamburg–London passage, nothing could have been more important to our pair than their own wisecracks (aimed at ladies as well as gentlemen) and their incessant peddling of tax-free booty; the comfort of their ticketholders appeared to come last. Efficiency seems to have preoccupied this company so pervadingly that inflight food service has vanished on domestic hops; beverages are decanted aloft, but the new system is to hand out lunchboxes at the airports to those about to climb aboard. The excuse is that this is necessitated by bigger passenger load factors and shorter flight times between points. Fie! Their schedules are approximately the same as they have been since the inception of jets. Thus, if Lufthansa truly believes this farcical reasoning, why does it serve food at all? Frankly, this reporter views it as a transparent hoodwink to cut down on passenger attention—a ploy motivated by penny-pinching and by the general decline of personnel initiative. Moreover, anyone who knows anything about aircraft design immediately recognizes this as a step to eliminate galleys aboard, thus gaining additional seating space. Shame on this carrier! The First-class "Senator," which we've never ridden, flies between German terminals and American points. An aura of *Gemütlichkeit* is allegedly added by beer service from a freshly tapped keg called *Dämmerschoppen* ("dusk-pint"). The barrel is rolled down the aisle on a cart also laden with smoked ham and pumpernickel. You may also sit in one of the *no-smoke* zones (where tobacco, not ham, is prohibited). Sorry, we just don't know how good or how bad its North Atlantic service is compared to the competition. One of these days we'll see. Lufthansa, incidentally, just has inaugurated a reduced-rate hotel plan that's split into 3 price categories and is available in 10 European countries; the savings are significant, so check with the airline before booking your independent accommodations. It might save you a bundle.

DRINKS   Most connoisseurs (if they weren't born in Burgundy, Bordeaux, or Champagne) agree that Germany makes the finest white wines of the world. With typically Teutonic attention to detail, every bottle of character bears its full pedigree on the label—type, year, district, grower, shipper, and often even the condition of the grape at the picking ("Spätlese" for fully ripe, "Beerenauslese" for overripe, etc.). "Riesling" is a generic term for any wine of the Riesling grape, as opposed to the Sylvan grape. Moselle, Rhine, Ahr, Franconia, Palatinate, and others are named for their specific districts or valleys, although technically they could be called Rieslings. Steinwein is harsh and rough; most visitors prefer others. Hock, derived from "Hochheimer," is erroneously used by many British drinkers as a blanket appellation for all Rhines and similar types; the vineyards for this are actually on the north bank of the Main.

Most Americans seem to be familiar with only one German name—Liebfraumilch. Practically speaking, there are 2 good bottles of this for 10 bad ones, because this banner covers *all* of the output of the Rheinhessen region.

Ask for Oppenheimer Schlossberg, Niersteiner Domthal, or Nackenheimer Rotenberg for delicious examples, and forget about most others. Among late offerings, the '76 pressings are among the finest in the lineage.

All sugarless types (Moselle, Ruwer, Saar) are best when young.

If you're a zillionaire, "Beerenauslese" and "Trockenbeerenauslese" are the topmost rungs of wine quality (see below); they're so difficult to produce and so limited in supply that you'll pay from $35 to $120 per bottle at any fine restaurant (a 1921 vintage brings about $225!). They're categories, not brand names.

If you're a plain millionaire, Schloss Johannisberger is the finest "regular" wine in the land; the best years run up to perhaps $45. Other winners, not as expensive, are Deidesheimer Kieselberg Riesling Auslese, Berncasteler Doctor, and Piesporter Lay. In the medium range, our favorite is Jesuitengarten Riesling Auslese, a Palatinate variety available at Frankfurt's Rheinpfalz Weinstuben (see "Restaurants") at about $2.50 per 3-glass-carafe.

But don't be dazzled or intimidated by those important-sounding names, because starting with the '71 vintages, the government uncorked 3 general classifications for every drop of nectar produced in the country and set official testing numbers for both of the top grades. The categories are: Table wines ("Tafelwein") for the lowliest entries; Quality wines ("Qualitätswein") for the middle-bung brands; and Quality wines with Award ("Qualitätswein mit Prädikat") for the choicest crushings. That last (and best) batch becomes, in ascending order: Kabinett, Spätlese, Auslese, and with the aforementioned Beerenauslese and Trockenbeerenauslese the kings. The penalty for slapping an exalted label on a lower class distillate? Loss of the right to have it tested by the pros, which automatically means condemnation to the cheaper Table wine vine. And please don't be put off, either, by that humble designation. We could tick off at least 8 other European nations that would trade half of their agricultural budgets for the ability to grow German Table grapes.

German "champagne," called "Sekt," is, in actuality, sparkling Rhine or Moselle wine. Remarkable strides have been made in recent years to improve its quality. Today, selected labels of the *brut* types have an urbane and noble character. Mumm Dry (no relative of the French brand of the same name) is an excellent candidate for your white; Henkell Rosé is a delightful pink nectar. But far too many others are still cloyingly sweet, less bubbly than their French originals, and repulsive to the knowledgeable international palate.

German beer is as appetizing as ever—and it's about 30¢ to 50¢ per large mug in the average place. Fritz guzzles almost 256 pints a year; blotter-mouthed Bavarians turn up their steins with an astonishing 353 pints apiece annually. The choice is vast. Despite Common Market urgings to create a weaker pan-European brew, German malt masters are determined to stick to their centuries-old traditions. There are Helles (light), Pilseners (light in color but stronger), Dunkles (dark), Weisse (extra light), served in Berlin and Bavaria during the summer only, Berliner Weisse (Berlin wheat-malt specialty which is light and lemony)—more varieties than the tourist can tilt a mug at. The Bockbier season is January to March; this beer is one of the most delicious of all. Best-known brews are those of Munich, Dortmund, Donaueschingen (Fuerstenberg), Nürnberg (Siechen, Tucher), Würzburg, and Kulmbach. (The last is famous for being frozen into an iceblock which packs a 9% alcoholic punch after the solidification!) As a curiosity, you might like to try a stein of Weihenstephan. This brewery, in Freising, has been running continuously for almost 950 years; the yeast in your potion first saw the light of day in the eleventh century.

Imported spirits are available everywhere. Popular brands of Scotch, rye, and U.S.-Canadian blends pour with a mirthful abandon in the population centers and resorts. These have become the white-collar tipples of Germany. (Schnapps and Kümmel, the former standbys, have correspondingly gone out of vogue.)

THINGS TO SEE Here, in order of popularity, are the sights which this year's visitor to Germany is most likely to seek out:

1. **Rhine excursions**.With the addition of the Amsterdam/Rotterdam–Basle/Frankfurt services to the traditional Düsseldorf–Cologne–Mainz runs, a choice of spending anything from a few hours to a fortnight on this greatest of western European rivers has been opened for the vacationer. Comfortable, modern steamers of the "White Fleet" offer full-day excursions, overnight round trips or inexpensive intermediate voyages. Unhappily, schedules are not always reliable—so sometimes you may spend longer than you wish in an undesirable port. The *Helvetia,* more luxurious than her sister ship *Europa,* the newer and better *Britannia, France, Deutschland,* and *Nederland* each plies the route between Rotterdam and Basle 3 times a month—5 days up (6 after mid-September), 4 days down. Then we have the 3500-passenger (yikes!) *Loreley* (which carried Queen Elizabeth some summers ago) and the newer 700-ton *Rhein;* with her sister, the *Drachenfels;* they ply the Cologne-Mainz express route daily between April and October (and may God help the 3499th ticketholder, who'll need a coating of grease to wiggle himself aboard). If you're making a solo journey, expect to share your cabin with someone (of the same gender, fortunately or unfortunately). Avid sightseers, particularly mature or elderly ones, like these runs; younger, more volatile ones sometimes find them monotonous and boring. If you're among the latter group, you might consider making the Cologne-Mainz run aboard the *Rheinpfeil*, a 64-passenger hydrofoil which cruises at 37 mph. Hold onto your hat! Most sailings (or those also linked into the Moselle) are scheduled between March and October, but more runs are being stitched into the winter pattern every year. In some cases, part way may be covered by rail on a combined arrangement.

If you start from Cologne, you may find it much, much wiser to debark at Rüdesheim or Assmannshausen. Low water levels in summer often delay dockings at the Wiesbaden or Mainz terminals as much as 3 hours. If you want to be sure of reaching your bed by a decent hour, hop off early and motor down to your destination. The previously mentioned Philipp Keller service in Frankfurt (see "Buses and Cars") will meet you.

2. **Berlin**, if conditions permit. (Please turn back, earlier in the book, to its independent section.)

3. **Bavarian castles**, particularly Neuschwanstein, Herrenchiemsee, Linderhof, and the Residence Palace at Würzburg. (Check the German Federal

Railways about its combined rail-bus tours during weekends in summer.)
From Munich there's an easy excursion to the Cloister of **Andechs**—first by
subway to Herrsching am Ammersee, then from the exit by bus to your
destination. It's a baroque joy! The neighboring restaurant can fill your mortal
coil while your eyes give feast to your soul. Inexpensive and splendid on a
sunny day.

4. **Churches** and **cathedrals** at Ulm, Würzburg, Munich, Freiburg, Mainz,
Worms, Speyer, Cologne, Bremen, Marburg, Limburg, Regensburg, Trèves,
and Aachen.

5. The **Neckar Valley** and Heidelberg.

6. The **Hag** development and "Böttcherstrasse" in Bremen.

7. The **medieval castles** along the Moselle (especially beautiful for driving
or for delightful loafing aboard one of the tiny steamers). The Rhine, Danube,
Ahr, Lahn, Main, and Weser are also studded with ancient fortresses.

8. The **"Black Forest Post"** (from Karlsruhe through the upper Black
Forest to Freiburg), the "Black Forest–Lake Constance Post" (from Freiburg
through the lower Black Forest to Constance), and the "German Alpine
Post" (from Lindau through the Allgäu Alps via Garmisch–Partenkirchen to
Berchtesgaden—summer only). These fine bus tours offer dirt-cheap rates of
6 pfennigs per kilometer, modern equipment, and magnificent scenery. The
"Romantic Road" tours (see "Hotels") between Würzburg and Füssen in the
Allgäu Alps (also summer only) and the "Castle Road" tours from Mann-
heim via Heidelberg and Rothenburg to Nürnberg are outstanding, too.

9. The **motorboat rides** on the Neckar between Heidelberg and Neckar-
steinach, on the Moselle between Coblenz and Cochem (mentioned above),
or Trier (summer only) and other points, and on the Danube between Passau
and Linz. Let's not forget, either, about the slaphappy raft rides on Salzach,
an Inn tributary, and on the Isar.

10. **Bayerischer Wald**, a 30,000-acre national park nestling along the
Czech border near Regen. This first legally designated wilderness in Germany
abounds with wolf, lynx, otter, red deer, bear, beaver, alpine marmot, and 2
rare species of owl (Ural and pygmy). Some captive fauna is available to lazy
shutterbugs.

Hitler's Eagle's Nest, atop Mt. Kehlstein at Berchtesgaden and again
owned by the State of Bavaria, receives hordes of tourists. Take the special
Bundes-Post bus up the safe but hair-raising mountain road to a point 450
feet from the summit—and then ride the brass-plated elevator through solid
rock up to the "Tea House." While the comforts are 2nd-rate, the Alpine
panorama should leave you breathless. Other Hochland flings? Steeplejacks,
free-balloonists, and edelweiss gatherers with greater stomach than your
craven correspondent will be pleased to know that more than 100 funiculars
and teleferics now await the hardy for conveyance to almost any pinnacle in
the land.

Son et Lumière ("Sound and Light") or similar spectacles have caught on
big in Germany. One outstanding example is at Schloss Herrenchiemsee, a
copy of Versailles Palace on an island in the Chiemsee, about 46 miles down
the fast autobahn from Munich. The castle is fully furnished with its original
treasures and illuminated by more than 4000 wax candles; chamber music is

played; the pools and gardens are on show, but Mad King Louis' (Ludwig II of Bavaria) pornographic pictures are not. Every Saturday evening from May to September; book in advance in American Express, Munich, or you won't get in; arrive before 5:30 P.M., after which the palace tours end for the day; no photography permitted.

On a completely different note is the museum in the crematory of **Dachau** concentration camp, a 45-minute subway and bus ride from Munich, where at least 30-thousand human beings were cremated. Surviving inmates, representing 21 nations, established this monument to atrocity. Documents, orders, and photographs relating to the torture and extermination of prisoners are displayed.

Finally there's the Richard Wagner Festival at Bayreuth during July and August, the Munich Opera Festival during the same period, concerts by the Berliner Philharmonic Orchestra the calendar round and more folk festivals, home festivals, jubilees, fairs, religious events, expositions, congresses, and conventions than anyone can shake a stick at—or attend. Ask the German National Tourist Association or your nearest German National Tourist Office (New York, Chicago, San Francisco, Montreal) for their excellent programs of these topical events. If you write for tickets, do so by late November; after that, it's often a gamble.

§TIPS: Weather forecasts, road conditions, and information on Germany and its people are broadcast in English and 7 other languages during the tourist season over the South German Radio Station in Stuttgart. They are beamed during the musical program from 10 A.M. to 10:45 A.M.

Note for hobbyists, efficiency experts, and industrial spies: Germany's "**Open House**" program flings wide the doors of hundreds of the nation's factories and workshops. If you want to see how your Porsche, Volkswagen, or Mercedes-Benz is glued together, how they sandpaper the lenses of your Zeiss-Ikon camera, or how those trained fork-tongued aardvarks lick the gum on the labels on all those bottles of German beer or wine, here's your chance. The German NationalTourist Information Office in New York will provide a long list of the names and addresses of these hospitable companies or ateliers. Naturally, your welcome will be warmer if you'll write ahead and advise them of your arrival date.

TIPPING In all German hotels there is an automatic service charge of 10% to 15% of the price of the room. Now it is usually lumped into your overall bill rather than itemized separately. For meal service in hotels and restaurants the service bite is 10% to 15%; it no longer must be noted on the overall billing. For drinks most anywhere a separate tax (*Getränkesteuer*) is levied, but it does not often appear on your tab; generally this is 10%, but in Munich and Stuttgart it is 20%; you're still expected to shell out something for the bartender, however.

Tip about what you would in New York. Remember the concierge, maid, washroom attendant, baggage porter, valet, room waiter, and barber, if you use them—all in very small amounts. Forget doormen and theater ushers unless you are feeling expansive, generous, or 3-martini-ish.

HOW TO BUY A CAMERA Here are some private tips from one of the world's most illustrious and respected photographic suppliers, gleaned from more than 40 years of direct experience in his famous establishment:

(1) Never buy it near the end of your visit.

(2) Tell your dealer what *kinds* of pictures you will want to take, so that he can advise you which model among the myriads of types is precisely the best one for your purposes.

(3) Give him sufficient time to explain all of its lore and details to you. Then, in front of his eyes, check all of its functions yourself.

(4) Read every word of the instruction booklet without delay.

(5) If you're puzzled about even the smallest point, return to him on the following day so that your understanding and familiarity become 100% complete.

(6) Be certain that all of your electrical sources are fresh—both when you buy and later. Whenever the batteries in automatic cameras, in light meters, and in flashguns are run down, they give incorrect readings.

(7) BEWARE OF THE CHEAPEST OFFER—especially from the discount-house rascals in Germany who are pushing for a quick sale with glib promises of "servicing" which later never materialize. Since it is almost impossible for the layman to spot most technical alterations, it is common practice for them to peddle models which are already out of production. High-grade German cameras and equipment are sold *ONLY* through legitimate, well-established shops; the discount houses are forced to dig up their merchandise elsewhere. Although you'll find these so-called bargains here and in various other European lands, you'd almost surely end up as the loser. Any photo apparatus which does not come directly from the factory does not carry a bona fide guarantee. Charges for repairs of unguaranteed purchases are very often shockingly high.

(8) Thus, be *sure* to patronize only a topflight expert who has a well-trained staff. Should repairs be necessary during the term of your international guarantee or later, he will instantly advise you how to get them done either without charge or at the lowest cost.

(9) The aim of the legitimate dealer is not to sell you the most expensive type, but the *right* type expressly for your own personal requirements. You can count upon his honesty, his candor, and his dependability throughout a lifetime of association. After all, as our friendly great specialist comments, "It has *got* to be this way. A completely satisfied client is any company's best and most profitable recommendation!"

THINGS TO BUY In *Frankfurt am Main*, one of the first places we always head for is that wonderful **J. A. Henckels**, now in 7 more German hubs, plus others outside the country. Almost no one disputes that the pert "Twins," trademark and colophon of this giant since 1731, symbolize the world's finest cutlery, bar none.

Rosenthal? **Studio Haus Gilbert** (Friedenstrasse 10, next to Frankfurter Hof Hotel) is our local magnet for this most famous of German china. Ask for Mr. Peter Klotzer.

Cameras and optical devices? **Foto-Koch** (Kaiserstrasse 26, Am Dorn-busch, and Frankfurt Airport) is by far the best in this area. Good variety; solid reputation; 1-day film processing. Director Mühler (Kaiserstrasse head-quarters) would happily help you with your problems. Bric-a-brac in semipre-cious minerals? A Houston wheeler-dealer warns us against the ethical stan-dards he found at **E. Behm** (Kaiserstrasse 4); we don't know the place. Kaiserstrasse is the toniest shopping street, despite a handful of tourist traps with junk souvenirs; most department stores and larger establishments are on Rossmarkt and Zeil.

In *Munich*, Söhnges (Briennerstrasse 7 and Kaufingerstrasse 34, next to Marienplatz; *Berlin* branches Kurfürstendamm 139, Reichsstrasse 83, Europa-Center, and "Forum Steglitz") is one of the 2 or 3 top optical complexes in the world today. This reporter wouldn't dream of buying his soft contact lenses anywhere else; they're unique.

Kohlroser (Maffeistrasse 14, near the Hotel Bayerischer Hof, across from American Express) is our favorite camera shop in southern Germany—not only because the stock is so extensive but also because Mr. Kohlroser and assistants Schindler, Holzmeier, and Schuermann are all so honest, so kindly, and so interested in doing the best possible job for each client. Again in the past year, we've had at least 3-dozen letters from readers of both our *Shopping Guide* and this *Travel Guide* about how they went out of their way to be helpful and thoughtful—an unusual trait in the extracold world of big-time German commerce. Kohlroser will refund the turnover tax (value added tax) of about 9% through the TAX FREE SHOP ORGANIZATION after the customs declaration form is returned. Every camera in the shop is guaranteed for a minimum of 12 months, even if shipped. On their shelves you'll find, among others, the new small Leika CL, Leika M5, Leikaflex SL2, Rollei 35S, Agfa, Kodak, Linhof, Hasselblad, new Minox 35EL, Fuji, Mamiya, Olympus, Nikon, Asahi, and Minolta lines, plus the Leitz, Bauer, Rollei, and Braun-Nizo Super 8 movie cameras; there are new pocket-size Zeiss binoculars, opera glasses, interchangeable lenses for German and Japanese cameras, automatic slide projectors, flea-size electronic computer flash units, and goodness knows what else; furthermore, the house provides 2-day service on Ektachrome. Sample prices at this writing: Full automatics, $80 to $600; Leica CL, $399; the freshly unveiled Minox 35 EL, $150; Rollei XF, $142; new small Agfa "pocket," $120; latest full automatic Super 8 movie cameras, less than ever before. Superb stocks, superb values—but the most important asset around Kohlroser's is that wonderfully gentle and sweet spirit of theirs. A shutter-bug's heaven!

Germany's biggest **Rosenthal** sales tycoon, the dashing private pilot and porcelain expert Dr. Hans Zoellner, is the son of the factory's original Techni-cal Managing Director (1892 to 1935). His spacious, beautifully decorated store offers the complete collection of the Rosenthal "3 C's"—china, crystal, and cutlery—as well as the best in table- and housewares from Arabia, Dansk, Peil, Royal Berlin and many more. Prices? An astonishing 50% *average* saving against the same merchandise at home! The Theatinerstrasse 8 shop (in the center, near City Hall) carries all Rosenthal Studio-Line products as well as the "Classic Rosenthal" dinner sets ($50 to $2000), gift items ($1 to

$600), plus a vast Hummel collection. Safe shipment guaranteed; huge export and mail-order business; Dr. and Mrs. Zoellner or Miss Oppel will be your guardian angels. None better.

Leather goods and travel aids? It's **Plaschke** (Brienner Strasse 11, a few steps from Kohlroser), which has steadily built up a sterling reputation in individually designed-and-crafted luggage. Fine in every respect.

Nymphenburg (Odenplatz 1) is Rosenthal's only German rival for Cadillac-class porcelains; exquisite. **Hans R. Rothmüller** (Briennerstrasse) is the most distinguished jeweler, with the most distinguished price tags, too. To soothe the Inner Man while She shops for crystal and other superior gift items, **Alois Dallmayr** (Dienerstrasse 14–15) is to dewy-fresh comestibles what Strasbourg is to fois gras. In this space we cannot even *begin* to outline the galore of goodies that awaits your lucky, lucky 5 senses. Ask warmhearted Mr. and Mrs. Willie for their cheerful guidance. Super! For handicrafts, **Wallach** (Residenzstrasse 3) has 2 floors packed to the rafters and a basement bulging with antiques. **Deutsche Werkstätten** (Briennerstrasse 54 and branch) is the marketplace of many independent Bavarian artisans, with accent on furniture, fabrics, lamps, and wooden paintings. No Flea Market in Munich; the so-called Farmer's Market *(Auer Dult)* runs its frenzied course 3 times per year—early April, early August, and October 15 to 23. It's a huge rummage sale with great fun; many a visitor has picked up fine antiques for a song or occasionally a valuable old painting. *Don't miss it* if you're within shooting distance during these special weeks.

Europe's largest underground shopping center—$4,200,000 in cost, 100% air-conditioned, 44 separate stores—swung into action in '72 beneath the Stachus, Munich's main square. Almost simultaneously the Marienplatz, in front of the Rathaus, became a pedestrian island for strollers or buyers.

Shopping streets? Brienner Strasse, Theatinerstrasse, and Maximilianstrasse are the most chichi. Kaufingerstrasse is a pedestrian's paradise. Leopoldstrasse—in fact, Schwabing in general—is not what it used to be, in our eyes.

Berlin establishments have already been covered in the independent chapter on this city.

Shopping hours? Recently standardized throughout the nation, thank goodness: 9 A.M. to 6:30 P.M. Monday through Friday, 9 A.M. to 2 P.M. on most Saturdays, but 9 A.M. to 4 P.M. on the first Saturday of every month.

This is a fair cross section of what you'll find in the rest of Germany. The above cities offer the greatest shopping range, the finest qualities, and the lowest prices on most purchases. Our suggestion would be to concentrate the bulk of your buying in these, and pick up elsewhere only the odd piece which happens to tickle your fancy.

§TIP: Outbound passengers for foreign destinations are eligible for duty-free, tax-free bargains in liquor, cigarettes, cigars, and French perfumes ONLY at the **Airport Shops** in *Frankfurt am Main*, *Hamburg*, *Munich*, *Cologne* and *Düsseldorf*. You won't save a penny on cameras, Rosenthal china, Offenbach leather, or any *German-made* goods, because they're sold here at the same prices as at all German stores.

Dedicated shophounds? Space is too tight here for further listings—so consult this year's extensively revised and up-to-the-minute edition of *Fielding's Shopping Guide to Europe* for more stores, more details, and more lore.

THINGS NOT TO BUY   Anything junky or sleazy, categories which embrace perhaps 25% of the merchandise available to you.

Don't buy nonstandard items in spas, resorts, small towns, villages, or hamlets. Big-city merchants get the break, which they pass along to you.

Women's clothes and hats are much more chic than they were, but in general they're *still* dull (compared to American, French, and other standards). Many of them, too, are tailored for stylish stouts.

The 300-day clock looks intriguing—but if you stare at it hard, it will probably go out of kilter. So delicate that even dusting might throw it off. Not recommended, unless you live in a deep cave.

Electrical equipment is usually wired for 220 volts, and when you plug it (round prongs, not flat stems as ours are) into the 110-volt current in the United States, it will do everything but work. Be sure the product is designed for *both* voltages (most of today's output is).

LOCAL RACKETS   Few rackets are tried on travelers in Germany. Most important is the tendency of unauthorized moneychangers to stick their customers with counterfeit bills.

As in England, the so-called key swindle is back. This is the one where a pickup in a bar or nightclub gives the key to "her apartment" to the sucker for a 50-mark "deposit," promising to meet him there later—but, when he arrives in a lather, he finds it's a tobacco warehouse or empty lot. Other similar slippery practices are described under "Nightclubs."

If you lock your suitcase, leave no valuables unwatched, and try not to look like the "Man Who Arrived This Morning," you should have no troubles. Most visitors find the Germans honest and straightforward.

INFORMATION ON GERMANY   With typical organizational ability and attention to detail, German travel experts set up such an outstanding new holidays program that they put to shame some larger colleagues.

Headquarters and fountainhead of the national and international network is the **German National Tourist Association** (Beethovenstrasse 69, *Frankfurt am Main*). Its General Manager is dynamic young Günther Spazier. Masses of color-illustrated booklets in English, French, German, and 7 other tongues, covering every region of the Federal Republic, are available at the Frankfurt apex or at any of its subordinate offices. These are often an enormous help in the selection of travel goals.

The branches in New York, Chicago, San Francisco, Montreal, Paris, London, Stockholm, Copenhagen, Amsterdam, Madrid, Brussels, Zürich, Rome, Vienna, Tokyo, Johannesburg, and Rio de Janeiro reflect this efficiency. The *New York* headquarters is at 630 Fifth Avenue; Manager Herman Krüger will solve your problems in a trice. In *Chicago*, the GNTO branch is at 104 South Michigan Ave., and the Manager is Hans J. Baumann; in *San Francisco* at 323 Geary St., with R. C. Warren holding the reins;

in *Montreal* at 47 Fundy, P. O. Box 417, Bonaventure, and Henning Schreiber the Canadian boss.

The **German Travel Association** (not to be confused with the official German National Tourist Association, which concerns itself only with promotion outside the homeland) has its own organization to aid the traveler. To date, more than 130 information centers—recognizable by a red plaque with a white *i*—have been accredited by it as worthy of serving the wayfarer. The bulk of these at present are concentrated in the Bavaria, Württemberg, Hesse, and Rhineland districts.

Matriculation at a German university, institute, or professional school? Try the **DAAD** (Deutscher Akademischer Austauschdienst), Kennedyallee 50, 532 Bad Godesberg; it's all at their fingertips, from Abaddon Philosophy to Zebra Zoology.

Greece

Here, with Rome, is 1 of the 2 glittering, shimmering fountainheads of our Western Civilization. Jounce merrily along the pulsing streets of its ancient capital: The golden shadow of Pericles is beside you. Climb the marblecapped Acropolis: You are standing beneath the pillars of mankind's Democracy. Look out to the Aegean: You are smelling the salty sea-swept drifts of early commerce. Watch a pair of brighteyed urchins running out their private marathon: You are experiencing the visible echo of the first Olympic Games, more than 27 centuries ago. At your feet, a white-robed thespian dons a tragic mask, then abruptly shifts to comedy. On your left, Socrates praises "the love of wisdom"—philosophy. On your right gathers a coterie of poets, musicians, architects, astronomers, painters, soldiers, lawyers, doctors, politicians, mathematicians. These were the seeds that germinated in the Plains of Attica and enriched the world. This is Greece. Never mind the origin of your own ancestors. You, with us, share the spirit, the soul, and the treasures of Hellenic heritage.

Not all of her myriad glories, however, are in the past. This year, fresh millions will make the cultural pilgrimage back to one of its main sources where the progeny of Sophocles are waiting to greet them. About 1/5th of the passports carried into this geographical Monument to the Mind will be American. Airliners will swoop in by the squadron to deposit their Icarian hordes on the gleaming tarmac. Twentieth-century Jasons will swagger aboard sleek white barks—plus a few Argonautical tubs—to sail for the dreamlands of Sappho. Islands will be routinely "discovered." The Muse of Inspiration now works overtime in the Greek National Tourist office.

This is a booming, throbbing, go-getting nation that won't even take GO for an answer.

In the past, surface travelers complained that Greece was "too far" or "too hard to get to." 'Tain't so any more! Several sleek, comfort-plus ferries now operate between Brindisi (Italy) and Patras. Stops at Corfu and Igoumenitsa; facilities ranging from airplane-type seats to Deluxe cabins for both day and overnight sojourns; drive-on-drive-off gangways; space for 150 or more cars; running every day of the week during summer, 6 days during fringe periods, and 3 days per week in winter. Additional routings reach Patras from Ancona. There is also piggyback railway service for autos through Italy, a sleeper-bus hookup between Naples and Brindisi in summer, and a viewful coastal highway at the threshold to Greece. The scenic drive now between Patras and the capital takes a mere 3 hours. This Aegean nation is rapidly becoming only a hop from the rest of the Continent for motorists.

CITIES *Athens* (Athinai) with its port of Piraeus (Peiraieus) is the largest, with almost 3-million people; as we mentioned, here's the birthplace and heart of Greek culture, a *must* for all visitors. The poet Palamas described her as "a diamond in the ring of the world." Millions of gallons of paint have been used in sprucing up the capital; Constitution Square, Omonia Square, and other landmarks have been revamped; 5 new public plazas have been opened; the Plaka district has been illuminated by lamps, another fillip of charm. Mount Lycabettus, its looming central hill, now has a cable railway zooming through a 225-yard tunnel which whisks sightseers from Plutarchou and Aristippou Sts. to its crown in 5 minutes. Up top, a restaurant and snack bar operate at full blast. Increased prosperity has brought along its usual handmaiden: Today's narrow streets are bumper-to-tailpipe with cars. *Thessaloniki* (Salonika), up on the Aegean near the Yugoslav border, is 2nd, with about 600 thousand; imposing station in this most important of railway junctions; superb dwelling space, especially in the new deluxe Macedonia Hotel (bid for a sea view here); fevered port with all the color of a nation in motion; heaps of modern buildings; heaps of Byzantine churches; excellent seafood restaurants plus many with international ovens; now becoming a hub for disciples of the sun who are pointed toward Chalkidiki or of excursionists bound for *Philippi* (near Cavalla) or *Pella*, where Alexander the Great was born. *Patras* (Patrai), the Brindisi ferry terminus on the road to Olympia, is 3rd with about 100-thousand—and that's about all. Of the major tourist attractions, *Rhodes* and *Corfu* are gorgeous; *Crete* and *Mykonos* will continue to be 2 of the most enchanting islands of the hemisphere, if the influx of rubbernecks doesn't spoil them (see "Greek Islands"). *Hydra*, a beachless, almost-bare rock, has become the regional bohemia. *Santorini*, a volcanic mass which arose from the sea about 2500 years ago, is believed by many to be the lost Atlantis (what, another?); it has interesting excavations, and a perilous cliff-ride side-saddle on a beleaguered donkey. *Corinth*, about 1¼ hours from Athens, comes up with ancient ruins and a famous canal; *Olympia* boasts the original Olympic Stadium and the breathtaking Hermes of Praxiteles (the '65 quake, which left 25% of the city in ruins, did not damage any of the famous antiquities housed in its museum); *Delphi*, site of the legendary Oracle, has its open-air theater of classic times, the Temple of Apollo, the Treasury of the Athenians and other famous monuments, a cluster of hotels, handwoven regional materials, and more Yankees per square inch than building stones (further information follows); *Mistra* offers magnificent Byzantine mosaics; *Mycenae, Epidaurus, Tiryns, Sparta, Kastoria, Mount Athos*, and the Aegean or Saronic Gulf sites of *Delos, Naxos, Poros, Spetsai*, and *Tinos* all have their special appeal, in one way or other. *Aegina*, with its Temple of Aphea, on the other hand, is almost torpid in its lassitude; since classical times it has been called "The Eyesore of the Piraeus."

If we were asked to choose our favorite travel targets in Greece, not counting Athens, we'd pick Rhodes, Corfu, Delphi, the Argolis tour (which includes Corinth, Epidaurus, and Mycenae), Hydra, and Mykonos—but this is merely a matter of personal taste, with which you might disagree.

MONEY Coins of 1, 2, 5, 10, and 20 drachmas are minted, plus 10-, 20-, and 50-lepta (½ drachma) pieces; notes for 50, 100, 500, and 1000 drachmas are in circulation. Right now a drachma is worth a little less than 3¢.

PRICES Medium by international standards. A representative cross section is as follows: shoes, $20 to $45; average lunch, $6 to $10; U.S. cigarettes, $1.40; drink in a nightclub, $7 to $12; nightclub dinner, including cocktail and wine, $25 to $30; drink in a bar, $1.50 to $2.50; man's custom-made suit, $200 to $250 (Greek material); to $350 (English material); woman's dress (Greek material), $120 to $150. These are press-deadline figures; by the time you get there, they might be slightly different since inflation has stalked the Greek economy more assiduously than that of any other European country.

ATTITUDE TOWARD TOURISTS The **Greek National Tourist Organization** recently limited hotel credits in order to get a leash on the nation's inflation. These shrewd watchdogs of your pocket and purse are well aware of the human tendency by a few avaricious rascals to take advantage of outlanders. Thus, they have proposed that hotel rates be posted in individual rooms and that those addling Greek, hen-scratched receipts be itemized in at least one foreign language. (So how's your Armenian?)

CUSTOMS AND IMMIGRATION The marble-white complex at the Athens' Hellenikon Airport, designed by the late Eero Saarinen, is a glorious feather in Greece's aesthetic cap. Newly expanded with 2 annexes exclusively for foreign flights, it is the most gracefully designed terminus in either Western Europe or the British Isles. Average respectably dressed North Americans are waved through the Customs formalities smilingly, speedily, and helpfully. Vagabonds from narcotics-producing nations, however, are often given careful scrutiny.

One pettiness which should be eliminated is the requirement that all foreign currency over $500 must be listed on a separate form—that is, if you expect to take this much or more out again. Greek money is limited to 750 drachmas either going out or coming in.

Although officials are tough if they have to be, treat them right and normally they'll beam.

HOTELS   For more comprehensive information on certain hostelries than space limitations permit here, interested travelers are referred to the annually revised *Fielding's Selected Favorites: Hotels and Inns, Europe* by our son, Dodge Temple Fielding. Its latest edition, in which a total of 300-odd favored possibilities were handpicked from the 4000-plus personally inspected, will be at your bookstore early this year.

At long last, thank Zeus, the innkeeping looms are weaving woofs of quality into the warped fabric of quantity. There are even touches of rich brocade among the myriad of stopping places in the nation's patchy patchwork blanket. Most of the new projects, naturally, are designed for the bargain-basement, white-sale traffic migrating from the cold, sunless, foggy-bottoms of Northern Europe. A number of existing houses and some of the newest rush-ups are unequivocally raddled for burlap peddlers. Trashy, low-level beds, spindly furnishings (tailored for the cramped dimensions of the rooms rather than the ample posteriors of nondiet nomads), skimpy rugs, bare walls, excruciatingly jarring taste, plus a woeful absence of concern for the scrub brush and the dust cloth, are clearly threads in the Hellenic tapestry.

In *Athens*, of course, you'll find the widest choice of lodgings; the cost range is highest here as well. *The Olympic champs garner close to $36 to $40 for singles, $50 to $65 for doubles, and $70 to $90 for suites. The next heat in the price marathon cross the finish line at $25 to $30 for loners, $35 to $40 for duos, and $45 and up for premium accommodations. The not-so-fleet-of-foot circle the track at $16 solo to $21 to $25 in tandem. At the back of the pack, $9 and $12 (singles and doubles) are the consolation prices—but in most of the latter, there's precious little consolation.*

The **King George** is a veritable treasure trove of *objets d'art*. Careful maintenance; Directoire lobby conforming harmoniously with the classic style; more than 500 paintings by prominent Greek artists on permanent exhibit throughout the public rooms, corridors, and bedchambers; Tudor Hall for penthouse dining (see "Restaurants") with its 12-table, alcove-lined grillroom adjoining; Empire-mood La Causette bar on the ground floor; flowers wherever you sniff. All bedchambers are comfortable; we prefer those on the upper 3 floors that face the rear. TV for rent; an encouraging evaporation of the plastic furniture-coverings of yore; increasingly kindhearted staff. Formerly guided by the late, great Connoisseur Dr. Basil S. Calcanis, and now under the regency of his spectacularly handsome son, and keen-eyed Manager George Papageorgio, here is a lovely haven for any artful lodger. During some season in the near future, these firebrands plan to open a Deluxe resort village called the **Sun Palace** at *St. Demitri,* on the way to Cape Sounion. It is to comprise 3 pools, 5 restaurants, and bungalow space for 770 visiting hearthsiders. Here's one to keep in mind for your Aegean holiday.

The **Grande Bretagne**, frequently the choice of the traditionalists rather than modernists, is famous all over the world as the "G.B." Enormous, high-ceilinged lobby warmed up with acres of tapestry; adjoining lounges humanized and defrosted; excellent, silken, relaxing bar; lovely dining room (with waltz orchestra), but ordinary cuisine; new cafeteria. Its imposing 8-story wing faces Constitution Square and the Acropolis; prize rooms are the

6th-level terraced perches overlooking the plaza; all floors redone, some in peach or avocado tones with teal carpets, zippy classical lines, marble baths, and lots of color; no radios is the house policy; warmer attention by desk personnel. In sum, here for your pleasure is a solid and generally comfortable *Greek-style* hotel, thanks to the tireless energies and talents of Owner Pericles Petracopoulos and General Manager George Canellos, a veteran of more than a ½-century with the organization.

The **Athens Hilton** is gracefully situated on a hillside overlooking the Royal Palace and the Parthenon, about 5 minutes by taxi from the heart of town, near the U.S. Embassy. The concept is grand and the line is clean; a roof-high linear tablet of carved Yanina marble sets the semiabstract architectural tone. Expansive 3-tier lobby; 500 comfortable-size units with balconies and beautiful black Carrara baths; suites of varying dimensions; native fabrics and warm colors; 2 interior courts in the ancient atrium manner. Completely air-conditioned; 75-table regional-style Taverna Ta Nissia downstairs appended by the attractive and informal pizzeria (the latter 7:30 P.M. to 2 A.M. only); 24-hour Byzantine Café for back-home soda-fountain snacks; Pan Bar for daytime libations; Top-of-the-Mark-type garden restaurant; Galaxy roof nightclub with sliding ceiling and inside-outside dancing; swimming pool and adjoining bar; shops galore. Try to book your room on the rear of the upper floors for less noise or to their front facing the Acropolis for one of the finest vistas in the capital.

The 400-room **Caravel** is too new and variable for our rankings at press time, but its statistics are impressive—from its rooftop pool, through its air-conditioned maze containing 2 bars, a Men's Club, a 24-hour cafeteria, a pizzeria, and a *taverna,* to its convention halls. (The sauna is not air-conditioned, by the way.) Sheraton, which once held the latchkeys, has turned them over to new managers whom we don't know.

In the 2nd file, the **Athénée Palace** offers decent, reasonably pleasant facilities. About 150 medium-size, clean, bright, carpetless bedchambers, all with small (or minuscule) bathrooms and some with balconies; slipcovers, not to our liking, used extensively but always crisp and fresh; noisy on the Stadium Street side; 2nd-floor mirror-clad restaurant and tiny lobby bar. We think Entrepreneur Spiros Damigos, the warm and treasured friend of so many thousands of U.S. gypsies including my Nancy and me, is trying hard in carrying forward his crusade of merit. We commend him and his march of progress.

The **King's Palace** is bustling and commercial. Excellent central location makes it almost an amendment to noisy Constitution Square; recently painted façade; dynamic troika-style teamsmanship by Executive Director John G. Vasdekis, Manager Mitropoulos, and Managing Director Takis Karadontis. June-to-October roof garden with eye-popping view and solarium but no pool; 150 superb, recently converted twins; other accommodations small and spiritless; all with baths or showers and piped music; all s-s-s-soundproofed against street clangor; quiet but viewless units on the Parliament side; air conditioning; housekeeping standards perking up notably. Excellent in a strictly-business way.

The 250 room **Royal Olympic**, located across from the Temple of Zeus (or

Jupiter, if you're a Roman), is owned and operated by the poised, young, hardworking Saki Papademetriou. Besides fresh rooms, the youngest annex includes the darkly handsome medieval Templar Grill and a convention hall. Whisper-soft, individually controlled air conditioning plus double-glazed windows as noise shields; magnificent oh-ing and ah-ing at Mt. Lycabettus and the Stadium; upper floor peeks at the Acropolis. Sounds of happy splashing from the beautified pool area; adjoining lobby, bar, and all-new photoriffic dining room, but cuisine generally not too distinguished. Bedchambers with full carpets; multichannel consoles for music and radio (including U.S. Armed Forces Network); wood, leatherette, or velvet headboards; colored tiles and gay towels in its well-appointed baths. Enthusiastically recommended because of its never-ending parade of improvements.

High over the city in the Kolonaki residential enclave, sits the majestically modern, 150-room **St. George Lycabettus**, opened in late '73. In this southern part of heaven, please try to book on the front for a sweeping Grecian panorama. Two-tiered rooftop pool; appending terraces with snack tables; L-shape lobby with many gracious touches; lower-level restaurant with appetizing color blends; intimate grill, plus a coffee shop that is a knockout for design and rendition; attractive Tony's Bar; bank, shop, hairdresser, and barber; garage (a car is useful since taxis are a bit of a problem to snag up here). The suites are striking; the normal twins are clean lined and charming but somewhat short on space for this category; the singles are neat and adequate. A splendid choice if you don't insist on a front-row ticket to the midcity traffic circle.

The **Amalia** (pronounced "Am-MAL-ia") is a jaywalk from the Royal Garden, one block from Constitution Square. Though raised from First-class to an official Deluxe standing, it still offers 98 fairly cramped rooms, all with bath or shower; individually controlled air conditioning; large windows; furnishings subdue-hued. Suite #603-4 nestles nicely in a corner; the lobby impressed us as being colder than a polar bear's toenail; the dining room and bar seem like hidden afterthoughts; Director Kokkinos has not, to our eyes at least, pumped in any new decorative BTU's to warm it up. Your free-lance reservations might be troublesome here, because group bids, of which there are many, receive A-plus priority.

The **Olympic Palace**, with its central and increasingly raucous site, opened in '59, but periodic refreshenings keep it pert. All 100 units come with bath or shower and wall-to-wall woofing-and-warping; radio, telephone, terrace, and air conditioning; the public rooms are charming. One nice, bright touch is provided by flowers on tables stationed along the carpeted hallways. We are especially fond of #608, a viewful double. Reminiscent of the Amalia and deserving of the same ranking even though rates run about 20% lower.

King Minos proffers a fancy brochure proclaiming the following: "Main hall spacious and impressing with King's Minos Palace of Knossos represented on its walls, welcomes you." Its architect, however, was more skillful than its copywriter. Clean structural scheme highlighted cleverly by marble and wood; indirect illumination; maintenance skidding notably on our latest look; 100% air-conditioned; beauty parlor and barbershop; 5-stool bar; next-door lounge with ornamental birdcage; balconies on all front units; reasonable tabs for reasonable living space. The housekeeper recieves a Minos from us; otherwise we'd score several pluses.

The **Esperia Palace**, a vassal under the King's Palace-Alfa scepter, shows continued improvement, although at certain peak periods we've had to crane our long necks over tour groups to see it. Classically restyled entrance and lobby; ingratiating Athineos Restaurant and cafeteria; large parquet-floor lounge; library and card room; blithe little bar. All its 185 zestlessly wallpapered accommodations with veranda and private bath, mostly with squat-down tubs; all ¾-bed singles (often sold for doubles) are for Gulliver's travels, but not yours; mock-walnut furnishings and blue-flowered cretonne bed-spreads with matching curtains; air-conditioned; the 2 upper floors (8th and 9th) are singles exclusively. Try to get a high perch for the view and to avoid the traffic din. Worthy for its drachmae. **Attica Palace** has an ideal address, a so-so oft-crowded downstairs, with the upper floors trying to carry the eye-appeal load. Pencil-thin aluminum-and-glass structure in central location; 100 loooong and narrow rooms with baths and showers; simple, long lobby up one flight. Noisy, but now much improved in its housekeeping standards. The **Pan**, a 10-story structure facing Constitution Square, simply didn't pan out to our expectations on our recent inspection. Sorry, but still nix.

The **Astor** originally popped up with 100 units; it found life so good that 33 rooms were added a few moons later. All offer bath, terrace, and air conditioning. Functional lobby and pleasant bar adjoining; cheerful, enlarged rooftop restaurant (functioning until midnight); efficiency bedrooms brightened by fresh paint, gay blankets and curtains, but no carpeting (synthetic flooring); conventional baths totaling 35%; other 65% (a nice one is #710) featuring 2-step tubs which will give you the feeling you're Rodin's *Thinker*. Manager Dimitrios Kokkeas provides golden value for silver coins.

The 350-unit **Stanley** is unabashedly aimed at package tourism—and it seems to be doing its job so well that already another wing is on the drawing boards. Sited on Karaiskaki Square with a pleasant greensward at its front door, it is too far from the hub of the city for most hikers to hoof it to the center. Attractive public rooms; top marks for the rooftop pool, solarium, and relaxing zone; lower scores for the utilitarian bedchambers; premium accommodations air chilled. Not terribly distant, at Omonia Square, the **Dorian Inn** is another fresh contender tailored for conducted tours. Three main columns mark its 13-story triangular ground plan, again with a swimmery at penthouse level, albeit smaller and more constricted because of its midtown address. All 150 rooms and 30 suites air-conditioned; restaurant, grill, bar, shop, the usual bag of tricks with few surprises. We repeat, both of these are more geared to mass migrations rather than to individual explorers.

The extra-clean, 110-room high-voltage **Electra**, sparking on Hermou Street near Constitution Square, crackles with a full bath count, full air conditioning, and ½ of its bedchambers facing inside; restaurant plus cafeteria. Thomas Sviriades, former Chief Receptionist of the Athénée Palace, is one of its owners. The cheeriness in décor, the finger-lickin' savor of its cookery, the perfect midtown situation for active travelers, the try-harder attitude of management and staff, and the low rates all meld to make this one a prize in the Athenian grab bag. Morning, noon, and night become this Electra.

The same Producer uncorked the **Electra Palace** in '73 up in the Plaka district. In addition to similar décor and similar bedchambers, he unhatched 150 feebly air-conditioned units all with private bath, a rooftop Eden overlooking the Acropolis, a garage, and a swimming pool.

The 200-chambered **Nina Palace** disclosed heaps of heartening potential on our recent inspection of its budding roof garden, pool, grill, and bar. Two-tiered lobby of 2-toned alabaster; mezzanine lounge, promenade, and writing cranny; unadorned dining room; alcove bar in warmer tones; cheerful Mexican nightclub; garage, hairdresser, and shops. We found the doubles to be better buys than the poorly designed suites. If operated correctly, this will probably be a winner for the drachmas.

The **Arethusa** bowed in enthusiastically in '72. This one comes up with a first-rate address near Constitution Square, a viewful roof garden, an inviting mezzanine cafeteria, and 87 quiet panel-windowed bedchambers with modern light-wood furnishings, radios, and individual air conditioning. Ask for any nest ending in "01" or "08"; while these are in the same moderate price range as the standard twins, they provide an extra dividend in scenery and space. Physically, we like the plant a lot.

The **Ava** is also a spry young sibling. Its mere 18 rooms cluster under a roof at 9 Lissikratous Street, which is more residential than commercial. Quite nice though tiny.

Even newer is a trio which will require time to mature. The massive 800-pillow **Titania**, near Omonia Square, is frigid in the most gelid context of a sleeping factory. It has all the basic ingredients—except warmth, in our opinion. The 90-room **Christina** is air-conditioned and comfortable, and seems to provide reasonably good service. Another 90-unit entry, **Heordion**, is sited on the lower slopes of the Acropolis; splendid views of the historic navel of western civilization from the upper 2 tiers on the back of the hotel. Bright accommodations which complement the charm of the public rooms. The last candidate holds the best promise in our estimation.

The **Galaxy** fills its spiral nebula with a wood-lined lobby, marble elevator bank, a mezzanine bar plus snack counter, a glass-lined but viewless restaurant, full-space air conditioning, a myriad of lounges and cozy corners, and a 108-room firmament twinkling with satellite efficiency. A stellar attraction for 4th-magnitude budgets.

The **Acropole Palace** is trying harder than an Olympic sprinter to match its Deluxe classification, but both shoelaces look loose to us. It caters almost exclusively to conducted-tour bookings and airline crews. Improved lobby; brightened public rooms; big bedchambers that seem rather gloomy to our eyes. Its chief assets are its A-plus table and a staff that seeks to please.

The **Sirene**, though a mile or so from the metropolitan fulcrum, is not very *sirene,* in our opinion. If fact, we found it very, very noisy. Characteristically modern throughout, with its finest feature the pool and snackery on its 7th plateau. Minilobby with small restaurant up a ½-flight; 103 bedrooms that we can almost guarantee won't live in your memory; wee baths with sitz tubs and cable-type showers. The price is not too high, but then neither are the rewards.

How the 10-story, 400-bunked **Ambassadeurs** achieved its First-class rank is a diplomatic mystery to this traveling envoy. Let us exercise the ultimate in protocol by merely avowing that we are personally not in accord with the official classification.

Marmara ("Marble Palace"), another link in the King's Palace-Alfa chain, is a good 10 minutes from midtown but still noisy. Blue-ceilinged lobby in white stonework enhanced by tearoom gallery; zipless bar; attractive dining room; fine modern kitchen. Of its 140 small units, 40 have no private facilities. To overstate things a mite, here's a Marmaramarvelous bet for the budgeteers.

The **Diomia** opened in '64 on a quiet, narrow lane about one block off Constitution Square. Two floors have been added to the original 71 units; all of its vaguely Danish-modern rooms have bath or shower and a little terrace; 50% are air-conditioned. Scandinavian-style lobby and minibar; airy dining salon; all public rooms with piped music; Snack Bar-Drink Bar a split level below the ground floor. We were pleased to see honest-to-goodness rugs and honest-to-goodness pictures in the bedchambers, warm touches provided by active Director Alex Carolos which are almost nonexistent among its confreres. On the other hand, we are becoming highly alarmed by the number of complaints we have been receiving concerning day-to-night maintenance here. Let's hope that it's only a temporary situation.

The **Athens Gate** recently swung open to welcome strollers along the Hellenic paths. The front units provide Olympian views of the Temple of Zeus. Ground-level public space limited, but plans include utilization of the 360° views from the rooftop; cookery said to be worthy; friendly service; clean. We must also check into the 150-unit **Golden Age**, which is not far from the Hilton. Lobby and cafeteria on ground floor; handsome dining salon and bar on mezzanine; all indications of a sound investment for your touristic dollar.

The **Atlantic** rattles 145 doorkeys; bath or shower with every unit, and some now air-chilled. Commercial and noisy; preponderance of conducted groups; cramped space; strictly functional; sparsely furnished. **El Greco**, if it is still functioning when you arrive, is no longer recommended. **Achillion** is reasonably well heeled, but we strongly suspect its mattresses are stuffed with prime-grade Greek marble. Although its situation is unattractive, this one is superior to most of its classification. **Alfa** has 98 accommodations, ½ with baths and ½ with showers. It also provides a restaurant, a bar, and a cocktail lounge; here is another under the King's Palace baton. Better downstairs than in the sleepers. The **Minerva Athens**, across from the King George, occupies the top 3 floors of an office building. All 60 rooms have bath; commercial, with a heavy traffic of local businessmen. In other countries, all of these would be considered Grade-C rather than Grade-A or B houses.

The 275-room, Class-C **Omonia** boasts a full bath-or-shower count but not much else to lift your spirits. Naturally, it's sited on the plaza from which it takes its name. There is one unquestionable asset: When the bill is tendered, no smelling salts will be needed for this Omonia. The nearby, smaller (only 56 rooms) **Pythagorion** has much more heart, in our opinion—and for almost the same outlay. Well run by Proprietor-Travel Agent John Stephanidis. A money saver. We missed the new **Ilisia** in the Hilton district, but we were told that it is worthy, too. **Lycabette**, on a quiet street, comes up with 50 rooms, 15 of which are loners, all with shower or bath. Air-cooled throughout;

Luculus Restaurant; chummy bar; nice lounge; well furnished; radio in every nest. Not bad—and happy for medium budgeteers. **Hermes,** on Apollonos Street, has unveiled 45 plain and inexpensive accommodations. Heaven-scent roof garden for summer dining; full pension plan pushed during peak periods. **Imperial** has no lobby—but it does have 21 door keys and an owner who is said to be especially pro-American. The **Xenophon**, on the N-1 highway north of town, is chiefly for motorists. For apartment dwelling, the **Riva** is a modestly priced but luxuriously outfitted retreat that we highly recommend. Our next choice in this category would be the **Delice**, in the Hilton district.

Suburban settings? The **Astir Palace** was constructed to lure shipowners, yachtsmen, and sybarites of all callings. Long, linear, modernistic structure standing majestically above the Vouliagmeni shores (15 miles from Athens); one façade flanked by a harbor for pleasure craft and the other by golden sand; handsome waterside Club House with restaurant, snack bar, and recreational facilities; 2 new pools for indoor-outdoor splashing; Glyfada golf course 5 miles away; dozens of bathing baylets opening into glittering Saronic Gulf. Hotel composed of an elegant classic-style restaurant, a rustic plank-ceilinged grill-cum-nightclub, 2 bars, sweeping vista-filled lounges, terraces, balconies, and luxurious fresh-looking appointments. Total of 147 accommodations, including some 2- and 3-room suites, each with a veranda and a glorious panorama. The 69 summer bungalows sprinkled below the hotel have been gracefully re-A-stirred—new ones with air conditioning, full kitchenettes, and even room service from the clubhouse; old ones with smart fresh colors, no air cooling, and nice, private, L-shape terraces. In winter we would prefer the hotel itself. Advance reservations *an absolute must,* since some bookings are made a year ahead. Another detriment is the noise factor from its proximity to the airport. Overall, we like it and laud it highly.

Astir Bungalows at *Glyfada Beach*, 10 minutes closer to town, is operated by the same company. It's more village-like in concept. Hillside perch dotted with 100 one-room chalets, 7 two-room, and 7 three-room villas; all with private bath or shower, refrigerator, wide flower-girt terraces, and central heating. Bigger units cozied-up with working fireplaces; room service; Asteria Tavern for let's-go-out diners; cocktail and snack bars; both rocky and sandy beaches at the bottom of the grassy slopes; pool and imbibery freshly a-bubble. Recommended for families or more thrifty travelers. The **Apollon Palace**, even nearer to town than the Astir Palace, opened in late '73 with 300 units that to us suggest prefabrication. Officially it is Deluxe, but we'd label it High First-class. Vast marblesque lobby; wide seafront terrace; 3 pools; restaurant with orchestra; 24-hour Coffee House. All doubles of standard dimensions; good baths; furnishing pleasant but not striking. That last comment might well serve to wrap up the entire hotel.

The gigantic resort complex known as **Sun Palace**, still under construction during our latest swing, is being created (and slowly) by the famed Calcanis family who operate the capital's King George. The luxury-category undertaking is 17 miles from the city on the Apollo Coast road. While the central hostelry of 250 rooms and at least one swimming pool plus a separate restaurant building are scheduled for next year's debut (bungalows, a marina, villas, roads, and more support facilities are to come later), our private guesstimate is that living will not be comfortable here until around 1979. This enormously ambitous venture ultimately will sprawl across 100 acres—much of which we will reinspect during the continuing development.

Not far away, a slightly less expensive miracle was taking shape under the name of **Cape Sounion Beach**, a First-class dream of Takis Karadontis, president of both the Greek and Athens Hotel Associations, and his radiant sister Ket. The panorama is plainly glorious; there's a huge pool beside the remains of a 2000-year-old silver mine; a 7-sided glass-enclosed bar adjoins its delightful restaurant; another dining salon plus a *taverna* also are available. When finally completed in a year or 2, it will comprise 400 rooms and 400 bungalows—virtually a village in itself. This one shows excellent promise.

The **Xenia**, formerly called the Lagonissi project, had plummeted to great depths before it was taken over by the National Tourist Office. Because of its situation on one of the most breathtaking headlands on this enchanting coast, it could be a marvelous money-mill. Personally, we much prefer its spacious beachside cottage accommodations to the cramped main-building lodgings. Most of the amenities are here for a tiptop holiday at reasonable prices. **Blue Spell**, closer to town, didn't bind us much. At the **Eden Beach** in *Saronis* (30 miles out), pick only a front chamber because the rear cubicles struck us as awful. The beds that we tested certainly didn't spring from any Eden we've visited, either. Austere seems to be this Adam's word for it. We haven't yet inspected the brand-new 220-room **PLM Porto Heli** in the district from which it takes its name (35 miles from Epidaurus with ferry connections to Athens). It is said to have a private beach, a swimming pool, and 2 restaurants. We'll see it soon.

Then there's the **Motel Belvedere Park** with its 80 one-room bungalows, all with shower and bath and varying somewhat in quality. This one is open all year, is directed by the amiable Mr. Papadopoulos, and comes up with a fresh wing, a penthouse luxury restaurant, a basement grill and bar, 2 swimming pools, and a lovely vista. Bed and breakfast only. Relaxing.

Porto Carras, near Thessaloniki, is the name of both a place and a resort created by shipowner John Carras. It is due to open this year and the scuttlebutt is that it will be huge, lovely, and deluxe. We'll pop in soon for a check.

Dedicated budgeteers? Since we're too bottlenecked here for additional entries, please consult our annually revised paperback *Fielding's Low-Cost Europe,* which lists scads more bargain hotels or pensions and money-saving tips for serious economizers.

FOOD When the Greeks try to cook like Frenchmen the results are usually disappointing if not disastrous. When they cook like Greeks they turn out interesting fare. In general, however, from the American point of view, the national culinary level is an adventure.

Regional dishes worth trying are Dolmades (grape leaves stuffed with meat, rice, onion, and seasonings); Souvlakia (a succulent facsimile of shish kebab, consisting of lamb, tomatoes, and peppers roasted on a spit); Moussaka (chopped meat baked with potato ,veal, eggplant, tomato sauce, cheese, eggs, and spices); the magnificent red mullet, finest in the 7 seas; kalamaraki (tenderized squid); octopus (so delicious it tastes like chicken-lobster); and the local langouste (clawless crayfish). These are merely samples; there's a large choice of other specialties.

We stumbled across one of our happiest food discoveries some years back. It's called Peïnerli, and it's a "sandwich" of crisp, succulent pizza dough shaped like a Viking ship containing your choice of fillers: cheese and tomato sauce, chopped meat and cheese, chopped meat and egg, ham and cheese, ham and egg, sausage and egg, fried egg and ground meat only—all huge, and all around $2.50. When it comes piping hot to the table, mix the fillers on the "deck" so they soak into the underside of the crust. Then eat the center out, and finally polish off the whole. **Y Pighi Eleftheriatis** ("The Source") at **Drossia**, 14 miles northeast of Athens, is the original creator and king of this dish. Here is an absolutely TERRIFIC treat—a happy drive for lunch on a benign day, very reasonable in price, and 102% worth the trip! Personally, we love everything about it and find it amazing that each successive yearly visit seems better than the last one! Since the success of "The Source," many less skillful imitators have sprung up in or around Drossia; for a switch, we tried a crowded pavilion-restaurant called the **Small Pines**; it was a big disappointment.

Not recommended is a little number called Kokoretsi, (sometimes spelled Cocoretzi), which is mushy intestines stuffed with liver, *very* fresh kidneys, and innards, half-baked by an apathetic fire. Because it's often as high as a kite, with a monstrously hideous aroma, we've turned kelly green on no less than 7 separate occasions over the years while trying to force it down; it happens to be the only recognized dish we've ever samlpled anywhere that we simply couldn't stomach before the 8th try.

Meal hours are generally from 7 P.M. to 10 P.M. for dinner. As in Egypt, Spain, or Portugal, the later the hour, the larger the crowd.

Caution: Drink water from the tap *only* in Athens, Rhodes, Delphi, Corfu, Crete, and Olympia, where it is safe; everywhere else, never touch anything but bottled water (wine is even safer). Under no circumstances should you drink milk unless you are *certain* it has been boiled; ice cream is similarly hazardous. Fruits, melons, and vegetables which grow in the ground should always be washed. In the larger centers, restaurateurs generally do this before serving such food. Don't worry about it in the good places in Athens, but when you buy them yourself or eat them in villages, this precaution must be taken.

§TIP: Whenever you tackle the flavorful little Greek clams called Thalassina, always squeeze a drop of lemon juice over each one before downing it; *if it doesn't wiggle when the juice hits it, leave it alone!*

RESTAURANTS Don't look for dining elegance in Greece; in routine establishments you're liable to find paper tablecloths, paper napkins, colorless furnishings, and panting waiters who'll toss successive courses at you as fast as Chinese Ping-Pong balls.

No traveler who enjoys maritime fare should be deprived of visiting the enormously colorful and delightful lineup of restaurants at the crescent-shape base for fishing boats in **Tourkolimano** ("Turkish Port"), across town near the harbor for private yachts. Almost all these moorings are still simple and unspoiled. In benign weather, go first across the street from the establishment of your choice to the awninged concrete strip directly over the water, to select your table. Then recross the boulevard, enter its front door, and select by the piece your shellfish (as many and as varied as you wish) from the aproned Poseidon in charge of this specialty. Next ask the proprietor to open the trove of stainless-steel drawers where the catches of the day lie in pristine freshness. Watch his scales as he weighs your picks; if he charges more than the Government-regulated 400 drachmae ($11) per kilo (2.2 lbs.), he's cheating you. (Lobster is officially about $17 per kilo.) Ask for Greek peasant salad on the side; garlic fans should bid for the piquant and unusual Skordalia sauce. Finally, head back to your table on the quai, order a San Rival Ouzo, ice, and water—and bask in peace and joy until the business of addressing the meal commands your attention. They are equally pleasant by day and by night. In the latter case, there's little activity until 9:30.

Along this non-Cannery Row, our favorite is **Paragadia**, where our latest delicious lunch for 4 including all of the above sips and forkings, and tips, came to nearly $40. **Zephiros** repeatedly has turned on high-tide comestibles for our fishing parties; the shell game here is especially deft and cunningly presented. **Kokkini Varka** ("The Red Boat") is much less polished, but still a winner. The balance, navigating from the southwest and moving northeast along this short avenue are **Mourayo, Prassina Trehandiria, Kamnires, Kanaris, Kymata, Kranai, Kailanis, Semiramis, Trata, Poseidonos, Kavos** and **Zorba's** (of course)—most of them good. Stroll down the line and choose for yourself. When the skies are clear, the thermometer is kind, and the place is right, here can be one of the most joyful experiences on your entire European itinerary.

Among the much more expensive and elegant institutions, **Dionysos**, at the foot of the Acropolis, is almost as important as the Parthenon to the tourist trade. Despite the drawbacks which you might or might not encounter, it is worth a visit, if only to dwell upon the 3000-year-old architectural vista. And how agreeable it is to watch the Sound and Light spectacles flickering on the historic next-door mountain as you dine! About 30 tables and alfresco terraces upstairs (best view); more below for snacks and libations; heavy-ish and often greasy international cuisine. Despite occasional service lapses plus a bothersome lack of acoustical soundproofing, most of the time we enjoy it a lot. Evenings it is nearly always jammed, so reserve well in advance; open 8 A.M. to 2 A.M. Costly for the nation, but exceptionally rewarding for those eyeful antiques outside. The newer, slightly less chic branch on Mt. Lycabettus also provides a feast for the hungry eye. (We recommend this Mt. Pentelicus view at lunchtime and the main restaurant's sea wonders after sunset.) Again the staff attitudes are ice-cold, but this seems minor compared to the glories surrounding you. A *must* for free-spending wayfarers.

The **Athens Hilton** presents formal or informal nutrition, depending upon your whim—and your whim may range from a chocolate ice-cream soda to Beluga caviar. Its Taverna Ta Nissia used to be such an outstanding gustatory landmark that we had trouble staying away from it. On our latest try, however, we were given a relentless hardsell pitch by the Maître, followed by servings of uninspired culinational wares—at Olympian price tags, too. The adjoining Pizzeria is an excellent bet for the classic Italian-style snack. *Open from 7:30 P.M. to 2 A.M. only.* Recommended if you're in the mood.

Tudor Hall, the penthouse oasis crowning the King George Hotel, offers a glamorous setting. Baronial 2-story room softly illuminated and richly paneled; solid bank of windows on one side and tiny terrace on the other; courteous attention on our most recent incognito try. Connoisseur Dr. Basil S. Calcanis has inaugurated a semi-separated Grill at one end which is strikingly different but equally tasteful in its décor; the white-capped chef here pits his Greek-style specialties against the international cuisine of his adjoining competitor; it is open at lunch and dinner 365 days per year. In both, you will find high culinary standards plus a magnificent panorama of the rooftops, Acropolis, and floodlit Parthenon. A superior choice for that Big Night Out.

The **Templar Grill** in the Royal Olympic is also strong on knightly charms —but this time at ground level. We've never seen it crowded, although we are told that it is skyrocketing up in Athens' social circles. Lip service? Could be, because our own dining experience here has not been too favorable.

Vladimir (12 Aristodimou St.), perched on a steep hillside a short climb from the Hilton, offers a curious but tempting mélange of Russian, Greek, French, and Oriental viands. To our surprise, even "American Hamburger" is offered as a main course. Terrace munching in rear garden during the warm months; immaculate kitchen; pleasant ambiance; on the expensive side for Greece.

For straight fare in more typical surroundings, **Facyo** occupies premises at 5 Efroniou St., also near the Hilton. The famous Kyrios Facyo, its aproned Turkish host, beams in avuncular radiance to bring happiness to his clients; although his English is sketchy, his eyes bespeak heart-deep kindness; if linguistic difficulties should occur, his maître commands our tongue. About 18 tables in a simply furnished square room; ornate, vividly colored, ancient-style Macedonian ceiling and murals; refrigerated display counters backed by shelves of bottles running the entire length of the right side; choose your appetizers from these cases; hot dishes in adjoining segment. Unelaborate but fun.

Papakia (5 Iridanou St.) means "The Duckling"—and its fowl deeds to us are dismal cookery of late and declining service standards. This once-ducky choice has now laid an egg, think we.

Yerofinika (10 Pindarou St.) has its entry through a narrow alley; 2-tier room with sun terrace on one side; similar-type display casement for selecting your vittles on the other; diet-busting dishes including desserts which deserve commendation by the Fat Men's Society. While we happen to have a reasonably strong preference for Facyo's, this one is also very good.

Three Brothers (7 Elpidos St.) is a fraternal import from Corfu. Nondescript, smokefilled front room chuckling gaily with lively parties of food-savvy Greeks (very few tourists on each of our several visits); passageway with bustling kitchen on the left; 14,926,344-calorie showcase of comestibles (pick your share before sitting down) on the right; garden-like sanctum to the rear containing perfectly awful seacoast paintings, lanterns, and maritime riggings. No English spoken; fish plates especially fresh and well prepared; not at all fancy; no fancy tariffs either. A winner in its fraternity.

Tabula, not far from the Hilton, yearns to be the leader among the young In Set. While it was distinctly "out" on our late visit, there is a definite eye appeal in this subterranean den. Maybe we hit it on an off night.

The **Steak Room** (4 Aeginitou St.) also is about 5-minutes' walk from the Hilton in the direction of the U.S. Embassy. Small narrow den with a busy bar to the left, pine ceiling; modern copper lamps; blue carpet; pink and green linens; only 12 tables, many of them filled with Americans. The most expensive cuts of steer are reasonably priced and come with a green salad and a baked potato or French fries; glasses of iced water appear automatically when clients are seated. Our muscle-girded T-bone would have evoked the envy of Joseph M. Palooka; it was flavorful, however. Passable, if your choppers have been filed into fine little points.

Down the line, **Zonar's** (9 Venizelou Ave.), one block from the Grande Bretagne, might be called the Greek Schrafft's; coffee shop, confectionery, tearoom, bar, and restaurant combined in a single operation under the Dionysos aegis; hot in summer; average in quality; popular with trippers. **Floca** continues to uphold its good reputation; café-restaurant aura; by local standards, prices on the high side. **Élysée** was a below-decks fastness with brick pillars, wrought iron chandeliers, green rush-bottomed chairs, and mediocre cookery on our night. The ground-level snack-and-pack shop works around the clock.

Corfu (almost next door to King's Palace Hotel) appeals more to the stomach than to the eye; simple, spotless, reasonable, and enormously popular. If you don't mind the rush-rush atmosphere, it can fill that tummy as satisfactorily as many far more costly addresses. **Delphi** (13 Nikis St.) is a midcity favorite among businessmen because of luscious lunches, tiny tabs, and ΦΑΣΤ service. The front segment is rustic in aura while the rearward enclave seeks to appear more refined. (It barely makes it.) The **Stagecoach** (6 Loukianou St.) aims to recreate them thar places like Laramie, Cheyenne, Laredo, Dodge City and such. Does a fittin' job, too, it does. Purty fine steaks, burgers, and chili through them swingin' doors. Easy on the moneybelt, too.

Now—would you be interested in experiencing one of the most unusual and fascinating meals of our travel lives? This is served at the little grocery-shop-restaurant called **Vassilena** (corner of Etolikon and Vitolion Sts., port of Piraeus, 20 minutes from the heart of Athens). About 14 tables in a clean but simple room, with scrubbed floors, towel-covered windows, wine bottles and canned tomatoes on shelves; the latest additions include central heating, new and more comfortable chairs, a polished mosaic floor, and a summer terrace —all equally modest. No menu is offered; you merely sit down and your waiter will start the 1-price, no-choice parade of 19 heavenly dishes which will take you 2½ hours to consume. On our last waddle away from these precincts we counted the following as only *part* of our meal: raw clams, herring, head cheese, milk cheese, shrimp, octopus, Dolmades, whiting, lobster, batterfried shrimp, garlic-treated Vienna sausages, red mullet, Tarama Salad, Moussaka, and oranges—not to mention lemon soup as the next-to-last course (following the accurate Oriental principle that it settles the stomach), plus the best home-cured olives we've ever eaten. Price of this gargantuan repast, including coffee and all the open wine you can pour down? Less than the cost of the wine alone if you were at home (actually, $5.82 on our latest check)! The patriarch died a while back, but English-speaking son George and sweet daughter-in-law Nelly carry on precisely in his spirit. We've touted this dark horse so heavily since 1957 that you might have to wait in line behind other adventurous Guidesters. *Dinner only;* closed every Sunday; reserve in advance. Please don't be detoured by the ridiculous deceit evinced by the people at the Concierge's desk at the Athens Hilton. When we asked them to make our reservation, they gratuitously chorused "We do not recommend this place. It's not any good." Since the restaurant is too small to give them a cut of your business, their attitude is easily explained—but don't YOU swallow this nonsense. An unforgettable gastronomic excursion, even to a vast percentage of steak-and-potato habitués.

For a less exotic but border-to-border change of atmosphere and diet, every U.S. traveler should pay at least one visit to a typical Greek *taverna.* (Ta Nissia in the Hilton is much too urbanely hoked up to be the Real McCoy.) These famous institutions, most of which operate on a cold-weather basis *only,* feature rôtisserie-type grills, hearty masculine menus, wine from huge barrels, folk music that is often deafening, and informal, family-style hospitality. Within the city (not the environs), most do not serve lunch; evening is the time to go. Probably the most elaborate is **Palia Athina** (4 Flessa St.). Reslicked rustic décor; orchestra and dancing; vague aura of a transplanted German *Bierstube;* outdoor frolics adjoining during summer. **The Seven Brothers Social Tavern** (39 Hiperidou St.), not to be confused with the aforementioned Three Brothers restaurant, now cocks an all-too-serious eye on the tourist trade. It does have a spotless kitchen but food that is strictly indifferent; go for nibbling and wine drinking, not for a heavy dinner; closed July and August. **Steki tou Yanni** (1 Trias St.) is a perpetual favorite—with good reason. Motif—if we can call it that—trending toward a shambling stew of reed mats, bamboo fixtures, pastel-washed stucco, eclectic odds-and-endless ends; clangorous, busy, and stuffy; leather-lunged singers backed up by iro-fingered guitarists; hustling service. The jumbled entrance is lip-smacking-dab in front of the usual food counter for picking your foodstuffs in typical Greek dining fashion. Here, however, unless you make an emphatic point of ordering just what you desire, a huge, multicourse, and perfectly wonderful set meal will appear automatically. We like it, for its type. **Xinou** (4 Geronta St.) gave us several of the best repasts of our very recent Plaka parades. To the eye, it's a tumbled-down shack divided vaguely into 3 rooms and a tree-covered patio. To the palate, it was a happy surprise. Plank ceilings; exposed pipes; coal stoves; the inevitable cretonne curtains; genre paintings on cracking walls. Its trio of musicians wander from room to room playing exquisite folk melodies with expressionless, Buster Keaton visages. Almost exclusively Greek clientele who loyally return night after night, era after era. The drill here is to try to snag a table early, pick your mouth-melting platters on an everybody-share-a-bite basis, and sit down to a feast fit for Olympians. Waiters, owners, chefs, cousins, almost anybody who is connected to this house and who loves food can be found in the working area husbanding the pots and pans while guests mill among them prodding the meats and asking serious questions. If you're not persnickety, we think you'll love it as much as we did. Very inexpensive for the rewards. Highly recommended. **New Vrahos** ("The Rock"), with appetizing regional dishes, offers high-spirited Plaka festivities; small band; show time at 11:15 P.M. and 1:15 A.M. The original building burned to bedrock recently and this is the replacement; it has the same management as before; ask for Owner-Maître Alex. Here's another which functions only in winter. **Taverna Ambrosia**, in the same district, strums up interesting cookery and live guitar music. **Vlachos** (also called Tarasa) is in the Old Town on the northern slope of the Acropolis; beautiful Athenian view from the summer terrace, but otherwise we found it dirty, dreary, and depressing. **Bacchus**, also Acropolis-neighbored, is drenched with atmosphere and foreigners; so-so, at best. **O Yeros tou Moria** was climbing back up on our latest visit after a short decline. Spicy fare and bouncy songs that make us clap our hands for this revival. **Psaropoulos** for fish and **George's** for steaks are bettable bets in the Glyfada district, about 9 miles from town. **Belle Maison** (Victoria Sq.), appeals to locals chiefly; they come to hear the guitar pickin's and to dine on its finger-lickin' vittles. **Erotokritos,** in the Plaka, is another popular target. **Kritiku** (24 Mnissikleous St.), in 4 rooms, is an escape from the sidewalk cracklings of Shishkebab. Along this same street there are more kebab joints than you can shake a shish at.

A pair of Frenchies? **L'Abreuvoir** and **Je Reviens** (51 and 49 Xenokratous St.) are next-door neighbors up in the Kolonaki district. Cuisine superb in both year round, but we like summer wiles at their parkside tables best of all.

Ever try a *bouzouki*? Nope, it's not a Greek firearm—just a stringed instrument that accompanies the roisterous dances expressing the gaiety bursting out of these wonderful, vigorous people. The devil-may-care custom of breaking cheap saucers when the excitement reached a climax was curtailed by Government edict after a flying splinter of crockery injured the eye of one onlooker a while back. More recently a reveler got 6 months in the pokey for becoming a berserk discus thrower after tippling his 3rd liter of wine. Economy-minded Bonifaces, who had charged per plate, also were discouraged from such profit-taking when promoters shoved stacks of porcelain in front of tourists, who then listlessly tossed the tableware onto the stages without a proper spontaneous reaction to the folkways. In a "black market" sense, authentic *bouzouki* fun and frenzy can still be found after the doors are officially closed and the police are courting the sandman. For this brand of high-stepping hilarity, you must ask a Greek night owl to take you to his favorite nest—but if you go, please sit well away from the stage or wear extra-thick skier's goggles to protect your eyes. **Fantis**, in the Plaka district, is fair, but we can't really forgive the management for spoofing up the evening with electronic musical assists. Our meal was routine-to-poor. One dancer carried a table clenched between his teeth—more tender, we'll wager, than our beefsteak. **Dilina** at distant *Glyfada* ranks in the top league at the moment. **Kalokerinou Taverna** (10 Kekropos St.) is open all year; it whips up yummy food, music, an occasional floor show, and an open terrace in the summertime. You might try the cabaret at **Mostrou Taverna** (Mnissikleous

St.), also in the Plaka district, which pulls at the strings of many an Athenian heart with its own show backed by the national folk music; we like this professional operation. Others in the dervish whirl include the popular **Palia Athina** (4 Fleesa St.) and **Plakiotiko Saloni** (15 Dedalou St.); both feature Greek cabaret. The **Epta Adelfia** (39 Hiperidou St.) and the **Erotokritos** (1 Erotokritou St.) romp in with long floor shows of a national character; as *tavernas* they draw a consistent following. The costly **Tower Suite**, 24 floors up in the Tower Building no longer provides *bouzouki;* it has gone international and added a dash of strip. Go to any of these for drinks (or if you can stand the snacks!) between 11 P.M. and about 5 A.M., when the last customer leaves. A *must* for local high jinks.

§TIP: As is the case with most night spots, they rise and fall rapidly—frequently disappearing altogether while we are rushing to get this perishable research fodder printed, bound up, and onto the bookseller's shelves. Athenian nighteries seem to be particularly fickle, so for your up-to-the-instant convenience and fun we're going to list the top *bouzouki* players and singers currently in vogue. If you can pinpoint where they are at the moment of your visit (with the help of some local tip-sheet or your concierge), we think you will derive heaps of musical lore in the shortest time. They are as follows: Bithikotsis, Hadji, Poulopoulos, Voskopoulos, Marinella, Moscholiou, Kokotas, Mitsakis, Tsitsanis, and Zabetas—and they're generally considered to be the Carusos of the troupe.

Game for game? Shoot arrow-straight for either the modest, galleried, shoplike **Zafiris** (4 Thespidos St.) or **The Rotunda** (2 Kapodistriou St.). If you target onto the former, top your boar, pheasant, partridge, or luscious pigeon with a dessert of quince jelly or a pool of golden honey flecked with walnut chips. Both are packed tighter than a Springfield's magazine. Good hunting!

Turkish tempters? The previously described **Facyo** (5 Efroniou St.) is the top of the fez. **Bosphorus** and **Yerofinika** are others. These dish up similar platters. A trio of Turkish Delight!

A yen for chopstickery? **Pagoda** (2 Bouscou St.) and **Mr. Yung's** (3 Lamahou St.) adhere to one of our favorite Oriental proverbs: "Spare the rib and spoil the customer." Both offer a wide array of platters. The former is part of a chain; while we've also sampled its link in Nairobi, we can assure you it is not worth the effort to try its sister entries in Beirut and Nicosia. The latter, Mr. Yung's, is more appealing to the eye, but its treatment of Eastern cuisine impressed us as being . . . well, bizarre. **Michiko** (27 Kydathineon St.) resides in a Plaka mansion where it pans out Japanese dainties plus continental fare. None will cause you to worship their ancestors.

Bagatelle (opposite the Hilton) might be your bag for Gallic creations; like many French dishes, it's on the expensive side.

Lunch or dinner excursions to the suburbs? Our top favorite—one which we make it a point never to miss—is to **Y Pighi Eleftheriatis** ('The Source') at *Drossia*, 14 miles northeast of the capital (Please turn back to the "Food" section, in which its magnificent Peïnerli, a 32nd cousin of pizza, is described in detail.) To us, here's practically an annual Holy Pilgrimage. **Pamela's**, 11 miles out at **Voula**, is ultrafashionable these days and nights. It's on the sea with bathing available and trio music (harp, guitar, piano) by starlight every day of the week. **Psaropolou**, facing the sea at **Glyfada**, is a handsome kettle of fish. Entrance terrace dotted with flowers; glass-lined, modern dining room; expensive for the region, but worth the angling. We're told that **Mooring**, in the Vouliagmeni marina, also serves up a wide variety of superb sea specialties at moor or less reasonable prices. *In all suburban tavernas, (1) drink wine or beer only, and (2) scrutinize the ceremony of weighing your fish to see that YOU aren't the critter being hooked.*

La Belle Hellene, in **Kifisia** (on the way to the mountain in Politea), nestles on a slope surrounded by exclusive surburban homes. Spacious patio with pines and a trout pool; covered terrace; stone and glass-lined dining room in L-shaped; floor-to-ceiling copper hearth; flame-lit lanterns on tables; small selection; friendly service; fair cuisine. High tariffs, but pleasant enough in good climate. These Alleghenies of Atticus also come up with **Blue Pine Farm**—yup, Blue Pine Farm—which is known for its hillbilly-Xerxes steaks. It is rustic, enchanting, and deservedly popular. Always reserve ahead. **Myrtia**, near the Stadium, is said to be another winner, but we missed it on our marathon.

Kira Maria, in the suburb of **Halandri**, tugs at the girthstrings as ardently as it pulls at the heartstrings. The surroundings are as alluring as are the mouthwatering Souvlakia and other charcoal specialities. Very recommendable for adventurers.

The coffee-bar business is percolating vigorously. A potful have bubbled up, some of which serve griddle sandwiches. One of the better blends is **Brazilian**, located in the Arcade at 3 Stadium St. You might try **American Bar and Restaurant** in Constitution Square; it's owned by a Greek-American who knows which side his burger is broiled on.

For dining suggestions in other parts of the land, consult TWA (now at Xenophontos St.). A list for the Delphi route follows separately.

Dedicated budgeteers? Since we're too bottlenecked here for additional entries, please consult our annually revised paperback, *Fielding's Low-Cost Europe,* which lists scads and scads of other bargain dining spots and money-saving tips for serious economizers.

NIGHTCLUBS The continuing popularity of the taverns has caused a nightclub debacle of major proportions. Of today's scepter bearers, **Galaxy** is one of the front-runners. Big time entertainment nightly; high but value-filled tabs; nearly always crowded. Be sure to reserve ahead. **Neraïda** (near Old Phaleron, 5 miles along the shore toward the airport) is a knockout. Top-flight cabaret of Greek stars plus top international names; space for about 700 revelers on alfresco evenings; richly plush and discreet interior facility for colder months; showtime at 11:30 P.M., with entertainment throbbing until the last holdout weaves homeward. The crowd is chic, the food is good, and the tariffs are costly by local standards. Go late for the liveliest whoops—and book your table in advance. Highly recommended. **Fantasia** is a lesser light, and we've already mentioned the **Tower Suite**. **Copacabana**, on Constitution Square, produces the biggest floor show of all. It's sort of a

Levantine version of any gin mill or bump-and-grind emporium one might find on Times Square. The geography changes, but the game's the same. **Athinea** offers winter-only dancing at 6 Venizelou Ave.; in summer it gallops to an enchanting open-air site at the racecourse. No cover charge; no cabaret; passable vittles; dinner reservations mandatory.

Discothèques? **Dolly's** (Kolonaki Square) draws the chichiest of the Young Executive Set. No membership required; filled to the scuppers always; up-to-the-second musical selections; reasonable tariffs for ample, honest quaffs. Platters also spin on the **Galaxy** floor of the Hilton and at **Architectoniki** (University St.). Down a jigger is **Whisky-à-Gogo**. **Nine Muses**, **Donald Scotch Club**, **V.I.P.'s**, and **Show Boat** wrap up the picture.

Lonely and masculine? **Las Vegas, Maxim, Flamingo, Flamenco**, or **Minuet**—call it what you wish!—is next to the Olympic Airways office on the main square (as we write these words, we have the hollow vision of its sign painter slapping out still another name-change); here's the most pleasant pickup spot, if you don't mind that 4:30 A.M. deadline until your companion is permitted to leave. Small show; one 30-day padlocking by the authorities for alleged overcharging; nothing special, but best-scrubbed of its type. **Mimosa** (5 Ionos St.) couldn't be more routine. Earlier in the evening (7:30 P.M. onward), **Apotsou** (University St.), **Number 17** (17 Voukourestiou St.), **Orphanides** (7 Venizelou Ave.), and **Zonar's** (9 Venizelou Ave.) are the best frequented spots for C_2H_5OH addicts. Most of this lot can be deadly dreary and zzzzzzip-less.

A spin on the wheel of fortune? At **Mount Parnes**, 3500 feet above Athens and 15 miles north of it, private interests have taken over the Greek National Tourist Office's 5-story fizzle. This modern Phoenix, built originally as a super-deluxe hotel with air conditioning, restaurant, recreation facilities and scores of other razzle-dazzlers designed to lure pilgrims away from the capital, went up in fiscal (flames) in 1969; it has now risen from its ashes in the form of a posh gambling casino. The cuisine is above average, the accommodations are comfortable, and for gamesters it can be an excellent target for an evening, a weekend, or the "full-house" treatment.

§TIPS: Practically every elaborate night spot in Athens requires its bar girls to stay until 4:30 or 5 A.M. Don't let them sucker you into buying extra drinks on the promise they'll sneak out earlier, because they can't.

Motorized prostitution, with taxi-girls in the true sense of the word, is still rolling on the Athens afterdark scene. Around midnight they pop out of cruising cabs and inveigle lone pedestrians to a bit of l'amour on wheels. Despite increased police surveillance, plenty of strangers are trapped-and-robbed on this pitch, so don't be tempted.

Be careful about Mickey Finns, companions who will disappear at the crucial moment, and other clip practices in the dives. Leave your getaway money in the hotel safe, drink bottled beer that is opened in front of your eyes, pay after each individual serving, and keep your dukes up every second; here is one of the roughest leagues in Europe.

TAXIS   Plentiful. Now that many of the wheezy rattletraps are being replaced, there's a whit more comfort. Standard rates of about 40¢ per mile;

24-hour service; a 5-drachma supplement at night. The average run from the center of Athens to the airport is around $3.50 Cabbies are seldom tipped, but if you wish to please them, give them a little something extra. Many additional hacks have come into the capital fleet recently, thus enlisting a brigade of greenhorns into the trade. Not once on our latest 2-week rounds did we find a driver who immediately knew an address—even when it was written out in Greek letters. (One genius, believe it or not, didn't even know how to locate Constitution Square!) Time after time we ran into utter confusion, so to allay at least a smidgen of the annoyance, check with your concierge first.

§TIP: When the meter in your taxi ticks, be sure it reads Drs. 8.50 as you set out; this is especially important for hacks in the curbside ranks outside the larger hotels. The GNTO (thank Zeus!) has finally cracked down on cabbies with "broken" or "out of order" meters; a few, however, may remain. Now a sinner stands to lose his license if he overcharges and is reported. He's both more careful and more sly these days—so *you* be wary too!

TRAINS   Improving generally, but still spotty in quality. The international expresses through Yugoslavia to Zürich, Paris, Ostend, Germany, or other European points are comfortable. There is good diesel railcoach service from Athens to Corinth, Olympia, Nauplia, or Tripolis, and from Athens to Levadia, Larissa, Salonika. The roadbed to the Peloponnesus is narrow-gauge and obviously rooted in a firm foundation of Jell-O. Travel by car (but be sure to read the "Hired Cars" warning below) or by bus if you can; the Pullman-coach buses are royal chariots by comparison. If you must take a train, *stick to First-class.*

AIRLINE   Olympic Airways is the sole domestic carrier. The current fleet consists of Boeing 707-384's, 727's, 720-B's, plus a pair of 747's, a twin-turbo prop Japanese YS-II, and an increasing hopper of choppers and lighter birds to lift travelers to the islands. There's a transatlantic link between New York and Athens nonstop, plus hops via Paris. This has more recently been augmented by termini in Chicago and Montreal. We haven't yet had a chance to climb aboard the transoceanic leg. Other international services, besides the European skein, run down through Africa and out to the Far East. Traffic to Rhodes had become so massive that, even with several dozen shuttles per week being operated, these harassed citizens would not ordinarily carry any passenger to the island who could not show a confirmed return ticket before his departure from Athens. In an effort to ease this situation, even more flights have been added.
We've used this line on numerous recent European or domestic flights. The earliest ones were superb, but the latest hops were fraught with rudeness from ground personnel, high-handed treatment from overburdened officials, or inexcusable neglect on land or aloft.

HIRED CARS AND MOTORING   Chauffeur-driven cars in Athens are one of the sorriest examples of legalized hijacking we've encountered anywhere in our wanderings. The iron fist of the Greek Government should bring down the wrath of outraged justice upon these wretches. To permit this gouging to continue means that, in the long run, Fair Hellas will suffer powerful backlash from disgusted and disenchanted visitors. Reforms are supposed to be on their way, but to play it as safely—and as economically— as possible, book your vehicle *only through one of the recognized and reputable local travel agencies,* such as **Hellenic Tours,** 3 Stadium St., where Mr. Nelson Melamed is director, or through General Manager Artemios Cotsifakis of **American Express** on Constitution Square. With the sound guidance of these individuals, you will at least know the established price beforehand. They have kindly offered to serve as special watchdogs for readers of this book.

§TIPS: Roads are not Greece's greatest selling point. On the mainland they are often rutted, washed out, snow-blocked, or mud-drenched. On the islands they frequently seem to vanish entirely. The scenery may be breathtaking everywhere, but take an extra-deep breath before setting out anywhere. The nation's 2 major highways run from Patras to Athens (limited access and a lovely 3-hour run) and from the capital north to Thessaloniki. The toll pike leading into Athens is very short, only 2 lanes wide in many places, and so poorly engineered as to be especially dangerous on rainy nights.

Don't start any motoring journey after dark. The countryside is so desolate that if a breakdown occurs you could be stranded till dawn. Trucks also begin their long hauls in the evenings; the major arteries are so clogged with them that they're almost sclerotic. Greek drivers—all too many new to the game —do not share our respect for the eyes of oncoming drivers; even buses and trucks contribute in this innocent discourtesy. (On one recently completed 66-mile hitch, we spent more than 2½ hours behind our wheel, due only to the dangers encountered from headlight-blindness.) It's a question of inexperience, not inconsideration.

DRINKS   Practically everything is available in unlimited quantities—from Scotch to blends to bourbons to you name it—at prices similar to those in America. Brandy is the national hard drink; Metaxa, sharply sweet, is the most popular; Camba, far dryer and smoother to our palate, is the closest contender; both cost $4 to $9 per bottle. Ouzo, bless its jaunty heart, is the national apéritif; it is a thaumaturge's cross between French Pernod, Javanese arrack, and Turkish raki, with a faint licorice flavor. Order Sans Rival brand *only* (its superiority to all others is fantastic); mix it with water plus lots, lots, lots and lots of ice; then when you sit and sip in that healing Greek sun, zip one errant thought our way. No Greek whisky is made, but Greek vermouth is quite drinkable. So is Greek beer, which is mighty refreshing on a hot summer's day; get a fix with "Fix" or an omega with "Alpha"—2 popular brews. Amstel, the Dutch beer, also is sudsing over the local market; it is made locally, not imported. Henninger beer has appeared, too.

Order your wine *aretsinto* ("without resin"), or your mouth will pucker so much you'll think you've eaten a basket of persimmons. In Homeric times the Greeks smeared the linings of their wine barrels with pine sap, a crude preservative. Over the centuries the people grew to like the turpentine flavor, and today's vintages are therefore deliberately resinated. But to the neophyte they taste like a blend of nail polish remover and deck enamel. Greek wine is properly poured from a brass mug; nowadays you'll also find it served in aluminum replicas. In *tavernas,* the protocol is to half-fill your cup, especially when quaffing the resinated ones. If you specify that you want *aretsinto,* they'll always find an unprocessed bottle of the same brand for you.

Among dry-to-medium white wines, Elissar (our personal preference), Cava Kamba, Pallini, St. Helena, Demestica, King, and Minos are especially favored. In a Solomonic court decision, the former King Minos brand, which came in either white-and-dry or red-and-medium, is now known as King and Minos respectively. Cava Boutari and Cava Naoussa reds (Burgundy-type) are heavyish but sound; both are good complements to extra-spicy or garlicky dishes. From Rhodes, Chevalier de Rhodes is quite passable. Mavrodaphni and Samos, sweet to very sweet, are favorites of the ladies. Outside this select group, Hellenic wines are without exception 2nd-rate to American and European tastes.

True to form in this land of straight brandy and ouzo, the cocktails are lethal except in the largest hotels.

TIPPING   Tip more than you usually do, because every penny is desperately needed. In luxury or First-class restaurants, although the 12% service charge is now included, add 5% on the *plate* for the waiter or maître and small change on the *table* for the busboys. In your hotel, give at least $1 to the concierge, 50¢ to the maid, 50¢ to the baggage porter, and 25¢ to the elevator operator. For special attention of any kind, raise the scale accordingly. They'll never ask you to remember them, but they'll be grateful if you do.

HAIRDRESSING   The shop in the **Acropole Palace** is now the number one in the capital; ask for Mr. Peter. **George**, at 5 Kanari St., also deserves a good send-off. Next comes **Angelo's**, permanently waving at 2 Amalia Ave. A shampoo, set, and manicure run about $12 to $16. Give $1.25 to the admiral of your waves, 50¢ to each of his crew, $1 to the manicurist, and you'll be generous. As for the **Hilton** shop, my Nancy comments that it seemed exactly the same as its sister in any other city: Adequate, rushed, no great shakes. In all these places, the staffs speak English. Ask your concierge to make your appointment in advance.

Men's haircuts are about $3 to $4 without tip. In hotels it's higher, naturally. The barber at the **Grande Bretagne** must have been thinking about bowling when he last trimmed my scanty locks, because if my head had been detachable he would have run up a string of 12 perfect strikes. Tote a large club or a sword cane here—or try another.

THINGS TO SEE   Classic attractions in or near *Athens*, include the National Archaeological Museum (priceless ancient treasures), Benaki Museum (more modern Greek and Levantine displays), the interesting Museum of War Souvenirs, the Byzantine Museum, the Ghennadios Library (Byzantine books, manuscripts, and art objects)—plus scads of world-famous ruins such as the Acropolis with its Parthenon (now under such serious siege from air pollution, spike heels, and jet vibrations that a study is underway to halt this twentieth-century corrosion; already pedestrians are prevented from entering the interior structures), Hadrian's Arch of Triumph, the Temple of Zeus, the Theater of Dionysius, the Stoa of Attalus, and others. Prices to all historical and cultural attractions draw $1.

Son et Lumière ("Sound and Light") spectacles are presented 3 times nightly between April 15 and October 15 at the **Acropolis**. More than 500 varicolored floodlights play over the site for 45 minutes per performance, accompanied by a musical score and a dialogue in English, French, or Greek. (Find out the time in advance for your language preference.) Not scheduled on full-moon evenings, 2 nights before, or 1 night after; seating on the hill of Pnyx; small entrance fee for a chair; even less for a cushion. The French sponsors turned over the whole $240,000 of equipment to the Greek National Tourist Organization, on completion of their contract.

The summertime concerts by the **Athens State Orchestra** or ancient drama performances in the **Herodus Atticus Theater** at the base of the Acropolis are wonderful. The combination of romantic antiquities and starlit nights is unforgettable.

Changing of the Guard at the Tomb of the Unknown Soldier is spectacularly colorful; Sunday morning only at 11 A.M. is the big ceremony, but every hour on the hour you may witness the less-glamorous starch.

The **Zappion Gardens** are renowned for art shows, held at intervals throughout the year.

Folk dancing takes place under the stars nightly from May to October, weather permitting, at the theater on the west flank of the Philopappus hill, across the Acropolis. Matinees on Wednesday and Sunday.

The **Epidaurus Drama Festival** (June and July) draws 50-thousand foreign spectators annually. Greek theater at its purest; marvelous acoustics; top-caliber stars. Don't miss it. Or, if you do, there are 45 others from which to choose throughout the land.

For more spirited cultural intake, there's the **September Wine Festival** in **Daphne**. All the free drink you can hold; said to be more exciting than a barrel of bromo.

Don't forget the **Aegean cruises**, ranging from 1 to 7 days, which can be enchanting if you pick the right vessel. (See "Greek Islands.")

More than a dozen trailer camps or tenting sites have been set up in various rural areas. Check the Automobile and Touring Club of Greece for further information.

§TIP: Most newspaper kiosks, hotel desks, and travel bureaus carry what might be called Greek *Cue* magazines; *The Week in Athens, What's on in Athens,* and *Tourist Week.* They're in English, and they're often free. Since employees of the newer hostelries are not always up on the latest doin's, these little publications are invaluable.

DELPHI   This classic sightseeing target, 105 miles from Athens, draws countless excursionists—and well it should, because few travel rewards in

Greece are richer. A now-abuilding cultural and spiritual center also may bring crusades of pilgrims and scholars to its majestic heights in the very near future. **Transportation** CHAT offers a bus tour for about $20, including lunch; the ride is 4 hours each way. Key Tours, the cooperative enterprise of Athens travel agencies, also provides worthy packages aboard air-conditioned Pullman coaches. Private operators base their tariffs on the number of passengers—and prices are positively cutthroat. For one person, the standard rate is from $150 to $200, depending on the size of the car; for 5 occupants the range is from $40 to $50 per head—for a simple one-day outing! There are magnificent vistas peppering this road; all buses pause frequently for picturetaking. Many visitors prefer to drive themselves at a leisurely pace and hire a guide when they arrive. The highway itself is not the best. **Points en route** The **Monastery of St. Luke** boasts a trove of outstanding eleventh-century mosaics. **Levadhia**, 1¼ hours out, comes up with a striking panorama of Mt. Parnassus and the Thebes Plain. Its principal restaurant, featuring the usual specialties plus peasant bread and beer, is unattractive. For sunny-day lunching, we much prefer the charming little establishment at Falling Water, on the edge of town. Scads of rug shops in this center, none of which seemed especially intriguing. **Arahova**, 6 miles before Delphi, nestles in a hillside; most of its homes are in Turkish style. In the mercantile district, we had the best luck at **Andreas N. Granitsiotos**; carpets range from $5 to $130; long-hair wool weaves are about $5 or less per pound; he also offers blankets and scarves. **Sights** The **Oracle**, **Museum**, and **Theater**—the why-and-wherefore of your trip, of course—are in the near suburbs of Delphi. On full-moon nights, scads of Athenians run up here to see the lovely phenomenon of moon beams on the ravine and the lower plain containing 5-million (!) olive trees. The reflections are such that it is impossible to discern where the land ends and the Gulf and Corinth begin. If you go, be sure to book a seafront room, of course. The settlement itself has 2000 permanent residents and is perched at an altitude of 2132 feet. **Hotels** The recently built, 100-room **Amalia** garners the local laurel wreath. Modernistic, wood-stone-and-glass-lined lobby, almost Danish in concept; lounge, dining room, and bar; efficient, color-toned bedchambers; air conditioning; small but light baths. Viewful, youthful, and you-ful. The **Xenia,** formerly called the Delphi and run by Spiros J. Damigos, offers a dining room with a wide terrace; a fresh lounge; 45 rooms, all with bath, and a view of the gulf; door numbers on tiles with flower patterns, a sweet touch; 4-story ranch-design construction; simple but tasteful. Down a peg, with identical rates, is **Vouzas**. Situated on the main thoroughfare; 60 units with 60 baths or showers; many outsiders with private terraces; roof restaurant with glorious sweep of the mountainscape; management by John Vouzas. Also good, but not quite up to the leaders. **Apollon** is Class-B, with 24 rooms and 4 baths; group tours predominate; 2nd-string. **Hermes** and **Baronos** are side-by-side; good vistas from both; okay. The **Parnassus** and **Pythia** are fair. **Castalia** is more frentic and less inviting; we found it smelly as well. Avoid all other lodgings in this area, because they're unlivable. The **Youth Hostel** is more fun than comfort—but, as old Plato said so gloomily, "If you've got youth, then who the hell cares?" **Restaurants** The **Amalia,** the **Xenia**, and the **Vouzas**, plus the 2 tourist pavilions (Mr.

Damigos has the **Belvedere**), are open all day; tea, sandwiches, and beer are served in the latter. Happy touring!

THINGS TO BUY At this writing, the Government is experimenting with seasonal schedules, *very* much subject to change: In summer, 7:45 A.M. to 2:45 P.M. (Mon., Wed., Sat.), 7:45 A.M. to 1:45 P.M. and 5 P.M. to 8 P.M. (Tue., Thu., Fri.); in winter, Monday through Friday from 8:30 A.M. to 1:30 P.M. and from 4 P.M. to 7:30 P.M. Everything is shut tight on Wednesday and Saturday afternoons; during the week only the kiosks, restaurants, and transportation offices are open during the long afternoon siestas.

As we go to the press, the shops below are still standing at their now-current addresses. However, midtown Athens is in such a turmoil of reconstruction that please don't be surprised by sudden relocations before your visit.

Furs? While furs are a terrific bargain, if you are not thoroughly conversant with their subtleties they can be terribly tricky to buy. That is why we suggest that you head straight for the 4-generations-old **J.A. Sistovaris & Sons, Inc.** (14 Voulis St., 4 Hermou St., and 9 Panepistimiou Sve., Athens), Greece's leading fur purveyors. Here is the largest house of its type in the nation, with the top name. Any of the Sistovaris' clan will happily assist you in showing their collection, which ranges from mink to broadtail to Persian lamb to leopard to their world-famous homegrown stone marten, and all kinds of foxes. Everything conforms to the high Sistovaris standards. Warning: Avoid *any* local guide or street "friend" who might insist on taking you to various "factories," or "showrooms," too many of which are fancied-up tourist traps; they'd make you a sucker for their commissions.

Handwoven ladies' clothes, regional crafts? **Levantis** (3 Nikis St.) is one of THE 2 quality places. Elias Levantis, an alumnus of Saks Fifth Avenue and 13 years of U.S. expertise, has designed ALL of the beautifully color-blended fabrics and models which comprise his exclusive 104-piece collection—each item individually named. *Don't miss it!* Supplementing his fascinating originals starting at $50, you'll find a lovely new line of his own washable cotton dresses in gay Hellenic patterns. He will custom-make in American sizes your choices of coats, capes, stoles, and slacks ensembles within 48 hours (if necessary) at the same prices. Also on hand are his famous adjustable golden belt, his uniquely created assembly of 67 different kombaloi ("worry beads") and the cream of the ceramic, ikon, copper, costume jewelry, and silk-scarf crop, plus other carefully selected temptations. Although the premises are small, it's miles, miles better than 98% of its competition.

Our other favorite is **Nikos and Takis** (10 Panepistimiou St., 10 Lisou St., and branches in Rhodes, Crete, Corfu, and Delphi). Their original and strikingly effective creations highlight the best of Byzantine and Classic Greek fashions—but with a sophistication and flair that is *so* special, *so* attractive, and *so* very much their own. Happily recommended.

Full honors for today's spectacular planet-wide renaissance of Greek gold jewelry in the international best-dressed set belong to one single genius—Ilias **Lalaounis**. In the capital he's at 6 Panepistimiou Ave., 12 Voukourestiou St., Athens Hilton, Tower of Athens, and G.B. Hotel; domestically you'll find branches on Mykonos, Corfu, and Rhodes; in Switzerland he displays at Greider's in Zürich and the Palace Hotel in St. Moritz, plus Bon Genie in Geneva. His herculean efforts are responsible for reviving the again-raging fashion for museum-style pieces that have enchanted ladies since the days (and nights) of Helen of Troy. His contemporary creations and interpretations—adored by chicly adorned women everywhere—comprise a vast collection of 18- and 22-karat gold treasures that is renewed constantly (the latest are 3 complete lines using movement as the theme). Bracelets, rings, earrings, necklaces, and pins identical to those forged in the Golden Age of Pericles wait to be worn in the Golden Age of You. The classical and Minoan-Mycenaean periods predominate, with their emphasis on lions, serpents, and other talismans of Ancient Greece; a 2nd line of eleventh-century Byzantine reproductions captivates more ornate feminine tastes. Prices? Amazingly low for such purity of gold and purity of craftsmanship. All staffers speak English, as does the Maestro himself. Here's ladyluck if we ever saw it!

Sterling creations? The **4 Lamda** (Tower of Athens, at Messogion and Sinopis streets) is another showcase for the ever-rich, ever-versatile talents of Mr. Lalaounis—but it owes its name and its inspiration to his young daughters Katerina, Dimitra, Maria, and Joanna. Sterling silver, crystal, plastic, and semiprecious stones are the media, and family genius is the catalyst. Inspired and inspiring.

Antiques? Exactly these same jet-setters and shipping heiresses also flock to the colorful and knowledgeable Constantine Haritakis, near the King's Palace Hotel. His shop is small but his friendships are global in extent. Icons are one of his specialties. Ask for the ebullient, English-speaking "Mr. Taca" in person.

Extraordinary rugs? **A. Karamichos & Co.** (3 Mitropoleos St. upstairs) for at least 400 years—probably a thousand!—has been the leading creator of Greece's *flokati*—gorgeous, fluffy, 100% virgin wool floor coverings. They're produced in western Thessaly where craftsmen have been weaving them since the age of Odysseus, washing them under the crystal cascades of clear mountain water, billowing the natural lustrous shag in the Aegean sun, and then sometimes dying them to radiant hues. Sold by weight—which provides a measure of their purity—these top-line Karamichos carpets are handloomed to last a lifetime. (The ones in our own home have given daily service only for a decade or so, but they look better today than when we bought them. Bred in water, literally, they have improved with both washing and wear.) Mr. Karamichos and Chief Assistant Eugene Alexander are so justly proud of their creations that, as far as we have learned, here is the sole dealer in the land who gives a money-back guarantee. It was also the sole *flokati* representative selected by the Government officially to exhibit at the Montreal Olympic Games. The top-quality handwoven beauties are kept exclusively here, because this connoisseur refuses to sell them to department stores or elsewhere. The extra-thick category (appropriately labeled Karamichos Anniversary Flokati) is the Rolls-Royce of the art. Tariffs are from $45 up. If miracles could happen, Karamichos is the only place we would know where you could buy a magic carpet. Just plain wonderful!

Greek handicrafts, souvenirs, paintings? **A. Martin's Attika Giftshops** (6

Constitution Sq., under the Attika Palace Hotel) is the largest institution of its type in the nation. Over 2000 different items—ranging from antiquities to brass incense burners to ceramic cups to copper shields to marble-based Parthenons to onyx pencil holders to wolf-sactal rugs to . . . well, you name it—can be found on its premises. Prices? One can pick between a $1.85 wine glass or a $850 handwoven Minoan-style carpet (mailing and packing included). Please don't miss the Art Corner, which boasts one of the most impressive and most versatile displays of bas-relief copper work and contemporary paintings found in Greece today. The motto of this fine, honest house is "You are not a customer, but a guest"—and we'll bet you'll agree once you are met by genial Proprietor Fred Martin, his lovely wife Litsa, or his 2 hardworking sons Taki and Tom. Open weekdays (during regular shopping hours) *and* Sunday (10 A.M. to 1:30 P.M.) in High Season. Happily recommended. At the **National Organization of Hellenic Handicrafts** (9 Mitropoleos St.), you'll find 2 floors of Greek-made wares. The assemblage impressed us as being somewhat limited and somewhat bizarre, in a disappointing way. **Attlaos** (3 Stadium St., in the Arcade) is considerably better than average. But in the regiments of "soovineer jernts" which brassily overcrowd the center of the city, so much crude, tasteless, claptrap junk is in evidence that we've lost all interest in it. No need to list more names, because in store after store you'll see exactly the same rubbish—except at the above-mentioned Levantis and possibly "**National Welfare Fund**" (24 Voukourestiou St.).

Pandrossou St. is the **Flea Market** of Athens—grand fun for the shophound. This tiny street is most certainly worth a look.

More copper articles? Take a stroll along Efestou St., for the darndest assortment of copper utensils and bric-a-brac you've probably ever seen—most at a song.

Reading matter? **Eleftheroudakis** (Nikis St., opposite the Post Office on Constitution Square) carries a mouth-watering supply of American and English books, originals and reprints, from the latest novels to a technical library any U.S. bookseller would be proud of. Hospitable, knowledgeable, kindly staff; tops for browsers. **Pandelides** (11 Amerikis St.) is also worthy for between-the-covers activities—literary variety.

Department stores? **The Minion** (Patissia St.), **Lambropoulos Bros.** (Aeolou and Stadium Sts.) and the **Athenee** (Stadium St.) are the national pacesetters. Unfortunately this field is slow when compared to the faster similar tracks in some of the larger lands abroad.

There are no taxes or duties on purchases by foreign visitors, regardless of the amounts involved.

Other good buys in Athens? Since space is too limited here, please consult this year's extensively revised, up-to-the-minute annual edition of our *Shopping Guide to Europe* for a number of additional tips and suggestions.

THINGS NOT TO BUY Shoddy inexpensive ready-made dresses or suits (improving through the rash of new Italian-style boutiques, but still not up to U.S. standards; some of the medium-price Greek ones are beauties, however); the cheaper ready-made Greek blouses (the Hellenic figure has narrow

shoulders and a huge bust); all imported merchandise except books, regardless of category (taxes and Customs duties add 200% *extra* to all foreign-
made cosmetics, as an extreme example).

LOCAL RACKETS   The one that blackened our eye on recent trips still
riles us—the chauffeur-driven car gouge. Please excuse us if we don't again
spell out the way this swindle works, since our blood pressure would run
550/250. You'll find it described, down to the last anguished tear, under
"Hired Cars." Also in Athens there has been a major influx of touts who
approach foreigners of both genders on the street, shake hands as effusively
as if they had been bosom pals for life, and then smooth-talk the suckers into
3rd-or-4th-rate shops (furs, especially). The only cure: Brush them off instantly, rudely, and *hard!* Outside of these, there are very few others. The
Greek people as a whole are extraordinarily honest and decent. They bargain
ardently (less ardently, however, than their Eastern neighbors), but once their
word is given, it is their bond. You'll find them as reliable as any Europeans,
and much more reliable than some.

INFORMATION ON GREECE   The U.S. fountainhead for tourist infor-
mation is the **National Tourist Organization of Greece**, 601 Fifth Ave., New
York 10017, N.Y. Your next best bet is to write to the Office of the Secretary-
General, **Greek National Tourist Organization**, Stadium St., Athens.

For actual travel *arrangements* (ticket, sightseeing, excursions, and the
like), for more than 2 decades we've continued to have perfect luck with
Hellenic Tours, 3 Stadium St., Athens. Director Nelson Malamed and his
charming wife Mary couldn't be kinder, nicer, or more efficient, and we
recommend this company heartily.

Finally, please turn to the "Yacht Chartering" section in the immediately
following "Greek Islands" chapter for important suggestions to protect
voyagers in this racket-infested industry.

Greek Islands

AND CRUISING

You really haven't seen Greece unless you've visited the islands. No 2 are alike. They are scattered in their infinite variety from the Ionian to Aegean Seas, and Crete dips down into the Mediterranean.

Although the larger targets are available by air as well as by sea, we recommend hands down that you, the discerning traveler, don your dark glasses with your widest-brim hat and head for a ship (be it cruise or chartered). *If you proceed with utmost caution in the selection of your vessel,* here can be one of the most heavenly experiences of your entire journey.

AEGEAN CRUISES   Since 1-to-14-day trips are available, plus special weekend jaunts, which should you choose? Every ship's officer and ship's social hostess with whom we've ever discussed this question corroborates our own conviction that the longer the Aegean voyage, the greater the rewards. When a sizable group of strangers is thrown together, only the fastest workers aboard are given enough time in a weekend or even in 4 days to sort out the fellow-passengers whose companionship beckons with the greatest fun. Therefore, following proper selection of your vessel and your stateroom, our most urgent recommendation is that you live it up at sea for one full week.

Next, as of now but subject to change, these itineraries, which begin and end at the Athens port-suburb of Piraeus, are virtually standard. The 3-day wanderer will probably head to Delos, Mykonos, Rhodes, Crete, and Santorini. The 4-day sailor is almost sure of stopping at Crete, Rhodes, and Mykonos, with pauses at such alternates as Kusadasi ("Island of Birds" in Asia Minor), Patmos, Hydra and/or Santorin. The 7-day pilgrim is even more certain—but not 100%—to disembark at Crete, Santorin, Rhodes, Alexandria, Delos, and Mykonos.

Next, depending upon your option, any day can be sailing day. Departures are usually scheduled for late afternoon or early evening. Long voyages weigh anchor between late morning and late afternoon. Current capacities vary between 200 and 750 berths. No company runs these cruises between the end of October and the middle of March. Most operators start later and end earlier.

For details and reservations on all of the vessels listed below, please consult splendidly efficient, all-knowing **Hellenic Tours**, 3 Stadium St., Athens, or your travel agent.

Last, on all of the good ones, you can expect to find stabilizers, full air conditioning, ample lounges, at least 2 bars, poor-to-fair institutional-style cuisine, a ship's hospital supervised by a doctor, a swimming pool (perhaps 5 postage stamps in breadth), a beauty parlor, a cinema, a sundeck (too often cruelly cramped), trap shooting, a nightclub with orchestra, and piped music. A few offer such extras as elevator, laundry service, telephones in the state-rooms (the *Jason* and a couple of others feature a 10-button system through-out), a sauna, and a small gymnasium.

However, barring the meager handful of costliest deluxe accommodations, you can also *count* on the fact that the miniaturization of your stateroom will dismay and disappoint you at first sight. This is why we beseech you to heed this special word of counsel: *Pare down your wardrobe to its absolute mini-mum before climbing up that gangplank,* because the storage space allotted to each routine excursionist is so sparse that it is absurd. Any good-natured hotelier in Athens would be happy to store your excess while you're afloat, either free of charge or for a trifling fee.

In all the ships which have earned our approval, *generally* you will find clean quarters, decent service, adequate but not opulent comfort, and tariffs commensurate with value received. But let's be mountain-brook-clear in stressing the word "generally," because the lack of consistency in the quality of these cruises—usually excellent but occasionally execrable—has given seri-ous grounds for many complaints to this *Guide*.

The Sun Line (now navigated by America's Marriott Corp.) has recently unveiled the reigning Queen of the Aegean, the 700-passenger *Stella Solaris.* This most sophisticated frog in the pond—lately refitted at a cost of $20,-000,000—is a beauty. Inside she has become an opulently lavish floating hotel with altered stateroom dimensions, a rich new stem-to-stern décor, and just about every amenity possible to imagine. She breaks the waves smoothly on the 7-day circuit in summer and brings happiness to Caribbean trippers in winter. For big-ship buffs, what a honey she is! We are equally fond of the tasteful and dignified *Stella Oceanis*, which roams the waters of the Mid-Med and the Aegean. Talk about dreamboats—these 2 have it.

The *Atlas,* formerly the comely *Ryndam*, is now the flagship of the Epirotiki Line. She, too, has been renovated almost totally. Her public rooms reflect the outstanding talents of Maurice Bailey—and there are many happy surprises, including such extras as a heated inside swimming pool (not count-ing the big one in the sun), a cinema, and a fastness of open deck space. Nearly all of her cabins are relatively spacious vis-à-vis much of her competition. Very sound, too.

The new, 4800-ton *Aquarius* has taken to the 7-day seaway, covering 11 ports including Turkey on her itinerary. Again designer Maurice Bailey conceived her interior garb. She has a swimming pool and nightclub, plus an intimacy evoked by her somewhat small capacity (280 voyagers). We haven't gone with her yet, but she is a popular lady who is known for good service.

We especially like the *Orion* for the comparative spaciousness of her cabins (the largest in the Aegean fleet) and her vast expanses of glass for better sightseeing. The Piraeus-Istanbul 7-day route is her beat in season. Although she carries only 143 vacationers, she has most of the amenities of her bigger colleagues, including air conditioning, stablizers, and a lot more. One of our leading favorites.

The *Galaxy* is slightly smaller. You'll find her spinning in 3- and 4-day orbits in her cool, steady, and sleek way. Especially amiable crew.

The new *Golden Odyssey* will spin her yarn this season. Built by Danes and managed by the Royal Cruise Line, this creation of modern shipbuilding art is already being touted as one of the finest ladies to take to sea. She roams in 12-day circuits, and from initial reports, we'd guess she'll be a very popular gal indeed.

The sea-green *Jason*, who hastens for the Epirotiki Line, continues her love affair with Turkey on the conventional 7-day run. She is imaginative in her ambiance and versatile in her facilities. If you can afford her best, the Castor and Polux suites on Apollo Deck are worth the extra investment. Next best are staterooms #A-1 to #A-6, equipped with tubs. Try #P-7 to #P-22 on D Deck for a less costly but satisfactory buy. We'd avoid E Deck (named "Nereus Deck" by the PR-minded owners) as we'd avoid sleeping in a bird-house. For this one-week cruise, she's high among the pacesetters.

The *Jupiter,* 3rd in size in the whole armada, is reported to have brought pride by her performance since she was totally renovated by the Epirotiki geniuses somewhat recently. She's a 3- and 4-day swinger with fine lines, which we have seen. Unhappily, we've not yet been aboard her.

Lower on our tide line comes the *Kentavros* (K Lines). Despite her ancient age of about 3 decades, she still skims at her normal 16 knots. Here's another split-week carrier with 3- and 4-day offerings. Her major conversion in '65 turned out to be salubrious in some ways and disappointing in others. But she's so well scrubbed, radiates such a happy aura, and is manned by such a good crew that Guidesters' reports have been cheerful.

Both the *Atlantis* (a sister to the *Jason* and the *Stella Oceanis*) and the *Illyria* (converted by her new Blue Aegean Sea Line skippers) are fresh debs on the 3-to-4-day circuits. Both are recommendable.

The *Poseidon* (Greek name) or *Neptune* (Latin name), the same ship that goes on 4-day swings, is one we haven't tried personally. We have had several complaints recently alleging that this line juggles reservations and cabins to better suit its load factors. True?

The 23,000-ton *Navarino,* formerly the *Gripsholm,* carries old-world nostalgia into new ports of call this season. The conversion came too late for us to incorporate in our rankings.

If hotel class vessels are not for you, the 620-ton *Meltemi II* slips her moorings at Corinth for 7-day classical Greece and Ionian Island loops including a stop at Itea (port of Delphi). Remodeled from a Yugoslavian coastal steamer, she's now in the heavy yacht class, albeit not a very luxurious one.

Reportedly a happy crew; superior cookery, according to the logs of many aboard; no swimming pool; no live music; all cabins outside and air-conditioned.

The *Saronic Star,* quite new in these waters, is our prime choice for one-day cruises from Piraeus to Aegina, Hydra, and Poros. Also very good are the *Meltemi I* and the *Marina,* but their ages put them below her class. The *Hermes* zips out to the same isles under the Epirotiki burgee. Rates run $25 or so, including lunch, for a sailing day that dawns at 8:30 A.M. and ends at 7 P.M. The *Romantica* (Chandris Cruises) offers weekend and 5-day excursions. She's not our glass of Greek wine. *Neither this one nor any other scheduled ship unlisted above—is recommended this year.*

RHODES   The "Isle of Roses" now has more tourist beds than Athens. (Astonishing, but true!) Yet the parade of hotels cheek-by-jowl à la Miami Beach has not seriously affected the basic charm of the capital or its environs. Battalions of buses? Yes. Regiments of new lodgings? Yes. Alien hordes of migratory invaders? Yes. But these have not made serious dents on the island's historic radiance. Its fascination remains intact. To call it "spoiled" is a canard.

Location? Largest of the Dodecanese Islands, roughly 16 miles off the Turkish coast and 280 air miles southeast of Athens. *Size?* 54 by 27 miles, shaped like an ocarina. *Population?* Nearly 70 thousand. *Cities?* **Rhodes** proper, with 30-thousand people, is the capital and the only important settlement. **Lindos**, a whitewashed village with its own Acropolis, is about an hour away. In fair weather this charming coastal hamlet is a *must* for sightseers despite the increasing influx of this century's worst examples of so-called architecture—visual pollution. *Connections?* From **Athens** (Piraeus): Overnight boat service which stops at other islands en route—simple and pretty rugged; from Athens airport 50 weekly Olympic Airways flights which take a little over an hour; from other islands twice per week. Caution: In peak periods, traffic is so heavy that normally you will be asked to show your confirmed return ticket before Olympic will permit you to board in Athens. A recent 600-yard runway extension enables larger airliners to fly in and out. Although this is calculated to relieve the pressure, we anticipate only greater congestion as the jumbo-jet-boom zooms. Even as you read this, a new, $10,000,000 airport is making its in-Rhodes 10 miles from the capital to accommodate legions of sight-and-sun-seers; possibly it will be functional by this simmertime. *People?* Lovely; very clean, overwhelmingly kind to Americans. With the influx of tourism, avarice and graspiness are beginning to raise their inevitable heads. *Best season?* Late spring or early fall. Summer is fine when the breezes blow, but when they don't, it can be hot; winter is comparatively mild, but some spells are unpleasant; prices from November through February in many hostelries have been slashed 50% as a spur to Off Season tourism.

Hotels For far more comprehensive information on certain hostelries than space limitations permit here, interested travelers are referred to the annually revised *Fielding's Selected Favorites: Hotels and Inns, Europe* by our Marco

Polo son, Dodge Temple Fielding. The latest edition, in which a total of 300-odd favored possibilities were handpicked from the 4000-plus personally inspected, will be at your bookstore early this year.

With its vast new wing, the **Grand Summer Palace** bows welcome to 800 courtiers, all of whom may make their individual splashes in any of 4 swimming pools, including 1 indoors for cooler months. Oases of snacking corners and alfresco lounges; nightclub-*taverna;* casino for year-round gambols from 7 P.M. to the wee hours. Some units with verandas facing gardens and pools; other seafront accommodations slightly more expensive; winter reductions about 50%. Its recent change of proprietorship over to the prestigious Astir group of Athens fame is certainly a harbinger of even better days ahead. The situation is its primary asset. The **Dionysos**, launched in 1970, is probably next. This also-superbly-sited youngster consists of 2 separate air-conditioned buildings, tennis courts, minigolf, and 3 swimming pools. The first structure, in the deluxe category, is limited to suites which offer a 2-bed room and bath, a sitting room, a kitchenette with refrigerator, and a big veranda also with a magnificent view of the sea. There is a garden cocktail bar plus an adjoining snack installation featuring regional specialites. The second structure is a complex which embraces the main dining room, the main bar, a cinema, a lecture hall, and a nightclub. The accommodations here, down one peg in the "A" category, are conventional in pattern but not in décor; refrigerators throughout are a thoughtful touch. Satisfactory in its bracket. The **Miramare Beach**, an ambitious project 3 miles from the city on the airport road, offers a new central edifice, 167 bungalows, a later 60-unit 2-story section, and a scattering of 3-to-4-room Deluxe cottages; its official category is Luxury. Beachfront ambiance in a lovely setting; swimming pool; atmospheric Greek *taverna* with regional specialties. The faded **Des Roses** is due to be uprooted and replanted by gardeners from the Bank of Greece who own it. Blossom time is unknown.

The young 11-story **Rodos Bay** looms up as one of the loftier buildings on the island, allegedly 30 feet higher than the vanished Colossus of Rhodian legend. (*Of course* you remember that this ancient statue was 100.206 feet tall!) Sited 2 miles out toward the airport, this entry fronts the beach from a slight rise. Rooftop saltwater pool; bar and restaurant sharing a twinkling tableau of southwest Turkey; cookery that's easy to forget (service can be forgetful, too); shops, tennis, minigolf, and sauna; *taverna*; nightclub; cavernous, granite-girt lobby punctuated by wooden beams and paved with gray marble; 28 relatively spartan but air-cooled bungalows; 35 split-level suites; 175 bedchambers with white stucco walls, pastel-tiled decking, telephones, baths or showers. Our favorites are the high-ceilinged duplexes on the 5th level. Heavy group traffic, especially by German vanguards in summer. The **Belvedere** is back in the middle of town. Biggish structure with an austere sense of modernity; 165 rooms, all with bath or shower; the fronts have terraces looking seaward, but the backs peer onto a truck route. The food to us was inedible. Despite the nice pool and tennis court, we'd call it a noisy bunker. Not for us. The midcity **Mediterranean** was awash with cheapjack tours and redolent with petroleum odors on our visit. Very pleasant sidewalk terrace but otherwise too commercial and crass for our taste. This same group has unveiled its neighboring **Rodos Palace Resort Complex** consisting of a deluxe tower hotel for 800 plus chalet accommodation for nearly as many. The Maurice Bailey décor makes handsome use of marble and panels, with ample space and the clever employment of trickling water to add a note of solace. Cheerpacked grill, huge restaurant, colorful nightclub, pink coffee shop, shops also for shopping. We think this one shows real sticking power. The sleek **Oceanis,** with a relaxed composure, is sited out near the Miramare. Inviting swimming pool; fair public rooms; air conditioning; well-appointed bedchambers. If you prefer a noncentral address (across the highway from the breakers), this is it. The youthful **Metropolitan Capsis**, across from the Dionysos, is an imposing structure. Roof garden, pool, sauna, and gym; seaview rooms with air conditioning; food and service geared to the throngs of tour registrants who roll in as waves to the shore. The vastly widened **Golden Beach** peers furtively at Mt. Filerimos across a narrow strand of sand. Modern, sawtoothed structure perfectly complemented by enough athletic paraphernalia to sponsor its own Olympic games; bath, telephone, and radio for every registrant. The **Cactus**, **Sirabas**, and **Ibiscus** line up side by side by side, revealing equal proclivities for provoking our professional boredom. The young **Chevaliers Palace** may lack an apostrophe, but it offers a chivalrous welcome to some 300 pilgrims and sun worshippers. Decoratively, it jousts merrily with its own image: flags, armor, chain mail, and other hokum of ages gone by. This modern castle is air-conditioned, too, Sir Everyman and Lady Fairweather. **Imperial** is almost viewless. The **Marie**? New-y, but phooey. **Thermai** bubbles in its own sylvan park. So-so. The **Plaza** is pleasant but hardly a Ritz. The **Park**'s best feature is its nightclub. **Spartalis** eschews the obligatory pension policy. The 3rd floor, claiming the finest rooms, is vintage '61; not all accommodations have bath or shower however. **Olympic** has 46 small rooms; front units have terraces; baths just a bit more spacious than bassinets; one block from the sea; gaudy lobby. **Cairo Palace**'s 111 rooms have baths or showers (13 singles excepted); restaurant and main hall brashly redecorated; this one caters heavily to Germans. The **Soleil** has 93 rooms, 41 baths, one newer wing, and a garden restaurant; it has finally roused itself sufficiently to add curtains to its windows. Many new Class C hotels have sprung up; to U.S. trippers, they're so basic they're scarcely worth mentioning. In the mountains, 30 miles distant, there is one choice—the **Elaphos**. No swimming pool and way-the-hell-and-gone up on a Grecian Alp. More for sea-sickened Hellenes than for sea-coasting North Americans. Seasonal only.

Restaurants Most hotels impose a full-pension plan, but a few independents have had the courage to serve the more adventurous public. **Kon-Tiki,** moored at the extension of a marina which overlooks a small bay, is the tightest little ship on the horizon, in this salt's opinion. All the nautical trimmings come with this one: Hurricane lamps, tarpaulins, ship's tackle, and the fetching charm of a cozy bark. Excellent regional cuisine, among the best we've had in Rhodes; sparkling cleanliness; friendly crew; reasonable tabs. Our pick of the fleet. **Oscar** is next. **Deluca** gave us wretched regional fare in something less than a hospital-clean atmosphere. The **Farm House**, a 3-minute walk from the Grand Hotel, is recommendable. Bamboo trappings;

sea-vista terrace in summer; open-kitchen hearthside in winter. Inexpensive, simple, and good. **Aira Mare** and **Maison Fleuri** rank high in the luxury category; the former is Greek, the latter French. **Anixis** is a medium-priced winner; **Kaliva** is a cutie by the sea. **Elli** is so-so for snacks. As for local *tavernas,* the colorful **Vrachos** huddles by the shore; it is haunted by burly sailor lads and assorted toughies. **Arapaki** is a worthy alternate. The **Yachting Club** sails in with alfresco service; forthright, unglamorous cuisine; fine view. The rebuilt **Park Rodini,** 2 miles from the center, comes up with music occasionally; agreeable for dancing; not too bad for a late bite and a nuzzle. Several **cafés** line the New Market; all are dirty and 3rd-class to our eyes. **Peristeri** is emphatically not recommended.

Night Life Nearly all of the Deluxe and First-class hotels have nightclubs that function from time to time. The **Miramare** spotlights dancing in the bar. **Rhodes By Night**, near the Miramare, is a gimmicky mock-fortress structure offering dining (fish specialties), dancing, cabaret, and no-seaview portholes. Summer patio; clean; festivities from 8 P.M. until the last Socratic barfly crawls out; open all year. Best of the circuit. Café-bars *(kafenion)* are popular, especially in the Old Town. In the New Town **Aketon** is tops, followed by **Trianon** and **Lindos**.

Things to See The site of one of the Seven Wonders of the World, the **Colossus** of Rhodes, which once straddled the harbor and which was destroyed by an earthquake in 224 B.C. (a group of sculptors and archaeologists plan to erect an aluminum replica of the original); a 1-hour tour of the ramparts and defenses of the **Old Town** (a *must* for every visitor), built by the Crusaders; the magnificent medieval **walled city** of the Knights Hospitalers of St. John of Jerusalem (today the Knights of Malta), with its castles, palaces, and fairy-tale ruins; the **Thermal Springs of Callithea,** 6 miles out, with Moorish architecture, a grotto restaurant, a spring house, 3 kinds of beneficial waters, and a discouraging array of 120—count 'em 120—toilets; the splendid cellar **Aquarium** with an amazing variety of rays, moray eels, turtles, brilliant starfish, and local sea denizens in a series of tanks; the somewhat overrated **Valley of Butterflies** at Petaloudes, 15 miles out, where clouds of pinkish-gray beauties rise by the thousands as you walk along the little cascades (season only). The young-in-legs may pedal about the capital on a rented bike for very soft-spoked rates. And for other types of sightseers, we've read that a nudist colony for 500 bare-skin buffs was to be undraped in the coastal region opposite the airport from the capital. Its announcement blithely stated, "The accommodations will consist of huts for two, planned so that the erection and placement takes into consideration the local topography and vegetation." Anyone for landscape gardening? Finally, try not to miss that aforementioned drive out to **Lindos**, an hour from your metropolitan doorstep. This ancient, lime-washed, seacoast village is nestled in a rugged meander of an age-old ravine. Park your car in the town square and take the 20-minute hike up the footpath to the cliff-high fortress and the quietly eroding sandstone Acropolis. The awe-inspiring vistas of the sapphire water, the cubistic white-on-white jumble of houses, the fishing harbor, the still lagoon in a bracelet of volcanic rock, and the far-ranging sweep of a golden sandy beach, are breathtaking. If you pack a picnic lunch, nibble and day-dream on the flower-covered slopes below the ramparts; you will be much happier than if you had dined at the handful of rawboned *tavernas* in the town. On the way down, take the path leading to the small but gemlike Byzantine chapel. Be sure to give a moderate tip to the 212-year-old woman who explains in perfect Greek just what every statue, painting, niche, and curlicue means (to her, not to you, unless you speak the language). If you *must* overnight, the **Pallas** and **Electra** boardinghouses are just about the only pads available; neither will bring fond memories of your nights at the Ritz. The drive back is over the same good but narrow route. For us, it was one of the high points of a very recent island odyssey.

Things to Buy For that marvelous Rhodes pottery, try **Icaros** first; retail store at 1 Museum Square, factory 1½ miles on the outskirts, and the leader of the industry. All sorts of animals in ceramics, from $1 to $6; large dolls in regional dress of various islands, from $4 to $12—what a gift! At the factory, we bought 6 Rhodian beer steins ($2.50 each) for shipment to our home in Mallorca, Spain; they arrived promptly and unbroken, and we're crazy about them; while shipping charges to U.S. could double these prices, they'd *still* be an extraordinary bargain. **Frarakis** (7 Museum St.) is probably the 2nd-best choice; same prices as Icaros, and some different specialties. **Papanikitas** (corner of Museum Square and Street of the Knights) is also good for similar things. For costume jewelry, try **George Stavrianakis** (2 shops—Hippocrates Square and 21 Ethnarchis Macarios St.): Rose of Rhodes earrings for $9.50—that sort of specialty. For 18- or 22-karat gold objects and other more costly items, **Lalos Louizidis** (French St. at the New Market), **Skiathitis** Bros. (just below Cairo Palace Hotel), and **Demetrius Anghelou** (Museum Square) are the best in the city. For embroidery, **Arapoudis** offers a collection of needlepoint, blouses, bridge sets, and children's local costumes. In general, we're very disappointed by what shopkeepers offer in Rhodes. Too much of it is sucker bait for the mass tourist trade.

Things Not to Buy A gigolo—of any size, shape, shade, or flavor. The Rhodes Rogue's Gallery is alive with more slippery critters than can be found in the Bronx Zoo's Reptile House. These Lothario Lukes, this island's indige-nous vipers, encourage Senseless Sallys to ply them with expensive talismans for their favors; then they seek kickbacks from some of the sleazier brand of shopkeepers. Even worse, these Strangeloves have been known to blackmail their naïve nymphs after the ladies have returned to hearth and home. The mayor asserts that a lass can usually recognize them by their English, Ger-man, or Swedish vocabularies which inevitably stress and restress, "I love you!"

Further Data Write or get in touch with the Director of Tourism, Rhodes; his office will send you a boatload of brochures and handle your travel puzzles.

Take a look at Rhodes; you won't be sorry. It's a delightful off-trail adven-ture for the inquisitive or the peace-seeking voyager.

CORFU   Here's a little charmer measuring 48 by 20½ miles and boasting 150-thousand residents—1/5th of them in the city proper. At its closest point, Albania—you can't swim over without a visa—is only ½ mile away. If you think you're seeing green spots before your eyes, you are, because this isle sprouts more than 5-million olive trees. (The color-blind might note in advance that the bigger species bear oranges!) Olive oil, the only industry that challenges tourism, has finally lost its lead against the mushrooming facilities for the traveler. Here is a floral paradise—the principal garden spot, in fact, of Greece. This is due chiefly to the abundance of rich soil and many little soft raindrops. The gentle atmosphere is scented by wildly rampant natural blossoms—wisteria, jasmine, dahlias, camellias, mimosa—Ferdinand's bull-heaven! The airport has been enlarged, but it still could use another notch or 2 in its belt; Olympic wings in domestically; a few jets swoop in on international runs; British Airways also has hammered out a link with London Town.

The Italy-Greece car ferries almost certainly will call again this year, from 3 to 7 days per week, depending upon the time of year. Smaller craft make daily runs to and from the Greek mainland. Generally, this sea-blessed community is more *mañana*-prone than Mallorca; it trails its Balearic rival's construction explosion by about a decade. *Corfu*, its capital and main port, has no commercial fishing interests whatever. The best swimming can be found at the Yacht Club; the Cavalieri Hotel can arrange it for you. *Dassia* (4 miles) splashes up next. *Paleokastritsa* (40 minutes) is packed with bathers; *Ermones* is pebbly; *Sidari* has sand, but it's an hour's drive; *Kanoni* (2 miles) is rocky and not too appealing. *Mon Repos*, in the town itself, isn't worth the effort.

Hotels   At *Kanoni,* 2½ miles from Corfu town, the famous Hilton chain just has forged a new link incorporating 300 rooms, 2 swimming pools, 2 tennis courts, and other vacation amenities—none of which we've seen, since it opened after we went to press. Ask your travel agent to fill you in on last-minute details if your interest is stimulated on this one. In town, **Corfu Palace**, in a beautiful garden setting, undoubtedly remains the Deluxe leader. Extensively reconstructed, this year it again will remain open around the calendar. Spacious, well-furnished rooms, all with bath and balcony; Albatros grill with cocktail pianotations and dancing until midnight; tantalizing cuisine under excellent Helvetian-trained chef; romantic setting embracing the enclave of a seawater swimming pool (the sea itself is not inviting here), cabanas, and snack bar; lovely barbecue dinners served once a week in warm months; indoor splasher, sauna, and gym projected. The respected Swiss Gauer experts command this one and the Miramare Beach. On the northwest coast 9 miles from the city, the Gauer group also opened the linear and low **Emones Beach**. Gorgeous site on a small mountain; golf links on one flank, pebble beach on another; spectacular pool with terrace and snackery overlooking this precinct of paradise; tennis court; inside-outside dining; 2 bars; lounge dominated by a massive pewter hearth; 30 air-conditioned rooms in main unit plus clusters of bungalows in 14 tiers blanketing the hillside. A gem among Greek resorts which we salute enthusiastically. Back in town, the plaza-sited **Cavalieri** now seems to be slipping a bit but it remains a fair enough port in a storm. This was once run by the dashing Count Spyro Flamburiari, who lately has been concentrating all his energy and considerable talents on the construction of the new and vast **Poseidon Beach** at *Nissaki*. This suburban sprawl ultimately will accomodate 600 "villagers" sheltered in all manner of dwelling space. We can't wait to see it. Beyond this one is the colorful **Nissaki Beach**, which is approached down a steep lane from above the hotel. Appealing taverna; active bar; pebble beach; pool; unspoiled site for romantic holidaymakers. **Corcyra Beach Hotel** perches bright and white on a slope above *Gouvia Bay* (5 miles from Corfu town); it faces the tiny islet of Vidos and St. George's Chapel on the promontory. Entrance beside a filling station to a stairstep main building; 20 bedchambers in the central complex; more than 100 bungalows; swimming pool plus 2 private beaches. Simple, clean, not at all expensive. Worth every drachma, if you don't mind holidaying with hordes of pilgrims from Europe's cloudy climes. **Castello Corfu**, converted from a private villa, offers a 30-room main building and a 26-room annex. Ownership by Emil Bouas, one of the most genial, obliging, and conscientious Bonifaces on the isle; most accommodations with bath; entrance via a narrow, winding lane; no pool but swimming club about a mile away. A restful haven. The **Kanoni**, one mile south of Corfu and just below the airline flight path, is a horizontal slab containing a restaurant-by-pool, 150 bedchambers (mostly twins) with balconies, cold-air-by-button, telephones, and baths. Adequate, if unoriginal. **Astor-Corfu** is on the noisy main street of the port. Dreary lobby; drearier rooms; only 50% private-bath count; beds so lumpy they'd fascinate holidaying phrenologists; chilly reception. Not recommended. For emergency use only, the **Swiss** and **Splendid** are dinky, with no private plumbing; Third class. In the suburbs, one hour from town, the attractive **Miramare-Beach** is the present front-runner in a homestretch challenge. Its 150 seaside bungalows are patterned after the Miramare Beach at Rhodes. Minigolf; trapshooting; water skiing; donkeys and carts; children's playground; "Miramarette" summer Fiats for hire; bus service to airport, dock or city; a meal and bathing exchange with the Corfu Palace is available to guests—but with that long, narrow road which is *so* crowded in summer we recommend that you stay put. The **Marbella Beach**, 12 miles south of town, is composed of 64 Moorish-style apartments, plus a huge main building, a discothèque-in-a-cave, and other dazzlers. The **Messonghi** reminds us of one of those WW II rest centers for shell-shocked troops. Large, unimaginative edifice wrapped around 462 sterile rooms; boringly traditional lobby; beach that only a shipwrecked Noel Coward could be grateful for. We weren't excited by it—or in it—or even around it. The neighboring, 4-story **Delfinia** is fair in amenities, but it's as groupy as a Cherokee Conclave. The **Eagli** has been refeathered; we don't like its site. The smaller **Oasis** is crassly commercial; it has a better location. Across the island, you'll find the **Mega** and the **Costa** in *Ypsos*; there are 2 tyke-size hostelries at *Zephyros*. The **Grand**, 10 miles west of the capital at *Glyfada* is one of the safest Corfu bets if you yearn for solitude and natural beauty. You'll find 210 air-cooled rooms, suites and apartments, each with its own bath, phone, and radio. At *Kondokali,* the First-class **Palace** is young and worthy; at *Dassia,* the **Chandris** offers both hotel and bungalow-downing; the **Kerkyra Golf** takes its name from its location; you'll probably enjoy it if you want to avoid crowds.

Restaurants (1) **La Lucciola**, (an ancient inn en route to *Paleokastritsa* with good Italian cookery), (2) **Moulin Vert** (in town; French and Greek specialties), (3) **Tripa** (*taverna* in an old country house at Cynopiastes), (4) **The Rock** (fabulous bay situation; disco activity, too), (5) **Xenia Paleokas-tritsa** (excellent seafare), (6) **Dionyssos** (Greek and international skillets).

Night Life The **Achilleion Casino** has brought a shaft of moonlight to the otherwise dreary afterdark situation. Within this Pompeiian-style oasis renovated to the toss of $1,000,000, you'll find roulette, baccarat, and boule; Entrepreneur Baron Hartman von Richthofen, the only surviving brother of the famous Red Baron of WW I, has older marbles spinning at Baden-Baden. Gaming rooms, nightclub, restaurant, and snack bar open from 5 P.M. to 4 A.M.; park and museum available from 9 A.M. to 1 P.M.; operates year round. Here are 3 straight passes by Lady Luck for Corfu, and a giant step for the farsighted oracles behind Greek tourism. **Bora-Bora** and **Koukouvaia** both feature disco dancing between the new port and *Kondokali*. **Nouveau** does a similer thing in the town.

Shopping The "Hurry-Hurry-Hurry!" class of tourist junk is predominant. Olive-wood bowls and canes made by prisoners make curious souvenirs. **Peroulis Brothers**, Esplanade, has a representative mélange of this merchandise; they also market filigree work, bracelets, and Venetian-style wares. Small silver boats bearing Corfu's heraldry and handwrought gold rings symbolizing the 7 Ionian Islands are available here, as well as at **Tantis Anthony** and **Ionas Spiros**. Ladies' wear? Try the **Royal Boutique**. Finally, for connoisseurs of the truly exotic, we recommend the island pride—delicious preserved kumquats and the sweet, strange, interesting kumquat liqueur—almost unknown in other parts of the world.

MYKONOS   This dazzling white islet in the Cyclades is tourist-conscious —but not spoiled. (To cite a charming example which amused us, the ancient bus that grinds up from the port to the town boasts a placard over the driver's seat proclaiming that your 6¢ fare can be charged to your Diner's Club credit card.) Aside from its topographical attractions and its 300 tiny churches (you may see 3 individual chapels side-by-side-by-side), it is most famous for its pet pelicans—Peter and 2 or 3 cronies who back up his Satchel-mouthed Highness as spares. Long, long ago the original bird, who flew in from the unknown, was credited as the talisman who relieved the islanders' financial woes. Just as Gibraltans pin their faith on their lucky Barbary Apes, the Mykonos folk believe they will prosper as long as a pelican is in residence to freeload on the community. Not too long ago a party of blackhearted scoundrels from a neighboring island snuck in and bird-napped Pete. Before this fowl deed was undone, the inhabitants were on the edge of the bloodiest Armageddon since Paris girl-napped Helen. *Area?* 32.5 square miles. *Population?* About 10-thousand. *Terrain?* Largely rocky. *Climate?* Usually windy but sunny. *Industries?* Fisheries and tourism. *Towns?* **Mykonos**, a small, charming village clustered in the center of a bowl-shape bay, is the only important one. *Beaches?* Excellent. The swimming is wonderful. *Things to see?* Practically nothing—and nearly everything. It is a town to stroll through. Since the roads are poor and they go almost nowhere, it stands to reason that there is practically no motor traffic. Greek Easter is nothing short of spectacular here. Don't be alarmed when you see the outdoor services at midnight, boys tippling in the belfries ready to haul on the bell cords, skyrockets going off, and the magnificently robed priest calling out "Christ is Risen!" while parishioners try to toss lighted firecrackers under his skirts. (Most of the explosives, not all, are wrapped in rope to prevent injury.) Then come processions, incense, plenty of imbibing throughout the holiday weekend, and so much lamb to eat that you'll think your hide is coming up in white fleecy tufts.

Hotels? No changes here. Since officials are worried about insufficient water supplies, an embargo was imposed on new construction. Thus what was, is —and probably will be for a long time to come. The **Xenia** is our favorite of the mini crop. It is on a promontory overlooking a bay, a picket line of windmills, and the white-on-white townlet of Mykonos. Comfortable, motel-like accommodations; abundant and sometimes even appetizing cookery; extremely nice people who run it. Our top choice for convenience and pleasure. The **Leto**, owned by the same company, nibbles at the edge of the main tour boat and fishing harbor, so bathing here is not the best. Its uninspired décor leaves us cold. The **Aphrodite**, about a 30-minute bus jog-and-jostle across to the desolate end of the island, maintains a romantic lonely vigil over some of the most breathtaking sea-and-landscapes in the Cyclades. Two beaches enfolding twin coves; 110 so-called bungalows which, in fact, are joined in one stair-step structure; all with bath and balcony facing the waves; swimming pool; tennis; ample recreation hubs for the groups to which it seems to cater; careless service, as might be expected in so remote a clime. The solitude is the thing here—good or bad. Shoppers will find it too far from town; peaceniks will probably love it.

Restaurants? The hotels will likely require that you have breakfast and one other meal with them. We pecked with the pet pelicans at both **Alefkandra** and **Fouskis**. Though the regional cookery was good at both, we prefer the former because of its sea view and beguiling, sail-covered open plaza. Every turn in the lane seems to have a café, so never fear starvation.

Night life? The very air lilts with Greek music wafting with forlorn softness from the myriad bars. The best places to weep or fall in love with its infatuating melodies are at the **Mykonos**—rush ceiling (the only thing hurried about it), dancing, and someone normally on hand to give informal instruction in the *bouzouki*. Next come the **Montparnasse** (go to the back room for more meaningful hand-holding), the **7 Seas** (near the harbor and strong on atmosphere), and **Meltemia** (quite a nice spot; close supervision by Managing Proprietor Vassiliou; house policy is to discourage gay assemblies under this roof). The **Remezzo** leads the discothèque file. It specializes in fluid sedations for the more sedate set, plus heavy breathing, sighs, and sips on its incredibly beautiful harborside patio. The **9 Muses** is much more of a swinger; it's recommendable for old married couples who are enjoying their 2nd week anniversary. Because lots more await, the fun is to wander and discover.

Excursions by sea? The most popular is the ½-hour voyage on stout fishing launches over to the small island of **Delos** with its extensive ruins, mosaics, and famous stone lions. Quickie trips can be had for peanuts, leaving at 9 A.M. from the main harbor and returning from the rocky uninhabited archaeological sites by lunchtime. *Other sightseeing?* Walking, drinking ouzo in the port, and viewing the **Mykonos Folklore Museum** overlooking the dock.

Shopping? Fabulous **Lalaounis** (see "Things to Buy" in the chapter on Greece) has a jewelry branch here. **Yannis Travassaros** turns lovely handwoven textiles into dresses and other items of feminine desire. The **Present Shop** weaves a tale of local blouses, jerkins, and yummy lump-knit sweaters; ask for John Nikoy. At the **Mykonos Art Shop**, in the port, Dimitri Vigliaris purveys some of the better quality souvenirs on the island. Prices are low by U.S. standards, and the merchants are not averse to engaging in the fine Greek pastime of bargaining.

Mykonos is unique. Since the aforementioned water shortage has placed a governor on its growth, it offers the rare mixture of rewards that so many vacationers seek but seldom find in combination: sun, sea, and relative solitude.

Clever, those pelicans!

CRETE This birthplace of Western Civilization, conquered and reconquered by numberless encroachers, is just beginning to undergo the expected invasion by camera-bearing legions from far shores. Here are some thumbnail gleanings: *Area?* With 3235 square miles, this is largest of the Greek islands. *Population?* About 440 thousand. *Terrain?* Mountainous and rocky. *Industries?* Olive oil, wine, nuts, citrus fruits, dairying, and small mineral workings. Raisins are the main export. *Culture?* Seat of the Minoan Empire; occupied by the Dorian Greeks, the Romans, the Genoese, the Venetians, the Turks, England, France, Russia, Italy, and other powers; strong Venetian influence today. *Towns?* **Heraklion** (sometimes called Castro), overnight by ship from Piraeus or by shuttles via Olympic Airways, is the principal port, a city with about 100,000 souls. **Canea** (Khania), considerably smaller, is the capital. Built in Italian style, its walls and ancient galley slips recall the Venetian period. It is today chiefly interested in its oranges, olive oil, and soap. There are no other communities of importance. *Things to see?* The tremendously exciting **Minoan Archaeological Museum** in *Heraklion*, one of the world's greatest; the thrilling labyrinthian **Royal Palace** at *Knossos*, about 15 minutes by car from Heraklion; the **Historical Museum** in *Heraklion*, with ancient, medieval, and Byzantine collections; the **Vrondisi Monastery**, 28 miles southeast of *Heraklion*; the ruins of the **palace** at *Phaistos*, on the south side of the island; the **Diktaion Cave**, where Rhea is said to have given birth to Zeus; the **ruins** of *Gouvnia*, a prehistoric agricultural town reminiscent of a smaller Pompeii; the mountain eagle's nest of **Sphakia**, with such a bloody history that the black shirt and kerchief of mourning became the regional costume. *Beaches?* *Malia*, closest to Heraklion, offers a small cove, windmills, banana plantations, and a tiny hotel too rugged for most Yankee sightseers. **Minos Beach**, 50 miles to the east, has the finest sands (but a mere 50 yards of the stuff), plus a 75-bungalow development on the style of the Miramare in Rhodes. Gaggles of gaga Guidesters have written in to say that these Minos cottages are genuine pluses for vacation joy. The local arithmetic also adds up to one of the better values in Greece.

Hotels? In **Heraklion** there is a tie for first place in our ratings between the **Atlantis** and the more centrally located **Astoria Capsis**; both sport swimming pools at their penthouse peaks. These would be followed by the **Astir** and then the **Xenia**. (Don't let any overzealous hackie sucker you into a 60-drachma ride way out to the Xenia Motel.) Next we'd select **El Greco** (isn't *that* a wonderful name?) over the **Knossos Beach**, even though the latter is convenient for exploring the Royal Palace.

Our out-of-town summer choices would run this way: At **Aghios Niko-laos**, the above-mentioned Minos Beach luxury complex; then the **Mirabello** and the **Hermes**; at **Elounda,** the Deluxe **Elounda Beach** setup; at **Creta Beach,** the **Creta Beach** and the **Electra**; at **Malia,** the **Ikaros Village**, the **Akti Sirinon**, and the **Malia Beach**; at **Hersonissos,** the **Creta Maris**; at **Gouvas,** the **Candia Beach**; and, finally, at **Stalis**, the **Blue Sea** (a grade-B motel).

Restaurants? When you are not hotel dining, the leading independent choices in **Heraklion** are the **Kostos** and the **Klimataria** followed by **Valkania** or **Maxims**. *Tavernas?* The **Alkion, L. Peripteron, Kastella**, and **S. Renata** are popular; the **Kallithea** and the **Aretoussa** feature the music of Crete while **Ariadni, Zorbas,** and **Stamna** lean more to the national idiom.

Nightclubs? **Heraklion**'s swingers usually can be found after dark at the **Castello**, the **Dionyssos**, the **Piper**, or the aforementioned **Ariadni**.

Shopping? **Zacharopoulos** in the Knossos Palace is worth exploring for jewelry and handicrafts. **Helen Kastrinojianni**, opposite the Heraklion Museum, also features local craft work plus attractive woven fabrics.

Information? Young Suraryanakis Evangelos at the Greek National Tourist Office is tops as an official source. Otherwise, write or visit J. C. Rassidakis, the personable, gentle expert who directs the **Creta Travel Bureau** (25th August St., Heraklion). He will plan your touring high spots, whistle up a self-drive car if desired, and in general be your genial guide.

Ireland

(see also Northern Ireland)

Ever heard of an entrancing, beguiling, little nation named Poblacht na hÉireann? Pronounce it "*Pub*lockt nah *Hair*-un," but call it the "Republic of Ireland" if you don't speak Gaelic. The country is free from English interference, economically and otherwise; this is a subject best left alone when there's an Irishman around. It's an island, of course, smaller than Pennsylvania but larger than South Carolina; you could drop its entire area into Lake Superior.

One-sixth of the seagirt—Northern Ireland, in the northeast—is also taboo as a conversational subject. Orangemen of Belfast heartily reciprocate this mutual distrust and suspicion. It's as different from the rest of Ireland as Morocco from Milwaukee, particularly since the tragic and bloody civil war erupted there to make it currently risky for residents and travelers alike. The majority of the populace of Antrim, Derry, and the northeastern counties is Protestant; in the Republic, 95% of the people are Catholic.

The Emerald Isle is a good name for it. See for yourself as you wing over the countryside. The fields are so green you might imagine you're wearing tinted glasses. The climate is mild, and to call it "moist" is like calling the Sahara Desert "dry." The summers are cool (50°–60°) and the winters are gentle (40°–50°). A bored newspaper editor with a sense of humor once ran this banner headline in August: "76° HEAT WAVE SWEEPS COUNTRY —THOUSANDS PROSTRATED!"

Here is the sod on which to relax. As *Time* stated so pungently, "The Irish have always cultivated the art of living, and they still have time and space for the slow perusal of race horses, the thoughtful consumption of stout, and the weighty disputation in rich, foamy periods that make English English seem like verbal porridge. . . . Ireland has in abundance the qualities that often seem to be disappearing elsewhere: kindliness, an unruly individualism, lack of snobbery, ease, style, and, above all, sly humor." National awareness of the value of foreign tourism hit the Man in the Street only recently, and the revolution since this awakening has been one of the most startling and gratifying developments we've ever witnessed in travel. This belated industrial revolution has created more than 400 new factories and 50-thousand new jobs. The fine Irish air is laced today with the sweet aroma of touristic success— a dollar-green that enhances their own lovely shade of Kelly. And coupled with this trend, the traveler finds that his dollar is threaded with spools of elastic. Dublin today—not to mention the even cheaper rural Irish targets— can provide the lowest-cost holiday in Europe. But if you want floor shows, superhighways, strip joints, recreation directors, subways, nightclubs, and the frenzied, taut scurrying of the mass-produced American vacation, here still isn't your answer. Ireland will offer you a good chair and invite you to enjoy what John Burroughs once called "the Beautiful Foolishness of Things." Should you be after medicine for overtired nerves—a gentle peace in simple surroundings with a people so warm you'll be on first-name terms in 5 minutes —this is your Arcadia, your Hesperides, your long-sought haven.

SHANNON INTERNATIONAL AIRPORT   Shannon is the airport, Rineanna (pronounced "Ry-nana") is the location, and Limerick is the town. You'll hear it called all 3; any of them will do. Because of the Government's huge investment in the terminus, it had balked at TWA's proposal to bring transatlantic flights down at Dublin (120 miles away); the American carrier has been successful in its landing bid, however. Transit passengers generally have time to refuel in its outstanding restaurant, to polish off a quickie at its friendly bar (amazingly low prices), and, *if not bound for Dublin or domestic points,* to load up with tax-free spirits, U.S. cigarettes, French perfumes, Swiss watches, English pewter, Irish linens, and other goodies at the Tax Free Airport Store. This one makes all other tax-free operations in all other European or U.K. airports look sick. The Liquors Department alone cheers money-conscious travelers to the tune of 3300 bottles per week; the Souvenirs Department, with ¼-million customers annually, does a turnover Macy's would envy; the Mail Order Department has been set up on a money-back-guarantee basis for Americans who cannot travel to Europe but who wish to share the soothing cost advantages. Write Manager Dick Scott, Shannon Mail Order Service, Shannon International Airport, Ireland, for the fine low-cost catalogue. Discounting perfumes, all bona fide gifts up to $10 in fair retail value are, at this writing but subject to change, free of U.S. duties. Absolutely reliable; money-back guarantees promptly honored. WHAT a bonanza for Christmas worriers—and who isn't?

   Airport moguls and the C.I.E. bus interests have pooled resources to offer a delightful 24-hour "Medieval Tour" for international wanderers—a worthy and interesting overnight stopover en route in either direction across the Atlantic. A highly sophisticated Guidester wrote to us, "I expected this to be the usual mechanical, touristy, gimmicky bore—but it was so fresh that I had a *lovely* time!" The all-expense fee of about $55 per person includes hotel room, transportation, and the usual—plus a colorful fifteenth-century banquet in the Great Hall of Bunratty Castle, during which a "Lord and Lady" are elected. Transients may enjoy the dinner, if space is available. Now this monument, with its reconstructed Irish village complex, with 6 cottages, a forge, and a souvenir shop to the rear, is open the calendar round. While here, please don't miss the unusually fetching fashions for both genders at the **Bunratty Cottage Shop** opposite the Castle. It is the loving creation of Designer Vonnie Reynolds, whose poise, polish, and charm warmly complement the wealth of her talent. While her own inspired styles are featured, you can also find a wide range of tweed and knit suits by Jimmy Hourihan, and beautiful pure-cotton crocheted blouses and other wearables pleasantly displayed in a cottage atmosphere. Highly recommended.

Two-to-six-day circuits, including this feudal feast and providing an even wider spectrum of Irish culture, also have been initiated; be sure to inquire for full details of the equally intriguing "Kinvara Tour" or about the week-long cruises on the River Shannon aboard the cleverly conceived 12-passenger "Floatels." (A sample 2-day voyage can be arranged for about $30 inclusive. Even the most wary of landlubbers may sign on for a cautious lunch and afternoon spin for only $15. Ship ahoy!) All are hugely successful; great fun.

Eye-popping evidence of the country's economic resurgence greets you right inside the gateposts. Shannon Development Co., under handsome Brendan O'Regan (the whiz kid who originally brought the Tax Free Airport Store into flower), has attracted an impressive industrial complex to the once stark and barren sandspit adjoining the runways. Stop to see it. Genial Genius O'Regan (who also operates the Bunratty Medieval Tours) is the essence of the new generation of go-getters who have rejuvenated Ireland overnight. It's exhilarating to witness pioneer p spirit and Celtic muscle in action.

For information about lodgings, turn to "Hotels."

CITIES   *Dublin*, first, foremost, and always. The world's 2nd largest brewery, widest main street, oldest Chamber of Commerce, tattler of tallest tales —and courtliest people. Settled by Danes in A.D. 852, it's the size of Seattle, with over ½-million people; quaint and colorful, it's a fascinating blend of bustling metropolis and dusty one-horse town. On Sunday nights, scores of citizens practice the homey ritual of visiting its candy shops. Here's a city that's as warm and engaging as her people. Museums, gorgeous parks, dance halls, movies, a million things to see—don't miss Dublin, if you can possibly get there. Her airport, once a sleepy bump on the heath, is atingle with activity as a result of improvements to accommodate large jets; a "red telephone" information service is in operation. Aer Lingus-Irish Airlines runs a 45-minute shuttle service from here to Shannon, and it also flies direct to various cities in England and on the Continent.

Cork City, the size of Schenectady, is 2nd in importance. It's on the River Lee, way down south; Blarney Castle is 6 miles from the center. Cork Airport is expected to increase tourist traffic to the Southern Counties by at least 25%. Because of its lusterless mien, heavy industries, lowgrade hotels and restaurants, and maddeningly narrow, complex, traffic-choked bridges and streets, here is our least favorite center on the Emerald Isle. Its citizens, however— Corkers to their core—radiate a special vitality that you'll adore. The small-boat harbor of *Crosshaven*, around the river's bend nearby, is much more scenic and tranquil for overnighting.

Limerick, previously mentioned, is 3rd. **Waterford**, near Cork, has a colorful harbor situation but aesthetically is rather grim and unattractive (topers will be pleased to observe it is the home of the Royal Liver Assurance Co.), **Galway**, capital of western Ireland, is the remaining city of consequence; here, as well, is an unprepossessing center. Look to the rural areas to find the true spirit of this hospitable and beautiful nation.

MONEY AND PRICES

Although Ireland issues its own currency, its denominations and their exchange rates are the same as those of Britain. Please turn back to the section on "Money and Prices" in our chapter on England for an explanation.

English and Irish pounds are acceptable anywhere in the country, but be sure to winnow your supply of Emerald Isle money before you leave since it is not spendable anywhere else.

Prices are spiraling upward steadily, but, because of a favorable exchange rate, our U.S. or Canadian dollars more than absorb the inflation. They now stand slightly below English levels. You can easily pay $15 for a big dinner in one of the 6 or 8 pacesetting restaurants—but *average* accommodations, food, shopping, and tourist facilities are generally quite reasonable.

ATTITUDE TOWARD TOURISTS

One of the warmest—and best-organized—receptions for today's foreign visitor. One master organization runs the show—**Bord Fáilte Éireann**. Director-General Joe Malone is its helmsman. The headquarters (Baggot Street Bridge, Dublin 2) inspects and classifies accommodations, trains professional staffs, assists resorts and hotels with financial grants up to 20% of renovation costs, maintains historic sites —solid groundwork for your touring pleasure. Since nearly ¼ th of the nation's external income derives from trippers, it is understandably persnickety about safeguarding its unspoiled scenic charms. And its recently inaugurated "Tidy Towns" competition is doing just that; derelict sites are being cleared, and roadside gardens are sprouting everywhere. The **Information Offices** (14 Upper O'Connell St. and 51 Dawson St.) courteously handle your itinerary problems, distribute reading material, and answer routine inquiries on anything from sports to theatrical events.

A "**Meet-the-Irish**" program enables visitors to meet people with like interests and to be invited into their homes. By writing to your nearest Irish Tourist office and stating your name, address, profession, hobbies, and age group along with the dates and places where you would like to have introductions, everything will be set up for you on arrival. But be sure to make application not less than one month in advance.

If your trip is still in the planning stage, touch base with the **Irish Tourist Office** at either 590 Fifth Ave., N.Y. 10036; 224 N. Michigan Ave., Chicago; 681 Market St., San Francisco; 7 King St. East, Toronto; or 2100 Drummond St., Montreal. Ask for the *International Reservations—Ireland* card and brochure, which list toll free numbers you may use to book rooms almost instantly in about 360 inns in Eire or Great Britain (also in North America).

CUSTOMS AND IMMIGRATION

Efficient, courteous, and accommodating. The list of dutiable articles is long, but it's one of the most sensible, flexible arrangements in existence. The visitor is allowed free entry with *a "reasonable" amount of all bona fide personal effects.* Few set limits; if the traveler plays fair, so do Customs men. They are fond of Americans. They'll greet you with a smile, and they'll generally run you through in a matter of seconds.

Certain items have maximums, and these you must watch: (1) 1000 cigarettes *or* 200 cigars *or* 2½ lbs. of tobacco *or* any combination of these not exceeding 2½ lbs.; (2) 1 quart of liquor; (3) 1 pint of perfume (has there ever been a whole pint of perfume?); (4) 2 bottles of wine; and (5) gifts for Irish friends not exceeding $57 in value.

Prohibited or dutiable articles include coffee extract (if they pick this up, you'll pay a 37½% Customs fee), saccharin (they're tough on this), unlicensed arms or ammunition, and narcotics, plumage, the usual contraband.

Now we are going to quote directly from an official source: "In theory, contraceptives are taboo in Ireland; however, one is allowed to bring into the country a limited amount for personal use." (The "limit" was not specified, nor any conceivable "use" other than "personal" described, so we will refrain from further comment.)

Finally, pig meat in any shape, form, or state of ripeness cannot be imported. If you *must* have your porker or pork, stick him or it down your shirt and button your vest.

Personal search is extremely rare.

§TIP: Never try to grease palms at the Irish frontiers, because there's a £200 fine for offering money to a Customs officer. It might work in France or Italy —but in Ireland it spells trouble in king-size capitals.

HOTELS   For far more comprehensive information on certain hostelries than space limitations permit here, interested travelers are referred to the annually revised *Fielding's Selected Favorites: Hotels and Inns, Europe* by Dodge Temple Fielding, our son—who also happens to have been stung by the bug of travel. Its latest edition, in which a total of 300-odd favored possibilities were handpicked from the 4000-plus personally inspected, will be at your bookstore early this year.

It's a sad fact that temperamentally the Irish—like Americans—aren't built to be first-rate hotelkeepers. You may disagree violently with this statement, but we doubt it. In the handful of leading international houses, you still should find top-grade attention although the touristic in-rush is gradually manifesting obvious strains even at this level; in the rest, organization is improving, but it's most often on the slaphappy side. Staff people everywhere, despite professional shortcomings, have hearts of pure gold; *always*—repeat, *always*—treat them as friends rather than servants, because they can tie you up in knots if they feel you're unduly lordly, snooty, or arrogant.

Ireland's Official Tourist Board has given the nation's hotels an enormous shot in the arm with grants up to 20% to any operator who wishes to build new bedrooms or install new bathrooms, and up to 33⅓% toward conversions to central heating. Even further investment incentive was provided when the Government sanctioned a 10% annual depreciation write-off on an industry-wide basis. The effects of this assistance are nuclear. Construction is booming throughout the nation. The breakthrough in the vexing shortage of decent accommodations is at last well in sight.

The Swan Ryan organization is now well set up to assist the carefree traveler whose funds are limited. Its first step was to build a chain of 4 major ultramodern hotels in **Killarney**, **Limerick**, **Galway**, and **Sligo**. While their public rooms vary in décor, most bedchambers, standard in every detail, offer small dimensions, a double bed, a single bed, a daybed, panoramic windows, and tiny baths. Their per-person rates are in the $8 to $12 range, depending upon the season and how you choose to snooze (singly or in tandem). Upon their inauguration, the company instituted its amazingly low-cost "Roamaround" travel schemes; these include fly-and-drive itineraries to Ireland, Scotland, and England, incorporating round-trip fares between 5 U.S. gateways and London, Prestwick, or Shannon, plus options galore once you alight. There's a discount for kiddies who are willing to allow Mom and Pop to share their room. Further information may be obtained from **Ryans Tours, Inc.**, 15 East 48th St., New York 10017, from 875 N. Michigan Ave., Chicago, Ill. 60611, from the London sales office at 150 New Bond Street, W1Y-ONU, or from the main office at 4 Lower Abbey St., Dublin 1. Because these links are widely dispersed from the northwest to the southeast of the island, the wanderer has the opportunity of carving out a giant sightseeing triangle which encompasses the major part of the nation. You will find cleanliness without luxury (no telephones, for example, and very limited room service, of course), you'll see eye-popping travel targets and miles of countryside if you opt for a set program (not counting the almost unlimited variety of beautiful side trips)—and you should find lots of fun in the process. The flexibility is so broad that Ryans can put wings on your transatlantic daydreams or link you into one of its adventures once you are on European soil (er, that is, sod).

We continue to be bowled over by the values being offered by this outstanding organization—the zeal and courtesy of its personnel, the high quality of its facilities in view of such minuscule outlays, the efficiency of its planning, the farsightedness of its administration, and the amount of grace in this vast operation that refuses to apply cattle-car attitudes to volume business. To us it is an extremely rare and equally refreshing experience to watch a profit-making company give so much back to the customer. What a blessing it would be for the industry if so many thousands of others would do only a fraction as well!

Another ingenious twist—this one more specialized—is the **Rent-An-Irish-Cottage** program which was launched by the Shannon Development Company (turn back to "Shannon International Airport"). Twelve units made their '69 debuts in **Ballyvaughan** (County Clare); 8 became operative in **Corofin** (County Clare) almost immediately afterward; a total of 84 will eventually dot the rural resort map of the West. These thatched-roof houses, extremely simple in execution and in furnishings, embody the flavor of a small, traditional farmhouse. Each contains a v-shape dining-living room with 2 single settee beds, a double-bedded room, a double-decker room, an attic double room, a small kitchen with electrical fittings, a tiny bathroom, kitchen utensils, crockery, cutlery, and several coin-operated heaters. Under overcrowded conditions, a family of 8 can be accommodated. The minimum rental must be for 7 nights; extra days are charged pro rata. The costs of food, drink, utilities, linens (other than bed clothing), and cleaning woman are not included. The basic rental ranges from about $65 to $80 per week, depending on the time of year. Although this is a far cry from opulent living, we wonder where else 8 individuals can find such a vacation for such a modest outlay.

Because Ireland is busting out all over, we've recently wrapped up a countrywide reinspection of its touristic facilities. Here are our latest ratings of its principal hotels—with some of which you and our local friends might howlingly disagree:

In **Dublin**, the stately **Shelbourne** is beloved by the Old Generation, and is gaining favor rapidly with the Young Guard as well. The British Trust Houses Forte organization owns it. The personable manager, Patrick Browne, who is maintaining the same personnel and policies, is trying hard against architectural roadblocks that are sometimes (not always!) very difficult. Here's the Dublin home of the nation's literati, the hunt-shoot-and-fish country squires, and the touring Boston Brahmins; authors from Thackeray to Elizabeth Bowen have fondly sung its praises in their books; the Constitution of the Irish Free State was framed within its venerable walls. Some of the innovations include its L-shaped air-conditioned duo-dining facility (music nightly in summer except Sun. and Mon.), a high-in-the-stirrups, neo-rustic Saddle Room spotlighting 3 separate ribs of beef (rare, medium, well done), a handsome Grill Bar with a long, chummy counter and 12 tables (amiable for drinks, light bites, and after-theater nibbles), and a parking lot for 50 cars. Newer 6-story wing; 3 large fresh suites, plus the honeymoon "sweeties"; overall total of 172 rooms and baths. Its Georgian façade commands a splendid view of St. Stephen's Green. A mellow fellow that's becoming more youthful by the year.

The century-old **Gresham**, which marked time for several listless seasons lately, finally is in the process of sprucing up. You'll find the rouge-tone Gandon Restaurant, the brick-pillared Hunting Lodge Grill with choir chairs and reminders of sports afield, an adjoining Swiss-style cocktail corner, the cellar-cited Malt for barrel-backed pubbery, the Tain ("Thawn") Coffee Shop with its burnished-gold sculpture of Celts at arms, air conditioning in all public rooms and a general pep-up of the bedchambers. If you are feeling extra-affluent, the quartet of penthouse Terrace Suites, with their sweeping panorama of the city, are exquisitely decorated with fine paintings, antiques, and tasteful bric-a-brac; they cost from $175 to $230 per day; #603-605, with its full-size built-in bar, large full kitchen with refrigerator, full stove, and complete equipment, open peat-burning fireplace, TV, and other lures, is one of the most beautiful hotel accommodations we have encountered in all our lives; as a grace note, clients in these opulent perches are attended by their own personal butler. Let's hope the proposed renovation program is prompt and thorough.

The new, 400-room, Deluxe **Burlington** seeks to blend traditional décor with modern comfort, a feat which it achieves handily because of the ample skills of veteran General Manager Michael Brennan. Airy lobby with busy adjoining bar and popular lounge; ground-floor Sussex Room, the hotel's premier restaurant; grill cum coffee shop; rooftop salon with heaping servings, live music, dancing, and lots of reveling youngsters; Annabel's red and gold acreage for disco-doin's; indoor pool, plus sauna and massage; nice staff throughout. The accommodations provide space, light, and efficiency, but very little inspiration. The 4 corner Presidential Suites are another story, of course; they are generously outfitted. Overall, it swings, but in a peculiarly sedate Irish manner.

The **Royal Hibernian** was built more than 200 years ago. Under its present ownership by the J. Lyons group and its experienced skippering by Michael Governey, formerly of the Old Ground in Ennis, this clipper is sailing sweetly again. The entrance, lounge, and dining rooms are gay and bright; there are a splendid kitchen and many renovated bedchambers. The Lafayette Restaurant features an expensive menu and sound cuisine, with varying regions of Gallic gastronomy highlighted on Saturday nights in winter; the Bianconi Grill-Bar seats 55 *bons vivants,* with snacks, wine, and beer available; the freshly turned, mod-style Rôtisserie accents more expensive grills than those of the Bianconi and is targeted for the young executive clientele; the Buttery Bar continues to draw the fashionable. Much better and steadily improving.

The twin-structured **New Jury's** (formerly the Intercontinental), impersonal and cool, was conceived and erected by this U.S.-based global chain to purvey every function of the twentieth-century efficiency hotel. Lobby and public areas in one building; sleeping accommodations in adjoining facility; clinical air somewhat warmed by the Dubliner (a charming pseudo-Victorian room with a bar on its far side), the decorative touches in its Embassy Grill, and the introduction of its Coffee Dock snack bar (80 seats; attractive muraled walls featuring ships of all ages; open from 6 A.M. to 5 A.M. year round). Its Martello Roof is a popular after-dark roost. Total of 315 units, divided almost equally between studio-type and conventional doubles; 2 large suites with bar, kitchen, TV, sitting room, and standard bedchamber. The bathrooms throughout are tiny. Service and cuisine are improving. Now quite good for its type.

The 124-room-and-bath **Royal Dublin**, opposite the Gresham, greets guests with a lobby painting of Sitric, the Viking king, and "raths" (plans) of fortresses in sandstone and pebble. Its Oyster Bar features bivalves shipped fresh from Galway Bay each dawn in season. Cool-tinged yet appealing grill, bar, and dining room; underground carpark; gray brick corridors; front units with balconette-bay windows; velvet headboards; matching curtains; emerald carpets; radios, telephones, and thermal shower taps; inviting Queen Gormley suite. Manager Hugh Margey has an excellent plant with which to work. Very young, but recommended with confidence.

Although the **Skylon**, about 10 minutes by car from both the airport and the center, sprang on the scene not long ago, it's due for another growing spree soon. It is a sister operation to the Tara Tower, the Montrose, and the Green Isle (see below). Low, rather extensive lobby with simple furnishings, piped music, and buried baby spotlights in an acoustic ceiling; bizarre hodge-podge bar-lounge with 13 swingable stools; intimate but clashing 007 Bar;

Grill-Bar with counter and tables, featuring low-price fare; fetching dining room with Cecil King murals and well-planned illumination; beauty parlor; sauna. Its 100 rooms and 100 baths are identical, with orange-striped wall-to-wall carpets and matching curtains, adequate but not spacious dimensions, terribly cramped baths, and insufficient storage space. We'd judge it as run-of-the-mill—but, comparatively speaking, not bad for the price.

Tara Tower, described to us by a bellhop as having "an evocative name for the Irish," refers to a hallowed spot in County Meath, 20 miles northwest of Dublin, which was the capital of the Celtic Empire and the site from which St. Patrick began his evangelizing mission in the fifth century. This newcomer could almost serve as a carbon copy of the Skylon. We were attracted by its grill with ship's lantern illumination, the shingle-roofed counter for lighter biting, and the purple dining room with globes and flowers. Pick a high waterfront unit; we'd judge it might render evocative moments for you, too —Irish or not.

The **Central** impresses us as being dull, dull, and duller.

The **Clarence** is rated "A" by the Tourist Board inspectors—but we wonder how in heaven's name it deserves it. Or as James Joyce might have opined: "?Htiw hcihw dne fo eht tebahpla od uoy esoppus yeht nageb"

Buswells is a mixed bag—and not the most glamorous one, at that. Georgian bar which hints more of a Chatham County (Ga.) courthouse; raspberry-and-white dining room; mélange of sleeping themes; baths that—no, that couldn't be a ring in the tub, or could it? Our lack of enthusiasm is Pullman-Bus size.

The **Crofton "Airport" Hotel** (quotation marks ours) is only 2 miles along the highway—actually closer to Dublin than to the terminus. We found it to be a halfheartedly, sloppily refurbished classic mansion onto which has been tacked a 5-floor modern wing. Currently it has 120 units; plans are underway to up this total to 200. To us, here is a battling May-December marriage. In view of its "A" tariffs, not recommended to the North American pilgrim.

The **Parkside**, as far as we Park Benchers are concerned, should be resolutely avoided.

A 250-unit **Holiday Inn** is slated for the downtown area, but it may be a while inn-coming.

On the outskirts you'll find the popular **Royal Marine Hotel** at *Dun Laoghaire* ("Done Leery"), on a harbor 6 miles south of the capital. Here's a viable candidate for pilgrims taking the 3-hour car-ferry hop to Holyhead. It is a gingerbread structure (vintage 1865) with high ceilings. On one recent Marine patrol, a lounge had been refurbished, a cute little Edwardian bar added, and 48 extra twin-bed units, all with private bath and shower have now followed suit. The Gay Nineties Charcoal grill offers excellent food, pleasant ambiance, and good service at reasonable prices; 5 acres of lawns and flowers; boating, swimming, yachting, sailing, golf, tennis, racing, hunting, and dancing; pick your weather carefully here. More popular with visitors from within the British Isles and conference clans than with Yankee colonists. Anthony McClafferty, its engaging manager, will give you a fine Irish welcome. The **Montrose**, which blossomed in '64 in the *Stillorgan* residential district, offers a vast panoply of sleeping combinations that can accommodate almost anything from an eremite to a Ringling Brothers troupe. Every unit with coin-operated TV and central heat; Belfield Grill for light appetites, open noon to midnight; noisy restaurant; huge bar; ballroom alternating as a leggy nightclub Saturdays and 2 other week-nights in season; 2 saunas; hairdresser and gift-shop-newsstand-book-counter; parking lot. Practical—especially if you happen to have a family à la Brigham Young's. The same organization guides the **Green Isle**, beside the Naas Road just off the Shannon turnpike 4 miles from the center. Its lodgings are split into 40 in its main building and 28 in its so-called motel section. Modern, often frenetic lobby blaring with public address announcements and staffed by flocks of pretty colleens with emerald minis and shamrock brooches; fresh dining room with oversize windows; cookery routine; lobby bar a nothing; 1200-seat ballroom with international cabaret on Saturday night. Most of the motel units have 2 conventional beds and 2 studios—far too snug for 4 adults. Although busload upon busload of tour groups stream in, the majority of its patronage is local. Not our dish, because (1) it is too far from the action and (2) it's clean but too impersonal and sterile to seduce us. North of Dublin town, 8 miles out, the **Portmarnock Country Club** is a fair-weather friend. Once the private estate of the Jameson whiskey moguls, it now offers terrace-dining, Moroccan-style cellar bar, open-air dancing (scheduled nights only), and seaside sports along the cheerless sand dunes. The lobby needs a capable decorator's hand. Terribly bleak in winter, but benign in summer. Go elsewhere if you're the restless type, as it's pretty remote. The **Grand** at *Malahide*, a 10-mile skip, has been decorated and enlarged. We didn't make the trek, because so many Dublin reports were discouraging.

The **International**, at the airport, has been taken over by Jury's. This one-story structure contains 150 units, a restaurant, and a Grill-Bar; it is air-conditioned and soundproofed by double panes. And that's that.

Irish town, village, or country hotels? Here are the key choices for the overseas wanderer, some excellent and some unprepossessing:

Achill (County Mayo, extreme west) offers the Grade-B **Achill Head Hotel,** which, after a decline, now seems to be bouncing back. The Great Southern chain's **Malaranny**, which lies at the entrance of Achill Island, splashes with a swimming pool. Only fair.

Adare (County Limerick, 10 miles southwest of Limerick City) is proud of its little **Dunraven Arms**—rightfully so. Within striking distance of Shannon Airport; décor of lovely antiques, soft colors, and serene character; staff polished and warmhearted; handsome dining room; Long Bar perfect for romancers; cuisine not up to its special ambiance. All 27 rooms and 17 baths unfancy but cheerful, comfortable, and absolutely spotless in maintenance; convenient as a shooting or hunting headquarters; 3 championship golf courses within driving distance, plus the 9-hole Adare Manor Links; fascinating Old World village. *Reserve in advance.* Here is still one of the very best country inns in the nation. Cheers and more cheers!

In *Athlone* (County Westmeath, halfway between Dublin and Galway on the main road), **Shamrock Lodge**, which a while back changed ownership, has a lovely homey feel about its premises and its personnel—that of a private house. Small, clean rooms with 4 private baths; fine lunch stop en route to

Ashford Castle. The **Prince of Wales**, in an easier-to-find central location, has been demolished, rebuilt, and redecorated—yet in the process its 45 nests were afforded a mere half-dozen baths. Not our version of farsighted innkeeping.

In **Ballynahinch** (County Galway), **Ballynahinch Castle** is smaller than its more famous neighbor, Ashford Castle, but from the sportsman's point of view it's even better. Excellent salmon and trout fishing, both river and lake. Recently acquired by a syndicate of wealthy American sportsmen who have no intention of spoiling the fun of its loyal clientele. Accommodations fair, at best. The nearby **Zetland Arms**, was built on a cost-no-object basis by the Guinness family and is one of the most luxuriously decorated fishing hotels in the nation. It is centered in more than 10-thousand acres of bog, lake, and estuary landscape for rough shoots and angling. Managing Director Edwards has created a very exclusive anglers' lodge for today's Isaac Waltons.

Ballyvaughan (County Clare)? **Gregan's Castle Hotel**, 4 miles from this coastal hamlet on the Lisdoonvarna road, was our happiest "find" on one very recent circuit. Seemingly, it's hell-and-gone from everywhere—but actually it's in beautiful country only 30 miles around the bay from Galway. (If you're proceeding northward, be sure, *doubly* sure, not to miss the glorious coastal drive along L54, one of the most magnificent ocean panoramas in the nation.) This gem was opened in '68 by an enterprising British couple who spent a great deal of money converting a desolate ruin to a gracious, tasteful country inn. Sited on a slight promontory, with a sweeping view of the countryside down to the distant bay; intimate Corkscrew bar; lovely Tudor-style dining room; outstanding cuisine; 2 Tudor lounges. Its 14 rooms, 6 with private bath, are named for Irish towns or counties instead of numbered; the "Tralee" double accommodation is our favorite. New Owners Peter and Moira Haden are making further improvements. Open from Easter to late November; book well ahead in season. Here is a joyously conceived, joyously operated gem for tranquillity seekers—or even as a target for lunch. Highly recommended on every count.

Bantry (County Cork, extreme southwest) has the **Ballylickey House,** situated in wild terrain for visitors who wish to relax. Not Deluxe, but adequately substantial. We haven't seen them, but a friendly American who resides in Ireland suggests the **West Lodge** and the **Bantry Motor Inn**. Thanks for the tips to us and fellow Guidesters! We'll banter with this Bantry band soon.

In **Bundoran** (County Donegal, northwest coast), the **Great Southern** is so superior that no #2, #3, #4, or #5 seems to stand between it and #6. Approximately 130 acres of treeless "parkland" bordering a small sand beach and rocky shoals; large, Victorian building serenely surrounded by an 18-hole championship golf course (free to guests); heated seawater pool; tennis court; putting green; lobby and lounge completely updated. Its 101 bedchambers and 68 baths are an Irish mulligan of good and poor; if you're a duo, try to maneuver yourselves into #115; although many of its accommodations are cramped and unappealing, all are clean. Not the Crown Jewel of its big chain—but damned good for this isolated simple resort. The **Hamilton** (Main St.) recently underwent alterations, but we haven't seen the changes. The **Central** (also Main St.) has applied scattered cosmetics to its weary mien, and a more efficient fire-prevention system has been installed. Nonetheless, we would take no delight in sleeping here.

In **Cahir** (pronounced "care," County Tipperary), **Cahir House** offers a skimpy Care Package in luxury but a small feast in rural-style welcome. There are no private baths for its 23 rooms. **Kilcoran Lodge Hotel** is 5 miles outward toward Cork. This one also radiates a happy family atmosphere. It has been spruced up considerably. Homey furnishings; spotlessly kept; flowers throughout; #10 our pick; try for your reservation in the shooting lodge from which it was converted, rather than in either wing. Better than its mate.

Carrickmacross (County Monaghan), despite its globally famous lace, has never picked up the stitches in its hotel-keeping. The best known is the **Nuremore**, which makes us shudder in reminiscence. Although it is located on a lovely 100-acre plot which faces a small lake and is encompassed by a golf course, it impresses us as being such a mishmash of new construction tacked onto a shabby old mansion that we wouldn't vacation here for all of the exquisite bridgecloths in the city. To cap our disappointment in its physical plant, our lunch in this officially rated class "A" house was Class Double Z in quality—one of the most appallingly bad meals we've ever had in any establishment during our many years of Irish roamings. (Even the *tea* was awful.) **Markey's Pub**, on the central drag, is said to be a better dining choice, notably for its inexpensive grills; in our opinion, it would have to labor awfully hard to be worse. **Sharley Arms**, on the main street, is in the "D" category. Chillingly barren as it is, we'd almost prefer it to the Nuremore. How we bleed for the poor wretches whose bosses send them to buy the products of this center!

In **Cashel** (County Tipperary, roughly ⅔rds along the Dublin–Cork highway) the **Cashel Palace** is a converted eighteenth-century bishop's manse. James Cox Brady has taken it over and is pouring in $'s and TLC by the Cashel bushel. Flawless appointments; sumptuous tranquillity; popular with equestrians; good Derby Kitchen Grill-Restaurant and the adjoining Derby Bar. Soul-soothing gardens and lawns; 20 rooms and 20 baths, all attractively done; #2, #7 and #1 are our favorites, in that order. Reserve early. Again our warm salutes. **Grant's Castle Hotel** fronts the main street with its venerable twin towers. Its 19 rooms and 2 baths are spartan. **Chez Hans**, in a converted church, is reported to provide choice meals for wanderers in this domain. For overnighting, the glass-lined **Cashel Inn** archly commands a winning hillside perch out of the town. Cool and simple in a modern mood, but more than ample for motoring transients. The view of the distant mist-cloaked castle is enough to take your b-r-e-a-t-h a-waaaay.

Castlebar (County Mayo) is a town we are always happy to pass through at the maximum speed limit. **Breaffy House**, about 2 miles out, was almost completely rebuilt after a fire; it now runs a bath for every unit. We're told that this mansion's former grimness is a shade of the past; our fingers are crossed. The **Travelers Friend Hotel** in town is no friend of this traveler. You can sleep much, much more comfortably elsewhere.

Cobh (County Cork)? Skip it.

Cong's Ashford Castle (County Mayo), with its dramatic setting on the shores of Lough Corrib, its turreted walls, and its baronial furnishings, is straight out of the pages of a fairy-tale book. It is a 4-hour drive from Dublin to this former home of the Guinness family, directly across the Emerald Isle to the Atlantic side. Recently it was purchased from Noel and Angela Huggard by an Irish consortium headed by John A. Mulcahy, an American who expanded the overall capacity while updating the creakier older segments. Fresh total of 77 accommodations, all with bath; sun lounge; extended dining salon. Substantial cuisine; extra charge for breakfast in your room (only Continental style offered, and then never on Sundays); strict dinner hour of 7 P.M. to 8:15 P.M.; laundry service only twice a week.

   Cork (County Cork), our least favorite Irish center, bobs up with a meager fishnet of decent lodgings. Neighboring Crosshaven, however, is a far better catch, so please see below.) **Arbutus Lodge** probably leads the uninspired parade, chiefly because of its better-than-average dining room (lined with oil paintings), it's friendly fireside bar, and it's amiable personnel. About 3-dozen bedchambers in a converted house that overlooks from its hillside perch the industrial muscle of Cork below; some private baths; mountains of chintz and other grandmotherly touches. Rather old-homey and certainly adequate. The 96-room **New Jury's** is also satisfactory. Pleasant, airy location a few minutes from the center; U-shape, 2-storied banks of standard rooms in 2 styles; ¾-bed twins (studio couch added) to accommodate 3 very close relatives; impersonal and utilitarian singles. Adequate space in sleeping sections; compact minibath; floor to ceiling windows; free cots for Young Fry. Although the cuisine could scarcely be more routine, the service is attentive, kind, and willing. The **Silver Springs**, also a short haul along the Dublin highway from the nexus, is a 7-tier, waffled structure of contemporary design. The Rank organization recently sold it to the Costelloe Group, and Manager Dermot Lovett is applying gobs of polish here. Modern lobby with Danish-style illumination and piped music; spectacular blue and white hexagonal dining room with large panes for its river view; Blarney Bar directly underneath, also hexagonal and also attractive; big carpark. All sleeping quarters quintagonal in shape to offer maximum vistas; dimensions on the small side; baths tiny and poorly executed. The housekeeper needed an administrative rocket, because the maintenance of many of the carpets and furnishings we saw was inexcusably slipshod; we'll hope for more sparkle now that the owner has changed. It shelters scads of conducted tours from North America, England, Northern Ireland, and France. The **Victoria**, with 77 rooms and 13 baths or showers, is central and commercial. Its Oak Room serves as the bar; redecoration of the lobby is now finished. Here is the traditional gathering place for local farmers and their wives and for Irish traveling salesmen. Pretty dreary. The **Imperial**, also on the main street, is a mercantile mix of a faded, hard-used plant with fresh paint and fresh carpeting here and there. The management claims that it is one of the oldest hotels in the country—and too much of it, unfortunately, looks it. No. The **Metropole**? On our latest checkup, the first sight of its filthy entrance and staircase from its river side discouraged us; only a few steps farther were needed to put us off completely. On the outskirts, the German-run **Cork Airport Motel** occupies 4 acres of a treeless hillside with a wonderful view. Postage-stamp lobby with glass-sided 10-table dining room adjoining and bar to rear; air-conditioned; central heating; piped music. Its 20 sleeping quarters, all standard, are Lilliputian, with trickle showers. The boldly lettered sign "No charge for Children, but nominal charge for cot in same room" swiveled our neck in a ludicrous double-take. Far, far, far from U.S. motel standards, but passable as a one-night shelter. **Ashbourne House** at *Glounthaune*, 6 miles along the Waterford road, is a converted private mansion which comes up with 23 rooms, 15 baths, and good cookery. Atmospherically, however, we don't think most Yankees would find themselves fond of it. Incidentally, Culinary Master Ernest Evans of the Towers in Glenbeigh (see below) is the Director mainly responsible in the operation of the **Blackrock Castle Restaurant**, on the lee at Tivoli. It was built in 1829 and taken over by Mr. Evans' group a while back. Admirals' Court Bar on top; all-stone Grand Banquet Hall below; classic à la carte menu; no entertainment; evenings only; closed Sunday; open all seasons. Although we haven't yet tried it, it is said to be one of the best dining places in the entire south. The **Grand Hotel** at *Crosshaven*, 12 miles from Cork, really would be our preferential port if we were to pause anywhere in the Cork environs. Coastal setting beside what claims to be "the oldest yacht club in the world" (Commodore Denis Doyle owns the hostelry; yachtsmen often rag him by calling it the Royal Doyle); starkly white, angular, 25-unit Victorian edifice; elegant entrance and dining room with rose carpets and moss walls; air-conditioned bar swathed in Williamsburg blue and white; bar overlooking modern indoor pool; hairdresser and barber. All chambers chat-up telephones, radios, and TV's; the majority draw baths; most scan Cork estuary and the river harbor; 2 suites are extra-inviting. Manager Doran and Assistant Vincent O'Sullivan run a tight ship which we personally find delightful.

Donegal (County Donegal) has such 2nd-rate contenders that our suggestion would be to push along to the Great Southern in Bundoran instead. Neither the **Central** nor the **National** impressed us one whit. We hear good things about the **Rathmullan House** in *Rathmullan* and the beachside **Sand House** in *Rossnowlagh*, but we've seen neither personally.

Dundalk (County Louth, directly south of the Northern Ireland border on the coastal highway) has 3 possibilities, none of them outstanding. The **Fairways**, a few miles to the south, would have our option here. Lounge with sweet little fireplace; large, bright dining room; small garden to the rear; 33 tiny units, 8 with bath. The upkeep is not what it might be; when we made our inspection, it could have benefited from a generous application of Air Sweetener. Nonetheless, it's better than passable. In town, the 22-room, 13 bath-or-shower **Derryhale** is a modified red-brick, bay-windowed private home boasting its own greenhouse. A lovely carved mahogany staircase is its principal asset. Cheerful dining quarters; comfortable, old-fashioned bar; nests which are clean but very basic in their furnishings. More popular among Irish businessmen than outlanders. **Ballymascanlon House**, about one mile down a side road north of the center, is enchanting from its exterior. Its long, winding entrance of well-tended lawns and gardens, its small watering pond for cows, and its steeds wandering in their green pastures whet the appetite for its handsome structure. But the current management takes too literally the Plunket family motto to "Make haste slowly." Inside we found it a heartbreaker. To us, its design, décor, and furnishings are a nightmarish mishmash of tastelessness and ugliness. Its owners have completed their new 50-unit hotel, the **Imperial** in Dundalk, with tour groups the main target. After our crushing disappointment in the original venture, we are wary of this yet unseen addition. This rural haven could be SUCH a gem with better administration and a hefty input of loving care!

In **Ennis** (County Clare; about 20 miles north of Shannon Airport) the **Old Ground** is a charmer. Its venerable interior has been smartened up radically. Mellowness of lobby typified by its well-rubbed grandfather clock and other serene antiques; lovely rose-hue, wallpapered dining room; Poets' Corner Bar with its slate floor, copper, ceramic casks, and old prints infinitely preferable to its brasher modern beverage rendezvous; 67 rooms with bath or shower, all redone and fresh; our preference, the older section; top-grade direction by Manager Richard Oldfield. Highly suitable in comfort, in staff morale, and in tone. The 40-unit **West County Inn** is essentially targeted for tour groups. Although it has been open for only a few short years, already we saw numerous ominous signs of wear. Its unappealing exterior does not correctly reflect its small-boned but livable interior. Large, large lobby; Grill and banqueting facilities; every accommodation with bath, radio, and adequate storage space; all very clean and all very clinical except for its warm staff friendliness. Far from special.

Galway 's (County Galway) lodgings would never send the late César Ritz into raptures. (Perhaps this is the biggest understatement in these Irish evaluations.) The **Great Southern** is far and away the local leader. Among its refurbishings is the Claddagh aerie complex—a Top-of-the-Mark-style installation which incorporates a penthouse Grill, cocktail bar, swimming pool, and sauna. The face-lifted Cois Farraige ("By the Sea") presents Irish entertainment in Season. General Manager Rory J. C. Murphy, and his staff are laboring mightily to raise the quality of this veteran—and they are succeeding. Not great by international standards, but pleasantly viable. The 100-room **Galway Ryan** is on the Limerick highway perhaps ¼-mile south of the center. Dramatic space-age main building, centered by white-brick, orange-chaired cockpit which is its sunken lounge; red-carpeted, purple-walled, white-chaired dining room divisible with sliding panel; tasteful low-ceilinged bar; piped music. Please be reminded that all of Ryan's enterprises are ingeniously keyed for the transient budgeteer. The 115-unit **Corrib Southern**, a relatively new star in the Great Southern cross, now glimmers in the local heavens. All accommodations with private bath; pool and sauna; probably a-comin' up with that usual brand of (Great) Southern Comfort. We'll nip in soon. The **Flannery Inn Motel**, about 400 yards south of the Galway Ryan, greets guests with a TV set fitted into the stone wall directly above the lobby fireplace, plum-colored lounge chairs, and a huge gilt-framed picture of a floating swan. To call it functional would be a gratuitous gilding of this chilly lily pond. The beach resort area of **Salthill**—only minutes from the center —might be summed up in 3 words: A cleaner Blackpool. The **Warwick Hotel**, with 70 rooms and 30 baths, is the best of the scruffy lot. The **Rio, Banba, Ardilaun House**, and its 29 other lodgings are not geared for North American vacationers unless they enjoy being pushed around by seething mobs, or unless they are in dire financial distress.

Glenbeigh (County Kerry), our favorite village on the Ring of Kerry, has 2 little treasures. One is operated by bearded, rotund, jolly Ernest Evans and the other by his mother; these enterprises are totally different in character. The **Towers**, thanks to Mr. Evans' gastronomic artistry, is celebrated from shore to shore for its extraordinary cuisine. After graduation from Lausanne's Hotel School and intensive study in the kitchens of Paris' George V, the Baur au Lac in Zürich, and other landmarks, he returned to this family-owned hostelry to repaint and refit it completely. Each year he travels to France to buy his own wines. A typical low-cost dinner menu offers 37 choices of sea-fresh marine dishes, country-fresh meat or fowl dishes, and garden fresh vegetables. This intimate, family-style haven is predominantly a center for sportsmen; one-week fishing or rough shooting parties including all living costs, gillies or guides, and all expenses except drinks, laundry, and tips, come to roughly $300 per person. Here is a gem of an Irish country hotel—simple, friendly in its welcome, and with personnel enchanting in their solicitude. The **Glenbeigh**, with its riot of flowers which catch the passerby's eyes, is a lovely 1½-century-old mansion which holds greater appeal for the ladies. Not only do its lobby and lounge also burst with blooms, but its shining brass, bright-yellow-upholstered furniture, and chuckling peat fire during colder days provide a cheerful welcome. With its large bay window overlooking the fine garden and lawns on the side, the dining room is a delight. The same loving attention has been lavished on the bedchambers; although some are quite small, all are different and all are attractively done in cretonnes and chintzes. The senior Mrs. Evans is a warm gentlewoman who patently adores her home and her clientele. Mr. Burglar is the manager. Almost without exception, the guests are as friendly as the staff. The charges are virtually identical in both. This spot unabashedly stole my Nancy's affection—and my deep admiration. Highly recommended for pilgrims in search of beauty and serenity.

In **Kenmare** (County Kerry), modernists should opt for either the expanding **Kenmare Bay** or **Riversdale House**. Traditionalists would probably be happier in the **Great Southern**.

Killarney and environs (County Kerry): **Dunloe Castle**, 9 miles out on the **Gap of Dunloe**, offers the greatest luxury and snob appeal of the region —but, in our opinion, in an uncomfortably self-conscious manner. It is not a castle; the original rooms were razed to make way for a totally modern 3-building complex with a magnificent sweep of the countryside. The large separate building opposite its entrance is its convention hall, the center of its many congresses; there's also a swimming pool, a sauna, and a hairdressing parlor. Burnished modern lobby; vast dining room seating 180; pleasant little grill adjoining; 12-stool, 4-table bar nicely done; spacious lounge up one flight. We prefer the so-called old wing, because of the warring colors in the "new." This 141-bedchamber, 8-suite extravaganza is operated by the same German entrepreneurs who run the Hotel Europe (see below); a large segment of its staff has been recruited from their fatherland. (One guest wrote us that she "had to look out the window to be sure I was in Killarney and not Kiel".) Far better for our own personal tastes is the newer, richly viewful, ever-friendly **Aghadoe Heights Hotel**, about 3 miles toward Tralee, where we enjoyed yet another spellbinding respite on a recent Kerry Ring-a-ling. Its hilltop setting offers a 360° sweep of the lakes and countryside—wow, WHAT a glorious situation! Rooftop restaurant and cocktail bar to take maximum advantage of its unique panorama; 35 rooms and 35 baths, all on the smallish side; proprietorship by Louis O'Hara, former General Manager of the Great Southern (see below). The cuisine, the warmhearted Hibernian attention and graceful service, the sink-in modern comfort, and the enrapturing solace of those fairyland hills and silvered lakes beckon our spirits so completely that we can hardly wait to return. We loved it—and we think you will too. The **Europe** is the harnessmate of Dunloe Castle. Stark, nearly treeless lakeside location, about 3½ miles from town; 3 dining salons, swimming pool near the boathouse; sauna; 8 suites and 200 rooms, all with bath or shower; bowling alley; Killarney Golf Course adjacent; fishing rights; adjoining bungalows not a part of its complex; enormous, well-used parade ground for trotting out the vast stable of horses. The bone in our throat here is that its tariffs are at identically the same rarefied levels as those of its more luxurious confrere. Here's a typical late-model city-slick hotel, the prototype of which can be found in dozens of booming international centers. Satisfactory for wayfarers who seek efficiency at very high prices with sparse charm or character. The ancient, urban **Great Southern** in town, has been given massive plastic surgery—so successfully that the patient is now much more beautiful than she ever was. The ornate, flavorful lobby, with its high ceilings, masses of filigree, and mélange of furniture, is as Celtic as a leprechaun. The bar alas, now has been updated and called The Punch Bowl; the huge, white dining room with its dome center overlooks green, green lawns. Grill moved downstairs; fetching little cocktail bar adjoining; stunning heated indoor pool and sauna for both genders in a separate building. A handful of extra accommodations have been created, and all of its so-tired rooms have been given the Benzedrine of central heating and redecoration in the style of the fresh wing. Management by bright, alert Denis Hurley. Busy, busy, busy—but oodles of flavor. **The Torc** (meaning "Boar Mountain") was called the Great Southern Inn when it was yet a suckling. This piglet is a cool motel-style structure just out of the city on the Cork highway. Of course it is the infant of the neighboring hotel which christened it with the former name (see above). The Generation Gap is tremendous, because its architecture is as clinical as a Saarinen-conceived hospital. Modern-as-next-week main building; hollow-square interior containing reception at entrance, bar to rear, dining room on other side and broad corridor, all enclosed by floor-to-ceiling glass. Piped music; heated pool; sauna; delicious food for its reasonable tabs. The adjoining bedrooms section displays better taste than the competitive Ryan's houses, but its luggage space and baths are inadequate for overseas guests. Okay for solo trippers or for couples, but a brannigan is virtually guaranteed when more adults are squeezed in. The 168-unit **Killarney Ryan** is a few hundred yards farther along the same road. Open-plan central block with reception, small bar, and lounge seating 100, shamrock-green dining room seating 200, and air conditioning; piped music; Telex; occasional evening entertainment in Season. The configurations and furnishings of the bedchambers are the same as in all of the Ryan enterprises (see earlier reference in "Hotels"). General Manager D. J. Bowe is a gentleman who fairly hops (or jigs) with Irish enthusiasm. Again, a value

for the bargain hunter. The sprawling **Castlerosse**, on the Kenmare Estate
1½ miles along the lake, is a frequent choice of golfers since an excellent
36-hole circuit is only a club-head away. Far from fancy, but ample comfort
for the dedicated sportsman. Manageress Miss Elizabeth McCarthy is a
sweet, friendly hostess. Swimming pool; tennis; bountiful table of salmon,
meats, and homegrown vegetables; car service available. Its 42 bedrooms,
including 3 oddly-designed "duplex suites," all have baths (no showers) which
are utilitarian but little more; one very nice hideaway cottage nearby. Pleasant
in the simple country style. **White Gates**, a cozy guesthouse on Muckross
Road, is big on warm half-timbered charm and small on its tabulations. A
winsome nest. The **International**, in the center, is a branch of the Trust
Houses Forte organization—and, as a rare, rare exception, the moguls of this
normally fine chain should hide their heads in shame to maintain this relic
as one of their own. Old, old house partially redone, with age wrinkles
showing too often through its cracks; air-conditioned dining room; 2 bars; 120
accommodations of routine-to-sad appearance and comfort, in our opinion;
groups, groups, and more groups by the score. Its mien is so listless and
tasteless that we believe its parent company is negligent in not infusing it
massively with financial plasma. If you go, don't book on the streetfront; it
is often the stuff of which insomnia is created. The **Three Lakes**, 500 yards
from the railway station, was launched only a while back, but its maintenance
was so slack to our eye that its inauguration could well have taken place in
the early fifties. Gloomy modern lobby and lounge; boxy 2-sided bar also
leading to lounge; unappealing dining room; routine cookery; carpark under
the building. All its chambers are studio-style, with the beds in opposite
corners; appended are tiny, sque-e-e-ze-in baths without showers. It is also
jammed to its rafters by groups during busy months. Very poor, say we. The
Cahernane, perhaps one mile along the Muckross road, occupies a 100-acre
park through which there is a long driveway to the century-old converted
mansion. One newish wing; only ground-level units with private baths; fine
staircase, fireplace, and other antiques in its lobby, plus the amiable Cellar Bar
with its handsome vaulted ceiling. Not exciting but fair enough if you pick
your room carefully. The **Lake**, 2 miles toward Muckross, is another rebuilt
mansion—this one very badly executed, in our judgment. It offers a lovely
view of the lake to the rear—but, as far as we're concerned, that's it. The
Muckross, 10 minutes from Killarney in the hamlet of the same name, borders the highway as closely as is possible. We found it to be clean, but, with
its 43 gloomy rooms, only 3 baths, and its funereal plastic flowers potted
around the lobby, we wouldn't advise it on a bet.

In *Kilkenny*, about 1½ hours from Dublin on the Cork road, the **New
Park** is a pleasant stopping spot for visitors to the city's castle and craft
center. Set on the edge of rich meadows and a lawn dotted by oaks, this
modern entry is very well run and genuinely inviting.

Kinsale (County Cork) boasts the long, rectilinear, harbor-sited **Trident**
as the leading contender in the port, with 40 rooms and 40 baths. This
waterfront quaysider, now flexed by the Costelloe Group's muscle, is also
headquarters for the Kinsale Sea Angling association. The best local bait for
salty-fisher types. Next in line is the Trust House Forte organization's 63-

room, 27-bath **Acton's**, an eighteenth-century building with small dimensions, undistinguished furnishings, and a gardenette plus a heated outdoor swimming pool. We wouldn't write home about either.

On the outskirts of *Leenane* (County Galway), the **Leenane** overlooks Killary Bay and the slopes of a handsome *pin* ("mountain"). Large, gracious lounge with comfortable brown chairs, grand piano, and fireplace; pert Killary Bar; simply furnished rooms in modern Irish with small storage space, cramped baths, and rather austere accouterments. Pleasant for a peaceful overnight or for a brief interlude of fishing and swimming at its nearby beaches. Season: Easter to October 1.

In *Letterkenny* (County Donegal) the 56-room, 56-bath **Ballyraine** opened not long ago. Although our schedule was too full to get up here during our latest rovings, reports about this house are favorable. We are told it is sited ¼-mile from town in a park setting, it is modern in execution, and its rooms are small. **Gallaghers**, in the center of the village, has 19 chambers and 2 baths; here is emergency shelter only.

Limerick City (County Limerick)? Please consult the section to follow on "Shannon Airport and vicinity" before deciding to stay in this center, because we think almost all of its hostelries are mediocre in quality. The 96-unit **New Jury's** leads the local pack of hobbled runners. Riverside situation; courtly stablemate of the Cork filly and the larger Dublin hotel; carbon copy of the former, with the same U-shape layout and central service building housing undistinguished restaurant, routine hideaway bar, and lounge. Chambermaid service and overall staff lassitude seem to be the areas drawing most howls from Guidesters; among the more illuminating was a thoughtful 7-point grumble which indicated to us that perhaps the chiefs of all major departments here need a few rockets; maybe the new ownership will be able to fire these needed pyrotechnics. In any case, its accommodations are unarguably the choicest to be found in this busy junction. The 7-story, 70-room, 70-bath **Royal George**, on the main street, completed a major reconstruction job recently. Small lobby with smartly turned-out Hall Porter; tiny, amusing Buccaneer Bar at street level; routine main bar up one flight. Bunkers a standard 12′x12′ in dimensions, which is obviously too snugglesome except for honeymooners; judicious employment of colors almost throughout. Still a long way from great—but an enormous renaissance. The budget-oriented **Ardhu Ryan** (turn back to the beginning of this section for a description of this chain) draws our 3rd-place ranking—a significant illustration of the paucity of attractive shelter here. Several years ago Mr. Ryan purchased Ardhu House, a Victorian relic in which gingerbread vied with old ladies. Immediately he modernized the interior of the original building (the demolition of which he is currently considering) and, on tight schedule, threw up a monolithic 6-story structure containing 168 of his standard bedrooms and baths; more recently these were augmented, bringing the new total up to 216 units. This complex is sited in an 8-acre park on the outskirts beside the airport highway. Because of the juxtaposition of hyper-moderna with Victoriana, maintenance appears to be slipshod when, in fact, it is satisfactory for the category. A good money-saver for the thinner-walleted traveler. **Cruises Royal Hotel**, in the center, is a moonshot from being Royal. Although a few revivifications have been applied in the public areas, its rooms are ultramini, with screamingly rippled, clashing carpets. Many low-level tour groups find shelter here, predominantly from the North of England. Our summary? To be avoided. The newer 80-room **Glentworth** is a better bet in this bracket. For the moment anyway, it is fresh and bubble-bright. The **Parkway Inn Motel**, one mile from the nexus on the Dublin highway, was opened in '67. Its bustling reception flanks one side of the entrance and the lounge-bar the other. Its units are cramped and, in our view, sleazy in appointments. So poorly conceived, in our opinion, that it is not recommended to the average North American tripper. For emergency pit stops, motorists might consider the **Two-Mile Motor Inn** or the **Green Hills**. While both are basic, we feel that we'd blow fewer gaskets in the former. Regarding **Hanrattys**, just off the main street, our evaluation dictates that we elide the first syllable and place emphasis upon the "ratty"—not literally so, but because of its scruffy carpets, tasteless mien, and low standard of facilities. Nix, nix, nix.

In *Louisburgh* (County Mayo), it's the **Old Head**. Seafaring readers will know our meaning when we write that in our opinion, it lives up to its name in a number of ways. Not recommended to any reader of this *Guide*.

Mullingar (County Westmeath) offers the **Greville Arms**, which is reported to be modest, clean, and good. When a Delaware friend of the *Guide* was so enchanted by its food that she wished to compliment the chef, up popped a merry Irishman who had been sent to Paris for his training! For idlers who wish to break the 4-hour drive between Galway and Dublin, here's apparently a satisfactory stop. The town's commercial—but the fly-casting is great at Lough Ennel, where Sweden's Crown Prince once dipped the royal line.

Oughterard (County Galway; 17 miles northeast of Galway city, directly across the lake from Ashford Castle at Cong) is a sweet hamlet with perhaps 500 inhabitants. The renewed, 33-room gardenfronted **Sweeney's** steals the cupcake in this village. It fairly oozes charm, conviviality, and tasteful homeyness. Two-century-old lounges; lawnside dining salon; tiny elevator; laced from cranny to nook with brassware, oil paintings, and highly polished hospitality. A cutie that is almost irresistible. The **Connemara Gateway Motor Inn,** operated by the Trust Houses Forte chain, is infinitely more commercial in tone. Modern, elongated structure of gray paneled concrete about a mile from the center, sited on 48 acres of lawns and pastoral land, with a view of Lough Corrib in the distance; functional lobby; lounge-bar with bright-orange plastic "leather" predominating; color-toned Grill open from noon to 10:30 P.M.; heated swimming pool brightened by umbrellas and complemented by a snack bar; putting green; croquet. All 48 twin-bed, green and yellow, studio-type units come with bath, clip shower (telephone style), electric kettle, coffee, tea, sugar, and 2 cups. It is open from Easter to October 1 only. The expanded **Egan's Lake Hotel**, where the action is, is not on the water but smack in the center of the settlement. Beguiling Mrs. Egan is normally on hand here, because Mr. Egan, who is an auctioneer, likes to follow the races. Although it is a hodgepodge in architecture and in furnishings, the copper and brass shine and the blue-flowered carpeting is cheerful. The aroma of beer faintly permeates the premises. Fishermen generally find this a happy haven. The 20-room, 8-bath **Corrib Hotel** is now owned and managed by Brian Walsh —and that's all we know about it, to our pained chagrin. At nearby **Clifden,** we hear that **Glenowen House** is similar to sweet little Sweeney's. That makes us doubly sorry to have missed it.

Parknasilla (County Kerry; roughly 35 miles from Killarney and 15 miles from Kenmare) has another **Great Southern** hotel that sits in a 200-acre park on the shores of an island-dotted Atlantic fjord. Lush subtropical vegetation nurtured by the Gulf Stream, which hits the coast at this point; azure cove with sweeping view of the bay, fronting rock-clad beach with patches of sand, and a toy wharf with its tiny boathouse; tennis, golf, deep-sea fishing, shoot-ing, pony trekking, boating, water skiing, swimming in the cove or in the glasslined pool; sauna; revamped bar; quiet and pleasant Manager Brendan Maher has spread new carpets, moved the reception, built a new lounge, spruced up furnishings, and provided all rooms with private bath. We rate this high on the Ring of Kerry for tranquil lazing in the region. Not far away at Tahilla Cove is a charming little **guesthouse;** limited accommodations; satisfactory food; quiet atmosphere.

Port-na-Blagh (north tip of County Donegal, at the top of Ireland), a charming little seaside resort with a sandy beach and polar-bear water, comes up with the **Port-na-Blagh** or **Shandon**—both friendly hostelries that provide satisfactory food and reasonable accommodations. Sheephaven Bay setting, which we happen to like but which some feel is bleak.

Rosapenna (see Port-na-Blagh for general location), the rebuilt **Rosapenna Hotel**, former estate of the Earl of Leitrim, provides 47 bedrooms and 40 baths. Set in a commanding position between Sheephaven and Mulroy Bays, on some of the most forlorn acreage in Ireland; 27-hole golf course just outside the door; private 3-mile sandy beach; cove-sited swimming pool; fishing, tennis, shooting, sailing, and pony trekking available. Season: March 26 to October 30.

Shannon Airport and vicinity, not including Limerick City (County Clare)? Within these few square miles, so much has been—and is— cooking that the most practical way for us to report the region is in a single cluster. Weathered-in passengers may take the 2- to 3-minute walk from the terminus to the **Shannon International**. Although the building looks drab, its interior is a happy surprise. Ownership by Bernard P. McDonough, who also operates Dromoland Castle and Clare Inn (see below); utilitarian lobby; 2 plain but comfortable lounges; pleasantly decorated small dining room; care-ful maintenance; 24-hour dry-cleaning; surprisingly quiet at night; open 365 days per year. Total of 126 rooms and 126 small baths with showers; 4 different decorating patterns, but all the same size and layout; unusually expensive rates for Ireland, as is S.O.P. in all the McDonough projects in the region. Although costly, excellent for transients. The **Shannon Shamrock**, 10 minutes toward Limerick, is as serene as a slumbering leprechaun. Long, low, ranch-style building in fieldstone; adjoining crafts center part of complex but inde-pendent of hotel; tiny reception area with souvenir counter under desk; jum-bled lounge; dining room with view of Bunratty Castle through its big picture windows. Its 84 rooms, all with bath and shower, are studio-style; their furnishings, tastelessly modern in tone, are somewhat bare and gimmicky. Although it is roughly half the price of the Shannon International, to us it offers less than half of its value and attraction. **Dromoland Castle**, near **Newmarket-on-Fergus**, is an 8-mile skip-and-jump from the airport. Guidesters seeking lavish living will find nothing in the nation to touch its princely opulence and imposing elegance. This baronial fief of the noble Inchiquins was purchased in '63 by the aforementioned American Midas, Bernard P. McDonough, who spent $3,000,000 to take it apart and to put it back together again. Grandiose park setting with teal-blue lake and a 9-hole golf course; tennis court, boating and hare coursing; fishing and shooting facilities available; beauty salon. Vast dimensions restyled in swashbuckling valiance by Leon Hegwood and Carlton Varney of Dorothy Draper & Co., Inc.; taste aggressive, but—unlike the job performed by the same experts in Brussels' Westbury Hotel—in our opinion, inspirationally appropriate to its milieu. Queen Anne annex connected by glassed-in corridor; cuisine akin to the Little Girl With The Curl; no à la carte. Our latest humdrum meal for 2, with a bottle of unexceptional wine (reflecting a national disregard for vintages and their care), came to more than $36 without tips; one entrée—at these prices, mind you, and from a total choice of just 3—was *corned beef and cabbage!* Kindly service; shy, smartly outfitted, well-trained staff effusing provincial Irish charm; 2 lovely lounges; cozy main bar the proud domain of friendly, alert, discreet Joe Higgins; second Bar downstairs as the after-dinner rendezvous, with 1 or 2 instrumentalists in High Season; between July 15 and September 15, full pension or demipension only; open from mid-March to October 31. The majority of its 67 rooms and 67 baths are spacious; a few mother-in-law rooms are uncomfortably small; avoid #11 and #12 at all costs. My Nancy and I prefer #201. We repeat, and re-repeat that its tariffs are moon-high. But for prosperous travelers who like their comfort in theatrically dramatic surroundings, here's Ireland's answer. The **Clare Inn**, a few hundred yards down the highway on a corner of the Dromoland estate, was launched in '68 by Mr. McDonough as supposedly "a less costly option." Nevertheless, our twin bill for a very recent overnight, breakfast, and our bland lunch reads out at over $50 in the Off Season! Hilltop situation; white building reminiscent of high-class motel; more subdued décor by the same firm; golf course privilege, fishing, and other facilities of its sister house extended to all guests; Olympic-size pool still being postponed on our visit because of a so-called water shortage (in Ireland?). Small but pleasant reception area; panoramic bar in tartan (where you'll be asked to have a sandwich and/or soup for lunch if you arrive in fringe seasons); 125-seat dining room with wild purple-and-rouge circus colorations; serene lounge and solarium in light greens and whites. Its 121 bedchambers in 4 different color schemes are large and handsomely furnished, and have walls so thin that you should ask for an isolated room if one is available. This venture depends heavily on high-bracket tour groups. A commercialized Dromoland Castle, without the fanfare—and priced way, way up in the fluffy clouds, too. The 133-room **Limerick Inn** is under the dynamic ownership of Tom Ryan. Six tall arches on the façade; stone and glass central entrance; floral decorative themes; ample living space; red-damask bar; apple-green restaurant with ginger-jar décor on the walls; basket-weave wool carpets; a high level of cheer everywhere. Possibly functioning for your arrival this season may be Roger Perret's white Georgian **Bunratty Hotel,** only a lance's heave from the Castle itself, the Folk Park, Durty Nelly's famous bar, and Vonnie Reynold's smart Bunratty Cottage Shop. One hundred rooms were being promised, and if plans run to form, this should provide sightseers with a center-stage address for the Green Isle's stellar attraction. Tell your travel agent to keep you posted on the opening date.

In *Sligo* (County Sligo) the **Great Southern** is still at an administrative crossroads. The existing structure will either be placed on the market or torn down for construction of a Great Southern Inn on its site, while the chain will build a brand-new Great Southern Hotel on the Dublin road about ½-mile from the center. General Manager Tim Corcoran, as genial as a St. Nicholas who has cut his calories to 1000 per day, will continue to be its Grand Panjandrum. Please make a last-minute check on its status. This plan holds excellent promise. The **Silver Swan**, inaugurated next to Hyde Bridge in the center, offers the soothing and pleasant sound of rushing waters on 2 sides. Air-conditioned lobby in clashing modern colors, with rugs woven with sufficient ships' wheels to equip a miniflotilla; horseshoe-shape bar; 2 carparks; some food smells where they shouldn't be during our late afternoon inspection. Total of 24 small rooms and 12 baths or showers; immaculately clean when we went through them. Quite good, but certainly not worth seeking out. The **Yeats Country Ryan** is 5½ miles out at *Rosses Point*, overlooking the bay. It is 200 yards from the County Sligo Golf Club (one of the best courses in the nation); guest cards are available to all clients. A fine beach (arctic-temperature ocean!) is a 5-minute walk from its doors. Lobby and lounge with gray and white brick walls plus tangerine carpeting; pleasantly retoned dining room in original Yeats House; bar attractively blended to conform with the modernity of the housing wing. A Grill-Bar sizzles and gurgles directly across the street. The rooms and their furnishings are identical to those of the other Ryan hostelries (see first part of this section). Another good buy for the thrifty traveler. **Ballincar House** is on a tangent to *Rosses Point*, perhaps 2 miles from the city. Though sited on a tranquil park, to us it does not look at all promising for discriminating Guidesters. **Sligo Jury's**, a sibling of the Dublin Jury's organization, opened recently on a 7-acre chunk of scenic Irish turf. From what we could see during its fitting out, the grand design is that of a motel, while it offers the facilities of a first-class hotel. There are 60 rooms, 60 baths, central heating, 2 restaurants serving reportedly good cuisine, 2 bars, and a number of interesting amenities. Near *Cliffoney*, about 15 miles to the north, the Mountbatten family's **Classiebawn Castle** is available for rent by parties (not individuals) for a minimum of 2 weeks in summer or 1 week in winter, except during the month of August when its owners are in residence. It sits atop a dune, with treeless, bushless sand radiating in every direction. From the outside it gave us such a stark, spooky impression that we think of it as Dracula's Castle-by-the-Sea. The interior, however, is reported to be old-fashioned, warm, and country-mansionish rather than castle-ish. There are 10 bedrooms and 5 baths. Its rates are for millionaires only. For further information, write to Secretary Gabrielle Gore-Booth, Lissadel House, County Sligo.

Tipperary (County Tipperary)? Yes, it's a long, long way. . . . but to us not worth it when you reach this colorless farming town. The **Royal** is clean, and its food smelled country-good. However, when we saw the royally rung-sprung chairs and the shrieking varieties of pinks on its ground floor, we were unnobly discouraged from parking here. It has 22 rooms and 1 bath. The **Tipperary**, with 18 chambers and its toilets down the hall, draws our even louder "No."

Tralee (County Kerry) has most of its appeal on the fringes of the town itself. Its beauty is in its name and in its famed "Rose" of song. Intimate, sylvan **Ballyseede Castle**, on a 300-acre estate, houses a mere 13 rooms beneath its crenels. Most come with private bath; the dining room is sunlit, as are the people who attend you; the bar is in red; the bridal suite features a canopied bed; all bay-windowed bedchambers are named, not numbered. Quite nice. The **Mount Brandon**, opened in '66, is employed by tour conductors as a sleeping factory. Its 164 small rooms with toilets and showers, tiny closets, and tiny baths demonstrated such inexcusably careless maintenance that we were openly dismayed. We think of it as being so barny and cold that we can still almost feel the chill winds blowing through it. Spare us forevermore, please! **Benners**, on the main street, bespeaks its 1¼-century of careful use. Sweet entrance with shining copper, plus peat fire burning in winter; neighborly bar to the right; old-fashioned lounge to the left; 56 grandfatherly rooms; 17 private baths. Clean, plain, friendly, and very Irish. Out on the Killarney road a few minutes by car, the modernistic **Earl of Desmond** commands an eyeful treasure of land, sea, and sky. Inside it is merely utilitarian, so we'd use it only as a touring base.

Tramore (County Waterford) has the completely rebuilt **Grand** and the expanded 90-room **Majestic**, both substantial veterans near the sea which are beloved by local vacationers.

Waterford (County Waterford) offers the newish **Tower Hotel**. It is routine-modern with a hodgepodge décor. We haven't seen the newer 100-room-and-bath **Ardree**, which is reported to be a very sound alternate.

Waterville (County Kerry) is a fishermen's paradise. And for super-deluxe sporting shelter, there's the inspired **Waterville Lake**, handsomely situated on the shores of island-studded Lough Currane. This American-owned company has also acquired the famous Butler's Pool, where one canny Irishman says the salmon have to jostle for position. Appropiate use of the scenery is only one winning feature; the building itself enhances the enchanting lake- and landscape with space concepts that are awesome. The sumptuousness both inside and out is a feast for the eyes. Bedchambers are look-alikes, but of its pair of suites we prefer #2 to #1. Unquestionably among the nation's finest. The promontory which you can see from here is uneasy host to the links- and loughside **Reenroe**, an awkward, commercial structure that also belongs in the Mulcahy net of Waterville Lake and Ashford Castle fame. We found it big and cold, with a personality that oppugns the lovely lay of the land. In the village, **Butler Arms**, a tiny nest for sportsmen, would be our choice of the modest candidates that line the single trail along the shore.

Westport (County Mayo) comes up with the **Belclare** as one of its 2 viable stops. The spruce main structure, atop a hill, has a lovely view of the lake. Tennis court; swimming pool; connecting wings of 46 units on left and banquet-conference center on right. Since we arrived just before its May 1 to September 30 season had started, our doorbell ringing roused nobody. But the curtains were up, so we prowled and peeped everywhere possible. Immaculate dining room and kitchen; white leather bar with black trim and fireplace; the sweet smell of success in its exterior and what we could see of its interior. We would not be surprised if here is indeed a winner. **Westport Jury's**, 2 miles from the center on the Castlebar road, was built by the Dublin Jury's group. Its split-level, crucifix-shape, ultramodern structure contains a restaurant, quick-service grill, bar, and 58 twin-bed rooms with bath, radio, and central heating. It's both efficient and comfortable. On the estate, there's a zoo; salmon fishing and equitation are available nearby.

In *Wexford* (County Wexford) the up-and-coming **Talbot** is building a name for its food and lodgings. The Chairman is accomplished, urbane Toddie O'Sullivan of Dublin's Gresham fame. Boxy, 6-story structure; carpeted, partitionable lounge; shopping arcade; spacious dining salon and adjoining patio; pine-paneled Pike Room Snackery; cozy cocktail cranny in mustard and green. Bedchambers, in a modern mode, come with phones, radios, and (praise be!) central heating; most have a diminutive bath. Next there's the family-style **Strand**, with good vittles and an indoor pool, followed by **Whites,** a mixture of new and old in a half-timbered coaching inn.

Additional possibilities, in the small-and-agreeable category, are the **Lake Hotel** in *Virginia* on serene Lough Ramor (County Cavan), which is a favorite of local "coarse" fishermen, and the **Park**, another Virginian, which is also reported as worthy (22 rooms, 7 baths, private golf course, lake view; management by Barry McDonnell). The new guiding hands in the **Renvyle House Hotel** (on the Connemara coast) are trying hard to keep up the old quality; the cuisine is now said to be exceptional and the standards are reputedly prime. **McFadden's** at *Gortahork* (County Donegal) is described by some raffish rovers from Charlotte, N.C., as "a little gem." Merrily run by Lilis and Bernie O'Leary, who'll "provide good comfort and good food for a good price." However, other rovers (perhaps not so raffish) disagree, pointing out that the food IS good but the rooms leave much to be desired. Will other Rashly Raffish Rovers please stand up?

Although we're familiar with hostelries not mentioned, these are the only ones known to us which we recommend to U.S. voyagers. They range from Limerick to Letterkenny in location, and from $11 to "up" in cost.

An indispensable item to carry along is the thin-lined guidebook, *Ireland —1977* Hotels and Guesthouses, which you can obtain free from the **Irish Tourist Offices** in New York, Chicago, San Francisco, and Toronto. More than 400 listings!

To assure yourself of a hot bath in many of the older hotels here, you may require (1) clairvoyance, (2) flexibility, and (3) dexterity. The first will enable you to divine when the water is warm enough, the second to bathe at precisely the hours you do not wish to, and the third to leap gazelle-like out of the shower when the hot changes to cold or warm to scalding (rare!).

The Irish Tourist Board issued a list of over 100 stopping places which furnish baby-sitting service up to midnight at rates ranging from 30¢ to 90¢

per hour. Since most already offer a 10% to 33⅓% discount for children under 10 years of age, this supervision of the Dr. Denton members of your party is a built-in bonus.

A "room only" charge—sans the customary breakfast inclusion—has been agreed to by 483 proprietors. A number of them have also dropped the tradition of multiplying the single rate by 2 to determine the double rate; these now offer a realistic concession.

Dedicated budgeteers? Since we're too bottlenecked here for additional entries, please consult our annually revised paperback, *Fielding's Low-Cost Europe,* which lists scads more bargain spots and money-saving tips for serious economizers.

FOOD AND RESTAURANTS   Irish cuisine is superb—so long as it involves grills, roast beef, steaks, salmon, or simple dishes. We're sad to report, however, that neither fancier fare nor vegetables are as well cooked or well presented as in the more food-conscious of European lands.

Odd Tidbits Department, Culinary Division: In the counties (not cities, generally), the man of the sod prefers his roast beef stone dead; if you like yours rare, specifically ask if they have it "underdone" when you order. As in Finland, normally tea is brewed in improper metal pots and nowhere could we find a tea strainer (don't these hardy folk have use for 'em?). Insomniacs will be cheered to know Sanka in percolator or drip-grind form (not powder) is available—and it makes magnificent Irish Coffee. Incidentally, this happy brew never tastes as wondrous in any other country, and why, we don't know. The same holds true for Guinness. Even though the English brewery is larger than the local one, we prefer the Irish product. England's harder water perhaps? Mashed potatoes are called "creamed potatoes"; paper napkins pop up even in some of the most elegant establishments. Milk is rich, plentiful, and pasteurized; soda fountains (called "cafés" or "milk bars") list such exotic items as Banana Split Joy, Chocolate Kiss Shake, and Melancholy Baby.

The **Gresham Hotel Hunting Lodge**, formerly the Grill and now a completely remodeled installation, has regained its rank as *Dublin*'s universally acknowledged pacemaker for dining (see "Hotels" for a fuller description). The Gandon Restaurant was refashioned so as not to spoil its familiar mien. Off-lobby situation; red-and-black décor, with waiters in matching shades; service infinitely better. Palms and salaams.

The **Shelbourne** divides its dining room in thirds. One leg is the Saddle Room, featuring pine paneling, a beamed ceiling, and an open grill; rib beef is carved (lunch and dinner, in 3 separate degrees: stunned, medium, and crispy). The Grill-Bar adjoining, for light bites and theatergoers' fare, is also engaging; 12 tables, counter with stools, good colors, reasonable prices. The 3rd section retains the conventional atmosphere, with Paul Hogarth illustrations and 3 handsome brass chandeliers. More expensive tabs; table d'hôte or à la carte selections; dancing; open until 12:30 A.M. A new bar was decanted more recently; snacks are available here. All are air-conditioned. All good.

The Lafayette Restaurant at the **Royal Hibernian** is now fine. Though its high-style furnishings and overbright illumination do not happen to appeal to us, the quality of its cookery is, for Ireland, at gastronomic level. This relatively costly rendezvous stages Gallic dinners drawn from varying regional specialties on Saturday nights in winter; its Bianconi Grill-Bar comes up with lighter and more reasonable comestibles; the rôtisserie falls between these extremes. For day-in-night-out dining, we would pick the last as one of the most rewarding corners of culinary excellence and consistency in the city. Nothing fancy, but darned good for quality, price, and atmosphere.

. **The Celtic Mews** (109a Lr. Baggot St.) is the most a-mewsing independent oasis, in our opinion. Host Joe Gray really knows the hospitality game; he also can produce an excellent and interesting meal. Ground-floor lounge with attic room for dining; wooden floors; candle illumination. Ours was an altogether enjoyable experience. Highly recommended. **Snaffles** (Leeson St.) is now perhaps even better in the gustatory department. Cellar location; 2 rooms with oil paintings, Chippendale chairs, Persian carpets, and a glow of mellowness. Our party's raw plaice and mousse, plus game paté, kidneys with mustard, and piquant tongue, were superb. The wines are expensive but choice and well maintained. Very good indeed. **Buck Whaley's**, a neighbor, tries to do a similar job, but we think it fails. **Sachs** is a newcomer to town, but already we are hearing high praise for its kitchen.

The **Soup Bowl** (2 Molesworth Place) is inconspicuously cupboarded behind its single red door. Cathy and Peter Powry are the prime movers at this one. Downstairs there are 3 tables in a living room ambiance with a fireplace and a large refrigerator; 10 more tables are up one flight; service is rather informal. Dinner only is served (8 P.M. to midnight); it is closed Sunday; be sure to reserve in advance. This *potage* is recommended for what it is.

A pleasant expedition is a ramble through the zoo at **Phoenix Park** and an inexpensive meal in its lovely setting of lawns and flowering shrubs; worth the trip when the sun is out. **Barnardo's** (19 Lincoln Place) is an Italian specialist with a bleak décor but appetizing dishes; reasonable. The **Golden Orient** (Leeson St.) is just the place for adventurers who'd enjoy exploring genuine Pakistani cookery. The newer Tandoori Rooms downstairs are said to be excellent.

For a light lunch, the Buttery in the **Royal Hibernian** is recommended; the management was granted special permission by London's Berkeley to duplicate the décor of the internationally famous original. The Coffee Dock at the **New Jury's** is middling. The **Berni Inn** is a promoter of olde-fashioned atmosphere with its grills; this is part of a chain.

Shopper's Special? Try **Le Savoir Faire** in Switzer's department store. Just refashioned, it is now more inviting than ever. Our recent noontime repast here was, without qualification, one of the best meals on our nationwide tour. You'll find high quality for its low, low prices; both a fixed menu and à la carte are available. *Ave!* (For even tighter budgets, Switzer's also operates a darned good cafeteria on the same floor.)

Pocket-size excursions? In nearby *Stillorgan*, a residential suburb, the **Beaufield Mews** offers antiques and nutrition to pilgrims who hunger for a quiet haven similar to our own popular northeastern Red Barns, White Turkeys, or Spinning Wheels. Softly illuminated converted stable; 2-or-3-choice menu nightly; operative 6:30 P.M. to 10:30 P.M., but never for lunch,

Sundays, bank holidays, or Christmas and Easter weeks. Oodles of charm. In **Howth**, a sweet little fishing village only 20 minutes north of midcity, the **Abbey Tavern** draws raves from almost every quarter. Old-style tavern to which a restaurant has been added; good cookery composed mostly of shellfish; other landed specialties also on tap; ballad-belting troubadours entertain nightly in the barnlike room to the rear. Mrs. Scott-Lennon is the proprietress. The C.I.E. transportation people run a weekday "Minstrel Tour" out here, which includes visits to the James Joyce Museum and other places associated with Irish literary giants; bookings through the C.I.E. office opposite the Gresham; cost for the haul, the vittles, the songs, and overnighting at the hotel is in the $50 range. Corny as it may sound, we think you will enjoy it as much as we did—and that was a lot. There's a more refined sort of seafood restaurant called the **King Sitric** (named for the famous ninth-century Viking sovereign of Dublin) around the corner on East Pier that's touted for it's fresh net-work. White facade looking to the harbor; upstairs bar done out preciously in florals and ruby; cheery sea-level restaurant with waiters in black tie. Both of these anchorages can be reached by bus from town. By taxi, the ride is about $5. **Sutton House** is also a satisfactory choice, according to local chums. Near *Sandyford*, a 6½-mile junket into the mountainscape, **Lamb Doyles Roadhouse** provides a glorious vista of the city and surrounding hills. Starkly modern structure with granite blocks, sheets of glass, panels of pine, and a purple and blue ambiance; lunch from 1 P.M. to 3 P.M.; dinner plus dancing from 7 P.M. to 11 P.M.; culinary standards only so-so. For sunny-day meanderings farther out, try the **Roundwood Inn**, which used to be called the **Wicklow Hills Hotel** (steak dishes and student balladeers) or the **Glenview Hotel** near *Bray*. For seasiding, *Dun Laoghaire* offers the gray-and-white **Mirabeau** facing the harbor (a neat house with superior kitchen crafts), **na Mara** (in a converted railway station but specializing in sea craft), and **Teddy's** (on the seawalk, rougher hewn, simpler cookery). This town makes an excellent excursion point for old or young salts. One run we really enjoy is the skip out to seaside *Malahide*, where **Johnny's** does its magic. Johnny and Eileen Oppermann are the Merlin-class magicians —and what a culinary show you'll receive! Downstairs hideaway in a Georgian town house; brick and stone walls; crackling fire; spluttering candles; peeking views of the open kitchen and busy, smiling Chef Johnny. The menu is small but truly select. Frankly, we love it. Closed Sunday and Monday. Out at *Killiney*, **Rolland** is the creation of Henri Rolland whose father, Pierre, cooked for palates named Kennedy, Nixon, de Gaulle, and MacMillan. The word is out that it is attractive not only to the eye, but to the taste as well. We'll try it next time in County Dublin.

The **Gresham** and the **Shelbourne** offer dancing from 1 to 5 nights per week, depending upon the season. For the younger set, there are many public dance halls similar to the Four Provinces or Crystal Ballroom, with no liquor but plenty of rock-'n'-roll; these jive joints, which have recently spilled over into scads of smaller Irish communities, have given birth to more than 200 "show bands" bearing such labels as the Rockets, the Jets, and the Monarchs. It's a rage—but if you're over 21, you'll feel 91 when you watch these kids in action.

PUBS As in England, the venerable color, serenity, and neighborliness of
Irish pubs are fast vanishing. Less and less are they companionable gathering
places for a pint, a quiet chat, and a game of darts. Explosively, these old-style
havens are undergoing a revolutionary change in character to become what
are called "Singing Pubs."

Younger people are the majority who frequent this mutation. Generally
speaking, the middle-aged and the elderly continue to maintain their loyalty
to the traditional-style establishments. When they die off, however, a centuries-old institution will virtually disappear with them.

Among the new genus in **_Dublin_**, **Gulliver's Inn** (67 New St.) was
launched to celebrate Jonathan Swift, who was the dean in St. Patrick's, just
around the corner. Red velvet cushions; only slightly cacophonic solos by
guitars and other instruments; terrible ventilation. Except for its lack of
dancing and psychedelic lights, it could be a disco. Probably the costliest—
and perhaps the noisiest—in the city. **Slattery's Terenure House** (Terenure
St.) consists of 3 sections in a large building. The first is a ground floor
lounge-bar which could be mistaken for an expanded version of a typical Irish
hotel installation. The 2nd is a spartan ground-floor bar for the serious male
toper. The 3rd is its _pièce de résistance:_ An upstairs cabaret-bar (small admission charge) which holds 400 revelers. Stage and orchestra; electric organ;
lone singers or small groups airing their adenoids in tandem; public address
system twisted up to its maximum. Friday and Saturday are its only scheduled
nights of operation. It is one million miles from the classic milieu for elbow-
bending. **William Searson** (42 Upper Baggot St.) is a suavely decorated
contemporary complex of 3 bars with lounges; while 2 are modern, the Public
Bar is done in fake turn-of-the-century. Crowded by students; known for the
fights (now less frequent) on its premises. In atmosphere, here could be a
cocktail lounge in any American city. **Bartley Dunne** (Mercer St.) offers an
unusually versatile selection of booze drawn from its wines-and-spirits shop
adjoining. Dim lighting; candles on tables; piped music (softly so, for a
change); 2 arched, cozy, corner rooms to rear which encourage romance. Also
popular among the Junior Set.

Classic types? The **Bailey** (Duke St.), for decades one of the city's most
celebrated haunts of the literati, fell into disrepute a few years back, but now,
thank goodness, it has been pleasantly revived. Ground-floor bar and diner;
inner Fish Bar with leather booths, slat-faced walls, and delicious sea delicacies; upstairs U-shape salon, again wood lined and touched up with old
mirrors and hanging plants. The air of conviviality is manifestly inviting; so
is the splendid quality of its foodstuffs. Richly recommended for blue-ribbon
pubbery. **Davy Byrnes** (Duke St.) draws more than its share of Intelligent
Young Dolls and Very Earnest Young Authors. The **Toby Jug** (South King
St., next to Gaiety Theatre) has a small, pleasant Lounge Bar in front and
Public bar to the rear. Its patrons can _talk_ in this typically plain milieu.
Neary's (Chatham St.), with a tiny cocktail bar on one side, is also friendly
and unpretentious; it is reminiscent of a U.S. corner tavern. **McDaid's** (Harry
St. off Grafton) doesn't seem as amusing as it used to be. **Peter's Pub** is
dullsville, in our opinion. **Jerry Dwyers**, the pungent but far from hygienic
center on Moore St. in the street market district, attracts playboys. **Mooney's**

Bars (several scattered branches) cater to a mixed group, predominantly male, of business executives, clerks, dockers, coal heavers—the hardworking Dubliner who drinks a Guinness rather than a cocktail.

Late bite? Try the Coffee Dock at the **New Jury's.**

Bar girls, taxi girls, pickups? Nothing like the Latin countries: No bordellos, no steerers, no blandly acknowledged immorality.

TAXIS, TRAINS, AND TRANSPORTATION Two fleets of radio-contact cabs—**National** and **Blue Cabs**. Dial 77-22-22 for the former; for the latter it's 76-11-11. The independents, recognizing competition, have perked up their cars and services, and even have a central telephone of their own (79-66-66). Call any of these and you'll have a taxi within 10 minutes, regardless of where you are.

Every company now uses meters. The minimum ride is about 60¢. *Tip heavily;* 3 pence is barely adequate for a minimum haul, and at least 5 pence should be given for anything greater.

With a rare display of savvy about "what-helps-tourism-helps-us-all," more than a dozen hoteliers and businessmen have become godfathers to **jarvies** (horse-drawn cabs) and refurbished them. (You'll hear, with pride, "I'm atellin' yez, Mister, eleeghant is the word fer it.") When you're doing the town, they'll give you the true feeling of *The Wearing of the Green*.

Jaunting cars (the Irish "dogcart," a one-horse affair) are lots of fun. In some places you can get them for as little as $3 per day. **Bicycles** cost perhaps a dollar for 8 hours, a fine investment. But the most exotic transportation available is in Cork—the **Gypsy Caravan**, a horse-drawn trailer capable of accommodating 4 persons. These brightly painted wagons are equipped with foam-rubber berths, a bottled-gas stove, heat, light, sheets, and blankets—and they're all yours for about $125 per week. You don't even need to know one end of the beastie from the other, because they'll cheerfully give you free lessons in harnessing and driving—something which you should accept as insurance against mishaps. Check the Irish Tourist Office for details.

Short-run trains are showing great improvement. The majority of the **Irish Railways'** local lines are now dieselized. Among the blue-ribbon runs, the *Enterprise Express* and the *Dublin-Cork Express* are outstanding. On the former, we had the most delightful train ride of one European circuit. The breakfast was a joy—piping hot scones, ham finger-sandwiches, fluffy cake, generous servings of coffee, and other temptations; the hostess couldn't have been sweeter or prettier; the schedule was nonstop. One odd little anomaly surprised us: The same drink in the same cozy little rolling bar costs considerably more in the North of Ireland than it does in Eire. Thus, to quote a cheerful and thrifty Irish friend, "the north-bound traveler is well advised to refresh himself early, and vice versa."

On hinterland hauls, the Irish Railways are still a far cry from their Swiss confreres. For a quiet trip ride First-class; for fun unrefined, ride Second.

Long-distance **bus** hauls—and some of the newer short-haul links—are as modern and speedy as our Greyhound routes. But when you climb aboard the average rural Irish bus, prepare yourself for An Experience. Many of them are primitive, most are crowded, most pick up passengers every 42 feet—but you'll get a kick out of your ride, and you'll probably arrive on time. The friendliness and banter are worth the price of admission.

The **C.I.E.** (35 Lower Abbey St., Tel.: 300777), a big-time organization with large and comfortable vehicles, many of them diesels, operates (1) 18 single-day sightseeing tours from the Central Bus Station; (2) 6-day round-robin tours; (3) a so-called Super Deluxe 6-day swing through the south in summer; (4) other 2- to 12-day offerings to various parts of the country. Americans are so fond of these C.I.E. road excursions they're sold out long in advance; your travel agent should make the earliest possible reservations to insure your space.

AIRLINES   Aer Lingus-Irish International Airlines is the promotional name of 2 operational divisions which share common management: Aerlinte Eireann for transatlantic service, and Aer Lingus for British and European runs. Until recently, the government limited the landing rights of all foreign carrier's except British Airways to Shannon Airport in the southwest region. After perhaps 2 decades of bitter controversy, TWA has at last been permitted to fly in and out of Dublin—a healthy competitive step forward for the convenience of the North American visitor.

These highborne Hibernians now fly the Boeing-747 jumbo on long runs —and they fill them with more seats than most any other carrier; 4 Boeing-707 pure jets do the work for 133 passengers per cabin. During the summer season these shuttle to London, making the run in 50 minutes. We've recently hopped off a New York–Dublin spin and our First-class physical facilities (*not* the wonderfully kind crew) did not impress us as favorably as on some more luxury-minded fleets. The Economy section is vast, absolutely enor-mous, and as pleasant and comfortable as the IATA straitjacket will allow (see "Let's Go By Plane"). The Deluxe segment, however, contained a mere 8 seats plus a galley; a forward cargo hold totally consumed the lounge (practically a standard offering on other intercontinental jets). We under-stand, furthermore, that there is no First Class whatever on the Montreal loop. Here's an operator that is frankly after the Economy trade; it does beautifully in this category. But it does not shoot for the higher-paying passenger; the cuisine suffers in variety and quality (and why not, with an incentive to feed a maximum of only 8 mouths per flight?); its leg-stretching areas were designed for leprechauns, not for long-boned Yankee-Doodlers (the seat itself is comfortable). But the service! Oh, those warm, kind, lovely, friendly, generous-hearted colleens!!! They are *marvelous*—and so is Aerlinte Eireann, IF you hold an Economy-class billet. Irish hospitality is renowned —and shure they don't be calling it "The Friendly Airline" as a mere bit of blarney!

The Aer Lingus leg is one of the most efficient feeder companies in modern aviation. Their passenger load factor is almost habitually the highest in com-mercial aviation—both domestically and between other nations. They just don't come safer, more wide-awake, or better.

DRINKS   As in Finland, the divisions concerning alcohol are radical. At one extreme, you'll find an exceptionally large percentage of heavy topers. At the other, the Pioneer Society, a fiercely dedicated temperance organization, has enlisted legions upon legions of the population; its male members may be spotted by its distinctive insignia worn as lapel buttons. Visit after visit, we are surprised to find so many fanatically vehement Drys in the nation where strangers are addressed perhaps faster and more frequently than in any other by the hospitable phrase, "D'ye want a drink?"

A taste of Irish whiskey is a must for drinkers. (One of its greatest salesmen was Brendan Behan, author of *The Hostage* and *The Quare Fellow*, plays which must have been written in Pot Still ink.) No potatoes at all; it's tripled distilled from grain (Scotch is merely twice distilled!). Put 70¢ on the bar, ask for "a half one," and up will come this unique, potent, and healing libation. There are 4 major distillers; John Jameson's (Holinshed's "Soverigne Liquor" at its finest), John Power's ("Enjoy that POWER!"), D. Williams at Tullamore ("Give Every Man His Dew!"), and Cork's, makers of Paddy Flaherty ("Will 'oo have a Paddy?" means your host is a true-blue Cork man). Crock O'Gold is our least favorite blend. There are also distillers of an illegal firewater called "poteen," a fairish glass of which will delicately lift the enamel from every molar in your mouth; this rural moonshine, the despair of legitimate whiskey producers and Government "reven-oors," is ubiquitous these days, because of too-high liquor taxes.

Scotch is plentiful; Canadian Club is obtainable in the better bars. Sparkling water is cheap by the split—and, if a bit of mild teasing may be permitted, who else but the hard-drinking Irish would produce a special size for the infants of the land, "Thwaites' Baby Soda"?

Guinness stout comes in extra (medium weight) and foreign export (doubly fortified). This brewery landmark, on which the original Arthur Guinness took a 1400-year lease, has merely another 1200 years to go before expiration; the same yeast strains have been continuously under cultivation and in use since its founding. Guided tours through the 63-acre plant, the 2nd largest of its type in the world, surpassed only by London's Park Royal operation, are offered at 11 A.M. and 3 P.M. Monday through Friday; children under 12 are not eligible, because the climax takes place in the sampling room (all free!). Many Americans prefer their stout diluted with beer or ale; most all like "Black Velvet" (50% Guinness and 50% champagne).

Beer flows in Niagaras, of course. The Harp brand twangs a tangy note. In your sweetest Irish tenor, warble for an extra-cold one. Otherwise it will be served to you at skin temperature.

Virtually from coast to coast, wines are limited in selection, secondary in quality, and poor in handling and presentation. Ireland apparently has a low priority at Bordeaux, Burgundy, Reims, and other vinelands because she has never been a major customer at these marketplaces. Due to the heavy influx today of German visitors and residents, the white grape is now beginning to apppear in greater quantity. But here, too, the Saxon elixirs are decidedly below the quality levels of the fatherland.

Irish coffee (also known as Gaelic coffee) is one of the pleasantest beverages possible to sample. To make it, add a jigger of Irish whiskey to ⅔rds of a glass of steaming black coffee; add sugar to taste; float thick, rich cream on the top without stirring, and sip slowly. It's wonderful. Just ask for it by name, and the waiter will bring you pure bliss in a glass.

For your after-dinner liqueur, Irish Mist is to Ireland what Drambuie is to Scotland. Interesting and different; increasingly popular.

There are bars, pubs, cocktail lounges, and licensed dining rooms everywhere. Today they drink (and how they do!) from 10:30 A.M. to 11:30 P.M., save for a 60-minute respite in the cities of Dublin and Cork that is universally and with good-humored irreverence called the "Holy Hour." Bar time is shorter on Sundays and St. Patrick's Day; it's bone dry on Christmas Day and Good Friday (except with meals, praise be!). St. Patrick's Day used to call for special foxiness, because the only whiskey openly sold in the nation was at the annual Ballsbridge Dog Show. They're still talking about the chap (some claim it was Brendan Behan) here who looked up from his glass, focused both bloodshot eyes on his surroundings, and growled in exasperation, "What stupid eejit let all these *demmed* dogs into a respectable pub like this?"

Ice for your nip? Plentiful in the cities, of course—but if you should ask for it deep in the countryside, your sweet rustic waitress is liable to say, "Shure and where would I find *that* at this time of the year?"

THINGS TO SEE   Too much to cover in this short space.

Dublin, of course. The Abbey Theatre, which cuddles the experimental Peacock Theatre in its basement, has inaugurated "A Night at the Abbey" happening. For approximately $10 you will be given a seat in the circle, a program, a glass of Guinness or a soft drink during the intermission, a light Theatre Supper of a cold meat salad, dessert, coffee, wine or beer in the Rooftop Reception room, and the counsel of a member of the artistic staff of the organization. This package is available from May through August only. The revitalized Gate Theatre, sired by the Abbey in 1928, specializes in an international repertory. Then, to skim the surface, you'll also find the Municipal Art Gallery (now proudly showing the Lane impressionist paintings), the National Gallery in Merrion Square (partially endowed by George Bernard Shaw), the Chester Beatty Library (really a repository of Middle and Far Eastern artifacts), St. Stephen's Green, Phoenix Park, Guinness's, the James Joyce Museum (appropriately sited in the Martello Tower in suburban Sandycove, where Joyce lived), the "Crusader's Corpse" in St. Michan's Church, the *Book of Kells* in Trinity College—the city is full of wonderful things.

In the countryside, the drive through the extreme **southwest** of the nation (*Bantry–Ballylicky–Kenmare* and around the legendary "Ring of Kerry" to *Killarney* or the nearby *Dingle Bay* where *Ryan's Daughter* was filmed) is particularly stirring, beautiful, and worth adventuring. The L54 *coastal* road up to *Ballyvaughan* (County Clare) is even more breathtaking. You will thrill to a parade of glorious seascapes and landscapes in wild and unforgettably impressive terrain. Remember, however, that most of the hotels in this area are closed during Off-Season.

And while in Killarney, don't miss the extraordinary excursion up the mountain road to "Ladies View" and "Moll's Gap." If you don't use your own car or take a conducted bus tour, you may proceed by jaunting cart, pony trap, or pony-*back* (if you're out of your orangutan mind) up, in, out and around, to the upper lake. Here, according to friendly and intrepid Bronxville Guidesters, a mediocre but filling picnic lunch may await you. Your return may then be made by big comfortable rowboats, with 4 brawny oarsmen pulling you down the 14-mile channel through the 3 lakes. This is a 6-hour trip. We took ours the easy way, by self-drive automobile.

The **west** of Ireland—**Galway**, **Mayo**, **Sligo**, and the islands off this coast (remember *Man of Aran?*)—offers spectacular geography, a fascinating breed of people and beauty that is even more pristine. The *Naomh Eanna,* a handsome little steamer, handles the Aran run. Arrival and departure times are such that you will have to spend 2 nights in Galway. The junket is 9 hours each way with only 1½ hours at the destination. If you can't spare that much time, regularly scheduled 20-minute flights zip out of Galway; they're very reasonably priced.

And speaking of flying, if you are in the Shannon area, try to arrange a visit to Bunratty Castle and the Folk Park. The idea of attending one of its medieval feasts may seem downright mawkish to cosmopolitan diners (indeed, the food might be termed "ho-cuisine"), but the building, grounds, costumes, and exquisite choir singing are so engaging that we think you will forgive the cornball aspects of such an obvious touristic ploy. This one really *is* rewarding and we recommend it strongly.

Perhaps the most famous single tourist landmark is **Blarney Castle**, near the city of **Cork** (75 miles from Shannon, 160 miles from Dublin). If you kiss the stone (admission now about 75¢; as with almost anything you make love to, the cost has gone up), be sure the man holding your feet is sober—as ours wasn't.

The Irish Tourist Office will give you travel details on every part of the country.

TIPPING   Something to watch: Most hotels in Ireland include a 12½% service charge in the bill; add 5% to this for taxes. The chambermaid should be given 10%. Hand taxi drivers about a dime for a 35¢ ride; large tips are expected because the rates are low. In ordinary restaurants, waiters should be tipped 15% to 20% of the bill; in the finer ones, 10% to 15% will do.

THINGS TO BUY   As in a number of countries abroad, the recently inaugurated Value Added Tax system deeply permeates the economic lives of the citizenry here. The version in Ireland requires that you pay from 6.75% to 19.5% extra on all purchases if used within its borders. To avoid this levy, instruct the merchant either (1) to direct substantial acquisitions in bond to your departing aircraft or ship, or (2) to forward them unaccompanied straight to your home. For mail-order customers, of course, no V.A.T. problem exists.

In **Dublin**, shopping hours are generally from 9:30 A.M. to 5:30 P.M., with Saturday closings at 1 P.M. In most other parts of the country, 1 P.M. closings are made on Wednesday instead of Saturday.

Tweeds are the best buy in the nation—gorgeous handwoven, 100%-wool Donegals. *Don't miss them.* Ready-made sport jackets for men are in the $45 to $60 range, and made-to-your-measure examples run only slightly higher. You can get the "Irish hacking cut" (which we prefer in the rougher materials), or the straighter lines of the conventional "American" concept (which will be more Irish than Yankee). Ladies will go mad at the bargains in piece goods; enough tweed for the finest suit in a wardrobe will run from $20 to $30. *Every inch is handloomed;* once a run is exhausted it can seldom be duplicated.

There are 2 specialists whose standing, merit, and reliability are so equal in every respect that we have to list them alphabetically: **Kevin & Howlin Ltd.** and **O'Beirne & Fitzgibbon Ltd**. The former has reopened at 31 Nassau St., 8 doors from its site for decades; the latter is at 14–15 Upper O'Connell St., next to the Gresham Hotel. We'd suggest you have a look at both, in order to find exactly the pattern, color, and texture which best strikes your fancy. Three choices are offered: (1) made-to-measure sport jackets, suits, slacks, and other wearables, (2) ready-mades, and (3) materials straight from the bolt, for adaptation by your own tailor or dressmaker. Every inch is handloomed, much of it in country cottages by gnarled oldsters whose weaving skills were learned a ½-century ago or more. When you purchase this cloth by the yard, *be sure to buy a sufficient quantity,* because each tweed bears its own distinct, recognizable difference from all others. They run from large, bold hounds-tooth checks that can be seen (and heard!) 23 miles away to soft, subtle hues so gently blended that a magnifying glass is necessary for full appreciation of their intertwinings. Many of the dyes are made from local berries grown in the farmyards. For travelers who desire custom-made garments at startling low tariffs when compared to those of individually cut and sewn creations in other lands, there are 2 options: Either stay long enough on the Olde Sod to allow time for their completion (the required period varies according to the season) or have them shipped home after the first trial fitting. The author found his all-time favorite piece of wearing apparel here—a Donegal jacket now hard-worn through 60 countries and still 100% serviceable. In ready-made items, tweed suits run from $100 up, tweed jackets are $70 to $76, tweed topcoats run from $90 to $100 and materials $7 per yard. You'll also find Irish sweaters of pure wool from $14, Irish-made cashmere sweaters and cardigans from $34 to $36; a very wide range of tweed hats and caps (some to match the jackets and suits) at $7 and $12 respectively; poplin and tweed ties also available. Made-to-measure garments, which naturally are very much prefer-able, cost only a trifle more. Sara and Noel Kevin, a charming mother-and-son team, will welcome you with heartwarming Irish friendliness and grace. O'Beirne and Fitzgibbon is considerably larger, with a greater selection on hand—but roughly speaking, prices fall within the same limits. This house does an enormous mail-order business in America; even though the U.S. duty on tweeds is 25%, it's *still* perhaps 50% cheaper to send direct to the source for a jacket which Tripler's or Brooks might sell for from $175 to $250. Finally, please spare the time to be shown the range of grand Irish shetland and cashmere sweaters. Twinkly-eyed Paddy O'Beirne and his handsome, magnetic son are your gentle bonifaces. Our urgent recommendation: Get your sport jackets custom made in the "hacking cut"—because these rough materials lend themselves far better to this traditional Irish style than to American models. Remember, too, that the tailoring on everything, particu-larly the ready-mades, is very Irish—exactly as it should be—so you cannot expect Fifth Avenue or Middletown lines. Don't miss these supervalues, because here's the only stop on your trip where they exist.

Handwoven, hand-knit, or hand-fashioned wearables? **Irish Cottage Industries Ltd.** (18 Dawson St., opposite the Hibernian Hotel) was established 50-odd years ago to encourage ancient Irish crafts. Glorious ladies' weight tweeds, individually designed and dyed in special I.C.I. hues; some are as light and soft as Bermuda cottons. In these exclusive weavings, chic handbags and a vast range of Aran knitwear from $33.10 as well as very light knitwear from $10.90, gossamer-weight blouses from $26.10, scarves, stoles, shawls, woolen hats, tams, and mittens. For men, tweed hats and caps, gnat-weight ties, Aran sweaters, and cardigans. For ladies, best high-fashion tailoring, plus good range of ready-to-wear suits, coats, capes, and skirts. Give cheers from us to genial Director John C. Cassidy and his attractive son. Truly fine.

Department stores? Historic **Switzer & Co. Ltd.** (Grafton St.), with over 70 shops on 5 floors, is one of the liveliest and savingest anywhere abroad. Ireland's largest selection of Waterford glass at ⅓rd less than U.S. prices; noble Royal Worcester, Doulton, Aynsley, and Wedgwood tableware; glittering Irish hand-cut crystal; chic Irish fashions plus prestigious imports from Wahls of Sweden, Gaston Jaunet, Aquascutum, Jaeger, and many more; trend-setting Man's Shop; Fabrics Shop with everything from Moygashel Linens to Sanderson prints to handwoven wool rugs; outstanding Irish Shop with dolls, leprechauns (we love our dear Sean and never travel without him), and scads of inexpensive souvenirs; magnificent silverware collection for use or investment; alert Information Bureau; open Saturday afternoons. Break for coffee, lunch in the alluring Savoir Fair Restaurant, or treat yourself to a hairdo in the bargain! What buys, what cash windfalls—and what a lovely fresh approach! If you can't find what you're after here, try **Brown, Thomas & Co.** almost directly opposite. It's not as alert or versatile, but its quality is also sound.

Your own coat of arms in decorative heraldry? **Mullins of Dublin Ltd.** at Heraldic House (O'Connell St.), like its London confrère, has long been a world leader in strikingly decorative heraldic plaques, parchments, scrolls, door knockers, car badges, blazer-pocket badges, and the like, hand-fashioned in your own family's coat of arms at startlingly low prices. Catalogue and major mail-order facilities with guaranteed delivery; Main Shop Manager Peter Kelly and Connell Gallagher your friendly mentors; unusually interesting, pride-inducing, and worthy.

Men's handmade footwear? It's still obtainable—provided the calendar means less than zero to you. The craft is a vanishing one, and a couple of decades from now it will probably no longer exist. A pair of shoes, in calf as soft as the proverbial baby's bottom, costs around $55; hunting boots and field boots, popular with Americans, go from $100 up. Delivery is sometimes measured in Light Years rather than months, weeks, or days—but they're well worth the long wait. Try the highest-ranking **Michael Edge** (11 Dame Court), where this author used to buy most of his personal supply. When he's not too pressed, he can complete orders in about 30 days; he'll come up with any style or color you desire—in fact (to quote him), "anything in the shoe line which covers the foot." **Tom Tutty** (Poplar Square, Naas, 20 minutes out on the Limerick Pike) is said to deliver more quickly, but we haven't tried his fleet-footwear. Every Thursday afternoon you can catch him at the Royal Dublin Hotel, where he takes fittings and orders. Isn't Ireland grand?

Antiques and bric-a-brac? **Butler** (Bachelor's Walk) has 3 different show-rooms, and they're all good in their own ways. Other leading choices are **Dooly** (Dawson St.), **Louis Wine** (Grafton St.), and **Naylor** (Liffey St.). If none of these prove fruitful, roam at random along Bachelor's Walk and Ormond Quay.

Haute Couture? Fashionable distaffers are talking ardently about **Mr. Ib Jorgensen** (24 Fitzwilliam Sq., with boutique on Molesworth St.). Both his lovely home and his boutique are worth visiting. In the latter, ask for Mrs. Rice or Mrs. Lumbert. Costly but excellent. **Anna Livia** (32 Dawson St.) caters to the more athletic Country Club Set; made-to-order coats, sports-wear, and accessories at reasonable tariffs; also good.

Royal Irish silver? Mr. and Mrs. Toddie O'Sullivan's magnificent private collection of old Irish silver, plus numerous others belonging to museums, are now being reproduced down to the faintest hallmark. And how *glorious* they are! Some of them are only $20 or $25. You'll find a representative display in **Brown, Thomas & Co.** or **Switzer & Co**. (see above) or in Altman's in New York (where you'll pay a lot more). Lovely, lovely, *lovely!*

Antique silver? The **Fine Arts Showroom** (South Anne between Grafton and Dawson) is now the leader. Splendid early Georgian Irish and English collection, plus fine furniture, paintings, jewelry, and porcelain. Young Mr. John O'Reilly is your man. **Weldon** (55 Clarendon St.) doesn't seem to us to be what it was before the death of Mr. Weldon, its proprietor. But his wife is carrying on, and it's still never a surprise to find a very choice item or 2 within these small premises.

Souvenirs as such are either very very good or horrid.

Dedicated shophounds? Space is too tight here for further listings—so consult this year's extensively revised and updated edition of *Fielding's Shopping Guide to Europe* for more stores, more details, and more lore.

PERSONAL SERVICES　　My Nancy prefers to have her hair tended in only 2 salons in Dublin: Helena Rubinstein of **Brown, Thomas & Co**. department store or the beauty shop at **Switzer's**. Both offer superior locks'-smiths.

LOCAL RACKETS　　Here's what the locals would call "a hot ticket"— the only racket, save the rare taxi driver's petty larceny, which we've ever come across here in more than 3 decades. Mr. John Warren, an Aus-tralian Guidester, ruefully reports, "I was walking down Grafton St., camera dangling and looking very much like a tourist. A man stopped me, said he had noticed me at the airport, and offered to buy me a drink, which I accepted. A little tipsy, he claimed to be celebrating the birth of a son that morning. After a few drinks, when he had me feeling very friendly, he said he must rush to the hospital to comply with visiting hours. Suddenly, discovering he had "lost" his wallet, he showed me his Identification Card and asked to borrow £10. The bartender, who had overheard, spotted his ID card as false and threw him out. Later a Garda (policeman) told me that 2 or 3 cases per month are being reported on this swindle by a small group who hook susceptible visitors."

The Irish may recklessly disregard facts with their characteristically pleasant blarney; aside from this harmless practice, they are 99.9999% an honest, squareshooting people.

Italy

The twentieth-century Italian is one of the *oldest* men on the face of the earth. He has seen everything. Before and since the founding of Rome, Etruscans, Greeks, Roman emperors, Carthaginians, Gauls, Normans, Lombards, Saracens, Spaniards, French, Austrians, Germans, and a few others have pushed him around. Centuries of continual crises have made him a moral and political realist, with a hedonistic reverence for good music, good wine, good love, and the pure pleasures of the senses.

His climate is as diverse as his landscape. Along the Italian Riviera, it's subtropical, similar to upper (not lower!) Florida at its most delightful. Around Sicily and the southern coast, you'll bask in typical Mediterranean surroundings. The Adriatic side is cooler than its western twin. The Po Basin, across the North, has frigid winters, very hot summers, and is periodically plagued by serious inundations. Around Rome, Naples, Pescara, Bari, and Taranto, conditions are fairly pleasant throughout the year. But keep out of the high Apennines and Alps from September to May, unless you've got skis. April to October are the best tourist months; at other times, "Sunny Italy" often just "ain't."

The people are just as sharply divided, too. Rome–Pescara might be designated as the Italian Mason-Dixon line. Broadly speaking (obviously there are tens of thousands of exceptions), the North is far more advanced than the South. Farms are tidier, streets are cleaner, schools are everywhere; Giovanni Doe is a better-dressed, better-educated man. He is taller and more slender than his deep-Mediterranean brother; generally he has a more stable temperament.

By comparison, Southern Italy, along with Sicily, Sardinia, and the lesser islands, is culturally and economically barren. It is officially called the *Mezzogiorno* ("noon" is the literal translation, but its application in this arcane geographical usage is, instead, "half"). Today's boom in land reclamation, transportation improvements, hotel construction, and added commercial responsibility is enormous. But agriculture still predominates. This Southern Sig. Doe retains more of the traditional Mediterranean features—but, curiously enough, you'll see scores of blond, blue-eyed Sicilians who are throwbacks to the Norman conquest of Roger I in A.D. 1060.

But if this sun-kissed nation presents apparent ethnic differences from its topmost shiny button in the north down to the southernmost tip of the Boot and beyond to seagirt Sicily, these are magnified 50 times over when all of its peoples, their parties, their guilds, their unions, their industries, their special flairs, and their proud regional egos come into kaleidoscopic focus in the capital. Leadership of such a divergent land—each segment with such a will of its own—is a near impossibility. Strikes of overwhelming magnitude and bewildering impact have become a way of life to a shocking degree. Since our notebooks, tapes, and typewriter ribbons are as incendiary as our thoughts of any such inflammatory outrages against any civilized society, we will not list here the seemingly endless pox of full-fledged strikes, the short but diabolically disruptive "hiccup" walkouts, and the rampant absenteeism —all of which have played and are playing such havoc with the majority of the populace as well as with you and with us, the innocent and well-meaning visitors. Suffice it to say that (1) the professional practitioners such as doctors, dentists, lawyers, and hospital personnel, (2) the State or municipal employees such as those in a governmental department (all except the cabinet minister himself), the police, public transportation, airports, the airline, post offices, sanitation, and more, and (3) tidal wave upon tidal wave in private enterprises such as factories, hotels, restaurants, shops—almost a case of you-name-it— now stage what has virtually become their annual Rite of Winter, Spring, Summer, or Fall. Although union leaders apparently take great pride in hitting their homeland by *almost one strike, somewhere, every day of the past 5 years,* others with more vision are far from jubilant. During the past decade, industry has lost 50 times more man-hours than were squandered in West Germany. Over the same span, 5 times as many businesses have been squeezed out of operation as in France. Since the petroleum crisis, the republic has edged dangerously close to civil bankruptcy. Severe austerity or further social unrest, therefore, almost certainly must follow. We could, but we won't, recite more of these appalling statistics.

This *Guide* is a guidebook and nothing more. We never have—and never will—take sides or pontificate on matters of internal policy, whether we personally condone or disagree. Nevertheless, as travel writers we are duty-bound to apprise our readers of the conditions they can expect to find and how these may add to or detract from their traveling pleasure.

We beseech you, therefore, to take a good long look at the day-to-day news bulletins and be alerted to these ever-threatening roadblocks to holiday fun. Naturally, with so many elements conspiring for recovery or ruination, we can't make any concrete predictions. We can only repeat our entreaty that you formulate your plans with wisdom and foresight, keeping in close touch with the international information media and the responsible judgment of your most alert and friendly travel agent.

Finally, if you do decide to tuck this scenically glorious Garden of Eden into your itinerary, here is one thoughtful bonus: In Rome, you can simply pick up a telephone and ask a dial-a-strike service just what is going to happen. Will mail be delivered? Will trains run? Will planes fly? The number is 85-85-45. A perfect solution—if there isn't a phone strike!

Despite the cities, the mountains, and the arid hills of the South, 68½-million acres of the land are agriculturally productive. Farming engages more than ⅓rd of the population.

Three independent domains, each with its separate leader, laws, diplomats, and other governmental facilities, function within the borders of Italy—the Vatican, the Sovereign Military Order of Malta, and the Republic of San Marino.

Patriarch of the Vatican is the Supreme Pontiff, Paul VI, Giovanni Battista Montini. His papal state of 108 acres and 890 people operates under extraterritorial rights; as spiritual head of the Catholic Church, he is responsible only to his tenets, his followers, and himself. Italian law guarantees him a yearly indemnity of approximately $700,000, a sum which remains unclaimed and unpaid; under the Lateran Pact, Italy also awards a fixed stipend to every parish priest in the land. But not all of their financial relationships, unfortunately, are this harmonious. The flag is white and yellow, charged with crossed keys and triple tiara. A complete coinage is struck every year; examine your change in Rome for Pius XII coins, because the early ones are already becoming collectors' items. (For further information on the Vatican, turn further along.)

The Sovereign Military Order of Malta (does the term "Knights of Malta" sound familiar?), with headquarters on via Condotti, and a villa—its demesne —on Aventine Hill in Rome, sends its own ambassadors to many Catholic countries, issues its own "SMOM" license plates, and performs many other functions of separate statehood. Its total population is 40—but it maintains a national air force of 50 planes! No coins or stamps have yet been issued, but both are planned as soon as technicalities can be cleared with the International Postal Union. It is smaller than Vatican City, but potent both ecclesiastically and politically. It used to be customary for sightseers up on the Aventine to peek through its famous "Keyhole" for a perfectly framed view of St. Peter's; now the Grand Chancellor has sadly informed our longtime New Canaan, Conn., friend who is a Magistral Knight that insufficient personnel are at hand to cope with casual visitors.

Visit these autonomies, if you can. It'll be hard to realize you're in self-supporting, self-governing foreign nations and not in Italy.

CITIES *Rome* (Roma) is said to have been founded in 753 B.C., when Romulus, son of the god Mars, yoked a bullock and a heifer to a plowshare, marked out a boundary, and built a wall. Be that as it may, the city has at least 2500 years of unparalleled cultural accomplishment. Larger than Philadelphia, it now totes up close to 3-million *Romani*. Most impressive of all is the Colosseum, which has been crumbling at such an alarming rate that in late '72 its entrance was barred by the City Fathers—but later partly reopened. Among the other leading landmarks are the Pantheon, the Arch of Titus, the Arch of Constantine. You'll find an easy grace, too, along the streets, in the buildings, everywhere, which only centuries of polite concourse can bring. But downtown congestion now is so incredibly bad that the city was moved to ban all vehicles from 5 of its main piazzas. The Traffic Commissioner has sealed off a whopping 25 acres in the Trevi Fountain district for pedestrians (hotel guests, residents, and employees excepted)—with the cool declaration that he will create 5 *more* "islands" of similar size in the center of the capital. Plenty of good hotels, nightclubs, and dining places (the top ones expensive even for Americans); a bustling railway terminus; excellent shops; enough churches and antiquities to wear out the Baedeker family; 3 theaters which screen films in English (ask your concierge). Leonardo da Vinci Airport, in the heart of the coastal fog belt 45 to 90 minutes and a $10 to $12 taxi ride from the metropolis, next to Zurich's Kloten is still possibly the most poorly planned and most frustratingly inefficient major international terminus in Europe; its new floor with 7 main exits and automated baggage delivery does little to alleviate the built-in chaos; avoid lunching or dining here at all costs. Among the better attractions are the St. Sebastian or St. Calixtus Catacombs (a New York-to-Chicago taxi ride from the center), the Cappuccini Chapel (walls and furniture of human bones), the Borghese Art Gallery, and the Palazzo Venezia (Mussolini's famous balcony). For about 10¢ the *Circolare Destra or Circolare Sinistra* streetcars, now labeled "29" or "30," will each give you the same fast-whirling circular grand tour of the city, clockwise or counterclockwise, without a guide; board them and leave them as you wish (the Colosseum is a convenient starting point); set out around 10 A.M. or 5 P.M., because otherwise the 4 daily rush-hour mobs will shred you into vermicelli.

Milan (Milano) is second, with 1¾-million people. It is the financial and industrial center of the nation, boasting 37% of all Italian businesses; with less than 1/25th of the country's population, it accounts for 1/5th of all wages and pays 24% of the national tax bill. Urbanity and sophistication are at their highest next to Rome; here is one of the most advanced cities in Europe, intellectually and technically—and, according to late surveys, also one of the most expensive. It's in the heart of Lombardy, up north near Switzerland (St. Moritz seems to be the weekend retreat of nearly every rich Milanese skier); Como, Maggiore, and other Italian lakes are only a hop, skip, and jump away. The Duomo, most famous landmark on the upper half of the Peninsula, concentrates 2300 statues and some of the world's finest stained glass in 2 treasure-filled acres. The Brera Gallery sets off its paintings with a unique display technique which delights the spectator. The Poldi Pezzoli Gallery, tiny but choice, is the cultural contribution of an unselfish private citizen; Botticelli's "Virgin" and a priceless collection of porcelains are found here. The air-conditioned Rinascente Department Store is one of the most modern establishments of its kind in Europe. Then, of course, there are Leonardo da Vinci's slowly fading "Last Supper," La Scala opera (don't miss its museum, open daily at specified times and during all performance intermissions), the

Museum of Modern Design in the Sforza Castle, and a host of other high points. Lots of factories including nearly 3000 U.S. firms; some slums, of course, but scads of interesting things for the outlander to see (tourism is growing dramatically here). Primarily commercial; un-Latin feeling of hustle and bustle.

As for **Naples** (Napoli), our affection for this 3rd city in the nation must continue to be a mixture of irritation and pity. With all her exquisite natural assets, this oppidum could be THE gemstone in the Tyrrhenian tiara, THE true mermaid of the majestic Italian coastline. Instead, gangsters have almost paralyzed her. The arteries which feed the metropolis contain holes in which an entire vehicle can disappear. Exploding sewers pockmark the terrain so that in some districts it bears a resemblance to Swiss cheese. Scores of people have been killed or injured, and several hundred have been forced to flee their homes in recent years because of these gaping rifts. The barricades surrounding them are untended, the lanterns are stolen, the wood is whisked away to be burned—resulting in mantraps which remain open for months on end. The taxi drivers, porters, boatmen, almost the entire skein of personnel who greet the vacationer have now gotten into the act. Vast armies of migrants, including us, are finding it no fun anymore. These baneful evils, combined with the very recent demise of all scheduled transatlantic passenger shipping, have slid stopover tourism into such a downward spiral that today there is only one truly fine hotel and not a single truly fine restaurant except at this hotel. The airport is a horror. It has deteriorated into a transient way station en route to or from its booming nearby island and mainland resorts. (Incidentally, please *never* be conned into the wretched one-day Rome–Naples–Sorrento–Rome bus excursions which are being so heavily touted by many concierges in the Eternal City; turn to the Rome section in "Hotels" for the inside facts about these nightmares.) The city is larger than Houston (about 1¼-million people). Her attractions include Vesuvius (take the INT excursion at 8:30 A.M. daily, from piazza Municipio 70, by bus and chair lift, straight to the top), the new digs at nearby Oplontis, one of the world's most magnificent bays, the Castel Sant'Elmo and the former monastery of San Martino, the San Carlo Opera House, 499 churches—a score of wonders, if one could only see them in peace. As a passing point for excursions to Pompeii, Capri, Ischia, Sorrento, Amalfi, and other places, it is vital; because of this trim-the-sucker attitude toward her visitors, however, to us it is a case of "See Naples and Drop Dead."

Turin (Torino), a serene metropolis in the Piedmont near the French border (readily discernible in the local dialect), currently rates 4th—but it has passed the million-mark and soon might capture Naples' 3rd-place crown. About 30-thousand *Torinesi* work in the Fiat auto works, largest plant in the world outside the Detroit area; the unique Museum of The Automobile, containing 370 vintage models, is fascinating. They are equally proud of their city's art treasures, Egyptology Museum (second most important in the world), Cinema Museum, former Royal Palace, and Palazzo del Lavoro. With one exception, its mediocre hotels are completely out of key. Despite a couple of excellent restaurants, generally the amenities for welcoming and comforting tourists are 2nd rate. To top this off, air pollution from her industries was so severe on our latest swoop that we could never recommend that any traveler with heart or respiratory ailments drive within even 10 miles of the amber, skyborne doughnut of filth benighting this city when a strong wind is not belting it away. Based on a strong Francophile influence, here is a way of life which, like Milan's, differs from that of the rest of Italy.

Genoa (Genova), 5th, is perhaps the least publicized and visited center in the country—a pity from the standpoint of the traveler, because it is colorful. We don't know why this old port is so neglected by holiday seekers. It became a jet-blown twentieth-century air-harbor as well when it constructed a huge platform over the water named (what else?) the Christopher Columbus Airport. Medium-range planes offer regular connections with London, Rome, and Milan, plus the Italian islands. Something is also being done about highway routes to the south; long tunnels hewn at unbelievable cost now make the approach easier. Fellow countrymen cite the Genoese as generous and friendly away from home, but niggardly and remote within their own borders. We haven't found this so, but we do agree with the charge that they lack the sartorial chic and glamour of the more cosmopolitan Milanese or sophisticated Roman.

Venice* (Venezia) is an absurd and wonderful dream. To protect themselves from the approach of armies by land, a group of staid and somber citizens many centuries ago carved for themselves a slice of sea and proceeded to erect buildings on top of the waves. This fantastic conglomeration of houses, churches, gardens, factories, streets, and squares rests on piles sunk deep into the mud. It has been called "a kind of poem in stone accidentally written by history on the waters." The main boulevard, most of the important arteries, and many of the small streets are paved with *acqua* instead of asphalt —and sometimes this H_2O bears no resemblance whatsoever to *Quelques Fleurs* or *Chanel No. 5*. Warning: Since taxis, buggies, rickshas, bicycles, roller skates, and all types of transportation which can't dance on the water are forbidden, in 48 hours of normal sightseeing the average visitor's backside will sag to within 2 inches of the ground. He can count on the *circolare* (in all other Italian towns a tram or bus, but here a boat), and that, with the vessels of about 600 gondoliers (about a dozen now motorized) and about 100 launch operators, is IT; the fastest of the *motoscafi* is the *diretto* variety. A special canal pares travel time between the Marco Polo airport and the center of town to 20 minutes. This terminus, built on reclaimed land, can accommodate only jets without full fuel loads at takeoff. **The Lido**, a separate settlement a few minutes away by Chris-Craft, offers a galaxy of summer attractions, capped by its famed Casino. When the white marbles of the roulette tables clatter to a halt at the end of the season, the management tucks them into a velvet case and paddles over to its smaller Cà Vendramin, in Venice proper, where the wheels and dice are set to spinning once again (ironically, in the villa where Richard Wagner died!). Scattered in the lagoon and envi-

---

*As a pigeon-footnote to this city, the fowl problem of a feathered population explosion is finally being solved. Hawkish city fathers are now exporting 100-thousand of them to any other hamlet requesting them, or setting squadrons free in the countryside.

rons are the smaller islands of Murano (glassware), Burano (lace), Torcello (fine Byzantine church), and Strà (site of Villa Pisani with its legendary frescoes). You can also take a summer cruise via the canals over to Padua aboard the riverbark *Il Burchiello;* for the return, we recommend hopping a bus. Venice's vaunted corruption, racketeering, political chicanery? Yes, but only in the highest circles (well, *mostly* in the highest circles). The city is tightly held in the palms of roughly 705 stalwarts—gondoliers, motor-launch operators, and guides—whose administrative spoils have been accused of outsmelling the Canale Scomenzera at high noon in August. If you're abroad during the right months, it would be a great mistake to miss one of the most unique—if one of the most venal—cities on the globe. Looking ahead to the year 1990—when, as we've already mentioned, it is estimated that this marvel of a metropolis will be ⅔rds submerged if something isn't begun immediately to save it—an emergency "sinking fund" was established by a concerned Roman Cabinet (8 governments have fallen since that time). With reference to our previous generalization, the Italian legislature has passed a bill which provides more than $480,000,000 to fight flooding, pollution, and decay. In addition, Dutch hydraulics experts have teamed up with Italian engineers to seek a lasting solution to the city's permanent wave problem. These specialists have checked the tides by employing removable barriers at the 3 sea entrances plus industrial controls within the lagoon. To their valiant and ingenious efforts, we say Good luck! *Salute!* and *Op Uw gezondheid!*

Florence is the Athens of Italy. Renovations and an aura of freshness have brightened her aspect immeasurably. The metropolis is aburst with works of art bearing such signatures as Fra Angelico, Michelangelo, Botticelli, Donatello, Ghiberti, Cellini, and Leonardo da Vinci. There are Giotto's historic Bell Tower; the shop-lined Ponte Vecchio; the opera house; the Medici Chapel; the fractured Brunelleschi dome (lately protected from traffic vibrations), the National Art Museum; the Uffizi (which is supposed to be enlarged, with auto traffic now banned in this vicinity on an experimental basis) and Pitti Palaces (2 of civilization's most fabulous centers of art); the Strozzi Palace (magnificent courtyard); the National Library; the renovated San Marco Gallery (Fra Angelico frescoes); the Bargello Museum (cameos, ivories, della Robbias), just about everything for travelers with a sense of the beautiful. It is situated in the heart of a chain of lovely hills; some Americans rate it as the pleasantest place in Italy. This center, too, is suffering from the traffic headaches that plague nearly every square foot of terra firma occupied by modern man; don't be surprised, therefore, if this year certain central districts are banned to auto beasties. If you like your painting, architecture, churches, and tombs—and if you don't mind the fact that every 2nd person you stumble across is a visitor (stumble *over*, too, since many of the youngsters now seem to live on the streets)—Florence is highly recommended, even though too many of her inhabitants are so *tired* of being hosts that their welcome is perfunctory and unsmiling.

Now let's run down the list of the most popular smaller centers, in alphabetical order:

Assisi is a wonderful little town—for about half a day, if you're average. That's enough time to admire the renowned Basilica of St. Francis, to be wooed fleetingly by its Romanesque romanticisms, and to drink in the view of the plains below. If you'd like a scholarly and pleasant guide, the brothers at the San Damiano Convent are beloved by many Americans; no charge, of course—just alms to the church, which are voluntary. Except for these, what you've got are substandard hotels (many of which aren't properly heated in chilly times), approximately 100 tourist-junk shops, and approximately 1000 other excursionists. Pretty overrated for lengthy lingering, but ideal for a passing flirtation.

Amalfi, an important maritime republic during the Middle Ages, is also the target of dozens of daily bus tours from Naples, which pause here for refreshment on the spectacular (but not too difficult) coastal drive between Salerno and Sorrento. Small, increasingly inviting village; handsome yet modest hotels; definitely worth a visit or even a stopover.

Bari, founded by the Illyrians and civilized by the Greeks, is the chief port and commercial mart on Italy's heel; next to Naples, it's the most important Peninsular city in the South. The crypt of St. Nicholas, patron saint of gift-giving and the inspiration of Santa Claus, is here (his symbol of 3 brass balls was later purloined by pawnbrokers). Leading attraction is the famous Levant Fair (18 days around mid-Sept.); otherwise it offers fair swimming, a few antiquities, below-average hotels and restaurants, and little of interest.

Bologna, boasting about 500-thousand residents, also has a Communist government; some call it "the buckle in the country's Red Belt," in this nation that burgeons with fellow-travelers—the biggest outside of the Communist bloc. It is better known as the seat of the oldest university in the world (the word "university" was invented here) and the richest, highest-caloried fodder of the nation. Lots of U.S. students in educational residence; dynamically busy, no-nonsense atmosphere; more than 20 miles of arcaded walks; leaning towers; splendid palaces designed by such masters as Palladio and da Vignola; 10 museums with treasures from Etruscan to modern times; National Gallery with works by 56 great painters, including Raphael's "St. Cecilia"; villa and mausoleum of Guglielmo Marconi; funicular to San Luca, 750-feet up. "Baloney" originated in Bologna; if you'd like to sample the original article, ask for Mortadella (the homemade version at world-famous Al Pappagallo is—literally—one of the most delicious food items, bar none, that we have ever tasted). Except for its cuisine and its art, not a top favorite with most outlanders. Incidentally, if you arrive by train, be certain to take the West (Oeste) exit—NOT the East (Este). There are no taxis at the latter. Este is very remote, requiring the time and money of a 15-minute trek plus a wasted tip to the porter.

Capri is the Jekyll and Hyde of Italian resorts. In summer it has become a cheap, flamboyant hive swarming with sexual partners of myriad persuasions, phony Bohemians, and off-the-record weekenders. Saturation point is reached around August 15, the midsummer holiday of Ferragosto, when a procession carrying a figure of the Madonna parades through the little central piazza. Off Season, however, it is as lovely as it ever was. Blue Grotto; funicular from main port to main village; chair lift to mountain peak; from May 1 to September 30, private cars banned from the tiny isle (fines for disobeying this rule can hop from $80 to $800); taxis and buses available throughout the year; one small, so-so beach at Marina Piccola; fast hydrofoil service (30 minutes) which skims atop the waves from Naples to Capri and returns in half the time of the less expensive—but much more crowded—regular service. In spring or fall you might love it; in summer, Elba (to the north) is a far better bet.

Elba, which Virgil called "The Generous Island," was Napoléon's home prior to his famous 100 days—and we wish it could be ours for 1000. To travelers in the know and in search of tranquillity rather than frenzy, it already has replaced Capri; the boom is zooming; the vanguard of trippers carry the banners of Sweden and Germany to its shores. Simple, primitive, unspoiled; glorious mountains, shimmering olive-toned landscape, breathtaking beaches; only 8 small towns, a dozen small villages, and a scattering of hamlets on this 30-mile home of 32-thousand people; hotels, restaurants, and night life (2 nightclubs now exist!) limited but adequate (see later); excellent, zippy 30-minute hydrofoil service between Piombino and Portoferraio 15 times per day, plus numerous regular ferry luggers; daily High Season link with Leghorn via the Isle of Capraia; excursions (100 minutes) to Corsica from mid-June onward; Aertaxi zips to and from the mainland; scenic route, reminiscent of the Amalfi Drive, touching 10 enchanting little hamlets. Health addicts oink around in therapeutic mud baths at the Terme of San Giovani —great for the complexion, but hard on laundry bills. For the panorama of a lifetime, take the rope-railway *("cabinova")* from Marciana to the 3100-foot peak of Monte Capanne. Nearby is the uninhabited rock known as Monte Cristo, the islet where the fabulous "Count" created by Alexandre Dumas found his buried treasure.

Ischia, less than 2 hours by ship from Naples or ½-hour by hydrofoil, is attractive, faddish, and a favorite of well-heeled pilgrims from many lands (particularly West Germans) for its health spas and sunshine. It's a volcanic island, where outcroppings of lava and pines abound; in character, atmosphere, and feel, it bears little or no resemblance to neighboring Capri. Its 3-wheel minitaxis are an amusing oddity—slow, noisy, but charging 50% or less of the standard vehicles' fares. Prices surprisingly high; scenically, less dramatic than Capri; spiritually, less enchanting than Elba: *never* go out of season, since the slothfulness is disturbed only by the buzzzzzz of a softly snoring volcano. Higher each year on our pleasure chart.

Messina has a fair shake of new or improved accommodations, lavish portions of squalor, ravenous wolf packs of mosquitoes, and a chronic shortage of mosquito netting. Here's a gem of a city—to miss.

Montecatini, 25 miles from Florence, catches much of the overflow when Florentine hotels are overbooked. To us it seems to be waning for North American pleasure seekers, but local hoteliers are making a valiant effort to reverse this tendency. The waters are famous for their beneficial effects on the liver. Within the immediate area are over 300 square miles of parks and gardens which tend to keep things cool during the hottest months.

Although ***Palermo*** is Italy's 6th city and Sicily's largest center, the lion's share of commerce is concentrated around ***Catania***, on the East Coast. Labeled by its promoters "The Golden Shell," it has some pleasant aspects, Moslem ruins, Norman traces, and baroque beginnings, but better-grade vacationing facilities are so limited that it's not worth a special journey. A weekly ferry service to Gela, Catania, and the island of Malta slices the wavelets. Overnight car-ferry connections with Naples (and other more distant points) are excellent aboard the vessels of either the Canguro or Tirrénia lines. Both services run clean, comfortable ships that can save 2 full days of driving over the desolate hills of southern Italy.

Perugia, like Assisi, draws such a flood of excursionists that its reception is noticeably jaded and mechanical. This ancient hill town is the site of the University for Foreigners, where scads of homesick scholars learn their basic Italian. The Collegio del Cambio has some fine frescoes, the National Gallery has some famous paintings, and the panorama of the valley is lovely.

Pisa, except for its legendary Leaning Tower, venerable Duomo, baptistery, and exquisite Gothic church by Nicola Pisano, is practically a zero for most tourists. June *(Giugno Pisano)* is best, when *Il Gioco del Ponte* (tug-of-war on the bridge) and other pageantry bring it alive.

Portofino has one of the dreamiest natural settings—a tiny, cliff-lined harbor of unsurpassing charm and intimacy, over which broods a castle (formerly owned by Countess Mumm but now in the hands of a British couple) and the Splendido Hotel. It's about 75 minutes by road from Genoa. Spring and fall are the best times to go; in summer it's often akin to Times Square, so crowded that the excursionists, the souvenir vendors, and the high proportion of Gay Boys nearly trip over one another along the quay. A *must* to visit—but pick your season.

Positano, in the opinion of many, is the star attraction of the Amalfi Drive and of the entire area near Naples. The houses of this highly paintable village climb straight down the mountainside, like mountain goats; so will you, every time you go for a swim in the sea. (Happily, many hotels now boast pools.) If you're planning an overnight in this region, it's a sensible stop.

Rapallo, a short hop from Genoa, is on the blatant side when the summer legions descend to shatter its days and nights. Typically crowded 2nd-rate oasis, closer to the taste of Europeans than Americans.

Ravello is above Amalfi, and it is almost as attractive—one of the more popular (and crowded) targets, in fact, on the Peninsula. Its Villa Rufolo gardens are famed (here Wagner was purportedly inspired to compose *Lohengrin),* its Hotel Caruso and Hotel Palumbo are agreeable, and its wines are well regarded by Italian connoisseurs (a viewpoint we personally cannot share).

Ravenna, halfway between Venice and Ancona, is a culture seeker's paradise—historically and artistically, one of the outstanding smaller sites of the Western world. No other city can compete with its wealth of Byzantine architecture or its unique mosaics. Ecclesiastical treasures; Dante's tomb; Theodoric's tomb; a scholar's heaven. Giant ENI rubber-and-fertilizer plant; indifferent hotels, limited touring facilities; 6 miles from the sea, on the Corsini Canal. Not for the fun-lover, but The Pearly Gates if you're serious-minded.

Rimini, on the Adriatic coast east of Florence, might be called the Atlantic City of Italy. Strictly a resort, May to September only: Jump-off spot for easy excursions to Ravenna and San Marino; fair restaurants and nightclubs; the

Malatestian Temple and the well-packed bikinis are the most remarkable attractions.

San Remo, 9 miles from the French border toward Nice, will still cost you plenty, but its sophistication has gone stale. Those once-resplendent trappings of leisure—casino, race track, golf course, and luxury hotels—now seem static and moth-eaten, because other resorts have pushed forward while this one has marked time. Okay for those who don't mind paying today's prices for yesterday's facilities. The top drawing card is still the annual Song Festival (late Jan.), but even here, political logrolling has driven away top talent. **Ospedaletti**, 3 miles away, is startlingly cheaper.

Santa Margherita has Smart hotels worthy of such a glittering resort, an interesting fish market and a pleasant situation on the water. It is booming today—perhaps because it can accommodate more visitors than lovely, neighboring Portofino.

Sardinia's most alluring siren for North Americans is the breathtakingly savage, beautifully sea-lapped **Costa Smeralda**, a 30-mile necklace of wild, lonely, *ponète*-blown coves whose principal landlord is the dedicated, hardworking Aga Khan. Along this glorious villa-specked littoral—more extensive, incidentally, than the entire Belgian seaboard—are no less than 80 powder-white, gemlike beaches. It's a land of twisted cork trees, soughing pines, and glistening juniper, with a boscage of rosemary that scents the Mediterranean sailor's wind. The angular mountains are of granite and basalt. The vales are dotted with nuraghi (prehistoric fortress-shape structures). Its primitive inhabitants speak a Low Latin, with dialect overtones of ancient Genoese, Lybian, Phoenician, Spanish, and Carthaginian. The inlets and quiet corners along this row are far too numerous to mention; a typical one has been described accurately as "a Pacific bay on a Brittany coast." There are 5 hotels of varying categories, co-crowned by the Aga Khan's magnificent Cala di Volpe and the equally luxurious cottage-style Pitrizza. Cuisine? Much of it is about as exciting as a hangnail. The local fare, based ponderously on pasta, is even worse. The yacht basin at **Porto Cervo** is one of the best and most scenic in the western world; the local marina, skipper's club, and nucleus of cozy-corner night spots swing with international celebrities, as well as with Everyday Jet Setters who wing in or cruise over from the nearby thickets of Rome. Winter, when only one hotel stays open to date, can be as lonely as a doxy at a Billy Graham revival—bringing just enough rawness to evoke avid interest in timetables. The easiest way is aboard His Highness' sleek, constantly expanding, turboprop airline, Alisarda, which calls regularly at Rome, Nice, and Milan from the home base, **Olbia**. Alitalia zips in daily from Milan and Rome to **Alghero** and **Cagliari**. The latter is hopelessly far away; the pull from the former is a tediously long ride. British Airways has a London link with Alghero. Passenger and car ferries steam 4 times a day in summer from the port of Rome (Civitavecchia) to Olbia and the adjoining **Golfo di Aranci**. A loop with Genoa is also possible aboard the *Canguro Rosso*, the so-called Red Kangaroo that hops with its pouchful of passengers between the north of Italy and Sardinia. We've recently bounded off of one of these vessels and recommend each ship in the Kangaroo fleet heartily. Genoese luggers drop anchor at both Olbia and **Porto Torres**. (The latter is about 80 miles from your hotel.) As islands go, the land of the Sards is so vast that if you head to this northeastern chip of emerald paradise, don't plan to land anywhere else but Olbia. When you alight, we think you'll agree that here is one of the most exquisite shorelines in Europe.

Siena offers a mesmeric passageway to the Renaissance; it is probably the only city in Italy to retain so much ancient charm. As an illustration, film makers found Verona's complexion had changed so radically over the years that they came here to shoot *Romeo and Juliet.* The Duomo, the Pinacoteca, and the Music Academy are musts; the capper is the spectacular Palio ("the world's craziest horse race"), a pageant climaxed by hell-for-leather riding in the huge piazza del Campo; this event is held twice annually on the Festivals of the Madonna, July 2 and August 16.

Sorrento—the town itself and *not* the tranquil enclaves established by clever innkeepers—is a brassy, artificial tourist trap. Fine setting; some excellent hotels and restaurants; we'd prefer, however, to spend the night in Coney Island—a community which might be raucous but which doesn't lure the suckers with this particular brand of "quaintness." Perhaps you'll disagree, because this is merely one opinion—but we loath the village even while we love many of its facilities.

Taormina, the garden spot of Sicily, caters mainly to the middle-aged sun-seeker. This increasingly tourist-conscious village (and what a pity it's so fast being spoiled!) sits on a headland almost 1000 feet above the outer Straits of Messina (above the bathing beach too, which is good to know in advance). The view of the town and sea from inside the Greco-Roman theater is one of the most inspiring anywhere; the summer concerts draw musicians from as far as Los Angeles. Mount Etna, the volcano of Ulysses, thrusts its snow-capped cone through the clouds to the rear; in '62 this off-again, on-again boiler ("on" in the spring of '71) built a new 120-foot hill beside its crater; CIAT will take you there on a fascinating all-day excursion. With the failure of a short-lived casino, all hopes for similar gamble-inos were likewise crapped out. Now the highlight of the city's social glitter is its annual David di Donatello Film Festival, Italy's most important event in the motion picture industry. It's usually held from the beginning of August for an 8-day period. Here's a great attraction you shouldn't miss if you're anywhere near these waters—but nail down your hotel space well in advance. Highly recommended. Strand-hounds, young and old, prefer to stay at Mazzarò Beach, directly below, to which there is a funicular. Naxus is also popular with coupon clippers (but not with us). Transportation hang-ups? Shoot arrow-straight to the CIT office on the main drag, where kindhearted Bureau Chief S. Marzullo will fix you up in a jiffy. Ask for him especially because he is a fun-filled and helpful friend of any Guidester. For more than 2 decades, the unofficial mayor, social arbiter, and spiritual *doge* of the town has been the American cosmopolite and *bon vivant,* Culver Sherrill.

Trieste is a cleaner-than-average town with friendlier-than-average citizens; some sightseeing attractions, but more commercial than touristic.

Verona, the city of Romeo and Juliet, provides a whirl of ancient byways, tiny piazzas, hill and valley vistas, an open market, superb opera at the open arena in summer or in its modern hall in winter, trade fairs galore, and an improving hotel picture. A charmer that you really should visit.

Finally, the *Italian Lake District* is a skein of pros and cons. The over all pattern gives us, at least, the impression the area is *still* somewhat over-rated. The scenery can be glorious, with Garda the largest and most enchant-ing lake, followed by Maggiore and Como. But offsetting panoramas of dra-matic mountains, peaceful shorelines, and cool blue waters are a number of drawbacks. Many of these waters are now so polluted that swimming is banned. The roads—narrow and serpentine—aren't built to accommodate the armadas of trucks, scooters, and pleasure vehicles that snarl them in summer. Nearly all its hotels are either as old hat as Grandpa's boater or as claptrappy modern as a $10-down Florida real estate development. The general quality of its restaurants runs from routine to mediocre to poor. The weather is benign for too few months, with the fringe seasons spoiled by unpredictable periods of cold and rain. Villa d'Este, at **Cernobbio** on Como, is an aristo-crat in the innkeeping peerage as is Villa Serbellone in **Bellagio**; more about these in the "Hotels" section to follow. **Gardone** is an excellent base of operations for Garda, because from here excursions or steamer trips can be made to **Desenzano**, **Sirmione**, **Malcesine**, up the Brenta Mountains in the Dolomites, and several other interesting alternatives. **Stresa** is the traditional hub (with Locarno, Switzerland) for **Maggiore**, and **Como** is a convenient starting point for **Bellagio, Menaggio**, and Villa Carlotta.

For information on other centers, consult the CIT (see later) or your local travel agent.

VATICAN CITY Standing on the side of a hill on the west bank of the Tiber, it is separated from Rome and Italy only by a wall. The Pope is absolute monarch, with full legislative, executive, and judicial powers.

Dominating the City is the Church of St. Peter, largest in the world and sited in the smallest independent state in the world. Close by is the Apostolic Palace, home of His Holiness and site of the famous Vatican Museum (55-room modern art section lately reopened). It is the biggest residential castle in existence, with 1400 rooms that cover some 13½-acres. Within are also the City Governor's Palace, a post office, a tribunal, a mosaic factory, a barracks, an observatory, a railway station, a power plant, a newspaper, a pharmacy, a TV station, and the superradio station over which are broadcast the Pope's messages to 6 continents. The construction of a new, self-service restaurant for visitors has been completed in the basement in front of the main picture gallery, with a tree-shaded terrace at ground-floor level. *Sampietrini* is the name given to those who maintain the Basilica but do not live here. The ranks of the famed Swiss Guard now number 54; for the first time since the Middle Ages, this colorful and elite corps, whose red, yellow, and blue pantaloons were designed by Michelangelo, has been phased out; their replacements are the plain-blue-uniformed Vatican *gendarmerie*.

St. Peter's is breathtaking. The dome, Michelangelo's work, is almost as high as the tallest Egyptian pyramid; from doorway to altar, you could tuck in the towers of New York's Waldorf-Astoria, with room to spare. In the museums, chapels, and libraries of the Vatican you'll find Raphaels, Mi-chelangelos, Peruginos, Botticellis, tapestries, liturgical vessels, priceless manuscripts. An elevator will whisk you to the base of the dome; from there you can climb the winding stairs to the pinnacle for a splendid view of the meandering Tiber and Rome. Then take the walk around the inside upper periphery, put an ear close to the wall, and listen to people talking hundreds of feet away. St. Peter's alone is worth a special trip from America. Please remember that the Sistine Chapel is closed to visitors on Saturday afternoon and Sunday as well as on holidays.

Audience with the Pope: The best way to arrange this is through a letter from your Bishop to Rt. Rev. Msgr. Benjamin Farrell, J.C.D., Casa di S. Maria dell'Umiltà, via dell'Umiltà 30. Small group or individual meetings are becoming more and more difficult to arrange, though His Holiness grants a few almost daily. Apply as soon as you arrive in Rome; the Casa is only 2 blocks from the Trevi Fountain, a bonus to sightseers who are in the area. We're also told that the Paulist Fathers at the Church of St. Susanna are extremely helpful in this respect.

On Wednesdays an enormous audience is held in St. Peter's for which tickets are usually available a day ahead, provided you don't require reserved seats. There are 3 classes: The first 2 permit you to sit in grandstand structures flanking the main altar, while the 3rd is simply admission for standing room. For tickets to this (as well as to the excavations beneath St. Peter's), apply to the same source mentioned above. Short gals should don their highest heels, or their view may be completely cut off. Thousands flock to these gatherings, so be sure to get there early! For special audiences *(Baciamano)*, ladies should wear black dresses, high necklines, long sleeves, and veils (now optional, but more courteous), while men should appear in dark suits with dark ties. Dress requirements for the Wednesday services are nearly as rigid, although they are constantly violated by scores of unknowing travelers. The Papal address is condensed and translated for the devout in English, French, German, and Spanish. The big assemblages are scheduled from October to July, moving to the summer residence in Castel Gandolfo from July to late September. Transportation to St. Peter's is provided at nominal cost; hotel pickup and round trip are available through SITA (the "coaching" arm of CIT), American Express, and Thomas Cook, also for relatively few lire.

§TIPS: Regardless of personal religious denominations, we feel that women should wear a veil or hat and long sleeves when visiting any Catholic house of worship. The widely publicized liberalization of the regulation concerning appropriate dress was erroneous, according to a Vatican spokesman. Thus, the long-standing respect for sartorial propriety should be exhibited in any Catholic sanctuary. If you don't have a hat, a handkerchief over the hair will do in a pinch. Women also should note that the Vatican line on the hemline expressly bars miniskirt and shorts wearers at the entrance to St. Peter's Basilica unless they agree to wear plastic raincoats lent to them by the attendants. If you aren't of this faith, you're not expected to kiss the papal ring or to follow such traditions as genuflection (a curtsy toward the altar).

Don't be startled by the collegelike cheers, loud handclapping, and ecstatic cries of "Viva Il Papa!" from European student priests and other spectators when the Pope is carried into the Basilica by the *uscieri.* It's unlike anything ever heard in America.

MONEY   You'll find metal coins for 5, 10, 50, 100, and 500 lire (the first 3 are not very commonly seen; the last, in silver, are collectors' items). Because of the currency "float," our press-time dollar conversions which follow will not be correct when you read them. A gold 10,000-lire "sequin" or "florin" is also available—a limited minting for ceremonial occasions. Folding money with a dollar-size dimension is being used for the 1000-lire ($1.20) and the 5000-lire ($6) bills. Newer issues have been printed for 50,000- and 100,000-lire ($60 and $120), with first-in-history 2000 lire and 20,000 lire notes ($2.40 and $24) making their debuts in '73.

PRICES   The cost of living is skyrocketing—for Italians. But for dollar-carrying North Americans, the purchasing power over the devalued lira is balm to the budget. The difference manifest in the past couple of seasons benefits most hard-currency voyagers by as little as 30%, running on up to nearly 50% for the most prosperous foreign-exchange-raters. Tariffs are rising, however. During Off Season, price levels drop slightly. (For guidelines to this year's hotel rates, please turn ahead to the "Hotels" section.)

ATTITUDE TOWARD TOURISTS   Tourism is a serious facet of Italian life and economy. Traditionally, it earns more foreign exchange than any other industry. With this size stake, the nation can ill afford to be anything but hospitable to guests from abroad. And that's just what you'll find, almost everywhere you go—hands in your pockets or out.

The national tourist office is called "ENIT." In New York, it is listed as the **Italian Government Travel Office**, 630 Fifth Avenue, N.Y. 10020. Dr. Emilio Tommasi mans the helm.

American Express and Cook's are weak in Italy, in our opinion (you might stoutly disagree). Their banking services are unparalleled, but we don't feel they're doing the *travel* job for which they have been famous for so many decades.

From intimate experience year after year and place after place as routine clients, our admiration and enthusiasm for the famous **Compagnia Italiana Turismo (CIT)** knows no bounds. We've used them annually since 1950, and they're so extraordinarily good they continue to amaze us. Normally, huge corporations such as this semiofficial giant (60 offices in Italy and 26 in foreign cities) have no business being so efficient, pleasant, and personalized. Here is most definitely the number one operator on the Continent.

No matter who you are, what budget you have, or how you plan to go, our sincere recommendation is this: Place at least the Italian section of your journey in the hands of CIT. You may work with them direct, through any of their branches, or through the offices listed below—or you may instruct your travel agent to turn over this portion to them, at no additional cost to anybody (they'll act as his European representative). In return, we'll practically guarantee they'll make your trip happier.

In addition to excellent facilities for *all* classes of independent travelers, CIT offers hundreds of guided tours to any point in the country, and to most of the Continent. For local excursions (Amalfi Drive, Vesuvius, night life of Rome, and dozens of others), they're versatile, dependable, and inexpensive.

The 60 CIT branches scattered all over the Italian map give the voyager an almost instantaneous service network for any problems which might pop up to plague him en route. Foreign offices in New York, South America, and most European capitals are also excellent; we tested their outlets in Paris, Brussels, and London on two recent trips, and they couldn't have been finer, in every detail.

Most of their guided tours are booked via SITA, the affiliated bus company created to supply deluxe bus transportation for the tourist. Most of their fleet is made up of fine, easy-riding "Roadmasters"—specially designed 36-seaters with a bar, a public-address system, individual reading lights, 2 drivers, a hostess, and the last word in cruising luxury. Tickets are valid for 60 days; you may climb on or off at your fancy, because stopovers are unlimited. You are seldom deposited at a station or terminal; wherever local laws permit curbside unloading, they'll go straight to your hotel. This is a good theory and it usually works well—but occasionally there are irritating delays while waiting for tardy tourists. Once in a blue moon, too, a hostess might line her purse by selling you a lunch ticket for more than it is worth; merely wait until you can see the menu in the restaurant to solve this one. And some of the guides talk too much about minor and uninteresting antiquities—slightly irritating when you're tired, a state which seems to come somewhat more easily on buses than on trains. In any case, you'll always be stimulated by a ride on SITA—and it will give you a happy inside look at the country. It goes just about everywhere. For self-drive automobiles, no other reliable agency is more reasonable (see "Cars").

If you want further information about CIT or SITA, ask your travel agent. If he doesn't happen to have the specific things you need, a letter to Mr. Tommaso Pucci, General Manager, CIT, or Dr. Aldo Amerio, President, CIT, piazza della Republica, Rome, should bring an immediate answer. These gentlemen are energetic, progressive, tops in their specialities. Foreign Manager Enzo Balzamo, a warm-hearted professional, can also be a Friend Indeed; his address is CIT, piazza della Republica, Rome. In Naples, perhaps the most noisomely difficult city in Western Europe to traverse, we never move without the peerless help of encyclopedically knowledgeable and incisive Branch Manager Dr. Amabile Fazi and CIT Guide-Interpreter Joseph Laudato, both of whom have saved us untold time and money for more than 25 years. In our opinion, at least, CIT is the finest big outfit in Europe to fend off travel headaches.

CUSTOMS AND IMMIGRATION   Easy and pleasant.

Tobacco is a state monopoly. Officially, you are allowed 400 cigarettes, their corresponding *weight* in cigars, or 500 grams (approximately 1 lb.) of pipe tobacco. Above this, the duty is about $3 per carton. (Incidentally, Italy now prohibits smoking in many public places, but generally this ukase is so casually applied that you might not know it even exists.) Two unsealed bottles of wine and one jug of spirits are permitted, as are (supposedly) all "normal personal effects." Carry your supplies in the right places, act like Little Lord Fauntleroy at the frontier, and they probably won't even bother to open one suitcase.

Money regulations have been tightening steadily. Today you aren't permitted to take out more than 50,000 lire.

Exports other than souvenirs are a different story. You can leave with all you want of silk shirts, silver lighters, costume earrings—the usual sort of stuff—but for vintage paintings (not modern ones), sculpture, tea services, china, and other purchases of this nature, you must obtain an Export License. This also applies to antiques—broadly interpreted, anything made from the dawn of creation to about A.D. 1900 (including Etruscan vases!). All works of art must be examined and cleared by the Belle Arti (Fine Arts Commission) —a sensible piece of legislation, because uncounted tons of Italy's most ancient and precious treasures have found their way in an unauthorized manner to other countries in the past. Your dealer will help you here; in a pinch, ask CIT to come to your rescue. In this department there is no joking —but the inspectors should receive you nicely.

HOTELS For far more comprehensive information on certain hostelries than space limitations permit here, interested travelers are referred to the annually revised *Fielding's Selected Favorites: Hotels and Inns, Europe* by our vastly traveled son, Dodge Temple Fielding. Its latest edition, in which a total of 300-odd favored possibilities were handpicked from the 4000-plus personally inspected, will be at your bookstore early this year.

Italy tucks in a mighty host of sleepyheads per night. Since the previously mentioned waves of strikes continue to fuel inflation, there's no telling at this writing when, if ever, they will taper off. Meanwhile the dollar's strength over the lira's weakness works in your behalf to provide you with greater value for the outlay. So-called inclusive billings often fail to include minizaps for sales taxes, service charges, special regional assessments, and such "extras" as cooling your epidermis in summer, warming it in winter, and keeping it clean year round (if you use the tub or shower down the corridor). Therefore, please never trust "official" quotations; they are most often only the start. *Always demand that hoteliers give you the total rate including all supplements before agreeing to sign the register.*

Concurrently, many places have sharply jacked up the prices of amenities such as drinks, laundry, and room service items. Your so-called "Continental Breakfast" of a small pot of miserable coffee, 2 rolls, and modest dollops of jam and butter now might go from $1.75 to $3 per person. Hence, do as the nationals do by stepping out to the nearest espresso bar for a savory cappuccino and 2 pieces of fluffy pastry for between 50¢ and 75¢.

In summer, a good double room in Rome will cost $35 to $60; 2 people can live in comparative opulence at the finest hotel for *$60 to $85;* expenses in tourist centers (including taxes upon taxes, service charges, extra charges, and the endless, endless *tipping) remain murderous.* In the small nontourist villages, of course, dwelling space will cost a lot less.

The State is now striving to raise hotel classification standards by boosting qualitative and basic plant equipment requirements. Here's a noble gesture we are watching with a careful (but jaundiced) eye.

The leprosy of the obligatory pension plan exists in epidemic proportions across Italy's hotelscape. Many of the nation's finest and most imposing hostelries—impeccably honest in all other conduct—have succumbed to this greedy, shady practice of forcing clients to pay for either 2 or 3 of their daily meals as an automatic part of the rental arrangement.

Dedicated budgeteers? As you will see, the listings which follow cover several hundred hostelries in all price categories. Because space limitations prevent us from making additional entries on this mile-long roster, please consult our annually revised paperback *Fielding's Low-Cost Europe*, which carries scads more bargain hotels, pensions, and money-saving tips in or for Italy's most important centers.

Below we rate these hotels according to our personal estimate of their comfort and satisfaction for today's average stateside visitor. Please remember this is simply our opinion; it differs in places from the official ranking, and plenty of people will disagree. Let's take it city by city, in alphabetical order:

In **Amalfi**, the **Santa Caterina** evokes sighs with a patio 150 feet above the sea. Redecorated units for 90 guests in the main building, plus accommodations for 30 more in villas spotted along the lemon grove slopes. Balconies for all; elevators to the beach plus newly rippling swimmery; well-prepared food with vegetables grown on the premises; service as crisp as the lettuce. The 50-sancta **Luna Convento**, owned and operated by the Barbaro brothers, is justly proud of its revamping; you'll find a lift from the street to the hotel, a pool, a fresh dining room and terrace, a summer-only nightclub, improving kitchen, and generally cooking on all burners nowadays. The **Cappuccini-Convento,** by far the most famous (a marble plaque here recalls the visit of "Enrico Wadsworth Longfellow"), has a fantastic setting in a twelfth-century monastery, but some time ago we found the administration so uninspired, the food so tasteless, the rooms so unattractively furnished, and the atmosphere so brashly geared for tourism that we did not care to overnight here. This one is due for a recheck. The **Pensione Sole** is a clean, quiet, family-run house with a bounty of comforts for its extra-low tariffs. Superb for the money. The **Excelsior** at **Porgerola**, a twisty 15 minutes up, teeters viewfully above the town. If awards are ever given for tranquillity, this one should win a Peace Prize. First-class category; modern ambiance in a sawtooth layout; all 90 seafront units have bath; most have private terrace. Administration and staff now improved; physical facilities are still above average. The Second-class **Residence** is no longer recommended. **Caleidoscopio**, about 2 miles from the center, overlooks (but is not on) the sea. Every room with bath or shower; all front accommodations with balconies; large pool; substantial cuisine supervised by Proprietor Anastasio Porpora; a happy choice, in a modest way, for travelers who seek calm. The well-situated **Miramalfi** is budget class, with a good building but mediocre food and service; it, too, has a concrete-lined swimmin' hole. Staircase construction with ample parking space at the uppermost rung; in another way a stare-case, too, because the view is outstanding. The First-category **Saraceno** courts posh pashas from its perch just below the highway at **Conca dei Marini.** Our preopening visitation revealed a cliff-hugging structure linked by mirrored elevator to a private beach and jammed-crammed with gimmickry. Whitewashed lobby and lounges with moor Middle Eastern memorabilia than Suleiman the Magnificent's tomb; vaulted restaurant-grill with tiled floor and—yep, you guessed it—the inevitable camel depicted on a mural; gilt cave-dwelling bar; lower-level pool and mini-chapel. In addition to the so-called "Royal Apartment," there are 60 adequately sized doubles with showers, chilled air, TV's, Frigobars, more Arabesque accouterments, and terraces fronting the foam. Service and cuisine? As big a mystery to us as the contents of dem 40 urns baked for oil. The nearby Second-class **Bellvue,** a 5-minute drive toward Positano, is a fair roadside spot—if you don't face that noisy roadside. It offers only 24 bedchambers, each with balcony, terrace, and bath or shower. Its bright, hardworking manager is doing a commendable job in converting this former pension into a full-blown resort hostelry. Good news for money-savers.

Bari : Skip it if you can and try for shelter at one of the coastal resorts farther south. This town is busy, jammed, and dirty. The **Palace** has 150 air-cooled rooms, all with bath or shower and most with terrace; back-alley location off the main traffic artery; garage. The best of a very poor lot. Next is the seaside **Nazioni,** a middle-age matron whose makeup and wardrobe have been totally renewed. (We'll bet *you'd* never know it, either.) In a lower category, the **Grand & Oriente** the **Victor,** the **Leon d'Oro,** and the **Windsor Residence** all reflect degrees of modernity or renovation. The Second-class **La Baia,** at nearby ***Palese***, is chiefly a luncheon excursion point, but it should be considered as a worthy alternative; private garden and beach; comfortable enough. All others not recommended. If you have time to drive 35 miles to ***Alberobello*** (halfway to Brindisi), you might enjoy **dei Trulli.** Thirty rooms in 20 unique, conical buildings called *trulli;* some accommodations with fireplaces and living rooms; swimming pool. This entire village of beehive-shape structures has been deemed a national monument.

Bellagio counts as one of its hospitality treasures the 100-room **Grand Hotel Villa Serbelloni,** a national monument that has operated as a hostelry since 1872, residing today in an enclave of land belonging to the Rockefeller Foundation. Lakeview terrace flanked by palm trees in its park; small sandy *lido* plus a heated pool; main salon with frescoed ceilings, parquet floor, and working fireplace; spectacular garden vista from the restaurant; outstanding kitchen with superb wines to complement the cuisine. Venetian and Florentine bedchambers come with home-style comfort, many have painted highlights, and about half boast waterfront reflections; only 4 feature balconies. Personally we prefer the north wing, especially suite #160, a corner choice. Proprietors Rudy Bucher and his wife keep this expensive pearl gleaming from April to October annually—so sparkling, in fact, that it is fit for a doge. A praiseworthy candidate by any measure.

Bologna this year leads off its parade with the Deluxe **Royal Carlton,** located near the station. Manager Piero Modena, a cherished friend who for years ran the Florence Excelsior like a dream, now is at the helm of this young and highly stylish cruiser. It couldn't have a better skipper and you couldn't be in better hands. The taste overall is an exquisite meld of modernity and tradition, with every comfort available and every convenience provided. Well run kitchen, excellent cave with the accent on Italian vintages, superb Royal Grill that is truly regal, handsome American bar backed by a breakfast room. Total of 250 bedchambers including 22 suites; colors varying from powder blue to cognac to olive green to salmon; extravagant artwork on which millions were spent by newspaper magnate Attilio Monti. Easily the city's leading light. Slightly dimmer is the lower-wattage **Internazionale**, a 2-part structure dating from the sixteenth century and 1972. Of its 140 units more than half are singles; both of these Monti hostelries come with ample garage space—an important factor in this cluttered town. Well below these comes the **Majestic Baglioni**, which doubles as a national museum. Marvelous ceilings; attractive public rooms; dark corridors; spotty maintenance for such an exclusive house. Fully air conditioned; bedchambers disappointingly flat; management changes so frequent that local wags say there is a new director every month instead of every year. **Residence Elite** started life in 1973 as an apartment house and has undergone a beneficial conversion for the traveler. Many suites, some with kitchenettes; charming restaurant with bottles in vitrines for décor; copious buffet popular with Bolognese. An elite treat. The **Garden** has an out-of-center situation, about 5 minutes by taxi from the city's heart; ocher-hued stucco building; glass-enclosed ground-floor portico surrounding a spacious greenery-filled courtyard (obviously the seed of its name); air conditioning on request; garage with service attendants. All 83 soundproofed bedchambers with radio and telephone; furnishings inclined to be rather spindly copies of provincial styles; functional but small baths, some with showers only. Recommended. The **Jolly**, facing the rail station, is more commercial in tone. Chilly ambiance; 2 dining rooms; spacious lounges; 200 units, all with bath; fully air-conditioned. Always booked solid by visiting salesmen, so be sure to nail down your reservation. **Milano-Excelsior**, also opposite the station, gets better every year under the hardworking management of Manager Eibenstein. His Reception Chief, Pier Luigi Pigrucci, is another friend of the traveler. Shiny dirt-free throughout; 109 bedrooms, all with radio, telephone, and bath; 6 very pleasant suites; ssssssoundproofed windows on the front side; amiable personnel who aim to please. This house owns the neighboring 108-room **Alexander**, also a solid value at an even lower tab. The Second-class **Roma,** which we'd place in a higher category, is a budgeteer's delight, particularly since it was partially renovated. Midtown situation, one block off the central piazza; hotel bus service to and from the station; covered parking area; intimate public rooms; 91 units, all with telephone and many with large private terrace; 55 baths or showers. Replete with good cheer and kindness. Substantial comfort at bargain prices. **Crest**, on the outskirts near the congress center, offers 164 clean and cheerfully simple shelters. All's here for a pleasant repose. Dropping to Third-class, the 17-room **Kennedy** is out of the center, but it is air-conditioned. We're told that **Tre Vecchi's** 92 cells are superior for its class, but as much has not been said about the service in its dining room. The **Fiera** is young but unexciting. The **Accademia** is about the same. The **Cristallo**? Never in a thousand years for this wayfaring stranger. The **Palace** is clean but too decrepit to consider. Other bottom-barrel choices are **San Donato**, **Nettuno**, and **Europa**.

Bolzano's upland valley offers the aging **Park Laurins**. This one is smack-dab in the middle of town, but it is peacefully embraced by tall shade trees and a somnolent garden with a private swimming pool. Its 120 accommodations and 4 suites claim many improved refurnishings plus a quantity of added baths; lovely terraces for breakfasting or bucolic lounging; open Easter to

October 1. If you opt for silence and the amenities of 1910, look no further. The faster-paced **Grifone**, under the same management and with the same rates, draws a livelier clientele. Three restaurants plus a large, coolish bar; 140 unfancy units and 65 baths; garniture in Tyrolean Baroque and Biedermeier. Tops for the young in heart. The flamboyant **Alpi** boasts 120 bedchambers— each with bath or shower. Ceramic-and-marble lobby, with Moorish ceiling; somewhat cramped dimensions; air conditioning; some nests with refrigerators. Flocks of continental group tours home in on this one. Slick, but not our pony glass of Strega. The **Scala** has taken admirable steps toward modernizing; the **Luna** also is enjoying a new phase. The **Citta** may delude you by its attractive public rooms—but our love affair with this house stops right there. Seldom have we seen such poorly maintained, dismal, and totally depressing "first-line" bedrooms in all of our Italian travels; only the restaurant's passable pasta keeps this one's head above water.

Brindisi, the ferry takeoff point for Greece, is an important but woefully inadequate, filthy and dregs-ridden crossroads for American motorists. If you've prepurchased your ferry passage—and we beg you to do this—plan to arrive only before departure time and overnight either aboard or almost anywhere else up or down the pike. This hub is a blotch on the touristic map. Dott. Norberto Rolandi of the city's tourist bureau naturally takes exception to these observations, but after still another inspection we still stand firmly behind our guns. Your choice here is between the **Internazionale** (on the sea) with 85 silo-stark, old rooms, all with bath or shower, or the even less appealing, centrally located **Jolly**. The others are Third-class and recommended only for Marine boot-camp aspirants. Please continue to watch out for pickpockets, dope peddlers, and flimflam artists. They run rampant on the streets, in the ticket agency lines, and at the port. We personally experienced an unsuccessful jostling by a light-fingered team of woman and 9-year-old son. We also witnessed other attempts here. Watch your car, too!

Capri captures many aristocratic hearts with the centrally located **Quisisana**, a product of and for the Establishment which never diminishes in its mandate for excellence. This enchantress is taking giant strides under the tireless hawk-eye of soft-spoken but razor-keen Director Roberto Ferraro. Lobby, grillroom, handsome English bar (with kindly Marcello on duty for almost 4 decades), nightclub, swimming pool, kitchen, shops—even the petunias were rearranged during one housecleaning. In summer, bid for the seafront units only; the back ones face the boisterously noisy footpath just off the town square. Here is solid, old-style, cool-tempered luxury at its tastefully zestful best—a hint of the Caesars, in fact. A tip of our *cappèllo* to Sig. Ferraro, to the supremely helpful Alfredo DiStefano (our pick as the number one concierge on Capri), and to all the staffers who keep this ship sailing so very smoothly.

For perhaps a younger, amorous clientele, the elegant little **Punta Tragara** could qualify as the honeymoon capital of the West. The burnt-ochre, villa-style hideaway was designed by Le Corbusier in 1927 and converted into a hotel in '73; a prohibition against animals and small children (under 12) insures tranquility. Graceful seaview thermal pool and salt water bath on cliff; adjoining bar and dining room; unusual, whimsical sunning tiers; Taverna disco-quarter for guests only; sumptuous interiors even though life is oriented to one of the most breathtaking stretches of Mediterranean coast one can find; glorious comfort-laden bedrooms and suites. Overall, here is a sneak preview of what paradise must be like—provided you've come with the right Adam or Eve. Open Easter until October 15. A delight!

The fresh **Luna** also beams with honors. Marvelous view of the Faraglioni cliff on the seaside and L-curving for a townscape panorama along the other shank; one of the quietest sites of any Capri hostelry; entrance via a 100-yard vine-covered path bordered by cascades of blossoms; full air conditioning; swimming pool. Top First-class (not Deluxe) category: 58 rooms; extra-good plumbing in all the better accommodations; somewhat clashy Italian provincial furnishings; generally more space than most new hotels can boast in this pinchpenny era; same Vuotto family ownership as the cozy little La Pineta and Flora (see below). Director Aldo Strina, its original architect and the owner's son-in-law, operates this Capri-cio. Recommended. The face-lifted **Tiberio Palace** commands a wonderful vista at one of the most convenient perches on the island; traditionally sound cuisine which we hope Proprietor Avino, a Neapolitan industrialist who enjoys this hosting as a sideline, will maintain; full-time direction by Anthony Ferraro, brother of the Quisisana chieftain. A revivified restaurant and bar; a sizzling grill-*pizzeria;* spick-and-span furniture throughout; air conditioning, radio, and TV. We observed more group traffic here recently than on earlier visits. **La Palma** stands in stacked-arcade fashion. This one is in the hands of Franco Ferraro, yet another brother in this fecund island tribe. Alfresco terrace for sipping and sunning; sauna-solarium complex; wide corridors; superb maintenance. All 80 amply proportioned chambers provide air conditioning, bath or shower, and phones; #126, a standard double, sparkles with a yellow-, blue-, and white-tiled floor, an expansive balcony, an outsize bureau, and a stocked Frigobar. This extensively refurbished hostel recently was elevated to First-class status; we concur in every department. The **Regina Cristina**, despite the attractive pool it shares with the Villa San Felice, seemed to us once more on our latest revisit to be marking time. Present total of 48 bedchambers, all with showers; 27 with terraces; high decibel level on our PTI (Package Tour Indicator); furniture either tiki or taki. Although one of our twin beds was comfortable, the other felt as though it might have been bought surplus from the Naples Flea Market. Right there, as Minnesota Fats would say, are your odds.

In a lower category, **La Pineta** is a sweetie. Excellent rooms, some even handsomer than those in the Quisisana; heaven-sent privacy; superb view from the heart of a pinewood facing the sea; lovely pool area with sauna and bar, just right for lunch, surrounded by 1- or 3-bedroom units; breakfast on your terrace (or in the nibble-nook if, saints forbid, it should be raining); beach strip at Marina Piccola with cabanas, provision for water sports and lunching facilities at Gloria's Ristorante delle Sirene. Migrations of notables have hidden away here, for very good reason. Young, alert Manager Costanzo is the perfect host who knows just when to leave you alone and how to make you feel at home under his happy roof. The sky-blue **Flora**, owned by the same Vuotto family, is just as nice, with exactly the same medium rates—but it's a smidgen less carefree and more formal. Both are recommended highly for tranquillity and comfort. **Scalinatella** resides next to La Pineta. It's just as melodic as the sound of its name. With the latest additions, it now embraces 12 suites with terrace, Frigobar, and safe, 16 doubles, 3 singles, air conditioning, no restaurant, an oooolala garden, a bar, a wide lobby, and the careful attention of Mario Morgano and his sons, Enrico and Nicole. For romancers only. **La Residencia**, next to the Regina Cristina, comes up with a floorload of late-model pads, plus the original 54 older rooms, 36 private baths, 16 balconies, traditional décor, and Mother Nature outside your window at her most exquisite. If you are maneuvered into the **La Romantica** annex, be sure to demand a front accommodation. Sound. The midvillage **Gatto Bianco**, with many added terraces, is a mélange of conventional and supermodern decorative concepts. Colorful, but becoming splashy—especially with its psychedelic nightclub called Splash.

Villa delle Syrene, in our revised opinion, is a borderline First-class hotel. New floor with 4 suites, large terraces, and simple décor; lounge with lemongrove vista; 20 rooms in neighboring annex; clean, attractive, recommendable. We are not so fond, however, of the **Bellavista**, a sister operation which we found dull by comparison. **Semiramis** is cheerful, bright, and dependable despite its growing legion of low-element Londoners. The pension **Villa Margherita**, with a lovely quiet garden at its entrance, a neat little lobby, and some excellent rooms with terrace and bath is an odds-on choice as a residence house; breakfast only. Pensione **Esperia** has been enlarged and modernized; sensible rates; very good. If you're watching the budget closely, **Villa Oreste** taps out 15 bedchambers and simple comfort for the price. So does the equally tiny **La Pazziele** with its splendid garden and thoughtful touches. **Florida** and **Floridiana** are hives for economy package tours—mostly from northern Europe. Not worth Tampa-ing. **Vittoria Pagano** is inexpensive and, for us, looks it in every way. Finally, the **Pensione Terminus** is a Third-class, pocket-size bargain if you don't mind parking at a busy, noisy midcenter address. Operation by the deAngelis family who own the popular La Campannina Restaurant downstairs. Recommendable to the hungry who are slightly hard of hearing.

The **Europa Palace**, in *Anacapri*, has a metropolitan rather than resorttype atmosphere; Buck Rogers modernity that somehow seems out of step with the eternal beauty of Mother Nature; shocking blue and orange hues softened by sprigs of flora; panoramic roof garden with bar service and periodic barbecues; Sans Souci nightclub; tennis court; swimming pool. Foremost in comfort rather than charm—but be sure, sure, *sure* to demand exactly the type of bedchamber you want, since some Guidesters have been sorely disappointed by casual reservations policies. **Caesar Augustus**, on a cliff 1000 feet above the sea, offers one of the most spectacular vistas we've found in any European hotel—and little else, in our most serious professional opinion. You may rightfully disagree with us, but our impression continues to be distinctly unfavorable. How sad, because it could be a stunner. The group-minded **San Michele**, almost across the road, has modern furnishings, a fabulous terrace, and the same disadvantage of this suburban location. A bus stop on the Anacapri–Capri route is immediately outside, however, and this transportation is easy, cheap, and frequent. Even though this resort is geographically more elevated than the town, it's still quite a comedown spiritually. Don't bother with any of the port-sited offerings at **Marina Grande**, they're ideal for sardine fishermen.

Cernobbio (**Lake Como**) is the seat of the world-famous **Villa d'Este.** Built in A.D. 1568 as a private residence for Cardinal Tolomeo Gallio and later occupied by the Dowager Empress of Russia, the Princess of Wales, the Princess Torlonia, and other notables, it has been operated as a hotel since 1873. About 110 ultraposh rooms in the main building; 51 magnificently comfortized ones in the neighboring annex; terrace restaurant; glorious setting; 4 tennis courts; nearby 18-hole golf course; new heated pool with 2-style saunas and gym plus a floating swimmery; outdoor restaurant for bathers; private beach; horses available; slot-car track; nightclub plus discothèque; woody new grill in the Sporting Club for informal meals; open early-April to late-October. One of the aristocrats of Italy and priced accordingly. The **Regina Olga** is geographically in the same league, but that's where the similarity stops with a jolt.

At **Como**, a highly inviting medium-priced stop is the **Barchetta Excelsior**, now popping its buttons with gleeful pride over its top-to-bottom renovation. Piazza location facing the water; modern building; sidewalk café; 57 sky-bright functional rooms, all with cramped baths or showers; very clean and now quite a good buy. The restaurant (closed Thursday) is perhaps the best in town, incidentally. **San Gottardo** has perked up some of its appurtenances; large, spotless, and so-so. The First-echelon **Como**, sited in the center, is said to be a sound bet for those who don't like too much Como-tion. **Metropole Suisse** is rising, even though its restaurant has risen and gone; it's Second-class. On the road to Villa d'Este, in a wretchedly noisy location, the **Villa Fiori** has been converted from a private home; Peninsular décor; passing-fair now, but long country miles to go. As for the Second-category **Continental**, to date our reader reports have not been encouraging.

Cortina d'Ampezzo boasts the palatial **Miramonti Majestic.** This one —now a link in a chain that was forged beside Lake Como's shores—is sited in an outskirts situation surrounded by a golf course, ski lifts, tennis facilities, ice and curling rinks, a swimming pool, and the well-tempered chords of an ever-present dance band after sunset. Extensive modernizations and more to come; ground floor totally restyled, now even more inviting than before; ambitious revampings of its 200 spacious accommodations, most with balcony and many with regadgeted baths; open mid-December to March, and June to September. Very good indeed. The **Cristallo Palace** is another fine choice. Except for a golf course, it has all the recreational features of the Miramonti, plus a rumpus room for the tykes. Complement of 110 rooms and 105 baths; most units with Tyrolean décor and painted florals; 90% with private balcony; operative December 20 to March 15, and June 15 to September 15. Not as chichi as the pacemaker, but in many ways warmer and more friendly. Down in the thick of the action, the **Savoia** is a merry address. Its 2 buildings, connected by a tunnel under the main street, confer the title as Cortina's biggest hostelry. Lively and gaily traditional. The **Corona**—picked by many discriminating wanderers—simply did not demonstrate the flair of a professional hotel operation to our experienced noses. Its patrons, the

Rimoldi brothers, have filled it with $1,280,000 worth of contemporary paint-
ings—many of which seemed as abstract as the current management. Chalet-
style exterior; 64 rooms; 40 with bath or shower. Perhaps you will crown this
Corona with more accolades than we did; personally, we found it as cold as
a Dolomite icicle on New Year's Eve. The midvillage **de la Poste** almost
surely will reappear this season, rebuilt after its disastrous fire of 1975. We'll
be anxious to see the new version. **Bellevue** seems to be skidding dramatically
in quality; no longer worth the tabs, we feel. **Europa**, under Cristallo Palace
aegis, remains open all year. Rooms about as tight as the inside of a ski boot;
good food in its below-stairs restaurant. A bit commercial in tone. **Splendid
Venezia,** just a few doors away, is a smart buy if you can snatch one of its
back-corner doubles with balcony. Fine for its category. The chalet-style
Menardi should be ranked in a higher official status, but the owner prefers
it to remain a quiet "sleeper" value at budget rates. Renewed dining room;
38 units in main house plus 10 in the annex; added furnishings and many
resplashed baths; spotless maintenance; savory vittles (so we're told). **Ampezzo** is another bargain, despite its growing age. The **Grand Hotel Tre Croci**
is 4 miles out, halfway to Lake Misurina and high in the hills. Here, for our
money, is certainly one of the kings of the Dolomites. Heaven-loads of peace
and upland tranquillity wreathed in mountain flowers and glorious vistas; ski
lift, pool, sauna, and gym; beauty and barbering facilities; tennis, hiking paths,
and cliff climbing. It is due to reopen this season after lengthy and extensive
reconstruction, which we'll bet will make it even more alluring than in former
times. Ably operated by climber-skier-bobsledder Otto Menardi, designer of
our Squaw Valley Olympic downhill slopes. If you're looking for a paradisia-
cal address about 1000 yards short of St. Peter's, don't fail to knock on these
pearly gates—but softly, please. Superb. If none of these suits you, there are
some 4 score more awaiting your choice. We've still not seen the 2 entrants
in nearby _Borca di Cadore_, but both, along with 263 one-family cottages,
a church, a supermarket, and sports facilities, sound worthy indeed for lire-
minded skiers or summer holidaymakers.

Elba offered a limited but colorful selection on our recent visit. The **Del
Golfo**, 20 minutes from the port at _Procchio_, wins many hearts. Beach
location with taxis readily available; 95 small- to medium-size accommodations in 6 different buildings; the nicest in the main structure and in the "New
Villa." Some split-level duplex apartments for families or single Texans; 2
tennis courts; extra-nice L-shape pool above beach; many sporting amenities
here or nearby; splendid kitchen for regaining those spent ergs. Energetic
Director Ernesto Nagy will be your friendly and thoughtful host. The **Désirée,** tucked around the neighboring cove, has similar architecture but a less
dramatic view. Pleasant décor; private beach and cabanas; nice garden; alfresco dining in season; very clean. Most of its 60 good-size rooms come with
shower or bath and balcony. A rewarding Second-class stop for budget-
conscious pilgrims. The **Renée** is only so-so, in our opinion. **La Perla** is
directly on the noisy highway. The **Hermitage at** _Biodola_ on a woodland
inlet is ready-made for honeymooners. Ranch-style building; expansive dining-terrace overlooking the swimming pool and beach. Accommodations in
12 varisize bungalow units (#98 is best if you've brought your Junior Patrol).

The biggest drawback here is lack of adequate room service; the manageress frankly confessed that this chore rankled the waiters when it was requested. A winner if you enjoy total privacy. **Darsena,** facing the dock in *Portoferraio*, is reasonably comfortable; every room with private bath and telephone; every front room with private terrace; medium bracket. The **Massimo,** in the same vicinity, is immediately opposite the ferry landing and subject to all the busyness therewith. All 60 old-fashioned rooms with toilet and shower; only for overnighting. Open all year. We found the 62-room-and-shower **Residence** very noisy; it stays open year round too. The **Picchiaie Residence** (no relation) comes up with bungalow-down comforts in 51 rooms; baths number 31; there are also tennis and a swimming pool. At *Magazzini,* 10 minutes away, the newish L-shape **Fabricia** provides a soothing bay view from its olive-grove situation. Pleasant pool; tennis court; hypermodern décor; animated Italian clientele mostly. Recommended only if you *parla Italiano.* At *Marina di Campo* **Marina 2** is still growing on its hilltop. Quiet sealess views; 80 balconied rooms; all amenities including a refrigerator in the bedchamber. Dining indoors, on a patio, or beside the pool; new nightclub and sauna; quite a tranquil haven. Not far away, **Iselba** features separate beachhouse cabins with individual terraces; pine-grove setting fronting a wide strand; 15 units (12 apartments) added to the former 50; 2 villas serve as annexes. Open mid-May to mid-October; agreeable. Nearby, the 75-unit **Villa Ottone** is set in its own park, with a 22-room colony of bungalows fringing the woodlands. Private pebble beach; tennis; glass-lined dining room; richly decorated bar; somewhat used in feeling, but adequate. The beach and sites are dreamy but the quality, in our opinion, is poor at both the Second-class **Bahia,** and the 119-unit (80% with bath) **Lacona** in *Cavoli.* The **Elba International,** initially called the Eurotel, in *Capoliveri,* near *Porto Azzurro,* has escaped us to date. The Second-class **Garden** on the gulf at *Schiopparello* has a sublimely quiet setting on a dark-sand beach. Too tour-group-minded to suit us. The former tiny-tot **Pension Valle Verde,** above the Désirée at *Marciana Procchio,* calls itself a hotel, but a rose by any other. . . . Not for plucking by this gardener. The **Grotte of Paradise,** across Portoferraio Bay, is a rebuilt villa with a maze of cabins and other outbuildings; pretty basic. *All or nearly all these are closed from roughly October to May;* during a recent winter, the only lodgings we could find were at the tiny **Ape Elbana,** which we now like somewhat better, but not much.

Florence? Here's our report from our recent on-the-scene rovings. In a 2-way tie for the number one Deluxe ranking come the Excelsior and the Savoy. (Alas, the fine old Grand has closed.) This duet is so neck-and-neck that your preference depends largely on your personal taste. Then we follow up with other stellar selections in this better-than-average hotel oasis.

The **Excelsior** has emerged from her major overhaul in sparking radiance. Her premises now boast suites among the loveliest in Europe, each outside charmer with its own massive penthouse terrace overlooking the Arno or a townscape of gloriously untouched antiquity; the cozy Belvedere Junior-Suite (the former proprietor's apartment, when it was privately owned) is one of the sweetest corners imaginable. Major portions of the 2nd floors rebuilt, with ultraposh button-poppers the "special Deluxe" units facing the river. The

Donatello Bar has a 3-split personality: Bar, paneled nook, and hearthside room, with 2 levels in damask; snack service on tap, plus an appetizing light lunch; excellent Concierge desk lorded by Giulio Taiuti;Manager Roberto Bucciarelli runs this 5-star show with vigor and savvy. Every one of its 220 rooms has bath or shower; full air conditioning; 50 units with multichannel radio, 20 with TV and 40 with Frigobars. Catering to so many Deluxe American independents and fancy tour-group clients, its cuisine and its atmosphere reflect an awareness of heavy U.S. patronage.

Lavishly refashioned at a Shah's ransom of $3,200,000, the 100-room **Savoy** now indisputably shares top honors with the Excelsior. Midtown *palazzo* expanded and totally renovated; high-ceiling corridors; spacious dimensions; new wall-to-wall carpeting; walnut, mahogany, or painted Venetian-style furnishings; liberal scattering of antiques and ancient chandeliers to augment the traditional atmosphere; bar and dining room rather heavy and old-fashioned. Hardworking Director Vittorio Spicciani keeps this house in perfect trim as a unique period piece in Italian architecture. Chief Concierge Joseph is a perfect St. Peter to wayfarers from abroad. Recommended with respect, confidence, and cheers.

The marble-entranced **Villa Cora** is situated in a park above the town; there's a fine dinner-only restaurant (flanked by a pool), a tavern, and 58 fully-bathed accommodations which are very beautifully furnished. The frescoed ceilings and public sancta are marvels of their time and a joy to observe. Manager Dante Poggiali heads a staff that is correct and courteous, but not particularly warm or cordial. Lovely it is.

The **Villa Medici** now seems to be losing its luster in our renewed opinion. More than 100 comfortable rooms, all with bath or shower, 5-channel radio consoles and TV plugs, 3 phones (2 to the outside and 1 for service only); à la carte year-round interior dining in the separately managed Lorenzaccio restaurant; poorly located, because of structural limitations; captivatingly landscaped street-level pool and garden with buffet lunch served. The back rooms and 7 penthouse perches, each dubbed and patterned after a flower, command the best view and most tasteful décor; air-conditioned. Manager Manlio Giardi has his work cut out for him. Same prices as the Excelsior.

In First-class, the **Jolly** maintains a firm footing at the entrance to Cascine Park. Unquestionably, the reasonable tariffs and contemporary luxury amenities give it a special demand status; its once-dubious future now looks a lot brighter under the management of Sig. Graziano. Spectacular, modernistic lobby; glorious 6th-floor roof garden for alfresco apéritifs, backed by 2 glass-fronted interior restaurants and bars for service year round; open-air 7th-floor pool and sun terrace, lovely for lazing; austere main dining room with open spit and a chef under the tallest cap in Tuscany. All 145 units with bath, air conditioning, piped music—each with furnishings executed by local artisans; 32 good-size front doubles with balcony, alcove, bathroom, and lavatory. As a guideline for preference when booking, the 3rd-floor units are modernistic in décor, while all other levels are traditional. Demipension is said never to be force-fed to the clients, but we'll believe it when we see it. This house is well architected in a comely twentieth-century fashion. The **Lungarno** is a beauty—and it's even more appealing since its tariffs have been trimmed slightly. The Augustus and the Continental (see below) hold part of the deed. Its fabulous situation beside the Arno, a few steps from the Ponte Vecchio, possibly makes it the most expensive real estate anywhere on the river. Original 40 rooms extended to 70; 22 suites, including one atop the thirteenth-century stone tower which provides the finest eyeful of Tuscany anywhere in town; some excellent balconied riverfront units; back rooms disgracefully small, as are many other pockets of this miniminded house; cozy bar but no restaurant. Very colorful, tasteful, and comfortable.

The air-conditioned **Kraft** is another winner. Roof terrace with panoramic view and swimming pool; good dining salon, with personable Maître Marino one of the tops in his trade; all rooms with bath and shower, plus pillowed headrests in the tubs; excellent service; units #132 and #232 are bright, airy doubles; #304 is a pleasant twin with balcony. We have a special admiration for Manager Mario Moschi. Another pearl beyond price: It's blessedly quiet. The hypermodernistic 140-room **Michelangelo** goes all out to say it is with it, *really* with it! Corridor floors, walls, even doors, are carpeted in the same gray-brown woof that cloaks the bedrooms; beds have sleek striped spreads; prints provide color; all in all it is a creature of its time—from small baths to a plenitude of panache. The 1961-vintage **Park Palace** is lord of its hilltop. Total of 21 units in main building and 9 in the annex; private baths and air conditioning throughout; swimming pool; downstairs Taverna restaurant and bar adjoining. While each ingredient is attractive, it doesn't seem to jell as a whole. Service can be poor; peak season here is only 2 summer months (open all year, nevertheless); we have our doubts about its future. You may prefer this for lunch rather than for overnight. The **Villa Belvedere** and the **Villa Park San Domenico** are special cases which we will discuss farther along. The **Minerva,** very central and with a pleasant piazza in front, comes up with 85 doubles with bath and 35 with shower; modern lobby; attractive restaurant with glassed-in garden; completely air-conditioned. Topside pool; interior wall surfacing of harsh and dismal marble-dust gesso; extra-cordial concierge; front units more spacious but noisy; newer wing, overlooking a quiet cloister, with cell-size sleeping quarters. Overall verdict? Fair. The extensively re-vamped **Astoria** has been taking lovely pills. Now the lobby has been re-shuffled, the capacity boosted to 90 rooms and 90 baths, air conditioning has been installed throughout, and independent garage facilities have been arranged. The palatial breakfast room is one of the most spectacular you'll see anywhere. (Instead of "Breakfast at Tiffany's," it reminds us of "Eggs Benedict in the Sistine Chapel.") Despite catering heavily to Northern European and other conducted tour groups, Manager Nobbio and his thoughtful staff put hospitality in first place. The **Plaza Lucchesi**, up the Arno near Santa Croce Church, has undergone a vast revamping. Fancied-up entrance in glass and brass; overall perk-up in maintenance. The reception, once scorchingly rude, has improved; on another test we again received nothing but kindness and cordiality from every staffer we encountered. Getting better—but slowly. The **Anglo-Americano,** under the helmsmanship of Manager Bandinelli, was whooooshed through by a construction hurricane. Modern elevator; 40 floral-tile baths (almost a full ratio now); 35 rooms refurnished; beds in gold leaf or white; serene. More a made-over homestead than a metropolitan hotel.

The **Capitol**, at the edge of town in the Automobile Club Building, opened in '61. Busy-street location; glass-and-steel block-style architecture; cellar restaurant with ugly muslin ceiling; heavy use of plastic wall sheathing; modern lounge; air-conditioned throughout; 60 doubles and 30 singles; all with bath or shower and most too small for our taste. Nice staff; tour groups often present. Satisfactory. **Aerhotel Baglioni** is now partially piloted by Alitalia, which has fluffed its wings in the process and aimed its appeal to flocks of groupies who swarm over in such numbers. The **Majestic** is modern, clean, and also infatuated by group movements in the touristic field. You'll need wheels to reach the **Monginevro**, which is way-the-hell-and-gone into the industrial sticks. Window-lined 10th-floor restaurant; full air conditioning; 91 units including 3 suites; all units with small bars; fronts with private balconies; linoleum flooring with throw rugs; Second-class price tags.

The fully air-chilled **Continental** is more tastefully tailored for its price than is its sister across the river. One of the most romantic little twelfth-century tower suites in Christendom; roof garden, plus bar and breakfast room; no dining facilities; plunked smack in the center of the city's worst traffic snarl. Not bad for pedestrians and the slightly deaf. The 71-room **Augustus** nestles beside its *sorella*, tucked slightly off the main drag. Again, no restaurant; sunken, Nordic-style modern bar under a gently arched white ceiling; self-control air conditioning (which aids as well in sound proofing); singles with showers; all twins with baths. **Londra**, inspired by the Minerva prophets, reshaped its main floor, bar, and public sanctuaries. Since it was fairly modern to begin with, the upper tiers have remained unshed. The **Principe** is perhaps worthy. Situated on the Arno, near the Grand; 2 additional floors bring the total to 24 rooms with bath; centrally air-conditioned; so-so. The **Umbria**, with its shady garden and air of sedate solitude, is a tranquil oasis. The **Columbus** is so far out along the Arno that a car is an absolute must—unless you can tolerate a long taxi ride every time you hop into the center. Attractive public areas; downstairs dining pit, plus window-lined breakfast and snack corner; multilevel bar; 105 air-conditioned bed-chambers and 72 private baths. One room we inspected was so bone-crushingly narrow it was just plain ludicrous. (When we stepped into the lavatory, our guide said proudly, "Here's one with a shower!" We asked, "Where?" Our companion replied. "Why, you're standing under it!") The column of units ending with the number "13" are the biggest; they are more than adequate for their bill. Very good, if you don't mind the tedious hike from the doin's and if you pick your nest carefully.

Here's how we score the rest of the pack: **Hotel de la Ville**, indeed convenient to the major sightseeing attractions (and nice, as well); **Ritz**, a perky youngster with chilled air but no restaurant; **Della Signoria**, satisfactory for bed and breakfast, and **Berchielli**, a remodeled *palazzo* with 84 charming rooms which mostly go pipeless. **Bonciani, Adriatico**, and **David** are not recommended.

Pensions? Our top laurels go to the lovely little **Hermitage** (Vicolo Marzio 1, at the bridgehead of the Ponte Vecchio) and to the demure **Mona Lisa** (Borgo Pinti 27). The former boasts a roof garden over 18 pleasant rooms and the latter is a fourteenth-century palace with as much charm as tradition. Both require full board. **Beacci** (via Tornabuoni 3) occupies 3 floors over an art gallery; it's quite comfortable. **Centrale** (via dei Conti 3) is clean and agreeable. **Villa Villoresi** (colonnata di Sesto Fiorentino, near the Florence exit of the Autostrada del Sole) is good for lengthy stays, but inconvenient for trippers-in-a hurry because it's 3 miles out; Countess Villoresi and her radiant daughter, Cristina, take great pride in their ancient homestead. **Villa Carlotta** (via Michele di Lando 3) perches on a hard-to-find hilltop; this hideaway is ideal for creative types who yearn to-get-away-from-it-all. **Villa Belvedere**, the leader of the smaller houses and 10 minutes from the center, offers a fine view of the city. The Perotto team (she is the daughter of the late owner) run this haven smoothly. Their pride-and-joy's 30 rooms all boast baths, air conditioning, and daily rubdowns; try for #26 or #36. The pool is an added bonus; half pension is required; it is closed December through February. Here is an especially outstanding choice for those seeking a friendly welcome, reasonable tariffs, and tranquillity. **Park San Domenico** nestles in a cypress forest toward *Fiesole*. Baronial appointments a bit faded but still in the Grand Tradition; 19 rooms with baths; one in which a Czar of Russia is said to have slumbered (in the bedroom, we assume). Manager Constantini and his family try constantinily to please.

After a short decline, **Villa La Massa**, the Deluxe country-estate-type hotel in neighboring *Candeli*, has now regained many of its earlier assets. The rooms are comfortable, immaculate, and tastefully furnished, due to the efforts of Owner Maria Broggini. Expanded dining salon; 2 improved kitchens; sleekly rustic, blue-clad-and-gold-gilt, October-to-May La Cave nightclub for cellar-brations; touch-ups numerous and well done. There's a tiny pool, and anglers can borrow the gardener's pole for compleat relaxation on the Arno banks. Many U.S. pilgrims are again enthusiastic about this sylvan nook. So are we as we pray that it continues its special mandate on grace and tranquillity. The best route to reach it is by the Viale Europa, not the Lungarno.

At *Fiesole*, 4 miles out of town, overlooking the Florentine valley, **Villa San Michele** is lord of its hillside. This one is a tastefully converted fifteenth-century monastery originally designed by Michelangelo. Splendid panorama; a guest book that boasts more blue blood than the registry for a royal coronation. Its 23 bedrooms, all with bath and all former cells, have been lavishly and comfortably outfitted for distinctly nonhirsuted disciples. Gentle, urbane Lucien Tessier and his sparkling Irish wife, Máire, are a charming and capable host-and-hostess team. Open March 20 to November 1. Here is a Deluxe bell ringer (sweetly muffled, of course). We were much more impressed by it on our most recent inspection than on many previous visits.

Genoa can be proud of the **Colombia-Excelsior**—classic, comfortable, and though expensive for this city, the lowest rates of any Deluxe hotel in Italy. This CIGA-operated house's major improvements, include the wood-paneled, extra-comfortable, maritime bar (which instantly became the social wheelhouse for local scuttlebutt among shipping moguls and knowledgeable voyagers alike); don't miss its vitrines of lost or donated cigarette lighters behind the counter; there's a new and winning off-lobby lounge. Other updatings comprise the extensive front-bedroom renovations, self-regulating air conditioning in all accommodations, restyled bathrooms which bring the plumbing ratio up to 1-to-1, many late-sprouting balconies, 100 Frigobars, a new telephone system, and a dining room with some of the finest ladlings in the region (please try the local specialty: Trenette Avvantaggiate al Pesto). Coupon-clippers should reserve #208-209, the so-called Ambassador's Suite; our pick of the twins is #111. Director Piero Coloru, merry and enormously efficient, is on the go ceaselessly to tighten up and improve this house. He has virtually no competition in the city. The **Savoy-Majestic**, which began a renovation program recently, is the front-runner's nearest challenger. Director Mauro Placido has reshaped most of the bedrooms, renewed the kitchen, refashioned the lobby, lounge, and bar, and generally spruced up his house. He has also been working assiduously on the adjoining **Londra Continentale,** turning on new baths throughout, new automatic elevators, a new passageway to the Savoy Restaurant, a zippier lobby, and a garden loggia with tables for drinks on the mezzanine. This one, too, is coming along smartly. The **Plaza-Corvetto**, centrally but quietly situated, provides appealing shelter with a small hint of luxury. Total of 100 renewed and attractive bedchambers, most with air cooling; 86 baths; bar and parking area. One caution: its whipper-snapper page boys (and even desk personnel) tend to leer lustfully at anything in skirts, so perhaps single ladies might feel uncomfortable here—but on somber second thought, they may even happen to prefer it. A little costly, but what's a gal to do in Genoa? The **Eliseo** seems to us to be slipping down in quality while creeping up in price. On the main piazza, the **Bristol** is a living period piece; the baths on the 2nd floor, for example, could be in a showcase of Italian design crafts; they are so dated, but so beautiful. Public rooms vary between tasteful opulence and gaudy neon color schemes in plastic textiles; its 6-person white Formica elevator must have been built for a dozen Goliaths —it is the biggest we've seen outside of the *U.S.S. Enterprise.* If you enjoy indoor tennis, push aside the easy chair in room #244 and you should have just about enough space. Perfect for any love match, even if your partner happens to be a long-distance track star. The **Park**, a dimestore-rococo villa on the corso Italia just across the road from the sea, is usually packed to the scuppers with sailors. Almost impossible to find a berth. The **City** is strictly functional; numbers ending in 23 or 28 are the better bets. Below these, we really can't recommend any. But for emergency use only, here are notations from our meanderings: The cold and dark **Milano-Terminus**, with ½-dozen updated rooms, is fair—or let's even say poor. **Aquila & Reale**, near the Colombia-Excelsior, would provide our roof only if the waterfront wharves were filled and no space remained in the bus station. We have seen dentists' waiting rooms with jollier-looking sad sacks than the ones we spied in this lounge. Never. **Italia-Minerva?** Nix. Best pensions are (1) **Simonini** (via Balbi) and (2) **La Principessa** (via Fieschi, in the "Small Skyscraper"); both are noisy, but both can be recommended. Unless you know Mr. Upjohn or someone else with a warehouse full of insecticides, better avoid the flop joints along the portside via Gramsci. If you check into one of these seamen's digs, you might come home with more itches than a Genoese Fido.

Ischia ? The enchanting **Regina Isabella** complex, 5 miles from Porto

d'Ischia at Lacco Ameno, is indeed a *Hôtel de Grande Classe International*
which triumphantly merits its membership in the ultraselective Prestige et
Tradition Groupment to which it has been elected. Three separate units
connect along the shore of a lovely bay. The nexus is the Queen Isabelle, with
118 rooms and 118 baths, a beautiful indoor-outdoor dining-room-terrace (jackets and ties required at dinner), 2 fine pools (one s-o-o-o charmingly blended
into a shaded grove with a natural islet of flowers and greenery in its center),
a soothingly elegant décor featuring a plethora of the most stunning tiles
we've ever seen in any hostelry anywhere, a gayly umbrella-ed beach, a
solarium, 2 TV rooms, a garage, a hairdressing salon and a barbershop,
sumptuous cuisine, and lots, lots more. The 2nd link in the chain is the
elaborate, computerized **Therme Regina Isabella e Santa Restituta**, the famous thermal baths for physical reinvigoration, nose and throat ailments,
gynecological cures, beauty treatments, and special gymnastics under the
supervision of medical specialists and an experienced staff. Then come the
sea-bordered pool and the Sporting Terrace, an urbane and enticing oasis
which offers a luxurious buffet at lunchtime. Still farther along, perched atop
a cliff perhaps 100 feet high, is the **Sporting Hotel**—15 suites only which
command the premium tariffs. Individual water-skiing or participation in a
special school; sailing; speedboating; golf driving range; minigolf; Mediterranean bowling; interchangeable meal plan with 4 other establishments; cosmopolitan clientele with North Americans peaking in midsummer. Handsome,
vibrant General Manager Harald L. Sellner deserves congratulatory salutes
for its patrician, immaculate mien, its ball-bearing organization, and its ever-
courteous staff. Closed from mid- or late October to mid- or late April.
Superb! The First-class **La Reginella** is situated on the town square in Lacco
Ameno; rooms only half as attractive as comparable accommodations on
Capri, at prices ⅓ higher; a poor value. In the Port, **Excelsior** seems to have
made a big comeback; private bathing beach; comfortable; clean; excellent
physical plant; nice pool. Now *the* choice within the town limits. The **Moresco**, across the street and on the beach, comes next. Moorish-style construction; charming gardens and ambiance punctuated with gay touches of color;
swimming pool; cozy bar and public rooms far more ingratiating than the
brash modernity of its bedchambers; 56 spotless units with baths and balconies or terraces; chilly management. Older Guidesters may like this one more
than do the youngbloods. The portside **Aragona Palace** evokes our most
vehement NO. Life begins here at 1 A.M.. For insomniacs only. **Grand Hotel
Punta Molino**, in the curve of the bay facing the Aragonian castle, is a worthy
alternate. Sweet gardens; small beach; good pool; routine bedchambers. Under the professional direction of Giorgio Stacchini, the **Jolly** has taken on a
decidedly upbeat character. Sixty units added, bringing the total to 220
refreshed or new nests; comfortable fittings in simple surroundings; TV, radio,
and Frigobar; grounds well landscaped; swimming pool that's covered and
heated for colder months. Twin lounges, a nightly movie, a piano bar, and
a new restaurant are welcome additions. A jovial salute to this Jolly entry.
The **Elma** resides in its own park at *Casamicciola*, with 65 seaview rooms
divided among 4 distinct but interlocked blocks. Large pool; tennis court;
thermal bath area (for guests) with doctor and nurses; bar with piano player;

films. Director Umberto Italiano sees to it that his kind staff provides dramatically more than what you might expect from a Second-class Superior hostelry. Superb value, in our opinion. The **Parco Aurora** has a fine location on the beach; it converted a neighboring villa into an annex; its accommodations, however, must have been designed for the smaller, less-obese offspring of dwarfs, because they're claustrophobic. The **Cristallo Palace,** about 5 minutes along the road toward Lacco Ameno, offers 85 rooms—most with baths, and all with balcony or terrace. Pleasant split-level patios for dining and sunning; nice seaview, but noisy locale; its screaming cretonne plastics might make your eyeballs bounce. The nearby beach is not recommended for swimming; take the bus service to San Montano, where lunch is available. Not bad if you wear welder's goggles. In Second class, the **Miramare e Castello** faces the castle from its beachfront location; renewed some time back; open March-October only; coming up in every sense. The **Regina Palace** and the **Floridiana** are also in this category; the latter has a "thermal" swimming pool. The **Ischia**, on a strip of seashore, is the bailiwick of an Italo-American *signora*. Simple, no-frills accommodations; 32 units, most with plumbing—and Holy Hephzibah, are *they* colorful! One room we winced at had pink walls, green doors, and a yellow bath. Okay for colorblind budgeteers. The best pension, in a walk, is **La Villarosa**; modern building in the port; antique décor; kindly staff; be sure to get a room on the 3rd or 4th floor, or you'll miss the view. The **San Pietro** pension, atop a glorious promontory, is wonderfully situated; total renovation a while back—and badly needed. The **Santa Caterina**, at **Forio,** on the west coast, also boasts a lovely location; a car is a must for beach or town hopping.

In **Milan**, there's a rich air of discrimination surrounding the **Principe e Savoia**. Exquisitely rebuilt and redecorated, this aristocrat takes the crown as one of Europe's finest Deluxe hotels. Loaded with antiques and ankle-deep carpeting; stunning ceiling-height-marble bathrooms, with 2-entrance split facilities and telephones; electrically raised Venetian blinds for all floor-length, wall-wide picture windows; 100% air-conditioned; stunningly handsome, intimate My Grill; adjoining enclosed terrace-garden; finely hewn bar extended into a conservatory style nookery, with one wall the original exterior stones of the building. The modern annex is quite different in tone but many guests prefer it to the traditional main address. Manager Mario Miconi, with the able assistance of Manlio de Min, is doing a notably outstanding job. Cheers and salutes to his urbane haven. The **Palace**, once considered almost outlandish by us in its striking modernity, has been warmed up so handsomely by young, energetic Manager Francesco Chiais that it is now becoming one of our favorite Milanese choices. Color schemes rehued to curry, brown, cranberry, and beige; architecture inspired by 3 different virtuosi in the field; 75% of the house renewed; lighting fixtures often hideous, but gradually being replaced; nicely prepared and presented cuisine in the Venetian style. Now restful and recommendable. The 335-unit **Hilton** extends a hearty welcome to contemporary travelers. Top-hatted doorman to greet you; delightful Trattoria da Pepi at mezzanine level, with fanciful food displays and an upbeat pasta-pack of peninsular gaiety; Music Club at penthouse height, with dancing from 9 P.M. to 2 A.M.; off-lobby London Bar; nursery for tot watching.

Twin units somewhat cramped but extra-brightly decorated; superb furnishings; paisley velvet spreads; radio, TV, massage vibrators; salons with refrigerators; all singles with French beds and ample room to move about (both in the *grand lit* and out of it). Baths throughout come with only one basin. The rates frankly are walloping. For those who can afford the tabs, it's a lovely address indeed, but our general impression is that most vacationers might find it too costly for the rewards. The **Excelsior Gallia** has put on some additional raiments. Now 100% air-conditioned; 280 rooms and 260 baths, all ample in size, adequate in comfort, and clean. The renewed 5th and 6th floors are best, in our opinion, as well as a few units in the older wing. Direct-dial phone system; full carpeting throughout; hushaby double-glaze windows; overall predominance of business registrants rather than holidaymakers. Red-blooded males will rocket straight up the walls at the soft, sultry voice purring the floor numbers through the automatic speakers in the elevators. RRRRRRRoooooowwwww! Same rates as the leader; good, but not *that* good —except for the sexy elevators we shuffled around in for 6 or 7 hours one recent afternoon. The young **Plaza** serves breakfast only, but its accomodations are among the nicest in the city. Futuristic, cantilevered lobby; heavy use of chrome and glass; semicircular bar; angular construction; interesting colors. A bit odd but we like it. The 200-room **Jolly President** mixes Empire highlights with an egg-crate ceiling in its lobby and lounge. Air-conditioned; small chambers with floor-to-ceiling windows; competently run in a commercial way. **Michelangelo** has set up his modern easel near the tracks and is highly touted by local *dilettanti.* The revitalized **Duomo** really shines in spots. The trick will be to find those spots. The duplex suites and "VIP rooms" would be our choices, so ask for these first and then request that they show you around if some other accommodation is desired. Manager Ghirardi has brought this one up commendably. In the **Continental**, the cavernous lobby was refurbished in a dull way; the Conti Grill (3 connecting rooms) is cozy and charming; the first-floor front accommodations were reworked, again with little imagination or flair; fully radioed; air-cooled; an old, old building, with narrow halls and structural limitations which are almost impossible to surmount. Though many La Scala artists still cling to the tradition of patronizing it—as Metropolitan Opera baritone Cornell MacNeil explains, "You almost *have* to stay here; it's the only place they'll look for you if you're a singer"—we'd call this commercial house just so-so, much to the consternation of Director Comm. Dott. Constantino Gallia, whom we respect deeply, but with whom we continue to disagree. The fresh, 150-room, glass-and-concrete **Nasco** is a product of our modern times, rendered smoothly in a chipper meld of Italo-Scandinavian concepts. Bar-lounge that doubles as a foyer; spring-green breakfast room; 7 color schemes; snug accommodations, but good ones. A lively candidate with numerous virtues. **Carlton Hotel Senato** offers 80 cramped but efficient bedchambers, all with bath, shower, stocked refrigerator, and micro-TV sets; facial tissues, shoeshiner, silent valet, scales, and other functional gimmicks; garage, restaurant, and bar; your quoted rate includes air conditioning, service charge, and taxes. Mercantile but convenient. The **Cavour** comes up with a handsome lobby, 100 appealing but smallish rooms, and 73 private baths. Choose your location on the courtyard side away from the clattering street; tub with every room, radiant heating here and there, and modest features in general; simple, modern tone; no great shakes, but okay for the price. The reasonably priced **Leonardo da Vinci**, 25 minutes out on the Bruzzano pike, offers 320 hotel rooms plus 1000 apartments. (Minimum stay in the latter is a month.) Indoor pool, 8 tennis courts, 2 saunas, 2 restaurants, 4 bars, disco nook, shopping arcade, hairdresser—actually, it is a hamlet unto itself. The free shuttle to town 24 times a day is a boon if you don't wish to drive.

More Milanese morsels? **De la Ville** boasts 93 baths for 104 breezy nests; soundproofed and sssssound for medium budgets. The **Andreola**, a toot from the station, has been refashioned in up-to-the-era stylings. The nearby **Splendido** is doing the same. **Francia Europa** seems to be on the wane, in our poll. No thanks. **Windsor** castles in behind the Principe e Savoia; it's a regal choice for its class. For the reasonable tariffs, we think you will find palatial rewards. **Marino alla Scala** waits in the wings of the opera stage; here's an untemperamental coloratura with a kind and helpful manager. **Manin**'s claim to fame are the Colombo brothers who own it and try to greet every guest by name; garden dining, air cooling, Telex, and proximity to the city's zoo are its fringe benefits. **Cavalieri** revamped 70 of its bread-and-butter boxes, but we find the attitudes here so crusty that we can't toast it. A penchant for pensions? The **Terminus** (via Vittorio Veneto 32) is a work of duel affection by Lydia and Mario Ferrari. So warm is their welcome and so loving their attention to their 68-room domain that we were ready to settle in inn-stantly. Even Brill, the dog, proffers a wag of greeting. **Casa Svizzera** (via San Raffaele 3) was reprogrammed with 75 units, 75 baths or showers, and 75 climate-control thermostats, but we still find it humdrum.

Fianlly, if you are a bird of passage, you might wish to wing in at one of the no-nonsense flyway perches in the Milan air space, either the **Aerotel Executive** by the airport or at the **Aerotel Fieramilano**, across from the fairgrounds. Both have clean lines, cheerful décor with modern lithos for artwork, and limited but adequate living space for transients.

Montecatini? **Grand Hotel e La Pace**, known as "La Patch-eh" to its international clientele, is slipping, we think, despite genial Proprietor Innocenti's heavy infusions of lire and love; 170 rooms, 170 baths; pool; April to October only. **Croce di Malta**, next down the line, has been extensively face-lifted; very good, too; April to November season. The April to October **Bella Vista Palace e Golf**, is smaller, but its reputation is comparable; cordial reception and atmosphere; extra-worthy cuisine. The **Ambasciatori** (formerly Cristallo Bonacchi) has changed hands and demeanor; it now has top-to-bottom air conditioning, a swimmery, and spring-sprung thermal bath. Sounds interesting. The **Nizza e Suisse** has been thoroughly remodeled and boosted up to First class. If you don't like these, there's a choice of more than 50 others in what has been facetiously called "Italy's Beachless Summer Miami Beach."

Naples? First to repeat a warning and a plea: *please* avoid as you would a plague the 1-day Rome–Naples–Sorrento–Rome bus excursion which is being pushed so mercilessly by so many concierges in the Eternal City; even though, as you will now read, the vast majority of Neapolitan accommodations are substandard, it's indefinitely more wise to tolerate one of them for a single overnight for the fastest sensible coverage of the same ground and more. Turn to Rome in the "Hotels" section for more details.

The **Excelsior**, operated by CIGA and directed by Milan-trained Dr. Massimo Rosati, who intimately knows his local ropes and their knots, is so far ahead of the pack here that no other house is in any way competitive with it. From the tallest eaves to the deepest wine cellar, it is a Koh-i-noor diamond which glitters dazzlingly over what has become virtually a derelict wasteland of hosteleries. Most of this plant has been exquisitely refurnished. About 60 bedchambers plus several sitting rooms and lounges redesigned by the famous Stigler (see CIGA hotels in *Venice*); all lodgings have been renewed in classic elegance; soundproof double windows (one glass nearly ½-inch thick!) on all sides; doubles #19 and #20 are first among equals. The cuisine is sumptuous; the service is flawless. Chief Concierge Cavotti and Maître Contiero are star professionals. This operation reflects solidity, tradition, and sound management. Here's the *only* quality hotel of the city—and it's even getting better. The **Royal,** also facing the bay, is gold and blue and glass; the clientele is very mixed, with heavy occupancy by NATO forces in winter; its nonofficial clientele is often alarmingly sleazy. Warm-weather penthouse pool; 10 floors against the Excelsior's 6, with both buildings the same overall height, which illustrates its cramped dimensions; all windows and glass doors have now been wind-proofed so that they no longer shake, rattle, and roll. A mass hostelry which packs 'em in and out at tariffs considerably lower than those of the Excelsior. The **Vesuvio** has lowered its tariffs—and well it should have done. Fully air-conditioned; tons of plastic and Formica; range of lodgings from Archaic to Zesty; tabs pegged at about half those of the leader. The effects of its aging and the diminished number of visitors to its city in recent years continue to deepen its slide. Saddening. **Santa Lucia**, next to the Excelsior, has given herself a general puffup since her takeover by the Royal interests. Once-proud dining room now sealed shut as an economy measure; sleeping lockers to the rear too barnacled for this old salt; we prefer the bayside #47 as a double stop. Director Morante and his kindly staff try very hard without notable success for their American guests. Becalmed. The youthful **Ambassador's Palace** just missed being called the *Grattacielo* ("Skyscraper"), but it does provide an altogether heebie-jeebie, knee-knocking sensation when the bay-borne winds make the edifice sway in the breeze; 16th to 30th floors of an office building, with a separate entrance. Commercial theater-like lobby and large banquet hall; desk crew largely unfamiliar with English on our latest try; 280 cramped, sparsely furnished rooms; all with bath or shower; ⅔rds with a sea view. Frequent changes of management, the latest top-hat being Sig. Gerardo Bertazzoni, who was again out when we called. The **Mediterraneo**, opened in '58, is downtown. Another large, streamlined, air-conditioned skyscraper; every room with bath or shower; most with bright tiled floors and sticky plastics; shoddy appointments and linens; 50-car underground garage; glorious panoramic roof, featuring a restaurant-sun terrace complex which is no great shakes in the food department; air-conditioning fee included in the overall bill; heavy South American traffic. A longtime chum warned us that the bar pulled a no-menu racket that prices your sandwich and drink at whatever the public will bear. Much too commercial and soulless for our liking. The **Majestic,** centrally located, offers a lovely view from the top 2 floors, a white marblesque lobby, and 120 rooms with bath or shower; air cooled; further chilling by Northern European tour groups; now breakfast only. Only fair. The century-old **Parker's Hotel**, above the city, has a passel of charms. The new owner-director has invested heavily in improvements. Seaview location not far from center; 100-car garage added; cookery far more appetizing. We like the distinctive #414 as a normal double or the split-level #211 for 2 women or 2 men (beds separated). Old-fashioned but superior to most of its younger colleagues. The **Britannique**, once part of Parker's, shares its vista with this veteran. Rated as Second class, its 91 rooms are fair; 57 with bath or shower; #344 is a good double. Both cater heavily and successfully to wholesale package occupancy. The opened, air-conditioned Second-class **Commodore** is the most popular address in the station area, perhaps because it's the only one in the vicinity with a bath or shower for every room. The **Turistico** provides sound budget renewals masterminded by Manager Lamborgese. It has no restaurant. Although the site is convenient and the food is good, the **Londra** should be used only in an emergency, in our opinion. Young wayfarers seem to enjoy the Second-category **Stadio**, near the San Paolo Stadium and municipal pool. Wardship by the clergy or a bolt of the same cloth; not restrictive in any sense. We think the **Domitiana**, on the same cinder track, is better, but both are too far out for most older shoppers or sightseers. The **San Germano**, in the same official class, is far along the pike toward the NATO base. Capacity of 83 rooms, 43 baths, and 40 showers. Viands above average; routinely modern; except for its distance, a value for your lire. The **Rex**, around the corner from the Excelsior, must have the kindest owners in the city. Why else would they rent rooms by the hour? For bargain hunters on wheels, the 100-bed **Motel AGIP** has rolled in on the outskirts. We've never inspected the **Commodore**; one experienced traveler has just reported that it's "the best Second-class bet in the city." Next time!

Cultural note: In the lesser Neapolitan hotels, near the station, solo male travelers used to be asked at the registration desk if they wanted a *letto caldo* (hot bed)—which was slang for a sponsored prostitute. We're told this is no longer done, but in Naples, who knows?

Parma ? Pretty cheesy. The extensively refurbished **Park Hotel Stendhal**, in the city, has a cheerful bar-lounge, a restaurant with perked-up cuisine, and 45 refashioned units with bath. **Palace Maria Luigia** is said to be fresh and a first-rate First-classer with a well-run dining room.

In ***Perugia***, the **Brufani** maintains a gimpy lead over a still more slew-footed field. Old, Old, Old World flavor; still renewing its rooms; central situation; management by Aldo Bottelli. Fair. The newer **Excelsior Lilli**, on an outlying hump of roadside terrain, is okay for desperate motorists who prefer modernity. The **Grifone**, of a similar ilk, would come next, but we're not overjoyed with either, although the last has been completely air-cooled and supposedly pepped up. The little **La Rosetta**, down the street from the Brufani, is a lot cheaper, and the vittles, for its category, are outstanding. So, we hear, are the renewed units. **Della Posta** and **Dei Priori** are both breakfast only.

Pisa now offers some decent additional stops. **Dei Cavalieri** is Neo-Italian-Modern, with 102 air-conditioned rooms, 102 respigoted baths, a bright-red American bar, and a redecorated restaurant which has drawn complaints from readers; pleasant but not plush. The **Mediterraneo** comes up with 105 spacious air-chilled rooms, all with radio and telephone, and ⅔rds with private bath; lantern-lit penthouse nightclub with recorded music. Not bad. The **Duomo**, almost at the foot of the Leaning Tower, has 90 air-conditioned rooms, 90 baths, cuisine which is also poor, a viewful roof terrace, avant-garde furnishings, and good drinks; First-class (not Deluxe); also fair accommodations at reasonable prices. The **Nettuno** is roomy but gloomy. The **Royal Victoria**, although it retains the furniture used by Queen Victoria when she stayed here, is light-years from regal. If it's summer, and if you wish to escape the crush of this tourist-gagged city, the **Golf** at *Tirrenia* (on the coast, 10 miles from the steps of the Tower) might be the answer to your vacation prayers. Pine grove situation just a mashie shot from the sea; adjoining golf course, tennis, swimming pool, and full resort amenities; modern tone with ornate fillips; all 100 units with bath, balcony, and air conditioning. Better than the sweltering hives of midtown Pisa. Also for motorists, the **California Motor Inn** was launched at Kilometre 338 of the via Aurelia National Highway—about one mile from the city. It consists of a cluster of 9 villas, each with 6 rooms, plus a restaurant, the usual services, and neon lighting à la jukebox; we haven't tried it, but Guidesters who have say they've been disappointed. From our visual inspection, it seemed far too modest for the comfort-conscious Americans bred on our own brand of clean and cozy motels.

Portofino's **Splendido**, perched on a mountainside, offers one of Europe's most gracious vistas—especially from its elegant glass-front dining salon, which is also the scene of such delicious cuisine (but alas, we found the maître uppity and the waiters slow paced.) A pool is undoubtedly splashing for your pleasure this year. Total of 80 units, 69 with small bath or shower; fresh carpeting and plastering throughout; first-floor accommodations the biggest; only 4 inside rooms; fine, rich appointments almost everywhere, but some beds are indeed sag-sacks. Structurally and from a landscaping point of view it's glorious; its human approach, which we have damned so roundly for so many years, has been flip-flopped for the better. We hope the new management will keep up the fine attention to hospitality and plant. The smaller **Nazionale**, in the village, is entirely refitted; now expanded to 56 rooms and 56 baths; simple, Second class, agreeable, and friendly; parking at an inconvenient distance; noisy in season. The poorly situated **San Giorgio** is under the same management, but that seems to be where the similarity ends. Not recommended. The **Piccolo**, the only remaining choice, is tiny; facilities perhaps too regional for the average American.

Positano poses prettily with its rock-ribbed, vine-clad **San Pietro**, girt by flowers, aproned by sea, and showered with love by Proprietor Attanasio and Manager Cinque. This canon takes its name from the chapel on its cliffside. Pool and tennis court due for your arrival; private beach; plant-lined restaurant with 2 grills and a pizza oven; exquisite taste in its clean-lined accommodations; floral displays rampant; balconies and terraces cushioned by bougainvillaea. Though it is officially rated First-class (and so priced, too!) the standards handily tip it over into the Deluxe bin as far as we're concerned.

A dream spot—but not from mid–Nov. until Easter when it shutters. **Le Sirenuse** also clings to a hillside, with 7 floors staggered in staircase fashion, and with the main entrance on the 4th; all living quarters facing the sea; door keys featuring a mermaid suffering a severe bellyache; *taverna* and barbecue sizzling brightly; private steps to the waves. The staff in this converted and enlarged family mansion, which used to mirror the merriment of its former clientele of painters and socialites, grew sour for a spell, but rebounded when the San Pietro began to draw off business. Very colorful to the eye and to the spirit. **Villa Franca**, down the scale, has a similar personality. All of these are intimate and oriented toward vacationers rather than transients. The **Royal**, a First-class entry, is not directly on the briny but its 5 levels offer an excellent vista; 7-minute walk from the center, with bus service available; elevator; 50 unadorned rooms, all with bath or shower and private balcony, radio, telephone; some units enlarged and modernized; nice pool. **Miramare** has a superb position over the sea, with a full panorama to the south; enchanting restaurant; 15 rooms with bath, in 2 buildings; glassed-in goldfish swim merrily in some of the bathroom windows while you bathe; facilities simple but adequate; good but not outstanding, except for the magnificent location; be prepared to climb steps until your ears turn cartwheels. The **Poseidon** is next; off-beach setting; 11-room addition facing the Gulf of Salerno; good parking space; fair cuisine; English-speaking staff; coming up strongly. The newer Second-category **Posa-Posa** is also away from the waves; it is very noisy. The quieter **Montemare**, with the same breathtaking sea view as the Miramare, is Second class, clean, and unpretentious; 15 rooms with bath or shower. **Pensione Conca d'Oro** garners 31 cheers for its 31 rooms with bath. A budget bet and a good one. On the beach, the **Covo dei Saraceni** sails away with salutes; also Second-class; convenient for bathing; pleasant. Low man on the local totem pole is the **Savoia**; heavy Italian trade. Motorists might like it because they can park in the little square nearby.

Rapallo awards its crown to the **Bristol**, 2 miles out along the Gulf of Tigullio. Sweeping reconditioning undertaken, but furnishings still suffer from cretonne-itis; fresh 5th floor, with 7 small cozy suites and kitchenettes; baths throughout; traditional atmosphere with moquettes in all accommodations; large seawater pool with direct elevator service (the automatic type) from building; private beach; spacious terraces; open-air restaurant; in the hands of Andrea Costa, better and better every day. **Aerotel** is a 50-room apartment house that rents by the day, week, or month. Appealing restaurant; bar; pool; gardens; excellent for its type. **Savoia** reminds us of an old crone with too much makeup; although seriously in need of a face-lifting, it is still popular with the nationals. **Europa** is also skidding. **Moderne et Royal** is now the leading hostelry in the so-called Superior Second class. The **Riviera**, with private balconies on its 4th floor and a total renovation job a while back, comes next in this category. **Astoria** boasts a glass-fronted entrance and not much more. **Bel Soggiorno**, on the coast, offers barely reasonable value to families. While the **Miramare** is a winner for food, it lacks spice in the bedroom stew. Thoughtful, nice people who run its basic plant very well indeed. With a generous bank loan, this could be one of the better bets in town. The **Eurotel** is air-conditioned; all rooms with balcony overlooking the deep blue; pool; garage. For pensions, try (1) **Bandoni** and (2) **Mignon-Posta.**

Ravello, a village 1000 feet above the sea, offers 2 choices and each is recommendable. **Palumbo**, a twelfth-century palace, has 40 units in the main building plus 2 annexes, respectively rated in Categories I and II. Handsome, whitehaired Swiss Director Vuilleumier runs this house very well. Daring color schemes; 20 private baths; rooms identified by the colored tilework as well as numbers; #28, #32, and #34 offer stunning 3-directional panoramas and plenty of breathing space. Both are for peace-loving pilgrims; the latter now seems a bit expensive for its amenities. **Caruso Belvedere**, a converted castle, has an enchanting garden and terraces, 26 old-fashioned rooms (some with fireplaces), and pure serenity. The 3 Caruso brethren are its friendly proprietors (one makes the house wine); even friendlier are the scrumptious Crespelle alla Caruso (ham and cheese filled crepes) and chocolate soufflé. The **Rufolo**, with exquisite gardens, is more modest. The 25-unit **Graal** is a Third-category sweetheart. If you can tolerate a tiny room with an elfin bath, you will be rewarded with the same eye-popping view as is offered by the 2 leaders—but at only about half the tariff. Owner Oliviero Palumbo makes the wine, his wife Anna makes the food, and 2 of their 6 children make the beds. Open the year round for thrifty wanderers with acumen. **Parsifal**, next to the C-B, is the leading pension. Thanks to the Patron Saint of Tired Travelers, a road now wiggles directly up to this highland enclave.

Rimini, now bloated by more than 60-thousand beds in nearly 1600 hotels and pensions, offers the gamut from gilded, silk-draped fourposters to Italian Boy Scout camp cots. The glutting continues apace. Warning: Since a serious water shortage has developed, we urgently suggest you select your shelter from the choices which follow. (The houses we list either maintain sizable water reserves or have special pumps for emergency dry spells; waterless periods usually occur in summer just before noon and last until well after dinnertime. An aqueduct plus an improved sewage system costing 11,000,-000,000 lire—*you* figure it out because we haven't got that many fingers and toes!—have been installed, but still there may be pockets which do not benefit from this essential element.) The **Grand** is the lone Deluxe offering. Here is a creaky personification of the fast-vanishing hotel tradition for which it is named. Tennis courts, private beach, hot-and-cold showers in bathing cabanas; lovely dining terrace; dancing in garden as well as in the cellar Lady Godiva nightclub; gorgeously furnished with fading appointments; full of art treasures; lower early-season rates make this a good buy; expensive later and worth it. This pacesetter is managed by Director Arpesella who is experimenting with winter operation as well as High Summerizations. We wish him *buona fortuna.* In First class, the starkly modern **Ambasciatori**, with every balconied room facing the sea, rules the roost. Private tract of Adriatic shoreline, plus spacious rooftop solarium; American Bar; cookery that is reported to be noteworthy (we've not tried it); piano lilts at lunch and dinner. Its 75 spare-size accommodations heavily accent glass; substantial but strictly basic comfort. The **Excelsior-Savoia** provides more bedroom space; insist on reservations in only the newer wing here, because the original section is far less agreeable. Arresting twentieth-century décor, reminiscent of the better designs of Miami Beach; push-buttons like crazy; indifferent cuisine; mannerly clientele; very satisfactory indeed. A newer one called **Bellevue** (What! Not "Bella Vista"?) is said to be the *bella* of Kennedy Square at the site of the former Lido. Ambasciatori patronage; 66 First-class rooms; 66 baths; air conditioning. Might be a winner. The beachside **Imperiale** comes up with 60 rooms, 100% bath-and-shower ratio, and a glass-wrapped, Top-of-the-Mark dining perch that is panoromantic by starlight. Still along the shore, the **Sporting**, with its red and yellow exterior, is now one of the better bets; rooftop solarium plus waterside cabanas; sound amenities; attractive to the eye; pleasant for Sporting types—indoor or outdoor. Management could be improved, say we. The **Corallo**, this one with a blue and pink skin, has turned into a gaudy corral, in our opinion. Perhaps the latest management will perk things up. Moving inland, the highly touted, 6-story **Abarth**, formerly called Palatino Imperatore, occupies a pine grove residential address several hundred yards from the Adriatic. Institutional and gelid to the marrow; 90 rooms, all with baths and balconies that stare directly onto the balconies of neighboring hotels and apartments. The **Atlantico**, again a fair trot from the sand fleas, offers a vast and wondrously viewful penthouse dining room; almost exclusively patronized by package migrations of charter groups from the North and East; little chance of fun for the loner. **Waldorf** towers up as the most modern inn in the area. A solid First-class choice. Other recent additions, all fair but none sparkling, include the **Amati**, **Baltimora**, **Adriaqueen** (wonderful name but sinking fast), and **Metropol**. Get 'em while they're hot, or they'll be cold turkey tomorrow! Of the Second-class shore havens, **Kursaal** leads the pack. Same ownership and similar architecture as the Ambasciatori. This hostelry offers a waterfront dining salon; all accommodations canted toward the breakers; 2-dozen private cabanas. Very good value. The **National** has solid resort-style amenities, reasonable tariffs; the food we're told is dull. The **Internazionale**, another horse in the Ambasciatori stable, is moving up impressively. Management still has some distance to go, however, think we. The **de Londres** is so-so, though recently modernized. The 40-room **Mocambo**, once in First-class, has been recategorized; formerly nothing special—and now even less. **Milano île de France** is a comfortable little budget bargain; here's the only stop along the Strand that stays open all seasons. The **Giulio Cesare** is blessed with an excellent situation and a compact, efficient plant. Management now improved. No restaurant. In-town shelter can be had year round at (1) the **Palace** (hotel-school management, clean basic appurtenances, friendly English-speaking staff) and (2) the **Napoleon** (room and breakfast only). **Biancamano**, a Second-class entry, is charming, and its plant is unusually good. The big bugaboo here is its absolutely horrible service. If someone would jack up the staff, this contender could compete handily with the higher-ranked Ambasciatori. Unless otherwise noted, *all the above are closed from October to March or April.* If you land in this area after nightfall or out of season, it is safer to stick it out in Rimini rather than push on to San Marino, because the latter has now fallen far behind in its innkeeping.

Rome? First a serious warning: Please don't be gulled by the local concierges—some of them, sad to say, in top-ranking hostelries—who are so strongly pushing the new 1-day Rome–Naples–Sorrento–Rome sightseeing excursions. Usually they depart at 7 A.M. and return at midnight, when the poor limp fish are spooned out of the vehicles. During this 17-hour marathon, only perhaps 3½ hours are passed on terra firma. Result: The victims absorb almost nothing of the character of the stopovers and are zombies during the debilitating hangover which long lingers. Greed is the motivating factor behind this high-pressure salesmanship, because the tour operators pay commissions of up to 50%. If you're in a tearing hurry for an infinitely more rewarding glimpse of these southern attractions, here's how to do it in the fastest and best way: Ride a morning TEE or *rapido* to Naples and check into a hotel. Take a round-trip afternoon bus excursion to Vesuvius and Sorrento. Reasonably early the next morning, board a hydrofoil (preferred) or conventional ship to Capri and/or Ischia; on certain days there are direct sea connections between these 2 island resorts. Then, in the late afternoon, glide back to Rome on another TEE or *rapido*. If your mandatory checkout time should interfere, store your baggage downstairs while you're finishing up your explorations. Fatigue? Normal. Coverage, comfort and enjoyment? No comparison!

Here is how we found the hotels on our latest exhaustive re-inspections:

The **Grand**, 100% air-conditioned, is the home of diplomats, dignitaries, and lovers of top traditional European hotelkeeping; urbane, spacious, and luxurious, it is the capital showcase of the CIGA chain. Each floor boasts an exotic Chinese-style nest with red lacquer and bamboo trim; also lately unveiled are 16 Junior Suites beguilingly turned out in golds and yellows, with rose fabrics and rice-paper walls; the Royal, Queen and Presidential superposh suites have been reexalted; some extra-modern units have been turned on for variety in décor; piped music, TV, and refrigerators are now operative in 100% of its accommodations. There's a Health Club with sauna, massage, barbering, and beauty-parlor facilities; the lobby and reception area lead to the Le Rallye bar and grill; the off-lobby Pavillon, in garden-conservatory style provides both liquid and light solid refreshments; the pasta-oriented Le Maschere Restaurant ("The Masks") evokes the fantasy of an operatic stage setting with soft guitar strummings and candlelit intimacy; there are high hopes of constructing a new floor with not more than 40 bedchambers and baths. Capable, distinguished directorship by Dott. Nico Passante, whose previous performance at the Europa e Brittania in Venice impressed us so mightily. Highest recommendation for this Grand old landmark.

The beautiful **Eden**, which first opened its doors in 1889, reveals not even the most minuscule trace of its age today. It commands a central situation atop a small ridge, with the added bonus that it overlooks the Villa Borghese and the Pincio Gardens. There are a smartly designed entrance, a tasteful lobby, a lovely skylit lounge in soft dewy hues, an adjoining library, and a suave, 2 tier breakfast room. The finial on the crown, where all other meals are now presented, is the penthouse terrace and bar with its marvelous, vista-rich sweep of the city, with romantic illumination, sliding windows designed to disappear vertically, and cascading bowers of greenery and flowers. The cuisine in all of these departments, not incidentally, is far above average; Silvio, the famous Chief Barman, is an international institution. Every accommodation in the house, including the 13 suites, has long been reconstructed and revivified; on our very recent visit, we were *delighted* by the arrestingly unusual urbanity and elegance, in subdued modern tones, of the large new crop which has just burst into bloom. Since it is located on a very noisy corner, *all windows* have been double glazed successfully to muffle the traffic sounds, and the 100% air-conditioning system is purring. Here's an almost paradisial Eden that serves its tempting apple—sans viper—to its rightfully loyal throng of modern Adams and their elegant Eves. Enthusiastically recommended.

The **Hassler**, favorite of so many Social Registerites and unobtrusively rich travelers, is expertly run by American Proprietress-Directress Carmen Wirth and skilled, ever-kind General Manager Nadio Benedetti; together they carry on its noble traditions. And speaking of nobility, its register reads like a catalogue of royalty, heads of state, and men-of-the-moment on almost any day of the year. The subtle homeyness here is hard to duplicate anywhere in the city. It offers a wonderful roof garden, 2 recently re-styled salons, a soothingly delightful reading room in soft greens, extra-smooth service, and, for our money, the best location in Rome (atop the Spanish Steps). Magnificent view from the upper floors; full air conditioning; all front units restyled; many widened by clever architectural techniques and built-in furnishings; hand-painted murals added to some walls; 9 compact but pleasantly furnished suites were redone a short time back; 3 prize junior suites and 3 choicest doubles have been added, all above the serene garden instead of the teeming street; #103 is fit for a shah—at the very least; #303-304 buys a magnificent view; #610 is also one of the best in the house, with lovely terrace, cozy ambiance, and a bird's-eye sweep of the center. Recommended with cheers.

P.S. Here, too, the Wirth-while foresightedness of its owner has created an apartment hideaway for seekers of more domestic coziness; this 30-unit, air-conditioned, ultra-luxurious poolsider is called **Maison Cassia Antica**. Drop a note to Mrs. Wirth or Director Roberto Antonucci for all the tantalizing details that space doesn't allow us to record here. The Hassler touch is a warranty of good taste.

The **Excelsior**, CIGA-owned cornerstone of via Veneto, is Rome's Community Center for well-heeled movie moguls, cloak-and-suiters, bet-a-thousand horse players, on-the-make nobility, and flashily attired fingersnappers who want action NOW. Celebrated ground-floor bar by Jansen of Paris; savory food; soundproof double windows wherever you peek; enlarged baths, including twin basins, separate nonskid tub and shower rooms; immaculate maintenance; very expensive; impeccable direction by Director Giancarlo Polesel. The only handicap here—a matter which has nothing to do with either Mr. Polesel's excellent administration or the quality of its facilities—is the brash, sloppily dressed, loudmouthed type of transient junketeer who has singled out the Excelsior as his Roman Domain.

At long, long last, the conveniently sited **Flora** is on the march again. After nearly a decade of sad decay, this establishment has finally pulled up its socks in a quiet but happily gratifying way. All of the public rooms and all of the bedchambers which we were shown (about 30 of them on 4 different floors) have been face-lifted. The overall maintenance is now excellent; the welcome couldn't have been more gracious; the cuisine in its ground-floor restaurant was pleasant but not memorable. There is a genteel aura in keeping with its classical décor. All of the bedrooms have high ceilings, quasi-portable-unit air conditioning, old-style plumbing fixtures (that work), plenty of closet space, and lots of Lebensraum. Many have parquet floors. Most are extremely comfortable. Better than we've seen it in many a season. Now strongly recommended.

The **Palazzo degli Ambasciatori** ("The Palace of the Ambassadors") is also on the jump, but the fiscal nutrients here have not been quite so manifest. All corridors renewed; more than 70% of the bedchambers winningly restyled; some heavily endowed with synthetic materials; 4th floor the latest to receive cosmetics; very good baths; 2 fine suites; #214 the most imposing. Otherwise it has pockets of old-fashioned furniture; drinks refrigerators come with all billets; air conditioning with individual controls, is throughout; alas, the grill has become a glorified snack bar and we saw other signs of economizing. An illustrious name, and now with ample charms to honor it properly. Congratulations to friendly Managing-Proprietor Aldo Della Casa, but we wish he would loosen up his purse strings on some niggling little aspects of his hotel management. In general, we like it.

For the typical U.S. visitor to the Eternal City, a splendid candidate is the **Mediterraneo**. It is not as luxurious as our pacesetting pack, but the management shows such alert interest in North American tastes and preferences, the rooms are so clean, and the staff is so friendly that most first-timers seem to feel more at home here than anywhere else in town. This enterprise is the star of the largest family-controlled hotel empire in Europe. Behind its tremendous success is Angelo Bettoja (pronounced Bet-toy-yah), who has recently resigned after several years on the firing line as the President of the Rome Hotel Association and whose beautiful wife is American. One block from both the central railway station and the airline terminus; 120-car garage—and *what* an asset that is here; 100% private bath count; entire floors redone, with new carpets, and upholstery phased in. This dynamic organization gobbled up the adjoining Hotel Urbe, which was razed and rebuilt to make this *alma mater* Rome's second largest hostelry; the upper 2 levels of this 5-story wing contain only compact apartment accommodations, each with a private kitchenette. You'll find greater lushness and plushness elsewhere, but not quite the same friendly attitude toward the transatlantic guest. Again, after just enjoying every moment of what was perhaps our 14th or 15th stay here, we reiterate that from Manager della Venezia, through the excellent Concierge team of Neri Martano and Dino Annibaldi, right down the line, they all do their best to honor the Bettoja slogan, "Every Guest Is a VIP"—and please believe that after 30 consecutive years of hard research travel for this *Guide,* my Nancy and I have learned enough to spot almost instantly the difference in the comparatively few places where we are known as reporters from the treatment accorded to virtually *"Every* Guest!"

The **Bernini Bristol** lately seems to have lost some of its head of steam. The earlier upliftings now are becoming dated. Nice restaurant overlooking the famous Bernini Fountain, full air conditioning, Telex, reception hall recast, refrigerators in all bedchambers. Most rooms small; more space and flair in units ending in "06" and "07"; 75% in contemporary décor with chestnut woodwork; 25% in older-style mahogany veneer; double windows installed wherever needed; clientele a mix of tour followers and independents. What it lacks, in our opinion today, is a dash of inspiration.

The no-longer-querulous **Quirinale** queues up about here. Germany's Steigenberger chain now has it manacled into its linkage. Management is by Robert Grübner. While many phantoms remain to be exorcised, this tired and rather cumbersome house is at last spotlessly clean. Fresh paint has been applied to every square centimeter of its interior walls and the courtyard façade; the entrance has been perked up; the kitchen restoked; 80% of the accommodations have been redecorated (baths included); the remainder have been refreshed; bid for a garden-side nest for greater P and Q. Still a problem is the staff attitude, which again on this visit ranged from indifferent to openly rude. Far from a Grand or an Eden or a Hassler, but zooming along remarkably under its present paper-bred handicaps.

The 200-unit **de la Ville**, a First-category house atop the Spanish Steps next to the Hassler, boasts an illustrious reputation and an ideal address. Its British landlord, the Grand Metropolitan chain, has poured in tons of capital to help it to realize its considerable potential. Quietly urbane lobby, uncluttered and uncommercial; kitchen moved to main floor adjoining new restaurant and close to Rotunda dining area; air conditioning deployed throughout; acres of new carpeting laid; muted gold draperies and spreads spread everywhere; dignified standard furnishings installed; 100% of its 50 new rooms plus its more venerable lodgings now with TV, radio, direct national and international dialing, and private bathing bins; bar-ettes placed in suites; reasonable rates for value received. In spite of the updatings, the personnel here simply murdered it for us. The concierge's gruffness to us, the reception's arctic chill, the sullenness of the maids and waiters over our 3 days and 2 nights of incognito trial, made us almost weep for the expensive renovations that this chain has thrown away in order to lure guests. Until there is a turnaround in client attention, with at least basic civility the order of the day, we are staying far, far away.

The youthful **Jolly**, fringing the Gardens, is to our eyes such a hideous architectural blight it astonishes us that Roman authorities ever permitted it to be built within the glorious Borghese enclave. Iron and concrete exterior that more closely resembles a modernistic factory than a hotel on the Eternal City's prime parcel of real estate; bronze-tinted windows; subterranean lobby, bar, and dining spread; 200 units in the twenty-first-century mood, all with a goodly supply of formica veneer, a microscopic bath and shower, a music console, a TV, and double-glaze windows. The balconied treetop accommodations are heaven-sent abodes of tranquillity. The service standards and cuisine in this backyard of princes are typically Jolly—the antonym of the name. (It has one of the lowest staff-to client ratios in the city for its category.) A mixed bagatelle in which the choice is left to you.

The 210-room **Parco dei Principi** is perfectly located near the Aviary of the Borghese Gardens, an 8-minute stroll from via Veneto. Aesthetically, however, our tastes just don't happen to jibe with those of Manager Vito Tine, or with some of his loyal and prestigious clients. Unattractive cluttered façade that struck us as downright ugly-duckling; standardized interior that never varies save in the arrangement of its white, black, or green color blends; immense, frigid lobby; clinical bar; enormous downstairs dining rooms for everyday patronage or for ceremonial occasions; air conditioning; skinny hear-through walls; spindly, modernistic, creaky furniture. A rustic snack bar and cabanas are snuggling next to its handsome irregular-shape outdoor pool. The ambitious proprietor also holds the front-door keys to 4 hostelries in Naples, 2 in Florence, 1 in Sorrento, and a 48% share in the capital's Flora. But the Deluxe rating and price scale he has wrangled for this one do not make a Deluxe hotel. Sorry, but we find this house starkly commercial, tonelessly bleak, and icily oriented for the businessman's world—not for merry pilgrims in search of alluring wiles.

The 400-room, air-conditioned, fully balconied **Cavalieri Hilton**, in a 15-acre park atop Monte Mario, adds its dazzle to the Latin scene with an 8-layer-cake structure facing the Vatican and the distant Alban Hills to the southeast. Our personal reaction—with which you might disagree 1000%—is that its public sections were poorly conceived and tastelessly architected, while its sleeping quarters, in striking contrast, are graceful, unusually spacious, tasteful, and outstandingly comfortable. Extensive gardens; penthouse La Pergola supper club plus alfresco terrace for dinner-dancing; pleasant, 185-seat Le Belle Arti dining room; mosaic-lined Coffee Shop; cocktail lounge at ground level; L'Ellisse nightclub featuring French specialties. All of the usual Hiltonia is here, including heated senior and junior pools, sauna—the works. A fair example of its type—if this is the type for which you are looking.

If a little voice tells you that the unappealing neo-Victorian building in front of you *can't* be the **Lord Byron**, please don't listen, for as soon as you step across the threshold you will realize instantly that you have come to the right place. You will hardly believe that you are in the same house. Its lobby, soothed by soft music, sets a complete change of mien and mood—from exterior fuddiness to interior sumptuousness. The appointments are stunning. The handsome American Bar, within sight of the reception desk, beckons alluringly. Down a short flight of stairs is the 9 table Le Jardin restaurant, which could be a set from an Antonioni masterpiece: glossy white walls warmed by pastel rose broadloom and cream-colored furniture. This tastefully avant-garde theme is carried upstairs through the intriguing maze of corridors and the 50 individually draped bedrooms. Although this Parioli-sited hostelry is a hefty hike from the Via Condotti and some of Rome's sights, it is a short stroll to the Villa Borghese gardens and the Via Veneto. We are particularly drawn to the tranquility and the parking space (!) here. We also like the personal attention devoted to guests by genial, hardworking Manager-Proprietor Amedeo Ottaviani and his courteous minions.

The **Leonardo da Vinci**, an artfully conceived modern-lined stunner, in some ways is aptly named. On its ground-floor walls hang more than $1,-000,000 worth of fine paintings collected by Owner-Architect Alfio Machini, who shares its proprietorship with his brother, Sig. Alvaro. Noncommercial, nonurban situation on the murmur-quiet via dei Gracchi; entrance flanked by awning-covered terraces for sipping and alfresco chatting; restaurant, grill, and bar; underground garage; 264 rooms, all with bath or shower plus refrigerators with packaged snacks; more units in blueprint. Accommodations generously equipped with 6-channel radios, princess-style telephones, single-button controls to extinguish or illuminate lights, Venetian fixtures, excellent furniture, tile flooring, double windows, and 100% air conditioning; superb taste throughout; maintenance improved under Manager Franco Citarella; very heavy play by groups. A fine plant with lots of potential.

The **Victoria** occupies a sedate but convenient location overlooking Borghese Gardens, around the corner from via Veneto. Very attractive clientele of professors, musicians, artists (and even a humble travel author or 2); 115 rooms with 115 baths; optional air conditioning up to 90%; some accommodations lovely and some more simple; all Guidesters provided with a complimentary copy of the *Rome Daily American* newspaper with their morning coffee (or their choice of 5 blends of tea); colorful roof-garden for sunbathing and sipping; French-tone restaurant in soft ocher, white, and Trianon gray; breakfast segment with damask-sheathed walls; half or full pension from April to October, at a reasonable rate for this city; superb concierge desk manned by the ever-friendly team of Gino, Nino, and Tony. Swiss-owned by Alberto H. Wirth; resident management by Hans Hürlimann, another product of the excellent Helvetian innkeeping tradition. Mr. Wirth has converted this antebellum building into a generally comfortable haven.

Sitea (opposite the Grand Hotel at via Vittorio Emanuele Orlando 90) is a Second-class hostelry with First-class comfort. Its progress has been so laudable that, without jack-rabbiting its prices unfairly or unduly, it now vies with the big fellows in more respects than simply value for money. Delightfully pleasant little dining room, bar, and lounges, all tastefull and immaculate; 40 small, spotless, well executed bedrooms and 22 baths; location bordering the action; savory snacks; parking garage. Its greatest asset is the extraordinary friendly, personalized welcome and care which warm-hearted Gianni (Johnny) DeLuca and his effervescent wife Shirley extend with such grace and sincerity. Tops in its class.

The graceful **Carriage** perhaps cruises more smoothly than any house of its class in the capital. This little-publicized preserve at the foot of the Spanish Steps—literally a few steps from Rome's most ultrafashionable shopping street, Via Condotti—was launched in 1970. Antiques, chandeliers, mirrors, brocades, and thick carpets adorn its foyer-style lobby, ornate salon, and TV lounge. This minicandidate has no restaurant and almost no other public amenities. However, its irreverent bar was formerly an alter in a seventeenth-century Sicilian church, and 2 panels on the wall come from an eighteenth-century library. All of the 25 sweetly appointed bedrooms come with bath, telephone, radio, floral wallpaper, combination bed-table-bar wagons, and curious triangularly shaped corner wardrobes. Fuchsia-tone #36 wins our prize among our twins, while rooftop #47, with its wraparound terrace, is a splendid single for the price. Your most powerful yearn here—stronger in daylight than in night—would probably be for sssssoundproofing. Proprietor-Manager Clemete Giuili and his English-speaking son, Elio, have instilled in their hard-working staff the same kindness with which they greet every guest. We tip our hat to this gentleman-hotellier, for his Carriage gives a welcome lift to many a weary wayfarer.

The **President**, near St. John Lateran Basilica, has steered a reasonable platform to its group-minded electorate. Diverting La Hacienda restaurant with colorful woven tablecloths, Andalusian paintings, Tiffany-style lamps, and a nibble nook devoted to authentic Castilian pizza; woody bar; colonial breakfast room; 170 bedchambers, 50% with bath, 50% with shower; 100% air-conditioned; 5-channel radio; attractive but somewhat spindly furniture. Slightly higher scale than elsewhere, but a fair reward if the platoons of Northern European package troops haven't secured the high ground.

The **Forum**, named for the Imperial Forum which it overlooks, is tucked into a small restored *palazzo*. Intimate, pleasant, wall-to-wall carpeted lobby; eighteenth-century décor; fully air-conditioned; double windows for sssssssilence; tasteful little roof-garden restaurant; interior dining salon for rain-outs; agreeably furnished bedchambers. Very appealing, but its eensie-weensie rooms and bathrooms and its offbeat location seem serious detractions to all but midget archaeologists.

The **Cardinal** began life circa A.D. 1400; recently it was renovated to the tune of $3,000,000. You'll find a mixture of comfort, color, and nitpicking drawbacks (such as unsoundproofed streetside units), but overall it is a fair bet for the outlay.

The **Caesar Augustus**, out near the site of Olympic Village, has a lovely roof garden which offers dining, dancing, and bar, with swimming pool in a raised segment directly above—and that's as far as its current assets go, in our opinion. It has given itself over almost entirely to block bookings nowadays. Not worth the 20-minute taxi journey either, we think.

To us the '72-vintage **Roma-St. Peter's Holiday Inn Hotel**, despite its half-hearted regional style splashes here and there, looks, sounds, and smells typical of just about any of the larger Holiday Inns anywhere in America. In general we'd call it as Italian as Mom's apple pie; when we look at its facilities and guests, are we in Rome or Chicago or Sioux City or Topeka or where? Its hillside address on the access road to Fiumicino International Airport carries a modest scenic advantage and a major practical disadvantage. While its view is pleasant but not half what we'd hoped to find, it is so far from the center through heavy traffic that we think of this establishment as being hell-and-gone in the outskirts—even though the brochure misleadingly claims that it's a 10 minute journey. (Could this figure have been based on driving conditions at midnight?) Scads of U.S. travelers abroad who are most comfortable in stereotyped lodgings totally familier to them find it pleasing. Others, including us, swear by the old maxim, "When in Rome, do as the Romans do."

A sister establishment, the **Parco dei Medici Roma-Aero Holiday Inn Hotel**, opened in '76 halfway along the airport road 7 miles from the city center and 7 miles from Fiumicino. It is sited on a desolate plain seemingly in the middle of nowhere—nowhere yet, but a massive business-apartment complex has started construction around it. Ugly concrete edifice containing bedrooms plus 1-story projection at ground level with entrance, c-o-l-d lobby, reasonably pleasant bar and cheerful dining room combining cafeteria and table service; menu heavily Italian but with a few items such as hamburger ($2.34) and banana split ($1.40); piped music endlessly in public areas; 2 attractive pools; tennis courts; convention facilities. Total of 337 standard doubles and 7 suites; habitations far more tasteful than in U.S. counterparts; ice and shoe shining machines on each floor. The same double-hellacious problem exists here: Should the client use a hideously expensive taxi or depend on the hourly shuttle bus to town and the terminus? Even if the guests have their own car, who in their right minds would want to brave the traffic nightmare in the metropolis? As far as we are concerned, here is one of the least desirable hostelries in the region in which we would ever stay, because its God-forsaken location is so inconvenient.

For those who look for extra value for less money, we recommend the **Massimo d'Azeglio**, now the number two of the Bettoja chain. Millions of lire were spent in a cellar-to-roof rebuilding and refurbishing project; this massive old-timer was torn apart and completely redesigned. All 300 good but unfancy rooms with private baths or showers; 100% air-conditioned; double windows to sssssssh street exposures, but some facets still noisy; modernized lobby; bar-ette; quiet, cozy, attractive, spiced-up dining room, with cuisine which is just plain *terrific* (top, top quality for decent prices). For category and tariffs, we just don't know anything in this city that can better it.

The 60-room **Eliseo** is located just off the top of via Veneto. Small entrance lobby; adjoining bar; expanded roof-garden restaurant; copper-sheathed rôtisserie. Clean but dreary, in our view; all narrow-guage units with bath and peignoir; air conditioning on request; some accommodations with small individual balconies. Okay, provided you draw one of the prime units rather than the several mother-in-law rooms. This same company operates the **Park**, a less expensive, 30-room-and-bath establishment in Parioli. Though quite a distance from the doin's, there's ample parking space for motorists, free bus service to town (the Eliseo's doorstep, to be exact), and the added bonus that all bedchambers face on a sleepy private garden. Happy for money-conscious tranquillity seekers.

The buff-colored, 250-room **Visconti Palace** provides comfortable modernistic shelter, trim uplifting décor, 2 restaurants, a roof garden (gone to seed on our visit) and an overall mien that would seem to attract groups. (Their rates certainly favor this trade.) Basically, we liked it. **Villa Pamphili**, about the same size, has a location convenient to the Vatican; otherwise it is too far out of the shopping center to suit us. Huge pool; 2 tennis courts; terrace dining plus main restaurant; fair amenities. **Midas Palace**, another contemporary of the 1975 crop, is about ⅓rd larger but similar in concept since the same firm also designed the Pamphili. It, too, boasts a large swimming pool. Not bad if you prefer lounging to gadflying around the town. Many groups.

The restyled, air-chilled **Boston**, almost in the shade of the Borghese bowers, is a mixture of Beacon Hill nabobery and baked-bean basics. Seventh-floor units with terraces, the aristocrats of the Back Bay Society; other accommodations so stark that iced codfish cartons would seem warm to us by comparison; interior dining room; woody bar. Overpriced, in our judgment, for its poorer bedchambers, but a fair value for the better nests. Your pick of the lock will be the key to the city in this Boston.

The **Ritz**, a flatiron-shape structure in the Parioli district, conscientiously tries to live up to its name. Cacophonous location but corner-to-cranny air conditioning hushing the din; walnut-paneled lobby; American bar; well-executed Louis XV furnishings; Louis XVI à la carte restaurant in old rose and mellow green; Tiffany Salon used by groups and diners from the adjoining

Sporting Hotel; beauty parlor and barbershop. Most accommodations large, distinctive, and peaceful, with ample closet space; a few such as #214 and #215 impossibly noisy; 6th-floor suites with private balcony; medium rates. If you're given a bad room, you're likely to share the angry evaluation of 2 Chattanooga, Tenn., VIPs that this house is "a bomb"; if you aren't perhaps you might find it agreeable but not outstanding.

The nearby **Residence Palace** is continuing to recover under the resident doctoring of Manager Raimondo Secco. The sanitation and maintenance standards have soared; more sparkle glitters hither and yon; air conditioning has been installed. While suggestions of skimpiness still prevail, this one is now quite recommendable if you prefer a suburban address.

Napoleon, a 10-minute walk from the station, has a piazza location in full view of a public market. All 100 units with bath or shower and "Massage Boy" bed vibrators; about half with radio; 40 singles; 2 tiny suites per floor; full air conditioning; tasteful traditional décor. Pleasant, if you don't mind the mélange of nationalities shepherded by Mr. Cook.

The **Michelangelo**, a few steps from the Basilica of St. Peter and the Vatican border, offers a fading modern tone and an ultra-efficiency motif. Scuff marks wherever we peeped; 100% artificially cooled; 200 rooms with dark "interior" full baths or showers; many chambers with floor-length glass doors or windows, but 50% with individual balconies; no spreads on beds; linoleum floors; the lobby and the stark, abstract-style restaurant have all the intimacy of Orwell's 1984. To us, it just barely passes muster for its official Category I.

The **Commodore** boasts 70 bedrooms with bath or shower, bright and clean appointments, a helpful staff kindling a friendly atmosphere, and a central setting. Year-round restaurant; air conditioning; 8 units with small balconies, 5 with sitting rooms, 23 singles; decent baths; quality furnishings; demipension not demanded. We like #608 as a cozy nest. Pleasant as a midtown haven.

The **Savoia**, also purchased by the Grand Metropolitan group (see the de la Ville above) recently was given a partial overhaul, but the results still leave us ice-ice-cold. Even the once-popular "Pub" now seems threadbare and shabby to us. Despite its fine location bordering via Veneto, we turn thumbs down.

The **Claridge**, on a tramline in the Parioli district, offers 200 air-conditioned, wallpapered rooms, all with bath or shower; small, rugless, severely modern décor that seems a bit pinchpenny in its rendition; high ratio of tiny individual terraces; chipper dining salon with patio for outdoor ruminations; efficient and friendly concierge and reception staffs; about 15 minutes from the center. Pretty good, despite the increasing aura of commercialism we detected.

The **Metropole** is another semifrigid lady to us. Air conditioning and double windows throughout; modern, plastic-chaired lobby, about as sterile as the inside of a Band-Aid box; lounge music nightly to raise the BTUs; 285 clean, uninspired rooms, in which you will know you're a stranger; monotonous bare floors broken only by tiny bedside rugs; functional, institutional dining room. To its official First-class rating, we'd still say ho-hum.

La Residenza, a few steps off the via Veneto at via Emilia 22, is a 3-star "discovery." It has only 27 rooms, most with bath but all with quiet home-spun charm; #25, #35, #51, and #55 are all sweet havens. Dining room closed in favor of snack service; restaurant with street entrance possibly on the drawing boards now; off-lobby bar; extra-kind Concierge Gustavo; Manager Maisano who is trying hard. Here's a darned good decently priced stop, with one of the most convenient (and even quiet!) locations in the Eternal City.

The **Panama** is okay now but it soon may require redredging to remove the silt of bygone years. Also tranquil and also as cozy as the back seat of a Fiat; colorful lobby; attractive restaurant, bar, and downstairs grill; parking area plus a small garage; 42 small, zestless rooms and 40 baths or showers, most overlooking a shady little garden; #101 the largest double; service unusually good for its informal style.

The **San Giorgio**, number 3 in the Bettoja Group, underwent exhaustive renovations; lobby and restaurant connection with the Massimo d'Azeglio; 200 rooms with baths, 25% of which are fresh; air-conditioned throughout, with double windows for quiet; 2 modern automatic elevators; bar with handsome Roman murals; lovely breakfast nook; all immaculate, and all modestly but amply furnished. Here's an excellent midtowner that has come up in price as it has risen in value.

The 60-unit **Lloyd** has a handsome exterior with orange-awning trim, a pleasant, amiable atmosphere, and an efficient English-speaking concierge. Small lobby with adjoining bar and balconette; restaurant now closed; most bedchambers large, but many lack warm, woman-touched décor; bath or shower with most rooms; some of the marble flooring is badly chipped. Worthy for lire-minded wanderers.

The refitted, fully air-conditioned **Sporting**, behind the Ritz (which owns it), has a Kelly-green steel-and-glass shell outside—and a similar coolness inside. Fresh entrance, lobby, streetfront restaurant; vitally needed garage; all 195 thimble-size bed-cells come with ultracramped bath or shower. Mostly for low-spending tour packs from Bremen to Brest.

The **Regina Carlton**, with its superb via Veneto address, was undergoing a refresher course in innkeeping and a total renovation on our latest tour. Hence, we cannot predict what will appear by the time of your visit. But the convenience of that location—wow!

Tiziano, former palace of Cardinal Pacelli (Pope Pius XII), has a noisy location and a mixed bag of airline-terminal and traditional trappings. Beautiful ancient stairwell; much needed new silver-and-crystal décor in lobby; some updatings; in general, furnishings not to our taste—and that would include those schoolhouse water fountains in the hallways; 52 high-ceiling units, almost all with bath or shower. If sleep comes hard, we'd advise an inside accommodation. Adequate.

The **Degli Aranci**, in a quiet residential district, is now in full bloom. Lovely dining terrace suspended in an orange bower; vague plans for converting a stable into a rustic restaurant; improved lobby and bars; 47 rooms with 80% bath count. The better accommodations can be plucked with private balconies for the same price as the lesser ones. Young, dynamic Manager

Franco Apruzzese is doing a first-rate job in making this little tree a pick of the orchard. Better and better.

The **Coliseum**, in the same tariff range, boasts a lovely lobby, slick-rustic lounge, a handsome breakfast corner, and 50 bedrooms with shower; the units are decorated in Castilian moods; each seems smaller than a Spanish fly. We fear space is so limited you might have to leave your extra socks or nighties downstairs. In addition, too many reports about its "surly, shabby service" (to quote their essence) and its "bus-tour mob scenes" have spoiled our enthusiasm. Perhaps its association with the Tiziano will bring more savvy administrative control—or perhaps it won't. Let's wait and see.

The **Giulio Cesare** provides a splendid view of the Vatican and the Borghese from its roof garden. Owner-Manager Vincent Pandolfi has panned out handsome salons, and many bedchambers that might seem frilly to some trippers. Not bad, however, for anyone whose tastes run to the delicate.

Anglo-Americano winks hello with an electric-eye door. Lobby with midnight-blue, textiled walls, plus lots of leather and wood. Upstairs the bedchambers and baths are so narrow that we'd bet you'd find it easier to squeeze between the hyphen in its name. Not for sturdy-framed Anglos or muscular Americanos, on our physiological scales.

The **Columbus**, in the shadow of St. Peter's and Vatican-owned, was once a convent. Its 115 rooms, 60 with bath or shower, are painfully impersonal, with furnishings that amplify their sterility; in doubles we prefer #345 or #221. Well maintained; a favorite journey's end for religious pilgrimages or tours from all over the world. For the ecclesiastically inclined only.

The **Majestic**, on via Veneto, comes up with a charming outdoor terrace for summer meals. But inside, the beauty fades. Hopes still high to add a new floor; 105 units with private bath (14 singles without); those ending in "20" featuring cozy bay-type balcony; clean but darkish atmosphere; puffy old chairs; similar clientele; air conditioning on request. Not for the young-at-heart.

The **Atlantico**, joined to the aforementioned Mediterraneo, has the advantages of Bettoja administration, full air conditioning, and a kindly staff. Its decorative features and general ambiance, however, are geared more to the European guest than to the Yankee Doodler.

The classic **Grande Albergo Plaza**, on the busy Corso (around the corner from the deluxe shopping oases of via Condotti), has changed only a whit, structurally or in décor, since it opened more than a century ago. Heavily patronized by the Italian "Establishment," with recent invasions by American tour groups; adequate maintenance; wall-to-wall air conditioning; 240 rooms and 200 private baths. We'd call it intriguing for some but loathsome for others. This one must be on you.

Mondial, ia block from the Commodore, has a chilly modernistic lobby, air conditioning in its restaurant and in a scattering of bedchambers, and an overall cast of stark functionality. The big exception to this motif is its warmhearted and ingratiating concierge. Sparkling clean and well maintained; dining block with fish-and-chicks tilework; 76 ample-size rooms, most with bath or shower; nail down an outside room. Okay but austere.

Up in the Parioli district, the **Parioli** provides 98 units, ⅔rds of them with private bath and fair but not special amenities. The **Hermitage** has an unlived-in feeling; 46 singles, 35 doubles, and 19 suites, all with private bath and air conditioning. It's spacious enough, but the violent color contrasts of flaming roses and poisonous cretonnes are eye-racking; heavy, stiff furniture; poorly engineered illumination; so amateurishly executed throughout that it isn't for us, despite the wondrous view from the top floors. One ameliorating gimmick is the free self-drive service in a bantam Fiat for any guest who signs the demipension pledge, with a radial limit of 18 miles from Rome proper and a daily allowance of 30 miles. The **Garden Roxy**, with nice terraces and an open-air restaurant, is otherwise going to seed, in our estimation; still on the Roxies this year. The **Fleming** is too remote for most holidaymakers; nevertheless it's constructing 2 floors and soon will have a capacity of 450; pool, air conditioning, and reportedly flavorful fare. The **Hotel dei Congressi**, near the World Exhibition, is used for—you guessed it—congresses.

Other Roman recommendations? The Bettoja-owned **Nord** tops this list with air-conditioned public rooms, a 70% bath count, and soothing tariffs that are attracting additional new flocks of dollarwise North American sparrows. **Palatino**, on the other wing, asks golden goose eggs for 213 roosts which seem to us to be furnished in Modern Mediocre. Groups galore. **Hotel Medici** (via Flavia 96) appeals in all ways but location. **Universo** comes on big, cold, and functional, while the **Moderno** go-goes traditional, noisy, and costly. **Rivoli** is routine. **Villa delle Rose** literally is a thorn in this traveler's side. **Minerva** to us seems outrageously overpriced for her favors.

Pensions? **Orsini** (via Virginio Orsini 4) leads this budget category. Quiet setting; immaculate garden and parking area; cared for care-essingly by the Mainoldis. **Home in Rome** (via Corsica 4) offers 14 rooms and half that number of baths on 2 clean floors of an apartment house. **Texas** (via Firenze 47) dispenses Lone Star-sized comforts at Rhode Island rates, including flavorful fare and magnificent martinis. *Reserve well in advance for any of these.* **Villa Le Terrazze** and **Santa Elisabetta** don't impress us at all. **Bellavista Milton** can never be *Paradise Regained. Fielding's Low-Cost Europe* lists dozens more.

Motorists? **Motel AGIP**, actually a 272-bed hotel 8 miles out on the via Aurelia, wins our rally as one of the most impressive operations of its type on the Continent. You also can place your money on **Raganelli**, about 500 yards away, and on the **Consul**, along the same route. **Béla Motel**, 10 miles out on via Cassia, has a pool, restaurant, bar, and 40 adequate units that are well priced for their value.

Villa Florio, a converted private mansion near the Frascati–Grottaferrata junction (perhaps 40 minutes out), used to be highly fashionable for country dining. Twenty tile-floored, cretonney rooms are also offered to travelers in search of serenity. Swimming pool; citified-rustic. Now the clientele is disturbingly mixed and the prices seem too high for what it offers.

Private car with interpreter-driver in Rome? Our foremost treasure in this field for many happy years has been an ever-faithful, ever-alert, ever-warm friend and factotum, **Dino Presciutti**, who for more than 2 decades has devotedly served Angelo Bettoja, perdurable president of the Rome Hotel

Association and proprietor of the famous Bettoja hotel chain, and his illustrious late father before him as the number-one escort and courier for their VIP guests. A range of Mercedes lead off his sizable stable. He personally or his associates may be engaged by you *well ahead of time* for airport transfers, ½-day, full-day, or longer city sightseeing or shopping, or private excursions to any point in Western Europe, the U.K., and Ireland. You may write to him c/o the Hotel Mediterraneo or telephone to him there or at his home (557–4367). His English is impeccable, his manner is gentle, and his driving is superb. We adore him.

San Remo, which we haven't rechecked for too long a lacuna, has become hotel poor. Unlike its vigorously competitive neighbors along the French Riviera, it has been hobbling along on its former glories. Now vast area revampings are in the works, including transposition of the railway line plus construction of a 4-mile seafront promenade and a private yacht harbor. The century-old **Royal**, queen of the resort, offers comfort but not luxury. Lovely vista with terraces, flower beds, tables, and pool marching down toward the sea; casino, opera, 18-hole golf course, Tennis Club, Yacht Club, Riding School, and water skiing within easy reach. Annual renovation quota of a mere 16 to 20 rooms; 15 suites and 130 bedchambers, nearly all with handsome marble baths (those dozens of corridor cupboards disguise the expanded plumbing facilities); the older accommodations are preferred by us here, since the newer ones are furnished in Italian-modern that is skimpy and garish. The **Savoia** now ranks as a *very* poor second. Grubby, spare furnishings for the price and category; small pool; North European tours rush in where others may fear to tread; closed October and November. In First-class, the **Miramare** commands a viewful seaside and palm-garden domain. Some units even better than some Deluxe nests, at a frond of the price; 70 rooms, including its *dépendance* in the greenery; recommendable kitchen; extra-cordial staff; closed end-September to December 20. Very good for the outlay. The imposing white-faced **Astoria**, across the avenue from the water, is less tasteful in décor; singles are the better bets here. The **Londra**, pick of many quick-rich Italians, displayed to our eyes gaudy flamboyance coupled with broken walls, cracked baseboards, and furniture suggestive of a hoochy-cooch act in a 2-bit flesh parlor. Not our taste—at least, in a hotel. The **Residence** we can live without. Entrance through the street-level garage; not much. **Grand Hotel des Anglais** was renewed, but we're still not sold on it. The central **Europa** is clean, commercial, and nice for what it is—which is "adequate." Here is a careful operation by an old-fashioned hotelier who knows his trade. The bright-white **Victoria-Roma** is fairly appealing; there is easy parking in front. The **Park** is not recommended. **Garisanda** is a well-sited pension. We'd far rather push along to the **Grand del Mare** near *Bordighera* (see below) than to stay in this withering resort. Otherwise, on Cape Nero, between *San Remo* and *Ospedaletti*, the very modern **Rocce del Capo** has another beautiful view and another swimming pool; private beach, nightclub, and restaurant; very Italian resorty in tone, with possibilities of so-so fun in season.

Santa Margherita's leading hoteliers are walloping each other purple in the scramble for first-place honors—but this is one shindy where our shillelagh stays peacefully with Grandma. For Classic Conservatives, the **Imperiale** is in a state of flux. Currently it offers a rococo turn-of-the-century building, a lushly refurbished décor in the Grand Tradition, a private park and gardens, a vista of Tigullio Bay, an open-air restaurant, a courteous staff. For Hilton buffs, the **Park Hotel Suisse** has arresting angular architecture of the ultramodern school, self-control air conditioning, a twisted-torso-shape seawater pool, and electric-bright color contrasts throughout; 75 smallish rooms, all with bath or shower; bay view and quiet hillside situation; interior and alfresco dining or imbibing; charcoal grill; you'll either like it or loathe it, depending upon your receptivity to its progressive ambiance. For Middle Grounders, the **Miramare**, on the beach, is a middle-age structure which has been modernized in a pleasant way under the guiding hand of Manager Paolo Bisconi, an alumnus of both London's Savoy and Florence's Villa Medici. Traditional tone retained but brightened; excellent baths in expensive *imported* opaline marble (why this was done in marble-rich Italy we'll never comprehend—but they are lovely); gardenside quietest in summer (important, since there's no air conditioning). Charming, intimate Shangrila winter nightclub, plus the waterside Barracuda for summer-izations; our recent meal here again was one of the finest of our Italian circuit—*but* one of the most expensive. Getting better and better. At half the outlay, the **Continental** cops all honors as one of the select bargain paradises along this stretch of coast. Wonderful perch nesting cozily in a park of southerly-exposed flora and palm; romantic private beach; open terrace for breakfast and dinner; simple dining room; 64 good-size bedchambers, including the expanded annex, all with private bath and seafront balcony. Operative year round—and, as we have commented, one of the best buys in the region. The Continental-owned **Regina Elena** is almost as good, but it is more modern and it lacks the marvelous situation of the Continental. So clean and bright that our eyes sparkled the remainder of the day after inspecting it; neat, and colorful, and trim in every aspect; glass-lined dining room under a geodesic dome; double-plate glass doors on all bedroom balconies; excellent management by the reigning Ciana family. Superb for the category. The **Laurin**, down a notch, operates under the Park Suisse aegis. It has been to the beauty parlor and now twinkles. The **Metropole**, while sound in basic amenities, is better geared to European tastes than to our own. Plank-wood floors and throw rugs; 50% bath ratio; #45 provides the nicest vista. Fair. **La Vela** ("The Sail") continues its well-deserved popularity. The **Tiguillio**, inside the city, is okay for budgeteers or for seaside vacationers who hate the sea.

Siena's prime offerings nestle in the surrounding hills. The **Park**, 1½-miles out, is a landed estate beautifully remodeled by the English-based Falcon Inn organization which reputedly spent almost $2,000,000 in updatings here recently. New pool, plumbing, and air conditioning; telephone system modernized and Telex added; many more freshets still to come from young, zealous Manager Mario Pescini. Numerous notables have basked in its sixteenth-century furnishings and quiet mien; capacity of 58 rooms, all with private bath; closed in winter. Glorious garden, private chapel, lift; tennis courts; terrace-restaurant; brisk climate; central heating. Tranquillizing and very recommendable indeed. The **Villa Scacciapensieri** ("Scatter Your Cares"), a careless mile or more from the center, has been transformed into a hostelry with 19 units in the Villa, 9 in the Villino, and 2 in the poolside Villetta; all accommodations are regaled with loving attention to detail; the dining room reflects the devotion to cuisine and wines of Francesco Pallasini, a connoisseur of heroic stature. (He conducts twice-weekly wine seminars in 4 languages here.) A truly international and discriminating clientele returns with regularity to this country estate. One good reason: Miss Nardi, the owner and a gracious hostess for more than 4 decades, shudders at the mention of mass tourism. She also shutters it tightly when winter winds blow. Enchanting. How we yearn to go back! The **Garden**, in Second-class, won our heart with its magnificent terrace view over the entire city. The spacious grounds are an asset for travelers with children. Just at the fringe of the old section, you'll find the dignified **Palazzo Ravizza**, Pian dei Mantellini 34. Flavorful ambiance punctuated by bookshelves, mounted guns, a concert grand, and similar touches; tearoom-bar that huddles cozily around an enormous fireplace; attractive wooden stools and chairs; 28 tastefully decorated rooms, 10 with bath; #20 is a quaint apartment overlooking the posies, with its own fireplace; demipension compulsory. Handily managed by Sig. DeSanti. The **Excelsior** has 140 rooms and 120 baths—plus, when we inspected it too far back, such poor maintenance that we couldn't recommend it. Improved? The **Continental** was icy-cold and equally uninspired, in our opinion. The **Minerva** is commercial. The 70-room **Moderno**, in the center, is Second-class; it was only so-so.

In **Sorrento** you will find Manager Osvaldo Coppola of **Acampora Travel**, a CIT affiliate, an extraordinarily resourceful and competent lifesaver in solving any lodgings or similar problems which might arise to plague you. He's our answer man in this town. The resort's most renowned stop is the antique, creaky **Excelsior Vittoria**, which stays open year-round. Its Old World furnishings are so quaint they're almost a Bemelmans caricature—but the staff are warm human beings instead of unsmiling robots. Ideal situation; parkland setting with large pool; relaxed atmosphere; excellent food; professional guidance by Ugo Fiorentino, who's a tiptop leader in his field. We enjoyed our latest stay and we think you will like this stop, too. The **Tramontano**, now the largest in Sorrento, creaked up to the big leagues a while back with some renovations. Now, alas, we think it's again fusty, musty, and a bit crusty. Forests of potted plants reminiscent of a Sidney Greenstreet set; dank corridors; frosted-glass doors; mix-and-match furniture; wheezing Model-T-outmoded radiators; full bath count; beach elevator; lackluster cuisine on our recent sampling. Overall, we'd say pretty poor. The **Parco dei Principi** is by the sands, with its entrance at the end of a verdant grove. Perfect setting; air conditioning; 105 good-size rooms with private baths and terraces. The saddening thing here is the pinchpenny attitude displayed in its clashy Formica-clad furnishings, in its frequent absence of pictures, in its stagnant-looking swimming pool on our look, and in its stark, Woolworthy décor. If this company would throw out the second-rate carpentry and replace it with what this house deserves—which it might never receive, since it is in the same chain as Rome's Parco dei Principi—here could be one of the most stylish leaders in the region. The **Royal**, proudly refitted expensively by Proprietor Renato Scarpato and Manager Antonino Esposito, has been taking giant strides—especially in its public sectors. The swimming pool and gardens are breathtaking. Attractive restaurant; 2 bars; bedchambers ranging from homey-plain to plain-period. Despite the generous infusions of lira, somehow the living quarters here lack heart, in our opinion—a commodity that money can't buy. The **Europa Palace** impressed us this time as sliding. Oldish entrance and lounge; beach 140 feet down by elevator, with snack bar and sun chairs; large accommodations and baths. Ho-hum. The **President**, governing on a pine-dotted hill overlooking the town, has credentials which include a heavily marbled rotunda lobby, a long lounge warmed by intricate tilework and Persian-style rugs, a sedate dining room adjoining an outside terrace, a woody bar in the mod mode, and a solarium-pool complex. As with the other late candidates in its ruling class, this one has gone on record as favoring classically modern furniture in its upstairs precincts, a bath in every room, and balconies with panoramas of Vesuvius, Ischia, and the azure Tyrrhenian Sea which might catch your breath. We vote a resounding "Yes." The arch-ridden **Hermitage**, far above the town on a pine-draped slope, is aptly named. This haven is about 15 minutes from the action. As quiet as a Trappist abbey; glorious kidney-shape pool, with a goiter-shape appendage for kiddies immediately adjoining; provincial-style dining room with a belt of windows overlooking the bay, the town, and the surrounding mountains; nonascetic furnishings that are also not very aesthetic; bath and spacious terrace with every accommodation. A supersilent retreat. Back in town, the 125-room, fully-balconied **Cesare Augusto** is 100 yards behind piazza Tasso; it's a beauty for modern metropolitan tastes rather than for resort-sort amenities. Kindhearted direction by Sig. Apreda; equally professional and conscientious staff; enormous dining salon with mediocre cookery; woody, almost Scandinavian, Taverna dei Mulini; ice-cool bar. Rooftop pool, plus solarium with snack service, with evening dancing on occasion and a sweeping command of some of the world's most enchanting real estate. Comfortable rooms with ceramic-tile floors; simple, clean-lined, fresh-looking trappings. Bid for the 4th or 5th floors, the only ones high enough for a sea view. Excellent, if you don't insist on a waterfront address. The flamingo-colored **Ambasciatori** enfolds 105 nests perched on a cliff over its own stretch of sand. Heavily wooded and tiled lobby in avocado; matching bar with sloping ceiling; airy seaview dining room with gleaming marble floor; lush enclosed garden; rippling pool; excellent maintenance throughout; cheerfully chirping desk flock. While all of the bedchambers are reasonably proportioned, their bathrooms are almost absurdly cramped; all sport balconies, with the 40% bordering the briny the most choice. Recommended. The **De La Ville** is steered by the Ambasciatori. Incongruously dull motor-lodge facade; spritely split-level lobby dappled with marble, wood, and foliage; green-tiled lounge with modish sink-in chairs and waffled ceiling; adjoining bar in the same theme; somewhat elegant restaurant with sconces set on creamy columns; sun terrace overlooking the Bay of Naples and the parent house 150 yards distant; rectangular pool with circular kiddie nook; densely planted flora out back. All 100 units come with bath or shower; most wear balconies; the front ones peep at the deep. A welcome Category I contender. The **Riviera**, another First-class wave watcher with an elevator to the beach, entered the scene in '69. Bleached plantation-like abode; spacious lobby and lounge festooned with silver ceiling fixtures and military-postured furniture; dining room warmed with original artwork; diminutive imbibery flanking an alfresco terrace; so-called VIP nightclub-discothèque; seawater swimmery. All cubicles offer full piping and balconies; all are stuffed with straitlaced accouterments; the loners provide more space per face than do the duos. We're told that it's open all year to tour traffic. The **Carlton** makes its bid with a tan and brown restaurant; chrome-a-somed bar; swimming pool; total of 70 boxes reachable via a closet-size elevator; pink candy-striped spreads on nonresiliant beds; bathrooms contusive for big-boned North Americans. In neighboring *Santagata*, the **Continental** is petaled with approximately the same level of inn-or-out facilities. The **Aminta**, on the "Green Ribbon Road," has a country mien. Enchanting locale deep in Neapolitan vineyards; modern Italianate lobby; inviting pool and sun terraces; attractive dining room with viewful fresh-air terrace; sparkling, shining, first-rate maintenance. All rooms and baths quite small; private balconies; furnishings adequate but not luxurious; reasonable rates. A restful haven for the world-weary. Don't bother with the nearby **Metropole**. **La Dania** is our favorite low-cost entry; ask for Signora Delizza. The remainder, in descending order, are the **Plaza** (dead center, with no view), **Regina** (now with restaurant; a favorite among Scandinavians), **Caravel** (70 rooms; swimming pool in garden; caters heavily to package tours from northern Europe), and **Minerva** (formerly a pension; good cookery in its restaurant; good splashing in its penthouse pool). Both the midtown **Michelangelo** and the neighboring **Flora** provide excellent shelter for moderate tariffs. The former seems more luxurious; the latter boasts a rooftop pool and sundeck. Alternates in this category might include the **Bellevue Syrene** and the more modest **Britannia**. The **Bristol** is a solid Second-class buy. Best position of all, with a terrific scenic scope; handsome floors made with local ceramics; cuisine extra-fine for the category; not plush in any sense, but the money's worth for any budgeteer. Finally, nestling on a mountainside 7 miles out of Sorrento on the Positano highway near *Meta,* the **Nastro Azzurro** offers 74 tiny rooms with bath or shower, a circular 2-part swimming pool, a thrilling command of the bay, and Second-class tariffs and facilities. Too quiet and too isolated for the average U.S. visitor, but sunny and airy for tranquillity seekers who don't mind being vastly outnumbered by Continental sun worshipers.

In *Spoleto*, the Second-class **Dei Duchi** usually has been considered the best. The **Clitunno** near the Teatro Nuovo, and the **Ferrovia** in the lower city, are the only other acceptable choices that we know about since we haven't had time to inspect the 18-room **Clarici Commercio**, a Third-category, tranquil abode with a hanging terrace. We have heard it praised, though. Most culture buffs drive in from other resort digs because this can be one of the hottest hollers in them thar hills.

Taormina leads off with the imposing **San Domenico Palace**, once a huge convent. This spectacular sixteenth-century landmark (a hotel since 1880) is perched on the rim of a 1000-foot cliff. Long, white-tiled pool decanted 3 terraces down into the flower-decked garden; Romanesque outdoor bar plus a cluster of changing cabins; fully air-conditioned; almost every suite, bed-chamber, and bath refurbished in excellent taste, each different from the next. Spacious rooms with magnificent vistas; extraordinarily fine Sassari tilework and 1984-style fixtures in most baths. General Manager Fredi Martini, who had done such a fine job of blowing the cobwebs from this once neglected relic, also has perked up the staff in every department. His Neapolitan wife, Mina, incidentally, is responsible for the magnificent gardens here. This remains indisputably the leading house on the island. The **Timèo**, which also nestles in a viewful position, is the only hotel within the town area. Old folks are so fond of this old-timer it is almost always full. Partial recent redecorating has brightened the dining room and bar while retaining a polished Victorian aura elsewhere. In sharp contrast to our fare cited directly above, our recent meal was superb, as was the service by cordial Maître Rocco Bambara and his gracious staff. Many chambers with flowered terraces overlooking (under-looking?) Mt. Etna; venerable antiques including many of the guests. A quiet, mannered bastion for its loyalists, where newcomers are also welcome. Open the year around.

The **Capotaormina** (its mouthful word springs from the cape of the same name), a large, crescent-shape structure, perches 150 feet high along the edge of the most advanced promontory on the coast, which blesses it with a sweep of the most breathtaking seascape of any major hostelry in the region. Totally contemporary design and ambiance; 200 air-conditioned rooms and baths, all but 12 with balcony, dressing-room enclave, and small refrigerator; 2 bars, one adjoining the pool; beauty parlor; boutique; sauna; underground garage for 80 cars and parking space above; convention facilities for 350; special elevator between guest floors and private beach in its own cove. This relatively mammoth entry initially sent earthquake shocks throughout the island, but now the populace stifles its yawns.

The air-conditioned **Diodoro Jolly** is an up-and-coming contender. Eyeful sea-and-volcano vista; 10-minute hike from town; modernistic furnishings; changed management (and, we hope, a new chef as well); facilities for alfresco dining and drinking; 300-seat inner salon with gold carpet, wooden beams, and green velvet chairs; huge swimming pool for summer and winter dipping; sauna; tennis court; all 102 diminutive units with private bath and big balcony; First-class rating for Deluxe physical standards (this commercially oriented chain bought it after it was built); improved service. One of the better links in this chain. Recommended. The **Bristol Park** is older in fashion. Similarly breathtaking panorama from a site that is neither in the village nor at the beach (a car would be an asset, but there's free minibus service to the shore); sprightly dining room with pink napery; pleasant terrace for breakfast and apéritifs; 100% air-conditioned; snail-like elevator. Every accommodation with its own attractive balcony; simply but tastefully furnished; demipension required in season. U.S. wanderbirds usually find this a happy nest. Its warm-hearted family touch is everywhere in evidence. The **Excelsior Palace** has been renewed to a degree, and that degree is enhanced because of air conditioning. In some respects nicer than the B-P; fair kitchen with deft service (no outdoor dining, sad to say); very noisy in the early morn when motorists and buses are pulling out. Still a mixed bag. The **Miramare**, pleasantly set at the outer limits, has been expanded; 60 tastelessly decorated rooms, nearly all with private bath; very clean; heated swimming pool; good food for the price; a summer house; somewhat under par for its category. If you book here in winter, you might wake up to find your whatsis icicled and navy blue. The **Méditerranée**, in a tranquil urban location, is a solid Second-class candidate. Modern; 70% air-conditioned; rooftop swimming pool; all rooms with bath or shower; most with terrace; good management; panoramic site. Less expensive, naturally. The **Continental**, a few yards away, offers an excellent position, many modern amenities, reportedly good food and service, and extraordinary popularity. No elevator, but full air cooling; 43 units with bath or shower, plus terrace or balcony. Director Renato di Pasquale is a young and personable administrator who keeps his house in good order. We were chilled by the **Imperial Palace**; now it's possibly the fate of the Danas whose tour agency acquired it for them. The year-round **Monte Tauro** vaguely resembles a bunker on its exterior. Top-level reception with outdoor, glassed-in elevator to wisk guests to their rooms on 8 floors below. Eager-to-please staff, many quite youthful; comfortable units with Frigobars, TV, and adequate dimensions. Okay for cliff dwellers. While the 33-room **Villa Paradiso** is officially designated a pension, we feel it offers comforts that few First-class hostelries do in this resort. Whitewashed salon divided by arches and gladdened by foliage; penthouse terrace restaurant; uninspired skilletry; extensive use of wrought iron; most perches with vistas of Mt. Etna, the public gardens, and the hamlet of Giardini. **Villa Riis** has just been totally refurbished. Now open all year. This charmer is well liked by just about everybody. **Villa S. Giorgio**, near the town border and the most tranquil haven in its category, does 10 of its 20 rooms handsomely, but the rest are stark. The industrious management here is doing everything possible to bring it up; a homespun sentiment at the entrance reads "The House of Peace." **Arathena** has 45 fully piped pads, and sits in a slumberful neighborhood. **Pensione Le Terrazze** is a fine old homestead on the Corso; appealing vista; economical; a favorite with junior U.S. diplomats. **Pensione Adele**, near the city hospital and the magnificent Culver Sherill estate, is tastefully accommodating in the style of a private home; some balconies; garage space, too. **Bel Soggiorno**, 7 minutes from the center through the public gardens, has perked up its 20 rooms and 14 baths; one of the most likable staffs in town. The **Sole-Castello**, in Second category, occupies a sensationally dramatic setting up and up and up on a peak overlooking the town, the bay, and the mountains on both sides of the hotel. Modern construction; 80% of accommodations with terrace; handsome dining patio in season; plastic-y furnishings in public rooms, but better taste in bedchambers; 40 units, nearly all with bath or shower. Passable. Down at *Mazzarò Beach*, a lazy 5-minute amble by car, big, Big, B I G things are happening. The **Mazzarò Sea Palace** has swung open its Deluxe portals at a site almost adjoining the funicular terminus (connected to this station by a tunnel). This ultramodern, high-cost entry features a round "superstructure" lounge for 360° pan-o-ramics, a restaurant with tinted glass and white molded tables, and a bar to match. Its 120 bedchambers, accommodating some 200 holidaymakers, are only a pillow's toss from the breakers. They have expansive terraces, quality twin beds, beige carpeting, and adjustable lighting. **Villa Sant' Andrea** is a sparkling anchorage with a light cargo of sea-soned wiles. Lovely garden terrace a tier above water level; dining patio and outdoor bar; 40 homey rooms, all with bath; 7-unit annex; nice clientele; open March to October. Just the retreat for sun-worship, park-strolling, sea-bathing, and lazing up a daydream, with the mainland just in view along the azure horizon. Mighty nice for a tranquil holiday. The Second-class, 43-room **Lido Méditerranée** and the centrally cited, but quiet, 59-unit **Vello d'Oro** are another pair of chicks. Make a last-minute check with your travel agent on this brood, because they promise to chirp prettily. The wide-angled **Holiday Inn**, while comfortable and sumptuously outfitted, seems to us more designed for package groups and congresses than for independent voyagers. Indoor-outdoor swimming facilities plus the Mediterranean itself; private beach; sauna and gym; tennis court; 280 bedchambers, limited in size. A U.S. import if we ever saw one, but still quite nice for those who Buy American. *Other hotels or pensions in the Taormina area are not recommended.*

In *Turin*, the Jolly chain took over and refashioned the famous **Excelsior Grand Hotel Principi di Piemonte**, formerly in the deluxe CIGA stable. Director Sergio Cappetta (who also oversees the Jolly Ambasciatori here) shuttered the restaurant, reduced the services, but freshened the décor. Now a hostelry appropriate for its targeted client—the businessman who wants simple comfort during a brief stay, no frills, Telax, telephones that work, and reasonably fast service. The **Jolly Ambasciatori** seems to function on approximately the same principle and, insofar as its audience is chiefly commercial, it serves its purpose very well indeed. Routine cuisine; TV added to bedchambers; some complaints concerning the beds here. Generally acceptable. The **Majestic**, also functional, inclines its decorative taste to its masculine following. Half its 100 units with air conditioning; streetsider with double-glazed windows; radio, Frigobar, and TV on request. Carefully maintained. The air-conditioned **Turin Palace**, opposite the station, has retained its old-fashioned grandeur in the public sections, but modernized its spacious sleepers in a tasteful and practical style. The arresting **City** is proud of its futuristic architecture—and well it should be, because it is an agreeable combination of comfort and imagination that required courage on the part of the proprietor. Engaging metal structures by Piero Cerato; rouge carpeting; twenty-first-century appointments that are at once soothing and exhilarating. Well done, say we—but *not* for traditionalists. Below these, the **Suisse Terminus** shocks the eye with its glaringly modern façade; regretfully inside we found it drab and charmless. **Grand Fiorina**, while central, certainly did not impress us as grand. **Sitea**? Some halfhearted refreshments, but the clashings of its appurtenances jarred us to our shins. The **Roma** is for emergencies only. If you like the odor of disinfectants, try the **Luxor**, which, incidentally, claims one of the damnedest, chummiest elevators we've just about ever ridden—it slaps the fanny *every* time on ingress and egress. Heaven for masochists. **Grande Ligure** will be shuttered for several seasons to undergo a complete overhauling. **AGIP**, the petroleum interest, has pumped up a sleeping station at the Milan exit of the autostrada. Also away from the city's polluted air, the imposing **Villa Sassi**, 4 miles out on the Genoa approach road, is a stately and tranquil haven for motorists who wish to avoid the industrial hubbub. Only 12 rooms in this 2-century-old mansion overlooking the river; 5-acre park setting; glorious dining room and terraces which are sometimes commandeered by banquet parties; bedchambers pleasant but not outstanding. A favorite hideaway for many let's-get-away-from-it-all Turinesi.

Venice and the *Lido* are the crown jewels of the Adriatic shore.

This city is the headquarters of the famous Grand Hotels of Italy Corporation—CIGA—which owns no less than 8 hotels plus the next-mentioned Palazzo del Giglio apartment complex in this region, in addition to other leaders in Rome, Florence, Milan, Genoa, Naples and Stresa. The Koh-i-noor diamond of the chain is the polished little **Gritti Palace** of Ernest Hemingway fame, just Across the River and Into the Trees from the gondola park. Now back in the skillful hands of our good friend Director Dr. Natale Rusconi, who returned after revitalizing Rome's Grand, this house traditionally has been one of the number one stopping places in the world. First, it is small, gladsome, and almost club-like. Second, nothing has been spared in décor, in staff (roughly 2 employees per guest, and they are extra-cordial and adept), in cuisine (one of the most celebrated chefs on the Continent), or in the attributes of pure luxury. Rooms and apartments on the top floor have been transformed into beautiful "penthouse-studios." The canalside units were later given a puffup; many, incidentally, come with stocked bar-type refrigerators; the entire house, of course, is air-conditioned. If expense is no object, try to reserve Suite #110; it's one of the finest hotel accommodations, in taste and in feeling, that we've seen anywhere. We've carried on a long and devoted love affair with this tiny gem of a hostelry, and are delighted to see that its former chieftain is maintaining all those qualities which have made it a masterpiece of innkeeping in the past.

Almost next door is the gorgeous **Palazzo del Giglio apartment colony** which we've already mentioned. It is an exquisite union of bright, joyful colors, modern comfort, carefully selected antiques, and works of art to complement the whole and create an enchanting homey atmosphere. Just 16 suites in varying sizes to accommodate couples or families or friendly migrants; full air conditioning plus TV, radio, beautifully equipped kitchens— the works. Laundry, maid, and other services available. The cheer, the privacy, the luxury, and the economics of this dandy little enclave make it almost irresistible for travelers who plan to stay a week or more in Venice. Administration by the Gritti people, who are always at the beck or phone-call of their neighboring apartment clients. We love it and recommend it highly to anyone looking for this particular milieu.

The stalwart, blissfully tranquil **Cipriani**, 5 minutes by water from St. Mark's Square, reigns on the island of Giudecca. This is the lifelong dream of Giuseppe Cipriani, founder and for perhaps 4 decades owner of world-famous Harry's Bar (see "Restaurants")—and it has been handsomely realized. His chief of day-to-day operations is Director Giuseppe Cecconi—and these 2 "Joes" are masters of their innkeeping ins-and-outs. Deluxe category; 100 air-conditioned, soundproofed rooms, all with private bath; 4th-floor units best; apartments "A," "B," or "C," all in the same line, with the same awe-inspiring vista, are fit for any twentieth-century doge. Peaceful situation overlooking the Lagoon; large pool (the *only* one at any Venetian hostelry) hugged by 2 arms of an arcade with service facilities, its own kitchen, boutiques, and a hairdressing salon; laundry with 12-hour express service. Chef Guiliano's cuisine is 5-star in every respect; indoor and terrace restaurants, with pension terms *not* required; free motor-launch shuttles, day and night continuously, to St. Mark's for all clients. Closed end of October to early April; lovely in every respect. Very warmly recommended.

The **Danieli Royal Excelsior** is CIGA's larger Deluxe offering, with greater mass appeal. Entirely air-conditioned; roughly 245 rooms in 3 separate structures, coupled by short passageways: The "Palace" building (architecturally gorgeous; double pane windows in front; refreshened décor; renewed public rooms and plumbing; 50 units on the quiet Rio del Vin side revamped and specially made furniture installed), the "New" building (less classic and also appealing; 80 refashioned bedchambers), and the "Danielino" building (more in tune with the conventional American viewpoint; use chiefly by groups; fronts with terrace); TV and radio plus many refrigerators added. Its General Manager is Sig. Alfredo Puricelli, who also runs the Excelsior Lido. Different in concept from the Gritti or the Cipriani, but still fine save for the debits we have outlined.

The Deluxe **Europa e Britannia** offers an extra feature in its sprawling construction; the guest can view the big canal from 4 sides. Beautiful garden restaurant ablossom; sweetly color-conditioned on the outside; fully air-conditioned on the inside. The Swiss-trained manager, Pierre Barrelet, has been assigned an excellent fief in the CIGA empire. Vast changes—all of them highly beneficial; same tariff range for a canalside double or a unit facing the Venetian Court. Now highly recommended.

The **Bauer Grünwald** has taken Beauty Pills. Now it also boasts a houseful of exquisite Medici-style furnishings moved from the former Grand. This significant coup has sparked even further cosmetology throughout the B-G by Manager Luigi Carussio. Ask to see the Shah's bed in #212 (provided the Shah is not in it); units ending in "52" or "53" cast wonderful glances at the canal; 80% of the building is air-conditioned. Public rooms boast a discreetly modern décor melding softly through a rich antique haze; splendid, Grand Canal terrace; roof garden; Czar-opulent Royal suite; ordinary accommodations "inside" and somewhat cramped; clean, very well run, expensive, and— less lively than most.

The **Luna**, Venice's oldest hotel (dating from 1474, but a religious retreat even prior to *that!),* buffed the finishing touches on its 10-year renovation program a while back. Now 100% air-conditioned; waterside bar on tiny canal facing the Royal Garden; 2 automatic elevators; comfortable bedchambers; most baths replete with marble. There are an attractive rose-toned dining room and open terrace in which ½-pension is a *must.* If you can, snag #154 for the view or #107 for its huge balcony with table and chairs. Director Carlo Valensin can be rightfully proud of this zenithing "Moon." Unusually good value.

The freshly restyled **Regina**, adjoining the Europa e Britannia and sharing the same kitchen and talented chef, is also under the administrative CIGA-wing. Smaller than its neighbor, but almost brighter in feeling; new lobby plus skylit salon; pleasant outdoor restaurant crowning the waves by the gondola rank; winter dining room with rejiggered brown-tone bar opposite; uniform standard accommodation; extra-nice terraced nests in #'s 552/554; demipension required for all canal-sited guests. An equitable buy that is glowing with esteem. The **Metropole** boasts an excellent address a few steps away from the ferry landing, facing the Lagoon. Canal entrance for gondolas and water taxis; complete air conditioning; sumptuous interior, a modern adaptation of the classic Venetian style; compact restaurant and American bar; generously outfitted bedchambers, most featuring jazzy blue headboards festooned with a metallic motif resembling a coat of arms. For situation and decoration, this rejuvenated house is loaded with appeal. Its service standards are another story. **Monaco**, now reperked with fresh carpets, multichannel radios, and given a handsome bamboo-toned bar, nestles dockside on the Grand Canal just across the walkway from Harry's Bar. Similar in size to the Regina; prices nearly the same; fully air-conditioned; the Frenchy accommodations with painted furniture best. Not bad at all. **La Fenice** is above the restaurant of the same name, but is not associated with it. Located in the wings of the famous Fenice Theatre. Cozy, elegant lounge with silk wall coverings; beautiful antique furnishings; no restaurant, but a bar 10-seconds away for thirsting Thespians; 63 rooms, most with bath but some of the "sitz" style; striped or pastel sheets to match the color scheme. Nice concierge named Paul Saccoman; low in cost, but high in rewards. Recommended within its Second-class ranking. The **Park,** quietly (sic) situated across from the railway station and city parking garages, has 100 medium-size rooms, the back ones facing Papadopoli Park. We applaud its straightforward comfort, its kind minions, and its homespun hospitality. Special tip: If you can handle your luggage, do not take a water taxi from the station. Instead of crossing the street, walk toward the Park Hotel, which is visible to the right as you exit. Within 3 minutes by foot you will find a public *motoscafo/vaporetto* stop with convenient transportation to all canalside hotels. Difference in price? For a taxi you are likely to shell out at least 7500 lire. The most you will pay by using public transportation is 120 lire—about 14¢. The 69-room-and-bath **Londra** is beginning to show its will to live. The pulse beat is quickening, we are pleased to report. Although we've changed our minds to conclude that the little **Patria Tre Rose** is somewhat less than a honey for the money, Guidesters' opinions are sharply divided on this one. **Cavalletto**, a property of the charming and brilliant Edward M. Masprone, son of the late Rafaele Masprone of the Gritti, has been mightily improved. Public rooms refashioned; 96 units, 85 with bath or shower; annex without private plumbing; commercial, but very worthy for its reasonable tariffs. The **Boston,** near St. Mark's Square, serves breakfast only, which means no forced pension or demipension; inexpensive and solid. **Ala** has 60 chirpy nests; only breakfast is required. Ala be praised! **Carpaccio**, on the Grand Canal, steps forward with a generous helping of flair for its bracket. Large rooms, generally clean; simply furnished; situation excellent; moderate terms; one of the best *quids* for your *quo* in the city. **Pensione Seguso**, fronting the Canale Della Giudecca, bobs up with 50 units, ½ with bath or shower; #23, facing the trees across the water, should double your pleasure. Top value. *Fielding's Low-Cost Europe* lists scads more.

Country living near Venice? The grimly fading **Villa Condulmer** (3 miles from **Mogliano** on the A-27 to V. Vento) is a 250-acre estate set in flat terrain. Big, sparsely furnished halls; 36 antiquated rooms, all with bath or shower; swimming pool lush with tropical greenery. This one is in dire need of a pep-up, in our opinion. If it ever receives same, it could be quite agreeable.

In **Asolo**, about 50 minutes out on the main Venice–Verona highway, you'll find the **Hotel Villa Cipriani**. This town was the celebrated former home of both Eleanora Duse and Robert Browning; the villa itself now belongs to the Guinness family. It is beautifully operated by Sig. Cipriani; 35 rooms all with private bath; 4 Deluxe suites; décor similar to the Venice Cipriani; huge garden; full pension—with à la carte menu! The Cipriani name is its own recommendation; here's a fine stop for lunch or for rest.

In the **Lido**, a few minutes by motorboat from Venice, you'll find the hotel which has made this island a legendary summer resort—the **Excelsior Palace**, guided by Director Alfredo Puricelli. The munificent CIGA war chest has provided a staggering $3,000,000 for revamping. A beach has been built, and it is more beautiful than ever. A pool also is splashing and a waterfront Taverna is sizzling. There are a beach bar and 360 luxury cabanas. The center of the main structure also was reconstructed; it includes bar and kitchen, plus 100 repiped bathrooms. Air conditioning murmurs throughout this 380-room house—but not at night during our visit, darn it. (You can't open the windows either because of the plague of mosquitoes.) The best units, in our opinion, are the cheerfully modernized ones on the ground level and the 5th and 6th floors. Emphasis is being placed on the creation of a vacation haven for the bright, the vigorous, and the Jet Setters of any age (as long as they're young at heart) in a campaign to wipe away its former image as a hermitage for the creaky in body and spirit. **Hotel Quattro Fontane** ("Four Fountains"), oppo-site the Casino, is officially categorized as Second class, but its accommoda-tions (especially in the newer 25-unit wing) are strictly First-class quality. The owner's wife, who is Danish, has contributed her taste to the décor. Tennis; live music; garden; open-air restaurant. *Always full, so reserve in advance.* Good within its league for its service, price, management, and ambiance; recommended. We also are reasonably fond of the 75-room **Villa Mabapa**, believe it or not, a contraction of Mamma, Bambino, and Papa, a reference to the Vianello tribe who run the place. Except for the location, which is far from the casino and other Lido action, this one competes favorably with the Four Fountains. **Grand Hotel des Bains**, perhaps due for revamping soon so check first, is gifted with a warmed seawater pool, 3 tennis courts at its Sporting Club, a discothèque, a bar, and full air conditioning. The rooms when we saw them, however, were still too old-fashioned and uncozy for us. Maintenance, on our visit, was plummeting. The **Adria Urania** and its neigh-boring **Villas—Nora** and **Ada**—are all beautifully managed by Mr. and Mrs. Biasutti. Back-street location, 5 minutes from *vapore* station; fronted by manicured garden; veranda dining; indoor fish restaurant with shells from Kenya and Mexico, nets, and Turkish lamps; many homey touches through-out. Sig. Biasutti claims, "My house is the only one in Europe that makes contractual provisions with its staff for short hair and long smiles." Quite true. In the same neighborhood, the **Riviera** also boasts an excellent staff, but the heavy group traffic slays some of its potential warmth. **Hungaria** is one of the worst hotels in the region, in our opinion—and that's quite a distinction when one considers the others which remain.

Verona boasts one of the most unusual hotels in the nation. The **Due Torri,** opened in late '58, is the hobby of a wealthy Italian couple, Dr. and Mrs. Enrico Wallner. They delegate its day-to-day administration to a professional manager. For more than 1000 years there has been some kind of inn, tavern, or hostel on this site (Mozart stopped here in 1770); after 80 years of its disuse, the Wallners have created a showplace. Within its rooms there are 50 different motifs of exact period-furniture combinations of the eighteenth and early nineteenth centuries, both Italian and French; a sufficient supply of excess antiques is in storage to equip 200 additional rooms! Dignity and richness everywhere; ultramodern lighting, plumbing, and technical facilities; cuisine vastly improved and very well presented; keen-eyed attention from Resident Manager Raimondo Giavarini; rates especially moderate for such opulence. Recommended for its unique ambiance. **Colomba d'Oro** was recently given a shampoo, shower, shave, and massage. First floor, 3rd story, restaurant, and breakfast room renewed; firm-sprung beds throughout; nice perky baths; brass lamps and flowered wallpaper installed; 60% air conditioning sealed-in silence with double windows; garage; Proprietor Tapparini provides a lot for your money. Fresh, clean, and tasteful. The **Grand** has been perked up brightly. Public rooms smartened; lobbyside patio sweet for summer dining; most ceilings so high you'll think you're sleeping in a square silo. Comfortable, nonetheless, and getting better. The **San Pietro** on the Autostrada exit from Venice and Milan, is so-so for go-slow motorists who prefer Verona from afar. Each unit with private balcony; most with bath or shower; clean as shining tile. The **San Luca,** in the Second file, comes up with First-class amenities. Alley situation, which detracts from its status but adds to its tranquillity; cool but appealing lobby with adjoining bar; mezzanine breakfast deck; rooftop solarium; good, modern air conditioning; extra-kind concierge and back-up staff. All 40 smartly appointed contemporary bedchambers with wall-to-wall carpets, muted color blends; and small but efficient baths. For its low rates and relatively high-style rewards, we think it's a sensible buy. **Accademia** now scores about C-minus in this same school by comparison. **Giulietta e Romeo,** as well as **Milano,** are also scholarly Second-class bets. For students, Tanzanian civil servants, or privates in the Yucatan army, the following 3 tag ends may be suitable—but we doubt it. **Europa** is functional; the language spoken here is seldom, if ever, uttered in Buckingham Palace. **Verona** offers less space than the inside of the "o" in its name. **Valverde** is young, but "young" is the only favorable adjective we can muster.

. For travelers to *Sicily, Sardinia, or the south of the Italian Peninsula* (plus a few spots in the north), the **Jolly Hotels** chain started out to be a godsend—but now we're not quite so sure. Count Marzotto, the hardworking textile magnate who founded it, soon relinquished his reins. Since they're no longer centrally operated, and quality and service are left to the discretion of the individual proprietors, in some houses the standards have become downright ragged. Another irritation are their grandiose announcements about additional links which, on investigation, turn out to be half-built or still on paper. Nevertheless, 50-odd establishments exist; most are located in lesser-known but attractive villages or areas sufficiently close to main roads to appeal to motorists. The Italian Government underwrites 33% of the financing. Facilities are *not* Deluxe; they're First-class by European ratings, *which means Second-class by American standards.* Each structure has a high bath-or-shower count, an American Bar, and comfortable but not elegant furnishings; a very few have swimming pools. Many rooms have signs suggesting you take your meals at the hotel. The food is sometimes (not always!) quite acceptable; terms are reasonable for complete pension. (Be sure to ask for this in advance, because otherwise you will not be given the special rate.) For simple accommodations off the beaten track (or in a few key cities), you still shouldn't go wrong with many of these if you don't expect too much. Typical examples are found at **Agrigento**, **Avellino**, **Benevento**, **Brindisi** (ugh!), **Cagliari**, **Castelvetrano**, **Catania**, **Erice**, **Ischia**, **Iglesias**, **Olbia**, **Oristano**, **Pescara**, **Salerno**, **Mantua**, **Messina**, **Palermo**, **Parma**, **Ravenna**, and **Trieste**. Your travel agent has a full listing.

For miscellaneous centers not covered above, here are the best-known stopping places—some fine, some routine, and some substandard: In **Abano,** the rebuilt **Orologio**, with 2 swimming pools and a private park, has recaptured first place. The **Trieste** would come next, followed in a lower category by the fresh **Savoia**, the **Columbia**, and **Bristol**. **Aosta** offers no luxury nests. **Europe,** the most modern, tops our list. Next comes **Couronne et Poste**, followed by the chalet-style **Valle d'Aosta**. The Rank organization of England may have completed its new entry by now; we're anxious to rank it. All are for serious skiers. **Argentario** region? See **Port'Ercole** for Il Pellicano. In **Agrigento,** it's (1) **Jolly**, (2) **Della Valle** (air-conditioned; amateurish management; fierce cookery). In **Alassio**, it's the **Mediterraneo** first, then the **Alfieri**. In **Arenzano**, that pleasant little fishing village 13 miles west of Genoa, the First-class **Residenza Punta San Martino** sits high on St. Martin's Cape; 2 pools, 9 holes of golf, tennis, restaurant, nightclub; despite these attractions, not suggested as a stopover for North Americans. In **Assisi,** the **Subasio** is best for the view, but the air-conditioned **Umbra** has the best rooms; **Windsor Savoia** and **Giotto** are both worthy. All are chilly in the cool months due to their high altitude and low heating standards. Near **Bordighera** (San Remo region), the **Grand del Mare** is unusual as a structure. To take advantage of the sea and to avoid highway disturbances, the building plus the pool area and surrounding park were jacked up onto struts while the land was filled in beneath. Entrance via an underground parking apron with open *pluvium;* stunning modernistic pool, with white metallic lily pads for diving or sunning; private beach; conservatory with 50-yard glass wall that rises or falls away to open air at the flick of a switch; 2 restaurants; Charleston nightclub with poolside portholes; 3-part bar; one wing of private apartments; 80 seafront rooms with modern or traditional decor (we prefer the latter); dull, dull, dull menu on our recent sampling. What a honey of a twenty-first-century hostelry this is! *Don't miss it* if you're in the vicinity—and be sure to tell Manager Luigi Scianda (for 16 years at the Grand in Rome) that you are a.Guidester. **Campo Carlo Magno**, in the Dolomites, offers the restful altitudinous **Golf Hotel**—with what else but a golf course! Ski lifts and everything for outdoor types; rustic lumber-lined dining room for hungry types; peaceful wood-paneled bedrooms for sleepy types. Almost always filled at Christmas and the first 3 weeks in August by year-ahead enthusiasts. This luxuriously rebuilt chalet-style nook high, high in the hills sounds heavenly. In *Catania*, the **Excelsior Grand** avoids the city's commercialism; 100% air-conditioned, when it works (you'll pay for it regardless!); somewhat gaudy neo-Italian rooms now with piped melodies; high prices for the region; cuisine that has slipped; not a Ritz or a Palace, but tops for the area. The **Central Palace** is central, but 'tain't no palace even though it's air-conditioned and open all year; noisy locale; rather amateurish concierge and slipshod maintenance on our recent peek. If you absolutely *must,* the split-level apartments with kitchenettes are the pick of the dismal pack. The 160-unit **Jolly** is busy-busy with tour groups; the **Costa** is simple but commercial. We haven't seen the new **Baia Verde**, a seasider a few miles out of town with a swimming pool and air cooling. Might be nice; the rocky coast is anyway. The **Plaja** is passable for strict economists. The **AGIP Motel**, at the Taormina road exit at Ognina, offers 45 rooms, all with shower; miserable maintenance; restaurant; bar; garage. All of these are mediocre or worse by international standards. *Laveno* offers nothing except the ferry. In *Malcesine*, the **Malcesine**, on the water's edge, has reportedly gone off; poor quality beds and cookery, so we're told. In *Maratea*, on the coast about 115 miles below Salerno, the **Santavenere**, which we've just visited, is a long white redoubt in a sylvan setting overlooking the sea on 3 sides. It was "discovered" for us by Helen King, our dear friend and former New York editor. Old-fashioned stylings with modern appointments; 44 units, half with sea view; medium-size pool; pebbled beach; cordial staff. The main floor is in the middle of the building—a neat arrangement which does away with the necessity of elevators and also avoids too close proximity of its private terraces. While the drinks were excellent, the food, though graciously served, was just so-so. Excellent for seekers of solitude. Open late May to late August. In *Menaggio*, the little town about an hour from Como, the **Grand Hotel Victoria** comes up with turn-of-the-century spaciousness, a lovely lake vista, 100 old-style rooms and 53 private baths with reluctant plumbing; so peaceful that surely none of its guests or staff has ever heard of the SST or U-235, and now becoming about as seedy as a Burpee hothouse. We don't like the **Grand Hotel e Menaggio**; starkly old hat and cheap tour groupy. The modernized Second-category **Bellavista** might be the pick of the lot; we haven't seen it since its renovation. In *Merano*, the **Bristol** is a combination of Milanese-modern and tradition styling. Here's the **GRAND** s-p-a-c-e concept in everything. Manager Hugo Dibiasi places a heavy accent on comfort and clean-line luxury. All 150 rooms and 20 suites with bath or shower; 80% with private balcony; rooftop garden solarium and blue-tiled heated pool; thermal baths; season from early April to late October. By miles the choicest in the Alto Adige region. The aging **Palace** has a fine location, a heavenly pool, and a fair degree of attractions, many coming from its kitchen. The contemporary **Eurotel**, open all year, is typical of the production-line variety of latter-day budget shelters. Our "normal" double (with space-saving Murphy beds) boasted no less than 52 panels, drawers, or sliding shelves, which amusingly made us feel we were sleeping in the inner coffer of a Chinese puzzle box. **Mirabella,** in a residential setting, is also operative all year. Converted Family mansion with thermal waters; somewhat grim public rooms; low bath ratio. Its attractive exterior does not follow through into the interior. The modernized **Bavaria** is quiet; it is said to serve good cookery too. The **Emma** is hostess almost exclusively to groups that benefit from its face-lifting and culinary specialties. Of the later crop, **Meranerhof** has recently moved up to first category; good cookery, too. The **Mignon** is not bad, either; it's also noted for its outstanding kitchen. The **Irma,** out in Maia Alta, is quite pleasant in a slightly lower bracket. In *Modena,* a friendly Ontario physician recommends the spotlessly antiseptic **Real-Fini**, which is under the TLC of Dr. Fini, M.D. Food and service come in for equal praise—and our Canadian correspondent enthusiastically prescribes his colleague's *spiritus* Rx elixir retorted from local nuts (be sure to sample this liquor, he pleads). *Lago d'Orta* is a lovely sightseeing drive, but we've found nothing recommendable for an overnight stay. *Omegna*, at its head, is a hideous steel-and-umbrella manufacturing center. In *Padua,* the **Storione** has been vastly updated and is now this town's runaway leader. Manager Maccio is giving this house his all. The commercial-minded **Plaza** is a substantial bet. These would be followed by the **Europa,** the centrally sited **Leon Bianco,** (with a good restaurant), the **Monaco, Biri,** and the **Grande Italia.** In *Palermo,* the residential **Grand Hotel Villa Igiea**, in its own back-o-town park by the sea, is a shining oasis in this hotel-poor region. It's rambling, aged, and cool—a traveler's reward. Seawater swimming pool; 100% air-conditioned; erratic service accentuated on our latest visit by one of the most irritating concierges we've ever encountered. The **Jolly**, severed from the sea by a wide avenue, nonetheless gets blasted by highway noise all NIGHT L-O-N-G. It's still better than much of the competition—especially if you're a heavy sleeper. **The Grande Hotel & delle Palma,** owned by the Villa Igiea, is a fair choice despite the fact that it's showing its age virtually everywhere. Midcity situation in the throbbing eye of the 4-wheel hurricane; overweening institutionality despite some recent renovations; air-cooling now cooing a Grandiose sigh of welcome relief; clean but zestless bedchambers; generally inviting baths with colorful tiles—and almost the *only* touch of hue-someness in the barnlike joint. If you stop, please ask to see the modest little corner where Wagner composed *Parsifal.* This stadium-size hideaway is sure to give you a Lohen-grin. Not our Ring, but perhaps you'll disagree. The **Mediterraneo, Ponte** and **Metropole** are barely acceptable. **Mondello Palace Hotel,** 7½ miles from the center, is Italian-modern in tone; First category; 70 rooms, baths, and showers, many with terraces; avoid the rear singles which open to a dust road; swimming; summer dancing; minigolf; garden; March through November. The **Sole** is worthy in Second class; so is the **Splendid La Torre in** *Mondello*. A Motel AGIP was recently completed; 200 beds; always clean; always a bargain. Out at *Solunto*, the bungalow-style **Zagarella** is a peaceful middle-bracket tie-up. In *Pallanza*, on Lake Como, the First-class **Grand-Majestic** occupies a noisy roadside site; another old dowager who needs paint pots and nourishing cream by the gallon; season only. At **Port'Ercole**, a harbor of *snobismo* on the Argentario promotory (opposite Orbetello, 103 miles north of Rome toward Grosseto), **Il Pellicano** is a beak full of charm. The Dutch Royal Family are within a Shell's throw, and they use its dining facilities frequently. Seaside location; Pompeiian-red manor house with a glorious patio for sipping and munching; novel pool; 18 original rooms, plus 5 cottages, and an 8-unit annex; fine, highly polished rusticity cooled by full air conditioning; expensive all-inclusive tariffs. There's an air of elegant hominess which we think any well-heeled, social-conscious, and peace-loving Guidester would adore. The village itself isn't much; its few hostelries are often inconvenienced by an inadequate water supply. The island of **Giglio** offers the First-class **Campese** with a glorious ½-mile sandy beach; packet boat transportation to-and-fro once daily; inviting, if silence is your meat. Back on the mainland, Porto Santo Stéfano offers the **Filippo II**, the best of an indifferent lot; the stone-faced **Don Pedro** isn't much either. **Calamoresca** comes up with 45 units and tubs, a pool, and a movie theater. Local chums award this nominee an Oscar; we'll preview it soon. For budgeteers, **Villa Letizia** (toward the "Pelican" at **Port-'Ercole**) is a beguiling 12-room pension with a private beach and lip-smacking vittles. In the same general vicinity, but northward along the Grosseto pike, the terra-cotta **La Corte del Butteri** at **Fonte-Blanda** (10 miles from Orbettello) is a rancho by the sea. Waterside restaurant; Tuscan cowboy bunkhouses in 2 stories; busy atmosphere, similar to an attractive motel on U.S. #1. In **Pugliano**, the Third-class **Ercolano** at the Funicular Station is useful for Vesuvius excursionists; renovated but still primitive; improved cuisine; wonderful view. In **Ragusa**, it's (1) San Giovanni (bed and breakfast only), (2) **Jonio** (more cosmopolitan), (3) **Mediterraneo**. In **Raito**, that alluring cliffside village 2½ miles from Salerno up the Corniche from the main Amalfi Drive, the First-class **Raito** is tip of the tops; good kitchen; recommended. The nearby **Lloyd's Baia** is also said to be a worthwhile stop, particularly since Lloyd modernized his premises. In **Ravenna** honors go to the modern, central **Bisanzio**; rather gaudy décor, but extra-sweet personnel for this tourist town and a superior restaurant. Second is the **Jolly**; also basic and sound. The **Argentario**, with 34 Class II piped chambers, may rank 3rd if what we hear is true. In **Riva del Garde**, on the north shore of Lake Garda, a reasonable hául from Trento or Brescia, a discriminating lady from New York's capital trilled the praises of the **du-Lac-et-du-Parc**—and, from its eye-popping brochure, well she might. First-class (not Deluxe); large, old-fashioned but renovated headquarters in wooded park; 200 rooms, mostly with bath; 40 bungalows; pool; tennis; private beach; much more. Her comments: "For serenity seekers, beautiful, charming, perfect in every way—and not too expensive." Warmest thanks, kind friend! In **Saint-Vincent**, the winter and summer resort in the Aosta region, the Deluxe **Billia** rules the roost; popular nightclub featured; one of Italy's best casinos connected by direct passageway. In **Salerno**, key feeder-point on the Autostrada, the **Grand Diana Splendid** is a small skyscraper, with an attractive roof restaurant and a modern ambiance; much better than it was. The second-place **Jolly,** on the seaside, has had a change in management, thank heavens, which has picked it up a bit, particularly in the scrubbing department; all units now have bath or shower and air conditioning; a revamped restaurant is in the works, we're told. Okay. Don't bother with any of the others. In **San Felice Circeo,** Rome's most exclusive escape hatch, the **Maga Circe** is the Old Reliable, with only 38 rooms. The **Neanderthal**, which has 57, is seasonal. The newer **Punta Rossa,** built into the cliffside, counts 25 bungalows with 45 chambers, each with private bath; pool; very restful. In **Santa Severa** (main road to Pisa, 32 miles from Rome), the **Maremonti** is a private residence transformed into an inn; private beach; not luxurious and not expensive; good simple rest spot near the capital.

   Sardinia's Costa Smeralda (see "Cities") is a $168,000,000 island development along 30 miles of the northeastern shoreline, largely sponsored by the Aga Khan. His pride is the glamorously rustic, **Cala di Volpe,** which nestles almost village-style by the sands of a glorious bay. His Highness gave French Master Architect Jacques Couelle a blank check to build anything he desired. This genius made one try, disliked what he did, destroyed the first structure, and began anew. To guarantee every detail would be "perfectly imperfect," Couelle supervised the laying of paving stones that do not quite join, braiding the cane so it does not appear uniform, processing the walls so they seem aged by the centuries. He "rusted," then "stopped" the oxidation of wrought iron. Bleaching, chipping, dusting, beating—he employed a trillion techniques to meld this composite into a creation of the highest form of distilled structural art, a place in which to live, to love, and to relax. Surrounding the pueblo enclave is a toy harbor. Here you will find hotel boats bobbing at their moorings, tennis courts, a huge glittering olympic swimming pool, and a parcel of what might be called beach-lets. Entrance across a bamboo-covered footbridge to a timber-toned lobby; main restaurant and bar under giant wooden beams and plaited stalks, both overlooking the teal waters and the 100-yard log pier; 44 rooms in the older segment, each in different dress (bid for these since the newer wing is only so-so and can be hotter). Rates are close to Deluxe standards anywhere in Italy—but, because of its relative isolation, the frolicking nightlife, the delicious drinks (try a Smeraldino Cocktail for a green-eyed thrill), the joyous pastimes, and the fun-filled ambiance of play-filled luxury, a pair of pilgrims could easily work through $150 per day, including normal meals (not caviar, plover's eggs, and the like). Occasional complaints about the concierge. You'll find a beauty salon, a barbershop, a duo of boutiques, and a warehouse full of peace and tranquillity. There's one all-encompassing word for this Eden—*fabulous!* **The Pitrizza**, also owned by the Aga Khan, is in the same Deluxe category. This one is nearer to the coastal heartbeat of **Porto Cervo**, a 10-minute panoramic ramble by car. Although it is more private in concept—a ½-dozen 4-to-8-person bungalows —it is equally glorious, equally comfortable, with the opulence of a potentate's diadem. Its lichen-flecked rock walls blend so harmoniously with the landscape that from several hundred yards away it can scarcely be seen. Each yard-thick roof of the villas and main building has been given a rich blanket of soil, an independent irrigation system, and a magnificent assortment of Mediterranean flowering plants and shrubs—a tour de force by Luigi Vietti. The pool, hewn from native cobble, first flows through hillside pockets and then cascades over a rocky weir into the sea. Central clubhouse with restaurant, bar, and coveside terrace; candlelight dinners twice weekly; dancing a regular feature; all chalets with air conditioning plus working fireplaces; individual patios under vine-draped, raw-wood lattices; stable-type doors; agrestic Sardinian handicrafts; colorful, nature-toned décor. As we mentioned earlier, all 3 Aga Khan hotels (including the lower-category Cervo described below) can provide a launch to whisk you and your sand-mates to any of the 80 heaven-kissed beaches along the 30-mile shore for a day of reclusive sunbathing; they will pick you up at any hour you specify. An 18-hole golf course designed by Trent Jones has finally teed off. These 2 are LOVER-LY; what better? The Rank-run, 100-room **Romazzino** has now moved up to the Deluxe bracket. It commands what we believe is the most scenic site of all —a hillside perch above a bay twinkling with salt-and-pepper islands. North Wing best for the view; modern lobby and lounge with ceramic "trees"; Juniper Bar; coolish dining salon; beachside "Wooden Leg" barbecue hutch; Alfonso's Pizzeria; private boat dock; hairdresser and barber; free baby-sitter service; Sunfish sailboats for rent; full range of water-sport facilities; newspaper kiosk and a few shops. Its generally spacious bedchambers have colorful tile floors and raffia carpets. Selected antique furnishings mixed with contemporary comfort-insurers; baths, showers, and individual peignoirs; private balconies; single bedsteads for a nunnery. For the healthy outlay, it's very good indeed; better suited to animated young folk than to older Grand Tour peace-seekers. The fully air-conditioned expanded **Cervo**, smack in the center of the port, is the nucleus of the social, boating, and nightlife whirl. It is the only area in the close-knit community that stays open year round; encompasses a marina, a swimming and barbecue area, restaurant, bar, supermarket, equestrian club, shopping arcade, plaza for star-sprinkled galas, real estate agency, post and telegraph office, and ultra-exclusive Yacht Club. If you've got a gleam in your eye and a jingle in your pocket, you're bound to pop into this merry complex to share the the action. Simpler accommodations than Cala di Volpe and Pitrizza; correspondingly lower price tags; same administrative aegis; more than adequate comfort; convivial people; usually full in season—and with good reason. Highly recommended. The nearby 80-room **Luci di la Muntagna,** with its distant view of Corsica, also hops with carefree abandon. Architecture that suggests it came out of a plaster-of-Paris mold; active floating jetty for sport boats (6 for rent by guests); good beach with free deck chairs and umbrellas; enlarged restaurant; rooftop solarium; swinging discothèque; all units with bath or shower; new swimming pool possibly underway; most with private balcony; narrow dimensions; 5 pastel color schemes. Except for the cell-size accommodations, here's a laudable medium-bracket candidate. The **Residence Liscia di Vacca** is nearby, Second-class, has swimming pool, and said to be pleasant for budget voyagers; we haven't dropped our anchor at its port-als. In the same category, the fresh 70-Kip **Cinesta** debuted recently; the 420-guest, First-class **Pervero** ("pear tree") teed off this year by the golf links; and, finally, the **Dolce Sposa** ("sweet wife") makes up more than 100 beds. Additional runners may be found along the shores (perhaps a ½-hour drive) and in a dreary town of *Olbia* but for the full galaxy of happy and/or luxurious resort-style living, we strongly recommend that you limit your selection to the established 5 (or possibly 6) stalwarts of the Costa Smeralda. In their separate and varying ways, they can fill almost *any* bill of holiday delight.

In *Sestriere*, the **Principe di Piemonte** is well liked for its skiing, dancing, and *joie de vivre* in season. The Fiat interests orginally bankrolled (and later sold) the towering cylindrical **Duchi d'Aosta**. It offers abundant comfort, excellent cuisine, and reasonable tariffs. Here's the favored winter shuggery of the fashionable Hawes clan of Elstree and Mallorca. **La Torre**, its twin, specializes in singles during the playful months. In *Sestri Levante* (about 30 miles south of Genoa), the far-and-away leader is **Grand Hotel dei Castelli** —3 linked castles which occupy their own high-perched peninsula up a first-gear-only road. Owner Queirolo's gorgeous antiques scattered through its 43 rooms and 6 suites—plus its exquisite panorama and good facilities— merit salutes and salaams. **Vis à Vis** is simple-modern but offers a fine bay setting for meditations and quiet pursuits. Pleased reports have come in about the sixteenth-century **Villa Balbi**; one twentieth-century wing; "fine service and food"; "excellent attention." In *Siracusa*, it's the **Jolly** for well-tempered Yanks or Rebs. The **Grand Hotel Villa Politi** has a marvelous site over an ancient quarry, but we found dismal maintenance, leaky plumbing, and erratic service. The **AGIP** motel, nearby, is one of this chain's better links. The **Park** is a so-so Second-class alternate. We'd suggest pulling on to Catania or even to Taormina for longer sojourns. In *Sirmione* (midway between Milan and Venice), the Peninsula town which juts out into Lake Garda, the First-class **Villa Cortina** overlooks the water from the center of a large park; tranquil and pleasant. The **Continental** is runner-up. Everything is seasonal here. *Stresa*'s pacesetters are **Des Îles Borromées** (operated by CIGA and smoothly managed by Vincenzo Schachner) and the **Regina Palace** (taken over by the Bossi family, formerly associated with the late Oscar Wirth in Rome's Hassler and Eden). The former, a Gay Nineties holdover, had its heyday about the time the *Titanic* went down; its redone bar looks both brash and apologetic in the bosom of this sprawling, last-century matron; it is spacious, well maintained, and comfortable. The latter, also Victorian down to its tearose toenails, has brilliant gardens, a lakeside terrace-restaurant with dancing, and the ghosts of countless waistcoat-and-bustle memories; here's a pleasant relic, too. The **Bristol**, next to Des Îles Borromées, is newer, clean, and on the small side. Capacity of 114 cramped but nicely turned-out units, 106 with private bath; savory cookery, jarring lobby; better taste upstairs. Not in the class with the 2 leaders. **Villa Aminta**, a converted mansion on the main pike, features a small "beach," a big, sparkling, glassed-in restaurant, an expansive terrace-garden for open-air dining, and an accomplished chef. Total of 35 adequate but diminutive rooms and baths; ask for the newer ones only. **Astoria** is plunk next door to the Regina Palace—a choice location. Tiresomely modern in tone; 100 accommodations in hair-raising colors; skimpy furnishings. Passable for a single night, if you're stuck. Save for Villa Aminta which runs year round, all the above are open only from April to October. In *Tremezzo*, the **Grand Hotel Tremezzo**, with its private little park and pool, is average but not outstanding; the **Bazzoni**, also on the lake, is okay for its lower category. In *Trieste*, **Excelsior Palace** is looking better after its renovation program. The **Jolly** evokes only the mildest chuckle of approval from us. The modest **Obelisco**, with its hillside location and nice staff, was also getting a facial when we came to call. The **Adriatico**, out at Grignano Bay, can be pleasant in season. Manager Pregazzi is making it zing. *Viareggio*'s leader is the 250-bed **Grand Hotel et Royal**, between the sea and pine woods. Open-air and indoor dining areas; American Bar; most units with bath or shower; weird combination of ultramodern and traditional décor, akin to finding an astronaut's helmet in a hansom cab. The 80-room-and-bath **Palace** also faces the waves; here are a lovely terrace, solarium, and panoramic vistas. Finally, in *Vicenza*, the **Jolly Campo Marzio** and the **Jolly Statione** (no restaurant) probably won't give you the jollies, but at least they may keep the raindrops from falling on your head.

Motels? **AGIP**, the Italian national petroleum monopoly (look for the sign of a black 6-legged dog on a yellow background), has taken over the project of *autostelli,* which it began with the Italian Automobile Club (ACI) some years ago. There are still a couple of dozen low-price ACI operations in southern Italy, but the AGIP Motels, with the air-conditioned showcases the 525-bed installation near *Milan*, the busy 272-bed installation outside *Rome* (see above), or the quieter and more luxurious queen of the chain at *Florence*, provide basic shelter for low lire. All have bath or shower; most offer a restaurant with simple food. (Regular gas stations of this network have no lodgings, but some offer full dining facilities or snack bars.) *Turin* and *Bologna* are additional offerings; other recent branches, mostly south of Naples, are also available, including one in *Palermo* and a scenic newer arrival on Pugnochiuso Bay at *Vieste*, near Foggia. For further information, write to the Società Esercizio Motels Italia, viale dell'Arte 72, EUR, in the capital. One possible irritant is truck noises at night, but most U.S. tourists are so tired after the day's dodge 'em games with Italian daredevils they couldn't care less.

§TIPS: Italian law requires that the basic rate plus service and taxes be posted in each room. Officialdom just winks at this statute.

Don't expect American-type air conditioning, because you'll rarely find it. Most hotels, including top international landmarks, turn off their systems from midnight to dawn—leaving you to stifle to catalepsy unless you open your windows before going to sleep. To us fresh-air fiends, this Latin quirk is completely incomprehensible.

FOOD Discounting the North, where rice is king, the average Italian exists on bread and pasta, the latter a word for which there is no literal translation. From the basic ingredient—wheat flour—spring dozens of variations: Ravioli (rectangular), fettuccine (ribbon-like), lasagne (flat), farfalle (butterflies), conchiglie (shells), ziti (large macaronis), and many others. Food authorities may squabble with this iconoclasm, but officially, at least, spaghetti is *not* pasta; it is classified as *grano duro* or "hard wheat." You may even run into the square—yep, *square*—spaghetti that is sweeping across Italian palates. It's called Spaghetti alla Chitarra; order it "con Pecorino," a stronger grated cheese than the usual Parmesan. We think it's a delicious variation on a belly-busting theme. Most pastas are served in gargantuan portions; after a dinner plate of this "appetizer," the visitor seldom can find room for the meat, potatoes, vegetables, salad, and dessert that follow.

Italian white truffles are the most scrumptious in the world—infinitely superior to the coarser black variety grown in France. Specially trained dogs are used in Alba, south of Turin, the global capital of this delicacy, to sniff out their earthen hiding places and to root them up. Like caviar, if eaten in quantity over several days, they are said to have an aphrodisiac effect. Some medical authorities such as Ole Doc Joe Raff go so far as to claim they have a sexually therapeutic power; he states that one of the early symptoms of loss of amorous prowess is   *

Risotto is marvelous, and has innumerable versions. The basis is towel-rubbed rice, simmered in bouillon or chicken broth until the kernels are dark and tasty. With this are mixed mushrooms, peppers, onions, saffron, butter, and cheese; veal, chicken, pork, lobster, beef. Other ingredients can then be added. Risotto alla Milanese is perhaps the most famous; we personally prefer the illegitimate brother of this simpler dish, the one with chunks of chicken, asparagus, browned onions, tomatoes, and peas, similar to Arroz con Pollo.

Polénta is a staple of the North. It's a cornmeal porridge, white or yellow, so heavy in texture that it stands up by itself. It isn't particularly interesting in taste, but its importance as a native food makes it worth a try. Don't order it in a first-class restaurant, however, or the waiter will probably throw you out! Incidentally, northern cooking leans heavily on butter; prime ingredient throughout the South is oil.

Italian pizza is conceded to be finer than its American cousin. (The taste is so different you might not agree at first.) Naples, the center, offers 27 types made in about 200 *pizzerie,* according to veteran foreign correspondent and pizza-hound Walter Hackett, our dear old friend and traveling companion. Essentially, it's a crisp, crunchy, flat pie, made of dough, fresh tomatoes, and cheese—but the seasonings vary from basil to orégano, and the additional alternates vary from fresh (not tinned) anchovies to mushrooms to mussels to clams to salami. Try Pizza Margherita—mozzarella, tomatoes, olive oil, and basil. Or try Pizza Calzone, with added cream cheese and salami; Calzone means "pants," referring to a half-moon flap of pastry which covers the top like a small tent. Both are delicious.

Prosciutto, dark spicy local ham served in wafer-thin slices, is an excellent cocktail appetizer. It's wonderful with fresh figs or a slice of melon—but be sure to order it "crudo" (raw), or they might serve it "cotto" (cooked).

Antipasti (salami, cheese, prosciutto, celery, egg, artichoke hearts, black olives, pimento, and other spicy foods) are the Italian hors d'oeuvres. The word means "against pasta," since its ingredients are usually so much lighter and cooler than the wheat-based dishes. Generally there's enough oil in one portion to run the engines of the *Queen Elizabeth 2* across the Atlantic.

Other specialities worth trying are Scampi alla Griglia (grilled crawfish resembling large grilled shrimp), sea crab cocktail (eat the delicate "coral" separately), Carpaccio (heavenly paper-thin slices of raw sirloin spiced with ground pepper and dashed with oil and vinegar), Cannelloni (pasta stuffed

*Failing eyesight. (We're glad to see that you recovered it.)

with pâté or other meats and baked in cheese and tomato sauce), Minestrone (delicious multivegetable soup with regional variations of added pasta, rice, etc.), Pollo alla Diavola (called "deviled chicken," but actually broiled with herbs), Scaloppine San Giorgio (veal stuffed with ham, cheese, and mushrooms; particularly fine at Venice's Royal Danieli), Pansoti con Salsa di Noce (a Genoese specialty of pasta with a walnut filling), and that king of desserts, Gâteau Saint-Honoré, purely Italian, despite its French name.

Oh—let's not forget that extraordinary Venetian crab, either. Listed as La Granservola, it's a lobster-size crawfish with tiny claws and a huge, meaty body. The favorite way to serve it is in the shell, reinforced with piquant seasonings. Venice is the center; summer is the season; try any good seafood restaurant for a succulent sample.

§TIPS: Stick to bottled water in rural or village areas of Italy. (In the larger cities, tap water is pure.) Popular sparkling brands are San Pellegrino and Crodo; Fiuggi is the best bet without gas (said to be *the* remedy for kidney stones—and just ask your physician what he thinks of THIS claim!); the almost-flat San Gemini, recommended by local physicians for bellyaches, is sold in pharmacies but not in bars.

Italian ice cream is now the best in Europe. It's safe in all big cities, because it has been pasteurized.

You may order half *(mezzo)* portions of spaghetti and similar pasta dishes —a useful gimmick for survival.

Scandals involving adulterated foods have raised the ire of authorities and consumers all the way down the Boot. Cheese made with dirt and banana peels, butter processed from donkey fats, spaghetti paste pressed from rotten eggs, pig fodder baked into loaves of bread, and even nastier rackets have been uncovered. The Government instigated a nationwide crackdown, with raids, confiscations, and shutdown orders in dozens of communities, followed by internationally publicized civil and criminal trials. In a recent typical scandal, a warehouse full of impounded wine (being held as grounds for adultery) vanished right from under official noses. Where had it gone? No one will tell, but some journals have hinted the defendant tapped the barrels in custody, sold the lot, and walked away with a fat profit, leaving not even the dregs of evidence for his prosecution!

If you don't outsmart 'em, Italian waiters will try to heap 24 courses on your table in 7 minutes flat. Your best Oneupmanship for this game is to order a single dish at a time—ONLY. Then you can enjoy piping-hot food throughout your meal—and drive them up the wall in frustration.

RESTAURANTS   Good restaurants in every city. Even the hamlets usually have at least one oasis where you'll find cuisine of high quality. Don't be startled by the down-to-earth simplicity which you'll find in many of them; with surprisingly few exceptions, the Italian entrepreneur concentrates on food rather than on fancy decorations.

Prices? Leaping lasagne and zooming ziti! As at home, the scale in the metropoli generally pole vaults over that in rural centers. However, posh resort stops often charge the same as their city-slick cousins. *Cafeteria-style* *trays pan out in the $2.50 range. Conventional fodder in the bulk of establishments listed below goes for $6 to $10, including house wine and tip. The star performers twinkle modestly at close to $14, glitter more noticeably at around $19, and sparkle openly for about $30. For hard-bitten budgeteers, a pizza is the most convenient and universal answer; it cuts from 75¢ a wedge to the same outlay for the entire π, depending on where you munch it. A bottle of respectable wine decants from $2.50 to $9. In doubtful feederies, be sure to check your bills carefully against the menu.*

Dedicated budgeteers? As you will see, the listings which follow cover at least 500 dining spots in all price categories. Since space limitations prevent further entries here, please consult our annually revised paperback, *Fielding's Low-Cost Europe,* which carries scores more bargain-level establishments and money-saving tips in and for Italy's most important centers.

Once again, let's proceed alphabetically, by cities:
Amalfi's best food can be had at the **Luna**, in our renewed judgment. **Santa Caterina** would be next. **Cappuccini** has the most spectacular view, but the cookery curled our hair into neat little rows of granny knots. **La Marinella**, on the beach, is the relaxed Poseidon for seafood specialties, since the operators catch their own catch for the skillets; it has ocean-floor-level prices, too. **Ciccio**, **Cielo e Mare**, **Lo Smeraldino**, **Lido Azzurro**, and **Flavio Gioia** are additional possibilities; they are untried by us.
Assisi's Hotel **Giotto** is the culinary choice followed closely by the **Umbria**. **Subasio Hotel** offers fixed meals or à la carte that are *not* prepared by Escoffier, but there's a magnificent vista; lots of bus excursionists. **La Taverna dell 'Arco** is the pick of independents. **Bibo** is tops for snacks.
In **Bari**, The pick of the midtowners are the **Mediovale La Taberna** and **La Vecchia Bari**. Suburban choices, however, have more appeal to us. Of these we prefer **La Sirenetta a Mare**, 4 miles out, with good sea specialties and dancing in the evening; run by the Vincenti tribe; closed Tuesdays. **Adriatico**, also featuring sea denizens, has improved; it's still far from great; shuttered on Fridays. **Grotto Regina**, at Terra a Mare, emerged from being shut down for refurbishing and enlargement by Comm. Giuseppe Calabrese; now it should be even a better bet than previously for mingling with the local chichis and hes. We've had good reports on **Marc Aurelio a Mare**, a 5-mile coastal drive to Lungomare N. Massaro Palase; fish and barbeques are its specialties. **La Pignata**, back in town, also serves finny fare of renown. Both **La Taverna** and **Taverna Verde** have fallen from our grace; no longer recommended.
In **Bologna**, Al Pappagallo (the "Parrot") is known from Zagreb to Zamboanga for its rich, ounce-manufacturing fare. Don't let its nonfancy mien deceive you for 2 seconds, because here, IF you hit it right, can be a happy experience. Unfortunately, this author and a host of Guide readers have been hitting it notably wrong these days. Our latest meal was—to be charitable—even more ordinary than any of our previous repasts. Despite this teetering, its reputation is weighty and its cookery is *so* right whenever it is right. Closed Friday.

Resteria Luciano (via Nazario Sauro 19), infinitely more steady in its skilletcraft, is now pushing Al Pappagallo mercilessly. On one recent circuit (incognito, as usual), this elf-size gem dished up one of the finest meals in that area. Please don't expect physical charm and eye appeal, because they are negligible. Two very plain rooms behind the kitchen; all 12 tables occupied almost exclusively by local citizenry; walls lined with Luciano's cooking diplomas and awards; the *maestà* delights in discussing in Italian the preparation of his triumphs; no English spoken. Start with his heavenly Manicaretto Garisenda (green pasta roll with lightly smoked ham and a grated Parmesan cheese garnish), and finish with his yumptious Merengo di Ponteassieve (an aerated and iced meringue dessert). Cheers and salutes to this splendid little gastronomic haven. **Nello** (via Montegrappa 2), sometimes known only by its street name, is composed of 3 levels, each with its own personality (we prefer the vaulted cellar with wine cradles and hanging meats); slow-footed but quick-tongued service which tends to push the house specialties—with good reason, since these are the best by far; now expensive; more than adequate for better than average regional dining. While **Tre Vecchi** (via dell'Indipendenza 47) has been modernized inside, its exterior remains the same. Your interior will probably not be treated quite as gently as before. More's the pity. **Don Rodrigo** (via della Zecca) features international cookery. It is popular with after-theater and post-operatic calorie hunters, as is **Don Quijote**. **Tre Galli d'Oro** ("Three Golden Cocks") and **Nerina** (behind Hotel Roma) come next. **Diana** is highpriced for Second class. For quality at lower cost, try **Al Contoncino** or **Antico Brunetti**. **Château Bellevue** is for summer excursionists; 15 minutes from the city, up the San Luca funicular; good vista and soothing ambiance on a nice day, but the pot-and-pan-man needs a few more lessons. **Fagiano** (via Calcavinazzi 2) is typical and cheap.

Bolzano's leader is the handsomely inviting Grill of the **Hotel Grifone**, which is intimate, colorful, and international in its appeal. Among the independents, **Wienerwald** is a link in the low-price ubiquitous European chain of the same name. The **da Cesare** is pretty good for regional platters. **Vesuvio** fires up crispy pizza; so does **Veruschka**. The **Caterpillar** wiggles up on the outskirts and it's worth a visit. After these, 'tain't much, McGee.

Brindisi? Bring your own picnic basket to this filth-ridden town—and we're not kidding. Everything we found here was either wretched in quality or served in such seemingly unsanitary surroundings that we settled for a boiled egg and bottled beer. Should hunger overcome you, the dining room of the **Hotel Internazionale**, along the port, is probably the best option of the scruffy lot. If you're heading for Greece on one of the sleek overnight ferries, you may be able to dine in one of the clean, bright cafeterias or relatively posh saloons aboard. Be extra-careful, however, because we presumably paid for vittles on one tub and received nothing—nor was there even food service for independent travelers. The oily-tongued ticket agents who clog the port area might promise champagne and nightingales' tongues flambé; we would have been satisfied with even a crust of bread and nonrancid butter on our miserable voyage. And while we're at it, let us again remind you to be extra-wary of pickpockets in the ticket agency line, on the streets, and in the bay district; if you can, always have someone in your family or party stand guard over your car. Even in the main square, broken windows and thefts are not uncommon. This is especially true for soft-top convertibles.

Capri's most famed establishment is 79-year-old Miss Gracie Fields' **La Canzone del Mare**, a chichi beach club at the foot of a cliff adjoining a small beach. Magnificent location; pool; bar; now lunch only; very, very swank, and very, very lovely. But that food, for those prices—ouch! One light noon-bite (Prosciutto, Cannelloni, ½-bottle of local wine, and Café Hag) came up in such ridiculously skimpy portions we actually laughed when they served it —but we stopped laughing fast when they handed us that tab. As one illustration, our minestrone here cost 1700 L. *vs.* 500 L. at La Capannina (below). If you're loaded with lire and eat a big breakfast first, this place is a dream. If you're poor and famished, you can find the same scenery for 50% less money at attractive little **Da Pietro** (also known as "Gloria's," for the titled Englishwoman who runs it) a short distance down the shore. Check first because it might have shuttered; if it is still functioning you're likely to find much better food these days than in a neighboring high-price spot called **Da Vincenzo delle Sirene**, so don't let yourself confuse them. All closed tight in winter.

Please refer back to "Hotels" for the **Punta Tragara**, such an enchanting spot that it is a wonder anyone can swallow. Nothing on Capri can touch it for elegance and plushness. The glorious 6-table terrace is Paradise South. Very costly; be sure to reserve.

La Capannina (via delle Botteghe 15) draws the island's top palms and salaams from our old-time, loyal, discriminating Guidesters and friends, Rose and Mortimer Sachs of Palm Beach, Florida. On a 4-week stay, they zeroed in for "at least 40 of our 60 meals." Here's their description: "The 3 charming, tiny inside dining rooms are lovely, and the patio is beautiful. The kitchen is the best equipped of any local restaurant. The house wine, from their own vineyards, is excellent. The prices, while not inexpensive, are competitive. If you shouldn't accept our unqualified recommendation for this spotless, colorful little gem, just check with Joan Crawford, Emilio Pucci, the Marchesa Rittinghausen—or the Shah of Iran, if you can reach him!" We've just come from a table test here and find the Sachs' report 105% correct. After receiving a topnotch apprenticeship in Palm Beach, young Antonio deAngelis took over from his late father. Antonio and Maître De Gennaro are on their toes. To make things even better, Antonio married Aurelia, the daughter of a maître in one of America's leading culinary establishments—and this provides an extra dividend of welcome for the traveler. Lira-for-lira this is our candidate for top value on the island. Bravo! Closed Thursday and 4 months in winter.

Ai Faraglioni, on the footpath called via Camerelle, was one of the happiest discoveries of a joy-filled island odyssey some time ago, but, alack and alas, more recently we've found it grimly disappointing in reception and culinary skills. Scenic, vedy-vedy social, immaculate, pleasant terraces for people watching, but far less enjoyable overall than it was on previous incognito samplings. **Da Gemma**, perhaps 50 steps up the arch-covered footpath from the Central Plaza, is the artists' and writers' favorite; 2 sections, one a year-round tavern and the other a seasonal patio; the former comprises a series of rooms enclosing an open, sunken kitchen. With Grottino (opposite side of the plaza) and La Capannina, Da Gemma vies for the most delicious regional cookery to be found on Capri. **O'Saraceno** made us feel claustrophobic—a totally unnecessary sensation in this isle of open vistas and space. The garden of the **Quisisana** is particularly attractive at night; for indoor munchers, its French restaurant has been lovingly done over in elegant tones. Much improved. **Casina delle Rose,** with its Taverna now operating during the evening, is coming up again under its improved management; check your bill to make certain no discrepancies exist with listed menu prices. **Grotto Verde**, near the funicular base in the port, is strongly *caprese*—rough but fun, with excellent typical cookery and reasonable tabs. If you don't expect anything but simplicity and honest fare, you'll probably enjoy it a lot. Closed Mondays. **La Pigna**, below the taxi rank off the main piazza, is a family operation which has everything going for it except the cookery. Glass-enclosed arcade flanked on 3 sides with cascades of greenery and flowers; superior white house wine; personable English-fluent waiter in Gennaro. Shame on the chef, say we. **Fontanella**, below the Hotel Ponta Tragara, is reported as very chic. Regretfully we went to dine there on the final evening of our latest visit and discovered that only lunch is served. Among the outdoor cafes most frequented at the cocktail hour, the **Caffé Caso** seems to draw the intelligentsia of the island while the **Gran Cafe Town and Country** attracts merely the affluent; **Piccolo Bar** is more for every *uomo;* a general audience goes here. **Tiberio**, which resides in the cellar of a local church is considered by many to be a tourist trap—perhaps just right, however, for a trappist tour.

At *Caserta*, the **Massa da Peppino** is a yummy choice for grills and regional pickings except on Monday. Out on the Capua-Naples main auto expressway, the **Autostrada Pavesi** has a good-quality air-conditioned restaurant. It's a godsend for the motorist in a hurry. **La Bomboniera** is ballyhooed for its bountiful bonbons; we found it only so-so.

In *Catania*, **La Tavernetta,** with its moderate tabs, has been perked up brightly. Modern structure plus alfresco terrace beside the sea. **Costazzurra,** near by, is reasonably sound. The **Alba**? One friend advises, "Simply ignore that it exists." Okay, done. **Forte Apache** dishes out local grub in a mock fortress; its chief hits bull's-eyes with his culinary arrows; a chuck wagon that's on the move. **Camst Sicilia**, across from the Bellini Gardens, is a neomodern cluster of eateries under one roof which are balm for brittle budgets. Airy dining section up front with a menu listing the daily special, perhaps 6 pastas, and 3 hot dishes; less expensive cafeteria to the rear with the chef's suggestions scrawled on a blackboard; more formal and costly repastery upstairs. Our green lasagna and ½-bottle of local wine hit the spot while tapping our wallet without pain. Cheerfully recommended.

In *Como*, first a warning: The **Funicolare Restaurant**, at the foot of the funicular, is NOT recommended by this *Guide*—but definitely, oh so definitely. In the town itself we're partial to the restaurant of the **Barchetta Excelsior** as well as to **Da Celestino** and **Imbarcadero**. A fascinating excursion can be had to **Locanda**, on the island of *Comacina*, which boasts romantic origins back to the early twelfth century. It is located across from the village of Sala Comacina, 20 minutes by road from Villa d'Este; athletic diners also can row in from Sporano or an oarsman can do the muscle work for you for about $1 round trip. The house (open February 1 to October 30) was built in 1963 by the state, it functions under management contract by experienced, gracious, English-speaking Benvenuto Puricelli. An abundant and flavorful fixed-price menu totals approximately $17 per person. The high point of the meal (only performed when the restaurant is full) is the Fire Rite—a bit of amiable hocus-pocus involving tinkling bells, flaming coffee, and a public taste test of the brew by a supposed virgin. While the *espresso* concoction might enjoy the flambé process, clients themselves are prohibited from smoking throughout all meals as house policy. Closed Tuesday. **Le Tout Paris**, at *Sala Comacina*, is said to be better than satisfactory for cuisine at prices that run anywhere from 30% to 40% under those of Locanda. Closed Wednesday. In *Rogaro*, the 12-table **Veluu**, opened in 1975 by Carlo Antonini, is recommended by 2 local connoisseurs who tell us that it is one of the most attractive, chic, and well-run oases in the lake district. Sited on the ground floor of Villa Antonini, the dining room overlooks Lake Como from atop its own peninsula. Accessible only by car; closed January. Sounds exceptional. The **Vapore Torno**, 15 minutes out at *Torno*, is another pacesetter for the region (Apr. to Sept. only). **Da Pizzi** offers 2 dining places—an expensive one, open summer only, and a small, typical one, open all year; we prefer the cookery in the little brother, even though it's less costly and less fancy. The **Negri** in *Pusiano,* 9 miles from Como on the Lecco highway, features freshly caught perch with risotto; very cheap, simple, and good. Under "Hotels" we've already mentioned **Villa Serbelloni** at *Bellagio*. Finally, don't forget that renowned but terribly costly **Villa d'Este** is only a skip-and-jump away at *Cernobbio;* here locals also rate the **Terzo Grotto** highly.

In *Cortina D'Ampezzo*, **El Toulà**, about 15 minutes toward *Pocol*, is a favorite of Smart Set diners; checkered table napery; darkness in tone; lightness in cuisine. **El Camineto**, a little farther along (turn right before *Pocol*), is smaller, also chichi, and also worthy. So is the family-run **Beppe Sello** for regional skilletry. **Al Foghèr** isn't what it used to be. **Ra Stua** also has slipped.

Elba ? Too long ago, we folded our napkins after a gastronomic waddle through this island. Here's what our taste buds told us then—and undoubtedly much has changed in today's wild touristic merry-go-round: (1) **Hotel del Golfo** in *Procchio*, where the chef knew his trade. Barbecue and grills on the beach from June 20 to September 20; excellent Bistecca alla Fiorentina; pizzeria sideline. (2) **La Sirene** in *Portoferraio* for solid cookery of the family, by the family, and for you; no-monkey-business décor. (3) The **Hermitage** in *Biodola*. (4) **La Marinella** for finny critters and lobster. (5) The seaside **Zi Rosa** at *Portoferraio,* a gem among pizzerie; Manager Fuochi is a charming and gracious mentor to Americans. Other choices are **Kon-Tiki, La Triglia**, and **Iselba** in *Marina di Campo* and **Ape Elbana** or **Taverna Giamaica**, both in *Portoferraio*. **Giappone**, on the square, is Third-class; typical and simple. *Most of these establishments are closed in winter.* Incidentally, the **Hotel Centrale** in *Piombino* (mainland port for Elba excursionists) is decently adequate, if you stick to fish, pasta, and cheese.

Florence boasts numerous worthwhile middle-bracket restaurants—but she had surprisingly few sophisticated tables for a city of her breeding and patrician flair. **Oliviero** (via delle Terme 51R) now comes closest to satisfying that need; it still falls far short, however, of many oases in the capital. Three-room string of nooks, the first containing a bar and melodious piano tinkler and the next pair for calories only. Flamingo-hued cloths on extra-tiny tables; matching banquettes; greengage textiled walls; coffered ceilings. Our steak was too well educated to retain any real flavor of beef, but our partner's Delizie de Vitella Mode du Chef (shaved veal in a delicate sauce of cream, parsley, a touch of garlic, and champagne) was succulent; the Tuscan house wine is superb. Very attentive service. Substantial, miles from cheap, and moderately elegant, but not a true aristocrat in any sense.

The famous **Sabatini** (via Panzani 41) is again off our list. Here, to us, is a self-inflated, overblown presumption of an institution that gained world renown on its once-solid merits. In fairness, some Guidesters take exception to this view, love it, and think we should have our head and tongue examined. We'd appreciate your comments if you go.

Buca Lapi (via del Trebbio 1) is the classic choice of visiting firemen; cellar décor, travel-poster motif, 22 individual table lamps hanging from ceiling; indifferent cookery on our tries; in our estimate, too tourist-slick and expensive for anybody except first-timers.

Doney (via Tornabuoni 11) has combined his operation into a 2-part restaurant, bar, pastry shop, take-away counter, and tearoom in the same building. One dining quadrant is à la carte only, with deluxe tariffs; a 2nd serves light lunches. Entire complex redecorated and air-conditioned; so beloved by U.S. trippers that the only Italians we saw were on the staff; good cookery and good drinks

Harry's Bar (lungarno Amerigo Vespucci 22R) is a Florentine landmark; it's only a long olive-pit throw from the Excelsior. Still small, still intimate, still cozy; still a *must* for everybody. Here's an utterly captivating nook with a limited but tempting menu, the most delicious American-style snacks and dishes in central Italy, and drinks concocted with such love (usually by Leo, the Chief Mixmaster) you'll think you're back in "21" in New York. Heirs to the business, Sergio and Roberto, maintain perfect control of the late Harry's splendid domain. It remains a joy, professionally, to watch these master hosts receive traveler after traveler with such warmth, kindness, and individual interest. Animated, cosmopolitan, fun; highest recommendation throughout. Closed Sundays and December 20 to January 15. Don't miss it.

For hotel dining, the **Excelsior**'s Chef Alzetta is especially gifted in his special preparation of chicken, Spaghetti alla Matriciana, and rice with truffles. The **Aerhotel Baglioni Roof**, lovely on a summer night, caters heavily now to packaged groups. Stupendous view of the city, cool green garden décor with more than 2000 plants; food passable only; dancing discontinued; June 1 to September 1 only.

Back to the independents again, **Giovacchino** (via dei Tosinghi 2) is noted for its roasts. Self-service downstairs; dancing on the upper level; so-so cookery, in our opinion; possibly a stronger appeal to Italian clientele. The similar-sounding **Giovannino** (Borgognissanti 93r, near the Grand) served us a listless lunch again recently. Still low on our poll. For the economy-minded, **Buca Mario** (piazza Ottaviani 16) will give you a good dinner for low tabs; 3 rooms in cellar; clean, attractive, and plain; heavy local trade; increasingly popular with Americans. As Bucas go, we prefer this one to the aforementioned Buca Lapi. **Nandina** (piazza Santa Trinità), a simple spot, has recently changed hands, so we must nip back for another test. The downstairs **Buca dell' Orafo** ("Goldsmith"), tucked in behind the Ponte Vecchoio, is a family *trattoria* with savory cookery. It has continued to improve to the point that it is now frequented by the elite of Tuscany and their guests. Only a dozen tables; no décor; specialties include Stracciatella alla Buccia di Limone, Petti di Pollo, Bistecca alla Fiorentina, Bollito, and Stracotto. An amiable choice. **Sostanza,** behind the Excelsior, at via del Porcellana, is a highly touted *trattoria* among Florentines. Rough, amusing atmosphere; go noonish for lunch or at 7 P.M. or 10 P.M. for dinner, to avoid the peak of the throng; otherwise it's frenzy in Firenze. Best bets were the breast of chicken, local beefsteak that is enormous and mouth-melting, and vegetable soup. A popular stop. **Le Cantine,** in Palazzo Pucci, has had a change in management; we'll check in again soon. **Sherwood** (via Torta 7) sits you in huge blossom booths that climb up, up, and awaaay, like Jack's beanstalk, while the waiters bee-buzz in and out. Youngsters seem to enjoy its nectar. **La Loggia,** at piazzale Michelangelo, is a municipally owned century-old former art gallery. Its dramatic hillside site commands a 180° panorama of the city. Alfresco terrace lunching or dining among portico columns or an open patio bordered by stone balustrade; about 90 tables; pleasant, small glassed-in restaurant for wintertime. As a capricious little fillip, you may ride by carriage to this happy spot via the American Express Night Tour. Enchanting—*if* a surfeit of tour groups doesn't spoil the atmosphere. Have the appetite of a ravenous panther? The stomach of a hippo? Head straight for **Otello** (recently moved but still near the station). A barrage of howitzers couldn't be noisier—but that Big Gun in the kitchen couldn't possibly mow you down with a more walloping charge of fodder even though it's only a shadow of its former self. Masses of antipasti on rolling carts; colossal servings from heaps of spit-roasted *tordi* (thrushes) to mountains of hocks; sweets in portions calculated to turn a Sinatra into a Gleason at one sitting; phenomenally large fruits, many of which could compete with a Spalding medicine ball. Even the pepper mills are 5-feet tall! Sit in the hut-style room and wear your Paul Bunyan earmuffs. It won't be the best meal you've ever devoured, but we'll bet you a wheel of Gorgonzola it'll probably be the biggest. Fairly cheap tariffs; Goshen for a glutton. **Al Girarrosto** (9/10 piazza Santa Maria Novella) specializes in wild bore, venison, pheasant, and other forest denizens in season, plus a variety of saddle-broken grills. Frustrated anglers may point a pinkie at the live trout tank in the window and be sure of a satisfying catch. Two pleasant but routinely decorated floors; painting exhibits which are changed fortnightly; in summer, sometimes more comfortable to dine in the cellar nook rather than outside. If you're game for game, draw a bead on this one. Recently enlarged. **La Bussola,** near the Straw Market, offers back-room seclusion, deft service, and inspired Lasagne alla Ferrarese amid photos of strippers and other "personalities of the world." Open midday and 6 P.M. to 2 A.M.; closed Monday; very easy on the wallet.

Al Campidoglio (via del Campidoglio 8R) *can* have fine vittles and service to match. But when it's crowded, it's a different story: hurry-hurry, busy-busy, gobble-gobble, brrrrp-brrrrp, damn-damn. **G. Nuti** (via Borgo San Lorenzo 24N) is a tiny pizza sanctuary where the pasta pleases. Perfect for a bite or a nip. The **Da Zi Rosa** (via Fossi 12) is a modest haven where niblets are more of an attraction than its heartier choices. Nice people, but the portions we had were so tiny our female companion joked she would slip her lunch into her compact and save it for a snack later. We found few clients —yet the telephone was so busy on our visit it sounded like a direct line to Hialeah. **Camillo** (borgo San Jacopo 57-59R) is again one of our favorite *trattorias*. Throngs of visiting U.S. buyers continue to pour in here by the score to feast on Owner Bruno's delicate software. The food is still delicious —about that there's no question—and, at last, the client is being given kinder attention than of yore. Very recommendable for its high-quality cuisine. **Mamma Gina**, a few doors away, was taken over by 3 former Sabatini waiters recently and totally redecorated; they revised its kitchen toward the provision of grills. We like it even more now than before. The flairful **Ringo's Bar**, on the same street (19r), is costly but popular for its chef's salad served in a jumbo goblet. Nice on a warm day. **Paoli**, set in a palace, is on the comeback trail. **Villa La Massa** (see "Hotels"), on the outskirts, should dish you up a well-presented meal, if it's an "on" day with the mercurial chef and crew; a happy renaissance. **Queen Victoria** whips up a sweet Hollywood version of an 1890's ice cream parlor; its upstairs restaurant section is of a lesser nobility, however. Also for lightish biting, the **Pub George & Dragon** (borgo Santissimi Apostoli 33R) comes up with succulent snack selections in cozy Victorian surroundings. Sandwiches at the bar at all hours; reserve a table upstairs for heavier nibblings; increasingly popular with a seemingly pixilated following of gay young men; ownership by Savino Pinchiorri and his bubbly, extra-friendly, French-born Anna; closed Monday. **Da Dino** is noted for its wines; we were not impressed by the grubby surroundings and mediocre cookery, however. **Celestino** is intimate, inexpensive, and worthy as a purveyor of Florentine platters. Closed Tuesdays. **13 Gobbi** ("13 Hunchbacks"), near the Grand, does it the Hungarian way. It does it well, too. Chinese chow? **Fior di Loto** is *it*—and *it* alone, since no others exist here. At **Fiesole**, an art center and hill town a few miles distant, **Mario**, on the main square, served the best fare locally. Very inexpensive; the view (why you came) does not exist. We prefer the upstairs dining room in winter and the courtyard garden in summer. **Aurora**, nearby, is okay if you can sit outside and gaze along the Arno valley; the interior dining cell is a downright horror, in our opinion. The **Blu Bar** faces the same direction; it's salubrious for sipping. **Raspanti**, farther out, overlooks a Tuscan vale on the reverse of the ridge—not the Arno and Florence side. Pretty fair in season, but we'd prefer to view the main event. Don't bother with **Il Mulinaccio**, a chuck-wagon-style poser that can be chucked out as far as we're concerned; big show, little value.

In **Genoa**, your best dining bet is now the **Colombia-Excelsior Hotel**. Yumptious regional specialties, plus a wide range of international dishes; set menu tariffs approximately the same as its rivals'—but far, far more savory; clean, deluxe surroundings and top-category service (see "Hotels"). Among the independents, **Pichin** (vico Parmigiani 6) is typical of the locale. Don't be led to the first small room at the right; be sure to march across the hall and past the kitchen into the larger quarters opposite the entrance, where you will find about 25 tables. Up a few steps is a cozier nook. Worthy grills and roll-cart barbecues; wonderful Capricious Salad; appetizing fruit and vegetable displays; à la carte only; becoming rather expensive. Simple—but still a solid value. **Margherita da Zeffirino** (via XX Settembre 20) is a more recent buzz among local cognoscenti. Some prefer the upstairs section, which offers live music; personally, we opt for the plain and rustic downstairs feedery. Vast open-for-the-eye wildlife refrigerator at entrance; yawning tile oven where the game sizzles gamely; boar, venison, or other season-only choices aboard a rolling "hot counter" to serve you at tableside. If your smile is contagious, bustling young Proprietor Luciano might send over a glass of Prunella at the end of your meal. Thumpingly expensive, but very good. **Olivo** (piazza Raibetta 15) is large, straightforward in its Genoese fare—but now, sadly, it seems to be plunging downhill. Here was once *the* favorite of the businessmen and the family trade in the Old City. Closed Thursday. **Mario** (via Conservatori del Mare 332) is a *trattoria* in the same tradition; virtually no décor; cookery on the heavy side; dull but recommendable. The spacious **Alfredo El Cucciolo** (via San Vincenzo) features a Tuscan kitchen and tabs that strike us as inflated for the return. **Selvatico**, on the seafront Corso Italia, plays its several tiers to a chic glowing audience who crowd it year round. The blame is usually aimed at Pappardelle alla Boscaiola, delicate fresh pasta with mushrooms and cream. What a yum-yum! **Della Santa** (via Indoratori 1) nips in about 10 tables; the husband (Prince Borromeo's former chef) is at the skillets and the wife is at your elbow; limited menu of international selections; slow service; closed Mondays; better and better and better. **Justino's Gran Grotto** (11R via Fiume) is strictly for the traveler who must count and double count every penny; too dismal to please most merrymaking pilgrims, despite the adequate quality of its wares. **Taverna del Mille**, in the Sturla district, is amusing as a change of pacers. Former stable; décor of saddles, tack, wagon-wheel fixtures, stone walls, and muskets; wine flagons and cups with the names of Garibaldi's G.I.'s; a dozen tables inside, plus an alfresco terrace for warm-weather dining; delicious Triada (3 types of pasta). Saddlebags of fun on our last visit, but later comers now say nay. **Punta Vagno** and **Orizzonte** have both just locked their doors. **Caprice**, on the promenade, remains unspectacular but solid. Good. On a sunny day, a 20-minute excursion to *Boccadasse* (literally: "Mouth of the City") is especially recommended; here are the last remnants of an ancient fishermen's village, over a small cove. **Vittorio al Mare** is the big dining place, with what might be termed a seafoam-green, chipped-plaster rig with superb seafood—especially on that airy outdoor terrace of a fine summer's day. Don't confuse this one with its namesake in midtown. **Italia** (farther out toward *Nervi*) offers 2 waterside levels, sweeping panoramic windows to soak up grand vistas of the Mediterranean, and assorted maritime effects. Some of its best effects will appear after you've sampled its seafood antipasto or its delicious risotto. Ummmmm. Many romantic-minded couples steal away from the city's gaze to goo-goo-eye here. Pleasant. Another fair-weather charmer is **La Rocca** at the mountaintop village of *San Rocca* *di Camogli*, a ½-hour drive toward Rapallo (turn right from Ruta before entering the tunnel). Magnificent view from 3 drinking-dining terraces; chic clientele who continue to come, despite the generally slipshod administration; medium-to-high tabs, reserve in advance during peak season; 9 A.M. to midnight; closed January and February. Fetching when the heavens are blue.

Ischia's highest quality cuisine is dispensed in the lovely outdoor-indoor terrace restaurant of the luxury **Hotel Reina Isabella**; an excellent buffet lunch is daily offered to sunseekers in its informal adjoining **Sporting Terrace**. Both are fondly recommended. **San Montano** at San Montano Beach is the number one independent oasis for the visitor; nothing on the island except the Reina Isabella can touch this waterside restaurant, which draws the cream of the yachting trade. Open-air ambiance; the green tagliatelle and Mediterranean "lobster" are terrific; tariffs on the expensive side; take your bathing suit, pick your weather, and your lunch should be a happy one. **La Lampara** we disliked, because the prices seemed steep and the choice of eatables limited; terrace over the bay; not for us, despite its attractive setting. The little **Duilio**, almost next door, is 50% cheaper, and the seafood is delicious; very primitive, with service that couldn't be more confused; fun nevertheless, if you're in the mood. The portside **Il Porticciuolo** specializes in piscatorial picken's. **Romantica** has slipped somewhat, according to our local rumormonger. We don't know it personally, however. **Da Michele**, a wooden shack and wooden platform directly on the beach, offers bathing-suit dining in summer only. Food? The customers stuff the bikinis better than the chef stuffs the Cannelloni, but who cares? **Di Massa** is *Ponté d'Ischia*'s best bet. Two excursions for a sunny-day lunch: **Trattoria Terre di Fuoco** above *Citara Beach* (20 minutes from the Port); unpretentious but viewful terrace dining, with volcano smoke curling about your toes; the specialty is rabbit, but fortunately there is also a selection of heftier critters. **O Padrone do Mare** is *Lacco Ameno*'s leading seafood emporium; we prefer the platters to the people here, however. The southside village of *Sant' Angelo* is renowned for its thermal baths in natural rock formations; 2 lava-grain beaches flank the causeway; the sand is so hot the ravenous can literally fry an egg on it (the ravenous with good teeth, that is); many German tour troups. **Pensione La Palma** might be a good stop here, but arrange your table and your menu in advance. Awning-covered terrace; beach and sea panorama; peaceful. Finally, this terrain is famous for its wine; friendly imbibing is the next-to-principal sport. Of the whites, we'd suggest D'Ambra Vini, the stronger Biancolella or Forastera. Among the reds, Pede E'Palumbo ("Pigeon Foot") is the choicest of the coop.

Merano offers little, because most hotels require full pension. **Andrea** is intimate and regional. **Forsterbräu** is a beer hall for budget pockets; *very* popular (they are also served who only stand and wait). Be sure to sample the Bauer Speck here—a thin-sliced Tyrolean-cured meat that is sheer heaven. **Villa Eden**, on the outskirts, is said to provide "refined" cuisine amid parkland greenery.

In *Milan*, **Savini** is not just fine, in our opinion, it is fantastic—seemingly better than before. Rendezvous of La Scala artists since Italian opera was in knee pants; slightly formal atmosphere; happy little bar; too-bright illumination. Truly outstanding operation by the Pozzi family, papa Angelo and son Renaldo, who speak good English. Closed Sunday. Our top recommendation in the city. **El Toulá** is elegant, friendly, and peopled with chic Milanese society. Location behind La Scala in the city's "Wall Street" district; spacious; gracious décor; advance reservation suggested, especially during the opera season. A handsome link in this chain operation. **Giannino** (via Antonio Sciesa 8) remains one of the truly great 5-star restaurants of Europe, although our latest visit left us with the feeling that it has gone off a bit. Several modern, handsome dining rooms; glassed-in kitchen and fascinating food displays; immaculate, charming decoration; initial reception sometimes lax, but table service usually (not always) attentive and thoughtful; direction by Elio; nutrition by Chef Mattraelli. Still recommendable. **St. Andrews** (via Sant' Andrea) is a First-category address that is beloved by locals. Mock-wood ambiance; central hearth the main decorative feature; bookcases on walls; leather chairs and love seats around low tables; subtle lighting from overhanging hooded lamps; rust carpets; lime-green textiles; profession-proud waiters in formal attire. The cookery was much better than average; it was much costlier than average, too. Our severest complaint, however, involves its deafening music that blares through the sound system—not only killing the otherwise pleasant surroundings, but virtually murdering any possibility of normal conversation. After we had started our meal, this cacophony forced us to throw in the sponge and escape to a quieter retreat. What a pity; this could be a gem.

La Nos ("The Walnut," at Via Amedei 2 in old Milan) is "camp" in a smooth, professional way—serious but zany. Diners walk through a long, art-filled corridor, up some stairs to the high-ceilinged restaurant, to find 2 main sections and 2 smaller nooks. Whirring fans; suspended Tiffany-style lamps; a church pulpit used as a bottle rack; a menu in the shape of a walnut tree. Décor seemingly assembled from Grandma's rummage sale; nevertheless it is homey and, surprisingly, most effective. Minstrels who look as if they've been wandering since Justinian's court play softly and pleasantly. Specialties focus upon Milanese skilletry—rather heavy and routine to our palate, but who cares? Ask for plump, jolly Proprietor Guido Roncoroni or sympathetic, mischievous Dino, who looks like a cross between Marcello Mastroianni and Dean Martin. Very popular among Milanese, but almost unknown to travelers; English spoken by all the efficient, friendly staff with whom we talked. Closed Sunday and August. Fun is the keynote.

Le Quattro Stagioni (the Four Seasons), about 20 minutes along the Autostrada, is a pleasant expedition on a sunny day or starlit night. Open-air dining in an attractive garden with fountain; kidney-shape tables; immaculate glassed-in kitchen; medium-lofty tabs. Try Pollo alla Creta, an herb-soaked bird of paradise; finish off with its La Grappe cheese from the Savoie—and sigh with bliss. A favorite for upper-crust Milanese family outings. **Giggi Fazi**, the Roman entrepreneur, has 2 places in the area—on piazza Risorgimento in the city, and a summer branch at via Lodovico Il Moro 167-169 in **Ronchetto delle Rane**—both disappointingly inferior to his original in the capital. The metropolitan one is big, bustling, and barren, with friendly waiters who ride you to decide what to order NOW—and, when it comes, to eat it NOW; dancing under bare-bulb lighting; just so-so NOW. The suburban one has been rebuilt and renamed **El Ronchett**. Neither is our platter of pasta.

Alfio (via Senato 31) is the happiest "discovery" of one of our recent Milanese busy-bee circuits—and this one is a honey that seems to get sweeter with each new buzz in our repollination flight. Midway down the entrance stairs you spy a huge open freezer shelf, overhung with garlands of fruits and vegetables and groaning with a magnificently colorful, diversified antipasto exhibit. The main dining room has a curved opaque skylight, living flora, lime-lemon-orange variations in napery, and bamboo walls. A few steps above this sanctum are 3 paneled sanctuaries with about 5 tables each; upstairs there's still another pair of regionally decorated bowers with 15 tables. The cuisine is excellent; the specialties are antipasti and fish, but a huge menu boasts almost everything that grows or wiggles; the prices are medium. We've been fond of this house for many years.

Taverna del Gran Sasso (pizzale Principessa Clotilde 8) looks like the warehouse on the MGM studio lot marked: "Storage #67, Italian Restaurant Scenery." And has it got it—*mamma mia!* Your eyeballs are poked by wagon wheels, garlic strands, corn clusters, brass pots, wine jugs, cheese wedges, cattle yokes, oaken barrels, sausage, hams, chickens, salamis, ceramics, breads, even a sewing machine—plus checkered tableclothes, natch. The dishes are chiefly from the Abruzzi province. We must confess we did not eat here; we merely stepped into the room and let our pores feed us by osmosis. Perhaps that's the way to do it.

Il Canneto, sometimes called Osteria del Vecchio Canneto (via Soferino 56), is the newer seafood version of Gran Sasso; it's under the same décor-happy ownership. Greetings to all comers with a foghorn and ship's whistle; cellar situation; huge room decked with brass musical instruments, an ocean-liner's anchor, sails, a winch, and fathoms of chain; singing waiters in ship-wreck costume; leviathan 16-course meal for a white bait price tag. The only items not from the briny deep are the pasta, the fruit, the wine, and the bib tucked under your proliferating chins. Snacks prohibited; only full feasts served. Cargoes of fun—but bring 6 famished friends along to help clean the platter.

The **Biffi** was restyled but not beefed up, in our opinion. Now it is a modern adaptation of an Edwardian snackery and is plugged into a subterranean music hall. The quality is typical of the high Doney-chain efforts, but it lost something in its new lyrics.

Famed and fine orchestra conductor David Blum waves his baton for **Boeucc Flavio** (piazza Belgioioso). We'll give this one a sounding on our own tuning forks soon. Thanks for the upbeat tip, Maestro!

Venturesome? Then don't miss **Scoffone Bottega del Vino** (via Victor Hugo 4), one of the most ancient wine houses in Italy. Scrumptious hot and cold dishes are available at a do-it-yourself counter or in a more modern cafeteria-style dining room in the rear. We much prefer the front segment with its painted walls and ceiling. Black dado, wrought-iron chandeliers, and earthy atmosphere. Our bottle of Barolo (a rich blood-red vintage from the Piedmont), slices of cold suckling pig, pickled vegetables, and floating mozza-rella (it should come in its whey when it is properly kept and served) were admirable straightforward fare. Prices are unbelievably low; the quality is extremely high. Hundreds of varieties of native wines await experimenting oenologists. Very plain—but just plain wonderful for what it is.

Hotel dining? The My Grill of the **Principe e Savoia** is a stunner. The adjoining L'Etoile is perfect for lighter cozy nibbles. The Rib Room of the **Hilton** sizzles with roast beef for penthouse rancheros. Its next-door Music Club is a danceable top spot for the evening. The **Palace Hotel Roof**, open May through October, is so up-to-date it might have been designed by Raymond Loewy; lovely terrace and view. We like it. The **Cavalieri** also has a pleasant roof garden in season. The Conty Grill of the **Continental,** a string of agreeably decorated little rooms, is nice for handholding.

Cheap, colorful Milanese restaurants? Very few, to our knowledge; the city is too busy and too industrial to support them. One simple, smooth, well-run pizzeria which makes our taste buds stand up and whistle is **Santa Lucia** (via San Pietro all'Orto 3). Walls flanked with perhaps 100 photos of film, opera, and entertainment personalities; open kitchen aft; immaculate surroundings; nobody we saw spoke English. Fine for wallet-watchers, with low-priced spaghetti (various sauces), pizza, prosciutto and salami in the buck-and-under league; dramatically mixed clientele, from sable to mink to let-out lapin; here's the Sardi's AND Reuben's of Milan. Operates nonstop from 9 A.M. to 3 A.M. Highly recommended. Among other popular lower-cost stops we found were **Wienevard**, in the Galleria (bar upstairs, tavern-type dining rooms in cellar; commercial in tone) and, in summer, the Italo-Austrian-rustic **Don Lisandar Birreria**, at via Manzoni 12A (patio with umbrellas but no grass or trees). The **Foyer**, on via Verdi, is said to be good for post-operatic tonsil-ticklers, but we missed it. Two of the leading *trattorie* are the world-famous **Bagutta** (via Bagutta 14) and the heavier-handed **La Tampa da Antonio** (via Laghetto 3); both cater to artists and local Bohemians. A Montana Guidester wrote, "**Al Ciovassino**, via Ciovassino 5, is excellent, with Italian food priced right, and untainted by tourists—tops in any man's country." We hied ourselves there immediately (it's down a small alley about 300 yards from La Scala) and found every word to be true. Two rooms; tempera paintings brightening the walls; kindly personnel who speak only Italian; hardy, belly-filling fare; closed Sunday. Salutes and thanks to this sage sagebrush epicure! Guidesters' letters, incidentally, trickle in constantly saying how delighted their authors are with the food, prices, and most of all, the warm reception provided by the owner, who has practically invented a new sign language to make himself understood to readers of this book. We are grateful to him and to you. **Collina Pistoiese** (via Amedei 1) is one station where the local soccer teams swallow hardy nutrients. It greets you with an entrance crammed with antipasto; then come 4 rooms, wooden arches, paintings, engravings, and a final scrimmage with perfectly wonderful regional cuisine and house wine, all for very moderate tabs. Closed Friday. Recommended. **Vecchia Osteria del Laghetto**, in the ghetto at via Festa del Perdono 1, is a handsome, rustic haven for games. **La Pantera**, at #12 on the same row, was a dismal, miserable, nauseating failure on every score when we sampled it. Not recommended by us no matter how heavily touted it may be locally or in the international press. Least expensive of all are the **Alemagna** snack bars, several of which are sprinkled through the city; clean, fast, and money-saving.

Montecatini 's 2 feederies of distinction are the **Centrale** (piazza del Popolo 20) and **Le Panteraie** (via delle Panteraie). The former is glamourless, with a no-nonsense atmosphere; some of Tuscany's best cookery in colorless surroundings. The latter is a short hop from the center, in a scenic area; swimming pool, dancing, solid fare, very agreeable in season; open May to October, and December to February only; recommended. A moderate price Tuscan house called **San Francisco** is said to be quite good; lunch only; top service; ask locally for directions. Ditto for **Tettuccio**.

Naples ? The late Ian Fleming, debonair creator of Secret Agent James Bond, said in one of his last books, "The American travel writer, Fielding, summed up Neapolitan cuisine: 'It runs,' he wrote, 'from high mediocre to just plain lousy.' I cannot improve on that." Back then we were complimented that this famous gastronome and cosmopolite agreed with our premise that no major city in Italy offered a larger percentage of dirtier, sloppier, or more disappointing restaurants vis-a-vis good ones. Now we regret to report that with the enormous falloff of tourism due to the total elimination of scheduled transatlantic passenger liners the culinary picture is even darker. Another contributing factor is that its numerous private clubs provide savory full meals for modest tariffs. Thus, with so much of both the transient and the moneyed-resident traffic drained off, scores of its public oases are tottering from fiscal drought.

The most consistently dependable choice for lunch or for dinner in the entire region is the **Hotel Excelsior**. All of the rigidly top-quality cookery, service, and hygienic standards maintained throughout the great CIGA chain are scrupulously observed here, with the consequence that the fare is uniformly excellent. Because Naples is the birthplace of the pizza, you'll find it on this menu—and *is* it delicious!?! The **Ambassadors' Palace** and the **Mediterraneo** offer superior views but we've found their viands sometimes villainous. The rest of the hotel pack have run-of-the-mill kitchens at best and abominable ones at worse. **La Sacrestia** (via Orazio 116), choicely positioned on a hillside 15 minutes from the center, draws bevies of smartly attired sophisti-cats. Main dining room with alcoves for diners who prefer the illusion of privacy with their seen-ery; neo-Baroque décor encompassing frosted ceiling beams, strategically placed tinted mirrors, paintings, and chandeliers; more intimate subterranean chamber with tiny bar, stucco walls, blue tile floor, and a scattering of tomes; outside terrace for viewing the crescent-shape metropolis while sampling the Assaggi ("Mixed Pastas to Test"); dignified but not warm service. While the Scazzetta (spinach or broccoli smothered in cheese and cream) and the seafood we tried were sound investments, our "Entrecôte alla Griglia " was a misnomer, because what appeared was a T-bone so thin that it could have been a snack for a Junior Girl Scout.

Don Pasquale, in our opinion, has been seriously scarred by its recent revolution. For a time it was closed. After its reopening, we feel that many of its former assets of charm, of succulence in cookery, and of other earlier drawing cards have faded to the point where we now regard it as a ho-hum target. Sad, sad, sad. . . .

Cantinone (via San Pasquale 56, at via dei Mille) seems popular with locals, but only so-so to us. Handsome décor featuring a colossal open grill facing the main room; 2 adjoining units separated by rough-wood lattices, hanging air-dried hams, smoked sausages, garlic garlands, and all the paraphernalia of Italian Rustic gimmickry; Pompeian-rouge and Capri-blue linens; rush-bottomed chairs; waiters in red and azure minismocks; appetizing selection of meats in 2 refrigerated vitrines flanking the chimney; wild goat the roast specialty. Service so rapid we'd bet you could get a minute-steak in 30-seconds flat—too fast, in fact. It's not a gastronomic shrine by any means.

Galeone is up, up, up, on Posillipo where it has become a favorite meeting perch among middle and top echelon businessmen. Lovely situation; vittles good but not distinguished; service alert. A medium-high flier.

The **Tiffany** (via Petrarca), too, is a steep taxi climb from midcity. It's also a steep ride back—and seldom have we squandered taxi fare so foolishly. Never again—not dinner, not lunch, not even breakfast at this Tiffany's ever, ever, ever, for us.

Da Ciro (via Santa Brigida 71–74) impressed us most recently as being in a decline. It was a sad disappointment this time.

Il Girarrosto (Fratelli Imperatore di via Scarlatti 180) is a tiny food shop with an even tinier restaurant attached. Very informal; excellent for snackery-smackery; Wednesday is its day off.

La Quercia ("The Oak"), on vicolo della Quercia near piazza Dante, is a favorite among princes, potentates, and the pasta peerage; it continues to draw favorable reports; no imported liquors are available in this *trattoria*; also locked up on Wednesday.

Giuseppone a Mare (discesa Capo Posillipo), on the sea perhaps 10 minutes from the center in the vicinity of Masaniello, is relaxing on a sunny day. Extra-fresh fish every day; average meal from $12.50 to $15 per person. Specialities of oysters and shellfish, vended from table to table by a blue-sweatered *ostricaro,* or "oysterman"; on the simple side in furnishings; open terrace; clean, bustling, busy; pizza a dream; not much English spoken; don't go on Wednesday. Watch out your check isn't loaded in petty amounts by the cashier or waiter. The **Pizzicato** (piazza Municipio) serves allegedly American-style refreshments, with pizza the feature upstairs; when we saw it, however, its cavernous premises were so grubby that they'd have taken away our appetite if their food already hadn't. We rate it as abominable.

Salvatore (Riviera di Chiaia 91) greets guests with a glassed-in sidewalk segment; behind that is a small vaulted room; both are heavily patronized luncheon nooks for neighborhood office workers. Acceptable Pizza Margherita, Prosciutto e Carciofini, and Vermicelli alla Vongole, though you'd probably be happier with a fish dish (say, Frittura di Pesce del Golfo). There's strolling entertainment by the Geriatric Brothers, who offer witty ditties in the local *lingua.* Fair to middling.

D'Angelo (15 minutes by taxi up the Vomero) couldn't be more gimmicky if it tried for the next 500 years. Glorious view, open terrace, good pizza—but such tourist-trap stridence leaves us not only stone cold but frozen stiff. Closed Tuesday. Our most unfavorite type of restaurant. **Le Arcate** (nearly next door at via Aniello Falcone 249), also large and barnlike, now exudes more zing. A discothèque now contributes to its youthful appeal. In this production-belt category, better geared for first-timers; also inactive on Tuesday.

In the Santa Lucia Basin (marine cove opposite the Excelsior and Vesuvio Hotels), except on Wednesday, **La Bersagliera** is still an unabashed tourist-hooker—but, regardless of this drawback, it is now definitely worth a visit. The waterside terrace is a delight, despite its pushy waiters. Spotlessly clean, enormous kitchen, which you may inspect; delicious Mozzarella Carrozza starter (cheese melted over a toasty carriage); tempting shellfish platters displayed on beds of chipped ice (but *please* don't eat them); fresh sea denizens on our try—so newly plucked from the Mediterranean they could shed an indignant sneer your way. Prices are on the high side, in line with the brutal official tariffs on piscatorial gastronomy around the shores of this coastal nation. Although it is sited in Naples' nucleus of huckster hideaways, this one seems to be king of the sea. Tip to sportsmen: Extending from the terrace townward are several outstanding competitive yacht clubs where the sleekest and latest Italian racing machines float. You're welcome to stroll down, take a peek—and lumber away lime with envy. **Zi Teresa**, through the binoculars of our observation ship, has been sinking. It exhibited a doorman dressed to resemble Horatio Hornblower, pushy waiters also in costume (local wags quip that that's why you pay more here than at Bersagliera), a table-hopping photographer, strolling musicians, grotto atmosphere (nets, lobster traps, Vesuvio blowing its stack, *et al.*), plus poor spaghetti, wretched saltimbocca, unasked-for mineral water and potatoes, a free glass of Liquore Galliano, and puffed-up tariffs on our recent revisit. We think Disney World is a universe better. **Transatlantico** was redecorated some time ago—or "resurrected" would be more accurate. The fabulous refashioning reportedly consumed all of $2000! Lots of fresh paint, awnings on the terrace, some brand-new light bulbs—what next? The locale is bewitching, but we've never been fond of its staff attitudes. As for the rest of them, we're fed up with the dirt, sham, the surly personnel, and the feeling of being clipped which always seems to come when we dine along this row.

Ercolano is a tiny, flavorful installation in a 3rd class hotel. The jovial boss, who speaks fractured English, decides what *you* eat in a warmly hospitable way. Can be fun if you're in the mood. **Damiani**, a hopping pizza emporium 9 miles up the Domiziana Route toward Rome, has facilities for swimming (day or night), including 250 cabanas; restaurant of sorts, plus bar; dancing on weekends; much frequented by U.S. officers and families in season; jumping on our visit. The neighboring **Löwenbräu Beer House** in the Londres (piazza Municipio) serves adequate but not outstanding German and American selections.

A 'O Re Burlone, above Gaeta Bay, comes on with a strong tourist-oriented, gimmick-riddled personality that is typical of other Remington Olmstead, Jr., properties. Inevitably the show, show, show, and more show is the thing. Some outlanders find it highly appealing; personally, we happen to regard it as a hoked-up trumpery, an opinion with which you might well disagree.

Padua? We'd bet on **Le Padovanelle**, on the outskirts, **Dotto**, and **Isola di Caprera**, in that order—but without much enthusiasm for any.

Palermo sets its most distinguished tables at **Gourmand's** (via Libertà). Mod-minded décor with a culinary display near the door; L-shape chamber;

tables lining the walls, separated at intervals of 3 by black-and-chrome dividers; sound-suppressing cork paneling; thick carpeting; silver-hued swivel
lamps reminiscent of beauty-parlor hair driers; fresh flowers everywhere;
adroit service; well-heeled clientele of businessmen and their ladies; steep but
value-received tabs. Spaghetti alla Gourmand's, with mozzarella blended into
the sauce, is a savory selection; so are many of the fish dishes as well as game
in season. Now one of the choicest palate-pleasers in the city. **Villa Igiea**'s
kitchen crew and service personnel at last seem to be snapping to attention.
The Great Hall atmosphere still constitutes a pleasant setting, and now with
the staff morale higher we are pleased to put it back on the "recommended"
list. **La Caprice** (via Cavour 42–44) is chic and so are the tariffs; bright yellow
décor; small bar by the entrance; canopied rear patio; smart. The newer
Charleston (piazzale Ungheria) is a similar flapper that has been dancing up
the rankings. Now considered by many to be tops in town. (This one migrates
to Mondello when the weather warms.) **La Stipa** (via Cavour 97, a block from
the waterfront) is a brick-lined den divided into 4 small segments by arches;
it is also one of the few truly fine, yet inexpensive, restaurants on Sicily.
Antipasto selections are made from the buckling table in the rear. These may
be followed by a superb Involtini (veal wrapped around mozzarella, ham,
bread crumbs, and parsley), filet in cream sauce with prosciutto and mushrooms, or the house specialty: Spaghetti Frutta di Mare (spaghetti laced with
savory sea-morsels and cooked piping hot in a bag). Unusually friendly service and memorable culinations. Closed Wednesday. **Al Gabbiano**, on the sea
at *Mondello*, caps them all for finny fare. Nice outdoor terrace for sun-day-
excursionists or weekly cooing moonshiners. **Gambero Rosso,** nearby, is
similar. In town, we'd pick the rusticky **Osteria Marinera,** only a toot from
the ferry port. **La Botte**, in *Monreale*, is said to be worthy. **Al Fico d'India**,
in the center of Palermo, is not, but NOT, in our opinion.

In *Perugia*, have a look at the better-known **Brufani** and the small,
less-expensive **La Rosetta**, only a block apart in hotels of the same name—
and decide for yourself. We're particularly fond of the high-quality service
and sound regional fare of the latter, and our latest check rekindled the
longtime romance; a number of Guidesters are unfond of the former, which
cocks a markedly greater commercial eye toward its numerous banquets and
receptions and which utilizes its Palace Room in winter and its Biblioteca in
summer whenever they're available for independent diners. The **Bibo** is popular; the **Excelsior Lilli** and the **Grifone** are especially interesting for their
typical local wines for a reasonable outlay.. The last is air-cooled.

Pisa fare leans to the unglamorous, even at the **Hotel dei Cavalieri** and
the newer **Hotel Duomo**. Wev've been able to find only one surefire candidate
in this area: the **Nettuno** at *Viareggio*, 15 minutes out by car. Harbor
location; semiopen kitchen; top quality dining; on the expensive side for Italy.
Well worth the ride. **Margherita** is reportedly well seeded for the pasta
playoff; it's still untested by us.

Pompeii? Ouch! Until recently, we'd rather have lunched on Ken-L-
Ration and Octagon soap than chance another crack at the **Ristorante Turis-
tico**, opposite the entrance to the ruins—but reports indicate it has improved.
Fervent prayers for (1) its success, if it has, and (2) you, if it hasn't. We are

told **Tiberio** is better. The former closes on Tuesday; the latter is open the week around.

In *Portofino*, **Il Pitosforo** holds the lead. Situation farthest out on the bayfront; 2 stories above street level, with a small interior restaurant, a 20-table, semiopen terrace, and a lovely view; service friendly, menu local and substantial; very expensive by local standards; try a bottle of Bianco Secco Portofino wine, dry and agreeable, with an amusing label. Best in the village. The **Nazionale** is tailored for tourists, but skillfully so; terrace-dining 20 yards from bay, smack in the center of things; better-than-average food; also expensive for region. The **Splendido Hotel** cuisine is Deluxe again in every respect, and its setting is magnificent. Our recent lunch was Splendido from soup, to service, to Saltimbocca. **Delfino**, around the bay between Nazionale and Il Pitosforo, has a modern kitchen, a plain décor, and a celebrity-starred clientele; seafood a specialty; far from cheap; cookery fair rather than outstanding. **La Gritta** is a Turkish-style bar replete with sports-car-height chairs, cushions, and diners in blue jeans; only for special tastes, which aren't ours.

In *Positano*, **Buca di Bacco** still is, and seems to be ever, the favorite. Better than ever. Discounting the local white wine, the **Hotel Sirenuse** sets a savory spread—but it costs and costs. **Taverna del Leone**, just past the Hotel San Pietro, keeps pounding pleasing pizzas till 2 A.M. **Tre Sorelle** is another pie-eyed protagonist. **Chez Black** and **Santa Caterina** get honorable mention from local chums; we were too wracked with ricotta to slice our way into either.

Rapallo has the air-conditioned, fern-lined **Da Fausto** (piazza Nuova Posta), the third successive enterprise operated by the celebrated host of the same name; arbor-styled booths give garden effect; the movie stars' favorite; expensive; ask for Signorina Rosanam, Fausto's pert, pretty, English-speaking daughter, who is usually on hand. The sea-sited **Sibelius** rolls in with coffee, tea, snacks, and some of the chicest clientele on the coast; a few Guidesters aver that it may be slipping. **Rosa Bianca** is wilting, too, according to our on-the-spot sources. **Tigullio's Rocks**, a later entry uphill between Rapallo and Chiavari, has a striking view of Tigullio Gulf; already popular. Pizzeria-type stops are a good alternative in this town, since none of the above places is gastronomically significant.

Ravello's feederies are almost entirely limited to the innkeepers' kitchens. Disgraceful!

Rimini hasn't a single establishment which can be called first-rate. The dining room of the **Grand Hotel** is its only Deluxe oasis. **Chez Vous**, nearby, is about the best independent *chez* in this sea-side district—but "best" being a relative word, we'd call it only slightly better than fair. In the city, **Vecchia Rimini** is the top choice, mostly for Adriatic fauna. L-shape room broken up by venetian-blind partitions; prices high for this unpretentious corner, but substantial quality and wide range offered; ask for Giovanni. **Da Bruno** (corso Umberto I 79) has a small terrace; inside, the walls crawl with the most jaundiced painted fish, lobsters, and fruit which ever turned this diner bilious-green by osmosis; beyond the immaculate kitchen, in the alley, an ancient bag at least 110 years old mumbles and mutters as she grills real fish over a battery of charcoal-filled buckets; they're a masterpiece of cookery, a delight to the palate, especially the *misto* (mixed) plate; little-to-no English is spoken. **Da Nello** is plain and also maritime. **Artists Tavern** is a boon for travelers who don't speak or read even their own language. No menu—just picture album into which you point your pinkie at your entrée. It consists of an open patio plus a grocery-lined inner sanctum. The chef might be a sculptor, but he certainly isn't an artist when it comes to gastronomy. The prices, not incidentally, are way, way, waaaay, too weighty for the featherweight rewards, in our opinion. **Nord Ouest-Club Nautico** (a pert little sailing center) is the pick-o-the-port for salty types. **Belvedere** (a 200-yard walk to the end of the pier) is another favorite mooring for brows that have borne more corporate tax problems than yachting caps; it conjures up visions of a Levantine Atlantic City to our naughty-cal peepers.

Rome has everything for every pocketbook and taste. Again 3 of our team have just fanned out to eat ourselves cross-eyed through the heart of its galaxy from gastronomy shrines to sleazy spaghetti slingers. Now that we have lumbered away from the last tables of this marathon and compared notes over triple Alka Seltzers, here are our evaluations of this year's culinary scene, with Peninsula-wide differences open for your disagreement:

For *international* fare, in descending order of preference our top kudos go to the quartet of Sans Souci, El Toulá, La Graticola del Jackie O' and St. Andrews.

In atmosphere, quality, variety and s-m-o-o-t-h-l-y polished service, **Sans Souci** (via Sicilia 20) has so steadily and unwaveringly continued to climb the poles of sophistication and savvy that we regard it without qualification as the reigning monarch. Convenient site a few steps from via Veneto; inspired ownership by Bruno Borghese; cunning, softly illuminated little bar in separate room at entrance; necklace of split-level nooks and crannies fetchingly strung with their walls in green, yellow, and white tapestries and their banquettes in handsome light leather; melodizing by singer-pianist with guitarist. Comprehensive, original menu offering outstandingly savory national and international dishes; equally laudable wines and other libations; splendidly trained service personnel; fleets of alluring tableside carts; cascades of flambé fireworks; dressy clientele; *dinner only* that should ring in at about $25 each with a good wine. First Maître Giancarlo Schianchi and Sommelier Nino are on top of your pleasure every second. If you hit it under normal conditions, from start to finish your spirits and your palate should be *sans souci* in this suave, chic, patrician establishment. Closed Mondays; always reserve in advance. Here, in our opinion, is absolutely *the* brass ring on the Roman merry-go-round.

El Toulà (via della Lupa 29) is a link in the chain that boasts colorful hideaways in Cortina and on the Costa Smeralda. It exudes a mellowed élan of tranquility and *haute cuisine* which attracts the quiet, burnished, old-moneyed aristocrats as its major clients. Here's a moss-green nookery where the walls are covered with velvet and the carpet is earth-hued; there are vegetables and flowers on the tiny tables; at night everything would dissolve in an instant if illumination were not by candles. Our heaven-sent Tagliatelle and South Tyrolean Sondbichilar white wine made us grateful for our chosen profession; moreover the final summation came as an additional blessing, it was so low by comparison with billings in other top-rank establishments in this and other capitals. The dominant theme here is subtle seduction. If that certain someone shares your mood, you'll probably love it, her, and everything in sight. Very, *very* chic and very, *very* good.

La Graticola del Jackie O' (Via Boncompagni 11, ½-block from via Veneto) consists of complementary twins. "The Grill," down one flight, is an elaborate, plushly decorated restaurant, while Jackie O' is a glittering ground-floor disco-nightclub. In one striking way it might be likened to Maxim's of Paris, because here for the moment (but for how long?) is the leading Italian showcase for theatrical personalities, gold-disk rock stars and other self-styled Beautiful People who come to see and to be seen. The manager told us that Mrs. Onassis has granted permission for the use of her name; we couldn't see if his fingers were crossed. Impressive canopy-corridored entrance; winding staircase to large, quietly voguish, segmented premises in tavern motif; immaculate open kitchen and king-size grill firing to greet clients as they step inside; discreet piped music; cunning 4-table adjoining bar due for expansion. The emphasis is on meats and switches to fish on Fridays. Our bill for our light dinners and rosé was $12.04 per appetite, but it could have run a lot higher with more costly choices. Go late, late, late—not before 10:30 ever—and reserve in advance; closed July 25 to August 25, but otherwise in action 7 days per week; *dinner only*. An important and interesting addition to the after-dark scene in the capital. Enjoy!

The smaller, more intimate, more reasonably priced **St. Andrews** (via Lazio 22/A, also ½-block from via Veneto) is in major contrast to the above trio. This little siren has the comfortable, cozy milieu of a select private club. Bar at entrance; 2 adjoining rooms; paneled walls with taseful modern paintings artfully placed; subtle to dark illumination with highlighted touches of greenery; deft, sophisticated client attention; limited but carefully chosen menu; good wine list. Its tariffs are suprisingly low for its stature, with the average all-inclusive check perhaps $12; our proprietary-label whisky was only $1.20 per drink, with Chivas and other premium brands at $1.80. Also *dinner only* from 8 P.M. to 1 A.M.; also go late; closed Monday. Director Turriziani is principally assisted by Barmen Vittorio and Stefano; they administer it as urbanely as if they were wearing silk gloves. A benison for weary wayfarers who wish to relax, to talk, and even to hold hands.

George's (via Marche 7) has now rocketed out of its temporary slump so brilliantly that save for one—and only one—obstacle, we would rank it with the aforementioned pacesetters. Frenchy rather than Italian in tone; satin-lined ceilings; lamps and flowers on tables; lovely garden terrace; smooth dinner music; attention now sharply honed. More popular than ever with the elegant element of midtown types (via Veneto is just a skip away); gourmet food shop lip-smack beside the canopied entrance. What puts our hair up is its tariffs—even considering the strong-dollar-weak-lira economy that weaves elastic into North American budgets these days. A moderate lunch can casually wave *ciao* to $50. Usually closed from August 10 to September 10. Getting better and better; now warmly recommended for quiet luxury at blue-ribbon prices.

Hosteria dell'Orso (via di Monte Brianzo 93), for more than three decades the unchallenged dining and/or dancing rendezvous on the Italian Peninsula, has lost its crown and deteriorated heartbreakingly. Founder Antonio Prantera, the genius who was president of the nation's 240-thousand-member Restaurant, Bar and Café Association for a quarter of a century, resold it in '76 to his handsome, charming nephew, Alessandro Basile, after the failure of the recent first buyer. It occupies Dante's fourteenth-century home, an official National Monument. The former ground-floor Blue Bar is now the Piano Bar, with a pianist and 2 guitarists; this is the only segment which was going well during our latest visit. Sig. Basile, who sadly admitted that the rest had dropped off sharply, nurtures ambitious plans. By the time you read this, the princely Borgia Room with its lapis lazuli pillars and gold utensils might —repeat, might—be reopened, as might La Cabala nightclub, which of yore entertained as great a number and variety of stellar celebrities as any oasis in the world. Lorenzo Galeazzi, Sig. Prantera's master chef of 20 years, reportedly will be reengaged. While the author was interviewing the new owner, another member of the Fielding team independently slipped inside without identification to test its standards; for a mediocre single dinner, his bill with tip was a whopping $48.16. Heavy group traffic helps to support this once-great institution which formerly accepted only the chic-est of the chic. While our most fervent good wishes ride for its comeback, regretfully we are so skeptical that we must wait and see.

For *Italian* fare, our numbers 1, 2, 3, 4, and 5 rankings go, with tongues slapping our chest, to **Cesarina** (via Piemonte 109–115). Here is one of Italy's greatest exponents of national cookery and since 1961 our favorite regional culinary pilgrimage in the Eternal City. Mamma Cesarina, a smiling Powerful Katrinka, drew acclaim for her Bologna establishment until she found communist interference intolerable and packed off to Rome. Now you'll probably see her standing in her immaculate open kitchen, pounding the pasta while waving instructions to the staff with her busy, muscular arms. Mama's cookery is just plain superb; noisy after 1:30 or 9 P.M., so go earlier if you prefer its more tranquil moods; ask for Maître Ivo (rhymes with "heave-ho"), whose smile and whose English are cheering. Be *sure* to try a tiny cup (not bowl) of Mamma's heavenly Passatelli first, followed by the tri-plate—bite-size samplings of 3 different types of pasta called Misto Cesarina—while sipping her Albana white wine from the North; you will go out of your mind about them, and that's a promise! After this, nibble her oh-so-delicious Giambella, a featherlight lemon-flavored cake dipped in the Albana before application to your soul. Beef Tartare aficionados normally bask with her Carpaccio— paper-thin slices of filet mignon with the perfectly complementary dressing and seasoning. In spite of the scads of fellow countrymen who have now "discovered" it (many of them, we blush to confess, through this *Guide*), salaams and salutes to every department. Closed in August and one night each week. Which evening? The evening Mamma wants to doll up for a date!

Now for the grab bag of the lesser plums and prunes. Good hunting!

Villa Miani is so special in character that tranquility seekers adore it and swingers loathe it. In '70 this magnificent pre-Roman estate atop Monte Mario, 20 to 40 minutes from the center on via Trionfale near the Hilton, was converted by an oil baron and his associates into a gastronomic oasis. As an introduction to its grandeur, the driveway from gate to doorsteps winds through parklands with small lakes for more than 1 kilometer. As you drink, dine, or wander through the numerous terraces of the commanding 3-story mansion or its vast gardens, Rome is breathtakingly at your feet. Although banquets and receptions are its main sources of income, individual patrons are welcomed and coddled with even a greater measure of grace and attentiveness. During the cooler months you may feast, often in semisolitary splendor, in a historic, colorful, fascinating *taverna* with gaily muralled arched ceilings. When you make your reservation, we urge that you ask Manager Roger Borella to arrange that you try its superexcellent antipasto, followed by the pasta specialties of either Ruote di Carro ("Carriage Wheel") or Crespelli and topped off by 3 Choix Flambée (pineapple, cherries, ice cream, and a secret sauce prepared and flamed at your table). Scrumptious! *Dinner only;* closed on Mondays. Especially when the moon is full, all of the ingredients of an unforgettable experience are here for the Quiet American connoisseur who brings his or her own companions.

Alfredo's used to be the most famous eating place of all, but its current complications are enough to baffle Perry Mason. Here's why: A man named Alfredo got tired of brandishing a couple of gold-plated spoons which were a gift from Douglas Fairbanks and Mary Pickford—so he sold his business to an assistant. He also sold his name; this first establishment is known as the **Original Alfredo alla Scrofa** (via della Scrofa 104); unconfirmed rumors were still floating around that it might close before the coming season. Then, bored by retirement, he opened a 2nd restaurant called the **Original Alfredo all-'Augusteo** (piazza Augusto Imperatore 30), which he ran until his death. Now his Garibaldian-mustachioed son Armando, who calls himself "Alfredo"—when he's not pumping himself up as the "King of Fettuccine"—has taken over. This newer operation impresses us as highly overpriced and distinctly tourist-happy, with cuisine which we thought was definitely substandard, and with tip-hungry musicians who panhandled from table to table in a very bold way. To lure Americans, just about every gimmick on the list seems to be there, including the corny hamming with the spoons when they mix the Fettuccine (the quality of which now also seems to us on the decline). The illumination is overbright, the noise level can be deafening, and the harem-scarem "service" we suffered on our recent round was straight out of a Chaplin scenario. This place is not for us—ever again. To round things off, there's one more candidate—the simple **Original Alfredo** in Trastevere, a so-so *trattoria* which is completely different in tone. Our meal here not long ago seemed to be below 2nd-rate, our tab contained a well-rounded clip, and when we sent it back for correction the new version was still loaded in favor of the proprietor. It boils down to this: Try alla Scrofa if you want action and pictures of movie stars; the service we have found is sometimes abominable. Try Trastevere for low-grade Italian fare at cheaper prices, particularly on a summer's night. Or try all'Augusteo if you can't live without it—but despite its popularity among first-time visitors to Rome, we cannot conscientiously recommend it to any friend of this *Guide.* Summary: Not one of them would be our candidate.

Girarrosto Toscano (via Campania 2), right off via Veneto facing the

Borghese's ponderous battlements, has become one of the more fashionable, and likewise costly, dining spots in town. Subterranean setting; 2 bright and cheery sancta with open rôtisserie near entrance; stucco vaulted ceiling; blond wood banquettes for perhaps 150 munchers; wine bottles ringing the room; waiters sometimes overefficient. The antipasto, presented on a massive platter, is a meal in itself; the meat-filled tortellini were excellent; so was our inch-thick Florentine steak (but remember, please, that the price of the steerage gets beefier in direct proportion to its weight). It is shuttered on Wednesday. Our toast to Host Martini for his happily blended Tuscan cocktail.

Osteria St. Ana (via della Penna 68) still radiates debutante grace. Cellar site with steps leading past a food display; long semidivided room (we prefer the pink-toned right side); paintings and sculpture adorning the stucco walls; white furniture. Our ravioli was served in a huge porridge bowl; our grilled quail was fair game; after the repast, a house *digestif* was offered free of charge. Maître Elio told us it was a composition of—hold your breath— Crème de Cacao, Tio Pepe sherry, French cognac, and Grand Marnier, floated with whipped cream and garnished with a cherry. (Horrible as it sounds, we were floored to find it *delicious!*) Closed Sunday.

Al Fogher ("The Forge," via Tevere 13/6) is the creation of the tall, ebullient Pina Deva, its owner and charmingly inventive directress-chef. This one is styled as a tasteful country home in which the hostess's personal touch is ubiquitous in both food and décor. Our turkey and braised beef were outstanding; the cold meat platter and the glazed fruit dessert were prettily presented. Rewarding as a change.

Domus Aurea (Giardini al Colle Oppio), rambling across a small hill overlooking the Coliseum, is similar in concept. Inviting open terrace for 150 diners, many of them from bus groups; air-conditioned interior salon; music nightly; sparkling kitchen producing so-so to ho-hum cookery. Easily accessible to midtown sightseers and panoRomantically rewarding. We like it, especially when our eyes are hungrier than our tummies.

Passetto (piazza Zanardelli 14) is a standby of the Old Guard. It retreated for a while, battled its way back, and now seems to waver between these 2 poles. Kind reception; warmhearted professional attention; boat-shape rolling cart containing shellfish and crustacean appetizers in nests of shaved ice; high quality ingredients; knowledgeable preparation. Should we have any quibble other than its variability, it would be that for some palates the cuisine might seem unusually bland by comparison with the usually sharper Italian flavorings.

Two ultracosmopolitan, cuisine-savvy Roman friends were startled that **Gino in Trastevere** (via della Lungaretta 85) was not in this roster that eagerly and kindly they invited us to lunch with them here without identifying us to the proprietors. Both chorused in advance that it is "the best seafood restaurant in the city"—and they may well be right. Clients are greeted at the door by a bountiful chilled display case of finny and shelled delights—so f-r-e-s-h and attractive that it could make an interesting still-life oil or photo study. Adjoining is a table with 13 large service platters of splendid antipasti, crowned by a huge whole "cheek" (yes, that's the term!) of blue-ribbon-class prosciutto. Simple, small, pleasant room with smiling minions; adjoining shaded miniterrace at lunch; entire small piazza dotted with tables and made merry by strolling guitarists on benign evenings; operated by beamingly hospitable, non-English-speaking brothers Enzo and Gino; average meal with wine in the $10 to $11 range; longish taxi ride but worth it. *Benissimo!*

Papa Giulio (19 via Giulia), the stable of a fifteenth-century palace that is now a national museum, offers more eye appeal than palate satisfaction. This Brobdingnagian manger is tricked out in Pompeian-red burlap and aqua blue; a great fireplace commands one sector. Our party of 4 enjoyed the antipasto, detested the quartet of entrées sampled, and bowed low in culinary homage to the platter of truly excellent crêpes Suzette. But since the main dishes are so poor, in our opinion, the frills mean little when one is being socked for the full meal—socked hard, too! Sorry, not our Papa any more.

The **"31" Al Vicario** (via Uffici del Vicario 31) has been handsomely revitalized by its Doney-chain owners. Four attractive rooms in beige and white; comfortable banquettes; thick carpets; rich textiles in salmon and complementing pastels; Picasso, Marini, and other modern-art treasures on the walls; outdoor patio dining during warm months; closed August. We hope it survives, because here is a genuine asset to refinement in Roman culinary circles.

The **White Elephant** (via Aurora 27) has lurched into a sinking spell, in our disheartened view. In décor, it is rich. Victorian bar and decorative touches; gilded dining room in stately Regency ambiance; sumptuous little gaslit nightclub downstairs. Our 3 latest rechecks revealed that old pachyderms *can* forget—cookery skills, at least.

The old-fashioned **Ranieri** (via Mario dei Fiori 26) has been a citadel of Italian comestibles since 1843. Until recently, its atmosphere was almost *too* mellow and its tempo *too* lento; now this serenity has vanished—especially at lunch, when its 3 small rooms are jammed with clients, resonant with the din of voices, and dominated by rushing waiters who dart so nimbly that they should be signed up by the New York Jets. This is one of the few worthy dining places within easy walking distance of the Spanish Steps; we are joyed to witness the recapture of its august reputation. Again to be respected. Do go for its dedication to good cuisine.

Mastrostefano is diagonally across from its famous 3-step neighbor (see below) but nowadays we think it deserves a higher rung on the dining ladder. Extensive 2-part terrace with rows of parasoled tables; one interior room modern and red, another classical and yellow; buzzing with nice-looking clients; outstanding cuisine; zealous attention. We like it very much, except on Mondays, when it closes.

Tre Scalini (piazza Navona 28) is named for the "Three Steps" which were immortalized by Garibaldi. Since all but walking traffic has been banned from this large and lovely square, it is a delight on a beautiful day or evening to sit under the awnings of the sidewalk "terrace" here and contemplate the magnificence of the Bernini Fountains as you eat. Inside you will find a flagstone-tiled floor, a small bar (perhaps the most leprous dry martinis in the nation), and brightish illumination. The **4 Fiumi**, a similar setup directly next door, does not meet Mastrostefano's or even Tre Scalini's quality standards by 3 long strides, in our judgment.

Capriccio (via Liguria 38) has sunk so low, in our view, that a return bout could only be a *capriccio*. Sad.

Da Bolognese (piazza del Popolo) is the favorite meeting place of lovely budding movie stars, gal painters, and gals in the Creative Arts! Their choice is well founded, because the cuisine is superb, the personnel are warm, and while the house isn't opulent in any respect, the prices are right. Here are our suggestions: Try its terrific Mortadella as the first course (the original version of our infinitely inferior U.S.-style baloney, to which don't forget to apply freshly ground pepper from the mill). Then, if you like the New England boiled dinner, try the Gran Carrello Misto di Bollito. If not, the Cotolette alla Bolognese (mixed fried meats) is a pleasant alternate. True-blue U.S. Senators and Yankees should take pleasure in opening their meal with ½-portion of Pasta e Fagioli (bean soup with pasta). The Rivera Rosé (from Bari, of all places!) is commended to you. Closed every Monday, willy-nilly; open the other 313 days of the year. Best in good weather on the terrace. Now—*please don't take dessert, coffee, or liqueurs here.* Move next door to the expensive, highly à la mode **Pasticceria Rosati**, find places on its large sidewalk terrace, and take your pick from its vast variety of homemade pastries, candies, other sweets of many types, or its versatile assortment of alcoholic and nonalcoholic beverages. On a sunny day it is heavenly to laze here almost within the shadows of the Bernini Fountain, the Ramsete Obelisk, and the 2 beautiful churches on Valadier Square, with the Borghese Gardens directly above.

We believe that the well-meaning and doubtless sincere traveler who wrote us that **Il Matriciano** (via del Gracchi 51–57) is replacing Da Bolognese as a magnet for the chic Roman set should be asked to stand in a corner and to recite, "A bum steer! A bum steer!" 100 times—but thank goodness honest opinion is a 100% free commodity. Our feeling is that to associate these 2 is to compare an aging hayburner with a sleek, staunch, dependable Alfa Romeo. Remote outlying location in workers' district with no scenic charms; sidewalk dining; superswift and cheerful attention. Our solo lunch, 3rd-rate in every regard, totaled $11.25 including tip—and the capper came when they presented us with an incorrect bill. This checkup was a sad disappointment, but who in the *épreuves* can win them all?

L'Eau Vive (via Monterone 85), formerly Il Ghiottone, was purchased in '70 by the French religious order of Working Missionaries of The Immaculate Virgin of the Poor, which has missions from Paris and Brussels all the way to the Congo and the Orient. The good sisters first stripped the walls of the 2 high-ceiling rooms of all appurtenances and then repainted them in pleasant but starkly plain horizontal bands of olive green, whitish green pastel, and brown. As a result, the only warm color touches remaining are the red tablecloths and the small flowers at their center. The "maître d'hotel," the "chef," and all of the waitresses are nuns who have taken the vows; in nationality, we noted 2 French, 2 South Vietnamese, 1 Congolese, and a number of others which we could not determine, all dressed in their regional civilian costumes. Petit bourgeois clientele; spotlessly clean; piped music; Italian and French the only Western languages spoken; impeccably handwritten menu and wine card; inexpensive tariffs; tiny couvert per person; tipping prohibited. Although this gracious, friendly, sympathetic, hardworking group tries very hard, it is painful to report that the overall result is amateurish and our cuisine (entirely based on France) was not very successful; 1 or 2 readers report better luck. How sincerely we wish we could recommend this labor of love!

Sabatini (vicolo Santa Maria 18) and **Giggi Fazi** (via Lucullo) both have become so variable in our several recent tests—ranging roughly between passable and unsatisfactory—that personally we've lost our enthusiasm for the pair.

Le Bistrot de Paris (via del Greci 5) caters to the Swank Set. Gaul lends its mood. *The* place to be seen on the Roman scene tonight; piano bar; high tabs. A bit faddistic, but okay.

Biblioteca del Valle (largo del Teatro Valle 9) has 2 sections: Restaurant on one side and pizza palace on the other, with music, dancing, some younger Italian folk, and often too many tourists in both. Premises partially renewed; food only fair during our latest rerun; atmosphere now the delight of foreign yokels; too few minions to cope with peak hours; closed June 15 to September 15 and on Fridays.

La Fontanella (largo Fontanella Borghese 86) is soundproofed and brightened by a mosaic in medieval motif; Proprietor Osvaldo, who pops in and out in his chef's whites, is beloved by Italians who know their vittles; this "Little Fountain" is not glamorous, but clean, attractive, and substantial. The Tuscan house specialty is truffles (it didn't have them, however, on our try when Florence restaurants did). Some disturbing ripples have flowed in from Guidesters about the waiters being cocky. Our latest recheck did not reveal this, but we were not as satisfied with the cookery as we had been in former years.

La Capricciosa (largo dei Lombardi 8) is a sound, budget-level *trattoria* for serious feeders. No bar; 3 clean dining rooms and one basement corner in modern tone; capriciousness that live music makes noisier; open 9 A.M. till after 2 A.M. every day of the year. The food is good, the ladles are generous, and the prices are right. What more could a hungry traveler want?

Taverna Flavia (via Flavia 9) lines its walls with photos of celebrated clients while lining its clients with celebrated cookery. Simple interior of several interlocking rooms; bottle-green color scheme; generally folksy service that usually functions perfectly, even though its English stops around the letter "d"; occasional staff waywardness; incessantly rising tariffs. Our recent samplings of pasta, White Truffles, Grilled Scampi, Sautéed Brains with a light garlic flavor, and the house wine were all above average. Again, there was a small error on our bill, but it was corrected instantly when we objected; be sure to practice your own arithmetic on your check. Here's a chummy reeler we think you might agree is worth a run. Blushingly, we admit that we like it.

Da Meo Patacca!!! (piazza dei Mercanti 30, in Trastevere) characteristically labels itself with 3 exclamation points. It couldn't be more shamelessly contrived for the visitors' trade—but it's great fun if you're in the mood. Even nontouring Italians flock in for the frolic and foodstuffs. The ground floor might be a Hollywood producer's concept of a converted Sicilian barn. It has been hung with great necklaces of onions, peppers, and dried corn, and stuffed with such gimmicks as ox yokes, a hand organ, a wine cart, copper peasantware, and other objects known among Helen Hokinson adherents as "picturesque." (Incidentally, we so loathe this overworked adjective that here, presented between quotation marks, is the only time you will suffer it in this *Guide.*) Rôtisserie grill and kitchen at one end; gadget-filled cellar down narrow stairway; large open summer terrace on one side. If you'll stick to Antipasto Misto, a double T-bone steak, fruit or cheese, an iced bottle of Verdicchio rosato (rosé), plus coffee and Sambuca con Mosche (anisette with "flies," which are whole coffee beans), you will dine royally for not excessive money; these are the best of its specialties. The proprietors are Remington Olmstead, Jr., a former musical-comedy singer from Pasadena, and his Italian wife, Diana. Go at night, because at lunch it is often overrun by wide-eyed gawkers on conducted tours; loud music by costumed performers (who seem never to be offstage) or by tip-fevered troubadours at your elbow. Very noisy, admittedly 100% cornball—but right now it's one of the most popular tourist meccas in the capital.

The newer **Da Ciceruacchio**, just in front, is also under the Olmstead key. Prison-lore motif, derived from its use as an Austrian hoosegow during the Risorgimento; bungling reception on our incognito revisit, keyed to the bus groups which thunder in rather than to individual clients who reserve in advance; overtly clippy musicians who had the gall to put 1000-lire banknotes on their guitars as a tip lure. It has been renewed in part, but it still looked second-rate and tatty to us; the food, moreover, was so downright awful to our taste buds that we did not consume more than a 1/3rd of any course we ordered. We were also overcharged on our bill, so all-in-all it's simply not for us—ever, ever, ever again. The same ringmaster owns a beach haven called **Aeneas Landing** on *Gaeta Bay*, 2½-hours south toward Naples, and **A 'O Re Burlone** (which we now know), a garden restaurant on a panoramic hilltop, which were launched under this same burgee. Of course they have their Olmsteadfast come-ons: 2-masted brigantines moored in the bay for customer-cruising—just the thing for our Sixth Fleeters on a busman's holiday.

L'Etichetta (piazza Nicosia), with new ownership, is a fresh fish find we hooked. Its buffet table buckled under dozens of denizens from the deep. Fat goldfish eyed us scornfully as we feasted on Gran Fritto Misto di Pesce and French rosé. Relatively undiscovered, which is a pity since it deserves a school of followers.

Coq d'Or (via Flaminia Vecchia 493, about a 10-minute taxi ride beyond Olympic Village) is a golden rooster that crows more and more for battery clientele. Its barnyard is in a 300-year-old palace. Main-floor bar dominated by gracious stone chimney; tabby-hued velvet walls; pliant leather stools; guitar lilts; upstairs dining room under a lovely painted rotunda; garden view through tower windows; several nooks for friendly persuasions; piano melodizing continued through dinner. For tranquilizing, here's almost a must on the suburban nightscape—if the waves of visitors don't break the spell.

La Csarda (via Magnanapoli 6) is a hearty haven if you hunger for Hungarian vittles and violins. **Il Buco** (via Sant'Ignazio 8) has delicious Tuscan steaks; no longer inexpensive but recommendable. **Al Girarrosto Fiorentino** (via Sicilia 44-48) is another Tuscany import; no decorative zing, but tempting kitchen offerings and ultrakind personnel. **La Vigna dei Cardinali** (piazzale Ponte MIL VIO 34) offered our party a garden in front, a fireplace in a vaulted room, dark timbers, a 22-dish antipasto of so-so quality, poor client attention, and an error on our tab. Nope, not for us.

Angelino a Tormargana (piazza Margana) spills in a semicircular pattern onto an ancient plaza, hiding itself halfheartedly behind screens, greens, and well-used umbrellas. Inside you'll find 2 rooms with yellow-and-white tile floors, not elaborate but cordial. If you walk to the rear to mix your own martinis (as we did), you'll see an immaculate kitchen, with smiling stout Mamma in a starched white uniform presiding over the stove. As you dine, an ingratiating family of white-to-tiger-colored cats will panhandle your excess dainties with dignity. Plain and warm in the inimitable local way; simple fare, well cooked; small portions. Quality-plus for the price.

In the low lire league, our number one favorite in Rome since 1950 has been **Scoglio di Frisio** (via Merulana 256). *(Please doublecheck its location after your arrival, because plans are well advanced on its shift to larger premises.)* It gets better every year. The Frisio's "Rock" motif is expressed in rough papier-mâché boulders which project from the walls as from the interior of a cave; fishnets, Bowery Art Shop murals, and stalactites pull hard against one another in polychromatic contrast. But whether you're a spelunker, a troglodyte, a fisherman, or an ordinary wanderer, we think the pizza (special oven hot in evenings only), the spaghetti with clam sauce, the filet of sole with peas, mushrooms, and olives (ask for "alla Frisio") are a dream. Bustling with battalions of papas, mammas, *bambini,* foreign residents, and hungry sightseers; 75% filled by Italian patrons—an indication of its value to homegrown palates. Many Vatican disciples bring American pilgrims here; Notre Dame alumni can often be found in a genial huddle. Neapolitan atmosphere; go for dinner, not lunch. Patron Augusto Rossi is an extraordinarily warm, gentle, and kind host to North Americans, whom he adores (and all of our team adore *him!*); handsome, smiling Maître Attilio has been his personable and efficient chief of staff for more than 20 years. What a bargain! Recommended with our tongues hanging out. Closed Monday.

Piperno a Monte Cenci (via Monte Cenci 9), a nonkosher pride of the Jewish-Italian ghetto of the Eternal City, has been famous since 1844 as The Artichoke Capital of the World; its specialty comes in Jewish style only (opened, flattened, and sautéed in some deliciously secret fashion). Following an atrophy of its standards, it was taken over by a vigorous and competent young couple who have improved it so dramatically that now at nearly every meal the house is full. Friendly, noisy, and bustling; old-fashioned furnishings; closed last half of August and various holidays; wine and beer only; we found it cheap, rewarding, and better than on any previous visit after our latest Exodus. **Giggetto** (portico d'Ottavia) is also said to be a winner when it comes to artichokes, as well as Scampi Gratinée, Canneloni, and its antipasto spread; ask for Olindo. **Tanenbaum**'s kosher food is supplied to airlines leaving from Rome—but some Americans who have been brought up on kosher cookery have found this menu simply doesn't stand up to their satisfaction. Of this fine ethnic kitchen, the only qualifying dishes we could discover this time were artichokes and fish. **Giovanni** (via Marche 19, directly in back of via Veneto) drew enthusiasm from several previous readers, so we hied ourselves there for a look. Here's a small, cramped, pleasant lunching or dining spot, with rushed but genial service, a high decibel level, well-prepared offerings, and medium tariffs. Verdict: Agreeable, but run-of-the-mill. **Al Circo Massimo** (via dei Cerchi 53) is about the same. L-shape room; cheeses, pots, and garlic suspended from rafters; bottle-glass windows; chummy atmosphere. Our fresh fish and quail were fair enough. **Tientsin** (via Capo le Case 55) has Chinese vittles which reasonably—but only reasonably —closely resemble American-Oriental. The décor is a perfectly horrid aqua-hued Cathay nightmare, highlighted by an internally illuminated pillar resembling a mammoth Chungking barber pole. Prices that won't hurt that yen, plus a 100-item menu of Eastern goodies. Recommended for the hungry whose vision ranges from 20/400 to 20/625.

The **Wiener Bierhaus** (via della Croce 22) is rated by aficionados of Bratwurst, Kaiserfleisch, Wiener Schnitzel, and similar specialties as one of the best beer halls in town, but after our latest revisit we're going to go for the ham hocks and that's about it. **Old Vienna** (via degli Artisti 25, about 200 yards from the Excelsior Hotel) has become a zestless pizza parlor, a turn which good Austrian burghers might well deplore.

Tempio d'Agrippa (pizza della Rotonda 14) is not recommended to Attila the Hun or any contemporary invader of this land. Our food was dreadful, our service worse, and our rotund bill topped a fiasco we still think is outrageous.

Among the *trattorie,* **Al Chianti** (via Ancona 17), also known as "Ernesto & Mario," has a Tuscan ambiance, with about 14 Lilliputian tables in Italian-rustic. Its motif employs enough raffia, straw, and flotsam to titillate the heart of Trader Vic. The substantial viands lose some of their savor under the high-pressure rush-act of the waiters. Nice tone for the price range. For the down-to-basic-earth Roman atmosphere, **Romolo** (via di Porta Settimiana 8 in Trastevere) is still popular among local socialities. Clean; big garden which once belonged to La Fornarina ("The Bakery Girl"), who was Raphael's mistress; sound food; low, low tariffs. **Cesaretto** (via Cesare Beccaria 3) is a workman's favorite; primitive but spotless; delicious spaghetti, Roman baby lamb, a complete meal with wine or beer for about the price of a movie. Nino speaks good English. Very, very plain, but tops for its class. **Da Mario** (via della Vite 64A) comes up with one room, one waiter, and onederful Tuscan cuisine; clean, inexpensive, and so crowded our elbows are still contused. **Augustea** (via della Frezza 5) offers 2 plant-lined rooms, a free fish dish to start, a good meal in the middle, and a gratis liqueur at the end. Seafood is the mainstay; closed Monday.

Even worthier is **L'Albanese** (via dei Serpenti 148), an unsung candidate we stumbled across while searching hungrily for a place to eat. This one is immaculately clean. Mosaic-tile floor; wine-shelved, half-paneled walls in the 10-table front room; small enclosed "terrace" to the rear; 7-table segment adjoining. No English is spoken, but they must have been double-jointed from the way they bent over backward to communicate. Although there are hundreds of similar places in the city, here's a pleasant, no-fireworks example when you forget your guidebook. Closed Sundays.

Something different? **Ambasciata d'Abruzzo** (via Pietro Tacchini 26), up in the Parioli district, provided us with one of the most fun-filled and tummy-filling experiences of a recent Italian circuit. Crammed to the rafters with laughing locals, a jovial proprietor, and his staff who keep bellowing, "Mangi,

mangi, mangi!" ("Eat, eat, eat!") and similar encouragements. Even as the host carries platters to his patronage, he spoons free bites to other clients along his happy route. The moment you sit down, a basket with 17 types of sausage is placed on your table, plus a cutting board, bread, cheese, and knives. Then you are given a stack of plates and told to take anything (and as much as you want) from the terraces of antipasto; we counted 35 different preparations on our visit, and were they ever deeeeelicious! These were all we could manage, but serious gourmands then go on to roasts, fowl, trout, and a menu so long that our vision blurred just glancing at it. Absolutely imperative to reserve in advance, especially on a Saturday afternoon when loyalists stand in the street waiting to grab a seat. The entrance, incidentally, is so narrow that you may squeeze in, but if you "Mangi, mangi, mangi!" as the man says, we'd bet you won't be able to squeeze out.

Snacks? Unfortunately there are NO truly authentic American-style nibble nooks available in the entire capital even though there has been some attempt at the pretense. **California** (via Bissolati) is superb for light bites even though its offerings are 99 + % Italian. The new owners have given it fresh, attractive raiments; the shaded sidewalk café is especially alluring. Our hamburger (ask for it between bread!) and ham sandwich were quite good in flavor but European in presentation and absurdly high in price for this market. Other tariffs that we studied also seemed exorbitant for the fare. Still, for quality it's the best, in our opinion. The **Piccadilly** (piazza Barberini) is a 1250-seat magnum opus which has grouped a snack bar, a cafeteria, 2 restaurants, an English-style pub, and a shop into a single complex. Sadly, its Old Glory-fications of our home-style cookery draw half-masted praise from us. Foreigners don't seem to go. **Nuovo Colony** ("New Colony," via Sicilia 45–47) was a disaster to us on our latest try; both the hamburger and the hot dog we resampled on these premises (which we used to love) were not only abysmal but to our taste execrable. Ugh—and double ugh. God save us there's a **Wimpy** on via Veneto. The **Luau** (via Sardegna 34) is in a state of flux this year.

Additional dining places of character are **La Cisterna in Trastevere** (via della Cisterna 13), which has facinating murals, miserable (to us) cookery, and psychologically impervious waiters in eighteenth-century livery, and **Andrea** (via Sardegna 26–28, a block behind the Flora Hotel), which should give you ample satisfaction at medium-to-high prices. **Nini** (via Borgognona 11) is *not* recommended.

Sunny day or starlit night? When "summer treads on heels of spring," the wise traveler follows the Roman custom of escaping to the suburbs for dining and entertainment. **Villa Florio** (see the final portion of "Hotels, Rome"), about 40 minutes from the capital near the Frascati-Grottaferrata junction, is beautifully executed as a country mansion with swimming pool ringed by tables, but it is now so expensive and the crowd is so mixed that we're no longer fond of it. But one we *are* fond of in the immediate vicinity is **Tuscolo** (via Anagnina 241, in Grottaferrata). Its dynastic proprietors seem to be the Italian equivalent of the Kennedy clan—the Blasi tribe, with mothers, fathers, sisters, brothers, brothers-in-law, cats, sisters-in-law, dogs, grandfathers, goldfish, grandmothers, sons, daughters, and grandchildren galore (20 or more, all told)—the 2-legged section of whom all pitch in to make this former pasta shop a roaring success as a restaurant. Now matured into 5 individual kitchens, 6 dining rooms, and 3 summer terraces, with the capacity of stuffing 500 tummies at 1 sitting. Open from 11 A.M. until well after midnight; closed Fridays; tykes under every 2nd foot; frequent weddings, confirmations, and other celebrations (most of them, probably, within the Blasi population). Good wholesome homegrown food, and good wholesome fun. **Il Fungo**, in the suburb of E.U.R. about 35 minutes from the Colosseum, features mushrooms on its menu. Perfectly situated in a watertank of Mussolini's former fair grounds; cuisine so-so in savor, but so-so-SOOO high in cost. Although opera star Mario del Monaco put on an adequate performance with this parvenu, our bill had mushroomed too fast to merit any applause.

Gina in *Fiumicino*, up the strand 1 mile from Ostia, is reported to be excellent. We went for a summer Sunday lunch (heaven help us, because ½-million people were swarming in the area!), but the place was too packed to get in. It is said to have its own fishing boat, the whole catch of which is used exclusively for its patrons. **Re Capriccio Marinaro da Vicenze e Ruggero**, a block or so from the beach, hits us as the number one in *Ostia*. Double-tier sidewalk row under awning; small room with closely gathered tables; immaculatey clean including kitchen and lavatories; display cooler with tempting variety of ex-nautical dwellers rooted from home for only a matter of hours; happy family atmosphere with merry decibel level. Through error, our cherished friend-driver Dino let slip our identity, so the patron instantly paraded a series of 14 very small test plates of his special prides. The ones we enjoyed the most were the Cannelloni 007 (top secret à la James Bond), the batter-fried Moscardini (please don't ask; just *try!*), and the savory prawns grilled to perfection. Pretensions? Who's joking? Our bill for 2 for this extraordinarily curious panorama of taste-nibbles including the wine was $16.10; the normal tariffs are markedly less expensive. A simple, very pleasant, no-nonsense goal when the day is balmy. **Corsetti**, just below Ostia at *Tor Vaianica*, is a beachside retreat which used to be our coastal favorite for scrumptious seafood. How saddened we were, however, on our latest fishing expedition here to detect what impressed us as frozen maritime fare. If this is true and if it is house policy, then the disaffection for this angler will be compleat. **L'Escargot** (out at Appia Antica 46 with a Roman address of Umiltà 34-35) has a farmhouse atmosphere. Timber ceiling strung with hams and salamis; calico napery and country lamps; fireplace; about 15 tables; photos of film notables and not-so-notables line the walls. Good but unspectacular food; such hospitable service that the client feels cheerfully relaxed; reasonable prices. We like the pipe-and-slipper comfort of the atmosphere here—and, after our recent try of the in-town candidate, we like that too. **Hostaria L'Archeologia** (139 via Appia Antica) is similar in tone. Cattle-shed restaurant with garden in the back; slow but kindly service; excellent fettuccine with foie gras. A sleepy family place that is nice if you seek relaxation and a simple value. **La Fattoria**, at the approaches to *Fiumicino*, is a happy little tip for dawdlesome air travelers. It offers especially nice garden dining in summer; the inside restaurant draped with sausages, hams, and the like. If your flight departure is delayed, this quiet corner might be just the spot to soothe those jet-frazzled nerves and to rescue you from those horrid restaurants in the terminus itself. **Casale**, at the 10-kilometer marker on via Flaminia, is a just-barely-converted peasant farm still replete with oil lamps, nestling ducks, and haystacks. No sign at entrance; service in barnyard alfresco setting or in 3 ancient storerooms; beamed ceilings and drying corn, peppers, garlic, and onions comprise the unwhitewashed décor. Large grill for roasting chickens or ½-lambs; large self-service antipasto table. Not a Brown Derby or a "21," but if you enjoy playing country Rube as much as we do on occasion, here's a dude's delight. Others of note are **San Callisto**, via Appia Antica 220 (traditional oasis on the old Appian Way), **Trattoria Pancrazio**, near *Campo dei Fiori* (a cave in the Teatro dei Pompeii excavations, always cool on blistering days)—plus, of course, Santa Maria in Trastevere. Here, on the square, you'll find **Galeassi**'s still drawing a now-fading number of movie and theatrical people after losing a percentage of them, a while back, to rival **Alfredo**'s across the square. **Piccolo Mundo** (via Aurora 39-B) also very central, promotes a celebrity reputation, but—an odd but legitimate question —were all of the clips and photos on the walls given by visitors to these precincts? Exceptionally considerate service and a star-rating reception. Amusing if you like crowds. **Checchino**, in the slaughterhouse district of *Testaccio*, is said to be interesting for meats. It's at the foot of a hill made from the rubble of Roman bricks and has some connection with the Academy of Italian Cuisine. Please excuse our vagueness on details since we didn't get by to test it; we are only mentioning it because this one sounded so curious to us. We'll become beefeaters very soon.

And let's not forget the ubiquitous cafés—an important part of the Roman scene, since professional and social lines are often drawn on the customer's choice of hangout. Americans swarm to the area so aptly christened "The Beach"—a name which has stuck as hard as the chewing gum under its sidewalk chairs. This is table-lined via Veneto, home or next-door neighbor of the U.S. Embassy and Consulate, the Excelsior, "the Ambassadors," and Flora hotels (among many). **Caffè Doney**, delight of tourists from Milwaukee, Madras, Manila, and Manchester since the Jurassic Age of travel, has undergone a curious phenomenon: Local celebrities and in-the-swim folk seem to be staying away in droves. We much, much prefer **Harry's Bar**, a 2-minute walk up and across the street to its farthest corner opposite the Hotel Flora. It has no connection with namesakes in other Italian hubs. The awninged sidewalk portion extends one full block. Inside is its comfortable clublike bar featuring platters of splendid appetizers called Tartina, as well as sandwiches on call; the dining room is quiet and elegant. Complete meals with good table wine in the $8 to $10 range served during normal hours; open for drop-in drinks and snacks from 10:30 A.M. to perhaps 2 A.M.; closed Sunday. To us this leaves all of the rest along "The Beach" way below the neap-tide marker; others prefer Doney's, Cafe de Paris, or Rosatti's, so you pays your money and takes your choice!

Downtown, **Caffè Greco** (via Condotti 86) is historically the revered haunt of painters, sculptors, authors, and people of the arts; Mark Twain liked it so much that you'll find his statue enshrined in this ancient building, now a national monument. **Babington** (piazza di Spagna 23) is beloved by the British; passable but miles from remarkable muffins and scones. There are dozens of interesting cafés—each with its distinctive clientele and aura.

Hotels? For elegant luxury lunching or dining, we're specially impressed by **Le Maschere**, that colorful delight in the Grand—a masterpiece of subtle theatrical lighting, live guitar serenades, melodic fountains, silky-smooth service, and truly fabulous pasta creations (38 types in all!). Our recent feast of Bresaola (dried beef appetizer), Pennette alla Boscaiola (a woodland wonder), and Maccaruni di Segni al Prosciutto (a style of fettuccine, not to be confused with macaroni) was sheer, unadulterated heaven. There's a pizza for every day of the week; black tie is requested for the galas each Friday. It's marvelous. We are also very fond of the brilliantly revivified panoramic Roof Garden at the **Eden**. For the maximum yield per lira to entice and charm the taste buds, the **Massimo d'Azeglio** has all the rest buffaloed. (You might disagree, of course, with this personal evaluation.) It is cozy, intimate, and cheerful; it will give you a superb meal in the classic Italian way. The house blue ribbons are won by its Sole Pirata (prepared with ham and black truffles), its Filet Mignon with Mustard Sauce, its Rigatoni Villa d'Este, and its Taglierini d'Azeglio. If you're still drooling, just wait until you try those pastries! No Roman candles or glamour, but if it's only food you're after, here's mouthwatering fare. For scenery, the winter-only roof at the **Hassler** provides excellent offerings in lovely surroundings; expensive. The **Excelsior** has improved notably; now fine.

In *San Remo*, the redecorated E. Phillips Oppenheim-era dining room of the gambling **Casino** will give you a seat over the Gulf; the **Royal,** with its Murano-glass ceiling and bouquet fixtures, will serve you more distinguished viands. Dancing in both. If you're after a savory regional meal at a more modest price, try **Au Rendez-Vous** (corso Matteotti 90); large, clean, bustling, and noisy; sterile décor without frills; the cuisine makes the difference. Recommended. **La Lanterna** faces town from a bend in a quay. Middling view of the harbor and the walls of a medieval jail; natural wood interior; front terrace for fair-weather munching; our recent bill concealed 2 chisels; the cookery now seems oriented strictly for routine tourist traffic. Better by leagues is the **Caravella**, ⅔rds of it in the waters. Wonderful maritime vista; tanks for selecting your tearful meal; be sure to try the fruit-of-the-sea cocktail, which is prepared at tableside. Very good, but pretty steep tariffs. **Pesce d'Oro** (corso Cavallotti 174) is about 2 miles toward Genoa on the via Aurelia route. No atmosphere; no view; snail-like service and whalelike tariffs for what you get. Ho-hum. At **Castel Doria**, the food is savory when the chef is in the mood, but at other times you'll take your chances. **U Nostromú** specializes in seafood; small terrace; dull. These last two seem to be slipping now. The **Capo Pino** at surf's edge is a bustling aboriginal warren. Entrance from the top; restaurant and bar, in terra-cotta red, 2 levels below the road; pool and terrace by the shore. Not much appeal for the average North American tripper. Finally, minutes before the Ventimiglia frontier crossing, you'll come across 2 possibilities. One is an unusually attractive oasis named **La Mortola**. Simple modern décor; terrace with view of bay; seafood specialties; whopping selection of perhaps 60 hors d'oeuvres (a meal in itself); friendly, accomplished service; open daily from 8 A.M. to 1 A.M., but closed all of June and July; across the road is the 22-room Hotel Eden, under the same management; very, very good. The other is **Gino** at *Piani di Vallecrosia*, which we've never tried.

Santa Margherita's top independent kitchen is **Dei Pescatori**, on the fringe of the yacht harbor. Long and narrow, with no outdoor service; fish, of course, is the specialty. **Nanni**, also harborside, is a venture of the New York Nanni's, who seem to have a winner on their hands; very popular with the boating crowd; we must drop our hook here soon. We'll also look in on the waterfront **La Posada**, recommended by thoughtful Atlanta readers. For hotel dining, the **Miramare** has one of the better chefs of the nation—but you'll pay plenty for his wares. There is also a summer nightclub restaurant of renown: **Capo di Nord-Est**, which is one mile out, and which is romantic for handholding. Seaside location, dancing, intermittent entertainment; pleasant, but more famous for its atmosphere than for its food. **Helios**, a flamingo-pink structure on the water, has a good vista and nice terrace, but Escoffier never slept here. The little Second-class **Taverna Brigantino** is nautical, simple, on the pagan side, and cheap.

Siena's culinary crown belongs to **Guido**, a stone-and-brick vault on the main street of the Old Town. Rugged rusticity lined with photos of opera and theatrical personalities. Spitted meats spinning over licking flames at the entrance; hardy fare that is superb for what it is; friendly service; reasonable tabs. We love it. The most famous tourist meccas are **Al Mangia** and **Alla Speranza**; both have outdoor terraces facing the magnificent piazza del Campo; both are colorful, but oh-so-geared for You Know Who. **Tre Cristi** is next. **La Taverna di Nello** is said to be worthy, but we haven't tried it. **La Campane** is the budget prince of the poor man's peerage.

In *Siracusa*, **Fratelli Bandiera**, with sidewalk tables, has an eyefilling command of the bay—and the best command of the stove. All are pretty routine.

Sorrento's accomplished chefs must be in hiding. **Della Favorita o'Parrucchiano** gets the leading vote, and that's in an election of gastronomic gnomes. Two tiers of charming, enclosed, viewless terraces lined with lemon and orange trees; amiable management. Closed Wednesday. **Peppino Francischiello** and the **Tripoli** are gaining more and more attention from other visitors—but certainly not from us. **La Minervetta** (via Capo 21) and a pension called **La Tonnarella** (a few steps away) both offer a cliffside sweep from open terraces on Capo di Sorrento; we think the food is wretched, but the surroundings are lovely. The latter has a elevator down to the sea. At the former, when we asked for a wine list, the waiter brought out the entire *cave* in his 2 hands: 5 half-bottles, all white, all foul, were all perfectly in tone with the culinary horrors foisted upon us here. For yachtsmen, the Marina del Cantone at *Nerano* boasts 3 waterfront moorings, all pretty rough but fair enough for salty types. The routine **Hotel Residence** is flanked to port by **Lo Scoglio** and to starboard by **Taverna Maria Grazzia**. Be sure to ask prices before ordering at the latter pair.

Taormina's hoteliers have so mercilessly jammed their Full-Pension needle into the innocent pilgrim that almost no appealing restaurants exist. **Da Angelo** (Corso Umberto 42), a local pacesetter, is reasonably pleasant in aura and viands—but please don't expect to walk away with angelic music in your ears. Closed on Tuesday. **Naumachie** (Corso Umberto 76–80) would be a solid little pasta and pizza parlor in most other centers of this size; here it's another of the leading independent lights. L-shape chamber with brick oven at a right angle; antipasto display near entrance; about 15 tables clothed in light blue or pink. Nine varieties of pizza, plus an equal number of spaghetti variations, are available. **Miosotis** is okay but not outstanding; Mondays are its rest time. **Cyclope** is run by 2 brothers who were formerly with the Excelsior. Tiny dining quarter; so-so vittles for the nonparticular. The renewed rustic-style **Pescatore**, directly in front of *Isola Bella* on the pike to Messina, is attractive when the sun is shining. The seafood cocktail is a selfish shellfish salad. At nearby *Mazzarò Beach*, **Villa Sant' Andrea** is a charmer for lunch; since it's a hotel restaurant, it's open every day. **La Griglia** resides haughtily and peacefully nearly 2-thousand feet above sea level and more than 1-thousand feet over Taormina at *Castelmola*, perhaps 20 minutes from town by car. Although there are other dining targets in this village, none comes close to matching either the fabulous land- and seascapes or the superb regional cuisine of this one. Here's a dedicated family operation, with matriarch Maria Intelisano and daughter-in-law Angela in the kitchen and sons Giorgio, Giuseppe, and Pancrasio serving clients with sincerity, warmth, and grace. Please be sure to try Bruschetti (crude toast with tomato and oil). It's open all year, all week in summer, and every day except Thursday in winter. A 3-V champ: Verve, vistas, and vittles.

In *Trieste*, **Nuovo Dante** (formerly Otello) was temporarily shuttered on our latest whirl. Hence, **Piccolo** temporarily and precariously becomes our ranking local pick. **Bottega del Vino** is a regional-style establishment inside San Guisto Castle, with music of sorts and dancing; open at night only. Greatly improved under tutelage of Mr. Valentino Lanzellotti, one of the great chefs of the older generation. **Birreria Forst Europa** is the restaurant of the well-known Forst Brewery. The latter 2 are on the down-to-earth side, but newcomers seem to like 'em.

Turin has fine gastronomy in addition to its fine vermouths. Our lead-off choice, **Cambio**, is in the Teatro Carignano building—Turin's opera house. Nineteenth-century aura featuring crystal chandeliers and velvet-swathed banquet rooms; good food, friendly staff, and decorous dining. **Tiffany** is intimate; added to its charm, you can count on well prepared cuisine. **Baccarat**, near Valentino Park, is modern in tone and superb in quality. **Muletto** is typical of the First-class establishments in the Piedmont area. **Al Gatto Nero** (corso Unione Sovietica 14), founded in '58, might take you until '78 to track down, but it's certainly well worth the search. Look for the small black cat on the door adjacent to an auto showroom. Entrance through a cozy bar; clublike atmosphere with red brick walls and hanging flora; open 12:30 P.M. to midnight. Reserve in advance. Its 2 owners hustle-and-scussle between the dining room and kitchen, but be patient about the slower-than-average service. Highly recommended. For economizing, **Ferrero**, opposite the station, is a solid choice, as are **Birreria Wuhrer, Cerro**, and **Fontana dei Francesi**; you can't go far wrong at **Taste Vin** or **Vecchia Lanterna**. La Cascine operates beside a small lake from June to September; beautiful flower garden;

dancing. Finally, please don't forget the lovely sylvan **Villa Sassi**, 4 miles out on the Genoa highway, in a heavenly park overlooking the Po. Perfect for a sunny-day excursion. Try their "Fritto Misto Villa Sassi." This one's a knock-out.

Venice, like Rome, offers everything. **Quadri** (piazza San Marco 120), in our opinion, is one of the better restaurants in Italy; it is also one of the oldest. Elegance and grace; tiny, open dining room at street level and chichi quarters upstairs; classic Venetian décor at its richest; busy at the lunch hour; very expensive indeed. Closed November through March. Our very recent recheck confirmed our recommendations from earlier visits. **Caffé Florian**, across the *piazza*, began life as far back as 1720. It offers 6 little rooms, each with its own entrance, plus 7 rows of outside tables; a 5-piece band gently massages the eardrums of anybody in the entire square. When certain popular cocktails are ordered, they're concocted and rattled up in a small shaker at your table by the friendly waiters. Closed Fridays except in summer. Our pick of the esplanade. **Lavena**, around the corner, is also noteworthy. **Harry's Bar** (San Marco 1323), where Mr. Hemingway's Colonel whiled away so many brooding hours, is a shrine and an apex for visiting firemen. It's a typical Class AAA, Big City gin mill, U.S.-style—intimate, friendly, sophisticated, and cheerful. Limited but excellent menu at high prices: hamburger (a whole meal in itself) about twice the price of a thick one back home; also cream of onion soup, club sandwich (huge) and other stateside delicacies. Arrigo, the alert and friendly son of Giuseppe Cipriani, is "Harry"; Roger is the bar maestro. **Harry's ***** Restaurant** twinkles happily above the Bar; 60 can be nourished in ***** style at one sitting; we've recently come from another sit-in with a batch of homemade ravioli and a plate of Scampi Carlina; if we could untangle our tongue from the carriage of our typewriter, we'd describe it leth lithp-ingly—but, since we can't, you'd better order it yourself. Always reserve in Season. Wonderful; getting better, better, and better.

Antico Martini, in the piazza facing the famous Teatro La Fenice, vies for top honors. Pleasant luxury-leaning interior with French curtains, gilt mirrors, and crystal fixtures; awning-covered plaza site for outdoor dining; excellent, kind, and professional service keenly hawk-eyed by Maître Diana. Our seafood cocktail was heavenly, but even more paradisial was our blessèd sole on a bed of rice garnished with red pepper and giblets, and topped by a light cream sauce faintly laced with curry. Please try these if you like 'em, although other dishes are equally praiseworthy. Dinner only; expensive but highly recommended on every score. (Incidentally, for those who wish to extend the evening, there's a pleasant nightclub in the back.)

For Italian dining and T-bone steaks cut to order, **Taverna La Fenice** (San Marco 1937) gets a blue ribbon, despite a few cavils from travelers. Our latest dinner here revealed a tremendous pickup in service standards. This judgment is based on watching other tables as well as our own. Handsome, timber highlights; covered terrace in summer; versatile kitchen; specialties very costly. We are happy to report an improvement. The **Caravella** (calle XXII Marzo) is even more costly, but in its way it is more beautiful, too, and the culinary preparations are excellent. Bar at entrance with ruby-red chairs at cozy tables; interior room on 2 tiers; wood-lined walls resembling an ancient bark; brass lamps set in velvet-upholstered vitrines imparting a soft glow; gay explosions of flowers everywhere, and all dew-fresh; mock-crystal drinking glasses; calico napkins. The parchment menu—and a big one it is—has prices for the host only. Specialties include: lobster, spaghetti Venetian-style (that's with a mixture of sautéed onions and anchovies which might be too seasoned for many palates), spider crab, and sole. Many concierges in town disrecommend this establishment, possibly because it does not pay off to attract clients, or possibly because it is admittedly high in price. We liked it, however, and we think you will as well. **Do Forni** (calle Specchiero 468) features young, urbane Proprietor-Chef Paties often at your tableside preparing the dishes for you personally—and mighty lip-smacking good they are, too. Two of the 3 rooms in medieval Venetian style; tented motif for summer dining; tariffs medium to expensive. Sample his Spaghetti all'Isolana and his Spiedino Do Forni Guarnito (a brochette of 7 meats). Closed Thursday but open every other day of the year. Superb. **A la Vecia Cavana** (Rio Terra SS. Apostoli) borders a canal; in the thirteenth century gondolas parked under its arches; we moored here recently and loved it. Savoy-trained Alberti Felice is the floorman who speaks perfect London-bred English; his brother Roberto does the cooking. Try their Sardine Saor (a local starter), the antipasto of fish, the Scampi alla Cavana (on a wooden skewer and yumptious), the Eel in Tomato Sauce, the Polenta on a shingle, the Grilled Salad, and the white wine of Verona. Ummmmm! If you're inquisitive, you can tell how many times Peter O'Toole has rung in by the number of bells missing from the bell wheel. He snatches one every visit. A bell ringer on our charts, too. **Trattoria La Colomba** (Frezzeria 1665) and, to a lesser degree, **Al Graspo de Ua** (San Bartolomeo 5094) offer similar attractions at the same cost; no terrace at the latter. The former, incidentally, is the well-known establishment displaying paintings on its walls and is not to be confused with the newer **Colombo**, which is also recommendable for its skilletry. **Antico Locanda Montin** (near the Ca'Rezzonico water-taxi landing at San Trovaso) is a favorite of ours from way back. Picture-lined, raw interior; vine-lined summer garden; simple cookery; basic tariffs; frequented by artists, nobility, and a grateful travel writer or two. **Al Peoceto Risorto** (calle Donzella 249) is not recommended. **Da Nico** (Frezzeria 1702) is also under management that has let it slip; still okay, but no longer a rave for bargain hunters. The nearby **Da Gianni** is a fair choice for pizza. **Cicci della Salute**, across the Canal from the Gritti Palace, is recommended to those on a tight budget. **Trattoria Madonna**, near the Rialto Bridge, is very popular, with commendable skilletcraft; one drawback for Americans may be the language barrier; so crowded it's nearly always a tough scramble to get in. Don't fall for the shameless photo racket here which comes on as a "gift" but which winds up soaking you for a pocketful of lire. Oh, oh, oh, HOW we hate ourselves for being suckered into this fastie! **Carbonera** didn't seem the same as it used to be, although it's trying hard for a comeback. Although **Trattoria Malamocco Venezia** teems with local residents, we didn't like the noisy atmosphere, the bustle of the waiters, or the house wine—but the bean soup, if not a bit cold, was tasty.

Al Teatro (on piazza Fenice adjoining Teatro La Fenice) still gets star ranking as the top pizzeria in town. The entrance room contains a counter, a bar, an open grill, and a frenzied trade; the second room offers about 15 tables, 24 ceiling lights, celebrity-photo-lined walls, and a cheerful, relaxed atmosphere; between the 2 is an open kitchen with a pizza oven that's home base for 16 types (available only during mealtimes, when the stoves are hot). Super for its category; we tout it heartily—but we don't tout the pestiferous photographer who works there.

Ice cream? The silkiest we've discovered is at **Todaro**, near the columns on S. Marco.

TIP: Do as the *cognoscenti* do, by dropping into the nearest bar at 11 A.M. for a glass of "ombra" (white wine) to sip while snacking on appetizers. The star of this show is **Enotica al Volto**, back of the Town Hall, where the owner offers over a thousand different vintages with a menu of the specialties featured that day. If you are as serious a connoisseur as he is, he would be delighted to open and to share one of his very special favorites with you. Closed Sunday.

Want a wonderful excursion on a bright day? For sophisticated dining at a jewel of a country inn, take a speedboat (35 minutes) to the island of Torcello and its lovely **Locanda Cipriani**. Same magic Cipriani aegis; peaceful terrace; 5 choices of menus of gourmet fare at fixed price in the highish area; please, please, ask Maître Gianni to bless you with *both* Gnocchis—Gnocchi Torcellano and a Gnocchi Santa Fosca—both featherlight, different in concept, and guaranteed taste treats; they're the finest we've ever savored. For fish dishes and risottos in colorful, cheerful, noisy surroundings, there's the famous **Da Romano** on Burano Island, roughly the same haul; full of local card players, artists, and characters.

Al Postiglone, at *Morocco*, is the newest venture of the Cipriani tribe, this one located 20 minutes from Venice on the Treviso pike. Alfresco terrace with about a dozen cocktail tables; interior salon separated by Moorish arches and glass; décor comprising browns and pale yellow, with splashes of spring colors; excellent staff; set menus between $5.50 and $7.50 with à la carte nudging $13 per person. Though it is new, its administration is so experienced that we think this one will soar.

Dining in the Lido? Our dear chum George Prade, worldwide Sales Manager for Mumm champagnes, who is even more sparkling and delightful than his noble products, advises us to head straight for the open-air restaurant of **Hotel Quattro Fontane** for its 50-dish antipasti "smörgåsbord" (accompanied by a bottle of Mumm's Cordon Rouge, of course). When this connoisseur labels any cuisine "at the top," *that,* hungry friends, is IT. Otherwise you might like the snackeries at the **Excelsior** or **Les Bains**.

Verona ? **Veronanticca** (via Sottoriva 10) now boasts the most sophisticated tables in town; the proprietors are Onofrio and Romeo Donadel. The mountainside **Re Teodorico** (5 minutes above the city) is tops physically but its kitchen is so-so. Approach along a fortress balcony bordered by 80-foot cypress giants; breathtaking outdoor terrace high above the sparkling meanders of the Adige River; peaceful silence broken only by the chiming of chapel bells, far below, from the tile-clad city. Big menu; fair food. You probably won't even notice its simple interior, because here is one of the loveliest perches on the European circuit. Open every day except

February's Fridays. The **12 Apostoli** offers a small colorful dining room in the Old City. Named in A.D. 1745 for the 12 friends who advised the founder to turn his butcher shop into a restaurant; arched ceiling; photo gallery of celebrities who have dined here over the past half century. The Proprietor-chef's family has operated the place continuously since 1904; cuisine well served and reasonably appetizing. Our bill was precise, but other Guidesters have run up against a different abacus here. **Pedavena** (piazza Brà 20), run by a big brewery, sloshes in modern sudsy duds. It has also lost its head, in our estimation. **Bragozzo,** near Juliet's Tomb, specializes in fish. Décor composed of the usual flotsam washed through a 5-part room; quite good for what it is. **Tre Corone** (piazza Brá 16), which pulls an international clientele, is not too spectacular. It's merely convenient.

Finally, roadside dining places of quality are making their appearance in Italy. As a result, excursionists or motorists can dine well without making unnecessary detours into city centers (see "Cars" below).

In other cities, ask the CIT office—or, even better, enjoy the fun of exploring for yourself.

Meal hours: In Rome and the South, breakfast, 7 A.M. to 9 A.M.; lunch, 1 P.M. to 3 P.M.; tea, late in the afternoon; dinner, 9:30 P.M. to 11 P.M.—and a midnight snack, usually in the nearest pizzeria. From Rome northward, dinner is often earlier.

NIGHTCLUBS The Italian nightclub usually blooms for about 6 months, and then dies of creeping boredom. Except for certain landmarks, the places which are crowded today might be boarding up their doors tomorrow—so take at least a part of the following with a grain of salt.

Rome? This warning is deadly serious. Avoid as you would hungry cobras nearly all of the wee-hour self-termed "glamour" spots clustered in the famous via Veneto area. With a handful of exceptions, a couple of which are listed below, they are grimy, garish, badly ventilated, dimly lit clip joints in which some of the sharpies on hand would pry the gold from their own grandmother's teeth if Granny were suddenly to become immobile.

The new **Jackie O'** (via Boncompagni 11, less than a block from via Veneto) is the most ostentatious dazzler. The best description we find for this is the single exclamation, "WOW!" Ground floor above La Graticola (see "Restaurants"); large room with walls and ceilings in shiny black plastic plus mirrors almost anywhere one double-looks; ultra modern tables and trimmings; small bar plus bandstand for 4 musicians; whisky $6.75 per cup all-in, with no cover charge; go very, very late. The with-it cinema, theatre, and rock-music, Big Name, Big Talk, Big I'm-Impressing-Everybody Set finds it Heaven Number Six; to us it is so super-ultra-overwhelmingly-blindingly spectacular (and loud!) that please give us cheese, radishes, and Glenfiddich in bed.

La Clef (via Marche 13, also near via Veneto), designed, built, and operated by tycoon Bruno Borghese of Sans Souci fame (see "Restaurants"), is the most elegant late-night drop-in oasis in the Eternal City. Here you will find a chic, cozy hand-holding rendezvous in a richly modern and discreet milieu. Subdued strains of a singer-pianist from 10 to 12; rock with dancing from 12 to 1; disco gyrations from 1 to 3:30; cover charge and first drink about $8.75;

subsequent drinks about $5; open end of September to end of June only. So skillfully conceived that the top of the night-owl society love it and flock here through Roman flyways.

La Cabala (via de Monte Brianzo 93), at once one of the most beautiful and volatile candidates in the Roman legions of the night, is presently suffering in the same limbo as Hostaria dell'Orso (see "Restaurants"), the mother operation. What an enchantress this place can be when it is operating smoothly. That is why we are hoping with all of our hearts that the current administration can upgrade it to the point where its once matchless standards are recaptured. Usually closed from June to mid-October.

L'Arciliuto (piazza Monte Vecchio 5) is the love nest created by the renowned musician, Enzo Samaritani. This talented young man won a wide and devoted following with his Italian guitar specialties and his renditions of ancient folk songs at the Blue Bar of the Hostaria dell'Orso. Now he has opened his own romantic den in a former studio of Raffaello. (Please note the great artist's fresco plastered into the arch just inside the entrance—a priceless windfall which Sig. Samaritani discovered through private research.) The inner structure has been left almost exactly as originally designed by the sixteenth-century Maestro. Vaulted ceiling; sienna-colored walls mellowed by flickering tapers; beige carpets; provincial woodwork. Soul-soothingly comfortable leather chairs and divans for sipping, listening, and between-song conversing; lutes and rare stringed instruments forming the decorative motif; piano for intermission tinkling or for accompanying the proprietor as he strums, chants, or softly whispers the melodies of Calabria, Sicily, and other provinces of his musical land. Excellent drinks; canapés available; suave service; honest accounting. We fell so hard for its relaxing ambiance, its sweetly poignant entertainment, its kind personnel, and its allure and grace that we now return often during our annual Roman roamings. Be sure to get *exact* directions before you set out, because it's in a hard-to-find, tiny courtyard about 3-minutes' walk from the Passetto restaurant. If you wish to reserve a table (it is small), telephone 65-94-19. Warmest endorsement in every regard for seekers of that tranquil but rewarding evening. We've picked up a rumor that this one might be closed. Please check locally on its veracity or lack of veracity.

Scarabocchio (piazza dei Ponziani 8), under new ownership, has capitalized on its living-room structure. Single sanctum; angular bar; ring of chairback stools around the piano occupying one corner and most of the spotlighting; champagne-colored velvet love seats and divans kneeling at squat tables; illuminated glass floor for dancing; subtle lighting; an audience that works strenuously at getting with it. Still hot, but cooling gradually.

Capriccio (via Liguria 38) is down in the depths of the restaurant of the same name. The bar at the entrance is stretched into a giant fishhook; the display-mezzanine resembles a Steuben casement; through the arches is the inner sanctum of red and gold. Small dance floor kept busy by a peppery band; popcorn-patrician patronage; whisky decanted for a King's Ransom. In our opinion, the insurmountable obstacle is that it lacks truly deluxe flair and charm in décor (see above). Just so-so.

Club 84 (via Emilia 84) is still plugged into the elegance circuit. Its prices are now among the costliest in this Eternally Expensive City. Year-round operation; L-shape, raucous, close, and intimate; small band; no cabaret; companions available but not graspy; slide projections of resort scenes. A nice spot and honest.

Gattopardo (via Mario dei Fiore 95A) mixes nutrients with its nightwork. Restaurant plus orchestra; not too expensive; this "Leopard's" lair is targeted to younger nimrods. Did we smell pot in the air? No—that couldn't be, now could it?

The highly advertised **Fascination** was handcuffed by the police sometime back after a fascinating shoot-em-up. It was given a reprieve and changed its name to **Chez Maxim**; that closed as well, and a new cabaret, **Il Carlino**, appeared, perhaps to replace the moniker with yet another. But no matter what it might be called this year, we'd exert extreme wariness. **La Tour Hassan** (via dei Serviti 28) is said to be an Arabian-style citadel offering worldwide slave-market companionship (Lonely Male Dept.), plus a highly touted floor show. Since we haven't yet hung our burnous here, we don't know how hard it might try to milk us itinerant camels from the open spaces of North America. Nothing would surprise us. The **1001**? One-thousand-and-one times, no.

To round out the nightscape, **Dave's** (in the Hotel Savoia) is a celebrity ringsider for winter sippers, and **Il Club** (piazza San Lorenzo in Lucina) is a disco-whip cracked by a Neopolitan maestro.

During the warm months, **"Brigadoon"** (about 8 miles along via Aurelia, not far from the big AGIP Motel) is the pacesetter in the alfresco circuit. Name bands and recording artists; First-class rather than Deluxe; in-and-outdoor dinner dancing; small cabaret; medium tabs and public. Balmy weather fun for the Non-U. The **Bagaglino** (via Due Macelli 75), is not for the average outlander any more, because comedy and satire in the Italian language have become its features.

As for the taxi-dance palaces which call themselves nightclubs, a 2nd serious caution! Generally speaking, there are 2 ironclad rules the sucker must learn through bitter experience: (1) If he sits with a "hostess," the only drink he can offer her is local "champagne" at perhaps $30 per bottle or imported champagne at perhaps $50 per bottle, and (2) no "hostess" may leave the establishment as much as 30 seconds before final closing time (3 A.M. in most joints, 4 A.M. in the New Florida). Time and again they might pull the hoary trick of silently slipping a bottle of bubbly up to your table as soon as you sit down with a taxi-girl—and, before you're aware of it, the wire is pulled, the cork is popped, and you're stuck with your "order" plus tip—because "it's too late to take it back, sir." If you're male, lonely, well heeled, and on the town, a cruise of the *hotel bars* along the via Veneto often brings quicker and less anguished results with far less energy and far, far less money (if you argue). But *don't be a chump for the steerers who lurk at the Excelsior Hotel entrance and along via Veneto.* If a huckster hands you a flyer and a smooth line of chatter, our advice would be to run-don't-walk in the opposite direction.

The **Mini Club** (via Emilia 48) functions on 2 floors with 2 separate bars and 2 independent coveys of pickups. This tiny microversion of the aforementioned Club 84 could use a bit more grooming, but its tariff levels run ⅓ to ½ of those at the pacesetters. No cover charge, no minimum, no stay-until-3-A.M.-policy.

Tonight's version of *la dolce vita* can be found—at fancy prices—at **Scacco Matto** ("Checkmate"), off the arty Piazza del Popolo. The address is via Ferdinando di Savoia 6. Mostly for the young.

Piper Club, far out at via Tagliamento 9, now features live bands and tapes along with its elaborate cabaret. The 2-dozen hostesses attend to a more mature and conservative clientele than in former years. First drink at $7.50; searching for an identity; not our bag but to each his own special thing.

In *Milan*, top honors for *summer* operation go to **Rendez-Vous**, newest venture of Rino Scrigna, who also owns Chez Maxim. Garden ambiance, with tables both inside and alfresco; good cabaret (for Milan!); dancing nightly; typical high-grade Scrigna attention to cuisine and service; frankly expensive by national standards. Unrivaled during the warm months. Should be patronized by gentlemen only. For *winter* shenanigans, **Astoria** (piazza Santa Maria Beltrade 2) is currently the most elegant. Rich, large, and brightly illuminated; entertainment and lively orchestra; tiny "music fee" but robust booze bill; companions available; closed June through August, when the staff migrates en masse to Nord-Est in Santa Margherita. **Caprice** (via Borgogna 5) takes the second tinsel-sprinkled popsicle. Longish room in varying reds, with bar at one end and dance floor at the other; dim lights; small show; house girls; closed summers; hard on the pocketbook, but not bad. **Maxime** (Galleria Manzoni) offers coral-velvet banquettes, double-candle lamps on tables, dancing, a modest cabaret, hostesses on tap, and lower beverage charges than those at Caprice. Closed summers, too. **Charlie Max** (via Marconi 2) woos young marrieds with exceptional nightclub cuisine, danceable orchestrations, and sane price tags. Recommendable for couples. **Number One** (via Annunciata) is the *numero uno* disco-hub at this instant; it's *very* expensive. For number two, we'd draw on **Bang-Bang** (via Molino delle Armi) followed by the **Old Fashion**, in the Park. **Nepentha** (near Plaza Hotel) has drawn outraged quacks from 2 well-traveled American-Mexican lovebirds who nest in Ireland; they report priceless menus and fowl greed that made them grouse at the supposed barnyard treatment. Black lacquer and Chinese red trim the ambiance; tableside whisky service at tabs that trim the plumage of fine-feathered night owls; it also operates in cagelike dimensions. This Stork, as with so many others of the same name, does not make us cackle. **Santa Tecla,** behind the Royal Palace, demonstrates its jazz interests through myriad record jackets on its walls. **Sans Souci** seems to have gone down; not recommended.

Florence's darkling hours are darkling even more; nightclubs are sparser and sparser in this city. The **Moulin Rouge**, on the outskirts along the river (a long taxi ride), can be pleasant during the chillier times. Draped ceiling with inset light boxes; bar with adjoining dance floor; comfortable banquettes and well-padded easy chairs; many good-looking ladies also well-padded and also easy; show that's strictly from Ted Mack's Amateur Hour. When the charitable waiter noticed we couldn't stomach the house's chemistry, he quietly (without even being asked) spirited it away and spirited back genuine *spiritus frumenti.* Very good—but we'd trust that bartender less than the *Peking People's Daily.* **Full Up** currently is the fullest straight discothèque. Comfortable and highly agreeable for its type. The **Jolly Club**, near the bridgehead of the Ponte Vecchio, comes up with a ceramic-lined entrance and tile-sided youngsters who jig hip-to-hip in jam-packed joviality. Fun for the striplings. So is the now snapped-up **Red Garter**; mostly for beer and teen revels. It's a perfect nest for youthful night hawks with extra-tight elastic in their own little garters—the ones around their wallets. The **River Club** retains its loyal oarsmen. Liquid fuel is the be-all of its being. **Arcadia** lifts spirits with its piano bar, cabaret, and disco doin's. Closed August 1 to September 15. The winter-only **Mach II** has become a membership club. Don't fret about exclusive entry policies, because if American Express will change your greenbacks into lire, we'd almost guarantee you'll qualify as an exalted card-carrier. **Al Pozzo di Beatrice** is a cozy cellar hive swarming with Bee-girls who hungrily buzz for honey in any sugar-daddy's sack. Its dark interior is bathed in a crimson haze; its colorful flooring and its huge pillar are the dominant decorative features. Open nightly at 10 P.M.; also open at 5 P.M. on holidays for tea-dancing—bags provided by the house. Be careful. **Pintor's** is no longer full of beans; closed mid-June to mid-September; not recommended.

Naples' after-dark attractions are generally honky-tonk and murderously expensive. The **Vesuvio Roof Garden** in the Hotel Vesuvio is the only truly noteworthy evening oasis in the city—and this one functions merely in the summer. **Pacuvio**, at a good site up on Orazio, is a solid, respectable, family-type establishment. Dinner from 9 P.M. until the cabaret begins at 11; short breaks until 1 A.M.; regional fare that is well above average. The only difficulty is that unless you understand the Italian spoken in the show, you'd probably be bored. Very agreeable otherwise. **Shaker** pours its beverages at half the price except on Thursday, when it's inoperative. Basically, it is a modern, amiable bar and cocktail lounge. Meals are also available. Not bad. Sportive gentlemen on the loose might find their pleasures (*and* their initial steps toward bankruptcy) in an amazing establishment called the **Antony Cabaret** (via Nazario Sauro, one block from the Excelsior); we use the word "amazing" because we have the feeling that the proprietor could wax fat on the profits of a total of 6 customers per night. Loaded with gobs when the 6th Fleet is in port; watch your wallet; watch your teeth. Obviously, we dislike this one with a passion. The **Snake Pit** (via Vittorio Emanuele 39) is *really* rugged, especially when the U.S. fleet is in; plenty of women, plenty of action, plenty of lowdown color; closed Monday. Except for serving us bum whisky from a quality bottle for our 2nd (not first) drink, this place seems to be on the level, but watch out for shady or downright crooked practices in other Neapolitan dives. Mickey Finns, pickpockets, and "rolling" are common.

Venice? Four suggestions: (1) the **Casino** at the Lido, with the only real floor show within miles. (2) **Chez Vous** at the Excelsior-Lido, offering all-out competition, (3) a drink, a dance, or a pitch at the **Antico Martini** or (4) go to bed with a good book. Pleasant dinner-dancing on the **Bauer-Grünwald** roof in season only. **Ai Musicanti** gives a first impression of a Bavarian beer hall that has suddenly been dipped in Italian schmalz (if you can imagine such a metaphor). Happy reception; strolling singers airing their adenoids over such unlikely old chestnuts as *The Colonel Bogey March;* outrageous, fun-loving flirtations from 9 to 10.30 by ersatz gondoliers who often gently pinch the posteriors of giggling female clients. Ninety percent for tour groups but so obviously contrived that who could care? A hoot. The **King's Club**, hard by the airport, is said to be the only fetching disco in the area. **Antico Pignolo** isn't even mildly recommended for the small hours; patronage of unhappy sailors who don't know any better.

Here are selected night spots in other centers: **Bari** : **Palace Hotel** and its **Tavernetta** (enlargements and renovations now completed; food served in latter.) **Bologna** : (1) **Esedra** (3 miles from town; snack bar, restaurant, and swimming pool; open day and night in summer; orchestra plus cabaret), (2) **Jolly Joker**, (3) **Black Shadow**, (4) **Shangri-la** (no show), and (5) **Fontanina** (1 mile out). **Capri**: Don't bother. **Club Number Two**, in a basement, has Reputation Number One for late cavortings; it costs multi-$$$. **Splash** hires a live band in season; ho-hum. **Catania** : Get a good night's rest. An insomniac? Okay: (1) **Al Castello**, (2) **Black and White**. **Number One**, 7 miles out at **Acistello,** is a teeny-bopping platter palace. G'night now. **Cortina d'Ampezzo** : **Bilbo Club** (formerly the Canadian Club) is THE place to be seen. Runners-up are the **Monkey Club** and the Miramonte Majestic's new **Tiger Club**. **Ballantine** and **Snoopy** will also wear out your dogs. **Elba**: (1) **Norman's Club** in Capannone, 3 kms from Portoferraio (long time we no see; open end of June to end of Sept.; lovely view; attractive décor; pizza and cold dishes only; not expensive), (2) **La Taverna** in Procchio (small band; pizza, and grills or sizzle; open to 6 A.M.), (3) **Club 6 Whisky a Gò Gò** in Capannone (records, teen-agers, low prices; typical), (4) **La Boîte** in Marciana Marina (waxworks and tapes only), (5) **Hobby Club** in **Porto Azzurro** (sea-bottom tabs; disk-o-doin's only). **Genoa**: (1) **Astoria** (first rate artists; gals available but not predatory; nice clientele), (2) **Caprice** (good shows; champagne bubbles at popping prices; your evening can easily cost $130), (3) **Moulin Rouge** (winter only; fair cabaret; a tough, brawly following; not much), (4) **Ragno d'Oro** (now mainly a beer house upstairs, with dancing on ground floor; also pretty rugged), (5) **Lucciola** (summer only; on the skids; a gyp, in our opinion), (6) **La Cambusa** (a sailors' joint; winter only; for that sinking feeling). **Scandinavian** and **New York** are still not recommended; both are forbiddingly tough. **Ischia**: (1) **Scotch**, (2) **La Lampara** (same owner as Scotch), and pick-your-place discos for the young. In the port area, mainly for wine and song, you'll find (1) **Vecchio Romano**, (2) **Giardino Degli-aranci**, (3) **Antonio**, (4) and **Nino**. **Portofino**: (1) **Carillion** (most chic; on the beach; cabaret in summer), (2) **La Potinière** (also on the shore; hatbox-size; season only; hardly worth it), (3) **La Gritta** (another go-go bar, this one with cushions on the floor; Lorenzo Raggio is its go-go proprietor), and (4) **Lo Scafandro Bar** (same ownership as the Carillon; chiefly for hippies). **Positano**: **Buca di Bacco** or **Africana** (15 minutes on the road to Amalfi; seaside perches; fun; the latter is a sea-filled cave in winter, but a real swinger for 90 days in summer). **Rapallo**: (1) **Le Roi** sits on a shaky throne. (2) **Porticciolo** caters to the under-30's—and we mean I.Q. So does the **Eden Club**. Between here and **Santa Margherita**, the grotto-style **Nord-Est** has become a community—high-spirited restaurant, boutique, and swinging discothèque

under its Swiss management; also tops is **S-M's Saltincielo** (waaaaay up above
the breakers). ***Riccione*** : **Villa Alta** (one of Italy's most romantic outdoor
settings). ***Rimini***: (1) The **Lady Godiva** (cellar of the Grand Hotel; lively
action; occasional appearances by the Lady-in-Buff herself), (2) **L'Altro
Mundo** (product of the Ambasciatori Hotel; sited near the airport, on the pike
to San Marino; seating for 2500, which makes it one of Europe's biggest
nighteries; "other-worldly" illuminations in the mod-mood; orchestra; ask for
Gilberto Amati or Luciano Pari; good for its mass-minded bracket), (3)
Embassy (mostly for dancing), (4) **Paradiso** (on the hill) now rebuilt, (5) **Las
Vegas** (dancing and show; clientele seemed questionable, to us), (6) **Safari** is
for mature gents on the prowl, (7) **La Lanterna**, on the hill near the airport,
offers live notes plus waxed ones. ***San Remo***: (1) **Boccaccio** (velvet-lined
walls and ceiling; burgundy hues; well-dressed, mannerly people), (2) **VIP's**
(below the Tourist Office; very, very good for dancing, romancing, and sipping), (3) **Casino**, (4) **Capo Nero**. The last 2 are pretty poor. ***Sorrento***: (1)
Taverna O'Caballero, (2) **2001**, and (3) **Tiffany**. For outdoor sipping, try the
Oriente Bar. ***Stresa***: (1) **Maxim's**, (2) **Pavon Doré**. ***Taormina***: (1) **La
Giara** (intimate dimensions; no show and no pickups except among patrons;
dancing), (2) **Sesto Acuto** (fourteenth-century building with mock-antique
décor; large rooms in somewhat heavy Spanish ambiance; small floor show
intermittently; hardly worth your effort), (3) **La Tavernetta** (intimate late-
hour drinking nook over the Mocambo Café). All are closed on Monday.
Turin: (1) **Chatam** (top clientele; not cheap), (2) **Moulin Rouge** (interna-
tional shows, striptease, B-girls, excellent rising-and-falling dance floor), (3)
Perroquet (expensive but good; many nonladies; cabaret), (4) **Estoril**.
Verona: **Astoria** isn't much, gang, but it's the only show in town except for
Bella Verona (the *bella* of the discothèque ball). ***Viareggio*** : **La Bussola** (at
Focette; a beehive for summer frolic under the stars; top Italian recording
names).
   For the nightclubs of other cities or regions ask the CIT, the ENIT, or the
concierge at the local hotel after your arrival. Don't trust the recommendations of taxi-drivers because (1) they're liable to get a cut from the doorman
for delivering the corpus, and (2) you're liable to be steered to a 3rd-rate clip
joint.
   The Merlin Law, like Camelot's magician for whom it is not named,
performed a latter-day miracle in Italy a while back by closing all houses of
prostitution. Senator Augusta Merlin, who forced the bill through after 10
years of yammering, got her comeuppance in the next election by being
demoted to the Chamber of Deputies. Scorecard since the "clean" life was
introduced: (1) About 550 houses closed; (2) some practitioners advertise in
newspapers as "masseuses" or "manicurists"; (3) more and more have become highway hitchhikers; (4) some have joined the curbstone coaxers who
often have to outrun police roundups; (5) an increasing number (estimated
at 3000 in the capital alone), sufficiently well-heeled or financed by "backers,"
have invested in autos to become so-called klaxon girls, vice-versa-ing motor
mores by picking up the males; (6) those with the greatest business acumen
discovered the telephone's less virtuous possibilities to become *ragazze squillo*
("call girls"), at tabs as stiff as $500 per night—or knight, as you will; (7) less

imaginative gals are hoofing places such as Genoa's waterfront "Sin Street" (via Gramsci), pose as hitchhikers at the edges of cities or towns (even a world-wise physician from Wynnewood, Pa., reported to us his droll amazement at finding an immense traffic jam generated by them near Rimini), or have interested themselves in anything else that attracts the species known as Homo *Sap*-iens; (8) the sale of hard-porn publications has flowered all across the nation. As a small sampling of how the prohibition flopped, *Lo Specchio,* the Italian weekly, found that more than 1-million prostitutes now ply their trade within the national borders, including 100-thousand in Rome; they work moviehouses, theaters, art shows, and business conventions; there are at least 2000 each Sunday at Rome's intercity soccer matches; deluxe lassies operate on crack express trains; others harbor on cruise ships; a few solicit on the national airline routes from Milan to Naples. The situation is so alarming that deadly serious consideration is being given right this minute to the repeal of this legislation and the return of officially licensed houses. Here's the important conclusion—one we hope amorous wanderers will strike in bronze. No thanks to the mercies of this Merlin Law, the VD rate has leaped more than 150% in a decade, *which currently gives Italy the highest incidence of social maladies (especially syphilis) in all of Europe.* 'Nuff said?

On a lighter note, Rome's tax collectors have started a new war to collect the municipality's rightful share of their incomes. An enterprising reporter outwitted his proofreader on the sedate *New York Times* with this somewhat startling quotation: "We'll look into the lucrative flesh trade," the City Hall source said grimly, "never mind how."

TAXIS The same old story: Scant when you want 'em and dozens when you don't. In every major center—especially during the late-afternoon-early-evening rush hours as well as whenever it rains—the street traffic moves incredibly slowly and remains incredibly chaotic. To avoid being stranded until you're wild with frustration, a simple and too-often-important trick is to memorize the bus numbers and general routes which pass by or near your hotel.

While most of the cabs are late models, a few could be relics of Garibaldi's march across Sicily (1860). The invasion of fleets of toy-size Fiat 850's is a mass phenomenon. These bouncy, perky little devils dart through traffic like hot-tailed lizards, and they'll probably scare the daylights out of you. With the exception of Florence and 1 or 2 other provincial hubs where tourists are gouged, they're reasonable in price. Since pets and wives are still free, we might insert the gentle reminder that a marriage certificate is handier to carry than a muzzle.

The fares are jumping so fast and so often that sometimes a legitimate boost is correctly added before the meters can be adjusted to tally it—usually 100 or 150 lire per ride. To avoid being conned (which nears attempted standard practice), be certain to look for the *official* notice which by law must be prominently displayed.

Important: *From 10 P.M. to 6 A.M., there is an extra charge per vehicle* (not per passenger). Some of the drivers would steal the pennies from a dead man's eyes—and their deliberate abuse of this surcharge is one of the most commonly practiced rackets of Italy. They'll argue, wheedle, bluster, and practically burst into tears—but just remember that when they play you for a sucker in this manner, you should simply hand them what's right and then tell them to buzz off. If things get really bad, demand they drive you to the nearest police station *(Questura,* pronounced "Kwes-too-rah," or to the Distretto di Polizia); 99% of the time this will shut them up instantly.

Equally important: *Be sure the meter is correctly set at the beginning of the ride* (particularly in Rome and a few other metropolises). Otherwise, especially in the via Veneto and piazza di Spagna areas, you might get stuck with the last rider's fare on top of your own.

Unless your driver is extraordinarily patient or kind, 15% should be his maximum tip.

TRAINS   A king-size headache for everybody.

The State Railways is unable to cope with the traffic volume and existing equipment is being overworked beyond the limits of safety. One major—repeat major—factor in swelling the virtually standard mob-scene nightmare is the countless thousands, thousands, thousands, and more thousands of free passes which Europe's most befuddled bureaucracy has passed out lavishly as if they were advertising throwaways distributed on a city sidewalk. In near-panic at this state of affairs, the Government earmarked funds for the modernization of rolling stock, track beds, and other hardware. Two-fifths is being invested in the South, where conditions are most critical of all. The tariff scale remains among the lowest in Europe. Incidentally, there are whispers in the roundhouse of 20% hike, so you may be digging a little deeper into your pockets to buy your tickets this season.

Your best chance of getting a seat is in First-class. *Make sure of it by reserving in advance, whenever reservations are possible.* If you have no reservations, and if you are leaving from the point where the train is made up or cars are being added, plan to arrive at the station 30 minutes before departure time, to assure yourself of a space when the gates are opened for entry. Rome, Milan, Turin, and Venice are almost always terminal points. In Second-class, there's an excellent chance you'll stand. First is definitely worth the difference. The so-called Lusso, with armchairs, is available on the 6-hour Rome–Milan *Settebello* ("Seven Times Beautiful"), which Italians describe as the finest train in the world. Restaurant service at your seat may be had on *La Freccia della Laguna* ("The Arrow of the Lagoon"), between Rome, Florence, Bologna, and Venice, and on the Rome–Genoa–Turin Express as well.

Some of the new single-compartment sleepers are the best around. The cheapest sleeping accommodation is called the *Carrozze Cuccette* (pronounced "Cah-ROT-zay Coo-CHET-tay")—ordinary coaches fixed up with bunks. Again—be certain to reserve them beforehand.

You may save money by buying a "free circulation" ticket (30 days of travel), a "circular" ticket (a minimum of 600 miles within 60 days), a "Per Manifestazione" ticket (for visitors who come to Italy for expositions, fairs, or other special events), or a "group" ticket (minimum of 4). And don't forget to check into the Eurailpass (see "Let's Be European").

AIRLINE   Alitalia Italian Airlines, as you undoubtedly know, is an official transportation arm of the nation. As such, it reflects much of the havoc of a government that has endured nearly 40 changes of administration during the past 3 decades or so. When it is functioning smoothly it likewise radiates a Latin grace and charm that can only bring passengers back again for more high-flying adventure.

Harnessing a fleet of Boeing 747's and DC-8's (mostly over the North Atlantic), Caravelles and DC-9's (for important European runs), Alitalia soars along as one of the largest commercial carriers in the world.

In the introduction of this chapter we have already delineated with agonizing detail the disruptive effects of Italy's rampant strike situation. The diabolical result of this all too often carries over into the aeronautical realm as well. Within the skein that is Alitalia, more than 20 separate unions are involved, and even when one of these syndicates decides to go out on a "wildcat," a "flash," or a "hiccup" protest, very frequently the entire line shuts down. Aviation being what it is, there is so much interdependence among the specialized divisions that one often cannot function safely without the others. As we write these words, the pilots are seeking a separate contract with the carrier; their union is so potent that in *one* month it forced Alitalia to scrub nearly 1/5th of its scheduled flights. Similer expressions of labor unrest have cost Alitalia as much as $2,500,000 a day, according to independent surveys.

As so many of these paralyzing issues are referred back to political paper-shufflers and assorted bumbling martinets, there's little that Alitalia can do to resolve its deeper problems until the administration in Rome itself is functioning properly.

In spite of this, however, Alitalia's administrative pilots at last seem to be climbing over the turbulence of a storm-bound government and operating more independently of the crippling bureaucrats. Studies are underway and programs are being implemented that we hope will unravel many of these earthborne glitches. The carrier again is recognizing that the passenger comes first. Strenuous efforts are being made to hack through the red tapes that have manacled so many domestic flights. Simultaneously, the entire system is about to experience an upgrading in quality. As one small example of the new thinking at Alitalia, the chefs do not believe that they can provide a wide assortment of top quality, well prepared pasta while aloft. Thus, even though it is much more expensive, in First class on the transatlantic passages you will find U.S. prime beef served in both directions on virtually every flight.

Though Alitalia cannot in one fell swoop overcome the handicaps imposed by years of Italy's political and economic chaos, it is ingeniously exploring routes around the thunderheads. Our hats are off to the enormous progress which it has forged on the long-range skyways, and may it keep up the slaying of snafus on the continental and domestic flyways as well.

DRINKS   Grappa, vermouth, and brandy are the national hard drinks. Grappa, popular in the North, is a raw, harsh, high-proof beverage made from the leftovers of the ordinary distillation process; it is considered horrid by most visitors, including us. By the terms of a Franco-Italian treaty, the brandy may no longer be called "cognac"; normally, it's as nectareous as Listerine.

Vecchia Romagna and René Briand are the only brands we can recommend. To the American who likes his Gordon's or Beefeater's, the gin is a magic carpet to the Al Capone days. Cocktails get progressively worse, province by province, from the Swiss border to Sicily. Local whiskies lift the hair straight off the drinker's pate, but some of the liqueurs (notably Strega and Aurum) are extremely palatable. One "discovery" which delights most visitors is Sambuca *(anisette)* when it is served *con mosche* (with "flies," which are floating coffee beans); delicious! Curiosity, The Power of Advertising Dept.: Hannun and Blumberg's *Brandies and Liqueurs of the World* (Doubleday, 1976) states, "Galliano is probably as well known in the United States as Bénédictine." Although it was first compounded in Livorno around 1900, just *try* to find this good product in the next Italian bar or bars you enter! Oceans of imported spirits are freely available; good Scotch runs anywhere from $10 to $15 per bottle.

Italy is a wine country. She has moved ahead of France as the largest producer in the world, even though the Gauls still drink more on a per capita basis; she dedicates 55% of her farmland to the glories of the grape. There are not many quality vintages, though, compared with France, Spain, and Germany; table wines are the specialty. But the prices! Top-drawer bottlings come to perhaps $10 or $12; everyday "cooking" varieties are yours for a fast $1 or $1.50. For special treasures, however, you can pay a miniransom. On a personal note, for more than 30 years we tried without success to run down the rare and legendary Brunello di Montalcino, which a number of otherwise authoritative oenologists in our library flatly call "the most expensive wine in the world." (It isn't. Certain nonancient Burgundies and Trocken-beerenausleses run considerably higher.) In '76 a cherished and generous Roman friend drew from his private cellar to end our quest—and, while it was splendid, this $40 delight lacked the body and ultimate velvetness of a vintage Romanée-Conti. Furthermore, you *could* pay as much as $450 for an 1888 Boindi-Santi, a robust Tuscan red!

Vinofeiters, who turn out 300-million gallons annually of adulterated or false wines, are a big headache despite recent crackdowns. If you'll recall the whisky-making scene in *Mister Roberts,* you should have an idea of their taste. Ingredients run the gamut from water, sugar, denatured alcohol, apple juice, potato juice, turnip juice, dried fig paste, curry, glycerine, or other chemical and coloring products—many of which are barred by law from human consumption. One of the most repulsive gimmicks is the use of ox blood—yes, ox blood—for the tinting of ruby-red. It sounds like a lot of trouble for a small profit, but the manufacturing costs are 1/5th of those of the true grape essence.

But something is finally being done about it. In addition to punitive court actions, the Government has readied a classification system similar to France's *appellation contrôlée.* Its regulations encompass geography, altitude, soil, humidity, color, acid content, and additives. Under these new labeling controls, "aged" means more than 2 years old and "reserve" signifies an elder citizen of 3 years or more. Only about 15% of vineyards in France come under the controlled-name status—and the same will be true here. Thus if you stick to the officially classified labels *only,* you'll know what's inside the bottle. If you don't, does a potion of ox blood bother your sensitivities?

If we were forced to drink 3 normally priced wines in Italy—one red, one white, and one rosé—to the exclusion of all others, here's what we'd pick:

> For the red—Valpolicella (Bolla)
> For the white—Soave Bertani
> For the rosé—Bolla

Bardolino (a red from Verona), Verdicchio (a white from the Adriatic slopes), and Rosatello (a rosé) are excellent alternatives; many prefer these, in fact, to the trio which we've selected as a matter of personal taste. Barolo, a rich ruby pressing from the Piedmont, is especially complementary to pecorino and other strong cheeses. The Lambrusco from Emilia and the Ricciotto from Verona are sparkling reds worthy of attention. Chianti, for us, is too harsh, too rough, and too acid for any dish containing less than 12 oz. of olive oil per person; perhaps you'll disagree. Antinori, however, is an excellent label in this category. All but one of the Italian rosés, including Bertolli and Rosatello, are downright poor when compared to the products of southern France. The exception is Bolla, made by peeling the grapes before fermentation; the bottle is identified by an attached plastic rose, and this brand is delicious. Sparkling Asti Spumante is the closest facsimile to champagne; the dry types can be forced down pleasantly, but the sweet ones are so cloying they might make you shudder. Booby prize in this department goes to the so-called Moscato of San Marino, popular along the Rimini Riviera; it is the most repulsive wine we have ever tasted.

For an apéritif, invariably we choose a deeeelicious elixir called Rosso Antico, which is spreading in fame with deserved rapidity up and down the Boot. It's sweeter and more gentle than Campari. Sip it *on the rocks,* not at pouring temperature. You might also wish to try either a Carpano "Punt e Mes" (characteristic bitter vermouth which we happen to find a delight) or a Cinzano (pronounced chin-ZAN-o) with soda, ice, and lemon peel on a hot day; they're national favorites which many travelers also adore. Or, if you really want to be European, ask for an "Americano"—sweet vermouth, bitter Campari, a dash of soda, and a lemon peel. If you like tart things, you'll probably find this refreshing.

§TIP: The best tonic in the world for overeating, flatulence, gas pains, picking yourself up off the floor when you've mixed oysters and bananas—practically any stomach ailment up to chilblains or ulcers—is an Italian bitters called Fernet Branca. The taste is horrible, but the effect is atomic. This hideous black liquid has saved my digestion and my temper on so many occasions that I now carry a small flask of it in my briefcase whenever I travel. Try any bar; less than soda pop.

TIPPING Aside from the hotels and restaurants, a nearly general 10%.

Hotels automatically add 18% to your bill for a "service charge." This is sometimes a racket, because the employees who have helped you don't always see it, despite union laws which insist that they must. Give the concierge from $1 per day extra (never exceeding a total of $7), and hand small amounts in person to your maid, baggage porter, room waiter, and valet, if you use them. At sit-down cafés, the tabs *always* include service, but many villains stamp the required *Servizio Compreso* so lightly it's almost illegible. In restaurants, a flat 15% is added to the bill; give your waiter half of the service charge in addition, never exceeding 800 lire.

Always tip everybody for small services, because Italians consider it gainfully earned income.

PERSONAL SERVICES   Italy has the best barbers and beauticians in the world; by actual statistics, one out of every 84 people in the country is involved in these occupations. A good haircut costs from $3 to $7; a shave from $2 to $3, and a shot of fancy after-shave lotion or hair tonic perhaps $1. Ladies can get "the works" (shampoo, wave, manicure) for $20.

Since the untimely death of its founder-owner and since its acquisition by Gillette, world-famous **Eve of Rome** (via Veneto 116) has climbed back from its temporary slump. Her personal friend Mrs. Winkler is running it well; ask for sweet Augusta, who was a protégé of the founder.

Elizabeth Arden has closed its Roman shop.

Attilio (stunning salons at the Excelsior Hotel and headquarters at piazza di Spagna 68) and **Spartaco & Ugo** (piazza di Spagna 51) are in the same exalted bracket. Both are equally reliable and fine.

In *Venice*, a New York Guidester recommends **Carol's**.

Tip about 2000 lire to the hairdresser, 1000 lire to the manicurist, and 500 lire to the others. That's plenty, so they say.

Italian doctors are renowned throughout Europe for their excellence. The better ones are as modern in techniques and practices as your good family physician or surgeon at home; complete stocks of American, English, Swiss, German, and local medicines are available in profusion. We were tremendously impressed by the thoroughness, efficiency, and skill with which Dr. Salvatore Mannino tackled assorted ailments of ours. We cannot embarrass Dr. Mannino by directly recommending his service to readers, because this would be a breach of his professional ethics; we can only say that if we should ever pick up anything from a hangnail to yaws in the Eternal City, he's 100% our man. New York-trained, he speaks perfect English. His office is via Lisbona 9; his office phone is 84 45 712, and his home phone (for emergency calls) is 32 74 562. Another topliner is the Yankee-born internist, Dr. Frank Silvestri. You'll find this personable stateside-schooled specialist, plus 3 of his English-speaking Italian colleagues, at the American Medical Center, via Ludovisi 36 (phone 464-143 or 485-706).

THINGS TO BUY   Silk, men's and ladies' wear, gloves, leather, jewelry, knitwear, silver and glassware and art and other treasures for the home, religious items, straw, shoes, camoes, *haute couture*, mosaics—and then *more* silk.

Before proceeding further, here are warnings to all friends of this *Guide* which hopefully will save them from being bilked:

• Every major tourist center in the nation is now plagued by armies of "steerers." If any well-dressed, charming, suave man or woman of *any* nationality (some even pose as Americans!) strikes up a conversation with you on the street, in a café, or elsewhere—and then smoothly suggests that you accompany them while they pick up a purchase, be measured for a fitting, or similar dodge—BE ON YOUR GUARD IMMEDIATELY. There is at least a 98% chance that, in gambling or carnival argot, they are "shills" whose game is to sucker innocent travelers into dishonest establishments which give them a commission on everything that their victims can be high-pressured into buying. One common ploy is to introduce themselves as a "Count," a "Countess," or a similarly phony title. Their fields of operation cover virtually every type of merchandise favored by outlanders. If you fall for their honeyed pitch, 50 gets you 1 that you'll be sorry.

• Be careful when you buy tortoiseshell objects. Be *certain* the item is made from a species which can be legally imported into the U.S. and into your state. Many tortoiseshell objects are made from endangered species; they would be confiscated and you might face stiff penalties. There is a clever plastic imitation in many supposedly reputable shops. The test is this: When held up to the light, portions of the plastic are nearly transparent, while the genuine article is always uniformly opaque. Neither material burns, although unscrupulous merchants will tell you that plastic *is* inflammable—and then apply a match to "prove" that you're getting the real McCoy.

• A kindly but rueful lady from Van Nuys, California, has reported a tale of woe which was new to us. In a second-line shop in Venice, she spotted the Bank of America credit-card sticker on its door and charged some glassware accordingly. When the wrong items were sent, she returned them—to learn that the store refused to accept the shipment. Then the Bank of America informed her (1) that this was not one of its accredited accounts and (2) that evidently these people dealt with a local bank which itself had extended the use of their credit facility. (Parenthetically, we must comment that this kind of hanky-panky cannot happen to American Express or Diner's Club clients.)

• For further tips on shady practices, please turn to the "Local Rackets" section at the end of this chapter.

Men's silk suits and specialties in **Rome**? **Brioni** (via Barberini 79) is a pacesetter for the American who wants the best—at very fair tariffs, too. It (1) collaborates directly with top textile manufacturers in producing exclusive Brioni silk, wool, cotton, and linen designs; (2) creates a complete parallel line of shoes, ties, and accessories to blend with the colors and stylings of all of its models; and (3) influences world style trends. Brioni today is Italy's oldest and most famous High Fashion center for men—as well as the only men's wear firm officially appointed by the Government to represent Italian styles abroad. For its burgeoning international network, Brioni has introduced a large ready-made line of splendid wools tailored by hand "Roman Style" at the Penne factory. Nobody else anywhere offers such a large collection of such exquisiteness. If you want to be conservative, the brilliant fashion king, Gaetano Savini-Brioni, will personally make you *très soigné* with the finest silk or wool suit sewed today. But if you really want to knock them out, choose one of their stunning black silk dinner coats or other custom-made beauties that are the Brioni trademark—silk blazers, slacks, shirts, pajamas, their marvelous collection of original ties, and other exclusives. Normal 3-to-4-day delivery on custom garments—much finer work at enormous savings over the U.S. scale. Ask for the gentlemanly and knowledgeable General Manager Dr. Ettore Perrone-Brioni or Edwin Mula, our special chum; their English is perfect. The Ladies' Boutique, run by the Maestro's daughter Gigliola, keeps your gal busy, happy, and in mischief; it offers beautiful knitwears and super made-to-measure dresses, coats, and suits in exciting fabrics. Super-super.

Angelo (via Bissolati 34/36, next to Pan Am, plus a new branch at piazza Trinità dei Monti 17-A, opposite the Hassler) is also magnificent. Handsome, talented, magnetic Angelo Vittucci, after 17 years of brilliant apprenticeship, went independent in 1963. With his equally gifted and personable partners, Aldo Uggeri and Carlo Ilari, he timorously opened their spacious and beautiful premises—to be bowled over by instantaneous success. And, with their taste, imagination, and own special magic, how well they deserve it! Gorgeous handworked suitings in silks, worsteds, tropicals, and others at competitive tariffs; striking sport jackets; our one-of-a-kind dinner coat and trousers inspiringly designed by Mr. Angelo himself; custom-made silk dressing gowns; custom-made silk slacks. Unique foulard linings; individually fashioned shirts; roughly 3-zillion exclusive tie patterns; all other haberdashery imaginable; finished delivery in 3 full working days. Mr. Angelo, Mr. Aldo, Mr. Carlo, and assistants are 100% bilingual. Also stupendous.

In this same luxury bracket, **Cucci**, **Caraceni**, **Battistoni**, and **Cifonelli** are all master cutters, too—but Brioni and Angelo have American-style savvy.

Others in this league? Caution: PICK CAREFULLY! Our closets are stuffed with single-purchase trial suits so heartbreakingly butchered that we couldn't wear them to a chihuahua fight. So move warily among the smaller, less famous, less costly cutters, because they're all too apt to victimize you.

Further to drive harder the crucially important words of warning directly above, which apply to both lady and gentleman buyers: in all custom-made garments, always, always, always find time for 3 fittings. A minimum of 2 fittings normally does not work; YOU would be the one who takes this chance. Never, never, never accept one fitting with subsequent forwarding to your home, because automatically you would be buying disappointment and grief.

Silks and other materials by the yard? **Galtrucco** (via del Tritone 14) has everything. Fine.

Jewelry and *objets d'art?* **Bulgari** (via Condotti 10) puts Cartier, Tiffany, Winston, and the rest of the million-dollar league to shame. Without overstating its position a particle, it is one of the most fabulous establishments in the world. On one side, you will find *the* Thousand and One Nights in jewels— treasures of such dazzling beauty that not even the legendary Scheherazade could find the proper words to describe their magnificence to King Shahriyar. On the other side, shoppers of our bracket meet a vast selection of things that are within almost everybody's price range—all in the exquisite Bulgari taste. Unique collections of diamonds, rubies, emeralds, and sapphires are profusely displayed, together with superb pearls, in a series of pieces that are unbelievably glorious. Wander at will through the biggest private assemblage of English and continental antique silver in Europe. Take your choice of the very rare old Chinese jades and hard stones . . . the Renaissance jewelry and sixteenth-century rock crystals . . . the fantastically crafted, historic, one-of-a-kind boxes and watches . . . enough to dizzy even the most experienced connoisseur. Whenever we make one of our frequent tours of these glittering premises, as we stroll, every successive island of beauty, cabinet by cabinet, seems to sit up and beg, "Look at ME next!" Such wonders are here that Maestro Sotirio Bulgari, who founded the firm in 1881, would surely thrill at his monument. The great, universally beloved Giorgio Bulgari died in 1966, but his handsome, urbane, painstakingly trained offspring, Gianni, Paolo, and Nicola, will greet you with traditional Bulgari warmth, patience, and expertise. Your browsing is welcomed, even if it is only to feast your eyes. So have a look—and we envy your dreams. (P.S.: For stay-at-home New Yorkers or afterthought vacationers, Bulgari has another jewel of a beauty spot in the Hotel Pierre at Fifth Ave. and 61st St.)

Gloves? We've long believed that the small, old-line specialist called **Catello d'Auria** (via Due Macelli 55) does the best job on the Italian Peninsula. It's about 2 blocks from the foot of the Spanish Steps—and be sure to double-check the name over the door, because confusion with several inferior shops in the vicinity would be easy. All that the d'Auria family has cared about since 1894 is making finer gloves than any other craftsmen—and to hell with chaise longues, air conditioning, perfumed receptionists, and over-inflated tariffs! Since every single piece is fashioned 15 or 20 feet from where you buy it, you can order any unorthodox style, color, material, or fillip that has ever nibbled at your subconscious, at no increase in cost—and prices are dirt cheap to begin with. As illustrations of its range, you'll find everything from wrist lengths to 24-inch lengths in ladies' daytime wear, a parade of virtually every conceivable dress style in gentlemen's wear, and exotica such as pearl-beaded, gold-embroidered creations which are eye-riveting. Our pets are the tailor-made models for kids from 2 to 12. Its extensive mail-order business to the States is proliferating more and more every year, so take home or write for their handy little free catalogue in English. Along the same line, if you should lose one d'Auria glove, you might wish to do what we have done at least a dozen times—tuck the other into an envelope, return it to the shop, and have a brand-new duplicate pair by airmail within a matter of days! Pleasant, kindly people; chic, reasonable, and dependable merchandise. If you like your gloves with sequins, diamonds, bananas, Hershey Bars, or any other trimmings, do as Barbara Stanwyck did and commission d'Auria to design 31 original patterns for your exclusive wear. It'll be a bargain!

Leather? **Gucci** (via dei Condotti 21) is indisputably the most plush. Its 2-floor premises are rich, its stocks are elegant but stratospheric in cost, and its sales staff is much more polite than it used to be. Branch on New York's 5th Avenue. **Fendi** (via Borgognona 36A, 38, 39, 4L, now a pedestrian mall), with 2 stores directly opposite each other, is a more down-to-earth candidate, as is **L. Righini** (via dei Condotti 76). We make our own personal purchases in both of these solid and reliable operations. **Tivoli Leathers** (via San Martino della Battaglia 60–66) is also fine.

Treasures for the home? Nearly anywhere, **Casa Danske** (via Francesco Crispi 87, just off via Veneto) is the closest we've ever found to being *the* dream shop of the North American hostess and host. Its new owner is the legendary Royal Copenhagen Porcelain Manufactory, which since 1775 has been spinning out its incredible fairyland of 100% hand-made, hand-painted masterpieces. In addition to those glorious porcelains, in this captivating little 4-story house you'll find a painstakingly selected collection of Georg Jensen ranging from his unique silver jewelry to his latest kitchen creations in cast iron, stainless steel, and wood, plus glassware, plus furniture, plus myriads of other wantables—the top-cream merchandise of Scandinavia at prices dramatically lower than at home. Winningly friendly Nordics, headed by Resident Co-Managers Mogens Lykkeberg and Ole Bang, will welcome you with Danish smiles. Please, please do yourself and us the favor of browsing through this gem!

Knitwear? Separates and unbelievably lighter-than-ever wool knits in bright, gay, vibrant colors are now the cachet and trademark of Europe's most famous and fashionable knitwear couturier and boutique, **Laura Aponte** (via Gesu e Maria 10)—and how American gals love'em! The weights are so fantastic that 6 complete outfits fit easily into a small weekend bag. You'll find tops galore to combine with full or Chanel-length or straight-pleated skirts, or trousers. Daytime woolen dresses; ankle-length dressy types; short skirts; long skirts; pants; pantsuits; tops; lots more. Her elegant and celebrated hand embroideries continue to be a unique attraction. Unlike most Roman shops, this one is normally open from 9 to 6, without a lunch break. Ask for the radiant Miss Aponte in person, or for the Misses Stefania or Mirella. *Salve!*

Trico (via delle Carozze) has a very fine name in this field, too. **Julian de Ville** (via Veneto 183) offers a less exciting line, but perhaps you might find it worth a look. **Alfredo's Knits** (51 piazza di Spagna), for reasons which we consider adequate, is NOT recommended by this book.

Haute couture? **Irene Galitzine** (fashion's most savvy reporter, Eugenia Sheppard, has lauded her as "one of Rome's major attractions, like the Forum or the Baths of Caracalla"), **Fontana**, **Tita Rossi**, **Zecca**, **Eleanora Garnett** and **Baratta** (branch in Rome, center in Milan) have the most exalted reputations; famous **Simonetta** and **Fabiani** caused a ruckus in the Government and in the trade by moving to Paris; **Capucci** and **Balestra** are rising; **Antonio De Luca** (via del Babuino 79)—terrific!—is our current personal favorite. Of course, **Emilio Pucci** is *the* designer for blouses or slacks. In the top couturiers, you'll be rocked $300 to $400 for an ordinary dress, $400 to $600 for an embroidered one, and up to $1500 for an evening gown. B-r-r-r! **Fantasia** (via Condotti 19) has lovely accessories at high tariffs, if you can stand the miserably bored and uninterested clerks.

Boutiques? Dozens upon dozens. **La Mendola** (piazza Trinità dei Monti 15, atop the Spanish Steps) is our '77 candidate as THE champion. Pennsylvania's Jack Savage and Illinois' Mike La Mendola, whose winning personalities and design genius spark their vast array of elegant exclusives, continue to enchant everybody from Ann Margret to Carol Burnett to great-name U.S. department-store buyers to Mrs. Size 18 America. In this delightfully cheerful, relaxed, and informal rendezvous, you'll find price levels for all budgets, with both ready-mades (free alterations by nimble, ingratiating Filippa) and custom-mades (2 to 7 days) at least 50% below chic U.S. resort tariffs. Their most famous specialties are the trademarked La Mendola prints on uncrushable lightweight silk and wool jersey, silk chiffon-Georgette, and crepes—oh la la!

These (plus solids) come in day dresses and suits, cocktail and evening wear, debutante gowns, a year-round cruise line, play and travel clothes, and fun-filled "at homes"—all with that inspired La Mendola dash, and nearly all either created for y-o-u or straight off-the-rack. One startler is their ingenious "magic dress" of pure silk jersey (for all ages and most occasions), which can be worn short or long, at your whim—and, without wrinkling, can be sent home in an airmail envelope! (Both of us are *c-r-a-z-y* about the 2 Nancy bought and wears as her husband's favorites.) Their frequent foreign fashion shows at the Bergdorf-Marshall Field level have taken them to such scattered centers as New York, Philadelphia, Cairo, Abu Dhabi and Tehran. It's remarkable to us how these experts so smartly and elegantly festoon 3 generations at once, without even blinking. Extra affection is lavished upon you 14's, 16's, 18's, and difficult figures. They are thoroughly experienced in shipping all over the world. Ask for Mr. Jack, Mr. Mike, or Mme. Anne (their Gal Friday)—and enjoy. Terrific!

Roberta (piazza di Spagna 30), described more fully in the "Venice" shopping section further along, is another honey, especially for its gorgeous handbags, luggage, and "coordinated" wearables. This one shouldn't be missed.

Because of space limitations in this book, information on other boutiques may be found in *Fielding's Shopping Guide to Europe*.

Shoes? For men, **Samo** (via Veneto 189, via del Tritone 204, and via Sistina 106) is the fleetest and most graceful runner in Italian footwear. For ladies, **Lily of Florence** (via Lombardia 38) is the exclusive purveyor of the famous Amalfi line; Mrs. Power, herself an American, is the gracious and warmhearted director of this new branch. Highly recommended. **Soré** (opposite Trevi Fountain at No. 97) is not as à la mode but it is more popularly priced.

Cameos, coral, and related items? **Giovanni Apa Co.**, the world's finest specialist (see "Excursion to Pompeii," which follows), has a handsome shop at piazza Navona 26-27 and a newer branch on the Tiburtina Road to *Tivoli* —both operated by the manly sons of this famous family. Incomparable.

Paintings and art, for pleasure and investment? **Gallerias Schneider** (Robert Schneider) and **Odyssia** (Miss Skouras), owned and operated by Americans, handle some of the top Italian painters. **L'Obelisco**, **Barcaccia**, and **Il Camino** are well known. There are now more than 50 galleries in the capital.

Antiques? Be careful! The local **Flea Market** operates on Sundays from 6 A.M. to midafternoon; it is a tourist trap to end all tourist traps. (The adjoining ½-mile strip of automotive parts shops might sell you YOUR missing hubcaps, because most of its merchandise is stolen.) If you absolutely *must* see it, go very, very early, as the dealers do—and don't buy any "genuine Etruscan" articles, because they're fakes. Via Giulia is a good street for general browsing; via dei Coronari is the lower-price center; piazza Fontanella Borghese also offers jewelry; the same plea for caution applies to both. So watch out for counterfeits, always bargain, and always take along an Italian friend to protect your interests.

The **Lion Bookshop** (via del Babuino 181) has large stocks of reading matter in our language. Look for the Lion Rampant outside, then go through the door and search hard for the showroom. Or try the **American Book Shop** (via delle Vite 57), which is also versatile.

Religious articles? **Al Pellegrino Cattolico** (via di Porta Angelica 83), across from St. Peter's, offers complete stock for the devout; they will have your rosaries blessed by the Pope and delivered to your hotel, at no extra fee. Honest, 100% dependable, and fine; none better.

Drugs, cosmetics, and toiletries? **Lepetit Farmacia** (corso Umberto 417) has the largest American and English assortment in the capital.

Bargain shopping area? **Via Cola di Rienzo**, across the river from piazza dei Popolo. Haggle hard!

In *Florence*, via Tornabuoni is the Fifth Avenue, via Porta Rossa is the 34th St., and Santa Maria is the Madison Avenue. Ponte Vecchio, the dramatic little shop-lined bridge, is limited to silver, embroideries, blouses, and specialty items. The **San Lorenzo "Central" Market** and the even more charming **"New" Market** (Porta Rossa and Santa Maria) are also good for strolling and casual shopping. The rather poor **Flea Market** (Piazza Ciompi) also operates from Monday through Saturday.

Straw wearables? For more than 4 decades the one-and-only **Emilio Paoli** (via Vigna Nuova 26R) has continued to create the world's most fascinating miracles in straw. Stunningly chic hand-crocheted Renaissance-design straw coats, long evening skirts, and dresses ($50 to $80)—in many models and colors, with coordinated purses; exclusive raffia handbags ($15 to $20); gay straw hats ($4 to $16); a garden of daisies, poppies, buttercups, etc.; intriguing Gift Dept; straw ties, animals, fruits, vegetables, and lots more. Every single article is original handwork, too! See Mrs. Alda, Miss Leda, or Mr. Ranieri. Great!

Ladies' shoes? **Lily of Florence** (borgo San Jacopo 20) is one of the best bets—and bargains!—within 7 leagues of the Arno. In 1966, Statesider Lily Power packed her bags in Seattle, Washington, and moved to the Boot; by 1969, the happy combination of her Italian heritage and her American savvy had established her as a dynamic, innovative leader in the field. Her shop is the sole distributor of world-famous Amalfi shoes; the dressier "Lily of Florence" line is also featured. All U.S. sizes; tariffs which run 30% to 50% less than those that you'd pay back home. Mrs. Power is now concentrating on her new Rome branch (via Lombardia 38); her son Lynn, her daughter Maria, and her daughter-in-law Rosemary will welcome you with grace. Terrific! **Romei**, the great boutique described almost immediately below, has opened an impressive and interesting new shop at Lungarno Acciaioli 32-R which focuses entirely on very chic footwear also at prices which are suprisingly refreshing for the quality. Proudly and exclusively it offers distinguished lines in U.S.-style lasts. Ask for blonde and beautiful Mrs. Victoria Romei. Definitely worth prowling by any feminine visitor. **Salvatore Ferragamo**, at Palazzo Feroni, is the only Florence outlet of some of the most renowned craftsmen globally in this field—but is it e-x-p-e-n-s-i-v-e!

Knitwear? The **Romei Boutique** (via Porta Rossa 77 *Red*) is a knockout. Most Americans adore the collections, because (1) in its own ways it's months ahead of competition, (2) its prices are so advantageous that you'd pay double in the States for the identical item, and (3) highest standards, taste, and flair are its watchwords. Exclusives on the full Mirsa (Marquesa di Gresy) and De Parisini silk-dress lines; wool knit models, including 2- and 3-piece wool-knit suits; costume coats and dresses; lovely silk-knit 1- and 2-piece dresses; gay matching silk print scarves; many other tempters. Mr. Loris or Mr. Victor will be your guides. Intriguing.

So is **Sonya** (Lungarno Acciaioli 26-R)—a sparkling *bijou* which is the highly successful creation and namesake of a bright, gay, young, enormously talented Californian. Everything here is designed and manufactured through her own virtuosity; all of her knits reflect the relaxed grace and elegance of the Golden State Look. Coordinates are one of her special pets. When you walk into her pert premises, please know that the function of the showroom is display; the bulk of her versatile stock is on instant call from the rear. Throughout her thriving export network in North America and elsewhere, the merchants add stiff markups to her merchandise—a b-i-g advantage to the visiting shopper who buys at the source, comparatively at wholesale discounts. This radiantly vivacious lady is so friendly that she's a font of sage advice to outlanders; her love of people is phenomenal. If she's out, ask for Dorothy or Anna. Not to be missed.

High-fashion leather? **John F.** (Lungarno Corsini 2)—both the venerable family firm and its personable entrepreneur—win the sweepstakes in a walk. Although the magnificent frescoed fifteenth-century ceiling and statuary in its section of the historic *palazzo* are ornately Florentine, it is small, happily intimate, and convivial. You'll find a broad and ultrafashionable range of classical and sport handbags from $20 up, as well as wallets, eyeglass cases, key cases, cigarette cases, and a trove of other accessories from $8 up—all in superb craftsmanship and all at ⅓ of their U.S. and Canadian prices! As a dividend, the large and lively Mail Order Department here is as busy as beavers in its daily shipments all over the world. John F. worked for a number of years in New York; since it gives him keen pleasure to assist all newcomers with great courtesy and interest, please don't fail to seek him out. What buys!

Italian handicrafts and majolica ceramics? **Soc. A. Menegatti & Co.** (Via Tornabuoni 79) and **S.E.L.A.N.** (Via Porta Rossa 107–113R) offer good browsing.

EXTRAORDINARY gifts for friends (or yourself)? **Balatresi** (Lungarno Acciaioli 22R) is so fascinatingly different that it shouldn't be missed by a-n-y-b-o-d-y. Lots of their treasures are 1-of-a-kind. Head first for their eye-popping alabaster collection: beautiful eggs (65¢), 15 kinds of fruit (90¢), decorative owls ($2 to $20), and unusual boxes ($6.90 to $24). Those who wish to splurge will find gorgeously hand-carved articles in rare varieties of this gleaming mineral—dishes, vases, boxes, animals, ashtrays—all created by skilled craftsmen exclusively for them. From the supplies dug from rich veins in their own mine, talented artisans fashion the celebrated brown onyx of Tuscany into contrasting types of trays, boxes, vases, and animals ($4 to $40). Also importantly featured are magnificent pieces in hard stones such as malachite, lapis lazuli, rodonite, and other specimens, as well as exquisite enamelware including the famous Fabergé reproductions ($5.50 to $58), hand-painted globes with a compact interior bar created solely for Balatresi by Maestro Giorgio, and a trove more. The crown jewels of their vast array are the gorgeous original works of art which are sold only here; a pair of prime examples are the striking ceramic sculptures of Fosco Martini and the wide selection of renowned Florentine mosaics (authenticated by signatures of the top experts in the field). Three more honest human beings than gentle, friendly Proprietor Umberto Balatresi, his lovely wife Giovanna, and his quietly engaging sister Daniela do not exist. Their guarantee is their sacred bond. As a bonus, these dedicated experts take delight in giving geology lessons on whatever objects intrigue their customers. Safe shipment assured to anywhere in the world. Hats in the air!

Silver? **Ugo Bellini** now has such tempting stocks that our President Joseph A. Raff, who has seen just about *everything*, couldn't resist an expensive "impulse" gift for his Judy on a recent visit here. **Peruzzi Bros.** (Ponte Vecchio, corner Borgo San Jacopo 2-4) is in the same class. Embroideries? **Mamma Galassi** (via Calimals 25R) is versatile and inexpensive; an especially good bet. As a second choice, the **Rifredi School of Embroidery** (via Carlo Bini 29), run by 2 nice gals, is a 10-minute ride from town; also a favorite with U.S. visitors. Galleries? **Masini** usually offers the best selection of paintings at reasonable tariffs; handsome salons on the Lungarno Corsini (entrance in the Riscasoli Palace on piazza Goldoni); excellent reputation. We like Arno (via della Vigna Nuova 73), too; ask for Miss Wanda Papini. Antiques? Via de' Fossi (cheaper) and via Maggio (more lire) are the best streets—but take care!

Since your chauffeur or guide will get a 10% rakeoff on your purchases in Florence if you don't claim it (this does *not* apply in Emilio Paoli, Ferragamo, Balatresi, Romei, Sonya, John F., Bellini, and 1 or 2 other top-drawer places, however), tell the shopkeeper firmly that "I've been sent by no one, I'm paying cash, and I expect the usual 10% discount!" And if you buy a hefty amount in any one store, always bargain!

In *Milan* the shops are closed on Monday mornings.

Franzi (via E. Teodoro Moneta 40) offers the finest medium-price leather.

Jesurum (via Monte Napoleone 14) has an enticing selection of dentelle and an exciting collection of shore fashions. Turn to "Venice" for more details.

Fabulous and famous **Roberta** (also see "Venice") operates a gorgeous branch at Pietro Verri 7. She has remodeled a quaint old stable and filled it with antique harnesses, hobbyhorses, perambulators, and other venerable treasures to set off her vast and unique merchandise—including her dee-lightful innovation—her SQUARE umbrella ($28 to $35)! Ask for her charming manageress Miss Sanda Bresner. Tops.

Galtrucco (via San Gregorio 29), on the central piazza near the Cathedral, is the combined Saks-Bergdorf-Macy for yard goods. Branch in Rome.

Baratta (via Monforte 2) dresses the lion's share of the most elegant men and women who patronize La Scala. This year he is easily the best in the North, and one of the top houses of the nation. Here's the only combined male-and-female custom-cut wearables house we've ever run across. Also branch in Rome.

La Rinascente, the big department store, is at via San Rafael 2 on Piazza Duomo.

Second-rate flea market? The **Fiera di Semigallia** (via Calatafini) every Sat. morning. Haggle your hardest!

Via Monte Napoleone is the local peak of chic. If you'll start on its lower end and stroll through the short pedestrian mall of via delle Spigna, and then cut back down via Manzoni, this U-shape trek will show you the choicest galaxy of merchandise in this center.

Naples has essentially limited pickings. While via Roma and via Chiaia are the most popular shopping stems, you'll find higher quality around piazza dei Martiri and along via Calabritto.

Try **Roberta** (via Calabritto 8, described at length in the "Venice" section) for top couture items displayed over 2 floors of elegant Neapolitan real estate; **Mario Valentino** (next door at #10) for fashionable shoes and bags; the **Ricciardi Boutique** (across the street at #15) which exclusively purveys the Micmac, Christian Aujard, and Aqualo lines; **Alinari** (a few doors down) for prints; **Spatarella** (at #1) for bargain purses; or **L'Angolo** (piazza dei Martiri 36) for attractive and unusual gift items. **M. Tramontano** (via Chiaia) has a big choice of brooches and buckles, plus more than 125-thousand different buttons. Cameos? Buy *all* your cameos at Apa (see following on the Naples–Pompeii highway) instead of in the city.

Antiques? The assortment at **Galleria d'Arte** (piazza dei Martiri 32) interested us the most; even an elaborately rococo sedan chair was at hand. All prices are fixed here. Aficionados should start at the National Museum and walk up via Constantinopoli or via D. Morelli and pick from the holes-in-the walls. No guarantees on reliability; occasional values; always bargain your head off with these smiling sharks.

The **Flea Markets** (corso Malta and corso Navara near the railway station) in the main are wretchedly junky.

Capri ? Most shops offer the same merchandise and the same high prices as Naples—with 7 laudable and conspicuous exceptions.

Sea Gull (via Roma 25) is just plain terrific. Here, as a starter, you will find the cream of the harvest from the top artists and craftsmen of Italy. Personable, knowledgeable owner Antonio Staiano and his delightful wife Helen— who is American—should be mighty proud of their taste, versatility, and decent tariffs. Galaxy of modern and traditional ceramics (fine copies of antique pieces); stunning Capodimonte chandeliers, ceramic animals, and figures by Neapolitan sculptor Nicco Venzo; alabaster; pewter; decorative plates and wall plaques; revered Ernestine chinaware, coffee and tea services; fabulous glass sculpture from Italy's leading designers; paintings by both internationally famous and local artists; exciting collection of fashion jewelry; more! Be *sure* to spot the sea-gull-decorated awnings. For armchair travelers on the West Coast, Sea Gull also has a nest in Carmel, California. Multilingual personnel; expert packing and shipping all over the world. Don't miss this one. It's a honey.

The other equally happy and special sparkler of which we're so fond is **La Campanina** (Discesa Quinisana 18, a minute down from the square). Warmly, expansively ebullient Founder-Owner Alberto Frederico brims with contagious *joie de vivre* for his sweet wife-partner Lina and their participating children, for his wide world of visitors whom he welcomes with the essence of openhearted Italian hospitality, and for his inspired original designs in chains, brooches, rings, earrings, bracelets, necklaces, charms, and other wantables—all priced impeccably fairly—which grace his small, elegant, trend-setting shop. Gold is his essential medium, often combined with coral and other flourishes; "The Bell" (its translated name), taken from an historic Caprese legend, is his creative cachet. His early years with the U.S. army instilled such a bond that annually he invites every American on the island to a lavish July 4 cocktail party. What a family! What treasures!

La Parisienne (on the square), featuring Livio di Simone's inspired appeal, is the acknowledged fashion arbiter for ladies. It is rumored that Mrs. Onassis and Mrs. William Paley are among its clients. Matching shirts, skirts, and pants at 50% of their Fifth Avenue tags are perhaps its best-known feature. Ask for Mme. Dria. Still expensive but very smart.

The other 4 stops we like are Oriane (via Camerelle, adjoining Hotel Quisisana), operated by an attractive English lass, Mrs. Anne Gargiullo, for handmade Capri silk and high-style boutique items; Canfora (opposite the Quisisana) for sandals; Yves Dupris (via Camerelle), with its men's shop across the street from its women's shop, for further boutique selections; and nearby Chantal, for chic clothes for Him.

For reasons we consider sufficient, the well-known Mariorita Shop in Anacapri is NOT recommended by this Guide.

Excursion to Pompeii ? The highway is loaded with souvenir shops and cameo vendors, most of which are not only second-rate but trashy. Only 2 places, as far as we know, offer top-class stocks and are reliable. While M. & G. Donadio is the largest and oldest, with a good reputation, the price tags here alarmed us—much too high, in our strictly personal opinion, to recommend it to our bargain-loving readers. For more than 25 years we've been convinced that the Giovanni Apa Co., at Torre del Greco, is head, shoulders, and carving awl above all competition. This venerable house, more than a century in business, is primarily a factory-wholesaler. This, plus the fact (as only one example) that the Apas personally go direct to sources in the 4 corners of the world to buy their own corals—take a look at the gorgeous shade called "Angel's Skin"!—accounts for their low tariffs. At sunlit benches, you may watch its 40 master carvers and 80 artisans fashion Madagascan, Mediterranean, or Caribbean conch shells into exquisite cameos and mount them in gold or silver settings. Silver-mounted brooches and pendants in exclusive (and heavenly) pink-and-white; large, prime cameo or intaglio (reverse-carved) cuff links; coral or cameo earrings. Lovely ladies' and men's semiprecious stones and rings (topazes, amethysts, and monster aquamarines). Beloved Patriarch Giovanni Apa is still the spry Grand Vizier; Giovanni Jr., Maurizio, Luciano, Ricardo, and Mario Jr., sons of the brother-founders, are brilliantly carrying this monument to new heights. Branches in Rome (piazza Navona 26-27), on the Tiburtina Road from Rome to Tivoli, and in Tivoli (main square). Highest recommendation.

Sorrento is the largest, greatest, and most celebrated center in the world for inlaid furniture and similer artistic accessories. The range of its products is astonishing. Literally they run into the hundreds. Utilizing skills which flowered here ages ago, every single piece from the most modest fruit basket to the most elaborate baroque highboy is 100% inset by hand. To see these displays is a unique shopping experience.

The cornucopia of exquisite, exclusive masterworks in the enormous 3-level showrooms of century-old, 400-employee **A. Gargiulo Jannuzzi** (center of main square) stops us in our tracks. After watching its maestros ply their complex crafts while articulate Libby Gorga explains their cunning techniques, visitors are better prepared to "oh" and to "ah" as they roam through the monumental collection of everything from dining sets to chests of drawers to ladies' desks to tea carts to 3-table nests to cigarette, music, jewelry, and cigar boxes to a plethora more; 86 different items run from $8 to $50. Beautiful, moderately priced embroidered table linen, blouses, handkerchieves, and the like, hand made in convents or by orphaned children, are its strong alternate magnet. Free brochures; worldwide shipment; guaranteed delivery; continuously open 365 days (summers until 10 P.M.). We salute gallantly intrepid Matriarch Gargiulo and sons Peppino and Apollo. Wonderful!

Smaller **Notturno**, nearby, opened its factory in '60 and its retail outlet in '75. Its $285 gaming table caught our eye as an especially interesting bargain. Director Pepe Ercolano and Assistant Michele Notumo have much to offer. More limited but also excellent. **Melanie** (Toni DiMaio) and **Cuomo** (father Frederico and son Carlo Cuomo) are dependable but even less versatile establishments which in general seemed to be costlier.

Please don't miss this distinct and fascinating tour de force if you're in Sorrento.

Venice is teeming with guides, concierges, gondoliers, and other fast operators hungry for commissions on your purchases. The usual bite is 20% to 25% on glass, and 15% on lace. As in Florence, don't tell even the concierge of your hotel where you're going, because he might climb on the phone when you're out the front door, tell the merchant that he sent you, and claim his rakeoff on *your* money. Thus, inform the shopkeeper immediately that nobody directed you to his establishment (except a guidebook or other disinterested source), that you're paying cash, and that you want the above scale of discounts for yourself. In this rotted, graft-infested community, the poor store owner is forced to pay somebody in order to exist—so why shouldn't it be you? And PLEASE DON'T BUY EVEN A 10¢ GLASS ARTICLE ON THE ISLAND OF MURANO. Our files groan under the blizzard of complaints from travelers who have been swindled here. Perhaps there are exceptions, but we trust ONLY Pauly or Salviati (see below).

To counter the fringe operators, the Chamber of Commerce and the legitimate old-line merchants set up the Venetian Crafts Association to guarantee both product quality and business ethics among its members; be sure to look for the Association's 4-leaf-clover symbol displayed in all these companies.

Pauly & Co. (headquarters at ponte dei Consorzi, plus 3 branches in center) and **Salviati & Co.** (San Gregorio 195) are world-famous for their fabulous glass; both are worth a buying trek from Timbuktu. The venerable Pauly Co. supplied most of Europe's Royal Houses before the war. Their products have won 25 Gold Medals, 16 Notable Award Prizes, 33 Award Diplomas, the French Legion of Honor, the Crown of Leopold, and the

Crown of Italy. In their archives, you'll find 800-thousand one-of-a-kind sketches of antique, classical, and modern patterns. A team of celebrated Glass Masters produces exclusively for them. Even though Pauly has 3 retail branches on Piazza San Marco, don't miss a tour of its Ponte dei Consorzi headquarters. Demonstration furnace and budget shop on ground floor; upstairs, you may wander at will through perhaps 20 glorious rooms full of treasures for the table, the home, and the eye.

Salviati, dean of the field, reached its centennial in '59—and in '63 it captured the celestial "Golden Compasses" award, the biannual "Oscar" presented for Italy's most noble designs in manufactured products. Their pioneering has had a profound influence on the evolution of glass all over the world—thanks to a team of designers and glassmakers to whom we owe the most select production of Murano riches. Salviati mosaic panels or murals have been commissioned by such widely scattered places as the Vatican, the Royal Palace of Siam, Windsor Castle, and California's Stanford University. This company also maintains 2 retail outlets on Piazza San Marco, but it would be a pity to miss their magnificent display mansion (free gondola across the Grand Canal from the Gritti Palace landing). In addition to 2 of the most exciting museum collections of ancient and modern glass in existence, plus a glass and metal sculpture exhibition by American Claire Falkenstein, you'll find a demonstration furnace, and you'll also revel in chamber after chamber of tableware, vases, candelabra, lamps, and other objects that shimmer as did the Pleasure Dome of Xanadu.

Both firms guarantee safe arrival to your home of everything they ship— and you can absolutely trust them on this. *Have limitless patience about shipment delays* (months are par for the course, due to Italian export red tape and the monumental backlog snarls at U.S. docks)—and be sure to find out approximate delivery costs to your area, because port brokers' fees are sometimes wicked through no fault of these good artisans. Please remember that *nobody* is permitted to pay U.S. Customs duties and handling before our American officials can evaluate these foreign purchases upon entry, so it is impossible for these companies to estimate the levy accurately. Whether you spend nothing, $1 for a string of beads, or $4000 for a set of spiderweb-and-thistledown champagne glasses, a visit to both these institutions is a must for any American shophound.

Ladies' handbags and stunning boutique items? Well! Wait until you enjoy **Roberta**'s fabulous creations! "Roberta" is the brilliant, charming Mrs. Giuliana Camerino, who started by making her unique handbags as a hobby during World War II, followed by opening an elf-size, sidestreet business, and meteorically became one of the top couture arbiters on the Continent. Her invention of the "coordinates" concept—designing, producing, and selling perfectly blended suits, jackets, raincoats, shoes, scarves, valises, umbrellas, and other articles externally to clothe The Complete Woman—has been pirated, less successfully, all over the world; each individual ensemble carries the basic leitmotif of one special handbag (her original love); the spirit of Venice is evident in even the smallest details. Her headquarters at Santa Maria Formosa 6123, down a by-lane, is surely worth a visit—but you will want to concentrate most of your time in her gloriously elegant, 4-story showplace at

Ascensione 1256, near piazza San Marco, which bears the accent of the best of rue du Faubourg-St.-Honoré. Its strikingly colorful décor, in turquoise-green and pink-green, is highlighted by fifteenth-century antiques on the ground floor and massive, ornate Sicilian box settees (resembling bedboards of the Medicis) on the next 2 floors; a bar reserved for her clients occupies the top. Chic hand-loomed, cut-velvet bags are her perennial bestsellers; her woven-leather exclusives are this year's mode. Her small, light, handsome "24 ore" suitcases, in antique Venetian velvets from $80 to $160, are eyebrow-raisers for air travelers. Many items for teen-agers; street-level boutique with lower prices. Previously mentioned year-round branches in Rome, Florence, Milan, Naples, Modena, and Bari; seasonal shops in Lido and Cortina d'Ampezzo. Don't miss this gem!

Exquisite Venetian jewelry? In quality, in fame, in the distinction of its worldwide clientele, the unchallenged King of this City of Palaces is **G. Nardi** (piazza San Marco 69-71, in the Arcades). Since 1920 it has specialized in designing and creating treasures in gold and precious stones, all handmade and all signed as originals with the Nardi name. Today 2 Nardi pieces at first glance are recognized and envied virtually everywhere: its fabulous "Othello, The Moor of Venice" pin ($200 to $4000), and its glorious triple-tiered ring which forms a bouquet of tulips. Its current fashion innovations are in enamel or "Angel Skin" (rose coral) surrounded by diamonds. Full line of gems, including mouth-watering antiques; new shop adjacent at No. 68 with exceptionally fine rarities; no purchase tax ever; open all year. Ask personally for the gentle Mr. Nardi Sr. or his equally engaging son Sergio; otherwise, try Messrs. Menegon or Zambon. Wonderful!

Lace and radiantly enticing beachwear? After much too long an absence, we've just returned to **Jesurum** (ponte Canonica 4310) to find a glorious revolution. This renowned centurion still purveys the best available traditional Venetian lace (many museum pieces). But under young, dynamic Mario Levi-Morenos, the lovely old palace now glows with the incandescent color splashes of a vast, vivid, and strikingly different assemblage of everything for the beach—trunks, bikinis, robes, shirts, skirts, slacks, dresses, accessories, and lots more for women or men. This innovator, or charming 31-year-staffer Mrs. Eugenia Graziussi, would welcome you smilingly. Branch in Milan. T-e-r-r-i-f-i-c!

Vogini (4 shops on 4 corners of San Marco-Ascensione) runs the gamut in fine leather goods.

Sicily, in general, is second-rate scavenging for visiting shophounds. **Taormina**'s best target is **Daneu** (corso Umberto 126) for island handicrafts; branch in Palermo; versatile and popular. **Giovanni Panorello** (corso Umberto) is worth skimming for antiques. **Giovanni Vadalà** (Corso Umberto 193-195) is an attractive boutique featuring Hermès, Burberry's, Yves St. Laurent, and others. Otherwise, the main street now seems one unbroken string of brassy tourist junk hovels. In **Palermo**, try **Salvatore Barraja** (same street) for variety items; **La Botteguccia** (piazza Ungheria) for boutique specialities, and **Eugenia Patella** (corso Vittorio Emanuele 474) for fine antiques. The **Daneu** branch (corso Vittorio Emanuele 452) accents antiques rather than the handicrafts of its Taormina headquarters. Via Maqueda, via

Rome, and via Ruggero Settimo are the buyer's best stamping grounds. *Catania*'s leading shopping streets are via Etnea and corso Sicilia. All are pretty disappointing.

Space limitations prevent further general listing in smaller centers, but here is one superspecial bet where we considered the values extraordinary: In **Genoa**, **A Alioto** (via Ippolito D'Aste 7-5) is the king of handmade fashion jewelry of many varieties. Nothing we've ever seen in Florence or the rest of Italy can begin to touch his craftsmanship in this line. Everything originally designed; stunning bracelets, necklaces, brooches, earrings, chains, charms, and more in both classic and modern, each bearing his own unique flair. Private 3rd-floor studio-apartment (#5) with door marked "A. Testa"; difficult to find, but not to be missed under any circumstances. Prices? The average creations run from an unbelievable $10 to $45. MARVELOUS! Also here in the Quarto section may be found an exotic curiosity: **Victor Salvi**, one of the 3 harp factories south of the Pearly Gates. In **Como**, it's silk, silk, silk, and more silk by the sail-length. Two landmarks vie for the leadership: Proprietor Ercole Moretti of **Seterie Moretti** (via Garibaldi 69) is assisted by 10 designers in the creation of his specialty of strikingly original prints; each pattern is limited to a maximum output of 10 pieces. Proprietoress Giovanna Rainoldi and her nephew Antonio of **Rainoldi** offer wearables at their piazza Cavor headquarters, plus bolt silks, sheets, and linens at their other two branches. The latter firm is closed Monday. Since the tariffs in both are virtually at wholesale levels, identical purchses cost appreciably more in almost any other retailer shop in Italy. Recommended. In *Ischia*, the **Dominique** chain (6 stores) carries outstanding boutique items at stiff quotations; **Filippo** (on the main street) is also expensive and fine for men's and women's slacks. The flock of others on corso Vittoria Colomare "import" their wares from Florence, Sorrento, and other mainland hubs. Sadly, this island has no significant specialty.

Other cities? Ask the local CIT Director *in person,* if he's available—not your hotel concierge, and most particularly not your sightseeing guide.

§TIP: Shopping hours differ. Wherever the *siesta* custom is observed (Rome, Naples, the South), most stores are open from 9 A.M. to 1 P.M. and 4 P.M. to 7 or 8 P.M. In the central and northern regions, however, there are so many local variations that it's wise to check first with the concierge of your hotel. (Everything is open at 3 P.M. in Milan, Turin, Genoa, and Bologna.)

Generally speaking, Venice and Milan are the most expensive cities in Italy. Genoa and Turin are ordinarily the next most costly. Rome and Naples usually run higher than Florence. Bologna is often surprisingly low.

All-night drugstores throughout Italy carry either an illuminated red cross or the word *Farmacia* in red. Many U.S. pharmaceuticals (manufactured in Italy) are available.

If you buy an Italian silver case in scrollwork for your Zippo lighter anywhere but in the top-liners, remember that (1) no matter how pretty it looks, the operating design is generally terrible; (2) it's liable to break sooner than you might think; and (3) you won't be able to ask the Zippo Co. to fix it. Why should they underwrite other workmen's products, when all their own so proudly carry that unique Zippo No-Charge Lifetime Guarantee?

§WARNING: We suppose that *somewhere* in the world there might be a mail carrier that is as total a disaster as the Italian Postal Service; based on our own dismal experience, however, we doubt it. Hard-pressed Italians and savvy visitors use commercial couriers such as Rome's Missori and Tavani (Viale M. Gelsomini 14) to deliver anything of the slightest importance. If you have absolutely no recourse but to use the mails, please *be sure* to register your letter or package before affixing the stamps. Keep a duplicate, if possible. Better still, save the item and drop it into the first mailbox you spot that is not on Italian soil.

Dedicated shophounds? Space is too tight here for further listings—so consult this year's annual edition of the vastly updated, purse-size edition of *Fielding's Shopping Guide to Europe* for many more stores, many more details, and much more a lore.

THINGS NOT TO BUY   Expensive "jewelry" (much of it is fake) except in reputable stores such as Bulgari (see "Things to Buy") or Sheffield on via Veneto in Rome; tortoiseshell or crocodile products (both endangered species, overstocked on Italian shelves); "antiques" or "old paintings" in small establishments (forgery is a thriving trade, and you must be a specialist); phony "Made in Switzerland" watches; mechanical gadgets such as fountain pens (they often break); *any* glass items on the island of Murano; women's shoes (except Lily of Florence, Romei, Samo's, Ferragamo's, or American lasts or casuals); cotton goods, except hand-blocked prints (danger of shrinkage); perfumes (too high); ready-made articles in general.

LOCAL RACKETS   In any small shop selling nonproprietary goods, *never take the first price;* offer them about half what they ask, and bargain from there. The larger and more chichi establishments are fairly well regulated; the "quaint" places are the ones geared to take advantage of tourists.

Restaurant checks are sometimes padded; smaller hotels will make "mistakes" on telephone calls you never made. A blight growing by skips and leaps is the rigged tabulating machines at the cashiers' desks of hotels, including various large and so-called respectable houses. Your statement printed in IBM-type figures will be meticulously itemized, often correctly—but the total will be hundreds or thousands of lire higher than the sum reached through pencil and paper. Add up every single item on every tab, wherever you go in Italy—and check your change everywhere, especially at Fiumicino Airport.

Pickpockets are not uncommon. Whenever you walk through an Italian train to the dining car, keep one arm over your wallet; these light-fingered gentry are so prevalent in the crowded corridors of Second-class coaches that the police have set up patrols on international expresses. Watch yourself in trams, buses, elevators, ticket lines, and all other crammed places such as at tourist attractions or at sightseeing targets (the Colosseum area is especially notorious; also please be extra careful anywhere in the port city of Brindisi).

And, ladies, now more than ever, beware of the "friendly" little caress. Fleet-footed swains often work in pairs—one for the pinch on the bottom and the other, simultaneously, to pinch the purse. The flattered ego is their fattest asset, so be girdled against all surprise touchings, no matter how gentle.

Along the same line, Italian talent for doing almost anything aboard a motorscooter has reached a new peak in pocketbook-snatching. The 2-wheeled bandit zips up, hooks the handbag in a flash from the lady's arm, and scampers away through traffic. Your 2 best countermoves: (1) follow age-old etiquette by letting the gentleman walk on the curbside or (2) go to your nearest elephant store and get a giant rubber band for a shoulder strap.

Beware of counterfeit lire. If there's a distinguishable watermark (star in a circle) on the 500-lire or 1000-lire note, or if it is noticeable on the left end of the 500 or 10,000 note, you are generally safe; to date, they haven't succeeded in forging this imprint. Traveler's checks have again become of keen interest to underground printers; recently a multimillion-dollar flummox was uncovered, with American Express as the victim.

As author Cele Wohl once put it, whenever you're approached by street Arabs to change your dollars into lire, "Say NO in loud English. It's the same in Italian." Exchange swindles sting lots of innocent travelers.

Another clever dodge is worked on motorists. Thieves ice-pick one tire of a parked car loaded with luggage. When the owner removes his possessions to lighten it and get at the spare, he is likely to line them up on the curb or shoulder. Quick as a flash, he has one less piece of baggage—and it's always the little one—the jewel box, briefcase, or handbag with traveler's checks in it.

Many filling station attendants will race to check your engine oil and tell you your sump needs 1 or 2 liters. Don't buy it! Wait a couple of minutes with the motor off for the oil to settle; then make sure he shoves the dipstick down the full distance. Examine the mark yourself, and watch the boy carefully so he won't wipe a false line onto the rod. Also hawk-eye that counter on gasoline tanks, so you won't be paying for more than you get.

The "gold watch" con game is back, too. If anybody asks you to "hold" 2 or 3 watches as "security" for a few moments, run for the nearest cop.

A well-traveled journalist told us of one they tried to pull on him in Naples: The menu switch. He ordered from one card, checked his bill, protested it—and was promptly shown a *second* menu, with a different scale of prices! When in this area and uncertain about any restaurant, require that they leave the original on your table.

We've also heard of a twentieth-century deception from our dear friend Captain Robert Mitchell, U.S.N., who with his lovely wife, Liz, discovered the ultimate ploy in this Italian bay-city marketplace. Since Neapolitan housewives often determine the freshness of the fish on the open stands by the luster of the eyes, some very shrewd mongers are now plopping drops of Murine into the peepers of yesterday's (or prior) catches. This world-famous cardiologist noted in his diagnosis: "They sure do sparkle, too!" Thank you, Doctor! (P.S.: Do you know the best way to avoid the nonstop racketeering in Naples? Get the next train to Rome—fast!)

Of all the groups of surly, devious, tip-hungry ruffians we've met in our travels, the Venetian gondoliers take our personal bobby prize. Make your deal in advance, watch them like eagles, and *don't be bluffed into giving in on any excess demands.* The photo racket (see "Restaurants") seems especially virulent in this town, so never say "yes" to a shutterbug unless you want an outrageously costly snapshot of you or yours.

Look out for La Scalpers at La Scala in Milan. They hang around the opera house on evenings or matinee days when performances are sold out—usually demanding double or triple the box-office prices. The correct prices for all categories of seating are listed on bill-boards in front of the theater. These jackals fast-talk that the posters omit fictitious taxes, supplements, and other charges. (Through a convenient mirror, we watched one dim-witted, know-it-all American sheared of 4000 lire, when the original ticket cost only 1800 lire.) Once inside, be wary of the ushers (they wear great necklaces of gold medallions). A favorite stunt is to sell foreigners a program just before curtain time —and then scoot to another balcony with the change from their big bills. A colleague from one of the other tiers then replaces him, after effecting the same bilk.

At the gates of Pompeii, a hawker sidled up to us and offered sets of photographs of the pornographic murals which are rarely shown to the public. If you're curious (and who isn't?), simply laugh at his first price of 10,000 lire; we got him down to 3000 and *still* paid too much! He'll also offer you small metal copies of Pompeiian phallic symbols. The purpose of the things? "To wear in the lapel, sir!"—and he was serious!

Finally, just across the frontier near Lake Como, the Swiss hamlet of Chiasso nods sleepily in the Alpine sun. It has a mere 7000 inhabitants. So why does it need 15 major banking houses? To handle the $900,000,000 that illegally flows out of Italy each year, of course. The smuggling of lire to greener economic pastures is a big business here and in several similar borderline confederacies. Italians are looking for more profits and greater security than they can find at home. Thus, the savvy Swiss are cashing in and so is Wall Street—at least that's how the rumor goes.

By and large, the Italians are much more honest than many Americans think. The great mass of her citizenry are simple, open, friendly, with a soft spot for the U.S. and its travelers. Every country has crooks; Italy suffers far more than most (perhaps the highest incidence of guile in the Western World) —but the majority remain upright, responsible, God-fearing people.

Liechtenstein

Liechtenstein, like Andorra, Luxembourg, Monaco, and San Marino, is a storybook land which frequently seems to get lost by European cartographers. But more Americans are discovering it every year, because this matchbox Principality is one of the last gentle, happy, unspoiled paradises on the face of a tired and cynical continent. Here are some rapid-fire jottings:

Vaguely the shape of Idaho (and about the size of an Idaho potato), this midget Elysium sprawls between the east bank of the Upper Rhine (near Lake Constance) and a towering range of 7000-foot peaks; it is the historic buffer state which separates Switzerland from Austria. St. Gall is only a hop, skip, and jump from the capital; Zürich is an easy morning's drive, and Innsbruck (Austria) isn't much farther by crack train. The main railway line to Vienna, one of central Europe's greatest arteries, cuts across the heartland and then passes on Austrian soil within rods of the bordering river (international transfer point: Buchs/SG, Switzerland).

Founded in 1719, it has proudly cherished its independence since then; the benevolent and popular Reigning Prince is Franz Joseph II. The national language is German, and the monetary unit is the Swiss franc. Here is 1 of the 4 European lands in which Catholicism is the state religion (others: Spain, Monaco, and Luxembourg). In a national referendum the men again recently rejected voting rights for women. Obviously, this miniland is seething with political unrest. Why else would it have put a new government in office—the 2nd change of ruling party in more than 4 decades? There is no standing military might; 40 policemen do the job of the army, navy, air force, and marines. There are no labor unions, no poverty, and practically no taxes (to discourage fugitives and financial-angle guys, however, citizenship papers are almost impossible to obtain). Crime is virtually unknown.

Industries include postage stamps, textiles, tools, sausage casings, false teeth (a big chomp in the economy!), and optical instruments; agriculture predominates. The postage stamps boast some of the finest engraving in the world; oddly enough, they have the same value to philatelists whether they're canceled or uncanceled.

Vaduz (pronounced Vah-dootz), the capital, crams 4020 (count 'em!) living human beings (national census: 23,000, composed of 14,000 citizens and 9000 foreigners) into one metropolis, if you can imagine such staggering overpopulation. **Schaan**, the national (not international) railway station, and handsome little **Triesenberg** are the only other villages of importance. In winter almost everyone and his ski partner evacuate the centers for the higher slopes. If you look carefully, you may recognize the royal sitzmark of Prince Philip, Prince Charles, or Princess Anne, who make this a scheduled winter wonderland.

HOTELS Let's consider the ones in Vaduz first. More about the Tourotel Gaflei and the Motel Waldeck later. The elfin **Sylva** (said to be cozy) at *Schaan* and the **Engel** (near the Austrian border at *Nendeln* and perhaps noisy) opened very recently.

The **Sonnenhof**, on the mountainside, easily captures top honors not only as the finest hostelry in the land, but also as one of the leading choices in the entire region—in or out of Liechtenstein. This is the happy domain of Emil Real, brother of the restaurateur Felix Real (see below) and his beautiful wife, Jutta (pronounced "Utah"). There is a lovely view from its front-facing rooms; the tranquillity is heavenly. This entire plant has been refreshed; a new glass-wrapped swimming pool and wood-wrapped sauna are fully operational; now, you'll find a dozen new suites, each with color TV. Wall-to-wall carpeting, excellent furniture, and many baths have been added; most accommodations offer small refrigerators filled with goodies for between-meal nibbling and stocked with champagne, beer, whisky, and local products at very reasonable prices. Since these warmhearted hoteliers try so hard to create a cozy, friendly "family" atmosphere, all guests are encouraged to enjoy their cups together in the homey main-floor lounge. Its extra-savory cookery is reserved for residents, which keeps the flavor up and the madding crowds down (another Real-istic guarantee of solace). Open all year; tons of bucolic charm; perfect for a rest, in every particular. *Wunderbar!*

The tiny perked-up **Real**, the centrally located brother of the Sonnenhof, is the 10-unit (5 singles, 5 doubles) extension of Liechtenstein's most celebrated restaurant. The staff's warmth of hospitality is truly overwhelming; okay for overnight, but perhaps a bit too noisy for a longer stay. The **Engel** (this one in town) is adequate rather than fancy. Busy-busy location; flower-lined balconies along front; ground-level beer-cellar-type den for dancing, plus Restaurant Français; 14 rooms and 10 baths or showers; fruit in bedchambers for evening snack; sparkling, clean, and appealing. Down a notch or two, the **Vaduzer Hof** comes up with 100 rooms, not enough private baths, many balconies, a warm little darkwood *Weinstube* and a blondwood *Bierstube*—plus music and dancing in summer. We saw evidence of slack maintenance. The petite **Adler**, also on a bustling street site, is well managed and gives good value; be warned, however, that little or no English is spoken. The **Old Castle Inn** evokes a British mood, nevertheless, with its pub and 10 bedchambers.

The 24-room economy-minded **Elite** is in midtown. Clean; breakfast only; nothing special. The ancient **Löwen** had only its captivating dining terrace overlooking the vineyards to recommend it when we peeked in, but since our last visit this attractively situated hostelry has been closed for thorough renovations. We'll be anxious to see it in its new raiments. **Motel In Liechtenstein**, 3 miles up from the center on an impressive mesa, commands a stunning panorama of the Rhine Valley. Improved management; wheelborne Americans enjoy its auto-matic convenience. Viewful dining room and terrace; 33 plastic-y units, all with bath or shower; a cozy stop for ramblers. **Hotel Meierhof**, closer to town on the same route, has a restaurant downstairs and 14 bedrooms above, including one deluxe double. Passable for serious budgeteers or summer-izing families who might enjoy the adult and kiddie pools in the back garden. High in the country, the inn in Masecha is ideal for students or hard-driven economy-seekers. The rebuilt **Schlössle** has stoked up a new sauna; it has the personality of an apartment dwelling rather than that of a full-scale hotel. The **Gasthof Samina** in *Triesenberg*, once an enchanting little spot, since its sale has become abysmal, in our opinion, in comfort and taste.

The mile-high, supermodern, 40-room **Tourotel Gaflei** reportedly consumed $1,500,000 before inauguration. Now it has been further enhanced by a swimming pool, a sauna, and minigolf links. Sweeping panorama of the hills sloping toward Triesenberg and the valley of the capital, ½-hour drive over a curvaceous lane; handsome, spacious public rooms, but small-gauge bedchambers; all units with private bath or shower, telephone, and radio; bowling alleys; basement bar; yards of terrace space for sun-soaking and oooo-ing and aaaaahhh-ing at the majestic mountains.

Up at *Malbun*, the restfully rustic **Gorfion** is heavenscent in summer and a snow haven in winter. Small, but what a little gem for sporting or lazing types! The **Alpen** would be our next choice; it is more modest, but it also has an enclosed swimming pool as well as personality and comfort. **Galina** is under new management, so we can't say much until we have another look. The sold-and-resold **Motel Waldeck** at *Gamprin*, near the Austrian border, debuted with 30 streamlined, narrow-dimension bedchambers, all with shower. Captivating setting as viewful as all outdoors. Practically since its outset, this one has been in a serious state of flux. Let's wait some more. A youth hostel is abuilding between Vaduz and Schaan, but more we cannot tell you. In most hotels and restaurants, you will find very few men on the staffs. The preponderance of female personnel hits the outsider smack in the eye— particularly if he's male. When we pointed this out to a friendly Vaduzer, he admitted with surprise that it was true and that most natives were not aware of it. "Rather nice, though, isn't it?" he commented. As our Irish friends would say, "That it *is,* indeed."

RESTAURANTS The **Hotel-Restaurant Real**, on the main square in *Vaduz* opposite the Telephone Office, is definitely first, foremost, and finest in the land. Our dear friend, the late Paul Gallico, world-famous author, traveler, and gourmet, lived in Liechtenstein for many years and dined here regularly; on a day-in, day-out basis, he called it one of the most consistently sound kitchens he knew in Europe. You'll almost always find the Reigning Family dining here on the cook's night off at the castle. (The Real brothers were decorated for their fantastic catering of the Royal Wedding not long ago —and perhaps you remember the Real plaudits for their participation in the Shah of Iran's national anniversary jubilee at Persepolis.) Small, sweet, not fancy; one of its working family will greet you with a smile and *"Grüss Gott!"* Outstanding are the terrine of smoked trout, the mousseline of turbot, lamb in herbs, Veal Steak Royal, and the Soufflé Glace Real. Patron Felix Real brings the best of his Maxim's of Paris experience to the skillets. Our recent lunch of smoked mountain trout and saddle of venison was a triumph of culinary artistry and joy. Highest recommendation.

Torkel, site of a 3-century-old wine press, is pleasant enough for the rustic-toned flavor of Old Liechtenstein.

The viewful **Hotel-Restaurant Engel** features a cellar with local musicians; the "Liechtenstein Polka," of which the residents are so proud, is rendered about every 6½ minutes. Here is the trysting place where lonely male may find lonely female when the moon comes over them thar mountains. **Schlössle** is the only other spot which fringed on after-dark gaiety.

Chez Fritz, less than 15 minutes by car from Vaduz, is in the Hotel Bahnhof at *Buchs* (Switzerland). This one used to be a treat, but our latest dinner was a sad disappointment. Our fish course was utterly limp and tasteless; our meat was on the verge of going sour. It's a 3-minute walk from the main station in case you're planning a rail stopover at this junction. Local friends tell us it has become like the little girl who had a little curl right in the middle of her forehead: very, very good or horrid. Another "foreign" alternate might be **Drei Könige** at *Sevelen*, on the Swiss side, too. Nothing fancy, but substantial.

The **Hotel Lattmann** or the rejuvenated **Grand Hotel Quellenhoff** in *Bad Ragaz*, 30 minutes by car across the Swiss border, are happy targets for a dinner excursion; take your pick. There is a beautiful golf course here, too. Both hostelries offer good cuisine and attention; both are expensive; the latter is closed in winter.

§TIP: Just after sunset, cast your eyes up to watch Franz Joseph's mountain-top castle. The kitchen of the fabulous Restaurant Real is 2000 feet directly down the cliff from this Alpine aerie. When the light is right, you can see the Prince reeling down a fishing line with a silver tray balanced at its end, for his evening meal. (We *told* you it's a fairy-tale land!)

THINGS TO BUY AND THINGS TO SEE   Go to any of the 3 outlets of the wonderful little **Tourist Office Quick** before spending one nickel or investigating one *Schloss* on a lone-wolf basis—because you're almost sure to find what you want at this fountainhead for foreign visitors. The 2 main shops are within shouting distance of each other in Vaduz (newest and smartest entry is between the Vaduzer Hof and the Hotel Engel), and the branch is located on the Liechtenstein-Austrian border opposite Feldkirch. All 3 are handy for changing currency, and all are open routine hours, lunch hours, weekends, *and* holidays. The proprietor, Baron Edward von Falz-Fein, is supercharged with enthusiasm for his work and hospitality for his guests; this lively nobleman, who masterminds the Principality's team at the Olympics, has fingers in every bowl of *Schlag* in the land. You'll find postage stamps, cuckoo clocks, silver, all sorts of attractive and cornball local memorabilia, Swiss watches, and cameras and photo accessories at German prices. Or if sightseeing is your interest, the Baron will organize a visit to the Stamp or Art Museums (be sure to view the Rubens paintings at the **Engländerbau**) and other high points, a drive up to Masecha, and later a mountain excursion to the lofty winter-sports resort of Malbun (5000 feet), with 7 hotels and 5 ski tows and a chair lift which zip up to 7500 feet for a fascinating survey of Austrian real estate to pop your eyes. As a warm-day alternative, he'll recommend a plunge in the ultramodern swimming pool between Vaduz and Schaan. Whatever you need during your stay, he either has it, will find it, or will fix it; Americans on tour often suggest that he change his name to "Baron Liechtenstein."

COST OF LIVING   Considerably less than in Switzerland, but not as low as in Austria. Full pension in a good hotel runs from about $17 to $32 per person per day; good restaurant meals can be had for $8.

As a final word, we're lastingly grateful to Paul Gallico for his friendly guidance and assistance on many past visits to this mountain paradise.

Luxembourg

Luxembourg is a Grand Duchy, a never-never land of castles, turrets, swords, gold braid—a twentieth-century Camelot with toy trimmings. Anno Domini 1963 marked its 1000th anniversary. There's a romantic sort of aimlessness about it, a feeling that nobody works (far from the truth!), that a glittering duke will dash around the next corner on a white charger, velvet cloak flying behind. If a citizen gets mad at his vested officials, he has only to dial 478-1 to hear a voice reply, "Good morning! The Government!" It's a happy, serene, fat little community of 337-thousand people; Chicago is said to boast more Luxembourgers than the homeland. It's a prosperous tyke, too; unemployment virtually doesn't exist and it is so fond of finance that there is one bank for every 1100 citizens in the Duchy. In the Middle Ages knights and barons controlled the destiny of the nation. Their homes were tremendous strongholds—fortresses the ruins of which dot the countryside at Vianden, Beaufort, Bourscheid, and other locales. They were responsible for dubbing the domain "The Land of Haunted Castles." The country takes its name from the tiny palace of Sigefroi, Count of Ardennes, who 10 centuries ago erected his "Lucilinburhuc" ("Little Castle") where the capital stands today. The mantle of State is worn today by Prince Jean, eldest son of the now retired Grand Duchess Charlotte. After settling the Kammerwald border dispute with Germany, and giving back 1200 acres, Luxembourg again boasts the easily remembered acreage total of 999 square miles. One-third of its inhabitants raise crops or cattle; everybody seems to get rich on the steel mills (7th largest in the world). The army (reduced in size from 2000 conscripts to 600 professionals) is receiving higher pay than ever before. Illiteracy is unknown. The country is 99% Roman Catholic, but there is such freedom of worship that all faiths joined with the Government to help a new rabbi set up his synagogue. There are 130 castles but no full-time university exists. Radio Luxembourg, which broadcasts in 5 languages to 10 countries, claims more than 50-million daily listeners, including 78% of the teen-agers in Great Britain. The nation's newest showpiece is the Luxembourg Theater at Limpertsberg, where opera, drama, and ballet reach their peaks. Although the official language is French (parliamentary directives, Government publications, etc.), the *operative* tongue is a jawbreaking dialect called Letzeburgesch. German is also common, but English, despite its recent acceleration, still lags far behind. Womens' Liberationists will be gratified to know that the Burgomaster of its key city is Colette Flesch, a clever gal who received her master's degree at Wellesley. Spend a few days in the capital, untouched by 12 wars, and you'll find yourself living the pages of an Anthony Hope novel.

One of the most striking vistas in the country is the after-dark illumination of the Petrusse Valley bed, which winds its way crookedly through the heart of the once-impregnable, 1000-year-old Luxembourg City, a bastion which covetous generals of yore labeled the "Gibraltar of the North." Clervaux, previously mentioned Vianden with its enormous Hall of the Knights, and several other historic castles in the hinterland are now beautified by the same technique. On many evenings until 11 P.M. in summer (the schedule varies) cleverly placed spotlights and floodlights give the medieval bridges, massive ramparts, towering spires, and greenery the ethereal glow of a Victorian fairy-tale illustration. Here, in this capsule, is one of the loveliest creations of nature and man.

The U.S. Legation became a full-fledged Embassy in '55. Affairs of State are conducted in an ancient, handsome building with a spacious terrace, overlooking the best part of the valley.

CURRENCY   *Within* the Grand Duchy, the Luxembourgian franc and the Belgian franc are equal and the Luxembourgian franc is interchangeable with the currencies of U.S., Great Britain, France, West Germany, and Italy. *When you leave, however, make sure that you've converted all your Luxembourgian notes to Belgian ones, because local bills are not generally accepted by other lands.*

TRAVEL INFORMATION   The U.S. wayfarer in search of further information will be welcomed by the friendly and helpful Anne Bastian of the **Luxembourg Tourist Information Office** at 200 East 42nd St., N.Y. 10017. The Embassy in Washington now routes all travel inquiries to her. In Luxembourg City there are 2 information offices; your hotel will direct you to either.

CUSTOMS AND IMMIGRATION   A glance at your passport, and you're smilingly waved through. If you want it stamped, as a souvenir, you'll have to ask for it!

HOTELS   In *Luxembourg City*, the **Cravat** has an overall view of the valley and all-over amenities. The Pétrusse corner boasts 20 spacious, carpeted, twin-bed nests plus 2 suites perched high over the river gorge. Cozy ground-floor café, still the social umbilicus of the city; rôtisserie added to the restaurant; lunch and dinner menu includes delicious smörgåsbord-type buffet at bargain tabs; popular bar at which the good Eddie reigns with his warming smile. This family house is managed by the 3rd-generation Fernand Cravat. Obviously not a Palace or a Ritz, but very pleasant indeed.

The **Kons** (place de la Gare), is in flux at the moment. A German bank recently purchased it and put in its own management, absorbing a lot of space in the public rooms for private lease and closing the bar in the process. Large, colorful restaurant with winter garden; many fine oils, prints, tableaux, and friezes in corridors and bedrooms; excellent appointments in French periods; gay, fresh, and uplifting. Inside accommodations surrounding a quiet patio courtyard with murmuring fountain; well-groomed and uniformed staff. This station hotel has successfully taken advantage of every legitimate engineering and design trick in the book to create an island of calm and midtown tranquillity.

Holiday Inns has entered its bid for bed-needy, bone-weary international barnstormers opposite the Common Market Center in outlying *Kirchberg*, perhaps 15 minutes from the train station. There's a restaurant, a swimming pool, 250 bedchambers, and ample parking for motorists. Pipes and phones in all single, double, and triple nests; tot-cots provided for a small extra charge; lofty tabs. Incidentally, if you wing in by Icelandic Airlines and are booked on to another destination, the "Stopover Program" is a giant-size aspirin for flight-weary travelers who watch their pennies. This package includes pickup service at the airport, delivery to the hotel, all meals, a room with private bath, a citywide sightseeing tour, and transportation back to the airport. Should you nod "yes" to this bonus plan, you may tuck in a good chunk of Luxembourg as a low-cost extra during High Season. Here's a happy value for bargain-seeking adventurers. The 150-unit **Aero Golf**, a First-class flier, revved up between the airport and—the golf course, natch. We plan a comprehensive pass on our next Luxembourgian loop, but for starters we hear from locals that it is better than the Holiday Inn. True? We'll soon see.

The 42-unit **El Dorado** is modern, neat, sparkly-clean, color-toned, spacious, and livable. A fresh restaurant recently was unwrapped. Refrigerators in every room vie with scales in every bathroom. (Management's dark sense of humor?) Highly recommended.

The **Central-Molitor** provides 35 centrally sited kips with bath and shower, plus fresh furnishings, wall-to-wall carpets, automatic telephone hookup with long distance pan-European network, private safes (we won't say where), double windows and soundproofed walls, shaver plugs (even beside the bed for lazy groomers—or grooms), bidets ("with hot and cold running water," reminds the administration proudly), automatic door openers, electronically controlled red warning lights that glow "Do Not Disturb" in the corridor, and many other button-poppers. Host Ernest Thill speaks perfect English and couldn't be kinder.

The 4-story **Rix**, an outgrowth of the successful Pavillion Royal restaurant which adjoins it, offers 20 bright accommodations which Proprietor Fernand Rix keeps rubbed to a state of immaculate polish. Crusty shell; simple lobby with high clerestory and brass chandelier; friendly main-floor bar; well-outfitted rooms with full carpeting; front units with balconies facing the treetops and a mini parking lot; rear accommodations supersilent for serious snoozers; small baths with excellent ventilation, bubbles for the tub, and wonderful

American-made adjustable showerheads. Clients are not required to dine at the owner's restaurant—but since it's the best in town, why not?

The **Alfa** (place de la Gare) has been refashioned from Alfa to omega, but we haven't read through its new alphabet. The 60-room **International** seems to have perked up somewhat, but we'd much prefer to spend $1 or $2 more for one of the previously described hostelries. On the outskirts, the **Euro-Parc,** about 5 minutes along the Route d'Echternach, is a low-octane pit stop for motorists. Chalet-style building; pool, play area, and private lake; camping ground with A-frame shelters; thatched-roof café-restaurant and dancing on occasion; simple accommodations with curtained-off baths. Not much when compared to the city slickers. The expanding **Novotel** group has just unveiled 120 units near here (at *Dommeldange*). It is more of a motel than a hotel, but satisfactory as simple shelter.

If it's country life you're after, the **Hôtel du Grand Chef** in *Mondorf-les-Bains* is an Arcadian dream. Situated beside the huge rose-filled Kurpark (state operated, with 40 types of water treatment); back garden along a 3-foot stream, called the Gander River, separating Luxembourg from France. Handsome, imposing structure with modern comforts; 35 units in the old wing and 15 newer ones with private balcony, reputed to serve some of the most satisfactory vittles in the land. A charmer in every respect. Closed in midwinter. The **Heintz Hôtel** in the lovely little town of *Vianden* personifies the gentle charm of Mme. Hansen, its owner. Thirty bedrooms, all with bath and private balcony (you may pay extra for the latter); decorative highlights include vaulted ceilings, timbers, and oodles of antiques. It's about 45 minutes from the capital, and it's the proud possessor of the only chair lift in the Grand Duchy—a low-cost ride to a forest-type chalet where you can have a drink on open-air terraces to spike the already intoxicating view. A former convent, here's one of the nation's oldest and most interesting buildings. Renewed salutes! The **Bel-Air** in *Echternach*, smartly remodeled and expanded, is a garden retreat for weekending. Locals praise the kitchen here. The **Airfield Hotel**, about a 3-minute walk from the terminus, has a country setting, simple amenities, a wide variety of dishes on its menu, a small bar, and a good location for a quick getaway.

Other havens? The **Euro** (not to be confused with the Euro-Parc above) is along the busy Route d'Arlon to Brussels. This one has décor to please any 40-year-old tot: drum stripes, checks, sworls, and animal wallpaper. The **Dany**, on this same road and with an antique carriage out front, is also good basic shelter. Its prize, however, is its charming little restaurant boasting charbroiled steaks, lamb on the spit, and other grills which pop right in front of your popping eyes. Expensive tabs here, but pizza and snacks are available in the Crazy Horse Bar, which adjoins the stables and is ricks of fun. For other rural hostelries, check with the Tourist Bureau or our Embassy.

FOOD AND RESTAURANTS Four of Luxembourg's restaurants are outstanding. Pavillon Royal and Au Gourmet are tops for city dining, and the Hôtel Hiertz's nookery in *Diekirch* plus Bonne Auberge at *Gaichel* (about 25 minutes from the center by car) get our top vote for rural excellence. The neighboring **Reisdorfer** is said to be in the same league; this may be, but we've never tried it.

Full meals in the top establishments should settle at $14 to $20, while the majority of feederies are perhaps $4 less.

Pavillon Royal gives the illusion of a suburban setting, despite its location on one of the main boulevards of the metropolis. Converted mansion set back from the traffic by a manicured gravel "garden"; front-porch patio for sips or summer sups; formal marblesque dining room, a bit on the stiff side, with false fireplace, high-back chairs, and a multicolored skylight; live fish and lobster bins, with seawater imported from Holland. Savory cuisine, although our grilled lobster had more vinegar than a Maine fisherman in Baa Haaba; count on snail-like attention if crowded; inoperative on Sundays, Christmas, all of August. Very sound indeed. **Au Gourmet**, a 60-second walk from the Cravat, seems to offer just a little more chic. Two main rooms plus a small nook to the rear, each decorated with wood panels, silk brocade, and pewter highlights; attractive chandelier; comfortable chairs. Versatile menu of game, specialties, and stock dishes comprising perhaps 75 choices; full wine card; somewhat understaffed, but when service finally comes, attentive, friendly, and professional. If the Ostend oysters are in season, please try them for the memory of this happily shellshocked traveler. Excellent. The **Cordial** is still on the comeback trail. Window-wrapped mezzanine in a commercial building, overlooking a routine square; packed at noon with somber businessmen; tops in food but bottoms in service. **Rôtisserie Ardennaise**, not related to the famed Brussels establishment of the same name, has a rustic ambiance. Bar semidivided by greenery; walls partially paneled; cartwheel light fixtures, provincial gimmicks. Despite the obviously touristic outlook, it is chiefly favored by locals who think franc-ly about their vittles. Certainly this is one of the best dining bargain spots in the nation. On one recent swing, when we ordered a simple Châteaubriand for 2, out came a post-office-size chunk of tender-sweet beef AND a colossal platter with side dishes containing French fries, braised endive, asparagus, carrots, peas, sautéed mushrooms, baked tomato au gratin, salad, bread, and a full boat of Béarnaise sauce. All of the extras came at no extra charge! For wholesale calorie shoppers, here's that Big Discount House in the Sky. Unusually rewarding for its type. We've had encouraging reports from local friends on the **Greiveldinger**, but because the believing is in the tasting, we'll soon spoon in.

The Second-class **Schintgen** still offers a laudable light meal (soup, meat or fish, potatoes, one vegetable, salad) for reasonable tariffs. Solid, unglamorous, dependable; good for its category. The **Roma**, featuring an Italian menu, is adequate. Our latest pasta-packing repast here wasn't at all bad for a modest kitchen. The glacially cool restaurant at the **Café du Commerce** is renowned for its *moules;* here's the only place in town that will mollify your appetite after midnight, an innovation which has been well received. Last, and in our opinion least, 2 centrally located **Wimpy** beaneries offer inexpensive, 98-item menus featuring such specialties as eggburgers, fishburgers, and pineappleburgers.

If you're the type who likes exploring, drive out to the **Hôtel Hiertz** in the sleepy town of *Diekirch* (half-an-hour north on Route 7). The small restaurant in this ultramodest hostelry was awarded a coveted 2-star rating in 1971 by the *Guide Michelin*—an honor almost unknown outside France. Emerald watersilk and wood-paneled walls; flowers and candles on tables; Limoges porcelain supplemented by tiny cloverleaf patterns on salmon-colored napery; smooth, friendly service. Among the outstanding selections our party chose from its limited menu were Quiche Ardennaise, pintade (guinea fowl), quail, parfait, and advocat pudding. Always reserve your table; we saw cars outside from Belgium, Germany, France, and even Japan. Verdict? Five tuneful forks vibrating with happiness for an outstanding dining experience.

Suburban or rural expeditions? The leader is the previously mentioned **Bonne Auberge**, located so close to the border it's almost an immigrant. Rural sophistication; cozy bar; split-level dining room in quarter-circle design with big windows; happy use of colors; Danish-style lamps. Definitely worth the 25-minute excursion, especially when the weather is benign. Now a few bedrooms have been added, if you *really* want to make a night of it. The **Hôtel du Grand Chef** in *Mondorf-les-Bains*, in the heart of the vineyard country, is convenient and pleasant for a short summertime safari. **Helene Klein's Restaurant** in *Hespérange*, about 15 minutes from the center is reported to offer sound cookery; she's the owner and chef; simple atmosphere; we've never tried it.

Three additional possibilities: Many dining places on the Moselle River are delightful, and king of them all is the **Hotel Simmer** in *Ehnen*. The simple, family-run **Hôtel Hallerbach** in *Haller* (northwest of Echternach) is also special; the *patron* rattles the skillets, and live trout are stored in his little aquarium.

Check these and all other country places before leaving the capital, because most of them close down when business is slow.

Be sure to treat yourself to some wild game in fall and winter. The supply of partridge, pheasant, venison, and wild hare is usually ample. The hare is smaller and sweeter than the Belgian variety. Our favorite is roast saddle of hare; the Luxembourgers seem to like theirs cooked, ears and all, in red wine. But the delight of delights—a dish fit for a palace—is Partridge Canapé—a fat little bird served whole on toast, with baby mushrooms and a sauce of pan juices to crown it. Just flip us that bunch of grapes, Juno, and move over!

If you want a weekend of forests, brooks, trails, peace, and quiet, you might like the aforementioned **Hotel Bel-Air** in *Echternach*. There's stream fishing and hiking for active souls, loafing for others. The building has been extensively renovated in a charming way; the locale is gorgeous and the reception is warmly hospitable. As an overnight stop, it is also highly recommendable.

§**TIPS**: Coffee is inordinately expensive in Luxembourg—often twice the price of a piece of pie.

If you enjoy the tactile sensation of green persimmons, then try Letzburger Kachke'ss (cooked and aged cottage cheese) for breakfast or with cocktails. It's a proud specialty of this ancient land. You may detest it (as we do), or you may love it—but one thing is certain: your breath will never allow you to forget your holiday in Luxembourg, forever and evermore.

NIGHTCLUBS Amateur Night at your local Benevolent Order of Snoozing Octogenarians just might be more exhilarating. **Splendid** is doubtless the

most sophisticated nightery in the entire Grand Duchy. You've seen its type
of acts if you've watched Ed Sullivan: tricycle-riding chimps, ventriloquists,
acrobats, "exotic" dancers (local schoolteachers?), a singing duo, and a quartet. Rouge walls supporting waffled ceiling; mosaic bar with stools so high
you'll think you're in the crow's nest of the *USS Enterprise*. It serves honest
libations with tariffs nearly as lofty. And here to us was a nightlife first: When
we politely shooed away a pair of resident B-girls, they scampered without
a single peep! The **Plaza** is second on this 5-step ladder. Quiet ambiance;
attractive décor with awnings and lanterns; 2nd-string show of 3rd-rate strippers and "singles"; similarly bashful barmaids who don't twist your drinking
arm. We thought, but were not sure, that we caught the flash of a speck of
bathtub enamel once when we tilted our glass. True? **Scorpion**, formerly
Charly's Bar, has become a discothèque, but we haven't seen the new critter.
As for a gin mill called **Chez Nous**, we dislike this one with a passion. For
sipping, snacking, and nuzzling, we much prefer to kick up our hoofs at the
Crazy Horse Bar at the aforementioned Dany Hotel. Here's *the* spot for
stalling around on a loose rein.

Cover these slowly and carefully, savoring each minute—because when
you've finished, you've had your whirl. Even though most residents of this
little Duchy go to bed with the chickens, so many outlanders from nearby
industrial, military, and administrative complexes crawl this circuit that these
jernts are sometimes quite lively—particularly on weekends.

TAXIS   Get them at the station. Standard rate for short hauls is about 85¢
per mile, but if your journey is a long one, it decreases considerably. Although
the jockeys wheel and deal for huge tips at the end of the ride, 15% is ample.
Cars are recent and good U.S. models. Drivers are generally more courteous
than they used to be.

AIRLINES   Luxair sprouted its wings in '62 with one Fokker "Friendship." The "Friendship" must have taken, because now there's another little
Fokker plus 2 Caravelles. These zip to-and-fro daily between the capital and
Amsterdam (via Brussels) and Paris, twice a day over to London, 5 times a
week to Frankfurt am Main, and twice a week to Nice and Palma de Mallorca, plus darts to Athens, Málaga and Tunis. Icelandic provides daily
service between New York, Chicago, Reykjavik, and Luxembourg at prices
below IATA rates; an associated carrier which could be called "Sunlandic"
but is actually International Air Bahama dashes 6 times a week between
Nassau and Luxembourg at similar bargain tariffs (see "Let's Go By Plane").
Finnair makes one circuit every 7 days between Helsinki–Göteborg–Luxembourg–Barcelona–Málaga.

DRINKS   Luxembourg has now thrown the gauntlet at Milwaukee, Munich, and Copenhagen. To keep pace with the output of its 7 local breweries,
each Luxembourger—man, woman, and child—downs an average of 33 gallons a year. Brother, *that's* living (with a head on it!). Possibly this deluge of
suds has helped to float away memories of the genuine absinthe which used
to be available in every bar. The present-day substitute uses anise as a base;

the wormwood elixir that put the squirm in the beverage has been banned. Beer remains the best buy: 50¢ for the biggest glass in Europe, and please keep in mind that every time you knock one down a local tot has that much less to guzzle to maintain the national quota. Tops in white wines (reds or rosés are not pressed in this land) for most American tastes is Gewürztraminer. Always ask for the '75 vintage, which is now the choicest year generally available. You might find extra pleasure in a Riesling called Wormeldange Nussbaum. Next comes Riesling Sylvaner (pale, light, and quite dry). The Muscat Othonel is too fruity and too sweet for most U.S. palates. Local gentry seem to prefer the fairly dry Riesling Wormeldange Koeppchen; ask for this one by the grower's name, the best of which bears the Madame Hartmann cachet. For a sparkling wine, either the St. Martin or the Bernard Massard brand is suitable for nonceremonious drinking; this first cousin to a *blanc de blancs* is quite drinkable. Additional local production—and it sounds like a tidal wave for such a little land—includes the 100-proof plum brandy (slivo-vitz-type) known as Quetsch, 2 others made from yellow plums called Prunelle and Mirabelle, and the Swiss-beloved, cherry-pit spirit: Kirsch. The numerous local imitations of French liqueurs are such distant relatives that they'd qualify as 14th stepcousins twice-removed.

§TIP: As a guarantee of quality and authenticity in selecting your wines, be sure to ask for those bottles with the "Marque Nationale" sticker. This control device assures you that what you order, you get.

CAPSULE JUNKETS Here are suggestions for covering some of the less-known treasures of this little Duchy. You can pick up a map when you get there, and the strange names of these off-trail places will make sense. All of these are one-day junkets, based on residence in Luxembourg City:

Drive to **Clervaux**, take lunch at the Hôtel Koener, continue to **Wiltz,** and backtrack to **Vianden**. From teatime at the Heintz Hôtel you're only 45 minutes from the bright lights.

Or visit the **Hamm Cemetery**, where so many of our soldiers, including General George S. Patton, are at peace—continue to the Moselle River, have lunch at Simmer's in **Ehnen**—and get back to the capital in time for coffee and cakes at Namur's, a ceremony you shouldn't miss.

Or amble out to **Echternach**, where on Whitsun Tuesday there's a renowned **Dancing Procession** which might be called the New York Garment District rumba (3 steps forward and 2 steps back). Splendid basilica, eighth-century tomb of St. Willibrord, and handsome forested surroundings. Then proceed to **Esch-sur-Sûre** (from its amusing pronunciation, known to local wits as "The Seventh Martini Village"), swim, motorboat, or laze above its hydroelectric dam, and return.

For a longer outing, run up to the **Hamm Cemetery** via the road to Saarbrücken. After this stop, continue for 3 miles, turn left at **Sandweiler,** and skip on to **Ehnen** for coffee at the Simmer. As you leave the hotel, turn right along the Moselle and motor on until you reach a stone gate with a huge champagne bottle at the entrance. This is the **St. Martin Cave**, where some of the nation's finest sparkling wine is sleeping—and where, for a trifling sum including a glass of bubbly, you may watch it snooze. It's a fascinating tour into the cliffside cellars; afterward, you can sit on the river terrace (with Germany only 50 yards away) and sip the house product at factory tariffs. Now push on to *Remich* and cut in to *Mondorf-les-Bains*, where you can stroll in the lovely rose gardens of the **Kurpark** or take a hydrotherapy treatment in the modern bathhouse. Have lunch at the Hôtel du Grand Chef (the backyard has a tiny footbridge to the other side of the fairyland stream, which is French soil). Perhaps you'll wish to linger longer in the parklands or in the thermal waters as an excuse to take tea and the scrumptious pastries at this same hotel. Then zip back to the capital by the main pike that passes through *Frisange* and *Hespérange.* It's a full circuit, but not tiring—and most rewarding for all it embraces.

For single-track gustatory excursions: Try for lunch or dinner (1) the **Hôtel Hiertz** at *Diekirch*, (2) the Hôtel du Grand Chef at *Mondorf-les-Bains*, (3) the Hôtellerie de Vieux Moulin near *Septfontaines*, on the Valley of the Seven Castles route, (4) the stops listed above.

At least take a look at *Larochette*, if you can. This lovely village is in the approaches of what is called the "Little Switzerland of Luxembourg," a beautifully wooded and hilly region with striking rock formations, between Consdorf, Echternach, and Beaufort. Here's a perfect example of the toy charm of the Grand Duchy.

Mallorca

If we were asked to select the 2 most stimulating and rewarding targets in Spain for the average U.S. visitor, we'd pick Mallorca (Majorca) and Madrid in one second—except from mid-June to mid-September in the former, when it is horribly overcrowded.

Mallorca, roughly 60 miles by 50 miles at its widest points, is the capital of the Balearic Islands (Menorca, Ibiza, Formentera, and scores of rock-dots). Lying almost exactly 100 miles southeast of Barcelona, it is as accessible, timewise, as Boston or Washington is from New York City—25 to 55 minutes by air (depending on the type of plane) or 8 to 9 hours by steamer. With its 5000-foot mountains, lush plains, magnificent beaches (France's famed Riviera imports these sands), benevolent climate, warmhearted people, colorful background, and comparatively reasonable (but fast-rising!) prices, it has become one of the most popular resorts on the Mediterranean. In 1950, approximately 100-thousand visitors came to soak up its sun; last year the total was 3-million-plus. In one 24-hour period during the August rush, 502 airplanes processed almost 48-thousand passengers at the Son San Juan jet-port—a world's record. On a similar day of frenzy, JFK Airport in New York processed its all-time high of about 18.5-thousand ticketholders, or *less than half of the Palma flood!*

July-August is High Season, with practically flawless weather. Spring and fall are lovely; May, June, September, and October, have more than enough balmy days to offset gray ones. November-December and March-April are chancy—sometimes glorious, sometimes awful; parts, but only parts, of January and February are very raw, chilly, and unpleasant. The legendary false spring called *Las Calmas de Enero* ("The Calms of January"), similar in nature to our Indian Summer, blankets the land for 2-to-3 weeks in heavenly weather. This title is incorrect, because sometimes it falls in February; no one can accurately forecast this blissful hiatus in advance. When it comes, the spellbinding perfume and blossoming of nearly 10-million almond trees attired in petals of pink or white are reasons enough to visit the island in Off Season. There's good swimming from late spring to middle fall only, unless you've got long white hair on your chest like a polar bear.

CITIES Mallorca has the profile of a goat's head: *Palma*, the capital, is at the mouth, *Sóller* is near the eye, and *Formentor* is on one of the horns. The heartbeat of the island lies in Palma, its only large center—approximately 250-thousand inhabitants, most of the good restaurants, hotels, nightclubs, shops, most of the frenzy. At the peak of the season (not so noticeably in the spring or fall), the capital is packed so tightly with French, English, German, and other nationals who are flown or motor-coached in on bargain tours like so many cattle, that it's grossly tinny and crass; strike out during July and August for the tiny villages, to find the real charm of the Balearics.

A PLACE IN THE SUN? La Capella, in *Santa Margarita* (about 1 hour from Palma), is so extra special—and this is a broad statement—that it sweeps all honors as the most distinguished stopping place in the Balearic Islands. The urbane and personable Count de Queylar accepts carefully screened reservations from discerning wayfarers who will not destroy the graceful atmosphere (thus children are not accepted) and who will make worthy his efforts as a gentle and erudite host. This imposing eighteenth-century manor (updated with every imaginable twentieth-century comfort) commands the highest hilltop on his 30-acre fief. Rural site offering distant views of Alcudia and Formentor Bays; 10 minutes to a sandy beach; terraces, patios, gardens, chapel, and a splendid swimming pool. Each couple is assigned a grand bedchamber and a sitting room; each has 2 baths and a house telephone; most have fireplaces. The tariffs of about $50 per person per day include excellent French-based cuisine, at least 8 servants, whatever is consumed in wines and spirits of all kinds, and the luxury of absolute peace in a glorious milieu. But in recent times the Count has continuously endeavored to sublease La Capella as a single unit during the peak travel months of July and August. Thus, if your footsteps should bring you to Mallorca at other times, in La Capella you would find a uniquely magnificent Old World oasis of elegant living.

HOTELS Now, let's come back to earth again. Mallorca has the highest concentration of hotels and pensions per capita *of any major resort area in the world*—Florida, Las Vegas, Capri, and the French Riviera included. Every shoe manufacturer, raffia potentate, and artichoke entrepreneur seems to have climbed aboard the construction bandwagon with visions of a quick peseta. the isle now has a grand total of *approximately 1500 hostelries*. Naturally, the facilities and service in most of this crop are amateurish in the extreme.

Don Jaime Enseñat Alemany, one of this industry's most highly respected leaders, has warned the Palma Chamber of Commerce that a minimum of 300-thousand more visitors must be wooed in order to support this tidal wave of building. If you stick to the establishments this Guide has winnowed for you below, your chances of a happy holiday will be increased. Another guideline might be the star system which the Government uses; it is explained under "Hotels" in the chapter on "Spain."

Because our rankings are primarily reportorial (*i.e.,* based on value-for-money plus standards of taste and service which we think will appeal to discriminating travelers of almost any financial means), we feel no compunction about downgrading or eliminating numerous "officially rated" top-grade houses which don't meet our own criteria for inclusion.

In this regard, independent travelers to Mallorca face an extraordinary situation. Tour-group operators have so engorged various districts by advance block booking of the vast majority of their hostelries for the entire season that we are compelled to slice away giant chunks of the island which we think would disappoint or disillusion North American fun-seekers. As typical examples, *Páguera* is now jammed almost exclusively with German and English trippers; *Arenal*, *Ca'n Pastilla*, *Ca'n Picafort*, *Cala Ratjada*, *Cala Millor*, and *Porto Cristo* host invasions of Teutonic armies; *Palma Nova* and *Santa Ponsa* tan the bleached hides of Scandinavian, Dutch, Belgian, and other northlandic sun worshipers.

So—with a lynching party on our doorstep bruiting its vociferous objections—we'll dive into an island summary that will highlight only what we believe, as professionals and residents, are the most rewarding treasure troves for your Mallorquin Odyssey.

The **Formentor** is practically a generic name for holiday relaxation. Recently, impressive improvements have been made by Don Miguel Buadas, its proprietor. The gleamiest dazzlers are its 2 exquisite swimming pools (one heated) tiled in Valencia-style patterns and sited in a palm grove almost at your doorstep. There's a wide-angle, panoramic lobby, colorful and airy; all the bedrooms are bright, cheerful, and tasteful. Additional wing and elevator, air-conditioning from portal-to-portal, a discothèque, spacious seaview terrace with an orchestra before and after dinner for open-air sipping and dancing (the same garden-girdled patio is utilized for apéritifs and Gala Nights); Beach Bar with upper deck featuring lunches or light refreshments and so round, so firm, so fully packed bikinis on its waterside perch; water-ski boats plus equitation; new additional tennis courts plus *frontón;* tiny bullring for mini-*corridas.* Other baubles include 17 suites (the prizes are gorgeous #238 and #338), 3 dining rooms, terraces, a modernized kitchen, and a movie theater with free films in English or Spanish 2-to-3 evenings per week. The setting is a pine mantle along a cliff-lined coast which is 10 times more beautiful than Capri. The bay is glorious, the water is unbelievably blue, and the beach offers magnificent sunning and lazing. Clientele? A condensed *Who's Who in the World.* London-Savoy-trained Concierge Francisco Borrás is a gem; so is Juanito, his leading assistant; so is Chief Barman Jaime. The cuisine has been improving and is now quite commendable, especially in the main building. (The clubhouse buffets are pleasant for midday dining, but don't compare in quality with the skilletry in the hotel itself.) Incidentally, the taxi ride to or from the capital or the airport takes about 90 minutes and costs around $20; the nearest fishing village, *Puerto de Pollensa*, which is also the telephone exchange, is a 15-minute drive. Better and better every year; warmly and highly recommended.

Son Vida, another threat to dominance in country living, nestles less than 15 minutes from Palma in a breathtaking mountaintop showcase. This totally converted castle has been renowned for centuries for its priceless collection of medieval arms. All its 175 nesting spots (leaning heavily toward suites and demisuites) have private bath and air conditioning; most come with private terrace; several honeymoon suites have been installed in the towers. The newest wing, which started flapping in '72, is feathered with 75 large doubles and the Must-Be-Seen-to-Be-Believed Imperial Suite, fitted with 2 bedrooms, 4 bathrooms, a wide-angle sitting room with dining area to accommodate 12, and a huge balcony overlooking the links. Other units, also facing the fairways and Palma Bay, boast Spanish-modern trappings, frigobars, and 3-part bathrooms which include separate ladies' boudoirs, bath and shower, and W.C. A gardenside coffee shop and 2 more luxury dining spreads also are perking here. *Pièce de résistance* of the house is the fantastic 250-foot terrace, partially awninged for outdoor dining, with the sweep of the city and the sea at your feet. Commodious fishhook-shape heated swimming pool with wading pool for small fry at one end; Snack Bar adjoining; spacious main dining salon leading to lively garden-type restaurant; 3 bars, library, and Grand Salon. While the cuisine has improved dramatically in recent months, it still draws some complaints; pay extra, if you can, for à la carte instead of the cost-included pension menu, and your fare will equal or better any table on the entire island. On the 1400-acre estate, you'll find tennis courts, a 10-horse stable, and an 18-hole golf course plus a handsome 19th-hole club. Savvy direction by veteran expert Salvador Palmada. Here's a serene haven for the wealthy traveler who seeks beauty, peace, and tranquillity.

In **Palma** proper, we continue for the nonce to tip our sombrero to the Victoria-Fénix combo, which recently was purchased by a largely commercial hotel chain, one of the biggest in the Balearics. This side-by-side winsome twinsome forms a delightful resort complex within itself. Embraced between the arms of these 2 elegant houses is an aquatic tropical paradise: a magnificent sky-blue swimming pool, a spectacular grand patio, plants, flowers, colorful awnings, Palm Springs type bar, snack service for bathers, and nightly cocktail dancing until 1 A.M. Both are under the able management of astute young Don Jaime Cortés. In the **Victoria** (everything is open to guests of both hotels), there is a bingo hall and even a movie theater where late-released films are regularly shown. Aside from the youthful 2-floor "annex," only the old Victoria name remains. The main building was razed and resurrected by the architect who did the Fénix (see below). Set-back entrance in a small parking apron; pleasantly inviting lobby with glass-enclosed wild-duck pond and fountain; 100% glass-walled stretch commanding the seaside fronts of the wide-girthed lounge, dining room, and leather-and-paneled bar; mammoth open terrace dotted with pine trees and flora, providing breakfasters with seagull's-eye view of the swimmers below. All of the 150 smartly outfitted bedchambers come with bath, air conditioning, and individual balcony; 115 bayside units and 35 facing the garden; suites that are strictly *ne plus ultra*. This siren stands imposingly over the Mediterranean as one of the best-equipped, best-managed, and most comfortable houses in Europe. Let's hope that the new proprietors keep it that way.

The **Fénix** is a knockout, too. Equally well administered; 100 rooms, all with bath, all air-conditioned, all soundproofed, and all with private terraces which face the bay a hop-and-a-flip below; 6 suites with fireplaces and double terraces also available. The décor is regional modern in flavor, and suave throughout with most of its revamping energies lately aimed at its public areas. Dining services lately reduced; bar enlarged; heated pool. This one may close again in midwinter, so check first if you're traveling then.

For sheer richness, nothing touches the young, $8,000,000, 150-room **Valparaiso**. $7,000,000 of its cost was won by the leather-mogul Alba brothers in a national lottery; they decided to stake their winnings on an upgraded level of luxury for Mallorca. Whether this represents a white knight in *hôtellerie* for the island or a white elephant for the Albas remains to be seen, but one thing is certain—it cannot be ignored. Where water is scarce, they've built a cascade and small lake at the terraced entrance (trucks refill it when evaporation makes this necessary); there's a vast ternate pool area adorned with bronze statues and showering fountains that are illuminated at night; inside there's another swimmery plus saunas for men and women (there's yet another large splasher just for the 180 staffers who live in their own luxury compound near the tennis courts). The view from its semiurban site above the town is breathtaking; one can hardly help being awed by the acres of polished marble on its floors, the textiles covering almost every wall throughout the building, the massive crystal chandeliers, the tooled leather, the reproduced Oriental lacquers, the smoked mirrors, the abundance of fine woolen carpets and spreads, and the schools of minions who render impeccable service. There are a formal dining room plus window-lined grill (where our meal was a costly culinary atrocity), a patio for outdoor snacking and imbibing, a 24-hour bar in the form of a ship's saloon, and a handsome discothèque in orange and black diagonal stripes. There are 3 styles of bedchambers: classic, which is inclined toward English, and 2 versions of Spanish (we prefer either of the latter); all come with balcony, air conditioning, compartmented baths, TV, and the very highest quality furnishings. Our bill for one night with dinner and breakfast for 2 totaled a little more than $85 without tips, stunningly expensive by Spanish standards but about on par with deluxe continental tariffs. Impressive it is; cozy it is not. But if you are looking for an almost Roman imperial setting, Mallorca now has one—all 5 stars' worth shining down on Palma from the hillsides.

The Deluxe-category **Nixe Palace** is uniformly carpeted and furnished in a contemporary motif. While better than she used to be, she is becoming increasingly tour-happy. From the peak of a terraced cliff about 10 minutes from the hub of the city, she towers over Cala Mayor beach (the only top-bracket hostelry in the immediate area that nibbles at the edge of a sandy shank). Attractive heated pool several levels down the flowered slope with daily buffet for swimmers; handsome main floor, including the English-style dining room (ethnically ironic, because this one also has adopted kosher cuisine), the adjoining treetops breakfast patio, the pine-paneled bar (highlighted by equestrian tack and partitioned from the lobby by a vitrine displaying pewter), the awning-shaded porch for alfresco sipping, and the richly outfitted nautical lounge. The entire building is air-conditioned, with individ-

ual controls in the bedchambers. The 35 spacious split-level units are by far
the best accommodations in this house; these come with private seafront
balcony, a solid glass wall for view, a wood one for decorative warmth, and
the ever-present, all-too-tiny-but-efficient interior baths. Our only major
demurrer is the vulgarity of so many of the conducted tour people she attracts.
Gracious, hard-trying personnel keynoted by keen-eyed Director Juan Tor-
tella. Now a solid contender.

The **Meliá Mallorca** opened in the spring of '54. Here is a place about
which few wayfarers remain neutral; in general, either they love it or they
loathe it. Two pleasant pools (one heated); refreshment patio and terraces;
vintage hyper-Meliá ambiance and décor; standard rooms either in terra cotta
or green motifs, all with bath, balcony, and 3-channel Muzak system and all
comparatively cramped; a few bayfront units which are larger, more expensive, and more comfortable. Large wing subsequently inaugurated; substandard *residencia* annex directly across the street, which we'd advise you to
avoid. Manager Don José Tur Olmo directs most of his efforts toward block
bookings made through this chain operation; 40% of the overall occupancy
now consists of Americans. Verdict? We think it's crassly and brashly institutional, but some travelers don't. Such violently mixed Guidesters' reactions
each year that this one must be on you.

The **De Mar**, about 10 minutes from the center in *Las Illetas*, became a
De-Mar-velous luxury house after it finally outlived its growing pains. Now,
however, a creeping mantle of uncertainty lined with an undercoat of commercialism has spoiled this one. It was built from scratch in the astonishing
period (for Mallorca) of 18 months; the hastiness of its construction is showing
from skin to core. To add to the slipping image, the grounds and public areas
vitally require more careful pruning. We haven't sampled its table personally,
but on our last check, we noticed that it also features kosher cooking. This
electrifyingly modern contestant—its daring brown ceramic exterior has
given it the nickname "Villa Chocolate"—sad to say is sailing more and more
into the lanes of group convoys from northern climes. Last year it was closed
during winter.

The **Maricel**, 15 minutes from the center, has an official 4-star rating
(instead of 5),but we like it so much we are including it high in our listings.
Extensive modernizations in which its traditional Old Mallorquin flavor has
been preserved; it evokes a clublike ambiance enhanced by a friendly staff and
heavy occupancy by a convivial British clientele. There's an attractive dining
room and lobby; the cuisine is substantial; modern kitchen; tennis court; no
sandy beach but sea bathing available; good swimming pool; 8 bungalows
refitted; all baths revamped. Hardworking Director Enrique Cabré radiates
true dedication in his supervision of this tasteful little haven. Pert but not
elegant. We love it.

La Cala, in the Cala Mayor district, is to us, with the Nixe Palace, the only
good hotel in Palma which fronts a full-fledged sand beach. All of this
hostelry's 64 modest, pleasant, thoughtfully designed rooms are with bath;
most seaside locations have their own little terraces. Private illuminated pool
if the beach is crowded; outdoor bar service; sweeping sun-terrace; lively
clientele. About 10 minutes from the center, closer to town than the neighbor-

ing Maricel; not to be confused with the **Hotel Cala Mayor**, which is inferior. Highly recommended for its category.

The 800-pillow **Bellver**, facing the bay from Palma's Paseo Maritimo, is a hard-bit victim of the touristic boom-bug. All 15 floors air-conditioned; swimming pool; cinema; nightclub; coffee shop; management by Marciano Paredes, a skilled professional. Conventions and mass bookings compose its roster of registrants, some of whom have complained of *very* impersonal service. Even more heartless, in our opinion, is the newer **Palas Atenea**, with a similar bayfront setting, the same pack-'em-in attitude, and the same administration. If you book one of its 400 look-alike cubicles you may experience how truly boring a hotel can be when—as we felt it was here—human caring is absent. The Hall Porter, however, seemed to be the lone contradiction to this on our incognito sleep-in.

For midtowners, the **Almudaina** is convenient for shophounds and city kittens who can take or leave the sea. Renovations, mostly in public areas, have left more pluses and minuses than are in a 4th-grade arithmetic primer. Rear perches above the 5th floor offer choice views of the cathedral and harbor; all stalls on the main drag (and we mean *drag*) are perfect if you thrill to the sound of clanging gear changes and screeching disc brakes. Grade for this semester? B-minus, but with Prof. José Luis Gaspart now running the class, we're expecting a *hotel cum laude* before too long.

Jaime I has good and bad points in its makeup. Lobby with 2 hilarious plaster lions to greet guests; staff unbelievably awkward; one added wing; coffer-and-beam-ceiling reception area; split-level dining room, with each stratum distinctive; hunting-den bar; nicely textiled cozy lounge; excellent 6th-floor maritime La Bitacora nightclub; steps to the rooftop, with pools for both parents and kiddies, a bar, and the sweeping vista of Palma and the port. All public rooms air-conditioned; some bedchambers with attractive bricked-in panels for "headboards"; ample luggage space; more-than-adequate comfort. If its personnel were given a few basic lessons in comportment, civilized manners, and the fundamentals of polite hotel-keeping, it could be a bargain-basement gem. But as it is, the tail wags the dog—and, believe us, this is the tail.

Saratoga, also for city dwellers, is amiably executed and not expensive. Three lounges and dining room adjacent to heated pool and balconied bedchambers above; another pool and bar topside; colorful contemporary furnishings; doubles with baths and singles with showers; better-than-average cookery. The room card states, "The Management appeals to the guests to use a correct dressing when passing at the dining room"—a hint of their earnest efforts to keep up its tone. Very goodly indeedly.

The **Jaime III** is sterile by comparison. Muted colors throughout with maroon and black predominating; public areas air-conditioned; 88 twins and only 2 singles; nice balconies overlooking a dry metropolitan gulch. Fair but far from exciting.

The **Capitol**, another candidate just off the main shopping street, is tucked away in a small plaza that echoes the traffic din all day but is reasonably tranquil when the sandman comes. Functional lobby, usually atitter and aclatter with achattering foreign tour groups; tasteless air-conditioned dining room in which the full-pension or half-pension gouge force-feeds every client; bedroom décor anything but capital. Clean, at least.

The **Constelación**, set on a hillside above the city, orbits within a galaxy of other 3-star and lesser planetoids. Extremely helpful and ever-smiling concierge; small pool and bar across a busy byway; glassed-in restaurant opposite reception; 28 twins, 12 singles, and penthouse suite more than adequate but not luxurious. It is so popular among both individual wanderers and tour clusters that it is nearly always filled to capacity.

The **Araxa** is styled in what might be called "Mallorquin Modern"— traditional island colors, materials, and furnishings combined with Willow-garden swimming pool; decorative lily pond; individual terraces; quiet location ½-mile from the center, away from the sea; medium rates. Although it's still bright and attractive, travelers with whom we've talked are far less enthusiastic than they used to be. Many tour groups.

Residencia Nacar is a budget diadem with its brightest gem the aforementioned young, energetic Director José Luis Gaspart. All 60 accommodations with bath and shower; 2 elevators; functional décor. A sterling buy at brass-tack prices.

The **Pensión Armadams**, with 30 rooms and 20 baths, has been moving along admirably. Another fine stop for economizers. **Residencia El Patio**, with 11 attractively outfitted bedchambers above the Deluxe restaurant of the same name, is also a happy but noisy nest for the thrifty. Some insist it is tops on the island for peseta value—but we don't go quite that far. All units with private bath (#10 has a 4-poster), but best of all is that discounted menu in the El Patio for hotel guests. Yum-yum!

For true peseta-thrifting, most of this next bundle offer simple shelter, cleanliness, reasonable comfort, and 3 meals a day for surprisingly low tariffs: **Infanta** (near the busy Plaza Gomila; nice garden with bar; for the more quiet types),**Yoga** (swimming pool, which can also be used for wise reflection; 40 cells for contemplation; 40 baths and showers for navel rinses; devoted staff of disciples), **Paraiso del Mar**, **Residencia Rosamar**, **La Portassa** (superb situation), **Pensión Menorquína** (architecture reminiscent of Gaudí; 25 rooms, all with private balcony, but only 3 with bath; Manager Francisco Bonmatí very helpful), and **Pensión Marblau** (50 units all with bath and many with terrace; musty; restaurant under separate direction).

Beach hotels in Palma proper? To reemphasize this important fact, only La Cala and Nixe Palace. For Mediterranean bathing otherwise the visitor must strike out for the boondocks. Here are our choices of the top resort centers and the most appealing hostelries on tap at each one:

Southwest of the metropolis, along the rockbound coast, *Cala Mayor*'s runner-up to the Nixe Palace (see earlier) is the **Emperatriz**. Private house converted quite some time ago into a Second-class hostelry; plastics throughout; small chambers; better for its grounds than its interior. The **Bristol** has become a mighty challenger. Public zones rezipped; dining salon in old *español* style; lounge with large hearth; restful patio *andaluz;* added furnishings. Coming on strong. **Impala** is not recommended to anyone we know or love. Its publicity brochures puff it up as heaven's gift to innkeeping, but all of its many facilities impressed us as being substandard.

In the nearby *Las Illetas* suburb, the **Bonanza**, with its neighboring (and cheaper) **Bonanza Playa**, is a happy corner of Mallorca. Two pools (one heated), minigolf links, and private beach; garden with ancient cloister décor; evening meals outdoors in summer; bar in bam-bamboo-boo tones; 10 Moorish-mooded "villas" on the grounds. This couplet is big stuff for the tour packagers, but very attractive and well maintained. We wish more independent voyagers would discover it because we think it is among the worthier coves on the coast. **Gran Albatros**, in the same bracket, has doubled its nests to 100 and otherwise regilded its cage. A private beach and heated swimmery make it a sound enough perch. Costly, not bad, but we prefer its competitor, the Bonanza. The Second-class **Bon Sol** is still more suited to European than American tastes, despite improvements and modernizations. Fair. The **Illetas** is disrecommended; far, far too amateurish, we think.

The **Bendinat**, 6 miles from the center in the same direction, was a delight on our last peek. Main building with 10 rooms, each with bath; 9 beguiling individual and duplex guest cottages adjoining; tennis, garden, billiards, private rock "beach"; lovely alfresco dining terrace. Reserve well in advance; popular among the English; groupy but nice.

The **Son Caliu** takes its name from the cove where it is sited. Nice beach plus pool; waterside snack bar; maintenance slipping perilously. Now accepting group bookings (mostly English) and in danger of overdeveloping, in our opinion.

Not far away, the **Punta Negra** distributes its dual personality of a 40-room hotel and 13 bungalows between the twin beaches at its doorsteps. Sea or pool swimming available; immaculate dining room with savory offerings; cozy in tone; a favorite among traveling Yanks and Rebs. Be sure to have confirmed reservations because it is deservedly popular and always jammed. Recommended.

Palma Nova, beyond the Bendinat turnoff on the Paguera highway, offers the **Comodoro** and the **Delfin Playa**, which are neck-and-neck for our number-one local slot. The former boasts a dreamy waterfront dining terrace, an indoor-outdoor poolside bar, and warm décor touched up with maritimeliness. Here's a joyful haven in a seedy little baylet. The latter, in sawtooth architecture, displays a captivating blend of man-made forms and nature. Broad stone staircase tiptoeing directly into the palm-lined swimming pool; greenery married to walls, pillars, and rock terracing; rich rustic Spanish decoration; fine-quality, comfort-conscious furnishings; public rooms air-conditioned; bedrooms that say "welcome," each with its own private balcony plus bath with seahorse towel rings. Thoughtfully masterminded as a good bet for any big fish who washes up on Palma Nova sands. Both First category; both youngsters; both open around the calendar; both recommended. The **Hawaii**, where your Martini may march up in a coconut shell, is passable at best. After our aloha in its depths, we'd prefer to pass it—but the travel agencies obviously don't. The 180-room **Cala Blanca** also woos migrations of package trippers from the graylands of Europe. Very nice physical plant, however, if you can boll-weevil your way in. The **Canaima** lacks aplomb. The basic facilities are here, but when viewed together, they fail to jell; the inclination to cut corners on the housekeeper's budget is noticeable. Some might like it; we're luke. The park-situated **Bermudas** seemed "shorts" on everything—particularly on its badly tailored maintenance; needs to pull up those knee-length socks. The **Playa** scared us out of our wits. A consortium of blue-ribbon psychiatrists might paw the dust just to meet the chap who painted those corridors. WOW! Go anytime between November 1 and February 28 (or 29th on leap years), because it is operative only from March 1 to October 31. All these hostelries have latched onto the best brochure artist on the island, and his lovely layouts might fool you. In compliment to his talents, we haven't seen anything slicker since our last greased-pig chase.

In *Magaluf*, the 15-story, cliff-sited **Coral Playa** is king of the mountain. All 200 sea-seeing bedchambers with terrace and private bath; cooled public rooms and heated swimming pool; dancing nightly in Season; good, sound direction by D. Francisco Capo. Very attractive. We haven't seen the **Cala Viñas**, but now that Great Britain's Trust Houses Forte group is holding its administrative reins, we'd bet this will be a house you can put your trust in. We'll see soon. The mammoth **Magaluf Park** seems like a skyscraping monument for groupies. It has space for 900 sun-seeking souls, plus 3 bars, 3 pools, and 3 times too many bulk bookings to suit us. The **Guadalupe** is a 500-room link in the ubiquitous Hotels Mallorquines chain, which runs the aforementioned Bellver, Palas Atenea, and 20 other hostelries on the island. This organization necessarily deals heavily with package tours. The **Flamboyan** caters 99% to pre-booked English clientele. Fully air-conditioned; renovated lobby, restaurant, and lounge; oodles of terraces; 2 bars; 78 units with bath; doubles with individual balcony. Flamboyan-t for the region. The 161-room **Pax,** while Second class, offers much more heart and warmth. Not directly on the water but across the road from it; nice heated pool; bar, salon, and dining room; Iberian-tone bedrooms, each with terrace and private bath; plenty of color and ripe with charms. Quiet and economical for the right traveler. Open April to mid-October. **Atlantic** registers low tide on our chart. Coney Island atmosphere in the Mediterranean sun. **El Caribe**, in the same category as the Pax, comes up with a better seaside situation, but with far less élan than its spiffier competitor. It's okay—but if you don't insist on the waves at your tootsies, we still prefer the Pax. The Meliá-run, gradually expanding **Apartotel** is for long-pausing pilgrims, and its added wing can hold more of them than ever.

At *Camp de Mar*, the First-class **Gran Hotel Camp de Mar** is the juiciest kernel on a rough cob. No-groups policy, a rarity; improved décor throughout; all units with bath and private terrace; swimming pool now abubbling. All in all, a corn borer. The **Playa**, one category lower, is more functional but far less appealing aesthetically—quite an achievement. **Villa Real** is even more uninteresting. And so is this entire beach, which is 2nd-rate compared to many other captivating coves, hillocks, and crannies of this romantic isle.

All of these (except, of course, La Capella) are within about a ½-hour radius of Palma.

Country hotels or hostelries farther out? The ultramodern, medium-price **Molins** at *Cala San Vicente* (2 toy coves near Pollensa, 1-hour from Palma) is an excellent bet. Perched on a hillside facing its little beach, its design is linear-boxlike—unattractive on the exterior but surprisingly cozy inside; 89 rooms, all with bath, radio, and independent terrace fronting the sea; beach bar and American bar, with friendly Tolo the excellent Mix-Master; swimming pool and sun terrace; tennis court and surrounding garden; air-conditioned public rooms. Sound cuisine; fine maître d'hôtel in Miguel; Concierge Tony couldn't be more willing. About half the price of the Formentor, and warmly recommended within its comfortable but not luxurious range.

The **Simar** is outfitted with tiny accommodations. Beautiful pool and recreational apron across the street; 30-room annex; beach restored and descending staircase laid; dining room stretched for sea view. Operative April to October only; coming up perkily. The 35-room **Cala San Vicente,** also seasonal, is routine; many English tour groups; so-so. The **Niú** is simple; newish but seedy-ish dining room and bar; low-low tariffs; accept only the most modern bedchambers in this pension. It is what it is. The **Hostal Mayol** has matured from its origins as a restaurant and swinging discothèque into a popular little inn. Clean, pleasant, basic amenities; informal, almost slaphappy atmosphere which can be fun if you're young enough. The cookery is still the best in the cove. Artist-Manufacturer-Tycoon Jaime ("Jimmy") Mayol, who ran it as a cheerful pastime and hobby and who is still often on hand to chat, couldn't be more affable. **Hostal Los Pinos,** on a hillside across from the Molins, is a converted private house which is householded by Anna and Juan Coll. As a former headwaiter, he understands attention to his guests and lavishes it on each one. A happy place. That green-tiled monstrosity is called (among other things) the **Don Pedro**. It caters largely to British trippers. Forget it—if you can.

For fun-and-games at a soothingly reasonable price level, *Puerto de Pollensa* offers the most—especially to unmarrieds and young-marrieds. This is the nearest village to Formentor; frequent boat service (a few pennies) to the Formentor beaches for swimming (poor bathing but beautiful bayside surroundings in the Puerto). The outskirting **Illa D'Or**, with its blendfully added wing, has our first slot now that the midtown **Daina** has gone over primarily to block bookings by a German travel agency. Remote situation at the end of the pine-lined sea path, about 10 minutes from town by foot; waterfront patio plus facilities for bay bathing and boating; snack bar for swimmers and shallow-draught skippers; poorly surfaced tennis court; handsome lounge; fresh dining room with improved cuisine served on annoyingly small tables; daily outdoor buffet in season; 120 accommodations, many of them new. Recommendable, if you don't mind its distance from the port action. The little **Sis Pins**, back in the village, has a homey personality. It also boasts one of the friendliest and most loyal staffs in the region. Improved seafront apron for swimming or sunbathing; better maintenance; earplugs suggested if you draw a rear window in summer; open all year; 10% reduction in Low Season. Good for its low price. The **Miramar** is improving again; repaved concrete tennis court served up; 16 rooms added; elevator service to both old and young wings; large, traditional, and barnlike, but at last on the go. Closed March to November. The whitewashed **Capri** draws a discriminating following within the heart of the village. Total of 33 comfortable rooms, all with bath and 1 with private balcony; amiable bar and terrace fronting the bay; one of the best values on tap. The **Eolo**, is also modern but shows premature wear. In any case, the Yorkshiremen singing around the piano don't seem to mind. The mammoth **Pollensa Park** is chiefly reserved for registrants on a private charter plan. **El Montelyn**, a block off the seafront, comes up with 32 charming apartments (some with oh-so-handy kitchenettes), a yummy snack bar, and a pool for residents. And not only that: the snack bar serves real, honest-to-goodness U.S.-style hamburgers and Neapolitan-style pizzas. Its delightfully hospitable hosting family, the Reuters, have stoked up a sauna and now spread their Swedish charm to guests most of the year round. Very comfortable, and fun. The **Raf** is a frequent choice of the Yachting Set; handy situation, a short roll from the main quay; genial administration and personnel; informal, basic, and a snug harbor. The **Carotti** specializes in tour groups; reasonably sound physical plant, but always so crammed you don't stand a chance of getting in. The **Bellavista** claims 42 rooms and 12 baths; almost all accommodations with private terrace; tiny dimensions; a staff that speaks Spanish only. Modest. The 32-unit **Marina** is colder than a sea urchin's bottom spine in mid-December. No, thanks. The **Pensión La Torre** doesn't send us either. **Pensión del Luz** is another chipper little budget haven which money-savers seem to enjoy. We like it, too. **Pensión Rex** and **Pensión Barcelona** are also designed for the peseta-pressed pilgrim. The 66-room **Uyal**, about a mile along the Alcudia road, draws heavy traffic from northern European lands. Seaside swimming and sunning terrace across the highway; salon and bar expanded; once chilly in approach and manner, but now unfreezing commendably. The impersonal **Pollentia** lacks flair or imagination. All these houses jump as madly as rabbit warrens during the summer.

In *Puerto Alcudia*, block bookings have now sewn up most of the High Season accommodations, but the area is recommendable because of its lovely, wide, sandy beach. Of the big ones, **Playa Esperanza** is possibly best. **Golf** is okay in the minor league and **Xara** is passable. The Moorish-influenced **Rocador** is 3rd. Stepped-terrace landscape; spacious rustic Ibiza-style sleepers; nice pool. **Cala Gran** grows grander by the season. The **Tucan** has 150 happy pads. Whucan use 'em? Yucan. **Costa del Sur** is also young, but most of its bookings are taken by travel agencies a year in advance. Among the pensions, **Ca'n Trujillo** is the leader, followed by the **Areil**, the **Oasis**, the **Hostal Romano**, the **Mistral**, and the **Las Vegas**. But again there's very little chance of nipping a kip in any of these, since German tour operators invariably nail them down solid from spring to late fall.

RESTAURANTS   There is a surprising variety on the island.

El Patio (just off Plaza Gomila, *Palma*) has long been one of the most famous landmarks of the Balearics. Its cane-lined walls are banked with photos and sketches of royalty, film stars, ambassadors, admirals, tycoons, and other notables from dozens of nations who have been nourished here. Its supervision is in the able hands of Don Marcos Pomar, son of the late founder.

In *Cala d'Or* you'll find one of the top restaurants on the island—**La Cuadra**, operated by bearded young Geoff, who is the best possible walking advertisement for his own interesting and unusual cookery. This is a fine target for a lunch excursion on a bonny day. Small, attractive premises with no view but with many original touches and colorful décor; noble assistance by his charming gal friend; expensive tabs which are merited; *reserve in advance.* Highly recommended. The **Cala d'Or Hotel**, with its attractive downstairs bar, inviting terrace, and winsome Mallorquin flavor is 2nd. Very chic clientele; skilletry highly regarded year after year. Traditionally the best bet for the moneyed traveler—but don't expect a "21."

La Caleta, next to the Alcina Hotel, is the ground-floor feedery in the apartment colossus that soars above. Immaculate entrance without any particular decorative motif; long bar leading to swimming-pool deck; huge upper terrace with tables for warm-weather munching; Bagatel-Lo Pub; plate-glassed, seafront interior dining room, with modern red-cushioned chairs, brass globe sconces, and terra-cotta floors. Very good reception; better attention from captains and waiters; now *the* gathering spot for VIPs. Prices about the same level as those of El Patio.

Don't be put off by the membership status of the **Club de Mar** yacht basin in the **Puerto Pi** section of Palma at the east end of the waterfront Paseo Maritimo boulevard. Three segments are open to the public in any case and for under $2 you can take out daily membership which entitles you to use the full club facilities; we'll wager that you'd be delighted by it. Some of the best cuisine on the island; stunning vista; handsome nautical rigging in blue and white. Please try to navigate into this splendid port—it's the salt of the sea!

Smaller, less expensive, and equally enticing is **Le Relais**, directly across the private street from the entrance to the Club. Through a little garden and up a flight of stairs you'll find a suavely decorated, broad-windowed, L-shape oasis in soothing blues and pastels. The food, with a number of authentic Mallorquin dishes scattered through the menu and sophisticatedly presented, is exemplary. So are the atmosphere, the welcome, and the attention. Urbane Captain Cecil Morrison has trimmed up this prized bark so smartly that it now draws aboard impressive segments of the island's Old Landed aristocracy. Still pricy but outstanding.

Mac's Cristina (Calle Pursiana 12, a hard-to-find street off Calle Argentina) is, if you hadn't guessed, run by Mac— and we'll bet you can't guess who Mac is. Well, she's about the winningest Philippine we've met this side of Manila. Her island cuisine, too, is something that will put a smile on your tummy. Please, p-l-e-a-s-e don't miss her Lumpia (an omelet-size, sweet-and-sour canape that's fit for the Pacific gods) or the Adobo (chicken and pork that have been marinated, then braised, then fried). There's a friendly beakful of a bar at the entrance, followed by a candlelit inner salon, which in turn is augmented by an inviting alfresco patio where you can linger over Mac's romantic inventions until dusk or dawn. Anybody who can't love this happy corner just can't love. The prices, incidentally, are unbelievably low for such a stunning culinary novelty and for such superlative quality. Now *dinner only* and closed Monday.

Inviting little **La Broche** (Calle Asprer 3, just off Av. Jaime III) is a happy choice since its Great Leap Forward under the direction of Frank Spapen, a Belgian who brought in his own French chef from Morocco (*sic*). Intimate, split-level bistro atmosphere; kitchen and dark-wood bar at entrance; perhaps 2 dozen tables; red-checkered cloths, candles, and fresh flowers; air conditioning; prompt, smooth, courteous service. Included among our last 4 feasts here were sole smothered in mushrooms and mussels, Boeuf Bourguignonne, Lobster Soufflé, and Soufflé Grand Marnier; the latter were as puffy and fluffy as clouds over Paris. Enthusiastically suggested for you *and* your wallet. Branches in **Puerto de Sóller** and **Puerto Andraitx**.

Samantha's (Plaza Mediterráneo) is attracting legions of transients from Nice to Nantucket, as well as a very loyal home-town following. Her décor is outstanding, not only in the small, discreetly sited bar, but in the diminutive, 25-table dining salon with its softly glowing Tiffany-style lamps. Our only demurrer here is the chef's odd penchant for undermining his own best efforts—as he did when our excellent Gigot of Lamb arrived with canned beans. When the skilleteer becomes as organized as the friendly and professional reception, this chic challenger should be truly worthy. Open from 1 P.M. to 3:30 P.M. and from 8 P.M. to midnight. Closed Sunday.

Outside of Palma proper, but still in the city's foraging zone, 2 spots enjoy great fame, but both, in our opinion, are slipping. One is informal; the other is not. The first is called **Foc i Fum** which means "Fire and Smoke" in Mallorquin. It is located in the hills backing Puerto Andraitx, about 15 minutes from Palma center. This was created by André Surmain, founder of the elegant Lutèce restaurant in New York, who has pulled up stakes and left it in the hands of his lovely but much overworked wife, Nancy. Dining in summer on 2 levels, both under the stars; gas-torch illumination; open kitchen; sun motif on place plates; wine chilled in wooden casks and served from Spanish drinking beakers; now hit-or-miss service. The set meal consists of your own selection of self-sliced viands from a huge wooden press draped with sausages and garnished with olives and other tidbits; then comes your choice of cold or hot soup; the main courses are chiefly variations on traditional Mallorquin classic dishes. You'll probably pay $15 per head. So far, summers only and evenings only, so be sure to reserve in advance. The more formal **Portanova** is located in an exclusive apartment complex of the same name, about 6 miles from Palma on the pike to Palma Nova. Its semicircular dining room affords a stunning bay view from its wide windows; furnishings were chosen in coincident taste with the twenty-first century, comfortable and trim without being aggressive and hard-lined; the attendance used to be one waiter for every client, but now this ratio has fallen off sharply. The menu is copious; the cookery is, to us at least, no long spectacular; the price is perhaps $20 per diner. This one is more dressy than Foc i Fum and it functions year round. Both used to be champions in their own way, but today we don't think they are worth the journey.

La Vileta, 15 minutes out, is a solid, steady, ever-dependable favorite to which we often happily return. It occupies a converted farmhouse which was taken over by Bob Edward's English father many years ago and in which this handsome, knowledgeable son is now the highly personable host. He offers a vast variety of British, French, and Spanish staples, from delicious Quiche Lorraine to Roast Lamb in Rosemary to Beef and Kidney Pie to Paella to a number of his own savory inventions. Of equal interest is the fact that the prices are right; the value is delivered for every peseta expended. Often when we're stuck about places in which we can relax and enjoy (incidently, there's a lovely open-air evening dining terrace in season), we'll turn to each other and say, "Let's go THERE!" Unpretentious, comfortable, and warmly friendly.

The new **Los Gauchos** (San Magin 78) rides in with approximate facsimiles of platters from the South American Chuckwagon. Cultivated pampered-pampas atmosphere spread over 2 small rooms with about 8 tables; savory grills; pseudo-Mexican dishes, flavorful though composed of local ingredients; attentive service with chief honcho Tomas Ruiz holding the reins. A novelty for Palma which seems to be catching on. Though of limited authenticity, our grub was quite recommendable.

The **Duksa Grill** (Paseo Mallorca 22, around the corner from Av. Jaime III) stands tummy-to-tummy with a same-ownership pub next door. Very attractive furnishings on 2 floors, warmhearted maître, and fare which almost (but not quite) lives up to the promise of its decorative flourish. We prefer the subterranean sanctum at dinner time.

The tiny, posh **El Horreo** provides a wondrous vista of the Palma bayscape through its plate-glass window wall. Deluxe interior and service; chilly cafeteria; pool and sun deck open to clients; trying hard. This one is located in the Neptuno building with the easiest entrance via the Plaza Mediterraneo. Satisfactory both by day or by eve.

Ca'n Sophie (better known as Chez Sophie at Apuntadores) is an *enfant de La Belle France*. Shortly after the original Sophie passed on, Odette (of embroidery fame) stitched a fine partnership with Chef Jean. The premises are still simple, spotlessly clean, and pervaded with the warmth and solicitousness which we have always found here. Our twosome repast, including onion soup, snails, sole, and green salad, was as fine an example of French-style home cooking as we've experienced in these parts, and at tabs that are almost a steal. Very solid and sound value. Closed Sunday.

Antonio's, near El Patio, dishes out lackluster fare at almost deluxe tariffs. Attractive surroundings, except for the unusually filthy carpets on our visit; more spacious than its neighbor; fumbling service. Not even the mildest threat to the frontrunners. **Ola's**, nearby, is okay as a steak joint for medium budgets. The menu contains almost anything that Ola himself enjoys—from Swedish meatballs to Mexican chili. Kooky but fun. **Penelope** (Progreso 39) is pleasant to the eye, but her cooking wouldn't lure this Odysseus home from any voyage.

La Casita (Calvo Sotelo 198) is the best American-style restaurant we've found during our 2-decades-plus residence on the island—and IS it a bargain!!! New Jerseyite Jim Mangin and his charming wife Denyse (who speaks perfect English) opened the doors of their sweet little haven in '68; after a year-long closing because of an illness in the family, they have now again parted the portals and are doing a deservedly popular business. Simply furnished room with 10 tables; service bar and immaculate kitchen to the rear; décor as cheerful as the restaurant's extremely friendly and warmhearted proprietors; cassette-taped mood music. Mrs. Mangin supervises the culinary department while her husband carries out his role as Chief Boniface, Chief Barman, Chief

Greeter, and Chief Hawkeye to oversee the comfort of each individual guest. Don't go here for just a hamburger or similar light bite, because it's not a snack bar; the versatile card features both specialties of the U.S. and a few deee-licious Gallic dishes snuck in by Madame. Because the chemical constituents of Spanish flour, dairy products, and other ingredients differ slightly from their stateside equivalents, it is impossible to duplicate the *exact* taste of the originals in a few of the items—but the Mangins are so skillful that they come mighty close! A substantial fixed meal with wine is yours for about $5.50 per appetite; if you decide to live it up by ordering à la carte, you might drop all of $7 or so. The hours are from 1 P.M. to 4 P.M. and 7 P.M. to midnight; it is closed on Tuesdays and for 30 days during January or February when the hardworking owners take their vacation. Advance reservations are advised during the season, especially on weekends. My Nancy and I will always be grateful to Mrs. Louis Schonceit (the universally beloved "Renée Carroll" of Sardi's fame) for tipping us off to this unostentatious little honey. We love it, too!

Galician fare? We're fond of the rough-and-ready **Casa Gallega** (Pueyo 6) in midcity. The ground-floor counter is always jammed; down here you'll also find a few tables; upstairs is for more formal dining. Some platters are heavenly (such as toasted, seasoned medallions of octopus or the tiny eels called *angulas* in oil and garlic), while others are merely excellent. Service can be impudent, but for such splendid gastronomy, try to forget it.

Sa Premsa (Plaza Obispo Berenguer de Palou 13, and branch on Calvo Sotelo) is an unfastidious, downright dirty wine cellar which also serves meals. Big, spartan, noisy; 252-gallon wine tuns ring the walls; service nonstop during the day and the evening. Burly atmosphere and miserable cookery. Nix. **Fonda de Puerto**, on the palm-lined Port Boulevard, blows both hot and chilly. On our latest try it was the latter; this one has very few pretenses in any case. Sidewalk terrace with perhaps 7 tables; simple dining room now made more chipper with gay ceramics and stucco booths. Fair. For fish only, you might want to hook into the ultrabasic **Lonja del Pescado Cantina** (also known as "Pósito de Pescadores" and "Casa Eduardo"), on the middle wharf. Upstairs location; open kitchen; 10-fathom plainness in furnishings (you must ask for a tablecloth if you dislike resting your elbows on fancy plastic); viewless terrace for summer customers; homespun service; bargain-basement tabs; little effort made to give it sparkle, élan, or a beatific glow. To get first crack at the daily catches from the boats that dock downstairs, the management offers the crews a special concession of 2 courses, fruit, and wine for about 50¢. **Portixol**, in the hotel of the same name, looks out on Palma harbor and asks: "Will our marine stew and lobsters, too, ever equal such a view?" Nay, say we!

Italian-French dishes? The recently enlarged **La Pizzeria** (Calle Bellver 22, in Torreno) tops all local contenders by a dozen leagues. Warm reception by tall, smiling Mme. Monique; sizzling-hot platters by Pierre, her mustachioed and stripe-shirted chef-husband; some of the best-tossed salads in the capital; meats so-so to *sí-sí;* terrace with checked tablecloths, candlelit jugs, and rustic country-tavern atmosphere. Here is a darned good restaurant—not a pizza joint, as its name implies. We go here often and enjoy it a lot.

Scandinavian? **Suarta Pannan** (Calle Brondo) is the midcity rendezvous of many Vikings. Spacious booths; chummy atmosphere; selected Nordic fare. Chinese? **Mandarin**, next to the Victoria, was a big disappointment to our chopsticks on an earlier probe, but more recently we've skewered into some passable delicacies here. Like our stick-handling: Off and on. Now no less than 3 competitors have recently opened; not one is worth the effort of going, in our opinion.

The **Bar Formentor**, smack in the center of town, *the* local gin mill, social axis, and home-away-from-home for nearly every American on the island. With its complete change of ownership and staff, however, it is fading by delivering less food and less good cheer for more money. Other light-biteries include **Kais** (on the Borne) **Cafeteria Nacar** (on the Jaime III), **Delta 107**, and **Moby Dick** in Palma Nova. **Yacht Ritz** (Borne) sails in with thin vittles for nickels and dimes. **Cafeteria Marqués** (Marqués de la Cenia 50) flips flavorful Finnish fare.

For luncheon or dinner excursions out of the capital on a sunny day, the fabulous **Son Vida** (15 minutes) offers the most spectacular view; order à la carte only, because the set meals are governed by price controls, which make them somewhat institutional; summer munching by the pool is an especially rewarding experience which we enjoy whenever possible. At *Palma Nova* (7 miles), along the route to Andraitx and conveniently sited near Marineland, **Mesón Son Caliu** bubbles with the delights of the island's regional décor and typical local cuisine, all overseen by Mallorquin Lorenzo Bosch and his British wife, Carol. The setting is sweetly romantic. Closed on Monday except for holidays; always reserve ahead in summer. **Baraka** also is very popular in this district. **Bon Aire**, in *Illetas*, is a fair family target for summer light biting, and loafing by its 4 pools. In the hinterland, the **Hotel Molins** (1 hour), the **Hotel Bendinat** (25 minutes), the **Hotel Villamil** (25 minutes), and **Ca'n Pacienci** (1 hour; see special note below) are the most rewarding. **Hostal Baviera** is charming when the tour-group mobs haven't commandeered it. **Ses Rotges** in *Cala Ratjada* (1 hour) has been improving of late. Now it's back among the favored haunts of the island. The **Ambassador**, just outside *Paguera*, is a pause that refreshes; extensive Deluxe (for Mallorca) menu; prices surprisingly low-key for such high-key cuisine; bleak setting, but a reward for the Inner Man. The **Hotel Cala d'Or** does *not* accept meal-only clients.

A novel dining notion? **Ca'n Pacienci**, in the northwest corner of the island, is a tiny *finca* ("farmhouse") tucked at the end of a short driveway about ⅓rd of the way from *Pollensa* to *Puerto de Pollensa*. The entrance bears a white wooden sign on the left of the main highway. Don't look for formality or uniformed waiters or even menus here. Direct your concierge to phone Pollensa 530-787 a day or 2 in advance to place your reservation and specify your selections. A tack-room bar features a double-faced fireplace which glows into this nook and the cozy dining room which adjoins. Theres also an alfresco garden area for dining or sipping. Extra-careful hosting by Norman and Phyllis Rose, the gracious English couple who own and run it. Here is a perfect target for a lunch *or* dinner excursion; fabulous Painter Michael Huggins' studio (see "Adventure in Art?") is only 3 minutes away. Closed Sunday.

In the daytime especially, you may prefer to launch into a light lunch and libation at **Ca'l Patró**, behind the Hotel Niu at *Cala San Vicente*. Inner and outer eateries keyed to nautical fare with nets and other fish-fetchers; well-stocked bar serving suds to see-worshipers from the beach; a few shells for typical coastal comestibles. Owned by the gentle, softspoken archon of artisanry and local handicrafts, Don Martin Vicens. A handsome kettle.

In *Pollensa* itself, our choices are **Ca'n Juan** and **Sant Jordi**. Both are adequate but not spectacular. P.S.: Parking in this village can generate a size-44 headache.

In *Puerto Pollensa*, the new **Stay**, beside the ferryboat landing, is a knockout by night and a buzz of marine activity by day. Until the dinner hour, you'll find a self-service snack bar, a cafeteria, and a lovely awning-clad or open westerly terrace. After dark diners sit inside or on the bayside embankment where sailing dingies tug at their moorings. Helmsman Don Miguel runs a tight ship; his crew is superb; his galley is first class; and his prices are appropriate for the quality wares he produces from the earth and the sea. We love it any time, any season. **La Lonja**, on the opposite quay, also is a popular dining lodestone in the region. The candlelit tables on the terrace are particularly salubrious on a summer's eve with the moon rising across the bay. Ask for Don Salvador or Don Juan, the coproprietors, both of whom speak American with their tongues and kindness with their souls-*meunière*. At the end of the same quay, the **Puerto Pollensa Yacht Club** turns on some Gallic delights in delightfully fresh surroundings. It is open to the public and prices are lower than at either of its harbormates. Ask for Jeanie or Olga. Very pleasant it is. **Ca Vostra** might please you if you're in the mood for an authentic traditional local feast. For the pick of finny denizens from the eastern end of Mallorca, Juan Petit Paris's **Bar Petit Paris** is unsurpassed. And why not, since this warmhearted entrepreneur owns and operates by far the largest fleet of fishing boats and passenger launches in the area? He, his spry señora, and their son Juan will give you their smiling welcome and never steer you wrong on their recommendations for the day. Plain surroundings, but a winner in maritime skilletry. The expansive **C'an Pep** earns its share of the year-round traffic. Pepe, the jovial *jefe,* does all of the buying, oversees the cooking, and greets the clients. His fish soup and his full-bodied Paella are especially laudable. **El Cano** is the new creation of a young Danish-German couple (Lisa and Johan) who offer different cuisine for the islanders, including a delicious smörgåsbord about once a month. **El Pozo**, for years the sophisticated pacesetter of the village, has now become the domain of an ex-employee of the Hotel Formentor. Although Sr. Luis has introduced a number of even more cosmopolitan touches (not listing prices on guest menus, for instance), at this writing serious problems remain in the kitchen and in the fact that he seems to be understaffed. We're pulling hard that he will soon grasp sufficiently firm control so that his venture no longer can be more appealing to the eye than to the palate. The **Chequered Flag** unfurls its victory banner along the road to Pollensa, 2 gear shifts from the center of town. Discreet mélange of racing and rustic themes that might be described as Indianapolitan-Mallorquin. Britain's Meg and Geoff Basden are 2 of the most warm and likable bonifaces on the island. Open daily in season.

Several manor houses (variously prefixed with the word *Son* or *Ca'n* in the island dialect) have been opened to the public with what we'd term, for want of a better word, "barbecue dining" as the feature. The farm fare is simple, but the fun and the food are genuine. Here are a few recommendable manorisms: The **Moli d'es Compte** ("The Count's Windmill") is situated on the main pike from *Palma* to *Puigpuñent*; **Son Gual** is on the same route; **Son Amar** is a 6-minute drive from the capital on the *Valldemosa* road; **Son Termes** stokes its stoves along the lane to *S'Esglaieta*; **Ses Cullidoras** resides at *Sollerich* on the way toward Oriente.

Our sunny-day excursion favorite—though the cuisine leaves heaps to be desired—is the cliff-high **Es Grau**, teetering 1000 feet above the Mediterranean, about 1 hour from Palma, 9 miles past Andraitx; head for the Mirador Ricardo Roca. Its sunset orientation glories with 35 terrace-sited tables plus 20 more in the interior salon. Service harried but kind; bus tours abounded. In July and August it's open from 8 A.M. to 10 P.M. closing 2 hours earlier the rest of the year. For eyeful, sighful, my-oh-myful sightseeing, this slice of heaven is tough to top.

NIGHTCLUBS In *Palma*, **Tito's** has emerged as one of the most spectacular showplaces on the European after-dark circuit today. *Don't miss it!* Two long shows nightly in season often feature some of the entertainment world's top talent. Magnificent, transparent, covered multitier patio (removable in summer); former winter club converted into chic inner sanctum; no entrance fee or minimum charge; first drink very steep, with future libations for much, much, much less; excellent orchestra for dancing and cabaret; well-dressed clientele. Entrepreneur Tony Ferrer is a ranking impresario in the nighttime leagues; few have mastered the nocturnal arts as well as this gentleman. Here's an attraction rivaled only by Pavillon in Madrid for warm-weather gaiety.

The **Tagomago**, in the Porto Pi area, is a very poor second, in our opinion. This converted, newly refashioned country farmhouse, with its huge, 4-tier, dimly lit garden, has a seating capacity of more than 1000 on its split-level summer terrace. Its founders are the Los Valldemosa (the top musical assemblage in the Balearics, who now appear at Jack El Negro's which is reviewed below); on our recent visit, the "show" consisted of one comedian who spoke for 66 nonstop minutes—every word of it in Spanish. Unattractive, red-lined, L-shape interior; savory spit-roasted chicken and other taste-ticklers; bouncy orchestra for dancing; youngish clientele; tabs about the same as the above Ti-totals. As at Tito's, *reserve in advance.*

My Own Place is columnist-commentator Riki Lash Lazaar's $60,000 investment in warm intimacy and fun—backed by a stunningly panoramic sweep of Palma Bay. The irrepressible Riki welcomes all guests and puts many on his radio show—with special speakers beamed into "MOP." Here is a delightful drop-in spot at any time from 7 P.M. to 3 A.M. for handholders, for lonely-spirits who are bored with institutional-style impersonality, and for nightowls who seek relaxed respite in a glorious setting. He is such a gracious host that you should have the feeling you're an honored member of his "club" within 5 minutes. Our only demurrer here concerns the libations, which we think could be a mite more potent. Cheers and salutes!

Jartan's is a notch down the scale; not too long on the Palma nightscape, but moving up steadily. **Jack El Negro's**, in Los Valldemosa's camp, is a big open-air establishment which offers a windmill, long bar, and small red-clothed tables with captain's chairs, plus a splendid view of the harbor. Young Antonio is the cheerful and obliging barman. Cool, clean, and recommended. **Kalcutta** runs a show plus dancing sequences. **Globo Rojo** features international cabaret and other typical nocturnal delights.

Rosales is a favorite of the middle-class Mallorquin family, often with kids and all; alfresco in warm weather; small cabaret aclatter with fairly good flamenco.

Palma has gone discothèque happy—and the throb of ones that we've recently inspected is still ricocheting off our rim-shot eardrums. At the top, **Barbarela** seems to be edging out **Alexandra's**. Both do their zingy thing in the latest mod mood. **Socaire**, in Tito's, is possibly the most attractive. The theme is nautical and lovely; the atmosphere is deluxe. The **Club de Mar** also draws skippers and mates for grog and reeling. **La Rueda Numero Uno** has rolled up as a big wheel in town for those on the night trail. **Zhivago** is the loudest. The entrance charge buys your first drink; the pre-Columbian décor *(sic)* has been mutated, but not muted, into a Russian theme. Side dishes of borsch and caviar, perhaps to steppe up the taste buds; occasional appearances by top English recording stars; fresh ventilation, but ambiance hotter than an 8-alarm fire. **Rodeito** is a much cozier swinger. So is **Tiffany**, which glitters with 2 bars and a series of raised and sunken dancing squares (the *décor,* that is). **The Lord Nilsson** seems to have recruited a shipload of followers. It's keener than most on promotion. **Crazy Daisy** and **Bavaria**, down the street from the Hotel Victoria, are back-to-back and belly-to-belly, mass-over-class jernts which we find crass. Entrance chit gets you a drink in either section. **Teacher's Whisky-A-Gogo** is a well-aired cave where you'll pay about $1.50 to enter and to sip the Iberia-bred drink included in this price (a Teacher's Highland Fling costs half as much again). So-so-A-Go-Go.

String pickin's? **The Guitar Center**, strums up regular musical evenings, beginning at 9:30, for serious but funloving aficionados of the instrument. We recently enjoyed a concert here by Gene and Francesca Raskin (composer and artists of the smash hits "Those Were The Days" and "Hello Love"). Other equally big-time greats of the musical whirl-d also pop in to add their talents to the sessions. Victorian-flea-market atmosphere. Highly recommended for sips and salubrious sounds.

TAXIS   Ah—*Those* Were The Days when the drivers used to be sweet-natured, helpful, and honest. Now, unfortunately, the tourist migration has made many of them sour, rude, and dishonest—even to the point, on occasion, of extracting their own tips. *Watch them carefully, and do not pay 1 céntimo more than the metered tariffs* (plus possibly any supplements which should be printed on a card which the driver can provide). If they object, demand they drive you to the nearest *comisaría.* Tip 5 to 10 pesetas for the average haul.

CAR HIRE   for self-drive autos, 1 and only 1 is recommended in the capital: **Empresa Garaje Vidal** (Av. A. Rosello 56); new or nearly new Seats (Spanish Fiat) and Renault Dauphines at moderate tariffs are the specialty. Owners

Don Andrès and Don Antonio Darder, cheerful and friendly brothers who speak English, will see you are given rapid, painless, and conscientious service. In other outfits you're likely to find grinding-gear jalopies or only motor scooters. Wild horses couldn't drag us on any of them. So many U.S. friends have had road failures, blowouts, and other troubles with inferior dealers—plus the fact local driving is so very hazardous for first-timers—that none is advised. You may hire a chauffeur-driven sedan from your hotel for perhaps $35 per day—not too bad if you split it with another couple. Personally, we often use a courteous, kindly pilot named **Antonio Jaime** (Reina M. Cristina 40, tel.: 12–444); his language facility is limited, but his heart is not. On the other side of the island, we are impressed with the kindness and efficiency of **Autos La Parra** (Calle Juan XXIII, Tel. 75, Puerto de Pollensa). It's owned and operated by a local consortium of young mechanics and hotel concierges; it's fleet of more than 80 SEATS is kept in tip-top condition. Please ask for Angel, Gregorio, or José-Maria. Recommended.

TIP: If you have any problems concerning car ownership in Spain (or Europe), shipment home of your lizzie, American technical specifications, or retirement abroad and the most economical way to go about licensing your family vehicles, go immediately to the previously mentioned Don Antonio Darder who makes an extra-special effort to help readers of this *Guide*. This gentleman has gone so far as to provide his personal office telephone number (Palma 21–75–60) for your convenience. His town headquarters, where he is the Ford agent, is **Motor Balear S.A.** at Aragon 2; the modern service center (Talleres Darder, with 53 mechanics, no less) is in the *Polygono* industrial suburb on Avenida Asima. For anything from Spanish tourist plates to a brass ooga-horn, this good friend and brilliant young administrator is the accelerator who will speed you to your destination with the least possible trouble.

TRAINS   Electric service to Sóller, and Lionel-size miniatures operated on diesel oil or almond shells to Inca, Manacor, and other points.

AIR AND SEA TRAVEL   **Iberia** provides most of the muscle in Mallorca's air bridge, lots of it stretching between Madrid or Barcelona and Palma. British Airways, SAS, Lufthansa, Swissair, KLM, Sabena, Air France, Air Algeria, and many more offer direct service from their respective capitals to Palma; some are summer only. Aviaco, an Iberia subsidiary, wings passengers around the islands and the mainland. We repeat: *Every flight on every airline is nearly always crowded;* nail down your tickets early, or you might be stuck for several frustrating days.

Son San Juan, the island's jet airport, is only 10 minutes from your Palma doorstep via the new multimilliondollar speedway. In season, the Saturday and Sunday crush when most charter flights arrive and depart (despite their own new detached building) must be seen to be believed. Great balls of lightning, WHAT a human zoo it becomes! The restaurants are wickedly overpriced and poor. Expect a somewhat disenchanting first impression of Mallorca.

Trasmediterránea has a sizable fleet of steamers which originate at Barcelona, Alicante, and Valencia and cover the major islands. There are noon and midnight summer sailings daily (except Thurs. and Sun., when the night run doesn't function) between Barcelona and Palma, less frequent winter service between Barcelona and Palma, a weekly run between Alicante and Palma (stepped up to 3 times per week from July to Sept.), a hitch linking Valencia and Palma 4 times every 7 days, thrice-weekly service between Ibiza and Palma year round, and once-a-week service between Valencia–Ibiza and Alicante–Ibiza. In addition, you'll find twice-weekly links between Palma and Menorca, plus a twice-a-week sailing between Alcudia (Mallorca) and Menorca. Finally, there's a more venerable gal between Palma and the rock-dot of Cabrera each Friday, year round.

Two good ships are in service between Palma and Barcelona. The *Juan March* and her sister, *Ciudad de Compostela,* are the slick chicks on the Balearic beat. Sometimes they alternate with their twins, *Santa Cruz de Tenerife* and *Los Palmas de Gran Canaria,* which normally frequent the Canary Island lanes. These beauties can accommodate as many as 750 passengers and 130 automobiles; they cruise at 21 knots. If you can afford it, book First-class cabins; they're worth the difference; on any of the other older steamers, ask for Deluxe or semi-Deluxe accommodations. The lounges in the younger barks are gracious; the food is ample, badly cooked, well served, and amazingly inexpensive; the bars are friendly. In summer, other ferries are brought in to supplement these graceful newcomers between Palma–Alicante and Palma–Valencia. Still newer equipment has been tied into the Málaga–Melilla–Almería loop, but these are lighter babies than the fleet's star performers.

The vessels to Ibiza and Mahón (Menorca) also soon will be replaced by smart cruisers.

Ybarra, the route of the "Blue Kangaroo," offers 7- to 8-hour Barcelona–Palma shuttles aboard the *Cabo San Sebastián,* a sleek hippity-hopper pouching up to 1000 passengers and 110 autos. It glides in each direction 3 times per week and from previous experience aboard "Kangaroo" Ships, we can recommend this one.

Naviera Aznar, represented by the personable and dynamic Miguel Puigserver of Palma, has inaugurated a roll-on ferry service between Alcudia and Port Vendres on the French Mediterranean. The modern carrier can take 750 passengers and 250 cars on the 10-hour voyage—a real time and energy saver for zips to and from the Continent.

Don't, for heaven's sake, take deck passage on *any* overnight sailing, regardless of circumstances. The bigger ships offer air-line style chairs (120 to 250 of them!) in enclosed dormitory-like salons; they're clean enough, but when full they're a jungle. The others sleep passengers in open, maritime discomfort. We repeat: Get a stateroom—it will provide you with a delightful cruise, in miniature, on the Mediterranean.

A minicruise? We recently disembarked from a delightful passage aboard one of the **DFDS Seaways** twin sister ships, *Dana Sirena* and *Dana Corona.* Departure was from our Mallorca home (Palma port), east to Genoa, and south to Patras on the northern Peloponnesus. In a nutshell, it was heaven on waves! These sparkling Danish drive-on car ferries (which take passengers

without wheels, too, of course) are so well designed, so beautifully maintained, and so smartly operated that here is one of the finest maritime bargains
we've found on the 7 seas. Versatile accommodations; superb Scandinavian
cuisine plus Italo-international cookery either in the pay-as-you-go deluxe
dining salons or in the cheerful cafeterias; tax-free gift shops; low-cost bars;
hairdressers; ample deck space. Although these function efficiently for continental motorists, in reality they add up to small but excellent cruise ships with
bargain rates for what they offer. Genoa is a particularly convenient base for
most European visitors. Recommended with heartiest salutes for a soul-
soothing interlude in anyone's journey.

Finally, a link between Marseille–Palma–Algiers has been forged for summer cruising aboard the French vessels *El Djeizair, Pte. de Cazalet,* and the
car ferry *Avenir.* (Caution: Many autos are stripped en route.) Check with
your travel agent for last-minute progress on these, as well as exact schedules
for the Europe-to-Africa runs.

DRINKS   Mallorquin specialties are *palo* (originally made from the bark
of the Peruvian quina tree), which is the islander's favorite beverage neat or
highball-style, and *anis* (the Tunel brand is marvelous). Try them both for
size; they cost pennies, and they're mighty interesting.

THINGS TO SEE   Our candidate for the number one sightseeing attraction used to be the **Caves of Drach** ("Dragon") at **Porto Cristo**, 40 miles
on good roads from the capital. Underground music that's now so corny
you'll probably have to stifle your giggles; a gimmicky boat ride on an eerie
underground lake; worth the time, if you don't get stuck in one of the
interminable queues which sometimes stack up at its water section. Bus
excursions from Palma at regular intervals. **Artá** also has awesome caves;
Campanet has them in miniature. Beyond Drach, about 4 miles toward
Cala Millor, you kiddies from 6 to 96 shouldn't miss the **Auto-Safari**, a
40-acre spread of flamingoes, swans, giraffes, rhinos, and 400 species of bush
animals which wander the fields as you drive by to nod good-day. The paved
route is almost 2 miles long; top speed is 6 mph.; passengers are prohibited
from leaving the protection of their cars. If you are in this region and love
God's critters as much as we do, this can be much more fun than a barrel
of Drachs.

Next most rewarding, in our opinion, is the junket to **Formentor**, with
a stop on the return trip to see the Mallorquin dancers at the little hamlet
of **Selva**. Best scenery and best dancers on the island. Regular excursions
Tuesdays and Fridays (other days in summer, too).

In the capital, the magnificent, privately financed, multimillion-dollar **Auditorium** is the most impressive cultural magnet of the Balearics. If you're
music-hungry, be sure to check the programs and schedules during the time
of your visit. Here's a fabulous *coup* for the island—and you!

In the north, the village of **Pollensa** sponsors a **Music Festival** during
July and August. Such virtuosi as Segovia, Szeryng, Spierer, Ricci, Rubinstein, Stern, and Richter have given full-evening concerts in the charming
art-filled cloister of the Santo Domingo Church. Any concierge on the island

probably can arrange tickets for you. The prices are laughably low and the rewards are memorably high.

Instant Iberia? Now you can wrap up Granada, Seville, Segovia—the whole shooting match—in one turn through Mallorca's **Spanish Village** ("Pueblo Español"), just outside Palma at **Son Dureta**. Architectural reproductions of typical or famous buildings—private homes, towers, mosques, chapels, patios, and more—from various periods and regions of the nation are represented in a well-constructed, permanent, $5,000,000 street scene. Wonderful! It's only 5 minutes from the center by bus. You'll also find artisan shops, craft stalls, bars, a so-so local-style restaurant and a flamenco nightclub. Here is a curiosity that, for peanuts, could save you pots of pesetas—*if* you don't like traveling (Heaven forbid!).

Marineland makes a glorious splash on the Costa den Blanes, a few minutes out of Palma on the Andraitx road. Trained sea lions, dolphins, and parrots, plus a zooful of other critters, are on hand for the splendid shows, the exhibits, or for just strolling around and chatting with the animal kingdom. Within this seaside compound are myriad recreational facilities, rides, play parks, a restaurant, a snack terrace, an aquarium—enough to keep mom, dad, and all the brood engaged for many happy hours. Public Relations Director Roberto Bennett knows very well that the best show on earth is the earth and its residents. Some of our globe's most lovable companions are here just waiting to extend a paw, a claw, or a flipper in everlasting friendship. Recommended, as one beastie to another.

Petra, about 1½ hours by car from the capital, offers a dot of territory which is an official part of the State of California—the house of the great Junipero Serra, who founded 21 missions on our West Coast and who changed the history of our Pacific area. The home is surprisingly small and sparsely furnished, but it reflects an interesting picture of eighteenth-century Mallorquin living; the nearby Museum Center of Studies contains paintings and books referring to this indomitable pioneer. If you've got time on your hands and adventure in your blood, you may take the Toonerville train (narrow gauge) which pokes through the heart of the island to this little village; culture-minded motorists find it a convenient detour en route to the Drach Caves excursion. Especially appealing to Californians.

Valldemosa, the monastery where George Sand and Chopin once wintered, is what we consider a 21-karat tourist trap. While this famous couple were here, there was such mutual antipathy between them and the natives that they left the island under a cloud; now, however, the shrewd locals have "re-created" (to use a kind word) a shrine to these beloved historical characters —almost 100% for foreigners, who swarm through the phonied-up premises by the thousands upon thousands. The view is magnificent; the overcommercial atmosphere isn't. Clever job of "reconstruction," though, so long as the spectator realizes the width of the gap between "legend" (to be kind again) and fact. Only 11 miles from Palma; plenty of bus trips that stop here and continue to Sóller, which is pleasant from a scenic point of view. If you're bored and hungry, zip over to the Valldemosa Country Club for a pastoral repast and a batch of tall cool drinks. Anyone may drop in for a meal or nip; you also may reserve in advance by telephoning 17100. Extra-nice if you hate sightseeing. Look for the signs, 2 miles out of the hamlet on the road to Bañalbufar. (Summer only).

The **Krekovic Collection**, devoted to Inca art and culture, is on display at **Son Fusteret**, about a mile from the center of Palma on Calle de Eusebio Estada, or the old road to Buñola. The subjects are monumental and (though the collection is specialized) are so linked to Hispano-American folklore that we think most travelers who have been lured to Iberia would appreciate this fascinating exhibition as much as we do. Open every day but Sunday.

The top **beaches** are at Formentor, Magaluf, Paguera, Cala d'Or, and San Vicente (beware of undertow at the latter during certain sea conditions).

A nip into North Africa? Viajes Iberia (see "Information and Assistance") flies day-long junkets to Algiers and Tunis (every day in season to the former and twice weekly to the latter); the planes are somewhat cramped and lumbering DC-6s, but it's a short flight. Our recent 9:15 A.M. to 6:30 P.M. hop to Algiers included visits to the Botanical Gardens, Casbah, a mosque, lunch at a resort outside the city, and an hour's shopping (goods are shoddy and expensive). Jumping the tour is not encouraged, but is permitted, if you want to prowl on your own; bring your best French or Arabic. The trip to Tunis is much the same; it includes lunch at the Hilton and some roamin' through Carthage. Cholera shots are required to reenter Spain. Different and fun.

INFORMATION AND ASSISTANCE The **Spanish Tourist Office** branch is on the Borne in *Palma*; Director José Luis González Sobral and his staff are friendly and knowledgeable. Since no bookings or itinerary arrangements can be made here, we always use **Agencia Schembri, Viajes Marsans**, or **Viajes Iberia** (not to be confused with Iberia Airlines; representative of American Express) for tickets or reservations. All three are dependable; see Don Juan Manera at Schembri, Sr. D. Martorell at Marsans, and Don Luis Linares at Iberia; all speak good English and are cordial in the extreme.

Come to Mallorca and the islands, if you can. To millions of overseas visitors, including us, who have already basked in their sun and their charms, they offer one of the outstanding travel targets of the world.

ADVENTURE IN ART? If you're headed toward Formentor or Puerto de Pollensa—or if you're seeking an unusual excursion—be sure to stop en route at the studio of Michael Huggins, the internationally renowned and beloved artist. Connoisseurs including German industrialist Gunther Sachs, opera-TV star Patrice Munsel, ICI tycoon Lord Clitheroe, former U.S. Ambassador Frederick Nolting, Mrs. Florence Kriendler and Brig. Gen. Malcolm K. Beyer of the "21" restaurant family, the Freddie Heinekens of Dutch brewing, the dancing Arthur Murrays, the Duchess of Windsor, Princess Pignatelli d'Aragón, and Impresario Stanley Black have snapped up his stunning work. No "abstract" dribs-and-drabs for *this* master; his luminous gold-leaf wonders, startling *trompe-l'oeil* realisms, and still lifes warm almost anyone's walls, eyes, and soul. (We know, because our own house is full of 'em!) Take the *inland* road to the "Big" Póllensa *(not the bay road to Puerto de Pollensa)*. Just past Pollensa and Km. Marker #53, the sign "CA'N

XINO" points up a tiny road to the right. If you telephone Pollensa 530386 for an appointment (please don't drop in unannounced), this charming Englishman and his beautiful wife will be happy to invite friends of this *Guide* for a chat and a look through the studio. Less than 1 hour from Palma; one of the happiest "finds" in this whole book.

PERSONAL SERVICES   Beauty parlor? My Nancy is happiest with the salon at the Hotel Victoria.

Sauna, massage, and physical beautification? **Don Abel González**, Spanish Olympic judoist and gymnast, master-muscles the handsomely rebuilt Therapeutic Institute of Obesity and Aesthetics (Monserrat 6). He also answers personal calls to the Victoria, Fénix, Son Vida, and Formentor hotels. Wet steam, dry steam, facials, electric or wax depilage, the works—all under medical direction. Three types of massage (aesthetic, athletic, and medical) are given by him and his 4 other experts for about $12. It is the only establishment of its type in the nation in which all services are individual and by appointment; ask your concierge to call 214452. This engaging and very competent young man is the best masseur we've met anywhere, including Scandinavia; he has pummeled the Fielding ménage and their guests for many years, and we're all very fond of him. A sure cure for tense, weary, or hung-over pilgrims.

Movies in English? Watch the *Bulletin* (see "Things to Buy") for the programs at **Cine Regina** (Teniente Mulet, Terreno). Usually middle-aged but classic films are shown. On that odd evening when you can't decide between the beach or the bar, see the Late-Late Show (9:30 P.M.) before you begin your night-beat beguine.

THINGS TO BUY   *Palma* is the shopping center; the choicest merchandise is here. If you cover the following shops, each tops in its specialty, you'll see the best Mallorca offers:

La Casa del Hierro (Calle Victoria 22) has striking wrought-iron bric-a-brac.

Casa Bonet is to needlework what the Rolls-Royce is to cars—except for its fantastic price values. The Spanish Art Commission recently permitted it to open its beautiful new headquarters at Puigdorfila 3 in Palma's heartland of National Historical Monuments; an outlet on the ground floor of the Hotel Palas Atenea (Paseo Maritimo) also has just opened its doors. For nearly a century, during which it was the official purveyor to the Spanish Royal Court, Casa Bonet has won consistently every Exposition Gold Medal in sight, and has spread the fame of Mallorquin hand embroidery all over the globe. The artistry of its 350 island specialists cannot be duplicated anywhere else today; its museum is an Aladdin's Cave of musical scores, Chinese calligraphy, and intricate etchings exquisitely duplicated by needle. The array of bridge sets, tablecloths, placemats, runners, and the like—every stitch done by hand, in plain or colorful patterns—is (adjective applied literally) sensational. And the monogrammed sheets—well! New pride of the house is its even-lower-price, exclusive, perfectly executed line of machine-made linens of highest quality; as one example of this unique Bonet process, a 118-x-72-inch tablecloth with

12 dinner-size napkins is only from about $54 as well as wash-and-wear from about $45 for the same size ($85 up in individual needlework). For men, one special suggestion for sartorial distinction: Class AAA linen handkerchiefs, *with your own signature or choice of 200 monogram styles, for around $2.50* —a $20 value on Fifth Avenue. Don Alfredo Bonet, the global King of Embroidery, masterfully reigns over his fabulous monarchy. Ask for Señorita Caty on the Hotel Palas Atenea premises. Lovely branches in Madrid and Marbella (see "Things to Buy" in chapter on Spain). Super-super.

Pearls? Caution!! There is only one—we repeat, *one*—founder, developer, and leader of this island industry, which this company has almost singlehand-edly made world-famous. The name is Perlas Majorica (don't confuse it with "Majorca" or "Mallorca")—and be SURE to look for its "Official Agency" seal. Others are rank imitators whose products might (and often do!) chip, fade, and lose their luster within weeks or months after purchase. But Perlas Majorica finally hit the jackpot in 1952 with a revolutionary discovery which so closely resembles genuine first-rank pearls that it's difficult for anyone but an expert to tell them apart. Their iridescence and luster are perfect and unalterable. They laugh at perfumes, humidity, perspiration, and changes of temperature. They come in bluish-white, cream-rose, and grayish-black. Every individual Perla Majorica carries a unique 5-year International Certificate of Guarantee which you may present in the U.S. or nearly 50 other countries. Their sizes, also flawless, run from 4 to 14 millimeters in diameter—offering so many hundreds of combinations either strung or in ear clips, pins, and rings that most U.S. pilgrims end up buying several pieces. And the prices! For *exactly* the same Perlas Majorica exported globally, you'll pay a piddling $24 to $85 here. If you're making an island excursion, don't fail to make the fascinating circuit of the factory at Vía Roma 52 or its new shop opposite, in **Manacor**, or alternately to stop in at the big, glittering, downtown retail store at Plaza Rector Rubi 8 (beware of steerers, imitators, and fakers in this city). But if your visit is limited to **Palma**, its lovely shop is at Av. Jaime III 11 (just off the Borne, the main street), where you should ask for sweet Manageress Antonia Girbau. While there, take a gander at the new line of Joyas Majorica, semiprecious stones set in silver. Yum, yum! But don't be a sucker for the oceans of cheap "Majorca pearls" you'll see everywhere; buy *only* Perlas Majorica to be safe.

Top jewelers? **Sanz** (Plaza Pio XII 26, at inland end of the central Borne Promenade) is Spain's traditional leader of the Classic School, with gorgeous things; it has branches in all principal Spanish cities, in France, and in New York. In Palma, you will be welcomed by 2 of the warmest, kindest, most delightfully friendly mortals on this Isle of the Calm—Director Don Francisco de la Torre and his sweet English assistant, Mrs. Lesley Thomas. **Plateria Mallorca** (Plaza Rosalio 4—ask for Bartolomé, José, or Thomas Miró) and **Gregory** (Avenida Jaime II plus Serrano 92 in **Madrid**) and down the scale from Sanz. In each you will find everything from inexpensive charms to pieces priced at an Emperor's ransom. All 3 merit their sterling reputations.

Enchanting Oriental handicrafts and boutiques? The **Manila** chain is the 12-year-old creation of Philippine gentlelady Mrs. Conchita Zethelius, who, at 45 after severe financial reverses, moved to Mallorca first to sell toys at $23 per month. From her original doll-size mart, through her genius she is now the endearing suzerain of a miniempire of 5 large and enormously successful shops. Twin hubs are the **Manila Import** sisters (Paseo Mallorca 4 and Av. Jaime III 6), proudly featuring exquisite Philippine, Taiwanese, Hong Kong, Chinese, Indian, and Thai placemats, women's blouses, Barong Tagalog shirts, laquered tea services, brass coffee tables, kimono-style dresses, jeweled elephants, and dozens of other beautiful Oriental treasures. **Manila High Selections** (Brossa 2) and ultra-exclusive **Manila Prestigio** (Tous y Maroto) are specialized boutiques. **Rodier** (Av. Jaime III 11) has the complete Spanish-manufactured Rodier sportswear line at 25% to 30% less than elsewhere in Europe. Astonishingly low prices; worldwide shipment; ask for the lovely "Mrs. Tina" in person. Heavenly, heavenly!

Unusual custom-made jewelry? **Pablo** Fuster of **Relojería Alemana** (Calle Colón 40) is the youngest man ever to win Spain's coveted National Handicrafts Award—and he deserves it, think we. Please don't miss this fine artist's display in his shop or in either the Hotel Palas Atenea or the Hotel Valparaiso. Cheers!

Spain's best leather? Incomparable **Loewe** (see "Things to Buy" in Madrid) has now opened a branch at Paseo del Generalíaimo.

Suède? After 25 years of research as residents of the island, we have yet to find one outlet which completely satisfies us. None of the much-touted factories and shops for antelope or suède in *Inca*, center of this industry, appeals to us much. Incidentally, most of the cheaper lines are so poorly dyed that the color will stain your hands and your body. You might be the rare, rare buyer who has the luck to benefit by hitting a once-in-a-blue-moon high-quality processing run; with 1 exception, so far we haven't. *Pink* (Av. Jaime III 15) has a reasonably smart display of coats and suits; they make all of the necessary alterations. The honest people here advise against buying black because it, too, runs. Our lone flower in this desert.

Glass? **Gordiola** (Calle Victoria 8) is internationally famous for its regional glassware of all types. After several years of small-town administration in big-town *Palma*, it pulled up its socks to a laudable degree. We are not yet certain that its packing procedures for shipment are up to scratch, but recent reports on this aspect are favorable. In any case, here is the finest quality and most outstanding selection on the island. As an alternate, a visit to the glass factory at *S'Esglaieta* (Valldemosa road) might well be worth your time. We do not like the prices, attitudes, or swarms of bus traffic at the much-advertised *Campanet* center.

Antiques? **Linares** (near the Cathedral) rules the roost. It is a branch of the celebrated Madrid pacesetter, and both its stocks and its physical plant are in exquisite taste. So far ahead that no competition on the island can touch it. Our special salutes go to its old Spanish pieces from $5 up.

Newspapers? The *International Herald Tribune* is available at better hotels and newsstands. More fun is the English-language, American-idiom *Mallorca Daily Bulletin.* It will probably be presented to you with your breakfast, or you'll find it at the hotel desk for the taking. If not, any kiosk will sell you this local, action-packed Clarion for a few pesetas. Jammed with island happenings; expert columnizing by gentle, universally esteemed "Benito" and irrepressibly fun-filled, charming Riki Lash Lazaar, whose My Own Place we describe so lovingly in the "Night Clubs" section; more habit-forming than "Peanuts." Although it might be a wee bit short on hard-news reportage, who cares? Here's a colorful souvenir of your Mallorquin meanderings.

Dedicated shophounds? Space is too tight here for further listings—so consult this year's vastly expanded and updated purse-size edition of *Fielding's Shopping Guide to Europe* for more stores, more details, and more lore.

Monaco

Monaco, 9 miles east of Nice, has a higher population density (over 40 thousand per square mile) and a smaller total area (370 acres, or 0.58 square miles) than any other nation in the world. It is just about half the size of New York's Central Park. The correct pronunciation is "MON-a-co," not "Mon-AH-co."

Ruled by members of the Grimaldi family since the late thirteenth century, it has been an independent state—almost unbelievable in Europe—since 1415. This remarkable dynasty—"Seigneurs" until 1621, when they became "Princes"—has reigned for more than 5½ centuries. Louis II died in 1949; his successor is a grandson whose name is familiar in deepest Idaho, Nepal, and the Congo—Prince Rainier III. This handsome young nobleman was called the World's Most Eligible Bachelor until his storybook romance and marriage with Grace Kelly—a royal fairytale, moreover, that since has produced a little prince (Albert) and 2 princesses (Caroline and Stéphanie).

The Principality is divided into 4 distinct sections: Old Monaco (a tiny antiquated village which sits on The Rock), La Condamine (home of many amiable Monégasques), Fontvieille (the new, expanding industrial complex), and Monte Carlo (named for Charles III in 1866). Don't confuse the last with the others, because Monte Carlo is a very small part of a very small land.

Each year 1½-million tourists come to the terraced hills and azure waters of Monaco, to play golf or tennis, to tie up their yachts, or to laze in the gentle sun by day and to dine, drink, dance, or gamble by night. The Monte Carlo Golf Club perches on the 2700-foot cap of neighboring Mont-Agel in France. Its 18 holes are scattered in the mountains in such a spectacular way that if the player carelessly stepped off the fairway to make a niblick shot, he might suddenly find himself doing a slow breast stroke in the sea. The Monte Carlo Country Club offers 20 championship tennis courts, several squash courts and practice courts, an attractive clubhouse, and the fabled "Easter Open Tennis

Tournament," one of the outstanding sports events of the year. For sailboat, motorboat, water-skiing, fishing, and skin-diving enthusiasts, the Yacht Club de Monaco has major interest. For skeet and electric-target fans, the Shooting Stand Rainier III is so fine that it's the site of the International Championship Meet in February.

In '67, as soon as the Royal Couple forced Aristotle Onassis to turn over all of his holdings in the mighty *Société des Bains de Mer,* which owns and operates 4 hotels, 18 restaurants, nightclubs, and the legendary Casino, Monte Carlo was launched on her glorious rebirth. A titanic national modernization plan was inaugurated, backed by the Prince's government and local private capital. Some 50 acres of new construction (1/6th of the country!) has been completed. To start, a great chunk of the 90-thousand square yards of avenue Princesse-Grace, reclaimed from the sea, is blooming as a flower-lined boulevard. An Olympic-caliber swimming pool has been excavated in front of the quai Albert Ier to supplement the terraced one at the Hôtel Métropole and the turquoise jewel at the Hôtel de Paris. Almost a score of new skyscrapers (some of them 30 stories tall) have been built. In conjunction with London sources, a 5-year, $72,000,000 project comprising the construction of 6 hotels, a 1000-seat conference center, a marina, restaurants, bars, swimming pools, shops, entertainment facilities, a tourist casino, a Disneyland-type operation, a dolphinarium, nightclubs, and underground parking, is in negotiation. Drilling crews spent 7 years burrowing a 2½-mile tunnel which now eliminates all surface railroad tracks from the landscape. A spankingly modern station has been unveiled, with a gleaming exposition hall and congress hotel spanning the former rail hub. The present harbor is being enlarged for major vessels, and a new yacht harbor and land site in Fontvieille is being carved out. A patch of Mediterranean has just been filled in for helicopter service to and from the Nice International Airport and the private landing strip at Cannes. More than 1-million acres of undersea ground will be converted into a ½-mile bathing beach, part of which will be a costly underwater "dam" to retain the sand for your tootsies. Loews, the American hotel chain, staked a $100,000,000 bet in unwrapping a 650-unit hotel-apartment complex here. The scope of the SBM's expansion activities, which currently involve 29 separate operations, is breathtaking. On its boards are 2 new hotels; an absolutely enormous new center for galas has been unveiled in the Larvotto area as a part of the reborn $7,000,000 Summer Sporting Club (with its own casino, of course). If you are a guest in an SBM hostelry, you may receive a "passport" admitting you to 5 Monte Carlo sports facilities free of charge. Here is an extraordinarily intelligent, vigorous, competent team which has already accomplished miracles and will soon be accomplishing many more.

The key to this revolutionary renaissance is the philosophy of the Crown. By seeking *selected* mass tourism (not the category of cheapjack, collarless racetrack touts and louts)—and by attracting the high-society group simultaneously—Monaco is having its cake and eating it too. It is superbly intelligent thinking which is bearing fruit in both directions. Prince Rainier and Princess Grace, who labor so tirelessly that they would exhaust the average business tycoon, merit hard-earned congratulations for their extraordinary vision and drive.

The economy has also blossomed into a diversity which old-timers find hard to believe. Chemicals, food products, chocolate, beer, plastics, precision instruments, beauty products, glass, ceramics, and printing now contribute between 25% and 30% of the total state revenue. Tourism and companion trades ante another 30%, stamps 8%, and taxes on tobacco and liquors, plus registration fees, provide the lion's share of the rest. The intake from the gambling concession, contrary to popular belief, makes up only about a 4% share—even when there's a good winning year. Unemployment is nonexistent. In '63, Rainier's new constitution gave women the vote—possibly a Grace-note.

The wheels of the world-famous Monte Carlo Casino, which start at 10 each morning (movie houses don't open until 2 P.M.!), have been spinning since 1856. Financially, over a long parade of consecutive years it came up in the red; now it is not only in the black, but it has taken on France's number-one casino in Cannes in blazing competition. Compared to the lush Lido in Italy or Viña del Mar in Chile—even to the neighboring municipal enterprise in Nice—it is still noticeably less glamorous. The French are shoveling their spare francs to the horses or to their own gaming tables, and the English, when they are not patronizing the diminishing British baizeworks, are enduring a period of tighter reined austerity. In general, international businessmen (many of them Italian) and the minimum-ante curiosity seekers have replaced the Russian princes and Imperial ladies of the glittering past. But it's still a *must* to every visitor, because in its heyday there was nothing in the world which approached it.

Radio Monte Carlo and Télé Monte Carlo, the national broadcasting and television stations, are powerful voices which are heard or seen throughout the Continent. A huge transmitter—said to be the world's most electronically potent commercial installation—is plugged in; oddly enough, France owns 83% and Monaco the remaining 17%.

Festivals, fireworks, dog shows, opera, ballet, fencing tournaments, international yacht races, swimming championships, lectures, the latest plays from Paris, religious pageants—these are but a few of the many activities and attractions.

Auto trials seem to hold a special fascination for the Monégasques. The *Grand Prix de Monaco,* first sponsored in 1929 by the national Automobile Club, continues to be the topranking race of all the *Courses dans la Cité.* It is run in May, and it counts toward the official world's driving championship. The annual *Rallye,* held around the last of January, is a particular favorite with Americans. Stock U.S. and European cars start from different points— Oslo, Glasgow, Lisbon, Athens, Frankfurt am Main, Paris, Warsaw, Monte Carlo itself—and "rally" along the way. Each has a handicap which brings him into the pack as the finish is approached. It is a contest of delicate timing and precision roadwork, not exclusively of speed. At the barrier in Monaco, climbing contests are then held on the Principality's steepest highways.

Water skiing is enormously popular; snow skiing may be enjoyed in the French mountains, a few hours away by car.

HOTELS In the **Hôtel de Paris**, one of the 2 or 3 pacesetters within hundreds of miles, the feathers are flying. The client-staff ratio has been reestablished at 1-to-1. In this rambling Edwardian structure are housed sumptuous apartments complete with servants' quarters, the Empire Room restaurant dominated by a colossal Gervais mural painted in 1909, and a cellar of 185-thousand bottles of fine wines (including 35-thousand bottles of vintage champagne). Four additional stories of luxury suites ("La Rotonde") are completely air-conditioned (the overall count is now 90%); illustrious Chef Sebastien Bonsignore's glass-wrapped Grill with its sliding roof and splashes of garnet and blue (dancing nightly) is so airy and elegant on its 8th-floor perch that you'll think you're dining on a superplush transatlantic liner; the entire ground floor and 90 bedchambers were entirely refurbished; the kitchen has been 100% modernized; the beauty salon and barbershop have been changed; a line of top-drawer boutiques glitter in the rear of the lobby. Another stunner is the huge, shell-roofed, oval, heated-seawater swimming pool niched on the cliffside, with its own tunnel connecting directly—the most artistically conceived year-round natatorium we have ever seen. This magnificent installation is augmented by 9 saunas, opulent dressing rooms, a separate bar, and a spacious terrace for swimming and sipping. Superb administration; very, very expensive, but you're almost certain to be wrapped in cotton. There's a wonderful aura of charm about this lively old girl.

The previously mentioned **Loews**, a small city in itself, dips its toes directly into the Mediterranean at the foot of the cliffs below the Grand Casino. It contains its own Las Vegas style gaming room, 3 spectacularly outfitted restaurants including the Folie Russe supper club with cabaret, 3 bars, a revamped discothèque (quite poor at first), a surprisingly small rooftop pool, sauna, boutiques, and terraces with every accommodation. The décor is almost dazzling in its effort to evoke zip, zest, and pizzazz throughout. General Manager Maurice Briquet has an arresting plant with which to work; to fill it he surely will have to take in many groups.

Another newcomer is the 100-unit **Mirabeau,** which is linked to an even larger apartment complex; both segments here face the sea, but some of the finest waterfronters gaze onto a new freeway overpass which occludes the Med. The hotel is graciously clad in costly raiments, reflecting the excellent taste of Swiss Manager Alexander Mehl. Cozy dining spread; superb service; just great, if it weren't for that darned pike's peek.

The **Hermitage,** owned by SBM, has rejoined the competitive fray with élan. Much to our delight, this weed-gone-to-seed has been totally revitalized in its Belle Époque tradition and is coming up curlicues. Revivified public areas; Princess Wing nobly living up to it Grace-cious name; vastly improved restaurant; 140 spic-and-costly nests radiating newborn glamour; gleaming brass beds; tasteful traditional trappings; modern, functional baths; full air conditioning. A bouquet to Manager Georges Maillet, who also cultivates the Old Beach. Heartily recommended, at long, long last.

The **Nouvel**, connected by tunnel under the avenue Princesse Alice, might be called a 100-room annex of the Hôtel de Paris—even though this is not officially correct. Every accommodation with bath, except the maids' rooms (which unfortunate clients are sometimes given in emergencies); all face the bay. *Don't let them shuttle you over here;* since the rates are identical, and since guests must make the cross-country hike to the de Paris dining room, Grill, or bar for their sustenance, most American travelers aren't at all happy in this area. There is talk that the SBM might redo it completely soon, but at this writing it is only talk.

The **Metropole** recently moved into Britain's Grand Metropolitan chain. Today this stately dowager's wrinkles are beginning to tattle on her. Nonetheless, while her makeup is peeling and her limbs are creaky, this grande dame retains many of her former charms. Fine restaurant with combo for dancing; summer bar on a tree-canopied patio; Amazon Bar for thirsting sea-gazers; lovely pool and sun terrace; 3 communicating villas-in-waiting for long-term suitors. Total of 20 suites handsomely done in Louis XV and XVI; 260 rooms which are comfortably bedded but in various stages of decline. Manager Jacques Simone should spruce up this lady posthaste. With her past glories in mind, he can't start soon enough to suit us.

Holiday Inn has unfurled its banner on Larvotto Beach. Ideal location beside the Sea Club; tassled plastic parasols fluttering on the tiny lido; year-round, heated, salt-water pool; lovely, elegant sea-foam-green public rooms; 320 air-chilled doubles with color TV and radio. Bid for a front room only, since the backs overlook a wall and a highway.

The **Old Beach** has 60 rooms (all with air conditioning and bath or shower), 7 bungalows, 200 dressing cabins, 144 cabanas, 34 private solaria, a restaurant, and 3 snack bars. Guests in all the *Société* hotels may use these facilities, but outsiders must pay an admission fee. Much better than it was.

In town, the **Bristol** tops our list of its less luxurious category. Penthouse glass-fronted restaurant with a breathtaking view of the port; sidewalk snackery for quick bites; 30 units with bath and 20 with shower, all with private balcony, full carpeting, and air conditioning; side doubles crushingly small and offering no vista; front twins larger, better, and boasting the azure Mediterranean as their picture windows. Clean and adequate, but less professional than its SBM contenders. Next down the line in appeal come the cold-hearted **Europe** (53 bedchambers with 20 facing or peeking at the sea; pleasant lobby, bar, and remodeled dining salon, but upstairs furnishings scruffy; some baths separated from sleeping areas by curtains only), the **Alexandra** (noisy, mid-nation perch; no restaurant; gaudy appointments; 60% bath/shower count; clean but achingly small-dimensioned), and the quietly situated **Rome** (residential location; more of an inn than a hotel; old-fashioned but well maintained furnishings and fine embroidered linens; attentive hosting by Mr. Bonvin; appealing and viewful for tranquillity seekers; we like it for what it is). The **Balmoral** also boasts a superb vista of the bay and some refashioning, but its rents are considerably higher. **La Réserve Suisse** is now worth considering. Commercially oriented with curtained showers and a fraternity-house atmosphere; very low rates, but hardly a swinger. The **Miramar**, on quai John F. Kennedy, comes up with 14 rooms that are almost in the mast riggings of the yachts tied up at its doorstep. These will seem huge if you've just rolled off your 30-foot sloop, but smallish if you're a landlubber; restaurant 25 steps away. Convenient for docksiders and now very good for its class. **Siècle**, near the station, is ideal for the student exile, but not much for the rest of us; snack bar and terrace restaurant for contemplating the world's problems over an inexpensive Pernod; fun if you're the right age and temperament.

RESTAURANTS Most spectacular, of course, is the **Black Jack Club**, with its big-name international cabaret; it is downstairs at the **Casino**. Go for dinner; the cuisine is good; the music (provided by a 16-piece honey-smooth orchestra during a recent repast) is so delightfully danceable you'll forget that anything such as a Rolling Stone ever existed in the perverse annals of primitive man. In the same class is the **International Sporting Club** (winter); the **Summer Sporting Club**, which now is comprised of the Maona, La Salle des Etoiles, Jimmy'z and Parady'z, plus the gaming rooms and recreation facilities is glamorous to look at, but is it ever expensive—and the food we sampled was not at all noteworthy (big notes, too!). The **Winter Sporting Club** (Dec. 20 to Easter) is open only for major events and entertainments; most fashionable is the Easter Bal Paré dinner, with Christmas, New Year's TV Festival, and Rallye evenings the runners-up. Another offering music at least part of the year is **des Ambassadeurs**. Among worthy hotel candidates, the aforementioned Folie Russe in **Loews** generates excitement and rubles with its high-cost cookery and cabaret; the Empire Room and the Grill of the **de Paris** are both outstanding. **Monte Carlo Beach** also has a luxury restaurant with a pleasant atmosphere. The **Bristol** is okay for cookery.

Rampoldi has fine cuisine, but those tabs—wow! Our flea-size lunch for 2 was gargantuanly priced; we're happy we weren't *really* hungry. Small, well-decorated, partitioned room; service that was professionally meticulous but so glacial, mechanical, and disinterested it chilled our gizzards; to us, this establishment seems to reflect a we-love-money-but-not-the-customers attitude. The cookery, however, is excellent.

Bec Rouge is almost as good, but here, too, the tariffs have jumped so high that we wondered if what we last consumed here was worth it. The slightly sterile atmosphere is softened by flowers; 22 tables inside; 15 on avenue St.-Charles for summer alfresco dining. On earlier visits, every single item on the menu that tickled our appetites had a supplemental charge. Now there's a fixed meal and a full carte of more than 30 items. Young, aggressive M. Roux is your pleasant host.

As for others, **Astoria** appealed to us for its quietly sophisticated ambiance and recommendable cuisine. Bar at the portal with a lone cream-color room farther back; our meal was reasonably priced and appetizing; the house Bordeaux was outstanding; we experienced good service, too. Worth a try. The **Vesuvio** is no big puff of smoke. On The Rock, the **Pinocchio** now seems to enjoy a rock-hard reputation. **La Chaumière**, near the Exotic Gardens, can be marvelous for Mother Nature's scenery but is low on man-made décor; it loads up with so many bus tours in summer that these scenic joys take 30th place. **St. Nicholas**, near the Royal Palace, tried to pass off on us canned paté of wild boar as the fresh variety. Our steak was so thin that it better belonged on a microscope slide in Lab. 32. Our shrimp were so tough that they almost out-musseled our choppers. We'll fill our gastronomic stocking elsewhere next time. The **International**, also close to the Regal Residence, is decked out in the rustic mood, highlighted by checkered tablecloths. We enjoyed its skillful skilletry and modest price tags. For Polynesian platters on wax as well as on porcelain, park your outrigger at **Jimmy'z**, next to **Maona** (exotic cookery) on the beach. This sassy South C's discothèque, named after New

Jimmy's in Paris, has as its guiding coxwain the same swaggering Régine. She also is responsible for **Parady'z** in the same Sporting Club complex. A New Orleans belle rings praise for **Belli**, which she calls "an unusually satisfactory and modestly sealed Italian entry." We'll decipher that semantic plateful on our next session behind the Monégasque napkins. **Brazil** is chiefly for snacks. **La Rascasse**, down at the moorings, served us a tongue-twisting lunch in grim surroundings; no English spoken; a favorite of Algerian immigrants; sinking fast. **La Calanque** is any angler's big catch for fish. One of the best of the finny tribe on the coast. L'Escale first changed its cuisine and its name to **Chinatown**, then moved to a modern site at the port while the **Mandarin** took over the original venue. Neither appealed to us one yuan's worth. **Le Dragon d'Or** is a tearoom with extra-tempting pastries—edible variety.

Light bites? The imposing **Café de Paris**, opposite the Hôtel de Paris adjoining the Casino, is your best bet. Its air-conditioned interior is modern and pleasant; its big alfresco terrace supports perhaps 75 tables; a string ensemble performs here even at *noon,* yet! (Is it the only snack bar in the world with live Bach and Beethoven?) Its specialty is onion soup, but there is a vast choice of hot and cold plates, salads, sandwiches, ice creams, pastries, and the like. Here is the most pleasant stop of its category in the Principality. **Le Drugstore** is the roundup point for the more lively cowboy-and-gal—in an innovation inspired, no doubt, by the fantastic success of its Parisian predecessors—everything from *le hamburger* (ouch!) to *le whisky* to *le parfum* to *les souvenirs corny,* but no pharmaceuticals; open 24 hours daily. Our recent brace of cheeseburgers and milkshakes totaled almost $9! We know where you can get a better *steer* for that kind of hay. **Crêperie**, up an alley near the Royal Palace, is a far better snackery, especially for its pizzas, sandwiches, and thin pancakes. Tables and benches; the wide variety of crêpes for very low tabs; pleasant family operation; open late; griddles of fun. **Pub Bahia** seems to be stealing the local thunder from **Tip Top**; very "in" at the instant. Alternatives are **Royalty** or **Le Roxy**, for the pick of the crop. The youthful, tiny, and attractive **Le Louisiane**, near the Bristol, at harborside, features sandwiches, drinks, and youthful romancing à la 1 glass and 2 straws.

Short excursion? The 10-minute run up to the **Hostellerie Jérôme** at *La Turbie* (in France) is a favorite of many Monégasques—and of ours too. Ancient stone house with a 10-table main room and a 4-table dogleg; tiny patio for sipping; ornately painted ceiling; great sprays of flowers and bowls of fruit; menus on huge leather-covered parchment broadsides. Our terrine, snails, grilled chicken, and vegetables were succulent, well prepared, and nicely presented; the 30-year-old Calvados was among the best we've sampled. Almost no view; open every day in summer; closed in November; between times, be sure to telephone from town first to see if anything's cooking. If you seek panaromantics at higher prices but with lower quality food, the restaurant of the **Hôtel Vistaëro**, at nearby *Roquebrune* (described in the "French Riviera" chapter), may be your candidate.

Pissaladìera, Socca, Pan Bagnat, and Tourta di Ge are among the food specialties. The "blond" Monaco beer, 4-quart steins of which are sold near the Gate of the Royal Palace, is known all over the world for its excellence.

NIGHT LIFE   The **Summer Sporting Club**, on a terrace over the sea, is by far the most chichi oasis during the warm months. During galas, 1200 guests are accommodated in this handsome (and expensive) social center. Now the terraced clubhouse is deftly screened by roof gardens. Its counterpart, the **International Sporting Club**, is opened on December 24, for the winter season only. The **Winter Sporting Club** has been previously mentioned. **Le Black Jack** at the Casino draws the elite of 6 continents. The **Empire Room** of the Hôtel de Paris is also smart, swank, and glittering. **Loews** features its own casino plus the doin's in its supper club and discothèque. **Chez Ali Baba** has an interestingly naked floor show when it functions (mostly around Christmas). The **Sea Club** is a discothéque, and what more can we say? The **St. Louis**, done up in American 1890's trappings is another one. It is small, clean, and recommended. Don't forget the previously mentioned **Jimmy'z**. For an informal beer, it's the **Bahia Pub**, the **English Pub**, or the **Tip Top**. Gentlemen on the prowl? If your quarry isn't sipping an ice-cream soda at **Le Drugstore,** she's possibly at the **Casanova**, a dark corner for snuggling, imbibing, and clapping dutifully whenever a bra hits the dust. Small band; honest drinks; so-called attractions which just bare-ly might attract a sheepherder fresh from Kara Kum, U.S.S.R. Finally the **Open Air Cinema**, miniskirting the Mediterranean, proudly advertises that it shows "100 films in 100 days"—but who wants to go to the movies in Monte Carlo?

DAY LIFE   The ubiquitous fêtes, galas, and sports already mentioned; the Prince's Palace (open to the public from July to Oct.; tapestries, art treasures, Napoleonic memorabilia, view of the bay); the National Museum (believe it or not, children will love it); the Oceanographic Museum (one of the world's oldest, finest, and most important, directed by Commandant Cousteau of underwater-exploration fame, with an extraordinary aquarium, a Deep Sea exhibition, and a magnificent collection of nautical wonders and formaldehideous freaks); the Zoological Acclimatization Center of Monaco (Prince Rainier III founded this project in '54, and it remains his favorite); the Museum of Prehistoric Anthropology (also entered through the Exotic Garden). Big concerts are given in the Court of the Prince's Palace during the summer. Finally, the gardens of the Principality are famous for their beauty —Casino, St. Martin (bordering the Oceanographic Museum), Parc Princesse Antoinette (olive trees millennia old), and the strange Exotic Garden itself (thousands of plants, from semidesert countries, which cling to the slopes of the mountain, flourishing in their new environment) Their climax comes with the Monaco Garden Club's International *Concours* of bouquets in May—a beautiful "do."

INFORMATION ON MONACO   This nation's excellent **Direction du Tourisme et des Congrès** couldn't be more cooperative. It will give you full information about the Principality, and furnish you with a raft of well-prepared maps, brochures, and booklets about Monaco, its environs, and foreign tourist centers of importance. Location: Smack in the center of Monte Carlo, at 2A boulevard des Moulins. Hours: Mon.-Sat., 9 A.M.-7 P.M.; Sun. and holidays, 9 A.M. to noon. The answer man for travelers is M. Louis Blanchi.

If you can't wait, go to 115 E. 64th St., and the Monaco Tourist Office will trigger golden Riviera reveries before you leave the sidewalks of Gotham.

CUSTOMS AND IMMIGRATION   None. Get a visa only if you want it as a souvenir in your passport; the cost is $1. Bring in a suitcase full of cigars, a barrel of whisky, a fortune in gold, and they're delighted!

Netherlands

Holland is such a tiny country that South Carolina, our fortieth state, covers twice as much ground; multiply the population of Brooklyn roughly by 5, and you'll have every living being within its borders. Yet this microscopic midget has enormous sinews; it is unequivocally a major power today.

The mixup on national terminology is still going on. They've been fighting about it since 1842, and there's still no decision in sight.

The Netherlands covers 11 national provinces, of which Holland is only a segment (this one divided into North and South counties); the Netherlanders are the people-as-a-whole, while the Hollanders, Zeelanders, Brabanders, and other local groups make up the country. "Dutch" is a generic term which means precisely nothing; the Germans are "Dutch" too, and that's why so many local burghers shudder when the word is applied.

Yet—Holland and Dutch are so deeply rooted that "the Netherlands" and "Netherlanders" are applied only by purists and the government. So here's our theory: While it's linguistically incorrect, common usage is a better criterion. Let's call the nation Holland and its people the Dutch or Hollanders.

Nearly ½ the land is below high-tide level. Were it not for her engineers, the nation would be 50% soil and 50% H_2O., twice daily. Water is the ever-present, ever-threatening problem. Since A.D. 1200, an estimated 1,400,000 acres have vanished into Davy Jones's locker. Of this, the Dutch have salvaged almost 1,300,000, acres. They've partially tamed it with fabulous chains of dikes, put it to work on 5000 miles of canals and pushed it back in reclamation projects which make Hoover Dam a merit-badge project for aspiring Boy Scouts. Recovery of the Zuiderzee, 1350 square miles of salt lakes, started in 1928 with the construction of the enclosing dike; many dams (the largest 18½ miles long), giant tidal sluices, huge "polders," 2000 pumping stations, and the latest scientific know-how have changed the face of the countryside. In an area nearly as large as Rhode Island, whole new villages have been created; fertile soil valued at $253,000,000 has been added to the national resources.

The Dutch climate is on a par with Ireland's. It's about as unattractive, for year-round living, as London or New York. There is a fair amount of sunshine —witness the phenomenal growth of a wide variety of plants—but when it's not making honest rain, you can bet a guilder to a dubbeltje that it's misty from the marshes or foggy from the sea. Average humidity is high; to us (but not to a Dutchman!) the sunbeams seem about as virile as a glass of French beer. Winters are colder than those in Eastern England; Utrecht, roughly in the center, has a January mean of 35°, a July mean of 62°. You'll be thankful for your tweeds about 300 days in the year.

Queen Juliana is a direct descendant of the Dutch George Washington (William the Silent), and she continues to be overwhelmingly popular. She is married to Prince Bernhard von Lippe-Biesterfeld, a gay and democratic nobleman who likes fast cars, planes, good entertainment, and wildlife (animal variety). The House of Orange, to which the Queen belongs, is one of the oldest and most respected hierarchies in the world.

Holland—as if you didn't know—is famous for its many flowers, which bloom until late fall. The best season is April to June. The village of Boskoop, with 700 nurseries, is the largest horticultural center in the world. Aalsmeer, 10 miles from Amsterdam, has weekday floral auctions which draw scores of fascinated tourists (see "Things to See"), plus a vast facility for experimental floristry and a government horticultural school. Within 20 miles of The Hague is the tulip center. Don't miss the Keukenhof Flower Exhibition if you're in Holland between about end-March and mid-May (dates subject to weather). It's a comfortable afternoon expedition from Amsterdam.

Last, don't forget that the Netherlands is a cradle of fine art. You'll find Rembrandt, Frans Hals, van Ostade, Jan Steen, van Goyen, Potter, van de Velde, Vermeer, van Gogh (not only has a new museum with his works been opened in Amsterdam, but if you get over to *Otterlo*, near Arnhem, you'll find 272 of his beauties in the little-known Kröller-Müller Museum), and scores of other famous Dutch painters, both past and very actively present. In Amsterdam, The Hague, and Rotterdam there are enough Rembrandts to warrant a holy pilgrimage. In music, its Concertgebouw Orchestra is world-renowned. Its ballet corps is on tiptoe status with the finest. In Delft, antiques take the limelight. For all cultural pursuits, here's a rich trove.

CITIES   *Amsterdam* lighted its 700th anniversary candle in 1975, but it is younger than ever in spirit. The city has much in common with Boston, Massachusetts. It has the same twisting little streets, funny little shops, and Dutch Renaissance or baroque buildings, but most striking of all is its blend of old and new; once the same in size as our Cod capital, it now is closer to

Cleveland in population. You can step from the Kalverstraat, the Boylston Street of Holland, and find yourself in sleepy by-lanes a few feet wide; in 3 or 4 seconds you'll lose 3 or 4 centuries. In '72 its main boulevard, Leidsestraat, was turned into a pedestrian mall. Construction of a subway system is currently under way both underground and underwater. Canals intersect the city at dozens of angles—so don't be surprised if you see a barge or two politely waiting for a traffic light at the local Copley Square. Yet this metropolis is so wide awake that more than 150 American companies have opened offices here during the past several years. The hotel picture has improved considerably. There are plenty of fine restaurants and lively nightclubs, crowded transport, attractions such as the magnificent State Museum (better known as the Rijksmuseum), the Municipal Museum, the aforementioned van Gogh Museum, Rembrandt's House, Royal Palace, the Concertgebouw, the Anne Frank House (having financial troubles), historical maritime and aviation displays, diamond-cutting workshops, pushcarts with raw herring, streamlined department stores, broad *grachten* lined with elms, the House of the Sculptured Heads—a wonderful panorama of color and beauty in majestic old Amsterdam. It's the financial center, the shopping center—and now, with hundreds of summertime youths huddling wherever the authorities permit, it is also a hippie epicenter. Don't miss it.

Rotterdam, the chief port and undisputedly the world's busiest harbor, used to be as lusty as San Francisco. Hitler's infamous "lesson" to the Dutch people—destruction by bombing of 25-thousand buildings within 20 minutes, without waiting for their answer to his ultimatum—carved it down temporarily to the size of Duluth, Minnesota. But the hardworking burghers, having completed their mammoth reconstruction program, are now expanding at an unbelievable pace. The results are astonishing (and humbling!). Ample accommodations; good restaurants; a splendid zoo; Boymans' van Beuningen Museum (very important collection, with paintings by Bosch, seventeenth-century landscape artists, a few by Rembrandt and van Gogh, and many modernists); Scheepvaart Museum (ship models); outstanding modern statuary, including the prizewinner by U.S. sculptor Naum Gabo. To cap this array, the De Doelen concert hall issues a grace note at the Schouwburgplein; this colossus is the biggest on the Continent; its novel profile rings the audience around the musicians. Four 1-mile-long tunnels under the Maas River (2 for vehicles, 1 for bicycles, and 1 for pedestrians) and a new subway have been completed recently, any of which make the Lincoln or Holland tubes look dingy; Groothandelsgebouw, the largest building in Western Europe, with 250 firms (nearly all wholesale companies), a 500-car garage, a 5000-wheel bicycle bin, and a 1-mile air-conditioned interior roadway; the 15-thousand-acre $200,000,000 Europoort project which now clears the Nieuwe Waterweg for 250-thousand-ton ships. The pile-driving frenzy of creating too many massive civic projects at once will madden travelers and residents alike for many earsplitting years to come. She has a bustling, busy, clangorous, commercial—and nautical—atmosphere. Not as interesting as Amsterdam, but worth a visit. P.S. to all engineers: There's absolutely no dam excursion like a zip out to the famous Delta Works, the DNA and RNA of the Netherlands. The best targets are nearby **Veere, Middelburg**, and **Zierikzee**. Fascinating!

The Hague hasn't Antoine's or the Sazarac cocktail, but it has close to the same number of people as New Orleans. Here is the seat of the Government; Amsterdam is often called the capital, but national laws are made in The Hague. The world-famous Peace Palace (meeting place for the Permanent Court of International Justice), the International Institute of Social Studies (in the former Royal Palace), the Palace in the Wood, and a number of royal retreats are all at The Hague. Good hotels, fair restaurants, the U.S. Embassy in its glacial Korte Voorhout building, crowded streetcars, conservative night life, the inevitable museums (Mauritshuis, for example), canals, parks, parks, more parks, and century-old elms.

Scheveningen (pronounced Skay-vah-ning-uh) is very close by. It's the big resort section on the beach, part of The Hague and about 10 minutes by car from the center. Concerts, minigolf, swimming, a jetty with 4 recreational "island" platforms crowned by a 135-foot crow's nest for observation; riding, nightclubs, soda-pop stands, American bowling alley; seasonal patronage but year-round hotels—the works. In many ways, it is the Atlantic City and the Virginia Beach of Holland. Like Washington, D.C., The Hague is a city of strangers—so unless you're a lobbyist, a celebrity, or a businessman with an ax to grind, you'll probably twiddle your thumbs with the other bewildered tourists. Go to The Hague for culture and to Scheveningen for laughs.

Utrecht, fourth ranking, is the geographic center; it's one of the oldest cities in the land. Dayton, Ohio, has the same population. As one typical example of its modern thinking, a huge construction program has modernized the rail center, developed a trade-fair site, filled in 2 major canals, and incorporated a new hotel and business buildings into a melded metropolitan scheme. The full project will continue until 1982. Its Hoog Catarijne shopping center is functioning and shouldn't be missed by anyone with an interest in urban planning. Well-maintained hotels, most on the commercial side; busy restaurants; up-to-the-minute facilities. A railway junction, a hub for religious life, science, communications, trade—some Dutch prefer it to its larger sisters. Americans often don't, because many find it somber and dull. Famous industrial Fair in March and September; among museums, (1) the Gold, Silver, and Clocks, (2) the Organ in the same building, (3) the Central, with ancient and modern works, and (4) the Railway exhibits are the best-known of its 14 candidates; in addition, 6 castle museums are within Utrecht Province. The cathedral is magnificent; the Vismarkt (fish market) is so unusual no one should miss it. And speaking of sea denizens, there's a wonderful Dolfinarium at *Harder-wijk*, where the lovely critters perform tricks; nearby is the 4-H'ers dream at the Flevohof agricultural exhibit. Finally, the Avifauna at *Alphen* is a delight for viewing our feathered friends; swans, rare geese, wood duck, plus other ornamental waterfowl and fluttery fellows occupy a Rhine-side park; fascinating!

Haarlem, population 168-thousand, has its points for some sightseers— the Frans Hals Museum, which can be seen by candlelight at various intervals, a great cathedral (St. Bavo with its famous organ), pure Dutch architecture, colorful gardens, and the beach resort of Zandvoort.

Other important centers are *Eindhoven, Groningen, Gouda, Alkmaar, Arnhem, Nijmegen, Maastricht, Leeuwarden, Breda, Leyden, Apeldoorn, Middelburg, 'S-Hertogenbosch, Valkenburg, Hil-*

versum, Delft, Dordrecht, Ede, Venlo, and ***Amersfoort***. Most of the rest are below 50 thousand in population, and many of them are charming. For further details, consult the Netherlands National Tourist Office, 576 Fifth Avenue, New York 10036, or in any major capital of Europe.

MONEY AND PRICES The Dutch use cents and guilders—100 of the former to 1 of the latter. The approximate values, including some of the nicknames similar to "nickel" and "quarter" at home, are:

	Dutch	*U.S.*		*Dutch*	*U.S.*
1	cent	= .40¢	1	kwartje	= 10¢
1	stuiver	= 2¢	1	guilder	= 40¢
1	dubbeltje	= 4¢	2½	guilders	= 100¢

The plural of guilder (also called the florin) is guldens in Dutch, guilders in English. A 10-guilder silver piece was struck to commemorate the Liberation; these are limited in number; they may be taken outside the country without restriction. The banknotes (see the 5-guilder bill) are among the most tastefully designed in the world.

In case anyone cares, 10 Dutch banks now issue standard traveler's checks to foreign visitors. You may buy them through your own bank before your departure from America.

The Dutch are among the most heavily taxed people in the world. As in France, hotels and food are the most expensive items, but taxis, trains, drinks, knickknacks, and tips are still more reasonable than their Chicago, San Francisco, or New York equivalents. Compared to your outlay in France, Finland, Belgium, Italy, Sweden, or Switzerland, you'll continue to spend less in Holland.

Regardless of the exchange rate, incidentally, the dollar hit a dolorous low in this Low Country recently. Pornographic antics have been reproduced on fake greenbacks, replacing both the Great Seal and the Father of Our Country. They are peddled mainly in Amsterdam's red-light district at approximately 80¢ per bill. How's *that* for devaluation?

ATTITUDE TOWARD TOURISTS Spiritually, a huge welcome mat, in neon lights. They want American tourists, not only for dollars, but for the deep kinship they feel with the American people.

The Netherlands National Tourist Office (NNTO) is one of the best-managed and smoothest-functioning agencies of its type on the Continent. Typical Dutch efficiency, attention to detail, and kindness are reflected by its Director General, Joop Strijkers. This is the fountainhead of Dutch tourism; there are branches in 8 major European centers. In New York, the address is 576 Fifth Avenue, and the Managing Director is J.G. Bertram. In San Francisco, it's 681 Market St., Room 941, with Manager C. K. Kammeyer behind the desk and the smile. In Toronto, your Dutch uncle is youthful Robert Al at suite 3310, Royal Trust Tower. If you plan to use Amsterdam as your European gateway, ask your local NNTO office about the "Stay on the House" program. It can save you a pocketful of guilders.

Working with NNTO are more than 450 local offices scattered throughout the Netherlands, supported mainly by local contributions. These are called **VVV**, and there is 1 for every Dutch hamlet which can show the census takers a population of more than 2 human beings, 3 dogs, and 5 cows. You'll find these offices everywhere, and they are an enormous help to the wanderer. **Amsterdam**'s VVVs are on Rokin 5 and opposite the Central Station—both in the highly capable hands of A. F. Luyken (other divisions at Schiphol Airport and Utrechtseweg); the **Rotterdam** branch, operated by Fred van Heezik, is at Stadhuisplein 19 (other booths at the station and Zuidplein); **The Hague** headquarters is at Nassauplein 31; a year-round office chugs away at the station; during the season it operates 3 additional information hubs in or fringing the city plus an office at **Scheveningen** on the central square.

The interesting program **"Get in Touch with the Dutch,"** run by the Amsterdam VVV, is similar to the Scandinavian operations. To meet your opposite number in his or her home and have a cozy look at family life after 8 P.M. in the Lowlands, apply in person for your application at Rokin 5.

The peak tourist season is June and July—but, if you're wise, you'll avoid the crush (and find still greater beauty!) by planning your trip for late spring (April is busier than June) or early fall.

CUSTOMS AND IMMIGRATION   Pleasant but thorough, in a mechanical routine. You're allowed 400 cigarettes free of duty, 1 bottle of liquor, and the ordinary concessions which are granted all over Europe—as long as you declare the items. In practice they will rarely bother any U.S. visitor with *reasonable personal* variances, as long as they're obviously for his own use.

Restraints on the importation and exportation of currencies, both foreign and domestic, have been abolished. Here is a lesson in economics which makes chimpanzees of certain highly touted financial wizards of other lands.

HOTELS   For far more comprehensive information on certain hostelries than space limitations permit here, interested travelers are referred to *Fielding's Selected Favorites: Hotels and Inns, Europe* by our Marco Polo son, Dodge Temple Fielding. The latest annual edition, in which a total of 300-odd favored possibilities were handpicked from the 4000-plus personally inspected, will be at your bookstore early this year.

In general, Dutch houses are seasonal, clean, and surprisingly high-priced; there's usually plenty of space in winter, but they get tight in warm weather. *Reserve in advance all year round in the capital and principal metropolises; in lesser towns, bulbtime and high summer are the thorniest periods.*

As is the case everywhere, service standards are on the decline. After 4 months of employment a worker can collect 80% of his salary for one year and 60% for the following one. Is it any wonder that staffs are so hard to obtain and retain?

In the less elaborate or smaller houses, furnishings are often old, and baths are at a premium. But you can be almost sure that your room was scrubbed minutes or hours before you got there, because the average Dutch hostelry shines like Mother Hubbard's cupboard.

Rates have risen not only sharply but shockingly. This year, with the normal inflation, you'll pay from $19 to $33 for a good single with bath, $30 to $48 for a good double with bath—plus 15% for service if you stay 5 nights or less. Second-class tariffs for the same categories average $17 to $25; breakfast is frequently included.

Amsterdam's hotel scene is blossoming quicker than a Maytide tulip patch. If you'll stick to the candidates listed below, you should enjoy the greatest comfort within each respective category.

The **de l'Europe** earns its laurels as one of the Continent's most elegantly sedate havens on the scene today. This patrician achieves the rare status of being stately without being stuffy. It nestles on the bank of one of the capital's busiest and most colorful canals. Main portals welcoming guests with a bright smile; Relais for quick bites, with sky-blue napery at counters and tables, sapphire carpets, and black leather seats; attractive glass-sheathed dining room with separate entrance, just a yardarm from the passing boats; complete refurnishing and freshening of the lobby in hues of seafoam green; impressive ½-million-bottle wine cellar. Now 100% of the rooms have been modernized, with the superb beds and excellent baths installed (twin basins; fluffy robes; sleek lines); 10 newer units with terraces; 10 redone in English style; many doubles turned into large singles. Manager Pieter Jennen is keeping up the good works. Among the Dutch-style hotels, here is *definitely* a front runner. Recommended.

Marriott introduced its initial European hotel effort by purchasing perhaps the prime piece of property in all of Holland. It then went on to unveil a sparkling (inside, not outside) air-conditioned physical plant that fairly crackles with new innkeeping concepts for the Continent. Personnel—from highly skilled General Manager Robert Small to stunning Hospitality Hostess Emmy Ettema—are young, vigorous, and eager to welcome you. Daring color blends evoking exhilaration and warmth simultaneously; cunning illumination throughout; vastly popular public rooms, among the most zestful in Amsterdam. Invitingly nautical Port O' Amsterdam specialty restaurant with novel ideas for the presentation and service of food; Dutch Inn for all-day vittles; below-decks Windjammer Bar for grog between mates (very matey it is); combo for dancing, a big drawing card for townspeople and guests alike. Bedchambers employ similar rich melds of cheerful hues and bold textiles; color TVs, featuring 2 closed-circuit films per day plus the normal schedules; 5 suites; paltry baths; book on the viewful Leidseplein side for one of the most enchanting canal-and-cityscape vistas in Europe. Here is a hostelry that not only does a job and does it well, but is truly fun to stay in. We wish Marriott continued success with its maiden European venture.

The 11-story, 276-room **Amsterdam Hilton** is another bellringer for contemporary-style dwelling and bright lights. A 100-unit Garden Wing augments the original capacity. Quiet but somewhat remote location; handsomely re-styled Amsterdam Grill with charcoal-broils and beef flown in from the U.S.; Pâtisserie café refashioned, showing silent films (à la Gotham) after 9 P.M.; natural oak Half Moon Bar; Juliana Discothèque in cellar. Subdued colors in bedrooms, highlighted with original Dutch paintings; spacious suites and demisuites; ungenerous twin-bedded doubles, but larger studio-twins; tiny, save-that-penny baths throughout, with awkwardly planned ventilation slots that usurp privacy. This landmark is an imposing thoroughbred in the Hilton bloodline.

Within the past few seasons, the world-famous **Amstel** has been bartered twice; the present owner is Britain's Grand Metropolitan chain, an expansion-minded company that has been buying up deluxe hostelries helter-skelter across the Continent. The library-mood La Rive restaurant is one of the most attractive intimate salons we've seen anywhere; the piano melodizing lends even more enchantment to its Amstelside setting. High ceilings; classic décor in public rooms; lobby and corridors restyled; 80 bedchambers rejuvenated; exceptionally warm and friendly personnel. Despite increasing competition, for the time being at least, this will probably remain one of the smarter gathering places for sophisticated tourists and socialites. We are keeping our fingers, toes, eyes, and ears crossed for the success of young General Manager van Heuvel, who is trying hard.

The **Apollo** boasts an occupancy of 445 souls in 230 rooms. Slate-floor lobby fronting the water; recent enlargement of the lounge and parking space; attractive warm-toned restaurant and adjoining Bodega; Coffee Shop in Scandinavian tones; underwater Le Poisson Rouge Bar with its fascinating aquarium filled with 21-karat goldfish. As if that weren't sufficient, the adjoining Apollo Sports Hall complex flexes in with a cinema, its own bar and terrace, and enough gymnastic equipment to weary an Olympic decathlon squad. Older semicircular segment containing single accommodations; some tiny twins which we hope will be made into spacious loners plus 2 suites that are enchanting for their waterway panaromantics; all units dressed up with modern-living design details; prices very reasonable for the javelin-sleek rewards. It is our hope the pulse will continue at the same beat under its recent switch to British doctoring by the Trust Houses Forte clinic.

The **Parkhotel** has been redecorated in a very impressive way. It reveals a fresh 81-unit wing, a refeathered main entrance plus 2 others, a garage (what a blessing!), a Scandinavian-tone French restaurant, a spacious Coffee Shop, the Queen's Bar in an English mood, smart lounges, a rash of restyled baths, and 5 duplex suites with kitchenettes. Lobby redone; run by gracious people who take their innkeeping cues from the gentle, everwatchful Managing Director J. van 't Hoenderdaal. Superb.

The **Victoria,** opposite the Central Station, also was sold not long ago by its local family ownership and tucked into the same English-leather portfolio as the Amstel and the American (next paragraph). Lobby and reception redesigned in light woods and warm textiles; cozy triplet lounge refashioned in lovely ancient tones, with tapestried walls and lowered oak-timbered ceiling, brown velvet chairs, and animal prints; open-hearth writing nook; 6-table Spanish Room for *comida* and candle beams; side-by-side Grill rebuilt, with air conditioning added; piano music nightly in both dining salons; demipension required. Uninspired but functional reconstruction of nearly all the 150 accommodations; décor mixed; some space limitations. Overall quite good.

The centrally situated **American** has been so sweepingly and dramatically revitalized by its generous Grand Metropolitan owners that virtually no trace of its antiquity remains inside. The exterior, however—a national monument reflecting a distinct period of Dutch architecture—is untouched. More than $3,500,000 in updatings have been poured into this house. Lobby smartly dressed in marble, sandstone, and fresh carpeting; stone reliefs added; ingratiating Europa dining room with a crackling iron hearth; all 185 units resparkled. Some so-called "suitettes" were constructed which feature a sitting area on the lower level and beds on a higher tier. We prefer these for space and the canalside rooms with arched windows for aesthetics. Moving up to the big leagues and now definitely a pennant contender.

The 380-room **Sonesta**, beside the Singel, Amsterdam's oldest canal, is the newest major hostelry to open in this city. Part of this modern structure incorporates 13 monument houses from the seventeenth century plus the ancient circular Lutheran Church (a tunnel links the latter to the hotel and will be used for congresses). A Rib Room specializes in grills; there's a coffee shop plus a "brown café" (local parlance for a dim tavern) where you can buy a meter (!) of beer for $3.50; you'll also find a bar and courtyard lounge; bedrooms are not too big. It was still enduring some teething pains on our early visit, so we are reserving judgment until we can get back for another look. It should be mature for your holiday, however.

The **Okura**, off the ways in '71, is the first major Japanese-owned-and-operated hotel on the Continent. This 23-story, contemporary-style structure strikes us as an impressive new tooth in Amsterdam's jagged skyline. (Some, however, disagree and liken it more to a sore thumb.) Busy but inhospitably sterile lobby with low ceilings and small pond (watch your footing when in the vicinity of the latter); Blue Sky penthouse restaurant with splendid uninterrupted panorama but French cuisine which to us stuttered in both skilletry and staff work; passable Chinese and Japanese eateries plus coffee shop; shopping arcade; saunas. While you might well take exception or exceptions, we hold 3 important cavils: First, we think that it is rather shockingly overpriced. Second, we find the dimensions of its accommodations uncomfortably tight for large-frame clients. Third, and most distressing, in all of our travel years we have never encountered such chaotic disorganization among the minions of any so-called luxury house as we did when we were here.

The **Memphis** might make you sing the blues when the bill comes, but it's a ragtime band for syncopated comforts and upbeat charm. No full restaurant, but Frenchy breakfast room and Sapphire Bar attractive for nibblers and sippers; reasonable elbowroom; deep-down, rest-provoking furnishings; lawn-thick wall-to-wall carpeting in forest green; pastel-stripe bed linens and gold-and-cream spreads; 5th-floor units with atelier windows. Except for its upper-octave prices, this combo plays a catchy and tuneful little number that has us humming. Plenty of brass, but not for tailgaters.

The cub named **Pulitzer** is not a front-page headliner, but after our recent week's review we would not hesitate to award it a prize for human interest among hostelries. Fourteen ancient houses have been charmingly joined in a multilevel composite—fine for all but the aged or infirm. Small modish lobby accented by antiques; dining room with open grill and so-so cookery; some units facing a garden court; others on a street; still more on a tiny canal a few blocks from the town's mainstreams. Décor boldly employing open timbers, rough brick walls, rugged textiles and daring colors; friendly but still unpolished personnel during our stay. Here's a refreshing change from the Hilton-Sheraton-Intercontinental versions of Old Glory-fications of which it is a vague copy in Old Dutch dress. Amusing. The new **Amster Centre** employed the same architectural technique of joining old houses under one roof. The formula is a sound one and these 110 bedrooms are also inviting. If we had our druthers, we'd pick the Pulitzer first in this type of hostelry.

The **Amsterdam Arthur Frommer** is an appealing complex of 13 weavers' homes which have been cleverly integrated into a single unit. Breakfast-only restaurant; Golden Age Bar where we found slapdash—nay, screwball!—service plus green "gas" lanterns; 90 Flemish-style rooms with bed vibrators. The only serious drawback we found here was its unremitting flow of U.S. traffic, often youthful and often objectionably raucous. Otherwise, we like this one a lot.

The careworn **Doelen** has changed its entrance and been given a few touchups, mostly on the 5th floor. In general, however, the restorative efforts impressed us as being superficial. Despite its central address and scattering of assets, we think that you will find better rewards for your guilders elsewhere.

The proprietor of the above house gave his name to the newer **Caransa**, which is crammed smack into the noisy nucleus of Rembrandtsplein. Parking is a major headache for motorists; even with its double-glaze windows, light sleepers may find it next to impossible successfully to court the sandman. All 66 units are doubles; all splash in with private bath and whoopee color schemes incorporating stripes or florals. The Plaza Restaurant is at street level; please pardon the terrible pun, but we find it totally pedestrian. More flairful in its modern dress than the dowager Doelen, but again overpriced on our scales for the payoff in contentment.

The tiny **Alexander** is a luxury dish lately conjured up by the famous Dikker & Thijs Restaurant, which it adjoins in panhandle fashion. Only 25 ultramodern rooms; plastic furnishings; grays and whites as backgrounds for explosions of bright and cheery pigments; phones, 4-channel radios, and alarm clocks; #'s 502 and 503 our favorite viewful doubles. Pleasant indeed as a blue-ribbon way station.

The **Carlton**? This one keeps rolling along in an unspirited fashion. Here's what you'll find: Updated 1st, 3rd, and 4th floors; bath or shower facilities for 100 units; many private refrigerators. Upstairs décor in either Louis XV à la Hollandaise, with off-white and cream shadings, or modern tints; original oils and watercolors lend zest. Five suites; smallish twin-bed doubles; midget baths; inadequate luggage space; if you're after Yankee-size elbowroom, you'll pay for it; there's bed-and-breakfast only. If you're booked here this season, doublecheck your dates and keep your fingers double-crossed—because legions of Guidesters have complained of careless reservations policies.

The **Port van Cleve**, which occupies 5 floors above the restaurant of the same name, has now passed the century mark. Midcity location; small lobby; ingratiating oak-panel-and-tile Old Dutch Inn bar. Overall, you'll find a clean, bright atmosphere in cramped dimensions; we heard vague rumblings about future building hopes; the singles atop offer excellent scanning of the city through their garret-style windows; suites #131 (with balcony) and #132 are the only nests for stretching in this entire structure, even though the latest 27-room addition features turn-around space. Only fair.

The even more elderly, eternally growing **Krasnapolsky** has paused in its expansion—at least momentarily. This accrued and reaccrued layer-by-layer structure continues to be a mish-mash. Bright, airy, antiseptic lobby and adjoining bar; 40-car garage—a vital asset in this midcity enclave. The suspended potted palms in its winter-garden restaurant made us feel like Luther Burbank catching a bite between experiments; cozier interior dining room in gilt and ecru, to offset it; listless cuisine, but top-form drinks, in its American Bar. Persistent word continues to class it in terms of its human relations as "an unfriendly Statler." So-so at best.

The **Schiller**, now owned by the Caransa across the plaza, is still supposed to undergo a thorough revamping. Since the only things that had materialized on our latest visit were new curtains, we'll believe it *if* we see it. Mr. Caranza and his associates have fed us so much claptrap about their "expansion" projects in the past that now we're from President Truman's State regarding their future "alterations."

The **Van Wehde**, adjoining hippiedom's Vondel Park at 8 Korte van Eegh-enstraat, is run by an amiable young couple who do their darndest to provide maximum comfort for economy travelers. New dining room; cherry-red central heating; 10 bedchambers and 2 baths. A fat reward for thin wallets. The 34-nest **Owl**, with breakfast only, is not bad for economizers. Bid for a quiet side if you toss and turn all night.

The **Crest** is in a special category. This $5,000,000, 15-story, 263-room former ESSO hotel is situated at the fringe of the city, about a 15-minute sprint from the Rembrandtsplein and 20 minutes from Schiphol Airport. Within the stalwart edifice are offices, full garage services plus indoor and outdoor covered parking, a jewelry shop with a diamond-polishing exhibit, a boutique, a barbershop, a beauty salon, and a newspaper kiosk. Spacious flagstone and wood-ribbed lobby; restaurant; cheery Pot Luck coffee corner; Dracs Bar. Brightly appointed bedchambers featuring wide windows, individual temperature controls, thick cranny-to-cranny carpeting, a silent valet with a built-in pants presser, an audio console with 12-channel selectivity, an automatic wake-up buzzer, a well-designed RCA "Bell Captain" refrigerator for do-it-yourself barflies, an occasional bouquet of fresh flowers, and small, efficient, "interior" baths. The 15-floor units boast balconies plus full-wall slide-away windows. The 600-unit, 18-story **Alpha**, across Europa Boulevard from the Crest in a shopping complex, is being sponsored jointly by the British Strand Hotels, and Holland's KLM Airlines. Doubles rent for about $45; we hear its reservations policies may be a bit cavalier; perhaps it's merely young and green as yet.

The **Schiphol Airport Hilton**, which made its inaugural hop in the fall of '72, is the only hostelry that is actually sited on the grounds of the flying field's complex—2 minutes from the terminal by shuttle bus. This sleek 204-unit haven for transients is so convenient to the key highway systems that guests can drive to Amsterdam, the Hague, or Rotterdam in jig time without bucking any big-city traffic. Air-conditioned and soundproofed throughout; exquisite indoor pool affording a scenic grace note to the glass-lined grillroom on a higher tier; sauna; coffee shop; on our test, cuisine beautifully presented, clumsily served, and neck-snappingly expensive (don't pant for the advertised roast beef at midday because it appears only after dusk); bristling with activity nearly the clock around. You'll pay generously for whatever you get.

While the 400-room **Schiphol Arthur Frommer** is sponsored by the author of *Europe On $10 A Day* and his associates, they actually have been charging approximately 3 times that amount per twin without meals. Its architecture (which to us resembles a sleeping factory) and its heavy patronage by groups dim our enthusiasm for this candidate. Much, much more attractive and chipper is the Amsterdam Arthur Frommer, in our opinion.

Sheraton Inn is a bit farther from the airport. It reflects an economizing mentality in its 170 bedchambers. Dark wood-lined bar; restaurant with leatherette chairs and suspended lamps; poor baths; air conditioning plus basic amenities. Manager Wim van Ingen is trying to do a lot on a low budget. This house and a twin Inn in *Geldrop* both charge modest rates for clean, basic shelter.

Four well-known establishments are *not* recommended by us this year. Here they are—and here's why: The **Slotania** is so far from the center of the city that the ride seems endless; small and unpretentious; definitely not worth the journey for the average U.S. tripper. The **Belfort** is off our list for the very same reasons. The **Euromotel E-9** and **Amsterdam Motel E-10**, both in the direction of Schiphol Airport, also don't thrill us.

Dedicated budgeteers? Since we're too bottlenecked here for additional entries, please consult this year's edition of our annually revised paperback, *Fielding's Low-Cost Europe*.

The Hague has been experiencing a hotel revolution. The leader, a fresh wind off the waves in the hospitality seas, is the stunningly modernistic **Promenade**. One drawback: It is so far into the outskirts that the site almost borders the neighboring resort of Scheveningen. We were fascinated to observe how successfully its administrators have blended Old World luxury with twentieth-century modernity while conjoining cold-eyed commercialism with intimacy and warmth—feats of innkeeping legerdemain that are close to impossible. Many fine art works lining the public rooms; grandly patrician glass-lined restaurant; Couperous Bar plus café terrace; attractive snackery; viewful and efficient bedrooms. Most of the staff seem to be fed on happiness pills because of their cheeriness. Your own car is virtually a *must* if you select this one. Our warmest recommendation.

Nearby, the slabular **Bel Air**, also a youngster, tries to match this local paragon, but to us the strong undertones of group tourism, remote service attitudes, and a less generous budget plainly show through the veneer. That's not to say it isn't comfortable; it is. Still, for approximately the same outlay, we would much prefer the Promenade, providing we had wheels.

In the city itself, the **Hotel des Indes** is the current leader. Soon it may have even firmer claims to the title since its new proprietor has been laving it open-handedly in florins. Its situation, plunk in the middle of Embassy Row, is a B-I-G plus. Its forest-green and red-checked Copper Kettle grill is enticing; its public rooms, while stately, tend toward the fusty; its bedchambers have a dated but spaciously relaxing aura. A midtown winner that is continuing to step up its pace.

The **Central** is the site of the House of Lords Restaurant, formerly the culinary pacesetter of The Hague. The **Park** has undergone a complete renaissance. Rooms much improved by keen-eyed Director William Bergmans. Now there's ample parking space available for clients' cars—a happy coup because of the hotel's narrow-street location, 1-way traffic, and bumper-to-bumper snarl. Try to secure one of its larger abodes when you reserve. Very good.

The hotels of **Scheveningen** are typically resort style: Built for the vacation trade, with an aura of gaiety and an air of nonpermanence about them. The **Europa** has just completed a renovation dust-up that added one brand-new wing. Fresh swimming pool, sauna, ladies' hairdresser, skittle alley; conference salons; garage and service station with direct elevator connection to your floor. Much improved. The **Badhotel** ("Bad" is Dutch for "bath," in case you're curious about this anomaly) is 1 block off the sea. Attractive cellar restaurant; ground-level feedery; bath-or-bad-tub-size rooms; so-so. The **Eurotel** is composed of apartments, which can be especially commodious for families on the move. Our personal preference in this cluster is the tiny, unostentatious, early-century-Dutch **Bali Hotel**, which is run in conjunction with the celebrated restaurant. Modest rooms; annex; spotless cleanliness; unattractive rococo exterior; fine bar, with Bob presiding; extremely friendly service; eye-poppingly sumptuous breakfasts. Aside from these fantastic morning feasts and rijsttafel (Indonesian cuisine—see later), no other meals are served; since most travelers prefer to explore for themselves for lunch and dinner, this isn't a drawback. No public rooms or lobby; and due to design limitations, the original building offers only 1 public bathroom per floor. But the fine newer *dépendance* in the adjoining building brings the room count up to 33, adding 8 doubles (all with bath) and 4 singles. *Reserve in advance* through Lou Elfring, the Proprietor. This little haven is so popular it's almost always fully booked weeks ahead.

The **Hoornwijck Motel** parks just outside The Hague at **Rijswijk** on the Rotterdam road. Taverne for cozy fireside and taper-lit meals. It is truckloads better now that it has been overhauled.

In **Rotterdam**, the 11-story, 275-room **Hilton** is a wee shade smaller than its Dutch uncle in Amsterdam. Two-level lobby linked by a white marble, free-form stairway; 420-capacity Gold Ballroom; MacGreggor Bar; woodily outfitted La Côte de Boeuf restaurant, where the menu plumps the rib roast as "what you came for," but which was not available for our grilling (a duplicate of the maddening experience we had at the Schiphol and Düsseldorf Hiltons); Winter Garden for dining and dancing, with flower-framed pool and lush greenery; freshly perked Coffee Shop, with above-average snacks but dregs-of-the-pot attention standards; Le Bateau discothèque spinning at a mooring beside the hotel. Both in this house and at the Amsterdam Hilton we were socked with an extra service charge to put through each transatlantic phone call. Why, then, were we also asked to pay 15% for staff attention? Manager Rudy Bausch is trying hard to meld the various elements into a harmonious whole.

The **Parkhotel** shows laudable managerial effort and expenditures. Every room was redone not long ago; despite the inhibiting effects of its vintage structure, some units (but not all) compare favorably with and even outclass the Hilton. There are a rebuilt entrance, a smart lobby, a separate reception desk, a very appealing dining room overlooking a 7000-tulip flower patch, and a café. The cane-ceilinged bar and adjoining lounge, beside the narrow Westersingel waterway, has been expanded, and the front garden has been terraced and dotted with umbrellas. Hard-driving direction by ever-helpful C. A. van Hout; improving steadily.

The **Atlanta** is shining after a million-dollar reconditioning and construction program. All public rooms revamped; popular horseshoe bar hung with paintings; 6th-floor units with private balconies; almost all baths remodeled, but a few old ones remain. Units on the 4th, 5th, and 6th levels with access to ice-cube machines in the corridors; other bedchambers offer ice buckets; TV available; some modernistic touches, such as leatherette bed headboards here and there. Manager E. F. Sack has at last got this one in the bag.

The **Central** has pounded and hammered its way up in our rankings. Entire ground floor ripped out, renewed, and beautified; café paneling retained at even greater expense than that tailored to match; bar in he-man tones; every bedroom totally refashioned and immaculately maintained; small baths throughout. Director Philipsen is an ultrawarm and kindly gentleman who exudes friendship; his staff reflects his concern for hospitality.

The conveniently located **Rijnhotel** is only passable to these observers, despite its stunning modernistic building. Singles hardly larger than closets, with baths about as cramped as iron lungs; panel-windowed, narrow-bedded doubles that should rightfully be singles. The architect who conceived this gleaming but benumbing dollhouse should be rapped on the knuckles and demoted to designing silos. The **Savoy** is a big, newish Second-class house keyed for the budget-minded European trade. The **Regina** is a hodgepodge of fading decorative themes and fading comforts. It's headed by P. Goosen. Large doubles so comfortable they're worth the price difference from the normal size; 10 apartments with soundproof ceilings and wall-to-wall carpeting; baths generally poor, some offering curtains (à la Marseille) instead of doors; charming Dutch café-bar; fine, glittering kitchen. No longer a relic, but lots more Goosen and zip-in' again needed. The **Savoy** impressed us as being studiously spiritless and institutional. Modern as a nose cone and just about as inspiring.

The **Euromotel**, 20 minutes out of town by the apron at the airport, is a sleek contender for motorists, birds in flight, and eremites. Richly decorated restaurant in the style of a Valais tavern; wonderful bar in subdued tones; modern rusticity in public rooms; full air conditioning. Its 100 units are divided into 60 hotel bedchambers with full bath and 40 motel accommodations with shower. Doubles facing a small canal and lake; singles fronting the jet-ways; soundproofing throughout; free bus to and from the terminal and the bright lights. For the first time in our researchings, we saw a fascinating prefabricated installation which combines refrigerator, wardrobe, drawer space, and a bin for storing luggage. Every room has one; it's quite an innovation. Although this venture is somewhat curious in all-around concept, it is clean, efficient, well managed, and very reasonable. Recommended.

The **Delta**, 6 miles out in the petro-industrial community of **Vlaardingen**, is unique. It is not only *on*—but literally *in*—the Maas River; just pour a libation, put your feet up, and view the fascinating restless maritime parade of hundreds of ships that silently slip by every day. Incidentally, here's the only luxury hotel in the world with insurance against ship collision.

Eindhoven is proud of its **Grand Hotel de Cocagne**, a 9-story glass-and-steel showplace erected by the Philips Electric colossus (and what else *is* Eindhoven but Philips?). Completely air-conditioned; large congress hall and 9 conference centers; attractive lounge banked by winter garden and restaurant; commodious Bodega for beer quaffers; 86 functional, decent-size units and 86 baths, but "convertible" singles cramped when they're employed as doubles. A slick operation primarily for the business trade. On the outskirts, the **Motel Eindhoven** is one of the finest motels not only in Holland, but in Europe. If you don't need to be in the town, this stop is a honey. At **Geldrop,** a **Sheraton Inn** recently was inn-cubated. Very simple, clean, basic, and economical.

In **Utrecht**, the **Des Pays-Bas** offers 40 rooms, 13 baths, and the most heart of all. **Smits**, with linoleum-covered floors, is last and least. Keep a weather eye open for the new **Holiday Inn**. It's at Jaarbeursplein 24, but more we cannot tell you.

The **Bouwes** at **Zandvoort** (15 miles from Amsterdam, near Haarlem) was gutted by fire 2 seasons back, and we don't know its present status or even if it will be rebuilt. The neighboring **Badhotel**, open year round, is a possible alternate. Three bars, restaurant, and casino; 48 tiny rooms with shower or bath; no great shakes, but it may jiggle more excitingly soon. The $2,000,000 **Bouwes Palace** boasts 19 stories and the championship among skyscrapers in this very Low Country. Total of 100 apartments and 48 rooms about the size of a gnat's eyecup; many of the former preempted by sea-fevered locals; indoor pool; sauna bath; penthouse restaurant somewhat more international under its Austrian direction.

Good reports from kindly readers have come in about the inn-like, lakeside **Hotel Plasmolen** at **Mook**. We haven't yet given Mook a look.

The one redeeming feature about **Volendam** is the **Hotel van Diepen**, which is thoroughly honest and legitimate, and which serves the local specialties better than anyplace else except perhaps the Spaander. More about these under "Restaurants" and the village itself in "Things to See."

Motels? You'll find 'em everywhere today. Once you are in Holland, the VVV can give you exact addresses along your route. Keep in mind that most will be a far cry from the plush types which grace American highways!

FOOD   The Dutch relish their food; their cuisine, at its best, is delicate, savory, and full of unexpected nuances. At its worst, however, it's torpid, greasy, overrich, and as heavy as U-235.

Under ideal circumstances, breakfast offers a choice of various breads, butter, cheese (always), tea or coffee, and sometimes a boiled egg or meat. The famous "Dutch Coffee Table" (sometimes a warm dish, then cold meats, cheese, fruits, and beverage) is the national lunch. Many people have a light afternoon tea, and dinner is always the heaviest meal of the day.

Typical Dutch dishes are also typically American: Steak with French fries and salad, asparagus with egg and butter sauce, boiled beef. More exotic are minced beef (rolpens) with fried apples and, in winter, curly cabbage and sausage, hotchpotch (hutspot), and that famous, wonderful pea soup. Oh oh OH, that delight of the last! Let the good local burghers save it for ice-skating time; we like this magnificent erwtensoep about 364 days of the year. It's loaded with spicy sausages and pork fat; it's as thick as diesel oil, as rich as supercondensed cream, as inert as infantry pancakes, and as indigestible as green sawdust—but is it good! Nearly everybody goes for this Polaris of the Lowlands Kitchen.

Tragedy: Nearly all of the glorious Dutch oysters, famous all over the world, are now as extinct as the dodo. Those enormous new dikes have changed the salinity and other constituents of the water, and most of the centuries-old oyster beds have already expired. Few are left, and these rare survivors are dying so fast you'd better eat all you can get of these historically savory bivalves before they're gone forever.

Some specialties of the Netherlands are herring (try Hollandse Nieuwe— "new" herring—springtime only, as an appetizer), smoked eels (excellent) and other fish; cheese; Deventer gingerbread, currant bread, small sugared fritters (poffertjes); mouth-melting chocolate (Droste and Van Houten are the best); a special caramel candy (Haagse Hopjes), and an unusual egg-flip concoction (Advocaat). Most of them are delicious.

The best bet of all—something no American should miss—is the world-famous rijsttafel (pronounced rye-staffel, and translated as rice table). This, for want of a more descriptive phrase, was the ceremonial feast of the Dutch colonists in Indonesia. The cuisine is like nothing most of us have ever sampled—vaguely Chinese, but with such major departures that it is unique in the annals of dining. The most recent ones we staggered through, at the Bali restaurants in both Amsterdam and Scheveningen, consisted of nearly 30 separate platters—platters, not dishes—and, washed down by a couple of steins of good Holland beer, it was worth all the dreams that later plagued us. Starve yourself all day; permit yourself only 1 order of Sateh Babi (spit-roasted pork on a stick in a delicious hot sauce) with your cocktails; when you sit down to face the dizzy array, put 2 spoonfuls of rice in the center of your plate and *limit yourself to 1 small taste of everything.* Otherwise, you're licked from the start. Highest recommendation of all for any visitor.

Skip lobster in Holland; 95% of the supply is imported these days, and it costs up to Rockefeller levels. Fresh or smoked salmon is in the same category.

If you're hungry at an odd hour of the day, try an Uitsmijter sandwich (translated as "Bouncer"). It's one of the 3 national types: Roast beef, ham, or veal (take your choice), with lots of trimmings, and a fried egg on top. A wonderful bedtime snack, if your stomach is a Bessemer converter.

RESTAURANTS   Expensive, but nothing like the costs in Belgium or France. In average places you'll pay $5 to $10 for a routine meal, but in the Deluxe restaurants it's easy to triple these minimums.

For your run-of-the-mill fare, stick to the smaller establishments. A Tourist Menu promotion, in which 400 restaurants have agreed to offer a 3-course meal for a top tariff of $4.50, is worth checking into if you're a bargain hunter. First-class hotels are steep; top restaurants are often sky high. If you're watching your pennies, there are many snack bars which serve good cafeteria-style food at low prices. You can point at the food instead of fighting the menu.

Amsterdam's leader for elegance today is the **La Rive**, overlooking the canal at the Amstel (see "Hotels"). The gracefulness of this library-style salon, its setting, and the taste manifest in the entire presentation of scene and cuisine, surely make it a water-and-landmark for discriminating travelers. Less posh, but more animated and colorful is the maritime-ly **Port O' Amsterdam** in the Marriott Hotel. It incorporated many North American concepts in its gastronomy that instantly clicked with the more fun-loving and adventurous Dutch. These ideas surely will be copied widely—a measure of the compliments it merits. The **Excelsior Room** of the Hotel de l'Europe is among the more sophisticated pleasure domes in the city.

As for independents, the city's pacesetter is the gaily adorned **De Gravenmolen** (Lijnbaanssteeg 5-7). And what a charmer it is! Two adjoining houses on an enchanting side street in the old center were converted into a restaurant-bar-tavern by personable Host Jan Gravendeel. Ground level for liquid refreshment and lighter bites; captivating upstairs linkage of rooms with paisley green walls, vermilion highlights, suspended plum-colored lamps over candlelit tables, brass sconces, comfortable barrelstave chairs, thick sea-blue carpets, and a joy-burst of flowers before each diner. Beautifully prepared cuisine, somewhat limited in variety but outstanding in quality; smooth, kindhearted service; reasonable tariffs for such sophisticated international gastronomy. If they're available, please have a go at the helium-light Quenelles or the delicious Terrine de Ris de Veau sprinkled with pistachio flakes. How we pray that this one continues with the same 5-star performance standards we experienced during its introductory seasons! Amen! Amen! The same people have opened **De Gravenplas**, a tiny waterside inn with a restaurant at *Langeraar,* which is a sweetie for a lunch or dinner excursion. Or perhaps an overnight?

Another *must* for the average American traveler is the previously mentioned **Bali** restaurant at Leidsestraat 95. This twin to the Scheveningen operation is even better than its world-famous sister. We've already reported our enthusiasm for its astonishing multi-plate rijsttafel in the section on "Food"; anyone who leaves Holland without enjoying this unique adventure in dining has missed the chance of a lifetime. One-flight up; recent extension which doubles its capacity; 100% air-conditioned; modern, pleasant rooms with orange awnings and bay windows; tiny, cozy, ever-jammed Balinese Bar; Javanese waiters in colorful headdresses; 18 female Javanese cooks in the immaculate kitchen; experienced leadership by Proprietor Max Elfring Jr., a friend and admired professional. Ask Max for "the works"; for about $13.50, they'll give you around 9 weeks' worth of vitamins; lesser choices run as low as $9 or so. And when the meal is finished, order one of their "Bali Mystery" cocktails (iced coconut milk, rum, and secret ingredients)—perfect for cutting and complementing this gargantuan repast. *Reserve in advance* (early the same day); despite its expansion there's almost always a hungry queue in the foyer. Marvelous fare; an unforgettable experience; highest possible recommendation.

The most famous restaurant in the Lowlands, the **Five Flies,** is now being operated by the Krasnapolsky Hotel interests. On our recent sampling, this marvelously decorated landmark—even under its improved management—was as bad as we have ever seen it. The cafeteria-type tableware (stainless utensils and cheap plastic salt-and-pepper shakers) might embarrass a Woolworth's basement; our meal was sad news for the palate; the bill was high for the return; the service was perfunctory when it wasn't entirely absent. Definitely not recommended.

The upstairs operation of **Dikker en Thijs** (Leidsestraat 82) is traditionally regarded by local burghers as the most distinguished epicurean center in the Netherlands. Although we wouldn't go nearly that far, our latest lunch here was a big improvement over our earlier disappointing experiences. Streetside main room with a small segment facing the canal; blond chairs, gold curtains, and silver candelabra; the general feeling that it requires a yet-to-be-found catalyst to tie together its coolish ingredients for genuine warmth, coziness, and elegance. The service, we concur, is among the finest you'll find in the region, but overall we're only medium-zealous in our praises. The less expensive **Café du Centre**, downstairs, has been enlarged by stretching one section into a long narrow corridor with red-and-white tablecloths and modern touches suitable for a snackery. It's always busy. The subterranean **Prinsenkelder**, part of the complex, shares its chef but not its menu with the alma mater. It's a long, Old-Worldly room with tile flooring, timbered ceiling, and manor-isms of a Pieter de Hoogh painting. Not Princely but a stout vassal nonetheless.

De Boerderij ("The Farm") is conveniently situated on a corner of the Leidseplein—and nearly every American traveler adores it. Intimate ambiance of banquettes, mosaic tiles, fireplace, copper skillets, and piped music; 2 floors, each with 7 tables; small rôtisserie; rotund, genial Proprietor Wunneberg, a Commander of the Cordon Bleu and the best portable advertisement for his own cooking, wanders around in his chef's cap to attend to the comfort of each guest. Medium-high prices and possibly the most savory European-style food in Amsterdam. Reserve a day in advance in High Season; closed Sunday and holidays. Cheers, cheers, and more cheers!

Molen De Dikkert, out on the Amsterdamseweg, is an amusing rural target. It is built into the base of a huge windmill. If you telephone 020-411378 (wear a glove when dialing) a vintage Rolls-Royce will be dispatched to pick up you and your party—a no-extra-cost service. Tavern atmosphere with weed-fiber blocks set into timbers; Delft theme in linens and china; red rush-bottom chairs; ultramodern bar that is totally out of context. The kitchen has improved notably now that Proprietor Goudsmit, who also owns the Memphis Hotel, has become the miller. The setting, the transportation gimmick, the occasional music for dancing, and the relaxing candlessence are enough to make an evening. Now that its cuisine is first-rate too, we warmly recommend it to seekers of the different.

The fine old-world precincts of the **Port van Cleve** (Nieuwe Zijds Voorburgwal 178) seem to be improving again, we are happy to report. Two floors: Bodega Bar for journalistically inclined visitors on one side of ground floor, opposite a big, barren, cafeteria-like chamber where waiters bawl your order to the counters as loudly as thirsty steers; somber dining room upstairs. The traditional come-on always has been beefsteak—24 separate varieties, from rump steak to double sirloin. They've been individually numbered in sequence since the founding in 1870; yours, if you try one, will probably bear a tag in the neighborhood of 5,000,000—and cross your fingers that it ends in triple zeros, because then all your wine is on the house.

The **Swarte Schaep** (Black Sheep), Korte Leidsedwarsstraat 24 directly off Leidseplein, is a delight to the eye. Rich atmosphere of polished rusticity, beams, candles, and copper and brassware; comfortable surroundings that enhance a romantic mood; acceptable cuisine at rather stately prices; service as soft-spoken as the mood. Pay a bit more for a moderate vintage wine rather than ordering the house variety, because the difference is significant. Distinctly rewarding if you prefer ambiance to alimentation.

The next-door **Bistro La Forge** is a handsome youngster which has bellows of style and lower tabs. Managerial headaches, however, still keep it variable in the cookery department. Double-tiered ground-floor restaurant with a grand fireplace commanding one wall; large captain's chairs and trappings that display a generous pocket; upstairs U-shape bar adjoining a second dining room. We hope it can become a high-stepper.

Good words are falling on our desk concerning **Claes Claesz**, which is avowed to be ultrachic these nights; also favored, this time by Latin tummies, is **Ristorante Mario**, an import from Turin. **Kelderhof** (Prinsengracht 494) is a newcomer that puts on a bold, rustic show with brick floors and walls, a fountain in the foyer, a long pine bar plus barrel tables, a larger inner sanctum with wicker chairs and a tavern atmosphere, and cookery that discloses a French pedigree. Fun, so let's hope it keeps up the initial pace. The **Bistro** at *Ouderkerk*, 10 minutes out beside the Amstel River, is pulsing with enthusiasm these days. So are we—in anticipation of a sampling *muy pronto*.

De Gouden Eeuw ("Golden Age", Keizersgracht 402) appeared to be one of the most chic culinary shrines in Europe—until we took our forks to our tongues. Open evenings only; enchanting eyefuls enhanced by tapers, mauve-pink linens, burgundy velour draperies, a hearth, and live piano, harpsichord, or guitar music; romantic twin-tier restaurant; makeshift bar downstairs; entrance always locked but a waiter answers when you ring the bell. Our Judy quipped that her Veau Fontainbleu, ushered from the kitchen with theatrical flourish, was "so hopelessly gucky that can the chef be a new bride?" And talk about poise! After it had been returned, the maître dropped her 2nd helping on the checkerboard carpet in full view of everyone. Disdainfully ignoring the carnage at his feet, he continued to her side with the platter and asked with perfect aplomb, "Any more potatoes, madam?" The wine list is very limited, but the prices are not. Our overall bill for 2 effectively dispatched

$40 to the Dutch economy. *Golden* is an age-old word, but *value* is another.

Les Quatres Canetons (IIII Prinsengracht) is "in" these days. The plant itself resembles a made-over bunker painted with mud, but the service is perfection, the cookery inclines favorably toward the French, and the presentation is above average (which also can be said for the prices). Okay, but it strikes us as just plain gloomy.

At last Amsterdam has a solstice-tide seafood purveyor in the **Neptunus** (Rokin 87). It is ironic that in this ocean-born-and-bred capital only modest fish houses (see the one below) existed prior to the arrival of this big catch. Walls of cork and wood; beamed ceiling with lantern beams for lighting; framed reproductions of ships; decorative helm; booths with dark-blue cushions; sky-blue napery; taped soft music. Poseidon's pals handsomely presented and carefully cooked; expert navigation by Skipper Choy and First Mate Gallis; large portions at whitebait prices. Swimmingly recommended for its net profits.

The **Oesterbar**, on the Leidseplein, up to now has been the favorite fish restaurant in Western Europe of an irreverent Dutch sidekick. He informed us, "I like the hygienic-looking tiled walls and the silly fishes that gaze at you with such tender eyes through the aquarium-windows." We recently returned their gaze and fed our guilt-ridden corpus with ungrateful sole. Perhaps we're just softies, because the food was delicious—but we get the Orwellean feeling that one day *we're* going to be in that tank, with some cocksure mackerel wearing a bib over his starched tucker and waiting for *his* victim. Excellent for any conscienceless palate. If you admire this one as much as we do, you'll also like the **Keyzer,** a sister operation in the wings of the Concertgebouw.

Het Begijntje (Begijnensteeg 6), in a tiny hideaway lane just off Kalverstraat near the Spui, is once again worth the considerable effort to find it. But before you begin the safari, may we suggest you take a Bokma (gin) or other spirituous drink at the world-famous **Hoppe**, a bar at the corner of Spui and Heisteeg which is the Amsterdam version of New York's P. J. Clarke's? The restaurant features a Spanish guitarist, candle illumination, terra-cotta tile floors, a U-shape configuration with a bar along one stem, an expensive menu, and a wine list glued around a magnum. Our meal was much better this latest try; we still found the mood pretentious, the former smart waiters replaced by prissy smart alecks, and Owner John Baaker overly familiar with his clients. Some will like it, while others will find the personnel too much to swallow. Count your change here.

Le Double W (Utrechtsedwarsstraat 107-109) is now just another steak joint, in our opinion. Its open grill crackles under a huge wrought-iron hood suspended by chain weights. Black and white cinder-block walls; lynx-eye lighting fixtures, plus candles; raffia placemats; menu etched onto a diptych 4-feet tall; wheelbarrow replete with raw vegetables; service sometimes by meatheads who easily might louse up an order for a hard-boiled egg. The same management used to operate the **Volendam,** on the canal facing the Marriott Hotel. It didn't shiver our timbers with delight although we did like the moody darkness of the adjoining Chelsea Bar and the handsome old leeboard sloop that is moored out front as a come-on. We don't know the ownership setup now, so we can't vouch for its quality.

Staying out late? The **Night Restaurant '66** (26 Reguliersgracht), a short totter from the club-girt Rembrandtsplein, yawns "Good Morning" at 10 P.M. and goes to sleep just before dawn. So-called French cuisine; atmosphere remotely Scandinavian in tone; low tabs. If it's late enough, and if you've imbibed enough, you probably won't even mind the food. **Dorrius** (Nieuwe Zijds Voorburgwal 336) is excellent for guilder-watching pilgrims. It is simple, traditional, and substantial; its 4-course lunch is more than a bargain. Closed Sunday. Very rewarding for its category. **Le Chat Qui Pelote** (Zeedijk 16), in the prostitution lane, is a deep, narrow feedery overlooking from its back windows a quiet waterway. The cuisine is not sensational, but it's adequate for the tariffs and it's fun as a curiosity. **Castell,** (Lijnbaansgracht 252-4), next to the famous Continental Bodega, specializes in grills and Indonesian Sates. Bar to the left of entrance; open 5 P.M. to 12:30 A.M.; closed Sunday; popular at first but slipping today.

Chow mein, chop suey, and the like? One of the better Chinese restaurants in Holland is **Lotus** (Binnen Bantammerstraat 5), smack in the heart of the colorful red-light district. Open kitchen, half of which is devoted to sino-savories, mainly from Canton; the other half is dedicated to Indonesian dishes. Low prices; immaculate split-level interior; interesting clientele. Recommended. Another good one is **Fong-Lie** (P.C. Hooftstraat 80). Owned and operated by a friendly and conscientious young couple; cleverly tiered small room for 40, as crowded as a fan-tan game when full; beer and wine only; 12 A.M. to 10 P.M. daily except Sunday and Monday. **Peking,** (Vijzelstraat 28) is more costly; it is also more northern in its culinary posture; some excellent gems bubble in its Soo-Gaw pots. Japanese? **Toga** (Weteringschans 128) wraps up nibbles from Nippon which some diners praise and others seem to abhor. We must give it a try personally soon.

Italian? **La Capannina** (Korte Leidsedwarsstraat 103) pounds out Neapolitan fare. Every bay-bred device imaginable hangs from the walls or ceiling; the dough is rolled, flung, battered, and kneaded in front of your eyes. This show alone is worth the $6.50 cost of an ordinary meal. We've had more educated Latin ladles in Düsseldorf. A better bet is **Mirafiori**, across from the Parkhotel; extra-palatable pastas, extra-friendly proprietor. **Roma,** on the Rokin, is modern but sterile in tone. Spanish? **La Cacerola** (Weteringstraat 41) is currently *en vogue;* you'll drop soothingly few pesetas if you take your *cena* here; the Dutch owner speaks perfect Castilian. Danish? *Skåls* to the **Kopenhagen** (Rokin 84). Low tabs for tiptop snacktime quality. Kosher Kookery? Give **Sandwich Shop Meyer** a flyer; no longer newish but still very Jewish; located by Nieuwmarkt 13. For bigger ruminations of these ethnic nutrients, **Ufaratsta** (Wouwermanstraat 27) has the blessings of the Amsterdam rabbinate—so who are we to argue?

Snacks? **Bodega Continental** (Lijnbaansgracht) is IT for sherry and nibbles between 11 A.M. and 7:30 P.M.; popular among Amsterdamers. **Plein 24** (Leidseplein) is just about perfect for quickie nourishment. Dutch style; very cheap; open until 1 A.M. **Pub O'Henry** (Rokin 89) is right-on for Union Jacks and Jills; it waves the flag from noon to 11 P.M. There's also a Wild West theme: Tossed sawdust on the floor; boar, deer, moose, and a bovinity of heads on the walls; toward dusk an old-fashioned pie-anner player rags out barroom melodies for all and sundry. **Van Dobben** (Korte Reguliersdwarsstraat 5-7-9, near the Rembrandtsplein) specializes in a bewildering variety of tempting sandwiches, plus a few soul-soothing soups. Simple; inexpensive. **Upstairs** (2 Grimburgwal) is a narrow room up a steep flight of stairs that were built in 1536. It serves pancakes (crêpes) only; the prices contradict the staircase; they won't make you puff.

Dedicated budgeteers? Since we're too bottlenecked here for additional entries, please consult this year's vastly revised and updated edition of our annually revised paperback, *Fielding's Super Economy Europe,* which lists scads more bargain dining spots and money-saving tips for serious economizers.

In **The Hague**, the hotels offer the best cuisine of all. For elegance, service, and clean-lined modernity, the **Promenade** is the pick of the pack. For intimacy, the Copper Kettle in the **Hotel des Indes** wins a loving cup. The House of Lords in the **Central** is making a sincere effort to rejoin the peerage these days. Among the independents, the midcity, 2-story **Garoeda** (18A Kneuterdijk), It spotlights Far Eastern delectations. Indonesian staff; a few European dishes; not expensive but very, very good. The **De Kieviet** (see below) provides sturdy competition in the Deluxe bracket. The **Saur** (Lange Voorhout 51), famous for fish specialties, is a runner-up; less costly, slow service, plain appointments; its snack bar has become *the* hangout for local Americans—but damned if we know why. **Royal** (Lange Voorhout 44) is rather dull; ultraconservative surroundings, a fine reputation, as giddy as lunching at the Union Club. The **Bistroquet** (same square at #98) is so popular that you must reserve in advance to enjoy its French preparations. **Nostalgia Restobar** (Javastraat 94) is a wacky hark back into yesteryear that amusingly resurrects Arts Nouveau and Deco in a sentimental mishmash. Upstairs there's a picture gallery. A curiosity that adventuresome voyagers will enjoy. **Chalet Suisse** (Noordeinde 123) is part of a chain; Swiss cookery in the Swiss manner, at medium tariffs. **In den Kleynen Leckerbeck** ("In the Little Gastronome"), Noordwal 1, counts exactly 14 tables. Clean, quaint Old Dutch motif; Lilliputian kitchen; tiny fireplace; they're especially proud of their Poulet Kiëv. A charmer. **Chez Eliza** (Hooikade 14-A) is gaining a following for its French skilletwork. **Roma** (Papestraat 22) wins *salutes* for its Italian creations. **Thousand And One Nights** (Bagijnestraat 24) features a whirling dervish in the kitchen who spins out Middle Eastern culinations. We've never puffed our hookah here. While **Tampat Senang** (Laan van Meerdervoort) is well regarded for its rijsttafel—most locals aver it is the best, in fact—we prefer the creaky sort of authenticity and easy aura of dear old Garoeda. You might disagree.

In **Wassenaar**, 3 miles from The Hague, **De Kieviet** is still a top favorite with the U.S. Embassy group and American residents. Completely rebuilt in an offbeat and less attractive way after being razed by fire; modern tavern décor, with corner tables placed so awkwardly that Your Waiter automatically becomes Your Friend; glassed-in fireplace rôtisserie; daylight terrace-dining in warm weather. Acceptable fare at very high tabs; always reserve in advance.

In **Scheveningen** (beach resort of The Hague), the **Paddock** now gets our vote for straight fodder; open all year. But if you have time for only 1 meal in this part of Holland, make it a rijsttafel at the aforementioned **Bali Restaurant** and Hotel (see "Food" and "Hotels"). This is the twin to the newer Bali in Amsterdam. You'll find more than a score of platters (not plates) of the same exotic delights—bland or pungent, sweet or spicy, light or filling, according to your personal tastes—for a surprisingly modest price. The bartender, Bob, is a wizard; terrace-dining in summer. Ask for Lou Elfring, the genial and knowledgeable Director. Always crowded; reserve the same day, for sure. Top recommendation to this institution.

In **Rotterdam**, please, please don't miss the fabulous tower, the **Euromast**, for your introductory meal. This 240-ton appendage crowns a 606-foot pylon; the effect is reminiscent of a giant up-ended swizzle stick. About 40-feet up there's a barnacle bulge that contains a working facsimile of a ship's bridge; a bluff, hearty merchant mariner is always on watch to explain its controls, instruments, and gadgets to young folk between 5 and 85. At the pinnacle of this aerie are 2 observation platforms from which you can gaze as far as 60 miles, plus an even newer Space Tower that revolves as it ascends. One-flight below are 2 restaurants—the tiered, popular-price mass feedery for budgeteers and the plush Rôtisserie for the middling-opulent voyager. Suave décor; kindly service by Maître J. A. Smithuis and his sturdy cohorts; variable cuisine. The view of the world's busiest harbor and the city is, of course, indescribably beautiful. Unique in the nation.

Coq d'Or (van Vollenhovenstraat 25) has its own cachet, too. We feel, however, that top attention comes only to those who are familiar to the house. In summer, there's a serene garden for alfresco repasting. Inside there's a barlike counter where medium-light dishes are offered to clients-in-a-hurry (goulash, chicken stew, tomato soup, and so on); a blackboard lists the choices. Extending from this is the candlelit dining room; formal dining upstairs, with ultrachic clientele and lilting piano melodies which set the exact mood craved by both your digestion and libido. If you pull any strings to be recognized or recommended, we think you might find it very pleasurable indeed. Closed Sunday.

The **Old Dutch Inn** (Rochussenstraat 20)—on the same tack—is the meeting place of Everyone Who Is Anyone in Rotterdam. It's large and exceedingly popular; the décor is very Old and very Dutch. Busy and noisy; rush-rush-rush service; waiters sweating so hard and running so fast they could be a Keystone Comedy act; atmosphere so frenetic it bursts the pleasure bubble. Go from 9:30 P.M. onward to duck this treadmill pace and to give the chef time to fold the sauces properly. The cookery fulfills the yearnings of Hollanders for rich, gooky sauces and zillion-calorie fare; it's oh-so-heavy-ugh-so-heavy, unless you precisely specify otherwise—and we mean precisely. Ground-floor coffee-room and balcony dining; higher-than-average prices. Hors d'oeuvres are sealed in transparent plastic before being passed out à la Free Lunch style. Closed Sunday. Packed for lunch and dinner.

In Den Rust Wat (Honingerdijk 96) is an outskirts cottage, vintage 1597. Enchanting single room in ancient rustic motif; careful service; magnificent fare for the region; delicious Snails Provençale and Pepper Steak; quality wines; startlingly cheap for the value. The name means "Bide-a-While" and the invitation couldn't be more sincere. We'd bide under its thatched roof any time.

The **Heineken Hoek** (Coolsingel 65) occupies the Holbein Huis premises and augments other Hoeks in Amsterdam and Antwerp. It was urgently recommended by an especially dear friend, who bursts into lyrical operatic arias whenever he describes the wonder, the beauty, the celestial zest of the beer they serve in this joint. The friend's name? Freddy Heineken, who makes the stuff. We'll treat him and his beautiful American-born Lucille of the bourbon empire—and who can top such a happy bourbon-and-beer "boiler-maker"?—to a mug or 5 of his product on our next visit if we can catch them in town.

The **Chalet Suisse** (Kievitslaan 31) can be very pleasant if you're in the mood for what it offers. Park surroundings; spacious chalet-style architecture; main floor rimmed by a rectangular balcony replete with scrubbed-wood tables and red-and-white striped curtains; waitresses in regional costume; tiered terrace in front for sunny-day dining or tippling; chummy bar inside. Gigantic 143-item menu with such Valais specialties as mountain wind-and-snow-cured beef; Swiss, French and Italian wines, as well. Packed solid at night; slow but friendly service; closed Sunday. Recommended.

Alpine flavor in both dishes and ambiance can also be found in the **Euro-Motel** Airport restaurant, while an inn-ermost atmosphere is available at the cozy **Herberg** (Kleiweg). **De Pijp** (Gaffelstraat 90) is about as rough as they come. Open kitchen at your elbow; no-nonsense cookery; 7 wooden tables pushed together in community fashion; flotsam décor; sawdust on its stone floor; superb cooking. A favorite of true-blue Rotterdamers and often difficult for outsiders to get inside. Not for fainthearts, but highly recommended.

The **Witte Paard** (White Horse), on the outskirts, compares unfavorably with a "country" restaurant in the suburbs of New York or Washington. The exterior blends rusticity, antiquity, and *haut décor* in properly eye-catching proportions—but the interior, at least to us, is a letdown. Not to our taste.

Genuine "country" atmosphere and charm? The well-known **De Beuken-hof**, in *Oegstgeest* (2 miles from Leyden), is elaborate and expensive in a slick-rustic manner; tap room, gardens, dining room, converted hayloft for larger parties, and the Beech Tree, for which it was named. Close to Amsterdam and now better under its new ownership. **De Deyselhof** at *Landsmeer,* nearer to Amsterdam and now only a 15-minute drive via the new tunnel, is so popular from Tuesday through Saturday (closed otherwise) that a reservation is an absolute *must.* Three segments for dining; 2 carriages inset into walls; open hearth and open hearts; pretty fair cuisine for blue-ribbon tabs. **Le Postillon de La Provence**, at *Laren,* about 15 miles from Amsterdam, is a rural enchantress. Busy grill; beamed ceiling; moss-green carpet; thick wooden tables; thick steaks, too, and delightful cuisine of all sorts. It is owned by the funloving J. P. De Wijs, former Resident Manager of the Amsterdam Hilton. In this bright young man's hands it has become a red-hot contender.

If you must go to *Volendam*, the city of the itching palm, the **Hotel van Diepen** serves an adequate meal. The best thing to order is fried eel, of which they are proudest; it sounds terrible, but you'll be surprised how flavorsome this delicate white meat can be. At the **Spaander Hotel**, our recent "coffee table" consisted of soup, hors d'oeuvres, a variety of meats and cheeses, a some-kind-of croquette, and a pot of coffee; it cost around $2, and it wasn't bad for such a modest snack. At the **Old Dutch**, a Lowlands hamburger with good old native French fries goes for about $1.50. Fair.

For the rest, why not explore? We've tried at least 7-dozen restaurants on our visits to the Netherlands, and while some were better than others, none was dirty and few were disappointing.

NIGHTCLUBS Plentiful. Everything from Persian Rooms to Times Square tourist traps to neighborhood taverns to honkytonks—the galaxy. You can sip champagne in your evening clothes at swank membership clubs, or you can drink beer while clutching your wallet in one of the most wide-open bordello districts in Europe. As mentioned earlier, this nation's liberal statutes have attracted some migrants. (One hotel we know suddenly, innocently found itself the site of an International Congress of Homosexuals—the most unconventional convention it ever unwittingly hosted. The fly boys wing in regularly for weekend flings.) With the tightening up of legal loopholes in England, France, and Germany, Holland has now become a temporary haven and safe harbor for Gay, hippie, Way Out, and Way Way Out sets. So don't be surprised at what you see—of *any* gender or nongender. In this freewheeling society, even the prices of narcotics are broadcast over the radio at specific times of the day.

In *Amsterdam*, **Blue Note** (Leidseplein area) is miles ahead as the top nightery open to you and me. Very good bands; tiny dance floor; 4 cozy bars; 20-minute cabaret; popular with parents and the Younger Set alike. If you're a middle-age smoothie, you've already seen 2 dozen like it; if you're 19 and in love, you'll be in company with plenty of similar couples. This one earns the parental okays of the local mammas and papas.

Whisky à Gogo is a jigger-size private club over the Blue Note, with three 14-seat bars and 4 Lilliputian tables. The member or guest-member may select a top brand of any potable, and it will be stored for him in his own locker. All subsequent soda, ice, and service is included in one single bill. If you're well dressed and reasonably sober, you may be invited up when you tap at the door. Operates from 10 P.M. to 4 A.M. (Sat. to 5 A.M.); very pleasant romancing spot (as long as you bring your own romance!).

Le Poisson Rouge, downstairs in the Apollo Hotel also draws moony types. It's not the grooviest, but if you're in that mood and with that someone, it can be a big, big catch.

Most fun of all, if you're bright-eyed, bushy-tailed, and young in spirit, is to bar-hop through Amsterdam's more typical small bistros. If you're a man and if you're alone, you should particularly enjoy this circuit—although wives often get a great kick out of it, too. We are especially fond of the cozy **Auberge Privé** (Leidseplein 8) which is not *private* except in mood, the **Bon Mariage** (Herengracht 338) for snuggles, wine, and cheese; then the sea-and-seeworthy **Boekanier,** at the yacht club (toward the airport), where you can sip and linger or even dine in easy chairs drawn up before a crackling fire; or, back in town, the ultra-intimate, ultra-Dutchy **Tapperij Gijsbrecht van Aemstel** (Herengracht 435), where romance is spun from dim light and liquids. **Frascati** (Nes 59) draws most of its following from the theatrical and TV sectors. All of these fall into the loosely classified category of "brown cafés"—lovers' or topers' nooks where *you* provide most of the wattage.

For the "in" crowd a quartet of swingers take the prize: (1) **Voom-Voom**, (2) **King's Club**, (3) **Club 67** and (4) **Zzazz**. The first boasts 2 bars, soft sofas, wooden timbers, and fair-priced libations. The second is sheathed with colored plexiglass partitions, mirrors, brass, and crystal; it spotlights an American-style unslipped-disk jockey. The third is spacious, modernistic, and loaded with booths; if the policy still holds, you can't enter if you're over 30. (We knew a 12-year-old shill who vouched for us.) The last features black and orange diagonals, a loud atmosphere, cheap drinks, and hot dogs. This one's whippery for whippersnappers. **Boeing** flies by night in the form of a 707 cabin. Odd but hardly jet-propelled. **Toy-Toy** next door, is dressed in vinyl and stocked with little Dutch stenographers. Pretty routine. **Revolution** revolves in fin de siècle moods; it didn't turn us on. **Rasputin** swings in with a zigzag brass-topped bar, molded plastic chairs, a long room, and few long faces.

In the Hand Holding Department, the atmosphere at the **Corrida Club** (Wagenstraat 2) turns peons into matadors. Tête-à-tête drinking; subdued and slightly faded décor; piano virtuoso Gé van Toorenburg plays the "Warsaw Concerto" or "Night and Day" better than Liberace. Closed Sunday; still good. **Zirbelstube** has the air of a ski-resort tavern; knotty pine by the kilometer; no tablecloths; whisky on tap, but wine is the usual beverage here; clean, animated, and attractive for a pause, except for its terrible ventilation. Jewish cabaret à la Minsky is available at **Li-La-Lo** (109 de Clercqstraat); services begin at 10 P.M.; we don't know their dishes from their knishes, because we've never said *L'Chayim* here. The **Caliente** (Lijnbaansgracht, just off the Leidseplein) has picked up a blistering batch of BTUs to become a very hot contender. Two bars flanking a circular dance floor; white wrought-iron appointments; candlelighting; plastic flowers by the synthetic grove; mild Mexican theme; good spirits in the glass and in the air; routine disrobing every quarter-hour on the belly button. *Saludos, amigos!* The hippie parlor known as the **Paradiso** is back again after a period in limbo. The government advises kids that they can't sleep here, but who can tell the difference? We were told that pot can be smoked but not sold. True? The **Carrousel** (Thorbeckeplein 20) features goofy dolls on the walls, bartenders who double in musical brass (as well as behind the brass rail), and worn surroundings which mean nothing to the clients who have come to listen and not to see. If you can still recall the era, or even the books, of F. Scott Fitzgerald, we think you'll enjoy the uninhibited, fun-filled atmosphere that seems almost anachronistic today. **Café de Paris** now is said to discourage male customers. We skirted it on our last whirl and from what we hear, we're not panting to get in. Early-to-bedders will probably relish the aforementioned **Continental Bodega**; excellent wines at cave-bottom prices; closing time is 7:30—that's P.M. not A.M.! Another one of this sort but even better is the **Heineken Hoek**, smack on the Leidseplein. It is built around copper brewing kettles. Very atmospheric.

Oosterling is yet another favorite for sip samplers; shades drawn at 6 P.M. normally, but not until 7 P.M. on Friday. **Courage** stays open later. **Boogaloo** is rather cheap—and we mean this in *every* sense of the word. For youngsters, **Tuf-Tuf,** in a tiny alley called Handboogsteeg, registers one of the highest tides in the Lowlands. Dutch-door (what else?) entrance; split-level arrangement; upper rank with bar and quiet corner for stoking with Coke; main stratum in saloon style with antique tram-car fixin's; lower pit for jiggers, terpsichorean variety, who display the latest disco-techniques; median age of customers about eighteen. A wonderful evening out for shavers who hardly know which end of a razor to pick up. **Lucky Star**, atwinkle dimly across from Club '67 in the heartbeat of town, has faded slowly. We have a feeling it is in an eclipse. The **Moulin Rouge** (5 Thorbeckeplein) puts on one of the splashiest promotions on the nightscape. Frankly, we wouldn't tilt with this red windmill for love or guilders. A beer draws a whopping head of around $2 per cup. We were amused by the alleged retort of a multimillionaire brewer who is said to have commented to the owner of the joint, "I'm glad you don't sell my product here, because as much as I like it, it's still not worth *that* much." Never again for us.

Looking for companionship? Try Sheherazade or practically any gin mill around the Rembrandtsplein or in the Seamen's Quarter (locally called the Zeedijk district). **Sheherazade** (2 blocks from the Rembrandtsplein at Wagenstraat 5) is currently the pick of the lot; 2 orchestras, dim lights, and Dutch hotshots fad-dancing; whisky which tasted to us as if it never saw the Scottish sunrise; dim, humid, seraglio lighting; no cover or minimum, but drinks run into money. Plenty of hostesses, and some of them fairly cute. The **Casablanca** is a rowdy *boîte:* entertainers, blaring music, crowds of sailors and their girl friends. In our best Canarsie manner, quite appropriate to the subject, let us leave this jernt lay: It ain't genteel—and it could be dangerous. **Max Pola,** just off the Leidseplein, is an amusing piano bar for after-dinner revels. Nice people, good drinks, tuneful entertainment by Max himself. Gentlemanly companionship? The **Bonaparte Club** gave us the impression that it lost some of its attracting power since its redecoration. Ex-prize fighter doorman; long bar for mixing; big pedestal booths for sit-down types; décor in what we'd term Hygienic Twentieth Century Empire. Appears to be popular with those who care. **Incognito** pulls in Jet Setters plus other flighty types of another disposition. More Empire décor; go late if you go-go. The **Privé** is another entry for the inner circle. Very successful as of the instant. Two others are the rage among the foreign elements; membership is required by all comers. With absolutely no vulgarity intended, we report their names and addresses simply as they are: **The Coc** (49-A Korte Leidsedwarsstraat) and **The Dok** (460 Singel). We're told that the former is the more "exclusive," and that both welcome the special planeloads of winged weekenders who fly in regularly from London, Berlin, and other more restrictive climes in search of freedom. Apparently they find it in abundance. (A National Tourist Office official disclosed that there are at least 15 such clubs in the city; he added that male mail requests for guidance to these spots are routinely answered.) Heterosexual onlookers are discouraged, of course.

The Seamen's Quarter is as blatant as New Orleans used to be—and, in the same way, an interesting and curious clock-stopper. Along Oude Zijds Voor-burgwal and in the neighborhood of Oudekerksplein (ironically, Old Church Place) are low-grade bars adjoining really low-grade cribs. Some of the cribs actually sport red lights. While this area may be relatively safe, if not lusty, please do not wander onto the Oude Zijds Achterburgwal, which can be extremely dangerous. Drugs are marketed openly and rough stuff does occur; even the police are unable to control the gangsterism that is bred by the narcotics trade. Be careful with your wallet and with what you drink (bottled beer, uncapped before you, is best). It's a wide open district—the last of a social phenomenon that vanished elsewhere in Europe 25 to 50 years ago.

The Hague? The **Rose & Orange** is a cheerful pub for the Mug Set. **Alexandra** strips on a regular basis; she offers a floor show, too.

The **7 Club**, up 1-flight and operated for adults, recently was reshaped by its new owners. Improved 7-upwards. **L'Étoile**, its downstairs hangout for teen-agers, has music to suit its clients; fairly good but far from outstanding. **Charlotte Chérie** is a cozy, 25-watt-bulb bar, made to order for hand holding; tiny band, tiny dance floor, nice bartenders, gals, gals, and more gals; pleasant drop-in stop for a quick drink. If none of these turns up anything savory, there are about 25 more hitching posts—mostly small, intimate bars with the omnipresent B-gals.

Scheveningen, the beach resort 15 minutes out via the high-speed thru-way, is a big drawing card for night types, who usually conclude their revels here. **Gretna Green** struck us as being the leader. Cozy, sophisticated ambiance; square bar; decorative forge for welding that coy "maybe" into a stain-less "yes"; small cabaret at intervals; just the hideaway for a pitch, a convivial cocktail, and warbling an intimate serenade of Gretna Greensleeves. **Joseph's Place** is a 1-flight-up, handsomely made-over cartwright's shop; a woody wagon-train with a paddock-bar will be your stablemate. This Joe likes the Place. **Tiffany's** offers a necklace of facets, each glittering with an agrestic polish, and each strung cheek-to-cheek by the collection of young gems and their janes beaded with pearls of perspiration. The trio occupy various sancta in the enormous Palace Gebouw. They share the same sovereign, similar low-price tithings, and an upbeat spirit that should make most beachcombers glow. All are recommended.

Rotterdam's night lights glimmer most invitingly at **El Amra**, a 3-minute toddle from the Hotel Atlanta in midcity. Intimate dimensions cunningly achieved by a hefty stone partition between its twin segments; bandstand backed by a hide-covered marquee; "showtime" a solo crooner; intimate dancing interspersed with fad-prancing the principal themes. Even though our familiarly labeled French cognac was poured out for a modest $2.50, some alchemist seemed to have gone to unheralded lengths to transmute our cupful from Gallic essences to local ingredients. Nevertheless, here's the "in"-ner-most spot in this Lowland Grenada. After that, we'd rate them this way: (2) **Bristol** (glass-lined round-robin nest; superb for late teen-types who don't mind the jam-up on the dance circle; watch your billings here); (3) **Casino de Paris** (2 dimly lighted rooms with candles in bottles; Undersea Bar with huge, garish, fake fish and a few eenie-weenie goldfish with inferiority complexes;

expanded Louis XVI Bar; band okay; whisky okay; sandwiches okay; good but not outstanding); (4) **Embassy Club** (newly refeathered as a cozy nest for nighthawks); (5) **La Bonanza** (circular realm under a giant spoked wheel on the ceiling; 2 bars; inner hub for the shortsighted, plus an outer raised ring for tierful gazing; legitimate whisky on our sip; international cabaret; scintillating strip by Mother Nature, despite the ladies' long acquaintance with Father Time); (6) **L'Ambassadeur** (becoming a tough hangout; peepers rank behind a plate-glass barrier; snacks-to-steaks available; show commences at 10:30 P.M., returning every hour until 3 A.M.).

Garden of Eden turned on a membership policy when it began specializing in films about Eve and her sinful progeny. Other less attractive, so-called respectable bars—the take-your-wife types—include **Top Hat, Atlantic, Plaza**, and **Coney Island.**

La Romantica (Witte de Withstraat 14) is a small, clean, coldly decorated room with harsh lighting and a lively neighborhood-tavern-style clientele; don't go out of your way. **La Roulette Bodega-Bar** (Schiedamsevest 146) offers watered-down Reno-type surroundings; **Oase** (Schilderstraat 24) also has music. Discothèque? **Le Bateau** rocks every night except Monday from 8 P.M. to 4 A.M. at an anchorage beside the Hilton. It's a happy bark. The **Dive Inn** and **De Wieck** compete for the same clientele.

If you're looking for riotous local color, a quick junket to Katendrecht ("The Cape" or Chinatown) is it. In this Seamen's Quarter, you'll find music, lights, and the fastest kind of action—after all, since a whole ship can be unloaded in a couple of hours these days, how much time can a poor sailor and his girl waste on discussions of Aristotelian philosophy? In the **Brooklyn Bar, Happy Times Bar, Neutral Bar, Pacific Bar, Tsong Kok Low's** chopstick emporium, and dozens of similar old-style saloons or cafés, you'll find dancing, boozing, grass-smoking (possibly), and skylarking in the raw. Lots of harpies on tap for company (some are perfect caricatures of Sadie Thompson). See this before midnight, if you're interested, with the swing through the legitimate nightclubs planned for later. Watch your watch and bankroll, drink bottled beer, and don't act like a tourist who has come to view the animals. They can be very rough indeed if they decide to make trouble.

For further entertainment information on other cities, consult the NNTO or any of the 450 VVV headquarters.

§TIP: Gambling has been approved officially in Holland, so gamesters soon may be able to play roulette and blackjack in several green baizeworks around the nation. Baccarat is due to follow after the casinos are established in Zandvoort, Valkenburg, and Scheveningen. Others in Arnhem/Nijmegen and Breda/Tilburg are proposed for future wheeling and dealing.

TAXIS　　We used to nourish the illusion Dutch cab drivers were more trustworthy than their colleagues in most other European lands. But now, on repeated recent visits, they cheated us blind—or tried to!—at least ¼th of the time. It's disappointing in a nation of such legendary integrity.

As for gratuities, the meter reading now includes the full legal tip. What a boon this is! When you jump in, be sure the flag is pulled down at the beginning—and at the end, be sure he doesn't roll the tabulations back to zero before you have a chance to *see for yourself* what they read. If he doesn't have a meter, always find out the cost before climbing aboard.

You'll find it difficult to hail a street cruiser; head for a taxi rank instead or for the nearest telephone in order to summon a cab.

TRAINS   Fast service, accurate schedules, high frequency. Among the world's most modern rolling stock, now 100% electric or diesel—but equipment still isn't sufficient to cope with the enormous traffic demands. During rush hours, you might stand all the way. Always ride First class, because distances are short, the price difference is trivial, and Second can be overcrowded.

Electric trains run from Amsterdam to The Hague every quarter hour; some have coffee bars. "D" and "TEE" trains (the latter are international) have adequate dining cars. Fares are extremely low. "D" trains charge an extra 80¢ at the ticket office or $1.20 on the rods, and they're worth it.

Watch out for the inland 1-day excursion ticket, because the return half expires as soon as the last train on the timetable of that night pulls out. The free publication, "Day Trips in Holland," available at the sales window of any station, has further information about this.

The best bet for serious riders (unless you have your Eurailpass) is the 8-day season ticket which is valid all over the Netherlands Railways network and on The Hague-Amsterdam bus. Use it until calluses appear on your nether regions—as often and as much as you like—for approximately $30 in First or $20 in Second class. Such money-savers as the Day Rover (24 hours for $10 or less), the Day Multi-Rover or "Meerman's Kaart" (designed for 2-to-6-person groups), and the Weekend or Evening Returns are also available. *Bring a passport photo if you want to be a "Rover" boy-or-girl.*

Porters are found only at the larger stations. A few—not all—possibly could be termed robbers. You must pay a set rate per piece, plus a tip—but don't give them more than a 20% gratuity, even if their bleats can be heard all the way to the Hook-of-Holland. They may be ordered in advance through a special postcard furnished by the railway. As we oafishly stare at the Dutch text and unintelligible blank spaces on the sample before us, however, we've decided we'd rather heft 800-lb. barbells than try to cope with this form.

AIRLINE   KLM is a colossus of aviation, with a sterling reputation and a magnificent overall record. In '73, an extensive survey by *Flight International* magazine named it as the safest commercial carrier in the 15 leading nations.

The company flies 7 Boeing 747 Jumbos, 7 DC-10-30's, 12 DC-8 jetliners and 11 "Super" versions of the same rocket on intercontinental routes, with 19 DC-9's earmarked for the European network. KLM's subsidiary, NLM Dutch Airlines, operates a domestic network using Fokker-27 Friendship turboprops to link Amsterdam, Eindhoven, Enschede, Groningen, and Maastricht.

Schiphol Airport, 7 miles from the center of Amsterdam, is home base for the KLM fleet. It's a monument to Dutch drainage skills that on this very spot in 1573 the navies of Spain and the Netherlands fought a sea battle! Should you approach the field via the Ringcanal dike road, you will see ships riding higher than your ground level—and before you take off on the runway, you'll be 14 feet below the adjoining canal.

In addition to being aesthetically pleasing in a sleek way, it is perhaps the best-planned and most efficient airline passenger facility in Europe today. Conveyor belts for luggage, rolling sidewalks, an ingenious message system for travelers, all types of restaurants, and a self-service tax-free shop are only a part of its twenty-first-century picture.

We recently stepped off a KLM 747 transatlantic crossing, and our long-time affection and respect for this carrier remain untarnished. The airmanship we witnessed was again a virtuoso performance. Every member of the cabin crew was warm, competent, and with-it; these genuinely eager-to-please professionals all reflected their painstakingly thorough training. The noncomestible amenities were far, far better than those we have found aboard Alitalia, Iberia, and a score of competitors; only SAS, Swissair, and 2 or 3 others of the 40-odd we've flown top them here, in our opinion. The cuisine aloft, in both presentation and preparation, was our only disappointment. All in all, the spirit and ambiance and expertise we again observed reinforce our belief that here indeed is a magnificent airline.

If you should ever find yourself tangled up with scheduling problems or other emergencies involving this fine carrier, take them to Charles L. Bulterman at KLM, 609 Fifth Ave., N.Y 10017.

Recommendation: A magnificent carrier. KLM has our complete respect, confidence, and admiration.

DRINKS   A bonanza in scope. Unknown brands of Scotch can be bought for about $9.50, with proprietary brands running up to $14.50-or-so; imported ryes, bourbons, gins, rum, Canadian Club, and others are well represented in the better shops, bars, and restaurants, at decent prices. And those good, GOOD Heineken and Amstel beers, bless their soothing souls, are about 50¢ per mug.

Dutch gin (they call it *jenever*) is for taste buds which can flash a college degree. It's colorless, volatile, aromatic, slightly bitter—a flavor you'll find in no other bottle in no other land. The "Oude Klare" is a dryer and more sophisticated type than the stronger, more highly flavored "Jonge." Our favorite brand is Bokma, available almost everywhere. Drink it from a shot glass; when you blow out your breath, be careful of that stranger's cigarette 20 feet away. (If proper form is followed, it will be served, instead, in a "tulip" glass—and your first sip must be slurped while the glass rests on the bar!) Never, never attempt to make a martini of it, as I did; the results curled my locks. It simply isn't made for mixing.

The liqueurs, over 40 varieties, are interesting. Ask for Bols or Hoppe products, which are dependable, while some imitations are not.

§TIPS: When the drinks are on you, say "Let's have a *borrel!*" It's the universal Dutch invitation; in Americanese, it translates "Got time for a short one, brother?"

The historical national toast is *"Op uw gezondheid,"* which means "To your good health." (Try not to pause after the first 2 words.) Most Dutchmen settle for a simple *"Proost"* before the elbow bends and a few use an affected *"Santé,"* derived from the French, *naturellement*.

Since brewers are usually given exclusive contracts, most Dutch restaurants sell only 1 brand of beer.

THINGS TO SEE   Before offering any positive suggestions on this subject, we hasten to inject a negative one: The once-classic tourist meccas of **Marken** (closed to auto traffic) and **Volendam** are not recommended today. We've again returned from a thoroughgoing tour of both these gimmick hubs, and this admonition, published annually in the *Guide* for the last 2 decades or so, now becomes even stronger. The Dutch Government has been laboring valiantly to knock some manners into these rotten-spoiled villagers and to root out the phony-baloney sham that has flummoxed so many foreign visitors—with some success in Volendam, and less in Marken. Our advice: Skip these traps and go to **Spakenburg** instead. Here's a hamlet where the folk dress and charm are far more genuine—and it's only a 60-minute drive from Amsterdam. Customary hours for wearing these togs is on Sundays around church-meeting time: 9 A.M. to 9:30 A.M. or 6:30 P.M. to 7 P.M. Or go on from Zwolle to **Giethoorn** (called "The Dutch Venice") and **Staphorst**, which is straight from a quaint old print. In both, be sure to obtain prior permission if you wish to photograph any of the inhabitants. These have been the real stuff, not hammy theatrical displays—but now even a few of these people are learning cornball tricks.

In **Amsterdam**, the first thing you should do is to take a boat ride (**rondvaart**) around the city—especially during the Festival (see below), when everything's ablaze with special illumination from 8:30 P.M. to midnight. For less than a dollar you can travel for 1¼ hours, and you'll treasure the barge pilot's view of the most intriguing canals. Along the Rokin, the Nassaukade, and the Damrak you'll find 4 or 5 lines, all controlled by the municipality. The boats leave at 30-minute intervals; they all have glass roofs. Here is a junket that is really fun. You'll see everything from the Blue Bridge to the Brewer's Canal to the red-light district. Candlelight cruises begin at 9:30 P.M. and last until 11:45 P.M., with a ½-hour port-o'-call at the Havenrestaurant; in this package you'll receive a glass of wine and a few bars of live music. The local VVV can get you aboard.

Next, no traveler should *dream* of missing the **Rijksmuseum**, with its unparalleled collection of Old Dutch masters; Rembrandt's "Night Watch" is, of course, its star attraction.

Rijksmuseum Vincent Van Gogh (Paulus Potterstr.) is devoted to the works of the master and to his friends and contemporaries, such as Gaugin, Manet, and Toulouse-Lautrec.

The nearby **Stedelijk** ("Municipal Museum," Paulus Potterstr. 13) offers a modern art panoply from Picasso to Chagall, Monet, Miró, Degas, Cézanne, Braque, Mondrian, Matisse, and Toulouse-Lautrec. The most illustrious American painter represented? Willem de Kooning whose name and heritage bring delight to local connoisseurs. It is operative from 9:30 A.M. to 5:30 P.M.

on weekdays and from 1 P.M. to 5 P.M. on Sunday. The gate toll is 60¢. Also the Stuff of Dreams.

Time out now for a breather? **Heineken Brewery** (Van der Helststr. 30) is the beeline target of battalions of thirsty visitors who are enamored of this zesty Golden Liquid. Go to the Stadhouderskade entrance Monday through Friday; shuttle into the staging area between 9 and 11 A.M. (only during the summer); its delicious beer with niblets of cheese await you at tour's end. Fanciful, filling, fun and also only 40¢.

The 4-story **Anne Frank House** (Prinsengracht 263), in which the martyred child wrote her 2-year diary before being discovered and killed by the Nazis, is in deep financial trouble. The Anne Frank Foundation, launched in '60 to keep the house open as a permanent monument to the dangers of political extremism, now charges 60¢ admission in order to maintain this cause. We believe that this symbol of courage in the face of inhumanity is worth an hour of your time and as many loose guilders as you can contribute beyond the modest entry fee.

Madame Tussaud's (Kalverstr. 156) is fashioned in the image of the famous London waxery. Open daily from 10 A.M. to 6 P.M. in winter but extended by several hours in summer.

Aspiring architects and perspiring rubbernecks may also find pleasure in one or more of the following: (1) **Royal Palace** (built as the town hall in 1662; perched on exactly 13,659 pilings; famous for van Helt Stockade's allegoric ceiling paintings; open daily from 1:30 to 4:30 P.M. between June 1 and the 3rd week in August, with a 20¢ gate fee for adults and half price for youngsters); (2) **Nieuwe Kerk** (late Gothic Church with wooden vaults and uniquely clustered columns); (3) **Oude Kerk** (consecrated in 1306; Iron Chapel which houses timeworn municipal documents; steeple carillon); (4) the **Waag** (completed in 1488; merchants weights-and-measures house until 1819; circular floorplan); (5) **Portuguese Synagogue** (early seventeenth-century structure; a haven for refugees from the Inquisition); and (6) the **Stock Exchange** (built in 1903; the earliest employment of structural iron).

The **Beguinage** (end of Begijnensteeg, off Kalverstraat) is a courtyard quadrangle of seventeenth-and eighteenth-century homes which will shunt you back 300-years. Here's a 3-star stroll that is known and enjoyed by far too few of us outlanders.

Finally, the **Mint Tower** (Muntplein), 3 blocks to the south, draws batteries of foreign-manned Roleiflexes. The nation's coin presses were hidden in its octagonal base after the French captured Utrecht in 1672. This one is a canalside charmer.

In June the **Holland Festival** is an enterprise sponsored by Amsterdam, The Hague, Rotterdam, and Scheveningen; this is a good time to plan to be in Holland. Most of the Festival revolves around music: Alternate or simultaneous dramas, concerts, opera, or ballet in various cities—something big every night—with an occasional film exhibition to change the pace. For reservations, either write direct to the Booking Office, Holland Festival, Centraal Bespreekbureau, Postbus 430, The Hague—or call by phone or in person at Honthorststraat 10, Amsterdam. The larger VVV bureaus also will set aside ducats for you, not only for Festival events but for major theatrical performances at other times as well.

There are many interesting excursions within shooting distance of Amsterdam. **Alkmaar** on a Friday morning between May and late September is a very happy one if the weather is good: The huge **cheese market** is running full blast until noon; it's colorful and surprisingly odorless. If you want to expand this into a fuller loop, start out early for **Monnikendam** and take your morning coffee in the ancient waterside **Stuttenburgh Inn** with its 199 music boxes and antique curiosities. Now move north along the sea route and through **Volendam** (driving straight through is enough), **Edam, Hoorn**, and on to **Enkhuizen** for a visit to the fine little **Zuiderzee Museum,** right at the water's edge. A pleasant lunch can be had at either the next-door Taveerne in de Meermin or the Hotel Het Wapen, around the corner and across the bridge. After lunch, make your way over to **Alkmaar** (at this hour, of course, you will have missed the busy morning market sales, but it's worth going, anyway) and then down to **Haarlem** for a tour of the small but impressive **Frans Hals Museum**. For a refresher, the tiny Ark pub, down an alley, is a modest, fun-filled, and incredibly old stop for a quick beer. (Engineers may want to continue to **Heemstede** for a look at working models of the fabulous drainage systems employed by Dutch experts since 1860. Plan about 30 minutes to watch the full process at this **Polder Museum** —a diversion we think will appeal only to the technically minded.) The drive back to Amsterdam is only 13 miles from this point, so with ease you're back in time for dinner.

Another fascinating circuit shoots out to **Aalsmeer** as a starter (10 miles southwest of Amsterdam). This is Holland's permanent flower center, both physically and financially; thousands of blooms from the surrounding countryside pour into this funnel daily, where they are sorted, selected, and sold at auction in 2 gigantic wholesale markets. Exquisite colors and varieties, many new to the U.S. amateur gardener; a lovely spectacle, which must be viewed before 11 A.M. on any weekday (not Sun.); Saturday and Tuesday are best, followed successively by Thursday, Wednesday, and Monday; Friday is poorest. While the auctioning goes from 8 A.M. to 11 A.M. except on Sunday, *go very early to enjoy the liveliest fun.* Now whiz down to **Gouda** (pronounced not as "GOO-da," but as "HOW-da"). On the plaza surrounding the Town Hall, with its contrasting red-and-white shutters and gold trim, dairy farmers sell their famous cheeses every Thursday morning from mid-May to mid- September; a smaller flower sale is held at the same place on Saturday. You can sip a coffee in the 400-year-old Hotel de Zalm, on the periphery of the main square, before pushing on to either **Woerden**, another cheese center (by the main highway), or to **Oudewater**. In the latter, ladies, you can be weighed on the town scales. If you register even 1 oz. more than the minimum for a true mortal, you will be given a certificate declaring that you are not a witch (they are presumed to weigh less than normal gals). Then, if hubby ever has the nerve to make a certain baseless and offensive accusation, just smile as you fan this document under his nose! Personally, we're in love with the tiny, tiny canalside path that ambles through Oudewater and stretches on to **Utrecht**. Should you seek an off-trail adventure that really takes you through the backwash farmlands of the nation, don't miss this sampling of bucolic charm at its pastoral best. Utrecht has her diversions (see "Cities"), but we prefer to skim along east to **Soesterberg** for lunch at the 't Zwaantje

("The Little Swan") before viewing the Royal Palace at nearby **Soestdijk.**
If you're feeling especially rich and your tummy can hold out, a lovely
alternative is the previously mentioned Kasteel De Hooge Vuursche at Baarn,
or the cheaper and also extremely good Herberg de Roskam ("Inn of the
Currycomb"), next to the Castle entrance on the Hilversum highway. Then
a 1-hour detour to **Muiden**, site of the beautifully preserved thirteenth-
century fortress of the same name, is rewarding (but be sure to check on the
exact closing time before leaving your hotel, because it varies with the season).
From here, you're only ½-hour from your welcome bedside and a short siesta
before dinner in the metropolis. As for other targets, **Zandvoort Beach** is
passable. Except for the memorabilia of the Pilgrim Fathers and the ethnological museum, **Leyden** is nothing special. **The Hague** has a couple of
excellent museums, the lively beach resort of **Scheveningen**, and a fairy-
tale wonder for kids and adults alike: **Madurodam**, the most amazing miniature city in existence. This modern-day Lilliput, condensed into approximately 4 acres, employing 2¼ miles of railway track, and illuminated by
44-thousand lights, is a complete community of castles, churches, homes,
shops, docks, airport—everything imaginable. And the thousands of details
are a perfect 1/25th of their normal scale. More than 1-million visitors promenade its 2-mile circuit annually. It's open from early April to early October,
including Sunday; the admission price is peanuts; 50% discount for under-
13ers; 7:30 P.M. to 10:30 P.M. closings, depending upon the month; restaurant
on premises; don't miss this unique attraction, whether you're 7, 17, or 70.
Rotterdam, slightly more than an hour from Amsterdam, has some glorious river views and some excellent harbor installations. Try the **VVV Sightseeing Tour**, operated several times daily from April through October at
about $3 per person. It takes 1¾ hours, and fans out from the VVV office;
this is the best. Or try one of the well-known **Spido** cruises of the fabulous
docks—1¼ hours on the briny, with frequent departures in both summer and
winter, and watertaxi service, all from the Willemsplein Landing Stage. Day
excursions to the aforementioned Delta works are also on tap for dedicated
polder peepers. As another choice, spins by car to the Mill District have been
inaugurated. The **Blijdorp Zoo**, perhaps the most modern in Europe, is also
a treat for Bronx Zoo fans—and who isn't? And the new "Lijnbaan" Shopping Center brings cheers from even Texas, California, or Florida gals. Further suggestions for Rotterdam may be found under "Cities."

If you are wandering near the German border, the **Netherlands Open Air
Museum** in **Arnhem** is the European cousin of the Jamestown and Stur-
bridge Village projects. As a wise New Jersey friend of the *Guide* comments,
". . . if travelers to Holland could see that—and only that—they'd have a true
idea of Dutch folklore." Plan on a good ½-day to roam this 82-acre park at
leisure; superior snack-type food available; open daily from April 1 to November 1; wonderful. The **War Museum** at **Overloon**, extensively modernized,
is also interesting. Here, on the site of one of the greatest tank battles of the
war, a 40-acre park has been set aside, on which has been assembled every
conceivable type of armored vehicle, artillery piece, small arm, automatic
weapon, mine, and war-making device that was used in the Liberation. The
Documentation Hall and the section on booby traps are especially note-

worthy. Admission is about $1 (children 25¢), and there are 2 fairly good restaurants in the woods surrounding the exhibits.

The finest trip in Holland—one of the most stimulating holidays in Europe —is the circuit of what we'll still call the *Zuiderzee* (the official name is now the "IJsselmeer"), with a stopoff at the wild and beautiful island of *Texel*. The Zuiderzee is a gigantic salt lake that indents the center of Holland's coastline all the way down to Amsterdam; now blocked off from the sea by an 18½-mile dam, hundreds of thousands of acres of valuable land have been recovered from it. See your travel agent for bus or private-car touring arrangements.

If you're driving your own automobile, you can make the Zuiderzee circle in 1 day of hard pushing—omitting Texel, of course. The short, quick round, however, is not recommended because the pace will knock you out. If you can spare 2 days, you must still skip Texel; in this case, by far the best place to spend the night is the Hotel van Gijtenbeek in *Zwolle*. Though deep in the rural district, its comfort is good. If you can spare 3 or even 4 days, you are in for a junket you'll never forget, for here's the real heart of Holland.

Two points to remember: (1) The Texel ferry accepts automobiles only on a first-come-first-served basis, and (2) sailing times change according to the season; check before leaving Amsterdam.

Hindeloopen, *Harderwijk*, *Urk*, *Giethoorn*, *Staphorst*, *De Cocksdorp*, *Deventer*, *Zutphen*, *Bronkhorst*, *Doesburg*, *Sneek*— truly, Holland is full of delightful hamlets as intriguing as their names.

TIPPING   Hotels take 15% automatically on stays less than 6 days (10% for longer visits); this includes bar tabs charged to your room. Waiters get 15% (nearly always included in your bill). Theater usherettes and washroom attendants deserve the Dutch equivalent of a dime at the most. A law bundles the gratuity into the hairdresser's chit. Railway porters expect 15% to 20% more than the set rate (25¢ per load). Give the hall porter in your hotel a few guilders when you check out; he works hard for you, and it's the usual thing to do. Give the maid or other staff people a few guilders, too, if you have had any special services.

In general, the Dutch are far less grabby than the French or Italians but not quite so unmercenary as the Norwegians or Danes. Use your judgment, and you'll get along famously.

THINGS TO BUY   Diamonds, Delft ware, Dutch crystal, Dutch silver, miniatures, handicrafts, art, antiques, and Indonesian bric-a-brac are the top specialties here.

In *Amsterdam*, the best shopping streets are Kalverstraat, Rokin, Heiligeweg, and Leidsestraat. The first 2 can be covered in perhaps 15 minutes of walking. Antique hounds will find about 30 establishments in Nieuwe Spiegelstraat for happy browsing. The Amstelveen Shopping Center is 5 minutes from Schiphol Airport.

While diamonds are still a bargain, if you aren't thoroughly conversant with their technical subtleties they can be terribly tricky to buy. That's why we suggest that you head straight for the oldest and most respected gem merchant in the Netherlands—the house of **Bonebakker** (Rokin 88). Don't let the elegance of their air-conditioned premises stop you, because their diamond prices aren't a single guilder—or even kwartje—higher than anywhere else. Your local sightseeing guide, operating from a very human desire for a commission, might insist on leading you by the ear to various "factories" —some of which are good, and some of which are fancied-up tourist traps. For actual buying, we'd far, far prefer to discuss our transaction with gem experts such as Adrian Bonebakker or his son Ferdinand (the 6th generation here), who lay the 185-year-old Bonebakker reputation on the table every time they display a stone to a client. This Amsterdam landmark was founded in 1792 by Adrianus Bonebakker. As Holland's number one jeweler, they carry a complete line of classic and contemporary jewelry, Patek Philippe and Ebel watches, and other sinfully appealing luxuries. Generally speaking, the Dutch are an outstandingly honest people. But, as in every nation in the world, there *are* some exceptions—and diamonds are so arcane and so important a purchase that, for your own protection, it's just simple common sense to do business with the best purveyor. They are exempt from the national 18% B.T.W. tax, too! Closed Monday until 1 P.M. Tops.

Delft ware has so many perils for the unwary that we always make doubly sure of what we're getting by going to **Focke & Meltzer** (Kalverstraat 152 and P.C. Hooftstraat 65), and nowhere else. Scads of claptrap fakes of the real thing are being peddled all over Holland. But at this treasure house, leader throughout the Lowlands since 1823 and now the most modern china-and-crystal shop on the Continent, there's no monkey business about the famous Delft imprint. A big choice of genuine pieces runs from $5 to $2000; all are hand-painted under the glaze. In addition to the characteristic blue ware, Delft also produces articles in green Delvert, rainbow-hued Polychroom, and the famous red, blue, and gold Pijnacker—all on display here (look for the unique pieces signed by Master Craftsmen Sanders, Glaudemans, or Van Willigen—*what* beauties!). Americans also like Holland's best-known crystal products: Leerdam's hand-blown and hand-cut, fluted-style glasses (from $25 to $300 per dozen). Also, the best crystal, china, glass, faïence, and earthenware from 22, repeat 22, European countries is on hand—Orrefors, Wedgwood, Waterford, Royal Copenhagen, Herend, and many others. These magnates also operate a strikingly handsome similarly streamlined branch at Venestraat 20 in *The Hague*, a second in neighboring *Scheveningen*, and a third at *Ryswyk*. In Amsterdam, ask the amicable Mr. Paul Meltzer to be your mentor; this friendly gentleman has a special kinship with—and affection for—Americans. This garden of wantables is terrific. Happy 154th anniversary!

Dutch-style gold, silver, miniatures, and other souvenir items, plus smaller diamonds? **Carel van Pampus b.v.** (Kalverstraat 56 and Nieuwendijk 140) is the perfect problem solver for the wanderer who wants overseas mementos which (1) won't break, (2) won't cost too much, and (3) won't take up too much space or weight in the luggage. Among his most popular features are the Old Dutch room with handsome silver miniature furniture, his colorful enameled silver tulip brooches, and his attractive Old-Dutch-style silver-tipped corks, spoons, miniatures, boxes, and similar articles which bear effective reproductions of paintings by Rembrandt, Jan Steen, and other venerated masters. His great collection of gold charms starts at only $10. The small gold earrings for pierced ears are lovely for the younger voyager. Conversely, you might find your exact design and price in a nice piece of gold jewelry or a string of van Pampus-imported Japanese cultured pearls. Most shoppers aren't aware of the facts that (1) unset diamonds (a large assembly is on display) are automatically sold tax-free and (2) all purchases valued at more than $450 are also tax-free if a reliable source such as this one will prove that you are exporting them. Electronic and quartz Seiko watches are big sellers here, too. Important: Higher quality merchandise is stocked at his main store, while less costly jewelry and his complete lines of watches (as well as his own watchmakers' workshop) are found at his branch at Nieuwendijk 140. Mr. van Pampus, the 3rd generation of his family to operate these small, personalized establishments—as well as one of his country's experts in diamonds—will greet you at the headquarters with a warm smile. So will his friendly staff. Traveler's checks, as well as the majority of the most widely used credit cards, are accepted. Outstanding in its field.

Modern paintings and art objects? **Kunsthandel Ina Broerse** (Nieuwe Spiegelstraat 57), occupying 3 floors in a seventeenth-century house, offers triweekly purchase-exhibitions of Dutch graphics, ceramics, wall hangings, small sculptures and more, in addition to some permanent examples of folk art. Mrs. Broerse has proudly launched a sizable branch in Schiphol Airport upstairs in the Tax Free zone which displays the works of 50 to 100 of her artists and artisans. Both establishments are of special interest.

Indonesian bric-a-brac? **M. L. J. Lemaire** (Prinsengracht 841) sells figures, masks, daggers, old Batik, all sorts of East Indian trophies. It's striking stuff —but wear your blue jeans and plumber's cap when you go, because we have the feeling the *patron* sets the prices from the cut of his customer's clothes.

Shopping elsewhere in Holland? This year's vastly revised and updated edition of *Fielding's Shopping Guide to Europe* lists the top picks in 4 other cities; sorry there's no room to carry them here.

National holidays? New Year's Day; Easter and Easter Monday; the Thursday of Ascension Day (10 days before Whitsunday); Whitmonday; April 30 (the Queen's Birthday); Christmas and the following day.

Shopping hours? Complicated as all get out. *Department and durables stores are closed until 1 P.M. on Monday;* on other days, they're usually open from between 8:30 or 9 A.M. to 5:30 or 6 P.M., including Saturday. Shops featuring consumer goods generally lock their doors on Wednesday afternoon; Barbers and many hairdressers pull their blinds on Tuesday. Many continue until 9 or 9:30 P.M. on Thursdays. There's a flock of other variables —so check before leaving your hotel.

§TIP: Bona fide nonresident departing passengers at Schiphol Airport (Amsterdam) *with destinations outside the Benelux countries* may save up to 60% on a raft of luxury items (liquors, tobacco, perfumes, binoculars, tape recorders, watches, toys, and a galaxy more) at its self-service Tax Free Shopping Center, largest on the Continent. Read its interesting brochure, available on the spot, before you buy. Here is the only enterprise at any airfield in Europe that makes careful distinctions between levied and unlevied merchandise for the benefit of the customer. Its liberalized policies are good news for the tripper. Our only carp—a serious one—is that so many of its stores are chronically out of stock of exactly the listed item or items upon which the traveler's heart is set. This is a frequent and frustrating disappointment, because you may visit the area *only* as you leave.

THINGS NOT TO BUY   Furs (only rabbits are raised in Holland); routine costume jewelry (expensive and dull); fine gloves (the heavy ones are okay, but the dress-up variety cost a mint for poor quality); perfumes (much cheaper and better in France); fine wines (astronomical); shoes (a different last from the American foot).

Otherwise, there's a torrent of good things for practically all your needs.

§REMINDER: Watch Delft imitations, for reasons described above.

LOCAL RACKETS   The Dutch are square shooters; 99.99% of them are too dignified and decent to stoop to chicanery. Aside from the occasional larcenous taxi driver, Marken, Volendam, and the Seamen's Quarter in Amsterdam or its equivalent in other cities (even Hollanders ask for trouble when they venture here), you'll encounter honesty and integrity. If you leave your bankroll and your Rolleiflex in your hotel room by mistake, you come back 99 times out of 100 to find both untouched. Try this for size in some of the Latin countries, and you'll see the contrast.

Northern Ireland

As you might have noticed during the 30 years that this *Guide* has been issued and annually revised, politics never play any part between its covers. Your safety and comfort, however, most definitely do. Hence, it is for these 2 considerations that we are deleting our chapter on this noble land until she is again blessed with peace and order. As soon as her venerable and copious joys can again be experienced without fear of accidental injury, please take for granted that we will be prompt in resuming our full reportage here. How we pray that the time will come soon, soon, soon when her beauties will flower once more for the legions of voyagers who are eager to alight on her lovely shores!

Norway

Europe's most northerly country is only the area of New Mexico, but it's so long and thin that distances are amazing. From top to bottom it stretches the same length as from New York to Omaha, Nebraska; from side to side, however, the average breadth—60 miles—can be covered in 2 hours' easy driving. The famous Skagerrak (same latitude as Scotland) separates it from Denmark; the northern tip rises far beyond the Arctic Circle.

There aren't many Norwegians. Except for Luxembourg and some other tots, it is the smallest major nation in Europe, yet it ranks 3rd in the world (behind Switzerland and Sweden) in per capita income. (The U.S. is now number 4.) Some economists predict Norway will move up to 2nd before the decade retires. This year the 4-million inhabitants will probably be outnumbered by the estimated 4½-million foreign fun-seekers (4,499,999, all with cameras to snap the incomparably spectacular terrain). Ethnologically, they're dyed-in-the-wool Nordics; 98.7% are of pure local stock, 0.7% are the 25-thousand Lapps, and 0.5% are miscellaneous; intermarriage is rare. Most of them are blond, stocky, muscular, healthy—with a zest for living rivaled only by the Danes.

Crook by crook, the coastline measures 12,500 miles—½ the earth's circumference, twisting through a 2 x 4 area—and most of it is islands and fjords. There's wonderful fishing everywhere; you can drop your hook off 150-thousand islands! (Look out! You might strike oil since the continental shelf here seems to be bubbling with petroleum deposits.)

The ideal way to see Norway is to visit all 4 types of terrain: The fjords, the mountains, the valleys, and the plains. The fjords are giant cracks in the earth's crust, where the sea runs along rock-walled corridors which are often a mile deep and a mile high. The big ones are on the west coast, facing Iceland, Greenland, and Canada. The mountains are scattered wherever you go; the valleys nestle peacefully in their shelter and in the depths of the great serrated plateau. The plains run from Oslo up to Lake Mjøsa, but the country is so rugged that only 5% of its land can be cultivated.

King Olav V succeeded the equally beloved King Haakon VII to the Norwegian throne in '57, and, as always, they continue to call this nation which celebrated the 160th birthday of its constitution in 1974, a constitutional monarchy. Realistically, however, it is just about as democratic as Denmark and Sweden. Social legislation includes unemployment relief, sickness and accident insurance, old-age pensions, housing projects, care of mothers and children, schools for the deformed, and heaven knows what. There's universal suffrage for every citizen over 20 years old. Education is free and compulsory from the ages of 7 to 16, and illiteracy is unknown. Transmission of venereal infection is a criminal offense. The endowed state religion is Evangelical Lutheran (96.8%), but all faiths are tolerated.

Don't worry about raccoon coats and red-flannel underwear; the Norwegian climate is duplicated in parts of Massachusetts. The Gulf Stream keeps it warm: In the summer, the means are 60° at Oslo, 50° on the Arctic Circle; in the winter, they're 24° at Oslo, 10° where Santa Claus comes from. The midnight sun above the 66th parallel makes daylight last for weeks. There's no real darkness, even in the south, from May to August. On the coast it rains so much you'll think you're in Waterville, Wash. Lots of flowers and cool green forests, too.

Norway and the Norwegians are fun. Even without its magnificent scenery, this land would always be a perfect country for tourists.

CITIES   *Oslo* is the biggest, gayest, most pulsating and colorful. It's the capital, chief port (which is saying a lot in this maritime nation), and hub of society. The population is 475-thousand; in area it is one of the largest cities of the world. Picture Norway as a human finger pointing downward; Oslo is on the inside tip, up from the crook of the first joint. Good hotels, excellent restaurants, 3 major airlines (SAS, Wiederoe, and Braathens SAFE), fine trains, mild climate, handsome men, beautiful women. Seven-seas' relics range from original Viking ships to the 1895 polar vessel *Fram* to the *Kon-Tiki* raft to the papyrus *Ra II*. The harbor is a sporting sailor's paradise; gunwale to gunwale are the finest ocean racers, sloops, ketches, yawls, schooners, yachts, and other dreamboats with the capacity to turn grown men into boys again. The highly imaginative Henie-Onstad Museum at Høvikodden (7 miles west of the city center) was donated by the late ice-skating queen and her shipowner husband, Niels Onstad—both born here but later U.S. residents. The area contains more than 200 contemporary paintings, plus a "pop" gallery in which local pop-ers show their stuff; facilities for ballet, concerts, and selected exhibitions, as well as a congress hall, a cinema, a restaurant, a cafeteria, an open-air theater-in-the-round, and an esplanade at the base of its fanlike terraces which stair-step down to the lip of tranquil Oslo Fjord. Here you will find Sonja Henie's massive trophy collection. The complex is a proud button-popper for the nation that spent millions of kroner in its creation. Interestingly, this lazily sprawling minimetropolis boasts so much elbowroom that the annual Holmenkollen ski race covers a 35-mile run and 2000 cows graze on tidy farms—all within the city limits! The landscape is gently rolling pasture land and plain—not typical of the terrain as a whole, which is rugged.

Bergen, who recently kindled up her 900th birthday candle, is at the base of the fingernail. She's on the Atlantic side, directly across from Oslo, and her population of 215 thousand makes this sprightly dowager the 2nd largest city in Norway. Don't miss this jovial matron of the seas; her medieval charm will captivate you by day and enchant you by night. There's a magnificent panorama from either the cable airway to Ulriken, highest of its 7 famous mountains, or the funicular to Fløien. There's a fish market where you can select your dinner while it is still swimming; there are turreted bastions, crazy little houses built before 1800, the Edvard Grieg shrine, the aquarium, the intriguing Maritime Museum (don't miss this one if you've got salt in your veins), an upbeat pace to improve a previously indifferent hotel picture, good restaurants, and good comfort. Shipbuilding, trade, and harbor activities keep most of the people busy; don't believe the legend that "it always rains in Bergen" —it is only 99% true, and then only in 10- or 15-minute spells. For local information, call on the Information Office of Tourism, on the square near the Bristol. Here's a clean, quaint seaport with a great deal to attract the traveler.

Trondheim, is third in importance. It's up the coast from Bergen, nestled in the wrinkles of the skin back of the first joint. Decatur, Illinois, is larger; timber, fish, and shipping are the chief industries. The cathedral is the finest of its kind in Scandinavia. Geographically, you'll find the setting delightful. It's on a fjord; the old name is "Nidaros," which means "Mouth of the River Nid"—and that's just what it is.

Stavanger, capital of the sardine industry and the size of Laredo, Texas, is fourth. The similarity does not end there, because its Tourist Office is continuing a Texas-like drive to which the thriving SAS Royal Atlantic and K.N.A. hotels—the former one of Scandinavia's best equipped—have made substantial contributions. Finally, this Texas-tyke claims oil, too—but hers resides beneath the waters of the North Sea. One dazzler is the express boat service to and from Bergen on the high-stepping *Westamaran*. Deep-sea excursions with the inviting guarantee of "No Catch—No Cash" and outings to the canyon-like Lysefjord by "Fjord Clipper" (motor launch) are available to while away one's time here. **Voss**, birthplace of Knute Rockne, presented to the University of Notre Dame a handsome memorial honoring this immortal in '62. Pilgrims to this burgeoning village will find a cableway and several ski lifts to haul an ever increasing number of Americans and Britons each snowtime; the trails for walking or slicing down the soft white hills are among the loveliest we've ever seen (be sure to go to the very top first). Impressive ancient church in the town square; fine headquarters for fjord motoring excursions or skiing patrols into the nearby wilderness; new après-ski activities for nocturnal upliftings, too. **Fredrikstad** is a tale of 2 cities: the New Town (35-thousand modern-minded citizens) and the Old Town (cobbled streets, moats, and surrounding fortress walls, 700 souls, all of whom celebrated its 400th birthday in '67). Here is the site of the famous Plus craft center (its ateliers are open to the public). **Kristiansand** is on the lower tip of the nation; it is a thriving ferry point for Denmark, England, Germany, and Holland. **Kristiansund** straddles 3 islands with connecting bridges. This center is a fishing port and the striking-out point for climbing tours to the Nordmøre Alps. Lovely to look at, but not much action. **Aalesund** is another calling spot for steamers on the Coastal Expressway. It, too, is built on islands; when your ship pauses here for its usual 2½-hour docking, a run up to the summit of Aksla Mountain (only 625 feet high, but with a restaurant affording a breathtaking view of the waterways) is about the only show in town. **Molde** is famed for her roses and her panorama of 87 alplike peaks. The historic mining town of **Röros** is a cross-country skier's paradise; miles of rolling slopeland which stay under good powder until the end of April; strictly for sportsmen who love it in winter and antiquarians who love it in summer.

Geilo is so special that it is very dear to our travel hearts. On the main railway line halfway between Oslo and Bergen, it offers 1 main street, a handful of cozy hotels snuggling above the valley, excellent food on virtually every table, and an intimate spirit of holiday frolic. Here, for our öre, is one of the most rewarding pockets of vacation cheer on the map of Norway. In the future it may vie with Zermatt, Zürs, Courchevel, and other chummy corners for Europe's upland Jet Set swingers. The ski runs are not as long as they are in the midriff of the Continent, and the cold (yet superdry) air may be too brittle for all except the hardiest outdoor types. But, as a let's-get-away-from-the-rabble resort, this tiny gem is hard to beat. Between Geilo Sport (our favorite) and Intersport, there are 800 pairs of excellent cross-country, down-hill and slalom hickories for rent, plus poles, boots, toboggans, motorized snow scooters, all types of ice skates (the municipal rink is open all winter), and curling equipment. The indoor pool splashes from 6 A.M. to 9 P.M. Crowning the peaks and serving as the nexus for winter pioneers or summer hikers is the gloriously panoramic Geilo Toppen. This glassbound restaurant and cafeteria is at the top of the main chair lift, midway between the village and the upper reaches of the mountain range. The local Tourist Office will happily arrange for rental of any tack or gear for any sport in them thar hills —from an adventure-filled hunting trip afoot, aski, or aboard a gasoline-pepped Snow Cat, to pony trekking on the moors, to trout fishing at any of the 40 nearby lakes or streams (license: $1.40 per day, $5 per week, or $8.40 for the full season). If you prefer your very own wood-lined, ultracomfortable chalet, Berg-Hansen Travel Bureau ("Things to See") or the Tourist Office can fix *that* too. By American, Swiss, or French standards, costs are relatively low. For a relaxing pause to refresh sagging spirits through unspoiled natural treasures, we'd be hard put to think of any better spot. Please go, if you can; we think you'll fall in love with it, just as we did a long time ago.

MONEY AND PRICES   The Norwegian currency units are the öre and krone. There are 100 öre to the krone; 1 krone is currently worth about 18¢.

Despite the nation's decision declining membership in the Common Market, the recent 5% upward monetary revaluation, and the "added-value" ("MOMS") tax waxings, Norway today is not too, too expensive for the U.S. vacationer—in rural areas, one of the least costly lands in the Western Hemisphere (Oslo and Bergen prices are spiraling upward). You are likely to share with many other visitors the surprise of how little you'll spend for luxurious living.

You may bring in an unlimited amount of Norwegian Kroner and take out up to 800 kroner, but all bills must be in units of 100 kroner or smaller. There is no limit on the import or export of *foreign* currencies by travelers.

ATTITUDE TOWARD TOURISTS

You, as a tourist, are part of a whopping source of income (in 6th place on the national budget). Nothing is spared to give you pleasure and to make you comfortable. The **Norway Travel Association** (Landslaget for Reiselivet i Norge, L.R.N. for short) is a large, beautifully managed organization subsidized by the Government and by commercial companies (hotels, airlines, etc.) who benefit from your visit. Its chief is the highly efficient Just Muus Falck. It publishes scores of free posters, booklets, and hotel guides; it turns the heat on the Parliament any time an existing law is a hardship for the traveler. These are the people to see when a doorknob is stuck or you want to buy a sperm whale; check with the Oslo Tourist Information Office (Munkedamsveien 15). They can either fix it or find it in minutes. These people want tourists, and they're all-out to get them.

Norwegian Information Service (facts about the country) is at 505 Fifth Avenue in New York, but the **Norwegian National Travel Office** (facts about travel) is on the 11th floor at 75 Rockefeller Plaza, N.Y. 10019. Per Prag is the director of the latter; he also handles promotion for Sweden, but don't whisper it around. You can count on officials of both offices to flash typical North Country smiles and to take care of your questions promptly and efficiently.

CUSTOMS AND IMMIGRATION

Unusually courteous and cooperative. Since Scandinavia operates as 1 community customs area, the only time you will be confronted with customs procedures is if Norway is your incoming or outgoing gateway. Even though the official takes his job seriously—and he's stern about important violations—you should get along famously with the average Norwegian inspector. The legal limit is 400 cigarettes, but an extra carton or 2 will probably get by, as they seldom count your supply. Two bottles of spirits will pass, so stick the rest of your stock in your overcoat pockets or in the conductor's lunchbox.

HOTELS

For far more comprehensive information on certain hostelries than space limitations permit here, interested travelers are referred to *Fieldings Selected Favorites: Hotels and Inns, Europe* by our son, Dodge Temple Fielding. The latest annually revised edition, in which a total of 300-odd favored possibilities were handpicked from the 4000-plus personally inspected, will be at your bookstore early this year.

In *Oslo*, 2 (Grand and Bristol) cater so heavily to Scandinavian loyalists that sometimes they're the devil for Americans to get into. The new and still-to-be-ranked **Scandinavia,** sponsored by SAS, currently is being run by the Western International chain. We'll have more on this one in our next edition. The **Grand**, like New York's Plaza in the pre-Hilton days, made its name in the Spacious Tradition. It still retains its generous dimensions. In other ways, however, it is moving toward more modern concepts under Director Borchgrevink, who formerly did such a wonderful job at the Park in Sandefjord. Today he boasts more than 300 rooms with bath, the shimmering new high-in-the-sky l'Étoile restaurant, a bar, health center, and rooftop swimming pool. Another tall feather in his headdress is the Bonanza, a pure-bred Arizona import serving U.S.-style meals from 8 P.M. to 2 A.M., plus entertainment and bar libations. Famous Speilsalen Restaurant ("Mirror Room") with music from 9 P.M. to 12:30 A.M.; paneled Grill, beguiling, but —alas and alack—dancing is not a feature. Palm court repruned; beautiful Karl Johan Suite with a chalked-oak salon, bar, refrigerator, and canopied bed. The fresh-wind administration is sweeping away the last remaining cobwebs and making the old plant bloom. We're more fond of this hostelry and the friendly people who run it than ever before. Recommended.

The smooth-sailing **Continental**, with its traditional high-tide hospitality, has been (and is being) so handsomely refitted that here is one of the proudest rigs in the port city. The oldest deck of this happy ship dates back a mere half-decade, with 20 staterooms restyled each year on a continuing, unceasing cycle—and based on a poll taken of guests' opinions of architectural renderings. Dining room expensively revamped, with panoramic windows added; Fortuna Pub Maritime Restaurant that is the absolute kingfishery of the North; glamorously chic hairdressing salon and barbershop; 8 units specifically for early-morning arrivals whose normal accommodations have not yet become available—another convenience provided by the ever thoughtful administrators. You'll find a marble-sheathed entrance, a pleasant breakfast room, an immaculate Grill, A refashioned Pavilion that is a café by day and a Frenchy *Boîte* by night, the sidewalk-level Theatercafeen, a ground-floor bar plus another one in marine motif, a first-rate Swiss chef who whips up palate-pleasing vittles, and friendly, capable management by Mathis Berge. Choicest niche—frankly, our favorite accommodation in Norway—is the 8th-floor, corner-situated Nautical Suite with terrace, TV, and beautifully executed décor; #723, which nods above the tree-shaded park, is almost as good. Solid comfort, superior facilities (in many cases, better than the other leading house), and warmhearted attention provided by the smoothly professional skippering of the perennially personable and gracious Mr. and Mrs. Caspar Brochmann, both of whom are adorable and adored. Beloved by most U.S. voyagers—for excellent reasons.

The **Bristol**, now under new ownership by a local realtor, is smart and fashionable. The building recently was renewed, melding its formerly disproportionate elements in a rounded unity. Now there is a new reception desk, the bully El Toro restaurant in the cellar, the late-hours Leopard Club for revels, and a Bristol of bristlings in the redecoration department. Full carpets throughout; Danish-style furnishings in most bedrooms; hessian wall coverings, plus attractive paintings. Let's see how this house develops under its new proprietorship.

The **Ambassadeur** is something special. No restaurant; no bar; new small pool and gym; space for 60 envoys, mainly in singles or suites. Reception and lounge area featuring an aquarium and an interesting weapons exhibit; unusually appealing apartments with tiny refrigerators, framed tapestries, dark wood décor, telephone, radio, bathrooms with scales, and many umbrella-clad private balconies. Each nest is extremely comfortable (#52 is our favorite). Not really a full-scale hotel, but amply luxurious for anyone who seeks a quiet hideaway without fanfare and without built-in meals. Top recommendation for its very particular category.

The recharged **Astoria** has zoomed up among the leaders. It now sparkles with a clean-lined modernistic lobby, 99 perky bedchambers, superb single accommodations, bath or shower with almost every unit, radio-music consoles, lockboxes, double doors, and a lawn of turquoise carpeting. Odd facts department: Every inch of furniture within this entire house was constructed from a single African bibinga tree—so please don't carve your initials in the desk top! A solid utility address.

The clean and attractive **K.N.A.** offers 140 rooms with ultrasmall baths or showers (some old-fashioned); handsome restaurant and bar; special children's menu; public rooms and 85 sleeping units refurnished in the past few years; radios in every bedchamber. Book into the *older* section, which has better furnishings and a cheerier mien; the newer wing offers less space and beds in tandem. There's a somewhat impersonal, commercial feel to this establishment; many conducted tour groups stop here. General Manager Richard Patterson, a Past President of the Norwegian Hotel and Restaurant Association, is a delightful fellow who runs his house, within its limitations, very well indeed. The **Nobel** has a tiny modern lobby which might put you off right from the start. Facilities: 61 rooms and 48 baths; breakfasts only. Norwegian regional furniture—some antiques, some reproductions; a few bedchambers with refrigerator; indifferent standards of service seem to be the greatest liability here. The **Carlton**, under new management, has zipped up the furnishings and widened the windows to give its 50 minuscule and somewhat drab chambers the illusion of greater space; lounge and bar; for budgeteers or stoutish snackers, the special lunch table ladles out 16 self-service selections, including 1 hot dish. Still miniature but taking the right hormones. The **Norum** boasts its air-conditioned Bar Bistro, which angles out to a tiny, popular 10-table restaurant with 4-language menu, acoustical ceiling, and warmly ingratiating atmosphere. The serene ambiance of this old-fashioned mansion is homespun; heavy patronage by Parliament members. Agreeable for travelers with children; 5 minutes by taxi from the center. The **Viking,** one of Scandinavia's largest hostelries, is operated by the Norwegian Dining Car Co. It offers 350 rooms with individual toilets and 50% of them with bath or shower; most are mite-size but brightly furnished; orchestra for nightly dancing; volume-turnover operation; shoeshine machine on each floor; 10-story expansion still only a dream—along with a carload of other mirages which give the kindly Reception Manager, Finn Tiller, nightmares of frustration and anxiety. A while back a "rationalization group" announced in a survey that house porters are excess baggage on the Viking payroll. Since they've been dumped, you may have to "rationalize" those suitcases from the taxi up to the desk. A mass-motivated mammoth at its massiest. The **West** has an outstanding chef in the quietly modern Coq d'Or restaurant; all bedchambers now with private bath; clean simplicity the theme of the sleeping units. The new 500-pillowed **Summer Hotel** (Storgt. 55) aptly operates only

June through Aug. on a low-tariff basis that should draw waves of budget travelers in season. Basic rates from $17 to $21 per person, with breakfast, in a double room; $23 in a single; cafeteria available; all units with shower and w.c. In summer-y? A saving. The SAS-sponsored **Globetrotter**, near the airport, resembles its SASsy sister operation of the same name in Copenhagen (see "Hotels" in "Denmark"). Veteran Inge Hellebust is at the controls. Its 150 cabins are more mindful of transient traffic than of long runners. The 250-pillow **Gyldenlöve**, in *Bogstadveien* behind the Palace, was given new raiments, but they seem to be heavy enough to be the costumery of an Ibsen play. The suites especially hark back to the Norway of Old even though they are virtually new. Okay for medium-budget historians.

The **Stefan**, a Mission Hotel once bone dry, went mad and daringly un-bunged the beer keg; fairly comfortable rooms but indifferent cookery. For motorists, the **Helsfyr** is the closest thing to a U.S.-styled "motel" in Norway. Operated by the Workers' Travel Association; 70 rooms; a few private baths; modest but cheerful décor. North of town, 15 minutes from center; pretty spartan. It has been given permission to unwrap an 18-story hostelry, but we have no further details on this entry. The 36-unit restyled **Atlantic** owned by the Astoria people, provides a similar scene, but with far fewer baths than the major house. Good taste prevails and the rates are low.

The **Holmenkollen Turisthotell** offers such specialized appeal it must be considered separately. It's 20 minutes by electric railway from Oslo's bright lights, on the mountainside bordering the celebrated ski jump; magnificent views are an asset; a covey of rooms have recently been modernized with unimaginative taste; only 20 have private bath and shower, but there are vague plans to add more; suite #312, with its private terrace and fantastic vista, is a honey. If you're a winter-sports fan or a nature lover who plans a visit of 5 days or longer, this might be just the dish; the average traveler-in-a-hurry, however, generally prefers to stay in the city.

Tariffs vary with the seasons. From May 1 to September 30, the top period, rates for the leading establishments in Oslo—Norway's most expensive city—are roughly $19 to $33 for a single, $33 to $46 for a double, and $45 to $88 for a suite—all quotations with bath. Breakfast ($4) is additional, of course —but no bandit "extras" as in Sweden. A special discount for children under 12 and a further one for those under 7 are universally offered. As we've already noted, hotel prices have spiraled flabbergastingly. In the hinterland, however, your dollar will stretch miles further. Almost all the best-known provincial hostelries will still give you a room and 3 meals for $30 per day—and in the north, they'll charge you even less.

Dedicated budgeteers? Since we're too bottlenecked here for additional entries, please consult our this year's edition of our annually revised, heavily updated paperback, *Fielding's Low-Cost Europe,* which lists scads more bargain hotels or pensions and money-saving tips for serious economizers.

Bergen's hotel offerings have soared in quality during recent seasons.
The sparkling 9-story **Norge** is now one of the finest houses in the entire North. Quietly modern lobby in marble tones; ground-floor dining and drinking complex consisting of the cozy Ole Bull with charcoal grills, the main

restaurant, the rôtisserie, the Hjørnet ("Corner") Pub in dark wood high-lighted with copper and brass fittings, the Karjolen Bar with barrel stools and oak appointments, the outdoor summer café, and the Baldakinen restaurant on the balcony floor; the Garden Room Restaurant operates in the banquet hall June through August, with dancing featured. Downstairs you'll find a discothèque, a snack bar, shops, a florist, a bank, and a built-in SAS terminal. All 240 bedrooms air-conditioned; 15 suites (the smaller ones on the lakeside feature a superb view); doubles all with a sitting area; warm furnishings that are timeless; many private balconies; smallish but well-equipped baths; 4-channel radio; direct-dialing telephones with message lamps. According to a number of Guidesters, this Big City atmosphere sometimes falls down in its Small Town service standards; on our very recent incognito stopover, it happened to be silky-smooth. Managing Director Finn Skjøren is a veteran who is a master at his craft. Urbane, sleek, and warmly recommended.

The **Bristol** has been taken over by a couple of banking houses which planned to unveil a totally new hostelry. For some strange reason the ground floor incorporates a bank. The grill-bar is reportedly a winner. Probably a sound investment for '77 maturity.

The **Grand Terminus**, only a 30-second chug from the station but still surprisingly quiet, has become more and more of a streamliner . For many travelers, however, its ownership by a religious order and consequent lack of alcohol automatically drop it a notch as a holiday haven. We've come from a dry run here and—though parched to the core—we couldn't have been more pleased with the comfort standards, the cleanliness, the flavorful décor, and the gentle goodheartedness and deep-down-warmth of the personnel. Every bedroom in soothing, homey themes; units ending in "10" offer the most space (our #210 was lovely); almost every accommodation has private bath or shower. Not a choice for seekers of bright lights and hoopla, but ideal for tranquil, solid shelter—*and* for kindness by the bushel. Greatly improved.

The 11-story **Orion** is due for a total revamping, with even a fresh staff to pep it up. Check to see if it is ready prior to your departure.

The **Neptun** is on the move. It will gain about 3-dozen well appointed units for this season. The young and aggressive Manager, Hans Bruarøy, is pouring out the ergs to keep up its appeal. Each of its older bedrooms has been 100% redecorated; all of them have showers. Corridors colorfully redone; large café 1-flight up from lobby transformed into a modernistic 100-seat restaurant. Coming along nicely.

The **Toms Hotel** has been refashioned. We'll have a full report soon. **Slottsgaarden,** on the same portside square as the Orion, is oriented to group traffic from European hubs. Nothing special. The **Strand** is coming up re-markably. Now quite satisfactory. **Pension Park**, without any baths, has the atmosphere of a private home—and a home without any baths. Good for very tight budgeteers. The **Fantoft**, a summer-only operation, now fans in 1672 occupants in 4 separate segments. Blocks A and C, comprising 216 and 288 rooms respectively, have private showers and w.c.'s; Blocks B and D are the latest additions. The **Hatleberg** specializes in student shelter from June 15 to August 31. Its curriculum reads: 420 bedchambers, all with shower and toilet; a "shared twin" for around $13-or-so with breakfast. (That's not bad if the twin is appealing and the toast is properly done.) For both, economy is the word.

The **Solstrand Fjord Hotel**, 11 miles out (a 20-minute drive to *Os*), draws rhapsodic praises from a discriminating and kindly pair of Fort Lauderdale pilgrims. Seafront situation; colorful traditional building plus modern connecting annex; blissful calm prevailing. They call their annex suite "perfect," the cuisine "excellent," and the place itself "absolutely wonderful." We can scarcely wait to dig in here for some happy relaxation. At nearby *Alversund,* the **Alver** fluffed up 50 new beds, plus new baths, none of which we've tried.

Stavanger is experiencing such a petroleum boom that advance reservations here are a must nowadays. The city boasts the handsomely appointed and immaculate **S.A.S. Royal Atlantic;** stay here if you can, because most travelers feel it's worth the price difference from the local competition. Its historically outfitted Mortepümpen Restaurant is also tops for the district; there are 3 other dining quarters on the premises. The 6-story **K.N.A. Ocean Hotel** offers smaller rooms, a less desirable location, and a less attractive ambiance; nevertheless, it's better than adequate. Toilet plus bath or shower with all 120 rooms; yummy cuisine with a variety of specialties in its Grill; pleasant penthouse restaurant with dancing nightly; owned by the Royal Norwegian Automobile Club. The newer 170-kip **Esso Motor Hotel** (perhaps renamed **Crest** by now) is sure to be giving this one wheel-to-wheel competition. The recently anointed **St.-Svithun**, a "Mission hotel" with space for 110 teetotaling disciples, is central and clerically austere; inexpensive and drier than a camel's instep.

In *Trondheim*, the **Prinsen** maintains a noble bearing. On a room-for-room basis its living units provide a high overall ratio of comfort and maintenance. Loaded with restaurants and snack facilities; somewhat commercial in feeling; doubles in the "01" series are largest; modern furnishings; many paintings; enormous wall-mounted 2-channel radios; plenty of luggage space. Capably managed and solid. The **Britannia** provides a handsome public face with its canopy entrance, flashy white marble reception desk, captivating Palmehaven Restaurant, modern breakfast room, and grand lounges. Newer wing with 50 units; 6 new suites; continual program of repainting. Not a bad investment, but its sleeping amenities are unappealing. The **Astoria** now has a complete change of raiments. We can't comment on it until we get the fresh facts for you, but local friends recommend it. The **Larssen** is a charmer for the price. Fresh lobby; pleasant dining room, up 1-flight, lined with paintings; cozy lounges; restaurant and beer tavern on main level. Very recommendable for its category. The **Phoenix** discloses a taste that does not jibe with ours; we find it heavy, dreary, and flaccid. **Tronderheimen**, across from the Prinsen, offers chambermaids in regional costume, a honey of a dining room with authentic appointments, and simplicity in its economy-price bedchambers. Fair. **Bondeheimen** is about the same, but with less color and flair; better for families on tight budgets. The **Bristol** has been totally destroyed by a fire, according to press-time reports. Sorry, but we don't know if it will be rebuilt. For motorists, there's an **ESSO** (also perhaps to be renamed **Crest** by the time of your arrival) just outside of town on E-6. The **Ambassador** is okay for bed and breakfast; its location down by the riverside is a special asset. The recently trundled-out 100-bed **Trondheim Youth Hostel**, on a hillock overlooking the sea, is one of the best of its type in Norway; dormitory style, of course, but clean as an Arctic breeze. The 98-room **Singsaker Studenthjem** and the 247-unit **Studentbyen Berg** are alternates.

Sandefjord, the one-time whaling city (this commerce once made its inhabitants the most affluent citizens per capita in Norway!), proudly boasts of its **Park Hotel**. This monument to Moby Dick and his descendants is so extravagantly constructed, so lavishly outfitted, and so generously maintained that it will never make a dime—and the beauty of it is that it was planned this way! As a result, here is not only one of Scandinavia's finest hostelries, but one of the top oases in all of northern Europe. For physical diversion there are the sliding-roof, saltwater, heated pool (with its very own grill and bar, no less), a gym for fisical fitniks, a solarium, bubble baths for effervescent therapy, keep-your-chin-up underwater massages, 2 saunas, a host of automatic pinsetter bowling alleys, golf links (20 minutes), motorboats (available at the Marina), for sightseeing, fishing, and fjord bathing, and a local hunting and fishing club where you can arrange to hook a salmon from late June through August. The main salon, the Restaurant (dancing nightly year round), the Bistro lounge (snacks, lunch, and sips), and the Jonas (a cellar hideaway where the freshmen-to-postgrad set congregate Sat. evenings). Stay only in the main building. Competent direction by friendly, experienced, Hans Smedsrud. The rebuilt **Klubben**, out at *Tønsberg*, is a mod-minded knockout these days. Umbrella-dotted and awning-shaded waterside terrace cracking with the snap of wind-kicked flags; stone-floor reception; window-lined dining spread with schoonerisms on the walls; double rooms with sitting areas; facilities for yachting, golf, congresses, and dancing nightly to combo music. A big plus for the region, so be sure to reserve well in advance.

Mountain and sports hotels? Let's hit several targets along the general path between Oslo and Bergen. First, in *Gol* (the surrounding station village is not very charming), **Per's Hotel** is a worthy contender. A better choice might be the **Sole** at *Noresund* (closer to the capital, nibbling charmingly on the shores of Lake Krøderen). Modern atmosphere hewn from a former doctor's residence; especially noteworthy for the breathtaking vista. Moving north to the vales of the Valdres district, the **Beito**, in the mountains above *Fagernes,* provides space for 140 guests in 70 rooms; 9 suites; full bath and shower count; air-conditioned; captivating view of Jotunheimen; run by a retired mink rancher and his urbane sons. In the mountains west of this village, the **Sanderstølen** has been colorfully rebuilt from the ashes of a serious fire. Upland gaiety at its sprightly best; 115 units, ½ with bath or shower; very sound. To the east, the **Spatind**, boasting 84 accommodations, all with bath, is smoothly operated by Mr. and Mrs. Stig Johansen. In Fagernes itself, **Fagernes** is the king.

In *Geilo* (see "Cities" for mention of our special love affair with this tot), the flashy-but-tasteful **Bardøla** now steals the local thunder for travelers with modern tastes. Situation on a hillside glen above the town; private ski ·lift; spacious; sleekly rustic public rooms and lounges; bar for salubrious slaking; glass-lined dining room with woody touches, cascading greenery; cellar nightclub bouncing mostly for the young and spry; down-in-the-cellar gameroom with minibilliards, minibowling, and a toyland of diversions to keep the Small Fry out of mischief (free supervision, baby-sitting, and scheduled programs for kiddie pastimes); superb His and Hers sauna facilities; beauty salon; large basement hall planned exclusively for skiers (individual racks for every resident; drying pegs for boots and wet togs; buckling-on platforms; tools and gimmicks galore); horseback riding available in summer; health center, gym, and solarium; swimming pool yet another lovely fluid asset. Total of 83 updated accommodations; most units with private bath; top quality appointments. Proprietors Egil and Elsa Walhovd have spent a treasure chest of kroner and love to expand this once-modest pension into a First-class (not Deluxe) enterprise. Traditionalists or family groups historically had opted for the aging **Holms**, at the fringe of the Geilohøgda (6-minute chair lift, plus T-bar for the lower ranges). It is getting younger by the hour, however, and we will be anxious to see its extensive late remodelings. New dining salon; annex converted into popular pub and discothèque; swimming pool, sauna, gymnasium, and sportsman bar surely ready for your visit. Accommodations for 120 guests, nearly all provided with private plumbing; outstanding cuisine; girth-busting daily buffet lunch that features a galaxy of meats, sweets, salads, and 34 different types of herring; nightly revels to work it off; soothing rates. The attractive couple who manage it, Bernhard and Lise Johannessen, speak perfect American and couldn't be nicer or more friendly. A fine bet for nature lovers—or any other type, for that matter; especially happy for children. The expanded **Highland** has windows scanning Lake Ustedalsfjord. Lobby in birchwood, with regional furnishings, 2 working fireplaces, and rugs on the walls; pleasing touches of a spinning wheel and antiques hither and thither; dining room in stone and wood; cafeteria to handle its ever increasing package-tour traffic; updatings in one wing; indoor swimmery; good cookery; small, spare bedchambers with linoleum floor coverings; poor baths. For Highland hilarity and dancing nightly, this entry—with the Bardøla and perhaps the rekindled Holms—is a magnet for the youthful and spirited wayfarer. The **Ro**, on the main drag, is lower in category; ground-floor cafeteria; pleasant Kro restaurant; not bad. **Geilo Pension** is fun for its Old Norway atmosphere; Young Norway romps in its downstairs discothèque; inexpensive gaiety. **Alpin**, on the outskirts, seemed stiff and flairless; heavy patronage by British trippers; routine. The **Geilo Hotel** refashioned its exterior, pepped up its lobby, and fluffed up 100 fresh pillows a while back. There's a modern flavor which we laud. Across the valley on a rocky plateau, engineers solved an alp's-worth of topographical problems and unveiled the **Sportel**, which has had its agonizing share of teething pains. Now it has been taken over by the Bardøla interests, so it has more of a sporting chance. It plays host to 150 guests in surroundings that accent the antique décor of the region. Also available is the adjoining colony of chalets. We'll be anxious to inspect this lovely complex on our next slalom run. Back in the vale, the **Youth Hostel** is clean, neat, and very cheap; mostly English-speaking youngsters occupy its bunks. At *Ustaoset* (7 miles west) the **Mountain Hotel** has been renewed from peak to foothills. Adjoining cafeteria-style **Three Reindeer Inn;** nightclub; grill; bar; 77 rooms with bath or shower; lowish rates. We'll try to climb this Mountain soon. In **Voss**, the 48-room-and-bath **Park Liland** tops our list. Year-round operation; only a 10-minute walk to the aerial cableway (don't miss the view from up there); main-street situation opposite a church built in A.D. 1150; recreational facilities including an orchestra nightly, 2 bars, a TV parlor, a bowling alley, billiards, and Ping-Pong. Unhappily, the bedchambers lack even a smidgen of decorative verve. The gabled **Fleischer's,** so close to the station that every guest should automatically be issued a pocket watch, a fob, and a lantern with his door key, is so old-fashioned in its main building and so modern in its 18-room annex that the contrast is startling. Be sure to snag the latter if you choochoo into this one. Its "motel" afterthought, across the pike, is targeted for budgeteers, families, and—we suppose—"motorists." The newer **Jarl**, at the lower end of town, appeals more to Europeans than to Statesiders; its latest wing might provide more State-liness, however; all rooms have showers. The **Youth Hostel**, 2 miles out, is another of the adequate Norwegian shelters for bottom-budget undergrads; again okay for its type. The **Motel Voss** is growing; it is now up to 80 beds. In **Stalheim**, the 100-unit **Stalheim** sweeps the local honors. Attractive lobby gladdened by rich woods and regional antiques; all rooms with bath; many beds set into nook-style alcoves. Many amenities, but its brightest feather is the awesome view down the Naerø Valley. The big drawback is its fleets of bus excursionists at lunchtime. Open mid-May to mid-September only.

In the fjord districts, the **Brakanes** at **Ulvik**—with its emerald lawn nipping at the skirt of the Hardangerfjord—is perhaps the most stunning of all. Long, white, fresh-looking building plus a set-back annex (take the former in preference to the latter); lovely waterside terrace; some front units looking straight down the ripples; limited living space; very popular with Americans; open mid-May to late September. Recommended. The **Hotel Ulvik**, functioning as late as Christmas, is chiefly for passersby rather than for lingerers. Many British guests; unpretentious but comfortable. The **Strand** is a frostbiter's delight. Step out of bed into a skiff or a sailing dinghy at your doorstep. If your ancestors were penguins, water skiing is also in the ice tap. Brrrrrr! The **Motel**, at **Øystese** outside the center, and also proud of its water-ways, has been slightly improved. The **Gudvangen**, farther up the pike, is better as a coffee stop or excursion target than for overnighting; too modest in mien for most Yankee and Canadian tastes. Another in this category, useful because of the scenic drive via Fossli to glory in the waterway and the Voringsfoss waterfall, is the **Vøringsfoss** at **Eidfjord**. Very basic accommodations; its high point is the hand-painted dining room rendered for free drinks by the famous Norwegian artist, Bergslien. Worth a detour for a nip and a peek. For wheelborne travelers, the Norheimsund Fjord is a comfortable stop with a convenient motel segment. In **Kinsarvik**, the 90-bed **Kinsarvik** is a nirvana for nature lovers. New and especially convenient for ferry passengers crossing the Hardanger to Kvanndal. In nearby **Lofthus**, the **Ullensvang** has undergone a beauty treatment that is a credit to its cosmetician—especially in the pool area. Each room faces the water; the citizens don regional costumes every Sunday. Fun, and now very solid. In the Sognefjord region, we'd pick the **Kvikne's** at **Balestrand** or the 190-bed **Sogndal** at **Sogndal**. Around the Nordfjord, **Yri's** at *Olden* now leads the pack; it's small, cozy, and the food is scrumptious. The **Alexandra**, also with a good kitchen, has pulled down most of its older limbs and built new ones. The drawback here is its bigness (space for 300 guests), which makes it something of a nordic beehive. For sightseeing, few can top the eagle's-nest **Videseter**, a new perch high, high, high, above the Vide Valley. Owner-Manager Erster has razed the former shell and erected a 50-room house, all with private baths. Now he's considering an even newer extension. Excellent for overnighting; an *olé* ing La Jolla Guidester tells us that "since the tour buses now generally stop here for lunch only, there is blissful quiet after they leave. The food is excellent, the lodgings most comfortable by U.S. standards, the staff attitudes unusually pleasant, the cocktails perfectly mixed—and, as you say, the panorama is fantastic. This place is seventh heaven!" Our thanks and skåls via the polar route, Californiaway! In the village of *Førde*, the **Sunnfjord** is shining with space for 220 Waltons keenly bent on early-morning angling. Hardy's of London has hooked up a fishing school here with $10,000 in equipment for use by guests, plus experts standing by with baited breath to show how to use it. All units have bath or shower; about $170 buys a week of shelter, food, instruction, and whatever you can catch. This season there's a new wing, a new indoor pool, a solarium, and more recreation rooms. This one gives our line a mighty big tug. In the Møre and Romsdal fjord district, the **Viking** at *Ørsta* is the newest, but the older standbys still attract settled vacationers through their smooth-running portals. These are the revamped **Union** at *Geiranger* (*what* a vista!), the updated **Alexandra** at *Molde*, and the **Grand Bellevue** at *Andalsnes*. The area is one of the most striking in Norway.

For our other selections in more remote crannies of the land, you might try the **Grand Nordic**, the 300-bed **Royal** which SAS pilots, and the more economical, youthful 53-room **Saga** way up in *Tromsø*, the **Gausdal** and the **Skeikampen** in *Tretten*, the excellent **Fefor** in *Vinstra*—and, slightly below these, the **Bergsjø** in *Al*, the freshly upgraded, 160-pillowed **Bolkesjø** in *Bolkesjø,* the **Brekkestranda** (split-log construction with rooms and even beds fashioned to scorn rectangular patterns) at *Brekke*, the **Dalseter** (with swimming pool) in *Espedal*, the **Sjusjøen** in the hills above *Lillehammer* or the rebuilt **Lande Mountain** with an indoor pool, the **Oppdal** in *Oppdal*, the **Rauland** in *Rauland*, and the new beachside **Selje** or the **Solfonn** in *Seljestad*. Further choices on anyone's list should include the **Grand** in *Kongsberg*, the **Røros Tourist Hotel** in *Røros*, the beautifully modernistic **City** in *Fredrikstad*, the **Hovden** at *Setesdal* (Hardanger Plateau), the **Elveseter** in *Leirvassbu*, the fresh **Caledonien** or the older **Ernst** in *Kristiansand*, the **Heimly Pension** in *Flåm*, and the renewed **Grand** in *Kristiansund*. *These are the cream-of-the-cream of their category in Norway; their average all-inclusive price is about $33 per day.*

An extra-special flight of fancy? Recently we enjoyed a marvelous adventure that gave us a huge slice of Norway in less than a day. We booked a 5-passenger Cessna-206 from Busy Bee Air Service (Haakon VII's gate 10, Oslo 1; Telex 6945) and zoomed north for slopeside landings on the mountains and frozen lakes, taking a coffee break at the **Eidsbugarden Hotel** and a delicious buffet lunch at the **Hotel Tyin**, on the sapphire-lapped shores from which it takes its name. (During cold months, the former is accessible only by plane, "weasel"—snow tractor—or dog sled.) The first is a barn-red complex composed of a small central building, a cottage (where the poet, Vinje, lived), and a toy chapel. The keys are attached to a shard of elk antler, the furniture is painted in provincial whimsy, the public rooms are rich in woods and local textiles, and the vistas are a delight. The latter is a rustic dream slumbering by mythical waters; one can even reach it by car in winter. This one is more modest for lingering, but cross-country skiers and tranquillity seekers adore it. At both, the rates are unbelievably cheap, averaging around $23 per day per person, including those table-bending feasts so common to this country. Split 4 or 5 ways, the plane-and-pilot fee of approximately $120 per hour is not so costly considering the stunning rewards, the unique thrills, and the ease of exploring a vast segment of the North within an hour's flight time of the capital. In summer, the aircraft can be rigged for amphibious landings. All-in-all, this loop was the high point of a recent research whirl and we recommend it with cheers to wayfarers with limited time and disciples of Mother Nature's exquisite charms.

FOOD   To the traveler's jaded palate, Norwegian food is simple, wholesome, and, in general, well prepared. Although the accent is on fish—hundreds of varieties, hundreds of tricky recipes—that doesn't mean they don't know a good beefsteak when they see one. As a rule, savvy Nordics avoid piscatorial delights on Monday. In a culture where the critter is no longer considered fresh if it is 5 hours out of the sea, any stored fish is regarded as old. Nets, by law, cannot be put down on Sundays; thus, the Saturday catch, while preserved on ice, meets with singular unenthusiasm.

Besides the savory ocean harvests, Norwegian specialties you may like are ptarmigan (mountain grouse), flatbread (crisp cracker thinner than a dime), multer (delicious, all-purpose dessert or jam made from yellow mountain cloudberries with a unique flavor), tyttebaer (known as "lingon" or cowberries to Swedes, this is a small, tart, red berry—a cranberry with a difference), local cheeses of Port du Salut type (not the goat's milk cheese which looks like kitchen soap and tastes like peanut butter), kreps (succulent, 2-inch freshwater crayfish), reindeer steak (dark red, fine flavor), whale steak (ugh!), and the Norwegian "sandwich," which will haunt you pleasantly wherever you go. Unless you order otherwise, your breakfast will consist of smoked salmon, herring with onions, cheeses, and other hardy delicacies served open-style on their fine bread—with one boiled egg and coffee on the side. It sounds like rugged fare, but you'll be surprised at how smoothly it cranks up your gears for the day.

Norway is a coffee-drinking nation; as in America, the tea is mediocre. It is also the biggest cheese-eating nation in the world; per capita, each Oslo citizen (infants-in-arms included in this statistic) packs away nearly 25 lbs. per year!

RESTAURANTS AND NIGHT LIFE   *Oslo* comes up this year with the greatest culinary variety in the nation, of course. Unfortunately, however, service standards universally do not match the caliber of the traditional Norwegian kitchen. Inflation, too, is beginning to erode quality; lower grades of meat, poorer vegetables, inferior oils, and other baser ingredients are too often being substituted for the exacting specifications of yore. Numerous independent restaurateurs—all struggling vainly to hold prices down—appear to be applying that line from H.M.S Pinafore, "Things are seldom what they seem./Skim milk masquerades as cream." Virtually all of the leading hotels, however, still regard their dining rooms as a client service or as loss-leaders—the best advertising they can provide to attract and retain their loyal followings. A conscientious hotelier accepts food-and-beverage losses as part of the overhead of running a fine establishment. Our best meals this trip were ordered in hotels—and they were infinitely better than most of the ones we experienced among the independents. In the capital, the **Continental** leads the pack by furlongs. The prices in the elegant Salon, in the colorful Theatre Cafeen, in the Pavilion, or in the newer Fortuna are very reasonable too (see "Hotels"). The **Grand's** Bonanza is great fun for merrymakers in search of hee-haw entertainment and Wild West atmosphere. Be sure to book your table here. It's Speilsalen ("Mirror Room") is patrician but dull by comparison with the saddlebags of conviviality produced by the Bonanza. High above Oslo, in the hotel's new wing, l'Étoile shines with a special radiance. From the moment it glittered above the horizon, townsfolk universally declared it to be first magnitude. The **Bristol** has the El Toro, which we haven't sampled. The **Astoria** is solid even though it can't turn on much glamour. The *West* had curried favor with gastronomes in its Coq d'Or segment, but the management has been changed here and we can't be sure that it will carry on as before. The **Norum** and the **Carlton** have praiseworthy chefs.

Among the go-it-aloners, **Frascati** (Stortingsgata 20, near the Continental Hotel) has been the traditional leader. Air conditioning in summer; charming little bar with Black Watch carpeting, marble tables, and red leather chairs; Burbanks of greenery and rustic touches of wrought iron; piano-Solovox music for dancing; friendly service; mediocre spiritless cookery. The new owner is trying to maintain its venerable name, but we're not yet convinced that he can achieve this goal.

Gallagher's Steak House (Karl Johansgate 10) was an authentic reproduction of its famous namesake in Manhattan when it opened a short while back. More recently it was sold and now it is hardly better than routine. The adjoining Pancake House was flipped into a flatter flapjack called the **Sir Winston Pizza House**. The pub-pizzeria personality just doesn't come off, in our opinion.

The 30-table interior of **Najaden** (on the island of Bygdøy and in the Ship Museum, 10 minutes by ferry from the Town Hall) oozes with Norwegian maritime décor; the service plates bear a map design from A.D. 1539; picture windows open to the fjord and the legendary Polar ship, *Fram*. The major meal (euphemistically called "lunch" by foreigners and consisting mainly of open sandwiches) is served from 11 A.M. to 7 P.M. À la carte service is available from 11 A.M. to 11:30 P.M.; you'll find a trio tootling nightly. Men must wear jackets after 7 P.M. Usually a winner.

The **3 Kokker** ("Three Cooks") is situated in the Indeks Hus, only a sardine's leap from the American Embassy. This modestly billed "food and winehouse" is under the careful skilleting skills of Hroar Dege, a well-known name in Norwegian culinary circles since the days of Harold I of the Yngling Dynasty. All interior fittings, table utensils, and furnishings are especially made for the restaurant. The rates are reasonable. Open 11 A.M. to midnight as a restaurant, becoming the sometimes-spirited Earl's Nightcap "bistro-tèque" from the witching hour until 4 A.M.; bar libations begin at 3 P.M.; closed Sundays.

Blom (Karl Johansgate 41, 2 blocks from Grand Hotel), a remodeled wine store, caters to artists, writers, and as many tourists as they can pack in. Big sandwich table with 30 varieties daily from 11 A.M. to 2 P.M.; other dishes, including 9 specialties, run an uneven gamut from topflight to poor. Rollicking fun, but not at all cheap; most visitors like its regional flavor.

In the colorful Strøget, a shopping mall, **King George Steakhouse**, with its adjoining Pub, is introduced by an open patio, a fountain, an antique coach, wagon wheels, and a few alfresco tables. Inside, the booths are set into horse stalls, each one honoring a great mount in equine history. The waiters sport nifty tartan waistcoats. Our grilled meat was not from one of the track-bred residents of the paddock, but it was tough enough to suggest it. We haven't yet seen the **Operaklubben**, which opened nearby, but we'll warble in soon.

Wessels Kro (Stortingsgata 4), near Frascati, is named for the eighteenth-century poet who wrote and imbibed in Oslo. Four interior segments in a row duplicate the pub-crawling haunts of the famous Norwegian literator and toper. Ground-floor back room recreating a street lined with timbered stucco walls and log-end flooring; intimate upstairs nook with tiny dormer windows overlooking the tavern "alley" below; 5 tables under a low ceiling; colored panes, plus stained-glass genre scenes in leaded panels; checked linens in moss, burnt-orange, and terra cotta. Enormous snack table for self-servers. Our meal was quite respectable for the modest outlay; the service was kind but somewhat fumbling. Open daily from 9:30 A.M. to 11 P.M.; always safer to reserve in advance. Interesting and likable.

La P'tite Cuisine (sometimes called Chez Ben Joseph) is a tricolorful entry in midtown. Two multihued parasols stuck into a pair of unbunged barrels at the entrance; a hyper-Gallic den of "In"-equity; smiling team of straw-boater-topped waiters in illustrated aprons to greet incomers with a parley-voo; red-white-and-blue paper streamers rippling from the low ceiling; French songs in the air; the usual runny wine-bottle candles placed on the usual checkered tablecloths; 3-foot-long breadsticks bristling from 2-foot-high crocks; quality declining noticeably and prices moving up steadily. Fun-loving Ben Joseph, a former staffer at the Waldorf Astoria, is the key to the cheerful élan of this house. But who eats élan?.

Jaquet's Bagatelle (Bygdøy Allé) costs perhaps two-thirds as much as better-known and fancier places, but its dishes are among the most savory under the Midnight Sun. Not well-known among U.S. explorers; no personal-ity whatever; frenetic service; favorites of budgeteers with educated palates are Crevettes à l'Indienne and Volaille à l'Indienne, both of which are yummy. Here's an exceptional value if you seek food and not frills.

Lanternen, on the Bygdøy waterfront, releases stacks of mouth-watering publicity about its "American" hamburgers and other "U.S." specialties. Unfortunately, however, the PR man isn't the cook. Not for us, after our samples.

If time hangs heavy on a Friday, an entertaining place for lunch is **Tostrup-Kjelleren**, opposite the Parliament Building, where many Ministers dine when the weekly Palace conference is over. Tempting Norwegian sandwiches; also open for dinner.

Pernille, the big open-air sidewalk café-restaurant, is a pleasant oasis for light refreshments—especially on a warm summer evening (but *only* if the subway construction at its doorstep has been completed by the time you emerge). Order a low-price cooler and laze under a gay parasol to watch the teeming movement in this hub of the city. The same Mueller chefs also own the **Konge Terrassen**, across from the Royal Palace, beside the Haakon VII Statue. Kingly setting for princely rewards.

The restaurant in the **Edvard Munch Museum** serves light and full meals. Big windows opening to the street and park; tiny dimensions; natural wood walls; orange tablecloths and black-leather-covered chairs; reasonable prices. Not at all special, but okay for Munching.

In *good weather only,* there are 4 lovely spots which should be considered. **Dronningen** ("The Queen") is the Royal Norwegian Yacht Club headquarters; it's at the end of a long concrete drive in Oslofjord, 10 minutes from the center. Built on piles; beautifully redecorated by Forum (see "Things To Buy"). Huge-windowed Sextant Bar in the upper reaches done in blues, reds, browns, and white, with a magnificent harbor view; topside Captain's Cabin. Norwegian décor; sea-level Boat Deck restaurant suspended just a bitt above the wavelets. After you've had some grog up in the spars, you may choose either galley for dinner. Delightful to the eye and to the seafaring spirit, but —sadly—a dismal shade of its former glories in the culinary department, owing chiefly to its seasonal operation and resultant staff problems. **Frogner-saeteren**, 25 minutes by funicular or 20 minutes by car up the mountain (1387 feet), is a municipally owned and privately operated sports-restaurant with a magnificent panorama from 2 tiers of open terraces; if you can tear your eyes loose from the succulent white grouse on your plate, you can see at least 20 miles down the Oslofjord on a clear day. Authentic Norwegian log house, interestingly decorated; crowded with skiers in winter and tourists in summer, so be sure to reserve ahead; gorgeous when the sun is shining or the stars are out. The century-old **Holmenkollen** is 20 minutes from the center and just below the hotel of the same name. Regional stained-wood exterior with wide windows and magnificent vista from its front terrace; cafeteria at one end with 40 tables and large hearth which usually works Sundays only; cozy dining room in the center, charmingly decorated; adjoining dining room at other end for overflow use in summer. The cafeteria begins operations at 11 A.M. and the dining room at noon; both shutter at midnight; snacks, apértifs, and beverages usually available on request on the outdoor patio. The view alone makes the excursion worthwhile. The **Henie-Onstad Museum** at Høvikodden can combine a multitude of treasures with your nutrients. In addition to the superb paintings and sculpture on exhibit, 4 concerts a week are given in the giant recording studio, there are ballet and folk dancing performances at the outdoor amphitheater, and when the fjord isn't frozen, summer travelers can wrap up the entire package with a pennies-only cruise from the city on stately ferryboats. There's a cafeteria with excellent inexpensive renderings that can be ruminated inside or on a huge open-air terrace. For the particulars on what's doing when you're in town, check with your Hall Porter. A sightseeing must.

Out at Fornebu Airport (a very short ride), the **Caravelle** whooshes in with rumors of some of the best gobblings in the region. We flew in and out with only a nibble in between, but that lip-smacker spoke volumes of cookbook lore. The chef does his homework.

Night life? The **Telle Complex** tells it best. Except for the aurora borealis, it offers the biggest spectrum in Norway. This operation includes the agreeable Café En Cocotte for French cuisine, the restyled Rainbow, which is brighter than ever, the Natt with disco doin's plus food and drink from 8 P.M. to 4 A.M. and the rebuilt Tyrolerkro—a full-to-bursting grab bag of entertainment, all under one roof. For a tough, low-down outing, **Rosekjelleren** (Klingenberg 5; 1 block from the Continental Hotel) might be made to order. Here is the magnet for Norwegian sailors on the loose; they put on their best suits, belt down several quick schnapps, and then stalk through its doors, loaded for bear (or bare?).

Membership spot? The **Down Town Key Club** (Universitetsgaten 26) is it, if you care to pick the lock. It has been given new tumblers in the shape of the Storyville, a New Orleans style restaurant with appropriate music, the smokey Moke Café, and the enlivened Up Town Bar, all with sharps and flats through the whee-whee hours. The leader of the "in" crowd in naughty old Oslo. The **Leopard Club** in the Bristol Hotel is a handsome cub. A spot worth checking on your next safari. **Château-Neuf** is a student nightclub; proof of this status is required, kids.

Finally, there's a wonderful beer cellar for the Norwegian student trade called **Dovrehallen** (or occasionally Studentkroa) at Storgata 22, 10 minutes from the Grand Hotel. Here the youngsters let off steam, and it's most definitely worth seeing—particularly between mid-May and mid-June, when the "russ" (those who hope to pass their exams) are sporting their striking red caps. See if you can arrange through your hotel director or travel agent (or a friendly sophomore) for admission to this members-only attraction, because it's worth the effort. Beer is the sole beverage; students' orchestra, occasional students' floor show, even students' "police" to keep order; drop in between 7:30 P.M. and 11:30 P.M., if you can work it, and you're in for a treat.

For feminine companionship, the **Ribo Restaurant** (just off City Square, 1 block below the Grand Hotel), the **Rosekjelleren**, and the **Telle Complex** usually offer the best opportunities in winter. Between 7 P.M. and 10 P.M. are the customary hours.

Dedicated budgeteers? Since we're too bottlenecked here for additional entries, please consult this year's edition of our annually revised paperback, *Fielding's Low-Cost Europe*, which lists scads more bargain dining spots and money-saving tips for serious economizers.

Bergen's best tables are set by her innkeepers—that is, if the recently reopened Bellevue doesn't resume its role as number one for both view and culinary artistry. Late hearsay reports indicate that it may be up to its former glories but we've yet to confirm or disconfirm them. Otherwise, the restaurants in the **Norge** lead the local scene (see "Hotels" for descriptions). The Grill is our favorite for décor, service, and cookery. The slickly barn-style dining room comes up with a tiered periphery for tables and grossly inept attention by waiters—who generally are far younger than the Junior Executive Set who pour in here. The Hjørnet Café is *the* spot to be seen snacking a snack; very popular. Also in the hotel venue, the **Bristol** is very likely to be better than ever. It has been totally revamped and its culinary standards always have been first-rate. The **Holberg Stuen** and the **Wessel Stuen**, under the same ownership, offer lower-cost, tavern-style edibles. Tip-top quality. **Chianti**, in the bus station, is a large, chilly, cafeteria-restaurant with a small menu and smaller appeal; don't bother. **Rosenkrantz** has plush, unimaginative décor and similar fare; dancing nightly; almost Swedish in its lack of zip. The **Orion Hotel** may be better under its new proprietors. **Holm's Discosteak** is masterminded by the everfresh and sparkling Gunvor and Anna-Carine Holm, whose enthusiasm is pervasive. We haven't seen it but the idea of combining a grill and a discothèque under one rollicking roof sounds like fun. Pretty young waitresses in red overalls, stucco walls, candlelight, limited menu but unlimited horizons for these 2 dashing Nordics. We wish 'em luck. **Fløien** (a 60¢ ride to the top of the funicular) comes up with a soul-soaring panorama of the city, the harbor, the mountains, and the sea. While the perked-up but still pedestrian décor is as dull as the cuisine, it wouldn't matter if Escoffier himself were slinging the hash here; you'll probably never remember a single bite, with that magnificent view to distract you. By all means, go —even to feed your spirits rather than your tummy. Closed in winter. The Teaterkafeen has become the **Willis**; the switch ushered in a new manager not too far back who came from the Norge; it should be better now. Budget dining? We stumbled across the **Café Hanseaten** on a late foray, and what a "discovery" this one is for the freshman wayfarer or the economy traveler with a pack of wolf-hungry cubs in tow! Portside location overlooking the boats and Fish Market; orange awnings; upstairs cafeteria where our ignorance of Norwegian didn't matter (all dishes are under glass); 2 modest rooms with strictly functional appointments. Our gigantic repast for 2 included soup, shrimp-on-toast, Røket Torsk (smoked cod), Fisk Pudding (fish loaf), delicious crêpes, peaches and whipped cream, beverages, and bread. Everything was so unusually savory that, had we fallen into the Bergensfjord afterward, it would have taken a 5-ton derrick to haul us out. What a feed, at what a low price! Top recommendation for its modest category. We hear praises for the gabled Hanseatic **Bryggen Tracteursted** and the Old Town's **Gamle Bergen Tracteursted**, neither of which we've tried, darn it.

Trondheim's independent leader is the suavely rustic **Naustloftet**, a 2-minute walk behind the Prinsen, at the edge of the harbor. Exterior hung with fishermen's lanterns, plus a tableau of seagoing gear above the entrance; subterranean cave with barrel tables and chairs for tapping another keg in cozy surroundings; ground-floor snack-den in pine, illuminated by gas lamps;

main restaurant in a beamed-roof upstairs sail loft; stained-glass windows, char-indigo and mulberry napery, working corner fireplace, wrought-iron fixtures, and a wide-ranging but sea-oriented menu in Norwegian. Skipper Martin Michalsen is a jovial host who loves to give 101% of his good cheer to his guests. We think you'll like it as much as we did. The **Tavern Inn**, facing the port on a hill in front of the Folk Museum, is a sweetie for cottage cookery and regional fare; open May to October only; worth a try. In the hotel bracket, the **Britannia**'s Palm Garden (Palmehaven) is renowned for its dancing, spirits, wine, and one of the leading kitchens in the environs. Its fountain setting, silky-green grass, plants, and built-in elegance contradict the northerly latitude in a pleasing way. The **Prinsen** consists of (1) Bar, (2) Bistro, (3) Restaurant (dancing), (4) Cafeteria, (5) Pâtisserie, (6) Theatre Grill, and (7) Bowling Inn. Locals love this well-managed Fun Factory. We are especially fond of the Theatre Grill. Entry via a spiral staircase to a 4-level nest; bar, glass-enclosed patio, and 2 candle-lit dining decks; bleached wood trappings; costumed waitresses; excellent piano background for your midnight sunsettings. The food is well prepared and nicely presented, but the service lacks polish. The **Astoria** and the **Bristol** are popular-priced.

  Stavanger 's **SAS Royal Atlantic Hotel** has a knockout dining spot in regional motif: Mortepūmpen ("The Haddock Pump"), where you sit surrounded by wooden "houses" in a "square" of Old Stavanger. Outstanding. The hotel's dining room is the smart spot for dancing, rivaled only by the top-floor restaurant of the **K.N.A. Hotel**. The Grill and the Bar of the latter, which we have still to see, have been described as "out of the ordinary for Norway." The **Korvetten** features a cozy beer and wine pub in the cellar, a snack-bitery at ground level, and table service 1-flight up.

  Fredrikstad 's best bet in the new town is the dining room of the **City Hotel** (be sure to wear a coat and tie, gentlemen). In the older section, we like (1) **Kongsten Fort** (almost exclusively for groups), (2) **Tamburen** (year round), and (3) either the **Stabbursloftet** or the **Gryta** (both outstanding cafeterias in Scandinavia's largest food center). At *Halden*, 30 miles away, **Fredriksten Kro** is a popular excursion target; it is open in summer only.

  Meal hours are cockeyed to American travelers. The residents eat a heavy New England-style breakfast at 8 A.M.; at noon they munch sandwiches at their office desks, working without interruption; at 5 P.M. they sit down to their big dinner, and from 9 P.M. to 9:30 P.M. they polish off their day with tea and more sandwiches. You can follow your own schedule, of course—but if you should be brave enough to try things the practical local way, hark to that rumble in your stomach until it's adjusted!

TAXIS   Most taxis are modern and comfortable. If you are in a hurry, ask your hotel porter to call one before you come downstairs, and allow 5 to 10 minutes for arrival.

  One hackie we met recently lamented, "Prices keep changing so fast that the hackies don't even have time to get their meters adjusted to the new rates!"

TRAINS   Very good and improving steadily. The Arctic route runs 796 miles straight up to Bodø in the Land of the Midnight Sun. There are about

2000 miles of track, entirely nationalized, in part electrified. The remainder of the main lines are operated with diesel-electrics. Excellent service, streamlined cars, clean compartments, polite conductors on the overnight run to Stockholm; on some of the short local hauls, similarly good-mannered conductors and much better equipment than in the past. Diners soon may be replaced by cafeteria cars and service carts on all segments rather than on only a few links.

§TIP: If you're traveling short distances (especially between Oslo and Bergen), pick Tourist class rather than First. Recently, when we booked on the former, we heard a terrific argument between an American lady and a conductor. Her travel agent had selected premium seating for her, but she preferred the economy cars. And she was right! The new Tourist units are brightly decorated and divided into smoking and nonsmoking departments; windows are wide; seats are the big airliner type that can be made to recline; you can also reserve one of these chairs at no extra cost if you're riding the rods within Norwegian borders. On the other hand, First class offers straight-backed bench-type accommodations 3 abreast facing forward and 3 abreast facing backward. When the runs are crowded, this affords far less privacy and comfort than on the less expensive wagons.

As in the rest of Scandinavia, be prepared to lug, lug, and lug ALL of your baggage until your biceps go spastic. Particularly in the hinterlands, this is no area for the physically infirm.

AIRLINE   See "Scandinavian Airlines System"

Braathens SAFE is independent and flies mostly within Norway. Equipment consists of a feathering of Fokker Fellowships and Fokker Friendships, plus Boeing 737's.

Main airports of Norway are Fornebu (15 minutes from the center of Oslo; now, at last, with baggage porters; fine SAS-catered Caravelle Restaurant), Gardermoen (now used chiefly for charters; far out of the capital), Flesland (25 minutes from Bergen), Sola at Stavanger, Vaernes (modern and well equipped; good cafeteria; too-damned-long 45-minute ride from Trondheim), Bodø (north of the Arctic circle), Vigra off Aalesund, Bardufoss, and Tromsø. The Far North route has been extended to Alta, Lakselv, and Kirkenes.

If you run into any SAS problems in this land, take them to Oslo and the line's efficient, energetic Norwegian Director of Public Relations, Odd Medboe, or his charming, patient colleague, Mrs. Signe Siebke. They're the perfect answer for any troubled voyager.

§TIPS: As just mentioned above in "Trains," the shocking dearth of baggage porters in Norway and the rest of Scandinavia is not only a tribulation to you, but presents a very real danger to heart patients and others with handicaps.

DRINKS   There's a government beverage control in Norway called the Vinmonopolet, and some of the vagaries imposed upon it (and the harried consumer!) by the legislature are the most mysterious in the travel world. John Law tells you how, where, when, and what you can drink; the regulations contradict themselves backward, forward, and sideways. Here are the rules, and please don't ask us to explain them. Over-the-counter drinks are dispensed *only* in Oslo, Bergen, Trondheim, Stavanger, 7 small towns and in the most popular tourist hotels of the hinterland. No spirits may be served before 1 P.M. on any occasion; if you order a highball at 11:45½ P.M. instead of before 11:45 P.M., you won't get it; not a single drop of anything stronger than wine is obtainable in any city on Sundays or holidays. Poor lambs who arrive unprepared often drop in the street from dehydration. Bottles up to any number, on the other hand, may be openly purchased in Vinmonopolet stores (big cities only between 10 A.M. and 5 P.M. on Mon., Tues., Wed., and Fri.; till 6 P.M. on Thurs.; and between 9 A.M. and 1 P.M. on Sat. and days prior to official holidays if these don't fall on Sun.). *Buy all liquor for weekend consumption or for any-day-off-the-beaten-track excursions before leaving Oslo or the key cities;* otherwise you're liable to be limited to beer and wine. And buy it during these special hours, because at any other time your hotel would be forced to charge 45% above their normal bottle price.

The selection of imported whiskies and liqueurs is large, and they cost from $11 to $23 per fifth; imported gins, $15; aquavit, $12.50. House-brand sherries are exceptionally fine. U.S. ryes and bourbons are available in fair quantity.

If you're a Dry Martini hound, Gordon's Gin is a third more expensive as a base than local Golden Cock gin—and 30 one-thirds better.

Linje Akevit or aquavit is the pride of Norwegian distillers, and distinctly palatable to most visitors. "Linje" means "line," and every bottle of this brand has been mellowed on a ship that has crossed the Equator. The action of the sea supposedly softens the aquavit. Always drink it with beer; this "keeps away the red nose," Norwegians say. (Danes say the opposite!)

But tie a stout cord to each ear to prevent your head from spinning à la DC-7 propeller before tackling a brand called Brennevin 60 Per Cent. It has the highest proof of any akevit or aquavit in the world—120. (The strongest proprietary Scotch, in comparison, is a schoolgirlish 86 proof.)

The most popular local liqueur is St. Halvard, a Bénédictine type worth trying. Claret is the national favorite in wines, and the stocks are fairly good. Beer drinkers should order the export type; the lighter ones are thin.

If you are on very good terms with a restaurateur, he may break the law for you by serving aquavit before 3 o'clock—but don't be surprised if it comes up purple. That's just a drop of Dubonnet added to fool the other diners!

The L.R.N. and other travel interests are working to have these ridiculous regulations repealed, but it continues to be an uphill fight. Visitors are still denied the simple pleasure of a glass of spirits when and where they choose. Through this policy, the nation loses tons of money and goodwill.

THINGS TO SEE   Everything you can. Get away from Oslo, which is beautiful but not typical; go north to Finnmark or west to the fjords, because you're not even scratching the surface of a magnificently scenic country if you don't.

If you drive your own car, please remember our previous admonition: Norwegian mountain roads (*e.g.,* Bergen–Oslo) can be hair-raising to vacationers who are timid about heights. One popular itinerary is the Peer Gynt

Way via the Gudbrand Valley between Lillehammer and Vinstra. If your nerves jangle from this above-the-tree-line jaunt, stop at the soul-soothing Skeikampen Hotel, mentioned earlier; it will restore your equilibrium with grace.

Your first step might be to check all your plans with our warm friend and the Good Samaritan for thousands of Guidesters, Geoffrey K. Ward, of the Berg-Hansen Travel Agency in Oslo. This fireball long ago volunteered to offer extra-cordial attention to readers of this book—and he has never failed either them or us.

One of the very best bets for the first-time visitor is the exciting, luxury "**Norwegian Fjord Line Tours**"—3 days for about $200—or 6 days on the "**Fjord Explorer Tours**" for about $330, all-inclusive (prices subject to slight alterations). Travel is by motorcoach and fjord steamers; stops are made at the number one mountain and fjord hotels (all offering private bath). In addition to fantastic scenery, there are all sorts of fascinating special events the ordinary traveler misses; on the longer circuit, for example, there's a mush out to the edge of Europe's largest ice field, lunch at an ancient farm, and much more. Route? Between Oslo and Bergen, *or* Bergen and Oslo; itineraries are duplicated, from either point of origin; departures for the 6-day round-robin from Oslo and Bergen on Tuesday and Saturday. The 3-day loops (daily departures in either direction) are extra-fine, of course, but the 6-day junkets include so much more that they're even better.

If you wish to strike out alone, the **Oslo–Flam–Stalheim–Norheimsund–Bergen–Oslo** circuit is possibly even more spectacular and rewarding for unescorted vacationers. This round trip can be done in 4 days, by train, boat, and bus, but extra time in Bergen would make it happier; logical en route stops would be the Fretheim Turisthotell at Flåm and the Stalheim at Stalheim. This can be done for perhaps $200, including everything—and it's a tour you will never regret. *If you drink, bring your own liquor supplies for weekends and offbeat stops on these itineraries.*

The Gold-Plate Special is a tour of **Finnmark**—the land of Norway's fairy tales, where Kriss Kringle picks up his reindeer, and where the sun shines at midnight during the bountiful, green summer. If we sound like an old-fashioned Rotarian-Baroque illustrated lecture, it is because our enthusiasm for this particular adventure is boundless. Hammerfest, 944 miles above the Arctic Circle, is the "highest" town in civilization—and the ultimate is reached via a 22-mile highway from the world's most northerly village of Honningsvåg to the North Cape itself. We feel that the vessels that ply these cold waters have considerably lower comfort standards than those ships steaming the more southerly lanes; therefore you might prefer air-and-overland transportation to cruising. Organized package tours have elicited an icy chill-factor from participants in some group plans, so be sure to select your agency with care if you cannot go it alone.

Please note that *everything must be set up long in advance.* Your 5-to 10-day look at the top of the world can be had for about $450. Stops can be made at comfortable and charming Guest Houses operated by the Norwegian Government in the best tradition of the hunting lodge—wines and spirits excepted —with good beds, tempting food, pleasant but simple décor, and efficient plumbing. During the day you can turn the clock back some 200 years; seek out the migrant Sames in their tent villages and watch them lasso reindeer; drive on well-surfaced roads over the treeless Vidda (highlands), the stark beauty of which is matched only by the steppes of Russia. You can drop a line in any stream and hook fresh-water salmon up to 50 lbs., trout up to 25 lbs., and several varieties of game fish which were completely strange to us.

An excellent independent itinerary is **Oslo–Tromsø–Lakselv–Karasjok–Hammerfest** ; it may be done in 3 ways. One tour of 6 to 8 days is by SAS plane to Lakselv, by hired car (about $50 per day for long hauls) to Karasjok and eventually to Hammerfest, from there by Norwegian coastal steamer (clean, comfortable, cheap) to Bodø or Trondheim, and by SAS plane back to Oslo. (We are especially fond of the Coastal Express vessels, which are practically the only year-round links between the south, the north, and the lovely points in between. Take one of these island-skirting voyages if you can. Apart from the food, which is mediocre, it's a real life dream that you will always remember.) Karasjok is the Lapp capital, a few miles from the Finnish border; if the weather is pleasant, you can hire a colorful river canoe with an outboard motor, as we did, and cruise through the wilderness to this remote frontier. If you have your car with you and enough time, another possibility would be to follow Route 6, the North Cape road, all the 1517 miles; this gets so monotonous toward the end that you'll be crawling up the wall.

With the exception of rented cars, prices in Finnmark are relatively low. The Guest Houses cost about $20 per night, meals and tips included. You'll need a warm coat, walking shoes, cap or beret, heavy socks, and (if female) a pair of woollies. The summer weather is generally warm and lovely, but sometimes that wind can be straight from the North Pole. Midwinter can also be surprisingly cheerful, despite the frosty nip. The hours of sunlight are brief, of course.

Do go to Finnmark or see those fjords farther south, no matter what. The Hardangerfjord, Sognefjord (fast boat service available), Sunnfjord, Geirangerfjord, and Nordfjord are so wonderful that any one of them will take your breath away.

§TIPS: The Oslo Travel Association set up a "**Know the Norwegians**" program to introduce visitors to English-speaking residents who share their business, cultural, or hobby interests. If you apply to this headquarters in advance, specifying your expected date of arrival, arrangements will be made for you to be taken into the bosom of a Norwegian family. July and August are the leanest months because so many local citizens are away on vacation. No appointments will be made until you show up in person. Free, of course, as a warming example of international brotherhood.

TIPPING   There's comparatively little tip-hunger in Norway. Restaurants include 15% for the waiters, so little more is needed. Hotels include a service charge of 15% which covers everybody except the Hall Porter (50¢ per day is generous). Barbers get 35¢ on a haircut; hairdressers get 10%; if waiters have been especially attentive, an extra 5% above the service charge on the bill is a good tip. Taxi drivers rate 10% and the hatcheck girl gets 30¢.

Baggage porters (IF you can find one!) charge 35¢ for hauling suitcases from the hotel lobby to the room. This amount is added to your bill. At checkout time, however, you must pay this extra trifle in cash.

THINGS TO BUY In *Oslo*, most U.S. shoppers seem to head for Norway Designs CNS, David-Andersen, and William Schmidt & Co. first, because that's where they find national specialties which have the greatest appeal for visitors.

Prize arts, crafts, and industrial designs? Before buying a single matchstick in Norway, your first investigatory stop should be at **Forum** (Rosenkrantz-gate 7, opposite the Hotel Bristol). Here's the 20+-year-old Permanent Sales Exhibition of the works of more than 130 of the nation's leading artists and artisans—a sweeping galaxy of furniture, silver, glass, ceramics, textiles, and other flawless creations, every piece with a fair price tag. It is a nonprofit enterprise. Managing Director Arne Remlov, N.I.L., A.I.D., is one of the world's most respected and distinguished interior designers. Every item in these beautiful showrooms has been judged and passed by the dedicated Mr. Remlov, who would have fits if there weren't a specific Foundation rule prohibiting the presence of what the Austrians call "kitsch" (ugly, impractical, or quick-buck pieces). In addition to the historic textiles and rugs, and the stoneware and ceramics from individual makers, specialties with the greatest appeal for most North American visitors include the cunning Hadeland crystal souvenir articles ($9), the lovely glass designs of Benny Motzfeldt ($7 up), the unique concepts in enamel ashtrays of Artist Bjørn Engø ($12 to $170), fine handwoven shawls and plaids ($10 to $57), Peter Omtvedt's hand-carved heads and ornaments recalling the Viking era, and carved teak trays, bowls, and other items by Rachel Weyergang ($1 to $60). Flat 16⅔% purchase-tax exemption; quick, safe delivery; helpful, kindly, English-speaking sales staff; branch at Airport Transit Hall. You couldn't find a happier lead-off point for your Norwegian shopping—so go to it, and good luck!

Den Norske Husflidsforening, popularly known as "Husfliden" (Møllergaten 4), has an old name. Large selection of painted or paint-it-yourself furniture; their own workshop; Director Gro Mollnes and Anette Solberg Andresen speak excellent English. Recommended.

Norwegian artisans have developed fine enameling to the point where not even Venetian or Florentine craftsmen can successfully compete with them. **David-Andersen** (Karl Johansgate 20), considered by many to be the leading house in the country, wrecks our budget every trip to Oslo with their irresistible enameled demitasse spoons ($10 to $18)—but that's individual softheadedness, because their enameled jewelry dessert spoons, cake forks, and enameled solid-silver salt-and-peppers are equally tempting. Another big draw is their original "Saga" collection of eleventh-century Viking jewelry facsimiles—brooches, bracelets, rings, earrings, pendants, and cuff links, from $12 to $30 per item. One exciting feature is their "Troll" collection of Norwegian jewelry—all in sterling silver, dotted with glittering stones from the high mountain mines of the west, and surprisingly inexpensive for their typical flair of elegance. Full line of handcrafted sterlingware, too, for the home. On every above-mentioned item there is a 16⅔% discount if mailed or sent to any foreign address and if the value totals more than $100. In enameling and silver, ask for Miss Dickens, and in jewelery, ask for Miss Aass or Mrs. Kjolberg —nice gals who know the whims of us Yankee buyers. Air-conditioned; branch in Bergen. Tops for gifts—to friends or to yourself.

Tostrup, across the street, also has an enviable reputation and sound merchandise—but we don't have quite the same enthusiasm for their displays as we do for David-Andersen's. Perhaps you'll disagree.

Regional souvenirs? **William Schmidt & Co.** (Karl Johansgate 41) has everybody licked in wearables and souvenirs of genuine Nordic flavor. Nothing—repeat, *nothing*—on its shelves is mass-produced. Most popular items are their wonderful sweaters and pullovers in Old Norwegian patterns—the largest selection, by far, on the Continent; ladies' models start at $57, men's at $59, and children's (the biggest seller) at $21, depending on size. Lovers of the unique may buy dramatic, long-lasting handbags, gloves, hats, ski boots, and other wearables in genuine seal, as well as attention-arresting reindeer-skin hats and slippers or reindeer knives. Ladies will find Schmidt's famous "Vams" ($77) and handwoven, silk-lined jackets ($50). Collectors of curiosa will find intriguingly sweet woodcut figurines and trolls. Feminine Small Fry will find dolls in beautiful native costumes to bring sparkle to their eyes (or to those of the young-in-heart, as well). For the home, you'll see hand-printed place mats in rose pattern, silver and enamel items, handwoven table runners in handsome variegated hues, pewter in profusion, and scads of other interesting things. There is a Schmidt branch at the modernized Fornebu Airport, which carries the full Schmidt range of merchandise and which is open 7 days per week from 7 A.M. to 10 P.M. Flat 16⅔% saving on all these items if they are mailed out of Norway; deliveries guaranteed. American Express, Diners Club, Master Charge, Bank America and Eurocard credit cards are welcome. Ask for Director T. Fjeld Fretheim or his daughters, Mrs. Ellen Hauge or Mrs. Elizabeth Syberg, the current Family Standard Bearers, who are most obliging. Highly recommended.

Sports equipment? **Marius Eriksen** (Ruselökkveien 5) is perhaps the best known. **Kaare Berntsen** (Universitetsgata 12) sets the pace in antiques, both for quality and price; smaller **Wangs Kunst** (Kristian IV's Gate 12) and **Hammerlunds Kunsthandel** (Tordenskjoldsgate 3) sometimes offer good rummaging as well. We're particularly fond of **Bergfjerdingen** (Damstredet 5); 2 elves' rooms with copper molds, wood, glass, pottery, and a big fireplace.

Furs? To our chagrin and with our all-around apologies, we still haven't revisited **Pels-Backer** (Kongensgate 31), the country's leading purveyor. We are told that Lars Backer, the 3rd-generation owner of this 1856 house, has vastly and successfully modernized both the premises and the flair of its stylings. Since 50% of the world's production of blue fox is indigenous to this land, here is the top specialty in its versatile line. We'll eagerly go back on our forthcoming Northern circuit.

Steen & Strøm, a department store, has a representative cross section of Norwegian retailing.

Finally, please DON'T MISS the **Shopping Bazaar**. The butchers' stalls in the historic brick firehouse behind the Cathedral (Church St. near Market Pl.) have been rebuilt into enchanting little shops. "**Husfliden**" has a branch here;

Oivind Modahl 's thumb-size jewelry quarters (Dronningensgate 27) boast an ingenious toothpick-size staircase to the consulting booth; at same address, **Skattekisten**'s antiques are under the eaves; additional attractions. Delightful place for browsing; fixed prices everywhere.

Bergen? For national handicrafts, the world-famous "**Husfliden**" (Vågsalmenning 3) has proudly sustained its reputation as Norway's leading center of home arts and crafts for over 8 decades. Full guarantee (and 16⅔% discount) on all foreign shipments; in headquarters ask for kindly Store Manager Karlsen; **Husfliden House** branch 200 yards away. Salutes!

Enameled silver and costume jewelry? **David-Andersen** (see "Oslo") has a branch here; Mr. Lytskjold speaks English.

Department stores? Try **Sundt** or **Kløverhuset** for the widest variety.

A flock of interesting silver and ceramics places are more or less clustered in the midtown area; they're worth an exploratory look.

⋅ Bergen's shops often close from Monday to Friday at 4:30 P.M. (7 P.M. on Thurs.), and on Saturday at 2 P.M.

Dedicated shophounds? Space is too tight here for further listings—so please consult this year's vastly revised and updated edition of *Fielding's Shopping Guide to Europe* for more stores, more details, and more lore.

§TIPS: Shopping hours in most of the larger cities (Bergen excepted) are 9 A.M. to 5 P.M. on weekdays and 9 A.M. to 1 to 3 P.M. on Saturday, with no noontime closings. Since the '76 introduction of the 40-hour week, many places stop at 1 P.M. on Saturday and others do not open before 10 A.M. on Monday. Everything is shuttered tight before Easter for a 7- to 10-day national vacation—as well as on 5 other holidays.

You'll need an export license for antiques.

Avoid the national Luxury Tax (16⅔%) by arranging with the merchant to ship important merchandise direct to your home.

THINGS NOT TO BUY Very little. Textiles (manufactured, not hand-loomed) still seem second-line, in general; leather goods are expensive and not worth it. Stick to arts and crafts, and you won't go wrong.

LOCAL RACKETS We found none. Norwegians are too proud to be petty.

Portugal

Gradually but assuredly Portugal's long winter of discontent is melting into a sunlit spring. A regeneration has begun.

Adjustment to post-revolutionary chaos largely has been achieved while new patterns of order are becoming fixed. Absorption of some 650,000 refugees from Angola and Mozambique has peaked; many of the former have returned to their homeland, and some of the latter are finding jobs and accommodations; both have created massive economic and housing problems in Lisbon and elsewhere, but the worst is now behind the tiny, almost impoverished nation—or so it would seem from our up-to-the-minute examination of this land of cork farms, rugged mountains, rolling plains, fourteenth-century hamlets, and cities of tomorrow.

To be sure, there remain tattered posters by the square mile—a blemishing, mottled legacy of electioneering which followed the fall of the old regime in April 1974. In an outburst of pluralistic enthusiasm, hardly a wall can be found throughout Portugal that does not reflect the expansive freedom of political expression. If it defaces buildings and monuments with painted slogans, graphic rant, and blatant rhetoric, at least it dignifies the newly won stature of a society released from suppression.

At this precise moment, Portugal is an interesting nation in a fascinating stage of development. It is a time of intoxication and unrelenting labor, of dialogues and dreams, of endless graffiti and ceaseless grappling with realities. Rarely can you find such open experimentation in government by an essentially peace-loving public. There are no shadows to threaten the tourist, no fears (on our just-completed circuit) to warrant the slightest anxiety. Numerous hallmarks of luxury and ease are beginning to reappear for the outlander and for the Portuguese as well. (To help pull through these troubled times, the United States recently donated $25,000,000 as an outright gift; Norway sent a small town of new prefabricated houses; more assistance and credits are trickling in.)

While inflation has roared on dolorously for the whole country—exacerbated by the painful burden of accepting so many African refugees—tariffs for the foreigner are still gratifyingly cheap. For superb seafood and improving shelter, you'll pay anywhere from a quarter to a half of the Continental outlay for similar rewards.

It is a dream country for hard-up connoisseurs because gold-plated elegance of the utmost refinement and taste can be purchased for bargain basement price tags.

Your hotel might be run by a "workers' committee" and your egg scrambled malevolently by a "kitchen commission," but through it all the Portuguese has not lost one iota of his warmth or of his vital fraternal affection that form the essence of his humaness. Moreover, he hasn't lost his sense of humor. In a bar where we very recently witnessed wretched service (obviously by "committee" greenhorns), someone had hung a sign poking fun at the whole system. In large hand-blocked letters that suggested political bombast, it screamed, "VOTE FOR THE TWO PARTY SYSTEM!" And then in smaller print it chuckled, "One on Friday and one on Saturday."

It is difficult to resist the enchantment of these new Europeans, these ancient navigators, these builders of a nation.

And what of the sunshine? It still blesses the Portuguese sky with its own special brilliance just as it illuminates the everlastingly mellow Portuguese smile.

CITIES *Lisbon* (Lisboa), as the capital and heartbeat of a small nation, was naturally where the red carnation revolution gathered all of its energy and entertained most of its political rallies. The result for today's tourist is an unbecoming panoply of aging posters, peeling placards, crumbling billboards, and credos painted on monuments and walls with aerosol sprays. On top of this, the nation (which means chiefly Lisbon itself) had to take in a huge number of refugees from former African territories. By the time of your visit most of these unfortunate displaced persons will have found housing and possibly even work so that the business of cleaning up the city and its surroundings can gain momentum. There are wonderful things to see here, and our suggestion to anyone who also is seeking comfort and luxury is to absorb them quickly and move on to the coastal and resort redoubts while giving the capital time to get its house in order. Two or three days for observing the sights, hearing some *fado* singing, and doing a bit of shopping should be adequate until the restoration is complete—probably in another year ot two.

Oporto (Porto) is second. This is the port-wine center in the north; larger than El Paso or Jersey City, there's plenty of bustling activity in this gateway to the sea. The town is built on a dome-shape hill; exits of a fine 2-tier bridge hit the riverbank at top and bottom levels. Local color abounds in Oporto, too; the scale of living is far simpler than it is in Lisbon. The cathedral (begun in the early twelfth century) and the Soares dos Reis Museum in the Carrancas Palace (its cavernous hulk stuffed with gold artifacts and paintings) are 2 goblets for culture sippers of this vintage city. As a base of operations for the traveler, it's ideal; excursions through the wine country, to Bom Jésus, to Braga, to Guimarães, and to dozens of fascinating villages can be made with a minimum of discomfort. These are especially popular in autumn, when the grapes are in harvest.

Funchal, third in importance, is covered separately in the "Madeira" section (see end of "Portugal" chapter).

Coimbra, the fourth city, is ancient, beautiful, and serene. It spreads itself lazily over one big hill, rising from the banks of the Mondego River to a dominant clock tower at its cap. The University is here; its library alone is worth a special trip for bibliophiles. The *fado* "April in Portugal" was originally a famous song to this hill town.

Setúbal, fifth in size, is a sardine-factory center within easy ride of Lisbon. The Church of Jesus, in which the pillars are twisted to resemble fishermen's ropes, is so curious it shouldn't be missed. Pleasant side trip from the capital —but a trip to **Sintra** is more civilized.

Estoril, **Cascais**, and **Figueira da Foz** are the best-known international seaside resorts. The strand of **Caparica**, the wooded bay of **Portinho d'Arrábida**, and the rustic harbor of **Sesimbra** are reminiscent of the French Riviera—but their tariffs, thank goodness, are not. **Obidos** recalls the majesty of a walled city now dozing amid lichen-flecked, Helios-warmed stones. The sunny **Algarve Coast**, from Sagres to Vila Real (Spanish frontier), offering some of Europe's finest beaches, has triggered the country's hottest touristic boom. The international-size Arabia Airport 2 miles west of Faro, capital of the region, is fully operational and efficient. Further information follows in "Hotels" *et seq.* The rest of Portugal is mostly small villages and hamlets.

MONEY AND PRICES

The monetary units are the centavo and escudo. Forget about the former. The smallest coin, 10 centavos, is about ½¢; 100 centavos make 1 escudo. The escudo itself is worth 3¢; there are coins of 10, 20, and 50 centavos; in escudo mintings there are units of 1, 2½, 5, 10, and 20; the notes are in 20, 50, 100, 500, and 1000 escudo denominations. The method of listing is a mild shock to new American visitors; the symbol "$" is placed *after* the escudos and *before* the centavos. Thus, 2 escudos and 50 centavos becomes 2$50—not $2.50; but the humble sum of 7½¢.

Lisbon prices are now among the lowest in Europe and they are even more agreeable in the provinces despite nationwide inflation. Your dollars will have more elastic in them here than in most Continental lands in 1977.

During this period of political upset, it would be wise not to change too many dollars into escudos at one time. Upon departure, convert all of your escudos back into dollars or some other currency that is readily negotiable elsewhere.

Credit cards, incidentally, are not accepted in many restaurants. Hotels will take most of the major cards, but if you plan to travel extensively you'd better bring along a stack of traveler's checks.

ATTITUDE TOWARD TOURISTS

Please come! That's the clarion call from official sources. To make it easier, this year you can even receive "Portugal on a Silver Platter"—a program in which 130 hotels on the mainland and on Madeira are participating. If Lisbon is used as a gateway by air or sea, you will be gifted with one free night for every four at a 5-star hotel which bears the bonus emblem. Other goodies include gasoline reductions, wine, gifts, handicrafts, free meals, shopping discounts, sightseeing, and slashed car rental fees.

The **Direction-General of Tourism** (Praça dos Restauradores 27) is the government tourism organization. This agency, under the hardworking directorship of Dr. Cristiano de Freitas, publishes voluminous travel literature, maintains a string of Information Offices, and assists the visitor in all possible ways. Because it's open every day of the week (Sun. 10 A.M. to 5 P.M.), and because English is spoken by nearly everyone, it makes an excellent mail delivery point. One of its major triumphs—and responsibilities—is the construction and maintenance of the renowned Portuguese *pousadas* and *estalagens;* these are the simple, plain, strategically located series of resthouse hotels especially designed for foreign traffic. The tariff is an astonishing $7 or so per person per day, including meals and wine of the region (the Pousada dos Loios, one of the few exceptions, charges about $12 while the tiptop rate is knocked down by the Pousada da Raínha Santa Isobel at Estremoz—all of $18 inclusive of 3 meals, service, and taxes); 5 days is the maximum permissible stay. They are scattered in such a manner that travelers on normal routes may usually sleep at one, take lunch at another, and spend the night at still another, thus avoiding the rigors of routine back-country lodgings; all are clean, comfortable, and cheap. If you need help with an industrial problem, the efficient Pedro de Vasconcelos, Secretary General of the **Portuguese Industrial Association** (F.I.L. in Alcântara) will cheerfully advise you. The **Portuguese National Tourist Office,** at 570 Fifth Ave., N.Y. 10036, is the national representative. And the head of this administration is the ever-helpful Nuno Almeida. Branches also are located at 3250 Wilshire Blvd. in Los Angeles and at The Palmer House in Chicago.

CUSTOMS AND IMMIGRATION The laws are the craziest in the world, but the men who carry them out are models of efficiency.

It's a "tolerance" system—with unique variations. Big items are charged by weight and not by classification. Inspectors often wink at minor infractions by the friendly traveler, but anyone foolish enough to get nasty, can be slapped down with a king's ransom in duty on all his belongings.

Dogs and cats must have officially stamped health certificates from the country of origin, in case anybody cares. Leave your white-mantled colobus at home because simians are forbidden visas!

HOTELS Enormous changes are in the works. As if the revolution were not bad enough for Portugal's innkeepers, along came the twin crises of Angola and Mozambique to heap Ossa upon Pelion. Many hotels were requisitioned in their entirety for housing refugees torn from their African homelands. Most of these unfortunate people were not accustomed to luxury living; many probably had never before seen the inside of a fine hotel. Their huddled presence has resulted in inordinate wear on both public rooms and facilities as well as on bedchambers. Throughout our recent visit, it was commonplace to see refugee children playing in wet bathing suits on the silk brocade furnishings of aristocratic lobbies. Almost nothing had been painted since April 1974; no repairs had been effected; nobody cared.

Now the tourist authorities *do* care and with enormous financial support from the treasury they are zealously hailing the painters, summoning the plasterers, and spiffing up the entire skein. Some houses will take longer to restore than others—this we have seen for ourselves on our just-ended countrywide tour. Thus, if you stick pretty closely to the stops we recommend on the following pages, we think you will receive the best accommodations and the warmest welcomes. As we mentioned in the introduction to this chapter, Lisbon was the hardest hit of any area, so if you are blocking off time on your Portuguese holiday calender, this year we suggest that you accord greater weight to the coastal resorts and rural oases which for the moment can provide more comfort and simple natural charm.

In **Lisbon**, the walk-away champ for 1977 is the tall, stately **Sheraton**. This one is excellent by any standards. It contains the glorious rooftop Panorama Restaurant and outdoor terrace which boast magnificent views. Below are the lush Alfama Grill, the intimate Taverna Bar, the Caravelle Coffee Shop, a heated swimming pool, a health club, a sauna, and 388 air-conditioned, comfortable, handsomely equipped suites or bedchambers. For meetings and/or banquets, a ballroom and 4 satellites hold from 20 to 630 clients. General Manager Joâo Mendes Leal should (but doesn't have time to) bust his buttons with pride in what is to us the best planned and most fetching house in the whole chain.

The **Tivoli**, completely refurbished and expanded, remains a showcase of professional innkeeping. This Portuguese version of an American operation is commercial in tone, but its airy, freshly revamped, and totally refurnished public rooms and its conservatively modern and well-maintained accommodations are so attractively done that impersonality is minimized. (A cricket that once inadvertently arrived in a shipment of flowers for the lobby is now a regular chirping feature here; in fact 2 fresh ones are delivered every week to sing a song of welcome.) An additional wing has raised its capacity to 320 units; an extended carpark and garage now function as a part of the blossoming Tivoli-Jardim complex (see below). All rooms have bath, radio, TV outlet, and air conditioning, and are very clean; color schemes vary, with some soothing and some aggressively extroverted; many baths are faced in handsome marble. There's a beautifully viewful rooftop terrace-grill-nightclub combination which overlooks the slope to the river, with a cheery fireplace for cool months and a patio for summer tippling. The service now is keen and friendly. The courtly and amiable Director Alfredo Coelho Fernandes merits bows for his upgrading of facilities. Very good and still improving, says this Jiminy Cricket. Just a hop skip and jump away, is the almost-adjoining, newer **Jardim**, which some loyalists even prefer to the mother patch. Set-back construction insuring extraquiet and insulation; independent reception desk; easy parking out front or in the cellar of the same building; orange and blue lounge; woody snack bar with a magnificent Lurçat tapestry; cozy dining room keyed up in white bricks; mezzanine bar; an abundance of posies from the rooftop solarium to the giant spray in the lobby; full air conditioning. All bedchambers equipped with comfortable beds, radios and piped music, bright, well-designed baths, full-length mirrors, and ample storage space; front units featuring wide balcony furnished with big cushioned chairs and a table; a few accommodations overlooking the lovely garden for which it was named. For tranquillity in the modern mood, stay here; for action and traditional surroundings, pick the Tivoli. Each is rewarding in its respective way.

Next comes the modernistic **Altis**, which gives us the impression of a Scandinavian hostelry transplanted intact to Iberia. Actually it is now being managed by the Méridien group of France. The lobby is a dark marble fastness dominated by a colossal metal Christus. Window-lined rooftop grill, candlelit by evening; adjoining S. Jorge Bar; appealing Girassol restaurant at treetop level; interior Herald Bar with piano tinklings from time to time. Some of the bedrooms are L-shaped and adequate in size while others are narrow-gauged. Décor leans to blond wood trim highlighted by tufted textiles in warm brown, orange and red. Basically this is a substantial address that can be enthusiastically recommended, especially during these times of inn-keeping hardship in the capital.

Both the world-famous **Ritz** and the once stately **Avenida Palace** are in such a state of flux that you might do better to choose one of our other offerings this year until they can recover from the ultraheavy occupation by African refugees. On our visit the former was badly worn, cheerless, and in need of a strong managerial hand. The latter was totally run down, but both officially deluxe houses expected to be at least partially renovated by this season. We would be surprised if they are.

The **Príncipe Real** seems to have survived the revolution in striking form. We commend its aplomb and durability. It comes up with a tranquil address in midcity, an unimpressive entrance and façade, and better public rooms than bedchambers. Hypercharming ground floor composed of a hearth-brightened lounge, a red-rooted bar and 3-table cocktail cranny, and—happiest of all—the warmhearted welcome of Sr. and Sra. José Rezende, proprietors who have poured their love into this peaceful little hideaway. Enchantingly panoramic 5th-floor breakfast room with 10 tables—a knockout; A-plus maintenance from cellar to rooftop; 24 units, each with private plumbing, wall-to-wall carpeting, odd-shape configurations, and bolts of clashing cretonnes; no radios, TV, or piped music. Except for the letdown in the sleeping segments, this one has its unique allure, which we heartily praise.

The **York House** (Rua das Janelas Verdes 32), a converted seventeenth-century monastery plus a much newer annex, is something very, very special. Homelike atmosphere within its cloistered confines; inconvenient suburban situation; hard-to-find, inconspicuous gate to white stone steps and ivied path; tiny reception area; intimate, half-tiled main dining room (ex-wine cellar uncasked for overflow); cozy bar. Reputedly excellent Portuguese specialties with French overtones; menu otherwise chiefly international in scope. Its delightful French-speaking proprietress, Madame Andrée Goldstein, is assisted by her French nephew and her American niece. As an informal and friendly hideaway, here is one of the best "pension" bets (if we can call this establishment a "pension") we have ever seen anywhere, but anywhere. Caution: Make reservations long, long, *long* in advance. Our highest recommendation in every respect, within its budget-price league.

The **Flórida** has taken on a commercial tone, but it is passable in our opinion. Portuguese textiles and regional hues throughout; lobby in gray, red, and blue, with adjoining wood-paneled bar; cool dining room facing plaza; Grill serving à la carte selections from 9 P.M. to 3 A.M.; umbrella-dotted terrace for breakfasting or imbibing now buffeted by more and more traffic noises. Fair.

The **Dom Carlos**, a semicircular house, nestles at the edge of a small park. In better times we could recommend it, but for the time being let's wait to witness its level of recovery.

The **Fénix** wings in with a split-level lobby warbling piped melodies, full air conditioning, a delightful Spanish-style Bodegón (taproom) with piano lilts, a smoothly conceived dining room with excellent cuisine, a commercial patina, inadequate elevator service, and tiny, tiny rooms in jocular colors with equally small baths. Clean, bright, and okay, except for its mercantile feel and overcramped design.

The **Embaixador** (Ambassador) and the **Diplomático** both require so much reconditioning that we wouldn't stay at either for the nonce. The **Penta**? One local wag cracked that service can be so awful that even the refugees complain.

The **Mundial** is very much in the middle of things—too much so, from the standpoint of noise. This house caters to conducted tours, to journalists, and to business people; it is well adapted for these specialized types of clientele. Its 146 rooms, all with bath, are slightly larger than those of the Embaixador (which isn't saying much). Pleasant roof-garden restaurant, with a panorama of the castle and the Old Town.

Plaza, centrally sited, is quiet and dignified. Vast recent improvements and reasonable maintenance; decent-size bedchambers flavorfully enhanced by old-fashioned furnishings; plug-in air conditioning ready on request for 50% of the house sockets. **Infante Santo** and **Lutecia** are too worn to wear well in our opinion.

The **Eduardo VII**, 10 minutes from the center, is largely dedicated to group traffic. Lobby small; private bath with all 95 rooms or suites; self-styled American Bar, plus full restaurant, on the 10th floor; some of the terraces open to a scenic spread of the city. New Manager Nogeira de Ameida is trying to weave in some zip. For a lower outlay, the **Miraparque**, a converted apartment house which operates pension style, offers clean but austere accommodations. The 35-room **Flamingo** is off our list for now. We hear that the **Lis** has become the Communist Party headquarters—it's not for this fellow traveler.

The **Presidente**, the **Jorge V**, and the **Impala** are all poor value for this year's Guidesters, in our view.

The **Príncipe**, **Reno** (adjoining), **Excelsior** (best of the lot) and **Capitol** are typical representatives of the flock of smaller havens that sprang up a few years ago to lure the mass influx of bygone holidaymakers. May they thrive again, because basically they do their jobs quite well. The older **Europa**, **Borges**, and **Metrópole** are all adequate, if you're a student or young and sturdy; the cookery is often their weakest point.

For a holiday in Portugal involving sun, swimming, dancing, all sports, old-fashioned loafing and/or big-league gaiety, Lisbon isn't your dish of tea. The experienced traveler, particularly during the hot months, splits his time between the capital and the neighboring **Costa do Sol** ("Sunny Coast"), a shoreline playground which extends from the city limits to Cascais and Praia do Guincho. (For our description of the fabulous and luxurious Hotel do Guincho, please see further along.) **Estoril**, 30 minutes out, is the center of the beehive. Exiled Kings (Italy), Regents (Hungary), and Pretenders (France, Spain) have lived here; enough Archdukes, Princes, Counts, Barons, and lesser fry lazed in its soft climate to fill a special supplement of *Almanach de Gotha;* as a publicity release once put it, "With over half of the Continent's deposed Monarchs, Pretenders to Thrones, and ex-Excellencies in residence, Estoril's post-office roster reads like a lengthy royal flush." The beach is good, the hotels are grim for the moment, the people fun, and the prices surprisingly low to the vacationer from the U.S. **Cascais**, next door, is quieter, generally less expensive and less chichi; rapidly vanishing local color; only so-so as a base, unless you install yourself in the delightful Hotel Cidadela (see below). **Sintra**, farther out, has the marvelous, old-world Hotel Palácio de Seteais (also see below).

Moving north from the capital along the shore road, the first major oasis you'll find is the **Motel Continental** at **Oeiras** (about 5 miles short of Estoril). Impressively sprawling complex; huge dining panoply consisting of a glass-wrapped café, restaurant, bar, and a prairie-size outdoor dining terrace viewing the waves; enormous swimming pool just above a rocky beach; playground (free) in groves behind the buildings; gigantic carpark at entrance. Tucked into the nearby woods is the 140-unit semicircular motel. All accommodations resembling small chalet-suites, with a tiny patch of lawn, a tiny garden path, a tiny patio, and a car slot or garage; plain furnishings; twin beds plus an upper bunk slung crosswise above their headboards; TV; kitchenette and refrigerator; small bath with shower and bidet. Groceries and other supplies are available at the miniature supermarket in the restaurant enclosure. Try to book on the seaside, not the parkside.

The **Praia Mar**, pried away from the water by a superhighway, suffers from its off-the-sea location, but boasts compensatory comforts and thoughtfully executed amenities. Entrance along a mosaic walk that creates an optical illusion of undulating waves (even when you're sober); modern, subdued ambiance; public rooms air-conditioned; splashworthy pool; large 8th-floor glassbound restaurant with a wonderful vista; 2 bars; lounges; small nightclub. Handful of little suites in its overall complement of 143 accommodations, all with private bath and most with balcony; confined dimensions; sparse furnishings over tile floorings. Except for its unfortunate situation, this one's basically sound. Personally, however, we prefer other choices directly on the waterside.

Estoril's hotels stack up this way to us this year:

The **Lennox Country Club** is a hotel—not a club, as its title implies. Here is a perfect little gem for golfers and tranquillity-seekers. It is just a chip shot from the center, on a narrow, peaceful uphill lie. Three buildings resembling a private-mansion complex (10 bedrooms in the main structure, 6 in the annex, and 5 apartments in the block around the corner); glassed-in dining room opening to a greensward and swimming pool with its own ranch-style imbibery; lounge with small bar (pour-your-own-drinks and write-your-own-bills policies); accommodations named for famous golf courses; except for 1 showered unit, all with private bath. Our favorite is the Lytham Room, with its sparkly fresh mien, sun balcony, and exceptionally lovely view. No tour groups ever; only residents and their guests permitted use of the public rooms, bars, pool, or cinema; complimentary shuttle services to airport, golf course, and docks; free, unlimited supply of house wines, bottled water, fruit, mid-morning coffee, afternoon tea, and a welter of other kindnesses. Write to Mr. or Mrs. D. C. Reid, the proprietors, or to Receptionist Jane Goddard *long* in advance, because the clientele consists chiefly of well-contented repeaters. Although officially it is rated 3rd among Estoril hostelries, those who thrive in this very special type of ambiance rank it higher. A Whole-in-One!

The colossal 19-story, 400-room **Estoril Sol**, Portugal's largest hotel, cranked open its glass portals in '65. Towering mightily near Cascais Bay, it dominates the skyline for miles around. For youngbloods, group leaders, and modernists, it also dominates the social life of the area. Its vast skein of entertainment or pastime facilities include a terraced Olympic-size pool, kiddy pond, artificial beach with tunnel access under the road, bowling lanes, Turkish bath, sauna, discothèque, 5 bars, a beauty parlor, barbershop, and 2 banquet-conference rooms for 1200. Ultracool marble-lined lobby; 10th floor nerve center with spacious lounge, panoramic restaurant with atrocious cuisine (on our sampling), bar, card nook, and ballroom; each level hued in different color schemes. The best accommodations for the money, in our opinion, are the 3 suites on the 19th floor—exceptional values when split among 4 to 6 occupants. Book away from the "front," because of the railroad and auto traffic noises. Service? Impersonal and institutional, with a long climb ahead.

The **Estoril Palácio**, the traditional and historic leader which was taken over by the government, has had such heavy occupation by refugees, that it will take at least another year to put it right (if you'll pardon the expression) again.

The little **Hotel Das Arcadas** was under the same ownership and management as the Palácio and consequently experienced a similar dreary fate.

The 84-room **Monte Estoril**, on a hillside overlooking the sea, must wait a while before we can recommend it again. The **Zenith** and the **Londres** are off our list in '77.

The **Cibra** is moving ahead with good ideas and deliberate speed. Its penthouse restaurant is a plus; the room count now is 89, all with bath and all seaside units with balconies. The waves sea-able only from the 3rd floor and above. This once-brash challenger is beginning to provide genuine value for your escudo. Much better.

The **Atlântico** is scissored from the sea by railway tracks. In defiance of its well-intentioned beauty treatment, the maintenance is so poor that paint is chipped and plaster is loose. The personnel we saw couldn't be more harried if they'd had chiggers and wore boxing gloves.

The massive and mass-minded, new, 350-room **Centra Estoril** exudes a chill factor that to us recalls mushes across the Yukon tundra. Perhaps you'll have another opinion.

The **Paris**, going on to only 4 decades, impresses us as having been untouched since the day Herbert Hoover took over from Calvin Coolidge.

In **Cascais**, 14 miles from Lisbon, the **Albatroz** is a tranquil retreat. A happy-family atmosphere (almost slaphappy really when the service is off) pervades the cliff-high 16-room manse, the lawn, the tea terrace, the fireside lounge, the breathtakingly situated dining salon, the bar, and every cranny of this amiable home. All units have a sea view, full bath, and individual décor, usually in woods and tartans; some offer small-arched windows providing a porthole effect; we prefer #1, #6, or #14. Quite good. **Cidadela** is unusual in concept and, we think, fair in execution. You may choose between hotel-style living or private apartment-style living with connecting-door units stretchable from 1-to-7-person occupancy. (A small but well-stocked downstairs supermarket can furnish the comestibles for your fully equipped kitchenette.) Inside-outside dining area; glass-fronted and poolside bars; large terrace adjoining main floor; beauty salon; 2 boutiques; garage and parking space. For the wayfarer in search of Portuguese P. & Q., this haven probably will be suitable to most trippers. The commercially oriented 59-room **Baía** unveiled its ultramodern barracks with a façade of balconies in '62. Beach boulevard front, on a heavily traveled, noisy corner; hoi polloi ground-floor café-terrace; romantic penthouse with bar; urbane 4th-floor dining room, with wraparound windows on 3 sides; bright, matchbox-size bedchambers, intelligently designed for maximum efficiency; bathrooms every inch of 5-feet long (not bad, if you're blessed with 5 feet and no torso). We think the **Nau** should be read "No " in our book. For traditionalists in search of flavor and charm, the little **Estalagem Solar Dom Carlos** has traditionally been a honey for the price. Lustrous garden restaurant; décor unusually beguiling.

At **Guincho**, 20 miles from Lisbon and 4 miles beyond Cascais, please don't miss the exquisite **Hotel do Guincho**, which commands one of the most glorious settings of any hostelry we have ever seen. Its cliff-high perch is flanked on either side by bowls of golden sand rising from the breakers up into the gorse-covered dunes. This thirteenth-century fortress is the most westerly point on the continent; it was restored in the sixteen-hundreds, but the latest updatings to comfortize this sparkling antique gem were effected without altering the original tone or structure to any appreciable degree. At a cost of more than $6,000,000 in redecoration, the 38-room *fortaleza* probably will never make money—anyway profit was never the intention here. Each room different, most with balcony, some large suites with fireplaces (pick #309, 310 or 312), all with air conditioning, many with carved vaulted stone ceilings, some furnishings dating back 350 years. Our very recent lunch in its elegant seafront dining room was nothing short of superb (see "Restaurants"), at a price that was remarkably cheap. By international standards, in fact, you will be flabbergasted by the ultralow tariffs for such baronial rewards. Perhaps by the time you arrive a new modern wing will be gestating next door, but we are sure that even when completed it will not be able to accommodate all of the business that will be rushing to its portals. Thus, be certain to reserve long in advance *summer or winter.* Our top recommendation for coastal navigators. The neighboring **Muchaxo** has 56 modest bedchambers (see "Food and Restaurants"). The **Estalagem** has 15 simple, clean rooms, and the same view but far less color. That's it.

In **Sintra**, the **Hotel Palácio de Seteais** has a wonderful setting, gorgeous gardens, lavish furnishings, and top-grade cuisine. Our recent visit convinced us that this gem has fully regained the earlier glories that had started to wane several seasons back. This former summer residence of the king was converted into what was hoped would be a superluxurious country inn. We are delighted to note that scores of Guidesters again are enjoying this fine establishment. Resident Manager Mario Joaõ is now giving this grande dame rejuvenation unguents—and they appear to be having a favorable effect. Hurrah!

The **Vale de Lobos**, 12 miles from Lisbon via Queluz and Belas, is a sleepy haven across a dry valley from *Sintra*. Its beautiful garden-landscape situation is fittingly enhanced by a sapphire-blue pool, tennis courts, and white wood trellises. Attractive windowed dining room with handsome wrought-iron and copper chandeliers; billiard parlor; skating rink; 30 small, uninspired rooms so jarringly out of key that they're for shut-eye only. In winter there's dancing, and all year there's robust outdoor huffing and puffing for those who enjoy huffing and puffing.

In *Azeitão*, also across the Tagus, there's the romantic little **Quinta das Torres**, a seventeenth-century palace. Some modern comforts, but the management scorns electricity in favor of petroleum lamps and open fireplaces, for authentic Old World atmosphere. Lovely park, courtyard, and lake swimming pool; 11 units, mostly suites, in different styles.

In *Sesimbra*, 45-minutes from Lisbon via the gloriously panoramic bridge, the **Hotel Do Mar** nestles 75 yards above the sea and this still-unspoiled fishing village. Vaguely Hawaiian-style construction, with buildings staggered up a hillside for successively better vistas of the bay; entrance at top, with access to 4 tiers of rooms and terraces; glassy crown composed of a 2-section restaurant with a sweeping view; its ambiance, smiling service, and seascape insure its evergreen popularity. Bar, at lobby level, in regional fabrics and woods, built on a man-made promontory, with an L-shape patio adjoining; sun roof; small nightclub; beauty parlor; 3 boutiques. At sea level, there's a hexagonal dining pavilion (season only), backed by 3 crescents of rooms; lovely circular swimming pool one plateau higher; smaller ringlet of water exclusively for children; trim lawns, plants, and shrubs. Total of 120 bedchambers, all with tiny bath, plus terrace facing the water; a ½-dozen suites extremely fetching in the local mood. Highly recommended (1) for sunbathers who want serenity in comfort, and (2) for a lunch excursion from Lisbon (be *sure* to reserve your table in advance). Ask your driver to go about ¼-mile past the hotel on the shore road for a peek at the beach and the fleet of typically colorful and interesting fishing boats.) Full, full, full from June 1 to late September.

In *Oporto* it's the **Infante de Sagres**. Full of thoughtful touches such as walnut "silent valets" and other fillips, plus an invigorated ambiance smacking of neo-Baroque elegance backed by bushels of escudos and TLC; well-run dining room with superior cuisine and an unusually fine maître; friendly staff led by "Let's-get-serious" Manager Vasco Seabra. We congratulate everyone involved in recrowning this lovely gal as the Queen of Oporto. The **Dom Henrique** stacks 100 modern units into the tallest (18 stories) edifice in the city; the views from the restaurant, bar, and terrace are enchanting; so are the rooms, except for their slightly cramped proportions. Recommended. The **Castor** is one we missed, but friends tell us it is worthy. The traditional-style

da Batalha is routine. The **Albergaria de São João** is a more inviting residence. The **Tuela** is a far-out budget bet with 45 fully piped chambers and a very kind staff. **Vitor** is now under the same house flag. The **Império** is not recommended by us this year.

In *Figueira da Foz*, the halfway point between Lisbon and Oporto, it's the **Grande**, across from the broad beach. Nothing else here is much good.

The *Algarve* district in the extreme south went through the throes of the nation's hottest real-estate boom just prior to the revolution, and just about every second fisherman and cork farmer in the region got up to his elbows in the innkeeping pot of gold. First, in wild popularity, then in total neglect, then with infusions of refugees, and finally with a mandate on normalcy returning to this zone, select addresses have appeared and disappeared swiftly. The mercurial pattern continues, but in general some of the best and most luxurious resort life of this hard-pressed little country can still be found down on this coast. The roads are narrow but excellent; the beaches are wide and often deserted; the water is cold and given to frequent undertows (swim only where there are lifeguards); the scenery is hauntingly serene when you escape from the pockets of Miami Beach architecture. The prices are very easy to take nowadays.

Moving toward Spain from the western littoral, *Sagres*—now an Iberian enclave of African refugees—offers the bluff-bound **Hotel da Baleeira**. Here is a case-in-point of the dramatic decline in one of our former stellar attractions. What a pity! It occupies perhaps the most breathtaking address along this rocky but romantic row, overlooking a *matelot's* cove and 70 miles of visible coastline. Awning-lined, glass-enclosed dining room. Sandy beach at the base of a cliff; summer nightclub a few steps below the main building; facilities for outdoor fishfries; rooftop solarium; sport shop; bar; TV room; terraces galore; swimming pool. Total of 105 units facing the sea, most with private balcony; backaching beds on our sleep-in; small baths disclosing several pieces of broken hardware during our ablutions; service and general household maintenance were inexcusably poor on our visit (and complaints of unchanged linen, unrepaired plumbing, and unhonored reservations are inundating us!). The local Workers' Committee had better snap to attention. Here is a handy starting point for your tour of South Portugal—but it is in grave danger of turning its former siren lures into a shipwreck of disasters. A word of warning: Since this promontory juts out as sharply as Dick Tracy's chin, harsh Atlantic gales slash uppercuts at it in the winter and fringe seasons. The building is simply *not* adapted to the colder and stormier months. The state-operated **Pousada Do Infante** has only 15 heavily booked accommodations with bath, many of which remain occupied by Angolans; the same is true of the newer 18-room **Estalagem das Descobertas**, set back 200 yards behind the cliffs. For serious budgeteers, the simple but spotless **Pensão Infante** in the village provides shelter and nutrients for peanuts per *noite*. *Lagos* offers the First-class **Meia Praia**. Stair-step structure facing the Atlantic from across railway tracks; 66 rooms with bath and balcony; narrow bedrooms with uninspired functional furnishings. Just so-so. For position, we prefer the tiny **Praia Dona Ana** around the curve of the coast, about 100 yards above a bathing cove; a mere dozen clean accommodations at lean tariffs. The

5-story, 70-room **Golfinho** is typical of the hurry-built hostelries in this area. Appealing vista from top-floor restaurant; maritimeliness bar at ground level; hairdresser; clam-size space concepts which are far too spare for long-staying holidaymaking; baths with "telephone"-type showers; all rooms with air conditioning and tiny balcony; book high for the view. Not bad, but not exciting either. The 122-room **Lagos** has some new features which we haven't seen. **São Cristóvão**, at the outskirts, is adequate for overnighting only; inexpensive and modern. Don't bother with the prefab cabins stuck up on the hillock beside the road to Sagres. This complex is billed as a "motel," but we erroneously took it for a gypsy campsite.

In *Alvor*, the deluxe **Alvor Praia** commands a heavenly cliff-high sweep above a rock and sand beach. Handsome white linear structure flanked by a decorative pond at its entrance and a heated variform swimming pool on its grassy seafront facade; spacious lobby highlighted by a mother-of-pearl multidisk bauble suspended over an interior lakelet; viewful restaurant, plus candle-lit grill with white brick and woody tones; excellent cuisine; snack bar; sauna; hairdressing and barber facilities; 25% reduction on green fees at the nearby golf club. Full air conditioning; 200 smallish balconied rooms; 16 very large suites; huge wardrobe closets; eversharp management by soft-spoken Ruy de Almeira, a dedicated pro. Tops in the immediate area for year-round seasiders. Within sight but farther inland, the **Penina Golf Hotel** remains one of the better golfing resort havens in Europe. Somewhat curious setting plunked just off the main highway, 2½-miles from the sea (an advantage for golfers who dislike the wicked Atlantic-borne winds); masterfully planned 18-hole links; curved pool in the garden; fully outfitted clubhouse downstairs in main building; sauna; 2 tennis courts. Marvelous interior appointments set amid modern Algarve architecture; wide, clean-lined lobby with sumptuous adjoining lounges; spacious dining room with 3 huge, 12-arm silver chandeliers; Monchique Grill with brass lanterns, touches of timber, and glass-covered rôtisserie; live music nightly. Total of 214 air-conditioned rooms, many with their own balcony. If you shun isolation, golfing, or just-getting-away-from-it-all, this spot most definitely is not geared for you. But if you are discriminating and if you take this sport seriously (with a healthy helping of luxury), Penina is still *the* place to tee off.

Praia da Rocha, with its savage red rocks (illuminated at night) and its faun-colored sand, is popping with pride over its 7-story, 180-room cliffside giant—the Deluxe-category, white-and-blue **Algarve**. A king's ransom has been poured into this flashy youngster, but somehow we feel the truly discriminating traveler would find it too showy, glossy, boisterous, and spectacularly Las Vegas in its concept. Almost every conceivable amenity has been crammed into its imposing hulk—from a solarium and sauna on the roof to one of the most glorious swimming pools we've seen on its lower grass-skirted terrace, plus another one for kiddies lower toward the sea. Azure-tile motif carried over into the interior; busy lobby frequently abustle with sun-and-fun-drenched Teutons and other northern heatniks; hyper-decorative dining room with highback chairs; abundance of nibble nooks and bars; nightclub; pool drinkery with a flowering garden on its roof; air-chilled throughout. Ordinary bedchambers are very good; almost all face the sea and have private balcony.

The suites, however, pull out all the architectural stops. Here are a few samples: The 6th-floor "Yachting" fleet harbors Scotch plaids, polished wood, brass hardware, and, naturally, nautical rig; 2 "Mirador" combos, called "Super-luxe," are isolated beside the rocks and feature minigolf links at their doorsteps; the "Presidential" is subdued, leathery, and masculine; the "Oriental" pad, in Ottoman overtones and Moorish moods, is clearly designed for the Caliph of Something-or-other; the "Esplanade" annex boasts individual gardens. The effort, the tremendous investment, and the extraordinarily high quality of the construction and appointments must surely be commended. The lower-category **Jupiter**, which orbits a few hundred yards away, is yet another asset to this tourist-minded hamlet. Groupy in feeling and more commercial in general; swimming pool at its entrance, too close to the street junction and traffic for comfort; shops bordering its ground-floor fringes; coolish restaurant; bowling alley, snack corner, and Boîte Jupiter discothèque usually packed with youngsters; Rotary meetings on Friday. All 144 bedrooms with private bath, comfortable blond-wood furniture, and appealing colors; 8 junior suites with TV; seaside and riverside units with balcony; radiant-type heating *and* cooling (a first on us). Satisfactory for its bracket. The plaza-sited **Rocha** is still resting after its renewal and expansion program a while ago. The 30-room **Bela Vista** is next in line, but it is largely devoted to sheltering refugees, as are the **Pensão Sol** and the **Estalagem São José**. *Portimão*, a busy fishing port, comes up with the **Globo,** smack in the center of town and smack in the middle of the government housing fever. The **Estalagem Miradoiro** might have more space for you now. The 12-room **Residência Dennis**, which is well run, is for bed-and-breakfast only. Fair enough for the low price and category. This center is too commercial, zestless, and mundane for most holidaymakers—especially since many top-quality oases have sprung up in the near vicinity. In *Albufeira*, the **Sol e Mar** rules the roost in the town proper. This entry is First-class rather than Deluxe. Ideal situation; cliff-hanging terrace for drinks over the sea; panoramic dining room; lounges, and bar; glorious sun patio; bouncy little Pescador Night Club; 72 rooms, all with private bath; warming decorator touches of brick-tile floors, rustic woodwork, and plaid textiles. We like it. **Estalagem do Cerro** comes up with 50 bedchambers between its main building and its annex; small dimensions, but efficiency in design to make the most of what you're given; air conditioning. Very sound. The **Baltum**, in a lower bracket, is small but passable for short-stopping. **Residências Boavista** is better for longer layovers or family stakeouts. Complex of 15 apartments, with 20 rooms later added; swimming pool; nightclub; shops; bar-restaurant combination; low rates. This one has had more than its share of growing pains—but if it gets hold of that rope, it could be a slick bell-ringer. Let's keep a hopeful ear tuned in on it. **Estalagem Sao Jorge**, 2 miles east of town, is okay as an overnight hitching post for motorists on the move; not near the sea, but adequate for sleeping. Also on the eastern wing but well outside of the town, the 130-room **Penta** resides on a terrace above the sea. Supermodern, verticular structure edging on a deep ravine; high-ceilinged lobby dominated by a clerestory in its pluvium; avant-garde sculpture and paintings in corridors and public rooms; red-toned grill; dining salon stair-stepping down to a poolside umbrella-shaded patio for midday munching; expensive à la carte niblets. All units in the sawtooth pattern with slide-away balcony doors; 12 bungalows for peace-niks. We've heard some hearty howls of complaint regarding the maintenance and service of late. The **Vilamoura** accents bungalow living in a sea-nipped stucco pueblo village. We suspect its chief appeal will be to golfers. Also in this subdivision called *Vilamoura*, we inspected the new and growing **Dom Pedro**, which ultimately may include a casino, a 1000-yacht marina, golfing, restaurants and bars, pools, tennis and squash courts, a movie theater, and shops. Overall, it impressed us as spare at this stage with few prospects of warming up as it matures. We'll see when things settle a bit.

In a settlement called *Vale do Lobo* (not to be confused with Vale de Lobos, which is 12 miles from Lisbon), the deb-like **Dona Filipa** is the inaugural Portuguese venture of the British Trust Houses Forte organization, which does such a sterling job within the British Isles. This is our favorite 19th-hole along the entire coast—but nongolfers might disagree since the action here centers on chip shots and tidbits of links lore. Upland perch on a 400-acre estate surrounded by the sea, a beautiful 27-hole golfing circuit, a clubhouse, tennis courts, and a growing urbanization with its own ready-made "village"; swimming pool; private beach backed by oxide-hued cliffs; summer disco-thèque; Moorish dining room; active bar. Comfortable complement of 125 bedrooms; private balconies with cutie-pie alcoves, chairs and a table; good baths; superb air conditioning that automatically shuts off when terrace doors are opened (those doors have screens, too). We prefer the Portuguese-style chambers to the conventional ones; the suites are also a joy. Director Pierre Vacher has a wonderful plant with which to work. Here's a teed-up winner in our Tournament of Champions, but again let us recommend it especially for the mashie set—not for city slickers in search of metropolitan pastimes. Also for golf as well as other outdoor diversions, the **Quinta do Lago**, 10 minutes along the pike at *Almansil*, is a luxurious apartment subdivision for visitors who are considering homesteading in the region. Advance booking is a must, and while the kips are available on a daily-rate basis, the concept obviously is for longer rentals. *Armação de Pêra*, a few miles away, the **Hotel do Garbe** is now beginning to show the first telltale signs of age. Glorious cliff-top situation; airy dining room; busy lounge and card room; chalet-style nightclub; tile-lined bar, open terrace for seaside dancing; hairdresser and barbershop. Colorful décor in all its 54 bedchambers; some studio suites with refrigerator. Becoming a family target for British trippers. A casino with adjoining restaurant is only a few minutes' walk from here; otherwise there's nothing else around except the crash of waves, the cry of gulls and a shuffle of idle refugees from the overcrowded billets nearby. *Praia da Quarteira*'s **Toca do Coelho** ("Rabbit Hole") is the coziest local hutch for basic comfort; 35 rooms with bath and terrace; seafront dining; very inexpensive; no English spoken by its ultrakind staff. The **Triangulo** is raw-boned simplicity. One ameliorating amenity is its skylit dining salon and adjoining loft bar; otherwise this contender is pretty grim. Again, you'll see foreign settlers by the droves. At *Faro*, the harborside **Eva** rules the port. It is a project of one of Portugal's most popular bus-tour companies. A former Quonset-shape annex that once housed herds of tour buses was converted into a well-designed Moorish-style nightclub with *fado;* a swimming pool plus an alfresco dining patio and bar have bubbled up on the roof. Total of 150 rooms, all with lovely terraces and nice baths; viewful indoor penthouse restaurant and grill; pleasant ground-floor bar and snack corner; hemline of shops at sidewalk level; free minibus hops to the Eva Villa, the hotel-owned beach site, and the nearby golf links; extra-good beds (that are almost too large for the rooms). Director Alberto Strazzera can feel assured that he has the best stop in this busy hub. The **Faro**, across the town square, used to be fair, but now we say nay. The **Albacor** serves breakfast only; clean; low tabs; so-so. The **Santa Maria,** behind the Faro, is a favorite stop for sun-seeking Teutons; routine, at best. *Vila Real*, with the neighboring beach resort of *Monte Gordo*, steers most of the Deluxe traffic to the **Vasco da Gama**. Management by Reinaldo Pimenta de Almeida. Wide beach of powder-soft sand; 2 pools; 2 tennis courts; 4-lane bowling center; minigolf; patio bar plus beach bar; dismal cuisine on our try; amiable nightclub with occasional cabarets; air conditioning in public rooms. Bedrooms come with radio, private balcony, and some of the most complicated bathroom plumbing we've seen outside an Apollo spaceship; be sure to select a seafront location, preferably in the newer wing. Naturally, you are bound to find teething pains in such a big project raised in such a remote clime—so don't look for perfection. Nearby, the same company has also put up a Second-class, 100-room house called **Das Caravelas**. Sparkling clean; attractive bedrooms; low rates; ask for Mr. Mascarenhas. Our recent meal here was a delight in every respect. The 95-room **Alcazar** is a wonderland of far-out modern architecture in its interior design. We find it agreeably diverting in the oddball way that some resort havens can be. How it wears and how it wears on you are something else to consider. **Dos Navegadores**, a 60-unit candidate, is cruising along comfortably. Not bad. The **Monte Gordo**, slightly nearer the breakers but with fewer amenities, is a former pension that grew and grew and grew. Strictly for budgeteers. **Catavento** is a residence tieup that is even more economical. In their respective categories, all the candidates are adequate. The beach is wonderful.

Now let's wrap up the rest of Portugal: In *Buçaco*, it's the flamboyant, gingerbread-on-gingerbread **Hotel Palace**, a state-owned former royal residence bordering on a magnificent forest; in *Coimbra*, the **Hotel Bragança,** 83 rooms with bath, and the **Astória**, with beds on a dais; in *Setúbal*, the 76-room **Esperança** or the hill-topping and historic **Estalagem de S. Filipe;** in *Nazaré*, the **Nazaré**, with fair-to-middling facilities and a delightful vista from its 5th-floor restaurant and 6th-floor roof garden-bar; in *Évora*, the **Planície** and the **Pousada Dos Loios**; in *Viana do Castelo*, the **Alfonso III** with its restaurant on the VIIth floor; in *Ericeira*, the 94-room **Hotel Turismo**; in *Abrantes*, the **de Turismo Abrantes**, every room with bath; in *Foz do Arelho*, the **do Facho**, directly over the beach; in *Curia*, the **Palace;** in *Espinho*, the **Palácio**; in *Luso*, the **Grande Hotel das Termas;** in *Leiria*, the modernistic, well-run, 55-unit **Eurosol**, with its panoramic 8th-floor restaurant and handy garage, or tiny, fresh **Estalagem Claras**; in *Ofir* (Fão), the agreeable little **Ofir**, and the 89-room motel-inn, **do Pinhal**, with cocktail lounge, 300-seat dining room, and 2 swimming pools or the tiny **Estalagem do Parque do Rio** where we haven't yet parqued our carquas; in *Matozin-*

hos, the **Pôrto do Mar**; in *Tomar*, the ultramodern and well-run **Dos Templários** and the 10-den **Estalagem de Santa Iria**; in *Caniçada*, it's the same-size **Pousada de Sao Bento** with its spectacular views of the town, dam, river, and national park; in *Estremoz*, it's the brilliantly restored **Pousada da Rainha Santa Isabel**; in *Elvas*, it's the **Pousada de Santa Luzia**; in *Vidago*, the **Palace**; in *Santarém*, the sad **Abidis**. Many of these are only a few seasons old, but in some cases where the government has requisitioned space for exiles from Angola and Mozambique, the wear and tear has been horrendous. Moreover, out in the provinces the recovery is likely to take longer than in the metropolitan and touristic tenderloins.

The *Azores* offer a widening choice. All the best, with 1 exception, have latched onto the name **Terra Nostra**. The top 2 are in *Furnas* and at *Santa Maria Airport* (**Hotel do Aeroporto de Santa Maria**), followed by the weakest cousin at *Ponta Delgada*; in the last, we hear that the **São Pedro** is a pleasant 30-room hostelry, but we've still to knock at this St. Peter's pearly gates. The **Angra** and **Estalagem da Serreta** in *Angra* are said to be acceptable; so is the **Fayal** at *Horta*. Finally, there's the First-class (not luxury) 40-room **Hotel do Infante**, which we've also not yet seen. Comfort is lacking in all other candidates.

All hotels in Portugal offer the visitor 3 plans: (1) Complete Pension (Pensão), (2) Room and Breakfast (Alojamento), and (3) Room only (Dormida). One catch: *the patron must always specify his choice, or he might be socked with Pensão.*

Incidentally, you should check with your hotel concierge before starting out on a sightseeing expedition if you are on the full-pension plan; special luncheon arrangements can often be made in outside restaurants in such cases, and all you have to pay then is the tip.

Dedicated budgeteers? Since we're too bottlenecked here for additional entries, please consult this year's edition of the vastly updated, annually revised paperback, *Fielding's Low-Cost Europe,* which lists scads of bargain hotels, pensions, and money-saving tips for serious economizers.

§TIP: If you're driving through rural Portugal, before departure be sure to get a list of the *pousadas* and *estalagems* (see "Attitude Toward Tourists") from your hotel concierge or the Direction-General of Tourism.

FOOD   Portuguese cuisine is delicious. It's not fiery, as one might expect on the Iberian Peninsula; neither is it doughy, with the accent on pasta. The French influence is pronounced; the eye is as important as the palate, and each course is garnished and presented to the diner in its most tempting and appetizing form. The cooking is good, if a bit on the bland side; the variety is bewildering. The wonderful fresh fruits of the sea you will probably find are more appealing than earth's bovinity. Steaks, whether boiled, blow-torched, or pounded, invariably turn up as a major challenge to modern dentistry. Cod is the staple of every coast and it appears in myriad forms; sole and all the brotherhood of the crustacean clan are also abundant; lobster (clawed or clawless) is snappingly expensive.

In some dining spots, mostly the regional ones, the cook has the habit of delicately pouring a 20-gallon drum of olive oil into the pan before dropping in your lamb chop. The taste isn't too bad, but it's rough as a knobkerrie on uninitiated stomachs. A few of these backwoods Escoffiers also pop whole garlic cloves into their creations as freely as walnuts. Whenever you step out of your international hotel or your chichi restaurant, remember 3 phrases: *sem azeite* ("without oil"), *com manteiga* ("with butter"), and *sem alho* ("without garlic"). You'll need them! You also may require *sem coentros* ("without coriander") which, when chopped and served *fresh* in various stews, seems to our repulsing palates to resemble a fetid first cousin of ipecac. It's bright green—exactly the virescent hue we turn whenever we accidentally run into a sprig.

Since Brazil is a cultural offshoot of Portugal, coffee is the pillar of almost everyone's diet. To the Yankee palate, the local version has the pungent overtones of that dark, glistening substance found at the bottom of the vat after an 800x15 Goodyear Suburban Snow Tire has been boiled in acid for 3 days. Actually, the quality is higher than can ordinarily be found in the U.S.; they simply don't blend it, that's all. Some travelers find the "Carioca" style the least lethal—equal parts of coffee and hot water; others like it *com leite* —coffee and milk, 50-50; after a heavy meal, most of us take it *claro* (plain) —but the wise follow the national custom of filling almost ⅓rd of the cup with sugar before application of the fluid to the larynx.

Cheese? Serpa, snappy and tangy, is outstanding, with plenty of character. Serra is a lighter, creamier version that is pure heaven as a complement to a glass of vintage port. Queijo fresco, a butter substitute with overtones of cottage cheese, is liked by many U.S. visitors.

The city water of Lisbon, Estoril, and Oporto is sweet and potable, *but do not trust it elsewhere*. Agua de Luso is the best-known bottled brand. To my Nancy and to me, somehow it tastes "wetter" and is more thirst-quenching than any other H_2O on the Continent. Darned if we know why!

RESTAURANTS In *Lisbon*, there's a big choice of restaurants. While few establishments merit Great or near-Great cuisine classification, the general standard is fair and prices are still agreeably low to North American pocketbooks. For extra-special short excursions from the capital, please note further along our reports on the Hotel do Guincho at *Guincho* and the Palácio de Seteais near *Sintra.*

Among the city's hotels the **Sheraton**'s Panorama is not only tops in altitude, but in 1977 it is also higher in quality than many independent challengers. The **Altis** also features a rooftop grillroom with a breathtaking view. The vista and cuisine at the **Tivoli** again are to be recommended this year. The famous **Ritz Grill** was a disappointment this time. The Bodegón of the **Fénix** presents crispy salads and light offerings in summer, but without a skyline bonus.

As for the **Aviz** (Rua Serpa Pinto, off Rua Garrett), here is a bright and shining gemstone. Premises 1-flight up; handsome oak-and-quilted-leather bar with globe sconces, velvet upholstered chairs, green brocade wall-coverings, and a small vitrine displaying a novel pocket-watch collection; 3 dining rooms, 1 in beryl and 2 in gold; sophisticated atmosphere; faultless service on our tries. Since Proprietor Rugeroni is seldom on the premises during service hours, be sure to ask for courtly, kindly, English-speaking Maître Espirito Silva, who is an extra-charming host. About $25, including wine, should do it up nicely for two.

The highly popular **Escorial** (Rua das Portas de Santo Antao 47-49) is modern in concept. One room with a counter and quick service; the other with wood walls, vertical metal strips, globe lamps on polished steel brackets, and fireman-red tablecloths. Drinks cart for premeal sippers; shellfish specialties; attractive and clever presentation (*e.g.*, shrimp cocktails served in a calyx that is then set into an ice-filled glass bowl and illuminated from the inside); whale-size tariffs (one Guidester sent us his bill covering a drink and 2 small seafood platters—$28. OUCH!); fairly respectable steaks; rushed but smooth service. Reserve ahead, but still expect to wait in a cramped corridor until a table is cleared. Recommended for cuisine but not for that quiet, low-cost evening out.

The nearby **Gambrinus** (Rua das Portas de Santo Antao 25) is an old-timer that remains right up at the front of the pack. Entry to a seafood display; long bar leading to a split-level, arch-ceilinged dining room. Handsomely brightened; principal wall featuring a colorful Portuguese abstract painting; 23 tables; extraordinarily agile service by Lisbon standards; well-prepared cuisine. The big drawback here is that its prices have skyrocketed to the point where we now see sparks; they're outlandish, in our opinion. This stalwart veteran is not in the Aviz class, naturally—but it is one of the better independents.

Chester (68 Rodrigo Fonseca, in the neighborhood of the Ritz) is a new steakhouse which appeals to the chic Young Executive Set. Cellar bar with bold, diagonally striped carpets; fresh airy lounge; ground-floor restaraunt to right of entrance, with wooden coffers and paneled walls; upper trim of green tapestry; ruby napery; maps of English counties on the walls; placemats recalling scenes from the U.K.; piped music; engaging touches such as candles floating in vases surrounded by flowers. The service was superb, but alas, our meat was tougher than buffalo shank (perhaps we should have ordered Châteaubriand). We heard about another popular grill house in the same district called **Numero Um** ("Number One"). We looked in and it seemed to be active and attractive, but we can't tell you anything about the cookery.

Tavares (Rua da Misericórdia 24) claims to be trying to recoup its former reputation as the leader, but it still has a long, long way to go. Why so many loyal Portuguese continue to speak in such rapturous tones about this one is a mystery to us. Even at its Old World best, we can find little excuse for the shabby entrance lounge, the unkempt carpets, the chipped walls, and the worn and squeaky furniture. We do like some of its ancient gilt mirrors (2 are blistered beyond the point of distinguished decadence), its chandeliers, and the nostalgia of bygone grace that is not-too-far gone. Our service was thoughtful and attentive but haughty in attitude; the wine was poorly presented to us; the room was noisy; our food was no better than ordinary; the bill was on the high side, by Lisbon standards. Not at all revered by this evaluator—but a local landmark.

Faz Figura (Rua do Paraiso 15-B) resides high in the Alfama district overlooking the harbor cranes and shipping channels of the Tagus River. Two rooms with leather Chesterfield banquettes, large windows, air conditioning, and a wonderfully posh clublike atmosphere; expansive 14-table open terrace with an awning for summer diners; exceptionally kind reception; attentive service. Our shrimp cocktail was delicious; the Steak Portuguese is cooked in a casserole with boiled potatoes and smoked ham; the tiny Squids Gratiné were lovely. Our enthusiastic recommendation for viewing and dining in the medium-budget category.

Pabe (Rua Duque de Palmela, 27-A) means "Pub"; decoratively, it is one of the most stylish establishments you'll find on either side of the English Channel. Half-timber exterior with stained-glass leaded windows; first room with open beams, pewter plates, rich woodwork; tables with inset metallic panels, and booths with antique lighting. We made the mistake of going to the rear chamber through the saloon doors, where the atmosphere is so refined as to suggest an Edwardian parlor. Our crêpes of shellfish were leaden and our partner's Sole Florentine was burned. We have a feeling that this could be one of the nicest spots in the capital if tiptop management took the helm. As it is, to us it is just another Pabe.

António (Rua Tomás Ribeiro 63), in the shadow of the Sheraton, is a corner site with two rooms; this time we prefer the one further back. Ink-block molded ceiling in blue and white; inset planter boxes; always busy with schools of hungry Portuguese who swim in for its excellent piscatorial preparations. You might appreciate the house specialty called Acorda, an airy pasta which resembles a marriage of a fallen soufflé and a damp omelette; it is made with whipped bread, egg, clams, shrimp, and black olives. A huge lunch for two with wine will hardly dent your budget for more than $15. Net worth to this fisherman.

La Gondola (Avenida de Berna 60) serves a savory selection, with emphasis on Italian dishes. Agreeable little summer garden; adequate cellar; glum waitresses; choice for a tranquil, unhurried lunch in serene surroundings, provided the nearby air traffic is using the east-west runway pattern not the north-south. In general, we're fond of this one.

Montes Claros, atop the hill of the same name, sits in a lovely park 10 minutes out, and offers a beguiling view. But that's all, in our opinion. Hardly worth the effort.

A Quintá ("The Farm"), atop the Santa Justa outdoor elevator in the heart of the city, serves small portions; if you're intensely hungry, a refill costs practically nothing. Selections including Hungarian goulash, steak-and-kidney pie, home-cured corned beef, and fluffy omelets; no pretensions, not the best ventilation, no crystal chandeliers, no heel-clicking headwaiters—just a friendly reception and a simple atmosphere. Closed Sunday.

Belcanto (Largo S. Carlos) comes up with 11 tables, red velvet banquettes, wood paneling, and a comfortable, unglamorous air. The bar is very popular with menfolk. Through the course of our meal we watched many lone ladies come in, sit down, and smoothly find companionship. The edibles are nothing to rave about, but some of the 2-legged dishes that sauntered in did indeed look appetizing. While we passed up the tarts here, the apéritif was delightful.

Cortador ("Butcher shop"), also known as "Oh Lacerda!", used to be one of our chops—but no longer, emphatically. On our last look at this steak house in which the clients pick their own cuts of meat, the atmosphere reeked of such contrived touristy "quaintness" and our meal was so substandard for the price that we're not going back. Too much a commercial proposition now, in our opinion, with too sharp an eye cocked for the Innocent Abroad.

Atrium (Rua de São Julião 86–106), expansively spread out in the shopping area, is a 3-in-1 restaurant, cafeteria, and self-service snackery, all done up in the modern mode and all shuttered on Sunday. Lunch only.

Budget dining? **A Primavera** (Travessa da Espera 34) is tiny, tiny, tiny. This one has 2 long tables and 1 small table, tiled walls, an open kitchen, and stools for seats. Closed Sunday; a whopping meal (including wine and service) in down-to-earth surroundings for a song; excellent for the type. **As Velhas** (Praça da Alegria 19) and **Oriental** (Rua São Julião 132), lunch only, also bat high in this league.

Snacks? First, please let us explain that the term is NOT the same to a Portuguese as it is to a Yank or a Canadian. In this country it signifies only that the service is more rapid than average. Thus, as one illustration, if you order a "Hamburger Flórida" at the Snack Bar of the **Hotel Flórida**, up will come a huge chopped steak smothered in onions and embraced by heaps of potatoes and trimmings (delicious, incidentally)—the same dish that would be served as a main course in the regular restaurant, but produced, instead, in short-order style. Sandwiches are almost nonexistent; nibbles are usually confined to sweets and coffee. So you'll probably wish to bear this in mind when you see the scores of "snack bars," many of which opened only yesterday. **Monumental**, near the garage entrance of the Ritz, is one of the better recent examples. **Galeto** is another. It's located on the Avenida da República, near the Praça do Duque de Saldanha, and it's one of the most popular stops in town. Other outstanding entries are **Derbi**, around the corner from the Pan Am office, the **Pique-Nique** (an appalling variation of a nostalgic English word), the **Noite e Dia** (which is open "Night and Day," near the Embaixador), and **Hippopótamo** charging in the basement of the Eduardo VII Hotel. **Bénard** (Rua Garrett 84) is a handy coffee shop for that break in the shopping routine. Lisbon's drugless drugstore, called **Sol a Sol** and situated far uptown on the Avenida da Liberdade, features a double-deck feedery amid 33 boutiques!

Fado. Last but far from least, no lively traveler should leave Lisbon without visiting one of the world-famous *fado* restaurants—birthplace and home of the heart-rending folk music so beloved by the people. These are the "taverns" (for want of a better word) where young girls in aprons or potbellied characters in sweaters will suddenly burst forth in these stylized, haunting, provocative laments. Informal atmosphere; adequate food; songs which will never leave you. *Reserve early everywhere.*

Lisboa à Noite (Rua das Gáveas 69) is a solid candidate that is (as of this writing) patronized almost exclusively by Lisbonites. It gets better every *noite* ("night"). Whitewashed den under arches; open tile-lined kitchen at one end; guitars and copperware on the walls. Croak hello to the caged raven in the back room; if he doesn't quoth you a welcome, amiable Maître

Antonio surely will. Solid local fare; pure *fado* renditions every 15 minutes after 11 P.M.; the soul-buffeting voice of Fernanda Maria; no gimmicks. We still prefer it to any in the city. Celebrated Haydn Conductor David Blum and his equally gifted singer-wife told us a while back that **Parreirinha d'Alfama** (Largo Chafariz de Dentro) is on an equal musical par; we've recently come from another session here, and the Professor and his Lady couldn't be more correct, although far more tourists roll in here than into our first choice. Overcrowding and poor ventilation seem to be its chief drawbacks. Otherwise very good. **A Severa**, on the same street, is the monotonously insistent choice of almost every concierge and taxi driver in town. They've got a point, at least concerning the musical renditions. **O Faia** (Rua da Barroca) is where you will hear everything from "My Bonnie Lies Over the Ocean" in Danish to very beautiful native songs. Don't eat here; we've already made this sacrifice for you. Our bill was incorrectly figured also, so be careful. **Tipóia** (Rua do Norte 100) is sadly sinking, in our opinion; but its prices would support the full cast of the Metropolitan chorus; such a downright clip we can no longer advise it. **Adega Mesquita** (Rua do Diário de Noticias 107) pans out favorable food and ample portions of its life blood—fine *fados*. **Timpanas** (Rua Gilberto Rola 22-24), offers dances, songs, and piano melodizing; not bad. **Herminia** (Rua da Misericórdia) belongs to a popular artist named Herminia Silva; local folk love her, but we're personally not so enamored. **Luso** (Travessa da Queimada), crawling with rubberneckers, not only leaves us prodigiously unenthusiastic, but it gives us the miseries. **O Forcado** (Rua da Rosa 221), not a Portuguese expletive, is yet another in the something-for-everybody category. The music is professional, but the gimmickry is overwhelming. Group pilgrimages seem to have sapped its viability. As for **Machado** (Rua do Norte 91), the most famous of all, we now consider it completely unacceptable. What a pity they felt it necessary to add all the cornball yocks to such fundamentally enchanting music. Folk dancing forms a large part of the evening here.

Dedicated budgeteers? Since space is much, much too tight for additional Lisbon entries, please consult this year's edition of our annually revised paperback, *Fielding's Low-Cost Europe,* which lists many other dining and entertainment spots and money-saving tips for serious economizers.

In *Estoril*, the **Palácio Hotel**, the **Casino** and the mammoth **Hotel Estoril Sol** are flawed by cookery which, in our opinion, ranges from miserable to execrable. **Tamariz,** on the beach, is pleasant on a sunny day—especially since the installation of the pool and locker rooms. Attractive dining terrace, plain interior; things often seem slightly on the grimy side here, but not enough to throw you. Santini's immaculate **Ice Cream Bar** adjoins; 10 flavors, all creamy. The **Estoril Country Club,** open to Palácio Hotel guests, is the luncheon favorite of golfers; wonderful view, lovely surroundings, fair food, waiters who always vex us with their surliness. The cliff-dwelling **A Choupana** in Sao Joao do Estoril will add to your gastronomic estoreel. Wide windows for coastscape vistas, courteous service, gentle-to-the-tummy but not outstanding cookery, and moderate tabs. This one gives us the impression of an upper-grade seaside roadhouse, if we may be permitted to mangle our language so liberally.

Cascais, next door to Estoril, offers **Pescador**, behind the fish market and a 2-minute stroll from the port; it is so superior to anything along the coast that it is worth a special trip from Lisbon to lunch or dine. Trappings of rough nautical life cover the walls; the atmosphere is refined but almost sporting in its informality; the attention can't be faulted for a place of its type; and the cuisine—both in preparation and volume—is stunning. Outstanding value in an outstanding fisherman's hut. On the same mall, **O Pipas**, a few doors further into town, is perhaps even more attractive in a gimmicky fashion, but personally we found the cookery fourth-rate by comparison—and at very little difference in price. The garlands of garlic, the false wine tuns on the walls, and the maritime come-ons somehow seemed artificial here. Quite popular, but not with the Fielding tribe. Also in the port area we would choose **Bal Varte** or **João Padeiro** over O Pipas. They don't give off the same fireworks, but they served us much better Atlantic harvests on our recent swing. Another solid contender is **Fim do Mundo** (End of the World). Tiny room, abristle with hustle and bustle; small bar to rear; indoor dining only. Service still friendly but hurried; be SURE to try the Fish Stew Fim do Mundo and the house cake with cream (chocolate frosting cloaking an almond and honey core)—yum, yum! **O Batel** (Travessa das Flores, opposite the fish market) is situated in a tiny courtlike square, also away from the sea. Two immaculate rooms (18 tables) divided by arches and colorful Portuguese draperies; beamed ceilings; beaming staff who fairly bust to please in their friendly but fractured English. Before dining at any of these, have a Pimm's Cup on the seaside terrace of the nearby **Albatroz** while watching the day's catch being fetched by lighter from the fishing trawlers. It will be a beautiful moment in any day; that we guarantee. The little garden at **Estalagem Solar Dom Carlos** and the 4th-floor glass-lined restaurant in the **Bala** are both charmers. **Retiro** has a dedicated following, too. **John Bull**, sitting behind the Baía Hotel, comes up with an authentic British pub atmosphere, but it is 100% Portuguese piloted, despite its name and ambiance. Two small rooms at ground level with paneling in such mellowed brown that it appears black; front segment carpeted and appointed with 2 or 3 overstuffed chairs and a sofa; back portion with a 3-stool-or-standup bar. Here is a friendly intimate pop-in spot for a cool drink and a chat. We're told that **Os Doze** is excellent, but that **Reijas** is "too noisy, too Americanized, and the waiters too inattentive." True?

A Taberna de Gil Vicente (Rua dos Navegantes 22-30) is high up in the town. The food is okay, but the tavern seemed too worn on our latest trial. **Aos 3 Porquinhos** ("The 3 Little Pigs") seems to be coming up again. The décor and denlike atmosphere are inviting; service has improved; far from our favorite but now securely on the scene. **Clube Naval** is typical of the better peninsular yacht clubs. It has the standard nautical aura, the standard setting over salt water and small craft, the standard inexpensive but adequate fare, and the standard spell for fresh-air lovers on lazy weekends when the sun is sparkling. We made it a point *not* to check if its facilities were limited to members, but no one ever quizzed us. Especially happy for vacationers with children. **Frango Real**, in midvillage on a busy street, means "Royal Chicken." The owner must be violently in love with a hen, because poultry is featured not only on the menu, but on the china, on the service plates, and in the murals all over the walls. Three pleasantly decorated rooms festooned with strands of garlic, clusters of onion, and other alluring lores; chef visible from sidewalk windows; rearward nook in garden-style, with backless benches. Justifiably popular; very satisfactory, especially when you're overcome by that fowl mood.

Tiny excursion? **Restaurante da Marinha**, in a pine grove a skip up the shore road (about 800 yards inland, via a secondary lane), is peacefully situated but noisy when crowded. Handsome swimming pool to one side; 3 walls of windows enfolding rough timbers, a farmhouse hearth, and colorful trimmings; seafood specialties, with a plenitude of other selections available; droves of yowling tots on Sundays and feast days. Out on the coastal pike toward Guincho, there are open stands where all types of fresh sea fare are grilled before you. Benches for seats, planks for tables; simplicity itself, but usually delicious. Take a sweater if you motor out in the evenings. A pocketful of small change should buy a feast.

On the road to *Sintra*, the historic **Queluz** (pronounced "Kayloosh") **Palace** is a peanut-size replica of Versailles. In its ancient, enormous scullery, the owners have built a full-scale restaurant called the "Cozinha Velha" ("Old Kitchen")—and that's exactly what it is. You'll see the original spits used for hundreds of years to roast whole oxen—plus enough utensils and gizmos in fine old copper to arouse larceny in the soul. Interesting and unusual; *Cozinha*-work adequate rather than exceptional.

In *Sintra*, we've already recounted our opinion of the **Palácio de Seteais** (see "Hotels"). It is definitely a worthwhile dining target again. Our recent twin lunch of melon, turbot in white wine, rabbit hunter-style, feather-light pastry, coffee, plus cocktails, a *vinho verde*, and a sip of Antigua brandy, came to only $17.50 including service (which, incidentally, was perfect). The entire experience is assuredly worth a midday excursion from Lisbon. Superb!

At *Praia do Guincho*, north of Cascais (remember the undertow along these beautiful shores is often so murderous that bathing is impossible), please treat yourself to a meal, a weekend, or lifetime at the converted fortress that is now **Hotel do Guincho** (see "Hotels"). Burnt-orange napery and pewter tones play polychromatic counterpoint with the sea and sky outside the plate glass windows. Elegance is the word, maintained in whispers by kind, English-speaking Maître Coelho. The cuisine was the finest of our recent nationwide tour and among the best we've sampled in Europe—all at a price that could hardly exceed $25 for two. Very highly recommended for discriminating voyagers. Much more informal, yet nearby, the combined **Muchaxo Restaurant** and **A Barraca Bar** are drawing knowledgeable excursionists from miles around. Vastly expanded facilities now seating 400 guests of all descriptions, economic brackets, nationalities, and sizes; swimming pool adjoining the rambling seaside structure. Service excellent and friendly; food also excellent for its inexpensive category. The dedicated and warmhearted host, handsome and charming Antonio Muchaxo, is the man who built this better mousetrap; he is drawing pilgrims from the 4 corners of the globe to his isolated work of love. It is packed to the scuppers when the weather is right. As for **Faroleiro**, it stank—literally—at the time we inspected it; no, with ringing sincerity. **Arriba**, on the seaside cliffs before you reach Guincho, is nice for sunning and poolside lounging, but for little else, we think.

Madeira restaurants are covered separately later.

Oporto offers the **Escondidinho** as its number one restaurant (high prices, so-so food) and the **Infante de Sagres** as its number one hotel dining room. The **Grande Hotel da Batalha** will never set the world afire with its culinary artistry, but it's fairly passable. The **Imperio** is for the birds, top branch to roots.

That's just about all for the country, as far as distinguished dining is concerned. Elsewhere (including the Azores), the traveler is usually safer if he sticks to his selected hotels and *pousadas* rather than risking the oil-heavy, garlic-heavy ministrations of more primitive tables.

NIGHTCLUBS Big-time entertainment and gaming regularly are dealt out in the **Casino** at *Estoril*—the world's largest without sleeping accommodations. Within this massive, modernistic, park-fronted structure, you will find: (1) A Las Vegas-type nightclub-restaurant with a surprisingly inexpensive (albeit mediocre) dinner from 9 P.M. to 1 A.M., featuring a floor show at 11:30 P.M. (talent drawn from the Continent and the British Isles), a prairie-size stage which ebbs and flows in independent segments, and a sizzling orchestra, (2) a small nightclub, (3) a cinema, (4) 2 bars, (5) a snack bar, and (6) the gambling rooms. The largest chamber-of-chance boasts 4 mammoth chandeliers, still another drinking rail and light-refreshment tables on the mezzanine. There are separate salons for baccarat, U.S.-style craps, boule, and a regiment of one-arm bandits for lovers of levers. Other pastimes include roulette, chemin de fer, blackjack, and French Bank. Limits vary; $3 minimum play at blackjack is one example. Your passport is required (no exceptions!) for admission to the gaming rooms; the entrance fee is perhaps $2.50 per person for a 2-day ticket, dropping per diem for longer subscriptions. Whether you bet $100 or nothing makes not a whit of difference.

Not to be outdone in the luring of gamboling gamblers, Casinos do Algarve, a private firm, opened 3-of-a-kind casinos at *Penina, Vilamoura*, and *Monte Gordo* on the sunny southern coast. The Penina operation, dubbed the Alvor Casino, is said to boast white, red, and black décor, 12 gaming tables (6 roulette, 2 blackjack, 2 baccarat, 1 French bank, and 1 craps), 60 American-made 1-arm-bandits, a 200-seat restaurant, and a nightly supper-club floor show. The other 2 entries should be awhirl by your arrival. Hours are from 5 P.M. to 3 A.M.; don't forget your passport.

Lisbon turns into an oversize country town as soon as dinner dishes are washed. Tourists are usually packed into the previously described *fado* haunts until midnight or so; locals generally roll in about 1 A.M., when the crowds are quieter and the singers can be heard better. This is the *real* nightlife of the nation, so please refer back to "Restaurants" for our latest recommendations.

For that elegant evening out, the **Carrousel** in the Hotel Ritz is not only the pacesetter, but it's also *the* lone entry in the thoroughbred class—smartly decorated in tasteful Ritz style. Street entrance only, with no direct hotel access; comfortable elegance; no show; dancing only; socially, tops, but expect to pay the piper handsomely.

Porao da Nau (Rua Pinheiro Chagas 1-D) has dancing as its big drawing card.

Nina (Rua Paiva de Andrada 11) is going stronger than ever. Bar with 2 friendly cats freeloading from the customers; separate counter, too; cavernous main room with free lancers who can leave at your bidding, plus about a dozen B-babes who probably are house property; small international cabaret (matinée from 6:30 P.M. to 7:30 P.M.; small show at 8 P.M.; reopens at 10 P.M.; more shows at 2 A.M. and 3:30 A.M.; closing 5 A.M.); untampered whisky and fair prices; don't trek there before 12:30 A.M. at the earliest. Above average for its type.

Maxime (Praça da Alegria 58) comes up with tatty surroundings, plenty of solo gals for solo gents, wheezy shows, seminudes (1:30 A.M. and 3:30 A.M.), souvenirs, and drinks that might sharpen your choppers to Mau-Mau proportions. (Ronsonol-on-the-rocks probably tastes more Scotch-like.) Our 1-word Maxime: Run!

Á Cave (Avenida Antonio Augusto de Aguiar 88) is *the* quick turnover den in the city. Instead of having to build up the boy-meets-girl rapport by the usual routine of soaking up a ½-dozen drinks, here the lone fox can storm in, sip 1 quickie, and toddle off with a vixen 5 minutes later. Cellar setup; peppery combo; no show; restaurant service if desired; tiny quaffs of questionable origin; packed with distaff opportunities; animated and worthy; go after midnight.

Fontória (across the square from Maxime) lures night-wandering moles into its sub-sub-sub-subterranean precincts. The door charge includes your first free sip of superbly suspicious so-called heather-dew. The high-ceilinged room is flanked by a 5-piece band at one end and a semipartitioned bar at the other. The premises teem with "hostesses" who could easily be entered in the Westminster Dog Show; all of them are *very* hungry; during our short visit we were approached for that "Cigarette, please?" no less than 5 times. Open from 10:30 P.M. to 5 A.M., 364 days per year (Holy Mon. is Hallelujah Day) —and how we bleed for that staff! Hardly worth it, unless you're a titanium prospector fresh from the volcanic craters of Zambia.

Barracuda (Rua da Misericórdia 12) changed its name and management a while back—but not, unfortunately, its dreary, dismal, drab mien. Up 1-flight to 3 separate rooms; dim lights, low ceilings, smoky air. The so-called Scotch pours for not too much per dram, but that's much too dram much for the redeye we received.

Hipopótamo (adjoining Hotel Eduardo VII) herds in the Student Set by their leather-lined eardrums. Combination snack bar (open all day) and dancing oasis (functioning until 2 A.M. *if* the traffic warrants it); records only; noise level only 3 bels lower than the amalgamated decibels of New York's subway. Closed Sunday; very inexpensive. For the beardless and braless only. The small **Ponderosa** (Avenida dos Estados Unidos da América) is now popular with teen types and the young-at-heart elders; again disks only. Other disco precincts include **Stone's** (Rua do Olival 1), where you'll pay about $3 minimum, the **Beat Club** (Rua Conde de Sabugosa 11F), where you can beat it up daily, even on Sunday, and **Archote** (Rua D. Filipe de Vilhena 6D), which is the lowest in cost and in value, too, in our opinion.

Caruncho (Lumiar district, about 20 minutes by car from the center) draws cub packs of seedlings. Weird but effective décor in suave Brazilian rusticity; huge clusters of trifurcated red lamps; tiny tables with stools; waiters in colorful farm-type garb; loud, sizzling combo; cheap drinks that must come from the lowest foothills of the Highlands. Though its name has the sound of a new American candy bar, it did not seem so sweet to us. Not worth the taxi fare.

Lisbon-in-the-raw? The rough joints proliferate at the docks, but Guidesters are advised 3 serious notes of caution: (1) always keep a weather-eye open in every direction to protect yourself (2) never be provoked into a fight, no matter how great the temptation, and (3) unescorted female curiosity seekers should stay the hell at home. **Texas Bar** is the "best" of the lot—if charity can stretch the adjective that far. Grimy, raucous, turn-of-the-century atmosphere with a wincingly ridiculous 3-piece combo; mixed mob from sailors to tramps to jetsam to the occasional pop-eyed tourist. We were solicited by positively, absolutely, totally, unqualifiedly the ugliest prostitute we have seen since those Gold-Tooth Gerties on the infamous 1-block Herbertstrasse in Hamburg's Reeperbahn—who was dead drunk, and who repeatedly asked for the mammoth sum of $2.63 for her services. (We bought her a drink and gave her 100 escudos at the bar, because she was *so* pitiful.) Our "Scotch" tasted as if the pharmacist's hand had slipped in balancing the percentages of rotgut brandy and caramel coloring; *order bottled beer only.* This Texas-on-the-Tagus is a lone star wrangler of the toughest order.

The **Ritz** (NO relation to the hotel) rates somewhere between 11th and 12th class, in our estimation. Merchant mariners in profusion; frequent brawls; stay away, or you might be paying the dentist for new bicuspids. Others for the brass-knuckled adventurer, all within a block or 2 of the Texas bar, are **Filadelfia**, **Arizona**, **Europa**, **Atlantic**, and **California**. The same cautionary measures apply in all of these.

Out of town, the **Monaco** on the *Estoril* highway seems to be doing a healthy business in the roadhouse manner, with dining, dancing, and romancing. Not earthshaking, by any means, but a nostalgic reminder of the Raccoon Coat Era. **Choupana** is another dine-and-dance haunt. The **Ronda** at *Monte Estoril* (halfway between Estoril and Cascais) has passed through as many hands as a World Series hot dog in the bleachers. Somehow, both still survive. At first glance, its red-and-black geometric décor is the exact physical rendering of the Armstrong Linoleum Sales Manager's nightmare after 3 Welsh rarebits; after you have a couple of Constantino brandies, however, it suddenly and miraculously takes on the aspect of a Dorothy Draper job. Dancing to tolerable music; no cabaret, thank fortune; quiet bar adjoining, with a view of the bay. Also, a discothèque called the "**31**" is spinning right next door.

Cascais has the **Canoa**, which leads the parade in the capital's suburbs; too-intimate dimensions; fishnet-y décor; June through October only; pacesetter for the chic, but not worth a special journey. The **Palm Beach**, on the water, has 2 faces. After sundown, this mecca for swimming is transformed into a nightclub. Outdoor terrace with colored lights and flowers; when this section is closed at 2 A.M., the clientele is moved en masse into the building for more dancing and a floor show. Also recommended. **Borsalino** has funny art deco outfittings, but it was sleepy and dull on our peep-in. **Van-Gogo** is the go-goingest pop-stop in town for (Dutch?) bop-hoppers. Typical, but good for its type. **Juliana's** is another which, by name alone, might appeal to Lowlanders. Fun and not expensive.

§TIPS: The old rule that B-girls couldn't leave before 5 A.M. has been eased in many dives. Many can be wooed out of most places as early as 3 A.M.— *but please don't be so foolhardy.* Now we'll tell you why.

Social note: Venereal disease is skyrocketing throughout the land as a result of soaring prostitution, very limited controls, and the pervading economic crises provoked by revolution and migrations of refugees teeming in from Angola and Mozambique. Commercial sex should be avoided like the plague that it is.

TAXIS   The Portuguese taxi driver is the wildest man, with the exception of the Japanese, who ever held the wheel of an automobile. You will die 10-thousand deaths on a 75¢ ride. Take smelling salts, 3 Nembutals, and a leather-covered club.

All cabs are metered and rates are cheap for the plethora of free thrills. If you're planning a sizable junket (Lisbon to Estoril, for example), your driver is required to give you 2 minutes of free waiting time for each kilometer of travel. *Set your price in advance on all out-of-town excursions;* here you must pay both ways, from cabstand all the way back to cabstand. Tip 4 escudos for the average distance; if longer, 15% will do fine. He cannot carry more passengers than the number stipulated over the meter; don't force him to do so, because he's then a sitting (or skittering) duck for a big fine. No supplements or extras after dark, but there is a small one for luggage (2 of our drivers never asked for it—the 3rd did).

TRAINS   Improving under a generous 10-year development program—but we'd still recommend that you avoid the railroads if you can fly. On the credit side, there are now many diesel locomotives and an impressive number of diesel "auto-coach" cars. On the debit side, some wood-burners remain on rural runs; drinking water is seldom carried; restaurant cars are sporadic and sparse.

We have not had a chance to climb aboard the Lisbon-Madrid overnight express, the *Lusitania,* but we are told it is superb for Iberian rail-riders. In addition to sleeping cars and *couchettes,* it sports wagons for carrying automobiles—a godsend for motorists who dread facing those pepper-hot Spanish highways.

It never hurts to take a supply of food and drink on domestic excursions —because you *might* get caught short without a diner.

AIRLINE   Transportes Aereos Portugueses (**TAP**), the official airline of the Department of Civil Aviation, rules the local skies unchallenged and wings to many other nations as well.

Bonus: U.S.-Lisbon round trippers on a 14-to-21-day excursion fare may fly to-and-from glorious Funchal, Madeira, for an extra $13 from the Portuguese capital!

In New York, TAP's address is 601 Fifth Ave.; the North American Director is the experienced António Parreira Pinto; Chicago, Los Angeles, San Francisco, Philadelphia, Washington, Boston, Newark, Cleveland, and Montreal also have reservations centers.

In the Azores, there's an interisland network covered by **SATA**, which operates 2 DH Doves. We've never flown it—but, for these short hauls, it is probably quite adequate.

Recommendation: TAP has an excellent record in the air. If we can fault it at all it is on the ground, where personnel don't seem to care a whit for their customers. We recently climbed aboard TAP on 5 different runs. Not only were we happily impressed by the knowhow of the pilots and cockpit crews, but our meals were delicious and the cabin service in each case was the ultimate in courtesy and kindness. It is fully as safe, as dependable, and as fine as any of the smaller European carriers.

DRINKS   Port is the major national wine, of course, and the canny Portuguese know how to cling to a good thing when they have it. Rarely will you find a superior type outside the country's boundaries; they export the poorer stuff and keep the choicest varieties for themselves.

There are 5 kinds of port: Vintage, Crusted, Ruby, Tawny, and White. Vintage, which takes 20 years to reach its prime, is the best; Crusted, never dated, is excellent; Ruby and Tawny (favorite of most travelers) are blends of up to 40 separate wines; White, light and pleasant, is the only type served before a meal (the rest are consumed at the end, with the cheese).

Madeira is the minor national wine—not as fashionable as it was when the clipper ships were sailing, but still as kind to the taste. It is the only one which thrives on motion, and it has the longest life of any. The 3 best types are Bual (our preference), Sercial (dry, characteristic flavor), and Malmsey (on the sweet side).

Portuguese table wines are most often no better than fair—although a few are delicious. Our candidates for leadership are Clarete, Ferreirinha (a very fine red), Quinta da Aguieira (excellent in red and white), Ermida (a delicate white), Vinho Verde Alvarinho (a refreshing young white that we think lends a cool magic to any lunchtime), Amarante (another "green" wine that is bitingly sharp and almost sour, but has an affinity for some fish platters), Gatão (available in small bottles; a white fruity, soft elixir that is "alive"), Quinta de Aveleda (*branco*, meaning white but also *verde*, meaning green or young), and Buçaco (supply rather severely restricted). Otherwise, there's Dão Cerejeira (red and quite dry). Among rosés, either the famous Mateus has improved or our taste has changed; it's tangy and dry, but of course it's a completely different critter from the bottlings of France's Provence. As for naturally sparkling choices, we think you might find Caves da Raposeira "Bruto" to be the most acceptable local substitute for champagne. Be warned, however, that most Portuguese bubbly is cloying and unpalatable. Last, there's always the wine of the country, in "open" servings; order this as *vinho da casa,* and remember that the law requires they furnish it with every table d'hôte (not à la carte) meal. Perhaps you'll disagree, but we feel that the table varieties of this land are among the least interesting on the Continent.

Brandy? Quite a few poor ones. The best we've sampled (and we confess that our experience in this area is limited) is Antigua, in a lovely tall, green fluted bottle. A brand named Constantino is seen frequently, but we now prefer the former.

All spirits except American whisky are available in profusion; all the King's Ransom you want for $17-or-so a bottle, and less desirable brands for slightly less. *Patronize only the largest and most reliable liquor shops, because a flood of imitation Scotch, flawlessly bottled and labeled, has hit Estoril and the tourist centers.*

Ginginha, the cherry liqueur first invented and distilled by local monks, couldn't be more Portuguese. Characteristic, curious, and worth a try.

Sagres and Skal have become the ranking beers. On recent tours, for some strange reason, we had repeated troubles with Imperial. At one hotel, for example, we had to ask for 3 bottles before finding one that was drinkable; at another, it took 2. Perhaps it's the fault of innkeepers who keep their supplies either too cold or for too long a period. When right, however, all these brews are excellent.

Eyebrow-lifting tidbit: You'll find no genuine colas in Portugal, because the authorities have made the profound discovery that the caffeine is injurious to national health (!). Synthetic substitutes are available (Nicol Cola, Canada Dry, *et al.*), but most of them are fierce. The prejudice against the quinine content in tonic water has finally been beaten down, however; gin-and-tonic lovers are no longer parched for Schweppes, Canada Dry, Ideal, or Hall. If you're a soft-drink fan, stick to those wonderful orangeades, which are at their peak in winter (harder to find in summer).

TIPPING In Portugal, as elsewhere, Americans are far more lavish than others. The current level is well below American standards.

Give taxi drivers 15% on top of the meter reading; hairdressers, 10 to 20 escudos; washroom attendants, 1 escudo; station porters, 5 escudos; and theater ushers, 2½ escudos. For waiters, add only 5% when service is included on the bill but 15% when it is not (usually it will not be included).

In general, the Portuguese themselves tip in peanut amounts, but as they are so strained economically, you will win their hearts and gratitude if you tip normally—which will seem generous to them.

THINGS TO SEE In our opinion, the most beautiful tourist sights in Lisbon and the suburbs are:

1. In *Lisbon*, the Coach Museum (a unique collection of vehicles; usually functioning 11 A.M. to 5 P.M. daily but closed Mon.; it was "temporarily" shuttered on our recent tour, so be sure to check if it has reopened), the Old Moorish Castle (Castelo de S. Jorge), and that part of the Old City adjoining the Castle. Go escorted to the latter, and in daylight; see the Popular Museum and a slice of life left over from the days of Columbus; the newish Gulbenkian

Museum offers Rembrandt, Rubens, and superb Middle Eastern artifacts (this alone can occupy a full day); the Tower of Belém (the sixteenth century starting block on the Tagus for many of the ancient explorers; it is now just as it was when built); Jerónimos Monastery (a breathtaking structure; burial place of Vasco da Gama, kings, poets, and Portuguese heroes); the neighboring Naval Museum; Sé Cathedral (a Romanesque resident of Lisbon since the middle fifteenth century; a trove of gold and silver objects can be viewed upon request). If you want to make the rounds with experts, the Star Travel Agency operates eyeful tours. Multilingual guides; daytime plus after-dark excursions; low tariffs.

2. **Sintra**, about an hour from the capital. Drive out through Estoril, then take the spectacularly beautiful mountain road through a national forest preserve (for a longer seaside route, go out to Guincho). When you near your goal, climb up and up through gardens and flowering camellia trees to the mammoth castle, straight from an illustrated fairy tale, perched on a peak. This was the summer home of the last kings of Portugal, and its medieval splendor is stunning. The road leads down past the old Moorish castle atop a neighboring crest to the little town in the valley. Some of the finest *quintas* (country estates) of Portugal are here, and they are a dream. Lunch at the splendid Hotel Palácio de Seteais; twin billing with a good wine will be about $16. Sintra also can be reached by train from Rossio Station in the capital; runs to and fro about every 30 minutes.

3. For a shorter outing, **Estoril**. We think it beats the Riviera during the summer (not in other seasons)—less crowded, less frenetic, friendlier reception, and cheaper tariffs. Gambling, swimming, yachting, golf, horseback riding, trapshooting, tennis, fishing, thermal baths, dancing—the works. Less than ½-hour by car or 45 minutes by Toonerville-type train (go First class *only)* from the center of Lisbon; dead in winter, spring, or fall.

4. The drive from Lisbon to **Setúbal** (see "Cities").

Elsewhere in Portugal your targets might be:

1. **Madeira**. Please turn to the section immediately following for information on this magic isle.

2. **Nazaré** (pronounced Nah-zar-ay), about 3 hours from Lisbon, is a colorful little fishing village and Portuguese summer resort of whitewashed houses, tourist-conscious fisherfolk, and narrow streets which all run down to the sea. Unfortunately, it is fast being ruined by the tidal flood of foreign rubberneckers. Legend ties the famous local tartan costumes to a crew of Scotsmen shipwrecked here centuries ago; you may buy this unique handwoven cloth along the beach. Wonderful swimming; fishing from sardine to fighting *carapau;* boats at reasonable rates. There's a funicular (when it works!) to the Sitio, or Upper Town, where you'll find a lighthouse, a church, and a glorious view. Lodgings? The **Hotel Nazaré** (see "Hotels") is the best of a routine lot. Go in spring or fall if you can, because it's so jammed during the hot months that lots of the fun is lost. Highly recommended—*if* you mind your calendar.

3. **Fátima**. Atop a mountain range called Serra d'Aire, this is the scene of the celebrated religious miracle—where the Virgin Mary appeared before 3 peasant children on repeated occasions during 1917. The site is 107 miles from Lisbon, a strenuous 1-day round trip. If you can talk your driver out of

his preoccupation with the horn button long enough to point out the brake pedal to him before departure, that's all to the good—because the roads are full of grades and curves. Or if you don't have a private car and don't like the frequent and easily available bus excursions (ask your hotel concierge about these), you may take the train which will deposit you within 15 miles of your goal, at a station now named Fátima, and run up the rest of the way by taxi. The *Sud-Express* (Paris-Lisbon) also stops daily at this point and is met by shuttle buses. If traveling locally by rail, it's wise to pack a lunch and thirst-quenchers. You may stay at the **Hotel de Fátima** (we've not yet seen this one, but readers tell us it's the choicest), the **Santa Maria** (also untested by us), the **Beato Nuno** (operated by the Carmelite Fathers; 8 rooms with bath, 60 with shower, 65 roomettes; many altars; English-speaking priest always on duty), the **Dominican Convent** (damp, expensive, not as clean as it might be), the 5 small pensions, or one of the 2 tiny hotels in the hamlet. *Unless you understand the Portuguese language, don't go on the 13th of May, June, July, August, or September;* on these dates, because of the crowds, the true spirit of the shrine will elude you, and you'll feel not only let down but lost. It distresses and dismays us to observe the increased parasitic commercialism that thrives at the outer fringes of this wondrous monument to faith. As in Lourdes and Montserrat, this aspect has grown so crass that some of the visitor's reverence is inevitably tempered. Magnificent new church and mammoth esplanade which will ultimately resemble the great plaza of Rome's St. Peter's; spectacular healing miracles have occurred at the Shrine. It's Catholic, of course, but travelers of Protestant, Jewish, and other faiths flock here, too. Despite its tinny, shoddy, mercantile edges, this should be seen by everybody, regardless of denomination.

4. The cathedral at *Batalha*, finest Gothic structure on the Peninsula.

5. *Évora*, a sleepy little town near the Spanish border, with the Temple of Diana, quaint monasteries, all sorts of things dating back to the Romans. Here is one of the keystones in the development of Portuguese history.

6. *Buçaco*, in the North. The King's hunting lodge has been converted into the grandiose, ultrarococo hotel which has been previously mentioned; excellent food; miles of fine walks, lovely location. A treat!

7. *Figueira da Foz*, the major seaside resort, 123 miles north of Lisbon. Splendid beach; imposing promenade; facilities include a gambling casino, a big open-air swimming pool, scads of hotels, pensions, and restaurants (mostly modest), a theater, and the usual summer attractions. Cheap, informal, and animated in season.

8. The *Algarve Coast*, the southernmost region of Portugal, now enjoying a fantastic touristic boom (see "Hotels" for details).

9. *Alcobaça*, on the Lisbon-Oporto road about 87 miles from the capital, with overtones of the classic French abbey. This huge Gothic monastery-church-cloister complex, begun in A.D. 1178, bears the architectural characteristics of the twelfth to fourteenth centuries.

10. The stark, terraced *Douro Valley*, the home of port wine.

These are merely suggestions. For further information, consult the Portuguese National Tourist Office in New York (or branches in Chicago and Los Angeles) or the Direction-General of Tourism in Lisbon.

THINGS TO BUY   Predictably, the pervasive fissions generated during Portugal's recent political trauma have seriously affected the production, quality and supplies of its merchandise for purchase. Although improvements are now proceeding swiftly, qualified observers forecast that normalcy will not be attained until sometime next year. However, some manufacturers and retailers weathered the tempest virtually intact—or at least intact to a viable degree. The leaders among these are listed below.

Gold is the best bet in the country. The law says that 18 or 19 karats is the minimum weight that can be sold over the counter. Of the many shops in **Lisbon**, the most reliable and interesting is **W. A. Sarmento**, Rua do Ouro 251 (bottom of the Santa Justa elevator), the nation's oldest and most respected specialist. This world-famous landmark was founded in 1870 by the original Wenceslau Sarmento. If your budget is limited, there is an almost bottomless display of alluring, intricately filigreed earrings, brooches, cuff links, and similar items, most of them in handworked, gold-plated silver—starting at an unbelievable $8 to $10. Equally tempting to most American lassies are Sarmento's 19¼-karat gold charms and natural sterling "costume" creations—a huge variety of subjects and designs in a very inexpensive price range. Because every article, no matter how modest, is fashioned in the Sarmento workshops, it is infinitely superior to the look-alike junk in the jungle of flashy tourist traps which soil the main streets of Lisbon. For the beauty lover who can afford to spend more, Sarmento points with pride to (1) its very important collection of sterling silver copies of masterpieces in the Portuguese Art Museum, (2) its rare collection of antique gold and antique jewelry copies, entirely made by hand, (3) its largest stocks of flatware, tea services, and other house silver on the Peninsula, (4) its dazzling gems, and (5) its carefully selected array of decorative bric-a-brac. American Express credit cards accepted; closed on Saturday afternoons. Be sure to ask for either of the Señhores Sarmento personally; no nicer, kinder, warmer, more helpful *cavalheiros* exist in this country. Solid as the Beira mountains.

Sereira (2nd floor, Rua S. Bernardo 108) is a joy to the clothes-conscious gal, to the fabric-happy hunter, and to the pilgrim in search of unusual and lovely touches for the home. Captivatingly gracious Senhora Sereira Amzalak reflects her flawless taste in every item and in her chic apartment-showroom. And those *stunning* hand-crocheted wantables! Suits run $155 to $180, coats are $186, and dresses to match are about $110, with a parade of less expensive items also on display. Just telephone 66–68–52 and these good people will open the door to welcome you. This small house is a "find"—and a jewel.

For Madeira embroideries, organdies, and tapestries, **Madeira Superbia** (Avenida Duque de Loulé 75A, and Rua Augusta 231, plus branches listed below) is again THE house in our unqualified opinion—and we've seen them all. Every piece of its richly wrought stocks comes direct from its venerable studios and "factory" in the island capital of Funchal. Four of their lures are their gay breakfast sets (1 mat and 2 napkins), ever-useful bridge sets, top-quality lunch sets, and oh-so-luxurious 8-piece dinner sets. In tableware, we are particularly fond of their delicate organdy squares (6 mats, 6 napkins). This progressive enterprise has expanded its range to include full lines of linen dresses, long evening dresses, and men's evening shirts (all Madeira-embroidered), linen blouses (Madeira-embroidered and appliquéd), fine handkerchiefs for both genders (with or without monogram), and daintily designed children's wearables. Colorful regional tapestries, into which every thread is hand-embroidered, have long been one of Madeira Superbia's most famous specialties. Low-priced examples which await your inspection are the floral needlepoint chair covers and squares for cushions. Ladies will find flocks of evening bags in both petit point and gros point. Householders will find a wide assortment of decorative tapestry rugs. Art connoisseurs will find rugs and wall hangings which are remarkably duplicated tapestry copies of the paintings of classic and contemporary masters. Lots more, too! At the main store, ask for helpful Miss Georgina or Miss Genovera. The Madeira Superbia branches are in **Lisbon**'s Hotel Ritz (Mrs. Teresa Rodrigues); and on rua Augusta (Miss Susana.); in **Estoril**'s Hotel Estoril Sol (Miss Elia Faria); and in **Faro** on the Algarve coast (José Rodrigues) Nobody as fine, highest recommendation.

Pavilhão da Madeira (Avenida da Liberdade 15) is also dependable, but to us, not in the same class. The **Madeira House** (Rua Augusta 131) impresses us as having become so commercial that we no longer like it at all.

Cork products are another favorite (and why shouldn't they be, in the country where the trees grow?). Local run-of-the-mill women's shoes have soles of this material; they're a great help on cobbled streets. Still the best source—but for the time being, sadly limited in variety and equally sadly run-down—is **Casa da Cortiças** (Rua da Escola Politécnica 4) presided over by a mellow-hearted, widely-beloved king of this specialty known as "Mr. Cork." Strictly a tourist enterprise, but worth a look for the sunniness of this legendary figure and with hopes that his inventory has again swelled by the time of your visit. Safe shipment is not guaranteed; always take insurance if you buy.

Ceramics and porcelains? Lovely, lovely stocks at **Vista Alegre** (Largo do Chiado 18). They're worth the attention of any foreign shophound. Small branch in the Hotel Ritz. Salutes to this one!

Portuguese handicrafts? **Triarte** (Avenida Sidónio Pais 4, downstairs in the Star-American Express shopping center) overflows with top-quality handmade articles from Viana do Castelo and surroundings—by far the best regional selection we have ever found in Lisbon.

Next in rank, but a big step down, is **Casa Regional da Ilha Verde** (Rua Paiva de Andrada 4). **Casa Quintao** (Rua Ivens 30) is known for its Beiriz and Arraiolos rugs. (The latter come ready-made or in $16 weave-it-yourself kits.) Additional selections of regional crafts can be plucked from **O'Local** (Rua Castilho 75A, near the Ritz), **Centro de Artesanato** (Rua Castilho 61), and **Avenidarte** (Avenida da Liberdade 224). The last two are proud of their abundance of wares.

Port wine? The State sponsored Institudô do Vinho do Porto (Port Wine Institute) used to be a treasure cave where 300 varieties were dispensed and sold, but now that a law to boost exports forbids the distribution of all rare or outstanding bottles within the land, it is no longer worth a visit.

Shopping hours vary slightly. You may be sure of one thing, though: Everybody puts up the shutters for lunch—so you might as well scratch the hours between noon (or 12:30 P.M. for a few diehards) and 3 P.M. off your schedule. In compensation, they don't nail down the doors again until 7 P.M. Saturday, thank goodness, is just about the same as any other day.

Dedicated shophounds? Space is too tight here for further listings—so consult this year's vastly revised and updated edition of *Fielding's Shopping Guide to Europe* ($3.95) for more stores, more details, and more lore.

THINGS NOT TO BUY Anything American, because it's 2 to 4 times what it costs in the States. Except in top shops, fabrics are another; they feel fine and are attractive to the eye—but the quality is poor, and the dyes are often not fast. Most ready-made apparel for both sexes is inferior; the prices are tempting, but the clothes become shapeless and shoddy in 10 or 12 wearings. Leave perfumes of all descriptions strictly alone—and don't touch gems, no matter how tempting they might seem, except in the tiny handful of proven houses such as Sarmento. Women's shoes are improving in both styling and lasting qualities, but with Portuguese leather-curing methods, caution is still advised.

HAIRDRESSERS Abundant, inexpensive, and usually quite good wherever you go. Your hotel hall porter will recommend a shop, but you won't do badly just picking one at random. For men, too, they all seem to know their trade and perform it well.

LOCAL RACKETS As a whole, the Portuguese are a simple, independent people, unversed in most of the slick and shady arts; while it's good business to have a resident along whenever you go shopping, don't worry about being fleeced if you go alone. Count your change, of course; there's always the occasional chiseler who gives back a handful of small coins in order to filch a few extras for himself. Don't buy a "swizs" (sic) watch from a street vendor. (You hardly need being warned of this old flimflam in the slicky-tricky tick-tock trade.) Most merchants will respect you as an American, just as you will respect their birthright—and chicanery is the exception rather than the rule.

Watch out for the counterfeit Scotch whisky (see "Drinks"). Patronize *only* the leading liquor dealers, preferably in Lisbon proper.

Women should walk with the latches of their pocketbooks turned toward themselves not outward. Also, with so many refugees unemployed, purse snatching is not uncommon nowadays.

MADEIRA As sweet as her wines, as soft as her sea zephyrs, as colorful as her bower-banked cliffs, she is one of Europe's last unspoiled outposts— and, thank goodness, she was scarcely touched by the negative effects of the revolution and its aftermath.

On "boat days," when the cruise ships anchor, she is overbustling and overexcited. But the moment they pull away, she reverts magically to her natural, easy-paced, utterly delightful enchantment and charm.

Here, to us anyway, is the uncontested Queen of the West Atlantic islands (there are 8)—far more ingratiating than the Canaries or the Azores, and likely to remain so, since the Government sternly controls expansion to prevent a touristic explosion. So far, this Gulf Stream Siren has deliberately restrained her capacity to a trifling 3000 hotel or pension beds—an interesting comparison, when one recalls that Mallorca has almost twice as many public hostelries as Madeira has public pillows. Until the Santa Catarina Airport was opened in 1964, 15 miles from the capital of Funchal, this semitropical Elysium was known chiefly to yachtsmen and to offbeat travelers. Now, however, the steadily growing whoosh of jets puts Lisbon only a brace of martinis away from the sunlit isle.

Now for some capsule facts to pinpoint this ocean fairyland: *Situation?* About an hour's flight by jet (2 hours by "prop") from Lisbon, north of the Canaries and 300 miles off the coast. *Inhabitants?* Her 280-thousand citizens are gentle, kind, warm, outgiving, generally with ripe-olive eyes that reflect their sunlight and inner tranquillity. *Climate?* Benign almost year round. The midwinter sweater-weather is only 15 degrees lower than the 78-degree mean of high summer. Early November to mid-December is supposed to be Off Season, but we love it then (good sun, a few scattered showers and frequent winds to freshen the foliage, and no tourist mobs). Dark clouds are most likely to linger in February—but where else in the European area (the Canaries are geographically African, of course) can one find such a salubrious aura and tempered clime during this period, when even Sicily and Greece are stormy and barren of enticements? *Topography?* A bastion of rocky cliffs, soaring hills, and lustrous vales which burst with fruits and gay flowers. Mountains peak at well over 6000 feet. Ridges crisscross her 35 miles of length and 14 miles of breadth. The around-the-island coastal road contains 2300 curves, with its longest straightaway exactly ¾ths of a mile. The profusion of wild and cultivated flora is breathtaking. Bananas, sugarcane, grains, blossoms, and tropical fruits blanket the rich earth near the coast. Thick forests mat and tint the higher reaches of the slopes. *Language?* Officially Portuguese, of course—but enough English is spoken in hotels, restaurants, and shops to ease your fears. *Connections?* Much easier than a few years ago. TAP flies Boeing 727 jets between Funchal Airport at the village of Santa Cruz and Lisbon. (The Las Palmas-Funchal leg is functioning, also, with the same aircraft.) By ship, frequent calls are made by big liners or cruisers steaming in from Lisbon or from distant ports. Portuguese steamship operators who can provide full details on prices, sailings, and amenities are Companhia Portuguesa de Transportes Maritimos, SARL, Avenida 24 de Julho 132, and Companhia Nacional de Navegação, Rua do Comércio 85; both are in Lisbon. *Social note?* One of the holdovers from British Colonial days is that Madeira is quite dressy. In *all* of the leading hotels, gentlemen *always* wear a tie and coat after nightfall; normally, you'll find more dinner jackets than business suits at Reid's. For ladies, cocktail dresses are a virtual must. But despite the casually formal atmosphere, after-dark life is quiet. Go to Madeira for relaxation, natural beauty, calm. Go elsewhere for "action."

Cities? **Funchal** is the heart and capital. To us, here is one of the world's most beautiful metropolises. Magnificent bay; home base for ⅓rd of the populace; houses stair-stepping up, up, up, up the mountainside. At night, its broad flank twinkles with myriad dots of light. Its dwellings accent the Portuguese addiction for vivid shadings and hues. The sidewalks are surfaced with intricately patterned small cobblestones—charming to the eye, but hell on ladies' high heels. The world-famous fireworks display every New Year's Eve illuminates the great crescent of the bay in stunning and awesome cascades of flame. For many weeks beforehand nearly every householder plots his own pyrotechnic wizardry for this thunderous 15-minute climax of his year. Prizes are awarded by the Municipality for the best presentations in various categories. Many cruise ships target their arrival for this time—and so should you, if at all possible.

Hotels? Two new hostelries for the Cap Garajau development, 450 feet above Funchal, probably will have joined the flock before you wing in. If you are interested in alighting here, be sure to check with TAP about the *free* Madeira passage as a bonus to your Lisbon ticket. The **Sotuma**, a whopper to house 500 holidaymakers, almost surely will be operative this season. The **Atlantic** and another center in the Matur subdivision are also on the probable list.

The century-old **Reid's**, one of the last of the Great Hotels of character, tradition, and personality (as opposed to the sleek look-alikes of today's production-belt school), is a little less glorious than before—but not by much. This flower-girt Eden is a resort-style pastoral haven for the traveler who seeks a hushabye corner of our busy world. Reconditioning and fresh construction have made a good part of this house princely. Commanding position crowning a promontory; gardens and pavilion bursting with blossoms; tennis court; private beach; seabathing pool; conventional pool with dancing on its aprons and a summer restaurant perched above; cozy Grill and adjoining bar high up; excellent cuisine. Complete facilities for fishing and skin diving from its own launches and speedboats (a very popular feature); total of 182 rooms, all with bath and many with private balcony; stay in the far, far nicer New Wing, if you can—and for heaven's sake avoid at all costs the sparse handful of so-called inland-view units in the Old Wing, because they are a a disgrace to a landmark of this distinction. Another debit is the recent sizable cut in the staff-client ratio, which in the long run is bound to affect its proud service standards, a fact echoed by an American couple who say the plant now is only resting on its laurels; sounds like Manager Henri Saldati has his work cut out for him. All in all, here is still a lovely escape for the careworn tranquillity-seeker, but we hope some new life can be pumped into it before it begins to founder seriously.

The **Madeira Hilton** (also called **Palácio**) opened on the outskirts of the action in '71 and then 3 years later announced that it was to terminate its management contract here. We are not sure for how long it will retain its former name—but it will honor all Hilton bookings, so we're told. This 9-level, twin-wing giant is shielded in front by a restaurant and an attractive heated pool. Most of its 260 pads are graced by balconettes facing the deep blue; their bathrooms, as usual, are too small. Among the most fetching features is the hand-holding atmosphere of its Viceroy Grill. Our early-bird stay here was thoroughly satisfactory, but how it functions from here out is anybody's guess. We'll try to nip by very soon.

The **Madeira-Sheraton** was decanted after we had departed for other shores. But we did climb through and over the partially constructed project back then and we did succeed in getting preliminary information. It is sited on a cliff around the cove from Reid's. At least one of its 3 pools outsplashes and outglitters the Hilton entries, but in our opinion it is not in the same league as the stunner at Reid's. Tennis; minigolf; Portuguese specialty grill and bar; panoramic cliff-edge nightclub; 300 accommodations, all with private balconies and terraces. The dimensions of every room we saw seemed notably stingier than those of either of its 2 major colleagues. We'll bet our shoes and shirts that the Long Knives are already flashing in a fiercely competitive battle with the other U.S. entry.

Holiday Inn also hung out its Welcome Shingle shortly after we had checked out of Reid's and the Hilton; this huge vacation complex has been developing for several years on the east side of the island, within sight and earshot of the Santa Catarina Airport, 15 twisty miles from Funchal. Fully air-conditioned; 2 restaurants; 8 bars; sizable nightclub; heated swimming pool plus 2 outdoor pools; health club with saunas, steam bath, massage and gymnasium; all of its somewhat uncomfortably small quarters with balcony overlooking the ocean and the hills.

Down the scale considerably, the **Santa Isabel** is also in the Modern Mood. Hillside, seafront location; roof garden with swimming pool, a huge viewful solarium, and a bar; smallish rooms; 10 suites with refrigerators; all with bath, shower, terrace, and ample closet space; Owner-Manager Jimmy Welsh keeps a steady hand on the throttle. The **Miramar** is good but not outstanding in any way. The **Savoy**, largest of all and still growing, occupies 2 acres of seaside terrain. Abundant routine amenities which are gobbled up in summer by the Touring Club of France. The first phase of a projected expansion to 350 units has already been achieved, with construction on Phase II possibly completed by the time you check in; 2 new swimming pools were also in the blueprint scheme. Here is a mass operation that teems with tour groups—all French in summer, and (in the past) 90% British in winter. Not our cup of Lipton's, but let's wait and see how these changes go. The **Monte Carlo**, teetering 900 feet up the mountainside, may have doubled its size for your arrival. Small, pleasant, outdoor terrace for breakfasting and apéritifs; vista-bound sun deck and swimming pool; dancing every evening (Wed. is Gala Night; Fri. is "folk" night); annex with 18 rooms; all 40 units with bath or shower; very sweet people operating this one. Simple, clean, and worth every escudo. Coming up smartly. The **New Avenue** couldn't be more British Colonial, down to its "Gentlemen's Cloak Room." Indefatigable plumbing; elderly ladies glued to its wicker chairs; 46 bedchambers with baths; plans afoot to raze the old girl and to pave up a completely New Avenue. As it stands, for arch-conservatives only. **Monte Rosa** and **Golden Gate**, both central, are too noisy and too bare for praise; the former is the choice for hard-driven budgeteers. Many pensions are on tap, and some are exceptionally nice. The best duet we saw was **Quinta Favila** (16 rooms, enchanting gardens, Old Portuguese décor, management by a kind Belgian lady) and **Quinta do Sol** (5 rooms, also charming).

Restaurants? Agreement is virtually universal that the **Grill Room of**

Reid's remains the most elegant dining establishment within 500 miles; its cuisine and its service still can't be equalled by the parvenus. The **Viceroy Grill** of the Madeira Palácio plays upon charming intimacy. Its motif is plaid with contemporary overtones; while the minions are gracious, we'd rate the kitchen as only fair. The **Sheraton** and **Holiday Inn** cookery remain untested by these footloose forks. The rooftop **Grill of the Hotel Savoy** gets the back of our professional hand. On our latest try, we found it gaudily accoutered, manned by brusque, rude, or slovenly personnel, and further spoiled by the low general caliber of this house's group traffic. Independent places? The **Casino**, which we used to evaluate as "the most chic night spot on the island," has changed so dramatically that now we are shocked straight to our toes. This time we found the ambiance dismal, the premises seedy, and the bare scattering of gamblers conspicuously listless. It had been our original intention to dine, to watch the floor show (still presented?), and to drop a modest number of chips on its tables—but after a quick inspection, we walked away with the very definite impression that this once-fine attraction has come upon hard times. No longer suggested. For regional fare without luxury, **A Seta** (Estrada do Livramento, 15 minutes out toward Monte) is a fun-filled little sweetie. Canary cages by entrance; about 2 dozen sparkling-clean wooden tables topped by place mats; pine ceiling; red shutters; 5-specialty menu. Our house-style shashlik was placed on a contraption unique to the island—it actually *hung* straight down over us; we were instructed to serve ourselves with our hands. The piping-hot fresh bread would cause a dieting saint to search his soul. Although it's not fancy, we fancy it very much indeed. **Club de Turismo da Madeira** (Estrada Monumental 179, about 10 minutes from the center) is less rustic and more sophisticated. Cliff-hanging site, with sheer drop to the sea; gorgeous vista; semiopen-air dining terrace by the pool, plus 10-table indoor dining room; lounges upstairs; lower level dressing cabins at bay height. The cookery is a far cry from Reid's, but quite good for the region; it's not expensive either. Ideal for quiet lunching on a sunny day. No club membership is necessary. Only 2 other places of note exist. One is the plainly decorated **Caravela** in the heart of the city, which comes up with a quasi-Madeirense menu (which we did not find appetizing) for its heavy Swedish patronage. The other is the **Vila Belo Mar**, which also thrilled us not—at those high prices, yet. As for all others, none is worth mentioning. Funchal offers a dreary lot, probably because nearly all of the hotels require full pension.

Sightseeing? If you'll forgive Madeira for its total lack of decent beaches (but not of water sports, which are listed below), a rapturous parade of other attractions is at your command. Most visitors give highest priority to trying the world-famous sleigh ride over the cobblestones of *Funchal*. Take a taxi up, up, and up to Terreiro da Luta. After drinking in the glorious panorama of the capital at your feet, climb aboard the wood-runnered sledge and bump down, down, down—2 miles of "tobogganing"—through the narrow and pictorial streets. There is absolutely no danger, because 2 or 3 men race alongside, guiding the clumsy vehicle in the proper direction (or pushing it whenever the going gets too slow). The price is about $3 per person. While it would never offer a thrill to a Cresta Run driver from St. Moritz—or even more than a mild tingle to an elderly spinster—it's fun, and it shouldn't be missed. If this isn't sufficient in the Curious Transportation Department, you may also hire bullock carts in the Avenida de Mar, near the pier, or mobile hammocks in such villages as Camacha, Santo da Serra, and Curral das Freiras. For motorboating along the coast, the Tourist Bureau's *Altair* and the craft belonging to the Golfinhos do Mar are available for charter. Within the hub there are 4 more traditional lures: (1) The Aquarium (in the Municipal Museum at Rua da Mouraria), (2) the Municipal Museum itself (regional and natural history), (3) Cruzes (antique art, with a fine orchid house adjoining), and (4) Arte Sacra (religious art). And don't forget about the Public Market, which is a ball if you see it sufficiently early in the day. Now—and please note this carefully—for any fortunate soul who is not subject to car sickness from the plethora of curves everywhere, it would be just as heinous a crime to limit his or her wanderings to Funchal as it would be for any visitor to Switzerland to see Geneva only. Our fervent recommendation would be to hie to Nortenha, the leading car-rental agency in the capital, and ask for Fernando da Silva (a brother, incidentally, of Francisco da Silva, the Assistant Manager of London's Savoy Hotel). Should he be out at the moment, one of his kindly English-speaking colleagues would take good care of you. While you will be offered your choice of perhaps 12 different sizes in 6 different makes, be certain to request a *small* model; we had perfect luck as an illustration, with a 2-seat MG-B. Then simply head in any direction with a picnic lunch. So most of the roads on this 35-x-14-mile island are narrow and rough? Begone, dull care! Actually, it would be sensible to discuss the main targets of interest with the Nortenha people or your hotel concierge before starting out, in order to select those which hold the greatest appeal for you. Personally, one of our 2 most delightful excursions was to **Porto Moniz** on the extreme northwest corner of the island—a *gorgeous* ½-day drive to a small, sleepy fishing village with the most spectacular natural pool that we have ever seen. The other was to **Curral das Freiras**, a tiny, primitive, fascinating hamlet cradled in a valley of towering peaks, where the vivid impression persisted that we were 3 days' journey from Lima, Peru, in the heart of the Andes; it was almost impossible to believe that this sanctuary from another century is less than 45 MINUTES from the bright lights of the Big City. Never will we forget our basket lunch in these incredible surroundings!

Beauty parlor? My Nancy's note to herself: "**Michelle Coiffeure** at Reid's Hotel (telephone: 2-30-01) is the best I found—because I liked it and looked no further." Wimmen!!!

Things to Buy? Many temptations. Let's capsule our findings: Embroideries, organdies, and tapestries are the finest purchases here. We recommend that the first stop of your shopping day be made at the Rua do Carmo 27-1 studios and "factory" of **Madeira Superbia**—and don't let that commission-hungry taxi driver or anyone else steer you to an inferior house. Up 1-flight; serene, old-fashioned ambiance; complex of large, plainly decorated rooms, in which are displayed for sale the scores of beautiful products made by this ranking establishment. For specific listings and prices, please turn back to the Madeira Superbia write-up in the "Lisbon" section. Unrivaled. If Madeira Superbia shouldn't happen to have the item you want, the friendly Mrs.

Santos at **Marghab** (Rua dos Ferreiros 165) might be able to come up with it. Also a top-drawer company, but considerably more expensive. Stunning handicrafts and decorators' pieces? **Casa do Turista** (Avenida do Mar, a 2-minute stroll from the Funchal Cathedral) beats all competition by a long country mile. There is nothing "turista" in its quietly elegant décor, its uniformly tasteful stocks, or its warmly courteous attention. Director Ramos is an unusually competent, progressive, go-getting executive, with immense personal charm and a perfect command of English; be sure to ask for him personally, because he delights in offering his clients advice and assistance. One of his prides is that, with the exception of the 80 brands of wines in his *porao,* every single article in the store can be sent to your home by parcel post —and its safe arrival is guaranteed. Don't miss this leader, either. Home furnishings and trimmings? **Decorama** (Rua Dr. Fernão 29) and **Cavres** (across the street) have the same ownership. The former stresses antique and souvenir merchandise, while its larger brother is more traditional. Both are worth a browse. Antiques? Try the basement of **Galerias da Madeira** (Rua do Bettencourt) for above-average values. The entrance is through a venerable embroidery shop (the wares of which intrigued us not), then down a flight of stairs. Haggle. Madeira wines? A call at the famous **Madeira Wine Association Lda.** used to be richly rewarding—but now that the Government has banned all sales of vintage Madeira within the borders of Portugal—permitting export commerce only—the selection at hand here is of such inferior quality that it's no longer worth your or our time. Department store? The "big" department store is **Maison Blanche**. It is entirely Victorian and small-townish in tone, quality, and styling. The personnel couldn't be sweeter. Main shopping street? Wander down Camacho for window-shopping the majority of the better establishments.

Go to Madeira if you can. Here is a still-unspoiled paradise (except on "boat days"), made by the Creator for lazing, sunning, strolling, browsing, and more lazing. To repeat, expect no fireworks of any description—except on New Year's Eve. Simply pause in its crystal air, amid its banks of flowers, so that your soul may soak up the tranquil contentment that will recharge your world-weary batteries. How we adore this Magic Isle!

SCANDINAVIAN AIRLINES
SYSTEM

In 1346, Denmark, Norway, and Sweden got together to discuss a Scandinavian Union. Six hundred years later they did something about it when, in 1946, they joined hands in the Scandinavian Airlines System—and it's just as remarkable as if Gimbel's said to B. Altman and Lord & Taylor, "Let's plunk all our merchandise on the same counter and sell it together!"

Credit is shared so scrupulously that 3 urchins couldn't divide a Hershey bar with greater solemnity or exactitude. The corporation chairmanship is revolved at yearly intervals; all crews represent 3 nationalities. The letterhead lists the partners in alphabetical order; the fuselage of each plane is emblazoned with 3 flags. And as the supreme Solomon's decision, *English* became the compromise official language!

The line now has 74 aircraft flying to 102 cities in 53 countries on 5 continents. SAS DC-10, DC-8, and 747B jet service cuts the sky time between New York and Copenhagen to slightly more than 7 hours, and between Los Angeles and the Danish capital to under 11 hours (about 9 from Seattle). The Chicago-Montreal-Copenhagen hookup has totaled only about 10 hours, while the nonstop Chicago speedster cuts off about 2 hours from that twice a week.

The SAS fleet consists of Boeing 747-B jumbos, DC-8's (in various stretched versions), and a flock of spunky DC-9's. The latest additions to the gleaming host of ultramodern newcomers is a gaggle of DC-10's. In all, the inventory of American-made aircraft and equipment on hand or on order is over the $1,000,000,000 mark—for 3 tiny countries who can muster only 17-million people among them!

Trunk routes fan out directly from the 3 Scandinavian capitals to (1) New York, (2) Montreal and the Midwest, (3) Seattle and Los Angeles, (4) South America (all the way down to Santiago), (5) Monrovia and Abidjan, (6) South Africa, (7) Tokyo, over the Pole and via Anchorage or along the speedy trans-Siberian route through Moscow, (8) Tokyo, along the southern route via India, (9) the spectacular Trans-Asian Express, on a straight line across the USSR to Bangkok, Singapore, and Jakarta, and (10) the West Indies. Coupled with Thai International, a sister fleet, SAS also delivers through service to Sydney via Bangkok. This summer, SAS plans to zoom nonstoppers between

JFK and Stavanger and Bergen in Norway. With combined equipment, every capital of Free Europe is now reached; so are various satellite countries, Moscow, and Leningrad. The pilots, predominantly Scandinavian (one of them a woman), are crackerjacks—or crackerjackies; in looks some of the hostesses are wholesomely rustic, while others beat Anita Ekberg to a frazzle.

The remarkable growth of SAS is based on service, more service, and still more service to its ticket holders—the brand of personal attention which makes the traveler come back on his next trip for another helping. It's just the right size—big enough to handle big things, but not too big to stop caring about its individual ticket holders. This interest in the passenger can't be touched, in our opinion, by any transatlantic competitor—consistently one of the finest we've found among the 43 international companies we've flown. Its Economy-class schedules are also just about unbeatable in the standard budget category—but naturally, as with all of the other IATA members, its hospitality here is somewhat hamstrung by the inhibiting specifications laid down by this worldwide air transport association (see "Let's Go By Plane"). Its kitchens still boast that no food is ever frozen, that every item is market fresh, and that diners are given the unique privilege of savoring such rare northern delights as Baltic salmon, Greenland shrimp, frikadeller, reindeer steak, and similar delicacies. Tickets may be purchased on the SAS Signature Plan (as well as on most credit cards); walk into the nearest branch office, fill out the form, and spread the cost of your journey over 6 to 24 months. For domestic hops, latecomers now can jump aboard and fork over the fare after they are seated. Within Scandinavia, incidentally, there are several special deals relating to family plans, senior citizens, business travelers, or sightseeing adventurers. You can check on these through SAS once you alight in the northlands.

The President of SAS is Knut Hagrup, the Norwegian engineer who conceived the polar route; he assumed command of the line after 23 years as head of SAS Operations. Other members of top management include Frede Eriksen (Danish), Kai Sotorp (Norwegian), and Yngve Wessman (Swedish).

The present General Manager of North American Operations is B. John Heistein, a Norwegian with vast experience as an American Express executive and SAS Veepee. If any special SAS problems or puzzles should befuddle you, drop a line to the able, scholarly, and graciously personable Sven Ralph Cohen, North American Director of Public Relations, who was lured from a similar role in the International Air Transport Association.

Safety record: Practically perfect. Minimum-safety standards set by SAS are, in our opinion, maximum-safety standards on several other well-known carriers. They seem to miss nothing, overlook nothing.

Recommendation: Complete. We continue to consider SAS virtually unbeatable—and, just as we've reported for many years in this *Guide,* its passenger service remains to us consistently among the most comfortable of the American or European carriers we fly.

Scotland

Scotland, second largest stockholder in the mighty business partnership of Great Britain Unlimited, combines so many contrasts on a single patch of earth that sometimes its visitors get the feeling they're touring a Hollywood movie lot. Within an area roughly the size of West Virginia, fjords, glens, moors, mountains, prairies, heaths, bogs, woodlands, rills, alpine lakes, and even Gulf Stream-nourished palm trees on its island of Arran—just about everything in the geography book except Himalayan ice bridges and Amazonian rain forests.

This scenic kaleidoscope, only 275 miles long and 150 miles wide, breaks down naturally into 3 divisions and several clusters of islands. The *Southern Uplands,* a brain-shape wedge between the English border and the Edinburgh-Glasgow line, stretch in a number of moorlike ranges from south to north—the Lowthers, Moorfoots, Cheviots, and others. Sheep-rearing and woolens keep these hardworking folk out of mischief; the fishing is extra-fine, because the Clyde, Tweed, and other rivers rise here. The *Central Lowlands,* that narrow band which belts the waist of the nation, contains ¾ths of Scotland's 5-million inhabitants and nearly all its heavy industries. Edinburgh, certain Clyde lochs and resorts, and the handful of its better attractions shouldn't be missed. Otherwise, this crowded ribbon, ravished by factories, is generally joyless for the tourist. The *Highlands,* on the other hand, are among the most glorious holiday areas in the world. These granite mountains and plains, split across the center by Loch Ness and Loch Lochy, sprawl over more than half the country's terrain. Inverness is the capital and Aberdèen is the major summer resort; grouse, deer, salmon, trout, ptarmigan, and hare abound in their purple moors, flashing streams, turquoise lakes, and cool forests. They're as different from the Central Lowlands as the lovely Pennsylvania Alleghenies are from the drab New Jersey industrial salt marshes. The

Hebrides, Shetlands, Orkneys, Skye, Arran, Bute, and other islands—each different, each fascinating to the off-trail explorer—round out the picture.

Halifax visitors please note: "Scotland" springs from "Scotia," as in "Nova Scotia"—literally, "the land of a tribe of Scots." When the Romans tried to rename the nation "Caledonia," there was almost another Battle of Cannai. These proud, stubborn, tough-fibered northerners have always worshiped liberty; their history flames with impassioned patriots of the stamp of William Wallace, Robert Bruce, and John Knox. In 1603, when Scottish King James VI succeeded Good Queen Bess on the throne of England, a Union of the Crowns was effected, which later gave the smaller nation a voice in the London government—but even today, many wearers of the plaid consider this a disaster ranking somewhere between the Great Whisky Famine of 1854 and Armageddon.

The Church of Scotland and the United Free Church (Presbyterian) joined hands in 1929, and their rigidly moral doctrines penetrate nearly every parlor from Lerwick in the Shetlands to Gretna Green in the south. You won't find nightclubs, bordellos, B-girls, or tolerated licentiousness in any form. On Sundays and religious holidays, you might as well be in Great Coco, Adaman Islands, as in Edinburgh, Glasgow, or any city here, because all that stirs is the electric current and dripping faucets. It's a constant source of amazement to Americans that the Scots can be brought up under such a bluenose code, in such a hard climate and in such cheerless, austere buildings—and still be among the warmest, wittiest, and sweetest people ever to walk on 2 legs.

Shipbuilding (down seriously in recent times), oil-rig manufacture for off-shore discoveries, textiles, brewing, pottery, marmalade, computers, bottled dew-of-the-heather—these are mere samples of this nation's powerful industrial complex. About 100-thousand men are employed in coal mines. Herring, cod, and whiting engage a flotilla of fishermen. The once-discarded prawns, now known as *scampi* (Italian for shrimp), are now a major catch. Scottish beef, considered by many gourmets to rival Chicago's best, comes from the famous Aberdeen Angus, Galloway, and Short Horn strains. (Sadly, as with premium grades of most commodities, the export market snatches so much that what remains for the local table often resembles filet of flintstone). Although Clydesdale draft horses and Shetlands, Highland, and Cheriot sheep are the traditional moneymakers, the country is gradually entering a bright new era of productivity and development. It's a working country, this one; from Ayr to Uyea, you'll find few loafers.

Finally, if you persist in referring to people, landscape, architecture, and local attractions as "Scotch," don't be surprised if your kilted companions lick their lips and rush away on "forgotten" appointments. It's "Scot," "Scotsman," "Scotswoman," or "Scottish," unless you're talking about (1) the whisky, or (2) a few oddball expressions such as "Scotch broth" that combine with a second word. Say "Scotch" only if you're thirsty!

CITIES   *Glasgow*, with nearly 1 million inhabitants, is the commercial capital of Scotland and the 3rd largest metropolis in Great Britain. Shipbuilding and engineering make her wheels turn; her famous cathedral dates back to 1197 and her University to 1450. The Kelvingrove Art Gallery, City Chambers, Hunterian Museum, Provand's Lordship 1471 house, Botanic Gardens, and Zoo are among her attractions; she has 50 public parks and 5 newspapers. The center of the city is currently undergoing a revolutionary face-lifting which will replace uninhabitable slums with longitudinal or skyscraping apartment dwellings and office buildings. These are laced nimbly through a skein of projects which include a hostelry sited at Anderston. Abbotsinch domestic airport has been revved up. It is now second only to London's Heathrow in its traffic of British skywaymen. The hotels, drab and mercantile until recently, are improving; a tough, rigidly enforced antismoke campaign is fast dispelling her one-time grim, grimy, and forbidden franchise on smog; her newly scrubbed face as well as her beautiful antiquities are at last being revealed in a more flattering light. Convenient jump-off point for many interesting excursions.

Edinburgh combines the old and the fresh with such charm that she's one of the most ingratiating cities on the travel map. Here's the political, judicial, and cultural capital of the nation. Her ½-million population is closest to Memphis', her climate to Seattle's. Two-thirds of her history is tied up in the "Royal Mile"—nearly a straight line from world-famous Edinburgh Castle to Holyrood Palace, incorporating such landmarks as the Shrine, the High Kirk (St. Giles's Cathedral), John Knox's House, the Canongate Tolbooth, Queen Mary's Bath, and a half-dozen of similar interest. Sir Walter Scott's "Dear 39" and the University of Edinburgh are musts. Princes Street, with its Scott Monument, National Gallery, Royal Scottish Academy, Scottish-American War Memorial, and smart shops is one of the handsomest thoroughfares in the world. Quiet atmosphere, except at Festival time every August; hotel situation radically better; excellent sports and spectator facilities, so-so restaurants, additional nightclubs, 2 modest gambling casinos that operate about as sheepishly as a Lothian herder; matronly, serene, beguiling. Cut your time in other metropolises to the bone and base yourself here.

Aberdeen, the size of Salt Lake City, successfully blends medieval mellowness with the gaiety of a modern seaside resort. There is also a new fever of prosperity as the region enjoys what might be termed a black-gold rush. She's situated on the banks of the Don and the Dee rivers and not far from the off-shore oil fields that are now being developed by the nation. Between the mouths of these streams, a 2-mile sandy beach has been dedicated to holidaymakers—perfect for Polar Club bathers who sprout walrus hair on limbs, back, and shoulders. Outstanding university, 8 lovely parks, spectacular Rubislaw granite quarry, venerable St. Machar's Cathedral; don't miss the Fish Market (now with guides), one of the most interesting in the United Kingdom.

Dundee, the jam and jute center, frowns down from a majestic site over the Firth of Tay; the bay-spanning bridge puts St. Andrews almost within a chip shot of this hub; it's industrial. So is **Hamilton**, and so is unsightly little **Clydebank**, with its foundries gradually tooling up for the petroleum trades of the nation. Attractive **Perth** and **Stirling**, both on the fringe of the Highland Hills, are standard favorites for antiquarians and sightseers; **Inver-**

ness, capital and one of the key touring centers of the Highlands, is typical of a tranquil provincial town.

Scottish architecture is so austere, angular, and utilitarian that her cities (with the exception of Edinburgh) and villages are aesthetically ungratifying. For warmth, color, and delight, look to her countryside and to the hearts of her people, instead.

MONEY AND PRICES

In practice but not in theory, all of Great Britain's floating currencies are mutually interchangeable. Below the border, only the Bank of England is authorized to issue money; in Scotland, no less than 4 Joint Stock Banks jealously guard their right to circulate their own legal tender. These notes are almost as bright and gay as Scottish tartans—a pleasure to carry and to use. The £5 English bill is technically not valid in Scotland—but any good Scotsman will change it, if only to be accommodating. However, it's sometimes difficult to change Scottish paper money back to English currency—especially in the London area.

Prices are practically on par with their British equivalents.

ATTITUDE TOWARD TOURISTS

The **Scottish Tourist Board**, with headquarters at 23 Ravelston Terrace, Edinburgh, does a phenomenal job for the traveler, in view of its limited size and budget. This Board of eminent Scots from all fields and walks of life minister to the nation's welfare.

The Board has completed various ambitious programs; now it's attacking new ones. Its main targets are the increase or betterment of accommodations for the traveler and the lengthening of the tourist season. It also encourages planners in other up-and-coming areas or in crowded established centers. Crofters and cottagers, as well, have been urged to make rooms available for visitors. Road improvement; new car ferries; natural resources further developed; ski lifts, additional fishing and shooting facilities, and other projects are being spotlighted.

For pamphlets or off-the-cuff information on anything from Edinburgh's Royal Mile to Sule Skerry to salmon fishing in Loch Lonachan, write, phone, or drop in at the **Information Centre**, 2 Rutland Place, in Edinburgh. These experts know everything worth knowing, and we certainly hope the reorganization under central (British) planning does nothing to up-set its present set-up.

France, England, and Italy could take lessons from this lively organization.

§TIPS: If you require any hard-to-get reservations or savvy guidance for places to hunt, golf, fish, ride, sail, or sightsee anywhere in this land, get in touch with our dear friend Bill Nicholson, **Tourist Promotion (Scotland)**, 36 Castle St., in Edinburgh. This brilliant gentleman almost single-handedly gave the country a tourist industry after he initiated Scotland's early promotional projects. Having retired, Bill just can't sit still when there are people to help, so he continues his genial services under the umbrella of his own personal company. He has a special warmth for *Guide* readers and no one knows Scotland more intimately or more comprehensively than this top-flight professional.

By phoning Edinburgh (031-) 246-8041 between May 1 and September 30, you'll get up-to-the-minute details on what to see and do—thanks to the STB-sponsored "Teletourist Service."

A plan whereby visitors may receive a 20% discount on many facilities during certain off-peak months may be offered again this year. Ask the STB about the "Highlands Holiday Ticket." Readers have not been too enthusiastic about it, but if you are still interested, the lookin' ain't much.

CUSTOMS AND IMMIGRATION   See "England." The regulations are the same.

HOTELS   For far more comprehensive information on certain places to stay than space limitations permit here, interested travelers are referred to the annually revised *Fielding's Selected Favorites: Hotels and Inns, Europe* by our son, Dodge Temple Fielding. The latest edition, in which a total of 300-odd favored possibilities were handpicked from the 4000-plus personally inspected, will be at your bookstore early this year.

Dramatic improvements have been made in key localities, particularly among the top-liners—but, speaking in general, too many are still too stiff, stark, and down-to-earth. The entry of pound-wise breweries into mass-market innkeeping is adding new yeast to the volume keg but little sparkle to the individual mug. In all too many cases, these hops-headed malt-masters are neglecting their bedchambers and service standards to pull more sudsy traffic into their taprooms. You'll find no nonsense about the average Scottish hostelry (not the front runners, however): It's a place to eat and sleep, just that.

You'll pay from $22 to $26 per person for bed-and-breakfast in the better group, and up to double this price in the Gleneagles league. Simple accommodations, especially in rural areas, can be had for as little as $12 per day.

§TIP: About breakfast: (1) Be sure to order it *before* 9:30 A.M.; otherwise you won't be able to coax a nibble until noontime, even if you starve. (2) Either gobble it down pronto or set all your plates on the night table. The shortage of serving trays throughout the British Isles invariably results in a visitation from your waiter about 10 minutes after his initial delivery. (3) Be prepared to shell out 5 New Pence supplement for munching in your room, instead of in the breakfast nook. Now—Good Morning to you!

In **Edinburgh**, the Railways-operated, group-minded, 230-room **Caledonian**, opposite Edinburgh Castle, is one of the top addresses in all Caledonia. From the exterior, this fortress-like landmark might be mistaken for a Scottish House of Usher; inside, however, the welcome is warmer. Plenty of private baths; some units terrific (the quietest face the abandoned station, not the Castle), some only good. There is dancing nightly (except Sun.) in the popular Pompadour; light meals are served in the cozy Laird's Lodge Coffee House, which sprouts into the lobby via a fresh lounge. A 51-unit wing and a 300-car parking lot have been spliced into the picture. Manager John Whittingham is doing a splendid job keeping this champ in trim. Palms and salaams to a hostelry of taste, flair, and charm.

P.S.: Here's a between-paragraph entertainment note: Both the Caledonian and the following "N.B." have "Scottish Nights"—national food specialties served up with generous helpings of piping-hot bagpipings and regional dancing by experts in authentic costume. These evenings are expensive by local standards, but the spirit, the fun, and the performance secure your investment. The former house brings out the skirls and the skillets on Tuesday, Thursday, and Saturday, while the latter kicks up its kilts on Monday, Wednesday, and Friday. The George (see below) also has joined in the merrymaking, so during the May-to-September period the visitor now has 3 choices. All are recommended. Great for a one-shot Highland fling.

The smartly run, 200-unit "N.B." (North British Station Hotel) is a solid teammate. Grand-mastered by sharpshooting A. S. Bonthron, who chipped in from the Turnberry golfing shrine; bright touches everywhere; sparkling-fresh Cleikum Restaurant and Bannatyne Bar replacing the formerly bleak Scots' Kitchen Grill; tiptop cuisine for tiptop tabs; Happy Sam's Bar for off-lobby chuckles and toping. Comfortable, cheer-livened sleeping quarters; pastel-ized suites; gardenside units the pick of the path; a truly outstanding Hall Porter in Mr. J. J. Petrie; mixture of commercial and touristic clientele. Better and better.

The George, now under the skilled management of dynamic, scalpel-keen John Ellerington, is a dramatically recovered patient. The full-scale rehabilitation not only includes revisions in the current facilities, but the grafting of 116 superb extra bedchambers which join the main building through bridge-work (all with private pipes), bringing the overall house count to 202 units. Split-level Perigord Room with all-you-can-eat, hot-and-cold-table selections; popular Restaurant des Ambassadeurs, featuring its traditionally yumptious roast-beef specialty and extra-smooth kindhearted service (which seems to permeate this hotel); dancing nightly. Its smart administration is successfully restoring much of its former finesse, charm, and grace.

If you have transportation, the outlying Post House is one of the most appealing modern addresses in the nation. It's a 10-minute drive from the center on the Corstorphine Road to Glasgow, raised above the highway and looking across rolling meadows toward the Pentland Hills. Excellent Ravelston Room restaurant festooned with local tapestries; inviting Honey Bear Buttery (that colossal statue is the beloved Wotjek, mascot of the Polish regiment that once was billeted in Edinburgh) bar and public quarters recalling the region's Celtic heritage; superb comfort in its well-appointed bedchambers. We are very fond of this Post House.

A little farther out on the same pike, the Royal Scot also opened in 1973. Physically it is more daring in concept, but we suspect that it will not wear as well as its contemporary rival. Wood has been handsomely melded into the free-form concrete structure providing warmth; tan- and beige-toned textiles enhance the humanizing process. Its many amenities were not all functioning on our visit due to a traffic slump, but overall this contender has got the goods to lure a following. Service probably will always be a problem at this remote site.

Back in town, the King James, yet another recent addition, is packing 'em in. The commercial atmosphere is softened by the richly adorned Stuart Restaurant which features a skillfully carved frieze, by the Queen's Lounge in green velvet with textile panels, and by the King's House for light lunching. The Coffee Pot pours over into a busy shopping mall. The smallish accommodations are thoughtfully outfitted. Okay as an up-to-date midtowner.

The tranquilly situated, 69-room **Roxburghe** retains far more of a family air than its busy-busy colleagues. Revampings from the cozy top-floor singles in garret style to the refreshed jousting-tent Consort Restaurant in the cellar (so-so cuisine and orchestra-dancing); traditional tones with Adam highlights lovingly preserved; top-form maintenance; first-rate attention by Willy, the hyperfriendly concierge; light, airy, flower-dotted dining room; captivating ground-floor cocktail bar (which we prefer for light dining as well as for sipping) in Victorianisms; self-serve luncheon buffet for a modest MacTab; cramped inside baths or shower compartments; some units perfectly designed for a mother-in-law with the sharpest tongue in the world. This one has been the favorite of many visiting performers, musicians, and gentle folk of the arts. Comfortable, homey, and still recommendable for its warmhearted personnel.

The 87-room **Carlton**, a Trust Houses Forte homestead across the bridge from the N.B., has sited its reception desk up 1-flight from the hurly-burly street. Entrance, lounge, and bar redecorated, with the entire remainder of the hotel due for a pep-up (no guarantees by us, because we've heard only promises, promises for the past several years); every unit with private bath; most with double-pane windows; corner bedchambers ending in "15" the largest. Our recent lunch here was one of the best we've had in any links of this chain, the fare of which, in general, is showing radical improvement over the standards of earlier years. Now well run, comfortable, and worth the price.

The **County**, more quietly situated, commanding the point of Abercromby Place and Dublin St., has furrowed a neater row in a hoedown revamping of its public rooms and most of its sleeping segments. Renewed entrance, reception, cocktail bar, dining room, and lounge; 50 so-so units; only 12 baths; #40 is our choice of doubles. Fair, if you can alight in one of its better nests.

The **Mount Royal** mounted a withers-to-bangtail regrooming program a while back. It's still far from qualifying as a thoroughbred, but on the county-fair circuit, the parlay isn't bad.

The partially redecorated **Scotia**, on Great King Street within 5 minutes' walk of the George, consists of 5 Georgian houses comprising 50 rooms with a quotient of 14 private baths. Guidance by brethren Reginald and Cyril Elliott; many young staffers, pleasant and forgivably amateurish. Modern, perked-up lounge and bar; good restaurant adorned with fine old paintings and gay red tableclothes; modest appointments including electric heaters; (try #33 for a pleasant back unit). We hope it continues to render top value for top dollars.

On the same street, the **Howard** now glows with renewed vigor. All 40 units pepped up and provided with private baths. Quite recommendable.

The **Rutland**, across from the Caledonian, offers viewful accommodations at 30% less than the outlay at the County. Proprietors Mr. and Mrs. Richmond are trying to convert its mercantile character into more of a family haven. Total of 19 rooms; no baths; bar and grill noisy after nightfall. Strictly for dedicated penny-watchers.

Several splendid havens have opened for travelers with special tastes or needs. Our personal favorite is **Dalhousie Castle**. The neighboring Jacobean Feast (see "Restaurants") is a highly bruited publicity come-on, but its soft-spoken luxury accommodations in a completely separate part of the fortress are absolute charmers. Henry IV held the castle in siege for 6 months and we could happily bivouac here for a lifetime—or at least a fortnight. All 24 units truly superb, but we are especially fond of Dalhousie Suite in the Tower or #22 up on the battlements (no elevator). Ask for Host Ian Dearmer. Something unique and spectacularly rewarding for twentieth-century day-and-knighthood. The official address is Bonnyrigg, Midlothian, a short haul from Edinburgh. Another winner is **Houstoun House** at *Uphall,* about 20 minutes by car from the bright lights. What a tranquil dreamland it is, too! This one is a converted mansion embraced with green lawn, guarded by a rolling 18-hole golf course. Proprietors Mr. and Mrs. Keith Knight are known by far-and-wide girths for their fine gastronomy, the best we've lately enjoyed in Scotland and high in the culinary rankings of Europe. Only set meals are offered. Virtually every dish is prepared by the owner-chef. Handsome, refined dining salons on the 1st floor; glass-lined, linkside lounge; vaulted whitewashed bar with deep soft divans and crackling fire in the chimney; 19 bedchambers with private bath (or one immediately adjoining); added wing with modern conventional décor. For reservations, write to the Knights, Houstoun House, Uphall, West Lothian, or if you want to telephone to book a table, the number is Broxburn 3831. One of the warmest recommendations in this book, but not at all for seekers of the fancy, the ritzy, or the pretentious. **Borthwick Castle**, 20 minutes from the capital at *Gorebridge*, is a cozy snuggery from which Mary Queen of Scots once escaped custody. She should have waited until it was refashioned because she would have changed her mind. From minstrel gallery to turrets, here's a tidy tower of taste and comfort. The **Forth Bridges Lodge**, at the headland of the famous firth, casts a commanding sweep over the wind-chafed waters. The views are breathtaking, but the whiffs from the Vat-69 distillery just below can be breathalizing when *those* cups runneth over. Efficiency-style bedchambers; 40 doubles; 20 more which can be stretched into trios; all with bath; some with TV (who could watch it with that magnificent sea outside your window?); each unit with its own teamaker set and all the fixin's; fair production-line-like food; similar service, but friendly. For motorists and wide-eyed wanderlusters. **Hawes Inn**, nearby at *South Queensferry*, is down by the water opposite the old pier. Here is where (room #13 to be exact) Robert Louis Stevenson blocked out the plot for *Kidnapped* and began writing the novel; it is also where Sir Walter Scott penned his *Balfour*. Only 7 bedchambers, 2 private baths, a darned good dining room, and a cozy cocktail lounge and bar nestle within the white walls and black enamel trim of this tiny hideaway. For nostalgics, excursionists, and overnight adventurers, but not for long stopovers—or Norman Mailers. The **Esso Hotel** (or **Crest**, if it has changed its name) is out in the same direction. Six floors of 120 lookalike cells; 6 so-called suites; 2 levels of public rooms; wide windows that don't allay the narrowness of the dimensions. Sheltering arms, but sterile ones. **Braid Hills**, south of town on Braid Road, weaves much more braided flair. Total of 70 units split equally between singles and twins; reasonable rewards; pleasant as a suburban address. **Cramond Inn** at *Cramond*, 5 miles from the hub (see "Restaurants") was an adorable sweetie on our last visit. **Ellersly House**, about 2 miles from the center on Ellersly Road, is now under the aegis of the Mount Royal, which perhaps will perk up its housekeeping standards. Garden situation and croquet green enhancing the converted private home; 27 sleeping units and 22 baths; 1 suite; elevator; large carpark; hotel shuttle to town available and inexpensive.

Glasgow now leads off with the modern, 9-story, 220-nest **Albany**. Its Four Seasons dining room is a delight for formality while the red-and-black Carvery sizzles with open banks of grills; a trapper's cabin hides in the cellar for light biting; accommodations throughout are well conceived and smartly attired. At last Glasgow has a big-city hostelry. The century-old **Central** is a property of British Railways. Scads of improvements, including vast technical revampings behind the scenes; Chief Hall Porter Bickerstaffe is one of the top pros in his profession; fearful street noises in some of its units. The high-style Malmaison Restaurant, in the Versailles mode, completes handily for local gastronomic honors. The **"N.B."** (another "North British" operated by the Railways) has also taken vanity pills. Chipper white façade; perky lobby carpets and curtains; bedrooms from top-to-bottom fluffed up; many baths modernized. Smarter in every respect. Both the comfortable, linear-structured **Grosvenor** and the freshly expanded **Pond**, each with 100 rooms, have been totally refashioned, while the 90-chamber **Ingram** has joined the fray and soon plans further restylings—which it vitally needs. The 116-unit **Royal Stuart,** opened in '65, dedicates ⅔rds of its accommodations to the lone traveler. Shamefully compact cells with tiny intercommunicating baths; air-conditioned and centrally heated; rooftop restaurant in prospect when funds appear. It is very popular, however. The small but tastefully contemporary **Tinto Firs** is a worthy stop for a brief layover. The Copper Grill is especially inviting; so are its 4 bars if you have an overwhelming thirst. For budgeteers, the **Lorne**, 15 minutes out of town, is sleek, and okay if you have wheels; the omnipresent Scottish brewers tapped this one.

The **Excelsior** (sometimes called the "Airport Hotel") at Abbotsinch domestic terminal renders topflight shelter and service. The **Silver Thread**, at nearby *Paisley*, is another youngster. Somehow its needlepoint did not weave us into its spell during our recent Scottish sewing bee.

The **Macdonald**, in Giffnock suburb about 10 minutes from midtown, is a favorite of wayfaring executives. Jumbled entrance; small lounge; paneled pub; simple, adequate, but showing wear. While still a Cunzie Neuk, 'tis nothing to hoot about, mon.

The **Campsie Glen**, in the settlement of the same name about 12 miles from Glasgow, roots in the country coombs. Quiet as the inside of a chinchilla muff and almost as pretentious; venerable country mansion with up-to-date décor; appalling concrete dining salon that reminds us of a beachhead bunker. Otherwise, the creature comforts are plentiful and satisfying.

For self-drivers, the **Newlands** (15 minutes from the center) is a honey for Scotland, despite its dearth of double accommodations. Tartan lobby; plasticy bar; all 34 rooms have sprightly décor and bath or shower; only 6 lodge 2 occupants; its young and winningly personable manager, Dennis Lynch, formerly of Edinburgh's Caledonian, should go a long way in his profession. A happy little haven that is warmly recommended.

Aberdeen, is in a state of cataclysmic flux—the antagonists being the "Squares" and the "Mods." A lot is happening up here in anticipation of the petroleum drilling offshore and the commerce this will develop. The **Station**, traditionally the doyenne of the dowager division, was a sad disappointment to us on our recent swing. Perhaps under Manager D. J. Tait it will begin to chuff. The expanded 113-room **Treetops**, on Springfield Road in the west end, struck us as a veritable orchard of goodies by comparison. Tranquil situation 5 minutes from the traffic nucleus; wide greensward in front; somnolent duck pond in the back garden; handsome dining room overseen by the former maître of the famous Royal Athenaeum; enormous menu and better-than-average cuisine for the region; long, inviting, lantern-lit bar sided by intimate tables and banquettes; fire-crackling lounge and TV nook. The **Royal Darroch** has a country address and country solace. Superb comfort. The cuisine is tiptop, too. The 100-unit **Sheraton Inn** has just opened, exchanging waves with the North Sea at its doorstep (innstep?) on Oldmeldrum Rd. Binnacle restaurant recalling clipper-ship times; 2 bars; extensive use of wood and dark timber tones; indoor swimming pool; 2 suites plus a clutch of simple but adequate accommodations. Its goal is not luxury and it achieves its more limited aims rather well. The **Caledonian**'s antiquated aura may be the headache of a new director. Its previous owners liquidated it, and the fresh team has moved in. Complete carpeting has been installed, and the entire plant refurnished. The **Dee Motel**, 1 mile out on the river and opposite the greyhound stadium, deserves mention along about here. A steady construction program now puts the overall count at 46 plain but bright bedchambers, each with shower and toilet. Three bars, including a snack corner; pine and brick décor; comfortable lounge; carport beneath every accommodation. Dee-lightful for mobile wayfarers. The mass-minded **Gloucester** has bashfully perked up with a few meek improvements. Redecorated dining room and lounges; some twins cheerful; dreary, perfectly horrid corridors lined with a maze of public toilet cabins. Total of 86 units and 4 private baths (extravagant plans to add ONE more of the latter—maybe!). Basic shelter *only* at times of dire distress. The **Imperial**, largest in the city, greets its guests with a tartan entrance and an off-lobby Regency-style dining room. Passable if you snag a decent bedchamber, but otherwise as grim as its neighborhood seems to be. The commercially oriented **Douglas,** run by the Gloucester people, has redone some of the arthritic bedrooms; they still seem zipless to us. Friendly Manager Gordon is its chief asset. If you're driving, the 40-room **Northern**, 10 minutes from the center and 5 from the airport, might fill the budgeteer's bill; cramped but chipper bedrooms in pastels with white furniture; only 4 baths; Lilliputian restaurant; jigger-size bar. A good little bet at the price. Northwest of here, 2 miles out of **Meldrum,** Robin Duff, the Laird of **Meldrum House**, is as respectful of his skillets as of his guests. Space for only 8 overnight couples, but 72 couverts for diners. Imposing graystone castle structure at the end of a drive lined with towering oaks and rhododendron shrubs; wide greensward at its door; a deluxe target for which you should certainly reserve in advance.

Perth's berths are mighty cozy in the rebuilt **Royal George**, a riverbank Trust Houses Forte member that was once the local haven of Queen Victoria. Nice views of the Tay and Perth Bridge; especially tempting grills in its restaurant; engaging Black Watch Bar; handsome lounges; 50 bedchambers; 18 baths; considerate service; solid in comfort; appealing in concept. Now a frontrunner in this city. The sparkling clean **Station Hotel**—ironic because both its exterior and the adjoining terminal buildings are still dismally gray from the chuff-chuff era—is also a sound bet. Midcity garden with lime-treed border; ambiance so cheerful you'll immediately feel your spirits lifting; lounge with plenty of Perthshire perk. The veteran Concierge, Tommy Anderson, could give lessons to IBM in efficiency; Barman Joe (at Gleneagles in summer) is one of the top mixers—of drinks AND of people—in the trade. From pastel doors, to teal-hued carpets, to cuisine, to the tiniest shining cranny in this house, we think you might be satisfied if you chug into this Station. Not as nicely situated as the Royal George, but very recommendable, indeed. The commercial, ultrabasic **Salutation**, in midtown, greets its guests with traffic noises about the level of a 3-gun salute. Routine. The **Isle of Skye,** at the bridgehead across the Tay, is an excellent nest for money-saving pilgrims. White stucco and wood façade; captivating Iron Hinges Cocktail Bar; Glenshee Ski Bar for buffet and snacks; Tudor dining room; firelit parlor; huge servings at high tea; added wing with best accommodations. The **Waverley** (next to the market) and the **Hunting Tower** (on the Crieff Road, 4 miles out) are other inexpensive stops.

In **Inverness**, the **Caledonian**, razed several seasons ago, reopened its portals to the tune of $1,500,000; 100 units with private bath; modern rather than traditional tone. Peppy, fun-filled atmosphere. The linkside and youthful **Kingsmills** is a mile from the center and only 10 minutes from the home of the Loch Ness Monster. Its ways are traditional while its amenities are modern. We recommend it if you have a car. The generously recharmed **Culloden House**, 6 miles out, is where Bonnie Prince Charlie was defeated in his attempt to capture the British throne for the Stuart kings. Never mind. We'll bet it will capture your heart and soul more than 2 centuries later. Everything about it bespeaks the easy comfort of Country Life. Back in town, the **Station** was old-maidenly when we saw her, yet her service standards are those of a hostess of breeding. Two dining rooms (we prefer the one in rouge tones); almost ⅓rd of its 71 units now with private plumbing; general upkeep fair. The **Glen Mhor**, overlooking the River Ness, is a warmhearted Nesstling spot. It rambles in houselike fashion, employs chenille and cretonne by the square mile, and creaks and squeaks from its welcoming floorboards. Call us addled, but we like it even for its faults. Not a Hilton, but who cares? The **Royal** may never live up to its promising moniker; it's a noble choice, however, for economizing vassals. A helpful Claremont, Calif., Guidester praised the **Palace**, with its quiet location on the Ness. We paddled up to its greystone portals and found a stately, old-timey, Establishmentarian establishment with 2 tall towers and tariffs not too steep for the ample comforts. The **Cummings,** with a fresh white façade and windows outlined in brown, is moving up in quality. Many private baths have been added, too. Now quite recommendable.

Braemar's leading house is the 60-room **Invercauld Arms**. Cheery appointments in the grandma context; top dining spot in town; closed to groups. One of the worthier stops in the area. The **Fife Arms** pipes in next. Open all year; migrations of bus tours pause here. Creaky. The newish, modern **Spittal** is an amiable lunch stop if you're running south through the **Devil's Elbow** (a satanic passage of highway). Inexpensive; tailored for budget ski buffs.

Dundee's champ is the **Angus**, a long, rectangular, glass-and-concrete heavyweight agraze in the city's blossoming shopping complex. Statleresque in tone; mezzanine restaurant with well-presented but institutional fare; handsome snack bar below lobby. A godsend for such a dismal industrial center. After this, and far below, there's the **Queens** (as somber, stern, and dull as Immanuel Kant) or the **Royal** (commercial, and bustling with marmalade moguls). Both of these are Trust Houses Forte entries; both, at last, are receiving a smattering of color, Clorox, and cheer.

St. Andrews tees off smartly with the **Old Course**, a member of the British Transport Hotels group which blankets the British Isles with top-grade oases. The handsome, sandstone-and-concrete, 74-room candidate debuted in '68 and it is easily a master in this tourney. The $2,000,000 project, bristling with balconies for lovely vistas, nuzzles only a pitch-and-putt from the 17th hole on its namesake, best-known of the 4 circuits at The Royal and Ancient Club; the back units overlook the flatter landscape of the Eden Course. Ground-level restaurant and bar, plus main dining room with balcony on the viewful 4th floor scanning the links, the bay, the seal islands, and the North Sea; wee Jigger Inn pub, in ancient style, adjoining the hotel for open-hearth merriment. Our recent rounds of golf and the tables couldn't have been more satisfying. Golf Clubs, even shoes, for rent; parking for 100 cars; most units in twin configuration; 6 singles and twice as many suites; full bath count. A straight-down-the-fairway winner on every score, according to our card. How we cheer a hard-hitting pro, because this shrine and fountainhead of world golfdom has traditionally missed par by 2-dozen strokes in its guestroom standards. Next, we would venture that the choice of most far-sighted swatters will be the tiny **Rufflets**—"farsighted," because its 20 bed-chambers (6 singles and 14 doubles) are almost always booked way, way in advance. Outskirts situation about 10 minutes by car to the tee; substantial cuisine; solid homespun comforts. A car is essential, in our opinion. The well-known **Scores**, on a hillock overlooking the course, is ideally situated. After seeming eons of lassitude, it is showing progress toward broad-spectrum improvement. Fresh entrance, reception foyer, and main-floor seafront lounge; redesigned bar; expanded mural-clad dining room; carpeting replaced throughout; bath count upped to 12 for 33 bedrooms. We prefer front units with their white furnishings and club-swinging spaciousness. Although its score is better, here is still a duffer in resort hotel circles. The 72-room, 25-bath **Rusack's**, bordering the links, is also feeling the shock of combat. It smacked on a new front door and buckets of pastel paint recently. Attractive lounge; agreeable dining room with asinine "no smoking" rule. Dismal doubles with bath; Easter to end-October only. Not terribly rich in honors in this amateur-level tournament. The **Golf**, a tyke-size offering at greenside, recently underwent a top-to-bottom reconstruction. Owner-Director Brewster has brewed up a linkside bar, an extra wing of rooms, and a widened dining salon. Homey atmosphere; not bad if you don't expect a Ritz. The once-passable **Imperial** today impresses us as having lost every shred of its former majesty. Pass it up. The 19-room **Reden**, in the university district, is one of the few houses that stays open year round—but there are no baths. Garden-side dining room; scarlet carpets; many windows and skylights; bright, airy and cheerful. Save it for warm months, and take your shower at the clubhouse because it can be very cool in winter. The ancient **Kinburn**, which also functions all year, is drably rickety. The **St. Andrews**, with the same sea-and-course view as Scores, has renewed its entrance and brightened its interior. Now pretty good as a moneysaver. But if you can afford U.S.-size tariffs, go to the Old Course and enjoy a holiday fit for a Player, a Nicklaus, or Y-O-U.

Other rural hotels for golfing, bathing, angling, or settin'? Now we're talking, because they're miles more pleasant and cheery than many of the soulless stone piles in the cities. Here are what we consider to be the best bets from your reporter's point of view:

Gleneagles Hotel at *Gleneagles*, Perthshire, 1½ hours from Edinburgh, is undoubtedly one of the top stopping places in the nation. Wonderful pastoral setting and lovely gardens; splendid golf facilities including three 18-hole championship courses, one full 9-hole course, one 18-hole pitch-and-putt circuit, and one 18-hole putting run; tennis, riding, and fishing; heated swimming pool and indoor games room; air-conditioned French Restaurant (High Season only); dancing weekday nights; renewed bar, massage parlor, the works. Central heating; TV in every room for lonely golf-widder-ladies; some accommodations plush; dozens of baths added. Its current manager is J. K. S. Bannatyne, the former chief of Edinburgh's leading Caledonian and an able administrator whom we admire greatly. Open April to end-October only. Highest recommendation.

The **Turnberry Hotel** at *Turnberry*, Ayrshire, 50 miles south of Glasgow and 15 miles from Ayr, is the favorite of the "Burns Country" excursionist, as well as many dyed-in-the-Shetland golfers. Each and every one of its 136 units now with private bath or shower plus TV sets throughout; entire structure renewed; color-matched textiles to offset the stark-white walls; fresh bar; complete revamping of lounges, dining room, heating system, virtually everything from cellar to eaves. The selected grounds sanctified for future British Open Golf Championships; tennis courts; indoor pool; dancing and movies; snooker room; minibus service to Prestwick and other getaway points; smoothly operated from check-in to *adios*. On a wonderfully relaxing golfing weekend here recently, we could discover only 2 minor flaws in an otherwise perfect sojourn: (1) the walls of our room were just skinny enough to admit normal noises from the adjoining chamber, and (2) the plentiful food was bland and institutional. Neither complaint, however, could ever discourage our yearn to return. (The **Cairndale** at *Dumfries*, less expensive, also draws heavily among the Bobbie Burns pilgrims.)

The **Marine Hotel** at *Troon*, Ayrshire, a quick skip from Prestwick Airport and 26 miles from Glasgow, offers an unprecedented 20 miles of golf courses in a row (whereon the British Open took place in '73). Almost 2-dozen units beautifully refashioned; lounge renewed; extended dining room with sea-and-links panorama; handsome cocktail bar with gold curtains; 70 rooms,

3 suites and 46 private baths. Dinner dancing Saturday nights (dress: black tie); friendly, sophisticated service under the watchful eye of Managing Director Keith Vilvandré. Also heaven for golf bugs, but becoming a frequent target for short-stay excursionists and package trippers.

The **Lochalsh Hotel** at *Kyle of Lochalsh*, 80 miles west of Inverness at the ferry point to the Isle of Skye, features an admirable view across the strait, modern appointments, and, for a change, genuine Scottish flavor and color. American bar; just 36 rooms, about ⅓rd with bath (we nabbed #20, on a corner); cookery reported to have fallen off alarmingly, but we can't say from personal experience; service also spare, according to other howls; book long, long, long in advance, because this mini-house is always crowded. And speaking of "mini," a veteran Park Ridge, Illinois, friend of the *Guide* wryly comments, "With the exception of a YMCA room, I have never seen a smaller accommodation than the one we drew." While it is open all year, the biggest crush comes during High Season when visitors are heading Skye-ward. Here is the most important way station en route. A good doctor from Oneonta, N.Y., praises the viewful **Balmacara**, 6 miles south of *Kyle*. It indeed sounds like a tiptop prescription for P & Q. Thanks, doctor.

The **Newton** in *Nairn*, 30 minutes northeast of Inverness on the Moray Firth, was described to us by a good Scotsman as "a civilized place"—and that it is. Here is a favorite quiet hideaway of prime ministers, industrial colossi, and Very Old Families. Vintage 1850 structure surrounded by fountained green and 35-acre parkland; castle architecture; 2 championship golf courses; tennis courts; trout and salmon fishing; central heating and open peat hearths; numerous lounges; cocktail bar oriented (or is it "occidented"?) toward the most glorious sunsets in the Highlands. One wing plus 2 suites were added; (#17-18 is the most imposing); the cuisine, which we've not sampled, is reportedly sound. Not posh, but deeply satisfying. We like it. The 59-room **Golf View** is bigger, more modest, and less expensive. Waterside situation; also with tennis facilities, also near the links; commendable cookery; attentive service; the best corner units are #106, 207, and 307. Both of these are seasonal only. The **Royal Marine**, with 48 kips, most with private plumbing, is the choice of a friendly leatherneck. We wonder why. It has snapped to attention and looks very trim indeed.

The **Buchanan Arms** at *Drymen*, Stirlingshire, is 5 miles from Loch Lomond, 36 miles from Glasgow, and 50 miles from Edinburgh. Country-house style; tartan carpets, colorful lounge, charming enclosed dining terrace; glass-sheathed rooftop cocktail lounge; 23 spotless rooms, 7 with private bath; cuisine inoffensive to mediocre to downright poor; management by French-born Pierre Bretenoux. Except for the unskilled skilletwork, our only other serious demurrer is the bedchamber décor, in which each piece of furniture seems locked in mortal aesthetic combat with the next. Okay, but no rave.

The turreted **Roman Camp Hotel**, on a 30-acre estate at *Callander* (38 miles due north of Glasgow, above Stirling), was the seventeenth-century hunting lodge of the Dukes of Perth. Library, lounge, magnificent gardens, fascinating tiny Gothic chapel; 16 bedrooms, nearly all with private or connecting bath; 1 eminently relaxable suite. The shocking-pink annex across the drive is less luxurious. Locals love it for its famous tea and scones. Closed in

winter; very good indeed; its charming English Manageress is aptly named
—Miss Perfect. Cheers and salutes.

Ardmay House in *Arrochar*, Dunbartonshire (75 minutes from Glasgow, on Loch Long) is a small Scottish country mansion under the direction of a pair of staunch Scots whom we are eager to meet. Heated, indoor
seawater (not freshwater) swimming pool—a genuine button-popper; home
atmosphere with now aging lochside cabin accommodations; beautiful setting; garden-fresh food from Ardmay Farm; special house blend of Ardmay
Heritage whisky; viewful dining room overlooking the torpedo testing range
(they're unarmed, of course); 18 bedchambers. Write early for space, because most (not all) U.S. nomads adore this unusual haven. The **Arrochar,**
with 33 rooms and baths, bloomed after our loop, but it's on our upcoming
Must Check list.

The **Golden Lion** at *Stirling*, Stirlingshire, 1 hour from Edinburgh, has
long been one of the most popular centers for excursionists to Loch Lomond,
the Trossachs, and the Southern Highlands. This old and famous house now
enjoys an 18-karat, $500,000 replating which includes a 58-room wing,
renewed reception area, restyled dining room, excellent reports now on its
cookery, Rose Bar and Thistle Lounge, revamped entrance, replaced beds,
built-in furniture, 1 late model elevator, and a carpark. This Lion is *really*
roaring—at a cost that might jolt you as a big cat's scratch. Recommended.
The **Sword**, on the outskirts, opens its scabbard for more diners than overnighters. 'Tain't much. About 20 minutes southwest, the 33-room efficiency-
modern **Falkirk Metropolitan** also is available as an en route stopping point.
Chiefly commercial, but suitable for the holiday trade.

The 57-unit **Grant Arms** has marched smartly to the fore at *Grantown-
on-Spey*, an easy hour's drive south from Inverness or Nairn. Boniface
Barry Rosier recently reinforced his garrison with such sterling spirit and
sterling pounds that its position as leader can now be taken for Grant-ed.
White-leather furniture commanding attention in the parade-ground-size
lounge. Winter-garden restaurant reconnoitering the Cromdale Hills; elaborate menu forecasting superior fare; expert service by Maître Rolf. You'll also
discover a licensed snackbar, a sauna, and a beauty parlor. Most of the private
quarters are color-keyed in matching curtains, bedspreads, tablecloths, and
wallpaper. Queen Victoria summed up her visit in 1860 with the notation
"Dinner very fair, all very clean." More than a century later, we can't top
it for candid commentary. Down the pike a way is the **Craiglynne Hotel**—
pure Walden for the nature lover, the sportsman, or the world-weary. Tumbling, salmon-full Spey only a toddle from your doorstep; daily (or overnight,
if you wish) pony trekking across fells and mountain slopes; shooting parties
arranged by Manager David Small; handy to golf courses and Cairngorm ski
slopes (special instructress for tots). Comfortable, eye-appealing public
rooms; regional food among the most savory in Scotland (our latest Haggis
and malt "gravy" were heavenly); hardy tartan bar with peat fire usually
smoldering; friendly, home-style service. **Nethybridge Hotel**, 15 minutes
south along the river at the hamlet of the same name, offers less zing in its
more ancient amenities. But fishermen go into ecstasies over its 6-mile reach
of private Spey. Strictly for dedicated anglers.

A new entry called **Tulchan Lodge** at *Advie* is writing a new deluxe chapter in the Spey River anthology. Shooting and angling rights plus all the comfort and convenience that humanity can divine will cost you close to $1500 per week per person. It is so special that we cannot devote more space to it except to recommend it to the sporting set.

Aviemore, the Inverness-shire ski town scratched out from bare foothills, is blossoming with Cairngorm candidates. This phenomenal site, Great Britain's $8,000,000 center of winter sport, might be a worthwhile skiing target for Britain's Union Jackrabbits and their snow bunnies who can't travel to the Continent for their muscle strain; for Yanks on hickories, however, we think it is not rewarding enough to warrant the transatlantic costs involved. Chairlifts, T-bars, and rope tows web the 4000-foot range; bowling, indoor bathing, curling, trout fishing, and dry-skiing facilities (nylon hills) are on tap; there's a community center complex with a restaurant and a huge theater. First king of the mountain was the Rank-wrought **Coylumbridge Hotel**, christened by the Duke of Edinburgh. Overall accommodations for 250 in "normal" bedchambers and 8-bunk double-decker "lodges"; mock-Swedish décor; restaurant, cafeteria, cocktail lounge, bar, snack corner, and nightclub; game room with slot-car racing; ski shop (rentals available); frequent movies (Rank, natch); enclosed covered swimming pool, ice rink; private fishing lake; horses and golf nearby; supervised nursery for the kiddies. Here's a fascinating experiment. The **High Range** has thrust up with 24 individual cedar-sided chalets and 8 private baths. Attractive sporting lounge with copper-hooded hearth; ski boutique; hairdresser; well maintained and recommendable. The new rambling 100-room **Post House** is a handsome offspring of the Trust Houses Forte group. It is sporting and familial, just the niche for informal fun seekers. The **Strathspey**, with curiously boxlike "tower" architecture, is completely out of harmony with the surrounding landscape, but so much in harmony with the times it has already had to build extra bedchambers. Rooms generally very small; cuisine above average for the region; service extra-kind; future bright and unlimited. The central **Badenoch** is a close carbon-copybook example of success breeding success. We're not so fond of it, but others seem to be. The nearby Spey Valley urbanization contains more dwelling space, but since we are not too fond of the entire range, the above represent what we consider to be the pick of the crop. All plan to remain open year round. Please don't even *think* of scaling these peaks in search of a St. Moritz or Sugarbush, because Aviemore is definitely still a raw, untried towhead among today's winter resorts. Praiseworthy for its valor, but so-so for its value.

Lomond Castle at *Balloch*, on 18 acres of Loch Lomond's shore (30 minutes from Glasgow), is a former private manor house—not a "castle." It's more of a restaurant (and a good one, too) than a hotel. Lovely garden parking-apron and entrance; ivy-sheathed stonework exterior; homey public nookeries; 14 pleasant but unspectacular rooms, with dressing tables cunningly arranged to block the views; only 3 baths. Small, semicircular dining room overlooks the water; the modernized bar shares its pastoral panorama; there's a wildly exciting bowling green for outdoor sportsmen plus water-skiing facilities for residents of polar ice caps. Mildly recommended. Closed end-October to the first week in April. As for the **Loch Lomond Hotel**, it strikes our professional soul as a Chamber of Horrors; personally, we'd rather bed down in a canoe. For most discriminating U.S. travelers, **Lomond Castle** wraps up the bearable lodgings in Balloch.

At *Banff*, the 30-room **Banff Springs** is the newest splasher. It is on a lonely bluff overlooking a magnificent stretch of sea and coast. The modern lines remind us of a suburban grade school; nevertheless its comfort is abundant. A car is a necessity, of course. Farther on, at *Cullen*, the **Seafield Arms** is a cozy nook in a cozy hamlet.

The **Dornoch Hotel** at *Dornoch*, in oddly named Sutherland (odd because Sutherland, with Caithness, is the most northerly tip of the mainland), gorges itself with tour packages. Now it is closed in winter. When we last rattled this doorknob, it was a stark building with many amenities; how long they will endure is a puzzle to us. We haven't yet noched-on-the-door of **Dornoch Castle**, which opened as a resort hotel some time back. This former palace of the Bishops of Caithness, overlooking the Firth, is said to have been attractively converted. Both offer the celebrated facilities of the Royal Dornoch Golf Club, plus loch-or-sea fishing, cold-water swimming, shooting, and deerstalking. Except during Highland Week (mid-May), when they buzz with activity, these are attuned to the nature lover. We hear praiseworthy lipservice concerning the nearby **Tongue**, cheeked in the townlet of the same name. A lady-of-London reader recommends it as a Victorian hunting and fishing retreat.

Pitlochry, Perthshire, offers 6 hotel choices—all routine—but this jumpoff point for the annual Games and for exploring the central Highlands can't be ignored because of its key geographical position. We'd pick the **Green Park**, ½-mile out of the center, as number one. Bankside situation nuzzling the Tummel River and man-made loch; lovely view of footbridge and majestic soaring mountains; yellow mansion with carved green eaves; comfortable but nonpalatial ambiance; the inevitable dressing table mirror slapped in front of almost every bedroom window. A tranquil slumberer which shutters from late October to the New Year. Baronial **Atholl Palace**, a colossal graystone eminence set in a hillside park, is a *pur sang* aristocrat. Since this could be one of the Great Houses of Scotland, we are delighted to hear that it is now being given the maintenance it deserves. Most rooms with private bath; many changes for the good. Everything is on the grand scale, including the tariffs. The next few years will be decisive for this noble blueblood. The now-sprinting **Hydro**, with 68 rooms but only 28 baths, has been making the waves crest in recent months. Enlarged dining salon; lounges redecorated; Saturday night dancing; fresh carpets everywhere; gay wallpaper and brightness sprinkled throughout. We like the corner turret accommodations the most. This Hydro is bubbling with sometimes-misplaced enthusiasm. The midvillage **Fisher's** used to be better for food than for sleeping comforts; however, we hear that there have been extensive renovations recently. **Scotland's**, another bustlebustle hive, also plays host to the mass market. The **Pine Trees** is more of a converted estate than an inn-and-out hotel. It pines away on a lovely 14-acre sweep of Perthshire—with nary a spirit in sight, except perhaps a wistful one (it's bone dry, alas). Please don't miss the chance to dip your hook in Pitlochry's legendary stream—Killiecrankie. Gear and license for the day may be obtained locally for minnow money. And who knows?—you may end up with a 40-lb. salmon! **Atholl Arms**, 7 miles north at *Blair Atholl*, is reportedly a worthy stop; we haven't seen it. The **Tilt,** another one on our futures list, is reported to be even better and more cheerful. **Crieff Hydropathic**, near *Crieff*—also in Perthshire—is said to be good for teen-agers, especially on holidays; inexpensive rates; many activities on tap, including horseback riding, Scottish dancing lessons, and a full program to keep them out of the shrubbery. Popular with oldsters, too.

Cardney House, near *Dunkeld* (Perthshire), is in a very special category. Cmdr. and Mistress MacGregor accept a few paying guests to live family-style in their exquisite home. The Laird, a retired naval officer, and his wife, an active concert singer, are a delightful couple, but they are *not* in the hotel business as such. Deerstalking, fishing, and shooting available on their 2000-acre estate; space for only 20 visitors. Arrange for your stay long in advance, because the MacGregors are often away. Superb for its type. **Dunkeld House** is more conventional in concept. Entrance via an arched stone gate; 1-mile drive through glorious Tay-side forest to the ocher-hued mansion; lawns of Karastan neatness and lush vegetation; 26 bedrooms and 20 baths; cuisine which struck us as no better than routine. As for our welcome, we might have been received with more warmth and common courtesy by our tax auditor than we were by Receptionist Miller and her cohorts. Fair, at best.

If you're dead set on staying in "Sir Walter Scott Country," the **Peebles Hydropathic** at *Peebles* is the logical selection. Sprawling structure with many recent redecorations; vast dining room, in which you're asked to use the same napkin for several successive meals; à la carte restaurant; cool, uninspired bar; dancing nightly. Recreational or health facilities include steam baths, massage parlor, swimming pool, 8 tennis courts, badminton, a pitch-and-putt course, Tweed River fishing, and nearby golf and horseback riding. Manager Pieter van Dijk is trying hard with an unwieldy and cumbersome plant, and his effort shows. Recommended. The sprightlier **Tontine** is younger in spirit. Fresh block of studio-style accommodations facing the river and Newby Uplands; older bedchambers more spacious; cozy, clean, and filled with warmhearted cheer. Manager P. A. Doig gives you a heaping handful for your New Pence. The **Park** is now colorful and inviting; it also has central heating. Both inexpensive, both for travelers younger than typical Hydrophiles, and both very pleasant indeed.

The traditionally front-running **Caledonian** in *Oban*, Argyll, has been taken over by a new group who are making the dust fly. Extensive modernizations are underway at last. Waterfront situation just a toot from the Hebridean ferry slips; old exterior; spacious public rooms; vista-oriented dining salon. Coming up with gratifying speed. The **Great Western**, beautifully perched on the Esplanade, seems to be wavering in the winds of change. Imposing gray-and-white Georgian building; viewful lochside command; glass-fronted terrace and adjoining Blue Sea Horse Bar; several switches in management recently. Here's a clear wait-and-see proposition in our book. The **Park**, nearby, is satisfactory in its amenities. The **Alexandra**, less appealing for comfort, in our opinion, boasts a better down-the-loch panorama; it is older in tone, despite recent refurbishings. The **Lancaster,** on the Esplanade, offers a magnificent vista! It operates all year. So does the **King's Knoll**, with its host Kilter Provost Mr. Spence. The **Columba** and the **Regent,** back at dockside, are for budget voyagers. The **Kings Arms** and the **Palace** used to be the only shelters open when winter winds blew. The latter, a temperance hotel, requires its cellmates to be in their rooms by II P.M. Unless you've been a long-term resident of a well-known address in Leavenworth, Kansas, we don't think you would feel at home in either. Incidentally, if you arrive late and plan to take the ferry to the Hebrides the next morning (very early), go right to the boat and sleep aboard. But PLEASE do us one favor, for sure: Do, do, *do* eat breakfast on the ship rather than in the hotel. The kippers served on these MacBraynes' ferries are easily among the best ever carried out of a smokehouse. What a treat!

Skeabost House, 5 miles out of *Portree*, Isle of Skye, is a lochside country estate converted into a restful nook for sporting or lazy types. Rough shooting, river salmon fishing, trout angling or sea fishing as easily arranged as that soothing whisky and soda in the firelit lounge. Total of 12 rooms and 1 private bath, plus 4 tiny nests and 2 baths in the cottage annex; lovely dining salon; inexpensive but tasteful furnishings; some handsome antiques. We suspect 3-day (or longer) stayers are preferred to overnighters. Soooooooo nice if you aren't looking for fireworks. The **Royal** now seems to be thriving and deserving of its great popularity. We must have a look soon. **Coolin Hills**, also in Portree, has 20 rooms, 2 private baths, and an unhappy mixture of genuine charm and crass modernisms. The **Sligachan** in *Sligachan* is renowned among mountain climbers. Since we spied flocks of slippers under the chairs by the entrance, we guessed most of the guests were high up in the heather. Only 1 of its 32 rooms comes with a private bath; #41 is especially appealing for its sea and mountain view; though we've had only coffee here, we're told the food is the tip of local culinary peaks. Owner Ian Campbell and Manageress Hunter do their competent best to maintain the comfortable air of informality and the homey flavor for which it is so well known. The **Marine Trident** at *Kyleakin* (ferry stop on Inner Sound) is a simple, clean port-o'-call with 25 units. Bright dining-sitting room; no central heating; no private baths; Mr. MacKenzie is the new owner. The **Dunvegan**, across the island, is a charmer. Its décor is simplicity itself, but somehow there's plenty of heart. Kind, thoughtful hosting by Mr. and Mrs. Robertson, who took it over after his retirement from London journalism. Now his Fleet Street pub is his tartan-clad, cellar Skye Bar, where Springbank Whisky, bottled specially for this house, is pleasantly decanted. Other attractions include pony trekking, fishing, sailing, sketching, painting, pottery instruction, and angling courses. Good food; autumnal color everywhere; 18 rooms and 2 private baths; #11 is a viewful double; end-September is the local festival period. The 24-unit **Uig**, in a hamlet called *Uig*, is said to evoke utterances of delight that resemble its name. We'll fly by this Skyeway soon. All these houses operate chiefly during the April-to-October season. *Be sure to have reservations confirmed before going off on a Skye-lark,* since available beds on the island probably total no more than 500.

As for other hostelries, the internationally famous **Marine Hotel** at *North*

Berwick, 20 miles from Edinburgh, is on the march again. This disciplined, taut, bright-eyed Marine—which stood so long at parade rest—is now snapping smartly to attention. **Blenheim House** is so tiny it's almost an afterthought; pleasant décor; savory à la carte selections; perky. The **Open Arms** at *Dirleton*, 3 miles from North Berwick, was only a fingerling, but recently it built up its biceps. On our recent peep, the cookery certainly opened our arms in a gesture of thanks. At *Fort William,* 2/3rds of the way between Inverness and Oban, imposing **Inverlochy Castle** steals not only all the local innkeeping thunder but, to an ever-growing number of devotées, it is now considered one of the brightest lightning bolts in the national welkin. Exquisitely appointed baronial estate surrounded by 50 acres of garden within 500 acres of farmland; only 18 supersumptuous luxury accommodations; skilled skilletry; blue-ribbon price tags; open May through October normally, but they will welcome special parties throughout the year if requests are made. Please reserve way, way, w-a-y in advance. Wonderful. The First-class **Milton** is a solid bet—but not for the victuals say several trippers. We hear the expanded (40 rooms, 40 baths), ranch-style **Croit Anna Motel,** 3 miles out, has become a close contender, with solid comfort and cookery—but we haven't wheeled in since the revampings. The **Alexandra** is much improved now that it has boosted its room count to 94 and spent a packet on modernizations. These are followed by the **Imperial** (for bareback riders only) and the Highland (bus groups galore). Down the pike at *Ballachulish* (ferry crossing), the **Ballachulish** comes up with home-style comfort, waterside dining, and year-round availability. Convenient, but hardly a New York Park Lane. The **Onich**, a few minutes away, offers lochs more color and charm. Stone-and-stucco house that grew, g-r-e-w, and G-R-E-W; 2 cheery bars; tartan-toned dining room with a reputation for savor; 20 well-appointed bedrooms, with hot and cold running water. Not bad. At nearby *Glencoe* (scene of the massacre of Macdonalds by Campbells), the **Kingshouse** is a pleasantly updated coaching inn at the edge of Rannoch Moor. The dining room is outstanding for the vicinity—that is, if the chef isn't a Campbell and you are a Macdonald. The **George & Abbotsford** in *Melrose*, near Galashiels (Roxburgh), drops its lure to fishermen and to scholars hooked on Sir Walter Scott. (He's buried at nearby Dryburgh Abbey.) Rights on the River Tweed to 4 private pools; groups never sheltered; 28 rooms and 7 baths; solid comfort with abundant touches of grace and charm; room #19, with 4 windows and a view of the ancient abbey, is our favorite. Very Scottish; recommended. Don't bother with **Waverley Castle**. It belongs to the Dark Ages, in our opinion. The **Bridge of Orchy Hotel** in *Argyll*, 20 miles from Loch Lomond, is much better now, according to a helpful Canadian reader. He reports friendly service and appealing cuisine. We haven't looked in for a while, so we are grateful for the tip. In the same county and just outside of *Strachur*, we stumbled across a cutie called **Creggans Inn**—and fell in love with its modest country charms. Its proprietor, Sir Fitzroy Maclean, Bt., is operating this honey of a haven for tranquillity seekers. Situation just across the shore road on Loch Fyne; panoramic lounge; public rooms cloaked in chintz; pleasant flower-papered dining salon; adjoining woody cocktail lounge; exceptional cuisine (Mrs. Maclean is the author of 2 best-selling cookbooks);

ingratiating summer veranda; cozy little bar in a rustic corner in the back of the house. Of its 24 rooms and 5 private baths, we're especially fond of #22, a garret-style double. Not posh by any stretch of the dollar or pound, but a peaceful little hermitage away from the cares of the mad, mad world. Recommended for doves. The **Loch Awe** features an awesome command of the lake of the same name. Pleasant baronial public rooms; 50 bedchambers but only 2 baths. Solace is dented almost every night when a bus tour unloads at its portals. Fair, at best. At *Inveraray*, the **Argyll Arms**, with its pier and grassy beach in front, is recommended for summer sojourns. The **George** is tops in winter, followed by **McBrides** at waterside. The **Taynuilt** is famous for its table, but the scenery is niggling and so are the accouterments. At the end of the Crinan Canal beyond Inverary in *Lochgilphead*, the **Cairnbaan** is a chalet-type perch which is a favorite of Alan Cameron, publisher of the widely read *Oban Times*. With his American wife, Jerry, he has trod the globe and knows its best amenities. Small dimensions but comfortable milieu; excellent beds; oil-fired central heating. The crowning glory here is the kitchen. In very few places throughout the British Isles have we witnessed such a vast and varied menu. The wine *carte* is also thoughtfully prepared and generous. Its management is by G. F. D. MacKay, who sports a kilt; the Polish chef is named Mr. Kluger. (Incidentally, the same company also owns the Crinan Hotel at the other end of the Canal; a meal interchange is possible.) Friendly Virgin Islanders write that prices here seem to rise inversely in relation to the sinking service attitudes; they wonder how long this house will remain a good value. We do too and will try to get by soon for another incognito inspection. In *Prestwick*, the seaside **Queen's** now rules the waves. Extensive redecorations and additions; nice stone-and-brick dining room, snug cocktail lounge; units #8 and #9 are good waterfront doubles. Improving. **Towans** (adjacent to the airport) can be recommended only for its main-building accommodations; the newer wing is so basic and shoddy it is downright depressing. The **Golden Eagle**, on the noisy main thoroughfare in town, was razed and then rebuilt. Fair. The proposed $2,100,000 hostelry which ultimately will join the new administration buildings at the airport, was still only a blueprint when we inquired. It will provide 150 units plus a floodlit golf course for sporting insomniacs—just a ground loop from the hangars. **Sundrum Castle Hotel**, 4 miles outside of *Ayr*, has been lightly spruced up to the point where its old and newer elements combine for the barest of comforts. Walls 3 yards thick; shooting, riding, and fishing available; 26 rooms; low bath count; open April to October. A sundrum that's the least humdrum of a sorry lot unless the city-cited **Caledonian** lives up to its advance publicity. This should be a 130-nest haven for modernists and a vitally needed breath of fresh Ayr for the region. The **Station Hotel** in town, with higher tariffs, was an abomination, in our judgment until the Reo Stakis group took it over and modernized it. Now all 36 units come with private bath. This is a reliable chain reaction. The **Savoy Park**, about the same size as Sundrum, boasts a residential situation, similar rents, and passable amenities.

Reports have winged in on several places we haven't yet been able to cover. The **Gordon Arms** at *Fochabers* in Speyside (main road to Inverness or Aberdeen) is more of a First-class pub than a hostelry; a kitchen described as "perfect"; extra-good shooting and fishing; 20 rooms; said to be a gem. The **Clansman** at *Brackla* (10 miles south of Inverness) has recently changed managerial hands. Fine panorama of Loch Ness; 26 bedchambers; paucity of private baths; should be quiet and pleasant. At *Elgin*, the **Eight Acres** reportedly reaps the finest harvest. The simple, country-style **Benleva** at *Drumnadrochit* (Inverness-shire) is the choice of a friendly Massachusetts Guidester; Proprietor Alexander Fox is reputed to be an extra-willing host. Sounds inviting. The late John Hannay, our beloved chum for donkey's years who was one of Britain's greatest shots, keenest sportsmen, and long the Vice-Chairman of London's Savoy Hotels Co. (Claridge's, Savoy, Berkeley, Connaught, etc.), warmly recommended the **Ednam House Hotel** in *Kelso*, about 43 miles southeast of Edinburgh. Former mansion of the Earl of Dudley; capacity of perhaps 35; bedroom, sitting room, 4 meals, radiant underfloor heating, and comfortable amenities; from your window you can watch the salmon leaping; ask for Manager Brooks. If this prestigious expert on innkeeping liked it so much, we'll go along 100%, sight unseen.

While an encouraging start has at last been made, most hotels of *Ayr*, *Wick* (the new 30-room **Mercury Inn** may be an exception), *Thurso*, and *Rothesay* could stand a great deal more refurbishing and modernization. Hundreds of American golfers stay in the previously delineated counties of St. Andrews or Ayr, to give 2 examples, every year—but this doesn't necessarily mean they're pleased by the unimaginative starkness (or downright grimness) which greets them. It's time hoteliers of these centers snapped out of their Old Lace thinking, loosened their purse strings, and offered the public the up-to-the-minute standards any traveler finds as routine in nearly every European country. Scotland is too enchanting a land to show this disappointing face to its friends and guests.

For information on other localities, consult the Scottish Tourist Board, or invest £1-plus-postage in *Where to Stay in Scotland,* their exhaustive annual guide to hotels and boardinghouses.

FOOD　　Never let misguided cookbook editors tell you (1) Scottish fare is heavy and coarse, or (2) Scottish specialties of gourmet rank are sparse. The Scots love the table, and their approach to it bears little resemblance to that of the English. It's a separate food culture—and to us, a more stimulating one.

Although few would deny their vegetables are often lumpy and sodden, the Scots are pastry-mad—and any nation famous for such scrumptious goodies must surely carry this delicate touch into other fields of cookery.

Specialties? No aspiring epicure should miss any of the following Scottish staples—and these are only a few: Haggis (see below); Scotch broth; Cock-a-leekie (chicken and leek soup); roasted or stewed grouse or ptarmigan; fresh trout, salmon, haddock, cod, or sole; Arbroath Smokies; kippers; fried herring in oatmeal batter, or grilled herring with mustard sauce; Findon Haddock (finnan haddie) with poached egg; scones; pancakes; oatcake; shortbread; heather honey; Black Pudding (oatmeal, blood, and seasonings); White Pudding (oatmeal base); Black Bun (chewy with raisins and ginger); marmalade; many, many more.

Meal hours: lunch, 12:30 P.M. to 2 P.M.; tea, 3:30 P.M. to 5 P.M.; dinner, 7

P.M. to 9 P.M. or later in summer, but 6 P.M. to 8 P.M. in winter. Chinese restaurants (you'll find 2 or 3 in almost every city today) usually operate until midnight, providing the only after-theater fare on any Main Street.

§TIP: No visitor can say he knows the real Scotland until he has gone through the Haggis Ceremony—a little gustatory adventure that is an ironclad requisite for every traveler of spirit. This national festival dish of oatmeal, assorted chopped meats, and spices must be specially prepared, but that's easy; just call any good hotel on your itinerary 1 day before you plan to arrive, and ask them to give you a Haggis with your dinner in place of the fish course. Be sure to order hot mashed turnips on the side, and be doubly careful not to forget what the Scots call the "gravy"—straight Scotch whisky sipped between bites, the *only* liquid that complements this fascinating dish. Maybe you'll love it (as we happen to), or maybe you'll loathe it—but we'll guarantee you'll find it sufficiently intriguing for that low-cost gamble of buying it.

RESTAURANTS Nearly every important independent dining place is a member of the British Hotel and Restaurant Association. Thus, it's revealing that accredited restaurants, tearooms, cafés, pubs, oyster bars, and snack bars in the country's 30,405 square miles cover a mere 8½ pages in this organization's directory.

By way of compensation for this, tabs are among the lowest in Britain. Full repasts in the finest establishments seldom exceed $16, with the majority charging tariffs in the $10 range.

When a Scot eats out, he almost automatically heads for a hotel. As a consequence, the Scottish restaurant, while blossoming notably, is still a foot-of-the-table institution. To fill the gap in a labor-short economy, you may find your kilted waiter purring in the purest Castilian, Sicilian, or even—as we discovered on our recent visit—in *Turkish!*

In *Edinburgh*, the "N.B." Grill (dancing on Sat. night) and the Pompadour (dancing nightly except Sun.) at the **Caledonian** are known for their excellent standards of cookery (see "Hotels" for information on "Scottish Nights" at these.) The Ambassadeurs at the **George** turns droves of visiting Americans into calorie-counters. A gargantuan portion of Aberdeen Angus roast beef, baked potato, Yorkshire pudding, and a large tossed salad will set you back surprisingly little per gastronomic ton (our latest tonnage for 2 couldn't have been better). Uncomfortable banquettes; swinging dance band nightly, rendering such hip tunes as "Nola" and "Glowworm"; a favorite with homesick Yankees. All of these serve lunch, but dinner is livelier. The **Café Royal & Oyster Bar** (17 W. Register St.) prides itself on its seafood— and well it should. It is masterfully administered by the George Hotel interests. Upstairs still inviting; public bar updated a while back (shoving it reluctantly into the modern world of the nineteenth century); exquisite cream and gold Crown Room; lower-cost Whip & Saddle paddock; overall capacity of 200 munchers; reservations a must before 10 P.M.; big à la carte menu; medium-high prices; closed Sunday; ask for Mr. Morgan or Mr. Murphy, 2 extragenial hosts. For culinary knowhow, this is one of the nation's best. The **Cavalier** (20 Abercromby Place) parries and thrusts with an elegant French businessman's club atmosphere; there wasn't a Roxanne in sight during our recent lunch. Burgundy-canopied bar and lounge; diminutive dining den with more private quarters farther back; bay windows; gold patterned wallpaper; moss carpeting; royal-blue ceiling trimmed with carved white wood; discreetly placed dueling swords; rolled parchment menus; adept, unobtrusive service. Our Salade Niçoise and Grilled Entrecôte with broccoli were Musketeer-size and fit for Cyrano's palate. Closed Sunday. A sprightly competitor in this mace-and-chain league. **Le Caveau** turns out French cuisine—usually at about $10 per *tête*. *Bon!* The **Doric Tavern** (15-16 Market St.) is on the Left Bank and might be a bit difficult to find; 12 tables with black-and-white-checked cloths; cozy, informal, "family" aura; food superior. The **Epicure** (10 Shandwick Place, around the corner from the Caledonian and next to the Scottish Tourist Board) offers a full bar with coffee lounge adjoining and 30 tables which are more frequently being filled by bus tourists. Our smoked salmon and Haggis were good, but other dishes, especially the vegetables, were a sodden mess. Nevertheless, for sampling, the proprietor will serve a special meal called "MacGregor's Own Scottish Dinner"; just order it by name, and up will come (in very small portions) a reasonable but unspectacular Cock-a-leekie soup, Scotch herring in oatmeal, Haggis with a nip of whisky, Scotch lamb, Scotch trifle, biscuits, Scotch cheese, and coffee (the last from the heathered meadows of Brazil)—all for an amazingly modest tariff. We'd recommend it chiefly to rush-rush travelers who do not have time to linger long enough to taste these Caledonian favorites one by one at other establishments. Okay, but no rave. **Hunter's Tryst** (Oxgangs Rd.), a delightfully cozy former coaching inn, once hosted Scott and Stevenson—and if their roast beef was as good as ours, they must have been regular customers. The name aptly embodies its romantic candlelit mien. A lover's tryst, too. The **Albyn** is the poorest bet we've ever stumbled across in the nation; they just about murdered our simple boiled potatoes, a culinary feat we had hitherto considered impossible; not recommended at all. For snacks or medium-price casual dining in bright-hued, cheerful surroundings, the little La Caravelle in the **"N.B."** Hotel is just the choice; this cozy ship knows how to please its many American friends—especially with the tempting "Scottish specialties" menu. Yum-yum! The Consort in the **Roxburghe** has an attractive theatrical ambiance with tented ceiling, striped textiles, and antlers for lighting fixtures. Food? Getting better, but still lacking finesse and flair. The **Abbotsford**, **Golf**, and **Beehive** are covered below, in "Pubs." The 2 top-floor dining rooms of the popular late-hour **Royale Chimes Casino** (3 Royale Terrace) furnish limited warm nutrients plus an assortment of snacks. The emphasis here is on what's on those groaning boards downstairs—namely, blackjack, chemin de fer, and roulette (service also by a pair of one-armed bandits). If you're looking for further action, check in at the **Carriage Club**. Ask your concierge for introductions. **MacVitties** (6 S. Charles St.) is like 4 department store eateries at one address—but without the department store. Upstairs Quick & Twenty lunch counter supplies honest portions of Haggis, omelets, and assorted grills, plus unlimited rolls and butter for bargain tabs. The adjoining Scottish Fare is a wee bit more formal and specializes in Trout in the Scot's Way (oatmealed). The Charlotte Rooms offer a daily cold buffet and piano lilts for the most discerning MacVittie-philes. The ground-floor self-service (Quick & Ten?) is ideal for shoppers on rollerskates. Hours vary among this quartet; all are shuttered on Sunday.

For elegant dining in the suburbs, please look back at our "Hotels" section for the description of **Houstoun House** at Uphall, which wins our bid as one of the top tables in the British Isles. After this, **Prestonfield House,** 10 minutes from your midtown doorstep, has been the prestige oasis. Here's a beautiful converted estate gentled by somnolent grace, fanning peacocks, and grazing lambs. Fireside bar for friendly persuasions; 4 bedrooms for visitors with slow digestion; large menu and generally excellent cuisine; chic clientele who find it wiser to reserve in advance. Hostess-Owner Mrs. Cunningham is a perfect delight, and Ernest, her earnest maître d'hôtel, will fly to meet your every whim. Open all year for lunch and dinner. Another little gem we've long favored is **Cramond Inn,** 5 miles (20 minutes by #41 bus) from the center, where the River Almond meets the Firth of Forth at *Cramond.* This 300-year-old village tavern and adjoining pub, winner of the nation's Pub of the Year Award in '72 (*1972,* that is!), is the hobby of one of Scotland's best-liked and most cosmopolitan tycoons, Lindsay Gumley; with loving attention he has restored every speck of its charm. Peat fireplace, low beams, dark oak, gay paintings; sweet bar with 12 seats; handsome lounge; cozy atmosphere. Specialties include Steak & Kidney Pie, Chicken & Ham Pie, Welsh Rarebit, lobster, crab, duck, goose, and Gumley-smoked salmon. plain country-style cookery; low tabs; Cramond bottled-and-labeled Burgundies, Bordeaux, and Champagnes imported direct from French vineyards; outstanding wine list. Caution: *8 tables and 25 persons are the dining limit here, so be sure to book your reservation before you go.* It has been much too long since we've unwound the world's cares here, and we're busting with eagerness to get back. The tiny Scandinavian-minded **Howgate Inn** (30 minutes out of the center) is another winner; rich dining on copper service; medium tabs for superior rewards. Swinging—that's how this gate rates inn our book. If you tire of Scots fare, the **House of Chow** is the local mandarin for Oriental chow-downing. The service is superb; the surroundings are decidedly untar-tanesque; the cookery is good by European "Eastern" standards; the prices are modest. Perfect as a change of pace. **Sik-Tek-Fok** also rates as a tong leader among Chinese feederies. **Jamils** is the local shrine for Indian palates. Although the people were kind and the dishes were acceptable, the physical appearance is off-putting. **Baba's,** which we haven't tried, might be better.

Don't forget the previously mentioned Jacobean Feast out at **Dalhousie Courte** (a part of the Castle) in *Bonnyrigg.* Eat with your fingers or a hunting knife; lusty singing by medieval troubadours; free double-decker bus service from Edinburgh Monday through Thursday; find your own way out and back Friday and Saturday; always book ahead. Inclusive banquet for about $14, and no tipping. These robust spectacles have become pretty popular all over—but not with gastronomes.

In *Glasgow*, the Malmaison at the **Central Hotel** is decorated à la Versailles. Separate entrance; 30 tables in 3 sections; high ceilings; suave ambiance; food on the upgrade. Also for hotel dining, the Four Seasons in the **Albany** is tops for style and grace. The Carvery here is also worthy for hungry beefeaters. **Casino-Restaurant Chevalier** (244 Buchanan St.) takes top dollar for late dining among the independents. Mr. Lion guards the door at ground level (say your hall porter sent you); handsome grill up 1-flight; nightly dancing on illuminated glass-paneled floor; active bar; ask for Maître Casavello. Gaming rooms on the 3rd tier with "21," boule, and roulette; friendly atmosphere (the *croupiers* are on a first-name basis with the regulars); rendez-vous of Glasgow's Young Executive Set. **Piccadilly**, another casino, is also a jackpot in the pots and pans department. The "**101**" (Hope St., directly across from the Central) and the **Grosvenor** (Gordon St.) are also popular favorites among the city's gentry; both recommended. We prefer the former for food and the latter for décor. **Guy's** closed its doors and then reopened them; our tummies were too packed to sample this one, though we hear it is once again liked by business and professional people. **Rogano Restaurant & Sea Food Bar** (11 South Exchange Place) is internationally renowned for its fish, crustaceans, and bivalves; not bad. **Ferrari** (10 Sauchiehall St.) offers continental-style dishes in a vaguely Bohemian atmosphere; sorry, but we feel this one has slipped. Finally, the **Whitehall** (51 West Regent St.) has a happily agreeable dining room upstairs and a pub and lunch bar (cold snacks only) below; pleasant, popular, and reasonable. A half-dozen Oriental flowers have blossomed but we were just too chop-chop-ed to pick up a chopstick on our latest round; all stay open late-ish. Outside of town (15 minutes by taxi), the **Lansdown Crescent** shines for the Bentley-Jaguar Set. Stable ambiance around a paving-stone courtyard; à la carte only; Mr. Defazzio is the Italian stablemaster. Although costly, it has thoroughbred tack and feed. Be sure to reserve your stall.

In **Aberdeen**, the famous old **Royal Athenaeum** is today's leader among independents. For local culinary achievement, it would be hard to match the consistently high-quality fare at both the **Station** and the aforementioned **Treetops** hotels. The former, a traditional front-runner, comes up with wood-paneled dining room and clean-lined decorator touches. The latter offers far more flair, modernity, and color; there's a vast menu of international favorites, fish, crustaceans, roasts, and grills; you'll even find a section devoted exclusively to curries. How well managed and well pruned is this Treetops! The **Chivas**, a jigger-size architectural Rob Roy stirred by the Chivas Regal whisky people, also draws praise from most customers. Once-fresh décor that could use another shake or 2; indirect lighting; huge map of Aberdeen to reorient you after that Scotch Mist; superskilled and extra-nice barman. From sip-to-sup, here's a First-class winner. The highly touted **Lengsteng Rooms** was a dismal disappointment to us on our incognito try—especially since seemingly every cab driver, concierge, and elevator operator we met in the city grew almost breathless at the sound of its name. Hard-to-find alley location on Bon-Accord Terrace, off Union St.; single wood-lined room with bar at one end; Swedish light fixtures; rushed service by an insufficient team of waiters; noisy atmosphere; poor wine list. Respectfully, therefore, a "no" —but perhaps it's better now. The **Steak House** is more our sort of stakeout. Rustic décor; many colorful touches. The **Egg & Bacon**, across from the Douglas Hotel, gets our vote for snacks and budget fare. A quartet of Chinese kitchens also have noodled in; the **Bamboo** on Union St. wasn't bad—but it wasn't good, either.

In **Inverness**, the rouge-red dining room of the **Station Hotel** puffs away with the honors. The rebuilt **Caledonian**, however, is a keen competitor. The **Carlton** heads the independent pack; restaurant and adjoining bar 1-flight above street level; not too inspiring. **Full Moon**, a Chinese contender, seemed in partial eclipse when we came dragon in; only so-so.

In **St. Andrews**, the penthouse bar and dining rooms of the **Old Course Hotel** are superb for views, service, and masterly cuisine. The upstairs spread of the **Niblick** often chips in with even better cookery; still, we're hooked on the panorama at our first choice. The **Grange**, an outskirts cottage, is better for atmosphere than for cookery. The **Commodore** is our runner-up. **Cross Keys** is a student pub.

Near **Braemar** (Perthshire), the **Dalmunzie Hotel** on the 6500-acre Spittal O'Glenshee estate has an altitude of 1200 feet, making it Great Britain's highest hostelry. While we haven't yet gotten up here (heavy snows blocked our try), its secluded location and facilities for tennis, golf, fishing, mountaineering, skiing, grouse shooting, and deerstalking sound promising, and its table is reputedly AAA. The **Spittal Hotel**, our alternate that icy day, is on the main route through Devil's Elbow; very satisfactory; no luxury.

In **Braemar**, it's the **Invercauld Arms**; in the **Drumnadrochit** environs, it's the **Lewiston Arms** or, according to a friendly Guidester, the **Benleva**; in **Fortingall**, it's the **Fortingall Hotel**, with its excellent wine list and oustanding cuisine (advance reservations essential); in **Pitlochry**, it's the previously mentioned **Fisher's**, where the food is more appealing than the furnishings; in **Drymen**, it's the previously mentioned **Buchanan Arms**; in **Perth**, it's the **Station Hotel**; in **Stirling**, it's **The Gateway** (Directors David and Mary Christie, themselves veteran travelers and international gourmets, cater to everything from the Argyll and Sutherland Highlanders annual Regimental Ball to the visiting Harlem Globetrotters) and the **Golden Lion** (see "Hotels"); in **Fort William**, it's the **Milton**. The **Open Arms** at **Dirleton** definitely is now worth trying; especially and deservedly popular on Sunday for lunch and dinner.

§TIP: New laws now sanction public drinking in Scotland on Sundays.

NIGHTCLUBS

NIGHTCLUBS   Zero. Weeknight dancing at some of the better hotels, but no cabarets, B-girls, hostesses, or ordinary after-dark action. Pickups must stay on the streets; they're not tolerated in even the less respectable bars.

When the sun goes down in Scotland, you've got your choice of hotel dancing, pub crawling, the handful of casinos in Edinburgh and Glasgow (plus disappointing discothèques, with a large but dreary early-closing nightery in many), or washing your drip-drys 5 or 6 times.

PUBS

PUBS   As in London and Dublin, the pub of yore is rapidly being replaced here by a hybrid that is part saloon and part discothèque. Today it's rare to find a thoroughbred stall where hairy-chested males gather for purposeful drinking. The oldest and best examples, physically unchanged for decades (when you can find one today), are rich with color, flavor, and charm. Routine neighborhood-corner-tavern examples, on the other hand, are often painfully plain and colorless.

Edinburgh offers several enchanting establishments. For the authentic feel of the Old City, the canopied rectangular bar and ornate woodwork of **The Abbotsford** (3 Rose St.) will transport you to mellow Victorian days. You may lunch here or nibble its snacks; noon to 2:30 P.M. and 5 P.M. to 10 P.M., and ask for Henry Kennedy; jam-packed on Saturday night; delightful. Equally beguiling is **The Volunteer Arms** ("Canny Man"), about a 15-minute taxi ride from the center at 237 Morningside Road. Its Public Bar is stuffed with mementos accumulated over nearly a century; on the sides are 3 small lounges, including 1 modernized that clashes with the venerable mood. Downstairs there are even gyrating go-go girls to further dispel the former authenticity. Go between 7 A.M. (if your liver functions at that hour) and 8 P.M.; Saturdays are best; ladies not welcomed at the bar, but a tiptoe peek from the door may satisfy their yen. The **Jolly Carter's** (Thistle St.) has a roughshod appearance in a studied way. **Tankard Lounge** (Rose St.) is a noisy playpen in which we saw many of the Gay Set. The **Chain Pier** (out at Newhaven docks) is a sailors' den, filled with the flotsam and jetsam of many a long voyage. **Scott's** (202 Rose St.) is a family institution with a loyal following. Miss Scott, long custodian of its private pewter mugs, has retired, but its popularity continues. Drinks only; an exceptionally amiable spot. The **Golf Tavern**, 10 minutes out at Brunstfield Links, faces the pitch-and-putt course of one of the world's oldest golfing centers. Sporting clientele; friendly Public Bar and higher-toned Cocktail Bar; separate entrance to the multistoried "Restaurant the 19th" upstairs, where you'll find 2 small rooms with 5 or 6 tables and passable fare. Lunch or beverages from noon to 2:15 P.M.; evenings from 5 P.M. to 10 P.M.; go Saturday, if possible. The **Beehive Inn** (20 Grassmarket) also has full meal service, plus dinner-dancing on Friday and Saturday from 8 P.M. to midnight; not quite the tang of the others, but reasonably amusing. The **Victoria and Albert** (Frederick St.) harks back to the good old days. There's a flavor we like a lot here; we hope it won't be destroyed by the encroachment of modernisms. **Bere & Byte** (across from the Caledonian and the Tourist Office) is a lodge-style snackery which, in our opinion, has matching food, furnishings, and flavor—all blah. The **Laughing Duck** specializes in German beer and atmosbeer.

In *Glasgow*, most pubs are so rough and rugged that you're liable to leave your front teeth with the sweepers. In **Lauder's** on Renfield St., though, you'll not only be safe but you'll probably enjoy it. Ladies shouldn't try it alone.

Aberdeen has the **King's Highway**, an old inn partially and unconvincingly restored in pseudo-Tudor. Ask directions from the hotel porter to this hard-to-find, drinking-for-drinking's-sake establishment.

If you're a Robert Burns devotee try **Poosie Nancy's** at *Mauchline* (60 miles from Edinburgh); it was one of his haunts—and of course he regularly composed songs and tippled in the **Globe Inn** at *Dumfries*, down by the English border.

TAXIS   When you first climb aboard one of Edinburgh's high-button-shoe-era Oxford taxis and see the driver pick up a microphone for broadcasting, it's about as unexpected as stumbling across a color TV on The Ark.

These Oxfords and most other cabs seat 5. You'll pay about $1.50 for the first mile, and there's no supplement for baggage *unless it rides in front with the chauffeur.* If the fare is $1 tip 10¢; if it's from $1 to $2, make it 15¢.

Drivers are generally courteous, friendly, and honest.

TRAINS Since Scotland is crosshatched by branches of the British Railways network, see "Trains" in the section on England. All facilities and equipment are pooled throughout the U.K. The popular Thrift-Tour Tickets and other bargains include the noted Circular Tours of Scotland, and MacBrayne's Steamer Services in the West Highlands and Western Isles. *As previously stated, most of these are sold only in North America.*

AIRLINES British Airways (see our evaluation in "England") and Caledonian, the Scottish International Airline, keep the local skies abuzz.

Prestwick, on the Firth of Clyde about 30 miles south of *Glasgow*, is the international airport. It's known to veteran airline captains as the only pea patch in the U.K. where weather conditions are never completely socked in. The modest facilities at *Edinburgh's* **Turnhouse** Airport are so overstuffed by the deluge of passengers that it brings to mind a size-46 man in a size-32 suit. For domestic traffic, *Glasgow's* **Abbotsinch** terminal has replaced the obsolete Renfrew field.

If you're covering ground in a hurry, BA flies to *Edinburgh*, *Aberdeen*, *Inverness*, *Campbeltown* (Kintyre, opposite North of Ireland), *Wick* (Caithness, on the northern tip), the *Isle of Islay*, the *Isle of Tiree,* the *Orkneys*, the *Shetlands*, and the *Hebrides*. The last time we heard, Glasgow-Edinburgh-London summer services totaled approximately 20 Vanguards a day.

DRINKS For nearly 500 years, distillers all over the civilized world have tried to imitate Scotch whisky. But even with identical ingredients and methods—for reasons which are unclear—no foreign-produced product has ever come within hat-tipping distance of the original.

This Most Seraphic of Solaces of Gentlemen, as Samuel Johnson put it, is classified into 5 types—4 geographical (Highland, Lowland, Islays, and Campbeltowns) and the 5th chemical (grain spirits for processing). Each is as different in flavor as U.S. rye from Canadian rye. North Americans overwhelmingly prefer the Highland category, because its peat-fire-dried malt adds the distinctive smoky tang to which they are accustomed.

After it is matured in casks for at least 3 years (usually 4 or 5), top-secret blending formulae are applied by each producer. The Scotch we drink in the States usually contains from 17 to 45 different whiskies.

The Royal Family of this kingdom are the pure Pot Still Malt runs which are *not* blended but remain in their virgin glow. Many Scots sip theirs with water; personally, we prefer it neat on a cold day; soda is universally considered to be a sacrilege, and ice is also not quite cricket. If you appreciate superb whisky and if you haven't run across it at home, don't leave Scotland without sampling this extraordinary potable. It's fit for the Gods. Tullmore is our favorite; Glenlivet, Glen Grant, and Glengarry are all better known and fine.

Ironically, it's sometimes a chore to find your familiar proprietary brand in the nation of its birth. Too much is exported.

Drambuie, that Isle of Skye nectar, is the national liqueur—proudly. Its base, of course, is Scotch, but the rest, except for mountains of sugar, is a secret. For saving his life during his attempt to regain the throne, Bonnie Prince Charlie gave the Laird of Mackinnon the recipe, and it's been guarded as carefully as the crown jewels since 1745. Don't miss this one either. (Incidentally, we put a bottle in our freezer at home—and it's *twice* as delicious at this cold, cold temperature.) Glayva, the second-string national liqueur, doesn't please our palate as warmly.

Scottish brewers build brass knuckles into many of their products. "Prestonpan's 12-Guinea Ale" (delicately referred to, when ordered, as "a wee heavy" or "a dump") is one of the strongest ales made; it's dark, thinnish, sweetish, and loaded with rubber truncheons as well. The cost is about 50¢ to 60¢, depending on the source—and be sure your hat is on tight!

Finally, in the States a socko TV advertising campaign persuaded us to buy a Caledonian bottled aperitif called Scotsmac which bears the subheading of "Wham's Dram." While we found the taste of this bizarre concoction tolerable but not sufficient to allure us for a second round, a description on its label made us sit straight up in amazement. Boldly it states "(You are drinking) a blend of Scotch malt and Scottish wine." Scottish *wine*? Whazzat again?

McEwan's, the most popular export ale, and Younger's, the leading beer, are on draft in the better pubs. Many Scots prefer mixing various types ("mild and heavy," etc.) rather than drinking them straight.

They love their dram and their glass in this land—and why shouldn't they, considering what they put in them?

§TIP: When you drink with a Scotsman, say "Slans-Jevah!" (phonetic spelling) instead of "Cheers!"—and watch his eyes sparkle with surprise at hearing his traditional Gaelic toast from the lips of a stranger.

THINGS TO SEE   *Edinburgh* is the traditional base for the traveler's Scotland. Nearly every visitor starts or finishes his Scottish explorations here. Turn back to "Cities" for more details.

The lower end of *Loch Lomond* buzzes like a flytrap with excursion buses, trailers, campers, and a zillion tourists in season. *Balloch*, at the southern tip, is euphemistically called the "Henley of Scotland." During the milder months, twice-daily steamer sailings across the loch originate from here; it's a 2½-to 3-hour trip each way, and a lovely one *if* the voracious mob doesn't dampen your pleasure. This region shouldn't be missed—but we strongly urge you to overnight elsewhere.

Provincial Scotland breaks down into 5 main areas: (1) the Trossachs, called the "Rob Roy" and "Lady-of-the-Lake Country" (which, like Lower Loch Lomond, is fast being spoiled by hordes of sightseers), (2) the "Burns Country," dominated by Ayr and Dumfries, (3) The Highlands, lord and master of Scottish grandeur, (4) the "Sir Walter Scott Country," from Edinburgh to the English border, and (5) the Isle of Skye and the Hebrides.

Since most American visitors to the Land of the Heather follow jet-propelled itineraries, we recommend this 2-day trip, with 1-day optional extension. We believe it encompasses the greatest cross section of landscape, history, beauty, and charm on the Scottish map. This 48-hour itinerary allows you to sample every type of terrain and view such major sights as Gleneagles, Loch Ness, Loch Lomond, Ben Nevis, and a score of others. Thousands of pilgrims undertake the bone-wearying haul by motor coach to **Inverness**, back to **Fort William** (3 hours), and then on to **Glasgow** (5 hours), a journey that would make misanthropes of Messrs. M. Polo and F. Magellan. So here's our "Short-Kilt Special"—a wee peek that somehow adds up to more:

Edinburgh is the beginning and end of your loop, and **Inverness**, capital of The Highlands, is your midway stop. One day before departure, if you've never tried a real Scottish Haggis (see "Food"), ask your porter to telephone the Station Hotel in Inverness and arrange that this traditional treat be waiting in place of the fish course of your dinner here; 24-hour notice is generally required, and the cost is perhaps $2.50 per portion. Then on the following morning, leave **Edinburgh** at 8:30 A.M., point the nose of your car toward **Stirling**, and get the lowlands along the Firth of Forth behind you as briskly as you can. At nearby **Doune**, there's an unthinkably ancient fortress-castle, if you're interested, plus a sports- and racing-car collection of the 1920's and '30's—but perhaps you'd rather push on to Gleneagles, Scotland's most fabulous hotel (closed Oct. to mid-Apr.) for a coffee break; this baronial country estate is something special. Then proceed to the Dewar's White Label town, **Perth**, for a friendly apéritif with Joe in the American Bar of the Station Hotel, followed by lunch in the dining room here (the food is the best in the area). Now cut northwest along the river valley through **Pitlochry**, **Blair Atholl**, along glorious **Glengarry**, through **Drumochter Pass** and the **Forest of Atholl** down to **Dalwhinnie**, and onward. (Mid-Apr. to early-Oct., the Pitlochry Festival Theatre draws culture-hungry crowds to its competent performances. Six plays ranging, say, from Shakespeare to Chekhov to Jean Anouilh to Noël Coward are presented Mon. through Sat.) By teatime, **Carrbridge** should loom up, and the simple, fishing-and-sporting Carrbridge Hotel should break out homemade dainties —high tea for about $1.25 per person. (We have been taken to task about this by an Englewood, N.J., Guidestress who tells us her waitress looked blank when asked for the special goodies. Perhaps these tidbits seem ordinary to those who serve them, but to us they were extra-special.) You might want to take in the **Landmark Visitors Center** which capsulizes Highland history and lore within one building and the surrounding grounds. It has its own restaurant plus shops. One hour after you're roadbound again, you'll be in **Inverness**, where the austere but adequate Station Hotel—and your Haggis, we hope!—is waiting.

The second day you take a different, even more spectacular, route. Start no later than 8 A.M. After leaving the "Ceud Mile Failté!" sign (Gaelic for "100,000 Welcomes!") behind at the city limits of Inverness, you loaf along the **Caledonian Canal** until it opens into **Loch Ness**—and as you parallel the 29 miles of this landmark, keep every eye in the car peeled for "Nesse," the fabled Loch Ness Monster! **Loch Lochy** is next—and then, 2 miles before **Spean Bridge**, you'll pass the famed **Commando Monument**, a stirring sight in a stirring location. Now it's time for coffee in the Milton Hotel in **Fort William**. Refreshed, stretching your legs almost in the shadow of Scotland's highest peak, **Ben Nevis**, you next take the bridge crossing at **Ballachulish**, then swoop across the magnificent **Rannoch Moor** and **Black Mount** to stop for lunch at the Royal Hotel in **Tyndrum**—again unimaginative food, but the only spot worth considering in the region. After the turnoff at **Crianlarich**, there's an interesting ride down **Glen Falloch** to the northern tip of **Loch Lomond**, and you now view this loch of song and story in its entirety all the way down to its termination at **Balloch**. Tea at the Buchanan Arms at **Drymen** will then be yours for the asking—and home you go to **Edinburgh**, in time for a well-earned dinner. Less than 400 miles, round trip—with about 4000 miles' worth of scenery!

For the 1-day extension, on the second morning of the trip, instead of driving to the Caledonian Canal, continue west and north from **Inverness** to **Beauly**, **Muir of Ord**, **Garve**, and **Braemore Forest**; turn off on A-832 around **Braemore Lodge**, go through **Dundonnell**, follow along the south shore of **Little Loch Broom** (not to be confused with Loch Broom and Ullapool to the north), and then sweep in a U-shape hook through **Aultbea, Poolewe, Gairloch**, and back along the lovely shores of **Loch Maree** to **Kinlochewe**. Turn southwest on A-890 at **Achnasheen**, and follow it to the turnoff for **Kyle of Lochalsh**, your destination. This is the ferry point for the **Isle of Skye** and its capital, **Portree**. (Fair warning: this routing is well off the beaten tourist-path, and a good part of the roads are secondary and small. But if you want unspoiled rural flavor and untouched scenic magnificence, this is it.) Round-trip bus excursions from **Inverness**, encompassing the enchanting **Isle of Skye**, operate selected days between May and September. On these we flatly guarantee a splendid case of fatigue.

On the third morning, take off early for the **Kyle of Lochalsh** ferry and continue along A-87 through **Dornie**, **Invershiel**, **Cluanie Br. Inn** and **Tomdoun** to **Invergarry**. At **Invergarry**, pick up the route down **Loch Lochy** described in our 2-day tour (to **Spean Bridge**, **Fort William**, **Loch Lomond**, and eventually to **Edinburgh**). The only thing you'll miss is Loch Ness, but honest to goodness, you'll never miss it.

These are fairly stiff hauls—but in 48 or 72 hours, you'll have a better cross section of the real Scotland than most travelers can get in a week.

Oban, a lovely little port, is one of the most convenient jumping-off points for scouting the Hebrides. Day excursions may be made to the islands of **Mull**, **Lismore**, and **Iona**. (The last is the birthplace of Scottish Christianity, where St. Columba preached, and where the first abbey has been restored.) Aboard the pleasant little lugger *King George V,* a tour of these dots can be linked up with a landing at Fort William. Even shorter skims aboard 12-passenger motor launches leave at scheduled intervals from the *Oban Times* slip and glide out to **Seal Island**. There you may stroll the beach and actually pet the animals for which the isle was named. Caledonian Mac-Braynes' Steamer Services also run a comfortable year-round short cruise through both Inner and Outer Hebridean points with the comfortable and cozy *Claymore*. Departures are at 7 A.M. on Monday, Wednesday, and Friday to **Tobermory** (where there's a sunken treasure ship) and then to **Coll**, **Tiree**, and **Barra** (the "Tight Little Island"), arriving in the evening at Loch Boisdale on **South Uist**. You may sleep aboard on the night before casting off. Since this craft accommodates as many as 50 automobiles, it is possible to drive off here (or take a bus) to **North Uist**, **Skye**, and **Kyle**, or to make your return along the same route, arriving at Oban before noon the next day. We think this is a well-rounded, economical, scenic composite for any wayfarer who does not wish to concentrate much time in any one area. The vessel is solid; the comfort is sound (her Deluxe cabins even have showers); the food is hardy and substantial; the price is right. Local wags who thirst for a sea voyage remark that MacBrayne's steamers are all beautifully equipped "with quite a few engines" (local parlance for "bars")—and that they are, mon!

THINGS TO BUY Scotland's best buy and most famous garment is knitwear. Of the scores upon scores of outlets we've perused, not one reaches knee-high to the **St. Andrews Woollen Mill**, adjoining the Old Course Pilmour Links at **St. Andrews**. Two charming, highly knowledgeable brothers, Robert and Raymond Philip, are so in love with their business that visitors are warmly encouraged to watch their 13-stage process of knitting Shetland or Fair Island sweaters or creation of other articles. Shetland pullovers in the $12 bracket; top name cashmeres in the $25 range, dipping for special bargains to $25 or so; tartan travel blankets, $12 to $17; sheepskins, $25; gorgeous double ones for $55; yard goods from $4 to $15; mohair throws at $25 and stoles for $10; many more choices, including cut-priced ends-of-batches, factory seconds, discontinued lines, and a category amusingly dubbed "Frustrated Exports." Personal checks for dollars accepted; free coffee offered; packing and mailing provided; closed on the Good Lord's Day (so is the Old Course). If you're anywhere nearby, *please don't miss it!*

In **Edinburgh**, our first stop is usually at **R. W. Forsyth Ltd**. (Princes St.), to hawkeye the latest tempters of this ranking department store. Export Dept. 1 flight up; ask for Mrs. Oliver; fine cross-section here.

Scottish Handicrafts? Two leaders. Baskets, pottery, knitwear, jewelry, printed textiles, stone carvings—the whole regional gamut is collected and sold by the **Scottish Crafts Centre** (Acheson House, Canongate); you may even have your family crest woven in tapestry here. Miss Ferguson, a charming national product, will assist you. Nonprofit **Highland Home Industries** (94 George St., plus 11 branches throughout the nation) provides the sales outlets for artisans from the Highlands and the Islands. Traditional handwoven tweeds, tartans, rugs, hand-thrown pottery, and allied handicrafts; good quality but fairly expensive; stylings rather routine.

Wm. Anderson & Son (19 George St.), Kilt Makers for the Royal Family and tailors of international fame, are also highly recommended for wearables.

Hamilton & Inches (87 George St.), the leading jeweler, features the striking local Cairngorm stones from about $10 up—a handsome curiosity. Brandy is the best color; you'll pay perhaps $80 for a large brooch in a gold setting. Tempting displays of Edinburgh thistle glass, Scottish silver, and English silver, too. Ian Inches is the expert to consult.

Antiques? In Scotland, most zealots look for Portobello pottery jugs, copper, and brass candlesticks; they're generally considered the prizes. **Henry's** (High St.) is *the* establishment for these and other treasures. **Wildman Brothers** (54 Hanover St.), operated by Sydney and Jack Wildman, is dependable for silver, jewelry, china, and the like.

In *Glasgow*, where there's at least an equal selection but fewer moneyed buyers, it's the branch of the above-mentioned **R. W. Forsyth Ltd.** (Renfield St.) for extra-fine Scottish wearables and generalia, **Frasers** (Buchanan St.) for furnishings and bric-a-brac, **R. G. Lawrie's** for souvenirs, **Moffet Muirhead & Co.** (132 Blythswood St.) for quality antiques, and **McGowans Glasgow Ltd.** (291 Sauchiehall St.) for furniture and potpourri items.

Sporting equipment? **Lillywhites**, the Abercrombie & Fitch counterpart for the British Isles and Europe, has a branch in Edinburgh. **Messrs. Fishing Tackle Ltd.** (35 Belmont St., *Aberdeen*) is now the most celebrated Scottish laird of rods and reels; Mr. Sharpe will be your personal Izaak Walton. The people at **John Dickson & Son** (21 Frederick St.) have been tying flies and freely dispensing sage advice since 1820. Equipment only (no clothes); branches in *Glasgow* and *Aberdeen;* very good indeed. *St. Andrews* is the place for golf clubs; ask the Club pro for the Master Maker.

River Tay pearls? *Perth*'s **A. & G. Cairncross**, the 101% reliable jewelry leader here, offers the best selection of this curiosity. Also found in scattered pockets of Scandinavia, this fresh-water variety is harder than the oriental type; because they're so rare, they are usually graduated. Interesting but expensive: pins start at $23, necklaces at $280, and the finest strand (kept in its vaults) is $4500. They are genuine seed pearls, not to be confused with "seeded" pearls. Tweeds and woolens? **Mairi Macintyre** in *Fort William* (branch on Esplanade in *Oban*) has glorious pastels; if you're within striking distance, don't miss her lovely things. Suède coats and jackets, sheepskin-lined? The well-known **Antartex** factory is on *Loch Lomond*, about 30 minutes from Glasgow; hand-knits available for men and women. *Pitlochry* possibilities? **Macnaughton**'s extra-large stocks of woolen manufactured products—skirts, coats, suits, ties, purses, and more—don't much impress us with their styling or tailoring, but perhaps you'll disagree. But we do think you'll like the unusually effective hand-loomed fabrics, tablemats, hangings, scarves, and other creations of **The Donavourd Hand Weavers**; they're a bit out of town, in a charmingly rebuilt coach house. For handicrafts, try **The Craftsman** at 21 Atholl Road. Antiques? **John Bell & Co.**, on Bridge St. in *Aberdeen*, probably has Scotland's most worthy collection; shudderfully high prices.

Shopping hours: Weekdays, 9 A.M. to 5:30 P.M., except Saturdays, 9 A.M. to 1 P.M. in the higher-class places. Second-class merchants stay open on Saturday afternoon, but close Tuesday afternoon.

THINGS NOT TO BUY Avoid the phony "white heather" peddled as a "rarity" (1 gives you 10 it's doctored), shun the typical tourist claptrap worth about half what is asked for it—and you should have happy shopping in Scotland.

HAIRDRESSERS **Green's**, on George St., is tops in *Edinburgh*, and **Stewart**, on Buchanan St., has them all licked in *Glasgow*—according to informants who still have hair. We're also advised that instead of patronizing most rural hairdressers it's better to tolerate that Wind-blown Shepherdess' Look until your return to the metropolis. For men, Professor Curry at the salon in **R. W. Forsyth Ltd**. (***Edinburgh***) won't cut your ears off (nor *talk* them off, either!).

LOCAL RACKETS   So startlingly unusual in this honest, decent, God-fearing land that when even a mild one pops up the citizenry explode. Some years ago, for instance, a red-hot newspaper hassle raged about (we quote) the "revolting spectacle" of certain "disreputable-looking characters" along the Trossachs highways, who were fast-talking tourists out of an occasional buck. "Dressed in a caricature of Highland clothing," one horrified critic stormed, "and playing the bagpipes badly, these individuals behave like Eastern mendicants!" This violent reaction against such minor chiseling is any traveler's guarantee of the high moral integrity he'll find among these wonderful Scots.

Spain

When our joints begin to creak and our bones grow weary, we're coming back to Spain for good.

Spain is California, Arizona, and Mexico on a huge canvas—with Colorado's towering mountains, Virginia's September sun, and Florida's dazzling blue waters thrown in for good measure. There's a balm, a warmth, a caress to Spain—a special *peace,* somehow; there's a constant feeling of beginning in a never-never land, where worry is part of the world left behind.

The country today is moving irremeably toward democratization, with a bicameral legislature and elected officials gradually replacing appointed ones. The cautious guidance of King Juan Carlos I is manifest in every aspect of social change. He is definitely at the helm of this ship of state—the charming Queen Sofía at his side—successfully navigating between the shoals of absolutism on the right and the agitated waters of an open society on the left. His seamanship so far has been masterful; moreover there are ample reasons to believe that he will continue to garner the confidence of his people and the highest respect of other nations.

Catholicism is the primary religion, but others are practiced openly and in complete freedom. Education is free and compulsory between the ages of 8 and 14. Limited military service is mandatory for able-bodied men. Girls, too, must work in social service for a 6-month period after they are 17 and before they are 35; married women are exempt. In 1967 the right to vote was extended to them for the first time.

Though Spaniards are more and more devoted to soccer these days, the age-old blood sport of bullfighting still draws a throng. This occurs despite the recent falloff in strength and quality of the fighting *toros.* Outlanders often are not so discerning and with tourism soaring and the number of *corridas* more than quadrupled over these boom years, breeders are no longer able to turn out sound, sure-footed animals. April to mid-October is the season; if you go, be sure to sit on the *sombra* (the shady side of the ring), or *sol y sombra* (half and half), not on the *sol* (sunny side). Ticket prices vary according to where you sit in relation to the sun, how close you are to the action, and who's fighting. They *cannot* be purchased far in advance; you'll have to wait until you're there, and then ask your hotel concierge the week of the *corrida*. The better placements are quite expensive.

There were again approximately 30-million visitors to Spain last year—with many Americans in the pack. This should permanently allay any lingering fears of unpleasant tourist conditions there—because *that* many smart U.S. voyagers simply can't be fooled. You'll eat good food, sleep in luxurious hotels, live with every imaginable comfort—and you'll pay less for it than in most other countries of Europe.

King Alfonso the Learned summed up his domain most lucidly and ably. Here's what you'll find today, just as he wrote in the thirteenth century:

"Spain has an overflowing abundance of every good thing . . . fruitful in crops, delicious with fruits, abounding in fish, rich in milk . . . plenteous in deer, well-stocked with horses, securely protected by castles, made glad by good wines, rejoicing in an abundance of bread . . . great wealth of minerals, silver and gold, precious stones and all kinds of marble, salt from land and sea and rock . . . lapis lazuli, ochre, clay, alum . . . sweet with honey and sugar, lighted with wax, seasoned with oil, and gay with saffron . . ."

CITIES AND REGIONS

Madrid, a city of more than 3-million people, is right smack in the middle of the country. It's the perfect hub of the wheel, with spokes radiating in every direction—physically, politically, and socially. In size it ranks just under Philadelphia; in temperature, hotels, food, and gracious living, it's hard to find an equal in Europe. May and October are the best months; midwinter is sometimes surprisingly cold, due to the city's situation and altitude. Although the Government moves to San Sebastián during the summer and many of the most interesting attractions shut down between August 1 and September 15, it's uncomfortably hot for only about 2 weeks per annum—and many hotels are now fully or at least partially air-conditioned. Increasing air pollution, however, is a menace that authorities are now trying to control. On a muggy afternoon your eyes may smart, but when the wind blows and the morning skies are a cornflower blue, they might tear in awe at Spain's glittering metropolitan diadem. We like Madrid at *any* time; it's a constant wonder and delight. To bypass it would be like visiting France without seeing Paris.

Barcelona, the second most densely populated city in the world, is second in importance—a point which any good Catalan will heatedly challenge. It's on the Mediterranean coast, northeast of Madrid, about 100 miles from the Pyrenees, sitting on a rich plain between 2 rivers and 2 towering mountains. The transportation links and the convenient situation make it a natural springboard for travel either way along the Spanish coast, up to the high hills, over to the Balearic Islands, or across the sea to the Riviera, Italy, and North Africa. Catalans feel a very special identity with their metropolis, which proudly produces so much of the nation's wealth. Artistic activities abound; although its cultural attractions are numerous (with contrasting wonders from the unthinkably ancient cathedral to the artist-endowed Picasso Museum to the fairyland of Gaudi's fantastically vast unfinished Temple), it conducts business in American style and is a huge commercial port. One detriment is the throat-rasping smog from its booming industries that occasionally blankets the metropolis. The sudden and welcome proliferation of new hotels, restaurants, and other up-to-date facilities to shove into the background the generally weary and worn ones has already totally changed its complexion vis-a-vis the comforts of the visitor. Now it has become a dramatically more desirable touristic target.

San Sebastián, the summer capital, is an Iberian Coney Island. Originally the Roman port of Easo, it has been Spain's most jam-packed bathing resort for centuries. Winning setting, with its semicircular bay flanked by twin mountains and backed by green hills; hotels and restaurants disappointingly substandard but improving; practically no ancient buildings or antiquities of note. Golf and horse racing at Lasarte; tennis at Ondarreta; plenty of jai alai, yachting, motor racing, and other sports; site of one of Europe's 4 most important annual Film Festivals. The City Fathers are fighting valiantly to lift the nationwide ban on gambling; they're anxious to build a casino which would be limited to patronage by foreigners, and which would rival the installation at neighboring Biarritz. The 66-foot-wide bridge between the respective Spanish and French border stations of Irún and Hendzye eases the formerly tortuous access from the north. La Concha ("The Seashell"), the world-famous beach, is imposingly attractive in its natural state—but from July to September it's worse than Sunday afternoon at Coney Island. Although its people are hospitable and ingratiating, it's such a disappointing travel target for most Americans that we'd advise skipping it.

Valencia has a special charm—but it's also not a favorite with most foreign travelers. Like Barcelona, it's so busy and so bustling that the atmosphere is more impersonal than in various cities of the interior—and, added to this, tourist facilities are meager. The city prefers to be an agricultural and shipping center. Its lifeline, water, is held in such reverence that the 1000-year-old Arab ceremony of electing a tribunal to regulate the flow to the orchards is still practiced and still recognized under the Spanish legal system. (You can see the judges in session every Thursday outside the Cathedral door.) There's a low-grade beach resort, 2 good hotels, 1 good nightclub, and a few points of antiquarian interest. But the twin high spots of the year—the famous *Fallas* fiesta on St. Joseph's Day (mid-Mar.) and the magnificent Battle of the Flowers (early Aug.)—shouldn't be missed by any U.S. vacationer who is footloose in Spain during these times; they both make the Carnival of Nice a tawdry, tinny, mechanical show in comparison. Be sure to arrange sleeping accommodations beforehand, however.

Seville is far more glorious, with its wealth of archeology and art. There are churches, convents, tombs, museums, and galleries on practically every block; orange trees line the winding streets, and in the parks are snow-white pigeons which will light on the head, shoulders, and arms of any traveler who'll spend 2¢ for birdseed. The *Feria,* held soon after Holy Week, is the biggest, most frenzied, most colorful traditional celebration in Spain. Every soul in town pulls out his regional dress from the mothballs, and for 144 dizzy hours all work is forgotten. This event alone is worth a special trip to Europe —but reserve your space months in advance, because every pallet in the district is sought after by the hordes of outside visitors.

Granada is lovely. In addition to the world-famous Alhambra and the Generalife, here's the International Command Post of the gypsies—many of whom live in comfortably furnished, electrically lit caves. Be careful of your money and personal possessions in this center; Spaniards won't touch 'em, but gypsies are among the most light-fingered gentry in the world.

Málaga, during the summer, is hot, crowded, and unimpressive—but the winter temperatures are so mild, comparatively speaking, that many sunworshipers flock down from the North to bask (or sometimes to shiver!) in its suburbs along the Costa del Sol or to hop the luxury *Ibn Batouta* ferry for a 5¼-hour trip to Tangier in Morocco. Its aeronautical welcome is much warmer now that the adobe terminal hut has been replaced by a modern building and control tower. There's also a slightly sunnier note in the hotel and restaurant scene. Nice setting at the foot of the mountain range, on the sea—but that's about all, touristically.

Cádiz has the drab commercialism of a port town. Its citizens spring from such mixed stock that they hardly look Spanish, as a group; the physical and psychological contrasts with neighboring Seville couldn't be broader or more striking. No fancy hotels, restaurants, or shops; not recommended for more than a passing visit.

Jerez da la Frontera, home of sherry and Iberian-style "cognac" (in Spanish, *coñac),* revolves around these palatable products to the exclusion of all other interests. Make the fascinating tour of one of the major *bodegas* (Gonzalez Byass, Terry, Pedro Domecq, Harvey's, Sandemann, Martin, or Williams) which extend all the way down to the oceanside village of **Puerto de Santa María** to see how these potables are produced; all are open from II A.M. to 2 P.M. daily, all are free, and all will load you with such samples of their wares that you'll be as stiff as a board by high noon. Charming little country town, with lots of color.

Córdoba beguiles us more on each successive visit—and we're darned if we can figure out why, because it's practically changeless. Its colossal Mezquita (1000-year-old mosque which is now the Cathedral) is one of the show places of the nation; its Romero de Torres collection (the twentieth-century eccentric who painted prostitutes as saints) is intriguing; its narrow streets in the Old Town and ghetto have color and charm. About 5 miles out, the fabulous ruins of the Medina Azahara are breathtaking; this palace (almost a mile long and more than a ½-mile wide) was built at the same time as the Mezquita, by the Caliph of Córdoba. The nearby Monasterio San Jerónimo (vintage 1405), with its enchanting primitive cloister, is also worth a visit; try to talk your way into its privately owned precincts. We did—and we loved it. Now we find it a rewarding stop—and we hope you will too.

Algeciras, traditional gateway to troubled Gibraltar, is a smaller Cádiz. The dusty, dreary shipping atmosphere of the town itself, which used to depress most voyagers, is gradually fading. In its environs, no fewer than 3 major tourist centers are either already perking or are preparing to lure merrymakers with sun, sea, sand, and salubrious *saludos.* There's also a hydrofoil link to Tangier (2¼ hours), which further enhances holiday rewards.

The island of **Mallorca** (Majorca), off Barcelona and Valencia in the sapphire Mediterranean, is so special that we give it its own chapter earlier in this book.

The **Costa del Sol** ("Sunny Coast"), with **Torremolinos**, **Marbella**, **El Rodeo** and other resort settlements strung along the 106-mile strip of seacoast on the Algeciras–Estepona–Málaga road, is geared to package tourism as well as to independent voyagers. The streets of Torremolinos and neighboring Málaga swarm in High Season with nonwriting writers, nonpainting painters, everyday sun-and-funseekers, and expatriates of a dozen nationalities. Contrary to her neighbors, Marbella is much more select and sedate; the sea bathing is excellent, the golf courses are perfect, and the atmosphere is sportingly chic. Rampant new construction in all categories from Deluxe to budget level has transformed hamlets, villages, and entire areas into an Iberian version of a Florida land boom. With so many hostelries writhing for attention, the newest trend is the low-cost apartment dwelling for 1-week-or-longer residence. Even some of the established houses have converted to this format, since taxes are lower and service standards are minimal. For do-it-yourself holidaymakers, however, this householding gimmick can represent a sizable saving in the Peseta Department. The region's nonstop activity will provide for the traveler a mélange of smart-to-poor hotels, restaurants, and other attractions. Definitely worth a visit provided you don't buck the mob from June to mid-September.

The **Costa Brava** ("Rugged Coast"), that rugged stretch of mountains, cliffs, and bays between Barcelona and the French border, has undergone a shocking transition. Here is today's story, and it is grim: (1) Thundering herds flood across its borders in bargain-basement charter groups to despoil its beautiful landscape. (2) With the exception of the justly celebrated Hostal de la Gavina at **S'Agaro** and 3 or 4 other stops, the hotels are miserable. In addition, only a handful are situated on scenic sites. Some sections of the "Rugged Coast" are more panoramic and breathtaking than the Amalfi Drive, but there are no lodgings on them. (3) Although a number of fine new trunk highways have materialized, the vast majority of the roads are still very narrow and serpentine. Loaded with buses, cars, trailers, motorbikes, scooters, campers, and heaven knows what else, they remain a single gigantic traffic snarl during the holiday months. Personally, we find so little of true value here that we have decided to peel this Spanish onion right off our research lists.

The **Canary Islands** have taken the same downward path. The climate is gloriously benign; most of the handsome population offer hearts and smiles of rare warmth and beauty; some of the scenic vignettes are magnificently spectacular. It so distresses us to see them ruined that we never wish to return. Therefore, please accept our apologies that further information about this erstwhile semitropical paradise must be sought elsewhere. To us, these islands have slid so far down the drain in terms of travel pleasure that today we do not consider them worth reporting in these pages.

The **Costa Blanca** ("White Coast"), the fancy touristic name for the coastline between Alicante and Valencia, is now being popularized to handle the overflow from the overcrowded Costa Brava. Still primitive in general, but the building spree has already added dramatically to its carbon-copy aspirations to duplicate its neighbor. To its credit, it has not quite achieved this goal —but another few seasons of gigantismic growth should make the mutation complete.

Toledo, **Segovia**, **El Escorial**, and excursion points from Madrid are covered in "Things to See."

Other favorites are **Sitges**, **Tarragona**, **Santander**, **Corunna** (La Coruña), **Salamanca**, **Valladolid**, and **Santiago de Compostela**. For further details on any of these, see the Spanish Tourist Office.

MONEY AND PRICES   The currency units are the céntimo and the peseta. The white metal céntimos are marked 10 (due for withdrawal soon) and 50; since 100 céntimos equal 1 peseta, consider them chicken feed without any real purchasing or tipping value. The peseta, currently about 68 to the dollar, has been minted in a coin series of 1 (yellow), 2½ (yellow), 5, 25, and 50 (all of alloy). A 100-peseta silver piece recently made its debut, but collectors are gobbling it up so fast you probably won't even see one. A new coin series with the visage of King Juan Carlos is due to appear soon. In bills, the present peseta denominations are 100, 500, and 1000—the last being worth only about $17.25, which is a curiously low maximum as a nation's exchange unit. Five pesetas are traditionally known as 1 "duro" ("hard"); in the hinterland, they still speak in terms of 3 duros or 10 duros, for example, instead of 15 pesetas or 50 pesetas.

In the cities Spain is still gratifyingly moderate by U.S. living-cost yardsticks; in the country, most prices are low enough to bring balm to your budgeting soul. If you stay in a top metropolitan hostelry, you'll pay about from $29 to $44 for a double room without meals; your dinner in a top restaurant should cost you from $13 to $23, including wines. If you strike out for the rural districts, you'll find excellent double accommodations with meals for as little as $15 apiece, and fine regional cuisine for $5 per person.

As for cashing personal checks where you aren't known, they are the kiss of death.

The traveler may now legally enter Spain with 50-thousand pesetas in local bank notes and an unlimited amount of foreign currency. On leaving, he may not take out more than 3000 pesetas.

ATTITUDE TOWARD TOURISTS   *Come*—in ones, twos, or millions! The economy is now so highly geared toward visitors that it would be in serious trouble without them. Minister of Information and Tourism, the dynamic, spirited Excmo. Sr. Don Leon Herrera Esteban, is handling an enormous responsibility with splendid results both for his nation and you, the guest in his land.

The **Spanish National Tourist Office** (Dirección General de Empresas y Actividades Turísticas) has its headquarters at Paseo del Generalísimo 39 and its Information office at Medinaceli 2 in **Madrid**. Much has been accomplished to ease the lot of the traveler.

The outstanding triumph has been the construction and operation of approximately 83 government-sponsored inns (*paradores,* hostels, mountain lodges, etc.)—one of the most farsighted touristic ventures in Europe. Their popularity is so enormous that the expansion program has to be pepped up. As a result, this year's adventurer will have a bevy of new ones at his disposal. These are practical, plain, clean hotels (not Deluxe), uniquely Spanish in design and furnishings, set up noncompetitively with private industry to open virgin tourist areas. Some of them are remodeled castles. The basic rate runs from about $6.50 to $15 per person, exclusive of meals, service, taxes, and extras. Visit or write to the Tourist office for a list of these colorful and reasonably priced vacation centers; they will handle your arrangements.

In the United States, there are official information branches in **New York** and **Chicago**. They are also in most European capitals, in Latin America, and in North Africa.

CUSTOMS AND IMMIGRATION   Always noisy, often slow, and sometimes extremely disorganized—but 99½% of the time, pleasant in their welcome-and-Godspeed to their guests. If anything, Spain is suffering only from the penalty of unbelievable success. Tourism has burgeoned so unpredictably and so outstripped even the wildest estimates that no matter how many facilities were constructed, they would be almost doomed to obsolescence before completion. The Madrid International Airport at Barajas and the Barcelona International Airport function in spectacularly modern buildings. In High Season, both are still packed tighter than a jar of Spanish olives. A new jetport, which would handle only international traffic, is being considered to relieve congestion at the former, but it's at least 3 years (or 12-million tourists) away. The fresh San Sebastián, Mallorca, and Málaga (incorrectly called "Torremolinos") airports also are modern but bursting in season. Studies are already under way on how all of these newcomers can be expanded or further zones be opened to siphon off some of the air pressure.

The officials at the counters are soldiers on detached service from the army, and their reception is usually bustling but kind. The Customs Chiefs at each post, on the other hand, are university graduates who have then been trained at a special government school. They are educated, highly intelligent gentlemen who generally couldn't be more helpful to the traveler. (At Son San Juan Airport and the Palma harbor in Mallorca, for example, the sunniness of Spain is reflected in the warm and gentle kindness of Don Juan Sard, Don Fernando de Diego Granda, Don Rafael Tauler, Don Miguel Suau, Don José Péréz, Don José Lopez, Don Sebastián Llobera, and Don Angel Gómez Torregrosa.) By choice, oddly enough, they prefer to alternate on straight 24-hour shifts without once closing their eyes! If you should run into trouble, don't try to settle it with the soldier who inspects your possessions; go straight to the top, where you should find a courteous, genial, and alert reception.

Cigarettes (2 cartons) and currency are the primary concern; approximately ½ pint of spirits and 1 "fifth" of wine are the official limits, but 2 *opened* bottles of whisky or hard liquor will usually pass. *Technically,* you'll be allowed the following quantities of the following items: 1 "still" camera with accessories and a maximum of either 5 *(sic!)* rolls of unexposed film or 12 plateholders; 1 portable noncommercial-type movie camera, up to 16 mm, with accessories and a maximum of 5 reels of unexposed film; 1 portable radio, not more than 13 lbs. in weight; 1 portable record player, with a maximum of 10 records; 1 portable musical instrument; 1 portable sound recorder; 1 portable typewriter under 17½ lbs. in weight; 1 pair of binoculars; various types of sporting equipment, including 2 shotguns and 300 cartridges of the same caliber (returnable bond and temporary import license required); 1 bicycle if used as transportation by the traveler (particulars to be entered in the passport); ½ pint of toilet water and a small quantity of perfume. As we emphasize above, these are the *legal* authorizations; in practice, you—and they—are likely to wind up in the deepest grasses of Left Field. And speaking of grass, *remember, the Spanish authorities are particularly harsh on anyone found with drugs in his or her possession—from hash all the way up (or down) to horse.* On some "permissible" things, don't be surprised if you not only fill out forms until the following Tuesday midnight, but also post a substantial bond which may be collected only on departure from the country. Any slick new American gadget is given special scrutiny, whether it's a light meter that doubles as a potato peeler or a bobby pin that plays "God Bless America"; if they suspect it's for business rather than for personal use, you're right on the griddle beside the pork *salchichas.* Contraceptive devices, Tampax-type supplies, and "the pill" are now openly sold.

Let none of this discourage you. Par for the course is a quick glance at 1 bag and automatic clearance of the others. Treat them right and they'll return your confidence.

Railway Customs officials are often more exacting than those at airports. Call the nearest branch of the Spanish State Tourist Office ("Turismo") in emergencies.

§TIP: *Never have yourself mailed any package of new articles from another country to Spain—and never send any gift to a Spanish friend without finding out first what the Customs duties will cost him.* The levy can be so wickedly stunning that it could easily turn *amigo* into *enemigo,* with you the innocent foe. This legal larceny creates bitter disgust in the minds of visitors who are hooked, and it's a scandal which the Government should clean up at once.

HOTELS For far more comprehensive information on certain hostelries than space limitations permit here, interested travelers are referred to the annually revised *Fielding's Selected Favorites: Hotels and Inns, Europe* by our travel-smitten son, Dodge Temple Fielding. The latest edition, in which a total of 300-odd favored possibilities were picked from the 4000-plus personally inspected, will be at your bookstore early this year.

In **Madrid**, they're wonderful: Plush, luxurious, clean, and with superb facilities and service. From a lodgings bottleneck a few years ago so many hotels have sprouted that the capital is now seriously overbuilt in its capacity for visitors. The boom season, which used to be 10 months, has been reduced to 6 or less. With such excessive competition, only the Ritz and a handful of other special ones are flourishing financially.

In the burgeoning array of newcomers which opened after our latest rounds or which may be flowering by the time you are ready for departure are Juan

Gaspart's 300-room, 5-star **Miguelangel** facing the Castellana, the 4-star, ultramodernistic **Los Galgos,** which is about the same size, the similar-in-tone **Alcazar** with 225 units, an 800-room Deluxe colossus on Calle O'Donnell, and another 300-roomer in the same category which is an offshoot of the hugely successful Plaza (see below). When these have had a chance to mature, we will put them into our rankings, but for the moment the following delineation comprises our current, up-to-the-minute capital classification.

The sparkling midcity **Villa Magna** is our *número uno* choice. Because this 5-star monument to Magna-ficence is the hobby of a banker, the expansiveness of the site, plus the plethora of luxury extras, ordinarily would be enough to give nightmares to any cost accountant in this Make-Every-Penny-Say-Uncle Era. Extravagant apron of garden fronting its set-back entrance; balconied 9-story structure of polished marble, glass, and stainless steel; breathtaking Carlos IV lobby by world-famous Jansen of Paris; opulent dining salon and Rue Royale restaurant; Mayfair Bar in English motif plus burgundy-banquetted Bonbonierre imbibery; aristocratic lounge; shops, hairdresser, and secretarial services; sauna; 350-car subterranean garage. All feathernests amply proportioned; tasteful textures of beige, blue, and seafoam green; comfortable cradles; 2 large easy chairs; double-glazed windows; summer and winter individual thermostats; radio and TV; compartmented baths with twin basins. Concierges Ovejero and Pacheco are tops in their trade. A bouquet to Director Antonio Lopera, formerly of the Ritz, later of Seville's Alfonso XIII, and always a friend to the traveler. A pearl that we recommend with cheers.

The patrician **Ritz** is quiet, elegant, smallish, and expensive. A $1,500,000 pepup and refreshening has manifested itself in bathroom modernizations, better closets, reupholstered furnishings, new curtains, carpeting, and bushels of behind-the-scenes alterations for Deluxe comfort. All of this was effected without disturbing the hotel's unique character. Managerial reins are in the expert hands of the Gran Señor of Spanish innkeeping, Don Alfonso Font, who is also Director of the Palace (see below). He, in our opinion, is one of the 3 greatest hotel men in the world—and he was elected first president of the 2400-member Spanish Hotel Association. The Maestro is ably assisted here by virtuoso Pablo Kessler. You'll find one of the most willing staffs on the Continent. They take the Ritz tradition so much to heart, however, that you shouldn't be surprised if they look you over for 2 or 3 days before admitting you to the family circle. If price is no object, Suite #111-112 is a dream. At least ¾ths of the building has now been air-conditioned and more is on the way. For the traveler who likes topflight living in luxurious surroundings, the Ritz is extraordinary.

The **Palace**, also superb, is one of Europe's largest hotels, with 800 rooms and 800 baths; the entire house is air-conditioned; most of the bathrooms have individual telephone, shower, and tub. The public rooms are spacious; the bar is famous as the most popular meeting place in the capital; there are all the small touches that give the guest maximum comfort and pleasure. Handsome entrance and baggage area; lobby touched up and 2 late-model elevators installed; gorgeous handwoven carpeting; gastronomy in the Grill far better than average; dining room cuisine fair; garage; telephone service still spotty but improving (this headache is due largely to the city exchange, not so much to the hotel); now completed $4,000,000 revivification program—and does it show! Not another Waldorf, New Yorker, or mass-production mecca; despite its size, the atmosphere is unfrenzied and the attention is individual. For the American voyager of taste, here is one of the leading Spanish-type hotels in Spain.

The gleaming white, 14-story, 250-room **Meliá Madrid** is the evolutionary zenith of Spain's most ubiquitous tour tycoon, bus operator, and private innkeeper. Don Pepe (José Meliá's nickname among his awe-struck minions) has added to the Madrid scene this gem so splendid it dazzles as a crown jewel of his mighty complex. The site, a few blocks beyond the Plaza Hotel in the cardiac zone of the capital's commerce center, is somewhat remote but not too hampering. Spacious lobby cleverly architected to kindle warmth in an essentially cool milieu; Don Pepe Grill up 1-flight, bigger, impersonal, less ingratiating Princesa Restaurant in the same level; Ebano ("Ebony") Bar with dimensions too open for intimacy; adjoining lounge; Bing-Bong Night Club (touted by the management as "A banging place in a booming town!"), with discothèque spinnings from 7:30 P.M. to 9:30 P.M. and live dance music from 10:30 P.M. to 3:30 A.M. It is 100% air-conditioned; there are other goodies galore. Rooms comparatively commodious, all with TV, refrigerator, piped music, tricky-but-practical luggage racks, wall-to-wall carpeting, and handsome fabrics; baths small but efficient; showers over nonskid tubs. The 3rd floor is devoted to a quintet of Deluxe suites, with a hand-picked staff to coddle their occupants; these are lovely. The "Gold Apartment," #303—a creation of world-famous Master Decorator Rafael García—is one of the most exquisitely conceived, strikingly beautiful, and delightfully comfortable hotel accommodations in which we have ever stayed. The cuisine is excellent; the welcome is friendly; the concierge and his staff are affable and willing. For standardized convenience, modern urbanity, and luxurious amenities in surroundings of contemporary good taste, this metropolitan stalwart shines on the Iberian Olympus.

The **Wellington** is fashionably moored on the fringes of sylvan Retiro Park. Largely because of the tireless efforts of Proprietor Baltasar Iban Valdés and General Manager José (Pepe) Losada, here is a challenger that comes on stronger and stronger *año* after *año*. Recently, this Wellington booted out virtually every wall, pipe, and switch on the premises and rebuilt 140 bedchambers, adding 7 suites with kitchenette; all 330 units now have air conditioning, taped music, TV, hand-stitched broadlooms, and attractive *seregrafía* tiles in the baths; dive into one facing the pool if you're looking for a springboard to dreamland. Lettuce-crisp dining room with superior fare and matching service; popular, wood-paneled El Fogón grill; banquet hall; terrace-topped swimmery (rare in Madrid); efficient phone exchange; 2 sprightly elevators; enlarged 100-car garage. A barrage of E's for efficiency, energy, élan, and esprit to this contender.

The **IFA Suite Hotel**, close by the halls of ivy in Madrid's University District, received its 5-star diploma in '71. Heavily marbled, graciously tapestried lobby and lounge; modish Valle Park restaurant; poolside meals in summer; El Faro bar; sinfully, nay, devilishly comfortable sauna; conference facilities; art gallery; souvenir shop. As its name foretells, all 135 units are single and double suites; all contain divans, TVs, carpeting, and well-outfitted marble baths with phones (some too with those dinky "telephone" showers); 4th-floor singles feature huge terraces. A sweet suitery in the suburbs with a distinction that's far from academic.

The 15-story, 1000-room **Meliá Castilla**, one of the most massive shelters abroad, is the aforementioned Don Pepe's grandest opus to date. This '70-vintage whopper is an "aparthotel" which he runs as a concession for a multitude of investors. We think he should have called it the Meliá Bunyan. Vast convention facilities for assembly of 2500 at a single roundup; kitchen capacity of 10-thousand hot meals per day (well, *warm* anyway); 3-level brick-toned Hidalgo Grill plus a cafeteria; attractive La Marisqueria seafood nook; everything under the sun for the wanderer, especially if he and she are business oriented. Despite efforts to the contrary, the lobby, the public rooms, and the ambiance are as *intime* as Grand Central Station. Upstairs, the pinched "efficiency" bedchambers each offer radio, TV, and an elfin bath. This monster is frankly designed and operated more and more for the conventioneer—and not the lavishly open-pursed one, either. Although it well accomplished what it has set out to do, many independent travelers such as we are put off by the chill factor which is ineradicable in any establishment of this size.

The sumptuous **Monte Real** is in a special category because of its outskirts situation at Calle Arroyo del Fresno 1—15 minutes out by taxi and just a potent mashie shot from Generalísimo Franco's country estate, El Pardo. Tennis courts; crescent-shape swimming pool; summer bar in Philippine motif; garden-bowered with bouquets of color; nearby golf course. Within, you'll find a pale-blue Frenchy dining room, a downstairs Grill with Signac and Matisse paintings (other oils by Murillo, Dali, and a trove of Impressionists displayed elsewhere), a nightclub, and other appurtenances. Recently enlarged; pleasant accommodations, all with radio, private terrace, and navel-deep wall-to-wall carpeting; duplex units with 2 bathrooms the premium retreats. The cuisine on our latest stopover was average, not extraordinary. For any well-capitalized traveler who wishes to avoid the cacophonous throb of big-city jitters, this is an elegant answer to a whisper-soft prayer.

The **Castellana**, formerly a Hilton ward, has been extensively regroomed and reattired since its recent adoption by Great Britain's Grand Metropolitan chain. Many bedchambers in the process of restyling or spankingly refreshened; *Intima* taper-lit restaurant with king-size buffet Saturday nights; adjoining Coffee Shop (7 A.M. to midnight) now perking; grill merged with ballroom. The brashness of its early-day decoration has now been toned down; the Patio Jardin, with its guitar strummings nightly, has been face-lifted for summer-izations. It boasts 2 popular bars, the rather high-priced Oxeito nook for *marisco* niblets from noon to midnight, new management by Miguel Ordóñez, who trained at London's Savoy, a competent concierge in Chief Alfredo Molero or his Assistant Jose de la Beompa, well-schooled reception people, and some of the finest switchboard operators in Spain. You'll also find an 80-car garage and other supplementary facilities. Moving up very smartly.

The suave, stainless-steel-and-marble-fronted, 200-room **Luz Palacio** stands 9 proud stories above a residential block of the Paseo de la Castellana. Totally air-conditioned; effective, gracious entrance and lobby; cleverly illuminated adjoining bar, cacophonous at cocktail-time; attractive food displays; evening dancing in the spacious yellow-hued dining room; careful maintenance once again, following a temporary bout with housemaid's knee; a pervading atmosphere of soft, modern luxury befitting its Deluxe station. Ample garage space and normal conveniences. All units with bath, shower, and radio, plus TV on request; predominance of smallish doubles, which they prefer to rent even to lone clients (statistics show 24 singles); 14 suites with generous bedrooms and parsimonious parlors; efficient, tasteful appointments which make courageous use of unusual color combinations. Capable direction by Ignacio Ramos, who has forged this into a stalwart shackle in the 13-link Interhotel chain. *Saludos* for its physical amenities.

The air-conditioned, 125-room **Mindanao** makes its Deluxe headquarters in the University District. We'd score it B-plus after our last-semester examination. Frequent recent changes in management; L-shape lobby in soft gold and browns; coolish Domayo restaurant with rouge pep-ups; deep carpets and soft music further to soften your tread; some highstepping in the evenings-only Club Mindanao; adjoining Coffee Shop; dimly lighted, lazy-S-form bar; somewhat uninviting P-shape swimming pool in the basement, with an adjoining bar and dressing rooms. Other fillips include separate "He" and "She" saunas. Predominance of twin units now that it has been expanded; a few suites and singles available; small bedchambers for stout rates; giddy wallpaper; namby-pamby taste in furnishings. Except for these few aesthetic and spatial drawbacks, here's one which we like.

The fully air-conditioned **Plaza**, One of Europe's tallest hotels, has a wonderful penthouse. On its 25th and 26th floors, you'll find dancing, a swimming pool, and roof-garden dining, plus an unparalleled view of the city; at teatime (7 P.M. to 9:30 P.M.), when 2 orchestras play, it is particularly popular. Spanish flavors both in décor and in its all à la carte cuisine; huge panoramic windows; a 5-man combo for dinner dancing from 10:30 P.M. onward; an urbane bar with a small lounge; no groups ever accepted in this area. Busy-busy lobby in bronze, wood, and leather motif; mezzanine refashioned; boutiques, a drugstore, and travel agency included; Scottish-tone, downstairs Coffee Shop; big dining room; semicircular bar in offbeat architecture; cheer-brightened corridors. Motorists have access to the 750-vehicle, 3-level underground garage across from the entrance—a BIG plus in this car-peted city. The king-size, 500-room frame contains 90 suites (29 duplex, featuring a tiny refrigerator and bar); none is elaborate, but for their layout, comfort, and garniture, they are among the best buys in the city. Increasingly commercial but still acceptable.

The **Eurobuilding** is composed of 2 attractive, angular edifices of laminated white marble. While the 8-story wing contains the posher pads, another 15-floor segment is devoted to more cost-conscious voyagers and convention groups. A quartet of restaurants, with the Balthasar, in Arabian reds, offering the most elegance; 4 distinctive bars; massive congress quarters; concourse of shops; sauna and garden-sited pools; barber and hairdresser; 700-car garage. Generous spread of 150 suites in the high-priced plush section; 450 bedchambers in the other block. Full air conditioning; balconettes; TV and piped music; pastel color schemes; modern furnishings; good baths. General Manager Mateo Bosch, an alumnus of the famous Victoria on Mallorca, keeps this swing-wing sizzler on its ever-true course. We'd buy a billet here anytime.

The 4-star **Sideral**, 50 yards from Retiro Park and 50 yards from the Prado, has been selected by both the deluxe Ritz and Palace as one of their favorite choices for overflow traffic. A basic anchorage in the widespread Mapotel chain since 1970; air-conditioned; conventional lobby with dimly illuminated snack bar to its rear; colorful but routine restaurant; large, attractive, gaily decorated, especially pleasant Bodega Castelana with roast lamb and suckling pig its specialties; garage for 50 cars; piped music. In general, we are even more enthusiastic about its 45 doubles and 5 singles upstairs than about its public precincts; in addition to a comfortable marble bath with 2 washbasins as adjuncts to the former, each boasts a small but cozy separate sitting room as well as an itty-bitty balcony done with charm. Salutes to this engaging shelter and to the sweet people who operate it!

Pintor-Goya, named, of course, for the great Spanish artist, makes its address appropriately at Goya 79, a brushstroke from picturesque Retiro Park and the Serrano shops. A tableau of tourist comforts fills its 9-story canvas. Lobby verdant with cascading flora; glass-hemmed garden; restful peacock-blue salon; small dining room that seems an afterthought; good barber; partly submerged garage. All 175 quarters are tastefully blessed with pleasing pastels, chilled air, and commodious baths. Tell your taxi driver you want the Pintor-*Goy*-ja. A sound and artfully conceived composition.

The **Suecia** ("Sweden"), conveniently sited behind the Cortes, is now only fair in our judgment. Except for the ground-level lobby, the first 4 floors of its building are occupied by Swedish offices (a bonus in silence for the upper tiers of bedchambers). Entrance on a tiny street; maintenance falling off, we think; sauna (men only); 66 small rooms, all with old-fashioned baths, all air-conditioned, and all with Swedish-style furnishings specially imported (after heroic Customs hassles) from the Land of the Reindeer; Bellman Restaurant. Here's a nonfancy operation.

Hotel Residencia Florida Norte opened its doors early in '73. Unusually handsome high-ceilinged lobby lined with light gray marble; strikingly lighted salon to right with coffee-brown wall-to-wall carpeting; harmonious furnishings, and huge Gobelins; Bar Goya on open mezzanine communicating with cafeteria; world-of-tomorrow subterranean restaurant; TV lounge; gift shop; hairdresser and barbershop; 100-slot garage. All of its 338 units come with air conditioning, taped melodies, and a Hiltonish brand of appeal; all but the smallest singles have an independent seating area and ample dimensions. Heavily patronized by group traffic. Director Luis Peiró has created one of the happiest recent additions to the Madrid hotellerie circle.

The **Emperatriz** was a total disappointment to us on our latest reinspection. We can't recommend it personally.

Don Quijote tilts in the bucolic meadows of the Cuidad Universiteria district, a 6-bit taxi ride from the action. Aluminum and glass micro-Hilton concept with a pseudo-Spanish flavor; indoor and outdoor swimming areas; sunken lounge dotted with brown and black overstuffed chairs; paneled bar in tasteful pastels; spotless 25-table restaurant opposite. The corridors linking the 8 singles, 84 doubles, and 8 suites on 4 floors are punctuated with artistic interpretations of you-know-who; the reading lamps are good; the firm beds are inscribed with quotations from . . . right, again. Often busy with local business-conference groups.

The **Principe Pío** is too routine to inspire much enthusiasm from us.

The **Sanvy** features an English Club (attractive as an extra residents' lounge), an American-style cafeteria with Spanish-slanted vittles, a ballroom, the violet-and-white Victor Bar-Discothèque, a beauty salon, and a barbershop. While few of these featherings appeal to our personal taste (we found them garish), we must commend the dedication of its proprietor. Pool still a popular puddle for Madrid's summer heatnicks; every unit with private plumbing; 4 suites on each of its 6 floors; no singles, but doubles rented at lower rates to lone wanderers. In general, not our pick, but suitable in the medium range.

The **Claridge**, a 3-star hostelry under the same administration as the Wellington, stands at Calle Conde de Casal 6, across Retiro Park. It's a long haul from the city's heartbeat. Corner situation rising 15 floors above the portals; 180 rooms, all with bath, shower, and air-conditioning; modern dogleg lobby with a coffee shop, a small food stall, and a cocktail lounge at the paw's end; noise level heightened by bar music; unfancy but adequate cellar dining room with open kitchen; dimensions inclined to be dwarfish. Director José Navarro serves as boniface to many groups; some readers like it, others aren't so keen on the staff attitudes. A bit remote geographically, but a worthwhile hideaway for the price.

The **Washington** and the **Menfis** both seem to us to be slipping.

The 50-room **Serrano** is only a hop from the U.S. Embassy and around the corner from one of the most fashionable shopping avenues in the city. Small, 1970-vintage structure with no restaurant, but a cozy pub with snacks; spotless chambers in contemporary Iberian motif; all doubles with Frigobar; administration by young, shy, and competent Don José Prados; extra-careful maintenance; eager and kindly staff.

The **Carlton**, in a noisy, unattractive situation beyond the railway station, is gradually becoming fuddy-duddy and spiritless. Zipless restaurant; 170 rooms with bath and 28 singles with shower only; taped music. Small dimensions with onionskin-paper-thin walls; plain, uninspired décor; it accepts some groups during the High Season, as well as much of the overflow from the Ritz and the Palace. Tolerable only.

The **Velázquez**, once regarded as a little masterpiece by this *Guide*, was in sore need of a major restoration on our latest study. Sorry, but we believe this Velázquez should not be exhibited in our gallery of desirables this season. Not recommended.

The **Colón** is a late entry with oodles of charm but handicapped by its location across Retiro Park from the main shopping district—not financially disastrous, however, because taxi fares in Spain are sherry-cheap. Monolithic construction with balconied façade shedding tiers from the 10th-floor down; main restaurant, grill, and a cluster of boutiques directly below; penthouse dining room, bar, and pool. All 170 units with air conditioning, bath, and radio; simple, fresh, functional décor that is kept sparkling clean; ample living space for the bracket; almost prohibitively sizable bookings from tour groupies, some of whom kept a Richmond newsman we know up till dawn. This one is in the same Colónnade as its namesake and the Regencia Colón in Barcelona. Except for its distance, normally a sound value for your peseta.

Residencia Marquina is operated by the owners of an adjoining movie theater (Calle Prim 11, off the Castellana near Av. José Antonio), in which the clients will find their hotel restaurant and cafeteria. Less than 2-dozen accommodations, but each with bedchamber, sitting room, and bath, plus space for a proposed kitchenette; full air chilling; sufficient luggage storage areas; slim elbowroom, in keeping with its reasonable tabs. The agreeable ambiance is better suited for long-term voyagers seeking a modest, unpretentious home-away-from-home. Reserve ahead, and don't expect cosmopolitan fireworks, because—like its address—it's Prim but not posh.

The 150-room **Alcalá**, near Retiro Park, is a quiet retreat with a small lobby-lounge and circular iron hearth, a better-than-average restaurant (under outside concession and with Basque specialties), cheerful halls, discreet lighting, and a kindly staff. Air conditioning throughout; dual-glaze windows on the front to blunt the din of the busy street; TV and piped music for further soothing. Narrow bedchambers with dark furniture, full-length mirrors, and walnut-paneled walls. Getting better each season and deserving of its higher turnover.

The **Mayorazgo** welcomes visitors with a Castilian lobby. It is soothingly and conveniently set back from the street. A fresh lounge, replete with fireplace and stained-glass windows, also offers a warm welcome. Units here are sized on the small side and range in ambiance from adequate to pleasant. Moving up.

The still-youthful, 6-floor **Residencia Bretón** has a pleasantly modern lobby from which a booze bar, snack bar, and breakfast nook are separated by screens. Among its 56 nests with bath, 10 of the singles contain limited plumbing. While this compact hostelry does not sparkle with much character or personality, we like it and hope you might too.

At the **Hotel Ecuestre** a vast palette of browns from sand to chocolate prevails from the lobby to the dining room to the upstairs corridors to the furniture and textiles of the accommodations and probably to the house cat (if there is one). Most of its 126 retreats (6 singles) are not only decent in size but present the *rara avis* of 2 closets; each has its viable bath which, even without the ring around the tubs, is brown. Lots of tour groups normally stomp these premises. Its 4 stars shine routinely but not brilliantly.

The **Cusco**, a newcomer quite a stretch from the center, wings in with 310 accommodations, none of which are singles. Large characterless lobby; no restaurant; brightly lit snack bar and café; clean and efficiently executed, but sterile and impersonal in tone and atmosphere. Heavy patronage by tour groups. So-so.

El Coloso, **Emperador**, and **Zurbano** are all off our list.

Pensions? Zillions, ranging in quality from superior to stinky. The best we've seen is **Residencia Castellana 60**, across from the sleek Hotel Castellana. It's popular as a semipermanent housekeeping headquarters for 2nd and

3rd magnitude movie luminaries billeted in the capital. The German proprietor keeps it bright and shiny. Total of 19 apartments, all with ample-size kitchenettes; no restaurant; breakfast only; concierge, porter, and maid service; short on charm, but popular and always packed. Practical for long-term stopovers. **Isamar** (Jorge Juan 32) is fair enough. So is **Gurtubay** (Calle Gurtubay 6); no English is uttered, however. **Apartamentos Quintana** (Quintana 22) caters only to visitors who will bide for a week or more. Its 56 small modern flats are neat; all offer a tiny kitchen, fireplace, terrace, bath, shower, private safe, and bookcases. Not bad, but we prefer the abovementioned Residencia Castellana 60. For older folk, **Pensión Galiano** (Alcalá Galiano 6) is a quietly charming and dignified pension. Each of its 19 rooms (17 of them doubles and all on 1 floor) with bath; spacious and well maintained; breakfast about 4 bits; only Spanish is spoken. Reserve well in advance. Worthwhile. The once-praised **Pensión Ferrer** (Ferrer del Río 6–8) has sunk so far down on our charts that we can no longer recommend it. Sorry. There are other pensions on other flights of the same building where you might find better pickin's. Also reported to be worth a try are Pensións **Claris** and **Palermo** (both at Plaza de las Cortes 4), **Easo** and **Mori** (both at Plaza de las Cortes 3), **Embajada** (Joaquín García Morato 5), **Gaos** (Mesonero Romanos 14), **Rosalía de Castro** (Campomanes 6), and **Guipuzcoana** (Av. José Antonio 44). **Hostal Amaya** (Av. José Antonio 12) seems to be going down for the count; 1—2—3—4—. Since sparse savings accrue with fewer meals or units without private plumbing, order the works.

The **Barajas**, on a hillock overlooking Madrid's busy airport, is a glorious perch for your capital fly-over. After our latest 4-day rest here, my Nancy and I are c-r-a-z-y about this house. Its director is veteran hotelier José María Carbó Jr. The 4-level, red-brick, linear structure contains 230 air-conditioned and jet-proof bedchambers, all with bath—and many with private balcony too. The wide-angle suites are extraordinarily appealing; these nests are equipped with TV sets, full dressing rooms, circular tubs, and bars. It also boasts the Toledo and El Porche restaurants (the latter is alfresco), El Patio Coffee Shop, Las Brisas Club (by the pool), Discothèque 747, a shaker of bars, a beauty salon, a sauna, a gymnasium, and convention facilities; a heated pool also gushes an invitation to relax. The prices make this one of the best luxury bargains on the entire Continent. As a *****-Deluxe springboard for high-diving (or sky-diving) air travelers, this one is a vitally needed addition on the touristic circuit. It also happens to be far-and-away the finest airport hotel we've seen on that side of the Atlantic—and perhaps even in the world. This one recently has been joined by its equally appealing 150-unit sister across the street. Marvelous!

Closer to town, the **Motel Osuna** is a vastly more modest but cheery operation. Its restaurant, lobby, lounge, and double tier of rooms overlook a lovely garden and swimming pool. A cutie for budgeteers in search of peace.

P.S. For Excursionists From Madrid: Now that the wonderful old **Felipe II** has been shuttered, the **Victoria Palace** is practically the only show in *El Escorial*—aside from the basilica, of course. Though it boasts a pool, it still doesn't make much of a splash with us.

Major Cities and Regions

Algeciras, the traditional gateway to troubled Gibraltar (closed off almost entirely to tourists, at this writing), offers the **Reina Cristina**. Gardens, tennis, minigolf, seabathing, beautiful heated pool, dancing, shopping, elbow-bending in its Patio Bar—all are on the premises or within easy reach. Cuisine which vies with the finest hotel fare in Spain; British ownership; staff as kind as ever on our recent stopover. We were especially fond of suites #246 and #346, which face the swimming pool; both have working fireplaces. Highly recommended as a haven of tranquility if you are booked into any of its better accommodations. **Octavio**, which debuted its 80 units in late '73, seems eager to please—and except for its urban situation facing the bus depot, we think it achieves that end pretty well. Airy mezzanine restaurant; classic furnishings with marble highlighting; soundproofed accommodations; eye-soothing blues, reds, greens, or gold predominating on each floor. A reasonable value. Nearby, **Las Yucas**, one year older, boasts a more recessed location but not quite the same élan. All 33 rooms with bath or shower, piped music, and air conditioning, and a few of them (such as the "01" and "09" series) with terraces. Groups win the restaurant while independent explorers are shunted over to the cafeteria—so how's *that* for revealing its priorities? **Guadacorte** resides at *Los Barrios*, on Algeciras Bay about 12 miles toward Sotogrande. It is also a '72 entry with many God-given assets in its favor. Man, however, has managed to infect the placid scene with a busy highway and a noxious petroleum cracking tower crowning the crest of a nearby knoll. Not bad for Aramco technicians on vacation leave from the Sahara.

Alicante: **Apartotel Meliá Alicante** is a massive semiresidential promotion containing 800 apartments. A lease-out arrangement permits the renting of these private cliff dwellings to the general public. Its sawtooth eminence fairly dominates the sprawling metropolis. Within its society are 2 heated pools, 3 restaurants (we like the scenic El Postiquet with its buffet), the bar El Acuario with fishes and travel writers humming along with tunes on the baby grand piano; hairdresser, newsstand, souvenir shop, and nightclub. Accommodations break down into 7 decorative styles. When reserving pick an odd-numbered key for a sea view; we also recommend the "61" type. Massive in concept—as Meliá's projects usually are. Then we'd select either the **Gran Sol** or the **Maya**. The former, in mid-city, offers a quiet lobby as a retreat from the frenetic street, a snack bar on the 26th floor, a sparkling and viewful bar-lounge, and pleasant, splendidly maintained kips, some of which proffer kitchenettes in their studio enclaves. The Maya, a 200-room, 10-story, chocolate-brown edifice overlooking Santa Barbara Castle, tilts heavily to an Aztec motif and tribal migrations from heap-big travel agencies. Ample facilities; 3 pools, tennis court, solarium; basement cafeteria; restaurant on first floor. Fatigue seems to be settling in at the **Carlton**, which has trotted itself out as host to too many a loyal Alicanter. The staff remains one of the most graceful and helpful in the region, but the plant itself could use a shot of rejuvenation. At the newish **Residencia Covadonga** your happiness will very likely depend upon your luck in drawing an acceptable bedroom. If you snag a spacious one facing the plaza and the Lucerios fountain, your stay might be delightful. Otherwise, we're not too sure. Next we'd pick the

108-room, air-conditioned **Leuka**, perched up the hill and away from the worst effects of the madding crowd. This would be followed by the **Cristal**, which, appropriately, is sheathed in "cristal" and reflects a fair amount of commercial chill. Like many glass houses, it's pretty colorless and brittle. The **Bernia**, on the other end of the synthetic ladder, leans decidedly toward plastics. Of the front-desk personnel whom we encountered, we doubt if one was older than 14. With normal luck, a few may have aged by the time you check in. The **Gran**'s sterling feature is its restaurant. Otherwise antiquity appears to be hounding its heels. The **Residencia Palas** and the **Hotel Palas** have more in common than name and management. Both also share our lack of enthusiasm as oases for weary camel drivers. In brief: A last resort.

Almería: See "Costa del Sol."

Barcelona provides a bedscape of comfort and variety:

The **Ritz** boasts a loyal following from all over the globe. It is in the hands of Don Salvador Palmada, who made the Hostal de la Gavina at S'Agaro (70 miles up the coast) world famous as virtually the only gem along the otherwise squalid Costa Brava and still at this writing the only 5-star Deluxe contender in all of Catalonia. He was also instrumental in polishing the facets of Mallorca's prestigious Son Vida. Gracious, ever-helpful Director Agustin Calonge boasts one of the most dedicated and efficient staffs in Europe; after my Nancy and Dodge headquartered here for a protracted period in '72 during my 100% successful eye operations in the globally revered Arruga Clinic, we adore their spontaneous sweetness and goodness even more. Most rooms are spacious, and all have private bath; Concierges Pablo and Pasqual are splendid professionals and human beings. Sr. Palmada acted with great wisdom, we think, in retaining his key personnel and in his decision to maintain the taste and Old World flavor of this imposing house while quietly streamlining its services and behind-the-scenes facilities. To traditionalists it is still number one; this year it's better than in many a Mediterranean moon. Still creaky in places— so let's hope your luck of the draw is good!

The newly expanded 250-room **Diplomatic**, also in the center, may have more appeal for modernists. Handsome Los Borrachos Grill with a full, rich menu, a wine bin, and piano music nightly; Restaurant Chez Diplomatic; snack plus drinking bar; The Scotch disco hub; writing room and sumptuous lounges; TV nook; barber and beauty salon; garage; travel agency; news kiosk; Telex hookup. The 10-story, setback structure contains a Tom Thumb swimming pool and solarium on the 8th level with beverage and light-bite service; office facilities available for businessmen who live out of a briefcase. The bedchambers are not a smidgen of the Ritz's size, but most are well appointed and thoughtfully conceived; we're especially fond of #1026, a clean-lined suite. Carrier heating and cooling system with individual controls; phones in rooms and baths; AM-FM radio consoles; double windows; TV in suites and in the excellent double units ending in "5". Manager J. Mercadal, former chief at the Manila (see below) and a retired blue-water skipper (sea below), has a sound ship to command; we hope he holds a steady course and a happy crew. Except for some frowns and a few signs of ineptitude from a desk clerk —check your bill and your change carefully—superior (for Barcelona) credentials on our Diplomatic mission of inspection.

Gran Hotel Calderon is a recent and welcome addition to the Barcelona innscape. Rooftop swimming pool with small bar and seperate solarium affording a magnificent view of the city; hypermodernistic entrance and lobby; extremely handsome, spacious mirrored lounge; cocktail nookery with comfortable upholstered chairs; calm, tasteful dining room; piped music wafting through the public sancta; 100% air-conditioned. All 244 rooms with bath, double basins, and your own TV; varying arrangements for its smallish accommodations; 20 nice but routine suites; rather dark décor. Not quite up to the Diplomatic in its newest wing, but nevertheless good for the price and category.

For business reasons we recently spent about 3 weeks at the **Avenida Palace.** We think the best way we can describe it is to liken it to that proverbial well-shined and comfortable old shoe. Suave, genial Don Juan Gaspart is its experienced, energetic, and watchful majesty. Concierge Luis Romeu and his colleagues are outstandingly courteous and efficient; most of the floor personnel are adept; every minion we met here was sweet and kind. Busy lobby in marble, glass, brass, and wood; listless dining room with glassed-in fountain and better than adequate cuisine; plain bar; air conditioning; immaculately maintained; blond-wood furnishings and white chenille spreads in all the bedchambers. Good solid solace without glamour at a purse-satisfying price.

The **Presidente**, in a very noisy locale, was generously endowed from basement to eaves with the accouterments of the twentieth century. Unfortunately, its modern-day construction techniques are already disclosing such telltale signs of severe overstrain and extensive "settling" that they alarm and distress us. This 15-story structure, off the main traffic lanes, is of white stone, steel, and glass; a small hook-shape swimming pool-terrace on the 9th floor overlooks another outdoor sipping patio at the 4th-floor level. Simple but smart glass-lined restaurant with ebony leather chairs, globe illumination, and a maritime mural; wood and tartan bar adjoining the spacious mezzanine lounge; tiny Concierge's desk which results in client logjams during rush hours; management by Miguel Cabré, who did a sparkling job with the more modest Manila. All of its 150 doubles and 8 suites come with individually controlled Carrier air conditioning. Ample dimensions (except in the expensive and inexcusably cramped suites); wide, wide windows commanding romantic vistas of townscape and bay; burgundy wall-to-wall carpeting, bright prints, and twin beds throughout; every bath with twin basins, separate toilet-bidet compartment, and frosted louvered window. This Presidente is fast losing our vote.

The 500-unit **Princesa Sofia** was inaugurated after our latest swing through Barcelona, so we haven't seen the finished product, which resides about 20 minutes from the airport. We did count, however, 4 restaurants, 2 saunas and gyms, plus a heated indoor-outdoor swimming pool. It looks promising. Indeed it does.

The 200-room **Colón** is scenically sited face-to-face with the ancient Cathedral in the Old City. Management by young and alert Sr. Oritz; all units claim air conditioning and private bath or shower; pleasant subterranean Carabela Restaurant; smartly renewed corridors with brass lamplights of low wattage; demisuites ending in #06 are among the best buys in the province. We are also fond of the quintet of 6th-floor units with wide-open terraces; they'll put you eyeball-to-eyeball with one of the oldest churches in Christendom. Handsome décor highlighted with velvet furnishings, gold-leaf mirrors, and lovely prints; maintenance could be picked up a bit in some quarters. Many European travelers of taste choose this one for its tranquility, grace, and homey atmosphere. Here's a "Columbus" worth discovering.

The **Derby** tipped its brimful of British mannerisms onto the Catalonian turf in '68. Residential location near Sears, a 5-minute taxi ride from the Paseo de Gracia; marble-floored lobby with crimson-carpeted staircase; Epsom restaurant; wood-hued hideaway bar. All 115 units with chilled air and warm baths; all in soothing tones. Not in the top winner's circle, but a dependable "place."

The **Manila** continues to climb. Now air-cooled for summer sufferers; Telex; rustic rooftop Grill with marvelous view; expanded Nautical Bar, plus opera-lounge nook displaying portraits of famous singing stars; reasonably spacious rooms with woody touches; Lilliputian baths boasting sterile-seal guarantees; reasonable return for a reasonable outlay. Helmsman Francisco Carbonell, former Assistant Manager at the Avenida Palace, has taken over with flair and enthusiasm. As Barcelona stogies go, here's a pretty good local-Manila wrapper.

The **Arycasa** offers many Deluxe features in keeping with its category, but the universally tiny dimensions of the physical plant are its most forbidding detractions. All units with radio, private safe, and air conditioning; a handful of suites with private terraces; décor vaguely in the Chippendale manner. Trying hard, but it still leaves us cold.

The **Residencia Córcega** is not recommended. **La Rotunda,** a 10-minute taxi ride from the center at the foot of Tibidabo Mountain, offers 71 suite-type units, all with kitchenette-cum-refrigerator, wall safe, and terrace; 25 have working fireplaces; sited with no view. The management hasn't scrimped either financially or operationally to ensure each guest's comfort. Drawbacks are (1) almost execrably low-grade cooking and (2) careless maintenance which could be remedied by application of a scrub brush and elbow grease. A good concept which needs more savvy administration.

Among the flock of lesser chicks, the **Barcelona** used to be one of the slickest. Now we find it molting pretty noticeably. The 60-unit **Regencia Colón,** near the Colón and with the same ownership, offers bare shelter at greatly reduced tariffs. Poor for view, but passable for peseta watchers. The **Cristal** is now so clouded, in our view, that we can't recommend it. The 76-room **Regente** offers better maintenance. Panoramic rooftop solarium, plus open terrace, restaurant, and tub-size swimming pool; newish restaurant at salon level; 2 floors with private balconies; well-outfitted bedchambers with individual air conditioners, 2 phones, door chimes, night bins for shoeshining, wall-to-wall carpeting, and cleverly designed bedlamps that won't disturb the other snoozer. Modern, functional, but too small in its twins for long-staying visitors; the singles, however, are ample. Director Rafael Bela gives a lot for the money; very pleasant for its type. The youthful **Balmora** is more of a residential stop than a full-blown hotel; parking facilities for motorists; passable as a midtown hitching post. The **Gaudi** had sunk to such abysmal depths on our latest inspection that under no circumstances is it now recommended by this *Guide*. The **Dante** kindles no inferno in our enthusiasm. Fair, but somewhat expensive for its unimaginative lodgings. The **Astoria,** the **Zenit,** the **Roma,** and the **Rallye** provoke only yawns in our moments of reflection.

Tibidabo Mountain rears its head over the city with 3 alternate entries. The **Florida**, with 54 rooms and baths, is near the top. Lovely view of the metropolis and the sea, but shoddy resort-style furnishings and poor upkeep; closed Off Season. **La Masía,** same ownership and crowning the peak, is category 1-B. Cretonne-y décor and bargain-basement fittings in its 29 units, all of which are located over its mass-production restaurant; simple and noisy. The **San Jerónimo**, at the Halfway mark, is fourth rate; not recommended to Yankee trippers. None of these, in our opinion, is worth the long haul from the doin's.

Up the pike a bit along the glutted *Costa Brava* (which, in general, we don't like or recommend), you'll find the world-famous **Hostal de la Gavina** at *S'Agaro*, about 70 miles from Barcelona. Almost 100% reconstructed or refurbished; the features receiving most of the beauty treatment include the entrance, elevators, Japanese garden, snack bar, Candlelight Room (elegant, intimate dining to piano lilts), and $25,000 oak-paneled, gold-leafed Louis XV Royal Suite. Beautiful lounges with antique furnishings; terrace-dining in season; high cuisine; 100 rooms and 16 suites, most with plush décor and bath; a few accommodations still small and simple; tennis courts and fair beaches. Its pool with cabanas and Snack Bar rivals any similar installation on the Mediterranean coast. The jewel of jewels in Catalonia; top rates and top quality. Splendid—as long as you don't mind the man-made horrors along its approach roads which spoil the area for us.

Bilbao's most up-to-date comfort salesman is the centrally sited, 4-star **Ercilla**, which complements its 350 fully bathed bedchambers with a restaurant and cafeteria, discothèque, sauna and massage facilities, beauty parlor, travel agency, souvenir shop, and car-hire service. Next comes the riverfront **Nervion**, with enough of a parking problem to unnerve arriving motorists. (Once you unload, however, it does have a garage.) Dark lounge; airy cafeteria; dining room with gracious bar; thoughtful space concepts which make this a sound buy for overnighting. The **Aranzazu** (meaning "Holly") is a fair tuck-inn, with ample-size bedchambers and an ingratiating staff. Its sister operation, the **Avenida**, doesn't tick over quite so well in our opinion. Perhaps this chain is concentrating its sights on the opening of its upcoming deluxe star on the Gran Via, the **Villa de Bilbao**. Keep your eyes alerted for this one because it might become the local pacesetter. Down the scale come the **Conde Duque**, facing the river near the Nervion, with small, clean, yet uninspired cubicles, the old-fashioned **Carlton** which has seen better days and nights, and, finally, the **Almirante**—a creaky bark that to us no longer has bite.

Cádiz will never be remembered for its hotels—or perhaps it will. They're miserable—so bad, in fact, that unless you *must* stop here, we sincerely recommend you pass it up and whip around the bay to overnight at the Hotel Fuentebravía in Puerto Santa María (description directly follows). The **Atlántico** is coming up, we're told, but we haven't seen it lately ourselves. What's left is the 65-kip **Francia y Paris**, which never thrilled us. Shelter can be found at the **Isecotel**, which turns on 120 apartments year round—mostly for French package tourists who don't seem to mind its abundant gloom.

Driving north from (or south to) *Tangier, Gibraltar,* or *Algeciras* via the coastal route? The **Hotel Fuentebravía** is near **Puerto Santa María** at the Rota border, a skip-and-a-jump from Jerez. Situated on a knoll commanding a beach, with Atlantic rollers for lullabies; lovely main building with a fresh dining room, bar, administrative section, modern-as-tomorrow kitchen. Papagallo Night Club, and a scattering of lodgings 1 level down; adjoining edifice with 90 comfortable doubles, each with bath and bay view; perfumed by 3 acres of flower gardens; 40 bathing cabins with shower; beauty salon; children's playroom; cluster of shops; 200-car garage; swimming pool. The friendly staff is on the youthful and inexperienced side, but normally it is eager and kind; the cuisine is interesting and varied, thanks to regularly imported chefs from other lands for "culinary months," when each specializes in his own national cookery. Our favorite accommodation is number 201, a double. We like this stop for its simple yet comfortable charm, and for the purebred, put-your-feet-up atmosphere which is evoked by Director José Luis Kutz and his delightful French wife, Monica. The barnlike **Playa de la Luz**, at **Rota,** on the other hand, is not recommended at all by this book. Mammoth production-belt-style dining room; huge courtyard walled in on 3 sides by single-story sleeping cells which were cramped and unattractive to us. Nix. Away from the sea, the stucco **Motel El Caballo Blanco** ("White Horse"), 1-mile south of **Puerto Santa María** on the Cádiz-Jerez highway, is a good-looking nag in the rapidly expanding Meliá stable. The contractors have been dutifully turning blueprints into footprints in the wet concrete here— a swift and extensive revamping of an already comfortable roadside haven. In bathing season, guests ride by horse and carriage to the beach, a 300-yard haul through groves of whispering pines. Whale-size swimming pool for the stay-at-homes; jungle gym for the tots; outdoor bar for the thirsting. Of its numerous individual bungalows with carports, a bevy are studio doubles, and the rest expand to accommodate 4 to 8. A reasonable alternative when the Fuentebravía is jammed.

Cartagena offers the sea-girt sporting paradise of **La Manga** with its 36 holes for golf, 15 clay or lawn tennis courts, marina and cove, clubhouse, and facilities for brief or extended holidays as well as for resident settlers. Our friend of many years, Herbert Jerosch, is the sparkplug of it all, and in this skilled professional's hands it could be nothing less than excellent. What a dream zone for sporting types—and at surprisingly low tariffs.

In *Córdoba*, the **Parador Nacional de la Arruzafa** comes as a tonic to trippers who count their greenbacks. This up-to-date link in the Spanish State Tourist Department's chain is startlingly deluxe for its rates. Gorgeous ambiance with sweeping plains of polished marble; 56 doubles; air conditioning and central heating; highly dunkable pool; telephone in every room *and* bath; private terraces overlooking the city and Guadalquivir Valley; kiddie-corner for children's dining. Here's a king-size value for anyone's money. A passable choice in the independent league is the **Meliá Córdoba**. Though its physique is handsome, its grooming looked slack to us. Enclosed dance terrace overlooking the swimming-pool patio; dining salons getting oldish; TV lounge;

every suite with a refrigerator; cunning desk-table tops which disguise the air-conditioning ducts. Only fair now, but maybe it will improve if and when it unveils its proposed 100-room annex. We'll see. Facing La Mesquita, the town's chief tourist attraction, **Residencia Maimonides** welcomes pilgrims with gracious arms, clean appointments, and a friendly mien. The Caballo Rojo snack stall subs for a fuller restaurant. All 1973-vintage chambers with private bath; plenty of living space; good taste on display from cranny to cranny. In short, a *mitzvah*. **El Cordobes** hops into the ring with a rooftop pool, terrace, and bar; a viewful patio; an attractive, somewhat spare lounge; a red and white diner in the cellar; 97 doubles, 6 singles; and a future that is clouded. A new proprietor recently placed his mantle over it, so what cape work he plans remains uncertain for the nonce. The **Gran Capitan**, a 4-Star '66 entry, offers the finest view imaginable of the railroad yard. Five-tiered structure enfolding 100 look-alike units; commercialized 2nd-floor reception; limp garlic-spiced restaurant; bar-lounge. Maintenance overall seemed pauce to us. That aside, our main demurrer here is the roundhouse location. The **Zahira** also excites us—to beat a retreat! Possible alternates include the **Selu,** the **Colón** and the **Marisa**, none of which we've carefully inspected.

La Coroña's prize is the recently renovated, portside **Finisterre**. The restaurant is so appealing that you will probably feel grateful for the 3 pools, gym, saunas, Turkish baths, tennis courts, basketball spread, skating rink, and playground. When you've completed the workout, the bedrooms are restful and sparkling clean. Warmly recommended. The **Atlantico** views the harbor through one eye and a lovely garden through the other. Modern tone in its 7 floors containing 200 bedchambers; 50% with Frigobars; cooler than our leading choice but certainly adequate. The beachfront **Riazor**'s sharpest feature is its excellent staff. Go here if you want a close-up of the ocean and kindhearted attention. Back in town, **Residencia España** seems more fit for traveling rope and hemp salesmen than for carefree holiday makers. Not exactly our splice of life.

Costa del Sol: First, a word of mild caution to visitors who undoubtedly will be taken by the beauty of this comely stretch of Iberian coast. It has grown faster than Jack's beanstalk, much of it on the basis of foreign vacationers who were lured into investing in the thousands of apartments, aparthotels, condominiums, clubs, communities, and other development arrangements which have burgeoned under the sun. Most of these are sound, worthwhile subdivisions, but a few are nothing more than slick, quick-money rackets in which swindlers offer guaranteed income to the buyer who sublets his dwelling. This is the bait. Later, when the entire building is sold out, comes the sting. The hotshots cash in their chips by selling off the parent company, thus leaving the tenant-proprietor with no viable guarantee, no maintenance contract, and—probably—no forwarding address for registering their squawks. In any nervous economy, bilkings are likely to occur; regretfully this seacoast is no exception. Our ominous tip is injected not to frighten would-be investors, but to help them enjoy the delights of Spain to the fullest. Now let's scan the sands of the Costa del Sol:

Almería: Known as the "Hollywood of Spain" because of its pure light, this has become the focal point of film folk from all over the celluloid world. And to coin showbiz terminology, the **Gran Hotel** is practically the only show in town. The modern edifice stands at the junction of the port's 2 main streets, offering a pool and, on our visit, a hefty ration of smugness from the pompous critters behind the desk. Not much else to recommend it. The **Costasol** didn't send us, either—except, perhaps, in the opposite direction. This could be followed by a tag-along list of hostelries such as the **Indalico**, the clean 40-room **Residencia Hairan, Hostal Guerry**, the **Embajador** (ugh!), and the unpolished **La Perla**. Good-bye, "Hollywood."

Málaga's 230-room, Deluxe **Málaga Palacio**, about which we have mixed sentiments, established a new and rather expensive standard of innkeeping in this coastal nexus—traditionally a 2nd-string watering hole compared to many other tourist centers in Spain. Surprisingly expensive and frequently kooky construction that scrimped on nothing—from woodwork to textiles, glassware, and linens; attractive lobby and lounges, more French than Iberian in tone; shopping bazaar; disco-cellar for all age groups; popular dark-paneled, brass-highlighted bar; coolish but urbane glass-lined, marble-pillared dining room, with now faltering cuisine; stunning rooftop swimming pool, with an apron for food service and a marvelous vista of the port, the sea, and the cathedral; fully air-conditioned. As one example of its tribulations, however, the sumptuous suites are so inefficiently designed that ours nearly drove us crazy. The smaller units seem to be the better buys; many doubles are pleasantly decorated and reasonably efficient (if you don't count the occasional pings in the pipes). Half of the guests here are in tour groups. Director-Proprietor Juan León Portillo has been directing a good percentage of his receipts back into the house, with substantial results already visible. Parking remains a headache despite an 80-car garage nearby. The best (if only) Palacio in town. (Out of the center we much prefer the Parador Nacional Gibralfaro, but more about that later.) The 44-unit **Residencia Bahía Málaga** is slipping; moreover we were unable to find a view of that famous *bahía* from any corner of the house that we inspected. Situation anchored on a busy street of commerce; ample space; all staterooms with baths. **Casa Curro** fits into the next slot in our today's rankings. Scruffy plant with rustic Spanish (what else?) dining room, plus another in simpler motif; complete air conditioning; all 49 sun-shy doubles with private bath. Routine but passable. **Los Naranjos** smiles at its namesake fruit trees (oranges) in its front garden. Cheerful, clean, and certainly adequate within its 3-star bracket. It serves only breakfast—and guess what juice? **Gaviota**, up a mile in the hills overlooking a verdant valley and the sea, is a winner for seekers of informality. Our only hope is that the urbanization at its doorstep does not spoil its former tranquil ambiance. Dining room kind of slaphappy, as everything here tends to be; outdoor mealtime terrace with one table sited under a vine-covered cupola; 27 rooms, mostly doubles, with baths; swimming pools; slopeside gardens; bar; a haven for flocks of French tourists in the hot months and for battalions of British in winter. **Hostal El Peñón** now seems to be sinking; too bad, because we had liked it. **Hostal Carlos V**, hard by the cathedral, offers sheltering arms, but not a smidgen more—no meals, no breakfast, not even coffee. It answers one need only—sleep. And that it can provide in pleasant surroundings. From

A-to-ZZZZzzzzzzz, A-okay. Inexpensive, too. The **Maestranza Apartotel**, on the other hand, puts its accent on its bar trade and cafeteria traffic. Somehow the accommodations wobble in 2nd best, in our opinion. Now we come to the **Las Vegas**. Now we leave the Las Vegas. That was quite enough, thank you. Let's scat back to that aforementioned government-run parador: For motorists, oooolala! There's a heavenly choice just 2 steps below the welkin and 10 minutes from the center of Málaga. This is the **Parador** section of the Gibralfaro complex (see "Restaurants"). Only a dozen rooms, but each features a special panoramic slice of Earth, Sea, and Sky; rustic décor; huge double accommodations; wide-angled terraces with folding louvered doors. So superior a value, with such a rewarding billion-dollar vista, that it's even worth renting a little car just to take advantage of this dreamland.

   Marbella, in our opinion, leads the pack of Costa del Sol resorts. Like all the others, it has skyrocketed in growth and popularity, but its maturity seems to have arrived more gracefully and its following seems more tasteful to us than the elbow-to-elbow mob scenes associated with many of the throng centers. For one thing, it is more spread out. The innkeeping aristocrat of this peerage, for instance, **Los Monteros**, is a delightfully ingratiating suburbanite which beckons only a ½-mile from the first tee of the famous Río Real course; free private bus to the greens; original stucco-and-wood structure surrounded by 3 lovely pools (one heated); newer Pavillon Mediterraneo complex with 50 hyperdeluxe units plus 7 suites; Abanico section in duplex form with splendid vistas (#'s 178, 278, and 378 are our choices); 7 superb tennis courts, and informal gardens; thatched-roof beach club, one of the loveliest in Southern Europe (with yet another natatorium, luxurious changing rooms palatial enough for either Caesar or Cleopatra, patio lunching, dining, and dancing in summer; beautifully conceived as a romantic shoreline niche away from the hotel itself); 5 excellent horses and acres of cantering space; quiet setting with babbling fountains and clinging vines; pleasantly rustic feeling with twentieth-century comforts. Dining at either the beach haven, the Sportsmen's Clubhouse, the Grill Room (open all year with piano music nightly), or the salon; the lavishly redecorated English Bar (orchestra every night) and a 2nd one in the hotel, plus another at the banks of the Med; management and staff fairly bubbling with kindhearted efficiency; friendly clubby atmosphere. Incidentally, if you require even more pampering, this same organization operates the interesting and luxurious **Incosol** medical institute with a capacity for 375 registrants in 193 rooms. Almost every physiotherapeutic device, dunk, shower, massage, heat, or cold treatment imaginable is here. Doctors, dentists, technicians, nurses, radiologists, caddies,—you name it, and Incosol probably can provide it. (Even to long-distance heart meters so that Doc can get a reading of your ticker when you chip into a sand trap on the 16th fairway!) A private hospital also will provide face-lifts, plastic surgery, and obesity regimens. It looked so good, in fact, that we can hardly wait to come down with something. *What* a holiday! Returning to the normal vacation diet, the **Marbella Hilton** is a fast 15-minute drive from Marbella itself. It was Uncle Conrad's first venture into a purely seasonal European beach atmosphere. This 150-foot-tall, 17-story, 270-room slab of eye-shocking architecture was taken over by the Hilton interests after previous proprietors decided to abandon their ambitious dreams. It is beset with drawbacks and blessed with advantages. Assets: Fantastic coastal vistas, especially from the upper levels; a beautifully designed swimming pool and covered terrace with snack service and a marine theme; a handsome interior court surrounded by boutiques, a hairdresser, a cosmetics corner, and a newsstand; much improved staff attitudes; free bus service 6 times daily to and from the center of town; a charming Moorish fountain in the center of the main patio; 3 tennis courts; 21 acres of estate with a vast palm and cypress grove spreading to a thatched-roof beach hut offering bar and nibble wares. Debits: An ill-planned, tunnel-like entrance that often leaves several cars choked up in a long waiting line; dinky bathrooms; the to us stupidly conceived, viewless, interior Los Naranjos Restaurant with grim colors, awful lighting, no à la carte, practically no choice of wines, slightly improved (to mediocre) cuisine on our last try, and such high prices for Spain that we winced. While the bedchambers themselves were appealing in a bland international manner (except for a few with hand-tooled leather headboards, you'd never know you were in Spain), General Manager Diego de Cossio has got such a plateful of travail ahead that we certainly don't envy him his task. Even though we feel this area vitally needs a hot professional jockey to spur up the local competition, we think that for the moment this challenger is too uncoordinated and too expensive for maximum enjoyment. Many dedicated Hiltonians will undoubtedly disagree. The **Marbella Club Hotel** is composed of 2 parts—the "New" and the original one. The promoter behind this enterprise is a certain Prince Alfonso Hohenlohe, an innkeeper who has spent a large portion of his career on the Costa del Sol and elsewhere in Spain. We prefer the "New" M.C.H. with its 120 rooms, its handsome beach baskery, and its myriad recreational facilities both on the premises and nearby. Décor varies between modern simplicity and mock Andalucian; 80% of all units with private terraces; ample space; better, in our opinion, as a lingering base than as an overnight stop. The original Marbella Club, further up the pike, stands on 11 acres of outskirts terrain. Our recent incognito stay here proved to be a mixed bag. Personnel in its tiny, drab reception area had progressed (?) from smartalecky attitudes to indifferent ones. The attractive but expensive grill, with its large windows, central hearth, clubby atmosphere, and canine corps of clients' pets on our visit, served us a savory smoked salmon and a wretched Chinese Fondue (were we not dog lovers, we might have slipped the latter under our table). Veranda Bar; a trophy room for more loving cupfuls; a beach retreat; a small pool plus aviary in a molting garden. The newer suites, with names such as 007, Holiday, Hollyday, Africa, and Gibraltar, are modernistic; the older cottages reflect Iberian traditions; rooms vary from spacious to cramped; all were clean; all seemed overpriced to us for the value returned. **Golf Hotel Nueva Andalucia** is the leading handicapper of a trio which also comprises the groupy **Nueva Andalucia Plaza** and the charmless **Torré de Andalucia**, which caters almost exclusively to golfers. Our choice in this threesome boasts only 14 doubles and 7 singles—plus 2 golf courses, the Las Naranjas Golf Club, a handsome pool, and such a loyal following of links buffs that advance reservations are an absolute must. Director Antonio Larrad is the man to write before you start to pack your tees. The remaining pair didn't excite us chiefly because their

larger size and mass tourism concepts have usurped so much of their personality. The **Golf Hotel Guadalmina**, near the hamlet of *San Pedro de Alcántara*, also is such a mecca for the mashie set that links addicts are often
required to book as far ahead as 1 year. Two courses at your doorstep plus
the clubhouse; riding; tennis; 3 pools (one heated) and cabanas; restyled
lobby; 100 rooms, each given a personality course and now very inviting
indeed; each with its own bath and balcony; 6 bungalows plus another privately owned cluster which is rapidly becoming a subdivider's paradise; varied cuisine in its restaurant; Grill air-conditioned; more informal than Los
Monteros. Tee-rrific for players who can also enjoy exchange privileges with
the Los Monteros and Atalaya courses. Dramatic changes occur so swiftly
on the coast that this one appears to be standing still in comparison with its
golfing partners. No longer a champion, but very much in the playoffs. The
massive **Don Pepe** is almost *forced* to be popular. This 250-room titan is a
landmark in the Meliá mass-construction mania. Aside from the nearby
mountains, it's the tallest thing around—and to us, it gives a vivid impression
of being architecturally out of joint (far less so, however, than does the newer
Hilton on the town's other flank). Vast list of resort amenities, including a
nice private beach, circular, all-weather pool, water sports, gardens, seasoned
Almirante Bar, El Farola grill in green and mocha, sauna bath, nursery,
hairdresser, shops, and scores of terraces for sunning by day or murmurs by
moonlight; 2 tennis courts (illuminated for love matches by night perhaps?)
and a movie theater reeled in. The General Manager is Francisco Somoggi;
his personable lieutenant is Sr. J. A. del Río; while the staff remains tiptop,
we now feel that group appeal is wearing it thin in places. Okay, but no rave.
We haven't yet inspected the brand-new **Marbella Inn**, adjoining *Puerto
Banus* with its tennis, golf, and bathing facilities on tap. We see, however,
that reservations can be made through the Holiday Inns organization, so you
might check with them. The mass-minded **Atalaya Park,** 9 miles toward
Algeciras, used to be a quiet suburban choice, but it is now growing so
rapidly that we've lost all our enthusiasm. It has tacked on a 7-story, 300-
room addition in the immediate vicinity—the dual segments romantically
referred to as "No. I" and "No. II." Lap-of-the-sea location, beauty and
health farm pamperings available; 18-hole golf circuit teed up; handsome
Clubhouse with a timber-lined restaurant, a snack bar at the first tee, lovely
lounges, and free bus service to and from the hotel; billiard room; bowling
alleys, swimming pool and bathers' restaurant; tennis, riding, and water-ski
facilities; snack bar, grill, and nightclub; shops; full air conditioning. All 200
rooms with bath and terrace; 25 bungalows for quieter vacationers or families.
This one seems to be losing its administrative grip while growing too big for
its beaches. Not for us. The homely **Skol** is slanted more toward apartment
than conventional hotel-room construction. **Estrella Del Mar** has a modern
aura sprinkled with antiques, antique reproductions, and scads of genuine
Teutonic reproductions in human form who are not quite antiques—yet.
Handsome rustic mien; expanded public rooms; restaurant in stucco, brick,
and wood; another recently uncorked; kitchen noises rattling across the
neighboring pool area (we could smell the *Kraut* stewing all the way out on
the highway); all sleeping units with decorative fireplaces. Reasonably good

choice if you *sprechen Deutsch.* **Cortijo Blanco** is a 107-room, patio-dappled, Andalusian structure. Ground-floor accommodations with a superb view of sun-soaking guests—*and* vice versa; demand upper storied units unless you're a chest-beating exhibitionist, because no goldfish ever commanded less privacy. Handsomer for landscape than for innscape. The **Pueblo Andaluz**, next door, has gobbled up the cottage concept spurned by Cortijo Blanco. Miniature village of about 100 tiny houses, all with private terraces and tiny baths; swimming pool and cabanas; Teheran Room for Middle Eastern vittles; managed by a deposed Persian prince who is also an art collector. A fairly amusing beat-the-heat stopover. It is shuttered in winter. **Las Chapas**, on the main highway in the settlement of *Las Chapas*, is a startler: The restaurant, bar, and some of its living quarters semienclose a tiny bull ring instead of the conventional patio. Some rough spots polished smooth by Manager Manolo Ramos Podadera; plain but passable décor; swimming pool; tennis courts; minigolf; on many Sundays, small but jet-powered cows are released to the *tienta,* and YOU can be the matador for free. Loews, the American innkeeper, plans to unveil 500 deluxe units and a beachfront golf course, so keep your eyes open and your clubs polished. **El Fuerte** and **Bellamar**, the only 2 major candidates in *Marbella*, itself, are simple and adequate. The former has had many renewals; pool now installed; tennis court; mini-golf; cool dining hall; comfortable but not inspired; open all year. The latter offers bareboned public rooms, dismal bedchambers and a pool; open March to October only. The Second-class **Artola**, in *Artola*, also bubbles up with a water hole (it looked about as clean as one), a tennis court, and a 7-hole (yes, 7!) golf course for abbreviated or lazy sportsmen. No frills, no thrills. The **Alhamar**, at *Calahonda*, is in the luxury bracket. Park setting with superb outdoor facilities and grounds; weary, gloomy, hangdog hutches as bedrooms; lovely, book-and-fireplace lounge with thick rug and stained-glass windows; listless dining room. Improving too slowly. The nearby **Calahonda** is newer, but too raw for U.S. wanderers. The **Guadalpin** and the **Río Verde**, both outside *Marbella* on the main pike to *Algeciras*, are emergency stops when everything else is jammed. Passable and inexpensive, but not for the long-term holidaymaker. **Santa Marta**, open April 1 to October 31, boasts horses, a private beach, a host of large, rebuilt bungalows—and solitude by the carload. Under the Pilotage of its judicious American owner, this *Santa* has been martyred, torn limb from limb, and finally resurrected. Cheery lounge; excellent dining room; air conditioning throughout; big bathrooms. Now a 4-star hermitage that we recommend to the welkin. Along the path to *Estepona,* the flowering **Golf El Paraiso**, in the Patio El Alcornocal development, is a knockout. Gary Player played a major part in the sporting side; international financier Col. Peter Sweet played his shares on the investment side. The melding of 2 such professional talents brings dividends directly to you, the traveler. Situation a ½-mile from the beach; heated pool plus children's paddler; 2 tennis courts; playground; revolving rooftop restaurant; discothèque; beauty center; space for nearly 400 guests in air-conditioned luxury nests. For the flavor of a Spanish village—as never was produced in any Spanish hamlet we've ever seen—this is an Iberian dream come true. A recommendation as warm as the *sol.* Otherwise in this vicinity, the **Estepona Club** is fair, at best. **El Mero** wiggles in with a fish-shape pool, an irregular-shape façade, and a goodly number of hourglass-shape clients tanning their velvet hides under the Spanish sunbeams. Two minutes from the breakers; pleasant glass-lined dining room air-conditioned; reasonable tariffs; open March to October. This Mero's not a bad catch. The nearby **Patricia** is. Its corridors remind us of the tunnel network in the heart of Gibraltar. At *Fuengirola*, the 243-room **Mare Nostrum** is a lifeless mass operation which conjures in our minds the image of an ogre's castle. Three turrets; naked light bulbs; crumbling plaster; pool, tennis, and jai alai. So grim it gives us the willies. Never our Nostrum, but ever our night-Mare. **Las Piramides**, unearthed in A.D. 1970, certainly gives this archaeologist pause to reconsider the follies of our time. Its twin middens are 10 stories tall; 4 apartment digs surround these; all feature pyramidal roofs in such incongruous pigments as to suggest mutiny among the painters of Ramses II. Lounge gaudied up with modish overhead lighting and Bell Époque ice-cream-parlor furniture—all in absolute disharmony to our peepers; blue-and-white candy-stripe feedery glazed with all the sticky charm of a half-spent lollipop; cutesy beige bar with glazed flowers, glazed shells, and our glazed eyes peeled upon them; gooey corridors lined with white slatted doors; baths blossoming with floral-patterned toilet-seat covers. Caravans of prebooked nomads unpack their camelbags here, but for us it's a blanket de-Nile to the independent bed-and-breakfast wanderer. Nothin dune. The **Torre Blanca**, 2 miles from the center, has an uncertain future. Construction has been completed on a recent peek, but it was not open. We suspect it will become an apartment cog in a free-wheeling-dealing-urbanization. **Somió** and **El Cid**, flanking the village on opposite approaches, are modest. We prefer the former. We don't like the **Florida** at all—too big, rambling, and unkempt.

Excursion point? If you're on wheels, try **El Campanario**, in the budding Sitio de Calahonda development near Mijas. Travel-weary appetites might be stimulated by a swim in its pool, a riding lesson, or a few sets of tennis on the subdivision's sparkling spread of Andalucia. Although the 15-table restaurant is stronger on gastronomy than it is on aesthetics, the versatile facility makes this a worthwhile target for Costa-hoppers. Splendid.

Last (but light years from least), the sumptuous **Sotogrande del Guadiaro** complex, a sportsman's paradise, has taken root. For physical attributes, almost nothing in the nation can touch it. Huge holdings of 3200 acres in view of the Rock of Gibraltar; magnificently manicured, cork-and-olive-tree studded, 18-hole championship course, plus smaller 9-hole circuit, both linkscaped by Trent Jones, the well-known American golf architect; ruggedly handsome membership-only Clubhouse with restaurant (very good cuisine on our sampling); 3 bars, pro shop, 2 boutiques, and L-shape heated pool; 200-yard-wide sandy beach sweeping for ½-mile along the private shoreline. The 46-room Tennis Club Hotel, open to the general public, with very comfortable inn-type atmosphere; pool, stable, a bull ring, tennis, its own 18-tee links, Frontón Club by the shore, shops, restaurant, and discothèque; movies in English; children (14 years and older) accepted here, but not in the other residential or recreational facilities. Total of 12 superdeluxe bungalows for members or for holders of cards to other recognized clubs throughout the world; charming décor; each spaciously designed with a working fireplace, a bath with flowered tiles, a comfortable sitting room, and a refrigerator but no kitchen. The main hotel (again limited to members or to the country-club set of other nations with what we'd guess to be the approved social credentials) is now open; golf-course situation; 120 rooms and every conceivable resort amenity. Now that improved administrative supervision is being restored, here again is one of Spain's best bets for any discriminating traveler's itinerary—provided, of course, that your reservation is accepted.

Torremolinos? Vast changes in this boom-boom-BOOM town. Both in the hamlet itself and along its coastal approaches, new hostelries until very recently were popping up as rapidly as bubbles in a pitch-pot. So many in this roiling caldron are house-of-cards affairs that the older generation of leaders, which gave way to these bright-and-shiny buttons for a while, have now come back into their own glory. Others that could not keep up with the double-time pace have converted to apartment dwellings. Many of the giant new structures, too, trend toward the residential concept—either renting their space, or leasing or selling it under a cooperative arrangement. For the tourist who plans to spend a week or longer, this can be a big money-saver, because (1) they are cheaper to run, (2) building codes are more relaxed than for hotels per se, and (3) service standards are low to nil. Typical rates in these can range from $85 per person per month (winter) including breakfast and house cleaning, to $200 for the same renderings in High Season. The very best we saw —and it stacked up well against any luxury hotel accommodation in the vicinity—drew $600 per month for a 3-bedroom spread (6 beds, no service). Within its living complex were 2 swimming pools, shops, gardens, and a minigolf course; the apartments all had telephones and were efficiently air-conditioned. Some of the leaders in this bracket are: (1) **Playamar** (our pick of this type on the coast; 21 15-floor buildings with 1000 units overall; a metropolis of fun, recreation, and relaxation at village-size price tags), (2) **La Nogalera** (excellent furnishings; accommodations of all sorts), (3) **Eurosol** (more metropolitan in concept), (4) **UTO Ring** (acquired from the Meliá stable but retaining the hyper-Español décor, cramped space, and lofty tariffs of yore), (5) **Alay** (smartly clean-lined; a refreshing production by José Sendra, one of the most likable and skillful innkeepers on the coast; the best buy around), (6) **Las Cascadas**, (7) **Aloha**, and (8) **El Congresso** (eventually to be a stack of 3500 units in 8 edifices looking like columns of Paul Bunyan's poker chips; a good bet, providing you get a map with your key). Since hotels are our chief concern, we did not overnight in any of these. But we did check their facilities, and all seemed to be more than satisfactory in their respective categories. For details, go further into these with your travel agent. We have a feeling you might turn up a rewarding nugget if you do.

At the city's airport gateway, **Holiday Inn** greets flyway inn-comers with 200 nests spread over 8 floors of white stucco. Spacious dining terrace overlooking pool complex and gardens (the beach here is rather punk); restful Andalusian décor with all-American undertones; cozy green-clad Retiro cafeteria; grill plus La Bodega restaurant; Corrida Bar in black and red. Accommodations featuring 2 double beds, wall-to-wall warp-and-woof, twin-sinked baths, and a generous cargo of U.S. comfort standards; the "16" series of suites is especially inviting. Service was sluggish on our investigation, but otherwise it passed every test as a recommendable Holiday stop. A dandy Yankee Doodler.

Back in town, among the "regular" hotel group, the **Tritón** has roared back to life after several years in the doldrums. Director Eloy Durán is polishing up the prongs, snapping the whip, and setting fires under staffers who had grown too complacent after its initial success. Always bid here for a garden unit, not one facing the fortress of apartments. This year's traveler will find seafront lounge and terrace, an appealing dance salon, an expanded and redecorated dining room, an improved bar, a reset hairdressing salon, a garage for 100 cars plus auto rentals and chauffeur service, 2 saunas, 2 tennis courts, a modern kitchen, a better heating and air-conditioning system, and a herculean revision of the palm haven and beach facilities which include a heated freshwater swimming pool, a salty dipper, an outdoor grill and cold buffet, and a shoreside bar. The cuisine is only slightly better than routine unless you ask Maître Antonio Fernandez to hawkeye the skillets for you; then it can shine. Dr. Durán deserves a double "E" for his Effort Española. Recommended once again.

The 106-room **Carihuela Palace** has a historic place in the sweepstakes record book. As it stood on our recent scouting, this was a crossbreed between a holiday retreat and a Westchester shopping mall. On one hand, you'll find a cafeteria, a movie theater, and souvenir counters in a split-level Spanish bazaar. On the other, are 2 pools (the beach is poor), surrounding gardens, a tennis court, an alfresco summer nightclub on weekends, a dining room, and amenities that are generally comfortable but are now in need of some sparkle. The cottage-style units at lawnside are particularly attractive; bid for a seaside unit (a little less noisy than those facing the road).

The 9-story **Riviera**, where your key is linked to a miniature anchor, comes up with many pleasant features. Private beach and seawater pool with overlooking dining room; terraced summer grill; cunning use of rocks, cactus, and fountains for landscaping and decoration; uncluttered, almost cool, public facilities; sauna; beauty salon and barbershop; parking lot plus covered garage; all 190 units and 8 suites with bath, private terrace, and air conditioning. Excellent Concierge team; well managed overall.

The **Meliá Torremolinos** is another barque in the Meliá fleet. It is also the largest structure on the coast—and you may *just* be able to see it if the buses which herd in front to deposit tour groups happen to move. Of its 183 weakly air-conditioned rooms, 70% face the sea and 30% curl around the pool (with more of the latter coming up soon). The lower deck is thickly larded with anchors, bottles, fishnets, and other maritime flotsam; gigantic 250-seat dining hall; 3 bars (including a charmer by the pool); 2 nightclubs; religious services every day at 5 P.M. plus Mass on Sunday. Sleeping accommodations are disturbingly cramped. As a space-and-money-saving device, the bathroom is separated from the bedroom by a wooden partition which starts 7 inches from the floor and rises 7 feet straight up—fascinating if you're either 6 inches or 8 feet tall. The front-office people we saw impressed us this time as cool, correct, efficient, but unfriendly. For the area, it's a pretty good bet.

The **Al-Andalus** now seems to be fading into the pack. Ownership by Salvador Palmada of S'Agaro fame; management by Don Juan Sanchez, whose family has the Palace in Las Palmas. Since it is located across the highway from the sea, we believe this is a better choice for winter than for summer. Red Room for à la carte meals and terpsichore; ground-level, mural-clad dining salon (where you may be seated with strangers if you don't insist on your own table); big trade nowadays with North American tour groups; garden dancing; rustic trappings and handwrought touches predominant in the décor; L-shape pool; tennis courts; balky central air conditioning that can be maddening when the highway racket grows particularly bothersome. Total of 8 suites, 18 singles, and 80 doubles, all with bath, private balcony, and sea view; 66-room annex; full pension required in High Season; cuisine so-so. We hope it can overcome its group-mindedness, because the basic substance here is very good.

The pity about the massive 400-unit **Cervantes** is that it could be so much better if its decorators had turned on more aesthetic éclat. As it stands, the halfhearted sprinkling of armor in its lounges suggests to us that a patrol of medieval mercenaries might have discarded a few pieces of hardware under the broiling Spanish sun and marched on. All of the recreational pluses are here, the rooms are of good size and have balconies, the public areas are well engineered, but the minuses in drab color schemes, enfeebled flair, and unenthusiastic maintenance counterweigh against the overall impression. Sorry, but it gives us a grand case of yawns.

The **Gran Hotel Nautilus** is beginning to surface from the depths. Glass-enclosed heated pool; tastefully redecorated seaview bar and lounge; indifferent cookery and dining-room service on our sampling; clean but cheerless marble corridors; billiard parlor, kiddy nook, tennis court, boutiques. Most of its accommodations have been revamped; these now sparkle. Assistant Manager Nicholas Beck's serious professionalism belies his years.

The 300-coop **Las Palomas**, a crescent-shape structure across from Al Andaluz, is functionally modern but chillingly sterile, in our view. The septagonal pool is nice for dunks; otherwise it doesn't raise a ripple from us.

The **Pez Espada** ("Swordfish") is housed in a large masonic slab. Precisely 100% of its 150 refurnished double accommodations with pipit-size baths offer an angular sea view. It is big and impersonal, with full air conditioning, large terraces. Grill Room with dancing, a nightclub, 4 bars, inviting pools (summer and winter), sauna bath, private beach (one of the best on the shore), tennis court, minigolf, water-skiing, and a garden with a tropical bar. General Manager Laffore and Catering Chief Moreira are working hard to give it more personality and zest. They seem have it zinging already.

In First-class, the 260-room **Alay** is a peach, but it is very costly for the bracket. This one was conceived by José Sendra, a professional hotelier who has done more for this coast than the peseta, the franc, the mark, or the krona. It is attached to both the 1000-capacity congress hall and the similarly styled Alay Apartments, mentioned earlier. Clean, modernistic lines blending with colorful adaptations of Moorish design; tropical dining room overlooking 1 of 2 swimming pools; cafeteria; Arabic bar; game room; boutiques, flower shop, and news kiosk; Rendez-vous nightclub under a crimson tent, with whimsical décor and paintings from the flea market; charming colonial lounge beneath a cascade of greenery; 100% air conditioning that's cooooooool. Some pads on the narrow side; we prefer the accommodations facing Málaga to those peeping at Torrebermeja. Always improving, but no longer as cheap as of yore.

In the next less-costly category, we are very fond of the inviting, 86-room **Tropicana**. Here is an informal atmosphere that is homey and cheerful. Its brightest baubles are the Trader Victorian dining room and the romantic pool that suggests (at least to us'n old Indian scouts) an attractive Seminole campsite. The kindness of the staff and the warmth of their attention show the epitome of Spanish hospitality. Director Miguel Romero and Maurice Beriro are among the most artful and cordial hosts on the coast. Adequate (but not sparkling) maintenance; comfortable rooms with good-looking rustic touches; appetizing meals. Recommended as a happy house with lots of heart. The **Torremora** is a fairway from the golf course along the Málaga highway. Private bus service to the links and nearby beach; 105 accommodations with bath and terrace; some units with wide awnings; colorful décor employing brick, tile-work, copper, and rough textiles; lovely willow-side pool, plus children's pond in the garden; usually loaded with British sun-seekers. Pleasant, despite its distance from the action. The **Siroco**, in a still lower tariff group, is an economy link for the same chain that operates the Tritón, the Emperatriz in Málaga, and the Las Chapas in Marbella. All 121 bedrooms with private bath; only 16 without individual balconies; swimming pool; tennis now lobbing. Though it lacks flair, here's certainly a bargain buy.

The ruggedly charming **Parador del Golf**, sponsored by the Spanish Tourist Office, is a better-than-par challenger to the top group for out-and-out living comfort (especially for golfers who don't mind taking a few extra swings at the sparrow-size mosquitos that strafe in from the neighboring swamp; now there's air conditioning, so they no longer attack by night); low, low tariff for a handsome double lodging. This 40-unit project, architected in the rustic *ranchero* style, occupies the center of an 18-hole golf course 5 miles out on the main road toward Málaga and beneath the Airport's approach lanes. Impressive circular swimming pool; attractive public rooms; outdoor dining May to September; no nightclub; heaps of caterwauling youngsters about on our tour; private beach 100 yards from the doin's; rough-hewn wooden planking in the bedchambers; motel atmosphere with do-it-yourself-dammit service standards. Here's a perfect hitching post for motorists, links buffs, or wayfaring families with leather-lunged kids. A value for the price—if you remember the citronella and earmuffs.

El Pinar, a 100-room First-category candidate a little closer to town, is slipping, in our opinion. Little English spoken; perversely inviting public rooms with rampant plastics, batteries of fireplaces, and a rabbit's warren of facilities in aimless disarray. Glassed-in dining room, topped by splendid circular terrace; swimming pool across the road. Its big drawbacks are the unappetizing pastiche of bedchambers and the transportation difficulties in peak periods.

The **Isabel** reclines gracefully behind the high-tide line, a short stroll south of the action. Rectangular 7-story mountainous structure; teardrop pool with garden; placid Moorish-tone lobby with brick and tile hearth; leather-padded bar; adjoining equestrian lounge. Cheerful restaurant with terra-cotta floor, iron chandeliers, and other Iberian touches; alfresco dining terrace; discothèque. A mere 40 units, mostly doubles with seaview terraces; some corner triples; North African garniture; heavy wooden furnishings, frigobars; large twin-basin bathrooms. A spacious ultra-clean haven; exceptional in its category.

The totally revamped **La Roca** was a pleasant rediscovery on a late Costa del Sol-searching. Attractive garden with swimming pool; private beach across the highway; a handful of bungalows for rent; hunting-lodge lounge and bar; 28 doubles with bath and terrace; 4 suites and 4 singles. Nice for its bracket. The 270-unit **Los Patos** and the neighboring **Aloha Playa** are a pair of production belt sleeping factories that might be placed on your "alternates" list. Fair but cool is our weather report. **Lloyd's** has been in a state of flux. Careworn semicircular building; a few added chambers, but that's about all; tasteless trappings; some might say that Rex, the mascot pooch, lives more sumptuously in his doghouse—but we wouldn't, necessarily. **Los Nidos**, in our estimation, is tolerable only to low-cost tour groups—or to specialists in abnormal psychology who could be driven loco by trying to figure out that startling, multigadgeted, bangle-clad, spiral, elliptical, vertical, tangential, metallic gismo in the lobby. Now it is expanding in a village concept. The **Amaragua** is a part of its scheme. West of town toward Algeciras, the **Delfín** seemed amateurish and overrun by tour groups; a quick-buck-turnover setup, if we ever saw one. The **Costa del Sol**, opposite, reflects a similar personality; it attracts many British guests. Also disenchanting is the **Mar Ymar**, which is a weirdy in its excruciating color-clashes in public rooms and gingerbready construction. Magnificent sea view, one of the best in the region; mediocre sleeping quarters with 10 more tacked on in 10 brand-new hues; angry reader reports about rude clerks. Not recommended, not if your eyes aren't écru-heliotrope-henna-periwinkle-sensitive. Perhaps its management will tone down the pigments and tone up the staff. The **Jorge V** should abdicate, in our judgment; a sleazy monarch, at least to us.

The **Blasón** blazes in with a reception arsenal stocked with armaments. Further along we found halls reeking with disinfectants, water-stained walls, exposed electrical wires over mirrors, and renditions of the Symphony for Horn, Brake, and Gear emanating from the street. Students of the bizarre may enhance their repertoire by checking into one of its triangular rooms or wriggling into a tub which can be entered only from one end (such is the structure of the bathroom). Groups galore—and you won't find us among 'em.

Granada? Our first choice is easily the state-operated **Parador San Francisco** up in the Alhambra complex itself. The building was originally an Arab palace and mosque; lately it was converted into a Franciscan convent and finally into a parador. ("Lately" in the Granadino's mind means circa 1492!) This officially declared National Monument is a unique repository for many of the region's greatest artists and artisans. It is literally crammed with rare iron and copper pieces, rugs, tiles, mosaics, and embroideries. Its 13 air-conditioned nests are always booked 6 months in advance. Just plain wonderful.

Among the privately owned hostelries, the **Luz de Grenada** provides by far the best accommodations and service we've experienced around this hub. The problem is that it's not in the city proper. This one is sited in a dreary outskirts locale that is okay for weary motorists but absolute zero for sightseers unless they want to roar in and out by taxi. Clean modern structure; spacious lobby with tentacles of lounges radiating from one side; masculine bar and wide-angle dining room up 2 flights; grill, plus a second bar on the roof, overlooking a *pueblo* complex below; delicious cuisine on our belly-busting luncheon; perfect attention from a well-trained squadron of maîtres and waiters; different ownership El Cadi disco on the premises. Bedrooms not too big, but thick in comforts and thin in price. If you can accept the transportation hang-up, we'd call this the tiptop independent buy in town and the most rewarding as well. Recommended for everything but its address. Then there's the much improved 250-room **Meliá Granada** in midtown. Public rooms renewed and painted in soothing hues; full air conditioning (a welcome noise muffler); plastics added everywhere possible; mediocre food; popular snack bar; ul-trakind staff; some bedchambers cramped (if you're bad humored) or cozy (if you're amorous). Very central and convenient for midtowners. The 133-unit **Alhambra Palace**, with perhaps the best position of all for sightseeing, seems to be responding at long last to the enthusiasm of its new management. Gervasio Elorza has wrought wonders in sweeping away cobwebs for the Chavarri brothers who originally owned this house; they dropped it for a dismal spell, and now have resumed ownership. Rooms perked up; full air cooling now; fresh facade. Portions remain dreary, but if they continue at the present rate, we predict that it will once again be a gem in the Andalusian diadem. No promises but lots of hopes. **Residencia Macia**, at the foot of the Alhambra, offers fresh, clean, attractive kips in the low-priced category. Splendid for money-savers. (The owners, incidentally, probably will have opened a 3-star competitor next to the Luz Granada by the time you alight.) **Brasilia** turns on its greatest appeal at the 7th floor, where the front accom-modations boast Sierra-view balconies. Midcity situation, sparkly, air-condi-tioned, and worthy for the outlay. The **Guadalupo** welcomes numerous groups to its Alhambra arms. If you can snag either #407 or #426 we think you will dance a *jota*. The **Los Angeles** seems so package-tour oriented and overpriced, in our opinion, that we say ho-hum to this one. While the person-nel were cordial and this hostelry is one of the 2 which has a pool, we think most pilgrims will share our boredom. **Colombia** is recommended only to homespun types and totally color-blind wayfarers. Nice, but WOW what pigments! French patrons predominate at the **Kenia**. They know a bargain when they see one. The unpretentious **Rallye** nudges bumpers with the Re-nault showroom. Lots of polish on this mini; compact prices too. Our kudos diminish respectively for the 60-room-and-bath **Sacromonte**, the older but similarly outfitted **Sudan**, and the chill-blown, commercial **Monte-carlo**. For budget-watchers, the youthful **Hostal Internacional** provides basic shelter. The location, however, put us off. Further down our list, the **Victoria** is noisy and the **Washington Irving** seems to have lost its muse. Both, at best, are just passable. **Hostal Carlos V** might serve in an emergency. But we pray one never occurs. Finally, the **Anacapri** and **Los Faisanes** are not recommended to any capricious fowl on the wing.

Jerez: This center of glorious sherry and Spanish *coñac* historically has been the absolute lees of the innkeeping cup. However, the '71 vintage, 65-room **Jerez** has finally banged out the bung to become the unquestioned area leader. Spanking-white 3-story structure; cool, steel-blue-carpeted reception and sunken lounge; clean, airy dining den (with uninspired fare) abutting an alfresco terrace and pool; chummy equestrian bar. Management seems to us to be riding on its laurels rather than high in the saddle. Stirrup-linked keys unlock pads with rust broadloom, stucco walls, Brobdingnagian twin beds sheathed in avocado spreads, and spacious bathrooms with long fluorescent lights, magnifying mirrors, lake-size tubs separated from the other conveniences, and towels you can practically get lost in; most chambers wear balconies. The newer, 2-star, 30-room **Mica** might be a worthy alternative if this one is fully booked. Otherwise, **Los Cisnes** ("The Swans"), for eons the local leader, is such an ugly duckling that we were again struck with horror that its céntimo-pinching direction has still done little or nothing to improve the amenities here. Among the remainder, the **Arenal**, a so-called luxury-class pension, is out-and-out poor. The 27-room **Imar** impressed us as ranging from depressing to downright sickening. Except for the Jerez, we'd prefer to curl up in a barrel at one of the local wine cellars than to sleep in any of the other public offerings here.

León: **Hostal de San Marcos** (building begun in 1530 and constructed for 2 centuries; now totally made over for Deluxe patronage; exquisite marriage of glass and stone; superb management; A-plus comfort; baronial interior; 258 rooms, each with private bath, telephone, and air conditioning; glorious melding of the life of the cloistered era with the comforts of the twentieth century. The main restaurant is open in summer only; the flamenco nightclub functions on fiestas and weekends. Director Enrique Gonzalez is a pro who knows his innkeeping P's and Q's from A to Z. The Spanish National Tourist authorities have every right to be superproud of this gemstone. The commercial **Conde de Luna** would have to rank next in our poll. All of the amenities are here; there's even a bit of flair from the decorators, but in comparison with the San Marcos, it is decidedly number two. **Quindos** is smaller and more modest with a corresponding drop in price tags. Adequate. Across the Bernesga River, the **Riosol** represents—to us, at least—a port only in times of raging storm. It struck us as drab and heavily used.

Oviedo boasts the majestic **Hotel de la Reconquista**, which incorporates within a *hospicio* (children's refuge) built by Carlos III a restored ancient chapel, a restaurant, grill, coffee shop, tearoom, and a host of hospitable nests for today's wayfaring pilgrims of any age. Fully air-conditioned for the heirs of yesteryear. Splendid. Halfway to León, the **Parador Nacional Puerto de Pajares** offers only 15 rooms (#9 is our favorite) plus a breathtaking balcony view of the Peña Uviña mountain range. Charming regional restaurant; no private baths; bedrock tariffs for solid rewards.

San Sebastián's spectacular topper is the cliff-high **Monte Igueldo**—so high up on that Monte, in fact, that it smiles down upon the lighthouse. It's a blessing to let's-get-away-from-it-all holiday-hounds who, like us, are unnerved by the din of the city. Ocean-wide lobby; glass-fronted lounge looking seaward; coolish bar nookery; starkly marblesque dining room with appealing vittles; 4th-floor pool; small shop; 121 rooms; corner units peering at the summer capital, the bay, and the unbelievably enchanting Basque coastline; full carpeting; full bath count. Service much improved by Manager José-María Casado. Access is via a private road (a sticker is put on your windshield so that you won't have to pay a toll each time) or on the funicular (also free for hotel guests). Open year round. It must be as windy as Dover, however, on a wintry day. Truly a wonder of architecture; sky-highly recommended as a stunning achievement.

The **Londres** is one of the slicker shell-ters along La Concha (the bayside beach), despite the coldly institutional fastnesses of plastic and Formica in its older bedchambers. Ask for one of the refashioned units, which are miles better, in our opinion. Now we do admire its overall atmosphere, brightened corridors, freshened and attractive wood-lined and flower-dotted dining room, and open seafront terrace for summer sipping. The staff attitudes seem to have soared, too, of late. Very worthy, indeed.

Also down at sea level, the old-fashioned **Maria Cristina** is in a special class. Five minutes from the beach; spacious and serene; creaky yet spotlessly clean; expansive grounds; traditional furnishings; in general, standing still. Its view of the once-lovely Urumea River has alas been disgracefully despoiled by paper-mill deposits that drift by in giant malodorous wads. Taut management; the people in attendance are fine. Youngbloods probably won't like this *grande dame,* but older pilgrims should find solace here.

The **San Sebastián** may be the newest hostelry in town, but in our notebook we've penned, "Blah on the outside; blah on the inside." The location is on a busy artery, but otherwise we say it's pretty bloodless. The glass-and-marble **Orly**, a First-class entry diagonally across from the Biarritz, offers better accommodations. Lobby at ground zero, 60 terraced units on floors 8 to 12, and private apartments (occasionally available) sandwiched between. Private garage; Snack Bar; utilitarian furnishings and claustrophobic dimensions. Not bad for small-boned economizers, but not special either. **Hispano-Americano** is smartening up keenly under the watchful guidance of Director Sr. D. Miguel Goñi. Multitudes of fresheners, including a flower-lined river-terrace for summer dining, a solarium, carpets, improved bathrooms, and relatively fresh paint everywhere. All 82 units with showers; full pension obligatory; now open the year around.

The **Biarritz** is always remembered by us for its almost frighteningly antique lobby. Razing plans were scotched in favor of a wait-a-while policy that was still waiting on our latest check. Sixth floor; the newest of an old lot; all levels retouched; plastic chairs and low beds introduced; full pension required. Pretty dreary to us. The 12-unit **Chomin**, above the restaurant of the same name, is a resident-style stop which might be ideal for families. Despite its association with the feedery below (see "Restaurants" section), it scorns the full-pension-required gouge. Two blocks from the sea; all bedchambers with bath; so-so maintenance, which is pitiful considering its potential. The **Codina**? As travel reporters who have long inspected hundreds of hotels annually, we cannot remember when we boggled in such shock and dismay as we did when we first toured through this one. Our latest investigation, however, notes a considerable swing toward better housekeeping standards. If you must stop here, pick the "9" series of rooms, which leads the grim parade. The 21-room **Parma** is bare-boned, but fair enough in a pinch. Along the pike at **Fuenterrabía**, the **Parador El Emperador** lights up 16 cells in the ancient fortress of Carlos V. Though the total number of accommodations is small, the rustic enchantment of the Middle Ages pervades the atmosphere. Also near the San Sebastián Airport, you'll discover the **Hostal Provincial de Jaizkibel**, a mountainside retreat which we found excellent for lunch; we prefer the parador for sleeping, however. At nearby **Renteria**, Hostal Lintzirin reverberates from the growl of highway traffic. Better than adequate facilities, but far from restful, unfortunately.

Santander hobbles in with the ultracommercial **Bahía** as its modest leader. It counts 250 tiny cubicles with baths, but we can't wax enthusiastic over any of 'em. At the beach sector, **Sardinero** is a renewed old-timer. **Maria Isabel** would be our next choice followed by the **Rhin**. Further out, at **Santillana del Mar**, headquarters for viewing the prehistoric cave paintings, the **Parador Gil Blas** is a sweet medieval complex in a wonderfully intimate dairying hamlet. Don't miss this touch of arcadia if you are within 100 miles of the village. **Los Infantes**, in the same settlement, will ultimately grow to a size of 50 rooms, blending old-world décor with modern times. Simple but nice. At **Fuente Dé**, along the route of the Picos de Europa mountains, the 10-unit **Refugio de Montaña** commands a spellbinding view of them thar *montañas*. More of a lodge than a full-blown hotel, but *what* an eyeful of Mother Nature!

Santiago de Compostela: The multimillion-dollar **Hostal de los Reyes Católicos** ("Hostel of the Catholic Kings"), underwritten by the government, is a fantastic architectural and decorative monument—so opulent, so grandiose, and so extravagantly conceived that it's a wonder to the eyes. Commercially, however, this all-season retreat must always remain, through this very lavishness, a Taj Mahal-size white elephant. Spacious public rooms, 4 dining salons, concert hall, auditorium, bar, and hairdresser; dancing nightly in both the nightclub and the grill. Now there are 150 units with bath, many expanded from smaller bedchambers; three 1-room suites that are slightly smaller than Candlestick Park; regal doubles; cuisine expensive and appealing; Chief Concierge José Calvo is a genial mentor. Worth a special detour to overnight here, because there's nothing else like it in Spain.

Seville is undergoing numerous changes. The Meliá chain just has forged 2 new links here (the luxury-class, 221-unit **Sevilla** and the more modest, 350-room **Parque**) which will be open for your visit this season. Until we can get by for a thorough check, we'd be happy with the sweet little **Doña Maria**. We also suspect that discriminating Guidesters will even compare it favorably with the prestigious dowagers of Seville. Midtown situation squinting at the Cathedral from the narrow Calle don Ramondo; vaulted lobby with brick pillars; restaurant in Moorish décor; rooftop swimming pool with bar and snack tables; 100% air-conditioned. Total of 50 doubles and 12 singles—and no 2 alike; full carpeting; 12 units with canopied beds; Simmons mattresses for all snoozers; attractive paintings; many baths with double basins; some with French doors leading to balconettes. The proprietor is the artfully motivated Marquis de San Juaquin; Manager Miguel Villegas, formerly of the Colón, runs the day-to-day show. Very tasteful; very comfortable; very highly recommended.

The youthful, 82-room, gaily terraced **Pasarela** stands face-to-face with the

Meliá Sevilla. It exudes good taste, modern tones, expensive garniture (marble trim in baths, as one small example), a garage (which is a blessing in this town), and such highlights as potted gardens hanging in front of your picture window. You'll also find a cafeteria for putting on weight and a sauna for taking it off. Well conceived by Santander Proprietor Don Manuel Peña. We like this entry. *Saludos!*

The 8-story, fully air-conditioned **Luz Sevilla** also is tuned to the tastes of modernists and Jet Settlers. This one boasts a collection of up-to-date international hotel amenities fused with undertones of Spanish flavor. Attractive soft-hued décor throughout; viewful rooftop summertime Grill, with dancing on weekends; alfresco apron for panaromantics; orchestra nightly; leathery bar with handsome wooden panels and tartan carpet; hearthside library; marblesque dining room, also with open terrace adjoining; solarium and children's pool. A boutique, an Avis car rental agency, barbershop, beauty parlor, and basement garage make up the panoply of fringe benefits. All bedchambers with piped music, bedside and bathroom phones; wall-to-wall carpeting; first-quality appointments; frigobars in all suites; units ending in "02" the most spacious. Highly recommended for its type, but impressively expensive by national standards.

The creaky yet historic **Alfonso XIII** ("thirteen" is pronounced "TRAY-thay") is almost a shrine for nostalgic visitors to Andalusia. The lobby is a museum of Spanish and Moorish art; the lavish workmanship, the specially baked tiles, the tapestries, and the $50,000 gold service for royalty will never be duplicated. Friendly concierge and staff; vastly improved cuisine; spotless cleanliness in a general aura of seeming decrepitude. Still one of the sights of Seville, but to us, very much in need of more up-to-the-era creature comforts and conveniences. **Nuevo Lar** swung open its 139 portals in '73, and this one has the necessary mod-cons. Marble lobby cheered by a small aquarium; restaurant for intimate dining near entrance; larger banquet hall up a flight; staff on the cool side but well trained. The bedchambers are meticulously maintained; patterns are at war with each other but the colors overall formed an amnesty pact; book units ending in "18" because they are much more spacious than others. Spiffy and neat. A treat.

The slightly larger **Maria Luisa** Park opened a year earlier on a scenic avenue across the river. One peek will assure you that it is very much in the twentieth century. If you want to cash in on a splendid view, bid for a frontside address with terrace. The rust-toned **La Macarena** blushes incarnadine beside the old wall of the city—a nice touristic touch that later seems merely tedious when you are saddled with the effort of getting to or from midtown. The glassed-in patio is a plus as is the rooftop, L-shape swimming pool. In sum, however, we think you can do better closer to the doin's than way out in the ruins.

The **Colón** has charged in with many spectacular gains recently. New entrance, new lobby, new desk plan, new bar; cleverly conceived Burladero Restaurant in *torero* style (even the plates bear a bullring design); huge dining room overlooking a lane of orange trees; masculine bar untouched; 100% air-conditioned; 261 bedrooms; some baths with double basins and bright floral patterns; well-equipped living space with huge wardrobes and silent valets; 7th-floor accommodations with private balconies (especially desirable in balmy winter weather, when they are in sunshine all day long). Director Don Pedro de Torres Gracía provides as much as any of the luxury-category innkeepers at half their blue-ribbon tariffs. This house has the feeling of a back-home Statler—cool, commercial, but efficient. Now a solid favorite of wayfaring Americans—for excellent reason. Superb for the money.

Many of the architectural features in the '73-vintage **Becquer** were salvaged from the razed *palacio* that stood on this site. Marble portal leading to an open lobby divided by wrought-iron screens; English bar; breakfast-only service; garage; Andalusian patio on first floor; 126 air-conditioned bedrooms. Sound returns in the medium-price range.

The **Christina**, directly across the plaza from the Alfonso XIII, evokes an air of somber commercialism. Appealing roof garden in summer, plus Bodega nightclub in basement, offering some of the best flamenco dancing and other entertainment in town; friendly personnel. Its chef, however, is in howling need of a refresher course in cooking school, poor fellow. In our personal judgment the beds are small and the furnishings tasteless; moreover we found the maintenance dragging. Lackluster to us. The off-beat **Murillo** is sited on a charming, lamplit, hard-to-find, pedestrian-only street (Lope de Rueda 3, 5, and 7) in the Old Town. Slaphappy, informal administration, overseen by funloving Proprietor Miguel Linares, a brother in the family that operates Spain's largest chain of art and antique shops. Colorfully decorated with pieces of his Linares collection; 64 small rooms with bath or shower; all front units with private balcony; best buys in the 14-suite annex. Cheerfully amusing; for the young-in-heart. To our distress, the **Inglaterra** is turning into one of those "big bustling establishments." It delivers 120 now-worn accommodations, the last installment looking onto a quiet interior garden. Sleek glassy entrance warmed somewhat by wood; 200-year-old tiles decorating the lobby and public areas; richly framed oil paintings; window-fronted dining room facing the active plaza; leathery bar stamped with the seals of 8 colleges of Oxford; a boutique. Curiously, this house features the most comfortable telephone booths we've ever dialed in our travel snoopings—2 easy chairs, artwork, glass doors, and antique phones. One decorative theme in all bedrooms: brownish-gold carpets, yellow-to-beige chenille spreads, carved wood headboards, black chairs, twin basins in baths plus a shower cap for milady. The suites, except for corner-sited #508, were unimpressive to us; all 5th floor units sport terraces, by the way. Fatigue seems to be setting in here.

Now let's round up our budget shelters: The **Reyes Catolicos** would be our pick of the low-cost havens; dining for registrants is at the Montecarlo. Then comes the unpretentious, Spanishy **Ducal**, followed by the aesthetically surprising **Don Paco**, which is a paean to pigments. Nice facilities and extra-sweet staffers, but why it hues its ode-ious path we'll never know. **Alcazar** also leans to passionate pink, salmon rouge, khaki brown, and pistachio green. Clean it is, however. The **Venecia** and the previously mentioned **Montecarlo** (dining room) are emergency hole-ups only. Incidentally, unless you're willing to take potluck as a boarder in a private house, *do not go for* Semana Santa *(Holy Week) or the* Feria *without a confirmed reservation from one of the above;* any other hotels are not, repeat *not*, recommended. Since you'll be forced illegally to pay double the normal rates wherever you stay during these jam-packed weeks, you might as well do so with a degree of cleanliness and comfort.

Toledo has skyrocketed in its hospitality offerings of late. The duet of national paradors make it unique in Spain, for nowhere else to our knowledge are there 2 in such a small area. The **Conde de Orgaz** affords the most glorious view of Toledo possible—especially from its summer terrace where you may also take lunch. By this season, it expects to boost its room count to 100 doubles, all with balcony. The nearby **Parador del Virrey Toledo** actually resides within the fourteenth-century Oropesa Castle—one of the most impressive we've seen in all of our travels. If you can snag some digs high in the older section, we think you will have found your castle in the Spanish sky. Fabulous—and that's a word we seldom employ. Among the privately operated houses, the **Hostal del Cardenal**, within the ramparts, stands turret and parapet above any other independent inn in sight. Fountains, hearths, flowers, elegant staircases, and a salon sheathed with intricately carved wood form a proud cloak of refinement for this newish but cleverly antiqued house. Two-tier restaurant (see "Restaurants") on opposite edges of a tree-shaded courtyard; suite, 3 singles, and 2-dozen doubles whisper their Castilian heritage; handsome, functional baths; gracious and ingratiating staff. Holy Toledo, *what* a bell ringer! **Carlos V** leads the also-rans; if you should hear strange sounds as you walk through the Tombs of the Spanish Kings in the Escorial, they might be wails of protest from this great Emperor for this calumny on his name. We'd rate it as Tenth-Class Miserable, but some Guidesters are pushing it up to Ninth Class. We won't quibble; we also won't stay there. **Alfonso VI**, with its updated interior and kind personnel, is a sounder bet today; even one of the suits of armor was crooning on our visit.

In *Valencia*, the Inhousa Company's **Astoria Palace** is *the* Big Time local operation. Total of 208 spacious but stark rooms; La Bruja nightclub; terrace dining-and-dancing; a chilly marblesque lobbyette, an uncozy lounge, an unattractive restaurant, and all of its accommodations air-conditioned. Improving staff attitudes; warming up nicely; better than ever. The ubiquitous Meliá group recently unveiled a challenger here. The 4-star, 129-room **Azafata** is its name, but, of course, we haven't had an opportunity to check it out as yet. Both promise keen competition to the older hostelries. The **Excelsior** is coming up once again—but there's still a long climb ahead. Fully air-conditioned with individual controls; American Bar with adjoining summer-winter terrace; 65 rooms and baths; 12 corner suites; fresh wall coverings and paint make it much brighter than it was, but nicks, chips, and sticking hardware still turn up with disturbing frequency. The ancient and seedy **Reina Victoria** has had a piecemeal renovation job that still lacks flair. Full bath count for its 92 units; some Charles Addams doubles at dwarfish tabs; traffic-choked location. Fair, but uninspired, in our opinion. Except for the **Renasa**'s situation at the edge of town near the soccer stadium, we think it is one of the better and newest hotel buys in Valencia. Fresh, Scandinavian, clean-lined personality that we can recommend cheeringly. The **Sorolla** is smack in the middle of the bright lights. It's pretty perky too, so if you prefer midtown to the suburbs, this should fill the bill for a modest outlay. The **Oltra** is basic; you can't go too far wrong, but we wish the housekeeper would swallow more vitamin B. The **Llar** largely lures lodgers in lumps; heavy group patronage; bustling, genial staff; clean modest surroundings. The starkness at the **Ingles** tingles our nerves. Bah. The **Alhambra** shouldn't fool you with its attractive lobby, because here the beauty is only skin deep, in our beady-eyed view. "Give a man a landscape and a passion," said Jesús Gómez Escardó, "and you give him everything!" That last word nicely sums up what this master host and his charming wife Doña Alicia provide the fortunate guests of the **Hotel Monte Picayo.** This hostelry is not actually within the city limits of hotel-poor Valencia, but 14 miles down the pike in *Puzol-Sagunto.* Sprawled over a large hill are the central building, 10 cottages, 12 swimming pools, and 2 championship tennis courts. The lobby is stunning in concept, unusual in design, and flawless in execution: It consists of 4 descending tiers, housing respectively the reception area, the library, the bar, and the lounge overlooking the cascading main pool. Within easy strolling distance are the Grill, the sauna, the shopping gallery, the discothèque, and the 46 hyper-sumptuous chambers in the principal edifice. More? Much, much, much more. Suffice it to say that what the extremely talented Gómez team has done with their landscape has become our passion too. Fabulous!

Out at *El Saler*, the **Parador Luis Vives** provides peaceful duals in the sun. All 40 accommodations doubles; clinical taste; pool fringing the golf links. Fair-ways. In *Torrente*, 14 miles from the port up a difficult 3rd-class road, the **Lido** is better as a dinner-and-dance stop than as an overnight hitch. For motorists, **La Pinada**, at kilometer stone 28 on the Zaragoza highway, has a pleasant pool, a routine restaurant, and so-so sleeping quarters. One thing to be said for this one: it's on the way *out* of town.

In *Vigo*, Spain's salty old girl of the north, the **Bahía de Vigo** leads the convoy. It's on the waterfront a few steps from the docks; there's a modern commercial atmosphere throughout; we liked the ocean-wide restaurant on the 2nd floor as well as the Corsair's Bar; all 106 staterooms come fully plumbed. Shipshape. The fresh **Niza** would rank next in the Vigo regatta, followed by the 3-star **Ensenada** and the beachfront **Samil Playa**, also a 3-star rating officially.

In the Vigo vicinity, the environs almost bristle with those wonderful Government-run paradors. Our pick of the neighboring trio is the **Conde de Gondomar** at *Bayona*. It nests in an L-shape fortress bathed by the same winds that drove the ships of Sir Francis Drake along these shores. Infinite variety of pastimes, sports, recreation—even a genuine dungeon in which to drop the kids when they get cantankerous. Then there's the 50-room **Parador Casa del Baron** in the town of *Pontevedra* (20 miles from Vigo). The situation is not so maritime, but the regional cuisine is seasoned by the sea. Finally, there's the **Parador de San Telmo** at *Túy* (17 miles from Vigo) which gazes at Portugal across the Rio Miño. It's a nice stop if you wish to dawdle a while longer in Spain before hopping the frontier.

Other Towns and Centers

Almuñécar: **Sexi** used to be a fine overnighter for coast-highway motorists from Alicante to Málaga or Algeciras, but now, to conform to its socio-logically significant name, it's noisy, the beds sag, and the whole operation looks rumpled. Except for the headwaiter, the staff is so rough-and-ready that it would be more at home rushing the growlers from the nearest saloon. The cuisine is worse than deplorable. Even Masters and Johnson would have found this un-Sexi number an uninteresting bust.

Benidorm seems to cater solely to German tourists. The wide sandy beach is a dream—one of the best on the Mediterranean—but, on every day during High Season here, it is just like Coney Island on the Fourth of July. The **Delfín** is the Deluxe catch of the school. Quiet waterside situation with a sleek residential ambiance; excellent pool; appealing restaurant; winsome cafeteria for light bites; simple furnishings; bid only for a room facing the sea. Recommended chiefly for being away from the hurly-burly. The **Corregidor Real** is in the same bracket. It's 1 block from the sea, in the center of town. This youngster opened all the stops and valves in its Spanish décor—so overdone, in our opinion, that it is touristy-gimmicky. Extensive use of wood, bricks, rough textiles, and colored glass; tiny pool with adjoining bar; nightclub; 35 rooms and 35 baths. All right if you go for *mucho, mucho, mucho* flash. Operative from March 1 to October 30. The triangular-shape **Glasor**, opened in '67, is efficient but coldish; snag a seaside unit, because the others can be deafeningly noisy. **Los Alamos** is also in the front line. **Les Dunes** has become so careworn its sparkle has gone, we're sad to say. Excellent midbeach situation; grimly pedestrian in taste. The **Brisa** also has become winded in the race. Now spavined, to our eyes. **Planesia**, on the mountain slope, provides a warm welcome from Reception Chief Andreas Guerrero, brother of our friend at Valencia's Royal. Although the remainder of the Benidormitories are not recommended at this writing, changes occur so rapidly here that it would be wise to make an up-to-the-instant check with your travel agent immediately before departure from the U.S.

Castellón de la Plana (Mediterranean coast, 39 miles north of *Valencia*): The beachside **Golf** features Seville-style architecture, with its modern accommodations embracing a wide open patio. Reportedly poor service which we didn't experience personally. The smaller **Turcosa** is said to provide better client attention, possibly because, as a year-round operation, the staff is more stable. We have a feeling this will soon become a boom zone for package tours from the cloudy northern climes of Europe.

Gandía: This expanded whistle stop between Alicante and Valencia offers the **Bayren** (2½ miles from the village; front rooms overlooking the swimming pool and the sea; quiet in Off Season; friendly personnel), the young **Residencia San Luis** (clean-lined and sound), the **Safari** (even younger), and the **Recati** (small, quiet, on the dunes; coming up once again)—plus a gaggle of alternates.

Huelva: The **Luz Huelva** might very well be the best in town. The fresh-faced **Residencia Tartessos** would be our next choice in a more modest category. The **Victoria** has a kind staff, good kitchen, and poor amenities. The **Motel Ferreira**, on the route to Portugal, is now barely passable for folk on the move; pool, restaurant, and bar; so poorly maintained that we've lost all enthusiasm.

Irún: **Colón** (125 rooms, 125 baths, Frou-Frou nightclub, so-called Txingudi

Balls Saloon which interested inquiries have revealed is a ballroom; pretty good). **Alcázar** has added 10 more modern rooms, but we suggest **San Sebastían** if Colón can't handle your reservation.

Jávea: The **Parador Costa Blanca** is about the only grace note in this otherwise humdrum backwater—well, actually it's a beachfront settlement about 25 miles from Gandia. The palm garden is nice, but the facilities for travelers are routine.

La Manga del Mar Menor: This spit of seashore, located approximately 15 miles fron Cartagena, has experienced a touristic boom of late, but it fails to raise a pimple of excitement on our flesh. Of the 100 or so hotels, our bouquets go to the **Luz Cavanna**, the **Galua**, and the **Entremares**, in that order. If you prefer to overnight in **Cartagena**, our choice for the moment is the **Cartagonova** with the **Mediterraneo** next; a soon-to-be-built newcomer, however, may change our ratings.

Lérida: The **Hostal de los Condes de Urgel** (34 rooms with baths, 2 suites; 2 dining rooms; bars, terraces, and some units with balcony; swimming pool; central air conditioning; members of American Express and Diner's Club; very recommendable en route stopover). The **Palacio** and **Nacional** are not worthwhile tie-ups, in our opinion.

Mojácar: Down on the coast about 50 miles from Almeria, this shoreliner boasts the **Parador de Los Reyes Catolicos**, not to be confused with the Hostal of the same name in northwestern Santiago de Compostela. The white modern complex soon will expand to 100 seafront units. Enormous pool; broad vistas; superb comfort; interesting textures—a common feature of the parador system. The neo-Moorish, 145-room **El Moresco** hangs on a cliff higher up toward the whitewashed town. The octagonal rooftop pool is a marvel; the bedchambers, however, were somewhat disappointing.

Murcia : The **Reina Victoria** is an Old World charmer. The 96-room **Galua** is a New World upstart we haven't yet seen.

Nerja : The **Parador** is tops for seaside lazing. The **Balcón de Europa** is also friendly and comfy. Both are for seekers of absolute tranquillity.

Pamplona : The 8-story, curvilinear **Hotel de los Tres Reyes**, with its 3 crowns shining over the fringes of the city, is a godsend in this shelter-poor community. Total of 176 units including 8 suites, each with private terrace, bath, telephone, and radio; all public rooms and bedchambers air-conditioned; summer swimming pool plus patio dancing; good food in its modern-tone restaurant; 3 bars; barbershop and beauty salon; garage for 125 cars. Director Angel M. Cazon justifies his first name for providing such comfort in this wasteland of innkeeping; Concierge Emilio González is a cherub. Recommended as the top stop within many a mile. **La Perla** remains barely adequate as the sentimental host of Hemingway *aficionados*. **Yoldi**, with about 50 units, must have been designed for Spanish anvil salesmen. Sorry, but it doesn't qualify—and neither do the rest of the ragged lot.

Ronda: The **Victoria** is much better now, and the food is surprisingly savory —but the road up from the coast, while improved, is still a motorist's trial.

Salamanca: **Gran**, **Monterrey** (both so-so only). **Residencia Universitaria**

Gran Vía at Rosa 4, has been urgently recommended by one of our readers (a U.S. university professor) who lived there all summer; budget-level.

Santiago de la Ribera (Murcia): Our old friend Emilio Portman, the veteran hotelier who operated such renowned landmarks as Mallorca's Formentor and Barcelona's Ritz, was in charge of **Hotel Los Arcos**, on the Mar Menor, when last we heard. His presence should automatically ensure the comfort of any voyager.

Segovia: **Las Sirenas** (noisy).

Sitges is a charming little fishing port 45 minutes down the coast from Barcelona's airport. It's packed in high summer with trippers from all lands. In fringe seasons, however, it is an ingratiating rest stop with good food, fair hotels, and seaside golfing. Within the town, the **Calípolis** is the leader. Amiable staff; reasonable cuisine; spacious rooms with balconies; simple suites; moderate tariffs. Clients may use the municipal pool and receive a 50% greens fees discount at the links. The **Terramar**, by the golf club and overlooking a ringlet harbor with private beach, is seasonal but good. Wedding-cake construction with flower-girt terraces for all seafront rooms; inner court with a decorative pond; tennis courts; horses available; water sports facilities; swimming pool and adjoining outdoor bar; institutional dining salon as big and cold as the Avalon Ballroom; large bedchambers; oddly shaped suites; mélange of furniture from Iberian Provincial to Grand Rapids Seconds. Not bad in a sprawling, multischematic way. The Scandinavian-style **Los Pinos** is modest and not without its charms—especially as exhibited by Proprietors Xavier Tort and Augustin Sans (formerly of Barcelona's Ritz) and Miss Trudi at the Reception Desk. **La Reserve** is a friendly little pension. The 40-unit **Platjador** is amateurish; it's strictly for econ-o-misers. The **Subur** is zipless; this one caters heavily to European migrants. The enchanting **Vallpineda** development is designed chiefly for householders, but perhaps a chalet can be rented for a holiday respite. Excellent swimming pool in an enclave of gardens; deluxe restaurant; fine bar; the peace of the country, broken only by the sound of tennis balls plopping on its 7 championship courts. A pleasant clublike hideaway, but not by the sea.

Tarragona's **Imperial Tarraco** stands above the main crossroads as tall as a modern, flag-decked fortress—but it is not imposing, except in its massiveness. Although easily the leader for accommodations, it seems such a tasteless a vacation stop that we can't imagine ourself in a merry mood choosing it as a holiday house. The **Lauria** is next, followed far down the list by the **Europa** or the **Paris**. None is really exciting.

Trujillo : **Conquistador** (the only stop worth considering).

Valdepeñas : Point your headlights straight for **Motel del Hidalgo**, now under the crack direction of José María Mateu of Palma's Meliá Mallorca fame, because the next-ranked **Paris** is for lumberjacks.

Vitoria: **Canciller Ayala** (Deluxe category; 200 rooms; by far the most imposing in the region). Avoid the **Frontón** (ouch!).

Zaragoza: **Corona de Aragón** provides space for 520 guests in Deluxe surroundings; 2 restaurants featuring American, French, and Spanish cuisine; excellent and colorful grill; active bar; patio, solarium, sippery, and swimming pool on the roof; dark but spacious bedchambers. Substantial and very well managed. Then come a covey of late-sprouting question marks: **Alfonso I** (120 rooms; reportedly nicely furnished), **Ramiro I**^{er} (60 units in Deluxe quality), **Don Quijote** (170 accommodations), and **Don Yo** (170 door keys). Bringing up the wagon train, we have **Gran** (200 rooms in classic style; public lounges and 1st-floor accommodations air-conditioned; some bedchambers sumptuous in an antique way; others so-so; about the poorest personnel attention we've found in any luxury hotel in this nation), **Goya** (Statleresque in atmosphere; 100 newer rooms, all air-conditioned; 60 older units revamped; 100% bath count; clean, fresh ambiance; garage), **Gran Vía** (31 cubicles, each with private shower; okay for peseta-pinchers), **Conde Blanco** (chiefly for motorists), **Centenario** (seemed downright scabrous to us; recommended for mouth-breathers who never hope to smell again), and **La Fuente** (even worse), **Oriente** (more recently built, but already in a class with the last 2).

These, as we've said, are the most popular. The majority of them pass the test.

Hotels which are *the best available* are as follows: *Albacete*, **Gran**, **Almería**, **Goya**, **Residencia Fátima**, and **Simón**; *Alfaro*, **Burgo Viejo** (and its wine museum); *Aranjuez*, the undelicious **Delicias**; *Burgos*, **Condestable**, **España**, or the later-model **Landa Palace** (delightful!); *Avila*, **Los Cuatro Postes** (superb view of the medieval town); *Cartagena*, **Mediterráneo** (miserable!); *Ciudad-Real*, **España**; *Gerona*, **Italianos**, **Peninsular**, or **Rex**; *Guadalajara*, **España**; *Motril*, **Mediterráneo** and all others (fierce!); *Oviedo*, **Principado**; *Port-Bou*, **Estación** (a true boo-boo); *Valladolid*, **Olid** (an entry by the Meliá chain) or **Conde Ansúrez** (supposedly Deluxe, but a big disappointment to us).

Off the mainland, 2 centers have become of paramount importance to every American who plans a trip to Spain. These are the Balearic Islands (Mallorca, Menorca, Ibiza, and others), and the Canary Islands (Gran Canaria, Tenerife, Fuerteventura, and others). Mallorca is covered in its separate chapter; see our evaluation of the Canaries earlier in this chapter.

Taxes, service charges, and state-controlled extras are heavy in all Spanish hotels. Now, in accordance with an official edict, you should automatically receive an all-inclusive quotation. Some which cater to the tourist trade are allowed to tack a flat 30% onto everything in sight during July, August, September, 15 days at Christmas, 15 days at Easter, and throughout Corpus Christi. There is always a 20% purchase tax on alcoholic beverages (spirits *and* wines), plus another 10% levy on meals or special menus. The standard service bite is 15% throughout the nation. Last but not least, every stop on your schedule will collect the Tourist Tax (for the development of tourism) of 2% on all bills over 100 pesetas.

Therefore, as a rough rule of thumb, figure that you are paying about 25% above the basic rate for these extras.

Beginning in '70, a Government rating system was applied to most shelters in the following way: for hotels (1 to 5 stars), for hostels and pensions (1 to 3), and for apartment-hotels (1 to 4); inns will not be given official magnitudes. The grades are based on the facilities offered, and State-issued plaques denoting the rank are displayed.

Spanish hotel tariffs are supposed to be controlled. Some of the legal ceilings, however, are so cruelly unrealistic that many innkeepers are caught in a disastrous price-squeeze by operating costs that have risen 100% or more over the past decade. As a countermeasure, now a newer law has been passed which has permitted luxury category houses the freedom to charge anything they wish while raising the tariffs of all other establishments by 10%—bad news for all of us. If you should feel that some grasping scoundrel is unfairly taking you for a ride, send your complaint (enclose the bill) to the sympathetic and brilliant Minister of Information and Tourism, who should see that legal action is taken.

Even with illegal paddings, however, you'll still find most (not all!) of Spain's hostelries among the cheapest in Europe.

§TIPS: There are practically no window screens in this land, because the Spanish believe they cut down air circulation and block the view. One hotel which installed a few as a test, received so many outraged protests that they had to take them out (!!). In summer, carry a fly swatter, kill the current crop of flies before retiring, and keep your blinds *closed* during the night. Otherwise, at 6:15 A.M. they will drive you out of your mind.

The telephone service in hotels all over Spain—even the best ones!—is almost sure to be terrible. Most of the operators don't speak English. Ask for your party by room number, because Anglo-Saxon names usually throw the switchboard people into tizzies—and never depend upon telephone messages being properly (1) transcribed or (2) delivered.

As in most of Europe, the sly devils generally switch off the air conditioning from the wee hours to about 7 A.M. Spain is one of the worst offenders.

Many Spanish hostelries take up the carpets from public rooms and corridors during the summer. This undoubtedly brings down the temperature by several degrees—but it looks like the dickens.

State law specifically and rigidly forbids unaccompained females to enter a man's hotel room (not suite!) after dark, regardless of circumstances. Don't invite her up for a drink; you'll be stopped at the elevator.

Dedicated budgeteers? Since we're too bottlenecked here for additional entries, please consult this year's edition of our annually revised paperback, *Fielding's Low-Cost Europe,* which lists scads more bargain hotels, pensions, and money-saving tips for serious economizers in Madrid.

FOOD Regional specialties are surprisingly good, and their varieties are enormous. But the manner of preparation is so stereotyped throughout the land (*e.g.,* whenever you order *Entremeses,* literally "between several dishes" or hors d'oeuvres, you'll get the identical portion of a lonely sardine, ham, cheese, tuna, olives, etc.), that the food tends to pall on American palates as soon as the novelty has worn off.

Don't confuse Spanish cuisine with Mexican cuisine; chili powder, tabasco peppers, and hot stuff of this nature are almost unknown in Iberia. Even the terminology differs: south of the border, a *tortilla* is a pancake-type dough which serves as bread, but in Spain it's the word for omelet, with another noun added to specify its type.

Except in a handful of international establishments, all cooking is done in strong olive oil—one full serving of which is guaranteed to entwine the stomach and gullet into a perfect clove hitch. To avoid Traveler's Complaint, insist that everything be *preparado en mantequilla* ("cooked in butter"). Salads, fruits, and fresh vegetables are safe wherever you go. Incidentally, it's *always* wiser to pass up milk and ice cream in smaller towns and hamlets.

Aside from straight meat and poultry, here are some of the favorites of visiting Yankees: langosta (the clawless local "lobster" which now puts a helluva bite on your wallet or purse), Paella (world-famous Valenciana specialty of rice, peppers, shellfish, chicken, saffron, etc., served in a huge frying pan), lenguado (sole, brother!), perdiz (small whole partridge, rich and savory), and centollo (tender, flavorful crab from the Bay of Biscay).

Roast lamb (cordero asado) and roast suckling pig (cochinillo) are generally the finest meats. Steaks? Generally speaking, forget 'em. By U.S. standards, the beef is mediocre; it's never "topped" with grain, and it's slaughtered either too young or after age 36.

In many places, chickens and turkeys taste as though 15 minutes of setting-up exercises, 10 times around the track, and an ice-cold shower had been a routine part of their before-breakfast training all the way from the egg to the chopping block. Some of them are athletic and stringy, with muscles like Joe Frazier's. In leading restaurants, however, they range from good to delicious.

Exquisite fruit of all varieties, including the world's best oranges (winter only); honey with the fragrance of rosemary, marjoram, and orange blossoms; almond, nougat, marzipan, and tons of confections. As for cheeses, the better types include the Tetilla (soft and greasy), Cabrales (fermented and piquant), Burgos (all cream), Asturias (smoked-cured), and Manchego. Try the last, which has been molded in matting and preserved in oil; it's our favorite. Your friends might avoid you for 2 weeks afterward, but it's worth the gamble.

To combat the rising prices of foodstuffs, municipalities were ordered by the Government to curtail "unnecessary" middlemen and their excessive profits. As a result, 40 community markets have been inaugurated in the capital, and others elsewhere. The State has also given financial assistance to a fast-spreading chain of supermarkets—which, curiously enough, are far less popular than anticipated. Apparently the Spanish housewife holds her gossip and personalized service more dear than those extra céntimos in savings.

Officialdom also has taken further steps to nip mounting inflationary trends by guaranteeing foreigners a full meal for about $1.50. This so-called Tourist Menu is also available in Deluxe establishments, but in these the maximum tariff has been set at about $6. Restaurants must indicate their category on their menus and other printed material: 4 forks for top-ranking houses straight down to 1 fork for Fourth-class feederies. Cafeterias are distinguished by cups: 3 for Special grade, 2 for First class, and 1 for Second class. Here's the rung-by-rung ladder of the rankings and corresponding top prices for your vittles: $1.50 for Fourth-class restaurants and Second-class cafeterias; $2 for First-class cafeterias; $2.75 for Special-class cafeterias; $3.50 for Third-class restaurants; $4 to $6 for the remaining groups, in their respective brackets. Don't expect nectar and froufrou, because your limited choices obviously won't be the most savory on the griddle (and it also won't endear you to the restaurateur). But it is an ironbound warranty from the Chief of State that you can visit this land and be fed for very close to these amounts. What you'll be asked to swallow, however, is another matter. If your tastes hover above ground level, you can expect to shell out about $8 per meal in most good feederies and $10 to $18 in the classiest calorie castles.

§TIPS: Drink bottled water always, even though the tap water of the major cities is sweet and potable. If you like it without bubbles, ask for Solares; if you wish bubbles, any *agua mineral* such as Vichy Catalán will do.

A thrifty retired Navy Captain from Pasadena purchases distilled water in the pharmacies *(Farmacia* in Spanish) at 5 times less than a liter ordered in a restaurant and half as much as Solares from the grocery store. Thanks for the tip, Skipper!

If it's late spring (May or June), don't miss the wild Aranjuez strawberries and orange juice, a dessert for the gods—or the equally Olympian Aranjuez asparagus.

RESTAURANTS Spanish meal hours call for heroic belt-tightening and self-discipline on the part of the visitor. By the time most Americans finally sit down to tackle the groceries, they're so faint from hunger that an O'Sullivan's Heel Belle Hélène would be gratefully welcomed.

Breakfast is at your option, generally as early as or late as you choose— and 99½% of the time, it will be served on a tray or cart in your bedroom (most downstairs food services are closed until noon). Lunch is from about 2 P.M. to 3:30 P.M.—so it might be 4:30 P.M. before you stagger away from the table to your siesta. Dinner usually starts at about 9:30 P.M. at the earliest —which often brings the dessert and demitasse swinging down the aisle after midnight. Carry your Hindu prayer book, emergency pemmican, and size-10 girdle to help you through those desolate premeal hours. (P.S. At this writing, the Government is considering bringing mealtimes more in line with other European clockwork, cutting out siestas, and employing reforms to reduce the rush-hour traffic and late store openings and closings. We'll have to see this in action before we'll believe it, however. *Arriba, España!*)

There are 2 leading restaurants in **Madrid**, both extraordinarily fine.

Sharing the head of the list is **Horcher's** (Alfonso XII 6)—suberb, intimate, and, of course, expensive. The late Otto Horcher, its founder and a legend in his own time, recently turned over full reins to his son, Moppi, who with Maître Cristobel forms a gracious hosting team. As in all of this nation's leaders, gentlemen must wear jackets and ties. In the guest books of the old Berlin era, which they'll gladly show you, you'll find a fabulous cross section of celebrities from Mae Murray to Thomas Edison to Charles Chaplin to 4 kings to the ambassadors of 20 nations. Its hours (starting at noon for lunch and at 8 P.M. for dinner) enable U.S. pilgrims to eat at their accustomed times, to avoid the later rush, and thus to benefit from superior service. Try the magnificent roast baby lamb (spring and early summer); if this isn't available, there's a galaxy of specialties which range from pressed duck, partridge or hare to Turkey Xavier to liver dumplings to Pineapple-Lobster Titus to goodness knows what—each with a masterful touch. And please, please cap your meal with a Horcher creation called Crêpes Sir Holten; here's one of *the* prize taste-sensations in Spain. Closed Sunday. Highest recommendation.

In exactly the same tip-of-the-top bracket is the **Jockey Club** (Amador de los Ríos 6) one of the Great Restaurants of the world. It is small (18 tables only), highly exclusive, and expensive; it is not a private club, as the name implies. Sr. Don C. Cortés, the proprietor, runs it with a velvet hand. Each dish—possibly, and ironically, with the lone exception of Crêpes Toledo—is a masterpiece of culinary art (note the presentation of each platter to the diner!), and the service is most often but not always wonderfully smooth. The menu is printed in English, Spanish, and French. Barman Pedro is a maestro. *Always crowded,* so arrange with your hotel concierge to book in advance. Closed all of August; open daily and Sunday, otherwise. Ask for Maître Gerardo (Herardo) or Manager Felix, both of whom speak English; Mr. Cortés himself knows the Latin languages only. The only demurrer here is that sometimes the "regulars" get too much good attention, while the new-comers are given the impression they're out in left field; when no table reservations are made at peak times, the neophyte almost surely will be shunted into the listless lofts upstairs, without even a hope of experiencing the Jockey that booted home such fame and fortune for its proprietor. Be that as it is, this establishment has the feel of New York's "21" with the intimacy of the Laurent. Go late (2:30 P.M. or 10:30 P.M.) to be fashionable. Highest recommendation, as well.

The 4-chambered **Zalacain** (Alvarez de Baena 4) is approached via an illuminated lawn off the Castellana. Rust-toned bar; textiled walls, some hung with game paintings; our sampling of the platters truly outstanding—even to the bread which is baked in its own ovens. Also at rest on Sunday plus all of August. Very appealing to all the senses. We consider it 2nd only to the celestial twins above and certainly one of the better bets in the capital.

Bajamar (Av. José Antonio 78), a few steps from the Plaza Hotel, is one of the better seafood restaurants we've hooked into on our trolling missions across the Continent. It is also one of the most expensive—and for Spain, that's saying something. Entrance beside a trout tank to a modernistic down-stairs complex; counter backed by a legion of smoked hams and drying meats; refrigerated display of shell shockers of enormous size and tantalizing fresh-ness. (Madrid, though the most inland of Spanish metropolises, is also one of the best for seafood, since the best catches arrive in less than 60 minutes by air from both the Mediterranean and Atlantic coasts.) Prices vary with the individual selections—depending upon weight, time of year, scarcity, and other variables. You can be sure, however, that in cost and in quality they are fathoms above anything you're likely to find in Iberia. Highly recom-mended for anglers with leviathan-size wallets. We're hungry to go back, despite the extraordinary tabs. **La Trainera** (Calle Lagasca) is another nook for nautical niceties; it's not as expensive as Bajamar, but not, we think, as good, either. *You* aren't the one getting hooked here.

Old-world dining? Try **Lhardi** (San Jerónimo 8), which is sequestered atop an antique bar and takeout shop. Dark interior; embossed leather walls; parquet floors; heavy framed mirrors, burgundy velure banquettes; globe lighting, ancient waiters in tails. The cuisine is less important than the distinctive atmosphere. Here is a delightfully unique holdover from a graceful era that we believe conservative diners will relish. Always reserve at least 24 hours ahead (48 hours is normally necessary to be sure of a table at peak seasons). A touch of Victoriana that we love.

The **Puerta de Moros** (Don Pedro 10) used to be a dining champion of the capital, but now, with its eye shifting toward group trade, we feel it may be slipping somewhat. Guests in this converted Conde de Riudom Palace ascend via an elevator or tread the massive ancestral staircase to one of the 4 salons —each with its own décor. Large, high-borne bar, plus 2-wheel rig to dispense beverages at your elbow; extensive Iberian menu on parchment broadside; pushy service; lambent piano melodies for evening meals, which we much prefer to the midday munching. Gastronomically and socially not in the same league as the Jockey Club, Horcher's, or Zalacain.

Breda (Castellana 78, directly opposite Hotel Luz Palacio), a spear carrier in the Las Lanzas group (see below), is usually packed tighter than a peperoni. Even so, we find it more relaxing than its older Lance-mate, where one sits funnybone-to-funnybone with the other patrons. Down the steps to a subdued and pleasant milieu; about 20 tables with blue-and-white napery; wooden garniture; acoustic-tile ceiling to hush the rush; leather chairs; too-frequent appearance of chipped china and our latest trial was marred by indifferent service. Careless attention can spoil some aspects of a meal, but now we feel that the sins of omission go deeper here. Disappointing.

Pazo (Reina Mercedes 6), the nostalgic heartbeat of romantic Gallicia in the capital, offers an elegant greeting with its dressed-stone façade, coach lamps, and Georgian windows. Marblesque English bar to the right of entrance foyer with green banquettes, hunting prints, and shelves of Toby mugs; large dining room pleasantly outfitted with homeland paintings, patterned carpet, and moss and coral tablecloths; intimate seating despite the spaciousness of the salon. Our party's seafood cocktail, medallions of octopus, croquettes, and grilled whitefish were uniformly succulent, revealing careful preparation; Rio Femar, an earthy, sparkling white wine, provided a spirited counterpoint to our nauticalories. Delightful.

Mayte Hostal (General Mola 285, a longish ride), named for its highly talented proprietress, pans in on more of Madrid's proliferating cinemagnates and actors every day. Candlelit, cozy-corner atmosphere in L-shape configuration; stand-up and sit-down bars; ubiquitous sketches, caricatures, and oils (that's Mayte herself on the back wall); flaming dishes and sauces whomped up at tableside; every platter we've ever sampled here ranks as a masterpiece of gastronomy. Its 15 specialties include goose with raspberries, lobster, Clams Meunière, steaks, smoked cheese, and Torron ice cream. A capital bet in the Spanish capital.

Escuadrón (Bárbara de Braganza 10) marches proudly on the Madrid battlefront. It has recruited a camp following of the local Social Set. Delightfully elegant mien punctuated with paper-white napery, ink-black armchairs, ruby-hued paisley carpet, partially canopied ceiling, high cottage windows, and a rouge leather bar where the Squadron halts. About 14 tables plus 1 small private dining room; our meal was truly superb on a recent mess call; closed in August. We have a feeling this bivouac will make the troops happy for a long time to come. 'Ten-SHUN!

At **Luculó,** a few doors from Kreisler Gallery (see "Things to Buy"), the eyes have it but not, unfortunately, the ayes or ahs of tummy satisfaction. See-and-be-seen atmospherics; textile-textured walls in floral green and blue; red lacquered panels; tubular sconces resembling stock-car exhaust pipes; striking abstract mural plus oil paintings; comfortable tomato-tinted leather chairs; pewter place plates—all repeated in a reflecting ceiling to double the agony or ecstacy, depending upon your taste. Our flawlessly served twin luncheon consisted of a viscid paté, sweetbreads languishing in a doughy swamp, rich house-specialty poached eggs, and enough cream blended into every dish to evoke the contented wraith of Elsie with each spoonful. Poor old Lucullus, we'd opine, would have met his churning point here. Mooooooo!

Club 31 (Alcalá 58) was launched back yonder in '59 as a less formal, less expensive sister of the famed Jockey Club (see above). The décor of wood-paneled walls and wood ceilings, with recessed soft illumination, is almost Swedish or Finnish in tone. Tiny, chic bar in front; main room with a cluster of good-size tables for expansionists. The range of its menu is prodigious. Open continuously from noon to 2 A.M. daily and Sunday; after-theater onion soup and grilled chicken a popular feature. Be sure to reserve in advance, because normally it is jammed. Usually—not always—excellent for its category and tariffs.

Another **Mayte**, this one in the **Commodore Hotel** (Plaza de la República Argentina) offers twin dining segments, one for resident guests only and the other for the general public. During the colder months you'll find a rôtisserie offering sportsman's targets of so-so quality (wild boar, partridge, venison, and the like in season), plus broiled steaks, flaming turbot, and similar passing-fare. In summer, the tables are moved directly onto the lawn of the large patio, illuminated by treetop lights and the open sky. Air conditioning; 2-level bar; swimming pool. The setting is attractive, but the cuisine, sad to say, is not as high-and-Mayte as at the above "Hostal".

The **Medinacelli** (del Prado 27, near Palace Hotel), a 4-fork venture, bordered the maximum 5 forks in ambiance, substance, and tariffs. Bar; L-shape dining room in subdued tones with suspended red Tiffany-style lamps over its 20-plus tables; good Iberian-international menu belying its name; 2 upstairs banquet settings convertable for overflow. If the eagerness of service and the chef's enthusiasm continue, here indeed willl be a medium-high-cost enterprise which delivers on every invested peseta.

Bellman, the *intime* restaurant of the Hotel Suecia, has been relocated within the same building—and somehow, sad to say, it seems to have lost something in the shift. Perhaps the paucity of the staff revealed it in a poorer light.

Las Lanzas (Espalter 10), previously mentioned as a more frenetic sister to the Breda, is still dear to the hearts of both resident Americans and Smart Set Spaniards. Steaks and chops spotlighted on the charbroiler; native selections also featured; well-intentioned but poorly trained waiters; service plates grossly chipped (as at the Breda; both must hire gorillas as dishwashers); other operating touches amateurish; prices now moving bullishly. While the management still has a lot to learn, it is trying hard—so we must rate this armory of "The Lances" a solid value in overcrowded surroundings.

Principe de Viana (Calle Doctor Fleming 7) is actually around the corner from its street address—a few steps from where your taxi stops. Ground-level lair divided by a stairwell; longer upstairs salon with green stained-glass windows; wooden walls and polished ceiling beams; blue and forest-tone carpeting. Our waitress, outfitted to resemble a secretary bird, for some unfathomable reason changed our silverware 3 times before a single calorie was brought to the table. How's *that* for service? Loved by locals, but our expensive meal did not warrant a return visit, unless to figure out that caper with the cutlery.

Poncio Pilato (Almirante 5) schemes its black-on-white theme around 4 Latin columns, flowers on 18 tables, gray-toned artwork, and a loyal conclave of satisfied legionnaires. This centurion was impressed by the menu of international dishes, the versatility of the chef, and the moderate prices for its imperial rank—all in all, a gustatory Roman circus! Though young, it holds every promise of becoming Eternal.

Casa Botín (Cuchilleros 17) is a tried-and-true standby, famous all over the world for its bullfighting guests and its roast suckling pig. This is the restaurant where Jake Barnes, hero of *The Sun Also Rises,* plays his last scene; Hemingway gave the place considerable attention in *Death in the Afternoon* as well. Cooking is still done in the original oven, dating from A.D. 1725. Be sure to order the Cordero Asado or the Cochinillo Asado because this baby lamb and this juicy little piglet are too good to miss. Little English is spoken; ask for Don Antonio, the hospitable son of the owner (and the 4th generation to be represented here), to translate your needs. Crowded by fellow tourists; reservations gladly accepted even though every table has been sold out ages ago; expect to wait (standing in a jammed passageway) for at least 45 minutes beyond the time of your booking unless you get there around 8-ish; the air conditioners dating from A.D. 1971 help in summer. Very reasonable; very Spanish; very plain. Definitely worth a visit if you're in the mood for atmosphere. This authentic landmark we *do* recommend—highly.

Alkalde (Jorge Juan 10) splits its multiple personality and waiters between upper and lower dining alcoves and brick-walled basement grottos. Chummy service; classical regional fare plus Basque and Chilean specialties; unique fish soup, a dream; many local patrons. Sound.

El Bodegón has just moved to a new site at Pinar 15, but aside from the physical trappings everything remains the same. The staff is professional but friendly; the food is substantial; high segments of Madrid society often may be found within its precincts. Certainly no Horcher's or Jockey Club, but pleasant.

José Luis (Rafael Salgado 11), hard by the football stadium, draws athletes, aficionados, Babbitts, and a mixed clan. Originally a neighborhood pub, it grew faster than Jack's beanstalk. Bar and 8 tables at entrance; main dining room down a few steps, clublike with paintings, diplomas, and a large bookcase; relaxed atmosphere brightened by mulberry touches; urbane food and attention; separate bar next door on mezzanine level; small glass-wrapped sidewalk restaurant; closed Sundays and August. Don José Luis loves to present little souvenirs to the ladies. Prices high but not exorbitant. Very, very good.

Other colorful worthies? Here's a triumvirate of amiable examples: **Casa Valentín** (headquartered at Calle San Alberto 3, just off Puerta del Sol) has opened 2 newer havens, each boasting the same belt-bruising fare. Its original entry has long been a bullfighters' favorite. Ground-floor, L-shape, standup bar (not set up for ladies), where the local gentry gorge themselves from the copious array of tidbits on display, trading jokes and tossing discarded shrimp husks on the floor; narrow stairway to the delightfully regional dining accommodations upstairs; medium-priced and especially beloved by first-timers. The second entry **Los Porches** (Paseo del Pintor Rosales 1), is active in summer only (June 1 to Sept. 30); appealing surroundings, happy ambiance, and excellent service. The last, **Nuevo Valentín** (Concha Espina, opposite the football stadium), is the most chic of the trio. Sidewalk dining at about 40 tables when old Sol is benign; small, intimate, red-leather bar to the right of the entrance; spacious dining room to the left with hunt-and-harvest scenes; leaded windows and walnut panels; although it's still rather *Nuevo*, this is definitely a heartwarming valentine. Our incognito reception, our meal, and our service were all excellent. Same eager and sympathetic attention at each address; same prices; same praise. All recommended—especially the *Nuevo*, which we found unusually rewarding.

Ruperto de Nola, topping the unusual Torres Blancas apartment building, is a recent addition to the Odd Night Out scene. Circular free-form room finished in a glazed white porcelain-like surface; basket-handle arched windows affording a splendid view of the city; perfect acoustics for a music hall but so reverberative for human voices that it is uncommonly (and uncomfortably) loud; posh red upholstery; massive food displays sometimes requiring 2 busboys to carry a single platter; better than average cuisine for higher than average tabs. Very Much In tonight in Madrid, but the clamor inside this mod-lined chatterbox and the theatrical performances in bringing out the food put us off. Perhaps you'll disagree and be more favorably impressed than we were.

Casa Paco (Puerta Cerrada 11), in the old part of town, zings with color for the eyes, peasant-style flavor for the tummy, and noise for the ears. Two floors (we prefer upstairs); always busy, if not hectic; steak's the main thing and it's usually ordered by weight; Cebón de Buey is also delicious, as are some of the seafood platters. Don't worry if the meat is not done quite well enough for you; the plates are literally oven-hot, so simply slice off a slab, touch it to your heavy porcelain platter, and it will be brown in a jiffy! We enjoyed it on our several recent eat-ins, but some travelers find its ambiance too, too "authentic" to suit them. Not for the squeamish.

Julián Rojo (Ventura de la Vega 5, a short hike from the Palace) is another tavern-type temple of taurine trauma. Again 2 stories; bright with bullfight pictures; skilletcraft not as skilled as of yore, on our recent test.

Both **La Corralada** (Villanueva 21) and **Aroca** (Plaza de los Carros 3)

impressed us as being as routine as a gaggle of other small, basic Iberian-style
feederies in the city. Neither is as easy on the bankroll as it physically appears.
The former is a favorite of the younger set. The fish in the latter is exceptionally fresh and savory, but its starkness and its slambang but well-meaning
service detract from our desire to return.

La Fragua (Ortega y Gasset 6) belongs to the same armory as the aforementioned Breda and Las Lanzas. Small, intimate, with sound service; similar
fare to that of "The Lances." It also gets the point.

Tranquilino (Jardines 3) calls itself an "Argentine Steak House"—even
though its steers are Spanish. The Buenos Aires proprietor has tried hard to
make it representative of his native land. Waiters and doorman in gaucho
dress and boots; tricked-up rustic décor in varnished rough wood and 2000-
volt green; 9 tables and tiny bar at street level and 18 tables in 2 rooms upstairs.
Your steak comes piping hot on a table-size charcoal brazier, and you eat it
from a rectangular scrubbed board bearing a recess for the savory barbecue-
type sauce. Our "Baby Beef" wasn't up to the standards of U.S. corn-fed
prime, of course (no Iberian beef ever can be)—but it was swallowable, just
the same. Service which couldn't be more cordial; soft, piped music on both
floors, featuring such gems of the pampas as "La Comparsita" and "Warsaw
Concerto." Despite its flamboyant color scheme, we like this place. Ask for
José Luis, who speaks English. We haven't yet tried its summer operation,
Glorieta Puerta de Hierro, with its adjoining children's park.

Mesón de San Javier (Calle del Conde 3) is a typical and ingratiating little
bodega on a tiny hard-to-find street. The whole baby chicken (when they
make it), stuffed with ham and roasted in butter, is worth clucking about.
Strangely enough, it's been renamed Chicken Temple Fielding; we wonder
why. For dessert, be sure to try Proprietor Denis' Crêpes Fabiola or the
strawberries flambé in season. No cocktails, no whisky, no gin; Spanish
brandy-and-soda, sherry, or a pitcher of house wine are priced in pennies.
Reserve in advance. Since it is a rough-and-ready den, ladies would probably
feel more comfortable with escorts. They're so honest in this place that an
amused Virginia lassie reports her waiter's whisper: "Everything is delicious
here except the coffee—so please don't order it!" Simple tavern, for the
down-to-earth traveler (and tea drinker!).

La Quinta del Sordo or "The Home of the Deaf One" (Sacramento 19),
once the Goya residence, is named for this great artist who lived in a sad
world of silence. Recently unveiled by Patrón Miguel Jimenes, formerly the
spark behind the abovementioned Mesón de San Javier; rustic cottage surroundings with snack bar in front, a wider expanse farther in, and 2 intimate
6-table quarters to the left; stone, timber, and hearthside atmosphere; soothingly low outlays for deliciously simple inlays. Lunchtime is quieter; dinner
is livelier. An enchanting little haven in every cranny.

El Ultimo Cuplé (Palma 51) means "The Last Tune," and it certainly
seemed to be croaking a swan song on our visit. Kind, hard-working staff in
dismal surroundings; tatterdemalion menus; geriatric combo wheezing out a
cacophony of melodies; more examples and more's the pity since the personnel seemed to be trying so hard. It's hymn time, we think.

La Grillade (Calle de Calatrava 32) is still striving to squeeze into the sophisticated inner circle. Downstairs site with speckled emerald carpet, acoustic ceiling (trying in vain to absorb the overly loud recorded music), candles, paintings, and an assortment of decorative effects that didn't jell to our aesthetic senses. Smooth service by waiters in red jackets; better than average cuisine; reasonable prices. A more intimate feeling suffuses the room after 10 P.M., when 2 guitarists begin to strum. Worth a try.

The **Gure-Etxea** (Plaza de la Paja 12), if you hadn't already guessed from the distinctive spelling of its name, is a serious Basque bailiwick. Diminutive working bar near entrance; tastefully decorated with lore of the northern province; varied menu; amiable service by waitresses from 1:30 P.M. to 4 and from 9 to midnight; closed Sundays. A beret-clad old-timer here told us that guests receive special attention if they address the proprietor by name—which just happens to be Ignacio Loinaz Echániz Galarraga Arrizabalaga Garmendia Alcorta Leunda Joaristi Zalacain Landa Mendizábal Aranguren Guruceta Elorza Elola Gurruchaga Egaña Soraluce Izaguirre Galdós Oyarzábal. Got that? If not, go anyway. It's fun.

Pazo de Monterrey (Alcalá 4), a *"restaurante-marisquería,"* gives a lot for the money. This bustling, modern, down-to-earth enterprise, with its bar and paper-littered floor-rail area (a Spanish custom where open appetizers are offered stand-up drinkers) separated by a partition from the tables, is proud of its fine variety of shellfish (*mariscos*) and well it should be; the special trencher-eater's platter (½ lobster, ½ giant crab, oysters, shrimp, and more) at about $10, alone cost more than everything consumed by my 2 other companions. Generous choice of briny and nonbriny dishes; h-u-g-e portions; unpolished but smiling attention; very popular, especially for lunch. If you're not seeking atmosphere, here's one hell of a good bargain in regional type fare.

Las Reses (Orfila 3) tucks its cookstoves into the crook of its L-shape configuration. Neo-Andalucian in atmosphere, employing Moor-or-less North African overtones; Spanish skilletry; well-prepared beef and lamb. We've nevir boasted over hour spelling abilities, but git a lode of there menyou entrees: "Yearling Cutler Mother-in-law Dish, Rib Steak Holher-in-law Dish, Pourtuguese Chiken, Scrambled Eegs with Mush-rooms, Mixeed Salid, Chees as Ordered, Whippes Creem and particulary Iris Coffee." Clozed Sundae. Wunderful!

Hogar Gallego (Plaza Comandante las Morenas 3), on the other fin, long one of Madrid's leading exponents of seafood, has been surfeited by its success —in our opinion, at least. Its charmless, overcrowded summer garden seems to go further to seed every year. We liked our latest fish soup, but the rest was for the sandcrabs. Typical fare of Galicia is also offered. Sorry, no longer for us.

Balthasar, in the basement of the Eurobuilding, draws mostly businessmen at midday. Cozy entry bar plus buffet on show; 28 tables divided into 2 segments by a beaded wooden screen; ample attention. The cuisine seemed more suited to satisfying the hungry diner rather than the discerning gourmet. Fair enough, however, if you're out at this neighborhood at mealtime.

El Púlpito (Plaza Mayor 9) is pleasant. It offers a wide selection from the Iberian market. Total of 28 tables on 2 floors; open kitchen at rear of ground-level section where you can watch the chefs at work; small bar and chilled

food display at entrance. Our salad was crisp and our thick steak was topped
with smoked ham and an egg! A bow to owner José Luis—plus a recommendation to you.

An identical ailment seems to have hit both **La Barraca** (Reina 29) and the
refashioned **Caves of Luis Candelas** (just off Plaza Mayor, below El Púlpito)
—namely, Too Many Tourists. We're convined they've gone much too far
overboard for the U.S. and foreign trade, and that their authentic flavor, once
so appealing, has been lost. Neither is recommended to any reader of this
year's *Guide*.

Riscal (Marqués de Riscal II) is also for the birds, not for us; we feel this
Riscal has miscal-culated, with fare and service unattractive. The **Urogallo**
(Calle Gavina 23) seemed to be a molting rooster on our latest peck around
the Madrid henhouse. Cock-a-doodle-don't.

Mesón del Segoviano (Cava Baja 35) is a student drinking house in the very
old traditions of Iberia. Doll-size rooms; noisy but fun; flamenco from time
to time; a 25-peseta gratuity to the wandering musicians will give you that
Andrew Carnegie glow. Start late, take a crowd, and drink only the bottled
Spanish *coñac* (not kegged). For the young in heart.

American and pseudo-American? **Foster's Hollywood** (Magallanes 1)
flashes back to a Silver Screen fantasyland which never was. Installed with
full treatment by shrewd Los Angeles entrepreneurs; bar and quick-lunch
facilities at entrance; back-to-back bar in Art Deco dining room with tables
and banquettes; list of 43 cocktails plus Root Beer, Irish Coffee, and Hot
Buttered Black Rum. Brown-Derby-style 80-item menu featuring many
dreamed-up "Filmland" concoctions; mainstays 7 varieties of ½-lb. and 8
varieties of ¼-lb. hamburgers; fixed daily 3-course meal including wine about
$6. Burgers extra-savory considering foreign climes; toasted sandwiches even
better; brownies poor; "Star-Spangled Banana Split" too formidable for us to
face. Open 365 days per year from 1:30 P.M. to 3 A.M. Very expensive in
comparison to competition, but miles above all in authenticity.

The **California** chain has 7 links, the largest and best at Goya 47. Far
plainer, noisier, busier, and cheaper than Foster's Hollywood; ground level
with stark modern blond walls, bare marble floors, full-length sit-down
counter, formica tables, and corner bar; big basement for overflow. Curious
parodies of U.S. quick-service food; only 14 sandwiches (no hamburgers or hot
dogs), but 146-plate galaxy in an astonishing mélange of Iberian offerings;
superfast personnel; masterfully organized. High-quality vittles for such low,
low outlays; well-mixed drinks; normally mobbed day and night by locals;
open 7 A.M. to 1:30 A.M. the calendar around. You'll save a bundle, but you'll
eat *a la Española*.

Lums (Alcalá 202), **Kentucky Fried Chicken** (Conde del Valle Suchil 20),
and **Helen's** (Generalísimo 90) should be rapped on the knuckles, in our
opinion, for purveying what we regard as such punk imitations of our national
kitchen. **Dolar** and the scads of others which now pepper the city shouldn't,
because they just don't know any better.

The **Drugstore**, a 3-minute walk from Kreisler's fine emporium on Serrano
(see "Things to Buy") is a mod-mooded lunch stop, discothèque, boutique
center, and—well, drugstore sans drugs. Counter or table service; fair ham-

burgers, sundaes, milk shakes, or other flip-siders. Fun, in a teenie-bopper way.

French? **Le Bistroquet** (Calle del Conde 4) resembles an MGM bistro right down to its checkered tablecloths and wax-dripped wine bottles with candles. Perhaps 20 tables, almost rim-to-rim; disturbingly loud piped music ("The Last Time I Saw Paris"?); limited *carte* featuring grilled meats and fish; Maître Pierre—er, Pedro—the soul of kindness. *Comme ci, comme ça.* **El Galeón** (Calle Velázquez 80) is another Frenchie.

German? **Edelweiss** (Jovellanos 7) serves a skimpy meal with fine German-type beer for matching tariffs. Herring in sour cream and onions (Arenque Crema); bratwurst with potato salad and sauerkraut; pumpernickel bread; Camembert; also many other non-Teutonic selections. Depressingly stark décor; harassed service; go very early or very late, because it's *always* overfull at meal hours, and they won't accept reservations. Branch in the country (see below).

Italian? **Alduccio Pizzeria** (Av. del Generalísimo Franco 38) is more of a *trattoria* than a full-scale restaurant. Simple surroundings on street level; 9 tables; bilious green ceiling and cotton-cloth wall coverings emblazoned with blue and gold churches; inexpensive; we licked our chops over its Tagliatelle and Lasagne. *Bene* for *pasta* hounds. **La Trattoria** (Plaza del Alamillo 8) is in a quiet sector of the Old Town. Nothing too special about it, in our opinion.

Chinese? Because many of the key vegetables which are necessities in classic Chinese cookery are not grown in the area, and because other standard ingredients are either too high priced or unobtainable in Spain, **El Buda Feliz** (Tudescos 6), **Chino Kowloon** (Travesía del Conte Duque 15), **House of Ming** (Castellana 74), **Mandarin** (Brasil 16), **Mei Ling** (Generalísimo 74), **Pagoda** (Leganitos 22), **Shanghai** (Leganitos 26) and a couple of others are forced to improvise combinations—some of them billed under familiar names—which are weird and occasionally unpleasant to these travelers' palates. It is virtually a culinary school of its own. House of Ming and Mandarin are especially well established. While we don't happen to enjoy them at all, scads of customers —especially residents—do.

Japanese? The **Mikado** (Calle Huesca 71) struts in with honors that would be a compliment to anyone's ancestors, considering its Iberian address. Excellent reception from its kind doorman, to the waitresses in the raiments of Nippon, to the courtly Manager Suzuki-San; Malacca lighting fixtures; extractor fans over several tables to draw off the cooking aromas; good fish-based soup; savory Tempura; fair Sukiyaki, within the limits possible with Spanish beef as the base. Its location in a building on the edge of town ($2 taxi ride) is its only major drawback. Our courteous bow of respect.

Philippine? **Sulú** (Av. Generalísimo 58) bills itself as a "steak house," but wait until you taste the delicious Misono, a specialty of the archipelago that is prepared not only *at* your table but *in* your table! What a delight—your exquisitely costumed chef-waitress melding the ingredients on a fire-hot grill around which you dine, the aromas drifting up into individual ventilator hoods. A ½-dozen such installations are here plus conventional settings for more continental cravings. Entrance through a shimmering, tinkling curtain of nacre medallions; additional mother-of-pearl decorative touches behind the handsome Malayan bar; sinfully appetizing curried niblets, *satés* (kebabs), and island delicacies; relaxing cane-back chairs augmenting the forest of malacca separators and rattan screens. Here's something exotic for the eye, ear, nose, and throat. A touch of joy to all the senses. **Casa Anselmo** (Plaza de las Salesas 7) is a newer, smaller, and lower-priced example of the same origin. How satisfactory it is we do not know.

Mexican? **¡¡A Todo Mexico!!** (San Bernardino 4) is an enticing segment in a group of 3 outlets which also include **Mexico Lindo** (Plaza de Ecuador 4) and **El Charo** (San Leonardo 3). The 3-language menu is 100% alike throughout. Bar; dining room to rear striking in vivid colors against white stucco; agile, amiable attention; open every day. B-i-g, c-o-o-l Margaritas; 10 set meals at painless prices; extravagant, extra-delicious Special Mexican Combination Platter with Guacamole on the side. These savvy pros offer the most genuine and tempting food of its genre that we have ever tried abroad. *¡Olé!*

Swiss? **Chalet Suizo** (Fernández de la Hoz 80) is an alpine facsimile where inordinate amounts of garlic and oil are foisted on fine Helvetian cuisine. An American and his Puerto Rican wife landlord this chalet-style venture; unfortunately, they've matched the Swiss décor far, far better than they've duplicated the fodder. Attentive, tidily groomed staff; not expensive. Too bad, but our reaction to this one is nix.

Danish? **Danica** (Canillas 96) is a small, lively bar-restaurant in gay national colors of red and white, so friendly in its personnel and clientele that it could be your Scandinavian club in Madrid. Warm, gracious, English-speaking Edith and Jorgen Hansen created it all with their own hands. Taped music; limited menu of 11 open sandwiches, 2 main courses, 4 desserts; very reasonable tarriffs. Unfortunately its distance from the center and small selection make this fun-filled little place a specialized target for hungry Danophiles.

Kosher? The **Sinai** (Príncipe 33, 1 flight up, and another at Av. José Antonio 29) answers the Diaspora with Sephardic cookery (based on the creations of the Jews who fled to Spain and Portugal), rather than the more familiar recipes of the Ashkenazim (those who went farther up into Europe, and who predominate in North America). The former will find *eppis essen,* but the latter should go only on *Donnershtick,* when the specialty is Couscous with chicken or lamb. Even more startling is the kosher Paella (mamma would faint at the very *thought*). If you're crossing the desert, there's an excellent take-away service—just right for a snack.

Moroccan? **Al Mounia** (Calle Recoletos 5) is the most authentic Maghrebian eatery we've seen since making the rounds of Casablanca's better spots a while back (the Shari family, your hosts, have another Eastern-Oriented oasis there). Finely detailed and exquisitely tiled Arabesque salon; 14 bright tables; waiters in ethnic habit; piped Middle Eastern melodies; excellent couscous, shish kebab, and other specialties from the lands of the Atlas; minaret-high, but worthy tabs. Salaams to the Chef, who labors with Allah's hand.

Further East? **Vihara** (Plaza Santa Bárbara 8) brings Hindu atmospherics from the hinterland of India. Curries form only a chapter, because its cookbook is fat and varied. Of its 3 segments, we prefer the downstairs "grotto". Quite good for its specialties. Recommended.

Tea? **Embassy Club** (Paseo de la Castellana 12) is a fashionable redezvous for upper-bracket *Madrileñas;* delicious watercress sandwiches, petits fours, and the like; go about 6 P.M.

The best hotel surroundings for lunching or dining in Madrid are found (in season) at the lovely garden of the **Ritz**; expensive as the devil; the Grill at the **Palace** (also very expensive) and the **Fénix** garden are also popular landmarks. The Rue Royale of the **Villa Magna** is trying to bring blue-ribbon French cuisine to the Spanish capital. Our inspection most assuredly disclosed that the décor will aid any digestion—Iberian or Gallic. Prices are close to those of Horcher's or the Jockey Club. We wish it, and you, *bonne chance.*

During the summer, the one place not to overlook is **Pavilion**, in Retiro Park. Open-air dining and dancing in a lovely setting; smooth, fast floor shows, which generally come up with excellent talent. Now tops in the city. The **Florida**, also in Retiro Park and also alfresco, takes second honors; same features and same prices; excellent as well. Nearby, the **Pinto** (Montalbán 9) trots out 14 tables, a bar, and Spanish home cooking by the friendly family that fills its feedbag. Nice and neighborly. **Villa Rosa**, 20 minutes out in the suburb of *Ciudad Lineal*, used to have a dreamy physical plant, stately trees, a swimming pool, and other lures to the eye. Then, through inept management, it hit the skids and deservedly dropped out of vogue. Now we hear that Sr. Luis Hernando Olives has remodeled it into shades of its former self. Sorry, we missed it this trip.

Beyond Barajas Airport, in the classically beautiful university town of *Alcalá de Henares*, the State-Tourist-Office-operated **Hostería del Estudiante** is a charming target for lunch or dinner when the weather is halcyon. Ancient, rustic baronial hall remodeled; typical Spanish fare; tabs so inexpensive your eyes will pop. This one is inside, with no garden facilities—but the settlement itself is delightful sightseeing bait.

For a Spanish-style Care package to prevent early-evening atrophy of hungry U.S. tummies, be absolutely certain to try the **tascas** (taverns) on or near the Calle de Echegaray—just an olive-pit's throw from the Palace Hotel. Here's where Madrid's lively hordes huddle for snacks and apéritifs from 7 P.M. to 10 P.M.

Each stop banners its own specialties. **La Casona**, which can pack in 400 nibblers, is noted for its potatoes and mushrooms. **La Chuleta** draws ham and *mariscos* (shellfish) fans. **Gayango** is renowned for its *bacalao* (cod), steaming casseroles of baby shrimp, oysters, and hot tamales. **Posada del Enano** comes up with a trove of *boquerones* (a very special anchovy); **O'Pote** serves delicious *vieiras* (scallops); **Motivos** offers *chanquetes* (oh-so-good sea minnows); **Espuela** purveys *pinchos morunos* (barbecues); **La Trucha** is good for heavier fare, and **Taverna Toscana** has other palate tempters. **Los Corsarios** (Calle de Barbieri 7) projects a swinging atmosphere beloved by the Younger Set; cellar-sited **Sésamo**, where the Fielding gypsies usually throw in the towel, features the reviving *Sol y Sombra* ("Sun and Shade," half anis and half Spanich *coñac).* Drink either the house wines or common sherry; beer is too filling, unless your surname is Tuborg, Carlsberg, Heineken or Schlitz. Scads more places may be explored in these Tidbit Alleys. They are very, very inexpensive, and they provide a scrumptious experience for travelers in ALL economic brackets. But please remember that dinner is still coming up!

Other Cities and Regions

Algeciras' only sensible choice is the **Reina Cristina**, with its lovely summer garden and soothing music, or the independent romantic siren on neighboring Getares Beach, with its fish so fresh they'll practically leap off the plate to insult you, its sardines grilled on an open fireplace, its big steaks, and its view of "The Rock" (Gibraltar) across the bay. Full pension guests of the hotel may dine at the first without extra charge. **El Cigarron. La Langosta**, with steaks, clawless lobster, other denizens of the sea, and good wine, is agreeable for its class. **La Cazuela**, cooks up open beams, nautical paintings, rugged country-textured flooring, and specialties of the briny. Not too bad when one really considers the alternatives. **La Sirena Dorada**, on the beach, happens to be one such alternative, in our book. **Mesón de Sancho** (20 minutes toward Cádiz) has sunk below sea level in our tide chart. Nix.

Alicante's leading choice, apart from the hotels which are not choice at all, is out at *La Albufereta*, a longish taxi jaunt from the center. It's called **Pizzeria Romana**, located on the Finca Las Palmeras, a private residence of the Decouty family, who have opened their ground floor as a 3-room Italian restaurant. The décor is just what you'd expect—right down to the red-checked curtains—and the cookery is a delight. Even though it's not Italian, please try the Mouclade Charentaise, which is heavenly. Tiptop, in any language. **Ranchito Vera Cruz**, at Playa San Juan, blows hot and cold, depending on the pair of proprietors who also blow hot and cold. Can be fun, if the boys are in the right mood.

Almeria: Please check under "Costa del Sol."

Barcelona's culinary pickin's are not as slim as they have been. Several notable additions within the past few seasons have perked up its table considerably. The Catalans—perhaps the most traveled Executive Set in all Spain—are demanding their due at last.

The Old World dining room in the **Hotel Ritz**, long a bell ringer for international kitchen craft, is the leading exponent of French *haute cuisine* in the city. High ceiling; classic mirrored walls; soothing piano lilts; faultless service reminiscent of bygone days; extensive (but not overextended) menu of traditional favorites; bountiful wine cellar. Our most recent repast here, set in the gentle and low-keyed ambiance often preferred by serious gastronomes, was perfect on all counts. Heartily recommended to any educated palate.

Atalaya (Av. Generalísimo Franco 523), in the penthouse of Catalonia's tallest building, turns on a spellbinding view of the metropolis and particularly of Antonio Gaudi's unfinished Sagrada Familia Cathedral (see "Things to See"). Stunning decorative complexions of purple, cyclamen pink, and white; attentive, knowledgeable staff; prices to match the sky-high locale; commensurate level of fare supervised by Chef Juan Méndez Raja. Although the menu, again, is not ponderous, it incorporates selected Spanish and French choices, focusing especially on fresh pickin's from local, Galician and Madrid markets. Both the restaurant and its underground bar and snackery are closed Sundays and during August, as are many restaurants in this city. Splendid management by Director Manuel Giménez. Head and shoulders above any other independent groundling. The same group operates the novel **Zacarias** (Av. Gen. Franco 477) which is sort of an Executive Set discothèque with calories added. Small menu, but well selected; suave presentation; dressy, expensive, and recommended to young marrieds who jingle and swing.

Via Veneto (Ganduxer 10-12) is the gemstone of the young and keen Sr. Don Oriol Regas, who, with his brother, has also cornered the chichi trade at their equally luxurious Bocaccio discothèque (see "Nightclubs"). Professional greeting by a liveried doorman who also parks your cars (rare in this country); small cocktail nook at entrance with a standup minibar; main dining room on 2 tiers; flowered carpets, *fin de siècle* décor lavender-hued globe fixtures; plum leather chairs and banquettes; about 20 tables and several back rooms for satellite service; flower-embraced silver candelabra. Imperial attention from a sharp-eyed battery of carefully trained waiters; staff sometimes inclined to affect snobbish airs now that its success with Catalonia's nabobbery is assured; general supervision by Director Juan Carlos Lopez, Maître Roberto, and Sr. Quenó. Grand presentation from merlon-cut melons, to stuffed feathered pheasants, to flaming crêpes. Our wishes for luck and prosperity here appear to have been answered with cornucopias of good fortune and pesetas. *Muchos saludos!*

Olivero's (Paseo de Gracia 44) was purchased by W. R. Grace & Co. which sunk more than $1,000,000 into a fruitless revivification program before throwing in the towel and getting rid of it. We do not know the identity of its new owner, but he has our sympathy. It is a 2-story complex with a snackbar on the street floor and a lavish, beautifully decorated luxury restaurant up one flight. We feel that this one is an elaborately festooned white elephant which is saddled by problems which appear to us to be virtually insoluable.

El Gran Gatopardo (Aribau 115) is a muscular "Great Leopard" that stalks a fashionable younger clientele. Though interesting in spots, overall we found it a bit pretentious. Burnt-orange terrycloth wall covering; comfortable black barrel chairs; lighting from cleverly conceived beige sconces; 12 tables on ground zero; 8 more on the mezzanine; electric humidors puffing up 9 varieties of stogies (4 from Havana); no music; adept waiters under the direction of Sr. Francisco. Our only demurrer in the skilletry department concerns the chef's cloyingly apparent sweet tooth; everything—even the vegetables— seemed to have been dusted with a dose of Jack Frost. A high-priced sweetie, but not for diabetics.

El Nicholas II (Av. de Sarriá 137-39), as you will have guessed, is a Slavic sanctuary for high-steppe-ing princes and princesses from Pinsk to Paramus. Low-beamed, Gothic-arched chambers with windows stained in turquoise and gold; blue-felt walls with color-coordinated velvet hangings, gray paneling, and icon lamps; 2-tier bar; subterranean dining room with separate alcove; pewter candlesticks on tables; soft piano-tations or tapes accompanying lunch, while a balalaika, violin, and vocalist immortalize the Volga at dinner. Luncheon is started with an evil-sounding but delicious house apéritif (Rasputin's Refresher) spirited with Campari, vodka, and Grand Marnier, plus open sandwiches of whitefish "caviar" and pâté. Our party's superb borsch, "capitalist" lobster, and filet à la Romanoff were tsar-iffic, as was the service, led by Maîtres Roig and Gonzalez. Open from 1 P.M. to 4 and 9 to 12; closed Sunday in summer and all of July and August. This one might have turned Ivan the Terrible into Constantine the Contented.

Reno (Tuset 27) is another member of the silk-stocking bracket. Air-conditioned heptagonal room, with suave décor highlighted by comfortable black banquettes, paneled walls, and oversize windows; 15 tables inside, plus 10 smaller ones on glassed-in sidewalk terrace; deft, discreet service which oh-so-smoothly tends toward the "hard sell" approach. Rele Surtido Nouilles Catalana ("mixed grill" of chicken, ham, pork, and *noisettes* of lamb, in a masterful sauce) was especially succulent. We happen to prefer it at lunch-time, because it's more crowded at nightfall. Ask for Maître José, the hand-some English-speaking son of the ever-watchful Proprietor Don Antonio Juliá. World-famous author and epicure Paul Gallico reports that he and his lovely Virginia "give full marks to it as a charmer without gastronomic excitement but with perfect cuisine and service." Although we don't go quite so far, it is practically a surefire gamble; better every year.

Quo Vadis (Calle Carmen 7) was a tip from our beloved Mallorquin neighbors, Helen and Jack Abbott, whose home-table gastronomy is second to none in Spain. Now that we've tried it, retried it, and love it, all our opinions concur 1000%. You'll find a decorative scheme employing stone-work and bright tones; a host of fast-paced, friendly, and excellent waiters; a free tiny pot of the chef's pâté at your request; succulent meats (our Porter-house was one of the best we've ever enjoyed in Spain); gigantic salads (e.g., 2 whole ears for an endive mix); buckle-bending desserts. The exceptionally high quality of the foodstuffs and the excellence of their preparation make it one of the truly fine "little" restaurants of Catalonia. Regional dishes, mostly; Patron Martin Forcada and his handsome son demand staff perfection; spot-lessly clean. Tip: The smooth verbal pitch here to order the costliest items (*French* oysters, crab, and the like) is an irritant. Skillet magic at gradually rising prices; closed Monday. The greatest and most expensive of its type in the metropolis—and worth every peseta in value.

Orotava (Consejo de Ciento 335) has been a favorite of loyal Catalonians for decades—so much so, in fact, that many regard it as their private club in Barcelona. Its personable Director-Proprietor, Sr. J. Luna, has served some of the greatest celebrities of the art, music, and literary worlds. Most, we would guess, have been of stellar rank, because the prices here are exception-ally high for the nation. One long room with a bar at front, separated by a curtain from 2 other segments behind; space for about 40 diners or lunchers; tile floors; whitewashed walls hung with oil paintings. The beaten-copper façade graphically depicts the wild game specialties that are featured inside. The service is swift and kind; the cuisine and the presentation are outstanding. A topflight bag, but bring along your money belt loaded with ammo.

Guría (Casa Nova 99), one of the most highly praised havens in its niche of the sky, is a complete enigma to us. Close friends swear their affection for us will dissolve unless we pronounce it the finest gastronomic center in Europe. Other knowledgeable Barceloneses wink and say that the owner's technique is a masterpiece of artifice. "Insiders" maintain that the luscious young waitresses are so craftily trained in coquettish wiles that the diner could stuff himself with bedsprings and not know the difference. Our recent incognito tests were a total shambles, from service to cookery. Rich oak paneling from front door to 2nd-story rafters; handsome bar at the entrance; warm hunting-lodge paintings; padded leather chairs; Basque specialties predominant. It's dealer's choice on this one.

Agut d'Avignon (Trinidad 3), tucked away in an obscure cul-de-sac off Calle Aviñó in the Old Town, is another regional bell ringer. Ramon Cabau, its mustachioed, energetic owner, carefully supervises the belfry of belles, including his daughter, who swing to your wishes in black mini-mini uniforms and pink aprons. Romantic 3-story residence divided into quintet of working segments; clean surroundings; simple interior highlighted by huge turn-of-the-century murals. Our party's Sopa al ¼ hora (fish soup), Pulpitos (infant squid), Tortilla de Trufas (truffle omelette), Habas a la Catalana (broadbean stew), and Anec amb Figues (duck with figs) were fit for a feast. Lunchtime jammed with businessmen (and occasionally Salvador Dali); dinner hours crowded with legions of society settlers; functioning 1 P.M. to 5 and 9 P.M. to 1 A.M.; closed Sundays, Christmas, and *Semana Santa* (Holy Week). *Saludos y olés!*

Epsom, in the lower paddock of the Hotel Derby (Loreto 25) is a worthy mount in the local sweepstakes. Wreath-like food display greeting hungry stallions and mares at the bottom of the stairs. Very sound tip sheet touting, Catalan and French entries, all of which are well groomed and priced to stay in the running. Proud silks, every one.

Carballeia (Reina Cristina 3) faces the port, unloading a cargo of similar nibblings in far more modest precincts. Possibly $5 have been invested in fancying up the joint, but the fins in the pan receive primary concern in this coaster. The long lines of happily anxious clients waiting to dine here vouch for the values. Kind, considerate service (daily Spanish stock-market report on each luncheon table); hosting by Sr. Ribas; extremely busy from 1:30 P.M.

Casa Bofarull-Los Caracoles Bodega (Escudillers 14) is colorful and charming, with so much regional flavor that many less hardy clients consider it unsavory. Not so at *all!* Caracoles means "snails"; this is the specialty, but everything under the sun is available. The entrance looks discouraging, but once inside, you pass the huge woodstove to find yourself in a small backroom, one of 3, with a balcony above. The walls are lined with wine casks, peppers, garlic clusters, and drying spices; the snail pattern is followed in the shape of the special bread. Daily recommendations of the chef are written on the back window, in bright chalk; all tables are generally full during the rush hours. The roast-chicken-on-a-spit is worthy of an award—which it once received in Paris (order *pechuga* if you want white meat). Menus are in 4 languages, including English—and their listed prices are still simple for this simple type of place. Use a cab instead of your own car, because the streets are too narrow. Beloved Founder-Owner Antonio Bofarull has passed to his reward, but his spirit remains to reward the customer—and so does his experienced and personable son, Don Feli. In our opinion, this down-to-earth oasis which has pleased hundreds of celebrities gives the most and the best for the money in the city. Open from 1:30 P.M. to 1:30 A.M. every day of the year.

Hogar Gallego (Layetana 5) is another no-nonsense vendor of very variegated victuals, the galaxy flavored with Galician gusto and none pegged to pop the top off your piggybank. Shellfish, which are the specialty here, have their own small stall near the door; the main dining room, mezzanine, and back area hold perhaps 60 tables; service is rushed but capable; our sea-fresh Centollos (spider crabs) were sheer gifts from the cool Atlantic. Open every day; reservations recommended for Sundays and holidays. YUMMY.

The **Hostal del Dimoni** (Antico Ampurdanes Herzegovino) is on our list for an upcoming trial. It's said to be amusing in a crackpot way.

Koldobika, behind the Ritz, spotlights Basque cookery. Conglomerate decorative themes. Heavy use of tiles; adroit waitresses; spotlessly scoured. The cuisine here has picked up so markedly that it's left us almost speechless (but *not* wordless!). It is extensively employed for local functions and family affairs. Now basking in its well-earned glory.

Udala (Sicilia 202) provides yet another bow to the gastronomy of the Pyrenees—and even less expensively than the above. Lobby entrance to the main chamber; upper sanctum with 8 more tables; bar with guayana wood stools; simple, clean décor; unobtrusive piped music. Our Pisto a la Bilbaína (scrambled eggs, tomatoes, and red and green peppers) was an unusual treat; so were the accompanying *sidra* (cider) and the follow-up glass of Karpy, the Basque version of Cointreau. Loli Martínez is the pretty Maîtresse; José Solozabal is the charming and knowledgeable owner. A deep tip of our beret to this house, its exceptional values, and kind staff.

La Pérgola (Av. María Cristina near Plaza España) faces Europe's largest colored fountain—an impressive display which, unfortunately, splashes only on Saturday and Sunday evenings during the colder months. Commodious premises with capacity of 500 noisy munchers or sippers, split 50-50 between ground floor and spacious terrace 1-flight up; popular with the masses (and the Iberian equivalent of our own drugstore cowboys) for lunch, tea, dinner, dancing, and nipping; cozy for its size; well illuminated; no cabaret. Never bother at teatime, because you'll think you are fighting your way through a January white sale at Macy's. So crowded on weekends that advance reservations are urged. Vitry isn't in the kitchen here, but the offerings are fair enough for the price bracket.

A la Menta (Plaza Manuel Girona 50, behind the Royal Palace) opened in this essentially residential area in '70. Long, narrow *marisco* (shellfish) bar on street level; downstairs segment of 3 rooms and perhaps 15 tables, plus an arresting display of raw vegetables, seafood, and fruit; rustic national décor; l-o-w tariffs for such hearty fare; smooth, cordial service by waiters Jaime and Isidro, who speak English. Open from 1:30 P.M. to 4:30 and from 8:30 to 1 A.M. every day except Christmas. More than worth the long taxi trot from the center.

La Bruxa Borracha, or "The Drunken Witch" (Sarria 15), is every bit as off-beat as its name, décor, and menu suggest. Three diminutive dens conjured with painted ceilings, red velvet, Tiffany lamps, old heavy portraits, pale-purple linen, and antiques in abundance, all of which meld into a savory brew.

The recipes of the spirit world bear such titles as "Garlic Soup Which Makes The Man Handsome" and "Feast of the Wizards" (a nineteenth-century concoction of snails in rabbit sauce); finish off with "The Cup of the Drunken Witch," combining pineapple, peach, flan, ice creams, sherbert, whipped cream, and rum cake served in a mortar bowl the size of Bela Lugosi's skull. Please ask that your wine be decanted into one of the 15 exquisite champagne glasses found in a Gerona convent *(convent???)*. Open from 1 P.M. to 4 and from 9 to, well, to the bewitching hour; closed Sunday from June to September. This bubble's definitely worth the toil and trouble.

Finesterre (Av. Gen. Franco 469) had perhaps the greatest fame, but to us it sadly lacks consistency. Some dinners we've eaten here have been quite good; at other times, the plates have been stone cold, the potatoes limp with cold grease, and the table service about as sloppy as that of a Tenth Avenue Coffee Pot. Good when good, but very poor when bad.

Petit Soley (Plaza Villa de Madrid 5) is a young and tiny entry; ample parking, for a change; open grill in center; roving guitar players at intervals; hot in summer; busy, noisy, and gay. The cookery is recommendable but not exciting. The only surprises are on the bills—unhappy ones.

For finny denizens in more characteristic surroundings, **Casa Costa**, in nearby *Barceloneta*, is a Catalan-style picnic pavilion that opens directly onto the beach. There's a baker's dozen of similar establishments along this row, but this one draws the knowledgeable brain-food seekers. Cheap prices; rough but friendly service; enormous kitchens with hefty blue-clad Mammas rattling the pans; savory preparations in the plebeian manner both here and in its modern annex; display stands in front with fish so fresh that it's polite to return their winks. Fun for first-timers.

The totally rebuilt **Restaurant de l'Ast**, on Miramar, offers a lovely view of the Barcelona Port, fine rôtisserie chicken *(Ast* means "Spit"), a charming terrace for fair-weather dining, soothing prices—and now its earlier intolerably nasty welcome has improved vastly. Once again, a treat.

In this same general vicinity, **La Torre de San Sebastián**, a cableway tower overlooking the harbor, comes up with crude seafare, low prices, an abundance of litter on the floor—but one of the most magnificent panoramas in the region. Go for the view only.

Casa Jordi (Passatge Marimón 18), an inexpensive family eatery, romps in with *porróns* of red wine on the tables and plates of fried whitings, Pa Torrat amb Oli i Domática (toasted peasant bread with olive oil and sliced tomatoes), local olives and other such nibblings delivered as soon as you are seated. We like this honest house and its owner, who trained at the fabulous Gleneagles in Scotland and scored a double birdie when he married a bonnie lassie and brought her home to open this braw *casa*.

Niu Guerrer (Plaza de Tetuán 6, about 4 blocks from the Ritz), is a long narrow establishment reached through a jumble of bars and checkrooms. Ceramic plates and pitchers on a dado under the ceiling; Catalan offerings on an expansive but not expensive menu; okay in an oddball way. **El Canario de la Garriga** (directly opposite the Ritz) is another comfortable, family-style nest. About 30 tables; another decorative collection of kilned platters, pots, and pitchers; happy waiters in plaid shirts; a gratis offering of *boquerones* (whitebait marinated in brine) to encourage your appetite. Although the prices are low and the food is substantial, we can't get too enthused over this one.

Tinell (Freneria 8–10), in the Gothic quarter, is convenient for visitors to the Cathedral. Small, simple bistro owned by the Sebastián Damunt family; 3 weensy dining dens; clean; economical; sound, wholesome cookery featuring game in season.

Italian? **Peppone** (Maestro Nicolau 2), a block-wide combination snackery and deluxe smackery, loses something in the Catalan translation. Both sections are large, effectively fitted with autumn-hue tablecloths, white chairs, black ceilings, and planter boxes; you'll also reflect on a mirrored wall, a tiered antipasto board fringed with fresh fruit, and rush-covered wine bottles. Attractive presentation dimmed somewhat by the rock music. Fair, but not too authentic in flavor—at least to our palate.

Spanish-style "American" hot dogs, hamburgers, griddle cakes, and the like? Dozens of modern-tone cafeterias have begun to sprout in the city. Catalonian attempts to imitate our light bites can sometimes be lauded for effort but almost never for results. Although the **Atalaya Cafeteria** is removed from the shopping area (Avenida Generalísimo Franco 523), it is worth the longer ride because here is by worlds and worlds the most attractive of the rather sorry lot we have inspected. This is sited in the basement of the city's tallest skyscraper and is under the same management as the ultrachic Atalaya Restaurant in the penthouse. The surroundings are rich and soothing; the fare is so far from what mother used to make that it won't even give you nostalgia for your corner drugstore. Nonetheless, if you play the Pretending Game here, you might like it. Sit at the bar area for reduced rates, because the dining area on the side has boosted prices by perhaps 10¢ or 15¢ on each item. **Kok d' Or** (Calle Balmes 149) is also physically attractive—but oh, that chef! Never again for us. **Le Pub** (Paseo de Gracia 44) does, indeed, show the trappings of Albion. However, its multinational combination of Spanish-made Yankee-style burgers in an English aura filled with a faintly French-sounding name adds up to a rather pale copy of the letters U-S-A. **Comedia Club** (next to the Avenida Palace Hotel), on the other griddle, pans out passable but far from memorable skilletry on its ground level. All breads and pastries baked on the premises. Upstairs restaurant not worth the climb, in our opinion. The **Treno** (in the Cristal Hotel) is also better than average for small appetites, but please remember that the average around here is pretty darned low. **Moka** (on the Rambla, opposite the flower market) perks out a snack area with steeper-tariffed grillroom beyond. Our beef was overseasoned; don't order vichyssoise unless you're accustomed to having it served hot (one of the damndest, most repulsive liberties we've ever seen taken with a classic recipe). To our cup, this Moka is a weak blend. **La Luna, Samoa,** and **Kansas** huddle under the same managerial wing. This is why we always now skip the lot. **Salón Rosa** (Paseo de Gracia) is popular with Spanish *señoras* (not *señoritas)* for tea. We walked into **Navarra** (Paseo de Gracia 2), pivoted on our first step, and walked right out. Navarra again. **Glaciar** (Plaza Real) is well catered and cheap, but hyper-Iberian in its notions on light-biting.

Bilbao? Fly arrow-straight to **El Txangurro** (Alda, Urquijo 74) with its fishnet trappings, paintings framed in portholes, waitresses in sailor's garb, friendly service, and daily harvest of fresh, fresh fish. We loved every nibble of the bait and urge you to take its hook, too. After this one, we like **Luciano** (Barrencalle 38 and 40, in the Old Town). When you strut down the alley, peek in at all the frenzied culinary commotion in the kitchen and be prepared to lick your chops. Polished timbers, brass chandeliers, and brick fireplace; well-groomed clientele; kindly welcome. And don't let war, depression, or lockjaw keep you from trying the fresh anchovies, the palate-cheering Changurro (Basques spell it as in the above restaurant; it's chopped crabmeat in its giant shell), the piping-hot stuffed red peppers, or the home-grown Tarta (cake). You'll gobble for hours and then float away light as a fine soufflé.

If it's summer, join the stream of pilgrims to **Santurce**, 3 miles out. Then follow the tradition by buying sardines direct from the fishing boats and taking them to the little *tascas* where they'll fry them for you in a special way. Order Chacolí (apple wine) and bread, roll up your sleeves—and you're already 50% a *Vasco!* A famous ritual.

Burgos comes up with the colorfully rustic **Hostal Landa**, 2 miles south of town on N–1, and the less attractive **Hostal del Cid**, north of the city limits on the same highway.

In **Cádiz**, here's how we'd rate 'em: (1) **El Telescopio** (casks of local flavor), (2) **El Anteojo** (simple, dirt-cheap, with some of the most savory prawns and filet of sole in the nation), (3) **El Sardinero** (spotless, unpretentious, and centrally located, with friendly staff), and (4) **Comedor Vasco** (*bodega*-type décor with U.S.-Greek-restaurant overtones, for winter dining). **Pasaje Andaluz** is getting better and better.

Córdoba now comes up with several rewarding choices—as long as you don't expect a "21." For color, **El Zoco**, owned by the Melía interests, is a stunner. This was an authentic Moorish market situated in the very heart of the ancient ghetto. In the basement (now a *bodega*), a nucleus of Jews kept their forbidden religion alive during the Inquisition; across the alley, in a state of wonderful preservation, is the oldest (only one small room) synagogue in Europe. In addition, this structure also houses the Museum of Bulls (Museo Taurino) for Córdoba. Several rooms strung throughout numerous levels of the complex; open patio for summer dining and viewing the evening flamenco dancing; lovely fountain bubbling throughout the performance. Not a gustatory shrine—very poor, in fact, for cookery—but a memorable experience for any holidaymaker's circuit. Tops in town as a touristic drawing card. For simple nutrients without as much theatrical and/or historical flair, the **Méson El Caballo Rojo** ("House of the Red Horse"), with its viewful summer terrace, and the **Méson del Conde** ("House of the Count") are recommendable; both are typical regional taverns. For a sunny-day excursion, **Castillo de la Albaida** is a modest but deserving choice. One mile out of town, on the road toward Trasierra; tranquilizing 270° vista of the plains and distant mountains; country manse atmosphere, with the best feature its open terrace for viewful munching; homespun service that can become over-busy-busy on weekends or holidays; steaks cooked "well done" unless you specify otherwise; our garlic soup was the best we had on that circuit (but it lingered for days, our friends tell us). No great fireworks, but it can kindle a cheerful ambiance if you're in the mood. For hotel fare, we hear that the **Córdoba Palace** has improved significantly in its skillet skills. In fact, the only flies in the *gazpacho* come from Guidesters who complain that swarms of winged critters attack at mealtimes on the open poolside terrace. Otherwise, this hotel seems to be taking giant strides in all directions. On our latest try, the dining room in the **Gran Capitan** combined fumbling service with sludgelike Stuffed Bull's Tail Cordoba.

La Coruña comes up with **Finesterre** for the leading hotel kitchen. Among the independents, we'd choose **Pornos** (*sic!*), **El Rápido, Abrego, Duna**, in that order—or a picnic shopped at **Aniceto Rodrigues**, at Cantón Pequeño 23, if you want to enjoy the countryside.

Costa del Sol: Let's start with *Almería*, where gastronomy certainly was not born, but where it is given a modest foothold at **El Rincón de Juan Pedro**. The décor makes no pretensions; it is purely and simply regional, clean, attractive, and relaxing. You could say exactly the same for the food. Open all year, too.

In *Fuengirola*, **Don Bigote** (½-mile out at Los Boliches) is the choice (except for the nearby **La Langosta**, where the food's fair, but the service kills it for us). Century-old former sardine-packing factory; Spanish-style bar and small hearthside lounge near entrance; 3 dining nooks seating a total of 250; the first, our favorite, lined with cozy raised alcoves on one side plus textured walls, ceiling beams, Mexican curtains, and Moorish lamps; 2-tiered alfresco terrace brimming with flowers. Roy Wykes, the mustachioed proprietor (Don Bigote means "Sir Mustache"), is your amiable host, while Vera, his whisker-less better half, cruises among the guests to see to their comfort and satisfaction. Our richly endowed Andalucian fish soup, perfectly spiced, was delightful; so was our guest's beef casserole, an honest, hearty dish well suited to the cool evening. We like this friendly and cheerful domain. Heading toward *Estepona*, **El Molino** is more culinary grist for your mill. The miller, incidentally, is Belgian—and do *those* folks know how to cook!

Marbella's waves have rolled up a crester on a hill about a mile from the Hilton. **La Hacienda Las Chapas**, at kilometer stone 200, is a white adobe structure composed of a small bar at its entrance leading to a T-shape room with a fireplace where the T is crossed. Beamed ceiling; bleached walls; terra-cotta floor; wooden tables; cushioned chairs; elegant place settings with gargantuan wineglasses. Our Roquefort Salad and veal baked in aluminum foil were superb, as were the Roast Partridge in Vine Leaves and Quail Flambé enjoyed by others in our party. Belgian Owner Paul Schiff has composed a melodious Suite for Gastronomes. Phone ahead (831 267 or 831 116) for reservations. Closed Mondays. Recommended. **El Platanal** ("The Banana Tree"), guided by Fun City Proprietor-Chefs Joe and Lois McDonnal, is said to peel off solid slices of roast beef. Its fronds were bound up for alterations when this tallyman strode by, but we hope to pick its fruit next round. Otherwise the region's most alluring siren is **Rascascio**, about 5 miles out toward Estepona. Hillside perch bowered with olive trees and bougainvillaea; farmhouse ambiance; house dazzlers include grills from the briny and from the prairie; the adjoining cowshed offers 45 small apartments for diners who may wish to parlay the evening into a fortnight (2-week minimum). Sound management by Enid Riddell (that lady who whispers sweet somethings to her sizzling grill). **La Tricicletta** (Buitrago 16) bounces in with baskets of atmosphere and eye appeal. Don't go for lunch, because it is never served. Your taxi will deposit you at the edge of a small plaza; follow the arrows through the shoulder-hugging alley and up to its low iron gate; enter a peaceful courtyard; to your immediate right, in a separate adjunct, is the bar. Wooden staircase leading to an L-shaped dining room; timbered gambrel roof, with windows in the treetops; taper illumination; check-patterned and gay solid-shaded tablecloths; rush-bottomed, black-lacquered chairs; simple décor oozing with charm. Extensive and daring menu (for Spain); joint ownership by an Irishman, an Englishman, another Belgian, and an American, who keep this 4-wheeler free-wheeling at a happy clip. Very good, indeed. **La Bonne Auberge**, on a residential street overlooking the lighthouse, boasts 2 dining rooms, a waterside terrace, and artillery barrages of kitchen noises. Stucco-and-beam interior; so-so cookery; French management. Better for viewing than for chewing. **Grillon** is another entry from Gaul; it's said to be better in Low Season, when service is a reality. **Charlemagne** tries to be French, too. **Las Picas** is not noteworthy. 'One of Madrid's leading restaurateurs, Horcher, has just opened **La Fonda** at Plaza de Cristo; though we have not yet seen it, this is sure to be one of the top choices here, too. Hotel dining everywhere is not too inspiring.

Out at fashionable *Puerto Banus*, Madrid's doge of dining, the remarkable Don Carlos Cortés of Clubs Jockey and "31" fame, has extended his capital gains to this coastal venue. The **Club 31** hosts 200 guests in the main establishment with seating for 26 more in a private salon. Décor similar to the Madrid "31"; cuisine and its cost also following suit; functioning 7 days per week save in November, when it shutters. Very chic; a new triumph for Sr. Cortés, who remains one of Spain's most illustrious arbiters of gastronomy.

Torremolinos has an indifferent lot. **Chez Lucien**, a few minutes out toward Málaga, is the most rewarding choice. Fine Lobster Thermidor and delicious soufflés; several French specialties on the menu; almost French prices too; service slipping on our latest tryout; if you don't order ahead, you're in for a long wait, sans bar or garden in which to sip your apéritif. Expensive but still a standard bearer. **Tortuga** (Calle San Miguel), which later lumbered onto the beach, is a popular novelty. Lobster bisque and sirloin steak are the best bets, we found. Ground-floor bar with fireplace and barrel chairs; 11-table upstairs dining room; babbling pool with rocks and greenery; aquarium with curious angelfish to envy your nibbling; rooftop kitchen, plus space for a small complement of alfresco diners. Rather high tabs, but the general quality is there. Even higher prices and much lower quality? Our advice is to miss the **Seven Seas** in the Eurosol apartment complex. Indoor orientation overlooking gardens; grim atmosphere that tries to be clubby. On our recent visit the bartender did not have Tio Pepe Sherry on hand; the service was fumbling; the cooking was strictly 2nd-rate to our tastes. **La Brocherie** (No. 704 in the La Nogelera apartotel) allegedly is Gay Liberation, South, according to an amused reader who said his party's Fruta del Mar, onion soup, roast lamb, and filet mignon were sssscrumptious. **Kings Club**, also in the Nogalera, seemed doomed to us. Almost empty almost every night —and we understand why. Here are 3 good reasons: the local ham with indifferent melon costs far too much, the Pepper Steak (not so peppery and hardly a steak) also is unfairly fared, in our opinion, and the Crêpes Suzette (absolutely repulsive on our taste test) might have come from an orphan tin. It's vedy,vedy snob-conscious and it's vedy, vedy lousy, for our pesetas. **La Grenouille** serves only light bites and beverages. The Moroccan patroness can often be found at the corner table, elegantly smoking a king-size cigarette held in her ringed fingers by an 8-inch-long ebony holder—and studiously reading a comic book. The **Napoli** dishes up typical Italian Cous-cous, not to mention North-African-style pizza. **Hong Kong** sounds the gong from 1 to 4 in the afternoon and from 7 to 12 in the evening, with you-know-what; we said yum-yum from egg rolls to Nasi Goreng to Sweet-and-Sour Pork. Recommended. The **Canton** can, too, but not nearly so well. **Mandarin** stokes up a 4-course Indonesian dinner that's not too bad. **Bali** (Plaza Andaluciá) spotlights the same cuisine with a second focus on Chinese fare. Tolerable. The **Bodegón** (Calle Cauce), with scarlet pillars, white walls, and bench seats, seems to be a happier hunting ground for rabbits than for carnivora. **El Cacique** waves a welcome with a surfside alfresco hut and a *pampas*-pampered inner sanctum. Argentine specialties such as Empanadas (meat pies), Berenjenas (cold pickled eggplant), and sirloin steak draw gastronomic gauchos from miles around. Inexpensive and different. **Antonio's** (Calle Bulto) highlights (no pun) a 9-candle holder producing enough molten wax to dwarf Mont Blanc. Packed to distraction in season, with the result that service can be appalling. Branches in Málaga and Nueva Andalucía. **Pedro's,** a complex of complex-ridden hippies, yippies, and kippies, on the main drag, is *the* haven for peroxide blondes (at least 3 sexes) who thrive on a fish-and-chips diet. Low prices and lower quality. The neighboring **V.I.P.** and **Bar Central** also cater to beatnix; go for drinks only, if that. **El Porrón** may cluck proudly over its spitted chickens and grilled steaks, but we don't crow at all. **Pogo's** is back in biz; snacks on the square—plaza, that is. **Caballo Blanco** (4 miles out) is serene, rustic, and simple. **Chez Mas**, a hut on the seaside across the highway, served us a delicious Shrimp Bisque and a Dorade with herbs for a minimum number of céntimos. Max Fognon, its proprietor, is French. Very raw in ambiance. **Torremuelle** (a few minutes toward Fuengirola) surrounds an ancient fort; a magnificent view surrounds you; mostly for snacks and pana-romantics. The **Bar Manolo,** just off the main plaza, is good in for seafood and *tapas* but dreadful for meat and eggs. **Victor**, on the midtown drag, is a shadow of its former self. For late afternoon snacks, **La Vina P.**, next door, offers a grimy counter loaded with grilled tidbits and shellfish goodies. Until after midnight, **El Goloso** (down an alley off the main square) flips up Crêpes Grand Marnier; hamburgers and hot dogs also on order for more plebian tastes. One *must* in this 90-proof hamlet is a predinner snort at a tiny Spanish pub called **Casa Quitapenas** (San Miguel 34), where potables are tapped from giant Ali Baba crocks; along about sundown, every second Iberian south of Bilbao pops in here for a quickie. Don't miss it. **Casa Prudencio** (Calle Carmen 43) has a better location than its chef deserves, at least in our view. Moonlight dancing by the sea during our visit; beamed ceiling; nautical dry-mounts; plain red tablecloths; decent service. Our Gaz-pacho, however, was poor; the Brochette Prudencio, an aquatic shish kebab, was fair at best; the wine reminded us of another liquid that's usually poured on open wounds. At least the bill here won't give your wallet lesions.

Granada? The dining room or the rooftop grill of the **Luz Granada Hotel** runs away with every trophy in town among private entrepreneurs. The service is suave; the cuisine is tops in the region; the prices are fair. Highest recommendation for both. The Moorish Grill at the **Alhambra Palace** has finally picked up a bit, but there's still a long way to go. Arched windows, pastel filigrees, hanging brass, trick mirrors; beguiling décor which, to us, is still wasted. The upstairs dining room seems even more faltering by compari-son. The garden at **Parador San Francisco** is lovely in good weather. The inside is pleasant, too. Since it is a Government-run kitchen, it is almost phenomenal that the quality is so lofty. Not a trace of institutionalism. Actually, we even prefer it to the privately operated competitors. For shellfish and finned fare, nothing tops reliable old **C'Unini**, behind the flower market. As usual in these harbors, the *marisco* bar is at ground level and the full restaurant is up in the spars. Fresh catches? Look at 'em wigglin! For similar nettings in more fancy surroundings, try **Méson de las Vidrerias**, where Granada shines through every stained-glass window. If you're trying to slim down, *puh-leeese* don't peek into the open kitchen. You'll gain 3 pounds just on a glance. Very popular. **Casa Salvador** whips up family atmospherics, simple cookery, simple surroundings, simple prices. Pure and simply, a win-ner—except on Fridays when it rests. **Los Manueles** occupies one entire street —every inch of Zaragoza 2 to 4, one of the shortest lanes in Iberia. Cheerful, basic, and busy. When you pay the reasonable tab, it will then be rubbed off the marble bar top where your waiter has chalked the summing up. Sum fun. We meticulously studied the menu at the **Mogambo** and were tempted to order the "Grab Custard." Our unshaven waiter, however, pointed to the "Han With Broad Beans", so we took that plus some "Roval Soup" and a slice of "Bread". What a han-hamded copyreader they've got, *n'est-ce paw?* For day-in-dine-out consistency, we always keep coming back to the **Sevilla,** where you'll see nothing spectacular and you'll swallow nothing spectacular. Nevertheless, for this city, it's darned good—and it seems to stay that way year after happy year. A lot of French, American, Spanish, and Granadinos agree. **Los Leones** couldn't be less colorful or less costly. **Alcaicería**, sup-posedly in the same category as the Sevilla, has spruced itself up, but its noisy, hurly-burly pace and upsie-downsie quality still turn us off.

Jerez, for some strange reason, seems almost a gastronomic desert. The **Hotel Jerez** is the exception, particularly in the steak department, which may be why about 60 Andalucian bicycle racers, their trainers, and the press had lunch there the same day we did. The area leader, indoors or on the sunny terrace. **El Bosque**, 1 km from the center along the Seville highway, remains the most famous candidate, but it was again a big disappointment to us on our latest trial. With sorrow, not recommended except for a drink in the garden. On a later recheck of Jerez, we were so desperate to find a good meal that we fell back upon a creaky old procedure which has worked well for us in the past: to stop 5 locals at random on the street and politely to ask, "Where can we find the best food in town?" To our surprise, each was vehement in his selection of a little midtown spot named **Joaquín** (Calle Ramón y Cajal 10). Only 8 tables; bar occupying ¼th of the room; spotlessly clean until the standup patrons begin dropping *marisco* shells, in the Iberian tradition. The fish soup was one of the best balanced, most delicate, most delicious that we have had of this nationally popular brew during our long residence in this nation. Please don't miss this masterpiece which is made *especially* for you, not laddled out of a mammoth cauldron. Stick to the sea-ways; the meats are strictly routine in quality; avoid the house wine. **Los Cisnes Hotel** has improved to the point of being tolerable. **La Vega** is fair as a cafeteria. The **San Francisco** is so-so. Others are worse.

La Coruña: Covered under C.

In *Málaga*, the State-operated **Hostería de Gibralfaro** (see "Hotels") offers one of the most stunning panoramas of any restaurant in Spain. It's atop Monte de Gibralfaro, 10 minutes out (about $2 each way, by taxi); heavenly terrace, especially at night; cuisine tasteless but prices reasonable; don't miss a trip up here. For excellent cookery and sophistication, on the other hand, the dining room of the **Palacio Hotel** is the patrician choice. Superb in every way on our very recent trial runs. The French-owned **Le Gourmet** now functions chiefly as a bar. *C'est la vie*. **La Algería** (Marín García 18) is busy, smoky, noisy, and animated; large standup bar at entrance and twin dining rooms to rear. One shocked Guidester once reported that he watched his waiter mix a salad—with his hands! (We're anxious to see how he prepares scrambled eggs.) For a sunny-day lunch, the seaside, pueblo-style **Antonio Martín**, near the bullring, is a relaxing noontime choice. Here you'll find the best general level of cookery in the town; sit only in the waterfront patio; its inside dining room seemed a mite less inviting and is always packed. Finny fare is best (especially the *chanquetes,* if they are running—inch-long white fish that resemble fat needles and are kissin' cousins to anemic eels); tabs are low; go early or reserve in advance. Very popular. Finally, the State Tourist Department has opened a charming little golf club 10 minutes from town on the Torremolinos road. It's called **Parador del Campo de Golf**. Terrace-dining in summer; same prices (and food) as other government-run inns; private beach 200 yards from clubhouse; you may rent clubs for a 9-hole round before lunch.

Marbella: See "Costa del Sol."

Oviedo is not exactly overrun with gastronomical shrines. After possibly the **Reconquistador Hotel**, you might try the **Pelayo, Marchica, Ronda**, or a sliced apple and local cheese.

Pamplona's pride and joy (and all of Spain can take a bow for this one) is **Le Mesón del Caballo Blanco**. This "House of the White Horse" was built by the city itself, with absolutely no reservations on the purse strings. Although only an architectural youngster, it appears to be 90; it is a perfect duplicate—sensitively rendered—of a fifteenth-century stone homestead. Ground floor Chacoli Bar offering rock-lined arches, smoked hams and sausages, bottle-glass windows, and a massive wine press; upstairs restaurant wrapped in timber and granite, with L-shape conformation in a split-level layout; inviting hearth with wrought-iron fixtures and coats of arms of ancient Navara; floors of brick and solid planking. The attentive waitresses are tricked out in polkadot blouses and velvet jerkins. Our meal of Trucha Navarra (local-style trout), Cordero en Chilindrón (heavenly roasted lamb), Cardo (a celery-like vegetable) and Cuajada de Urdiain (sugared-and-iced sheep's milk yoghurt which, unlikely as it might sound, is a taste treat) was superb. Very inexpensive for what one receives. Under the administrative aegis of the Hotel de los Tres Reyes, it is beautifully managed as a regional oasis. Salutes and hearty, "Well Dones!" to the genii behind this one. Recommended with cheers. **Hostal del Rey Noble**, also known as "Las Pocholas," takes the midtown honors. More cosmopolitan ambiance; 2 dining rooms; beamed ceilings; pleasant but not visually ex-citing in the same way as the Caballo Blanco; broad menu selection; high prices for the district. A solid second. **Iruña**, also central and very nearby, is next. Highly touted by locals, but we've never lifted our fork here.

In *San Sebastián*, **Salduba** (long a fishermen-district favorite) is a de-lightfully rustic siren who beckons to hungry wayfarers of all callings. It also rates as our number one catch in this seaside city. The 2 floors contain stalwart beams of timber, wagon-wheel chandeliers, fat pigtails of plaited garlic, copperware, red-checked linens, and giant candles in wrought-iron braces. The young waitresses seem to find the recipes for foreign cocktails a bit mysterious—but ooooolala-di-da-di-da, when they toted out that repast of Sopa de Pescado (fish soup), Sole Meunière, Changuro al Horno (baked deep-water crab), and Crema de Espinacas (creamed spinach)! Our taste buds took off faster than a Saturn V booster. It is superb in the honest manner of a native feedery. If you *must* dine deluxe style, you might not like it, but if you let your palate master your aesthetics, we think you will find this a nutritious and enriching experience in every way. Recommended as one of the tops of its type in Iberia. The **Chomin** (downstairs in the inn of the same name, near the Codina Hotel) is a more sophisticated offering, despite its Basque chalet exterior. Nondescript international interior with polished wood and marble trimmings; about 25 tables plus a working bar; open terrace for summer-izations; medium-to-high tariffs; Neptune's dishes far more savory than the meats on our visit; professional service eagle-eyed by English-speaking Maître Paco. Not as good as it was, in our opinion, but still worth a try. **Azaldegui** (Miraconcha 23), we are sad to report, has slipped dangerously into a tideless backwater. Hillside situation with unspectacular ocean view; decoration that has gone zipless; 12-table terrace in summer; main dining room in 3 sections, with tiny bar at one end. Its service is now more frenzied than a Le Mans pit stop. Regrettably, our Lobster Thermidor tasted almost *au gratin,* while our partner's Sole Au Gratin seemed to have been baked in a Thermidor sauce. Prices higher than ever; to us, no longer a value for those rich, rich tabs. **Casa Nicolasa** (Aldamar 4) still commands the greatest fame locally. On our round, the cookery was still coming up commendably. Side-street location; 3 small, austere rooms; well-dressed diners as busily achatter as monkeys. They still serve Canard à l'Orange with the duck *boiled* (a "First" for us—and we pray a "Last"!), so some clients must enjoy this abomination. Otherwise the cuisine is more and more pleasantly honed. Expensive for the region, but now a better bet. But please remember: If you still order that seethed quacker soaking in its bath of pure Portland cement, THAT canard is on you, chum. On your first balmy day, don't miss **Cumbre Monte Ulía** (10-minute ride to the top of Monte Ulía) for a glorious panorama of the city, bays, and La Concha at your feet; immaculate dining room with mirror-sheen floor, pink and yellow linens, and waitresses in regional costumes; 50-table hedge-ringed terrace with low stone wall slopeside, so that you can soak up the view. Better-than-average culinary standards. A *must* in good weather. The *Monte Igueldo* complex is a fortresslike structural mélange, with an enormous ballroom, movie theater, children's playground, zoo, restaurant, and bar. Funicular for pedestrians and toll road for motorists: 40 tables for cocktails; promenade-terrace; unfancy dining room with limited menu; we haven't tried the food. Here's an alpine Yankee Stadium that is glutted with every form, shape, and manner of humanity during the Travel World Series from May to October. Worth a look, but take your Louisville Slugger to beat your path through the throng. The deluxe **Monte Igueldo Hotel** is tranquil, of course. We never found time to sample its cuisine. The vista is enchanting, so for this alone it is recommendable. The **Club Gudamendi** on Carretera del Barrio de Igueldo is perched around the shoulder of the same mountain. Terrace-dining in local country-club atmosphere; splendid position, but routine heavy-on-oil kitchen. In *Pueblo de Igueldo*, the family-style **Recondo** leads with a strong challenge from **Mendi Sorotz**, in the town square.

Back at sea level again, the **Royal Club Náutico**, at the apex of the Concha, is a ferryboat-shape building that doubles as a restaurant and nightclub. Park outlook from the "stern"; 2 "decks" with inside and outside tables; roofed, open-sided "sundeck" for floor show and dancing; cool and pleasant in summer, as long as your gastronomy isn't too choosy at the moment. For bistro-type nourishment in the Old City, **Casa Rodil** (Esterline 8) is a worthy excursion. Bright yellow, coral, and natural-wood décor; menu in Spanish and French; crustacean specialties of Langostinos (prawns), Bisque de Cigalas (lobster-type soup first enriched by the shells and then strained), and Crab Centollo (Biscay Bay delight); ask for Don Manuel. Pleasant but not exceptional. **España** is more colorful, typical, and earthy. Tiny, covered patio in season; nakedly stark furnishings; local workers happily tilting its Spanish-version pinball machines or intent on card games at its marble bar-tables. Look for the cheerful, fun-loving Basque *patrón*, Don Ignacio, or his pert English-speaking daughter, Señorita María Coro. As authentic and flavorful as a cask of pungent sherry. **La Cueva** (plaza de la Trinidad) boasts a scenic niche in the Old Quarter. It's a bar that grew up to become a specialty corner. Fun.

For 3 rough-and-ready seafood dens, try **Aita Mari** ("Father Mari" in Basque), just 50 yards from the fishing boats at Calle Puerto 23 and **Juanito Kojua** (pronounced "Coo-ow") at #14 on the same street. The former has 3 levels with stone walls, wooden dados, tile floors, and lip-smacking specialties. The latter has 2 dining areas in a sterile, brightly lit, wardroom atmosphere. **Restaurante Eguía**, just a sardine's leap away, works both sides of its narrow street from the same kitchen. Bar, snack room, and perspiring chef in the economy division.

Snack Bars? Try the **Rivoli** (near Hotel Continental). Modern lunchroom personality; nibble counter in front; dining hall to the rear; low prices; English menu offering everything from "water melon juice" to "a piece of sponge cake." Other good bets are **Dover** (2 branches), **Big Ben** (Alvenida 3), **California** (Hernani 17) and **Mónaco** (Av. de España 27). For The Cup That Cheers, **Bar Bosque, Café Paris**, and **Madrid** are the most popular.

Outside of town about 4 miles, *Rentería* offers the **Panier Fleuri**, where the Fombellida family has been stoking the ovens since 1920. Its shaded garden is inviting in summer. The interior, with its turn-of-the-century décor, sheds 2 tiers of delight in winter. Happily recommended. About 6 miles from the airport and a ½-mile off the main pike, you may find the **Atamitx**, in the Barrio Ugaldetxo of *Oyarzun*. Split-log construction; communal bench seating; 2 separate grills (fish and meats); rough and ready and lots of fun. Finally, at *Orio*, **José Marí** is the pick of the local sweets. A couple of other chocolate covered Orios reside in the main plaza, but we always dunk with José Marí.

Santander is composed of 3 gastronomic syllables: The prefix is **Puerto;** the middle-fix is **Vivero**; the suffix is **Casa Valentin**. And that spells *San-tan-der.*

In *Segovia*, the **Mesón de Cándido** (on the main plaza) is practically a national institution. Even the enthusiastic local police—if they see a hungry look in your eye—will automatically steer you to this address before you can say "boo." Several room levels; stupendous roast piglet and roast lamb; colorful, not too expensive, and fine. A number of Guidesters have squawked about higher lunch tabs for their drivers than for themselves. Service is fast, if not abrupt. As a souvenir, you'll be given a tiny earthenware jug announcing in Spanish that it was stolen from this house. *Phone for your table in advance.* **El Abuelo** ("The Grandfather") is a characteristic cellar, unspoiled, with a cobblestone floor, low ceilings, and poor old "Grandpa" in a cage in one corner; its suckling pig is just worth oinking about. Basic.

Seville will never exactly outdazzle Paris as a Temple of Gastronomy; there's an old Spanish saying that the people of Andalusia think too much about living to waste time on food, and it couldn't be truer. The number-one restaurant of the city—and a notable exception to the Andalusian adage—is the Burladero in **Hotel Colón**. Attractive décor designed to pique the interest of bullfight aficionados; comfortable, handsome appointments, extensive menu, outstanding viands, stiff prices for the region. Ask for Maîtres Luis Noval or Rafael Carrillo. Locally unrivaled. It had been rumored that the same interests would open a million-dollar restaurant next to the Cathedral, possibly to be named **Méson del Moro**. Keep your eyes open for this newcomer because it sounds terrific. By tradition, next in line has been the **Hostería del Prado,** on the Prado de San Sebastián; we used to be fond of this one, but then we went off it for a spell; now we like it again for regional cookery and *tapas*. Then flows the **Rio Grande**, perched on the far bank of the Guadalquivir beside the San Telmo Bridge. Intimate maroon-tone cocktail area near entrance effectively ruined by a cold food display; elegant dining room divided by glass and wrought iron, accented with globe lamps, oil portraits, and potted plants; massive windows abutting a summer-only alfresco terrace; adroit service; well-scrubbed restrooms. Our recent repast here turned up a mixed bag: garlic soup that couldn't have been better and a sirloin that tasted as if it had once lined Joe Frazier's punching bag; the accompanying potatoes, tomatoes, and carrots were not tepid—they were downright cold and so, at that point, were we. **La Muralla**, in La Macerena Hotel, jams its tables too much together. The chef's hand was heavy on our sampling. So-so. **Casa Senra** (Becquer 25, a 15-minute taxi hop from the center), formerly the sloppiest, grubbiest, dirtiest, most dreadful dump that ever delighted Sevillanos, their guests, and us with superb culinations—has cleaned itself up. Entrance bar for premeal libations and mariscos; stucco dining alcoves; beamed ceiling; polished marble floor; wooden tables covered with clean tartan cloths; comfortable chairs replacing old stools and benches; waiters in white jackets; air conditioning. The cookery is still as scrumptuous as ever, particularly the seafood specialties flown in daily. The grills are also prime —so is our Grade-A recommendation. **Los Alcazares** (Miguel Manara 10) is an unpretentious eatery dividing its 11 tables between 2 floors. Seascape murals and bullfight posters decorating the upstairs segment; chummy service; student minstrels sometime roll in after 10. The hot garlic soup and partridge in sherry casserole are inexpensive but worthy selections. Next down the step-ladder is **La Raza**, at the entrance to María Luisa Park—but unfortunately facing the traffic rather than the greenery. Identical menus, tariffs, and ownership as Hostería del Prado; appetizing steaks—for Spain, that is. In summer, this one has the edge on its harness mate. **Luna Parque**, across the street, also stares obsessively at the thoroughfare rather than at Mother Nature. (*You* figure 'em out.) Décor jarringly disjointed by a cold-box placed in the dining room; professional service; fair cuisine. Open all 4 seasons—as if anyone here cared about blossom time. **Bodegón Torre del Oro** (Calle Santander 29, a 3-minute stroll from the Alfronso XIII), has a noisy beerhall ambiance, savory Pechuga Vileroi (a chicken-breast specialty), fairly reasonable tariffs, and a no-non-sense approach to skilletry. Fun, if you're in a rollicking mood. **Los Corales** (Sierpes 102) draws almost as many tourists as flies; there were plenty of both during our last visit. Central location; friendly reception and service; food and drink so-so; seafood is best; medium-to-high prices; colorful décor, in a contrived way. Just fair. **Manolo Bar** (Pasaje del Duque) offers good cookery and good service; covered terrace; medium-to-low price bracket; popular. **Casa Luis** (Paseo de Colón 6) is very plain, very cheap, and very characteristic; service standards sinking radically with its too-easy success; sidewalk terrace, hideous artwork in dining room, beautifully tiled bar adjoining. **Pescadería Málaga** (Calle O'Donnell) specializes in fried fish; typical. So does the **Bar Colon**, but it's exceptionally raw in character. **Restaurant los Monos** or **Juliá** (Plaza de México) has an attractive but overbusy garden. Inside, its 1000-seat dining fastness reminds us of a cheap snack-stop on the old U.S. No. 1. Locals are attracted by its *feria*-type décor and regional fare. Nothing special. The newish **El Fogon** (Habana 8) turned us off with its window display of dead fish and meat. Somehow it all looked deader than recent expiration would have it. No thanks.

Sitges, an hour's drive south of Barcelona and worthwhile as an excursion target from the Catalonian capital, boasts the superb little **Mare Nostrum**, one of our favorite fair-weather choices in the province. Awning-topped, umbrella-dotted apron across from the seaside promenade; interior units split into a bar and a dining nook lined with paintings; delicious shrimp cocktail served on an open plate, with the sauce mixed before your eyes; carefully and intelligently prepared filets of sole, done either in simple butter or with an almond garnish; Crema de Mariscos soup that is just out of this glittering world; good meats, too—but we inevitably come back for the piscatorial delights. These, with a cold bottle of Las Campanas *rosado* (the best Spanish rosé), should put the glow of romance into any cheeks. Courteous service by the same staff year after happy year; tabs slightly higher than most medium-range candidates in the nation. We love it day or night. **El Greco**, also on the front, provides an extensive menu of well-treated comestibles. It, too, is best for outdoor dining when the climate is benign. **Fragata**, near the lovely seaside chapel and the fishermen's wharf, serves decent drinks and culinations, but the prices knocked us for a loup (if you'll pardon our finny pun). The service is often careless and care-less. The **Brasa**, downstairs in the **Hotel Calípolis**, is an amusing stop for snacks, club-platters, and light meals late in the evening; it swings in season. The **Baxeroe** in nearby *Villa Nueva* gave us sole food fit for the gods. Always filled with loyalists. **El Velero** is so unattractive you'd never believe that its array of pastries could mutilate your diet with second helpings. A sweetie for sweets, but a misery for main courses. The **Valpeneda** development (see "Hotels") is pleasant by sunlight or by moonbeams. Inland valley situation; modern, clubby atmosphere; tennis courts; swimming pool; bars; outdoor-indoor dining; operated by the Fragata concession. If you scoot down here from Barcelona, try to make it during the fringe seasons, because it's a colossal hassle in midsummer.

Torremolinos: See "Costa del Sol."

Toledo has been offering a disappointing selection. **Hotel del Cardenal** has an enchanting garden, a marvelous arbor-covered dining-terrace, a cleverly "aged" 2-story restaurant (we prefer the upper level), and a score of attractive features—but the food we ate, course by course, and the so-called service we experienced could only be termed appalling by us. Our Garlic Soup was greasy; the Navarra Trout was very poor; the lamb was tasty but tough and dry. Lovely setting; shocking maintenance and undisciplined staff on our visit; zipless vittles. **Venta del Aire** has very little charm, no view to speak of, and service which we'd hardly call the world's most agreeable; in addition, so many flies appeared to enjoy its full-pension plan on our last visit that it seemed a pity to interfere with their feeding. Both establishments are loaded, but loaded, with tourists in season. Try the parador; it's bound to be better.

Valencia offers little. **Viveros** (Jardines del Real), our first choice, has unglamorous but substantial cookery and slow service. The same company operates the newer **Les Graelles** (Paseo de la Alameda), where we dined very, very well in lovely surroundings. The offspring, in fact, now seems even better —and certainly it's more attractive than the alma mater. **Ateneo**, on Plaza Caudillo, probably turns on better cookery more consistently. Cafeteria plus a rather overwhelming old-world restaurant. Stuffy in its mood, but reliable in its quality. For dinner only, **Casa de Lee** includes a few Oriental dishes among its Iberian selections. Whacky but fun. Across the street, **Mesón de Marisquero** specializes in fruit of the sea, cleanliness, good value, and friendly service. What else could one ask? **Lara** (Calle Paz 46) comes up with a small dance floor, intimate corners, and palate-tickling atmosphere; not bad. **Lionel,** facing the Plaza Caudillo, is genteel, discreet, and chicly intimate. The cuisine is French, *mais oui!* Closed Sunday. **Mesón del Conde** (Calle de José Iturbi 18) has 2 brick-and tile-lined rooms and 15 blue-and-white-robed tables. Waiters in tartans and waistcoats; attentive service; low tabs; many Italian selections have slipped onto its Spanish menu. *Muchas bene!* **La Gran Parrilla** (Calle Marqués del Turia 10) features an open kitchen and a respectable menu. **Palas Fesol** (Hernán Cortés 9) is plain and inexpensive; budgeteers like this one, but we feel that it has been slipping lately. **O'Lano's Basque** (Calle San Martín) boasts a bar, restaurant, and O'Lano's élan; amusing at night because O'Lano is such a character; this one gets better every visit. If you're restless, if the day is lovely, and if you don't mind participating in a mob scene, **La Pepica** (Playa Levante) is right on the beach (10 minutes by taxi from the center). It's simple, cheap, Spanish, and busy as a minny in a minnow hatch. Lunch is preferable; so popular that a hotel has recently been added; the food —well. . . . **Las Arenas**, farther down the street, has better fare but less character; same management as **Café Noel** (Calle Ruzafa). **La Marcelina**, also by the water, is pleasant for a lazy daytime, maritime meal; ask for Paco. The **Club Náutico** is directly on the wharf overlooking the port entrance. From your table you can toss a line to that passing boatswain. Outdoor terrace and glassed-in, flower-lined dining salon; separate bar; wonderful seafood, especially shellfish; courteous service; physically raw in appearance; teeming with local folk in season; inexpensive. A happy choice if you wish to flee the bustling city. Finally, if you are outward bound from the airport, we think that the **Azafata Hotel Grill**, off Route 111, is better than any terminal cookery (that phrase is almost 100% accurate) you are likely to ingest before you fly.

Zaragoza has dozens of bars for tidbits—but a paucity of full-fledged restaurants. The **Savoy** (good service, clashing décor, fair prices) and the **Laguna** (we prefer this one) are the only candidates serving international cuisine. For strictly regional cookery in colorful Aragón surroundings, the **Mesón del Carmen** is tops. Busy-beehive atmosphere; U-shape room with nibbler-and-sipper's bar down one side and tables down the other; smoky; full of rich Spanish life and vitality; excellent skilletcraft in the manner they know best; reasonable tariffs. Recommended as your first shot in this way station. The nutrition complex at the new **Hotel Corona de Aragón** includes the Moorish-striped Albarracín Grill for spit roastings, the Bearn Restaurant on the mezzanine for international fare, the modernistic Formigal for coffee-shop wares (plus take-away service), and Piccadilly's Bar for sips and snacks. We are especially fond of the grillroom here.

Mallorca? See its independent chapter, listed alphabetically.

For information on restaurants in other localities, consult the Spanish Tourist Offices everywhere—or ask your hotel concierge.

Dedicated budgeteers? Since we're too bottlenecked here for additional entries, please consult this year's vastly updated edition of our annually revised paperback, *Fielding's Low-Cost Europe,* which lists scads more bargain dining spots and money-saving tips for serious economizers in Madrid and Torremolinos.

NIGHTCLUBS   Since most neophytes to **Madrid** usually want to see the world-famous and historic flamenco dancers, let's open the curtain with a sampling of the most prominent names currently on stage.

Corral de la Morería (Morería 17) means "Corral of Happiness"—and, for most first-timers, it lives up to its joyful moniker. L-shape main room with small stage occupied by 8-shape ladies and handsome, swarthy male dancers; about 10 performers on our night, all much more attractive than those in other flamenco parlors (cross your fingers that the dynamic Lucero Tena will be there on your night); corner bar; capacity for about 80 show-viewers; popular for dinner; food miles from great, but edible; your first libation painfully high and your later ones less; untampered spirits in our glasses. It's best to go late to avoid the bus excursions. Tops for its type for zing and fire, although sometimes short on artistry and polish.

Café de Chinitas (Torija 7), a long room with green textiled walls and a stage at one end, today resembles an elegant Spanish salon, but the original café was a far more modest Malaguenian *tablao* of the 1850's. Red-framed portraits of renowned matadors; tomato- and avocado-colored bar; chairs, tables, and other trimmings carrying out the Andalucian motif. Smaller flamenco ensemble than at the Corral; performances better conceived but far less spontaneous; excellent costumery; top guitarists and singers; honest drinks; no groups. Eminently rewarding for a sophisticated evening, but we prefer the Corral's spirit-of-the-moment.

Zambra (Ruiz de Alarcón 7, around the corner from the Ritz Hotel) seems to be regaining its snap; it is still in the mainstream of Madrid's night scene. Many new faces in the administration, entertainment, and service ranks; tiny music-hall layout, with about 2-dozen tables placed for excellent viewing of the heeling and clapping onstage; stifling lack of ventilation on our latest wheeze-in; 3 shows, with the best from 11 P.M. to 12:30 A.M.; others from 12:30 A.M. to 1:30 A.M. and 1:30 A.M. to 3 A.M. Good whisky at much higher prices than those at the Corral—which makes your first drink startlingly expensive. Once more the Zambra of yore; worth a peek if you are an aficionado of this school—and if you don't mind the jam-up of foreign tourists.

Las Brujas ("The Witches") is situated at Calle Norte 165 in the Old Town, a narrow street that's hard to find and virtually impossible for parking. Dogleg bar at entrance facing a huge blue-and-white mural; l-o-o-o-n-g arched main room to the rear resembling a Quonset hut and recalling the tunnel from Grand Central to 125th Street; 200-seat capacity at 40 tables; small stage way up front with about 20 wee (if you're in the back) performers; intermittent shows from 11:30 P.M. to 3:30 A.M. Don't go for dinner, even though it's served. Drinks in the Corral price league, but our so-called White Label tasted suspiciously gray. As in the above establishments, there are no B-girls. Don't go out of your way for this one.

Torres Bermejas (Mesonero Romanos 15), formerly the Taberna Gitana, has perhaps the most attractive setup of all. The ceiling is coffered in gold; the walls are brightened by Moorish tiles; a sweet little loggia bedecks a corner beside the raised stage; numerous small package-groups tumble in; our drinks were legitimate. The service matches the artistry of the performers—enthusiastic but not too professional. (Strangely enough, flamenco dancing can be enhanced by this ironic fault, since its essence is spontaneity.) You may see grime, traces of amateurism, and undercurrents of organized tourism here, but basically we think it is rewarding if only to absorb the fundamental richness of the Arabic décor. Recommended.

Villa Rosa (Plaza Santa Ana 15), on our swing, was being bruited by nearly every concierge and hackie we met in the city as being the hottest stomper in town. To us, its *belle époque* interior and hyper-theatrical stagings simply didn't ring true. Dining commencing at 9:30 P.M.; main show at 11; operative until 3:30 A.M. We don't mean it unfairly when we say that we don't like it, but that's the way we call it when that's the way we see it. Perhaps you'll be more indulgent than we are.

Madrid's nightscape is now pulsing with the beat of discothèques. **La Boîte** is tonight's chichi panjandrum. White-brick façade with globe sconces; green paisley textiled walls; gilded mirrors; *fin-de-siècle* paintings; danceable music; steepish tabs. Sophisticated as a cool perch for night owls and their fine-feathered birdies. Don't, incidentally, confuse this with the "Boite-Theatre" rage now sweeping Madrid. **Ales** (Veneras 6) is one example of these softly lit dens where music, drink, and light drama are offered—of course, *only in Spanish.* These are a far cry from the disco-scene with which we now continue. **Bocaccio,** which debuted in '72, is owned by the 2 brothers who run its solid namesake in Barcelona (see below). Huge, even for a big city discothèque; turn-of-the-century thematics on ground level; more "with it" substrata for dancing (just follow the decibels); attractive patrons; good live bands; expensive but unadulterated libations. This one is deservedly popular, but we wonder what will happen when its novelty wears off. **Tartufo** is becoming one of our faithful standbys. Clubby upstairs atmosphere exuded by only 3 intimate tables flanking a working fireplace; lower-level rectangular den with smallish dance floor and excellent lighting displays; couples-only admission policy; authentic Highland dew and other nectars. In a word: tasteful. **Long Play,** which had been spinning along famously prior to our visit, seemed to have slowed to about 15 rpm when we inspected it for labeling purposes. It's run by Diego Martin, the best-known deejay in town; other than that personality, we found it a very standard platter indeed—except, perhaps, for the drinks, which were too teeny to bop for us. **Carnaby St.** and the **Royal Bus** traffic in miniskirted and hot-pantsed twisters. **Stone's** and the **J&J** are a pair of challengers that come on strong if the crowd is right. As always with this type of establishment, these might be in one minute and out the next.

Among the "respectable" places in *Madrid* which are fun for everybody, the leader tonight is **El Biombo Chino** (Isabel La Católica 6), a former movie house which was converted into a fairly attractive reeler without cinematics. Alluring entrance, with flowers and plants and running water bordering the stairs; balcony with handsome bar and a few tables at street level; main seating area and dance floor 1-flight down; grade-B B-girls on our night. Sizzling orchestra of 14 to 16 musicians; cabaret not an extravaganza but excellent in quality; libations priced at levels similar to those in New York and Los Angeles ginmills. Clean, pleasant, and decent.

Flamingo (Av. José Antonio 34) draws a lively young clientele, well-dressed, well-mannered, and nonbeatnik. Good Italian band and soignée gal vocalist; Scotch at reasonable tabs; spacious bar. Especially recommended to the College Set.

Bali Hai (Flora Alta 8) is a South Sea-soned cellar specializing in Polynesian nutrients, both in the glass and on the plate. Some exotic beverages sipped out of distinctive containers through 2-foot-long straws; décor suggesting a Malayan longhouse; high-backed Malacca chairs; waiters in glossy dinner jackets; enough flotsam and jetsam on the walls, hanging from the ceilings, and stuffed into vitrines to evoke the envy of Old Vic—Old *Trader* Vic, that is. Superb combo on our visit. We also were pleased with the samplings of Oceanic, Chinese, Japanese, and Indian tidbits that we exchanged among the members of our party who dined and danced here. Highly recommended for romancers.

In winter, **Cubaclu** (Virgen de la Alegría 9, near the bullring) swings best to a Latin beat; dancing; low tabs; weekends are the jumpingest if you love humanity. **Camagüey** (Desengaño 16, just off the Gran Vía) does not extend invitations to the ball, but the atmosphere is nice, the music is excellent, the cookery is recommendable, and the drinks are good; go late. **Alazán** (in the Castellana) impressed us as being a fleecing corral. Many young people prefer **Club Castelló** (Castelló 24), which is open from 6 P.M. to 9 P.M. and from midnight to 2:30 A.M. Many older ones prefer **Larré** (in the Castellana). The latter is more of a convivial drinking spot. **Canesteros** (Calle Barbieri 3) is recommended by a kindly Palo Alto lady who opines that "the dancing and singing were rendered with grace and spirit." Thanks for the tip.

In summer, fly straight as a swallow to **Pavi** (Retiro Park). When the climate is benign, no other place in the capital can touch it. Garden dining-and-dancing under the stars; high-class floor show; cuisine far below the Jockey Club-Horcher's bracket. Worth the fairly steep outlay, if only as a Madrid memory to take home and nurse during those bleak nights in January. **Florida** (Paseo de Coches del Retiro) also hits the cash register with a firm finger; newish décor; almost as fine.

For Men Only, **Micheleta** (Costanilla de Los Angeles 20) is now patronized by the cream of the Spanish demimonde—and some of them are gorgeous. It's a sizable establishment, decorated in a discreet and agreeable way. At least ⅝ths of the band must suffer from congenital tone deafness, however, because the music is a triumph in atrociousness. Strictly for amorous gents with well-lined wallets—and, for heaven's sake, DON'T make the stupid blunder of taking your wife here or to the others mentioned below, because somebody might spit on her for brashness.

Casablanca (Plaza del Rey 7, across from the Circus) is still popular. Stage show of 20 performers; 10-piece orchestra; ballroom layout with a slide-away stage; sleazy; dismal, cornball in its overall personality. We encountered a big-change gouge by the cigarette girl. No admission charge, but sobering tariff for The Cup That Cheers; go about 12:30 A.M. Hostesses galore, both at the balcony bar and at the downstairs tables—many of them in wool sweaters that cry for a strong deodorant. Open all year, except Holy Week. This one, we'd guess, is a prime target for hicks happily down from the Asturian hills.

Another candidate in this men-only group is the big, impressive **Pasapoga** (Av. José Antonio 37), which is more lavish than Micheleta or Casablanca. The "hostesses" are now back, after being banned in an effort to raise its tone.

Good cabaret; the usual nightclub junk sold from table to table; closed August.

Down the list about a dozen pegs is the **Folies** (Paz 11-13), a busy, barnlike mecca of starry-eyed lassies fresh from the farms. Unsophisticated and not very interesting. Entertainment 2nd-string. The **Lido** has been renewed; we missed it on our fling.

Feminine solace may also be found in the early evening at **Chicote's** and **El Abra** (opposite each other on Av. José Antonio).

Stay away from a joint called **York Club**. Its B-girls are the brassiest vultures I've ever seen in the capital; they're all honor students in How To Take The Visiting Sucker. Although our party emerged unscathed, we wouldn't have been surprised if they'd tried to slip us Mickey Finns. **Moulin Rouge**, **Las Palmeras**, and **Congo Club** are traps which are also firmly *not* advised.

Sipping and friendly persuasions? **Hermitage Bar,** in the Eurobuilding, lights up a warm, living-room ambiance in which to heal the day's wounds or seal more positive alliances. Sumptuous divans; unusual silver lamps with smoked shades; soft-spoken gentlemanly staff; a soothing mood. The nearby **San Francisco**, another hospitable haven, comes on with 3 whole floors, English-speaking personnel, many Yanks at the brass rail or at tables, and drinks mixed in the back-home fashion. The **Wahine** (Serrano 80) whistles up Polynesian tempters à la Trader Vic's, but that's where the comparison falls out of its long boat. The bar in the center is low tide on our plumbline; the backwater atoll behind it is a more in-tune lagoon for your paddling.

In *Barcelona*, the Smart Set highsteps smartly out to the **Bocaccio** (Muntaner 505), which is owned by the Regas tribe of Via Veneto fame (see Barcelona "Restaurants" and Madrid's nightclubs, above). Chic clientele of well-dressed discothèque-niks; crimson color scheme with Art Nouveau trimmings; Tiffany lamps and glasses in that artisan's latest bamboo pattern; well-paced music that even permits fuddy-duddy fox-trotters such as us to get in an occassional jog. Here's an elegant entry that vies with this brand of night spot almost anywhere on the Continent. Top recommendation for its type. Next is **Los Tres Molinos** (end of Av. Gen. Franco). This "Three Windmills" offers interior, patio, and teatime dancing; poor cookery; same ownership as La Pérgola; highish prices; flamenco entertainment at times; no bar girls (as such); open year round. These are followed by—*at this instant only*—**Baccara, Ciro's, Snob**, and **Le Clochard**; way, way up at Fun Fair, a peer titled **Lord Black** turns on unusual flicks on midsummery eves.

The hottest corner for *winter* play is the sophisticated, modern **Papagayo**, a subterranean living room (or Junior Executive Suite). Mustard-colored easy chairs; gaming-table bar; superb orchestra during our Bar-ce-lone-rangerings; no show; reasonable tabs. Elegant, suave, and pleasant for this mercantile city. **Las Vegas**, where local socialites gambol, sip, jiggle, and yak, places second in this hierarchy. *Nouvelle vague* singer, usually French; fairly expensive; no pickups. Closed during the *caliente* months. **Shangri-La** (Muntaner 492) is an infant sired by the Las Vegas owners. Dancing but no cabaret. The **Planeta 2001** was enjoying all the praise of a newborn babe on our inaugural orbit. The highlight here is in your highball—an illuminated drinking glass that is now blinking in several other Iberian darkspots. We'll be able to judge this flash in the panorama better next solstice. After you've closed this one (*if* you're single that evening), down your nightcap at **Chez Charley** while sizing up the battalions of distaff talent.

Next, here's a rundown, starting at the top, of the hustle-for-bustle gin mills: The air-conditioned **Emporium** (Muntaner 4) has improved—but, although it now offers the best show and draws the nicest clientele in its league, we always expect to be greeted at the portal by Texas Guinan or P. T. Barnum. This one's for the big-spending butter-and-olive trade; too rich for our blood. **Jardines Granada** is supremely uninteresting, as is **Andalucía de Noche** (Rambla). The **Kit-Kat** (Escudillers, in the Old Quarter) is a night-club-cum-discothèque-cum-cafeteria-cum-snack-bar, with 27 tables, sterile furnishings, and limp atmosphere; forget it. The nearby **New York** is reported to be far, far better; we haven't yet commuted to this Gotham. **El Brindis** (Plaza Real) is a sailors' favorite; routine dancing spot, apparently not clip (but don't bank on it). **Pan Am's** is about the same; don't let this local Juan Trippe you up, because it has nothing to do with the airline of the same name; allegedly, from reports, a fly-by-night operation. **Barcelona de Noche**, **La Macarena**, and **Venta Eritaña** are not, repeat not, recommended; the customer has about as much of a break in these as he would get on an old-fashioned carnival midway.

Jamboree (Plaza Real) is a rock-em-and-sock-em jazz joint for listening and jam sessions. Here's where nearly every visiting big-name musician jumps when he's in town.

Flamenco? The best we've found is at **Los Tarantos**, next to the Jamboree and under the same ownership. V-shape room with a raised platform at the bottom of the V; ambiance that tries valiantly to resemble a gypsy camp; lantern illumination; continuous shows from 10 P.M. to 3 A.M.; every performer a serious artist in this ethnic specialty. To us, certainly worth the outlay for its music and terpsichore.

Bodega del Toro (Conde del Asalto 103) also can be a delight to lovers of this form of Iberian art—as long as they (1) have flaps on their pockets, and (2) learn the Spanish word for "no" (it is "NO!"). Attractive mien; small stage; no food; terrific musicians and performers; painfully expensive for the Catalan league. Watch out for this smoothly executed swindle here: after 10 or 12 gypsies have come to your table to show their stuff, they'll coolly invite themselves to 1 or 2 rounds of drinks at your expense—and suddenly you'll wake up with a $100 tab clutched in your moist palm. To avoid this slick charade, your best protection is to glue yourself to the bar from the time you enter; you can see and hear all the doin's from there. Gaiety and excitement if you hit it right—but don't trust even your own brother here or in *any* of the gypsy joints in the Old Quarter, because they're expert in flimflam. Closed Monday.

Straight discing? They are, in descending order: **Metamorfosis** (Calle Beethoven—*sic*!), **Mix** (Urgel 10), **La Lechuza** (Tuset 1), **Le Clochard** (Muntaner 492), and **Lord Black** (Parque Montjuich).

Nightlife is beginning to perk afresh along the Calle Tuset. Among the newcomers is the downstairs **La Cova del Drac**, the upstairs **El Drug Store** with music and entertainment at stiffish tabs, **El Doblón**, **Runner's Club**, and **Club Gotarda** (opposite the José Antonio monument). **Baccarra** and **Bori y Fontesta** are said to be fun places. Catalan friends recommend each for its respective character—but more we cannot tell you.

For cocktails (8 P.M. to 10:30 P.M.), there's the **Marfil**, where just about everybody goes for that casual drink—or to meet that "model." In conformance with many other establishments, it's divided into 2 sections; one bar is for men only (in the Spanish sense), and the other is for "respectable" clients. Ho-hum. On our recent round, we were again told that even better-looking babes inhabit the **Bar Club**. When we investigated, the clientele consisted of 1 lone, toad-faced inebriate who was heaving his hulk away from the sauce counter; we had another look later—almost exactly the same scene. The Scotch Bar at the recently turned **Key Club** is now developing a loyal young clan.

The **Bikini** (Av. Gen. Franco 571) is a ranch-style building with superior garden for minigolf, dancing, and imbibing. Pleasant décor of glass, blond wood, wall lights in brick blocks; inexpensive tariffs. We have the feeling that this is more for young-fry local taste than for tourist taste, but perhaps you'll disagree.

In the shank of the evening, **La Masia** really rocks. It's a few minutes out of town (Av. Gen. Franco at Esplugas); from the outside, it looks like a country house, but the inside has tables, a dance floor, a bar, hard-working musicians, a serious-minded chef, and 86-proof clients. Just the place to go after that 3rd or 4th brandy-and-soda, when the world is encased in a gentle rosy glow. Your wife might lap up this one, too. No show.

Tropical and **Capri**, summer entries at nearby *Gavá* (9 miles out), are so 2nd-string in quality that your drive would be wasted. Starseekers, however, enjoy them for the swimming.

Something very special? **Salòn García Ramos** (San Elias 42 bis; be *sure* to get directions from your concierge, because few cabbies know it) is a rare "find." The entrance is via a garden gate, basement staircase, and then through a narrow passage to a simple cellar vault. Here is Don García's shrine to Spanish folk and classical music—to poetry from Lorca to unknowns, to study by worshipful students (who bring their instruments and are permitted to play), to nonbeatnik respect for sentiment and art. Although he may pour the drinks, turn the lights up and down, and greet incoming guests, the Master is not a nightclub operator. While he recites in his native tongue only, you will learn his meanings through his eyes and his gestures, even if you don't understand a spoken word. Plain, plain room; paintings, rosaries, and guitars on the walls; creaky to outright broken chairs; a simple but honest atmosphere, with low-price drinks to match. If you are at the door and hear him performing, please enter quietly and wait for him to seat you. (He also respects his neighbors, even to the point of asking that you speak softly on the streets surrounding his haven.) This we promise: If you approach this gentleman's studio with respect and in seriousness, you might be rewarded with one of the deeply spiritual experiences of your life. Highest recommendation.

In *Valencia*, the **Club Internacional** (Ribera 4), formerly the Drink Club, now wins the cup. Vaguely oval zinc bar; sophisticated inner sanctum with single acts twice nightly; professional service; pleasant bar girls who are not too aggressive. Okay. **Sala Stop** (F. Esteve 4), a red-lit, barn-like dance hall, charges $5 for entry. Some B-gals on "reserve." Pretty routine. Number three is **La Bruja**, in the **Astoria Hotel**; best band for dancing, cold ambiance, but popular. **Mocambo** (Sangre 9), in midtown, is open year round. Air conditioning; bar to the right of its arcade entrance; one main salon in tearoom disguise, frosted with a baker's dozen of tarts; legitimate drinks; much improved. Festivities begin at 11:45 P.M.; main show at 1:15 A.M.; mock flamenco that is more Holyoke, Mass., than Andalusia. Lone males may enjoy it here. As for the rest, **Club Simun** (Sta. Clara 5) is a pale carbon copy of our first choice; in the shank of the evening it's a disco hub, later it's a routine night roost; **Brunos** (Riberas 8) and **Zambra** (Ribero 16) are ho and hum, respectively.

Seville's leading exponent of flamenco is the **Patio Andaluz** (Plaza del Duque 4) which is keenly challenged by the **Patio Sevillano** (Paseo de C. Colón 11a) both owned by the enterprising Juan Cortés and Matías Garrado. Both offer excellent *tablao,* clean surroundings, and a polka-dot nebula of whirling Andalusian atmospherics for the $7.50 entry fee. A duo that we have no hesitation in recommending. **La Cochera** (Av. de Menéndez Villajos) dances close on the heels of the first pair—it might even have fractionally more chic. Highest marks to the flamen-corps; rustic bar and restaurant in front serving regional fare; 3-alcove back room under a beamed ceiling; raised platform for the excellent young dancers and singers; honest drinks. The management was so grateful for the business that it gave the 2nd drink gratis to his appreciative guests. But don't count on that every time. For crisp, authentic flamenco and a full evening's entertainment (albeit somewhat tourist-oriented), we give orchids to this one. **Turin** (Asunción 21), reputedly very popular, was shuttered at 1 A.M. when we rolled by. Unfortunately we never got back. **La Trocha** was about to move its *taberna* to another site during our visit, so again we draw a blank. For economy night-owling, **Garbanzo Palace** (Menéndez Pelayo 18), which means "Chick Pea Palace" is a sweet pea, as far as we're concerned. A lot of locals seem to agree. Fun and folksy. Among the discothèques, the well-run **Petrarca** (M. Carmelo 10) is the fastest spinner. **El Dragon Rojo** (Betis 60) is also near the top of the pops. We are fond of its fireplace lounge and the small illuminated fountain which provide a modicum of relaxation. The **Melody**, near Petrarca, is not recommended. Neither is **Los Gallos**. As for bars, the **Siete Puertas** ("Seven Doors") is now only a drinking parlor; gentlemen of the old school are advised to don a suit of armor before venturing inside, in order to protect themselves from the harpies who, if still there—we're quite serious—will grasp them in a startlingly indecent manner as soon as they step up to the bar. In our travels, we've never come across such openly and persistently predatory trollops. (If you *do* go look out for that blonde with the hangnail.) Across the pike, are the **Ta-Ca-Ta** and **La Vaquita**, which are routine, followed by **Maxime** and **Desirée**. **La Marina** sometimes zings for that lonely forlorn male who gets his kicks by holding hands with a gold-toothed wench. (You *know* the cost of gold these days!) **Valentino**? Forget it.

In *Granada*, gypsy dancing has become a disgusting racket. The sucker is levied the fixedprice for a package deal, and the tour operator then selects the cave which will yield the most profit for the least effort. Average performance less than 30 minutes; "artists" so untalented no top operation would hire them (the best migrate to Madrid, Barcelona, or Seville); 1 free eyedropper of rotgut *manzanilla* for "refreshments"; spectators packed in too tight for anyone to escape before completion of the show. You'll be sorry if you don't avoid this travesty; it's a cosmic low in tourist-racketeering. Satisfy that yen at **Zincale** (Sacromonte 19) which is one of the notable exceptions to the otherwise sorry scene. Private audiences may watch Mario Maya's artistry in cozy studio surroundings from 7 P.M. to 3 A.M. any day but Sunday. This one we *do* recommend. Away from the city, there are the nightly 2-hour performances at the poolside **Jardines Neptuno**, where the entrance fee of $7.50 includes one quaff and the show. The flamenco sessions in **Las Cuevas de las Golondrinas** (advance notice necessary) have been sterilized, dehumanized, and left bereft of any cultural significance. As a curiosity, however, they still may be worth a jaunt. **Rey Chico** (in Alhambra) turned on an embarrassingly miserable show during our night beat. Not recommended. The **Granada Night Tour** offers an amusing cross section of this slice of Andalusia. Unfortunately, the quality of its folkways was so low as to be termed pathetic by us. We are reminded regretfully that the derivation of the word *gyp* comes from *gypsy*.

Bilbao is big on bars (about 125 in its Bario Chino district, which is perfectly safe and fun to see). **Trana, El 7, Gaucho, San Remo**, and **New York** are a few better examples. **Guria, Lasa, Machimbenta**, and **Changurro** are the leading nightclubs.

Málaga's nightscape is unusually dreary, since most of the action is siphoned off by the insomniacs farther along the Costa del Sol. The bar of the **Malaga Palacio** is the top spot for sipping before dinner. **El Troubador,** under Canadian proprietorship, is best for later libations. The **Pigalle** dishes out a modern ambiance; pepper-hot band and cabaret, and a bevy of placid B-girls. **La Taverna de Gitanas** is another challenger; typical mien; medium prices; well ventilated; the city's best flamenco.

In *Marbella*, El Serrallo, in the **Hotel Don Pepe**, gets the biggest play from the tourist traffic. Far-out Far Eastern motif dimly illuminated by 3 giant snowflakes; Mediterranean-blue carpeting, matching velvet settees; and cream-colored leather hassocks; brass tables; dance floor, but no cabaret. Best of an almost nonexistent lot. The **Hilton** lounge seemed dull and spiritless on our recent try. Perhaps it will perk up when you bounce by. **Bar oo**, is ringed by local Social Circles. Small talk is so minimal here that this is how it got its unusual name. Proprietor Menchou, a character whose personality is about as unobtrusive as the Rock of Gibraltar, has parlayed this duet of zeros into a peseta mill. Definitely "in." **Playboy**, near San Pedro de Alcántara, is a routine beach discothèque. **Platero** now takes 2nd honors from the **Pagoda** for flamenco performances. A follow-up to the Madrid operation of the same name, the **Nido de Arte de Don Jaime**, has opened on Rodeo Beach. Highly recommended. An experiment called the **Crazy Gambas** was operating sporadically, so it may have folded by the time you pull in. Be sure to check locally, if you are handicapped with masochistic tendencies.

Torremolinos lives for sunset. Its nocturnal pastimes come in all classes, sizes, shapes, colors, genders, and nongenders. **Long Play** is the suave émir of the disco set. Brown velour walls; oval dance pad; L-shape bar; discreet lighting shining on discreet clientele. A quality roost for birds and roosters. The Parrilla of the **Pez Espada** is zesty, especially on Friday nights (see "Hotels"). **El Madrigal,** in the Sol y Mar urbanization (main pike toward Algeciras), is luring droves of merrymakers from the city lights. International shows; 2 orchestras which seem to own more microphones and electronic assists than Radio City Music Hall; regularly scheduled flamenco presentations. Well respected. The **Blue Note** seems to be fading. **Jaleo** goes in for groups, flamenco, and organized fun. Routine but always packed. **Piper's** is a subterranean, multilevel monument to Pandemonium. It's dotted with 3 bars and a seemingly endless number of tiny dance floors, all connected by twisting, graded aisles and decorated with used auto parts and other geegaws screwed into its vibrating walls. This one reminds us of a complicated rat maze we observed back in Experimental Psych. 10; the smart rodents quickly found their way out—the others went crazy. **Tabu** is for a more mature and better-heeled crowd. Modest door bite includes the first drink; effective racing-past-the-stars videonics; comfortable copper-clad bar at rear; lively yet thoughtfully modulated music. Improving. **Cleopatra,** almost next door, is another contender in the sophisti-category. Rectangular chamber with small square for gyrators; revolving, reflecting-"eye" chandelier; paneled and padded libations counter stacked with all-purpose champagne glasses, flanked by a huge sun disk; waiters in Egyptian tunics. Hieroglyphics, sphinxes, and other pharaoh-panalia are set amid these sands of time and run through the hourglass as follows: dance music from 9:30 to 11:30, floor show ending at midnight, rock rhythms and a Charlie Chaplin film until 1:15, second floor show, food service from 2 to 3 A.M., followed by psychedelic melodies until the 4:30 closing. Ideal for an Arabian Knight and his harem mate. **Tiffany's** keeps a cote of doves within its pounding walls. Oh, how we mourn for these sleepless feathered creatures! **Pedro's** a beatnik den on the main drag, attracts the most informal sartorial getups anywhere. Swinging, blues-y modern music in the downstairs lair; 3 tiers of banquettes suggesting padded baseball bleachers; our generous drinks of politely termed "Scotch" never saw the Highlands. Fun, (1) if you've never worn a girdle or a tie—or (2) if you've worn both at the same time. The chairs at the next door **VIP** are more comfortable; ditto for everything else. **Top-Ten** is now a better tieup for teen types. **El Dorado**, with medium prices, has throngs of jeans-clad whippersnappers undulating to the tattoo of the lastest record hits; Whisky-à-Go-go-go atmosphere that's gone, man, but gone. **Barbarela** seemed round, raucous, and far too rowdy and rapacious a gal to us for what she offers; we heard she's tripping (but *not* the light fantastic). The ground-floor bar of the **Tortuga** restaurant is a favorite watering spot for young middle-agers (16 to 22 years old, *à la* Torremolinos); legitimate beverages; woody atmosphere; Impresaria Daix, a peroxide blonde with a voice reminiscent of B. S. Pully's, is the soul of hospitality. **Betty's Club** usurped 15 minutes of our lives; we begrudge each of them. Ditto for the dark, dingy **Bier Keller.**

Other drinking spots? Plenty. But first a word of caution. Many of the watering holes in this tourist-glutted town have succumbed to the very un-

Spanish practices of fleecing customers and stocking bathtub booze, not to mention more nefarious misdemeanors. We therefore urge you to be on your guard in any questionable nook and to be doubly watchful around the Begoña area. A buxom barmaid at the **Jockey Club** offered us a filly as a groom's companion for the evening. Lots more were seemingly available in this paddock. The **Galloping Major** apparently plays host to seafarers judging by the *USS Nathan Hale, Andrew Jackson,* and other Sixth Fleet plaques on its whitewashed walls. Small stuccoed and beamed room; stone floor; large bar; Spy prints; crossed cavalry swords; clashing chairs with floral jackets; pubby atmosphere. Tranquil, cozy, clean, and honest. **Don Quijote, Chocolate Café, La Province, Moulin Rouge, Di Do, El Ancle, Samba, Corazón, El Refugio, Sportsman,** and **Ye-Ye,** all within tooting range of a police whistle from Begoña Passage, were still ladling out the sauces when we tiptoed through the seedy *begoñas,* but there's no guarantee in this weed patch as to how many will be pruned away by the time you test your green thumb. A final suggestion: In all but the top-line hotels, pay for your drinks and snacks the moment they are served to you. This simple precaution might save you from winding up the evening resembling the Trojan priest in the Laocoön statue.

Almería's rundown runs rapidly from the **Playboy** through **Chapina** to **Hoango** (ugh!). Out of town, the **Baroque** and the **Aguadulce** may keep the fireflies awake—but not us, sad to say.

Sitges (an hour or less south of Barcelona) starts the night with the **Monaco**. Dancing from 10 P.M. until your sandals need resoling; entrance fee pays for first drink; peppery 6-piece band; fun atmosphere for young folk. **Mi Borito-Jo** ("My Donkey And I") clops up next. The **Brasa,** below the Hotel Calípolis, is the late-night gathering spot for that final nuzzle and sip. This town is jammed with a zillion bars—none of which will remind you of New York's Algonquin.

Benidorm fluctuates wildly, with openings and shutterings every instant. When we last looked—about 7½ minutes ago—**Granada** was the top stop for Spanish and international-style cabaret. The **Corregidor Real Hotel** boasts a nightclub that's among the front-runners. **La Parilla**, outside of town, is the most intimate haven for dancing and starlight persuasions. Then there's the inevitable **Whisky-A-Gogo**, of course. And there are also at least 25-thousand additional places where a thirst can be quenched—all routine and uninspiring.

The nighteries of *San Sebastián* are the epitome of boredom. Rated from V to Z, they run (1) **La Perla** (on the beach and only a summer operation), (2) **Tennis Club** (closed in winter), (3) **Royal Club Náutico** (see "Restaurants"), (4) **Trinquete** (converted country house with flat music and flatter pickups), (5) **Igueldo** (mountain ballroom for mass entertainment; see "Restaurants").

Alicante seems to specialize in after-darkness ennui. **El Duende**, in the Hotel Carlos, and **Taifa**, in the Mélia, try, but, oh my, how we yawn! The **Albany** is less of a wheeze than the **Chamonix**; both could heal the woes of chronic insomniacs. Outside the city limits, **Playboy** and **Paraiso** knit up the ravell'd sleave of care with stunning efficiency. If you're like this reporter, you'll yearn for the sunrise.

Zaragoza's nocturnouts include (1) **Cancela** (3 sections: bar, cabaret, and flamenco stage), (2) **Cosmos** (routine), and (3) **Venus** (summer terrace; shows; 1 mile outside the city). All require a moderate minimum.

For other centers, ask the Spanish Tourist Office branches or your hotel concierge. And be careful, because clip joints are a céntimo a dozen, particularly in the South—or nearly anywhere the traveler finds gypsies.

§TIPS: Most nightclubs boom after midnight. In the majority, you'll pay an admission charge of $2 to $5 per person; cover or minimum charges are not unusual. Drink prices are often murder; in discothèques nowadays they ask as much as $3 to $6.50 per cup. Stick to brandy instead of whisky, if you can force it down; Scotch costs a mint, and it's probably counterfeit anyway; rye and bourbon are almost unknown, although they are beginning to appear in the larger centers.

TAXIS   Fares inching up far too frequently and fast, but still relatively cheap. Despite some new fleets in the larger cities, unbelievably old rattletraps are still sometimes found in the provinces. The "micro-taxis," approved for scooting around Madrid's streets, can slice 25% from your transportation bill. Give a 10% tip for an ordinary run; a night surcharge is added almost everywhere. An airport pickup in the capital now costs 375 pesetas. When entering the cab, *always check whether the flag is pulled down on the meter to the reading of not more than 25 pesetas.* (And don't hail a *gran turismo* hack that doesn't have a meter.) Some of these robbers have conveniently poor "memories." Either they'll (1) "forget" to zero the meter from the last haul, so you'll pay the previous passenger's ride as well as your own, or (2) "forget" to haul down the flag at all, so that at the end you can be snared with that rusty swindle of a double or triple "estimated" fare. On our recent capital rounds, we were victimized 6 times by roundabout route-takers rather than short direct-line drivers; numerous attempts also were made at shortchanging us. Larceny is increasing among this once-honest group, particularly in Madrid, Barcelona, and Palma—and it's all the fault of too-generous tourists like us. If you should ever run into trouble with any of them, don't pay a cent more than you should. Just demand that he drive you to the nearest *comisaría* (police station)—an order that will *always* settle his bleats.

AIRLINES   There are nominally 2: (1) **Iberia**, the state-owned carrier, and (2) Aviación y Comercio S.A., called **Aviaco**. The first now controls the second, but they will continue to fly under separate burgees. They exchange aircraft, however, on certain routes. Two others, **Spantax** and **Aerlype**, are employed solely in charter and cargo work.

Aviaco, as well as the flying public, benefits from this arrangement—in one sense. Its safety record was so spotty that we refused to ride this carrier before the takeover. Now we will. Currently, Aviaco plies partly on a nonscheduled basis to Nice, Tangier, Algiers, Oran, Mallorca, Minorca, various points on the Spanish mainland, and up to Brussels.

Iberia is a small colossus—and a haughty one, due solely to the fact that they've got just too damned much business. They employ the most modern aircraft internationally; locally, most of the time you'll find good equipment too. Maintenance, from a technical standpoint, is first-rate, but the fleet does work hard.

Service? Oh, *how* it varies! On several earlier transatlantic loops we've experienced sun-drenched Spanish charm both on the ground and while aloft. On one recent round-trip between Palma de Mallorca and New York, however, we could easily understand why our desk is spread with complaints from Guidesters who seem to have shared our bad luck on their overocean flights. Our food in Tourist Class was plainly inedible; the hostesses were kind but inept (even with no more than 18 passengers aboard); frequently the cocky stewards were too busy flirting with the stewardesses to attend to their passengers; the ground staff at Kennedy couldn't be bothered to offer us the smallest courtesies. (All of the terminal's baggage lockers were occupied or broken, but Iberia would not watch over our hand luggage for us while we ran some errands at the airport. Swissair, a few doors away, gladly volunteered to keep an eye on it.) When our flight was delayed for more than 3 hours for mechanical reasons, we had to *demand* a meal ticket as midnight approached. Any progress reports or announcements made to the waiting travelers had to be sought by the passengers themselves and passed on to their colleagues, prompting one wag to dub the line *"Siberia."* Never was a drink offered us nor was there an apology for all of the inconveniences from the ground supervisor, the desk staff, or the pilot or crew. In addition, one of our pieces of luggage—in such a meager cargo—was lost (but subsequently recovered). From our latest circuit, we'd venture that segments of Iberia are beginning to take their customers too much for granted. This is so untypical of the Spanish personality that we hope its directors will cast a stern eye on the few negligent staffers who need their knuckles rapped.

Point-to-point in Spain, where the company has a virtual monopoly, we're happy to report marked improvement. They've installed beverage-and-snack facilities on most longer hops (tea, Coke, beer, etc. for a nominal sum; sandwiches, sherry, brandy, vermouth, and whisky for a bit more). This and other innovations show an interest in the regional traveler's welfare—a praiseworthy trend.

On the other hand, some of the metropolitan ticket offices (not flight crews) still have some of the most boorish, peremptory personnel we have ever come across in the aviation industry. In many cases, it seems to be a "don't-care-and-don't-bother-us" attitude—and this is a pity, because these people are Spain's ambassadors to thousands of visiting foreigners, and their lack of courtesy is totally un-Spanish. To be fair, however, not all Iberia's office employees fall into the indifferent category. The chiefs of the ground staffs at the airports in Palma de Mallorca, Barcelona, and Madrid, as 3 shining examples, always seem to go beyond the line of duty in kindness and consideration for the passenger. They are wonderful. If the overworked desk clerks can't give you satisfaction, just ask for the *jefe* and chances are he will smooth your flight path admirably.

Recommendation: Iberia will get you there, with efficient, safe flying. International services vary widely, with transatlantic flights largely in need of better, sharper administration and much more carefully trained, much less lazy hostesses. In sum, we think it's shake-up time at the Spanish national carrier.

§TIPS: Charter your own airplane? Conducted tours, freight shippers, private merrymakers, or businessmen-in-a-hurry may choose their own go-anywhere air taxi from the reliable, well-maintained **Spantax** fleet of DC-6's, DC-3's, Beechcraft, and Pipers.

An American company called **Aerlype** also renders the same service with 3- or 5-place Aztecs and Comanches. Forty insular and peninsular cities are on the docket; since we know no more about this outfit, make "contact" either through your travel agent or directly (Aerlype, Torre de Madrid, Madrid).

DRINKS Sherry, the national wine, comes in 7 major types, some with a number of subclassifications; like port (Portugal), it is always bottled blended rather than "straight." Call it Jerez (pronounced HAIR-eth), and drink it whenever you'd normally reach for a Coke at home. Through the revolving *solera* system of mixing, the old and the new vintages are combined to produce a product which is always standard. Years ago, a small inner circle of British pukka sahibs made superdry sherry a mark of social elegance in England; this foible, based on snobbism far more than on actual taste, quickly spread to America. During our residence in Spain, not only have we been weaned away from the Manzanillas, Finos, and other salty, acrid varieties, but we've also converted number of our overseas house guests through a simple 2-glass experiment. If you'd like to try this for yourself, line up an order of Tio Pepe next to an order of Long Life (or Dry Sack, in a Pinch) —and your palate will instantly decide which pleases you more. Tio Pepe ("Uncle Joe" in Spanish) has the big reputation and international markets, but it's too saline and puckery for our maximum enjoyment; Long Life (or any similar Oloroso blend) is old, soft, and golden, with just enough dryness and richness of body to give true delight. Perhaps you'll disagree, of course, because this is strictly a minority opinion—but why not give it a whirl?

Spanish red table wines are perhaps the most underrated of any in Europe. Countless gallons flow over the border each year to be sold as "French" types in France and elsewhere. Most of these reds resemble Burgundies rather than Bordeaux in their heaviness and fullness; the whites, not as fine, are most often too sweet for the U.S. taste; every so-called rosé we've ever tried (except the Las Campanas, René Barbier, and Señorio de Sarria brands, which are in such short supply you probably won't find them) has been just plain awful.

If we were forced to pick out 1-of-a-kind for comparatively expensive daily consumption, we'd take Marqués de Riscal for our red, Monopole for our white, Cepa de Oro for our Chablis, and N.P.U. for our Spanish "champagne." Viña Pomal and Federico Paternina "Ollauri" also used to be superior rubies in their "Reserva" class, but their quality has fallen off shockingly since the flood of well-heeled tourists inundated Spain. All the "Reserva" and "Gran Reserva" types have deteriorated, in fact. Since there is no official *Appellation Controlée* (as in France) to police the producers, any Juan Doe or John Smith can fill a bottle with 1964 rotgut, label it impressively as "Gran

Reserva 1929," and place it on public sale! We make no specific accusations against any specific companies in this text—but we *do* wish to point out this very curious anomaly. Binisalem Franja Roja '53 is terrific, if you can get it. Cepa Rhin and Viña Sol are nearly the only other whites we've found which even approach dryness. In Cordoba, however, be sure to pick a local *montilla* called "medio de veinte-quatro" ("a half of 24"); it is so light it cannot travel even to other Spanish cities. (The barman will think you're El Cordobés, himself!) Aside from N.P.U., the "champagnes" range from sweet to cloying to sick-making. You'll pay from $2 to $5 for all of these save the N.P.U., which runs perhaps $7.50 per bottle.

During the summer, be sure to sample the cooling, refreshing wine punch called Sangría. Choose your own base (red, white, or champagne); it will be served in a pitcher with orange slices, lemon slices, seltzer, sugar, and usually a tiny glass of cognac for flavor. Available anywhere at any mealtime; light, delicate, and delicious. Dubonnet and Campari are also popular in warm weather.

At long last, bourbon is now available in many of the larger and better hotels, restaurants, and bars in the major cities. Rye drinkers, too, have found their luck is turning; Canadian Club, Seagram's, and other such nectars are now raising their noble hats behind Spanish bars. Prices nip up at about $10 per bottle in the marketplace.

Scotch? Importation taxes were given a colossal jump in '68, because so many Spaniards are now drinking it that there is a surplus in various locally produced beverages. Most of it is genuine, but in nightclubs and other places you might still run into counterfeits—filthy tasting!—smuggled in from Tangier. Thus, even a small pouring of either the honest or dishonest product will cost you plenty. A few years ago, Iberian highlanders from Segovia succeeded in producing a first-cousin facsimile of the barley brew. It is called DYC (pronounced as in Tracy). Unfortunately, its vogue has been so great the distillers are now turning it out too quickly, with less and less flavor of the better grade Scotian dew. Despite this crass commercialism, throughout this nation call for this brand to save your money and your taste buds. A fifth costs around $9. If DYC doesn't please you (and quite possibly it won't), switch to Fundador *coñac* for your highball; Fundador is by far the leading choice among visiting Americans, because it's the only truly dry, champagne-type brandy on the local market. You'll pay perhaps 60¢ per glass or about $3.50 per bottle in the average bar or grocery shop. (It's around $12 in the States, now that it is sold on our side of the Atlantic.) Spaniards like Carlos I, Gonzalez Byass Lepanto, Larios 1866, and similar distillates, but they're much too rich and too heavy for the typical stranger.

Liqueurs? Just name your favorite, and chances are good that they'll have it. Any big bar stocks at least 30 or 40 varieties.

Beer? Tuborg's and Carlsberg's golden elixirs have hurdled the frontier, as a result of a commercial exchange with Denmark. Their incomparable tang has saved the lives of tens of thousands of visiting Scandinavians, Britons, Americans, and beachcombing travel writers, including Temple H. Fielding. Imports of fine Dutch Heineken are also trickling in, and both Guinness and Pripps (Swedish) have set up their own Iberian plants. There are now 40 breweries spread over 25 of Spain's provinces, and the elasticity of the suds is more stretchable daily. Almost everyone agrees that San Miguel has taken over the leadership among domestic labels. This Philippines-based company bottles it in Lérida and Málaga on their true Pilsner formula; available nearly everywhere; light, creamy, and refreshing, but a shy, wispy Campfire Girl compared to those Grand Old Maestros from Denmark.

For soft drinks, Coca-Cola, Pepsi-Cola and Fanta are omnipresent, even in the smallest villages; ginger ale and Schweppes tonic water and bitter lemon (other brands are fierce) can be had from place to place; lemonade *(limonada)* and orangeade *(naranjada)* are wonderful in winter but not so good in summer; *horchata,* a milky beverage made from a native root, has an almondy flavor which is highly pleasing.

§TIP: Cuba Libre (rum and cola) fans will blanch at this tipple here, because the mixer is always compounded for the infinitely sweeter tooth of the Spaniard. Thus, if you're North American, be sure that the barman adds at least 10 drops of tart Rose's Lime Juice (or a similar product) to create the balance to which you're accustomed. Otherwise, it's sickening.

THINGS TO SEE Topographically, the country is like an insipid picture in a million-dollar frame. The center is filled with scenery that is comparatively dull and monotonous; the border and coastal areas are normally (but not always) spectacular and brilliant. That is why you should try to get down as far as *Valencia*, *Granada*, *Málaga*, *Seville*, or *Cádiz* if you want sun, or up as far as *Bilbao* or *San Sebastián* if you want the full impact of the Pyrenees.

Mallorca in the Balearic Islands is, to our minds, the best single regional choice of the American who is willing to pick the right season. See the independent section, earlier in this *Guide,* for details.

In *Madrid*, one of the first stops for any art lover is, quite naturally, **El Prado** (closed Mon. but open every other day of the week and from 10 A.M. to 1:30 P.M. Sun.). With its staggering treasures of El Greco, Velázquez, Goya, Murillo, Botticelli, da Vinci, Tintoretto, Rubens, Van Dyck, and dozens of others, we consider this, as a matter of personal taste only, the number one art gallery of the world—despite its bad hanging and poor lighting. Alarmingly, the increasing pollution of the capital's air and the oral and skin emissions of up to 10-thousand visitors per day are making its 2500 paintings "ill," according to Curator Xavier de Salas who has continued to issue this warning—so far unheeded—over his lengthy tenure. (A proper air conditioning system would cost 10 times his total annual budget.) In addition to this there's the **Royal Palace** (open mornings and afternoons), the **Pardo Palace**, the not-to-be-missed **Museo de Lázaro Galdeano**, the fascinating **Rastro** ("Thieves' Market"—try it on Sunday morning, bargain for everything, and be careful about pickpockets!), **University City** with its **Museum of Contemporary Art** (or another one at Calvo Sotelo 20), the **National Archaeological Museum**—all the Baedeker wonders rolled into one, for which local guidebooks are available at hotels or the Tourist Office. The **Wax Museum** in the Central Colón delights kiddies and parents alike. Cortés, the Conquistadores,

Cervantes, Romeo and Juliet, El Cordobés, Louis Armstrong, Einstein, Rasputin, Wild West movie sets, and scores more, all backgrounded with appropriate music, are represented. Hours are 10:30 to 1:30 and 4 to 10: open
Sundays without that midday siesta. To cap it off, an extra sight most travelers
never see is the remarkable collection of the celebrated **Pedro Chicote**. The
good Don Pedro and his officials call it a museum; if that is correct, it is our
all-time favorite institution of antiquities and "art." Under one roof, Spain's
most famous caterer has assembled nearly 7500 full bottles, all different,
containing all types of liquor known to modern man. The market value of this
amazing display is at least $250,000; the famous, from royalty to movie stars,
have donated exotic types to the project. Admittance by card only, so beg any
and all Spanish contacts for an introduction to this greatest collection of
spirits on the globe.

Surroundings of Madrid? Bus excursions are operated on various days of
the week to 5 popular suburban targets; again check with your concierge for
schedules and details. **Toledo**, 44 miles to the south, has often been called
"the most perfect and brilliant record of genuine Spanish civilization." Most
unfortunately, however, it has become one of Europe's biggest and worst
tourist traps. The setting is magnificent, the **Cathedral** is a treasure house of
art, **El Greco's** house is routinely interesting (his best works have gone
elsewhere)—but so many souvenir hawkers and curbstone promoters greet
the swarming armies of sightseers that the atmosphere is increasingly tinny,
mechanical, and cheap. *Don't buy a single piece of merchandise in this city;*
the sharks who run some of the supposedly most respectable shops charge up
to 40% more than you'll pay in Madrid for the identical item. (We must
interject a personal note here: Since we first published this admonition in '56,
the excursion guides have lost so many commissions from these Toledo
sharpies that they've launched a major campaign against this book, our
personal integrity, and once, with an anonymous death threat sent by some
hotheaded paranoid, against our life. Some of them, for example, have "stood
there and watched with their own eyes" while Madrid shopkeepers "bribed"
me with "$5000 in cash" to "keep the business from leaving the capital."
Because the Spanish State Tourist Office and I are eager to crack down on
these vipers, any reports of this type of incident—date, time, name of bus
company, and name or description of the guide, forwarded to me personally
at Formentor, Mallorca, Spain—will help us a lot.) **El Escorial**, 31 miles out,
has Philip II's famous castle-monastery filled with paintings, books, royal
tombs, and royal antiquities. **Valle de los Caidos** ("Valley of the Fallen"),
Generalísimo Franco's tombsite and monument to casualties on *both* sides of
the Spanish Civil War, is so breathtaking in concept and so colossal in scope
that it might be straight from the time of the Pharaohs. A mountain of rock,
topped by a cross 500-feet high and 300 feet across the arms (elevator inside),
has been converted into a gigantic basilica and great nave large enough to hold
4 good-size churches with space to spare; you'll find the 8 magnificent Tapestries of the Apocalypse, an 800-foot crypt, an exquisitely carved transept, a
cloister, a monastery, a novitiate, an ecclesiastical study center, and a hostel.
The valley itself, scooped out, landscaped, and crisscrossed with concrete
highways, holds more than 1-million people. It's an engineering and aesthetic

marvel which will thrill spectators for centuries to come. Approximately 30 miles from the capital; ATESA buses cover both Los Caidos and neighboring Escorial for honest fares that include the usual third-rate lunch. But don't let the quality of any meal interfere with your journey here, because to miss it would be like going to Rome and skipping St. Peter's or the Colosseum. **Avila**, 70 miles to the northwest of El Escorial, is a fairy-tale city from a distance, with 86 towers and a medieval wall rising starkly from the landscape; when you've seen this, however, you've had the frosting and top 2 layers of the cake —because there's nothing especially spectacular inside.

Our enthusiastic preference goes to the **Segovia–La Granja** tour—by far the most rewarding itinerary of this group, in our opinion. If you're on your own, you can easily pause for an inspection of the "Valley of the Fallen," which is en route. Then continue on via the road that tunnels 1½ miles under the Guadarrama Mountain Range; the small toll is negligible for a look at this engineering marvel. Segovia, 60 miles from the capital, couldn't be more Castilian in flavor, with moats, castles, a marvelous **Roman aqueduct** (now in need of structural muscle), the renowned **Zuloaga Museum of Ceramics** (which most travelers especially enjoy), and the internationally famous **Mesón de Cándido** restaurant (see "Restaurants" for precautionary words). On the return trip, an alternate routing that is not far out of the way will put you in storybook La Granja, the "Spanish Versailles," with its fountains, gardens, summer palace, and the nation's finest tapestry collection. Beautiful mountain drive one way and interesting plains drive the other; not yet too spoiled by the legions of rubbernecks who invade Toledo and dampen its charms.

In **Barcelona**, you may choose from the **Fine Arts Museum** (Medieval, Renaissance, Baroque Paintings and Sculpture), **Archeological Museum** (prehistory of the Moorish invasion), the **Natural History Museum** (stuffed animals and specialized 7000-volume library), the **Scenic Art Museum** (theatrical memorabilia in a Gaudí-designed building), the **Numismatic Museum** (coins of all periods), the **Municipal Museum of Music** (musical instruments, manuscripts, and effects of celebrated composers), the **Maritime Museum** (ship models and nautical lore), and other displays. The **Modern Art Gallery** features collections of nineteenth- and twentieth-century paintings, sculpture, and drawings; even more timely, the expanding **Picasso Gallery** was inaugurated in a fifteenth-century palace; it houses early paintings and sketches, later experiments in ceramics, plus the artist's 2 gifts of his assembled personal collection totaling more than 2000 works done between the ages of 9 and 22, plus a set of canvases finished when he was 36. Antiquary hounds may visit, under the street, the excavations of the original city as it stood from Christ's time to A.D. 400. Antonio Gaudí's **Templo Expiatorio de la Sagrada Familia**, a colossal, 1/5-completed (it was started in 1882) cathedral which resembles a 300-foot tall tower of gingerbread, is a must. Architecture buffs have been arguing about this edifice for nearly a century; you'll find it wondrous or a nightmare, but certainly you won't be apathetic. There are a fairly good **Zoo**, a **Terrarium**, and an **Aquarium** The Young and the Brave have great fun riding the aerial railway and the junior-size spider-web-constructed Ferris wheel on **Mount Tibidabo**. As for the world-famous Monastery of **Montser-**

rat, about 30 miles out, you'll find a glorious vista—but like Lourdes, it is now so rotten spoiled by fringe commercialism that it is a disgrace. Our advice is to stay away.

Costa del Sol ? Maybe something, maybe nothing yet. André Poulsen's copy of Copenhagen's Tivoli possibly will have cranked into action by the time you arrive. Plans envisioned a huge park holding $5,000,000 worth of eateries, rideries, galleries, strolleries, and other replicas of dignified (*not* Coney Island) Danish amusements. Mr. Poulsen's Playground would also include free Andalusian folk dancing shows and a Wild West town. Admission would be set at only about a quarter. Let's cross our fingers that this exciting and ambitious program will open and meet with instant success.

For sightsseeing information on any of the above—and more—drop in for a chat with friendly, English-speaking Director Alejandro Fieijal of the Spanish State Tourist Department's branch at Av. José Antonio 658.

Festivals? Nearly every city, town, and village has its own *fiesta.* The majority are in summer, but there are also spectacular celebrations in spring and fall. Far, far too many even to begin to list in these pages—but drop a line to your nearest official Spanish outlet (see "Attitude Toward Tourists") for their free booklet, *Festivales de España*—and for other details.

The Spanish National Tourist Office can also furnish you with more than 70 gratis publications covering the principal sights of every region.

TRAINS Improving notably. We've recently sampled the sleeper from Madrid–Cadiz–Madrid, and we were pleasantly surprised that the Wagons-lits' comfort standards have been boosted to match those in almost any country of Free Europe today. There are still many horribly rough patches in the roadbed, but now at least there are some smooth ones too. Our 2 dinners in the restaurant cars were well prepared and served with deftness and grace.

Border-to-major-city and major-city-to-major-city schedules are quite comfortable—but be sure to pick the best expresses only. The *Talgo,* which formerly ran only from Irún to Madrid, now has another section which makes the Barcelona–Madrid connection in 9 hours, a cut of 4 hours in travel time; on the Barcelona half of the run, the tracks are still so mismated that you'll sympathize with the ice cubes of a cocktail shaker.

Passenger fares are very modest by U.S. standards. Luxury train and sleeping-car tickets were reduced to levels just below airline prices, in order to woo tourists back to the rails.

You can save 27% by buying a blanket ticket called a *kilométrico,* but this means you must ride a minimum of 1850 miles within 3 months, or that 2 of you must ride 2500 miles within 4 months. Saints preserve us! For Lionel fans only. The Eurailpass is a better bet—if you're traveling in other countries as well.

An enormous reconstruction program will eventually eliminate washboard roadbeds and replace the chicken-coop passenger coaches. More than half the steam-engine fleet has already been retired. By this year *in theory,* all locomotives are supposed to be electric or diesel-electric, with 1400 miles of trackage powered by current. But as a precaution, we repeat: Take most long-distance trains and carefully selected excursions with impunity; otherwise go by private car, hand-picked bus, or airplane.

BUSES ATESA also offers a bewilderingly extensive network of motor-coach tours for the visitor who wants to cover the greatest amount of territory for his dollar.

From our latest information, there are 10 fixed all-inclusive deluxe tours, 2 so-called Slow Motion tours, scores of optional-combination itineraries, and a galaxy of city or suburban sightseeing excursions. As typical illustrations of some of the hauls: A week-long Andalusian tour from Madrid to Granada–Torremolinos–Seville–Córdoba and back to Madrid; a 5-day version of almost the same itinerary; a 9-day Iberian swing encompassing the capital at both ends and Salamanca, Viseu, Fátima, Lisbon, Seville, Antequera, and Granada in between; a castle sweep of 3 days' duration in the Madrid region; a Moroccan caravan departing from Tangiers for 7 days of nomading between Rabat, Casablanca, Marrakesh, Meknès, Fez, Xauen, Tetuán, and returning to Tangiers. Schedules and routes will probably be altered when the spring timetables are released—but this is a general idea. Prices are at hubcap levels. Vehicles are 29-, 34-, or 40-seaters with radio, individual lights, public-address system, reclining chairs, 2 drivers, and a multilingual interpreter-guide; those on southern routes are air-conditioned. Tickets are issued for full or partial journeys, but preference is for applicants who want the whole thing. Baggage is limited to 66 lbs.

American readers who took these trips recently showed sharply mixed reactions. Some felt they were the greatest joy—and travel bargain—of their entire European junket. Others angrily reported disorganization and don't-care attitudes of personnel. It looks as if the success or failure of the individual run depends upon the caliber of the Tour Conductor; if you're lucky, you'll get a good one who will give utmost satisfaction—but if you draw a lemon, most of the fun might be spoiled. In any case, you'll stop at all interesting landmarks, stay at good regional hotels, eat at adequate restaurants, shop as you please, relax with somebody else doing the driving—and your transportation, room with bath, food, service charges, tips, guide fees, entrance fees to national monuments, and everything else comes to the grand total of perhaps $35 per day.

One drawback is certain, however: The bumpy highways throughout Spain. As a result, the shock absorbers and springs on your carriage were probably worn out one week after it came off the assembly line. Wheel bases are short, and seating is usually done by alphabet, so if your moniker is Mr. Zitzbach, you'll probably be seated right over those hard-pressure Goodyears. Pilgrims with lumbar ailments are often in misery from the moment the driver shuts the door—and once you're off and running, there's practically no turning back (no pun intended).

TIPPING Give your taxi driver from 5% to 10% of the fares. Hotels extract their own service charge, usually 15%; to this, add the following: Baggage porter, 15 pesetas per person per suitcase; maid, 40 pesetas per day; room waiter, if used, 50 pesetas per day; concierge, minimum of 50 pesetas per day, not exceeding $5 per week, unless special services have been rendered; valet, if used, 15 pesetas per call. Restaurant waiters should be given 5% to 10% over and above the check, depending upon the quality of the attention. Theater ushers get 5 pesetas—or 10 pesetas if you are generous.

The people aren't as grabby as the Italians or the French; you'll like their independence and their effort to do a good job without the tip as the primary consideration.

PERSONAL SERVICES   Sick in Spain? **Madrid** 's splendid **British-American Hospital** is at Calle del Límite 1 in the quiet University district (phone: 2-34-67-00). Its cheerful building contains the latest in modern equipment. English-speaking doctors and English nurses are on duty 24 hours a day; bilingual telephone operators will answer your call the clock around. Everything is here, from an up-to-the-minute operating theater, a maternity wing, an X-ray Department, an Iron Lung, an extensive laboratory, and all out-patient facilities on a nonstop basis; ambulance service is always available. Joint Honorary Presidents are the American Ambassador and the British Ambassador. If you need medical attention, this outstanding nonprofit institution will bring you solace, comfort, and expert attention. One of the finest small hospitals on the Continent.

Hairdressers? In **Madrid**, **Elizabeth Arden** (Plaza Independencia 4) usually does a chic job for U.S. ladies; telephone Directress Mercedes Muñoz at 2-76-64-00, and try to make an appointment with Alfonso, if he's still there. Open 10 A.M. to 7 P.M. without a lunch break; closed August and holidays. Most larger hotels also have competent services. The Palace utilizes the **Fortes** shop (Calle Serrano 63); ask for Srta. Conchita, and you'll look elit-a; its main enterprise is reliable, too. Always telephone first, since closing hours and days of operation are likely to vary from season to season.

THINGS TO BUY   Embroidery items, *haute couture,* handcrafted silk blouses and lingerie, handicrafts, paintings, fabrics for home use, ceramics, gloves, selected (not all) leather goods, mantillas, wrought iron, inlaid wood boxes, colognes, straw work, casual shoes, canned truffles, delicacies.

First and foremost, a warning: Wherever you wander in today's Iberia, please be extremely leery of most of the so-called "factories" or shops where tour guides might lead you. The commissions they collect on *your* purchases from *your* outlay normally average 25%; in such notorious traps as Toledo, the bus guide, the local guide, and the driver skim off up to a total of 50%(!). You'd be wise to comparison shop and then to patronize ONLY reliable independent merchants such as those listed below.

Embroidered linens and needlework? **Casa Bonet** (see "Mallorca" and "Marbella"), the world's mightiest name and greatest exponent in this field —which sells its exquisite handworked pieces at prices still so low you won't believe 'em—has a branch in **Madrid** at Zurbano 67 (about 200 yards from the Castellana. All its glorious Palma stocks are available. (1) Make this your first stop, (2) ask for English-speaking Miss Soledad, and (3) DON'T MISS IT!!

Spain is still a paradise for the affluent clothes-conscious gal. Only the

wealthy, however, can now afford to patronize the Big League Iberian houses
—**Pertegaz, Herrera y Ollero, Pedro Rodriguez, Miguel Rueda, Lino,** and
a few others; prices have shot up to the point where they're staggering in
contrast to less-touted labels. If you're rolling in that green stuff, you'll get
handsome and well-made merchandise, but you'll pay almost as much as you
do in Paris, Rome, or elsewhere.

Men's suits? **Ongard** (Av. José Antonio 34), **Cutuli** (San Jeronimo 29),
González y García (Barquillo 9), **Gregorio Ruiz** (Zorilla 23) and **Marcelo**
(San Jeronimo 5) are all well known and respected. Average suit: Around
$225. **G. Cristóbal** (Castellana 53) garbs such handsomely turned-out friends
of ours as 2 successive Joint Spanish Mission American Major Generals,
former Castellana Director Herb Jerosch, and Galeria Kreisler (see below)
Proprietor Ed Kreisler—all of whom have independently sung its praises to
us. We've not yet tried this establishment, but the craftsmanship, as displayed
on these smartly attired cosmopolites, indicates that here indeed is one of
Spain's finest stylists. Please remember, though, that in general the craftsmanship in this nation suffers when compared to that of Italy's maestros—but the
costs are much, much less.

Handcrafted silk blouses and lingerie? **Srta. Emilia de Valeiras** (apartment
at Diego de León 39) whose mother was the official seamstress to the Royal
Court, continues the tradition with her carefully fashioned things. Lacework,
baby clothes, and other items also available. Warmly recommended.

Spanish handicrafts, tasteful top-quality souvenirs, paintings galore?
Kreisler (Serrano 19), the skyrocketing Permanent Spanish Exhibition, is any
visiting shopper's dream. Don't confuse it with shoddy, inferior imitations
which pay rakeoffs and which are rife. In these regal, spacious, and sumptuous air-conditioned premises, Ohio fireball Edward Kreisler has assembled
the most arrestingly attractive handmade creations of thousands of artisans
—the finest collection of Spanish crafts and gifts in the world. More than 65%
of his stocks are otherwise unobtainable—and what you don't find he'll have
made up for you! For normal buyers and collectors for investment, here is the
largest and most complete assemblage of Lladro porcelain on sale anywhere,
including editions limited to 700 to 1500 pieces before the molds are broken,
at 3 to 4 times less than Stateside tariffs. You'll find Toledo Damascene
jewelry (up to 40% under what the Toledo merchants charge on the spot),
Majorica pearls with original Eduardo clasps, ceramics, placemats, linens,
ladies' handbags, brassware, copperware, wrought iron, wood carvings, dolls,
solid silver or gold charms—just about everything except Don Juan's magic
wand. Low, low prices; important values; expert packing even for shipment
by camelback to Samarkand. **Galeria Kreisler**, an intertwined enterprise,
displays and sells the best of Spanish figurative (representational) graphics
and sculpture in the basement and figurative oils and art throughout the
ground floor. It is an internationally famous trove. Don't let any greedy taxi
driver give you the guff that *the* Permanent Spanish Exhibition is "out of
business." Just drop into the one-and-only Kreisler complex and say hello to
its jet-propelled director for us. Open all year. Highest recommendation.

Galeria Kreisler Dos (Hermosilla 8, about 75 yards away) fills out the
spectrum by exhibiting the abstract, avant-garde creations of *every* leading

Spanish artist on a regular basis. (These differ completely, of course, from the figurative school shown in the aforementioned headquarters.) They range from the oils, graphics, and sculptures of such masters as Miró, Picasso, and Juan Gris, to those of virtually all talents of special note within Iberia, to those of the younger group who show exceptional promise to pay later dividends. Most are permanently represented in Madrid's National Museum of Contemporary Art and in prodigious foreign showcases. Despite the tremendous renaissance in Spanish art, it is still much less costly than French, Italian, American, and other *oeuvres.* Nowhere in existence is there anything comparable.

Furniture, fabrics, and stunning decorative items for the home? **Artespaña** (Hermosilla 14, plus several branches in the city) is Iberia's answer—and a good one—to Denmark's Illums Bolighus. Its range of merchandise varies as much as the tiptop quality varies little. Chic? Indeed. Expensive? And how! Ask for courteous Mr. Cardof.

Superb jewelry? **Luis Sainz** (Av. José Antonio 13) is the Cartier of Spain; branches in **Barcelona, Palma, Biarritz, Paris,** and **New York**. Extra fine.

Books? **Miessner Libreros** (José Ortega y Gasset 14) probably offers Madrid's most versatile stocks.

Leather goods? Far and away the number one house in the nation is **Loewe** (main stores: Av. José Antonio 8 and splendid redecorated and enlarged Serrano 26). Since its founding in 1846, the original Don Enrique Loewe Roessberg's modest 18-worker establishment has expanded to 2 factories, 19 deluxe salons, and 800 employees. In the process, it has earned an unsolicited Appointment to the former Spanish Royal Court, gold medals in international expositions, and the 24-karat reputation for producing some of the most striking works of art in the industry today. Handbags, briefcases, air luggage, vanity cases, all types of jewel boxes, writing pads, suède and leather jackets and coats, gloves, shoes, frames, scrapbooks, wallets, billfolds, diaries, cigarette boxes, flasks, gaming sets, address and memo pads, every kind of small executive-type gift—all are here, and all so carefully fashioned that each piece has the style, flair, and finish of a fine jewel. Write to its central offices (Barquillo 13, Madrid) for any desired general or specific information concerning its network or its articles; your query would be welcomed. Loewe's latest triumph is its 2 dazzling new branches in **London** (see "England"). Other branches in **Madrid** (Palace Hotel), **Barcelona** (Paseo de Gracia 35 and Hotel Presidente), **San Sebastián** (Miramar 2 y 3), **Granada** (Hotel Alhambra Palace), **Bilbao** (Gran Via 39), **Seville** (Plaza Nueva 12 and Hotel Alfonso XIII), **Valencia** (Av. Poeta Querol 7), **Córdoba** (Parador Nacional de la Arruzafa), **Las Palmas de Gran Canaria** (Santa Catalina Hotel), and **Palma de Mallorca** (Paseo del Generalísimo 14). Legendary.

Superior Spanish shotguns, hunting accessories, and a galaxy of other sporting goods? **Viana** (Serrano 68, opposite Sears Roebuck) offers just about everything there is to shoot, reel, roll, throw, kick, or wear in the purlieu of sport. Covering nearly the entire right wall of the ground floor is a small forest of 12-, 16-, and 20-gauge shotguns—a glittering tribute to the age-old Iberian craftsmanship that long has drawn sighs of envy from foreign gunsmiths and sighs of ecstasy from discerning collectors. Prices? At least 50% less than comparable stocks fetch on English, Belgian, German, or Swiss racks. A Nimrod's nirvana.

Colognes, cosmetics, and miscellany? **Alexandre** (corner of Av. José Antonio and San Luis) has every cosmetic product and bottled scent available locally. Since several French perfumers make cologne in Spain—Guerlain, for example—the prices are excitingly aromatic to any shopper's nose.

Wrought iron? Reindeer teeth? Curry combs for canaries? The "Thieves' Market," **El Rastro**, offers a fascinating jumble of junk—some good, some dreadful. Go from 10 A.M. to 2 P.M. on Sunday morning, and leave all your valuables (including passport!) in your hotel. Its so-called antique stores are also open on weekdays, when it isn't of quite such vital interest to the pickpockets and other ruffians.

Liquors? Yours for a song, in straw jugs, matador bottles, señora bottles, all shapes and sizes. One quart per person (21 or over) is the limit, back home.

In **Barcelona**, the **Paseo de Gracia** between Plaza Cataluña and the Diagonal has the best (and most expensive!) shops; if you stroll along each side in turn, you'll probably find what you're after, in the highest quality. For local color, try the U-shape walk from **Plaza de Piño** through **Calle Petritxol,** around the corner of **Puerta Ferrisa** to **Galleries Malda**, and back again to Plaza de Piño. This street offers a gaggle of shoes, watches, candy, and staple items. **Loewe** (Paseo de Gracia 35) has no rivals for handbags and traditional Spanish leather goods.

American tourists do not need export licenses if their purchases total 25-thousand pesetas (about $450), or less. This applies to goods which are carried at departure or subsequently shipped. If this amount is exceeded, however, a license is mandatory.

Most stores close between 1 P.M. and 4 or 4:30 P.M.—but the Government's effort to eliminate the *siesta* might alter this slightly by the time you arrive.

Dedicated shophounds? Space is too tight here for further listings—so consult this year's vastly revised and updated edition of *Fielding's Shopping Guide to Europe* for many more stores in more Spanish centers, more details, and more lore.

THINGS NOT TO BUY   Spanish shawls. The only real Spanish shawls are antiques from China. This has become a tourist racket; prices have sky-rocketed to heights that only a naïve visitor would pay. Handkerchiefs are often sleazy and expensive except in wonderful Bonet (see "Madrid" and "Mallorca" sections, and please remember that it has opened a gorgeous branch in Marbella). Beware also of the metal of the cheaper varieties of handbags or costume jewelry; it might tarnish all too soon.

LOCAL RACKETS   The Barcelona docks are one of the rare places in Spain where the traveler must be wary. Porters sometimes overcharge; local ship's personnel, especially stevedores who load tourist automobiles aboard steamers, sometimes demand fantastic tips; certain cartage companies who transfer heavy baggage to hotels or connecting transportation centers run up enormous charges. Even as far back as 1954 (!), one of the latter, a firm named

Placido, billed a well-known U.S. novelist $25 for hauling 1 trunk and some light suitcases from the waterfront to the Ritz, a distance of a few blocks. Make your deal first, and be careful.

Watch *any* transaction *anywhere* with a gypsy. You can count on magnificent honesty from most Spaniards, but the gypsy lives by trickery.

"Ronson" and "Omega" lighters (asking price: $3), "Parker" pens (asking price: $9), and other "branded" merchandise are hawked by sidewalk sharpies in the cafés of the larger cities. It's all sucker bait, counterfeited in illicit Tangier factories—and it's guaranteed not to work.

The taxi-meter racket (described in "Taxis") is becoming more widespread and virulent. Madrid and Palma are the biggest trouble spots.

Keep an eye peeled for pickpockets in streetcars, buses, and crowded areas in Madrid, Barcelona, and the tourist centers. They and motorized bandits have sharply increased during the past few seasons. Many of them, naturally, are gypsies.

Forbid the shoeshine boys on the street to apply any kind of dye (not wax polish) or to change your heels. If you don't, you'll be sorry later.

Spanish integrity is 99.99% universal; as a nation and a people, you'll find far less thievery, far less cheating, and far less chicanery than in Italy, France, or most of the world—sad to say, even than in America. Discounting the gypsies, the moral standards are not only admirable but splendid.

A final word about Spain in general: After you reach Spanish soil, you might well understand the feeling of restfulness, warmth, beatitude, peace, that we have described. It's there, like a magic spell—and we hope you'll find it as we do.

Sweden

Most of us picture Sweden—especially Lapland—as a rugged, rocky, wind-swept country, where the good-natured, fair-haired stalwarts milk reindeer, drink Swedish Punch, battle the cruel elements, and never take off their red-flannel underwear.

Not on your life! It's a land of lakes and streams; much of it is flatter than Ohio. Thousands of pools and rivulets glitter on the placid, green landscape of the south; the summer sun there is warm, fields burst with ripe, golden wheat, and gentle pastures are brilliant with flowers. One-tenth of the population tills the dark soil on these plains, the coastal terraces, the lake shores, and the northern valleys; in this balmy bottomland climate, warmed by the Gulf Stream, everything flourishes from peas to sugar beets to long-stemmed roses. The mountains, sentinels shared with Norway, rise in the north and west.

Swedish stock is as undiluted as Kentucky's best thoroughbreds: about 8-million pure Nordics against 500-thousand Finns, Lapps, Czechs, Greeks, Italians, and others. Lutheran Protestantism is far and away the dominant religion, but the 98% national participation is a loaded statistic; unless you declare yourself otherwise, you're automatically a member of the Church of Sweden. There's complete freedom of worship; education and military service are compulsory and universal.

Democracy and socialization have far outstripped America. This northern wonderland also happens to be one of the most "capitalistic" nations on the globe (above the per capita income in the U.S.)—while still being the most civic-conscious of major free-world countries. To support this, taxes are now so murderous that someone with a salary of $16,000 takes home only $7890.

Some by-products of this State paternalism are startling or amusing to the stranger. Few jails in Sweden have iron bars—yet it's a crime to get drunk. Smoking is relatively low on a per-capita basis, but legislation is now going through to virtually create a nonsmoking nation over the next decade or so. Labor is extremely strong—yet management relations are so enlightened that there have been only a handful of strikes since World War II. Any Swede under 20 who has a job but doesn't behave himself is required to pay room and board at home, upon his parents' request. No country in Europe is better suited for tourists—as tourists are beginning to discover.

CITIES   *Stockholm* is a miniature New York, Washington, Chicago, Los Angeles, and Podunk rolled into one and transported to Scandinavia. Somewhat larger than Washington, it has 665-thousand people, 3 railroad stations, an excellent hotel picture, plenty of restaurants and shops, wonderful relics; and the Rotary Club meets on Tuesdays! The 5-block, glass-and-concrete, "New Manhattan" business complex, with small skyscrapers, terraced gardens, and garages (6 floors underground), has risen on the site of outmoded houses in the Klara District. The paralyzing shortage of adequate housing has been given A-1 priority by the government. Suburban apartments at last are becoming available—and at *what* a cost! This 700-year-old city of islands is spick-and-span, modern, efficient and beautiful to the eye.

Göteborg (Gothenburg), pronounced "YOTE-ah-borg," celebrated its 350th anniversary in '71. This ancient seat, Sweden's busiest port, is second in importance—about the size of Newark, N.J. It's on the west coast, seaward. There are many historic canals here, and the Göta River ends the famous Göta inland waterway which winds cross-country to Stockholm. Several hotels are available. Dining spots are now more engaging than before. There are ample tourist facilities. The city is an interesting one, and the inland boat ride across the peninsula is a relaxing and pleasant journey. You can fly back to Stockholm by fast, frequent SAS service.

Malmö is third. It's right on the tip, closest to Germany and Denmark. This is the jumping-off point for excursions to the Swedish châteaux country; there are at least 200 fine ones from the sixteenth and seventeenth centuries. Five major hotels, 1 outstanding restaurant in a restored ancient house, plenty of shops, and plenty of bustle; 6 miles of quays, Sweden's biggest man-made harbor, and one of Scandinavia's largest and most modern theaters are here. Immaculate and comfortable ferryboats make the crossing to Copenhagen in 1½ hours, and 36 hydrofoil services per day in both directions nip the time to a mere 35 minutes.

The rest of the "cities" are hamlets, bucolic and charming. Visit Stockholm first, then branch out to *Visby,* the *Lake Siljan District* in Dalarna (Tällberg, Rättvik, Mora), the *West Coast,* the glassworks districts of *Kalmar* and *Växjö* (in the latter, the House of Emigrants commemorates the centennial of the first wave of the U.S. migration), *Lapland,* or *Östergötland,* which are the best bets for tourists.

MONEY AND PRICES   The öre and the krona (plural: kronor) are the media of exchange. The krona is worth about 23¢, or 4.4 kronor to $1, so here's your scale: 100 öre = 1 krona—approximately 23¢. Silver coins come in 10, 25, 50 öre, and 1, 2, and 5 kronor values; notes are in 5, 10, 50, 100, 1000, and 10,000 kronor values.

Prices are more inflated than was Phileas Fogg's famous balloon. To counter the shockingly costly welfare program, a 17.7% National Consumers' Tax has been slapped onto everything from clothes to comestibles to construction to curling irons. (Rents are excepted). While the capital's sidewalks are benevolently heated by the Government to melt their winter snows, a housewife who skips along them to her butcher pays $6 a lb. for steak; her beleaguered husband in his favorite tavern can drown his economic sorrows for 70¢ to $1.15 for a beer or up to $3.80 for a gin and tonic! Laundry bills are so bleaching that it is almost cheaper to purchase all new garments—*if* you buy them in some *other* country, that is. It is little wonder that Stockholm has won the UN's Dubious Achievement Award, after Tokyo, as the most expensive major city in the world. And since the labor unions walked away with a 2-year, 20% wage hike, Svend Doe and Sweden's visitors can count on a sharp further upward spiral in living expenses. Tonight's solitary dinner in a top restaurant will lighten your wallet from $15 to $24, including beverages. A hotel room for 2 in a leading establishment will bid *adiós* to another $30 to $57. Even a short taxi ride will tick off $2.50-or-so. Prices in the provinces, however, are refreshingly lower. Moreover, there are good, simple, almost-reasonable facilities everywhere in the land for the traveler who must watch his budget.

ATTITUDE TOWARD TOURISTS   Five separate organizations fly the banners of welcome for foreign visitors, and each tackles its special phase with earnestness, intelligence, and efficiency.

The **Stockholm Tourist Association**, directed by Fritz Alm, operates inquiry bureaus at Hamngatan 27, the headquarters in Sweden House, at Värtahamnen and Skeppsbron (landing stages of Finland steamers), and at the Stockholm City Hall, plus a mobile unit with telephone. Enough? Its hotel booking office functions year-round in the Central Railway Station. Finally, it sponsors the intriguing "Sweden at Home" program for the benefit of overseas guests: You are invited for an evening with a local family which shares your professional interests, hobbies, or other mutual bonds—in their house, without fees or considerations of any kind. Merely fill out the form with your personal particulars, and they'll cross-check their files for exactly the right host. It's the kind of hospitality—and heartwarming contact—which money can't buy.

The **Swedish Tourist Board,** also in Sweden House, is the master organization and moving force in the promotion of international understanding through travel. It maintains 11 branch offices in foreign capitals, publishes many useful pamphlets and brochures, and coordinates all official activities in the field. If you're a journalist, radio commentator, television producer, author, photographer, movie cameraman—anything to do with any aspect of the press—go to this enterprise for sound advice and invaluable local assistance.

The **Swedish Institute for Cultural Relations** handles foreign-study groups (labor, management, religious, farmers, teachers, social workers, professional associations, and similar units); **Reso** (Travel and Holiday Organization of the Popular Movements) not only operates 1 First-class and 4 budget-price hotels in the capital, major oases in Malmö, Jönköping, and Göteborg, and about a dozen bottom-price resort centers in the hinterland, but it also makes available a whopping number of private homes in Stockholm for workers, students, and low-income vacationers, Swedes or foreigners.

In America, **Scandinavian National Tourist Offices** are at 75 Rockefeller Plaza, N.Y. 10019 and at 3600 Wilshire Blvd., Los Angeles, Calif. 90010. They will plan your trip, answer your questions, do everything but make your actual reservations. Here are the places, too, for further information on Reso, study-group facilities, and other special data.

Make certain you have advance reservations before venturing to Sweden.

The Stockholm Tourist Association sponsors "Miss Tourist," a telephone voice in the capital to give you fresh-off-the-griddle facts on local events of interest. Just dial 22-18-40. The daily newspapers also print a section summarizing the international scoop in English. It's darned good, too.

The Stockholm Tourist Association is also behind the selection of a "Hostess Queen" each year to charm VIPs who visit. Tenure of office for queens, who must combine brains *and* beauty, has been notably short. To the anguish of their business-minded sponsors, the barrage of matrimonial offers is so wearing that the reigning beauty seems to succumb 46 seconds after her coronation.

CUSTOMS AND IMMIGRATION

One of the best in Europe. You'll be received, quizzed, stamped, inspected, approved, and through the gate while your head is still spinning. The inspectors are thorough, quick, and alert. Load-your-own-baggage carts have been installed in the major airports. Incomers must choose the green (no) lane or the red (yes) lane, depending on whether they have anything to declare. Let that ol' conscience be your guide!

You may bring in 2 liters of liquor; 400 cigarettes are free, with a duty of 3¢ per cigarette for any over this number. Since American varieties sell for $1.25 and up per pack in Sweden, it's cheaper to carry your entire supply. They won't go through your pockets (unless you look like a pusher); innocent visitors are treated like ladies and gentlemen.

There is no import limit on foreign funds, but the maximum in *Swedish* currency which may be brought in or carried out is 6000 kronor.

Incoming motorists must be able to produce (1) a valid driver's license, (2) proper registration, and (3) evidence that their insurance policy conforms with the national compulsory coverage.

HOTELS

For far more comprehensive information on certain hostelries than space limitations permit here, interested travelers are referred to the annually revised *Fielding's Selected Favorites: Hotels and Inns, Europe* by our son, Dodge Temple Fielding. The latest edition, in which a total of 300-odd favored possibilities were picked from the 4000-plus personally inspected, will be in your bookstore early this year.

Stockholm's choices are the most varied, of course.

The **Grand** is under the same administrative aegis as the Strand and Carlton Hotel interests (see below). Beautiful location; enviable physical plant; bedchambers modernized and expensively comfortized. Its glassed-in verandas now function all year. Bar and restaurant in summery colors; revamped Spegelsalen ("Hall of Mirrors"), barely altered in overall effect; excellent Candlelight Dinner on Wednesday nights, patterned after the Royal's in Copenhagen (see "Restaurants"); dancing every night except Monday in its Royal roost; 355 rooms and baths; radios added throughout; TV in all sancta. Our choice of quarters are the "50's" (#150 through 650), which are delightful; superposh Suite #338-39-40 was designed by Count Bernadotte. Service standards, once the big bugaboo here show significant improvement.

Sheraton popped the cork on its 476-bubble magnum on New Year's Day, 1971. It's a 9-story, $13,000,000 midcity slicker. Banquet and conference facilities for 425 big dealers; chilly lobby, in contrast to its warmhearted accommodations; Telex; on-the-spot banking; expense-accounter room rates; high quota of attaché cases among its luggage checkins. Orange-highlighted Royal Blue restaurant, regionally patterned Dalecarlia Room, cocktail lounge, and coffee shop; sauna for boiling away those sins. Top-floor balconied units the premium spreads; 6 lakefront suites; many twins with 2 double beds; teal, rouge, and other rich colors blending in modern themes; TV plus superb music console; fully carpeted; small but well-equipped baths. Overall, this is a fine example of the American mood.

The elderly **Strand**, in midtown facing the water, emerged from a costly and long-term beauty treatment which makes her lovely to behold—when the lazybones housekeepers get off their ashcans and on their broomsticks. Soothing lobby in white marble, warmly touched up with dark woods and rich color; popular Maritime Restaurant and dice-cup-size casino; elegant main-floor dining room and adjoining bar nook; convenient snack haven dishing up savory and inexpensive short-order selections from midday to dusk. Most of the 112 units with 2 types of showers plus a full bath (ours had a ring around it, and it wasn't 14-karat, either). We're also sad to report that we were given (1) pushy, almost crude, attention in the Maritime Restaurant and (2) snail-paced neglect in our room. New staff for key commands began work here after our latest visit—and this could perk it up immensely. Recommended for its physical amenities only, until we can test this contender under its maturing leadership.

The **Foresta**, now a licensed member of the Ramada Inns chain, is a 10-minute cab ride from the center. Here's an interconnected unit with shelter for 400 guests within 4 separate buildings (a 5-story transient hotel with singles, doubles, and suites, all with bath and balcony; a still expanding aparthotel with 1–3 rooms, 1-month minimum occupancy, or shorter stays permissible in its 30 latest nests!; the Milles Hall with theater, banquet, and conference facilities; and a reborn miniature Gothic castle with restaurants). At night, from the big bridge to Stockholm's center, this house is especially alluring in its illumination, reminiscent of a dream sequence from Disney World. Pleasant, clean-lined lobby; heliport and roof terraces; 30 lovely fresh suites surrounding the city's only hotel swimming pool. Varisize accommodations on the penultimate level (the top tier is best) have appealingly furnished sitting rooms, complete kitchenettes, TV, 6-channel radio, and splendid terraces. Our only criticisms are (1) the smallness of some of the standard quarters, (2) a gaggle of chambermaids who seem shy on elbow grease, and (3) its distance from the doin's.

The **Diplomat** presents itself with elegant up-to-date credentials housed within a classic downtown structure. Tearoom plus a dining salon for groups. An inviting green-tinted bar serves up snacks. The overall decorative scheme ranges from Swedish birch freshets to English oaken warmth. While some of its accommodations are truly patrician, this house (which is expanding) needs a bit more time to jell. Otherwise most appealing.

The 240-room **Park** greets its guests with a lemon-colored lobby which adjoins a salty maritime restaurant and a merry-time bar. Excellent sauna; kitchenettes available; service still immature but trying. If you can snag a sleeper overlooking the lovely Humlegården you will be rewarded with a majestic sylvan tableau smack in the center of the city.

Across this same greensward stands the youthful **Anglais**. Façade dotted by flaming gas lamps; dark Andalusian-style lobby in ceramic tones; candle-brightened ground-floor rôtisserie with forest-green leather chairs; bar open at 1 P.M.; enclosed court accessible to 1st-level guests; restaurant with piano music nightly; tiny roulette room. The bedchambers feature chestnut furnishings, matching jalousie-doors leading to private balconies, well-equipped efficiency baths with barbaric ventilation slots under the doors rather than built into an interior system; other fillips include 5-channel radio, electric alarm clocks, silent valets, TV available for a price (free in the suites), and pencil-thin spotlights at the doors for key fumblers. Chief Concierge Frödin mans the desk here. In physical appearance, this stripling is handsome indeed—but client attention, as everywhere, is extremely slack in this highly welfared state.

The 11-story **Continental** is a Reso chain-link forged close by the main station in midtown. Handsome lobby; large-but-cozy, low-ceilinged, wraparound Café on the mezzanine overlooking the entrance hall; quick-service cafeteria in the cellar by the subway exit; Steak House; gorgeous split-level, split-personality dining room in blacks, golds, and reds, ingeniously highlighted by striking use of Orrefors glass insets on pillars and lamps for decorative effect; bank, travel agency, beauty parlor, underground station, and garage. Seven types of rooms, all with wood floor-to-ceiling panels backing the beds, and offbeat employment of textiles and colors; sliding partitions to separate sitting and sleeping areas in the demisuites; all baths supermicroscopic; baggage stowage adequate for business travelers but far too small for overseas voyagers. Commercial and solid.

The vast 380-unit **Amaranten** is one of the largest hostelries in Sweden—and one of the best investments for your travel dollar that we've found in this city if you can weather its tempest of convention and other groups. Noncentral but not inconvenient location (subway station in the block); spacious lobby with a colorful textile montage on one wall; adjoining brasserie with room dividers, hanging lamps, and excellent cafeteria-type food service; sumptuous restaurant with booths and an amusing centerpiece divan in 4 segments; cocktail lounge blending gold leaf and tavern tones; colossal photo blowups in corridors depicting the beauties of the North—some of them very curvaceous indeed. For a medium-budget establishment, we continue to be impressed by a service attitude that equaled if not bettered many of the Deluxe entries in this metropolis. Very highly recommended for its category.

A sister candidate, the **Reisen**, was given a new gown and coif not long ago. She's a stunner, too—a pert, fresh-faced gamin made over from the linkage of 3 seventeenth-century houses. Lobby and new bar facing the water; guestrooms incorporating the rugged brick walls of the original structures; cellar with 2 saunas, a swimming pool, and a vaulted clubroom. The dining quadrant overlooks the harbor; there's the Clipper Club on the ground floor; and for private parties the saloon of a ship has been reconstructed inside the hotel. Director Olle Asp is doing a splendid job of milling maximum value into your travel dollars. Our port-o-call couldn't have been more rewarding in comfort-kindness-and-consideration per krona.

The **Carlton** is radically improved. At least 90% of its rooms have been entirely rebuilt and refurnished under the discerning eye of Manager Jakob Jonker. The balance, plus the corridors, have been spruced up in varying degrees. A total of 115 offer private bath, and the remainder have private toilet but no tub or shower. Three suites with TV and 2 baths each; entrance and lobby fully modernized; ground-floor lounge enlarged and redecorated; cocktail bar added. There's a beauty parlor at your disposal, the British-overtoned Carlton Inn for quick meals, and a modern kitchen. Accommodations on the cramped side, all offering simple but practical Swedish furniture, radio, and TV-for-hire. Now less expensive than the Strand, but still not as cheery, in our opinion. Much better than ever before, however.

Holiday Inn provides 200 shelters out at *Alvsjö*. The **Birger Jarl** is a bit larger; it's also a youthful contender.

In number of beds but not of rooms, the **Palace** is one of the larger hotels in the city. It occupies 4 floors of a fringe-area commercial building (the premises of a local automobile dealer); with such ample garage space, its main occupancy target is the motorist. There are 230 accommodations with 175 baths, of which the 38 so-called Motel Rooms are triumphs of architectural planning for children, elves, or midgets. Restaurant, self-service cafeteria, snack bar, Finnish bath, beauty parlor, barbershop, rentable TV, and other facilities; clean, utilitarian décor. This one is more for automobilists with kids or Scandinavian businessmen who travel by car than for tourists with an eye toward elbowroom and the plushier type of comfort.

The **Mornington**, like the Palace, is situated in one section of a commercial building—this time on the 4th, 5th, and 6th floors. All its 82 rooms have TV for hire, radio, and radiant heating; 60 come with bath and 20 with shower; the singles are tiny, but the doubles offer workable living space. Star attractions are its 3 demisuites with good baths, more *Lebensraum,* permanently installed TV sets, and amazingly practical wardrobes with "dishrack" drawers (becoming more and more popular with efficiency experts). Not terribly exciting overall.

The **Malmen**, owned by the municipality and operated by Reso, is a streamlined, starkly modern factory of mass-production tourism; dining salon refashioned nicely; Club Malmen stoked up for night owls; 265 minuscule, painfully clean rooms, all with radio, automatic awakening bell, and toilet; many showers added lately; tandem-style beds in all doubles and triples; service for *minimum* essentials only (guests must shine own shoes on machine in lobby); relatively speaking, in this costly hotel economy, a money-saving bet for students or dusty-footed budgeteers but most certainly not for Americans in search of the amenities. The **Stockholm** occupies the 6th and 7th floors of an office building; lovely view; some bedchambers agreeable and some shoebox-size; breakfast room but no restaurant. Manager Wally Frisack is pleasant, competent, and hard-toiling. More a sleeping convenience than a full-blown hotel. The **Plaza** operates on the 5th to 7th floors of a business structure; bright little lobby, small but cheerful accommodations, quiet location, no bar; agreeable roof-garden restaurant; 40 bedrooms; no great shakes, but tolerable. The **Wellington**, with its white-hot sauna, sails nicely under the skippering of Margaretha Kvistgaard. Small but trim, it seems to be moving smartly into the winds of fortune. The **Alexandra**, with 75 singles and 25 twins, is another relative newcomer. Its prices are medium-low. Fair enough for the outlay. The **Bromma**, near the domestic airport, offers 143 accommodations within its main building (better) and annex. Maximum doubles at reasonable tabs; baths mostly the sit-down type; fair amenities, but too far out for most visitors to the big city. Nearby, the **Flyghotellet** is reasonable enough as a medium-priced landing field. The **Flamingo** might be termed a supermarket hostelry. No porters, so you load your luggage into a grocery cart provided in the lobby and wheel your cargo to your bin; no reception minions even to show you to your address. Restaurant, grill, bar, and cocktail lounge similarly impersonal; clean, ultramodern, and oh-so-sterile. To us, this Flamingo is strictly a 1-legged critter. The **Sjöfartshotellet** waddles in with a quick-frozen lobby, a nautical dining room, and monotonous corridors. Within the 6 stories are 183 modern, utilitarian rooms with glass-front masks; efficient for group bookings, but not to our tastes. The **Jerum** and the **Domus**, now redecorated, are students' dormitories in winter and equally sterile, institutional-style hotels in summer. The **Frälsningsarmén's** (Salvation Army's) **Hotell** is open to both genders; very cheap, and better than most YMCA's or YWCA's in the States. Dry, of course. The 146-room **Kristineberg**, about 10 minutes out in a residential district, lacks zip, zest, or zing, in our opinion. Too dowdy for most merrymakers. **Esso** has dropped the checkered flag on a 153-cylinder competitor at *Ulriksdal*, north of the city, and yet a newer racer on the route to Arlanda. Finally, there's the **Gyllene Ratten Motel**, 4 miles south, as well as a covey of new entries farther out (see below).

Dedicated budgeteers? Since we're too bottlenecked here for additional entries in Stockholm, please consult this year's vastly updated edition of our annually revised paperback, *Fielding's Low-Cost Europe*, which lists more bargain places to stay and money-saving tips for serious economizers.

Saltsjöbaden, the renowned beach resort 25 minutes by train from the capital, is proud of its venerable **Grand**—and rightly so. Administration by the same Grand masters (Strand and Carlton, too) as in Stockholm; waterfront situation; 100 rooms, each with bath or shower; now redone almost from the ground up, in excellent taste; cookery reportedly in poorer taste; often frequented by the Senior Citizenry; 2 bars, TV room, table tennis, so-called casino roulette; sauna; nearby facilities for swimming, yachting, tennis, golf, water skiing, plus winter sports.

Göteborg has the **Park Avenue**, our candidate as one of the leading hotels of the nation. Modern, fresh, attractive décor; wonderful Lorensberg Restaurant with top-talent floor show and dancing every evening but Sunday; delightfully cozy, beguiling Belle Avenue Grill; anchovy-size Tidbit Room with light fare for budgeteers; mezzanine bar and snack loggia; self-service breakfasts at rates that won't curdle your café au lait. Vast opulent new wing; new sauna and pool; new sky bar and Panorama tearoom; of all the twins, ¼th have private verandas; top floor (10th) is entirely in elegant balconied large suites; 9 small suites are one of the best values in Sweden; all accommodations are newly furnished and appointed, with a keen eye toward comfort and convenience. Our only nitpick is the dismal lobby décor, which remains the same year after year. We haven't yet seen the 323-room **Scandinavia,** but we hear that it leans heavily toward the convention trade. For modernists, the newish Reso-owned, 10-story, crescent-shape **Opalen** is as fresh as a fjord breeze. The designers, thank goodness, did not make the same boudoir design bumbles here that were made in the Stockholm Continental (see earlier comments). Careful planning of the bedchambers, in fact, gives these comfortable and tasteful accommodations the edge over the cool-tempered public rooms. Clerestory restaurant that has been given a warmup treatment (dancing except Sun.); popular Bodega Cafeteria with trencherman servings; quick-lunch den converting to a roulette rank at nightfall; hairdressing and barber facilities. All 230 rooms with well-equipped baths (good ventilation, soap flakes, peignoirs, Kleenex, bidets). There are artful touches in the displays of twentieth-century tapestries and the handicraft vitrines in the corridors. Here's a thoughtfully conceived and clean-lined haven that the young-in-spirit should undoubtedly enjoy. Somewhat commercial, but a sound and solid second; highly recommended. The **Rubinen**, under the same Reso proprietorship, stands a few doors away from the Park Avenue. Although its prices are higher, it is Swedish miles below the leader in quality and performance, in our opinion. The 400-room **Europa** is a recent major addition to the city. Two dining quadrants; a bar; gym, sauna, and pool; pedestrian passage connecting it to the Ostra Nordstan shopping mall. We'll check it out soon. **Three Crowns** proffers 172 accommodations all with faucets (in bath or shower), a restaurant, cafeteria, a sauna, a garage, and bedchambers textiled in blue hues —royal, no doubt. We'll be anxious to seek our first audience here next swing. **Eggers** is next—but it may not be for long. Its proposed renovation has been scuttled; hopes of moving to an entirely new site are now troubling the owner's slumber. Current total of 88 rooms and only 16 baths; friendly, cheery personnel; well maintained and sprightly, despite its century-plus of wear. Lodge *only* in the more modern bedchambers here, because the others are scrambled Eggers. The **Ritz**, across from the railway switchyard but nevertheless quiet, is now run by the Salvation Army. They keep it brighter than a Christmas glockenspiel. Restaurant unveiled a while back; very, very good, clean shelter for the bargain hunter who rolls in thirstless. The **Carl Johan Hotel**, plus the **OK** and the **Hallarna**, are new ones on us. The last has 92 units; from the brochure before us, it seems to be a reasonably appealing efficiency camp for motorists who tire at the E3-E6 junction. The **Excelsior** is a fair bet for budget-conscious families; a handful of baths on tap; also sparkling. There's another **Esso** at the entrance from the Malmö highway; it's a pit stop for traffic shunners. Cozy restaurant; modern comfort. At *Kungälv*, 13 miles north of Göteborg, the 130-room **Fars Hatt** wears the sylvan crown. Two comfortable wings and a swimming pool; 2 saunas, tennis, bowling, and a golf course nearby; 2 popular restaurants and an active bar. Very solid accommodations. as a motel-type stop, we love it.

Malmö has had a storm of new or recent hotel constructions and renovations, but her 2-century-old matrons still steal their share of the thunder. The modern architectural syndromes of spacelessness and iceberg-chill in functionality result from this city's greater interest in businessmen than in tourists. The **Savoy**, mellow, charming, and carefully maintained, has an enviable location overlooking the canal and maritime docks. Cozy, popular Grill and gracious dining room, both noteworthy for cuisine; biggest banquet facilities in South Sweden (again for its heavy business clientele); hodgepodge building pattern containing 100 bedchambers and 65 baths, all with hip-pocket closet dimensions. Director Lars Lendrop and his live-wire art-collecting wife do a fine job here. The Reso-run, mercantile **St. Jörgen**, canonized in '64, is a sterling example of the modern crop. Centrally situated and thoughtfully planned; built-in tranquillity surrounding 2 garden courts, effectively designed restaurant and cafeterias, cocktail lounge, and coffee bar; dancing every night but Monday in the Tavernan, which doubles in daytime as a breakfast den and quick-lunch snackery; roulette room where you can play for your meal chits; sauna and gymnasium. Total of 304 accommodations, including 23 singles and 5 doubles with shower only (1 day is the maximum permissible stay in the former, due to a health ordinance governing windowless rooms), 5 suites, and doubles with a full array of convenience features. Very good for jet-age tastes. The **Kramer** was owned by a brewery, but now it's under its own head. It still carries on as a traditional Malmö address. Pleasant lounge; large dining salon; 2 nightclubs; handsome bar in mahogany tones plus the Pub. A penthouse lords over 4 suites plus 100 lesser pads with 64 baths; each floor features a different shade of linens. Newly renovated and better. The 180-unit, supermodernistic **Scandinavia** provides a surprising amount of elbowroom for a contemporary north-country enterprise. Beguiling roof garden; cheery restaurant, bar, and casino; sauna and gymnasium; billiard parlor; 44 bowling lanes (site of the '67 World Championship); all bedchambers with 2 windows, alarm clock, radio, telephone, silent valet, and full bath, plus telephone-style shower in each; soothing color schemes. Some 30 apartments rent cheaply by the week or month. Especially recommendable for families, athletes on holiday, or ten-pin addicts. **Teaterhotellet**, across from the National Theater, the **Plaza,** and the Reso-operated **Arkaden** are all pretty routine. Near the airport, adjoining the racetrack, is the ultrabasic **Jägersro Motell**. At nearby *Hässleholm* we hear the **Stadhotellet** is a useful address (since the town is an important junction). You might also pick either of the **Esso motels** in the area. They're consistently high-octane.

Lysekil, 2 hours north of Göteborg just off the trunk road to Oslo (Norway), has the well-known seaside **Lysekil**. Travelers tell us this merry little house has 50 rooms, some with bath and all with private toilet; 3 restaurants, a nightclub, a bar, and a gaming room adjoin. Facilities are amiable without being plush. In this very Swedish summer mecca, you'll find fishing (no licenses or restrictions), an open-air cafeteria on the beach, an Aqualung Diving School, an International Youth Club, teen-agers dancing nightly at the Al Fresco restaurant, a Carnival in mid-August, and other drawing cards. It sounds like fun.

Båstad recently enjoyed a touristic boom period. **Tylösand** (the seaside resort on a cape facing Denmark, 5 miles from Halmstad on the Malmö-Göteborg road) comes up with a cluster of summery hotel buildings, several bungalows for transients, 1 restaurant seating 550, 2 smaller dining establishments, Finnish steam baths, a wonderful beach (cold water—brrr!), and 27-hole golf courses, tennis courts, dancing, and many other attractions. Main plant open mid-June to mid-August; stay at the **Tylösands Havsbad**, best in the community. At **Halmstad**, the **Hallandia** and **Stenwinkeln** are new-ish; we don't yet know either. For pilgrims from Denmark, the *Europafergen* makes the daily ferry run between Grenå and Varberg. At neighboring **Falkenberg**, the seafront **Strandbaden** is dramatically avant-garde in architectural concept. For honeymooners, the favorite is **Gyllene Uttern**, 1½ miles south of the village of **Gränna** on the Stockholm–Jönköping–Malmö route. Two hotels (1 First class, 1 for country living); Tudor-style architecture; grass growing on the roofs; lake view; guest cottages with 1-or-more bedrooms, a bath, and a sitting room; exquisite Wedding Chapel to make it legal; lovely setting and enchanting décor; not overexpensive. May to September only. Just the dish for lovebirds who want bucolic scenery and less-than-zero chatter from anybody.

Linköping (pronounced "Lin-shoe-ping") produces the delightful little **Frimurarehotellet**, provincial but comfortable. Its newer section is best; there's a bath provided with every unit. Good dining room under a slat roof; ancient Grill with hunting scenes in stained-glass windows; chef laboring happily under a copper hood; off-lobby bar. Inviting in a clubby fashion. The 100-room **Rally Motel** is just a fair bet for motorists. We've recently Rallied here again and found it now basic-to-skimpy, but entirely suitable for what it is. Squash court, Finnish bath, barbershop, grill-restaurant, and 24-hour coffee shop with help-yourself snack bar; all but the loners have bath. **Esso** is also on the scene with 96 gleaming reasons to pause for the night. In the center, the **Stora** is adequate for emergency shelter if all else is filled.

In industrial-minded **Jönköping**, the waterside **Stora Hotellet** rules the wavelets. Dining room facing Vättern Lake; newer wing with more comfort but less vista than the older portion; total of 130 rooms and 82 private baths. The better choice for traditionalists. The Reso-built **Portalen**, in the middle of town, is for pilgrims who prefer sleek modern lines and strict functionality. Restaurant with giant chunks of carved wood (we ate lunch here, so we'd guess the food *must* be better at the Stora); summer garden and dining patio; Bodega Cafeteria; full Reso panoply of gadgets, including TV, radio, piped music, clock, phone, and an ingenious window-blind system (set inside Thermopane glass for controlling light to any desired gradient). Its cramped layout is its chief drawback. Still fair for overnighting, but not longer. The **Esso** and **MHF** motels might even be better for wayfarers on the go. Adequate space in the latter is MHF—Mighty Hard to Find. We don't know about the **Ramada** entry here.

In *Norrköping*, the **Standard** has been completely rebuilt around 182 fresh rooms, making it the local banner entry. The **Stora**, opposite, is clean and extremely well maintained for its modest category; pleasant winter and summer dining rooms; maritime cocktail lounge with portholes; small casino and bar. For medium budgeteers. The **Ritz**, with its revamped façade and lobby, dates back to '35 in one wing and to '65 in the other; book into the "other" only; no restaurant. **Mobilen,** 1 mile out of the center, is U-shape, with the reception desk and a cafeteria at one end and a restaurant on the second flank; textiles in rich burnt colors; interior brick walls; 2 beds and a folding divan in each of its 42 accommodations; efficiency baths. Fine as a motel-type stop. **Esso** is another, of course; it pumps up 150 units.

In the Dalarna province, there are 3 prime regional targets. *Tällberg* has by far the most color and charm with its mountainside spread, lake view, pine groves, and scattering of turkey-red cottages in the lap of Siljan forests. Its silent mystique is periodically upset in High Season by reindeer-like herds of tourists. *Rättvik* also radiates lure, but it is more urban and physically less enticing. The outskirts should not be overlooked. *Leksand* is relatively commercial and dull; not worth the transatlantic fare to see it, but if you are in the area it has its points. As for hotels in this birch-and-pine heartland, here's our detailed town-by-town breakdown: In *Tällberg,* the **Greens** boasts lovely buildings and an enchanting situation. In many respects—especially physical allures—it reeks with Dalecarlian appeal from its gables to its tables; dozens of nooks for cozy chats; Rumpus Room; tiny Picasso lounge; seventeenth-century library with a twentieth-century TV set; brass place settings in its viewful woody dining room; sweet young hostesses; indoor-outdoor swimming pool with temperature control; minigolf and badminton. All rooms (named, not numbered) now have tub or shower and new furnishings; "Gesunda," with its arched ceiling, sublime little balcony, warming hearth, and gay colors, is our personal pick; open all year except 1 week before Christmas. The **Dalecarlia Turisthotell** offers 80 rooms, only 28 baths, and a nearby annex with 50 additional units for conducted tour groups. Its tiny sixteenth-century reception hall is engaging; very large glass-fronted dining room with a heavenly command; earthly dancing once or twice weekly throughout the year; casino; bar; mini-bowling. This one demonstrates a certain flair for mass appeal, suburban-style—but it is spectrums below the Greens for sheer color. The **Långbergsgården**, a farmstead occupying 10 hilltop acres of ancient cattle-grazing land, boasts 55 rooms—25 in the main building and 30 in sleepy little cottages dotting the rumpled terrain. Poma-type ski lift for winter sports; 3 chalets, which Americans seem to love for their peaceful seclusion. Our recent visit convinced us it is indeed making progress, but we'd be happier—and so would you—if the pace were quicker. *Rättvik* 's leader is the **Siljansborg**, in which families and throngs of children unwind and frolic. With the amiable management here, small wonder it boasts one of the most loyal followings outside of Drottningholm Palace.

Suburban location; spellbinding lake vista; excellent cuisine; pleasant accommodations; service that delights the visitor. In general, its greatest appeal is for post-30-year-olds and under-10-year-olds; some of the nation's most distinguished, mature-but-not-elderly Swedes swear by this sylvan haven with its kindhearted staff and special values. Not luxurious, but overflowing with gentle warmth and hospitality—*and* kids. **Persborg**, also out of the hurly-burly and fronting the lake, offers 38 rooms and 13 baths or showers in its rambling main structure, plus 3 annexes with 13, 4, and 17 units (5 with bath or shower); the outside *dépendances* are much cheaper, of course. All bed-chambers are tight-dimensioned, ultraclean, and routinely furnished; those with plumbing have the tiniest baths outside of Lilliput; friendly personnel; also very pleasant. The **MHF** motel's 36 doubles are woefully weensie. *Leksand* (about 6 miles from Tällberg) has as its leader the ancient 40-room **Trekullor**. The **Furuliden** might come next, but we must review the scene again to be sure. The **Siljansnäs** (on the lake, 9 miles west) lists a pool, sauna, curling, and scenery, plus 30 rooms, 22 baths, and 20 balconies. At *Mora*, the **Mora Hotel** deserves mention; 75 moorings; 25 baths. We haven't yet seen the **Siljan**; 37 units with toilet and TV; 9 with shower; sauna. The celebrated **Sälens Högfjällshotell** at *Sälen* has an annex that functions during the summer. The main house will operate only in the winter season and will be rented to private sources during the warm months; more about this in "Things to See."

Visby's leaders are (1) **Snäckgärdsbaden**, and (2) **Visby**, rebuilt and enlarged some years ago. The former has a pool, minigolf, badminton, and dancing during the evening; its big drawback is its paucity of private baths; June 1 to August 31 only. The latter comes up with a considerably higher bath count; open June through August.

Touring by car or dogsled? U.S.-style motels are springing up like crocuses, all over Sweden. Ten examples, plus a bumper crop of unknowns that we hear are worth a gambol: (1) **Fleninge Motell**, 6 miles from the Elsinore (Denmark)–Hëlsingborg ferry, offers every room with bath, radio, and waking alarm; restaurant and cafeteria; adjoining service station; no tipping permitted; sponsorship of the Union of Temperance Drivers of Sweden. (2) **MHF Motel**, 1½ miles north of *Hëlsingborg*'s Central Station, has 45 rooms, each with shower, toilet, TV, radio, and ownership-management which will never bestow its Good Conduct Medal on the villain who writes this *Guide*. (3) **Stadshotellet** at *Värnamo*, about halfway between Stockholm and Malmö on National Highway E-4, features superadvanced Swedish décor and furnishings; TV, radio, waking alarm, and bath or shower in every room; spacious, fully licensed restaurant with smörgåsbord; breakfast room, bar, and hairdresser; starkly modern in tone. (4) *Stockholm*'s entry is the **Gyllene Ratten** ("Golden Steering Wheel"), 4 miles south of the city at the intersection of the Södertäljevägen and Vantörsvägen highways; 1-story building straight out of "Progressive Industrial Architects' Journal," commercial enough to be a Seventh Avenue Community Center; 109 rooms (some twins, some studios, some bunks); 98 baths; grill, bar, and dining room; car-servicing facilities. (5) **Rally Hotel** in *Linköping* has been previously described. (6) So has **Jägersro**, near *Malmö*. (7) And so has the **Mobilen** at *Norrköping*.

(8) **Stad** at **Karlstad**, while not technically a motel, is a perfect rest point for motorists rolling between Stockholm and Göteborg or Oslo. One Illinois Guidester raves about his Louis XVI suite, huge bath, and Deluxe appointments. "Our daughter," he writes, "had a double room the size of a tennis court, beautifully furnished . . ." (9) Going north from Göteborg to Fredrikstad (Norway), the **Carlia Gästis** at **Uddevalla** has chilblains; still, it's reasonable. (10) Further up near the frontier, the **Laholmen** is the best stop in **Strömstad**; low-cliff situation; good restaurant; summer only. **Stadshotell** is almost the only winter choice; not much.

Now for that bevy of question marks: The **Esso** petroleum interests have pumped up nearly a score-and-10 spiffy roadsiders strung out across the nation. Ask at any filling station in its Swedish fraternity for brochures on the rest stops. Most that we have inspected have been excellent in facilities, but often lacking in service and culinary polish. In general, we can recommend them to Happy Motorists. Otherwise, **Vätterleden**, 11 miles north of Jönköping, has 52 units, most with shower and TV, and low tariffs which include breakfast and service. **Stadt Ljungby**, at **Ljungby**, features 20 bedchambers all with bath or shower. **Terraza**, also at **Ljungby**, boasts 75 rooms, some with full bath and some with only shower and toilet. At **Sandviken**, the **Eos** is reported to be a pleasant budget stop by a reader from Haifa who paused here. Up in the far north, **Blå Aveny**, in the university town of **Umeå**, has 80 rooms with bath; restaurant seating 220 munchers; nightclub, casino, sauna, gymnasium, and garage. Sounds excellent for this north port. In **Kiruna,** 90 miles north of the Polar Circle, the **Ferrum** provides shelter plus drinks in the Midnight Sun Lounge. P.S.: Since the sun doesn't set here in June and July, don't try to anticipate the cocktail hour by watching the shadows.

For information on hotels or motels in other parts of Sweden, consult your travel agent or the Swedish National Tourist Office.

Practically every small town and resort has comfortable pensions which charge $14 to $18 per day, all meals included. To get pension terms you must stay a minimum of 3 days. The **Swedish Tourist Board** can send you a folder and fill you in on details. *What* a buy in contrast with the costly general level here!

Youth Hostels are in operation between June 1 and September 1; of these 185 shelters ranging from farmhouses to historic buildings, only 21 are open year round (exception: Dec. 23 to Jan. 2). Rates are about $2 to $4 per night for members during the summer, with a 35¢ supplement from September to June; meals are $1.35 to $3. Little English is spoken in this circuit. Hitchhiking is sternly discouraged in Sweden. For information write to **Svenska Turistföreningen** (Swedish Touring Club), Fack, S-10380, Stockholm 7. *Fielding's Low-Cost Europe* isn't too bad, either, on its student economizings in the Stockholm area.

§TIP: The Swedes (and Finns) promote the bonanzarific **Hotellcheck** plan that can save up to 30% of your holiday expenses. It works this way: Your coupon book is valid for 4 days (and can be extended from 1-to-4 more) at any time during June, July, and August, as well as from any Friday afternoon to any Monday morning between September 1 and May 31. There are no restrictions on your itinerary or your time spent in any of the participating hostelries; bed-and-breakfast is included; a number of independent restaurants have also climbed aboard this budgeteer's bandwagon. For its pamphlet and other details, consult your travel agent, the Swedish National Tourist Office, or Hotellcheck Center (Box 21048, S-100 31, Stockholm 21).

FOOD A black and white picture. When restaurant fare is good, it's superb —but when it's not good, it's often heavy, tasteless, larded with grease, and unimaginative. Top cooks use sensitive fingers and palates as delicately as angels; routine cooks use muscle-bound thumbs and fists. We've never found a land where the contrast between fine eating places and greasy spoons is so apparent.

Until a few seasons ago, smörgåsbord was nearly extinct in its own homeland, mostly because restaurateurs found they could heap up bigger piles of kronor from straight dining. At that time, thanks to the blessed grace of Tore Wretman, the unchallenged king of his nation's restaurateurs, these oh-so-heavenly, delightfully groaning banquet boards then began reappearing. This gastronomic saint reversed the trend by appealing to national pride to offer this feast which is so genuinely Swedish that no one else can even palely imitate it.

After 2 years of experimentation, Mr. Wretman designed what we dubbed the "Miracle Table." This oval masterpiece eliminates all the fancy folded napkins, floral patterns, doodads, and gimmicks which clutter up working efficiency. Its 40 trays and bowls of varying sizes, all beautifully inset and rigidly controlled from freezing to simmering temperatures, permit the diner to peruse the *full* display at a glance and then to dive into his choices. It is topped by a crockery decanter built to dispense 6 varieties of snaps. This smörgåsbord goes full blast at the Operakällaren and the Stallmästaregarden restaurants (see following section), weekdays from noon to 3 P.M. and Sundays and holidays (if no change occurs by the time of your feast) from noon to 8 P.M. Don't miss it! Elsewhere in the capital, this type of service can be found at the Grand Hotel (in summer on the Veranda, in winter in the Winter Garden), at Ulriksdals Wärdshus, at Solliden in **Skansen** (11:30 A.M. to 3 P.M.), at the Grand Hotel in **Saltsjöbaden**, and at several scattered oases —and *remember, it's always lunch, never dinner.* Some city restaurants offer its items individually on small plates, tailored to the customer's girth and pocketbook; these are known as *assietter.*

Cardinal rule with smörgåsbord: Eat all fish on the 1st plate, meats on the 2nd, and hot appetizers on the 3rd (optional). Never mix fish and meat.

As a curiosity, try the delicious tiny crayfish called *kräftor*—a freshwater toyland lobster. It's expensive—20 for about $18—but you'd be wrong to miss this important ceremonial dish of Swedish homes; the season is early August. Odd facts department: Since a disease recently killed many local crayfish, a fresh crop is being bred from those of our own Lake Tahoe.

Then there is *strömming,* dwarf Baltic herring. The Swedish cook boils, fries, pickles, pounds, and minces it, makes croquettes, fishburgers, and canapés of it—serves it in every conceivable fashion except raw, at which the good housewives draw the line. One popular presentation is 2 fillets, back-to-back, with parsley between—a herring sandwich, in effect. There is also plenty of the inevitable (and we think scrumptious) smoked eel. But the very best, in our opinion, is the juicy, delicately sweet salmon trout.

Sweden has no special meal hours. Most people lunch from 12 to 2 P.M., dine from 5 P.M. to 8 P.M. (afternoon tea is not popular), and later "sup" on snacks—but restaurants are open continuously during the day and evening. *Your large meal (whether lunch or dinner) might cost up to $18 to $24, with the average perhaps $11 to $15.* Be prepared for a bricklayer's breakfast.

RESTAURANTS For dining without dancing, **Stockholm**'s most celebrated and distinguished institution is **Restaurant Riche**. Enclosed sidewalk dining terrace with big windows and flower boxes; eighteenth-century French-influenced décor, plush and opulent; superelegant Riche Bar at entrance, where gold-leaf frescoes go mad; service notably fast and deft; ask for Manager Hedman or Maître Andersson. Our number one candidate within the city. Its intimate Theatre Grill, with a separate entrance, has been refashioned with apple-red upholstery, glass-and-gold partitions in a window-box effect, and with synthetic marble pillars and matching tables. Our meal was served much more professionally on our latest curtain raiser, but $96 for a very light 4-person dinner with 2 bottles of routine German wine strikes us as simply too much—even as good as it was.

Another *must* for the food (and interior-decoration) lover is **Stallmästare-garden** ("Royal Stablemaster's House"), 15 minutes by taxi from the center. Enchanting patio garden, made glad by cool pools, tiny waterfalls, and flowers; dining pavilion on lake (view blocked by the SAS terminal); previously described (see "Food") 40-dish smörgåsbord at lunch only on weekdays but up to 8 P.M. on Sunday (again, if still open on the Sabbath; presentation not as imposing as that in the Operakällaren; excellent flame-lit Grill for conventional dining); lovely atmosphere and urbane fare. Open all year, but a sunny day in summer is happiest. Laurie Nilsson will take fine care of you. A gustatory and aesthetic *must.*

The landmark **Operakällaren** is part of the Royal Opera House. An *opus magnum* it is—and seldom have we viewed such an impressive and awesomely efficient complex. *Fin de siècle* décor; Grill, American bars, sidewalk café; tiny Snack Bar adjoining the traditional Opera Bar; glass-enclosed, 400-seat banquet hall; beautiful firelight effect from gas flares surrounding the 2nd floor; fantastic wine cellars; the *pièce de résistance* is an ultraplush oasis facing the sea, complete with rainproof terrace for the warmer months. The tariffs, frankly, are 14-karat. Manager Jan Ling will welcome you warmly; Swiss Chef Werner Vögeli's hands are famed for their delicate touch. Technically and aesthetically, this one is a marvel.

The capital's diners display an affinity for going underground. While about a dozen subterranean haunts now exist, we'd rate the 3 leading deluxe establishments in the following way—in descending order, of course: (1) First, we remain true to the **Fem Små Hus** ("Five Small Houses"), all of 'em tucked into a cellar and sub-cellar in an Old Town-House. Vaulted ceilings; a firelit bar with antique furnishings; red tablecloths; candles in copper hurricane lamps; old timbers and bricks for richness. The selections are limited to several types of herring for starters, followed by grills. Our meal was satisfactory, but we were overcharged by $3 on our bill. The bar, quite naturally, is utilized to encourage drinking while guests are waiting for their tables; from our personal experience, however, we saw numerous tables ready inside. We wonder, therefore, if this isn't just a ploy—and, if so, a clumsy one—to extract a few extra kronor from its innocent trade. Extremely engaging atmosphere, but the attitude toward the client might border on being naughty. (2) **Aurora** could be almost a carbon copy in physical makeup. Italianate entrance; rustic interior; fowl suspended from ceiling rods; dull bar; also jammed with the Young Executive Set and their chic oh-so-lovelies. Most agreeable potluck on our try, too. (3) **Diana** is the newest of the Old Towners and very popular it is.

The ultramod **Cosmopolite**, in midcity opposite the N.K. Department Store, whips out exceptional value for moderate to medium-high tariffs. On the main glass-lined level, it adjoins a fascinating boutique filled with craft and tableware products of Swedish design or artisanship; these are on sale or can be ordered. Handsome place-settings reflecting the finest national skills— from beautiful wine goblets, to handloomed textiles, to the leather chairs on which you sit. Superb presentation that is not luxury category, but is certainly appealing; delicious cuisine (our plate of warm garnished *gravadlax* was heavenly); rushed service that tries to please. And please don't miss a peek or a nibble or a sip in the lower-tariffed downstairs wine restaurant. Waiters wear black smocks, smoke curls from the cigarettes of lingering newspaper readers, and the quality is tops for tavern-type snacks. We're very fond of every department in this cosmopolitan candidate.

Le Gourmet is becoming more attractive by the moment. Director Peter Schück is a serious gastronome and oenophile (take a look at his wine association certificates and cups at the desk). Mirror Room with rich woods and smoked and etched glass; main quadrant recently given the warm-up treatment; superb gourmet menus at startlingly low tariffs; quick lunches and snackery nibbles also available. This one is a bargain in almost any category for discriminating ingestion. Firmly recommended.

The famous old Bacchi Wapen finally bit the dust and has phoenixed as the **New Bacchi**. It reopened with different ownership and style after our departure, so we can't tell you more. Sorry. **Adam and Mari**, on a small island in the heart of the city, has a warm-weather terrace, somber accouterments, and a sturdy French kitchen; 2 orchestras; no cabaret; singles abound; currently open all year, for a change. **Piazza Opera**, formerly the Tessin, has been pounded into a pizza parlor. The **Strand Hotel** comes up with a doublebarrel threat to the waistlines of gastronomic sightseers. Its Maritim ("Maritime") Grill, stunningly decorated, is noted for seafood specialties which are culinary triumphs; stunningly high tariffs; service that can border on downright rudeness. Its main dining room, spacious in dimension, is imaginatively operated. Change of management here, so we hope it will perk up the poor Strand-brand staffing into a bandstand show. The **Grand**'s elegant Winter Garden is unique during the cold months. Candlelight Dinners from 6 P.M.

to 10 P.M. every Wednesday shouldn't be missed. In this frenetic world of rush and clatter, here's a truly civilized and sophisticated isle of calm. Six-string ensemble melodizing continuously for diners or dancers; rich, soft Andalusian atmosphere; long, lean tapers and ruby-shaded table lamps; azaleas in planter boxes; lovely pods of greenery growing in strategic corners; elegant, well-dressed clientele, many in black tie and evening dress. The service is so smoothly professional it was the best we experienced (incognito, of course) on our latest Swedish soirées. We loved it, and we wish it every continued success. The Royal Room here has revels every night except the Lord's. All dining and drinking oases in this hostelry are thumpingly expensive. The **Alexandra** has become second-rate on our scale; the clientele seemed to be slipping, too; the food we had here was strictly for Lake Mälaren ducks; open every day on the calendar.

Berns, in the heart of the capital, is one of Europe's most vast and imposing feederies; 1470 customers can be served simultaneously. After entering through the Red Room, decorated with memorabilia of Swedish Literary Immortal August Strindberg, you're given the choice of the French Verandah (Montparnasse décor), the Roulette Room for penny-ante gaming (once the Chinese Restaurant, which has now moved to Kornhamnstorg in the Old Town), or the main dining room (music, balconies, high ceilings, barn-size). In '64 it celebrated its centennial with 100 consecutive days of Eartha Kitt, Marlene Dietrich, and other luminaries on stage. The star-gazing continues year-after-light-year. Always booked tight for major shows, so please reserve well in advance for opening nights or when headliners are in town. In the past, this mass-production mecca came up repeatedly with the dullest meals we've ever eaten in the North, but the quality of our latest dinner and an earlier lunch on the Terrace was excellent. Usually closed June through August. Tops for the Big Night Out.

In the less expensive category, **Cattelin** is a traditional standby. Simple, friendly atmosphere, not chichi; full of socialites, artists, students, civil servants, and assorted Characters; rôtisserie grill to rear; seafood annex; open all year. **Stortorgskällaren** ("Cellar by the Market") is located, quite naturally, on the Great Square in Old Town. It offers a cozy ambiance with 24 candlelit tables; at the street-level entrance, you'll find a bar and 2 small dining rooms for overflow trade. Unelaborate and agreeable. **Östermalmskällaren**, in Storgatan adjoining the colorful Östermalmstorg flower market, budded as a twin-unit bower with unusual intimacy for hand-holding dining. It is not in the luxury category. Open every day; 2 rooms divided by wooden columns with a total of perhaps 45 tables; deftly decorated and cleverly planned so that each grouping seems in its own cosmos; exceptionally cunning illumination; front portion with handsome large window; rear rookery (better at dinner hours) in darker shades; soooooothing piano musings at night. Striking textile mural of the region dominating one wall; small open rôtisserie and peekable glassed-in kitchen; delightfully kind, alert staff. Here's one of the happiest "discoveries" of a late tour. Highly recommended. **Restaurant Promenade** is central, opposite Humlegården Park; help-yourself selections; now rekindled after a sputtering spell. The **Östergök** ("Eastern Cuckoo") romantically draws its name from the myth that when this feathery herald is heard from the east, your spirits will be cheered. Ours were, among its heavy wooden tables, dim lamplit glow, and sweet-rustic atmosphere. Swedish cottage fare of outstanding quality; reasonable tabs; closed Sundays and all of July. Chirpy. By the way, the adjoining **fish restaurant** is becoming one of the city's most popular evening gathering spots. **Pizzeria Capri** is cheery for peninsular pickin's. The **Stekhuset Falstaff**, a 10-minute taxi jaunt to Tegeluddsvägen 90, is the latest rage among local beefeaters. Low-ceilinged room with 2 adjacent annexes; terra-cotta tile flooring; highly polished enamel-red chairs; blue, green, and black placemats; black-handled utensils; azure paper napkins; busy, gas-flame rôtisserie sizzling sirloins, T-bones, chops, and filets. The menu is a do-it-yourself multiple-choice ticket on which you note the type, weight, and preparation of your cut. While we were steer-ed here by a friendly posse of meat-minded trailblazers, our hefty twin bill for a couple of medium-rare ranch rovers and house wine did not incite us to sing "Home on the Range." Truthfully, we were happy to mosey on down the line. Maybe your lasso will be luckier.

Pubs? Two are unusually inviting. **Player's Inn** crackles with a hearth in the middle one of its 3 adjoining salons. The ceiling is oak, and so is the atmosphere. The food is incidental. **Tudor Arms**, slightly less refined, is turned out in half-timber and white stucco. A young throng parades through every evening for steak-and-kidney pie, roast beef, and other publican pamperings. Neither is for purposeful dining, but both are fun.

Now for a pair of highflying, low-value novelties: The enchanting aerial vista from **Gondolen**, an altitudinal barque above the Old Town, will almost make you forget that miserable fodder on your plate. Our good friend, Swedish gourmet and world traveler Georg Sylvander, claims this panorama has synthesized his personal rule: "Never eat seriously at any spot where there is a magnificent view!" Mr. Sylvander couldn't be more right—at least about this one. Book a window table on a sunny day; go only when you're not hungry. The next is the **Kaknästornet**, 360 feet up in the TV tower which looms above the Djurgarden. Entrance costs peanuts per adult; it's free for young tots accompanied by oldsters. Indoor and outdoor sightseeing terraces for oooohing and ahhhing from 9 A.M. to midnight; glass-lined restaurant functioning from 11:45 A.M. to the bewitching hour; topographical maps, a telescope, and a tape-recorded guide service on tap on top; an ultrascenic, multilingual hostess to orient your hawk-eyeing. If that basement-level cuisine served way up in the stratosphere doesn't get you, then surely the elevators will. They rocket aloft and plummet down at more than 15 feet per second (among the speediest in Europe). Here is certainly a tourist attraction that's TVriffic—but we wish that the food were . . . ulp . . . excuse us, please. Others? Oh—let's not forget the spotless, efficient **I.C.A. "Ringbaren"** chain, while we're up; moderate-price cafeterias plus table-service outlets; excellent value for budgeteers. This company also sponsors **Brända Tomten** (originally an antique shop). What we saw of **Conti** didn't impress us very much—but we got there too late to make a fair judgment. For Mexican crafts, you might want to try **El Sombrero**. Its North-of-the-Border *jefe* is William Clauson, a troubadour who rode over the frontier from Ashtabula, Ohio, and who speaks perfect "Swenglish." We haven't sampled his skillet skills.

For other dining possibilities, see "Nightclubs."

In addition to the previously mentioned Stallmästaregården, there are several likely targets in the suburbs; pick your weather for any of these. **Djurgårdsbrunns Wärdshus**, behind Skansen in the famous Deer Park (15 minutes from the city), is an eighteenth-century, Gustavian-style house with an attractive table-and-awning-lined flagstone patio—perched on the banks of a placid canal. In summer it turns on a special boat cruise plus coffee in the park for about $17 per passenger. Rather nice except for its occasionally fluctuating libations billings. **Solliden**, nearby, is slightly cheaper and caters to a mass trade. Enormous recent improvement, thanks to the perspiration, plasma, and lachrymal outpourings of Manager Lennart Lindgren. Now a delightful choice for a sunny day; recommended with salutes. **Drottningholms Wärdshus**, near the castle of the same name, is gaining a following. The décor is rich with intimate appeal and charm; the cookery is above average—but then so are the tariffs. If you don't mind a 25-minute train ride, the aforementioned **Grand Hotel** in *Saltsjöbaden* serves a splendid smörgåsbord on Sunday noons. **Ulriksdals Wärdshus** at *Solna* (10 minutes from Stockholm, near Ulriksdal Palace), a lacy filigreed wood and window-paned country mansion built in 1868, is popular summer and winter. Small porch at entrance for cocktails and chitchat; glass-sided 25-table dining room in gay pastels; enchanting bucolic view; appealing upstairs for private parties and banquets. Our recent sampling of the Swedish national feast was nothing more than smörgåsboredom; it's served weekdays between noon and 3 P.M. and Sundays from noon to 7 P.M. More for eye appeal and sylvan leisure than for palate satisfaction.

In the miscellaneous category, that 1713-vintage cellar called **Den Gyldene Freden** ("The Golden Peace") has color galore—*and* now there's a lot more quality mixed into the pigments. Different helmsman who has it sailing even more smoothly than before; ground-floor salon in tavern style; cellar portions cozier for evenings; one segment bisected from end to end by a single community table; excellent service from staffers in regional costumes; prices very reasonable and eatables improving; now worth a visit for those who want a fashionable place to dine and sane value-packed billings; closed in July. For fish, **Sturehof** (center of town) has the most exalted finny reputation; English pub added; midnight closing. For shoppers, the summer-only, high-up open-air terrace at the **NK Department Store** has one of the finest views in midtown, plus a self-service cafeteria; very popular and very good; winter lunchrooms, too. The **Lille Köbenhavn**, across the street, specializes in Danish goodies; moderate tabs; a hit at midday. For students, **Minerva** has a Parisian bistro décor, a Swiss chef, and great élan; closed mid-June to mid-August; hot as hades, but lots of laughs.

For sky travelers, the **Flygrestaurangen** at Bromma (Stockholm's domestic airport) has zoomed up like an Apollo spacecraft—not in height (it is a mere 1-flight climb), but in quality. It has been enlarged and has even added Polynesian pannings which are said to be South Pacific-ing. Caviar is flown in from Teheran, canvasback ducks from America, and 58 other specialties from about 30 SAS-serviced countries—so how international can a restaurant get? Open from 11 A.M. to 11 P.M.; à la carte only. A SASsy little number. At Arlanda, the international terminus, **Jetorama** is a nourishing corner.

Dedicated budgeteers? Since we're too bottlenecked here for additional entries in Stockholm, please consult this year's vastly updated edition of our annually revised paperback, *Fielding's Super Economy Europe*, which lists more bargain dining spots and money-saving tips for serious economizers.

In **Göteborg**, the **Park Avenue Hotel** is a knockout—marvelous! THE place on Sweden's West Coast; attention courteous but staffing insufficient; chic, lively, fashionable, and delightful. The cozy, beguiling **Belle Avenue Grill** is also highly recommended; no music. The **EuropaKällaren** in the **Europa**, untested by us, has a sound reputation locally. Among the independents, the best known is **Henriksberg**, 10 minutes from the center. It reopened with completely new fittings; glorious view of the harbor and busy cargo cranes; recent expansion onto the veranda; dancing downstairs in the nautical Kajutan Room in season; friendly, fast, and deft service. The showpiece platters, pretty side dishes, and desserts are among the most imaginative we've seen anywhere, with flowers cunningly blended; try the lovely, scrumptious figs with ice cream, whipped cream, Grand Marnier, and a great big tulip to cap them! Our chief objection is the tariffs, which, in our opinion, are plainly rapacious. The **White Corner**, a 2-minute walk from the Rubinen, is much less costly. For hardy, unfancy fare, we think it is also much better. Ground-level snack center, bar, and popular-price restaurant; ruggedly handsome downstairs Grill, with steaks the feature; crackling rôtisserie and hearth at one end; comfortable armchairs and booths; blue- and gray-checked table-cloths; pewter place plates; illumination by candles; excellent service by waiters who present the meat choices on plaques. We romped through the house specialty, a superbly aged T-bone accompanied by a baked potato and salad, while our dinner partner chomped happily on a tender sirloin; both were agreeable to the taste and appetizing to the eye. Highly recommended—especially downstairs. The **Masthugget** is another good buy. Self-service and table attention; modernistic décor; decent tabs. A treasure island for budgeteers in this Land of the Disappearing Kronor. The **Opalen**'s restaurant-nightclub swings with Junior Executive Suiteniks and nice lone ladies hoping for action. Our meal was grim, but the animated atmosphere makes up for almost any kitchen sins. Okay—if you're just learning to handle a Gillette, and if you've just grabbed a snack somewhere else. The **Valand** is comprised of a series of rooms that includes the main dining salon, the Little London, a congenial bar, the Club Alexander, and a small upstairs Casino (where you can risk your all in its penny-ante play). **Restaurant Sofus** has scuttled its warm-weather nightclub after midnight; it's okay for earlybirds.

In summer only (May to mid-Sept.), there are 2 popular choices. The **Liseberg**, in Liseberg Amusement Park, is lively; good food and band, top artistic attractions; medium tariffs. **Långedrag**, in the Yacht Harbor 15 minutes by taxi, offers a glorious view of the Göteborg Inlet and its heavy ship traffic; spacious in size; production-belt vittles and reasonable prices; worth trying if the day is sunny.

Malmö's best bet is the **Kockska Krogen**, the vaulted cellar of Jörgen Kock's palace. (He was the city's powerful mayor in the fifteenth century, when the port was Danish.) The Savoy interests have restored it at a cost of $770,000. As an example of authentic period architecture, we'd call it an *absolute sightseeing must;* it's a happy haven for gastronomy as well. One main sanctum with several radiating brick-arched rooms; wonderful cheese bar at the entrance for munching with beer or wine while you wait for your table; shipment-home service for anything on the 28-item dairy tempter; benches with stuffed coffee bags for cushions; interior units with comfortable banquettes; leather-backed armchairs with brass studs; wooden place platters and bread plates; candles in wrought-iron bases; rich brown carpet to warm away the basement chill. The menu is in Swedish, but a maître in chef's costume helps with the translations; food bills—presented in a music box—are very reasonable for the quality. A fabulous tourist attraction that rings true, without the slightest spoilage by gimmicks. Highest recommendation for this city. Another worthwhile eye-pleaser, providing a panoramic view of the town and of Copenhagen (across the sparkling strait), is the penthouse **Kronprinsen**, a Top-of-the-Mark spellbinder crowning a residential structure. This is South Sweden's space platform. It contains a garage, a 2nd-floor nightclub, and enough ground-level shops to keep your wife busy until you're hungry again. Heavy food odors; cuisine not special; clientele drawn from every quarter; go for the vista and the relaxing ambiance, not for the cookery. **Residens Schweizeri** (near the Savoy) is a happy choice for lunch and pastry; Proprietor Marcel Laurent has created a highly popular Swiss House here. Among the hotels, it's the **Savoy**, the **Kramer**, the **St. Jörgen**, and the **Scandinavia**, in that order. In nearby *Skanör* a few minutes from Falsterbo, **Gästgifvaregard** offers the perfect village diversion for city-tired travelers. Cozy old house converted into a restaurant in 1910; 3 rooms inside a flag-lined building; geese by the gaggle greet the guests; white-hatted chef doing wonders with each and every goose. Try this and the smoked eel (the latter cut with sheep shears and presented on a special server with scrambled eggs and rye crisp). Another treat is a delicious bitters called Malört, extracted from a local plant. Same Lendrop administration that sails the Malmö Savoy; lovely for a fair-weather excursion.

§TIP: If meals are served in both the bar and the dining room of any establishment, choose the bar. It's usually far cheaper.

NIGHTCLUBS

In '66 all nightclubs, as such, were banned. The legislative Do-Gooders limited late-evening operations to selected establishments which offered alcoholic beverages and dancing. These were permitted to operate 6 nights per week. The curfew was set at 2 A.M.; drink service stopped ½-hour earlier. Later the Stockholm (or is it "Stockhold"?) City Council held another Bluenose conclave, and the massive liberalizations are these: On special application, licensed restaurants may stay open until the wicked hour of 3 A.M.; alcohol must cease to flow at 2:30 A.M. And that's that!

The **Bolaget** is bowling 'em over in the capital aisles these nights. It was recommended to us by our dear friend, the ever-keen, highly perceptive Gordon McLendon, who has tipped us (and you) off on a number of superb entries in this guidebook. This versatile swinger's haven spins from 7 P.M. to 3 A.M. every day of the week; the midnight show spotlights local and international artists; tinklings in the Pianobar ripple from 8 P.M. till closing; dancing trips in from 10 P.M. to 2 A.M. While the normal restaurant dinner chomps standard bites out of your wallet, the segment called The Wreck provides simple nutrients for becalming tariffs. Its go-getting Bonifaces are Gun and Sten Holmquist, a double-barreled Sten-Gun combination of blond pulchritude, intelligence, hospitality, and youthful vigor. With that magical McLendon backing, we give this one enthusiastic huzzahs of praise. We wish it continuing success.

The new **Hamburger Börs** seems to be a hot-dawg contender, presenting such headline relish as Sammy Davis, Jr., and other top bananas of show biz. **Berns** gets its share of big spenders too. This house still pours out first-class gin-mill talent. Mini-Lido type atmosphere; nominal cover charge; food improving. Some semblance of movement might be found in the **Strand Hotel** ("entertainment" in quotes) and perhaps at the previously mentioned **New Bacchi**. **Club Opera** is popular for dancing. **Adam & Mari**, operative only a few days each week, is fair for dinner dancing, but the Royal in the **Grand Hotel** is more consistent. **Golden Days** throbs with British piano and banjo pickin's on the merry mock-stern of a ship. **Konstnärshuset** and **Alexandra's** (a discoperation) plus a molting covey of pipits, warble for a woeful wayworn welter of night hunters. **Baldakinen, Baldakinens Pelarsal, Cirkeln**, and **Hasselbacken** also draw an array of thwarted insomniacs. Among the discothèques which have popped up recently, the **Top Club** in the Eden Hotel is fair for young fry; **Golden Circle** rings in with pop music; **Engelen**, a converted pharmacy, stirs out beer only with a dash of jazz for members—but you probably can wiggle in. **Bobbadilla**, an Old Town cellar haunt for youngsters, was wheeling gaily on our latest spin of the platters (it closed and then reopened), followed by the **Manzanilla**. The **Gazell** isn't worth the leap. The rebuilt **Berzeliiterrassen** has widened its scope. Now it offers invitations to the dance every night except Monday year round; meals and wines added; good orchestra; college-age travelers can usually find partners here. **Stampen** is great fun for Dixieland rebs like us'ns. The ceiling and walls are hung with whimsical junk items: an upside-down Christmas tree, a bib-and-tucker, a baby carriage, and one of the most forlorn sights we've ever seen—a stuffed dog. Only beer is served along with some of the happiest sounds in the North. Top recommendation for the carriage trade to toe-tapping tailgaters. For gents on the prowl, amost any nightery can be a happy hunting ground.

In **Göteborg**, the Mirabelle in the **Park Avenue Hotel** is among the best in the North. Don't miss it. The **Opalen** also swings for the Younger Set. The previously mentioned **Valand** is next in line. Our favorite night-galloping Göteborger tells us that **Krokodil** is now very "in," but we haven't checked it personally as yet. The **Adam & Eve** is not recommended, even to Beelzebub.

Looking for action in *Malmö*? Get thee to Copenhagen is our advice.

You won't feel faint and giddy from the mad revelry of Swedish night life. Isn't this a stunning paradox, in such a socially and sexually liberal society?

TAXIS Taxis are plentiful; most are recent American cars. The minimum rate is fairly low—but the meter goes up like a skyrocket. A trip across Stockholm can cost you $4 or more. "Ledig" means "For Hire." When you can spot this on his flag, he's yours.

As in many other countries, scores of jockeys "don't happen to have change"—trusting you'll let them pocket the difference. Watch this racket.

For Stockholm sightseers, here's soothing news for the budget: For about $5 you can buy a 3-day, unlimited-travel ticket valid on all buses and subways, including the lines to Drottningholm Castle and Lidingö Island.

TRAINS Superior. There's a continuous program to hitch up new "comfort" cars with double-deck domes and posh up-to-date amenities. First-class smoking compartments often come equipped with twin banquettes of 3 seats each, plus a table flanked by 2 sink-in adjustable armchairs—all in the same roomy, handsome, and practical salon area. Other compartments (always including Second class) are conventional but also relaxing and well designed. Many trains feature half-coach snack bars instead of full-fledged dining cars. They're immaculately clean; limited menus in 4 languages; soft drinks, wine, export beer, tea, and coffee are the only beverages; the food attracts the eye but is lackluster to the palate.

The Swedish Railways, known as "SJ" (Statens Järnvägar), operates 95% of the nation's railroads, 22% of its buses, and 5% of its highway freight, plus a network of travel offices. For the visitor who wants to see a lot and whose funds are limited, SJ and its Danish, Norwegian, and Finnish counterparts offer (1) train "circular tours" around Scandinavia (interrupt your journey wherever you wish, and save 10%-25%), (2) a sliding scale of prices which decrease as the distance increases (if you buy all your tickets at once, this arrangement will earn dollars for you), and (3) a 50% discount during summer—regardless of nationality—for anyone older than 65. The Eurailpass sold in the U.S. is accepted in this land. Fares are low; sleepers are very cheap.

AIRLINE See "Scandinavian Airlines System."

DRINKS Package sales today are unrestricted. The Swede is the world's 2nd-thirstiest tippler, lining up at the counter right behind the Yugoslav. You may buy unlimited amounts of whatever you choose at any State liquor store from 9 A.M. to 6 P.M. on weekdays and from 9 A.M. to 1 P.M. on Saturdays, but you may be asked to show some form of identification that bears a mugshot (your passport, parole card, or International Driver's Permit will do). Restaurants keep the corks out of the bottles from noon until closing time.

Scotch, Canadian Club, English gin, French cognac—you'll find a wonderful variety at the official dispensaries—at prices that will provide you with a presip hangover. Levies are frankly lethal.

Aquavit, the national drink, is also called "snaps," "brännvin," and "aqua vitae." But no matter by what name it slides down the gullet, there's enough heat in 1 glass to turn all the radiators in the Empire State Building cherry red. The base is potatoes, grain, or an extraction of *wood* alcohol! It is flavored with berries, seeds, leaves, herbs, flowers, and spices. Drink it well chilled with smörgåsbord (not with the entrée or by itself), gulp the potion in 2 or 3 swallows (don't sip!), and chase it quickly with 5 or 10 gallons of beer. The best brand, to our taste, is Åhus, which is closest to that King of Scandinavian

Good Cheer, Denmark's Aalborg. Swedes prefer others, such as Överste (slightly spiced, slightly sweet) or O.P. (aroma of cumin).

Swedish Punch is a happy beverage. The ingredients are Java arrack and a special rum; float Remy Martin or another good French cognac on top of the glass; you'll find a drink fit for the gods. Expensive but worth it.

Beer comes in the following 4 grades (based on their alcohol content): *Starköl* (4.5%), *Mellanöl* (3.6%), *Pilsner* (2.8%), and *Lättöl* (1.8%). One Swedish wag quips that the first leaves you in no doubt as to whether you are drinking beer and the last in some doubt as to whether you're drinking water. Pripps and Skål are the most popular brands for middle-of-the-road drinkers (not drivers). Now that the government controls the nation's largest brewery, topers fear this heralds the introduction of weaker brews as a move to curb alcoholism throughout Sweden. (Next year the *Mellanöl* variety will be banned with only the weaker brew available in grocery stores; state-controlled outlets, however, will continue to peddle stronger suds to adult buyers.) Teetotallers already are employing the euphemism "people's beer" as a temperance label for the watered-down version.

§TIP: Beware of inferior Swedish gins or aquavits; some of the less reputable brands are distilled from cellulose. It's always wise to insist on Gordon's for your martinis (only a bit more), because 2 or 3 of these innocent little wood-alcohol cocktails—believe me!—will jar you into a state which only a qualified physician or mortician can distinguish from rigor mortis.

SKÖL (or SKÅL)   See under "Denmark." The same applies here, only more so; the formalities are far more rigidly observed.

THINGS TO SEE   In *Stockholm*, **Drottningholm Palace** is particularly impressive. This used to be the favorite royal winter residence of the king, the most beautiful of royal homes, with Gobelin tapestries scattered around like bathroom rugs. The adjoining **Court Theater**, untouched since 1766, is still very much in use; several times per week beginning in May performances "De l'Époque" are featured. See it if you can; 20 minutes by bus, or 50 minutes by frequent steamers.

In **Östermalmstorg**, the public market in the center of the city, you'll find vegetables, flowers, practically every kind of fish from minnows to sperm whales—the works. Quite a deal.

Djurgarden (Deer Park) shouldn't be missed. It's the island home of world-famous Skansen: A magnificent open-air museum with authentic farms, a zoo, a Lapp camp, Nordic antiquities, and great natural beauty. Speaking of pulchritude, a young lovely named "Miss Skansen" will meet you at the information booth (inside at Bollnästorget) in regional costume any day in June, July, or August at 11 A.M., 1 P.M., 3 P.M., or 5 P.M. to give you up-to-the-minute developments on everything from the concerts to the folk dancing to the performances by international artists to the teen-age dance fests to the feeding time of the 4-footed critters. Free, too! It is 7 minutes from the city by Bus No. 47 or No. 67. If possible (and if the weather is benign), plan to have lunch at either Stallmästaregården (a short drive), Djurgårdsbrunns

Wärdshus (behind Skansen), Solliden (in the Park) or Ulriksdals Wärdshus; see "Restaurants" for details.

Social Tours, in-depth study programs in the arts, sciences, business, and social welfare, offer the foreign visitor a rare opportunity to see how the Scandinavian people live. Highlights might include a visit to a family in a suburban housing project, a lakeside children's camp, or an ultramodern home for the aged. Operated between June 1 and August 31; programs range from several days to several weeks; stimulating, educational, and different. Just telephone Stockholm 111142, and the Tourist Sightseeing Organization will set up a swing through 2 apartments (one for retired people), a church, and 2 suburban shopping centers.

Packaged **motorcoach excursions** include the 2 "Grand City" Tours, the nonstop City Tour, an Evening loop, and a day-long trip to Uppsala and Sigtuna. Motorboat outings include the Grand Scenic Tour Under the Bridges, the Royal Canal Tour, the Archipelago Tour, and a waterborne version of the Evening Tour. Prices vary from $2.50 to $8 for the capital sightseeing to around $21 for the all-day Uppsala-Downsala-Sigtuna circuit. Most operate in summer only. Tickets may be purchased at any travel bureau or leading hotel.

A marvel that is a *must* for every visitor, regardless of age, gender, or aesthetic disposition, is the seventeenth-century warship *Wasa,* which was salvaged intact from the 110-foot depths of Stockholm Harbor in '61. Divers with powerful water-jets pumped 6 tunnels beneath her hull, through which several thousand feet of 6-inch cable were threaded to hoist her out of the mud and face up to the surface—one of the most complicated undersea salvage projects ever undertaken. She occupies a site of honor in a provisional building near the Nordic Museum and Skansen. She's in a remarkable state of preservation for her 3½ centuries—mostly due to the cold, cold waters in which she lay.

The **Stockholm Student Reception Service** welcomes foreign undergraduates with dances, movies, lectures, sightseeing tours, picnics, and other events during 2 months of the summer vacations. It also puts out a revised pamphlet listing activities available to foreign students. Check in for your copy at Sweden House (Kungsträdgården Park).

In the **suburbs of Stockholm**, dozens of resorts and maritime beachscapes afford the visitor fascinating glimpses of coastal Sweden. You may charter a fishing boat and crew to poke at your whimsy through Stockholm's archipelago of 25-thousand islands and skerries. Anglers must have fishing licenses (easy to obtain) before they are allowed to wet a line. Green shores, smiling beaches, pastures and groves, sunbaked isles, and foaming bays; a delight.

Should you proceed independently, go by commercial steamer and return by rail or bus. *Saltsjöbaden*, a short ride from the city, is the best known beach; take your bathing suit and plan on luncheon at the local Grand Hotel. If you are young, rugged, and want to get away from the crowds of this popular resort, get off the Saltsjöbaden train at the station nearest *Erstaviksbadet*, a wooded beach with fewer people and wonderful swimming. You used to have to undress behind a tree, a matter that was supremely unimportant to everybody but yourself. Now cabins have been provided for the modest.

Sandhamn, the largest yachting center, has perhaps the best bathing of all; the boat leaves about 10 A.M. and returns about 7 P.M., and the ride takes 3½ hours each way—a long haul but definitely worth it. **Vaxholm** is a pretty trip and excellent for a quiet lunch. Swimmers can take a dip at nearby **Eriksö**.

Away from Stockholm, there are dozens of organized expeditions that range far afield. The 7-day Lapland Tour mushes from June 19 to August 7. Also available is the 6-day junket to Copenhagen and Oslo from Stockholm's home plate; on this there's a special reduction for Eurailpass holders. Reso sponsors any number of treks from 2 to 21 days to fit almost any wanderer's whims or budget, including visions of Scandinavian coastal areas, Norwegian fjords and mountains, lake districts, the Isle of Gotland, Western Scandinavia, capital cities, and many other tempters. Your travel agent has details on all of these—and more.

If these don't appeal to you, a quick tour of **Östergötland** might. About 3 hours by train from Stockholm, on the main line to Copenhagen, it's Sweden in a capsule, with rolling fields, sweeping forests, lovely lakes, and miniature mountains. High point to most visitors here is the excursion on the Göta, or Kinda, canal—charming at first but quite dull after the novelty has worn off. You can also play golf, sail on the lakes, fish for salmon or char, go to horse races or county fairs, or do practically anything you like. This is rural living, but it is usually busy and always urbane.

Farther down in **Skåne** Sweden's southernmost province, the late Dag Hammarskjöld's farm near Löderup is open to visitors during summer months. The lovely white farmhouse, with its enclosed cobbled courtyard, reflects this great mediator's wide cultural interests and world travels. All of his personal possessions are here. It is a fascinating stop—one well worth a detour.

Sharing the same bucolic enticements, but much more familiar to Americans, is **Dalarna** province. This round requires at least 2 days, and preferably 4. Here, too, there's not much excitement, but you'll get a glimpse of a way of life different from anything else in Scandinavia. Go first to **Rättvik** (4 to 5 hours from Stockholm)—and then proceed, if you like, to the entrancing little village of **Tällberg**, beloved of so many of Sweden's overseas guests. Lodgings in this Lake Siljan District (Tällberg, Rättvik, Leksand, and Mora) have been previously listed and rated in the "Hotels" section; most are not elegant, but comfort is there.

From Rättvik it is 3 hours by car or hotel bus to the strikingly different terrain around **Sälen**. Here are the high mountains and deep valleys of the West. The previously mentioned Sälens Högfjällshotellet, the best mountain-resort hotel in the nation, is open to the public only in winter. Skiing conditions are nearly perfect. You'll find good food, magnificent scenery, bus excursions to Norway, and every convenience to which you are accustomed. Of the 110 rooms, 74 have private bath—a high percentage for rural Sweden. An alternative is Hotel Högfjället at **Storlien**, situated on an Alpine plateau near the Norwegian border. Its 246 rooms and 41 baths make it Scandinavia's

largest resort hostelry; tiny accommodations; modern décor; unusually happy
for children.

Want a full day's excursion to keep the tykes out of mischief? Drive east
to **Lake Storsjön** and search for the Swedish brother of the Loch Ness
Monster, which was sighted again recently by 4 workmen. King Oscar I long
ago commissioned an official hunting party, and his ancient beast-snaring
equipment can be seen in the Östersund City Museum. Accounts vary about
this uncaught but oft-seen fellow. Some say he's black, others say he's brown.
Some measure his length at 15 feet, some swear he's not an inch under 70 feet.
But they ALL agree on one observation: He wears a *very* sinister smile.

Or how about a cruise? Steamers depart from Stockholm bound for the
semi-autonomous **Åland Islands**, halfway to Finland. The 8-hour round
trip costs under $10 and you can fill up on tax-free stores aboard, sights galore,
and a pretty fair smörgåsbord on some of the ferries. Inquire locally for
details.

The world-famous glass center of **Orrefors**, just off the main east-coast
highway between Denmark and Stockholm (220 miles north of Hälsingborg),
is an especially interesting little detour for motorists. Here you may watch
master glassblowers turn out exquisite products. Alternate choices might be
at Kosta, Boda, or Strömbergshyttan in the same district.

Skokloster, which dominates a large lake about ¾ths of the way toward
Uppsala from Stockholm, is one of the most magnificent palaces in the
hemisphere. It was built in the mid-seventeenth century for Field Marshal
Carl Gustaf Wrangel—and the gorgeous interiors bear witness to the splendor
of Sweden's Golden Age as a major power. If you're wheeling toward the
University City, this one is more than worth the short turnoff to any rover
who appreciates its special type of beauty and magnificence.

No tourist should miss **Visby**. This insular capital, the only walled town
in northern Europe, is one of the most worthy sights in Scandinavia. You'll
find Viking remains such as you have never seen before; occasionally you'll
see traces of Minoan, Greek, and Roman cultures. The wall is about 2 miles
in circumference; there are 100 churches which stood before Shakespeare
donned his first pair of long trousers. Now Visby is a vacation center. Broad
beaches, good bicycling, good tennis, gorgeous scenery; impressive musical
drama, *Petrus de Dacia,* presented during July and August in the medieval
cathedral ruin of St. Nicholas. The Snäckgärdsbaden and the Stadshotellet,
its leading hostelries, have been mentioned in the "Hotels" section. One night
from Stockholm by boat, or about 50 minutes by SAS (5 flights daily from
June through Aug.; more on the weekends).

TIPPING   Most restaurants automatically add 13% to the bills. In hotels,
a 15% service charge appears when it has not already been included in the
room rate (virtually all the prestige houses now bury it in your bill). Give
hatcheck girls 1 krona and taxi drivers 10% of the fare. The hall porter in the
hotel gets a separate bite on top of your automatic service charge; it's not
customary locally to tip him when you check out unless he has given special
service to you. Railway porters (identified by *Stadsbud* on their caps) in
Stockholm's Central Station charge about 60¢ to tote 1 or 2 bags between the
train and the taxi stand; each additional piece is around 30¢.

THINGS TO BUY   Glass, ceramics, silver, handicrafts, cutlery, modern furniture, boutique items, and trick matches.

The merchandise is a knockout; so are some (not all) of the prices. Never bargain. Merchants have bigger bank accounts than you have, and they couldn't care less if you "leave it lay." Jensen silver and Royal Copenhagen porcelain are heavily represented, and they sell for less in Denmark.

In **Stockholm**, the outstanding specialist for Orrefors, Kosta, and other Swedish glass is named exactly that—**Svenskt Glas** (Birger Jarlsgatan 8). It is a small, exquisite, Tiffany-style establishment which has supplied the Royal Families of Sweden, Denmark, and the United Kingdom for more than 40 years—as well as regiments of foreign guests such as you and us. The dazzling advantage here for Yankee shoppers is that with ALL costs included— purchase price, shipping, insurance, and U.S. Customs duties—*you'll still pay about half the American retail price for precisely, identically the same articles.* This is also why so many U.S. and Canadian executives are ordering so heavily here or in their equally chic branch in **Lucerne** (see "Switzerland") for their *business* gifts. What fantastic bargains!! Since the factories nudge up the tariffs all too frequently, the figures quoted below might not be to the penny—but the differences would be too slight to vex you. The most popular category among our overseas pilgrims is their tableware: 4 types of glasses, 12 of each shape, from $180 to $1800 complete. Engraved art crystals run from $16 up. Colored, multilayered, one-of-a-kind pieces start at $40, and they're gorgeous. Highball, Old Fashioned, Martini, and other barware can be had from $25 per dozen up. Again this year, in collaboration with the World Wildlife Fund, Svenskt Glas is producing a limited line of animal sculptures of endangered species—and a substantial portion of each purchase price is being contributed to the W.W.F. (how typical of this fine, forward-looking house!). And how beautifully they will monogram or crest your crystal! Export packing by carefully trained specialists; Mail Order Dept. smoothly operated by Ingemar Nilson (ideal for gifts); 15% discount on all foreign shipments. Excellent English spoken by the entire staff; ask for the gentlemanly, kindly Owner-Manager, Anders Borg, who speaks excellent English and who is usually on the floor—or for Miss Martensson, if Mr. Borg happens to be taking a breather. Here is *the* target for discerning shophounds!

Ceramics and china? **Gustavsbergs Utställning** (Birger Jarlsgatan 2) is a charmer, with grace, gaiety, and gladness in its gorgeous table and decorative products. See cordial Mrs. Marie-Louise Eggers, the Showroom Manager.

Swedish silver and gold in all price ranges? Our respect for—and fondness for!—**Kurt Decker AB** at Biblioteksgatan 12 flame brighter on our every return to this Garden of Wantables. A silver or gold charm from its b-i-g assortment, from $1 or $5? A setting of its unique flatware or an impressive coffee service, both of which are enjoying such tremendous popularity in North America today? A piece from the largest Georgian silver collection in the nation, at $20 to $12,000? A half-dozen gifts of its best-selling silver wine-bottle drip stoppers, at only $5.50 each? Plate, sterling, yellow or white gold, platinum, rare gems—such friendliness glows here that you'll be welcomed with exactly the same cordiality if you browse or if you splurge. P-l-e-a-s-e see one unique new creation: The exciting new rock-crystal "headlight" ring ($90). In '61, genial Director Decker, an English and German diplomate in gemology, sold his ⅓rd interest in Sweden's largest jewelry chain (42 outlets) to go on his own here; as you'll see, it's his joy, his fun, and his occupational passion. Try to chat personally with him or with Mr. Apfel. Wonderful!

Department stores? **NK**, which we recommended unreservedly for 20 years as one of the world's greatest department stores, continues to worry and puzzle us. All we *do* know is that, after our latest painstaking inspection, we were disappointed by what we saw. Obviously, it is still the leader in Sweden, despite our assessment that it isn't what it used to be. **PUB**, a cooperative, is lower-level and less interesting; **Åhléns** (Klarabergsgatan/Drottninggatan), somewhat less central, is one of the biggest and very modern; **MEA** has almost no appeal for many outlanders, including us.

Swedish handicrafts? **Svensk Hemslöjd** (Sveavägen 44) is the marketing center for the handwrought creations of Sweden's best artisans. The shy sweetness of Directress von Münchow will charm you. A fairyland. **Nordkalottshopen** (Birger Jarlsgatan 35) stocks souvenirs from Lapland; **Panduro Hobby** (Kungsgatan 32) offers the raw materials from which you can create your own Scandinavian arts and crafts.

Shopping Center? **Hötorgscity** ("Haymarket") has been launched near the Concert Hall. Architecture of tomorrow; central patio for refreshments; some (not all) top merchants represented here.

Evening or Sunday buying? The **Hötorget Station** (subway) and **Central Station** (basement) feature a cluster of merchandisers open until 10 P.M. daily, plus Sunday afternoon and evening.

Shopping hours: 9:30 A.M. to 6 P.M. on weekdays except Saturday; on Saturday, 9 A.M. to 2 P.M. (most big stores). Many merchants remain open until 7 P.M. on Monday and Friday. There's no noontime closing.

§TIPS: Be careful about (1) delivery *within Sweden* of gold or silver articles, chocolate, carpets, liquor, or furs (arrange for airport, ship, or foreign delivery to save the 15% Value Added Tax—and *keep your sales slip to show at departure,* or you might not get your stuff!), (2) perfumes, cigarettes, and similar luxury imports (heavy duties make them prohibitively expensive). The mandatory rule requiring Export Licenses for purchases over $500 has been lifted for tourists.

Dedicated shophounds? Space is too tight here for further listings in Stockholm, Malmö, and Göteborg—so please consult this year's totally updated edition of *Fielding's Shopping Guide to Europe* for data on more cities, more stores, more details, and more lore.

THINGS NOT TO BUY　　Swedish quality is renowned. In integrity of merchandise, you won't get stung. Price is the major consideration.

LOCAL RACKETS　　"Racket" is too harsh a word for this accepted (but fast vanishing) local custom—but it *is* disturbing to poor yokels like us who get caught by it. A very few hotels (*not* including Stockholm's Grand, Strand, Carlton, and other large ones) still might quote you a bed charge which doesn't include other taken-for-granted necessities—and bang goes your budget! Therefore, always worm the *total* rate out of the hotelier before you check in, even if it pains his soul to tell you. Fortunately, this system is increasingly rare.

Aside from this trifle, you'll leave with strong admiration for Swedish ethics. With amazingly few exceptions, Swedes are an honest, reliable, decent people.

Switzerland

If a group of scientists were given 50-trillion dollars, atomic power, and instructions to carve from the earth's surface a tourists' paradise, they'd probably just point to Switzerland, shrug their shoulders, and say, "Why build another?"

Switzerland has everything. It's got mountains, lakes, snow, the sort of thing you've been taught to expect, of course—but it's also got electric trains, castles, old-age pensions, fondue, wild ibex, and, with few exceptions, one of the most honorable collection of human beings on the globe.

This country, almost twice the size of Massachusetts, has often been called "a nation of hotelkeepers"; if said without scorn, there's truth in it. The tourist industry is a key business which occupies more than 190-thousand citizens. Over 20-million foreign visitors are registered in hotels each year. Yet Swiss travelers are so peripatetic that foreign nations retrieve more than half of the total income spent in Switzerland by all of us outlanders!

In religious division, there are 48% Reformed Protestants, 49% Roman Catholics, and 3% in other denominations—with freedom of worship for all sects. Military training is compulsory for all males at the age of 20; paradoxically, you'll probably see more and better soldiers here and in Sweden than in most other tourist lands in Europe. If the alarm is sounded anywhere up in them thar Alps, more than 600-thousand troops can be mobilized within a mere 48 hours. As mod-minded Minutemen, the alert Swiss stock their guns and field gear in their own homes. Unemployment is almost nil. Quite a few of the residents still are from abroad. The recent referendum to expel ⅓rd of the foreigners living in the nation was rejected by the cautious electorate —but only narrowly.

Amazing people: To the eye, there are enormous regional differences, but at the core there is a stubborn and admirable sameness. The Italian Swiss in the South (Lugano, Locarno) seem the softest, gayest, and merriest; the

French Swiss in the West (Geneva, Lausanne) seem the liveliest, most peripatetic, and most volatile; the Alamannic Swiss in the East (Zürich, Berne, Basle, Lucerne, St. Gall) seem the most wooden and humorless in social relationships. Yet under the surface they all share one characteristic that dominates everything: they are *Swiss*, down to their toenails.

CITIES *Zürich* is the largest; it's about the size of Phoenix; commerce, industry, and culture are centered here. You'll find the leading banks and insurance companies; biggest shops, factories, markets; excellent hotels, restaurants, and amusements; unlike the outlying towns, the distinct hustle and bustle of a metropolis. From the tops of the encircling hills, the city is a stunning sight: Villas and gardens stretch down to the silvery inland sea, with snowcapped mountains always in the background. The people of this metropolis are supposed to be the greatest boasters in the country—and why not, when 1 out of 275 residents is a millionaire (so who sneezes at millionaires in Swiss francs)? Actually, they prefer to be called the "superrich." Make Zürich and Geneva your excursion centers, for everything worth seeing in the nation can be covered from these 2 bases. If you can, plan to be in Zürich in June; the month-long Festival here is one of the most famous on the Continent.

Basle, a cultured dowager who is so cosmopolitan that she shares her roots with both France and Germany, is also a major financial center. The confluence of these social and economic wellsprings provides the city with a unique richness that discriminating voyagers appreciate. The Kunstmuseum, as one outstanding example, offers such variety, not to mention quality, that it alone warrants a visit to this center; its many antiquities, its Holbein collection plus 21 other museums, its university (which was in operation before Columbus weighed anchor), its zoo, its extraordinary chemical plants, and its skyline on the Rhine are additional lures for adventurers. The Carnival in February or the Swiss Industries Fair in April are said to be interesting; we've not yet seen either.

Berne, the capital, is one of the few undestroyed medieval cities of Europe, and it's charming. The Aare River divides it twice, in a horseshoe, and the turreted buildings on its banks look like an illustration from *Grimm's Fairy Tales*. The world's oldest and largest horological puppet show every hour in its historic Clock Tower; famous fifteenth-century Bear Pits, housing the city's traditional mascots; excellent hotels, fine little shops, covered sidewalks, winding streets (many of them now experiencing an experimental traffic ban), an almost rural atmosphere; 18-hole golf course 11 miles out, with clubhouse, restaurant, and pool. In conformity with its medium geographical position, the people are medium humorless and medium austere.

Geneva is beautiful—and full of tourists. The lake is fantastically blue (except for the sparkling white plume of the world's tallest fountain—the Jet d'Eau). The atmosphere is French, the buildings are handsome, the gardens are bursting with color, and the streets are a blaze of Ferrari-red, Porsche-silver, DB-green and other hues of the international Sporting Set. If you want gaiety, action, and familiar faces, it's a fine place as a base for western operations.

Lausanne is another popular center for holidays in French Switzerland.

On the south slopes of hills which gradually fall away to Lake Geneva, it is sheltered. The climate is unusually beguiling, with a record of 1912 hours of sunshine per year. Its university and schools are world-famous. It offers good sports, entertainment, and food, along with the world's shortest subway, the new and queer Musée de l'Art Brut, a generally well-ordered aura, and the homes of many international celebrities.

Lucerne, with the deserved slogan of *"Living* Lucerne," has the greatest influx of Americans of any Swiss city, town, or hamlet. Its traditional star attractions are the Lion Monument, the year-round Glacier Gardens with its museum, the covered bridge, and the famous August-September International Music Festival. Its 2 pet mountains are supplemented by a scenic 18-hole golf course, a fascinating Transport Museum (historic and/or modern locomotives, cars, airplanes, plus a steamer; a star-bright planetarium has twinkled on the scene and there's a restaurant) and a suspension cable-car system to the top of Mt. Pilatus. In town, the sparklingly refreshed Kursaal-Casino spins for penny-ante gamesters (boule only), dancers, and diners. The Casino Chalet stirs in a dash of local flavor with fondue, local color with flag-throwers, and local sounds with yodelers. As in Florence, tourism makes 99% of its wheels go around; into this center of 70-thousand inhabitants, from 10- to 30-thousand foreigners pour *daily* off the boats, trains, and cars; there are now at least 80 hotels with 5500 beds. If you're a first-tripper, naturally you won't want to miss the landmark. But hit it in the spring or fall, if you can —because in peak season it's so jammed with sightseers that its atmosphere, normally so alluring, becomes tinny, mechanical, and production-belt in feeling.

St. Moritz, roughly 6000 feet high, is the most celebrated winter resort —and a delightful summer resort, too. It is a cluster of 4 small communities strung along a mountain valley like glistening pearls on a green or white string; the Village, the Spa, St. Moritz-Suvretta, and St. Moritz-Champfèr are its components. Winter is very elegant and sophisticated, while summer is more sedate (and ideal for children). Its closest competitor is Gstaad, where the fashionable people are generally confined to Palace Hotel clients or to the relatively small private-chalet group. Downtown, this minority is vastly outnumbered by the medium or budget economic groups. But not so in St. Moritz, which is still decidedly The Queen, despite its accelerating influx of packaged tours and clubmanship festivities. Train, bus, and air-taxi connections with most principal cities; nearly 60 hotels and pensions, from superplush to a-song-and-a-few-francs a day; scores of restaurants, from chichi, black-tie establishments to holes-in-the-wall; probably the most fabulous winter sports facilities of the world, from the Cresta toboggan run (Gunter Sachs is considering freezing up another one) to the Olympic bobsled run to Olympic ski jumps to ice rinks to almost 3-score ski routes to curling at the Kulm and the Carlton; helicopter service for skiers or sightseers, plus ski-plane airport on a glacier, plus an aerial cableway extension to 11-thousand feet which combine to hustle a capacity of 19-thousand snow-bunnies up the slopes every hour; championship regattas for summer sailors; tennis; dancing, fashion shows, bridge tournaments, lectures, concerts, horse races on frozen lake surfaces, ice parades, "skeleton" races, every imaginable type of social activity; handsome terrain, not as breathtaking as Zermatt or even Arosa, but more pruned and polished; like Biarritz and Cannes, one of the most sophisticated and lively vacation focal points on the European continent. Despite some low-priced accommodations, in general it is extremely expensive—but worth every penny if you can afford it.

Arosa, 68 miles to the north, is a spellbinder for looks, but not a lass with quite the same patrician panache as St. Moritz. Her surrounding hills are peopled by funloving Swiss and by an increasing flood of newly prosperous German visitors. Numerous woodland trails, ski slopes, ski lifts, aerial cableway, and chair hoists; a cross-country ski school at Maran; glorious 2-hour excursion up to 7600 feet over the famous Arlenwald Circle by horse-drawn sleigh; summer 9-hole golf course, horseback riding, tennis, fishing, rowing, Alpine bathing "beach"; improving hotels, where you'll also take most of your meals.

Interlaken is the most fun if you hanker for nostalgia. The real-life clock seems to have stopped back when this century was in diapers. Speaking of timepieces, it has a noteworthy Flower Clock; the legendary view of the Jungfrau from the hotels lining the Höheweg, the annual Mozart Festival, and medieval Unterseen are other reasons to be here. Hop the funicular up the Harder Kulm, go to the Ibex Preserve, and take the circle trip to the Jungfraujoch (Lauterbrunnen and Kleine Scheidegg, returning via Grindelwald) —marvelous! As one gateway to the hauntingly beautiful Bernese Oberland, pause only briefly here while reserving most of your time for the majesty of the hills. The drive from Berne to Grindelwald and Lucerne via Interlaken threads along the shores of 5 lakes and through innumerable Alpine vistas. The environs are what count, not the town. Major efforts, such as the addition of a community swimming pool, the teeing up of a golf course, and the inauguration of open-air plays in summer, are being made to change this Victorian dowager's spots and to promote her as a convention center—an operation involving the same basic problems, it seems to us, as transforming a Boy Scout camp into an Alpine Las Vegas.

Grindelwald, 13 miles up the valley from Interlaken, is a tiny toenail on the foothills of the magnificent Bernese Oberland. Europe's longest chair lift will set you atop the point called First for a fantastic First-hand view of the spires above and the Lilliput below. A rack-railway scrambles up the 2-mile-high Jungfraujoch to the loftiest station in the Alps. Flanking this is the infamous "North Wall," that formidable barrier of stone and ice that has taken the lives of so many climbers. The Eiger and Jungfrau are next door. Three transportation hookups now link the most important round-the-valley slopes into a skier's dream-come-true. The usual accouterments are thoughtfully provided by The Lord and His angels for hiking, skiing, fishing (the last in the glacially formed Lütschinen River); man-made facilities for heated-pool swimming, tennis, and sleigh-riding; 35 hotels or pensions. Her granite-bound people often seem as closed and forbidding as a snow-sealed crevasse —extremely reserved, ingrown, and of a suspicious nature. Once they know someone, they are warm and cordial. But at first sight they impress many travelers as among the least outgoing, least personally attractive regional groups in the nation.

Locarno, the lowest city in Switzerland (with only a 600-foot elevation), is an ideal stop for the traveler to or from Italy. It has a lovely setting on the shores of Lake Maggiore; the Ticinese here are among the most warmhearted and hospitable people in Europe. Reasonably good accommodations and fine restaurants; one of the scariest (absolutely safe!) cable-car ascents in the Alps; several swimming pools down by the Lido plus one covered dippery; plenty of good shops; International Film Festival in August; friendly atmosphere.

Lugano, down the line a bit, is also on the lakeside, backstopped by the mountains. It has been taking giant strides recently to improve its hospitality facilities. The bustling modern Congress Center herds conventioneers from all over the world. One of its biggest drawing cards is the gambling casino and cut-price shopping area of Campione d'Italia ("Sample of Italy"), almost directly across the lake by frequent ferry service—an isolated chunk of Italian territory, 1.8 square miles in area. The steamer excursion to Gandria is mobbed in summer. About 160 hotels or pensions, almost all of them on the jump; funiculars, chair lifts, and cable cars galore. One thing which shouldn't be missed is the fabulous Thyssen collection of Goya, El Greco, Holbein, Dutch masters, and Italian Renaissance artists which is housed in a private museum adjoining this family's villa; unfortunately, it is open to the public for only a few hours on weekends and holidays—but catch it if you can. A waterside hub that's becoming increasingly popular with Americans; it's best seen around the Easter holiday period, in our opinion.

In *Gstaad*, the international set does most of its dining, dancing, drinking, gossiping, and wife-swapping in the merry surroundings of the famed Palace Hotel—but it retreats to privately owned or rented chalets for its beauty sleep, indoor acrobatics, and repairs. Beautiful setting in an open valley which absorbs more hours of sunlight than many of its competitors; slick-rustic atmosphere with everything from Karl Brunner ski pants to bargain-basement chinos and rummage-sale caps on its crowded main artery; golf course, riding academy, and 50 mountain lifts; helicopter service to the higher grounds; annual Yehudi Menuhin Festival; if you stay within its moneyed precincts, allegro, expensive, and chichi. Seasons: mid-December to March, and mid-June to mid-October.

Leysin is just the opposite—a fast-developing winter sports mecca for budgeteers that is 13 miles by road or 4 by rail from the lake-level junction of Aigle. Admirable location on the same type of sun-catching slopes, with a glorious panorama below; téléferic to the tip of the Oldenhorn; a score of simple, not very attractive hotels; restaurants equally plainly adorned for clients with consumptive pocketbooks; heavy patronage by economy-minded Swiss and English *en famille;* 50 sky-car "gondolas."

Montreux, in grandma's day a Main Station on the Grand Tour and later an unwitting victim of overpopularity by the Follow-the-Leader Set, is bouncing back through her forward-looking and lively luring of the big-fish traveler. With the opening of the conference and exhibition center, conventions inevitably headquarter here in winter, fall, and early spring. The Casino includes a stunning array of restaurants, night spots, a movie house, and a recording studio. You'll find dancing, gambling and other gambols at the Pavillon, opposite the Palace Hotel. You should also take in the dramatically medieval Castle of Chillon, the lakeside promenades and roads, the heated pool, the International Television Symposium (late May), the Jazz Festival (mid-June), and the annual "September Musical." The Great St. Bernard Tunnel (coupling Germany's autobahn and Italy's Autostrada) continues to make it a mob scene in high season, but during the less frenetic months, it is much more pleasant than it used to be.

Villars, near Montreux, is just off the main artery to Italy. It is not to be confused with the smaller Villars-sous-Mont, near Bulle. You'll find plenty to do in both seasons. During the summer, this mile-high vale offers golf, minigolf, tennis, swimming (one pool with salt water, no less!), horseback riding, bowling, and curling or skating on artificial rinks. Winter pastimes including skiing over 25 miles of runs made accessible by 12 miles of mechanical aids, an ice center, hockey, sleigh-riding, and the other usual snowtime pursuits. French tourists (and their language) predominate, followed by Belgians, and a handful of British twice a year—with just a few Americans so far. Impressive Sports Center where you can order a snack or a pair of skates or a bowling ball or a slot to park your car; prices within the complex are very reasonable. All categories of hotels for all categories of wallets.

Crans-Montana is experiencing a boom. From a resident population of around 3500 in the sleepy Off Season, the crescent of hills which has lengthened on both ends of town can accommodate some 25-thousand sun-worshippers or snow-bunnies—many of them luscious weekday widows whose husbands join them for weekend frolics. If you don't mind alpine traffic jams, Crans, with its environs, can be a jovial swinger for a highland fling. This recently "discovered" Valais perch, 5000 feet above sea level in a glittering chalice, deserves a ranking a few rungs below St. Moritz and Gstaad. Virtually every major resort amenity is available: a championship golf course, heated swimming pools, horses, a casino, a theater, helicopter service, curling, and enough ski lifts (32 on our latest count, capable of hauling up 16-thousand people an hour) and runs to befuddle an athletic centipede. Costs run high, now that the spark of fashion has been kindled. *Anzère*, nearby, is a newly developing chick that may represent a challenge in a few seasons.

Zermatt ? Here, a full mile above sea level and 2 miles below the tips of towering Monte Rosa, you will find one of the most breathtaking creations of Providence. For snow-buffs, it is Heaven on Skis: 18 slopes ranging up to more than 6½ miles, with an altitude differential of over 5700 feet; 30 lifts totaling nearly 30 miles in length in 6 varieties of transport; almost 75 miles of officially maintained ski courses, plus oodles of deep-powder zones for off-trail adventurers; toboggan runs; skating and curling facilities; seasonal trails to the rooftop of the world; a Hollywood director's Elysium of photographic possibilities (don't forget your ultraviolet or skylight filter, Cecil). Narrow-gauge trains pull from Visp to Zermatt in 65 minutes with 14 hauls a day each way. An auto route from Visp stops just outside the village (maintaining the traditional no-motor-driven-vehicle policy within town limits; expansive parking facilities are now at Täsch, 4 miles below Zermatt). The Vergers have wound up a fine modern chopper as an aid to mountain rescue and as a lure to well-heeled go-it-alone skiers. (Since local medical facilities are limited, we'd highly recommend chartering it should a serious injury occur; it's well worth the outlay as an airborne ambulance.) To cope with the explosion in tourism, new hotels, pensions, and shelters of every description are popping up as fast as ants at a picnic. Its holidaymakers are now derived from the broader base of the American ski club and European vacation populace, with fewer socialites and more youthful informality. Summer is a lovely time to come, too, because it turns into an arcadian upland garden of wildflowers, rippling streams, and clear blue light. Here at the top of the world is The Great Architect at His most majestic.

Winterthur? The skillful and witty scrivener, John Justin Smith, writing in the prestigious *San Francisco Chronicle,* recently chided us for omitting this art and cultural center from our text. By George, he's right! Though we've often passed through the charming ancient town, we've somehow never lingered here. Our keen-eyed journalistic colleague commends museums, castles, exhibits—treasures galore which we must get by to see—and will very soon.

Vevey, **Bürgenstock**, **Neuchâtel**, **Lenzerheide-Valbella**, **Klosters** (with electrically heated lake water for bathers), **Pontresina**, **Saas Fee, Davos-Platz**—the list of pleasant stopoffs is almost endless. Clean hotels (and good relaxing) in all. The Swiss National Tourist Office has scads of fine folders and brochures on any region or almost any single spot you might select.

MONEY AND PRICES   The Swiss franc is the most stable currency in Europe. This year, what with inflation's spiral, your U.S. greenbacks will look considerably paler than they did a while ago. In rough terms, you can count on getting about 2.5 swiss francs for every dollar. A stamping of cupronickel 2-franc, 1-franc and 50-centime pieces is now circulating, while the older, intrinsically more valuable coinage is being withdrawn.

Compared to the rest of the Continent, Switzerland is pretty steep for the American traveler. Its consumer price index recently vaulted up by 8%, the biggest peacetime jump on record. Most imports and many living essentials are more costly than in the United States. Nevertheless, the values are unquestionably there, either in quantity (*e.g.,* food) or in quality (*e.g.,* workmanship).

§TIP: Don't cash in all your Swiss bank notes when you leave the country. They're stronger than dollars all over Europe.

ATTITUDE TOWARD TOURISTS   Since ¼th of the national investment is tied up in tourism, the Swiss are all-out to cater to the visitor. The **Swiss National Tourist Office** is a whopping enterprise; no country in the world can match it for size or spread. They have the most voluminous, most readable collection of free guidebooks we've ever seen. Their architects are studying 44 vacation centers street by street, hotel by hotel, and room by room, planning new partitions and bathrooms as far ahead as A.D. 2001.

General Manager of the worldwide SNTO network is Dr. Werner Kämpfen. While this gentleman's mind, body, and soul are totally devoted to visitors to his land, please don't hoist your troubles onto this busy executive's doorstep. Instead, if any extraordinary situation should arise while you are in Switzerland, communicate with the Press and Public Relations Director at Talacker 42 (phone: 23-57-13), in the Sihlporte district of Zürich (business and airlines area)—but, for heaven's sake, don't bother him either about inconsequentials.

By all means visit one of their branches before or during your trip. The **New York** office, at 608 Fifth Ave, is under the aegis of Bruno Baroni; in the **San Francisco** bureau at 661 Market St. that Golden Gate-way is now swung by Willy Isler; A modest subagency also functions with Chris Zoebeli manning the deck at 106 S. Michigan Ave. in **Chicago**; Max Lehmann is Switzerland's man in **Toronto**. Many cities in Latin America have SNTO representatives; so does practically every capital of Europe. And every Swiss town, no matter how small, has its "**Verkehrsverein**," Tourist Promotion, or Official Enquiry Office. They'll give you free expert advice.

CUSTOMS AND IMMIGRATION
Polite and well organized. In addition to personal effects, officially you may take in the usual 400 cigarettes *or* 100 cigars *or* 1 lb. of pipe tobacco (the once-down-trodden female who was permitted only cigarettes may now bring in as many stogies or pipe loads as papa), 2 cameras and unlimited unexposed film (overseas visitors only), typewriter, ½ liter of perfume in an opened bottle, 1 sewing machine, 1 baby carriage—the same general exceptions which apply through most of Europe. Either 1 bottle of spirits plus a bottle of wine *or* 2 bottles of wine are also allowed (don't forget that all this is per person). Pilgrims under 17 are forbidden to import ANY alcoholic beverages or ANY tobacco products. Unofficially, however, it would be surprising if they were to ignore the oral declaration of any average U.S. visitor and ask him to open even 1 bag. Merchandise in normal quantities may be shipped home without special permit or license, and it is not subject to export duty. All the inspectors speak English, and most of them are meticulously polite and correct. You should find a pleasant reception.

§TIP: Never forward a package of new articles to yourself from any country to Switzerland—and never mail a gift to a Swiss friend without first checking the Customs duties. We shipped a small box of miscellaneous trivia to ourselves at Zürich (writing supplies, film, a couple of spare Zippo lighters) and walked into a bill of $40—more than we had originally paid for the stuff. Used clothing, however, is free.

HOTELS
For far more comprehensive information on certain hostelries than space limitations permit here, interested travelers are referred to the annually revised *Fielding's Selected Favorites: Hotels and Inns, Europe* by Dodge Temple Fielding, our peripatetic son. The latest edition, in which a total of 300-odd favored possibilities were handpicked from the 4000-plus personally inspected, will be at your bookstore early this year.

You'd expect to find outstanding accommodations in this "nation of hotelkeepers" (said again without derision), and you most certainly do. Most of Switzerland's 8000-plus stopping places for transients are models of comfort, cleanliness, and efficiency; elevators work, maids don't talk your ear off, breakfast comes so hot it burns your gullet. Not only is the Swiss hotel manager an institution from Buenos Aires to Birmingham, but the Swiss concierge is such a fixture that many of the current crop are the 4th or 5th generation in the trade.

While the capacity is skyrocketing, the service headaches have grown to Mr. Aspirin's king-size proportions. As previously stated, the Swiss employment rate is so high that 50% to 75% of today's innkeeping staffs are foreigners.

Prices vary considerably. Probably 80% feature American plan (room, board, and basic tips included in the bill). On this arrangement (3 meals plus lodging), you'll pay between $26 and $48 per person per day. Deluxe metropolitan hotels and resorts such as St. Moritz double, triple, or even quadruple these figures. As a median guideline, however, we'd peg a good twin accommodation with bath in a substantial Swiss address at around $38, plus service and taxes but usually inclusive of continental breakfast.

Most visitors to urban (not rural) communities find the full-pension arrangement unsatisfactory; every adventurous U.S. pilgrim agrees that it is boring to take *all* meals in one place. The standard European practice used to be room and breakfast—a pattern still being followed in some of the better and less greedy hostelries. If you're in a city, *ask for the demipension plan,* which is about 20% less than full pension, and which gives you the option of eating some of your meals elsewhere. In resorts during peak season, you probably can't get it; many popular provincial centers insist on 3 squares only for all guests.

Here is our personal rating, in order of desirability, of the top Swiss houses. As with all personal evaluations, there's plenty of room for disagreement.

Arosa has been fevered by a reconstruction epidemic over the last few seasons. The results for today's merrymakers? A-rosy. In the upper crust of these snowfields, 3 houses—each with its own personality and appeal—are outstanding. The **Tschuggen** is stunning if your taste chooses the slalom run for modernity. Proprietors Julie and Armin Wyssmann have invested a shah's ransom in creating a holiday nucleus that glitters almost as brightly as any contender in the Swiss Alps. The public rooms are vast and handsomely outfitted; there's a pool on the roof, plus a sauna, massage parlor, and panoramic snackery; there's a full ski shop in the basement, a zinging discothèque, a bowling center, and a sweet little *Stübli* where a warning on a gigantic cowbell advises "Whoever rings buys a round!" The dining room is airy; the grill adjoining the ballroom-bar is inviting; there's dancing to an orchestra every night. The twentieth-century bedchambers—replete with every conceivable comfort while providing hectares of space—focus their wide-angle windows on a Kodak kingdom of natural beauty. Instead of the snowflake emblems worn by its staffers, you might just as well imagine buttons proclaiming that "We Try Harder"—because they truly do! For physical amenities here is a blooded patrician of the peerage. The **Kulm**, older in years but younger in spirit, has been refreshed throughout and given a brand-new wing. The feeling is one of an alpine chalet done up in discriminating personal taste. There's enough whoop-de-do per hour here to make a Catskill social director hide in terror. Sparkplug of this jovial case of internal combustion is the debonair Hans Leu (rightfully rhymns with "joy"), an alumnus of Zürich's fabulous Dolder Grand (and, we suspect, also a graduate of Barnum & Bailey, Disneyland, and Tinker Toys Inc.). Here, too, the tireless holidaymaker will find the supercharged range of recreational facilities. Glass-sheathed swimming pool with tickling water jets; sauna; solarium; bowling; old bar moved to the "entertainment area"; most major ski runs at your doorstep; ice rink; an American-style grill with yumptious beef imported from the U.S.; lounges, games and events galore. For high-stepping gaiety, throw away your Miltowns and check in here. Exhaustedly recommended. The **Park** captures the crown for pure alpine esthetics. The woodwork, the carefully hewn polite rusticity, the costumed staffers, the mandate on coziness—all conspire to give this house a mellow glow of a deluxe Arcadia. Unfortunately, however, its situation in a viewless bottomland and its extremely heavy patronage by German-speaking guests possibly make this the least appealing of the Big Three for fun-seeking Yanks and Rebs. A knockout to the eye, but merely a light jab to the the entertainment torso, in our opinion. Perhaps you'll disagree. The **Prätschli**, product of a successful architect turned hotelier, is away from the center in its own hillside domain. Proprietor Graessly, a well-intentioned hobbyist, seems to extend greetings to more Teutonic clients than to any other nationality, so again we think that wayfarers who speak only English might not find it as convivial as the multinational enclaves of the Tschuggen and the Kulm. The **Hof Maran**, also on the Prätschli slopes, turns on 75 rooms, half of which claim private baths. The vivacious will find a 9-hole golf course, ice skating, tennis, children's recreation, skiing, and curling (outdoor variety, unfortunately). Dining room, grill, cafeteria, and separate restaurant; comfortable bedchambers for indoor curling (fortunately) with ample space and good baths. Proprietor Traber has a warm affection for Americans. Recommended. The **Bellevue** is an excellent bet—franc-ly speaking. Keen administration by friendly, hard-driving Fredy Hold; attractive Arven Restaurant downstairs; cozy bar-lounge; orchestra for après-ski terpsichore; 75 balconied rooms and 66 baths; try for its corner units. Very good. The **Valsana** draws a lively young set; its bar glows with robust revelers when the snowflakes fall; there's a pool to add to the splash. Fun, but don't sleep here. The totally refashioned **Alexandra** offers space for 200 sleepyheads, but we've not yet snoozed among them. The **Savoy** is 50% renewed —and that's the better half; don't even *look* at the other half. The middle-age **Seehof** has had her face lifted; 78 rooms and 40 baths; now okay. For the economy-minded, the **Merkur** might be just the thing. **Des Alpes** is a foothill of its former self. **Excelsior** has begun to come up again since its restyling; all 80 units with bath; swimming pool. Showing promise. The **Central** is also very worthy, now that is has repaneled its bedchambers; it is noted for its kitchen. Many Arosa hotels are closed during part of April, all of May, part of June, and all of November; exceptions are 10 Second-class hostelries and 15 boardinghouses which operate throughout the year, most of which are simple, clean, and comfortable.

Basle recently uncorked 3 new hostelries, all of them high-caliber in tone and much needed in this busy cultural and commercial center. They are the

450-pillow **Hilton**, run by Director Urs Hitz, the **Mot-Hotel Europe** for 250 voyagers, and the **Basel**, which resides in the heart of the Old Town. Until we can check these newcomers out personally, we'll continue to recommend the **Euler**, near the station. Its massive redecoration program has been enormously successful, providing banquet facilities, an underground passage connected to the new subway, a basement cafeteria, a spacious carpark and the rear courtyard. Management by the former owner of a local restaurant who hopefully will keep up its fine reputation for gastronomy. The **Drei Könige** ("Three Kings"), founded in A.D. 1026, is Switzerland's oldest hotel. It used to be our favorite (yep, far more recently than in the eleventh century). Sadly, the antique touches which gave it its particular charm have now been almost totally erased; its now-modernized units seem flat and uninteresting by comparison, although the refreshened riverfront units still offer a wondrous view. Streetside rooms newly air-conditioned, with triple-plate glass installed to ssssssh the traffic din, but still so far from adequate that earplugs are provided by every bed. Cuisine? We still receive too many complaints from Guidesters to satisfy us that Manager Amberg's fresh restaurant is doing much better than of yore; we'll be anxious to give the skillets another taste test. The staff attitudes have picked up commendably in recent months. This venerable house impresses us as being overpriced for land-view locations—but, for its better offerings overlooking the Rhine, here is certainly the Three Kings of the local mountain. The youthful **Alban-Ambassador** still seems to be searching for its portfolio. This one appears to lack a strong executive to guide it, in our judgment. Air-conditioned public rooms; modernistic rôtisserie and grillroom; bar; sauna; hairdresser and barber; minigolf; automated parking facility with slots keyed to the driver's room number. Airy units, each with stocked refrigerator; radios and alarm clocks throughout; small baths; frequent complaints of staff negligence. The 200-room **International** has been taking pep pills; it has become a much higher octane operation. Plenty of color in the Modern Convention Hotel approach; 50% renovated; keyed strongly toward conventioneers; pool, sauna, and gymnastic facilities almost surely flexing their brawny muscles; main dining room, plus a new feedery; full air conditioning; a few viewless cubicles; others crackling with flair. Young Director R. F. Gasteyger is doing a first-rate job here. Very good in the medium-to-high bracket. The **Schweizerhof**, more than a century old, has been updated recently. Rates hover in the welkin zones for the earthy rewards; #36 is one of its best maximum twins. Okay, but a bit steep. **Victoria-National** welcomes guests with an artful lobby depicting scenes from the local zoo, the fish market, the festival, and the tower. Limited in space but very clean; 40% with bath and shower; double-glazed windows on the noisier front; 5th-floor units with balconies on the façade. Warming up. The youthful, cozily conceived **Alexander** boasts many winning charms. Each floor has its rooms named for cities; town maps of their individual namesakes are in each bedchamber—an inexpensive but clever means of smashing institutionality to smithereens. The restaurant has been outfitted in weathered timber impacted in white stucco and dressed with farm implements; the cooking focuses on provincial recipes. Space limitations are a problem, but they are so cloaked in attractiveness that for brief stopovers we don't think you'll mind. We like it for its type. **Drachen** is a candidate in the contemporary crop of functional houses. Its 40 narrow-dimension rooms are skillfully planned. All have air conditioning, radio, rental TV outlet, private strongbox built into the floor of the wardrobe, and courtside situation for added quiet; tiny baths. A good value. **Excelsior**, under the same management, recently added 2 dining salons and possibly has already begun its proposed total overhaul of the structure. Busy-busy-busy, with a Shell gas pump at the front door. The **Bernina**, under new direction, has 30 chambers and a modest mien. The **Alfa** is adequate for autoists shunting between Germany and Zürich; for others, it is too far out.

In *Berne*, we're always deeply fond of the ever-luxurious, 130-room **Schweizerhof**, with no view but with the most convenient location for shoppers. This house blends the fabulous Gauer-family antique collection with up-to-the-minute streamlining in living facilities; each hallway, for example, offers almost priceless collections from different periods (3rd floor in seventeenth century, 4th all-Swiss floor with ancient rifles, harness, a sleigh, *et al.*) —while each of the staff carries a short-wave "Walkie-Talkie" locator. When you pick up the phone in your room it automatically switches off the radio, turning it on again when you put down the receiver! One of the most captivating innovations is the Simmental Stube, a dining salon of a fine old house that was dismantled and reassembled to the last splinter as a cozy restaurant; moreover, there's the Arcady Snack-Bar, with entrances to both the hotel and the appendant Gübelin jewelry arcadia, and an underground tunnel to the Berne station where there is ample covered parking space for motorized clients. The outstanding Horseshoe Grill adjoins. General Manager Urs Schaerer, young, alert, and intelligent; Concierge Louis Achermann surely one of the best in Europe; a few suites with 2 tubs and 2 showers in the same bathroom; if you're a wealthy Easterner or a poverty-stricken Texan, cross your fingers for one of the trio of apartments (#110, #210, #310); book away from the main street if you are a light sleeper. The favorite hotel abroad of scores of Yankee travelers. The 200-room **Bellevue-Palace**, high on the riverbank, has a beautiful view of the Alps and a décor which a much smarter friend advises us includes "Directoire, Biedermeier, and Louis XVI in the Arabesque fashion of Queen Marie-Antoinette." Many oriental businessmen now use it as their occidental headquarters. Big sun-front dining terrace, commanding the valley; *Chaîne des Rôtisseurs* chef (Western Hemisphere Division) whose touch is perfection; suave and friendly concierge and service; scads of thoughtfully executed amenities. The majority of bedchambers are spacious, in superb taste throughout. Proprietor Jost Schmid and his lovely Swedish wife Margit, who picked up the family reins here, are fast revolutionizing this landmark into one of the top hostelries on the European map. Elegant, excellent—an all-out recommendation if the grand concept is your preference.

The **Metropole** may be short on bedroom space, but its public sancta are a cheering delight. Colorful, woody Brasserie with beer-wagon theme, Vieux Moulin grill with a working waterwheel, gaily decorated President-Club bar. Lots of fun in an altogether odd-ball fashion—which we'll bet foreign visitors will love. The midtown **Savoy**, oh-so-handily located, cooks up the corner Burgunderstube as the most appealing unit of its 5-part dining setup. Of its

71 bedrooms, 25 have full-tub baths, 25 have showers, and all have essential plumbing and radios; just a few attractive accommodations are available (#230 is an example). Heavy South American trade in summer. A good commercial house, better designed for business people than for vacationers. The new **Alfa** has a snack bar and a restaurant within its poured-concrete hull. Efficiency is the word, but this gets dressed up nicely in the bedchambers. Book the larger doubles for comfort and away from the busy Seilerstrasse for peaceful slumber. The **Nydeck** is an inexpensive choice in the city's antique district. Very nice people running it; spare but prim; especially good for singles. **Bären** romps in with 60 rooms, 30 baths, and 30 showers; bright décor; its only fancy quarters are #215, #315, and #415. Adequate. The **Krebs** is sprightly and very clean; 42 rooms, 4 baths, and 5 showers; breakfast only; a value for the price. The **Wächter Mövenpick** is in the same bracket; #209 is a pleasant wood-lined twin. The **Regina**, 10 minutes from the center in a residential section, is also petite; breakfast is the only meal; good bet when the kids are along. The centrally sited **Bristol** is colorful in a modern plaid-and-plastic fashion. Not bad for modest budgets and breakfast-only over-nighters. The **City** has just experienced an urban renewal program which we haven't seen. The **Stadthof** claims no lobby at all. But it *does* boast a Swiss-style Grill with rôtisseries and a mini-mini-mini-bar that are cute. The many-many-many mini-mini-mini rooms might be okay for elves, but not for our personal full fathom of flesh. The **Continental** can easily be missed. The **Arca** is a good bet for skinny-pursed-and-bodied budgeteers; very small cells.

Bürgenstock? There's no place like it in the world. This 500-acre sky empire over the Lake of Lucerne (25 minutes from Lucerne proper) must be seen to be believed. A bronzed, good-looking magnate named Fritz Frey would need an alpenstock to count the Swiss francs spent to blast, carve, and whittle the top of his private Alp into a Deluxe resort. The result is eye-popping—the mountain vacationist's dream. Three hotels (the palatial **Grand**, the plush **Palace**—with every suite and bedroom now beautifully redecorated —and the more moderate **Park**), all hung with Van Dycks, Brueghels, Tintorettos, and the like, and all with a magnificent view; Mountain Inn for light refreshments at the 3000-foot peak, reached by one of Europe's fastest and highest elevators; 6-minute funicular to lakeshore bathing and quay for the 100-passenger Bürgenstock yacht; Guest Club entertainment center; night-club; the world's most exclusive 9-hole Golf Club (Mr. Frey is its ONLY member, but he'll permit you to play); championship tennis courts; fine heated Alpine swimming pool with dancing at Poolside Café; and Underwater Bar for oglers; Golf Grill, Sporting Club, 2 orchestras, gala evenings, concerts, shopping center, beauty parlor, fashion shows, private chapel—this cloud-kissed community offers just about everything but harp solos by the neighboring angels. Recent complaints by Guidesters, however, center on a heavier play from package tours than in previous years and a rather stingy attitude of chambermaids concerning towels and fresh linens. Soon it will have completed an athletic club with an indoor pool (white marble set amid black marble terraces), a sauna, massage facilities (dry as well as underwater types), and a restaurant—all reached via a tunnel leading to a cliffside elevator. An ancient Tavern has been remodeled and turned on for Burgenstockbrokers. Season: May to October for the Grand Park, and June to October for the Palace; everything shut tight in winter. As always, recommended with cheers.

Crans-Montana stands tall with the sleekly rustic **Royal**, overlooking a fir-flecked 9-hole golf course. Viewful, hearth-warmed main-floor lounges, bar, and dining room lined with glass; charming, lodgelike Caveau du Roy for Valais cheese specialties; cordial administration by Manager Gédéon Barras. All 80 havens with bath or shower; 50 bedchambers facing south, each with sunny balcony. Very sound. The **Golf** chips in with a tranquil setting at the edge of the major links. From your doorstep it's a putt to the first tee, a 5-minute hike to the ski lift, a totter for a splash in the covered swimming pool, and an hourly wait between bus shuttles to the village. This one is the social heartbeat of the hillfolk, but to us it looks as if it will soon need some spiffing up up in them thar hills, folks. The extensively remodeled **Excelsior** is managed by André Barras, cousin of the Royal's emperor. Modern lounge; nice bar; convenient playroom; balconies on the southern exposure; fresh-to-the-eye but cramped dimensions in the latest segment. Not bad. **Des Mélèzes,** an 8-iron shot from the Golf Club, is also on par. Here's an eagle in comfort for budgeteers. The **Rhodania** and **Richelieu** offer similar amenities in big sprawling houses at higher basic rates. Okay, but not raves. The former has the better chef, not to mention the sweet-toothed barman who dumped 6 (!) cherries into our Old Fashioned. The **Etoile** is agreeable for accommodations. The modern little **City** provides one of the best hotel kitchens in the region, for our money. The **Robinson** and the **Mont Blanc** are the best of the year-round operations. **De l'Etrier**, a good-looking A-frame structure in wood, comes up with 150 door keys for rentals on a monthly (perhaps on a weekly) basis. Tiny bar; no lounge; pool; superior for its type of apartment-hotel complex. The **Beau Séjour** and the **Eurotel** are adequate; many check into these because of their swimmeries. There are 3-dozen additional hotels or pensions on this mountain perch, plus a throng of guesthouses and apartment dwellings which are available. Most of the bigger ones are strictly seasonal. At **Montana** itself, the most impressive edifice for miles around is called Supercrans—and as an apartment citadel with a swimming moat that is just what it is. Super! The **Ambassador**, also with an aquatic spread, is a chalet-style beaut. **Anzère**, a budding resort nearby, can provide additional kips in its tiny but ultracozy **Hotel de Masque**. It remains a quiet village that is bound to wake up and roar very soon.

In **Davos**, the **Belvedere** is one of the brightest lights of the Alps. Many-balconied, block-long building; fresco-walled dining salon with carved wood ceiling and brick arcade; 2-level peasant-style Grill; play lounge for tots; 200 units and 120 baths. The top floor, named Bel-Étage, is limited to suites—and they are lovely. This one is owned by Toni Morosani, whose son is now in full managerial command. Most American ski buffs are as happy as seal pups here. The **Derby** also gleams with an inviting warmth. Approximately the same tariff level; chic clientele; atmospheric Palüda Grill; sauna and health center; its 145 bedrooms and 68 baths have been given a thorough renovation. Also recommended. The **Schweizerhof**, a Belvedere property, has reopened after a total renovation, plus addition of a Bel-Étage (see above), balconies for its southern façade, and an indoor pool. It should be another winner in the best Morosani tradition. The **Flüela**, next to the railway terminal, has effected many new bedroom improvements, with additional goodies in the shape of uplifted public areas, a sizzling grill, a pool, a gym, and other recreational facilities. The **Post**, another in the Belvedere stable, swings with fun and frolic. There's a pool and a dapper 25-apartment wing called the Pöstli. This Post is now a solid stake. We hear welkins of praise for the ever-expanding **Sunstar-Park** and for the renewed and scenically sited **Wald-hotel Bellevue**, which is aptly named. Both sound mighty inviting. The **Europe** is a popular action station with the Young Set. It's noisy; perhaps the food could stand improvement. **Seehof**, with its La Bohème night spot, is a good bet for the spry. The **Des Alpes**, a young entry on the main drag, has small accommodations; breakfast only. One Guidester who did not enjoy her stay at the Belvedere highly recommends the **National**, which we've not seen recently. We'll pop in on our next hillclimb. In *Dorf*, the Seehof is best known for its romantic Bohème nightclub.

In *Geneva*, the century-old **Richemond** is a prizewinning nominee. There are an informality and warmth here which do not exist in other top-category hotels in formal, correct Switzerland. Direct credit for this can be traced to Jean Armleder, the supercharged proprietor, of the 3rd successive family generation to hold this post; he is aided by his son, Victor. Almost 90% of the establishment is furnished with traditional Continental softness and appeal. Some units lately redone in Directoire style; a bevy of accommodations in sleek-rustic moods for more masculine tastes; a handful of less elaborate, small billets with daybeds, radio, wall-safe, additional telephone in the bathroom, and other twentieth-century innovations which are cheerful, utilitarian, and slightly sterile in aura. The Presidential Suite #407, with gold-silk walls, lovely blending colors, and refrigerator, is the chief-of-the-stately ticket; suite #510 is the largest in the house. For alfresco dining, the open-air terrace and adjoining sidewalk café, both bursting with flowers, were attractively remodeled; Le Gentilhomme grill-bar, with its music and sophisticated clientele, has recently undergone a top-hat-to-spats sprucing up; better than ever before, this one remains the smartest cocktail and dining spot in the metropolis. The Millionaire's Club, a cellar music-lounge for members, can be visited by those who receive a special card from the desk. Parking space has been obtained for 350 cars within 100 yards of the hotel. A superduper Phantom V Rolls Royce and a Mercedes Pullman limousine are at guests' disposal for airport or station pickup and excursions—a unique, silk-stocking fillip in this city. Highly recommended.

The **President** bills itself as "Le Premier Palais de l'Europe." Our own doorpost-to-rooftop reinspection indicates that after years of mellowing, this establishment is finally achieving status in the opulence circuit even though it now accepts a limited number of group tours. Lakeside setting in an unhappy location for shoppers or sightseers; dazzling white marble façade; a much improved French Restaurant, with adjoining bar, Grill, Tearoom, and cocktail retreat; rich, rich downstairs décor a startling contrast of Gobelin tapestries, showy period pieces, and Lunar Missile modernity; lounge with sliding roof; 100-car garage. The handful of apartments, 20 suites, and 270 rooms all have bath, radio, 2 or 3 telephones, private short-wave signal reception, and floor-to-ceiling windows. Bedroom rates as well as food prices are shockingly high. Very costly, but appealing to many nabobs.

The **des Bergues** functions smoothly under the sharp-eyed guidance of Manager Emile Soutter and his equally hardworking English wife. Updated reception area and uplifted lobby; several dozen handsome units added; corridors brightened in the newest wing; floral wallpaper smoothed on, plus the addition of velvet upholstery, radios in night tables, padded headboards, and thermal taps in new baths; 2 bars; main dining room with balconied tables overlooking the lake spillway; Amphitryon restaurant, very popular with the Diplomatic Set; bustling Snack Bar; superb Concierge in Léon Wellinger and his assistant, Paul. Traditional gathering place of Swiss bankers, coupon-clippers, and The Oldest Families.

The **Beau Rivage**, adjoining the Richemond, now is sailing to even more promising horizons under the helmsmanship of Director Fred Mayer and a tip-top crew composed of his wife, son, and daughter-in-law; Concierge Zunino also maintains a trim deck. Mr. M's fresh baubles include a stunning restaurant and the 2-tier Louis XIII Puss-in-Boots rôtisserie, an English-style piano-bar, a fine kitchen with Chef Leheu of Paris's famed Taillevent, a canopied terrace for dining under infrared heating lamps when the air is chilly, and a restyled 1st floor in Louis XVI vestments. There's also a cozy corner cafeteria for summerizations. All back units—many of them among the most attractively comfortable rooms in Switzerland—are preening proudly this year; the lakefronters are due next for revamping. Coming up and up and up, with good taste and carloads of flair except in some of its sleeping space.

The **de la Paix** is one of the most distinguished smaller hotels in the nation. Lakefront situation; dignified lobby; restaurant *à la français;* TV now in every haven; gay touches splashed throughout; colored tiles, up-to-the-minute fixtures, and scales added to practically all bathrooms. While some of its lodgings are small, others are so spacious that Prince Rainier and Princess Grace chose de la Paix on one state visit. Worldwide reputation meriting every iota of its fame.

The glistening 400-room, steel-and-concrete **Intercontinental** is a 16-story giant located about 5 minutes along the Lausanne Speedway. Immense marbleized lobby, 1-flight up by escalator, now liberated from much of its initial chill; rich, cunningly decorated Les Continents Restaurant for international fare; Café Le Voltaire in chevrons-and-heart pattern for snacks; expanded downstairs dining spread; crimson Le Carnaval Supper Club for rooftop dancing and occasional cabaret (operative 7 P.M. to 2 A.M. and closed Mon.). Our recent luncheon in Les Continents was beautifully presented, expertly served, and carefully prepared; the cost was surprisingly low for the delicious rewards. You'll also find a main-floor cocktail lounge, a galaxy of shops (including one dandy tempter called "Watches of Geneva"), a heated swimming pool with adjoining bar, a 170-car underground garage, and full air conditioning. Standard upstairs décor highlighted by green and orange; elf-size baths; reserve high for the best views. Georges Desbaillets, the former sultan of the Istanbul Hilton and a native *fils* of Geneva, seems to be warming this house up commendably. Now recommended.

Du Rhône, with an excellent riverside situation, comes on stronger and stronger as a zesty cosmopolitan address for globe-trotters. On our recent incognito stay, we could only find reasons to commend Director R.A. Lendi and his go-getting team of administrators. Clearly, however, it remains a commercial operation with a big-city temperament. Now the entire accommodation skein has been updated, a fresh wing fluffed up, carpets spread to add warmth and cheer, old baths modernized with phones in each, all suites renewed, the telephone system given direct dialing, TV put into all rooms, and a parking lot opened for 60 cars. The restaurant and Le Neptune grill (closed weekends) are popular gathering spots nowadays, and not without reason. There's a busy-busy atmosphere with lounges a-chatter with clients from all 4 corners of the earth. Now strongly recommended to readers who seek action, comfort, and modernity.

The Deluxe **La Réserve** recently was taken under the management aegis of the Richemond, which gives it a double bonus in travelers' rewards. This ultra-quiet rural beauty dominates a spruce-dotted, 8-acre domain near the outskirting hamlet of Bellevue; it is pedestaled upon a setback garden hummock severed from the lake by the Lausanne autoroute. Open-space-concept lobby livened by ceramic butterflies; window-lined split-level dining room with a glorious view of lawn and trees; French chef who is justifiably stirring jealousy in many Geneva kitchens (La Réserve also now has an enviable Chinese restaurant which is independently operated); wide terrace adjoining for summer pastimes; richly outfitted, ruby-toned bar; ocher-hued coffee shop; beauty parlor; heated swimming pool and 4 tennis courts. All bedchambers with private loggia, bath, shower, radio and TV; color-keys in blue, green, and orange; some 3-person units available in its 60-room total. Both cuisine and dwelling space come at premium rates. From what we could see, this sylvan *réserve* boasts many alluring features that the city slickers can never provide. (Indeed, in summer it almost gives the impression of being a country club rather than a hotel.) The Armleder clan has put together an enchanting package which General Manager Roland Klinger maintains in high polish.

Back in town, **La Résidence** has been perking up. There's a rejuvenated lobby plus an enlarged restaurant and bar, all brightened sparklingly by lots of plate glass and mirrors. Its 140 bedrooms are being refashioned at a rate of about 20 per season; the contrast between the renewed and the older units is vivid. Recommended *if* you draw one of the better lodgings. The **d'Angleterre**, boasting a restyled entrance, lobby, and reception area, offers 66 soundproofed rooms, all with private bath, most of them amply dimensioned. Pleasant setting, with its excellent dining sections fronting the waterside; keen management by Robert O. Bucher; friendly people; vague plans for further updatings; heartily endorsed as one of the best candidates in its medium-price category. The **Balzac** is youthful and First-class; its restaurant, bar, and brasserie are independent; there's private parking in the adjoining Gulf station. All 40 unusually large bedrooms with efficiency bath or shower; comfortable armchairs or divans in some units; a few dressing alcoves; night tables with radios and telephones; TV on request; wide-angle windows affording townscape vistas. This Balzac pens out an entertaining *Human Comedy*. The **Cornavin** has added garage facilities near its portals, a new lobby, fresh lounges and public rooms, and group bookings by the score. Warmhearted

Concierge Gottfried Rudisuhli always finds time to chat with his guests and make them feel welcome to his city. Prices very reasonable; not bad if you say "okay" to the station area. The **Metropole** (to us, at least) is a seedy relic. The Rhone-sited **Ambassador**, on the quai des Bergues, a newcomer to the hotelscape, was somewhat of a disappointment to us. Woody lounge with modernistic padded easy chairs; corner restaurant and bar; 90 contemporary-style bedrooms, all fully carpeted but extremely small and with virtually no baggage space; tiny baths, and 28 units with only w.c.'s. The brochure looks better than the real thing. The **Bristol** opened recently and is reported to be doing very well. Pleasant brown-and-yellow toned restaurant overlooking the square; tartanesque bar; well-appointed suites and bedrooms. Manager Cirafici, who moved from the Beau Rivage, has a sturdy young plant to nurture. The **Royal** is even newer, and from the publicity we've seen it seems to offer top-quality modernity and comfort. **Ramada** also has joined the fray. Both of these have about 250 rooms. We'll check them soon.

The pert little **Grand-Pré** is the economy-class triumph of the resourceful Armleder family of Richemond fame. All 85 units tiny but tastefully outfitted; singles in front and doubles in back; only 6 singles without bath or shower; no restaurant. There's a crisp, happy atmosphere here, generated and maintained by Director Pierre Gentinetta, whom we admire for his professional skill and staff command. Excellent for budgeteers. The **Century** impressed our Judy as a house designed almost exclusively for male patronage. All sizes, shapes, and lines for mascu-linear appeal are here, without a single dainty frill. Large, gracious lobby with comfortable chairs functionally arranged; 140 rooms with 120 baths or showers; 50% of the accommodations with he-man kitchenettes; a number of American companies keep year-round apartments here. Deservedly popular. The **California** has a chummy cellar bar and a roof-garden snackery. All 67 Mini-Modern units with bath or shower; 7 with kitchen facilities plus dining counter; 25 others with kitchenettes only (we saw no ventilators); lovely, delicious, noble combination of colors that would warm and gladden any Princeton Tiger's heart (orange and black, *mais oui*). But so Many, Many, Many groups thunder through it that we felt lost as footloose independents. The **Du Midi** boasts an excellent central address, a spiral entrance stairway beside a gurgling fountain, the cellar Carnotzet for fondue, a sidewalk terrace, a breakfast room, and 82 accommodations, all with bath or shower, a refrigerator, radio, telephone, alarm clock, scales, and an air of no-nonsense functionality. Very solid for the modest outlay; highly favored by us. The newly expanded 165-room, marble-fronted **Méditerranée** is in high tide nowadays. Efficient modernistic concept; French-style les Quatre Saisons restaurant with abundant salad choices and seasonal accent on vegetables; active cellar L'Armailli Carnotzet open nightly except Monday, with 3-piece Swiss combo and regional cookery; sun-dappled breakfast nook; coffee shop; bar; sauna; nearby carpark; well-outfitted chambers (with refrigerators) with back views of Lac Léman and the Jet d'Eau. It is clean, smooth, and on the hop. The **De Berne** was initially planned as a haven for tour groups. Expansive lobby with acres of space for luggage; full air conditioning; breakfast room and snack center on main floor; improved hallways; peanut-shell quarters, each packed with telephone, radio, red and white furniture, and private bath. Sorry, but we don't exactly Berne with enthusiasm for it. The **Windsor**, across the street, offers 56 bedchambers. Small lounge, small bar, small cells, small recommendation. The **Excelsior,** a station hotel, has space for 75 snoozers with very thin wallets. Fair shelter if you don't expect Riche-mond rewards. The **Rivoli**'s sleeping quarters are even more minuscule. Okay for businessmen with very brief briefcases. The youngish **Phenicia** offers 56 cubicles with garish décor, bath or shower, radio, and just enough space to stretch out. Clean but lean. The **Époque**, which faces it, is 2 years older and 2 well worn. Weensie restaurant off the lobby; 60 functional units with showers; not Epoque-shattering by any stretch of the imagination. **La Tourelle**, at **Vésenaz** nestles in a homey parkland setting; with its lake view, it can be just the ticket for thrift-minded tranquillity seekers of taste. Skip the **Lido**; an all-night bakery next door might knead your dollars into doughnuts as far as sleeping is concerned. The Deluxe **Regent**, a Japanese entry, is scheduled to land this year near the airport. Both the new **Hotel 33** and **Air Escale** are heavily boarded by airline crews. Out at neighboring **Petit-Lancy** we hear fond praise for the comforts and cuisine of the tiny **Hostellerie de la Vendée**, but personally we haven't tried it.

Only 11 miles across the border from Geneva (20 minutes by the Speedway), **Divonne-les-Bains** offers resort thermal-spa facilities, 3 aging but adequate hotels, an 18-hole golf course, a racetrack, occasional polo matches, and the richest gambling facilities in Gaul. The Casino—with roulette, baccarat, American games (including craps), boule, and chemin de fer—is the town's main attraction and almost its reason for being. Both the Hotel du Golf and the Parc (formerly called Chicago) now come under the escutcheon of the Rothschilds. The **du Golf** has a lovely garden situation, a barnlike ambiance brightened with sparkly hues of fresh paint, and a number of fainthearted, cost-conscious renovations. All 100 bedrooms come with private bath; 50% have been renewed. We felt a notable lack of warmth throughout. Be sure to have confirmed reservations here; also check your bills carefully. The pool, shared with the Parc, is large and very handsome. The **Parc** is really an antique annex of the former. Its unretouched mien has more charm than that of the principal house, but wherever it is old (going on its 13th decade), it is downright decrepit. No restaurant; 50 of its 100 units with private bath; June through September only; rumors rife that it may be razed for an apartment site. The 3rd possibility, **Château de Divonne,** is just outside of town on a commanding perch. It is a beautifully maintained structure dating from the second half of the eighteenth century. Captivating terrace for settin', starin', and rockin' those blues away; 40 period rooms; 25 baths; open June to September. This Divonne world is as tranquil as the inside of a bubble, so don't expect fireworks. Recommended only for lazing, gazing, and gaming.

Grindelwald 's queenly choice is the **Grand Hotel Regina**, rejuvenated by dashing Fred Krebs and his hotelier clan on a cost-is-no-object basis. This year they will cut the ribbon on a blue-ribbon annex—a luxury chalet-style edifice with 9 luxury suites, open fireplaces, color TV, and even some baths with tubs for twosomes and a view of the Eiger. His 300-piece collection of antique local prints (on display throughout) alone has consumed a small Alp of francs. The exterior remains gingerbready—but inside there has been a revolution. Numerous standard units restyled with built-in furniture and hip-deep wall-to-wall carpets; plenty of flowers around; big, open-air, heated pool with colorful umbrellas on lawn, against one of the most glorious Alpine backdrops imaginable; adjoining Health Pavilion with a covered pool, sauna, massage parlor, and clubroom. Folklore Fondue Dinner Parties every Monday featuring a yodeling quartet (delightful in winter after a community sleigh ride); Candlelit Dinner Dances every Thursday night in summer, with occasional floor shows; Sunday Tea Dances in winter. "La Ferme" ("The Farm") nightclub with huge open *Alphütte* fireplace, charcoal grill, and the sizzling sounds of a discothèque; Sports Bar. One happy Englishman summed it up simply: "Every time we visit the Grand Hotel Regina we find some added touch of comfort, some new thoughtful kindness, some extra little luxury which one doesn't normally find in *any* resort hotel." Hats off to this talented, hardworking host! The 80-room **Adler,** also teetering above the deep valley, is a chalet-style structure. Garden, tennis, Ping-Pong; glorious vistas from the dining room-lounge-bar combination and the open terrace. Its modernistic and tasteless furnishings are a handicap to the warm, wood-lined rooms; 45 very minuscule baths; amiable personnel. Very sound. **Belvedere** has the usual resort appurtenances without a speck of unusual flair. The indoor pool and sauna are welcome splashes. **Parkhotel Schönegg** offers cozy public rooms—especially the rustic down-1-flight Gydis Bar—but bedchambers that are much too snug. Many caressing touches including those (dictated by the dimensions) that you're bound to get constantly from your snoozing companion. Too tiny but sweet. **Schweizerhof** (like the Schönegg, on the "wrong" side of the road) is an inn that grew "out." Moderate renovations begun, but ho-hum except for its interior natatorium and sauna facilities. For budgeteers, **Bel-Air Eden**, next to the Regina, is spic, span, and snappy. We consider it superior for the modest outlay. **Bernerhof Garni**, adjoining the Central Wolter, is also a tidy choice for tidy, uncluttered wallets. Noisy, but a pretty good buy.

Gstaad offers the **Palace** as a traditional attraction. This castle-style building, Swiss flags flying from its truncated ramparts, dominates the village. It draws an ultrachic, sophisticated, international clientele, which is bolstered by fashionable residents of opulent chalets who make it their social fulcrum; many guests wear black tie every night at dinner. The lobby and many of its public rooms are conservative rather than high-borne. Exceptions include: (1) The *wonderful* Maxim's Room, which blooms on Saturday nights only. The world's greatest headliners are either on the stage or in the audience. (2) The suave Grill-Bar with dancing nightly, presided over by André, one of Europe's most famous and beloved dispensers. (3) The pleasant, charming, well-executed dining salon. Veteran-Proprietor-Director Ernest Scherz keeps hthese running as smoothly, as quietly, and as sumptuously as a Rolls-Royce Mulliner-Park Ward convertible. Hi-Fi Club in basement for teen-agers or young marrieds, jumping from 4 to 6:30 P.M. and from 8 P.M. to 1 A.M.; large skating rink, curling, 2-lane "automatic" bowling, tennis, heated pool, beauty parlor, and table tennis room; instructors for all sports; sauna and massage; within call (off premises), everything from golf to riding to ski lifts to mumblety-peg. Of a total of 230 bedchambers, the majority have bath or shower; the best doubles end with "25". It is very expensive, but only a few francs higher than its nearest competition (and *infinitely* worth the difference). Here certainly is one of this globe's finest mountain hotels, suavely and savvily run by Herr Scherz, his delightful wife Silvia, and their 2 stalwart sons. Top recommendation.

The **Parkhotel** occupies its own hilltop. Somewhat stuffy public rooms; natural-wood bar-grill in the cellar (athwart a slope); the 2-table Cave Romande is the dividing hyphen between the latter units. Well maintained, with pots of new cosmetics applied—but, except for its situation and the cellar installation we have described, it's so fuddy-duddy that here is a Giant Step down from the Palace in elegance, quality, and flair (but not in tariffs). Open mid-December to late March, and early June to late September. The **Bellevue**, at the approach to the village and structurally similar to the Parkhotel, is set in its own garden just off the main highway. We have the feeling this one caters heavily and somewhat impersonally to mass tourism. Also seasonal. The **Alpina**, near the Palace but on higher ground, has been refurbished and scrubbed up of late. A 70-bed wing and a few baths recently added; run-of-the-mill décor with spare provincial zest. In season the **Olden** is appealing more as a merry perch for night owls than for its lodgings. Miss Hedy, known far and wide as "the Dinah Shore of the Piano," is the magnetic English-speaking proprietress; she's a Hedy charmer. Attractive café and restaurant; popular La Cave for cellar-brations; 25 simple bedchambers and 4 baths that are no better than routine in any regard—but here's the 5th-ranking house in Gstaad. **Post-Rössli** offers a total of 50 rooms; 7 of which are in an annex; good cuisine; homey atmosphere. The location is noisy but handy (no taxi required to get to the doin's), and the price is right. The little **Chalet Christiania** is breakfast-only; clean, well situated, and inexpensive. **Bernerhof**, a toot from the railroad station, is, in our opinion, a gloomy mass-production sleeping factory for the European tour-group mobs. Not recommended for Americans. In a special category, the **Chesery** is an exquisitely executed chalet-style building with 3 handsome dining areas—but with a total of only 1 suite and 3 double rooms for overnighting. Its 4 accommodations are tastefully and imaginatively done in what might be punned as late Cantonese. Although it is chic, expensive, and fine—albeit with a high decibel level at night—we'd still be far, far happier parking our tired tootsies at the Palace. If this one had more door keys, however, it would definitely rate as #2 in the region. A friendly M.D. from Philadelphia sent us a brotherly Rx for the **Sporthotel Rütti**, operated by the Villiger family. It's a couple of minutes out of the center and sounds just the medicine for quieting jangled nerves and face-lifting sagging spirits into robust smiles. Thank you, Doctor! At *Chateau-d'Oex*, 8 miles away, we hear mighty alluring reports about the **Chalet du Bon Accueil**. This new one on us is our goof in inadequate coverage, for which our faces are red in embarrassment. This omission will be rectified.

In *Interlaken*, most of the accommodations are strictly Swiss-Resort-Traditional: Gables, cupolas, crystal chandeliers, terraces, red plush, Louis Quinze via Basle or Grand Rapids. Along hotel row, which fronts the main park for several blocks, the Splendid, Victoria-Jungfrau, Schweizerhof (razed by fire while in the process of renovation), Belvedere, Royal St. Georges,

Beau-Rivage (bus parties by the scores), and Du Lac line up stiffly, primly, and austerely, almost tippet-to-tippet. Shades of Grandma's day! To us, the sight is like viewing a bikini-clad beauty contest of octogenarians. The 180-pillow **Métropole** is a renewed chick which must be shaking up the old biddies. It boasts an indoor pool, a sauna, heaps of entertainment facilities, oodles of drinking and snacking corners, plus the welcome hint of fresh innkeeping ideas. We must see this babe on our next visit. The **Victoria-Jungfrau**, partially redecorated back yonder in '58, has the weightiest reputation; excellent for its style; many groups, but these served in a separate dining salon; recommended. The **Beau-Rivage**, near the Interlaken-Ost station, is painfully plain in some of its accommodations and painlessly fine in some of its others; savory à la carte temptations and excellent dining-room service; bitter howls from Guidesters who tell us that the bed-and-bathroom linens aren't changed often enough and that it is time for the fumigators to pay a call here. The family-style **Krebs** has a variety of rooms, and a friendly welcome; complaints have been received concerning the limitations of its menu. The mother and sister of the renowned Krebs clan operate an 80-room, 20-bath companion called the **Bellevue**, in the old part of town; the traveling McKennys report identically excellent cuisine, a lovely garden, good service, plenty of towels, taut management; they should know. The **Belvedere**, however, is not recommended; reports of surly desk personnel would keep us away. The **Bernerhof** and **Eurotel** top our agenda for our next go-around. The former, however, is on the bottom of the list of a kindly Clearfield, Pa., Guidester who wails that she could find "more amenities in a railroad station than in room #48." Perfect holiday community for travelers between 80 and 120 years of age.

In *Klosters*, the **Silvretta** and the Vereina stand Alp-high above local competition with the newer Pardenn challenging hard. At the former, under progressive-thinking Giorgio Rocco's 1-man administrative reign, sleeping quarters have been renewed throughout and vast sums were poured into a top-to-bottom modernization program. Recently added baubles include the handsome Charcoal Grill Rôtisserie with its small dance floor, a coffee bar, and the charming, split-level Five-to-Five club. Hotel now operating in winter only; current total of 115 rooms and 85 baths; elastic pension plan to suit the appetite of either the robust athlete or the relaxed lounge lizard; dining privileges, with meal vouchers, at the ski restaurant on the $6,000,000 Madrisa slopes development—a wonder of landscape engineering designed for sports lovers; indoor pool possibly now a-gurgling in the south court of the building. Mr. Rocco knows his business. Better every year—but expensive. The 100-room **Vereina** has zoomed up with such dramatic improvement over the past few seasons that it now shares our top billing. Father-and-son team of Anton and Stephan Diethelm fret personally over the needs of every client. Baronial atmosphere in public rooms ndand lounges; dancing in season (live orchestra) in the Grisons-style Caveau; adjoining dining room; warmhearted pub-grill with live lobsters and other seafood; Scotch Bar in tartan, with a piano tinkling during the busy hours; tennis courts; ski school at the back doorstep. Most of the accommodations come with private bath; about ⅓rd have their own balcony (the views overlooking the slopes are superb); the southwestern units, with wood paneling, are excellent; #23 is a double with a single annex—a perfect combo for a couple with a small child. Most units extra-spacious and comfortable; swimming pool newly bubbling. All-in-all, a happy feeling pervades this wholesome family retreat. The **Pardenn**, the first major new entry in Klosters in far too long, indisputably steals the local thunder for modernistic good looks. Long, balconied, 5-story building bordered by slate walks, 2½ acres of south-side lawns, and luxurious flower beds; broad terraces; copper-hooded open grill; open or glass-bound heated swimming pool, depending on the season; sauna plus beauty and health facilities; bar-lounge; sumptuous suites; spacious twin units with seating alcoves; same Graessly proprietorship as the Prätschli in Arosa and the Elite in Geneva. Excellent for physical assets—and definitely among the frontrunners. Hans Guler's **Chesa Grischuna**, another highland jewel, exudes a rustic-style ambiance so delightful it would mellow the crustiest of Philadelphia lawyers. Total of 30 accommodations in knotty-pine *arvenholz* style (5 with bath and 3 with shower), including a 14-room (6 with bath) annex with larger bedchambers —and that's all! But if you'll search the premises, you'll also uncover a restaurant, subterranean bowling lanes, a sportsman's bar, music, and barrels of animation. Here indeed is a pint-size prodigy. The 30-room **Alpina**, a short glide from the station, offers cozy shelter. Old-fashioned lounge-bar; ground-floor restaurants where Proprietor-Chef Hermann Bolliger pans out masterly vittles; small dining salon à la Louis XV; attractive, well-maintained units, all with radio and telephone; warmhearted staff. Good value. **Guler's Weisskreuz** is chiefly for groups; it's a white-hot money-saver for budget pilgrims, however.

In *Lausanne*, the **Beau Rivage** in the Ouchy district (5 minutes from the center) still gets a palm and a salaam—but the Lausanne Palace is now giving it a battle. Director-General Walter O. Schnyder (pronounced "Schneeder") and Directress Irmgard Muller, both internationally respected hoteliers, have supervised its $2,000,000 reconstruction cycle—and today's results are terrific. Almost all the one-time Victorian stuffiness of this landmark has gently been eased out, without disturbing its gracious atmosphere. A $650,000 conversion of a staff house into a guest annex containing 3 duplex suites is under way. Its 3 wings have been melded into one smoothly functioning composite. One superdeluxe $40,000 duplex apartment (sitting room, 2 double bedrooms, 2 baths, maid's room, and private stairway) is operative; enchanting Grill (closed Mon. and for lunch); expanded bar; corridors beautified. Lovely gardens which require 8 full-time gardeners and 2 year-round flower arrangers; tennis courts; automatic laundry; 80-car garage. One of the very top hotels of Switzerland.

The aforementioned **Lausanne Palace**, born an aristocrat many decades ago, continues to reveal its *pur sang* breeding. All accommodations in the Palace Building have now been refurbished; the Grill has bounced back with such flair that it is one of the 2 most fashionable hotel restaurants in the city —superb both in visual appeal and culinary performance. The Brummell Night Club is operated by an independent company. The connecting Beau Site Building has been made ready for your Beau Site-seeing, adding 50 rooms to the overall total plus shops by Pucci, Ferragamo, Saint Laurent, and

Gerard, plus a sleekly modern barber and beauty salon, plus a sauna and massage parlor, plus a new bar and garden court, plus, plus, . . . plus! Many accommodations feature shadowless reading lamps, pillow-side command consoles for adjusting everything in the room except your bedfellow, electric blinds, infrared bathroom heating and piped music as you bathe, Frigobars, thermal taps, and—wow!—we're breathless. You might be, too, when you see this palatial Palace. Magisterial management by E. L. ("Milo") Niederhauser, former secretary of the International Hotel Association; Concierge Ernest is the perfect Answerman for your Lausanne needs. The ingredients in this elegant, salubrious sanctuary are now manifestly alluring. Also highly recommended.

Despite its heavily geriatric clientele and its overstuffed public areas, we also have a high regard for the **Royal Savoy**. Modernized entrance to this old-fashioned baronial establishment; 120 of its 135 rooms with baths; restaurant overlooking garden; bar; 2 conference quadrants; swimming pool plus skating rink and tennis courts 200 yards away. The staffers are especially warm and kind here. At long last the **Mirabeau** is clean and comfortable; central location and traditional in tone. Ask for a waterside room on the 4th floor; these are the quietest and most viewful. Also fresh from the beautician come the **De la Navigation** and the **Du Parc**; we hear both are stunners but we've seen neither personally. The **Carlton** boasts 55 face-lifted units, all with private bath; try for #310–11, a corner suite; its refurbished Le Richelieu Grill is a favorite of peripatetic royalty; the Ascot Bar is spirited; friendly, ever-helpful Concierge Peter is a BIG plus for keen-eyed Director André L. Chollet. Sound in a cozy way. The **Victoria** greets incomers with a lovely Lurçat tapestry behind the reception desk. Attractive Le Paddock nightclub; snack bar; 65 units, most with bath and some with rubber executive chairs and padded headboards that smelled to us like gymnasium wrestling mats on a hot day; #311 is a pleasant garden-sited double in traditional style. We like this one—except for a few of those isolated appurtenances. The **de la Paix** recently added 36 new units with bath; bid for one of these if you check in. The mercantile **Terminus**, opposite the Central Station, has redesigned its entrance and inaugurated a Renaissance Salon; recent bar, lounge, and breakfast nook as well; 80 modern rooms with bath or shower. The **Continental**, also hard by the station, chugs in with 123 pleasantly modern bedchambers. Within its slick core are Le Beaujolais Restaurant for French cuisine and grills, the Lobster Bar with critters from the aquarium yours for the choosing, the Snack Bar, and the Basement Brasserie; there are also a downstairs shooting gallery and a bowling alley. Front units air-conditioned; 5th-floor attic rooms spun up as demisuites; décor highlighted with paneling or stonework in soft brown, yellow, or orange tones. Convenient, comfortable, and functional; better for Hiltonites than for Old Worlders. The **City**, a Georges Fassbind holding, is plain, stark, and distressingly plastic-ridden. Bare lobby; narrow but fresh-looking corridors; bright accommodations with new furniture; 70 bedchambers with only 18 full baths and 4 showers. Popular among students and the parsimonious. The **Alpha**, formerly called Des Palmiers, a clean, rapidly expanding 270-bed house, has also been taken over by Mr. Fassbind; glazed-concrete lobby; cellar-situated Carnotzet for raclette, fondue, and other Alpine specialties; ground-level Calèche restaurant for more conventional dining; extensive bedroom revampings with wide windows, colorful linens, radios (which we like) and nonclosing closets, low beds, and eensie baths (which we don't like). A fair bet for tolerant trippers. The newly arrived **Parking**, yet another Fassbinder, officially is rated as First-class. Space for more than 200 parkers, about 300 yards from the main station. Its 2 restaurants serve up French cuisine plus specialties such as Fondue Bacchus and Malayan Curry. Another foreign entry on our visit was Memphis Slim —on the keyboard. The **Bellerive**, a converted apartment house, offers a micro-lobby, a black-red-blue-yellow-brown-white miniature bar, and 38 tiny, cramped, functional, sterile bedchambers; not the nest for tall, rangy, or long-shanked Americans. The 104-room **Novotel** opened very recently; it boasts a grill and a swimming pool, but more we cannot tell you. The revamped **Château d'Ouchy** is a bulky antique whose site dates back to the twelfth century. Today all bedchambers come with shower and private bath; some accommodations only slightly smaller than Burning Tree Golf Course. Tourist-oriented, but different. Long ago, the mighty Beau Rivage (see above) absorbed the next-door Lutétia et Florissant, invested $500,000 in a modernization program, and renamed it **La Résidence.** All the 60 rooms in both buildings of this First-class entry have baths, showers, and double washbasins. Sharp-eyed Walter O. Schnyder has generously donated his charming wife as the manageress of this domain. Ideal for quiet types or well-behaved family groups; salutes as a restful haven.

In *Leysin* the **Grand Hôtel** is biggest and best—and probably one of the only hostelries in the world with its very own railway station. Game room, indoor pool, tennis, bar with dancing; its Carnotzet, *the* local hangout, is often merry. Sleeping space for 250 clients; furnishings too spartanlike for our taste. The undisputed local leader—but a poor relative to the number one houses in scores of other Swiss resorts. **Central-Résidence** turns on an indoor swimmin' hole, a loggia-terrace with every room, a kitchenette, and a full bath count. A youngster with plenty of pepper. **La Mésange** offers a colorful, chipper lobby; an extremely cozy dining room with wide windows framing its L-shape; very small bedrooms, and 2 private baths. Imaginative despite its structural limitations. **Les Orchidées** is a small, sharply angled, pastel-hued edifice dropping downhill from the main road. Bland, zingless furnishings and décor in its public rooms and 25 bedchambers. So-so. The **Eden** we don't know from overnighting, but its view is lovely. **Mont-Riant** nestles by the edge of the forest. All front units with balconies; outstanding cuisine; otherwise routine. **La Paix**, with its trim chalet exterior, is in a somewhat noisy location; friendly staff and atmosphere; tiny, tiny bedchambers. **La Primevère** is simple; it does have a good kitchen. **Relais**, in First class, is comfortable. The remainder are so bareboned that most U.S. visitors would probably be happier spending the night under a spruce.

In *Locarno*, the **Palma au Lac** celebrates more than a century of gracious living, growing mellower every year. Its *haute cuisine* is internationally famous—for excellent reason. Byronic setting; focal point for high-life and action; terrace dining by the shore in season; friendly bar with piano lilts nightly; attractive French-style restaurant; elegant Coq d'Or Grill with gold flatware, candelabra, and a 14-karat ambiance; courteous reception and staff attitudes. Proprietor Bolli, aided by Assistant Manager Michael Bolli, is a warmhearted and devoted hotelier whose avuncular cheer seems to permeate his house. He has lately waved his magic wallet to make it even more radiant. There's an indoor heated pool, a private strip of lakeside beach, a sauna, a barbershop and beauty salon; many new suites have been unveiled. (Those we've inspected are gorgeous.) All front units with full bath and balcony; back units now about 50% with full plumbing; most rooms are adequate to spacious. Concierge Giuseppe Bass will sort out most any problem. All-in-all, this one beams—and we think you might, too, when you check in. Top recommendation. The spacious **Esplanade** (Aubonne Section) offers a lovely lake view, open-air dining, dancing, a heated pool, a restyled lobby, vans of new furniture, and a rekindled spirit that has it glowing radiantly. The new house policy is to encourage longer, more relaxing visits rather than the brief sojourns so common to big-city hostelries. It is managed by Ulrich Schattner, with his guidance provided by the superlative Hangartner team, famed far and wide for their earlier Dolder Grand magic in Zürich and their present direction of the Palace Hotel in St. Moritz. Here is a bucolic country address to keep in mind, especially if you are on a lazy trip by car to or from Italy. The **Park**—for a change, this one *does* occupy an honest-to-goodness park in the city—has bounced back with such vim and Vigoro that it plucks a pretty orchid. Its turquoise pool is a perfect color meld with the stately braces of peacocks which strut in iridescent splendor at its brim. If you are an avid naturalist who seeks Edwardian amenities in twentieth-century Europe, you might enjoy unpacking your trowel, hoopskirts, and spats here. For tranquillity seekers, it's an Eden, but for high-spirited youngbloods accustomed to more razzmatazz, we don't believe this one would swing with more than a minuet. The **Reber**, along the promenade where the Palma au Lac also resides, seems to have grown cooler on our charts. Swimming pool a-bubbling; tennis courts; nightclub next to the Grill; 3rd and 4th floors featuring private refrigerators, safes, and furnishings that are a cross between classic and avant-garde; balconies jutting from each waterside unit; corridors sheathed in mock-wood; baths cramped and poorly executed. When you register, try to snag #208, a wide-angled older type double which is 10% cheaper than the latest wingers—and we think better. The rates are in the same general bracket as our top choice, but the rewards are not so high, in our opinion. The adjoining **Pavilion Reber** offers 14 rooms and 14 baths—a pleasant outbuilding with motel privacy but hotel-room service. Better every year. The **Orselina**, at the top of the funicular winking down at the slope, the town, and Maggiore, is a honey of a perch for tranquillity seekers. Kips for 100 relaxers who can probably be heard zzzzz-ing on any quiet afternoon. The modernistic **Muralto**, only a puff from the station, overlooks the lake from its midcity perch. Within its shell is a snack center, a terrace restaurant, a heated pool, a metropolitan post office, a newsstand, 2 levels of shops, and an arcade. The décor is a blend of twentieth-century and earlier themes; which, paradoxically, meld well. Spankingly clean and eye-stimulating; bar and refrigerator in lakefront units; good baths with twin basins; huge towels; service primarily for do-it-yourselfers. For what it is, we like it. The

Quisisana's best feature is its waterside dining room. Much better dwelling space now, too. The **Rondinella** proudly boasts a covered swimming pool; pleasant bedchambers, but a rawboned and unappetizing restaurant that is somehow quite popular; we've never sampled the skilletcraft. The **Remorino** provides space for 44 sleepers; full bath ratio; breakfast only. The **Beau Rivage** has been refashioned, but it will never make the cover of *Vogue*. The **Excelsior**, next to the Tennis Club, serves up 25 rooms with bath or shower, clean, unadorned simplicity, amateurish management, and budget-bracket tariffs; sun worshipers will revel in its roof-garden solarium. The **Belvédère** impresses us as a potentially desirable way-stop which is going to seed—and we wish it were otherwise. The tiny **Alexia Garni**, on the Station Square at Locarno-Muralto, offers breakfast only; Ticino-style lobby, about a dozen rooms in a private house, economy prices. **Zücherhof** is even more simple. The **Motel Losone**, 5 minutes' drive from the center toward Ascona, doesn't send us—except, perhaps, farther down the pike.

Want a real adventure in this region? Try the **Cardada Hotel**, 4500 feet up the Cardada Alp via one of the most hair-raising rides by suspension railway ever sweated by the acrophobic traveler. The view is unbelievable from this little hostelry; if you're not a sissy about cliff-hanging, a night here will be an experience you'll never forget.

In *Lucerne*, the fresh-faced **Grand National** ranks among the key stopping places of the nation for appointments, luxury, and attention to the guest. Its high-spirited cordial director, Eric Glattfelder, is injecting even greater turn-of-the-century elegance and twentieth-century vitality into this grande dame. Capacity of 208 rooms and 140 renewed baths; savory food in its perked-up restaurant and sumptuous festival hall; noisy street side now hushed by double-pane windows; open March 15 to November 1 only; expensive and fine. The **Palace** has rebounded so dramatically from its earlier listlessness that young-in-heart deluxe wayfarers might enjoy it even more than the somewhat austere Grand National. Swinging Intimo nightclub, reshaped in split-level with ruby and sapphire tones, *belle époque* fixtures, Lautrec prints, and the ambiance of a soft-spoken discothèque; all public rooms totally overhauled, corridors brightened and beautified; refreshed Mignon-Grill and bar; nearly every bedchamber and bath spiffed up, most of them boasting fabric wall coverings underlined with foam-rubber matting for silent nights; raw-silk curtains usually mated to upholstered headboards; a handful of mother-in-law rooms (aren't *all* mothers-in-law a handful?) The new modern-style wing plus a pool and a sauna are on the futures list. With its enviable setting on the lakeside promenade, we think more and more Americans of taste will flock to its doorstep. Now open year round. The **Schweizerhof** claims an excellent lakefront location. Fuddy-duddy features, fossilized furnishings, and flagrant fustiness are strategically offset by up-to-date trappings and occasional revisions. In the new wing, every accommodation is air-conditioned, double doors are installed, and all appurtenances have been reupholstered or replaced. The older wing still suffers from geriatric miseries. Why in heaven's name doesn't it perk up its bar and throw out the cheap carney-show candy game machine in its lobby? We are still hoping that the dust will begin to fly, now that the Hauser family proprietors are—after disgracefully shameless years of delay—speaking franc-ly. The **Carlton-Tivoli** is still being extensively remodeled by Director Fritz Furler, who is aided in the day-to-day operations by veteran Marco Hefti. Entire façade modernized; roof-garden restaurant with lakeside dining in addition; Grill and expanded terrace recently unveiled; kitchen recooked not long ago; oodles of bedrooms refashioned; 3 luxury suites, 120 rooms, and a full bath count; high incidence of refurnishings and updatings including the addition of TV and refrigerators for many units. Private bathing and water skiing; 4 tennis courts; dancing in 1 of its 2 popular bars. Now a very good bet at the price—*if* you hit the right location. The **Astoria**, an 8-story establishment on the main Pilatusstrasse thoroughfare, has been renovated and given a lobby on the street level. (Previously guests signed in near the roof line.) A much better arrangement in a much better house. The midcity **Monopol & Metropole** has been completely revamped in a spiffy way. Good medium-price dining room; busy bar; 5th-floor units never given to groups; #314 especially pleasant twin in Tirolean theme. Solid value. The **Montana,** 250 feet above the Palace, is reached by funicular or road. Glass-and-aluminum entrance tacked onto a period piece; 75 rooms and 45 baths; most units with balcony; 80% of them face the lake; we're fond of #114; closed in winter. Fair. The sweet little **Luzernerhof** has cozy rooms and picture windows with Venetian blinds; improved lobby, reception, and bar; new 12-room annex; good dining salon consistently serving up some of the yummiest cuisine in the region; all accommodations so clean and bright that they cheer the soul. The **Wilden Mann** also offers one of the leading restaurants in the city; fresh-as-Swiss-cream kitchen and modernized dining facilities; meal-exchange program with the Carlton-Tivoli and the Gütsch (see below); 2 small, quiet penthouse suites with terraces overlooking a charming crazy quilt of roofs; 20 bedchambers face-lifted and 24 baths installed; antique-style décor in this architectural joining of 7 tiny houses. Now under the management of Walter Arndt. We've never stayed at the **Royal**, but it looks adequate for its category; closed November to Easter. The **Hermitage**, 5 minutes out at Seeburg, impressed us as quite an investment for the noise, the discomfort, and the inconvenience that one might encounter for even the very low rates; creaky old section; loud, road-sited, modern annex. Not recommended by this book under any circumstances. The twelfth-century **Balances & Bellevue** is in a special category. Pilgrims with a penchant for antiquity might feel they're stepping right into a Brueghel landscape here (or, if they're lodged facing the street, into a boiler factory which clangs until 1 A.M. or 2 A.M.). Romantic painted façade commanding the Weinmarkt (Wine Market Square) and the River Reuss, on the more tranquil postern side; décor predictably flounced in velvets, tapestries, and similarly fussy froufrou; warm, attractive Zur Ratslaube dining room with abundant art work, red curtains, and chain-held chandeliers; enchanting vine-lined terrace that will level you, eyeball-to-eyeball, with inquisitive swans. When Zur Ratslaube overflows its capacity, clients may take their meals in the mural-clad Rotes Gatter, in which hangs a portrait of this very room painted 8 centuries ago. Total of 80 bedchambers; 50 private baths; 16 single units; try ample-size #37 for a more expensive accommodation or #10 for a satisfactory smaller nest. If your beard measures 9 feet, and if you can tolerate the correct but sometimes disagreeable-to-wayfarers current management, we think you might adore this gentle, venerable escape from the Missile Era. The comfortably revamped **Gütsch** is also in a singular bracket in our reporter's notebook. This interesting castle-like structure is located 5 minutes above the city, with an enchanting vista of the lake and the huddle of pitched roofs below. Authentic iron battle masks flanking the entrance, plus such decorative carry-overs inside as lances, suits of armor, and mounted deer heads; swimming pool in the forest garden; open patio with terrace-nibbling in summer; 2 dining rooms; dancing nightly in the rustic hall; wine cellar with Fondue service. Its 45 gaily recast rooms include 4 extra-charming duplex apartments in split-level arrangement for intimate hideaways, some units with four-poster beds, open ceiling beams, soft carpeting, and the atmosphere of a medieval fortress; now there's an excellent private bath with every accommodation. Taking giant strides under new Manager Ralph Alder. Here's a manorial haven for the right type of overknighter. Down by the lake again, the **Seeburg**, with space for about 100 Seeburgers, opened its portals recently, then added an annex to augment its capacity. All units canted toward the water; all with bath or shower and balcony; 3 restaurants. We got the impression that its main target is touring parties rather than individual wayfarers. The **de la Paix** has undergone a peaceful revolution. It still doesn't suffer from aggressive tendencies, but the pool is a cool fillip.

Lugano's 150-plus hotels and pensions have changed radically over the past few seasons. Our recent harvest of notes shifts the ratings extensively. In the town, the lakeside **Eden** has been given a shower of delights. It is now vivaciously colorful and modernistic. Sunbursts, arcs, glowing beads, bangles, painted rainbows, dyed leather, cheery textiles, sprightly plastics, and other gladsome inspirations of fanciful artistry give this house a decorative character unmatched anywhere in contemporary Europe. Totally upbeat lobby in cool, whimsical tones; fairytale lounge with coral sink-in seats matching the carpets; canary-yellow breakfast room dolloped by orbital disks; grill ringed by circular patterns; ultra-hip turquoise snack bar; adjoining waterside terrace for dining, sipping, or dancing; heated pool plus another one filled with salt (*sic*) water—in landlocked Switzerland. Bedchambers also flairfully attired, with balcony, radio consoles, TV, and refrigerator; predominating schemes of olive, blue, or red. This one now stays open year round. It's a must for Peter Maxiamatic Modernists. In the nearby shoreside village of *Morcote,* the **Olivella Au Lac** scoops clean-lined luxury into a parfait of tranquillity. Viewful French restaurant; tavern-style snackery; amusing nightclub (watch out for those chairs that resemble a shark's mouth); glass-fronted indoor swimmery plus garden-sited pool; massage and beauty parlors; nursery. The bedchambers are smart but not spectacular; comfort standards range nearer to superior First class than to Deluxe. Very worthy as a hideaway, if you don't mind the distance from the center. Back in the city, the **Splendide-Royal** now has been given a spiffing up and a watering down—the latter via an indoor domed and skylighted natatorium. Classic resort mien, with all the traditional appurtenances; noisy location on main boulevard facing lake (a disadvantage shared by all other major hostelries except the Arizona); waterfront bar. Try to get accommodations on the 3rd or 4th floors, which are the most modern in mood. Open all year. The **Europa** has also been on the jump. Very recently restyled and updated; modernized dining room; adjoining outdoor patio with bubbling fountain and awning arcade; heated covered pool with hanging garden and bar; service occasionally rankling; parking for 50 cars; street-level shops and Café Boulevard where snack-meals appear. Sleeping accommodations are pleasant; front corner doubles are best; well liked by upper-echelon tour groups. Proprietor Rolf Fassbind is especially fond of Americans. Recommended. The **Bellevue au Lac**'s now-completed renovation program has nobly reglamorized this fading dowager. Lobby completely updated; tasteful dining salon plus open-air grill; bar; most rooms converted to modern tone; color TV on request (but we prefer the lake view from the balconies); extra-efficient kitchen; all units now with private bath. Much improved and now staying open for all seasons. The 60-room **Arizona**, high on a hill overlooking the town and the water, is a friendly and comfortable oasis for the weary motorist. Curious but intriguing Jet Age architecture; all rooms with bath or shower, balcony, and angular walls in irregular directions. It has now been purchased by the bright-eyed and bright-idea-ed Eden gardeners who plan to add splashes of a new pool plus other dashes of pepper very soon. Offbeat but surprisingly pleasing. The ultramodern **Du Lac**, hard by the water, has been totally revivified. Floating swimming pool bobbling at the edge of its own sandy beach; managed smoothly by Mr. Corrado Kneschaurek. Very pleasant. **La Residenza**, a tawny newcomer, serves breakfast only, but it also serves up tennis courts, a pool, and a beach. The **Select**, also just hatched, is one we haven't inspected personally. The cream-colored **Motel Vezia**, 10 minutes along the St. Gothard highway, is a steadily improving possibility for the roadbound. Adjoining restaurant; heated pool—red-hot sauna, too; low rates; 150 beds; most units with bath or shower. Tip-top administration by Roland and Rosemarie Wilke, formerly of the Arizona. The **Excelsior** shelters 100 souls per night—not with much inspiration, either, in our view. The **Plaza** is a bargain, considering its competition. About 2 blocks from the lake; 33 small, functional rooms, all with radio and bath or shower; bed-and-breakfast only; open year round. The **Schmid** in *Paradiso* (foot of the San Salvatore funicular) is said to be clean, quiet, and comfortable; rates are low for its full-pension rewards. We'll look in soon. In the district, the **Admiral** sails in as an imposing member of the local flotilla. Very trim indeed. The **De la Paix** also seems to be a relaxing medium-price oasis in this suburb. The **Commodore**, a converted apartment house, is now sailing under the burgee of Manager J.P. Crettaz, formerly of Portugal's excellent Penina Golf Hotel. This one has a fine situation and many up-to-date riggings to recommend it. A sister operation, the **De la Paix** in *Lugano Paradiso*, provides a heated open-air pool which is available to visiting Commodores and Doras. Both sound very nice for their category. We must also size up the park-bound **Villa Castagnola** in outlying *Cassarate* and the **Ring** apart-hotel in neighboring *Bissone*; both boast swimming facilities.

In *Montreux*, the **Palace**, under the wing of Director Alfred Frei, is worth the francs in value. New entry and lobby; new *Salle de spectacles;* new coffee nook, bar, shopping arcade, and glass-lined elevators to the restaurant level; kitchen rebuilt; virtually all of its 270 rooms now totally freshened, with the best facing the lake and with balcony; automatic phone system; lovely pool with Bather's Bar and cabanas. Commendable on every score. The 170-room-and-bath, chain-operated **Eurotel** makes a vigorous splash with an indoor-outdoor pool plus sauna and massage facilities; 3 handsome dining areas; many units with kitchenette; rooms ending with "5" featuring lakefront balcony. For modernists who prefer sleekness and dash in their architecture to strict conventionality, here's the lone choice in town. The **Excelsior**, on the lake, is blessed by blissful vistas and the lively ownership of Mr. and Mrs. Fritz Liechti. Almost every room has been cunningly redone; additional major works also have been wrapped up, including a new lobby, bar, expansion of the Grill and terrace, redecoration of the dining room (with delicious food as a standard bonus), a new wing of apartments with its own pool, sauna, and sporting club. The southwest corner doubles (rooms #116, 136, 156, 176, 196) are extra-beguiling in taste, brightness, charm, livability, and space. Cheers to this imaginative and energetic duo for their valiant revolution. The **National** has also been given the works in its beauty treatment. Proprietor Frei forked out a virtual fortune in completely refurbishing this 100-year-old house. Lobby and public sections agreeably redone; appetizing à la carte Restaurant Français plus the Panoramic dining salon; fresh-as-droplets garden-sited pool; service and cuisine reported excellent; total of 60 units and 46 baths, with the best on the front. Long-stayers should be sure to order the units with the big baths; the small ones are passable only for overnighters. Mr. Frei has made great strides with this architecturally difficult plant. Now creditably on the ball. The **Golf** doesn't shoot its par; uninspired and lackluster, despite some earnest perkup touches such as the repainting of its façade; the adjoining **Villa Arizona** offers 12 modern rooms and baths that we prefer to those in the main operation. Both houses lunch and dine in the wooded, rustic Fromagerie (you can guess the specialties). The **Eden** had her face made up and opened a new entrance, new bars, new restaurants, and 105 new bedchambers. The style is fresh but traditional. Fair. Other worthy choices include the smallish **Bonivard**, the somewhat larger **Europe** (different from the Eurotel), the 100-pillowed **Helvétie**, and the massive **Grand-Territet** (in the district from which it takes its name). Budget bets? It's extremely difficult to scout out inexpensive lodgings here, due to heavy all-year pressures on available accommodations. But these which follow are our favorites: **Hôtel de Londres**, on the main highway, is well maintained, popular, and very successful. **Pension Wilhelm**, well situated on the rue de Marché, is immaculate; not too many private baths for its 60-bed capacity. **Pension Masson**, next to the Castle of Chillon, is slowly being modernized; it's a long, long hike from the city: **Les Iris** (in the village of *Chernex*, 10 minutes up the mountain) is family-style, with a captivating view; sweet, quiet, old-shoey. Also above the city in panoramic *Glion sur Montreux*, the **Victoria Glion** apparently has made numerous recent improvements including the addition of a swimming pool. Manager Toni Mittermair respectfully submits that our earlier writeup was outdated and incorrect. In reply to this gentleman's demurrer, we will refrain from all comments about his hostelry until we can offer a full report after a full inspection. As for **Des Alpes Vaudoises** here, it was shuttered temporarily on our recent attempt to inspect it.

Pontresina's **Schlosshotel** skis away with the crown in this winter wonderland. There's an indoor pool, one of the finest in Europe, with a fully mirrored wall reflecting the snow-draped Alps through floor-to-ceiling windows; it's a sapphire gem. Clientele mostly German; 15 suites; 170 beds and 80 baths. Panorama Bar with mountain view; disco-hub called Club Nr. 1, also with orchestra; enchanting Marie Louise Relais for afternoon tea and à la carte dining; Candlelight Dinner Dances plus Ballroom Galas with floor shows; bowling, minigolf, children's playroom; adjoining skating and curling rinks; lovely open terrace for lunch and sunbathing, with separate bar; Rustic Tavern and Fondue Grill for regional or seasonal specialties; hotel bus service to St. Moritz (2 miles) every hour until late evening. Expensive, of course. Pontresina is neither as fortunately situated nor as animated as is next-door St. Moritz, but this beautiful project is making inroads on its international society trade. A delight. The nearby **Kronenhof-Bellavista** seems tacky compared to its elegant peer—especially when you first see that huge, ridiculous illuminated crown on top of its domed rotunda. Swimming pool its greatest pride; about 175 rooms; low bath count; furnishings generally not very attractive; one of the best kitchens in the valley; almost exclusive patronage by rootin' Teutons on snowbound holidays. Only $5 or so cheaper than the Schloss, but a whopping difference in quality. The Swiss-rustic **Schweizerhof** has been renewed; it now appears totally modernized. Cheery, hardy-fare restaurant with cheese specialties; greater variety of nationalities on its register than many other houses in the district; kind service. Solid, stolid, and recommendable. The **Sport Hotel** has polished off an extensive renovation program, adding the Nordiska bar in the process. Big doubles; we like #11, #45, #82, and #122 as extra-spacious twins. Coming up rapidly. The **Walther** has finally been spruced up. We like the spruce in the new Clubhütte nightclub, too. **Engadinerhof** is trying to make improvements. Bedrooms still so-so on our inspection; restaurant going strong. The **Atlas** reformed its world; it now stays open winter and summer. For budgeteers, the village-edge **Steinbock**, owned by the Walther-Palace, is now very pleasant. **Bernina**, also outlying, has an amiable ambiance but tiny bedchambers. No rave. The breakfast-only **Palü** is so modern in tone that it seems almost Scandinavian. Small bedrooms but appealing public corners. Not bad for its type.

St. Moritz? Go between December 1 and April 15 or mid-June to end-September, because these are the seasons. For the lively sophisticate, there is only a single pacesetter, the **Palace**—to us, one of the finest resort hotels of its type we have seen in the world. The building is Wedding Cake, with nothing left off in the way of spires, V-shape gimmicks, and architectural frosting which could possibly be glued or screwed on. Inside, however, it is a triumph of urbanity which brings sunlight to the soul. Direction of this upland paradise is in the incomparably skilled hands of Georges Hangartner, the Master Hotelier who put Zurich's Dolder Grand on the charts of all discriminating global navigators. He works hand-in-hand with the Badrutt brothers, Andrea and Hansjurg, whose family practically founded St. Moritz as a holiday center. The swimming pool, glassbound and set among rocks and a waterfall, might qualify as the 8th wonder of the hotel world. A marine bar overlooks it from the mezzanine. "Regular" bar with dancing and nonstop zip;

elegant little Renaissance Bar, a hideaway for quiet cocktailing and gossiping late at night; "Grand" bar always with the swingingest bands in Europe; Engadiner *Stubli* for more easygoing merriment; *intime* à la carte Grill; regular restaurant; King's Club discothèque full, full, FULL (reserve in the morning); superb service throughout, with client-staff ratio at 1-to-1. Total of 300 rooms, most with bath and all furnished in classic-style comfort and livability; extra-sumptuous suites and 70 units recently restyled with superdeluxe appointments; south side completely balconied; sauna and masseuse; gymnastics and swimming instruction, plus a tennis coach; the only hotel we've inspected which offers decently organized bridge games and tournaments; every plush facility imaginable. A new annex has been opened across the street with a shopping arcade, a floor of "sports type" rooms for youngsters on limited allowances, and a top tier with 3 large apartments for longer lingerers; copious staff and garage space also are tucked into this new petit palace. Sparkling, bright, chichi, social, and usually full. Highest recommendation.

The **Kulm**, a mainstay of tradition and fun, is currently managed by friendly and energetic Heinz Hunkeler who with his sparkling wife Erika did such a magnificent job at Venice's Bauer Grünwald. Extensive recent revampings; restyled East Wing, providing more than 60 spacious, airy, gaily attired units with bath. An Olympic-size heated pool has made its splash in affiliation with the Carlton-Kulm Sporting Club; it's *lovely* for lunch on a warm sunny day; a covered pool and sauna also have added a further dash of merriment. Extra-savory cuisine (our Fettuccine was the best we've devoured in the nation); ballroom, bar, grill, snack-bar, sun terrace, music, 300 beds and about 175 baths. Superb, especially in its newer sleeping segments.

The **Carlton** recently underwent a change in management and ownership, so we must look in this season to find out what plans are afoot. Entire lobby in modernistic tones; Grill-Bar refreshed as well; attractive lounge for dancing. Dining room cookery not up to the standards of the Grill on our samplings. We'll have a new report next edition.

Suvretta-House, a short bus ride (or longish hike) from the center, has been moving alps with its $2,500,000 Suvretta-House-party. She is becoming one of the loveliest ladies of the Engadin. This now-glamorous landmark occupies its own distinguished niche as the ideal family-type hotel. The huge, sprawling structure, perched on its own mountainside with its own spectacular vista, is a totally self-sustaining resort community. Everything is here: The Suvretta ski runs, the Suvretta ski lifts, the Suvretta ski school (40 instructors), the Suvretta skating rinks, the Suvretta stables, and Suvretta nursery, the Suvretta curling rinks—a complete plant for every holiday need, including a glass-lined swimming pool, brightly facing the sunny south. Free bus service to the village every 30 minutes. Handsome wood-lined entrance hall; arched corridors; exquisite nightclub in rouge hue with gold trim; bars everywhere you tipple. Attractive dining room with topflight skilletry, lovely diningterrace, tennis courts, bowling, private club for regional residents, splendiferous boutiques by Celine of Paris and Pucci, playgrounds, orchestras, many social events and galas; garage; vast staff quarters; 325 rooms and 250 baths. Manager Müller pilots this jumbo with skill and grace.

The **Monopol** is a midtowner that has been zooming up dramatically. It is now being managed by Mr. and Mrs. Hans Strässle. Woody Grischuna Grill, filled with animated couples dancing nightly to its peppery combo; adjoining Bärengraben room for specialties, fondues, and other hippy dips; rustic bar popular with chattering bench-sitters; 1 floor plus a covered rooftop pool recently added; solid comfort, pleasant décor, ample space in most accommodations; some units too cramped, however. Concierge Lorenz is so pro-Yankee you'd think he was a presidential candidate. Tariffs hovering between those of the middle bracket and the luxury entries; excellent for the outlay; getting better every year.

In medium-price stops, the **Post** (1 block from the Palace) gets an armload of laurels. Mme. Spiess, for half-a-century active in the hotel and its owner for 3 decades, has posted all of her dedication to her beloved house. It is an exceptional value. Caution: Between seasons, when the Big Four are closed, quotations are jacked up to the Deluxe category. If you can promote one of these choice accommodations for yourself, you should be both snug and satisfied. The strikingly modern **Cristallo** crystallizes all of the dramatic splashes of color, New Wave furnishings, and production-belt concepts that might be found in any equally soulless counterpart in Santiago, Stockholm, or Syracuse. Central location; standard hotel amenities plus hydrotherapy facilities and Finnish mud baths; small bedrooms and tiny baths. Overall, to us at least, it seems as cool as *cristallo*. The **Schweizerhof** has been recently revamped to the tune of nearly $1,000,000. New top floor; restyled dining room; handsome Stübli offering Swiss dishes that vary daily; Sunday night buffet; Scotch Bar; picnic club on the Suvretta slope; wood-lined Grill. Good space, and getting better every season. The newer midcity **Hauser** features a restaurant-tearoom at ground level and 50 wood-toned, brightly decorated bedchambers above. Pert, reasonable, and fun. Then there's the rather expensive **Chantarella**, halfway up Corviglia in lofty isolation; full of terraces, sports chatter, gaggles of easygoing old-timers taking their ease in easy chairs, and hot buttered rum; 110 units, many facing south; open-air restaurant; skating and curling rinks; principally for ski enthusiasts and dedicated relaxers. The **Calonder**, at the edge of the village, offers about 70 rooms and 24 baths; most have recently been redone, and 30 have radio; cozy, appealing Caprice Grill; pleasant bar and lounge; not operated during the dead months; amiable—and we hope it stays that way under its new owners. The **Steffani**, in Class 1-B, has its amusing modernized Malibu discothèque; self-service cafeteria; cozy Cresta Bar; bowling, terrace-dining, other features. There's a new penthouse level; most other nests have been refluffed; a garage adjoins; very central and swinging in its youthful way. The **La Margna** and the **Bernasconi** (very, very outstanding restaurant in the last; Herbert von Karajan, royalty, and quiet types often slip in here for tranquil stopovers) are small and economy-level. **Languard**, our choice of the *garni* bets, is where we once spent 2 weeks of a delightful ski holiday. Same view as the Palace; a family-run and family-feeling hideaway which we loved. The **Bernina** is in the same league. Finally, the old-style but well-outfitted and well-situated **Belvédère** also serves only breakfast; solid bedchamber comforts; small indoor pool; reasonable tariffs. Not at all bad as a respectable money-saver.

In *Villars*, a 30-minute drive from Montreux, the **Sporting** has been totally renewed. It may top the local list, but we won't know until we check in on our next rounds. The **Eurotel** is also new; likewise we haven't seen it. Circumstances have prevented us from getting up here recently, but we'll review this scene soon. **Grand Hôtel du Parc** boasts a woodland setting and a 1932 exterior. Lobby and public rooms warmly inviting; cute minibar; cheerful, airy dining room; 2-lane bowling center and intimate nightclub downstairs; indoor pool 2 curling *pists* and 2 ski lifts. Good taste; skimpy portions sometimes in the cookery; the same parsimonious trait is carried into its 100 pastel-shaded bedrooms. **La Renardière** is composed of 4 separate chalets; heavy French and Belgian patronage who praise its table; fair enough. The viewful **Montesano**, across the Arveyes line on the main road outside the village, resembles the top 2 strata of a 6-layer wedding cake. Entrance via the second coating of icing; clean, sound, and somewhat refashioned by the funloving son of its late proprietor. Developing an upbeat flair. The **Curling** has been given a new curl, wave, manicure, and set. We like the dining room; the bar is a bit overdone and corny. Very sporting. **Marie-Louise** is due for another check by us now that it has new management. In the budget bracket, **Garni Ecureuil** is a honey for its category. Help-yourself-to-your-own-key policy in both its main building (vintage '62) and its older chalet; charmingly cozy dining room with highland specialties; 19 housekeeping "apartments" which are a wonderful buy for 2 people (perfect for long do-it-yourself ski holidays). Genial, enterprising Owner-Manager Charles Seeholzer speaks some English. Closed May and November. Highest recommendation for its type; here is a true "find." The **Chalet Henriette** wiggles in with a polished-rustic exterior that is trim and attractive. Many interior improvements; baths and showers recently tapped on; skillets attended by Proprietor Huguet, who is reported to be a deft chef. A cutie if intimacy is your bag. Also acceptable are the **Richemont, Du Soleil**, and **Chamossaire**.

Zermatt, capped by the Matterhorn, is surely the most scenically exciting resort in the nation. This highland hamlet has mushroomed so fast that we must divide its lodgings into what we call the "Classic Old-Timers" and the "Neomodern Newcomers"—in general, 2 utterly different groupings in mood, architecture, and range of facilities. Here there is no competitive situation of the U.S.-style Hiltons *vs.* the European-style Excelsiors, because nothing resembling an American-conceived hostelry has yet moved into the picture.

The first cluster offers all of the Swiss vintage-traditional earmarks, including the gingerbread. It runs from the best, most spacious, most renowned hostelries to horrors left over from Grandma's epoch. The second is almost universally of the chalet genre (a good example is the exceptionally friendly Alex described below) some built yesterday, with smaller rooms, fewer amenities, more informality, and cheaper tariffs. This class ranges from comfortable contemporary inns (colorful ambiance in modern tone) to jerry-built real estate speculations in which few overseas travelers would find vacation happiness. Let's consider them separately, so that you may satisfy your own personal needs, preferences, and budgets.

"Classic Old-Timers"? The **Mont Cervin** (French for "Matterhorn") for decades has been the most famous hotel of the Canton. More than ever, it deserves that honor. Recently it instituted big changes which include a new reception zone, lobby, lounge, an exquisite residents' bar, conference facilities, injections of cheer and color everywhere, a six-pack of new units in the main building, and a clutch of "romantic" rooms in the original Villa Margharita section. Manager Wolfgang Pinkwart has moved over here from the Monte Rosa (see below) and is doing a commendable job in every respect. It boasts a covered swimming pool plus sauna and massage facilities—a proud feather in its alpine cap. Escargot minibar; main Rendez-Vous interior bar, jammed to the scuppers after nightfall; vastly improved adjoining nightclub also so packed in season that even a midget peri without a table reservation couldn't be shoe-horned in. The skillet-work is good in the main, but the High Season Friday night buffets are nothing short of spectacular—among the finest seen anywhere in Europe today. The spirit, flair, and overall sense of renaissance in this house are thrilling. Better and better.

The **Zermatterhof**, owned by the town's citizens, presents as its face the most professional hotel exterior of all. Handsome, modern entrance into an immaculately pruned lobby; split-level lounge a casebook example of period gentility; L-shape dining room with one leg old-fashioned and the other brightly blended (a curious combination which comes off). The redesigned ground-floor U-shape section, fronting lawn and street, contains (1) the cozy, glass-wrapped, exquisitely executed Grill with an open rôtisserie in its far corner, (2) an ultramodern café with live and discothèque music and eye-jiggling raspberry banquettes, divided from the Grill by yellow and green curtains, (3) a new urbane dining salon, and (4) a sterile, brassy rotunda bar. The 100 rooms, half of the total lately freshened, come with 60 full-tub baths; ⅔rds of them sport appealing Swiss-rustic décor, with burnished and slightly darkened natural wood ceilings, doors, bedboards, wardrobes, and trim; ⅓ rd have a pleasant classic mien; all offer the identical yardsticks of quality and upkeep. General Manager German (pronounced "Gurman" and formerly the Grill Maître) is the efficient and instantly likable Boniface.

The **Seilerhaus**, across the street and only slightly less expensive, is the newest entry in the Seiler stable. Technically, because it debuted in '59, it isn't a Classic Old-Timer—but except in its Stube, the atmosphere is so routine and un-Swiss that it could have been transplanted from Kankakee, Kensington, or Kokomo. Now the façade has been brightened and top and back units are being modernized. The ground floor is occupied by a post office, independent shops, a tiny lobby, a small sun terrace, and a clean-lined but unexciting 140-seat dining room offering a 4-course menu (wide choices), plus snacks. The Otto Furrer-Stube, a basement nook, is described in "Restaurants." In general, a mixture but a good one.

The **Schweizerhof**, to us at least, evokes a coldly commercial aura. Coolish foyer; dining room and bar markedly on the arctic side; 30-room annex (simple, no private baths, built in '61) connected to main building; 49 units, 43 baths, all cramped, and all utterly without character or charm, in our opinion, despite some very recent updatings. No resort ambiance, except in the garb of the guests; so humdrum in appointments and tone that the traveling salesman of legend would feel at home. Same ownership as the National-Bellevue.

The **Monte Rosa**, an antebellum Seiler period piece, was born in 1853 and given its latest major remodeling in '71 (that's 1971). Today it flowers with bouquets of appeal without any serious loss of character. Smallish lobby and 3 lounges; sweet, sweet 4-table, 7-stool bar; low-ceilinged 100-seat dining room. More than 2-dozen fresh bedchambers plus a flush of new baths. Manager Urs Keller continues to coddle this lady of classic breeding. A lovely rejuvenation.

The **Beau-Site** is a Grand Old Warrior, which has been made a speck more youthful through an outside cleaning, an interior pep-up, and the addition of a swimming pool. Its adjoining chalet has been sold to become the not-unpleasant **Garni Christen**. Half of the **National-Bellevue** has been razed to become a shop; the new Bellevue portion which replaces it is now better than the National segment. While the director tries hard, his staff seems to us to be one of the least disciplined clubs in the majors.

"**Neomodern Newcomers**"? The sweetly running **Alex** is winning so many hearts—including our own—that we are tossing away all considerations of prestige and vastness to include it among the Big Boys. Here's a charmer—and *what* a buy! It is sited on a viewful but hard-to-find perch down a narrow lane, 1 block from the railroad station. Overgrown chalet-motif building; captivating rustic lounge and hyperactive lobby-bar; 7 suites that are beauts; Matterhorn-view bedchambers freshly updated or totally redone; vast, variform indoor swimming pool with waterside service of snacks and beverages; saunas (both of these and the pool are free for hotel guests); smallest units energized with the addition of sitting alcoves. Main-level breakfast room perhaps refashioned for this season; exceptional Tavern Chez Alex in cellar, delightfully regional in dress, with old beams and all the trimmings (please see "Restaurants" for our culinary kudos). The rooms are outstandingly good for the price bracket: bright, well conceived, immaculate, and larger than those of many more costly houses. Sweater-clad Alex Perren, a 4th-generation mountain guide who lost a foot in a rockslide in '59, is the cheerful, smiling, attractive personality who will go all out for your welcome and comfort. His delightful wife and helpmate, smiling Gisela, is another sugar-coated bonus in personality. Sometimes they get so enthusiastic that they overbook; so be sure, sure, sure your reservation has cast-iron confirmation spikes nailed into it. To us, here is the number-one money-saving value in Zermatt.

The **Tenne**, behind the station and connected to the well-established restaurant of the same name, burst on the scene with notable flair a short while ago. Lobby with coffered ceilings (painted in scenes of Zermatt's history), ruby velvets, emerald-green divans, and sapphire carpet; dining in the restaurant if desired; 28 superbly comfortable, spotless, and sumptuous bedrooms—all with bath and radio, except for 2 singles with showers only; 14 units with balcony facing the Matterhorn; top-floor accommodations cozied-up with lots of wood; baths chippered with flowered tiles; some 4-person spreads. Shuttered October and November. Highly recommended.

The **Walliserhof**, a Zermatt landmark, at last seems to be regaining that old zing of yore. Recently it renewed its public sancta and every one of its bedchambers in a mood of upland rusticity. All now come with bath (many of 'em new, too) or shower, phone, radio, and Frigobar; many feature wooden ceilings. Guests are admitted gratis to the Mont Cervin swimmery. The grill has been resizzled and the Weinstube remains one of the most popular social hubs of the Valais—making this truly a *Walliser-hof.* The weekly buffet during ski season is mighty alluring—and its flavor lives up to its stunning eye appeal. Proprietor Theo Welschen and Manager Arnold Frei turn on a zesty fry of highland nutrition for any plainsman's soul. Always abuzz with frolicsome holiday-makers.

Alpenblick, closest to the Matterhorn, is at the extreme edge of the settlement about 10 minutes by Shank's Mare from the hub. Lovely open terrace to one side (20 tables; drinks, snacks, or full meals), with a magnificent unbroken sweep of this mountain whenever weather smiles; glassed-in terrace facing the street; large dining room without distinction; 25 cramped and characterless rooms with dwarf-size baths; overall raw-new air that doesn't send us. Cuisine very poor at our lunch-for-1; often full to the rafters with French clients—and the language preference here reflects it. For the difference from the leaders, not worth it to us—except for that glorious view on the Matterhorn side. The young **Nicoletta** was funded by a local bonesetter and is operated by Werner Seeholzer, a pleasant, well-meaning professional who appears to be having headaches shaking down his staff into a polite and helpful service crew. Lovely view-bound rôtisserie with one of the crustiest maîtres we've ever encountered anywhere; coolish dining room; happy Carnotzet; game segment; ideal location for skiers—equidistant from all major lifts. It adjoins a midtown supermarket and popular-price cafeteria; it turns on a solarium, a pool, and a sauna; the rooms are large and superbly furnished; the colors add vim; the baths are carpeted. Pretty good for a modern hotel—and we'll wager a franc that there will always be an M.D. on call. The 59-room **Bristol** features dancing in its neo-gothic cellar grill, a favorite spot for après-ski romancers. Minisize cells, most with bath or shower. Fair pickin's for small-boned clients. **La Couronne**, with a good situation at the end of the river bridge across from the Zermatterhof, is a '61 chalet-style candidate. Old Zermatt Restaurant-Bar-Grill and hairdressing salon in front (count your change extra-carefully in the former); general taste harder, less ingratiating, and more clashy-in-colors than in the Alex; rooms smaller and less attractive, with 2 exceptions only; cold, uninviting restaurant. Not as good a bet, by a long shot, as the much cheaper, better furnished, more comfortable rival we've just mentioned. The **Christiania**, important because of the chair lift at its doorstep, seemed too slaphappy in its administration to suit us. Adequate plant and a proper kitchen for its expanded dining facilities, but we simply didn't tune into its wavelength. Adjoining swimming pool, sauna, fitness center, and an apartment-hotel. The **Perren** is neither new nor old—except for its fresh-as-spring *garni* wing. On the river; routine furnishings and rooms. Just so-so, if that. The small, bland **Rhodania** is, in our opinion, much, much too tall in the Pocketbook Department to worry its competition. Not recommended.

In the budget category, all of the following are *Garni* (breakfast only), but full meals can be arranged in most of them, on separate terms. In this group, the side-by-side **Eden & Rex** form a twin combo under the same administration. They are joined in the middle and share an excellent indoor pool. Unusually large accommodations, many with balcony and all with breathtaking Alpine vista; public rooms and corridors highlighted with copperware, spinning wheels, and regional touches; new chalet-annex nearby plus sauna. Nice. The **Jägerhof** is run by Mr. and Mrs. Victor Perren; he's one of the most popular young ski instructors on hickories. Clean, airy, informal, and recommendable for the sweet people who operate it. The mid-village **Darioli** has no lobby, but its tiny grill and *Stubli* weave a gypsy spell. Peasant-style furniture in bedrooms; attic units without bath; simple, but winsome. **De la Poste**, operated by American Karl Ivarsson, is globally noted for its discothèque complex in the cellar. We prefer the nonsleeping quarters to the kips. Overall, however, the operation strikes us as slaphappy, if not downright amateurish. But that's just our personal impression. The **Derby**, on the main street next to the Walliserhof, sprouts typical upland architecture. Sizable restaurant on ground floor that is intimate, low-ceilinged, and pleasant; open-air terrace service a few steps above the milling throng on the road; bedrooms tiny, tidy, and cheerful, with baggage space sufficient for 1 small attaché case; appealing, nevertheless, in their fully paneled walls, small streetside balconies, and color touches. Noisy in front, of course. The **Slalom** is the rear section of La Couronne (see above). Same modern aura but cheaper, smaller, and more corner-cutting; no elevator; 24 rooms and 3 private baths; one bedchamber with badly balding rugs, but the others fairly well maintained. Okay, but surely not special. The **Biner** is okay. Chummy staff here. The **Chesa Valese** is a warm, cozy 30-room villa with 6 baths, 6 showers, many balconies, and a feeling of "Welcome Home." Very ingratiating in its quiet fashion. The **Excelsior** and the **Aristella** are newish production-line plants à la Chalet School of architecture and appointments; these are also passable for their category. The barnlike **Bahnhof**, a summer bunker for rough-and-ready climbers, is as raw as they come. The prices are ultrabasic, too. Shelter here often means 6 to a room and "Everybody up at dawn!"

Finally, down at the neighboring hamlet of *Täsch*, there are several entries which have come to flower or are budding. Travelers with cars sometimes prefer to live here because of the enormous parking lot. We think it is decidedly 5th-rate by comparison with Zermatt. We imply no scare tactic whatsoever when we report that avalanches have tumbled into this region in years gone by.

In *Zürich*, the **Dolder Grand** has a mountainside location, 10 minutes by car from the heart of the city; breathtaking panorama; viewful crescent-shape dining salon, occasionally occupied nowadays by groups; 200 rooms and 200 baths. While suite #315-316 is outstanding, #368-369 in one Tower is our favorite among favorites, one of the snuggest nests we've inspected in many a palace. A splendid new Royal Suite should be ready for this year's noble voyager, too. Excellent and costly simultaneous translation facilities in the convention center headquarters; spacious gardens and woods; 9-hole golf course and tennis courts nearby in private club. We look forward to meeting new Manager Raoul de Gendre, who has acquired some of his professional experience in the U.S.

The **Baur au Lac** boasts a superb downtown lakeside setting. We were happily impressed on our latest bower-to-Baur inspection. This year you'll find an impressive Men's Club (where captains of industry can indulge their fancies with everything from the latest stock market quotations to a private secretary); in its cellar is the Diagonal Discothèque; there's an excellent telephone system throughout, a boutique plus barbering and hairdressing salons, air conditioning for the public rooms, and a panoply of posh accommodations. You'll snooze in a velour-upholstered bed, park your luggage on slide-out shelves, and use an improved bathroom (still smallish, but equipped with dressing tables and illuminated mirrors for the ladies). Now all of the accommodations come with private bath and the oldest units have been brought up to the quality level of the newest ones. We think you will enjoy the generally perked-up comfort. One of its brightest, gayest, most charming assets—untouched, thank goodness—is the delightful Grill-Bar, which is *always* jammed after dark; don't miss it! Now resplendent in fresh sheen and glitter, this midcity Deluxe inn is fast regaining its traditional place in the sun.

Down a notch to First-class, the air-conditioned **Eden au Lac** is a splendid house. It turns out the most savory and imaginative fare we've tried in any Swiss hotel in its category—as well as many of its more exalted brethren. If any visitor here misses what is called "The Gourmet's Menu" (which varies every 2 weeks to conform with the season's best and freshest offerings), he ought to have his head examined. The aura, bathed in a Trianon gray, is on the old-fashioned side, in a nostalgically serene way; the 53 rooms, all with bath or shower, are comfortable, but you mustn't expect luxury; many have been repowdered and some have been given air conditioning. Young, friendly Rudi and Hanni Bärtschi comprise the managerial team and they are delightful. Service unusually attentive; ratio of 1 staffer to 1 client; some personnel here as long as 30 years; checkout time of 2 P.M. strictly observed; upper-case clientele who return with migratory regularity. We like the lake view, the flowers and fruit in the rooms, the delicious meals, and the aging grace of this mellow house. Not for mods; those who seek a tranquil niche will find a home-sweet-home-away-from-home. The **Carlton-Elite** is smack in the center. Its Pub, decorated with saddles, bridles, and raw bricks, is more popular than ever even though we found the service in it worse than ever. It is sited in a charming little cul-de-sac. Colorful Locanda Ticinese Italian-Swiss tavern; attractive Flower Terrace for open-air summer meals; communal plus private bar for guests; 10 split-level accommodations in natural wood and textile motif, with color TV, refrigerator, "silent valets," twin washbasins, and up-to-the-minute gadgetry; other units on the smallish side, with wall-to-wall carpeting and modernistic tone. The restaurant ideas, as sired by Mövenpick and as evinced by the Pub, are unusually imaginative. Even if you don't overnight, please sample the sippets of this salubrious stall. The sapling **Waldhaus Dolder** splits its structure between apartments and rooms for transients while sharing its mountain address with its neighboring alma mater, the Dolder Grand. It is a 10-story *éminence grise* (gray concrete) which is First class, not Deluxe. Engagingly decorated restaurant and dining sectors; grill under iron hood with leaded glass and outfitted with woodsman's tools; Dolderbahn Bar for nostalgics; glass-lined pool area that can be opened in summer; sauna. Bedchambers as well as the longer-rental apartments rely heavily on formica and other coolish effects. Space is ample; comfort is abundant; tranquility is assured; flair seems to be in short supply within the dwelling areas. We suspect families will find it perfect for their needs. **Zum Storchen**, which occupies one of the better midcity situations, zuuums in with a timber-lined waterside rôtisserie, a dining terrace over the water, a soulless bar with piano-tations, and an alp of aid from Chief Concierge Roth. Total of 80 rooms, all with radio and telephone, and most with bath or shower; singles facing the town; the choicest streamside doubles #323 and #423, (often held for loyal clients); demipension required in summer. Unless you snag one of its prime accommodations, we think you can do better elsewhere. Out of midcity, the all-*nova* **Nova Park** is emphatically for mods. Far Out *is* the term for it; not that the facade would clue you in; that's Dullsville. But inside it swings. Wild color combinations in the lobby; public rooms jazzy with paintings and sculpture. Music (some piped, some live) filtering everywhere—from busy lounges, to the woody self-service restaurant, to another nook where a piano player tickles the keys, to any of several feederies, one of which contains executive chairs and individual TV sets tuned into the stock-market quotations; pages wandering the halls and corridors in Courrèges-type costumes; extensive conference facilities plus a fitness center. Of its 360 accommodations all seemed cramped to us, but the so-called "Executive Doubles" provide the highest dividend in space per dollar. The "Dreamland Suites" truly must be seen to be believed. Shag carpeting covers the floor, walls, ceiling, and much of the built-in furniture (2 come in burgundy and 2 in blue); they feature dozens of pinpoint lights glinting romantically through the textiles à la El Morocco; the bed (in repose) is sunken, but can be made to rise, fall, or angle at a button's touch; a huge 2- (maybe 3-) person bathtub —also sunken and unseparated from the bedroom—beckons Dreamlanders to roll out of their mechanized bunk and into their own azure Mediterranean (or Red Sea, if you pick one of the wine-dark suites); overall the space is rather limited (not that a lot will be required by clients who bid for these) and the prices are almost out of sight. When we asked our guide if these apartments were popular sellers, his reply was, "Well, it takes a special kind of guest to request them." He can say *that* again. Our lunch was fair but not better; the cocktails were good; the service was poor. Later we saw a client carrying his own dirty laundry to the front desk and were told that this was SOP, as no valet pickup existed. Some travelers might extract a giggle out of the whole experience, but at the blue-ribbon price tags it demands we would feel as if the joke were on us. Not for traditionalists by any stretch of the wallet. The **Zurich**, on the other hand, impressed us as being just as commercial but much more artfully so. Handy, scenic location overlooking the river and a magnificent townscape; waterfront restaurant with cyclopean ceiling lights; inviting Tourne Broche Grill; bar, pool, gym, shops, garage; handsomely furnished bedchambers, again with a heavy inclination toward white formica surfaces; color-brightened baths. Somehow this brand of subdued modernity appeals to us much more than that espoused by the N-P. Also costly by local standards. In general, recommended. The railbird's **Ascot** is near one of the train stations. Tastefully refashioned; front rooms with balconies and deck chairs; 2nd floor Bel Étage with special flavor; 6 suites (2 with kitchens) in velvet, silk, and flowered décor; 60 rooms, all with bath, radio, and most with picture windows; many with color TV; enlarged lobby; high-in-the-stirrups, rouge-toned, intimate Jockey Club restaurant (microwave kitchen); sidewalk café; busy Turf Bar. Nobel Prize on the Bel Étage is #215 with rust carpets, gold curtains and a button beside the bed to raise or lower him or her (or both) to any desired position; if *this* becomes boring, another button lowers a mirrored panel across the room to disclose a TV set. Lilliputian but pleasant. The rather costly **Bellerive au Lac** recently polished off a major renovation program. Attractive but somewhat commercial lobby, dining room, and new bar; handsome wildlife paintings by Hug throughout the house; all baths restyled, remaining small but efficient. Singles are the best values; the twins seemed high to us. The **Atlantis**, 15 minutes by taxi from the center, is sited in a suburban office complex. Swissair is a major stockholder; consequently many of its passengers alight here. Spacious lobby in Scandinavian motif; 2-tier rôtisserie plus intimate pinewood *Stubli;* bar toned up in green leather; adjoining nightclub; glass-fronted swimming pool covered by a sail; sauna with snoozzzzable easy chairs; hair dressing salon; fine Grieder boutique; Avis agency plus garage. The well-furnished rooms are efficient in the modern theme, highlighted by photomurals of the airline's destinations and generously outfitted with phones at bedside and in the bath; radios and TV (some in color and all with remote-control switches), refrigerators, infrared heat lamps; ample space; individual terraces. The penthouse units are especially laudable. There's plenty of zing per cubic foot here. But despite the fact that a hotel bus goes to and from the city 6 times per day, we believe that many independent travelers will find it unhappily remote as a holiday headquarters. How we'd like to be wrong! Back in town, the **Europe** glows with Old World charm and crackles with twentieth-century convenience. Winningly attractive French-provincial lobby; beverage salon under crystal, embraced by ruby velour walls; patterned corridors; delightful accommodations with such touches as rheostat lighting, humidifiers, refrigerators, electric bed controls plus radio-TV consoles, air conditioning, wall safes, silent valets, shaving mirrors, drying racks in baths and much more—even to bowls of fruit placed in the rooms. Number 52 is a superb corner double; we also like #46 or any unit ending in "6." Excellent as an intimate hideaway. The nearby **Opera**, behind its namesake, is now performing, but so far we've missed the show. It looked promising, however. **St. Gotthard**, 1 block from the main station, is in a district we don't like. This landmark is best known for its Hummer ("Lobster") Bar, its cosmopolitan sidewalk café on the Bahnhofstrasse, and its rebasted Rôtisserie; its 110 rooms show commendable improvement plus a notable trend toward gaiety and decorative flair. The newer wing of 28 bedchambers twinkles with white brick, rustic textiles, rich wood, and floral patterns. Some units have their own refrigerators. Coming up smartly and now recommended. The neighboring **Glockenhof** isn't bad as a family stop, though many package groups pause here. The **Continental**, a glass-and-steel edifice that started life as an office building, retains a certain hangover haze of its commercial origins. All pads with radio, bath or shower, and makeshift closets; full air conditioning; attractive restaurants serving unusually high-grade cuisine. For a shelter without frills but all the necessities and many comforts, this one is very satisfactory indeed. The **Savoy**, oldest in town, is scheduled to reappear next year—its ancient facade intact—after a hyper-costly reconstruction jamboree by its banking proprietors. We await the deluxe rejuvenation with glee. The 56-room **Rigihof**, en route to the Dolder, is a converted apartment house on a clangorous street. Full bath count; homey atmosphere; for budgeteers and travelers with children. The **Kindli**, with no views from its inner-canyon site in midtown, is, in our evaluation, a conglomeration of good and bad. You pays your money and you takes your choice. **Chesa Rustica**, at Limmatquai 70, is as cute as they come for tiny inn-type hostelries. The cookery in the restaurant, grill, or bar is lip-smacking, too. The **Krone**, originally built on the Limmat Quai in A.D. 1599, has had a $250,000 top-to-bottom alteration job. But after our recent shocking encounter with its director and his wife, 2 of the rudest people we've ever had the displeasure—personally or professionally—to meet, we cannot recommend this house or its restaurant to any traveler of discrimination or taste. How this couple ever got into the hospitality field is a wonder to this grieving reporter. A thousand times no for this old krone. The **Adler**, with 50 rooms and 18 baths, is fair. The **Butterfly**, with cocoon-size cells, is better suited in dimensions to the flocks of Oriental clients who patronize it. Cramped. The **Schweizerhof** has made some vague attempts at restylings. Even though we admire Manager Rudolf Muhlberg's penny-stretching efforts to reclaim it from dreariness, we think he needs a bigger budget to do the job properly. Pretty dull. The **Alexander,** across the lake in *Thalwil* and not to be confused with one of the same name in Zurich proper, has been taken over by new interests since our latest Zürich rounds, so we'll reserve comment until we can check in again. A car is a must, however. The **Ermitage,** 10 minutes by car at the lakeside suburb of Küsnacht, would be a pleasant little haven if its tariffs were in closer conformity to its value. Here's the residential wing of the well-known restaurant of the same name, with 28 small, modestly furnished rooms and 28 baths; tranquil and agreeable setting; inconvenient location for the traveler-in-a-hurry. We like this house, but we can't help but feel it is glaringly overpriced when its amenities are compared to those of the Dolder or Baur au Lac. Finally, the 50-room **Waldorf**—with astorian tabs for double occupancy—did not seem worth the outlay. Not recommended. For weatherbound air travelers, the youthful **Airport Hilton** roars in with top-flight public quarters, a viewful swimming pool and sun deck, and a newer wing of 125 rooms. Fabulous Sutter's Grill that's a gold mine for beef-hungry U.S. prospectors; honky-tonk piano music nightly; salubrious dark-toned Bonanza Bar; Coffee Shop maintaining a spur of Old West flavor; bedchambers adequate but not up to the flair of the lobby and restaurant décor. Manager Albert Grieder may sincerely believe that the gold-tinted plate-glass bedroom windows are see-through *only* from the inside out, but after we'd paraded through the parking lot one night, we can advise more than a dozen female registrants that he is delightfully wrong. Recommended. Across the highway, the fortress-like **Holiday Inn** is linked in gray concrete massiveness to the Mövenpick complex, its Swiss dining partner. The sister **Inn** at neighboring *Regensdorf* has somewhat more architectural style, but both are intended to be only functional flyway-stations. Our recent meal in the Appenzeller Stube of the airport entry was quite tasty and lots of fun. Well done for what they are, but somehow both give us the feeling of being in a Las

Vegas "Strip" hotel rather than on European soil. **Hotel Airport** (5 minutes from the jet blast and 20 minutes from the city) offers 47 adequately appointed units for one-nighters. All accommodations with bath or shower; attractive 9-tabled Grill Room; green-and-wine-plaid restaurant; pleasing main-floor bar; ask for Manager Gehrig. Good for its purpose.

At *Horgen*, on the south side of Zürich Lake 10 miles from the city, the gleaming youthful **Seehotel Meierhof** has whipped off its peignoir to reveal its saucy shape. Sleek lines, as streamlined as a Playmate; viewful rooftop La Rôtisserie l'Horizon adjoining the cocktail lounge; public restaurant and snack bar; lovely no-extra-cost indoor pool, with slide-away glass panels, agurgling round the calendar (open until 10 P.M.); infrared ready room for palefaced pilgrims, plus open-air solarium for the genuine article; beauty parlor and barbershop; gift center, bank, and 90-car garage on the preserve. Total of 140 smallish doubles and suites, each with private bath, TV, radio, 2 phones, and your own stocked refrigerator—everything from a fifth of Ballantine's to a magnum of Pommery. Management by Hans Zürcher, whom we haven't met. One novel convenience is its very own speedboat, which shuttles to and from Zürich's principal piers. Say *sí-sí* for the Zürich-see-side (despite the rail line in front), because it's the most see-worthy at this See-hotel.

Out at *Oerlikon*, a suburb in the direction of the airport, we found the vast **International** about as institutional as they can come. The pool and sauna on the top floor and the Panorama Grill on the penultimate level are its highest points in every sense.

Leading hotels in other centers of Switzerland are as follows:

Adelboden : **Nevada-Palace** (with pool and sauna).

Appenzell : (1) **Hecht**, (2) **Säntis**.

Arbon : **Metropol** (lakeside house with roof garden and heated pool).

Ascona : (1) The youthful and scenic **Sasso Boretto** (a beaut with pool and sauna; directed by Hans Hollenstein, an experienced professional), (2) **Europe au Lac** (modern Italian motif; 2 sides of triangular construction face lake; private beach and swimming pool; closed Nov. through mid-Mar.; excellent cuisine; happy resort choice).

Bad Ragaz : (1) **Grand Hotel Quellenhof** (indoor swimming pool for hotel residents only; 18-hole golf course; rambling, classic spa style, with 2 main buildings; closed between seasons; setting and region reminiscent of Interlaken; lovely for serenity), (2) **Grand Hotel Hof Ragaz** (also with an indoor splasher). (3) **Touring Mot-Hotel Schloss Ragaz** (conventional hotel, with motel in gardens; good but not luxurious).

Braunwald : **Alpenblick** (Glarus Alpine viewing; good food).

Bulach : **Goldener Kopf**.

Cully : **Auberge du Raisin**, 6 miles from Lausanne, a story-village hostelry run by the Gauer interests of Berne; ground-floor restaurant; heart of the Swiss vineyard country.

Flims : **Parkhotel Waldhaus** (with swimmery), followed by the **Adula** (also with pool) and the **Schweizerhof**.

Fribourg : (1) **De la Rose** (nightclub; 80 rooms, all with bath). (2) **Duc**

Bertold (outstanding architecture; lovely appointments; top cuisine). (3) **Elite** (small and, well, elite).

Gottlieben : **Drachenburg** is known for its table.

Kreuzlingen (junction of Rhine and Boden See): The very modern **Schweizerland** draws high praise from a merry Sarasota couple. Front rooms with fine lake view; worthy restaurant; 3 bowling alleys; sounds delightful.

Lac Champex (above Orsières): **Alpes et Lac** (a Cleveland reader calls this "the best spot of our trip"; this refurbished house has been in the same family since 1888, and it is now run by young Mme. Meilland).

Lenzerheide-Valbella (2 toy villages snuggling together in a mile-high Grisons' valley): (1) **Kurhaus**, (2) **Schweizerhof**. The new **Post-Hotel** (Valbella) might well knock the spots off the traditional leaders here. Cozy rustic appointments; handsome Grill, lounges, and terraces; indoor glass-wrapped swimming pool; all units with bath or shower; southside ones with private balcony. We also hear fond words about the nearby **Guarda Val**, another youngster and one we haven't checked personally. The **Valbella Inn** (with pool), the **Sporthotel Happy Rancho**, and **Sunstar** all win orchids from ski-buff Guidesters, too.

Merligen : **Beatus** (on Lake Thun midway between Thun and Interlaken; modern in concept; indoor pool; 140 rooms with baths and balconies; private beach; opened in '61; this one's an absolute peach; definitely worth a detour to pause here).

Morat : **Le Vieux Manoir** (old manor house at shore's edge facing the mountains; said to be perking up smartly in the hands of Manager Hans Scheerrer) or **Hotel du Bateau** (lakeview and lake-based cuisine; Navy Club for dancing).

Morges : **Hotel du Lac** (and it's smack on the *lac*). Other choices: **Mont Blanc au Lac** or **La Couronne**.

Neuchâtel : (1) **Beaulac** (efficiency type, built on wonderful lakeside position; 40 small rooms with tiny baths, showers, and radio, plus 6 with toilet only; open-air-terrace dining, private jetty "beach"; coolly efficient). (2) **Terminus** has a new chief conductor who is pouring on the steam; now chugging along happily. (3) **Touring** has a café but no restaurant. We haven't seen the new 240-bed **Eurotel**, but we'd bet on it anyway since things are so spare hereabouts. The **Central** and **Beaux-Arts** are clean but routine.

Nyon : **Hostellerie of the XVI Century**. Also **Du Clos de Sadex** or possibly the **Des Alpes** and the **Beau Rivage**.

Rapperswil : (1) **Schwanen** (up-to-date rooms overlooking the Lake of Zürich; food, service, and bar above average; medium prices; unruffled and good); (2) **Du Lac**, (3) **Speer**, and (4) **Hirschen**—all 3 routine.

Rigi Kaltbad : A sport center called the **Hostellerie Rigi** has replaced the Grand Hotel which burned down several years ago; indoor pool for winter paddlers; spacious "dispersal" construction rather than "compressed" architecture of conventional hostelries; sounds revolutionary.

Rossinière : the living antique, **Grand Chalet**, steals the Vaudois thunder locally.

St. Gall area : (1) **Walhalla** (opposite railroad station; newish and commercial; clean as a moon rocket; fresh entrance to ground floor, popular,
café-style Stadtrestaurant; Chez Caroline restaurant, with gas burners on
tables, up 1-flight). (2) **Hecht** (management by Willi and Roland Studer;
rooms modernized; 50% with bath or shower, excellent downstairs Grill
under arches; adjoining bar, beguiling for romantic persuasions; watch
this one take off under the jet-fired inspiration of that Studer fuel). (3)
the refashioned **Metropol** (across from the terminal; 36 rooms, all with
full bath or shower). (4) **Im Portner** (café on ground floor; rooms neat
and clean; Mr. and Mrs. H. U. Egli-Moser are trying hard; we hear that
their labors are paying dividends). At neighboring ***Gossau***, the modernized **Ochsen** is tops. The tiny **Rössli Flawil**, 8½ miles from St. Gall,
offers a pleasant restaurant, public rooms, and extra-basic bedchambers;
operated by the chef-owner; 8 rooms and 3 baths; 20 minutes by secondary road; a little country inn that you might adore, but don't expect a
Schweizerhof. In ***Wil***, chug straight into the futuristic-styled **Derby
Bahnhof**.

Samedan : **Bernina** (cozy; good for families; superior cuisine; home-style
service; reasonable prices), possibly followed by **Clubhotel Quadratscha
Des Alpes**.

Seengen: **Schlosshotel Brestenberg** (on a hummock overlooking the peaceful Hallwilersee, a lake that's an hour's drive from Zürich; lovely woodland castle; comfortable for rural lazing).

Sierre : Either the **Europe** or the **Atlantic**; both newish.

Sils Maria : **Waldhaus**, then maybe **La Magna** or **Maria**.

Solothurn : The well-appointed, pension-priced **La Couronne**.

Tarasp : **Kurhaus Tarasp** first, then the **Hotel Tarasp**.

Unterwasser : The **Sternen** shines brightest for the sporting crowd.

Vevey : (1) **Les Trois-Couronnes** (million-dollar modernization program
finished; 100 rooms and 100 baths; handsome, ample-sized, and luxurious
in parts; big dining-terrace and redesigned entrance; ask for #66 if
you're splurging; great character and charm in this veteran). (2) **Du Lac**
has been bought by the same interests; a modernization program has
been wrapped up. At ***Mont Pelerin***, above Vevey, **Le Mirador** is a
viewful repose for peaceful wayfarers—only 90 of 'em since it is bent on
limiting expansion while lengthening quality. Refashioning program
which ate through $5,000,000; reportedly fine cuisine in the grill or
Fontainebleau Room (reserve ahead); pool and saunas splashing and
stoking up; additional rooms in adjoining chalets. A major stamping
from the founder of Pennsylvania's Franklin Mint who recently took it
over. Already becoming known to discriminating travelers, so be sure to
book well in advance.

Villeneuve : **Byron** (big villa-esque mansion overlooking the garden, the
swimming pool, and the lake; grill-restaurant; only 5 minutes from Montreux).

Vitznau : **Parkhotel** (dipping now going on in its pool).

Wengen : **Hirschen** is rather commercial; it has a pool, nightclub, and
shopping center. At ***Wildhaus,*** the **Acker** is perhaps the leader of the

Toggenburg Valley; the panorama restaurant, Alphütten bar, and sporting comfort draw many repeaters to its door.

Winterthur : (1) **Garten** (much improved recently). (2) **Krone** (not what it was).

These are the most famous of their regions—some palatial, some unpretentious, some mediocre.

For less-known stops, consult your travel agent or the *Swiss Hotel Guide;* the most expensive listings in it are generally the best, although in a few instances this does not hold true.

Most hotels give a 50% reduction for children 1 to 6 years old, and a 30% reduction for children between the ages of 6 and 12.

Check your meal arrangements carefully; if you eat in an outside restaurant you may be paying for 2 dinners instead of 1.

Dedicated budgeteers? Since we're too bottlenecked here for additional entries, please consult our annually revised paperback, *Fielding's Low-Cost Europe,* which lists scads more bargain hotels or pensions and money-saving tips for serious economizers.

FOOD AND RESTAURANTS

Switzerland has a superb cuisine; it's not all chocolate and cheese, as many visitors suppose. A cold buffet of chicken, duck, roast beef, ham, smoked pork, sausage, and pressed meats is commonly served at lunch; at dinner, you name it and it's yours. Some hotels don't serve hot meals after 9 P.M., so check up on yours if you plan to be late.

Fondue is as local as baked beans in America; don't miss it, if you like cheese. It's a vague Welsh rarebit made with white wine, into which you dunk (and swab) chunks of sweet bread. When the opposite sex shares this dish, Swiss tradition dictates that the one who loses the bread off the fork owes the men (or the ladies) a kiss; offenders beyond kissing age must buy the company a bottle of wine (no instances recorded). From Valais comes raclette, another melted cheese dish even more delicious than fondue.

As for straight cheeses, our favorites are Alpenzieger (Glarus), a sharp, tangy blend seasoned with green herbs; Vacherin du Mont d'Or, a winter product with the viscosity of Liederkranz—and that fine Gruyère.

Sausage is a national specialty, and each region has its own types. The big, fat Zürich version, a bologna with a Napoleonic complex, is one of the most succulent. Even more famous is the St. Gall Bratwurst. Order *any* kind of sausage—*any* time—with the fluffy, hashed-brown potatoes called Rösti, and you are in for a deeeeee-licious treat. Other typical offerings of this region include Geschnetzeltes nach Zurcher Art (thin-sliced veal with a cream sauce). Zürcher Leberspiessle (liver strips with sage seasoning, spit-roasted and served with beans), or Ratsherrentopf (mixed grill on a bed of rice or noodles).

Dinner in top places runs perhaps $15 without wine; prepared blue-plate specials can be had for about $6.50. At the other end of the scale, both the tearooms and the Mövenpick restaurants (an interesting combination of drugstore and cosmopolitan cookery, with branches in key cities) offer snacks and light meals for $4.50 or so. It's simply a matter of choosing your own category and spending what you please, because the range is ample. Prices are generally lowest in small villages or at train-depot eateries.

Granted that Swiss cooking lacks the inventiveness and delicacy of French cooking, few countries offer better day-in and day-out fare.

Arosa's **Central**, bound neatly in Arven wood, features regional dishes from the Grisons. The **Kursaal** (Casino) comes up with 3 bars, 2 orchestras, and vittles. Most appetites are shackled to their hotel pension plans. While the **Tschuggen** and other major hotels don't require registrants to dine in the house, most smaller ones do. The **Kulm**, more informal in the hotel or at its amusing tavern by the ice rink, has the top cuisine, in our franc opinion. Its steaks are prime. The **Park** is handsome; now the cookery and service are coming up, too. The bars of the **Posthotel** and the **Carmenna** hop to lively lilts in season. The grill of the **Savoy** is a gem for eye appeal, as is the Relais de Champagne in the **Valsana**.

In *Basle*, the watch-ful **Rôtisserie de l'Horloge** in the main Swiss Industries Fair Building (Mustermesse) is distinguished; a bit more jubilant than its neighboring horological exhibit; now run by our old friend Jean-Pierre Gagneaux (and how we hope his radiant wife is on hand when you roll in). Expensive and fun. The redecorated Rhy-Stube is now the **Paprika** (next to Drei Könige); the **Schützenhaus** ("Ranger's House") has color, but we haven't assayed the skillet skills since it changed its manager; **Seiler's Ress-lirytti** is happily made-up in merry-go-round décor, but the cookery on our try seemed to come from a House of Horrors kitchen; the **Walliser-Kanne** is rustic and attractive; the **Casino** has a new look and a new manager. On a benign day, you might try the extremely variable but eye-appealing **Schloss Binningen**, in a park setting a few minutes from the center. It's a renovated thirteenth-century castle (Junior Prince size), with a small Wine Garden at its entrance, a *Gaststube* in its front room, an enchanting medieval-style *Trinkstube* upstairs (private parties only), a quiet and intimate dining room, and a knockout of a terrace for warm-weather dining (lunch or dinner). The cookery could be improved, but the atmosphere makes it worth the short ride. Medium expensive. In hotel circles, the **Euler** still walks off easily with the epicurean honors, while the **Drei Könige** ("Three Kings") still draws complaints from Guidesters. Pauls' **Red Ox Grill** and the **Golden Dragon Chinese Restaurant** are delightfully cozy and charming, and their cookery is delicious. We haven't sampled the **Goldner Sternen**, but we will soon.

In *Berne*, the Simmental Stube and the famous Horseshoe Grill of the **Schweizerhof**, both backstopped by renowned Chef Ernesto Schlegel (so prized that he is a member of the hotel's Board of Directors!), are unquestionably above everything else in the city limits. The former is the dining room of an old mansion, transplanted intact. The Horseshoe Grill has *gemütlich* dimensions, versatile menu, wine list so staggering that the printing probably costs a bottle per copy, and artful drink blending; huge, juicy steaks with corn-on-the-cob (!) year round. The tip of the top. The lovely dining terrace of the **Hotel Bellevue-Palace** is also a front-runner; eye-popping menu and 100-thousand-bottle wine cellar; high gastronomy; alp-high recommendation. The Cercle Munz, downstairs, is popular for regional specialties. **Charley's**

Beef Corner slices into you-know-what on its main floor, which resembles a woody sort of brasserie. Excellent grills, steak sandwiches, and huge bowls of mixed salad for surprisingly moderate tabs. Our service could have been better, but the atmosphere doesn't seem to require highly trained minions. Downstairs is the Cadillac discothèque in upbeat modern tones, a den for young executives and their cuties. A successful package. So is the popular priced **Chutrasco**, an Argentinian chain-bred hoofer that appears with frequency in German grazing grounds these days. The **Galaxy**, rigged out as a ship, nets a fair catch of water-bred denizens. **Mistral** blows in with the cuisine of Provence served in an ancient cellar. Vaulted brick ceiling, stone walls, terra-cotta floors, hanging lanterns plus fat spluttery candles on polished dark-wood tables. The ground floor breezes in with a nice bar and lounge for lighter refreshments and freshets of conversation. Even more antique is the 400-year-old **Klötzlikeller**, a typical subterranean student hangout. **Harmonie** captures a similar choir of warblers. **Della-Casa** (Schauplatzgasse 16) presents a listless café at street level, but an ingratiating, low-ceiling, wood-lined restaurant above. Soft lights; leaded windows; planter boxes; menu with selections ranging from Zarzuella to Calf's Knuckles; wine card covering the slopes of the Valais (Switzerland) to the flats of Benisalem (Mallorca). Aside from watching our waitress nibble at leftovers from guests' trays, we enjoyed our meal. Say we, *bene!* Closed Sunday. For Swiss specialties, we used to be devoted to the rustic, simple, inexpensive Taverne Valaisanne of the **Hotel Hirschen**, a few steps from the abovementioned Schweizerhof. That love affair is finished, alas. Too bad. **Le Vieux Manoir** ("The Old Manor House") in *Morat*, 16 miles out on the Lausanne Road, is said to be recovering its long-lost chic. The new management perhaps has the right formula; we hope so, because it is a lovely site. Back in *Berne*, **Restaurant Räblus** (Zeughausgasse 3, near the Clock Tower) is Gallic in accent. Upstairs dining room; simple décor with wine bottles; downstairs bar with pianist; flaming specialties are featured. Cleverly merchandised atmosphere that is more convincing than the cuisine. Fun and—happily—open until 1 A.M. Monday through Saturday; closed Sunday. **Menotti's Ratskeller** (Gerechtigkeitsgasse 81) is about as Ratskellery as the Eiffel Tower—which isn't situated in a cellar, either. Cuisine basically French, with a few Italian dishes (Pappagallo Bolognese, Fritto Misto, and the like) thrown in for spice; extra-creditable wine list; menu available in English; waiters amiably accommodating. The décor is undistinguished Swiss-modern, with the only notable departure the stuffed beaver which greets you at the door with paws outstretched. They try hard—but a good French bistro does exactly the same thing better. Closed Mondays. **Le Dézaley** is the budget choice of a Helvetian friend who knows his calories; we've never set tongue to fondue here, but we accept his verdict with alacrity. **Kornhauskeller** is a baronial German-type beer cellar, dominated by a massive wine barrel and made glad (evenings only) with an oomp-pah band; trencherman's fare, substantial cookery, horrible service, moderate tariffs; try the home-grown Berner Platte; recommended to sausage-and-sauerkraut fans. **Du Théâtre** is celebrated for its kitchen; we find it excruciatingly dull, despite its fine viands and practiced attention. The famous **Mövenpick** chain now boasts 4 capital branches, and "capital" they are, as drop-in feederies. They all sport the usual handsome décor and the characteristically huge range of prices. The one with the Gade Restaurant is tops, in our opinion. The **Café Rudolf** is routine but agreeable. The **Commerce**, a bistro that serves Spanish fare, is noted locally for its Paella, its Arroz Marinera (fish soup), and other Iberian exports cooked up by Enrique Ros. The 10-table room is about as sullen as a squid's glare, but the cuisine sparkles if you hanker for Spanish calories. If you ride the rods this season, you may want to sample the wares at any of the **Railway Station Restaurants** in midtown; they chug up with variety, savor, and boilers of steam. There's a self-service snackery at track level; the conventional dining platforms are upstairs. Out at *Worb* the **Lowen** roars pridefully about its lion shares of local fares, according to a transplanted New England reader who now lives in Berne. We look forward to our first feast—and thanks for the tip.

In *Brig*, the little **Guntern** has again picked up hearteningly. Other meritorious restaurants are absent here. The **Couronne Hotel** is the most satisfactory substitute.

Buchs offers **Chez Fritz**, described in the "Liechtenstein" chapter.

Crans-Montana nourishes most of its visitors either in its hotel dining rooms or in private chalets. Among the independents, only one really shines: the **Channe Valaisanne**. Typical foodstuffs and preparation of the Valais (as the name implies); raclette and fondue always steaming invitingly; functioning year round. As stolid as the mountains which surround it. **Rôtisserie de la Reine** offers an impressive international table ably lorded by Max Léonard. We enjoyed our meal; our eyes enjoyed the surroundings. In hotel circles, we'd pick the **Royal** if we were trying to impress Ursula Andress or the **City** if we were interested in cookery; the latter is modest. The **Sporting** is THE spot for dancing and for displaying the creations of the Paris fashion command. Rustic Upper Rhône décor; food mediocre but stunningly expensive; ties and jackets required on gentlemen. Chic as can be, but much, much better for *after*-dinner persuasions, in our opinion. **Le Français**, more informal, is usually more fun for the uninhibited. Other night stops include **The Club,** the **Pub, 400 Coups**, and **Whisky-A-Gogo**, which hop according to the season and the crowd on that particular evening.

In *Davos*, try chicken curry and other Oriental specialties at **Meierhof**. The **Waldhotel-Bellevue** cops the honors for scenery; the kitchen is notable, too.

Geneva's Le Gentilhomme at the **Hôtel Richemond** still unquestionably has the top cuisine and most fashionable clientele in the city. As an alternative, the open-air terrace-restaurant here, with its connected sidewalk café, comes up with thousands of flowers, skillful after-dark illumination, and music piped from Le Gentilhomme; a happy focal point for visitors and residents alike, from breakfast to after-theater snacks; U.S.-styled table d'hôte lunch (consommé, hamburger-steak platter, ice cream) for hurried trippers, plus self-service hors d'oeuvres table. To us, the only faux pas here is the totally incomprehensible permissiveness of admitting jacketless and tieless patrons at noon. In the main Banquet Room, already famous for the ability of its 5 tons of walls to recess into the floor at the touch of a button, an amazing sliding ceiling has been installed. The Amphitryon Room at the

Hôtel des Bergues now draws heavily from the diplomatic corps to sample its pleasant ambiance, deft service, and good food. The **Puss 'n Boots** of the Beau Rivage is recommendable, too, Superb reception, service, and presentation; scalloped ceiling over panels; lovely faïence earthenware; first-rate sommelier. Try the Tarte aux Poires Genevoise, a local sweet that we richly enjoyed. The view from the **La Réserve** dining room is enchanting. Our lunch was pleasant, too, but it wasn't cheap. Now that the Richemond has assumed its management, it is even better than before. Down one flight, **Tse Fung** is the best Chinese restaurant we have ever found in Switzerland—and it vies for our top ranking in all Europe. Elegant setting, furnishings, and tableware; large selection of Cantonese, Peking, and Shanghai specialties, beautifully prepared; open 365 days for lunch and dinner. More expensive than average Cathay establishments, but infinitely better in its suavity and quality. Fine! As for straight restaurants, our happiest stop in the city is **Le Béarn** (quai de la Poste 4); it remains as good as ever. *Fin-de-siècle* décor; paneled walls with red "silk" that is actually plaster; 9 tables in front; larger room to the rear for overflow traffic. In addition to the superb dishes with their accent on French gustation, both my Nancy and our Judy *again* almost swooned over the mashed potatoes here, declaring once more that they were the best either of our gals had ever tasted. (Our Tío Pepe also loved 'em, and agrees that no one can put a patch on this potato patch.) All-out recommendation for. this little gem; *don't miss it!* Next in line is **L'Or du Rhône** (place du Cirque 1). Here's a rôtisserie-type establishment with an open fireplace where steaks and chicken-on-the-spit are broiled by white-capped Patron Fiechter, in full view of the guest; the bar in front, as impersonal as an airport waiting room, is neither fish nor fowl. Old Tavern authenticity, not Olde Taverne phoniness; advance reservations mandatory for dinner. Two Detroit friends of the *Guide* lyrically praise the artfulness of the martinis and the cuisine here, but they knock the lack of ventilation in which the temperature is upped by the (1) heaters on the service tables, (2) candles on the dining tables, and (3) physical heat produced by the customers who jam it. They are absolutely correct about its Turkish-bath aura when filled—but still recommended, despite the owner's parsimony in not installing a proper air-circulation system. **Au Fin Bec** (rue de Berne 55) is an unpretentious old-timer to which Genevois flock, especially in game season. Enclosed-garden entrance; begonia-bowered, arch-lined, tree-covered patio for fair-weather meals, plus 3 inside dining rooms; neighborhood drop-in atmosphere; warm attention dispensed by Hostess Mme. Janet and her staff of aproned waitresses. Our substantial dinner for 4 (hors d'oeuvres, woodcock, kidneys in white wine, and Blanc de Blancs '61) was a treat at around $16 per tummy. Around October (or later, if in season), order as a curiosity the large celerylike vegetable called "cardon," which is a house specialty. No patrons received after 2 P.M. or 10 P.M.—a rigid rule—so plan accordingly. Plain but beckoning. The **Park de Budé**, near the Intercontinental, is a deluxe entry nurtured by Victor Armleder, son of the city's leading hotel scion. Entrance alcove with easy chairs for premeal libations; up a 1/2-story to the sail-loft where a dozen tables complete the picture; marine décor theme; superb fish; perfect service on our boarding. The same family oversees the many facets of the **La Coupole** complex, a linkage of several sprightly feederies within a midtown office building. Its 22 backgammon tables (free) along with frequent tournaments are its backbone. These are fleshed out so enticingly that it is just as alluring for nonplayers. Striped bar at entrance packed during peak hours with a mélange from the ultrachic to the semidemimonde; suave Backgammon Bar where the dice quietly roll and where clients relax in comfortable chairs to sip their perfectly blended drinks; reasonably priced Swiss-rustic dining room with temptingly prepared vittles and a business clientele at lunch; swingingest action in both bars from 5 to 8, continuing in the gaming areas from 10 to 1; closed Sunday and Christmas week. A merry and meritorious fun spot which we highly recommend. The Belle-Époque-styled **La Rotonde Coffee Shop** at rue du Mont Blanc 3, which is open from 7 A.M. to midnight except on Monday, is okay for light bites and beverages. The atmosphere is better than the kitchen work. The well-known **Mövenpick** has one of its ubiquitous superrestaurants on place de la Fusterie. Another, on the right bank, is proclaimed to be the biggest and most modern in Switzerland; we dined on excellent roast beef here recently; while the Yorkshire Pudding looked authentic, we secretly think the pastry chef is a spy from Lancaster. Incidentally, the payment system at the production-line stand-up snack bar defies the most exquisite brand of Soviet bureaucracy; its complicatedness borders on the comic (if you're not hungry or in a rush to eat). **Don Quijote** (rue de Berne 1), opposite the station, is a touch of old Granada. Central "wishing well" in the handsome wood- and iron-highlighted upstairs restaurant for tossing your loose change, which the 78 gypsy-fingered Spanish staffers divvy up on holidays; street-floor snack bar; medium-expensive, savory Iberian dishes; Cellar Taverna de Sancho Panza; well patronized by a well-groomed clientele. Ask for Director Don Thomas. *Olé!* We're told that **Le Catalan** (route de Florissant) is even better nowadays. Said to be "less slick but with superior food." We'll sample it soon. The **Mére Royaume** (rue Corps-Saints 4), dating back to 1602, seems to be bouncing back to life under the Armleder leadership. (They took it over more recently than in the early seventeenth century.) Our *omble* (lake fish) in butter sauce was not good, *it was fantastic!* Chummy brick and timber personality enhanced by kind, efficient service, moderate prices, and splendid value in the culinary output. **La Perle du Lac**, on the lake, has a lovely terrace, and an impressively agreeable alfresco atmosphere. Closed when winter winds blow. The **Port Gitana Grill**, 1-mile farther along, has a shorefront setting and satisfactory viands; small cabaret; numbingly expensive, in our opinion. **Auberge Communale de Confignon** (10 minutes by taxi in the Confignon suburb) served us the best steak of our entire Swiss loop recently. Simple, long building on a hillock overlooking town; huge delicious cuts of steer; fast service; outstanding quality for medium-to-low tariffs. Highly recommended for purposeful beefeaters. **Lion d'Or**, about the same distance to Cologny, is also bully. Lakefront windows; pine-lined dining room; outdoor terrace for sipping; magnificent grills; friendly attention by Maître Jean Romello. Be sure to top off your repast with a "lie"—not a falsehood, but a glass of Genevoise firewater concocted from the by products of the grape. Very hardy and good. **Le Mazot** (Hôtel d'Alleves, near American Express) has gone flamboyant, with flambeaux and chafing dishes galore; piano player and genial aura; the lovely bar upstairs is knee-deep in Persian rugs, and from here you can gaze down at the diners and glory in the precipitous alpine cleavages below. Our service was quick, firm, and proper, but lacking in warmth; the cuisine was passable (except for the fish, which was notably poor). It might kindle some glow if (1) your lucky star is with you, and (2) you wrap your beard in a wet napkin to prevent starting a holocaust.

The **Bar Américain and Grill** (in the Cornavin Station) offers 7 interesting regional menus from 11 A.M. to 1 A.M. The restaurant proper, with heavy yellow curtains and fetching mien, is faintly reminiscent of a small, smart East Side New York bistro. **Café-Crémerie La Clémence** (Bourg-de-Four 20) is a tumultuous churn of male students, newspaper snoopers, and soapbox orators; worth seeing if you take your earmuffs. **Café-Restaurant de la Pointe** (rue Jargonnant 3) is known for its Steak au Poivre; inexpensive and amusing. **À l'Olivier de Provence** (rue Jacques-Dauphin 13) is an outstanding family-run enterprise; 14 tables, paper napery, candle illumination, and fanny-firmer kitchen chairs; savory calves' liver and big-casseroled Potatoes au Gratin are the top attractions here; reserve in advance; popular and worthy. **La Pescaille** (15 av. Henri Dunant) is a bit out of the center, but our seafood adventure here was well worth the taxi hop. Warm reception; careful attention by waiters in waistcoats; cheerful décor in its one-room precinct. Prices float up to the higher tide levels of Geneva dining, but we'd say it's top value for top dollar. At **Roberto's** (rue de la Madeleine) the upstairs restaurant is more elegant than the ground-level station. Outstanding Italian savor for relatively low cost. Closed Monday. From the Land of the Rising Sun? **Yamakawa** (rue Henri Blanvalet 3) is simplicity itself, in the finest traditions of the Orient. The Japanese chef provides about 6-dozen dishes of superb quality for an audience that is at least 80% Nipponese. The price tags certainly reflect that nation's booming economy. Our meal of 2 portions of raw fish appetizers, Sukiyaki, and Sake totaled around $35. Rich tabs for rich rewards. Chinese chomping? Our first choice would be, of course, the aforementioned **Tse Fung**, but after it would come **Celeste Empire** (rue Tour-Maîtresse), where the ambiance can be hectic, followed by **Fleur de Ming** (rue de Port)—and, at the tail of the dragon, the **Auberge des Trois Bonheurs** (rue de la Cité 29). **Wimpy** has rolled out 4 stations in the city for budget biters. Finally, this *Guide* must continue to withhold its endorsement of **Le Chandelier**; to our distress (and perhaps we are again partially responsible), this once-charming little haven impressed us on our latest visit as a slick, commercial, tourist-motivated operation; now heartily disrecommended, despite murmurs it may be trending upward again.

Sunny day? There's a tiny bistro at *Chambésy s/Genève*, about 15 minutes from the center of Geneva (start along the Lausanne highway and turn off up the mountain). The name is **Relais de Chambésy**; it's at the hub of the village; there's a tree-shaded terrace with 7 or 8 tables; the atmosphere is bustling and friendly. Don't fail to try their 2 specialties, Entrecôte (steak) with a mustard sauce and the light, mouth-watering Sabayon to settle the meat. (The sliced ham is also delicious.) **L'Auberge du Grand-Lancy**, 2 miles from the center, is utilitarian rather than social; game and fish specialties; quite expensive; closed Mondays and most of July; also agreeable when skies are clear. The **Restaurant du Parc des Eaux-Vives**, across the far waters on the lake bank opposite the Richemond Hôtel, is an impressive graystone château which the city owns. Iron gate entrance; lovely landscaping with the Geneva Tennis Club courts behind; portal canopied with a blue- and white-striped baldachin; umbrella-lined terrace for tea or apéritif sippers, without food service; 6 huge windows in the main dining room with magnificent views of the water and the distant UN enclave. The quality of the gastronomy is now spiraling upward, so that it stands today as one of the city's more sophisticated and worthwhile dining targets. **Pavillon de Ruth**, a lakefront venture at the previously mentioned *Cologny* (2 miles), works continuously from March to December 15; we wish the cookery was as satisfying as the scenery. Pity. **Carnotzet** (Lausanne road) is a sprawling outdoor-indoor establishment with a perfectly wonderful spread of Lake Léman and Geneva; delightful as a drop-in spot for coffee or refreshments when the air is balmy. **Rôtisserie du Lac** at *Coppet* (also Lausanne road) has been entirely renovated. Indoor dining room with fireplace and beamed ceiling, lakeside terrace; rôtisserie in summer; horseshoe-shape, Scottish tartan bar upstairs, with piano background music; 8 bedchambers and 4 baths; Chef-Owner René Gottraux speaks no English, but his daughter is a linguist. Very fashionable these days among the smart set of the metropolis who swarm in by car or boat; if your gastronomy isn't fussy and your wallet is verdant with greenbacks, you'll find this a beguiling retreat. Variable. Our beloved friend Georges Prade, Prince of the Mumm Champagnes interests, tipped us off that **Auberge des Grands Bois** at *Buchillon* (2 exits short of Lausanne on the auto route, near Ste. Sulpice) turns out some of the best lake-fish cookery in the nation. He was right again, of course. The trout, perch, and *omble* (deep-water critters) are heavenly, the prices are relatively low, and the drive into the country is lovely. Typically rustic atmosphere with no pretensions; the proprietress is the mother of André, the world-famous bar chief of the Palace Hotel in Gstaad. Very popular, so do call ahead to reserve. Another food-savvy friend, David Blum, the famous conductor who adds a grace note to this *Guide* from time-to-time, recommends the **Gothard** in *Chêne Bourg*. We so frequently concur with this gentleman on matters of cuisine that we can suggest it to you without a personal trial. Finally, if you're outward bound, the dining complex at the *Airport* is interesting for jet-watchers and A-okay for tummy-teasers. Economy counter and tables on the same tier as the public observation deck; Le Circle Bar and the elegant Rôtisserie 1-flight up; exactly the same vistas in both; satisfactory culinary productions for the corresponding price levels. Recommendable if you're on the run, but not worth a special safari if you're stationed in town.

In *Grindelwald*, the **Gasthof Steinbock**, opposite the Hotel Adler, takes top honors in our survey. Bustling, no-nonsense, bare-floored, Swiss-modern eatery with a 3-language menu and close ventilation; drinks served at your table; no bar; portions so H-U-G-E they might daunt a grizzly bear. When we first boggled over the platters set before other diners, we shuddered—but, to our surprise, our Wiener Schnitzel and its trimmings were light and well cooked. Piano and accordion in evening; occasional yodeling and regional entertainment. Best in the village for its category; recommended. The adjoining **Alkoholfreies Restaurant Zur Alten Post** is a mountain-style T-room for T-totalers. You'll never get that alpenglow here, but if it is tidbits you fancy, this teeny tapless tavern should suit you to that T. **Rendez-vous** offers the Hungry Man a starvation menu: sandwiches and pastries only. But the Thirsty Man or Dancing Man will leave replete. Lovely small open terrace with sweeping panorama for sunny-day sipping; a cute little spot. The **Regina** wears the undisputed crown in the hotel regency; it offers *haute cuisine* at prices that don't bite back. **Spinne** is the evening mecca of teen-agers who dance with Spinne-tingling abandon. One combo upstairs challenges another downstairs—so when it goes, man, it really GOES. Anyone over 21 should pack along his ski poles and earmuffs. At "**First**," the last stop on the 7220-foot-high chair lift, there's a simple restaurant and terrace for plain fare and fantastic viewing. Never mind the provisions; you'll never see what's on your plate, anyway.

Gstaad 's chic-to-chic leader, naturaly, is the **Palace Hotel**, where black-tie attire is not at all uncommon every evening. Conservative raiment in dining room décor; ultratasteful Maxim's Room for Saturday nights only and its superluxurious galas; suave Grill-Bar with dancing in the afterglow, with André acting as Master of Libations. Sophisticated international clientele are drawn here as flies to orange-blossom honey. Fashionable, opulent, and sound in service, cuisine, and ambiance. Tops. The **Chesery** also attracts its own disciples from the Social Set. Midvillage setting; more of a food-and-fun complex than a hotel (only 3 double rooms and 1 suite). From the bottom up, there are the cellar Carnotzet with isolated pockets for quiet nibbling and a bar to one side, a ground-floor nightclub with music and quaffing counter, a 2nd-floor, 6-table Fondue Stubli cozy in coral, yellow, and green, and an adjoining 7-table Grill with an open rôtisserie sizzling at one end. All decorations in imaginative "Cantonese." (Again, ouch!) Very appealing. The hilltop-high **Parkhotel** features its own intimate Bar-Grill in natural wood and regional fixin's, plus the tiny 2-table Cave Romande which is a darling. The **Olden** is a swinger—chiefly because of the attractive English-speaking proprietress, Miss Hedy, known far and wide as "the Dinah Shore of the piano." Café in front; L-shape restaurant farther in for 80 munchers, sippers, tea-dancers, or 9 P.M.-to-1 A.M. highsteppers; special Swiss evenings with yodeling and local attractions on Fridays; La Cave, in intimate connecting links downstairs, with hot roasts and cool melodies, plus a next-door skittles court. Extensive menu and semialtitudinous prices; perfect for merry night owls or the keyboard Shore Patrol.

Interlaken is interlocked with hotel dining rooms almost exclusively. If you're a renegade like us (and many local residents), you'll break step and hop over to the little **Hotel Bären**, near the post office. Our recent Bratwurst, Rösti (Swiss-style hashed-brown potatoes), and draft beer were all superior in preparation and quality. A new fillip for filling up is its Swiss meal consisting of Fondue, Brienzlig (fried lake fish), Bratwurst mit Rosti or, some other main course, salad, and a dessert of ice cream and cake topped with hot chocolate sauce—just the thing for dieters. Exceptionally fine service, too! Ask for either of the Proprietors Frei. Yum-yum.

Lausanne offers several attractive oases. The Grill at the **Beau Rivage** boasts a mighty reputation. Decorated in Florentine style; maximum of 75 clients; twin piano lilts; dancing; very expensive; *evenings only and closed on Mondays.* The **Lausanne Palace** Grill, completely remodeled and refreshened, is superb. Classic, quiet room attuned for opulent dining; comfortable chairs and ample elbowroom so that your sweet nothings can't be eavesdropped by the next table; urbane service; spiraling rôtisserie to nudge your taste buds gently; cozy bar adjoining. A happy rebirth. **Rôtisserie de la Grappe d'Or**, under the direction of Michel Wilhelm, is the pacemaker among the independent restaurants. Enormous open grill, from which come some of the tiniest servings outside of a Harz Mountain aviary; beamed ceilings, and sophisticated rustic ambiance which has picked up even more crispness, color, and charm. *Entre-nous* atmosphere; well-schooled, attentive staff who prefer to perform for the clients whom they know best; sommelier who stirs his martinis black-and-blue to an untimely death; many of the choicest selections limited to 2-person portions; priced for guests with big fat, unnumbered accounts in those big, fat Swiss banks. The presentation of the cuisine—as evinced by the clever rolling apéritif cart, for example—is far more eye-appealing than that of many of France's greatest gastronomic shrines; its quality, however, suffers somewhat by comparison. Here's a professionally operated oasis which most well-heeled tourists adore far more than do many local Swiss. M. Girardet's **Hotel de Ville** in the tiny hamlet of *Crissier* is now one of the most talked about shrines on the continent— certainly a recommendation, but so much in demand that you must book at least a week in advance. We won't describe the somewhat dull interior because we heard that it was due for some redecoration after our departure. The cuisine is undoubtedly dazzling, so if you want to give it a whirl, dial Crissier 34•15•14 and hope for the best—which you'll surely receive if you do get in. The **Voile d'Or** ("Golden Sail"), formerly the Centre de l'Hôtellerie, is a unique jammer beginning to heed the helm. Beautiful reed-lined lakeshore situation; pleasant split-level lounge, bar, and restaurant in stonework and Douglas fir, with icicle-thin ceiling fixtures in serpentine pattern; rope carpets, and scatter rugs; orange-and-white-fringed umbrellas dotting the snack terrace. It's highly variable, according to local friends who go more frequently than we do. Le Beaujolais in the **Continental Hotel** turns on a reasonable meal for the outlay. The uninterested, slow service, however, reduces the pleasure of the overall experience, according to one cosmopolite who has been several times. Le Calèche, ground floor in the **Alpha Hotel**, is fun for rusticity in the city. Steaks of all dimensions and cuts; cafeteria-style service; downstairs Carnotzet for cheese-whizzing. Fair returns for the outlay; very popular. Down the line comes the more modest **Pomme de Pin** (Cité Derrière 15), with its renowned chicken specialties, also good, but far from cheap. **Aux Trois Tonneaux** ("3 Barrels") is taverny, with intimate dimensions and limited menu; we enjoyed our recent meal of stuffed mushrooms and steak. Proprietor Boss, we're happy to say, is rolling out the barrels again. Pleasant for lodge-type dining. **Chez Charles**, (rue des Mousquines) has been totally re-chezed; simple family diner; low-cost for high quality. Ironically our podiatric plates were alive with frogs' legs and pig's feet; we sho' 'nuff ankled away happily from our Franco-American soul food. **Café du Jorat** (place de l'Ours 1) is famed for fabulous fondue-fondling; recommended. **Mandarin** (avenue du Théâtre 7) wins our fortune cookie for Chinese delights. **La Cravache**, a pub next to the Palace Hotel, is simple and cozy for a nip 'n sip.

Sunny day or starlit evening? The Gauer interests of Berne's Schweizerhof took over the **Hotel du Raisin** at *Cully*, between Lausanne and Montreux. They revivified this small-town tavern, furnished it with covered wooden banquettes, and touched it up appealingly in other respects. Worth a visit for its hearthside dining, but a bit expensive. The **Major Davel Restaurant**, down the slope at water's edge—a combination of café, bar, and restaurant—seems even better. Fish specialties, with Filet de Poisson Belle Meunière and Truite du Lac Poché Hollandaise both delicious; Chicken Curry for 2 is a piquant alternative. Other stops of interest along the shore are **Auberge de l'Onde** at *St.-Saphorin* (rendezvous of artists and authors), **Restaurant Le Monde** at *Grandvaux* (vineyards and a glorious view; RESERVE IN ADVANCE), and **Chez Pitch Restaurant** at *Pully* (open all year, with reservations also a *must* in season). Finally, the celebrated **Swiss Chalet** of the Brussels World's Fair was reassembled at *Signal de Sauvabelin*, 1800 feet above the city. It presents a magnificent Alpine panorama, with the blue Léman waters at its feet.

In *Leysin*, locals informed us that the **Mésange Hotel** offered the best cookery. When we hied ourselves there, we found it plain substantial, inexpensive, and good. The Carnotzet of the **Grand Hôtel** changes its specialty twice a week. Fun. Of the independents, **Prafandaz** for fondue is the big cheese in the local pot, followed by **L'Horizon** and perhaps **Le Leysin**.

Locarno's Feed Box Special is **I Due Gatti-Las Gatos**, perched at 1400 feet on a mountainside just past the hamlet of Brione, 15 or 20 minutes from your hotel. To get up to it, be sure to use the Orselina route, and be sure to take a bug-size Fiat instead of a Cadillac, because the road is narrow. Open terrace with breath-catching panorama; Spanish specialties (including a Catalonian-speaking cat named Muchacho), plus French and Italian dishes; excellent cookery. The setting alone is worth the price of admission. Or if you're in the mood for an even more striking panorama (plus that spine-chilling cable-car ride!), the **Cardada Hotel**, 4500 feet up an alp, is swell for lunch. While the food is nothing special, the cost is negligible and the vista will thrill you.

In town, the **Campagna Ristorante & Grotto** has 4 rooms, 2 fireplaces, and a tavernish architecture; terrace with stone tables for summer dining; modest prices and simple furnishings; typical Ticinese atmosphere. **Da Emilio,** between La Palma and Reber Hotels on the lakeside promenade, strikes us as slipping seriously; its future is alleged to be in doubt, so check before setting out. The **Oldrati**, on the main square, has a masculine, ground-floor, "modernistic" tavern and an upper-level, tea-roomy restaurant. Glorious view. Among the hotels, **La Palma au Lac** draws highest kudos from many leading epicurean societies (14 in 1 swoop recently!)—and we most heartily concur. Proprietor Bolli and his chef both received Diplomas of Honor and Medals in 3 successive World Congresses of Gastronomy, among others. Try to make it when a buffet is scheduled if you also want to give your eyes a feast (usually once a week in Season). The **Esplanade** is agreeable. Both feature alfresco dining in season. **Du Lac** is amply rewarding for the moderate tabs. **Caverna degli Dei** has more of a cave-born nightclub atmosphere than that of a full-blown restaurant. Maritime specialties; dancing nightly; a few hotel rooms for weary revelers. Routine, but it's almost the only late stop in town. The Grotto Grill in the **Grand** is said to be amusing, but we haven't crept in. At **Brissago** (beyond Ascona), the **Giardino**, in an ancient town house, came up with a loftier reputation than foodstuffs on our recent sampling. Perhaps you'll have better luck.

In **Lucerne**, **Old Swiss House** remains the first choice for a refined and colorful repast, thanks to the tireless hard work of urbane Proprietor Willy Buholzer as General Factotum, his equally indomitable wife, Hanny, and brother Kurt who rattles the skillets in the kitchen. As evidence of its years of success, it has even had to rearrange the entrance and expand the capacity (while maintaining the air of upland intimacy). Its décor and ambiance are still Overdone Swiss, with too much aimed toward the tourist trade (waitresses in costume, antique crucifixes, and the like)—but here is such a tight ship that the cuisine is excellent, the service kind, and the welcome warm. The price scale is substantial by national (not U.S.) standards. It gives us great pleasure to recommend this one as the best independent dining place of the city. Don't expect a Tour d'Argent, but it is way, way above the average for this Canton. Reservations mandatory in season. Lonesome for home? Try the delicious, unfancy wares at the **Luzernerhof**. The Dittli family can fill our bill any morning, noon, or night with their honest creations. Here vegetables taste like vegetables; food tastes like food; there's no trickery. The service is so sweet that the waitresses urge you to finish the huge portions; the dining room is attractive; the prices are very reasonable. What traveler could ask for more? Highly recommended. Next, the **Wilden Mann** features Châteaubriand steaks and similar belt-busting fare; tavern motif in one segment; sleeker, more international lines in another; slipping a bit on our scales. **Schwanen** is schwimmin' handsomely under the aegis of Director Urs Lauper. We must get back for another sampling at the **Stadtkeller**, which a local friend stoutly avows is one of the better attractions in the city. Swiss music, Swiss food, Swiss alpenhorn tooting from special stage—almost more Swiss than the Swiss, to please its big foreign trade. This city lives for the tourist in season and here is one of its magnets. Other new entrys for sampling include the **Hofbräuhaus** and the **Braukeller**. The Lapin Restaurant hops in the **Hôtel de la Paix**. Split-level dining room in sleek rustic-modern; waitresses in provincial costumes; moving-color-slide gismo for selecting your dishes; some counter service; choice of 7 types of sausage, the house specialty; our Bratwurst and Rösti were delicious. The owner's wife is a sister in the Real family who conjure up such culinary magic in Liechtenstein's leading gastronomic haven. A budgeteer's delight. The **Li Tai Pe Chinese Restaurant** (Furrengasse 14), has been converted into a Jade Pavilion of the Orient by hardworking Robert and Margaret Chi Tsun. (He was the former number one diplomatic aide to Gen. Chiang Kai-shek.) Breathtaking collection of rare Cathay artworks; 5 Far Eastern cooks mind the Soo-Gaw pots; savory cuisine and lovely presentation. If you're a party of 4, be sure to order the Peking specialty variously called Chrysanthemum Pot or Chue Hua Kuo or Steamboat; this cauldron of Oriental treasures is, as far as we know, unequalled in Europe. It must be ordered 1 day ahead; we venture this would be one of the memorable feasts of a lifetime. Top recommendation. **Raben** (in the old part of town) is an upstairs rôtisserie with 9 tables, beamed ceilings, tapestries, crossbows, and leather casements; worth a try. **Galliker's** is redolent of an English pub atmosphere. Hardy fare for these hardy Alpine rancheros; Pot au Feu seems to be the favorite choice. Bully for it. For light but full meals, **Café Arcade** is just the ticket; inside tables, plus a ringlet of alfresco *couverts* bordering the waterside and the Open Market; excellent pastries; Mrs. Helfenstein speaks English. Colorful as a ham-and-eggery. **Da Peppino** works up Italian specialties. *Buono!* Calories afloat? Try the good ship **William Tell**, moored in front of the American Express office. It carries a cargo of tea, snacks, and full repasts. *Bon voyage!*

Lugano's best used to be the **Hotel Splendide-Royal**, but it has been colorfully upstaged by the flairfully renewed **Eden** (see "Hotels"). Full meals or snacks are available at the latter. The **Capo San Martino**, on the main highway to Italy, is on a promontory which is medium-high over the water; vast terrace service; clean; cheaper and quieter; very popular for lunching and gazing.

Within the city, **Bianchi** now brooks no pretenders to its independent crown. It is old-fashioned and solid, with gold-silk walls, high ceilings, a fireplace, and no-nonsense fare. Recommended to the hungry Inner Man, if not to the Glamor Seeker. In *Vezia*, 2 miles out, **Villa Recreatio**, open all year, is equally satisfying. **Galleria,** in an arcade off via Vegezzi, comes up with almost comparable vittles at similar tariffs, according to a well-fed Evanston Guidester. We don't know it personally, but we will. **Orologio** is beginning to tick again; okay if you're a VIP or known to the management, so be sure to have your concierge shovel it on before strutting in. (This irks us, but that's the way the cookie crumbles.) **Grotto del Renzo**, 3 miles into the hills toward *Sorengo*, is pleasant for typical fare.

Montreux offers as our number one nomination **L'Hostellerie de Caux**, about 20 minutes up into the hills from the center via a lovely, curvy, but well-made road. Chalet exterior; illuminated trout tank at the door; L-shape main restaurant; adjoining terrace with about 15 tables; good but not dazzling view. Slick-rustic interior with 10 pale-raspberry-clad sites, a large fireplace, semibeamed ceiling, a bar, and a not-so-pastoral TV set in one corner. Cuisine excellent; savory fixed meals; specialties include "A La Broche" of Porterhouse for 4 persons, to Jambon à l'Os for 1 person to grilled steaks for twin munching; wine cellar of no less than 10-thousand bottles. The service and the ambiance are delightful. Young, charming, English-speaking Monsieur and Madame Charles Rust are the *patrons,* and they take warm personal care of their clients; ask for them. Closed mid-November to mid-December, and Tuesdays except in July and August. Highly recommended. **Le Vieux Montreux**, opened in '63, is our prize candidate within the city limits. Antique coach at entrance; restaurant down 1-flight in a late-fifteenth-century wine cellar; tiny bar with old timbers and inches of atmosphere; inner sanctum under a long narrow archway, with an open rôtisserie and a grandfather clock dominating either end. Red napery, piped music, ancient pots and pans decorating the walls; especially popular at night, when its 16 tables are candle-lit. Very attractive indeed; also recommended. **Le Montagnard** ("The Mountain Man") is our third choice. About 15 minutes up by taxi you'll find this former old stable, hand-transformed by Hans Odermatt personally, who did most of the carpentry, the masonry, and the perspiring. Another chalet mien, also of '63 vintage; not much of an outside view, but oozing with color and charm. The main hall is a split-level woody area with a slate-roofed bar to one side (note especially the all-wood clock at the door). Lights in brass bells, old-fashioned farm implements, chamois pelts, waiters in regional costumes, a mural, a loft, and several tables outside for warm-weather dining complete the picture. Don't fail to try "riz montagnard," the big specialty of the house; it's superdelicious. Herr Odermatt, with beard, a huge chef's cap, mountain knickers, and perfect English with a strong Australian accent (!), is a charmer. Liveliest in the evening; very good. **Manoire**, a third Alpine alternate about 4500 feet up on the Col de Jaman (a normal 40-minute ride from Montreux) is another typical highland nest. Open-air rôtisserie; simple fare-of-the-country well prepared; snowed in during much of the winter; the very narrow asphalt road has now been remade, but it remains scary for acrophobes. Now back to the town itself: The recently and lavishly redecorated restaurant of the municipality-sponsored **Casino** is extra-pleasant on a sunny day. Poolside situation; lovely sweeping terrace; routine cookery; heavy draw from the younger set. Its adjoining glassbound nightclub—stunningly remodeled with Matterhorns of Swiss francs—is the biggest font of cabaret entertainment and gala evening pastimes. Worth a gambol. So is **La Vieille Ferme**, in more rustic tones, as well as **La Bavaria** if you want to summon up another regional mood. **Montreux-Plage** is the only local feedery with a patio directly on the water. Locals say it has a *"dans le vent"* atmosphere. Not gourmet level, but quite acceptable for motorists—or hungry long-distance swimmers from Geneva. We hear avid praise for both **La Locanda** and for **La Rouvenaz**, neither of which we've tried. Our sources, however, are reliable. The **Museum Club** is a tenth-century structure restored into a Ratskeller by the Montreux Tourist Office. It's the perfect drop-in spot for a hogshead of wine during the season. Fat red candles sputtering on planked tables; fat red burghers sipping and sputtering in their chairs (capacity of up to 220 for banquets); open for dancing, yodeling, and mountain fun from June to September. The entry fee includes all the wine you can pour past your larynx; go around 9 P.M.; you are welcome to take along your wine glass as a free souvenir. The Mayfair Pub in the **Hôtel Splendid** has a central location with plenty of parking space across the main street. We haven't tried it since the change. The Tavern at the **Castle of Chillon** has an interesting atmosphere—but oh! oh! oh! that cookery! We've recently tried it again, and it was just plain atrocious. A spirited and observant couple from St. Petersburg, who based in this city for several months, call the cuisine of the **Eden au Lac** (downstairs oasis of the Hotel Eden, separately operated and not to be confused with the main dining room), "the best we had in Switzerland." They continue: "Here's an informal, almost American atmosphere; bright cheerful décor; close view of the lake, waterfront Quay of the Flowers, and the passing promenaders—a revelation to automobile-enthralled Americans like us. Maître Cornelius Brower will beamingly create Crêpes Copacabana on request. He sprinkles powdered coffee on the crêpes, marries Crème de Cacao with the cream and butter sauce, and finally, flames cognac expertly. Then· he lavishes the yummy production over generous scoops of coffee ice cream and flourishes it proudly upon the table." Forgive the droplets of water which wrinkle this page; they accidentally slipped from our salivary glands as we wrote this. Closed from October to April, so damn, damn, damn our luck for *again* mushing in during its hiatus! The same Floridians also recommend **Les Narcisses**, a small village inn above the hub at Chamby. Their advice: "Choose a clear day, eat and drink slowly, and savor the meaning of *la belle Suisse.* "

At **Morges**, the somewhat overrated **Chez Felicie** rôtisserie will stuff you with as many dozen grilled chickens as you can swallow in one sitting; upstairs and downstairs dining rooms. Both the **Mésange** and the **Léman** are recommendable.

Neuchâtel 's blue-ribbon bet is **Des Halles**, now totally renovated and under new direction. It has a classic French personality in·one portion, a brasserie in another. The steamship, **Le Vieux Vapeur**, docked in the harbor, is a cargo of delights for nautical nibblers. **Du Théâtre**, **Beau-Rivage**, and **St. Honoré** are substantial; on a sunny day, the lakeside terrace of the ultramodern **Beaulac Hotel** offers a lovely setting. **Buffet de la Gare**, believe it or not, is darned good for your francs. And so is the restaurant of the **Hotel Beaux-Arts**. We're told that **La Grappa** and the **Hôtel Auvent** out at *Boudevilliers* are okay, but we've tried neither. In *Saint-Blaise*, **Au Boccalino** does nice things for Italian cookery; it is 3 miles out of town.

In *St. Gall*, the stucco-and-timber **Walliserkeller** is the local mecca for regional dishes such as fondues, raclette, and other cheese-whizzes. Taverny atmosphere with plates as wall-sconce reflectors, hanging lanterns, a charcoal grill, and a smoky air; extensive menu. Good, as long as you know what it is. The Grill downstairs in the **Hecht Hotel** offers a more elegant mood under its arched ceiling. Cozy bar adjoining; wrought-iron fixtures; well-wrought piano melodies nightly. Very pleasant indeed. **Baratella** is an Italian *trattoria* that many wanderers like. **Seeger Bar-Tea Room** (plus discothèque on the first floor) is busy and amiable around the Lipton's hour—but stay away on Saturday nights, because so many customers are in the pot that they jam its spout.

St. Moritz offers several possibilities. The local "21" is **Chesa Veglia**, owned by the Palace Hotel's Badrutt brothers, but operated by Village Mayor Hans Gartmann and his wife. Here's a glorified Engadine chalet with a marvelous (yet low-price) pizzeria, 2 bowling alleys, and a perfectly delightful life-size wooden horse. Heart of the enterprise is the vastly more exclusive, dressy, and expensive Chadafö Grill. Aside from the tariffs, the only difference between this room and the others seems to be the use of charcoal here, while the adjoining nooks utilize electric ovens and grills; the vegetables are given identical treatment throughout; there is piano melodizing in the Chadafö, with dancing featured elsewhere. All couverts must be reserved at least 24 hours in advance (48 hours on High Season weekends). Even for an après-ski Neapolitan nibble in the cellar, it is almost impossible to snag a table between 4 P.M. and 7 P.M. Our blue-ribbon meal was only fair—not memorable. (Our accountant remembers it, however, and never fails to remind us.) On the other hand, the Grill at the **Palace Hotel** (advance reservations advised) was infinitely more rewarding on our recent tries. Outstandingly superb cuisine, suave service, and good cheer; highest recommendation in every regard. The grill at the **Kulm** also is a marvel for gastronomy, but it is not as elegant to the eye—nor is it intended to be. For less lofty, utilitarian dining, nothing we've found in the valley can touch the little Cascade Restaurant in the **Hotel Bernasconi**. We supped here regularly during a recent fortnight's ski holiday—and each meal surpassed the last. Not a Grand or a Ritz in atmosphere, but clean, ingratiating, and intimate. Dress including anything from the rainbows of sportswear to suits, ties, and frocks; lovely presentation by highly skilled, friendly Maître Ruoso Manlio; consistent culinary cunning. It would be a disservice to single out any dish as being especially succulent, since everything we tried during our 2 weeks was mouthwatering. So popular that day-ahead bookings are a *must* in winter; same-day notice is advised at other times. This charmer evokes Cascades of happy memories and fond wishes. The Grischuna in the **Hotel Monopole** is fun. Separate niche for Swiss cheese specialties; bench bar; dancing nightly; prices medium-high; cookery satisfactory but not startling. The Caprice Grill in the **Calonder** is more *intime* and less costly. The always-jammed **Calèche Cafe,** in the center, left this reporter stone cold when it was last checked. We'll have another look soon. **Salastrains** is halfway up the slope; snacks for skiers; packed tightly on sunny days; stem in at noon for lunch and begin schussing earlier for maximum pleasure. **Acla-Clavadatsch** is the nearby alpside hut for Schweizerhof guests. Outdoor grills; piano player by the hearth; noontime only; meal chits in lieu of francs; a chummy bonus if you are staying in this hotel. **Corviglia Club**, mecca of society sportsmen, is catered by the Chesa Veglia and the aforementioned Hans Gartmann. It is restricted to members and their guests; uncrackable, unless you're invited. Lunch expedition on a balmy day? The trip up the **Diavolezza aerial railway** to 8800 feet can be enormous fun, if your company is as nice as ours was. It's a leap-and-a-skip past Pontresina, a drive which takes perhaps 20 minutes. At the top, the panorama from the terrace of the mountain restaurant called **Abeba** is fabulous. You'll eat locomotive-size hot dogs and typical farmer fare—and love it. In **Pontresina** itself, the **Sarazena** tries to be the chief of the chic clique; the effort was in vain, on our peek.

Verbier's best tables—and prettiest, too—are in the rustic **Ecurie** of the Hotel Ermitage. Our recent repast was delightful at medium-high prices.

Villars offers scant facilities for the gastronome. There are few restaurants as such—most vittles are swallowed in the dining rooms of the leading hostelries or the pubs. Of the latter group, **Sporting** is the champ. Its Tisonier segment turns on the most *haute* cuisine, while there are nooks for grills, pizzas, and wines, and even a nightclub for the strong in spirit. Fine open terrace for snacks; terpsichorean frivolities at teatime and from 9 P.M. to 1 A.M.; many big-name performers engaged from time to time; occasional cabaret. Here's a real swinger. **Alpe-Fleurie**, opposite the station and adjoining the hotel of the same moniker, occupies a laggard's 2nd place. Ground floor divided between its ordinary feedery (paper "tablecloths") and an equally simple nightclub (cloth tablecloths); go between 11 P.M. and 2 or 3 in the morning; routine cooking. Informal and inexpensive. The **Central**, just above the artificial Ice Rink, is a different ball of cheese: Carnotzet-type, with 6 red-checked tables; raclette the specialty; adjoining café with valley view; disco-center now pulsating to work off the carbohydrates. Busy and fun. For chalet fixin's, the **Chez-Gollut** at *Frience* and the **Refuge** at *Solalex* raise the roofs of most discerning mouths—with pleasure, that is. **Mon Repos** in *Arveyes* does a commendable job with its Italian cookery.

In *Zermatt*, **Tenne** steals the local thunder for decorative allure. Here, surprisingly to our ever-curious eyes, is one of the most visually enjoyable restaurants we have ever found in Switzerland. Main 11-table dining room in . miniature medieval court-and-cloister architecture; alcove seating; big crackling-wood grill and service board on one side; casement windows; central covered atrium, 2 stories high, with zodiacal mural on the ceiling and an organist's perch ¾ths of the way up; adjoining bar cunningly carrying out the same motif, with inverted-V roof, walls in ancient timbers, and 8 of the damnedest, most puzzling (and most uncomfortable) bar stools we've ever bucked—small saddles, affixed to the floor, which actually ROCK!!! Upstairs, via a rope-banister staircase, are 2 more rooms—a grill with blue-and-white textile touches and a weathered-and-woody den that is strikingly attractive. The immaculate, well-equipped, and expensive kitchen is in the cellar. The expensive menu features Grills à la Broche. Specialties: Sirloin à l'Os Café de Paris, Porterhouse or Châteaubriand for 2, roast rack of lamb, and many other tempters; ample-but-not-large wine list. Dress optional, from ski togs to Brioni's most chic (as is customary in Zermatt these days). When it is busy, the poor service can spoil the fun of an entire evening. Otherwise, we remain a loyalist. Taverne Chez Alex, the cellar of the **Hôtel Alex**, is a cutie. Rusticity by the carload, with old beams, Alpine architecture, and the flavor of the hills; menu selections are small but choice. For day-in-night-out dining, nothing in the valley can touch it with a 10-foot slalom pole. The tip of the topmost peak for its category. The slick-rustic Otto Furrer-Stube—named for the famous mountain guide who was killed—is the popular cellar haunt of the **Seilerhaus**. Entrance from the street or from the hotel; its scant 16 tables nearly always packed to the scuppers; small bar behind arches; glasswrapped terrace; air-conditioned, but still hot; redolent with food smells; a severely overworked staff; cookery that impressed us as too costly for the so-so rewards. A big name locally, but only fair by national guidelines. **Chez Gaby** is strong on eye-appeal, but Gaby's place is a witch to date. Miserable reservations policy on every one of our numerous tries; poor reception when you finally do make it. Ground-floor dining room dominated by a green tile-topped table; open rôtisserie; upstairs bar with more settings; an earnest chef (Gaby himself) who often apologizes for the staff shortcomings in a hospitable way. Okay for grills, but *what* a production to get in. The back-o-town **Spycher** features a tiny intimate quadrant in the back of a multisection room. Lodge décor; typically overheated, as only the Swiss can overheat a restaurant. We found our platters too heavily sprinkled with Aromat, a flavor accenter, on our latest try. The **Bambi**, at the lower end of town, is not only attractive to the aesthetic senses, but here we've repeatedly had one of the best shish kebabs we've ever savored anywhere in Europe. Add to that its comparatively low prices and the sweet family service, and Bambi becomes a teriffic buy. Personally, we go back frequently and love it. The **Stockhorn**, near the Eden & Rex, is quite a warm and cozy nook today. Ski instructor Émile Julen is the owner, and his taste for winter sport, climbing, and good solid cookery is reflected on its walls and tables. Ropes, crampons, picks and other lore of the mountains for décor; intimate ground-level dining room plus a charming dark raclette *Stube* in the cellar. Now definitely recommendable for its type. The **Couronne** is best for après-ski *Glühwein* and snacks when the slopes have been retired for the day. The **Walliserkanne,** next to the Walliserhof, is in no way associated with Theo Welschen's hotel interests. Not at all special. The **Mont Cervin** whets your appetite with predinner libations in the Rendez-Vous Bar or with prelunchtime nips at the tiny streetside Escargot bar. Handsome, nonaggressive dining room with wholesome well-cooked fare. Very pleasant, indeed. The Grill of the **Zermatterhof** is an exquisitely polished oasis. Intimate, elegant, glass-wrapped; open rôtisserie crackling in one far corner; yumptious cuisine. A café with live and recorded music is partitioned from this high-style aristocrat by green and yellow curtains; in this section are banquettes of rasping raspberry hue and a more informal air. Sound, solid and recommendable. The **Walliserhof** boasts both its locally popular *Gaststube* up front (regional décor and dishes to match) and its sprightly modern, glass-bound restaurant to the rear, where the weekly buffet is truly splendid. Each has its appeal, depending upon your mood. The **Alpenblick**, a 10-minute hike toward the Matterhorn, unveils a perfectly splendid panoramic terrace, but perfectly atrocious victuals.

Finally, you might try **Elsie's place**. This Zermatt personality, who presided at the Rendez-Vous Bar of the Mont Cervin for 25 seasons, opened her own little haven opposite the church, a few steps from the Hotel Zermatterhof. In this very ancient house you'll find 6 tables, a small semicircular bar, knotty walls, casement windows, and a friendly atmosphere. Elsie's prides: Irish coffee (very costly but *delicious*), ham and eggs, hot dogs, other light snacks, and all beverages (which can sometimes taste foreign indeed to U.S.-bred sippers). Closed May, October, and November; otherwise it goes full blast from 10 A.M. to midnight, 7 days a week.

In *Zug*, world-travelers Maria and Jack Pearson praise the cozy little **Aklin am Zytturm** to the high blue-Swiss heavens. If this food-savvy twosome say it's good, we're already jumping to give it a try. We made a special foray out here one Thursday only to discover that this is the exact day it closes for a rest. Instead, we lumbered down to the **Hecht**, at lakeside, and pouted until we were presented with a marvelous fish platter, a glorious waterfront panorama, and a delightful wedge of Kirschtorte that melted away the last vestiges of regret. What the Hecht!—we'll recommend both. The **Rathaus** is okay for light bites and atmosphere and the **Ochsen** leads the hotel herd.

Zürich's most fashionable oasis is the Grill Room of the **Baur au Lac**. The dining room of the **Dolder Grand** also has a fine reputation; under its new change of management we must try it again. We're told that groups are beginning to appear in these lovely precincts. True? **Kronenhalle** (Ramistrasse 4) again came up with such impeccable cookery that we again lick our chops in reminiscence. Two floors; old-fashioned ambiance, enlivened by the Picassos, Dalis, and Matisses on the walls; rendez-vous of journalists, authors, painters, and people in the arts; medium prices and food that would delight the original Lucius Licinius Lucullus in regeneration; miserably rushed service that nearly always borders on negligence; go early for dining or later for tippling, because more and more stern (and justified!) complaints are reaching us from discriminating Guidesters. One of the coziest, most tastefully decorated, most beguiling bars in Helvetia directly adjoins; Chief Mixologist Paul Nuesch is the bonded spirit of friendship to many an American traveler, according to our warmhearted amigos Annette and Bert Parks; be sure to have your cocktails and/or liqueurs and coffee here. Paul Gallico once called this one of the nation's top 2 restaurants; we don't go quite that far, but we also cheer. A discovery if you hit it right, despite its undermanned staff.

Seiler's Ermitage, once our favorite, suffered a seizure of doldrums for many months—but now it is coming up to full sail again. Lovely lakeside country-house situation at Küsnacht-Zürich, 10 minutes by car or motorboat from the center; graduated terraces for fair-weather dining, and picture-windowed interior for inclement days or evenings; garden concerts by Viennese trio in season. The turtle-slow service and ragged cookery which so disappointed us several visits ago showed striking and gratifying improvement on our later cloak-and-dagger try. We believe Dr. Seiler has at last found the remedy to restore its once-radiant bloom, and that his attractive haven will soon be a joy to the soul again. Shuttered December 15 to February 15.

Haus zum Rüden (Limmatquai), built in 1295 and restored in 1936, preserves the charm of the traditional Guild House. Proprietor Peter Halter and his lovely wife offer a friendly welcome. Handsome furnishings, fair cooking, and adequate service. Still solid, but lately we've developed a fondness for the ancient guild of the hat weavers, **Zunfthaus zur Waag** (Münsterhof 8) which is in a more colorful antique square. Upstairs dining rooms with leaded windows, cream-colored panels, thick carpeting, candles and flowers on tables, and ultrakind attention by staffers who have a limited facility with English. The grilled meats are hewn from rancher's dreams. We'll eat our hat if you don't agree. And a tip of that reportorial *chapeau* to Zurich businessman-gourmet Reini Willi for originally introducing it to us way back in the thirteenth century. If you like these, then **Schmiden Zunft** and **Kaiser's Reblaube** (Goethe Stübli) are more names to jot down in your Zurich notebook. The **Kropf**, just off Paradeplatz, goes back before the turn of the century—as perhaps do some of its big buxom waitresses who bellow orders across the hall to its kitchen. Wooden floors, wonderful no-nonsense cooking, low prices, jovial in the best tradition of an honest tavern-type hideaway. Filled with Swiss. (Privately, one of our favorite corners in Zurich.) For beef served in a more North American manner, steer yourself directly to **Jacky's Stapferstube** (Culmanstrasse 43); it's nothing fancy for the peepers. Stucco walls; low-timbered ceiling; electrified "gas" lamps plus candles; a beautiful shrimp cocktail, an oh-so-succulent entrecôte for 2, herb-tinged spinach, garlic-flavored pasta (spatzle), and tiptop service. Reserving ahead is a *must* in this simple steakery. Italian restaurants have become very popular in

Zürich, due to the influx of *paesani* into the region. **Casa Ferlin** (Stampfenbachstrasse 38), sometimes called Chiantiquelle, has the biggest name. Wall panels of red damask; ceiling decorated with ceramic denizens of the Mediterranean; delicious Fettuccine; adept service. The owner sometimes plays the organ—sometimes too loudly. To us, the chief demurrer with this *casa* is its price scale. Not quite so *buono* is the more modest **Piccoli** (Rotwandstrasse 48). The Veronese proprietor is the host, as well as the hunter who often shoots the game which is served; his wife commands the skillets with exquisite grace. Quick-paced service; clientele frequently composed of Italian luminaries and other celebrities who slip in secretly for a nibble hidden from the public gaze; simple surroundings. **Trattoria Toscana** (Fraumünsterstrasse 14, a 5-minute stroll from the Baur au Lac) certainly provides effulgent cheer for the eye. The furniture is gaily painted, bright panels depict orange trees, mini-Tiffany lamps illuminate the warm tables, and mirrors are framed in Della Robbia ceramics. The cookery, however, was decidedly 2nd-rate on our 2-person sampling. Moreover the kitchen refuses to whomp up any pasta after 1:30 P.M. (it begins lunch at 11:30 A.M.!), so if you have not ordered fairly early then you are out of luck. Our maître and our waiter were the twin souls of discourtesy—we suppose because we arrived for our table at 1:15 P.M., requested an apéritif, and expected to follow this single libation with a meal. We were thus scolded by our Italian minion: "In Zürich you eat like the military—ON TIME!" Not with this mess sergeant, we don't. Never again. Too bad, too, because it could be a charmer. **Osteria Fiorintina** dishes out more attractiveness in its *osteria* corner than it does in its big, coolish café. The ravioli was good but our other commestibles seemed pedestrian. The **Silver Ranch** (245 Letzigraben), is not a favorite of ours. Vegetarian munching? **Gleich** (9 Seefeldstrasse) is as slick as a polished tomato. It is very attractive, modern in manner, and fully soundproofed to tone down the clack of healthy teeth crunching crispy-krinkly carrot steaks. The service is superb; our very recent meal here was so surprisingly delectable that we returned on a later day to enjoy an even better one. It has become extremely popular, especially at noon. Highly recommended. Closed Sunday. **Hiltl** (Sihlstrasse 26–28) is another leaf in this botanical brotherhood. Its fashion is also modern now that it has been restyled and the cuisine is top-of-the-stalk. Ground-floor for groundling cookery; upstairs featuring an Indian plate, but in either place please finish your graze with the delicious mango ice cream. In the "Hotels" section, we've already called attention to the gloriously palate-soothing "Gourmet's Menu" at the **Eden au Lac**; please don't miss this unique treat. The Hummer ("Lobster") Bar of the **Hotel St. Gotthard** is appealing, but the stew of confusion in its neighboring Bouillabaisse segment was bumbling from soup to NUTS! What a pathetic circus! For snacks and light fare; don't pass up the Pub in the previously described **Carlton-Elite**; it's a smasher. Across the street, the **Investor's Club** markets light refreshment along with ticker-tape replay of the stock market report. Savvy hostesses help you with your share selections, give advice, and answer your bids. Please don't step on a gnome, however. The face-lifted **Kranzler-Huguenin**, offers nibbly meals only, in a "grand-café" setting. The ancient **Veltliner Keller**, now operated by Mr. Jonkmanns, seems to be even better than before. **Töndury's Widder** spreads over several separate rooms on 4 floors of a venerable residence; intimate dimensions, excellent cuisine, routine tariffs; book in advance; praiseworthy for the bracket. Go to **Walliser-Keller** only for fondue; very Swiss. The **Krone** (Limmatquai 88) is definitely NOT recommended for reasons already described under "Hotels." We're not especially fond of the **Shiffstube**, either, but the people are nice and the piano music is tranquillizing. **Hong Kong** rings our gong for Oriental skills. Ueli Prager's remarkable **Mövenpick** chain now has 6 outlets in Zürich (others in Geneva, Lausanne, Berne, and Lucerne). The most elaborate example is in Dreikönighaus ("Three Kings' House") on Beethovenstrasse; here, as in the previously described Geneva operations, you'll find everything from standup facilities to the Deluxe Baron de la Mouette Rôtisserie-Grill. Efficiency-plus; each superior for its level and purpose. **Old Fashion** (Fraumünsterstrasse 15) is under the aegis of Olga Hefti; comfortable, friendly, Swiss-pub style; for lunching, dining, or quaffing. Finally, no sweet-toothed traveler should miss the wonderful **Sprüngli Confiserie** on Paradeplatz; as in Demel in Vienna, here's sugar, spice, and everything extra *extra* nice in pastries, snacks, beverages, and candies; eretail shop on one side and refreshments on the other; main outlet of the celebrated Lindt chocolates, to us the best in the world; yum, YUM, YUM!

Two excursions? The 20-minute drive to the **Eichmühle** in *Wädenswil* affords a scenic lakeview jaunt to an enchanted fairy-tale cottage where Magician–Chef Paul Wannenwetsch conjures up some exquisite creations from his cauldrons. Leave yourself in the hands of the master and we'll bet that you'll agree with us that he cooks with a wand instead of a skillet. Closed Tuesday; be sure to reserve ahead. Another target might be the aptly named **Solitude** in *Küsnacht*, about 15 minutes from the center of Zürich. It is a simple farmhouse with several interior dining nookeries plus a 6-table front terrace where you'll often find golfers from the nearby links trying to erase the memory of their scorecards. Roast chicken is the star of the unpretentious menu, either crisply done with fried potatoes and creamed corn or in a savory almond sauce. Not even the cluck-cluck of happy diners can disturb the Solitude.

Dedicated budgeteers? Since we're too bottlenecked here for additional entries, please consult our annually revised paperback, *Fielding's Low-Cost Europe,* which lists scads more bargain dining spots and money-saving tips for serious economizers.

NIGHTCLUBS Reading from west to east, the after-dark picture grows dim, dimmer, and dimmest.

Berne is now glutted with cheapy, boring dance bars that cropped up to allay the loneliness of its thousands of foreign workers. American tourists would feel decidedly out of place in them. Outside of these, the town's hottest burner is the **Mocambo**. Its Scotch Bar is at street level; reasonably attractive and very busy on Saturday night. Main enterprise in the cellar; spacious, multitiered sanctum, wrapped on 3 sides by tables at the balcony stratum; small bar in one corner. Dramatic Braille-provoking cell with 1-watt illumination and blue-and-white paneling; 5-piece band, with organ-inspired music straight off the corncob; dance floor more jammed than a Virginia turkey farm in early November. Hour-long cabaret at 10 P.M. and midnight, said to be good for Switzerland (since this rockabye atmosphere put us to sleep, we didn't see it). Legitimate whisky; damsels aflutter, but nobody pecked at us for free drinks. For Helvetia, very good. **Chikito** (within a block of Mocambo geographically, but perhaps 10 blocks down in quality) draws a younger crowd; in its slightly lighter gloom, we glimmed only 2 or 3 old men of 27 or 28. The ground level has become a discothèque while the bumping and grinding wheezes along in the cellar. The **Babalu** bounced in after our night-beat along the Gurtengasse; 2 bars adjoin, including the local **Playboy Club.** The **Happy Light**, a disco-spinner in the Casino, also was switched on recently. **Cadillac** shifts nightly into a dine-and-dancery.

In **Geneva**, the number one gathering place for the socialite and sophisticate is the handsomely regroomed Le Gentilhomme at the **Hôtel Richemond;** no show, casual dancing; cocktails, gourmet dining, and Diors the main attractions. **Le Club 58** and **The Pussy Cat Saloon** share a common entrance; turn left for the former, right for the latter. Admission chomp on weekends; Edwardian interior with patterned carpeting on walls; rouge and black color scheme; excellent strips, similar to the Crazy Horse in Paris. Better for Him than for Her. The **Griffin's** is one of the most fashionable discothèques in the land. It's private, but membership can be purchased; frequently, generous Proprietor Bernard Grobet or Maître Joe Panarinfo invite newcomers to join on a gratis basis. Highly stylized, modernistic downstairs retreat; adjoining rustic dining room serving from 8 P.M. to dawnish (meats are best); very comfortable surroundings; music in the twentieth-century mood, but hardly reminiscent of Glen Miller. For its type, one of the better examples on the Continent. **La Tour**, a split-level cave with alternating combos, draws a similar clientele of youngbloods and nonacidhead hippies. Crowded dance floor; good ventilation; attentive service. Worth a Tour. **Ba-Ta-Clan**, wickedly fashioned in Frenchy tones, grinds out set after set of seminude shows, with short intermissions, often billed as "The Most Risqué Striptease in Europe"; strange sort of sexy ambiance; Tom Thumb tables in music-hall arrangement; weekend admission bite; whisky legitimate on our latest sip; B-girls tougher than Popeye and slipperier than Olive Oyl; for any gent under the age of 165, the ripest cabaret in Switzerland. **Maxim's** swings in with an ornate glass, brass, and iron entrance; wood and burgundy tones in its cellar salon; multilevel seating for better views of the jugglers, strippers, and crooners; standard tariff. Much better under its new owner. **Moulin Rouge** made our party see red; here's one windmill we'd like to tilt without pulling a single punch. Never again for us. **Le Grillon** is agreeable for dancing; perky combos; small cabaret at 11 P.M. **Le Baladin**, nearby, is chiefly for terpsichore; there's no show. **Piccadilly** is smaller, more *intimo,* and okay for avoiding that certain someone; a bit of strip-for-kip; everything closed (and clothed) Sunday. **Mylord** is a disko-haunt for youngsters. **Chez Monique** is 4th-rate. Finally, **rue des Étuves**, 200 yards east of Hôtel du Midi, is lined with amusing workmen's cafés.

Lausanne has the lavish **Tabaris**, which is on the rise again after a few slack seasons. Rich furnishings, good-size cabaret, yummy B-girls, the usual. **Metropole** and **Paradou** are less plush enterprises, with floor shows and routine appurtenances—some of whom might accept an invitation to the prance. **Brummell,** the nightery in the cellar of the Lausanne Palace, has no affiliation with the hotel. The management is enjoined from using "Lausanne Palace" in any of its publicity. Independent entrance from the street; art-theater-type foyer; textiled walls in lavender and blends; L-shape, softly illuminated, split-level room; striptease, now the house specialty, is an act curiously titled Le Snack. The **Scotch** provides individual lockers for its loyal patrons' bottles; Young Marrieds like this one for hand-holding. **Bagatelle** attracts the Young Unmarrieds; name bands always; operated by the Tabaris people. **Johnnie's** comes up with black leather furniture, a mosaic floor, canned music, and fairly reasonable tabs; we saw no B-girls. **Le Paddock** is for side-saddle hand-holding, loose reins, and informal prancing. The **Château d'Ouchy** offers darkling revels indoors only now that the garden has been pruned from its vine. For action along different lines, go to *Divonne-les-Bains* or across the lake to the casino at *Évian* (France); steamer service to the latter all 4 seasons.

Lucerne isn't the wildest town, either. The expansively modernized **Kursaal-Casino** may provide a mild tingle, if you like to bet nickels; you'll find more things to do and nicer places to do them here today or tonight; now it's operative year round. The **Dupont** is slightly better than it was, which still isn't saying much. **Kakadu,** when we peeked in, was *really* rocking. The flashier set were getting their kicks by blowing the paper envelopes off the drinking straws. Yipes! **Hazyland** is mainly for dancing. The Palace Hotel offers the **Intimo** for sophisticats to a-mews themselves. The **Adler** is a disco hub.

In *Zürich*, the night spots can now stay open until the wicked hour of 2 A.M., following a referendum in which—for the first time—women were allowed to vote. The all-male electorate previously had turned down the proposal—twice. Long live the *Frauenverein!*

Until the nocturnal wheels really start rolling and new challengers enter the nightscape, your most lively choices (partners often available, if desired) are (1) **Mascotte,** (2) **Café de la Terrasse,** and (3) **Hazyland,** for a barn-dance atmosphere. **Birdwatcher's Club** in the Simplon Hotel is a quiet, elegant lounge where nighthawks preen for their well-feathered chicks. **Red House** and **La Puce** also are colorful contenders. We haven't seen the new **Downtown** but we hear it incorporates a Mexican restaurant called Santa Fe at ground level. *Buena Suerté!* Discothèques? The **Queen Anne Club** (Kreuzstrasse) is the first public offering in the region. It's only a few steps from the Eden au Lac and Bellerive au Lac hotels, and it's amazingly fancy for Zürich. The **Boîte de Nuit** is the spinner of Jo Roland, the famous chansonnier. Musical shows nightly; elegant clientele; very à la mode. **La Ferme,** a rustic disco-very owned by the Trattoria Toscana, can be barns of fun. **Golden Life** also glitters for the same lifestylists. **Blackout** blinks near the airport.

As for other Swiss cities, towns, and villages—have you written the folks or read any good books lately?

§TIPS: Hostesses are required to stay on the premises until closing time; if they leave before this, they lose their jobs. The B-girls are house employees who get a cut on every drink the customer buys; most complain of "stomach trouble" which only champagne (not whisky) will soothe; most start gently with a ½-bottle of bubbly and work up quickly into the $40-per-jug-per-20-minutes league. The customary gratuity runs from $30 to $125; the majority are of French, German, or Austrian rather than Swiss birth.

In Zürich (where else?), do-gooders have taken to spraying streetwalkers with stink-bombs to put them out of action for at least several hours at a time. These self-appointed vigilantes also stand sentinel and record license numbers of cruising cars, write letters to the wives of amorous gentlemen, and act as neighborhood wardens to suppress the ladies at their trade. The 630 registered paramours (probably twice as many if you count moonlighters) now must function only between 8 P.M. and 3 A.M., chiefly in the Old Town, along the Limmat River, and in the shadows of the cathedral. (Current rates mount from 150 to 250 francs per motorized rendezvous). The movement recalls to our mind the following lines by John Vance Cheney:

> The happiest heart that ever beat
> Was in some quiet breast
> That found the common daylight sweet,
> And left to Heaven the rest.

TAXIS   Rather expensive. Both the full-size cabs and the smaller *Kleintaxis* charge at the same rate. Limousines are more, of course.

Geneva has opened a **Taxi Telephone Center**. Simply dial 165, and one of a fleet of 150 cars will be at your disposal. In *Berne*, it's 24-24-24; in *Zürich*, it's 44-44-41.

After many disappointments by chiselers in big citys, at airports, and in chic resorts, we make it a habit to count our change and to check into any supplements before paying them. We're especially watchful when we take a cab from the vicinity of Zürich station. Intercity fares are also inexcusably rigged, by common consent.

It's smart to use buses for short hauls in any Swiss city; conductors, usually English-speaking, will steer you to your destination in a friendly way—and you'll save plenty.

TRAINS   Excellent. The SBB's (or CFF's, if you prefer the French initials of the German) national network is 100% electrified; they run like Swiss watches. They usually keep their split-second schedules; they are usually clean; they usually go like a bat out of Hilvetia. One of the fastest runs is made by the noon flier from Geneva to Zürich.

A total of 260 First-class and 230 Second-class coaches, all of a radically improved design, have been placed in service. Now 50 new *couchette* coaches (6 daytime seats converting to 6 sleep-in-your-clothes berths in each unit) have been added to the Basle–Vienna, Zürich–Rome and other hauls. These are on the unfancy side, but they save money.

The food in the dining cars (many modernized, with air conditioning added) is both inexpensive and excellent. Breakfast (ham and eggs—the works) costs $4-or-so; lunch and dinner are about $7 anywhere in Switzerland for twice the price. Service is polite, fast, and efficient except on crowded mainliners (*e.g.*, Zürich–Geneva), when they'll sometimes make you stand up for your sandwich and drink instead of deigning to disturb an empty table that has been set up for a full meal.

Ticket prices are quite reasonable considering the value received for your franc. (Those francs, incidentally, can be dropped directly into automatic ticket dispensing machines—a timesaving innovation that is beginning to blanket the nation.)

There are 5 classifications—and knowing what each does is important. First is the **ordinary** variety, full fare for 1-way trips. Validity varies between 2 days and 2 months, depending upon the run. Purely routine.

Second is the **round-trip** ("Return Rail") class, a 25% saving on the cost of 2 single rides. Good for 10 days; validity may be extended for another 7 or 14 days for a slight extra charge.

Third is the **Holiday Card**. It can be issued only outside of Switzerland in 8-day, 15-day, or 1-month versions which allow you to travel at will around the country on rails, by steamer, on postal motor-coaches, or up and down numerous cableways. The savings can be tremendous for anyone who plans to move around a lot. Check with your travel agent or any branch of the Swiss National Tourist Office.

Fourth is the combination of **Half-Fare Season Ticket** and Supplementary Vouchers. The basic unit here costs only in the vicinity of a dollar a day; it will take you to most of the principal tourist targets. For off-trail points, mostly in the mountain areas, you may purchase as many Supplementary Vouchers as your itinerary requires. These are sold in "days"—5 for $30 (First class) or $20 (Second class), or 10 on a prorated scale. Once equipped with both of these, you can ride for unlimited mileage at 50% of the standard fare on 3125 miles of Federal trackage and lake routes, 144 private railways, 9 private steamship lines, and unlimited postal motor coaches (this sentence has made us reach for our vitamins). They're obtainable only at railway stations (2-to-24 hours' notice) or through travel agents *within Switzerland*. Please remember that your passport photo must be submitted with your application. For further details, see the man at the window.

Fifth is the **Party type**. Groups of 10 to 24 persons get a 25% reduction. If most of your in-laws are with you, take advantage of the 35% discount for parties of 25 or more. Validity is for 2 months, and if more than 15 adults travel together, the tour conductor may ride free.

But don't forget first to look into the Eurailpass if you are touring other countries as well.

An interesting statistic: If the 5000 bridges and 700 tunnels of the Swiss Federal Railways were stretched out in a line, they would reach over 275 miles.

§TIPS: An excellent time-, sweat-, profanity-, and worry-saver is to arrange with your hotel concierge (give him at least 1 hour's advance notice) for your luggage to be shipped separately in the baggage car of the train—usually the same one or ones that you ride. This is a *wonderful* help, particularly if you must make changes (Geneva to St. Moritz, for example, involves 2). Very inexpensive and 99½% dependable.

Old trick: Buy a Second-class ticket and waltz over the landscape in deluxe style, highball in hand—by riding all the way in the dining car.

Children under 6 years of age ride as guests of the conductor and engineer; children from 6 to 16(!) pay ½-fare. Men of 65 or over and women who will confess to 62 years of age may buy ½-fare tickets valid for 12 months. When applying for this Senior Citizens' privilege ask for the "Season Ticket for the Aged"—and we wonder who the 14-year old public relations stripling was who gave it *that* name!

AIRLINE On our latest business trek to the States via **Swissair** from Zürich to N.Y. (we've stopped counting our air crossings over 34 years), when my Nancy and I stepped off the SR-747 at JFK, we agreed that here was the most perfect transatlantic flight we'd ever enjoyed—and we knew it was good not just because we are travel writers, but because of our painstaking research to learn the reactions of other passengers aboard. The nonstop vitality and friendliness of the cabin crew, the superb First-class cuisine (which also looked mighty appetizing in Economy class), the felicitous surprise touches, the superb behind-the-scenes organization—all seemed so excessively good to be true that we promptly booked our return with this same company to reassure ourselves that this hadn't been a freak. It wasn't. Our eastbound trip was again equally outstanding in every fine detail. Any carrier in the world, no matter how good, inevitably must come up with one sour flight now and then. But it is our belief that Swissair, like a luxury Swiss watch, almost consistently is in the top of the pack in giving to its customers extra comfort and happiness.

"Quality, not quantity" is the motto it lives by—and that's why, in our most thoughtful opinion, here is indeed one of the finest carriers in the air. With such peak standards in passenger and technical operations, it's small wonder most of its customers are "repeaters" or "regulars."

This year's fleet consists of Boeing 747Bs and DC-10s which service the North Atlantic between New York, Chicago, Boston, Montreal, and 2 Swiss gateways—Geneva and Zürich. The DC-10 and the DC-8 are employed on many North and South Atlantic passages plus routings to the Far East and Africa. Spin the globe and pick a destination. Unless your finger lands on Central America, New Zealand or Australia, Swissair can fly you there on a Jumbo, a DC-10 or -9 or -8, or a carrier pigeon.

Within the country, the skies are always busy with shuttles from and to Zürich, Geneva, and Basle.

The Swissair Director for North America is now Reynold Schwab. (He replaces our long-term chum on this beat, Dr. Hugo Mayr, who has moved along to pilot the airline's worldwide foreign operations out of Zürich.) If any special (not routine) problems involving the organization should arise, take them straight to Mr. Schwab at the Swiss Center, 608 Fifth Ave., N.Y. 10020. You may count upon his most interested and helpful personal attention.

Recommendation: We recommend Swissair unreservedly as a careful, efficient airline, with fine equipment, superservice within IATA limits, superior food, and pilots who know how to fly. We love it, and we hope you will too.

There are 3 major international airports—Kloten (6 miles from Zürich), Cointrin (3 miles from Geneva), and Blotzheim (4 miles from Basle). The fourth, near Berne, has been phased out by Swissair and replaced by an airline bus service between Zürich and the capital. As a spicy point of interest, the Kloten terminus was named for a neighboring village; sturdy Swiss burghers fainted like flies when an amused Hollander told them the startlingly vulgar Dutch translation of this word—but it wasn't changed to "Helvetia Airport," as planned, because too many announcement pamphlets had already been printed!

DRINKS   Everything is available including absinthe (illegal), at prices slightly below those in the United States. Popular brands of Scotch cost about $10 per fifth; Canadian Club sells for about the same; imported gins and ryes are less. Supplies are ample. Highballs run from $1.80 to $2.75, and most of the bartenders could do just as well with a medicine dropper as they do with their jigger glasses.

Swiss wines? Almost any wine lover can instantly set them apart from good French, Spanish, or Italian vintages, even when blindfolded. They have a unique character of their own: A freshness, a slight effervescence, a distinct tang to the tongue which is missing from all others. They take learning before true enjoyment can come. Most should be ordered young.

The majority of visiting Americans seem to prefer Johannisberg as their white and Dôle as their red. You'll always be reasonably safe if you order either of these sound old standbys. Personally, we happen to prefer the Cortaillod of Neuchâtel to the Dôle, but that's merely a matter of taste. Other satisfactory types, at random, are Oeil de Perdrix (Geneva area), Maienfelder, Altstätter, and Churer-Schiller (St. Gall and the Grisons), Mont d'Or, Dézaley, and St. Saphorin (Lavaux), Fendant and Torrenté-Château la Tour (Valais), and Cru de Champréveyres or the sparkling whites of Bienne or Neuchâtel. Here are the best of the land.

Swiss beer is cheap and plentiful. Swiss brewers seem to make an ideal potion for invalids, old ladies, and nursing mothers. All brands I have tried share a watery, Milquetoast spinelessness—but perhaps the tangy Tuborg, Carlsberg, Heineken and other beer made for Men rather than for Brownies has spoiled me. The Cardinal brand seems to embody the most zing. Naturally, this is an individual reaction with which you may disagree. Dixie drinkers, however, may draw a draught of southern comfort from a brew called Beauregard. The label slogan reads "SPECIALE BLONDE, SPEZIAL HELL." Saddleup, Genruhl! Dat South's gonna rise agin'!

For teetotalers, the noncarbonated, natural white or red grape juice called Grapillon is wonderfully refreshing; about 50¢, but be sure it's served icy cold. Apfelsaft is a pleasant and soft apple cider; the milk-based Rivella product is still taking the country by storm. Domestic cola types are preferred to U.S. colas by many Swiss, mainly for reasons of thrift.

Kirsch, made from the juice of compressed cherry pits, is the national hard drink. It is to fondue what an embrace is to a lover. Don't miss a sample of this fiery, rather bitter spirit, especially with cheese or fruit.

Pear liqueur is equally characteristic and even more delicious. Pear brandy (Eau de Vie de Poire Pure) has oversize vertebrae and bulging biceps. Shut your eyes, take a sip, and then blow—IF you can (but not near a lighted candle, please).

The most astonishing Swiss liqueur is Appenzeller Alpenbitter. Appenzell is the town and Alpenbitter is the product—"Alpine Bitters," made up of the essences of 67 different flowers and roots. In taste it is vaguely reminiscent of gin-and-tonic consumed in a perfume factory, but don't let this stop you from sampling a genuine curiosity among potables.

Another flag-waving oddity is the so-called Marmot Chocolat Suisse—in taste a kissin' cousin of Crème de Cacao, with tiny cubes of extrasuave milk chocolate floating in the upper half of the bottle. All it needs is cheese and a wristwatch in the bottom half to make it 200% Swiss.

Absinthe, long banned by the Government, is bootlegged all over the land. The base is wormwood elixirs; Pernod, as most travelers know it, is the watered-down version. You'll find it in almost every rural inn or tavern—but the proprietor must trust you before he'll serve you, just as in the U.S. speakeasy days. Ask for it with sugar and water; it will probably be dispensed in a porcelain beer mug to fool the police. The price is about $1.50 per glass; treat it with utmost respect, because the "proof" is sometimes 120 or 136 against the 100 proof of the strongest ryes and bourbons in the States.

THINGS TO SEE We're tempted to throw in the sponge on this subject, since Switzerland offers exactly 19,999,999 exciting things to see or do.

Among the classic targets, our favorite-of-favorites is *Zermatt*. For our reasons why, please check back in the "Cities" section toward the beginning of this chapter.

St. Moritz wears its own proud crown—for polish, for chichi, and for glamour rather than for comparatively natural simplicity. Here is the ski ground and playground of the elite of 4 continents (see "Cities" *et seq.*); among the newer attractions are the teleferic extension to the 11-thousand-foot Piz Corvatsch, the St. Moritz Helicopter Service, and the Freddie Wissel Air Taxi Service which, similar to the "eggbeater" outfit just mentioned, deposits its sporting clientele on loftly glaciers and peaks no funicular or teleferic can reach. Let's not forget, too, the aerial cableway to neighboring Diavolezza; we've already suggested a lunch excursion here in "Food and Restaurants." Its combined "lifts" can tote 19-thousand visitors per hour to the summits. The tourist can visit St. Moritz with very little money in his pocket—physically possible although realistically unwise. But if your wallet is loaded for bear and your aspirations loaded for lion (social species), this should be happily rewarding hunting ground.

Arosa carries a coronet, as well (see "Cities" *et seq.*). Beautiful setting; all facilities; so jam-packed in season that only those who like crowds should tackle it. If you should need any help here, the hardworking, alert local Tourist Chief, Werner Grob, is a mighty good man to see or to know; he does his job with utmost efficiency, and he's always ready with expert assistance.

Near *Lugano* at Melide (lake bridge on main highway from Italy; same village with La Romantica Hotel-Restaurant), a unique exhibition called

Swissminiatur has already wooed more than a million spectators. Towns, hamlets, castles, mountains, automatic railways, remote-control steamers, and other real-life things are reproduced in exact dimensions and detail, on a scale of 1 to 25. Surely worth a stop if you're staying in Lugano or driving the southern route—or if you're an elf. The sport centers of *Carona* and *Bedano*, both nearby, are now catching on, too.

Sion sires a $187,000 *Son et Lumière* spectacle. Elaborate electronic apparatus, including 194 floodlights and 6-track stereophonic equipment, project it on the 2 high hills of Tourbillon and Valère, which form a dramatic background to the city. Season only; daily program starting at 9 P.M. and lasting slightly less than 1 hour. For daylight pastimes, it provides everything from sixth-century castles and churches to glacier landings by mountain pilots.

Most Americans in Switzerland make what might be called the Swiss Baedeker Circuit—that classic, old-fashioned swing made by their parents, grandparents, and neighbors before them, through such dependable travel chestnuts as Geneva, Lucerne, Interlaken, Montreux, and Lausanne. All these places are very attractive, as millions of footweary travelers will testify. But so many people have trod this path for so many years that the freshness is gone, and the welcome is often hollow and professional.

If you're after a region which few U.S. vacationers know and which hasn't been "civilized" beyond repair, the 2-day or 3-day circuit from *Zürich* through the Principality of *Liechtenstein* and *La Suisse Orientale* (Nordostschweiz or Northeast Switzerland) is an enchanting choice. Spend your first night in *Vaduz*, the capital of this rustic little border state on the Rhine (see separate section); the second night might be spent in *St. Gall*, where the hotel situation has improved. If you stop here, there will be time for a look at neighboring *Appenzell*, the Abbey Library, and other points of interest. And the return to Zürich should be made around the other leg of the loop, through *Romanshorn*, *Kreuzlingen*, *Stein am Rhein*, *Schaffhausen*, *Winterthur*, and *Effretikon*—with a pause at *Neuhausen*'s Rhine Falls if you're not in too much of a hurry. Full information on this off-trail territory can be obtained from any Swiss National Tourist Office branch or the Tourist Office Quick in Vaduz. Quiet rather than spectacular beauty; recommended to old-timers rather than first-trippers.

From *Zürich*, should time be too pressing for such extensive coverage; a junket to the aforementioned Rhine Falls makes an interesting 1-day safari; you may lunch comfortably in the ancient Sonne Restaurant at *Stein am Rhein*—or take the repast at the Fischerzunft in *Schaffhausen* (excellent cuisine), with tea at Stein.

There are 23 well-equipped mineral spas in the country. *St. Moritz* (see previous comments) is the highest in altitude—and possibly in price. *Baden Ragaz-Pfäfers*, and *Tarasp-Schuls-Vulpera* are characteristic. Each is a center for particular types of illness; some are purely for rest and relaxation. The Swiss National Tourist Office publishes a free Pocket Guide about them.

August 1 is the big Swiss national holiday—the Bundesfeiertag—with bonfires and dancing all over the country. Annual folk festivals include Good Friday at *Mendrisio*, Camellia at *Locarno*, Blessing of the Alpine Pastures at *Lötschental*, and Escalade at *Geneva*. *Zürich* pops its fuses twice: once during the traditional Spring Festival of Sechseläuten, when Old Man Winter (a mammoth dummy stuffed with fireworks) is publicly burned at the stake, and again during the June Festival weeks, with concerts, opera, exhibitions, theater, and other gala events. *Lucerne* toots its whistle from mid-August to early September, with enough concerts, choirs, plays, and cultural exhibits to make you positively unlivable to your friends, neighbors, and even casual acquaintances at home. *St. Gall* also blows off the lid at the end of June *every second year,* when 9000 children march through the streets in the biennial Children's Festival, consuming as they go the legendary 29 miles of Bratwurst; check during the spring of your particular journey.

The **Jungfrau** and *Interlaken*; the **Schilthorn** and the high surrounding triad corona seen from *Mürren*; the **Lake of Constance** with its castles, orchards, and quaint villages; the **Grisons**, land of 150 valleys; **Bürgenstock;** the **Bernese Oberland**, with its lakes, glacial valleys, and high-Alpine landscape; the **Jura**; the **Valais**—everywhere in Switzerland you'll find something quaint and beautiful.

TIPPING An automatic service charge of 15% across-the-board in all Deluxe and First-class hotels is in operation. Most other hostelries now get 15% as well. Tip the rest of the hotel people as previously indicated. Porters will tell *you* how much you owe them; taxi drivers, especially the resort robbers, shouldn't get a penny more than 10%. Leave something extra for the maid; all of them knock themselves out to keep your room extra clean.

BUYING A WATCH In *Fielding's Shopping Guide to Europe,* we have outlined our ratings of the watches of the 29 leading Swiss manufacturers and what we term the *"23 Musts"* which we believe every potential customer should know before making any purchase in this special field. Sorry, but our space here is too limited to attempt to tackle this complex and lengthy area, even in condensation.

After comparing the stocks and prices of probably all the major dealers in the land, we're stuck on an outstanding pair—one for the Ford-Oldsmobile type of buyer, and the other for the Rolls-Cadillac league.

With the widest variety—from dependable, low-cost to precision luxury timepieces—in existence, and a globewide guarantee service, **Bucherer** is the largest and best-known watch retailer in the world. Any visitor to Switzerland —particularly the first-timer—who misses a look-see here loses a one-and-only shopping experience. The headquarters is in *Lucerne,* where you will find 3 separate escalatored sales floors with a choice of 60-thousand different items. There are 4 branches in the *Zürich* area, plus others in *Geneva*, *Lausanne*, *Basle*, *Locarno*, *Lugano*, *Interlaken*, *Bürgenstock*, *St. Moritz*, *Davos*, and *New York*. One of the primary reasons they give such enormous values is that they manufacture their own watches from the movement up. Sample rounded-out prices, all subject to small changes: Men's waterproof wrist models from $24 and waterproof automatics from $40; ladies' types from $28; ring watches from $33; cover models from $38; travel or musical alarms from $25; cuckoo clocks from $20; 400-day clocks from

$50. In their expensive line, you'll see (1) jeweled pieces from $220 to $20,000; (2) the celebrated Rolex gallery, including the famous Day-Date, the "Cellini" series, and the sensational new Submariner Sea Dweller among others; the high-precision, Government-tested Bucherer Chronometer starting around $73; (3) For-The-Twenty-First-Century-Man, the super-accurate, electronic-age quartz watch from $120 (Bucherer was the only retail shop in the nation to participate in its development); (5) For-The-Purple-Only, Piaget dazzlers styled with faces of precious stones, the most ingenious of which is the $1600 gentleman's automatic that is one of the thinnest of its class ever made. Lots, lots, lots more, too! Our personal favorite is the Vulcain "Cricket" wrist-alarm, which for a quarter of a century has been our indispensable eye-opener, flight-catcher, appointment-nudger, and pest-shedder. The Gift Department is packed with goodies such as sweet music boxes. The jewelry range spans from the inexpensive Charms Department to all price categories in their eye-popping yellow and white gold articles (traditional and boutique). New styles are constantly being added by their large design group, who specialize in diamond solitaires and loose gems such as emeralds and rubies. In the *Lucerne* hub (the best bet because of its mammoth inventory), you will find a multilingual sales staff of over 100 people. Tops for the budget, normal, and fatter-than-normal pocketbook.

Since 1854, **Gübelin**'s dynamic spirit of creation has inspired the industry and continued to add to its reputation as Europe's most honored citadel for quality in its field. With its beautiful headquarters at Schweizerhofquai 1 in *Lucerne* expanded into a chain of elegantly impressive branches in *Zürich, Geneva, Lugano, Berne, Basle, St. Moritz, Bürgenstock*, and *New York* (745 5th Ave.), for more than a century cosmopolites have basked in the jump given them by the revolutionary design coups of these magicians. Always characteristically ahead, its latest line has been developed to kindle special appeal in people with youthful tastes. Its newest assemblage of accessories, a stunning collection of rings, is the *ne plus ultra* of simplicity and purity of line. In discreet and patrician harmony with its unique and arresting clips, brooches, and necklaces also inspired for tomorrow, today they are glittering cachets among the International Set. Watches of all descriptions, including Patek Phillipe, Audemars Piguet, Omega, and Gübelin (what finer?), are yours for the picking among its large, varied, but painstakingly selected stocks; so are its remarkable electronic quartz models. Again, here is an impressive collection of clocks of all descriptions. (As a personal sidelight, for more than 2 decades, individually or collectively we have always carried and relied upon its handsome, ingenious, compact, 8-day, 21-jewel travel alarms encased in smartly tooled leather.) This institution, founded before the American Civil War, is owned and directed by Dr. E. Gübelin, a research member of America's Gemological Institute and Britain's Gemological Association who is a world-famous specialist in, and author about, precious stones, and by watch virtuoso Walter Gübelin, who shares equal celebrity in his own vast sphere. Prices? Nary a worry! Whether you seek an inexpensive timepiece or a jewel of exceptional value, just walk straight in. You'll never find another treasure-house displaying such masterworks as this one does.

In conclusion, there is this to be noted: No American or Japanese watch can meet the quality of the best creations of these Swiss master workmen. Because standards are so high and costs are comparatively low, the traveler who goes home without a good Swiss timepiece on his wrist and 2 or 3 inexpensive ones in his bag for gifts hasn't made the most of his fine opportunity. The U.S. Customs has no limit on the number of watches you may bring in for personal use, but there are restrictions on the *number of certain brand names* allowable. So check before stocking up.

§TIPS: Don't bargain. Prices are rigid.
Experts say that your watch will Live Longer and Stay Younger if you'll (1) rest it on the bedside table while you're sleeping, and (2) wind it in the morning instead of at night. (Getting-up time is fairly constant with most people, but bedtime is apt to vary—and results are better if it's wound at the same hour.) Self-winders should be worn 24 hours a day in order to maintain a constant level of tension on the mainspring.

OTHER THINGS TO BUY   Swiss chocolates, high-fashion specialities, Tidstrand blankets and stylings, ski pants and winter sporting goods, hand embroideries, cameras and photo supplies, handicrafts, jade, leather goods, Swedish glass (yes, Swedish glass), art objects, Swiss Army knives.
Always, our first and last errands on Swiss soil are to load up twice on what we consider the finest chocolates in the world—**Lindt's**. Ubiquitous Lindt & Sprüngli are traditionally Switzerland's number one craftsmen of their art. For chocolate-loving or gift-minded travelers who wish to take Lindt's home, its vast, extra-delicious selection ranges from 2¢ to $9. Sadly, *no candies containing alcohol are passed by U.S. Customs.*
Geneva? Before sailing forth on any point-to-point shopping expedition here, we most strongly urge that every visiting tally-ho hunter set his or her comparative bearings at **Bon Genie** (rue de Marche 34), the 5-story headquarters of the celebrated luxury specialty-store chain which markets close to 100-thousand different types of ladies', men's, and children's fashions and accessories annually. Tycoons Jean-Jacques and Michel Brunschwig faithfully expand on the dictum established by their grandfather in 1891: "Mode, Quality, and Price." It is not a sales machine; within its harmoniously decorated, softly illuminated, intimate premises; they insist that each customer is welcomed as an individual. In addition to its mammoth stocks of originals or other Swiss creations, it harbors glamorous boutiques or departments where you will find the products of Gucci (Italian leather), Louis Vuitton (French luggage), Ilias Lalaounis (gold jewelry; see "Greece"), Pierre Cardin (French men's wear), Estee Lauder (U.S. cosmetics), Braemar (Scottish cashmere), Christian Dior (lingerie), and other foreign stars. Branches in *Lausanne, Vevey,* and *Fribourg.* Long one of Switzerland's undisputed style setters.
Le Grand Passage, formerly the largest department store of the city, was razed by such a terrible conflagration that only its facade was left standing. The damage was estimated at up to $20,000,000. Whether or not it will reopen this year is unknown to us at press time.

Au Chalet Suisse (place du Lac 1) specializes in lovely Appenzell embroidery, organdy and lace table settings, blouses, children's dresses, and dozens of inexpensive textile oddments. Kind, English-speaking staff; Miss Colette is especially helpful. Very good.

The biggest drugstore in the world? **Pharmacie Principale** now surpasses Rexall's in Los Angeles as the record breaker. Everything from dried pimpernel flowers to maternity garments to miniature chamois to neon-lit bikinis—you name it. If you look hard enough, you'll also find toiletries and medicines.

Lucerne is the apex of Switzerland's most lively, prominent, and dynamic photographic enterprise, which also happens to be the most popular with the U.S. shutterbug—the **Weber Group.** If you seek (1) honesty and reliability, (2) quality and versatility, (3) top-drawer advice, and (4) top-drawer service, here's your perfect answer. North Americans flock to it because energetic, sympathetic Mr. Weber and his young, capable, multilingual staff radiate the warmth, patience, and enthusiasm that instantly put the shopper on a personal basis. Largest and best selection of all leading cameras; worldwide service certificate with every purchase; bottomless stocks of lenses and binoculars; color transparencies and prints galore; film of all categories from just about everywhere; one-day delivery on color printing. For full service, try the renewed and expanded **Weber b/Bahnhof** (opposite Station), the center which carries all photographic supplies, **Weber Victoria Ltd.** (Pilatusstrasse 18), or **Central Photo & Optics** (Hertersteinstrasse 47), the pacesetter for high-quality Zeiss sunglasses and general optical aids). Casual browsers will find a treasure trove at the large, modern **Tefora Ltd.** ("Te" for television, "fo"for foto, and "ra" for radio, at Grendel 8), which tempts with electric or electronic equipment, souvenirs, and the like in addition to its photo lines. All of the handpicked, painstakingly trained Weber managers are vastly knowledgeable and vastly eager to help you with their advice. If your problem is an especially puzzling one, Paul Weber himself is usually on tap in this city, so do not hesitate to ask for this ranking expert in person. Should time be too short or should you forget something, any of this Group will rush whatever you require anywhere on the globe—and the best part of it is that you can depend upon the renowned Weber service, just as have so many other thousands upon thousands of its delighted clients. Absolutely unrivaled.

Swedish glass? Since Switzerland is Central Europe's most heavily trammeled crossroads for overseas visitors, we want to make darned certain that no lover of exquisite glassware misses this crystal opportunity. **Svenskt Glas** has tenderly unwrapped its first shop outside of its homeland, tucked snug in the middle of the Old Town just a few steps from Bucherer, Gübelin, and the Schweizerhofquai. What a canny move this is! You will find exactly the same globally famous, globally revered selections of Orrefors and Kosta table-tinklers, beauty-ware, and household sparklers that radiate on their Swedish shelves. Furthermore, with all costs included—that's purchase price, shipping, insurance, and U.S. customs duties—you'll still pay *about half of the North American retail cost for precisely the same articles.* Ask for Manageress Doris Christen or her assistant, Miss Jacquelin Curti—and then pick up a goblet to skål your own good fortune in finding this outlandishly felicitous bargain in Switzerland. More details in the Swedish chapter, of course.

Zürich? If you want to find some honest-to-goodness regional craftsman-ship instead of souvenir-stand junk, **Schweizer Heimatwerk** might warm your shopping soul. There are 5 shops. The headquarters is at Rudolf Brun-Brücke (formerly called Urania-Brücke). The branches are at the National Bank Building (a few steps away); at the Zürich Airport, at Hinterlauben in *St. Gall*, and at Hauptgasse in *Stein am Rhein*. In all you will encounter only the finest handwrought products from Alpine farm families and small artisans all over the national map. Original costumes of the Swiss cantons, for both children and children-at-heart, range between $40 and $100; colorful Toggenburger wooden articles are $2.50 to $25; hand-painted provincial ceramics start at $1.90; woodcarvings run from $10 to $30. Dolls in at least 30 different styles of national dress are tagged from $4 to $20. Handloomed textiles in gay patterns are stocked in profusion for about $15 per meter, or in ready-cut Hasli sets or Hasli aprons from $4.50 to $18. Fondue dishes, Swiss Army knives, music boxes, all kinds of doilies, leather-belted-and-decorated cowbells, carved wooden masks from the Alps, carved cookie forms, Swiss semiprecious stones set in silver or gold, minerals for collectors, peasant toys, basketware—this is only the beginning. We'd suggest that you try the Rudolf Brun-Brücke center first, and then skip over to the neighboring Bank Building shop for what you might have missed. Ask for Manageress Miss Hagenbuch in the former and Manageress Miss Gassmann in the latter. And when you have examined this most exciting harvest of exclusively Swiss rural treasures in existence, have you finished your adventure in this basic purlieu? For your sake we hope not and here's why:

Remarkable Director Wettstein has recently applied his decades of special-ized expertise to purchase, to expand, and masterfully to streamline **Spindel** ("Spindle," St. Peterstrasse 11, off Bahnhofstrasse 31), founded in 1937 by local social-minded ladies. His taste and professionalism have converted this 3-story structure into one of the best commercial assemblages of *international* handwrought arts and crafts from every European nation. Italian and Ger-man handloomed materials and hand-printed aprons ($3.50 up); Romanian and Polish table rugs; English, French, Sardinian, Danish, and Czech tradi-tional and modern ceramics ($1 up); Portuguese, French, and Italian pewters, wonderful array of Finnish and German toys ($1.20 up); Icelandic and Norwegian homespun knitwear ($7.50 up); many, many other transcontinen-tal as well as Swiss delights, Your oracle here is Manageress Miss Hartung. A fascinating crossroads of far-flung cultural triumphs which pops the eyes!

Leather goods? **Mädler AG** (Bahnhofstrasse 26, at Paradeplatz) is the Swiss and Austrian headquarters of this illustrious, historic, and widely re-nowned chain. This fine old house, launched in Leipzig by gifted patriarch Moritz Mädler in 1850, evacuated itself from East Germany after World War II. In the process, the government stripped all but 3 of its then-bulging assets: Its priceless name, traditions, and skills. In 1951 it launched its first new venture here in Zürich; since then, through the artistry and flair of its crea-tions, the network has proliferated. Awaiting you in these precincts is a sumptuous scope of creamy-smooth suitcases, small luggage, carry-on bags, handbags, vanity cases, briefcases, similar articles, and scores of strikingly beautiful, hard-to-find gift items. The workmanship is exquisite; the modes.

have a special cachet; the quality is superlative; the cost range is appealing. Patrician and chic Ms. Stephanie Mädler, who personally does all of the designing and styling, would bring geysers of pride to Founder Herr Moritz. Superb!

High fashion and all accessories? The **Grieder** department-specialty stores have often been called "The Neiman-Marcus of Europe." They are emphatically THE trend setter in eastern Switzerland. Grieder designs are so exclusive that, even with their fine ready-mades, there is almost no chance of ever running across a duplicate. In their imposing headquarters on Paradeplatz, worth the careful coverage of every fashion-conscious visitor, you'll be regaled by *haute couture* lounges, a fur department, a fetching shoeshop, beauty parlors, a men's section, a galaxy of textile departments—even a smashing boutique, rightfully named VIVA, for your teens and 'tweens (feminine *and* masculine, too!) who want to be "in." Handsome, brilliantly talented Peter Grieder is ably carrying on his grandfather's tradition of Quality First, combining his personal U.S. coast-to-coast practical retailing experience with the brilliant mercantile heritage of his forebears. In addition to several outlets in or close to Zürich (the aforementioned downtown nexus and branches in the Glatt Shopping Center and Zurich Airport), Mr. Grieder also operates emporiums in **Bürgenstock, Lucerne,** and **St. Moritz**. Exceptional in every particular.

Stunningly chic Greek gold jewelry? Legendary tastemaker **Ilias Lalaounis** has launched a dazzling display of his masterpieces at Grieder's in Zürich (above paragraph) and at Bon Genie on rue du Marché in Geneva. Please turn back to "Greece" for details which should make your mouth water.

Sublime Chinese art objects? **The Jade Dragon Ltd.** (Talstrasse 16, a few steps from Hotel Baur au Lac) is a connoisseurs' treasure trove. While for the most part the prize harvest of individual glories in this smallish haven is very, very expensive and very, very beautiful, it also offers a variety of enchanting selections at prices which thou and we, as average acolytes, can afford. The most precious articles appeal only to collectors. Although it specializes in celestial jade bowls, egg-shell-fashioned plates, necklaces, scepters, pendants, animals, and other masterworks, visitors can find anything from ivory-topped gourd cricket cages (worn from the lapel, they chirp!) to Mongolian milk bowls to lacquered Mandarin chain cases to cloisonné teapots. Its old and modern Chinese and Tibetan Jewelry includes rings ($20 to $80), earrings and brooches ($32 to $80), bracelets ($12 to $1200) and much more. Delightful Manageress Miss Rosemary Spring will welcome you warmly. P-l-e-a-s-e make this breathtaking pilgrimage!

Elsewhere in Switzerland: Swiss embroideries and handworked appliqués have been famous for centuries; so have the St. Gall linens and organdies, the most distinguished in Europe. For the best values and most tasteful stocks, try the nearest **Sturzenegger** store. Headquarters are in **St. Gall** (Poststrasse 17); home base for the mills that make those gorgeous materials; branches are located in **Zürich, Lucerne, Berne, Basle, Crans sur Sierre, Davos, Interlaken, Montreux, St. Moritz,** and **Zermatt**.

Since 1896 prodigious **Tidstrand of Sweden** has been unchallenged as the greatest designer and manufacturer of blankets and allied products in existence, with worldwide distribution limited to only the most illustrious speciality shops and department stores. Tax difficulties have now forced this hallowed institution to move to **Martigny**, a short 35 minutes from Lausanne, where it is opening a warehouse and showroom for its exquisitely hued blankets, throws, shawls, skirts, ensembles and more, plus a new knockout line of chic *après-ski* and sportswear. A warehouse visit here would be definitely to your advantage. Ask for Mrs. Giroud-Tidstrand in person. Number I among the global élite.

Swiss ski pants can't be surpassed—and **Kalten Brunner** in **Davos** and **Rufener** in **Grindelwald** are the Nina Ricci or Brioni of the field.

Antiques? **Antiquities Moinat**, in **Rolle** (Vaud), is Switzerland's most famous dealer; closed Sunday and Monday. Traditional hunting grounds are **Schlüsselgasse** (around St. Peter's Church) in **Zürich**, rue de la Cité, **Grand Rue**, and **rue'Hôtel-de-Ville** in **Geneva**, Cheneau de Bourg in **Lausanne**, and **Kramgasse** in **Berne**.

Main shopping streets? Here's a quick rundown: In **Geneva**, the long stretch named at various points **rue de la Confédération**, **rue du Marché**, **rue de la Croix**, and **rue de Rive** is the hub. Also try the **rue du Rhône**. In **Zürich** it's the **Bahnhofstrasse**; in **Lausanne**, the **rue de Bourg**; in **Berne**, **Spitalgasse** and **Marktgasse** (railway station to Clock Tower).

Shopping hours? During the tourist influx, so varied that there's no good rule-of-thumb. They open anywhere from 7 to 8:30 A.M.; some fold up for lunch anywhere from 12-or-12:30 P.M. to 1:30-or 2 P.M., while some stay open all day; most (not all) close at 6:30 P.M. on weekdays and midday or 5 P.M. on Saturdays; some are open evenings and Sunday mornings in summer. In winter, however, nearly every shopkeeper in the nation goes home between noon and 2 P.M on Saturday.

Dedicated shophounds? Space is too tight here for further listings—so consult this year's vastly revised and updated edition of *Fielding's Shopping Guide to Europe* for more stores, more details, and more lore.

THINGS NOT TO BUY   Quality is the byword in Switzerland. You won't like most of the music boxes, ashtrays marked "Souvenir of the Alps," and other cheap junk made for the tourist trade; you will like the "legitimate" items made for the Swiss people.

Prices will be your worry, not quality. Lace, for example, is gorgeous—but compared to the cost at Maria Loix or other top Belgian purveyors, it's absolutely highway robbery. Break it down to American currency; if the item is worth it, well and good. You may be sure that anything you buy will stand up, *if* you can afford it.

LOCAL RACKETS   Solely among a scattering of Swiss taxi drivers have we ever found any dishonesty in this nation. The only other reader-complaints we've ever had about Swiss ethical patterns were on a similar minor subject: the Kurtax (at Interlaken, for example, you're given a little shopping brochure issued by the merchants in return for this extra tax which is automatically slapped on your hotel bill). These are trifles. Switzerland is one of the most honest and upright communities on the globe today.

Curious sidelight: The integrity of the famous "Swiss Made" stamp on wristwatches was recently subjected to a crass indignity with the discovery of floods of Italian-wrought phonies on the *Swiss* market—each one bearing proud Helvetian trademarks. These fakes, worth $2.30 apiece, were peddled for between $34.50 and $46! Italian authorities have now cracked down on the bogus workshop and its *tempus fugitives.* Nevertheless, avoid all street-hawkers' "bargains" in timepieces, no matter how tempting.

Now that you have read all about all of the countries in Free Europe and the wonders they have to offer for your vacation pleasure, as final steps we have rounded up the latest available data, as of our press time, on getting there and back. Please honor our request which follows, however, for a last-minute checkout of the transatlantic portion of your journey with your travel agent or the other suggested sources. And as our Spanish friends say, *"¡Vaya con Dios!"*

Let's Go By Plane

(With a Special Report on the Supersonic Concorde)

Can you believe it? Something *good* is happening! *And* it's happening at last in the airline industry, where it is rare indeed that the general public gets a break. Credit for this goes straight-as-a-jet to the charter operators; these are the pioneering business dynamos who have been scrambling relentlessly to rake down the tariffs for transatlantic passage.

By and large, the scheduled airlines (that is, the big boys that you know right off by name) have done their dreary best to keep prices sky-high. When the traveler responded to this malevolence by moving over to charters (or "supplemental" carriers in trade lingo), the airlines snapped to attention by initiating their very own charter services; now the latter in most cases are in the black while many of the "skeds" are still dripping with red ink.

Let's face it, anybody with money or a reasonable line of credit can purchase an airline ticket at the established rate. What most voyagers want to know is how they can fly to their destinations cheaper than by the Economy or First-class methods. Thus, we're going to put the cartel-like regular passage on the shelf until later and initially examine the money-saving virtues of charters. There are a jillion types, so let's boil that spaghetti bowl down to the basic strands.

First, we have the recently created **One-stop Tour Charter (OTC)** and it sweeps in with a multitude of blessings. A spokesman for the Civil Aeronautics Board, which approved the plan, called it "a victory for the consumer." Another stated, "The rules represent the most significant step the agency has ever taken in regard to charter transportation."

To illustrate the contrast between regular scheduled service and the OTC, let's set up a typical case: If you want to fly from New York to Paris for a week's holiday, the *cheapest* unrestricted ticket you can buy for the round-trip is in the neighborhood of $750. Add your hotel bill to that and you've pretty nearly kissed away at least $1000, probably closer to $1200.

Under the OTC system you can have the same 7-day vacation, *including your hotel,* and your minimum outlay will be about $360! (You can spend more, of course, if you want a suite or similar luxury accommodation and, naturally, you can stay longer than a week if you wish to.) The cheapest discount fare for the plane ticket alone is around $375 for the same destination; moreover, that ticket must be purchased 60 days in advance of departure and is good only Off Season. OTC bookings can be made 30 days ahead of transatlantic flights and are good any time of year. Later, even this time will probably be reduced.

Second, by the time you are ready to soar aloft, the aviation authorities possibly will have approved the **Advance Booking Charter (ABC)** plan which would provide inexpensive passage without the requirement of ground arrangements or other services which now are a part of the OTC program. The discounted fares would become available if the passenger signed up for the flight 30 days prior to departure. Moreover, the ticket price would be a fixed one regardless of the quantity of people who fly with you; this differs from the Travel Group scheme which we will discuss below. As we write this, a firm decision has not been handed down to us groundlings, so be sure to check with your travel agent for the latest data.

Third, we have the **Inclusive Tour Charters (ITC)** which meld low-cost flying with a tour package. Generally, these are more costly than the OTCs as you must call at three different destinations. Under this system there is no hard-and-fast reservations deadline, so if you act quickly and have a bit of luck you can often travel very cheaply just where you want to go and at your greatest convenience. A romantic fillip here is the option of exchanging cruise ship accommodation for your hotel portion and linking your holiday into an air-and-sea adventure.

Fourth, **Travel Group Charter (TGC)**, while only handling your flight arrangements, is rather demanding on the prepayment (60 days before you climb aboard) and on the deposit you must lay down (at least 25% for any booking you make earlier than 2 months ahead). Obviously, this is designed for a determined sort of tripper who is going to get somewhere no matter what. If the wayfarer can't travel on the specified date, then his entire outlay is risked. The regulations do include some elastic, however. It's acceptable to substitute another name for your own if an emergency pops up, but most vacationers already have such frayed nerves by the time they are ready for a holiday that they don't want to shop for a surrogate merrymaker who can leave at a moment's notice for Zagreb.

Finally we have the Affinity Charters, which probably will be phased out as the TGCs, the ABCs, the OTCs and others in this alphabet soup take hold. The "Affinity" clause binds passengers into a club, a class, or an organization of some kind (often contrived) just for the purpose of cheap block bookings on an airliner. Now that the codes have broken down somewhat due to the more liberal plans, the affinity packaging may expire or at least be reduced in importance.

As for regular scheduled air passage, the transatlantic fares continue to rise, climbing 6% across the board this year after zooming up by 4% and 16% two seasons before.

A round trip between New York and London is (as of our press time) $1225 in First class, dropping to $808 in Economy during the High Season. (During the shoulder weeks and in winter there is a significant falloff in prices, but for illustrative purposes we'll only quote the peak periods to give you an idea of what's available.) Next comes the 14-to-21-day Excursion fare at $630; you are allowed 4 extra stopovers in Europe and there is a surcharge for flying on weekends. The 22-to-45-day Excursion at $523 permits no stops other than your destination; the weekend supplement may be added. There is also a 22-to-45-day APEX ticket which requires that you pay for your trip 2 months before departure date. If you leave and return via Canada, the APEX bite can be purchased for approximately $435 round trip at the peak period. IATA carriers advertise fares (called GITs) which include ground arrangements, tours, car rentals, and such, but these are so complicated and subject to so much change that you'd better discuss them with your travel agent.

The ever-popular Youth Fare had been abandoned from the U.S. to Europe 2 seasons back, sending squadrons of youngsters up to Canada to hop aboard cheap transatlantic flights. At this writing, it has been reinstated and the lowest tariff we can find between New York and London is $410 round trip, rising to $436 in the fringe season, and peaking at $493 during the busiest summer weeks. You'll have to inquire whether this one is still on by the time you are ready to take off for Europe.

As you can see, prices and conditions change rapidly in this bruisingly competitive marketplace.

If you have read the early pages of "Let's Get Ready," you already know that the international airlines are treating you as a prize boob. We are convinced not only that *scheduled* transatlantic fares for the individual traveler are shamefully overpriced, but that the long-standing cat's cradle of limitations, regulations, restrictions, and counterrestrictions is an affront to you as a paying passenger as well as an insult to you as a human being.

Throughout the industry, "cattle-car thinking" is king. Privately, nearly every aviation bigwig talks in terms of "push 'em on, pack 'em solid, push 'em off, and to hell with 'em."

This attitude would be defensible regarding Economy class—*if* a rapid, frill-less passage were to be offered at a rock-bottom economy rate. But to jam vacationers into seats so miserably tiny that they'd make most motor-coach operators throw up their hands in horror, to service a vast number of passengers with a grossly inadequate sprinkling of exhausted attendants, and to charge such inexcusably lofty independent fares for a transatlantic trip under these conditions seems to us, at least, like legalized rapacity—especially since coach excursions, round trip between New York and California, cover nearly the same mileage at such an amazingly lower cost.

For this premium price, the passenger has every right to expect a comfortable, relaxed ride—and in most cases, he just isn't getting it. Some token effort now is being made to grant full-fare customers a modicum of greater attention over the cut-rate traveler, but so far these extras include special luggage markers or identity tags and perhaps an additional square centimeter of exposed incisor when the airline clerk smilingly checks you in and charges you for overweight.

The airlines themselves, with their governments (who own approximately 60% of the roster), are solely and completely culpable for high rates and so-so rewards. Their front is the International Air Transport Association (commonly called IATA), a cartel whose 108 members in 84 countries carry close to 90% of the world's air traffic, and which has until recently dictated every sentence in the foreign rule book to every scheduled transatlantic operator except Icelandic and Air Bahama.

Its original goals—to promote safety, to standardize ticketing procedures, to act as a global clearing house in interline bookkeeping, to synchronize landing rights in multiple hundreds of far-flung airports, and collectively to shoulder dozens of other technical functions which each carrier would otherwise be forced to undertake individually—were and are not only noble but so indispensable that, without it or a similar body, today's world of the skies would be in unthinkable chaos. Then, however, it radically and shockingly overstepped these objectives by becoming a price-fixing autocracy with a stranglehold on the framework of the industry.

IATA rigidly prescribes the number of allowable inches of "pitch" front to back between the seat banks (which boils down, by simple arithmetic, to the size of your chair), the number of cabin attendants who may serve you, the kind of hand baggage you'll be permitted to carry free, even the specifications for the sandwiches you may eat—in essence, just about everything that you touch or that touches you, either at the ground termini or during your flight. Its members have successfully ganged up to standardize all important passenger facilities and activities at the same level—and at that level, sad to say, is production-belt mediocrity.

IATA represents itself as a "voluntary" alliance which "unanimously" enacts all regulations and fares pertinent to its membership, after approval by the various States. This description stretches the actuality to the limits of charity.

If 1 or 2 or 8 or even a dozen of its smaller members should demand a showdown on any specific issue, and should stand up unflinchingly against the powerhouse, they would eventually end up with 2 options: (1) to surrender "voluntarily" and "unanimously," or (2) to get out of the organization, practically as of 60 seconds ago. The glue which holds everybody so rigidly in line, and which pastes together some of the astonishing compromises among power blocs which have emerged from its conferences, is the universal, pathological fear of a price war in the air.

Among current bones of fierce contention between members attempting to arrive at unanimity are the following: (1) The replacement of baggage weighing with a piece-count system. Most travelers do not realize that the jet, unlike the piston-driven airplane, can soar aloft and carry to its destination just about every ounce that physically can be stuffed aboard it. Because of this, the more enlightened operators are eager to save the time of their passengers and ground personnel by running luggage through without the red tape of adding up the poundages of each bag on their counter scales. But opponents—and there are many—decry the loss of what, all too often, is gratuitously phony revenue. It has been reported that in a recent 12-month period one major company "earned" *more than $8,000,000 in excess baggage fees*

—so why, reason its officials, should we be crazy enough to give THAT up? (2) Withdrawal of the multistop ticketing which has permitted voyagers to tuck as many as 19 cities into their itineraries at no extra cost. (The surface excuse here is the amount of paperwork involved in booking circuitous routings. Factually, when you buy passage to Rome, as one example, you are paying for and are entitled to 5136 miles of air travel from JFK. Few are aware that a ticket covers distance as well as delivery to an explicit city. Whether or not the tripper utilizes those air miles, he or she must still pay for them —and pay plenty.)

From your standpoint and ours, one evil is the preoccupation of the IATA carriers with so many expensive, energy-consuming side issues that, all too frequently, the tail wags the dog. They weep and wail about their "inadequate" profits, yet continue to shovel up to 28% of their *gross* incomes into what they euphemistically call "Sales." Their advertising bill for the North Atlantic route alone annually runs more than $45,000,000, but this is a fleabite compared to their multimillion-dollar investments in such extraneous fields as the travel-agency business, the packaged-tour business, the automobile rental business, the hotel business, the publishing business, the giveaway business, and the Fifth-Avenue-glamour-real-estate business. We believe this causes them to lose sight, at least partially, of their primary function: To transport the voyager from one point to another, with maximum interest in his or her welfare and happiness.

The 2nd evil springs from too many fingers in too small a pie. In a typical year more than 7.3-million empty seats will cross the North Alantic—that's the equivalent of 25 jumbos per day flying devoid of occupants. The North Atlantic route has turned into a dogfight, with far too few passengers to go around.

The 3rd evil, from the buyer's side of the fence, is today's overdominance of IATA in its role as buyer's collective whipping boy for the major operators of the industry. If a ticketholder complains about the eye-jolting tariff he pays, the discomfort of the seat he rides in, or just about any irritation, the airline will deftly double-talk about "IATA regulations" (*"We* don't like it, either, but they force us to do it!")—when the blame lies squarely at its own doorstep.

THE SUPERSONIC CONCORDE   Here, unquestionably, is a bird for disciples of flight—graceful *pur sang* aviation from lift-off to landing.

Though necessarily expensive (20% over First-class for equivalent mileage) and not designed to provide the same wide-angle comforts you'll find aboard larger aircraft, the benefits of alighting absolutely fresh at your destination and in half the time expended on subsonic jets are puissant, joyful, and incontestable.

Our own very recent transatlantic dash between Paris and Washington was an escape into the future. During 3 hours and 43 minutes of jetting, 2 hours and 52 minutes were at supersonic levels. All slower readings were necessitated by passage over populated areas where Air France and British Airways throttle back to reduce the risk of sonic showers below. (Actually, military planes skim above the North American Continent on approximately 1000 supersonic missions a day and nobody seems to notice.)

Strictly speaking, the Concorde is selling speed. Confident that this is the warranted commodity that droop-snoots assuredly provide while airborne, every erg is expended on terra firma to shave milliseconds off check-in time, baggage handling, customs, processing, and boarding. These have become so ultra-efficient and so smoothly coordinated, we'd wager that no chief of state could be transferred from throne room to gangway with greater swiftness than that accorded any ordinary ticketholder darting from midcity to tarmac. V-V-VIP lounges are available, where friends or clients may enter—and become appropriately impressed; there are phones, seas of beverages, magazines and smiles by the heavenful; bulky coats are hung on racks and loaded neatly into cabin stowage; there's a special tax-rebate desk for travelers who have made purchases abroad. For the hurry-up voyager, in other words, all systems are "go."

Inside the craft, the configuration places passengers two-by-two on either side of a central aisle. These are not the largest airline seats aloft, but for a man of normal build they are comfortable. There are free headsets for multi-channel music (no films are shown as there is insufficient time), a few airline souvenirs, and a bustle of winsome silk-clad hostesses and amiable stewards securing overhead luggage bins and tucking everyone in for ascent.

The taxi shunt to the end of the runway is rigid, reminding us of the suspension of a hot fighter plane; the guttural rush of wind from the engines does not seem noisy to us, only different in quality and perhaps even more agreeable than the shrieks of some conventional jets. Portholes are small and too high for easy viewing; they are about the size of a breakfast waffle. So what? At 60,000 feet almost the only visible elements are cloud scud below and the dusky cobalt blue of the nether reaches of space.

Takeoff is powerful, assured, as steep as that of any other commercial aircraft. The whoosh of air we noted at runway level has vanished to become a steady throaty whir. The skipper then introduces us to the digital read-out panel on the forward bulkhead which records Concorde's phenomenal haste in hundredths of a Mach (650 mph). There is no sensation of speed, however, even when crossing sound barriers. Rather, it is one of delicacy in the handling of the plane itself, as if the pilot were effectively reining in a splendid wild mustang that would like to prance across the prairies of the sky. Straight-and-level flight, in fact, is perfection itself—so stable that when our Concorde pushed over the Mach II mark, we observed that nobody in the cabin even paused in their appreciation of the caviar canapés to witness this miracle of 20th century aviation.

Clearly, Concorde has built-in shortcomings—as one might expect of a highly bred sprinter that forsakes girth for leanness and bulk for speed. As the galleys are tiny, the cuisine appers limited in quality and in presentation. The rest rooms also encourage comparisons with life aboard a submarine. If the food trolley is in the aisle, you might have to dawdle in the corridor until you can move fore or aft; there is no space to pass.

But whatever niggling inconveniences may be encountered, these were more than atoned for by the exquisite swiftness of the journey itself. Alighting Stateside, we emerged as fresh as if we had come from a long movie—and why not, since we landed 2 hours *before* we took off? (This is due, of course, to the time differential between continents.) Our clothing was unwrinkled; we felt no fatigue whatsoever, and there were no side effects except a sensation of extraordinary thirst which persisted for maybe 3 hours more.

The usual Concorde ground wizards whisked us to our connecting flight, fielded all nitpicks with luggage and transportation, and politely bid us *adieu*. Perhaps they didn't realize it at the time, but they were actually waving "hello"—Concordially, of course.

In our judgment, it's the wave of the future.

LOST BAGGAGE Don't start worrying—not yet. Most luggage is recovered by the owner within 24 hours of loss. While airlines permit 7 days for notification, you should report your miseries while you are still at the airport. If you are with a tour, then collar your group leader as soon as you are aware that your bindle has not followed you to your hotel. Some airlines, when they know they cannot retrieve the pieces quickly, provide emergency overnight kits to defrocked travelers; others hand out modest sums of money for basic necessities.

A "property irregularity" form must be filled in describing all the particulars of your anguished loss. If you put some identification inside your suitcase, it will help tremendously should the outside tag have been ripped off. You are required nowadays to have your own personal luggage card on every piece. (All airlines, incidentally, have keys to every sort of luggage; rest assured that Customs also will be having a look inside; this is also why you should be absolutely candid in reporting that extra bottle of Scotch or perfume that you may have tucked in among your sweaters.) If it finds your baggage, the carrier will deliver it to you promptly.

After a week has passed and your caboodle still hasn't been located, you should then begin the process of extracting a settlement. Our experience has been that you won't get anything near like the value of your carryall or wardrobe (not to mention valuables such as cameras or jewely—which should have been among hand luggage anyway.) With great luck, the airline *might* be badgered into shelling out the limit—which is based on the weight recorded on your ticket and set at $20 per kilo. Usually, however, you'll receive much less. (We were once offered $25 for a suitcase and contents worth nearly $650 and after going to the top of the executive ladder managed to pry only $50 out of the company!)

The best protection, in other words, is your own insurance policy.

BUMPING or BOUNCING These are the names of an increasingly widespread game played by airlines which use you as the ball. It goes like this: The 747 that's supposed to wing you to, say, Paris has 352 seats. Because Carrier X knows from experience that a number of people with reservations will be "no-shows," it covers itself when its loads reach capacity by overselling perhaps 20 extra passages. (Usually airline officials figure that 10% of the registrants on the computer won't arrive at the airport.) Sure enough, 19 inconsiderate individuals fail to appear—but what if you are customer number 353? "Sorry," says the clerk, "no more room." You have been bumped, bounced, and flounced.

What to do?

Know your "fly-rights" and use them.

The CAB has ruled that provided you hold a confirmed reservation plus a properly validated ticket and have shown up on schedule, the airline must deliver you to your overseas destination by other means *within 4 hours* of your planned arrival time. If unable to do so, it is required to give you at least partial compensation, depending upon the distance, of not less than $25 or more than $200, plus free passage on the next available flight. This is *in addition* to the price of your original ticket, which you can turn in for a 100% refund. Moreover, you must be paid this "denied boarding compensation" within 24 hours; if you aren't, you have 90 days in which to file a claim. So if you get the bounce, for heaven's sake don't stamp off muttering darkly about seeing your lawyer.—Stay right there and insist that you be given the CAB's printed regulation on the subject as well as the necessary forms you must fill out to collect this penalty. (This applies, of course, only within the USA, before or after international flights.)

As you may recall, public troubleshooter Ralph Nader once got bumped, sued the airline for damages, took the shindy to the Supreme Court, and won the day—a decision which suggests that even the CAB provisions to guarantee your privileges are perhaps insufficient. If this juridical stance is current, then we suppose bumping per se might be considered a fraudulent misrepresentation. In either case, if you *do* get bumped and you do display defiance plus a knowledge of the portentous intimidations at your disposal, we'll bet our wings that any wise airline official will quickly break into a righteous and gelid sweat, yielding mercurially to almost any of your demands for comfort and coddling. For more information on bouncing and other helpful hints for the airborne pilgrim, write to the Office of Consumer Affairs, Civil Aeronautics Board, Washington, D.C. 20428, and ask for the pamphlet, "Air Travelers' Fly-Rights." It could reward you with justifiable dividends and save you from jumbo-size headaches. Complaints about carriers also should be addressed to the CAB. (And possibly Mr. Nader?)

WHERE TO SIT   Despite advertising claims about their silence aloft, the fans of the enormous jet engines, combined with the slipstream whooshing past at 575 mph, cannot entirely be filtered out. So if there's a choice, sit as far *to the front* as you can. The farther back you are, the louder the impact you'll hear (and feel!) from the exhausts.

Twelve doctors at an International Symposium on Health and Travel issued the flat recommendation that you sit *amidships* (midpoint of the cabin), *on the right-hand side of the plane,* if your stomach does nip-ups in flight. They found that the young, fat, overtired passenger who rides by day on the left side, immediately aft of the wing, has the greatest inclination toward queasiness—while the thin, 30-year-old male who travels by night on the center-right is least likely to reach for that wax-paper bag. Incidentally, one other conclusion: "The smug attitude of the nonsensitive traveler toward his less fortunate companions," the kindly doctors scolded, "is in itself a frequent incitement to nausea."

§**SPECIAL TIPS:** Circadian rhythm is not the Kurdish sex cycle; it is, quite simply, the built-in body clock regulating our daily time phases. When this is thrown out of whack, we get "dysrhythmia," the time disorientation commonly known as "jet lag." It isn't the flying itself which causes the problem. It is the combination of super speed and the tendency to continue normal activity, or even to increase it, in the differing east-west time zones—in other words, the defying of our biological clock settings. Swallowing a highball when your stomach tells you it's breakfast-time is an obvious case in point.

Wise wayfarers can do a lot to combat "jet lag" with (1) adequate preflight rest, (2) intelligent consumption of food and alcohol prior to climbing aboard, (3) comfortable clothing (ladies should *never* don sausage-tight undergarments, while men should loosen their ties and belts), and (4) regular intervals of physical unkinking. The fetal-minded IATA constrictions in Economy-class seating scientifically have been found to be villainous after 2 hours aloft. But Dr. Daniel Gormley, a kindhearted specialist from Maplewood, Missouri, offers an easy solution. The Good Doctor urges long-haul passengers to stroll up or down the aisle (easily done on the 747's) every hour or so, just to keep the circulation moving and to prevent the blood from "pooling." In the Concorde (see above), the expired time aloft is so brief and the air is so fresh that we experienced no fatigue or lag whatsoever.

Formality is out. Relax and be yourself. In hot weather take off your jacket and put on a pair of bedroom slippers. If they're carried aboard, ask for a pair of those cute little "flight socks," compliments of the line. There is a lot of air to cover, and it's your money you're spending, so why not enjoy it?

Fasten your seat belt immediately, because takeoffs and landings can be frisky. All wise passengers wear it loosely engaged throughout the journey; this can be vitally important insurance against various types of emergencies.

FOOD   Sometimes the food could be hotter—that's a common failing—but airlines feed their international passengers far better than their domestic ones. For travelers of the Jewish faith, kosher meals are available on many Air France, El Al, KLM, Swissair, Sabena, SAS, and TWA schedules which originate in New York. They are prepared by Borenstein Caterers and bear the seal of approval of the Union of Orthodox Jewish Congregations of America.

GENERAL LORE FOR THE AIRWISE   Here's a quick roundup of facts and suggestions for *all* airborne trippers, regardless of the type of aircraft they happen to fly:

Ask for (or reach for) a pillow, as soon as you sit down.

For the occasional passenger who suffers serious inbred physiological annoyance from changes in altitude, the Air Force's "valsalva" technique will probably do the trick. It is *only* recommended to those who do *not* suffer from any kind of ear trouble. If you're normal, however, just close your mouth, squeeze tightly on your nostrils with thumb and forefinger—as you might when cannonballing into a swimming pool—and then try your damnedest to "exhale" through your ears. This usually takes a bit of practice. You might turn the color of a Mexican fire engine the first time you try it. Relief, however, is instantaneous, and this simple system will free you forever from dependence on those maybe-yes—maybe-no candy baskets. Infants should be given their bottles on takeoffs and landings. If you have a cold, *open your mouth* when you blow your nose—or you might be shopping around for a new pair of eardrums.

Ask "Eee Tee Aay, please?" to learn when you are expected to arrive. ETA is "Estimated Time of Arrival," a flier's term; maybe you'll impress your beautiful hostess with your encyclopedic knowledge of aviation language!

All modern aircraft are fitted with a radar "eye" that constantly scans meteorological conditions up to 150 miles ahead. This permits the captain to avoid potentially dangerous or uncomfortable weather patches.

For picture-taking, avoid reflection by aiming your camera at an angle to the window. If conditions for color photography are normal and your filmspeed rating is 32 A.S.A. or better, you can use a shutter speed as slow as 1/50th of a second with an f 8 setting. And don't take flash pictures at takeoff; you might scare the pants or panties off a dozen of your neighbors.

Your return flight from Europe will probably take longer than your eastbound passage because of the prevailing westerly winds.

One blight is the airport departure tax, now frequently being incorporated in the overall ticket cost. Many European lands now demand from 80¢ to $5 per passenger for the privilege of bidding adieu to their terminals—a farewell which registers as the height of inhospitality. Our own House Ways and Means Committee has now followed the trend with a $3 levy on all international air passengers; the funds will be used to help finance a $14-billion airport improvement program throughout this decade.

THE LINE YOU ARE FLYING　Here are some quick facts about the international airlines of North America and Iceland. European carriers on the Atlantic run include Aer Lingus-Irish International, Air France, Alitalia, British Airways, Iberia, TAP-Portugal, KLM-Royal Dutch, Lufthansa, Olympic, Sabena, Austrian Airlines, Scandinavian Airlines System, Finnair, and Swissair. Look for these under the country of their origin.

Trans World Airlines, Inc. (TWA): TWA's far-flung network spans 36 U.S. cities and 18 overseas centers. From its U.S. gateways, it carries more transatlantic traffic than any of its competitors.

The superstars of TWA's international fleet are the giant Boeing 747 and the Boeing 707.

Keen-minded Charles C. Tillinghast, Jr., is the wing commander; he's the line's Board Chairman and Chief Executive Officer. President and Chief Airline Executive is C. E. Meyer, Jr.

TWA's landed-gentry subsidiary, Hilton International, totes up 65 hotels in 40 foreign countries, thus assuring travelers of down-to-earth comfort almost anywhere they alight.

The Trans World Flight Center at Kennedy is a study in convenience and efficiency. Flight Wing One handily accommodates the jumbo jets. It also boasts integrated health, immigration, and Customs inspection facilities, allowing international passengers direct access to continuing domestic flights.

Each gate has its own comfortable waiting room in which ticketholders may relax before entering the planes via telescopic Jetways which protect them from exposure to the weather. TWA's fleet of 707's is equipped with carry-on-luggage compartments for international flights, an innovation that TWA pioneered earlier domestically.

TWA's plush Trans World Service includes an upper deck lounge for First-class passengers with economy sections boasting the cleverly designed "Twin" Seat, a TWA "first." When the center seat is not occupied, its back drops down, its armrests go up, and the occupant can rest and relax in dimensions approaching those for First-class passage.

Dining choices include 5 entrées in First-class, with a choice of 3 meals in economy. A salute to the carrier's culinary capabilities was recently received in the form of the coveted Golden Plate Award of the International Foodservice Manufacturers Association. The award, presented for outstanding contributions to the U.S. food service industry, marks yet another "first" for TWA. Issued to Dieter H. Buehler, director of dining and catering services, it marks the first time an individual associated with an airline has been chosen for the honor. The award was based on the airline's high level of food service, its innovation in service approaches and maintenance of service standards.

In-flight entertainment aboard TWA includes a choice of 2 top-quality films, either "mature" or "general." Special audio/stereo entertainment is provided by way of 9 channels with choices ranging from contemporary music to timely topics on the special "Executive Report" channel.

No-smoking areas are located in the First-class and economy sections of the aircraft. The airline was first to configure its entire fleet in such fashion. A special "Business Zone," located in the forward part of the economy section, has been set aside, load permitting, on transatlantic 747 flights primarily for the business traveler who wishes to work or sleep uninterrupted, in a quiet, relaxed atmosphere.

Safety record? When you climb aboard that painstakingly maintained TWA job, you're riding one of the planes which won award after award from the National Safety Council. And it should reassure you even more to know that the jet pilots who fly the President of the United States are given their refresher courses at the TWA Training Center.

Recommendation: Here's one of the best-equipped, best-maintained, and best-experienced carriers. To most international travelers this trio of star qualities shows up vividly.

Pan American World Airways, Inc. (Pan Am): This colossus of commercial aviation has an unparalleled record for pioneering new routes, planes, technical advances, and legislation. Starting as a Caribbean and Latin American trailblazer in the '20s, its flying boats were the first scheduled aircraft to bridge the Pacific and later the Atlantic.

Today Pan Am's Clippers wing along on many of their familiar routes as well as on some that TWA handled previously—all part of a cooperative program to reduce operating costs and to conserve aviation fuel.

The traditional First-class "President Special" designation is now gradually being dropped and more area identification is being used, such as "Trans-Atlantic Service" or "Pacific Service," many times in conjunction with the line's new tag "Pan Am's World." Furthermore, this carrier has cut to 30 passengers the capacity of its First-class sections on 747's and has turned the extra space into dining areas seating 14 high-flying g-astronomes. Our own experiences aboard Pan Am's 747-airships (these Jumbos have turned the language backward by decades while turning the clock forward by comfort) embodied the epitome of travel's more graceful moments. The cabin crews were alert and kind, the culinary preparations and presentations were superb by airline standards, and our particular flight was a joy in every thoughtful detail. We relished every mile.

Economy-class, though rigidly standardized by IATA, is more varied, too. There's a choice of 3 meals, with some unusual creations such as Chicken Alfredo, a pasta platter, beef and mushroom pie, the Kabejaufilet (cod in dill sauce) and Sauerbraten.

Pan Am's elliptical 16-gate "Worldport" terminal "brings the plane to the passenger" at Kennedy International Airport. Luggage can be checked in at curbside and Customs matters dispatched within the very same building. Voyagers board at fuselage level beneath a cantilever roof. It is a $150,000,000 architectural marvel, the most beautiful and efficient structure of its type we've seen. It has recently been enlarged to 5 times its original size, with 52 check-in positions and rooftop parking (short-term) for 400 cars.

Pan Am can provide many other services in addition to air transportation. Its Inter-Continental Hotels Corporation is one of the world's largest hotel chains—totalling some 83 properties in 55 countries. "Panamac," the reservations system, can book hotel rooms and make car rentals globally. Pan Am also has a wide variety of tours to Europe.

For passengers arriving in New York to join transatlantic Pan Am flights, free helicopter service is provided by New York Airways from New York and LaGuardia Airports to JFK. Pan Am has its own passenger check-in center at La Guardia where passengers are bussed, also gratis, to Kennedy.

Recommendation: The quality of the aircraft, the soundness of the mainte-nance, the skill of the pilots, and the competence on the mechanical side can't be topped by any airline in the world. Its First-class service holds its own with just about anything in the Atlantic skies.

National Airlines: To expand its grid which started in 1934 between St. Petersburg and Daytona Beach and proliferated to encompass 42 cities on the East, Gulf, and Pacific Coasts, National became the 3rd American transatlan-tic flag bearer in '70 by inaugurating a daily flight in both directions—now exclusively with DC-10s—between Miami and London. Because the engines are so quiet and emit so little smoke, the DC-10 is known as the "Good Neighbor Jet."

One of the greatest comforts enjoyed by the 247 clients whom each accom-modates is the extra width of its body. This advantage has made possible more highly personalized attention from the attendants. It has also created space for a large galley on the lower deck which is accessible by elevator from the main cabin. All food is prepared and arranged for display here. This facilitates the speed of its conveyance by carts to everyone, as well as faster tray pickups. It also éliminates all traces of cooking odors.

Stereo and movies are offered as optional fillips, the latter introducing a radically different cartridge system which is much less noisy than its predecessors.

From Florida, dinner in First class begins with assorted hors d'oeuvres, foie gras, Beluga caviar, iced vodka, soup, and either hothouse Bibb or Caesar salad. Among the main courses which may be chosen are Châteaubriand with mushroom trimmings, Lobster Thermidor, roast duck with plum sauce, or rack of lamb. Before landing in London, an English breakfast with champagne is a standard feature, including eggs cooked to order, fresh fruit and cream, or a Continental breakfast is available. A real hee-haw is the popcorn served with the movies. In Economy class, filet mignon or breast of chicken in sesame with plum sauce are the culinary foundations. Here, too, the breakfast spread is varied and abundant. On the return passage the lunch menus are equally imaginative, topped by international snacks before landing.

Personally, we haven't crossed the Atlantic aboard National, although we have flown it domestically and like it very much; the scattered evaluations we've so far received on this over-the-sea leg from kindly Guidesters almost without exception have been favorable. They are too few, however, to constitute even a reasonable solid basis for any vicarious observations we would choose to advance on its pluses and minuses. How do its personnel, its service, its cuisine, its maintenance aloft of the lavatories, and its supervision of all of the details pertinent to the happiness of the airborne vacationer stack up with the performances of compatriots TWA and Pan Am, as well as such outstanding rivals as Swissair, SAS, British Airways, KLM, and others? Sorry, but we can't say. That's why all impressions you may wish to send us about your crossing or crossings via National would be welcomed with eagerness and gratitude.

Air Canada (AC): This carrier, formerly known as Trans Canada Air Lines or TCA, started in '37 with two 10-passenger monoplanes, 71 employees, 122 air miles to service, and nothing in its pockets. Now it employs 21,000 people, wings over 86,000 unduplicated miles, and jingles with approximately $900,-000,000 in operating revenue. Last year it carried 11-million customers to 31 destinations in Canada, 10 in the U.S., 12 in Europe, and 10 in the Caribbean. The all-jet fleet counts 122 modern aircraft of various sizes.

We've had the pleasure of riding AC only once in our lives (Montreal to New York), but plenty of readers report that its long-haul Atlantic service is splendid in every detail.

Canadian Pacific Air (CP Air): This air arm of the world's mightiest independent transportation body was energized in 1942, by the amalgamation of 10 "bush" services in western and northern Canada.

In 3 decades it has mushroomed almost unbelievably. Today it boasts a 57-thousand-mile route pattern which links all major cities in Canada with 5 continents. CP Air has 7 daily round trips in each direction between

Vancouver, Toronto and Montreal—serving intermediate cities en route. It also boasts 2 hops per day between Vancouver and San Francisco.

Its DC-8 and Boeing 747 jetliners whoosh all over the world, while Boeing 737-200 short/medium jets zip to and fro. You may also hear a sextet of Boeing 727's in the crisp Canadian air. In addition, a $24,000,000 overhaul to the Vancouver base has been completed. The overseas routes extend through Hong Kong and Tokyo; Shanghai and Peking (yet to be inaugurated); Sydney, Fiji, and Honolulu; Mexico City; Lima, Santiago, and Buenos Aires; Amsterdam, via the polar route and North Atlantic, Lisbon, Madrid, Rome, and Milan, plus Athens and Tel Aviv.

We first hopped CP Air up to Great Slave Lake in Northwest Territories many, many moons ago, and ever since, our admiration has been profound. Our Good Neighbors up North can fly like angels. They should, because they're among the most experienced, most careful, most reliable air experts around.

Icelandic Airlines-Loftleidir (LL): Every scheduled company except Icelandic (and IAB) belongs to IATA (see beginning of this chapter)—and, as we've emphasized, IATA dictates 100% standard rates, down to the same penny, for all its members. Icelandic, however, has always stubbornly and courageously preferred autonomy. Because it has refused to join IATA, this holdout can charge its passengers as little or as much as it pleases—and you can count on the fact that you will always pay *much* less in comparison.

Here is a wonderful bargain for any economy-minded vacationer. Icelandic and International Air Bahama have joined in a unique "marriage of the Arctic and Tropics," representing each other worldwide and offering low fares and big savings to Luxembourg, whether you fly from Icelandic's New York and Chicago gateways or IAB's Nassau port.

Don't get the notion that here is a slapdash, 1-horse operation that flies tattered old candidates for the boneyard. It's a substantial, serious venture, with carefully maintained equipment, multimillion-dollar annual revenue, a nearly 700-million annual passenger mileage, U.S.-trained pilots, a high proportion of American personnel, and an ultramodern 218-room hotel.

In safety standards it has the full approval of the U.S. Civil Aeronautics Board. Up to this writing LL's safety record is flawless.

Icelandic celebrates its 25th anniversary of regularly scheduled transatlantic service this year. It flies an all-jet fleet of DC-8's, with 250-seat "stretched" versions on the New York- or Chicago–Luxembourg routes.

Low-fare bus and rail service link Luxembourg with Paris, Frankfurt, Cologne, and other major cities—but if you want to linger in the Grand Duchy for 1–3 days, Icelandic provides bargain stopover tours. LL also flies Oslo-Copenhagen-Stockholm and London-Glasgow from New York (some linking into Chicago), with one-hour stopovers in Iceland. You also can book the European hops aboard 727s operated out of Keflavik by Flugfelag Islands (FI), a sister company. Fares on the Scandinavian and British legs are identical to those of IATA lines, but with an important extra fillip. Passengers on these routes can enjoy one of the world's great travel bargains—layovers in Iceland, for 1 to 3 days, at a *maximum* of $15 a day including double room with bath in a First-class hotel, 2 meals daily (including delicious smörgå sbord luncheons) the first 2 days, breakfast on the 3rd day, sightseeing trips on the first 2 days, and transfers between airport and hotel. Children aged 2 to 12 pay half price. Regular summer rates on these stopovers, for Luxembourg-bound passengers, are $40 for 24 hours, $75 for twice as long, and $97 for 3 days as of our press time, but can be expected to rise slightly by the time you wing in. Adventurous ski buffs can take advantage of LL's bargain winter hickory runs in the homeland and to Geilo (see what we think of this northern slice of heaven in our "Norway" chapter). Additional offerings include youth fares (through age 23), affinity packages allowing different return dates, 1- and 2-week ski runs via Luxembourg to Austria, France, and Switzerland; summer escorted motorcoach romps of 2 and 3 weeks via Luxembourg to countries in western and eastern Europe; and Saga Discovery escorted summer loops which include Norway, Sweden, Denmark, Finland, and Iceland. Also popular are the winter weekend hops from New York to Iceland, and a series of Iceland Adventure summer tours—more than 20 packages to Iceland (pony treks, camping, geology and nature expeditions, salmon fishing), Greenland, and the Faroe Islands (about as off-the-beaten-path as you can get).

You won't find pink orchids aboard Icelandic, although the airline does serve complimentary wines and cognac with its full-course meals—but you will find a real value for the price—and please visit Iceland on one of the stopover plans or longer tours.

International Air Bahama: Since '68 this carrier has been affiliated with Icelandic as another big money-saver. Its DC-8 fan-jets, piloted by American million-mile captains and serviced by expertly trained multilingual hostesses, soar 6 times per week between Nassau (capital of the Bahamas) and Luxembourg, on 8-hour schedules. Since Nassau is only 30 minutes by air from Miami, here is an especially attractive bargain for residents of the southern states—as well as an exciting routing. IAB's year-round tariffs from Nassau to Luxembourg are roughly the same as Icelandic's, but there is no surcharge for weekend departures. Kids from 2 to 12 are charged 1/2-fare, and infants under 2 get aboard for 10%. The free baggage allowance for everyone except babies is 66 lbs.—22 lbs. over the IATA Economy-class limit. All meals, cocktails, champagne and other wines are gratis. If connections should snarl you up in Luxembourg for an overnight, the company will give you good hotel accommodations without charge, provided you make your request when you buy your ticket. IAB offers the same low-cost tours from Luxembourg as does Icelandic: 2- and 3-week car-and-rail packages all year and 1-week packages in winter, escorted 2- and 3-week summer motor-coach tours to countries in western and eastern Europe, and 1- and 2-week ski tours to Austria, France, and Switzerland. For further details, consult your travel agent or write direct to International Air Bahama, 25 S.E. Second Ave., Miami, Fla. 33131, or to any office of Icelandic Airlines.

WARNING! On both Icelandic and International Air Bahama, the load factors during certain seasons are so overwhelming that reservations foul-ups and outright booking blunders by inept ground personnel inevitably occur. Some of this results from oversold aircraft, since we are now receiving frequent complaints from ticketholders who claim they were bumped from their flights. On these two, please be *extra*-sure to have *all* of your travel arrangements confirmed—*in writing*—and, as on every other carrier, *reconfirm 72 hours before takeoff.* This tip may save you a bundle of money and a skullful of headaches!

Air India: Having learned to pamper maharajas in its pioneer days, this soundly managed and reliable long-line carrier tries to offer (with fair but not outstanding success, in our judgment) the transatlantic tripper an extra measure of plushiness. Its Boeing jetliners ply between (1) New York and London, Paris, Prague, Geneva, Frankfurt, Beirut, Cairo, Nairobi, and (2) Moscow, Singapore, and Sydney (Australia). A twice-weekly "express" links New York and New Delhi, via London and Moscow. Delhi, Bombay, and Calcutta are the company's Asian focal points. Its multimillion-mile pilots are U.S.- and British-trained. All Air India's jet skippers have had several months of tutelage in America.

Aircraft interiors reflect the rich coloring of the nation. Multilingual stewards, stewardesses, and sari-clad hostesses dispense exotic hors d'oeuvres and sweetmeats. Gourmet-class continental cuisine and a range of beverages are offered.

We recommend it highly for technical competence.

Ethiopian Airlines (EAL): We did our East African teething on this carrier, and it is impossible to express our delight in witnessing, as we did recently between 3 European cities, a safari-cum-Indian-Ocean cruise, a flying tour of East Africa, and an every-day-in-the-air 2-week domestic network romp aboard DC-6's and DC-3's, the fantastic growth and sophistication it has undergone. As a reporter for *Reader's Digest, Saturday Evening Post,* and other U.S. media, we bounced with its Texas pilots over the exotic terrain of Ethiopia, Eritrea, and the Somalilands when the line was lucky if it could snag 2 other paying passengers. (Once, in stocking feet, we even crawled over a cargo of $1,000,000 of Maria Theresa thalers before flying with them to Aden, Arabia.)

Today, this stalwart is beautifully equipped and skillfully manned—flamboyantly attired outside, gorgeously decorated inside, and hospitality-enriched by attractive English-speaking hostesses in native *shamas.* Its pride of *simbas* consists of Boeing 707 jets, Boeing 720-B's, DC-6B's, DC-3's, 3 Bell helicopters, and 6 training planes. TWA boosted it into the air during its early days, but now, except for occasional consultations, it runs its own show smoothly and very nearly independently. As a sample, Ethiopian provides service that is simply out of this world. Incidentally, it has the only aircraft maintenance center on African soil which has been certified by the U.S. Federal Aviation Authority as meeting or surpassing 100% of its demanding standards. From its European termini of Paris, Frankfurt, Rome, and Athens, you may be whisked over 27-thousand miles of awesome scenery—all the way to Shanghai in the East, to Nairobi and Dar es Salaam in the South, and to Lagos (across the Sahara) and Accra in the West. Africa is its specialty—and it is strictly à la mode all the way. Grab EAL wherever you can—on any of 3 continents—because here is the best small airline that we have ever enjoyed in our travel lives, globally, and certainly the Vanguard of birds over Africa.

El Al Israel Airlines: Here's one, regrettably, which we've still missed to date—but reports from all sources (except the Syrians) also couldn't be better.

Like Ethiopian, El Al is said to concentrate extra-heavily on passenger comfort and service, which may account for its having the highest load factor of all North Atlantic carriers.

Nonstop Boeing 747 and 707 jets, between New York and Tel Aviv—the longest scheduled commercial haul offered by any international carrier—fly 2 Atlantic-European crossings daily in peak season. Flight time is an amazing 10 hours and 20 minutes. It is the only carrier zipping nonstop both to and from Israel.

These blue-and-white birds also cover such ports-o'-call as London, Amsterdam, Brussels, Munich, Frankfurt, Geneva, Copenhagen, Vienna, Zürich, Paris, Marseille, Rome, Athens, Istanbul, Teheran, Bucharest, Nairobi, and Johannesburg.

El Al is also pushing for reduced air fares. *Mazel tov!*

Obviously these Israelis are doing a big job.

Miscellaneous: **Austrian Airlines**, as you may remember from the chapter on that country, is a well-run fleet. We've recently logged some flight time over the Continent on this carrier and look forward to our first transoceanic Viennese waltz as soon as possible. **TAP** streams Portugal's proud burgee over the Atlantic to New York and to 33 other cities in 14 other nations. The slogan that "We're big enough to take you to 4 continents but small enough to pamper you on a 747" is very well said. We have flown this carrier between European points perhaps 25 or 30 times—and, broadly speaking, we have very much liked everything we have seen. Its safety record and its amenities are excellent. Now that it is offering its own particular brands of skill along the primary skyway of the Western World, we're eager to try this long-range innovation. At this writing, the military has taken over the controls, but we'd guess that this is a temporary administrative measure until the government itself plots out a true course for the nation. The Russians have said *"da"* to the Atlantic and **Aeroflot** hops it once a week with a 120-passenger IL-62 between Moscow and New York, via Montreal. We haven't sampled its caviar —not *nyet.* **CSA** (its Czech mate) has twice-weekly probes to Prague with New York en passant. Bratislava and Amsterdam can also be ports-o'-call for the IL-62's, plus more than 50 cities on 4 continents. **Japan Air Lines** jumps daily from either London or Paris springboards to New York. Mexico's **Aero Mexico** says *sí-sí* to Miami 3 times a week from Paris and Madrid. These 3, too, are new on us.

FINAL TIPS   Memorize immediately the names of your hostesses or stewards. As a wise lass from American Airlines writes, "If the passenger takes the time to learn them, you'd be surprised how greatly increased her or his service would be, not to mention how pleased the attendants would be."

From your milk of human kindness, please give the airlines a break by not duplicating reservations on international runs. No-Show is a tough enough problem on shorties of the Boston-New York or Detroit-Cleveland class—but when a transatlantic hop is involved, it *really* hits their pocketbooks. If more Europe-bound pilgrims would do this, it would arrest their realistic but unforgivable recourse of overbooking almost all aircraft because of the deluge of last-minute cancellations.

IATA's carriers have tightened up on check-in deadlines. Because time and space on the apron, on runways, and along the air lanes is at a premium, travelers are warned that they must strictly adhere to the check-in time noted on their ticket envelopes.

During wintertime in Europe, always be prepared for delayed takeoffs, diversions to strange airports, and outright cancellations of flights—especially in the northern countries, mountain countries, British Isles, and the Benelux countries. Fog and smog are major problems, and flying weather is often terrible.

Don't ever play your portable radio in the cabin of any aircraft. It is liable to interfere with the plane's radio navigation systems and thus endanger the safety of the flight. This is now an international law.

Hand-carry all your film since x-ray inspection devices could alter its properties. If it is extra-extra valuable, special ray-proof containers exist for professionals who fly frequently.

Don't accept unopened gifts or packages to take on your flight unless you would trust the giver with your life. The 1972 midair explosion aboard an El Al jetliner (which miraculously made it back to Rome without an injury on board) was caused by a "present" handed before departure to 2 English girls by their newly found Arab "boyfriends." Although the airlines are doing everything possible to screen arms and explosives, there are still fanatical killers who recklessly use innocent humanity to gain publicity for their political causes.

In the unlikely event that you are skyjacked, do precisely what you are told by the crew or security officer. Stay calm. Skyjackers generally are not on suicide missions; because their normal goals are attention and money, you stand an excellent chance of getting off the plane with nothing more than frazzled nerves and time lost. Heroics, on the other hand, might harm not only you, but also place in jeopardy your fellow passengers.

If you are Europe-bound from the hinterlands of the U.S., and your domestic plane lands at either Newark or LaGuardia Airports, you are entitled to free helicopter transfer to Kennedy—a novel experience for many air travelers and a big bonus in time, money, and convenience.

N.Y. Airways Helicopter Service winds up chopper hops between the Wall Street heliport and JFK.

Keep the "Health Alert Notice" given to you at JFK or other international gateways in your purse or wallet for 6 weeks. If you become ill during this period, give the card to your doctor so that he can begin tracing the name and address of your particular microbe.

Here are 5 wise and important suggestions from a wise and important Corpus Christi Guidester who has flown his own airplanes for more than 30 years and with whom we are anxious to tilt glasses in gratitude for his thoughtfulness:

¶Whenever possible, choose the carrier with the greatest number of backup planes on tap at the airport of departure. When an immediate replacement is available your delay is minimized should mechanical problems ground the scheduled ship.

¶Try to choose a flight originating at the airport of departure. Then you'll never be penalized by time lags picked up by your bird en route from Hong Kong.

¶Always study alternate schedules so that if there is a foulup you can have your ticket endorsed to another airline. It is pathetic to see travelers impatiently sitting around awaiting a tardy plane when all they have to do is to walk a few yards and book with another company at no extra cost.

¶Always pick daylight over night flights. After 3 or 4 hours of disturbed dozing on the latter, you'll need to go to bed at least part of the next day.

¶If possible, avoid flying between major cities abroad on Saturdays and Sundays—particularly in High Season. Every major foreign airport is swamped on weekends with charter flights that throw "normal" flight schedules hopelessly akilter. Example: On a London—Rome shuttle, our takeoff was delayed for 71 minutes. Before landing, we flew the holding pattern over Fiumicino for another 53 minutes. The endless parade of charters, which almost always originate and terminate their 1-or 2-week tour packages to other countries on these 2 days, was the sole villain.

Temple Fielding Travel Award

On the occasion of this guidebook's 30th anniversary, its author, editors and staff have elected to look forward to the vast evergreen future of travel and tourism rather than backward into the achievements of the past three decades.

Therefore we are proud to dedicate this opportunity to the inauguration of the new and perpetuating TEMPLE FIELDING TRAVEL AWARD.

The 1977 recipient of this trophy—to honor the advancement of frontiers in commerce and tourism—is the Concorde aircraft itself, which is being operated in its first full year of regular service by Air France and British Airways.

To the Concorde:

The Temple Fielding Travel Award
for 1977.

Congratulations!

Index

Carrickmacross, Ireland, 551
Cars, *see* Motorcars
Cartagena, Spain, 941, 963, 965
Casamicciola, Italy, 609–610
Cascais, Portugal, 844
 hotels, 849, 851
 nightclubs, 868–869
 restaurants, 864–865
Caserta, Italy, 657
Cashel, Ireland, 551
Cassarate, Switz., 1083
Castel Gondolfo, Italy, 591
Castellón de la Plana, Spain, 962
Castelvetrano, Italy, 644
Castemola, Italy, 688
Castlebar, Ireland, 551
Castle Combe, England, 214, 228
Catania, Sicily, 586, 587, 697
 hotels, 644, 645
 restaurants, 657
 shopping, 718
Cauterets, France, 391
Cavalla, Greece, 498
Cavoli, Elba, 603
Celebrity Service, Inc., 73
Celle, Germany, 433, 446–447, 455
Cemeteries, American Military, 74
Ceramics, buying
 Denmark, 182, 183, 190
 Greece, 524, 533
 Italy, 713
 Netherlands, 810
 Norway, 839, 840, 841
 Portugal, 875
 Scotland, 917
 Spain, 1019
 Sweden, 1051
 Switzerland, 1133
Cernobbio, Italy, 590, 601, 658
Chalfont Saint Peter, England, 261
Chalkidiki, Greece, 498
Chambésy s/Genève, Switz., 1106–1107
Chambord, France, 388
 Château, 385
Chamonix, France, 316, 334, 365
Champillon, France, 339
Chandris Cruises, 529
Chantilly, France, 383
Charité-sur-Loire, France, 388
Chartres, France, 383
Chartre-sur-le-Loire, France, 389
Chartwell House, England, 273
Châteaubriant, France, 386
Châteaulin, France, 334
Château du Lude, France, 385
Château d'Oex, Switz., 1074
Château-la-Vallière, France, 390
Chateaulin, France, 334
Châteauneuf-sur-Loire, France, 386
Château-Thierry, France, 383
Châteaux Country, France, 384–390
 hotels, 386–388

restaurants, 388–390
 sightseeing, 384–386
 tourist information, 386
  Châteaux of the Loire, guide, 384
  sightseeing tours, 383, 384
Château Country, Sweden, 1024
Chatsworth House, England, 273
Chaumont Château, France, 386
Chaumont-sur-Loire, France, 390
Checks, personal, 42, 50
Cheltenham, England, 228
Chêne Bourg, Switz., 1107
Chennevières-sur-Marne, France, 361
Chenonceaux, France, 385, 389
Cherbourg, France, 334
Chernex, Switz., 1084
Chester, England, 216–217, 262, 274
Cheverny, France, 385, 386, 389
Chiasso, Switz., 721
Chichester, England, 275
Chillon, Castle of, Switz., 1059
Chinaware, buying
 Austria, 105
 Denmark, 183–184
 England, 280–281
 Finland, 311
 France, 399
 Germany, 151, 493–494
 Ireland, 575, 576
 Italy, 708
 Netherlands, 810
 Portugal, 875
 Sweden, 1052
Chinon, France, 386, 388
Chippenham, England, 213, 230–231
Chipping Campden, England, 227, 276
CIT, bus company, 592–593
Cigarettes
 Customs and, 39, 50, 53
  See also under Tobacco
Cinq-Mars-la-Pile Château, France, 386
Citara Beach, Italy, 663
Ciudad Lineal, Spain, 979
Ciudad-Real, Spain, 965
Civil Aeronautics Board (CAB), 1144
Classiebrawn Castle, Ireland, 562
Cleeve Hill, England, 228
Clervaux, Luxem., 728, 734
Clifden, Ireland, 560
Cliffoney, Ireland, 562
Climate, 69
Clocks, *see* watches and clocks
Clothing
 buying, *see* Apparel, buying
  See also Furs; Gloves; Shoes
Cluanie Brae, Scotland, 916
Clydebank, Scotland, 887
Clywd Valley, Wales, 230
Cobh, Ireland, 551
Cobham, England, 262
Coblenz, Germany, 434, 455, 490

Mon Repos, Greece, 534
Monaco, 30, 765–773
 Customs, 773
 gambling casino, 766, 767
 helicopter service, 766
 hotels, motel, 767–769
 nightlife, 772
 restaurants, 770–771
 shopping, 772
 sightseeing, 767, 772
 tourist information, 772–773
 trains, 61
Moncontour Château, France, 386
Mondello, Sicily, 646, 670
Mondorf-les-Bains, Luxem., 730, 732,
 735
Mondsee, Austria, 102
Money, 42, 49–50
 *Fielding's Quick Currency and
 Metric Converter*, 42–43
 foreign, conversion of, 41–42
 personal checks, 42, 50
 Pre-Paks, 42
 tipping, 55–56
 traveler's checks, 50
Monnikendam, Neth., 807
Monreale, Sicily, 671
Mont-Agel, France, 765
Montana-Vármala, Switz., 1067
Montargis, France, 338
Montbard, France, 363
Montbazon, France, 386–387, 388
Mont-de-Marsan, France, 338
Monte Carlo, Monaco, 765
 gambling casino, 766, 767
 hotels, 766, 767–769
 nightlife, 772
 restaurants, 770–771
 shopping, 772
 sightseeing, 772
 tourist information, 772–773
Montecatini, Italy, 586, 612, 667
Monte Estoril, Portugal, 868
Monte Gordo, Portugal, 857, 866
Monte Igueldo, Spain, 994
Montélimar, France, 365
Montgeoffroy Château, France, 386
Montoire Château, France, 386
Montoire-sur-le-Loire, France, 390
Mont Pelerin, Switz., 1099
Montpellier, France, 338
Montreuil-Bellay Château, France, 386
Montreux, Switz., 1058–1059, 1128
 hotels, 1083–1084
 restaurants, 1112–1114
 shopping, 1134
Mont-St.-Michel, France, 338, 392–
 393
Montsoreau Château, France, 386
Mook, Neth., 788
Mora, Sweden, 1035, 1049
Morat, Switz., 1098, 1102
Morcote, Switz., 1082

Moretonhampstead, England, 221, 263
Moreton-in-Marsh, England, 227, 263
Morges, Switz., 1098, 1114
Morocco, Italy, 691
Moselle River Valley, Germany, 433,
 489, 490
Motels, 71
 See also under names of cities and
 countries
Motorcars, 62–65
 buying abroad, 64, 154
 Customs and, 64
 gasoline, 66
 insurance, 63, 64, 65
 International Driving Permit, 62
 "piggyback" service for, 64–65
 rental, 63–64
 shipping overseas, 62–63, 282
 *See also under names of cities
 and countries*
Motorcoach travel, *see* Bus travel
Motril, Spain, 965
Mougins, France, 419
Mount Athos, Greece, 499
Muiden, Neth., 808
Muir of Ord, Scotland, 916
Mulhouse, France, 388
Mullingar, Ireland, 559
Mull Island, Scotland, 916
Munich, Germany, 430–431, 486, 588
 festivals, 430, 491
 hotels, 438–441
 motorcar rental, 486
 nightclubs, 480–482
 restaurants, 460–465
 shopping, 430–431, 493–494
 sightseeing, 430, 464, 490
Murano (island), Italy, 584, 716
Murcia (Santiago de la Ribera), Spain,
 963
Mürren, Switz., 1129
Mycenae, Greece, 499
Mykonos (island), Greece, 498, 499,
 523, 526, 536–538

Naestved, Denmark, 160
Nairn, Scotland, 898
Namur, Belgium, 111
Nancy, France, 338
Nantes, France, 315, 338
Naples, Italy, 578, 582, 587, 720
 bus tours, 582–585
 food, 652
 hotels, motel, 612–614
 nightclubs, 696
 restaurants,667–669
 shopping, 712–713, 717, 718
 sightseeing, 582
Narbonne, France, 338
National Airlines, 1148–1149
Nauplia, Greece, 517
Naxos, Greece, 499

BETWEEN GUIDEBOOK
AND READER 1947–1977

Birthdays are a time for merrymaking, so in that spirit of fun this Guidebook sets out to further that tradition.

As a newly born publication who began gestating as early as 1946, I was still pretty slim at birth; weighed in at only 427 pages, double spaced, in big type, and bulked out on the heaviest bond paper available to the publishing industry. My parent, the hopelessly naïve author who took undue credit for my early success, had to be forgiven for some obvious shortcomings (especially in geography) because my first edition—a volume on *European* travel, mind you—for some unearthly reason contained chapters on Ethiopia, Egypt, and Mid-East Aviation! (I suppose these romantics get carried away.)

So with apologies neither to history nor historian, let's take a nostalgic peek into the album of time and see what tourism was all about 30 years ago.

FIELDING'S TRAVEL GUIDE
EXCERPTS FROM THE
1947 EDITION

GENERAL COMMENTS: Aircraft loads are made up thirty hours and ten hours before flight, on a basis of maximum bad weather. If the sun shines at takeoff, there's room for as many as three extra passengers . . . At this writing, two-way passage and confirmed hotel reservations must be secured by all tourists (not businessmen) *before* a passport can be issued . . . Trans World Airline, whose legal name is still Transcontinental & Western Air, Inc. . . . You'll see plenty of arguments along the streets of Europe, but almost none of them will be fistfights. They'll throw rocks, hug, bite, kick, knee, scratch, or scream bloody murder—anything but a simple, lethal right cross to the opponent's jaw. They fight like girls, because they don't know pugilism. . . . Film: No color film whatsoever, but plenty of black-and-white in the larger cities. Take your own supply as insurance. Gaevert (probably misspelled) is a European brand I had especially good luck with . . .

BELGIUM: But once you get in, you'll find the hotels clean, luxurious, efficient; average price is $4.50 to $5.50 . . .

DENMARK: A typical platter I had, called "Delicious for Two," contained lamb cutlet, chicken, duck, kidney, lamb liver, sausages, mushrooms, and pâté de fois gras—and this was an appetizer! . . .

ENGLAND: Typical slyness is found in the sign posted by a golf club. "Any player whose ball rolls beyond the red flag designating the zone of an unexploded bomb in the ground may take one stroke with a new ball without penalty." . . .

FRANCE: The American will wear a sleezy $2.98 outfit in which the French girl wouldn't be caught dead; it's the $20 kind, or she'll up and make herself a luxurious duplicate by hand! . . . France has rolled along for twelve hundred years; and she's done it without much emphasis on soap. . . . If you want something like the Waldorf-Astoria, Blackstone, or Shoreham, you'll pay $7-$10, plus 15% service. . . .

GERMANY: To enter Germany these days you need the patience of Job, the loyalty of Jonathan, Martha's willingness to serve, plus a wife in the U.S. Congress. It can and is done, of course, but you'll be 186 years old before your permissions are cleared. . . .

GREECE: The porter in the Grande Bretagne indignantly waved aside my tip (he was semistarved) "because your great nation is a best friend of Greece." . . .

IRELAND: Watch your profanity in Ireland. After one or two cusswords, they had me talking like little Lord Fauntleroy. They just don't like it. . . .

ITALY: Mussolini's cult of more-offspring-for-the-state was a crime against her geography and economy. You'll still see traces of this worship of polygenesis wherever you go. You'll usually be asked, for example, how many *bambini* you have. If you say "One," you'll get a mild frown; "Three" brings a polite smile, "Five" a handclasp, and "Seven" a joyous thump between the shoulder blades. . . .

LUXEMBOURG: Prices and Rooms: $1.75-$3 single, $3-$6 double. Meals: $1.25-$2 for a dinner costing $20 in Spain, $15 in Portugal, and $10 in France . . .

NETHERLANDS: Ordinary stockings (neither silk nor nylon) have been on sale an hour or two per week, in the largest department stores; until recently, it took one year's supply of coupons for an entire family to buy father one suit of clothes . . .

NORWAY: From sad experience, I cannot overstress the importance of advanced reservations in Norway. I cabled Oslo's Bristol five weeks ahead of my visit; when I arrived, the harassed clerk laughed at my naïveté, suggesting that next time I let him know five *months* in advance . . .

PORTUGAL: Before Dr. Salazar took the reins of government, tuberculosis and syphilis were major menaces to the health of his people . . .

SPAIN: As stated in the introduction, the law requires that tourists spend a minimum of $12.50 daily for two weeks—about as hard as sitting in a chair or eating a 1¢ ice cream cone . . .

SWEDEN: A law has been passed limiting smörgasbord to three choices per person—no more groaning tables of their world-famous appetizers . . .

SWITZERLAND: I do not dare quote the value of the Swiss franc, because there are rumors that the U.S. dollar is soon to be further devaluated in Switzerland. . . .

AND THE YEAR 2007?

And what about 30 years from now? We expect to be going stronger than ever and probably will have expanded to include volumes in greater depth on individual countries, pre-packaged backgrounders on ethnological and historic aspects of the trip you are planning, plus all of the technological delivery systems which science will provide through miniaturization, electronic wizardry, incapsulation, and fields yet to be pioneered. Most likely your wristwatch and your television set will be major receptors of information into which we will link our services. Already scientists are far along the road to programming watches to contain vast amounts of information that you will need while in transit or in a memory bank which you will carry with you.

The airlines—probably they will be pooled into only one or several transportation systems three decades from now—are experimenting with voice-print ticket requisitions whereby you may be able to summon up all of the tour options and their respective prices on your home television screen, plus views of typical hotel rooms and scenes of areas which may interest you. The voice-print will be coordinated with your international credit card and, when it is confirmed that your bank balance is sufficient, your ticket is issued automatically. You will ride to the airport on a monorail or some other high-speed land transportation, your luggage will be taken from you at the town terminal, and you will board a hypersonic, solid-fuel aircraft designed and manufactured by several nations for their mutual use. This plane will fly in the neighborhood of Mach IV, which is approximately 2600 mph; it will shrink a transatlantic flight to approximately an hour. In several capitals and resorts you will be staying in hotel-club accommodations arranged through a travel federation to which you belong and in which you own shares. Pollution will be greatly reduced due to the extensive use of solar tidal energy production.

The character of travel, too, will be different in that much of the affluent world by the year 2000 will have "seen" the major sites, but now will be striving to "know" the countries and the people they visit. "Activity" tours (such as submarine exploration and Atlantis digs), which are just beginning to form a trend in 1977, will be diminishing and instead people will travel abroad to take courses actually on the scene of their principal interests. Emphasis will be on "in-depth" studies, while first-time sightseers in the older sense of the 1950's, 60's, and 70's will just be planning weekend trips to space platforms for another view of earth and our universe while scientists will have inaugurated the first enriched-atmosphere settlements on Mars.

Blue-skying—or pink-skying? Perhaps, but the Fielding team will be taking notes for *next* year's edition.